THE AMERICAN PAGEANT

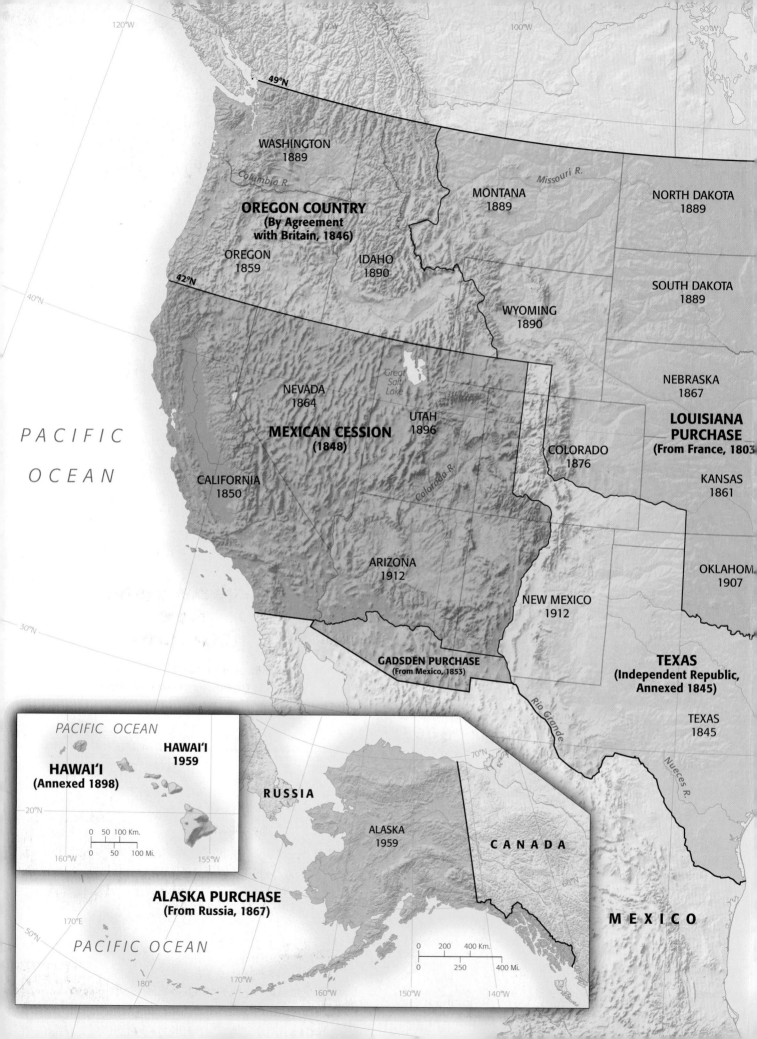

PACIFIC
OCEAN

49°N

WASHINGTON
1889

Columbia R.

OREGON COUNTRY
(By Agreement
with Britain, 1846)

OREGON
1859

42°N

MONTANA
1889

Missouri R.

NORTH DAKOTA
1889

IDAHO
1890

SOUTH DAKOTA
1889

WYOMING
1890

NEVADA
1864

Great
Salt
Lake

NEBRASKA
1867

MEXICAN CESSION
(1848)

UTAH
1896

LOUISIANA
PURCHASE
(From France, 1803)

COLORADO
1876

KANSAS
1861

CALIFORNIA
1850

Colorado R.

ARIZONA
1912

NEW MEXICO
1912

OKLAHOM
1907

GADSDEN PURCHASE
(From Mexico, 1853)

TEXAS
(Independent Republic,
Annexed 1845)

Rio Grande

TEXAS
1845

Nueces R.

PACIFIC OCEAN

HAWAI'I
1959

HAWAI'I
(Annexed 1898)

0   50 100 Km.

0   50   100 Mi.

160°W   155°W

20°N

50°N

170°E

PACIFIC OCEAN

180°

RUSSIA

70°N

ALASKA
1959

CANADA

60°N

ALASKA PURCHASE
(From Russia, 1867)

0   200   400 Km.

0   250   400 Mi.

MEXICO

170°W   160°W   150°W   140°W

CANADA

Lake Superior

Lake Michigan

Lake Huron

Lake Erie

Lake Ontario

St. Lawrence R.

MAINE
1820

VT.
1791

N.H.

MASS.

CONN.

R.I.

MINNESOTA
1858

WISCONSIN
1848

MICHIGAN
1837

NEW YORK

IOWA
1846

ILLINOIS
1818

INDIANA
1816

OHIO
1803

PENNSYLVANIA

NEW
JERSEY
1790

MASON-DIXON LINE

WEST
VIRGINIA
1863

DELAWARE

MARYLAND

THIRTEEN COLONIES

MISSOURI
1821

KENTUCKY
1792

VIRGINIA

2010

Mississippi R.

THE ORIGINAL UNITED STATES
(By Treaty with Britain, 1783)

THE ORIGINAL

36°30'N
MISSOURI
COMPROMISE
LINE

ARKANSAS
1836

TENNESSEE
1796

NORTH
CAROLINA

SOUTH
CAROLINA

MISSISSIPPI
1817

ALABAMA
1819

GEORGIA

LOUISIANA
1812

(Seized from Spain,
1810, 1813)

Gulf of Mexico

FLORIDA
(By Treaty with
Spain, 1819)

FLORIDA
1845

BAHAMAS

ATLANTIC

OCEAN

N

Territorial Growth
of the
United States

1820 Date of states admission to the Union

● Geographic center of population by decade

0	150	300 Km.
0	150	300 Mi.

CUBA

DOMINICAN
REPUBLIC

HAITI

PUERTO RICO
(Acquired from
Spain, 1898)

VIRGIN IS.
(Acquired from
Denmark, 1916–1917)

19°N

PUERTO RICO

VIRGIN
ISLANDS

18°N

68°W

67°W

66°W

65°W

0	25	50 Km.
0	25	50 Mi.

AP® Edition

THE
AMERICAN PAGEANT

A History of the American People

FIFTEENTH EDITION

David M. Kennedy
Stanford University

Lizabeth Cohen
Harvard University

CENGAGE
Learning®

Australia • Brazil • Japan • Korea • Mexico • Singapore • Spain • United Kingdom • United States

CENGAGE
Learning®

The American Pageant, **Fifteenth Edition**
AP® Edition
Kennedy/Cohen

Senior Publisher: Suzanne Jeans

Senior Sponsoring Editor: Ann West

Senior Development Editor:
 Margaret McAndrew Beasley

Assistant Editor: Megan Chrisman

Editorial Assistant: Patrick Roach

Managing Media Editor: Lisa Ciccolo

Marketing Communications Manager:
 Glenn McGibbon

Marketing Program Manager: Caitlin Green

Marketing Coordinator: Lorreen R. Towle

Senior Content Project Manager:
 Carol Newman

Senior Art Director: Cate Rickard Barr

Senior Print Buyer: Sandee Milewski

Senior Rights Acquisition Specialist:
 Jennifer Meyer Dare

Production Service/Compositor:
 Lachina Publishing Services

Photo Researcher: Picture Research
 Consultants

Text Designer: Diane Beasley

Cover Designer: Cabbage Design

Cover Image: Figurehead of Columbia from the
 prow of the ship Benmore, ca. 1870/
 Mariner's Museum, Newport News, VA,
 photo by Jason Copes

Associate Content Developer, Advanced
 and Elective Products Program:
 Ashley Bargende

Senior Media Developer, Advanced and
 Elective Products Program: Philip Lanza

Editorial Coordinator, Advanced and Elective
 Product Programs: Jean Woy

For product information and technology assistance, contact us at
Cengage Learning Customer & Sales Support, 1-888-915-3276.
For permission to use material from this text or product,
submit all requests online at **www.cengage.com/permissions.**
Further permissions questions can be e-mailed to
permissionrequest@cengage.com.

Library of Congress Control Number: 2011943904

AP Edition:

ISBN-13: 978-1-111-83106-6

ISBN-10: 1-111-83106-8

Cengage Learning
200 First Stamford Place, 4th Floor
Stamford, CT 06902
USA

Cengage Learning is a leading provider of customized learning solutions with office locations around the globe, including Singapore, the United Kingdom, Australia, Mexico, Brazil and Japan. Locate your local office at **international.cengage.com/region.**

Cengage Learning products are represented in Canada by Nelson Education, Ltd.

For your course and learning solutions, visit **www.cengage.com.**

To find online supplements and other instructional support, please visit **www.cengagebrain.com.**

National Geographic Learning/Cengage Learning is pleased to offer our college-level materials to high schools for Advanced Placement®, honors, and electives courses. To contact your National Geographic Learning representative, please call us toll-free at 1-888-915-3276 or visit us at http://ngl.cengage.com/.

Printed in the United States of America
5 6 7 8 17 16 15 14

X003200918909V

ABOUT THE AUTHORS

David M. Kennedy is the Donald J. McLachlan Professor of History Emeritus and Co-Director of The Bill Lane Center for the Study of the North American West at Stanford University, where he has taught for four decades. Born and raised in Seattle, he received his undergraduate education at Stanford and did his graduate training at Yale in American Studies, combining the fields of history, economics, and literature. His first book, *Birth Control in America: The Career of Margaret Sanger* (1970), was honored with both the Bancroft Prize and the John Gilmary Shea Prize. His study of the World War I era, *Over Here: The First World War and American Society* (1980; rev. ed., 2005), was a Pulitzer Prize finalist. In 1999 he published *Freedom from Fear: The American People in Depression and War, 1929–1945*, which won the Pulitzer Prize for History, as well as the Francis Parkman Prize, the English-Speaking Union's Ambassador's Prize, and the Commonwealth Club of California's Gold Medal for Literature. At Stanford he teaches both undergraduate and graduate courses in American political, diplomatic, intellectual, and social history, as well as in American literature. He has received several teaching awards, including the Dean's Award for Distinguished Teaching and the Hoagland Prize for Excellence in Undergraduate Teaching. He has been a visiting professor at the University of Florence, Italy, and in 1995–1996 served as the Harmsworth Professor of American History at Oxford University. He has also served on the Advisory Board for the PBS television series, *The American Experience*, and as a consultant to several documentary films, including *The Great War*, *Cadillac Desert*, and *Woodrow Wilson*. From 1990 to 1995 he chaired the Test Development Committee for the Advanced Placement United States History examination. He is an elected Fellow of the American Academy of Arts and Sciences and of the American Philosophical Society and served from 2002 to 2011 on the board of the Pulitzer Prizes. Married and the father of two sons and a daughter, in his leisure time he enjoys hiking, bicycling,

river-rafting, flying, sea-kayaking, and fly-fishing. He is currently writing a book on the American national character.

Lizabeth Cohen is the Howard Mumford Jones Professor of American Studies in the history department of Harvard University. In 2007–2008 she was the Harmsworth Professor of American History at Oxford University. Previously she taught at New York University (1992–1997) and Carnegie Mellon University (1986–1992). Born and raised in the New York metropolitan area, she received her A.B. from Princeton University and her M.A. and Ph.D. from the University of California at Berkeley. Her first book, *Making a New Deal: Industrial Workers in Chicago, 1919–1939* (1990), won the Bancroft Prize in American History and the Philip Taft Labor History Award, and was a finalist for the Pulitzer Prize. In 2008 it was reissued in a second edition with a new introduction. Her article "Encountering Mass Culture at the Grassroots: The Experience of Chicago Workers in the 1920s" (1989) was awarded the Constance Roarke Prize of the American Studies Association. Her most recent book, *A Consumers' Republic: The Politics of Mass Consumption in Postwar America* (2003), explored how an economy and culture built around mass consumption shaped social life and politics in post–World War II America. An article related to this book, "From Town Center to Shopping Center: The Reconfiguration of Community Marketplaces in Postwar America" (1996), was honored as the best article in urban history by the Urban History Association and received the ABC-CLIO, America: History and Life Award for the journal article that most advances previously unconsidered topics. She is currently writing a book, *Saving America's Cities: Ed Logue and the Struggle to Renew Urban America in the Suburban Age*, on urban renewal in American cities after World War II. At Harvard, she teaches courses in twentieth-century American history, with particular attention to the intersection of social and cultural life and politics, and in 2011 she was named the Interim Dean of the Radcliffe Institute for Advanced Study. Before attending graduate school, she taught history at the secondary level and worked in history and art museums. She continues to help develop public history programs for general audiences through museums and documentary films. She is married to an historian of modern France, with whom she has two daughters. For leisure, she enjoys swimming and bicycling with her family, watching films, and reading fiction.

Thomas A. Bailey (1903–1983) was the original author of *The American Pageant* and saw it through its first seven editions. He taught history for nearly forty years at Stanford University, his alma mater. Long regarded as one of the nation's leading historians of American diplomacy, he was honored by his colleagues in 1968 with election to the presidencies of both the Organization of American Historians and the Society for Historians of American Foreign Relations. He was the author, editor, or co-editor of some twenty books, but the work in which he took most pride was *The American Pageant*, through which, he liked to say, he had taught American history to several million students.

BRIEF CONTENTS

Part One

Founding the New Nation

C. 33,000 B.C.E.–1783 C.E.

Part Two

Building the New Nation

C. 1776–1860

Part Three

Testing the New Nation

1820–1877

Part Four

Forging an Industrial Society

1865–1909

Part Five

Struggling for Justice at Home and Abroad

1901–1945

Part Six

Making Modern America

1945 TO THE PRESENT

APPENDIX

CONTENTS

Part One

Founding the New Nation
C. 33,000 B.C.E.–1783 C.E.
2

1   New World Beginnings   33,000 B.C.E.–1769 C.E.   4

The geology of the New World • Native Americans before Columbus •
Europeans and Africans • Columbus and the early explorers • The ecological
consequences of Columbus's discovery • The conquest of Mexico • Spain
builds a New World empire

2   The Planting of English America   1500–1733   24

England on the eve of empire • The expansion of Elizabethan England • The
planting of Jamestown, 1607 • English settlers and Native Americans •
The growth of Virginia and Maryland • England in the Caribbean • Settling
the Carolinas and Georgia

Part Two

Building the New Nation
c. 1776–1860
156

Part Three

Testing the New Nation
1820–1877
336

Part Four

Forging an Industrial Society
1865–1909
486

26 The Great West and the Agricultural Revolution
1865–1896

27 Empire and Expansion   1890–1909

Part Five

Struggling for Justice at Home and Abroad
1901–1945
636

Part Six

❖◆❖

Making Modern America
1945 to the Present

828

You will find many additional text-wide resources, including a complete annotated **Suggested Readings** bibliography, a **Glossary of People to Know**, and **An American Profile: The United States and Its Peoples in Comparative Perspective**, on *The American Pageant* website found at www.cengagebrain.com

MAPS

FIGURES

TABLES

PREFACE

This fifteenth edition of *The American Pageant* reflects our continuing collaboration to bring the most recent scholarship about American history to the broadest possible student audience, while preserving the readability that has long been the *Pageant*'s hallmark. We are often told that the *Pageant* stands out as the only American history text with a distinctive personality. We define its leading characteristics as clarity, concreteness, a strong emphasis on major themes, integration of a broad range of historical topics into a coherent and clutter-free narrative, attention to a variety of interpretive perspectives, and a colorful writing style leavened, as appropriate, with wit. That personality, we strongly believe, is what has made the *Pageant* both appealing and useful to countless students for more than five decades.

Our collaboration on the *Pageant* reflects our respective scholarly interests, which are complementary to a remarkable degree. David Kennedy is primarily a political and economic historian, while Lizabeth Cohen's work emphasizes social and cultural history. Together, we have once again revised the *Pageant* chapter by chapter, even paragraph by paragraph, guided by our shared commitment to tell the story of the American past as vividly and clearly as possible, without sacrificing a sense of the often sobering seriousness of history, and of its sometimes challenging complexity.

Goals of *The American Pageant*

Like its predecessors, this edition of *The American Pageant* seeks to cultivate in its readers the capacity for balanced judgment and informed understanding about American society by holding up to the present the mirror and measuring rod that is the past. The division of the book into six parts, each with an introductory essay, encourages students to understand that the study of history is not just a matter of piling up mountains of facts, but is principally concerned with discovering complex patterns of change over time and organizing seemingly disparate events, actions, and ideas into meaningful chains of cause and consequence. The narrative propels the story, but throughout, we bring in voices from the past to encourage critical thinking. Boxed quotes help students hear the language of real people who experienced historical events.

"Examining the Evidence" features give students an opportunity to deepen their understanding of the historical craft by conveying how historians develop interpretations of the past through research in many different kinds of primary sources. Here students learn to investigate a wide range of historical documents and artifacts: correspondence between Abigail and John Adams in 1776, and what it reveals about women's place in the American Revolution; the Gettysburg Address and the light it sheds not only on President Lincoln's brilliant oratory but also on his vision of the American nation; a letter from a black freedman to his former master in 1865 that illuminates his family's experience in slavery as well as their hopes for a new life; the manuscript census of 1900 and what it teaches us about immigrant households on the Lower East Side of New York at the dawn of the twentieth century; and a new kind of architectural structure—the shopping mall—and how it changed both consumers' behavior and politicians' campaign tactics after World War II. Working with primary sources such as these helps prepare students for the challenging Document-Based Questions that they will encounter on the AP® U.S. History exam.

Thus, the book's goal is not to teach the art of prophecy but the much subtler and more difficult arts of seeing things in context, of understanding the roots and direction and pace of change, and of distinguishing what is truly new under the sun from what is not. The study of history, it has been rightly said, does not make one smart for the next time, but wise forever.

We hope that the *Pageant* will help to develop the art of critical thinking in its readers, and that those who use the book will take from it both a fresh appreciation of what has gone before and a seasoned perspective on what is to come. We hope, too, that readers will take as much pleasure in reading *The American Pageant* as we have had in writing it.

Changes in the AP® Fifteenth Edition

As in past revisions, we have updated and streamlined the text narrative, with some reorganization of content and expansion of the discussion of social and economic history.

Cultural History

This edition also offers markedly deeper explorations of the cultural innovations, artistic movements, and intellectual doctrines that have engaged and inspired Americans and shaped the course of American history.

AP® and Advanced Placement Program® are trademarks registered and/or owned by the College Board, which was not involved in the production of, and does not endorse, this product.

We believe that works of the imagination are an organic part of the larger historical picture, and that they both reflect and mold the society that gives rise to them. Readers will accordingly find substantially enhanced treatment of transcendentalism in Chapter 15, of post–Civil War literature and art in Chapter 25, the transnational spread of artistic "modernism" in Chapter 31, and late-twentieth-century letters, art, and architecture in Chapters 37 and 42. We have also added a new "Thinking Globally" essay on twentieth-century modernism and a new "Makers of America" feature on the Beat Generation of the 1950s. In all cases we have closely tied the discussion of these cultural and intellectual developments to the broader social and political contexts of which they were integral parts.

Global Context

We have also further expanded the *Pageant*'s treatment of the global context of American history. Today, political leaders, capital investment, consumer products, rock bands, the Internet, and much else constantly traverse the globe. But even before sophisticated technology and mass communication, complex exchanges among peoples and nations around the world deeply shaped the course of American history. Students will frequently encounter in these pages the people, ideas, and events that crossed national borders to influence the experience of the United States. They will also be invited to compare salient aspects of American history with developments elsewhere in the world. We believe that a full understanding of what makes America exceptional requires knowing about other societies, and knowing when and why America's path followed or departed from that taken by other nations.

Within each chapter, both text and graphics help students compare American developments to developments around the world. Railroad building, cotton production, city size and urban reform strategies, immigration, automobile ownership, the economic effects of the Great Depression, women's participation in voting and the work force, the cultural and artistic phenomena of modernism and postmodernism, and much more should now be understood as part of world trends, not just as isolated American experiences. New boxed quotes bring more international voices to the events chronicled in the *Pageant*'s historical narrative. Updated "Varying Viewpoints" essays reflect new interpretations of significant trends and events, emphasizing, when appropriate, their global contexts.

We have revised and expanded the "Thinking Globally" essays. Two such essays within each of the *Pageant*'s six parts present different aspects of the American experience contextualized within world history. Readers learn how developments in North America were part of worldwide phenomena, be it the challenge to empire in the eighteenth century, the rise of socialist ideology in the nineteenth century, or the globalization that followed World War II. Students also see how key aspects of American history—such as participating in the slave trade and its abolition, making a revolution for independence, creating a more united modern state in the mid-nineteenth century, and struggling to survive the Great Depression and World War II—were encountered by other nations but resolved in distinctive ways according to each country's history, cultural traditions, and political and economic structures.

Visual and Pedagogical Support

This edition also gives renewed attention to teaching strategies and pedagogical materials aimed at helping students deepen their comprehension of American history. Much new visual material—documentary images, graphs, and tables—illuminates complex and important historical ideas. Readers will also find redesigned maps with topographical detail and clear labeling to better communicate the text's analytical points. Key terms are printed in bold in each chapter and defined in a glossary at the end of the book. Every chapter concludes with an expanded chronology and a list of readable books to consult "To Learn More." (A fuller, chapter-by-chapter annotated bibliography suitable for deeper research is provided on the student Web site.) In addition, a list of the chapter key terms and a list of "People to Know"—created to help students focus on the most significant people introduced in that chapter—appear at the end of each chapter to help students review chapter highlights. Both lists are also included on the student Web site with expanded definitions. A revised Appendix contains annotated copies of the Declaration of Independence and Constitution and key historical events and dates such as admission of the states and presidential elections. On the Web site (located at www.cengagebrain.com), students will also find an extensive visual profile of the United States with charts and graphs illustrating many aspects of the American historical experience as well as comparisons to other nations. See the Supplements section below for a complete description of the many materials found there. It is our hope that readers will view our Web site as an exploratory laboratory enhancing *The American Pageant*'s text.

Chapter-by-Chapter Revision Details

Chapter 4—expanded Thinking Globally essay "The Atlantic Slave Trade, 1500–1860"

Chapter 7—new material on women's role in the Revolutionary War

Chapter 8—new material in Varying Viewpoints essay "Whose Revolution?"

Chapter 9—new material in Varying Viewpoints essay "The Constitution: Revolutionary or Counterrevolutionary?"

Chapter 10—new material on conflicts over government powers

Chapter 13—updating of voter turnout data

Chapter 15—new material on art and architecture in "Artistic Achievements" section; new material on romanticism and Margaret Fuller; new boxed quote from Washington Irving in "The Blossoming of a National Literature" section

Chapter 16—expanded Thinking Globally essay "The Struggle to Abolish Slavery"

Chapter 19—new material in Varying Viewpoints essay "The Civil War: Repressible or Irrepressible?"

Chapter 21—new material in Varying Viewpoints essay "What Were the Consequences of the Civil War?"

Chapter 25—new material on realism, naturalism, and regionalism, including Henry James, Edith Wharton, Theodore Dreiser, Kate Chopin, and Henry Adams, in "Literary Landmarks" section; under "Artistic Triumphs," new brief discussions of Thomas Eakins, Winslow Homer, and Frederick Law Olmsted

Chapter 31—new material on Ernest Hemingway, Gertrude Stein, T. S. Eliot, Ezra Pound, Robert Frost, Carl Sandburg, Sinclair Lewis, William Faulkner, and Eugene O'Neill; new boxed quotes from Mencken and Henry van Dyck and Faulkner; new Thinking Globally essay on modernism

Chapter 37—new material in "A Cultural Renaissance" section on abstract expressionism, Frank Lloyd Wright, Louis Kahn, John Updike, John Cheever, Gore Vidal, J. D. Salinger, Richard Wright, Harper Lee, Ralph Ellison, Robert Penn Warren, Flannery O'Connor; new boxed quotes from Allen Ginsburg and Arthur Miller; new Makers of America essay "The Beat Generation"

Chapter 41—new discussion of the Great Recession, the election of 2010, and the troubled Obama presidency

Chapter 42—new material on postmodernist thought, architecture, music, visual arts, literature, and film; new boxed quote from Twyla Tharp; new image of senior female military officer

AP® Test Preparation

This edition offers many opportunities to work with primary sources and features that will give students a test preparation advantage. The book begins with an overview on how to prepare for the AP® U.S. History exam and what to expect in particular from the exam, including test-taking strategies and examples for the different types of questions asked. A Correlation Guide provides *American Pageant*, Fifteenth Edition page references for the themes and topics found in the College Board's Course Description for United States History. With the help of teachers, these correlations will allow students to pinpoint exactly what they need to read in the textbook to make sure they are well prepared to take the exam.

Each chapter of the text ends with a review section containing a set of multiple-choice questions similar to those found on the AP® examination. Revised by Stacie Berman of Edward R. Murrow High School, Brooklyn, New York, these questions provide an opportunity for students to test their understanding of the chapter and practice answering the types of questions they will find on the U.S. History exam. Students will also have an opportunity to practice essay writing for the Document-Based Questions (DBQs) and free-response questions. Fifteen practice DBQs and eighteen practice free-response questions are included at the end of the book. The DBQs were written, edited, and reviewed by Tim Greene of Jersey Shore Area High School, Jersey Shore, Pennsylvania, and they closely follow the *Pageant's* narrative structure, with at least two questions for each of the textbook's six major sections. The questions are intended to help students use historical thinking skills to analyze and review major themes in those sections. The DBQs were designed to become more challenging as students advance through the text. The beginning exercises include five primary source documents; the later exercises include up to eleven documents. This progression will allow students to gain confidence in working with a relatively small number of documents in the earlier exercises before going to those that offer the same number of documents as an actual AP® U.S. History exam. The eighteen free-response questions were also revised by Tim Greene. Like the DBQs, these questions have been chosen to match the narrative structure of the text and to cover the major time periods and themes of the course.

Supplements Available with *The American Pageant, Fifteenth Edition*

Teacher Resources

Everything you need to teach the Advanced Placement U.S. History course with *The American Pageant*, AP® Edition can be found on a single Web site, using one single sign-on (SSO). Register at http://login.cengage.com and add *The American Pageant*, AP® 15th Edition to your bookshelf to get instant access to most of the resources described below.

Instructor Companion Site The protected AP® U.S. History teaching materials contained here include the

Teacher's Resource Guide, answers to the end-of-chapter multiple-choice questions, guidance and sample essays for the free response questions found at the end of the student text, customizable Microsoft® PowerPoint® slides of lecture outlines and images from the text; and JoinIn® PowerPoint® slides with clicker content.

Teacher's Resource Guide Written by Warren Hierl of the Career Center, Winston-Salem, North Carolina, this manual is based on the college Instructor's Resource Manual. It contains focus questions, chapter themes, chapter summaries, suggested lecture or discussion topics, additional class topics, character sketches with questions for class discussion, and "Makers of America" activities. Additionally, select chapters have activities on the great debates in American history, thus expanding and asking questions about the "Varying Viewpoints." Material developed just for AP® teachers includes an introduction to teaching the course, a pacing guide, and AP® Focus sections for each chapter of the text that relate chapter topics to likely AP® exam questions. The Teacher's Resource Guide also includes answers to the text's end-of-chapter multiple-choice questions as well as guidance and sample essays for the free-response questions found at the end of the student text.

AP® Teacher's Resource DVD with ExamView® and JoinIn® This dual-platform, all-in-one multimedia resource includes the Teacher's Resource Guide; a Test Bank that includes short-answer, multiple-choice, and essay questions; Microsoft® PowerPoint® slides of both lecture outlines and images and maps from the text that can be used as offered or customized by importing personal lecture slides or other material; and JoinIn® PowerPoint® slides with clicker content. Also included is ExamView, an easy-to-use assessment and tutorial system that allows teachers to create, deliver, and customize tests in minutes. Teachers can build tests with as many as 250 questions using up to 12 question types, and using ExamView's complete word-processing capabilities, they can enter an unlimited number of new questions or edit existing ones.

A printed version of the Test Bank, called the **Quizbook**, is also available to teachers using *The American Pageant*, AP® Fifteenth Edition.

WebTutor™ on Blackboard® and WebTutor™ on WebCT® With WebTutor's text-specific, preformatted content and total flexibility, teachers can easily create and manage their own custom course Web site. WebTutor's course management tool gives teachers the ability to provide virtual office hours, post syllabi, set up threaded discussions, track student progress with the quizzing material, and much more. For students, WebTutor offers real-time access to a full array of study tools, including animations and videos that bring the book's topics to life, plus chapter summaries, glossary flashcards, practice quizzes, and Web links. Ask your sales representative about available discounts.

Aplia™ Aplia™ is an online interactive learning solution that improves comprehension and outcomes by increasing student effort and engagement. Founded by a professor to enhance his own courses, Aplia provides automatically graded assignments with detailed, immediate explanations and innovative teaching materials. Our easy-to-use system has been used by more than 1,000,000 students at over 1,800 institutions. Chapter assignments developed specifically for *The American Pageant* include map- and content-based questions for each chapter, as well as primary source activities grouped around important topics. A course management system allows teachers to post announcements, upload course materials, host student discussions, e-mail students, and manage the gradebook. Teachers receive personalized support from a knowledgeable and friendly support team, who also offer assistance in customizing assignments to teacher course schedules. Ask your sales representative about available discounts.

Student Resources

Fast Track to a 5: Preparing for the AP® United States History Examination Written by Stacie Berman, Edward R. Murrow High School, Brooklyn, New York, and Mark Epstein, Greenwich High School, Greenwich, Connecticut, this is a test preparation manual keyed to the fourteenth and fifteenth editions of *The American Pageant*. It includes an introduction to the student, a diagnostic test, review sections with questions, and two complete practice tests in AP® format. It can be purchased with a text or separately.

Student Guidebook This tool is available in printed form. Written by John Irish of John Paul II High School in Plano, Texas, the Guidebook offers a variety of useful practice exercises to help students prepare for class and for exams. Features include a checklist of learning objectives and glossary terms to help students review the chapter; sections of questions including true/false, multiple-choice, identification, matching people, places, and events, putting things in order, and matching cause and effect; questions to help students develop historical skills and map mastery; and a final review section that allows students to apply what they have learned in the chapter. Ask your sales representative about available discounts.

Book Companion Site *The American Pageant* Web site features an assortment of resources to help students master the text content. The Web site includes glossaries, flashcards, crossword puzzles, tutorial quizzes authored by Jason Ripper of Everett Community College, Web links, and annotated bibliographies. Available at www.cengagebrain.com.

CourseMate Cengage Learning's CourseMate for *The American Pageant*, AP® Fifteenth Edition provides additional interactive learning, study, and exam preparation tools that support the printed textbook. The CourseMate site includes an integrated ebook, quizzes, flashcards, videos, and EngagementTracker, a first-of-its-kind tool that monitors student engagement in the course. In addition, this CourseMate website provides an online version of *FastTrack to a 5: Preparing for the AP® United States History Examination*, including review material and interactive multiple choice quizzes and diagnostic and practice tests. Ask your sales representative about available discounts.

CL eBook This interactive multimedia ebook links out to rich media assets such as video and MP3 chapter summaries. Through this ebook, students can also access self-test quizzes, chronology exercises, primary source documents with critical thinking questions, and interactive (zoomable) maps. Ask your sales representative about available discounts.

Additional Resources

Print Reader Program Cengage Learning publishes a number of readers, some containing exclusively primary sources, others a combination of primary and secondary sources, and some designed to guide students through the process of historical inquiry. *The American Spirit* Volumes I and II are print, primary source readers compiled and edited by David M. Kennedy and designed specifically to accompany *The American Pageant*. Visit www.cengage.com/history for a complete list of readers.

CourseReader for U.S. History CourseReader offers a way for teachers to build customized online readers for their courses. Selecting documents from a rich database of primary and secondary sources, including many from the Gale collections, teachers can create their own reader to match the specific needs of their course. An Editor's Choice developed just for AP® courses for *The American Pageant* provides a useful starting point. Go to www.cengage.com/coursereader for more information, and ask your sales representative about available discounts.

Acknowledgments

Many people have contributed to this revision of *The American Pageant*. Foremost among them are the countless students and teachers who have written unsolicited letters of comment or inquiry. We have learned from every one of them, and we encourage all readers to offer us suggestions for improving future editions. In particular, we wish to thank the following reviewers who gave us important feedback throughout the development of the fifteenth edition:

Jose Garcia, University of Central Florida
David Price, Santa Fe Community College
John Rawlins, Bowling Green State University
Lorna Rinear, Regis College
Jim Rogers, Louisiana State University at Alexandria
Kevin Sims, Cedarville University
Phyllis Soybel, College of Lake County
Joseph Zelasko, Mount Union College

We would also like to thank reviewers of the previous edition:

David Barber, University of Tennessee at Martin
Robert Berta, Northern Kentucky University
Timothy Buckner, Troy University
Cynthia Clark, University of Texas at Arlington
Matt Cone, Plano Senior High School, Plano, Texas
Will Corprew, Broome Community College
Charles Cox, Bridgewater State College
Chris Drake, Houston Community College
David Fitzpatrick, Washtenaw Community College
Christine Flood, University of North Carolina at Greensboro
Nancy Gentile Ford, Bloomsburg University
Ray Gunn, University of Utah
Neil Hamilton, Spring Hill College
Marc Horger, Ohio State University
Ronald Huetter, Suffolk County Community College
Gary Huey, Ferris State University
Don Jacobson, Oakton Community College
Jon Timothy Kelly, West Valley College
Paul Kelton, University of Kansas
Nonie Kouneski, Southwest High School, Minneapolis, Minnesota
Stacy Kowtko, Spokane Community College
Tim Lehman, Rocky Mountain College
Scott Lingenfelter, Roosevelt University
Robert Mayer, Kean University
Kenneth Millen-Penn, Fairmont State University
Sharon Musher, Richard Stockton College of New Jersey
Michael Namorato, University of Mississippi
Bridget Nimmer, Wauwatosa West High School, Wauwatosa, Wisconsin
Deanne Nuwer, University of Southern Mississippi
Jane O'Steen, Leesburg High School, Leesburg, Florida
Keith Pomakoy, Adirondack Community College
David Rayson, Normandale Community College
Lewie Reece, Anderson University

Marc Rodriguez, University of Notre Dame
Clyde Root, Bethel College
Horacio Salinas, Laredo Community College
Aldorigo Scopino, Central Connecticut State University
Karen J. Smith, Columbia Southern University
Robert St. Clair, Central Virginia Community College

Several people deserve special mention for their assistance:

Bob Burns, Valley Christian High School
Annika Christensen, Barnard College

Adrian Finucane, University of Kansas
Maria Ponomarenko, Stanford University
Scott Spillman, Stanford University
Daniel C. Wewers, Yale Law School

Our warm thanks to each of them.

David M. Kennedy
Lizabeth Cohen

Correlation of Themes for U.S. History AP® Course
to *The American Pageant*, 15th Edition

Theme	Correlation to the pages of *The American Pageant*
American Diversity The diversity of the American people and the relationships among different groups. The roles of race, class, ethnicity, and gender in the history of the United States.	66–67, 137, 293–294, 347–348, 528–529, 550–551, 562–563, 575–584, 683–684, 724, 867–868, 904–906, 930–931, 992–996, 1011
American Identity Views of the American national character and ideas about American exceptionalism. Recognizing regional differences within the context of what it means to be an American.	57–58, 95–96, 230–231, 234, 236–237, 252–253, 268–269, 270–271, 273–274, 284–285, 374–375, 422–423, 560–561, 870–871
Culture Diverse individual and collective expressions through literature, art, philosophy, music, theater, and film throughout U.S. history. Popular culture and the dimensions of cultural conflict within American society.	90–91, 94–95, 161, 324–332, 396–398, 565–567, 568–570, 715–716, 717, 719, 720–724, 880–883, 884–887, 910–914, 1007–1011
Demographic Changes Changes in birth, marriage, and death rates; life expectancy and family patterns; population size and density. The economic, social, and political effects of immigration, internal migration, and migration networks.	256–259, 276–277, 278–284, 500–501, 539–549, 575–584, 703–704, 767, 862, 903, 992, 995, 996, 1000–1007, 1005
Economic Transformations Changes in trade, commerce, and technology across time. The effects of capitalist development, labor and unions, and consumerism.	14, 31–34, 60–62, 64–65, 115, 285, 288–291, 292, 293–301, 302–304, 512–530, 531, 532–536, 537, 862–864
Environment Ideas about the consumption and conservation of natural resources. The impact of population growth, industrialization, pollution, and urban and suburban expansion.	278–281, 285, 288–290, 295–296, 338, 340–341, 514–517, 523–525, 539–545, 549–550, 580, 594–595, 650–651, 652–653, 654–655
Globalization Engagement with the rest of the world from the fifteenth century to the present: colonialism, mercantilism, global hegemony, development of markets, imperialism, and cultural exchange.	14–15, 27–28, 64, 83–84, 114–115, 302–304, 513, 608–610, 611, 616–617, 620–623, 627–630, 632, 842–843, 991–992
Politics and Citizenship Colonial and revolutionary legacies, American political traditions, growth of democracy, and the development of the modern state. Defining citizenship; struggles for civil rights.	113–115, 134–137, 138, 139, 152–153, 156–157, 158–160, 172–174, 177–178, 181–182, 895–898, 899, 900, 903–906, 910–914
Reform Diverse movements focusing on a broad range of issues, including anti-slavery, education, labor, temperance, women's rights, civil rights, gay rights, war, public health, and government.	317–318, 319, 349–350, 352–353, 354–357, 396–398, 530–533, 536–537, 564, 646–647, 895–898, 899, 900, 903–906, 910–914

Theme	Correlation to the pages of *The American Pageant*
Religion The variety of religious beliefs and practices in America from prehistory to the twenty-first century; influence of religion on politics, economics, and society.	22, 37, 41–44, 45–46, 53–55, 86–88, 98, 157, 309–310, 374–375, 549, 551–553, 580–581, 709–710, 951–953
Slavery and Its Legacies in North America Systems of slave labor and other forms of unfree labor (e.g., indentured servitude, contract labor) in American Indian societies, the Atlantic World, and the American South and West. The economics of slavery and its racial dimensions. Patterns of resistance and the long-term economic, political, and social effects of slavery.	12, 14, 17, 33–35, 38, 61–62, 63, 64–65, 66–67, 68–69, 70, 81, 83, 340–350, 381–383
War and Diplomacy Armed conflict from the precolonial period to the twenty-first century; impact of war on American foreign policy and on politics, economy, and society.	29, 98, 100–107, 124–125, 128–130, 132–151, 224–231, 244, 245, 368–377, 421–427, 429, 431–434, 678–694, 807–814

Correlation of Topics for U.S. History AP® Course
to *The American Pageant*, 15th Edition

Topic	Correlation to the pages of *The American Pageant*
1. Pre-Columbian Societies	
A. Early inhabitants of the Americas	5–10
B. American Indian empires in Mesoamerica, the Southwest, and the Mississippi Valley	5–7, 8–10
C. American Indian cultures of North America at the time of European contact	8–10, 28–31, 36–37
2. Transatlantic Encounters and Colonial Beginnings, 1492–1690	
A. First European contacts with American Indians	14–15, 28–31, 36–37, 47–48
B. Spain's empire in North America	15–19, 20–22
C. French colonization of Canada	98–100
D. English settlement of New England, the Mid-Atlantic region, and the South	24–28, 31–32, 34–40, 41–44, 53–59
E. From servitude to slavery in the Chesapeake region	38, 60–62, 63–64
F. Religious diversity in the American colonies	32, 35, 41–44, 45–46, 53–55, 73, 86–88
G. Resistance to colonial authority: Bacon's Rebellion, the Glorious Revolution, and the Pueblo Revolt	50, 61–62
3. Colonial North America, 1690–1754	
A. Population growth and immigration	78–80
B. Transatlantic trade and the growth of seaports	83–85
C. The eighteenth-century back country	79–80
D. Growth of plantation economies and slave societies	38, 60–70
E. The Enlightenment and the Great Awakening	87–88, 188
F. Colonial governments and imperial policy in British North America	114–128
4. The American Revolutionary Era, 1754–1789	
A. The French and Indian War	104–112
B. The Imperial Crisis and resistance to Britain	113—131
C. The War for Independence	122–131, 132–155
D. State constitutions and the Articles of Confederation	162–168
E. The federal Constitution	168–179, 181–182
5. The Early Republic, 1789–1815	
A. Washington, Hamilton, and shaping of the national government	181–184, 190, 192–193
B. Emergence of political parties: Federalists and Republicans	186, 198–201
C. Republican Motherhood and education for women	159–160, 313–314
D. Beginnings of the Second Great Awakening	307, 308–310, 313, 314, 348, 396
E. Significance of Jefferson's presidency	202–218, 222–223
F. Expansion into the trans-Appalachian West; American Indian resistance	148–149, 219–220, 233–234
G. Growth of slavery and free Black communities	157–158, 234, 235, 338–352
H. The War of 1812 and its consequences	224–231, 244, 245
6. Transformation of the Economy and Society in Antebellum America	
A. The transportation revolution and creation of a national market economy	157, 296–304
B. Beginnings of industrialization and changes in social and class structures	285–295

PREPARING FOR THE AP® EXAM

*A*dvanced Placement is a challenging yet stimulating experience. Whether you are taking an AP® course at your school or you are working on AP® independently, the stage is set for a great intellectual experience. As the school year progresses and you burrow deeper and deeper into the course work, you can see the broad concepts, movements, conflicts, resolutions, and personalities that have shaped the history of the United States. Fleshing out those forces with a growing collection of nuances is exciting. More exciting still is recognizing references to those forces in the media.

But as spring approaches and the College Board examination begins to loom on the horizon, Advanced Placement can seem downright intimidating given the enormous scope and extent of the information that is required to score well. If you are intimidated by the College Board examination, you are certainly not alone.

The best way to deal with an AP® examination is to master it, not let it master you. If you manage your time effectively, you will eliminate one major obstacle—learning a considerable amount of material. In addition, if you can think of these tests as a way to show off how your mind works, you have a leg up: attitude *does* help. If you are not one of those students, there is still a lot you can do to sideline your anxiety. Focused review and practice time will help you master the examination so that you can walk in with confidence and get a 5.

Before the Exam

By February, long before the exam, you need to make sure that you are registered to take the test. Many schools take care of the paperwork and handle the fees for their AP® students, but check with your teacher or the AP® coordinator to make sure that you are on the list. This is especially important if you have a documented disability and need test accommodations. If you are studying AP® independently, call AP® Services at the College Board for the name of the local AP® coordinator, who will help you through the registration process.

The evening before the exam is not a great time for partying. Nor is it a great time for cramming. If you like, look over class notes or drift through your textbook, but concentrate on the broad outlines, not the small details, of the course. The evening before the exam *is* a great time to get your things together for the next day. Sharpen a fistful of no. 2 pencils with good erasers for the multiple-choice section of the test; set out several black or dark-blue ballpoint pens for the free-response questions; get a watch, as no cell phones are allowed in the testing room. Get a piece of fruit or a snack bar and a bottle of water for the break; make sure you have your Social Security number and whatever photo identification and admission ticket are required. Then relax. And get a good night's sleep. An extra hour of sleep is more valuable than an extra hour of study.

On the day of the examination, make certain to eat breakfast—fuel for the brain. Studies show that students who eat a hot breakfast before testing get higher grades. Be careful not to drink a lot of liquids, necessitating trips to the bathroom during the test. You need energy to power you through the test—and more. You will spend some time waiting while everyone is seated in the right room for the right test. That's before the test has even begun. You will be given a 15-minute break between Section I and Section II; the U.S. History exam lasts for over 3 hours. So be prepared for a long morning. You do not want to be distracted by a growling stomach or hunger pangs.

Be sure to wear comfortable clothes, taking along a sweater in case the heating or air-conditioning is erratic—and by all means wear your lucky socks if you have some.

Now go get a 5.

AP® and Advanced Placement Program® are trademarks registered and/or owned by the College Board, which was not involved in the production of, and does not endorse, this product.

TAKING THE AP® U.S. HISTORY EXAM

The AP® U.S. History exam consists of two sections: Section I has eighty multiple-choice questions. Section II, Part A, is a document-based question (DBQ). Section II, Part B and Part C, each have two free-response questions; you will be required to write an essay on one of the two questions in each of those parts. You will have 55 minutes for the multiple-choice portion of the test. Answer sheets for the multiple-choice questions are collected, and you will be given a 15-minute break. You then have 60 minutes for the DBQ—15 minutes for reading the documents and 45 minutes for writing the essay. You are given 70 minutes to write two essays you select from the free-response questions that make up Parts B and C. Keep an eye on your watch. Watch alarms are not allowed.

The College Board has identified twelve themes that run through a U.S. History course: *American Diversity*—how ethnicity, race, gender, and class have shaped the nation; *American Identity*—a variety of thoughts on American exceptionalism; *Culture*—the arts and their power to describe both cultural cohesion and cultural conflict; *Demographic Changes*—how population shifts have affected the way the nation developed; *Economic Transformations*—the development of American capitalism through changes in commerce, labor relations, and technology; *Environment*—the tension between using, conserving, and protecting natural resources; *Globalization*—the growing political, economic, and cultural connections between the U.S. and other nations; *Politics and Citizenship*—the elaboration of the American political system; *Reform*—various governmental or grassroots attempts to correct wrongs or improve American life; *Religion*—the impact of religious thought and expression on U.S. History; *Slavery and Its Legacies in North America*—forms of forced servitude and their social, economic, and political impact; *War and Diplomacy*—how war has transformed the nation itself and its relationship with the world. A theme won't appear in every chapter of the textbook, but it will turn up over and over again in the course. For example, Reform played a big role in the Constitutional Convention, in the 1830s and 1840s, during Reconstruction, and into the twentieth century in the form of the progressive movement, the New Deal, and the Great Society. The themes can give you a real assist in writing free-response essays; they provide the big idea, which you support with your historical facts.

This text provides you with many sample questions for the different types of questions asked on the AP® exam. A set of multiple-choice questions follows each chapter of the text. If you take a few minutes to answer the questions after reading each chapter, you'll test yourself on the main points of the chapter *and* get some nice practice on the AP® questioning style.

At the end of this book you'll find a complete set of document-based questions and free-response essay questions. Your instructor may assign certain questions or you may want to try some on your own.

But before you tackle any of these, you might want to read the sections that follow on test-taking strategies for each question type.

Strategies for the Multiple-Choice Section

Here are some rules of thumb to help you work your way through the multiple-choice questions:

- **Scoring** There are five possible answers for each question. Each correct answer is worth 1 point, and there is no penalty for an incorrect answer. Therefore, you should answer every question, even if you have to guess. Some students go through the questions quickly, answering the ones they know, and then go back to the questions they were unsure about. If you do this, make sure to skip the correct lines in the answer sheet.
- **Read the question carefully** Pressured for time, many students make the mistake of reading the questions too quickly or merely skim them. By reading a question carefully, you may already gain some idea about the correct answer. You can then look for it in the responses. Careful reading is especially important in EXCEPT questions.
- **Eliminate any answer you know is wrong** You can write on the multiple-choice questions in the test book. As you read through the responses, draw a line through any answer you know is wrong.
- **Read all of the possible answers, then choose the most accurate response** AP® exams are written to test your precise knowledge of a subject. Sometimes

there are a few probable answers but one of them is more specific. For example, a question dealing with the Open Door policy in 1899 may have an answer that seems correct: "It sought to promote U.S. interests overseas." However, there may be an even better answer, one that is more specific to the topic: "To provide the U.S. access to trade in Asia."

- **Avoid absolute responses** These answers often include the words *always* or *never*. For example, the statement "Jefferson always rejected the Hamiltonian economic program" is an overstatement in that Jefferson never attempted to eliminate one of the key features of Hamilton's economic program, the Bank of the United States.

- **Mark and skip tough questions** If you are hung up on a question, mark it in the margin of the question book. You can come back to it later if you have time. Make sure you skip that question on your answer sheet too.

Types of Multiple-Choice Questions

There are various kinds of multiple-choice questions. Here are some suggestions for how to approach each kind:

Classic/Best Answer Questions

This is the most common type of multiple-choice question. It simply requires you to read the question and select the most correct answer. For example:

1. All money bills originate in
   (A) the executive branch.
   (B) the Senate.
   (C) the House of Representatives.
   (D) the judicial branch.
   (E) the State Department.

ANSWER: **C.** This is a question that has only one correct answer. The Constitution provides for all money bills to originate in the House of Representatives.

EXCEPT Questions

In the EXCEPT question, all of the answers are correct but one. The best way to approach these questions is as true/false. Mark a T or F in the margin next to each possible answer. There should be only one false answer, and that is the one you should select. For example:

1. All of the following were advantages of the Union in the Civil War EXCEPT that
   (A) it needed only to fight a defensive war.
   (B) it was more industrialized than the South.
   (C) it had a larger population.

   (D) it had a more developed railway system than the South.
   (E) it had a stronger navy than the South.

ANSWER: **A.** The North had to conquer the South and therefore could not wage a defensive war. Options B–E are advantages of the Union.

List and Group Questions

In this type of question, there is a list of possible answers, and you must select the answer that contains the correct group of responses. These questions look hard, but you can simplify them by crossing out items from the list and then eliminating them in the answers below. For example:

1. According to the Constitution, as amended, which of the following is directly elected by the people?

To approach the question, draw a line through choice I, because the president and vice president are not elected directly but are chosen by the Electoral College. Then cross out any response that contains choice I.

~~I. The president and vice president~~
II. Members of the House of Representatives
III. Justices of the Supreme Court
IV. Senators

~~(A) I and II~~
(B) II and III
~~(C) I, II and III~~
~~(D) I and IV~~
(E) II and IV

Continue to cross out items that are wrong and the responses that contain them. Justices of the Supreme Court are appointed, not elected. Draw a line through III and answer (B), which contains choice III. Now you have narrowed down the possible responses to one.

ANSWER: **E.** Under the Constitution, including the Seventeenth Amendment, which provides for the direct election of senators, members of the House of Representatives and Senate are elected directly.

Chart/graph questions

These questions require you to examine the data on a chart or graph. While these questions are not difficult, spending too much time interpreting a chart or graph may slow you down. To avoid this problem, first read the question and all of the possible answers so that you know what you are looking for. Before you look at the graph, you may be able to eliminate some obviously incorrect responses. For example:

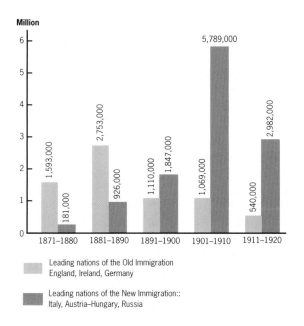

Leading nations of the Old Immigration
England, Ireland, Germany

Leading nations of the New Immigration::
Italy, Austria–Hungary, Russia

1. Which of the following statements does the graph above best support?
   (A) Immigration remained at the same level from 1871 to 1920.
   (B) The period 1871–1880 witnessed the largest immigration of New Immigrants in the late nineteenth century.
   (C) Most immigrants came from Italy and Germany.
   (D) Between 1911 and 1920 approximately 3 million immigrants came from England, Ireland, and Germany.
   (E) The period 1891–1900 was the first decade in the late nineteenth century in which the number of New Immigrants exceeded the number of Old Immigrants.

ANSWER: **E.** After analyzing the graph, option A can be eliminated because the measurement bars are not level in *any* period. Option B is incorrect because the total number of New Immigrants in 1871–1880 is the lowest of any decade represented. Option C is incorrect in that there is no way to tell from the graph what percentage of the immigrants came from a specific country. Option D is incorrect because this decade was actually the low point of immigration from England, Ireland, and Germany (540,000 contrasted with 2,928,000 in the period 1911–1920). Option E therefore is correct because the bar for New Immigrants is higher for the first time than the bar for Old Immigrants.

Political Cartoon Questions

These questions require you to interpret a political cartoon. Every political cartoon contains symbolism and a point of view. Examine the cartoon before you read the question and possible responses to determine what each part of the drawing represents and to identify the artist's viewpoint. For example:

THE BIG STICK IN THE CARIBBEAN SEA

1. What is the viewpoint expressed in the above cartoon?
   (A) The United States rejected the Roosevelt Corollary to the Monroe Doctrine.
   (B) Under Roosevelt the United States allowed European nations to take part in the colonization of South America.
   (C) Roosevelt brought the Caribbean under the control of the United States.
   (D) Roosevelt was protecting the Caribbean nations from U.S. intervention.
   (E) The United States in the early twentieth century began removing its military control of the Caribbean.

ANSWER: **C.** Roosevelt actually strengthened the Monroe Doctrine with his Roosevelt Corollary. Therefore, A and B are incorrect because one of the primary purposes of the Monroe Doctrine and the Roosevelt Corollary was to prevent European intervention in the Western Hemisphere. Because the United States consistently intervened in South American affairs, answers D and E are incorrect.

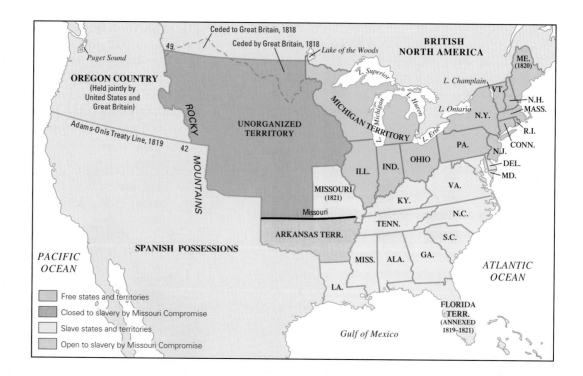

Interpreting a Map

For history students, maps are used to describe not just geography but social and political organization as well. Asked to interpret a map, you can pick up a lot of information just by looking at the key.

1. The map above shows the United States
   (A) at the end of the Revolutionary War.
   (B) following the end of the Mexican-American War.
   (C) after all of the eastern Native American tribes had been moved to reservations in the West.
   (D) after the passage of the Missouri Compromise.
   (E) at the outbreak of the Civil War.

ANSWER: **D.** At the end of the Revolutionary War the United States comprised the thirteen original colonies; therefore answer A is incorrect. B is incorrect for several reasons, foremost being the absence of Texas and the Mexican Cession on the map. There is no information on the map that indicates it has anything to do with Native American removal; thus answer C is incorrect. Answer E is incorrect because, although the map indicates free and slave states, it does not show states, such as California, Arkansas, Texas, and Oregon, that were present in 1861, when the Southern states began to secede.

Free-Response Questions

You are required to write essays for three free-response questions on the U.S. History examination. Section II, Part A, presents the Document-Based Question. It is mandatory. For the DBQ, you are given 15 minutes for reading the documents and organizing your material and 45 minutes for writing the essay. Section II, Parts B and C, has two standard free-response questions in each. You will be asked to write on one from Part B and one from Part C. You will have a total of 70 minutes for writing these two essays. Keep in mind that all free-response questions are likely to incorporate more than one of the College Board's twelve themes.

The Document-Based Question

The DBQ is considered by many students to be the most complex and challenging component of the AP® examination. As its name implies, the DBQ presents you with a wide variety of primary-source information in the form of ten or more documents. Primary sources are contemporaneous with a time period or event, and they include everything from maps, political cartoons, photographs, and illustrations to speeches, essays, books, documentaries, and editorials. Documents will *not* be taken from secondary sources, such as textbooks.

DBQ questions run the gamut from basic "why" and "explain" questions to "support or refute" and "how and why" questions. All free-response essays require you to utilize your knowledge of the topic, but with the DBQ your essay needs to be grounded on the documents. Your goal is to demonstrate your ability to tease out the thrust and substance of each document and then combine this information with your own general knowledge in an analytical and evaluative essay. The following are necessary for writing a quality DBQ essay:

- Background—your own knowledge of the topic
- Analysis—your ability to interpret and explain the documents
- Synthesis—your ability to blend your outside information with the information provided in the documents to explain an issue

There are fifteen DBQ practice questions at the end of this textbook. This includes thirteen DBQs from the fourteenth edition, with two new questions that were prepared for the fifteenth edition.

Take a look at an abbreviated DBQ, one that contains only four documents for explanation purposes.

(Remember, the DBQ for an AP® examination includes at least twice as many documents as we are using in this sample. You will have the opportunity to practice on full DBQs when you work on the DBQ practice questions at the end of your textbook.)

Question: Using the documents provided and your knowledge of the period, write an answer to the following question:

Analyze the factors that determined the degree of success that labor unions had in securing the goals that American workers desired during the years 1865–1900.

Document A: The Address of the National Labor [Union] Congress to the Working Men of the United States

Andrew C. Cameron, August, 1867

The question of all others which at present engrosses the attention of the American workman, and, in fact, the American people, is the proposed reduction of the hours of daily labor and the substitution of the eight- for the ten-hour system. . . . As might have been expected, the employing capitalists, aided by a venal press, have set up a howl of rage and protested the adoption of such [an] innovation. . . .

There are, probably, no organizations upon the nature of which so much ignorance exists, even among workingmen, or against which such persistent and systematic opposition has been urged, as trades unions. . . . [T]heir establishment has been beneficial to the community in general and the working classes in particular. . . .

Source: Excerpted from The Annals of America, *Vol. 10*

Document B: The Preamble to "The Constitution of the Knights of Labor," adopted 3 January 1878

[We] submit to the world the objects sought to be accomplished by our organization. . . .

. . .

2. To secure to the toilers a proper share of wealth they create. . . .

. . .

6. . . . the adopting of measures providing for the health and safety of those engaged in mining, manufacturing, or building pursuits.

. . .

11. The prohibition of the employment of children in workshops, mines, and factories. . . .

. . .

14. The reduction of the hours of labor to eight per day, so that the laborers may have more time for social enjoyment and intellectual improvement. . . .

Source: Excerpted from The Annals of America, *Vol. 10*

Document C: Earnings, Expenses and Conditions of Workingmen and Their Families

No. 51 [Family number], Machinist, American [birthplace]

EARNINGS

Of father	$540
Of mother	255
Of son, aged sixteen	255
Total	$1050

CONDITION

Family numbers 10—parents and eight children, five girls and three boys, aged from two to sixteen. Four of the children attend school. Father only works 30 weeks in the year, receives $3 per day for his services. They live in a comfortably furnished house, of 7 rooms, have a piano, take an interest in society and domestic affairs, are intelligent, but do not dress very well. Their expenditures are equal, but do not exceed their income. Father belongs to trades union, and is interested and benefited by and in it.

FOOD

Breakfast—Bread, meat and coffee.
Dinner—Bread, meat, vegetables and tea.
Supper—Bread, meat, vegetables and coffee.

COST OF LIVING

Rent	$300
Fuel	50
Meat	100
Groceries	200
Clothing	160
Boots and shoes	50
Dry goods	25
Books, papers, etc.	15
Trades union	10
Sickness [insurance]	50
Sundries	90
Total	$1050

No. 112 [Family number], Coal Miner, American [birthplace]

EARNINGS

Of father	$250

CONDITION

Family numbers 7—husband, wife, and five children, three girls and two boys, aged from three to nineteen years. Three of them go to the public school. Family live in 2 room tenement, in healthy locality, for which they pay $6 per month rent. The house is scantily furnished, without carpets, but is kept neat and clean. They are compelled to live very economically, and every cent they earn is used to the best advantage. Father had only thirty weeks work during the past year. He belongs to trades union. The figures for cost of living are actual and there is no doubt the family lived on the amount specified.

FOOD

Breakfast—Bread, coffee and salt meat.
Dinner—Meat, bread, coffee and butter.
Supper—Sausage, bread and coffee.

COST OF LIVING

Rent	$72
Fuel	20
Meat	20
Groceries	60
Clothing	28
Boots and shoes	15
Dry goods	20
Trades union	3
Sickness [insurance]	10
Sundries	5
Total	$253

Source: 1884, Illinois Bureau of Labor Statistics, Third Biennial Report, 1884 (excerpted from Hollitz, Thinking Through the Past, 2nd ed., Boston: Houghton Mifflin Co.)

Document D: Debs's Claim is Puerile: Violence the Strikers' Main Reliance to Insure Success

President Debs of the American Railway Union, President Gompers of the American Federation of Labor, and other labor leaders who are responsible for strikes, have repeatedly affirmed that during the present [Pullman] strike and in strikes in the past[,] all violent acts were done by men [who were] not strikers. . . . When several persons were shot by the United States troops, he claimed none of them was a member of the American Railway Union and instanced this fact to prove that the strikers were not the ones who were committing overt acts [of violence] . . . and are not accountable for the bloodshed, arson, destruction of property in other ways, hindrance to business, and other losses which the [state] always suffers when a big strike is in progress.

That the contrary is true is proved beyond cavil [frivolous objection] by reference to the history of every big strike ever ordered in this country. In a railway strike success can only be achieved by the forcible detention of trains . . . , and the forcible detention of trains means rioting, and perhaps bloodshed.

. . .

It is because Debs and his ilk cannot, and know they cannot, achieve their communistic ends by the ballot or in any other lawful way that they resort to the use of hurled rocks, blows with clubs, shots fired from ambush, and all the other base acts of a relentless and bloodthirsty guerilla warfare.

Source: New York Times, *11 July 1894 (excerpted from the* Times *through Proquest, an electronic database*

Steps in organizing and structuring the DBQ essay:

Step 1: Brainstorm ideas that relate to the question.
Step 2: Consider a structure for your response.
Step 3: Analyze each document. What is the meaning of the document? What or who is the source—the Supreme Court, a presidential candidate, a labor leader, a capitalist? The source provides important clues to the position being put forth in the document. As you analyze the meaning or significance of the document, jot down margin notes—generalizations that relate to the document. For example:

- **Margin note for Document A** Address to the NLU (National Labor Union) in support of the eight-hour day.
- **Margin note for Document B** Extract from the Knights of Labor constitution regarding higher wages, improved working conditions, and a shortened workday.
- **Margin note for Document C** Bureau of Labor Statistics cost-of-living figures for union members equals the amount paid in salary for the machinist, slightly less for the coal miner.
- **Margin note for Document D** Criticism of claim by Eugene Debs, president of the American Railway Union, that acts of violence were not perpetrated by union members and that Debs's union was interfering with the railroads. Suggestion that Debs is communistic.

When you begin to map out your essay, remember that the DBQ calls for a synthesis of the document information and your own knowledge of the topic. With that in mind, start with your own knowledge that the period 1865–1877 was characterized by tensions between labor and the business owners, or capitalists. You will need to point out the conditions—low pay and dangerous work environments—faced by workers. Documents A, B, and C provide the grist for this point; you might note that the sources for Documents A and B were partisan, while the source for Document C was nonpartisan. To assess the level of success for workers in achieving their objectives, you will need to address factors—in this case, obstacles—such as the role played by government in assisting the capitalist class put down strikes (for example, the Railroad Strike of 1877); the influx of millions of immigrants, which drove down wages; and the methods used by businesses and government to undermine union efforts. As you discuss these features, you should refer to the documents that support your own analysis. For example, the degree of success for the American workers in general and unions specifically was in part determined by the attitudes expressed in Document D, which portrays unions as violent. This turned public opinion against labor unions, therefore limiting their success.

Do not wait until you've read the documents to develop your own personal knowledge. Even before reading the documents, take a few minutes to brainstorm information that you can recall about the topic. If time permits, organize this information so that you can construct the essay while incorporating the documents into the essay. When the document information is similar to what you have brainstormed, present that knowledge as it is expressed in the documents. Possibly the document material can be used to help you analyze other issues.

Structure of a Free-Response Essay

In writing a free-response essay, whether a DBQ or a general free-response essay, you need the following:

- A well-developed thesis that sums up your perspective
- An effective analysis and appropriate use of information
- A lucidly cogent essay that is well structured and lucidly written

Below is one model for organizing your thoughts in preparation for writing the free-response and DBQ essays:

Thesis (opinion)
Supporting Arguments (major reasons, to be developed in the body paragraphs, that defend or support your thesis)
Structured Body Paragraphs
- *Topic Sentence*
  - supports the thesis
  - introduces the topic of the paragraph
- *Historical and Factual Information*
  - facts
  - details
  - statistics
  - quotes
- *Analysis*
  - explains the separate parts of your arguments
  - explains the significance of the information you present as it relates to the thesis

Framing the Debate To demonstrate an understanding of the complexity of the issue or question, you need to show that you are aware of both sides of the argument or perspective. This frames the debate for the reader. Thus in the introduction, you want to present the "other" view—the one you are *not* supporting. Make certain, however, that you do not develop the other perspective so fully that the reader is unclear about your thesis. Your objective is to convince the reader that you have a strong thesis and that it is well developed with historical information and analysis.

Outlining For each essay in Section II, the AP® examination has built in time for you to develop an outline.

Time spent on your outlines is important for a number of reasons:

- It prevents you from writing an essay that is unorganized because you begin writing whatever comes into your head at the moment.
- It helps you determine your perspective on the issue. If after completing an outline you realize that your information tends to support one view over the other, then this is the perspective you should develop.
- It provides you with a brief brainstorming opportunity before writing the essay.

Once you have outlined your essay, it is time to put pen to paper. Remember that examination readers are looking for a clear thesis backed up with specifics. Concentrate on setting out accurate information in straightforward, concise prose. You cannot mask vague information with elegant prose.

The questions at the end of your book will give you a good sense of the kinds of questions asked on the AP® U.S. History exam.

A Free-Response Question and Three Sample Essays

Having established the ingredients of a free-response answer, let us now look at three essays—one excellent (grade: 9), one good (grade: 6), and one poor (grade: 3). Comments following each essay explain ways in which each essay succeeded or failed. All three essays respond to the following free-response question:

> Question: Analyze the extent to which compromise was no longer possible between the North and South by the 1850s.

Sample Essay 1

By the time Abraham Lincoln was elected president in 1860, the time for compromise between the North and South had passed. Lincoln's election was the spark that ignited secession. Throughout the antebellum period political leaders had attempted to preserve the Union through compromise and by maintaining the political balance in the Senate. As early as the Constitutional Convention there were indications that the conflicting economies and cultures of the regions would ultimately have to be resolved, either through ongoing political compromise or through war. As late as 1858, just two years before secession, Lincoln had said "a house divided against itself cannot stand." The outbreak of the Civil War was the tragic resolution to the sectional differences and the inability to maintain two different economic, political, and cultural systems under one government.

Territorial expansion played a significant role in straining sectional relations because it involved the debate over the expansion or containment of slavery. In 1820 Congress seemed to have resolved this problem when it passed the Missouri Compromise, which prevented the expansion of slavery north of the 36° 30´ line. For a time, Congress was able to balance representation in the Senate by admitting both a slave state and a free state into the Union. For example, Missouri, a slave state, was admitted at the same time as Maine, a free state.

Compromise could only address the symptoms of the problem; it could not resolve the basic economic, moral, and cultural differences, especially because the two regions had completely different economic systems dominated by opposing dominant social, economic, and political classes: the planter-slaveholder in the South and the industrial capitalist in the North. Economically, Northern manufacturers and the Northern economy required a protective tariff, internal improvements, and a national bank to facilitate commerce, whereas the South wanted low tariffs, state banks, and was opposed to internal improvements. The North's economy and culture rested on the wage-labor system, which was, of course, inconsistent with the South's slave economy and culture. Both sought to expand their systems for a variety of reasons: politically the North and South quarreled over the extension of slavery because the addition of a new slave state or free state meant greater political representation in Congress. This in turn meant that either region, if given the political advantage, could pass legislation that affected not only the future expansion of slavery, but other burning political issues as well, such as the tariff.

Furthermore, the North maintained that the Union had been established as a contract between the people of the United States. Southern political leaders responded that the Union was the result of a compact between the states, and that a state had the authority to nullify federal laws and even secede from the Union. These conflicting political theories made compromise even more difficult to achieve because the South claimed to have the authority to reject any federal law it deemed unconstitutional or a threat to states' rights.

Added to this was the role of Northern abolitionists and Southern defenders of slavery whose justifications for or against the peculiar institution added a moral element to the already significant differences. Thus by the time Congress passed the Kansas-Nebraska Act in 1854 and the Supreme Court handed down the *Dred Scott* decision in 1857, the possibility of maintaining the Union became increasingly tenuous.

Politically, by the 1850s the two major political parties represented, for the most part, different sections: the Democrats articulated the South's objectives, whereas the Republicans represented an adversarial view. Up until the election of Lincoln, the presidency was occupied either by a Southerner or a Northerner who tended to favor the South's position. Lincoln, a Republican and an advocate of the containment of slavery, represented to the South that the executive branch would now become an obstacle to the South's political objectives, and that its political and economic influence would therefore wane over time. Thus, by the 1850s, conditions for secession were already present, and the time for compromise had, for all intents and purposes, passed.

Comment This essay effectively outlines the divisions that prevailed between the North and South in the antebellum period. While it by no means completely addresses the issue, given the time constraint (35 minutes) it successfully indicates that while Lincoln's election was the event that finally shattered the Union, deep social, economic, and political divisions had already been festering for decades. The writer articulates the view that the Civil War was the result of irreconcilable differences that could no longer be resolved through compromise. Although listing the features of the *Dred Scott* case would certainly help, the writer successfully synthesizes selective historical content with effective analysis to support the thesis. Grade: 9 (Excellent)

Sample Essay 2

Although there were many disputes, differences, and events that made compromise in the decades before the 1850s very difficult, political leaders such as Clay and Calhoun were able to work out solutions that politically resolved the differences between North and South and therefore prevented secession and war. Unfortunately the nation's political leaders were not up to the task in the 1850s. As early as the Constitutional Convention the Framers developed solutions to sectional problems such as the Three-fifths Compromise and the Assumption Bill. In the early nineteenth century, with tensions high over the attempt to expand or limit the spread of slavery, congressional leaders were able to work out the Missouri Compromise, which defined where slavery could and could not expand. In 1850 the United States could have experienced civil war had not political leaders worked out the Compromise of 1850, which strengthened the Fugitive Slave Act in the South's favor but allowed California to enter as a free state. True, the *Dred Scott* decision effectively eliminated the Missouri Compromise, but political leaders such as Senator Stephen Douglas could not create compromises that would reduce tensions. Instead, they offered the controversial Kansas-Nebraska Act.

The idea of popular sovereignty made compromise almost impossible because Congress could no longer establish areas where slavery could expand and where it could not. Besides, the Kansas-Nebraska Act further enforced the Fugitive Slave Act, which angered Northerners immensely. The only thing holding the Union together at this point was the hope on the part of the South that it could in the future continue to expand slavery. Lincoln, who was opposed to the expansion of slavery, concerned the South so much that no one in 1860 could find any way to compromise. With Lincoln's election the South seceded. But it didn't have to come to that. The nation's political leaders had failed to do what their predecessors in Congress had been able to achieve: effective compromises.

Comment This essay has a clear thesis: the nation's political leaders in the 1850s were responsible for failing to reduce or resolve the sectional tensions through effective compromises that earlier political leaders had accomplished. The writer cites several important political compromises. The scope of this essay could be broader, however, in that the author does not incorporate the role of territorial expansion into the discussion. Further, the discussion is limited in that no clear differences between the sections are established. Thus the essay focuses only on the controversy over the expansion of slavery and not on its economic and political consequences for the sections. It also depicts the Compromise of 1850 as a workable solution that had no subsequent repercussions. In fact the North was outraged by the Fugitive Slave component of the act. There is also a factual error: the Kansas-Nebraska Act did not strengthen the Fugitive Slave Act. An explanation of popular sovereignty would also add to the quality of this essay. Nevertheless, the writer exhibits a good understanding of the topic and uses information that sustains the thesis throughout the essay. Grade: 6 (Good)

Sample Essay 3

Compromise in the 1850s was impossible because the North and South no longer wanted to negotiate. They believed that only through war would their differences be settled. The Missouri Compromise was more effective than the Kansas-Nebraska Act. It prevented war, whereas the Kansas-Nebraska Act made war more possible. Popular sovereignty was not an effective solution either. Now slavery could spread anywhere and the North would be opposed to this. Lincoln was opposed to the spread of slavery, but he was not willing to break up the Union for it. Therefore a better solution to the problem could not be found. If Lincoln opposed the spread of slavery, what other option did the South have but to leave the Union? Also, the North and South viewed slavery differently. The North opposed it as inhumane, but the South claimed it was an institution that benefited both Southern whites and slaves. Had the Framers at the Constitutional Convention addressed the issue of slavery, future generations would not have to find solutions and compromises to this problem. But even if Congress did work out compromises, such as the Missouri Compromise, no one could determine what the Supreme Court would do, such as the *Dred Scott* case. Lincoln's election was not the cause of the war. True, he was a Northerner, but so were other presidents. Put simply, neither the North nor the South favored compromise by the 1850s because they could not resolve their political differences.

Comment This essay is weak in a number of areas. While it has a thesis, it is rudimentary; the thesis is not developed in the essay effectively. The writer strings together generalizations that have little connection to one another. Important issues are not explained. For instance, the writer contends that the Missouri Compromise was more effective than the Kansas-Nebraska Act but does not explain how or why the former prevented war. This essay lacks focus, analysis, and sufficient historical information to defend the thesis. Grade: 3 (Poor)

Sail, sail thy best, ship of Democracy,
Of value is thy freight, 'tis not the Present only,
The Past is also stored in thee,
Thou holdest not the venture of thyself alone, not of
    the Western continent alone,
Earth's résumé entire floats on thy keel, O ship, is
    steadied by thy spars,
With thee Time voyages in trust, the antecedent
    nations sink or swim with thee,
With all their ancient struggles, martyrs, heroes, epics,
    wars, thou bear'st the other continents,
Theirs, theirs as much as thine, the destination-port
    triumphant. . . .

                    Walt Whitman
        "Thou Mother with Thy Equal Brood," 1872

Part One

Founding the New Nation

ca. 33,000 B.C.E.–1783 C.E.

The European explorers who followed Christopher Columbus to North America in the sixteenth century had no notion of founding a new nation. Neither did the first European settlers who peopled the thirteen English colonies on the eastern shores of the continent in the seventeenth and eighteenth centuries. These original colonists may have fled poverty or religious persecution in the Old World, but they continued to view themselves as Europeans, and as subjects of the English king. They regarded America as but the western rim of a transatlantic European world.

Yet life in the New World made the colonists different from their European cousins, and eventually, during the American Revolution, the Americans came to embrace a vision of their country as an independent nation. How did this epochal transformation come about? How did the colonists overcome the conflicts that divided them, unite against Britain, and declare themselves at great cost to be an "American" people?

They had much in common to begin with. Most were English-speaking. Most came determined to create an agricultural society modeled on English customs. Conditions in the New World deepened their common bonds. Most colonists strove to live

lives unfettered by the tyrannies of royal authority, official religion, and social hierarchies that they had left behind. They grew to cherish ideals that became synonymous with American life—reverence for individual liberty, self-government, religious tolerance, and economic opportunity. They also commonly displayed a willingness to subjugate outsiders—first Indians, who were nearly annihilated through war and disease, and then Africans, who were brought in chains to serve as slave labor, especially on the tobacco, rice, and indigo plantations of the southern colonies.

But if the settlement experience gave people a common stock of values, both good and bad, it also divided them. The thirteen colonies were quite different from one another. Puritans carved tight, pious, and relatively democratic communities of small family farms out of rocky-soiled New England. Theirs was a homogeneous world in comparison to most of the southern colonies, where large landholders, mostly Anglicans, built plantations along the coast from which they lorded over a labor force of black slaves and looked down upon the poor white farmers who settled the backcountry. Different still were the middle colonies stretching from New York to Delaware. There

The Town of Secota, Engraving, by Theodore de Bry, 1590, after John White Painting John White was an English watercolorist who accompanied the first English expedition to Roanoke Island (later parts of Virginia) in 1585. His paintings faithfully recorded the Indian way of life that was now imperiled by the arrival of the Europeans. The New York Public Library/Art Resource, NY/Art Resource, NY

2

diversity reigned. Well-to-do merchants put their stamp on New York City, as Quakers did on Philadelphia, while out in the countryside sprawling estates were interspersed with modest homesteads. Within individual colonies, conflicts festered over economic interests, ethnic rivalries, and religious practices. All those clashes made it difficult for colonists to imagine that they were a single people with a common destiny, much less that they ought to break free from Britain.

The American colonists in fact had little reason to complain about Britain. Each of the thirteen colonies enjoyed a good deal of self-rule. Many colonists profited from trade within the British Empire. But by the 1760s, this stable arrangement began to crumble, a victim of the imperial rivalry between France and Britain. Their struggle for supremacy in North America began in the late seventeenth century and finally dragged in the colonists during the French and Indian War from 1756 to 1763. That war in one sense strengthened ties with Britain, since colonial militias fought triumphantly alongside the British army against their mutual French and Indian enemies. But once the French were driven from the North American continent, the colonists no longer needed Britain for protection. More important still, after 1763 a financially overstretched British government made the fateful choice of imposing taxes on colonies that had been accustomed to answering mainly to their own colonial assemblies. By the 1770s issues of taxation, self-rule, and trade restrictions brought the crisis of imperial authority to a head. Although as late as 1775 most people in the colonies clung to the hope of some kind of accommodation short of outright independence, royal intransigence soon thrust the colonists into a war of independence that neither antagonist could have anticipated just a few years before.

Eight years of revolutionary war did more than anything in the colonial past to bring Americans together as a nation. Comradeship-in-arms and the struggle to shape a national government forced Americans to subdue their differences as best they could. But the spirit of national unity was hardly universal. One in five colonists sided with the British as "Loyalists," and a generation would pass before the wounds of this first American "civil war" fully healed. Yet in the end, Americans won the Revolution, with no small measure of help from the French, because in every colony people shared a firm belief that they were fighting for the "unalienable rights" of "life, liberty, and the pursuit of happiness," in the words of Thomas Jefferson's magnificent Declaration of Independence. Almost two hundred years of living a new life had prepared Americans to found a new nation.

Library of Congress

Philadelphia, Corner of Second and High Streets Delegates to the Constitutional Convention in 1787 gathered in Philadelphia, the largest city in North America, a vivid symbol of the rise of American society from its precarious beginnings at Jamestown and Plymouth nearly two centuries earlier.

Chapter 1

New World Beginnings

33,000 B.C.E.–1769 C.E.

*I have come to believe that this is a mighty continent which was hitherto
unknown. . . . Your Highnesses have an Other World here.*

CHRISTOPHER COLUMBUS, 1498

Several billion years ago, that whirling speck of dust known as the earth, fifth in size among the planets, came into being.

About six thousand years ago—only a minute in geological time—recorded history of the Western world began. Certain peoples of the Middle East, developing a written culture, gradually emerged from the haze of the past.

Five hundred years ago—only a few seconds figuratively speaking—European explorers stumbled on the Americas. This dramatic accident forever altered the future of both the Old World and the New, and of Africa and Asia as well (see Figure 1.1).

✷ The Shaping of North America

Planet earth took on its present form slowly. Some 225 million years ago, a single supercontinent contained all the world's dry land. Then enormous chunks of terrain began to drift away from this colossal landmass, opening the Atlantic and Indian Oceans, narrowing the Pacific Ocean, and forming the great continents of Eurasia, Africa, Australia, Antarctica, and the Americas. The existence of a single original continent has been proved in part by the discovery of nearly identical species of fish that swim today in long-separated freshwater lakes throughout the world.

Continued shifting and folding of the earth's crust thrust up mountain ranges. The Appalachians were probably formed even before continental separation, perhaps 350 million years ago. The majestic ranges of western North America—the Rockies, the Sierra Nevada, the Cascades, and the Coast Ranges—arose much more recently, geologically speaking, some 135 million to 25 million years ago. They are truly "American" mountains, born after the continent took on its own separate geological identity.

By about 10 million years ago, nature had sculpted the basic geological shape of North America. The continent was anchored in its northeastern corner by the massive **Canadian Shield**—a zone undergirded by ancient rock, probably the first part of what became the North American landmass to have emerged above sea level. A narrow eastern coastal plain, or "tidewater" region, creased by many river valleys, sloped gently upward to the timeworn ridges of the Appalachians. Those ancient mountains slanted away on their western side into the huge midcontinental basin that rolled downward to the Mississippi Valley bottom and then rose relentlessly to the towering peaks of the Rockies. From the Rocky Mountain crest—the "roof of America"—the land fell off jaggedly into the intermountain Great Basin, bounded by the Rockies on the east and the Sierra and Cascade ranges on the west. The valleys of the Sacramento and San Joaquin Rivers and the Willamette–Puget Sound trough seamed the interiors of present-day California, Oregon, and Washington. The land at last met the foaming Pacific, where the Coast Ranges rose steeply from the sea.

Nature laid a chill hand over much of this terrain in the Great Ice Age, beginning about 2 million years ago. Two-mile-thick ice sheets crept from the polar regions to blanket parts of Europe, Asia, and the

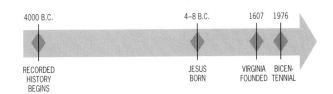

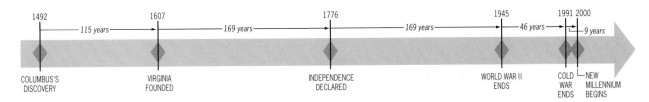

FIGURE 1.1 The Arc of Time

Americas. In North America the great glaciers carpeted most of present-day Canada and the United States as far southward as a line stretching from Pennsylvania through the Ohio Country and the Dakotas to the Pacific Northwest.

When the glaciers finally retreated about 10,000 years ago, they left the North American landscape transformed, and much as we know it today. The weight of the gargantuan ice mantle had depressed the level of the Canadian Shield. The grinding and flushing action of the moving and melting ice had scoured away the shield's topsoil, pitting its rocky surface with thousands of shallow depressions into which the melting glaciers flowed to form lakes. The same glacial action scooped out and filled the Great Lakes. They originally drained southward through the Mississippi River system to the Gulf of Mexico. When the melting ice unblocked the Gulf of St. Lawrence, the lake water sought the St. Lawrence River outlet to the Atlantic Ocean, lowering the Great Lakes' level and leaving the Missouri-Mississippi-Ohio system to drain the enormous midcontinental basin between the Appalachians and the Rockies. Similarly, in the West, water from the melting glaciers filled sprawling Lake Bonneville, covering much of present-day Utah, Nevada, and Idaho. It drained to the Pacific Ocean through the Snake and Columbia River systems until diminishing rainfall from the ebbing ice cap lowered the water level, cutting off access to the Snake River outlet. Deprived of both inflow and drainage, the giant lake became a gradually shrinking inland sea. It grew increasingly saline, slowly evaporated, and left an arid, mineral-rich desert. Only the Great Salt Lake remained as a relic of Bonneville's former vastness. Today Lake Bonneville's ancient beaches are visible on mountainsides up to 1,000 feet above the dry floor of the Great Basin.

✪ Peopling the Americas

The Great Ice Age shaped more than the geological history of North America. It also contributed to the origins of the continent's human history. Though recent (and still highly controversial) evidence suggests that some early peoples may have reached the Americas in crude boats, most probably came by land. Some 35,000 years ago, the Ice Age congealed much of the world oceans into massive ice-pack glaciers, lowering the level of the sea. As the sea level dropped, it exposed a land bridge connecting Eurasia with North America in the area of the present-day Bering Sea between Siberia and Alaska. Across that bridge, probably following migratory herds of game, ventured small bands of nomadic Asian hunters—the "immigrant" ancestors of the Native Americans. They continued to trek across the Bering isthmus for some 250 centuries, slowly peopling the American continents (see Map 1.1).

As the Ice Age ended and the glaciers melted, the sea level rose again, inundating the land bridge about 10,000 years ago. Nature thus barred the door to further immigration for many thousands of years, leaving this part of the human family marooned for millennia on the now-isolated American continents.

Time did not stand still for these original Americans. The same climatic warming that melted the ice and drowned the bridge to Eurasia gradually opened ice-free valleys through which vanguard bands groped their way southward and eastward across the Americas. Roaming slowly through this awesome wilderness, they eventually reached the far tip of South America, some 15,000 miles from Siberia. By the time Europeans arrived in America in 1492, perhaps 54 million people

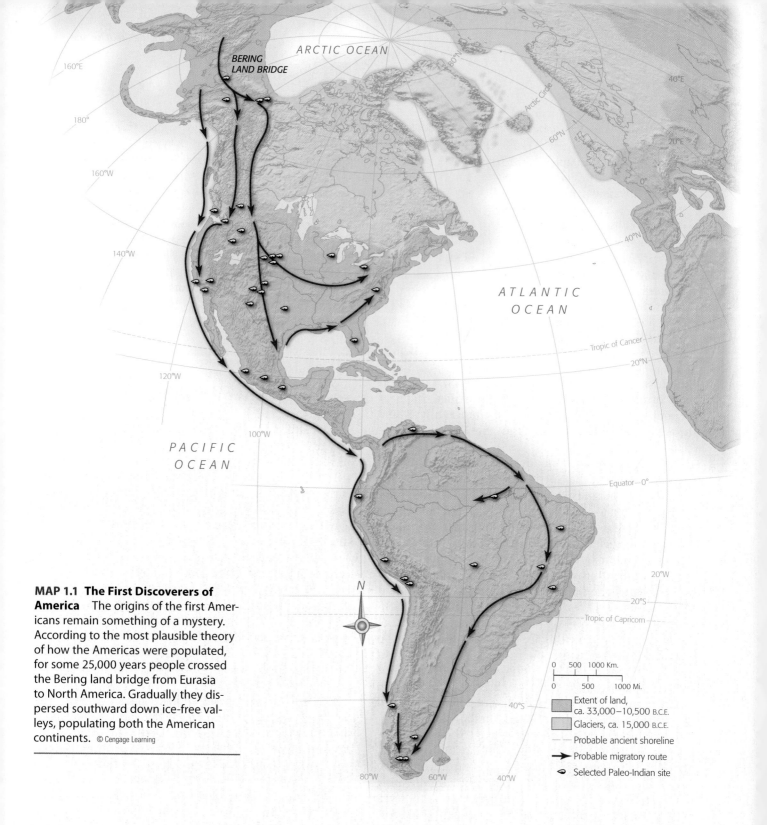

MAP 1.1 The First Discoverers of America The origins of the first Americans remain something of a mystery. According to the most plausible theory of how the Americas were populated, for some 25,000 years people crossed the Bering land bridge from Eurasia to North America. Gradually they dispersed southward down ice-free valleys, populating both the American continents. © Cengage Learning

inhabited the two American continents.* Over the centuries they split into countless tribes, evolved more than 2,000 separate languages, and developed many diverse religions, cultures, and ways of life.

Incas in Peru, Mayans in Central America, and **Aztecs** in Mexico shaped stunningly sophisticated civilizations. Their advanced agricultural practices, based primarily on the cultivation of maize, which is Indian corn, fed large populations, perhaps as many as 20 million in Mexico alone. Although without large draft

*Much controversy surrounds estimates of the pre-Columbian Native American population. The figures here are from William M. Denevan, ed., The Native Population of the Americas in 1492, rev. ed. (Madison: University of Wisconsin Press, 1992).

Making Sense of the New World

This map from 1546 by Sebastian Münster represents one of the earliest efforts to make geographic sense out of the New World (*Nouus Orbis* and *Die Nüw Welt* on the map). The very phrase *New World* suggests just how staggering a blow to the European imagination was the discovery of the Americas. Europeans reached instinctively for the most expansive of all possible terms—*world*, not simply *places*, or even *continents*—to comprehend Columbus's startling report that lands and peoples previously unimagined lay beyond the horizon of Europe's western sea.

Gradually the immense implications of the New World's existence began to impress themselves on Europe, with consequences for literature, art, politics, the economy, and, of course, cartography. Maps can only be *representations* of reality and are therefore necessarily distortions. This map bears a recognizable resemblance to modern mapmakers' renderings of the American continents, but it also contains gross geographic inaccuracies (note the location of Japan—*Zipangri*—relative to the North American west coast) as well as telling commentaries on

what sixteenth-century Europeans found remarkable (note the Land of Giants—*Regio Gigantum*—and the indication of cannibals—*Canibali*—in present-day Argentina and Brazil, respectively). What further clues to the European mentality of the time does the map offer? In what ways might misconceptions about the geography of the Americas have influenced further exploration and settlement patterns?

National Archives of Canada

animals such as horses and oxen, and lacking even the simple technology of the wheel, these peoples built elaborate cities and carried on far-flung commerce. Talented mathematicians, they made strikingly accurate astronomical observations. The Aztecs also routinely sought the favor of their gods by offering human sacrifices, cutting the hearts out of the chests of living victims, who were often captives conquered in battle. By some accounts more than 5,000 people were ritually slaughtered to celebrate the crowning of one Aztec chieftain.

✳ The Earliest Americans

Agriculture, especially corn growing, accounted for the size and sophistication of the Native American civilizations in Mexico and South America. About 5000 B.C.E. hunter-gatherers in highland Mexico developed a wild grass into the staple crop of corn, which became their staff of life and the foundation of the complex, large-scale, centralized Aztec and Incan civilizations that eventually emerged. Cultivation of corn spread across the Americas from the Mexican heartland. Everywhere it was planted, corn began to transform nomadic hunting bands into settled agricultural villagers, but this process went forward slowly and unevenly.

Corn planting reached the present-day American Southwest as early as 2000 B.C.E. and powerfully molded Pueblo culture. The Pueblo peoples in the Rio Grande valley constructed intricate irrigation systems to water their cornfields. They were dwelling in villages of multistoried, terraced buildings when Spanish explorers made contact with them in the sixteenth century. (*Pueblo* means "village" in Spanish.)

Corn cultivation reached other parts of North America considerably later. The timing of its arrival in different localities explains much about the relative rates of development of different Native American peoples (see Map 1.2). Throughout the continent to the north and east of the land of the Pueblos, social life was less elaborately developed—indeed "societies" in the modern sense of the word scarcely existed. No dense concentrations of population or complex **nation-states** comparable to the Aztec empire existed in North America outside of Mexico at the time of the Europeans' arrival—one of the reasons for the relative

Corn Culture This statue of a corn goddess from the Moche culture of present-day coastal Peru, made between 200 and 600 B.C.E., vividly illustrates the centrality of corn to Native American peoples, a thousand years before the rise of the great Incan and Aztec empires that the Europeans later encountered.

Bildarchiv Preussischer Kulturbesitz/Art Resource, NY

ease with which the European colonizers subdued the native North Americans.

The Mound Builders of the Ohio River valley, the Mississippian culture of the lower Midwest, and the desert-dwelling Anasazi peoples of the Southwest did sustain some large settlements after the incorporation of corn planting into their ways of life during the first millennium C.E. The Mississippian settlement at **Cahokia**, near present-day East St. Louis, was at one time home to as many as twenty-five thousand people. The Anasazis built an elaborate pueblo of more than six hundred interconnected rooms at Chaco Canyon in modern-day New Mexico. But mysteriously, perhaps due to prolonged drought, all those ancient cultures fell into decline by about 1300 C.E.

The cultivation of maize, as well as of high-yielding strains of beans and squash, reached the southeastern Atlantic seaboard region of North America about 1000 C.E. These plants made possible **three-sister farming**, with beans growing on the trellis of the cornstalks and squash covering the planting mounds to retain moisture in the soil. The rich diet provided by this environmentally clever farming technique produced some of the highest population densities on the continent, among them the Creek, Choctaw, and Cherokee peoples.

The Iroquois in the northeastern woodlands, inspired by a legendary leader named Hiawatha, created in the sixteenth century perhaps the closest North American approximation to the great empires of Mexico and Peru. The Iroquois Confederacy developed the political and organizational skills to sustain a robust military alliance that menaced its neighbors, Native American and European alike, for well over a century (see "Makers of America: The Iroquois," pp. 36–37).

But for the most part, the native peoples of North America were living in small, scattered, and impermanent settlements on the eve of the Europeans' arrival. In more settled agricultural groups, women tended the crops while men hunted, fished, gathered fuel, and cleared fields for planting. This pattern of life frequently conferred substantial authority on women, and many North American native peoples, including the Iroquois, developed matrilineal cultures, in which power and possessions passed down the female side of the family line.

MAP 1.2 North American Indian Peoples at the Time of First Contact with Europeans   Because this map depicts the location of various Indian peoples *at the time of their first contact with Europeans*, and because initial contacts ranged from the sixteenth to the nineteenth centuries, it is necessarily subject to considerable chronological skewing and is only a crude approximation of the "original" territory of any given group. The map also cannot capture the fluidity and dynamism of Native American life even before Columbus's "discovery." For example, the Navajo and Apache peoples had migrated from present-day northern Canada only shortly before the Spanish first encountered them in the present-day American Southwest in the 1500s. The map also places the Sioux on the Great Plains, where Europeans met up with them in the early nineteenth century—but the Sioux had spilled onto the plains not long before then from the forests surrounding the Great Lakes. The indigenous populations of the southeastern and mid-Atlantic regions are especially difficult to represent accurately in a map like this because pre-Columbian intertribal conflicts had so scrambled the native inhabitants that it is virtually impossible to determine which groups were originally where. © Cengage Learning

Cahokia This artist's rendering of Cahokia, based on archaeological excavations, shows the huge central square and the imposing Monk's Mound, which rivaled in size the pyramids of Egypt.

Unlike the Europeans, who would soon arrive with the presumption that humans had dominion over the earth and with the technologies to alter the very face of the land, the Native Americans had neither the desire nor the means to manipulate nature aggressively. They revered the physical world and endowed nature with spiritual properties. Yet they did sometimes ignite massive forest fires, deliberately torching thousands of acres of trees to create better hunting habitats, especially for deer. This practice accounted for the open, parklike appearance of the eastern woodlands that so amazed early European explorers.

But in a broad sense, the land did not feel the hand of the Native Americans heavy upon it, partly because they were so few in number. They were so thinly spread across the continent that vast areas were virtually untouched by a human presence. In the fateful year 1492, probably no more than 4 million Native Americans padded through the whispering, primeval forests and paddled across the sparkling, virgin waters of the continent north of Mexico. They were blissfully unaware that the historic isolation of the Americas was about to end forever, as the land and the native peoples alike felt the full shock of the European "discovery."

✸ Indirect Discoverers of the New World

Europeans, for their part, were equally unaware of the existence of the Americas. Blond-bearded Norse seafarers from Scandinavia had chanced upon the northeastern shoulder of North America about 1000 C.E. They landed at a place near L'Anse aux Meadows in present-day Newfoundland that abounded in wild grapes, which led them to name the spot Vinland. But no strong nation-state, yearning to expand, supported these venturesome voyagers. Their flimsy settlements consequently were soon abandoned, and their discovery was forgotten, except in Scandinavian saga and song.

For several centuries thereafter, other restless Europeans, with the growing power of ambitious governments behind them, sought contact with a wider world, whether for conquest or trade. They thus set in motion the chain of events that led to a drive toward Asia, the penetration of Africa, and the completely accidental discovery of the New World.

Christian crusaders must rank high among America's indirect discoverers. Clad in shining armor, tens of thousands of these European warriors tried from the eleventh to the fourteenth century to wrest the Holy Land from Muslim control. Foiled in their military assaults, the crusaders nevertheless acquired a taste for the exotic delights of Asia. Goods that had been virtually unknown in Europe now were craved—silk for clothing, drugs for aching flesh, perfumes for unbathed bodies, colorful draperies for gloomy castles, and spices—especially sugar, a rare luxury in Europe before the crusades—for preserving and flavoring food. Europe's developing sweet tooth would have momentous implications for world history.

The luxuries of the East were prohibitively expensive in Europe. They had to be transported enormous distances from the Spice Islands (Indonesia), China, and India, in creaking ships and on swaying camel back. The journey led across the Indian Ocean, the Persian Gulf, and the Red Sea or along the tortuous caravan routes of Asia or the Arabian Peninsula, ending at the ports of the eastern Mediterranean (see Map 1.3).

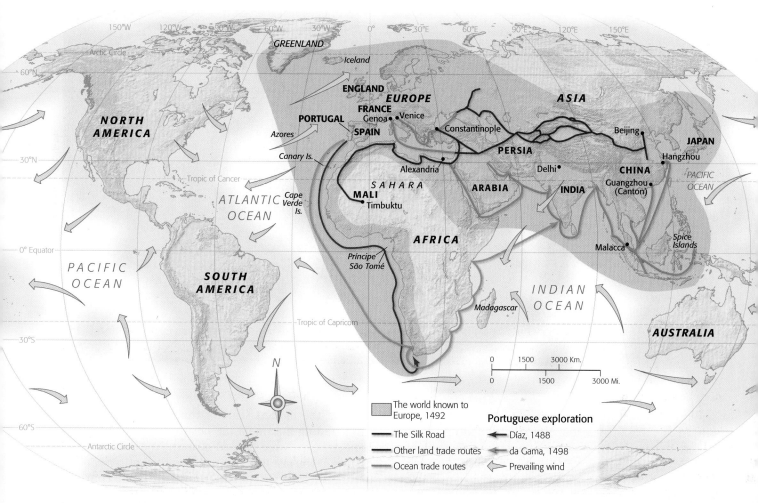

MAP 1.3 The World Known to Europe and Major Trade Routes with Asia, 1492
Goods on the early routes passed through so many hands along the way that their
ultimate source remained mysterious to Europeans. © Cengage Learning

Muslim **middlemen** exacted a heavy toll en route. By the time the strange-smelling goods reached Italian merchants at Venice and Genoa, they were so costly that purchasers and profits alike were narrowly limited. European consumers and distributors were naturally eager to find a less expensive route to the riches of Asia or to develop alternate sources of supply.

✴ Europeans Enter Africa

European appetites were further whetted when foot-loose Marco Polo, an Italian adventurer, returned to Europe in 1295 and began telling tales of his nearly twenty-year sojourn in China. Though he may in fact never have seen China (legend to the contrary, the hard evidence is sketchy), he must be regarded as an indirect discoverer of the New World, for his book, with its descriptions of rose-tinted pearls and golden pagodas, stimulated European desires for a cheaper route to the treasures of the East.

These accumulating pressures eventually brought a breakthrough for European expansion. Before the middle of the fifteenth century, European sailors refused to sail southward along the coast of West Africa because they could not beat their way home against the prevailing northerly winds and south-flowing currents. About 1450, Portuguese mariners overcame those obstacles. Not only had they developed the **caravel**, a ship that could sail more closely into the wind, but they had discovered that they could return to Europe by sailing northwesterly from the African coast toward the Azores, where the prevailing westward breezes would carry them home.

The new world of sub-Saharan Africa now came within the grasp of questing Europeans. The northern shore of Africa, as part of the Mediterranean world, had been known to Europe since antiquity. But because

Marco Polo Passing Through the Strait of Hormuz This illustration, from the first printed edition of *The Travels of Marco Polo* in 1477, shows the traveler crossing the Persian Gulf between the Arabian Peninsula and Persia (present-day Iran).

Bibliotheque Nationale, Paris, France/The Bridgeman Art Library

sea travel down the African coast had been virtually impossible, Africa south of the forbidding Sahara Desert barrier had remained remote and mysterious. African gold, perhaps two-thirds of Europe's supply, crossed the Sahara on camelback, and shadowy tales may have reached Europe about the flourishing West African kingdom of Mali in the Niger River valley, with its impressive Islamic university at Timbuktu. But Europeans had no direct access to sub-Saharan Africa until the Portuguese navigators began to creep down the West African coast in the middle of the fifteenth century.

The Portuguese promptly set up trading posts along the African shore for the purchase of gold—and slaves. Arab flesh merchants and Africans themselves had traded slaves for centuries before the Europeans arrived. The slavers routinely charged higher prices for captives from distant sources, because they could not easily flee to their native villages or be easily rescued by their kin. Slave brokers also deliberately separated persons from the same tribes and mixed unlike people together to frustrate organized resistance. Thus from its earliest days, slavery by its very nature inhibited the expression of regional African cultures and tribal identities.

The Portuguese adopted these Arab and African practices. They built up their own systematic traffic in slaves to work the sugar plantations that Portugal, and later Spain, established on the African coastal islands of Madeira, the Canaries, São Tomé, and Principe. The Portuguese appetite for slaves was enormous and

dwarfed the modest scale of the pre-European traffic. Slave trading became a big business. Some forty thousand Africans were carried away to the Atlantic sugar islands in the last half of the fifteenth century. Millions more were to be wrenched from their home continent after the discovery of the Americas. In these fifteenth-century Portuguese adventures in Africa were to be found the origins of the modern **plantation** system, based on large-scale commercial agriculture and the wholesale exploitation of slave labor. This kind of plantation economy would shape the destiny of much of the New World.

The seafaring Portuguese pushed still farther southward in search of the water route to Asia. Edging cautiously down the African coast, Bartholomeu Dias rounded the southernmost tip of the "Dark Continent" in 1488. Ten years later Vasco da Gama finally reached India (hence the name "Indies," given by Europeans to all the mysterious lands of the Orient) and returned home with a small but tantalizing cargo of jewels and spices.

Meanwhile, the kingdom of Spain became united—an event pregnant with destiny—in the late fifteenth century. This new unity resulted primarily from the marriage of two sovereigns, Ferdinand of Aragon and Isabella of Castile, and from the brutal expulsion of the "infidel" Muslim Moors from Spain after centuries of Christian-Islamic warfare. Glorying in their sudden strength, the Spaniards were eager to outstrip their Portuguese rivals in the race to tap the wealth of the

SEYLLOU DIALLO/AFP/Getty Images

TSGT Justin D. Pyle, USAF/Wikimedia Commons

Gorée Island Slave Fortress From this holding station off the coast of Senegal, thousands of African captives passed through the "Door of No Return" into a lifetime of slavery in the New World.

ocean navigation. In Spain a modern national state was taking shape, with the unity, wealth, and power to shoulder the formidable tasks of discovery, conquest, and colonization. The dawn of the Renaissance in the fourteenth century nurtured an ambitious spirit of optimism and adventure. Printing presses, introduced about 1450, facilitated the spread of scientific knowledge. The mariner's compass, possibly borrowed from the Arabs, eliminated some of the uncertainties of sea travel. Meanwhile, across the ocean, the unsuspecting New World innocently awaited its European "discoverers."

Onto this stage stepped Christopher Columbus. This skilled Italian seafarer persuaded the Spanish monarchs to outfit him with three tiny but seaworthy ships, manned by a motley crew. Daringly, he unfurled the sails of his cockleshell craft and headed westward. His superstitious sailors, fearful of venturing into the oceanic unknown, grew increasingly mutinous. After six weeks at sea, failure loomed until, on October 12, 1492, the crew sighted an island in the Bahamas. A new world thus swam within the vision of Europeans.

Columbus's sensational achievement obscures the fact that he was one of the most successful failures in history. Seeking a new water route to the fabled Indies, he in fact had bumped into an enormous land barrier blocking the ocean pathway. For decades thereafter explorers strove to get through it or around it. The truth gradually dawned that sprawling new continents had been discovered. Yet Columbus was at first so certain that he had skirted the rim of the "Indies" that he called the native peoples Indians, a gross geographical misnomer that somehow stuck.

Indies. To the south and east, Portugal controlled the African coast and thus controlled the gateway to the round-Africa water route to India. Of necessity, therefore, Spain looked westward.

✸ Columbus Comes upon a New World

The stage was now set for a cataclysmic shift in the course of history—the history not only of Europe but of all the world. Europeans clamored for more and cheaper products from the lands beyond the Mediterranean. Africa had been established as a source of cheap slave labor for plantation agriculture. The Portuguese voyages had demonstrated the feasibility of long-range

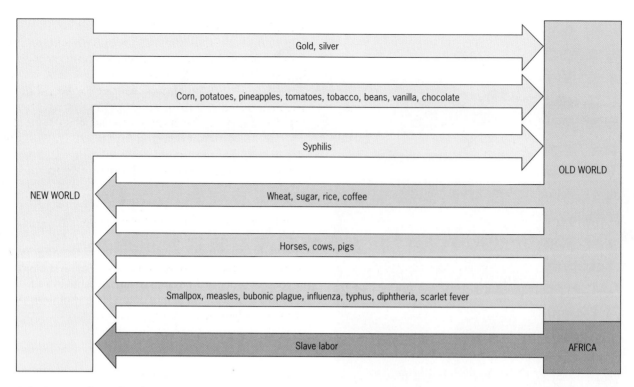

FIGURE 1.2 The Columbian Exchange   Columbus's discovery initiated the kind of explosion in international commerce that a later age would call "globalization."

Columbus's discovery would eventually convulse four continents—Europe, Africa, and the two Americas. Thanks to his epochal voyage, an interdependent global economic system emerged on a scale undreamed-of before he set sail. Its workings touched every shore washed by the Atlantic Ocean. Europe provided the markets, the capital, and the technology; Africa furnished the labor; and the New World offered its raw materials, especially its precious metals and its soil for the cultivation of sugar cane. For Europeans as well as for Africans and Native Americans, the world after 1492 would never be the same, for better or worse.

✵ When Worlds Collide

Two ecosystems—the fragile, naturally evolved networks of relations among organisms in a stable environment—commingled and clashed when Columbus waded ashore. The reverberations from that historic encounter—often called the **Columbian exchange** (see Figure 1.2)—echoed for centuries after 1492. The flora and fauna of the Old and New Worlds had been separated for thousands of years. European explorers marveled at the strange sights that greeted them, including exotic beasts such as iguanas and "snakes

with castanets" (rattlesnakes). Native New World plants such as tobacco, maize, beans, tomatoes, and especially the lowly potato eventually revolutionized the international economy as well as the European diet, feeding the rapid population growth of the Old World. These foodstuffs were among the most important Indian gifts to the Europeans and to the rest of the world. Perhaps three-fifths of the crops cultivated around the globe today originated in the Americas. Ironically, the introduction into Africa of New World foodstuffs like maize, manioc, and sweet potatoes may have fed an African population boom that numerically, though not morally, more than offset the losses inflicted by the slave trade.

In exchange the Europeans introduced Old World crops and animals to the Americas. Columbus returned to the Caribbean island of Hispaniola (present-day Haiti and the Dominican Republic) in 1493 with seventeen ships that unloaded twelve hundred men and a virtual Noah's Ark of cattle, swine, and horses. The horses soon reached the North American mainland through Mexico and in less than two centuries had spread as far as Canada. North American Indian tribes like the Apaches, Sioux, and Blackfeet swiftly adopted the horse, transforming their cultures into highly mobile, wide-ranging hunter societies that roamed the grassy Great Plains in pursuit of the shaggy buffalo. Columbus

The Scourge of Smallpox This Peruvian infant, depicted about 1700, was ravaged by the dread European disease and placed in a crude quarantine.

also brought seedlings of sugar cane, which thrived in the warm Caribbean climate. A "sugar revolution" consequently took place in the European diet, fueled by the forced migration of millions of Africans to work the canefields and sugar mills of the New World.

Unwittingly, the Europeans also brought other organisms in the dirt on their boots and the dust on their clothes, such as the seeds of Kentucky bluegrass, dandelions, and daisies. Most ominous of all, in their bodies they carried the germs that caused smallpox, yellow fever, and malaria. Indeed, Old World diseases would quickly devastate the Native Americans. During the Indians' millennia of isolation in the Americas, most of the Old World's killer maladies had disappeared from among them. But generations of freedom from those illnesses had also wiped out protective antibodies. Devoid of natural resistance to Old World sicknesses, Indians died in droves. Within fifty years of the Spanish

arrival, the population of the Taino natives in Hispaniola dwindled from some 1 million people to about 200. Enslavement and armed aggression took their toll, but the deadliest killers were microbes, not muskets. The lethal germs spread among the New World peoples with the speed and force of a hurricane, swiftly sweeping far ahead of the human invaders; most of those afflicted never laid eyes on a European. In the centuries after Columbus's landfall, as many as 90 percent of the Native Americans perished, a demographic catastrophe without parallel in human history. This depopulation was surely not intended by the Spanish, but it was nevertheless so severe that entire cultures and ancient ways of life were extinguished forever. Baffled, enraged, and vengeful, Indian slaves sometimes kneaded tainted blood into their masters' bread, to little effect. Perhaps it was poetic justice that the Indians unintentionally did take a kind of revenge by infecting the early explorers with syphilis, injecting that lethal sexually transmitted disease for the first time into Europe.

✳ The Spanish *Conquistadores*

Gradually, Europeans realized that the American continents held rich prizes, especially the gold and silver of the advanced Indian civilizations in Mexico and Peru. Spain secured its claim to Columbus's discovery in the **Treaty of Tordesillas** (1494), dividing with Portugal the "heathen lands" of the New World (see Map 1.4). The lion's share went to Spain, but Portugal received compensating territory in Africa and Asia, as well as title to lands that one day would be Brazil.

Spain became the dominant exploring and colonizing power in the 1500s. In the service of God, as well as in search of gold and glory, Spanish *conquistadores* (conquerors) fanned out across the Caribbean and eventually onto the mainland of the American continents (see "Makers of America: The Spanish *Conquistadores*," pp. 18–19). On Spain's long roster of notable deeds, two spectacular exploits must be headlined. Vasco Nuñez Balboa, hailed as the discoverer of the Pacific Ocean, waded into the foaming waves off Panama in 1513 and boldly claimed for his king all the lands washed by that sea (see Map 1.5). Ferdinand Magellan started from Spain in 1519 with five tiny ships. After beating through the storm-lashed strait off the tip of South America that still bears his name, he was slain by the inhabitants of the Philippines. His one remaining vessel creaked home in 1522, completing the first circumnavigation of the globe.

Other ambitious Spaniards ventured into North America. In 1513 and 1521, Juan Ponce de León explored Florida, which he at first thought was an island. Seeking gold—and probably not the mythical

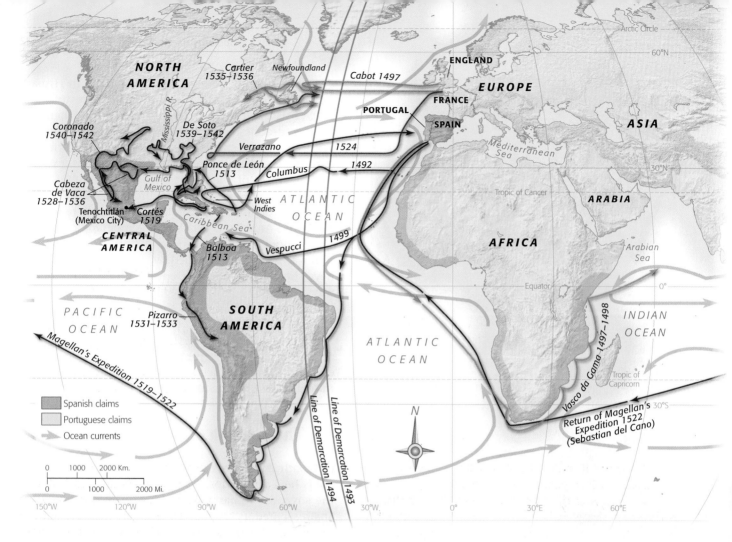

MAP 1.4 Principal Voyages of Discovery Spain, Portugal, France, and England reaped the greatest advantages from the New World, but much of the earliest exploration was done by Italians, notably Christopher Columbus of Genoa. John Cabot, another native of Genoa (his original name was Giovanni Caboto), sailed for England's King Henry VII. Giovanni da Verrazano was a Florentine employed by France. © Cengage Learning

"fountain of youth"—he instead met with death by an Indian arrow. In 1540–1542 Francisco Coronado, in quest of fabled golden cities that turned out to be adobe pueblos, wandered with a clanking cavalcade through Arizona and New Mexico, penetrating as far east as Kansas. En route his expedition discovered two awesome natural wonders: the Grand Canyon of the Colorado River and enormous herds of buffalo (bison). Hernando de Soto, with six hundred armor-plated men, undertook a fantastic gold-seeking expedition during 1539–1542. Floundering through marshes and pine barrens from Florida westward, he discovered and crossed the majestic Mississippi River just north of its junction with the Arkansas River. After brutally mistreating the Indians with iron collars and fierce dogs, he at length died of fever and wounds. His troops secretly disposed of his remains at night in the Mississippi, lest the Indians exhume and abuse their abuser's corpse.

Meanwhile in South America, the ironfisted conqueror Francisco Pizarro crushed the Incas of Peru in 1532 and added a huge hoard of booty to Spanish coffers. By 1600 Spain was swimming in New World silver, mostly from the fabulously rich mines at Potosí in present-day Bolivia, as well as from Mexico. This flood of precious metal touched off a price revolution in Europe that increased consumer costs by as much as 500 percent in the hundred years after the mid-sixteenth century. Some scholars see in this ballooning European money supply the fuel that fed the growth of the economic system known as **capitalism**. Certainly, New World bullion helped transform the world economy. It swelled the vaults of bankers from Spain to Italy, laying the foundations of the modern commercial banking system. It clinked in the purses of merchants in France and Holland, stimulating the spread of commerce and manufacturing. And it paid for much of the burgeon-

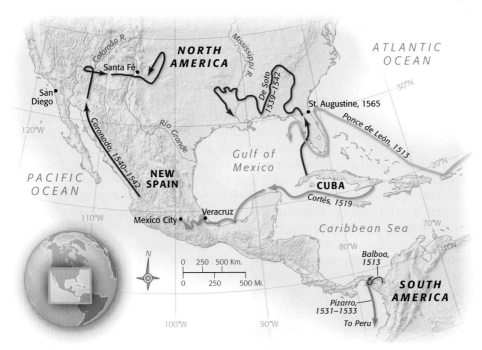

MAP 1.5 Principal Early Spanish Explorations and Conquests Note that Coronado traversed northern Texas and Oklahoma. In present-day eastern Kansas, he found, instead of the great golden city he sought, a drab encampment, probably of Wichita Indians. © Cengage Learning

ing international trade with Asia, whose sellers had little use for any European good except silver.

The islands of the Caribbean Sea—the West Indies as they came to be called, in yet another perpetuation of Columbus's geographic confusion—served as offshore bases for the staging of the Spanish invasion of the mainland Americas. Here supplies could be stored, and men and horses could be rested and acclimated, before proceeding to the conquest of the continents. The loosely organized and vulnerable native communities of the West Indies also provided laboratories for testing the techniques that would eventually subdue the advanced Indian civilizations of Mexico and Peru. The most important such technique was the institution known as the ***encomienda***. It allowed the government to "commend," or give, Indians to certain colonists in return for the promise to try to Christianize them. In all but name, it was slavery. Spanish missionary Bartolomé de Las Casas, appalled by the *encomienda* system in Hispaniola, called it "a moral pestilence invented by Satan."

✦ The Conquest of Mexico

In 1519 Hernán Cortés set sail from Cuba with sixteen fresh horses and several hundred men aboard eleven ships, bound for Mexico and for destiny. On the island of Cozumel off the Yucatán Peninsula, he rescued a Spanish castaway who had been enslaved for several years by the Mayan-speaking Indians. A short

distance farther on, he picked up the female Indian slave Malinche, who knew both Mayan and Nahuatl, the language of the powerful Aztec rulers of the great empire in the highlands of central Mexico. In addition to his superior firepower, Cortés now had the advantage, through these two interpreters, of understanding the speech of the native peoples whom he was about to encounter, including the Aztecs. Malinche eventually learned Spanish and was baptized with the Spanish name of Doña Marina.

Near present-day Veracruz, Cortés made his final landfall. Through his interpreters he learned of unrest within the Aztec empire among the peoples from whom the Aztecs demanded tribute. He also heard alluring tales of the gold and other wealth stored up in the legendary Aztec capital of Tenochtitlán. He lusted to tear open the coffers of the Aztec kingdom. To quell his mutinous troops, he boldly burned his

Bartolomé de Las Casas (1474–1566), a reform-minded Dominican friar, wrote The Destruction of the Indies *in 1542 to chronicle the awful fate of the Native Americans and to protest Spanish policies in the New World. He was especially horrified at the catastrophic effects of disease on the native peoples:*

❝Who of those in future centuries will believe this? I myself who am writing this and saw it and know the most about it can hardly believe that such was possible.❞

In 1492, the same year that Columbus sighted America, the great Moorish city of Granada, in Spain, fell after a ten-year siege. For five centuries the Christian kingdoms of Spain had been trying to drive the North African Muslim *Moors* ("the Dark Ones," in Spanish) off the Iberian Peninsula, and with the fall of Granada they succeeded. But the lengthy *Reconquista* had left its mark on Spanish society. Centuries of military and religious confrontation nurtured an obsession with status and honor, bred religious zealotry and intolerance, and created a large class of men who regarded manual labor and commerce contemptuously. With the *Reconquista* ended, some of these men turned their restless gaze to Spain's New World frontier.

At first Spanish hopes for America focused on the Caribbean and on finding a sea route to Asia. Gradually, however, word filtered back of rich kingdoms on the mainland. Between 1519 and 1540, Spanish *conquistadores* swept across the Americas in two wide arcs of conquest—one driving from Cuba through Mexico into what is now the southwestern United States, the other starting from Panama and pushing south into Peru. Within half a century of Columbus's arrival in the Americas, the *conquistadores* had extinguished the great Aztec and Incan empires and claimed for church and crown a territory that extended from Colorado to Argentina, including much of what is now the continental United States.

The military conquest of this vast region was achieved by just ten thousand men, organized in a series of private expeditions. Hernán Cortés, Francisco Pizarro, and other aspiring conquerors signed contracts with the Spanish monarch, raised money from investors, and then went about recruiting an army. Only a small minority of the *conquistadores*—leaders or followers—were nobles. About half were professional soldiers and sailors; the rest comprised peasants, artisans, and members of the middling classes. Most were in their twenties and early thirties, and all knew how to wield a sword.

Diverse motives spurred these motley adventurers. Some hoped to win royal titles and favors by bringing new peoples under the Spanish flag. Others sought to ensure God's favor by spreading Christianity to the pagans. Some men hoped to escape dubious pasts, and others sought the kind of historical adventure experienced by heroes

Conquistadores, ca. 1534 This illustration for a book called the *Köhler Codex of Nuremberg* may be the earliest depiction of the *conquistadores* in the Americas. It portrays men and horses alike as steadfast and self-assured in their work of conquest.

Granger Collection

ships, cutting off any hope of retreat. Gathering a force of some twenty thousand Indian allies, he marched on Tenochtitlán and toward one of history's most dramatic and fateful encounters.

As Cortés proceeded, the Aztec chieftain Moctezuma sent ambassadors bearing fabulous gifts to welcome the approaching Spaniards. These only whetted the *conquistador's* appetite. "We Spanish suffer from a strange disease of the heart," Cortés allegedly informed the emissaries, "for which the only known remedy is gold." The ambassadors reported this comment to Moctezuma, along with the astonishing fact that the

newcomers rode on the backs of "deer" (horses). The superstitious Moctezuma also believed that Cortés was the god Quetzalcoatl, whose return from the eastern sea was predicted in Aztec legends. Expectant yet apprehensive, Moctezuma allowed the *conquistadores* to approach his capital unopposed.

As the Spaniards entered the Valley of Mexico, the sight of the Aztec capital of Tenochtitlán amazed them. With 300,000 inhabitants spread over ten square miles, it rivaled in size and pomp any city in contemporary Europe. The Aztec metropolis rose from an island in the center of a lake, surrounded by floating gardens of

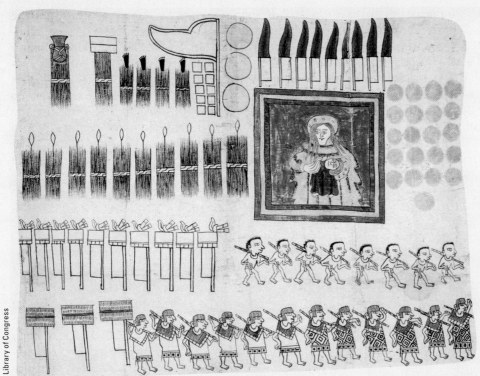

An Aztec View of the Conquest, 1531 Produced just a dozen years after Cortés's arrival in 1519, this drawing by an Aztec artist pictures the Indians rendering tribute to their conquerors. The inclusion of the banner showing the Madonna and child also illustrates the early incorporation of Christian beliefs by the Indians.

of classical antiquity. Nearly all shared a lust for gold. As one of Cortés's foot soldiers put it, "We came here to serve God and the king, and also to get rich." One historian adds that the *conquistadores* first fell on their knees and then fell upon the aborigines.

Armed with horses and gunpowder and preceded by disease, the *conquistadores* quickly overpowered the Indians. But most never achieved their dreams of glory. Few received titles of nobility, and many of the rank and file remained permanently indebted to the absentee investors who paid for their equipment. Even when an expedition captured exceptionally rich booty, the spoils were unevenly divided: men from the commander's home region often received more, and men on horseback generally got two shares to the

infantryman's one. The *conquistadores* lost still more power as the crown gradually tightened its control in the New World. By the 1530s in Mexico and the 1550s in Peru, colorless colonial administrators had replaced the freebooting *conquistadores*.

Nevertheless, the *conquistadores* achieved a kind of immortality. Because of a scarcity of Spanish women in the early days of the conquest, many of the *conquistadores* married Indian women. The soldiers who conquered Paraguay received three native women each, and Cortés's soldiers in Mexico—who were forbidden to consort with pagan women—quickly had their lovers baptized into the Catholic faith. Their offspring, the "new race" of *mestizos*, formed a cultural and a biological bridge between Latin America's European and Indian races.

extraordinary beauty. It was connected to the mainland by a series of causeways and supplied with fresh water by an artfully designed aqueduct.

Moctezuma treated Cortés hospitably at first, but soon the Spaniards' hunger for gold and power exhausted their welcome. "They thirsted mightily for gold; they stuffed themselves with it; they starved for it; they lusted for it like pigs," said one Aztec. On the **noche triste** (sad night) of June 30, 1520, the Aztecs attacked, driving the Spanish down the causeways from Tenochtitlán in a frantic, bloody retreat. Cortés then laid siege to the city, and it capitulated on August

13, 1521. That same year a smallpox epidemic burned through the Valley of Mexico. The combination of conquest and disease took a grisly toll. The Aztec empire gave way to three centuries of Spanish rule. The temples of Tenochtitlán were destroyed to make way for the Christian cathedrals of Mexico City, built on the site of the ruined Indian capital. And the native population of Mexico, winnowed mercilessly by the invader's diseases, shrank from some 20 million to 2 million people in less than a century.

Yet the invader brought more than conquest and death. He brought his crops and his animals, his

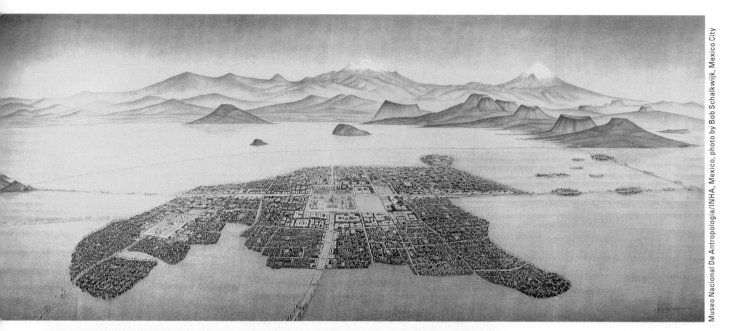

Artist's Rendering of Tenochtitlán   Amid tribal strife in the fourteenth century, the Aztecs built a capital on a small island in a lake in the central Valley of Mexico. From here they oversaw the most powerful empire yet to arise in Mesoamerica. Two main temples stood at the city's sacred center, one dedicated to Tlaloc, the ancient rain god, and the other to Huitzilopochtli, the tribal god, who was believed to require human hearts for sustenance.

language and his laws, his customs and his religion, all of which proved adaptable to the peoples of Mexico. He intermarried with the surviving Indians, creating a distinctive culture of **mestizos**, people of mixed Indian and European heritage. To this day Mexican civilization remains a unique blend of the Old World and the New, producing both ambivalence and pride among people of Mexican heritage. Cortés's translator, Malinche, for example, has given her name to the Mexican language in the word *malinchista*, or "traitor." But Mexicans also celebrate Columbus Day as the *Dia de la Raza*—the birthday of a wholly new race of people.

✦ The Spread of Spanish America

Spain's colonial empire grew swiftly and impressively. Within about half a century of Columbus's landfall, hundreds of Spanish cities and towns flourished in the Americas, especially in the great silver-producing centers of Peru and Mexico. Some 160,000 Spaniards, mostly men, had subjugated millions of Indians. Majestic cathedrals dotted the land, printing presses turned out books, and scholars studied at distinguished universities, including those at Mexico City and Lima, Peru, both founded in 1551, eighty-five years before Harvard, the first college established in the English colonies.

But how secure were these imperial possessions? Other powers were already sniffing around the edges of the Spanish domain, eager to bite off their share of the promised wealth of the new lands. The upstart English sent Giovanni Caboto (known in English as John Cabot) to explore the northeastern coast of North America in 1497 and 1498. The French king dispatched another Italian mariner, Giovanni da Verrazano, to probe the eastern seaboard in 1524. Ten years later the Frenchman Jacques Cartier journeyed hundreds of miles up the St. Lawrence River.

To secure the northern periphery of their New World domain against such encroachments and to convert more Indian souls to Christianity, the Spanish began to fortify and settle their North American borderlands. In a move to block French ambitions and to protect the sea-lanes to the Caribbean, the Spanish erected a fortress at St. Augustine, Florida, in 1565, thus founding the oldest continually inhabited European settlement in the future United States.

In Mexico the tales of Coronado's expedition of the 1540s to the upper Rio Grande and Colorado River regions continued to beckon the *conquistadores* northward. A dust-begrimed expeditionary column, with eighty-three rumbling wagons and hundreds of grumbling men, traversed the bare Sonora Desert from Mexico into the Rio Grande valley in 1598. Led by Don Juan de Oñate, the Spaniards cruelly abused the Pueblo

Museo Nacional De Antropologia/INHA, Mexico, photo by Bob Schalkwijk, Mexico City

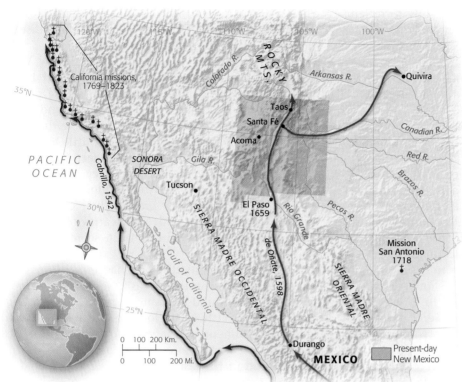

MAP 1.6 Spain's North American Frontier, 1542–1823

© Cengage Learning

The Granger Collection, New York

peoples they encountered. In the **Battle of Acoma** in 1599, the Spanish severed one foot of each survivor. They proclaimed the area to be the province of New Mexico in 1609 and founded its capital at Santa Fé the following year (see Map 1.6).

The Spanish settlers in New Mexico found a few furs and precious little gold, but they did discover a wealth of souls to be harvested for the Christian religion. The Roman Catholic mission became the central institution in colonial New Mexico until the missionaries' efforts to suppress native religious customs provoked an Indian uprising called **Popé's Rebellion** in 1680. The Pueblo rebels destroyed every Catholic church in the province and killed a score of priests and hundreds of Spanish settlers. In a reversal of Cortés's treatment of the Aztec temples more than a century earlier, the Indians rebuilt a *kiva*, or ceremonial religious chamber, on the ruins of the Spanish plaza at Santa Fé. It took

Arrival of Cortés, with Dona Marina, at Tenochtitlán in 1519 This painting by a Mexican artist depicts Cortés in the dress of a Spanish gentleman. His translator Malinche, whose Christian name was Marina, is given an honorable place at the front of the procession. She eventually married one of Cortés's soldiers, with whom she traveled to Spain and was received by the Spanish court.

nearly half a century for the Spanish fully to reclaim New Mexico from the insurrectionary Indians.

Meanwhile, as a further hedge against the ever-threatening French, who had sent an expedition under Robert de La Salle down the Mississippi River in the 1680s, the Spanish began around 1716 to establish settlements in Texas. Some refugees from the Pueblo uprising trickled into Texas, and a few missions were established there, including the one at San Antonio later known as the Alamo. But for at least another century, the Spanish presence remained weak in this distant northeastern outpost of Spain's Mexican empire.

To the west, in California, no serious foreign threat loomed, and Spain directed its attention there only belatedly. Juan Rodriguez Cabrillo had explored the California coast in 1542, but he failed to find San Francisco Bay or anything else of much interest. For some two centuries thereafter, California slumbered undisturbed by European intruders. Then in 1769 Spanish missionaries led by Father Junipero Serra founded at San Diego the first of a chain of twenty-one missions that wound up the coast as far as Sonoma, north of San Francisco Bay. Father Serra's brown-robed Franciscan friars toiled with zealous devotion to Christianize the three hundred thousand native Californians. They gathered the seminomadic Indians into fortified missions and taught them horticulture and basic crafts. These "mission Indians" did adopt Christianity, but they also lost contact with their native cultures and often lost their lives as well, as the white man's diseases doomed these biologically vulnerable peoples.

The misdeeds of the Spanish in the New World obscured their substantial achievements and helped give birth to the **Black Legend**. This false concept held that the conquerors merely tortured and butchered the Indians ("killing for Christ"), stole their gold, infected them with smallpox, and left little but misery behind. The Spanish invaders did indeed kill, enslave, and infect countless natives, but they also erected a colossal empire, sprawling from California and Florida to Tierra del Fuego. They grafted their culture, laws, religion, and language onto a wide array of native societies, laying the foundations for a score of Spanish-speaking nations.

Clearly, the Spaniards, who had more than a century's head start over the English, were genuine empire builders and cultural innovators in the New World. As compared with their Anglo-Saxon rivals, their colonial establishment was larger and richer, and it was destined to endure more than a quarter of a century longer. And in the last analysis, the Spanish paid the Native Americans the high compliment of fusing with them through marriage and incorporating indigenous culture into their own, rather than shunning and eventually isolating the Indians as their English adversaries would do.

Chapter Review

KEY TERMS

Canadian Shield (4)
Incas (6)
Aztecs (6)
nation-states (8)
Cahokia (8)
three-sister farming (8)
middlemen (11)
caravel (11)
plantation (12)
Columbian exchange (14)

Tordesillas, Treaty of (15)
conquistadores (15)
capitalism (16)
encomienda (17)
noche triste (19)
mestizos (20)
Acoma, Battle of (21)
Popé's Rebellion (21)
Black Legend (22)

PEOPLE TO KNOW

Ferdinand of Aragon
Isabella of Castile
Christopher Columbus
Francisco Coronado
Francisco Pizarro
Bartolomé de Las Casas
Hernán Cortés

Malinche (Doña Marina)
Moctezuma
Giovanni Caboto (John Cabot)
Robert de La Salle
Father Junipero Serra

TO LEARN MORE

Mark A. Burkholder and Lyman L. Johnson, *Colonial Latin America* (2000)

Alfred W. Crosby, Jr., *The Columbian Exchange: Biological and Cultural Consequences of 1492* (1972)

Jared Diamond, *Guns, Germs, and Steel: The Fates of Human Societies* (1998)

Tom Dillehay, *The Settlement of the Americas: A New Prehistory* (2000)

J. H. Elliott, *Empires of the Atlantic World* (2006)

Steven W. Hackel, *Children of Coyote, Missionaries of Saint Francis: Indian-Spanish Relations in Colonial California, 1769–1850* (2005)

Hugh Honour, *The New Golden Land* (1975)

Alice Beck Keyhoe, *America Before the European Invasions* (2002)

Anthony Pagden, *Peoples and Empires: A Short History of European Migration, Exploration, and Conquest, from Greece to the Present* (2003)

Andrés Reséndez, *A Land So Strange: The Epic Journey of Cabeza de Vaca* (2007)

John Thornton, *Africa and Africans in the Making of the Atlantic World, 1400–1800* (1992)

David J. Weber, *Bárbaros: Spaniards and Their Savages in the Age of Enlightenment* (2005)

A complete, annotated bibliography for this chapter—along with brief descriptions of the People to Know—may be found on the American Pageant website. The Key Terms are defined in a Glossary at the end of the text.

CHRONOLOGY

ca. 33,000–8000 B.C.E.	First humans cross into Americas from Asia
ca. 5000 B.C.E.	Corn is developed as a staple crop in highland Mexico
ca. 4000 B.C.E.	First civilized societies develop in the Middle East
ca. 1200 B.C.E.	Corn planting reaches present-day American Southwest
ca. 1000 C.E.	Norse voyagers discover and briefly settle in northeastern North America Corn cultivation reaches Midwest and southeastern Atlantic seaboard
ca. 1100 C.E.	Height of Mississippian settlement at Cahokia
ca. 1100–1300 C.E.	Christian crusades arouse European interest in the East
1295	Marco Polo returns to Europe
late 1400s	Spain becomes united
1488	Dias rounds southern tip of Africa
1492	Columbus lands in the Bahamas
1494	Treaty of Tordesillas between Spain and Portugal
1498	Da Gama reaches India Cabot explores northeastern coast of North America for England
1513	Balboa claims all lands touched by the Pacific Ocean for Spain
1513, 1521	Ponce de León explores Florida
1519–1521	Cortés conquers Mexico for Spain
1522	Magellan's vessel completes circumnavigation of the world
1524	Verrazano explores eastern seaboard of North America for France
1532	Pizarro crushes Incas
1534	Cartier journeys up the St. Lawrence River
1539–1542	De Soto explores the Southeast and discovers the Mississippi River
1540–1542	Coronado explores present-day Southwest
1542	Cabrillo explores California coast for Spain
1565	Spanish build fortress at St. Augustine
late 1500s	Iroquois Confederacy founded, according to Iroquois legend
ca. 1598–1609	Spanish under Oñate conquer Pueblo peoples of Rio Grande valley
1609	Spanish found New Mexico
1680	Popé's Rebellion in New Mexico
1680s	French expedition down Mississippi River under La Salle
1769	Serra founds first California mission, at San Diego

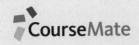
CourseMate

Go to the CourseMate website at **www.cengagebrain.com** for additional study tools and review materials—including audio and video clips—for this chapter.

AP® Review Questions for Chapter 1

1. The first European explorers reached the region that would become the Americas
   (A) more than 300 years ago.
   (B) about 400 years ago.
   (C) more than 500 years ago.
   (D) at least 600 years ago.
   (E) more than 600 years ago.

2. What proof has led researchers to conclude that the earth once contained a single continent?
   (A) There are identical species of fish in freshwater lakes across the globe.
   (B) There are similar types of mountain ranges around the world.
   (C) All the areas that are now separate regions were similarly impacted by the glaciers 10 million years ago.
   (D) Ethnic groups in one part of the world can trace their ancestry to people in completely different countries.
   (E) There are similar forms of vegetation in many nations.

3. What is the dominant theory about how the first people arrived in what we now call North America?
   (A) Native peoples long existed here.
   (B) They traveled in rafts and simple boats.
   (C) They walked as far as they could, then sailed or swam the rest of the way.
   (D) They walked across a land bridge from Eurasia to North America.
   (E) The first North Americans were Vikings who stayed.

4. The Incans (Peru), Mayans (Central America), and Aztecs (Mexico) owe the development of their sophisticated early civilizations to
   (A) the blessings of their many gods.
   (B) agriculture, particularly the cultivation of corn or maize.
   (C) early mathematics and mathematicians.
   (D) advanced early architecture.
   (E) political systems based on nation-states.

5. What was three-sister farming?
   (A) Small women-run farms that were common in some Native American cultures
   (B) An early farming cooperative in which three different tribal groups planted and harvested crops together
   (C) An agricultural method in which corn, beans, and squash were grown together
   (D) An effort originating in the southwest in 2000 C.E. to develop crops that would yield a more nutritious diet
   (E) The Iroquois inheritance system in which property and possessions passed from one generation to the next through the matrilineal (or mother's) line

6. Native Americans did NOT make a major imprint on the land they used for all of the following reasons EXCEPT they
   (A) feared changing it would impact their survival.
   (B) lacked the means to dramatically manipulate the land.
   (C) were spread in small groups across the continent.
   (D) revered nature and endowed it with spiritual properties.
   (E) had no desire to alter the landscape.

7. Which of these reasons did NOT drive the Europeans' exploration that led to "discovery" of the New World?
   (A) The desire to expand their empires and power
   (B) The quest for a cheaper route to the East
   (C) Spreading Christianity
   (D) Finding an alternate trade source for spices, sugar, and other expensive Eastern goods
   (E) Population surges and land shortages

8. The plantation system was first developed
   (A) in the American southern colonies.
   (B) by Portuguese explorers in West Africa.
   (C) by various tribal societies in Africa.
   (D) in the Chesapeake colonies.
   (E) by Native Americans.

9. All of the following events in the fifteenth century set the stage for the dramatic and unexpected discovery of the New World EXCEPT
   (A) increasingly successful long-distance voyages by explorers.
   (B) Spain's rising prominence, wealth, and power.
   (C) competition between European nations to colonize new land.
   (D) wars between rival European countries.
   (E) greater use of the compass.

10. What was the Columbian exchange?
    (A) Columbus's agreement with King Ferdinand and Queen Isabella
    (B) The diseases the Europeans brought to the Americas
    (C) A trade network Columbus established with Native Americans
    (D) The development of sugar plantations in the Caribbean for the European market
    (E) The transfer of plants, animals, culture, and diseases that occurred after Columbus's voyage

11. In the Treaty of Tordesillas, Spain
    (A) declared all New World territories as its own.
    (B) banned conquered Muslims from returning to its territories.
    (C) divided up the so-called New World with Portugal.
    (D) agreed not to enter the slave trade.
    (E) granted to Portugal control of West African silver mines.

12. Some scholars see the origins of modern capitalism in New World discoveries of precious metals for all of the following reasons EXCEPT that
    (A) they decreased the cost of consumer goods dramatically.
    (B) they stimulated surplus money supplies.
    (C) they laid the foundation for the development of the banking system.
    (D) they stimulated the spread of commerce and manufacturing.
    (E) they financed much of the international trade with Asia.

13. Spanish conquistadores, traveling to the New World, hoped to gain all of the following EXCEPT
    (A) noble or royal titles.
    (B) God's favor.
    (C) gold.
    (D) a fresh start.
    (E) the chance to organize an army.

14. Which of the following men was NOT an explorer for Spain?
    (A) Francisco Pizarro
    (B) Hernán Cortés
    (C) Giovanni Caboto
    (D) Juan Ponce de León
    (E) Francisco Coronado

15. How did the end of the Ice Age affect the peopling of the Americas?
    (A) It allowed settlers to explore new waterways.
    (B) It created new opportunities for African migration.
    (C) It allowed settlers to roam east and south, reaching all points of the continent.
    (D) It prevented future mass migration to the Western Hemisphere.
    (E) It opened the land bridge from Eurasia to the Americas.

16. The Spanish empire in America imported Old World culture and ideas by doing all of the following EXCEPT
    (A) building universities.
    (B) using the printing press to publish written work.
    (C) erecting cathedrals and Christianizing Native Americans.
    (D) fusing Spanish and native cultures through marriage.
    (E) shunning and isolating the Native Americans.

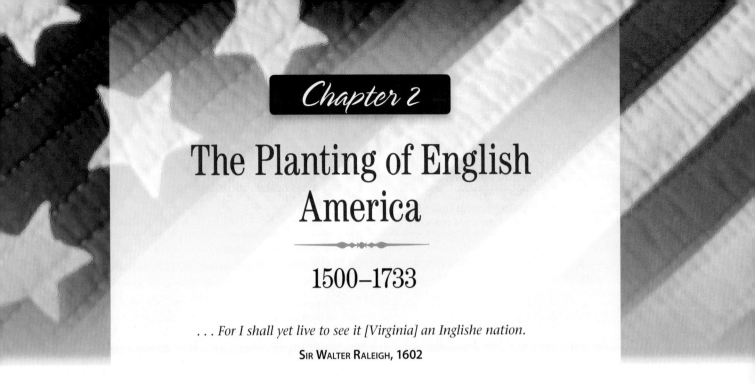

Chapter 2

The Planting of English America

1500–1733

. . . For I shall yet live to see it [Virginia] an Inglishe nation.

SIR WALTER RALEIGH, 1602

As the seventeenth century dawned, scarcely a hundred years after Columbus's momentous landfall, the face of much of the New World had already been profoundly transformed. European crops and livestock had begun to alter the very landscape, touching off an ecological revolution that would reverberate for centuries to come. From Tierra del Fuego in the south to Hudson Bay in the north, disease and armed conquest had cruelly winnowed and disrupted the native peoples. Several hundred thousand enslaved Africans toiled on Caribbean and Brazilian sugar plantations. From Florida and New Mexico southward, most of the New World lay firmly within the grip of imperial Spain.

But north of Mexico, America in 1600 remained largely unexplored and effectively unclaimed by Europeans. Then, as if to herald the coming century of colonization and conflict in the northern continent, three European powers planted three primitive outposts in three distant corners of the continent within three years of one another: the Spanish at Santa Fé in 1610, the French at Québec in 1608, and, most consequentially for the future United States, the English at Jamestown, Virginia, in 1607.

✦ England's Imperial Stirrings

Feeble indeed were England's efforts in the 1500s to compete with the sprawling Spanish Empire. As Spain's ally in the first half of the century, England took little interest in establishing its own overseas colonies. Religious conflict also disrupted England in midcentury, after King Henry VIII broke with the Roman Catholic Church in the 1530s, launching the English **Protestant Reformation**. Catholics battled Protestants for decades, and the religious balance of power seesawed. But after the Protestant Elizabeth ascended to the English throne in 1558, Protestantism became dominant in England, and rivalry with Catholic Spain intensified.

Ireland, which nominally had been under English rule since the twelfth century, became an early scene of that rivalry. The Catholic Irish sought help from Catholic Spain to throw off the yoke of the new Protestant English queen. But Spanish aid never amounted to much; in the 1570s and 1580s, Elizabeth's troops crushed the Irish uprising with terrible ferocity, inflicting unspeakable atrocities upon the native Irish people. The English crown confiscated Catholic Irish lands and "planted" them with new Protestant landlords from Scotland and England. This policy also planted the seeds of the centuries-old religious conflicts that persist in Ireland to the present day. Many English soldiers developed in Ireland a sneering contempt for the "savage" natives, an attitude that they brought with them to the New World.

✦ Elizabeth Energizes England

Encouraged by the ambitious Elizabeth I (see Table 2.1), hardy English buccaneers now swarmed out upon the shipping lanes. They sought to promote the twin goals of Protestantism and plunder by seizing Spanish treasure ships and raiding Spanish settlements, even though England and Spain were technically at peace. The most famous of these semipiratical "sea dogs" was

© The Gallery Collection/Corbis

Elizabeth I (1533–1603), by George Gower, ca. 1588 In this "Armada Portrait" of Queen Elizabeth I, the artist proclaims her the Empress of the World. She was accused of being vain, fickle, prejudiced, and miserly, but Elizabeth proved to be an unusually successful ruler. She never married (hence, the "Virgin Queen"), although many romances were rumored and royal matches schemed.

the courtly Sir Francis Drake. He swashbuckled and looted his way around the planet, returning in 1580 with his ship heavily ballasted with Spanish booty. The venture netted profits of about 4,600 percent to his financial backers, among whom, in secret, was Queen Elizabeth. Defying Spanish protest, she brazenly knighted Drake on the deck of his barnacled ship.

The bleak coast of Newfoundland was the scene of the first English attempt at colonization. This effort collapsed when its promoter, Sir Humphrey Gilbert, lost his life at sea in 1583. Gilbert's ill-starred dream inspired his gallant half-brother Sir Walter Raleigh to try again in warmer climes. Raleigh organized an expedition that first landed in 1585 on North Carolina's **Roanoke Island**, off the coast of Virginia—a vaguely defined region named in honor of Elizabeth, the "Virgin Queen." After several false starts, the hapless Roanoke colony mysteriously vanished, swallowed up by the wilderness.

These pathetic English failures at colonization contrasted embarrassingly with the glories of the Spanish Empire, whose profits were fabulously enriching Spain. Philip II of Spain, self-anointed foe of the Protestant Reformation, used part of his imperial gains to amass an "Invincible Armada" of ships for an invasion of England. The showdown came in 1588, when the lumbering Spanish flotilla, 130 strong, hove into the English Channel. The English sea dogs fought back. Using craft that were swifter, more maneuverable, and more ably

manned, they inflicted heavy damage on the cumbersome, overladen Spanish ships. Then a devastating storm arose (the "Protestant wind"), scattering the crippled Spanish fleet.

The rout of the **Spanish Armada** marked the beginning of the end of Spanish imperial dreams, though Spain's New World empire would not fully collapse for three more centuries. Within a few decades, the Spanish Netherlands (Holland) would secure its

In the years immediately following the defeat of the Spanish Armada, the English writer Richard Hakluyt (1552?–1616) extravagantly exhorted his countrymen to cast off their "sluggish security" and undertake the colonization of the New World:

❝There is under our noses the great and ample country of Virginia; the inland whereof is found of late to be so sweet and wholesome a climate, so rich and abundant in silver mines, a better and richer country than Mexico itself. If it shall please the Almighty to stir up Her Majesty's heart to continue with transporting one or two thousand of her people, she shall by God's assistance, in short space, increase her dominions, enrich her coffers, and reduce many pagans to the faith of Christ.**❞**

TABLE 2.1 The Tudor Rulers of England*	
Name, Reign	**Relation to America**
Henry VII, 1485–1509	Cabot voyages, 1497, 1498
Henry VIII, 1509–1547	English Reformation began
Edward VI, 1547–1553	Strong Protestant tendencies
"Bloody" Mary, 1553–1558	Catholic reaction
Elizabeth I, 1558–1603	Break with Roman Catholic Church final; Drake; Spanish Armada defeated

*See Table 3.1, p. 48, for a continuation of the table.

Sir Walter Ralegh (Raleigh) (ca. 1552–1618), 1588
A dashing courtier who was one of Queen Elizabeth's favorites for his wit, good looks, and courtly manners, he launched important colonizing failures in the New World. For this portrait, Raleigh presented himself as the queen's devoted servant, wearing her colors of black and white and her emblem of a pearl in his left ear. After seducing (and secretly marrying) one of Queen Elizabeth's maids of honor, he fell out of favor but continued his colonial ventures in the hopes of challenging Catholic Spain's dominance in the Americas. He was ultimately beheaded for treason.

The Granger Collection, New York

independence, and much of the Spanish Caribbean would slip from Spain's grasp. Bloated by Peruvian and Mexican silver and cockily convinced of its own invincibility, Spain had overreached itself, sowing the seeds of its own decline.

England's victory over the Spanish Armada also marked a red-letter day in American history. It dampened Spain's fighting spirit and helped ensure England's naval dominance in the North Atlantic. It started England on its way to becoming master of the world oceans—a fact of enormous importance to the American people. Indeed England now had many of the characteristics that Spain displayed on the eve of its colonizing adventure a century earlier: a strong, unified national state under a popular monarch; a measure of religious unity after a protracted struggle between Protestants and Catholics; and a vibrant sense of nationalism and national destiny.

A wondrous flowering of the English national spirit bloomed in the wake of the Spanish Armada's defeat. A golden age of literature dawned in this exhilarating atmosphere, with William Shakespeare, at its forefront, making occasional poetical references to England's American colonies. The English were seized with restlessness, with thirst for adventure, and with curiosity about the unknown. Everywhere there blossomed a new spirit of self-confidence, of vibrant patriotism, and of boundless faith in the future of the English nation. When England and Spain finally signed a treaty of peace in 1604, the English people were poised to plunge headlong into the planting of their own colonial empire in the New World.

✶ England on the Eve of Empire

England's scepter'd isle, as Shakespeare called it, throbbed with social and economic change as the seventeenth century opened. Its population was mushrooming, from some 3 million people in 1550 to about 4 million in 1600. In the ever-green English countryside, landlords were "enclosing" croplands for sheep grazing, forcing many small farmers into precarious tenancy or off the land altogether. It was no accident that the woolen districts of eastern and western England—where Puritanism had taken strong root—supplied many of the earliest immigrants to America. When economic depression hit the woolen trade in the late 1500s, thousands of footloose farmers took to the roads. They drifted about England, chronically unemployed, often ending up as beggars and paupers in cities like Bristol and London.

This remarkably mobile population alarmed many contemporaries. They concluded that England was burdened with a "surplus population," though present-day London holds twice as many people as did all of England in 1600.

At the same time, laws of **primogeniture** decreed that only eldest sons were eligible to inherit landed estates. Landholders' ambitious younger sons, among them Gilbert, Raleigh, and Drake, were forced to seek their fortunes elsewhere. Bad luck plagued their early, lone-wolf enterprises. But by the early 1600s, the **joint-stock company**, forerunner of the modern corporation, was perfected. It enabled a considerable number of investors, called "adventurers," to pool their capital.

Peace with a chastened Spain provided the opportunity for English colonization. Population growth provided the workers. Unemployment, as well as a thirst for adventure, for markets, and for religious freedom, provided the motives. Joint-stock companies provided the financial means. The stage was now set for a historic effort to establish an English beachhead in the still uncharted North American wilderness.

✳ England Plants the Jamestown Seedling

In 1606, two years after peace with Spain, the hand of destiny beckoned toward Virginia. A joint-stock company, known as the **Virginia Company** of London, received a charter from King James I of England for a settlement in the New World. The main attraction was the promise of gold, combined with a strong desire to find a passage through America to the Indies. Like most joint-stock companies of the day, the Virginia Company was intended to endure for only a few years, after which its stockholders hoped to liquidate it for a profit. This arrangement put severe pressure on the luckless colonists, who were threatened with abandonment in the wilderness if they did not quickly strike it rich on the company's behalf. Few of the investors thought in terms of long-term colonization. Apparently no one even faintly suspected that the seeds of a mighty nation were being planted.

The **charter** of the Virginia Company is a significant document in American history. It guaranteed to the overseas settlers the same rights of Englishmen that they would have enjoyed if they had stayed at home. This precious boon was gradually extended to subsequent English colonies, helping to reinforce the colonists' sense that even on the far shores of the Atlantic, they remained comfortably within the embrace of traditional English institutions. But ironically, a century and a half later, their insistence on the "rights of Englishmen" fed hot resentment against an increasingly meddlesome mother country and nourished their appetite for independence.

Setting sail in late 1606, the Virginia Company's three ships landed near the mouth of Chesapeake Bay,

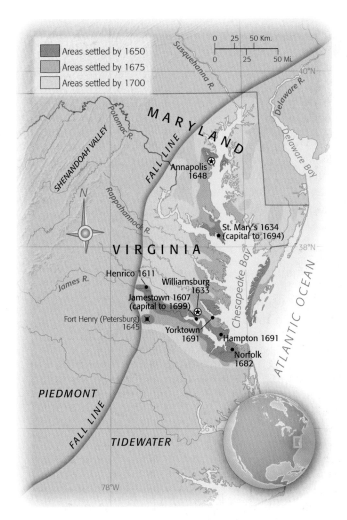

MAP 2.1 Early Maryland and Virginia © Cengage Learning

where Indians attacked them. Pushing on up the bay, the tiny band of colonists eventually chose a location on the wooded and malarial banks of the James River, named in honor of King James I. The site was easy to defend, but it was mosquito-infested and devastatingly unhealthful. There, on May 24, 1607, about a hundred English settlers, all of them men, disembarked. They called the place **Jamestown** (see Map 2.1).

The early years of Jamestown proved a nightmare for all concerned—except the buzzards. Forty would-be colonists perished during the initial voyage in 1606–1607. Another expedition in 1609 lost its leaders and many of its precious supplies in a shipwreck off Bermuda. Once ashore in Virginia, the settlers died by the dozens from disease, malnutrition, and starvation. Ironically, the woods rustled with game and the rivers flopped with fish, but the greenhorn settlers, many of them self-styled "gentlemen" unaccustomed to fending for themselves, wasted valuable time grubbing for nonexistent gold when they should have been gathering provisions.

George Percy (1580–1631) accompanied Captain John Smith on his expedition to Virginia in 1606–1607. He served as deputy governor of the colony in 1609–1610 and returned to England in 1612, where he wrote A Discourse of the Plantation of Virginia *about his experiences:*

❝Our men were destroyed with cruel diseases as swellings, burning fevers, and by wars, and some departed suddenly, but for the most part they died of mere famine. There were never Englishmen left in a foreign country in such misery as we were in this new discovered Virginia.❞

Virginia was saved from utter collapse at the start largely by the leadership and resourcefulness of an intrepid young adventurer, Captain John Smith. Taking over in 1608, he whipped the gold-hungry colonists into line with the rule "He who shall not work shall not eat." He had been kidnapped in December 1607 and subjected to a mock execution by the Indian chieftain Powhatan, whose daughter Pocahontas had "saved" Smith by dramatically interposing her head between his and the war clubs of his captors. The symbolism of this ritual was apparently intended to impress Smith with Powhatan's power and with the Indians' desire for peaceful relations with the Virginians. Pocahontas became an intermediary between the Indians and the settlers, helping to preserve a shaky peace and to provide needed foodstuffs.

Still, the colonists died in droves, and living skeletons were driven to desperate acts. They were reduced to eating "dogges, Catts, Ratts, and Myce" and even to digging up corpses for food. One hungry man killed, salted, and ate his wife, for which misbehavior he was executed. Of the four hundred settlers who managed to make it to Virginia by 1609, only sixty survived the "starving time" winter of 1609–1610.

Diseased and despairing, the remaining colonists dragged themselves aboard homeward-bound ships in the spring of 1610, only to be met at the mouth of the

The authorities meted out harsh discipline in the young Virginia colony. One Jamestown settler who publicly criticized the governor was sentenced to

❝be disarmed [and] have his arms broken and his tongue bored through with an awl [and] shall pass through a guard of 40 men and shall be butted [with muskets] by every one of them and at the head of the troop kicked down and footed out of the fort.❞

Ætatis suæ 21. A°. 1616.

Maioaks als Rebecka daughter to the mighty Prince Powhatan Emperour of Attanoughkomouck als Virginia converted and baptized in the Christian faith, and Wife to the wor.ⁱ¹ Mr. Tho: Rolff.

National Portrait Gallery, Smithsonian/Art Resource, NY

Pocahontas (ca. 1595–1617) Taken to England by her husband, she was received as a princess. She died when preparing to return, but her infant son ultimately reached Virginia, where hundreds of his descendants have lived, including the second Mrs. Woodrow Wilson.

James River by a long-awaited relief party headed by a new governor, Lord De La Warr. He ordered the settlers back to Jamestown, imposed a harsh military regime on the colony, and soon undertook aggressive military action against the Indians.

Disease continued to reap a gruesome harvest among the Virginians. By 1625 Virginia contained only some twelve hundred hard-bitten survivors of the nearly eight thousand adventurers who had tried to start life anew in the ill-fated colony.

✦ Cultural Clashes in the Chesapeake

When the English landed in 1607, the chieftain Powhatan dominated the native peoples living in the James River area. He had asserted supremacy over a few dozen small tribes, loosely affiliated in what somewhat grandly came to be called Powhatan's Confederacy. The English colonists dubbed all the local Indians, somewhat inaccurately, the Powhatans. Powhatan at first may have considered the English potential allies in his struggle to extend his power still further over his

Indian rivals, and he tried to be conciliatory. But relations between the Indians and the English remained tense, especially as the starving colonists took to raiding Indian food supplies.

The atmosphere grew even more strained after Lord De La Warr arrived in 1610. He carried orders from the Virginia Company that amounted to a declaration of war against the Indians in the Jamestown region. A veteran of the vicious campaigns against the Irish, De La Warr now introduced "Irish tactics" against the Indians. His troops raided Indian villages, burned houses, confiscated provisions, and torched cornfields. A peace settlement ended this **First Anglo-Powhatan War** in 1614, sealed by the marriage of Pocahontas to the colonist John Rolfe—the first known interracial union in Virginia.

A fragile respite followed, which endured eight years. But the Indians, pressed by the land-hungry whites and ravaged by European diseases, struck back in 1622. A series of Indian attacks left 347 settlers dead, including John Rolfe. In response the Virginia Company issued new orders calling for "a perpetual war without peace or truce," one that would prevent the Indians "from being any longer a people." Periodic punitive raids systematically reduced the native population and drove the survivors ever farther westward.

In the **Second Anglo-Powhatan War** in 1644, the Indians made one last effort to dislodge the Virginians. They were again defeated. The peace treaty of 1646 repudiated any thought of assimilating the native peoples into Virginia society or of peacefully coexisting with them. Instead it effectively banished the Chesapeake Indians from their ancestral lands and formally separated Indian from white areas of settlement— the origins of the later reservation system. By 1669 an official census revealed that only about two thousand Indians remained in Virginia, perhaps 10 percent of the population the original English settlers had encountered in 1607. By 1685 the English considered the Powhatan peoples extinct.

A Carolina Indian Woman and Child, by John White The artist was a member of the Raleigh expedition of 1585. Notice that the Indian girl carries a European doll, illustrating the mingling of cultures that had already begun. Granger Collection, New York

> *The wife of a Virginia governor wrote to her sister in England in 1623 of her voyage:*
>
> **❝For our Shippe was so pestered with people and goods that we were so full of infection that after a while we saw little but throwing folkes over board: It pleased god to send me my helth till I came to shoare and 3 dayes after I fell sick but I thank god I am well recovered. Few else are left alive that came in that Shippe.❞**

It had been the Powhatans' calamitous misfortune to fall victim to three Ds: disease, disorganization, and disposability. Like native peoples throughout the New World, they were extremely susceptible to European-borne maladies. Epidemics of smallpox and measles raced mercilessly through their villages. The Powhatans also—despite the apparent cohesiveness of "Powhatan's Confederacy"—lacked the unity with which to make effective opposition to the comparatively well-organized and militarily disciplined whites. Finally, unlike the Indians whom the Spaniards had encountered to the south, who could be put to work in the mines and had gold and silver to trade, the Powhatans served no economic function for the Virginia colonists. They provided no reliable labor source and, after the Virginians began growing their own food crops, had no valuable commodities to offer in commerce. The natives, as far as the Virginians were concerned, could be disposed of without harm to the colonial economy. Indeed the Indian presence frustrated the colonists' desire for a local commodity the Europeans desperately wanted: land.

✴ The Indians' New World

The fate of the Powhatans foreshadowed the destinies of indigenous peoples throughout the continent as the process of European settlement went forward. Native Americans, of course, had a history well

Carolina Indians German painter Philip Georg Friedrich von Reck drew these Yuchi Indians in the 1730s. The blanket and rifle show that trade with the English settlers had already begun to transform Native American culture.

Det Kongelige Bibliotek or The Royal Library in Copenhagen, Denmark

before Columbus's arrival. They were no strangers to change, adaptation, and even catastrophe, as the rise and decline of civilizations such as the Mississippians and the Anasazis demonstrated. But the shock of

Benjamin Franklin (1706-1790) in a 1753 letter to Peter Collinson commented on the attractiveness of Indian life to Europeans:

❝When an Indian child has been brought up among us, taught our language and habituated to our customs, yet if he goes to see his relations and make one Indian ramble with them, there is no persuading him ever to return. [But] when white persons of either sex have been taken prisoners by the Indians, and lived awhile among them, though ransomed by their friends, and treated with all imaginable tenderness to prevail with them to stay among the English, yet in a short time they become disgusted with our manner of life, and the care and pains that are necessary to support it, and take the first good opportunity of escaping again into the woods, from whence there is no reclaiming them.❞

large-scale European colonization disrupted Native American life on a vast scale, inducing unprecedented demographic and cultural transformations.

Some changes were fairly benign. Horses—stolen, strayed, or purchased from Spanish invaders—catalyzed a substantial Indian migration onto the Great Plains in the eighteenth century. Peoples such as the Lakotas (Sioux), who had previously been sedentary forest dwellers, now moved onto the wide-open plains. There they thrived impressively, adopting an entirely new way of life as mounted nomadic hunters. But the effects of contact with Europeans proved less salutary for most other native peoples.

Disease was by far the biggest disrupter, as Old World pathogens licked lethally through biologically defenseless Indian populations. Disease took more than human life; it extinguished entire cultures and occasionally helped shape new ones. Epidemics often robbed native peoples of the elders who preserved the oral traditions that held clans together. Devastated Indian bands then faced the daunting task of literally reinventing themselves without benefit of accumulated wisdom or kin networks. The decimation and forced migration of native peoples sometimes scrambled them together in wholly new ways. The Catawba nation of the southern Piedmont region, for example, was formed from splintered remnants of several different groups uprooted by the shock of the Europeans' arrival.

Trade also transformed Indian life, as traditional barter-and-exchange networks gave way to the temptations of European commerce. Firearms, for example, conferred enormous advantages on those who could purchase them from Europeans. The desire for firearms thus intensified competition among the tribes for access to prime hunting grounds that could supply the skins and pelts that the European arms traders wanted. The result was an escalating cycle of Indian-on-Indian violence, fueled by the lure and demands of European trade goods.

Native Americans were swept up in the expanding Atlantic economy, but they usually struggled in vain to control their own place in it. One desperate band of Virginia Indians, resentful at the prices offered by British traders for their deerskins, loaded a fleet of canoes with hides and tried to paddle to England to sell their goods directly. Not far from the Virginia shore, a storm swamped their frail craft. Their cargo lost, the few survivors were picked up by an English ship and sold into slavery in the West Indies.

Indians along the Atlantic seaboard felt the most ferocious effects of European contact. Farther inland, native peoples had the advantages of time, space, and numbers as they sought to adapt to the European incursion. The Algonquins in the Great Lakes area, for instance, became a substantial regional power. They bolstered their population by absorbing various surrounding bands and dealt from a position of strength with the few Europeans who managed to penetrate the interior. As a result, a British or French trader wanting to do business with the inland tribes had little choice but to conform to Indian ways, often taking an Indian wife. Thus was created a middle ground, a zone where both Europeans and Native Americans were compelled to accommodate to one another—at least until the Europeans began to arrive in large numbers.

✶ Virginia: Child of Tobacco

John Rolfe, the husband of Pocahontas, became father of the tobacco industry and an economic savior of the Virginia colony. By 1612 he had perfected methods of raising and curing the pungent weed, eliminating much of the bitter tang. Soon the European demand for tobacco was nearly insatiable. A tobacco rush swept over Virginia, as crops were planted in the streets of Jamestown and even between the numerous graves. So exclusively did the colonists concentrate on planting the yellow leaf that at first they had to import some of their foodstuffs. Colonists who had once hungered for food now hungered for land, ever more land on which

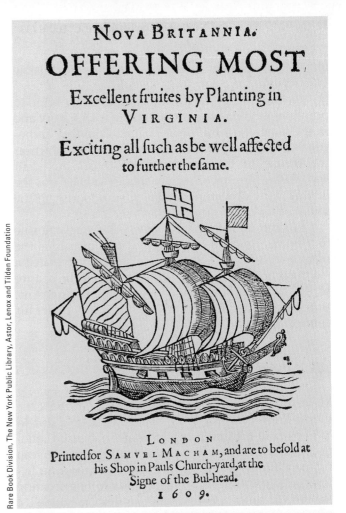

NOVA BRITANNIA.
OFFERING MOST
Excellent fruites by Planting in
VIRGINIA.

Exciting all such as be well affected
to further the same.

LONDON
Printed for SAMVEL MACHAM, and are to besold at
his Shop in Pauls Church-yard, at the
Signe of the Bul-head.
1609.

Advertisement for a Voyage to America, 1609

to plant ever more tobacco. Relentlessly, they pressed the frontier of settlement up the river valleys to the west, abrasively edging against the Indians.

Virginia's prosperity was finally built on tobacco smoke. This "bewitching weed" played a vital role in putting the colony on firm economic foundations. But tobacco—King Nicotine—was something of a tyrant. It was ruinous to the soil when greedily planted in successive years, and it enchained the fortunes of Virginia to the fluctuating price of a single crop. Fatefully, tobacco also promoted the broad-acred plantation system and with it a brisk demand for fresh labor.

In 1619, the year before the Plymouth Pilgrims landed in New England, what was described as a Dutch warship appeared off Jamestown and sold some twenty Africans. The scanty record does not reveal whether they were purchased as lifelong slaves or as servants committed to limited years of servitude. However it transpired, this simple commercial transaction planted the seeds of the North American slave system. Yet blacks were too costly for most of the hard-pinched white colonists to acquire, and for decades few were brought to Virginia. In 1650 Virginia counted but three hundred blacks, although by the end of the century blacks, most of them enslaved, made up approximately 14 percent of the colony's population.

Representative self-government was also born in primitive Virginia, in the same cradle with slavery and in the same year—1619. The Virginia Company authorized the settlers to summon an assembly, known as the **House of Burgesses**. A momentous precedent was thus feebly established, for this assemblage was the first of many miniature parliaments to flourish in the soil of America.

As time passed, James I grew increasingly hostile to Virginia. He detested tobacco, and he distrusted the representative House of Burgesses, which he branded a "seminary of sedition." In 1624 he revoked the charter of the bankrupt and beleaguered Virginia Company, thus making Virginia a royal colony directly under his control.

✵ Maryland: Catholic Haven

Maryland—the second plantation colony but the fourth English colony to be planted—was founded in 1634 by Lord Baltimore, of a prominent English Catholic family. He embarked upon the venture partly to reap financial profits and partly to create a refuge for his fellow Catholics. Protestant England was still persecuting Roman Catholics; among numerous discriminations, a couple seeking wedlock could not be legally married by a Catholic priest.

Absentee proprietor Lord Baltimore hoped that the two hundred settlers who founded Maryland at St. Marys, on Chesapeake Bay, would be the vanguard of a vast new feudal domain. Huge estates were to be awarded to his largely Catholic relatives, and gracious manor houses, modeled on those of England's aristocracy, were intended to arise amidst the fertile forests. As in Virginia, colonists proved willing to come only if offered the opportunity to acquire land of their own. Soon they were dispersed around the Chesapeake region on modest farms, and the haughty land barons, mostly Catholic, were surrounded by resentful back-country planters, mostly Protestant. Resentment flared into open rebellion near the end of the century, and the Baltimore family for a time lost its proprietary rights.

Despite these tensions Maryland prospered. Like Virginia, it blossomed forth in acres of tobacco. Also like Virginia, it depended for labor in its early years mainly on white indentured servants—penniless persons who bound themselves to work for a number of years to pay their passage. In both colonies it was only in the later years of the seventeenth century that black slaves began to be imported in large numbers.

Lord Baltimore, a canny soul, permitted unusual freedom of worship at the outset. He hoped that he would thus purchase toleration for his own fellow worshipers. But the heavy tide of Protestants threatened to submerge the Catholics and place severe restrictions on them, as in England. Faced with disaster, the Catholics of Maryland threw their support behind the famed **Act of Toleration**, which was passed in 1649 by the local representative assembly.

Maryland's new religious statute guaranteed toleration to all Christians. But, less liberally, it decreed the death penalty for those, like Jews and atheists, who denied the divinity of Jesus. The law thus sanctioned less toleration than had previously existed in the settlement, but it did extend a temporary cloak of protection to the uneasy Catholic minority. One result was that when the colonial era ended, Maryland probably sheltered more Roman Catholics than any other English-speaking colony in the New World.

✵ The West Indies: Way Station to Mainland America

While the English were planting the first frail colonial shoots in the Chesapeake, they also were busily colonizing the islands of the West Indies. Spain, weakened by military overextension and distracted by its rebellious Dutch provinces, relaxed its grip on much of the Caribbean in the early 1600s. By the mid-seventeenth century, England had secured its claim to several West Indian islands, including the large prize of Jamaica in 1655.

Sugar formed the foundation of the West Indian economy. What tobacco was to the Chesapeake, sugar cane was to the Caribbean—with one crucial difference. Tobacco was a poor man's crop. It could be planted easily, it produced commercially marketable leaves within a year, and it required only simple processing. Sugar cane, in contrast, was a rich man's crop.

African slaves destined for the West Indian sugar plantations were bound and branded on West African beaches and ferried out in canoes to the waiting slave ships. An English sailor described the scene:

"The Negroes are so wilful and loth to leave their own country, that have often leap'd out of the canoes, boat and ship, into the sea, and kept under water till they were drowned, to avoid being taken up and saved by our boats, which pursued them; they having a more dreadful apprehension of Barbadoes than we can have of hell."

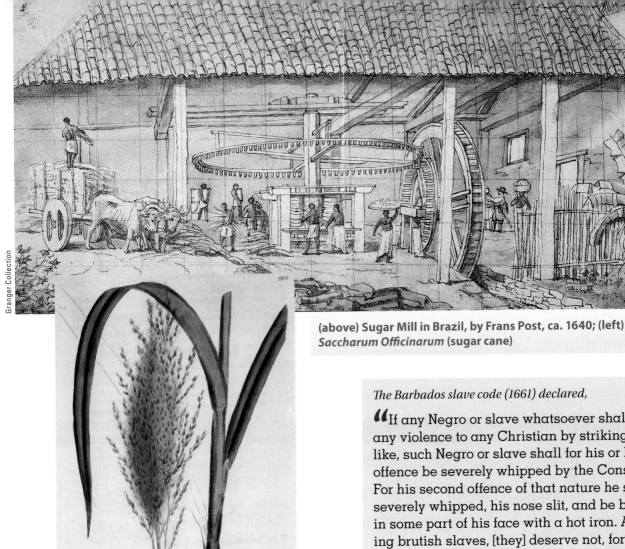

Saccharum officinarum

(above) **Sugar Mill in Brazil, by Frans Post, ca. 1640; (left)** *Saccharum Officinarum* **(sugar cane)**

The Barbados slave code (1661) declared,

"If any Negro or slave whatsoever shall offer any violence to any Christian by striking or the like, such Negro or slave shall for his or her first offence be severely whipped by the Constable. For his second offence of that nature he shall be severely whipped, his nose slit, and be burned in some part of his face with a hot iron. And being brutish slaves, [they] deserve not, for the baseness of their condition, to be tried by the legal trial of twelve men of their peers, as the subjects of England are. And it is further enacted and ordained that if any Negro or other slave under punishment by his master unfortunately shall suffer in life or member, which seldom happens, no person whatsoever shall be liable to any fine therefore."

It had to be planted extensively to yield commercially viable quantities of sugar. Extensive planting, in turn, required extensive and arduous land clearing. And the cane stalks yielded their sugar only after an elaborate process of refining in a sugar mill. The need for land and for the labor to clear it and to run the mills made sugar cultivation a capital-intensive business. Only wealthy growers with abundant capital to invest could succeed in sugar.

The sugar lords extended their dominion over the West Indies in the seventeenth century. To work their sprawling plantations, they imported enormous numbers of enslaved Africans—more than a quarter of a million in the five decades after 1640. By about 1700, black slaves outnumbered white settlers in the English West Indies by nearly four to one, and the region's population has remained predominantly black ever since. West Indians thus take their place among the numerous children of the African diaspora—the vast scattering of African peoples throughout the New World in the three and a half centuries following Columbus's discovery.

To control this large and potentially restive slave population, English authorities devised formal "codes" that defined the slaves' legal status and their masters' prerogatives. The notorious **Barbados slave code** of 1661 denied even the most fundamental rights to slaves and gave masters virtually complete control over their laborers, including the right to inflict vicious punishments for even slight infractions.

The profitable sugar-plantation system soon crowded out almost all other forms of Caribbean agriculture. The West Indies increasingly depended on the North American mainland for foodstuffs and other basic supplies. And smaller English farmers, squeezed out by the greedy sugar barons, began to migrate to the newly founded southern mainland colonies. A group of displaced English settlers from Barbados arrived in Carolina in 1670. They brought with them a few enslaved Africans, as well as the model of the Barbados slave code, which eventually inspired statutes governing slavery throughout the mainland colonies. Carolina officially adopted a version of the Barbados slave code in 1696. Just as the West Indies had been a testing ground for the *encomienda* system that the Spanish had brought to Mexico and South America, so the Caribbean islands now served as a staging area for the slave system that would take root elsewhere in English North America.

⭐ Colonizing the Carolinas

Civil war convulsed England in the 1640s. King Charles I had dismissed Parliament in 1629, and when he eventually recalled it in 1640, the members were mutinous. Finding their great champion in the Puritan-soldier Oliver Cromwell, they ultimately beheaded Charles in 1649, and Cromwell ruled England for nearly a decade. Finally, Charles II, son of the decapitated king, was restored to the throne in 1660.

Colonization had been interrupted during this period of bloody unrest. Now, in the so-called Restoration period, empire building resumed with even greater intensity—and royal involvement (see Table 2.2). Carolina, named for Charles II, was formally created in 1670, after the king granted to eight of his court favorites, the Lords Proprietors, an expanse of wilderness ribboning across the continent to the Pacific. These aristocratic founders hoped to grow foodstuffs to provision the sugar plantations in Barbados and to export non-English products like wine, silk, and olive oil.

Carolina prospered by developing close economic ties with the flourishing sugar islands of the English West Indies. In a broad sense, the mainland colony was but the most northerly of those outposts. Many original

TABLE 2.2 The Thirteen Original Colonies

Name	Founded by	Year	Charter	Made Royal	1775 Status
1. Virginia	London Co.	1607	1606 / 1609 / 1612	1624	Royal (under the crown)
2. New Hampshire	John Mason and others	1623	1679	1679	Royal (absorbed by Mass., 1641–1679)
3. Massachusetts	Puritans	ca. 1628	1629	1691	Royal
Plymouth	Separatists	1620	None		(Merged with Mass., 1691)
Maine	F. Gorges	1623	1639		(Bought by Mass., 1677)
4. Maryland	Lord Baltimore	1634	1632	___	Proprietary (controlled by proprietor)
5. Connecticut	Mass. emigrants	1635	1662	___	Self-governing (under local control)
New Haven	Mass. emigrants	1638	None		(Merged with Conn., 1662)
6. Rhode Island	R. Williams	1636	1644 / 1663	___	Self-governing
7. Delaware	Swedes	1638	None	___	Proprietary (merged with Pa., 1682; same governor, but separate assembly, granted 1703)
8. N. Carolina	Virginians	1653	1663	1729	Royal (separated informally from S.C., 1691)
9. New York	Dutch	ca. 1613			
	Duke of York	1664	1664	1685	Royal
10. New Jersey	Berkeley and Carteret	1664	None	1702	Royal
11. Carolina	Eight nobles	1670	1663	1729	Royal (separated formally from N.C., 1712)
12. Pennsylvania	William Penn	1681	1681	___	Proprietary
13. Georgia	Oglethorpe and others	1733	1732	1752	Royal

Carolina settlers, in fact, had emigrated from Barbados, bringing that island's slave system with them. They also established a vigorous slave trade in Carolina itself. Enlisting the aid of the coastal Savannah Indians, they forayed into the interior in search of captives. The Lords Proprietors in London protested against Indian slave trading in their colony, but to no avail. Manacled Indians soon were among the young colony's major exports. As many as ten thousand Indians were dispatched to lifelong labor in the West Indian canefields and sugar mills. Others were sent to New England. One Rhode Island town in 1730 counted more than two hundred Indian slaves from Carolina in its midst.

In 1707 the Savannah Indians decided to end their alliance with the Carolinians and to migrate to the backcountry of Maryland and Pennsylvania, where a new colony founded by Quakers under William Penn promised better relations between whites and Indians. But the Carolinians determined to "thin" the Savannahs before they could depart. A series of bloody raids all but annihilated the Indian tribes of coastal Carolina by 1710.

After much experimentation, rice emerged as the principal export crop in Carolina. Rice was then an exotic food in England; no rice seeds were sent out from London in the first supply ships to Carolina. But rice was grown in Africa, and the Carolinians were soon paying premium prices for West African slaves experienced in rice cultivation. The Africans' agricultural skill and their relative immunity to malaria (thanks to a genetic trait that also, unfortunately, made them and their descendants susceptible to sickle-cell anemia) made them ideal laborers on the hot and swampy rice plantations. By 1710 they constituted a majority of Carolinians.

Moss-festooned Charles Town—also named for the king—rapidly became the busiest seaport in the South. Many high-spirited sons of English landed families, deprived of an inheritance, came to the Charleston area and gave it a rich aristocratic flavor. The village became a colorfully diverse community, to which French Protestant refugees, Jews, and others were attracted by religious toleration.

Nearby, in Florida, the Catholic Spaniards abhorred the intrusion of these Protestant heretics. Carolina's frontier was often aflame. Spanish-incited Indians brandished their tomahawks, and armor-clad warriors of Spain frequently unsheathed their swords during the successive Anglo-Spanish wars. But by 1700 Carolina was too strong to be wiped out.

✹ The Emergence of North Carolina

The wild northern expanse of the huge Carolina grant bordered on Virginia. From the older colony there drifted down a ragtag group of poverty-stricken outcasts

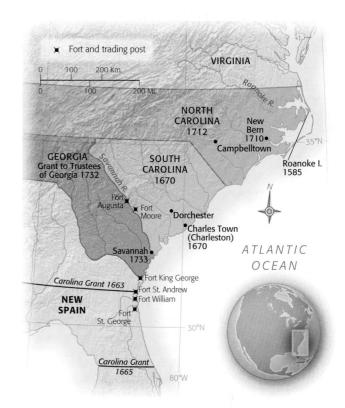

MAP 2.2 Early Carolina and Georgia Settlements
© Cengage Learning

and religious dissenters. Many of them had been repelled by the rarefied atmosphere of Virginia, dominated as it was by big-plantation gentry belonging to the Church of England. North Carolinians, as a result, have been called "the quintessence of Virginia's discontent." The newcomers, who frequently were "**squatters**" without legal right to the soil, raised their tobacco and other crops on small farms, with little need for slaves.

Distinctive traits developed rapidly in North Carolina. The poor but sturdy inhabitants, regarded as riffraff by their snobbish neighbors, earned a reputation for being irreligious and hospitable to pirates. Isolated from neighbors by raw wilderness and stormy Cape Hatteras, "graveyard of the Atlantic," the North Carolinians developed a strong spirit of resistance to authority. Their location between aristocratic Virginia and aristocratic South Carolina caused the area to be dubbed "a vale of humility between two mountains of conceit." Following much friction with governors, North Carolina was officially separated from South Carolina in 1712, and subsequently each segment became a royal colony (see Map 2.2).

North Carolina shares with tiny Rhode Island several distinctions. These two outposts were the most democratic, the most independent-minded, and the least aristocratic of the original thirteen English colonies.

ell before the crowned heads of Europe turned their eyes and their dreams of empire toward North America, a great military power had emerged in the Mohawk Valley of what is now New York State. The **Iroquois Confederacy**, dubbed by whites the "League of the Iroquois," bound together five Indian nations—the Mohawks, the Oneidas, the Onondagas, the Cayugas, and the Senecas (see Map 2.3). According to Iroquois legend, it was founded in the late 1500s by two leaders, Deganawidah and Hiawatha. This proud and potent league vied initially with neighboring Indians for territorial supremacy, then with the French, English, and Dutch for control of the fur trade. Ultimately, infected by the white man's diseases, intoxicated by his whiskey, and intimidated by his muskets, the Iroquois struggled for their very survival as a people.

The building block of Iroquois society was the long-house. This wooden structure deserved its descriptive name. Only twenty-five feet in breadth, the longhouse stretched from eight to two hundred feet in length. Each building contained three to five fireplaces, around which gathered two nuclear families consisting of parents and children. All families residing in the long-house were related, their connections of blood running exclusively through the maternal line. A single long-house might shelter a woman's family and those of her mother, sisters, and daughters—with the oldest woman being the honored matriarch. When a man married, he left his childhood hearth in the home of his mother to join the longhouse of his wife. Men dominated in Iroquois society, but they owed their positions of prominence to their mothers' families.

As if sharing one great longhouse, the five nations joined in the Iroquois Confederacy but kept their own separate fires. Although they celebrated together and shared a common policy toward outsiders, they remained essentially independent of one another. On the eastern flank of the league, the Mohawks, known as the Keepers of the Eastern Fire, specialized as middlemen with European traders, whereas the outlying Senecas, the Keepers of the Western Fire, became fur suppliers.

After banding together to end generations of violent warfare among themselves, the Five Nations vanquished their rivals, the neighboring Hurons, Eries,

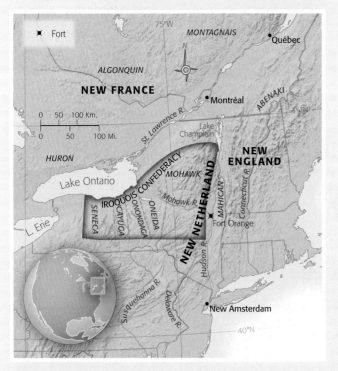

MAP 2.3 Iroquois Lands and European Trade Centers, ca. 1590–1650 © Cengage Learning

An Iroquois Canoe   In frail but artfully constructed craft like this, the Iroquois traversed the abundant waters of their confederacy and traded with their neighbors, Indians as well as whites.

The Longhouse (Reconstruction)   This photo shows a modern-day reconstruction of an Iroquois Indian longhouse typical of the kind built by many tribes in the Northeastern United States and parts of Canada. Bent saplings and sheets of elm bark made for sturdy, weathertight shelters. Longhouses were typically furnished with deerskin-covered bunks and shelves for storing baskets, pots, fur pelts, and corn.

and Petuns. Some other tribes, such as the Tuscaroras from the Carolina region, sought peaceful absorption into the Iroquois Confederacy. The Iroquois further expanded their numbers by means of periodic "mourning wars," whose objective was the large-scale adoption of captives and refugees. But the arrival of gun-toting Europeans threatened Iroquois supremacy and enmeshed the confederacy in a tangled web of diplomatic intrigues. Throughout the seventeenth and eighteenth centuries, they allied alternately with the English against the French and vice versa, for a time successfully working this perpetual rivalry to their own advantage. But when the American Revolution broke out, the confederacy could reach no consensus on which side to support. Each tribe was left to decide independently; most, though not all, sided with the British. The ultimate British defeat left the confederacy

in tatters. Many Iroquois, especially the Mohawks, moved to new lands in British Canada; others were relegated to reservations in western New York.

Reservation life proved unbearable for a proud people accustomed to domination over a vast territory. Morale sank; brawling, feuding, and alcoholism became rampant. Out of this morass arose a prophet, an Iroquois called Handsome Lake. In 1799 angelic figures clothed in traditional Iroquois garb appeared to Handsome Lake in a vision and warned him that the moral decline of his people must end if they were to endure. He awoke from his vision to warn his tribespeople to mend their ways. His socially oriented gospel inspired many Iroquois to forsake alcohol, to affirm family values, and to revive old Iroquois customs. Handsome Lake died in 1815, but his teachings, in the form of the Longhouse religion, survive to this day.

Although northern Carolina, unlike the colony's southern reaches, did not at first import large numbers of African slaves, both regions shared in the ongoing tragedy of bloody relations between Indians and Europeans. Tuscarora Indians fell upon the fledgling settlement at New Bern in 1711. The North Carolinians, aided by their heavily armed brothers from the south, retaliated by crushing the Indians in the **Tuscarora War**, selling hundreds of them into slavery and leaving the survivors to wander northward to seek the protection of the Iroquois. The Tuscaroras eventually became the Sixth Nation of the Iroquois Confederacy. In another ferocious encounter four years later, the South Carolinians defeated and dispersed the **Yamasee Indians**.

With the conquest of the Yamasees, virtually all the coastal Indian tribes in the southern colonies had been utterly devastated by about 1720. Yet in the interior, in the hills and valleys of the Appalachian Mountains, the powerful Cherokees, Creeks, and Iroquois (see "Makers of America: The Iroquois," pp. 36–37) remained. Stronger and more numerous than their coastal cousins, they managed for half a century more to contain British settlement to the coastal plain east of the mountains.

✷ Late-Coming Georgia: The Buffer Colony

Pine-forested Georgia, with the harbor of Savannah nourishing its chief settlement, was formally founded in 1733. It proved to be the last of the thirteen colonies to be planted—126 years after the first, Virginia, and 52 years after the twelfth, Pennsylvania. Chronologically Georgia belongs elsewhere, but geographically it may be grouped with its southern neighbors.

The English crown intended Georgia to serve chiefly as a **buffer**. It would protect the more valuable Carolinas against vengeful Spaniards from Florida and against the hostile French from Louisiana. Georgia indeed suffered much buffeting, especially when wars broke out between Spain and England in the European arena. As a vital link in imperial defense, the exposed colony received monetary subsidies from the British government at the outset—the only one of the "original thirteen" to enjoy this benefit in its founding stage.

Named in honor of King George II of England, Georgia was launched by a high-minded group of philanthropists. In addition to protecting their neighboring northern colonies and producing silk and wine, they were determined to carve out a haven for wretched souls imprisoned for debt. They were also determined, at least at first, to keep slavery out of Georgia. The ablest of the founders was the dynamic soldier-statesman James Oglethorpe, who became keenly interested in prison reform after one of his friends died in a debtors' jail. As an able military leader, Oglethorpe repelled Spanish attacks. As an imperialist and a philanthropist, he saved "the Charity Colony" by his energetic leadership and by heavily mortgaging his own personal fortune.

The hamlet of Savannah, like Charleston, was a melting-pot community. German Lutherans and kilted Scots Highlanders, among others, added color to the pattern. All Christian worshipers except Catholics enjoyed religious toleration. Many missionaries armed with Bibles and hope arrived in Savannah to work among debtors and Indians. Prominent among them was young John Wesley, who later returned to England and founded the Methodist Church.

Georgia grew with painful slowness and at the end of the colonial era was perhaps the least populous of the colonies. The development of a plantation economy was thwarted by an unhealthy climate, by early restrictions on black slavery, and by demoralizing Spanish attacks.

✷ The Plantation Colonies

Certain distinctive features were shared by England's southern mainland colonies: Maryland, Virginia, North Carolina, South Carolina, and Georgia. Broadacred, these outposts of empire were all in some degree devoted to exporting commercial agricultural products. Profitable staple crops were the rule, notably tobacco and rice, though to a lesser extent in small-farm North Carolina. Slavery was found in all the plantation colonies, though only after 1750 in reform-minded Georgia. Immense acreage in the hands of a favored few fostered a strong aristocratic atmosphere, except in North Carolina and to some extent in debtor-tinged Georgia. The wide scattering of plantations and farms, often along stately rivers, retarded the growth of cities and made the establishment of churches and schools both difficult and expensive. In 1671 the governor of Virginia actually thanked God that no free schools or printing presses existed in his colony.

All the plantation colonies permitted some religious toleration. The tax-supported Church of England became the dominant faith, though it was weakest of all in nonconformist North Carolina.

These colonies were in some degree expansionary. "Soil butchery" by excessive tobacco growing drove settlers westward, and the long, lazy rivers invited penetration of the continent—and continuing confrontation with Native Americans.

Chapter Review

KEY TERMS

Protestant Reformation (24)

Roanoke Island (25)

Spanish Armada (25)

primogeniture (27)

joint-stock company (27)

Virginia Company (27)

charter (27)

Jamestown (27)

First Anglo-Powhatan
   War (29)

Second Anglo-Powhatan
   War (29)

House of Burgesses (32)

Act of Toleration (32)

Barbados slave code (33)

squatters (35)

Iroquois Confederacy (36)

Tuscarora War (38)

Yamasee Indians (38)

buffer (38)

PEOPLE TO KNOW

Henry VIII

Elizabeth I

Sir Francis Drake

Sir Walter Raleigh

James I

Captain John Smith

Powhatan

Pocahontas

Lord De La Warr

John Rolfe

Lord Baltimore

Oliver Cromwell

James Oglethorpe

Hiawatha

CHRONOLOGY

1558	Elizabeth I becomes queen of England
ca. 1565–1590	English crush Irish uprising
1577	Drake circumnavigates the globe
1585	Raleigh founds "lost colony" at Roanoke Island
1588	England defeats Spanish Armada
1603	James I becomes king of England
1604	Spain and England sign peace treaty
1607	Virginia colony founded at Jamestown
1612	Rolfe perfects tobacco culture in Virginia
1614	First Anglo-Powhatan War ends
1619	First Africans arrive in Jamestown Virginia House of Burgesses established
1624	Virginia becomes royal colony
1634	Maryland colony founded
1640s	Large-scale slave-labor system established in English West Indies
1644	Second Anglo-Powhatan War
1649	Act of Toleration in Maryland Charles I beheaded; Cromwell rules England
1660	Charles II restored to English throne
1661	Barbados slave code adopted
1670	Carolina colony created
1711–1713	Tuscarora War in North Carolina
1712	North Carolina formally separates from South Carolina
1715–1716	Yamasee War in South Carolina
1733	Georgia colony founded

TO LEARN MORE

Ira Berlin, *Generations of Captivity: A History of African American Slaves* (2003)

———, *Many Thousands Gone: The First Two Centuries of Slavery in North America* (1998)

Kathleen Brown, *Good Wives, Nasty Wenches, and Anxious Patriarchs: Gender, Race, and Power in Colonial Virginia* (1996)

Colin G. Calloway, *New Worlds for All: Indians, Europeans, and the Remaking of America* (1997)

Ralph Davis, *The Rise of the Atlantic Economies* (1973)

Jack P. Greene, *Pursuits of Happiness: The Social Development of Early Modern British Colonies and the Formation of American Culture* (1988)

April Lee Hatfield, *Atlantic Virginia: Intercolonial Relations in the Seventeenth Century* (2004)

Edmund S. Morgan, *American Slavery, American Freedom* (1975)

David B. Quinn, *England and the Discovery of America, 1481–1620* (1974)

Daniel K. Richter, *Facing East from Indian Country: A Native History of Early America* (2003)

Nancy Shoemaker, *A Strange Likeness: Becoming Red and White in Eighteenth-Century North America* (2004)

Alan Taylor, *American Colonies: The Settling of North America* (2001)

Camilla Townsend, *Pocahontas and the Powhatan Dilemma* (2004)

A complete, annotated bibliography for this chapter—along with brief descriptions of the People to Know—may be found on the American Pageant website. The Key Terms are defined in a Glossary at the end of the text.

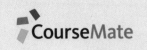

Go to the CourseMate website at **www.cengagebrain.com** for additional study tools and review materials—including audio and video clips—for this chapter.

AP® Review Questions for Chapter 2

1. Why did England show little interest in colonizing the New World during most of the 1500s?
   (A) Its navy was too weak.
   (B) It saw little promise in the colonies.
   (C) It didn't want to compete with its ally Spain.
   (D) Internal problems were overwhelming its government.
   (E) It considered the Americas a savage wilderness.

2. The event that signaled the beginning of the end for the Spanish empire in the New World was
   (A) the crumbling of its internal economy.
   (B) the defeat of the Spanish Armada.
   (C) repeated and successful looting of Spanish ships by English pirates and seamen.
   (D) a series of rebellions in its American colonies.
   (E) a new war with England.

3. The English first attempted colonization in the Americas in
   (A) Roanoke, Virginia.
   (B) Plymouth.
   (C) Newfoundland.
   (D) Jamestown.
   (E) Nova Scotia.

4. Which of the following did NOT influence the dramatic rise of England's colonization efforts in the early 1600s?
   (A) Population growth in England
   (B) English land shortages
   (C) Peace between Britain and Spain
   (D) Promised rewards for explorers from the crown
   (E) Desire for religious freedom

5. What makes the Virginia Company charter such a significant document to American history?
   (A) It guaranteed Jamestown colonists citizenship rights equal to those of Englishmen.
   (B) It outlined the goals and rules of the new colony.
   (C) It established colonial boundaries and outlined the region's power structure.
   (D) It sought a new and shorter trade route to the Orient.
   (E) It was a predecessor to the modern corporation.

6. What single cause was responsible for the death of so many Jamestown settlers in the early years?
   (A) Hazardous weather conditions
   (B) Attacks by Indians
   (C) Crop devastation
   (D) Homesickness
   (E) Starvation

7. After the arrival of Europeans in North America, which of the following did NOT negatively impact Native American cultural life?
   (A) Disease
   (B) The introduction of horses
   (C) Trade
   (D) Land
   (E) Intermarriage

8. The primary labor source for the early development of the plantation colonies of Virginia and Maryland was
   (A) families who settled the area.
   (B) indentured servants.
   (C) slaves brought from Africa.
   (D) prisoners.
   (E) second and third sons of English lords.

9. The Acts of Toleration (1649) granted Marylanders
   (A) the right to self-government.
   (B) legal sanction for importing African slaves.
   (C) the ability to export products that would directly compete with British goods.
   (D) freedom of Christian worship.
   (E) protection from hostile Indians.

10. The struggling Virginia economy was ultimately saved by
    (A) peace treaties with local Native American nations.
    (B) the slave trade.
    (C) rice cultivation.
    (D) an influx of large numbers of new settlers.
    (E) the development of tobacco.

11. The purpose of slave codes was to
    (A) limit the rights and behavior of Negro slaves.
    (B) outline how many slaves could be imported to the colonies.
    (C) regulate the slave trade.
    (D) prevent the excessive discipline or abuse of slaves.
    (E) legalize slavery in the colonies.

12. Which of these was NOT a reason for the founding of Georgia?
    (A) To protect northern English colonies from encroachment by Spain
    (B) To provide a second chance for those imprisoned for debt
    (C) To become a stronghold for the slave trade
    (D) To produce silk and wine there
    (E) To serve as an outpost for missionaries

13. The Iroquois became powerful in the 1500s and 1600s by
    (A) building strong relationships with colonists.
    (B) merging with other branches and tribes.
    (C) relying on a strong patrilineal social structure.
    (D) fostering tribal independence.
    (E) developing a strong trade network with European settlers.

14. Which of the following traits were NOT shared by all of England's plantation colonies (Maryland, Virginia, the Carolinas, and Georgia)?
    (A) Development and export of staple crops
    (B) Slavery
    (C) Aristocratic social hierarchy
    (D) Religious tolerance
    (E) The birth of large urban port cities

15. Which of the following effects of excessive planting in England's southern colonies contributed to westward expansion during colonial times and beyond?
    (A) Soil butchery
    (B) Search for new trade routes
    (C) Drought conditions
    (D) Lack of subsistence farming
    (E) Overproduction of cash crops

16. English settlers exerted their power over the Native Americans in all of the following ways EXCEPT by
    (A) radically altering the economy and means of commerce.
    (B) spreading European diseases against which Native Americans were powerless.
    (C) defeating various Native American tribes in armed combat.
    (D) destroying Native American customs in the Great Lakes area.
    (E) imposing European ideas about property and land ownership.

Chapter 3

Settling the Northern Colonies

1619–1700

God hath sifted a nation that he might send Choice Grain into this Wilderness.

WILLIAM STOUGHTON [OF MASSACHUSETTS BAY], 1699

Although colonists both north and south were bound together by a common language and a common allegiance to Mother England, they established different patterns of settlement, different economies, different political systems, and even different sets of values—defining distinctive regional characteristics that would persist for generations. The promise of riches—especially from golden-leaved tobacco—drew the first settlers to the southern colonies. But to the north, in the fertile valleys of the middle Atlantic region and especially along the rocky shores of New England, it was not worldly wealth but religious devotion that principally shaped the earliest settlements.

✴ The Protestant Reformation Produces Puritanism

Little did the German friar Martin Luther suspect, when he nailed his protests against Catholic doctrines to the door of Wittenberg's cathedral in 1517, that he was shaping the destiny of a yet unknown nation. Denouncing the authority of priests and popes, Luther declared that the Bible alone was the source of God's word. He ignited a fire of religious reform (the "Protestant Reformation") that licked its way across Europe for more than a century, dividing peoples, toppling sovereigns, and kindling the spiritual fervor of millions of men and women—some of whom helped to found America.

The reforming flame burned especially brightly in the bosom of John Calvin of Geneva. This somber and severe religious leader elaborated Martin Luther's ideas

in ways that profoundly affected the thought and character of generations of Americans yet unborn. **Calvinism** became the dominant theological credo not only of the New England Puritans but of other American settlers as well, including the Scottish Presbyterians, French Huguenots, and communicants of the Dutch Reformed Church.

Calvin spelled out his basic doctrine in a learned Latin tome of 1536, entitled *Institutes of the Christian Religion*. God, Calvin argued, was all-powerful and all-good. Humans, because of the corrupting effect of original sin, were weak and wicked. God was also all-knowing—and he knew who was going to heaven and who was going to hell. Since the first moment of creation, some souls—the elect—had been destined for eternal bliss and others for eternal torment. Good works could not save those whom **predestination** had marked for the infernal fires.

But neither could the elect count on their predetermined salvation and lead lives of wild, immoral abandon. For one thing, no one could be certain of his or her status in the heavenly ledger. Gnawing doubts about their eternal fate plagued Calvinists. They constantly sought, in themselves and others, signs of **conversion**, or the receipt of God's free gift of saving grace. Conversion was thought to be an intense, identifiable personal experience in which God revealed to the elect their heavenly destiny. Thereafter they were expected to lead "sanctified" lives, demonstrating by their holy behavior that they were among the "visible saints."

These doctrines swept into England just as King Henry VIII was breaking his ties with the Roman Catholic Church in the 1530s, making himself the head of

41

the Church of England. Henry would have been content to retain Roman rituals and creeds, but his action powerfully stimulated some English religious reformers to undertake a total purification of English Christianity. Many of these **Puritans**, as it happened, came from the commercially depressed woolen districts (see p. 26). Calvinism, with its message of stark but reassuring order in the divine plan, fed on this social unrest and provided spiritual comfort to the economically disadvantaged. As time went on, Puritans grew increasingly unhappy over the snail-like progress of the Protestant Reformation in England. They burned with pious zeal to see the Church of England wholly de-catholicized.

The most devout Puritans, including those who eventually settled New England, believed that only "visible saints" (that is, persons who felt the stirrings of grace in their souls and could demonstrate its presence to their fellow Puritans) should be admitted to church membership. But the Church of England enrolled all the king's subjects, which meant that the "saints" had to share pews and communion rails with the "damned." Appalled by this unholy fraternizing, a tiny group of dedicated Puritans, known as **Separatists**, vowed to break away entirely from the Church of England.

King James I, a shrewd Scotsman, was head of both the state and the church in England from 1603 to 1625. He quickly perceived that if his subjects could defy him as their spiritual leader, they might one day defy him as their political leader (as in fact they would later defy and behead his son, Charles I). He therefore threatened to harass the more bothersome Separatists out of the land.

✳ The Pilgrims End Their Pilgrimage at Plymouth

The most famous congregation of Separatists, fleeing royal wrath, departed for Holland in 1608. During the ensuing twelve years of toil and poverty, they were increasingly distressed by the "Dutchification" of their children. They longed to find a haven where they could live and die as English men and women—and as purified Protestants. America was the logical refuge, despite the early ordeals of Jamestown, and despite tales of New World cannibals roasting steaks from their white victims over open fires.

A group of the Separatists in Holland, after negotiating with the Virginia Company, at length secured rights to settle under its jurisdiction. But their crowded *Mayflower*, sixty-five days at sea, missed its destination and arrived off the stony coast of New England in 1620, with a total of 102 persons. One had died en route—an unusually short casualty list—and one had been born and appropriately named Oceanus. Fewer than half of the entire party were Separatists. Prominent among the nonbelongers was a peppery and stocky soldier of fortune, Captain Myles Standish, dubbed by one of his critics "Captain Shrimp." He later rendered indispensable service as an Indian fighter and negotiator.

The Pilgrims did not make their initial landing at Plymouth Rock, as commonly supposed, but undertook

Plymouth Plantation
Carefully restored, the modest village at Plymouth looks today much as it did nearly four hundred years ago.

Picture Research Consultants & Archives

a number of preliminary surveys. They finally chose for their site the shore of inhospitable Plymouth Bay. This area was outside the domain of the Virginia Company, and consequently the settlers became squatters. They were without legal right to the land and without specific authority to establish a government.

Before disembarking, the Pilgrim leaders drew up and signed the brief **Mayflower Compact**. Although setting an invaluable precedent for later written constitutions, this document was not a constitution at all. It was a simple agreement to form a crude government and to submit to the will of the majority under the regulations agreed upon. The compact was signed by forty-one adult males, eleven of them with the exalted rank of "mister," though not by the servants and two seamen. The pact was a promising step toward genuine self-government, for soon the adult male settlers were assembling to make their own laws in open-discussion town meetings—a vital laboratory of liberty.

The Pilgrims' first winter of 1620–1621 took a grisly toll. Only 44 out of the 102 survived. At one time only 7 were well enough to lay the dead in their frosty graves. Yet when the *Mayflower* sailed back to England in the spring, not a single one of the courageous band of Separatists left. As one of them wrote, "It is not with us as with other men, whom small things can discourage."

God made his children prosperous, so the Pilgrims believed. The next autumn, that of 1621, brought bountiful harvests and with them the first Thanksgiving Day in New England. In time the frail colony found sound economic legs in fur, fish, and lumber. The beaver and the Bible were the early mainstays: the one for the sustenance of the body, the other for the sustenance of the soul. Plymouth proved that the English could maintain themselves in this uninviting region.

The Pilgrims were extremely fortunate in their leaders. Prominent among them was the cultured William Bradford, a self-taught scholar who read Hebrew, Greek, Latin, French, and Dutch. He was chosen governor thirty times in the annual elections. Among his major worries was his fear that independent, non-Puritan settlers "on their particular" might corrupt his godly experiment in the wilderness. Bustling fishing villages and other settlements did sprout to the north of Plymouth, on the storm-lashed shores of Massachusetts Bay, where many people were as much interested in cod as God.

Quiet and quaint, the little colony of Plymouth was never important economically or numerically. Its population numbered only seven thousand by 1691, when, still charterless, it merged with its giant neighbor, the Massachusetts Bay Colony. But the tiny settlement of Pilgrims was big both morally and spiritually.

William Bradford (1590–1657) wrote in Of Plymouth Plantation,

❝ Thus out of small beginnings greater things have been produced by His hand that made all things of nothing, and gives being to all things that are; and, as one small candle may light a thousand, so the light here kindled hath shone unto many, yea in some sort to our whole nation.❞

✴ The Bay Colony Bible Commonwealth

The Separatist Pilgrims were dedicated extremists—the purest Puritans. More moderate Puritans sought to reform the Church of England from within. Though resented by bishops and monarchs, they slowly gathered support, especially in Parliament. But when Charles I dismissed Parliament in 1629 and sanctioned the anti-Puritan persecutions of the reactionary Archbishop William Laud, many Puritans saw catastrophe in the making.

In 1629 an energetic group of non-Separatist Puritans, fearing for their faith and for England's future, secured a royal charter to form the Massachusetts Bay Company. They proposed to establish a sizable settlement in the infertile Massachusetts area, with Boston soon becoming its hub. Stealing a march on both king and church, the newcomers brought their charter with them. For many years they used it as a kind of constitution, out of easy reach of royal authority. They steadfastly denied that they wanted to separate from the Church of England, only from its impurities. But back in England, the highly orthodox Archbishop Laud snorted that the Bay Colony Puritans were "swine which rooted in God's vineyard." The **Massachusetts Bay Colony** was singularly blessed. The well-equipped expedition of 1630, with eleven vessels carrying nearly a thousand immigrants, started the colony off on a larger scale than any of the other English settlements. Continuing turmoil in England tossed up additional enriching waves of Puritans on the shores of Massachusetts in the following decade. During the **Great Migration** of the 1630s, about seventy thousand refugees left England (see Map 3.1). But not all of them were Puritans, and only about twenty thousand came to Massachusetts. Many were attracted to the warm and fertile West Indies, especially the sugar-rich island of Barbados. More Puritans came to this Caribbean islet than to all of Massachusetts.

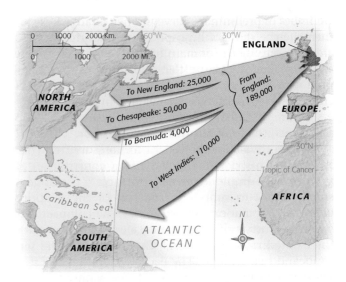

MAP 3.1B The Great English Migration, ca. 1630–1642 Much of the early history of the United States was written by New Englanders, who were not disposed to emphasize the larger exodus of English migrants to the Caribbean islands. When the mainland colonists declared independence in 1776, they hoped that these island outposts would join them, but the existence of the British navy had a dissuading effect. © Cengage Learning

MAP 3.1A Sources of the Puritan "Great Migration" to New England, 1620–1650 The shaded areas indicate the main sources of the migration. © Cengage Learning

✶ Building the Bay Colony

Many fairly prosperous, educated persons immigrated to the Bay Colony, including John Winthrop, a well-to-do pillar of English society, who became the colony's first governor. A successful attorney and manor lord in England, Winthrop eagerly accepted the offer to become governor of the Massachusetts Bay Colony, believing that he had a "calling" from God to lead the new religious experiment. He served as governor or deputy governor for nineteen years. The resources and skills of talented settlers like Winthrop helped Massachusetts prosper, as fur trading, fishing, and shipbuilding blossomed into important industries, especially fish and ships. The Massachusetts Bay Colony rapidly shot to the fore as both the biggest and the most influential of the New England outposts.

Massachusetts also benefited from a shared sense of purpose among most of the first settlers. "We shall be as a city upon a hill," a beacon to humanity, declared Governor Winthrop. The Puritan bay colonists believed that they had a covenant with God, an agreement to build a holy society that would be a model for humankind.

These common convictions deeply shaped the infant colony's life. Soon after the colonists' arrival, the franchise was extended to all "freemen"—adult males who belonged to the Puritan congregations, which in time came to be called collectively the Congregational Church. Unchurched men remained voteless in provincial elections, as did all women. On this basis about two-fifths of adult males enjoyed the franchise in provincial affairs, a far larger proportion than in contemporary England. Town governments, which conducted much important business, were even more inclusive. There all male property holders, and in some cases other residents as well, enjoyed the priceless boon of publicly discussing local issues, often with much heat, and of voting on them by a majority-rule show of hands.

Yet the provincial government, liberal by the standards of the time, was not a democracy. The able Governor Winthrop feared and distrusted the "commons" as the "meaner sort" and thought that democracy was the "meanest and worst" of all forms of government. "If the people be governors," asked one Puritan clergyman, "who shall be governed?" True, the freemen annually elected the governor and his assistants, as well as a representative assembly called the General Court. But only Puritans—the "visible saints" who alone were eligible for church membership—could be freemen. And according to the doctrine of the covenant, the whole purpose of government was to enforce God's laws—which applied to believers and nonbelievers alike. Moreover, nonbelievers as well as believers paid taxes for the government-supported church.

Religious leaders thus wielded enormous influence in the Massachusetts "Bible Commonwealth." They powerfully influenced admission to church membership by conducting public interrogations of persons claiming to have experienced conversion. Prominent among the early clergy was fiery John Cotton. Educated at England's Cambridge University, a Puritan citadel, he emigrated to Massachusetts to avoid persecution for his criticism of the Church of England. In the Bay Colony, he devoted his considerable learning to defending the government's duty to enforce religious rules. Profoundly pious, he sometimes preached and prayed up to six hours in a single day.

But the power of the preachers was not absolute. A congregation had the right to hire and fire its minister and to set his salary. Clergymen were also barred from holding formal political office. Puritans in England had suffered too much at the hands of a "political" Anglican clergy to permit in the New World another unholy union of religious and government power. In a limited way, the bay colonists thus endorsed the idea of the separation of church and state.

The Puritans were a worldly lot, despite—or even because of—their spiritual intensity. Like John Winthrop, they believed in the doctrine of a "calling" to do God's work on earth. They shared in what was later called the "Protestant ethic," which involved serious commitment to work and to engagement in worldly pursuits. Legend to the contrary, they also enjoyed simple pleasures: they ate plentifully, drank heartily, sang songs occasionally, and made love mostly monogamously. Like other peoples of their time in both America and Europe, they passed laws aimed at making sure these pleasures stayed simple by repressing certain human instincts. In New Haven, for example, a young married couple was fined twenty shillings for the crime of kissing in public, and in later years Connecticut came to be dubbed "the Blue Law State." (It was so named for the blue paper on which the repressive laws—also known as "sumptuary laws"—were printed.)

Yet, to the Puritans, life was serious business, and hellfire was real—a hell where sinners shriveled and shrieked in vain for divine mercy. An immensely popular poem in New England, selling one copy for every twenty people, was clergyman Michael Wigglesworth's "Day of Doom" (1662). Especially horrifying were his descriptions of the fate of the damned:

> *They cry, they roar for anguish sore,*
> *   and gnaw their tongues for horrour. But get away*
> *   without delay,*
> *   Christ pitties not your cry:*
> *   Depart to Hell, there may you yell, and roar*
> *   Eternally.*

✵ Trouble in the Bible Commonwealth

The Bay Colony enjoyed a high degree of social harmony, stemming from common beliefs, in its early years. But even in this tightly knit community, dissension soon appeared. Quakers, who flouted the authority of the Puritan clergy, were persecuted with fines, floggings, and banishment. In one extreme case, four Quakers who defied expulsion, one of them a woman, were hanged on the Boston Common.

A sharp challenge to Puritan orthodoxy came from Anne Hutchinson. She was an exceptionally intelligent, strongwilled, and talkative woman, ultimately the mother of fourteen children. Swift and sharp in theological argument, she carried to logical extremes the Puritan doctrine of predestination. She claimed that a holy life was no sure sign of salvation and that the truly saved need not bother to obey the law of either God or man. This assertion, known as ***antinomianism*** (from the Greek, "against the law"), was high heresy.

Brought to trial in 1638, the quickwitted Hutchinson bamboozled her clerical inquisitors for days, until she

Anne Hutchinson, Dissenter Mistress Hutchinson (1591–1643) held unorthodox views that challenged the authority of the clergy and the very integrity of the Puritan experiment in the Massachusetts Bay Colony. An outcast in her day, she has been judged a heroine in the eye of history. This statue in her honor, erected in the nineteenth century, now graces the front of the Boston, Massachusetts, Statehouse. Secretary of Commonwealth of Massachusetts State House/Picture Research Consultants & Archives eventually boasted that she had come by her beliefs through a direct revelation from God. This was even higher heresy. The Puritan magistrates had little choice but to banish her, lest she pollute the entire Puritan experiment. With her family, she set out on foot for Rhode Island, though pregnant. She finally moved to New York, where she and all but one of her household were killed by Indians. Back in the Bay Colony, the pious John Winthrop saw "God's hand" in her fate.

More threatening to the Puritan leaders was a personable and popular Salem minister, Roger Williams. Williams was a young man with radical ideas and an unrestrained tongue. An extreme Separatist, he hounded his fellow clergymen to make a clean break with the corrupt Church of England. He also challenged the legality of the Bay Colony's charter, which he condemned for expropriating the land from the Indians without fair compensation. As if all this were not enough, he went on to deny the authority of civil government to regulate religious behavior—a seditious blow at the Puritan idea of government's very purpose.

Their patience exhausted by 1635, the Bay Colony authorities found Williams guilty of disseminating "newe & dangerous opinions" and ordered him banished. He was permitted to remain several months longer because of illness, but he kept up his criticisms. The outraged magistrates, fearing that he might organize a rival colony of malcontents, made plans to exile him to England. But Williams foiled them.

✖ The Rhode Island "Sewer"

Aided by friendly Indians, Roger Williams fled to the Rhode Island area in 1636, in the midst of a bitter winter. At Providence the courageous and far-visioned Williams built a Baptist church, probably the first in America. He established complete freedom of religion, even for Jews and Catholics. He demanded no oaths regarding religious beliefs, no compulsory attendance at worship, no taxes to support a state church. He even sheltered the abused Quakers, although disagreeing sharply with their views. Williams's endorsement of religious tolerance made Rhode Island more liberal than any of the other English settlements in the New World, and more advanced than most Old World communities as well.

Those outcasts who clustered about Roger Williams enjoyed additional blessings. They exercised simple manhood suffrage from the start, though this broad-minded practice was later narrowed by a property qualification. Opposed to special privilege of any sort, the intrepid Rhode Islanders managed to achieve remarkable freedom of opportunity.

Other scattered settlements soon dotted Rhode Island. They consisted largely of malcontents and exiles, some of whom could not bear the stifling theological atmosphere of the Bay Colony. Many of these restless souls in "Rogues' Island," including Anne Hutchinson, had little in common with Roger Williams—except being unwelcome anywhere else. The Puritan clergy back in Boston sneered at Rhode Island as "that sewer" in which the "Lord's debris" had collected and rotted.

Planted by dissenters and exiles, Rhode Island became strongly individualistic and stubbornly independent. With good reason "Little Rhody" was later known as "the traditional home of the otherwise minded." Begun as a squatter colony in 1636 without legal standing, it finally established rights to the soil when it secured a charter from Parliament in 1644. A huge bronze statue of the "Independent Man" appropriately stands today on the dome of the statehouse in Providence.

✖ New England Spreads Out

The smiling valley of the Connecticut River, one of the few highly fertile expanses of any size in all New England, had meanwhile attracted a sprinkling of Dutch and English settlers. Hartford was founded in 1635 (see Map 3.2). The next year witnessed a spectacular

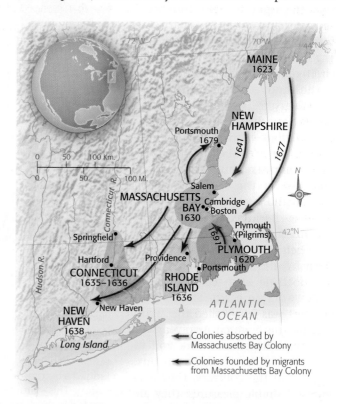

MAP 3.2 Seventeenth-Century New England Settlements
The Massachusetts Bay Colony was the hub of New England. All earlier colonies grew into it; all later colonies grew out of it. © Cengage Learning

beginning of the centuries-long westward movement across the continent. An energetic group of Boston Puritans, led by the Reverend Thomas Hooker, swarmed as a body into the Hartford area, with the ailing Mrs. Hooker carried on a horse litter.

Three years later, in 1639, the settlers of the new Connecticut River colony drafted in open meeting a trailblazing document known as the **Fundamental Orders**. It was in effect a modern constitution, which established a regime democratically controlled by the "substantial" citizens. Essential features of the Fundamental Orders were later borrowed by Connecticut for its colonial charter and ultimately for its state constitution.

Another flourishing Connecticut settlement began to spring up at New Haven in 1638. It was a prosperous community, founded by Puritans who contrived to set up an even closer church-government alliance than in Massachusetts. Although only squatters without a charter, the colonists dreamed of making New Haven a bustling seaport. But they fell into disfavor with Charles II as a result of having sheltered two of the judges who had condemned his father, Charles I, to death. In 1662, to the acute distress of the New Havenites, the crown granted a charter to Connecticut that merged New Haven with the more democratic settlements in the Connecticut Valley.

Far to the north, enterprising fishermen and fur-traders had been active on the coast of Maine for a dozen or so years before the founding of Plymouth. After disheartening attempts at colonization in 1623 by Sir Ferdinando Gorges, this land of lakes and forests was absorbed by Massachusetts Bay after a formal purchase in 1677 from the Gorges heirs. It remained a part of Massachusetts for nearly a century and a half before becoming a separate state.

Granite-ribbed New Hampshire also sprang from the fishing and trading activities along its narrow coast. It was absorbed in 1641 by the grasping Bay Colony, under a strained interpretation of the Massachusetts charter. The king, annoyed by this display of greed, arbitrarily separated New Hampshire from Massachusetts in 1679 and made it a royal colony.

✴ Puritans Versus Indians

The spread of English settlements inevitably led to clashes with the Indians, who were particularly weak in New England. Shortly before the Pilgrims had arrived at Plymouth in 1620, an epidemic, probably triggered

Rhode Island Historical Society

Attack on a Pequot Fort During the Pequot War of 1637, engraving by J. W. Barber, 1830 This was the first war between natives and Europeans in British North America. It culminated in the Puritan militia's vicious burning out and slaughtering of nearly three hundred Pequot men, women, and children. The defeat of the Pequots eliminated armed resistance to the new settlements of New Haven and Guildford. The Connecticut Valley would not see significant "Indian troubles" again for forty years, when the Indians of New England united in their final stand against the encroachments of English settlers, King Philip's War.

by contact with English fishermen, had swept through the coastal tribes and killed more than three-quarters of the native people. Deserted Indian fields, ready for tillage, greeted the Plymouth settlers, and scattered skulls and bones provided grim evidence of the impact of the disease.

In no position to resist the English incursion, the local Wampanoag Indians at first befriended the settlers. Cultural accommodation was facilitated by Squanto, a Wampanoag who had learned English from a ship's captain who had kidnapped him some years earlier. The Wampanoag chieftain Massasoit signed a treaty with the Plymouth Pilgrims in 1621 and helped them celebrate the first Thanksgiving after the autumn harvests that same year.

As more English settlers arrived and pushed inland into the Connecticut River valley, confrontations between Indians and whites ruptured these peaceful relations. Hostilities exploded in 1637 between the English settlers and the powerful Pequot tribe. Besieging a Pequot village on Connecticut's Mystic River, English militiamen and their Narragansett Indian allies set fire to the Indian wigwams and shot the fleeing survivors. The slaughter wrote a brutal finish to the **Pequot War**, virtually annihilated the Pequot tribe, and inaugurated four decades of uneasy peace between Puritans and Indians.

Lashed by critics in England, the Puritans made some feeble efforts at converting the remaining Indians to Christianity, although Puritan missionary zeal never equaled that of the Catholic Spanish and French. A mere handful of Indians were gathered into Puritan "praying towns" to make the acquaintance of the English God and to learn the ways of English culture.

The Indians' only hope for resisting English encroachment lay in intertribal unity—a pan-Indian alliance against the swiftly spreading English settlements. In 1675 Massasoit's son, Metacom, called King Philip by the English, forged such an alliance and mounted a series of coordinated assaults on English villages throughout New England. Frontier settlements were especially hard hit, and refugees fell back toward the relative safety of Boston. When the war ended in 1676, fifty-two Puritan towns had been attacked, and twelve destroyed entirely. Hundreds of colonists and many more Indians lay dead. Metacom's wife and son were sold into slavery; he himself was captured, beheaded, and drawn and quartered. His head was carried on a pike back to Plymouth, where it was mounted on grisly display for years.

King Philip's War slowed the westward march of English settlement in New England for several decades. But the war inflicted a lasting defeat on New England's Indians. Drastically reduced in numbers, dispirited, and disbanded, they thereafter posed only sporadic threats to the New England colonists.

✳ Seeds of Colonial Unity and Independence

A path-breaking experiment in union was launched in 1643, when four colonies banded together to form the **New England Confederation**. The **English Civil War** was then deeply distracting old England, throwing the colonists upon their own resources. The primary purpose of the confederation was defense against foes or potential foes, notably the Indians, the French, and the Dutch. Purely intercolonial problems, such as runaway servants and criminals who had fled from one colony to another, also came within the jurisdiction of the confederation. Each member colony, regardless of size, wielded two votes—an arrangement highly displeasing to the most populous colony, Massachusetts Bay.

The confederation was essentially an exclusive Puritan club. It consisted of the two Massachusetts colonies (the Bay Colony and bantam-sized Plymouth) and the two Connecticut colonies (New Haven and the scattered valley settlements). The Puritan leaders blackballed Rhode Island as well as the Maine outposts. These places, it was charged, harbored too many heretical or otherwise undesirable characters. Shockingly, one of the Maine towns had made a tailor its mayor and had even sheltered an excommunicated minister of the gospel.

Weak though it was, the confederation was the first notable milestone on the long and rocky road toward colonial unity. The delegates took tottering but long-overdue steps toward acting together on matters of intercolonial importance. Rank-and-file colonists, for their part, received valuable experience in delegating their votes to properly chosen representatives.

Back in England the king had paid little attention to the American colonies during the early years of their planting. They were allowed, in effect, to become semiautonomous commonwealths. This era of benign neglect was prolonged when the crown, struggling to retain its power, became enmeshed during the 1640s in civil wars with the parliamentarians.

But when Charles II was restored to the English throne in 1660 (see Table 3.1), the royalists and their Church of England allies were once more firmly in the saddle. Puritan hopes of eventually purifying the old English church withered. Worse, Charles II was determined to take an active, aggressive hand in the management of the colonies. His plans ran headlong against the habits that decades of relative independence had bred in the colonists.

Deepening colonial defiance was nowhere more glaringly revealed than in Massachusetts. One of the king's agents in Boston was mortified to find that royal orders had no more effect than old issues of the London *Gazette*. Punishment was soon forthcoming. As a slap at Massachusetts, Charles II gave rival Connecticut in 1662 a sea-to-sea charter grant, which legalized the

TABLE 3.1 The Stuart Dynasty in England*

Name, Reign	Relation to America
James I, 1603–1625	Va., Plymouth founded; Separatists persecuted
Charles I, 1625–1649	Civil wars, 1642–1649; Mass., Md. founded
(Interregnum, 1649–1660)	Commonwealth; Protectorate (Oliver Cromwell)
Charles II, 1660–1685	The Restoration; Carolinas, Pa., N.Y. founded; Conn. Chartered
James II, 1685–1688	Catholic trend; Glorious Revolution, 1688
William & Mary, 1689–1702 (Mary died 1694)	King William's War, 1689–1697

*See p. 26 for predecessors; p. 101 for successors.

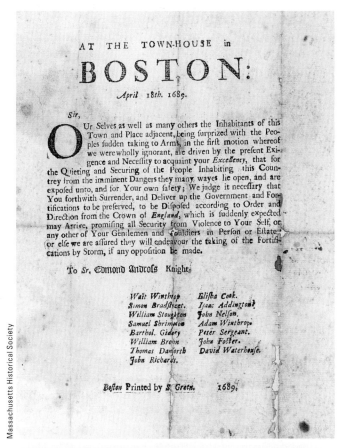

Massachusetts Historical Society

Massachusetts State Archives

Sir Edmund Andros (1637–1714); a Boston Broadside Urging Him to Surrender, 1689 After being expelled from New England, Andros eventually returned to the New World as governor of Virginia (1692–1697).

MAP 3.3 Andros's Dominion of New England © Cengage Learning

squatter settlements. The very next year, the outcasts in Rhode Island received a new charter, which gave kingly sanction to the most religiously tolerant government yet devised in America. A final and crushing blow fell on the stiff-necked Bay Colony in 1684, when its precious charter was revoked by the London authorities.

✸ Andros Promotes the First American Revolution

Massachusetts suffered further humiliation in 1686, when the **Dominion of New England** was created by royal authority (see Map 3.3). Unlike the home-grown New England Confederation, it was imposed from London. Embracing at first all of New England, it was expanded two years later to include New York and East and West Jersey. The dominion also aimed at bolstering colonial defense in the event of war with the Indians and hence, from the imperial viewpoint of Parliament, was a statesmanlike move.

More importantly, the Dominion of New England was designed to promote urgently needed efficiency in the administration of the English **Navigation Laws**. Those laws reflected the intensifying colonial rivalries of the seventeenth century. They sought to stitch England's overseas possessions more tightly to the motherland by throttling American trade with countries not ruled by the English crown. Like colonial peoples everywhere, the Americans chafed at such confinements, and smuggling became an increasingly common and honorable occupation.

At the head of the new dominion stood autocratic Sir Edmund Andros, an able English military man, conscientious but tactless. Establishing headquarters in Puritanical Boston, he generated much hostility by his open affiliation with the despised Church of England. The colonists were also outraged by his noisy and Sabbath-profaning soldiers, who were accused of teaching the people "to drink, blaspheme, curse, and damn."

Andros was prompt to use the mailed fist. He ruthlessly curbed the cherished town meetings; laid heavy restrictions on the courts, the press, and the schools; and revoked all land titles. Dispensing with the popular assemblies, he taxed the people without the consent of their duly elected representatives. He also strove to enforce the unpopular Navigation Laws and suppress smuggling. Liberty-loving colonists, accustomed to unusual privileges during long decades of neglect, were goaded to the verge of revolt.

The people of old England soon taught the people of New England a few lessons in resisting oppression. In 1688–1689 they engineered the memorable **Glorious (or Bloodless) Revolution**. Dethroning the despotic and unpopular Catholic James II, they enthroned the Protestant rulers of the Netherlands, the Dutch-born William III and his English wife, Mary II, daughter of James II.

When the news of the Glorious Revolution reached America, the ramshackle Dominion of New England collapsed like a house of cards. A Boston mob, catching the fever, rose against the existing regime. Sir Edmund Andros attempted to flee in women's clothing but was betrayed by boots protruding beneath his dress. He was hastily shipped off to England.

Massachusetts, though rid of the despotic Andros, did not gain as much from the upheaval as it had hoped. In 1691 it was arbitrarily made a royal colony, with a new charter and a new royal governor. The permanent loss of the ancient charter was a staggering blow to the proud Puritans, who never fully recovered. Worst of all, the privilege of voting, once a monopoly of church members, was now to be enjoyed by all qualified male property holders.

England's Glorious Revolution reverberated throughout the colonies from New England to the Chesapeake. Inspired by the challenge to the crown in old England, many colonists seized the occasion to strike against royal authority in America. Unrest rocked both New York and Maryland from 1689 to 1691, until newly appointed royal governors restored a semblance of order. Most importantly, the new monarchs relaxed the royal grip on colonial trade, inaugurating a period of "**salutary neglect**" when the much-resented Navigation Laws were only weakly enforced.

Yet residues remained of Charles II's effort to assert tighter administrative control over his empire. More English officials—judges, clerks, customs officials—now staffed the courts and strolled the wharves of English America. Many were incompetent, corrupt hacks who knew little and cared less about American affairs. Appointed by influential patrons in far-off England, they blocked the rise of local leaders to positions of political power by their very presence. Aggrieved Americans viewed them with mounting contempt and resentment as the eighteenth century wore on.

✵ Old Netherlanders at New Netherland

Late in the sixteenth century, the oppressed people of the Netherlands unfurled the standard of rebellion against Catholic Spain. After bloody and protracted fighting, they finally succeeded, with the aid of Protestant England, in winning their independence.

The seventeenth century—the era of Rembrandt and other famous artists—was a golden age in Dutch history. This vigorous little lowland nation finally emerged as a major commercial and naval power, and then it ungratefully challenged the supremacy of its former benefactor, England. Three great Anglo-Dutch naval wars were fought in the seventeenth century, with as many as a hundred ships on each side. The sturdy Dutch dealt blows about as heavy as they received.

The Dutch republic also became a leading colonial power, with by far its greatest activity in the East Indies. There it maintained an enormous and profitable empire for over three hundred years. The Dutch East India Company was virtually a state within a state and at one time supported an army of 10,000 men and a fleet of 190 ships, 40 of them men-of-war.

Seeking greater riches, this enterprising company employed an English explorer, Henry Hudson. Disregarding orders to sail northeast, he ventured into Delaware Bay and New York Bay in 1609 and then ascended the Hudson River, hoping that at last he had chanced upon the coveted shortcut through the continent. But, as the event proved, he merely filed a Dutch claim to a magnificently wooded and watered area.

Much less powerful than the mighty Dutch East India Company was the Dutch West India Company, which maintained profitable enterprises in the Caribbean. At times it was less interested in trading than in raiding and at one fell swoop in 1628 captured a fleet of Spanish treasure ships laden with loot worth $15 million. The company also established outposts in Africa and a thriving sugar industry in Brazil, which for several decades was its principal center of activity in the New World.

New Netherland, in the beautiful Hudson River area, was planted in 1623–1624 on a permanent basis (see Map 3.4). Established by the Dutch West India Company for its quick-profit fur trade, it was never more than a secondary interest of the founders. The company's most brilliant stroke was to buy Manhattan Island from the Indians (who did not actually "own" it) for virtually worthless trinkets—twenty-two thousand acres of what is now perhaps the most valuable real estate in the world for pennies per acre.

New Amsterdam—later New York City—was a company town. It was run by and for the Dutch company,

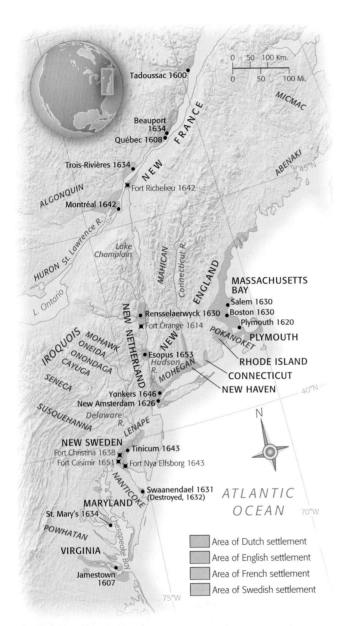

MAP 3.4 Early Settlements in the Middle Colonies, with Founding Dates © Cengage Learning

Area of Dutch settlement
Area of English settlement
Area of French settlement
Area of Swedish settlement

Courtesy, The Henry Francis du Pont Winterthur Museum

A Woman, by Gerret Duyckinck This portrait, painted between 1690 and 1710, depicts a prosperous woman in colonial New York. Her elegant dress of silk and lace, coral jewelry, and Chinese fan, and the Turkish rug beneath her arm, testify to the luxurious tastes and ties to international markets common among the "Hudson River lords."

in the interests of the stockholders. The investors had no enthusiasm for religious toleration, free speech, or democratic practices; and the governors appointed by the company as directors-general were usually harsh and despotic. Religious dissenters who opposed the official Dutch Reformed Church were regarded with suspicion, and for a while Quakers were savagely abused. In response to repeated protests by the aggravated colonists, a local body with limited lawmaking power was finally established.

This picturesque Dutch colony took on a strongly aristocratic tint and retained it for generations. Vast feudal estates fronting the Hudson River, known as **patroonships**, were granted to promoters who agreed to settle fifty people on them. One patroonship in the Albany area was slightly larger than the later state of Rhode Island.

Colorful little New Amsterdam attracted a cosmopolitan population, as is common in seaport towns. Twenty-three Jews arrived in 1654, refugees from religious persecution in Catholic Brazil—a harbinger of the city's later reputation as a haven for the homeless and the harried. A French Jesuit missionary, visiting in the 1640s, noted that eighteen different languages were being spoken in the streets. New York's later babel of immigrant tongues was thus foreshadowed.

✴ Friction with English and Swedish Neighbors

Vexations beset the Dutch company-colony from the beginning. The directors-general were largely incompetent. Company shareholders demanded their dividends, even at the expense of the colony's welfare. The Indians, infuriated by Dutch cruelties, retaliated with horrible massacres. As a defense measure, the hard-pressed settlers on Manhattan Island erected a stout wall, from which Wall Street derives its name.

New England was hostile to the growth of its Dutch neighbor, and the people of Connecticut finally ejected intruding Hollanders from their verdant valley. The Swedes also trespassed on Dutch preserves, from 1638 to 1655, by planting the anemic colony of New Sweden on the Delaware River (see Map 3.4). This was the golden age of Sweden, during and following the Thirty Years' War of 1618–1648, in which its brilliant King Gustavus Adolphus had carried the torch for Protestantism. This outburst of energy in Sweden caused it to enter the costly colonial game in America, though on something of a shoestring.

Resenting the Swedish intrusion on the Delaware, the Dutch dispatched a small military expedition in 1655. It was led by the ablest of the directors-general, Peter Stuyvesant, who had lost a leg while soldiering in the West Indies and was dubbed "Father Wooden Leg" by the Indians. The main fort fell after a bloodless siege, whereupon Swedish rule came to an abrupt end. The colonists were absorbed by New Netherland.

New Sweden, never important, soon faded away, leaving behind in later Delaware a sprinkling of Swedish place names and Swedish log cabins (the first in America), as well as an admixture of Swedish blood.

✴ Dutch Residues in New York

Lacking vitality, and representing only a secondary commercial interest of the Dutch, New Netherland lay under the menacing shadow of the vigorous English colonies to the north. In addition, it was honeycombed with New England immigrants. Numbering about one-half of New Netherland's ten thousand souls in 1664, they might in time have seized control from within.

The days of the Dutch on the Hudson were numbered, for the English regarded them as intruders. In 1664, after the imperially ambitious Charles II had granted the area to his brother, the Duke of York, a strong English squadron appeared off the decrepit defenses of New Amsterdam. A fuming Peter Stuyvesant, short of all munitions except courage, was forced to surrender without firing a shot. New Amsterdam was thereupon renamed New York, in honor of the Duke of York. England won a splendid harbor, strategically located in the middle of the mainland colonies, and the stately Hudson River penetrating the interior. With the removal of this foreign wedge, the English banner now waved triumphantly over a solid stretch of territory from Maine to the Carolinas.

The conquered Dutch province tenaciously retained many of the illiberal features of earlier days. An autocratic spirit survived, and the aristocratic element gained strength when certain corrupt English governors granted immense acreage to their favorites. Influential land-owning families—such as the Livingstons and the De

New Amsterdam, 1664 The future metropolis, already a bustling port, is shown here as it was in the year that the English took over New Netherland and renamed it New York.

Collection of the New York Historical Society

Quakers in the Colonial Era   Quakers, or Friends, were renowned for their simplicity of architecture, dress, manner, and speech. They also distinguished themselves from most other Protestant denominations by allowing women to speak in Quaker meetings and to share in making decisions for the church and the family.

Lanceys—wielded disproportionate power in the affairs of colonial New York. These monopolistic land policies, combined with the lordly atmosphere, discouraged many European immigrants from coming. The physical growth of New York was correspondingly retarded.

The Dutch peppered place names over the land, including Harlem (Haarlem), Brooklyn (Breuckelen), and Hell Gate (Hellegat). They likewise left their imprint on the gambrel-roofed architecture. As for social customs and folkways, no other foreign group of comparable size has made so colorful a contribution. Noteworthy are Easter eggs, Santa Claus, waffles, sauerkraut, bowling, sleighing, skating, and *kolf* (golf)—a dangerous game played with heavy clubs and forbidden in settled areas.

✸ Penn's Holy Experiment in Pennsylvania

A remarkable group of dissenters, commonly known as **Quakers**, arose in England during the mid-1600s. Their name derived from the report that they "quaked" when under deep religious emotion. Officially they were known as the Religious Society of Friends.

Quakers were especially offensive to the authorities, both religious and civil. They refused to support the established Church of England with taxes. They built simple meetinghouses, congregated without a paid clergy, and "spoke up" themselves in meetings when moved. Believing that they were all children in the sight of God, they kept their broad-brimmed hats on in the presence of their "betters" and addressed others with simple "thee"s and "thou"s, rather than with conventional titles. They would take no oaths because Jesus had commanded, "Swear not at all." This peculiarity often embroiled them with government officials, for "test oaths" were still required to establish the fact that a person was not a Roman Catholic.

The Quakers, beyond a doubt, were a people of deep conviction. They abhorred strife and warfare and refused military service. As advocates of passive resistance, they would turn the other cheek and rebuild their meetinghouse on the site where their enemies had torn it down. Their courage and devotion to principle finally triumphed. Although at times they seemed stubborn and unreasonable, they were a simple, devoted, democratic people, contending in their own high-minded way for religious and civic freedom.

William Penn, a wellborn and athletic young Englishman, was attracted to the Quaker faith in 1660, when only sixteen years old. His father, disapproving, administered a sound flogging. After various adventures in the army (the best portrait of the peaceful Quaker has him in armor), the youth firmly embraced the despised faith and suffered much persecution. The courts branded him a "saucy" and "impertinent" fellow. Several hundred of his less fortunate fellow Quakers died of cruel treatment, and thousands more were fined, flogged, or cast into dank prisons.

Penn's thoughts naturally turned to the New World, where a sprinkling of Quakers had already fled, notably to Rhode Island, North Carolina, and New

In a Boston lecture in 1869, Ralph Waldo Emerson (1803–1882) declared,

❝ The sect of the Quakers in their best representatives appear to me to have come nearer to the sublime history and genius of Christ than any other of the sects.**❞**

Jersey. Eager to establish an asylum for his people, he also hoped to experiment with liberal ideas in government and at the same time make a profit. Finally, in 1681, he managed to secure from the king an immense grant of fertile land, in consideration of a monetary debt owed to his deceased father by the crown. The king called the area Pennsylvania ("Penn's Woodland") in honor of the sire. The modest son, fearing that critics would accuse him of naming it after himself, sought unsuccessfully to change the name.

Pennsylvania was by far the best advertised of all the colonies. Its founder—the "first American advertising man"—sent out paid agents and distributed countless pamphlets printed in English, Dutch, French, and German. Unlike the lures of many other American real estate promoters, then and later, Penn's inducements were generally truthful. He especially welcomed forward-looking spirits and substantial citizens, including industrious carpenters, masons, shoemakers, and other manual workers. His liberal land policy, which encouraged substantial holdings, was instrumental in attracting a heavy inflow of immigrants.

✴ Quaker Pennsylvania and Its Neighbors

Penn formally launched his colony in 1681. His task was simplified by the presence of several thousand "squatters"—Dutch, Swedish, English, Welsh—who were already scattered along the banks of the Delaware River. Philadelphia, meaning "brotherly love" in Greek, was more carefully planned than most colonial cities and consequently enjoyed wide and attractive streets.

Penn farsightedly bought land from the Indians, including Chief Tammany, later patron saint of New York's political Tammany Hall. His treatment of the native peoples was so fair that the Quaker "broad brims" went among them unarmed and even employed them as baby-sitters. For a brief period, Pennsylvania seemed the promised land of amicable Indian–white relations. Some southern tribes even migrated to Pennsylvania, seeking the Quaker haven. But ironically, Quaker tolerance proved the undoing of Quaker Indian policy. As non-Quaker European immigrants flooded into the province, they undermined the Quakers' own benevolent policy toward the Indians. The feisty Scots-Irish were particularly unpersuaded by Quaker idealism.

Penn's new proprietary regime was unusually liberal and included a representative assembly elected by the landowners. No tax-supported state church drained coffers or demanded allegiance. Freedom of worship was guaranteed to all residents, although Penn, under pressure from London, was forced to deny Catholics and Jews the privilege of voting or holding office.

Penn's Treaty, by Edward Hicks The peace-loving Quaker founder of Pennsylvania made a serious effort to live in harmony with the Indians, as this treaty-signing scene illustrates. But the westward thrust of white settlement eventually caused friction between the two groups, as in other colonies.

Gilcrease Museum, Tulsa, Oklahoma

The death penalty was imposed only for treason and murder, as compared with some two hundred capital crimes in England.

Among other noteworthy features, no provision was made by the peace-loving Quakers of Pennsylvania for a military defense. No restrictions were placed on immigration, and naturalization was made easy. The humane Quakers early developed a strong dislike of black slavery, and in the genial glow of Pennsylvania some progress was made toward social reform.

With its many liberal features, Pennsylvania attracted a rich mix of ethnic groups. They included numerous religious misfits who were repelled by the harsh practices of neighboring colonies. This Quaker refuge boasted a surprisingly modern atmosphere in an unmodern age and to an unusual degree afforded economic opportunity, civil liberty, and religious freedom. Even so, "**blue laws**" prohibited "ungodly revelers," stage plays, playing cards, dice, games, and excessive hilarity.

Under such generally happy auspices, Penn's brainchild grew lustily. The Quakers were shrewd businesspeople, and in a short time the settlers were exporting grain and other foodstuffs. Within two years Philadelphia claimed three hundred houses and twenty-five hundred people. Within nineteen years—by 1700—the colony was surpassed in population and wealth only by long-established Virginia and Massachusetts.

William Penn, who altogether spent about four years in Pennsylvania, was never fully appreciated by his colonists. His governors, some of them incompetent and tactless, quarreled bitterly with the people, who were constantly demanding greater political control. Penn himself became too friendly with James II, the deposed Catholic king. Thrice arrested for treason, thrust for a time into a debtors' prison, and afflicted by a paralytic stroke, he died full of sorrows. His enduring monument was not only a noble experiment in government but also a new commonwealth. Based on civil and religious liberty, and dedicated to freedom of conscience and worship, it held aloft a hopeful torch in a world of semidarkness.

Small Quaker settlements flourished next door to Pennsylvania. New Jersey was started in 1664 when two noble proprietors received the area from the Duke of York. A substantial number of New Englanders, including many whose weary soil had petered out, flocked to the new colony. One of the proprietors sold West New Jersey in 1674 to a group of Quakers, who here set up a sanctuary even before Pennsylvania was launched. East New Jersey was also acquired in later years by the Quakers, whose wings were clipped in 1702 when the crown combined the two Jerseys in a royal colony.

Swedish-tinged Delaware consisted of only three counties—two at high tide, the witticism goes—and

was named after Lord De La Warr, the harsh military governor who had arrived in Virginia in 1610. Harboring some Quakers, and closely associated with Penn's prosperous colony, Delaware was granted its own assembly in 1703. But until the American Revolution, it remained under the governor of Pennsylvania.

✴ The Middle Way in the Middle Colonies

The middle colonies—New York, New Jersey, Delaware, and Pennsylvania—enjoyed certain features in common.

In general, the soil was fertile and the expanse of land was broad, unlike rock-bestrewn New England. Pennsylvania, New York, and New Jersey came to be known as the "bread colonies," by virtue of their heavy exports of grain.

Rivers also played a vital role. Broad, languid streams—notably the Susquehanna, the Delaware, and the Hudson—tapped the fur trade of the interior and beckoned adventuresome spirits into the backcountry. The rivers had few cascading waterfalls, unlike New England's, and hence presented little inducement to milling or manufacturing with water-wheel power.

A surprising amount of industry nonetheless hummed in the middle colonies. Virginal forests abounded for lumbering and shipbuilding. The presence of deep river estuaries and landlocked harbors stimulated both commerce and the growth of seaports, such as New York and Philadelphia. Even Albany, more than a hundred miles up the Hudson, was a port of some consequence in colonial days.

The middle colonies were in many respects midway between New England and the southern plantation group. Except in aristocratic New York, the landholdings were generally intermediate in size—smaller than in the plantation South but larger than in small-farm New England. Local government lay somewhere between the personalized town meeting of New England and the diffused county government of the South. There were fewer industries in the middle colonies than in New England, more than in the South.

Yet the middle colonies, which in some ways were the most American part of America, could claim certain distinctions in their own right. Generally speaking, the population was more ethnically mixed than that of other settlements. The people were blessed with an unusual degree of religious toleration and democratic control. Earnest and devout Quakers, in particular, made a compassionate contribution to human freedom out of all proportion to their numbers. Desirable land was more easily acquired in the middle colonies than in New England or in the tidewater South. One result

Examining the Evidence

A Seventeenth-Century Valuables Cabinet

In 1999 a boatyard worker on Cape Cod and his sister, a New Hampshire teacher, inherited a small (20-pound, 16½-inch-high) chest that had always stood on their grandmother's hall table, known in the family as the "Franklin chest." Eager to learn more about it, they set out to discover the original owner, tracing their family genealogy and consulting with furniture experts. In January 2000 this rare seventeenth-century cabinet, its full provenance now known, appeared on the auction block and sold for a record $2.4 million to the Peabody Essex Museum in Salem, Massachusetts. No less extraordinary than the price was the history of its creator and its owners embodied in the piece. Salem cabinetmaker James Symonds (1636–1726) had made the chest for his relatives Joseph Pope (1650–1712) and Bathsheba Folger (1652–1726) to commemorate their 1679 marriage. Symonds carved the Popes' initials and the date on the door of the cabinet. He also put elaborate S curves on the sides remarkably similar to the Mannerist carved oak paneling produced in Norfolk, England, from which his own cabinetmaker father had emigrated. Behind the chest's door are ten drawers where the Popes would have kept jewelry, money, deeds, and writing materials. Surely they prized the chest as a sign of refinement to be shown off in their best room, a sentiment passed down through the next thirteen generations even as the Popes' identities were lost. The chest may have become known as the "Franklin chest" because Bathsheba was Benjamin Franklin's aunt, but also because that identification appealed more to descendants ashamed that the Quaker Popes, whose own parents had been persecuted for their faith, were virulent accusers during the Salem witch trials of 1692.

Christies Images, Inc.

was that a considerable amount of economic and social democracy prevailed, though less so in aristocratic New York.

Modern-minded Benjamin Franklin, often regarded as the most representative American personality of his era, was a child of the middle colonies. Although it is true that Franklin was born a Yankee in puritanical Boston, he entered Philadelphia as a seventeen-year-old in 1720 with a loaf of bread under each arm and immediately found a congenial home in the urbane, open atmosphere of what was then North America's biggest city. One Pennsylvanian later boasted that Franklin "came to life at seventeen, in Philadelphia."

By the time Franklin arrived in the City of Brotherly Love, the American colonies were themselves "coming to life." Population was growing robustly. Transportation and communication were gradually improving. The British, for the most part, continued their hands-off policies, leaving the colonists to fashion their own local governments, run their own churches, and develop networks of intercolonial trade. As people and products crisscrossed the colonies with increasing frequency and in increasing volume, Americans began to realize that—far removed from Mother England—they were not merely surviving, but truly thriving.

Varying Viewpoints
Europeanizing America or Americanizing Europe?

The history of discovery and colonization raises perhaps the most fundamental question about all American history. Should it be understood as the extension of European civilization into the two continents of the New World or as the gradual development of uniquely "American" cultures? An older school of thought tended to emphasize the Europeanization of America. Historians of that persuasion paid close attention to the situation in Europe, particularly England and Spain, in the fifteenth and sixteenth centuries. They also focused on the exportation of the values and institutions of the mother countries to the new lands in the western sea. Although some historians also examined the transforming effect of America on Europe, this approach, too, remained essentially Eurocentric.

More recently, historians have concentrated on the distinctiveness of America. The concern with European origins has evolved into a comparative treatment of European settlements in the New World. England, Spain, Holland, and France now attract more attention for the divergent kinds of societies they fostered in America than for the way they commonly pursued Old World ambitions in the New. The newest trend to emerge is a transatlantic history that views European empires and their American colonies as part of a process of cultural cross-fertilization affecting not only the colonies but Europe and Africa as well.

This less Eurocentric approach has also changed the way historians explain the colonial development of America. Rather than telling the story of colonization as the imposition of European ways of life through "discovery" and "conquest," historians increasingly view the colonial period as one of "contact" and "adaptation" between European, African, and Native American ways of life. Scholars, including Richard White, Alfred Crosby, William Cronon, Karen Kupperman, and

Timothy Silver, have enhanced understanding of the cultural as well as the physical transformations that resulted from contact. An environment of forests and meadows, for example, gave way to a landscape of fields and fences as Europeans sought to replicate the agricultural villages they had known in Europe. Aggressive deforestation even produced climatic changes, as treeless tracts made for colder winters, hotter summers, and earth-gouging floods. Ramon Gutierrez's *When Jesus Came, the Corn Mothers Went Away* (1991) has expanded the colonial stage to include interactions between Spanish settlers and Native Americans in the Southwest.

J. H. Elliott's magisterial work *Empires of the Atlantic World* (2006) makes brilliant use of the comparative approach to illuminate the worlds of the British and Spanish Empires. Spain had a grand imperial plan that it pursued with notable consistency: exclude Jews and Moors (Muslims) from its domains, convert the native peoples to Catholicism, follow military conquest with military rule, and eventually defer to colonial elites for the orderly administration of its possessions. Britain had no comparably systematic plan. It showed relatively little interest in converting the Indians, tolerated all kinds of immigrants to its colonies, long left them alone to cultivate institutions of self-government and representative democracy, and when it eventually tried to tighten its imperial grip, pressured local elites into open revolt. The two empires left consequential and contrasting legacies of political stability in the United States and chronic political turmoil in Latin America. As one reviewer summarized the argument, "George Washington could draw on an inherited political culture, whereas [the great Latin American liberator] Simón Bolívar had to invent one."

The variety of American societies that emerged out of the interaction of Europeans, Africans, and Native Americans is now well appreciated. Early histories by esteemed historians like Perry Miller exaggerated the extent to which the New England Puritan experience defined the essence of America. Not only did these historians overlook non-English experiences, but they failed to recognize the diversity in motives, methods, and consequences that existed even within English colonization. The numbers alone tell an interesting story. By 1700 about 220,000 English colonists had immigrated to the Caribbean, about 120,000 to the southern mainland colonies, and only about 40,000 to the middle Atlantic and New England colonies (although by the mid-eighteenth century, those headed for the latter destination would account for more than half of the total).

Studies such as Richard S. Dunn's *Sugar and Slaves* (1972) emphasize the importance of the Caribbean in early English colonization efforts and make clear that the desire for economic gain, more than the quest for religious freedom, fueled the migration to the Caribbean islands. Similarly, Edmund S. Morgan's *American Slavery, American Freedom* (1975) stresses the role of economic ambition in explaining the English peopling of the Chesapeake and the eventual importation of African slaves to that region. Studies by Bernard Bailyn and David Hackett Fischer demonstrate that there was scarcely a "typical" English migrant to the New World. English colonists migrated both singly and in families, and for economic, social, political, and religious reasons.

Recent studies have also paid more attention to the conflicts that emerged out of this diversity in settler populations and colonial societies. This perspective emphasizes the contests for economic and political supremacy within the colonies, such as the efforts of the Massachusetts Bay elite to ward off the challenges of religious "heretics" and the pressures that an increasingly restless lower class put on wealthy merchants and large landowners. Nowhere was internal conflict so prevalent as in the ethnically diverse middle colonies, where factional antagonisms became the defining feature of public life.

The picture of British colonial North America that is emerging from all this new scholarship is of a society unique—and diverse—from inception. No longer simply Europe transplanted, British America by 1700 is now viewed as an outgrowth of many intertwining roots—of different European and African heritages, of varied encounters with native peoples and a wilderness environment, and of complicated mixtures of settler populations, each with its own distinctive set of ambitions.

Chapter Review

KEY TERMS

Calvinism (41)

predestination (41)

conversion (41)

Puritans (42)

Separatists (42)

Mayflower Compact (43)

Massachusetts Bay Colony (43)

Great Migration (43)

antinomianism (45)

Fundamental Orders (47)

Pequot War (47)

King Philip's War (48)

New England Confederation (48)

English Civil War (48)

Dominion of New England (49)

Navigation Laws (49)

Glorious (or Bloodless) Revolution (50)

salutary neglect (50)

patroonships (51)

Quakers (53)

blue laws (55)

PEOPLE TO KNOW

Martin Luther

John Calvin

William Bradford

John Winthrop

Anne Hutchinson

Roger Williams

Massasoit

Metacom (King Philip)

Charles II

Sir Edmund Andros

William III

Mary II

Henry Hudson

Peter Stuyvesant

Duke of York

William Penn

CHRONOLOGY

1517	Martin Luther begins Protestant Reformation
1536	John Calvin of Geneva publishes *Institutes of the Christian Religion*
1620	Pilgrims sail on the *Mayflower* to Plymouth Bay
1624	Dutch found New Netherland
1629	Charles I dismisses Parliament and persecutes Puritans
1630	Puritans found Massachusetts Bay Colony
1635–1636	Roger Williams convicted of heresy and founds Rhode Island colony
1635–1638	Connecticut and New Haven colonies founded
1637	Pequot War
1638	Anne Hutchinson banished from Massachusetts colony
1639	Connecticut's Fundamental Orders drafted
1642–1648	English Civil War
1643	New England Confederation formed
1650	William Bradford completes *Of Plymouth Plantation*
1655	New Netherland conquers New Sweden
1664	England seizes New Netherland from Dutch East and West Jersey colonies founded
1675–1676	King Philip's War
1681	William Penn founds Pennsylvania colony
1686	Royal authority creates Dominion of New England
1688–1689	Glorious Revolution overthrows Stuarts and Dominion of New England

TO LEARN MORE

Patricia Bonomi, *A Factious People: Politics and Society in Colonial New York* (1971)

Timothy H. Breen, *Puritans and Adventurers* (1980)

Jon Butler, *Awash in a Sea of Faith: Christianizing the American People* (1990)

John Demos, *The Unredeemed Captive: A Family Story from Early America* (1994)

David Hall, *Worlds of Wonder, Days of Judgment: Popular Religious Belief in Early New England* (1989)

Japp Jacobs, *The Colony of New Netherland: A Dutch Settlement in Seventeenth-Century America* (2009)

Donna Merwick, *The Shame and the Sorrow: Dutch-Amerindian Encounters in New Netherland* (2006)

Edmund S. Morgan, *Roger Williams: The Church and State* (1967)

Jenny Hale Pulsipher, *Subjects unto the Same King: Indians, English, and the Contest for Authority in Colonial New England* (2005)

Christina Snyder, *Slavery in Indian Country: The Changing Face of Captivity in Early America* (2010)

Harry Stout, *The New England Soul: Preaching and Culture in Colonial New England* (1986)

A complete, annotated bibliography for this chapter—along with brief descriptions of the People to Know—may be found on the American Pageant website. The Key Terms are defined in a Glossary at the end of the text.

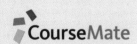

CourseMate Go to the CourseMate website at **www.cengagebrain.com** for additional study tools and review materials—including audio and video clips—for this chapter.

AP® Review Questions for Chapter 3

1. All of the following were tenets of Calvinism EXCEPT that
   (A) God is all-knowing and all-powerful.
   (B) by doing good deeds in this life, people could earn a place in God's kingdom in the afterlife.
   (C) it was predetermined which souls would go to heaven.
   (D) only during conversion might one receive a sign that he or she had been saved.
   (E) human beings were weak and prone to sin.

2. Separatists were Puritans who broke away because they
   (A) disliked the fact that all English subjects, regardless of piety, were automatically church members.
   (B) were unhappy with the total abandonment of formerly Catholic rituals in the Protestant Reformation.
   (C) felt that some members compromised their faith through alliances with King James I.
   (D) thought the Church of England had become corrupt.
   (E) saw new opportunities to begin a church of their own in the so-called New World.

3. Why did the Separatists who fled London for Holland eventually settle in the New World?
   (A) They were impressed by tales of great riches already discovered in English settlements.
   (B) England enticed them to the colonies with promises of religious freedom and assistance.
   (C) They were worried about the "Dutchification" of their children and wanted to practice their religion as English citizens.
   (D) They were enticed by friends and relatives who already relocated to the colonies.
   (E) They envisioned great financial opportunities for husbands and sons through an alliance with the Virginia Company.

4. The Mayflower Compact is significant because it
   (A) was the first constitution in the English colonies.
   (B) guaranteed religious freedom to all settlers.
   (C) was a first step toward colonial self-government.
   (D) included signatures of men and women who arrived on the Mayflower.
   (E) granted each settler 50 acres of land.

5. The colony founded by the Pilgrims in Plymouth Bay was
   (A) immediately successful.
   (B) at war from the start with native populations.
   (C) so ravaged by its first winter that many settlers abandoned the colony and returned home.
   (D) prosperous within a year, based on a bountiful harvest.
   (E) led by a series of corrupt, poorly educated men.

6. What did Massachusetts governor John Winthrop mean when he said, "We shall be as a city upon a hill"?
   (A) He envisioned the Massachusetts Bay Company as becoming the most economically successful British colony.
   (B) He hoped the colony would become a holy society that would serve as a model for people everywhere.
   (C) He was referring to Boston as the city where elite, wealthy, and well-educated people would settle and set an example for other colonists.
   (D) He was describing Boston as the seat of English colonial government.
   (E) He wanted the colony to provide public education for all citizens and believed an educated populace was the key to success in all colonies.

7. What was the single most important qualification for voting, above all others, in the provincial governments of the Massachusetts Bay Colony?
   (A) Land ownership
   (B) Male status
   (C) English citizenship
   (D) Tax-paying status
   (E) Church membership

8. Today, both Anne Hutchinson and Roger Williams are considered heroes for all of these reasons EXCEPT that they
   (A) challenged Puritan orthodoxy.
   (B) were exiled for their beliefs.
   (C) inspired dissent within the Puritan Church.
   (D) founded successful colonies elsewhere.
   (E) questioned colonial customs and practices.

9. How did Indians resist English encroachment on their land?

   (A) By forging intertribal alliances

   (B) By agreeing to convert to the Puritan faith

   (C) By seeking peaceful, cooperative use of the land

   (D) By arranging marriages between Indians and settlers

   (E) By seeking assistance from sympathetic colonists and Englishmen

10. Established in 1686, the Dominion of New England was

    (A) the name given to the colonial militia.

    (B) England's attempt to consolidate and better control its northeastern colonies.

    (C) the first colonial confederation stressing independent self-rule.

    (D) a religious organization established by the colonists to replace the Church of England.

    (E) a charter company that was granted settlement rights to the areas that would become Maine and New Hampshire.

11. The Dutch colony of New Netherland finally became the English colony New York as a result of

    (A) increased English immigration and settlement in the region.

    (B) the mismanagement and bankruptcy of the Dutch West India Company.

    (C) the inability of the Dutch to defend the colony against Indian attacks and encroachment by other European settlers.

    (D) the sale of the colony to England by the Dutch West India Company.

    (E) a battle by the English against Dutch forces in New Amsterdam.

12. Which of the following statements about the Pennsylvania colony is NOT true?

    (A) It was founded by William Penn as a haven for Quakers.

    (B) Organizers widely advertised to draw prospective settlers from several European countries.

    (C) Relations between early colonists and Indians were initially tense.

    (D) Its founder wanted to experiment with liberal forms of government.

    (E) Generous land policies attracted large numbers of immigrants.

13. The middle colonies—New York, New Jersey, Delaware, and Pennsylvania—all had which of the following traits in common?

    (A) Rich, fertile soil that enabled the region to produce and export vast quantities of grain

    (B) A population that was less ethnically and religiously mixed than other regions

    (C) Soil that was typically rocky and often difficult to farm

    (D) Landholdings that were generally small in size

    (E) Few industries or port cities for trade with England and other colonies

14. What were blue laws?

    (A) Legal codes that regulated who could vote

    (B) Laws that determined which religions would be permitted to settle in a given region

    (C) The rules that guided how large a tract of land a person would receive

    (D) Codes that regulated acceptable social behavior

    (E) Tariffs placed on certain imported goods

15. The Mayflower Compact, Fundamental Orders of Connecticut, and First Frame of Government in Pennsylvania are all evidence of

    (A) adherence to religious law in the colonies.

    (B) democracy in the British colonies.

    (C) early American criminal and civil laws.

    (D) colonists' desire for freedom from Great Britain.

    (E) peace treaties between colonists and Native Americans.

16. The middle colonies are considered by some to be the most American part of America for all of the following reasons EXCEPT that

    (A) the population was more ethnically mixed than in other regions.

    (B) there was an unusual degree of religious tolerance.

    (C) desirable land was more available than in the south and New England.

    (D) economic and social democracy prevailed in most areas.

    (E) settlers avoided purchasing and using slave labor.

Chapter 4

American Life in the Seventeenth Century

1607–1692

Being thus passed the vast ocean, and a sea of troubles before in their
preparation . . . , they had now no friends to wellcome them,
nor inns to entertaine or refresh their weatherbeaten bodies, no
houses or much less towns to repaire too, to seeke for succore.

WILLIAM BRADFORD, *OF PLYMOUTH PLANTATION*, CA. 1630

As the seventeenth century unfolded, the crude encampments of the first colonists slowly gave way to permanent settlements. Durable and distinctive ways of life emerged as Europeans and Africans adapted to the New World and as Native Americans adapted to the newcomers. Even the rigid doctrines of Puritanism softened somewhat in response to the circumstances of life in America. And though all the colonies remained tied to England, and all were stitched tightly into the fabric of an Atlantic economy, regional differences continued to crystallize, notably the increasing importance of slave labor to the southern way of life.

✹ The Unhealthy Chesapeake

Life in the American wilderness was nasty, brutish, and short for the earliest Chesapeake settlers. Malaria, dysentery, and typhoid took a cruel toll, cutting ten years off the life expectancy of newcomers from England. Half the people born in early Virginia and Maryland did not survive to celebrate their twentieth birthdays. Few of the remaining half lived to see their fiftieth—or even their fortieth, if they were women.

The disease-ravaged settlements of the Chesapeake grew only slowly in the seventeenth century, mostly through fresh immigration from England. The great majority of immigrants were single men in their late teens and early twenties, and most perished soon after arrival. Surviving males competed for the affections of the extremely scarce women, whom they outnumbered nearly six to one in 1650 and still outnumbered by three to two at the end of the century. Eligible women did not remain single for long.

Families were both few and fragile in this ferocious environment. Most men could not find mates. Most marriages were destroyed by the death of a partner within seven years. Scarcely any children reached adulthood under the care of two parents, and almost no one knew a grandparent. Weak family ties were reflected in the many pregnancies among unmarried young girls. In one Maryland county, more than a third of all brides were already pregnant when they wed.

Yet despite these hardships, the Chesapeake colonies struggled on. The native-born inhabitants eventually acquired immunity to the killer diseases that had ravaged the original immigrants. The presence of more women allowed more families to form, and by the end of the seventeenth century the white population of the Chesapeake was growing on the basis of its own birthrate. As the eighteenth century opened, Virginia, with some fifty-nine thousand people, was the most populous colony. Maryland, with about thirty thousand, was the third largest (after Massachusetts).

✹ The Tobacco Economy

Although unhealthy for human life, the Chesapeake was immensely hospitable to tobacco cultivation.

Profit-hungry settlers often planted tobacco to sell before they planted corn to eat. But intense tobacco cultivation quickly exhausted the soil, creating a nearly insatiable demand for new land. Relentlessly seeking fresh fields to plant in tobacco, commercial growers plunged ever farther up the river valleys, provoking ever more Indian attacks.

Leaf-laden ships annually hauled some 1.5 million pounds of tobacco out of Chesapeake Bay by the 1630s and almost 40 million pounds a year by the end of the century. This enormous production depressed prices, but colonial Chesapeake tobacco growers responded to falling prices in the familiar way of farmers: by planting still more acres to tobacco and bringing still more product to market.

More tobacco meant more labor, but where was it to come from? Families procreated too slowly to provide it by natural population increase. Indians died too quickly on contact with whites to be a reliable labor force. African slaves cost too much money. But England still had a "surplus" of displaced workers and farmers, desperate for employment. Many of them were young men who had fled the disastrous slump in the cloth trades that hit England in the early seventeenth century. Others were tenants who had been forced from their modest farms when landlords "enclosed" ever more acreage for sheep grazing. Making their way

> *An agent for the Virginia Company in London submitted the following description of the Virginia colony in 1622:*
>
> **❝**I found the plantations generally seated upon mere salt marshes full of infectious bogs and muddy creeks and lakes, and thereby subjected to all those inconveniences and diseases which are so commonly found in the most unsound and most unhealthy parts of England.**❞**

from town to town in search of wages, they eventually drifted into port cities like Bristol and London. There they boarded ship for America as **indentured servants**, voluntarily mortgaging the sweat of their bodies for several years (usually four to seven) to Chesapeake masters. In exchange they received transatlantic passage and eventual "freedom dues," including an ax and a hoe, a few barrels of corn, a suit of clothes, and perhaps a small parcel of land.

Both Virginia and Maryland employed the **headright system** to encourage the importation of servant workers. Under its terms, whoever paid the passage of a laborer received the right to acquire fifty acres of land. Masters—not the servants themselves—thus reaped the benefits of landownership from the headright system. Some masters, men who already had at least modest financial means, soon parlayed their investments in servants into vast holdings in real estate. They became the great merchant-planters, lords of sprawling riverfront estates that came to dominate the agriculture and commerce of the southern colonies. Ravenous for both labor and land, Chesapeake planters brought some 100,000 indentured servants to the region by 1700. These "white slaves" represented more than three-quarters of all European immigrants to Virginia and Maryland in the seventeenth century.

Indentured servants led a hard but hopeful life in the early days of the Chesapeake settlements. They looked forward to becoming free and acquiring land of their own after completing their term of servitude. But as prime land became scarcer, masters became increasingly resistant to including land grants in "freedom dues." The servants' lot grew harsher as the seventeenth century wore on. Misbehaving servants, such as a housemaid who became pregnant or a laborer who killed a hog, might be punished with an extended term of service. Even after formal freedom was granted,

E English of Reighly In Efex nº 2

Granger Collection

Early Tobacco Advertising   Crude woodcuts like this one were used to identify various "brands" of tobacco—one of the first products to be sold by brand-name advertising.

penniless freed workers often had little choice but to hire themselves out for pitifully low wages to their former masters.

Frustrated Freemen and Bacon's Rebellion

An accumulating mass of footloose, impoverished freemen drifted discontentedly about the Chesapeake region by the late seventeenth century. Mostly single young men, they were frustrated by their broken hopes of acquiring land, as well as by their gnawing failure to find single women to marry.

The swelling numbers of these wretched bachelors rattled the established planters. The Virginia assembly in 1670 disfranchised most of the landless knockabouts, accusing them of "having little interest in the country" and causing "tumults at the election to the disturbance of his majesty's peace." Virginia's Governor William Berkeley lamented his lot as ruler of this rabble: "How miserable that man is that governs a people where six parts of seven at least are poor, endebted, discontented, and armed."

Berkeley's misery soon increased. About a thousand Virginians broke out of control in 1676, led by a twenty-nine-year-old planter, Nathaniel Bacon. Many of the rebels were frontiersmen who had been forced into the untamed backcountry in search of arable land. They fiercely resented Berkeley's friendly policies toward the Indians, whose thriving fur trade the governor monopolized. When Berkeley refused to retaliate against a series of brutal Indian attacks on frontier settlements, Bacon and his followers took matters into their own hands. They fell murderously upon the Indians, friendly and hostile alike, chased Berkeley from Jamestown, and put the torch to the capital. Chaos swept the raw colony, as frustrated freemen and resentful servants—described as "a rabble of the basest sort of people"—went on a rampage of plundering and pilfering.

As this civil war in Virginia ground on, Bacon suddenly died of disease, like so many of his fellow colonists. Berkeley thereupon crushed the uprising with brutal cruelty, hanging more than twenty rebels. Back in England Charles II complained, "That old fool has put to death more people in that naked country than I did here for the murder of my father."

The distant English king could scarcely imagine the depths of passion and fear that **Bacon's Rebellion** excited in Virginia. Bacon had ignited the smoldering resentments of landless former servants, and he had pitted the hardscrabble backcountry frontiersmen against the haughty gentry of the tidewater plantations. The rebellion was now suppressed, but these tensions remained. Lordly planters, surrounded by a still-seething sea of malcontents, anxiously looked about for less troublesome laborers to toil in the restless tobacco kingdom. Their eyes soon lit on Africa.

Colonial Slavery

More than 7 million Africans were carried in chains to the New World in the three centuries or so following Columbus's landing (see "Thinking Globally: The Atlantic Slave Trade, 1500–1860," pp. 64–65). Only about 400,000 of them ended up in North America, the great majority arriving after 1700. Most of the early human cargoes were hauled to Spanish and Portuguese South America or to the sugar-rich West Indies.

Africans had been brought to Jamestown as early as 1619, but as late as 1670 they numbered only about 2,000 in Virginia (out of a total population of some 35,000 persons) and about 7 percent of the 50,000 people in the southern plantation colonies as a whole. Hard-pinched white colonists, struggling to stay alive and to hack crude clearings out of the forests, could not afford to pay high prices for slaves who might die soon after arrival. White servants might die, too, but they were far less costly.

Drastic change came in the 1680s. Rising wages in England shrank the pool of penniless folk willing to gamble on a new life or an early death as indentured servants in America. At the same time, the large planters were growing increasingly fearful of the multitudes of

Nathaniel Bacon (ca. 1647–1676) assailed Virginia's Governor William Berkeley (1606–1677) in 1676

"for having protected, favored, and emboldened the Indians against His Majesty's loyal subjects, never contriving, requiring, or appointing any due or proper means of satisfaction for their many invasions, robberies, and murders committed upon us.**"**

For his part, Governor Berkeley declared,

"I have lived thirty-four years amongst you [Virginians], as uncorrupt and diligent as ever [a] Governor was, [while] Bacon is a man of two years amongst you, his person and qualities unknown to most of you, and to all men else, by any virtuous act that ever I heard of. . . . I will take counsel of wiser men than myself, but Mr. Bacon has none about him but the lowest of the people.**"**

An Indentured Servant's Contract, 1746

Legal documents, such as this contract signed in Virginia in 1746, not only provide evidence about the ever-changing rules by which societies have regulated their affairs, but also furnish rich information about the conditions of life and the terms of human relationships in the past. This agreement between Thomas Clayton and James Griffin provides a reminder that not all indentured servants in early America came from abroad. Indentured servitude could be equivalent to an apprenticeship, in which a young person traded several years of service to a master in exchange for instruction in the master's craft. Here Clayton pledges himself to five years in Griffin's employ in return for a promise to initiate the young man into the "Mystery" of the master's craft. Why might the master's trade be described as a "mystery"? From the evidence of this contract, what are the principal objectives of each of the parties to it? What problems does each anticipate? What obligations does each assume? What does the consent of Clayton's mother to the contract suggest about the young man's situation?

Special Collections, John D. Rockefeller, Jr. Library, The Colonial Williamsburg Foundation

Special Collections, John D. Rockefeller, Jr. Library, The Colonial Williamsburg Foundation

The Atlantic Slave Trade, 1500–1860

For more than three centuries following Columbus's discovery, slave merchants crammed some 11 million African men, women, and children into the holds of ships and carried them like common cargo to the New World. Roughly 2 million souls perished mid-voyage before confronting the agonies and indignities of slavery in the Americas. As Map 4.1 shows, some 400,000 enslaved Africans came ashore in North America, while the overwhelming majority were destined for South America and the Caribbean.

European and American slave traders reaped enormous profits from this human trafficking, as did the African warlords who sold their hapless captives into lifelong bondage. British, French, Portuguese, Dutch, and New England slavers stuffed their ships to capacity with little regard for the health or comfort of their suffering cargo. One enslaved boy, Olaudah Equiano, later wrote of his constant fear during the voyage that his tormenting captors would murder him, as they did several others before his young eyes. Equiano survived, but the hideous conditions aboard those floating hells killed countless Africans and deeply traumatized many others.

Slave trading fed off the insatiable European appetite for sugar, as well as for tobacco, cotton, and other New World products that both Europeans and Americans craved. Marketing human beings on such a vast scale required the complicity not only of warlords and sailors but also of bankers and stevedores, planters and tailors, shopkeepers and bakers, and finally tea drinkers, smokers, and a host of middlemen on four continents.

Once purchased by their New World masters, slaves faced a life of ceaseless, unpaid toil. Though conditions varied across the vast slave dominion that stretched from Brazil to North America, most slaves had few if any legal rights. The Caribbean and Deep South sugar plantations in particular demanded notoriously man-killing, backbreaking labor.

Slavery in the Americas continued to gain importance, and human imports from Africa peaked in the late eighteenth century. Only in the nineteenth century, beginning with Britain in 1807, did nations in Europe and the

An African Slave Coffle   Yoked and bound, these men, women, and children were on their way to a coastal slave market, where they would be herded aboard ship for the Americas.

Library of Congress

MAP 4.1 Main Sources and Destinations of African Slaves, ca. 1500–1860 More than three centuries of the "African Diaspora" scattered blacks throughout the New World. Britain's North American colonies (the future United States) constituted the extreme northern periphery of this system, receiving about 400,000 of the nearly 10 million arrivals, the great majority of whom ended up in the West Indies and Brazil. © Cengage Learning

Americas begin to outlaw the international slave trade (see "The Struggle to Abolish Slavery," pp. 354–355). After Congress banned further slave importations to the United States in 1808, a flourishing internal market developed. Masters in the upper South bred slaves for sale on the rapidly expanding cotton frontier in the Old Southwest. Europeans, as well as Americans in the "free states," lent indirect support to that domestic slave trade as they continued to consume slave-produced goods. Slavery would not finally be abolished in the United States until 1863.

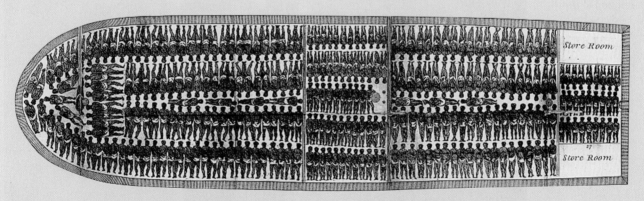

The "Middle Passage" The "middle passage" referred to the transatlantic sea voyage that brought slaves to the New World—the long and hazardous "middle" segment of a journey that began with a forced march to the African coast and ended with a trek into the American interior. Granger Collection

potentially mutinous former servants in their midst. By the mid-1680s, for the first time, black slaves outnumbered white servants among the plantation colonies' new arrivals. In 1698 the **Royal African Company**, first chartered in 1672, lost its crown-granted monopoly on carrying slaves to the colonies. Enterprising Americans, especially Rhode Islanders, rushed to cash in on the lucrative slave trade, and the supply of slaves rose steeply. More than ten thousand Africans were pushed ashore in America in the decade after 1700, and tens of thousands more in the next half-century. Blacks accounted for nearly half the population of Virginia by 1750. In South Carolina they outnumbered whites two to one.

Most of the slaves who reached North America came from the west coast of Africa, especially the area stretching from present-day Senegal to Angola. They were originally captured by African coastal tribes, who traded them in crude markets on the shimmering tropical beaches to itinerant European—and American—flesh merchants. Usually branded and bound, the captives were herded aboard sweltering ships for the gruesome **middle passage**, on which death rates ran as high as 20 percent. Terrified survivors were eventually shoved onto auction blocks in New World ports like Newport, Rhode Island, or Charleston, South Carolina, where a giant slave market traded in human misery for more than a century.

A few of the earliest African immigrants gained their freedom, and some even became slaveowners themselves. But as the number of Africans in their midst increased dramatically toward the end of the seventeenth century, white colonists reacted remorselessly to this supposed racial threat.

Earlier in the century, the legal difference between a slave and a servant was unclear. But now the law began to make sharp distinctions between the two—largely on the basis of race. Beginning in Virginia in 1662, statutes appeared that formally decreed the iron conditions of slavery for blacks. These earliest "**slave codes**" made blacks *and their children* the property (or "chattels") for life of their white masters. Some colonies made it a crime to teach a slave to read or write. Not

The Slave Ship Albatross, 1846 This eyewitness painting captures the dankness, gloom, and despair that reigned in the slaver's cargo hold.

National Maritime Museum, London

Granger Collection Foundation

RICE CULTURE ON THE OGEECHEE, NEAR SAVANNAH, GEORGIA.—Sketched by A. R. Waud.—[See Page 5.]

Rice Cultivation in the Colonial South Rice growing, imported from Africa along with African slaves to work the swampy rice fields, made South Carolina the rice basket of the British Empire.

even conversion to Christianity could qualify a slave for freedom. Thus did the God-fearing whites put the fear of God into their hapless black laborers. Slavery might have begun in America for economic reasons, but by the end of the seventeenth century, it was clear that racial discrimination also powerfully molded the American slave system.

✦ Africans in America

In the deepest South, slave life was especially severe. The climate was hostile to health, and the labor was life-draining. The widely scattered South Carolina rice and indigo plantations were lonely hells on earth where gangs of mostly male Africans toiled and perished. Only fresh imports could sustain the slave population under these loathsome conditions.

Blacks in the tobacco-growing Chesapeake region had a somewhat easier lot. Tobacco was a less physically demanding crop than those of the deeper South. Tobacco plantations were larger and closer to one another than rice plantations. The size and proximity of these plantations permitted the slaves more frequent contact with friends and relatives. By about 1720 the proportion of females in the Chesapeake slave population had begun to rise, making family life possible. The captive black population of the Chesapeake area soon began to grow not only through new imports but also through its own fertility—making it one of the few slave societies in history to perpetuate itself by its own natural reproduction.

Native-born African Americans contributed to the growth of a stable and distinctive slave culture, a mixture of African and American elements of speech, religion, and folkways (see "Makers of America: From African to African American," pp. 68–69). On the sea islands off South Carolina's coast, blacks evolved a unique language, *Gullah* (probably a corruption of *Angola*, the African region from which many of them had come). It blended English with several African languages, including Yoruba, Igbo, and Hausa. Through it many African words have passed into American speech—such as *goober* (peanut), *gumbo* (okra), and *voodoo* (witchcraft). The ringshout, a West African religious dance performed by shuffling in a circle while answering a preacher's shouts, was brought to colonial America by slaves and eventually contributed to the development of jazz. The banjo and the bongo drum were other African contributions to American culture.

Slaves also helped mightily to build the country with their labor. A few became skilled artisans—carpenters, bricklayers, and tanners. But chiefly they performed the sweaty toil of clearing swamps, grubbing out trees, and other menial tasks. Condemned to life under the lash, slaves naturally pined for freedom. The **New York slave revolt** that erupted in 1712 cost the lives of nine whites and caused the execution of twenty-one blacks, some of them burned at the stake over a slow fire. A **South Carolina slave revolt** erupted in 1739 when more than fifty resentful blacks along the **Stono River** tried to march to Spanish Florida, only to be stopped by the local militia. But in the end, enslaved Africans in the South proved to

Dragged in chains from West African shores, the first African Americans struggled to preserve their diverse heritages from the ravages of slavery. Their children, the first generation of American-born slaves, melded these various African traditions—Guinean, Igbo, Yoruba, Angolan—into a distinctive African American culture. Their achievement sustained them during the cruelties of enslavement and has endured to enrich American life to this day.

With the arrival of the first Africans in the seventeenth century, a cornucopia of African traditions poured into the New World: handicrafts and skills in numerous trades; a plethora of languages, styles of music, and cuisines; even rice-planting techniques that conquered the inhospitable soil of South Carolina. It was North America's rice paddies, tilled by experienced West Africans, that introduced rice into the English diet and furnished so many English tables with the sticky staple.

These first American slaves were mostly males. Upon arrival they were sent off to small isolated farms, where social contact with other Africans, especially women, was an unheard-of luxury. Yet their legal status was at first uncertain. A few slaves were able to buy their freedom in the seventeenth century. One, Anthony Johnson of Northampton County, Virginia, actually became a slaveholder himself.

But by the beginning of the eighteenth century, a settled slave society was emerging in the southern colonies. Laws tightened; slave traders stepped up their deliveries of human cargo; large plantations formed. Most significantly, a new generation of American-born slaves joined their forebears at labor in the fields. By 1740 large groups of slaves lived together on sprawling plantations, the American-born outnumbered the African-born, and the importation of African slaves slowed.

Forging a common culture and finding a psychological weapon with which to resist their masters and preserve their dignity were daunting challenges for American-born slaves. Plantation life was beastly, an endless cycle of miserable toil in the field or foundry from sunup to sundown. Female slaves were forced to perform double duty. After a day's backbreaking work, women were expected to sit up for hours spinning, weaving, or sewing to clothe themselves and their families. Enslaved women also lived in constant fear of sexual exploitation by predatory masters.

Yet eventually a vibrant slave culture began to flower. And precisely because of the diversity of African peoples represented in America, the culture that emerged was a uniquely New World creation. It derived from no single African model and incorporated many Western elements, though often with significant modifications.

UNITED STATES SLAVE TRADE.
1830.

Library of Congress

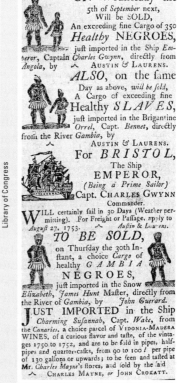

Charleston Library Society

(above) Africans Destined for Slavery This engraving from 1830 is an example of antislavery propaganda in the pre–Civil War era. It shows hapless Africans being brought ashore in America under the whips of slave traders and, ironically, under the figurative shadow of the national Capitol.
(right) Advertisements for Slave Sales in Charleston, South Carolina, 1753 Charleston had the largest slave market in the colonies.

(left) Yarrow Mamout, by Charles Willson Peale, 1819   When Peale painted this portrait, Mamout was over one hundred years old. A devout Muslim brought to Maryland as a slave, he eventually bought his freedom and settled in Georgetown. **(right) The Emergence of an African American Culture**   In this scene from the mid-nineteenth century, African Americans play musical instruments of European derivation, like the fiddle, as well as instruments of African origin, like the bones and banjo—a vivid illustration of the blending of the two cultures in the crucible of the New World.

Slave religion illustrates this pattern. Cut off from their native African religions, most slaves became Christians but fused elements of African and Western traditions and drew their own conclusions from Scripture. White Christians might point to Christ's teachings of humility and obedience to encourage slaves to "stay in their place," but black Christians emphasized God's role in freeing the Hebrews from slavery and saw Jesus as the Messiah who would deliver them from bondage. They also often retained an African definition of heaven as a place where they would be reunited with their ancestors.

At their Sunday and evening-time prayer meetings, slaves also patched African remnants onto conventional Christian ritual. Black Methodists, for example, ingeniously evaded the traditional Methodist ban on dancing as sinful: three or four people would stand still in a ring, clapping hands and beating time with their feet (but never crossing their legs, thus not officially "dancing"), while others walked around the ring, singing in unison. This "ringshout" derived from African practices; modern American dances, including the Charleston, in turn derived from this African American hybrid.

Christian slaves also often used outwardly religious songs as encoded messages about escape or rebellion. "Good News, the Chariot's Comin'" might sound like an innocent hymn about divine deliverance, but it could also announce the arrival of a guide to lead fugitives safely to the North. Similarly, "Wade in the Water" taught fleeing slaves one way of covering their trail. The "Negro spirituals" that took shape as a distinctive form of American music thus had their origins in *both* Christianity and slavery.

Indeed much American music was born in the slave quarters from African importations. Jazz, with its meandering improvisations and complex syncopations and rhythms, constitutes the most famous example. But this rich cultural harvest came at the cost of generations of human agony.

Charleston, South Carolina   Founded in 1680, Charleston grew to become the bustling seaport pictured in this drawing done in the 1730s. Charleston was by then the largest city in the mostly rural southern colonies. It flourished as a seaport for the shipment to England of slave-grown Carolina rice.

be a more tightly controlled labor force than the white indentured servants they gradually replaced. No slave uprising in American history matched the scale of Bacon's Rebellion.

✦ Southern Society

As slavery spread, the gaps in the South's social structure widened. The rough equality of poverty and disease of the early days was giving way to a defined hierarchy of wealth and status in the early eighteenth century. At the top of this southern social ladder perched a small but powerful covey of great planters. Owning gangs of slaves and vast domains of land, the planters ruled the region's economy and virtually monopolized political power. A clutch of extended clans—such as the Fitzhughs, the Lees, and the Washingtons—possessed among them horizonless tracts of Virginia real estate, and together they dominated the House of Burgesses. Just before the Revolutionary War, 70 percent of the leaders of the Virginia legislature came from families established in Virginia before 1690—the famed "first families of Virginia," or "FFVs."

Yet, legend to the contrary, these great seventeenth-century merchant-planters were not silk-swathed cavaliers gallantly imitating the ways of English country gentlemen. They did eventually build stately riverfront manors, occasionally rode to the hounds, and some of them even cultivated the arts and accumulated distinguished libraries. But for the most part, they were a hard-working, businesslike lot, laboring long hours over the problems of plantation management. Few problems were more vexatious than the unruly, often surly, servants. One Virginia governor had such difficulty keeping his servants sober that he struck a deal allowing them to get drunk the next day if they would

only lay off the liquor long enough to look after his guests at a celebration of the queen's birthday in 1711.

Beneath the planters—far beneath them in wealth, prestige, and political power—were the small farmers, the largest social group. They tilled their modest plots and might own one or two slaves, but they lived a ragged, hand-to-mouth existence. Still lower on the social scale were the landless whites, most of them luckless former indentured servants. Beneath them were those persons still serving out the term of their indenture. Their numbers gradually diminished as black slaves increasingly replaced white indentured servants toward the end of the seventeenth century. The oppressed black slaves, of course, remained enchained in society's basement.

Few cities sprouted in the colonial South, and consequently an urban professional class, including lawyers and financiers, was slow to emerge. Southern life revolved around the great plantations, distantly isolated from one another. Waterways provided the principal means of transportation. Roads were so wretched that in bad weather funeral parties could not reach church burial grounds—an obstacle that accounts for the development of family burial plots in the South, a practice unlike anything in old England or New England.

✦ The New England Family

Nature smiled more benignly on pioneer New Englanders than on their disease-plagued fellow colonists to the south. Clean water and cool temperatures retarded the spread of killer microbes. In stark contrast to the fate of Chesapeake immigrants, settlers in seventeenth-century New England *added* ten years to their life spans by migrating from the Old World. One settler claimed that "a sip of New England's air is better than a whole draft of old England's ale." The first generations of Puritan colonists enjoyed, on the average, about seventy years on this earth—not very different from the life expectancy of present-day Americans.

In further contrast with the Chesapeake, New Englanders tended to migrate not as single individuals but as families, and the family remained at the center of New England life. Almost from the outset, New England's population grew from natural reproductive increase. The people were remarkably fertile, even if the soil was not.

Early marriage encouraged the booming birthrate. Women typically wed by their early twenties and produced babies about every two years thereafter until menopause. Ceaseless childbearing drained the vitality of many pioneer women, as the weather-eroded colonial tombstones eloquently reveal. A number of the largest families were borne by several mothers, though claims about the frequency of death in childbirth have probably been exaggerated. But the dread of death in the birthing bed haunted many women, and it was small wonder that they came to fear pregnancy.

New England early acquired a reputation as a healthy environment. Urging his fellow Englishmen to emigrate to the Massachusetts Bay Colony in 1630, the Reverend John White described New England (somewhat fancifully) as follows:

"No country yields a more propitious air for our temper than New England. . . . Many of our people that have found themselves always weak and sickly at home, have become strong and healthy there: perhaps by the dryness of the air and constant temper[ature] of it, which seldom varies from cold to heat, as it does with us. . . . Neither are the natives at any time troubled with pain of teeth, soreness of eyes, or ache in their limbs."

A married woman could expect to experience up to ten pregnancies and rear as many as eight surviving children. Massachusetts governor William Phips was one of twenty-seven children, all by the same mother. A New England woman might well have dependent children living in her household from the earliest days of her marriage up until the day of her death, and child raising became in essence her full-time occupation.

The longevity of the New Englanders contributed to family stability. Children grew up in nurturing environments where they were expected to learn habits of obedience, above all. They received guidance not only from their parents but from their grandparents as well. This novel intergenerational continuity has inspired the observation that New England "invented" grandparents. Family stability was reflected in low premarital pregnancy rates (again in contrast with the Chesapeake) and in the generally strong, tranquil social structure characteristic of colonial New England.

Still other contrasts came to differentiate the southern and New England ways of life. Oddly enough, the fragility of southern families advanced the economic security of southern women, especially of women's property rights. Because southern men frequently died young, leaving widows with small children to support, the southern colonies generally allowed married women to retain separate title to their property and gave widows the right to inherit their husbands' estates. But in New England, Puritan lawmakers worried that recognizing women's separate property rights would undercut the unity of married persons by acknowledging conflicting interests between husband and wife. New England women, therefore, usually gave up their property rights when they married. Yet in contrast to old England, the laws of New England made secure provision for the property rights of widows—and even

Worcester Art Museum, Gift of Mr. & Mrs. Albert W. Rice

Mrs. Elizabeth Freake and Baby Mary   This portrait of a Boston mother and child in about 1674 suggests the strong family ties that characterized early New England society.

among the very few permissible grounds for divorce. Adultery was another. Convicted adulterers—especially if they were women—were whipped in public and forced forever after to wear the capital letter "A" cut out in cloth and sewed on their outer garments—the basis for Nathaniel Hawthorne's famous 1850 tale *The Scarlet Letter.*

✴ Life in the New England Towns

Sturdy New Englanders evolved a tightly knit society, the basis of which was small villages and farms. This development was natural in a people anchored by geography and hemmed in by the Indians, the French, and the Dutch. Puritanism likewise made for unity of purpose—and for concern about the moral health of the whole community. It was no accident that the nineteenth-century crusade for abolishing black slavery—with Massachusetts agitators at the forefront—sprang in some degree from the New England conscience, with its Puritan roots.

In the Chesapeake region, the expansion of settlement was somewhat random and was usually undertaken by lone-wolf planters on their own initiative, but New England society grew in a more orderly fashion. New towns were legally chartered by the colonial authorities, and the distribution of land was entrusted to the steady hands of sober-minded town fathers, or "proprietors." After receiving a grant of land from the colonial legislature, the proprietors moved themselves and their families to the designated place and laid out their town. It usually consisted of a meetinghouse, which served as both the place of worship and the town hall, surrounded by houses. Also marked out was a village green, where the militia could drill. Each family received several parcels of land, including a woodlot

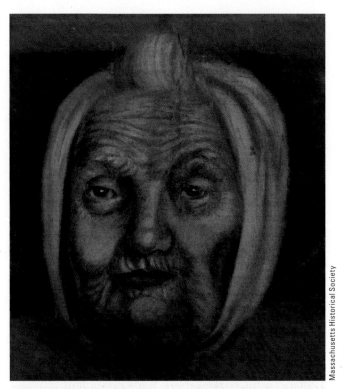

Mary Mirick Davie (1635–1752)   This woman exemplified the longevity of New Englanders. She bore nine children, buried three husbands, and was still performing household tasks past the age of one hundred.

Massachusetts Historical Society

extended important protections to women within marriage.

"A true wife accounts subjection her honor," one Massachusetts Puritan leader declared, expressing a sentiment then common in Europe as well as America. But in the New World, a rudimentary conception of women's rights as individuals was beginning to appear in the seventeenth century. Women still could not vote, and the popular attitude persisted that they were morally weaker than men—a belief rooted in the biblical tale of Eve's treachery in the Garden of Eden. But a husband's power over his wife was not absolute. The New England authorities could and did intervene to restrain abusive spouses. One man was punished for kicking his wife off a stool; another was disciplined for drawing an "uncivil" portrait of his mate in the snow. Women also had some spheres of autonomy. Midwifery—assisting with childbirths—was a virtual female monopoly, and midwives often fostered networks of women bonded by the common travails of motherhood. One Boston midwife alone delivered over three thousand babies.

Above all, the laws of Puritan New England sought to defend the integrity of marriages. Divorce was exceedingly rare, and the authorities commonly ordered separated couples to reunite. Outright abandonment was

The Massachusetts School Law of 1647 stated,

❝It being one chief project of the old deluder, Satan, to keep men from the knowledge of the Scriptures, as in former times by keeping them in an unknown tongue, it is therefore ordered that every township in this jurisdiction, after the Lord has increased them [in] number to fifty householders, shall then forthwith appoint one within their town to teach all such children as shall resort to him to write and read, whose wages shall be paid either by the parents or masters of such children, or by the inhabitants in general.❞

for fuel, a tract suitable for growing crops, and another for pasturing animals.

Towns of more than fifty families were required to provide elementary education, and roughly half of the adults knew how to read and write. As early as 1636, just six years after the colony's founding, the Massachusetts Puritans established Harvard College, today the oldest corporation in America, to train local boys for the ministry. Only in 1693, eighty-six years after staking out Jamestown, did the Virginians establish their first college, William and Mary.

Puritans ran their own churches, and democracy in **Congregational Church** government led logically to democracy in political government. The town meeting, in which the adult males met together and each man voted, was a showcase and a classroom for democracy. New England villagers from the outset gathered regularly in their meetinghouses to elect their officials, appoint schoolmasters, and discuss such mundane matters as road repairs. The town meeting, observed Thomas Jefferson, was "the best school of political liberty the world ever saw."

✴ The Half-Way Covenant and the Salem Witch Trials

Yet worries plagued the God-fearing pioneers of these tidy New England settlements. The pressure of a growing population was gradually dispersing the Puritans onto outlying farms, far from the control of church and neighbors. And although the core of Puritan belief still burned brightly, the passage of time was dampening the first generation's flaming religious zeal. About the middle of the seventeenth century, a new form of

sermon began to be heard from Puritan pulpits—the **jeremiad**. Taking their cue from the doom-saying Old Testament prophet Jeremiah, earnest preachers scolded parishioners for their waning piety. Especially alarming was the apparent decline in conversions—testimonials by individuals that they had received God's grace and therefore deserved to be admitted to the church as members of the elect.

Troubled ministers in 1662 announced a new formula for church membership, the **Half-Way Covenant**. This new arrangement modified the "covenant," or the agreement between the church and its adherents, to admit to baptism—but not "full communion"—the children of baptized but not-yet-converted existing members. (On "conversion," see p. 41.) By conferring partial membership rights in the once-exclusive Puritan congregations, the Half-Way Covenant weakened the distinction between the "elect" and others, further diluting the spiritual purity of the original settlers' godly community.

The Half-Way Covenant dramatized the difficulty of maintaining at fever pitch the religious devotion of the founding generation. Jeremiads continued to thunder from the pulpits, but as time went on, the doors of the Puritan churches swung fully open to all comers, whether converted or not. This widening of church membership gradually erased the distinction between the "elect" and other members of society. In effect, strict religious purity was sacrificed somewhat to the cause of wider religious participation. Interestingly, from about this time onward, women were in the majority in the Puritan congregations.

Women also played a prominent role in one of New England's most frightening religious episodes. A group of adolescent girls in Salem, Massachusetts, claimed to

The Free Library of Philadelphia

A Colonial Primer Religious instruction loomed large in early colonial schools. This eighteenth-century textbook from Germantown, Pennsylvania, taught lessons of social duty and Christian faith, as well as reading and writing.

Matthew Hopkins Witch Finder Generall

My Imps names are

Holt

1 Ilemauzar
2 Byewackett

Jarmara

Sacke & Sugar

3 Pecke in the Crowne
4 Griezzell Greedigutt

Newes

Vinegar tom

Correctly Copied from an extreme Rare Print in the Collection of J. Bindley Esqr.

Publifh'd as the Act directs March 20 1792 by J. Caulfield London

Bettmann/Corbis

Matthew Hopkins's Witch Finder Hopkins was a seventeenth-century English witch-hunter whose techniques included watching suspects to see if diabolical creatures, in the form of common animals, fed on the alleged witch's blood. He also urged that suspected witches be bound hand and foot and tossed in a pond. The innocent, he claimed, would sink (and often drown), while the guilty would float to the surface. His methods brought death to hundreds of women, men, and children in eastern England in the 1640s.

have been bewitched by certain older women. A hysterical "witch hunt" ensued, leading to the legal lynching in 1692 of twenty individuals, nineteen of whom were hanged and one of whom was pressed to death. Two dogs were also hanged.

Larger-scale witchcraft persecutions were then common in Europe, and several outbreaks had already flared forth in the colonies—often directed at property-owning women. But the reign of horror in Salem grew not only from the superstitions and prejudices of the age but also from the turmoil of the wars with the Indians, as well as the unsettled social and religious conditions of the rapidly evolving Massachusetts village. Most of the accused witches came from families associated with Salem's burgeoning market economy; their accusers came largely from subsistence farming

families in Salem's hinterland. The **Salem witch trials** thus reflected the widening social stratification of New England, as well as the fear of many religious traditionalists that the Puritan heritage was being eclipsed by Yankee commercialism.

The witchcraft hysteria eventually ended in 1693 when the governor, alarmed by an accusation against his own wife and supported by the more responsible members of the clergy, prohibited any further trials and pardoned those already convicted. Twenty years later a penitent Massachusetts legislature annulled the "convictions" of the "witches" and made reparations to their heirs. The Salem witchcraft delusion marked an all-time high in the American experience of popular passions run wild. "Witch-hunting" passed into the American vocabulary as a metaphor for the often dangerously irrational urge to find a scapegoat for social resentments.

✖ The New England Way of Life

Oddly enough, the story of New England was largely written by rocks. The heavily glaciated soil was strewn with countless stones, many of which were forced to the surface after a winter freeze. In a sense the Puritans did not possess the soil; it possessed them by shaping their character. Scratching a living from the protesting earth was an early American success story. Back-bending toil put a premium on industry and penny-pinching frugality, for which New Englanders became famous. Traditionally sharp Yankee traders, some of them palming off wooden nutmegs, made their mark. Connecticut came in time to be called good-humoredly "the Nutmeg State." Cynics exaggerated when they said that the three stages of progress in New England were "to get on, to get honor, to get honest."

The grudging land also left colonial New England less ethnically mixed than its southern neighbors. Non-English immigrants were less attracted to a site where the soil was so stony—and the sermons so sulfurous.

Climate likewise molded New England, where the summers were often uncomfortably hot and the winters cruelly cold. Many early immigrants complained of the region's extremes of weather. Yet the soil and climate of New England eventually encouraged a diversified agriculture and industry. Staple products like tobacco did not flourish, as in the South. Black slavery, although attempted, could not exist profitably on small farms, especially where the surest crop was stones. No broad, fertile expanses comparable to those in the tidewater South beckoned people inland. The mountains ran fairly close to the shore, and the rivers were generally short and rapid.

And just as the land shaped New Englanders, so they shaped the land. The Native Americans had left an early imprint on the New England earth. They traditionally beat trails through the woods as they migrated seasonally for hunting and fishing. They periodically burned the woodlands to restore leafy first-growth forests that would sustain the deer population. The Indians recognized the right to *use* the land, but the concept of exclusive, individual *ownership* of the land was alien to them.

The English settlers had a different philosophy. They condemned the Indians for "wasting" the earth by underutilizing its bounty and used this logic to justify their own expropriation of the land from the native inhabitants. Consistent with this outlook, the Europeans felt a virtual duty to "improve" the land by clearing woodlands for pasturage and tillage, building roads and fences, and laying out permanent settlements.

Some of the greatest changes resulted from the introduction of livestock. The English brought pigs, horses, sheep, and cattle from Europe to the settlements. Because the growing herds needed ever more pastureland, the colonists were continually clearing forests. The animals' voracious appetites and heavy hooves compacted the soil, speeding erosion and flooding. In some cases the combined effect of these developments actually may have changed local climates and made some areas even more susceptible to extremes of heat and cold.

Repelled by the rocks, the hardy New Englanders turned instinctively to their fine natural harbors. Hacking timber from their dense forests, they became experts in shipbuilding and commerce. They also ceaselessly exploited the self-perpetuating codfish lode off the coast of Newfoundland—the fishy "gold mines of New England," which have yielded more wealth than all the treasure chests of the Aztecs. During colonial days the wayfarer seldom got far from the sound of the ax and hammer, or the swift rush of the ship down the ways to the sea, or the smell of rotting fish. As a reminder of the importance of fishing, a handsome replica of the "sacred cod" is proudly displayed to this day in the Massachusetts Statehouse in Boston.

The combination of Calvinism, soil, and climate in New England made for energy, purposefulness, sternness, stubbornness, self-reliance, and resourcefulness. Righteous New Englanders prided themselves on being God's chosen people. They long boasted that Boston was "the hub of the universe"—at least in spirit. A famous jingle of later days ran,

> *I come from the city of Boston*
> *The home of the bean and the cod*
> *Where the Cabots speak only to Lowells*
> *And the Lowells speak only to God.*

New England has had an incalculable impact on the rest of the nation. Ousted by their sterile soil, thousands of New Englanders scattered from Ohio to Oregon and even Hawaii. They sprinkled the land with new communities modeled on the orderly New England town, with its central green and tidy schoolhouse, and its simple town-meeting democracy. "Yankee ingenuity," originally fostered by the flinty fields and comfortless climate of New England, came to be claimed by all Americans as a proud national trait. And the fabled "New England conscience," born of the steadfast Puritan heritage, left a legacy of high idealism in the national character and inspired many later reformers.

✹ The Early Settlers' Days and Ways

The cycles of the seasons and the sun set the schedules of all the earliest American colonists, men as well as women, northerners as well as southerners, blacks as well as whites. The overwhelming majority of colonists were farmers. They planted in the spring, tended their crops in the summer, harvested in the fall, and prepared in the winter to begin the cycle anew. They usually rose at dawn and went to bed at dusk. Chores might be performed after nightfall only if they were "worth the candle," a phrase that has persisted in American speech.

Women, slave or free, on southern plantations or northern farms, wove, cooked, cleaned, and cared for children. Men cleared land; fenced, planted, and cropped it; cut firewood; and butchered livestock as needed. Children helped with all these tasks, while picking up such schooling as they could.

Life was humble but comfortable by contemporary standards. Compared to most seventeenth-century Europeans, Americans lived in affluent abundance. Land was relatively cheap, though somewhat less available in the planter-dominated South than elsewhere. In the northern and middle colonies, an acre of virgin soil cost about what American carpenters could earn in one day as wages, which were roughly three times those of their English counterparts.

"Dukes don't emigrate," the saying goes, for if people enjoy wealth and security, they are not likely to risk exposing their lives in the wilderness. Similarly, the very poorest members of a society may not possess even the modest means needed to pull up stakes and seek a fresh start in life. Accordingly, most white migrants to early colonial America came neither from the aristocracy nor from the dregs of European society—with the partial exception of the impoverished indentured servants.

Crude frontier life did not in any case permit the flagrant display of class distinctions, and seventeenth-century society in all the colonies had a certain simple

Life and Death in Colonial America, by Prudence Punderson Note the artist's initials, "P.P.," on the coffin. This embroidery suggests the stoic resolve of a colonial woman, calmly depicting the inevitable progression of her own life from the cradle to the grave.

sameness to it, especially in the more egalitarian New England and middle colonies. Yet many settlers, who considered themselves to be of the "better sort," tried to recreate on a modified scale the social structure they had known in the Old World. To some extent they succeeded, though yeasty democratic forces frustrated their full triumph. Resentment against upper-class pretensions helped to spark outbursts like Bacon's Rebellion of 1676 in Virginia and the uprising of Maryland's Protestants toward the end of the seventeenth century. In New York animosity between lordly landholders and aspiring merchants fueled **Leisler's Rebellion**, an ill-starred and bloody insurgence that rocked New York City from 1689 to 1691.

For their part, would-be American blue bloods resented the pretensions of the "meaner sort" and passed laws to try to keep them in their place. Massachusetts in 1651 prohibited poorer folk from "wearing gold or silver lace," and in eighteenth-century Virginia a tailor was fined and jailed for arranging to race his horse—"a sport only for gentlemen." But these efforts to reproduce the finely stratified societies of Europe proved feeble in the early American wilderness, where equality and democracy found fertile soil—at least for white people.

Chapter Review

KEY TERMS

indentured servants (61)
headright system (61)
Bacon's Rebellion (62)
Royal African Company (66)
middle passage (66)
slave codes (66)
New York slave revolt (67)
South Carolina slave revolt (Stono River) (67)
Congregational Church (73)
jeremiad (73)
Half-Way Covenant (73)
Salem witch trials (74)
Leisler's Rebellion (76)

PEOPLE TO KNOW

William Berkeley
Nathaniel Bacon
Anthony Johnson

CHRONOLOGY

1619	First Africans arrive in Virginia
1625	Population of English colonies in America about 2,000
1636	Harvard College founded
1662	Half-Way Covenant for Congregational Church membership established
1670	Virginia assembly disfranchises landless freemen
1676	Bacon's Rebellion in Virginia
1680s	Mass expansion of slavery in colonies
1689–1691	Leisler's Rebellion in New York
1692	Salem witch trials in Massachusetts
1693	College of William and Mary founded
1698	Royal African Company slave trade monopoly ended
1700	Population of English colonies in America about 250,000
1712	New York City slave revolt
1739	South Carolina slave revolt

TO LEARN MORE

Virginia DeJohn Anderson, *Creatures of Empire: How Domestic Animals Transformed America* (2004)

William Cronon, *Changes in the Land* (1983)

John Demos, *Entertaining Satan* (1982)

———, *A Little Commonwealth: Family Life in Plymouth Colony* (1970)

David Hackett Fischer, *Albion's Seed: Four British Folkways in America* (1989)

Patrick Griffin, *The People with No Name: Ireland's Ulster Scots, America's Scots Irish, and the Creation of a British Atlantic World, 1689–1764* (2001)

Kenneth Lockridge, *New England Town: Dedham* (1970)

Mary Beth Norton, *In the Devil's Snare: The Salem Witchcraft Crisis of 1692* (2002)

Daniel Blake Smith, *Inside the Great House: Planter Family Life in Eighteenth-Century Chesapeake Society* (1980)

Laurel T. Ulrich, *Good Wives: Image and Reality in the Lives of Women in Northern New England, 1650–1750* (1982)

Daniel Vickers, *Farmers and Fishermen: Two Centuries of Work in Essex County, Massachusetts, 1630–1850* (1994)

A complete, annotated bibliography for this chapter—along with brief descriptions of the People to Know—may be found on the American Pageant website. The Key Terms are defined in a Glossary at the end of the text.

CourseMate

Go to the CourseMate website at **www.cengagebrain.com** for additional study tools and review materials—including audio and video clips—for this chapter.

AP® Review Questions for Chapter 4

1. Early colonists in the Chesapeake struggled with all of the following EXCEPT
   (A) a shorter life expectancy than other regions.
   (B) strange and debilitating new diseases.
   (C) land that was difficult to farm.
   (D) significantly more men than women.
   (E) lack of stable family structure.

2. What were freedom dues?
   (A) Farm implements, clothes, and sometimes land given to former indentured servants
   (B) Fees paid by former criminals to start a new life in the English colonies
   (C) The cost of passage for anyone moving from England to the colonies
   (D) The system that gave fifty acres of land to anyone paying the passage of workers to the Chesapeake
   (E) An agreement to work for seven years in exchange for passage to the colonies

3. Bacon's Rebellion was triggered by
   (A) new and heavy taxes in the backcountry.
   (B) land shortages and Indian policies.
   (C) a severe depression in the seventeenth century.
   (D) government mismanagement.
   (E) a slave uprising led by Nathaniel Bacon.

4. What was the middle passage?
   (A) The middle part of a ship, in which slaves were transported from Africa to the Americas
   (B) Slave ships that were bound for the middle colonies
   (C) The cost of transporting slaves from Africa to the New World
   (D) The transatlantic journey that brought slaves to the Americas
   (E) The organized breeding of slaves in the lower South for sale in the upper South

5. Slave codes had all of the following qualities EXCEPT that
   (A) the codes differentiated slaves from servants along racial lines.
   (B) they made all slaves the property of their white owners for life.
   (C) they made it illegal to teach a slave to read or write.
   (D) there were no provisions allowing for slaves to be freed.
   (E) they were first implemented in the Carolinas.

6. What is Gullah?
   (A) A slave language
   (B) A method of rice cultivation widely used in the Carolinas
   (C) A West African religious dance
   (D) A type of African bongo drum
   (E) A rice-based dish

7. The Stono Rebellion was
   (A) as large and devastating as Bacon's Rebellion.
   (B) an example of slaves' anger at their treatment and permanent servitude.
   (C) a slave revolt that erupted in New York in 1712.
   (D) a labor strike by African American bricklayers, carpenters, and tanners.
   (E) successful at reversing many of the restrictive slave codes.

8. All of the following are true about early slaves EXCEPT that
   (A) early slaves were primarily men.
   (B) slaves initially worked on small, isolated farms.
   (C) some early slaves were able to buy their freedom.
   (D) slave imports continued to outnumber American-born slaves well into the late 1700s.
   (E) slaves on plantations had greater social contact with each other.

9. How did slaves adapt the Christian religion to make it their own?
   (A) They rejected the notion of heaven.
   (B) They conducted services in their native languages.
   (C) They infused their worship with singing and dancing.
   (D) They merged African gods with the Christian God.
   (E) They accepted Christian scriptural interpretations for their servitude.

10. The largest social group of white Virginians were
    (A) plantation owners.
    (B) merchants.
    (C) indentured servants.
    (D) landless whites.
    (E) small farmers.

11. The early Puritans in New England lived
    (A) a few years longer than their counterparts in England.
    (B) almost as long as Americans today.
    (C) barely past the age of fifty.
    (D) not more than two years in the harsh New England climate.
    (E) the same number of years as their counterparts in the Chesapeake.

12. Why did New England leaders block women from retaining separate property and inheriting their husband's estates the way southern women did?
    (A) They feared that the family unity would be undermined.
    (B) They worried that women would hoard land needed for the region's economic development.
    (C) New Englanders were concerned that property ownership would keep women from marrying.
    (D) They believed the courts should handle these matters.
    (E) They felt widows were well protected under their laws.

13. All of the following statements about the witchcraft hysteria and trials in Salem in the 1690s are true EXCEPT that
    (A) they started when a group of teenage girls claimed that older women in town had cast spells on them.
    (B) property-owning women were often the targets.
    (C) those accused of witchcraft were never exonerated.
    (D) the witchcraft hysteria was driven by growing social and religious tension.
    (E) twenty people and two dogs were executed as witches.

14. How did New England settlers' ideas about land differ from those of the Indians they encountered?
    (A) The Indians used the land for farming, while the English wanted it for livestock.
    (B) The English believed in staying in one place until the soil was depleted, then moving on.
    (C) The Indians did not believe land could be privately owned.
    (D) New England colonists built their economy around staple crops.
    (E) The English relied on slave labor to help develop New England colonies.

15. Which of the following geographic features most contributed to New England settlers' seeking new land in the West?
    (A) Cold climate
    (B) Large forests
    (C) Access to waterways
    (D) Sterile soil
    (E) Stony coastlines

16. What was NOT a difference between southern and New England society?
    (A) Southerners depended on African slaves, while the New England climate made slaveowning impractical.
    (B) The expansion of settlements in the Chesapeake region was random, but New England society grew in an orderly fashion.
    (C) Southern life revolved around the plantation; life in New England revolved around the church and community.
    (D) Southerners emphasized farming over all other pursuits, while New Englanders viewed education as essential.
    (E) Southerners' devotion to religion decreased over time, while New Englanders remained devout throughout the colonial period.

Chapter 5

Colonial Society on the Eve of Revolution

1700–1775

Driven from every other corner of the earth, freedom of thought and the right of private judgment in matters of conscience direct their course to this happy country as their last asylum.

SAMUEL ADAMS, 1776

The common term thirteen original colonies is misleading. Britain ruled thirty-two colonies in North America by 1775, including Canada, the Floridas, and various Caribbean islands. But only thirteen of them unfurled the standard of rebellion. A few of the nonrebels, such as Canada and Jamaica, were larger, wealthier, or more populous than some of the revolting thirteen. Why, then, did some British colonies eventually strike for their independence, while others did not? Part of the answer is to be found in the distinctive social, economic, and political structures of the thirteen Atlantic seaboard colonies—and in the halting, gradual appearance of a recognizably *American* way of life.

★ Conquest by the Cradle

Among the distinguishing characteristics that the eventually rebellious settlements shared was lusty population growth. In 1700 they contained fewer than 300,000 souls, about 20,000 of whom were black. By 1775, 2.5 million people inhabited the thirteen colonies, of whom about half a million were black. White immigrants made up nearly 400,000 of the increased number, and black "forced immigrants" accounted for almost as many again. But most of the spurt stemmed from the remarkable natural fertility of all Americans, white and black. To the amazement and dismay of Europeans, the colonists were doubling their numbers every twenty-five years. Unfriendly Dr. Samuel Johnson, back in England, growled that the Americans were

multiplying like their own rattlesnakes. They were also a youthful people, whose average age in 1775 was about sixteen.

This population boom had political consequences. In 1700 there were twenty English subjects for each American colonist. By 1775 the English advantage in numbers had fallen to three to one—setting the stage for a momentous shift in the balance of power between the colonies and Britain.

The bulk of the population was cooped up east of the Alleghenies, although by 1775 a vanguard of pioneers had trickled into the stump-studded clearings of Tennessee and Kentucky. The most populous colonies in 1775 were Virginia, Massachusetts, Pennsylvania, North Carolina, and Maryland—in that order. Only four communities could properly be called cities: Philadelphia, including suburbs, was first with about 34,000 residents, trailed by New York, Boston, and Charleston. About 90 percent of the people lived in rural areas.

★ A Mingling of the Races

Colonial America was a melting pot and had been from the outset. The population, although basically English in stock and language, was picturesquely mottled with numerous foreign groups (see Map 5.1).

Heavy-accented Germans constituted about 6 percent of the total population, or 150,000, by 1775. Fleeing religious persecution, economic oppression, and the ravages of war, they had flocked to America in the early 1700s and had settled chiefly in Pennsylvania. They belonged to several different Protestant sects—primarily Lutheran—and thus further enhanced the religious diversity of the colony. Known popularly but erroneously as the Pennsylvania Dutch (a corruption of the German word *Deutsch*, for "German"), they totaled about one-third of the colony's population. In parts of Philadelphia, the street signs were painted in both German and English.

These German newcomers moved into the backcountry of Pennsylvania, where their splendid stone barns gave—and still give—mute evidence of industry and prosperity. Not having been brought up English, they had no deep-rooted loyalty to the British crown, and they clung tenaciously to their German language and customs.

The Scots-Irish, who in 1775 numbered around 175,000, or 7 percent of the population, were an important non-English group, although they spoke English. They were not Irish at all, but turbulent Scots Lowlanders. Over many decades, they had been transplanted to northern Ireland, where they had not prospered. The Irish Catholics already there, hating Scottish Presbyterianism, resented the intruders and still do—the source of many of the modern-day "troubles" in the Northern Ireland province of Ulster. The economic life of the Scots-Irish was severely hampered, especially when the English government placed burdensome restrictions on their production of linens and woolens.

Early in the 1700s, tens of thousands of embittered Scots-Irish finally abandoned Ireland and came to America, chiefly to tolerant and deep-soiled Pennsylvania. Finding the best acres already taken by Germans and Quakers, they pushed out onto the frontier, making them among the first settlers of the American West. There many of them illegally but defiantly squatted on unoccupied lands and quarreled with both Indian and white owners. When the westward-flowing Scots-Irish tide lapped up against the Allegheny barrier, it was deflected southward into the backcountry of Maryland, down Virginia's Shenandoah Valley, and into the western Carolinas. Their often rickety settlements bore the marks of Scots-Irish restlessness. Whereas their German neighbors typically erected sturdy homes and cleared their fields meticulously, the Scots-Irish satisfied themselves with floorless, flimsy log cabins. As befitted an uprooted, questing people, they chopped down trees, planted crops between the stumps, exhausted the soil swiftly, and moved on.

Already experienced colonizers and agitators in Ireland, the Scots-Irish proved to be superb frontiersmen, though their readiness to visit violence on the Indians repeatedly inflamed the western districts. By the mid-eighteenth century, a chain of Scots-Irish settlements lay scattered along the "great wagon road," which

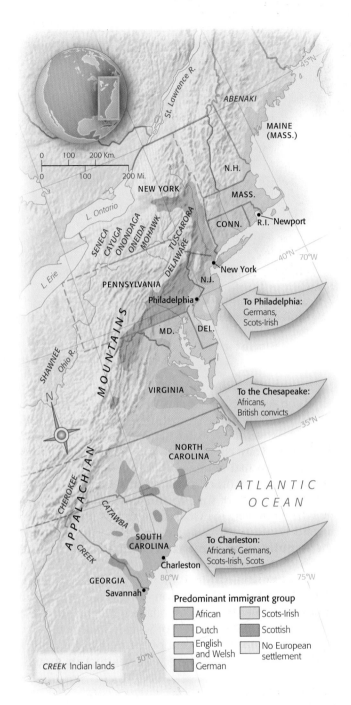

MAP 5.1 Immigrant Groups in 1775 America was already a nation of diverse nationalities in the colonial period. This map shows the great variety of immigrant groups, especially in Pennsylvania and New York. It also illustrates the tendency of later arrivals, particularly the Scots-Irish, to push into the backcountry. © Cengage Learning

hugged the eastern Appalachian foothills from Pennsylvania to Georgia.

It was said, somewhat unfairly, that the Scots-Irish kept the Sabbath—and all else they could lay their

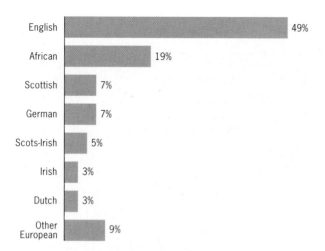

FIGURE 5.1 Ethnic and Racial Composition of the American People, 1790 Based on surnames. (Source: Adapted from the American Council of Learned Societies, "Report of Committee on Linguistic and National Stocks in the Population of the United States," 1932. Percentages total more than 100 percent due to rounding.)

hands on. Pugnacious, lawless, and individualistic, they brought with them the Scottish secrets of whiskey distilling and dotted the Appalachian hills and hollows with their stills. They cherished no love for the British government that had uprooted them and still lorded over them—or for any other government, it seemed. They led the armed march of the **Paxton Boys** on Philadelphia in 1764, protesting the Quaker oligarchy's lenient policy toward the Indians, and a few years later spearheaded the **Regulator movement** in North Carolina, a small but nasty insurrection against eastern domination of the colony's affairs. Many of these hotheads—including the young Andrew Jackson—eventually joined the embattled American revolutionaries. All told, about a dozen future presidents were of Scots-Irish descent.

Approximately 5 percent of the multicolored colonial population consisted of other European groups.

The young Frenchman Michel-Guillaume Jean de Crèvecoeur (1735–1813) wrote of the diverse population in about 1770,

❝ They are a mixture of English, Scotch, Irish, French, Dutch, Germans, and Swedes. From this promiscuous breed, that race now called Americans have arisen. . . . I could point out to you a family whose grandfather was an Englishman, whose wife was Dutch, whose son married a French woman, and whose present four sons have now four wives of different nations.**❞**

These embraced French Huguenots, Welsh, Dutch, Swedes, Jews, Irish, Swiss, and Scots Highlanders—as distinguished from the Scots-Irish. Except for the Scots Highlanders, such hodgepodge elements felt little loyalty to the British crown. By far the largest single non-English group was African, accounting for nearly 20 percent of the colonial population in 1775 and heavily concentrated in the South.

The population of the thirteen colonies, though mainly Anglo-Saxon, was perhaps the most mixed to be found anywhere in the world (see Figure 5.1). The South, holding about 90 percent of the slaves, already displayed its historic black-and-white racial composition. New England, mostly staked out by the original Puritan migrants, showed the least ethnic diversity. The middle colonies, especially Pennsylvania, received the bulk of later white immigrants and boasted an astonishing variety of peoples. Outside of New England, about one-half the population was non-English in 1775. Of the fifty-six signers of the Declaration of Independence in 1776, eighteen were non-English and eight had not been born in the colonies.

As these various immigrant groups mingled and intermarried, they laid the foundations for a new multicultural American national identity unlike anything known in Europe. The French settler Michel-Guillaume Jean de Crèvecoeur saw in America in the 1770s a "strange mixture of blood, which you will find in no other country," and he posed his classic question, "What then is the American, this new man?" Nor were white colonists alone in creating new societies out of diverse ethnic groups. The African slave trade long had mixed peoples from many different tribal backgrounds, giving birth to an African *American* community far more variegated in its cultural origins than anything to be found in Africa itself. Similarly, in the New England "praying towns," where Indians were gathered to be Christianized, and in Great Lakes villages such as Detroit, home to dozens of different displaced indigenous peoples, polyglot Native American communities emerged, blurring the boundaries of individual tribal identities.

✸ The Structure of Colonial Society

In comparison to contemporary Europe, eighteenth-century America seemed like a shining land of equality and opportunity—with the notorious exception of slavery. No titled nobility dominated society from on high, and no pauperized underclass threatened it from below. Most white Americans, and even a handful of free blacks, were small farmers. Clad in buckskin breeches, they owned modest holdings and tilled them with their own hands and horses. The cities contained a small class of skilled artisans, with their well-greased leather aprons, as well as shopkeepers, tradespeople, and some unskilled day laborers. The most remarkable feature of the social ladder was its openness. An ambitious colonist, even a former indentured servant, could rise from a lower rung to a higher one, a rare step in old England.

Yet in contrast with seventeenth-century America, colonial society on the eve of the Revolution was beginning to show signs of stratification and barriers to mobility that raised worries about the "Europeanization" of America. The gods of war contributed to these developments. The armed conflicts of the 1690s and early 1700s had enriched a number of merchant princes in the New England and middle colonies. They laid the foundations of their fortunes with profits made as military suppliers. Roosting regally atop the social ladder, these elites now feathered their nests more finely. They sported imported clothing and dined at tables laid with English china and gleaming silverware. Prominent individuals came to be seated in churches and schools according to their social rank. By mid-century the richest 10 percent of Bostonians and Philadelphians owned nearly two-thirds of the taxable wealth in their cities.

The plague of war also created a class of widows and orphans, who became dependent for their survival on charity. Both Philadelphia and New York built almshouses in the 1730s to care for the destitute. Yet the numbers of poor people remained tiny compared to the numbers in England, where about a third of the population lived in impoverished squalor.

In the New England countryside, the descendants of the original settlers faced more limited prospects than had their pioneering forebears. As the supply of unclaimed soil dwindled and families grew, existing landholdings were repeatedly subdivided. The average size of farms shrank drastically. Younger sons, as well as daughters, were forced to hire out as wage laborers, or eventually to seek virgin tracts of land beyond the Alleghenies. By 1750 Boston contained a large number of homeless poor, who were supported by public charity and compelled to wear a large red "P" on their clothing.

In the South the power of the great planters continued to be bolstered by their disproportionate ownership of slaves. The riches created by the growing slave population in the eighteenth century were not distributed evenly among the whites. Wealth was concentrated in the hands of the largest slaveowners, widening the gap between the prosperous gentry and the "poor whites," who were more and more likely to become tenant farmers.

In all the colonies, the ranks of the lower classes were further swelled by the continuing stream of indentured servants, many of whom ultimately achieved

A South Carolina Advertisement for Slaves in the 1760s Note the reference to these slaves' origin on West Africa's "Rice Coast," a reminder of South Carolina's reliance on African skill and labor for rice cultivation. Note, too, that half the slaves were said to have survived smallpox and thus acquired immunity from further infection—and that care had been taken to insulate the others from a smallpox epidemic apparently then raging in Charleston.

prosperity and prestige. Two became signers of the Declaration of Independence.

Far less fortunate than the voluntary indentured servants were the paupers and convicts involuntarily shipped to America. Altogether, about fifty thousand "jayle birds" were dumped on the colonies by the London authorities. This riffraff crowd—including robbers, rapists, and murderers—was generally sullen and undesirable, and not bubbling over with goodwill for the king's government. But many convicts were the unfortunate victims of circumstances and of a viciously unfair English penal code that included about two hundred capital crimes. Some of the deportees, in fact, came to be highly respectable citizens.

Least fortunate of all, of course, were the black slaves. They enjoyed no equality with whites and dared not even dream of ascending, or even approaching, the ladder of opportunity. Oppressed and downtrodden, the slaves were America's closest approximation to Europe's volatile lower classes, and fears of black rebellion plagued the white colonists. Some colonial legislatures, notably South Carolina's in 1760, sensed the dangers present in a heavy concentration of resentful slaves and attempted to restrict or halt their importation. But the British authorities, seeking to preserve the supply of cheap labor for the colonies, especially the West Indies sugar plantations, repeatedly vetoed all efforts to stem the transatlantic traffic in slaves. Many North American colonists condemned these vetoes as morally callous, although New England slave traders benefited handsomely from the British policy. The cruel complexity of the slavery issue was further revealed when Thomas Jefferson, himself a slaveholder, assailed the British vetoes in an early draft of the Declaration of Independence, but was forced to withdraw the proposed clause by a torrent of protest from southern slavemasters.

✸ Clerics, Physicians, and Jurists

Most honored of the professions was the Christian ministry. In 1775 the clergy wielded less influence than in the early days of Massachusetts, when piety had burned more warmly. But they still occupied a position of high prestige.

Most physicians, on the other hand, were poorly trained and not highly esteemed. Not until 1765 was the first medical school established, although European centers attracted some students. Aspiring young doctors served for a while as apprentices to older practitioners and were then turned loose on their "victims." Bleeding was a favorite and frequently fatal remedy; when the physician was not available, a barber was often summoned.

Epidemics were a constant nightmare. Especially dreaded was smallpox, which afflicted one out of five persons, including the heavily pockmarked George Washington. A crude form of inoculation was

introduced in 1721, despite the objections of many physicians and some of the clergy, who opposed tampering with the will of God. Powdered dried toad was a favorite prescription for smallpox. Diphtheria was also a deadly killer, especially of young people. One epidemic in the 1730s took the lives of thousands. This grim reminder of their mortality may have helped to prepare many colonists in their hearts and minds for the religious revival that was soon to sweep them up.

At first the law profession was not favorably regarded. In this pioneering society, which required much honest manual labor, the parties to a dispute often presented their own cases in court. Lawyers were commonly regarded as noisy windbags or troublemaking rogues; an early Connecticut law classed them with drunkards and brothel keepers. When future president John Adams was a young law student, the father of his wife-to-be frowned upon him as a suitor because of his chosen profession.

✸ Workaday America

Agriculture was the leading industry, involving about 90 percent of the people. Tobacco continued to be the staple crop in Maryland and Virginia, though wheat cultivation also spread through the Chesapeake, often on lands depleted by the overgrowth of tobacco. The fertile middle ("bread") colonies produced large quantities of grain, and by 1759 New York alone was exporting eighty thousand barrels of flour a year. Seemingly the farmer had only to tickle the soil with a hoe, and it would laugh with a harvest. Overall, Americans probably enjoyed a higher standard of living than the masses of any country in history up to that time.

Fishing (including whaling), though ranking far below agriculture, was rewarding. Pursued in all the American colonies, this harvesting of the sea was a major industry in New England, which exported smelly shiploads of dried cod to the Catholic countries of Europe. The fishing fleet also stimulated shipbuilding and served as a nursery for the seamen who manned the navy and merchant marine. A bustling commerce, both coastwise and overseas, enriched all the colonies, especially the New England group, New York, and Pennsylvania (see Map 5.2). Commercial ventures and land speculation, in the absence of later get-rich-quick schemes, were the surest avenues to speedy wealth. Yankee seamen were famous in many climes not only as skilled mariners but as tightfisted traders. They provisioned the Caribbean sugar islands with food and forest products. They also hauled Spanish and Portuguese gold, wine, and oranges to London, to be exchanged for industrial goods, which were then sold for a juicy profit in America.

Cotton Mather (1663–1728), Puritan clergyman and avid scientist, became frustrated with Boston residents' opposition to inoculation during the Boston smallpox epidemic of 1721. He wrote to a doctor friend,

"Never till now was that rule contested, of two evils, choose the least. . . . I would ask them whether it be not a most criminal ingratitude unto the God of Health, when He has acquainted us with a most invaluable method of the saving of our lives from so great a death, to treat with neglect and contempt, and multiply abuses on them who thankfully and in a spirit of obedience to Him, embrace His blessings? **"**

Codfishing in Newfoundland, 1738 Early European explorers were awed by the enormous schools of cod on the Grand Banks off Newfoundland. Fish were so numerous that they sometimes impeded the progress of sailing vessels. By the eighteenth century, New Englanders were aggressively exploiting the apparently limitless Grand Banks fishery, drying and salting huge catches for export to Europe and the West Indies. More than two centuries later the accumulated predation of generations of overfishing has depleted the once-fabulous Grand Banks cod population.

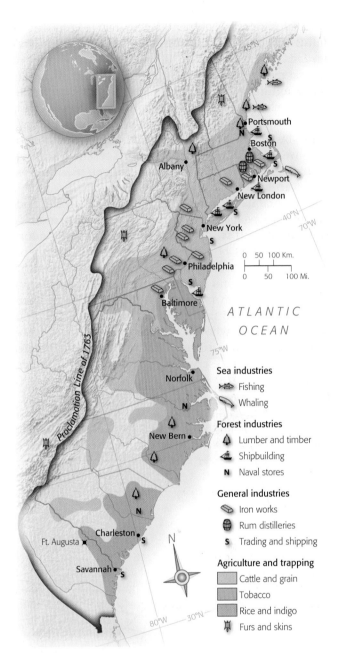

MAP 5.2 The Colonial Economy By the eighteenth century, the various colonial regions had distinct economic identities. The northern colonies grew grain and raised cattle, harvested timber and fish, and built ships. The Chesapeake colonies and North Carolina were still heavily dependent on tobacco, whereas the southernmost colonies grew mostly rice and indigo. Cotton, so important to the southern economy in the nineteenth century, had not yet emerged as a major crop. © Cengage Learning

The so-called **triangular trade** was infamously profitable, though small in relation to total colonial commerce (see Map 5.3). A skipper, for example, would leave a New England port with a cargo of rum and sail to the Gold Coast of Africa. Bartering the fiery liquor with African chiefs for captured African slaves, he would proceed to the West Indies with his sobbing and suffocating cargo sardined below deck. There he would exchange the survivors for molasses, which he would then carry to New England, where it would be distilled into rum. He would then repeat the trip, making a handsome profit on each leg of the triangle.

Manufacturing in the colonies was of only secondary importance, although there was a surprising variety of small enterprises. As a rule, workers could get ahead faster in soil-rich America by tilling the land. Huge quantities of "kill devil" rum were distilled in Rhode Island and Massachusetts, and even some of the "elect of the Lord" developed an overfondness for it. Handsome beaver hats were manufactured in quantity, despite British restrictions. Smoking iron forges, including Pennsylvania's Valley Forge, likewise dotted the land and in fact were more numerous in 1775, though generally smaller, than those of England. In addition, household manufacturing, including spinning and weaving by women, added up to an impressive output. As in all pioneering countries, strong-backed laborers and skilled craftspeople were scarce and highly prized.

In early Virginia a carpenter who had committed a murder was freed because his woodworking skills were needed.

Lumbering was perhaps the most important single manufacturing activity. Countless cartloads of fresh-felled timber were consumed by shipbuilders, at first chiefly in New England and then elsewhere in the colonies. By 1770 about four hundred vessels of assorted sizes were splashing down the ways each year, and about one-third of the British merchant marine was American-built.

Colonial naval stores—such as tar, pitch, rosin, and turpentine—were highly valued, for Britain was anxious to gain and retain a mastery of the seas. London offered generous bounties to stimulate production of these items; otherwise Britain would have had to turn to the uncertain and possibly hostile Baltic areas. Towering trees, ideal as masts for His Majesty's navy, were marked with the king's broad arrow for future use. The luckless colonist who was caught cutting down this reserved timber was subject to a fine. Even though there were countless unreserved trees and the blazed ones

were being saved for the common defense, this shackle on free enterprise engendered considerable bitterness.

Americans held an important flank of a thriving, many-sided Atlantic economy by the dawn of the eighteenth century. Yet strains appeared in this complex network as early as the 1730s. Fast-breeding Americans demanded more and more British products—yet the slow-growing British population early reached the saturation point for absorbing imports from America. This trade imbalance raised a question: how could the colonists sell the goods to make the money to buy what they wanted in Britain? The answer was obvious: by seeking foreign (non-British) markets.

By the eve of the Revolution, the bulk of Chesapeake tobacco was filling pipes in France and in other European countries, though it passed through the hands of British re-exporters, who took a slice of the profits for themselves. More important was the trade with the West Indies, especially the French islands. West Indian purchases of North American timber and foodstuffs provided the crucial cash for the colonists to continue to make their own purchases in Britain. But

MAP 5.3 Colonial Trade Patterns, ca. 1770 Future president John Adams noted about this time that "the commerce of the West Indies is a part of the American system of commerce. They can neither do without us, nor we without them. The Creator has placed us upon the globe in such a situation that we have occasion for each other." © Cengage Learning

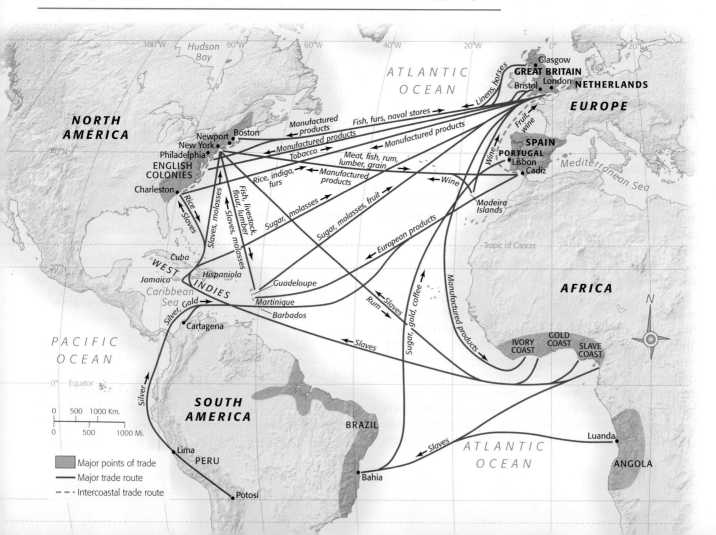

in 1733, bowing to pressure from influential *British* West Indian planters, Parliament passed the **Molasses Act**, aimed at squelching North American trade with the *French* West Indies. If successful, this scheme would have struck a crippling blow to American international trade and to the colonists' standard of living. American merchants responded to the act by bribing and smuggling their way around the law. Thus was foreshadowed the impending imperial crisis, when headstrong Americans would revolt rather than submit to the dictates of the far-off Parliament, apparently bent on destroying their very livelihood.

✦ Horsepower and Sailpower

All sprawling and sparsely populated pioneer communities are cursed with oppressive problems of transportation. America, with a scarcity of both money and workers, was no exception.

Not until the 1700s did roads connect even the major cities, and these dirt thoroughfares were treacherously deficient. A wayfarer could have rumbled along more rapidly over the Roman highways in the days of Julius Caesar, nearly two thousand years earlier. It took young Benjamin Franklin nine long, rain-drenched days in 1720 to journey from Boston to Philadelphia, traveling by sailing sloop, rowboat, and foot. News of the Declaration of Independence in 1776 reached Charleston from Philadelphia twenty-nine days after the Fourth of July.

Roads were often clouds of dust in the summer and quagmires of mud in the winter. Stagecoach travelers braved such additional dangers as tree-strewn roads, rickety bridges, carriage overturns, and runaway horses. A traveler venturesome enough to journey from Philadelphia to New York, for example, would not think it amiss to make a will and pray with the family before departing.

Where man-made roads were wretched, heavy reliance was placed on God-grooved waterways. Population tended to cluster along the banks of navigable rivers. There was also much coastwise traffic, and although it was slow and undependable, it was relatively cheap and pleasant, at least in fair weather.

Taverns sprang up along the main routes of travel, as well as in the cities. Their attractions customarily included such amusements as bowling alleys, pool tables, bars, and gambling equipment. Before a cheerful, roaring log fire, all social classes would mingle, including the village loafers and drunks. The tavern was yet another cradle of democracy.

Gossips also gathered at the taverns, which were clearinghouses of information, misinformation, and rumor—frequently stimulated by alcoholic refreshment

Sign of the Pine Tree Inn, 1768 Inns like Joseph Read III's in Lisbon, Connecticut, not only provided food, drink, shelter, and entertainment for colonial Americans but also were raucous arenas for debating political issues. This sign, with its circular yellow orb (sun) over a pine tree, may have been intended as a veiled reference to the Sons of Liberty, an extralegal resistance organization that had adopted as its symbol the Liberty Tree. The date of 1768 coincided with the British enactment of the Townshend Acts, which ignited a new wave of colonial resistance to British rule.

and impassioned political talk. A successful politician, like the wire-pulling Samuel Adams, was often a man who had a large alehouse fraternity in places like Boston's Green Dragon Tavern. Taverns were important in crystallizing public opinion and proved to be hotbeds of agitation as the revolutionary movement gathered momentum.

TABLE 5.1 Established (Tax-Supported) Churches in the Colonies, 1775*

Colonies	Churches	Year Disestablished
Massachusetts (incl. Maine)	Congregational	1833
Connecticut		1818
New Hampshire		1819
New York	Anglican (in New York City and three neighboring counties)	1777
Maryland	Anglican	1777
Virginia		1786
North Carolina		1776
South Carolina		1778
Georgia		1777
Rhode Island	None	
New Jersey		
Delaware		
Pennsylvania		

*Note the persistence of the Congregational establishment in New England.

TABLE 5.2 Estimated Religious Census, 1775

Name	Number	Chief Locale
Congregationalists	575,000	New England
Anglicans	500,000	N.Y., South
Presbyterians	410,000	Frontier
German churches (incl. Lutheran)	200,000	Pa.
Dutch Reformed	75,000	N.Y., N.J.
Quakers	40,000	Pa., N.J., Del.
Baptists	25,000	R.I., Pa., N.J., Del.
Roman Catholics	25,000	Md., Pa.
Methodists	5,000	Scattered
Jews	2,000	N.Y., R.I.
EST. TOTAL MEMBERSHIP	1,857,000	
EST. TOTAL POPULATION	2,493,000	
PERCENTAGE CHURCH MEMBERS	74%	

An intercolonial postal system was established by the mid-1700s, although private couriers remained. Some mail was handled on credit. Service was slow and infrequent, and secrecy was problematic. Mail carriers, serving long routes, would sometimes pass the time by reading the letters entrusted to their care.

✴ Dominant Denominations

Two "established," or tax-supported, churches were conspicuous in 1775 (see Table 5.1): the Anglican and the Congregational. A considerable segment of the population, surprisingly enough, did not worship in any church. And in those colonies that maintained an "established" religion, only a minority of the people belonged to it (see Table 5.2).

The Church of England, whose members were commonly called Anglicans, became the official faith in Georgia, North and South Carolina, Virginia, Maryland, and a part of New York. Established also in England, it served in America as a major prop of kingly authority. British officials naturally made vigorous attempts to impose it on additional colonies, but they ran into a stone wall of opposition.

In America the Anglican Church fell distressingly short of its promise. Secure and self-satisfied, like its parent in England, it clung to a faith that was less fierce and more worldly than the religion of Puritanical New England. Sermons were shorter; hell was less scorching; and amusements, like Virginia fox hunting, were less scorned. So dismal was the reputation of the Anglican clergy in seventeenth-century Virginia that the College of William and Mary was founded in 1693 to train a better class of clerics.

The influential Congregational Church, which had grown out of the Puritan Church, was formally established in all the New England colonies, except independent-minded Rhode Island. At first Massachusetts taxed all residents to support Congregationalism but later relented and exempted members of other well-known denominations. Presbyterianism, though closely associated with Congregationalism, was never made official in any colonies.

Ministers of the gospel, turning from the Bible to this sinful world, increasingly grappled with burning political issues. As the early rumblings of revolution against the British crown could be heard, sedition flowed freely from pulpits. Presbyterianism, Congregationalism, and rebellion became a neo-trinity. Many leading Anglican clergymen, aware of which side their tax-provided bread was buttered on, naturally supported their king.

Anglicans in the New World were seriously handicapped by not having a resident bishop, whose presence would be convenient for the ordination of young ministers. American students of Anglican theology had to travel to England to be ordained. On the eve of the

Benjamin Franklin's (1706–1790) Poor Richard's Almanack contained such thoughts on religion as these:

"A good example is the best sermon."

"Many have quarreled about religion that never practiced it."

"Serving God is doing good to man, but praying is thought an easier service, and therefore more generally chosen."

"How many observe Christ's birthday; how few his precepts! O! 'tis easier to keep holidays than commandments.**"**

Revolution, there was serious talk of creating an American bishopric, but the scheme was violently opposed by many non-Anglicans, who feared a tightening of the royal reins. This controversy poured holy oil on the smoldering fires of rebellion.

Religious toleration had indeed made enormous strides in America, at least when compared with its halting steps abroad. Roman Catholics were still generally discriminated against, as in England, even in officeholding. But there were fewer Catholics in America, and hence the anti-papist laws were less severe and less strictly enforced. In general, people could worship—or not worship—as they pleased.

✷ The Great Awakening

In all the colonial churches, religion was less fervid in the early eighteenth century than it had been a century earlier, when the colonies were first planted. The Puritan churches in particular sagged under the weight of two burdens: their elaborate theological doctrines and their compromising efforts to liberalize membership requirements. Churchgoers increasingly complained about the "dead dogs" who droned out tedious, over-erudite sermons from Puritan pulpits. Some ministers, on the other hand, worried that many of their parishioners had gone soft and that their souls were no longer kindled by the hellfire of orthodox Calvinism. Liberal ideas began to challenge the old-time religion. Some worshipers now proclaimed that human beings were not necessarily predestined to damnation and might save themselves by leading a life of good works. Most threatening to the Calvinist doctrine of predestination was **Arminianism**, named after the Dutch theologian Jacobus Arminius, who preached that individual free will, not divine decree, determined a person's eternal

fate, and that *all* humans, not just the "elect," could be saved if they freely accepted God's grace. Pressured by these "heresies," a few churches grudgingly conceded that spiritual conversion was not necessary for church membership. Together, these twin trends toward clerical intellectualism and lay liberalism were sapping the spiritual vitality from many denominations.

The stage was thus set for a rousing religious revival. Known as the **Great Awakening**, it exploded in the 1730s and 1740s and swept through the colonies like a fire through prairie grass. The Awakening was first ignited in Northampton, Massachusetts, by a tall, delicate, and intellectual pastor, Jonathan Edwards. Perhaps the deepest theological mind ever nurtured in America, Edwards proclaimed with burning righteousness the folly of believing in salvation through good works and affirmed the need for complete dependence on God's grace. Warming to his subject, he painted in lurid detail the landscape of hell and the eternal torments of the damned. "Sinners in the Hands of an Angry God" was the title of one of his most famous sermons. He believed that hell was "paved with the skulls of unbaptized children."

Edwards's preaching style was learned and closely reasoned, but his stark doctrines sparked a warmly sympathetic reaction among his parishioners in 1734. Four years later the itinerant English parson George Whitefield loosed a different style of evangelical preaching on America and touched off a conflagration of religious ardor that revolutionized the spiritual life of the colonies. A former alehouse attendant, Whitefield was an orator of rare gifts. His magnificent voice boomed sonorously over thousands of enthralled listeners in an open field. One of England's greatest actors of the day commented enviously that Whitefield could make audiences weep merely by pronouncing the word *Mesopotamia* and that he would "give a hundred guineas if I could only say 'O!' like Mr. Whitefield."

Triumphally touring the colonies, Whitefield trumpeted his message of human helplessness and divine omnipotence. His eloquence reduced Jonathan Edwards to tears and even caused the skeptical and thrifty Benjamin Franklin to empty his pockets

Jonathan Edwards (1703–1758) preached hellfire, notably in one famous sermon:

" The God that holds you over the pit of hell, much as one holds a spider or some loathsome insect over the fire, abhors you, and is dreadfully provoked. His wrath toward you burns like fire; he looks upon you as worthy of nothing else but to be cast into the fire.**"**

into the collection plate. During these roaring revival meetings, countless sinners professed conversion, and hundreds of the "saved" groaned, shrieked, or rolled in the snow from religious excitement. White-field soon inspired American imitators. Taking up his electrifying new style of preaching, they heaped abuse on sinners and shook enormous audiences with emotional appeals. One preacher cackled hideously in the face of hapless wrongdoers. Another, naked to the waist, leapt frantically about in the light of flickering torches.

Orthodox clergymen, known as **old lights**, were deeply skeptical of the emotionalism and the theatri-cal antics of the revivalists. **New lights**, on the other hand, defended the Awakening for its role in revi-talizing American religion. Congregationalists and Presbyterians split over this issue, and many of the believers in religious conversion went over to the Bap-tists and other sects more prepared to make room for emotion in religion. The Awakening left many last-ing effects. Its emphasis on direct, emotive spirituality seriously undermined the older clergy, whose author-ity had derived from their education and erudition. The schisms it set off in many denominations greatly increased the number and the competitiveness of American churches. It encouraged a fresh wave of mis-sionary work among the Indians and even among black slaves, many of whom also attended the mass open-air revivals. It led to the founding of "new light" centers of higher learning such as Princeton, Brown, Rutgers, and Dartmouth. Perhaps most significant, the Great Awakening was the first spontaneous mass movement of the American people. It tended to break down sec-tional boundaries as well as denominational lines and contributed to the growing sense that Americans had of themselves as a single people, united by a common history and shared experiences.

✸ Schools and Colleges

A time-honored English idea regarded education as a blessing reserved for the aristocratic few, not for the unwashed many. Education should be for leadership, not citizenship, and primarily for males. Only slowly and painfully did the colonists break the chains of these ancient restrictions.

Puritan New England, largely for religious rea-sons, was more zealously interested in education than any other section. Dominated by the Congregational Church, it stressed the need for Bible reading by the individual worshiper. The primary goal of the clergy was to make good Christians rather than good citi-zens. A more secular approach was evident late in the

George Whitefield Preaching
Americans of both genders and all races and regions were spellbound by Whitefield's emotive oratory.

Private Collection/Bridgeman Art Library Ltd.

The College of New Jersey at Princeton, 1764 Later known as Princeton University, it was chartered in 1746 by the Presbyterian Synod, though open to students of all religious persuasions. The fourth college to be founded in British North America, it met in Elizabeth and Newark, New Jersey, until a gift of ten acres of land precipitated a move to Princeton in 1756. All classes were held in the large building, Nassau Hall. Here the Continental Congress met for three months during the summer of 1783, making Princeton for a short time the capital of the nation. This copper engraving, based on a drawing by one of Princeton's earliest students, was part of a series of college views that reflected colonial Americans' growing pride in institutions of higher learning.

eighteenth century, when some children were warned in the following verse:

> *He who ne'er learns his A.B.C.*
> *Forever will a blockhead be.*
> *But he who learns his letters fair*
> *Shall have a coach to take the air.*

Education, principally for boys, flourished almost from the outset in New England. This densely populated region boasted an impressive number of graduates from the English universities, especially Cambridge, the intellectual center of England's Puritanism. New Englanders, at a relatively early date, established primary and secondary schools, which varied widely in the quality of instruction and in the length of time that their doors remained open each year. Back-straining farm labor drained much of a youth's time and energy.

Fairly adequate elementary schools were also hammering knowledge into the heads of reluctant "scholars" in the middle colonies and in the South. Some of these institutions were tax-supported; others were privately operated. The South, with its white and black population diffused over wide areas, was severely handicapped by geography in attempting to establish an effective school system. Wealthy families leaned heavily on private tutors.

The general atmosphere in the colonial schools and colleges continued grim and gloomy. Most of the emphasis was placed on religion and on the classical languages, Latin and Greek. The focus was not on experiment and reason, but on doctrine and dogma.

The age was one of orthodoxy, and independence of thinking was discouraged. Discipline was quite severe, with many a mischievous child being sadistically "birched" with a switch cut from a birch tree. Sometimes punishment was inflicted by indentured-servant teachers, who could themselves be whipped for their failures as workers and who therefore were not inclined to spare the rod.

College education—at least at first in New England—was geared toward preparing men for the ministry. After all, churches would wither if a new crop of ministers was not adequately trained to lead the region's spiritual flocks. Annoyed by this exclusively religious emphasis, many well-to-do families, especially in the South, sent their boys abroad to acquire

John Adams (ca. 1736–1826), the future second president, wrote to his wife,

❝ The education of our children is never out of my mind. . . . I must study politics and war that my sons may have the liberty to study mathematics and philosophy. My sons ought to study mathematics and philosophy, geography, natural history, naval architecture, navigation, commerce, and agriculture, in order to give their children a right to study painting, poetry, music, architecture, statuary, tapestry, and porcelain.**❞**

TABLE 5.3 Colonial Colleges

Name	Original Name (if Different)	Location	Opened or Founded	Denomination
1. Harvard		Cambridge, Mass.	1636	Congregational
2. William and Mary		Williamsburg, Va.	1693	Anglican
3. Yale		New Haven, Conn.	1701	Congregational
4. Princeton	College of New Jersey	Princeton, N.J.	1746	Presbyterian
5. Pennsylvania	The Academy	Philadelphia, Pa.	1751	Nonsectarian
6. Columbia	King's College	New York, N.Y.	1754	Anglican
7. Brown	Rhode Island College	Providence, R.I.	1764	Baptist
8. Rutgers	Queen's College	New Brunswick, N.J.	1766	Dutch Reformed
9. Dartmouth (begun as an Indian missionary school)		Hanover, N.H.	1769	Congregational

a "real"—meaning a refined and philosophical—education in elite English institutions.

For purposes of convenience and economy, nine local colleges were established during the colonial era (see Table 5.3). Student enrollments were small, numbering about two hundred boys at the most; and at one time a few lads as young as eleven were admitted to Harvard. Instruction was poor by present-day standards. The curriculum was still heavily loaded with theology and the "dead" languages, although by 1750 there was a distinct trend toward "live" languages and other modern subjects. A significant contribution was made by Benjamin Franklin. He had never attended college but played a major role in launching what became the University of Pennsylvania, the first American college free from denominational control.

✴ A Provincial Culture

When it came to art and culture, colonial Americans were still in thrall to European tastes, especially British. The simplicity of pioneering life had not yet bred many homespun patrons of the arts. One aspiring painter, John Trumbull (1756–1843) of Connecticut, was discouraged in his youth by his father's chilling remark, "Connecticut is not Athens." Like so many of his talented artistic contemporaries, Trumbull was forced to travel to London to pursue his ambitions. Charles Willson Peale (1741–1827), best known for his portraits of George Washington, ran a museum, stuffed birds, and practiced dentistry. Gifted Benjamin West (1738–1820) and precocious John Singleton Copley (1738–1815) succeeded in their ambitions to become famous painters, but like Trumbull they had to go to England to complete their training. Only abroad could

they find subjects who had the leisure to sit for their portraits and the money to pay handsomely for them. Copley was regarded as a Loyalist during the Revolutionary War, and West, a close friend of George III and official court painter, was buried in London's St. Paul's Cathedral.

Architecture was largely imported from the Old World and modified to meet the peculiar climatic and religious conditions of the New World. Even the lowly log cabin was apparently borrowed from Sweden. The red-bricked Georgian style, so common in the pre-Revolutionary decades, was introduced around 1720 and is best exemplified by the beauty of now-restored Williamsburg, Virginia.

Colonial Craftsmanship In the "Pennsylvania Dutch" country, parents gave daughters painted wooden chests to hold their precious dowry linens at marriage. The horsemen, unicorns, and flower patterns on this dower chest confirm its origins in Berks County, Pennsylvania. Granger Collection

"The Magnetic Dispensary," ca. 1790 This British painting made sport of the era's faddish preoccupations with electricity. Following Franklin's experiments, static electricity, generated here by the machine on the right, was employed for "medicinal" purposes as well as for tingling entertainments.

Colonial literature, like art, was generally undistinguished, and for many of the same reasons. One noteworthy exception was the precocious poet Phillis Wheatley (ca. 1753–1784), an enslaved girl brought to Boston at age eight and never formally educated. Taken to England when twenty years of age, she published a book of verse and subsequently wrote other polished poems that revealed the influence of Alexander Pope. Her verse compares favorably with the best of the poetry-poor colonial period, but the remarkable fact is that she could overcome her severely disadvantaged background and write any poetry at all.

Versatile Benjamin Franklin, often called "the first civilized American," also shone as a literary light. Although his autobiography is now a classic, he was best known to his contemporaries for ***Poor Richard's Almanack***, which he edited from 1732 to 1758. This famous publication, containing many pithy sayings culled from the thinkers of the ages, emphasized such homespun virtues as thrift, industry, morality, and common sense. Examples are "What maintains one vice would bring up two children"; "Plough deep while sluggards sleep"; "Honesty is the best policy"; and "Fish and visitors stink in three days." *Poor Richard's* was well known in Europe and was more widely read in America than anything except the Bible. Dispensing witty advice to old and young alike, Franklin had an incalculable influence in shaping the American character.

Science, rising above the shackles of superstition, was making some progress, though lagging behind that of the Old World. A few botanists, mathematicians, and astronomers had won some repute, but Benjamin Franklin was perhaps the only first-rank scientist produced in the American colonies. Franklin's spectacular but dangerous experiments, including the famous kite-flying episode proving that lightning was a form of electricity, won him numerous honors in Europe. But his mind also had a practical turn. Among his numerous inventions were bifocal spectacles and the highly efficient Franklin stove. His lightning rod, perhaps not surprisingly, was condemned by some stodgy clergymen who felt it was "presuming on God" by attempting to control the "artillery of the heavens."

✵ Pioneer Presses

Stump-grubbing Americans were generally too poor to buy quantities of books and too busy to read them. A South Carolina merchant in 1744 advertised the arrival of a shipment of "printed books, Pictures, Maps, and Pickles." A few private libraries of fair size could be found, especially among the clergy. The Byrd family of Virginia enjoyed perhaps the largest collection in the colonies, consisting of about four thousand volumes. Bustling Benjamin Franklin established in Philadelphia the first privately supported circulating library in America, and by 1776 there were about fifty public libraries and collections supported by subscription.

Hand-operated printing presses cranked out pamphlets, leaflets, and journals. On the eve of the Revolution, there were about forty colonial newspapers, chiefly weeklies that consisted of a single large sheet folded once. Columns ran heavily to somber essays, frequently signed with such pseudonyms as *Cicero*, *Philosophicus*, and *Pro Bono Publico* ("For the Public Good"). The "news" often lagged many weeks behind the event, especially in the case of overseas happenings, in which the colonists were deeply interested. Newspapers proved to be a powerful agency for airing colonial grievances and rallying opposition to British control.

A celebrated legal case, in 1734–1735, involved John Peter Zenger, a newspaper printer. Significantly, the **Zenger trial** arose in New York, reflecting the tumultuous give-and-take of politics in the middle colonies, where so many different ethnic groups jostled against one another. Zenger's newspaper had assailed the corrupt royal governor. Charged with seditious libel, the accused was hauled into court, where he was defended by a former indentured servant, now a distinguished Philadelphia lawyer, Andrew Hamilton. Zenger argued that he had printed the truth, but the bewigged royal chief justice instructed the jury not to consider the truth or falsity of Zenger's statements; the mere fact of printing, irrespective of the truth, was enough to convict. Hamilton countered that "the very liberty of both exposing and opposing arbitrary power" was at stake. Swayed by his eloquence, the jurors defied the bewigged judges and daringly returned a verdict of not guilty. Cheers burst from the spectators.

The Zenger decision was a banner achievement for freedom of the press and for the health of democracy. It pointed the way to the kind of open public discussion required by the diverse society that colonial New York already was and that all America was to become. Although contrary to existing law and not immediately accepted by other judges and juries, in time it helped establish the doctrine that true statements about public officials could not be prosecuted as libel. Newspapers were thus eventually free to print responsible criticisms of powerful officials, though full freedom of the press was unknown during the pre-Revolutionary era.

Andrew Hamilton (ca. 1676–1741) concluded his eloquent plea in the Zenger case with these words:

❝The question before the court and you, gentlemen of the jury, is not of small nor private concern. It is not the cause of a poor printer, nor of New York alone, which you are now trying. No! It may, in its consequence, affect every freeman that lives under a British government on the main [land] of America. It is the best cause. It is the cause of liberty.**❞**

✸ The Great Game of Politics

American colonists may have been backward in natural or physical science, but they were making note-worthy contributions to political science.

The thirteen colonial governments took a variety of forms. By 1775 eight of the colonies had royal governors, who were appointed by the king. Three—Maryland, Pennsylvania, and Delaware—were under proprietors who themselves chose the governors. And two—Connecticut and Rhode Island—elected their own governors under self-governing charters.

Practically every colony utilized a two-house legislative body. The upper house, or council, was normally appointed by the crown in the **royal colonies** and by the proprietor in the **proprietary colonies**. It was chosen by the voters in the self-governing colonies. The lower house, as the popular branch, was elected by the people—or rather by those who owned enough property to qualify as voters. In several of the colonies, the backcountry elements were seriously underrepresented, and they hated the ruling colonial clique perhaps more than they did kingly authority. Legislatures, in which the people enjoyed direct representation, voted such taxes as they chose for the necessary expenses of colonial government. Self-taxation through representation was a precious privilege that Americans had come to cherish above most others.

Governors appointed by the king were generally able men, sometimes outstanding figures. Some, unfortunately, were incompetent or corrupt—broken-down politicians badly in need of jobs. The worst of the group was probably impoverished Lord Cornbury, first cousin of Queen Anne, who was made governor of New York and New Jersey in 1702. He proved to be a drunkard, a spendthrift, a grafter, an embezzler, a religious bigot, and a vain fool, who was accused (probably inaccurately) of dressing like a woman. Even the best appointees had trouble with the colonial legislatures, basically because the royal governor embodied a bothersome transatlantic authority some three thousand miles away.

The colonial assemblies found various ways to assert their authority and independence. Some of them employed the trick of withholding the governor's

Junius, the pseudonym for a critic (or critics) of the British government from 1768 to 1772, published a pointed barb in criticizing one new appointee:

❝It was not Virginia that wanted a governor but a court favorite that wanted a salary.**❞**

The Hunting Party, New Jersey   Fox hunting began as a necessity in the colonies, where farmers on foot tried to keep foxes from overrunning the countryside. By the eighteenth century it had become an organized sport among the well-to-do, mounted on horseback. George Washington was famed as an ardent fox hunter, breeding his own hounds and importing a fine hunting wardrobe from England. Huntsmen wore scarlet coats to be easily visible, even in the depths of the forest, and cork-lined black hats for protection from low hanging branches or a fall.

salary unless he yielded to their wishes. He was normally in need of money—otherwise he would not have come to this godforsaken country—so the power of the purse usually forced him to terms. But one governor of North Carolina died with his salary eleven years in arrears.

The London government, in leaving the colonial governor to the tender mercies of the legislature, was guilty of poor administration. In the interests of simple efficiency, the British authorities should have arranged to pay him from independent sources. As events turned out, control over the purse by the colonial legislatures led to prolonged bickering, which proved to be one of the persistent irritants that generated a spirit of revolt.*

Administration at the local level was also varied. County government remained the rule in the plantation South; town-meeting government predominated in New England; and a modification of the two developed in the middle colonies. In the town meeting, with its open discussion and open voting, direct democracy functioned at its best. In this unrivaled cradle of self-government, Americans learned to cherish their privileges and exercise their duties as citizens of the New World commonwealths.

Yet the ballot was by no means a birthright. Religious or property qualifications for voting, with even stiffer qualifications for officeholding, existed in all the colonies in 1775. The privileged upper classes, fearful of democratic excesses, were unwilling to grant the ballot to every "biped of the forest." Perhaps half of the adult white males were thus disfranchised. But because of the ease of acquiring land and thus satisfying property requirements, the right to vote was not beyond the reach of most industrious and enterprising colonists. Yet somewhat surprisingly, eligible voters often did not exercise this precious privilege. They frequently acquiesced in the leadership of their "betters," who ran colonial affairs—though always reserving the right to vote misbehaving rascals out of office.

---

*Parliament finally arranged for separate payment of the governors through the Townshend taxes of 1767, but by then the colonists were in such an ugly mood over taxation that this innovation only added fresh fuel to the flames.

By 1775 America was not yet a true democracy—socially, economically, or politically. But it was far more democratic than England and the European continent. Colonial institutions were giving freer rein to the democratic ideals of tolerance, educational advantages, equality of economic opportunity, freedom of speech, freedom of the press, freedom of assembly, and representative government. And these democratic seeds, planted in rich soil, were to bring forth a lush harvest in later years.

✷ Colonial Folkways

Everyday life in the colonies may now seem glamorous, especially as reflected in antique shops. But judged by modern standards, it was drab and tedious. For most people the labor was heavy and constant—from "can see" to "can't see."

Food was plentiful, though the diet could be coarse and monotonous. Americans probably ate more bountifully, especially of meat, than any people in the Old World. Lazy or sickly was the person whose stomach was empty.

Basic comforts now taken for granted were lacking. Churches were not heated at all, except for charcoal foot-warmers that the women carried. During the frigid New England winters, the preaching of hellfire may not have seemed altogether unattractive. Drafty homes were poorly heated, chiefly by inefficient fireplaces. There was no running water in the houses, no indoor plumbing, and probably not a single bathtub in all of colonial America. Candles and whale-oil lamps provided faint and flickering illumination. Garbage disposal was primitive. Long-snouted hogs customarily ranged the streets to consume refuse, while buzzards, protected by law, flapped greedily over tidbits of waste.

Amusement was eagerly pursued where time and custom permitted. The militia assembled periodically for "musters," which consisted of several days of drilling, liberally interspersed with merrymaking and flirting. On the frontier, pleasure was often combined with work at house-raisings, quilting bees, husking bees, and apple parings. Funerals and weddings everywhere afforded opportunities for social gatherings, which customarily involved the swilling of much strong liquor.

Winter sports were common in the North, whereas in the South card playing, horse racing, cockfighting, and fox hunting were favorite pastimes. George Washington, not surprisingly, was a superb rider. In the nonpuritanical South, dancing was the rage—jigs, square dances, the Virginia reel—and the agile Washington could swing his fair partner with the best of them.

Other diversions beckoned. Lotteries were universally approved, even by the clergy, and were used to raise money for churches and colleges, including Harvard. Stage plays became popular in the South but were frowned upon in Quaker and Puritan colonies and in some places forbidden by law. Many of the New

The Popular Game of Billiards Most likely brought over by Dutch and English settlers, billiards provided amusement in local taverns throughout the colonies. By the nineteenth century, Americans, like the British and French who had long dominated the sport, had become obsessed with these games of cues and balls. The most popular form of pool, eight ball, was not invented until 1900.

Library of Congress

England clergy saw playacting as time-consuming and immoral; they preferred religious lectures, from which their flocks derived much spiritual satisfaction.

Holidays were everywhere celebrated in the American colonies, but Christmas was frowned upon in New England as an offensive reminder of "Popery." "Yuletide is fooltide" was a common Puritan sneer. Thanksgiving Day came to be a truly American festival, for it combined thanks to God with an opportunity for jollification, gorging, and guzzling.

By the mid-eighteenth century, Britain's several North American colonies, despite their differences, revealed some striking similarities. All were basically English in language and customs, and Protestant in religion, while the widespread presence of other peoples and faiths compelled every colony to cede at least some degree of ethnic and religious toleration. Compared with contemporary Europe, they all afforded to enterprising individuals unusual opportunities for social mobility. They all possessed some measure of self-government, though by no means complete democracy. Communication and transportation among the colonies were improving. British North America by 1775 looked like a patchwork quilt—each part slightly different, but stitched together by common origins, common ways of life, and common beliefs in toleration, economic development, and, above all, self-rule. Fatefully, all the colonies were also separated from the seat of imperial authority by a vast ocean moat some three thousand miles wide. These simple facts of shared history, culture, and geography set the stage for the colonists' struggle to unite as an independent people.

Varying Viewpoints
Colonial America: Communities of Conflict or Consensus?

*T*he earliest historians of colonial society portrayed close-knit, homogeneous, and hierarchical communities. Richard Bushman's *From Puritan to Yankee* (1967) challenged that traditional view when he described colonial New England as an expanding, opening society. In this view the colonists gradually lost the religious discipline and social structure of the founding generations as they poured out onto the frontier or sailed the seas in search of fortune and adventure. Rhys Isaac viewed the Great Awakening in the South as similar evidence of the erosion of the social constraints and deference that once held colonial society together. Unbridled religious enthusiasm, directed by itinerant preachers both North and South, encouraged the sort of quest for personal autonomy that eventually led Americans to demand national independence.

Other scholars have focused on the negative aspects of this alleged breakdown in the traditional order, particularly on the rise of new social inequalities. Social historians like Kenneth Lockridge have argued that the decline of cohesive communities, population pressure on the land, and continued dominance of church and parental authority gave rise to a landless class, forced to till tenant plots in the countryside or find work as manual laborers in the cities. Gary Nash, in *The Urban Crucible* (1979), likewise traced the rise of a competitive, individualistic social order in colonial cities, marking the end of the patronage and paternalism that had once bound communities together. Increasingly, Nash contended, class antagonisms split communities. The wealthy abandoned their traditional obligations toward the poor for more selfish capitalistic social relations that favored their class peers. The consequent politicization of the laboring classes helped motivate their participation in the American Revolution.

Some scholars have disputed that "declension" undermined colonial communities. Christine Heyrman, in particular, has argued in *Commerce and Culture* (1984) that the decline of traditional mores has been overstated; religious beliefs and commercial activities coexisted throughout the late seventeenth and early eighteenth centuries. Similarly, Jack Greene has suggested that the obsession with the decline of deference has obscured the fact that colonies outside of New England, like Virginia and Maryland, actually experienced a consolidation of religious and social authority throughout the seventeenth and eighteenth centuries, becoming more hierarchical and paternalistic.

Like Greene, many historians have focused on sectional differences between the colonies, and the peculiar nature of social equality and inequality in each. Much of the impetus for this inquiry stems from an issue that has long perplexed students of early America: the simultaneous evolution of a rigid racial caste system alongside democratic political institutions. Decades ago, when most historians came from Yankee stock, they resolved the apparent paradox by locating the seeds of democracy in New England. The aggressive independence of the people, best expressed by the boisterous town meetings, spawned the American obsession with freedom. On the other hand, this view holds, the slave societies of the South were hierarchical, aristocratic communities under the sway of a few powerful planters.

More recently some historians have attacked this simple dichotomy, noting many undemocratic features in colonial New England and arguing that while the South may have been the site of tremendous inequality, it also produced most of the Founding Fathers. Washington, Jefferson, and Madison—the architects of American government with its foundation in liberty—all hailed from slaveholding Virginia. In fact, nowhere were republican principles stronger than in Virginia. Some scholars, notably Edmund S. Morgan in *American Slavery, American Freedom* (1975), consider the willingness of wealthy planters to concede the equality and freedom of all white males a device to ensure racial solidarity and to mute class conflict. In this view the concurrent emergence of slavery and democracy was no paradox. White racial solidarity muffled animosity between rich and poor and fostered the devotion to equality among whites that became a hallmark of American democracy. Historians of Latin America point out that other New World societies, like Brazil and Mexico, had far sharper class divisions than the British colonies, with lasting consequences for their social integrity and political stability.

Few historians still argue that the colonies offered boundless opportunities for inhabitants, white or black. But scholars disagree vigorously over what kinds of inequalities and social tensions most shaped eighteenth-century society and contributed to the revolutionary agitation that eventually consumed—and transformed—colonial America. Even so, whether one accepts Morgan's argument that "Americans bought their independence with slave labor" or those interpretations that point to rising social conflict between whites as the salient characteristic of colonial society on the eve of the Revolution, the once-common assumption that America was a world of equality and consensus no longer reigns undisputed. Yet because one's life chances were still unquestionably better in America than in Europe, immigrants continued to pour in, imbued with high expectations about America as a land of opportunity.

Chapter Review

KEY TERMS

Paxton Boys (80)
Regulator movement (80)
triangular trade (83)
Molasses Act (85)
Arminianism (87)
Great Awakening (87)
old lights (88)

new lights (88)
Poor Richard's Almanack (91)
Zenger trial (92)
royal colonies (92)
proprietary colonies (92)

PEOPLE TO KNOW

Michel-Guillaume Jean de Crèvecoeur
Jacobus Arminius
Jonathan Edwards
George Whitefield

John Trumbull
John Singleton Copley
Phillis Wheatley
John Peter Zenger

CHRONOLOGY

1693	College of William and Mary founded
1701	Yale College founded
1721	Smallpox inoculation introduced
1732	First edition of Franklin's *Poor Richard's Almanack*
1734	Jonathan Edwards begins Great Awakening
1734–1735	Zenger free-press trial in New York
1738	George Whitefield spreads Great Awakening
1746	Princeton College founded
1760	Britain vetoes South Carolina anti–slave trade measures
1764	Paxton Boys march on Philadelphia Brown College founded
1766	Rutgers College founded
1768–1771	Regulator protests
1769	Dartmouth College founded

TO LEARN MORE

Bernard Bailyn, *The Peopling of British North America* (1986)

Richard L. Bushman, *From Puritan to Yankee: Character and Social Order in Connecticut, 1690–1765* (1967)

———, *King and People in Provincial Massachusetts* (1985)

John Butler, *Becoming America: The Revolution Before 1776* (2000)

Olaudah Equiano, *Equinao's Travels* (1789)

Benjamin Franklin, *Autobiography* (1868)

James Henretta, *The Evolution of American Society, 1700–1815* (1973)

Rhys Isaac, *Landon Carter's Uneasy Kingdom: Revolution and Rebellion on a Virginia Plantation* (2004)

Jill Lepore, *New York Burning* (2005)

Marcus Rediker, *Between the Devil and the Deep Blue Sea: Merchant Seamen, Pirates, and the Anglo-American Maritime World, 1700–1750* (1987)

Gordon Wood, *The Americanization of Benjamin Franklin* (2004)

A complete, annotated bibliography for this chapter—along with brief descriptions of the People to Know—may be found on the American Pageant website. The Key Terms are defined in a Glossary at the end of the text.

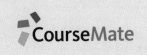

Go to the CourseMate website at **www.cengagebrain.com** for additional study tools and review materials—including audio and video clips—for this chapter.

AP® Review Questions for Chapter 5

1. What were the political ramifications of the surging population growth in the American colonies from 1700 to 1775?
   - (A) The number of colonies more than doubled from six to thirteen.
   - (B) The ratio of American colonists to English subjects dramatically declined.
   - (C) There were massive food shortages in the colonies.
   - (D) The immigrant population surpassed that of those born in the colonies.
   - (E) More people moved from the countryside to the growing cities.

2. All of the following statements are true about Scots-Irish immigrants to Pennsylvania EXCEPT that
   - (A) they were the first to settle the American West.
   - (B) they were not actually of Irish descent.
   - (C) many of them united with the American revolutionaries.
   - (D) they brought with them the know-how for whiskey distilling.
   - (E) they were tolerant of local Indians.

3. The ethnic diversity of the eighteenth-century American colonies is significant because it
   - (A) paved the way for a new, multicultural American identity.
   - (B) fueled heightened tensions within the colonies.
   - (C) made unity against the British difficult to accomplish.
   - (D) resulted in eighteen non-English signatories to the Declaration of Independence.
   - (E) caused the eventual rift between northern and southern colonies.

4. Which of these did NOT contribute to the increasing social stratification and declining opportunities for social mobility in pre-Revolutionary America?
   - (A) The growth of slavery in the Chesapeake
   - (B) The emergence of a wealthy merchant class
   - (C) Declining supplies of unclaimed land in New England
   - (D) The rising number of convicts sent to the colonies
   - (E) The impact of the wars of the 1690s and 1700s

5. Despite the constant threat of smallpox, American colonists resisted inoculation mainly because
   - (A) vaccines were rare and untested.
   - (B) doctors were poorly trained.
   - (C) ministers regarded inoculation as tampering with God's will.
   - (D) home remedies worked well in fighting and treating the virus.
   - (E) several prominent citizens had survived the disease.

6. Which of the following was the surest path to quick wealth in eighteenth-century America?
   - (A) Commerce and land speculation
   - (B) Tobacco farming
   - (C) Wheat cultivation
   - (D) Fishing
   - (E) Buying and selling slaves

7. The term *triangular trade* describes
   - (A) the three main staple crops that each colonial region relied on for trade: grain in the North, tobacco in the Chesapeake, and rice in the South.
   - (B) the exportation of colonial goods to other European countries through British middlemen.
   - (C) rum sent from New England to trade for slaves in Africa, who were then exchanged for molasses in the West Indies that could be sold back to New England.
   - (D) the trade network that included Indian fur traders, West Indian sugar growers, and British merchants.
   - (E) the notion of the East and West Indies as part of the broader American system of commerce.

8. The single most important manufacturing activity in the colonies in the 1770s was
   - (A) blacksmithing.
   - (B) lumbering.
   - (C) rum and whiskey production.
   - (D) carpentry.
   - (E) iron making.

9. What did Parliament hope to accomplish with the Molasses Act (1733)?
   (A) Cut off American trade with the French West Indies
   (B) Generate new revenue from the colonies
   (C) Install tariffs on goods not sent through England first
   (D) Stifle growing colonial commercial independence
   (E) Dramatically reduce whiskey and rum production

10. In the early eighteenth century, the Puritan religion declined for all of the following reasons EXCEPT
    (A) decreased interest in its complicated doctrines and long sermons.
    (B) disapproval of its efforts to loosen church membership requirements.
    (C) liberal challenges to older ideas about salvation.
    (D) increased tithing (taxing) of church members.
    (E) heightened support for Arminian assumptions about free will.

11. Which of these did NOT result from the Great Awakening?
    (A) The authority of older clergy was called into question.
    (B) Many new churches were established.
    (C) A new wave of Christian missionaries attempted to convert Indians and slaves.
    (D) Several colleges and universities were founded.
    (E) A heightened sense of sectional and regional differences developed.

12. Early college education in New England was designed to
    (A) prepare young men to become ministers.
    (B) educate future leaders.
    (C) create an enlightened citizenry.
    (D) teach boys to read and write.
    (E) encourage more men to enter the professions (law, medicine, etc).

13. Which of these is NOT numbered among Benjamin Franklin's many contributions to America?
    (A) Poor Richard's Almanack
    (B) Inventions
    (C) Scientific experiments
    (D) Writing the Declaration of Independence
    (E) The first public library

14. The Zenger case is significant for
    (A) making sedition illegal.
    (B) establishing freedom of the press.
    (C) guaranteeing backcountry residents equal representation in colonial governments.
    (D) ensuring taxation through proper representation.
    (E) linking voting rights and officeholding to property ownership.

15. Which of the following figures played a crucial role in developing American character?
    (A) Phillis Wheatley
    (B) Jonathan Edwards
    (C) Benjamin Franklin
    (D) John Trumbull
    (E) John Adams

16. All of the following are true about education and religion in the colonies EXCEPT that
    (A) most universities were founded by a specific religious group.
    (B) the majority of the faculty at each college comprised church officials.
    (C) the curriculum usually emphasized religion, Latin, and Greek.
    (D) college education was geared toward preparing men for the ministry.
    (E) families that disagreed with the emphasis on religion sent sons abroad for their education.

Chapter 6

The Duel for North America

1608–1763

A torch lighted in the forests of America set all Europe in conflagration.

VOLTAIRE, CA. 1756

As the seventeenth century neared its sunset, a titanic struggle was shaping up for mastery of the North American continent. The contest involved three Old World nations—England,* France, and Spain—and it unavoidably swept up Native American peoples as well. From 1688 to 1763, four bitter wars convulsed Europe. All four of those conflicts were world wars. They amounted to a death struggle for domination in Europe as well as in the New World, and they were fought on the waters and soil of two hemispheres. Counting these first four clashes, nine world wars have been waged since 1688. The American people, whether as British subjects or as American citizens, proved unable to stay out of a single one of them. And one of those wars—known as the Seven Years' War in Europe and sometimes as the French and Indian War in America—set the stage for America's independence.

✴ France Finds a Foothold in Canada

Like England and Holland, France was a latecomer in the scramble for New World real estate, and for basically the same reasons. It was convulsed during the 1500s by foreign wars and domestic strife, including the frightful clashes between Roman Catholics and Protestant **Huguenots**. On St. Bartholomew's Day, 1572, over ten thousand Huguenots—men, women, and children—were butchered in cold blood.

A new era dawned in 1598 when the **Edict of Nantes**, issued by the crown, granted limited toleration to French Protestants. Religious wars ceased, and in the new century France blossomed into the mightiest and most feared nation on the European continent, led by a series of brilliant ministers and by the vainglorious King Louis XIV. Enthroned as a five-year-old boy, he reigned for no less than seventy-two years (1643–1715), surrounded by a glittering court and scheming ministers and mistresses. Fatefully for North America, Louis XIV also took a deep interest in overseas colonies.

After rocky beginnings, success finally rewarded the exertions of France in the New World. In 1608, the year after the founding of Jamestown, the permanent beginnings of a vast empire (see Map 6.1) were established at Québec, a granite sentinel commanding the St. Lawrence River. The leading figure was Samuel de Champlain, an intrepid soldier and explorer whose energy and leadership fairly earned him the title "Father of New France."

Champlain entered into friendly relations—a fateful friendship—with the nearby Huron Indian tribes. At their request, he joined them in battle against their foes, the federated Iroquois tribes of the upper New York area. Two volleys from the "lightning sticks" of the whites routed the terrified Iroquois, who left behind three dead and one wounded. France, to its sorrow, thus earned the lasting enmity of the Iroquois tribes. They thereafter hampered French penetration of the Ohio Valley, sometimes ravaging French settlements and frequently serving as allies of the British in the prolonged struggle for supremacy on the continent.

---

*After the union of England and Scotland in 1707, the nation's official name became "Great Britain."

The government of New France (Canada) finally fell under the direct control of the king after various commercial companies had faltered or failed. This royal regime was almost completely autocratic. The people elected no representative assemblies, nor did they enjoy the right to trial by jury, as in the English colonies.

The population of Catholic New France grew at a listless pace. As late as 1750, only sixty thousand or so whites inhabited New France. Landowning French peasants, unlike the dispossessed English tenant farmers who embarked for the British colonies, had little economic motive to move. Protestant Huguenots, who might have had a religious motive to migrate, were denied a refuge in this raw colony. The French government, in any case, favored its Caribbean island colonies, rich in sugar and rum, over the snow-cloaked wilderness of Canada.

✦ New France Fans Out

New France did contain one valuable resource: the beaver. European fashion-setters valued beaver-pelt hats for their warmth and opulent appearance. To adorn the heads of Europeans, French fur-trappers ranged over the woods and waterways of North America in pursuit of beaver. These colorful *coureurs de bois* ("runners of the woods") were also runners of risks—two-fisted drinkers, free spenders, free livers and lovers. They littered the land with scores of place names, including Baton Rouge (red stick), Terre Haute (high land), Des Moines (some monks), and Grand Teton (big breast).

Singing, paddle-swinging French *voyageurs* also recruited Indians into the fur business. The Indian fur flotilla arriving in Montréal in 1693 numbered four hundred canoes. But the fur trade had some disastrous drawbacks. Indians recruited into the fur business were decimated by the white man's diseases and debauched by his alcohol. Slaughtering beaver by the boatload also violated many Indians' religious beliefs and sadly demonstrated the shattering effect that contact with Europeans wreaked on traditional Indian ways of life.

Pursuing the sharp-toothed beaver ever deeper into the heart of the continent, the French trappers and their Indian partners hiked, rode, snowshoed, sailed, and paddled across amazing distances. They trekked in a huge arc across the Great Lakes, into present-day Saskatchewan and Manitoba; along the valleys of the Platte, the Arkansas, and the Missouri; west to the Rockies; and south to the border of Spanish Texas (see Map 6.2). In the process they all but extinguished the beaver population in many areas, inflicting incalculable ecological damage.

MAP 6.1 France's American Empire at Its Greatest Extent, 1700 © Cengage Learning

Québec Scene, by Jean-Baptiste-Louis Franquelin, ca. 1699 (detail) The metal cooking pot and the Indians' clothing and blankets show the Native Americans' growing reliance on European trade goods.

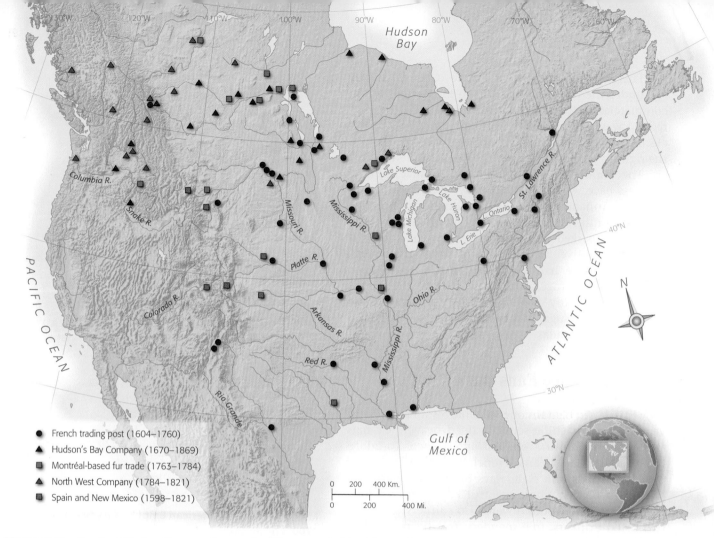

MAP 6.2 Fur-Trading Posts To serve the needs of European fashion, fur-traders pursued the beaver for more than two centuries over the entire continent of North America. They brought many Indians for the first time into contact with white culture. © Cengage Learning

- ● French trading post (1604–1760)
- ▲ Hudson's Bay Company (1670–1869)
- ■ Montréal-based fur trade (1763–1784)
- ▲ North West Company (1784–1821)
- ■ Spain and New Mexico (1598–1821)

French Catholic missionaries, notably the Jesuits, labored zealously to save the Indians for Christ and from the fur-trappers. Some of the Jesuit missionaries, their efforts scorned, suffered unspeakable tortures at the hands of the Indians. But though they made few permanent converts, the Jesuits played a vital role as explorers and geographers.

Other explorers sought neither souls nor fur, but empire. To thwart English settlers pushing into the Ohio Valley, Antoine Cadillac founded Detroit, "the City of Straits," in 1701. To check Spanish penetration into the region of the Gulf of Mexico, ambitious Robert de La Salle floated down the Mississippi in 1682 to the point where it mingles with the Gulf. He named the great interior basin "Louisiana," in honor of his sovereign, Louis XIV. Dreaming of empire, he returned to the Gulf three years later with a colonizing expedition of four ships. But he failed to find the Mississippi delta, landed in Spanish Texas, and in 1687 was murdered by his mutinous men.

Undismayed, French officials persisted in their efforts to block Spain on the Gulf of Mexico. They planted several fortified posts in what is now Mississippi and Louisiana, the most important of which was New Orleans (1718). Commanding the mouth of the Mississippi River, this strategic semitropical outpost also tapped the fur trade of the huge interior valley. The fertile Illinois country—where the French established forts and trading posts at Kaskaskia, Cahokia, and Vincennes—became the garden of France's North American empire. Surprising amounts of grain were floated down the Mississippi for transshipment to the West Indies and to Europe.

✶ The Clash of Empires

The earliest contests among the European powers for control of North America, known to the British colonists as **King William's War** (1689–1697) and **Queen Anne's War** (1702–1713) (see Table 6.1), mostly pitted British colonists against the French *coureurs de bois*, with both sides recruiting whatever Indian allies they could. Neither France nor Britain at this stage considered America worth the commitment of

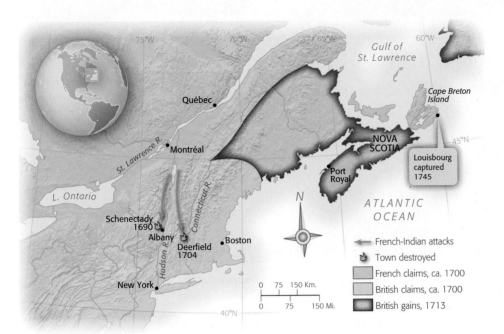

MAP 6.3 Scenes of the French Wars The arrows indicate French-Indian attacks. Schenectady was burned to the ground in the raid of 1690. At Deerfield, site of one of the New England frontier's bloodiest confrontations, invaders killed fifty inhabitants and sent more than a hundred others fleeing for their lives into the winter wilderness. The Indian attackers also took over one hundred Deerfield residents captive, including the child Titus King. He later wrote, "Captivity is an awful school for children, when we see how quick they will fall in with the Indian ways. Nothing seems to be more taking [appealing]. In six months' time they forsake father and mother, forget their own land, refuse to speak their own tongue, and seemingly be wholly swallowed up with the Indians." © Cengage Learning

large detachments of regular troops, so the combatants waged a kind of primitive guerrilla warfare. Indian allies of the French ravaged with torch and tomahawk the British colonial frontiers, visiting especially bloody violence on the villages of Schenectady, New York, and Deerfield, Massachusetts (see Map 6.3). Spain, eventually allied with France, probed from its Florida base at outlying South Carolina settlements. For their part the British colonists failed miserably in sallies against Québec and Montréal but scored a signal victory when they temporarily seized the stronghold of Port Royal in Acadia (present-day Nova Scotia).

Peace terms, signed at Utrecht in 1713, revealed how badly France and its Spanish ally had been beaten (see Map 6.4). Britain was rewarded with French-populated Acadia (which the British renamed Nova Scotia, or New Scotland) and the wintry wastes of Newfoundland and Hudson Bay. These immense tracts pinched the St. Lawrence settlements of France, foreshadowing their ultimate doom. A generation of peace ensued, during which Britain provided its American colonies with decades of "salutary neglect"—fertile soil for the roots of independence.

By the treaty of 1713, the British also won limited trading rights in Spanish America, but these later involved much friction over smuggling. Ill feeling flared up when the British captain Robert Jenkins, encountering Spanish revenue authorities, had one ear sliced off by a sword. The Spanish commander reportedly sneered, "Carry this home to the King, your master, whom, if he were present, I would serve in like fashion." The victim, with a tale of woe on his tongue and a shriveled ear in his hand, aroused furious resentment when he returned home to Britain.

The **War of Jenkins's Ear**, curiously but aptly named, broke out in 1739 between the British and the

TABLE 6.1 Later English Monarchs*

Name, Reign	Relation to America
William III, 1689–1702	Collapse of Dominion of New England; King William's War
Anne, 1702–1714	Queen Anne's War, 1702–1713
George I, 1714–1727	Navigation Laws laxly enforced ("salutary neglect")
George II, 1727–1760	Ga. founded; King George's War; Seven Years' War
George III, 1760–1820	American Revolution, 1775–1783

*See pp. 26 and 48 for earlier monarchs.

Chief of the Taensa Indians Receiving La Salle, March 20, 1682, by George Catlin, 1847–1848 Driven by the dream of a vast North American empire for France, La Salle spent years exploring the Great Lakes region and the valleys of the Illinois and Mississippi Rivers. This scene of his encounter with an Indian chieftain was imaginatively recreated by the nineteenth-century artist George Catlin.

Spaniards. It was confined to the Caribbean Sea and to the much-buffeted buffer colony of Georgia, where philanthropist-soldier James Oglethorpe fought his Spanish foe to a standstill.

MAP 6.4 North America After Two Wars, 1713 © Cengage Learning

Territorial claims
- British
- French
- Spanish

This small-scale scuffle with Spain in America soon merged with the large-scale War of Austrian Succession in Europe (see Table 6.2), and came to be called **King George's War** in America. Once again, France allied itself with Spain. And once again, a rustic force of New Englanders invaded New France. With help from a British fleet and with a great deal of good luck, the raw and sometimes drunken recruits captured the reputedly impregnable French fortress of Louisbourg, which was on Cape Breton Island and commanded the approaches to the St. Lawrence River (see Map 6.3).

When the peace treaty of 1748 handed Louisbourg back to their French foe, the victorious New Englanders were outraged. The glory of their arms—never terribly lustrous in any event—seemed tarnished by the wiles of Old World diplomats. Worse, Louisbourg was still a cocked pistol pointed at the heart of the American continent. France, powerful and unappeased, still clung to its vast holdings in North America.

✦ George Washington Inaugurates War with France

As the dogfight intensified in the New World, the Ohio Valley became the chief bone of contention between the French and British. The Ohio Country was the critical area into which the westward-pushing British colonists would inevitably penetrate. For France it was also the key to the continent that the French had to retain, particularly if they were going to link their Canadian holdings with those of the lower Mississippi Valley. By the mid-1700s, the British colonists, painfully aware of these basic truths, were no longer so reluctant to bear the

TABLE 6.2 The Nine World Wars

Dates	In Europe	In America
1688–1697	War of the League of Augsburg	King William's War, 1689–1697
1701–1713	War of Spanish Succession	Queen Anne's War, 1702–1713
1740–1748	War of Austrian Succession	King George's War, 1744–1748
1756–1763	Seven Years' War	French and Indian War, 1754–1763
1778–1783	War of the American Revolution	American Revolution, 1775–1783
1793–1802	Wars of the French Revolution	Undeclared French War, 1798–1800
1803–1815	Napoleonic Wars	War of 1812, 1812–1814
1914–1918	World War I	World War I, 1917–1918
1939–1945	World War II	World War II, 1941–1945

burdens of empire. Alarmed by French land-grabbing and cutthroat fur-trade competition in the Ohio Valley, they were determined to fight for their economic security and for the supremacy of their way of life in North America.

Rivalry for the lush lands of the upper Ohio Valley brought tensions to the snapping point. In 1749 a group of British colonial speculators, chiefly influential Virginians, including the Washington family, had secured shaky legal "rights" to some 500,000 acres in this region. In the same disputed wilderness, the French were in the process of erecting a chain of forts commanding the strategic Ohio River. Especially formidable was Fort Duquesne at the pivotal point where the Monongahela and Allegheny Rivers join to form the Ohio—the later site of Pittsburgh.

In 1754 the governor of Virginia ushered George Washington, a twenty-one-year-old surveyor and fellow Virginian, onto the stage of history. To secure the Virginians' claims, Washington was sent to the Ohio Country as a lieutenant colonel in command of about 150 Virginia militiamen. Encountering a small

Anne S. K. Brown Military Collection, Brown University Library

New Englanders Capture Louisbourg, 1745   When the final peace settlement of 1748 returned this fortress to France, the American colonists felt betrayed by their British masters.

detachment of French troops in the forest about forty miles from Fort Duquesne (see Map 6.5), the Virginians fired the first shots of the globe-girdling new war. The French leader was killed, and his men retreated. An exultant Washington wrote, "I heard the bullets whistle, and believe me, there is something charming in the sound." It soon lost its charm.

The French promptly returned with reinforcements, who surrounded Washington in his hastily constructed breastworks, Fort Necessity. After a ten-hour siege, he was forced to surrender his entire command in July 1754—ironically the fourth of July. But he was permitted to march his men away with the full honors of war.

With the shooting already started and in danger of spreading, the British authorities in Nova Scotia took vigorous action. Understandably fearing a stab in the back from the French **Acadians**, whom Britain had conquered in 1713, the British brutally uprooted some four thousand of them in 1755. These unhappy French deportees were scattered as far south as Louisiana, where the descendants of the French-speaking Acadians are now called "Cajuns" and number nearly a million.

✴ Global War and Colonial Disunity

The first three Anglo-French colonial wars had all started in Europe, but the tables were now reversed. The fourth struggle, sometimes known as the **French and Indian War**, began in America. Touched off by George Washington in the wilds of the Ohio Valley in 1754, it rocked along on an undeclared basis for two years and then widened into the most far-flung conflict the world had yet seen—the **Seven Years' War**. It was fought not only in America but in Europe, in the West Indies, in the Philippines, in Africa, and on the ocean. The Seven Years' War was a seven-seas war (see Map 6.6).

In Europe the principal adversaries were Britain and Prussia on one side, arrayed against France, Spain, Austria, and Russia on the other. The bloodiest theater was in Germany, where Frederick the Great deservedly won the title of "Great" by repelling French, Austrian, and Russian armies, often with the opposing forces outnumbering his own three to one. The London government, unable to send him effective troop

MAP 6.5 The French and Indian War in North America, 1754–1760 © Cengage Learning

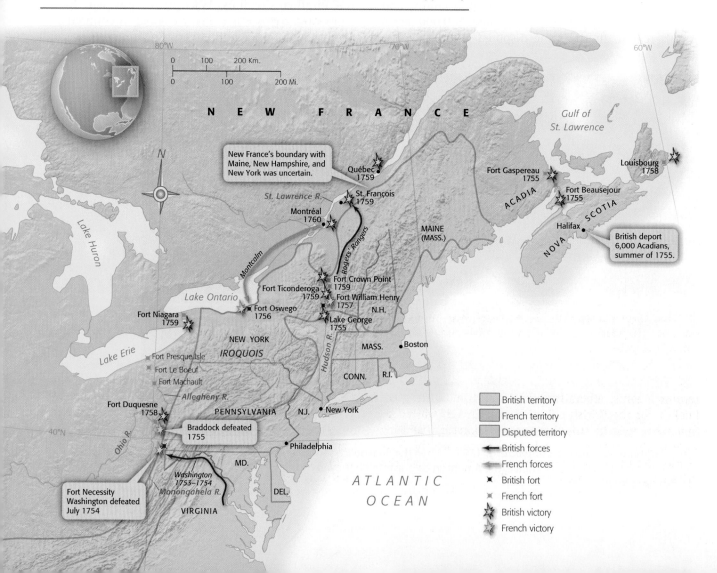

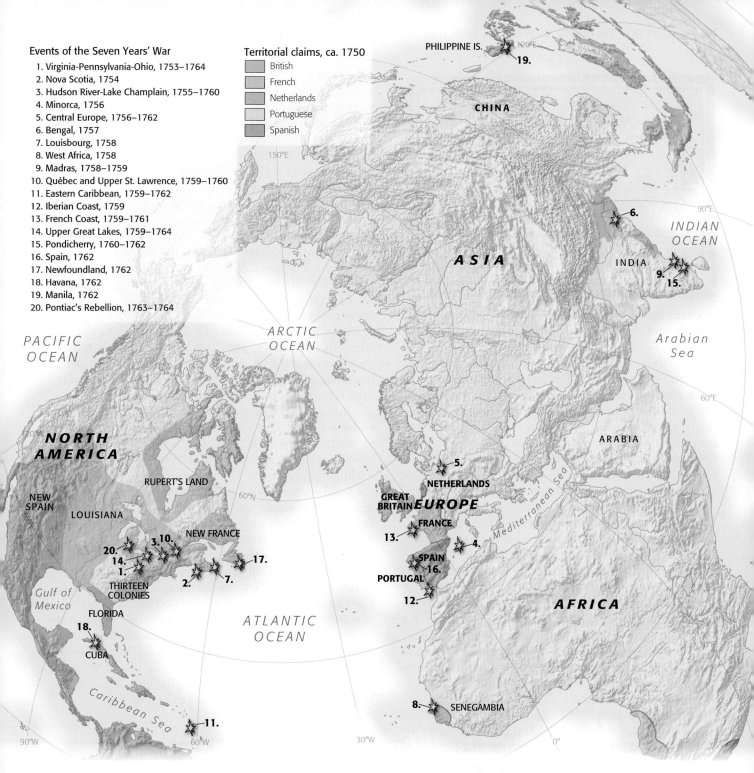

Events of the Seven Years' War

1. Virginia-Pennsylvania-Ohio, 1753–1764
2. Nova Scotia, 1754
3. Hudson River-Lake Champlain, 1755–1760
4. Minorca, 1756
5. Central Europe, 1756–1762
6. Bengal, 1757
7. Louisbourg, 1758
8. West Africa, 1758
9. Madras, 1758–1759
10. Québec and Upper St. Lawrence, 1759–1760
11. Eastern Caribbean, 1759–1762
12. Iberian Coast, 1759
13. French Coast, 1759–1761
14. Upper Great Lakes, 1759–1764
15. Pondicherry, 1760–1762
16. Spain, 1762
17. Newfoundland, 1762
18. Havana, 1762
19. Manila, 1762
20. Pontiac's Rebellion, 1763–1764

Territorial claims, ca. 1750

- British
- French
- Netherlands
- Portuguese
- Spanish

MAP 6.6 Global Scale of the Seven Years' War   Among the first of the truly "world wars" of the modern era, the Seven Years' War sucked in several nations who did battle around the globe. © Cengage Learning

reinforcements, liberally subsidized him with gold. Luckily for the British colonists, the French wasted so much strength in this European bloodbath that they were unable to throw an adequate force into the New World. "America was conquered in Germany," declared Britain's great statesman William Pitt.

In previous colonial clashes, the Americans had revealed an astonishing lack of unity. Colonists who were nearest the shooting had responded much more generously with volunteers and money than those enjoying the safety of remoteness. Even the Indians had laughed at the inability of the colonists to pull

Famous Cartoon by Benjamin Franklin Delaware and Georgia were omitted.

Library of Congress

together. Now, with musketballs already splitting the air in Ohio, the crisis demanded concerted action.

In 1754 the British government summoned an intercolonial congress to Albany, New York, near the Iroquois Indian country. Travel-weary delegates from only seven of the thirteen colonies showed up. The immediate purpose was to keep the scalping knives of the Iroquois tribes loyal to the British in the spreading war. The chiefs were harangued at length and then presented with thirty wagonloads of gifts, including guns.

The longer-range purpose at Albany was to achieve greater colonial unity and thus bolster the common defense against France. A month before the congress assembled, ingenious Benjamin Franklin published in his *Pennsylvania Gazette* the most famous cartoon of the colonial era. Showing the separate colonies as parts of a disjointed snake, it broadcast the slogan "Join, or Die."

Franklin himself, a wise and witty counselor, was the leading spirit of the **Albany Congress**. His outstanding contribution was a well-devised but premature scheme for colonial home rule. The Albany delegates unanimously adopted the plan, but the individual colonies spurned it, as did the London regime. To the colonists, it did not seem to give enough independence; to the British officials, it seemed to give too much. The disappointing result confirmed one of Franklin's sage observations: all people agreed on the need for union, but their "weak noddles" were "perfectly distracted" when they attempted to agree on details.

✳ Braddock's Blundering and Its Aftermath

The opening clashes of the French and Indian War went badly for the British colonists. Haughty and bullheaded General Edward Braddock, a sixty-year-old officer expe-

rienced in European warfare, was sent to Virginia with a strong detachment of British **regulars**. After foraging scanty supplies from the reluctant colonists, he set out in 1755 with some two thousand men to capture Fort Duquesne. A considerable part of his force consisted of ill-disciplined colonial militiamen ("buckskins"), whose behind-the-tree methods of fighting Indians won "Bulldog" Braddock's professional contempt.

Braddock's expedition, dragging heavy artillery, moved slowly. Axmen laboriously hacked a path through the dense forest, thus opening a road that was later to be an important artery to the West. A few miles from Fort Duquesne, Braddock encountered a much smaller French and Indian army. At first the enemy force was repulsed, but it quickly melted into the thickets and poured a murderous fire into the ranks of the redcoats. In the ensuing battle, George Washington, an energetic and fearless aide to Braddock, had two horses shot from under him, and four bullets pierced his coat. Braddock himself was mortally wounded. The entire British force was routed after appalling losses.

Inflamed by this easy victory, the Indians took to a wider warpath. The whole frontier from Pennsylvania to North Carolina, left virtually naked by Braddock's bloody defeat, felt their fury. Scalping forays occurred within eighty miles of Philadelphia, and in desperation the local authorities offered bounties for Indian scalps: $50 for a woman's and $130 for a warrior's. George Washington, with only three hundred men, tried desperately to defend the scorched frontier.

The British launched a full-scale invasion of Canada in 1756, now that the undeclared war in America had at last merged into a world conflict. But they unwisely tried to attack a number of exposed wilderness posts simultaneously, instead of throwing all their strength at Québec and Montréal. If these strongholds had fallen, all the smaller outposts to the west would have withered for lack of riverborne supplies. But the British ignored such sound strategy, and defeat after defeat tarnished their arms, both in America and in Europe.

✳ Pitt's Palms of Victory

In the hour of crisis, Britain brought forth, as it repeatedly has, a superlative leader—William Pitt. A tall and imposing figure, whose flashing eyes were set in a hawklike face, he was popularly known as the "Great Commoner." Pitt drew much of his strength from the common people, who admired him so greatly that on occasion they kissed his horses. A splendid orator endowed with a majestic voice, he believed passionately in his cause, in his country, and in himself.

In 1757 Pitt became a foremost leader in the London government. Throwing himself headlong into his task, he soon earned the title "Organizer of Victory."

View of the Taking of Québec, 1759 On the night of September 13, British forces scaled the rocky cliffs of Québec and defeated the French army defending the city. The following year, Montréal, France's last bastion in North America, surrendered. Fighting continued in the Caribbean, Europe, and the Philippines for two more years, until the Treaty of Paris was signed in 1763, eliminating France as a colonial power in North America.

He wisely decided to soft-pedal assaults on the French West Indies, which had been bleeding away much British strength, and to concentrate on the vitals of Canada—the Québec-Montréal area. He also picked young and energetic leaders, thus bypassing incompetent and cautious old generals.

Pitt first dispatched a powerful expedition in 1758 against Louisbourg. The frowning fortress, though it had been greatly strengthened, fell after a blistering siege. Wild rejoicing swept Britain, for this was the first significant British victory of the entire war.

Québec was next on Pitt's list. For this crucial expedition, he chose the thirty-two-year-old James Wolfe, who had been an officer since the age of fourteen. Though slight and sickly, Wolfe combined a mixture of dash with painstaking attention to detail. The British attackers were making woeful progress when Wolfe, in a daring night move, sent a detachment up a poorly guarded part of the rocky eminence protecting Québec. This vanguard scaled the cliff, pulling itself upward by the bushes and showing the way for the others. In the morning the two armies faced each other on the Plains of Abraham on the outskirts of Québec, the British under Wolfe and the French under the Marquis de Montcalm. Both commanders fell, fatally wounded, but the French were defeated and the city surrendered.

The **Battle of Québec** in 1759 ranks as one of the most significant engagements in British and American history. When Montréal fell in 1760, the French flag had fluttered in Canada for the last time. By the peace settlement at Paris (1763), French power was thrown completely off the continent of North America, leaving behind a fertile French population that is to this day a strong minority in Canada. This bitter pill was sweetened somewhat when the French were allowed to retain several small but valuable sugar islands in the West Indies and two never-to-be-fortified islets in the Gulf of St. Lawrence for fishing stations. A final blow came when the French, to compensate their luckless Spanish ally for its losses, ceded to Spain all trans-Mississippi Louisiana, plus the outlet of New Orleans. Spain, for its part, turned Florida over to Britain in return for Cuba, where Havana had fallen to British arms (see Map 6.7).

Great Britain thus emerged as the dominant power in North America, while taking its place as the leading naval power of the world.

✵ Restless Colonists

Britain's colonists, baptized by fire, emerged with increased confidence in their military strength. They had borne the brunt of battle at first; they had fought bravely alongside the crack British regulars; and they had gained valuable experience, officers and men alike. In the closing days of the conflict, some twenty thousand American recruits were under arms.

The French and Indian War, while bolstering colonial self-esteem, simultaneously shattered the myth of British invincibility. On Braddock's bloody field, the "buckskin" militia had seen the demoralized regulars huddling helplessly together or fleeing their unseen enemy.

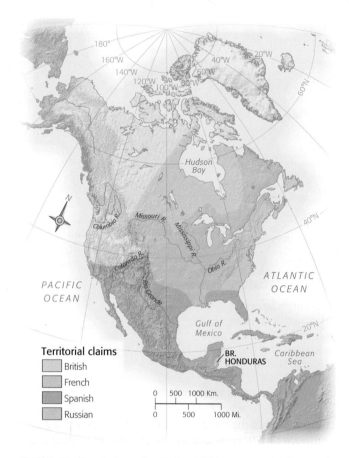

MAP 6.7A North America Before 1754
© Cengage Learning

MAP 6.7B North America After 1763 (after French losses) © Cengage Learning

Ominously, friction had developed during the war between arrogant British officers and the raw colonial "boors." Displaying the contempt of the professional soldier for amateurs, the British refused to recognize any American militia commission above the rank of captain—a demotion humiliating to "Colonel" George Washington. They also showed the usual condescension

The Reverend Andrew Burnaby, an observant Church of England clergyman who visited the colonies in the closing months of the Seven Years' War, scoffed at any possibility of unification (1760):

❝ . . . for fire and water are not more heterogeneous than the different colonies in North America. Nothing can exceed the jealousy and emulation which they possess in regard to each other. . . . In short . . . were they left to themselves there would soon be a civil war from one end of the continent to the other, while the Indians and Negros would . . . impatiently watch the opportunity of exterminating them all together.**❞**

of snobs from the civilized Old Country toward the "scum" who had confessed failure by fleeing to the "outhouses of civilization." General Wolfe referred to the colonial militia, with exaggeration, as "in general the dirtiest, most contemptible, cowardly dogs that you can conceive." Energetic and hard-working American settlers, in contrast, believed themselves to be the cutting edge of British civilization. They felt that they deserved credit rather than contempt for risking their lives to secure a New World empire.

British officials were further distressed by the reluctance of the colonists to support the common cause wholeheartedly. American shippers, using fraudulent papers, developed a golden traffic with the enemy ports of the Spanish and French West Indies. This treasonable trade in foodstuffs actually kept some of the hostile islands from starving at the very time when the British navy was trying to subdue them. In the final year of the war, the British authorities, forced to resort to drastic measures, forbade the export of all supplies from New England and the middle colonies.

Other colonists, self-centered and alienated by distance from the war, refused to provide troops and money for the conflict. They demanded the rights and

Detroit, 1794 A key French outpost from 1701 to 1760, Detroit fell to Britain during the Seven Years' War. The British remained at Detroit even after the American War of Independence, exciting bitter resentment in the infant American Republic (see pp. 166–167).

privileges of Englishmen, without the duties and responsibilities of Englishmen. Not until Pitt had offered to reimburse the colonies for a substantial part of their expenditures—some £900,000—did they move with some enthusiasm. If the Americans had to be bribed to defend themselves against a relentless and savage foe, would they ever unite to strike the mother country?

The curse of intercolonial disunity, present from early days, had continued throughout the recent hostilities. It had been caused mainly by enormous distances; by geographical barriers like rivers; by conflicting religions, from Catholic to Quaker; by varied nationalities, from German to Irish; by differing types of colonial governments; by many boundary disputes; and by the resentment of the crude backcountry settlers against the aristocratic bigwigs.

Yet unity received some encouragement during the French and Indian War. When soldiers and statesmen from widely separated colonies met around common campfires and council tables, they were often agreeably surprised by what they found. Despite deep-seated jealousy and suspicion, they discovered that they were all fellow Americans who generally spoke the same language and shared common ideals. Barriers of disunity began to melt, although a long and rugged road lay ahead before a coherent nation would emerge.

✦ War's Fateful Aftermath

The removal of the French menace in Canada profoundly affected American attitudes. While the French

hawk had been hovering in the North and West, the colonial chicks had been forced to cling close to the wings of their British mother hen. Now that the hawk was killed, they could range far afield with a new spirit of independence.

The French, humiliated by the British and saddened by the fate of Canada, consoled themselves with one wishful thought. Perhaps the loss of their American empire would one day result in Britain's loss of its American empire. In a sense the history of the United States began with the fall of Québec and Montréal; the infant Republic was cradled on the Plains of Abraham.

The Spanish and Indian menaces were also now substantially reduced. Spain was (temporarily) eliminated from Florida, although entrenched in Louisiana and New Orleans, and was still securely in possession of much of western North America, including the vast territory from present-day Texas to California. As for the Indians, the Treaty of Paris that ended the Seven Years' War dealt a harsh blow to the Iroquois, Creeks, and other interior tribes. The Spanish removal from Florida and the French removal from Canada deprived the Indians of their most powerful diplomatic weapon—the ability to play off the rival European powers against one another. In the future the Indians would have to negotiate exclusively with the British.

Sensing the newly precarious position of the Indian peoples, the Ottawa chief Pontiac in 1763 led several tribes, aided by a handful of French traders who remained in the region, in a violent campaign to drive the British out of the Ohio Country. **Pontiac's uprising** laid siege to Detroit in the spring of 1763 and

MAP 6.8 British Colonies at End of the Seven Years' War, 1763 This map, showing the colonies thirteen years before the Declaration of Independence, helps to explain why the British would be unable to conquer their offspring. The colonists were spreading rapidly into the backcountry, where the powerful British navy could not flush them out. During the Revolutionary War, the British at one time or another captured the leading colonial cities—Boston, New York, Philadelphia, and Charleston—but the more remote interior remained a sanctuary for rebels. © Cengage Learning

Legend (within map):
- European settlement before 1700
- European settlement 1700–1763
- Frontier, 1763
- Proclamation Line of 1763
- Pontiac's uprising, 1763

eventually overran all but three British posts west of the Appalachians, killing some two thousand soldiers and settlers.

The British retaliated swiftly and cruelly. Waging a primitive version of biological warfare, one British commander ordered blankets infected with smallpox to be distributed among the Indians. Such tactics crushed the uprising and brought an uneasy truce to the frontier. His bold plan frustrated, Pontiac himself perished in 1769 at the hands of a rival chieftain. As for the British, the bloody episode convinced them of the need to stabilize relations with the western Indians and to keep regular troops stationed along the restless frontier, a measure for which they soon asked the colonists to foot the bill.

Land-hungry American colonists were now free to burst over the dam of the Appalachian Mountains and flood out over the verdant western lands. A tiny rivulet of pioneers had already trickled into Tennessee and Kentucky; other courageous settlers made their preparations for the long, dangerous trek over the mountains.

Then, out of a clear sky, the London government issued its **Proclamation of 1763**. It flatly prohibited settlement in the area beyond the Appalachians, pending further adjustments (see Map 6.8). The truth is that this hastily drawn document was not designed to oppress the colonists at all, but to work out the Indian problem fairly and prevent another bloody eruption like Pontiac's uprising.

But countless Americans, especially land speculators, were dismayed and angered. Was not the land beyond the mountains their birthright? Had they not, in addition, purchased it with their blood in the recent war? In complete defiance of the proclamation, they clogged the westward trails. In 1765 an estimated one thousand wagons rolled through the town of Salisbury, North Carolina, on their way "up west." This wholesale flouting of royal authority boded ill for the longevity of British rule in America.

The Seven Years' War also caused the colonists to develop a new vision of their destiny. With the path cleared for the conquest of a continent, with their birthrate high and their energy boundless, they sensed that they were a potent people on the march. And they were in no mood to be restrained.

Lordly Britons, whose suddenly swollen empire had tended to produce swollen heads, were in no mood for back talk. Puffed up over their recent victories, they were already annoyed with their unruly colonial subjects. The stage was set for a violent family quarrel.

Chapter Review

KEY TERMS

Huguenots (98)
Edict of Nantes (98)
coureurs de bois (99)
voyageurs (99)
King William's War (100)
Queen Anne's War (100)
War of Jenkins's Ear (101)
King George's War (102)
Acadians (104)
French and Indian War (Seven Years' War) (104)
Albany Congress (106)
regulars (106)
Québec, Battle of (107)
Pontiac's uprising (109)
Proclamation of 1763 (111)

PEOPLE TO KNOW

Louis XIV
Samuel de Champlain
Edward Braddock
William Pitt
James Wolfe
Pontiac

CHRONOLOGY

1598	Edict of Nantes (repealed in 1685)
1608	Champlain colonizes Québec for France
1643	Louis XIV becomes king of France
1682	La Salle explores Mississippi River to the Gulf of Mexico
1689–1697	King William's War (War of the League of Augsburg)
1702–1713	Queen Anne's War (War of Spanish Succession)
1718	French found New Orleans
1739	War of Jenkins's Ear

1744–1748	King George's War (War of Austrian Succession)
1754	Washington battles French on frontier Albany Congress
1756–1763	Seven Years' War (French and Indian War)
1755	Braddock's defeat
1757	Pitt emerges as leader of British government
1759	Battle of Québec
1763	Peace of Paris Pontiac's uprising Proclamation of 1763

TO LEARN MORE

Fred Anderson, *Crucible of War: The Seven Years' War and the Fate of Empire in British North America, 1754–1766* (2001)

David Armitage, ed., *The British Atlantic World, 1500–1800* (2002)

Colin G. Calloway, *The Scratch of a Pen: 1763 and the Transformation of America* (2006)

David Dixon, *Never Come to Peace Again: Pontiac's Uprising and the Fate of the British Empire in North America* (2005)

Elizabeth Mancke and Carole Shammas, eds., *The Creation of the British Atlantic World* (2005)

Jane T. Merrit, *At the Crossroads: Indians and Empires on a Mid-Atlantic Frontier, 1700–1763* (2007)

Paul David Nelson, *William Tryon and the Course of Empire: A Life in British Imperial Service* (1990)

Carolyn Podruchny, *Making the Voyageur World: Travelers and Traders in the North American Fur Trade* (2006)

James Pritchard, *In Search of Empire: The French in the Americas, 1670–1730* (2004)

Peter Silver, *Our Savage Neighbors: How Indian War Transformed Early America* (2007)

A complete, annotated bibliography for this chapter—along with brief descriptions of the People to Know—may be found on the American Pageant website. The Key Terms are defined in a Glossary at the end of the text.

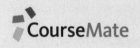

Go to the CourseMate website at **www.cengagebrain.com** for additional study tools and review materials—including audio and video clips—for this chapter.

AP® Review Questions for Chapter 6

1. What kept France from exploring the New World until the late sixteenth century?
   - (A) Lack of interest by the crown
   - (B) Ill-fated missions by early English settlers
   - (C) Foreign wars and internal conflicts
   - (D) The cost of financing an expedition
   - (E) Fear of repercussions from Spain and England

2. What decision did French explorer Samuel de Champlain make that had long-term negative consequences for France's conquest of the New World?
   - (A) He established Quebec as the capital of New France.
   - (B) He befriended the Huron Indians.
   - (C) He befriended the Iroquois.
   - (D) He drove out English settlers in the region.
   - (E) He antagonized Spanish and English explorers.

3. How did the government of the French colonies differ from that of the English colonies?
   - (A) The French colonies were run entirely by the crown.
   - (B) The French colonies established governments that were completely independent of the crown.
   - (C) Commercial companies had control over the French colonies.
   - (D) Colonists were granted a wide range of rights, including trial by jury.
   - (E) Settlers established a representative form of government elected by the people.

4. Settlement of the French colonies in New Canada grew very slowly until 1750 for all of the following reasons EXCEPT that
   - (A) there was plenty of available land for those who wanted it in their French homeland.
   - (B) Protestant Huguenots were prohibited from immigrating to the French colonies.
   - (C) the government focused on developing its Caribbean colonies.
   - (D) Canada's cold, snowy climate presented a difficult challenge.
   - (E) consumer demand for New France's main export, beaver skins, had dropped off considerably.

5. Which of the following was NOT a principal motivation for French exploration of territory beyond New France in the eighteenth century?
   - (A) Converting Indians to Christianity
   - (B) Keeping English settlers from moving into the nearby Ohio Valley
   - (C) Seeking new beaver supplies
   - (D) Thwarting Spain's attempts to claim land north of Mexico
   - (E) Difficulties with local native populations

6. After two wars for control of North America, in 1713, England and France signed a peace treaty that granted
   - (A) Acadia, Newfoundland, and Hudson Bay to the British.
   - (B) Acadia, Newfoundland, and Hudson Bay to the French.
   - (C) Maine and the Ohio Valley to France.
   - (D) Louisiana to the British.
   - (E) limited trading rights in Spanish Florida to the French.

7. All of the following Anglo-French colonial wars began in Europe EXCEPT
   - (A) King William's War.
   - (B) the French and Indian War.
   - (C) the War of Austrian Succession.
   - (D) Queen Anne's War.
   - (E) the War of Jenkins's Ear.

8. How did George Washington start the global war in 1754 that would later come to be known as the Seven Years' War?
   - (A) Washington forcibly relocated thousands of French Acadians from the area known as Nova Scotia to other French territories.
   - (B) Washington claimed, for his family, the same Ohio territory where the French had built Fort Duquesne.
   - (C) Washington's men killed a French military leader on the outskirts of Fort Duquesne.
   - (D) Washington recklessly attacked French forces without a battle plan.
   - (E) Washington sent an insulting letter to French leaders in the Ohio territory.

9. Prompted by the British to promote greater intercolonial unity and defense during the French and Indian War, the Albany Congress failed in its attempts to establish colonial home rule because
   (A) not all colonies sent representatives to Albany.
   (B) colonists felt it did not offer enough independence.
   (C) English authorities deemed such efforts illegal.
   (D) colonists were unwilling to fund the venture.
   (E) colonists wanted to preserve their individuality and did not see the need for union.

10. How did British leader William Pitt earn the nickname "Organizer for Victory"?
    (A) He shifted the failing British military strategy toward Quebec and Montreal.
    (B) He relied on the experience of older generals to lead.
    (C) He forced France to hand over to Spain its southernmost territories.
    (D) He trained colonists for military service.
    (E) He convinced colonists to donate funds for the war.

11. The intercolonial disunity that prevailed during the French and Indian War was caused by all of the following conditions EXCEPT
    (A) the prevalence of conflicting religions.
    (B) an enormous sense of geographic distance from one colony to the next.
    (C) varied nationalities.
    (D) differences about the continuation of slavery.
    (E) class tensions.

12. Colonists came away from their experience of the French and Indian War feeling
    (A) confident in their military might.
    (B) the desire for England to better safeguard its colonies.
    (C) increasingly concerned about Indian attacks.
    (D) a greater sense of oneness with their British compatriots.
    (E) eager to break off ties with England.

13. What key strategic tool did the Indians lose as a result of the war's outcome and the Treaty of Paris?
    (A) Alliances with Quakers and Christian missionaries
    (B) French and Spanish protection against the British
    (C) Strategic trading posts
    (D) Control of vital frontier territory
    (E) The ability to play rival European countries against each other

14. The Proclamation of 1763
    (A) exacted burdensome taxes from the colonists to finance England's war debts.
    (B) granted some frontier territory to Native Americans.
    (C) prohibited colonists from settling beyond the Appalachians.
    (D) established royal governors in the colonies.
    (E) made Florida a British territory.

15. In which of the following pairs is the second event a result of the first?
    (A) British triumph over Pontiac's Rebellion → the Proclamation of 1763
    (B) British invasion of Canada → end of the French and Indian War
    (C) the Albany Congress → desire for independence in the colonies
    (D) Queen Anne's War → King William's War
    (E) Louis XIV ascends the throne → conflict between France and Spain

16. Why was the French and Indian War a global war?
    (A) European nations, including France, Britain, and Spain, were among the belligerents.
    (B) The British attempted to persuade Native Americans to attack France.
    (C) It was a continuation of long-standing hostilities between Britain and France.
    (D) The war in America incited conflicts between other nations around the world.
    (E) Other nations mediated the peace settlement between the nations at war.

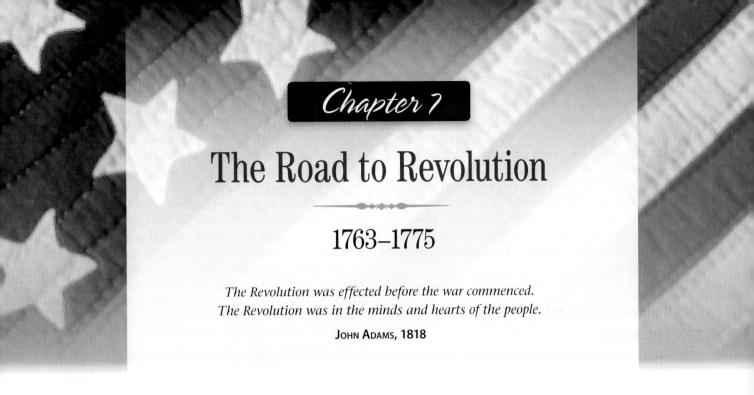

Chapter 7

The Road to Revolution

1763–1775

The Revolution was effected before the war commenced.
The Revolution was in the minds and hearts of the people.

JOHN ADAMS, 1818

Victory in the Seven Years' War made Britain the master of a vastly enlarged imperial domain in North America. But victory—including the subsequent need to garrison ten thousand troops along the sprawling American frontier—was painfully costly. The London government therefore struggled after 1763 to compel the American colonists to shoulder some of the financial costs of empire. This change in British colonial policy reinforced an emerging sense of American political identity and helped to precipitate the American Revolution.

The eventual conflict was by no means inevitable. Indeed, given the tightening commercial, military, and cultural bonds between colonies and mother country since the first crude settlements a century and a half earlier, it might be considered remarkable that the Revolution happened at all. The truth is that Americans were reluctant revolutionaries. Until late in the day, they sought only to claim the "rights of Englishmen," not to separate from the mother country. But what began as a squabble about economic policies soon exposed irreconcilable differences between Americans and Britons over cherished political principles. The ensuing clash gave birth to a new nation.

✴ The Deep Roots of Revolution

In a broad sense, America was a revolutionary force from the day of its discovery by Europeans. The New World nurtured new ideas about the nature of society, citizen, and government. In the Old World, many humble folk had long lived in the shadow of graveyards that contained the bones of their ancestors for a thousand years past. Few people born into such changeless surroundings dared to question their social status. But European immigrants in the New World were not so easily subdued by the scowl of their superiors. In the American wilderness, they encountered a world that was theirs to make afresh.

Two ideas in particular had taken root in the minds of the American colonists by the mid-eighteenth century: one was what historians call **republicanism**. Looking to the models of the ancient Greek and Roman republics, exponents of republicanism defined a just society as one in which all citizens willingly subordinated their private, selfish interests to the common good. Both the stability of society and the authority of government thus depended on the virtue of the citizenry—its capacity for selflessness, self-sufficiency, and courage, and especially its appetite for civic involvement. By its very nature, republicanism was opposed to hierarchical and authoritarian institutions such as aristocracy and monarchy.

A second idea that fundamentally shaped American political thought derived from a group of British political commentators known as **radical Whigs**. Widely read by the colonists, the Whigs feared the threat to liberty posed by the arbitrary power of the monarch and his ministers relative to elected representatives in Parliament. The Whigs mounted withering attacks on the use of patronage and bribes by the king's ministers—symptoms of a wider moral failure in society that they called "corruption," in the sense of rot or decay. The Whigs warned citizens to be on guard against corruption and to be eternally vigilant against possible conspiracies to denude them of their hard-won liberties. Together, republican and Whig ideas predisposed the

American colonists to be on hair-trigger alert against any threat to their rights.

The circumstances of colonial life had done much to bolster those attitudes. Dukes and princes, barons and bishops were unknown in the colonies, while property ownership and political participation were relatively accessible. The Americans had also grown accustomed to running their own affairs, largely unmolested by remote officials in London. Distance weakens authority; great distance weakens authority greatly. So it came as an especially jolting shock when Britain after 1763 tried to enclose its American colonists more snugly in its grip.

✴ Mercantilism and Colonial Grievances

Britain's empire was acquired in a "fit of absentmindedness," an old saying goes, and there is much truth in the jest. Not one of the original thirteen colonies except Georgia was formally planted by the British government. All the others were haphazardly founded by trading companies, religious groups, or land speculators.

The Female Combatants, 1776 Britain is symbolized as a lady of fashion; her rebellious daughter, America, as an Indian princess. Their shields of Obedience and Liberty seem mutually exclusive standards. Compare this cartoon with the one on p. 151.

The British authorities nevertheless embraced a theory, called **mercantilism**, that justified their control over the colonies. Mercantilists believed that wealth was power and that a country's economic wealth (and hence its military and political power) could be measured by the amount of gold or silver in its treasury. To amass gold or silver, a country needed to export more than it imported. Possessing colonies thus conferred distinct advantages, since the colonies could both supply raw materials to the mother country (thereby reducing the need for foreign imports) and provide a guaranteed market for exports.

The London government looked on the American colonists more or less as tenants. They were expected to furnish products needed in the mother country, such as tobacco, sugar, and ships' masts; to refrain from making for export certain products, such as woolen cloth or beaver hats; to buy imported manufactured goods exclusively from Britain; and not to indulge in bothersome dreams of economic self-sufficiency or, worse, self-government.

From time to time, Parliament passed laws to regulate the mercantilist system. The first of these, the Navigation Law of 1650, was aimed at rival Dutch shippers trying to elbow their way into the American carrying trade. Thereafter all commerce flowing to and from the colonies could be transported only in British (including colonial) vessels. Subsequent laws required that European goods destined for America first had to be landed in Britain, where tariff duties could be collected and British middlemen could take a slice of the profits. Other laws stipulated that American merchants must ship certain "enumerated" products, notably tobacco, exclusively to Britain, even though prices might be better elsewhere.

British policy also inflicted a currency shortage on the colonies. Since the colonists regularly bought more from Britain than they sold there, the difference had to be made up in hard cash. Every year gold and silver coins, mostly earned in illicit trade with the Spanish and French West Indies, drained out of the colonies, creating an acute money shortage. To facilitate everyday purchases, the colonists resorted to butter, nails, pitch, and feathers for purposes of exchange.

Currency issues came to a boil when dire financial need forced many of the colonies to issue paper money, which swiftly depreciated. British merchants and creditors squawked so loudly that Parliament prohibited the colonial legislatures from printing paper currency and from passing indulgent bankruptcy laws—practices that might harm British merchants. The Americans grumbled that their welfare was being sacrificed for the well-being of British commercial interests.

The British crown also reserved the right to nullify any legislation passed by the colonial assemblies if such

Paul Revere, 1786 by John Singleton Copley, Museum of Fine Arts, Boston, Gift of Joseph W. Revere, William B. Revere and Edward H. R. Revere

Paul Revere, by John Singleton Copley, ca. 1768 This painting of the famed silversmith-horseman challenged convention—but reflected the new democratic spirit of the age—by portraying an artisan in working clothes. Note how Copley depicted the serene confidence of the master craftsman and Revere's quiet pride in his work.

laws worked mischief with the mercantilist system. This royal veto was used rather sparingly—just 469 times in connection with 8,563 laws. But the colonists fiercely resented its very existence—another example of how principle could weigh more heavily than practice in fueling colonial grievances.

✵ The Merits and Menace of Mercantilism

In theory the British mercantile system seemed thoroughly selfish and deliberately oppressive. But the truth is that until 1763, the various Navigation Laws imposed no intolerable burden, mainly because they were only loosely enforced. Enterprising colonial merchants learned early to disregard or evade troublesome restrictions. Some of the first American fortunes, like that of John Hancock, were amassed by wholesale smuggling.

Americans also reaped direct benefits from the mercantile system. If the colonies existed for the benefit of the mother country, it was hardly less true that Britain existed for the benefit of the colonies. London

Adam Smith (1723–1790), the Scottish "Father of Modern Economics," frontally attacked mercantilism in 1776:

❝ To prohibit a great people, however, from making all that they can of every part of their own produce, or from employing their stock and industry in the way that they judge most advantageous to themselves, is a manifest violation of the most sacred rights of mankind.**❞**

paid liberal bounties to colonial producers of ship parts, over the protests of British competitors. Virginia tobacco planters enjoyed a monopoly in the British market, snuffing out the tiny British tobacco industry. The colonists also benefited from the protection of the world's mightiest navy and a strong, seasoned army of redcoats—all without a penny of cost.

But even when painted in its rosiest colors, the mercantile system burdened the colonists with annoying liabilities. Mercantilism stifled economic initiative and imposed a rankling dependency on British agents and creditors. Most grievously, many Americans simply found the mercantilist system debasing. They felt used, kept in a state of perpetual economic adolescence, and never allowed to come of age. As Benjamin Franklin wrote in 1775,

> *We have an old mother that peevish is grown;*
> *She snubs us like children that scarce walk alone;*
> *She forgets we're grown up and have sense of our own.*

Revolution broke out, as Theodore Roosevelt later remarked, because Britain failed to recognize an emerging nation when it saw one.

✵ The Stamp Tax Uproar

Victory-flushed Britain emerged from the Seven Years' War holding one of the biggest empires in the world—and also, less happily, the biggest debt, some £140 million, about half of which had been incurred defending the American colonies. To justify and service that debt, British officials now moved to redefine their relationship with their North American colonies.

Prime Minister George Grenville first aroused the resentment of the colonists in 1763 by ordering the British navy to begin strictly enforcing the Navigation Laws. He also secured from Parliament the so-called **Sugar Act** of 1764, the first law ever passed by that body for raising tax revenue in the colonies for the crown. Among various provisions, it increased the duty on foreign sugar imported from the West Indies. After

The Boston Gazette *declared in 1765,*

❝A colonist cannot make a button, a horseshoe, nor a hobnail, but some snooty ironmonger or respectable buttonmaker of Britain shall bawl and squall that his honor's worship is most egregiously maltreated, injured, cheated, and robbed by the rascally American republicans.❞

bitter protests from the colonists, the duties were lowered substantially, and the agitation died down. But resentment was kept burning by the **Quartering Act** of 1765. This measure required certain colonies to provide food and quarters for British troops.

Then in the same year, 1765, Grenville imposed the most odious measure of all: a **stamp tax**, to raise revenues to support the new military force. The Stamp Act mandated the use of stamped paper or the affixing of stamps, certifying payment of tax. Stamps were required on bills of sale for about fifty trade items as well as on certain types of commercial and legal documents, including playing cards, pamphlets, newspapers, diplomas, bills of lading, and marriage licenses.

Grenville regarded all of these measures as reasonable and just. He was simply asking the Americans to pay a fair share of the costs for their own defense, through taxes that were already familiar in Britain. In fact, the British people for two generations had endured a stamp tax far heavier than that passed for the colonies.

Yet the Americans were angrily aroused at what they regarded as Grenville's fiscal aggression. The new laws did not merely pinch their pocketbooks. Far more ominously, Grenville also seemed to be striking at the local liberties they had come to assume as a matter of right. Thus some colonial assemblies defiantly refused to comply with the Quartering Act, or voted only a fraction of the supplies that it called for.

Worst of all, Grenville's noxious legislation seemed to jeopardize the basic rights of the colonists as Englishmen. Both the Sugar Act and the Stamp Act provided

English statesman Edmund Burke (1729–1797) warned in 1775,

❝Young man, there is America—which at this day serves for little more than to amuse you with stories of savage men and uncouth manners; yet shall, before you taste of death, show itself equal to the whole of that commerce which now attracts the envy of the world.❞

for trying offenders in the hated **admiralty courts**, where juries were not allowed. The burden of proof was on the defendants, who were assumed to be guilty unless they could prove themselves innocent. Trial by jury and the precept of "innocent until proved guilty" were ancient privileges that British people everywhere, including the American colonists, held most dear.

And why was a British army needed at all in the colonies, now that the French were expelled from the continent and Pontiac's warriors crushed? Could its real purpose be to whip rebellious colonists into line? Many Americans, weaned on radical Whig suspicion of all authority, began to sniff the strong scent of a conspiracy to strip them of their historic liberties. They lashed back violently, and the Stamp Act became the target that drew their most ferocious fire.

Angry throats raised the cry "No taxation without representation." There was some irony in the slogan, because the seaports and tidewater towns that were most wrathful against the Stamp Act had long denied full representation to their own backcountry pioneers. But now the aggravated colonists took the high ground of principle.

The Americans made a distinction between "legislation" and "taxation." They conceded the right of Parliament to legislate about matters that affected the entire empire, including the regulation of trade. But they steadfastly denied the right of Parliament, in which no Americans were seated, to impose taxes on Americans. Only their own elected colonial legislatures, the Americans insisted, could legally tax them. Taxes levied by the distant British Parliament amounted to robbery, a piratical assault on the sacred rights of property.

Grenville dismissed these American protests as hairsplitting absurdities. The power of Parliament was supreme and undivided, he asserted, and in any case the Americans *were* represented in Parliament. Elaborating the theory of "virtual representation," Grenville claimed that every member of Parliament represented all British subjects, even those Americans in Boston or Charleston who had never voted for a member of Parliament.

The Americans scoffed at the notion of virtual representation. And truthfully, they did not really want direct representation in Parliament, which might have seemed like a sensible compromise. If they had obtained it, any gouty member of the House of Commons could have proposed an oppressive tax bill for the colonies, and the outvoted American representatives, few in number, would have stood bereft of a principle with which to resist.

Thus the principle of no taxation without representation was supremely important, and the colonists clung to it with tenacious consistency. When the British replied that the sovereign power of government could not be divided between "legislative" authority in London and "taxing" authority in the colonies, they forced the Americans to deny the authority of Parliament altogether and to begin to consider their own political independence. This chain of logic eventually led, link by link, to revolutionary consequences.

✷ Forced Repeal of the Stamp Act

Colonial outcries against the hated stamp tax took various forms. The most conspicuous assemblage was the **Stamp Act Congress** of 1765, which brought together in New York City twenty-seven distinguished delegates from nine colonies. After dignified debate the members drew up a statement of their rights and grievances and beseeched the king and Parliament to repeal the repugnant legislation.

The Stamp Act Congress, which was largely ignored in England, made little splash at the time in America. Its ripples, however, began to erode sectional suspicions, for it brought together around the same table leaders from the different and rival colonies. It was one more halting but significant step toward intercolonial unity.

More effective than the congress was the widespread adoption of **nonimportation agreements** against British goods. Woolen garments of homespun became fashionable, and the eating of lamb chops was discouraged so that the wool-bearing sheep would be allowed to mature. Nonimportation agreements were in fact a promising stride toward union; they spontaneously united the American people for the first time in common action.

Mobilizing in support of nonimportation gave ordinary American men and women new opportunities

John Dickinson (1732–1808), a lawyer and popular essayist, advocated a middle-of-the-road response to the new British revenue acts of the 1760s that appealed to most colonists at the time:

❝ The constitutional modes of obtaining relief are those which I wish to see pursued on the present occasion. . . . We have an excellent prince, in whose good disposition we may confide. . . . Let us behave like dutiful children who have received unmerited blows from a beloved parent. Let us complain to our parent; but let our complaint speak at the same time the language of affliction and veneration.**❞**

to participate in colonial protests. Many people who had previously stood on the sidelines now signed petitions swearing to uphold the terms of the consumer boycotts. Groups of women assembled in public to hold spinning bees and make homespun cloth as a replacement for shunned British textiles. Such public defiance helped spread angry resistance throughout American colonial society.

Sometimes violence accompanied colonial protests. Groups of ardent spirits, known as **Sons of Liberty** and **Daughters of Liberty**, took the law into their own hands. Crying "Liberty, Property, and No Stamps," they enforced the nonimportation agreements against violators, often with a generous coat of tar and feathers. Patriotic mobs ransacked the houses of unpopular officials, confiscated their money, and hanged effigies of stamp agents on liberty poles.

Shaken by colonial commotion, the machinery for collecting the tax broke down. On that dismal day in

Protesting the Stamp Act Even common household wares in the 1760s testified to the colonists' mounting rage against the Stamp Act. Many people in Britain sympathized with the Americans—and sought to profit from their anger, as this English-made teapot demonstrates. National Museum of American History, Smithsonian Institution, Behring Center

1765 when the new act was to go into effect, the stamp agents had all been forced to resign, and there was no one to sell the stamps. While flags flapped at half-mast, the law was openly and flagrantly defied—or, rather, nullified.

England was hard hit. America then bought about one-quarter of all British exports, and about one-half of British shipping was devoted to the American trade. Merchants, manufacturers, and shippers suffered from the colonial nonimportation agreements, and hundreds of laborers were thrown out of work. Loud demands converged on Parliament for repeal of the Stamp Act. But many of the members could not understand why 7.5 million Britons had to pay heavy taxes to protect the colonies, whereas some 2 million colonists refused to pay for only one-third of the cost of their own defense.

After a stormy debate, Parliament in 1766 grudgingly repealed the Stamp Act. Grateful residents of New York erected a leaden statue to King George III. But American rejoicing was premature. Having withdrawn

Public Punishment for the Excise Man, 1774 This popular rendering of the punishment of Commissioner of Customs John Malcomb shows him tarred and feathered and forcibly "paid" with great quantities of tea. From the Liberty Tree in the background dangles the threat of hanging, all for attempting to collect duties in Boston.

Courtesy of the John Carter Brown Library at Brown University

the Stamp Act, Parliament in virtually the same breath provocatively passed the **Declaratory Act**, reaffirming Parliament's right "to bind" the colonies "in all cases whatsoever." The British government thereby drew its line in the sand. It defined the constitutional principle it would not yield: absolute and unqualified sovereignty over its North American colonies. The colonists had already drawn their own battle line by making it clear that they wanted a measure of sovereignty of their own and would undertake drastic action to secure it. The stage was set for a continuing confrontation. Within a few years, that statue of King George would be melted into thousands of bullets to be fired at his troops.

✷ The Townshend Tea Tax and the Boston "Massacre"

Control of the British ministry was now seized by the gifted but erratic Charles ("Champagne Charley") Townshend, a man who could deliver brilliant speeches in Parliament even while drunk. Rashly promising to pluck feathers from the colonial goose with a minimum of squawking, he persuaded Parliament in 1767 to pass the **Townshend Acts**. The most important of these new regulations was a light import duty on glass, white lead, paper, paint, and tea. Townshend, seizing on a dubious distinction between internal and external taxes, made this tax, unlike the stamp tax, an indirect customs duty payable at American ports. But to the increasingly restless colonists, this was a phantom distinction. For them the real difficulty remained taxes—in any form—without representation.

Flushed with their recent victory over the stamp tax, the colonists were in a rebellious mood. The impost on tea was especially irksome, for an estimated 1 million people drank the refreshing brew twice a day.

The new Townshend revenues, worse yet, were to be earmarked to pay the salaries of the royal governors and judges in America. From the standpoint of efficient administration by London, this was a reform long overdue. But the ultrasuspicious Americans, who had beaten the royal governors into line by controlling the purse, regarded Townshend's tax as another attempt to enchain them. Their worst fears took on greater reality when the London government, after passing the Townshend taxes, suspended the legislature of New York in 1767 for failure to comply with the Quartering Act.

Nonimportation agreements, previously potent, were quickly revived against the Townshend Acts. But they proved less effective than those devised against the Stamp Act. The colonists, again enjoying prosperity, took the new tax less seriously than might have been expected, largely because it was light and indirect.

Library of Congress

Two Views of the Boston Massacre, 1770 and 1856   Both of these prints of the Boston Massacre were art as well as propaganda. Paul Revere's engraving (left) began circulating within three weeks of the event in March 1770, depicting not a clash of brawlers but armed soldiers taking aim at peaceful citizens. Absent also was any evidence of the mulatto ringleader, Crispus Attucks. Revere wanted his print to convince viewers of the indisputable justice of the colonists' cause. By the mid-1850s, when the chromolithograph (right) circulated, it served a new political purpose. In the era of the abolitionist movement, freedman Crispus Attucks held center place in the print, which portrayed his death as an American martyr in the revolutionary struggle for freedom.

They found, moreover, that they could secure smuggled tea at a cheap price, and consequently smugglers increased their activities, especially in Massachusetts.

British officials, faced with a breakdown of law and order, landed two regiments of troops in Boston in 1768. Many of the soldiers were drunken and profane characters. Liberty-loving colonists, resenting the presence of the red-coated "ruffians," taunted the "bloody backs" unmercifully.

A clash was inevitable. On the evening of March 5, 1770, a crowd of some sixty towns-people began taunting and throwing snowballs at a squad of ten redcoats. The Bostonians were still angry over the death of an eleven-year-old boy, shot ten days earlier during a protest against a merchant who had defied the colonial boycott of British goods. Acting apparently without orders, but nervous and provoked by the jeering crowd, the troops opened fire and killed or wounded eleven citizens, an event that became known as the **Boston Massacre**. One of the first to die was Crispus Attucks, described by contemporaries as a powerfully built runaway "mulatto" and a leader of the mob. Both sides were in some degree to blame, and in the subsequent trial (in which future president John Adams served as defense attorney for the soldiers), only two of the redcoats were found guilty of manslaughter. The soldiers were released after being branded on the hand.

Giving new meaning to the proverbial tempest in a teapot, a group of 126 Boston women signed an agreement, or "subscription list," that announced,

❝We the Daughters of those Patriots who have and now do appear for the public interest . . . do with Pleasure engage with them in denying ourselves the drinking of Foreign Tea, in hopes to frustrate a Plan that tends to deprive the whole Community of . . . all that is valuable in Life.**❞**

✴ The Seditious Committees of Correspondence

By 1770 King George III, then only thirty-two years old, was strenuously attempting to assert the power of the British monarchy. He was a good man in his private morals, but he proved to be a bad ruler. Earnest, industrious, stubborn, and lustful for power, he surrounded himself with cooperative "yes men," notably his corpulent prime minister, Lord North.

Samuel Adams about 1722 by John Singleton Copley, Museum of Fine Arts, Boston. Deposited by the City of Boston, L-R 30-76c. Photograph © 2008 Museum of Fine Arts, Boston

Samuel Adams (1722–1803) A second cousin of John Adams, he contributed a potent pen and tongue to the American Revolution as a political agitator and organizer of rebellion. He was the leading spirit in hosting the Boston Tea Party. A failure in the brewing business, he was sent by Massachusetts to the First Continental Congress of 1774. He signed the Declaration of Independence and served in Congress until 1781.

Fenimore Art Museum, Cooperstown, New York

Portrait Traditionally Said to Be That of Abigail Adams (1744–1818) The wife of Revolutionary War leader and future president John Adams, she was a prominent Patriot in her own right. She was also among the first Americans to see, however faintly, the implications of revolutionary ideas for changing the status of women.

The ill-timed Townshend Acts had failed to produce revenue, though they did produce near-rebellion. Net proceeds from the tax in one year were a paltry £295, while in that same year Britain's military costs in the colonies had mounted to £170,000. Nonimportation agreements, though feebly enforced, were pinching British manufacturers. The government of Lord North, bowing to various pressures, finally persuaded Parliament to repeal the Townshend revenue duties. But the three-pence toll on tea, the tax the colonists found most offensive, was retained to keep alive the principle of Parliament's right to tax the colonies.

Flames of discontent in America continued to be fanned by numerous incidents, including the redoubled efforts of the British officials to enforce the Navigation Laws. Resistance was further kindled by a master propagandist and engineer of rebellion, Samuel Adams of Boston, a cousin of John Adams. Unimpressive in appearance (his hands trembled), he lived and breathed only for politics. His friends had to buy him a presentable suit of clothes when he left Massachusetts

on intercolonial business. Zealous, tenacious, and courageous, he was ultrasensitive to infractions of colonial rights. Cherishing a deep faith in the common people, he appealed effectively to what was called his "trained mob."

Samuel Adams's signal contribution was to organize in Massachusetts the local **committees of correspondence**. After he had formed the first one in Boston during 1772, some eighty towns in the colony speedily set up similar organizations. Their chief function was to spread the spirit of resistance by exchanging letters and thus keep alive opposition to British policy. One critic referred to the committees as "the foulest, subtlest, and most venomous serpent ever issued from the egg of sedition."

Intercolonial committees of correspondence were the next logical step. Virginia led the way in 1773 by creating such a body as a standing committee of the House of Burgesses. Within a short time, every colony had established a central committee through which it could exchange ideas and information with other colonies. These intercolonial groups were supremely significant in stimulating and disseminating sentiment in favor of united action. They evolved directly into the first American congresses.

✴ Tea Brewing in Boston

Thus far—that is, by 1773—nothing had happened to make rebellion inevitable. Nonimportation was weakening. Increasing numbers of colonists were reluctantly paying the tea tax, because the legal tea was now cheaper than the smuggled tea, even cheaper than tea in England.

A new ogre entered the picture in 1773. The powerful British East India Company, overburdened with 17 million pounds of unsold tea, was facing bankruptcy. If it collapsed, the London government would lose heavily in tax revenue. The ministry therefore decided to assist the company by awarding it a complete monopoly of the American tea business. The giant corporation would now be able to sell the coveted leaves more cheaply than ever before, even with the three-pence tax tacked on. But many American tea drinkers, rather than rejoicing at the lower prices, cried foul. They saw this British move as a shabby attempt to trick the Americans, with the bait of cheaper tea, into swallowing the principle of the detested tax. For the determined Americans, principle remained far more important than price.

If the British officials insisted on the letter of the law, violence would certainly result. Fatefully, the British colonial authorities decided to enforce the law. Once more, the colonists rose up in wrath to defy it. Not a single one of the several thousand chests of tea shipped by the East India Company ever reached the hands of the consignees. In Philadelphia and New York, mass demonstrations forced the tea-bearing ships to return to England with their cargo holds still full. At Annapolis, Marylanders burned both cargo and vessel, while proclaiming "liberty and Independence or death in pursuit of it." In Charleston, South Carolina, officials seized the tea for nonpayment of duties after intimidated local merchants refused to accept delivery. (Ironically, the confiscated Charleston tea was later auctioned to raise money for the Revolutionary army.)

Only in Boston did a British official stubbornly refuse to be cowed. Massachusetts governor Thomas Hutchinson had already felt the fury of the mob, when Stamp Act protesters had destroyed his home in 1765. This time he was determined not to budge. Ironically, Hutchinson agreed that the tea tax was unjust, but he believed even more strongly that the colonists had no right to flout the law. Hutchinson infuriated Boston's radicals when he ordered the tea ships not to clear Boston harbor until they had unloaded their cargoes. Sentiment against him was further inflamed when Hutchinson's enemies published one of his private letters in which he declared that "an abridgment of what are called English liberties" was necessary for the preservation of law and order in the colonies—apparently confirming the darkest conspiracy theories of the American radicals.

On December 16, 1773, roughly a hundred Bostonians, loosely disguised as Indians, boarded the docked ships, smashed open 342 chests of tea, and dumped their contents into the Atlantic, an action that came to be known as the **Boston Tea Party**. A crowd of several hundred watched approvingly from the shore as Boston harbor became a vast teapot. Donning Indian disguise provided protesters with a threatening image—and a convenient way of avoiding detection.

Library of Congress

The Boston Tea Party, December 16, 1773 Crying "Boston harbor a teapot this night," Sons of Liberty disguised as Indians hurled chests of tea into the sea to protest the tax on tea and to make sure that its cheap price did not prove an "invincible temptation" to the people.

Ann Hulton (d. 1779?), a Loyalist, described colonial political divisions and her hopes and fears for her own future in a letter she sent to a friend in England in 1774:

“ Those who are well disposed towards Government are termed Tories. They daily increase & have made some efforts to take the power out of the hands of the Patriots, but they are intimidated & overpowered by Numbers. . . . However I don't despair of seeing Peace & tranquility in America, tho' they talk very high & furious at present. **”**

Tea was the perfect symbol to rally around as almost every colonist, rich or poor, consumed this imported, caffeinated beverage.

Reactions varied. All up and down the eastern seaboard, sympathetic colonists applauded. Referring to tea as "a badge of slavery," they burned the hated leaves in solidarity with Boston. But conservatives complained that the destruction of private property violated the law and threatened anarchy and the breakdown of civil decorum. Hutchinson, chastened and disgusted with the colonies, retreated to Britain, never to return. The British authorities, meanwhile, saw little alternative to whipping the upstart colonists into shape. The granting of some measure of home rule to the Americans might at this stage still have prevented rebellion, but few British politicians were willing to swallow their pride and take the high road. The perilous path they chose instead led only to reprisals, bitterness, and escalating conflict.

✪ Parliament Passes the "Intolerable Acts"

An irate Parliament responded speedily to the Boston Tea Party with measures that brewed a revolution. By huge majorities in 1774, it passed a series of acts designed to chastise Boston in particular, and Massachusetts in general. They were branded in America as "the massacre of American Liberty."

Most drastic of all was the Boston Port Act. It closed the tea-stained harbor until damages were paid and order could be ensured. By other "**Intolerable Acts**"—as they were called in America—many of the chartered rights of colonial Massachusetts were swept away. Restrictions were likewise placed on the precious town meetings. Contrary to previous practice, enforcing officials who killed colonists in the line of duty could now be sent to Britain for trial. There, suspicious Americans assumed, they would be likely to get off

scot-free. Particularly intolerable to Bostonians was a new Quartering Act, which gave local authorities the power to lodge British soldiers anywhere, even in private homes.

By a fateful coincidence, the "Intolerable Acts" were accompanied in 1774 by the **Quebec Act**. Passed at the same time, it was erroneously regarded in English-speaking America as part of the British reaction to the turbulence in Boston. Actually, the Quebec Act was a good law in bad company. For many years the British government had debated how it should administer the sixty thousand or so conquered French subjects in Canada, and it had finally framed this farsighted and statesmanlike measure. The French were guaranteed their Catholic religion. They were also permitted to retain many of their old customs and institutions, which did not include a representative assembly or trial by jury in civil cases. In addition, the old boundaries of the province of Québec were now extended southward all the way to the Ohio River.

The Quebec Act, from the viewpoint of the French Canadians, was a shrewd and conciliatory measure. If Britain had only shown as much foresight in dealing with its English-speaking colonies, it might not have lost them.

But from the viewpoint of the American colonists as a whole, the Quebec Act was especially noxious. All the other "Intolerable Acts" slapped directly at Massachusetts, but this one had a much wider range. By sustaining unrepresentative assemblies and denials of jury trials, it seemed to set a dangerous precedent in America. It alarmed land speculators, who were distressed to see the huge trans-Allegheny area snatched from their grasp (see Map 7.1). It aroused anti-Catholics, who were shocked by the extension of Roman Catholic jurisdiction southward into a huge region that had once been earmarked for Protestantism—a region about as large as the thirteen original colonies. One angry Protestant cried that there ought to be a "jubilee in hell" over this enormous gain for "Popery."

✪ Bloodshed

American dissenters responded sympathetically to the plight of Massachusetts. It had put itself in the wrong by the violent destruction of the tea cargoes; now Britain had put itself in the wrong by brutal punishment that seemed far too cruel for the crime. Flags were flown at half-mast throughout the colonies on the day that the Boston Port Act went into effect, and sister colonies rallied to send food to the stricken city. Rice was shipped even from faraway South Carolina.

Most memorable of the responses to the "Intolerable Acts" was the summoning of the **First Continental**

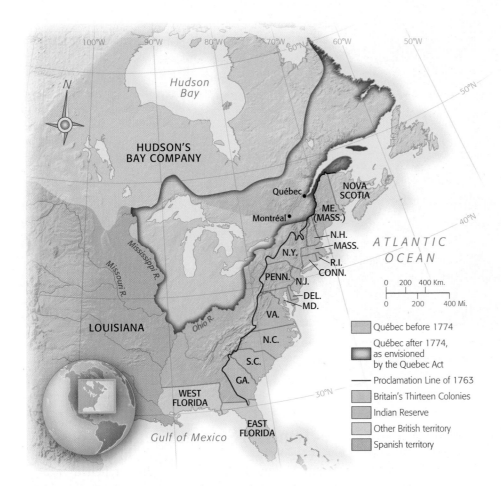

MAP 7.1 Québec Before and After 1774 Young Alexander Hamilton voiced the fears of many colonists when he warned that the Quebec Act of 1774 would introduce "priestly tyranny" into Canada, making that country another Spain or Portugal. "Does not your blood run cold," he asked, "to think that an English Parliament should pass an act for the establishment of arbitrary power and Popery in such a country?" © Cengage Learning

Congress in 1774. It was to meet in Philadelphia to consider ways of redressing colonial grievances. Twelve of the thirteen colonies, with Georgia alone missing, sent fifty-five well-respected men, among them Samuel Adams, John Adams, George Washington, and Patrick Henry. Intercolonial frictions were partially melted away by social activity after working hours; in fifty-four days George Washington dined at his own lodgings only nine times.

The First Continental Congress deliberated for seven weeks, from September 5 to October 26, 1774. It was not a legislative but a consultative body—a convention rather than a congress. John Adams played a stellar role. Eloquently swaying his colleagues to a revolutionary course, he helped defeat by the narrowest of margins a proposal by the moderates for a species of American home rule under British direction. After prolonged argument the Congress drew up several

dignified papers. These included a ringing Declaration of Rights, as well as solemn appeals to other British American colonies, to the king, and to the British people.

The most significant action of the Congress was the creation of **The Association**. Unlike previous nonimportation agreements, The Association called for a complete boycott of British goods: nonimportation, nonexportation, and nonconsumption. Yet it is important to note that the delegates were not yet calling for independence. They sought merely to repeal the offensive legislation and return to the happy days before parliamentary taxation. If colonial grievances were redressed, well and good; if not, the Congress was to meet again in May 1775. Resistance had not yet ripened into open rebellion.

But the fatal drift toward war continued. Parliament rejected the Congress's petitions. In America

A View of the Town of Concord, ca. 1775 Redcoats here drill on the Concord Green, near where colonial militiamen would soon repel their advance on stores of rebel gunpowder.

chickens squawked and tar kettles bubbled as violators of The Association were tarred and feathered. Muskets were gathered, men began to drill openly, and a clash seemed imminent.

In April 1775 the British commander in Boston sent a detachment of troops to nearby **Lexington and Concord**. They were to seize stores of colonial gunpowder and also to bag the "rebel" ringleaders, Samuel Adams and John Hancock. At Lexington the colonial "Minute Men" refused to disperse rapidly enough, and shots were fired that killed eight Americans and wounded several more. The affair was more the "Lexington Massacre" than a battle. The redcoats pushed on to Concord, whence they were forced to retreat by the rough and ready Americans, whom Emerson immortalized:

> *By the rude bridge that arched the flood,*
> *Their flag to April's breeze unfurled,*
> *Here once the embattled farmers stood,*
> *And fired the shot heard round the world.**

The bewildered British, fighting off murderous fire from militiamen crouched behind thick stone walls, finally regained the sanctuary of Boston. Licking their wounds, they could count about three hundred casualties, including some seventy killed. Britain now had a war on its hands.

---

*Ralph Waldo Emerson, "Concord Hymn."

✷ Imperial Strength and Weakness

Aroused Americans had brashly rebelled against a mighty empire (see "Thinking Globally: Imperial Rivalry and Colonial Revolt," pp. 126–127). The population odds were about three to one against the

The great conservative political theorist and champion of the American cause Edmund Burke made a stirring speech in Britain's House of Commons in 1775, pleading in vain for reconciliation with the colonies:

❝As long as you have the wisdom to keep the sovereign authority of this country as the sanctuary of liberty . . . they will turn their faces towards you. . . . Slavery they can have anywhere; freedom they can have from none but you. This is the commodity of price, of which you have the monopoly. This is the true Act of Navigation, which binds to you the commerce of the colonies, and through them secures to you the wealth of the world. Deny them this participation of freedom, and you break that sole bond which originally made, and must still preserve, the unity of the empire.**❞**

rebels—some 7.5 million Britons to 2.5 million colonists. The odds in monetary wealth and naval power overwhelmingly favored the mother country.

Britain then boasted a professional army of some fifty thousand men, as compared with the numerous but wretchedly trained American militia. George III, in addition, had the treasury to hire foreign soldiers, and some thirty thousand Germans—so-called Hessians—were ultimately employed. The British enrolled about fifty thousand American Loyalists and enlisted the services of many Indians, who though unreliable fair-weather fighters, inflamed long stretches of the frontier. One British officer boasted that the war would offer no problems that could not be solved by an "experienced sheep herder."

Yet Britain was weaker than it seemed at first glance. Oppressed Ireland was a smoking volcano, and British troops had to be detached to watch it. France, bitter from its recent defeat, was awaiting an opportunity to stab Britain in the back. The London government was confused and inept. There was no William Pitt, "Organizer of Victory," only the stubborn George III and his pliant Tory prime minister, Lord North.

Many earnest and God-fearing Britons had no desire whatever to kill their American cousins. William Pitt withdrew a son from the army rather than see him thrust his sword into fellow Anglo-Saxons struggling for liberty. The English Whig factions, opposed to Lord North's Tory wing, openly cheered American victories—at least at the outset. Aside from trying to embarrass the Tories politically, many Whigs believed that the battle for British freedom was being fought in America. If George III triumphed, his rule at home might become tyrannical. This outspoken sympathy in Britain, though plainly a minority voice, greatly encouraged the Americans. If they continued their resistance long enough, the Whigs might come into power and deal generously with them.

Britain's army in America had to operate under endless difficulties. The generals were second-rate; the soldiers, though on the whole capable, were brutally treated. There was one extreme case of eight hundred lashes on the bare back for striking an officer. Provisions were often scarce, rancid, and wormy. On one occasion a supply of biscuits, captured some fifteen years earlier from the French, was softened by dropping cannonballs on them.

Other handicaps loomed. The redcoats had to conquer the Americans; restoring the pre-1763 status quo would be a victory for the colonists. Britain was operating some 3,000 miles from its home base, and distance added greatly to the delays and uncertainties arising from storms and other mishaps. Military orders were issued in London that, when received months later, would not fit the changing situation.

America's geographical expanse was enormous: roughly 1,000 by 600 miles. The united colonies had no urban nerve center, like France's Paris, whose capture would cripple the country as a whole. British armies took every city of any size, yet like a boxer punching a feather pillow, they made little more than a dent in the entire country. The Americans wisely traded space for time. Benjamin Franklin calculated that during the prolonged campaign in which the redcoats captured Bunker Hill and killed some 150 Patriots, about 60,000 American babies were born.

✴ American Pluses and Minuses

The revolutionaries were blessed with outstanding leadership. George Washington was a giant among men; Benjamin Franklin was a master among diplomats. Open foreign aid, theoretically possible from the start, eventually came from France. Numerous European officers, many of them unemployed and impoverished, volunteered their swords for pay. In a class by himself was a wealthy young French nobleman, the Marquis de Lafayette. Fleeing from boredom, loving glory and ultimately liberty, the "French gamecock" was made a major general in the colonial army at age nineteen. His commission was largely a recognition of his family influence and political connections, but the services of this teenage general in securing further aid from France were invaluable.

Other conditions aided the Americans. They were fighting defensively, with the odds, all things considered, favoring the defender. In agriculture, the colonies were mainly self-sustaining, like a kind of Robinson Crusoe's island. The Americans also enjoyed the moral advantage that came from belief in a just cause. The historical odds were not impossible. Other peoples had triumphed in the face of greater obstacles: Greeks against Persians, Swiss against Austrians, Dutch against Spaniards.

Yet the American rebels were badly organized for war. From the earliest days, they had been almost fatally lacking in unity, and the new nation lurched forward uncertainly like an uncoordinated centipede.

General Washington's (1732–1799) disgust with his countrymen is reflected in a diary entry for 1776:

"Chimney corner patriots abound; venality, corruption, prostitution of office for selfish ends, abuse of trust, perversion of funds from a national to a private use, and speculations upon the necessities of the times pervade all interests.**"**

Imperial Rivalry and Colonial Revolt

In 1765 tax revolts exploded almost simultaneously in both Britain's and Spain's New World empires. In Boston the hated Stamp Act sparked riots and inspired a campaign to boycott British goods. At virtually the same moment in Quito (in present-day Ecuador), a two-mile-high Spanish colonial city nearly twice the size of Boston, surging crowds ransacked the local tax collector's office. Among other demands, they insisted that "pure" Spaniards leave Quito unless they had married into the native Creole (New World–born white) or indigenous Indian communities. Spanish officials restored order by force of arms, but antitax agitation continued to smolder everywhere in Spanish America. "There is no American," a Quito lawyer remarked, "who does not reject any novelty whatsoever in the management of taxation"—a sentiment that resonated as strongly in Philadelphia as in Mexico City.

Things soon got worse. Madrid's New World imperial authority was shaken to the core in 1781 when another tax revolt erupted in New Granada (present-day Colombia). By that time, the British colonials' War of Independence in North America was in its fifth year.

Intensifying imperial rivalry fueled events on both the American continents. Until the mid-seventeenth century, the three great Old World powers—England, France, and Spain—had largely confined their competition to struggles over boundaries and religious affiliation on the European continent. But after the Treaty of Westphalia in 1648 brought a truce to the wars of religion that had racked Europe for decades (the Thirty Years' War), great-power competition began to shift overseas. The faraway New World imperial outposts of Britain, Spain, and France now became pawns in a global struggle for mastery in Europe.

The Seven Years' War (1756–1763) ushered in a still more ferocious cycle of imperial conflict. Britain succeeded in expelling France from North America, but victory brought the burdens of managing vast new territories as well as the prospect of fresh confrontations with Native Americans threatened by westward expansion. Spain, France's erstwhile ally, grew increasingly wary of the newly invigorated and ambitious British Empire, which threatened Spanish interests at sea and along the sketchy borderlands that separated the two powers' imperial domains. As the risks and costs of imperial competition soared, London and Madrid adopted the same strategy: pressure the colonies to pay their share. New taxes and customs duties followed, along with more energetic efforts to collect them. To imperial officials like Britain's Prime Minister George Grenville or Madrid's "visitor general" to New Spain, José Gálvez, such reforms seemed not only

Collection of Martha Davidson

Tupac Amaru II   A Peruvian national hero, Tupac Amaru II is memorialized to this day with his portrait on the nation's currency.

De Español, y Mestiza, Castiza.

Couple with Child by Miguel Cabera This eighteenth-century portrait of a Mexican family illustrates the common intermarriage of Europeans and Indians in the Spanish New World. The ethnic complexity of Spanish America kept colonists there from uniting against imperial authorities as successfully as their northern neighbors.

reasonable but in tune with Enlightenment ideas about efficient administration. To colonial subjects these new policies were an anathema, a flagrant offense to their fundamental rights as colonial subjects.

But why did revolts against these new imperial policies kindle a full-fledged war for independence in the British colonies but not in Spanish America—at least not until Napoleon's invasion of Spain in 1808 hurled the Spanish Empire into tumult?

The role of rich and powerful allies provides part of the answer. The North American rebels could count on Britain's French and Spanish enemies to tender financial as well as military support. Spanish American anticolonial rebels had no such allies in London or Paris, which saw little prospect of unraveling the Spanish Empire and were already fully engaged on opposite sides of the American War of Independence.

The demographic composition of the two empires furnishes another part

of the answer. Spanish America was badly riven by sharp ethnic and racial divisions. The Spanish court had long encouraged the relatively few Spaniards who settled in the New World to intermarry with the local inhabitants. By the eighteenth century, the Spanish colonies had become a complex, tension-ridden mosaic of European, Creole, *mestizo*, and Indian peoples and cultures. When in 1780 the self-proclaimed Incan royal descendant Tupac Amaru II rebelled against Spanish rule, he at first attracted Creoles, but they bolted as the movement radicalized, and his rebellion was soon cruelly crushed.

To be sure, the British North American colonists had their ethnic differences, too, but many fewer. They had nurtured a culture of exclusion, rejecting intermarriage with Indians and blacks and banishing Indians to the wilderness. And they faced no Indian threat on the scale of Tupac Amaru II's uprising.

Inherited political traditions also played different roles. British settlers enjoyed long-standing institutions of political representation. They had brought with them from the mother country devotion to individual rights and the privilege of legal assembly that, when revolution came, gave their cause the kind of legitimacy that comes from time-honored habits. It was precisely the violation of those rights and privileges that "taxation without representation" seemed to threaten. Spanish colonists had representative institutions, too, but in Spain's much more autocratic imperial scheme, local assemblies lacked the authority, autonomy, and legitimacy they had come to enjoy in the British domains. North American colonists asserted their right to self-government on the basis of their historic rights as British subjects, a claim that was much more difficult to make in the absolutist monarchy of the Spanish Empire.

Gilbert du Motier, Marquis de Lafayette (1757–1834), by Joseph Boze, 1790 This youthful French officer gave to America not only military service but some $200,000 of his private funds. He returned to France after the American Revolution to play a conspicuous role in the French Revolution.

Even the Continental Congress, which directed the conflict, was hardly more than a debating society, and it grew feebler as the struggle dragged on. "Their Congress now is quite disjoint'd," gibed an English satirist, "Since Gibbits (gallows) [are] for them appointed." The disorganized colonists fought almost the entire war before adopting a written constitution—the Articles of Confederation—in 1781.

Jealousy everywhere raised its hideous head. Individual states, proudly regarding themselves as sovereign, resented the attempts of Congress to exercise its flimsy powers. Sectional jealousy boiled up over the appointment of military leaders; some distrustful New Englanders almost preferred British officers to Americans from other sections.

Economic difficulties were nearly insuperable. Metallic money had already been heavily drained away. A cautious Continental Congress, unwilling to raise anew the explosive issue of taxation, was forced to print "Continental" paper money in great amounts. As this currency poured from the presses, it depreciated until the expression "not worth a Continental" became current. One barber contemptuously papered his shop with the near-worthless dollars. The confusion proliferated when the individual states were compelled to issue depreciated paper money of their own.

Inflation of the currency inevitably skyrocketed prices. Families of the soldiers at the fighting front were hard hit, and hundreds of anxious husbands and fathers deserted. Debtors easily acquired handfuls of the quasi-worthless money and gleefully paid their debts "without mercy"—sometimes with the bayonets of the authorities to back them up.

A Thin Line of Heroes

Basic military supplies in the colonies were dangerously scanty. While many families and towns did own firearms—widespread militia service meant men needed weapons for training—the colonists had long relied heavily on Britain for troops, armaments, and military subsidies during expensive wars against Indians, France, and Spain. The rebels were caught in an unavoidable trap: at the very moment that the supply of British funds and war materiel evaporated, the cost of home defense mounted. Sufficient stores of gunpowder, cannon, and other armaments (let alone ships to transport them) could not be found. Among the reasons for the eventual alliance with France was the need for a reliable source of essential military supplies.

Other shortages bedeviled the rebels. At **Valley Forge**, Pennsylvania, shivering American soldiers went without bread for three successive days in the cruel winter of 1777–1778. In one southern campaign, some men fainted for lack of food. Manufactured goods also were generally in short supply in agricultural America, and clothing and shoes were appallingly scarce. The path of the Patriot fighting men was often marked by bloody snow. At frigid Valley Forge, during one anxious period, twenty-eight hundred men were barefooted or nearly naked. Woolens were desperately needed against the wintry blasts, and in general the only real uniform of the colonial army was uniform raggedness. During a grand parade at Valley Forge, some of the officers appeared wrapped in woolen bedcovers. One Rhode Island unit was known as the "Ragged, Lousy, Naked Regiment."

American militiamen were numerous but also highly unreliable. Able-bodied American males—perhaps several hundred thousand of them—had received rudimentary training. But poorly trained plowboys could not stand up in the open field against professional British troops advancing with bare bayonets. Many of these undisciplined warriors would, in the words of Washington, "fly from their own shadows." At the same time, deadly smallpox outbreaks ravaged the army, further weakening forces.

The Flutist, by Brazilla Lew   This portrait is believed to be that of an African American fifer in the Revolutionary War. Lew was a veteran of the Seven Years' War who had marched to Ticonderoga and served in the army a full seven years as frontline soldier, fifer, and drummer. In 1775, at the age of thirty-two, he fought at Bunker Hill as an enlistee in the 27th Massachusetts Regiment. A resident of Chelmsford, Massachusetts, he was said to have taught all twelve of his children to play musical instruments.

Women played a significant part in the Revolution. Many maintained farms and businesses while their fathers and husbands fought. Large numbers of female **camp followers** accompanied the American army, cooking and sewing for the troops in return for money and rations. One Massachusetts woman dressed in men's clothing and served in the army for seventeen months.

A few thousand regulars—perhaps seven or eight thousand at the war's end—were finally whipped into shape by stern drillmasters. Notable among them was an organizational genius, the salty German Baron von Steuben. He spoke no English when he reached America, but he soon taught his men that bayonets were not for broiling beefsteaks over open fires. As they gained experience, these soldiers of the Continental line more than held their own against crack British troops.

Enslaved blacks hoped that the Revolutionary crisis would make it possible for them to secure their own liberty. On the eve of the war in South Carolina, merchant Josiah Smith, Jr., noted such a rumor among the slaves:

❝[Freedom] is their common Talk throughout the Province, and has occasioned impertinent behavior in many of them, insomuch that our Provincial Congress now sitting hath voted the immediate raising of Two Thousand Men Horse and food, to keep those mistaken creatures in awe.**❞**

Despite such repressive measures, slave uprisings continued to plague the southern colonies through 1775 and 1776.

Blacks also fought and died for the American cause. Although many states initially barred them from militia service, by war's end more than five thousand blacks had enlisted in the American armed forces. The largest contingents came from the northern states with substantial numbers of free blacks.

Blacks fought at Trenton, Brandywine, Saratoga, and other important battles. Some, including Prince Whipple—later immortalized in Emanuel Leutze's famous painting "Washington Crossing the Delaware" (see p. 143)—became military heroes. Others served as cooks, guides, spies, drivers, and road builders.

African Americans also served on the British side. In November 1775 Lord Dunmore, royal governor of Virginia, issued a proclamation promising freedom for any enslaved black in Virginia who joined the British army. News of Dunmore's decree traveled swiftly. Virginia and Maryland tightened slave patrols, but within one month, three hundred slaves had joined what came to be called "Lord Dunmore's Ethiopian Regiment." In time thousands of blacks fled plantations for British promises of emancipation. When one of James Madison's slaves was caught trying to escape to the British lines, Madison refused to punish him for "coveting that liberty" that white Americans proclaimed the "right & worthy pursuit of every human being." At war's end the British kept their word, to some at least, and evacuated as many as fourteen thousand "Black Loyalists" to Nova Scotia, Jamaica, and England.

Morale in the Revolutionary army was badly undermined by American profiteers. Putting profits before patriotism, they sold to the British because the invader could pay in gold. Speculators forced prices sky-high, and some Bostonians made profits of 50 to 200 percent on army garb while the American army was freezing at Valley Forge. Washington never had as many as twenty thousand effective troops in one place at one time, despite bounties of land and other inducements. Yet if the rebels had thrown themselves into the struggle with zeal, they could easily have raised many times that number.

The brutal truth is that only a select minority of the American colonists attached themselves to the cause of independence with a spirit of selfless devotion. These were the dedicated souls who bore the burden of battle and the risks of defeat. Seldom have so few done so much for so many.

Chapter Review

KEY TERMS

republicanism (113)
radical Whigs (113)
mercantilism (114)
Sugar Act (115)
Quartering Act (116)
stamp tax (116)
admiralty courts (116)
Stamp Act Congress (117)
nonimportation agreements (117)
Sons of Liberty (117)
Daughters of Liberty (117)
Declaratory Act (118)
Townshend Acts (118)

Boston Massacre (119)
committees of correspondence (120)
Boston Tea Party (121)
"Intolerable Acts" (122)
Quebec Act (122)
First Continental Congress (122)
The Association (123)
Lexington and Concord, Battles of (124)
Valley Forge (128)
camp followers (128)

PEOPLE TO KNOW

John Hancock
George Grenville
Charles ("Champagne Charley") Townshend
Crispus Attucks
George III

Lord North
Samuel Adams
Thomas Hutchinson
Marquis de Lafayette
Baron von Steuben
Lord Dunmore

CHRONOLOGY

1650	First Navigation Laws to control colonial commerce
1696	Board of Trade assumes governance of colonies
1763	Seven Years' War (French and Indian War) ends
1764	Sugar Act
1765	Quartering Act Stamp Act Stamp Act Congress
1766	Declaratory Act
1767	Townshend Acts New York legislature suspended by Parliament
1768	British troops occupy Boston

1770	Boston Massacre All Townshend Acts except tea tax repealed
1772	Committees of correspondence formed
1773	British East India Company granted tea monopoly Governor Hutchinson's actions provoke Boston Tea Party
1774	"Intolerable Acts" Quebec Act First Continental Congress The Association boycotts British goods
1775	Battles of Lexington and Concord

TO LEARN MORE

R. B. Bernstein, *Thomas Jefferson* (2003)

Timothy H. Breen, *The Marketplace of Revolution: How Consumer Politics Shaped American Independence* (2004)

David Hackett Fischer, *Paul Revere's Ride* (1994)

Sylvia R. Frey, *Water from the Rock: Black Resistance in a Revolutionary Age* (1991)

Woody Holton, *Forced Founders: Indians, Debtors, Slaves, and the Making of the American Revolution in Virginia* (1999)

Pauline Maier, *From Resistance to Revolution: Colonial Radicals and the Development of American Opposition to Britain, 1765–1776* (1972)

David McCullough, *John Adams* (2001)

Robert Middlekauff, *The Glorious Cause: The American Revolution, 1763–1789* (2005)

Edmund S. Morgan and Helen M. Morgan, *The Stamp Act Crisis* (1953)

Joseph C. Morton, *The American Revolution* (2003)

Ray Raphael, *A People's History of the American Revolution* (2001)

Walter Stahr, *John Jay: Founding Father* (2005)

Alfred F. Young, *The Shoemaker and the Tea Party* (1999)

A complete, annotated bibliography for this chapter—along with brief descriptions of the People to Know—may be found on the American Pageant website. The Key Terms are defined in a Glossary at the end of the text.

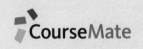

Go to the CourseMate website at **www.cengagebrain.com** for additional study tools and review materials—including audio and video clips—for this chapter.

AP® Review Questions for Chapter 7

1. The republican and Whig ideologies that English colonists embraced by the mid-eighteenth century included all of the following tenets EXCEPT that
   (A) power should be centralized within the monarchy.
   (B) citizens should put the public good ahead of their self-interest.
   (C) a functioning society is based on the virtue of its citizenry.
   (D) self-sufficiency, courage, and civic involvement are crucial for republican societies.
   (E) hierarchical governments breed corruption.

2. Which of the following circumstances did NOT influence America's attitudes about rights and the nature of government by the 1750s?
   (A) The aristocracy that was common in England never took hold in the colonies.
   (B) Property ownership and political participation was more easily accessible in the colonies.
   (C) Colonists had become accustomed to running things for themselves, with little interference from the crown.
   (D) Colonies universally embraced religious toleration.
   (E) The vast ocean expanse that distanced England from the colonies also weakened its ability to exert its authority.

3. Britain's relationship with its colonies was based on mercantilism, the theory that
   (A) wealth is power, and colonies could be used to enrich the mother country.
   (B) colonies should develop independent trade so as not to financially burden the mother country.
   (C) commerce should be allowed to develop, uninhibited by government interference.
   (D) England had the right to tax and regulate the colonies as it saw fit.
   (E) the colonies should become economically self-sufficient within twenty-five years of settlement.

4. The colonists detested the mercantilist system for all of these reasons EXCEPT that
   (A) it kept them in a state of economic dependency.
   (B) it caused a currency surplus.
   (C) England nullified any laws passed by colonial governments that interfered with the mercantilist system.
   (D) it restricted how American goods could be transported or sold.
   (E) it required the colonies to buy certain goods only from Britain.

5. In what ways did mercantilism benefit the colonists?
   (A) England provided subsidies for surplus crops.
   (B) Mercantilism helped several colonial merchants become wealthy.
   (C) It elevated some colonists to positions of political power.
   (D) It stimulated American wool manufacturing.
   (E) Britain granted them certain trade monopolies and protected them militarily.

6. To raise money to cover debts incurred in the Seven Years' War and to reassert authority over its North American colonies, Britain passed and enforced all of the following measures EXCEPT the
   (A) Navigation Acts.
   (B) Sugar Act.
   (C) Intolerable Act.
   (D) Quartering Act.
   (E) Stamp Act.

7. Americans responded to Britain's many new taxes in the 1760s with the line, "No taxation without representation." What did this mean exactly?
   (A) That Americans wanted to have representatives in Parliament before they would accept tax legislation passed there
   (B) That only colonial legislatures could tax the colonies
   (C) That colonists would accept virtual representation in fiscal matters
   (D) That Parliament put the needs of citizens in England above those of its colonists
   (E) That the king was the ultimate representative, and therefore, exclusively held the power to tax

8. Which of these protests against the Stamp Act was most effective in ultimately securing its repeal?
   (A) The Stamp Act Congress of 1765
   (B) Petitions to Parliament
   (C) Nonimportation agreements
   (D) Violent protests
   (E) Refusal to pay the tax

9. British colonists were outraged by the Townshend Act for all of the following reasons EXCEPT that
   (A) it sought to skirt the issue of taxation by imposing "duties" instead.
   (B) it taxed many of their favorite imported goods.
   (C) monies collected under the act would pay the salaries of royal officials.
   (D) it included a provision to close any colonial port that did not pay the duties.
   (E) it was yet another example of taxation without representation.

10. The Boston Massacre, which occurred on March 5, 1770, describes
    (A) a protest in which colonists burned Governor Thomas Hutchinson's house to the ground.
    (B) a standoff between colonists and redcoats that resulted in the deaths of eleven Bostonians.
    (C) a mob protest in which two dozen British soldiers were killed.
    (D) the first military battle between the Sons of Liberty and the British.
    (E) the dumping of 342 chests of imported tea and other goods into Boston harbor.

11. What was the most significant role of the Committees of Correspondence?
    (A) Writing broadsides
    (B) Encouraging women's participation in boycotts and rebellions
    (C) Building momentum for a complete break with England
    (D) Seeking every colony's participation in the first American Congress
    (E) Organizing local letter-writing campaigns to fortify colonial resistance to British policies

12. Why did tea become the focus of protests against British policies that ended with the Boston Tea Party in 1773?
    (A) The price of tea had skyrocketed under the British East India Company's trade monopoly.
    (B) Colonists resented England's attempt to force only one tea source on them.
    (C) Tea touched the lives of colonists from every social class.
    (D) It was England's leading export.
    (E) Colonists could easily go without tea.

13. The First Continental Congress met in 1774 principally to
    (A) strategize ways to redress colonial grievances.
    (B) declare the colony's independence from England.
    (C) outline a new national government for the future United States.
    (D) organize a colonial army.
    (E) enlist the support of other countries in their conflict with England.

14. Both Britain and Spain pressured their colonies with new taxes to help pay their share of the Seven Years' War, but reaction to these policies led to a war for independence only among British colonists for all of the following reasons EXCEPT that
    (A) Britain had rich and powerful enemies that colonists could tap for assistance.
    (B) Spanish colonies were far more ethnically and racially divided.
    (C) British settlers were accustomed to more liberal local governments than those in Spain and its colonies.
    (D) rights were a central component of British notions of citizenship.
    (E) British colonists had established local militias from the earliest days of settlement.

15. Which of the following lists is chronologically accurate?
    (A) Stamp Act, Boston Tea Party, Intolerable Acts, Townshend Acts
    (B) Sugar Act, Boston Massacre, The Association, Intolerable Acts
    (C) Stamp Act, Boston Tea Party, Lexington and Concord, First Continental Congress
    (D) Sugar Act, Townshend Acts, Boston Tea Party, First Continental Congress
    (E) Declaratory Act, Quebec Act, Boston Massacre, Quartering Act

16. At the beginning of the Revolutionary War, British victory seemed certain because
    (A) the British were more familiar with the terrain on which the fighting occurred.
    (B) Britain boasted a professional army of fifty thousand men.
    (C) the British cause was morally justified.
    (D) the Whigs and Tories were united in their goals for the American colonies.
    (E) Britain had the support of other European nations.

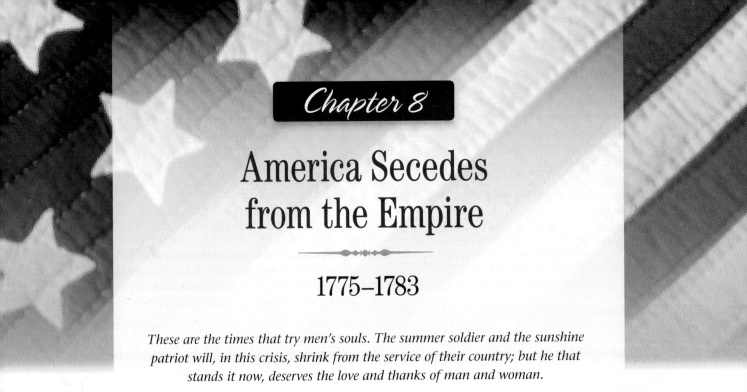

Chapter 8

America Secedes from the Empire

1775–1783

These are the times that try men's souls. The summer soldier and the sunshine patriot will, in this crisis, shrink from the service of their country; but he that stands it now, deserves the love and thanks of man and woman.

THOMAS PAINE, DECEMBER 1776

*B*loodshed at Lexington and Concord in April of 1775 was a clarion call to arms. About twenty thousand musket-bearing "Minute Men" swarmed around Boston, there to coop up the outnumbered British.

The **Second Continental Congress** met in Philadelphia the next month, on May 10, 1775, and this time the full slate of thirteen colonies was represented. The conservative element in Congress was still strong, despite the shooting in Massachusetts. There was still no well-defined sentiment for independence—merely a desire to continue fighting in the hope that the king and Parliament would consent to a redress of grievances. Congress hopefully drafted new appeals to the British people and king—appeals that were spurned. Anticipating a possible rebuff, the delegates also adopted measures to raise money and to create an army and a navy. The British and the Americans now teetered on the brink of all-out warfare.

✪ Congress Drafts George Washington

Perhaps the most important single action of the Congress was to select George Washington, one of its members already in an officer's uniform, to head the hastily improvised army besieging Boston. This choice was made with considerable misgivings. The tall, powerfully built, dignified Virginia planter, then forty-three, had never risen above the rank of a colonel in the militia.

His largest command had numbered only twelve hundred men, and that had been some twenty years earlier. Falling short of true military genius, Washington would actually lose more pitched battles than he won.

But the distinguished Virginian was gifted with outstanding powers of leadership and immense strength of character. He radiated patience, courage, self-discipline, and a sense of justice. He was a great moral force rather than a great military mind—a symbol and a rallying point. People instinctively trusted him; they sensed that when he put himself at the head of a cause, he was prepared, if necessary, to go down with the ship. He insisted on serving without pay, though he kept a careful expense account amounting to more than $100,000. Later he sternly reprimanded his steward at Mount Vernon for providing the enemy, under duress, with supplies. He would have preferred instead to see the enemy put the torch to his mansion.

The Continental Congress, though dimly perceiving Washington's qualities of leadership, chose more wisely than it knew. His selection, in truth, was largely political. Americans in other sections, already jealous, were beginning to distrust the large New England army being collected around Boston. Prudence suggested a commander from Virginia, the largest and most populous of the colonies. As a man of wealth, both by inheritance and by marriage, Washington could not be accused of being a fortune-seeker. As an aristocrat, he could be counted on by his peers to check "the excesses of the masses."

Washington at Verplanck's Point, New York, 1782, Reviewing the French Troops After the Victory at Yorktown, by John Trumbull, 1790 This noted American artist accentuated Washington's already imposing height (six feet two inches) by showing him towering over his horse. Washington so appreciated this portrait of himself that he hung it in the dining room of his home at Mount Vernon, Virginia.

✯ Bunker Hill and Hessian Hirelings

The clash of arms continued on a strangely contradictory basis. On the one hand, the Americans were emphatically affirming their loyalty to the king and earnestly voicing their desire to patch up difficulties. On the other hand, they were raising armies and shooting down His Majesty's soldiers. This curious war of inconsistency was fought for fourteen long months—from April 1775 to July 1776—before the fateful plunge into independence was taken.

Gradually the tempo of warfare increased. In May 1775 a tiny American force under Ethan Allen and Benedict Arnold surprised and captured the British

garrisons at Ticonderoga and Crown Point, on the scenic lakes of upper New York. A priceless store of gunpowder and artillery for the siege of Boston was thus secured. In June 1775 the colonists seized a hill, now known as **Bunker Hill** (actually Breed's Hill), from which they menaced the enemy in Boston. The British, instead of cutting off the retreat of their foes by flanking them, blundered bloodily when they launched a frontal attack with three thousand men. Sharpshooting Americans, numbering fifteen hundred and strongly entrenched, mowed down the advancing redcoats with frightful slaughter. But the colonists' scanty store of gunpowder finally gave out, and they were forced to abandon the hill in disorder. With two more such victories, remarked the French foreign minister, the British would have no army left in America.

Even at this late date, in July 1775, the Continental Congress adopted the **Olive Branch Petition**, professing American loyalty to the crown and begging the king to prevent further hostilities. But following Bunker Hill, King George III slammed the door on all hope of reconciliation. In August 1775 he formally proclaimed the colonies in rebellion; the skirmishes were now out-and-out treason, a hanging crime. The next month he widened the chasm when he sealed arrangements for hiring thousands of German troops to help crush his rebellious subjects. Six German princes involved in the transaction needed the money (one reputedly had seventy-four children); George III needed the men. Because most of these soldiers-for-hire came from the German principality of Hesse, the Americans called all the European mercenaries **Hessians**.

News of the Hessian deal shocked the colonists. The quarrel, they felt, was within the family. Why bring in outside mercenaries, especially foreigners who had an exaggerated reputation for butchery?

Hessian hirelings proved to be good soldiers in a mechanical sense, but many of them were more interested in booty than in duty. For good reason they were dubbed "Hessian flies." Seduced by American promises of land, hundreds of them finally deserted and remained in America to become respected citizens.

✯ The Abortive Conquest of Canada

The unsheathed sword continued to take its toll. In October 1775, on the eve of a cruel winter, the British burned Falmouth (Portland), Maine. In that same autumn, the rebels daringly undertook a two-pronged invasion of Canada. American leaders believed, erroneously, that the conquered French were explosively restive under the British yoke. A successful assault on Canada would add a fourteenth colony, while depriving Britain of a valuable base for striking at the colonies

Granger Collection

Battle of Bunker Hill, June 17, 1775 This British engraving conveys the vulnerability of the British regulars to attacks by the American militiamen. Although a defeat for the colonists, the battle quickly proved a moral victory for the Patriots. Outnumbered and outgunned, they held their own against the British and suffered many fewer casualties.

in revolt. But this large-scale attack, involving some two thousand American troops, contradicted the claim of the colonists that they were merely fighting defensively for a redress of grievances. Invasion northward was undisguised offensive warfare.

This bold stroke for Canada narrowly missed success (see Map 8.1). One invading column under the Irish-born General Richard Montgomery, formerly of the British army, pushed up the Lake Champlain route and captured Montréal. He was joined at Québec by the bedraggled army of General Benedict Arnold, whose men had been reduced to eating dogs and shoe leather during their grueling march through the Maine woods. An assault on Québec, launched on the last day of 1775, was beaten off. The able Montgomery was killed; the dashing Arnold was wounded in one leg. Scattered remnants under his command retreated up the St. Lawrence River, reversing the way Montgomery had come. French Canadian leaders, who had been generously treated by the British in the Quebec Act of 1774, showed no real desire to welcome the plundering anti-Catholic invaders.

Bitter fighting persisted in the colonies, though most Americans continued to disclaim a desire for

independence. In January 1776 the British set fire to the Virginia town of Norfolk. In March they were finally forced to evacuate Boston, taking with them the leading friends of the king. (Evacuation Day is still celebrated annually in Boston.) In the South the rebellious colonists won two victories in 1776—one in February against some fifteen hundred Loyalists at Moore's Creek Bridge in North Carolina, and the other in June against an invading British fleet at Charleston harbor.

✷ Thomas Paine Preaches Common Sense

Why did Americans continue to deny any intention of independence? Loyalty to the empire was deeply ingrained; many Americans continued to consider themselves part of a transatlantic community in which the mother country of Britain played a leading role; colonial unity was poor; and open rebellion was dangerous, especially against a formidable Britain. Irish rebels of that day were customarily hanged, drawn, and quartered. American rebels might have fared no better.

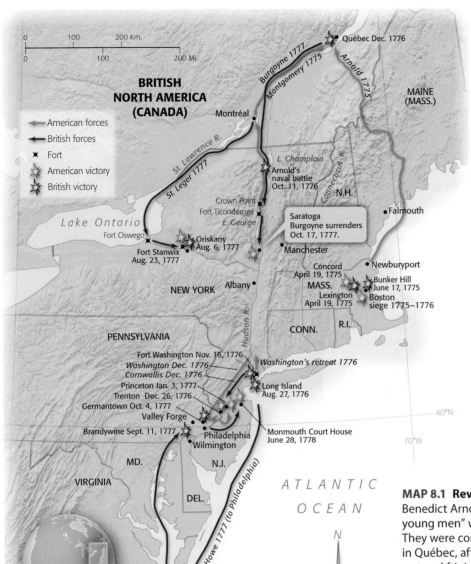

MAP 8.1 Revolution in the North, 1775–1776
Benedict Arnold's troops were described as "pretty young men" when they sailed from Massachusetts. They were considerably less pretty on their arrival in Québec, after eight weeks of struggling through wet and frigid forests, often without food. "No one can imagine," one of them wrote, "the sweetness of a roasted shot-pouch [ammunition bag] to the famished appetite." © Cengage Learning

As late as January 1776—five months before independence was declared—the king's health was being toasted by the officers of Washington's mess near Boston. "God save the king" had not yet been replaced by "God save the Congress."

Gradually the Americans were shocked into recognizing the necessity of separating from the crown. Their eyes were jolted open by harsh British acts like the burning of Falmouth and Norfolk, and especially by the hiring of the Hessians.

Then in 1776 came the publication of ***Common Sense***, one of the most influential pamphlets ever written. Its author was the radical Thomas Paine, once an impoverished corset-maker's apprentice, who had come

over from Britain a year earlier. He began his incendiary tract with a treatise on the nature of government and eloquently anticipated Thomas Jefferson's declaration that the only lawful states were those that derive "their just powers from the consent of the governed." As for the king, whom the Americans professed to revere, he was nothing but "the Royal Brute of Great Britain." *Common Sense* became a whirlwind best seller. Within a few months the astonishing total of 120,000 copies were sold.

Paine flatly branded the shilly-shallying of the colonists as contrary to "common sense." Nowhere in the physical universe did the smaller heavenly body control the larger one. So why should the tiny island of

In Common Sense *Thomas Paine (1737-1809) argued for the superiority of a republic over a monarchy:*

" The nearer any government approaches to a republic the less business there is for a king. It is somewhat difficult to find a proper name for the government of England. Sir William Meredith calls it a republic; but in its present state it is unworthy of the name, because the corrupt influence of the crown, by having all the places in its disposal, hath so effectively swallowed up the power, and eaten out the virtue of the house of commons (the republican part of the constitution) that the government of England is nearly as monarchical as that of France or Spain.**"**

Thomas Paine, by Auguste Millière

Britain control the vast continent of America? Paine's pen went a long way toward convincing the American colonists that their true cause was independence rather than reconciliation with Britain—not least because without independence, they could not hope for foreign assistance. Paine could thus be said to have drafted the foundational document not only of American independence, but of American foreign policy as well.

✷ Paine and the Idea of "Republicanism"

Paine's passionate protest was as compelling as it was eloquent and radical—even doubly radical. It called not simply for independence, but for the creation of a new kind of political society, a *republic*, where power flowed from the people themselves, not from a corrupt and despotic monarch. In language laced with biblical imagery familiar to common folk, he argued that all government officials—governors, senators, and judges—not just representatives in a house of commons, should derive their authority from popular consent.

Paine was hardly the first person to champion a republican form of government. Political philosophers had advanced the idea since the days of classical Greece and Rome. Revived in the Renaissance and in seventeenth-century England, republican ideals had uneasily survived within the British "mixed government," with its delicate balance of king, nobility, and commons. Republicanism particularly appealed to British politicians critical of excessive power in the hands of the king and his advisers. Their writings found a responsive audience among the American colonists, who interpreted the vengeful royal acts of the previous

decade as part of a monarchical conspiracy to strip them of their liberties as British subjects. Paine's radical prescription for the colonies—to reject monarchy and empire and embrace an independent republic—fell on receptive ears.

The colonists' experience with governance had prepared them well for Paine's summons to create a republic. Many settlers, particularly New Englanders, had practiced a kind of republicanism in their democratic town meetings and annual elections, while the popularly elected committees of correspondence during 1774 and 1775 had demonstrated the feasibility of republican government. The absence of a hereditary

The French philosopher Abbé Raynal (1713-1796) wrote in 1770,

" If any fortunate revolution should take place in the world, it will begin in America. . . . It will become the asylum of our people who have been oppressed by political establishments, or driven away by war.**"**

aristocracy and the relative equality of condition enjoyed by landowning farmers meshed well with the republican repudiation of a fixed hierarchy of power.

Most Americans considered citizen "virtue" fundamental to any successful republican government. Because political power no longer rested with the central, all-powerful authority of the king, individuals in a republic needed to sacrifice their personal self-interest to the public good. The collective good of "the people" mattered more than the private rights and interests of individuals. Paine inspired his contemporaries to view America as fertile ground for the cultivation of such civic virtue.

Yet not all Patriots agreed with Paine's ultra-democratic approach to republicanism. Some favored a republic ruled by a "natural aristocracy" of talent. Republicanism for them meant an end to hereditary aristocracy, but not an end to all social hierarchy. These more conservative republicans feared that the fervor for liberty would overwhelm the stability of the social order. They watched with trepidation as the "lower orders" of society—poorer farmers, tenants, and laboring classes in towns and cities—seemed to embrace a kind of runaway republicanism that amounted to radical "leveling." The contest to define the nature of American republicanism would noisily continue for at least the next hundred years.

✳ Jefferson's "Explanation" of Independence

Members of the Philadelphia Congress, instructed by their respective colonies, gradually edged toward a clean break. On June 7, 1776, fiery Richard Henry Lee of Virginia moved that "these United Colonies are, and of right ought to be, free and independent states." After considerable debate, the motion was adopted nearly a month later, on July 2, 1776.

The passing of Lee's resolution was the formal "declaration" of independence by the American colonies, and technically this was all that was needed to cut the British tie. John Adams wrote confidently that ever thereafter, July 2 would be celebrated annually with fireworks. But something more was required. An epochal rupture of this kind called for some formal explanation. An inspirational appeal was also needed to enlist other British colonies in the Americas, to invite assistance from foreign nations, and to rally resistance at home.

Shortly after Lee made his memorable motion on June 7, Congress appointed a committee to prepare a more formal statement of separation. The task of drafting it fell to Thomas Jefferson, a tall, freckled, sandy-haired Virginia lawyer of thirty-three. Despite his youth, he was already recognized as a brilliant writer,

The American signers of the Declaration of Independence had reason to fear for their necks. In 1802, twenty-six years later, George III (1738–1820) approved this death sentence for seven Irish rebels:

❝. . . [You] are to be hanged by the neck, but not until you are dead; for while you are still living your bodies are to be taken down, your bowels torn out and burned before your faces, your heads then cut off, and your bodies divided each into four quarters, and your heads and quarters to be then at the King's disposal; and may the Almighty God have mercy on your souls.❞

and he measured up splendidly to the awesome assignment. After some debate and amendment, the **Declaration of Independence** was formally approved by the Congress on July 4, 1776. It might better have been called "the Explanation of Independence" or, as one contemporary described it, "Mr. Jefferson's advertisement of Mr. Lee's resolution."

Jefferson's pronouncement, couched in a lofty style, was magnificent. He gave his appeal universality by invoking the "natural rights" of humankind—not just British rights. He argued persuasively that because the king had flouted these rights, the colonists were justified in cutting their connection. He then set forth a long list of the presumably tyrannous misdeeds of George III. The overdrawn bill of indictment included imposing taxes without consent, dispensing with trial by jury, abolishing valued laws, establishing a military dictatorship, maintaining standing armies in peacetime, cutting off trade, burning towns, hiring mercenaries, and inciting hostility among the Indians.*

Jefferson's withering blast was admittedly one-sided. He acted, in effect, as a prosecuting attorney, and he took certain liberties with historical truth. He was not writing history; he was making it through what has been called "the world's greatest editorial." He owned many slaves, and his affirmation that "all men are created equal" was to haunt him and his fellow citizens for generations.

The formal Declaration of Independence cleared the air as a thundershower does on a muggy day. As Paine had predicted, and as events were to prove, foreign assistance could now be solicited with greater hope of success. Those Patriots who defied the king were now rebels, not loving subjects shooting their way into reconciliation. They must all hang together, Franklin is said to have grimly remarked, or they would all hang

---

*For an annotated text of the Declaration of Independence, see the Appendix.

A Revolution for Women? Abigail Adams Chides Her Husband, 1776

In the midst of the revolutionary fervor of 1776, at least one woman—Abigail Adams, wife of noted Massachusetts Patriot (and future president) John Adams—raised her voice on behalf of women. Yet she apparently raised it only in private—in this personal letter to her husband. Private documents like the correspondence and diaries of individuals both prominent and ordinary offer invaluable sources for the historian seeking to discover sentiments, opinions, and perspectives that are often difficult to discern in the official public record. What might it suggest about the historical circumstances of the 1770s that Abigail Adams confined her claim for women's equality to this confidential exchange with her spouse? What might have inspired the arguments she employed? Despite her privileged position and persuasive power, and despite her threat to "foment a rebellion," Abigail Adams's plea went largely unheeded in the Revolutionary era—as did comparable pleadings to extend the revolutionary principle of equality to blacks. What might have accounted for this limited application of the ideas of liberty and equality in the midst of a supposedly democratic revolution?

Massachusetts Historical Society

King George III of England (1738–1820), by Johann Zoffany, 1771   America's last king, he was a good man, unlike some of his scandal-tainted brothers and sons, but a bad king. Doggedly determined to regain arbitrary power for the crown, he antagonized and then lost the thirteen American colonies. During much of his sixty-year reign, he seemed to be insane, but recently medical science has found that he was suffering from a rare metabolic and hereditary disease called porphyria.

separately. Or, in the eloquent language of the great declaration, "We mutually pledge to each other our lives, our fortunes and our sacred honor."

Jefferson's defiant Declaration of Independence had a universal impact unmatched by any other American document. This "shout heard round the world" has been a source of inspiration to countless revolutionary movements against arbitrary authority. Lafayette hung a copy on a wall in his home, leaving beside it room for a future French **Declaration of the Rights of Man**—a declaration that was officially born thirteen years later.

✴ Patriots and Loyalists

The War of Independence, strictly speaking, was a war within a war. Colonials loyal to the king (**Loyalists**) fought the American rebels (**Patriots**), while the rebels also fought the British redcoats (see "Makers of America: The Loyalists," pp. 140–141). Loyalists were derisively called "Tories," after the dominant political factions in Britain, whereas Patriots were called "Whigs," after the opposition factions in Britain. A popular definition of a Tory among the Patriots betrayed bitterness: "A Tory is a thing whose head is in England, and its body in America, and its neck ought to be stretched."

Like many revolutions, the American Revolution was a minority movement. Many colonists were apathetic or neutral, including the Byrds of Virginia, who sat on the fence. The opposing forces contended not only against each other but also for the allegiance and support of the civilian population. In this struggle for the hearts and minds of the people, the British proved fatally inept, and the Patriot militias played a crucial role. The British military proved able to control only those areas where it could maintain a massive military presence. Elsewhere, as soon as the redcoats had marched on, the rebel militiamen appeared and took up the task of "political education"—sometimes by coercive means. Often lacking bayonets but always loaded with political zeal, the ragtag militia units served as remarkably effective agents of Revolutionary ideas. They convinced many colonists, even those indifferent to independence, that the British army was an unreliable friend and that they had better throw in their lot with the Patriot cause. They also mercilessly harassed small British detachments and occupation forces. One British officer ruefully observed that "the Americans would be less dangerous if they had a regular army."

Loyalists, numbering perhaps 16 percent of the American people, remained true to their king. Families often split over the issue of independence: Benjamin Franklin supported the Patriot side, whereas his handsome illegitimate son, William Franklin (the last royal governor of New Jersey), upheld the Loyalist cause. The Loyalists were tragic figures. For generations the British in the New World had been taught fidelity to the crown. Loyalty is ordinarily regarded as a major virtue—loyalty to one's family, one's friends, one's country. If the king had triumphed, as he seemed likely to do, the Loyalists would have been acclaimed patriots, and defeated rebels like Washington would have been disgraced, severely punished, and probably forgotten.

Many people of education and wealth, of culture and caution, remained loyal. These wary souls were satisfied with their lot and believed that any violent change would only be for the worse. Loyalists were also more numerous among the older generation. Young people make revolutions, and from the outset energetic, purposeful, and militant young people surged forward—figures like the sleeplessly scheming Samuel

In late 1776 Catherine Van Cortlandt wrote to her husband, a New Jersey merchant fighting in a Loyalist brigade, about the Patriot troops who had quartered themselves in her house. "They were the most disorderly of species," she complained, "and their officers were from the dregs of the people."

Like the Van Cortlandts, many Loyalists thought of themselves as the "better sort of people." They viewed their adversaries as "lawless mobs" and "brutes." Conservative, wealthy, and well educated, Loyalists of this breed thought a break with Britain would invite anarchy. Loyalism made sense to them, too, for practical reasons. Viewing colonial militias as no match for His Majesty's army, Loyalist pamphleteer Daniel Leonard warned his Patriot enemies in 1775 that "nothing short of a miracle could gain you one battle."

But Loyalism was hardly confined to the well-to-do. It also appealed to many people of modest means who identified strongly with Britain or who had reason to fear a Patriot victory. Thousands of British veterans of the Seven Years' War, for example, had settled in the colonies after 1763. Many of them took up farming on two-hundred-acre land grants in New York. They were loath to turn their backs on the crown. So, too, were recent immigrants from non-English regions of the British Isles, especially from Scotland and Ireland, who had settled in Georgia or the backcountry of North and South Carolina. Many of these newcomers, resenting the plantation elite who ran these colonies, filled the ranks of Tory brigades such as the Volunteers of Ireland and the North Carolina Highlanders, organized by the British army to galvanize Loyalist support.

Other ethnic minorities found their own reasons to support the British. Some members of Dutch, German, and French religious sects believed that religious tolerance would be greater under the British than under the Americans, whose prejudices they had already encountered. Though Native American groups had varied responses to the war, many fought on the side of the British, expecting that their treaties with the Empire would protect their land claims.

Thousands of African Americans also joined Loyalist ranks in the hope that service to the British might offer an escape from bondage. British officials encouraged that belief. Throughout the war and in every colony, some African Americans fled to British lines, where they served as soldiers, servants, laborers, and spies. Many of them joined black regiments that specialized in making small sorties against Patriot militias. In Monmouth, New Jersey, the black Loyalist Colonel Tye and his band of raiders became legendary for capturing Patriots and their supplies.

As the war drew to an end in 1783, the fate of black Loyalists varied enormously. Many thousands who came to Loyalism as fugitive slaves managed to find a way to freedom, most notably the large group who won British passage from the port of New York to Nova Scotia. Other African American Loyalists suffered betrayal. British general Lord Charles Cornwallis abandoned over four thousand former slaves in Virginia, and many black Loyalists who

Tough Times for Loyalists Under the shadow of the tar bucket and bag of feathers shown in the upper right background, these Virginia Loyalists were roughly handled by a club-wielding crowd of Patriots.

Loyalists Through British Eyes   This British cartoon depicts the Loyalists as doubly victimized—by Americans caricatured as "savage" Indians and by the British prime minister, the Earl of Shelburne, for offering little protection to Britain's defenders.

boarded ships from British-controlled ports expecting to embark for freedom instead found themselves sold back into slavery in the West Indies.

White Loyalists faced no threat of enslavement, but they did suffer travails beyond mere disgrace: arrest, exile, confiscation of property, and loss of legal rights. Faced with such retribution, some eighty thousand Loyalists fled abroad, mostly to Britain and the maritime provinces of Canada, where they became known as the United Empire Loyalists. Some settled contentedly as exiles, but many, especially those who went to Britain, where they had difficulty becoming accepted, lived diminished and lonely lives—"cut off," as Loyalist Thomas Danforth put it, "from every hope of importance in life . . . [and] in a station much inferior to that of a menial servant."

But most Loyalists remained in America, where they faced the special burdens of reestablishing themselves in a society that viewed them as traitors. Some succeeded remarkably despite the odds, such as Hugh Gaine, a printer in New York City who eventually reopened a business and even won contracts from the new government. Ironically, this former Loyalist soldier published the new national army regulations authored by the Revolutionary hero Baron von Steuben. Like many former Loyalists, Gaine reintegrated himself into public life by siding with the Federalist call for a strong central government and powerful executive. When New York ratified the Constitution in 1788, Gaine rode the float at the head of the city's celebration parade. He had, like many other former Loyalists, become an American.

Adams and the impassioned Patrick Henry. His flaming outcry before the Virginia Assembly—"Give me liberty or give me death!"—still quickens patriotic pulses.

Loyalists also included the king's officers and other beneficiaries of the crown—people who knew which side their daily bread came from. The same was generally true of the Anglican clergy and a large portion of their congregations, all of whom had long been taught submission to the king.

Usually the Loyalists were most numerous where the Anglican Church was strongest. A notable exception was Virginia, where the debt-burdened Anglican aristocrats flocked into the rebel camp. The king's followers were well entrenched in aristocratic New York City and Charleston, and also in Quaker Pennsylvania and New Jersey, where General Washington felt that he was fighting in "the enemy's country." While his men were starving at Valley Forge, nearby Pennsylvania farmers were selling their produce to the British for the king's gold.

Loyalists were least numerous in New England, where self-government was especially strong and mercantilism was especially weak. Rebels were the most numerous where Presbyterianism and Congregationalism flourished, notably in New England. Invading British armies vented their contempt and anger by using Yankee churches for pigsties.

The Loyalist Exodus

Before the Declaration of Independence in 1776, persecution of the Loyalists was relatively mild. Yet they were subjected to some brutality, including tarring and feathering and riding astride fence rails.

After the Declaration of Independence, which sharply separated Loyalists from Patriots, harsher methods prevailed. The rebels naturally desired a united front. Putting loyalty to the colonies first, they regarded their opponents, not themselves, as traitors. Loyalists were roughly handled, hundreds were imprisoned, and a few noncombatants were hanged. But there was no wholesale reign of terror comparable to that which later bloodied both France and Russia during their revolutions. For one thing, the colonists reflected Anglo-Saxon regard for order; for another, the leading Loyalists were prudent enough to flee to the British lines.

About eighty thousand loyal supporters of George III were driven out or fled, but several hundred thousand

Art Gallery, Williams Center, Lafayette College

New York Patriots Pull Down the Statue of King George III Erected after the repeal of the Stamp Act in 1766, this statue was melted down by the revolutionaries into bullets to be used against the king's troops.

Washington Crossing the Delaware, by Emanuel Gottlieb Leutze, 1851   On Christmas Day, 1776, George Washington set out from Pennsylvania with twenty-four hundred men to surprise the British forces, chiefly Hessians, in their quarters across the river in New Jersey. The subsequent British defeat proved to be a turning point in the Revolution, as it checked the British advance toward Philadelphia and restored American morale. Seventy-five years later, Leutze, a German American immigrant who had returned to Germany, mythologized the heroic campaign in this painting. Imbued with the liberal democratic principles of the American Revolution, Leutze intended his painting to inspire Europeans in their revolutions of 1848. To that end, he ignored the fact that the Stars and Stripes held by Lieutenant James Monroe was not adopted until 1777; that Washington could not possibly have stood so long on one leg; that the colonists crossed the Delaware at night, not during the day; and that no African American would have been present. What Leutze did capture was the importance of ordinary men in the Revolutionary struggle and the tremendous urgency they felt at this particular moment in 1776, when victory seemed so elusive.

or so of the mild Loyalists were permitted to stay. The estates of many of the fugitives were confiscated and sold—a relatively painless way to help finance the war. Confiscation often worked great hardship, as, for example, when two aristocratic women were forced to live in their former chicken house for leaning Toryward.

Some fifty thousand Loyalist volunteers at one time or another bore arms for the British. They also helped the king's cause by serving as spies, by inciting the Indians, and by keeping Patriot soldiers at home to protect their families. Ardent Loyalists had their hearts in their cause, and a major blunder of the haughty British was not to make full use of them in the fighting.

✶ General Washington at Bay

With Boston evacuated in March 1776, the British concentrated on New York as a base of operations. Here was a splendid seaport, centrally located, where the king could count on cooperation from the numerous Loyalists. An awe-inspiring British fleet appeared off New York in July 1776. It consisted of some five hundred ships and thirty-five thousand men—the largest armed force to be seen in America until the Civil War. General Washington, dangerously outnumbered, could muster only eighteen thousand ill-trained troops with which to meet the crack army of the invader.

Disaster befell the Americans in the summer and fall of 1776. Outgeneraled and outmaneuvered, they were routed at the **Battle of Long Island**, where panic seized the raw recruits. By the narrowest of margins, and thanks to a favoring wind and fog, Washington escaped to Manhattan Island. Retreating northward, he crossed the Hudson River to New Jersey and finally reached the Delaware River with the British close at his heels. Tauntingly, enemy buglers sounded the fox-hunting call, so familiar to Virginians of Washington's day. The Patriot cause was at low ebb when the rebel remnants fled across the river after collecting all available boats to forestall pursuit.

The wonder is that Washington's adversary, General William Howe, did not speedily crush the demoralized American forces. But he was no military genius, and he well remembered the horrible slaughter at Bunker Hill, where he had commanded. The country was rough, supplies were slow in coming, and as a professional soldier, Howe did not relish the rigors of winter campaigning. He evidently found more agreeable the bedtime company of his mistress, the wife of one of his subordinates—a scandal with which American satirists had a good deal of ribald fun.

Washington, who was now almost counted out, stealthily recrossed the ice-clogged Delaware River. At **Trenton**, on December 26, 1776, he surprised and captured a thousand Hessians who were sleeping off the effects of their Christmas celebration. A week later, leaving his campfires burning as a ruse, he slipped away and inflicted a sharp defeat on a smaller British detachment at Princeton. This brilliant New Jersey campaign, crowned by these two lifesaving victories, revealed "Old Fox" Washington at his military best.

✴ Burgoyne's Blundering Invasion

London officials adopted an intricate scheme for capturing the vital Hudson River valley in 1777. If successful, the British would sever New England from the rest of the states and paralyze the American cause. The main invading force, under an actor-playwright-soldier, General John ("Gentleman Johnny") Burgoyne, would push down the Lake Champlain route from Canada. General Howe's troops in New York, if needed, could advance up the Hudson River to meet Burgoyne near Albany. A third and much smaller British force, commanded by Colonel Barry St. Leger, would come in from the west by way of Lake Ontario and the Mohawk Valley.

British planners did not reckon with General Benedict Arnold. After his repulse at Québec in 1775, he had retreated slowly along the St. Lawrence River back to the Lake Champlain area, by heroic efforts keeping an

In this sermon, published in the Pennsylvania Gazette *on April 18, 1778, a minister decried the brutality of the British army:*

❝ The waste and ravage produced by this unhappy war are every where felt. Wherever our foes pervade, ruin and devastation follow after them; or rather, they march in their front, and on their right, and on their left, and in their rear they rage without controul. No house is sacred; no person secure. Age or sex, from blooming youth to decrepit age, they regard or spare not. And in the field, how many of our countrymen and friends have fallen?❞

army in the field. The British had pursued his tattered force to Lake Champlain in 1776. But they could not move farther south until they had won control of the lake, which, in the absence of roads, was indispensable for carrying their supplies.

While the British stopped to construct a sizable fleet, the tireless Arnold assembled and fitted out every floatable vessel. His tiny flotilla was finally destroyed after desperate fighting, but time, if not the battle, had been won. Winter was descending, and the British were forced to retire to Canada. General Burgoyne had to start anew from this base the following year. If Arnold had not contributed his daring and skill, the British invaders of 1776 almost certainly would have recaptured Fort Ticonderoga. If Burgoyne had started from this springboard in 1777, instead of from Montréal, he almost certainly would have succeeded in his venture. (At last the apparently futile American invasion of Canada in 1775 was beginning to pay rich dividends.)

General Burgoyne began his fateful invasion with seven thousand regular troops. He was encumbered by a heavy baggage train and a considerable number of women, many of whom were wives of his officers. Progress was painfully slow, for sweaty axmen had to chop a path through the forest, while American militiamen began to gather like hornets on Burgoyne's flanks.

General Howe, meanwhile, was causing astonished eyebrows to rise. At a time when it seemed obvious that he should be starting up the Hudson River from New York to join his slowly advancing colleague, he deliberately embarked with the main British army for an attack on Philadelphia, the rebel capital. As scholars now know, he wanted to force a general engagement with Washington's army, destroy it, and leave the path wide-open for Burgoyne's thrust. Howe apparently assumed that he had ample time to assist Burgoyne directly, should he be needed.

General Washington, keeping a wary eye on the British in New York, hastily transferred his army to the vicinity of Philadelphia. There, late in 1777, he was defeated in two pitched battles, at Brandywine Creek and Germantown. Pleasure-loving General Howe then settled down comfortably in the lively capital, leaving Burgoyne to flounder through the wilds of upper New York. Benjamin Franklin, recently sent to Paris as an envoy, truthfully jested that Howe had not captured Philadelphia but that Philadelphia had captured Howe. Washington finally retired to winter quarters at Valley Forge, a strong, hilly position some twenty miles northwest of Philadelphia. There his frostbitten and hungry men were short of about every-thing except misery. This rabble was nevertheless whipped into a professional army by the recently arrived Prussian drillmaster, the profane but patient Baron von Steuben.

Burgoyne meanwhile had begun to bog down north of Albany, while a host of American militiamen, scenting the kill, swarmed about him. In a series of sharp engagements, in which General Arnold was again shot in the leg at Québec, the British army was trapped. Meanwhile, the Americans had driven back St. Leger's force at Oriskany. Unable to advance or retreat, Burgoyne was forced to surrender his entire command at **Saratoga** on October 17, 1777, to the American general Horatio Gates.

Saratoga ranks high among the decisive battles of both American and world history. The victory immensely revived the faltering colonial cause. Even more important, it made possible the urgently needed foreign aid from France, which in turn helped ensure American independence.

✦ Revolution in Diplomacy?

France, thirsting for revenge against Britain, was eager to inflame the quarrel that had broken out in America. Stripped of its North American colonies, Britain would

After concluding the alliance, France sent a minister to America, to the delight of one Patriot journalist:

❝Who would have thought that the American colonies, imperfectly known in Europe a few years ago and claimed by every pettifogging lawyer in the House of Commons, every cobbler in the beer-houses of London, as a part of their property, should to-day receive an ambassador from the most powerful monarchy in Europe.❞

presumably cease to be a front-rank power. France might then regain its former position and prestige, the loss of which in the recent Seven Years' War rankled deeply. For their part, the American revolutionaries badly needed help in the struggle to throw off the British yoke. The stage seemed set for the embattled new nation to make its diplomatic debut by sealing an alliance with France against the common British foe.

Yet just as they stood for revolutionary political ideas at home, the rebellious Americans also harbored revolutionary ideas about international affairs. They wanted an end to colonialism and mercantilism. They strongly supported free trade and freedom of the seas. They hoped to substitute the rule of law for the ancient reliance on raw power to arbitrate the affairs of nations. (When the new Republic's great seal proclaimed "a new order for the ages"—*novus ordo seculorum* in Latin— the sentiment was meant to apply to international as well as domestic affairs.) The Continental Congress in the summer of 1776 had accordingly drafted a **Model Treaty** to guide the American commissioners it was about to dispatch to the French court. One of the treaty's chief authors, John Adams, described its basic principles: "1. No political connection. . . . 2. No military connection. . . . 3. Only a commercial connection."

For a nascent nation struggling to secure its very existence, these were remarkably self-denying restrictions. Yet they represented an emerging school of thought, popular among enlightened figures in both Europe and America, that deemed history to have reached a momentous turning point when military conflict would be abandoned and the bonds of mutual commercial interest would guarantee peaceful relations among states. Many critics then and later have derided this dream of an imminent golden age as hopelessly naive and impractically utopian; yet it infused an element of idealism into American attitudes toward international affairs that has proved stubbornly persistent.

When wily old Benjamin Franklin arrived in Paris to negotiate the treaty with France, he was determined that his very appearance should herald the diplomatic revolution the Americans hoped to achieve. In his clothing and demeanor, he affected a persona that deliberately violated every norm of diplomatic behavior. Instead of the customary ceremonial sword, he toted only a plain white walking stick. Forsaking ermined robes and fancy wigs, he sported homespun garments and a simple cap of marten fur. "Figure me," he wrote to a friend, "very plainly dress'd, wearing my thin grey strait Hair, that peeps out under my only Coiffure, a fine Fur Cap, which comes down my Forehead almost to my Spectacles. Think how this must appear among the Powder'd Heads of Paris." He shocked the royal court, besotted as it was with pomp

Benjamin Franklin in His Fabled Cap He left school at age ten and became a wealthy businessman, a journalist, an inventor, a scientist, a legislator, and preeminently a statesman-diplomat. He was sent to France in 1776 as the American envoy at age seventy, and he remained there until 1785, negotiating the alliance with the French and helping to negotiate the treaty of peace. His fame had preceded him, and when he discarded his wig for the fur cap of a simple "American agriculturist," he took French society by storm. French aristocratic women, with whom he was a great favorite, honored him by adopting the high *coiffure à la Franklin* in imitation of his cap. Réunion des Musées Nationaux/Art Resource, NY

and protocol. But ordinary Parisians adored him as a specimen of a new democratic social order, devoid of pretense and ornament. When Franklin embraced and kissed the famed French philosopher Voltaire in a Paris theater, the spectators applauded wildly. Meanwhile, the diplomatic game intensified.

After the humiliation at Saratoga in 1777, the British Parliament belatedly passed a measure that in effect offered the Americans home rule within the empire. This was essentially all that the colonials had ever asked for—except independence. If the French were going to break up the British Empire, they would have to bestir themselves. Franklin now played skillfully on French fears of Anglo-American reconciliation. On February 6, 1778, France offered the Americans a treaty of alliance. It did not conform exactly to the terms of the Model Treaty Franklin had brought with him—an early example of practical self-interest trumping abstract idealism in America's conduct of foreign affairs. Against

its better judgment, the young Republic concluded its first entangling military alliance and would soon regret it. But the treaty with France also constituted an official recognition of America's independence and lent powerful military heft to the Patriot cause. Both allies bound themselves to wage war until the United States had fully secured its freedom and until both agreed to terms with the common enemy. With those pledges, the American Revolutionary War now became a world war.

✷ The Colonial War Becomes a Wider War

England and France thus came to blows in 1778, and the shot fired at Lexington rapidly widened into a global conflagration. Spain entered the fray against Britain in 1779, as did Holland. Combined Spanish and French fleets outnumbered those of Britain, and on two occasions the British Isles seemed to be at the mercy of hostile warships.

The weak maritime neutrals of Europe, who had suffered from Britain's dominance over the seas, now began to demand more respect for their rights (see Table 8.1). In 1780 the imperious Catherine the Great of Russia took the lead in organizing the **Armed Neutrality**, which she later sneeringly called the "Armed Nullity." It lined up almost all the remaining European neutrals in an attitude of passive hostility toward Britain. The war was now being fought not only in Europe and North America, but also in South America, the Caribbean, and Asia.

To say that America, with some French aid, defeated Britain is like saying "Daddy and I killed the bear." To Britain, struggling for its very life, the scuffle in the New World became secondary. The Americans deserve credit for having kept the war going until 1778, with secret French aid. But they did not achieve their independence until the conflict erupted into a multipower world war that was too big for Britain to handle. From 1778 to 1783, France provided the rebels with guns, money, immense amounts of equipment, about one-half of America's regular armed forces, and practically all of the new nation's naval strength.

France's entrance into the conflict forced the British to change their basic strategy in America. Hitherto they could count on blockading the colonial coast and commanding the seas. Now the French had powerful fleets in American waters, chiefly to protect their own valuable West Indies islands, but in a position to jeopardize Britain's blockade and lines of supply. The British, therefore, decided to evacuate Philadelphia and concentrate their strength in New York City.

TABLE 8.1 Britain Against the World

Britain and Allies	Enemy or Unfriendly Powers	
Great Britain Some Loyalists and Indians 30,000 hired Hessians *(Total population on Britain's side: ca. 8 million)*	Belligerents *(Total population: ca. 39.5 million)*	United States, 1775–1783 France, 1778–1783 Spain, 1779–1783 Holland, 1779–1783
		Ireland (restive)
	Members of the Armed Neutrality (with dates of joining)	Russia, 1780 Denmark-Norway, 1780 Sweden, 1780 Holy Roman Empire, 1781 Prussia, 1782 Portugal, 1782 Two Sicilies, 1783 (after peace signed)

In June 1778 the withdrawing redcoats were attacked by General Washington at Monmouth, New Jersey, on a blisteringly hot day. Scores of men collapsed or died from sunstroke. But the battle was indecisive, and the British escaped to New York, although about one-third of their Hessians deserted. Henceforth, except for the Yorktown interlude of 1781, Washington remained in the New York area hemming in the British.

✯ Blow and Counterblow

In the summer of 1780, a powerful French army of six thousand regular troops, commanded by the Comte de Rochambeau, arrived in Newport, Rhode Island. The Americans were somewhat suspicious of their former enemies; in fact, several ugly flare-ups, involving minor bloodshed, had already occurred between the new allies. But French gold and goodwill melted hard hearts. Dancing parties were arranged with the prim Puritan maidens; one French officer related, doubtless with exaggeration, "The simple innocence of the Garden of Eden prevailed." No real military advantage came immediately from this French reinforcement, although preparations were made for a Franco-American attack on New York.

Improving American morale was staggered later in 1780, when General Benedict Arnold turned traitor. A leader of undoubted dash and brilliance, he was ambitious, greedy, unscrupulous, and suffering from a well-grounded but petulant feeling that his valuable services were not fully appreciated. He plotted with the British to sell out the key stronghold of West Point, which commanded the Hudson River, for £6,300 and an officer's commission. By the sheerest accident, the plot was detected in the nick of time, and Arnold fled to the British. "Whom can we trust now?" cried General Washington in anguish.

The British meanwhile had devised a plan to roll up the colonies, beginning with the South, where the Loyalists were numerous (see Map 8.2). The colony of Georgia was ruthlessly overrun in 1778–1779; Charleston, South Carolina, fell in 1780. The surrender of the city to the British involved the capture of five thousand men and four hundred cannon and was a heavier loss to the Americans, in relation to existing strength, than that of Burgoyne was to the British.

Warfare now intensified in the Carolinas, where Patriots bitterly fought their Loyalist neighbors. It was not uncommon for prisoners on both sides to be butchered in cold blood after they had thrown down their arms. The tide turned later in 1780 and early in 1781, when American riflemen wiped out a British detachment at King's Mountain and then defeated a smaller force at Cowpens. In the Carolina campaign of 1781, General Nathanael Greene, a Quaker-reared tactician, distinguished himself by his strategy of delay. Standing and then retreating, he exhausted his foe, General Charles Cornwallis, in vain pursuit. By losing battles but winning campaigns, the "Fighting Quaker" finally succeeded in clearing most of Georgia and South Carolina of British troops.

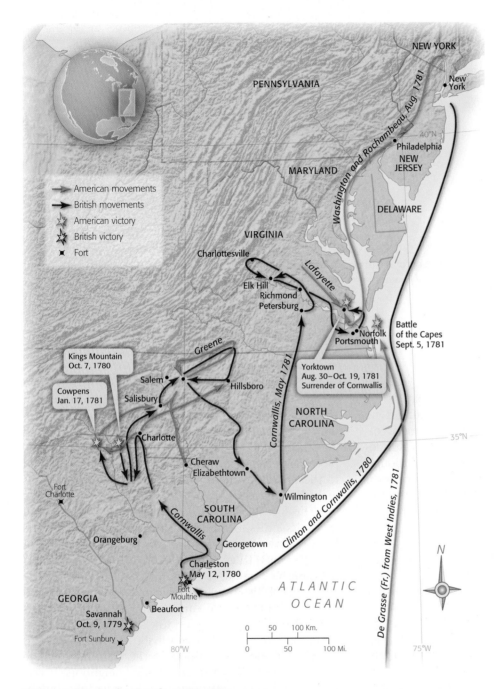

MAP 8.2 War in the South, 1780–1781 © Cengage Learning

✴ The Land Frontier and the Sea Frontier

The West was ablaze during much of the war. Indian allies of George III, hoping to protect their land, were busy with torch and tomahawk; they were egged on by British agents branded as "hair buyers" because they paid bounties for American scalps. Fateful 1777 was known as "the bloody year" on the frontier. Although

two nations of the Iroquois Confederacy, the Oneidas and the Tuscaroras, sided with the Americans, the Senecas, Mohawks, Cayugas, and Onondagas joined the British. They were urged on by Mohawk chief Joseph Brant, a convert to Anglicanism who believed, not without reason, that a victorious Britain would restrain American expansion into the West. Brant and the British ravaged large areas of backcountry Pennsylvania and New York until checked by an American force in 1779. In 1784 the pro-British Iroquois were forced to

Joseph Brant, by Gilbert Stuart, 1786 Siding with the British, this Mohawk chief led Indian frontier raids so ferocious that he was dubbed "monster Brant." When he later met King George III, he declined to kiss the king's hand but asked instead to kiss the hand of the queen.

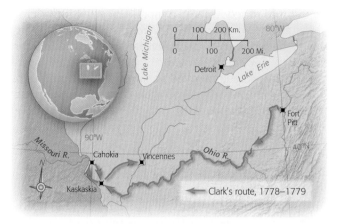

MAP 8.3 George Rogers Clark's Campaign, 1778–1779
© Cengage Learning

sign the **Treaty of Fort Stanwix**, the first treaty between the United States and an Indian nation. Under its terms the Indians ceded most of their land.

Yet even in wartime, the human tide of westward-moving pioneers did not halt its flow. Eloquent testimony is provided by place names in Kentucky, such as Lexington (named after the battle) and Louisville (named after America's new ally, Louis XVI).

In the wild Illinois country, the British were especially vulnerable to attack, for they held only scattered posts that they had captured from the French. An audacious frontiersman, George Rogers Clark, conceived the idea of seizing these forts by surprise. In 1778–1779 he floated down the Ohio River with about 175 men and captured in quick succession the forts Kaskaskia, Cahokia, and Vincennes (see Map 8.3). Clark's admirers have argued, without positive proof, that his success forced the British to cede the region north of the Ohio River to the United States at the peace table in Paris.

America's infant navy had meanwhile been laying the foundations of a brilliant tradition. The naval establishment consisted of only a handful of nondescript ships, commanded by daring officers, the most famous of whom was a hard-fighting young Scotsman, John Paul Jones. As events turned out, this tiny naval force never made a real dent in Britain's thunderous fleets. Its chief contribution was in destroying British merchant shipping and thus carrying the war into the waters around the British Isles.

More numerous and damaging than ships of the regular American navy were swift **privateers**. These craft were privately owned armed ships—legalized pirates in a sense—specifically authorized by Congress to prey on enemy shipping. Altogether over a thousand American privateers, responding to the call of patriotism and profit, sallied forth with about seventy thousand men ("sailors of fortune"). They captured some six hundred British prizes, while British warships captured about as many American merchantmen and privateers.

Privateering was not an unalloyed asset. It had the unfortunate effect of diverting manpower from the main war effort and involving Americans, including Benedict Arnold, in speculation and graft. But the privateers brought in urgently needed gold, harassed the

Baron von Steuben (1730–1794), a Prussian general who helped train the Continental Army, found the Americans to be very different from other soldiers he had known. As von Steuben explained to a fellow European,

❝ The genius of this nation is not in the least to be compared with that of the Prussians, Austrians, or French. You say to your soldier, 'Do this' and he doeth it; but I am obliged to say, 'This is the reason why you ought to do that,' and then he does it. ❞

enemy, and raised American morale by providing victories at a time when victories were few. British shipping was so badly riddled by privateers and by the regular American navy that insurance rates skyrocketed. Merchant ships were compelled to sail in convoy, and British shippers and manufacturers brought increasing pressure on Parliament to end the war on honorable terms.

✴ Yorktown and the Final Curtain

One of the darkest periods of the war was 1780–1781, before the last decisive victory. Inflation of the currency continued at full gallop. The government, virtually bankrupt, declared that it would repay many of its debts at the rate of only 2.5 cents on the dollar. Despair prevailed, the sense of unity withered, and mutinous sentiments infected the army.

Meanwhile, the British general Cornwallis was blundering into a trap. After futile operations in Virginia, he had fallen back to Chesapeake Bay at **Yorktown** to await seaborne supplies and reinforcements. He assumed Britain would continue to control the sea. But these few fateful weeks happened to be one of the brief periods during the war when British naval superiority slipped away.

The French were now prepared to cooperate energetically in a brilliant stroke. Admiral de Grasse, operating with a powerful fleet in the West Indies, advised the Americans that he was free to join with them in an assault on Cornwallis at Yorktown. Quick to seize this opportunity, General Washington made a swift march of more than three hundred miles to the Chesapeake from the New York area. Accompanied by Rochambeau's French army, Washington beset the British by land, while de Grasse blockaded them by sea after beating off the British fleet. Completely cornered, Cornwallis surrendered his entire force of seven thousand men on October 19, 1781, as his band appropriately played "The World Turn'd Upside Down." The triumph was no less French than American: the French provided essentially all the sea power and about half of the regular troops in the besieging army of some sixteen thousand men.

Stunned by news of the disaster, Prime Minister Lord North cried, "Oh God! It's all over! It's all over!" But it was not. George III stubbornly planned to continue the struggle, for Britain was far from being crushed. It still had fifty-four thousand troops in North America,

Battle of the Chesapeake Capes, 1781 A young French naval officer, Pierre Joseph Jennot, sketched what is probably the only depiction of the epochal sea battle by a participant. The British and French fleets first engaged on September 5 and for two days chased each other while drifting one hundred miles south. On September 8 the French turned back northward and occupied Chesapeake Bay, cutting off General Cornwallis, ashore in Yorktown, from support and escape by sea. When General Washington, with more French help, blocked any British retreat by land, a doomed Cornwallis surrendered.

The Huntington Library & Art Collections, San Marino, California including thirty-two thousand in the United States. Washington returned with his army to New York, there to continue keeping a vigilant eye on the British force of ten thousand men.

Fighting actually continued for more than a year after Yorktown, with Patriot–Loyalist warfare in the South especially savage. "No quarter for Tories" was the common battle cry. One of Washington's most valuable contributions was to keep the languishing cause alive, the army in the field, and the states together during these critical months. Otherwise a satisfactory peace treaty might never have been signed.

✵ Peace at Paris

After Yorktown, despite George III's obstinate eagerness to continue fighting, many Britons were weary of war and increasingly ready to come to terms. They had suffered heavy reverses in India and in the West Indies. The island of Minorca in the Mediterranean had fallen; the Rock of Gibraltar was tottering. Lord North's ministry collapsed in March 1782, temporarily ending the personal rule of George III. A Whig ministry, rather favorable to the Americans, replaced the Tory regime of Lord North.

Three American peace negotiators had meanwhile gathered at Paris: the aging but astute Benjamin Franklin; the flinty John Adams, vigilant for New England interests; and the impulsive John Jay of New York, deeply suspicious of Old World intrigue. The three envoys had explicit instructions from Congress to make no separate peace and to consult with their French allies at all stages of the negotiations. But the American representatives chafed under this directive. They well knew that it had been written by a subservient Congress, with the French Foreign Office indirectly guiding the pen.

France was in a painful position. It had induced Spain to enter the war on its side, in part by promising to deliver British-held Gibraltar. Yet the towering rock was defying frantic joint assaults by French and Spanish troops. Spain also coveted the immense trans-Allegheny area, on which restless American pioneers were already settling.

Blundering George III, a poor loser, wrote this of America:

❝Knavery seems to be so much the striking feature of its inhabitants that it may not in the end be an evil that they become aliens to this Kingdom.**❞**

In 1800 the Prussian statesman Friedrich von Gentz (1764–1832) published an essay titled "Origins and Principles of the American Revolution, Compared with the French." In it he argued that

❝the Americans escaped the most dangerous of all the rocks, which in our times threatens the founders of any revolution: the deadly passion for making political experiments with abstract theories and untried systems.**❞**

John Quincy Adams (1767–1848) translated von Gentz's work into English, because, he said,

❝it rescues [the American] revolution from the disgraceful imputation of having proceeded from the same principles as the French.**❞**

France, ever eager to smash Britain's empire, desired an independent United States, but one independent in the abstract, not in action. It therefore schemed to keep the new Republic cooped up east of the Allegheny Mountains. A weak America—like a horse sturdy enough to plow but not vigorous enough to kick—would be easier to manage in promoting French interests and policy. France was paying a heavy price in men and treasure to win America's independence, and it wanted to get its money's worth.

But John Jay was unwilling to play France's game. Suspiciously alert, he perceived that the French could not satisfy the conflicting ambitions of both Americans and Spaniards. He saw signs—or thought he did—indicating that the Paris Foreign Office was about to betray America's trans-Appalachian interests to satisfy those of Spain. He therefore secretly made separate overtures to London, contrary to his instructions from Congress. The hard-pressed British, eager to entice one of their enemies from the alliance, speedily came to terms with the Americans. A preliminary treaty of peace was signed in 1782; the final peace, the next year.

By the **Treaty of Paris** of 1783, the British formally recognized the independence of the United States. In addition, they granted generous boundaries, stretching majestically to the Mississippi on the west, to the Great Lakes on the north, and to Spanish Florida on the south. (Spain had recently captured Florida from Britain.) The Yankees, though now divorced from the empire, were to retain a share in the priceless fisheries of Newfoundland. The Canadians, of course, were profoundly displeased.

The Americans, on their part, had to yield important concessions. Loyalists were not to be further persecuted, and Congress was to *recommend* to the state legislatures that confiscated Loyalist property be restored. As for the debts long owed to British creditors, the states vowed to put no lawful obstacles in the way of their collection. Unhappily for future harmony, the assurances regarding both Loyalists and debts were not carried out in the manner hoped for by London.

As for Britain, its acceptance of defeat in North America eventually paid enormous strategic dividends. Persisting in the colonial conflict might well have bled Britain dry. But shutting down the war against the Americans enabled London to rebuild its army and navy and eventually prevail in its titanic struggle with Napoleon—and to become the preeminent world power in the nineteenth century.

✷ A New Nation Legitimized

Britain's terms were liberal almost beyond belief. The enormous trans-Appalachian area was thrown in as a virtual gift, for George Rogers Clark had captured only a small segment of it. Why the generosity? Had the United States beaten Britain to its knees?

The key to the riddle may be found in the Old World. At the time the peace terms were drafted, Britain was trying to seduce America from its French alliance, so it made the terms as alluring as possible. The shaky Whig ministry, hanging on by its fingernails for only a few months, was more friendly to the Americans than were the Tories. It was determined, by a policy of liberality, to salve recent wounds, reopen old trade channels, and prevent future wars over the coveted trans-Appalachian region. This farsighted policy was regrettably not followed by the successors of the Whigs.

In spirit, the Americans made a separate peace—contrary to the French alliance. In fact, they did not. The Paris Foreign Office formally approved the terms of peace, though disturbed by the lone-wolf course of its American ally. France was immensely relieved by the prospect of bringing the costly conflict to an end and of freeing itself from its embarrassing promises to the Spanish crown.

The Reconciliation Between Britannia and Her Daughter America (detail) America (represented by an Indian) is invited to buss (kiss) her mother. Compare this cartoon with the one on p. 114. Mirium and Ira D. Wallach Division of Art, Prints and Photographs, The New York Public Library. Astor, Lenox and Tilden Foundations.

America alone gained from the world-girdling war. The British, though soon to stage a comeback, were battered and beaten. The French savored sweet revenge but plunged headlong down the slippery slope to bankruptcy and revolution. The Americans fared much better. Snatching their independence from the furnace of world conflict, they began their national career with a splendid territorial birthright and a priceless heritage of freedom. Seldom, if ever, have any people been so favored.

Varying Viewpoints
Whose Revolution?

*H*istorians once assumed that the Revolution was just another chapter in the unfolding story of human liberty—an important way station on a divinely ordained pathway toward moral perfection in human affairs. This approach, often labeled the "Whig view of history," was best expressed in George Bancroft's ten-volume *History of the United States of America*, published between the 1830s and 1870s.

By the end of the nineteenth century, a group of historians known as the "imperial school" challenged Bancroft, arguing that the Revolution was best understood not as the fulfillment of national destiny, but as a constitutional conflict within the British Empire. For historians like George Beer, Charles Andrews, and Lawrence Gipson, the Revolution was the product of a collision between two different views of empire. While the Americans were moving steadily toward more self-government, Britain increasingly tightened its grip, threatening a stranglehold that eventually led to wrenching revolution.

By the early twentieth century, these approaches were challenged by the so-called progressive historians, who argued that neither divine destiny nor constitutional quibbles had much to do with the Revolution. Rather, the Revolution stemmed from deep-seated class tensions within American society. Once released by revolt, those tensions produced a truly transformed social order. Living themselves in a reform age when entrenched economic interests cowered under heavy attack, progressive historians like Carl Becker insisted that the Revolution was not just about "home rule" within the British Empire, but also about "who should rule at home" in America, the upper or lower classes. J. Franklin Jameson took Becker's analysis one step further in his influential *The American Revolution Considered as a Social Movement* (1926). He claimed that the Revolution not only grew out of intense struggles between social groups, but also inspired many ordinary Americans to seek greater economic and political power, fundamentally democratizing society in its wake.

In the 1950s the progressive historians fell out of favor as the political climate became more conservative. Interpretations of the American Revolution as a class struggle did not play well in a country obsessed with the spread of communism, and in its place arose the so-called consensus view. Historians such as Robert Brown and Edmund Morgan downplayed the role of class conflict in the Revolutionary era, but emphasized that colonists of all ranks shared a commitment to certain fundamental political principles of self-government. The unifying power of ideas was now back in fashion almost a hundred years after Bancroft.

Since the 1950s two broad interpretations have contended with each other and perpetuated the controversy over whether political ideals or economic and social realities were most responsible for the Revolution. The first, articulated most prominently by Bernard Bailyn, has emphasized ideological and psychological factors. Focusing on the power of ideas to foment revolution, Bailyn argued that the colonists, incited by their reading of seventeenth-century and early-eighteenth-century English political theorists, grew extraordinarily (perhaps even exaggeratedly) suspicious of any attempts to tighten the imperial reins on the colonies. When confronted with new taxes and commercial regulations, these hypersensitive colonists screamed "conspiracy against liberty" and "corrupt ministerial plot." In time they took up armed insurrection in defense of their intellectual commitment to liberty.

A second school of historians, inspired by the social movements of the 1960s and 1970s, revived the progressive interpretation of the Revolution. Gary Nash, in *The Urban Crucible* (1979), and Edward Countryman, in *A People in Revolution* (1981), pointed to the increasing social and economic divisions among Americans in both the urban seaports and the isolated countryside in the years leading up to the Revolution. Attacks by laborers on political elites and expressions of resentment toward wealth were taken as evidence of a society that was breeding revolutionary change from within, quite aside from British provocations. Some of these arguments have continued into more recent scholarship; Woody Holton, in *Forced Founders* (1999), argues that pressures exerted by the presence of Indians, slaves, and poor whites forced the Virginia elite onto the road toward independence.

While the concerns of the progressive historians echo in these socioeconomic interpretations of the Revolution, the neoprogressives have been more careful not to reduce the issues simplistically to the one-ring arena of economic self-interest. Instead, they have argued that the varying material circumstances of American participants led them to hold distinctive versions of republicanism, giving the Revolution a less unified and more complex ideological underpinning than the idealistic historians had previously suggested. The dialogue between proponents of "ideas" and "interests" has gradually led to a more nuanced meeting of the two views.

In another recent trend, scholars have taken a more transatlantic view of the Revolution's origins, asking when and how colonists shifted from identifying as "British" to viewing themselves as "American." Fred Anderson has argued that long before rebellion, the Seven Years' War (1756–1763) helped create a sense of American identity apart from Britain. Still other historians, such as T. H. Breen, argue that British nationalism actually intensified in the colonies over the course of the eighteenth century, as economic and cultural ties between Britain and North America strengthened through increased trade and the migration of ideas with the growth of print culture. Only when colonists realized that the British did not see them as equal imperial citizens, entitled to the same rights as Englishmen, did American nationalism emerge and Americans rebel. Taking a broader global view, David Armitage has argued that the American Declaration of Independence had an impact far beyond the British Atlantic world, shaping rhetoric of countries claiming their independence into the following century and beyond.

Chapter Review

KEY TERMS

Second Continental Congress (132)
Bunker Hill, Battle of (133)
Olive Branch Petition (133)
Hessians (133)
Common Sense (135)
Declaration of Independence (137)
Declaration of the Rights of Man (139)
Loyalists (139)
Patriots (139)
Long Island, Battle of (144)
Trenton, Battle of (144)
Saratoga, Battle of (145)
Model Treaty (145)
Armed Neutrality (146)
Fort Stanwix, Treaty of (149)
privateers (149)
Yorktown, Battle of (150)
Paris, Treaty of (151)

PEOPLE TO KNOW

Ethan Allen
Benedict Arnold
Richard Montgomery
Thomas Paine
Abigail Adams
Richard Henry Lee
Lord Charles Cornwallis
William Howe
John ("Gentleman Johnny") Burgoyne
Benjamin Franklin
Comte de Rochambeau
Nathanael Greene
Joseph Brant
George Rogers Clark
Admiral de Grasse

CHRONOLOGY

1775	Battles of Lexington and Concord
	Second Continental Congress
	Americans capture British garrisons at Ticonderoga and Crown Point
	Battle of Bunker Hill
	King George III formally proclaims colonies in rebellion
	Failed invasion of Canada
1776	Paine's *Common Sense*
	Declaration of Independence
	Battle of Trenton
1777	Battle of Brandywine
	Battle of Germantown
	Battle of Saratoga
1778	Formation of French-American alliance
	Battle of Monmouth
1778–1779	Clark's victories in the West
1781	Battle of King's Mountain
	Battle of Cowpens
	Greene leads Carolina campaign
	French and Americans force Cornwallis to surrender at Yorktown
1782	North's ministry collapses in Britain
1783	Treaty of Paris
1784	Treaty of Fort Stanwix

TO LEARN MORE

David Armitage, *The Declaration of Independence: A Global History* (2007)

T. H. Breen, *American Insurgents, American Patriots: The Revolution of the People* (2010)

Robert M. Calhoon, *The Loyalists in Revolutionary America* (1973)

Caroline Cox, *A Proper Sense of Honor: Service and Sacrifice in George Washington's Army* (2004)

Joseph J. Ellis, *His Excellency: George Washington* (2004)

David Hackett Fischer, *Washington's Crossing* (2004)

James H. Hutson, *John Adams and the Diplomacy of the American Revolution* (1980)

Linda K. Kerber, *Women of the Republic: Intellect and Ideology in Revolutionary America* (1980)

Wim Klooster, *Revolutions in the Atlantic World: A Comparative History* (2005)

Mary Beth Norton, *The British-Americans: The Loyalist Exiles in England* (1972)

———, *Liberty's Daughters: The Revolutionary Experience of American Women* (1980)

Cassandra Pybus, *Epic Journeys of Freedom: Runaway Slaves of the American Revolution and Their Global Quest for Liberty* (2006)

Alan Taylor, *The Divided Ground: Indians, Settlers, and the Northern Borderland of the American Revolution* (2006)

A complete, annotated bibliography for this chapter—along with brief descriptions of the People to Know—may be found on the American Pageant website. The Key Terms are defined in a Glossary at the end of the text.

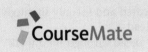

Go to the CourseMate website at **www.cengagebrain.com** for additional study tools and review materials—including audio and video clips—for this chapter.

AP® Review Questions for Chapter 8

1. What was the principal reason that the Second Continental Congress selected George Washington to head the army in 1775?
   - (A) They valued his leadership abilities.
   - (B) He had an impressive military track record.
   - (C) They wanted to squelch tensions between the colonies.
   - (D) He was willing to serve without pay.
   - (E) He was an aristocrat.

2. The Olive Branch Petition was
   - (A) England's attempt to end the war with the colonies.
   - (B) England's contract to hire German soldiers—called Hessians by Americans—to halt the colonial rebellion.
   - (C) a last-ditch effort by the Continental Congress to urge King George to end the hostilities.
   - (D) German soldiers shifting sympathies from the British to the Americans.
   - (E) an agreement between England and Native Americans that the latter would remain neutral.

3. Why did the colonial army invade and seek to conquer Canada in late 1775?
   - (A) They thought the British soldiers were most vulnerable there.
   - (B) They hoped to add it as a fourteenth colony.
   - (C) They wanted to establish Canada as a military base of operations.
   - (D) They hoped to secure France's support for the colonial cause.
   - (E) They wanted to eliminate the Roman Catholic regime there.

4. Even as they engaged in battles in 1775 and 1776, Americans continued to resist total independence from England for all of the following reasons EXCEPT that
   - (A) their loyalty to England was deeply ingrained.
   - (B) they enjoyed their status as part of a transatlantic community in which Britain was a leader.
   - (C) there was little colonial unity.
   - (D) they feared repercussions from Great Britain.
   - (E) they needed British protection from other potential invading nations.

5. Who was the first person to propose that the colonies become completely independent of England?
   - (A) Thomas Jefferson
   - (B) Samuel Adams
   - (C) Thomas Paine
   - (D) John Adams
   - (E) George Washington

6. In republican governments
   - (A) power flows from the people.
   - (B) monarchy, aristocracy, and commons share power equally.
   - (C) all people are considered equal.
   - (D) self-interest can be marshaled for the greater good.
   - (E) authority resides exclusively with the king.

7. What is meant by "a natural aristocracy of talent"?
   - (A) That only men of noble birth should lead
   - (B) That only the best-educated and socially situated men were qualified to lead
   - (C) That anyone could get ahead through hard work
   - (D) That the good of the majority mattered above the welfare of individuals
   - (E) That republican forms of government should replace monarchies

8. In the Declaration of Independence, Thomas Jefferson listed all of the following as reasons for severing ties with England EXCEPT
   - (A) imposing taxes without consent.
   - (B) eliminating trial by jury.
   - (C) establishing a military dictatorship.
   - (D) granting religious tolerance to Roman Catholics and others.
   - (E) cutting off trade.

9. Which of the following could NOT be said about Loyalists, who did not want to break from England?
   - (A) They were wealthy elites who considered Patriots to be lawless brutes.
   - (B) They believed no army could surpass the might of the British military.
   - (C) Some were British veterans of the Seven Years' War who relocated to America.
   - (D) They included new immigrants who resented the plantation elite.
   - (E) A large majority were African American current and former slaves.

10. In terms of supporting the Revolution, most colonists were initially
    (A) Patriots.
    (B) neutral.
    (C) Loyalists.
    (D) militia volunteers.
    (E) fearful.

11. What is the military significance of Washington crossing the Delaware on Christmas Day in 1776 and later surprising the Hessians at Trenton and Princeton, New Jersey?
    (A) It was the Patriots' first victory.
    (B) He was able to pick up new recruits and expand his army there.
    (C) The victories proved life-saving to the colonists' cause.
    (D) It led to the capture of British General Howe.
    (E) It enabled the Patriots to keep New England from being attacked and isolated by the British.

12. The Battle of Saratoga proved vitally important to the American cause because
    (A) it encouraged France to provide much-needed military aid.
    (B) the impressive British general Burgoyne perished in combat.
    (C) Britain surrendered, and the Revolution was won.
    (D) it boosted the morale of the Patriots.
    (E) it brought France, Spain, and Germany into the conflict on the side of the Americans.

13. Which of the following was NOT among America's goals for revolutionizing international affairs after its battle for independence?
    (A) Ending colonialism
    (B) Ending mercantilism
    (C) Promoting free trade
    (D) Instituting freedom of the seas
    (E) Forging military alliances

14. The Treaty of Fort Stanwix was
    (A) the first treaty between the United States and an Indian nation.
    (B) the peace treaty that ended the Revolution and created an independent United States.
    (C) an agreement between the British and four Iroquois nations in which they joined forces against the American revolutionaries.
    (D) a deal between France and Spain, in which the latter would gain Gibraltar should England lose.
    (E) the agreement negotiated by Benjamin Franklin that brought France into the Revolution on the side of the Americans.

15. Why have women's rights activists historically regarded Abigail Adams as a heroine when there was no full-fledged women's movement in America until the 1840s?
    (A) She was one of a few women to play a role in the Revolutionary War.
    (B) She urged her prominent husband, John Adams, to consider women's rights in the development of independent America.
    (C) She was outspoken in her fight for women's rights despite the lack of a movement.
    (D) She personally appealed to the Second Continental Congress to include women in the Declaration of Independence.
    (E) She symbolized equal partnership in marriage and fought for the right to vote.

16. The Revolutionary War became a global conflagration because all of the following countries played a role EXCEPT
    (A) France.
    (B) Spain.
    (C) Denmark-Norway.
    (D) Russia.
    (E) Poland.

Part Two

Building the New Nation

1776–1860

*B*y 1783 Americans had won their freedom. Now they had to build their country. To be sure, they were blessed with a vast and fertile land, and they inherited from their colonial experience a proud legacy of self-rule. But history provided scant precedent for erecting a republic on a national scale. No law of nature guaranteed that the thirteen rebellious colonies would stay glued together as a single nation, or that they would preserve, not to mention expand, their democratic way of life. New institutions had to be created, new habits of thought cultivated. Who could predict whether the American experiment in government by the people would succeed?

The feeble national government cobbled together under the Articles of Confederation during the Revolutionary War soon proved woefully inadequate to the task of nation building. In less than ten years after the Revolutionary War's conclusion, the Articles were replaced by a new Constitution, but even its adoption did not end the debate

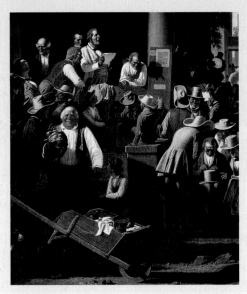

over just what form American government should take. Would the president, the Congress, or the courts be the dominant branch? What should be the proper division of authority between the federal government and the states? How could the rights of individuals be protected against a potentially powerful government? What economic policies would best serve the infant Republic? How should the nation defend itself against foreign foes? What principles should guide foreign policy? Was America a nation at all, or was it merely a geographic expression, destined to splinter into several bitterly quarreling sections, as had happened to so many other would-be countries?

After a shaky start under George Washington and John Adams in the 1790s, buffeted by foreign troubles and domestic crises, the new Republic passed a major test when power was peacefully transferred from the conservative Federalists to the more liberal Jeffersonians in the election of 1800. A confident President Jefferson proceeded boldly to

The Verdict of the People (detail) This election-day crowd exudes the exuberant spirit of the era of Andrew Jackson, when the advent of universal white male suffrage made the United States the modern world's first mass participatory democracy. Yet the black man with the wheelbarrow, literally pushing his way into the painting, is a pointed reminder that the curse of slavery still blighted this happy scene. George Caleb Bingham, *The Verdict of the People* (detail), Courtesy Saint Louis Art Museum expand the national territory with the landmark Louisiana Purchase in 1803. But before long Jefferson, and then his successor, James Madison, were embroiled in what eventually proved to be a fruitless effort to spare the United States from the ravages of the war then raging in Europe.

America was dangerously divided during the War of 1812 and suffered a humiliating defeat. But a new sense of national unity and purpose was unleashed in the land thereafter. President Monroe, presiding over this "Era of Good Feelings," proclaimed in the Monroe Doctrine of 1823 that both of the American continents were off-limits to further European intervention. The foundations of a continental-scale economy were laid, as a "transportation revolution" stitched the country together with canals and railroads and turnpikes. Settlers flooded over those new arteries into the burgeoning West, often brusquely shouldering aside the native peoples. Immigrants, especially from Ireland and Germany, flocked to American shores. The combination of new lands, new labor, and revolutionary new technologies like the telegraph and the railroad fed the growth of a market economy, including the commercialization of agriculture and the beginnings of the factory system of production. Old ways of life withered as the market economy drew women as well as men, children as well as adults, blacks as well as whites, into its embrace. Ominously, the slave system grew robustly as the production of cotton, mostly for sale on European markets, exploded into the booming Southwest.

Meanwhile, the United States in the era of Andrew Jackson gave the world an impressive

Women Weavers at Work (detail) These simple cotton looms heralded the dawn of the Industrial Revolution, which transformed the lives of Americans even more radically than the events of 1776. Slater Mill, Pawtucket R.I.

lesson in political science. Between roughly 1820 and 1840, Americans virtually invented mass democracy, creating huge political parties and enormously expanding political participation by enfranchising nearly all adult white males. Nor was the spirit of innovation confined to the political realm. A wave of reform and cultural vitality swept through many sectors of American society. Utopian experiments proliferated. Religious revivals and even new religions, like Mormonism, flourished. A national literature blossomed. Crusades were launched for temperance, prison reform, women's rights, and the abolition of slavery.

By the second quarter of the nineteenth century, the outlines of a distinctive American national character had begun to emerge. Americans were a diverse, restless people, tramping steadily westward, eagerly forging their own nascent Industrial Revolution, proudly exercising their democratic political rights, impatient with the old, in love with the new, testily asserting their superiority over all other peoples—and increasingly divided, in heart, in conscience, and in politics, over the single greatest blight on their record of nation making and democracy building: slavery.

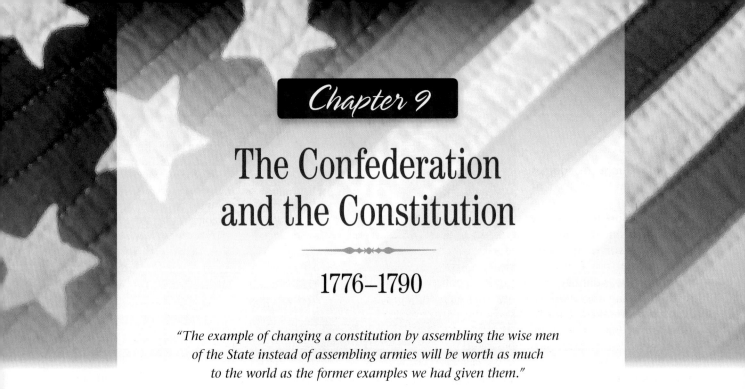

Chapter 9

The Confederation and the Constitution

1776–1790

"The example of changing a constitution by assembling the wise men of the State instead of assembling armies will be worth as much to the world as the former examples we had given them."

THOMAS JEFFERSON 1789

The American Revolution was not a revolution in the sense of a radical or total change. It did not suddenly and violently overturn the entire political and social framework, as later occurred in the French and Russian Revolutions. What happened was accelerated evolution rather than outright revolution. During the conflict itself, people went on working and praying, marrying and playing. Many of them were not seriously disturbed by the actual fighting, and the most isolated communities scarcely knew that a war was on.

Yet some striking changes were ushered in, affecting social customs, political institutions, and ideas about society, government, and even gender roles. The exodus of some eighty thousand substantial Loyalists robbed the new ship of state of conservative ballast. This weakening of the aristocratic upper crust, with all its culture and elegance, paved the way for new, Patriot elites to emerge. It also cleared the field for more egalitarian ideas to sweep across the land.

✖ The Pursuit of Equality

"All men are created equal," the Declaration of Independence proclaimed, and equality was everywhere the watchword. Most states reduced (but usually did not eliminate altogether) property-holding requirements for voting. Ordinary men and women demanded to be addressed as "Mr." and "Mrs."—titles once reserved for the wealthy and highborn. Employers were now called

"boss," not "master." In 1784 New Yorkers released a shipload of freshly arrived indentured servants, on the grounds that their status violated democratic ideals; by 1800 servitude was virtually unknown. Most Americans ridiculed the lordly pretensions of Continental Army officers who formed an exclusive hereditary order, the **Society of the Cincinnati**. Social democracy was further stimulated by the growth of trade organizations for artisans and laborers. Citizens in several states, flushed with republican fervor, also sawed off the remaining shackles of medieval inheritance laws, such as primogeniture, which awarded all of a father's property to the eldest son.

A protracted fight for separation of church and state resulted in notable gains. Although the well-entrenched Congregational Church continued to be legally established in some New England states, the Anglican Church, tainted by association with the British crown, was humbled. De-anglicized, it re-formed as the Protestant Episcopal Church and was everywhere **disestablished**. The struggle for divorce between religion and government proved fiercest in Virginia. It was prolonged to 1786, when freethinking Thomas Jefferson and his co-reformers, including the Baptists, won a complete victory with the passage of the **Virginia Statute for Religious Freedom**. (See Table 5.1, on established churches, on p. 86.)

The egalitarian sentiments unleashed by the war likewise challenged the institution of slavery. Philadelphia Quakers in 1775 founded the world's first antislavery

The impact of the American Revolution was worldwide. About 1783 a British ship stopped at some islands off the East African coast, where the natives were revolting against their Arab masters. When asked why they were fighting, they replied,

❝America is free, Could not we be?❞

society. Hostilities hampered the noxious trade in "black ivory," and the Continental Congress in 1774 called for the complete abolition of the slave trade, a summons to which most of the states responded positively. Several northern states went further and either abolished slavery outright or provided for the gradual emancipation of blacks. Even on the plantations of Virginia, a few idealistic masters freed their human chattels—the first frail sprouts of the later abolitionist movement.

But this revolution of sentiments was sadly incomplete. No states south of Pennsylvania abolished slavery, and in both North and South, the law discriminated harshly against freed blacks and slaves alike. Emancipated African Americans could be barred from purchasing property, holding certain jobs, and educating their children. Laws against interracial marriage also sprang up at this time.

Why, in this dawning democratic age, did abolition not go further and cleanly blot the evil of slavery from the fresh face of the new nation? The sorry truth is that the fledgling idealism of the Founding Fathers was sacrificed to political expediency. A fight over slavery would have fractured the fragile national unity that was so desperately needed. "Great as the evil [of slavery] is," the young Virginian James Madison wrote in 1787, "a dismemberment of the union would be worse." Nearly a century later, the slavery issue did wreck the Union—temporarily.

The Revolution enhanced the expectations and power of women as wives and mothers. As one "matrimonial republican" wrote in 1792,

❝I object to the word 'obey' in the marriage-service because it is a general word, without limitations or definition. . . . The obedience between man and wife, I conceive, is, or ought to be mutual. . . . Marriage ought never to be considered a contract between a superior and an inferior, but a reciprocal union of interest, an implied partnership of interests, where all differences are accommodated by conference; and where the decision admits of no retrospect.**❞**

Massachusetts Historical Society

Elizabeth "Mumbet" Freeman (ca. 1744–1829), by Susan Anne Livingston Ridley Sedgwick, 1811 In 1781, having overheard Revolutionary-era talk about the "rights of man," Mumbet sued her Massachusetts master for her freedom from slavery. She won her suit and lived the rest of her life as a paid domestic servant in the home of the lawyer who had pleaded her case.

Likewise incomplete was the extension of the doctrine of equality to women. Some women did serve (disguised as men) in the military, and New Jersey's new constitution in 1776 even, for a time, enabled women to vote. But though Abigail Adams teased her husband, John, in 1776 that "the Ladies" were determined "to foment a rebellion" of their own if they were not given political rights, most of the women in the Revolutionary era were still doing traditional women's work.

Yet women did not go untouched by Revolutionary ideals. Central to republican ideology was the concept of **civic virtue**—the notion that democracy depended on the unselfish commitment of each citizen to the public good. And who could better cultivate the habits of a virtuous citizenry than mothers, to whom society entrusted the moral education of the young? Indeed the selfless devotion of a mother to her family was often cited as the very model of proper republican behavior. The idea of "**republican motherhood**" thus took root, elevating women to a newly prestigious role as the special keepers of the nation's conscience. Educational opportunities for women expanded, in the expectation that educated wives and mothers could better cultivate the virtues demanded by the Republic in their husbands, daughters, and sons. Republican women now bore crucial responsibility for the survival of the nation.

✯ Constitution Making in the States

The Continental Congress in 1776 called upon the colonies to draft new constitutions. In effect, the Continental Congress was actually asking the colonies to summon themselves into being as new states. The sovereignty of these new states, according to the theory of republicanism, would rest on the authority of the people. For a time the manufacture of governments was even more pressing than the manufacture of gunpowder. Although the states of Connecticut and Rhode Island merely retouched their colonial charters, constitution writers elsewhere worked tirelessly to capture on black-inked parchment the republican spirit of the age.

Massachusetts contributed one especially noteworthy innovation when it called a special convention to draft its constitution and then submitted the final draft directly to the people for ratification. Once adopted in 1780, the Massachusetts constitution could be changed only by another specially called constitutional convention. This procedure was later imitated in the drafting and ratification of the federal Constitution. Adopted almost a decade before the federal Constitution, the Massachusetts constitution remains the longest-lived constitution in the world.

The newly penned state constitutions had many features in common. Their similarity, as it turned out, made easier the drafting of a workable federal charter when the time was ripe. In the British tradition, a "constitution" was not a written document, but rather an accumulation of laws, customs, and precedents. Americans invented something different. The documents they drafted were contracts that defined the powers of government, as did the old colonial charters, but they drew their authority from the people, not from the royal seal of a distant king. As *written* documents the state constitutions were intended to represent a *fundamental* law, superior to the transient whims of ordinary legislation. Most of these documents included bills of rights, specifically guaranteeing long-prized liberties against later legislative encroachment. Most of them required the annual election of legislators, who were thus forced to stay in touch with the mood of the people. All of them deliberately created weak executive and judicial branches, at least by present-day standards. A generation of quarreling with His Majesty's officials had implanted a deep distrust of despotic governors and arbitrary judges.

In all the new state governments, the legislatures, as presumably the most democratic branch of government, were given sweeping powers. But as Thomas Jefferson warned, "173 despots [in a legislature] would surely be as oppressive as one." Many Americans soon came to agree with him.

The democratic character of the new state legislatures was vividly reflected by the presence of many members from the recently enfranchised poorer western districts. Their influence was powerfully felt in their several successful movements to relocate state capitals from the haughty eastern seaports into the less pretentious interior. In the Revolutionary era, the capitals of New Hampshire, New York, Virginia, North Carolina, South Carolina, and Georgia were all moved westward. These geographical shifts portended political shifts that deeply discomfited many more conservative Americans.

✯ Economic Crosscurrents

Economic changes begotten by the war were likewise noteworthy, but not overwhelming. States seized control of former crown lands, and although rich speculators had their day, many of the large Loyalist holdings were confiscated and eventually cut up into small farms. Roger Morris's huge estate in New York, for example, was sliced into 250 parcels—thus accelerating the spread of economic democracy. The frightful excesses of the French Revolution were avoided, partly because cheap land was easily available, and because America had so few deeply entrenched landed aristocrats to be overthrown. It is highly significant that in the United States, economic democracy, broadly speaking, preceded political democracy.

A sharp stimulus was given to manufacturing by the prewar nonimportation agreements and later by the war itself. Goods that had formerly been imported from Britain were mostly cut off, and the ingenious Yankees were forced to make their own. Ten years after the Revolution, busy Brandywine Creek, south of Philadelphia, was turning the water wheels of numerous mills along an eight-mile stretch. Yet America remained overwhelmingly a nation of soil-tillers.

Economically speaking, independence had drawbacks. Much of the coveted commerce of Britain was still reserved for the loyal parts of the empire. American ships were now barred from British and British West Indies harbors. Fisheries were disrupted, and bounties for ships' stores had abruptly ended. In some respects the hated British Navigation Laws were more disagreeable after independence than before.

New commercial outlets, fortunately, compensated partially for the loss of old ones. Americans could now trade freely with foreign nations, subject to local restrictions—a boon they had not enjoyed in the days of mercantilism. Enterprising Yankee shippers ventured

Examining the Evidence

Copley Family Portrait, ca. 1776–1777

A portrait painting like this one by John Singleton Copley (1738–1815) documents physical likenesses, clothing styles, and other material possessions typical of an era. But it can do more than that. In the execution of the painting itself, the preeminent portrait painter of colonial America revealed important values of his time. Copley's composition and use of light emphasized the importance of the mother in the family. Mrs. Copley is the visual center of the painting: the light falls predominantly on her, and she provides the focus of activity for the family group. Although Copley had moved to England in 1774 to avoid the disruptions of war, he had made radical friends in his hometown of Boston and surely had imbibed the sentiment of the age about "republican motherhood"—a sentiment that revered women as homemakers and mothers, the cultivators of good republican values in young citizens. What other prevailing attitudes, about gender and age, for example, might this painting reveal?

John Singleton Copley, The Copley Family, Andrew W. Mellon Fund, image courtesy of the Board of Trustees, National Gallery of Art, Washington, D.C.

boldly—and profitably—into the Baltic and China Seas. In 1784 the *Empress of China*, carrying a valuable weed (ginseng) that was highly prized by Chinese herb doctors as a cure for impotence, led the way into the East Asian markets.

Yet the general economic picture was far from rosy. War had spawned demoralizing extravagance, speculation, and profiteering, with profits for some as indecently high as 300 percent. State governments had borrowed more during the war than they could ever hope to repay. Runaway inflation had been ruinous to many citizens, and Congress had failed in its feeble attempts to curb economic laws. The average citizen was probably worse off financially at the end of the shooting than at the start.

The whole economic and social atmosphere was unhealthy. A newly rich class of profiteers was noisily conspicuous, whereas many once-wealthy people were left destitute. The controversy leading to the Revolutionary War had bred a keen distaste for taxes and encouraged disrespect for the majesty of the law generally. John Adams had been shocked when gleefully told by a horse-jockey neighbor that the courts of justice were all closed—a plight that proved to be only temporary.

Western Merchants Negotiating for Tea in Hong Kong, ca. 1800 Yankee merchants and shippers figured prominently in the booming trade with China in the late eighteenth century. Among the American entrepreneurs who prospered in the China trade was Warren Delano, ancestor of President Franklin Delano Roosevelt.

✦ A Shaky Start Toward Union

What would the Americans do with the independence they had so dearly won? The Revolution had dumped the responsibility of creating and operating a new central government squarely into their laps.

Prospects for erecting a lasting regime were far from bright. It is always difficult to set up a new government and doubly difficult to set up a new type of government. The picture was further clouded in America by leaders preaching "natural rights" and looking suspiciously at all persons clothed with authority. America was more a name than a nation, and unity ran little deeper than the color on the map.

Disruptive forces stalked the land. The departure of the conservative Tory element left the political system inclined toward experimentation and innovation. Patriots had fought the war with a high degree of disunity, but they had at least concurred on allegiance to a common cause. Now even that was gone. It would have been almost a miracle if any government fashioned in all this confusion had long endured.

Hard times, the bane of all regimes, set in shortly after the war and hit bottom in 1786. As if other troubles were not enough, British manufacturers, with dammed-up surpluses, began flooding the American market with cut-rate goods. War-baby American industries, in particular, suffered industrial colic from such ruthless competition. One Philadelphia newspaper in 1783 urged readers to don home-stitched garments of homespun cloth:

> *Of foreign gewgaws let's be free,*
> *And wear the webs of liberty.*

Yet hopeful signs could be discerned. The thirteen sovereign states were basically alike in governmental structure and functioned under similar constitutions. Americans enjoyed a rich political inheritance, derived partly from Britain and partly from their own homegrown devices for self-government. Finally, they were blessed with political leaders of a high order in men like George Washington, James Madison, John Adams, Thomas Jefferson, and Alexander Hamilton.

✦ Creating a Confederation

The Second Continental Congress of Revolutionary days was little more than a conference of ambassadors from the thirteen states. It was totally without constitutional authority and in general did only what it dared to do, though it asserted some control over military affairs and foreign policy. In nearly all respects, the thirteen states were sovereign, for they coined money, raised armies and navies, and erected tariff barriers. The legislature of Virginia even ratified separately the treaty of alliance of 1778 with France.

Shortly before declaring independence in 1776, Congress appointed a committee to draft a written constitution for the new nation. The finished product was the **Articles of Confederation**. Adopted by Congress in 1777, it was translated into French after the Battle of Saratoga so as to convince France that America had a genuine government in the making. The Articles were not ratified by all thirteen states until 1781, less than eight months before the victory at Yorktown.

The chief apple of discord was western lands. Six of the jealous states, including Pennsylvania and Maryland, had no holdings beyond the Allegheny Mountains. Seven, notably New York and Virginia, were favored with enormous acreage, in most cases on the basis of earlier charter grants. The six land-hungry states argued that the more fortunate states would not have retained possession of this splendid prize if all the other states had not fought for it also. A major complaint was that the land-rich states could sell their trans-Allegheny tracts and thus pay off pensions and other debts incurred in the common cause. States without such holdings would have to tax themselves heavily to defray these obligations. Why not turn the whole western area over to the central government?

Unanimous approval of the Articles of Confederation by the thirteen states was required, and land-starved Maryland stubbornly held out until March 1, 1781. Maryland at length gave in when New York surrendered its western claims and Virginia seemed about to do so. To sweeten the pill, Congress pledged itself to dispose of these vast areas for the "common benefit." It further agreed to carve from the new public domain not colonies, but a number of "republican" states, which in time would be admitted to the Union on terms of complete equality with all the others. This extraordinary commitment faithfully reflected the anticolonial spirit of the Revolution, and the pledge was later fully redeemed in the famed Northwest Ordinance of 1787 (see Map 9.1).

Fertile public lands thus transferred to the central government proved to be an invaluable bond of union.

MAP 9.1 Western Land Cessions to the United States, 1782–1802

© Cengage Learning

The states that had thrown their heritage into the common pot had to remain in the Union if they were to reap their share of the advantages from the land sales. An army of westward-moving pioneers purchased their farms from the federal government, directly or indirectly, and they learned to look to the national capital, rather than to the state capitals—with a consequent weakening of local influence. Finally, a uniform national land policy was made possible.

✹ The Articles of Confederation: America's First Constitution

The Articles of Confederation—some have said "Articles of Confusion"—provided for a loose confederation or "firm league of friendship." Thirteen independent states were thus linked together for joint action in dealing with common problems, such as foreign affairs. A clumsy Congress was to be the chief agency of government. There was no executive branch—George III had left a bad taste—and the vital judicial arm was left almost exclusively to the states.

Congress, though dominant, was severely hobbled. Each state had a single vote, so that some sixty-eight thousand Rhode Islanders had the same voice as more than ten times that many Virginians. All bills dealing with subjects of importance required the support of nine states; any amendment of the Articles themselves required unanimous ratification. Unanimity was almost impossible, and this meant that the amending process, perhaps fortunately, was unworkable. If it had been workable, the Republic might have struggled along with a patched-up Articles of Confederation rather than replace it with an effective Constitution.

The shackled Congress was weak—and was purposely designed to be weak. Suspicious states, having just won control over taxation and commerce from Britain, had no desire to yield their newly acquired privileges to an American parliament—even one of their own making.

Two handicaps of Congress were crippling. It had no power to regulate commerce, and this loophole left the states free to establish different, and often conflicting, laws regarding tariffs and navigation. Nor could Congress enforce its tax-collection program. It established a tax quota for each of the states and then asked them please to contribute their share on a voluntary basis. The central authority—a "government by supplication"—was lucky if in any year it received one-fourth of its requests.

The feeble national government in Philadelphia could advise and advocate and appeal. But in dealing with the independent states, it could not command or coerce or control. It could not act directly upon the

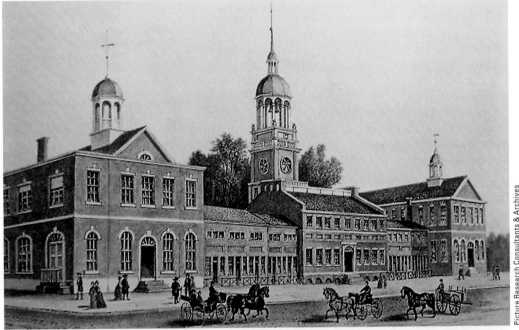

Independence Hall, Philadelphia, 1776 Originally built in the 1730s as a meeting place for the Pennsylvania colonial assembly, this building witnessed much history: here Washington was given command of the Continental Army, the Declaration of Independence was signed, and the Constitution was hammered out. The building began to be called "Independence Hall" in the 1820s and is today a major tourist destination in Philadelphia.

Picture Research Consultants & Archives

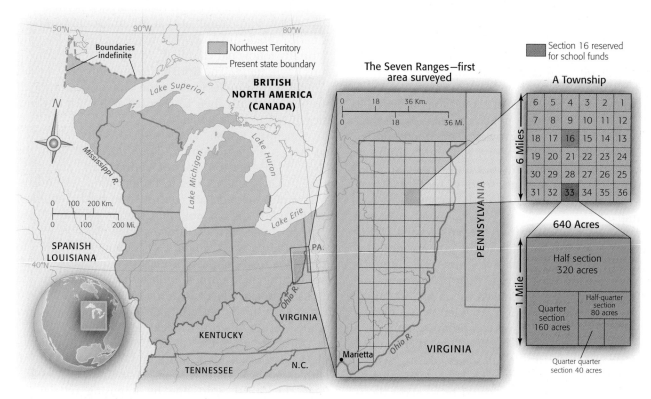

MAP 9.2 Surveying the Old Northwest Under the Land Ordinance of 1785 Sections of a township under the Land Ordinance of 1785. © Cengage Learning

individual citizens of a sovereign state; it could not even protect itself against gross indignities. In 1783 a group of mutinous Pennsylvania soldiers, whose pay was in arrears, marched to Philadelphia and made a threatening demonstration in front of Independence Hall. After Congress appealed in vain to the state for protection, its members fled to safety at Princeton College in New Jersey. The new Congress, with all its paper powers, was even less effective than the old Continental Congress, which had wielded no constitutional powers at all.

Yet the Articles of Confederation, weak though they were, proved to be a landmark in government. They were for those days a model of what a loose confederation could be. Thomas Jefferson enthusiastically hailed the new structure as the best one "existing or that ever did exist." To compare it with the European governments, he thought, was like comparing "heaven and hell." But although the Confederation was praiseworthy as confederations went, the troubled times demanded not a loosely woven *con*federation but a tightly knit federation. This involved the yielding by the states of their sovereignty to a completely recast federal government, which in turn would leave them free to control their local affairs.

In spite of their defects, the anemic Articles of Confederation were a significant steppingstone toward the present Constitution. They clearly outlined the general powers that were to be exercised by the central government, such as making treaties and establishing a postal service. As the first written constitution of the Republic, the Articles kept alive the flickering ideal of union and held the states together—until such time as they were ripe for the establishment of a strong constitution by peaceful, evolutionary methods. Without this intermediary jump, the states probably would never have consented to the breathtaking leap from the old boycott Association of 1774 to the Constitution of the United States.

✷ Landmarks in Land Laws

Handcuffed though the Congress of the Confederation was, it succeeded in passing supremely farsighted pieces of legislation. These related to an immense part of the public domain recently acquired from the states and commonly known as the **Old Northwest**. This area of land lay northwest of the Ohio River, east of the Mississippi River, and south of the Great Lakes.

The first of these red-letter laws was the **Land Ordinance of 1785** (see Map 9.2). It provided that the acreage of the Old Northwest should be sold and that the proceeds should be used to help pay off the national debt. The vast area was to be surveyed before sale and settlement, thus forestalling endless confusion and lawsuits. It was to be divided into townships six miles square, each of which in turn was to be split into thirty-six sections of one square mile each. The sixteenth section of each township was set aside to be sold for the benefit of the public schools—a priceless gift to education in the Northwest. The orderly settlement of the Northwest Territory, where the land was methodically surveyed and titles duly recorded, contrasted sharply with the chaos south of the Ohio River, where uncertain ownership was the norm and fraud was rampant.

Even more noteworthy was the **Northwest Ordinance** of 1787, which related to the governing of the Old Northwest. This law came to grips with the problem of how a nation should deal with its colonies—the same problem that had bedeviled the king and Parliament in London. The solution provided by the Northwest Ordinance was a judicious compromise: temporary tutelage, then permanent equality. First, there would be two evolutionary territorial stages, during which the area would be subordinate to the federal government. Then, when a territory could boast sixty thousand inhabitants, it might be admitted by Congress as a state, with all the privileges of the thirteen charter members. (This is precisely what the Continental Congress had promised the states when they surrendered their lands in 1781.) The ordinance also forbade slavery in the Old Northwest—a path-breaking step, though it exempted slaves already present.

The wisdom of Congress in handling this explosive problem deserves warm praise. If it had attempted to chain the new territories in permanent subordination, a second American Revolution almost certainly would have erupted in later years, fought this time by the West against the East. Congress thus neatly solved the seemingly insoluble problem of empire. The scheme worked so well that its basic principles were ultimately carried over from the Old Northwest to other frontier areas.

✦ The World's Ugly Duckling

Foreign relations, especially with London, remained troubled during these anxious years of the Confederation. Britain resented the stab in the back from its rebellious offspring and for eight years refused to send a minister to America's "backwoods" capital. London suggested, with barbed irony, that if it sent one, it would have to send thirteen.

Britain flatly declined to make a commercial treaty or to repeal its ancient Navigation Laws. Lord Sheffield,

whose ungenerous views prevailed, argued persuasively in a widely sold pamphlet that Britain would win back America's trade anyhow. Commerce, he insisted, would naturally follow old channels. So why go to the Americans hat in hand? The British also officially closed their profitable West Indies trade to the United States, though the Yankees, with their time-tested skill in smuggling, illegally partook nonetheless.

Scheming British agents were also active along the far-flung northern frontier. They intrigued with the disgruntled Allen brothers of Vermont and sought to annex that rebellious area to Britain. Along the northern border, the redcoats continued to hold a chain of trading posts on U.S. soil, and there they maintained their fur trade with the Indians. One plausible excuse for remaining was the failure of the American states to honor the treaty of peace in regard to debts and Loyalists. But the main purpose of Britain in hanging on was probably to curry favor with the Indians and keep their tomahawks lined up on the side of the king as a barrier against future American attacks on Canada.

All these grievances against Britain were maddening to patriotic Americans. Some citizens demanded, with more heat than wisdom, that the United States force the British into line by imposing restrictions on their imports to America. But Congress could not control commerce, and the states refused to adopt a uniform tariff policy. Some "easy states" deliberately lowered their tariffs in order to attract an unfair share of trade.

Spain, though recently an enemy of Britain, was openly unfriendly to the new Republic. It controlled the mouth of the all-important Mississippi, down which the pioneers of Tennessee and Kentucky were forced to float their produce. In 1784 Spain closed the river to American commerce, threatening the West with strangulation. Spain likewise claimed a large area north of the Gulf of Mexico, including a part of West Florida, granted to the United States by the British in 1783. At Natchez, on disputed soil, it held an important fort. It also schemed with the neighboring Indians, grievously antagonized by the rapacious land policies of Georgia and North Carolina, to hem in the Americans east of the Appalachians. Spain and Britain together, radiating their influence out among resentful Indian tribes, prevented America from exercising effective control over about half of its total territory (see Map 9.3).

Even France, America's comrade-in-arms, cooled off now that it had humbled Britain. The French demanded the repayment of money loaned during the war and restricted trade with their bustling West Indies and other ports.

Pirates of the North African states, including the arrogant Dey of Algiers, were ravaging America's Mediterranean commerce and enslaving Yankee sailors. The

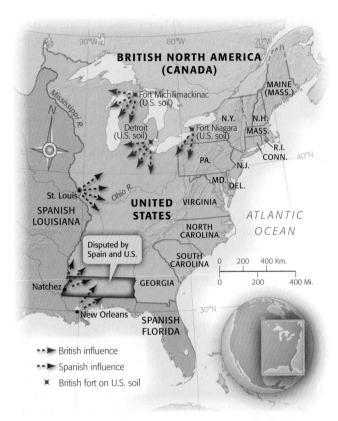

MAP 9.3 Main Centers of Spanish and British Influence After 1783 This map shows graphically that the United States in 1783 achieved complete independence in name only, particularly in the area west of the Appalachian Mountains. Not until twenty years had passed did the new Republic, with the purchase of Louisiana from France in 1803, eliminate foreign influence from the east bank of the Mississippi River. Much of Florida remained in Spanish hands until the Adams-Onís Treaty of 1819 (see p. 239–240). © Cengage Learning

British purchased protection for their own subjects, and as colonists the Americans had enjoyed this shield. But as an independent nation, the United States was too weak to fight and too poor to bribe. A few Yankee shippers engaged in the Mediterranean trade with forged British protection papers, but not all were so bold or so lucky.

John Jay, secretary for foreign affairs, derived some hollow satisfaction from these insults. He hoped they would at least humiliate the American people into framing a new government at home that would be strong enough to command respect abroad.

✴ The Horrid Specter of Anarchy

Economic storm clouds continued to loom in the mid-1780s. The requisition system of raising money was breaking down; some of the states refused to pay anything, while complaining bitterly about the tyranny of "King Congress." Interest on the public debt was piling up at home, and the nation's credit was evaporating abroad.

Individual states were getting out of hand. Quarrels over boundaries generated numerous minor pitched battles. Some of the states were levying duties on goods from their neighbors; New York, for example, taxed firewood from Connecticut and cabbages from New Jersey. A number of the states were again starting to grind out depreciated paper currency, and a few of them had passed laws sanctioning the semiworthless "rag money." As a contemporary rhymester put it,

> *Bankrupts their creditors with rage pursue;*
> *No stop, no mercy from the debtor crew.*

An alarming uprising, known as **Shays's Rebellion**, flared up in western Massachusetts in 1786. Impoverished backcountry farmers, many of them Revolutionary War veterans, were losing their farms through mortgage foreclosures and tax delinquencies. Led by Captain Daniel Shays, a veteran of the Revolution, these desperate debtors demanded that the state issue paper money, lighten taxes, and suspend property takeovers. Hundreds of angry agitators, again seizing their muskets, attempted to enforce their demands.

Massachusetts authorities responded with drastic action. Supported partly by contributions from wealthy citizens, they raised a small army. Several skirmishes occurred—at Springfield three Shaysites were killed, and one was wounded—and the movement collapsed. Daniel Shays, who believed that he was fighting anew against tyranny, was condemned to death but was later pardoned.

Shays's followers were crushed, but the nightmarish memory lingered on. The Massachusetts legislature soon passed debtor-relief laws of the kind Shays had championed, seemingly confirming Thomas Jefferson's fear of "democratic despotism." "An elective despotism was not the government we fought for," Jefferson wrote. The outbursts of Shays and other distressed debtors struck fear in the hearts of the propertied class, who began to suspect that the Revolution had created a monster of "mobocracy." Unbridled republicanism, it seemed to many of the elite, had fed an insatiable appetite for liberty that was fast becoming license. Civic virtue was no longer sufficient to rein in self-interest and greed. It had become "undeniably evident," one skeptic sorrowfully lamented, "that some malignant disorder has seized upon our body politic." If republicanism was too shaky a ground upon which to construct a new nation, a stronger central government would provide the needed foundation. A few panicky citizens even talked of importing a European monarch to carry on where George III had failed.

Library of Congress

Debtors Protest, 1787   This drawing done on the eve of the writing of the U.S. Constitution features a farmer with a plow, a rake, and a bottle complaining, "Takes all to pay taxes." The discontent of debt-rich and currency-poor farmers alarmed republican leaders and helped persuade them that the Articles of Confederation needed to be replaced with a new constitution.

How critical were conditions under the Confederation? Conservatives, anxious to safeguard their wealth and position, naturally exaggerated the seriousness of the nation's plight. They were eager to persuade their fellow citizens to amend the Articles of Confederation in favor of a muscular central government. But the poorer states' rights people pooh-poohed the talk of anarchy. Many were debtors who feared that a powerful federal government would force them to pay their creditors.

Yet friends and critics of the Confederation agreed that it needed some strengthening. Popular toasts were "Cement to the Union" and "A hoop to the barrel." The chief differences arose over how this goal should be attained and how a maximum degree of states' rights

Social tensions reached a fever pitch during Shays's Rebellion in 1787. In an interview with a local Massachusetts paper, instigator Daniel Shays (1747–1825) explained how the debt-ridden farmers hoped to free themselves from the demands of a merchant-dominated government. The rebels would seize arms and

"march directly to Boston, plunder it, and then ... destroy the nest of devils, who by their influence, make the Court enact what they please, burn it and lay the town of Boston in ashes."

could be reconciled with a strong central government. America probably could have muddled through somehow with amended Articles of Confederation. But the adoption of a completely new constitution certainly spared the Republic much costly indecision, uncertainty, and turmoil.

The nationwide picture was actually brightening before the Constitution was drafted. Nearly half the states had not issued semiworthless paper currency, and some of the monetary black sheep showed signs of returning to the sound-money fold. Prosperity was beginning to emerge from the fog of depression. By 1789 overseas shipping had largely regained its place in the commercial world. If conditions had been as grim in 1787 as painted by foes of the Articles of Confederation, the move for a new constitution would hardly have encountered such heated opposition.

A Convention of "Demigods"

Control of commerce, more than any other problem, touched off the chain reaction that led to a constitutional convention. Interstate squabbling over this issue had become so alarming by 1786 that Virginia, taking the lead, issued a call for a convention at Annapolis, Maryland. Nine states appointed delegates, but only five were finally represented. With so laughable a showing, nothing could be done about the ticklish question of commerce. A charismatic New Yorker, thirty-one-year-old Alexander Hamilton, brilliantly saved the convention from complete failure by engineering the adoption of his report. It called upon Congress to summon a convention to meet in Philadelphia the next year, not to deal with commerce alone, but to bolster the entire fabric of the Articles of Confederation.

Congress, though slowly and certainly dying in New York City, was reluctant to take a step that might hasten its day of reckoning. But after six of the states had seized the bit in their teeth and appointed delegates anyhow, Congress belatedly issued the call for a convention *"for the sole and express purpose of revising"* the Articles of Confederation.

Every state chose representatives, except for independent-minded Rhode Island (still "Rogues' Island"), a stronghold of paper-moneyites. These leaders were all appointed by the state legislatures, whose members had been elected by voters who could qualify as property holders. This double distillation inevitably brought together a select group of propertied men— though it is a grotesque distortion to claim that they shaped the Constitution primarily to protect their personal financial interests. When one of them did suggest restricting federal office to major property owners, he was promptly denounced for the unwisdom of "interweaving into a republican constitution a veneration for wealth."

A quorum of the fifty-five emissaries from twelve states finally convened at Philadelphia on May 25, 1787, in the imposing red-brick statehouse. The smallness of the assemblage facilitated intimate acquaintance and hence compromise. Sessions were held in complete secrecy, with armed sentinels posted at the doors. Delegates knew that they would generate heated differences, and they did not want to advertise their own dissensions or put the ammunition of harmful arguments into the mouths of the opposition.

The caliber of the participants was extraordinarily high—"demigods," Jefferson called them. The urgency of the crisis induced the ablest men to drop their personal pursuits and come to the aid of their country. Most of the members were lawyers, and most of them fortunately were old hands at constitution making in their own states.

George Washington, towering austere and aloof among the "demigods," was unanimously elected chairman. His enormous prestige, as "the Sword of the Revolution," served to quiet overheated tempers. Benjamin Franklin, then eighty-one, added the urbanity of an elder statesman, though he was inclined to be indiscreetly talkative in his declining years. Concerned for the secrecy of their deliberations, the convention assigned chaperones to accompany Franklin to dinner parties and make sure he held his tongue. James Madison, then thirty-six and a profound student of government, made contributions so notable that he has been dubbed "the Father of the Constitution." Alexander Hamilton, then only thirty-two, was present as an advocate of a super-powerful central government. His five-hour speech in behalf of his plan, though the most eloquent of the convention, left only one delegate convinced—himself.

Rising Sun Symbol at the Top of Washington's Chair
This brass sun adorned the chair in which George Washington sat during the Constitutional Convention. Pondering the symbol, Benjamin Franklin observed, "I have the happiness to know it is a rising and not a setting sun."
Independence National Historic Park

Most of the fiery Revolutionary leaders of 1776 were absent. Thomas Jefferson, John Adams, and Thomas Paine were in Europe; Samuel Adams and John Hancock were not elected by Massachusetts. Patrick Henry, ardent champion of states' rights, was chosen as a delegate from Virginia but declined to serve, declaring that he "smelled a rat." It was perhaps well that these architects of revolution were absent. The time had come to yield the stage to leaders interested in fashioning solid political systems.

✴ Patriots in Philadelphia

The fifty-five delegates were a conservative, well-to-do body: lawyers, merchants, shippers, land speculators, and moneylenders. Not a single spokesperson was present from the poorer debtor groups. Nineteen of the fifty-five owned slaves. They were young (the average age was about forty-two) but experienced statesmen. Above all, they were nationalists, more interested in preserving and strengthening the young Republic than in further stirring the roiling cauldron of popular democracy.

The delegates hoped to crystallize the last evaporating pools of Revolutionary idealism into a stable political structure that would endure. They strongly desired a firm, dignified, and respected government. They believed in republicanism but sought to protect the American experiment from its weaknesses abroad and excesses at home. In a broad sense, the piratical Dey of Algiers, who drove the delegates to their work, was a Founding Father. They aimed to clothe the central

Alexander Hamilton (1755–1804) clearly revealed his preference for an aristocratic government in his Philadelphia speech (1787):

❝All communities divide themselves into the few and the many. The first are the rich and wellborn, the other the mass of the people. . . . The people are turbulent and changing; they seldom judge or determine right. Give therefore to the first class a distinct, permanent share in the government. They will check the unsteadiness of the second, and as they cannot receive any advantage by change, they therefore will ever maintain good government.❞

Thomas Jefferson (1743–1826), despite his high regard for the leaders at the Philadelphia convention, still was not unduly concerned about Shaysite rebellions. He wrote in November 1787,

❝What country before ever existed a century and a half without a rebellion? . . . The tree of liberty must be refreshed from time to time with the blood of patriots and tyrants. It is its natural manure.**❞**

authority with genuine power, especially in controlling tariffs, so that the United States could wrest satisfactory commercial treaties from foreign nations. The short-sighted hostility of the British mercantilists spurred the constitution framers to their task, and in this sense the illiberal Lord Sheffield was also a Founding Father.

Other motives hovered in the Philadelphia hall. Delegates were determined to preserve the union, fore-stall anarchy, and ensure security of life and property against dangerous uprisings by the "mobocracy." Above all, they sought to curb the unrestrained democracy rampant in the various states. "We have, probably, had too good an opinion of human nature in forming our confederation," Washington concluded. The spec-ter of the recent outburst in Massachusetts was espe-cially alarming, and in this sense Daniel Shays was yet another Founding Father. Grinding necessity extorted the Constitution from a reluctant nation. Fear occupied the fifty-sixth chair.

✹ Hammering Out a Bundle of Compromises

Some of the travel-stained delegates, when they first reached Philadelphia, decided upon a daring step. They would completely *scrap* the old Articles of Confed-eration, despite explicit instructions from Congress to *revise*. Technically, these bolder spirits were determined to overthrow the existing government of the United States (see Table 9.1) by peaceful means.

A scheme proposed by populous Virginia, and known as "the large-state plan," was first pushed for-ward as the framework of the Constitution. The **Vir-ginia Plan**'s essence was that representation in both houses of a bicameral Congress should be based on population—an arrangement that would naturally give the larger states an advantage.

Tiny New Jersey, suspicious of brawny Virginia, countered with "the small-state plan." The **New Jersey Plan** provided for equal representation in a unicameral Congress by states, regardless of size and population, as under the existing Articles of Confederation. The weaker states feared that under the Virginia scheme, the stronger states would band together and lord it over the rest. Angry debate, heightened by a stifling heat wave, led to deadlock. The danger loomed that the conven-tion would unravel in complete failure. Even skeptical old Benjamin Franklin seriously proposed that the daily sessions be opened with a prayer by a local clergyman.

After bitter and prolonged debate, the **Great Com-promise** of the convention was hammered out and agreed upon. A cooling of tempers came coincidentally with a cooling of the temperature. The larger states were conceded representation by population in the House of Representatives (Art. I, Sec. II, para. 3; see the Appen-dix), and the smaller states were appeased by equal rep-resentation in the Senate (see Art. I, Sec. III, para. 1). Each state, no matter how poor or small, would have two senators. The big states obviously yielded more. As a sop to them, the delegates agreed that every tax bill or revenue measure must originate in the House, where population counted more heavily (see Art. I, Sec. VII, para. 1). This critical compromise broke the logjam, and from then on success seemed within reach.

TABLE 9.1 Evolution of Federal Union		
Years	**Attempts at Union**	**Participants**
1643–1684	New England Confederation	4 colonies
1686–1689	Dominion of New England	7 colonies
1754	Albany Congress	7 colonies
1765	Stamp Act Congress	9 colonies
1772–1776	Committees of Correspondence	13 colonies
1774	First Continental Congress (adopts The Association)	12 colonies
1775–1781	Second Continental Congress	13 colonies
1781–1789	Articles of Confederation	13 states
1789–1790	Federal Constitution	13 states

Signing of the Constitution of the United States, 1787 George Washington presided from the dais as the Constitutional Convention's president. At a table in the front row sat James Madison, later called the Father of the Constitution, who recorded the proceedings in shorthand. Daily from 10 A.M. to 3 P.M., from late May through mid-September 1787, the fifty-five delegates wrangled over ideas for a new federal government.

The final Constitution was short, not least because it grew out of the Anglo-American **common law** legal tradition, which made it unnecessary to be specific about every conceivable detail. It mostly provided a flexible guide to broad rules of procedure, rather than a fixed set of detailed laws. The original (unamended) Constitution contained just seven articles and ran to about ten printed pages. Elsewhere, where **civil law** traditions prevailed, constitutions took the form of elaborate legal codes and were often strikingly lengthy. India's constitution, for example, which came into force in 1950, contains almost four hundred articles and runs to nearly two hundred pages.

In a significant reversal of the arrangement most state constitutions had embodied, the new Constitution provided for a robust—though still legally restrained—executive in the presidency. The framers were here partly inspired by the example of Massachusetts, where a vigorous, popularly elected governor had suppressed Shays's Rebellion. The president was to have broad authority to make appointments to domestic offices—including judgeships—as well as veto power over legislation. Yet presidential power was far from absolute. The president, as commander in chief, was granted the power to wage war, but Congress retained the crucial right to *declare* war—a division of responsibilities that

has been an invitation to conflict between president and Congress ever since.

The Constitution as drafted was a bundle of compromises; they stand out in every section. A key compromise was the method of electing the president indirectly by the Electoral College, rather than by direct means. While the large states would have the advantage in the first round of popular voting, as a

Dr. James McHenry (1753–1816), a delegate from Maryland to the Constitutional Convention of 1787, took notes on the arguments made for and against the drafting of a new constitution:

"Gov. Randolph observed that the confederation is incompetent to any one object for which it was instituted. The framers of it wise and great men; but human rights were the chief knowle[d]ge of the times when it was framed so far as they applied to oppose Great Britain. Requisitions for men and money had never offered their form to our assemblies. None of those vices that have since discovered themselves were apprehended."

state's share of electors was based on the total of its senators and representatives in Congress, the small states would gain a larger voice if no candidate got a majority of electoral votes and the election was thrown to the House of Representatives, where each state would have, for this purpose only, just a single vote (see Art. II, Sec. I, para. 2). Although the framers of the Constitution expected election by the House to occur frequently, it has happened just twice, in 1800 and in 1824.

Sectional jealousy also intruded. Should the voteless slave of the southern states count as a person in apportioning direct taxes and in according representation in the House of Representatives? The South, not wishing to be deprived of influence, answered "yes." The North replied "no," arguing that, as slaves were not citizens, the North might as logically demand additional representation based on its horses. As a compromise between total representation and none at all, it was decided that a slave might count as three-fifths of a person. Hence the memorable, if arbitrary, **three-fifths compromise** (see Art. I, Sec. II, para. 3).

Most of the states wanted to shut off the African slave trade. But South Carolina and Georgia, requiring slave labor in their rice paddies and malarial swamps, raised vehement protests. By way of compromise, the convention stipulated that the slave trade might continue until the end of 1807, at which time Congress could turn off the spigot (see Art. I, Sec. IX, para. 1). It did so as soon as the prescribed interval had elapsed. Meanwhile, all the new state constitutions except Georgia's forbade overseas slave trade.

✴ Safeguards for Conservatism

Heated clashes among the delegates have been overplayed. The area of agreement was actually large; otherwise the convention would have speedily disbanded. Economically, the members of the Constitutional Convention generally saw eye to eye; they demanded sound money and the protection of private property. Politically, they were in basic agreement; they favored a stronger government, with three branches and with checks and balances among them—what critics branded a "triple-headed monster." Finally, the convention was virtually unanimous in believing that manhood-suffrage democracy—government by "democratick babblers"—was something to be feared and fought.

Daniel Shays, the prime bogeyman, still frightened the conservative-minded delegates. They deliberately erected safeguards against the excesses of the "mob," and they made these barriers as strong as they dared. The awesome federal judges were to be appointed for life. The powerful president was to be elected *indirectly* by the Electoral College; the lordly senators were

> One of the Philadelphia delegates recorded in his journal a brief episode involving Benjamin Franklin, who was asked by a woman when the convention ended,
>
> **❝Well, Doctor, what have we got, a republic or a monarchy?❞**
>
> The elder statesman answered,
>
> **❝A republic, if you can keep it.❞**

to be chosen *indirectly* by state legislatures (see Art. I, Sec. III, para. 1). Only in the case of one-half of one of the three great branches—the House of Representatives—were qualified (propertied) citizens permitted to choose their officials by *direct* vote (see Art. I, Sec. II, para. 1).

Yet the new charter also contained democratic elements. Above all, it stood foursquare on the two great principles of republicanism: that the only legitimate government was one based on the consent of the governed, and that the powers of government should be limited—in this case specifically limited by a written constitution. The virtue of the people, not the authority of the state, was to be the ultimate guarantor of liberty, justice, and order. "We the people," the preamble began, in a ringing affirmation of these republican doctrines.

At the end of seventeen muggy weeks—May 25 to September 17, 1787—only forty-two of the original fifty-five members remained to sign the Constitution. Three of the forty-two, refusing to do so, returned to their states to resist ratification. The remainder, adjourning to the City Tavern, celebrated the toastworthy occasion. But no members of the convention were completely happy about the result. They were too near their work—and too weary. Whatever their personal desires, they finally had to compromise and adopt what was acceptable to the entire body, and what presumably would be acceptable to the entire country.

✴ The Clash of Federalists and Antifederalists

The Framing Fathers early foresaw that nationwide acceptance of the Constitution would not be easy to obtain. A formidable barrier was unanimous ratification by all thirteen states, as required for amendment by the still-standing Articles of Confederation. But since absent Rhode Island was certain to veto the Constitution, the delegates boldly adopted a different scheme. They stipulated that when nine states had

TABLE 9.2 Strengthening the Central Government	
Under Articles of Confederation	**Under Federal Constitution**
A loose confederation of states	A firm union of people
1 vote in Congress for each state	2 votes in Senate for each state; representation by population in House (see Art. I, Secs. II, III)
Vote of 9 states in Congress for all important measures	Simple majority vote in Congress, subject to presidential veto (see Art. I, Sec. VII, para. 2)
Laws administered loosely by committees of Congress	Laws executed by powerful president (see Art. II, Secs. II, III)
No congressional power over commerce	Congress to regulate both foreign and interstate commerce (see Art. I, Sec. VIII, para. 3)
No congressional power to levy taxes	Extensive power in Congress to levy taxes (see Art. I, Sec. VIII, para. 1)
Limited federal courts	Federal courts, capped by Supreme Court (see Art. III)
Unanimity of states for amendment	Amendment less difficult (see Art. V)
No authority to act directly upon individuals and no power to coerce states	Ample power to enforce laws by coercion of individuals and to some extent of states

registered their approval through specially elected conventions, the Constitution would become the supreme law of the land in those states ratifying (see Art. VII).

This was extraordinary, even revolutionary. It was in effect an appeal over the heads of the Congress that had called the convention, and over the heads of the legislatures that had chosen its members, to the people—or those of the people who could vote. In this way the framers could claim greater popular sanction for their handiwork. A divided Congress submitted the document to the states on this basis, without recommendation of any kind.

The American people were somewhat astonished, so well had the secrets of the convention been concealed. The public had expected the old Articles of Confederation to be patched up; now it was handed a startling new document in which, many thought, the precious jewel of state sovereignty was swallowed up (see Table 9.2). One of the hottest debates of American history forthwith erupted. The **antifederalists**, who opposed the stronger federal government, were arrayed against the **federalists**, who obviously favored it.

A motley crew gathered in the antifederalist camp. Its leaders included prominent revolutionaries like Samuel Adams, Patrick Henry, and Richard Henry Lee. Their followers consisted primarily, though not exclusively, of states' rights devotees, backcountry dwellers, and one-horse farmers—in general, the poorest classes (see Map 9.4). They were joined by paper-moneyites and debtors, many of whom feared that a potent central government would force them to pay off their debts—and at full value. Large numbers of antifederalists saw in the Constitution a plot by the upper crust to steal power back from the common folk.

Richard Henry Lee (1732–1794), a prominent antifederalist, attacked the proposed constitution in 1788:

"'Tis really astonishing that the same people, who have just emerged from a long and cruel war in defense of liberty, should now agree to fix an elective despotism upon themselves and their posterity.**"**

The same year, prominent Patriot Patrick Henry (1736–1799) agreed that the proposed constitution endangered everything the Revolution had sought to protect:

" This constitution is said to have beautiful features; but when I come to examine these features, Sir, they appear to me horridly frightful: Among other deformities, it has an awful squinting; it squints towards monarchy: And does not this raise indignation in the breast of every American? Your President may easily become King: Your Senate is so imperfectly constructed that your dearest rights may be sacrificed by what may be a small minority; . . . Where are your checks in this Government?**"**

Silver-buckled federalists had power and influence on their side. They enjoyed the support of such commanding figures as George Washington and Benjamin Franklin. Most of them lived in the settled areas along the seaboard, not in the raw backcountry. Overall, they

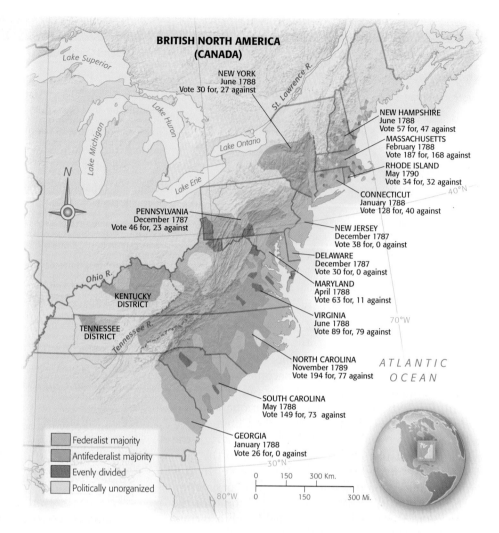

**BRITISH NORTH AMERICA
(CANADA)**

NEW YORK
June 1788
Vote 30 for, 27 against

NEW HAMPSHIRE
June 1788
Vote 57 for, 47 against

MASSACHUSETTS
February 1788
Vote 187 for, 168 against

RHODE ISLAND
May 1790
Vote 34 for, 32 against

CONNECTICUT
January 1788
Vote 128 for, 40 against

PENNSYLVANIA
December 1787
Vote 46 for, 23 against

NEW JERSEY
December 1787
Vote 38 for, 0 against

DELAWARE
December 1787
Vote 30 for, 0 against

MARYLAND
April 1788
Vote 63 for, 11 against

VIRGINIA
June 1788
Vote 89 for, 79 against

**KENTUCKY
DISTRICT**

**TENNESSEE
DISTRICT**

NORTH CAROLINA
November 1789
Vote 194 for, 77 against

SOUTH CAROLINA
May 1788
Vote 149 for, 73 against

GEORGIA
January 1788
Vote 26 for, 0 against

Federalist majority

Antifederalist majority

Evenly divided

Politically unorganized

ATLANTIC OCEAN

0   150   300 Km.

0   150   300 Mi.

MAP 9.4 The Struggle over Ratification This mottled map shows that federalist support tended to cluster around the coastal areas, which had enjoyed profitable commerce with the outside world, including the export of grain and tobacco. Impoverished frontiersmen, suspicious of a powerful new central government under the Constitution, were generally antifederalists. © Cengage Learning

were wealthier than the antifederalists, more educated, and better organized. They also controlled the press. More than a hundred newspapers were published in America in the 1780s; only a dozen supported the antifederalist cause.

Antifederalists voiced vehement objections to the "gilded trap" known as the Constitution. They cried with much truth that it had been drawn up by the aristocratic elements and hence was antidemocratic. They likewise charged that the sovereignty of the states was being submerged and that the freedoms of the individual were jeopardized by the absence of a bill of rights. They decried the dropping of annual elections for congressional representatives, the erecting of a federal stronghold ten miles square (later the District of Columbia), the creation of a standing army, the omission of any reference to God, and the highly questionable procedure of ratifying with only two-thirds of the states. A Philadelphia newspaper added that Benjamin Franklin was "a fool from age" and George Washington "a fool from nature."

✴ The Great Debate in the States

Special elections, some apathetic but others hotly contested, were held in the various states for members of the ratifying conventions (see Table 9.3). The candidates—federalist or antifederalist—were elected on the basis of their pledges for or against the Constitution.

With the ink barely dry on the parchment, four small states quickly accepted the Constitution, for they had come off much better than they expected. Pennsylvania, number two on the list of ratifiers, was the first large state to act, but not until high-handed irregularities had been employed by the federalist legislature in calling a convention. These included the forcible seating of two antifederalist members, their clothes torn and their faces red with rage, in order to complete a quorum.

Massachusetts, the second most populous state, provided an acid test. If the Constitution had failed in Massachusetts, the entire movement might easily have bogged down. The Boston ratifying convention at first

TABLE 9.3 Ratification of the Constitution

State	Date	Vote in Convention	Rank in Population	1790 Population
1. Delaware	Dec. 7, 1787	Unanimous	13	59,096
2. Pennsylvania	Dec. 12, 1787	46 to 23	3	433,611
3. New Jersey	Dec. 18, 1787	Unanimous	9	184,139
4. Georgia	Jan. 2, 1788	Unanimous	11	82,548
5. Connecticut	Jan. 9, 1788	128 to 40	8	237,655
6. Massachusetts (incl. Maine)	Feb. 7, 1788	187 to 168	2	475,199
7. Maryland	Apr. 28, 1788	63 to 11	6	319,728
8. South Carolina	May 23, 1788	149 to 73	7	249,073
9. New Hampshire	June 21, 1788	57 to 46	10	141,899
10. Virginia	June 26, 1788	89 to 79	1	747,610
11. New York	July 26, 1788	30 to 27	5	340,241
12. North Carolina	Nov. 21, 1789	195 to 77	4	395,005
13. Rhode Island	May 29, 1790	34 to 32	12	69,112

contained an antifederalist majority. It included grudging Shaysites and the aging Samuel Adams, as suspicious of government power in 1787 as he had been in 1776. The assembly buzzed with dismaying talk of summoning another constitutional convention, as though the nation had not already shot its bolt. Clearly the choice was not between this Constitution and a better one, but between this Constitution and the creaking Articles of Confederation. The absence of a bill of rights alarmed the antifederalists. But the federalists gave them solemn assurances that the first Congress would add such a safeguard by amendment, and ratification was then secured in Massachusetts by the rather narrow margin of 187 to 168.

Three more states fell into line. The last of these was New Hampshire, whose convention at first had contained a strong antifederalist majority. The federalists cleverly arranged a prompt adjournment and then won over enough waverers to secure ratification. Nine states—all but Virginia, New York, North Carolina, and Rhode Island—had now taken shelter under the "new federal roof," and the document was officially adopted on June 21, 1788. Francis Hopkinson exulted in his song "The New Roof":

Huzza! my brave boys, our work is complete;
The world shall admire Columbia's fair seat.

But such rejoicing was premature so long as the four dissenters, conspicuously New York and Virginia, dug in their heels.

✴ The Four Laggard States

Proud Virginia, the biggest and most populous state, provided fierce antifederalist opposition. There the college-bred federalist orators, for once, encountered worthy antagonists, including the fiery Patrick Henry. He professed to see in the fearsome document the death warrant of liberty. George Washington, James Madison, and John Marshall, on the federalist side, lent influential support. With New Hampshire about to ratify, the new Union was going to be formed anyhow, and Virginia could not very well continue comfortably as an independent state. After exciting debate in the state convention, ratification carried, 89 to 79.

New York also experienced an uphill struggle, burdened as it was with its own heavily antifederalist state convention. Alexander Hamilton at heart favored a much stronger central government than that under debate, but he contributed his sparkling personality and persuasive eloquence to whipping up support for federalism as framed. He also joined John Jay and James Madison in penning a masterly series of articles for the New York newspapers. Though designed as propaganda, these essays remain the most penetrating commentary ever written on the Constitution and are still widely sold in book form as ***The Federalist***. Probably the most famous of these is Madison's *Federalist* No. 10, which brilliantly refuted the conventional wisdom of the day that it was impossible to extend a republican form of government over a large territory.

Banner Paraded by the Society of Pewterers in New York City, 1788 This silk banner was carried by members of the Society of Pewterers in a parade in New York City, on July 23, 1788, to celebrate the impending ratification of the United States Constitution by New York State. The enthusiasm of these craftsmen for the Constitution confirms that not all federalists were well-to-do.

New York finally yielded. Realizing that the state could not prosper apart from the Union, the convention ratified the document by the close count of 30 to 27. At the same time, it approved thirty-two proposed amendments and—vain hope—issued a call for yet another convention to modify the Constitution.

Last-ditch dissent developed in only two states. A hostile convention met in North Carolina, then adjourned without taking a vote. Rhode Island did not even summon a ratifying convention, rejecting the Constitution by popular referendum. The two most ruggedly individualist centers of the colonial era—homes of the "otherwise minded"—thus ran true to form. They were to change their course, albeit unwillingly, only after the new government had been in operation for some months.

The race for ratification, despite much apathy, was close and quite bitter in some localities. No lives were lost, but riotous disturbances broke out in New York and Pennsylvania, involving bruises and bloodshed. There was much behind-the-scenes pressure on delegates who had promised their constituents to vote against the Constitution. The last four states ratified, not because they wanted to but because they had to. They could not safely exist outside the fold.

✦ A Conservative Triumph

The minority had triumphed—twice. A militant minority of American radicals had engineered the military Revolution that cast off the unwritten British constitution. A militant minority of conservatives—now embracing many of the earlier radicals—had engineered the peaceful revolution that overthrew the inadequate constitution known as the Articles of

A Triumphant Cartoon This cartoon appeared in the *Massachusetts Centinel* on August 2, 1788. Note the two laggards, especially the sorry condition of Rhode Island.

Confederation. Eleven states, in effect, had seceded from the Confederation, leaving the two still in, actually out in the cold.

A majority had not spoken. Only about one-fourth of the adult white males in the country, chiefly the propertied people, had voted for delegates to the ratifying conventions. Careful estimates indicate that if the new Constitution had been submitted to a manhood-suffrage vote, as in New York, it would have encountered much more opposition, probably defeat.

Conservatism was victorious. Safeguards had been erected against mob-rule excesses, while the republican gains of the Revolution were conserved. Radicals such as Patrick Henry, who had ousted British rule, saw themselves in turn upended by American conservatives. The federalists were convinced that by setting the drifting ship of state on a steady course, they could restore economic and political stability.

Yet if the architects of the Constitution were conservative, it is worth emphasizing that they conserved the principle of republican government through a redefinition of popular sovereignty. Unlike the antifederalists, who believed that the sovereignty of the people resided in a single branch of government—the legislature—the federalists contended that every branch—executive, judiciary, and legislature—effectively represented the people. By ingeniously embedding the doctrine of self-rule in a self-limiting system of checks and balances among these branches, the Constitution reconciled the potentially conflicting principles of liberty and order. It represented a marvelous achievement, one that elevated the ideals of the Revolution even while setting boundaries to them. One of the distinctive—and enduring—paradoxes of American history was thus revealed: in the United States, conservatives and radicals alike have championed the heritage of republican revolution.

Two Massachusetts citizens took opposite positions on the new Constitution. Jonathan Smith, a farmer unsympathetic to Shays's Rebellion of 1787, wrote,

❝I am a plain man, and I get my living by the plow. I have lived in a part of the country where I have known the worth of good government by the want of it. The black cloud of Shays rebellion rose last winter in my area. It brought on a state of anarchy that led to tyranny. . . . When I saw this Constitution I found that it was a cure for these disorders. I got a copy of it and read it over and over. . . . I don't think the worse of the Constitution because lawyers, and men of learning, and moneyed men are fond of it. [They] are all embarked in the same cause with us, and we must all swim or sink together.**❞**

Amos Singletary (1721–1806), who described himself as a "poor" man, argued against the Constitution:

❝We fought Great Britain—some said for a three-penny tax on tea; but it was not that. It was because they claimed a right to tax us and bind us in all cases whatever. And does not this Constitution do the same? . . . These lawyers and men of learning and money men, that talk so finely and gloss over matters so smoothly, to make us poor illiterate people swallow down the pill. . . . They expect to be the managers of the Constitution, and get all the power and money into their own hands. And then they will swallow up all us little folks, just as the whale swallowed up Jonah!**❞**

Varying Viewpoints

The Constitution: Revolutionary or Counterrevolutionary?

*A*lthough the Constitution has endured for over two centuries as the basis of American government, historians have differed sharply over how to interpret its origins and meaning. The so-called Nationalist School of historians, writing in the late nineteenth century, viewed the Constitution as the logical culmination of the Revolution and, more generally, as a crucial step in the God-given progress of Anglo-Saxon peoples. As described in John Fiske's *The Critical Period of American History* (1888), the young nation, buffeted by foreign threats and growing internal chaos, with only a weak central government to lean on, was saved by the adoption of

a more rigorous Constitution, the ultimate fulfillment of republican ideals.

By the early twentieth century, however, the progressive historians had turned a more critical eye to the Constitution. Having observed the Supreme Court of their own day repeatedly overrule legislation designed to better social conditions for the masses, they began to view the original document as an instrument created by elite conservatives to wrest political power away from the common people. For historians like Carl Becker and Charles Beard, the Constitution was part of the Revolutionary struggle between the lower classes (small farmers, debtors, and laborers) and the upper classes (merchants, financiers, and manufacturers).

Beard's *An Economic Interpretation of the Constitution of the United States* (1913) argued that the Articles of Confederation had protected debtors and small property owners and displeased wealthy elites heavily invested in trade, the public debt, and the promotion of manufacturing. Only a stronger, more centralized government could protect their extensive property interests. Reviewing the economic holdings of the Founding Fathers, Beard determined that most of those men were indeed deeply involved in investments that would increase in value under the Constitution. In effect, Beard argued, the Constitution represented a successful attempt by conservative elites to buttress their own economic supremacy at the expense of less fortunate Americans. He further contended that the Constitution was ratified by default, because the people most disadvantaged by the new government did not possess the property qualifications needed to vote—more evidence of the class conflict underlying the struggle between the federalists and the antifederalists.

Beard's economic interpretation of the Constitution held sway through the 1940s. In the 1950s, however, this analysis fell victim to the attacks of the "consensus" historians, who sought explanations for the Constitution in factors other than class interest. Scholars such as Robert Brown and Forrest McDonald convincingly disputed Beard's evidence about delegates' property ownership and refuted his portrayal of the masses as propertyless and disfranchised. They argued that the Constitution derived from an emerging consensus that the country needed a stronger central government.

Scholars since the 1950s have searched for new ways to understand the origins of the Constitution. The most influen-

tial work has been Gordon Wood's *Creation of the American Republic* (1969). Wood reinterpreted the ratification controversy as a struggle to define the true essence of republicanism. Antifederalists so feared human inclination toward corruption that they shuddered at the prospect of putting powerful political weapons in the hands of a central government. They saw small governments susceptible to local control as the only safeguard against tyranny. Federalists, on the other hand, believed that a strong, balanced national government would rein in selfish human instincts and channel them toward the pursuit of the common good. Alarmed by the indulgences of the state governments, the federalists, James Madison in particular (especially in *Federalist* No. 10), developed the novel ideal of an "extensive republic," a polity that would achieve stability by virtue of its great size and diversity. This conception challenged the conventional wisdom that a republic could survive only if it extended over a small area with a homogeneous population. In this sense, Wood argued, the Constitution represented a bold experiment—the fulfillment, rather than the repudiation, of the most advanced ideas of the Revolutionary era—even though it emanated from traditional elites determined to curtail dangerous disruptions to the social order.

Several recent studies have revived the progressive approach, focusing on the turmoil of the period. David Waldstreicher's *Slavery's Constitution* (2009) argues for the importance of slavery in the creation of the Constitution, even though it was not addressed by name in the text. Another recent treatment, Woody Holton's *Unruly Americans* (2008), argues that despite the antidemocratic tendencies of the framers, they were forced to create what was ultimately a radical document due to pressures from nonelites.

Chapter Review

KEY TERMS

Society of the Cincinnati (158)

disestablished (158)

Virginia Statute for Religious Freedom (158)

civic virtue (159)

republican motherhood (159)

Articles of Confederation (163)

Old Northwest (165)

Land Ordinance of 1785 (165)

Northwest Ordinance (166)

Shays's Rebellion (167)

Virginia Plan (170)

New Jersey Plan (170)

Great Compromise (170)

common law (171)

civil law (171)

three-fifths compromise (172)

antifederalists (173)

federalists (173)

The Federalist (175)

PEOPLE TO KNOW

Lord Sheffield

Daniel Shays

Patrick Henry

CHRONOLOGY

1774	First Continental Congress calls for abolition of slave trade
1775	Philadelphia Quakers found world's first anti-slavery society
1776	New Jersey constitution temporarily gives women the vote
1777	Articles of Confederation adopted by Second Continental Congress
1780	Massachusetts adopts first constitution drafted in convention and ratified by popular vote
1781	Articles of Confederation put into effect

1783	Military officers form Society of the Cincinnati
1785	Land Ordinance of 1785
1786	Virginia Statute for Religious Freedom Shays's Rebellion Meeting of five states to discuss revision of the Articles of Confederation
1787	Northwest Ordinance Constitutional Convention in Philadelphia
1788	Ratification by nine states guarantees a new government under the Constitution

TO LEARN MORE

Richard Bushman, *The Refinement of America: Persons, Houses, Cities* (1992)

Ron Chernow, *Alexander Hamilton* (2004)

Joseph Ellis, *Founding Brothers: The Revolutionary Generation* (2001)

Joanne Pope Melish, *Disowning Slavery: Gradual Emancipation and "Race" in New England, 1780–1860* (1998)

John Ragosta, *Wellspring of Liberty: How Virginia's Religious Dissenters Helped Win the American Revolution and Secured Religious Liberty* (2010)

Jack Rakove, *James Madison and the Creation of the American Republic* (2002)

———, ed., *The Federalist: The Essential Essays, by Alexander Hamilton, James Madison, and John Jay* (2003)

David Szatmary, *Shays' Rebellion* (1980)

David Waldstreicher, *Slavery's Constitution: From Revolution to Ratification* (2009)

Gordon S. Wood, *The Radicalism of the American Revolution* (1991)

A complete, annotated bibliography for this chapter—along with brief descriptions of the People to Know—may be found on the American Pageant website. The Key Terms are defined in a Glossary at the end of the text.

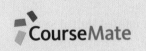

Go to the CourseMate website at **www.cengagebrain.com** for additional study tools and review materials—including audio and video clips—for this chapter.

AP® Review Questions for Chapter 9

1. The American Revolution is most accurately described as
   - (A) a total upheaval of colonial society.
   - (B) highly disruptive to work, social, cultural, and economic life in the colonies.
   - (C) a violent overthrow of the existing political framework.
   - (D) more of an evolution than a revolution.
   - (E) a war that reached far into even the most isolated communities.

2. The aftermath of the American Revolution triggered all of the following social changes EXCEPT that
   - (A) property requirements for voting were eliminated.
   - (B) trade and labor organizations were founded and grew.
   - (C) inheritance laws were restructured so that all property would go to a family's eldest son.
   - (D) a movement for the separation of church and state gained momentum.
   - (E) efforts to abolish slavery began in the North.

3. What is meant by the term *republican motherhood*?
   - (A) Women as shapers of future citizens
   - (B) Women as vital supporters of the revolutionary cause
   - (C) New opportunities for women as future educators
   - (D) The special responsibility elected officials' wives have to set an example for other women
   - (E) The justification for giving women voting rights

4. The state constitutions that were drafted beginning in 1776 had all of the following traits in common EXCEPT
   - (A) a Bill of Rights.
   - (B) limited legislative powers.
   - (C) annual election of legislators.
   - (D) little authority for the executive branch.
   - (E) a weak judiciary.

5. Economically, most Americans after the Revolution were
   - (A) much better off financially than they were before the war.
   - (B) worse off than before the war.
   - (C) still heavily importing British goods.
   - (D) in roughly the same financial position as before the war.
   - (E) rapidly shifting from farming to manufacturing.

6. What single issue nearly kept several colonies from refusing to sign the Articles of Confederation?
   - (A) Slavery
   - (B) The organization of the federal government
   - (C) Taxation
   - (D) States' rights
   - (E) Western lands

7. Although a landmark in government, why were the Articles of Confederation ultimately replaced with the U.S. Constitution?
   - (A) The Articles gave each state just one vote in Congress regardless of size.
   - (B) The Articles required a unanimous vote of all states to amend them.
   - (C) The Articles gave Congress no power to regulate commerce or to enforce taxation.
   - (D) The Articles forced states to sacrifice too much of their authority to a central government.
   - (E) The Articles prevented Congress from making treaties.

8. Passed by the Confederation Congress, the Northwest Ordinance of 1787
   - (A) detailed how western lands would be divided into towns.
   - (B) banned slavery in the Old Northwest.
   - (C) allowed colonies to become states once they contained thirty thousand residents.
   - (D) permanently placed the West under the authority of the federal government.
   - (E) called for the sale of western lands to cover the national debt.

9. The United States faced all of the following problems with foreign nations under the Articles of Confederation EXCEPT that
   - (A) Britain declined to repeal the Navigation Laws.
   - (B) France restricted the United States' trade with its colonies in the West Indies.
   - (C) Latin American nations refused United States' imports.
   - (D) Spain closed the Mississippi River to American commerce.
   - (E) North African pirates enslaved American sailors.

10. Which of the following best describes Shays's Rebellion?
    (A) A protest by debt-ridden farmers who were losing their land to foreclosures
    (B) A violent uprising between backcountry settlers, merchants, and Native Americans
    (C) A conflict over heavy taxes on farm products
    (D) A battle over the border between Vermont and British Canada
    (E) A clash over duties imposed by neighboring states on each other's goods

11. The man nicknamed "the father of the Constitution" was
    (A) Thomas Paine.
    (B) Thomas Jefferson.
    (C) George Washington.
    (D) Alexander Hamilton.
    (E) James Madison.

12. Which of the following was NOT among the reasons for revising the Articles of Confederation at the 1787 meeting of state delegates in Philadelphia?
    (A) Gaining better control over commerce
    (B) Curbing unlimited democracy practiced in several states
    (C) Strengthening the central government
    (D) Protecting existing institutions, including slavery
    (E) Safeguarding the union from uprisings

13. The Constitution that was drafted in 1787 contained all of the following compromises that secured its final passage EXCEPT
    (A) a strong central government.
    (B) a president elected by the people.
    (C) counting slaves as three-fifths persons.
    (D) closing the slave trade by 1807.
    (E) lifetime appointments for federal judges.

14. All of the following are true statements about the anti-Federalists EXCEPT that
    (A) they were opposed to a strong central government as outlined in the Constitution.
    (B) revolutionary leaders, including Samuel Adams, Patrick Henry, and Richard Henry Lee, joined their ranks.
    (C) they claimed the Constitution was drawn up by the wealthy to protect their interests.
    (D) they opposed adding a Bill of Rights to the Constitution.
    (E) their position was challenged in articles penned by Alexander Hamilton, John Jay, and James Madison.

15. The Articles of Confederation can be viewed as a reaction to life as British colonies because
    (A) the national government was composed of a legislative branch with representatives from the states, similar to the British Parliament.
    (B) all men were given equal rights, as stated in the Declaration of Independence.
    (C) it constructed a weak national government in response to Americans' fears of monarchy and tyranny.
    (D) the national government could tax the states and the people with majority approval in the national Congress.
    (E) the national government could make treaties and establish a postal service, continuing the unity forged during the Revolution.

16. The Constitution created a government unlike any in the world at the time because it
    (A) combined self-rule and a self-limiting system of checks and balances, allowing for liberty and order.
    (B) created the first democracy in history with no mention of the monarchs or dynasties prevalent in Europe.
    (C) allowed the states to maintain their individual identities and independence while the national government played a minor role.
    (D) took steps to abolish slavery in the future.
    (E) went into effect with the support of a minority of the population.

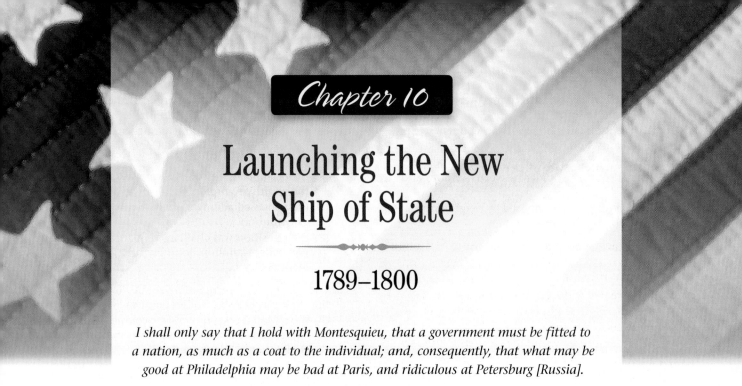

Chapter 10

Launching the New Ship of State

1789–1800

I shall only say that I hold with Montesquieu, that a government must be fitted to a nation, as much as a coat to the individual; and, consequently, that what may be good at Philadelphia may be bad at Paris, and ridiculous at Petersburg [Russia].

ALEXANDER HAMILTON, 1799

America's new ship of state did not spread its sails to the most favorable breezes. Within twelve troubled years, the American people had risen up and thrown overboard both the British yoke and the Articles of Confederation. A decade of lawbreaking and constitution smashing was not the best training for government making. Americans had come to regard a central authority, replacing that of George III, as a necessary evil—something to be distrusted, watched, and curbed.

The finances of the infant government were likewise precarious. The revenue had declined to a trickle, whereas the public debt, with interest heavily in arrears, was mountainous. Worthless paper money, both state and national, was as plentiful as metallic money was scarce. America's precarious national security was also threatened by the wars that rocked Europe in the wake of the French Revolution of 1789—an event that also roiled domestic politics in the fledgling United States. In the face of all those difficulties, the Americans were brashly trying to erect a republic on an immense scale, something that no other people had attempted and that traditional political theory deemed impossible. The eyes of a skeptical world were on the upstart United States.

Even after the battles over adoption of the Constitution, conflict continued to rage about the nature of government. Some, such as Thomas Jefferson and James Madison, supported a limited government. Others, such as George Washington and Alexander Hamilton, hoped to extend the powers of the government in order to create institutions that could strengthen the new country. The political fights of the Washington and Adams years made for a contentious start to the early Republic.

✵ Growing Pains

When the Constitution was launched in 1789, the Republic was continuing to grow at an amazing rate. Population was doubling about every twenty-five years, and the first official census of 1790 recorded almost 4 million people. Cities had blossomed proportionately: Philadelphia numbered 42,000, New York 33,000, Boston 18,000, Charleston 16,000, and Baltimore 13,000.

The French statesman Anne Robert Jacques Turgot (1727–1781) had high expectations for a united America:

❝ This people is the hope of the human race. . . . The Americans should be an example of political, religious, commercial and industrial liberty. . . . But to obtain these ends for us, America . . . must not become . . . a mass of divided powers, contending for territory and trade.**❞**

America's population was still about 90 percent rural, despite the flourishing cities. All but 5 percent of the people lived east of the Appalachian Mountains. The trans-Appalachian overflow was concentrated chiefly in Kentucky, Tennessee, and Ohio, all of which were welcomed as states within fourteen years. (Vermont preceded them, becoming the fourteenth state in 1791.) Foreign visitors to America looked down their noses at the roughness and crudity resulting from ax-and-rifle pioneering life.

People of the western waters—in the stump-studded clearings of Kentucky, Tennessee, and Ohio—were particularly restive and dubiously loyal. The mouth of the Mississippi, their life-giving outlet, lay in the hands of unfriendly Spaniards. Smooth-talking Spanish and British agents, jingling gold, moved freely among the settlers and held out seductive promises of independence. Many observers wondered whether the emerging United States would ever grow to maturity.

Washington for President

George Washington, the esteemed war hero, was unanimously drafted as president by the Electoral College in 1789—the only presidential nominee ever to be honored by unanimity. His presence was imposing: 6 feet 2 inches, 175 pounds, broad and sloping shoulders, strongly pointed chin, and pockmarks (from smallpox) on nose and cheeks. Much preferring the quiet of Mount Vernon to the turmoil of politics, he was perhaps the only president who did not in some way angle for this exalted office. Balanced rather than brilliant, he commanded his followers by strength of character rather than by the arts of the politician.

Washington's long journey from Mount Vernon to New York City, the temporary capital, was a triumphal procession. He was greeted by roaring cannon, pealing bells, flower-carpeted roads, and singing and shouting citizens. With appropriate ceremony, he solemnly and somewhat nervously took the oath of office on April 30, 1789, on a crowded balcony overlooking Wall Street, which some have regarded as a bad omen.

Washington soon put his stamp on the new government, especially by establishing the cabinet. The Constitution does not mention a cabinet (see Table 10.1); it merely provides that the president "may require" written opinions of the heads of the executive-branch departments (see Art. II, Sec. II, para. 1 in the Appendix). But this system proved so cumbersome, and involved so much homework, that cabinet meetings gradually evolved in the Washington administration.

At first only three full-fledged department heads served under the president: Secretary of State Thomas

Washington Honored This idealized portrait symbolizes the reverential awe in which Americans held "the Father of His Country."

Jefferson, Secretary of the Treasury Alexander Hamilton, and Secretary of War Henry Knox.

The Bill of Rights

The new nation faced some unfinished business. Many antifederalists had sharply criticized the Constitution drafted at Philadelphia for its failure to provide guarantees of individual rights such as freedom of religion and trial by jury. Many states had ratified the federal Constitution on the understanding that it would soon be amended to include such guarantees. Drawing up a bill of rights headed the list of imperatives facing the new government.

Amendments to the Constitution could be proposed in either of two ways—by a new constitutional convention requested by two-thirds of the states or by a two-thirds vote of both houses of Congress. Fearing that a new convention might unravel the narrow federalist victory in the ratification struggle, James Madison determined to draft the amendments himself. He then guided them through Congress, where his intellectual

TABLE 10.1 Evolution of the Cabinet		
Position	Date Established	Comments
Secretary of state	1789	
Secretary of treasury	1789	
Secretary of war	1789	Loses cabinet status, 1947
Attorney general	1789	Not head of Justice Dept. until 1870
Secretary of navy	1798	Loses cabinet status, 1947
Postmaster general	1829	Loses cabinet status, 1970
Secretary of interior	1849	
Secretary of agriculture	1889	
Secretary of commerce and labor	1903	Office divided, 1913
Secretary of commerce	1913	
Secretary of labor	1913	
Secretary of defense	1947	Subordinate to this secretary, without cabinet rank, are secretaries of army, navy, and air force
Secretary of health, education, and welfare	1953	Office divided, 1979
Secretary of housing and urban development	1965	
Secretary of transportation	1966	
Secretary of energy	1977	
Secretary of health and human services	1979	
Secretary of education	1979	
Secretary of veterans' affairs	1989	
Secretary of homeland security	2002	

and political skills were quickly making him the leading figure.

Adopted by the necessary number of states in 1791, the first ten amendments to the Constitution, popularly known as the **Bill of Rights**, safeguard some of the most precious American principles. Among these are protections for freedom of religion, speech, and the press; the right to bear arms and to be tried by a jury; and the right to assemble and petition the government for redress of grievances. The Bill of Rights also prohibits cruel and unusual punishments and arbitrary government seizure of private property.

To guard against the danger that enumerating such rights might lead to the conclusion that they were the only ones protected, Madison inserted the crucial Ninth Amendment. It declares that specifying certain rights "shall not be construed to deny or disparage others retained by the people." In a gesture of reassurance to the states' righters, he included the equally significant Tenth Amendment, which reserves all rights not explicitly delegated or prohibited by the federal Constitution "to the States respectively, or to the people."

By preserving a strong central government while specifying protections for minority and individual liberties, Madison's amendments partially swung the federalist pendulum back in an antifederalist direction. (See Amendments I–X.)

The first Congress also nailed other newly sawed government planks into place. It created effective federal courts under the **Judiciary Act of 1789**. The act organized the Supreme Court, with a chief justice and five associates, as well as federal district and circuit courts, and established the office of attorney general. New Yorker John Jay, Madison's collaborator on *The Federalist* papers and one of the young Republic's most seasoned diplomats, became the first chief justice of the United States.

✴ Hamilton Revives the Corpse of Public Credit

The key figure in the new government was still smooth-faced Treasury Secretary Alexander Hamilton, a native of the British West Indies. Hamilton's genius was unquestioned, but critics claimed he loved his adopted country more than he loved his countrymen. Doubts about his character and his loyalty to the republican experiment always swirled about his head. Hamilton regarded himself as a kind of prime minister in Washington's cabinet and on occasion thrust his hands into the affairs of other departments, including that of his archrival, Thomas Jefferson, who served as secretary of state.

A financial wizard, Hamilton set out immediately to correct the economic vexations that had crippled the Articles of Confederation. His plan was to shape the fiscal policies of the administration in such a way as to favor the wealthier groups. They, in turn, would gratefully lend the government monetary and political support. The new federal regime would thrive, the propertied classes would fatten, and prosperity would trickle down to the masses.

The youthful financier's first objective was to bolster the national credit. Without public confidence in the government, Hamilton could not secure the funds with which to float his risky schemes. He therefore boldly urged Congress to "fund" the entire national debt "at par" and to assume completely the debts incurred by the states during the recent war.

Funding at par meant that the federal government would pay off its debts at face value, plus accumulated interest—a then-enormous total of more than $54 million. So many people believed the infant Treasury incapable of meeting those obligations that government bonds had depreciated to ten or fifteen cents on the dollar. Yet speculators held fistfuls of them, and when Congress passed Hamilton's measure in 1790, they grabbed for more. Some of them galloped into rural areas ahead of the news, buying for a song the depreciated paper holdings of farmers, war veterans, and widows.

Hamilton was willing, even eager, to have the new government shoulder additional obligations. While pushing the funding scheme, he urged Congress to assume the debts of the states, totaling some $21.5 million.

The secretary made a convincing case for **assumption**. The state debts could be regarded as a proper national obligation, for they had been incurred in the war for independence. But foremost in Hamilton's thinking was the belief that assumption would chain the states more tightly to the "federal chariot." Thus the secretary's maneuver would shift the attachment of wealthy creditors from the states to the federal government. The support of the rich for the national administration was a crucial link in Hamilton's political strategy of strengthening the central government.

States burdened with heavy debts, like Massachusetts, were delighted by Hamilton's proposal. States

The Granger Collection, New York

Alexander Hamilton (1755–1804), by John Trumbull, 1792 He was one of the youngest and most brilliant of the Founding Fathers, who might have been president but for his ultraconservatism, a scandalous adultery, and a duelist's bullet. Hamilton favored a strong central government with a weak legislature to unify the infant nation and encourage industry. His chief rival, Thomas Jefferson, who extolled states' rights as a bulwark of liberty and thought the United States should remain an agricultural society, regarded Hamilton as a monarchist plotter and never forgave him for insisting that "the British Govt. was the best in the world: and that he doubted much whether any thing short of it would do in America."

with small debts, like Virginia, were less charmed. The stage was set for some old-fashioned horse trading. Virginia did not want the state debts assumed, but it did want the forthcoming federal district*—now the District of Columbia—to be located on the Potomac River. It would thus gain in commerce and prestige. Hamilton persuaded a reluctant Jefferson, who had recently come home from France, to line up enough votes in Congress for assumption. In return, Virginia would have the federal district on the Potomac. The bargain was carried through in 1790.

---

*Authorized by the Constitution, Art. I, Sec. VIII, para. 17.

✵ Customs Duties and Excise Taxes

The new ship of state thus set sail dangerously overloaded. The national debt had swelled to $75 million owing to Hamilton's insistence on honoring the outstanding federal and state obligations alike. Anyone less determined to establish such a healthy public credit could have sidestepped $13 million in back interest and could have avoided the state debts entirely.

But Hamilton, "Father of the National Debt," was not greatly worried. His objectives were as much political as economic. He believed that within limits, a national debt was a "national blessing"—a kind of Union adhesive. The more creditors to whom the government owed money, the more people there would be with a personal stake in the success of his ambitious enterprise. His unique contribution was to make a debt—ordinarily a liability—an asset for vitalizing the financial system as well as the government itself (see Figure 10.1).

Where was the money to come from to pay interest on this huge debt and run the government? Hamilton's first answer was customs duties, derived from a tariff. Tariff revenues, in turn, depended on a vigorous foreign trade, another crucial link in Hamilton's overall economic strategy for the new Republic.

The first **tariff** law, imposing a low tariff of about 8 percent on the value of dutiable imports, was speedily passed by the first Congress in 1789, even before Hamilton was sworn in. Revenue was by far the main goal, but the measure was also designed to erect a low protective wall around infant industries, which bawled noisily for more shelter than they received. Hamilton had the vision to see that the Industrial Revolution would soon reach America, and he argued strongly in favor of more protection for the well-to-do manufacturing groups—another vital element in his economic program. But Congress was still dominated by the agricultural and commercial interests, and it voted only two slight increases in the tariff during Washington's presidency.

Hamilton, with characteristic vigor, sought additional internal revenue and in 1791 secured from Congress an **excise tax** on a few domestic items, notably

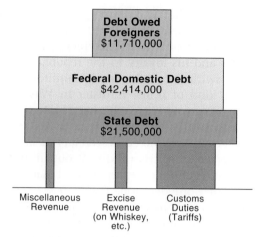

FIGURE 10.1 Hamilton's Financial Structure Supported by Revenues

whiskey. The new levy of seven cents a gallon was borne chiefly by the distillers who lived in the backcountry, where the wretched roads forced the farmer to reduce (and liquefy) bulky bushels of grain to horseback proportions. Whiskey flowed so freely on the frontier in the form of distilled liquor that it was used for money.

✵ Hamilton Battles Jefferson for a Bank

As the capstone for his financial system, Hamilton proposed a bank of the United States. An enthusiastic admirer of most things English, he took as his model the Bank of England. Specifically, he proposed a powerful private institution, of which the government would be the major stockholder and in which the federal Treasury would deposit its surplus monies. The central government not only would have a convenient strongbox, but federal funds would stimulate business by remaining in circulation. The bank would also print urgently needed paper money and thus provide a sound and stable national currency, badly needed since the days when the Continental dollar was "not worth a Continental." The proposed bank would indeed be useful. But was it constitutional?

Jefferson, whose written opinion on this question Washington requested, argued vehemently against the bank. There was, he insisted, no specific authorization in the Constitution for such a financial octopus. He was convinced that all powers not specifically granted to the central government were reserved to the states, as provided in the about-to-be-ratified Bill of Rights (see Amendment X). He therefore concluded that the states, not Congress, had the power to charter banks. Believing that the Constitution should be interpreted "literally"

One of the most eloquent tributes to Hamilton's apparent miracle working came from Daniel Webster (1782–1852) in the Senate (1831):

❝He smote the rock of the national resources, and abundant streams of revenue gushed forth. He touched the dead corpse of public credit, and it sprung upon its feet.❞

AN EXCISEMAN. *Carrying off two Kegs of Whiskey, is pursued by two farmers, intending to tar and feather him. he runs for 'Squire Vultures to divide with him; but is met on the way by his evil genius who claps an hook in his nose. leads him off to a Gallows. where he is immediately hanged.*

The Whiskey Boys   The cartoonist clearly favored the Pennsylvania rebels who resisted Hamilton's imposition of an excise tax on whiskey.

or "strictly," Jefferson and his states' rights disciples zealously embraced the theory of "strict construction."

Hamilton, also at Washington's request, prepared a brilliantly reasoned reply to Jefferson's arguments. Hamilton in general believed that what the Constitution did not forbid it permitted; Jefferson, in contrast, generally believed that what it did not permit it forbade. Hamilton boldly invoked the clause of the Constitution that stipulates that Congress may pass any laws "necessary and proper" to carry out the powers vested in the various government agencies (see Art. I, Sec. VIII, para. 18). The government was explicitly empowered to collect taxes and regulate trade. In carrying out these basic functions, Hamilton argued, a national bank would be not only "proper" but "necessary." By inference or implication—that is, by virtue of "implied powers"—Congress would be fully justified in establishing the Bank of the United States. In short, Hamilton contended for a "loose" or "broad" interpretation of the Constitution. He and his federalist followers thus evolved the theory of "loose construction" by invoking the "elastic clause" of the Constitution—a precedent for enormous federal powers.

Hamilton's financial views prevailed. His eloquent and realistic arguments were accepted by Washington, who reluctantly signed the bank measure into law. This explosive issue had been debated with much heat in Congress, where the old North-South cleavage still lurked ominously. The most enthusiastic support for the bank naturally came from the commercial and financial centers of the North, whereas the strongest opposition arose from the agricultural South.

The **Bank of the United States**, as created by Congress in 1791, was chartered for twenty years. Located in Philadelphia, it was to have a capital of $10 million, one-fifth of it owned by the federal government. Stock was thrown open to public sale. To the agreeable surprise of Hamilton, a milling crowd oversubscribed in less than two hours, pushing aside many would-be purchasers.

✦ Mutinous Moonshiners in Pennsylvania

The **Whiskey Rebellion**, which flared up in southwestern Pennsylvania in 1794, sharply challenged the new national government. Hamilton's high excise tax bore harshly on these homespun pioneer folk. They regarded it not as a tax on a frivolous luxury but as a burden on an economic necessity and a medium of exchange. Even preachers of the gospel were paid in "Old Monongahela rye." Rye and corn crops distilled into alcohol were more cheaply transported to eastern markets than bales of grain. Defiant distillers finally erected whiskey poles, similar to the liberty poles of anti–stamp tax days in 1765, and raised the cry "Liberty and No Excise." Boldly tarring and feathering revenue officers, they brought collections to a halt.

President Washington, once a revolutionary, was alarmed by what he called these "self-created societies." With the hearty encouragement of Hamilton, he summoned the militias of several states. Anxious moments followed the call, for there was much doubt as to whether men in other states would muster to crush a rebellion in a fellow state. Despite some opposition, an army of about thirteen thousand rallied to the colors, and two widely separated columns marched briskly forth in a gorgeous, leaf-tinted Indian summer, until knee-deep mud slowed their progress.

When the troops reached the hills of western Pennsylvania, they found no insurrection. The "Whiskey Boys" were overawed, dispersed, or captured. Washington, with an eye to healing old sores, pardoned the two small-fry convicted culprits.

Attorney Hugh Henry Brackenridge (1748-1816) mediated between the Whiskey Rebels and the town of Pittsburgh. He later wrote of the hated excise tax,

"I saw the operation to be unequal in this country. . . . It is true that the excise paid by the country would be that only on spirits consumed in it. But even in the case of exports, the excise must be advanced in the first instance by the distiller and this would prevent effectually all the poorer part from carrying on the business. I . . . would have preferred a direct tax with a view to reach unsettled lands which all around us have been purchased by speculating men.**"**

The Whiskey Rebellion was minuscule—some three rebels were killed—but its consequences were mighty. George Washington's government, now substantially strengthened, commanded a new respect. Yet the foes of the administration condemned its brutal display of force—for having used a sledgehammer to crush a gnat.

✷ The Emergence of Political Parties

Almost overnight, Hamilton's fiscal feats had established the government's sound credit rating. The Treasury could now borrow needed funds in the Netherlands on favorable terms.

But Hamilton's financial successes—funding, assumption, the excise tax, the bank, the suppression of the Whiskey Rebellion—created some political liabilities. All these schemes encroached sharply upon states' rights. Many Americans, dubious about the new Constitution in the first place, might never have approved it if they had foreseen how the states were going to be overshadowed by the federal colossus. Now, out of resentment against Hamilton's revenue-raising and centralizing policies, an organized opposition began to build. What once was a personal feud between Hamilton and Jefferson developed into a full-blown and frequently bitter political rivalry.

National political parties, in the modern sense, were unknown in America when George Washing-

ton took his inaugural oath. There had been Whigs and Tories, federalists and antifederalists, but these groups were factions rather than parties. They had sprung into existence over hotly contested special issues; they had faded away when their cause had triumphed or fizzled.

The Founders at Philadelphia had not envisioned the existence of permanent political parties. Organized opposition to the government—especially a democratic government based on popular consent—seemed tainted by disloyalty. Opposition to the government affronted the spirit of national unity that the glorious cause of the Revolution had inspired. The notion of a formal party apparatus was thus a novelty in the 1790s, and when Jefferson and Madison first organized their opposition to the Hamiltonian program, they confined their activities to Congress and did not anticipate creating a long-lived and popular party. But as their antagonism to Hamilton stiffened, and as the amazingly boisterous and widely read newspapers of the day spread their political message, and Hamilton's, among the people, primitive semblances of political parties began to emerge.

The two-party system has existed in the United States since that time (see Table 10.2). Ironically, in light of early suspicions about the very legitimacy of parties, their competition for power has actually proved to be among the indispensable ingredients of a sound democracy. The party out of power—"the loyal opposition"—traditionally plays the invaluable role of the balance wheel on the machinery of government, ensuring that politics never drifts too far out of kilter with the wishes of the people.

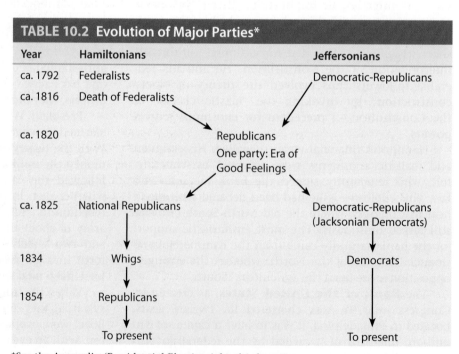

TABLE 10.2 Evolution of Major Parties*

Year	Hamiltonians		Jeffersonians
ca. 1792	Federalists		Democratic-Republicans
ca. 1816	Death of Federalists		
ca. 1820		Republicans One party: Era of Good Feelings	
ca. 1825	National Republicans		Democratic-Republicans (Jacksonian Democrats)
1834	Whigs		Democrats
1854	Republicans		
	To present		To present

*See the Appendix (Presidential Elections) for third parties.

Erich Lessing/Art Resource, NY

The Execution of Queen Marie Antoinette, 1793 The bloody excesses of the notorious guillotine disgusted many Americans and soured them on the promises of the French Revolution.

✴ The Impact of the French Revolution

When Washington's first administration ended in early 1793, Hamilton's domestic policies had already stimulated the formation of two political camps—Jeffersonian Democratic-Republicans and Hamiltonian Federalists. As Washington's second term began, foreign-policy issues brought the differences between them to a fever pitch.

Only a few weeks after Washington's inauguration in 1789, the curtain had risen on the first act of the French Revolution. (See "Thinking Globally: Two Revolutions," pp. 188–189.) Twenty-six years were to pass before the seething continent of Europe collapsed into a peace of exhaustion. Few non-American events have left a deeper scar on American political and social life. In a sense the French Revolution was misnamed: it was a historic, global revolution that sent tremors through much of the Western world and beyond.

In its early stages, the upheaval was surprisingly peaceful, involving as it did a successful attempt to impose constitutional shackles on Louis XVI. The American people, loving liberty and deploring despotism, cheered. They were flattered to think that the outburst in France was but the second chapter of their own glorious Revolution, as to some extent it was. Only a few ultraconservative Federalists—fearing change,

reform, and "leveling" principles—were from the outset dubious or outspokenly hostile to the "despicable mobocracy." The more ardent Jeffersonians were overjoyed.

The French Revolution entered a more ominous phase in 1792, when France declared war on hostile Austria. Powerful ideals and powerful armies alike were on the march. Late in that year, the electrifying news reached America that French citizen armies had hurled back the invading foreigners and that France had proclaimed itself a republic. Americans enthusiastically sang "The Marseillaise" and other rousing French

British political observer William Cobbett (1763–1835) wrote of the frenzied reaction in America to the death of Louis XVI,

❝Never was the memory of a man so cruelly insulted as that of this mild and humane monarch. He was guillotined in effigy, in the capital of the Union [Philadelphia], twenty or thirty times every day, during one whole winter and part of the summer. Men, women and children flocked to the tragical exhibition, and not a single paragraph appeared in the papers to shame them from it.❞

Two Revolutions

On July 14, 1789, a howling mob stormed the Bastille—a dank Parisian prison described by the Marquis de Lafayette as France's "fortress of despotism"—killed half a dozen soldiers, and paraded the severed heads of its commanding officer and the mayor of Paris throughout the city. The French Revolution was thus bloodily launched. Bastille Day is still celebrated as France's national birthday, just as Americans celebrate the Fourth of July.

The roots of the two Revolutions were thickly intertwined. To defray the cost of the war that had ousted France from North America in 1763, Britain had levied new taxes on its colonists, provoking them to revolt in 1776. In turn, aiding the rebellious Americans forced the French government to seek new revenues, lighting the fuse that led to the political explosion in Paris in 1789.

Even more notable was the intellectual commonality between the upheavals. The ideas that inspired the American and French revolutionaries grew from the common heritage of radical eighteenth-century Enlightenment thinking about equality, freedom, and the sovereignty of the people. The French Declaration of the Rights of Man (1789) deliberately echoed Thomas Jefferson's Declaration of Independence (1776) when it said that "men are born and remain free and equal in rights," among which were "liberty, property, security, and resistance to oppression." Many French thinkers openly credited the American Revolution as the inspiration for their own. As the American revolutionary Thomas Paine remarked to George Washington, "The principles of America opened the Bastille." Indeed, in many ways the French were even more radi-

cal than the Americans; their Revolution abolished slavery (temporarily), something the Americans failed to do for almost one hundred years more.

And yet the American and French Revolutions unfolded in dramatically different ways and left vastly different legacies. The Americans largely disarmed after winning their independence; allowed some eighty thousand hard-core Loyalists to depart without suffering grievous retribution (see "Makers of America: The Loyalists," pp. 140–141); peacefully resumed their habits of worship, toil, and governance; and proceeded to draft the U.S. Constitution, under which they have lived, with amendments, for more than two centuries. The American revolutionaries, in short, secured the fruits of their Revolution fairly easily, while the French struggled through ghastly bloodshed to ultimate failure—an

Storming the Bastille, 1789   This event signaled the outbreak of the French Revolution.

Réunion des Musées Nationaux/Art Resource, NY

outcome that haunted European politics for at least a century thereafter.

Revolutionaries in France had to grapple with the constant threats of counterrevolution at home and armed intervention from abroad. As a result, they soon descended into grisly violence, including the execution of some forty thousand Frenchmen in the notorious Reign of Terror of 1793–1794, the guillotining of the king and queen, and preemptive attacks on neighboring countries. They stripped the Catholic Church of its property and privileges, briefly experimented with a new state religion called the Cult of Reason, and eventually conceded supreme power to a brash young general, Napoleon Bonaparte, who convulsed all of Europe in the name of "liberty, equality, and fraternity." Napoleon was finally defeated at the Battle of Waterloo in 1815, after which the Bourbon monarchy was restored to the throne.

Why did these two great eruptions, sprung from a shared chain of events and espousing almost identical political philosophies, fare so differently? Many scholars have found the answer in the countries' markedly different pre-Revolutionary histories. France's Revolution confronted implacably entrenched adversaries in the landed nobility and the clergy. Those two "estates," as they were called, clung tenaciously to their ancient privileges, as did the princes and potentates who ruled in all the countries on France's borders. To succeed, the French Revolution had to concentrate power in the hands of a state powerful enough to extinguish its internal enemies and to forestall foreign intervention as well. Those stark necessities help account for the fact that down to the present day, central governments are stronger in almost all European societies than in the United States.

The Americans faced no such obstacles. They had no aristocracy worthy of the name, no church with the kind of influence that the Catholic Church commanded in France, and no menacing neighbors to fear. They had the luxury of being able to focus on limiting the power of the state, not enlarging it. Theirs was largely a *colonial* conflict, whereas France had to endure a *class* conflict. Not until Reconstruction following the Civil War would Americans confront a comparable task of mustering sufficient power to uproot and permanently extinguish an entire social order.

It has been said that to mount a revolution is "to murder and create." What was exceptional about the American revolutionaries was that they were spared the necessity to murder. The American Revolution grew not from abstract ideas, but from the preceding two centuries of American experience. It was less a revolution in the usual sense than a consolidation of already well-established norms, values, and behaviors. Alexander Hamilton understood that crucial point when he wrote to the Marquis de Lafayette in 1789, "I dread the reveries of your *philosophic* politicians."

The Key to the Bastille, Mount Vernon, Virginia   The Marquis de Lafayette instructed Thomas Paine, his American Revolutionary War comrade, to deliver the key to the liberated Bastille to George Washington. It hangs to this day in the entry hall of Washington's home at Mount Vernon, Virginia, a lasting symbol of the deep affinity between the French and American Revolutions.   Mount Vernon Ladies' Association

Revolutionary songs, and they renamed thoroughfares with democratic flair. King Street in New York, for example, became Liberty Street, and in Boston, Royal Exchange Alley became Equality Lane.

But centuries of pent-up poison could not be purged without baleful results. The guillotine was set up, the king was beheaded in 1793, the church was attacked, and the head-rolling **Reign of Terror** was begun. Back in America, God-fearing Federalist aristocrats nervously fingered their tender white necks and eyed the Jeffersonian masses apprehensively. Lukewarm Federalist approval of the early Revolution turned, almost overnight, to heated talk of "blood-drinking cannibals."

Sober-minded Jeffersonians regretted the bloodshed. But they felt, with Jefferson, that one could not expect to be carried from "despotism to liberty in a feather bed" and that a few thousand aristocratic heads were a cheap price to pay for human freedom.

Such approbation was shortsighted, for dire peril loomed ahead. The earlier battles of the French Revolution had not hurt America directly, but now Britain was sucked into the contagious conflict. The conflagration speedily spread to the New World, where it vividly affected the expanding young American Republic. Thus was repeated the familiar story of every major European war, beginning with 1688, that involved a watery duel for control of the Atlantic Ocean. (See Table 6.2 on p. 103.)

✷ Washington's Neutrality Proclamation

Ominously, the Franco-American alliance of 1778 was still on the books. By its own terms, it was to last "forever." It bound the United States to help the French defend their West Indies against future foes, and the booming British fleets were certain to attack these strategic islands.

Many Jeffersonian Democratic-Republicans favored honoring the alliance. Aflame with the liberal ideals of the French Revolution, red-blooded Jeffersonians were eager to enter the conflict against Britain, the recent foe, at the side of France, the recent friend. America owed France its freedom, they argued, and now was the time to pay the debt of gratitude.

But President George Washington, levelheaded as usual, was not swayed by the clamor of the crowd. Backed by Hamilton, he believed that war had to be avoided at all costs. Washington was coolly playing for enormous stakes. The nation in 1793 was militarily feeble, economically wobbly, and politically disunited. But solid foundations were being laid, and American cradles were continuing to rock a bumper crop of babies. Washington wisely reasoned that if America could avoid the broils of Europe for a generation or so, it would then be populous enough and powerful enough to assert its maritime rights with strength and success. Otherwise it might invite catastrophe. The strategy of delay—of playing for time while the birthrate fought America's battles—was a cardinal policy of the Founding Fathers. It was based on a shrewd assessment of American strengths and weaknesses at this critical moment in the young Republic's history. Hamilton and Jefferson, often poles apart on other issues, were in agreement here.

Accordingly, Washington boldly issued his **Neutrality Proclamation** in 1793, shortly after the outbreak of war between Britain and France. This epochal document not only proclaimed the government's official neutrality in the widening conflict but also sternly warned American citizens to be impartial toward both armed camps. As America's first formal declaration of aloofness from Old World quarrels, Washington's Neutrality Proclamation proved to be a major prop of the spreading isolationist tradition. It also proved to be enormously controversial. The pro-French Jeffersonians were enraged by the Neutrality Proclamation, especially by Washington's method of announcing it unilaterally, without consulting Congress. The pro-British Federalists were heartened.

Debate soon intensified. An impetuous, thirty-year-old representative of the French Republic, Citizen Edmond Genêt, had landed at Charleston, South Carolina. With unrestrained zeal he undertook to fit out privateers and otherwise take advantage of the existing Franco-American alliance. The giddy-headed envoy—all sail and no anchor—was soon swept away by his enthusiastic reception by the Jeffersonian Republicans. He foolishly came to believe that the Neutrality Proclamation did not reflect the true wishes of the American people, and he consequently embarked upon unneutral activity not authorized by the French alliance—including the recruitment of armies to invade Spanish Florida and Louisiana, as well as British Canada. Even Madison and Jefferson were soon disillusioned by his conduct. After he threatened to appeal over the head of "Old Washington" to the sovereign voters, the president demanded Genêt's withdrawal, and the Frenchman was replaced by a less impulsive emissary.

Washington's Neutrality Proclamation clearly illustrates the truism that self-interest is the basic cement of alliances. In 1778 both France and America stood to gain; in 1793 only France. Technically, the Americans did not flout their obligation because France never officially called upon them to honor it. American neutrality in fact favored France. The French West Indies urgently needed Yankee foodstuffs. If the Americans had entered the war at France's side, the British fleets would have blockaded the American coast and cut off those essential supplies. America was thus much more useful to France as a reliable neutral provider than as a blockaded partner-in-arms.

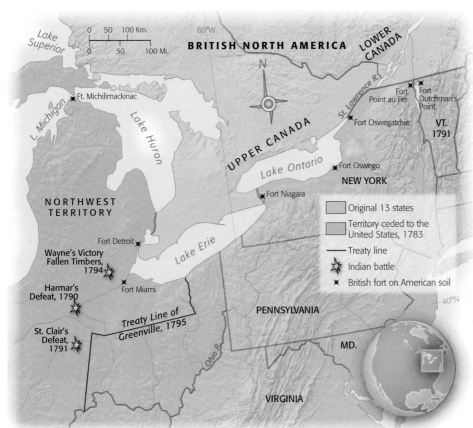

MAP 10.1 American Posts Held by the British and British-American Clashes After 1783 © Cengage Learning

✦ Embroilments with Britain

President Washington's far-visioned policy of neutrality was sorely tried by the British. For ten long years, they had been retaining the chain of northern frontier posts on U.S. soil, all in defiance of the peace treaty of 1783 (see Map 10.1). The London government was reluctant to abandon the lucrative fur trade in the Great Lakes region and also hoped to build up an Indian buffer state to contain the ambitious Americans. British agents openly sold firearms and firewater to the Indians of the Miami Confederacy, an alliance of eight Indian nations who terrorized Americans invading their lands. Little Turtle, war chief of the Miamis, gave notice that the confederacy regarded the Ohio River as the United States' northwestern, and their own southeastern, border. In 1790 and 1791, Little Turtle's braves defeated armies led by Generals Josiah Harmar and Arthur St. Clair, killing hundreds of soldiers and handing the United States what remains one of its worst defeats in the history of the frontier.

But in 1794, when a new army under General "Mad Anthony" Wayne routed the Miamis at the **Battle of Fallen Timbers**, the British refused to shelter Indians fleeing from the battle. Abandoned when it counted by their red-coated friends, the Indians soon offered Wayne the peace pipe. In the **Treaty of Greenville**, signed in August 1795, the confederacy gave up vast tracts of the Old Northwest, including most of present-day Indiana and Ohio. In exchange the Indians received a lump-sum payment of $20,000, an annual annuity of $9,000, the right to hunt the lands they had ceded, and, most important, what they hoped was recognition of their sovereign status. Although the treaty codified an unequal relationship, the Indians felt that it put some limits on the ability of the United States to decide the fate of Indian peoples.

On the sea frontier, the British were eager to starve out the French West Indies and naturally expected

Thomas Paine (1737–1809), then in France and resenting George Washington's anti-French policies, addressed the president in an open letter (1796) that reveals his bitterness:

❝And as to you, sir, treacherous in private friendship (for so you have been to me, and that in the day of danger) and a hypocrite in public life, the world will be puzzled to decide, whether you are an apostate or an imposter; whether you have abandoned good principles, or whether you ever had any.❞

Signing the Treaty of Greenville, 1795 Following General Wayne's victory at the Battle of Fallen Timbers in 1794, the Miami Indians surrendered their claims to much of the Old Northwest.

the United States to defend them under the Franco-American alliance. Hard-boiled commanders of the Royal Navy, ignoring America's rights as a neutral, struck savagely. They seized about three hundred American merchant ships in the West Indies, impressed scores of seamen into service on British vessels, and threw hundreds of others into foul dungeons.

These actions, especially impressment, incensed patriotic Americans. A mighty outcry arose, chiefly from Jeffersonians, that America should once again fight George III in defense of its liberties. At the very least, it should cut off all supplies to its oppressor through a nationwide embargo. But the Federalists stoutly resisted all demands for drastic action. Hamilton's high hopes for economic development depended on trade with Britain. War with the world's mightiest commercial empire would pierce the heart of the Hamiltonian financial system.

✷ Jay's Treaty and Washington's Farewell

President Washington, in a last desperate gamble to avert war, decided to send Chief Justice John Jay to London in 1794. The Jeffersonians were acutely unhappy over the choice, partly because they feared that so notorious a Federalist and Anglophile would sell out his country. Arriving in London, Jay gave the Jeffersonians

further cause for alarm when, at the presentation ceremony, he routinely kissed the queen's hand.

Unhappily, Jay entered the negotiations with weak cards, which were further sabotaged by Hamilton. The latter, fearful of war with Britain, secretly supplied the British with the details of America's bargaining strategy. Not surprisingly, Jay won few concessions. The British did promise to evacuate the chain of posts on U.S. soil—a pledge that inspired little confidence, since it had been made before in Paris (to the same John Jay!) in 1783. In addition, Britain consented to pay damages for the recent seizures of American ships. But the British stopped short of pledging anything about *future* maritime seizures and impressments or about supplying arms to Indians. And they forced Jay to give ground by binding the United States to pay the debts still owed to British merchants on pre-Revolutionary accounts.

Jay's unpopular pact, more than any other issue, vitalized the newborn Democratic-Republican party of Thomas Jefferson. When the Jeffersonians learned of Jay's concessions, their rage was fearful to behold. The treaty seemed like an abject surrender to Britain, as well as a betrayal of the Jeffersonian South. Southern planters would have to pay the major share of the pre-Revolutionary debts, while rich Federalist shippers were collecting damages for recent British seizures. Jeffersonian mobs hanged, burned, and guillotined in effigy that "damn'd archtraitor, Sir John Jay." Even George

Washington's huge popularity was compromised by the controversy over the treaty.

Jay's Treaty had other unforeseen consequences. Fearing that the treaty foreshadowed an Anglo-American alliance, Spain moved hastily to strike a deal with the United States. **Pinckney's Treaty** of 1795 with Spain granted the Americans virtually everything they demanded, including free navigation of the Mississippi, the right of deposit (warehouse rights) at New Orleans, and the large disputed territory of western Florida. (See Map 9.3 on p. 167.)

Exhausted after the diplomatic and partisan battles of his second term, President Washington decided to retire. His choice contributed powerfully to establishing a two-term tradition for American presidents.* In his **Farewell Address** to the nation in 1796 (never delivered orally but printed in the newspapers), Washington strongly advised the avoidance of "permanent alliances" like the still-vexatious Franco-American Treaty of 1778. Contrary to general misunderstanding, Washington did not oppose all alliances, but favored only "temporary alliances" for "extraordinary emergencies." This was admirable advice for a weak and divided nation in 1796. But what is sound counsel for a young stripling may not apply later to a mature and muscular giant.

Washington's contributions as president were enormous, even though the sparkling Hamilton at times seemed to outshine him. The central government, its fiscal feet now under it, was solidly established. The West was expanding. The merchant marine was plowing the seas. Above all, Washington had kept the nation out of both overseas entanglements and foreign wars. The experimental stage had passed, and the presidential chair could now be turned over to a less impressive figure. But republics are notoriously ungrateful. When Washington left office in 1797, he was showered with the brickbats of partisan abuse, quite in contrast with the bouquets that had greeted his arrival.

✦ John Adams Becomes President

Who should succeed the exalted "Father of His Country"? Alexander Hamilton was the best-known member of the Federalist party, now that Washington had bowed out. But his financial policies, some of which had fattened the speculators, had made him so unpopular that he could not hope to be elected president. The Federalists were forced to turn to Washington's vice president, the experienced but ungracious John Adams,

*Not broken until 1940 by Franklin D. Roosevelt and made a part of the Constitution in 1951 by the Twenty-second Amendment. (See the Appendix.)

John Adams, by John Singleton Copley, 1783 When he entered Harvard College in 1751, Adams intended to prepare for the ministry, but four absorbing years of study excited him about other intellectual and career possibilities: "I was a mighty metaphysician, at least I thought myself such." Adams also tried his hand at being a mighty scientist, doctor, and orator. Upon graduation he became a schoolmaster but soon decided to take up the law.

a rugged chip off old Plymouth Rock. The Democratic-Republicans naturally rallied behind their master organizer and leader, Thomas Jefferson.

Political passions ran feverishly high in the presidential campaign of 1796. The lofty presence of Washington had hitherto imposed some restraints; now the lid was off. Cultured Federalists like Fisher Ames referred to the Jeffersonians as "fire-eating salamanders, poison-sucking toads." Federalists and

Although Thomas Jefferson (1743–1826) and John Adams hardly saw eye to eye, Jefferson displayed grudging respect for Adams in a piece of private correspondence in 1787:

"He is vain, irritable, and a bad calculator of the force and probable effect of the motives which govern men. This is all the ill which can possibly be said of him. He is as disinterested as the Being who made him.**"**

Democratic-Republicans even drank their ale in separate taverns. The issues of the campaign, as it turned out, focused heavily on personalities. But the Jeffersonians again assailed the too-forceful crushing of the Whiskey Rebellion and, above all, the negotiation of Jay's hated treaty.

John Adams, with most of his support in New England, squeezed through by the narrow margin of 71 votes to 68 in the Electoral College. Jefferson, as runner-up, became vice president.* One of the ablest statesmen of his day, Adams at sixty-two was a stuffy figure. Sharp-featured, bald, relatively short (five feet seven inches), and thickset ("His Rotundity"), he impressed observers as a man of stern principles who did his duty with stubborn devotion. Although learned and upright, he was a tactless and prickly intellectual aristocrat, with no appeal to the masses and with no desire to cultivate any. Many citizens regarded him with "respectful irritation."

---

*The possibility of such an inharmonious two-party combination in the future was removed by the Twelfth Amendment to the Constitution in 1804. (See the Appendix.)

The crusty New Englander suffered from other handicaps. He had stepped into Washington's shoes, which no successor could hope to fill. In addition, Adams was hated by Hamilton, who had resigned from the Treasury in 1795 and who now headed the war faction of the Federalist party, known as the "High Federalists." The famed financier even secretly plotted with certain members of the cabinet against the president, who had a conspiracy rather than a cabinet on his hands. Adams regarded Hamilton as "the most ruthless, impatient, artful, indefatigable and unprincipled intriguer in the United States, if not in the world." Most ominous of all, Adams inherited a violent quarrel with France—a quarrel whose gunpowder lacked only a spark.

✷ Unofficial Fighting with France

The French were infuriated by Jay's Treaty. They condemned it as the initial step toward an alliance with Britain, their perpetual foe. They further assailed the pact as a flagrant violation of the Franco-American Treaty of 1778. French warships, in retaliation, began to seize defenseless American merchant vessels, altogether about three hundred by mid-1797. Adding insult to outrage, the Paris regime haughtily refused to receive America's newly appointed envoy and even threatened him with arrest.

President Adams kept his head, temporarily, even though the nation was mightily aroused. True to Washington's policy of steering clear of war at all costs, he tried again to reach an agreement with the French and appointed a diplomatic commission of three men, including John Marshall, the future chief justice.

The XYZ Affair When President Adams's envoys to Paris were asked to pay a huge bribe as the price of doing diplomatic business, humiliated Americans rose up in wrath against France. Here an innocent young America is being plundered by Frenchmen as John Bull looks on in amusement from across the English Channel.

The Lilly Library, Indiana University

Preparation for War to Defend Commerce: The Building of the Frigate *Philadelphia* In 1803 this frigate ran onto the rocks near Tripoli harbor, and about three hundred officers and men were imprisoned by the Tripolitans (see Map 11.2 on p. 211). The ship was refloated for service against the Americans, but Stephen Decatur led a party of men that set it afire.

Adams's envoys, reaching Paris in 1797, hoped to meet with Charles Maurice de Talleyrand, the crafty French foreign minister. They were secretly approached by three go-betweens, later referred to as X, Y, and Z in the published dispatches. The French spokesmen, among other concessions, demanded an unneutral loan of 32 million florins, plus what amounted to a bribe of $250,000, for the privilege of merely talking with Talleyrand.

These terms were intolerable. The American trio knew that bribes were standard diplomatic devices in Europe, but they gagged at paying a quarter of a million dollars for mere talk, without any assurances of a settlement. Negotiations quickly broke down, and John Marshall, on reaching New York in 1798, was hailed as a conquering hero for his steadfastness.

The **XYZ Affair** sent a wave of war hysteria sweeping through the United States, catching up even President Adams. The slogan of the hour became "Millions for defense, but not one cent for tribute." The Federalists were delighted at this unexpected turn of affairs, whereas all except the most rabid Jeffersonians hung their heads in shame over the misbehavior of their French friends.

War preparations in the United States were pushed along at a feverish pace, despite considerable Jeffersonian opposition in Congress. The Navy Department was created; the three-ship navy was expanded; the United States Marine Corps was reestablished (originally created in 1775, the Marine Corps had been disbanded at the end of the Revolutionary War). A new army of ten thousand men was authorized (but not fully raised).

Bloodshed was confined to the sea, and principally to the West Indies. In two and a half years of undeclared hostilities (1798–1800), American privateers and men-of-war of the new navy captured over eighty armed vessels flying the French colors, though several hundred Yankee merchant ships were lost to the enemy. Only a slight push, it seemed, might plunge both nations into a full-dress war.

✦ Adams Puts Patriotism Above Party

Embattled France, its hands full in Europe, wanted no war. An outwitted Talleyrand realized that to fight the United States would merely add one more foe to his enemy roster. The British, who were lending the Americans cannon and other war supplies, were actually driven closer to their wayward cousins than they were to be again for many years. Talleyrand therefore let it be known, through roundabout channels, that if the Americans would send a new minister, he would be received with proper respect.

This French furor brought to Adams a degree of personal acclaim that he had never known before—and was never to know again. He doubtless perceived that a full-fledged war, crowned by the conquest of the Floridas and Louisiana, would bring new plaudits to the Federalist party—and perhaps a second term to himself. But the heady wine of popularity did not sway his

The firmness of President John Adams (1735–1826) was revealed in his message to Congress (June 1798):

"I will never send another minister to France without assurances that he will be received, respected, and honored as the representative of a great, free, powerful, and independent nation.**"**

final judgment. He, like other Founding Fathers, realized full well that war must be avoided while the country was relatively weak.

Adams unexpectedly exploded a bombshell when, early in 1799, he submitted to the Senate the name of a new minister to France. Hamilton and his war-hawk faction were enraged. But public opinion—Jeffersonian and reasonable Federalist alike—was favorable to one last try for peace.

America's envoys (now three) found the political skies brightening when they reached Paris early in 1800. The ambitious "Little Corporal," the Corsican Napoleon Bonaparte, had recently seized dictatorial power. He was eager to free his hands of the American squabble so that he might continue to redraw the map of Europe and perhaps create a New World empire in Louisiana. The afflictions and ambitions of the Old World were again working to America's advantage.

After a great deal of haggling, a memorable treaty known as the **Convention of 1800** was signed in Paris. France agreed to annul the twenty-two-year-old marriage of (in)convenience, but as a kind of alimony the United States agreed to pay the damage claims of American shippers. So ended the nation's only peacetime military alliance for a century and a half. Its troubled history does much to explain the traditional antipathy of the American people to foreign entanglements.

John Adams, flinty to the end, deserves immense credit for his belated push for peace, even though he was moved in part by jealousy of Hamilton. Adams not only avoided the hazards of war, but also unwittingly smoothed the path for the peaceful purchase of Louisiana three years later. He should indeed rank high among the forgotten purchasers of this vast domain. If America had drifted into a full-blown war with France in 1800, Napoleon would not have sold Louisiana to Jefferson on any terms in 1803.

President Adams, the bubble of his popularity pricked by peace, was aware of his signal contribution to the nation. He later suggested as the epitaph for his tombstone (not used), "Here lies John Adams, who took upon himself the responsibility of peace with France in the year 1800."

✵ The Federalist Witch Hunt

Exulting Federalists had meanwhile capitalized on the anti-French frenzy to drive through Congress in 1798 a sheaf of laws designed to muffle or minimize their Jeffersonian foes.

The first of these oppressive laws was aimed at supposedly pro-Jeffersonian "aliens." Most European immigrants, lacking wealth, were scorned by the aristocratic Federalist party. But they were welcomed as voters by the less prosperous and more democratic Jeffersonians. The Federalist Congress, hoping to discourage the "dregs" of Europe, erected a disheartening barrier. They raised the residence requirements for aliens who desired to become citizens from a tolerable five years to an intolerable fourteen. This drastic new law violated the traditional American policy of open-door hospitality and speedy assimilation.

Two additional **Alien Laws** struck heavily at undesirable immigrants. The president was empowered to deport dangerous foreigners in time of peace and to deport or imprison them in time of hostilities. Though defensible as a war measure—and an officially declared war with France seemed imminent—this was an arbitrary grant of executive power contrary to American tradition and to the spirit of the Constitution, even though the stringent Alien Laws were never enforced.

The "lockjaw" **Sedition Act**, the last measure of the Federalist clampdown, was a direct slap at two priceless freedoms guaranteed in the Constitution by the Bill of Rights—freedom of speech and freedom of the press (First Amendment). This law provided that anyone who impeded the policies of the government or falsely defamed its officials, including the president, would be liable to a heavy fine and imprisonment. Severe though the measure was, the Federalists believed that it was justified. The verbal violence of the day was unrestrained, and foul-penned editors, some of them exiled aliens, vilified Adams's anti-French policy in vicious terms.

Many outspoken Jeffersonian editors were indicted under the Sedition Act, and ten were brought to trial. All of them were convicted, often by packed juries swayed by prejudiced Federalist judges. Some of the victims were harmless partisans, who should have been spared the notoriety of martyrdom. Among them was Congressman Matthew Lyon (the "Spitting Lion"), who had earlier gained fame by spitting in the face of a Federalist. He was sentenced to four months in jail for writing of President Adams's "unbounded thirst for ridiculous pomp, foolish adulation, and selfish avarice." Another culprit was lucky to get off with a fine of $100 after he had expressed the wish that the wad of a cannon fired in honor of Adams had landed in the seat of the president's breeches.

Congressional Pugilists
Satirical representation of Matthew Lyon's fight in Congress with the Federalist representative Roger Griswold.

The Sedition Act seemed to be in direct conflict with the Constitution. But the Supreme Court, dominated by Federalists, was of no mind to declare this Federalist law unconstitutional. (The Federalists intentionally wrote the law to expire in 1801, so that it could not be used against them if they lost the next election.) This attempt by the Federalists to crush free speech and silence the opposition party, high-handed as it was, undoubtedly made many converts for the Jeffersonians.

Yet the Alien and Sedition Acts, despite pained outcries from the Jeffersonians they muzzled, commanded widespread popular support. Anti-French hysteria played directly into the hands of witch-hunting conservatives. In the congressional elections of 1798–1799, the Federalists, riding a wave of popularity, scored the most sweeping victory of their entire history.

✯ The Virginia (Madison) and Kentucky (Jefferson) Resolutions

Resentful Jeffersonians naturally refused to take the Alien and Sedition Acts lying down. Jefferson himself feared that if the Federalists managed to choke free speech and free press, they would then wipe out other precious constitutional guarantees. His own fledgling political party might even be stamped out of existence. If this had happened, the country might have slid into a dangerous one-party dictatorship.

Fearing prosecution for sedition, Jefferson secretly penned a series of resolutions, which the Kentucky legislature approved in 1798 and 1799. His friend and fellow Virginian James Madison drafted a similar but less extreme statement, which was adopted by the legislature of Virginia in 1798.

Both Jefferson and Madison stressed the compact theory—a theory popular among English political philosophers in the seventeenth and eighteenth centuries. As applied to America by the Jeffersonians, this concept meant that the thirteen sovereign states, in creating the federal government, had entered into a "compact," or contract, regarding its jurisdiction. The national

In 1800 James Callender (1758–1803) published a pamphlet that assailed the president in strong language. For blasts like the following tirade, Callender was prosecuted under the Sedition Act, fined $250, and sentenced to prison for nine months:

❝ The reign of Mr. Adams has, hitherto, been one continued tempest of *malignant* passions. As president, he has never opened his lips, or lifted his pen, without threatening and scolding. The grand object of his administration has been to exasperate the rage of contending parties, to calumniate and destroy every man who differs from his opinions. . . . Every person holding an office must either quit it, or think and vote exactly with Mr. Adams.❞

government was consequently the agent or creation of the states. Since water can rise no higher than its source, the individual states were the final judges of whether their agent had broken the "compact" by overstepping the authority originally granted. Invoking this logic, Jefferson's Kentucky resolutions concluded that the federal regime *had* exceeded its constitutional powers and that with regard to the Alien and Sedition Acts, "nullification"—a refusal to accept them—was the "rightful remedy."

No other state legislatures, despite Jefferson's hopes, fell into line. Some of them flatly refused to endorse the Virginia and Kentucky resolutions. Others, chiefly in Federalist states, added ringing condemnations. Many Federalists argued that the people, not the states, had made the original compact, and that it was up to the Supreme Court—not the states—to nullify unconstitutional legislation passed by Congress. This practice, though not specifically authorized by the Constitution, was finally adopted by the Supreme Court in 1803 (see pp. 208–210).

The **Virginia and Kentucky resolutions** were a brilliant formulation of the extreme states' rights view regarding the Union—indeed more sweeping in their implications than their authors had intended. They were later used by southerners to support nullification—and ultimately secession. Yet neither Jefferson nor Madison, as Founding Fathers of the Union, had any intention of breaking it up; they were groping for ways to preserve it. Their resolutions were basically campaign documents designed to crystallize opposition to the Federalist party and to unseat it in the upcoming presidential election of 1800. The only real nullification that Jefferson had in view was the nullification of Federalist abuses.

✵ Federalists Versus Democratic-Republicans

As the presidential contest of 1800 approached, the differences between Federalists and Democratic-Republicans were sharply etched (see Table 10.3). As might be expected, most federalists of the pre-Constitution period (1787–1789) became Federalists in the 1790s. Largely welded by Hamilton into an effective group by 1793, they openly advocated rule by the "best people." "Those who own the country," remarked Federalist John Jay, "ought to govern it." With their intellectual arrogance and Tory tastes, Hamiltonians distrusted full-blown democracy as the fountain of all mischiefs and feared the "swayability" of the untutored common folk.

Hamiltonian Federalists also advocated a strong central government with the power to crush democratic excesses like Shays's Rebellion, protect the lives and estates of the wealthy, subordinate the sovereignty-loving states, and promote foreign trade. They believed that government should support private enterprise but not interfere with it. This attitude came naturally to the merchants, manufacturers, and shippers along the Atlantic seaboard, who made up the majority of

TABLE 10.3 The Two Political Parties, 1793–1800	
Federalist Features	**Democratic-Republican (Jeffersonian) Features**
Rule by the "best people"	Rule by the informed masses
Hostility to extension of democracy	Friendliness toward extension of democracy
A powerful central government at the expense of states' rights	A weak central government so as to preserve states' rights
Loose interpretation of Constitution	Strict interpretation of Constitution
Government to foster business; concentration of wealth in interests of capitalistic enterprise	No special favors for business; agriculture preferred
A protective tariff	No special favors for manufacturers
Pro-British (conservative Tory tradition)	Pro-French (radical revolutionary tradition)
National debt a blessing, if properly funded	National debt a bane; rigid economy
An expanding bureaucracy	Reduction of federal officeholders
A powerful central bank	Encouragement to state banks
Restrictions on free speech and press	Relatively free speech and press
Concentration in seacoast area	Concentration in South and Southwest; in agricultural areas and backcountry
A strong navy to protect shippers	A minimal navy for coastal defense

Thomas Jefferson at Natural Bridge, by Caleb Boyle, ca. 1801 A great statesman, Jefferson wrote his own epitaph: "Here was buried Thomas Jefferson, Author of the Declaration of Independence, of the Statute of Virginia for Religious Freedom, and Father of the University of Virginia."

Federalist support. Farther inland, few Hamiltonians dwelled.

The hinterland was largely anti-Federalist territory. Leading the anti-Federalists, who came eventually to be known as Democratic-Republicans or sometimes simply Republicans, was Thomas Jefferson. His rivalry with Hamilton defined the archetypal conflict in American political history. The two leaders appealed to different constituencies and expressed different theories of society, politics, and diplomacy.

Lanky and relaxed in appearance, lacking personal aggressiveness, weak-voiced, and unable to deliver a rabble-rousing speech, Jefferson became a master political organizer through his ability to lead people rather than drive them. His strongest appeal was to the middle class and to the underprivileged—the "dirt" farmers, the laborers, the artisans, and the small shopkeepers.

Liberal-thinking Jefferson, with his aristocratic head set on a farmer's frame, was a bundle of inconsistencies. By one set of tests, he should have been a Federalist, for he was a Virginia aristocrat and slaveowner who lived in an imposing hilltop mansion at Monticello. A so-called traitor to his own upper class, Jefferson cherished uncommon sympathy for the common people, especially the downtrodden, the oppressed, and the persecuted. As he wrote in 1800, "I have sworn upon the altar of God eternal hostility against every form of tyranny over the mind of man."

Jeffersonian Republicans demanded a weak central regime. They believed that the best government was the one that governed least. The bulk of the power, Jefferson argued, should be retained by the states. There the people, in intimate contact with local affairs, could keep a more vigilant eye on their public servants. Otherwise a dictatorship might develop. Central authority—a kind of necessary evil—was to be kept at a minimum through a strict interpretation of the Constitution. The national debt, which he saw as a curse illegitimately bequeathed to later generations, was to be paid off.

Jeffersonian Republicans, themselves primarily agrarians, insisted that there should be no special privileges for special classes, particularly manufacturers. Agriculture, to Jefferson, was the favored branch of the economy and formed the foundation of his political thought. "Those who labor in the earth are the chosen people of God," he said. Most of his followers naturally came from the agricultural South and Southwest.

Above all, Jefferson advocated the rule of the people. But he did not propose thrusting the ballot into the hands of *every* adult white male. He favored government *for* the people, but not by *all* the people—only by those white men who were literate enough to inform themselves and wear the mantle of American citizenship worthily. Universal education would have

Thomas Jefferson's vision of a republican America was peopled with virtuous farmers, not factory hands. As early as 1784, he wrote,

❝While we have land to labor then, let us never wish to see our citizens occupied at a workbench, or twirling a distaff.... For the general operations of manufacture, let our workshops remain in Europe.... The mobs of great cities add just so much to the support of pure government, as sores do to the strength of the human body.❞

to precede universal suffrage. The ignorant, he argued, were incapable of self-government. But he had profound faith in the reasonableness and teachableness of the masses and in their collective wisdom when taught.

Landlessness among American citizens threatened popular democracy as much as illiteracy, in Jefferson's eyes. He feared that propertyless dependents would be political pawns in the hands of their landowning superiors. How could the emergence of a landless class of voters be avoided? The answer, in part, was by slavery. A system of black slave labor in the South ensured that white yeoman farmers could remain independent landowners. Without slavery, poor whites would have to provide the cheap labor so necessary for the cultivation of tobacco and rice, and their low wages would preclude their ever owning property. Jefferson thus tortuously reconciled slaveholding—his own included—with his more democratic impulses.

Yet for his time, Jefferson's confidence that white, free men could become responsible and knowledgeable citizens was open-minded. He championed their freedom of speech, for without free speech, the misdeeds of tyranny could not be exposed. Jefferson even dared to say that given the choice of "a government without newspapers" and "newspapers without a government," he would opt for the latter. Yet no other American leader, except perhaps Abraham Lincoln, ever suffered more foul abuse from editorial pens; Jefferson might well have prayed for freedom *from* the Federalist press.

Differences over foreign policy defined another sharp distinction between Hamilton and Jefferson.

Hamilton looked outward and eastward. He sought to build a strong national state that would assert and expand America's commercial interests. "No Government could give us tranquility and happiness at home," he declared, "which did not possess sufficient stability and strength to make us respectable abroad." Foreign trade, especially with Britain, was a key cog in Hamilton's fiscal machinery, and friendship with Britain was thus indispensable. Jeffersonian Republicans, unlike the Federalist "British boot-lickers," were basically pro-French. They earnestly believed that it was to America's advantage to support the liberal ideals of the French Revolution, rather than applaud the reaction of the British Tories. Jefferson, in effect, faced inward and westward. His priorities were to protect and strengthen democracy at home, especially in the frontier regions beyond the Appalachians, rather than flex America's muscles abroad.

So as the young Republic's first full decade of nationhood came to a close, the Founders' hopes seemed already imperiled. Conflicts over domestic politics and foreign policy undermined the unity of the Revolutionary era and called into question the very viability of the American experiment in democracy. As the presidential election of 1800 approached, the danger loomed that the fragile and battered American ship of state, like many another before it and after it, would founder on the rocks of controversy. The shores of history are littered with the wreckage of nascent nations torn asunder before they could grow to a stable maturity. Why should the United States expect to enjoy a happier fate?

Chapter Review

KEY TERMS

Bill of Rights (182)
Judiciary Act of 1789 (182)
funding at par (183)
assumption (183)
tariff (184)
excise tax (184)
Bank of the United States (185)
Whiskey Rebellion (185)
Reign of Terror (190)
Neutrality Proclamation (190)

Fallen Timbers, Battle of (191)
Greenville, Treaty of (191)
Jay's Treaty (193)
Pinckney's Treaty (193)
Farewell Address (193)
XYZ Affair (195)
Convention of 1800 (196)
Alien Laws (196)
Sedition Act (196)
Virginia and Kentucky resolutions (198)

PEOPLE TO KNOW

George Washington
Alexander Hamilton
Louis XVI
Edmond Genêt
Little Turtle

"Mad Anthony" Wayne
John Jay
John Adams
Charles Maurice de Talleyrand

CHRONOLOGY

1789	Constitution formally put into effect Judiciary Act of 1789 Washington elected president French Revolution begins Declaration of the Rights of Man (France)
1790	First official census
1791	Bill of Rights adopted Vermont becomes fourteenth state Bank of the United States created Excise tax passed
1792	Washington reelected president
1792–1793	Federalist and Democratic-Republican parties formed
1793	Louis XVI beheaded; radical phase of French Revolution France declares war on Britain and Spain Washington's Neutrality Proclamation Citizen Genêt affair

1794	Whiskey Rebellion Battle of Fallen Timbers Jay's Treaty with Britain
1795	Treaty of Greenville: Indians cede Ohio Pinckney's Treaty with Spain
1796	Washington's Farewell Address
1797	Adams becomes president XYZ Affair
1798	Alien and Sedition Acts
1798–1799	Virginia and Kentucky resolutions
1798–1800	Undeclared war with France
1800	Convention of 1800: peace with France

TO LEARN MORE

Joanne Freeman, *Affairs of Honor: National Politics in the New Republic* (2001)

Francois Furstenberg, *In the Name of the Father: Washington's Legacy, Slavery, and the Making of a Nation* (2006)

Frank Lambert, *The Barbary Wars: American Independence in the Atlantic World* (2005)

Michael Merrill and Sean Wilentz, eds., *The Key of Liberty: The Life and Democratic Writings of William Manning, "A Laborer," 1747–1814* (1992)

Jeffrey L. Pasley, *"The Tyranny of Printers": Newspaper Politics in the Early American Republic* (2001)

Jeffrey L. Pasley, Andrew W. Robertson, and David Waldstreicher, eds., *Beyond the Founders: New Approaches to the Political History of the Early American Republic* (2004)

Bernard Schwartz, *The Great Rights of Mankind: A History of the American Bill of Rights* (1991)

Thomas P. Slaughter, *The Whiskey Rebellion: Frontier Epilogue to the American Revolution* (1986)

Robert W. Smith, *Keeping the Republic: Ideology and Early American Diplomacy* (2004)

Alan Taylor, *William Cooper's Town: Power and Persuasion on the Frontier of the Early American Republic* (1995)

Gordon Wood, *Empire of Liberty: A History of the Early Republic, 1789–1815* (2009)

Robert E. Wright, *Hamilton Unbound: Finance and the Creation of the American Republic* (2002)

A complete, annotated bibliography for this chapter—along with brief descriptions of the People to Know—may be found on the American Pageant website. The Key Terms are defined in a Glossary at the end of the text.

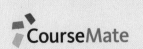

Go to the CourseMate website at **www.cengagebrain.com** for additional study tools and review materials—including audio and video clips—for this chapter.

AP® Review Questions for Chapter 10

1. All of the following are true statements about the Bill of Rights EXCEPT that it
   (A) is the first ten amendments to the Constitution.
   (B) gives to the federal government all powers not specifically designated in the Constitution.
   (C) protects personal liberties such as freedom of speech, religion, and the right to bear arms.
   (D) was added at the insistence of, and as a compromise with, anti-Federalists.
   (E) prevents the government from arbitrarily seizing private property.

2. Why did Secretary of the Treasury Alexander Hamilton want the federal government to assume state debts accumulated during the American Revolution?
   (A) He hoped to end the practice of speculating.
   (B) He supported fiscal policies that aided the masses.
   (C) He wanted to prove the federal treasury was solid enough to handle the debt.
   (D) He hoped to shift wealthy creditors' obligations and allegiances from the states to the federal government.
   (E) He wanted to put the new republic on more solid financial ground.

3. Leaders chose a site along the Potomac River for the nation's capitol city (ultimately, Washington, D.C.) in 1790 because
   (A) it was centrally located between northern and southern states.
   (B) it was close to the homes of several leaders, including President George Washington and Secretary of State Thomas Jefferson.
   (C) it would ensure that Virginia would vote in favor of Hamilton's plan for federal assumption of state war debts.
   (D) its strategic location would ensure the collection of customs and duties needed to pay down the national debt.
   (E) its river location made it easily accessible by various transportation routes.

4. Which of the following was NOT part of Hamilton's economic program for the new nation?
   (A) Protecting well-to-do manufacturing interests
   (B) Establishing a national bank
   (C) Setting an excise tax
   (D) Limiting the power of the central government
   (E) Creating a sound monetary policy

5. The "loose construction" interpretation of the Constitution refers to the notion that
   (A) in carrying out its duties, the central government can take any measure not specifically prohibited by the Constitution.
   (B) all powers not expressly given to the central government belong to the states.
   (C) the judiciary branch should be the final voice in interpreting the law.
   (D) Congress may pass only those laws and take only those actions deemed necessary to conduct the business of the United States.
   (E) the central government can only act as defined by the Constitution.

6. The Whiskey Rebellion is most significant because
   (A) it marked the first tax rebellion against the new republic.
   (B) distillers were successful in their push to have the government repeal its tax on whiskey.
   (C) it included many former veterans of the American Revolution.
   (D) it was the first protest to make its case without violence.
   (E) it led to the strengthening and increased credibility of Washington's government.

7. Which were the first two political parties in America?
   (A) Federalists and anti-Federalists
   (B) National Republicans and Democratic Republicans
   (C) Democratic-Republicans and Federalists
   (D) Whigs and Tories
   (E) Democrats and Whigs

8. What was the main reason that leaders in the newly formed United States were suspicious of the formation of political parties?
   (A) They feared such divisiveness might trigger another revolution.
   (B) They were not accustomed to the long-term existence of political parties.
   (C) They considered sustained opposition to government antithetical to unity and the functioning of a republic.
   (D) They believed parties to be seedbeds of corruption.
   (E) They worried that party politics would interfere with the functioning of government.

9. George Washington's 1793 Neutrality Proclamation in the conflict between France and England is significant for all of the following reasons EXCEPT that it
   (A) launched America's isolationist foreign policy tradition.
   (B) was based on an accurate assessment of America's military and diplomatic strengths and weaknesses.
   (C) marked a departure from the Franco-American Alliance of 1778.
   (D) united Federalists and Jeffersonians around a single cause.
   (E) actually served the French more than American entry into the war might have.

10. Which of these was NOT among the many responses to Jay's Treaty with Britain in 1794?
    (A) Outrage by southerners, Jeffersonians, and the French
    (B) A surge in President Washington's popularity
    (C) Increased interest by Spain in a treaty of its own with America
    (D) Mob riots and demonstrations
    (E) Britain agreeing to pay damages for seizing American ships

11. Americans were angered by the XYZ Affair with France because
    (A) they likened it to a bribe rather than respectable diplomacy.
    (B) the French refused to compensate American merchants for goods seized in their ships.
    (C) the French diplomatic minister sent American ambassadors home.
    (D) French importers had blocked American commerce from entering Europe.
    (E) French officials arrested America's diplomatic envoy John Marshall.

12. What move did John Adams make in 1800 that paved the way for the Louisiana Purchase in 1803?
    (A) He launched a crucial military battle that led to victory against French leader Napoleon Bonaparte.
    (B) He accepted a second invitation to negotiate a treaty with the French.
    (C) He authorized the government purchase of foreign land bordering American states.
    (D) He joined forces with the British against France.
    (E) He moved to purchase Florida from the Spanish.

13. The Alien and Sedition laws were intended to accomplish all of the following EXCEPT
    (A) silence critics of the Federalist government.
    (B) target immigrant voters.
    (C) grant the president the right to deport foreigners.
    (D) boost the power and popularity of Jeffersonian Democratic-Republicans.
    (E) raise residency requirements for citizenship.

14. What was the most fundamental difference between the Federalist party and the Jeffersonian Democratic-Republicans?
    (A) Jeffersonians felt that only the talented elite should lead; Federalists embraced the masses.
    (B) Federalists tended to be located along the Atlantic seaboard; Jeffersonians inhabited rural and backcountry regions.
    (C) Jeffersonians tended to be slaveowners; Federalists were largely opposed to slavery.
    (D) Federalists embraced commercial interests; Jeffersonians saw farming as the hallmark of the nation's economy.
    (E) Federalists advocated for a strong central government; Jeffersonians promoted states' rights.

15. Why did Thomas Paine declare, "The principles of America opened the Bastille"?
    (A) Both revolutions were built upon the ideals of liberty and equality.
    (B) America and France went through period of intense violence after their revolutions.
    (C) Both revolutions immediately produced strong, powerful leaders.
    (D) Americans' refusal to adhere to their alliance with France sparked a long, deadly war.
    (E) Both nations were spurred to action because the mother country levied unfair taxes.

16. Events in Europe drew the United States into world affairs in all of the following ways EXCEPT that
    (A) British naval practices in the West Indies led to the extremely unpopular Jay's Treaty.
    (B) The prospect of an Anglo-American alliance frightened Spain, leading to Pinckney's Treaty.
    (C) Improved relations with Britain led to the XYZ Affair and the buildup of the navy.
    (D) Napoleon's quest for European domination led to the end of the Franco-American alliance.
    (E) British and French impressments led to an era of complete isolation in the United States.

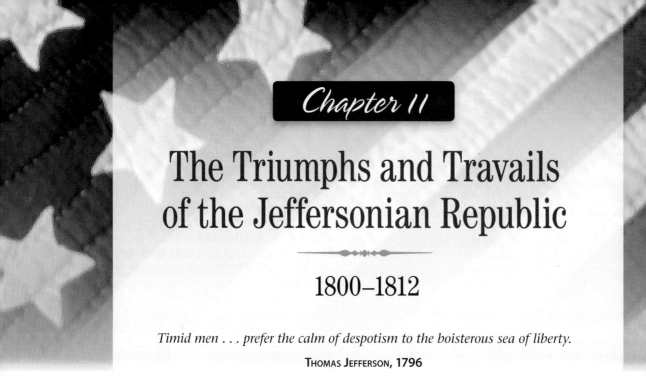

Chapter 11

The Triumphs and Travails of the Jeffersonian Republic

1800–1812

Timid men . . . prefer the calm of despotism to the boisterous sea of liberty.

THOMAS JEFFERSON, 1796

In the critical presidential contest of 1800, the first in which Federalists and Democratic-Republicans functioned as two national political parties, John Adams and Thomas Jefferson again squared off against each other. The choice seemed clear and dramatic: Adams's Federalists waged a defensive struggle for strong central government and public order. Their Jeffersonian opponents presented themselves as the guardians of agrarian purity, liberty, and states' rights. The next dozen years, however, would turn what seemed like a clear-cut choice in 1800 into a messier reality, as the Jeffersonians in power were confronted with a series of opportunities and crises requiring the assertion of federal authority. As the first challengers to rout a reigning party, the Republicans were the first to learn that it is far easier to condemn from the stump than to govern consistently.

✦ Federalist and Republican Mudslingers

In fighting for survival, the Federalists labored under heavy handicaps. Their Alien and Sedition Acts had aroused a host of enemies, although most of these critics were dyed-in-the-wool Jeffersonians anyhow. The Hamiltonian wing of the Federalist party, robbed of its glorious war with France, split openly with President Adams. Hamilton, a victim of arrogance, was so indiscreet as to attack the president in a privately printed pamphlet. Jeffersonians soon got hold of the pamphlet and gleefully published it.

The most damaging blow to the Federalists was the refusal of Adams to give them a rousing fight with France. Their feverish war preparations had swelled the public debt and had required disagreeable new taxes, including a stamp tax. After all these unpopular measures, the war scare had petered out, and the country was left with an all-dressed-up-but-no-place-to-go feeling. The military preparations now seemed not only unnecessary but also extravagant, as seamen for the "new navy" were called "John Adams's Jackasses." Adams himself was known, somewhat ironically, as "the Father of the American Navy."

Thrown on the defensive, the Federalists concentrated their fire on Jefferson himself, who became the victim of one of America's earliest "whispering campaigns." He was accused of having robbed a widow and her children of a trust fund and of having fathered numerous mulatto children by his own slave women. (Jefferson's long-rumored intimacy with one of his

The Reverend Timothy Dwight (1752–1817), president of Yale College, predicted that in the event of Jefferson's election,

❝the Bible would be cast into a bonfire, our holy worship changed into a dance of [French] Jacobin phrensy, our wives and daughters dishonored, and our sons converted into the disciples of Voltaire and the dragoons of Marat.❞

Washington and Jefferson Compared, 1807 This pro-Federalist, anti-Jefferson cartoon accuses Jefferson of sympathizing with French Revolutionary despotism.

slaves, Sally Hemings, has been confirmed through DNA testing. See "Examining the Evidence," p. 205.) As a liberal in religion, Jefferson had earlier incurred the wrath of the orthodox clergy, largely through his successful struggle to separate church and state in his native Virginia. Although Jefferson did believe in God, preachers throughout New England, stronghold of Federalism and Congregationalism, thundered against his alleged atheism. Old ladies of Federalist families, fearing Jefferson's election, even buried their Bibles or hung them in wells.

✹ The Jeffersonian "Revolution of 1800"

Jefferson won by a majority of 73 electoral votes to 65 (see Map 11.1). In defeat, the colorless and presumably unpopular Adams polled more electoral strength than he had gained four years earlier—except for New York. The Empire State fell into the Jeffersonian basket, and with it the election, largely because Aaron Burr, a master wire-puller, turned New York to Jefferson by the narrowest of margins. The Virginian polled the bulk of his strength in the South and West, particularly in

those states where universal white manhood suffrage had been adopted.

Decisive in Jefferson's victory was the three-fifths clause of the Constitution. By counting three-fifths of the slave population for the purposes of congressional and Electoral College representation, the Constitution gave white southern voters a bonus that helped Jefferson win the White House. Northern critics fumed that Jefferson was a "Negro President" and an illegitimate embodiment of the "slave power" that the southern states wielded in the nation.

Jeffersonian joy was dampened by an unexpected deadlock. Through a technicality Jefferson, the presidential candidate, and Burr, his vice-presidential running mate, received the same number of electoral votes for the presidency. Under the Constitution the tie could be broken only by the House of Representatives (see Art. II, Sec. I, para. 2). This body was controlled for several more months by the lame-duck Federalists, who preferred Burr to the hated Jefferson.* Voting in the

---

*A "lame duck" has been humorously defined as a politician whose political goose has been cooked in the recent elections. The possibility of another such tie was removed by the Twelfth Amendment in 1804 (see the Appendix). Before then, each elector had two votes, with the second-place finisher becoming vice president.

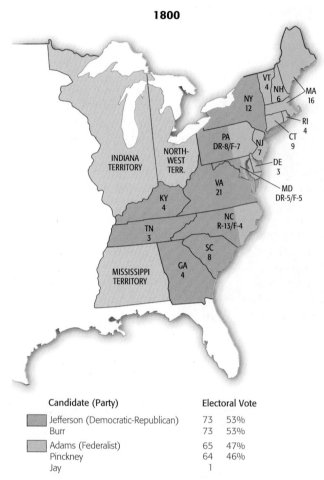

1800

Candidate (Party)		Electoral Vote	
Jefferson (Democratic-Republican)		73	53%
Burr		73	53%
Adams (Federalist)		65	47%
Pinckney		64	46%
Jay		1	

MAP 11.1 Presidential Election of 1800 (with electoral vote by state) New York was the key state in this election, and Aaron Burr helped swing it away from the Federalists with tactics that anticipated the political "machines" of a later day. Federalists complained that Burr "travels every night from one meeting of Republicans to another, haranguing . . . them to the most zealous exertions. [He] can stoop so low as to visit every low tavern that may happen to be crowded with his dear fellow citizens." But Burr proved that the price was worth it. "We have beat you," Burr told kid-gloved Federalists after the election, "by superior *Management*." © Cengage Learning

House moved slowly to a climax, as exhausted representatives snored in their seats. The agonizing deadlock was broken at last when a few Federalists, despairing of electing Burr and hoping for moderation from Jefferson, refrained from voting. The election then went to the rightful candidate.

John Adams, as fate would have it, was the last Federalist president of the United States. His party sank slowly into political oblivion and ultimately disappeared completely in the days of Andrew Jackson.

Jefferson later claimed that the election of 1800 was a "revolution" comparable to that of 1776, and

> *A Philadelphia woman wrote her sister-in-law about the pride she felt on the occasion of Thomas Jefferson's inauguration as third president of the United States in 1801:*
>
> **❝**I have this morning witnessed one of the most interesting scenes a free people can ever witness. The changes of administration, which in every government and in every age have most generally been epochs of confusion, villainy and bloodshed, in this our happy country take place without any species of distraction, or disorder.**❞**

historians have sometimes referred to the **Revolution of 1800**. But the election was no revolution in the sense of a massive popular upheaval or an upending of the political system. In truth, Jefferson had narrowly squeaked through to victory. A switch of some 250 votes in New York would have thrown the election to Adams. Jefferson meant that his election represented a return to what he considered the original spirit of the Revolution. In his eyes Hamilton and Adams had betrayed the ideals of 1776 and 1787. Jefferson's mission, as he saw it, was to restore the republican experiment, to check the growth of government power, and to halt the decay of virtue that had set in under Federalist rule.

No less "revolutionary" was the peaceful and orderly transfer of power on the basis of an election whose results all parties accepted. This was a remarkable achievement for a raw young nation, especially after all the partisan bitterness that had agitated the country during Adams's presidency. It was particularly remarkable in that age; comparable successions would not take place in Britain for another generation. After a decade of division and doubt, Americans could take justifiable pride in the vigor of their experiment in democracy.

✦ Responsibility Breeds Moderation

"Long Tom" Jefferson was inaugurated president on March 4, 1801, in the swampy village of Washington, the crude new national capital. Tall (six feet two and a half inches), with large hands and feet, red hair ("the Red Fox"), and prominent cheekbones and chin, he was an arresting figure. Having spent five years as U.S. minister to France (1784–1789), he was fluent in French and a sophisticated, cosmopolitan "citizen of the world," yet he never lost the common touch. Believing that the

The Thomas Jefferson–Sally Hemings Controversy

Debate over whether Thomas Jefferson had sexual relations with Sally Hemings, a slave at Monticello, began as early as 1802, when James Callender published the first accusations and Federalist newspapers gleefully broadcast them throughout the country. Two years later this print, titled "A Philosophic Cock," attacked Jefferson by depicting him as a rooster and Hemings as a hen. The rooster, or cock, was also a symbol of Revolutionary France. Jefferson's enemies sought to discredit him for personal indiscretions as well as radical sympathies. Although he resolutely denied having an affair with Hemings, the

charge that at first seemed to be only a politically motivated defamation refused to go away. In the 1870s two new oral sources of evidence came to light. Madison Hemings, Sally's next-to-last child, claimed that his mother had identified Jefferson as the father of all five of her children. Soon thereafter James Parton's biography of Jefferson revealed that among Jefferson's white descendants, it was said that his nephew had fathered all or most of Sally's children. In the 1950s several large publishing projects on Jefferson's life and writings uncovered new evidence and inspired renewed debate. Most convincing

was Dumas Malone's calculation that Jefferson had been present at Monticello nine months prior to the birth of each of Sally's children. Speculation continued throughout the rest of the century, with little new evidence, until scientific advances made possible DNA testing of the remains of Jefferson's white and possible black descendants to determine paternity. Two centuries after Callender first cast aspersions on Jefferson's morality, cutting-edge science helped establish the high probability that Jefferson had fathered Sally's youngest son and the likelihood that he was the father of all of her children.

A PHILOSOPHIC COCK

'Tis not a set of features or complexion
Or tincture of a Skin that I admire

Courtesy, American Antiquarian Society

customary pomp did not befit his democratic ideals, he spurned a horse-drawn coach and strode by foot to the Capitol from his boardinghouse.

Jefferson's inaugural address, beautifully phrased, was a classic statement of democratic principles. "The will of the majority is in all cases to prevail," Jefferson declared. But, he added, "that will to be rightful must be reasonable; the minority possess their equal rights, which equal law must protect, and to violate would be oppression." Seeking to allay Federalist fears of a bull-in-the-china-closet overturn, Jefferson ingratiatingly intoned, "We are all Republicans, we are all Federalists." As for foreign affairs, he pledged "honest friendship with all nations, entangling alliances with none."

With its rustic setting, Washington lent itself admirably to the simplicity and frugality of the Jeffersonian Republicans. In this respect it contrasted sharply with the elegant atmosphere of Federalist Philadelphia, the former temporary capital. Extending democratic principles to etiquette, Jefferson established the rule of pell-mell at official dinners—that is, seating without regard to rank. The resplendent British minister, who had enjoyed precedence among the pro-British Federalists, was insulted.

As president, Jefferson could be shockingly unconventional. He would receive callers in sloppy attire—once in a dressing gown and heel-less slippers. He started the precedent, unbroken until Woodrow Wilson's presi-

Litchfield Historical Society

Litchfield Historical Society

Mrs. Benjamin Tallmadge and Son Henry Floyd and Daughter Maria Jones; Colonel Benjamin Tallmadge and Son William Tallmadge, by Ralph Earl, 1790
The Tallmadges were among the leading citizens of Litchfield, a Federalist stronghold in the heavily Federalist state of Connecticut. Colonel Benjamin Tallmadge served with distinction in the Revolutionary War, became a wealthy merchant and banker, and represented his state in Congress from 1801 to 1817. Mary Floyd Tallmadge, like her husband, came from a prominent Long Island family. The opulence of the Tallmadges' clothing and surroundings in these paintings abundantly testifies to the wealth, and the social pretensions, of the Federalist elite. Note the toy carriage near the feet of the Tallmadge daughter—a replica of the actual, and elegant, carriage owned by the Tallmadge family.

Jefferson Inaugural Pitcher, 1801 This memento from the election of 1800 immortalized President Thomas Jefferson's words, "We are all Republicans, we are all Federalists," which turned out to be more hopeful than true. Jefferson was portrayed in the plain attire he favored, shunning the sartorial pretensions affected by many Federalists, such as the elegantly dressed Tallmadges shown on p. 206. Collection of Janice L. and David J. Frent

Thomas Jefferson's Polygraph, 1806 Jefferson's study reflected his fondness for ideas and inventions. One of his favorite devices was this polygraph, which Jefferson used to make copies of the letters he penned. It was patented in London in 1803. Jefferson acquired one the following year. "From sun-rise to one or two o'clock," he noted, "I am drudging at the writing table." Jefferson wrote almost 20,000 letters in his lifetime. He told John Adams that he suffered "under the persecution of letters," calculating that he received 1,267 letters in the year 1820, "many of them requiring answers of elaborate research, and all to be answered with due attention and consideration." The polygraph allowed him to keep duplicates of his letters, which he tied into bundles organized alphabetically and chronologically. Jefferson was thereby able to locate any given letter and even send for a particular one when he was away from his Monticello home.

dency 112 years later, of sending messages to Congress to be read by a clerk. Personal appearances, in the Federalist manner, suggested too strongly a monarchical speech from the throne. Besides, Jefferson was painfully conscious of his weak voice and unimpressive platform presence.

As if compelled by an evil twin, Jefferson was forced to reverse many of the political principles he had so vigorously championed. There were in fact two Thomas Jeffersons. One was the scholarly private citizen, who philosophized in his study. The other was the

President John F. Kennedy (1917–1963) once greeted a large group of Nobel Prize winners as

❝the most extraordinary collection of talent, of human knowledge, that has ever been gathered together at the White House, with the possible exception of when Thomas Jefferson dined alone.❞

harassed public official, who made the disturbing discovery that bookish theories worked out differently in the noisy arena of practical politics. The open-minded Virginian was therefore consistently inconsistent; it is easy to quote one Jefferson to refute the other.

The triumph of Thomas Jefferson's Democratic-Republicans and the eviction of the Federalists marked the first party overturn in American history. The vanquished naturally feared that the victors would grab all the spoils of office for themselves. But Jefferson, in keeping with his conciliatory inaugural address, showed unexpected moderation. To the dismay of his office-seeking friends, the new president dismissed few public servants for political reasons. **Patronage**-hungry Jeffersonians watched the Federalist appointees grow old in office and grumbled that "few die, none resign."

Jefferson quickly proved an able politician. He was especially effective in the informal atmosphere of a dinner party. There he wooed congressional representatives while personally pouring imported wines and serving the tasty dishes of his French cook. In part

The toleration of Thomas Jefferson (1743–1826) was reflected in his inaugural address:

❝If there be any among us who would wish to dissolve this Union or to change its republican form, let them stand undisturbed as monuments of the safety with which error of opinion may be tolerated where reason is left free to combat it.**❞**

Jefferson had to rely on his personal charm because his party was so weak-jointed. Denied the power to dispense patronage, the Democratic-Republicans could not build a loyal political following. Opposition to the Federalists was the chief glue holding them together, and as the Federalists faded, so did Democratic-Republican unity. The era of well-developed, well-disciplined political parties still lay in the future.

✷ Jeffersonian Restraint

At the outset Jefferson was determined to undo the Federalist abuses begotten by the anti-French hysteria. The hated Alien and Sedition Acts had already expired. The incoming president speedily pardoned the "martyrs" who were serving sentences under the Sedition Act, and the government remitted many fines. Shortly after the Congress met, the Jeffersonians enacted the new naturalization law of 1802. This act reduced the unreasonable requirement of fourteen years of residence to the previous and more reasonable requirement of five years.

Jefferson actually kicked away only one substantial prop of the Hamiltonian system. He hated the excise tax, which bred bureaucrats and bore heavily on his farmer following, and he early persuaded Congress to repeal it. His devotion to principle thus cost the federal government about a million dollars a year in urgently needed revenue.

Swiss-born and French-accented Albert Gallatin, "Watchdog of the Treasury," proved to be as able a secretary of the Treasury as Hamilton. Gallatin agreed with Jefferson that a national debt was a bane rather than a blessing and by strict economy succeeded in reducing it substantially while balancing the budget.

Except for excising the excise tax, the Jeffersonians left the Hamiltonian framework essentially intact. They did not tamper with the Federalist programs for funding the national debt at par and assuming the Revolutionary War debts of the states. They launched no attack on the Bank of the United States, nor did they repeal the mildly protective Federalist tariff. In later years they embraced Federalism to such a degree as to

recharter a bigger bank and to boost the protective tariff to higher levels.

Paradoxically, Jefferson's moderation thus further cemented the gains of the "Revolution of 1800." By shrewdly absorbing the major Federalist programs, Jefferson showed that a change of regime need not be disastrous for the defeated group. His restraint pointed the way toward the two-party system that was later to become a characteristic feature of American politics.

✷ The "Dead Clutch" of the Judiciary

The "deathbed" **Judiciary Act of 1801** was one of the last important laws passed by the expiring Federalist Congress. It created sixteen new federal judgeships and other judicial offices. President Adams remained at his desk until nine o'clock in the evening of his last day in office, supposedly signing the commissions of the Federalist "**midnight judges**." (Actually only three commissions were signed on his last day.)

This Federalist-sponsored Judiciary Act, though a long-overdue reform, aroused bitter resentment. "Packing" these lifetime posts with anti-Jeffersonian partisans was, in Republican eyes, a brazen attempt by the ousted party to entrench itself in one of the three powerful branches of government. Jeffersonians condemned the last-minute appointees in violent language, denouncing the trickery of the Federalists as open defiance of the people's will, expressed emphatically at the polls.

The newly elected Republican Congress bestirred itself to repeal the Judiciary Act of 1801 the year after its passage. Jeffersonians thus swept sixteen benches from under the recently seated "midnight judges." Jeffersonians likewise had their knives sharpened for the scalp of Chief Justice John Marshall, whom Adams had appointed to the Supreme Court (as a fourth choice) in the dying days of his term. The strong-willed Marshall, with his rasping voice and steel-trap mind, was a cousin of Thomas Jefferson. Marshall's formal legal schooling had lasted only six weeks, but he dominated the Supreme Court with his powerful intellect and commanding personality. He shaped the American legal tradition more profoundly than any other single figure.

Marshall had served at Valley Forge during the Revolution. While suffering there from cold and hunger, he had been painfully impressed with the drawbacks of feeble central authority. The experience made him a lifelong Federalist, committed above all else to strengthening the power of the federal government. States' rights Jeffersonians condemned the crafty judge's "twistifications," but Marshall pushed ahead inflexibly on his Federalist course. He served for about thirty days under a Federalist administration and thirty-four years under the administrations of Jefferson and subsequent presidents. The Federalist party died out, but Marshall lived on, handing down Federalist decisions serenely for many more years. For over three decades, the ghost of Alexander Hamilton spoke through the lanky, black-robed judge.

One of the "midnight judges" of 1801 presented John Marshall with a historic opportunity. He was obscure William Marbury, whom President Adams had named a justice of the peace for the District of Columbia. When Marbury learned that his commission was being shelved by the new secretary of state, James Madison, he sued for its delivery. Chief Justice Marshall knew that his Jeffersonian rivals, entrenched in the executive branch, would hardly spring forward to enforce a writ to deliver the commission to his fellow

John Marshall by Fevret de Saint Memin, 1801 Duke University Archives

John Marshall on Assuming the Chief Justiceship, 1801 Depicted here as a young man, Marshall was destined to serve on the Supreme Court for thirty-four years and deeply molded constitutional law. Born in a log cabin on the Virginia frontier, he attended law lectures for just a few weeks at the College of William and Mary—his only formal education. Yet Marshall would go on to prove himself a brilliant chief justice. One admiring lawyer wrote of him, "His black eyes . . . possess an irradiating spirit, which proclaims the imperial powers of the mind that sits enthroned therein."

In his decision in Marbury v. Madison, *Chief Justice John Marshall (1755–1835) vigorously asserted his view that the Constitution embodied a "higher" law than ordinary legislation and that the Court must interpret the Constitution:*

❝ The Constitution is either a superior paramount law, unchangeable by ordinary means, or it is on a level with ordinary legislative acts, and like other acts, is alterable when the legislature shall please to alter it.

"If the former part of the alternative be true, then a legislative act contrary to the constitution is not law; if the latter part be true, then written constitutions are absurd attempts, on the part of the people, to limit a power in its own nature illimitable. . . .

"It is emphatically the province and duty of the judicial department to say what the law is. . . .

"If, then, the courts are to regard the Constitution, and the Constitution is superior to any ordinary act of the legislature, the Constitution, and not such ordinary act, must govern the case to which they are both applicable.❞

Federalist Marbury. He therefore dismissed Marbury's suit, avoiding a direct political showdown. But the wily Marshall snatched a victory from the jaws of this judicial defeat. In explaining his ruling, Marshall said that the part of the Judiciary Act of 1789 on which Marbury tried to base his appeal was unconstitutional. The act had attempted to assign to the Supreme Court powers that the Constitution had not foreseen.

In this self-denying opinion, Marshall greatly magnified the authority of the Court—and slapped at the Jeffersonians. Until the case of **Marbury v. Madison** (1803), controversy had clouded the question of who had the final authority to determine the meaning of the Constitution. Jefferson in the Kentucky resolutions (1798) had tried to allot that right to the individual states. But now his cousin on the Court had cleverly promoted the contrary principle of "judicial review"—the idea that the Supreme Court alone had the last word on the question of constitutionality. In this landmark case, Marshall inserted the keystone into the arch that supports the tremendous power of the Supreme Court in American life.*

---

*The next invalidation of a federal law by the Supreme Court came fifty-four years later, with the explosive *Dred Scott* decision (see pp. 403–404).

Marshall's decision regarding Marbury spurred the Jeffersonians to seek revenge. Jefferson urged the impeachment of an arrogant and tart-tongued Supreme Court justice, Samuel Chase, who was so unpopular that Republicans named vicious dogs after him. Early in 1804 impeachment charges against Chase were voted by the House of Representatives, which then passed the question of guilt or innocence on to the Senate. The indictment by the House was based on "high crimes, and misdemeanors," as specified in the Constitution.*

Yet the evidence was plain that the intemperate judge had not been guilty of "high crimes," but only of unrestrained partisanship and a big mouth. The Senate failed to muster enough votes to convict and remove Chase. The precedent thus established was fortunate. From that day to this, no really serious attempt has been made to reshape the Supreme Court by the impeachment weapon. Jefferson's ill-advised attempt at "judge breaking" was a reassuring victory for the independence of the judiciary and for the separation of powers among the three branches of the federal government.

✦ Jefferson, a Reluctant Warrior

One of Jefferson's first actions as president was to reduce the military establishment to a mere police force of twenty-five hundred officers and men. Critics called it penny-pinching, but Jefferson's reluctance to invest in soldiers and ships was less about money than about republican ideals. Among his fondest hopes for America was that it might transcend the bloody wars and entangling alliances of Europe. The United States would set an example for the world, forswearing military force and winning friends through "peaceful coercion." Also, the Republicans distrusted large standing armies as standing invitations to dictatorship. Navies were less to be feared, as they could not march inland and endanger liberties. Still, the farm-loving Jeffersonians saw little point in building a fleet that might only embroil the Republic in costly and corrupting wars far from America's shores.

But harsh realities forced Jefferson's principles to bend. Pirates of the North African Barbary States (see Map 11.2) had long made a national industry of blackmailing and plundering merchant ships that ventured into the Mediterranean. Preceding Federalist administrations, in fact, had been forced to buy protection. At the time of the French crisis of 1798, when Americans were shouting, "Millions for defense but not one cent for tribute," twenty-six barrels of blackmail dollars were being shipped to piratical Algiers.

War across the Atlantic was not part of the Jeffersonian vision—but neither was paying tribute to a pack of pirate states. The showdown came in 1801. The pasha of Tripoli, dissatisfied with his share of protection money, informally declared war on the United States by cutting down the flagstaff of the American consulate. A gauntlet was thus thrown squarely into the face of Jefferson—the noninterventionist, the pacifist, the critic of a big-ship navy, and the political foe of Federalist shippers. He reluctantly rose to the challenge by dispatching the infant navy to the "shores of Tripoli," as related in the song of the U.S. Marine Corps. After four years of intermittent fighting, marked by spine-tingling exploits, Jefferson succeeded in extorting a treaty of peace from Tripoli in 1805. It was secured at the bargain price of only $60,000—a sum representing ransom payments for captured Americans.

Small gunboats, which the navy had used with some success in the **Tripolitan War**, fascinated Jefferson. Pledged to tax reduction, he advocated a large number of little coastal craft—"Jeffs" or the "mosquito fleet," as they were contemptuously called. He believed these fast but frail vessels would prove valuable in guarding American shores and need not embroil the Republic in diplomatic incidents on the high seas.

About two hundred tiny gunboats were constructed, democratically in small shipyards where votes could be made for Jefferson. Often mounting only one unwieldy gun, they were sometimes more of a menace to the crew than to the prospective enemy. During a hurricane and tidal wave at Savannah, Georgia, one of them was deposited eight miles inland in a cornfield, to the derisive glee of the Federalists. They drank toasts to American gunboats as the best in the world—on land.

✦ The Louisiana Godsend

A secret pact, fraught with peril for America, was signed in 1800. Napoleon Bonaparte induced the king of Spain to cede to France, for attractive considerations, the immense trans-Mississippi region of Louisiana, which included the New Orleans area.

Rumors of the transfer were partially confirmed in 1802, when the Spaniards at New Orleans withdrew the right of deposit guaranteed America by Pinckney's Treaty of 1795 (see p. 193). Deposit (warehouse) privileges were vital to frontier farmers who floated their produce down the Mississippi to its mouth, there to await oceangoing vessels. A roar of anger rolled up the mighty river and into its tributary valleys. American pioneers talked wildly of descending upon New

---

*For impeachment, see Art. I, Sec. II, para. 5; Art. I, Sec. III, paras. 6, 7; Art. II, Sec. IV in the Appendix.

MAP 11.2 The Barbary States of North Africa and the Burning of the Frigate *Philadelphia*, 1804 The Tripolitan pirates had captured the U.S. ship *Philadelphia* (see p. 195) and were preparing to use it against the Americans. In a daring exploit that ensured his lasting fame, twenty-four-year-old U.S. naval officer Stephen Decatur slipped into the harbor of Tripoli and burned the frigate to the waterline, denying it to the pirates. © Cengage Learning

The Burning of the Frigate Philadelphia in Tripoli Harbor by Nicolino Calyo (detail) The Mariners Museum, Newport News, Virginia

to seek allies, contrary to the deepening anti-alliance policy.

Hoping to quiet the clamor of the West, Jefferson moved decisively. Early in 1803 he sent James Monroe to Paris to join forces with the regular minister there, Robert R. Livingston. The two envoys were instructed to buy New Orleans and as much land to its east as they could get for a maximum of $10 million. If these proposals should fail and the situation became critical, negotiations were to be opened with Britain for an alliance. "The day that France takes possession of New Orleans," Jefferson wrote, "we must marry ourselves to the British fleet and nation." That remark dramatically demonstrated Jefferson's dilemma. Though a passionate hater of war and an enemy of entangling alliances, he was proposing to make an alliance with his old foe, Britain, against his old friend, France, in order to secure New Orleans.

At this critical juncture, Napoleon suddenly decided to sell all of Louisiana and abandon his dream of a New World empire. Two developments prompted his change of mind. First, he had failed in his efforts to reconquer the sugar-rich island of Santo Domingo (Haiti), for which Louisiana was to serve as a source of foodstuffs. Rebellious enslaved Africans, inspired by the French Revolution's promises of equality, and ably led by the gifted Toussaint L'Ouverture ("The Opener"), had struck for their freedom in 1791. Their revolt was ultimately broken. But then the island's second line of defense—mosquitoes carrying yellow fever—had swept away thousands of crack French troops. After the **Haitian Revolution**, Santo Domingo could not be had, except perhaps at a staggering cost; hence there was no need for Louisiana's food supplies. "Damn sugar, damn coffee, damn colonies!" burst out Napoleon. Second, Bonaparte was about to end the twenty-month

Orleans, rifles in hand. Had they done so, the nation probably would have been engulfed in war with both Spain and France.

Thomas Jefferson, both pacifist and anti-entanglement, was again on the griddle. Louisiana in the senile grip of Spain posed no real threat; America could seize the territory when the time was ripe. But Louisiana in the iron fist of Napoleon, the preeminent military genius of his age, foreshadowed a dark and blood-drenched future. The United States would probably have to fight to dislodge him; and because it alone was not strong enough to defeat his armies, it would have

The Granger Collection, New York

Toussaint L'Ouverture (ca. 1743–1803) A self-educated ex-slave and military genius, L'Ouverture was finally betrayed by the French, who imprisoned him in a chilly dungeon in France, where he coughed his life away. Indirectly, he did much to set up the sale of Louisiana to the United States. His slave rebellion in Haiti also (briefly) established the first black government in the New World, striking fear into the hearts of slaveowners throughout the Western Hemisphere.

Events now unrolled dizzily. The American minister, Robert Livingston, pending the arrival of Monroe, was busily negotiating in Paris for a window on the Gulf of Mexico at New Orleans. Suddenly, out of a clear sky, the French foreign minister asked him how much he would give for all of Louisiana. Scarcely able to believe his ears (he was partially deaf anyhow), Livingston nervously entered upon the negotiations. After about a week of haggling, while the fate of North America trembled in the balance, treaties were signed on April 30, 1803, ceding Louisiana to the United States for about $15 million.

When news of the bargain reached America, Jefferson was startled. He had authorized his envoys to offer not more than $10 million for New Orleans and as much to the east in the Floridas as they could get. Instead they had signed three treaties that pledged $15 million for New Orleans, plus an immeasurable tract entirely to the west—an area that would more than double the size of the United States. They had bought a wilderness to get a city.

Once again the two Jeffersons wrestled with each other: the theorist and former strict constructionist versus the democratic visionary. Where in his beloved Constitution was the president authorized to negotiate treaties incorporating a huge new expanse into the union—an expanse containing tens of thousands of Indian, French, Spanish, and black inhabitants? There was no such clause. Yet Jefferson also perceived that the vast domain now within his reach could form a sprawling "empire of liberty" that would ensure the health and long life of America's experiment in democracy.

Conscience-stricken, Jefferson privately proposed that a constitutional amendment be passed. But his friends pointed out in alarm that in the interval Napoleon, for whom thought was action, might suddenly withdraw the offer. So Jefferson shamefacedly submitted the treaties to the Senate, while admitting to his associates that the purchase was unconstitutional.

lull in his deadly conflict with Britain. Because the British controlled the seas, he feared that he might be forced to make them a gift of Louisiana. Rather than drive America into the arms of Britain by attempting to hold the area, he decided to sell the huge wilderness to the Americans and pocket the money for his schemes nearer home. Napoleon hoped that the United States, strengthened by Louisiana, would one day be a military and naval power that would thwart the ambitions of the lordly British in the New World. The predicaments of France in Europe were again paving the way for America's diplomatic successes.

In accepting the Louisiana Purchase, Jefferson thus compromised with conscience in a private letter:

"It is the case of a guardian, investing the money of his ward in purchasing an important adjacent territory; and saying to him when of age, I did this for your good; I pretend to no right to bind you; you may disavow me, and I must get out of the scrape as I can; I thought it my duty to risk myself for you.**"**

The senators were less finicky than Jefferson. Reflecting enthusiastic public support, they registered their prompt approval of the transaction. Land-hungry Americans were not disposed to split constitutional hairs when confronted with perhaps the most magnificent real estate bargain in history—828,000 square miles at about three cents an acre.

✦ Louisiana in the Long View

Jefferson's bargain with Napoleon was epochal. Overnight he had avoided a possible rupture with France and the consequent entangling alliance with England. With the **Louisiana Purchase**, America secured at one bloodless stroke the western half of the richest river valley in the world and further laid the foundations of a future major power. The ideal of a great agrarian republic, as envisioned by Jefferson, could now be realized in the vast "Valley of Democracy." At the same time, the transfer established valuable precedents for future expansion: the acquisition of foreign territory and peoples by purchase and their incorporation into the Union not as vassal states but on a basis of equal membership. This was imperialism with a new and democratic face, as French Louisianans learned when the Washington government agreed to accept their legal code based on French civil law, rather than English common law. To this day Louisiana state law, uniquely in the American system, retains vestiges of its French origins. Indian peoples within the purchase area would not prove so fortunate.

The purchase also contributed to making operational the isolationist principles of Washington's Farewell Address. Avoiding entangling alliances had been only an ideal to be pursued, rather than a realistic policy, so long as America had potentially hostile and powerful neighbors. By removing virtually the last remnant of significant European power from the North American continent, the United States was now at liberty to disengage almost entirely from the ancient system of Old World rivalries.

The enormous extent of the new area was more fully unveiled by a series of explorations under Jefferson's direction. In the spring of 1804, Jefferson sent his personal secretary, Meriwether Lewis, and a young army officer named William Clark to explore the northern part of the Louisiana Purchase. Lewis and Clark's **Corps of Discovery** ascended the "Great Muddy" (Missouri River) from St. Louis and spent the winter of 1804–1805 with the Mandan Indians in present-day North Dakota. Then, aided by the Shoshone woman Sacajawea, the thirty-three adventurers (one had died from illness in Iowa, the group's only casualty)

Meriwether Lewis Lewis is portrayed in this painting as he looked on his return from the great expedition through the Louisiana Purchase and the West.

struggled across the northern prairies and through the Rockies, finally descending the Columbia River to the Pacific coast.

Lewis and Clark's two-and-one-half-year expedition yielded a rich harvest of scientific observations, maps, knowledge of the Indians in the region, and hair-raising wilderness adventure stories. On the Great Plains, they marveled at the "immense herds of buffalo, elk, deer, and antelope feeding in one common and boundless pasture." Lewis was lucky to come back alive. When he and three other men left the expedition to explore the Marias River in present-day western Montana, a band of teenage Blackfoot Indians, armed with crude muskets by British fur-traders operating out of Canada, stole their horses. Lewis foolishly pursued the horse thieves on foot. He shot one marauder through

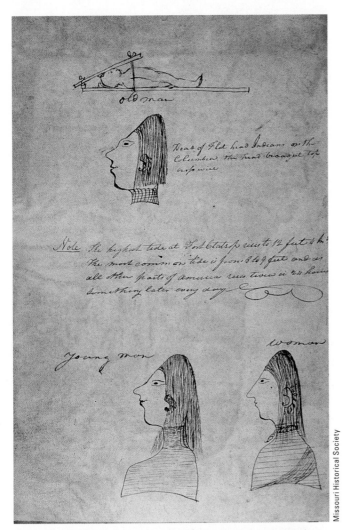

Missouri Historical Society

Chinook Indians, ca. 1805 William Clark served as the artist and cartographer of the Lewis and Clark expedition. Here he sketched the skull-molding practice that inspired Lewis and Clark to call these Indians "Flatheads." These people were distinct from the present-day Flathead Indians of Montana, who got their name from the French.

Gifts from the Great White Chief Among the objectives of the Lewis and Clark expedition was to establish good relations with the Indians in the newly acquired Louisiana Purchase. The American explorers presented all chiefs with copies of these medals, showing President Jefferson on one side and the hands of an Indian and a white man clasped in "peace and friendship" under a crossed "peace pipe" and hatchet on the other. All chiefs also received an American flag and a military uniform jacket, hat, and feather. Courtesy, The American Numismatic Society

the belly, but the Indian returned the fire. "Being bareheaded," Lewis later wrote, "I felt the wind of his bullet very distinctly." After killing another Blackfoot and hanging one of the expedition's "peace and friendship" medals around the dead man's neck as a warning to other Indians, Lewis and his terrified companions beat it out of the Marias country to rejoin the main party on the Missouri River.

The explorers also demonstrated the viability of an overland trail to the Pacific. Down the dusty track thousands of missionaries, fur-traders, and pioneering settlers would wend their way in the ensuing decades, bolstering America's claim to the Oregon Country. Other explorers also pushed into the uncharted West.

Zebulon M. Pike trekked to the headwaters of the Mississippi River in 1805–1806. The next year Pike ventured into the southern portion of Louisiana Territory, where he sighted the Colorado peak that bears his name.

✸ The Aaron Burr Conspiracies

In the long run, the Louisiana Purchase greatly expanded the fortunes of the United States and the power of the federal government. In the short term, the vast expanse of territory and the feeble reach of the government obliged to control it raised fears of secession and foreign intrigue (see Map 11.3).

Aaron Burr, Jefferson's first-term vice president, played no small part in provoking—and justifying—such fears. Dropped from the cabinet in Jefferson's second term, Burr joined with a group of Federalist extremists to plot the secession of New England and New York. Alexander Hamilton, though no friend of Jefferson, exposed and foiled the conspiracy. Incensed, Burr challenged Hamilton to a duel. Hamilton deplored the practice of dueling, by that date illegal in several states, but felt his honor was at stake. He met Burr's challenge at the appointed hour but refused to fire. Burr killed Hamilton with one shot. Burr's pistol blew the brightest brain out of the Federalist party and destroyed its one remaining hope of effective leadership.

His political career as dead as Hamilton's, Burr turned his disunionist plottings to the trans-Mississippi

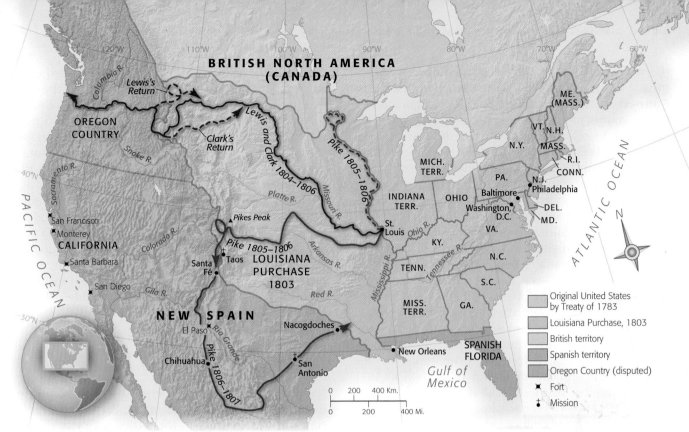

MAP 11.3 Exploring the Louisiana Purchase and the West Seeking to avert friction with France by purchasing all of Louisiana, Jefferson bought trouble because of the vagueness of the boundaries. Among the disputants were Spain in the Floridas, Spain and Mexico in the Southwest, and Great Britain in Canada. © Cengage Learning

West. There he struck up an allegiance with General James Wilkinson, the unscrupulous military governor of Louisiana Territory and a sometime secret agent in the pay of the Spanish crown. Burr's schemes are still shrouded in mystery, but he and Wilkinson apparently planned to separate the western part of the United States from the East and expand their new confederacy with invasions of Spanish-controlled Mexico and Florida. In the fall of 1806, Burr and sixty followers floated in flatboats down the Mississippi River to meet Wilkinson's army at Natchez. But when the general learned that Jefferson had gotten wind of the plot, he betrayed Burr and fled to New Orleans.

Burr was arrested and tried for treason. In what seemed to the Jeffersonians to be bias in favor of the accused, Chief Justice John Marshall, strictly hewing to the Constitution, insisted that a guilty verdict required proof of overt acts of treason, not merely treasonous intentions (see Art. III, Sec. III). Burr was acquitted and fled to Europe, where he urged Napoleon to make peace with Britain and launch a joint invasion of America. Burr's insurrectionary brashness demonstrated that it was one thing for the United States to purchase large expanses of western territory but quite another for it to govern them effectively.

★ A Precarious Neutrality

Jefferson was triumphantly reelected in 1804, with 162 electoral votes to only 14 votes for his Federalist opponent. But the laurels of Jefferson's first administration soon withered under the blasts of the new storm that broke in Europe. After unloading Louisiana in 1803, Napoleon deliberately provoked a renewal of his war with Britain—an awesome conflict that raged on for eleven long years.

For the first two years of war a maritime United States—the number one neutral carrier since 1793—enjoyed juicy commercial pickings. But a setback came in 1805. At the Battle of Trafalgar, one-eyed Horatio Lord Nelson achieved immortality by smashing the combined French and Spanish fleets off the coast of Spain, thereby ensuring Britain's supremacy on the seas. At the Battle of Austerlitz in Austria—the Battle of the Three Emperors—Napoleon crushed the combined Austrian and Russian armies, thereby ensuring his mastery of the land. Like the tiger and the shark, France and Britain now reigned supreme in their chosen elements.

Unable to hurt each other directly, the two antagonists were forced to strike indirect blows. Britain ruled the waves and waived the rules. The London government, beginning in 1806, issued a series of **Orders in Council**. These edicts closed the European ports under French control to foreign shipping, including American, unless the vessels first stopped at a British port. Napoleon struck back, ordering the seizure of all merchant ships, including American, that entered British ports. There was no way to trade with either nation without facing the other's guns. American vessels were, quite literally, caught between the Devil and the deep blue sea.

Even more galling to American pride than the seizure of wooden ships was the seizure of flesh-and-blood American seamen. **Impressment**—the forcible enlistment of sailors—was a crude form of conscription that the British, among others, had employed for over four centuries. Clubs and stretchers (for men knocked unconscious) were standard equipment of press gangs from His Majesty's man-hungry ships. Some six thousand bona fide U.S. citizens were impressed by the "piratical man-stealers" of Britain from 1808 to 1811 alone. A number of these luckless souls died or were killed in His Majesty's service, leaving their kinfolk and friends bereaved and embittered.

Britain's determination was spectacularly highlighted in 1807, in what came to be known as the *Chesapeake* **affair**. A royal frigate overhauled a U.S. frigate, the *Chesapeake*, about ten miles off the coast of Virginia. The British captain bluntly demanded the surrender of four alleged deserters. London had never claimed the right to seize sailors from a foreign warship, and the American commander, though totally unprepared to fight, refused the request. The British warship thereupon fired three devastating broadsides at close range, killing three Americans and wounding eighteen. Four deserters were dragged away, and the bloody hulk called the *Chesapeake* limped back to port.

Britain was clearly in the wrong, as the London Foreign Office admitted. But London's contrition availed little; a roar of national wrath went up from infuriated Americans. Jefferson, the peace lover, could easily have had war if he had wanted it.

★ The Hated Embargo

National honor would not permit a slavish submission to British and French mistreatment. Yet a large-scale foreign war was contrary to the settled policy of the new Republic—and in addition it would be futile. The navy was weak, thanks largely to Jefferson's antinavalism,

The Prairie Dog Sickened at the Sting of the Hornet, 1806 In this anti-Jefferson satire criticizing his negotiations for the purchase of West Florida in 1804, Napoleon, in the form of a hornet, stings Jefferson and makes him "cough up" $2 million in gold coins—the amount of the secret appropriation that Jefferson sought from Congress. The negotiations eventually failed.

Launching of the Ship *Fame*, by George Ropes, Jr., 1802 Jefferson's embargo throttled thriving New England shipyards like this one, stirring bitter resentment.

and the army was even weaker. A disastrous defeat would not improve America's plight.

The warring nations in Europe depended heavily upon the United States for raw materials and foodstuffs. In his eager search for an alternative to war, Jefferson seized upon this essential fact. He reasoned that if America voluntarily cut off its exports, the offending powers would be forced to bow, hat in hand, and agree to respect its rights.

Responding to the presidential lash, Congress hastily passed the **Embargo Act** late in 1807. This rigorous law forbade the export of all goods from the United States, whether in American or foreign ships. More than just a compromise between submission and shooting, the embargo embodied Jefferson's idea of "peaceful coercion." If it worked, the embargo would vindicate the rights of neutral nations and point to a new way of conducting foreign affairs. If it failed, Jefferson feared the Republic would perish, subjugated to the European powers or sucked into their ferocious war.

The American economy staggered under the effect of the embargo long before Britain or France began to bend. Forests of dead masts gradually filled New England's once-bustling harbors; docks that had once rumbled were deserted (except for illegal trade); and soup kitchens cared for some of the hungry unemployed. Jeffersonian Republicans probably hurt the commerce of New England, which they avowedly were trying to protect, far more than Britain and France together were doing. Farmers of the South and West, the strongholds of Jefferson, suffered no less disastrously than New England. They were alarmed by the mounting piles of unexportable cotton, grain, and tobacco. Jefferson

seemed to be waging war on his fellow citizens rather than on the offending foreign powers.

An enormous illicit trade mushroomed in 1808, especially along the Canadian border, where bands of armed Americans on loaded rafts overawed or overpowered federal agents. Irate citizens cynically transposed the letters of "Embargo" to read "O Grab Me," "Go Bar 'Em," and "Mobrage," while heartily cursing the "Dambargo."

Jefferson nonetheless induced Congress to pass iron-toothed enforcing legislation. It was so inquisitorial and tyrannical as to cause some Americans to think more kindly of George III, whom Jefferson had berated in the Declaration of Independence. One indignant New Hampshirite denounced the president with this ditty:

> *Our ships all in motion,*
> *Once whiten'd the ocean; They sail'd and return'd with*
> *a Cargo;*
> *Now doom'd to decay*
> *They are fallen a prey, To Jefferson, worms, and*
> *EMBARGO.*

The embargo even had the effect of reviving the moribund Federalist party. Gaining new converts, its leaders hurled their nullification of the embargo into the teeth of the "Virginia lordlings" in Washington. In 1804 the discredited Federalists had polled only 14 electoral votes out of 176; in 1808, the embargo year, the figure rose to 47 out of 175. New England seethed with talk of secession, and Jefferson later admitted that he felt the foundations of government tremble under his feet.

A Federalist circular in Massachusetts against the embargo cried out,

"Let every man who holds the name of America dear to him, stretch forth his hands and put this accursed thing, this Embargo from him. Be resolute, act like sons of liberty, of God, and your country; nerve your arm with vengeance against the Despot [Jefferson] who would wrest the inestimable germ of your Independence from you— and you shall be *Conquerors!!!*"

An alarmed Congress, yielding to the storm of public anger, finally repealed the embargo on March 1, 1809, three days before Jefferson's retirement. A half-loaf substitute was provided by the **Non-Intercourse Act**. This measure formally reopened trade with all the nations of the world, except the two most important, Britain and France. Though thus watered down, economic coercion continued to be the policy of the Jeffersonians from 1809 to 1812, when the nation finally plunged into war.

Why did the embargo, Jefferson's most daring act of statesmanship, collapse after fifteen dismal months? First of all, he underestimated the bulldog determination of the British, as others have, and overestimated the dependence of both belligerents on America's trade. Bumper grain crops blessed the British Isles during these years, and the revolutionary Latin American republics unexpectedly threw open their ports for compensating commerce. With most of Europe under his control, Napoleon could afford to tighten his belt and go without American trade. The French continued to seize American ships and steal their cargoes, while their emperor mocked the United States by claiming that he was simply helping them enforce the embargo.

More critically, perhaps, Jefferson miscalculated the unpopularity of such a self-crucifying weapon and the difficulty of enforcing it. The hated embargo was not continued long enough or tightly enough to achieve

Rivals for the presidency, and for the soul of the young Republic, Thomas Jefferson and John Adams died on the same day—the Fourth of July, 1826—fifty years to the day after both men had signed the Declaration of Independence. Adams's last words were

" Thomas Jefferson still survives."

But he was wrong, for three hours earlier, Jefferson had drawn his last breath.

the desired results—and a leaky embargo was perhaps more costly than none at all.

Curiously enough, New England plucked a new prosperity from the ugly jaws of the embargo. With shipping tied up and imported goods scarce, the resourceful Yankees reopened old factories and erected new ones. The real foundations of modern America's industrial might were laid behind the protective wall of the embargo, followed by nonintercourse and the War of 1812. Jefferson, the avowed critic of factories, may have unwittingly done more for American manufacturing than Alexander Hamilton, industry's outspoken friend.

✶ Madison's Gamble

Following Washington's precedent, Jefferson left the presidency after two terms, happy to escape what he called the "splendid misery" of the highest office in the land. He strongly favored the nomination and election of a kindred spirit as his successor—his friend and fellow Virginian, the quiet, intellectual, and unassuming James Madison.

Madison took the presidential oath on March 4, 1809, as the awesome conflict in Europe was roaring to its climax. The scholarly Madison was small of stature, light of weight, bald of head, and weak of voice. Despite a distinguished career as a legislator, he was crippled as president by factions within his party and his cabinet. Unable to dominate Congress as Jefferson had done, Madison often found himself holding the bag for risky foreign policies not of his own making.

The Non-Intercourse Act of 1809—a watered-down version of Jefferson's embargo aimed solely at Britain and France—was due to expire in 1810. To Madison's dismay, Congress dismantled the embargo completely with a bargaining measure known as **Macon's Bill No. 2**. While reopening American trade with all the world, Macon's Bill dangled what Congress hoped was an attractive lure. If either Britain or France repealed its commercial restrictions, America would restore its embargo against the nonrepealing nation. To Madison the bill was a shameful capitulation. It practically admitted that the United States could not survive without one of the belligerents as a commercial ally, but it left determination of who that ally would be to the potentates of London and Paris.

The crafty Napoleon saw his chance. Since 1806 Britain had justified its Orders in Council as retaliation for Napoleon's actions—implying, without promising outright, that trade restrictions would be lifted if the French decrees disappeared. Now the French held out the same half-promise. In August 1810 word came from Napoleon's foreign minister that the French decrees

Library of Congress

Britain and France Divide Up the World, 1805   The great-power rivalry symbolized here by British prime minister William Pitt and French emperor Napoleon wreathed the planet in years of warfare. When it ended with Napoleon's final defeat in 1815, Britain was the unchallenged mistress of the world's oceans.

might be repealed if Britain also lifted its Orders in Council. The minister's message was deliberately ambiguous. Napoleon had no intention of permitting unrestricted trade between America and Britain. Rather, he hoped to maneuver the United States into resuming its embargo against the British, thus creating a partial blockade against his enemy that he would not have to raise a finger to enforce.

Madison knew better than to trust Napoleon, but he gambled that the threat of seeing the United States trade exclusively with France would lead the British to

Insisted the editor of Niles' Weekly Register *(June 27, 1812),*

❝ The injuries received from France do not lessen the enormity of those heaped upon us by *England*. . . . In this 'straight betwixt two' we had an unquestionable right to select our enemy. We have given the preference to *Great Britain* . . . on account of her more flagrant wrongs. ❞

repeal their restrictions—and vice versa. Closing his eyes to the emperor's obvious subterfuge, he accepted the French offer as evidence of repeal. The terms of Macon's Bill gave the British three months to live up to their implied promise by revoking the Orders in Council and reopening the Atlantic to neutral trade.

They did not. In firm control of the seas, London saw little need to bargain. As long as the war with Napoleon went on, they decided, America could trade exclusively with the British Empire—or with nobody at all. Madison's gamble failed. The president saw no choice but to reestablish the embargo against Britain alone—a decision that he knew meant the end of American neutrality and that he feared was the final step toward war.

✵ Tecumseh and the Prophet

Not all of Madison's party was reluctant to fight. The complexion of the Twelfth Congress, which met late in 1811, differed markedly from that of its predecessor. Recent elections had swept away many of the older "submission men" and replaced them with young hotheads, many from the South and West. Dubbed **war hawks** by

The Battle of the Thames, 1813 Here the Shawnee leader Tecumseh stood his ground against the superior American force and died. A gifted organizer and military chieftain, he had denounced the tribal custom of torturing prisoners and opposed the practice of allowing any one tribe to sell land that, he believed, belonged to all Indians.

their Federalist opponents, the newcomers were indeed on fire for a new war with the old enemy. The war hawks were weary of hearing how their fathers had "whipped" the British single-handedly, and they detested the man-handling of American sailors and the British Orders in Council that dammed the flow of American trade, especially western farm products headed for Europe.

Western war hawks also yearned to wipe out a renewed Indian threat to the pioneer settlers who were streaming into the trans-Allegheny wilderness. As this white flood washed through the green forests, more and more Indians were pushed toward the setting sun.

Two remarkable Shawnee brothers, Tecumseh and Tenskwatawa, known to non-Indians as "the Prophet," concluded that the time had come to stem this onrushing tide. They began to weld together a far-flung confederacy of all the tribes east of the Mississippi, inspiring a vibrant movement of Indian unity and cultural renewal. Their followers gave up textile clothing for traditional buckskin garments. Their warriors forswore alcohol, the better to fight a last-ditch battle with the "paleface" invaders. Rejecting whites' concept of "ownership," Tecumseh urged his supporters never to cede land to whites unless all Indians agreed.

Meanwhile, frontiersmen and their war-hawk spokesmen in Congress became convinced that British "scalp buyers" in Canada were nourishing the Indians' growing strength. In the fall of 1811, William Henry Harrison, governor of Indiana Territory, gathered an army and advanced on Tecumseh's headquarters at the junction of the Wabash and Tippecanoe Rivers in present-day Indiana. Tecumseh was absent, recruiting supporters in the South, but the Prophet attacked Harrison's army—foolishly, in Tecumseh's eyes—with a small force of Shawnees. The Shawnees were routed and their settlement burned.

The **Battle of Tippecanoe** made Harrison a national hero. It also discredited the Prophet and drove Tecumseh into an alliance with the British. When America's war with Britain came, Tecumseh fought fiercely for the redcoats until his death in 1813 at the Battle of the Thames. With him perished the dream of an Indian confederacy.

When the war hawks won control of the House of Representatives, they elevated to the Speakership thirty-four-year-old Henry Clay of Kentucky (1777-1852), the eloquent and magnetic "Harry of the West." Clamoring for war, he thundered,

"I prefer the troubled sea of war, demanded by the honor and independence of this country, with all its calamities and desolation, to the tranquil and putrescent pool of ignominious peace.**"**

In a speech at Vincennes, Indiana Territory, Tecumseh (1768?-1813) said,

"Sell a country! Why not sell the air, the clouds, and the great sea, as well as the earth? Did not the Great Spirit make them all for the use of his children?**"**

William Henry Harrison (1773-1841), Indian fighter and later president, called Tecumseh

"one of those uncommon geniuses who spring up occasionally to produce revolutions and overturn the established order of things. If it were not for the vicinity of the United States, he would perhaps be founder of an Empire that would rival in glory that of Mexico or Peru.**"**

✦ Mr. Madison's War

By the spring of 1812, Madison believed war with Britain to be inevitable. The British arming of hostile Indians pushed him toward this decision, as did the whoops of the war hawks in his own party. People like Representative Felix Grundy of Tennessee, three of whose brothers had been killed in clashes with Indians, cried that there was only one way to remove the menace of the Indians: wipe out their Canadian base. "On to Canada, on to Canada" was the war hawks' chant. Southern expansionists, less vocal, cast a covetous eye on Florida, then weakly held by Britain's ally Spain.

Above all, Madison turned to war to restore confidence in the republican experiment. For five years the Republicans had tried to steer between the warring European powers, to set a course between submission and battle. Theirs had been a noble vision, but it had brought them only international derision and internal strife. Madison and the Republicans came to believe that only a vigorous assertion of American rights could demonstrate the viability of American nationhood—and of democracy as a form of government. If America could not fight to protect itself, its experiment in republicanism would be discredited in the eyes of a scoffing world. One prominent Republican called the war a test "to determine whether the republican system adopted by the people is imbecile and transient, or whether it has force and duration worthy of the enterprise." Thus, not for the last time, did war fever and democratic idealism make common cause.

Madison asked Congress to declare war on June 1, 1812. Congress obliged him two weeks later—the first of just five times in all of American history that Congress has formally exercised its constitutional power to declare war (see Art. I, Sec. VIII, para. 11). The vote in the House was 79 to 49 for war, in the Senate 19 to 13. The close tally revealed deep divisions over the wisdom of fighting. The split was both sectional and partisan. Support for war came from the South and West, but also from Republicans in populous middle states such as Pennsylvania and Virginia. Federalists in both North and South damned the conflict, but their stronghold was New England, which greeted the declaration of war with muffled bells, flags at half-mast, and public fasting.

Why should seafaring New England oppose the war for a free sea? The answer is that pro-British Federalists in the Northeast sympathized with Britain and resented the Republicans' sympathy with Napoleon, whom they regarded as the "Corsican butcher" and the "anti-Christ of the age." The Federalists also opposed the acquisition of Canada, which would merely add more agrarian states from the wild Northwest. This, in turn, would increase the voting strength of the Jeffersonian Republicans.

The bitterness of New England Federalists against "Mr. Madison's War" led them to treason or near-treason. They were determined, wrote one Republican versifier,

> *To rule the nation if they could,*
> *But see it damned if others should.*

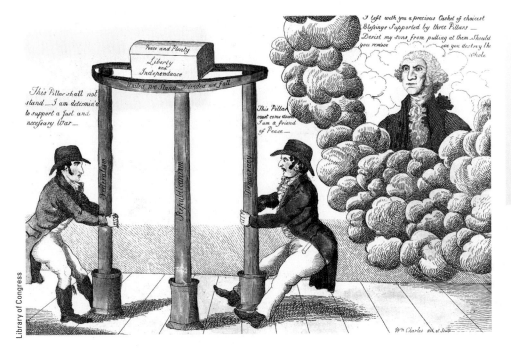

The Present State of Our Country Partisan disunity over the War of 1812 threatened the nation's very existence. The prowar Jeffersonian at the left is attacking the pillar of federalism; the antiwar Federalist at the right is trying to pull down democracy. The spirit of Washington warns that the country's welfare depends on all three pillars, including republicanism.

Library of Congress

New England gold holders probably lent more dollars to the British Exchequer than to the federal Treasury. Federalist farmers sent huge quantities of supplies and foodstuffs to Canada, enabling British armies to invade New York. New England governors stubbornly refused to permit their militias to serve outside their own states. In a sense America had to fight two enemies simultaneously: old England and New England.

Thus perilously divided, the barely United States plunged into armed conflict against Britain, then the world's most powerful empire. No sober American could have much reasonable hope of victory, but by 1812 the Jeffersonian Republicans saw no other choice.

Chapter Review

KEY TERMS

Revolution of 1800 (204)
patronage (207)
Judiciary Act of 1801 (208)
midnight judges (208)
Marbury v. *Madison* (209)
Tripolitan War (210)
Haitian Revolution (211)
Louisiana Purchase (213)
Corps of Discovery (213)

Orders in Council (216)
impressment (216)
Chesapeake affair (216)
Embargo Act (217)
Non-Intercourse Act (218)
Macon's Bill No. 2 (218)
war hawks (219)
Tippecanoe, Battle of (219)

PEOPLE TO KNOW

Thomas Jefferson
Sally Hemings
Albert Gallatin
John Marshall
Samuel Chase
Napoleon Bonaparte
Robert R. Livingston
Toussaint L'Ouverture
Meriwether Lewis

William Clark
Sacajawea
Aaron Burr
James Wilkinson
James Madison
Tecumseh
Tenskwatawa ("the Prophet")

CHRONOLOGY

1791	Toussaint L'Ouverture launches Haitian Revolution
1800	Jefferson defeats Adams for presidency
1801	Judiciary Act of 1801
1801–1805	Naval war with Tripoli
1802	Revised naturalization law Judiciary Act of 1801 repealed
1803	*Marbury* v. *Madison* Louisiana Purchase
1804	Haiti emerges as first independent black republic Jefferson reelected president Impeachment of Justice Chase
1804–1806	Lewis and Clark expedition

1805	Peace treaty with Tripoli Battle of Trafalgar Battle of Austerlitz
1805–1807	Pike's explorations
1806	Burr treason trial
1807	*Chesapeake* affair Embargo Act
1808	Madison elected president
1809	Non-Intercourse Act replaces Embargo Act
1810	Macon's Bill No. 2 Napoleon announces (falsely) repeal of blockade decrees Madison reestablishes nonimportation against Britain
1811	Battle of Tippecanoe
1812	United States declares war on Britain

TO LEARN MORE

Catherine Allgor, *Parlor Politics* (2000)

Stephen E. Ambrose, *Undaunted Courage* (1996)

Joseph Ellis, *American Sphinx: The Character of Thomas Jefferson* (1997)

John Ferling, *Adams vs. Jefferson: The Tumultuous Election of 1800* (2004)

Thomas Fleming, *The Louisiana Purchase* (2003)

Donald R. Hickey, *Don't Give Up the Ship! Myths of the War of 1812* (2006)

Peter P. Hill, *Napoleon's Troublesome Americans: Franco-American Relations, 1804–1815* (2005)

Donald Jackson, *Thomas Jefferson and the Stony Mountain: Exploring the West from Monticello* (1981)

Jon Kukla, *A Wilderness So Immense* (2003)

Marshall Smelser, *The Democratic Republic, 1801–1815* (1968)

Anthony Wallace, *Jefferson and the Indians* (1999)

Gary Wills, *Negro President: Thomas Jefferson and the Slave Power* (2003)

A complete, annotated bibliography for this chapter—along with brief descriptions of the People to Know—may be found on the American Pageant website. The Key Terms are defined in a Glossary at the end of the text.

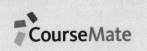

Go to the CourseMate website at **www.cengagebrain.com** for additional study tools and review materials—including audio and video clips—for this chapter.

AP® Review Questions for Chapter 11

1. What was the most decisive factor that helped Thomas Jefferson win the 1800 presidential election?
   (A) His support of agrarian interests
   (B) The three-fifths compromise
   (C) New York's electoral votes
   (D) Anger that Adams failed to declare war on France
   (E) The Alien and Sedition Acts

2. Jefferson considered his election in 1800 a "revolution" because
   (A) he won by a landslide.
   (B) it represented a rejection of states' rights advocates.
   (C) it marked a return to the values of 1776.
   (D) it proved that American democracy worked.
   (E) he advocated an end to partisanship.

3. In office, Jefferson surprisingly only eliminated which one of the following Federalist programs?
   (A) Assumption of states' Revolutionary War debts
   (B) The Bank of the United States
   (C) The protective tariff
   (D) Funding the national debt
   (E) The excise tax

4. Which of the following is NOT true about the Judiciary Act of 1801?
   (A) It resulted in the appointment of William Marbury to the Supreme Court.
   (B) It created sixteen new federal judges.
   (C) Jefferson and other Republicans condemned it as a Federalist court-packing scheme.
   (D) It was repealed the following year.
   (E) Adams used the act to appoint "midnight judges" on his last day in office.

5. The case of *Marbury* v. *Madison* (1803) is significant because it
   (A) reinforced the importance of the Constitution as the bulwark of national law.
   (B) gave the Supreme Court the authority to interpret the Constitution.
   (C) said only states can determine the validity of federal laws.
   (D) overturned the Judiciary Act of 1801.
   (E) renewed the charter of the Bank of the United States.

6. What was the main reason Jefferson reduced the size of the military when he became president?
   (A) He wanted to balance the budget.
   (B) He believed that militaries could not be trusted.
   (C) He regarded a large military as an unnecessary expense.
   (D) He feared being pulled into European conflicts.
   (E) He wanted the United States to be an example for the rest of the world through peaceful coercion.

7. Napoleon Bonaparte ultimately abandoned his vision of a New World empire and agreed to sell Louisiana to the United States for all of the following reasons EXCEPT that
   (A) he failed to conquer Santo Domingo, a necessary first step.
   (B) he feared that Britain, with control of the seas, would wrest control of Louisiana from the French.
   (C) he hoped to prevent a U.S.-British alliance against France.
   (D) he feared America might seize it militarily.
   (E) he hoped the United States would become powerful enough to thwart Britain.

8. Which of the following can NOT be said about the Louisiana Purchase?
   (A) It made U.S. isolationism possible.
   (B) It required a constitutional amendment for the purchase to be completed.
   (C) It set precedents for further expansion.
   (D) It more than doubled the size of the United States.
   (E) Its 828,000 square miles cost $10 million.

9. Lewis and Clark's expeditions were primarily designed to
   (A) be a scientific and geographic study of the Louisiana territory.
   (B) explore opportunities for further conquest of territories held by Mexico and Spain.
   (C) establish U.S. dominance over Indian populations in the region.
   (D) forge trade links with French, Indian, and Spanish settlers in the region.
   (E) search for gold and other valuable minerals.

10. Why did former vice president Aaron Burr challenge former treasury secretary Alexander Hamilton to a duel in 1804?
    (A) Hamilton revealed Burr's plan to entice New England and New York to secede.
    (B) Hamilton had accused Burr of corruption while in office.
    (C) Burr discovered that Hamilton had tried to provoke war with France.
    (D) Burr planned to reveal Hamilton's scheme to create a new confederacy from the new western territories.
    (E) Hamilton had encouraged Jefferson to drop Burr from his cabinet during his second term in office.

11. In the years before the War of 1812, what was impressment?
    (A) Blocking American ships from entering French and British ports
    (B) The seizure of neutral ships by warring nations
    (C) The capture and forced military service of American seamen by the British
    (D) A prohibition on the export of American goods
    (E) The resale of seized American goods by the warring nations of Britain and France

12. Jefferson's embargo strategy to get England and France to honor American neutrality in the years before the War of 1812 ultimately failed for all of the following reasons EXCEPT that he
    (A) underestimated British resistance and determination.
    (B) overestimated the importance of American goods overseas.
    (C) did not consider that other countries would step in to fill England and France's import needs.
    (D) did not foresee the massive nationwide protests by American citizens.
    (E) did not factor in the difficulty of enforcing the embargo at home.

13. Which of the following was NOT among the forces that pushed President James Madison to war with Britain in 1812?
    (A) England's arming of hostile Indians along the American frontier
    (B) British reinforcement of its Orders in Council
    (C) The rise to power of pro-war representatives in Congress
    (D) The need to assert American nationhood and rights
    (E) A desire to restore America's credibility on the world stage

14. The region that did NOT support the declaration of war against the British was
    (A) New England.
    (B) the South.
    (C) the West.
    (D) the middle Atlantic states.
    (E) the Chesapeake.

15. Politicians' struggle to maintain and strengthen their parties' influence can best be seen in
    (A) Jefferson allowing the Alien and Sedition Acts to expire during his administration.
    (B) Adams's appointment of "midnight judges" at the end of his term.
    (C) Marshall's establishment of judicial review in *Marbury* v. *Madison*.
    (D) Aaron Burr challenging Alexander Hamilton to a duel.
    (E) Jefferson's support for the Embargo Act in the era preceding the War of 1812.

16. Why was the War of 1812 a culmination of long-standing hostilities between the United States and Britain?
    (A) Britain refused to acknowledge American independence despite the terms of the Treaty of Paris.
    (B) The United States continued to persecute Loyalists who remained in the country, despite British protests.
    (C) The British practices of impressment and supporting Native Americans against the United States were issues during Washington's presidency.
    (D) Britain, adhering to mercantilist philosophy, refused to allow other European nations to trade with the United States.
    (E) New Englanders' support for Britain was a divisive force in the United States.

Chapter 12

The Second War for Independence and the Upsurge of Nationalism

1812–1824

The American continents . . . are henceforth not to be considered as subjects for future colonization by any European powers.

PRESIDENT JAMES MONROE, DECEMBER 2, 1823

The War of 1812 was an especially divisive and ill-fought war. There was no burning national anger, as there had been in 1807 following the *Chesapeake* outrage. The supreme lesson of the conflict was the folly of leading a divided and apathetic people into war. And yet, despite the unimpressive military outcome and even less decisive negotiated peace, Americans came out of the war with a renewed sense of nationhood. For the next dozen years, an awakened spirit of nationalism would inspire activities ranging from protecting manufacturing to building roads to defending the authority of the federal government over the states.

✸ On to Canada over Land and Lakes

On the eve of the War of 1812, the regular army was ill-trained, ill-disciplined, and widely scattered. It had to be supplemented by the even more poorly trained militias, which were sometimes distinguished by their speed of foot in leaving the battlefield. Some of the ranking generals were semisenile heirlooms from the Revolutionary War, rusting on their laurels and lacking in vigor and vision.

Canada became an important battleground in the War of 1812 because British forces were weakest there (see Map 12.1). A successful American offensive

might have quashed British influence among the Indians and garnered new land for settlers. But the Americans' offensive strategy was poorly conceived. Had the Americans captured Montreal, the center of population and transportation, everything to the west might have died, just as the leaves of a tree wither when the trunk is girdled. But instead of laying ax to the trunk, the Americans frittered away their strength in the three-pronged invasion of 1812. The trio of invading forces that set out from Detroit, Niagara, and Lake Champlain were all beaten back shortly after they had crossed the Canadian border.

By contrast, the British and Canadians displayed energy from the outset. Early in the war, they captured the American fort of Michilimackinac, which commanded the upper Great Lakes and the Indian-inhabited area to the south and west. Their brilliant defensive operations were led by the inspired British general Isaac Brock and assisted (in the American camp) by "General Mud" and "General Confusion."

When several American land invasions of Canada were again hurled back in 1813, Americans looked for success on the water. Man for man and ship for ship, the American navy did much better than the army. In comparison to British ships, American craft on the whole were more skillfully handled, had better gunners, and were manned by non-press-gang crews who were burning to avenge numerous indignities. Similarly, the

American frigates, notably the *Constitution* ("Old Ironsides"), had thicker sides, heavier firepower, and larger crews, of which one sailor in six was a free black.

Control of the Great Lakes was vital, and an energetic American naval officer, Oliver Hazard Perry, managed to build a fleet of green-timbered ships on the shores of Lake Erie, manned by even greener seamen. When he captured a British fleet in a furious engagement on the lake, he reported to his superior, "We have met the enemy and they are ours." Perry's victory and his slogan infused new life into the drooping American cause. Forced to withdraw from Detroit and Fort Malden, the retreating redcoats were overtaken by General Harrison's army and beaten at the Battle of the Thames in October 1813.

Despite these successes, the Americans by late 1814, far from invading Canada, were grimly defending their own soil against the invading British. Napoleon's European adversaries had vanquished him—temporarily, as it turned out—in mid-1814 and had exiled the dangerous despot to the Mediterranean isle of Elba. The United States, which had so brashly provoked war behind the protective skirts of Napoleon, was now left to face the music alone. Thousands of Britain's victorious veteran redcoats began to pour into Canada from the Continent.

Assembling some ten thousand crack troops, the British prepared in 1814 for a crushing blow into New York along the familiar lake-river route. In the absence of roads, the invader was forced to bring supplies over the Lake Champlain waterway. A weaker American fleet, commanded by the thirty-year-old Thomas Macdonough, challenged the British. The ensuing battle was desperately fought near Plattsburgh on September 11, 1814, on floating slaughterhouses. The American flagship at one point was in grave trouble. But Macdonough, unexpectedly turning his ship about with cables, confronted the enemy with a fresh broadside and snatched victory from the fangs of defeat.

The results of this heroic naval battle were momentous. The invading British army was forced to retreat. Macdonough thus saved at least upper New York from conquest, New England from further disaffection, and the Union from possible dissolution. He also profoundly affected the concurrent negotiations of the Anglo-American peace treaty in Europe.

✶ Washington Burned and New Orleans Defended

A second formidable British force, numbering about four thousand, landed in the Chesapeake Bay area in August 1814. Advancing rapidly on Washington, it easily dispersed some six thousand panicky militiamen at Bladensburg ("the Bladensburg races"). The invaders then entered the capital and set fire to most of the public buildings, including the Capitol and the White House. But while Washington burned, the Americans at Baltimore held firm. The British fleet hammered Fort McHenry with their cannon but could not capture the city. Francis Scott Key, a detained American anxiously watching the bombardment from a British ship, was inspired by the doughty defenders to write the words

Bettmann/Corbis

***Constitution* and *Guerrière*, 1812** The *Guerrière* was heavily outweighed and outgunned, yet its British captain eagerly—and foolishly—sought combat. His ship was destroyed. Historian Henry Adams later concluded that this duel "raised the United States in one half hour to the rank of a first-class Power in the world." Today the *Constitution*, berthed in Boston harbor, remains the oldest actively commissioned ship in the U.S. Navy.

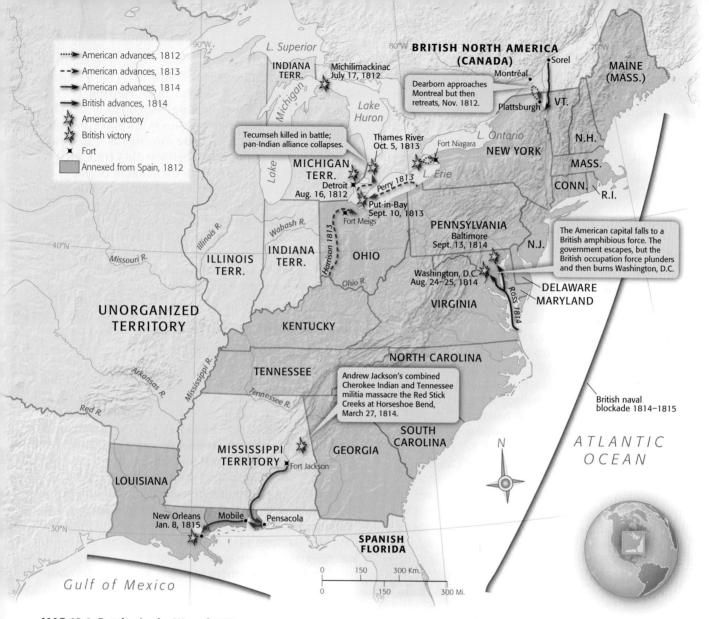

MAP 12.1 Battles in the War of 1812 © Cengage Learning

of "The Star-Spangled Banner." Set to the tune of a saucy English tavern refrain, the song quickly attained popularity.

A third British blow of 1814, aimed at New Orleans, menaced the entire Mississippi Valley. Gaunt and hawk-faced Andrew Jackson, fresh from crushing the southwest Indians at the Battle of Horseshoe Bend, was placed in command (see Map 12.5 on p. 241). His hodgepodge force consisted of seven thousand sailors, regulars, pirates, and Frenchmen, as well as militiamen from Louisiana, Kentucky, and Tennessee. Among the defenders were two Louisiana regiments of free black volunteers, numbering about four hundred men. The Americans threw up their entrenchment, and in the words of a popular song,

Behind it stood our little force—
None wished it to be greater;

For ev'ry man was half a horse,
And half an alligator.

The overconfident British, numbering some eight thousand battle-seasoned veterans, blundered badly. They made the mistake of launching a frontal assault, on January 8, 1815, on the entrenched American riflemen and cannoneers. The attackers suffered the most devastating defeat of the entire war, losing over two thousand, killed and wounded, in half an hour, as compared with some seventy for the Americans. It was an astonishing victory for Jackson and his men.

News of the American victory in the **Battle of New Orleans** struck the country "like a clap of thunder," according to one contemporary. Andrew Jackson became a national hero as poets and politicians lined up to sing the praises of the defenders of New Orleans. It hardly mattered when word arrived that a peace treaty had been

The Fall of Washington, or Maddy in Full Flight President Madison ("Maddy") was forced into humiliating withdrawal from the capital in 1814, when British forces put the torch to Washington, D.C.

Andrew Jackson (1767–1845) appealed to the governor of Louisiana for help recruiting free blacks to defend New Orleans in 1814:

"The free men of colour in [your] city are inured to the Southern climate and would make excellent Soldiers. . . . They must be for or against us—distrust them, and you make them your enemies, place confidence in them, and you engage them by every dear and honorable tie to the interest of the country, who extends to them equal rights and [privileges] with white men."

signed at Ghent, Belgium, ending the war two weeks before the battle. The United States had fought for honor as much as material gain. The Battle of New Orleans restored that honor, at least in American eyes, and unleashed a wave of nationalism and self-confidence.

Its wrath aroused, the Royal Navy had finally retaliated by throwing a ruinous naval blockade along America's coast and by landing raiding parties almost at will. American economic life, including fishing, was crippled. Customs revenues were choked off, and near the end of the war, the bankrupt Treasury was unable to meet its maturing obligations.

✹ The Treaty of Ghent

Tsar Alexander I of Russia, feeling hard-pressed by Napoleon's army and not wanting his British ally to fritter away its strength in America, had proposed mediation between the clashing Anglo-Saxon cousins as early as 1812. The tsar's feeler eventually set in motion the machinery that brought five American peacemakers to the quaint Belgian city of Ghent in 1814. The bickering group was headed by early-rising, puritanical John Quincy Adams, son of John Adams, who deplored the late-hour card playing of his high-living colleague Henry Clay.

Confident after their military successes, the British envoys made sweeping demands for a neutralized Indian buffer state in the Great Lakes region, control of the Great Lakes, and a substantial part of conquered Maine. The Americans flatly rejected these terms, and the talks appeared stalemated. But news of British reverses in upper New York and at Baltimore, and increasing war-weariness in Britain, made London more willing to compromise. Preoccupied with redrafting Napoleon's map of Europe at the **Congress of Vienna** (1814–1815) and eyeing still-dangerous France, the British lion resigned itself to licking its wounds.

The **Treaty of Ghent**, signed on Christmas Eve, 1814, was essentially an armistice. Both sides simply agreed to stop fighting and to restore conquered territory. No mention was made of those grievances for which America had ostensibly fought: the Indian menace, search and seizure, Orders in Council, impressment, and confiscations. These discreet omissions have often been cited as further evidence of the insincerity of the war hawks. Rather, they are proof that the Americans had not managed to defeat the British. With neither side able to impose its will, the treaty negotiations—like the war itself—ended as a virtual draw.

Relieved Americans boasted "Not One Inch of Territory Ceded or Lost"—a phrase that contrasted strangely with the "On to Canada" rallying cry at the war's outset.

✦ Federalist Grievances and the Hartford Convention

Defiant New England remained a problem. It prospered during the conflict, owing largely to illicit trade with the enemy in Canada and to the absence of a British blockade until 1814. But the embittered opposition of the Federalists to the war continued unabated.

In a letter to her friend Mercy Otis Warren, Abigail Adams (1744–1818) fretted that the British were taking advantage of Americans' disagreement over the War of 1812:

❝We have our firesides, our comfortable habitations, our cities, our churches and our country to defend, our rights, privileges and independence to preserve. And for these are we not justly contending? Thus it appears to me. Yet I hear from our pulpits, and read from our presses, that it is an unjust, a wicked, a ruinous, and unnecessary war. . . . A house divided upon itself—and upon that foundation do our enemies build their hopes of subduing us.**❞**

As the war dragged on, New England extremists became more vocal. A small minority of them proposed secession from the Union, or at least a separate peace with Britain. Ugly rumors were afloat about "Blue Light" Federalists—treacherous New Englanders who supposedly flashed lanterns on the shore so that blockading British cruisers would be alerted to the attempted escape of American ships.

The most spectacular manifestation of Federalist discontent was the ill-omened **Hartford Convention**. Late in 1814, when the capture of New Orleans seemed imminent, Massachusetts issued a call for a convention at Hartford, Connecticut. The states of Massachusetts, Connecticut, and Rhode Island dispatched full delegations; neighboring New Hampshire and Vermont sent partial representation. This group of prominent men, twenty-six in all, met in complete secrecy for about three weeks—December 15, 1814, to January 5, 1815—to discuss their grievances and to seek redress for their wrongs.

In truth, the Hartford Convention was actually less radical than the alarmists supposed. Though a minority of delegates gave vent to wild talk of secession, the convention's final report was quite moderate. It demanded financial assistance from Washington to compensate for lost trade and proposed constitutional amendments requiring a two-thirds vote in Congress before an embargo could be imposed, new states admitted, or war declared. Most of the demands reflected Federalist fears that a once-proud New England was falling subservient to an agrarian South and West. Delegates sought to

Massachusetts, Connecticut, and Rhode Island Contemplate Abandoning the Union, engraving by William Charles, 1814 This anti-Federalist cartoon shows Great Britain welcoming back its "Yankee boys" with open arms, promising them "plenty molasses and codfish, plenty of goods to smuggle, honours, titles, and nobility into the bargain."

The Hartford Convention or *LEAP NO LEAP.*

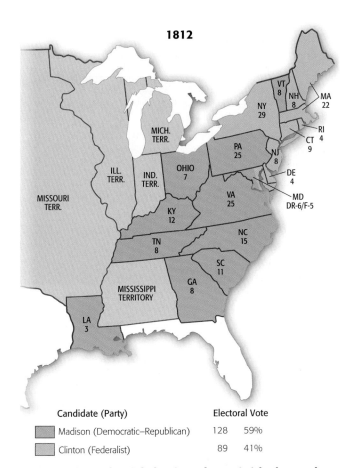

1812

Candidate (Party)		Electoral Vote	
Madison (Democratic–Republican)		128	59%
Clinton (Federalist)		89	41%

MAP 12.2 Presidential Election of 1812 (with electoral vote by state) The Federalists showed impressive strength in the North, and their presidential candidate, DeWitt Clinton, the future "Father of the Erie Canal," almost won. If the 25 electoral votes of Pennsylvania had gone to the New Yorker, he would have won, 114 to 103. © Cengage Learning

The War of 1812 won a new respect for America among many Britons. Michael Scott, a young lieutenant in the British navy, wrote,

"I don't like Americans; I never did, and never shall like them. . . . I have no wish to eat with them, drink with them, deal with, or consort with them in any way; but let me tell the whole truth, nor fight with them, were it not for the laurels to be acquired, by overcoming an enemy so brave, determined, and alert, and in every way so worthy of one's steel, as they have always proved.**"**

never again to mount a successful presidential campaign (see Map 12.2).

Federalist doctrines of disunity, which long survived the party, blazed a portentous trail. Until 1815 there was far more talk of nullification and secession in New England than in any other section, including the South. The outright flouting of the Jeffersonian embargo and the later crippling of the war effort were the two most damaging acts of nullification in America prior to the events leading to the Civil War.

✦ The Second War for American Independence

The War of 1812 was a small war, involving about 6,000 Americans killed or wounded. It was but a footnote to the mighty European conflagration that had been ignited by the French Revolution and Napoleon's imperial ambitions. In 1812, when Napoleon invaded Russia with about 500,000 men, Madison tried to invade Canada with about 5,000 men. But if the American conflict was globally unimportant, it had huge consequences for the United States.

The Republic had shown that it would take sword in hand to resist what it regarded as grievous wrongs. Other nations developed a new respect for America's fighting prowess. Naval officers like Perry and Macdonough were the most effective type of negotiators; the hot breath of their broadsides spoke the most eloquent diplomatic language. America's emissaries abroad were henceforth treated with less scorn. In a diplomatic sense, if not in a military sense, the conflict could be called the Second War for American Independence.

A new nation, moreover, was welded in the roaring furnace of armed conflict. Sectionalism, now identified with discredited New England Federalists, was dealt a black eye. The painful events of the war glaringly revealed, as perhaps nothing else could have done, the

abolish the three-fifths clause of the Constitution (which allowed the South to count a portion of its slaves in calculating proportional representation), to limit presidents to a single term, and to prohibit the election of two successive presidents from the same state. This last clause was aimed at the much-resented "Virginia dynasty"—by 1814 a Virginian had been president for all but four years in the Republic's quarter-century of life.

Three special envoys from Massachusetts carried these demands to the burned-out capital of Washington. The trio arrived just in time to be overwhelmed by the glorious news from New Orleans, followed by that from Ghent. As the rest of the nation congratulated itself on a glorious victory, New England's wartime complaints seemed petty at best and treasonous at worst. Pursued by the sneers and jeers of the press, the envoys sank away in disgrace and into obscurity.

The Hartford resolutions, as it turned out, were the death dirge of the Federalist party. The Federalists were

The White House and Capitol, by Anthony St. John Baker, 1826 This watercolor painting reveals the rustic conditions of the early days in the nation's capital. The President's House (now called the White House), on the left, was designed by Irish-born James Hoban and built between 1792 and 1800 in the neoclassical style. It has been the residence of every president since John Adams. When Thomas Jefferson moved into the house in 1801, he worked with architect Benjamin Henry Latrobe to expand it, creating two colonnades that were meant to conceal stables and storage. In 1814, during the War of 1812, the British Army set the President's House ablaze, destroying the interior and charring much of the exterior. Reconstruction began almost immediately, and President James Monroe moved into a partially finished house in 1817. The Capital dome is visible in the background on the right. It, too, burned in 1814. Its rebuilding, not completed until 1830, was overseen by Boston's Charles Bulfinch.

folly of sectional disunity. In a sense the most conspicuous casualty of the war was the Federalist party.

War heroes emerged, especially the two Indian-fighters Andrew Jackson and William Henry Harrison. Both of them were to become president. Left in the lurch by their British friends at Ghent, the Indians were forced to make such terms as they could. They reluctantly consented, in a series of treaties, to relinquish vast areas of forested land north of the Ohio River.

Manufacturing prospered behind the wooden wall of the British blockade. In both an economic and a diplomatic sense, the War of 1812 bred greater American independence. The industries that were thus stimulated by the fighting rendered America less dependent on Europe's workshops.

Canadian patriotism and nationalism also received a powerful stimulus from the clash. Many Canadians felt betrayed by the Treaty of Ghent. They were especially aggrieved by the failure to secure an Indian buffer state or even mastery of the Great Lakes. Canadians fully expected the frustrated Yankees to return, and for a time the Americans and British engaged in a floating arms race on the Great Lakes. But in 1817 the **Rush-Bagot agreement** between Britain and the United States

severely limited naval armament on the lakes. Better relations brought the last border fortifications down in the 1870s, with the happy result that the United States and Canada came to share the world's longest unfortified boundary—5,527 miles long.

After Napoleon's final defeat at Waterloo in June 1815, Europe slumped into a peace of exhaustion. Deposed monarchs returned to battered thrones, as the Old World took the rutted road back to conservatism, illiberalism, and reaction. But the American people were largely unaffected by these European developments. Turning their backs on the Old World, they faced resolutely toward the untamed West—and toward the task of building their democracy.

✦ Nascent Nationalism

The most impressive by-product of the War of 1812 was a heightened nationalism—the spirit of nation-consciousness or national oneness. America may not have fought the war as one nation, but it emerged as one nation. The changed mood even manifested itself in the birth of a distinctively national literature. Washington

Irving and James Fenimore Cooper attained international recognition in the 1820s, significantly as the nation's first writers of importance to use American scenes and themes. School textbooks, often British in an earlier era, were now being written by Americans for Americans. In the world of magazines, the highly intellectual *North American Review* began publication in 1815—the year of the triumph at New Orleans. Even American painters increasingly celebrated their native landscapes on their canvases.

A fresh nationalistic spirit could be recognized in many other areas as well. The rising tide of nation-consciousness even touched finance. A revived Bank of the United States was voted by Congress in 1816. A more handsome national capital began to rise from the ashes of Washington. The army was expanded to ten thousand men. The navy further covered itself with glory in 1815 when it administered a thorough beating to the piratical plunderers of North Africa. Stephen Decatur, naval hero of the War of 1812 and of the Barbary Coast expeditions, pungently captured the country's nationalist mood in a famous toast made on his return from the Mediterranean campaigns: "Our country! In her intercourse with foreign nations may she always be in the right; but our country, right or wrong!"

✶ "The American System"

Nationalism likewise manifested itself in manufacturing. Patriotic Americans took pride in the factories that had recently mushroomed forth, largely as a result of the self-imposed embargoes and the war.

When hostilities ended in 1815, British competitors undertook to recover lost ground. They began to dump the contents of their bulging warehouses on the United States, often cutting their prices below cost in an effort to strangle the American war-baby factories in the cradle. The infant industries bawled lustily for protection. To many red-blooded Americans, it seemed as though the British, having failed to crush Yankee fighters on the battlefield, were now seeking to crush Yankee factories in the marketplace.

A nationalist Congress, out-Federalizing the old Federalists, responded by passing the path-breaking **Tariff of 1816**—the first tariff in American history instituted primarily for protection, not revenue. Its rates—roughly 20 to 25 percent on the value of dutiable imports—were not high enough to provide completely adequate safeguards, but the law was a bold beginning. A strongly protective trend was started that stimulated the appetites of the protected for more protection.

Nationalism was further highlighted by a grandiose plan of Henry Clay for developing a profitable home market. Still radiating the nationalism of war-hawk days, he threw himself behind an elaborate scheme known by 1824 as the **American System**. This system had three main parts. It began with a strong banking system, which would provide easy and abundant credit. Clay also advocated a protective tariff, behind which eastern manufacturing would flourish. Revenues gushing from the tariff would provide funds for the third component of the American System—a network of roads and canals, especially in the burgeoning Ohio Valley. Through these new arteries of transportation would flow foodstuffs and raw materials from the South and West to the North and East. In exchange, a stream of manufactured goods would flow in the return direction, knitting the country together economically and politically.

Architect of the Capitol

Henry Clay (1777–1852), by John Neagle, 1843 This painting hangs in the corridors of the House of Representatives, where Clay worked as a glamorous, eloquent, and ambitious congressman for many years. Best known for promoting his nationalistic "American System" of protective tariffs for eastern manufactures and federally financed canals and highways to benefit the West, Clay is surrounded here by symbols of flourishing agriculture and burgeoning industries in the new nation.

Persistent and eloquent demands by Henry Clay and others for better transportation struck a responsive chord with the public. The recent attempts to invade Canada had all failed partly because of oath-provoking roads—or no roads at all. People who have dug wagons out of hub-deep mud do not quickly forget their blisters and backaches. An outcry for better transportation, rising most noisily in the road-poor West, was one of the most striking aspects of the nationalism inspired by the War of 1812.

But attempts to secure federal funding for roads and canals stumbled on Republican constitutional scruples. Congress voted in 1817 to distribute $1.5 million to the states for internal improvements, but President Madison sternly vetoed this handout measure as unconstitutional. The individual states were thus forced to venture ahead with construction programs of their own, including the Erie Canal, triumphantly completed by New York in 1825. Jeffersonian Republicans, who had gulped down Hamiltonian loose constructionism on other important problems, choked on the idea of direct federal support of intrastate internal improvements. New England, in particular, strongly opposed federally constructed roads and canals, because such outlets would further drain away population and create competing states beyond the mountains.

Nationalist Pride, ca. 1820 Nationalist sentiments swelled in the wake of the War of 1812, as Americans defined their country's very identity with reference to its antimonarchical origins.

✦ The So-Called Era of Good Feelings

James Monroe—six feet tall, somewhat stooped, courtly, and mild-mannered—was nominated for the presidency in 1816 by the Republicans. They thus undertook to continue the so-called Virginia dynasty of Washington, Jefferson, and Madison. The fading Federalists ran a candidate for the last time in their checkered history, and he was crushed by 183 electoral votes to 34. The vanquished Federalist party was gasping its dying breaths, leaving the field to the triumphant Republicans and one-party rule.

In James Monroe, the man and the times auspiciously met. As the last president to wear an old-style cocked hat, he straddled two generations: the bygone age of the Founding Fathers and the emergent age of nationalism. Never brilliant, and perhaps not great, the serene Virginian with gray-blue eyes was in intellect and personal force the least distinguished of the first eight presidents. But the times called for sober administration, not dashing heroics. And Monroe was an experienced, levelheaded executive, with an ear-to-the-ground talent for interpreting popular rumblings.

Emerging nationalism was further cemented by a goodwill tour Monroe undertook early in 1817, ostensibly to inspect military defenses. He pushed northward deep into New England and then westward to Detroit, viewing en route Niagara Falls. Even in Federalist New England, "the enemy's country," he received a heartwarming welcome; a Boston newspaper was so far carried away as to announce that an "Era of Good Feelings" had been ushered in. This happy phrase has been commonly used since then to describe the administrations of Monroe.

The **Era of Good Feelings**, unfortunately, was something of a misnomer. Considerable tranquility and prosperity did in fact smile upon the early years of Monroe, but the period was a troubled one. The acute issues of the tariff, the bank, internal improvements, and the sale of public lands were being hotly contested.

Boston's Columbian Centinel *was not the only newspaper to regard President Monroe's early months as the Era of Good Feelings. Washington's* National Intelligencer *observed in July 1817,*

❝Never before, perhaps, since the institution of civil government, did the same harmony, the same absence of party spirit, the same national feeling, pervade a community. The result is too consoling to dispute too nicely about the cause.❞

Picture Research Consultants & Archives

Fairview Inn or Three Mile House on Old Frederick Road, by Thomas Coke Ruckle, ca. 1829 This busy scene on the Frederick Road, leading westward from Baltimore, was typical as pioneers flooded into the newly secured West in the early 1800s.

Sectionalism was crystallizing, and the conflict over slavery was beginning to raise its hideous head.

The Panic of 1819 and the Curse of Hard Times

Much of the goodness went out of the good feelings in 1819, when a paralyzing economic panic descended. It brought deflation, depression, bankruptcies, bank failures, unemployment, soup kitchens, and overcrowded pesthouses known as debtors' prisons.

This was the first national financial panic since President Washington took office. Many factors contributed to the catastrophe of 1819, but looming large was overspeculation in frontier lands. The Bank of the United States, through its western branches, had become deeply involved in this popular type of outdoor gambling.

Financial paralysis from the panic, which lasted in some degree for several years, gave a rude setback to the nationalistic ardor. The West was especially hard hit. When the pinch came, the Bank of the United States forced the speculative ("wildcat") western banks to the wall and foreclosed mortgages on countless farms. All this was technically legal but politically unwise. In the eyes of the western debtor, the nationalist Bank of the United States soon became a kind of financial devil.

The **panic of 1819** also created backwashes in the political and social world. The poorer classes—the one-suspender men and their families—were severely strapped, and in their troubles was sown the seed of Jacksonian democracy. Hard times also directed attention to the inhumanity of imprisoning debtors. In extreme cases, often overplayed, mothers were torn from their infants for owing a few dollars. Mounting agitation against imprisonment for debt bore fruit in remedial legislation in an increasing number of states.

Growing Pains of the West

The onward march of the West continued; nine frontier states had joined the original thirteen between 1791 and 1819. With an eye to preserving the North-South sectional balance, most of these commonwealths had been admitted alternately, free or slave. (See Admission of States in the Appendix.)

Why this explosive expansion? In part it was simply a continuation of the generations-old westward movement, which had been going on since early colonial days. In addition, the siren song of cheap land—"the Ohio fever"—had a special appeal to European immigrants. Eager newcomers from abroad were beginning to stream down the gangplanks in impressive numbers, especially after the war of boycotts and bullets. Land exhaustion in the older tobacco states, where the soil was "mined" rather than cultivated, likewise drove people westward. Glib speculators accepted small down payments, making it easier to buy new holdings.

The western boom was stimulated by additional developments. Acute economic distress during the embargo years turned many pinched faces toward the setting sun. The crushing of the Indians in the Northwest and South by Generals Harrison and Jackson pacified the frontier and opened up vast virgin tracts of land. The building of highways improved the land routes to the Ohio Valley. Noteworthy was the

Cumberland Road, begun in 1811, which ran ultimately from western Maryland to Illinois. The use of the first steamboat on western waters, also in 1811, heralded a new era of upstream navigation.

But the West, despite the inflow of settlers, was still weak in population and influence. Not potent enough politically to make its voice heard, it was forced to ally itself with other sections. Thus strengthened, it demanded cheap acreage and partially achieved its goal in the **Land Act of 1820**, which authorized a buyer to purchase eighty virgin acres at a minimum of $1.25 an acre in cash. The West also demanded cheap transportation and slowly got it, despite the constitutional qualms of the presidents and the hostility of easterners. Finally, the West demanded cheap money, issued by its own "wildcat" banks, and fought the powerful Bank of the United States to attain its goal (see "Makers of America: Settlers of the Old Northwest," pp. 236–237).

✶ Slavery and the Sectional Balance

Sectional tensions, involving rivalry between the slave South and the free North over control of the beckoning West, were stunningly revealed in 1819. In that year the territory of Missouri knocked on the doors of Congress for admission as a slave state. This fertile and well-watered area contained sufficient population to warrant statehood. But the House of Representatives stymied the plans of the Missourians by passing the incendiary

Antislavery Propaganda in the 1820s These drawstring bags are made of silk and transfer-printed with "before" and "after" scenes of slavery. On the left bag, an African woman cradles her baby; on the right one, the grieving mother is childless and in chains, while slaves are being whipped in the background. These bags were purchased at an abolitionist fair, held to raise money for the antislavery movement. Purses and the like sold well at these events because women were prominent in the movement. The Daughters of the American Revolution Museum, Washington, D.C. Loan of Boston, Tea Party Chapter

Tallmadge amendment. It stipulated that no more slaves should be brought into Missouri and also provided for the gradual emancipation of children born to slave parents already there. A roar of anger burst from slaveholding southerners. They were joined by many depression-cursed pioneers who favored unhampered expansion of the West and by many northerners, especially diehard Federalists, who were eager to use the issue to break the back of the "Virginia dynasty."

Southerners saw in the Tallmadge amendment, which they eventually managed to defeat in the Senate, an ominous threat to sectional balance. When the Constitution was adopted in 1788, the North and South were running neck and neck in wealth and population. But with every passing decade, the North was becoming wealthier and also more thickly settled—an advantage reflected in an increasing northern majority in the House of Representatives. Yet in the Senate, each state had two votes, regardless of size. With eleven states free and eleven slave, the southerners had maintained equality. They were therefore in a good position to thwart any northern effort to interfere with the expansion of slavery, and they did not want to lose this veto.

The future of the slave system caused southerners profound concern. Missouri was the first state entirely west of the Mississippi River to be carved out of the Louisiana Purchase, and the Missouri emancipation amendment might set a damaging precedent for all the rest of the area. Even more disquieting was another possibility. If Congress could abolish the **peculiar institution** in Missouri, might it not attempt to do likewise in the older states of the South? The wounds of the Constitutional Convention of 1787 were once more ripped open.

Burning moral questions also protruded, even though the main issue was political and economic balance. A small but growing group of antislavery agitators in the North seized the occasion to raise an outcry against the evils of slavery. They were determined that the plague of human bondage should not spread further into the untainted territories.

✶ The Uneasy Missouri Compromise

Deadlock in Washington was at length broken in 1820 by the time-honored American solution of compromise—actually a bundle of three compromises. Courtly Henry Clay of Kentucky, gifted conciliator, played a leading role. Congress, despite abolitionist pleas, agreed to admit Missouri as a slave state. But at the same time, free-soil Maine, which until then had been a part of Massachusetts, was admitted as a separate state. The balance between North and South was thus kept at twelve states each and remained there for fifteen years. Although Missouri was permitted to retain slaves, all

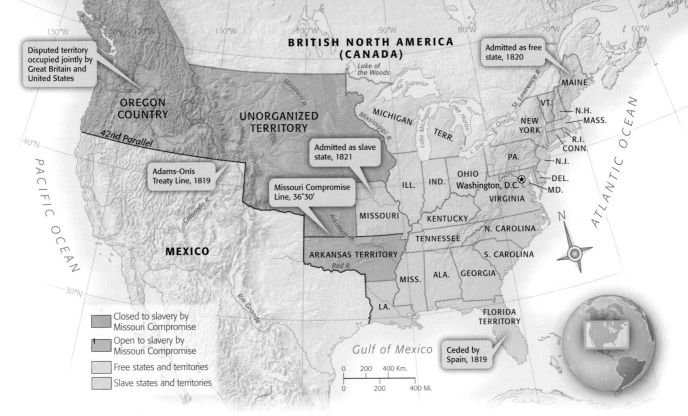

MAP 12.3 The Missouri Compromise and Slavery, 1820–1821 Note the 36° 30′ line. In the 1780s Thomas Jefferson had written of slavery in America, "Indeed I tremble for my country when I reflect that God is just; that his justice cannot sleep forever; that . . . the Almighty has no attribute which can take side with us in such a contest." Now, at the time of the Missouri Compromise, Jefferson feared that his worst forebodings were coming to pass. "I considered it at once," he said of the Missouri question, "as the knell of the Union." © Cengage Learning

future bondage was prohibited in the remainder of the Louisiana Purchase north of the line of 36° 30′—the southern boundary of Missouri (see Map 12.3).

This horse-trading adjustment was politically even-handed, though denounced by extremists on each side as a "dirty bargain." Both North and South yielded something; both gained something. The South won the prize of Missouri as an unrestricted slave state. The North won the concession that Congress could forbid slavery in the remaining territories. More gratifying to many northerners was the fact that the immense area north of 36° 30′, except Missouri, was forever closed to the blight of slavery. Yet the restriction on future slavery in the territories was not unduly offensive to the slave-owners, partly because the northern prairie land did not seem suited to slave labor. Even so, a majority of southern congressmen still voted against the compromise.

Neither North nor South was acutely displeased, although neither was completely happy. The **Missouri Compromise** lasted thirty-four years—a vital formative period in the life of the young Republic—and during that time it preserved the shaky compact of the states. Yet the embittered dispute over slavery heralded the future breakup of the Union. Ever after,

the morality of the South's "peculiar institution" was an issue that could not be swept under the rug. The Missouri Compromise only ducked the question—it

While the debate over Missouri was raging, Thomas Jefferson (1743–1826) wrote to a correspondent,

"The Missouri question . . . is the most portentous one which ever yet threatened our Union. In the gloomiest moment of the revolutionary war I never had any apprehensions equal to what I feel from this source. . . . [The] question, like a firebell in the night, awakened and filled me with terror. . . . [With slavery] we have a wolf by the ears, and we can neither hold him nor safely let him go."

John Quincy Adams (1767–1848) confided to his diary,

"I take it for granted that the present question is a mere preamble—a title-page to a great, tragic volume."

The Old Northwest beckoned to settlers after the War of 1812. The withdrawal of the British protector weakened the Indians' grip on the territory. Then the transportation boom of the 1820s—steamboats on the Ohio, the National Highway stretching from Pennsylvania, the Erie Canal—opened broad arteries along which the westward movement flowed.

The first wave of newcomers came mainly from Kentucky, Tennessee, and the upland regions of Virginia and the Carolinas. Most migrants were rough-hewn white farmers who had been pushed from good land to bad by an expanding plantation economy. Like Joseph Cress of North Carolina, they were relieved to relinquish "them old red filds" where you "get nothing," in return for acres of new soil that "is as black and rich you wold want it." Some settlers acquired land for the first time. John Palmer, whose family left Kentucky for Illinois in 1831, recalled his father telling him "of land so cheap that we could all be landholders, where men were all equal." Migrants from the South settled mainly in the southern portions of Ohio, Indiana, and Illinois.

As Palmer testified, the Old Northwest offered southern farmers an escape from the lowly social position they had endured as nonslaveholders in a slave society. Not that they objected to slavery or sympathized with blacks. Far from it: by enacting Black Codes in their new territories, they tried to prevent blacks from following them to paradise. They wanted their own democratic community, free of rich planters and African Americans alike.

If southern "Butternuts," as these settlers were called, dominated settlement in the 1820s, the next decade brought Yankees from the Northeast. They were as land-starved as their southern counterparts. A growing population had gobbled up most of the good land east of the Appalachians. Yankee settlers came to the Old Northwest, especially to the northern parts of Ohio, Indiana, and Illinois, eager to make the region a profitable breadbasket for the Atlantic seaboard. Unlike the Butternuts, who wanted to quit forever the imposing framework of southern society, northerners hoped to re-create the world they had left behind.

Conflict soon emerged between Yankees and southerners. As self-sufficient farmers with little interest in producing for the market, the southerners viewed the northern newcomers as inhospitable, greedy, and excessively ambitious. "Yankee" became a term of reproach; a person who was cheated was said to have been "Yankeed." Northerners, in turn, viewed the southerners as

Newcom Tavern, Dayton, Ohio Built in 1796, Newcom Tavern was a typical way station for the pioneers flowing into the newly secured Old Northwest in the early 1800s. Today it is Dayton's oldest building.

Building the Erie Canal A major engineering feat, the Erie Canal created an artificial waterway through upstate New York from the Hudson River to the Great Lakes, allowing people and goods to move to and from the Old Northwest more quickly and cheaply.

uncivilized, a "coon dog and butcher knife tribe" with no interest in education, self-improvement, or agricultural innovation. Yankees, eager to tame both the land and its people, wanted to establish public schools and build roads, canals, and railroads—and they advocated taxes to fund such progress. Southerners opposed all these reforms, especially public schooling, which they regarded as an attempt to northernize their children.

Religion divided settlers as well. Northerners, typically Congregationalists and Presbyterians, wanted their ministers to be educated in seminaries. Southerners embraced the more revivalist Baptist and Methodist denominations. They preferred poor, humble preacher-farmers to professionally trained preachers, whom they viewed as too distant from the Lord and the people. As the Baptist preacher Alexander Campbell put it, "The scheme of a learned priesthood . . . has long since proved itself to be a grand device to keep men in ignorance and bondage."

Not everyone, of course, fitted neatly into these molds. Abraham Lincoln, with roots in Kentucky, came to adopt views more akin to those of the Yankees than the southerners, whereas his New England–born

archrival, Stephen Douglas, carefully cultivated the Butternut vote for the Illinois Democratic party.

As the population swelled and the region acquired its own character, the stark contrasts between northerners and southerners started to fade. By the 1850s northerners dominated numerically, and they succeeded in establishing public schools and fashioning internal improvements. Railroads and Great Lakes shipping tied the region ever more tightly to the Northeast. Yankees and southerners sometimes allied as new kinds of cleavages emerged—between rich and poor, between city dwellers and farmers, and, once Irish and German immigrants started pouring into the region, between native Protestants and newcomer Catholics. Still, echoes of the clash between Yankees and Butternuts persisted. During the Civil War, the southern counties of Ohio, Indiana, and Illinois, where southerners had first settled, harbored sympathizers with the South and served as a key area for Confederate military infiltration into the North. Decades later these same counties became a stronghold of the Ku Klux Klan. The Old Northwest may have become firmly anchored economically to the Northeast, but vestiges of its early dual personality persisted.

did not resolve it. Sooner or later, Thomas Jefferson predicted, it will "burst on us as a tornado."

The Missouri Compromise and the concurrent panic of 1819 should have dimmed the political star of President Monroe. Certainly both unhappy events had a dampening effect on the Era of Good Feelings. But smooth-spoken James Monroe was so popular, and the Federalist opposition so weak, that in the presidential election of 1820, he received every electoral vote except one. Unanimity was an honor reserved for George Washington. Monroe, as it turned out, was the only president in American history to be reelected after a term in which a major financial panic began.

✴ John Marshall and Judicial Nationalism

The upsurging nationalism of the post-Ghent years, despite the ominous setbacks concerning slavery, was further reflected and reinforced by the Supreme Court. The high tribunal continued to be dominated by the tall, thin, and aggressive Chief Justice John Marshall. One group of his decisions—perhaps the most famous—bolstered the power of the federal government at the expense of the states. A notable case in this category was *McCulloch* **v.** *Maryland* (1819). The suit involved an attempt by the State of Maryland to destroy a branch of the Bank of the United States by imposing a tax on its notes. John Marshall, speaking for the Court, declared the bank constitutional by invoking the Hamiltonian doctrine of implied powers (see p. 185). At the same time, he strengthened federal authority and slapped at state infringements when he denied the right of Maryland to tax the bank. With ringing emphasis, he affirmed "that the power to tax involves the power to destroy" and "that a power to create implies a power to preserve."

Marshall's ruling in this case gave the doctrine of **loose construction** its most famous formulation. The Constitution, he said, derived from the consent of the people and thus permitted the government to act for their benefit. He further argued that the Constitution was "intended to endure for ages to come and, consequently, to be adapted to the various crises of human affairs." Finally, he declared, "Let the end be legitimate, let it be within the scope of the Constitution, and all means which are appropriate, which are plainly adapted to that end, which are not prohibited, but consist with the letter and spirit of the Constitution, are constitutional."

Two years later (1821) the case of *Cohens* **v.** *Virginia* gave Marshall one of his greatest opportunities to defend the federal power. The Cohen brothers, found guilty by the Virginia courts of illegally selling lottery tickets, appealed to the highest tribunal.

Virginia "won," in the sense that the conviction of the Cohens was upheld. But in fact Virginia and all the individual states lost, because Marshall resoundingly asserted the right of the Supreme Court to review the decisions of the state supreme courts in all questions involving powers of the federal government. The states' rights proponents were aghast.

Hardly less significant was the celebrated "steamboat case," *Gibbons* **v.** *Ogden* (1824). The suit grew out of an attempt by the State of New York to grant to a private concern a monopoly of waterborne commerce between New York and New Jersey. Marshall sternly reminded the upstart state that the Constitution conferred on Congress alone the control of interstate commerce (see Art. I, Sec. VIII, para. 3). He thus struck with one hand another blow at states' rights, while upholding with the other the sovereign powers of the federal government. Interstate streams were cleared of this judicial snag; the departed spirit of Hamilton may well have applauded.

✴ Judicial Dikes Against Democratic Excesses

Another sheaf of Marshall's decisions bolstered judicial barriers against democratic or demagogic attacks on property rights.

The notorious case of *Fletcher* **v.** *Peck* (1810) arose when a Georgia legislature, swayed by bribery, granted 35 million acres in the Yazoo River country (Mississippi) to private speculators. The next legislature, yielding to an angry public outcry, canceled the crooked transaction. But the Supreme Court, with Marshall presiding, decreed that the legislative grant was a contract (even though fraudulently secured) and that the Constitution forbids state laws "impairing" contracts (Art. I, Sec. X, para. 1). The decision was perhaps most noteworthy as further protecting property rights against popular pressures. It was also one of the earliest clear assertions of the right of the Supreme Court to invalidate state laws conflicting with the federal Constitution.

A similar principle was upheld in the case of *Dartmouth College* **v.** *Woodward* (1819), perhaps the best remembered of Marshall's decisions. The college had been granted a charter by King George III in 1769, but

When Supreme Court chief justice John Marshall died, a New York newspaper rejoiced:

❝ The chief place in the supreme tribunal of the Union will no longer be filled by a man whose political doctrines led him always ... to strengthen government at the expense of the people. ❞

Daguerreotype of Daniel Webster (1782–1852), by Southworth and Hawes Premier orator and statesman, Webster served many years in both houses of Congress and also as secretary of state. Often regarded as presidential timber, he was somewhat handicapped by an overfondness for good food and drink and was frequently in financial difficulties. His devotion to the Union was inflexible. "One country, one constitution, and one destiny," he proclaimed in 1837.

the democratic New Hampshire state legislature had seen fit to change it. Dartmouth appealed the case, employing as counsel its most distinguished alumnus, Daniel Webster ('01). The "Godlike Daniel" reportedly pulled out all the stops of his tear-inducing eloquence when he declaimed, "It is, sir, as I have said, a small college. And yet there are those who love it."

Marshall needed no dramatics in the *Dartmouth* case. He put the states firmly in their place when he ruled that the original charter must stand. It was a contract—and the Constitution protected contracts against state encroachments. The *Dartmouth* decision had the fortunate effect of safeguarding business enterprise from domination by the state governments. But it had the unfortunate effect of creating a precedent that enabled chartered corporations, in later years, to escape the handcuffs of needed public control.

If John Marshall was a Molding Father of the Constitution, Daniel Webster was an Expounding Father. Time and again he left his seat in the Senate, stepped downstairs to the Supreme Court chamber (then located in the Capitol building), and there expounded his Federalistic and nationalistic philosophy before the supreme

bench. The eminent chief justice, so Webster reported, approvingly drank in the familiar arguments as a baby sucks in its mother's milk. The two men dovetailed strikingly with each other. Webster's classic speeches in the Senate, challenging states' rights and nullification, were largely repetitious of the arguments that he had earlier presented before a sympathetic Supreme Court.

Marshall's decisions are felt even today. In this sense his nationalism was the most tenaciously enduring of the era. He buttressed the federal Union and helped to create a stable, nationally uniform environment for business. At the same time, Marshall checked the excesses of popularly elected state legislatures. In an age when white manhood suffrage was flowering and America was veering toward stronger popular control, Marshall almost single-handedly shaped the Constitution along conservative, centralizing lines that ran somewhat counter to the dominant spirit of the new country. Through him the conservative Hamiltonians partly triumphed from the tomb.

✵ Sharing Oregon and Acquiring Florida

The robust nationalism of the years after the War of 1812 was likewise reflected in the shaping of foreign policy. To this end, the nationalistic President Monroe teamed with his nationalistic secretary of state, John Quincy Adams, the cold and scholarly son of the frosty and bookish ex-president. The younger Adams, a statesman of the first rank, happily rose above the ingrown Federalist sectionalism of his native New England and proved to be one of the great secretaries of state.

To its credit, the Monroe administration negotiated the much-underrated **Anglo-American Convention** of 1818 with Britain. This pact permitted Americans to share the coveted Newfoundland fisheries with their Canadian cousins. This multisided agreement also fixed the vague northern limits of Louisiana along the forty-ninth parallel from the Lake of the Woods (Minnesota) to the Rocky Mountains (see Map 12.4). The treaty further provided for a ten-year joint occupation of the untamed Oregon Country, without a surrender of the rights or claims of either America or Britain.

To the south lay semitropical Spanish Florida, which many Americans believed geography and providence had destined to become part of the United States. Americans already claimed West Florida, where uninvited American settlers had torn down the hated Spanish flag in 1810. Congress ratified this grab in 1812, and during the War of 1812 against Spain's ally, Britain, a small American army seized the Mobile region. But the bulk of Florida remained, tauntingly, under Spanish rule (see Map 12.5).

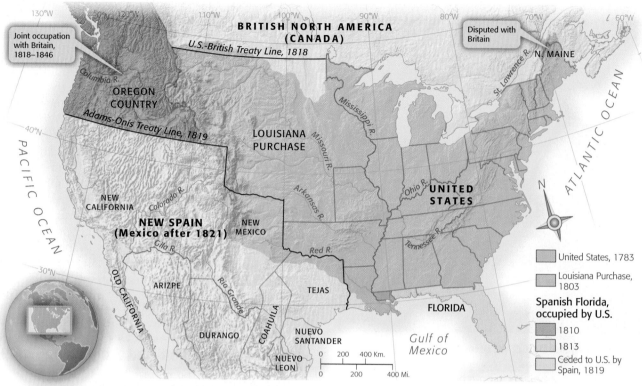

MAP 12.4 U.S.-British Boundary Settlement, 1818 Note that the United States gained considerable territory by securing a treaty boundary rather than the natural boundary of the Missouri River watershed. The line of 49° was extended westward to the Pacific Ocean under the Treaty of 1846 with Britain (see p. 368). © Cengage Learning

MAP 12.5 The Southeast, 1810–1819 © Cengage Learning

An epidemic of revolutions now broke out in South America, notably in Chile (1810), Venezuela (1811), and Argentina (1816), and Americans instinctively cheered the birth of these sister republics, though the checkered histories of the Latin democracies soon provided grounds for disappointment. But the upheavals in the southern continent forced Spain to denude Florida of troops in a vain effort to squelch the rebels. General Andrew Jackson, idol of the West and scourge of the Indians, saw opportunity in the undefended swamplands. On the pretext that hostile Seminole Indians and fugitive slaves were using Florida as a refuge, Jackson secured a commission to enter Spanish territory, punish the Indians, and recapture the runaways. But he was to respect all posts under the Spanish flag.

Early in 1818 Jackson swept across the Florida border with all the fury of an avenging angel. He hanged two Indian chiefs without ceremony and, after hasty military trials, executed two British subjects for assisting the Indians. He also seized the two most important Spanish posts in the area, St. Marks and then Pensacola, where he deposed the Spanish governor, who was lucky enough to escape Jackson's jerking noose.

Jackson had clearly exceeded his instructions from Washington. Alarmed, President Monroe consulted his

Historic Hudson Valley, Tarrytown, New York

Andrew Jackson (1767–1845), by Jean François de Vallée, 1815 This portrait of Jackson as a major general in the U.S. Army was painted by a French artist living in New Orleans. It is one of the earliest surviving portraits of Jackson and depicts him at a time when he was known for his stern discipline, iron will ("Old Hickory"), and good luck.

cabinet. Its members were for disavowing or disciplining the overzealous Jackson—all except the lone wolf John Quincy Adams, who refused to howl with the pack. An ardent patriot and nationalist, the flinty New Englander took the offensive and demanded huge concessions from Spain.

In the mislabeled **Florida Purchase Treaty** of 1819 (also known as the **Adams-Onís Treaty**), Spain ceded Florida, as well as shadowy Spanish claims to Oregon, in exchange for America's abandonment of equally murky claims to Texas, soon to become part of independent Mexico. The hitherto vague western boundary of Louisiana was made to zigzag northwesterly toward the Rockies to the forty-second parallel and then to turn due west to the Pacific, dividing Oregon from Spanish holdings.

The Menace of Monarchy in America

After the Napoleonic nightmare, the rethroned autocrats of Europe banded together in a kind of monar-chical protective association. Determined to restore the good old days, they undertook to stamp out the democratic tendencies that had sprouted from soil they considered richly manured by the ideals of the French Revolution. The world must be made safe *from* democracy.

The crowned despots acted promptly. With complete ruthlessness they smothered the embers of popular rebellions in Italy (1821) and in Spain (1823). According to the European rumor factory, they were also gazing across the Atlantic. Russia, Austria, Prussia, and France, acting in partnership, would presumably send powerful fleets and armies to the revolted colonies of Spanish America and there restore the autocratic Spanish king to his ancestral domains.

Many Americans were alarmed. Naturally sympathetic to democratic revolutions, they had cheered when the Latin American republics rose from the ruins of monarchy. Americans feared that if the European powers intervened in the New World, the cause of republicanism would suffer irreparable harm. The physical security of the United States—the mother lode of democracy—would be endangered by the proximity of powerful and unfriendly forces.

The southward push of the Russian bear, from the chill region now known as Alaska, had already publicized the menace of monarchy to North America. In 1821 the tsar of Russia issued a decree extending Russian jurisdiction over one hundred miles of the open sea down to the line of 51°, an area that embraced most of the coast of present-day British Columbia. The energetic Russians had already established trading posts almost as far south as the entrance to San Francisco Bay. (Fort Ross—"Ross" is a corruption of "Russian"—still stands today on the coast of Sonoma County, California.) The fear prevailed in the United States that the Russians were planning to cut the Republic off from California, its prospective window on the Pacific.

Great Britain, still Ruler of the Seas, was now beginning to play a lone-hand role on the complicated international stage. In particular, it recoiled from joining hands with the continental European powers in crushing the newly won liberties of the Spanish Americans. These revolutionaries had thrown open their monopoly-bound ports to outside trade, and British shippers, as well as Americans, had found the profits sweet.

Accordingly, in August 1823 George Canning, the haughty British foreign secretary, approached the American minister in London with a startling proposition. Would the United States combine with Britain in a joint declaration renouncing any interest in acquiring Latin American territory, and specifically warning the European despots to keep their harsh hands off the Latin American republics? The American minister,

President Monroe Thinking Globally Surrounded by his cabinet, the president is depicted explaining the Monroe Doctrine. Secretary of State John Quincy Adams is the first on the left; Secretary of War John C. Calhoun is the third from the right.

✴ Monroe and His Doctrine

The tenacious nationalist, Secretary Adams, was hard-headed enough to be wary of Britons bearing gifts. Why should the lordly British, with the mightiest navy afloat, need America as an ally—an America that had neither naval nor military strength? Such a union, argued Adams, was undignified—like a tiny American "cockboat" sailing "in the wake of the British man-of-war."

Adams, ever alert, thought that he detected the joker in the Canning proposal. The British feared that the aggressive Yankees would one day seize Spanish territory in the Americas—perhaps Cuba—which would jeopardize Britain's possessions in the Caribbean. If Canning could seduce the United States into joining with him in support of the territorial integrity of the New World, America's own hands would be morally tied.

A self-denying alliance with Britain would not only hamper American expansion, concluded Adams, but it was unnecessary. He suspected—correctly—that

the European powers had not hatched any definite plans for invading the Americas. In any event the British navy would prevent the approach of hostile fleets because the South American markets had to be kept open at all costs for British merchants. It was presumably safe for Uncle Sam, behind the protective wooden petticoats of the British navy, to blow a defiant, nationalistic blast at all of Europe. The distresses of the Old World set the stage once again for an American diplomatic coup.

The **Monroe Doctrine** was born late in 1823, when the nationalistic Adams won the nationalistic Monroe over to his way of thinking. The president, in his regular annual message to Congress on December 2, 1823, incorporated a stern warning to the European powers. Its two basic features were (1) noncolonization and (2) nonintervention.

Monroe first directed his verbal volley primarily at the lumbering Russian bear in the Northwest. He proclaimed, in effect, that the era of colonization in the Americas had ended and that henceforth the hunting season was permanently closed. What the great powers had they might keep, but neither they nor any other Old World governments could seize or otherwise acquire more.

At the same time, Monroe trumpeted a warning against foreign intervention. He was clearly concerned with regions to the south, where fears were felt for the fledgling Spanish American republics. Monroe bluntly directed the crowned heads of Europe to keep their hated monarchical systems out of this hemisphere. For its part the United States would not intervene in the war that the Greeks were then fighting against the Turks for their independence.

✹ Monroe's Doctrine Appraised

The ermined monarchs of Europe were angered at Monroe's doctrine. Having resented the incendiary American experiment from the beginning, they were now deeply offended by Monroe's high-flown declaration—all the more so because of the gulf between America's pretentious pronouncements and its puny military strength. But though offended by the upstart Yankees, the European powers found their hands tied, and their frustration increased their annoyance. Even if they had worked out plans for invading the Americas, they would have been helpless before the booming broadsides of the British navy.

Monroe's solemn warning, when issued, made little splash in the newborn republics to the south. Anyone could see that Uncle Sam was only secondarily concerned about his neighbors, because he was primarily concerned about defending himself against future invasion. Only a relatively few educated Latin Americans knew of the message, and they generally recognized that the British navy—not the paper pronouncement of James Monroe—stood between them and a hostile Europe.

In truth, Monroe's message did not have much contemporary significance. Americans applauded it and then forgot it. Not until 1845 did President Polk revive it, and not until midcentury did it become an important national dogma.

Even before Monroe's stiff message, the tsar had decided to retreat. This he formally did in the **Russo-American Treaty** of 1824, which fixed his southernmost limits at the line of 54° 40'—the present southern tip of the Alaska panhandle (see Map 12.6).

The Monroe Doctrine might more accurately have been called the Self-Defense Doctrine. President Monroe was concerned basically with the security of his own country—not of Latin America. The United States has never willingly permitted a powerful foreign

MAP 12.6 The West and Northwest, 1818–1824 The British Hudson's Bay Company moved to secure its claim to the Oregon Country in 1824, when it sent a heavily armed expedition led by Peter Skene Ogden into the Snake River country. In May 1825 Ogden's party descended the Bear River "and found it discharged into a large Lake of 100 miles in length"—one of the first documented sightings by white explorers of the Great Salt Lake. (The mountain man Jim Bridger is usually credited with being the first white man to see the lake.)

© Cengage Learning

nation to secure a foothold near its strategic Caribbean vitals. Yet in the absence of the British navy or other allies, the strength of the Monroe Doctrine has never been greater than America's power to eject the trespasser. The doctrine, as often noted, was just as big as the nation's armed forces—and no bigger.

The Monroe Doctrine has had a long career of ups and downs. It was never law—domestic or international. It was not, technically speaking, a pledge or an agreement. It was merely a simple, personalized statement of the policy of President Monroe. What one president says, another may unsay. And Monroe's successors have ignored, revived, distorted, or expanded the original version, chiefly by adding interpretations. Like ivy on a tree, it has grown with America's growth.

But the Monroe Doctrine in 1823 was largely an expression of the post-1812 nationalism energizing the United States. Although directed at a specific menace in 1823, and hence a kind of period piece, the doctrine proved to be the most famous of all the long-lived offspring of that nationalism. While giving voice to a spirit of patriotism, it simultaneously deepened the illusion of isolationism. Many Americans falsely concluded, then and later, that the Republic was in fact insulated from European dangers simply because it wanted to be and because, in a nationalistic outburst, Monroe had publicly warned the Old World powers to stay away.

Chapter Review

KEY TERMS

War of 1812 (224)
New Orleans, Battle of (226)
Congress of Vienna (227)
Ghent, Treaty of (227)
Hartford Convention (228)
Rush-Bagot agreement (230)
Tariff of 1816 (231)

American System (231)
Era of Good Feelings (232)
panic of 1819 (233)
Land Act of 1820 (234)
Tallmadge amendment (234)
peculiar institution (234)
Missouri Compromise (235)

McCulloch v. *Maryland* (238)
loose construction (238)
Cohens v. *Virginia* (238)
Gibbons v. *Ogden* (238)
Fletcher v. *Peck* (238)
Dartmouth College v. *Woodward* (238)

Anglo-American Convention (239)
Florida Purchase Treaty (Adams-Onís Treaty) (240)
Monroe Doctrine (242)
Russo-American Treaty (243)

PEOPLE TO KNOW

Isaac Brock
Oliver Hazard Perry
Thomas Macdonough

Francis Scott Key
James Monroe
George Canning

TO LEARN MORE

Jeremy Black, *The War of 1812 in the Age of Napoleon* (2009)

George Dangerfield, *The Awakening of American Nationalism, 1815–1828* (1965)

R. David Edmunds, *Tecumseh and the Quest for Indian Leadership* (1984)

David Heidler, *Old Hickory's War: Andrew Jackson and the Quest for Empire* (2003)

James E. Lewis, *The American Union and the Problem of Neighborhood* (1998)

Arand Otto Mayr and Robert C. Post, eds., *Yankee Enterprise: The Rise of the American System of Manufactures* (1981)

Drew R. McCoy, *The Last of the Fathers: James Madison and the Republican Legacy* (1989)

Dexter Perkins, *A History of the Monroe Doctrine* (1955)

Jack N. Rakove, *James Madison and the Creation of the American Republic* (1990)

Robert Remini, *Henry Clay: Statesman for the Union* (1991)

A complete, annotated bibliography for this chapter—along with brief descriptions of the People to Know—may be found on the American Pageant website. The Key Terms are defined in a Glossary at the end of the text.

CHRONOLOGY

1810   *Fletcher* v. *Peck* ruling asserts right of Supreme Court to invalidate state laws deemed unconstitutional

1811   Venezuela declares independence from Spain

1812   United States declares war on Britain
Madison reelected president

1812–1813   American invasions of Canada fail

1813   Battle of the Thames
Battle of Lake Erie

1814   Battle of Horseshoe Bend
Napoleon exiled to Elba
British burn Washington, D.C.
Battle of Plattsburgh
Treaty of Ghent signed ending War of 1812

1814–1815   Hartford Convention
Congress of Vienna

1815   Battle of New Orleans
Napoleon's army defeated at Waterloo

1816   Second Bank of the United States founded
Protectionist Tariff of 1816
Argentina declares independence from Spain
Monroe elected president

1817   Rush-Bagot agreement limits naval armament on Great Lakes
Madison vetoes internal improvements bill

1818   Jackson invades Florida
Chile, in rebellion since 1810, declares independence from Spain
Anglo-American Convention

1819   Panic of 1819
Spain cedes Florida to United States in Adams-Onís Treaty
McCulloch v. *Maryland*
Dartmouth College v. *Woodward*

1820   Missouri Compromise
Missouri and Maine admitted to Union
Land Act of 1820
Monroe reelected

1821   *Cohens* v. *Virginia*
Austria intervenes to crush popular uprising in Italy

1823   France intervenes to suppresses liberal government in Spain
Secretary Adams proposes Monroe Doctrine

1824   Russo-American Treaty
Gibbons v. *Ogden*

1825   Erie Canal completed

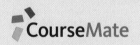
CourseMate

Go to the CourseMate website at **www.cengagebrain.com** for additional study tools and review materials—including audio and video clips—for this chapter.

AP® Review Questions for Chapter 12

1. The three decisive battles that turned the War of 1812 in the Americans' favor were
   (A) Montreal, Detroit, and Niagara.
   (B) Louisiana, Kentucky, and Tennessee.
   (C) Erie, New England, and New Orleans.
   (D) New England, Baltimore, and New Orleans.
   (E) New York, Washington, and New Orleans.

2. Which of the following was NOT true of the Battle of New Orleans?
   (A) It made Andrew Jackson a national hero.
   (B) It occurred two weeks before the war ended.
   (C) It restored America's sense of honor.
   (D) Its outcome triggered the British blockade of America's coastline.
   (E) It was England's most devastating loss in the war.

3. Encouraged by the Russian tsar, the 1814 Treaty of Ghent
   (A) ended the fighting and restored the territories.
   (B) forced England to compensate America for impressments and confiscated property during the war.
   (C) demonstrated America's decisive victory against the British.
   (D) granted England a neutralized Indian buffer zone in the Great Lakes.
   (E) gave part of Maine to England.

4. Which of the following statements does NOT describe the Hartford Convention of 1814?
   (A) It strengthened the position of the Federalist party.
   (B) It sought to remove the three-fifths compromise from the Constitution.
   (C) It included the threat of secession by northern states.
   (D) It featured demands for Washington to help compensate New England merchants for wartime financial losses.
   (E) It sought a two-thirds vote in Congress for placing embargoes, admitting new states, and declaring war.

5. Although globally unimportant, the War of 1812—dubbed "the Second War for American Independence"—was vitally important to the United States for all of the following reasons EXCEPT that it
   (A) inspired a new nationalism in the United States.
   (B) created greater respect for America's military might in the rest of the world.
   (C) increased a naval presence to protect the Great Lakes.
   (D) stimulated the development of American manufacturing.
   (E) led to Indian treaties that ceded large sections of the region north of the Ohio River to the United States.

6. What is being described by the term *the American system*?
   (A) The revitalization of fiscal policy under the Bank of the United States
   (B) The implementation of tariffs in 1816 to protect American industries from cheap imports
   (C) A campaign to develop and bring greater democracy to the West
   (D) A three-tiered program to promote America's home markets
   (E) The notion that improving transportation was the central government's responsibility

7. The "Era of Good Feelings" refers to
   (A) the exuberance Americans felt in the years after the War of 1812.
   (B) the presidency of James Monroe.
   (C) America's economic boom in the postwar years.
   (D) the end of party infighting between the Federalists and the Republicans.
   (E) the end of sectional tensions.

8. The first national financial crisis, the panic of 1819, was caused primarily by
   (A) surplus production of American-made goods.
   (B) economic downturns in Europe that began to reach American shores.
   (C) overspeculation in western lands.
   (D) a mortgage crisis.
   (E) a massive federal wartime debt.

9. All of these factors pushed new settlers toward the West, beginning in the 1820s, EXCEPT
    (A) the United States' military action against Native Americans opening up new land to settlement.
    (B) the rapid development of transportation networks along canals and other inland waterways.
    (C) increasing numbers of new immigrants streaming into America and moving westward rather than settling on the coast.
    (D) soil depletion, particularly in tobacco country.
    (E) promises of free government land.

10. What did the Missouri Compromise (1820) seek to accomplish?
    (A) Preserving the Union from the threat of southern secession
    (B) The eventual abolition of slavery
    (C) Admitting Missouri to the Union as a free state
    (D) Allowing each new western state to decide the slavery question for itself
    (E) Maintaining the balance between free and slave states

11. As chief justice of the Supreme Court, John Marshall made a lasting impact in several decisions that
    (A) increased the power of the states.
    (B) reinforced the doctrine of loose construction regarding the Constitution.
    (C) gave the states the right to alter contracts.
    (D) interpreted the Constitution along strict constructionist lines.
    (E) checked the excesses of business and the federal government.

12. Which of the following did NOT lead to the U.S. acquisition of Florida from Spain?
    (A) Revolutions in Central and South America
    (B) Rumors that Seminole Indians and fugitive slaves were using Florida as a refuge
    (C) Raids by Andrew Jackson
    (D) America's offer to purchase the state for $5 million from Spain
    (E) A treaty in which America agreed to cede Texas claims in exchange for Florida

13. What move made the United States most fearful of new colonization in its territories in the 1820s?
    (A) British expansion into Oregon
    (B) Spanish presence in Florida
    (C) Russian expansion beyond Alaska
    (D) British efforts to crush the newly freed Spanish South American territories
    (E) England's encroachment into Newfoundland fishing regions

14. The primary significance of the Monroe Doctrine (1823) is that
    (A) it outlined noncolonization and nonintervention mandates regarding the Americas and beyond.
    (B) it was incorporated into international law.
    (C) it led to a treaty and new boundary arrangements with the Russian tsar regarding Alaska.
    (D) its flexibility permitted reinterpretation by succeeding presidents.
    (E) it was instantly adopted as national doctrine.

15. Although it signified that the United States was becoming a world power, the Monroe Doctrine upheld the ideals of Washington's Farewell Address because
    (A) Monroe knew that Great Britain would support the United States in cases of European encroachment.
    (B) it promoted commercial relationships between the United States and several Latin American nations.
    (C) it was created during the Era of Good Feelings and was not the result of political posturing.
    (D) Monroe pledged that the United States would not involve itself in European matters.
    (E) Latin American revolutions were inspired by the American Revolution.

16. The War of 1812 helped to develop American identity for all of the following reasons EXCEPT that
    (A) Andrew Jackson became a prominent national figure.
    (B) it started the early industrial revolution in the United States.
    (C) Francis Scott Key wrote "The Star Spangled Banner," which became the national anthem.
    (D) it led to the birth of a distinctively national literature.
    (E) Washington, D.C., was restored as an even more impressive national capital.

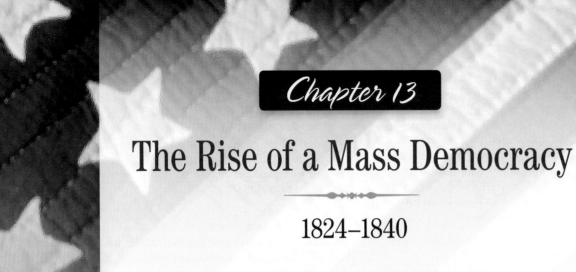

Chapter 13

The Rise of a Mass Democracy

1824–1840

In the full enjoyment of the gifts of Heaven and the fruits of superior industry, economy, and virtue, every man is equally entitled to protection by law; but when the laws undertake to add to those natural and just advantages artificial distinctions . . . and exclusive privileges . . . the humble members of society—the farmers, mechanics, and laborers . . . have a right to complain of the injustice of their government.

ANDREW JACKSON, 1832

The so-called Era of Good Feelings was never entirely tranquil, but even the illusion of national consensus was shattered by the panic of 1819 and the Missouri Compromise of 1820. Economic distress and the slavery issue raised the political stakes in the 1820s and 1830s. Vigorous political conflict, once feared, came to be celebrated as necessary for the health of democracy. New political parties emerged. New styles of campaigning took hold. A new chapter opened in the history of American—and world—politics, as many European societies began haltingly to expand their electorates and broaden democratic practices. The American political landscape of 1824 was similar, in its broad outlines, to that of 1796. By 1840 it would be almost unrecognizable.

The deference, apathy, and virtually nonexistent party organizations of the Era of Good Feelings yielded to the boisterous democracy, frenzied vitality, and strong political parties of the Jacksonian era. The old suspicion of political parties as illegitimate disrupters of society's natural harmony gave way to an acceptance, even a celebration, of the sometimes wild contentiousness of political life.

In 1828 an energetic new party, the Democrats, captured the White House. By the 1830s the Democrats faced an equally vigorous opposition party, the Whigs. This two-party system institutionalized divisions that had vexed the Revolutionary generation and came to constitute an important part of the nation's checks and balances on political power.

New forms of politicking emerged in this era, as candidates used banners, badges, parades, barbecues, free drinks, and baby kissing to "get out the vote." Voter turnout rose dramatically. Only about one-quarter of eligible voters cast a ballot in the presidential election of 1824, but that proportion doubled in 1828, and in the election of 1840 it reached 78 percent. Everywhere people flexed their political muscles.

✸ The "Corrupt Bargain" of 1824

The last of the old-style elections was marked by the controversial **corrupt bargain** of 1824. The woods were full of presidential timber as James Monroe, last of the Virginia dynasty, completed his second term. Four candidates towered above the others: John Quincy Adams of Massachusetts, highly intelligent, experienced, and aloof; Henry Clay of Kentucky, the gamy and gallant "Harry of the West"; William H. Crawford of Georgia, an able though ailing giant of a man; and Andrew Jackson of Tennessee, the gaunt and gutsy hero of New Orleans.

All four rivals professed to be "Republicans." Well-organized parties had not yet emerged; their identities were so fuzzy, in fact, that South Carolina's John C. Calhoun appeared as the vice-presidential candidate on both the Adams and Jackson tickets.

The results of the noisy campaign were interesting but confusing. Jackson, the war hero, clearly had the

Nelson-Atkins Museum of Art, Kansas City, Missouri. Purchase: Nelson Trust, 54-9. Photograph by Jamison Miller

Canvassing for a Vote, by George Caleb Bingham, 1852 This painting shows the "new politics" of the Jacksonian era. Politicians now had to take their message to the common man.

strongest personal appeal, especially in the West, where his campaign against the forces of corruption and privilege in government resonated deeply. He polled almost as many popular votes as his next two rivals combined, but he failed to win a majority of the electoral vote (see Table 13.1). In such a deadlock, the House of Representatives, as directed by the Twelfth Amendment (see the Appendix), must choose among the top three candidates. Clay was thus eliminated, yet as Speaker of the House, he presided over the very chamber that had to pick the winner.

The influential Clay was in a position to throw the election to the candidate of his choice. He reached his decision by process of elimination. Crawford, recently felled by a paralytic stroke, was out of the picture. Clay hated the "military chieftain" Jackson, his archrival for the allegiance of the West. Jackson, in turn, bitterly resented Clay's public denunciation of his Florida foray in 1818. The only candidate left was the puritanical

Adams, with whom Clay—a free-living gambler and duelist—had never established cordial personal relations. But the two men had much in common politically: both were fervid nationalists and advocates of the American System. Shortly before the final balloting in the House, Clay met privately with Adams and assured him of his support.

Decision day came early in 1825. The House of Representatives met amid tense excitement, with sick members being carried in on stretchers. On the first ballot, thanks largely to Clay's behind-the-scenes influence, Adams was elected president. A few days later, the victor announced that Henry Clay would be the new secretary of state.

The office of secretary of state was the prize plum then, even more so than today. Three of the four preceding secretaries had reached the presidency, and the high cabinet office was regarded as an almost certain pathway to the White House. According to Jackson's supporters, Adams had bribed Clay with the position, making himself, the people's second choice, the victor over Jackson, the people's first choice.

Masses of angry Jacksonians, most of them common folk, raised a roar of protest against this "corrupt bargain." The clamor continued for nearly four years. Jackson condemned Clay as the "Judas of the West," and John Randolph of Virginia publicly assailed

TABLE 13.1 Election of 1824			
Candidates	**Electoral Vote**	**Popular Vote**	**Popular Percentage**
Jackson	99	153,544	42.16%
Adams	84	108,740	31.89
Crawford	41	46,618	12.95
Clay	37	47,136	12.99

the alliance between "the Puritan [Adams] and the black-leg [Clay]," who, he added, "shines and stinks like rotten mackerel by moonlight." Clay, outraged, challenged Randolph to a duel, though poor marksmanship and shaky nerves rendered the outcome bloodless.

No positive evidence has yet been unearthed to prove that Adams and Clay entered into a formal bargain. Clay was a natural choice for secretary of state, and Adams was both scrupulously honest and not given to patronage. Even if a bargain had been struck, it was not necessarily corrupt. Deals of this nature have long been the stock-in-trade of politicians. But the outcry over Adams's election showed that change was in the wind. What had once been common practice was now condemned as furtive, elitist, and subversive of democracy. The next president would not be chosen behind closed doors.

✦ A Yankee Misfit in the White House

John Quincy Adams was a chip off the old family glacier. Short, thickset, and billiard-bald, he was even more frigidly austere than his presidential father, John Adams. Shunning people, he often went for early-morning swims, sometimes stark naked, in the then-pure Potomac River. Essentially a closeted thinker rather than a politician, he was irritable, sarcastic, and tactless. Yet few individuals have ever come to the presidency with a more brilliant record in statecraft, especially in foreign affairs. He ranks as one of the most successful secretaries of state, yet one of the least successful presidents.

A man of scrupulous honor, Adams entered upon his four-year "sentence" in the White House smarting under charges of "bargain," "corruption," and "usurpation." Fewer than one-third of the voters had voted for him. As the first "minority president," he would have found it difficult to win popular support even under the most favorable conditions. He did not possess many of the usual arts of the politician and scorned those who did. He had achieved high office by commanding respect rather than by courting popularity. In an earlier era, an aloof John Adams had won the votes of propertied men by sheer ability. But with the dawning age of backslapping and baby-kissing democracy, his cold-fish son could hardly hope for success at the polls.

While Adams's enemies accused him of striking a corrupt bargain, his political allies wished that he would strike a few more. Whether through high-mindedness or political ineptitude, Adams resolutely declined to oust efficient officeholders in order to create vacancies for his supporters. During his entire administration, he removed only twelve public servants from the federal payroll. Such stubbornness caused countless

President John Quincy Adams (1767–1848), Daguerreotype by Phillip Haas, 1843 Adams wrote in his diary in June 1819, nearly six years before becoming president, "I am a man of reserved, cold, austere, and forbidding manners: my political adversaries say, a gloomy misanthropist, and my personal enemies an unsocial savage."

Adams followers to throw up their hands in despair. If the president would not reward party workers with political plums, why should they labor to keep him in office?

Adams's nationalistic views gave him further woes. Much of the nation was turning away from post-Ghent nationalism and toward states' rights and sectionalism. But Adams swam against the tide. Confirmed nationalist that he was, Adams, in his first annual message, urged upon Congress the construction of roads and canals. He renewed George Washington's proposal for a national university and went so far as to advocate federal support for an astronomical observatory.

The public reaction to these proposals was prompt and unfavorable. To many workaday Americans grubbing out stumps, astronomical observatories seemed like a scandalous waste of public funds. The South in particular bristled. If the federal government should take on such heavy financial burdens, it would have to continue the hated tariff duties. Worse, if it could meddle in local concerns like education and roads, it might even try to lay its hand on the "peculiar institution" of black slavery.

Adams's land policy likewise antagonized the westerners. They clamored for wide-open expansion and resented the president's well-meaning attempts to curb feverish speculation in the public domain. The fate of the Cherokee Indians, threatened with eviction from their holdings in Georgia, brought additional bitterness. White Georgians wanted the Cherokees out. The ruggedly honest Adams attempted to deal fairly with the Indians. The Georgia governor, by threatening to resort to arms, successfully resisted the efforts of the Washington government to interpose federal authority on behalf of the Cherokees. Another fateful chapter was thus written in the nullification of the national will— and another nail was driven in Adams's political coffin.

✴ Going "Whole Hog" for Jackson in 1828

Andrew Jackson's next presidential campaign started early—on February 9, 1825, the day of John Quincy Adams's controversial election by the House—and it continued noisily for nearly four years.

Even before the election of 1828, the temporarily united Republicans of the Era of Good Feelings had split into two camps. One was the National Republicans, with Adams as their standard-bearer. The other was the Democratic-Republicans, with the fiery Jackson heading their ticket. Rallying cries of the Jackson zealots were "Bargain and Corruption," "Huzza for Jackson," and "All Hail Old Hickory." Jacksonites planted hickory poles for their hickory-tough hero; Adamsites adopted the oak as the symbol of their oakenly independent candidate.

Jackson's followers presented their hero as a rough-hewn frontiersman and a stalwart champion of the common man. They denounced Adams as a corrupt aristocrat and argued that the will of the people had been thwarted in 1825 by the backstairs "bargain" of Adams and Clay. The only way to right the wrong was to seat Jackson, who would then bring about "reform" by sweeping out the "dishonest" Adams gang.

Much of this talk was political hyperbole. Jackson was no frontier farmer but a wealthy planter. He had been born in a log cabin but now lived in a luxurious manor off the labor of his many slaves. And Adams, though perhaps an aristocrat, was far from corrupt. If anything, his uncompromising morals were too elevated for the job.

Mudslinging reached new lows in 1828, and the electorate developed a taste for bare-knuckle politics.

Adams would not stoop to gutter tactics, but many of his backers were less squeamish. They described Jackson's mother as a prostitute and his wife as an adulteress; they printed black-bordered handbills shaped like coffins, recounting his numerous duels and brawls and trumpeting his hanging of six mutinous militiamen.

Jackson men also hit below the belt. President Adams had purchased, with his own money and for his own use, a billiard table and a set of chessmen. In the mouths of rabid Jacksonites, these items became "gaming tables" and "gambling furniture" for the "presidential palace." Criticism was also directed at the large sums Adams had received over the years in federal salaries, well earned though they had been. He was even accused of having procured a servant girl for

Rachel Jackson A devoted wife who did not live to become first lady, Rachel died a month after the election of 1828. Andrew Jackson was convinced that his enemies' vicious accusations that she was a bigamist and an adulteress had killed her. The more complicated truth was that Andrew Jackson had married Rachel Robards confident that her divorce had been granted. Two years later, when they discovered to their dismay that it had not been, they made haste to correct the marital miscue. Granger Collection the lust of the Russian tsar—in short, of having served as a pimp.

On voting day the electorate split on largely sectional lines. Jackson's strongest support came from the West and South (see Map 13.1). The middle states and the Old Northwest were divided, while Adams won the backing of his own New England and the propertied "better elements" of the Northeast. But when the popular vote was converted to electoral votes, General Jackson's triumph could not be denied. Old Hickory had trounced Adams by an electoral count of 178 to 83. Although a considerable part of Jackson's support was lined up by machine politicians in eastern cities, particularly in New York and Pennsylvania, the political center of gravity clearly had shifted away from the conservative eastern seaboard toward the emerging states across the mountains.

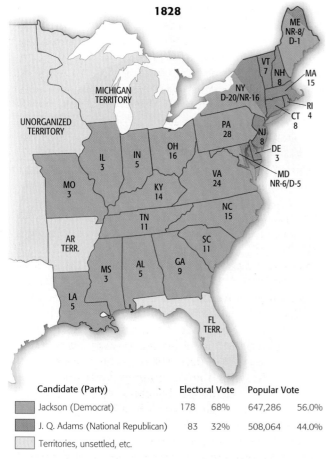

1828

Candidate (Party)		Electoral Vote		Popular Vote	
Jackson (Democrat)		178	68%	647,286	56.0%
J. Q. Adams (National Republican)		83	32%	508,064	44.0%
Territories, unsettled, etc.					

MAP 13.1 Presidential Election of 1828 (with electoral vote by state) Jackson swept the South and West, whereas Adams retained the old Federalist stronghold of the Northeast. Yet Jackson's inroads in the Northeast were decisive. He won twenty of New York's electoral votes and all twenty-eight of Pennsylvania's. If those votes had gone the other way, Adams would have been victorious—by a margin of one vote. © Cengage Learning

One anti-Jackson newspaper declared,

❝General Jackson's mother was a Common Prostitute, brought to this country by the British soldiers! She afterwards married a MULATTO man with whom she had several children, of which number GENERAL JACKSON is one.**❞**

✹ "Old Hickory" as President

The new president cut a striking figure—tall, lean, with bushy iron-gray hair brushed high above a prominent forehead, craggy eyebrows, and blue eyes. His irritability and emaciated condition resulted in part from long-term bouts with dysentery, malaria, tuberculosis, and lead poisoning from two bullets that he carried in his body from near-fatal duels. His autobiography was written in his lined face.

Jackson's upbringing had its shortcomings. Born in the Carolinas and early orphaned, "Mischievous Andy" grew up without parental restraints. As a youth he displayed much more interest in brawling and cockfighting than in his scanty opportunities for reading and spelling. Although he eventually learned to express himself in writing with vigor and clarity, his grammar was always rough-hewn and his spelling original, like that of many contemporaries. He sometimes misspelled a word two different ways in the same letter.

The youthful Carolinian shrewdly moved "up West" to Tennessee, where fighting was prized above writing. There—through native intelligence, force of personality, and powers of leadership—he became a judge and a member of Congress. Afflicted with a violent temper, he early became involved in a number of duels, stabbings, and bloody frays. His passions were so profound that on occasion he would choke into silence when he tried to speak.

The first president from the West, the first nominated at a formal party convention (in 1832), and only the second without a college education (Washington was the first), Jackson was unique. His university was adversity. He had risen from the masses, but he was

In 1824 Thomas Jefferson (1743–1826) said of Jackson,

❝When I was President of the Senate he was a Senator; and he could never speak on account of the rashness of his feelings. I have seen him attempt it repeatedly, and as often choke with rage. His passions are no doubt cooler now . . . but he is a dangerous man.**❞**

English novelist Charles Dickens (1812–1870) traveled to the United States just a few years after Alexis de Tocqueville (see "Thinking Globally: Alexis de Tocqueville on Democracy in America and Europe," pp. 252–253). He had his own views on the implications of America's vaunted "equality":

❝ The people are all alike too. There is no diversity of character. They travel about on the same errands, say and do the same things in exactly the same manner, and follow in the same dull cheerless round. All down the long table there is scarcely a man who is in anything different from his neighbor.**❞**

not one of them, except insofar as he shared many of their prejudices. Essentially a frontier aristocrat, he owned many slaves, cultivated broad acres, and lived in one of the finest mansions in America—the Hermitage, near Nashville, Tennessee. More westerner than easterner, more country gentleman than common clay, more courtly than crude, he was hard to fit into a neat category.

Jackson's inauguration seemed to symbolize the ascendancy of the masses. "Hickoryites" poured into Washington from far away, sleeping on hotel floors and in hallways. They were curious to see their hero take office and perhaps hoped to pick up a well-paying office for themselves. Nobodies mingled with notables as the White House, for the first time, was thrown open to the multitude. A milling crowd of rubbernecking clerks and shopkeepers, hobnailed artisans, and grimy laborers surged in, allegedly wrecking the china and furniture and threatening the "people's champion" with cracked ribs. Jackson was hastily spirited through a side door, and the White House miraculously emptied itself when the word was passed that huge bowls of well-spiked punch had been placed on the lawns. Such was "the inaugural brawl."

To conservatives this orgy seemed like the end of the world. "King Mob" reigned triumphant as Jacksonian vulgarity replaced Jeffersonian simplicity. Faint-hearted traditionalists shuddered, drew their blinds, and recalled with trepidation the opening scenes of the French Revolution.

✷ The Spoils System

Once in power, the Democrats, famously suspicious of the federal government, demonstrated that they were not above striking some bargains of their own. Under Jackson the **spoils system**—that is, rewarding

political supporters with public office—was introduced into the federal government on a large scale. The basic idea was as old as politics. Its name came later from Senator William Marcy's classic remark in 1832, "To the victor belong the spoils of the enemy." The system had already secured a firm hold in New York and Pennsylvania, where well-greased machines ladled out the "gravy" of office.

Jackson defended the spoils system on democratic grounds. "Every man is as good as his neighbor," he declared—perhaps "equally better." As this was believed to be so, and as the routine of office was thought to be simple enough for any upstanding American to learn quickly, why encourage the development of an aristocratic, bureaucratic, officeholding class? Better to bring in new blood, he argued; each generation deserved its turn at the public trough.

Washington was due, it is true, for a housecleaning. No party overturn had occurred since the defeat of the Federalists in 1800, and even that had not produced wholesale evictions. A few officeholders, their commissions signed by President Washington, were lingering on into their eighties, drawing breath and salary but doing little else. But the spoils system was less about finding new blood than about rewarding old cronies. "Throw their rascals out and put our rascals in," the Democrats were essentially saying. The questions asked of each appointee were not "What can he do for the country?" but "What has he done for the party?" or "Is he loyal to Jackson?"

Scandal inevitably accompanied the new system. Men who had openly bought their posts by campaign contributions were appointed to high office. Illiterates, incompetents, and plain crooks were given positions of public trust; men on the make lusted for the spoils—rather than the toils—of office. Samuel Swartwout, despite ample warnings of his untrustworthiness, was awarded the lucrative post of collector of the customs of the port of New York. Nearly nine years later, he "Swartwouted out" for England, leaving his accounts more than a million dollars short—the first person to steal a million from the Washington government.

But despite its undeniable abuse, the spoils system was an important element of the emerging two-party order, cementing as it did loyalty to party over competing claims based on economic class or geographic region. The promise of patronage provided a compelling reason for Americans to pick a party and stick with it through thick and thin.

✷ The Tricky "Tariff of Abominations"

The touchy tariff issue had been one of John Quincy Adams's biggest headaches. Now Andrew Jackson felt

Thinking Globally

Alexis de Tocqueville on Democracy in America and Europe

On May 11, 1831, a twenty-six-year-old Frenchman, Alexis de Tocqueville, stepped ashore in New York City and began his fateful acquaintance with Andrew Jackson's America. For nine months he visited the cities of the Atlantic seaboard from Boston to Washington, trekked west to Detroit, and floated down the Ohio and Mississippi Rivers to New Orleans, keenly observing the American scene. Four years later he published the first volume of his monumental work *Democracy in America*. It remains to this day probably the most insightful analysis of American society ever written and provides an indispensable starting point for understanding both the nature of modern democracy and the American national character.

Tocqueville was born in the French Revolutionary era, and he witnessed the so-called July Revolution in France in 1830, which widened the French electorate. He was following closely the agitation in Britain for a broader, more democratic franchise, which culminated in the landmark Reform Bill of 1832. He also knew of the several independent democratic republics that had blossomed in Latin America as the disruptions of the Napoleonic Wars weakened Spain's imperial grip: Venezuela proclaimed its independence in 1811, Argentina in 1816, Chile in 1818, Mexico and Peru in 1821. (Brazil declared its independence from Portugal in 1822, but remained a monarchy until becoming a republic in 1889.) Those events convinced him that democracy was the irresistible wave of the future, but he was far less certain about what that democratic future might mean for human happiness, political stability, and social justice. Thus he studied America to understand Europe's—indeed the world's—fate. "In America I saw more than America," he wrote. "I sought there the image of democracy itself . . . in order to learn what we have to fear or to hope from its progress."

He announced his central insight in his book's first sentence: "Among the novel objects that attracted my attention during my stay in the United States, nothing struck me more forcibly than the general equality of condition among the people." (He acknowledged the gross inequality of slavery, but he considered slavery to be something that was "peculiar to America, not to democracy.") The "primary fact" of equality, he argued, exercised a "prodigious influence on the whole course of society."

It is easy to understand why the scale and pervasiveness of American equality made such an impression on Tocqueville. Mass democratic participation was already a well-established fact when he arrived. Almost 1.2 million voters—nearly 50 percent of the adult white male population—had cast their ballots in the election that brought Jackson to the White House in 1828. In contrast, France's July Revolution had enfranchised fewer than 200,000 propertied males, less than 1 percent of the total population, in 1830. And Britain's Reform Bill of 1832 would extend voting rights only to some 800,000 male property holders—in a country with 50 percent more people than the United States.

Tocqueville repeatedly remarked on the seething, restless energy that American equality unleashed, and he speculated on two possible futures for the United States. They might be called, respectively, the *centripetal* and *centrifugal* scenarios.

In the first scenario, Tocqueville thought that the doctrine of equality might breed a suffocating conformity that would eventually invoke the power of the state to enforce a stern and repressive consensus—the kind of "tyranny of the majority" that had worried Founders like James Madison. Tocqueville thought he saw signs that such a future was already emerging. "I know of no country in which there is so little independence of mind and real freedom of discussion as in America," he wrote.

In the second scenario, equality might foster radical *individualism*, a word that Tocqueville coined to capture the unique psychology he encountered everywhere in America. "As social conditions become more equal," he wrote, people "acquire the habit of always considering themselves as standing alone, and they are apt to imagine that their whole destiny is in their own hands." In this case, gnawing individual loneliness and even social anarchy might define America's future. "Democracy makes every man forget his ancestors," Tocqueville wrote. "It throws him back forever upon himself alone and threatens in the end to con-

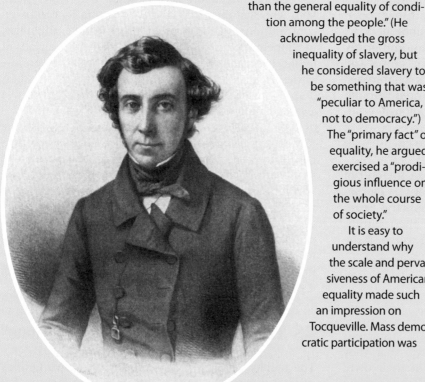

Alexis de Tocqueville (1805–1859) Granger Collection

252

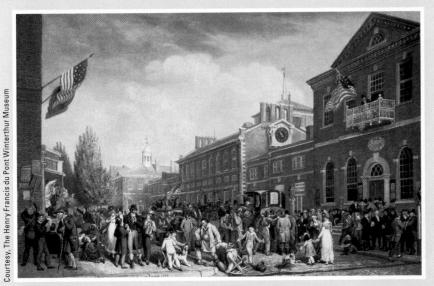

Election Day in Philadelphia, by John Lewis Krimmel, 1815 The German immigrant Krimmel recorded as early as 1815 the growing popular interest in elections that would culminate in Jacksonian democracy a decade later. Although politics was serious business, it also provided the occasion for much socializing and merriment. Even disfranchised free blacks, women, and children turned out for the festivities on election day.

fine him entirely within the solitude of his own heart."

Tocqueville noted several factors that mitigated both of those grim prospects and held American democracy in a healthy balance: the absence of hostile countries on its borders; a vigorously free press; robust voluntary associations (especially churches and political parties); and, crucially, "habits of the heart," which sustained a sense of civic belonging and responsibility. But Tocqueville raised troubling questions about whether those factors would prove durable. If not, what would the ultimate fate of democracy be?

Ironically, today the United States has markedly *lower* rates of political participation than many other countries, especially those in Europe (see Table 13.2). Can it be that America—the pioneering mass democracy that served as Tocqueville's laboratory and his window on the future—has proved to be less fertile soil for the development of democracy than the Old World societies with which he compared it in the 1830s?

TABLE 13.2 Voter Turnout by Country, 1840–2008

	1840		1900		1960	2008
	Percentage of Voting-Age Population*	Percentage of Eligible Voters[†]	Percentage of Voting-Age Population	Percentage of Eligible Voters	Percentage of Voting-Age Population	Percentage of Voting-Age Population[‡]
United States	30 (1841)	79 (1841)	34	73	63	58 (2008)
United Kingdom	4 (1842)	58 (1842)	14 (1902)	49 (1902)	77 (1958)	58 (2005)
France	1	79	33 (1898)	76 (1898)	68 (1961)	77 (2007)
Germany	—	—	26	68	87	72 (2005)
Japan	—	—	—	—	71 (1958)	67 (2005)
Mexico	—	—	—	—	52	64 (2006)

*Voting-age population includes individuals of any race and both genders. For France and the United Kingdom, individuals over the age of twenty are included in population estimates. For the United States, the voting-age population is an approximation of the total population over age twenty-one.

[†]Virtually all blacks and all women were ineligible to vote in the United States. Landholding requirements severely limited eligibility in the United Kingdom and France.

[‡]The voting age was reduced to eighteen in the United States, France, the United Kingdom, and Germany in the second half of the twentieth century. The voting age in Mexico was eighteen for both the 1958 and 2000 elections. The voting age in Japan is twenty.

(Sources: *Historical Statistics of the United States*, vol. 5; *State, Economy and Society in Western Europe, 1815–1975*; *International Historical Statistics, 1750–2005: Europe*; and *International Institute for Democracy and Electoral Assistance*.)

South Carolina Belle Sewing Palmetto Cockade The "Tariff of Abominations" of 1828 drove many people in South Carolina—the "Palmetto State"—to flirt with secession. Anti-tariff protesters wore palmetto blossoms, real or sewn from fabric, to symbolize their defiance of the federal law. The blue cockade indicated support for the ordinance of nullification. Granger Collection; Inset: Collection of McKissick Museum, University of South Carolina

expecting to be defeated, which would give a black eye to President Adams. To their surprise, the tariff passed in 1828, and Andrew Jackson inherited the political hot potato.

Southerners, as heavy consumers of manufactured goods with little manufacturing industry of their own, were hostile to tariffs. They were particularly shocked by what they regarded as the outrageous rates of the Tariff of 1828. Hotheads branded it the "Black Tariff" or the **Tariff of Abominations**. Several southern states adopted formal protests. In South Carolina flags were lowered to half-mast. "Let the *New* England beware how she imitates the *Old*," cried one eloquent South Carolinian.

Why did the South react so angrily against the tariff? Southerners believed, not illogically, that the "Yankee tariff" discriminated against them. The bustling Northeast was experiencing a boom in manufacturing, the developing West was prospering from rising property values and a multiplying population, and the energetic Southwest was expanding into virgin cotton lands. But the Old South was falling on hard times, and the tariff provided a convenient and plausible scapegoat. Southerners sold their cotton and other farm produce in a world market completely unprotected by tariffs but were forced to buy their manufactured goods in an American market heavily protected by tariffs. Protectionism protected Yankee and middle-state manufacturers. The farmers and planters of the Old South felt they were stuck with the bill.

his predecessor's pain. Tariffs protected American industry against competition from European manufactured goods, but they also drove up prices for all Americans and invited retaliatory tariffs on American agricultural exports abroad. The middle states had long been supporters of protectionist tariffs. In the 1820s influential New Englanders like Daniel Webster gave up their traditional defense of free trade to support higher tariffs, too. The wool and textile industries were booming, and forward-thinking Yankees came to believe that their future prosperity would flow from the factory rather than from the sea.

In 1824 Congress had increased the general tariff significantly, but wool manufacturers bleated for still-higher barriers. Ardent Jacksonites now played a cynical political game. They promoted a high-tariff bill,

John C. Calhoun (1782–1850), leader of South Carolina's offensive to nullify the Tariff of 1832, saw nullification as a way of preserving the Union while preventing secession of the southern states. In his mind he was still a Unionist, even if also a southern sectionalist:

❝I never use the word 'nation' in speaking of the United States. I always use the word 'union' or 'confederacy.' We are not a nation, but a union, a confederacy of equal and sovereign states.❞

During the crisis of 1832, some of his South Carolina compatriots had different ideas. Medals were struck off in honor of Calhoun, bearing the words, "First President of the Southern Confederacy."

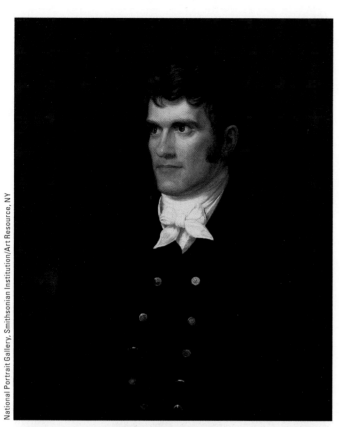

John C. Calhoun (1782–1850), by John Trumbull, 1827
Calhoun was a South Carolinian, educated at Yale. Beginning as a strong nationalist and Unionist, he reversed himself and became the ablest of the sectionalists and disunionists in defense of the South and slavery. As a foremost nullifier, he died trying to reconcile strong states' rights with a strong Union. In his last years, he advocated a Siamese-twin "dual presidency," probably unworkable, with one president for the North and one for the South. His former plantation home is now the site of Clemson University.

But much deeper issues underlay the southern outcry—in particular, a growing anxiety about possible federal interference with the institution of slavery. The congressional debate on the Missouri Compromise had kindled those anxieties, and they were further fanned by an aborted slave rebellion in Charleston in 1822, led by a free black named Denmark Vesey. The South Carolinians, still closely tied to the British West Indies, also knew full well that their slaveowning West Indian cousins were feeling the mounting pressure of British abolitionism on the London government. Abolitionism in America might similarly use the power of the government in Washington to suppress slavery in the South. If so, now was the time, and the tariff was the issue, to take a strong stand on principle against all federal encroachments on states' rights.

South Carolinians took the lead in protesting against the "Tariff of Abominations." Their legislature went so far as to publish in 1828, though without formal endorsement, a pamphlet known as *The South Carolina Exposition*. It had been secretly written by John C. Calhoun, one of the few topflight political theorists ever produced by America. (As vice president, he was forced to conceal his authorship.) *The Exposition* denounced the recent tariff as unjust and unconstitutional. Going a stride beyond the Kentucky and Virginia resolutions of 1798, it bluntly and explicitly proposed that the states should nullify the tariff—that is, they should declare it null and void within their borders.

✵ "Nullies" in South Carolina

The stage was set for a showdown. Through Jackson's first term, the nullifiers—"nullies," they were called—tried strenuously to muster the necessary two-thirds vote for nullification in the South Carolina legislature. But they were blocked by a determined minority of Unionists, scorned as "submission men." Back in Washington, Congress tipped the balance by passing the new Tariff of 1832. Though it pared away the worst "abominations" of 1828, it was still frankly protective and fell far short of meeting southern demands. Worse yet, to many southerners it had a disquieting air of permanence. The **Nullification Crisis** deepened.

South Carolina was now nerved for drastic action. Nullifiers and Unionists clashed head-on in the state election of 1832. "Nullies," defiantly wearing palmetto ribbons on their hats to mark their loyalty to the "Palmetto State," emerged with more than a two-thirds majority. The state legislature then called for a special convention. Several weeks later the delegates, meeting in Columbia, solemnly declared the existing tariff to be null and void within South Carolina. As a further act of defiance, the convention threatened to take South Carolina out of the Union if Washington attempted to collect the customs duties by force.

Such tactics might have intimidated John Quincy Adams, but Andrew Jackson was the wrong president to stare down. The cantankerous general was not a

---

At a Jefferson Day dinner on April 13, 1830, in the midst of the nullification controversy, President Andrew Jackson (1767–1845) offered a toast:

❝Our federal Union: It must be preserved.❞

John C. Calhoun rose to his feet to make a countertoast:

❝To the Union, next to our liberty, most dear.❞

diehard supporter of the tariff, but he would not permit defiance or disunion. His military instincts rasped, Jackson privately threatened to invade the state and have the nullifiers hanged. In public he was only slightly less pugnacious. He dispatched naval and military reinforcements to the Palmetto State, while quietly preparing a sizable army. He also issued a ringing proclamation against nullification, to which the governor of South Carolina, former senator Robert Y. Hayne, responded with a counterproclamation. The lines were drawn. If civil war was to be avoided, one side would have to surrender, or both would have to compromise.

Conciliatory Henry Clay of Kentucky, now in the Senate, stepped forward. An unforgiving foe of Jackson, he had no desire to see his old enemy win new laurels by crushing the Carolinians and returning with the scalp of Calhoun dangling from his belt. Although himself a supporter of tariffs, the gallant Kentuckian therefore threw his influence behind a compromise bill that would gradually reduce the Tariff of 1832 by about 10 percent over a period of eight years. By 1842 the rates would be back at the mildly protective level of 1816.*

The **compromise Tariff of 1833** finally squeezed through Congress. Debate was bitter, with most of the opposition naturally coming from protectionist New England and the middle states. Calhoun and the South favored the compromise, so it was evident that Jackson would not have to use firearms and rope. But at the same time, and partly as a face-saving device, Congress passed the **Force Bill**, known among Carolinians as the "Bloody Bill." It authorized the president to use the army and navy, if necessary, to collect federal tariff duties.

South Carolinians welcomed this opportunity to extricate themselves from a dangerously tight corner without loss of face. To the consternation of the Calhounites, no other southern states had sprung to their support, though Georgia and Virginia toyed with the idea. Moreover, an appreciable Unionist minority within South Carolina was gathering guns, organizing militias, and nailing Stars and Stripes to flagpoles. Faced with civil war within and invasion from without, the Columbia convention met again and repealed the ordinance of nullification. As a final but futile gesture of fist-shaking, it nullified the unnecessary Force Bill and adjourned.

Neither Jackson nor the "nullies" won a clear-cut victory in 1833. Clay was the true hero of the hour, hailed in Charleston and Boston alike for saving the country. Armed conflict had been avoided, but the fundamental issues had not been resolved. When next the "nullies" and the Union clashed, compromise would prove more elusive.

*For the history of tariff rates, see the Appendix.

✴ The Trail of Tears

Jackson's Democrats were committed to western expansion, but such expansion necessarily meant confrontation with the current inhabitants of the land. More than 125,000 Native Americans lived in the forests and prairies east of the Mississippi in the 1820s. Federal policy toward them varied. Beginning in the 1790s, the Washington government ostensibly recognized the tribes as separate nations and agreed to acquire land from them only through formal treaties. The Indians were shrewd and stubborn negotiators, but this availed them little when Americans routinely violated their own

William L. Clements Library, University of Michigan

Jackson the "Great Father" An anonymous cartoonist satirizes Jackson's alleged compassion for the Indians, but in fact his feelings toward Native Americans were complicated. He made ruthless war on the Creeks as a soldier, but he also adopted a Creek Indian son (who died of tuberculosis at the age of sixteen). At least in part, his motives for pursuing Indian removal stemmed from his concern that if the Indians were not removed from contact with the whites, they would face certain annihilation.

The "Trail of Tears" In the fall and winter of 1838–1839, the U.S. Army forcibly removed about fifteen thousand Cherokees, some of them in manacles, from their ancestral homelands in the southeastern United States and marched them to Indian Territory (present-day Oklahoma). Freezing weather and inadequate food supplies led to unspeakable suffering. The escorting troops refused to slow the forced march so that the ill could recover, and some four thousand Cherokees died on the 116-day journey.

covenants, erasing and redrawing treaty line after treaty line on their maps as white settlement pushed west.

Many white Americans felt respect and admiration for the Indians and believed that they could be assimilated into white society. Much energy therefore was devoted to "civilizing" and Christianizing the Indians. The Society for Propagating the Gospel Among Indians was founded in 1787, and many denominations sent missionaries into Indian villages. In 1793 Congress appropriated $20,000 for the promotion of literacy and agricultural and vocational instruction among the Indians.

Although many tribes violently resisted white encroachment, others followed the path of accommodation. The Cherokees of Georgia made especially remarkable efforts to learn the ways of the whites. They gradually abandoned their seminomadic life and adopted a system of settled agriculture and a notion of private property. Missionaries opened schools among the Cherokees, and the Indian Sequoyah devised a Cherokee alphabet. In 1808 the Cherokee National Council legislated a written legal code, and in 1827 it adopted a written constitution that provided for executive, legislative, and judicial branches of government. Some Cherokees became prosperous cotton planters and even turned to slaveholding. Nearly thirteen hundred black slaves toiled for their Native American

masters in the Cherokee nation in the 1820s. For these efforts the Cherokees—along with the Creeks, Choctaws, Chickasaws, and Seminoles—were numbered by whites among the "Five Civilized Tribes."

All this embrace of "civilization" apparently was not good enough for whites. In 1828 the Georgia legislature declared the Cherokee tribal council illegal and asserted its own jurisdiction over Indian affairs and Indian lands. The Cherokees appealed this move to the Supreme Court, which thrice upheld the rights of the Indians. But President Jackson, who clearly wanted to open Indian lands to white settlement, refused to recognize the Court's decisions. In a callous jibe at the Indians' defender, Jackson allegedly snapped, "John Marshall has made his decision; now let him enforce it."*

Feeling some obligation to rescue "this much injured race," Jackson proposed a bodily removal of the remaining eastern tribes—chiefly Cherokees, Creeks, Choctaws, Chickasaws, and Seminoles—beyond the Mississippi. Emigration was supposed to be voluntary

---

*One hundred sixty years later, in 1992, the state government of Georgia formally pardoned the two white missionaries, Samuel Austin Worcester and Elihu Butler, who figured prominently in the decision Jackson condemned. They had been convicted of living on Cherokee lands without a license from the state government of Georgia. They had served sixteen months at hard labor on a chain gang and later had accompanied the Cherokees on the "Trail of Tears" to Oklahoma.

One survivor of the Indians' forced march in 1838–1839 on the "Trail of Tears" to Indian Territory, farther west, remembered,

❝One each day, and all are gone. Looks like maybe all dead before we get to new Indian country, but always we keep marching on. Women cry and make sad wails. Children cry, and many men cry, and all look sad when friends die, but they say nothing and just put heads down and keep on toward west. . . . She [his mother] speak no more; we bury her and go on.❞

because it would be "cruel and unjust to compel the aborigines to abandon the graves of their fathers." Jackson evidently consoled himself with the belief that the Indians could preserve their native cultures in the wide-open West.

Jackson's policy led to the forced uprooting of more than 100,000 Indians. In 1830 Congress passed the **Indian Removal Act**, providing for the transplanting of all Indian tribes then resident east of the Mississippi (see Map 13.2). Ironically, the heaviest blows fell on the Five Civilized Tribes. In the ensuing decade, countless Indians died on forced marches—notably the Cherokees along the notorious **Trail of Tears**—to the newly established Indian Territory, where they were to be "permanently" free of white encroachments. The Bureau of Indian Affairs was established in 1836 to administer relations with America's original inhabitants. But as the land-hungry "palefaces" pushed west faster than anticipated, the government's guarantees went up in smoke. The "permanent" frontier lasted about fifteen years.

Suspicious of white intentions from the start, Sauk and Fox braves from Illinois and Wisconsin, ably led by Black Hawk, resisted eviction. They were bloodily crushed in the **Black Hawk War** of 1832 by regular troops, including Lieutenant Jefferson Davis of Mississippi, and by volunteers, including Captain Abraham Lincoln of Illinois.

MAP 13.2 Indian Removals, 1830–1846 © Cengage Learning

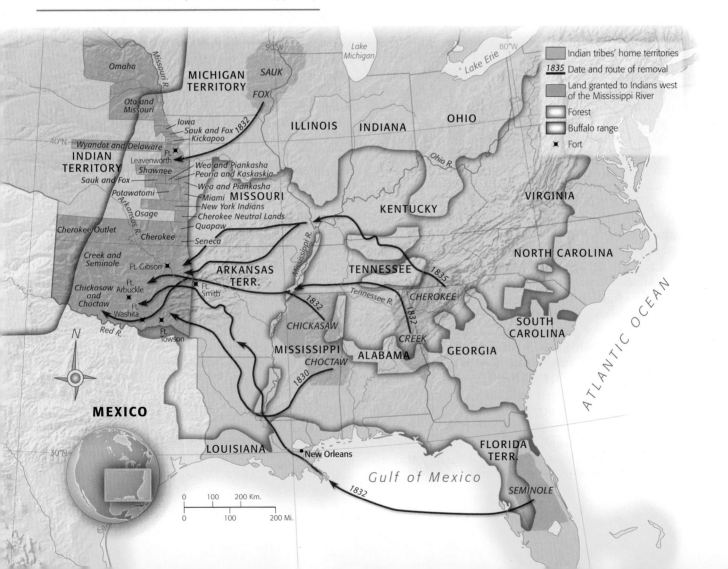

Black Hawk and His Son Whirling Thunder, by John Wesley Jarvis, 1833 Chief Black Hawk and his son are depicted here in captivity. After their surrender in the Black Hawk War of 1832, they were put on public display throughout the United States.

In Florida the Seminole Indians, joined by runaway black slaves, retreated to the swampy Everglades. For seven years (1835–1842), they waged a bitter guerrilla war that took the lives of some fifteen hundred soldiers. The spirit of the Seminoles was broken in 1837, when the American field commander treacherously seized their leader, Osceola, under a flag of truce. The war dragged on for five more years, but the Seminoles were doomed. Some fled deeper into the Everglades, where their descendants now live, but about four-fifths of them were moved to present-day Oklahoma, where several thousand of the tribe survive.

✷ The Bank War

President Jackson did not hate all banks and all businesses, but he distrusted monopolistic banking and overbig businesses, as did his followers. A man of virulent dislikes, he came to share the prejudices of his own West against the "moneyed monster" known as the Bank of the United States.

What made the bank a monster in Jackson's eyes? The national government minted gold and silver coins in the mid-nineteenth century but did not issue paper money. Paper notes were printed by private banks. Their value fluctuated with the health of the bank and the amount of money printed, giving private bankers considerable power over the nation's economy.

No bank in America had more power than the Bank of the United States. In many ways the bank acted like a branch of government. It was the principal depository for the funds of the Washington government and controlled much of the nation's gold and silver. Its notes, unlike those of many smaller banks, were stable in value. A source of credit and stability, the bank was an important and useful part of the nation's expanding economy.

But the Bank of the United States was a private institution, accountable not to the people, but to its elite circle of moneyed investors. Its president, the brilliant but arrogant Nicholas Biddle, held an immense—and to many unconstitutional—amount of power over the nation's financial affairs. Enemies of the bank dubbed him "Czar Nicolas I" and called the bank a "hydra of corruption," a serpent that grew new heads whenever old ones were cut off.

To some the bank's very existence seemed to sin against the egalitarian credo of American democracy. The conviction formed the deepest source of Jackson's opposition. The bank also won no friends in the West by foreclosing on many western farms and draining "tribute" into eastern coffers. Profit, not public service, was its first priority.

The **Bank War** erupted in 1832, when Daniel Webster and Henry Clay presented Congress with a bill to renew the Bank of the United States' charter. The charter was not set to expire until 1836, but Clay pushed for renewal four years early to make it an election issue in 1832. As Jackson's leading rival for the presidency, Clay, with fateful blindness, looked upon the bank issue as a surefire winner.

Clay's scheme was to ram a recharter bill through Congress and then send it on to the White House. If Jackson signed it, he would alienate his worshipful western followers. If he vetoed it, as seemed certain, he would presumably lose the presidency in the forthcoming election by alienating the wealthy and influential groups in the East. Clay seems not to have fully realized that the "best people" were now only a minority and that they generally feared Jackson anyhow.

The recharter bill slid through Congress on greased skids, as planned, but was killed by a scorching veto from Jackson. The "Old Hero" declared the monopolistic bank to be unconstitutional. Of course, the Supreme Court had earlier declared it constitutional in the case of *McCulloch* v. *Maryland* (1819), but Jackson acted as though he regarded the executive branch as superior to the judicial branch. The old general growled privately, "The Bank . . . is trying to kill me, but I will kill it."

Jackson's veto message reverberated with constitutional consequences. It not only squashed the bank bill

In Mother Bank's Sickroom Pro-bank men Henry Clay, Daniel Webster, and John C. Calhoun consult on the grave illness that is causing Mother Bank to cough up her deposits. While Nicholas Biddle, president of the Bank of the United States, ministers to the patient, U.S. president Andrew Jackson looks on with pleasure.

but vastly amplified the power of the presidency. All previous vetoes had rested almost exclusively on questions of constitutionality. But though Jackson invoked the Constitution in his bank-veto message, he essentially argued that he was vetoing the bill because he personally found it harmful to the nation. In effect, he was claiming

for the president alone a power equivalent to two-thirds of the votes in Congress. If the legislative and executive branches were partners in government, he implied, the president was unmistakably the senior partner.

Henry Clay's political instincts continued to fail him. Delighted with the financial fallacies of Jackson's message but blind to its political appeal, he arranged to have thousands of copies printed as a campaign document. The president's sweeping accusations may indeed have seemed demagogic to the moneyed interests of the East, but they made perfect sense to the common people. The bank issue was now thrown into the noisy arena of the presidential contest of 1832.

Banker Nicholas Biddle (1786–1844) wrote to Henry Clay (August 1, 1832) expressing his satisfaction:

“I have always deplored making the Bank a party question, but since the President will have it so, he must pay the penalty of his own rashness. As to the veto message, I am delighted with it. It has all the fury of a chained panther biting the bars of his cage. It is really a manifesto of anarchy . . . and my hope is that it will contribute to relieve the country of the domination of these miserable [Jackson] people.**”**

✴ “Old Hickory” Wallops Clay in 1832

Clay and Jackson were the chief gladiators in the looming electoral combat. The grizzled old general, who had earlier favored one term for a president and rotation in office, was easily persuaded by his cronies not to rotate himself out of office. Presidential power is a heady brew and can be habit-forming.

The ensuing campaign was raucous. The "Old Hero's" adherents again raised the hickory pole and bellowed, "Jackson Forever: Go the Whole Hog." Admirers of Clay shouted, "Freedom and Clay," while his detractors harped on his dueling, gambling, cockfighting, and fast living.

Novel features made the campaign of 1832 especially memorable. For the first time, a third party entered the field—the newborn **Anti-Masonic party**, which opposed the influence and fearsome secrecy of the Masonic order. Energized by the mysterious disappearance and probable murder in 1826 of a New Yorker who was threatening to expose the secret rituals of the Masons, the Anti-Masonic party quickly became a potent political force in New York and spread its influence throughout the middle Atlantic and New England states. The Anti-Masons appealed to long-standing American suspicions of secret societies, which they condemned as citadels of privilege and monopoly—a

note that harmonized with the democratic chorus of the Jacksonians. But since Jackson himself was a Mason and publicly gloried in his membership, the Anti-Masonic party was also an anti-Jackson party. The Anti-Masons also attracted support from many evangelical Protestant groups seeking to use political power to effect moral and religious reforms, such as prohibiting mail delivery on Sunday and otherwise keeping the Sabbath holy. This moral busybodiness was anathema to the Jacksonians, who were generally opposed to all government meddling in social and economic life.

A further novelty of the presidential contest in 1832 was the calling of national nominating conventions (three of them) to name candidates. The Anti-Masons and a group of National Republicans added still another innovation when they adopted formal platforms, publicizing their positions on the issues.

Henry Clay and his overconfident National Republicans enjoyed impressive advantages. Ample funds flowed into their campaign chest, including $50,000 in "life insurance" from the Bank of the United States.

Fistfight Between Old Hickory and Bully Nick, 1834 An aged President Andrew Jackson faces off against the bank's director, aristocratic Nicholas Biddle. Comically presented as sparring pugilists undressed in the style of the popular sport, the two are assisted by their seconds, Daniel Webster and Henry Clay for Biddle, Vice President Martin Van Buren for Jackson.

Most of the newspaper editors, some of them "bought" with Biddle's bank loans, dipped their pens in acid when they wrote of Jackson.

Yet Jackson, idol of the masses, easily defeated the big-money Kentuckian. A Jacksonian wave again swept over the West and South, surged into Pennsylvania and New York, and even washed into rock-ribbed New England. The popular vote stood at 687,502 to 530,189 for Jackson; the electoral count was a lopsided 219 to 49.

✯ Burying Biddle's Bank

Its charter denied, the Bank of the United States was due to expire in 1836. But Jackson was not one to let the financial octopus die in peace. He was convinced that he now had a mandate from the voters for its extermination, and he feared that the slippery Biddle might try to manipulate the bank (as he did) so as to force its recharter. Jackson therefore decided in 1833 to bury the bank for good by removing federal deposits from its vaults. He proposed depositing no more funds with Biddle and gradually shrinking existing deposits by using them to defray the day-to-day expenses of the government. By slowly siphoning off the government's funds, he would bleed the bank dry and ensure its demise.

Removing the deposits involved nasty complications. Even the president's closest advisers opposed this seemingly unnecessary, possibly unconstitutional, and certainly vindictive policy. Jackson, his dander up, was forced to reshuffle his cabinet twice before he could find a secretary of the Treasury who would bend to his iron will. A desperate Biddle called in his bank's loans, evidently hoping to illustrate the bank's importance by producing a minor financial crisis. A number of wobblier banks were driven to the wall by "Biddle's Panic," but Jackson's resolution was firm. If anything, the vengeful conduct of the dying "monster" seemed to justify the earlier accusations of its adversaries.

But the death of the Bank of the United States left a financial vacuum in the American economy and kicked off a lurching cycle of booms and busts. Surplus federal funds were placed in several dozen state institutions—the so-called **pet banks**, chosen for their pro-Jackson sympathies. Without a sober central bank in control, the pet banks and smaller "wildcat" banks—fly-by-night operations that often consisted of little more than a few chairs and a suitcase full of printed notes—flooded the country with paper money.

Jackson tried to rein in the runaway economy in 1836, the year Biddle's bank breathed its last. "Wildcat" currency had become so unreliable, especially in the West, that Jackson authorized the Treasury to issue a **Specie Circular**—a decree that required all public lands to be purchased with "hard," or metallic, money. This drastic step slammed the brakes on the speculative boom, a neck-snapping change of direction that contributed to a financial panic and crash in 1837.

But by then Jackson had retired to his Nashville home, hailed as the hero of his age. His successor would have to deal with the damage.

✯ The Birth of the Whigs

New political parties were gelling as the 1830s lengthened. As early as 1828, the Democratic-Republicans of Jackson had unashamedly adopted the once-tainted name "Democrats." Jackson's opponents, fuming at his ironfisted exercise of presidential power, condemned him as "King Andrew I" and began to coalesce as the Whigs—a name deliberately chosen to recollect eighteenth-century British and Revolutionary American opposition to the monarchy.

The Whig party contained so many diverse elements that it was mocked at first as "an organized incompatibility." Hatred of Jackson and his "executive usurpation" was its only apparent cement in its formative days. The Whigs first emerged as an identifiable group in the Senate, where Clay, Webster, and Calhoun joined forces in 1834 to pass a motion censuring Jackson for his single-handed removal of federal deposits from the Bank of the United States. Thereafter, the Whigs rapidly evolved into a potent national political force by attracting other groups alienated by Jackson: supporters of Clay's American System, southern states' righters offended by Jackson's stand on nullification, the larger northern industrialists and merchants, and eventually many of the evangelical Protestants associated with the Anti-Masonic party.

Whigs thought of themselves as conservatives, yet they were progressive in their support of active government programs and reforms. Instead of boundless territorial acquisition, they called for internal improvements like canals, railroads, and telegraph lines, and they supported institutions like prisons, asylums, and public schools. The Whigs welcomed the market economy, drawing support from manufacturers in the North, planters in the South, and merchants and bankers in all sections. But they were not simply a party of wealthy fat cats, however dearly the Democrats wanted to paint them as such. By absorbing the Anti-Masonic party, the Whigs blunted much of the Democratic appeal to the common man. The egalitarian anti-Masons portrayed Jackson, and particularly his New York successor Martin Van Buren, as imperious aristocrats. This turned Jacksonian rhetoric on its head: now the Whigs claimed to be the defenders of the common

Satiric Bank Note, 1837

Political humor can take more forms than the commonly seen caustic cartoon. Occasionally historians stumble upon other examples, such as this fake bank note. A jibe at Andrew Jackson's money policies, it appeared in New York in 1837 after Jackson's insistence on shutting down the Bank of the United States resulted in the suspension of specie payments. The clever creator of this satiric bank note for six cents left little doubt about the worthlessness of the note or Jackson's responsibility for it. The six cents payable by the "Humbug Glory Bank"—whose symbols were a donkey and a "Hickory Leaf" (for Old Hickory)—were redeemable "in mint drops or Glory at cost." The bank's cashier was "Cunning Reuben," possibly an anti-Semitic allusion to usurious Jewish bankers. Can you identify other ways in which this document takes aim at Jackson's banking policies? What symbols did the note's creator assume the public would comprehend?

Collection of the New York Historical Society

man and declared the Democrats the party of cronyism and corruption.

The Election of 1836

The smooth-tongued and keen-witted vice president, Martin Van Buren of New York, was Jackson's choice for "appointment" as his successor in 1836. The hollow-cheeked Jackson, now nearing seventy, was too old and ailing to consider a third term. But he was not loath to try to serve a third term through Van Buren, something of a "yes man." Leaving nothing to chance, Jackson carefully rigged the nominating convention and rammed his favorite down the throats of the delegates. Van Buren was supported by the Jacksonites without wild enthusiasm, even though he had promised "to tread generally" in the military-booted footsteps of his predecessor.

As the election neared, the still-ramshackle organization of the Whigs showed in their inability to nominate a single presidential candidate. Their long-shot strategy was instead to run several prominent "favorite sons," each with a different regional appeal, and hope to scatter the vote so that no candidate would win a majority. The deadlock would then have to be broken by the House of Representatives, where the Whigs might have a chance. With Henry Clay rudely elbowed aside, the leading Whig "favorite son" was heavy-jawed General William Henry Harrison of Ohio, hero of the Battle of Tippecanoe (see p. 220). The fine-spun schemes of the Whigs availed nothing, however. Van Buren, the dapper "Little Magician," squirmed into office by the close popular vote of 765,483 to 739,795, but by the comfortable margin of 170 to 124 votes (for all the Whigs combined) in the Electoral College.

Big Woes for the "Little Magician"

Martin Van Buren, eighth president, was the first to be born under the American flag. Short and slender, bland and bald, the adroit little New Yorker has been described as "a first-class second-rate man." An accomplished strategist and spoilsman—"the wizard of Albany"—he was also a statesman of wide experience in both legislative and administrative life. In intelligence, education, and training, he was above the average of the presidents since Jackson. The myth of his mediocrity sprouted mostly from a series of misfortunes over which he had no control.

From the outset the new president labored under severe handicaps. As a machine-made candidate, he incurred the resentment of many Democrats—those who objected to having a "bastard politician" smuggled into office beneath the tails of the old general's military coat. Jackson, the master showman, had been a dynamic type of executive whose administration had resounded with furious quarrels and cracked heads. Mild-mannered Martin Van Buren seemed to rattle about in the military boots of his testy predecessor. The people felt let down. Inheriting Andrew Jackson's mantle without his popularity, Van Buren also inherited the ex-president's numerous and vengeful enemies.

Van Buren's four years overflowed with toil and trouble. A pair of short-lived rebellions in Canada in 1837, mostly over political reform but aggravated by unregulated immigration from the United States, stirred up ugly incidents along the northern frontier and threatened to trigger war with Britain. The president's attempt to play a neutral game led to the wail "Woe to Martin Van Buren!" The antislavery agitators in the North were also in full cry. Among other grievances, they were condemning the prospective annexation of Texas (see p. 268).

Worst of all, Jackson bequeathed to Van Buren the makings of a searing depression. Much of Van Buren's energy had to be devoted to the purely negative task of battling the panic, and there were not enough rabbits in the "Little Magician's" tall silk hat. Hard times ordinarily blight the reputation of a president, and Van Buren was no exception.

✵ Depression Doldrums and the Independent Treasury

The **panic of 1837** was a symptom of the financial sickness of the times. Its basic cause was rampant speculation prompted by a mania of get-rich-quickism. Gamblers in western lands were doing a "land-office business" on borrowed capital, much of it in the shaky currency of "wildcat banks." The speculative craze spread to canals, roads, railroads, and slaves.

But speculation alone did not cause the crash. Jacksonian finance, including the Bank War and the Specie Circular, gave an additional jolt to an already teetering

The Long Bill Americans who bought on credit, confident that they could make their payments later, were caught off guard by the panic of 1837. Customers like the one shown here found themselves confronted with a "long bill" that they could not pay, particularly when the banks holding their savings collapsed.

Cincinnati Museum Center—Cincinnati Historical Society Library

structure. Failures of wheat crops, ravaged by the Hessian fly, deepened the distress. Grain prices were forced so high that mobs in New York City, three weeks before Van Buren took the oath, stormed warehouses and broke open flour barrels. The panic really began before Jackson left office, but its full fury burst about Van Buren's bewildered head.

Financial stringency abroad likewise endangered America's economic house of cards. Late in 1836 the failure of two prominent British banks created tremors, and these in turn caused British investors to call in foreign loans. The resulting pinch in the United States, combined with other setbacks, heralded the beginning of the panic. Europe's economic distresses have often become America's distresses, for every major American financial panic has been affected by conditions overseas.

Hardship was acute and widespread. American banks collapsed by the hundreds, including some "pet banks," which carried down with them several million in government funds. Commodity prices drooped, sales of public lands fell off, and customs revenues dried to a rivulet. Factories closed their doors, and unemployed workers milled in the streets.

The Whigs came forward with proposals for active government remedies for the economy's ills. They called for the expansion of bank credit, higher tariffs, and subsidies for internal improvements. But Van Buren, shackled by the Jacksonian philosophy of keeping the government's paws off the economy, spurned all such ideas.

The beleaguered Van Buren tried to apply vintage Jacksonian medicine to the ailing economy through his controversial "Divorce Bill." Convinced that some of the financial fever was fed by the injection of federal funds into private banks, he championed the principle of "divorcing" the government from banking altogether. By establishing a so-called independent treasury, the government could lock its surplus money in

vaults in several of the larger cities. Government funds would thus be safe, but they would also be denied to the banking system as reserves, thereby shriveling available credit resources.

Van Buren's "divorce" scheme was never highly popular. His fellow Democrats, many of whom longed for the risky but lush days of the "pet banks," supported it only lukewarmly. The Whigs condemned it, primarily because it squelched their hopes for a revived Bank of the United States. After a prolonged struggle, the Independent Treasury Bill passed Congress in 1840. Repealed the next year by the victorious Whigs, the scheme was reenacted by the triumphant Democrats in 1846 and then continued until the Republicans instituted a network of national banks during the Civil War.

✴ Gone to Texas

Americans, greedy for land, continued to covet the vast expanse of Texas, which the United States had abandoned to Spain when acquiring Florida in 1819. The Spanish authorities wanted to populate this virtually unpeopled area, but before they could carry through their contemplated plans, the Mexicans won their independence, in 1821. A new regime in Mexico City thereupon concluded arrangements in 1823 for granting a huge tract of land to Stephen Austin, with the understanding that he would bring into Texas three hundred American families. Immigrants were to be of the established Roman Catholic faith and upon settlement were to become properly Mexicanized.

These two stipulations were largely ignored. Hardy Texas pioneers remained Americans at heart, resenting the trammels imposed by a "foreign" government. They were especially annoyed by the presence of Mexican soldiers, many of whom were ragged ex-convicts.

Energetic and prolific, Texan Americans numbered about thirty thousand by 1835 (see "Makers of America: Mexican or Texican?" pp. 268–269). Most of them were law-abiding, God-fearing people, but some of them had left the "States" only one or two jumps ahead of the sheriff. "G.T.T." (Gone to Texas) became current descriptive slang. Among the adventurers were Davy Crockett, the famous rifleman, and Jim Bowie, the presumed inventor of the murderous knife that bears his name. Bowie's blade was widely known in the Southwest as the "genuine Arkansas toothpick." A distinguished latecomer and leader was an ex-governor of Tennessee, Sam Houston. His life had been temporarily shattered in 1829 when his bride of a few weeks left him and he took up transient residence with the Arkansas Indians, who dubbed him "Big Drunk." He subsequently took the pledge of temperance.

Samuel ("Sam") Houston (1793–1863) After a promising career in Tennessee as a soldier, lawyer, congressman, and governor, Houston became the chief leader and hero of the Texas rebels. Elected to the U.S. Senate and the governorship of Texas, he was forced into retirement when his love for the Union caused him to spurn the Confederacy in the Civil War.

The pioneer individualists who came to Texas were not easy to push around. Friction rapidly increased between Mexicans and Texans over issues such as slavery, immigration, and local rights. Slavery was a particularly touchy topic. Mexico emancipated its slaves in 1830 and prohibited the further importation of slaves into Texas, as well as further colonization by troublesome Americans. The Texans refused to honor these decrees. They kept their slaves in bondage, and new American settlers kept bringing more slaves into Texas. When Stephen Austin went to Mexico City in 1833 to negotiate these differences with the Mexican government, the dictator Santa Anna clapped him in jail for eight months. The explosion finally came in 1835, when Santa Anna wiped out all local rights and started to raise an army to suppress the upstart Texans.

✦ The Lone Star Rebellion

Early in 1836 the Texans declared their independence, unfurled their Lone Star flag, and named Sam Houston commander in chief. Santa Anna, at the head of about six thousand men, swept ferociously into Texas. Trapping a band of nearly two hundred pugnacious Texans at the **Alamo** in San Antonio, he wiped them out to a man after a thirteen-day siege. The Texans' commander, Colonel W. B. Travis, had declared, "I shall never surrender nor retreat. . . . Victory or Death." A short time later, a band of about four hundred surrounded and defeated American volunteers, having thrown down their arms at **Goliad**, were butchered as "pirates." All these operations further delayed the Mexican advance and galvanized American opposition.

"Come and Take It" This mosaic, done in 1959 by Bert Rees of Austin, Texas, shows one of the defenders' cannon, as well as their legendary battle flag of defiance.

Friends of the Governor's Mansion

The Battle of the Alamo, 1836
Long celebrated in song and story, the battle was a military defeat but a spiritual victory for the Texas rebels, whose annihilation to a man inspired others and led eventually to independence from Mexico.

Slain heroes like Jim Bowie and Davy Crockett, well-known in life, became legendary in death. Texan war cries—"Remember the Alamo!" "Remember Goliad!" and "Death to Santa Anna!"—swept up into the United States. Scores of vengeful Americans seized their rifles and rushed to the aid of relatives, friends, and compatriots.

General Sam Houston's small army retreated to the east, luring Santa Anna to **San Jacinto**, near the site of the city that now bears Houston's name (see Map 13.3). The Mexicans numbered about thirteen hundred men, the Texans about nine hundred. Suddenly, on April 21, 1836, Houston turned. Taking full advantage of the Mexican siesta, the Texans wiped out the pursuing force and captured Santa Anna, who was found cowering in the tall grass near the battlefield. Confronted with thirsty bowie knives, the quaking dictator was speedily induced to sign two treaties. By their terms he agreed to withdraw Mexican troops and to recognize the Rio Grande as the extreme southwestern boundary of Texas. When released, he repudiated the agreement as illegal because it had been extorted under duress.

MAP 13.3 The Texas Revolution, 1836   General Houston's strategy was to retreat and use defense in depth. His line of supply from the United States was shortened as Santa Anna's lengthened. The Mexicans were forced to bring up supplies by land because the Texas navy controlled the sea. This force consisted of only four small ships, but it was big enough to do the job. © Cengage Learning

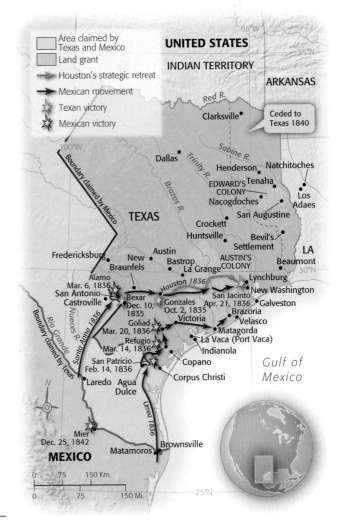

*M*oses Austin, born a Connecticut Yankee in 1761, was determined to be Spanish—if that's what it took to acquire cheap land and freedom from pesky laws. In 1798 he tramped into untracked Missouri, still part of Spanish Louisiana, and pledged his allegiance to the king of Spain. He was not pleased when the Louisiana Purchase of 1803 restored him to American citizenship. In 1820, with his old Spanish passport in his saddlebag, he rode into Spanish Texas and asked for permission to establish a colony of three hundred families.

Austin's request posed a dilemma for the Texas governor. The Spanish authorities had repeatedly stamped out the bands of American horse thieves and squatters who periodically splashed across the Red and Sabine Rivers from the United States into Spanish territory. Yet the Spanish had lured only some three thousand of their own settlers into Texas during their three centuries of rule. If the land were ever to be wrestled from the Indians and "civilized," maybe Austin's plan could do it. Hoping that this band of the "right sort" of Americans might prevent the further encroachment of the buckskinned border ruffians, the governor reluctantly agreed to Austin's proposal.

Upon Moses Austin's death in 1821, the task of realizing his dream fell to his twenty-seven-year-old son, Stephen. "I bid an everlasting farewell to my native country," Stephen Austin said, and he crossed into Texas on July 15, 1821, "determined to fulfill rigidly all the duties and obligations of a Mexican citizen." (Mexico declared its independence from Spain early in 1821 and finalized its agreement with Austin in 1823.) Soon he learned fluent Spanish and was signing his name as "Don Estévan F. Austin." In his new colony between the Brazos and Colorado Rivers, he allowed "no drunkard, no gambler, no profane swearer, no idler"—and sternly enforced these rules. Not only did he banish several families as "undesirables," but he ordered the public flogging of unwanted interlopers.

Austin fell just three families short of recruiting the three hundred households that his father had contracted to bring to Texas. The original settlers were still dubbed the "Old Three Hundred," the Texas equivalent of New England's Mayflower Pilgrims or the "First Families of Virginia." Mostly Scots-Irish southerners from the trans-Appalachian frontier, the Old Three Hundred were cultured folk by frontier standards; all but four of them were literate. Other settlers followed, from Europe as well as America. Within ten years the "Anglos" (many of them French and German) outnumbered the Mexican residents, or *tejanos*, ten to one and soon evolved a distinctive "Texican" culture. The wide-ranging horse patrols organized to attack Indian camps became the Texas Rangers; Samuel Maverick, whose unbranded calves roamed the limitless prairies, left his surname as a label for rebellious loners who refused to run with the herd; and Jared Groce, an Alabama planter whose caravan of fifty covered wagons and one hundred slaves arrived in 1822, etched the original image of the larger-than-life, big-time Texas operator.

The original Anglo-Texans brought with them the old Scots-Irish frontiersmen's hostility to authority. They ignored Mexican laws and officials, including restrictions against owning or importing slaves. When the Mexican government tried to impose its will on the Anglo-Texans in the 1830s, they took up their guns. Like the American revolutionaries of the 1770s, who at first demanded only the rights of Englishmen, the

José Antonio Navarro (1795–1871) A native of San Antonio, Navarro signed the Texas declaration of independence in 1836.

Texas State Library and Archives Commission

These events put the U.S. government in a sticky situation. The Texans, though courageous, could hardly have won their independence without the help in men and supplies from their American cousins. The Washington government, as the Mexicans bitterly complained, had a solemn obligation under international law to enforce its leaky neutrality statutes. But American public opinion, overwhelmingly favorable to the Texans, openly nullified the existing legislation. The federal authorities were powerless to act, and on the day before he left office in 1837, President Jackson even extended the right hand of recognition to the Lone Star Republic, led by his old comrade-in-arms against the Indians, Sam Houston.

West Side Main Plaza, San Antonio, Texas, by William G. M. Samuel, 1849 (detail)
Even after annexation, Texas retained a strong Spanish Mexican flavor, as the architecture and activities here illustrate.

Texans began by asking simply for Mexican recognition of their rights as guaranteed by the Mexican constitution of 1824. But bloodshed at the Alamo in 1836, like that at Lexington and Concord in 1775, transformed protest into rebellion.

Texas lay—and still lies—along the frontier where Hispanic and Anglo-American cultures met, mingled, and clashed. In part the Texas Revolution was a contest between those two cultures. But it was also a contest about philosophies of government, pitting liberal frontier ideals of freedom against the conservative concept of centralized control. Stephen Austin sincerely tried to "Mexicanize" himself and his followers—until the Mexican government grew too arbitrary and authoritarian. And not all the Texas revolutionaries were "Anglos." Many *tejanos* fought for Texas independence—seven perished defending the Alamo. Among the fifty-nine signers of the Texas declaration of independence were several Hispanics, including the *tejanos* José Antonio Navarro and Francisco Ruiz. Lorenzo de Zavala, an ardent Mexican liberal who had long resisted the centralizing tendencies of Mexico's dominant political party, was designated vice president of the Texas republic's interim government in 1836. Like the Austins, these *tejanos* and Mexicans had sought in Texas an escape from overbearing governmental authority. Their role in the revolution underscores the fact that the uprising was a struggle between defenders of local rights and the agents of central authority as much as it was a fight between Anglo and Mexican cultures.

Many Texans wanted not just recognition of their independence but outright union with the United States. What nation in its right mind, they reasoned, would refuse so lavish a dowry? The radiant Texas bride, officially petitioning for annexation in 1837, presented herself for marriage. But the expectant groom, Uncle Sam, was jerked back by the black hand of the slavery issue. Antislavery crusaders in the North were opposing annexation with increasing vehemence. They contended that the whole scheme was merely a conspiracy cooked up by the southern "slavocracy" to bring new slave pens into the Union.

At first glance a "slavery plot" charge seemed plausible. Most of the early settlers in Texas, as well as

American volunteers during the revolution, had come from the states of the South and Southwest. But scholars have concluded that the settlement of Texas was merely the normal and inexorable march of the westward movement. Most of the immigrants came from the South and Southwest simply because these states were closer. The explanation was proximity rather than conspiracy. Yet the fact remained that many Texans were slaveholders, and admitting Texas to the Union inescapably meant enlarging American slavery.

✳ Log Cabins and Hard Cider of 1840

Martin Van Buren was renominated by the Democrats in 1840, albeit without terrific enthusiasm. The party had no acceptable alternative to what the Whigs called "Martin Van Ruin."

The Whigs, hungering for the spoils of office, scented victory in the breeze. Pangs of the panic were still being felt, and voters blamed their woes on the party in power. Learning from their mistake in 1836, the Whigs united behind one candidate, Ohio's William Henry Harrison. He was not their ablest statesman—that would have been Daniel Webster or Henry Clay—but he was believed to be their ablest vote-getter.

The aging hero, nearly sixty-eight when the campaign ended, was known for his successes against Indians and the British at the Battles of Tippecanoe (1811) and the Thames (1813). Harrison's views on current issues were only vaguely known. "Old Tippecanoe" was nominated primarily because he was issueless and enemyless—a tested recipe for electoral success that still appeals today. John Tyler of Virginia, an afterthought, was selected as his vice-presidential running mate.

The Whigs, eager to avoid offense, published no official platform, hoping to sweep their hero into office with a frothy huzza-for-Harrison campaign reminiscent of Jackson's triumph in 1828. A dull-witted Democratic editor played directly into Whig hands. Stupidly insulting the West, he lampooned Harrison as an impoverished old farmer who should be content with a pension, a log cabin, and a barrel of hard cider—the poor westerner's champagne. Whigs gleefully adopted honest hard cider and the sturdy log cabin as symbols of their campaign. Harrisonites portrayed their hero as the poor "Farmer of North Bend," who had been

William Henry Harrison Home, Grouseland, Indiana

Harrison and Tyler Campaign Kerchief, 1840 As the two-party system came into its own by 1840, presidential elections became more public contests. Lively campaigns used banners, posters, flags, and other paraphernalia like this kerchief to whip up voters' support. Log Cabin Whigs took particular interest in attracting female supporters. They gathered up women at campaign stops, supplied them with Harrison kerchiefs for waving at key moments, and included them conspicuously in events. Although women could not vote, they had moral influence on their menfolk that the Whigs hoped to tap.

called from his cabin and his plow to drive corrupt Jackson spoilsmen from the "presidential palace." They denounced Van Buren as a supercilious aristocrat, a simpering dandy who wore corsets and ate French food from golden plates. As a jeering Whig campaign song proclaimed,

> *Old Tip, he wears a homespun shirt, He has no ruffled shirt, wirt, wirt.*
> *But Matt, he has the golden plate, and he's a little squirt, wirt, wirt.*

The Whig campaign was a masterpiece of inane hoopla. Log cabins were dished up in every conceivable form. Bawling Whigs, stimulated by fortified cider, rolled huge inflated balls from village to village and

Martin Van Buren Gags on Hard Cider   This 1840 "pull-card" shows Van Buren on the left as an aristocratic fop sipping champagne. When the right-hand card was pulled out, Van Buren's face soured as he discovered that his "champagne" was actually hard cider. The cartoonist clearly sympathized with Van Buren's opponent in the 1840 presidential election, William Henry Harrison, who waged the famous "log cabin and hard cider" campaign.

state to state—balls that represented the snowballing majority for "Tippecanoe, and Tyler too." In truth, Harrison was not lowborn, but from one of the FFVs ("First Families of Virginia"). He was not poverty-stricken. He did not live in a one-room log cabin, but rather in a sixteen-room mansion on a three-thousand-acre farm. He did not swill down gallons of hard cider (he evidently preferred whiskey). And he did not plow his fields with his own "huge paws." But such details had not mattered when General Jackson rode to victory, and they did not matter now.

The Democrats who hurrahed Jackson into the White House in 1828 now discovered to their chagrin that whooping it up for a backwoods westerner was a game two could play. Harrison won by the surprisingly close margin of 1,274,624 to 1,127,781 popular votes, but by an overwhelming electoral margin of 234 to 60. With hardly a real issue debated, though with hard times blighting the incumbent's fortunes, Van Buren was washed out of Washington on a wave of apple juice. The hard-ciderites had apparently received a mandate to tear down the White House and erect a log cabin.

Although campaigners in 1840 did their best to bury substantive issues beneath the ballyhoo, voters actually faced a stark choice between two economic visions of how to cope with the nation's first major depression.

Whigs sought to expand and stimulate the economy, while Democrats favored retrenchment and an end to high-flying banks and aggressive corporations.

★ Politics for the People

The election of 1840 conclusively demonstrated two major changes in American politics since the Era of Good Feelings. The first was the triumph of a populist democratic style. Democracy had been something of a taint in the days of the lordly Federalists. Martha Washington, the first First Lady, was shocked after a presidential reception to find a greasy smear on the wallpaper—left there, she was sure, by an uninvited "filthy democrat."

But by the 1840s, aristocracy was the taint, and democracy was respectable. Politicians were now forced to curry favor with the voting masses. Lucky indeed was the aspiring office seeker who could boast of birth in a log cabin. In 1840 Daniel Webster publicly apologized for not being able to claim so humble a birthplace, though he quickly added that his brothers could. Hopelessly handicapped was the candidate who appeared to be too clean, too well dressed, too grammatical, too highbrowishly intellectual. In truth, most

The County Election, by George Caleb Bingham, 1851–1852
The artist here gently satirizes the drinking and wheeling and dealing that sometimes marred the electoral process in the boisterous age of Jacksonian politics.

Saint Louis Art Museum, Gift of Bank of America

high political offices continued to be filled by "leading citizens." But now these wealthy and prominent men had to forsake all social pretensions and cultivate the common touch if they hoped to win elections.

Snobbish bigwigs, unhappy over the change, sneered at "coonskin congressmen" and at the newly enfranchised "bipeds of the forest." To them the tyranny of "King Numbers" was no less offensive than that of King George. But these critics protested in vain. The common man was at last moving to the center of the national political stage: the sturdy American who donned coarse trousers rather than buff breeches, who sported a coonskin cap rather than a silk top hat, and who wore no man's collar, often not even one of his own. Instead of the old divine right of kings, America was now bowing to the divine right of the people.

✴ The Two-Party System

The second dramatic change resulting from the 1840 election was the formation of a vigorous and durable two-party system. The Jeffersonians of an earlier day had been so successful in absorbing the programs of their Federalist opponents that a full-blown two-party system had never truly emerged in the subsequent Era of Good Feelings. The idea had prevailed that parties of any sort smacked of conspiracy and "faction" and were injurious to the health of the body politic in a virtuous republic. By 1840 political parties had fully come of age, a lasting legacy of Andrew Jackson's and Martin Van Buren's tenaciousness.

Both national parties, the Democrats and the Whigs, grew out of the rich soil of Jeffersonian republicanism, and each laid claim to different aspects of the republican inheritance. Jacksonian Democrats glorified the liberty of the individual and were fiercely on guard against the inroads of "privilege" into government.

Whigs trumpeted the natural harmony of society and the value of community, and were willing to use government to realize their objectives. Whigs also berated those leaders—and they considered Jackson to be one—whose appeals to self-interest fostered conflict among individuals, classes, or sections.

Democrats clung to states' rights and federal restraint in social and economic affairs as their basic doctrines. Whigs tended to favor a renewed national bank, protective tariffs, internal improvements, public schools, and, increasingly, moral reforms such as the prohibition of liquor and eventually the abolition of slavery.

The two parties were thus separated by real differences of philosophy and policy. But they also had much in common. Both were mass-based, "catchall" parties that tried deliberately to mobilize as many

President Andrew Jackson advised a supporter in 1835 on how to tell the difference between Democrats and "Whigs, nullies, and blue-light federalists." In doing so, he neatly summarized the Jacksonian philosophy:

❝ The people ought to inquire [of political candidates]—are you opposed to a national bank; are you in favor of a strict construction of the Federal and State Constitutions; are you in favor of rotation in office; do you subscribe to the republican rule that the people are the sovereign power, the officers their agents, and that upon all national or general subjects, as well as local, they have a right to instruct their agents and representatives, and they are bound to obey or resign; in short, are they true Republicans agreeable to the true Jeffersonian creed?❞

voters as possible for their cause. Although it is true that Democrats tended to be more humble folk and Whigs more prosperous, both parties nevertheless commanded the loyalties of all kinds of Americans, from all social classes and in all sections. The social diversity of the two parties had important implications. It fostered horse-trading compromises *within* each party

that prevented either from assuming extreme or radical positions. By the same token, the geographical diversity of the two parties retarded the emergence of purely sectional political parties—temporarily suppressing, through compromise, the ultimately uncompromisable issue of slavery. When the two-party system began to creak in the 1850s, the Union was mortally imperiled.

Varying Viewpoints
What Was Jacksonian Democracy?

Aristocratic, eastern-born historians of the nineteenth century damned Jackson as a backwoods barbarian. They criticized Jacksonianism as democracy run riot—an irresponsible, ill-bred outburst that overturned the electoral system and wrecked the national financial structure.

In the late nineteenth and early twentieth centuries, however, another generation of historians came to the fore, many of whom had grown up in the Midwest and rejected the elitist views of their predecessors. Frederick Jackson Turner and his disciples saw the western frontier as the fount of democratic virtue, and they hailed Jackson as a true hero sprung from the forests of the West to protect the will of the people against the moneyed interests, akin to the progressive reformers of their own day. In his famous 1893 essay, "The Significance of the Frontier in American History," Turner argued that the United States owed the survival of its democratic tradition to the rise of the West, not to its roots in the more conservative, aristocratic East.

When Arthur M. Schlesinger, Jr., published *The Age of Jackson* in 1945, however, the debate on Jacksonianism shifted dramatically. Although he shared the Turnerians' admiration for Jackson the democrat, Schlesinger cast the Jacksonian era not as a sectional conflict, but as a class conflict between poor farmers, laborers, and noncapitalists on the one hand, and the business community—epitomized by the Second Bank of the United States—on the other. In Schlesinger's eyes the Jacksonians justifiably attacked the bank as an institution dangerously independent of democratic oversight. The political mobilization of the urban working classes in support of Jackson particularly attracted Schlesinger's interest.

Soon after Schlesinger's book appeared, the discussion again shifted ground and entirely new interpretations of Jacksonianism emerged. Richard Hofstadter argued in *The American Political Tradition and the Men Who Made It* (1948) that Jacksonian democracy was not a rejection of capitalism, as Schlesinger insisted, but rather the effort of aspiring entrepreneurs to secure laissez-faire policies that would serve their own interests against their entrenched, and monopolistic, eastern competitors. In *The Jacksonian Persuasion* (1957), Marvin Meyers portrayed the Jacksonians as conservative

capitalists, torn between fierce commercial ambitions and a desire to cling to the virtues of the agrarian past. In an effort to resolve this contradiction, he argued, they lashed out at scapegoats like the national bank, blaming it for the very changes their own economic energies had unleashed. Lee Benson contended in *The Concept of Jacksonian Democracy* (1961) that the political conflicts of the Jacksonian era did not correspond so much to class divisions as to different ethnic and religious splits within American society. Using new quantitative methods of analysis, Benson found no consistent demarcations—in class, occupation, or region—between the Jacksonians and their rivals. Local and cultural issues such as temperance and religion were far more influential in shaping political life than the national financial questions analyzed by previous historians.

In the 1980s Sean Wilentz and other scholars began to resurrect some of Schlesinger's argument about the importance of class to Jacksonianism. In *Chants Democratic* (1984), Wilentz maintained that Jacksonian politics could not be properly understood without reference to the changing national economy. Artisans watched in horror as new manufacturing techniques put many of them out of business and replaced their craftsmanship with the unskilled hands of wage laborers. To these anxious small producers, America's infatuation with impersonal institutions and large-scale employers threatened the very existence of a republic founded on the principle that its citizens were virtuously self-sufficient. Thus Jackson's attack on the Bank of the United States symbolized the antagonism these individuals felt toward the emergent capitalist economy and earned him their strong allegiance.

The scholarly cycle came full circle with the publication of Charles Sellers's *The Market Revolution: Jacksonian America, 1815–1846* (1991). In many ways this ambitious synthesis offered an updated version of Schlesinger's argument about class conflict. American democracy and free-market capitalism, according to Sellers, were not twins, born from the common parentage of freedom and opportunity, reared in the wide-open young Republic, and mutually supporting each other ever since. Rather, Sellers suggested, they were really adversaries, with Jacksonians inventing mass democracy in order to hold capitalist expansion in check. Like Schlesinger's thesis, Sellers's interpretation provoked a storm of controversy. To supporters, the concept of the "market revolution" (see p. 302) provided a useful organizing tool for seeing social, cultural, political, and economic transformations as interdependent. To critics, Sellers's book suffered from a hopelessly romantic view of preindustrial society and a pronounced ideological bias. In an era of tightly contested elections, they argued, no party could expect to prevail by appealing exclusively to rich or poor along class lines.

Published a decade and a half later, *What Hath God Wrought: The Transformation of America, 1815–1848* (2007), Daniel Walker Howe's equally sweeping synthesis of the period, took a different view of the relationship between commercialization and democracy. Howe argued that mass political participation did not emerge as an antidote to the crushing yoke of industrialization; rather, it evolved out of the same forces that drove market expansion—the "twin revolutions" in transportation and communications. Advances in

printing and the proliferation of newspapers were prerequisites for mass political parties, which depended on the largely partisan press to publicize their platforms and rally support. The turnpikes, canals, and railroads that delivered local goods to increasingly distant markets also carried ministers to far-off parishes, setting off a religious revival that helped transform the political landscape. New churches, representing a multiplicity of faiths, created venues for debates on issues ranging from abolition to women's rights, issues that were intentionally kept out of the halls of Congress. Howe argued that Jackson's supporters did not object to new commercial opportunities. At the same time that Jackson worked to dismantle the Bank of the United States, he also funded transportation projects in the territories to promote westward expansion and built harbors along the eastern seaboard to fuel international trade. According to Howe, Jacksonians welcomed commerce, but they disagreed with Whigs over the *direction* of development, favoring a more agrarian, atomized economy.

Chapter Review

KEY TERMS

corrupt bargain (246)

spoils system (251)

Tariff of Abominations (254)

Nullification Crisis (255)

compromise Tariff
    of 1833 (256)

Force Bill (256)

Indian Removal Act (258)

Trail of Tears (258)

Black Hawk War (258)

Bank War (259)

Anti-Masonic party (261)

pet banks (262)

Specie Circular (262)

panic of 1837 (264)

Alamo (266)

Goliad (266)

San Jacinto, Battle of (267)

PEOPLE TO KNOW

John Quincy Adams

Andrew Jackson

Denmark Vesey

John C. Calhoun

Black Hawk

Nicholas Biddle

Daniel Webster

Henry Clay

Martin Van Buren

Stephen Austin

Sam Houston

Santa Anna

William Henry Harrison

TO LEARN MORE

Glenn C. Altschuler and Stuart M. Blumin, *Rude Republic: Americans and Their Politics in the Nineteenth Century* (2001)

Andrew Burstein, *The Passions of Andrew Jackson* (2003)

Daniel Feller, *The Jacksonian Promise, 1815–1840* (1995)

Michael D. Green, *The Politics of Indian Removal* (1982)

Daniel Walker Howe, *What Hath God Wrought: The Transformation of America, 1815–1848* (2007)

Louis P. Masur, *1831: Year of Eclipse* (2001)

David Andrew Nichols, *Red Gentlemen and White Savages: Indians, Federalists, and the Search for Order on the American Frontier* (2008)

Lynn Hudson Parsons, *The Birth of Modern Politics: Andrew Jackson, John Quincy Adams, and the Election of 1828* (2009)

Merrill D. Peterson, *The Great Triumvirate: Webster, Clay, and Calhoun* (1987)

Alexis de Tocqueville, *Democracy in America* (1835, 1840)

Harry L. Watson, *Liberty and Power: The Politics of Jacksonian America* (1990)

A complete, annotated bibliography for this chapter—along with brief descriptions of the People to Know—may be found on the American Pageant website. The Key Terms are defined in a Glossary at the end of the text.

CHRONOLOGY

1822	Vesey slave conspiracy in Charleston, South Carolina
1823	Mexico opens Texas to American settlers
1824	Lack of electoral majority for presidency throws election into House of Representatives
1825	House elects John Quincy Adams president
1828	Tariff of 1828 ("Tariff of Abominations") Jackson elected president *The South Carolina Exposition* published
1830	Indian Removal Act July Revolution in France
1831–1832	Alexis de Tocqueville tours United States
1832	"Bank War"—Jackson vetoes bill to recharter Bank of the United States Reform Bill in Britain expands electorate Tariff of 1832 Black Hawk War Jackson defeats Clay for presidency

1832–1833	South Carolina nullification crisis
1833	Compromise Tariff of 1833 Jackson removes federal deposits from Bank of the United States
1836	Bank of the United States expires Specie Circular issued Bureau of Indian Affairs established Battle of the Alamo Battle of San Jacinto Texas wins independence from Mexico Van Buren elected president
1837	Seminole Indians defeated and eventually removed from Florida United States recognizes Texas republic but refuses annexation Panic of 1837
1838–1839	Cherokee Indians removed on "Trail of Tears"
1840	Independent treasury established Harrison defeats Van Buren for presidency

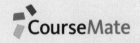
CourseMate

Go to the CourseMate website at **www.cengagebrain.com** for additional study tools and review materials—including audio and video clips—for this chapter.

AP® Review Questions for Chapter 13

1. What is meant by the term *corrupt bargain* in reference to the 1824 presidential election?
   (A) The selection of the president by the House of Representatives rather than the popular vote
   (B) Efforts by Andrew Jackson's campaign to bribe members of the House of Representatives to vote for their candidate
   (C) An alleged private deal between John Quincy Adams and Henry Clay to ensure Adams's presidency
   (D) John C. Calhoun's ability to run for vice president on both the Adams and Jackson tickets
   (E) The arbitrary elimination of the fourth-placed candidate from consideration of the presidency by the House of Representatives

2. John Quincy Adams was largely an unpopular president for all of the following reasons EXCEPT that he
   (A) replaced existing officeholders with his political supporters.
   (B) supported federal construction of roads and a national university.
   (C) sought to curb land speculation in the West.
   (D) was seen as having stolen the 1824 election.
   (E) was unwilling to court or campaign for public approval.

3. Which of these statements about the election of 1828 is NOT true?
   (A) The two main contenders were both Republicans.
   (B) Adams refused to engage in the negative campaign tactics that Jackson used.
   (C) Jackson's campaign depicted him as the champion of the common man.
   (D) It revealed a shift in political power toward new states west of the eastern seaboard.
   (E) The vote in the middle states was split between both candidates.

4. In his famed book about his tour through America, *Democracy in America*, Frenchman Alexis de Tocqueville was most impressed by
   (A) the persistence of slavery in America.
   (B) the roughhewn character of President Andrew Jackson.
   (C) the nation's bustling cities and commercial centers.
   (D) America's emerging industrialization.
   (E) the general equality of the American people.

5. What was the major significance of the spoils system, as employed by Andrew Jackson?
   (A) It enabled him to revitalize the federal government with new appointees.
   (B) It paved the way for him to expand the powers of the presidency and presidential appointees.
   (C) It became an important tool of the emerging two-party system.
   (D) It revealed the potential for scandal and corruption in American politics.
   (E) It led to the first case of embezzlement against the government.

6. Southerners hated the so-called Tariff of Abominations (1828) for all of the following reasons EXCEPT that they
   (A) felt it favored the North.
   (B) feared it would lead the federal government to intervene in slavery.
   (C) had little manufacturing and had to purchase the items affected by the tariff.
   (D) thought it would stall their thriving economy.
   (E) felt the government was overstepping its authority.

7. In simplest terms, the Nullification Crisis that began with South Carolina in 1828 describes
   (A) the state's attempt to block passage of the Tariff of Abominations in Congress.
   (B) South Carolina's effort to declare the tariff void within its borders.
   (C) a protest by several southern states to prevent the tariff from being collected.
   (D) the first time the South threatened to secede.
   (E) efforts in Congress to remove the most hated sections of the tariff in subsequent legislation.

8. What was the Cherokee strategy for dealing with white encroachment?
   (A) Violent resistance
   (B) Accommodation
   (C) Intermarriage with white settlers
   (D) Voluntary relocation
   (E) Negotiating treaties and land sales

9. The Trail of Tears is best described as
   (A) the Seminoles' seven-year guerrilla warfare in Florida to protect their land.
   (B) the practice of negating Indian treaties to allow for white encroachment on Indian land.
   (C) the forced march of the Five Civilized Tribes from their eastern homelands to resettlement in the West.
   (D) the bloody Indian resistance in the Black Hawk War to eviction by white settlers.
   (E) the promise by the U.S. government to create a permanent Indian homeland on the frontier.

10. Which of these was NOT among Andrew Jackson's reasons for vetoing the bill to recharter the Bank of the United States in 1832?
    (A) He hated monopolies.
    (B) He felt the bank had too much control over the nation's economy.
    (C) He considered it to be unconstitutional.
    (D) He thought the bank was potentially harmful to the nation.
    (E) He wanted to win over wealthy voters from the North and East in his reelection campaign.

11. The election of 1832 changed the face of American politics by
    (A) beginning the tradition of nominating conventions.
    (B) expanding the power of the presidency.
    (C) creating presidential "war chests" (campaign contributions).
    (D) demonstrating the power of the Electoral College versus the popular vote.
    (E) showing the power of voting blocs and interest groups.

12. The primary cause of the Panic of 1837 was
    (A) the bank crisis.
    (B) widespread speculation and get-rich-quick schemes.
    (C) the Specie Circular.
    (D) economic crises in Europe that expanded to America.
    (E) excessive government tariffs and subsidies.

13. The Texas Revolution and independence posed a thorny issue for the United States because
    (A) almost all of the revolutionaries were Americans.
    (B) the U.S. government had lent money and munitions to support the rebels.
    (C) Texans sought annexation by the United States.
    (D) it fueled a battle between Spain and Mexico.
    (E) Santa Anna threatened to move the battle onto U.S. soil.

14. What was the main difference between the Whigs and Democrats, the two parties that took hold in the late 1820s and 1830s?
    (A) Democrats tended to be wealthier; Whigs were typically more mainstream.
    (B) Democrats focused on the common good; Whigs celebrated individual freedom and self-interest.
    (C) Democrats favored states' rights; Whigs sought federal involvement, including tariffs, schools, internal improvements, and a national bank.
    (D) Democrats tended to be from the North and Old West; Whigs were often from the South and newer western territories.
    (E) Democrats were typically farmers; Whigs were primarily merchants.

15. John C. Calhoun stated, "I never use the word 'nation' in speaking of the United States. I always use the word 'union' or 'confederacy.' We are not a nation, but a union, a confederacy of equal and sovereign states." Which action exemplifies this philosophy?
    (A) Advocating a "dual presidency" in which the North and South were represented
    (B) Accepting the vice-presidential nomination in the election of 1828
    (C) Working in Congress to create compromises to deal with the slavery issue
    (D) Cooperating with Henry Clay on a South-West alliance
    (E) Authoring the South Carolina Exposition and Protest

16. All of the following tensions existed between American settlers in Texas and the Mexican government EXCEPT that
    (A) Mexico abolished slavery, but Americans insisted upon bringing slaves into Texas.
    (B) Americans expected to live by their own rules and resented the Mexican military presence.
    (C) The majority of American settlers were Christian, but not Catholic as required by Mexico.
    (D) Mexico expected significant industrial output from settlers who planted little.
    (E) Mexico permitted 300 American families to settle; 30,000 people, including some fugitives, arrived.

Chapter 14

Forging the National Economy

1790–1860

The progress of invention is really a threat [to monarchy].
Whenever I see a railroad I look for a republic.

RALPH WALDO EMERSON, 1866

The new nation bounded into the nineteenth century in a burst of movement. New England Yankees, Pennsylvania farmers, and southern yeomen all pushed west in search of land and opportunity, soon to be joined by vast numbers of immigrants from Europe, who also made their way to the country's fast-growing cities. And not only people were in motion. Newly invented machinery boomed the cultivation of crops and the manufacture of goods, while workers labored ever longer, harder, and faster. Better roads, faster steamboats, farther-reaching canals, and ribboning railroad lines all moved people, foodstuffs, raw materials, and manufactured goods from coast to coast, from Gulf to Great Lakes, and from American shores to the wider world. The prodigious momentum of burgeoning American capitalism gave rise to an economy that was remarkably dynamic, market driven, continentally scaled, and internationally consequential.

✴ The Westward Movement

The rise of Andrew Jackson, the first president from beyond the Appalachian Mountains, exemplified the inexorable westward march of the American people. The West, with its raw frontier, was the most typically American part of America. As Ralph Waldo Emerson wrote in 1844, "Europe stretches to the Alleghenies; America lies beyond."

The Republic was young, and so were the people—as late as 1850, half of Americans were under the age of thirty. They were also restless and energetic, seemingly

always on the move, and always westward. One "tall tale" of the frontier described chickens that voluntarily crossed their legs every spring, waiting to be tied for the annual move west. By 1840 the "demographic center" of the American population map had crossed the Alleghenies (see Map 14.1). By the eve of the Civil War, it had marched across the Ohio River.

Legend portrays an army of muscular axmen triumphantly carving civilization out of the western woods. But in reality life was downright grim for most pioneer families. Poorly fed, ill-clad, housed in hastily erected shanties (Abraham Lincoln's family lived for a year in a three-sided lean-to made of brush and sticks), they were perpetual victims of disease, depression, and premature death. Above all, unbearable loneliness haunted them, especially the women, who were often cut off from human contact, even their neighbors, for days or even weeks, while confined to the cramped orbit of a dark cabin in a secluded clearing. Breakdowns and even madness were all too frequently the "opportunities" that the frontier offered to pioneer women.

Frontier life could be tough and crude for men as well. No-holds-barred wrestling, which permitted such niceties as the biting off of noses and the gouging out of eyes, was a popular entertainment. Pioneering Americans, marooned by geography, were often ill-informed, superstitious, provincial, and fiercely individualistic. Ralph Waldo Emerson's popular lecture-essay "**Self-Reliance**" struck a deeply responsive chord. Popular literature of the period abounded with portraits of unique, isolated figures like James Fenimore Cooper's heroic Natty Bumppo and Herman Melville's restless

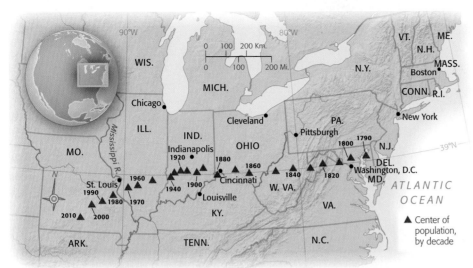

MAP 14.1 Westward Movement of Center of Population, 1790–2010 The triangles indicate the points at which a map of the United States weighted for the population of the country in a given year would balance. Note the remarkable equilibrium of the north-south pull from 1790 to about 1940, and the strong spurt west and south thereafter. The 1980 census revealed that the nation's center of population had at last moved west of the Mississippi River. The map also shows the slowing of the westward movement between 1890 and 1940—the period of heaviest immigration from Europe, which ended up mainly in East Coast cities. © Cengage Learning

Captain Ahab—just as Jacksonian politics aimed to emancipate the lone-wolf, enterprising businessperson. Yet even in this heyday of "rugged individualism," there were important exceptions. Pioneers, in tasks clearly beyond their own individual resources, would call upon their neighbors for logrolling and barn raising and upon their governments for help in building internal improvements.

✦ Shaping the Western Landscape

The westward movement also molded the physical environment. Pioneers in a hurry often exhausted the land in the tobacco regions and then pushed on, leaving behind barren and rain-gutted fields. In the Kentucky bottomlands, cane as high as fifteen feet posed a seemingly insurmountable barrier to the plow. But settlers soon discovered that when the cane was burned off, European bluegrass thrived in the charred cane-fields. "Kentucky bluegrass," as it was somewhat inaccurately called, made ideal pasture for livestock—and lured thousands more American homesteaders into Kentucky.

The American West felt the pressure of civilization in additional ways. By the 1820s American fur-trappers were setting their traplines all over the vast Rocky Mountain region. The fur-trapping empire was based on the **rendezvous** (French for "meeting") system. Each summer, traders ventured from St. Louis to a verdant Rocky Mountain valley, made camp, and waited for the trappers and Indians to arrive with beaver pelts to swap for manufactured goods from the East. This trade thrived for some two decades; by the time beaver hats had gone out of fashion, the hapless beaver had all but disappeared from the region. Trade in buffalo robes also flourished, leading eventually to the virtually total annihilation of the massive bison herds that once blanketed the western prairies. Still farther west, on the California coast, other traders bought up prodigious quantities of sea-otter pelts, driving the once-bountiful otters to the point of near-extinction. Some historians have called this aggressive and often heedless exploitation of the West's natural bounty **ecological imperialism**.

Yet Americans in this period also revered nature and admired its beauty. Indeed the spirit of nationalism fed a growing belief in the uniqueness of the American wilderness. Searching for the United States' distinctive characteristics in this nation-conscious age, many observers found the wild, unspoiled character of the land, especially in the West, to be among the young nation's defining attributes. Other countries might have impressive mountains or sparkling rivers, but none had the pristine, natural beauty of America, unspoiled by human hands and reminiscent of a time

Major Dougherty's Indian Agency on the Missouri River, by Karl Bodmer, 1833   The Swiss-born and Paris-trained artist Karl Bodmer painted this scene while accompanying German Prince Maximilian on his expedition across the American West. From St. Louis, the party traveled up the Missouri River by steamboat under the protection of John Jacob Astor's Fur Company. Bodmer painted scenes along the way, especially of Indians and their surroundings. Trading posts like this one both promoted commerce with the Indians and served settlers heading west.

before the dawn of civilization. This attitude toward wilderness became in time a kind of national mystique, inspiring literature and painting, and eventually kindling a powerful conservation movement.

George Catlin, a painter and student of Native American life, was among the first Americans to advocate the preservation of nature as a deliberate national policy. In 1832 he observed Sioux Indians in South Dakota recklessly slaughtering buffalo in order to trade the animals' tongues for the white man's whiskey. Appalled at this spectacle and fearing for the preservation of Indians and buffalo alike, Catlin proposed the creation of a national park. His idea later bore fruit with the creation of a national park system—the world's first—beginning with Yellowstone Park in 1872.

⭐ The March of the Millions

As the American people moved west, they also multiplied at an amazing rate. By midcentury the population was still doubling approximately every twenty-five years, as in fertile colonial days (see Figure 14.1).

By 1860 the original thirteen states had more than doubled in number: thirty-three stars graced the American flag. The United States was the fourth most pop-

ulous nation in the western world, exceeded only by three European countries—Russia, France, and Austria.

Urban growth continued explosively. In 1790 there had been only two American cities that could boast populations of twenty thousand or more souls: Philadelphia and New York. By 1860 there were forty-three, and about three hundred other places claimed over five thousand inhabitants apiece. New York was the metropolis; New Orleans, the "Queen of the South"; and Chicago, the swaggering lord of the Midwest, destined to be "hog butcher for the world."

Such overrapid urbanization unfortunately brought undesirable by-products. It intensified the problems of smelly slums, feeble street lighting, inadequate policing, impure water, foul sewage, ravenous rats, and improper garbage disposal. Hogs poked their scavenging snouts about many city streets as late as the 1840s. Boston in 1823 pioneered a sewer system, and New York in 1842 abandoned wells and cisterns for a piped-in water supply. The city thus unknowingly eliminated the breeding places of many disease-carrying mosquitoes.

A continuing high birthrate accounted for most of the increase in population, but by the 1840s the tides of immigration were adding hundreds of thousands more. Before this decade immigrants had been flowing in at a rate of sixty thousand a year, but suddenly

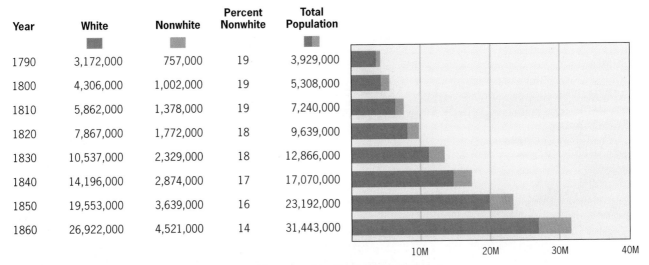

Year	White	Nonwhite	Percent Nonwhite	Total Population
1790	3,172,000	757,000	19	3,929,000
1800	4,306,000	1,002,000	19	5,308,000
1810	5,862,000	1,378,000	19	7,240,000
1820	7,867,000	1,772,000	18	9,639,000
1830	10,537,000	2,329,000	18	12,866,000
1840	14,196,000	2,874,000	17	17,070,000
1850	19,553,000	3,639,000	16	23,192,000
1860	26,922,000	4,521,000	14	31,443,000

FIGURE 14.1 Population Increase, Including Slaves and Indians, 1790–1860 Increasing European immigration and the closing of the slave trade gradually "whitened" the population beginning in 1820. This trend continued into the early twentieth century.

the influx tripled in the 1840s and then quadrupled in the 1850s. During these two feverish decades, over a million and a half Irish, and nearly as many Germans, swarmed down the gangplanks (see Table 14.1). Why did they come?

The immigrants came partly because Europe seemed to be running out of room. The population of the Old World more than doubled in the nineteenth century, and Europe began to generate a seething pool of apparently "surplus" people. They were displaced and footloose in their homelands before they felt the tug of the American magnet. Indeed at least as many people moved about *within* Europe as crossed the Atlantic. America benefited from these people-churning changes but did not set them all in motion. Nor was the United States the sole beneficiary of the process: of the nearly 60 million people who abandoned Europe

in the century after 1840, about 25 million went somewhere other than the United States.

Yet America still beckoned most strongly to the struggling masses of Europe, and the majority of migrants headed for the "land of freedom and opportunity." There was freedom from aristocratic caste and state church; there was abundant opportunity to secure broad acres and better one's condition. Much-read letters sent home by immigrants—"America letters"—often described in glowing terms the richer life: low taxes, no compulsory military service, and "three

TABLE 14.1	Irish and German Immigration by Decade, 1830–1900	
Years	Irish	Germans
1831–1840	207,381	152,454
1841–1850	780,719	434,626
1851–1860	914,119	951,667
1861–1870	435,778	787,468
1871–1880	436,871	718,182
1881–1890	655,482	1,452,970
1891–1900	388,416	505,152
TOTAL	3,818,766	5,000,519

A German immigrant living in Cincinnati wrote to his relatives in Germany in 1847,

❝A lot of people come over here who were well off in Germany but were enticed to leave their fatherland by boastful and imprudent letters from their friends or children and thought they could become rich in America. This deceives a lot of people, since what can they do here? If they stay in the city they can only earn their bread at hard and unaccustomed labor. If they want to live in the country and don't have enough money to buy a piece of land that is cleared and has a house then they have to settle in the wild bush and have to work very hard to clear the trees out of the way so they can sow and plant. But people who are healthy, strong, and hard-working do pretty well.❞

Mouth of the Platte River, 900 Miles Above St. Louis, by George Catlin, 1832
Catlin's West unfolded as a vast panorama of flat, open space peopled only by the Indians shown in the foreground. Catlin believed that capturing the unending prairie on canvas required a new aesthetic, the sublime horizontal, and an acceptance of a landscape bereft of man-built features, without "anything rising above the horizon, which was a perfect straight line around us, like that of the blue and boundless ocean."

meat meals a day." The introduction of transoceanic steamships also meant that the immigrants could come speedily and cheaply. The journey to the United States now took ten or twelve days, instead of ten or twelve weeks on a sailing vessel, and was much less expensive than a voyage to more distant immigrant destinations such as Australia, Argentina, or South Africa. The United States also received a far more diverse array of immigrants than did other countries. Argentina, for example, had a higher proportion of immigrants relative to its population than did the United States, but they came mostly from Spain and Italy. In contrast, the United States beckoned to immigrants from dozens of different nations.

✦ The Emerald Isle Moves West

Ireland, already groaning under the heavy hand of British overlords, was prostrated in the mid-1840s. A terrible rot attacked the potato crop, on which the people had become dangerously dependent, and about one-fourth of them were swept away by disease and hunger. Starved bodies were found dead by the roadsides with grass in their mouths. All told, about 2 million perished.

Tens of thousands of destitute souls, fleeing the Land of Famine for the Land of Plenty, flocked to America in the "Black Forties." Ireland's great export has been population, and the Irish take their place beside the Jews and the Africans as a dispersed people (see "Makers of America: The Irish," pp. 282–283).

These uprooted newcomers—too poor to move west and buy the necessary land, livestock, and equipment—swarmed into the larger seaboard cities. Noteworthy were Boston and particularly New York, which rapidly became the largest Irish city in the world. Before many decades had passed, more people of Hibernian blood lived in America than on the "ould sod" of Erin's Isle.

The luckless Irish immigrants received no red-carpet treatment. Forced to live in squalor, they were rudely crammed into the already vile slums. They were scorned by the older American stock, especially "proper" Protestant Bostonians, who regarded the scruffy Catholic arrivals as a social menace. Barely literate "Biddies" (Bridgets) took jobs as kitchen maids. Broad-shouldered "Paddies" (Patricks) were pushed into pick-and-shovel drudgery on canals and railroads, where thousands left their bones as victims of disease and accidental explosions. It was said that an Irishman lay buried under every railroad tie. As wage-depressing competitors for jobs, the Irish were hated by native workers. "No Irish Need Apply" was a sign commonly posted at factory gates and was often abbreviated to NINA. The Irish, for similar reasons, fiercely resented the blacks, with whom they shared society's basement. Race riots between black and Irish dockworkers flared up in several port cities, and the Irish were generally cool to the abolitionist cause.

The friendless "famine Irish" were forced to fend for themselves. The **Ancient Order of Hibernians**, a semisecret society founded in Ireland to fight rapacious landlords, served in America as a benevolent society, aiding the downtrodden. It also helped to spawn the **Molly Maguires**, a shadowy Irish miners' union that rocked the Pennsylvania coal districts in the 1860s and 1870s.

The Irish tended to remain in low-skill occupations but gradually improved their lot, usually by acquiring modest amounts of property. The education of children was cut short as families struggled to save money to purchase a home. But for humble Irish peasants, cruelly cast out of their homeland, property ownership counted as a grand "success."

Politics quickly attracted these gregarious Gaelic newcomers. They soon began to gain control of

Margaret McCarthy, a recent arrival to America, captured much of the complexity of the immigrant experience in a letter she wrote from New York to her family in Ireland in 1850:

" This is a good place and a good country, but there is one thing that's ruining this place. The emigrants have not money enough to take them to the interior of the country, which obliges them to remain here in New York and the like places, which causes the less demand for labor and also the great reduction in wages. For this reason I would advise no one to come to America that would not have some money after landing here that would enable them to go west in case they would get no work to do here. **"**

An early-nineteenth-century French traveler recorded his impressions of America and Ireland:

" I have seen the Indian in his forests and the Negro in his chains, and thought, as I contemplated their pitiable condition, that I saw the very extreme of human wretchedness; but I did not then know the condition of unfortunate Ireland. **"**

powerful city machines, notably New York's **Tammany Hall**, and reaped the patronage rewards. Before long, beguilingly brogued Irishmen dominated police departments in many big cities, where they now drove the "Paddy wagons" that had once carted their brawling forebears to jail.

American politicians made haste to cultivate the Irish vote, especially in the politically potent state of New York. Irish hatred of the British lost nothing in the transatlantic transplanting. As the Irish Americans increased in number—nearly 2 million arrived between 1830 and 1860—officials in Washington glimpsed political gold in those emerald green hills. Politicians often found it politically profitable to fire verbal volleys at London—a process vulgarly known as "twisting the British lion's tail."

✵ The German Forty-Eighters

The influx of refugees from Germany between 1830 and 1860 was hardly less spectacular than that from Ireland. During these troubled years, over a million and a half Germans stepped onto American soil (see "Makers of America: The Germans," pp. 286–287).

The bulk of them were uprooted farmers, displaced by crop failures and other hardships. But a strong sprinkling were liberal political refugees. Saddened by the collapse of the democratic revolutions of 1848, they had decided to leave the autocratic fatherland and flee to America—the brightest hope of democracy.

Germany's loss was America's gain. Zealous German liberals like the lanky and public-spirited Carl Schurz, a relentless foe of slavery and public corruption, contributed richly to the elevation of American political life.

Unlike the Irish, many of the Germanic newcomers possessed a modest amount of material goods. Most of them pushed out to the lush lands of the Middle West, notably Wisconsin, where they settled and established model farms. Like the Irish, they formed an influential body of voters whom American politicians shamelessly

For a generation, from 1793 to 1815, war raged across Europe. Ruinous as it was on the Continent, the fighting brought unprecedented prosperity to the long-suffering landsmen of Ireland, groaning since the twelfth century under the yoke of English rule. For as Europe's fields lay fallow, irrigated only by the blood of its farmers, Ireland fed the hungry armies that ravened for food as well as territory. Irish farmers planted every available acre, interspersing the lowly potato amongst their fields of grain. With prices for food products ever mounting, tenant farmers reaped a temporary respite from their perpetual struggle to remain on the land. Most landlords were satisfied by the prosperity and so relaxed their pressure on tenants; others, stymied by the absence of British police forces that had been stripped of manpower to fight in Europe, had little means to enforce eviction notices.

But the peace that brought solace to battle-scarred Europe changed all this. After 1815 war-inflated wheat prices plummeted by half. Hard-pressed landlords resolved to leave vast fields unplanted. Assisted now by a strengthened British constabulary, they vowed to sweep the pesky peasants from the retired acreage. Many of those forced to leave sought work in England; some went to America. Then in 1845 a blight that ravaged the potato crop sounded the final knell for the Irish peasantry. The resultant famine spread desolation throughout the island. In five years more than a million people died. Another million sailed for America.

Of the emigrants, most were young and literate in English, the majority under thirty-five years old. Families typically pooled money to send strong young sons to the New World, where they would earn wages to pay the fares for those who waited at home. These "famine Irish" mostly remained in the port cities of the Northeast, abandoning the farmer's life for the dingy congestion of the urban metropolis.

The disembarking Irish were poorly prepared for urban life. They found progress up the economic ladder painfully slow. Their work as domestic servants or construction laborers was dull and arduous, and mortality rates were astoundingly high. Escape from the potato famine hardly guaranteed a long life to an Irish American; a gray-bearded Irishman was a rare sight in nineteenth-century America. Most of the new arrivals toiled as day laborers. A fortunate few owned boardinghouses or saloons, where their dispirited countrymen sought solace in the bottle. For Irish-born women, opportunities were still scarcer; they worked mainly as domestic servants.

But it was their Roman Catholicism, more even than their penury or their perceived fondness for alcohol, that earned the Irish the distrust and resentment of their native-born, Protestant American neighytIrish immigrants was the parish. Worries about safeguarding their children's faith inspired the construction of parish schools, financed by the pennies of struggling working-class Irish parents.

If Ireland's green fields scarcely equipped her sons and daughters for the scrap and scramble of economic life in America's cities, life in the Old Country nevertheless had instilled in them an aptitude for politics. Irish Catholic resistance against centuries of English Anglican domination had instructed many Old Country Irish in the ways of mass politics. That political experience readied them for the boss system of the political "machines" in America's northeastern cities. The boss's local representatives met each newcomer soon after he landed in America. Asking only for votes, the machine supplied

Collection of the New York Historical Society

Outward Bound, the Quay at Dublin, 1854 Thousands fled famine in Ireland by coming to America in the 1840s and 1850s.

St. Patrick's Day Parade in America, Union Square, ca. 1870   This painting shows a St. Patrick's Day parade in New York City. The religious festival was celebrated with greater fanfare in America than in Ireland itself, as Irish immigrants used it to boost their ethnic solidarity and assert their distinctive identity in their adopted country.

coal in wintertime, food, and help with the law. Irish voters soon became a bulwark of the Democratic party, reliably supporting the party of Jefferson and Jackson in cities like New York and Boston. As Irish Americans like New York's "Honest John" Kelly themselves became bosses, white-collar jobs in government service opened up to the Irish. They became building inspectors, aldermen, and even policemen—an astonishing irony for a people driven from their homeland by the nightsticks and bayonets of the British police.

wooed. But the Germans were less potent politically because their strength was more widely scattered.

The hand of Germans in shaping American life was widely felt in still other ways. The Conestoga wagon, the Kentucky rifle, and the Christmas tree were all German contributions to American culture. Germans had fled from the militarism and wars of Europe and consequently came to be a bulwark of isolationist sentiment in the upper Mississippi Valley. Better educated on the whole than the stump-grubbing Americans, they warmly supported public schools, including their *Kindergarten* (children's garden). They likewise did much to stimulate art and music. As outspoken champions of freedom, they became relentless enemies of slavery during the fevered years before the Civil War.

Yet the Germans—often dubbed "damned Dutchmen"—were occasionally regarded with suspicion by their old-stock American neighbors. Seeking to preserve their language and culture, they sometimes settled in compact "colonies" and kept aloof from the surrounding community. Accustomed to the "Continental Sunday" and uncurbed by Puritan tradition, they made merry on the Sabbath and drank huge quantities of an amber beverage called *bier* (beer), which dates its real popularity in America to their coming. Their Old World drinking habits, like those of the Irish, spurred advocates of temperance in the use of alcohol to redouble their reform efforts.

✦ Flare-ups of Antiforeignism

The invasion by this so-called immigrant "rabble" in the 1840s and 1850s inflamed the prejudices of American "nativists." They feared that these foreign hordes would outbreed, outvote, and overwhelm the old "native" stock. Not only did the newcomers take jobs from "native" Americans, but the bulk of the displaced Irish were Roman Catholics, as were a substantial minority of the Germans. The Church of Rome was still widely regarded by many old-line Americans as a "foreign" church; convents were commonly referred to as "popish brothels."

Roman Catholics were now on the move. Seeking to protect their children from Protestant indoctrination in the public schools, they began in the 1840s to construct an entirely separate Catholic educational system—an enormously expensive undertaking for a poor immigrant community, but one that revealed the strength of its religious commitment. They had formed a negligible minority during colonial days, and their numbers had increased gradually. But with the enormous influx of the Irish and Germans in the 1840s and 1850s, the Catholics became a powerful religious group. In 1840 they had ranked fifth, behind the

Crooked Voting A bitter "nativist" cartoon charging Irish and German immigrants with "stealing" elections.

Granger Collection

Baptists, Methodists, Presbyterians, and Congregationalists. By 1850, with some 1.8 million communicants, they had bounded into first place—a position they have never lost.

Older-stock Americans were alarmed by these mounting figures. They professed to believe that in due time the "alien riffraff" would "establish" the Catholic Church at the expense of Protestantism and would introduce "popish idols." The noisier American "nativists" rallied for political action. In 1849 they formed the Order of the Star-Spangled Banner, which soon developed into the formidable American party, more commonly known as the **Know-Nothing party**, a name derived from its secretiveness. "Nativists" agitated for rigid restrictions on immigration and naturalization and for laws authorizing the deportation of alien paupers. They also promoted a lurid literature of exposure, much of it pure fiction. The authors, sometimes posing as escaped nuns, described the shocking sins they imagined the cloisters concealed, including the secret burial of babies. One of these sensational books—Maria Monk's ***Awful Disclosures*** (1836)—sold over 300,000 copies.

Even uglier was occasional mass violence. As early as 1834, a Catholic convent near Boston was burned by a howling mob, and in ensuing years a few scattered attacks fell upon Catholic schools and churches. The most frightful flare-up occurred during 1844 in Philadelphia, where the Irish Catholics fought back against the threats of the "nativists." The City of Brotherly Love did not quiet down until two Catholic churches had been burned and some thirteen citizens had been killed and fifty wounded in several days of fighting. These outbursts of intolerance, though infrequent and generally localized in the larger cities, remain an unfortunate blot on the record of America's treatment of minority groups.

Immigrants were undeniably making America a more pluralistic society—one of the most ethnically and racially varied in the history of the world—and perhaps it was small wonder that cultural clashes would occur. Why, in fact, were such episodes not even more frequent and more violent? Part of the answer lies in the robustness of the American economy. The vigorous growth of the economy in these years both attracted immigrants in the first place and ensured that, once arrived, they could claim their share of American wealth without jeopardizing the wealth of others. Their hands and brains, in fact, helped fuel economic expansion. Immigrants and the American economy, in short, needed one another. Without the newcomers, a preponderantly agricultural United States might well have been condemned to watch in envy as the **Industrial Revolution** swept through nineteenth-century Europe.

✶ Creeping Mechanization

A group of gifted British inventors, beginning about 1750, perfected a series of machines for the mass production of textiles. This harnessing of steam multiplied the power of human muscles some ten-thousandfold and ushered in the modern factory system—and with it, the so-called Industrial Revolution. It was accompanied by a no-less-spectacular transformation in agricultural production and in the methods of transportation and communication.

The factory system gradually spread from Britain—"the world's workshop"—to other lands. It took a generation or so to reach western Europe, and then the United States. Why was the youthful American Republic, eventually to become an industrial giant, so slow to embrace the machine?

For one thing, land was cheap in America. Land-starved descendants of land-starved peasants were not going to coop themselves up in smelly factories when they might till their own acres in God's fresh air and sunlight. Labor was therefore generally scarce, and enough nimble hands to operate the machines were hard to find—until immigrants began to pour ashore in the 1840s. Money for capital investment, moreover, was not plentiful in pioneering America, whose Industrial Revolution, like that of many a developing country in later centuries, awaited an influx of foreign capital—which in turn awaited assurance of secure property rights, sufficient infrastructure, an adequate work force, and political stability. Without such capital, raw materials lay undeveloped, undiscovered, or unsuspected.

The Republic was one day to become the world's leading coal producer, but much of the coal burned in colonial times was imported all the way from Britain.

The young country also had difficulty producing goods of high enough quality and cheap enough cost to compete with mass-produced European products. Long-established British factories in particular provided cutthroat competition. Their superiority was attested by the fact that a few unscrupulous Yankee manufacturers, out to make a dishonest dollar, stamped their own products with fake English trademarks.

The British also enjoyed a monopoly of the textile machinery, whose secrets they were anxious to hide from foreign competitors. Parliament enacted laws, in harmony with the mercantile system, forbidding the export of the machines or the emigration of mechanics able to reproduce them.

Although a number of small manufacturing enterprises existed in the early Republic, the future industrial colossus was still snoring. Not until well past the middle of the nineteenth century did the value of the output of the factories exceed that of the farms.

✶ Whitney Ends the Fiber Famine

Samuel Slater has been acclaimed the "Father of the Factory System" in America, and seldom can the paternity of a movement more properly be ascribed to one person. A skilled British mechanic of twenty-one, he was attracted by bounties being offered to British workers familiar with the textile machines. After memorizing the plans for the machinery, he escaped in disguise to America, where he won the backing of Moses Brown, a Quaker capitalist in Rhode Island. Laboriously reconstructing the essential apparatus with the aid of a blacksmith and a carpenter, he put into operation in 1791 the first efficient American machinery for spinning cotton thread.

The ravenous mechanism was now ready, but where was the cotton fiber? Handpicking one pound of lint from three pounds of seed was a full day's work for one slave, and this process was so expensive that American-made cotton cloth was relatively rare.

etween 1820 and 1920, a sea of Germans lapped at America's shores and seeped into its very heartland. Their numbers surpassed those of any other immigrant group, even the prolific and often-detested Irish. Yet this Germanic flood, unlike its Gaelic equivalent, stirred little panic in the hearts of native-born Americans because the Germans largely stayed to themselves, far from the madding crowds and nativist fears of northeastern cities. They prospered with astonishing ease, building towns in Wisconsin, agricultural colonies in Texas, and religious communities in Pennsylvania. They added a decidedly Germanic flavor to the heady brew of reform and community building that so animated antebellum America.

These "Germans" actually hailed from many different Old World lands, because there was no unified nation of Germany until 1871, when the ruthless and crafty Prussian Otto von Bismarck assembled the German state out of a mosaic of independent principalities, kingdoms, and duchies. Until that time, "Germans" came to America as Prussians, Bavarians, Hessians, Rhinelanders, Pomeranians, and Westphalians. They arrived at different times and for many different reasons. Some, particularly the so-called Forty-Eighters—the refugees from the abortive democratic revolutions of 1848—hungered for the democracy they had failed to win in Germany. Others, particularly Jews, Pietists, and Anabaptist groups like the Amish and the Mennonites, coveted religious freedom. And they came not only to America. Like the Italians later, many Germans sought a new life in Brazil, Argentina, and Chile. But the largest number ventured into the United States.

Typical German immigrants arrived with fatter purses than their Irish counterparts. Small landowners or independent artisans in their native countries, they did not have to settle for bottom-rung industrial employment in the grimy factories of the Northeast and instead could afford to push on to the open spaces of the American West.

In Wisconsin these immigrants found a home away from home, a place with a climate, soil, and geography much like central Europe's. Milwaukee, a crude frontier town before the Germans' arrival, became the "German Athens." It boasted a German theater, German beer gardens, a German volunteer fire company, and a German-English academy. In distant Texas, German settlements like New Braunfels and Friedrichsburg flourished. When the famous landscape architect and writer Frederick Law Olmsted stumbled upon these prairie outposts of Teutonic culture in 1857, he was shocked to be "welcomed by a figure in a blue flannel shirt and pendant beard, quoting Tacitus." These German colonies in the frontier Southwest mixed high European elegance with Texas ruggedness. Olmsted described a visit to a German household where the settlers drank "coffee in tin cups upon Dresden saucers" and sat upon "barrels for seats, to hear a Beethoven symphony on the grand piano."

These Germanic colonizers of America's heartland also formed religious communities, none more distinctive or durable than the Amish settlements of Pennsylvania, Indiana, and Ohio. The Amish took their name from their founder and leader, the Swiss Anabaptist Jacob Amman. Like other Anabaptist groups, they shunned extravagance and reserved baptism for adults, repudiating the tradition of infant baptism practiced by most Europeans. For this they were persecuted, even imprisoned, in Europe. Seeking escape from their oppression, some five hundred Amish ventured to Pennsylvania in the 1700s, followed by three thousand in the years from 1815 to 1865.

"Little Germany" Cincinnati's "Over-the-Rhine" district in 1887.

Cincinnati Museum Center—Cincinnati Historical Society Library

Another mechanical genius, Massachusetts-born Eli Whitney, now made his mark. After graduating from Yale, he journeyed to Georgia to serve as a private tutor while preparing for the law. There he was told that the poverty of the South would be relieved if someone could only invent a workable device for separating the seed from the short-staple cotton fiber. Within ten days, in 1793, he built a crude machine

In America they formed enduring religious communities—isolated enclaves where they could shield themselves from the corruption and the conveniences of the modern world. To this day the German-speaking Amish still travel in horse-drawn carriages and farm without heavy machinery. No electric lights brighten the darkness that nightly envelops their tidy farmhouses; no ringing telephones punctuate the reverent tranquility of their mealtime prayer; no ornaments relieve the austere simplicity of their black garments. The Amish remain a stalwart, traditional community in a rootless, turbulent society, a living testament to the religious ferment and social experiments of the antebellum era.

Marriage Plate, Bucks County, Pennsylvania, ca. 1806   The Germans who settled the "Pennsylvania Dutch" communities in the eighteenth century preserved ancient traditions of handicraft and art, as exemplified by this whimsical "marriage plate" made by a sixteen-year-old potter named John Leidy. The inscription reads, "Rather would I single live than the wife the breeches [trousers] give." 1895-78 John Leidy I, Dish, 1797, Philadelphia Museum of Art: Gift of A.C. Harrison, 1895

Jean Louis Atlan/Sygma/Corbis

Amish Country, Near Lancaster, Pennsylvania   For more than two centuries, the Amish people have preserved their traditional way of life.

called the **cotton gin** (short for engine) that was fifty times more effective than the handpicking process.

Few machines have ever wrought so wondrous a change. The gin affected not only the history of America but that of the world. Almost overnight the raising of cotton became highly profitable, and the South was tied hand and foot to the throne of King Cotton. Human bondage had been dying out, but the

287

Courtesy Gore Place Society, Waltham, Mass

© Bettmann/Corbis

Francis Cabot Lowell's Mill, Waltham, Massachusetts, 1826 and Cotton Industry; Carding, Drawing, and Roving; Engraving, 1835   Built in 1814, Lowell's mill (left) was a marvel of manufacturing efficiency. It combined all phases of production, including spinning and weaving, under one roof. The mill's labor force (right) was composed primarily of young women from the local farming communities.

insatiable demand for cotton reriveted the chains on the limbs of the downtrodden southern blacks.

South and North both prospered. Slave-driving planters cleared more acres for cotton, pushing the Cotton Kingdom westward off the depleted tidewater plains, over the Piedmont, and onto the black loam bottomlands of Alabama and Mississippi. Humming gins poured out avalanches of snowy fiber for the spindles of the Yankee machines, though for decades to come the mills of Britain bought the lion's share of southern cotton. The American phase of the Industrial Revolution, which first blossomed in cotton textiles, was well on its way.

Factories at first flourished most actively in New England, though they branched out into the more populous areas of New York, New Jersey, and Pennsylvania. The South, increasingly wedded to the production of cotton, could boast of comparatively little manufacturing. Its capital was bound up in slaves; its local consumers for the most part were desperately poor.

New England was singularly favored as an industrial center for several reasons. Its narrow belt of stony soil made farming difficult and hence made manufacturing attractive. A relatively dense population provided labor and accessible markets, shipping brought in capital, and snug seaports made easy the import of raw materials and the export of the finished products. Finally, the rapid rivers—notably the Merrimack in Massachusetts—provided abundant water power to turn the cogs of the machines. By 1860 more than 400 million pounds of southern cotton poured annually into the gaping maws of over a thousand mills, mostly in New England.

✦ Marvels in Manufacturing

America's factories spread slowly until about 1807, when there began the fateful sequence of the embargo, nonintercourse, and the War of 1812. Stern necessity dictated the manufacture of substitutes for normal imports, while the stoppage of European commerce was temporarily ruinous to Yankee shipping. Both capital and labor were driven from the waves onto the factory floor, as New England, in the striking phrase of John Randolph, exchanged the trident for the distaff. Generous bounties were offered by local authorities for homegrown goods, "Buy American" and "Wear American" became popular slogans, and patriotism prompted the wearing of baggy homespun garments. President Madison donned some at his inauguration, where he was said to have been a walking argument for the better processing of native wool.

But the manufacturing boomlet broke abruptly with the peace of Ghent in 1815. British competitors unloaded their dammed-up surpluses at ruinously low prices, and American newspapers were so full of British advertisements for goods on credit that little space was left for news. In one Rhode Island district, all 150 mills were forced to close their doors, except the original Slater plant. Responding to pained outcries, Congress provided some relief when it passed the mildly protective Tariff of 1816—among the earliest political contests to control the shape of the economy.

As the factory system flourished, it embraced numerous other industries in addition to textiles. Prominent among them was the manufacturing of firearms, and here the wizardly Eli Whitney again appeared with an extraordinary contribution. Frustrated in his earlier efforts to monopolize the cotton gin, he turned to the mass production of muskets for the U.S. Army. Up to this time, each part of a firearm had been hand-tooled, and if the trigger of one broke, the trigger of another might or might not fit. About 1798 Whitney seized upon the idea of having machines make each part, so that all the triggers, for example, would be as much alike as the successive imprints of a copperplate engraving. Journeying to Washington, he reportedly dismantled ten of his new muskets in the presence of skeptical officials, scrambled the parts together, and then quickly reassembled ten different muskets.

The principle of interchangeable parts was widely adopted by 1850. It gave rise to a host of other innovations, including Samuel Colt's fabled revolver, and it ultimately became the basis of modern mass-production, assembly-line methods. It gave to the North the vast industrial plant that ensured military preponderance over the South. Ironically, the Yankee Eli Whitney, by perfecting the cotton gin, gave slavery a renewed lease on life, and perhaps made the Civil War more likely. At the same time, by popularizing the principle of interchangeable parts, Whitney helped factories to flourish in the North, giving the Union a decided advantage when that showdown came.

The sewing machine, invented by Elias Howe in 1846 and perfected by Isaac Singer, gave another strong boost to northern industrialization. The sewing machine became the foundation of the ready-made clothing industry, which took root about the time of the Civil War. It drove many a seamstress from the shelter of the private home to the factory, where, like a human robot, she tended the clattering mechanisms.

Each momentous new invention seemed to stimulate still more imaginative inventions. For the decade ending in 1800, only 306 patents were registered in Washington; but the decade ending in 1860 saw the

© Bettmann/Corbis

Collection of Matthew Isenburg

The Growth in Cotton Production and Consumption Whitney's gin made possible the mass cultivation of upland, or short-stable, cotton, which was unprofitable to raise when its seeds had to be laboriously removed by hand. As cotton production pushed farther south and west, taking slavery with it, it provisioned a growing northern textile industry. The young girl in this daguerreotype is dressed in inexpensive American-made calico, or printed cotton cloth, as shown here. The availability of plentiful, cheap cloth vastly expanded women's wardrobes.

Said Abraham Lincoln (1809–1865) in a lecture in 1859,

❝ The patent system secured to the inventor for a limited time exclusive use of his invention, and thereby added the fuel of interest to the fire of genius in the discovery and production of new and useful things.❞

Ten years earlier Lincoln had received patent no. 6469 for a scheme to buoy steamboats over shoals. It was never practically applied, but he remains the only president ever to have secured a patent.

amazing total of 28,000. Yet in 1838 the clerk of the **Patent Office** resigned in despair, complaining that all worthwhile inventions had been discovered.

Technical advances spurred equally important changes in the form and legal status of business organizations. The principle of **limited liability** aided the concentration of capital by permitting the individual investor, in cases of legal claims or bankruptcy, to risk no more than his own share of the corporation's stock. Fifteen Boston families formed one of the earliest investment capital companies, the Boston Associates. They eventually dominated the textile, railroad, insurance, and banking business of Massachusetts. Laws of "free incorporation," first passed in New York in 1848, meant that businessmen could create corporations without applying for individual charters from the legislature.

Samuel F. B. Morse's telegraph was among the inventions that tightened the sinews of an increasingly complex business world. A distinguished but poverty-stricken portrait painter, Morse finally secured from Congress, to the accompaniment of the usual jeers, an appropriation of $30,000 to support his experiment with "talking wires." In 1844 Morse strung a wire forty miles from Washington to Baltimore and tapped out the historic message, "What hath God wrought?" The invention brought fame and fortune to Morse, as he put distantly separated people in almost instant communication with one another. By the eve of the Civil War, a web of singing wires spanned nearly the entire continent, revolutionizing news gathering, diplomacy, and finance.

Thus, by the time of the fabled London World's Fair in 1851, known as the Great Exhibition, American products were prominent among the world's commercial wonders. Fairgoers crowded into the dazzling Crystal Palace to see McCormick's reaper, Morse's telegraph, Colt's firearms, and Charles Goodyear's vulcanized rubber goods.

✴ Workers and "Wage Slaves"

One ugly outgrowth of the factory system was an increasingly acute labor problem. Hitherto manufacturing had been done in the home, or in the small shop, where the master craftsman and his apprentice, rubbing elbows at the same bench, could maintain an intimate and friendly relationship. The Industrial Revolution submerged this personal association in the impersonal ownership of stuffy factories in "spindle cities." Around these, like tumors, the slumlike hovels of the "wage slaves" tended to cluster.

Clearly the early factory system did not shower its benefits evenly on all. While many owners grew plump, working people often wasted away at their workbenches. Hours were long, wages were low, and meals were skimpy and hastily gulped. Workers were forced to toil in unsanitary buildings that were poorly ventilated, lighted, and heated. They were forbidden by law to form labor unions to raise wages, for such cooperative activity was regarded as a criminal conspiracy. Not surprisingly, only twenty-four recorded strikes occurred before 1835.

Especially vulnerable to exploitation were child workers. In 1820 a significant portion of the nation's industrial toilers were children under ten years of age. Victims of factory labor, many children were mentally blighted, emotionally starved, physically stunted, and even brutally whipped in special "whipping rooms." In Samuel Slater's mill of 1791, the first machine tenders were seven boys and two girls, all under twelve years of age.

By contrast, the lot of most adult wage workers improved markedly in the 1820s and 1830s. In the full flush of Jacksonian democracy, many of the states granted the laboring man the vote. Brandishing the ballot, he first strove to lighten his burden through workingmen's parties. Eventually many workers gave their loyalty to the Democratic party of Andrew

One observer in 1836 published a newspaper account of conditions in some of the New England factories:

❝ The operatives work thirteen hours a day in the summer time, and from daylight to dark in the winter. At half past four in the morning the factory bell rings, and at five the girls must be in the mills.... So fatigued ... are numbers of girls that they go to bed soon after receiving their evening meal, and endeavor by a comparatively long sleep to resuscitate their weakened frames for the toil of the coming day.❞

Courtesy of the Museum of Connecticut History

Collection of E. R. Fisher

Coexistence of the Craftsman's Shop and the Factory, 1860 These two images recorded workers laboring in very different kinds of work places in the same year. The painting, "The Wheelwright's Shop," by Edwin Tryon Billings (right), captures the survival of a small-scale, intimate shop producing hand-made wheels for carts and carriages. The daguerreotype (left) shows an operator working the Lock Frame Jigging Machine in Samuel Colt's state-of-the-art Hartford, Connecticut, gun factory. As different as they were, both jobs required skill and focus.

Jackson, whose attack on the Bank of the United States and against all forms of "privilege" reflected their anxieties about the emerging capitalist economy. In addition to such goals as the ten-hour day, higher wages, and tolerable working conditions, they demanded public education for their children and an end to the inhuman practice of imprisonment for debt.

Employers, abhorring the rise of the "rabble" in politics, fought the ten-hour day to the last ditch. They argued that reduced hours would lessen production, increase costs, and demoralize the workers. Laborers would have so much leisure time that the Devil would lead them into mischief. A red-letter gain was at length registered for labor in 1840, when President Van Buren established the ten-hour day for federal employees on public works. In ensuing years a number of states gradually fell into line by reducing the hours of working people.

Day laborers at last learned that their strongest weapon was to lay down their tools, even at the risk of prosecution under the law. Dozens of strikes erupted in the 1830s and 1840s, most of them for higher wages, some for the ten-hour day, and a few for such unusual goals as the right to smoke on the job. The workers usually lost more strikes than they won, for the employer could resort to such tactics as the importing of strikebreakers—often derisively called "scabs" or "rats," and often fresh off the boat from the Old World. Labor long raised its voice against the unrestricted inpouring of wage-depressing and union-busting immigrant workers.

Labor's early and painful efforts at organization had netted some 300,000 trade unionists by 1830. But such encouraging gains were dashed on the rocks of

Violence broke out along the New York waterfront in 1836 when laborers striking for higher wages attacked "scabs." Philip Hone's (1780–1851) diary records,

❝ The Mayor, who acts with vigour and firmness, ordered out the troops, who are now on duty with loaded arms. . . . These measures have restored order for the present, but I fear the elements of disorder are at work; the bands of Irish and other foreigners, instigated by the mischievous councils of the trades-union and other combinations of discontented men, are acquiring strength and importance which will ere long be difficult to quell.**❞**

The Invention of the Sewing Machine

Historians of technology examine not only the documentary evidence of plans and patents left behind by inventors, but surviving machines themselves. In 1845 Elias Howe, a twenty-six-year-old apprentice to a Boston watchmaker, invented a sewing machine that could make 250 stitches a minute, five times what the swiftest hand-sewer could do. A year later Howe received a patent for his invention, but because the hand-cranked machine could only stitch straight seams for a short distance before requiring resetting, it had lim-

ited commercial appeal. Howe took his sewing machine abroad, where he worked with British manufacturers to improve it, and then returned to America and combined his patent with those of other inventors, including Isaac M. Singer. Hundreds of thousands of sewing machines were produced beginning in the 1850s for the commercial manufacture of clothing, books, shoes, and many other products and also for home use. The sewing machine became the first widely advertised consumer product. Due to its high cost, the Singer

company introduced an installment buying plan, which helped place sewing machines in most middle-class households. Why was the sewing machine able to find eager customers in commercial workshops and home sewing rooms alike? How might the sewing machine have changed other aspects of American life, such as work patterns, clothing styles, and retail selling? What other advances in technology might have been necessary for the invention of the sewing machine?

National Museum of American History, Smithsonian Institution, Behring Center

hard times following the severe depression of 1837. As unemployment spread, union membership shriveled. Yet toilers won a promising legal victory in 1842. The supreme court of Massachusetts ruled in the case of **Commonwealth v. Hunt** that labor unions were not

illegal conspiracies, provided that their methods were "honorable and peaceful." This enlightened decision did not legalize the strike overnight throughout the country, but it was a significant signpost of the times. Trade unions still had a rocky row to hoe, stretching

The Sewing Floor of Thompson's Skirt Factory, 1859 The burgeoning textile industry provided employment for thousands of women in antebellum America—and also produced the clothes that women wore. This view of a New York City shop in 1859 illustrates the transition from hand-sewing (on the right) to machine-stitching (on the left). It also vividly illustrates the contrast between the kinds of "sewing circles" in which women had traditionally sought companionship to the impersonal mass-production line of the modern manufacturing plant. Note especially the stark exhortation on the wall: "Strive to Excel."

ahead for about a century, before they could meet management on relatively even terms.

✷ Women and the Economy

Women were also sucked into the clanging mechanism of factory production. Farm women and girls had an important place in the preindustrial economy, spinning yarn, weaving cloth, and making candles, soap, butter, and cheese. New factories such as the textile mills of New England undermined these activities, cranking out manufactured goods much faster than they could be made by hand at home. Yet these same factories offered employment to the very young women whose work they were displacing. Factory jobs promised greater economic independence for women, as well as the means to buy the manufactured products of the new market economy.

"**Factory girls**" typically toiled six days a week, earning a pittance for dreary, limb-numbing, earsplitting stints of twelve or thirteen hours—"from dark to dark." The Boston Associates, nonetheless, proudly pointed to their textile mill at Lowell, Massachusetts, as a showplace factory. The workers were virtually all New England farm girls, carefully supervised on and off the job by watchful matrons. Escorted regularly to church from their company boardinghouses and forbidden to form unions, they had few opportunities to share dissatisfactions over their grueling working conditions.

But factory jobs of any kind were still unusual for women. Opportunities for women to be economically self-supporting were scarce and consisted mainly of nursing, domestic service, and especially teaching. The dedicated Catharine Beecher, unmarried daughter of a famous preacher and sister of Harriet Beecher Stowe, tirelessly urged women to enter the teaching profession. She eventually succeeded beyond her dreams, as men left teaching for other lines of work and schoolteaching became a thoroughly "feminized" occupation. Other work "opportunities" for women beckoned in household service. Perhaps one white family in ten employed servants at midcentury, most of whom were poor white, immigrant, or black women. About 10 percent of white women were working for pay outside their own homes in 1850, and estimates are that about 20 percent of all women had been employed at some time prior to marriage.

The vast majority of workingwomen were single. Upon marriage they left their paying jobs and took up

A woman worker in the Lowell mills wrote a friend in 1844,

"You wish to know minutely of our hours of labor. We go in [to the mill] at five o'clock; at seven we come out to breakfast; at half-past seven we return to our work, and stay until half-past twelve. At one, or quarter-past one four months in the year, we return to our work, and stay until seven at night. Then the evening is all our own, which is more than some laboring girls can say, who think nothing is more tedious than a factory life.**"**

York, Pennsylvania, Family with Negro Servant, ca. 1828 This portrait of a Pennsylvania family presents a somewhat idealized picture of the home as the woman's sphere. The wife and mother sits at the center of activity; while she reads to the children, the husband and father stands by somewhat superfluously. A black servant cares for an infant in the corner, suggesting the prosperous status of this household.

their new work (without wages) as wives and mothers. In the home they were enshrined in a **cult of domesticity**, a widespread cultural creed that glorified the customary functions of the homemaker. From their pedestal, married women commanded immense moral power, and they increasingly made decisions that altered the character of the family itself.

Women's changing roles and the spreading Industrial Revolution brought some important changes in the life of the nineteenth-century home—the traditional "women's sphere." Love, not parental "arrangement," more and more frequently determined the choice of a spouse—yet parents often retained the power of veto. Families thus became more closely knit and affectionate, providing the emotional refuge that made the threatening impersonality of big-city industrialism tolerable to many people.

Most striking, families grew smaller. The average household had nearly six members at the end of the eighteenth century but fewer than five members a century later. The "fertility rate," or number of births among women ages fourteen to forty-five, dropped sharply among white women in the years after the Revolution and, in the course of the nineteenth century as a whole, fell by half. Birth control was still a taboo topic for polite conversation, and contraceptive technology was primitive, but clearly some form of family limitation was being practiced quietly and effectively in countless families, rural and urban alike. Women undoubtedly played a large part—perhaps the leading part—in decisions to have fewer children. This newly assertive role for women has been called "domestic feminism," because it signified the growing power and independence of women, even while they remained wrapped in the "cult of domesticity."

Smaller families, in turn, meant child-centered families, since where children are fewer, parents can lavish more care on them individually. European visitors to the United States in the nineteenth century often complained about the unruly behavior of American "brats." But though American parents may have increasingly spared the rod, they did not spoil their children. Lessons were enforced by punishments other than the hickory stick. When the daughter of novelist Harriet Beecher Stowe neglected to do her homework, her mother sent her from the dinner table and gave her "only bread and water in her own apartment." What Europeans saw as permissiveness was in reality the consequence of an emerging new idea of child-rearing, in which the child's will was not to be simply broken, but rather shaped.

In the little republic of the family, as in the Republic at large, good citizens were raised not to be meekly obedient to authority, but to be independent individuals who could make their own decisions on the basis of internalized moral standards. Thus the outlines of the "modern" family were clear by midcentury: it was small, affectionate, and child-centered, and it provided a special arena for the talents of women. Feminists of a later day might decry the stifling atmosphere of the nineteenth-century middle-class white home, but to many women of the time, it seemed a big step upward from the conditions of grinding toil—often alongside men in the fields—in which their mothers had lived.

✵ Western Farmers Reap a Revolution in the Fields

As smoke-belching factories altered the eastern skyline, flourishing farms were changing the face of the West. The trans-Allegheny region—especially the Ohio-Indiana-Illinois tier—was fast becoming the nation's breadbasket. Before long it would become a granary to the world.

Pioneer families first hacked a clearing out of the forest and then planted their painfully furrowed fields to corn. The yellow grain was amazingly versatile. It could be fed to hogs ("corn on the hoof") or distilled into liquor ("corn in the bottle"). Both these products could be transported more easily than the bulky grain

itself, and they became the early western farmer's staple market items. So many hogs were butchered, traded, or shipped at Cincinnati that the city was known as the "Porkopolis" of the West.

Most western produce was at first floated down the Ohio-Mississippi River system, to feed the lusty appetite of the booming Cotton Kingdom. But western farmers were as hungry for profits as southern slaves and planters were for food. These tillers, spurred on by the easy availability of seemingly boundless acres, sought ways to bring more and more land into cultivation.

Ingenious inventors came to their aid. One of the first obstacles that frustrated the farmers was the thickly matted soil of the West, which snagged and snapped fragile wooden plows. John Deere of Illinois in 1837 finally produced a steel plow that broke the stubborn soil. Sharp and effective, it was also light enough to be pulled by horses, rather than oxen.

In the 1830s Virginia-born Cyrus McCormick contributed the most wondrous contraption of all: a mechanical mower-reaper. The clattering cogs of McCormick's horse-drawn machine were to the western farmers what the cotton gin was to the southern planters. Seated on his red-chariot reaper, a single husbandman could do the work of five men with sickles and scythes.

No other American invention cut so wide a swath as the **McCormick reaper**. It made ambitious capitalists

McCormick's Miraculous Reaper This illustration shows an early test of Cyrus McCormick's mechanical reaper near his home in Virginia in 1831. The reaper was best suited, however, to the horizonless fields of wheat on the rolling prairies of the Midwest. By the 1850s McCormick's Chicago factory was cranking out more than twenty thousand reapers a year for midwestern farmers.

Chicago History Museum

McCormick Reaper Works, 1850s Contrast this hectic scene of "mass production" with the simple workplace depicted in "The Wheelwright's Shop" on page 291.

Wisconsin Historical Society

out of humble plowmen, who now scrambled for more acres on which to plant more fields of billowing wheat. Subsistence farming gave way to food production for both domestic and foreign markets, as large-scale ("extensive"), specialized, cash-crop agriculture came to dominate the trans-Allegheny West. With it followed mounting indebtedness, as farmers bought more land and more machinery to work it. Soon hustling farmer-businesspeople were annually harvesting a larger crop than the South—which was becoming self-sufficient in food production—could devour. They began to dream of markets elsewhere—in the mushrooming factory towns of the East or across the faraway Atlantic. But they were still largely landlocked. Commerce moved north and south on the river systems. Before it could begin to move east-west in bulk, a transportation revolution would have to occur.

✣ Highways and Steamboats

In 1789, when the Constitution was launched, primitive methods of travel were still in use. Waterborne commerce, whether along the coast or on the rivers, was slow, uncertain, and often dangerous. Stagecoaches and wagons lurched over bone-shaking roads. Passengers would be routed out to lay nearby fence rails across muddy stretches, and occasionally horses would drown in muddy pits while wagons sank slowly out of sight.

Cheap and efficient carriers were imperative if raw materials were to be transported to factories and if finished products were to be delivered to consumers. On December 3, 1803, a firm in Providence, Rhode Island, sent a shipment of yarn to a point sixty miles away, notifying the purchaser that the consignment could be expected to arrive in "the course of the winter."

A promising improvement came in the 1790s, when a private company completed the Lancaster Turnpike in Pennsylvania. It was a broad, hard-surfaced highway that thrust sixty-two miles westward from Philadelphia to Lancaster. As drivers approached the tollgate, they were confronted with a barrier of sharp pikes, which were turned aside when they paid their toll. Hence the term **turnpike**.

The Lancaster Turnpike proved to be a highly successful venture, returning as high as 15 percent annual dividends to its stockholders. It attracted a rich trade to Philadelphia and touched off a turnpike-building boom that lasted about twenty years. It also stimulated western development. The turnpikes beckoned to the canvas-covered Conestoga wagons, whose creakings heralded a westward advance that would know no real retreat.

Western road building, always expensive, encountered many obstacles. One pesky roadblock was the noisy states' righters, who opposed federal aid to local projects. Eastern states also protested against being bled of their populations by the westward-reaching arteries.

Westerners scored a notable triumph in 1811 when the federal government started construction of the National Road, also known as the Cumberland Road, in honor of its starting point in Cumberland, Maryland. Although construction was interrupted by the War of 1812 and by states' righters' complaints about federal grants for internal improvements, the road reached

Mississippi in Time of Peace, by Mrs. Frances Flora Bond Palmer, 1865 By the mid-nineteenth century, steamboats had made the Mississippi a bustling river highway—as it remains today.

Vandalia, Illinois, 591 miles to the west, in 1839. Later extensions brought it from Baltimore, on Chesapeake Bay, to the banks of the Mississippi River in St. Louis.

The steamboat craze, which overlapped the turnpike craze, was touched off by an ambitious painter-engineer named Robert Fulton. He installed a powerful steam engine in a vessel that posterity came to know as the *Clermont* but that a dubious public dubbed "Fulton's Folly." On a historic day in 1807, the quaint little ship, belching sparks from its single smokestack, churned steadily from New York City up the Hudson River toward Albany. It made the run of 150 miles in 32 hours.

The success of the steamboat was sensational. People could now in large degree defy wind, wave, tide, and downstream current. Within a few years, Fulton had changed all of America's navigable streams into two-way arteries, thereby doubling their carrying capacity. Hitherto keelboats had been pushed up the Mississippi, with quivering poles and raucous profanity, at less than one mile an hour—a process that was prohibitively expensive. Now the steamboats could churn rapidly against the current, ultimately attaining speeds in excess of ten miles an hour. The mighty Mississippi had met its master.

By 1820 there were some sixty steamboats on the Mississippi and its tributaries; by 1860 about one thousand, some of them luxurious river palaces. Keen rivalry among the swift and gaudy steamers led to memorable races. Excited passengers would urge the captain to pile on wood at the risk of bursting the boilers, which all too often exploded, with tragic results for the floating firetraps. When the steamer *Sultana* blew up in April 1865, the explosion killed seventeen hundred passengers, including many Union prisoners of war being repatriated to the North.

Chugging steamboats played a vital role in the opening of the West and South, both of which were richly endowed with navigable rivers. Like bunches of grapes on a vine, population clustered along the banks of the broad-flowing streams. Cotton growers and other farmers made haste to take up and turn over the now-profitable soil. Not only could they float their produce out to market, but, hardly less important, they could ship in at low cost their shoes, hardware, and other manufactured necessities.

✴ "Clinton's Big Ditch" in New York

A canal-cutting craze paralleled the boom in turnpikes and steamboats (see Map 14.2). A few canals had been built around falls and elsewhere in colonial days, but ambitious projects lay in the future. Resourceful New Yorkers, cut off from federal aid by states' righters,

MAP 14.2 Major Rivers, Roads, and Canals, 1825–1860 © Cengage Learning

themselves dug the **Erie Canal**, linking the Great Lakes with the Hudson River. They were blessed with the driving leadership of Governor DeWitt Clinton, whose grandiose project was scoffingly called "Clinton's Big Ditch" or "the Governor's Gutter."

Begun in 1817, the canal eventually ribboned 363 miles. On its completion in 1825, a garlanded canal boat glided from Buffalo, on Lake Erie, to the Hudson River and on to New York harbor. There, with colorful ceremony, Governor Clinton emptied a cask of water from the lake to symbolize "the marriage of the waters."

The water from Clinton's keg baptized the Empire State. Mule-drawn passengers and bulky freight could now be handled with thrift and dispatch, at the dizzy speed of five miles an hour. The cost of shipping a ton of grain from Buffalo to New York City fell from $100 to $5, and the time of transit from about twenty days to six.

Ever-widening economic ripples followed the completion of the Erie Canal. The value of land along the route skyrocketed, and new cities—such as Rochester and Syracuse—blossomed. Industry in the state boomed. The new profitability of farming in the Old Northwest—notably in Ohio, Michigan, Indiana, and Illinois—attracted thousands of European immigrants to the unaxed and untaxed lands now available. Flotillas of steamships soon plied the Great Lakes, connecting with canal barges at Buffalo. Interior waterside villages like Cleveland, Detroit, and Chicago exploded into mighty cities.

Other profound economic and political changes followed the canal's completion. The price of potatoes in New York City was cut in half, and many dispirited New England farmers, no longer able to face the ruinous competition, abandoned their rocky holdings and went elsewhere. Some became mill hands, thus speeding the industrialization of America. Others, finding it easy to go west over the Erie Canal, took up new farmland south of the Great Lakes, where they were joined by thousands of New Yorkers and other northerners. Still others shifted to fruit, vegetable, and dairy farming. The transformations in the Northeast—canal consequences—showed how long-established local market structures could be swamped by the emerging behemoth of a continental economy. And as American products began to flow into international markets, even far-off Europeans began to feel the effects of America's economic vitality. Before long, Italian and Polish peasants, displaced from their marginal farms by the arrival of cheap American grains, would come to America to build new lives.

✦ The Iron Horse

The most significant contribution to the development of such an economy proved to be the railroad. It was fast, reliable, cheaper than canals to construct, and not frozen over in winter. Able to go almost anywhere, even through the Allegheny barrier, it defied terrain and weather. The first railroad appeared in the United States in 1828, and new lines spread with amazing swiftness. Andrew Jackson rode to his first presidential inauguration in 1829 in a horse-drawn carriage. At the end of his second term, eight years later, he departed from Washington in a railway car. By 1860, on the eve of the Civil War, the United States boasted thirty thousand miles of railroad track, three-fourths of it in the rapidly industrializing North (see Map 14.3).

At first the railroad faced strong opposition from vested interests, especially canal backers. Anxious to protect its investment in the Erie Canal, the New York legislature in 1833 prohibited the railroads from carrying freight—at least temporarily. Early railroads were also considered a dangerous public menace, for flying sparks could set fire to nearby haystacks and houses, and appalling railway accidents could turn the wooden "miniature hells" into flaming funeral pyres for their riders.

Railroad pioneers had to overcome other obstacles as well. Brakes were so feeble that the engineer might miss the station twice, both arriving and backing up. Arrivals and departures were conjectural, and numerous differences in gauge (the distance between the rails) meant frequent changes of trains for passengers. In 1840 there were seven transfers between Philadelphia and Charleston. But gauges gradually became standardized, better brakes did brake, safety devices were adopted, and the Pullman "sleeping palace" was introduced in 1859. America at long last was being bound together with braces of iron, later to be made of steel.

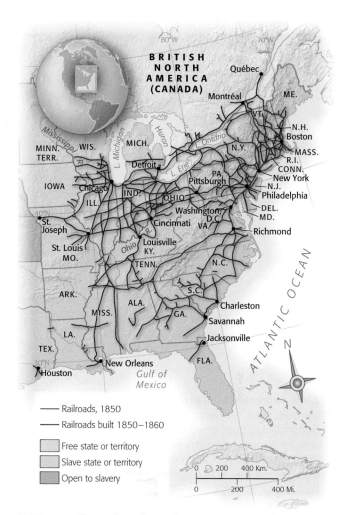

MAP 14.3 The Railroad Revolution Note the explosion of new railroad construction in the 1850s and its heavy concentration in the North. © Cengage Learning

✦ Cables, Clippers, and Pony Riders

Other forms of transportation and communication were binding together the United States and the world. A crucial development came in 1858 when Cyrus Field, called "the greatest wire-puller in history," organized a joint Anglo-American-Canadian venture to stretch a cable under the deep North Atlantic waters from Newfoundland to Ireland. Although this initial cable went dead after three weeks of public rejoicing, a heavier cable laid in 1866 permanently linked the American and European continents.

The United States merchant marine encountered rough sailing during much of the early nineteenth century. American vessels had been repeatedly laid up by the embargo, the War of 1812, and the panics of 1819 and 1837. American naval designers made few contributions to maritime progress. A pioneer American steamer, the *Savannah*, crept across the Atlantic in 1819,

Poster-Timetable for Baltimore & Susquehanna Railroad, 1840 Advertising the Baltimore & Susquehanna's train schedule alone was not sufficient to get passengers to their destinations. A typical trip often entailed coordinating legs on other railroad lines, stagecoaches, and canal boats.

Chariot of Fame **Clipper Ship, by Duncan McFarlane, 1854**

MAP 14.4 Main Routes West Before the Civil War Mark Twain described his stagecoach trip to California in the 1860s in *Roughing It*: "We began to get into country, now, threaded here and there with little streams. These had high, steep banks on each side, and every time we flew down one bank and scrambled up the other, our party inside got mixed somewhat. First we would all be down in a pile at the forward end of the stage, . . . and in a second we would shoot to the other end, and stand on our heads. And . . . as the dust rose from the tumult, we would all sneeze in chorus, and the majority of us would grumble, and probably say some hasty thing, like: 'Take your elbow out of my ribs!—can't you quit crowding?'" © Cengage Learning

but it used sail most of the time and was pursued for a day by a British captain who thought it afire.

In the 1840s and 1850s, a golden age dawned for American shipping. Yankee naval yards, notably Donald McKay's at Boston, began to send down the ways sleek new craft called **clipper ships**. Long, narrow, and majestic, they glided across the sea under towering masts and clouds of canvas. In a fair breeze, they could outrun any steamer.

The stately clippers sacrificed cargo space for speed, and their captains made killings by hauling high-value cargoes in record times. They wrested much of the tea-carrying trade between the Far East and Britain from their slower-sailing British competitors, and they sped thousands of impatient adventurers to the goldfields of California and Australia.

But the hour of glory for the clipper was relatively brief. On the eve of the Civil War, the British had clearly won the world race for maritime ascendancy with their iron tramp steamers ("teakettles"). Although slower and less romantic than the clipper, these vessels were steadier, roomier, more reliable, and hence more profitable.

No story of rapid American communication would be complete without including the Far West. By 1858 horse-drawn overland stagecoaches, immortalized by Mark Twain's *Roughing It*, were a familiar sight. Their dusty tracks stretched from the banks of the muddy Missouri River clear to California (see Map 14.4).

Even more dramatic was the **Pony Express**, established in 1860 to carry mail speedily the two thousand lonely miles from St. Joseph, Missouri, to Sacramento,

As late as 1877, stagecoach passengers were advised in print,

❝Never shoot on the road as the noise might frighten the horses. . . . Don't point out where murders have been committed, especially if there are women passengers. . . . Expect annoyances, discomfort, and some hardships.❞

California. Daring, lightweight riders, leaping onto wiry ponies saddled at stations approximately ten miles apart, could make the trip in an amazing ten days. These unarmed horsemen galloped on, summer or winter, day or night, through dust or snow, past Indians and bandits. The speeding postmen missed only one trip, though the whole enterprise lost money heavily and folded after only eighteen legend-leaving months.

Just as the clippers had succumbed to steam, so were the express riders unhorsed by Samuel Morse's clacking keys, which began tapping messages to California in 1861. The swift ships and the fleet ponies ushered out a dying technology of wind and muscle. In the future, machines would be in the saddle.

✴ The Transport Web Binds the Union

More than anything else, the desire of the East to tap the West stimulated the **transportation revolution**. Until about 1830 the produce of the western region drained southward to the cotton belt or to the heaped-up wharves of New Orleans. The steamboat vastly aided the reverse flow of finished goods up the watery western arteries and helped bind West and South together. But the truly revolutionary changes in commerce and communication came in the three decades before the Civil War, as canals and railroad tracks radiated out from the East, across the Alleghenies and into the blossoming heartland. The ditch-diggers and tie-layers were attempting nothing less than a conquest of nature itself. They would offset the "natural" flow of trade on the interior rivers by laying down an impressive grid of "internal improvements."

The builders succeeded beyond their wildest dreams. The Mississippi was increasingly robbed of its traffic, as goods moved eastward on chugging trains, puffing lake boats, and mule-tugged canal barges. Governor Clinton had in effect picked up the mighty Father of Waters and flung it over the Alleghenies, forcing it to empty into the sea at New York City. By the 1840s the city of Buffalo handled more western produce than New Orleans. Between 1836 and 1860, grain shipments

through Buffalo increased a staggering sixtyfold. New York City became the seaboard queen of the nation, a gigantic port through which a vast hinterland poured its wealth and to which it daily paid economic tribute.

By the eve of the Civil War, a truly continental economy had emerged. The principle of division of labor, which spelled productivity and profits in the factory, applied on a national scale as well. Each region now specialized in a particular type of economic activity. The South raised cotton for export to New England and Britain; the West grew grain and livestock to feed factory workers in the East and in Europe; the East made machines and textiles for the South and the West.

The economic pattern thus woven had fateful political and military implications. Many southerners regarded the Mississippi as a silver chain that naturally linked together the upper valley states and the Cotton Kingdom. They would become convinced, as secession approached in the 1850s, that some or all of these states would have to secede with them or be strangled. But they would overlook the man-made links that increasingly bound the upper Mississippi Valley to the East in intimate commercial union. Southern rebels would have to fight not only Northern armies but the tight bonds of an interdependent continental economy. Economically, the two northerly sections were conjoined twins.

✴ The Market Revolution

No less revolutionary than the political upheavals of the antebellum era was the **market revolution** that transformed a subsistence economy of scattered farms and tiny workshops into a national network of industry and commerce (see Map 14.5). Greater mechanization and a more robust market-oriented economy raised new legal questions about winners and losers. How tightly should patents protect inventions? Should the government regulate monopolies? Who should own the technologies and networks that made America hum in the 1840s and 1850s?

Under Chief Justice John Marshall, the U.S. Supreme Court vigilantly protected contract rights by requiring state governments to grant irrevocable charters. Monopolies easily developed, as new companies found it difficult to break into markets. After Marshall died in 1835, the climate began to change and the winds of economic opportunity blew more freely. When the proprietors of Boston's Charles River Bridge (which included Harvard College) sued the owners of the new Warren Bridge for unconstitutionally violating their original contract, the new chief justice, Roger B. Taney, sided with the newcomers and argued that "the rights of the community" outweighed any exclusive corporate rights. Taney's decision opened new entrepreneurial channels and encouraged greater competition. So did the passage of more liberal state incorporation laws beginning in the 1830s, granting investors the benefit of "limited liability" if their companies were sued or went bankrupt.

As more and more Americans—mill workers as well as farmhands, women as well as men—linked their economic fate to the burgeoning market economy, the self-sufficient households of colonial days were transformed. Most families had once raised all their own food, spun their own wool, and bartered with their neighbors for the few necessities they could not make themselves. In growing numbers they now scattered to work for wages in the mills, or they planted just a few crops for sale at market and used the money to buy goods made by strangers in far-off factories. As store-bought fabric, candles, and soap replaced homemade products, a quiet revolution occurred in the household division of labor and status. Traditional women's work was rendered superfluous and devalued. The home itself, once a center of economic production in which all family members cooperated, grew into a place of refuge from the world of work, a refuge that became increasingly the special and separate sphere of women.

Revolutionary advances in manufacturing and transportation brought increased prosperity to all Americans, but they also widened the gulf between the rich and the poor. Millionaires had been rare in the early days of the Republic, but by the eve of the Civil War, several specimens of colossal financial success were strutting across the national stage. Spectacular was the case of fur-trader and real estate speculator John Jacob Astor, who left an estate of $30 million on his death in 1848.

Cities bred the greatest extremes of economic inequality. Unskilled workers, then as always, fared

MAP 14.5 Industry and Agriculture, 1860 Still a nation of farmers on the eve of the Civil War, Americans had nevertheless made an impressive start on their own Industrial Revolution, especially in the Northeast. © Cengage Learning

Chicago, 1857 A modest village of a few hundred souls in the 1830s, Chicago was a teeming metropolis just two decades later—one of the fastest-growing cities in the world. A food and livestock processing center and transportation hub, it served the vast farming area of the western plains, a remarkably productive agricultural region and breadbasket to the world.

worst. Many of them came to make up a floating mass of "drifters," buffeted from town to town by the shifting prospects for menial jobs. These wandering workers accounted at various times for up to half the population of the brawling industrial centers. Although their numbers were large, they left little behind them but the homely fruits of their transient labor. Largely unstoried and unsung, they are among the forgotten men and women of American history.

Many myths about "social mobility" grew up over the buried memories of these unfortunate day laborers. Mobility did exist in industrializing America—but not in the proportions that legend often portrays. Rags-to-riches success stories were relatively few.

Yet America, with its dynamic society and wide-open spaces, undoubtedly provided more "opportunity" than did the contemporary countries of the Old World—which is why millions of immigrants packed their bags and headed for New World shores. Moreover, a rising tide lifts all boats, and the improvement in overall standards of living was real. Wages for unskilled workers in a labor-hungry America rose about 1 percent a year from 1820 to 1860. This general prosperity helped defuse the potential class conflict that might otherwise have exploded—and that did explode in many European countries.

The famed English writer Charles Dickens (1812–1870) traveled to the United States in 1842 and was sharply critical of certain aspects of the national character:

❝Another prominent feature is the love of 'smart' dealing which gilds over many a swindle and gross breach of trust; many a defalcation [embezzlement], public and private; and enables many a knave to hold his head up with the best, who well deserves a halter.**❞**

Chapter Review

KEY TERMS

"Self-Reliance" (276)

rendezvous (277)

ecological imperialism (277)

Ancient Order of Hibernians (281)

Molly Maguires (281)

Tammany Hall (281)

Know-Nothing party (284)

Awful Disclosures (284)

Industrial Revolution (285)

cotton gin (287)

Patent Office (290)

limited liability (290)

Commonwealth v. Hunt (292)

factory girls (293)

cult of domesticity (294)

McCormick reaper (295)

turnpike (296)

Erie Canal (298)

clipper ships (301)

Pony Express (301)

transportation revolution (302)

market revolution (302)

PEOPLE TO KNOW

Samuel Slater

Eli Whitney

Elias Howe

Isaac Singer

Samuel F. B. Morse

John Deere

Cyrus McCormick

Robert Fulton

DeWitt Clinton

Cyrus Field

John Jacob Astor

CHRONOLOGY

ca. 1750	Industrial Revolution begins in Britain
1791	Samuel Slater builds first U.S. textile factory
1793	Eli Whitney invents cotton gin
1798	Whitney develops interchangeable parts for muskets
1807	Robert Fulton's first steamboat Embargo spurs American manufacturing
1811	Cumberland Road construction begins
1817	Erie Canal construction begins
1825	Erie Canal completed
1828	First railroad in United States
1830s	Cyrus McCormick invents mechanical mower-reaper
1834	Anti-Catholic riot in Boston
1837	John Deere develops steel plow
1840	President Van Buren establishes ten-hour day for federal employees
1842	Massachusetts declares labor unions legal in *Commonwealth* v. *Hunt*

ca. 1843–1868	Era of clipper ships
1844	Samuel Morse invents telegraph Anti-Catholic riot in Philadelphia
1845–1849	Potato famine in Ireland
1846	Elias Howe invents sewing machine
1848	First general incorporation laws in New York Democratic revolutions collapse in Germany
1849	American, or Know-Nothing, party formed
1851	London World's Fair
1852	Cumberland Road completed
1858	Cyrus Field lays first transatlantic cable
1860	Pony Express established
1861	First transcontinental telegraph
1866	Permanent transatlantic cable established

TO LEARN MORE

John Bodnar, *The Transplanted: A History of Immigrants in Urban America* (1985)

Christopher Clark, *Social Change in America: From the Revolution Through the Civil War* (2006)

Thomas C. Cochran, *Frontiers of Change: Early Industrialism in America* (1981)

Hasia Diner, *Erin's Daughters in America* (1983)

David H. Hounshell, *From the American System to Mass Production, 1800–1932: The Development of Manufacturing Technology in the United States* (1984)

Paul E. Johnson, *Sam Patch, the Famous Jumper* (2003)

Gerard Koeppel, *Bond of Union: Building the Erie Canal and the American Empire* (2009)

Bruce Levine, *The Spirit of 1848: German Immigrants, Labor Conflict, and the Coming of the Civil War* (1992)

David Nye, *Consuming Power: A Social History of American Energies* (1998)

Michael O'Malley, *Keeping Watch: A History of American Time* (1996)

Augustus J. Veenendaal, *American Railroads in the Nineteenth Century* (2003)

A complete, annotated bibliography for this chapter—along with brief descriptions of the People to Know—may be found on the American Pageant website. The Key Terms are defined in a Glossary at the end of the text.

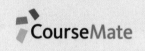

Go to the CourseMate website at **www.cengagebrain.com** for additional study tools and review materials—including audio and video clips—for this chapter.

AP® Review Questions for Chapter 14

1. The first national park, Yellowstone, was the product of
   (A) an emerging conservation movement that began in the 1830s.
   (B) a desire to make access to some western lands available to the entire public.
   (C) an effort to keep miners from exploiting and abandoning the soil there.
   (D) President Harrison's love of nature.
   (E) early overcrowding of people and animals on western lands.

2. What was the main factor contributing to rapid population growth in the 1840s and beyond?
   (A) Widespread immigration
   (B) Increased imports of slaves
   (C) Rising birthrates
   (D) Improved health
   (E) Acquisition of new territories

3. All of the following contributed to an increased influx of new immigrants to America in the nineteenth century EXCEPT that
   (A) Europe was running out of room for its rapidly expanding population.
   (B) new technologies made transatlantic travel faster and cheaper.
   (C) letters from American loved ones beckoned family to join them.
   (D) companies seeking workers offered lucrative incentives.
   (E) America was perceived as the land of opportunity.

4. Why did Irish immigrants embrace machine politics in the cities where they settled?
   (A) The machines offered much-needed cash in exchange for Irish votes.
   (B) The machines aided struggling newcomers with free coal, food, and legal advice.
   (C) They pledged to fight anti-Irish prejudice and bigotry.
   (D) The Irish were unaccustomed to politics, and machines provided an easy initiation.
   (E) Political machines helped Irish immigrants acquire land.

5. German immigrants to America differed from the Irish in all of the following ways EXCEPT that
   (A) German immigrants tended to be poorer.
   (B) many Germans left their homeland for political reasons.
   (C) Germans settled in the MidWest rather than eastern cities.
   (D) Germans became outspoken opponents of slavery.
   (E) only a minority of Germans were Roman Catholic.

6. Which of these was NOT a cause for the antiforeign or nativist movement that emerged in the 1840s and 1850s?
   (A) Fear that immigrants would drive wages down and compete for jobs
   (B) Concern that increased immigration would drive up land prices
   (C) Rampant anti-Catholicism
   (D) Fear that foreigners would outnumber native-born Americans
   (E) Concern that immigrants would outvote native-born Americans

7. Americans lagged behind the British in industrializing largely because they
   (A) feared they could not compete with the quality of British manufacturing.
   (B) preferred to import rather than manufacture goods.
   (C) associated the factory system with the worst qualities of European society.
   (D) were not interested in shifting from hand-made goods.
   (E) lacked the capital and infrastructure necessary to support the factory system.

8. Who is considered the father of the American factory system?
   (A) Moses Brown
   (B) Eli Whitney
   (C) Samuel Slater
   (D) Francis Cabot
   (E) Isaac Singer

9. New England was well suited to becoming an industrial center for all of the reasons below EXCEPT that
   (A) its land was too rocky and difficult to farm.
   (B) its dense population provided a ready labor force and customer base for factory-produced goods.
   (C) its seaports made importing raw materials and exporting finished goods easier.
   (D) its fast-flowing rivers provided the perfect power source for factory cogs.
   (E) it was hardest hit by the lack of imported goods during the War of 1812.

10. Despite poor working conditions, there were only twenty-four recorded strikes before 1835. Why?
    (A) It was against the law for workers to organize for better wages.
    (B) Often poor, workers could not afford to walk off their jobs.
    (C) Many of the workers were children.
    (D) Workers used their newly acquired right to vote to effect change instead.
    (E) Workers distrusted group activism and preferred to act as individuals.

11. The nineteenth century *cult of domesticity* is best defined as the
    (A) idea that women should determine family size.
    (B) belief that women should only work as household help, maids, and cooks.
    (C) notion that upon marriage, women should leave their paid jobs.
    (D) celebration of women's roles within the home.
    (E) new innovations that simplified housework and freed up women's time.

12. What most facilitated the emergence of the trans-Allegheny region (Ohio-Indiana-Illinois tier) as the nation's leading grain producers?
    (A) Rapid settlement of the West
    (B) Southern demand for food products
    (C) New farming technologies
    (D) A steady labor stream fueled by immigration
    (E) The push of Indians off the land and further west

13. Robert Fulton's development of the steamboat was significant for all of the following reasons EXCEPT that it
    (A) helped fuel further development of the West.
    (B) relied on making the best use of currents.
    (C) shortened travel time and lowered costs.
    (D) transformed streams into two-way transportation arteries.
    (E) facilitated trade with interior and southern regions.

14. Which of these did NOT play a role in stimulating U.S. economic growth and connections to the broader world?
    (A) The rise of railroads
    (B) The Pony Express
    (C) The development of canals
    (D) The market revolution
    (E) The emergence of steam

15. The invention of the cotton gin in 1793 contributed to the Civil War nearly seventy years later because
    (A) it renewed the demand for slaves in the South.
    (B) it indirectly spurred industrialization in New England.
    (C) British mills bought the majority of cotton produced in the South.
    (D) King Cotton eventually made up 60 percent of U.S. imports.
    (E) tobacco became a secondary cash crop.

16. Which of the following was NOT a change brought on by the Erie Canal?
    (A) The cost of shipping grain decreased sharply.
    (B) New cities in upstate New York blossomed.
    (C) The population of New England skyrocketed.
    (D) The Great Lakes took on a new importance for trade.
    (E) Local markets lost business to continental behemoths.

Chapter 15

The Ferment of Reform and Culture

1790–1860

*We [Americans] will walk on our own feet; we will work
with our own hands; we will speak our own minds.*

RALPH WALDO EMERSON, "THE AMERICAN SCHOLAR," 1837

A third revolution accompanied the reformation of American politics and the transformation of the American economy in the mid-nineteenth century. It consisted of a diffuse yet deeply felt commitment to improve the character of ordinary Americans, to make them more upstanding, God-fearing, and literate. Some high-minded souls were disillusioned by the rough-and-tumble realities of democratic politics. Others, notably women, were excluded from the political game altogether. As the young Republic grew, increasing numbers of Americans poured their considerable energies into an astonishing variety of religious revivals and reform movements.

Reform campaigns of all types flourished in sometimes bewildering abundance. There was not "a reading man" who was without some scheme for a new utopia in his "waistcoat pocket," claimed Ralph Waldo Emerson. Reformers promoted better public schools and rights for women, as well as miracle medicines, polygamy, celibacy, rule by prophets, and guidance by spirits. Societies were formed against alcohol, tobacco, profanity, and the transit of mail on the Sabbath. Eventually overshadowing all other reforms was the great crusade against slavery (see pp. 348–349).

Many reformers drew their crusading zeal from religion. Beginning in the late 1790s and boiling over into the early nineteenth century, the Second Great Awakening swept through America's Protestant churches, transforming the place of religion in American life and sending a generation of believers out on their missions to perfect the world.

✦ Reviving Religion

Church attendance was still a regular ritual for about three-fourths of the 23 million Americans in 1850. Alexis de Tocqueville declared that there was "no country in the world where the Christian religion retains a greater influence over the souls of men than in America." Yet the religion of these years was not the old-time religion of colonial days. The austere Calvinist rigor had long been seeping out of the American churches. The rationalist ideas of the French Revolutionary era had done much to soften the older orthodoxy. Thomas Paine's widely circulated book ***The Age of Reason*** (1794) had shockingly declared that all churches were "set up to terrify and enslave mankind, and monopolize power and profit." American anticlericalism was seldom that virulent, but many of the Founding Fathers, including Jefferson and Franklin, embraced the liberal doctrines of **Deism** that Paine promoted. Deists relied on reason rather than revelation, on science rather than the Bible. They rejected the concept of original sin and denied Christ's divinity. Yet Deists believed in a Supreme Being who had created a knowable universe and endowed human beings with a capacity for moral behavior.

Deism helped to inspire an important spinoff from the severe Puritanism of the past—the Unitarian faith, which began to gather momentum in New England at the end of the eighteenth century. **Unitarians** held that God existed in only *one* person (hence *uni*tarian), and not in the orthodox Trinity (God the Father, God the Son, and God the Holy Spirit). Although denying the deity of Jesus, Unitarians stressed the essential goodness of human nature rather than its vileness; they proclaimed their belief in free will and the possibility of salvation through good works; they pictured God not as a stern Creator but as a loving Father. Embraced by many leading thinkers (including Ralph Waldo Emerson), the Unitarian movement appealed mostly to intellectuals whose rationalism and optimism contrasted sharply with the hellfire doctrines of Calvinism, especially predestination and human depravity.

A boiling reaction against the growing liberalism in religion set in about 1800. A fresh wave of roaring revivals, beginning on the southern frontier but soon rolling even into the cities of the Northeast, sent the **Second Great Awakening** surging across the land. Sweeping up even more people than the First Great Awakening (see p. 87) almost a century earlier, the Second Awakening was one of the most momentous episodes in the history of American religion. This tidal wave of spiritual fervor left in its wake countless converted souls, many shattered and reorganized churches, and numerous new sects. It also encouraged an effervescent evangelicalism that bubbled up into innumerable areas of American life—including prison reform, the temperance cause, the women's movement, and the crusade to abolish slavery.

The Second Great Awakening was spread to the masses on the frontier by huge "camp meetings." As many as twenty-five thousand people would gather for an encampment of several days to drink the hellfire gospel as served up by an itinerant preacher. Thousands of spiritually starved souls "got religion" at these gatherings and in their ecstasy engaged in frenzies of rolling, dancing, barking, and jerking. Many of the "saved" soon backslid into their former sinful ways, but the revivals boosted church membership and stimulated a variety of humanitarian reforms. Responsive easterners were moved to do missionary work in the West with Indians, in Hawaii, and in Asia.

Methodists and Baptists reaped the most abundant harvest of souls from the fields fertilized by revivalism. Both sects stressed personal conversion (contrary to predestination), a relatively democratic control of church affairs, and a rousing emotionalism. As a frontier jingle ran,

The devil hates the Methodists
Because they sing and shout the best.

Powerful Peter Cartwright (1785–1872) was the best known of the Methodist "circuit riders," or traveling frontier preachers. This ill-educated but sinewy servant of the Lord ranged for a half-century from Tennessee to Illinois, calling upon sinners to repent. With bellowing voice and flailing arms, he converted thousands of souls to the Lord. Not only did he lash the Devil with his tongue, but with his fists he knocked out rowdies who tried to break up his meetings. His Christianity was definitely muscular.

Bell-voiced Charles Grandison Finney was the greatest of the revival preachers. Trained as a lawyer, Finney abandoned the bar to become an evangelist

Religious Camp Meeting, by J. Maze Burbank, 1839 At huge, daylong encampments, repentant sinners dedicated themselves to lives of personal rectitude and social reform. Fire-and-brimstone preachers like the one depicted here inspired convulsions, speaking in tongues, and ecstatic singing and dancing among the converted. Out of this religious upheaval grew many of the movements for social improvement in the pre–Civil War decades, including the abolitionist crusade.

Old Dartmouth Historical Society/New Bedford Whaling Museum

Oberlin College Archives, Oberlin, Ohio

Charles Grandison Finney (1792–1875), 1834 The charismatic Finney appears here at age forty-two, at the height of his career as an evangelist. A mesmerizer of audiences, he was said to have converted over a half million people. In 1834, Finney had just led a series of enormously successful revivals in cities along the Erie Canal. The next year he would establish a theology department at the newly founded Oberlin College in Ohio, where he helped train a generation of ministers and served as president from 1851 to 1866.

after a deeply moving conversion experience as a young man. Tall and athletically built, Finney held huge crowds spellbound with the power of his oratory and the pungency of his message. He led massive revivals in Rochester and New York City in 1830 and 1831. Finney preached a version of the old-time religion, but he was also an innovator. He devised the "anxious bench," where repentant sinners could sit in full view of the congregation, and he encouraged women to pray aloud in public. Holding out the promise of a perfect Christian kingdom on earth, Finney denounced both alcohol and slavery. He eventually served as president of Oberlin College in Ohio, which he helped to make a hotbed of revivalist activity and abolitionism.

A key feature of the Second Great Awakening was the feminization of religion, in terms of both church membership and theology. Middle-class women, the wives and daughters of businessmen, were the first and

In his lecture "Hindrances to Revivals," delivered in the 1830s, Charles Grandison Finney (1792–1875) proposed the excommunication of drinkers and slaveholders:

"Let the churches of all denominations speak out on the subject of temperance, let them close their doors against all who have anything to do with the death-dealing abomination, and the cause of temperance is triumphant. A few years would annihilate the traffic. Just so with slavery. . . . It is a great national sin. It is a sin of the church. The churches by their silence, and by permitting slaveholders to belong to their communion, have been consenting to it. . . . The church cannot turn away from this question. It is a question for the church and for the nation to decide, and God will push it to a decision."

most fervent enthusiasts of religious revivalism. They made up the majority of new church members, and they were most likely to stay within the fold when the tents were packed up and the traveling evangelists left town. Perhaps women's greater ambivalence than men about the changes wrought by the expanding market economy made them such eager converts to piety. It helped as well that evangelicals preached a gospel of female spiritual worth and offered women an active role in bringing their husbands and families back to God. That accomplished, many women turned to saving the rest of society. They formed a host of benevolent and charitable organizations and spearheaded crusades for most, if not all, of the era's ambitious reforms.

Denominational Diversity

Revivals also furthered the fragmentation of religious faiths. Western New York, where many descendants of New England Puritans had settled, was so blistered by sermonizers preaching "hellfire and damnation" that it came to be known as the **Burned-Over District**.

Millerites, or Adventists, who mustered several hundred thousand adherents, rose from the superheated soil of the Burned-Over District in the 1830s. Named after the eloquent and commanding William Miller, they interpreted the Bible to mean that Christ would return to earth on October 22, 1844. Donning their go-to-meeting clothes, they gathered in prayerful assemblies to greet their Redeemer. The failure of Jesus to descend on schedule dampened but did not destroy the movement.

Like the First Great Awakening, the Second Great Awakening tended to widen the lines between classes

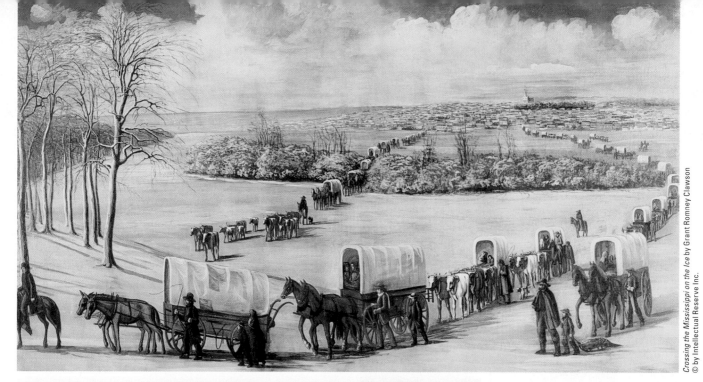

Mormon Trekkers Crossing the Mississippi on the Ice Driven out of Illinois after the murder of founder Joseph Smith in 1844, the Mormons wintered near Council Bluffs, Iowa Territory, before beginning the long overland trek to Utah.

and regions. The more prosperous and conservative denominations in the East were little touched by revivalism, and Episcopalians, Presbyterians, Congregationalists, and Unitarians continued to rise mostly from the wealthier, better-educated levels of society. Methodists, Baptists, and the members of the other new sects spawned by the swelling evangelistic fervor tended to come from less prosperous, less "learned" communities in the rural South and West.

Religious diversity further reflected social cleavages when the churches faced up to the slavery issue. By 1844–1845 both the southern Baptists and the southern Methodists had split with their northern brethren over human bondage. The Methodists came to grief over the case of a slaveowning bishop in Georgia, whose second wife added several household slaves to his estate. In 1857 the Presbyterians, North and South, parted company. The secession of the southern churches foreshadowed the secession of the southern states. First the churches split, then the political parties split, and then the Union split.

✳ A Desert Zion in Utah

The smoldering spiritual embers of the Burned-Over District kindled one especially ardent flame in 1830. In that year Joseph Smith—a rugged visionary, proud of his prowess at wrestling—reported that he had received some golden plates from an angel. When deciphered,

they constituted the Book of Mormon, and the Church of Jesus Christ of Latter-Day Saints (the **Mormons**) was launched. It was a native American product, a new religion, destined to spread its influence worldwide.

After establishing a religious oligarchy, Smith ran into serious opposition from his non-Mormon neighbors, first in Ohio and then in Missouri and Illinois. His cooperative sect antagonized rank-and-file Americans, who were individualistic and dedicated to free enterprise. The Mormons aroused further anger by voting as a unit and by openly but understandably drilling their militia for defensive purposes. Accusations of polygamy likewise arose and increased in intensity, for Joseph Smith was reputed to have several wives.

Continuing hostility finally drove the Mormons to desperate measures. In 1844 Joseph Smith and his brother were murdered and mangled by a mob in Carthage, Illinois, and the movement seemed near collapse. The falling torch was seized by a remarkable Mormon Moses named Brigham Young. Stern and austere in contrast to Smith's charm and affability, the barrel-chested Brigham Young had received only eleven days of formal schooling. But he quickly proved to be an aggressive leader, an eloquent preacher, and a gifted administrator. Determined to escape further persecution, Young in 1846–1847 led his oppressed and despoiled Latter-Day Saints over vast rolling plains to Utah as they sang "Come, Come, Ye Saints."

Overcoming pioneer hardships, the Mormons soon made the desert bloom like a new Eden by means of

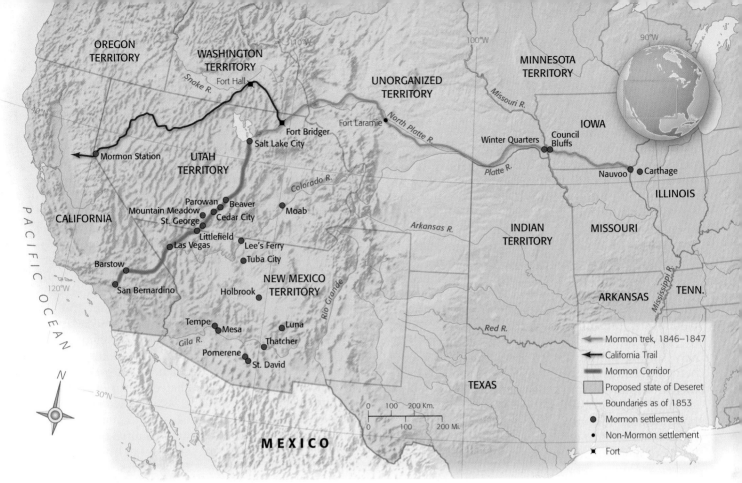

MAP 15.1 The Mormon World   After Joseph Smith's murder at Carthage in 1844, the Mormons abandoned their thriving settlement at Nauvoo, Illinois (which had about twenty thousand inhabitants in 1845), and set out for the valley of the Great Salt Lake, then still part of Mexico. When the Treaty of Guadalupe Hidalgo (see p. 371) in 1848 brought the vast Utah Territory into the United States, the Mormons rapidly expanded their desert colony, which they called Deseret, especially along the "Mormon Corridor" that stretched from Salt Lake to southern California.   © Cengage Learning

ingenious and cooperative methods of irrigation. The crops of 1848, threatened by hordes of crickets, were saved when flocks of gulls appeared, as if by a miracle, to gulp down the invaders. (A monument to the seagulls stands in Salt Lake City today.)

Semiarid Utah grew remarkably. By the end of 1848, some five thousand settlers had arrived, and other large bands were to follow them (see Map 15.1). Many dedicated Mormons in the 1850s actually made the thirteen-hundred-mile trek across the plains pulling two-wheeled carts.

Under the rigidly disciplined management of Brigham Young, the community became a prosperous frontier theocracy and a cooperative commonwealth. Young married as many as twenty-seven women—some of them wives in name only—and begot fifty-six children. The population was further swelled by thousands of immigrants from Europe, where the Mormons had established a flourishing missionary movement.

A crisis developed when the Washington government was unable to control the hierarchy of Brigham Young, who had been made territorial governor in 1850. A federal army marched in 1857 against the Mormons, who harassed its lines of supply and rallied to die in their last dusty ditch. Fortunately the quarrel was finally adjusted without serious bloodshed. The Mormons later ran afoul of the antipolygamy laws passed by Congress in 1862 and 1882, and their unique marital customs delayed statehood for Utah until 1896.

Polygamy was an issue of such consequence that it was bracketed with slavery in the Republican national platform of 1856:

"It is both the right and the imperative duty of Congress to prohibit in the Territories those twin relics of barbarism—Polygamy and Slavery."

✸ Free Schools for a Free People

Tax-supported primary schools were scarce in the early years of the Republic. They had the odor of pauperism about them, since they existed chiefly to educate the children of the poor—the so-called ragged schools. Advocates of "free" public education met stiff opposition. A midwestern legislator cried that he wanted only this simple epitaph when he died: "Here lies an enemy of public education."

Well-to-do, conservative Americans gradually saw the light. If they did not pay to educate "other folkses brats," the "brats" might grow up into a dangerous, ignorant rabble—armed with the vote. Taxation for education was an insurance premium that the wealthy paid for stability and democracy.

Tax-supported public education, though miserably lagging in the slavery-cursed South, triumphed between 1825 and 1850. Hard-toiling laborers wielded increased influence and demanded instruction for their children. Most important was the gaining of manhood suffrage for whites in Jackson's day. A free vote cried aloud for free education. A civilized nation that was both ignorant and free, declared Thomas Jefferson, "never was and never will be."

The famed little red schoolhouse—with one room, one stove, one teacher, and often eight grades—became the shrine of American democracy. Regrettably, it was an imperfect shrine. Early free schools stayed open only a few months of the year. Schoolteachers, most of them men in this era, were too often ill-trained, ill-tempered, and ill-paid. They frequently put more stress on "lickin'" (with a hickory stick) than on "larnin'." These knights of the blackboard often "boarded around" in the community, and some knew scarcely more than their older pupils. They usually taught only the "three Rs"—"readin', 'ritin', and 'rithmetic." To many rugged Americans, suspicious of "book larnin'," this was enough.

Reform was urgently needed. Into the breach stepped Horace Mann (1796–1859), a brilliant and idealistic graduate of Brown University. As secretary of the Massachusetts Board of Education, he campaigned effectively for more and better schoolhouses, longer school terms, higher pay for teachers, and an expanded curriculum. His influence radiated out to other states, and impressive improvements were chalked up. Yet education remained an expensive luxury for many communities. As late as 1860, the nation counted only about a hundred public secondary schools—and nearly a million white adult illiterates. Black slaves in the South

The Country School, by Winslow Homer, 1871   Stark and simple by latter-day standards, the one-room schoolhouse nevertheless contributed richly to the development of the young Republic.

Saint Louis Art Museum, Museum Purchase

Abraham Lincoln (1809–1865) wrote of his education (1859),

❝ There were some schools so-called [in Indiana], but no qualification was ever required of a teacher beyond 'readin', writin' and cipherin' to the rule of three. . . . There was absolutely nothing to excite ambition for education. Of course, when I came of age I did not know much. Still, somehow, I could read, write and cipher to the rule of three, but that was all. I have not been to school since. The little advance I now have upon this store of education, I have picked up from time to time under the pressure of necessity. I was raised to work, which I continued till I was twenty-two. ❞

were legally forbidden to receive instruction in reading or writing, and even free blacks, in the North as well as the South, were usually excluded from the schools.

Educational advances were aided by improved textbooks, notably those of Noah Webster (1758–1843), a Yale-educated Connecticut Yankee who was known as the "Schoolmaster of the Republic." His "reading lessons," used by millions of children in the nineteenth century, were partly designed to promote patriotism. Webster devoted twenty years to his famous dictionary, published in 1828, which helped to standardize the American language.

Equally influential was Ohioan William H. McGuffey (1800–1873), a teacher-preacher of rare power. His grade-school readers, first published in the 1830s, sold 122 million copies in the following decades. *McGuffey's Readers* hammered home lasting lessons in morality, patriotism, and idealism.

✦ Higher Goals for Higher Learning

Higher education was likewise stirring. The religious zeal of the Second Great Awakening led to the planting of many small, denominational, liberal arts colleges, chiefly in the South and West. Too often they were academically anemic, established more to satisfy local pride than genuinely to advance the cause of learning. Like their more venerable, ivy-draped brethren, the new colleges offered a narrow, tradition-bound curriculum of Latin, Greek, mathematics, and moral philosophy. On new and old campuses alike, there was little intellectual vitality and much boredom.

The first state-supported universities sprang up in the South, beginning with North Carolina in 1795.

Federal land grants nourished the growth of state institutions of higher learning. Conspicuous among the early group was the University of Virginia, founded in 1819. It was largely the brainchild of Thomas Jefferson, who designed its beautiful architecture and who at times watched its construction through a telescope from his hilltop home. He dedicated the university to freedom from religious or political shackles, and modern languages and the sciences received unusual emphasis.

Women's higher education was frowned upon in the early decades of the nineteenth century. A woman's place was believed to be in the home, and training in needlecraft seemed more important than training in algebra. In an era when the clinging-vine bride was the ideal, coeducation was regarded as frivolous. Prejudices also prevailed that too much learning injured the feminine brain, undermined health, and rendered a young lady unfit for marriage. The teachers of Susan B. Anthony, the future feminist, refused to instruct her in long division.

Women's schools at the secondary level began to attain some respectability in the 1820s, thanks in part to the dedicated work of Emma Willard (1787–1870). In 1821 she established the Troy (New York) Female Seminary. Oberlin College, in Ohio, jolted traditionalists in 1837 when it opened its doors to women as well as men. (Oberlin had already created shock waves by admitting black students.) In the same year, Mary Lyon established an outstanding women's school, Mount Holyoke Seminary (later College), in South Hadley, Massachusetts. Mossback critics scoffed that "they'll be educatin' cows next."

Adults who craved more learning satisfied their thirst for knowledge at private subscription libraries or,

An editorial in the popular women's magazine Godey's Lady's Book *in 1845, probably written by editor Sarah Josepha Hale (1788–1879), argued for better education for women as a benefit to all of society:*

❝ The mass of mankind are very ignorant and wicked. Wherefore is this? Because the mother, whom God constituted the first teacher of every human being, has been degraded by men from her high office; or, what is the same thing, been denied those privileges of education which only can enable her to discharge her duty to her children with discretion and effect. . . . If half the effort and expense had been directed to enlighten and improve the minds of females which have been lavished on the other sex, we should now have a very different state of society. ❞

Oberlin College Archives, Oberlin, Ohio

The Women Graduates of the Oberlin College Class of 1855 Oberlin was the first coeducational institution of higher education in the United States, accepting women in 1837, two years after it had welcomed African Americans. Feminists continued to press for coeducation, and by 1872 ninety-seven American universities accepted women. At some of these institutions, however, such as Radcliffe College of Harvard University and Barnard College of Columbia University, women were educated in associated schools, not alongside male students.

increasingly, at tax-supported libraries. House-to-house peddlers also did a lush business in feeding the public appetite for culture. Traveling lecturers helped to carry learning to the masses through the **lyceum** lecture associations, which numbered about three thousand by 1835. The lyceums provided platforms for speakers in such areas as science, literature, and moral philosophy. Talented talkers like Ralph Waldo Emerson journeyed thousands of miles on the lyceum circuits, casting their pearls of civilization before appreciative audiences.

Magazines flourished in the pre–Civil War years, but most of them withered after a short life. The *North American Review*, founded in 1815, was the long-lived leader of the intellectuals. *Godey's Lady's Book*, founded in 1830, survived until 1898 and attained the enormous circulation (for those days) of 150,000. It was devoured devotedly by millions of women, many of whom read the dog-eared copies of their relatives and friends.

✴ An Age of Reform

As the young Republic grew, reform campaigns of all types flourished in sometimes bewildering abundance. Some reformers were simply crackbrained cranks. But most were intelligent, inspired idealists, usually touched by the fire of evangelical religion then licking through the pews and pulpits of American churches. The optimistic promises of the Second Great Awakening inspired countless souls to do battle against earthly evils. These modern idealists dreamed anew the old Puritan vision of a perfected society: free from cruelty, war, intoxicating drink, discrimination, and—ultimately—slavery. Women were particularly prominent in these reform crusades, especially in their own struggle for suffrage. For many middle-class women, the reform campaigns provided a unique opportunity to escape the confines of the home and enter the arena of public affairs.

In part the practical, activist Christianity of these reformers resulted from their desire to reaffirm traditional values as they plunged ever further into a world disrupted and transformed by the turbulent forces of a market economy. Mainly middle-class descendants of pioneer farmers, they were often blissfully unaware that they were witnessing the dawn of the industrial era, which posed unprecedented problems and called for novel ideas. They either ignored the factory workers, for example, or blamed their problems on bad habits. With naive single-mindedness, reformers sometimes applied conventional virtue to refurbishing an

In presenting her case to the Massachusetts legislature for more humane treatment for the mentally ill, Dorothea Dix (1802–1887) quoted from the notebook she carried with her as she traveled around the state:

❝*Lincoln.* A woman in a cage. *Medford.* One idiotic subject chained, and one in a close stall for seventeen years. *Pepperell.* One often doubly chained, hand and foot; another violent; several peaceable now. . . . *Dedham.* The insane disadvantageously placed in the jail. In the almshouse, two females in stalls . . . ; lie in wooden bunks filled with straw; always shut up. One of these subjects is supposed curable. The overseers of the poor have declined giving her a trial at the hospital, as I was informed, on account of expense.❞

older order—while events hurtled them headlong into the new.

Imprisonment for debt continued to be a nightmare, though its extent has been exaggerated. As late as 1830, hundreds of penniless people were languishing in filthy holes, sometimes for owing less than one dollar. The poorer working classes were especially hard hit by this merciless practice. But as the embattled laborer won the ballot and asserted himself, state legislatures gradually abolished debtors' prisons.

Criminal codes in the states were likewise being softened, in accord with more enlightened European practices. The number of capital offenses was being reduced, and brutal punishments, such as whipping and branding, were being slowly eliminated. A refreshing idea was taking hold that prisons should reform as well as punish—hence "reformatories," "houses of correction," and "penitentiaries" (for penance).

Sufferers of so-called insanity were still being treated with incredible cruelty. The medieval concept had been that the mentally deranged were cursed with unclean spirits; the nineteenth-century idea was that they were willfully perverse and depraved—to be treated only as beasts. Many crazed persons were chained in jails or poor-houses with sane people.

Into this dismal picture stepped a formidable New England teacher-author, Dorothea Dix (1802–1887). A physically frail woman afflicted with persistent lung trouble, she possessed infinite compassion and willpower. She traveled some sixty thousand miles in eight years and assembled her damning reports on insanity and asylums from firsthand observations. Though she never raised her voice, Dix's message was loud and clear.

© Collection of the New York Historical Society

National Portrait Gallery, Smithsonian Institution/Art Resource, NY

(left) The Stepping Mill, Auburn Prison, New York, 1823; (right) Portrait of Dorothea Dix by Samuel Bell Waugh, 1868 Reformers like Dorothea Dix believed that idleness was a scourge and prescribed rigorous exercise regimens for prisoners. At the experimental prison in Auburn, chained prisoners were obliged to turn this wheel for long periods of time.

Her classic petition of 1843 to the Massachusetts legislature, describing cells so foul that visitors were driven back by the stench, turned legislative stomachs and hearts. Her persistent prodding resulted in improved conditions and in a gain for the concept that the demented were not willfully perverse but mentally ill.

Agitation for peace also gained momentum in the pre–Civil War years. In 1828 the American Peace Society was formed, with a ringing declaration of war on war. A leading spirit was William Ladd, who orated when his legs were so badly ulcerated that he had to sit on a stool. His ideas were finally to bear some fruit in the international organizations for collective security of the twentieth century. The American peace crusade, linked with a European counterpart, was making promising progress by midcentury, but it was set back by the bloodshed of the Crimean War in Europe and the Civil War in America.

✴ Demon Rum—The "Old Deluder"

The ever-present drink problem attracted dedicated reformers. Custom, combined with a hard and monotonous life, led to the excessive drinking of hard liquor, even among women, clergymen, and members of Congress. Weddings and funerals all too often became disgraceful brawls, and occasionally a drunken mourner would fall into the open grave with the corpse. Heavy drinking decreased the efficiency of labor, and poorly safeguarded machinery operated under the influence of alcohol increased the danger of accidents occurring at work. Drunkenness also fouled the sanctity of the family, threatening the spiritual welfare—and physical safety—of women and children.

After earlier and feebler efforts, the **American Temperance Society** was formed in Boston in 1826. Within a few years, about a thousand local groups sprang into existence. They implored drinkers to sign the temperance pledge and organized children's clubs, known as the "Cold Water Army." Temperance crusaders also made effective use of pictures, pamphlets, and lurid lecturers, some of whom were reformed drunkards. A popular temperance song ran,

> *We've done with our days of carousing,*
> *Our nights, too, of frolicsome glee;*
> *For now with our sober minds choosing,*
> *We've pledged ourselves never to spree.*

The most popular anti-alcohol tract of the era was T. S. Arthur's melodramatic novel, *Ten Nights in a Barroom and What I Saw There* (1854). It described in shocking detail how a once-happy village was ruined by Sam Slade's tavern. The book was second only to Stowe's *Uncle Tom's Cabin* as a best seller in the 1850s, and it enjoyed a highly successful run on the stage. Its

Signing the Pledge, Lithograph, 1846
Temperance reformers decried many evils of alcohol, but they fulminated especially against its corrupting influence on family life. Here a former drinker pledges to abstain hereafter, while his hopeful wife and children look on.

Granger Collection, New York

touching theme song began with the words of a little girl:

> *Father, dear father, come home with me now,*
> *The clock in the belfry strikes one.*

Early foes of Demon Drink adopted two major lines of attack. One was to stiffen the individual's will to resist the wiles of the little brown jug. The moderate reformers thus stressed "temperance" rather than "teetotalism," or the total elimination of intoxicants. But less patient zealots came to believe that temptation should be removed by legislation. Prominent among this group was Neal S. Dow of Maine, a blue-nosed reformer who, as a mayor of Portland and an employer of labor, had often witnessed the debauching effect of alcohol—to say nothing of the cost to his pocketbook of work time lost because of drunken employees.

Dow—the "Father of Prohibition"—sponsored the so-called **Maine Law of 1851**. This drastic new statute, hailed as "the law of Heaven Americanized," prohibited the manufacture and sale of intoxicating liquor. Other states in the North followed Maine's example, and by 1857 about a dozen had passed various prohibitory laws. But these figures are deceptive, for within a decade some of the statutes were repealed or declared unconstitutional, if not openly flouted.

It was clearly impossible to legislate thirst for alcohol out of existence, especially in localities where public sentiment was hostile. Yet on the eve of the Civil War, the prohibitionists had registered inspiring gains. There was much less drinking among women than earlier in the century and probably much less per capita consumption of hard liquor.

Stellar Suffragists Elizabeth Cady Stanton (left) and Susan B. Anthony (right) were two of the most persistent battlers for rights. Their National Woman Suffrage Association fought for women's equality in courts and workplaces as well as at the polls. © Bettmann/Corbis

Women in Revolt

When the nineteenth century opened, it was still a man's world, both in America and in Europe. A wife was supposed to immerse herself in her home and subordinate herself to her lord and master (her husband). Like black slaves, she could not vote; like black slaves, she could be legally beaten by her overlord "with a reasonable instrument." When she married, she could not retain title to her property; it passed to her husband.

Yet American women, though legally regarded as perpetual minors, fared better than their European cousins. French visitor Alexis de Tocqueville noted that in his native France, rape was punished only lightly, whereas in America it was one of the few crimes punishable by death.

Despite these relative advantages, women were still "the submerged sex" in America in the early part of the century. But as the decades unfolded, women increasingly surfaced to breathe the air of freedom and self-determination. In contrast to women in colonial times, many women now avoided marriage altogether—about 10 percent of adult women remained "spinsters" at the time of the Civil War.

Gender differences were strongly emphasized in nineteenth-century America—largely because the burgeoning market economy was increasingly separating women and men into sharply distinct economic roles. Women were thought to be physically and emotionally weak, but also artistic and refined. Endowed with finely tuned moral sensibilities, they were the keepers of society's conscience, with special responsibility to teach the young how to be good and productive citizens of the Republic. Men were considered strong but crude, always in danger of slipping into some savage or beastly way of life if not guided by the gentle hands of their loving ladies.

The home was a woman's special sphere, the centerpiece of the "cult of domesticity." Even reformers like Catharine Beecher, who urged her sisters to seek employment as teachers, endlessly celebrated the role

What It Would Be If Some Ladies Had Their Own Way The men in this antifeminist cartoon are sewing, tending the baby, and washing clothes. The scene seemed absurd then, but not a century later.

Stock Montage

of the good homemaker. But some women increasingly felt that the glorified sanctuary of the home was in fact a gilded cage. They yearned to tear down the bars that separated the private world of women from the public world of men.

Clamorous female reformers—most of them white and well-to-do—began to gather strength as the century neared its halfway point. Most were broad-gauge battlers; while demanding rights for women, they joined in the general reform movement of the age, fighting for temperance and the abolition of slavery. Like men, they had been touched by the evangelical spirit that offered the promise of earthly reward for human endeavor. Neither foul eggs nor foul words, when hurled by disapproving men, could halt women heartened by these doctrines.

The women's rights movement was mothered by some arresting characters. Prominent among them was Lucretia Mott, a sprightly Quaker whose ire had been aroused when she and her fellow female delegates to the London antislavery convention of 1840 were not recognized. Elizabeth Cady Stanton, a mother of seven who had insisted on leaving "obey" out of her marriage ceremony, shocked fellow feminists by going so far as to advocate suffrage for women. Quaker-reared Susan B. Anthony, a militant lecturer for women's rights, fearlessly exposed herself to rotten garbage and vulgar epithets. She became such a conspicuous advocate of female rights that progressive women everywhere were called "Suzy Bs."

Other feminists challenged the man's world. Dr. Elizabeth Blackwell, a pioneer in a previously forbidden profession for women, was the first female graduate of a medical college. The talented Grimké sisters, Sarah and

Angelina, championed antislavery. Lucy Stone retained her maiden name after marriage—hence the latter-day "Lucy Stoners," who follow her example. Amelia Bloomer revolted against the current "street sweeping" female attire by donning a short skirt with Turkish trousers—"bloomers," they were called—amid much bawdy ridicule about "Bloomerism" and "loose habits." A jeering male rhyme of the times jabbed,

> *Gibbey, gibbey gab*
> *The women had a confab*
> *And demanded the rights*
> *To wear the tights*
> *Gibbey, gibbey gab.*

Unflinching feminists met in 1848 in a memorable **Woman's Rights Convention at Seneca Falls**,

When early feminist Lucy Stone (1818–1893) married fellow abolitionist Henry B. Blackwell (1825–1909) in West Brookfield, Massachusetts, in 1855, they added the following vow to their nuptial ceremony:

"While acknowledging our mutual affection by publicly assuming the relation of husband and wife, yet in justice to ourselves and a great principle, we deem it a duty to declare that this act on our part implies no . . . promise of voluntary obedience to such of the present laws of marriage, as refuse to recognize the wife as an independent, rational being, while they confer upon the husband an injurious and unnatural superiority.**"**

Dress as Reform

Among the many social movements that swept nineteenth-century America, dress reform emerged in the 1840s as a critique of materialism and the constraints that fashion imposed on women. Medical professionals, social reformers, and transcendentalist intellectuals all argued that corsets constricting vital organs and voluminous skirts dragging along garbage-strewn streets unfairly restricted women's mobility, prevented women from bearing healthy children, and even induced serious sickness and death. The "Bloomer costume" depicted in this illustration from *Harper's New Monthly Magazine* in 1851 included Turkish-style trousers, a jacket, and a short overskirt that came to the knees. Named after reformer Amelia Bloomer (1818–1894), who publicized the new style in her magazine, *The Lily*, the bloomer dress was first adopted by utopian communities such as the Owenites in New Harmony, Indiana, and the Oneidans in New York. Radical social critic Henry David Thoreau also advocated rational dress as a way of rejecting the artificial desires created by industrialization. But while applauded by reformers, new-style dress was viciously ridiculed by mainstream society, as this print demonstrates. Critics claimed that women blurred gender distinctions by adopting "male" attire, endangering the family and even American civilization. After only a decade, practitioners gave up wearing bloomers in public, adopting plain and simplified clothing instead. But Owenites, some Mormons, women's rights advocates, farmers, and travelers on the overland trail continued to wear bloomers in private. How did dress reform intersect with other religious and social movements of the era? Why did bloomers upset so many antebellum Americans? Have there been other historical eras when new styles of dress came to symbolize broader social change?

© Bettmann/Corbis

New York. The defiant Stanton read a "Declaration of Sentiments," which in the spirit of the Declaration of Independence declared that "all men and women are created equal." One resolution formally demanded the ballot for females. Amid scorn and denunciation from press and pulpit, the Seneca Falls meeting launched the modern women's rights movement.

The crusade for women's rights was eclipsed by the campaign against slavery in the decade before the Civil War. Still, any white male, even an idiot, over the age of twenty-one could vote, while no woman could. Yet women were gradually being admitted to colleges, and some states, beginning with Mississippi in 1839, were even permitting wives to own property after marriage.

⭐ Wilderness Utopias

Bolstered by the utopian spirit of the age, various reformers, ranging from the high-minded to the "lunatic fringe," set up more than forty communities of a co-operative, communistic, or "communitarian" nature. Seeking human betterment, a wealthy and idealistic Scottish textile manufacturer, Robert Owen, founded in 1825 a communal society of about a thousand people at **New Harmony**, Indiana. Little harmony prevailed in the colony, which, in addition to hard-working visionaries, attracted a sprinkling of radicals, work-shy theorists, and outright scoundrels. The colony sank in a morass of contradiction and confusion.

Brook Farm in Massachusetts, comprising two hundred acres of grudging soil, was started in 1841 with the brotherly and sisterly cooperation of about twenty intellectuals committed to the philosophy of transcendentalism (see p. 327). They prospered reasonably well until 1846, when they lost by fire a large new communal building shortly before its completion. The whole venture in "plain living and high thinking" then collapsed in debt. The Brook Farm experiment inspired Nathaniel Hawthorne's classic novel *The Blithedale Romance* (1852).

A more radical experiment was the **Oneida Community**, founded in New York in 1848. It practiced free love ("complex marriage"), birth control (through "male continence," or *coitus reservatus*), and the eugenic selection of parents to produce superior offspring. This curious enterprise flourished for more than thirty years, largely because its artisans made superior steel traps and Oneida Community (silver) Plate (see "Makers of America: The Oneida Community," pp. 322–323).

Various communistic experiments, mostly small in scale, have been attempted since Jamestown. But in competition with democratic free enterprise and free land, virtually all of them sooner or later failed or changed their methods. Among the longest-lived sects were the **Shakers**, founded in England in 1747 and brought to America in 1774 by Mother Ann Lee. She moved her tiny band of followers to upstate New York—the first of a score or so of American Shaker communities. The Shakers attained a membership of about six thousand in 1840, but since their monastic customs prohibited both marriage and sexual relations, they were virtually extinct by 1940.

Harvesting, by Olof Krans, ca. 1896 The Shakers' emphasis on communal work and separation of the sexes was captured in this painting of the Bishop Hill Colony in Illinois. Krans, born in Sweden, arrived at Bishop Hill with his family in 1850 when he was twelve. Trained as a housepainter, he turned later in life to recording on canvas the simplicity of daily life that he remembered from his youth.

Bishop Hill State Historic Site, Illinois Historic Preservation Agency

Collection of the New York Historical Society

American Museum of Natural History

(left) Passenger Pigeons, by John Audubon; (right) John J. Audubon (1785–1851)
An astute naturalist and a gifted artist, Audubon drew the birds of America in loving detail. Ironically, he had to go to Britain in the 1820s to find a publisher for his pioneering depictions of the unique beauty of American wildlife. Born in Haiti and educated in France, he achieved fame as America's greatest ornithologist. The passenger pigeons shown here once numbered in the billions in North America but were extinct by 1900, thanks to aggressive hunting and trapping. This was perhaps the greatest mass slaughter of wildlife in history.

✴ The Dawn of Scientific Achievement

Early Americans, confronted with pioneering problems, were more interested in practical gadgets than in pure science. Jefferson, for example, was a gifted amateur inventor who won a gold medal for a new type of plow. Noteworthy also were the writings of the mathematician Nathaniel Bowditch (1733–1838) on practical navigation and of the oceanographer Matthew F. Maury (1806–1873) on ocean winds and currents. These writers promoted safety, speed, and economy. But as far as basic science was concerned, Americans were best known for borrowing and adapting the findings of Europeans.

Yet the Republic was not without scientific talent. The most influential American scientist of the first half of the nineteenth century was Professor Benjamin Silliman (1779–1864), a pioneer chemist and geologist who taught and wrote brilliantly at Yale College for more than fifty years. Professor Louis Agassiz (1807–1873), a distinguished French Swiss immigrant, served for a quarter of a century at Harvard College. A path-

breaking student of biology who sometimes carried snakes in his pockets, he insisted on original research and deplored the reigning overemphasis on memory work. Professor Asa Gray (1810–1888) of Harvard College, the Columbus of American botany, published over 350 books, monographs, and papers. His textbooks set new standards for clarity and interest.

Lovers of American bird lore owed much to the French-descended naturalist John J. Audubon (1785–1851), who painted wildfowl in their natural habitat. His magnificently illustrated *Birds of America* attained considerable popularity. The Audubon Society for the protection of birds was named after him, although as a young man he shot much feathered game for sport.

Medicine in America, despite a steady growth of medical schools, was still primitive by modern standards. Bleeding remained a common cure and a curse as well. Smallpox plagues were still dreaded, and the yellow fever epidemic of 1793 in Philadelphia took several thousand lives. "Bring out your dead!" was the daily cry of the corpse-wagon drivers.

John Humphrey Noyes (1811–1886), the founder of the Oneida Community, repudiated the old Puritan doctrines that God was vengeful and that sinful mankind was doomed to dwell in a vale of tears. Noyes believed in a benign deity, in the sweetness of human nature, and in the possibility of a perfect Christian community on earth. "The more we get acquainted with God," he declared, "the more we shall find it our special duty to be happy."

That sunny thought was shared by many early-nineteenth-century American utopians (a word derived from Greek that slyly combines the meanings of "a good place" and "no such place"). But Noyes added some wrinkles of his own. The key to happiness, he taught, was the suppression of selfishness. True Christians should possess no private property—nor should they indulge in exclusive emotional relationships, which bred jealousy, quarreling, and covetousness. Material things and sexual partners alike, Noyes preached, should be shared. Marriage should not be monogamous. Instead all members of the community should be free to love one another in "complex marriage." Noyes called his system "Bible Communism."

Tall and slender, with piercing blue eyes and reddish hair, the charismatic Noyes began voicing these ideas in his hometown of Putney, Vermont, in the 1830s. He soon attracted a group of followers who called themselves the Putney Association, a kind of extended family whose members farmed five hundred acres by day and sang and prayed together in the evenings. They sustained their spiritual intensity by submitting to "Mutual Criticism," in which the person being criticized would sit in silence while other members frankly discussed his or her faults and merits. "I was, metaphorically, stood upon my head and allowed to drain till all the self-righteousness had dripped out of me," one man wrote of his experience with Mutual Criticism.

The Putney Association also indulged in sexual practices that outraged the surrounding community's sense of moral propriety. Indicted for adultery in 1847, Noyes led his followers to Oneida, in the supposedly more tolerant region of New York's Burned-Over District, the following year. Several affiliated communities were also established, the most important of which was at Wallingford, Connecticut.

The Oneidans struggled in New York until they were joined in the 1850s by Sewell Newhouse, a clever inventor of steel animal traps. The manufacture of Newhouse's traps, and other products such as sewing silk and various types of bags, put the Oneida Community on a sound financial footing. By the 1860s Oneida was a flourishing commonwealth of some three hundred people. Men and women shared equally in all the community's tasks, from field to factory to kitchen.

The members lived under one roof in Mansion House, a sprawling building that boasted central heating, a well-stocked library, and a common dining hall, as well as the "Big Hall," where members gathered nightly for prayer and entertainment. Children at the age of three were removed from direct parental care and raised communally in the Children's House until the age of thirteen or fourteen, when they took up jobs in the community's industries. They imbibed their religious doctrines with their school lessons:

I-spirit
With me never shall stay,
We-spirit
Makes us happy and gay.

Oneida's apparent success fed the utopian dreams of others, and for a time it became a great tourist attraction. Visitors from as far away as Europe came to picnic on the shady lawns, speculating on the sexual secrets that Mansion House guarded, while their hosts fed them strawberries and cream and entertained them with music.

But eventually the same problems that had driven Noyes and his band from Vermont began to shadow their lives at Oneida. Their New York neighbors grew increasingly horrified at the Oneidans' licentious sexual

The Founding Father John Humphrey Noyes (1811–1886)

Granger Collection

Mansion House A sprawling, resplendent building, it formed the center of the Oneida Community's life and was a stunning specimen of mid-nineteenth-century architectural and engineering achievement.

practices, including the selective breeding program by which the community matched mates and gave permission—or orders—to procreate, without regard to the niceties of matrimony. "It was somewhat startling to me," one straight-laced visitor commented, "to hear *Miss* _____ speak about her baby."

Yielding to their neighbors' criticisms, the Oneidans gave up complex marriage in 1879. Soon other "communistic" practices withered away as well. The communal dining hall became a restaurant, where meals were bought with money, something many Oneidans had never used before. In 1880 the Oneidans abandoned communism altogether and became a joint-stock company specializing in the manufacture of silver tableware. Led by Noyes's son Pierrepont, Oneida Community, Ltd., grew into the world's leading manufacturer of stainless steel knives, forks, and spoons, until foreign competition forced it into bankruptcy in 2006. As for Mansion House, it still stands in central New York, but it now serves as a museum and private residence. Ironically, what grew from Noyes's religious vision was not utopia but a mighty capitalist corporation that finally succumbed to the "creative destruction" that is capitalism's essence.

A Bag Bee on the Lawn of Mansion House The fledgling community supported itself in part by manufacturing bags. Men and women shared equally in the bag-making process.

An outbreak of cholera occurred in New York City in 1832, and a wealthy businessman, Philip Hone (1780–1851), wrote in his diary for the Fourth of July,

❝ The alarm about the cholera has prevented all the usual jollification under the public authority. . . . The Board of Health reports today twenty new cases and eleven deaths since noon yesterday. The disease is here in all its violence and will increase. God grant that its ravages may be confined, and its visit short.**❞**

People everywhere complained of ill health—malaria, the "rheumatics," the "miseries," and the chills. Illness often resulted from improper diet, hurried eating, perspiring and cooling off too rapidly, and ignorance of germs and sanitation. "We was sick every fall, regular," wrote the mother of future president James Garfield. Life expectancy was still dismayingly short—about forty years for a white person born in 1850, and less for blacks. The suffering from decayed or ulcerated teeth was enormous; tooth extraction was often practiced by the muscular village blacksmith.

Self-prescribed patent medicines were common (one dose for people, two for horses) and included Robertson's Infallible Worm Destroying Lozenges. Fad diets proved popular, including the whole-wheat bread and crackers regimen of Sylvester Graham. Among home remedies was the rubbing of tumors with dead toads. The use of medicine by regular doctors was often harmful, and Dr. Oliver Wendell Holmes declared in 1860 that if the medicines, as then employed, were thrown into the sea, humans would be better off and the fish worse off.

Victims of surgical operations were ordinarily tied down, often after a stiff drink of whiskey. The surgeon then sawed or cut with breakneck speed, undeterred by the piercing shrieks of the patient. A priceless boon for medical progress came in the early 1840s, when several American doctors and dentists, working independently, successfully employed laughing gas and ether as anesthetics.

✸ Artistic Achievements

As early as the 1770s, Revolutionary Americans anticipated that a great cultural flourishing would accompany America's political awakening. Optimistic commentators spoke of the "rising glory" of America, sharing the British philosopher George Berkeley's prediction in 1752 that "westward the course of empire takes its way . . . time's noblest offspring is its last." But while American political thought sparkled with originality, the nation's earliest cultural forays proved less than spectacular. Flush with political independence, Americans strained to achieve cultural autonomy and create a national art worthy of their aspirations.

Architecturally, America chose to imitate Old World styles rather than create indigenous ones. Early national builders articulated a plain **Federal Style** of architecture that borrowed from classical Greek and Roman examples and emphasized symmetry, balance, and restraint. Public buildings incorporated a neoclassical vocabulary of columns, domes, and pediments to suggest venerable ancient models for America's novel republican experiment. Charles Bulfinch's design of the Massachusetts State House (1798) and Benjamin Latrobe's early-nineteenth-century additions to the U.S. Capitol and President's House (now White House) showcased this neoclassical obsession.

A remarkable **Greek Revival** came between 1820 and 1850, partly stimulated by the heroic efforts of the Greeks in the 1820s to wrest independence from the "terrible Turk." Popularized in pattern books for carpenters, plain and porticoed Greek Revival houses proliferated across America, especially in New York's Burned-Over District and the Old Northwest. About midcentury strong interest developed in a revival of medieval Gothic forms, with their emphasis on pointed arches, sloped roofs, and large, stained-glass windows.

Talented Thomas Jefferson, architect of revolution, was one of the ablest American architects of his generation. Inspired by the sixteenth-century Venetian architect Andrea Palladio, Jefferson's Virginia hilltop home, Monticello, arose as perhaps the most stately mansion in the nation and an iconic example of the Palladian style. Jefferson also modeled Richmond's new state capitol on an ancient Roman temple, the Maison Carrée, which he had visited while minister to France. The quadrangle of the University of Virginia at Charlottesville, another of Jefferson's creations, remains one of the finest examples of neoclassical architecture in America.

Early American painting also struggled to find a distinctive national style. Imitative portraiture and history painting predominated in the late eighteenth century, as American artists attempted to cover their provincial culture with a civilizing veneer. Painting suffered from the dollar-grabbing of a raw civilization; from the hustle, bustle, and absence of leisure; from the lack of a wealthy class to sit for portraits—and then pay for them. Some of the earliest painters, including Benjamin West, were enticed to go to England, where they found both training and patrons. America exported artists and imported art.

Painting, like the theater, also suffered from the Puritan prejudice that art was a sinful waste of time—and often obscene. John Adams boasted that "he would not give a sixpence for a bust of Phidias or a painting by Raphael." When Edward Everett, the eminent Boston scholar and orator, placed a statue of Apollo in his home, he had its naked limbs draped.

Competent painters nevertheless emerged. Gilbert Stuart (1755–1828), a restless Rhode Islander and one of the most gifted of the early group, wielded his brush in Britain in competition with the best artists. Returning to America in 1793, he produced several portraits of Washington, all of them somewhat idealized and dehumanized. (One of them appears on the familiar one-dollar bill.) Truth to tell, by the time he posed for Stuart, the famous general had lost his natural teeth and some of the original shape of his face. Charles Willson Peale (1741–1827), a Marylander, painted some sixty portraits of Washington, who patiently sat for about fourteen of them. John Trumbull (1756–1843), who had fought in the Revolutionary War, recaptured its heroic scenes and spirit on scores of striking canvases.

After the War of 1812, American painters turned increasingly from human portraits and history paintings to pastoral mirrorings of local landscapes. In America's vast wilderness the new nation's painters finally found their distinctive muse. The **Hudson River school** of the 1820s and 1830s excelled in this type of romantic art. Its leading lights, British-born Thomas Cole and New Jerseyan Asher Durand, celebrated the raw sublimity and grand divinity of nature.

Cole's canvases, including *The Oxbow* (1836), portrayed the ecological threat of human encroachment on once-pristine environments. His masterpiece five-part series *The Course of Empire* (1833–1836) depicted the cyclical rise and fall of human civilization—a powerful analogy for nineteenth-century Americans anxious about industrialization and expansion. Around midcentury a group of "luminist" painters, including German-born Albert Bierstadt, dramatically and sometimes fancifully rendered majestic natural landscapes in the same romantic tradition.

At the same time, new technologies reframed the artistic landscape. Portrait painters gradually encountered some unwelcome competition from the invention of a crude photograph known as the daguerreotype, perfected about 1839 by a Frenchman, Louis Daguerre. Cheap and easily reproducible lithographs, most notably from the New York City firm of Currier and Ives, offered picturesque scenes and city views to millions of consumers.

Music was slowly shaking off the restraints of colonial days, when the prim Puritans had frowned upon nonreligious singing. Rhythmic and nostalgic "darky" tunes, popularized by whites, were becoming immense hits by midcentury. Special favorites were the uniquely American **minstrel shows**, featuring white actors with blackened faces playing stock plantation characters. (For the survival of blackface performance into the twentieth century, see "Examining the

Virginia State Capitol, 1785–1788 With the coming of the American Revolution, Virginia Governor Thomas Jefferson urged that the state capital move from Williamsburg to Richmond. There he designed a new, neoclassical capitol building inspired by the Maison Carrée, an exceedingly well-preserved Roman temple in Nîmes, France. The Virginia State Capitol became the Capitol of the Confederacy during the Civil War.

The Oxbow, by Thomas Cole, 1836 This rendering of the oxbow of the Connecticut River near Northampton, Massachusetts, after a thunderstorm is considered one of Cole's (1801–1848) masterpieces. A leader of the so-called Hudson River school, Cole wandered on foot over the mountains and rivers of New York State and New England, making pencil studies from which he painted in his studio during the winter. He and other members of this group transformed their realistic sketches into lyrical, romantic celebrations of the beauty of the American wilderness.

Evidence: *The Jazz Singer*, 1927," p. 717.) "Dixie," later adopted by the Confederates as their battle hymn, was written in 1859, ironically in New York City by an Ohioan. The most famous southern songs, also ironically, came from a white Pennsylvanian, Stephen C. Foster (1826–1864). His one excursion into the South occurred in 1852, after he had published "Camptown Races" (1850), "Old Folks at Home" (1851), and "Oh! Susanna" (1848), the anthem of California gold-rushers. Foster made a valuable contribution to American folk music by capturing the plaintive spirit of the slaves. An odd and pathetic figure, he finally lost both his art and his popularity and died in a charity ward after drowning his sorrows in drink. Lacking adequate copyright protections, songwriters in this era earned pennies, not profits.

✷ The Blossoming of a National Literature

"In the four quarters of the globe," sneered a British critic of 1820, "who reads an American book, or goes to an American play, or looks at an American picture or statue?" Like their sisterly artistic pursuits, early American literary efforts also fell short of initial expectations. Despite an unusually literate population, post-Revolutionary America imported or plagiarized much of its "polite" reading matter from Britain.

Busy conquering a continent, Americans poured most of their creative efforts into practical outlets. Praiseworthy were political essays, like *The Federalist* (1787–1788) of Hamilton, Jay, and Madison; pamphlets, like Tom Paine's *Common Sense* (1776); and political orations, like the masterpieces of Daniel Webster. In the category of nonreligious books published before 1820, Benjamin Franklin's *Autobiography* (1818) is one of the few that achieved genuine distinction. His narrative is a classic in its simplicity, clarity, and inspirational quality. Even so, it records only a fragment of "Old Ben's" long, fruitful, and amorous life.

After 1820 a confident cohort of young American authors finally began to answer the call for an authentic national literature. Their rise corresponded with the wave of nationalism following the War of 1812 and the arrival of **romanticism** on American shores.

Conceived as a reaction against the hyper-rational Enlightenment, romanticism originated in the revolutionary salons of continental Europe and England. In direct contrast to neoclassicism, romanticism emphasized imagination over reason, nature over civilization, intuition over calculation, and the self over society. Emotion, expression, and experimentation were core values. Upsetting the restrained, clocklike universe of the eighteenth-century *philosophes*, nineteenth-century romantics elevated primal nature in all its sublime and picturesque glory. They celebrated human potential and prized the heroic genius of the individual artist. Infused with romantic energy, American literature flowered in the mid-nineteenth century as never before.

Washington Irving (1783–1859), born in New York City, was the first American to win international recognition as a literary figure. Steeped in the traditions of New Netherland, he published in 1809 his amusing *Knickerbocker's History of New York*, with its "local color" caricatures of the Dutch. When the family business failed, Irving was forced to turn to the goose-feather pen. In 1819–1820 he published *The Sketch Book*, which brought him immediate fame at home and abroad. Combining a pleasing style with delicate charm and quiet humor, he used English as well as American themes and included such immortal Gothic tales as "Rip Van Winkle" and "The Legend of Sleepy Hollow." Europe was amazed to find at last an American with a feather in his hand, not in his hair. Later turning to Spanish locales and biography, Irving did much to interpret America to Europe and Europe to America. He was, said the Englishman William Thackeray, "the first ambassador whom the New World of letters sent to the Old."

James Fenimore Cooper (1789–1851) followed on Irving's coattails and gained world fame making New World themes respectable. Expelled from Yale, he eventually married into a wealthy family and settled down on the New York frontier. Reading one day to his wife from an insipid English novel, Cooper remarked in disgust that he could write a better book himself. His wife challenged him to do so—and he did.

After an initial failure, Cooper launched an illustrious career in 1821 with his second novel, *The Spy*—an absorbing tale of the American Revolution. His stories of the sea were meritorious and popular, but his fame rests most enduringly on his five *Leatherstocking Tales*, featuring a dead-eye rifleman named Natty Bumppo, a solitary and self-reliant hero who mingles easily with nature's "noble savages" in stirring adventures like *The Last of the Mohicans* (1826). Cooper's novels sold well to Europeans, some of whom came to think of all American people as born with tomahawk in hand. Actually Cooper's deepest theme was an exploration of the viability and destiny of America's republican experiment; he contrasted the undefiled purity of "natural men," children of the untrammeled wilderness, with the artificiality and corruption of modern civilization. Cooper's emblematic tales of the vanishing frontier offered literary analogues of the Hudson River school's visual landscapes.

Along with Irving and Cooper, the third member of New York's trailblazing Knickerbocker Group was the belated Puritan William Cullen Bryant (1794–1878), transplanted from Massachusetts. At age sixteen he wrote the meditative and melancholy "Thanatopsis" (published in 1817), which was one of the first high-quality poems produced in the United States. Critics could hardly believe that it had been written on "this side of the water." Although Bryant continued with poetry, he made his living by editing the influential *New York Evening Post*. For over fifty years, he set a model for journalism that was dignified, liberal, and conscientious.

✴ Trumpeters of Transcendentalism

A golden age in American literature dawned in the second quarter of the nineteenth century, when an amazing outburst shook New England. One of the mainsprings of this literary flowering was **transcendentalism**, especially around Boston, which preened itself as "the Athens of America."

The transcendentalist movement of the 1830s resulted in part from a liberalizing of the straightjacket Puritan theology. It also owed much to foreign influences, including the German romantic philosophers and the religions of Asia. The transcendentalists rejected the prevailing empiricist theory, derived from John Locke, that all knowledge comes to the mind through the senses. Truth, rather, "transcends" the senses: it cannot be found by observation alone. Every person possesses an inner light that can illuminate the

Washington Irving's (1783–1859) popular folktale "Rip Van Winkle" (1819) offered a shrewd allegory for the dramatic changes sweeping the early Republic. In this short story, the fictional Rip sleeps through the American Revolution. Upon awakening after twenty years, he finds his fellow village people

❝haranguing vehemently about rights of citizens—election—members of congress—liberty—Bunker's hill—heroes of seventy-six—and other words, that were a perfect Babylonish jargon to the bewildered Van Winkle.**❞**

highest truth and put him or her in direct touch with God, or the "Oversoul."

These mystical doctrines of transcendentalism defied precise definition, but they underlay concrete beliefs. Foremost was a stiff-backed individualism in matters religious as well as social. Closely associated was a commitment to self-reliance, self-culture, and self-discipline. These traits naturally bred hostility to authority and to formal institutions of any kind, as well as to all conventional wisdom. Finally came a romantic exaltation of the dignity of the individual, whether black or white—the mainspring of a whole array of humanitarian reforms.

Best known of the transcendentalists was Boston-born Ralph Waldo Emerson (1803–1882). Tall, slender, and intensely blue-eyed, he mirrored serenity in his noble features. Trained as a Unitarian minister, he

early forsook his pulpit and ultimately reached a wider audience by pen and platform. He was a never-failing favorite as a lyceum lecturer and for twenty years took a western tour every winter. Perhaps his most thrilling public effort was a Phi Beta Kappa address, **"The American Scholar,"** delivered at Harvard College in 1837. This brilliant appeal was an intellectual declaration of independence, for it urged American writers to throw off European traditions and delve into the riches of their own backyards.

Hailed as both a poet and a philosopher, Emerson was not of the highest rank as either. He was more influential as a practical philosopher and public intellectual. Through his fresh and vibrant essays he enriched countless thousands of humdrum lives. Catching the individualistic mood of the Republic, he stressed self-reliance, self-improvement, self-confidence, optimism,

National Portrait Gallery, Smithsonian Institution/Art Resource, NY

Portrait of Washington Irving and His Literary Friends at Sunnyside, 1864 This apocryphal gathering of America's founding generation of writers, many of them now sadly unread, was imagined to take place in the library of Washington Irving's Hudson River home. Surrounding Irving, seated in the armchair at center, are fourteen accomplished creators of history, philosophy, fiction, and poetry: (seated, left to right) William Gilmore Simms, Fitz-Greene Halleck, William Hickling Prescott, Irving, Ralph Waldo Emerson, James Fennimore Cooper, George Bancroft; (standing, left to right) Henry Theodore Tuckerman, Oliver Wendell Holmes, Nathaniel Hawthorne, Henry Wadsworth Longfellow, Nathaniel Parker Willis, James Kirke Paulding, William Cullen Bryant, John Pendleton Kennedy. The portrait itself represented a collaborative effort of artists. Felix Octavius Carr Darley did the original drawing, with the help of photographs taken by Matthew Brady. Christian Schussele made a four-by-six-foot oil painting of the scene and Thomas Oldham Barlow rendered it as a steel-plate engraving for distribution to a wide public.

In 1849 Henry David Thoreau (1817–1862) published "Resistance to Civil Government" (later renamed "On the Duty of Civil Disobedience"), asserting,

"All men recognize the right of revolution; the right to refuse allegiance to and to resist the government, when its tyranny or its inefficiency are great and unendurable. But almost all say that such is not the case now. . . . I say, when a sixth of the population of a nation which has undertaken to be the refuge of liberty are slaves, and a whole country is unjustly overrun and conquered by a foreign army, and subjected to military law, I think that it is not too soon for honest men to rebel and revolutionize. What makes this duty more urgent is the fact, that the country so overrun is not our own, but ours is the invading army."

In 1958 civil rights leader Martin Luther King, Jr. (1929–1968) connected his theory of nonviolent resistance to Henry David Thoreau's pedigree:

"At this point [in the planning of the 1955 Montgomery, Alabama, bus boycott] I began to think about Thoreau's *Essay on Civil Disobedience.* I remembered how, as a college student, I had been moved when I first read this work. I became convinced that what we were preparing to do in Montgomery was related to what Thoreau had expressed. We were simply saying to the white community, 'We can no longer lend our cooperation to an evil system.'"

and freedom, though he also criticized American triumphalism of the Jacksonian brand. By the 1850s he was an outspoken critic of slavery, and he ardently supported the Union cause in the Civil War.

Henry David Thoreau (1817–1862) was Emerson's close associate—a poet, a mystic, a transcendentalist, and a nonconformist. Condemning a government that supported slavery, he refused to pay his Massachusetts poll tax and was jailed for a night.* A gifted prose writer, he is well known for *Walden: Or Life in the Woods* (1854). The book is a record of Thoreau's two years of simple existence in a hut that he built on the edge of Walden Pond, near Concord, Massachusetts. *Walden* epitomized the romantic quest for isolation from society's corruptions. A stiff-necked individualist, Thoreau believed that he should reduce his bodily wants so as to gain time to pursue truth through study and meditation. Thoreau's *Walden* and his essay "On the Duty of Civil Disobedience" (1849) exercised a strong influence in furthering idealistic thought, both in America and abroad. His writings later encouraged Mahatma Gandhi to resist British rule in India and, still later, inspired the development of American civil rights leader Martin Luther King, Jr.'s thinking about nonviolence.

Precocious Margaret Fuller (1810–1850) befriended Emerson around the time of his Phi Beta Kappa address in 1837 and soon joined the Boston circle of transcendentalists. She edited the movement's journal, *The Dial,*

for two years after its founding in 1840. In the same year, she launched her series of "Conversations," or paid seminars designed to promote scholarly dialogue among local elite women (and some invited men). Known for her sparkling conversational wit, Fuller also wrote prolifically. In 1845, she published *Woman in the Nineteenth Century,* a powerful critique of gender roles and an iconic statement of the budding feminist movement. After an influential stint as literary editor of Horace Greeley's *New York Tribune,* Fuller sailed for Europe and eventually took part in the struggle to bring unity and republican government to Italy. She died tragically in a shipwreck off New York's Fire Island while returning to the United States in 1850.

Bold, brassy, and swaggering was the open-collared figure of Brooklyn's Walt Whitman (1819–1892). In his famous collection of poems *Leaves of Grass* (1855), he gave free rein to his gushing genius with what he called a "barbaric yawp." His landmark "Song of Myself," with its unabashed first-person speaker, celebrated the romantic artist-hero in free verse. Highly emotional and unconventional, Whitman dispensed with titles, stanzas, rhymes, and at times even regular meter. He located divinity in commonplace natural objects (e.g., leaves of grass) as well as the human body. Whitman even handled sex with shocking frankness, although he laundered his verses in later editions, and his book was banned in Boston.

Whitman's *Leaves of Grass* was at first a financial failure. The only three enthusiastic reviews that it received were written by the author himself—anonymously. But in time the once-withered *Leaves of Grass,* revived and honored, won for Whitman an enormous following in both America and Europe and gained him the informal title "Poet Laureate of Democracy." Singing with transcendental abandon of his love for the masses, he caught the exuberant enthusiasm of an

---

*The story (probably apocryphal) is that Emerson visited Thoreau at the jail and asked, "Why are you here?" The reply came, "Why are you *not* here?"

Louisa May Alcott (1832–1888) This color lithograph printed by Louis Prang in 1888 made Alcott's image accessible to her many loyal readers. In search of independence for herself and financial security for her family, Alcott worked as a seamstress, governess, teacher, and housemaid until her writing finally brought her success. Her much-loved, largely autobiographical novel *Little Women* has remained in print continuously from 1868 until our own day.

© Bettmann/Corbis

expanding America that had turned its back on the Old World:

> All the Past we leave behind;
> We debouch upon a newer, mightier world, varied world;
> Fresh and strong the world we seize—world of labor and
>   the march—
> Pioneers! O Pioneers!

Here at last was the native art for which critics had been crying.

✳ Glowing Literary Lights

Certain other literary giants were not actively associated with the transcendentalist movement, though not completely immune to its influences. Professor Henry Wadsworth Longfellow (1807–1882), who for many years taught modern languages at Harvard College, was one of the most popular poets ever produced in America. Handsome and urbane, he lived a generally serene life, except for the tragic deaths of two wives, the second of whom perished before his eyes when her dress caught fire. Writing for the genteel classes, he was adopted by the less cultured masses. His wide knowledge of European literature supplied him with many themes, but some of his most admired narrative poems—*Evangeline* (1847), *The Song of Hiawatha* (1855),

and *The Courtship of Miles Standish* (1858)—were based on American traditions. Immensely popular in Europe, Longfellow was the first American ever to be enshrined in the Poets' Corner of Westminster Abbey.

A fighting Quaker with piercing dark eyes, John Greenleaf Whittier (1807–1892) was the uncrowned poet laureate of the antislavery crusade. Less talented as a writer than Longfellow, he was vastly more important in influencing social action. His abolitionist poems cried aloud against inhumanity, injustice, and intolerance, against

> The outworn rite, the old abuse,
> The pious fraud transparent grown

Undeterred by insults and the stoning of mobs, Whittier helped arouse a callous America on the slavery issue. He also left behind a legacy of "local color" sketches and verse dedicated to his native New England.

Many-sided professor James Russell Lowell (1819–1891), who succeeded Professor Longfellow at Harvard, ranks as one of America's better poets. He was also a distinguished essayist, literary critic, and diplomat, as well as editor of Boston's *Atlantic Monthly* and *North American Review*—a diffusion of talents that hampered his poetical output. Lowell is remembered as a political satirist in his *Biglow Papers*, especially those of 1846–1848 opposing the Mexican War. Written partly as poetry in the Yankee dialect, the *Papers* condemned in blistering terms the alleged slavery-expansion designs of the Polk administration.

Two women writers whose work remains enormously popular today also sprouted from this New England literary soil. Louisa May Alcott (1832–1888) grew up in Concord, Massachusetts, in the bosom of transcendentalism, alongside neighbors Emerson, Thoreau, and Fuller. Her philosopher father Bronson Alcott occupied himself more with ideas than with earning a living, leaving his daughter to write *Little Women* (1868) and other books to support her mother and sisters. Not far away in Amherst, Massachusetts, poet Emily Dickinson (1830–1886) lived as a recluse but created her own original world through precious gems of poetry. Her seclusion was but an extreme example of the romantic artist's desire for social remove. In deceptively spare language and simple rhyme schemes, Dickinson explored universal themes of nature, love, death, and immortality. Although she hesitated during her lifetime to publish more than a dozen of her poems, when she died, nearly two thousand of them were found among her papers and eventually made their way into print.

The most noteworthy literary figure produced by the South before the Civil War was novelist William Gilmore Simms (1806–1870). Quantitatively, at least, he was great: eighty-two books flowed from his ever-moist pen, winning for him the title "the Cooper of the South." His favorite themes, captured in titles like *The Yemasee* (1835) and *The Cassique of Kiawah* (1859), dealt with the southern frontier in colonial days and with the South during the Revolutionary War. Enormously popular in his own day, Simms ardently promoted southern literature and won the esteem of many northern writers, including Irving, Bryant, and Herman Melville, among others. Yet his national and international reputation suffered after the Civil War, no doubt due to his overt proslavery and secessionist sentiments.

✦ Literary Individualists and Dissenters

Not all writers in these years believed so keenly in human goodness and social progress. A clique of contrary-minded authors plumbed the darker realms of human experience, exploring pain, fear, and grief, along with the supernatural and the subconscious. Edgar Allan Poe (1809–1849), who spent much of his youth in Virginia, was an eccentric genius. Orphaned at an early age, cursed with ill health, and married to a child-wife of thirteen who fell fatally ill of tuberculosis, he suffered hunger, cold, poverty, and debt. Failing at suicide, he took refuge in the bottle and dissipated his talent early.

Poe was a gifted lyric poet, as the mesmerizing rhythms of "The Raven" (1845) attest. A master stylist, he also excelled in the short story, especially of the Gothic horror type, in which he shared his alcoholic nightmares with fascinated readers. If he did not invent the modern detective story, he at least set new high standards in tales like "The Murders in the Rue Morgue" (1841).

Poe was fascinated by the ghostly and ghastly, as in "The Fall of the House of Usher" (1839) and other stories. Obsessed with romantic antiheroes on the verge of mental disintegration, he reflected a morbid sensibility distinctly at odds with the usually optimistic tone of American culture. Partly for this reason, Poe has perhaps been even more prized by Europeans than by Americans. His brilliant career was cut short when he was found drunk in a Baltimore gutter and shortly thereafter died.

Two other writers reflected the continuing Calvinist obsession with original sin and with the never-ending struggle between good and evil. In somber Salem, Massachusetts, writer Nathaniel Hawthorne (1804–1864) grew up in an atmosphere heavy with the memories of his Puritan forebears and the tragedy of his father's premature death on an ocean voyage. His masterpiece was *The Scarlet Letter* (1850), which describes the Puritan practice of forcing an adulteress to wear a scarlet "A" on her clothing. The tragic tale chronicles the psychological effects of sin on the guilty heroine Hester Prynne, a classic romantic outcast, and her secret lover Arthur Dimmesdale, the father of her baby and a minister of the gospel in Puritan Boston. In *The Marble Faun* (1860), Hawthorne dealt with a group of young American artists who witness a mysterious murder in Rome. The book explores the concepts of the omnipresence of evil and the dead hand of the past weighing upon the present.

Herman Melville (1819–1891), an orphaned and ill-educated New Yorker, went to sea as a youth and served eighteen adventuresome months on a whaler. "A whale ship was my Yale College and my Harvard," he wrote. Jumping ship in the South Seas, he lived among cannibals, from whom he providently escaped uneaten. His exotic tales of the South Seas were immediately popular, but his masterpiece, *Moby Dick* (1851), was not. This epic novel is a complex allegory of good and evil, told by its narrator Ishmael in terms of the conflict between a whaling captain, Ahab, and a giant white whale, Moby Dick. The monomaniacal Captain Ahab, having lost a leg to the marine monster, lives only for revenge. His deterministic pursuit finally ends when Moby Dick rams and sinks Ahab's ship, leaving only one survivor. The whale's exact identity and Ahab's motives remain obscure. In the end the untamed sea, like the terrifyingly impersonal and unknowable universe of Melville's imagination, simply rolls on.

Capturing a Sperm Whale, painted by William Page from a sketch by C. B. Hulsart, 1835   This painting and Melville's *Moby Dick* vividly portray the hazards of whaling. Despite the dangers, it proved to be an important industry from colonial times to the end of the nineteenth century.

Moby Dick was widely ignored at the time of its publication; people were accustomed to more straightforward and upbeat prose. A disheartened Melville continued to write unprofitably for some years, part of the time eking out a living as a customs inspector in New York City, and then died in relative obscurity. Ironically, his brooding masterpiece about the mysterious white whale had to wait until the more jaded twentieth century for readers and for proper recognition.

✸ Portrayers of the Past

A distinguished group of American historians was emerging at the same time that other writers were winning distinction. Energetic George Bancroft (1800–1891), who as secretary of the navy helped found the Naval Academy at Annapolis in 1845, has deservedly received the title "Father of American History." He published a spirited, superpatriotic history of the United States to 1789 in six (originally ten) volumes (1834–1876), a work that grew out of his vast researches in dusty archives in Europe and America.

Two other historians are read with greater pleasure and profit today. William H. Prescott (1796–1859), who accidentally lost the sight of an eye while in college, conserved his remaining weak vision and published classic accounts of the conquest of Mexico (1843) and Peru (1847). Francis Parkman (1823–1893), whose eyes were so defective that he wrote in darkness with the aid of a guiding machine, penned a brilliant series of volumes beginning in 1851. In epic style he chronicled the struggle between France and Britain in colonial times for the mastery of North America.

Early American historians of prominence were almost without exception New Englanders, largely because the Boston area provided well-stocked libraries and a stimulating literary tradition. These writers numbered abolitionists among their relatives and friends and hence were disposed to view unsympathetically the slavery-cursed South. This "made in New England" interpretation dominated the writing of American history until the close of the nineteenth century, when pressure for national reconciliation overcame regional bias. "The history of the United States has been written by Boston," one pro-southern historian bitterly complained, "and largely written wrong."

Varying Viewpoints
Reform: Who? What? How? and Why?

Early chronicles of the antebellum period universally lauded the era's reformers, portraying them as idealistic, altruistic crusaders intent on improving American society.

After World War II, however, some historians began to detect selfish and even conservative motives underlying the apparent benevolence of the reformers. This view described the advocates of reform as anxious, upper-class men and women threatened by the ferment of life in antebellum America. The pursuit of reforms like temperance, asylums, prisons, and mandatory public education represented a means of asserting "social control." In this vein, one historian described a reform movement as "the anguished protest of an aggrieved class against a world they never made." In Michael Katz's treatment of early educational reform, proponents were community leaders who sought a school system that would ease the traumas of America's industrialization by inculcating business-oriented values and discipline in the working classes.

The wave of reform activity in the 1960s prompted a reevaluation of the reputations of the antebellum reformers. These more recent interpretations found much to admire in the authentic religious commitments of reformers and especially in the participation of women, who sought various social improvements as an extension of their function as protectors of the home and family.

The scholarly treatment of abolitionism is a telling example of how reformers and their campaigns have risen and fallen in the estimation of historians. To northern historians writing in the late nineteenth century, abolitionists were courageous men and women so devoted to uprooting the evil of slavery that they were willing to dedicate their lives to a cause that often ostracized them from their communities. By the mid-twentieth century, an interpretation more favorable to the South prevailed, one that blamed the fanaticism of the abolitionists for the Civil War. But as the racial climate in the United States began to change during the 1960s, historians once again showed sympathy for the abolitionist struggle, and by the end of the twentieth century abolitionist men and women were revered as ideologically committed individuals dedicated not just to freeing the enslaved but to saving the moral soul of America.

Scholars animated by the modern feminist movement have inspired a reconsideration of women's reform activity. It had long been known, of course, that women were active participants in charitable organizations. But not until Nancy Cott, Kathryn Sklar, Mary Ryan, and other historians began to look more closely at what Cott has called "the bonds of womanhood" did the links between women's domestic lives and their public benevolent behavior fully emerge. Carroll Smith-Rosenberg showed in her study of the New York Female Moral Reform Society, for example, that members who set out at first to convert prostitutes to evangelical Protestantism and to close down the city's many brothels soon developed an ideology of female autonomy that rejected male dominance. When men behaved in immoral or illegal ways, women reformers claimed that they had the right—even the duty—to leave the confines of their homes and actively work to purify society. More recently, historians Nancy Hewitt and Lori Ginzberg have challenged the assumption that all women reformers embraced a single definition of female identity. Instead they have emphasized the importance of class differences in shaping women's reform work, which led inevitably to tensions within female ranks. Giving more attention to the historical evolution of female reform ideology, Ginzberg has also detected a shift from an early focus on moral uplift to a more class-based appeal for social control.

Historians of the suffrage movement have emphasized another kind of exclusivity among women reformers—the boundaries of race. Ellen DuBois has shown that after a brief alliance with the abolitionist movement, many female suffrage reformers abandoned the cause of black liberation in an effort to achieve their own goal with less controversy. Whatever historians may conclude about the liberating or leashing character of early reform, it is clear by now that they have to contend with the ways in which class, gender, and race divided reformers, making the plural—*reform movements*—the more accurate depiction of the impulse to "improve" that pervaded American society in the early nineteenth century.

Most recently, historians of all kinds of reform have highlighted the transatlantic dimensions of these movements. American reformers corresponded with and adopted ideas from their European counterparts, participating in waves of reform that extended well beyond the shores of the United States.

Chapter Review

KEY TERMS

The Age of Reason (307)

Deism (307)

Unitarians (307)

Second Great
    Awakening (308)

Burned-Over District (309)

Mormons (310)

lyceum (314)

American Temperance
    Society (316)

Maine Law of 1851 (317)

Woman's Rights Conven-
    tion at Seneca Falls (318)

New Harmony (320)

Brook Farm (320)

Oneida Community (320)

Shakers (320)

Federal Style (324)

Greek Revival (324)

Hudson River school (325)

minstrel shows (325)

romanticism (326)

transcendentalism (327)

"The American
    Scholar" (328)

PEOPLE TO KNOW

Peter Cartwright

Charles Grandison Finney

Joseph Smith

Brigham Young

Horace Mann

Dorothea Dix

Neal S. Dow

Lucretia Mott

Elizabeth Cady Stanton

Susan B. Anthony

Lucy Stone

Amelia Bloomer

Robert Owen

John J. Audubon

Stephen C. Foster

James Fenimore Cooper

Ralph Waldo Emerson

Henry David Thoreau

Walt Whitman

Henry Wadsworth
    Longfellow

Louisa May Alcott

Emily Dickinson

Edgar Allan Poe

Nathaniel Hawthorne

Herman Melville

Francis Parkman

TO LEARN MORE

Robert Abzug, *Cosmos Crumbling: American Reform and the Religious Imagination* (1994)

Anne M. Boylan, *The Origins of Women's Activism: New York and Boston, 1797–1840* (2002)

Nathan O. Hatch, *The Democratization of American Christianity* (1989)

Joseph Hawes, *Children in Urban Society* (1971)

Daniel Walker Howe, *What Hath God Wrought: The Transformation of America, 1815–1848* (2007)

Paul Johnson, *A Shopkeeper's Millennium: Society and Revivals in Rochester, New York, 1815–1837* (1978)

Joseph F. Kett, *Rites of Passage: Adolescence in America* (1976)

Spencer Klaw, *Without Sin: The Life and Death of the Oneida Community* (1993)

Sally G. McMillen, *Seneca Falls and the Origins of the Women's Rights Movement* (2008)

Steven Mintz and Susan Kellogg, *Domestic Revolutions: A Social History of American Family Life* (1988)

William Rorabaugh, *The Alcoholic Republic* (1979)

Caroline Winterer, *The Culture of Classicism: Ancient Greece and Rome in American Intellectual Life, 1780–1910* (2002)

A complete, annotated bibliography for this chapter—along with brief descriptions of the People to Know—may be found on the American Pageant website. The Key Terms are defined in a Glossary at the end of the text.

CHRONOLOGY

1747 Shaker movement founded in Manchester, England

1770s First Shaker communities established in New York

1794 Thomas Paine publishes *The Age of Reason*

1795 University of North Carolina founded

1800 Second Great Awakening begins

1819 Jefferson founds University of Virginia

1819–1820 Irving publishes *The Sketch Book*

1821 Emma Willard establishes Troy (New York) Female Seminary

1825 New Harmony commune established

1826 American Temperance Society founded
Cooper publishes *The Last of the Mohicans*

1828 Noah Webster publishes dictionary
American Peace Society founded

1830 Joseph Smith founds Mormon Church
Godey's Lady's Book first published

1830–1831 Finney conducts revivals in eastern cities

1835 Lyceum movement flourishes

1836 Cole's *The Oxbow* debuts

1837 Oberlin College admits female students
Mary Lyon establishes Mount Holyoke Seminary
Emerson delivers "The American Scholar" address

1840 London antislavery convention refuses to recognize female delegates

1841 Brook Farm commune established

1843 Dorothea Dix petitions Massachusetts legislature on behalf of the insane

1845 Poe publishes "The Raven"

1846–1847 Mormon migration to Utah

1848 Seneca Falls Woman's Rights Convention held
Oneida Community established
Foster's "Oh! Susanna" debuts

1850 Hawthorne publishes *The Scarlet Letter*

1851 Melville publishes *Moby Dick*
Maine passes first law prohibiting liquor

1854 Thoreau publishes *Walden*

1855 Whitman publishes *Leaves of Grass*

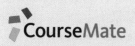 **CourseMate**

Go to the CourseMate website at **www.cengagebrain.com** for additional study tools and review materials—including audio and video clips—for this chapter.

AP® Review Questions for Chapter 15

1. As embraced by many of the Founding Fathers, Deism
   (A) emphasized that a person's fate was predestined and known only by God.
   (B) was rooted in strict adherence to the Bible.
   (C) celebrated God's hand in the daily workings of the world.
   (D) stressed that God created the world but trusted the moral capacity of human beings to run it.
   (E) embraced Original Sin and Christ's divinity.

2. Which of the following is NOT a true statement about the Second Great Awakening?
   (A) It was a religious movement that led to the reorganization of many existing churches and the founding of new sects.
   (B) It drew new converts from massive camp or revival meetings.
   (C) It had its greatest appeal to men, who constituted the majority of new religious adherents.
   (D) It inspired several reform movements.
   (E) It widened existing class and regional divisions.

3. The term *Burned-Over District* refers to
   (A) parts of western New York that were inundated with sermoners preaching hellfire and damnation.
   (B) factory districts in New England that were ravaged by fires in the early 1800s.
   (C) disillusionment in certain parts of the Northeast when Christ's second coming did not occur as predicted.
   (D) sections of the frontier that were overwhelmed with multiple revivals.
   (E) regions of New England that were overcrowded, overgrown, and increasingly run-down.

4. Who founded the Mormon religion (Church of Jesus Christ of Latter-Day Saints)?
   (A) Brigham Young
   (B) Joseph Smith
   (C) Charles Finney
   (D) Peter Cartwright
   (E) William Miller

5. Despite early resistance to public education, once established it was advanced by all of the following reforms EXCEPT
   (A) increasing manhood suffrage.
   (B) campaigns for better schoolhouses and higher pay for teachers.
   (C) efforts to keep children in school for longer terms.
   (D) improvements in textbooks.
   (E) the expanding number of public schools nationwide.

6. Why was there a lag in founding women's colleges and other secondary institutions until after the 1820s?
   (A) Lack of funding
   (B) Fear that education would make women unfit for marriage
   (C) Discomfort with women and men in similar institutions
   (D) The fact that educating women was against many religious principles
   (E) The fact that secondary education for women was against the law in many states

7. The reformer Dorothea Dix is best known for
   (A) championing the mentally ill.
   (B) temperance.
   (C) abolition.
   (D) educational reform.
   (E) labor reform.

8. Reformers blamed alcohol consumption—Demon Drink—for all of the following EXCEPT
   (A) corruption of women.
   (B) degradation of the family.
   (C) decrease in church participation.
   (D) disruption of American society by immigrants.
   (E) decline in worker productivity.

9. What is the significance of Seneca Falls in 1848?
   (A) The rise of the universal suffrage movement
   (B) The beginning of the abolition movement
   (C) The birth of the industrial revolution
   (D) The advent of the women's rights movement
   (E) The start of a dress reform crusade

10. Which of the following was NOT among the many Utopian communities that sprang up in the early to mid-nineteenth century?
    (A) Oneida
    (B) Brook Farm
    (C) Quakers
    (D) Shakers
    (E) New Harmony

11. The main spark in the flowering of a truly American form of literature was the
    (A) emerging consumer culture in the 1820s.
    (B) upswing in nationalism after the War of 1812.
    (C) intensifying rivalry with Britain.
    (D) improvement in publishing techniques.
    (E) rising literacy rates in America.

12. The transcendentalist movement of the 1830s
    (A) celebrated the power of the individual spirit.
    (B) embraced the communal influences of the church and other institutions.
    (C) believed that human beings attain knowledge through the five senses.
    (D) argued that laws and government were the key to social order.
    (E) put the greater good ahead of the individual's needs.

13. All of the following American authors celebrated the human potential for goodness and progress in their work EXCEPT
    (A) John Greenleaf Whittier.
    (B) Louisa May Alcott.
    (C) Henry David Thoreau.
    (D) Henry Wadsworth Longfellow.
    (E) Edgar Allan Poe.

14. Who is considered the "father of American history"?
    (A) Francis Parkman
    (B) George Bancroft
    (C) William Prescott
    (D) Herman Melville
    (E) Ralph Waldo Emerson

15. A major difference between the Great Awakening and Second Great Awakening was that
    (A) the Second Great Awakening encompassed a return to Catholic and Jewish ideals.
    (B) the Second Great Awakening manifested in reform movements that attempted to dramatically change American society.
    (C) the Great Awakening was unsuccessful at reviving religious fervor.
    (D) the Great Awakening was much larger in scope than the Second Great Awakening.
    (E) the population targeted by the Second Great Awakening was less diverse than during colonial times.

16. Advancements in American arts and culture resulted from all of the following EXCEPT
    (A) interest in the revival of Gothic forms.
    (B) surging nationalism after the War of 1812.
    (C) the idea that truth "transcends" the senses.
    (D) greater emphasis on education in the South.
    (E) foreign influences, including German romanticism.

Part Three

Testing the New Nation

1820–1877

The Civil War of 1861 to 1865 was the awesome trial by fire of American nationhood, and of the American soul. All Americans knew, said Abraham Lincoln, that slavery "was somehow the cause of this war." The war tested, in Lincoln's ringing phrase at Gettysburg, whether any nation "dedicated to the proposition that all men are created equal . . . can long endure." How did this great and bloody conflict come about? And what were its results?

American slavery was by any measure a "peculiar institution." Slavery was rooted in both racism and economic exploitation, and depended for its survival on brutal repression. Yet the American slave population was the only enslaved population in history that grew by means of its own biological reproduction—a fact that suggests to many historians that conditions under slavery in the United States were somehow less punitive than those in other slave societies. Indeed a distinctive and durable African American culture managed to flourish under slavery, further suggesting that the slave regime provided

some "space" for African American cultural development. But however benignly it might be painted, slavery still remained a cancer in the heart of American democracy, a moral outrage that mocked the nation's claim to be a model of social and political enlightenment. As time went on, more and more voices called more and more stridently for its abolition.

The nation lived uneasily with slavery from the outset. Thomas Jefferson was only one among many in the founding generation who felt acutely the conflict between the high principle of equality and the ugly reality of slavery. The federal government in the early Republic took several steps to check the growth of slavery. It banned slavery in the Old Northwest in 1787, prohibited the further importation of slaves after 1808, and declared in the Missouri Compromise of 1820 that the vast western territories secured in the Louisiana Purchase were forever closed to slavery north of the state of Missouri. Antislavery sentiment even abounded in the South in the immediate post-Revolutionary

Returning from the Cotton Fields in South Carolina African American slaves planted and picked virtually all the cotton that formed the foundation of the nineteenth-century southern economy. The white South ferociously defended its "peculiar institution" of slavery, which ended at last only in the fires of the Civil War. Saint Louis Art Museum, Gift of Bank of America

The 1st Virginia Regiment   These Virginia militiamen were photographed in 1859 while attending the trial of the abolitionist John Brown for treason against the State of Virginia. Two years later their regiment formed part of the Confederate army that struck for southern independence.

years. But as time progressed, and especially after Eli Whitney's invention of the cotton gin in the 1790s, the southern planter class became increasingly dependent on slave labor to wring profits from the sprawling plantations that carpeted the South. As cotton cultivation spread westward, the South's stake in slavery grew deeper, and the abolitionist outcry grew louder.

The controversy over slavery significantly intensified following the war with Mexico in the 1840s. "Mexico will poison us," predicted the philosopher Ralph Waldo Emerson, and he proved to be distressingly prophetic. The lands acquired from Mexico—most of the present-day American Southwest, from Texas to California—reopened the question of extending slavery into the western territories. The decade and a half that followed the Mexican War—from 1846 to 1861—witnessed a series of ultimately ineffective efforts to come to grips with that question, including the ill-starred Compromise of 1850, the conflict-breeding Kansas-Nebraska Act of 1854, and the Supreme Court's inflammatory decision in the *Dred Scott* case of 1857. Ultimately, the slavery question was settled by force of arms, in the Civil War itself.

The Civil War, as Lincoln observed, was assuredly about slavery. But as Lincoln also repeatedly insisted, the war was about the viability of the Union as well and about the strength of democracy itself. Could a democratic government, built on the principle of popular consent, rightfully deny some of its citizens the same right to independence that the American revolutionaries had exercised in seceding from the British Empire in 1776? Southern rebels, calling the conflict "The War for Southern Independence," asked that question forcefully, but ultimately it, too, was answered not in the law courts or in the legislative halls but on the battlefield.

The Civil War unarguably established the supremacy of the Union, and it ended slavery as well. But as the victorious Union set about the task of "reconstruction" after the war's end in 1865, a combination of weak northern will and residual southern power frustrated the goal of making the emancipated blacks full-fledged American citizens. The Civil War in the end brought nothing but freedom—but over time, freedom proved a powerful tool indeed.

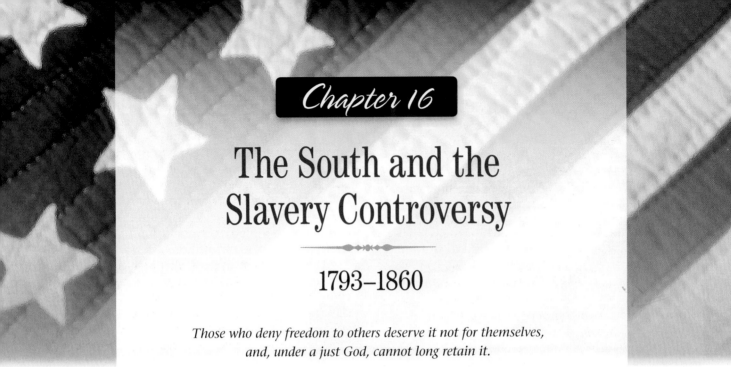

Chapter 16

The South and the Slavery Controversy

1793–1860

*Those who deny freedom to others deserve it not for themselves,
and, under a just God, cannot long retain it.*

ABRAHAM LINCOLN, 1859

At the dawn of the Republic, slavery faced an uncertain future. Touched by Revolutionary idealism, some southern leaders, including Thomas Jefferson, were talking openly of freeing their slaves. Others predicted that the iron logic of economics would eventually expose slavery's unprofitability, speeding its demise.

But the introduction of Eli Whitney's cotton gin in 1793 scrambled all those predictions. Whitney's invention made possible the wide-scale cultivation of short-staple cotton. The white fiber rapidly became the dominant southern crop, eclipsing tobacco, rice, and sugar. The explosion of cotton cultivation created an insatiable demand for labor, chaining the slave to the gin and the planter to the slave. As the nineteenth century opened, the reinvigoration of southern slavery carried fateful implications for blacks and whites alike—and threatened the survival of the nation itself.

✪ "Cotton Is King!"

As time passed, the Cotton Kingdom developed into a huge agricultural factory, pouring out avalanches of the fluffy fiber. Quick profits drew planters to the loamy bottomlands of the Gulf states. As long as the soil was still vigorous, the yield was bountiful and the rewards were high. Caught up in an economic spiral, the planters bought more slaves and land to grow more cotton, so as to buy still more slaves and land.

Northern shippers reaped a large part of the profits from the cotton trade. They would load bulging bales of cotton at southern ports, transport them to England, sell their fleecy cargo for pounds sterling, and buy needed manufactured goods for sale in the United States. To a large degree, the prosperity of both North and South—and of England, too—rested on the bent backs of enslaved bondsmen.

So did the young nation's growing wealth. Cotton accounted for half the value of all American exports after 1840, and export earnings provided much of the capital that stoked the Republic's economic growth. The South produced more than half of the entire world's supply of cotton—a fact that held foreign nations in partial bondage. Britain was then the leading industrial power. Its most important single manufacture in the 1850s was cotton cloth, from which about one-fifth of its population, directly or indirectly, drew its livelihood. About 75 percent of this precious supply of fiber came from the white-carpeted acres of the South.

Southern leaders were fully aware that Britain was tied to them by cotton threads, and this dependence gave them a heady sense of power. In their eyes "Cotton was King," the gin was his throne, and the black bondsmen were his henchmen. If war should ever break out between North and South, northern warships would presumably cut off the outflow of cotton. Fiber-famished British factories would then close their gates, starving mobs would force the London government to break the blockade, and the South would triumph. Cotton was a powerful monarch indeed.

✦ The Planter "Aristocracy"

Before the Civil War, the South was in some respects not so much a democracy as an oligarchy—or a government by the few, in this case heavily influenced by a planter aristocracy. In 1850 only 1,733 families owned more than one hundred slaves each, and this select group provided the cream of the political and social leadership of the section and nation. Here was the mint-julep South of the tall-columned and white-painted plantation mansion—the "big house," where dwelt the "cottonocracy."

The planter aristocrats, with their blooded horses and Chippendale chairs, enjoyed a lion's share of southern wealth. They could educate their children in the finest schools, often in the North or abroad. Their money provided the leisure for study, reflection, and statecraft, as was notably true of men like John C. Calhoun (a Yale graduate) and Jefferson Davis (a West Point graduate). They felt a keen sense of obligation to serve the public. It was no accident that Virginia and the other southern states produced a higher proportion of front-rank statesmen before 1860 than the "dollar-grubbing" North.

But even in its best light, dominance by a favored aristocracy was basically undemocratic. It widened the gap between rich and poor. It hampered tax-supported public education, because the rich planters could and did send their children to private institutions.

A favorite author of elite southerners was Sir Walter Scott, whose manors and castles, graced by brave Ivanhoes and fair Rowenas, helped them idealize a feudal society, even when many of their economic activities were undeniably capitalistic. Southern aristocrats, who sometimes staged jousting tournaments, strove to perpetuate a type of medievalism that had died out in Europe—or was rapidly dying out.* Mark Twain later accused Sir Walter Scott of having had a hand in starting the Civil War. The British novelist, Twain said, aroused the southerners to fight for a decaying social structure—"a sham civilization."

The plantation system also shaped the lives of southern women. The mistress of a great plantation commanded a sizable household staff of mostly female slaves. She gave daily orders to cooks, maids, seamstresses, laundresses, and body servants. Relationships between mistresses and slaves ranged from affectionate to atrocious. Some mistresses showed tender regard for their bondswomen, and some slave women took pride in their status as "members" of the household. But slavery strained even the bonds of womanhood. Virtually no slaveholding women believed in abolition, and relatively few protested when the husbands and children of their slaves were sold. One plantation mistress

---

*Oddly enough, by legislative enactment, jousting became the official state sport of Maryland in 1962.

Erich Lessing/Art Resource, NY

Interior of the Cotton Bureau in New Orleans, by Edgar Degas, 1873 Although this painting dates from 1873, French impressionist painter Edgar Degas (1834–1917) captured the insouciant self-confidence of cotton traders in the pre–Civil War era. As cotton cultivation spread into the new states of the trans-Appalachian Southwest, the entire Cotton Kingdom paid tribute to New Orleans, Queen City of the South, and the port through which millions of cotton bales flowed out to British textile mills.

Harvesting Cotton This Currier & Ives print shows slaves of both sexes harvesting cotton, which was then "ginned," baled, carted to the riverbank, and taken by paddle wheeler downriver to New Orleans for shipment to New England or overseas.

Granger Collection

harbored a special affection for her slave Annica but noted in her diary that "I whipt Annica" for insolence.

✦ Slaves of the Slave System

Unhappily, the moonlight-and-magnolia tradition concealed much that was worrisome, distasteful, and sordid. Plantation agriculture was wasteful, largely because King Cotton and his money-hungry subjects despoiled the good earth. Quick profits led to excessive cultivation, or "land butchery," which in turn caused a heavy leakage of population to the West and Northwest.

The economic structure of the South became increasingly monopolistic. As the land wore thin, many small farmers sold their holdings to more prosperous neighbors and went north or west. The big got bigger and the small smaller. When the Civil War finally erupted, a large percentage of southern farms had passed from the hands of the families that had originally cleared them.

Another cancer in the bosom of the South was the financial instability of the plantation system. The temptation to overspeculate in land and slaves caused many planters, including Andrew Jackson in his later years, to plunge in beyond their depth. Although the black slaves might in extreme cases be fed for as little as ten cents a day, there were other expenses. The slaves represented a heavy investment of capital, perhaps $1,200 each in the case of prime field hands, and they might deliberately injure themselves or run away. An entire slave quarter might be wiped out by disease or even by lightning, as happened in one instance to twenty ill-fated blacks.

Dominance by King Cotton likewise led to a dangerous dependence on a one-crop economy, whose price level was at the mercy of world conditions. The whole system discouraged a healthy diversification of agriculture and particularly of manufacturing.

Southern planters resented watching the North grow fat at their expense. They were pained by the heavy outward flow of commissions and interest to northern middlemen, bankers, agents, and shippers. True souls of the South, especially by the 1850s, deplored the fact that when born, they were wrapped in Yankee-made swaddling clothes and that they spent

Thomas Jefferson (1743–1826) wrote in 1786,

"What a stupendous, what an incomprehensible machine is man! Who can endure toil, famine, stripes, imprisonment & death itself in vindication of his own liberty, and the next moment . . . inflict on his fellow men a bondage, one hour of which is fraught with more misery than ages of that which he rose in rebellion to oppose."

Unlike George Washington, Jefferson freed only a couple of his slaves in his will; the rest were sold to pay off his large debts.

Basil Hall (1788–1844), an Englishman, visited part of the cotton belt on a river steamer (1827–1828). Noting the preoccupation with cotton, he wrote,

"All day and almost all night long, the captain, pilot, crew, and passengers were talking of nothing else; and sometimes our ears were so wearied with the sound of cotton! cotton! cotton! that we gladly hailed a fresh inundation of company in hopes of some change—but alas! . . . 'What's cotton at?' was the first eager inquiry. 'Ten cents [a pound],' 'Oh, that will never do!'"

the rest of their lives in servitude to Yankee manufacturing. When they died, they were laid in coffins held together with Yankee nails and were buried in graves dug with Yankee shovels. The South furnished the corpse and the hole in the ground.

The Cotton Kingdom also repelled large-scale European immigration, which added so richly to the manpower and wealth of the North. In 1860 only 4.4 percent of the southern population was foreign-born, as compared with 18.7 percent for the North. German and Irish immigration to the South was generally discouraged by the competition of slave labor, by the high cost of fertile land, and by European ignorance of cotton growing. The diverting of non-British immigration to the North caused the white South to become the most Anglo-Saxon section of the nation.

✦ The White Majority

Only a handful of southern whites lived in Grecian-pillared mansions. Below those 1,733 families in 1850 who owned a hundred or more slaves were the less wealthy slaveowners (see Figure 16.1). They totaled in 1850 some 345,000 families, representing about 1,725,000 white persons. Over two-thirds of these families—255,268 in all—owned fewer than ten slaves each. All told, only about one-fourth of white southerners owned slaves or belonged to a slaveowning family.

The smaller slaveowners did not own a majority of the slaves, but they made up a majority of the masters. These lesser masters were typically small farmers. With the striking exception that their households contained a slave or two, or perhaps an entire slave family, the style of their lives probably resembled that of small farmers in the North more than it did that of the southern planter aristocracy. They lived in modest farmhouses and sweated beside their bondsmen in the cotton fields, laboring callus for callus just as hard as their slaves.

Beneath the slaveowners on the population pyramid was the great body of whites who owned no

slaves at all. By 1860 their numbers had swelled to 6,120,825—three-quarters of all southern whites. Shouldered off the richest bottomlands by the mighty planters, they scratched a simple living from the thinner soils of the backcountry and the mountain valleys (see Maps 16.1 and 16.2). To them the riches of the Cotton Kingdom were a distant dream, and they often sneered at the lordly pretensions of the cotton "snobocracy." These red-necked farmers participated in the market economy scarcely at all. As subsistence farmers, they raised corn and hogs, not cotton, and often lived isolated lives, punctuated periodically by extended socializing and sermonizing at religious camp meetings.

Some of the least prosperous nonslaveholding whites were scorned even by slaves as "poor white trash." Known also as "hillbillies," "crackers," or "clay eaters," they were often described as listless, shiftless, and misshapen. Later investigations have revealed that many of them were not simply lazy but sick, suffering from malnutrition and parasites, especially hookworm.

All these whites without slaves had no direct economic stake in the preservation of slavery, yet they were among the stoutest defenders of the slave system. Why? The answer is not far to seek.

The carrot on the stick ever dangling before their eyes was the hope of buying a slave or two and of parlaying their paltry holdings into riches—all in accord with the "American dream" of upward social mobility. They also took fierce pride in their presumed racial superiority, which would be watered down if the slaves were freed. Many of the poorer whites were hardly better off economically than the slaves; some, indeed, were not so well-off. But even the most wretched whites could take perverse comfort from the knowledge that they outranked someone in status: the still more wretched African American slave. Thus did the logic of economics join with the illogic of racism in buttressing the slave system.

In a special category among white southerners were the mountain whites, more or less marooned in the

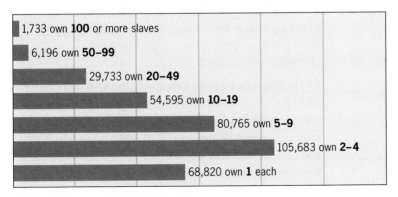

FIGURE 16.1 Slaveowning Families, 1850 More than half of all slaveholding families owned fewer than four slaves. In contrast, 2 percent of slaveowners owned more than fifty slaves each. A tiny slaveholding elite held a majority of slave property in the South. The great majority of white southerners owned no slaves at all. © Cengage Learning

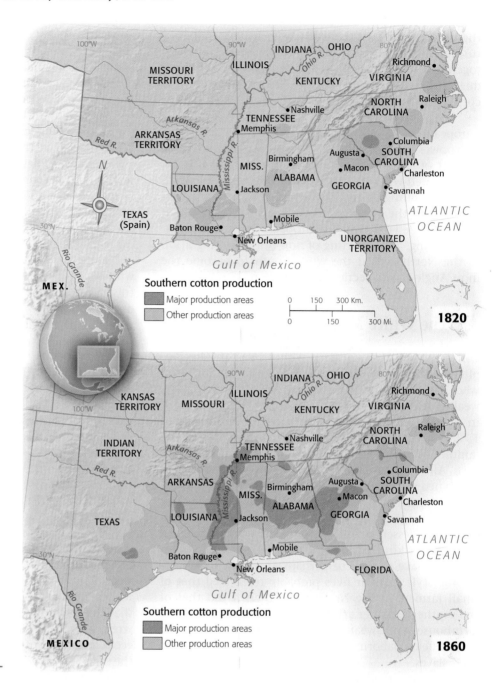

MAP 16.1 Southern Cotton Production and Distribution of Slaves, 1820 © Cengage Learning

valleys of the Appalachian range that stretched from western Virginia to northern Georgia and Alabama. Civilization had largely passed them by, and they still lived under spartan frontier conditions. They were a kind of living ancestry, for some of them retained Elizabethan speech forms and habits that had long since died out in Britain.

As independent small farmers, hundreds of miles distant from the heart of the Cotton Kingdom and rarely if ever in sight of a slave, these mountain whites had little in common with the whites of the flatlands. Many of them, including future president Andrew Johnson of Tennessee, hated both the haughty

"Arthur Lee, Freeman," petitioned the General Assembly of Virginia in 1835 for permission to remain in the state despite a law against the residency of free blacks. After asserting his upstanding moral character, he implored,

❝He therefore most respectfully and earnestly prays that you will pass a law permitting him on the score of long and meritorious service to remain in the State, together with his wife and four children, and not force him in his old age to seek a livelihood in a new Country.❞

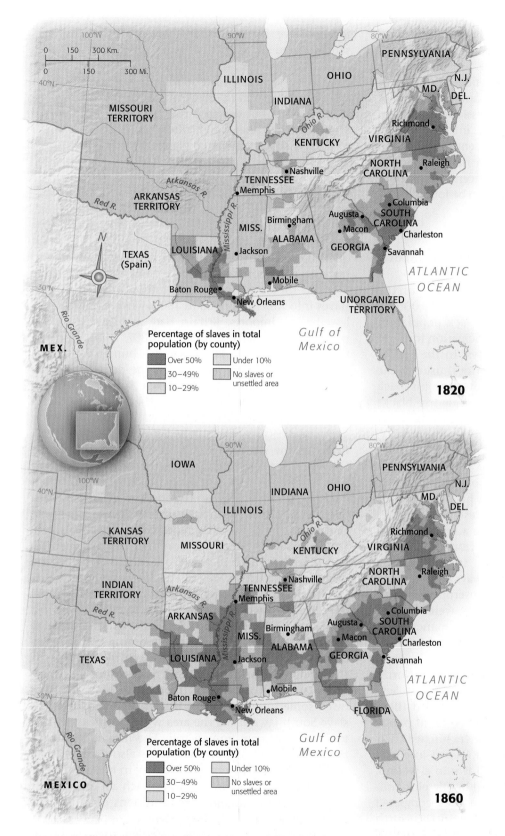

MAP 16.2 Southern Cotton Production and Distribution of Slaves, 1860 The philosopher Ralph Waldo Emerson, a New Englander, declared in 1856, "I do not see how a barbarous community and a civilized community can constitute a state. I think we must get rid of slavery or we must get rid of freedom." © Cengage Learning

planters and their gangs of blacks. They looked upon the impending strife between North and South as "a rich man's war but a poor man's fight."

When the war came, the tough-fibered mountain whites constituted a vitally important peninsula of Unionism jutting down into the secessionist Southern sea. They ultimately played a significant role in crippling the Confederacy. Their attachment to the Union party of Abraham Lincoln was such that for generations after the Civil War, the only concentrated Republican strength in the solid South was to be found in the southern highlands.

✴ Free Blacks: Slaves Without Masters

Precarious in the extreme was the standing of the South's free blacks, who numbered about 250,000 by 1860. In the upper South, the free black population traced its origins to a wavelet of emancipation inspired by the idealism of Revolutionary days. In the deeper South, many free blacks were mulattoes, usually the emancipated children of a white planter and his black mistress. Throughout the South were some free blacks who had purchased their freedom with earnings from labor after hours. Many free blacks owned property, especially in New Orleans, where a sizable mulatto community prospered. Some, such as William T. Johnson, the "barber of Natchez," even owned slaves. He was the master of fifteen bondsmen; his diary records that in June 1848 he flogged two slaves and a mule.

The free blacks in the South were a kind of "third race." These people were prohibited from working in certain occupations and forbidden from testifying against whites in court. They were always vulnerable to being hijacked back into slavery by unscrupulous slave traders. As free men and women, they were walking examples of what might be achieved by emancipation and hence were resented and detested by defenders of the slave system.

Free blacks were also unpopular in the North, where about another 250,000 of them lived. Several states forbade their entrance, most denied them the right to vote, and some barred blacks from public schools. In 1835 New Hampshire farmers hitched their oxen to a small schoolhouse that had dared to enroll fourteen black children and dragged it into a swamp. Northern blacks were especially hated by the pick-and-shovel Irish immigrants, with whom they competed for menial jobs. Much of the agitation in the North against the spread of slavery into the new territories in the 1840s and 1850s grew out of race prejudice, not humanitarianism.

Antiblack feeling was in fact frequently stronger in the North than in the South. The gifted and eloquent former slave Frederick Douglass, an abolitionist and self-educated orator of rare power, was several times mobbed and beaten by northern rowdies. It was sometimes observed that white southerners, who were often suckled and reared by black nurses, liked the black as an individual but despised the race. The white northerner, on the other hand, often professed to like the race but disliked individual blacks.

✴ Plantation Slavery

In society's basement in the South of 1860 were nearly 4 million black human chattels. Their numbers had quadrupled since the dawn of the century, as the booming cotton economy created a seemingly unquenchable demand for slave labor. Legal importation of African slaves into America ended in 1808, when Congress outlawed slave imports. Britain had abolished the slave trade (but not slavery itself) in 1807, a milestone in the continuing struggle to establish human rights as a principle of international law. In the decades thereafter, the Royal Navy's **West Africa Squadron** seized hundreds of slave ships and freed thousands of grateful captives. Yet despite that effort, as many as 3 million enslaved Africans were shipped to Brazil and the West Indies in the several decades after 1807. In the United States, the price of "black ivory" was so high in the years before the Civil War that uncounted thousands of blacks were smuggled into the South, despite the death penalty for slavers. Although several slave traders were captured, southern juries repeatedly acquitted them. Only one slave trader, N. P. Gordon, was ever executed, and this took place in New York in 1862, the second year of the Civil War.

Ironically, the suppression of the international slave trade fostered the growth of a vigorous *internal* slave trade, as upper South states like Virginia became major sources of supply for the booming cotton economy of the Deep South. Most of the increase in the slave population in the United States came not from imports, but from natural reproduction—a fact that owed something to the accident of geography that the slave South lay outside the area where tropical diseases took such a grisly human toll. The natural reproduction of enslaved African Americans also distinguished North American slavery from slavery in more southerly New World societies and implied much about the tenor of the slave regime and the conditions of family life under slavery in the United States.

Above all, the planters regarded their slaves as investments, into which they had sunk nearly $2 billion of their capital by 1860. Slaves were the primary form of wealth in the South, and as such they were cared for as any asset is cared for by a prudent capitalist.

Musee de l'Homme, Paris/RMN/Art Resource, NY

Stanley B. Burns, M.D. and The Burns Archive

A Market in People (left) Held captive in a net, a slave sits on the Congo shore, waiting to be sold and shipped. (right) Once in the United States, slaves continued to be treated like commodities. This woman suffers the humiliation of an inventory number pinned to her dress, most likely for her sale at a slave auction or transport to a new owner.

Accordingly, they were sometimes, though by no means always, spared dangerous work, like putting a roof on a house. If a neck was going to be broken, the master preferred it to be that of a wage-earning Irish laborer rather than that of a prime field hand, worth $1,800 by 1860 (a price that had quintupled since 1800). Tunnel blasting and swamp draining were often consigned to itinerant gangs of expendable Irishmen because those perilous tasks were "death on niggers and mules."

Slavery was profitable for the great planters, though it hobbled the economic development of the region as a whole. The profits from the cotton boom sucked ever more slaves from the upper to the lower South, so that by 1860 the Deep South states of South Carolina, Florida, Mississippi, Alabama, and Louisiana each had a majority or near-majority of blacks and accounted for about half of all slaves in the South.

Breeding slaves in the way that cattle are bred was not openly encouraged. But thousands of blacks from the soil-exhausted slave states of the Old South, especially tobacco-depleted Virginia, were "sold down the river" to toil as field-gang laborers on the cotton frontier of the lower Mississippi Valley. Women who bore thirteen or fourteen babies were prized as "rattlin' good breeders," and some of these fecund females were promised their freedom when they had produced ten. White masters all too frequently would force their attentions on female slaves, fathering a sizable mulatto population, most of which remained enchained.

Slave auctions were brutal sights. The open selling of human flesh under the hammer, sometimes with cattle and horses, was among the most revolting aspects of slavery. On the auction block, families were separated with distressing frequency, usually for economic reasons such as bankruptcy or the division of "property" among heirs. The sundering of families in this fashion was perhaps slavery's greatest psychological horror. Abolitionists decried the practice, and Harriet Beecher Stowe seized on the emotional power of this theme by putting it at the heart of the plot of her acclaimed 1852 novel, *Uncle Tom's Cabin.*

In 1852 Maria Perkins, a woman enslaved in Virginia, wrote plaintively to her husband about the disruption that the commercial traffic in slaves was visiting upon their family:

"I write you a letter to let you know of my distress my master has sold albert to a trader on Monday court day and myself and other child is for sale also and I want you to let hear from you very soon before next cort if you can I dont know when I dont want you to wait till Christmas I want you to tell Dr Hamelton and your master if either will buy me they can attend to it know and then I can go after-wards I dont want a trader to get me they asked me if I had got any person to buy me and I told them no they took me to the court houste too they never put me up a man buy the name of brady bought albert and is gone I dont know whare they say he lives in Scottesville my things is in several places some is in staunton and if I should be sold I dont know what will become of them I dont expect to meet with the luck to get that way till I am quite heart sick nothing more I am and ever will be your kind wife Maria Perkins.**"**

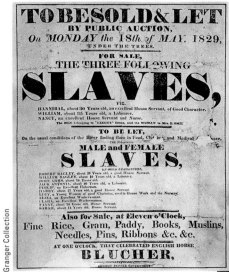

A Slave Auction Abraham Lincoln said in 1865, "Whenever I hear anyone arguing for slavery, I feel a strong impulse to see it tried on him personally."

✴ Life Under the Lash

White southerners often romanticized about the happy life of their singing, dancing, banjo-strumming, joyful "darkies." But how did the slaves actually live? There is no simple answer to this question. Conditions varied greatly from region to region, from large plantation to small farm, and from master to master. Everywhere, of course, slavery meant hard work, ignorance, and oppression. The slaves—both men and women—usually toiled from dawn to dusk in the fields, under the watchful eyes and ready whip-hand of a white overseer or black "driver." They had no civil or political rights, other than minimal protection from arbitrary murder or unusually cruel punishment. Some states offered further protections, such as banning the sale of a child under the age of ten away from his or her mother. But all such laws were difficult to enforce, since slaves were forbidden to testify in court or even to have their marriages legally recognized.

Floggings were common, for the whip was the substitute for the wage-incentive system and the most visible symbol of the planter's mastery. Strong-willed slaves were sometimes sent to **breakers**, whose technique consisted mostly in lavish laying on of the lash. As an abolitionist song of the 1850s lamented,

> *To-night the bond man, Lord*
> *Is bleeding in his chains;*
> *And loud the falling lash is heard*
> *On Carolina's plains!*

But savage beatings made sullen laborers, and lash marks hurt resale values. There are, to be sure, sadistic monsters in any population, and the planter class contained its share. But the typical planter had too much of his own prosperity riding on the backs of his slaves to beat them bloody on a regular basis.

By 1860 most slaves were concentrated in the **black belt** of the Deep South that stretched from South Carolina and Georgia into the new southwest states of Alabama, Mississippi, and Louisiana. This was the region of the southern frontier, into which the explosively growing Cotton Kingdom had burst in a few short decades. As on all frontiers, life was often rough and raw, and in general the lot of the slave was harder here than in the more settled areas of the Old South.

A majority of blacks lived on larger plantations that harbored communities of twenty or more slaves. In some counties of the Deep South, especially along the lower Mississippi River, blacks accounted for more than 75 percent of the population. There the family life of slaves tended to be relatively stable, and a distinctive African American slave culture developed. Forced separations of spouses, parents, and children were evidently more common on smaller plantations and in the upper South. Slave marriage vows sometimes proclaimed, "Until death or *distance* do you part."

With impressive resilience, blacks managed to sustain family life in slavery, and most slaves were raised in stable two-parent households. Continuity of family identity across generations was evidenced in the widespread practice of naming children for grandparents or adopting the surname not of a current master, but of a forebear's master. African Americans also displayed their African cultural roots when they avoided marriage between first cousins, in contrast to the frequent

Louisiana State Museum

Louisiana State Museum

The Cruelty of Slavery Slaveowners used devices like this collar with bells to discipline and patrol their slaves. This female slave shown toiling in New Orleans has such a collar riveted around her neck, designed to prevent her from hiding from her master or escaping.

intermarriage of close relatives among the ingrown planter aristocracy.

African roots were also visible in the slaves' religious practices. Though heavily Christianized by the itinerant evangelists of the Second Great Awakening, blacks in slavery molded their own distinctive religious forms from a mixture of Christian and African elements. They emphasized those aspects of the Christian heritage that seemed most pertinent to their own situation—especially the captivity of the Israelites in Egypt. One of their most haunting spirituals implored,

> *Tell old Pharaoh*
> *"Let my people go."*

And another lamented,

> *Nobody knows de trouble I've had*
> *Nobody knows but Jesus*

African practices also persisted in the **responsorial** style of preaching, in which the congregation frequently punctuated the minister's remarks with assents and amens—an adaptation of the give-and-take between caller and dancers in the African ringshout dance.

✦ The Burdens of Bondage

Slavery was intolerably degrading to the victims. They were deprived of the dignity and sense of responsibility that come from independence and the right to make choices. They were denied an education, because reading brought ideas, and ideas brought discontent. Many states passed laws forbidding their instruction, and perhaps nine-tenths of adult slaves at the beginning of the Civil War were totally illiterate. For all slaves—indeed for virtually all blacks, slave or free—the "American dream" of bettering one's lot through study and hard work was a cruel and empty mockery.

Not surprisingly, victims of the "peculiar institution" devised countless ways to throw sand in its gears. When workers are not voluntarily hired and adequately compensated, they can hardly be expected to work with alacrity. Accordingly, slaves often slowed the pace of their labor to the barest minimum that would spare them the lash, thus fostering the myth of black "laziness" in the minds of whites. They filched food from the "big house" and pilfered other goods that had been produced or purchased by their labor. They sabotaged expensive equipment, stopping the work routine altogether until repairs were accomplished. Occasionally they even poisoned their masters' food.

The slaves also universally pined for freedom. Many took to their heels as runaways, frequently in search of a separated family member. A black girl, asked if her mother was dead, replied, "Yessir, master, she is dead, but she's free." Others rebelled, though never successfully. In 1800 an armed insurrection led by a slave named Gabriel in Richmond, Virginia, was foiled by informers, and its leaders were hanged. Denmark Vesey, a free black, led another ill-fated rebellion in Charleston, South Carolina, in 1822. Also betrayed by informers, Vesey and more than thirty followers were publicly strung from the gallows. In 1831 the semiliterate Nat Turner, a visionary black preacher, led an uprising that slaughtered about sixty Virginians, mostly women and children. Reprisals were swift and bloody, and **Nat Turner's rebellion** was soon extinguished.

An especially dramatic episode involved the enslaved Africans who rebelled aboard the Spanish slave ship *Amistad* in 1839. They seized command of the vessel off the coast of Cuba and attempted to sail back to Africa, but were driven ashore on Long Island. After two years of imprisonment and several trials, former president John Quincy Adams finally secured their

Slave Nurse and Young White Master Southern whites would not allow slaves to own property or exercise civil rights, but, paradoxically, they often entrusted them with the raising of their own precious children. Many a slave "mammy" served as a surrogate mother for the offspring of the planter class.

Missouri Historical Society

Abby Aldrich Rockefeller Folk Art Collection, Williamsburg, VA

Slaves Being Marched from Staunton, Virginia, to Tennessee, by Lewis Miller, 1853 In this folk painting of slaves in transit from the upper South to the new cotton lands of the lower South, couples travel together and children accompany parents. In reality the forced movement of slaves often involved the painful separation of family members.

Tag Identifying Slaves and Free Blacks in Charleston All slaves in Charleston, South Carolina, were reminded of their status as property by the tags they were forced to wear, marked with their skills—such as porter or mechanic or carpenter—and the year the tag was issued. After 1848 even free blacks had to wear tags, ensuring that no African American could be anonymous in the city. The badge above was issued to a freed slave in Charleston, South Carolina, sometime after 1848. The American Numismatic Society

freedom in a brilliant, moving argument before the U.S. Supreme Court in 1841, and the Africans returned to the British colony of Sierra Leone, in West Africa.

The dark taint of slavery also left its mark on whites. It fostered the brutality of the whip, the bloodhound, and the branding iron. White southerners increasingly lived in a state of imagined siege, surrounded by potentially rebellious blacks inflamed by abolitionist propaganda from the North. Their fears bolstered an intoxicating theory of biological racial superiority and turned the South into a reactionary backwater in an era of progress—one of the last bastions of slavery in the Western world. The defenders of slavery were forced to degrade themselves, along with their victims. As Booker T. Washington, a distinguished black leader and former slave, later observed, whites could not hold blacks in a ditch without getting down there with them.

✦ Early Abolitionism

The inhumanity of the "peculiar institution" gradually caused antislavery societies to sprout forth. Abolitionist sentiment first stirred at the time of the Revolution, especially among Quakers (see Map 16.3). Because of the widespread loathing of blacks, some of the earliest abolitionist efforts focused on transporting blacks bodily back to Africa. The **American Colonization Society** was founded for this purpose in 1817, and in 1822 the Republic of **Liberia**, on the fever-stricken West African coast, was established for former slaves. Its capital, Monrovia, was named after President Monroe. Some fifteen thousand freed blacks were transported there over the next four decades. But most blacks had no wish to be transplanted into a strange civilization after having become partially Americanized. By 1860 virtually all southern slaves were no longer Africans, but native-born African Americans, with their own distinctive history and culture. Yet the colonization idea appealed to some antislaveryites, including Abraham Lincoln, until the time of the Civil War.

In the 1830s the abolitionist movement took on new energy and momentum, mounting to the proportions of a crusade. American abolitionists took heart in 1833 when their British counterparts, inspired by the redoubtable William Wilberforce, a member of Parliament and an evangelical Christian reformer whose family had been touched by the preaching of George Whitefield (see Chapter 5), unchained the slaves in the West Indies (see "Thinking Globally: The Struggle to Abolish Slavery," pp. 354–355). (Wilberforce University in Ohio, an African American college that later sent many missionaries to Africa, is named for him.)

As with Wilberforce, the religious spirit of the Second Great Awakening now inflamed the hearts of many American abolitionists against the sin of slavery. Prominent among them was lanky, tousle-haired Theodore Dwight Weld, who had been evangelized by Charles

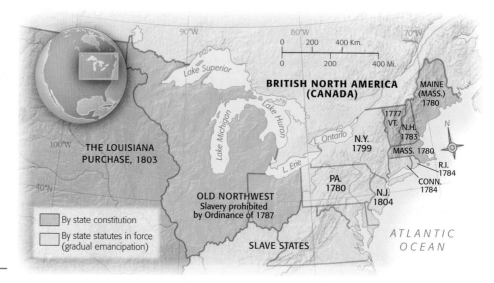

MAP 16.3 Early Emancipation in the North © Cengage Learning

Grandison Finney in New York's Burned-Over District in the 1820s. Self-educated and simple in manner and speech, Weld appealed with special power and directness to his rural audiences of untutored farmers.

Spiritually inspired by Finney, Weld was materially aided by two wealthy and devout New York merchants, the brothers Arthur and Lewis Tappan. In 1832 they paid his way to Lane Theological Seminary in Cincinnati, Ohio, which was presided over by the formidable

ANTI-SLAVERY EVENTS

DURING THE YEAR ENDING 5TH MARCH

1863.

AM I NOT A MAN AND A BROTHER

AM I NOT A WOMAN AND A SISTER

" Can we behold, unheeding,
Life's holiest feelings crush'd ;—
While *Woman's* heart is bleeding,
Shall *Woman's* voice be hush'd ?"

Boston Athenaeum

"Am I Not a Man and a Brother? Am I Not a Woman and a Sister?" A popular appeal.

Lyman Beecher, father of a remarkable brood, including novelist Harriet Beecher Stowe, reformer Catharine Beecher, and preacher-abolitionist Henry Ward Beecher. Expelled along with several other students in 1834 for organizing an eighteen-day debate on slavery, Weld and his fellow "Lane Rebels"—full of the energy and idealism of youth—fanned out across the Old Northwest preaching the antislavery gospel. Humorless and deadly earnest, Weld also assembled a potent propaganda pamphlet, *American Slavery as It Is* (1839). Its compelling arguments made it among the most effective abolitionist tracts and greatly influenced Harriet Beecher Stowe's *Uncle Tom's Cabin*.

✹ Radical Abolitionism

On New Year's Day, 1831, a shattering abolitionist blast came from the bugle of William Lloyd Garrison, a mild-looking reformer of twenty-six. The emotionally high-strung son of a drunken father and a spiritual child of the Second Great Awakening, Garrison published in Boston the first issue of his militantly antislavery newspaper, ***The Liberator***. With this mighty paper broadside, Garrison triggered a thirty-year war of words and in a sense fired one of the opening barrages of the Civil War.

Stern and uncompromising, Garrison nailed his colors to the masthead of his weekly. He proclaimed in strident tones that under no circumstances would he tolerate the poisonous weed of slavery, but would stamp it out at once, root and branch:

I will be as harsh as truth and as uncompromising as justice. . . . I am in earnest—I will not equivocate—I will not excuse—I will not retreat a single inch—and I WILL BE HEARD!

Bellegrove Plantation, Donaldsville, Louisiana, Built 1857

The sugar-growing Bellegrove Plantation—on the banks of the Mississippi River ninety-five miles north of New Orleans—was laid out on a grander scale than many southern plantations. In this rendering from an advertisement for Bellegrove's sale in 1867, the planter John Orr's home was identified as a "mansion," and quarters for his field hands proved extensive: twenty double cabins built for slaves (now for "Negroes") and a dormitory, described in the ad but not pictured here, housing 150 laborers. Because of the unhealthy work involved in cultivating sugar cane, such as the constant digging of drainage canals to keep the cane from rotting in standing water, many planters hired immigrant (usually Irish) labor to keep their valuable slaves out of physical danger. The presence of a hospital between the slave cabins and the mansion indicates the very real threat to health. The layout of Bellegrove reflects the organization of production as well as the social relations on a sugar plantation. The storehouse where preserved sugar awaited shipping stood closest to the Mississippi River, the principal transportation route, whereas the sugar house, the most important building on the plantation, with its mill, boilers, and cooking vats for converting syrup into sugar, dominated the canefields. Although the "big house" and slave quarters stood in close proximity, hedges surrounding the planter's home shut out views of both sugar production and labor. Within the slave quarters, the overseer's larger house signified his superior status, while the arrangement of cabins ensured his supervision of domestic as well as work life. What else does the physical layout of the plantation reveal about settlement patterns, sugar cultivation, and social relationships along the Mississippi?

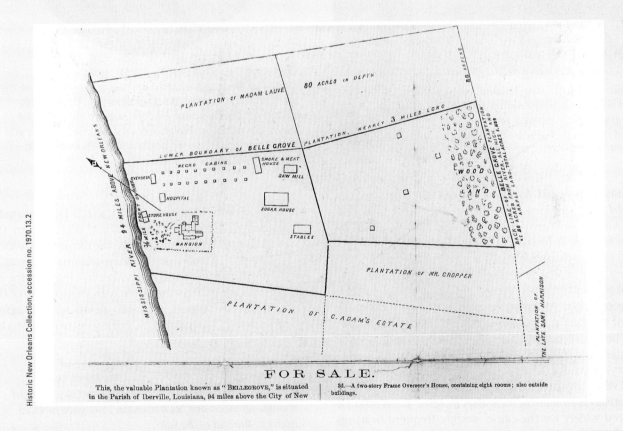

FOR SALE.

This, the valuable Plantation known as "BELLEGROVE," is situated in the Parish of Iberville, Louisiana, 94 miles above the City of New

3d.—A two-story Frame Overseer's House, containing eight rooms; also outside buildings.

Other dedicated abolitionists rallied to Garrison's standard, and in 1833 they founded the **American Anti-Slavery Society**. Prominent among them was Wendell Phillips, a Boston patrician known as "abolition's golden trumpet." A man of strict principle, he would eat no cane sugar and wear no cotton cloth, since both were produced by southern slaves.

Black abolitionists distinguished themselves as living monuments to the cause of African American freedom. Their ranks included David Walker, whose

Sojourner Truth Also known simply as "Isabella," she held audiences spellbound with her deep, resonant voice and the religious passion with which she condemned the sin of slavery. This photo was taken about 1870.

National Portrait Gallery, Smithsonian Institution/Art Resource, NY

Frederick Douglass (1817?–1895) Born a slave in Maryland, Douglass escaped to the North and became the most prominent of the black abolitionists. Gifted as an orator, writer, and editor, he continued to battle for the civil rights of his people after emancipation. Near the end of a distinguished career, he served as U.S. minister to Haiti. Onondaga Historical Association

incendiary ***Appeal to the Colored Citizens of the World*** (1829) advocated a bloody end to white supremacy. Also noteworthy were Sojourner Truth, a freed black woman in New York who fought tirelessly for black emancipation and women's rights, and Martin Delany, one of the few black leaders to take seriously the notion of the mass recolonization of Africa. In 1859 he visited West Africa's Niger Valley seeking a suitable site for relocation.

The greatest of the black abolitionists was Frederick Douglass. Escaping from bondage in 1838 at the age of twenty-one, he was "discovered" by the abolitionists in 1841 when he gave a stunning impromptu speech at an antislavery meeting in Massachusetts. Thereafter he lectured widely for the cause, despite frequent beatings and threats against his life. In 1845 he published his classic autobiography, ***Narrative of the Life of Frederick Douglass***. It depicted his remarkable origins as the son of a black slave woman and a white father, his struggle to learn to read and write, and his eventual escape to the North.

Douglass was as flexibly practical as Garrison was stubbornly principled. Garrison often appeared to be more interested in his own righteousness than in

the substance of the slavery evil itself. He repeatedly demanded that the "virtuous" North secede from the "wicked" South. Yet he did not explain how the creation of an independent slave republic would bring an end to the "damning crime" of slavery. Renouncing politics, on the Fourth of July, 1854, he publicly burned a copy of the Constitution as "a covenant with death and an agreement with hell" (a phrase he borrowed from a Shaker

Frederick Douglass (1817?–1895), the remarkable ex-slave, told of Mr. Covey, a white owner who bought a single female slave "as a breeder." She gave birth to twins at the end of the year:

❝At this addition to the human stock Covey and his wife were ecstatic with joy. No one dreamed of reproaching the woman or finding fault with the hired man, Bill Smith, the father of the children, for Mr. Covey himself had locked the two up together every night, thus inviting the result.**❞**

After hearing Frederick Douglass speak in Bristol, England, in 1846, Mary A. Estlin wrote to an American abolitionist,

❝[T]here is but one opinion of him. Wherever he goes he arouses sympathy in your cause and love for himself. . . . Our expectations were highly roused by his narrative, his printed speeches, and the eulogisms of the friends with whom he has been staying: but he far exceeds the picture we had formed both in outward graces, intellectual power and culture, and eloquence.**❞***

*From Clare Taylor, ed., *British and American Abolitionists: An Episode in Transatlantic Understanding* (Edinburgh University Press, 1974), p. 282.

condemnation of marriage). Critics, including some of his former supporters, charged that Garrison was cruelly probing the moral wound in America's underbelly but offering no acceptable balm to ease the pain.

Douglass, on the other hand, along with other abolitionists, increasingly looked to politics to end the blight of slavery. These political abolitionists backed the Liberty party in 1840, the Free Soil party in 1848, and eventually the Republican party in the 1850s. In the end, most abolitionists, including even the pacifistic Garrison himself, followed the logic of their beliefs and supported a frightfully costly fratricidal war as the price of emancipation.

High-minded and courageous, the abolitionists were men and women of goodwill and various colors who faced the cruel choice that people in many ages have had thrust upon them: when is evil so enormous that it must be denounced, even at the risk of precipitating bloodshed and butchery?

✴ The South Lashes Back

Antislavery sentiment was not unknown in the South, and in the 1820s antislavery societies were more numerous south of the **Mason-Dixon line*** than north of it. But after about 1830, the voice of white southern abolitionism was silenced. In a last gasp of southern questioning of slavery, the Virginia legislature debated and eventually defeated various emancipation proposals in 1831–1832. That debate marked a turning point. Thereafter all the slave states tightened their slave codes and moved to prohibit emancipation of any kind, voluntary or compensated. Nat Turner's rebellion in 1831 sent a

*Originally the southern boundary of colonial Pennsylvania.

wave of hysteria sweeping over the snowy cotton fields, and planters in growing numbers, recollecting the massive slave revolt that had erupted in Haiti in the 1790s, slept with pistols by their pillows. Although Garrison had no demonstrable connection with the Turner conspiracy, his *Liberator* appeared at about the same time, and he was bitterly condemned as a terrorist and an inciter of murder. The State of Georgia offered $5,000 for his arrest and conviction.

The nullification crisis of 1832 further implanted haunting fears in white southern minds, conjuring up nightmares of black incendiaries and abolitionist devils. Jailings, whippings, and lynchings now greeted rational efforts to discuss the slavery problem in the South.

Proslavery whites responded by launching a massive defense of slavery as a positive good. In doing so, they forgot their own section's previous doubts about the morality of the "peculiar institution." Slavery, they claimed, was supported by the authority of the Bible and the wisdom of Aristotle. It was good for the Africans, who were lifted from the barbarism of the jungle and clothed with the blessings of Christian civilization. Slavemasters strongly encouraged religion in the slave quarters. A catechism for blacks contained such passages as

Q. Who gave you a master and a mistress?
A. God gave them to me.
Q. Who says that you must obey them?
A. God says that I must.

White apologists also claimed that master-slave relationships really resembled those of a family. On many plantations, especially those of the Old South of Virginia and Maryland, this argument had a certain plausibility. A slave's tombstone bore this touching inscription:

JOHN:
A faithful servant:
  and true friend:
Kindly, and considerate:
Loyal, and affectionate:
The family he served
Honours him in death:
But, in life they gave him love:
For he was one of them

Southern whites were quick to contrast the "happy" lot of their "servants" with that of the overworked northern wage slaves, including sweated women and stunted children. The blacks mostly toiled in the fresh air and sunlight, not in dark and stuffy factories. They did not have to worry about slack times or unemployment, as did the "hired hands" of the North. Provided with a jail-like form of Social Security, they were cared for in sickness and old age, unlike northern workers, who were set adrift when they had outlived their usefulness.

These curious proslavery arguments only widened the chasm between a backward-looking South and a

The Struggle to Abolish Slavery

When slaves in the French Caribbean colony of Saint-Domingue, inspired by the Revolutionary fervor that had seized mainland France, rose up and demanded "liberty, equality, and fraternity" for themselves, they became, in 1794, the first enslaved people in the New World to win their freedom. They went on to proclaim their independence from France in 1804 by creating the Republic of Haiti. Meanwhile, in 1802, Napoleon had reinstated slavery in what remained of his Caribbean empire. It would take another revolution in France, in 1848, to secure permanent emancipation throughout the French Caribbean.

Table 16.1 documents the long, 250-year struggle to abolish slavery throughout the world. Agitators outraged by the scourge of human bondage and committed to ending it, known as abolitionists, shared antislavery sentiments and strategies across national boundaries. From the late seventeenth through the mid-nineteenth century, British and American abolitionists wove dense networks of mutual support. They shared writings, lecturers, and funding and jointly sponsored conferences such as the World's Anti-Slavery Convention of 1840 in London, which became famous for inspiring the American women's rights movement when it refused to seat female delegates.

But the political fortunes of abolitionist movements, and hence the timing of the longed-for day of freedom, varied sharply from nation to nation. In France emancipation was twice tied to revolutions. In Great Britain massive citizens' petition campaigns, orchestrated by venerable lifelong abolitionist leaders such as William Wilberforce, brought enormous popular pressure to bear on the government. Parliament eventually responded by outlawing the slave trade in 1807 and then, three days before Wilberforce died in 1833, prohibiting slavery itself throughout most of the British Empire.

The antislavery impulse in the United States sprung from a variety of sources. Some abolitionists opposed the brutality of the trade in human beings because they idealistically believed that the end of slavery was tied directly to humanity's progress. Others wished for the economic and labor systems in the South to more closely resemble northern models of free labor. Ideas about what might come after abolition were similarly diverse; while some hoped that former slaves might continue to work in their communities, others supported colonization, the repatriation of freemen to countries in Africa.

In the United States as in Britain, abolitionism became a robust social

Granger Collection

World's Anti-Slavery Convention, London, 1840 The convention assembled antislavery advocates from around the world, but it refused to seat female delegates. Women were allowed to observe, but not to take part in, the official proceedings. The frustrations of the unseated American representatives led to the historic Woman's Rights Convention at Seneca Falls, New York, in 1848 (see p. 318) movement, propelled not least by women and free blacks. The issue had first become highly politicized in the 1770s, though during the Constitutional Convention delegates had chosen not to ban slavery in the new United States. By the 1830s, debates had heated up again as abolitionists objected to the expansion of slavery into the growing western territories of the country. But the roots of the "peculiar institution" in the United States ran wide and deep. Even though the American slave trade was ended in 1808, a widespread internal trade continued, and it took the Union's victory in a bloody Civil War in 1865 to eradicate slavery once and for all. Elsewhere in the Americas, enslaved peoples secured their freedom gradually and, in stark contrast to the United States, peacefully. Emancipation typically became possible only after the achievement of independence from Spain, where abolitionism never gained much traction. Cuba, still a Spanish colony into the 1890s, was among the last places in the New World to set its slaves free.

TABLE 16.1 Comparative Abolition of Slavery

Country	Date Abolished	Notes
Mexico	1829	The slave trade was prohibited in 1824, but slavery itself was not abolished until 1829, eight years after Mexico gained independence from Spain.
Great Britain	1833	The slave trade was ended in 1807, but slavery was not abolished until 1833. The abolition of slavery did not apply to British India, where slavery persisted until 1860.*
France	1848	Slavery was first abolished in 1794 but was reestablished by Napoleon Bonaparte in 1802. In 1848 the Second Republic replaced the July Monarchy and abolished slavery in all French colonies.
Bolivia	1851	All slaves born since independence (1825) were freed in 1831, but slavery was not abolished entirely until 1851.
Ecuador	1852	At the time of independence in 1821, all children born to slaves after that date were declared free, but slavery persisted until 1852.
Peru	1854	At the time of independence in 1821, all children born to slaves after that date were declared free, but slavery was not abolished entirely until 1854.
Argentina	1854	Emancipation, first begun in 1813, was completed in 1854.
Venezuela	1854	Gradual emancipation began when independence was fully secured in 1821, but slavery was not completely abolished until 1854.
Russia	1861	Peter the Great first abolished slavery in 1723 by converting household slaves into serfs. Tsar Alexander II freed Russia's 22 million serfs in 1861.
Netherlands	1863	Slavery was abolished in all Dutch colonies.
United States	1865	The slave trade was ended in 1808, but slavery was not abolished entirely until after the Civil War, with the ratification of the Thirteenth Amendment. Slavery was abolished earlier in the North, in the decades after the Revolution, often through gradual emancipation.
Paraguay	1869	Gradual emancipation began in 1842, but slavery was not abolished until 1869.
Cuba	1886	Gradual emancipation began in 1870; the Spanish government freed the remaining slaves in 1886.
Brazil	1888	The slave trade was abolished in 1851. A gradual emancipation law was first passed in 1871, but slavery was not abolished entirely until 1888.
Korea	1894	State-owned slaves were emancipated in 1801. Although slavery was formally abolished in 1894, it persisted in some regions until the 1930s.
China	1949	The emperor abolished slavery toward the end of the Xing dynasty, in 1910, but it persisted until the communist government proclaimed abolition in 1949.
Saudi Arabia	1962	Slavery was abolished under pressure from the United Nations and moderate Arab states.
Yemen	1962	Leaders of the newly proclaimed Yemen Arab Republic abolished slavery after overthrowing the imamate in 1962.

*The British East India Company had sovereignty over India until 1858, when the British government took over—and abolished slavery shortly thereafter.

[Sources: Martin A. Klein, *Historical Dictionary of Slavery and Abolition* (2002); Robert Fogel, *Without Consent of Contract* (1994); Herbert Klein, *African Slavery in Latin America and the Caribbean* (1986); Edward Alpers, Gwyn Campbell, and Michael Salman, eds., *Slavery and Resistance in Africa and Asia* (2005); Jerome Alan Cohen, R. Randle Edwards, and Fu-mei Chang Chen, *Essays on China's Legal Tradition* (1980).]

In Defense of Slavery This pair of illustrations contrasts the supposedly benevolent slave regime of the South with the harshness of working life in England, where starvation wages and unemployment blighted workers' lives. Apologists for slavery frequently invoked this comparison between allegedly paternalistic slavemasters and the uncaring capitalists who captained the Industrial Revolution.

forward-looking North—and indeed much of the rest of the Western world. The southerners reacted defensively to the pressure of their own fears and bristled before the merciless nagging of the northern abolitionists. Increasingly the white South turned in upon itself and grew hotly intolerant of any embarrassing questions about the status of slavery.

Regrettably, also, the controversy over free people endangered free speech in the entire country. Piles of petitions poured in upon Congress from the antislavery reformers, and in 1836 sensitive southerners drove through the House the so-called **Gag Resolution**. It required all such antislavery appeals to be tabled without debate. This attack on the right of petition aroused the sleeping lion in the aged ex-president, Representative John Quincy Adams, and he waged a successful eight-year fight for its repeal.

Southern whites likewise resented the flooding of their mails with incendiary abolitionist literature. Even if blacks could not read, they could interpret the inflammatory drawings, such as those that showed masters knocking out slaves' teeth with clubs. In 1835 a mob in Charleston, South Carolina, looted the post office and burned a pile of abolitionist propaganda. Capitulating to southern pressures, the Washington government in 1835 ordered southern postmasters to destroy abolitionist

material and called on southern state officials to arrest federal postmasters who did not comply. Such was "freedom of the press" as guaranteed by the Constitution.

✭ The Abolitionist Impact in the North

Abolitionists—especially the extreme Garrisonians—were for a long time unpopular in many parts of the North. Northerners had been brought up to revere the Constitution and to regard the clauses on slavery as a lasting bargain. The ideal of Union, hammered home by the thundering eloquence of Daniel Webster and others, had taken deep root, and Garrison's wild talk of secession grated harshly on northern ears.

The North also had a heavy economic stake in Dixieland. By the late 1850s, southern planters owed northern bankers and other creditors about $300 million, and much of this immense sum would be lost—as, in fact, it later was—should the Union dissolve. New England textile mills were fed with cotton raised by the slaves, and a disrupted labor system might cut off this vital supply and bring unemployment. The Union during these critical years was partly bound together with cotton threads, tied by lords of the loom in collaboration with the so-called lords of the lash. It was not surprising that strong hostility developed in the North against the boat-rocking tactics of the radical antislaveryites.

Repeated tongue-lashings by the extreme abolitionists provoked many mob outbursts in the North, some led by respectable gentlemen. A gang of young toughs broke into Lewis Tappan's New York house in 1834 and demolished its interior, while a crowd in the street cheered. In 1835 Garrison, with a rope tied around him, was dragged through the streets of Boston by the so-called Broadcloth Mob but escaped almost miraculously. Reverend Elijah P. Lovejoy of Alton, Illinois, not content to assail slavery, impugned the chastity of Catholic women. His printing press was destroyed four times, and in 1837 he was killed by a mob and became "the martyr abolitionist." So unpopular were the antislavery zealots that ambitious politicians, like Lincoln, usually avoided the taint of Garrisonian abolition like the plague.

Yet by the 1850s the abolitionist outcry had made a deep dent in the northern mind. Many citizens had come to see the South as the land of the unfree and the home of a hateful institution. Few northerners were prepared to abolish slavery outright, but a growing number, including Lincoln, opposed extending it to the western territories. People of this stamp, commonly called "free-soilers," swelled their ranks as the Civil War approached.

Varying Viewpoints
What Was the True Nature of Slavery?

By the early twentieth century, the predictable accounts of slavery written by partisans of the North or South had receded in favor of a romantic vision of the Old South conveyed through popular literature, myth, and, increasingly, scholarship. That vision was persuasively validated by the publication of Ulrich Bonnell Phillips's landmark study, *American Negro Slavery* (1918). Phillips made three key arguments. First, he claimed that slavery was a dying economic institution, unprofitable to the slaveowner and an obstacle to the economic development of the South as a whole. Second, he contended that slavery was a rather benign institution and that the planters, contrary to abolitionist charges of ruthless exploitation, treated their chattels with kindly paternalism. Third, he reflected the dominant racial attitudes of his time in his belief that blacks were inferior and submissive by nature and did not abhor the institution that enslaved them.

For nearly a century, historians have debated these assertions, sometimes heatedly. More sophisticated economic analysis has refuted Phillips's claim that slavery would have withered away without a war. Economic historians have demonstrated that slavery was a viable, profitable, expanding economic system and that slaves constituted a worthwhile investment for their owners. The price of a prime field hand rose dramatically, even in the 1850s.

No such definitive conclusion has yet been reached in the disputes over slave treatment. Frank Tannenbaum's classic comparative study, *Slave and Citizen* (1947), argued that slavery was more humane in Latin America than in the United States, leaving a legacy of less sharply defined racial castes there. Beginning in the late 1950s, historians came increasingly to emphasize the harshness of the U.S. slave system. One study, Stanley Elkins's *Slavery* (1959), went so far as to compare the "peculiar institution" to the Nazi concentration camps of World War II. Both were "total institutions," Elkins contended, which "infantilized" their victims.

More recently, scholars such as Eugene Genovese have moved beyond debating whether slavery was kind or cruel. Without diminishing the deprivations and pains of slavery, Genovese has conceded that slavery embraced a strange form of paternalism, a system that reflected not the benevolence of southern slaveholders, but their need to control and coax work out of their reluctant and often recalcitrant "investments." Furthermore, within this paternalistic system, black slaves were able to make reciprocal demands of their white owners and to protect a "cultural space" of their own in which family and religion particularly could flourish. The crowning paradox of slaveholder paternalism was that in treating their property more humanely, slaveowners implicitly recognized the humanity of their slaves and thereby subverted the racist underpinnings upon which their slave society existed.

The revised conceptions of the master-slave relationship also spilled over into the debate about slave personality. Elkins accepted Phillips's portrait of the slave as a childlike "Sambo" but saw it as a consequence of slavery rather than a congenital attribute of African Americans. Kenneth Stampp, rejecting the Sambo stereotype, stressed the frequency and variety of slave resistance, both mild and militant. A third view, imaginatively documented in the work of Lawrence Levine, argued that the Sambo character was an act, an image that slaves used to confound their masters without incurring punishment. Levine's *Black Culture and Black Consciousness* (1977) shares with books by John Blassingame and Herbert Gutman an emphasis on the tenacity with which slaves maintained their own culture and kin relations, despite the hardships of bondage. Most recently, historians have attempted to avoid the polarity of repression versus autonomy. They assert the debasing oppression of slavery, while also acknowledging slaves' ability to resist the dehumanizing effects of enslavement. For example, Walter Johnson's *Soul by Soul* (1999) details the horrors of the slave market but explains the multitude of ways that enslaved people could influence their own sale and position. The challenge before historians today is to capture the vibrancy of slave culture and its legacy for African American society after emancipation, without diminishing the brutality of life under the southern slave regime.

A new sensitivity to gender, spurred by the growing field of women's history, has also expanded the horizons of slavery studies. Historians such as Elizabeth Fox-Genovese, Jacqueline Jones, and Catherine Clinton have focused on the ways in which slavery differed for men and women, both slaves and slaveholders. Enslaved black women, for example, had the unique task of negotiating an identity out of their dual responsibilities as plantation laborer, even sometimes caretaker of white women and children, and anchor of the black family. By tracing the interconnectedness of race and gender in the American South, these historians have also shown how slavery shaped conceptions of masculinity and femininity within southern society, further distinguishing its culture from that of the North.

Scholarship on slavery continues to grow. The newest work by Philip D. Morgan and Ira Berlin has drawn attention to how both the institution of slavery and the experience of the enslaved changed over time. They have contended that slavery was far from monolithic. Rather, it adapted to particular geographic and environmental factors, which influenced the diet and work routines of slaves and shaped the degree of autonomy in family life and culture that slaves were able to carve out. Slavery also changed from one generation to the next. As southern slaveholders responded to new social and economic conditions, they gradually altered the legal status of slaves, making slavery a hereditary condition, outlawing manumission in many places, rendering freedom for the enslaved increasingly difficult to attain, and placing onerous restrictions on the work opportunities and mobility of free African Americans. One of the most recent and overarching syntheses of Atlantic slavery, David Brion Davis's *Inhuman Bondage* (2008), stresses the dehumanization inherent to slavery, especially in harsh New World systems.

Chapter Review

KEY TERMS

West Africa Squadron (344)

breakers (346)

black belt (347)

responsorial (348)

Nat Turner's rebellion (348)

Amistad (348)

American Colonization
   Society (349)

Liberia (349)

The Liberator (350)

American Anti-Slavery
   Society (351)

Appeal to the Colored Citizens of the World (352)

Narrative of the Life of Frederick Douglass (352)

Mason-Dixon line (353)

Gag Resolution (356)

PEOPLE TO KNOW

William T. Johnson

Nat Turner

William Wilberforce

Theodore Dwight Weld

William Lloyd Garrison

David Walker

Sojourner Truth

Martin Delany

Frederick Douglass

TO LEARN MORE

Erskine Clarke, *Dwelling Place: A Plantation Epic* (2005)

Frederick Douglass, *Narrative of the Life of Frederick Douglass* (1845)

John Hope Franklin, *From Slavery to Freedom* (8th ed., 2000)

John Craig Hammond, *Slavery, Freedom, and Expansion in the Early American West* (2007)

Anya Jabour, *Scarlett's Sisters: Young Women in the Old South* (2007)

Julie Roy Jeffrey, *The Great Silent Army of Abolitionism: Ordinary Women in the Antislavery Movement* (1998)

Walter Johnson, *Soul by Soul: Life Inside the Antebellum Slave Market* (2001)

Stephanie McCurry, *Masters of Small Worlds: Yeoman Households, Gender Relations, and the Political Culture of the Antebellum South* (1995)

Melton Alonza McLaurin, *Celia, a Slave* (1991)

Joshua Rothman, *Notorious in the Neighborhood: Sex and Families Across the Color Line in Virginia, 1787–1861* (2003)

James B. Stewart, *Holy Warriors* (1976)

Gavin Wright, *Slavery and American Economic Development* (2006)

A complete, annotated bibliography for this chapter—along with brief descriptions of the People to Know—may be found on the American Pageant website. The Key Terms are defined in a Glossary at the end of the text.

CHRONOLOGY

1793 Whitney's cotton gin transforms southern economy

1800 Gabriel slave rebellion in Virginia

1807 Britain abolishes slave trade

1808 Congress outlaws slave trade
Royal Navy forms West Africa Squadron

1817 American Colonization Society formed

1820 Missouri Compromise

1822 Vesey slave rebellion in Charleston, South Carolina
Republic of Liberia established in Africa

1829 Walker publishes *Appeal to the Colored Citizens of the World*

1831 Nat Turner slave rebellion in Virginia
Garrison begins publishing *The Liberator*

1831–1832 Virginia legislature debates slavery and emancipation

1833 British abolish slavery in West Indies
American Anti-Slavery Society founded

1834 Abolitionist students expelled from Lane Theological Seminary

1835 U.S. Post Office orders destruction of abolitionist mail
"Broadcloth Mob" attacks Garrison

1836 House of Representatives passes "Gag Resolution"

1837 Mob kills abolitionist Lovejoy in Alton, Illinois

1839 Weld publishes *American Slavery as It Is*
Slave revolt aboard *Amistad*

1845 Douglass publishes *Narrative of the Life of Frederick Douglass*

1848 Free Soil party organized

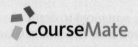

Go to the CourseMate website at **www.cengagebrain.com** for additional study tools and review materials—including audio and video clips—for this chapter.

AP® Review Questions for Chapter 16

1. From the outset, the U.S. government grappled with the uncomfortable question of slavery in all of the following legal measures EXCEPT the
   (A) Northwest Ordinance in 1787.
   (B) constitutional ban on slave imports beginning in 1808.
   (C) Missouri Compromise in 1820.
   (D) Nonimportation Act of 1807.
   (E) Compromise of 1850.

2. What single event halted idealistic discussions in the early republic about the eventual end of slavery?
   (A) The War of 1812
   (B) The invention of the cotton gin
   (C) The election of slaveholding presidents like Washington and Jefferson
   (D) The explosion of tobacco as an export crop
   (E) The Congressional Gag Order

3. Which of these economic woes was NOT associated with cotton cultivation in the plantation South?
   (A) A concentration of wealth, economic resources, and power in fewer and fewer hands
   (B) Excessive land cultivation and soil depletion
   (C) Overspeculation in land and slaves
   (D) Increasing vulnerability to a volatile world market
   (E) Rising numbers of new immigrants seeking to profit from the land

4. Nearly three-quarters of all white southerners by 1860
   (A) owned no slaves.
   (B) owned slaves.
   (C) cultivated cotton.
   (D) were connected to the plantation system.
   (E) lived in or around the Appalachian Mountains.

5. Which of the following is NOT a true statement about free blacks in antebellum America?
   (A) Some owned slaves and property.
   (B) They shared the same voting and other rights as white men everywhere.
   (C) Some purchased their freedom by working after hours for extra money.
   (D) Southern freedmen were at risk for being captured and re-enslaved.
   (E) They were often despised more in the North than in the South.

6. The number one form of wealth in the South was
   (A) land.
   (B) slaves.
   (C) cotton crops.
   (D) tobacco crops.
   (E) inheritance.

7. Considered one of the most traumatic aspects of slavery, forced separations of loved ones happened most frequently on
   (A) small plantations in the upper South.
   (B) large plantations in the upper South.
   (C) large plantations in the Deep South.
   (D) small plantations in the Deep South.
   (E) farms and plantations of all sizes.

8. Slaves worked to undermine masters and regain some margin of autonomy—however small—in all of the following ways EXCEPT by
   (A) slowing down the pace of their work.
   (B) taking food from masters' kitchens and gardens.
   (C) destroying homes and crops.
   (D) pilfering household and other goods from masters' homes.
   (E) sabotaging equipment.

9. What was the result of the slave uprising aboard the *Amistad* in 1839?
   (A) Slaves commandeered the ship and successfully returned to Africa.
   (B) Slaves who rebelled were sentenced to death.
   (C) Slave rebels ultimately won their freedom in court.
   (D) It led to the passage of slave codes in the South.
   (E) The conflict led to a fire that claimed the lives of all passengers and destroyed the ship.

10. The earliest antislavery efforts focused mainly on
    (A) immediate and complete emancipation.
    (B) gradually freeing the slaves over a period of years.
    (C) transporting slaves to their own colony within the region that would become the United States.
    (D) aiding slave rebellions and uprisings.
    (E) exporting slaves back to Africa.

11. How did the two great abolitionists, former slave Frederick Douglass and northern white businessman William Lloyd Garrison, differ in their strategy for ending slavery?

    (A) Douglass believed the North should break away from the slaveholding South; Garrison did not.

    (B) Garrison renounced political remedies; Douglass embraced them.

    (C) Garrison sought the violent overthrow of slavery; Douglass did not.

    (D) Douglass made incendiary speeches; Garrison appealed more to reason, principle, and integrity.

    (E) Douglass was prone to theatrics; Garrison was known for his impassioned speeches.

12. The wave of hysteria following Nat Turner's rebellion produced all of the following results EXCEPT that it

    (A) made white southern slaveholders more fearful of slaves and hostile toward them.

    (B) fueled the passage of strict slave codes.

    (C) halted discussions about ending slavery in southern states.

    (D) breathed new life into the abolitionist movement in the South.

    (E) inspired pro-slavery advocates to defend slavery as a positive good.

13. Which of these was NOT offered as a defense of slavery?

    (A) That it was a positive good, supported by the Bible

    (B) That slaves were treated as family members

    (C) That it was good for Africans, who were inferior people

    (D) That slaves were better treated and cared for than northern factory workers

    (E) That slavery provided blacks with minimal education in reading and writing

14. The main reason that much of the North did NOT initially embrace abolitionism or support it until the 1850s was that

    (A) the northern economy was tightly bound to that of the South.

    (B) most northerners disliked the lecturing, protests, and other tactics employed by abolitionists.

    (C) northerners were not yet sure whether slave or paid labor would drive industrialization.

    (D) territorial expansion had not yet become a major concern for the North.

    (E) northerners considered slavery a matter for the states to decide.

15. How did abolition in the United States differ from the process in other parts of the Americas?

    (A) The United States abolished slavery long before most nations in Latin America.

    (B) Violent slave revolts in other nations were integral to abolitionists' cause.

    (C) Slavery was abolished in Latin America before the nations became independent.

    (D) The United States promised emancipated slaves land and compensation.

    (E) Abolition in the United States was the result of the bloodiest war in American history.

16. Southern society, more than other parts of the United States, resembled British society because

    (A) there was a small, distinct planter aristocracy.

    (B) state legislatures had one house in which seats were inherited.

    (C) leading voices in the South fought for abolition.

    (D) elite southerners favored the writing of Sir Walter Scott.

    (E) women controlled the social activities in their homes.

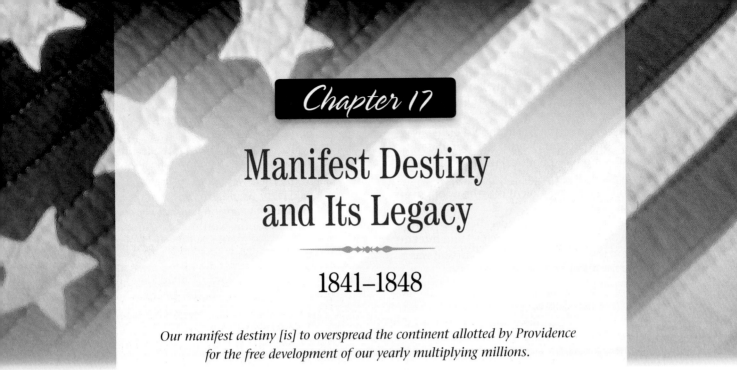

Chapter 17

Manifest Destiny and Its Legacy

1841–1848

*Our manifest destiny [is] to overspread the continent allotted by Providence
for the free development of our yearly multiplying millions.*

JOHN L. O'SULLIVAN, 1845*

*T*erritorial expansion dominated American diplomacy and politics in the 1840s. Settlers swarming into the still-disputed Oregon Country aggravated relations with Britain, which had staked its own claims in the Pacific Northwest. The clamor to annex Texas to the Union provoked bitter tension with Mexico, which continued to regard Texas as a Mexican province in revolt. And when Americans began casting covetous eyes on Mexico's northernmost province, the great prize of California, open warfare erupted between the United States and its southern neighbor. Victory over Mexico added vast new domains to the United States, but it also raised thorny questions about the status of slavery in the newly acquired territories—questions that would be answered in blood in the Civil War of the 1860s.

⭐ The Accession of "Tyler Too"

A horde of hard-ciderites descended upon Washington early in 1841, clamoring for the spoils of office. Newly elected President Harrison, bewildered by the uproar, was almost hounded to death by Whig spoilsmen.

The real leaders of the Whig party regarded "Old Tippecanoe" as little more than an impressive figurehead. Daniel Webster, as secretary of state, and Henry Clay, the uncrowned king of the Whigs and their ablest spokesman in the Senate, would grasp the helm. The aging general was finally forced to rebuke the

overzealous Clay and pointedly remind him that he, William Henry Harrison, was president of the United States.

Unluckily for Clay and Webster, their schemes soon hit a fatal snag. Before the new term had fairly started, Harrison contracted pneumonia. Wearied by official functions and plagued by office seekers, the enfeebled old warrior died after only four weeks in the White House—by far the shortest administration in American history, following by far the longest inaugural address.

The "Tyler too" part of the Whig ticket, hitherto only a rhyme, now claimed the spotlight. What manner of man did the nation now find in the presidential chair? Six feet tall, slender, blue-eyed, and fair-haired, with classical features and a high forehead, John Tyler was a Virginia gentleman of the old school—gracious and kindly, yet stubbornly attached to principle. He had earlier resigned from the Senate, quite unnecessarily, rather than accept distasteful instructions from the Virginia legislature. Still a lone wolf, he had forsaken the Jacksonian Democratic fold for that of the Whigs, largely because he could not stomach the dictatorial tactics of Jackson.

Tyler's enemies accused him of being a Democrat in Whig clothing, but this charge was only partially true. The Whig party, like the Democratic party, was something of a catchall, and the accidental president belonged to the minority wing, which embraced a number of Jeffersonian states' righters. Tyler had in fact been put on the ticket partly to attract the vote of this fringe group, many of whom were influential southern gentry.

---

*Earliest known use of the term *Manifest Destiny*, sometimes called "Manifest Desire."

Yet Tyler, high-minded as he was, should never have consented to run on the ticket. Although the dominant Clay-Webster group had published no platform, every alert politician knew what the unpublished platform contained. And on virtually every major issue, the obstinate Virginian was at odds with the majority of his adoptive Whig party, which was pro-bank, pro–protective tariff, and pro–internal improvements. "Tyler too" rhymed with "Tippecanoe," but there the harmony ended. As events turned out, President Harrison, the Whig, served for only 4 weeks, whereas Tyler, the ex-Democrat who was still largely a Democrat at heart, served for 204 weeks.

✯ John Tyler: A President Without a Party

After their hard-won, hard-cider victory, the Whigs brought their not-so-secret platform out of Clay's waistcoat pocket. To the surprise of no one, it outlined a strongly nationalistic program.

Financial reform came first. The Whig Congress hastened to pass a law ending the independent treasury system, and President Tyler, disarmingly agreeable, signed it. Clay next drove through Congress a bill for a "Fiscal Bank," which would establish a new Bank of the United States.

Tyler's hostility to a centralized bank was notorious, and Clay—the "Great Compromiser"—would have done well to conciliate him. But the Kentuckian, robbed repeatedly of the presidency by lesser men, was in an imperious mood and riding for a fall. When the bank bill reached the presidential desk, Tyler flatly vetoed it on both practical and constitutional grounds. A drunken mob gathered late at night near the White House and shouted insultingly, "Huzza for Clay!" "A Bank! A Bank!" "Down with the Veto!"

The stunned Whig leaders tried once again. Striving to pacify Tyler's objections to a "Fiscal Bank," they passed another bill providing for a "Fiscal Corporation." But the president, still unbending, vetoed the offensive substitute. The Democrats were jubilant: they had been saved from another financial "monster" only by the pneumonia that had felled Harrison.

Whig extremists, seething with indignation, condemned Tyler as "His Accidency" and as an "Executive Ass." Widely burned in effigy, he received numerous letters threatening him with death. A wave of influenza then sweeping the country was called the "Tyler grippe." To the delight of Democrats, the stiff-necked Virginian was formally expelled from his party by a caucus of Whig congressmen, and a serious attempt to impeach him was broached in the House of Representatives. His entire cabinet resigned in a body, except Secretary of State Webster, who was then in the midst of delicate negotiations with England.

The proposed Whig tariff also felt the prick of the president's well-inked pen. Tyler appreciated the necessity of bringing additional revenue to the Treasury. But old Democrat that he was, he looked with a frosty eye on the major tariff scheme of the Whigs because it provided, among other features, for a distribution among the states of revenue from the sale of public lands in the West. Tyler could see no point in squandering federal money when the federal Treasury was not overflowing, and he again wielded an emphatic veto.

Chastened Clayites redrafted their tariff bill. They chopped out the offensive dollar-distribution scheme and pushed down the rates to about the moderately protective level of 1832, roughly 32 percent on dutiable goods. Tyler had no fondness for a protective tariff, but realizing the need for additional revenue, he reluctantly signed the **Tariff of 1842**. In subsequent months the pressure for higher customs duties slackened as the country gradually edged its way out of the depression. The Whig slogan, "Harrison, Two Dollars a Day and Roast Beef," was reduced by unhappy Democrats to "Ten Cents a Day and Bean Soup."

✯ A War of Words with Britain

Hatred of Britain during the nineteenth century came to a head periodically and had to be lanced by treaty settlement or by war. The poison had festered ominously by 1842.

Anti-British passions were composed of many ingredients. At bottom lay the bitter, red-coated memories of the two Anglo-American wars. In addition, the genteel pro-British Federalists had died out, eventually yielding to the boisterous Jacksonian Democrats. British travelers, sniffing with aristocratic noses at the crude scene, wrote acidly of American tobacco spitting, slave auctioneering, lynching, eye gouging, and other unsavory features of the rustic Republic. Travel books

Frances Trollope (1780–1863), an English writer disillusioned by the failure of a utopian community she had joined in Tennessee, wrote scathingly of the Americans in 1832,

❝Other nations have been called thin-skinned, but the citizens of the Union have, apparently, no skins at all; they wince if a breeze blows over them unless it be tempered with adulation.❞

The Land of Liberty, 1847 This British cartoon reflected the contemptuous view of American culture, politics, and diplomacy that was common in early-nineteenth-century Britain.

Granger Collection

penned by these critics, whose views were avidly read on both sides of the Atlantic, stirred up angry outbursts in America.

But the literary fireworks did not end there. British magazines added fuel to the flames when, enlarging on the travel books, they launched sneering attacks on Yankee shortcomings. American journals struck back with "you're another" arguments, thus touching off the "Third War with England." Fortunately, this British-American war was fought with paper broadsides, and only ink was spilled. British authors, including Charles Dickens, entered the fray with gall-dipped pens, for they were being denied rich royalties by the absence of an American copyright law.*

Sprawling America, with expensive canals to dig and railroads to build, was a borrowing nation in the nineteenth century. Imperial Britain, with its

*Not until 1891 did Congress extend copyright privileges to foreign authors.

overflowing coffers, was a lending nation. The well-heeled creditor is never popular with the down-at-the-heels debtor, and the phrase "bloated British bond-holder" rolled bitterly from many an American tongue. When the panic of 1837 broke and several states defaulted on their bonds or repudiated them openly, honest Englishmen assailed Yankee trickery. One of them offered a new stanza for an old song:

> *Yankee Doodle borrows cash,*
> *Yankee Doodle spends it,*
> *And then he snaps his fingers at*
> *The jolly flat [simpleton] who lends it.*

Troubles of a more dangerous sort came closer to home in 1837 when a short-lived insurrection erupted in Canada. It was supported by such a small minority of Canadians that it never had a real chance of success. Yet hundreds of hot-blooded Americans, hoping to strike a blow for freedom against the hereditary enemy, furnished military supplies or volunteered for armed service. The Washington regime tried arduously, though futilely, to uphold its weak neutrality regulations. But again, as in the case of Texas, it simply could not enforce unpopular laws in the face of popular opposition.

A provocative incident on the Canadian frontier brought passions to a boil in 1837. An American steamer, the **Caroline**, was carrying supplies to the insurgents across the swift Niagara River. It was finally attacked on the New York shore by a determined British force, which set the vessel on fire. Lurid American illustrators showed the flaming ship, laden with shrieking souls, plummeting over Niagara Falls. The craft in fact sank short of the plunge, and only one American was killed.

This unlawful invasion of American soil—a counterviolation of neutrality—had alarming aftermaths. Washington officials lodged vigorous but ineffective protests. Three years later, in 1840, the incident was dramatically revived in the state of New York. A Canadian named McLeod, after allegedly boasting in a tavern of his part in the *Caroline* raid, was arrested and indicted for murder. The London Foreign Office, which regarded the *Caroline* raiders as members of a sanctioned armed force and not as criminals, made clear that his execution would mean war. Fortunately, McLeod was freed after establishing an alibi. It must have been airtight, for it was good enough to convince a New York jury. The tension forthwith eased, but it snapped taut again in 1841, when British officials in the Bahamas offered asylum to 130 Virginia slaves who had rebelled and captured the American ship **Creole**. Britain had abolished slavery within its empire in 1833, raising southern fears that its Caribbean possessions would become Canada-like havens for escaped slaves.

✦ Manipulating the Maine Maps

An explosive controversy of the early 1840s involved the Maine boundary dispute. The St. Lawrence River is icebound several months of the year, as the British, remembering the War of 1812, well knew. They were determined, as a defensive precaution against the Yankees, to build a road westward from the seaport of Halifax to Québec. But the proposed route ran through disputed territory—claimed also by Maine under the misleading peace treaty of 1783. Tough-knuckled lumberjacks from both Maine and Canada entered the disputed no-man's-land of the tall-timbered Aroostook River valley. Ugly fights flared up, and both sides summoned the local militia. The small-scale lumberjack clash, which was dubbed the **Aroostook War**, threatened to widen into a full-dress shooting war.

As the crisis deepened in 1842, the London Foreign Office took an unusual step. It sent to Washington a nonprofessional diplomat, the conciliatory financier Lord Ashburton, who had married a wealthy American woman. He speedily established cordial relations with Secretary Webster, who had recently been lionized during a visit to Britain.

The two statesmen, their nerves frayed by protracted negotiations in the heat of a Washington summer, finally agreed to compromise on the Maine boundary (see Map 17.1). On the basis of a rough, split-the-difference arrangement, the Americans were to retain some 7,000 square miles of the 12,000 square miles of wilderness in dispute. The British got less land but won the desired Halifax-Québec route. During the negotiations the *Caroline* affair, malingering since 1837, was patched up by an exchange of diplomatic notes.

An overlooked bonus sneaked by in the small print of the same treaty: the British, in adjusting the U.S.-Canadian boundary farther west, surrendered 6,500 square miles. The area was later found to contain the priceless Mesabi iron ore of Minnesota.

✦ The Lone Star of Texas Shines Alone

During the uncertain eight years since 1836, Texas had led a precarious existence. Mexico, refusing to recognize Texas's independence, regarded the Lone Star Republic as a province in revolt, to be reconquered in the future. Mexican officials loudly threatened war if the American eagle should ever gather the fledgling republic under its protective wings.

The Texans were forced to maintain a costly military establishment. Vastly outnumbered by their Mexican foe, they could not tell when he would strike again. Mexico actually did make two halfhearted raids that, though ineffectual, foreshadowed more fearsome efforts. Confronted with such perils, Texas was driven to open negotiations with Britain and France, in the hope of securing the defensive shield of a protectorate. In 1839 and 1840, the Texans concluded treaties with France, Holland, and Belgium.

Britain was intensely interested in an independent Texas. Such a republic would check the southward surge of the American colossus, whose bulging biceps posed a constant threat to nearby British possessions in the New World. A puppet Texas, dancing to strings pulled by Britain, could be turned upon the Yankees. Subsequent clashes would create a smokescreen diversion, behind which foreign powers could move into the Americas and challenge the insolent Monroe Doctrine. French schemers were likewise attracted by the hoary game of divide and conquer. These actions would result, they hoped, in the fragmentation and militarization of America.

Dangers threatened from other foreign quarters. British abolitionists were busily intriguing for a foothold in Texas. If successful in freeing the few blacks there, they presumably would inflame the nearby slaves of the South. In addition, British merchants regarded Texas as a potentially important free-trade area—an offset to the tariff-walled United States. British manufacturers likewise perceived that those vast Texas plains constituted one of the great cotton-producing areas of the future. An independent Texas would relieve British looms of their chronic dependence on American fiber—a supply that might be cut off in time of crisis by embargo or war.

MAP 17.1 Maine Boundary Settlement, 1842 © Cengage Learning

St. Louis in 1846, by Henry Lewis   Thousands of pioneers like these pulling away from St. Louis said farewell to civilization as they left the Mississippi River and headed across the untracked plains to Oregon in the 1840s.

✦ The Belated Texas Nuptials

Partly because of the fears aroused by British schemers, Texas became a leading issue in the presidential campaign of 1844. The foes of expansion assailed annexation, while southern hotheads cried, "Texas or Disunion." The pro-expansion Democrats under James K. Polk finally triumphed over the Whigs under Henry Clay, the hardy perennial candidate. Lame duck president Tyler thereupon interpreted the narrow Democratic victory, with dubious accuracy, as a "mandate" to acquire Texas.

Eager to crown his troubled administration with this splendid prize, Tyler deserves much of the credit for shepherding Texas into the fold. Many antislavery Whigs feared that Texas in the Union would be red meat to nourish the lusty "slave power." Aware of their opposition, Tyler despaired of securing the needed two-thirds vote for a treaty in the Senate. He therefore arranged for annexation by a joint resolution. This solution required only a simple majority in both houses of Congress. After a spirited debate, the resolution passed early in 1845, and Texas was formally invited to become the twenty-eighth star on the American flag.

Mexico angrily charged that the Americans had despoiled it of Texas. This was to some extent true in 1836, but hardly true in 1845, for the area was no longer Mexico's to be despoiled of. As the years stretched out, realistic observers could see that the Mexicans would not be able to reconquer their lost province. Yet Mexico left the Texans dangling by denying their right to dispose of themselves as they chose.

By 1845 the Lone Star Republic had become a danger spot, inviting foreign intrigue that menaced the American people. The continued existence of Texas as an independent nation threatened to involve the United States in a series of ruinous wars, both in America and in Europe. Americans were in a "lick all creation" mood when they sang "Uncle Sam's Song to Miss Texas":

> *If Mexy back'd by secret foes,*
> *Still talks of getting you, gal;*
> *Why we can lick 'em all you know*
> *And then annex 'em too, gal.*

What other power would have spurned the imperial domain of Texas? The bride was so near, so rich, so fair, so willing. Whatever the peculiar circumstances of the Texas Revolution, the United States can hardly be accused of unseemly haste in achieving annexation. Nine long years were surely a decent wait between the beginning of the courtship and the consummation of the marriage.

Thomas J. Green (1801–1863), who served as a brigadier general in the Texas Revolution, published a pamphlet in 1845 to make the case for American support of an independent Texas:

❝ Both the government of the United States and Texas are founded upon the same political code. They have the same common origin—the same language, laws, and religion—the same pursuits and interests; and though they may remain independent of each other as to government, they are identified in weal and wo'—they will flourish side by side and the blight which affects the one will surely reach the other. **❞**

✪ Oregon Fever Populates Oregon

The so-called Oregon Country was an enormous wilderness. It sprawled magnificently west of the Rockies to the Pacific Ocean, and north of California to the line of 54° 40'—the present southern tip of the Alaska panhandle. All or substantial parts of this immense area were claimed at one time or another by four nations: Spain, Russia, Britain, and the United States.

Two claimants dropped out of the scramble. Spain, though the first to raise its banner in Oregon, bartered away its claims to the United States in the so-called Florida Treaty of 1819. Russia retreated to the line of 54° 40' by the treaties of 1824 and 1825 with America and Britain. These two remaining rivals now had the field to themselves.

British claims to Oregon were strong—at least to that portion north of the Columbia River. They were based squarely on prior discovery and exploration, on treaty rights, and on actual occupation. The most important colonizing agency was the far-flung Hudson's Bay Company, which was trading profitably with the Indians of the Pacific Northwest for furs.

Americans, for their part, could also point pridefully to exploration and occupation. Captain Robert Gray in 1792 had stumbled upon the majestic

In winning Oregon, the Americans had great faith in their procreative powers. Boasted one congressman in 1846,

❝Our people are spreading out with the aid of the American multiplication table. Go to the West and see a young man with his mate of eighteen; after the lapse of thirty years, visit him again, and instead of two, you will find twenty-two. That is what I call the American multiplication table.❞

Columbia River, which he named after his ship; and the famed Lewis and Clark expedition of 1804–1806 had ranged overland through the Oregon Country to the Pacific. This shaky American toehold was ultimately strengthened by the presence of missionaries and other settlers, a sprinkling of whom reached the grassy Willamette River valley, south of the Columbia, in the 1830s. These men and women of God, in saving the soul of the Indian, were instrumental in saving the soil of Oregon for the United States. They stimulated interest in a faraway domain that countless Americans had earlier assumed would not be settled for centuries.

Pundt and Koenig's General Store, Omaha City, Nebraska, 1858 Settlers bound for Colorado and California stopped here for provisions before venturing farther west across the open plains. The Huntington Library & Art Collections, San Marino, California

Scattered American and British pioneers in Oregon continued to live peacefully side by side. At the time of negotiating the Anglo-American Convention of 1818 (see pp. 239–240), the United States had sought to divide the vast domain at the forty-ninth parallel. But the British, who regarded the Columbia River as the St. Lawrence of the West, were unwilling to yield this vital artery. A scheme for peaceful "joint occupation" was thereupon adopted, pending future settlement.

The handful of Americans in the Willamette Valley was suddenly multiplied in the early 1840s, when "Oregon fever" seized hundreds of restless pioneers. In increasing numbers, their creaking covered wagons jolted over the two-thousand-mile Oregon Trail as the human rivulet widened into a stream.* By 1846 about five thousand Americans had settled south of the Columbia River, some of them tough "border ruffians," expert with bowie knife and "revolving pistol."

The British, in the face of this rising torrent of humanity, could muster only seven hundred or so subjects north of the Columbia. Losing out lopsidedly in the population race, they were beginning to see the wisdom of arriving at a peaceful settlement before being engulfed by their neighbors.

A curious fact is that only a relatively small segment of the Oregon Country was in actual controversy by 1845. The area in dispute consisted of the rough quadrangle between the Columbia River on the south and east, the forty-ninth parallel on the north, and the Pacific Ocean on the west. Britain had repeatedly offered the line of the Columbia; America had repeatedly offered the forty-ninth parallel. The whole fateful issue was now tossed into the presidential election of 1844, where it was largely overshadowed by the question of annexing Texas.

✴ A Mandate (?) for Manifest Destiny

The two major parties nominated their presidential standard-bearers in May 1844. Ambitious but often frustrated Henry Clay, easily the most popular man in the country, was enthusiastically chosen by the Whigs at Baltimore. The Democrats, meeting there later, seemed hopelessly deadlocked. Van Buren's opposition to annexing Texas ensured his defeat, given domination of the party by southern expansionists. Finally party delegates trotted out and nominated James K. Polk of Tennessee, America's first "dark-horse" or "surprise" presidential candidate.

Polk may have been a dark horse, but he was hardly an unknown or decrepit nag. Speaker of the House of Representatives for four years and governor of Tennessee for two terms, he was a determined, industrious, ruthless, and intelligent public servant. Sponsored by Andrew Jackson, his friend and neighbor, he was rather implausibly touted by Democrats as yet another "Young Hickory." Whigs attempted to jeer him into oblivion with the taunt "Who is James K. Polk?" They soon found out.

The campaign of 1844 was in part an expression of the mighty emotional upsurge known as **Manifest Destiny**. Countless citizens in the 1840s and 1850s, feeling a sense of mission, believed that Almighty God had "manifestly" destined the American people for a hemispheric career. They would irresistibly spread their uplifting and ennobling democratic institutions over at least the entire continent, and possibly over South America as well. Land greed and ideals—"empire" and "liberty"—were thus conveniently conjoined.

Expansionist Democrats were strongly swayed by the intoxicating spell of Manifest Destiny. They came out flat-footedly in their platform for the "Reannexation of Texas"[†] and the "Reoccupation of Oregon," all the way to 54° 40'. Outbellowing the Whig log-cabinites in the game of slogans, they shouted "All of

---

*The United States had given up its claims to Texas in the so-called Florida Purchase Treaty (Adams-Onís Treaty) with Spain in 1819 (see p. 240).

Manifest Destiny: A Caricature The spirit of Manifest Destiny swept the nation in the 1840s, and threatened to sweep it to extremes. This cartoon from 1848 lampoons proslavery Democratic presidential candidate Lewis Cass as a veritable war machine, bent on the conquest of territory ranging from New Mexico to Cuba and even Peru.

---

*The average rate of progress in covered wagons was one to two miles an hour. This amounted to about one hundred miles a week, or about five months for the entire journey. Thousands of humans, in addition to horses and oxen, died en route. One estimate is seventeen deaths a mile for men, women, and children.

Westward the Course of Empire Takes Its Way This romantic tribute to the spirit of Manifest Destiny was commissioned by Congress in 1860 and may still be seen in the Capitol.

Oregon or None." (The slogan **"Fifty-four forty or fight"** was not coined until two years later, in 1846.) They also condemned Clay as a "corrupt bargainer," a dissolute character, and a slaveowner. (Their own candidate, Polk, also owned slaves—a classic case of the pot calling the kettle black.)

The Whigs, as noisemakers, took no backseat. They countered with such slogans as "Hooray for Clay" and "Polk, Slavery, and Texas, or Clay, Union, and Liberty." They also spread the lie that a gang of Tennessee slaves had been seen on their way to a southern market branded with the initials J. K. P. (James K. Polk).

On the crucial issue of Texas, the acrobatic Clay tried to ride two horses at once. The "Great Compromiser" appears to have compromised away the presidency when he wrote a series of confusing letters. They seemed to say that while he personally favored annexing slaveholding Texas (an appeal to the South), he also favored postponement (an appeal to the North). He might have lost more ground if he had not "straddled," but he certainly alienated the more ardent antislaveryites.

In the stretch drive, "Dark Horse" Polk nipped Henry Clay at the wire, 170 to 105 votes in the Electoral College and 1,338,464 to 1,300,097 in the popular column. Clay would have won if he had not lost New York State by a scant 5,000 votes. There the tiny antislavery **Liberty party** absorbed nearly 16,000 votes, many of which would otherwise have gone to the unlucky Kentuckian. Ironically, the anti-Texas Liberty party, by spoiling Clay's chances and helping to ensure the election of pro-Texas Polk, hastened the annexation of Texas.

Land-hungry Democrats, flushed with victory, proclaimed that they had received a mandate from the voters to take Texas. But a presidential election is seldom, if ever, a clear-cut mandate on anything. The only way to secure a true reflection of the voters' will is to hold a special election on a given issue. The picture that emerged in 1844 was one not of mandate but of muddle. What else could there have been when the results were so close, the personalities so colorful, and the issues so numerous—including Oregon, Texas, the tariff, slavery, the bank, and internal improvements? Yet this unclear "mandate" was interpreted by President Tyler as a crystal-clear charge to annex Texas—and he signed the joint resolution three days before leaving the White House.

✯ Polk the Purposeful

"Young Hickory" Polk, unlike "Old Hickory" Jackson, was not an impressive figure. Of middle height (five feet eight inches), lean, white-haired (worn long), gray-eyed, and stern-faced, he took life seriously and drove himself mercilessly into a premature grave. His burdens were increased by an unwillingness to delegate authority. Methodical and hard-working but not brilliant, he was shrewd, narrow-minded, conscientious, and persistent. "What he went for he fetched," wrote a contemporary. Purposeful in the highest degree, he developed a positive four-point program and with remarkable success achieved it completely in less than four years.

One of Polk's goals was a lowered tariff. His secretary of the Treasury, wispy Robert J. Walker, devised a tariff-for-revenue bill that reduced the average rates of the Tariff of 1842 from about 32 percent to 25 percent. With the strong support of low-tariff southerners, the **Walker Tariff** bill made its way through Congress,

TABLE 17.1 House Vote on Tariff of 1846

Region	For	Against
New England	9	19
Middle states	18	44
West and Northwest	29	10
South and Southwest	58	20
TOTAL	114	93

though not without loud complaints from the Clayites, especially in New England and the middle states, who cried that American manufacturing would be ruined (see Table 17.1). But these prophets of doom missed the mark. The Walker Tariff of 1846 proved to be an excellent revenue producer, largely because it was followed by boom times and heavy imports.

A second objective of Polk was the restoration of the independent treasury, unceremoniously dropped by the Whigs in 1841. Pro-bank Whigs in Congress raised a storm of opposition, but victory at last rewarded the president's efforts in 1846.

The third and fourth points on Polk's "must list" were the acquisition of California and the settlement of the Oregon dispute (see Map 17.2).

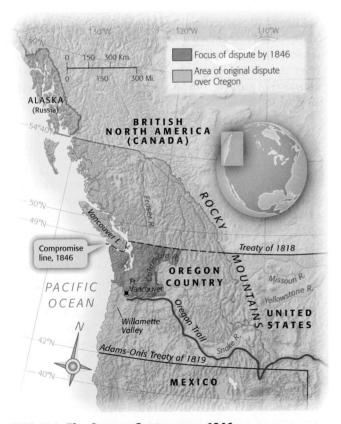

MAP 17.2 The Oregon Controversy, 1846   © Cengage Learning

"Reoccupation" of the "whole" of Oregon had been promised northern Democrats in the campaign of 1844. But southern Democrats, once they had annexed Texas, rapidly cooled off. Polk, himself a southerner, had no intention of insisting on the 54° 40' pledge of his own platform. But feeling bound by the three offers of his predecessors to London, he again proposed the compromise line of 49°. The British minister in Washington, on his own initiative, brusquely spurned this olive branch.

The next move on the Oregon chessboard was up to Britain. Fortunately for peace, the ministry began to experience a change of heart. British anti-expansionists ("Little Englanders") were now persuaded that the Columbia River was not after all the St. Lawrence of the West and that the turbulent American hordes might one day seize the Oregon Country. Why fight a hazardous war over this wilderness on behalf of an unpopular monopoly, the Hudson's Bay Company, which had already "furred out" much of the area anyhow?

Early in 1846 the British, hat in hand, came around and themselves proposed the line of 49°. President Polk, irked by the previous rebuff, threw the decision squarely into the lap of the Senate. The senators speedily accepted the offer and approved the subsequent treaty, despite a few diehard shouts of "Fifty-four forty forever!" and "Every foot or not an inch!" The fact that the United States was then a month deep in a war with Mexico doubtless influenced the Senate's final vote.

Satisfaction with the Oregon settlement among Americans was not unanimous. The northwestern states, hotbed of Manifest Destiny and "fifty-four forty-ism," joined the antislavery forces in condemning what they regarded as a base betrayal by the South. Why *all* of Texas but not *all* of Oregon? Because, retorted the expansionist Senator Benton of Missouri, "Great Britain is powerful and Mexico is weak."

So Polk, despite all the campaign bluster, got neither "fifty-four forty" nor a fight. But he did get something that in the long run was better: a reasonable compromise without a rifle being raised.

✶ Misunderstandings with Mexico

Faraway California was another worry of Polk's. He and other disciples of Manifest Destiny had long coveted its verdant valleys, and especially the spacious bay of San Francisco. This splendid harbor was widely regarded as America's future gateway to the Pacific Ocean.

The population of California in 1845 was curiously mixed. It consisted of perhaps thirteen thousand sun-blessed Spanish Mexicans and as many as seventy-five thousand dispirited Indians. There were fewer than

Fort Vancouver, Oregon Country, ca. 1846   Fort Vancouver, on the Columbia River near its confluence with the Willamette River, was the economic hub of the Oregon Country during the early years of settlement. Founded as a Hudson's Bay Company fur-trading outpost, the fort was handed over to the Americans when Britain ceded the Oregon Country to the United States in 1846.

a thousand "foreigners," mostly Americans, some of whom had "left their consciences" behind them as they rounded Cape Horn. Given time, these transplanted Yankees might yet bring California into the Union by "playing the Texas game."

Polk was eager to buy California from Mexico, but relations with Mexico City were dangerously embittered. Among other friction points, the United States had claims against the Mexicans for some $3 million in damages to American citizens and their property. The revolution-riddled regime in Mexico had formally agreed to assume most of this debt but had been forced to default on its payments.

A more serious bone of contention was Texas. The Mexican government, after threatening war if the United States should acquire the Lone Star Republic, had recalled its minister from Washington following annexation. Diplomatic relations were completely severed.

Deadlock with Mexico over Texas was further tightened by a question of boundaries. During the long era of Spanish Mexican occupation, the southwestern boundary of Texas had been the Nueces River. But the expansive Texans, on rather far-fetched grounds, were claiming the more southerly Rio Grande instead. Polk, for his part, felt a strong moral obligation to defend Texas in its claim, once it was annexed.

The Mexicans were far less concerned about this boundary quibble than was the United States. In their eyes all of Texas was still theirs, although temporarily in revolt, and a dispute over the two rivers seemed pointless. Yet Polk was careful to keep American troops out of virtually all of the explosive no-man's-land between the Nueces and the Rio Grande, as long as there was any real prospect of peaceful adjustment.

The golden prize of California continued to cause Polk much anxiety. Disquieting rumors (now known to have been ill-founded) were circulating that Britain was about to buy or seize California—a grab that Americans could not tolerate under the Monroe Doctrine. In a last desperate throw of the dice, Polk dispatched John Slidell to Mexico City as minister late in 1845. The new envoy, among other alternatives, was instructed to offer a maximum of $25 million for California and territory to the east. But the proud Mexican people would not even permit Slidell to present his "insulting" proposition.

✵ American Blood on American (?) Soil

A frustrated Polk was now prepared to force a showdown. On January 13, 1846, he ordered four thousand men,

On June 1, 1860, less than a year before he became president, Abraham Lincoln (1809-1865) wrote,

" The act of sending an armed force among the Mexicans was unnecessary, inasmuch as Mexico was in no way molesting or menacing the United States or the people thereof; and . . . it was unconstitutional, because the power of levying war is vested in Congress, and not in the President.**"**

under General Zachary Taylor, to march from the Nueces River to the Rio Grande, provocatively near Mexican forces. Polk's presidential diary reveals that he expected at any moment to hear of a clash. When none occurred after an anxious wait, he informed his cabinet on May 9, 1846, that he proposed to ask Congress to declare war on the basis of (1) unpaid claims and (2) Slidell's rejection. These, at best, were rather flimsy pretexts. Two cabinet members spoke up and said that they would feel better satisfied if Mexican troops should fire first.

That very evening, as fate would have it, news of bloodshed arrived. On April 25, 1846, Mexican troops had crossed the Rio Grande and attacked General Taylor's command, with a loss of sixteen Americans killed or wounded.

Polk, further aroused, sent a vigorous war message to Congress. He declared that despite "all our efforts" to avoid a clash, hostilities had been forced upon the country by the shedding of "American blood upon the American soil." A patriotic Congress overwhelmingly voted for war, and enthusiastic volunteers cried, "Ho for the Halls of the Montezumas!" and "Mexico or Death!" Inflamed by the war fever, even antislavery Whig bastions melted and joined with the rest of the nation, though they later condemned "Jimmy Polk's war." As James Russell Lowell of Massachusetts lamented,

Massachusetts, God forgive her,
She's akneelin' with the rest.

In his message to Congress, Polk was making history—not writing it. Like many presidents with ambitious foreign-policy goals, he felt justified in bending the truth if that was what it took to bend a reluctant public toward war. If he had been a historian, Polk would have explained that American blood had been shed on soil that the Mexicans had good reason to regard as their own. A gangling, rough-featured Whig congressman from Illinois, one Abraham Lincoln, introduced certain resolutions that requested information as to the precise "spot" on American soil where American blood had been shed. He pushed his **spot resolutions** with such persistence that he came to be known as the "spotty Lincoln," who could die of

"spotted fever." The more extreme antislavery agitators of the North, many of them Whigs, branded the president a liar—"Polk the Mendacious."

Did Polk provoke war? California was an imperative point in his program, and Mexico would not sell it at any price. The only way to get it was to use force or wait for an internal American revolt. Yet delay seemed dangerous, for the claws of the British lion might snatch the ripening California fruit from the talons of the American eagle. Grievances against Mexico were annoying yet tolerable; in later years America endured even worse ones. But in 1846 patience had ceased to be a virtue, as far as Polk was concerned. Bent on grasping California by fair means or foul, he pushed the quarrel to a bloody showdown.

Both sides, in fact, were spoiling for a fight. Feisty Americans, especially southwestern expansionists, were eager to teach the Mexicans a lesson. The Mexicans, in turn, were burning to humiliate the "Bullies of the North." Possessing a considerable standing army, heavily overstaffed with generals, they boasted of invading the United States, freeing the black slaves, and lassoing whole regiments of Americans. They were hoping that the quarrel with Britain over Oregon would blossom into a full-dress war, as it came near doing, and further pin down the hated *yanquis*. A conquest of Mexico's vast and arid expanses seemed fantastic, especially in view of the bungling American invasion of Canada in 1812.

Both sides were fired by moral indignation. The Mexican people could fight with the flaming sword of righteousness, for had not the "insolent" Yankee picked a fight by polluting their soil? Many earnest Americans, on the other hand, sincerely believed that Mexico was the aggressor.

✴ The Mastering of Mexico

Polk wanted California—not war. But when war came, he hoped to fight it on a limited scale and then pull out when he had captured the prize. The dethroned Mexican dictator Santa Anna, then exiled with his teenage bride in Cuba, let it be known that if the American blockading squadron would permit him to slip into Mexico, he would sell out his country. Incredibly, Polk agreed to this discreditable intrigue. But the double-crossing Santa Anna, once he returned to Mexico, proceeded to rally his countrymen to a desperate defense of their soil.

American operations in the Southwest and in California were completely successful (see Map 17.3). In 1846 General Stephen W. Kearny led a detachment of seventeen hundred troops over the famous Santa Fe Trail from Fort Leavenworth to Santa Fe. This sun-baked outpost, with its drowsy plazas, was easily captured. But before Kearny could reach California, the fertile province was won. When war broke out, Captain John C. Frémont, the dashing explorer, just "happened" to be there with several dozen well-armed men. In helping to overthrow Mexican rule in 1846, he collaborated with American naval officers and with the local Americans, who had hoisted the banner of the short-lived **California Bear Flag Republic**.

General Zachary Taylor meanwhile had been spearheading the main thrust. Known as "Old Rough and Ready" because of his iron constitution and incredibly unsoldierly appearance—he sometimes wore a Mexican straw hat—he fought his way across the Rio Grande into Mexico. After several gratifying victories, he reached **Buena Vista**. There, on February 22–23, 1847, his weakened force of five thousand men was attacked by some twenty thousand march-weary troops under Santa Anna. The Mexicans were finally repulsed with extreme difficulty, and overnight Zachary Taylor became the "Hero of Buena Vista." One Kentuckian was

heard to say that "Old Zack" would be elected president in 1848 by "spontaneous combustion."

Sound American strategy now called for a crushing blow at the enemy's vitals—Mexico City. General Taylor, though a good leader of modest-sized forces, could not win decisively in the semideserts of northern Mexico. The command of the main expedition, which pushed inland from the coastal city of Veracruz early in 1847, was entrusted to General Winfield Scott. A handsome giant of a man, Scott had emerged as a hero from the War of 1812 and had later earned the nickname "Old Fuss and Feathers" because of his resplendent uniforms and strict discipline. He was severely handicapped in the Mexican campaign by inadequate numbers of troops, by expiring enlistments, by a more numerous enemy, by mountainous terrain, by disease, and by political backbiting at home. Yet he succeeded in battling his way up to Mexico City by September 1847 in one of the most brilliant campaigns in

MAP 17.3 Major Campaigns of the Mexican War © Cengage Learning

American military annals. He proved to be the most distinguished general produced by his country between the Revolution and the Civil War.

✵ Fighting Mexico for Peace

Polk was anxious to end the shooting as soon as he could secure his territorial goals. Accordingly, he sent along with Scott's invading army the chief clerk of the State Department, Nicholas P. Trist, who among other weaknesses was afflicted with an overfluid pen. Trist and Scott arranged for an armistice with Santa Anna, at a cost of $10,000. The wily dictator pocketed the bribe and then used the time to bolster his defenses.

Negotiating a treaty with a sword in one hand and a pen in the other was ticklish business. Polk, disgusted with his blundering envoy, abruptly recalled Trist. The wordy diplomat then dashed off a sixty-five-page letter explaining why he was not coming home. The president was furious. But Trist, grasping a fleeting opportunity to negotiate, signed the **Treaty of Guadalupe Hidalgo** on February 2, 1848, and forwarded it to Washington.

The terms of the treaty were breathtaking. They confirmed the American title to Texas and yielded the enormous area stretching westward to Oregon and the ocean and embracing coveted California. This total expanse, including Texas, was about one-half of Mexico. The United States agreed to pay $15 million for the land and to assume the claims of its citizens against Mexico in the amount of $3,250,000 (see "Makers of America: The Californios," pp. 374–375).

Polk submitted the treaty to the Senate. Although Trist had proved highly annoying, he had generally followed his original instructions. And speed was imperative. The antislavery Whigs in Congress—dubbed "Mexican Whigs" or "**Conscience Whigs**"—were denouncing this "damnable war" with increasing heat. Having secured control of the House in 1847, they were even threatening to vote down supplies for the armies in the field. If they had done so, Scott probably would have been forced to retreat, and the fruits of victory might have been tossed away.

Another peril impended. A swelling group of expansionists, intoxicated by Manifest Destiny, was clamoring for all of Mexico. If America had seized it, the nation would have been saddled with an expensive

War News from Mexico, by Richard Caton Woodville The newfangled telegraph kept the nation closely informed of events in far-off Mexico.

Early in 1848 the New York Evening Post *demanded,*

"Now we ask, whether any man can coolly contemplate the idea of recalling our troops from the [Mexican] territory we at present occupy . . . and . . . resign this beautiful country to the custody of the ignorant cowards and profligate ruffians who have ruled it for the last twenty-five years? Why, humanity cries out against it. Civilization and Christianity protest against this reflux of the tide of barbarism and anarchy."

Such was one phase of Manifest Destiny.

and vexatious policing problem. Farseeing southerners like Calhoun, alarmed by the mounting anger of antislavery agitators, realized that the South would do well not to be too greedy. The treaty was finally approved by the Senate, 38 to 14. Oddly enough, it was condemned both by those opponents who wanted all of Mexico and by opponents who wanted none of it.

Victors rarely pay an indemnity, especially after a costly conflict has been "forced" on them. Yet Polk, who had planned to offer $25 million before fighting the war, arranged to pay $18,250,000 after winning it. Cynics have charged that the Americans were pricked by guilty consciences; apologists have pointed proudly to the "Anglo-Saxon spirit of fair play." A decisive factor was the need for haste, while there was still a responsible Mexican government to carry out the treaty and before political foes in the United States, notably the antislavery zealots, sabotaged Polk's expansionist program.

✦ Profit and Loss in Mexico

As wars go, the Mexican War was a small one. It cost some thirteen thousand American lives, most of them taken by disease. But the fruits of the fighting were enormous.

America's total expanse, already vast, was increased by about one-third (counting Texas)—an addition even greater than that of the Louisiana Purchase. A sharp stimulus was given to the spirit of Manifest Destiny, for as the proverb has it, the appetite comes with eating.

The Mexican War proved to be the blood-spattered schoolroom of the Civil War. The campaigns provided priceless field experience for most of the officers destined to become leading generals in the forthcoming conflict, including Captain Robert E. Lee and Lieutenant Ulysses S. Grant. The Military Academy at West Point, founded

in 1802, fully justified its existence through the well-trained officers. Useful also was the navy, which did valuable work in throwing a crippling blockade around Mexican ports. A new academy at Annapolis had just been established by Navy Secretary and historian George Bancroft in 1845. The Marine Corps, in existence since 1798, won new laurels and to this day sings in its stirring hymn about the "Halls of Montezuma."

The army waged war without defeat and without a major blunder, despite formidable obstacles and a half-dozen or so achingly long marches. Chagrined British critics, as well as other foreign skeptics, reluctantly revised upward their estimate of Yankee military prowess. Opposing armies, moreover, emerged with increased respect for each other. The Mexicans, though poorly led, fought heroically. At Chapultepec, near Mexico City, the teenage lads of the military academy there (*los niños*) perished to a boy.

Long-memoried Mexicans have never forgotten that their northern enemy tore away about half of their country. The argument that they were lucky not to lose all of it, and that they had been paid something for their land, has scarcely lessened their bitterness. The war also marked an ugly turning point in relations between the United States and Latin America as a whole. Hitherto, Uncle Sam had been regarded with some complacency, even friendliness. Henceforth, he was increasingly feared as the "Colossus of the North." Suspicious neighbors to the south condemned him as a greedy and untrustworthy bully, who might next despoil them of their soil.

Most ominous of all, the war rearoused the snarling dog of the slavery issue, and the beast did not stop yelping until drowned in the blood of the Civil War. Abolitionists assailed the Mexican conflict as one provoked by the southern "slavocracy" for its own evil purposes. As James Russell Lowell had Hosea Biglow drawl in his Yankee dialect,

> *They jest want this Californy*
> *So's to lug new slave-states in*
> *To abuse ye, an' to scorn ye,*
> *An' to plunder ye like sin.*

In line with Lowell's charge, the bulk of the American volunteers were admittedly from the South and Southwest. But, as in the case of the Texas Revolution, the basic explanation was proximity rather than conspiracy.

Quarreling over slavery extension also erupted on the floors of Congress. In 1846, shortly after the shooting started, Polk had requested an appropriation of $2 million with which to buy a peace. Representative David Wilmot of Pennsylvania, fearful of the southern "slavocracy," introduced a fateful amendment. It stipulated that slavery should never exist in any of the territory to be wrested from Mexico.

In 1848 the United States, swollen with the spoils of war, reckoned the costs and benefits of the conflict with Mexico. Thousands of Americans had fallen in battle, and millions of dollars had been invested in a war machine. For this expenditure of blood and money, the nation was repaid with ample land—and with people, the former citizens of Mexico who now became, whether willingly or not, Americans. The largest single addition to American territory in history, the Mexican Cession stretched the United States from sea to shining sea. It secured Texas, brought in vast tracts of the desert Southwest, and included the great prize—the fruited valleys and port cities of California. There, at the conclusion of the Mexican War, dwelled some thirteen thousand Californios—descendants of the Spanish and Mexican conquerors who had once ruled California.

The Spanish had first arrived in California in 1769, extending their New World empire and outracing Russian traders to bountiful San Francisco Bay. Father Junipero Serra, an enterprising Franciscan friar, soon established twenty-one missions along the coast (see Map 17.4). Indians in the iron grip of the missions were encouraged to adopt Christianity and were often forced to toil endlessly as farmers and herders, in the process suffering disease and degradation. These frequently maltreated mission Indians occupied the lowest rungs on the ladder of Spanish colonial society.

Upon the loftiest rungs perched the Californios. Pioneers from the Mexican heartland of New Spain, they had trailed Serra to California, claiming land and civil offices in their new home. Yet even the proud Californios had deferred to the all-powerful Franciscan missionaries until Mexico threw off the Spanish colonial yoke in 1821, whereupon the infant Mexican government turned an anxious eye toward its frontier outpost.

Mexico now emptied its jails to send settlers to the sparsely populated north, built and garrisoned fortresses, and, most important, transferred authority from the missions to secular (that is, governmental) authorities. This "secularization" program attacked and eroded the immense power of the missions and of their

Dance of Native Californians at San Francisco de Assis Mission, 1816, by Ludwig Choris   In the sixty years that they operated, the twenty-one California missions employed 142 priests and baptized 87,787 Indians. Missions became a combination of churches, towns, schools, farms, factories, and prisons.

The Landowner and His Foreman, by Julio Michard, 1839 This California ranchero's way of life was soon to be extinguished when California became part of the United States in 1848 and thousands of American gold-seekers rushed into the state the following year.

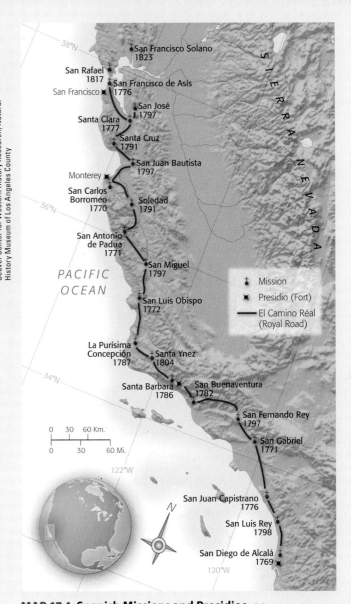

MAP 17.4 Spanish Missions and Presidios © Cengage Learning

Franciscan masters—with their bawling herds of cattle, debased Indian workers, millions of acres of land, and lucrative foreign trade. The frocked friars had commanded their fiefdoms so self-confidently that earlier reform efforts had dared to go no further than levying a paltry tax on the missions and politely requesting that the missionaries limit their floggings of Indians to fifteen lashes per week. But during the 1830s, the power of the missions weakened, and much of their land and their assets was confiscated by the Californios. Vast *ranchos* (ranches) formed, and from those citadels the Californios ruled in their turn until the Mexican War.

The Californios' glory faded in the wake of the American victory, even though in some isolated places they clung to their political offices for a decade or two. Overwhelmed by the inrush of Anglo gold-diggers— some eighty-seven thousand after the discovery at Sutter's Mill in 1848—and undone by the waning of the pastoral economy, the Californios saw their recently acquired lands and their recently established political power slip through their fingers. When the Civil War broke out in 1861, so harshly did the word *Yankee* ring in their ears that many Californios supported the South.

By 1870 the Californios' brief ascendancy had utterly vanished—a short and sad tale of riches to rags in the face of the Anglo onslaught. Half a century later, beginning in 1910, hundreds of thousands of young Mexicans would flock into California and the

Southwest. They would enter a region liberally endowed with Spanish architecture and artifacts, bearing the names of Spanish missions and Californio *ranchos*. But they would find it a land dominated by Anglos, a place far different from that which their Californio ancestors had settled so hopefully in earlier days.

Storming the Fortress of Chapultepec, Mexico, 1847 The American success at Chapultepec contributed heavily to the final victory over Mexico. One American commander lined up several Irish American deserters on a gallows facing the castle and melodramatically dropped the trapdoors beneath them just as the United States flag was raised over the captured battlement. According to legend, the flag was raised by First Lieutenant George Pickett, later immortalized as the leader of "Pickett's charge" in the Civil War Battle of Gettysburg, 1863.

The disruptive Wilmot amendment twice passed the House, but not the Senate. Southern members, unwilling to be robbed of prospective slave states, fought the restriction tooth and nail. Antislavery men, in Congress and out, battled no less bitterly for the exclusion of slaves. The **Wilmot Proviso** never became federal law, but it was eventually endorsed by the legislatures of all but one of the free states, and it came to symbolize the burning issue of slavery in the territories.

In a broad sense, the opening shots of the Mexican War were the opening shots of the Civil War. President Polk left the nation the splendid physical heritage of California and the Southwest but also the ugly moral heritage of an embittered slavery dispute. "Mexico will poison us," said the philosopher Ralph Waldo Emerson. Even the great champion of the South, John C. Calhoun, had prophetically warned that "Mexico is to us the forbidden fruit . . . the penalty of eating it would be to subject our institutions to political death." Mexicans could later take some satisfaction in knowing that the territory wrenched from them had proved to be a venomous apple of discord that could well be called Santa Anna's revenge.

Chapter Review

KEY TERMS

Tariff of 1842 (361)

Caroline (362)

Creole (362)

Aroostook War (363)

Manifest Destiny (366)

"Fifty-four forty or fight" (367)

Liberty party (367)

Walker Tariff (367)

spot resolutions (370)

California Bear Flag Republic (371)

Buena Vista, Battle of (371)

Guadalupe Hidalgo, Treaty of (372)

Conscience Whigs (372)

Wilmot Proviso (376)

PEOPLE TO KNOW

John Tyler   Winfield Scott
James K. Polk   Nicholas P. Trist
Stephen W. Kearny   David Wilmot
John C. Frémont

CHRONOLOGY

1837	Canadian rebellion and *Caroline* incident
1839	Aroostook War breaks out over Maine boundary
1840	Antislavery Liberty party organized
1841	Harrison dies after four weeks in office Tyler assumes presidency
1842	Webster-Ashburton treaty
1844	Polk defeats Clay in "Manifest Destiny" election
1845	United States annexes Texas
1846	Walker Tariff Independent treasury restored United States settles Oregon dispute with Britain United States and Mexico clash over Texas boundary Kearny takes Santa Fe Frémont conquers California Wilmot Proviso passes House of Representatives
1846–1848	Mexican War
1847	Battle of Buena Vista Scott takes Mexico City
1848	Treaty of Guadalupe Hidalgo

TO LEARN MORE

William Cronon, *Nature's Metropolis: Chicago and the Great West* (1992)

Iris Engstrand et al., *Culture y Cultura: Consequences of the U.S.-Mexican War, 1846–1848* (1998)

John Mack Faragher, *Sugar Creek: Life on the Illinois Prairie* (1986)

Sam W. Haynes and Christopher Morris, eds., *Manifest Destiny and Empire: American Antebellum Expansionism* (1997)

Robert W. Johannsen, *To the Halls of the Montezumas: The Mexican War in the American Imagination* (1985)

Theodore J. Karamanski, *Fur Trade and Exploration: Opening the Far Northwest, 1821–1852* (1983)

James McCaffrey, *Army of Manifest Destiny: The American Soldier in the Mexican War* (1992)

Dale Morgan, ed., *Overland in 1846: Diaries and Letters of the California-Oregon Trail* (1963)

Martha Sandweiss, *Print and Legend: Photography and the American West* (2002)

Michael L. Tate, *Indians and Emigrants: Encounters on the Overland Trails* (2006)

Richard Bruce Winders, *Crisis in the Southwest: The United States, Mexico, and the Struggle over Texas* (2002)

A complete, annotated bibliography for this chapter—along with brief descriptions of the People to Know—may be found on the American Pageant website. The Key Terms are defined in a Glossary at the end of the text.

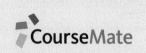 Go to the CourseMate website at **www.cengagebrain.com** for additional study tools and review materials—including audio and video clips—for this chapter.

AP® Review Questions for Chapter 17

1. What distinguished William Henry Harrison's presidency?
   (A) It was plagued by tensions between western settlers and Native Americans.
   (B) It was the shortest on record.
   (C) It was marked by hard drinking.
   (D) It was undermined by venomous Whig party politics.
   (E) It was the first time a frontiersman held the United States' highest office.

2. What prompted fiercely loyal Whigs to denounce their leader, President John Tyler, as "His Accidency"?
   (A) His veto of bills to establish a national bank
   (B) His refusal to sign the Tariff of 1842
   (C) His height and natural clumsiness
   (D) His perceived ineptitude as president
   (E) His inability to keep his entire cabinet from resigning

3. Tyler was considered by contemporaries as a "Democrat in Whig clothing" for all of the following reasons EXCEPT that he
   (A) supported states' rights over a nationalist agenda.
   (B) disliked protective tariffs.
   (C) favored federal funding of internal improvements like roads and canals.
   (D) opposed a national bank.
   (E) rejected the idea of turning profits from the sale of western lands over to the states.

4. In the 1830s, America's relationship with Britain was marked by all of the following EXCEPT
   (A) a borrower-lender status.
   (B) a constant state of being on the brink of war.
   (C) a series of compromises.
   (D) ongoing boundary disputes.
   (E) tension over tariffs.

5. The U.S.-British tension over the Maine-Canada boundary that nearly sparked a war was finally settled in 1842 by
   (A) granting the entire area in question to the Americans.
   (B) granting the entire area in question to the British.
   (C) dividing the area equally between both nations.
   (D) adjusting the Canadian border so that the United States gained an additional 6,500 square miles.
   (E) adjusting the Canadian border so that the British gained thousands of miles of U.S. territory.

6. Which of the following did NOT influence the decision to annex Texas, the Lone Star Republic, to the United States in 1845?
   (A) Fear that Texas's continued independence made America vulnerable
   (B) The belief that Mexico would not be able to reclaim its lost Texas territory
   (C) Increasing British interest in Texas
   (D) Pressure from southern states to annex Texas, ideally as a slave territory
   (E) Whig campaigning in the 1844 election on the promise of annexing Texas

7. Manifest Destiny is best described as
   (A) a sense of mission to ultimately eliminate slavery from U.S. soil.
   (B) the goal of expelling all foreign influences from American borders so that the nation could fully develop as a republic.
   (C) the notion that America was ordained by God to spread its democratic institutions beyond its existing borders.
   (D) America's push toward becoming a commercial nation and world power.
   (E) a phrase coined by Henry Clay to justify pushing the British further back into Canada.

8. How was the question of the Oregon boundary finally resolved between the United States and Britain?
   (A) Britain peacefully settled for the proposed line of 49°.
   (B) America threatened war with England over settling the boundary at the Columbia River.
   (C) Polk pushed his 1844 campaign promise of the 54° 40' line until Britain agreed.
   (D) The two nations agreed to continue jointly occupying the region as they had for decades.
   (E) American settlers in the territory attacked small clusters of British until they withdrew into Canada.

9. All of the following fanned the flames that led to the U.S. war with Mexico EXCEPT
   (A) Polk's desire for California.
   (B) Britain's offer to purchase California from Mexico.
   (C) a dispute over where the Texas border with Mexico actually lay.
   (D) Mexico's anger at the U.S. annexation of its territory in revolt, Texas.
   (E) American bloodshed at the hands of Mexican troops along the Rio Grande.

10. What was Polk's real goal once the battle with Mexico began?
    (A) To end the fighting once he captured California
    (B) To conquer all of Mexico's land claims north of the Nueces River
    (C) To use Santa Anna to betray—and help the United States annex—Mexico
    (D) To keep Mexico from regaining Texas and advancing into the United States
    (E) To take Mexico City

11. The Treaty of Guadalupe Hidalgo, which ended the U.S. war with Mexico, included all of the following terms EXCEPT that it
    (A) confirmed that Texas belonged to the United States.
    (B) gave the United States all of the territory to the Pacific, including California.
    (C) required the United States to assume the land claims against Mexico made by U.S. citizens.
    (D) required that the United States pay $25 million for its land acquisitions, primarily California.
    (E) granted to the United States nearly one-half of all the land formerly held by Mexico.

12. Who were the Californios?
    (A) The original inhabitants of the land later called California
    (B) The descendants of Spanish and Mexican conquerors who once ruled the region
    (C) Christian missionaries who sought to convert local Indians along the Pacific Coast
    (D) Mexican prisoners released from jail and sent to settle California
    (E) The name given to U.S. settlers who moved into the territory acquired after the war with Mexico

13. From a domestic standpoint, which of these was NOT a product of the war with Mexico?
    (A) A significant loss of life and a weakening of the U.S. army
    (B) Training the military officials who would eventually become leaders in the Civil War
    (C) Pushing the slavery debate into the foreground
    (D) Weakening U.S. relations with Latin America
    (E) Increasing the geographic size of the United States by one-third

14. Symbolically important, the 1846 Wilmot Proviso stated that
    (A) slavery should never be established in the territories acquired from Mexico.
    (B) each new territory in the land acquired from Mexico should decide the slave issue for itself.
    (C) slavery in the United States should end by a specified date.
    (D) the number of slave and free states should remain equal and balanced.
    (E) southern states would make no effort to influence the further course of slavery in the territories.

15. John C. Calhoun stated, "Mexico is to us the forbidden fruit . . . the penalty of eating it would be to subject our institutions to political death." How did this statement prove to be correct?
    (A) Northerners took control of the newly acquired land, limiting the South's power.
    (B) European nations regarded the United States as an aggressor.
    (C) The controversy resulting from gaining new land led to the Civil War.
    (D) The United States went into debt after paying millions of dollars for the Mexican Cession.
    (E) The president gained too much power with the addition of new territories.

16. All of the following accomplishments from the 1840s are examples of America fulfilling its Manifest Destiny EXCEPT
    (A) gaining land that would become New Mexico and Arizona from Mexico.
    (B) lowering tariff rates.
    (C) annexing Texas.
    (D) formally acquiring land in Oregon Country.
    (E) acquiring gold-rich California.

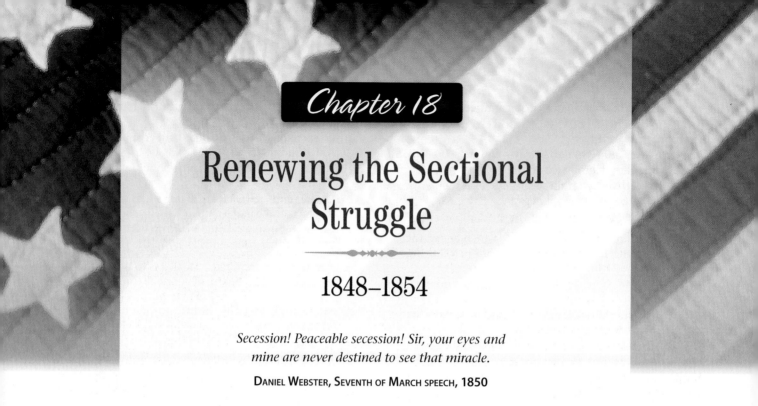

Chapter 18

Renewing the Sectional Struggle

1848–1854

*Secession! Peaceable secession! Sir, your eyes and
mine are never destined to see that miracle.*

Daniel Webster, Seventh of March speech, 1850

The year 1848, highlighted by a rash of revolutions in Europe, was filled with unrest in America. The Treaty of Guadalupe Hidalgo had officially ended the war with Mexico, but it had initiated a new and perilous round of political warfare in the United States. The vanquished Mexicans had been forced to relinquish an enormous tract of real estate, including Texas, California, and all the area between. The acquisition of this huge domain raised anew the burning issue of extending slavery into the territories. Northern antislaveryites had rallied behind the Wilmot Proviso, which flatly prohibited slavery in any territory acquired in the Mexican War. Southern senators had blocked the passage of the proviso, but the issue would not die. Ominously, debate over slavery in the area of the Mexican Cession threatened to disrupt the ranks of both Whigs and Democrats and split national politics along North-South sectional lines.

★ The Popular Sovereignty Panacea

Each of the two great political parties was a vital bond of national unity, for each enjoyed powerful support in both North and South. If they should be replaced by two purely sectional groupings, the Union would be in peril. To politicians, the wisest strategy seemed to be to sit on the lid of the slavery issue and ignore the boiling beneath. Even so, the cover bobbed up and down ominously in response to the agitation of zealous northern abolitionists and impassioned southern "fire-eaters."

Anxious Democrats were forced to seek a new standard-bearer in 1848. President Polk, broken in health by overwork and chronic diarrhea, had pledged himself to a single term. The Democratic National Convention at Baltimore turned to an aging leader, General Lewis Cass, a veteran of the War of 1812. Although a senator and diplomat of wide experience and considerable ability, he was sour-visaged and somewhat pompous. His enemies dubbed him General "Gass" and quickly noted that *Cass* rhymed with *jackass*. The Democratic platform, in line with the lid-sitting strategy, was silent on the burning issue of slavery in the territories.

But Cass himself had not been silent. His views on the extension of slavery were well known because he was the reputed father of **popular sovereignty**. This was the doctrine that stated that the sovereign people of a territory, under the general principles of the Constitution, should themselves determine the status of slavery.

Popular sovereignty had a persuasive appeal. The public liked it because it accorded with the democratic tradition of self-determination. Politicians liked it because it seemed a comfortable compromise between the free-soilers' bid for a ban on slavery in the territories and southern demands that Congress protect slavery in the territories. Popular sovereignty tossed the slavery problem into the laps of the people in the various territories. Advocates of the principle thus hoped to dissolve the most stubborn national issue of the day into a series of local issues. Yet popular sovereignty had one fatal defect: it might serve to spread the blight of slavery.

✶ Political Triumphs for General Taylor

The Whigs, meeting in Philadelphia, cashed in on the "Taylor fever." They nominated frank and honest Zachary Taylor, the "Hero of Buena Vista," who had never held civil office or even voted for president. Henry Clay, the living embodiment of Whiggism, should logically have been nominated. But Clay had made too many speeches—and too many enemies.

As usual, the Whigs pussyfooted in their platform. Eager to win at any cost, they dodged all troublesome issues and merely extolled the homespun virtues of their candidate. The self-reliant old frontier fighter had not committed himself on the issue of slavery extension. But as a wealthy resident of Louisiana, living on a sugar plantation, he owned scores of slaves.

Ardent antislavery men in the North, distrusting both Cass and Taylor, organized the **Free Soil party**. Aroused by the conspiracy of silence in the Democratic and Whig platforms, the Free-Soilers made no bones about their own stand. They came out foursquare for the Wilmot Proviso and against slavery in the territories. Going beyond other antislavery groups, they broadened their appeal by advocating federal aid for internal improvements and by urging free government homesteads for settlers.

The new party assembled a strange assortment of new fellows in the same political bed. It attracted industrialists miffed at Polk's reduction of protective tariffs. It appealed to Democrats resentful of Polk's settling for part of Oregon while insisting on all of Texas—a disparity that suggested a menacing southern dominance in the Democratic party. It harbored many northerners whose hatred was directed not so much at slavery as at blacks and who gagged at the prospect of sharing the newly acquired western territories with African Americans. It also contained a large element of "Conscience Whigs," heavily influenced by the abolitionist crusade, who condemned slavery on moral grounds. The Free-Soilers trotted out wizened former president Van Buren and marched into the fray, shouting, "Free soil, free speech, free labor, and free men." These freedoms provided the bedrock on which the Free-Soilers built their party. They condemned slavery not so much for enslaving blacks but for destroying the chances of free white workers to rise up from wage-earning dependence to the esteemed status of self-employment. They argued that only with free soil in the West could a traditional American commitment to upward mobility continue to flourish. If forced to compete with slave labor, more costly wage labor would inevitably wither away, and with it the chance for the American worker to own

General Zachary Taylor (1784–1850) This Democratic campaign cartoon of 1848 charges that Taylor's reputation rested on Mexican skulls.

property. As the first widely inclusive party organized around the issue of slavery and confined to a single section, the Free Soil party foreshadowed the emergence of the Republican party six years later.

With the slavery issue officially shoved under the rug by the two major parties, the politicians on both sides opened fire on personalities. The amateurish Taylor had to be carefully watched, lest his indiscreet pen puncture the reputation won by his sword. His admirers puffed him up as a gallant knight and a Napoleon, and sloganized his remark, allegedly uttered during the Battle of Buena Vista, "General Taylor never surrenders." Taylor's wartime popularity pulled him through. He harvested 1,360,967 popular and 163 electoral votes, as compared with Cass's 1,222,342 popular and 127 electoral votes. Free-Soiler Van Buren, although winning no state, polled 291,263 ballots and apparently diverted enough Democratic strength from Cass in the crucial state of New York to throw the election to Taylor.

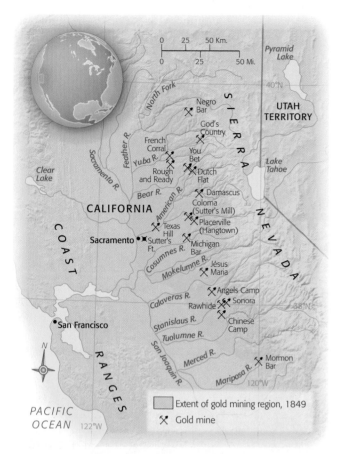

MAP 18.1 California Gold Rush Country Miners from all over the world swarmed over the rivers that drained the western slope of California's Sierra Nevada. Their nationalities and religions, their languages and their ways of life, are recorded in the colorful place names they left behind.

© Cengage Learning

⚒ "Californy Gold"

Tobacco-chewing President Taylor—with his stumpy legs, rough features, heavy jaw, black hair, ruddy complexion, and squinty gray eyes—was a military square peg in a political round hole. He would have been spared much turmoil if he could have continued to sit on the slavery lid. But the discovery of gold on the American River near Sutter's Mill, California, early in 1848, blew the cover off (see Map 18.1).

A horde of adventurers poured into the valleys of California. Singing "O Susannah!" and shouting "Gold! Gold! Gold!" they began tearing frantically at the yellow-graveled streams and hills. A fortunate few of the bearded miners "struck it rich" at the "diggings." But the luckless many, who netted blisters instead of nuggets, probably would have been money well ahead if they had stayed at home unaffected by "gold fever," which was often followed by more deadly fevers. The most reliable profits were made by those who mined

A married woman wrote from the California goldfields to her sister in New England in 1853,

> **❝**i tell you the woman are in great demand in this country no matter whether they are married or not you need not think strange if you see me coming home with some good looking man some of these times with a pocket full of rocks. . . . it is all the go here for Ladys to leave there Husbands two out of three do it there is a first rate Chance for a single woman she can have her choice of thousands i wish mother was here she could marry a rich man and not have to lift her hand to do her work.**❞**

the miners, notably by charging outrageous rates for laundry and other personal services. Some soiled clothing was even sent as far away as the Hawaiian Islands for washing. Many of the "forty-niners" who flopped in California kept chasing their dream of gold in even more distant places, notably Australia in 1851.

The **California gold rush** attracted tens of thousands of people to the future Golden State almost overnight, completely overwhelming the one-horse territorial government. A distressingly high proportion of the newcomers were lawless men, accompanied or followed by virtueless women. A contemporary song ran,

> *Oh what was your name in the States?*
> *Was it Thompson or Johnson or Bates?*
> *Did you murder your wife,*
> *And fly for your life?*
> *Say, what was your name in the States?*

An outburst of crime inevitably resulted from the presence of so many miscreants and outcasts. Robbery, claim jumping, and murder were commonplace, and such violence was only partly discouraged by rough vigilante justice. In San Francisco, from 1848 to 1856, there were scores of lawless killings but only three semilegal hangings.

A majority of Californians, as decent and law-abiding citizens needing protection, grappled earnestly with the problem of erecting an adequate state government. Privately encouraged by President Taylor, they

The idea that many ne'er-do-wells went west is found in the Journals *(January 1849) of Ralph Waldo Emerson (1803–1882):*

> **❝**If a man is going to California, he announces it with some hesitation; because it is a confession that he has failed at home.**❞**

Placer Miners in California Cheap but effective, placer mining consisted of literally "washing" the gold out of surface deposits. No deep excavation was required. This crew of male and female miners in California in 1852 was using a "long tom" sluice that washed relatively large quantities of ore.

drafted a constitution in 1849 that excluded slavery and then boldly applied to Congress for admission. California would thus bypass the usual territorial stage, thwarting southern congressmen seeking to block free soil. Southern politicians, alarmed by the Californians' "impertinent" stroke for freedom, arose in violent opposition. Would California prove to be the golden straw that broke the back of the Union?

✦ Sectional Balance and the Underground Railroad

The South of 1850 was relatively well-off. It then enjoyed, as it had from the beginning, more than its share of the nation's leadership. It had seated in the White House the war hero Zachary Taylor, a Virginia-born, slaveowning planter from Louisiana. It boasted a majority in the cabinet and on the Supreme Court. If outnumbered in the House, the South had equality in the Senate, where it could at least neutralize northern maneuvers. Its cotton fields were expanding, and cotton prices were profitably high. Few sane people, North or South, believed that slavery was seriously threatened where it already existed below the Mason-Dixon line. The fifteen slave states could easily veto any proposed constitutional amendment.

Yet the South was deeply worried, as it had been for several decades, by the ever-tipping political balance. There were then fifteen slave states and fifteen free states. The admission of California would destroy the delicate equilibrium in the Senate, perhaps forever. Potential slave territory under the American flag was running short, if it had not in fact disappeared.

A Stop on the Underground Railroad Escaping slaves could be hidden in this small upstairs room of Levi and Catharine Coffin's House in Newport, Indiana. The beds were moved in front of the door to hide its existence. The Levis were Quakers from North Carolina who, during twenty years in Newport, helped more than 2,000 fleeing slaves safely reach Canada—and freedom.

Harriet Tubman (on left) with Some of the Slaves She Helped to Free John Brown called her "General Tubman" for her effective work in helping slaves escape to Canada on the Underground Railroad. During the Civil War, she served as a Union spy behind Confederate lines. Herself illiterate, she worked after the war to bring education to the freed slaves in North Carolina.

Agitation had already developed in the territories of New Mexico and Utah for admission as nonslave states. The fate of California might well establish a precedent for the rest of the Mexican Cession territory—an area purchased largely with southern blood.

Texas nursed an additional grievance of its own. It claimed a huge area east of the Rio Grande and north to the forty-second parallel, embracing in part about

MAP 18.2 Texas and the Disputed Area Before the Compromise of 1850 © Cengage Learning

Disputed area

Present-day state boundaries

half the territory of present-day New Mexico (see Map 18.2). The federal government was proposing to detach this prize, while hot-blooded Texans were threatening to descend upon Santa Fe and seize what they regarded as rightfully theirs. The explosive quarrel foreshadowed shooting.

Many southerners were also angered by the nagging agitation in the North for the abolition of slavery in the District of Columbia. They looked with alarm on the prospect of a ten-mile-square oasis of free soil thrust between slaveholding Maryland and slaveholding Virginia.

Even more disagreeable to the South was the loss of runaway slaves, many of whom were assisted north by the **Underground Railroad**. This virtual freedom train consisted of an informal chain of "stations" (antislavery homes), through which scores of "passengers" (runaway slaves) were spirited by "conductors" (usually white and black abolitionists) from the slave states to the free-soil sanctuary of Canada.

The most amazing of these "conductors" was an illiterate runaway slave from Maryland, fearless Harriet Tubman. During nineteen forays into the South, she rescued more than three hundred slaves, including her aged parents, and deservedly earned the title "Moses." Lively imaginations later exaggerated the reach of the Underground Railroad and its "stationmasters," but its importance was undisputed.

By 1850 southerners were demanding a new and more stringent fugitive-slave law. The old one, passed by Congress in 1793, had proved inadequate to cope with runaways, especially since unfriendly state authorities failed to provide needed cooperation. Unlike cattle thieves, the abolitionists who ran the Underground

Railroad did not gain personally from their lawlessness. But to the slaveowners, the loss was infuriating, whatever the motives. The moral judgments of the abolitionists seemed, in some ways, more galling than outright theft. They reflected not only a holier-than-thou attitude but a refusal to obey the laws solemnly passed by Congress.

Estimates indicate that the South in 1850 was losing perhaps 1,000 runaways a year out of its total of some 4 million slaves. In fact, more blacks probably gained their freedom by self-purchase or voluntary emancipation than ever escaped. But the principle weighed heavily with the slavemasters. They rested their argument on the Constitution, which protected slavery, and on the laws of Congress, which provided for slave-catching. "Although the loss of property is felt," said a southern senator, "the loss of honor is felt still more."

✸ Twilight of the Senatorial Giants

Southern fears were such that Congress was confronted with catastrophe in 1850. Free-soil California was banging on the door for admission. "Fire-eaters" in the South were voicing ominous threats of secession. In October 1849 southerners had announced their intention to convene the following year in Nashville, Tennessee, to consider withdrawing from the Union. The failure of Congress to act could easily mean the failure of the United States as a country. The crisis brought into the congressional forum the most distinguished assemblage of statesmen since the Constitutional Convention of 1787—the Old Guard of the dying generation and the young gladiators of the new. That "immortal trio"—Clay, Calhoun, and Webster—appeared together for the last time on the public stage.

Henry Clay, now seventy-three years of age, played a crucial role. The "Great Compromiser" had come to the Senate from Kentucky to reprise the role he had played twice before, in the Missouri and nullification crises. The once-glamorous statesman—though disillusioned, enfeebled, and racked by a cruel cough—was still eloquent, conciliatory, and captivating. He proposed and skillfully defended a series of compromises. He was ably seconded by thirty-seven-year-old Senator Stephen A. Douglas of Illinois, the "Little Giant" (five feet four inches), whose role was less spectacular but even more important. Clay urged with all his persuasiveness that the North and South both make concessions and that the North partially yield by enacting a more feasible fugitive-slave law.

Senator John C. Calhoun, the "Great Nullifier," then sixty-eight and dying of tuberculosis, championed the South in his last formal speech. Too weak to deliver it himself, he sat bundled up in the Senate chamber, his eyes glowing within a stern face, while a younger colleague read his fateful words. "I have, Senators, believed from the first that the agitation on the subject of slavery would, if not prevented by some timely and effective measure, end in disunion." Although approving the purpose of Clay's proposed concessions, Calhoun rejected them as not providing adequate safeguards for southern rights. His impassioned plea was to leave slavery alone, return runaway slaves, give the South its rights as a minority, and restore the political balance. He had in view, as was later revealed, an utterly unworkable scheme of electing two presidents, one from the North and one from the South, each wielding a veto.

Calhoun died in 1850, before the debate was over, murmuring the sad words, "The South! The South! God knows what will become of her!" Appreciative fellow citizens in Charleston erected to his memory an imposing monument, which bore the inscription "Truth, Justice, and the Constitution." Calhoun had labored to preserve the Union and had taken his stand on the Constitution, but his proposals in their behalf almost undid both.

Daniel Webster next took the Senate spotlight to uphold Clay's compromise measures in his last great speech, a three-hour effort. Now sixty-eight years old and suffering from a liver complaint aggravated by high living, he had lost some of the fire in his magnificent voice. Speaking deliberately and before overflowing galleries, he urged all reasonable concessions to the South, including a new fugitive-slave law with teeth.

As for slavery in the territories, asked Webster, why legislate on the subject? To do so was an act of sacrilege, for Almighty God had already passed the Wilmot Proviso. The good Lord had decreed—through climate, topography, and geography—that a plantation economy, and hence a slave economy, could not profitably exist in the Mexican Cession territory.* Webster sanely concluded that compromise, concession, and sweet reasonableness would provide the only solutions. "Let us not be pygmies," he pleaded, "in a case that calls for men."

If measured by its immediate effects, Webster's famed **Seventh of March speech** of 1850 was his finest. It helped turn the tide in the North toward compromise. The clamor for printed copies became so great that Webster mailed out more than 100,000, remarking that 200,000 would not satisfy the demand. His tremendous effort visibly strengthened Union sentiment. It was especially pleasing to the banking and commercial centers of the North, which stood to lose millions of dollars by secession. One prominent Washington banker canceled two notes of Webster's totaling $5,000

---

*Webster was wrong here; within one hundred years, California had become one of the great cotton-producing states of the Union.

Ralph Waldo Emerson, the philosopher and moderate abolitionist, was outraged by Webster's support of concessions to the South in the Fugitive Slave Act. In February 1851 he wrote in his journal,

❝I opened a paper to-day in which he [Webster] pounds on the old strings [of liberty] in a letter to the Washington Birthday feasters at New York. 'Liberty! liberty!' Pho! Let Mr. Webster, for decency's sake, shut his lips once and forever on this word. The word *liberty* in the mouth of Mr. Webster sounds like the word *love* in the mouth of a courtesan.**❞**

and sent him a personal check for $1,000 and a message of congratulations.

But the Free-Soilers and abolitionists, who had assumed Webster was one of them, upbraided him as a traitor, worthy of bracketing with Benedict Arnold. The poet John Greenleaf Whittier lamented,

> *So fallen! so lost! the light withdrawn*
> *Which once he wore!*
> *The glory from his gray hairs gone*
> *For evermore!*

These reproaches were most unfair. Webster had long regarded slavery as evil but disunion as worse.

✦ Deadlock and Danger on Capitol Hill

The stormy congressional debate of 1850 was not finished, for the Young Guard from the North were yet to have their say. This was the group of newer leaders who, unlike the aging Old Guard, had not grown up with the Union. They were more interested in purging and purifying it than in patching and preserving it.

William H. Seward, the wiry and husky-throated freshman senator from New York, was the able spokesman for many of the younger northern radicals. A strong antislaveryite, he came out unequivocally against concession. He seemed not to realize that compromise had brought the Union together and that when the sections could no longer compromise, they would have to part company.

Seward argued earnestly that Christian legislators must obey God's moral law as well as man's mundane law. He therefore appealed, with reference to excluding slavery in the territories, to an even "higher law" than the Constitution. This alarming phrase, wrenched from its context, may have cost him the presidential nomination and the presidency in 1860.

As the great debate in Congress ran its heated course, deadlock seemed certain. Blunt old President Taylor, who had allegedly fallen under the influence of men like "Higher Law" Seward, seemed bent on vetoing any compromise passed by Congress. His military ire was aroused by the threats of Texas to seize Santa Fe. He appeared to be doggedly determined to "Jacksonize" the dissenters, if need be, by leading an army against the Texans in person and hanging all "damned traitors." If troops had begun to march, the South probably would have rallied to the defense of Texas, and the Civil War might have erupted in 1850.

✦ Breaking the Congressional Logjam

At the height of the controversy in 1850, President Taylor unknowingly helped the cause of concession by dying suddenly, probably of an acute intestinal disorder. Portly, round-faced Vice President Millard Fillmore, a colorless and conciliatory New York lawyer-politician, took over the reins. As presiding officer of the Senate, he had been impressed with the arguments for conciliation, and he gladly signed the series of compromise measures that passed Congress after seven long months of stormy debate. The balancing of interests in the **Compromise of 1850** was delicate in the extreme (see Table 18.1).

The struggle to get these measures accepted by the country was hardly less heated than in Congress. In the northern states, "Union savers" like Senators Clay, Webster, and Douglas orated on behalf of the compromise. The ailing Clay himself delivered more than seventy

TABLE 18.1 Compromise of 1850	
Concessions to the North	**Concessions to the South**
California admitted as a free state	The remainder of the Mexican Cession area to be formed into the territories of New Mexico and Utah, without restriction on slavery, hence open to popular sovereignty
Territory disputed by Texas and New Mexico to be surrendered to New Mexico	Texas to receive $10 million from the federal government as compensation
Abolition of the slave trade (but not slavery) in the District of Columbia	A more stringent fugitive-slave law going beyond that of 1793

speeches, as a powerful sentiment for acceptance gradually crystallized in the North. It was strengthened by a growing spirit of goodwill, which sprang partly from a feeling of relief and partly from an upsurge of prosperity enriched by California gold.

But the "fire-eaters" of the South were still violently opposed to concessions. One extreme South Carolina newspaper avowed that it loathed the Union and hated the North as much as it did Hell itself. A movement in the South to boycott northern goods gained some headway, but in the end the southern Unionists, assisted by the warm glow of prosperity, prevailed.

In June 1850 the assemblage of southern extremists met in Nashville, ironically near the burial place of Andrew Jackson. The delegates not only took a strong position in favor of slavery but condemned the compromise measures then being hammered out in Congress. Meeting again in November after the bills had passed, the convention proved to be a dud. By that time southern opinion had reluctantly accepted the verdict of Congress.

Like the calm after a storm, a second Era of Good Feelings dawned. Disquieting talk of secession subsided. Peace-loving people, both North and South, were determined that the compromises should be a "finality" and that the explosive issue of slavery should be buried. But this placid period proved all too brief.

✵ Balancing the Compromise Scales

Who got the better deal in the Compromise of 1850? The answer is clearly the North (see Map 18.3). California, as a free state, tipped the Senate balance permanently against the South. The territories of New Mexico and Utah were open to slavery on the basis of popular sovereignty. But the iron law of nature—the "highest law" of all—had loaded the dice in favor of free soil. Southerners urgently needed more slave territory to restore the "sacred balance." If they could not carve new states out of the recent conquests from Mexico, where else might they get them? The Caribbean was one answer.

Even the apparent gains of the South rang hollow. Disgruntled Texas was to be paid $10 million toward discharging its indebtedness, but in the long run this was a modest sum. The immense area in dispute had been torn from the side of slaveholding Texas and was almost certain to be free. The South had halted the drive toward abolition in the District of Columbia, at least temporarily, by permitting the outlawing of the slave *trade* in the federal district. But even this move was an entering wedge toward complete emancipation in the nation's capital.

Most alarming of all, the drastic new **Fugitive Slave Law** of 1850—"the Bloodhound Bill"—stirred

Granger Collection

Henry Clay Proposing the Compromise of 1850 This engraving captures one of the most dramatic moments in the history of the United States Senate. Vice President Millard Fillmore presides, while on the floor sit several of the "Senatorial Giants" of the era, including Daniel Webster, Stephen A. Douglas, and John C. Calhoun.

up a storm of opposition in the North. The fleeing slaves could not testify in their own behalf, and they were denied a jury trial. These harsh practices, some citizens feared, threatened to create dangerous precedents for white Americans. The federal commissioner who handled the case of a fugitive would receive five dollars if the runaway were freed and ten dollars if not—an arrangement that strongly resembled a bribe. Freedom-loving northerners who aided the slave to escape were liable to heavy fines and jail sentences. They might even be ordered to join the slave-catchers, and this possibility rubbed salt into old sores.

So abhorrent was this "Man-Stealing Law" that it touched off an explosive chain reaction in the North. Many shocked moderates, hitherto passive, were driven into the swelling ranks of the antislaveryites. When a runaway slave from Virginia was captured in Boston in 1854, he had to be removed from the city under heavy federal guard through streets lined with sullen Yankees and shadowed by black-draped buildings festooned with flags flying upside down. One prominent Bostonian who witnessed this grim spectacle wrote that "we went to bed one night old-fashioned, conservative, Compromise Union Whigs and waked up stark mad Abolitionists."

The Underground Railroad stepped up its timetable, and infuriated northern mobs rescued slaves from their pursuers. Massachusetts, in a move toward nullification suggestive of South Carolina in 1832, made it a penal offense for any state official to enforce the new federal statute. Other states passed "personal liberty laws," which denied local jails to federal officials and otherwise hampered enforcement. The abolitionists rent the heavens with their protests against the man-stealing statute. A meeting presided over by William Lloyd Garrison in 1851 declared, "We execrate it, we spit upon it, we trample it under our feet."

Beyond question, the Fugitive Slave Law was an appalling blunder on the part of the South. No single irritant of the 1850s was more persistently galling to both sides, and none did more to awaken in the North a spirit of antagonism against the South. The southerners in turn were embittered because the northerners would not in good faith execute the law—the one real and immediate southern "gain" from the Great Compromise. Slave-catchers, with some success, redoubled their efforts.

Should the shooting showdown have come in 1850? From the standpoint of the secessionists, yes; from the standpoint of the Unionists, no. Time was fighting for

MAP 18.3 Slavery After the Compromise of 1850 Regarding the Fugitive Slave Law provisions of the Compromise of 1850, Ralph Waldo Emerson declared in May 1851 at Concord, Massachusetts, "The act of Congress . . . is a law which every one of you will break on the earliest occasion—a law which no man can obey, or abet the obeying, without loss of self-respect and forfeiture of the name of gentleman." Privately he wrote in his journal, "This filthy enactment was made in the nineteenth century, by people who could read and write. I will not obey it, by God." © Cengage Learning

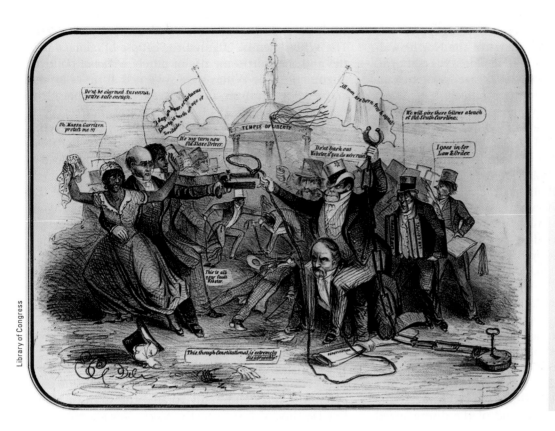

Library of Congress

Protesting the Fugitive Slave Law, 1850 The cartoonist makes bitter sport of the hated law and heaps scorn on Daniel Webster, on his hands and knees at the right, who voted for the law as part of the Compromise of 1850. The outspoken abolitionist William Lloyd Garrison is depicted much more favorably on the left.

the North. With every passing decade, this huge section was forging further ahead in population and wealth—in crops, factories, foundries, ships, and railroads.

Delay also added immensely to the moral strength of the North—to its will to fight for the Union. In 1850 countless thousands of northern moderates were unwilling to pin the South to the rest of the nation with bayonets. But the inflammatory events of the 1850s did much to bolster the Yankee will to resist secession, whatever the cost. This one feverish decade gave the North time to accumulate the material and moral strength that provided the margin of victory. Thus the Compromise of 1850, from one point of view, won the Civil War for the Union (see Map 18.4).

✸ Defeat and Doom for the Whigs

Meeting in Baltimore, the Democratic nominating convention of 1852 startled the nation. Hopelessly deadlocked, it finally stampeded to the second "dark-horse" candidate in American history, an unrenowned lawyer-politician, Franklin Pierce, from the hills of New Hampshire. The Whigs tried to jeer him back into obscurity with the cry "Who is Frank Pierce?" Democrats replied, "The Young Hickory of the Granite Hills."

Pierce was a weak and indecisive figure. Youngish, handsome, militarily erect, smiling, and convivial, he had served without real distinction in the Mexican War. As a result of a painful groin injury that caused

him to fall off a horse, he was known as the "Fainting General," though scandalmongers pointed to a fondness for alcohol. But he was enemyless because he had been inconspicuous, and as a prosouthern northerner, he was acceptable to the slavery wing of the Democratic party. His platform revived the Democrats' commitment to territorial expansion as pursued by President Polk and emphatically endorsed the Compromise of 1850, Fugitive Slave Law and all.

The Whigs, also convening in Baltimore, missed a splendid opportunity to capitalize on their record in statecraft. Able to boast of a praiseworthy achievement in the Compromise of 1850, they might logically have nominated President Fillmore or Senator Webster, both of whom were associated with it. But having won in the past only with military heroes, they turned to another, "Old Fuss and Feathers" Winfield Scott, perhaps the ablest American general of his generation. Although he was a huge and impressive figure, his manner bordered on haughtiness. His personality not only repelled the masses but eclipsed his genuinely statesmanlike achievements. The Whig platform praised the Compromise of 1850 as a lasting arrangement, though less enthusiastically than the Democrats.

With slavery and sectionalism to some extent soft-pedaled, the campaign again degenerated into a dull and childish attack on personalities. Democrats ridiculed Scott's pomposity; Whigs charged that Pierce was the hero of "many a well-fought *bottle*." Democrats cried exultantly, "We Polked 'em in '44; we'll Pierce 'em in '52."

Luckily for the Democrats, the Whig party was hopelessly split. Antislavery Whigs of the North swallowed Scott as their nominee but deplored his platform, which endorsed the hated Fugitive Slave Law. The current phrase ran, "We accept the candidate but spit on the platform." Southern Whigs, who doubted Scott's loyalty to the Compromise of 1850 and especially the Fugitive Slave Law, accepted the platform but spat on the candidate. More than five thousand Georgia Whigs— "finality men"—voted in vain for Webster, although he had died nearly two weeks before the election.

General Scott, victorious on the battlefield, met defeat at the ballot box. His friends remarked whimsically that he was not used to "running." Actually, he was stabbed in the back by his fellow Whigs, notably in the South. In addition, Free Soil party candidate John P. Hale, senator from New Hampshire, siphoned off northern Whig votes that might have gone to Scott. Hale walked away with a respectable 5 percent of the popular vote. The pliant Pierce won in a landslide, 254 electoral votes to 42, although the popular count was closer, 1,601,117 to 1,385,453.

The election of 1852 was fraught with frightening significance, though it may have seemed tame at the time. It marked the effective end of the disorganized Whig party and, within a few years, its complete death. The Whigs' demise augured the eclipse of *national* parties and the worrisome rise of purely *sectional* political alignments. The Whigs were governed at times by the crassest opportunism, and they won only two presidential elections (1840, 1848) in their colorful career, both with war heroes. They finally choked to death trying to swallow the distasteful Fugitive Slave Law. But their great contribution—and a noteworthy one indeed— was to help uphold the ideal of the Union through their electoral strength in the South and through the eloquence of leaders like Henry Clay and Daniel Webster. Both of these statesmen, by unhappy coincidence, died during the 1852 campaign. But the good they had done lived after them and contributed powerfully to the eventual preservation of a *united* United States.

✴ Expansionist Stirrings South of the Border

The intoxicating victory in the Mexican War, coupled with the discovery of gold in California just nine days before the war's end, reinvigorated the spirit of Manifest Destiny. The rush to the Sierra Nevada goldfields

MAP 18.4 The Legal Status of Slavery, from the Revolution to the Civil War © Cengage Learning

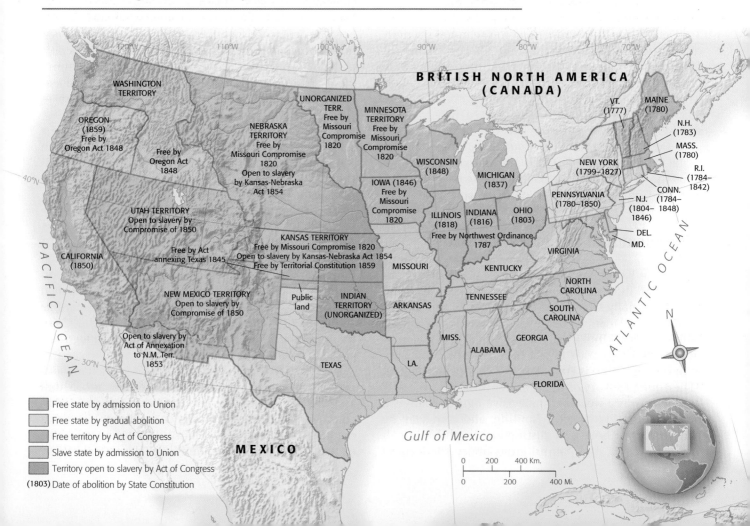

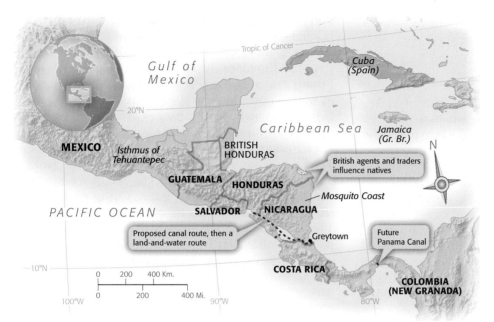

MAP 18.5 Central America, ca. 1850, Showing British Possessions and Proposed Canal Routes Until President Theodore Roosevelt swung into action with his big stick in 1903, a Nicaraguan canal, closer to the United States, was generally judged more desirable than a canal across Panama. © Cengage Learning

aroused particular concerns about the fate of Central America. Since the days of Balboa, this narrow neck of land had stimulated dreams of a continuous Atlantic-to-Pacific transportation route that would effectively sever the two American continents (see Map 18.5). Whoever controlled that route would hold imperial sway over all maritime nations, especially the United States.

Increasing British encroachment into the area—including the British seizure of the port of San Juan del Norte (renamed Greytown) on Nicaragua's "Mosquito Coast"—drove the governments of both the United States and New Granada (later Colombia) to conclude an important treaty in 1848. It guaranteed the American right of transit across the isthmus in return for Washington's pledge to maintain the "perfect neutrality" of the route so that the "free transit of traffic might not be interrupted." The agreement later provided a fig leaf of legal cover for Theodore Roosevelt's assertion of American control of the Panama Canal Zone in 1903. It also led to the construction of the first "transcontinental" railroad. Completed in 1855 at a cost of thousands of lives lost to pestilence and accident, it ran forty-eight miles from coast to coast through the green hell of the Panamanian jungle. A full-blown confrontation with Britain was avoided by the **Clayton-Bulwer Treaty** in 1850, which stipulated that neither America nor Britain would fortify or seek exclusive control over any future isthmian waterway (later rescinded by the Hay-Pauncefote Treaty of 1901; see p. 628).

Southern "slavocrats" cast especially covetous eyes southward in the 1850s. They lusted for new slave territory after the Compromise of 1850 seemingly closed most of the Mexican Cession to the "peculiar institution." In 1856 a Texan proposed a toast that was drunk with gusto: "To the Southern republic bounded on the north by the Mason and Dixon line and on the South by the Isthmus of Tehuantepec [southern Mexico], including Cuba and all other lands on our Southern shore." Nicaragua beckoned beguilingly. A brazen American adventurer, William Walker, tried repeatedly to grab control of this Central American country. (He had earlier tried and failed to seize Baja California from Mexico and turn it into a slave state.) Backed by an armed force recruited largely in the South, he installed himself as president in July 1856 and promptly legalized slavery. One southern newspaper proclaimed to the planter aristocracy that Walker—the "gray-eyed man of destiny"—"now offers Nicaragua to you and your slaves, at a time when you have not a friend on the face of the earth." But a coalition of Central American nations formed an alliance to overthrow him. President Pierce withdrew diplomatic recognition, and the gray-eyed man's destiny was to crumple before a Honduran firing squad in 1860.

Sugar-rich Cuba, lying just off the nation's southern doorstep, was also an enticing prospect for annexation. This remnant of Spain's once-mighty New World empire already held a large population of enslaved blacks, and it might be carved into several states, restoring the political balance in the Senate. President Polk had considered offering Spain $100 million for Cuba, but the proud Spaniards replied that they would sooner see the island sunk into the sea than in the hands of the hated Yankees.

Rebuffed as buyers, some southern adventurers now undertook to shake the tree of Manifest Destiny. During 1850–1851 two "filibustering" (from the Spanish *filibustero*, meaning "freebooter" or "pirate") expeditions, each numbering several hundred armed men, descended upon Cuba. Both feeble efforts were repelled,

The first platform of the newly born (antislavery) Republican party in 1856 lashed out at the Ostend Manifesto, with its transparent suggestion that Cuba be seized. The plank read,

"Resolved, That the highwayman's plea, that 'might makes right,' embodied in the Ostend Circular, was in every respect unworthy of American diplomacy, and would bring shame and dishonor upon any Government or people that gave it their sanction.**"**

and the last one ended in tragedy when the leader and fifty followers—some of them from the "best families" of the South—were summarily shot or strangled. So outraged were the southerners that an angry mob sacked Spain's consulate in New Orleans.

Spanish officials in Cuba rashly forced a showdown in 1854, when they seized the American steamer *Black Warrior* on a technicality. Now was the time for President Pierce, dominated as he was by the South, to provoke a war with Spain and seize Cuba. The major powers of Europe—England, France, and Russia—were about to become bogged down in the Crimean War and hence were unable to aid Spain.

An incredible cloak-and-dagger episode followed. The secretary of state instructed the American ministers in Spain, England, and France to prepare confidential recommendations for the acquisition of Cuba. Meeting initially at Ostend, Belgium, the three envoys drew up a top-secret dispatch, soon known as the **Ostend Manifesto**. This startling document urged that the administration offer $120 million for Cuba. If Spain refused, and if its continued ownership endangered American interests, the United States would "be justified in wresting" the island from the Spanish.

The secret Ostend Manifesto quickly leaked out. Northern free-soilers, already angered by the Fugitive Slave Law and other gains for slavery, rose up in wrath against the "manifesto of brigands." The shackled black hands of Harriet Beecher Stowe's Uncle Tom, whose plight had already stung the conscience of the North, now held the South back. The red-faced Pierce administration hurriedly dropped its reckless schemes for Cuba. The slavery issue thus checked territorial expansion in the 1850s.

✴ The Allure of Asia

The acquisition of California and Oregon had made the United States a Pacific power—or would-be power. How could Americans now tap more deeply the supposedly rich markets of Asia? Rivalry with the British

lion once again played a role. Britain had recently humbled China in the **Opium War**, fought to secure the right of British traders to peddle opium in the Celestial Kingdom. At the war's conclusion in 1842, Britain gained free access to five so-called treaty ports, as well as outright control of the island of Hong Kong (where it remained for another century and a half). Prodded by Boston merchants fearful of seeing Britain horn in on their lucrative trade with China, President Tyler thereupon dispatched Caleb Cushing, a dashing Massachusetts lawyer-scholar, to secure comparable concessions for the United States. Cushing's four warships arrived at Macao, in southern China, in early 1844, bearing gifts that included a weathervane and a pair of six-shooters.

Impressed by Cushing's charm and largesse—and also eager for a counterweight to the meddlesome British—silk-gowned Chinese diplomats signed the **Treaty of Wanghia**, the first formal diplomatic agreement between the United States and China, on July 3, 1844. Cushing was interested in commerce, not colonies, and he secured some vital rights and privileges from the Chinese. "Most favored nation" status afforded the United States any and all trading terms accorded to other powers. "Extraterritoriality" provided for trying Americans accused of crimes in China before American officials, not in Chinese courts. (Cushing was prompted to seek this particular immunity by the memory of a seaman on a U.S. vessel who had been strangled to death by Chinese authorities for what was apparently the accidental drowning of a Chinese woman.) American trade with China flourished thanks to Cushing's treaty, though it never reached the proportions his backers had dreamed of. More immediately important was the opportunity it opened for American missionaries, thousands of whom soon flooded prayerfully through the treaty ports to convert the "heathen Chinese." Fatefully, America had now aligned itself with the Western powers that chronically menaced China's cultural integrity. All of them would one day reap a bitter harvest of resentment.

Success in China soon inspired a still more consequential mission to pry open the bamboo gates of Japan. After some disagreeable experiences with the European world, Japan, at about the same time Jamestown was settled, withdrew into an almost airtight cocoon of isolationism and remained there for more than two centuries. The long-ruling warrior dynasty known as the Tokugawa Shogunate was so protective of Japan's insularity that it prohibited shipwrecked foreign sailors from leaving and refused to readmit Japanese sailors who had been washed up on foreign shores. Meanwhile, industrial and democratic revolutions were convulsing the Western world, while Japan remained placidly secluded. By 1853 Japan was ready to emerge from its self-imposed quarantine.

In 1852 President Millard Fillmore dispatched to Japan a fleet of warships commanded by Commodore Matthew C. Perry. The brother of the hero of the Battle of Lake Erie in 1813, Perry prepared diligently for his mission, voraciously reading about Japan, querying whalers about Pacific Ocean currents, and collecting specimens of American technology with which to impress the Japanese. His four awesome, smoke-belching "black ships" steamed into Edo (later Tokyo) Bay on July 8, 1853, inciting near-panic among the shocked Japanese. After tense negotiations, during which Perry threatened to blast his way ashore if necessary, Perry stepped onto the beach, preceded by two conspicuously tall African American flag bearers. From elaborately carved gold-trimmed boxes, Perry produced silk-bound letters requesting free trade and friendly relations. He handed them to the wary Japanese delegation and then tactfully withdrew, promising to return the following year to receive the Japanese reply.

True to his word, Perry returned in February 1854 with an even larger force of seven men-of-war. Once again he combined bluster and grace, plying the Japanese with gifts, including a miniature steam locomotive and 350 feet of track. With this display of pomp and bravado, he persuaded the Japanese to sign the landmark **Treaty of Kanagawa** on March 31, 1854. It provided for proper treatment of shipwrecked sailors, American coaling rights in Japan, and the establishment of consular relations. Perry had inserted only a commercial toe in the door, but he had cracked Japan's two-century shell of isolation wide-open. Within little more than a decade, the "Meiji Restoration" would end the era of the Shogunate and propel the Land of the Rising Sun headlong into the modern world—and an eventual epochal military clash with the United States.

✦ Pacific Railroad Promoters and the Gadsden Purchase

Acute transportation problems were another legacy of the Mexican War. The newly acquired prizes of California and Oregon might just as well have been islands some eight thousand miles west of the nation's capital. The sea routes to and from the Isthmus of Panama, to say nothing of those around South America, were too long. Covered-wagon travel past bleaching animal bones was possible, but slow and dangerous. A popular song recalled,

> *They swam the wide rivers and crossed the tall peaks,*
> *And camped on the prairie for weeks upon weeks.*
> *Starvation and cholera and hard work and slaughter,*
> *They reached California spite of hell and high water.*

Feasible land transportation was imperative—or the newly won possessions on the Pacific Coast might break away. Camels were even proposed as the answer. Several score of these temperamental beasts—"ships of the desert"—were imported from the Near East, but mule-driving Americans did not adjust to them. A transcontinental railroad was clearly the only real solution to the problem.

Railroad promoters, both North and South, had projected many drawing-board routes to the Pacific

Commodore Matthew Perry in Japan, 1853 Among Perry's gifts to the Japanese was a miniature railway, complete with engine, cars, and track, which made a vivid impression on the Japanese artist who created this work.

MAP 18.6 The Gadsden Purchase, 1853 © Cengage Learning

Coast. But the estimated cost in all cases was so great that for many years there could obviously be only one line. Should its terminus be in the North or in the South? The favored section would reap rich rewards in wealth, population, and influence. The South, losing the economic race with the North, was eager to extend a railroad through adjacent southwestern territory all the way to California.

Another chunk of Mexico now seemed desirable, because the campaigns of the recent war had shown that the best railway route ran slightly south of the Mexican border. Secretary of War Jefferson Davis, a Mississippian, arranged to have James Gadsden, a prominent South Carolina railroad man, appointed minister to Mexico. Finding Santa Anna in power for the sixth and last time, and as usual in need of money, Gadsden made gratifying headway. He negotiated a treaty in 1853, which ceded to the United States the **Gadsden Purchase** for $10 million (see Map 18.6). The transaction aroused much criticism among northerners, who objected to paying a huge sum for a cactus-strewn desert nearly the size of Gadsden's South Carolina. Undeterred, the Senate approved the pact, in the process shortsightedly eliminating a window on the Sea of Cortez.

No doubt the Gadsden Purchase enabled the South to claim the coveted railroad with even greater insistence. A southern track would be easier to build because the mountains were less high and because the route, unlike the proposed northern lines, would not pass through unorganized territory. Texas was already a state at this point, and New Mexico (with the Gadsden Purchase added) was a formally organized territory, with federal troops available to provide protection against marauding tribes of Indians. Any northern or central railroad line would have to be thrust through the unorganized territory of Nebraska, where the buffalo and Indians roamed.

Northern railroad boosters quickly replied that if organized territory were the test, then Nebraska should be organized. Such a move was not premature, because thousands of land-hungry pioneers were already poised on the Nebraska border. But all schemes proposed in Congress for organizing the territory were greeted with apathy or hostility by many southerners. Why should the South help create new free-soil states and thus cut its own throat by facilitating a northern railroad?

Douglas's Kansas-Nebraska Scheme

At this point in 1854, Senator Stephen A. Douglas of Illinois delivered a counterstroke to offset the Gadsden thrust for southern expansion westward. A squat, bull-necked, and heavy-chested figure, the "Little Giant" radiated the energy and breezy optimism of the self-made man. An ardent booster for the West, he longed to break the North-South deadlock over westward expansion and stretch a line of settlements across the continent. He had also invested heavily in Chicago real estate and in railway stock and was eager to have the Windy City become the eastern terminus of the proposed Pacific railroad. He would thus endear himself to the voters of Illinois, benefit his section, and enrich his own purse.

A veritable "steam engine in breeches," Douglas threw himself behind a legislative scheme that would enlist the support of a reluctant South. The proposed Territory of Nebraska would be sliced into two territories, Kansas and Nebraska (see Map 18.7). Their status regarding slavery would be settled by popular sovereignty—a democratic concept to which Douglas and his western constituents were deeply attached. Kansas, which lay due west of slaveholding Missouri, would presumably choose to become a slave state. But Nebraska, lying west of free-soil Iowa, would presumably become a free state.

Douglas's Kansas-Nebraska scheme flatly contradicted the Missouri Compromise of 1820, which had forbidden slavery in the proposed Nebraska Territory north of the sacred 36° 30′ line. The only way to open the region to popular sovereignty was to repeal the ancient compact outright. This bold step Douglas was now prepared to take, even at the risk of shattering the uneasy truce patched together by the Compromise of 1850.

Many southerners, who had not conceived of Kansas as slave soil, rose to the bait. Here was a chance to gain one more slave state. The pliable President Pierce, under the thumb of southern advisers, threw his full weight behind the Kansas-Nebraska Bill.

But the Missouri Compromise, then thirty-four years old, could not be brushed aside lightly. Whatever Congress passes it can repeal, but by this time the North had come to regard the sectional pact as almost as sacred as the Constitution itself. Free-soil members of Congress struck back with a vengeance. They met their match in the violently gesticulating Douglas, who was the ablest rough-and-tumble debater of his generation. Employing twisted logic and oratorical

Library of Congress

Douglas Hatches a Slavery Problem   Note the already hatched Missouri Compromise, Squatter Sovereignty, and Filibuster (in Cuba), and the about-to-hatch Free Kansas and Dred Scott decision. So bitter was the outcry against Douglas at the time of the Kansas-Nebraska controversy that he claimed with exaggeration that he could have traveled from Boston to Chicago at night by the light from his burning effigies.

MAP 18.7 Kansas and Nebraska, 1854   The future Union Pacific Railroad (completed in 1869) is shown. Note the Missouri Compromise line of 36° 30′ (1820). © Cengage Learning

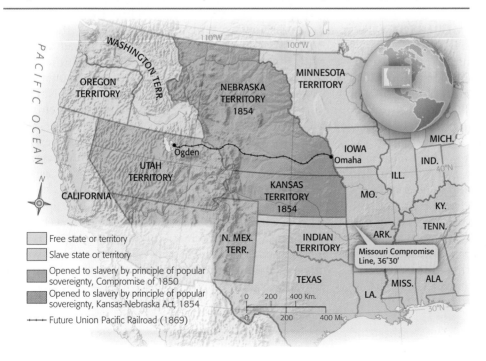

Free state or territory

Slave state or territory

Opened to slavery by principle of popular sovereignty, Compromise of 1850

Opened to slavery by principle of popular sovereignty, Kansas-Nebraska Act, 1854

Future Union Pacific Railroad (1869)

fireworks, he rammed the bill through Congress, with strong support from many southerners. So heated were political passions that bloodshed was barely averted. Some members carried a concealed revolver or a bowie knife—or both.

Douglas's motives in prodding anew the snarling dog of slavery have long puzzled historians. His personal interests have already been mentioned. In addition, his foes accused him of angling for the presidency in 1856. Yet his admirers have argued plausibly in his defense that if he had not championed the ill-omened bill, someone else would have.

The truth seems to be that Douglas acted somewhat impulsively and recklessly. His heart did not bleed over the issue of slavery, and he declared repeatedly that he did not care whether it was voted up or down in the territories. What he failed to perceive was that hundreds of thousands of his fellow citizens in the North *did* feel deeply on this moral issue. They regarded the repeal of the Missouri Compromise as an intolerable breach of faith, and they would henceforth resist to the last trench all future southern demands for slave territory. As Abraham Lincoln said, the North wanted to give to pioneers in the West "a clean bed, with no snakes in it."

Genuine leaders, like skillful chess players, must foresee the possible effects of their moves. Douglas predicted a "hell of a storm," but he grossly underestimated its proportions. His critics in the North, branding him a "Judas" and a "traitor," greeted his name with frenzied boos, hisses, and "three groans for Doug." But he still enjoyed a high degree of popularity among his following in the Democratic party, especially in Illinois, a stronghold of popular sovereignty.

✵ Congress Legislates a Civil War

The **Kansas-Nebraska Act**—a curtain-raiser to a terrible drama—was one of the most momentous measures ever to pass Congress. By one way of reckoning, it greased the slippery slope to Civil War.

Antislavery northerners were angered by what they condemned as an act of bad faith by the "Nebrascals" and their "Nebrascality." All future compromise with the South would be immeasurably more difficult, and without compromise there was bound to be conflict.

Henceforth the Fugitive Slave Law of 1850, previously enforced in the North only halfheartedly, was a dead letter. The Kansas-Nebraska Act wrecked two compromises: that of 1820, which it repealed specifically, and that of 1850, which northern opinion repealed indirectly. Emerson wrote, "The Fugitive [Slave] Law

> *Massachusetts senator Charles Sumner (1811–1874) described the Kansas-Nebraska Bill as "at once the worst and the best Bill on which Congress ever acted." It was the worst because it represented a victory for the slave power in the short run. But it was the best, he said prophetically, because it*
>
> **❝** annuls all past compromises with slavery, and makes all future compromises impossible. Thus it puts freedom and slavery face to face, and bids them grapple. Who can doubt the result?**❞**

did much to unglue the eyes of men, and now the Nebraska Bill leaves us staring." Northern abolitionists and southern "fire-eaters" alike saw less and less they could live with. The growing legion of antislaveryites gained numerous recruits, who resented the grasping move by the "slavocracy" for Kansas. The southerners, in turn, became inflamed when the free-soilers tried to control Kansas, contrary to the presumed "deal."

The proud Democrats—a party now over half a century old—were shattered by the Kansas-Nebraska Act. They did elect a president in 1856, but he was the last one they were to boost into the White House for twenty-eight long years.

Undoubtedly the most durable offspring of the Kansas-Nebraska blunder was the new Republican party. It sprang up spontaneously in the Middle West, notably in Wisconsin and Michigan, as a mighty moral protest against the gains of slavery. Gathering together dissatisfied elements, it soon included disgruntled Whigs (among them Abraham Lincoln), Democrats, Free-Soilers, Know-Nothings, and other foes of the Kansas-Nebraska Act. The hodgepodge party spread eastward with the swiftness of a prairie fire and with the zeal of a religious crusade. Unheard-of and unheralded at the beginning of 1854, when the nativist Know-Nothings instead seemed to be the rising party of the North, it elected a Republican Speaker of the House of Representatives within two years. Never really a third-party movement, its wide wingspan gave it flight overnight as the second major political party—and a purely sectional one at that.

At long last the dreaded sectional rift had appeared. The new Republican party would not be allowed south of the Mason-Dixon line. Countless southerners subscribed wholeheartedly to the sentiment that it was "a nigger stealing, stinking, putrid, abolition party." The Union was in dire peril.

Chapter Review

KEY TERMS

popular sovereignty (378)

Free Soil party (379)

California gold rush (380)

Underground Railroad (382)

Seventh of March
   speech (383)

Compromise of 1850 (384)

Fugitive Slave Law (385)

Clayton-Bulwer Treaty (389)

Ostend Manifesto (390)

Opium War (390)

Wanghia, Treaty of (390)

Kanagawa, Treaty of (391)

Gadsden Purchase (392)

Kansas-Nebraska Act (394)

PEOPLE TO KNOW

Lewis Cass

Zachary Taylor

Harriet Tubman

Millard Fillmore

Franklin Pierce

William Walker

Caleb Cushing

Matthew C. Perry

CHRONOLOGY

1844 Caleb Cushing signs Treaty of Wanghia with
   China

1848 British seize port of San Juan del Norte in
   Nicaragua
   Treaty of Guadalupe Hidalgo ends Mexican War
   Taylor defeats Cass and Van Buren for presidency

1849 California gold rush

1850 Fillmore assumes presidency after Taylor's death
   Compromise of 1850, including Fugitive Slave
   Law
   Clayton-Bulwer Treaty with Britain

1851 Australian gold rush

1852 Pierce defeats Scott for presidency

1853 Gadsden Purchase from Mexico

1854 Commodore Perry opens Japan
   Ostend Manifesto proposes seizure of Cuba
   Kansas-Nebraska Act repeals Missouri Compro-
   mise of 1820
   Republican party organized

1856 William Walker becomes president of Nicaragua
   and legalizes slavery

1868 Meiji Restoration in Japan

TO LEARN MORE

William J. Cooper, *Liberty and Slavery: Southern Politics to
   1860* (1983)

David H. Donald, Jean H. Baker, and Michael F. Holt, *The
   Civil War and Reconstruction* (rev. ed., 2001)

Kenneth S. Greenberg, *Masters and Statesmen: The Political
   Culture of American Slavery* (1985)

Keith P. Griffler, *Frontline of Freedom: African Americans
   and the Forging of the Underground Railroad in the Ohio
   Valley* (2004)

Bruce Levine, *Half Slave and Half Free: The Roots of the Civil
   War* (1992)

James M. McPherson, *Battle Cry of Freedom: The Civil War
   Era* (1988)

David M. Potter, *The Impending Crisis, 1848–1861* (1976)

Richard H. Sewell, *A House Divided: Sectionalism and Civil
   War, 1848–1860* (1988)

Robert Trennert, *Alternative to Extinction: Federal Indian
   Policy and the Beginnings of the Reservation System,
   1846–1851* (1975)

**A complete, annotated bibliography for this chap-
ter—along with brief descriptions of the People to
Know—may be found on the American Pageant
website. The Key Terms are defined in a Glossary
at the end of the text.**

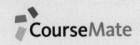

Go to the CourseMate website at
www.cengagebrain.com for
additional study tools and review
materials—including audio and
video clips—for this chapter.

AP® Review Questions for Chapter 18

1. The doctrine of popular sovereignty, as embraced in the mid-nineteenth century, is best defined as
   (A) placing the power of the federal government above that of states.
   (B) giving the people of a territory or state the right to decide the slavery issue for themselves.
   (C) the notion that government is subject to the will of the people.
   (D) allowing Congress to decide the issue of slavery prior to admitting a new state.
   (E) putting the good of the majority ahead of individual desires.

2. Who were the Free-Soilers?
   (A) A political faction in the South that embraced slavery in the territories
   (B) A political group supporting the rights of squatters to keep the land they developed in the West
   (C) A northern-based political party that supported the Wilmot Proviso and banning slavery in the territories
   (D) An abolitionist political party that sought the immediate end of slavery and the granting of land plots to freedmen
   (E) A political coalition of farmers that sought to curb the excesses of industrial development

3. Which of these statements is NOT true about the California gold rush of 1849?
   (A) It made many "forty-niners" rich.
   (B) It fueled lawlessness in the California territory.
   (C) It led Californians to seek rapid admission as a state.
   (D) It sent tens of thousands into the territory and overwhelmed state government and resources.
   (E) It reignited the slavery debate.

4. The Underground Railroad is best defined as a
   (A) group of businessmen seeking monopoly control over the burgeoning railroad industry.
   (B) secret network of slaveowners who banded together to recapture runaway slaves.
   (C) black market for trade goods designed to circumvent protective tariffs.
   (D) network of safe places that hid runaway slaves on their journey north to freedom.
   (E) system for illegally smuggling slaves from Africa into the United States after 1808.

5. Which of these agreements was NOT part of the Compromise of 1850, which kept the Union together?
   (A) California was admitted as a free state.
   (B) New Mexico and Utah were allowed to decide the slave question independently.
   (C) A more severe fugitive slave law was enacted.
   (D) Texas received $10 million from the federal government for ceding some of its land to New Mexico.
   (E) Slavery was abolished in the District of Columbia.

6. The Fugitive Slave Law of 1850 was hated in the North for all of the following reasons EXCEPT that
   (A) it denied slaves the right to testify on their own behalf.
   (B) northerners who helped slaves escape could receive heavy fines and jail terms.
   (C) southerners could require compensation from the federal government for runaway slaves that were not found.
   (D) northerners could be required to help recapture runaway slaves.
   (E) commissioners would receive lower compensation for declaring a runaway slave "free" than they would for declaring him or her a "fugitive."

7. What was the major significance of the presidential election of 1852?
   (A) It proved a triumph for the Compromise of 1850.
   (B) It marked the beginning of the end for the Whig party.
   (C) It put America's first "dark horse" candidate in the White House.
   (D) It launched a new Era of Good Feelings across the nation.
   (E) It pitted two war heroes against each other as candidates for America's highest office.

8. The United States and New Grenada (Columbia) signed a vital treaty in 1848 that
   (A) gave the United States the right to travel across the isthmus in exchange for its military neutrality.
   (B) provided the United States with exclusive use of the isthmus in exchange for military defense of New Grenada.
   (C) broke ground on what would become the Panama Canal.
   (D) united the two countries against incursions into Central America by England and other European powers.
   (E) welcomed U.S. expansion into Central America in exchange for assistance with new transportation systems.

9. What made the Ostend Manifesto so controversial?
   (A) It represented an attempt at U.S. expansion into Asian territories.
   (B) It demonstrated northern interests to block the further acquisition of slave territories.
   (C) It was a secret plan to buy, or take, Cuba by the United States.
   (D) It had the backing of Spain, France, and England.
   (E) It was a declaration of war if Spain did not release the captured American ship *Black Warrior*.

10. The importance of the Treaty of Wanghia (1844) was that it
    (A) gave the United States access to Japanese markets.
    (B) banned tariffs on U.S. imports to Japan and China.
    (C) granted the United States coaling rights in Japan.
    (D) gave China the right to try Americans accused of crimes in China in Chinese courts.
    (E) was the first formal treaty and trade agreement between China and the United States.

11. Why was the Gadsden Purchase such a contentious issue?
    (A) The $5 million purchase price was outrageously high.
    (B) It furthered southern designs on locating a transcontinental railroad there.
    (C) It would add a new slave territory and ultimately tip the balance between free and slave states.
    (D) It sparked a renewed debate about the process for admitting new territories and states.
    (E) It further eroded U.S.-Mexico relations.

12. The main push behind discussions about building a transcontinental railroad in the mid-1800s was the
    (A) need to boost the southern economy.
    (B) need to create jobs and pull the nation out of an economic depression.
    (C) goal of connecting the Pacific Coast territories with the rest of the nation.
    (D) desire for new markets for northern manufactured goods.
    (E) goal of stimulating midwestern development.

13. The Kansas-Nebraska Act heightened sectional tensions between the North and South in all of the following ways EXCEPT that it
    (A) repealed the revered Missouri Compromise.
    (B) divided Nebraska into two territories that would decide the slavery question independently.
    (C) heightened antislavery fervor in the North.
    (D) led northerners to resist further compromise with the South.
    (E) led to further enforcement of the Fugitive Slave Act in the North.

14. Which of the following is NOT a true statement about the rise of the Republican party in the mid-1850s?
    (A) The bulwark of its support was below the Mason-Dixon line.
    (B) It drew dissatisfied Whigs, Democrats, Free-Soilers, and Know-Nothings.
    (C) It symbolized the increasing sectionalism that was leading the nation toward civil war.
    (D) The party first emerged in the Midwest in protest to the Kansas-Nebraska Act.
    (E) Within two years, the party held the position of Speaker of the House of Representatives.

15. All of the following indicate that the idea of Manifest Destiny would extend beyond the North American continent EXCEPT
    (A) the "secret" offer to purchase Cuba.
    (B) trade agreements with China.
    (C) Commodore Perry opening Japan.
    (D) conflict with Britain in Central America.
    (E) the Gadsden Purchase.

16. Why was the Compromise of 1850 a great feat in American political history?
    (A) It solved the nation's problems in a way that most of the country accepted.
    (B) Great statesmen worked within the system, creating separate legislation that together became the compromise.
    (C) It preserved the Missouri Compromise line and kept the balance of power in the Senate.
    (D) It settled the nation's slavery issues in that era, preventing the need for future compromise.
    (E) Congress and President Taylor worked together to help the nation overcome a potentially disastrous crisis.

Chapter 19

Drifting Toward Disunion

1854–1861

*A house divided against itself cannot stand. I believe this government
cannot endure permanently half slave and half free.*

ABRAHAM LINCOLN, 1858

The slavery question continued to churn the cauldron of controversy throughout the 1850s. As moral temperatures rose, prospects for a peaceful political solution to the slavery issue simply evaporated. Kansas Territory erupted in violence between proslavery and antislavery factions in 1855. Two years later the Supreme Court's incendiary *Dred Scott* decision extended formal protection to slavery in all the territories of the West. Attitudes on both sides progressively hardened. When in 1860 the newly formed Republican party nominated for president Abraham Lincoln, an outspoken opponent of the further expansion of slavery, the stage was set for all-out civil war.

★ Stowe and Helper: Literary Incendiaries

Sectional tensions were further strained in 1852, and later, by an inky phenomenon. Harriet Beecher Stowe, a wisp of a woman and the mother of a half-dozen children, published her heartrending novel ***Uncle Tom's Cabin***. Dismayed by the passage of the Fugitive Slave Law, she was determined to awaken the North to the wickedness of slavery by laying bare its terrible inhumanity, especially the cruel splitting of families. Her wildly popular book relied on powerful imagery and touching pathos. "God wrote it," she explained in later years—a reminder that the deeper sources of her antislavery sentiments lay in the evangelical religious crusades of the Second Great Awakening.

The success of the novel at home and abroad was sensational. Several hundred thousand copies were published in the first year, and the totals soon ran into the millions as the tale was translated into more than a score of languages. It was also put on the stage in "Tom shows" for lengthy runs. No other novel in American history—perhaps in all history—can be compared with it as a political force. To millions of people, it made slavery appear almost as evil as it really was.

When Mrs. Stowe was introduced to President Lincoln in 1862, he reportedly remarked with twinkling eyes, "So you're the little woman who wrote the book that made this great war." The truth is that *Uncle Tom's Cabin* did help start the Civil War—and win it. The South condemned that "vile wretch in petticoats" when it learned that hundreds of thousands of fellow Americans were reading and believing her "unfair" indictment. Mrs. Stowe had never witnessed slavery at first hand in the Deep South, but she had seen it briefly during a visit to Kentucky, and she had lived for many years in Ohio, a center of Underground Railroad activity.

Uncle Tom, endearing and enduring, left a profound impression on the North. Uncounted thousands of readers swore that henceforth they would have nothing to do with the enforcement of the Fugitive Slave Law. The tale was devoured by millions of impressionable youths in the 1850s—some of whom later became the Boys in Blue who volunteered to fight the Civil War through to its grim finale. The memory of a beaten and dying Uncle Tom helped sustain them in their determination to wipe out the plague of slavery.

Harriet Beecher Stowe (1811–1896), 1853 This oil portrait of Stowe was painted a year after she published *Uncle Tom's Cabin*. Her pen helped to change the course of history. National Portrait Gallery, Smithsonian Institution/Art Resource, NY

Granger Collection

"The Book That Made This Great War" Lincoln's celebrated remark to author Harriet Beecher Stowe reflected the enormous emotional impact of her impassioned novel.

The novel was immensely popular abroad, especially in Britain and France. Countless readers wept over the kindly Tom and the angelic Eva, while deploring the brutal Simon Legree. When the guns in America finally began to boom, the common people of England sensed that the triumph of the North would

In the closing scenes of Harriet Beecher Stowe's novel, Uncle Tom's brutal master, Simon Legree, orders the $1,200 slave savagely beaten (to death) by two fellow slaves. Through tears and blood, Tom exclaims,

❝'No! no! no! my soul an't yours, Mas'r! You haven't bought it,—ye can't buy it! It's been bought and paid for, by one that is able to keep it,—no matter, no matter, you can't harm me!' 'I can't,' said Legree, with a sneer; 'we'll see,— we'll see! Here, Sambo, Quimbo, give this dog such a breakin' in as he won't get over, this month!'**❞**

spell the end of the black curse. The governments in London and Paris seriously considered intervening in behalf of the South, but they were sobered by the realization that many of their own people, aroused by the "Tommania," might not support them.

Another trouble-brewing book appeared in 1857, five years after the debut of Uncle Tom. Titled ***The Impending Crisis of the South***, it was written by Hinton R. Helper, a nonaristocratic white from North Carolina. Hating both slavery and blacks, he attempted to prove by an array of statistics that indirectly the nonslaveholding whites were the ones who suffered most from the millstone of slavery. Unable to secure a publisher in the South, he finally managed to find one in the North.

Helper's influence was negligible among the poorer whites to whom he addressed his message. Yet the South's planter elite certainly took note of Helper's audacity, which fueled their fears that the nonslaveholding majority might abandon them. *The Impending Crisis of the South*, with its "dirty allusions," was banned in the South and fed to the flames at book-burning parties. In the North untold thousands of copies, many

Harriet Beecher Stowe, *Uncle Tom's Cabin*

As works of fiction, novels pose tricky problems to historians, whose principal objective is to get the factual record straight. Works of the imagination are notoriously unreliable as descriptions of reality, and only rarely is it known with any degree of certainty what a reader might have felt when confronting a particular fictional passage or theme. Yet a novel like Harriet Beecher Stowe's *Uncle Tom's Cabin* had such an unarguably large impact on the American (and worldwide) debate over slavery that historians have inevitably looked to it for evidence of the mid-nineteenth-century ideas and attitudes to which Stowe appealed. The passage quoted here is especially rich in such evidence—and even offers an explanation for the logic of the novel's title. Stowe cleverly aimed to mobilize not simply her readers'

sense of injustice but also their sentiments on behalf of the antislavery cause. Why is the *cabin* described here so central to Stowe's novel? What sentimental values does the cabin represent? What is the nature of the threat to those values? What

does it say about nineteenth-century American culture that Stowe's appeal to sentiment succeeded so much more dramatically in exciting antislavery passions than did the factual and moral arguments of many other (mostly male) abolitionists?

> THE February morning looked gray and drizzling through the window of Uncle Tom's cabin. It looked on downcast faces, the images of mournful hearts. The little table stood out before the fire, covered with an ironing-cloth; a coarse but clean shirt or two, fresh from the iron, hung on the back of a chair by the fire, and Aunt Chloe had another spread out before her on the table. Carefully she rubbed and ironed every fold and every hem, with the most scrupulous exactness, every now and then raising her hand to her face to wipe off the tears that were coursing down her cheeks.
>
> Tom sat by, with his Testament open on his knee, and his head leaning upon his hand ; — but neither spoke. It was yet early, and the children lay all asleep together in their little rude trundle-bed.
>
> Tom, who had, to the full, the gentle, domestic heart, which, woe for them ! has been a peculiar characteristic of his unhappy race, got up and walked silently to look at his children.
>
> "It's the last time," he said.

Albert and Shirley Small Special Collections, University of Virginia Library

---

in condensed form, were distributed as campaign literature by the Republicans. Southerners were further embittered when they learned that their northern brethren were spreading these wicked "lies." Thus did southerners, reacting much as they did to *Uncle Tom's Cabin*, become increasingly unwilling to sleep under the same federal roof with their hostile Yankee bedfellows.

✦ The North-South Contest for Kansas

The rolling plains of Kansas had meanwhile been providing an example of the worst possible workings of

popular sovereignty, although admittedly under abnormal conditions.

Newcomers who ventured into Kansas were a motley lot. Most of the northerners were just ordinary westward-moving pioneers in search of richer lands beyond the sunset. But a small part of the inflow was financed by groups of northern abolitionists or free-soilers. The most famous of these antislavery organizations was the **New England Emigrant Aid Company**, which sent about two thousand people to the troubled area to forestall the South—and also to make a profit. Shouting "Ho for Kansas," many of them carried the deadly new breech-loading Sharps rifles, nicknamed "Beecher's Bibles" after the Reverend Henry Ward Beecher (Harriet

Beecher Stowe's brother), who had helped raise money for their purchase. Many of the Kansas-bound pioneers sang John Greenleaf Whittier's marching song (1854):

> We cross the prairie as of old
> The pilgrims crossed the sea,
> To make the West, as they the East,
> The homestead of the free!

Southern spokesmen, now more than ordinarily touchy, raised furious cries of betrayal. They had supported the Kansas-Nebraska scheme of Senator Douglas with the unspoken understanding that Kansas would become slave and Nebraska free. The northern "Nebrascals," allegedly by foul means, were now apparently out to "abolitionize" *both* Kansas and Nebraska.

A few southern hotheads, quick to respond in kind, attempted to "assist" small groups of well-armed slaveowners to Kansas. Some carried banners proclaiming,

> Let Yankees tremble, abolitionists fall,
> Our motto is, "Give Southern Rights to All."

But planting blacks on Kansas soil was a losing game. Slaves were valuable and volatile property, and foolish indeed were owners who would take them where bullets were flying and where the soil might be voted free under popular sovereignty. The census of 1860 found only 2 slaves among 107,000 souls in all Kansas Territory and only 15 in Nebraska. There was much truth in the charge that the whole quarrel over slavery in the territories revolved around "an imaginary Negro in an impossible place."

Crisis conditions in Kansas rapidly worsened (see Map 19.1). When the day came in 1855 to elect members of the first territorial legislature, proslavery "border ruffians" poured in from Missouri to vote early and often. The slavery supporters triumphed and then set up their own puppet government at Shawnee Mission. The free-soilers, unable to stomach this fraudulent conspiracy, established an extralegal regime of their own in Topeka. The confused Kansans thus had their choice between two governments—one based on fraud, the other on illegality.

Tension mounted as settlers also feuded over conflicting land claims. The breaking point came in 1856 when a gang of proslavery raiders, alleging provocation, shot up and burned part of the free-soil town of Lawrence. This outrage was but the prelude to a bloodier tragedy.

✦ Kansas in Convulsion

The fanatical figure of John Brown now stalked upon the Kansas battlefield. Spare, gray-bearded, and ironwilled, he was obsessively dedicated to the abolitionist cause. The power of his glittering gray eyes was such, so he claimed, that his stare could force a dog or cat to slink out of a room. Becoming involved in dubious dealings, including horse stealing, he moved to Kansas from Ohio with part of his large family. Brooding over the recent attack on Lawrence, "Old Brown" of Osawatomie led a band of his followers to Pottawatomie Creek in May 1856. There they literally hacked to pieces five surprised men, presumed to be proslaveryites. This terrorist butchery besmirched the free-soil cause and brought vicious retaliation from the proslavery forces.

MAP 19.1 Bleeding Kansas, 1854–1860 "Enter every election district in Kansas . . . and vote at the point of a bowie knife or revolver," one proslavery agitator exhorted a Missouri crowd. Proslavery Missouri senator David Atchison declared that "there are 1,100 men coming over from Platte County to vote, and if that ain't enough we can send 5,000— enough to kill every Goddamned abolitionist in the Territory." © Cengage Learning

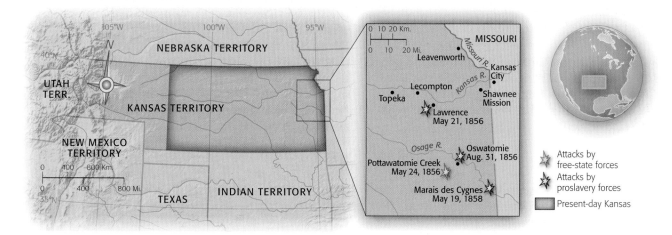

John Brown (1800–1859) This daguerreotype of the militant abolitionist Brown tells a tale of two men, the sitter and the photographer. It was taken in 1847 when Brown was running a wool-brokerage house in Springfield, Massachusetts, and working closely with other New England abolitionists, including Frederick Douglass. Brown made his way to the Hartford studio of free black photographer Augustus Washington, who was the son of an Asian woman and a former black slave and well known in abolitionist circles. Six years later, Washington would close his successful studio and take his family to Liberia, convinced that American blacks would do better in their own country in Africa than as free men in the United States (see pp. 349–350).

Civil war in Kansas thus erupted in 1856 and continued intermittently until it merged with the large-scale Civil War of 1861–1865. Altogether, the Kansas conflict destroyed millions of dollars' worth of property, paralyzed agriculture in certain areas, and cost scores of lives.

Yet by 1857 Kansas had enough people, chiefly free-soilers, to apply for statehood on a popular-sovereignty basis. The proslavery forces, then in the saddle, devised a tricky document known as the **Lecompton Constitution**. The people were not allowed to vote for or against the constitution as a whole, but for the constitution either "with slavery" or "with no slavery." If they voted against slavery, one of the remaining provisions of the constitution would protect the owners of slaves already in Kansas. So whatever the outcome, there would still be black bondage in Kansas. Many free-soilers, infuriated by this ploy, boycotted the polls. Left to themselves, the proslaveryites approved the constitution with slavery late in 1857.

The scene next shifted to Washington. President Pierce had been succeeded by the no-less-pliable James Buchanan, who was also strongly under southern influence. Blind to sharp divisions within his own Democratic party, Buchanan threw the weight of his administration behind the notorious Lecompton Constitution. But Senator Douglas, who had championed true popular sovereignty, would have none of this semipopular fraudulency. Deliberately tossing away his strong support in the South for the presidency, he fought courageously for fair play and democratic principles. The outcome was a compromise that, in effect, submitted the entire Lecompton Constitution to a popular vote. The free-soil voters thereupon thronged to the polls and snowed it under. Kansas remained a territory until 1861, when the southern secessionists left Congress.

President Buchanan, by antagonizing the numerous Douglas Democrats in the North, hopelessly divided the once-powerful Democratic party. Until then, it had been the only remaining *national* party, for the Whigs were dead and the Republicans were sectional. With the disruption of the Democrats came the snapping of one of the last important strands in the rope that was barely binding the Union together.

✴ "Bully" Brooks and His Bludgeon

Bleeding Kansas also spattered blood on the floor of the Senate in 1856. Senator Charles Sumner of Massachusetts, a tall and imposing figure, was a leading abolitionist—one of the few prominent in political life. Highly educated but cold, humorless, intolerant, and egotistical, he had made himself one of the most disliked men in the Senate. Brooding over the turbulent miscarriage of popular sovereignty, he delivered a blistering speech titled "The Crime Against Kansas." Sparing few epithets, he condemned the proslavery men as "hirelings picked from the drunken spew and vomit of an uneasy civilization." He also referred insultingly to South Carolina and to its white-haired senator Andrew Butler, one of the best-liked members of the Senate.

Hot-tempered Congressman Preston S. Brooks of South Carolina now took vengeance into his own hands. Ordinarily gracious and gallant, he resented the insults to his state and to its senator, a distant cousin. His code of honor called for a duel, but in the South one fought only with one's social equals. And had not the coarse language of the Yankee, who probably would reject a challenge, dropped him to a lower order? To Brooks, the only alternative was to chastise the senator as one would beat an unruly dog. On May 22, 1856, he approached Sumner, then sitting at his Senate desk, and pounded the orator with an eleven-ounce cane until it broke. The victim fell bleeding and unconscious to the floor, while several nearby senators refrained from interfering.

Sumner had been provocatively insulting, but this counteroutrage put Brooks in the wrong. The House of Representatives could not muster enough votes to expel the South Carolinian, but he resigned and was triumphantly reelected. Southern admirers deluged Brooks with canes, some of them gold-headed, to replace the one that had been broken. The injuries to Sumner's head and nervous system were serious. He was forced to leave his seat for three and a half years and go to Europe for treatment that was both painful and costly. Meanwhile, Massachusetts defiantly reelected him, leaving his seat eloquently empty. Bleeding Sumner was thus joined with bleeding Kansas as a political issue.

The free-soil North was mightily aroused against the "uncouth" and "cowardly" "Bully" Brooks. Copies of Sumner's abusive speech, otherwise doomed to obscurity, were sold by the tens of thousands. Every blow that struck the senator doubtless made thousands of Republican votes. The South, although not unanimous in approving Brooks, was angered not only because Sumner had made such an intemperate speech but because it had been so extravagantly applauded in the North.

The Sumner-Brooks clash and the ensuing reactions revealed how dangerously inflamed passions were becoming, North and South. It was ominous that the cultured Sumner should have used the language of a

Regarding the Brooks assault on Sumner, the Illinois State Journal, *one of the more moderate antislavery journals, declared,*

❝Brooks and his Southern allies have deliberately adopted the monstrous creed that any man who dares to utter sentiments which they deem wrong or unjust, shall be brutally assailed.**❞**

One of the milder southern responses came from the Petersburg *(Virginia)* Intelligencer:

❝Although Mr. Brooks ought to have selected some other spot for the altercation than the Senate chamber, if he had broken every bone in Sumner's carcass it would have been a just retribution upon this slanderer of the South and her individual citizens.**❞**

barroom bully and that the gentlemanly Brooks should have employed the tactics and tools of a thug. Emotion was displacing thought. The blows rained on Sumner's head were, broadly speaking, among the first blows of the Civil War.

✦ "Old Buck" Versus "The Pathfinder"

With bullets whining in Kansas, the Democrats met in Cincinnati to nominate their presidential standard-bearer of 1856. They shied away from both the weak-kneed President Pierce and the dynamic Douglas. Each was too indelibly tainted by the Kansas-Nebraska Act.

SOUTHERN CHIVALRY — ARGUMENT VERSUS CLUB'S.

Library of Congress

Preston Brooks Caning Charles Sumner, 1856
Cartoonist John Magee of Philadelphia depicted Brooks's beating of Sumner in the Senate as a display of southern ruthlessness in defending slavery, ironically captioned "southern chivalry."

Know-Nothing Banner, 1856 The Know-Nothing Party feared that slavery and other sectional issues were blinding Americans to the real danger in their midst—uncontrolled immigration and foreign influence. The Party ran ex-President Millard Fillmore for president in 1856, using banners like this one to alert voters to the threat presented by recent Irish and German immigrants, many of them Catholic.

NATIVE.AMERICANS.

BEWARE OF

FOREIGN.INFLUENCE

The delegates finally chose James Buchanan (pronounced by many Buck-anan), who was muscular, white-haired, and tall (six feet), with a short neck and a protruding chin. Because of an eye defect, he carried his head cocked to one side. A well-to-do Pennsylvania lawyer, he had been serving as minister to London during the recent Kansas-Nebraska uproar. He was therefore "Kansas-less," and hence relatively enemyless. But in a crisis that called for giants, "Old Buck" Buchanan was mediocre, irresolute, and confused.

Delegates of the fast-growing Republican party met in Philadelphia with bubbling enthusiasm. "Higher Law" Seward was their most conspicuous leader, and he probably would have arranged to win the nomination had he been confident that this was a "Republican year." The final choice was Captain John C. Frémont, the so-called Pathfinder of the West—a dashing but erratic explorer-soldier-surveyor who was supposed to find the path to the White House. The black-bearded and flashy young adventurer was virtually without political experience, but like Buchanan he was not tarred with the Kansas brush. The Republican platform came out vigorously against the extension of slavery into the territories, while the Democrats declared no less emphatically for popular sovereignty.

An ugly dose of antiforeignism was injected into the campaign, even though slavery extension loomed largest. The recent influx of immigrants from Ireland and Germany had alarmed "nativists," as many old-stock Protestants were called. They organized the American party, also known as the Know-Nothing party because of its secretiveness, and in 1856 nominated the lackluster ex-president Millard Fillmore. Antiforeign and anti-Catholic, these superpatriots adopted the slogan "Americans Must Rule America." Remnants of the dying Whig party likewise endorsed Fillmore,

and they and the Know-Nothings threatened to cut into Republican strength.

Republicans fell in behind Frémont with the zeal of crusaders. Shouting "We Follow the Pathfinder" and "We Are Buck Hunting," they organized glee clubs, which sang (to the tune of "The Marseillaise"),

Arise, arise ye brave!
And let our war-cry be,
Free speech, free press, free soil, free men,
Fré-mont and victory!

"And free love," sneered the Buchanan supporters ("Buchaneers").

Mudslinging bespattered both candidates. "Old Fogy" Buchanan was assailed because he was a bachelor: the fiancée of his youth had died after a lovers' quarrel. Frémont was reviled because of his illegitimate birth, for his young mother had left her elderly husband, a Virginia planter, to run away with a French adventurer. In due season she gave birth to John in Savannah, Georgia—further to shame the South. More harmful to Frémont was the allegation, which alienated many bigoted Know-Nothings and other "nativists," that he was a Roman Catholic.

Spiritual overtones developed in the Frémont campaign, especially over slavery. The Independent, *a prominent religious journal, saw in Frémont's nomination "the good hand of God." As election day neared, it declared,*

"Fellow-Christians! Remember it is for Christ, for the nation, and for the world that you vote at this election! Vote as you pray! Pray as you vote!"

✦ The Electoral Fruits of 1856

A bland Buchanan, although polling less than a majority of the popular vote, won handily (see Map 19.2). His tally in the Electoral College was 174 to 114 for Frémont, with Fillmore garnering 8. The popular vote was 1,832,955 for Buchanan to 1,339,932 for Frémont, and 871,731 for Fillmore.

Why did the rousing Republicans go down to defeat? Frémont lost much ground because of grave doubts as to his honesty, capacity, and sound judgment. Perhaps more damaging were the violent threats of the southern "fire-eaters" that the election of a sectional "Black Republican" would be a declaration of war on them, forcing them to secede. Many northerners, anxious to save both the Union and their profitable business connections with the South, were thus intimidated into voting for Buchanan. Innate conservatism triumphed, assisted by so-called southern bullyism.

It was probably fortunate for the Union that secession and civil war did not come in 1856, following a Republican victory. Frémont, an ill-balanced and second-rate figure, was no Abraham Lincoln. And in 1856 the North was more willing to let the South depart in peace than in 1860. Dramatic events from 1856 to 1860 were to arouse hundreds of thousands of still-apathetic northerners to a fighting pitch.

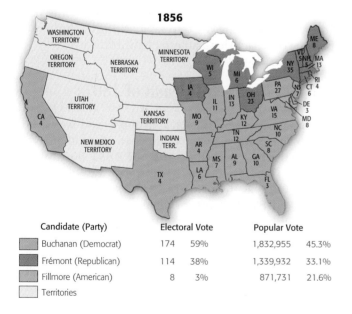

1856

Candidate (Party)	Electoral Vote		Popular Vote	
Buchanan (Democrat)	174	59%	1,832,955	45.3%
Frémont (Republican)	114	38%	1,339,932	33.1%
Fillmore (American)	8	3%	871,731	21.6%
Territories				

MAP 19.2 Presidential Election of 1856 (electoral vote by state) The fateful split of 1860 was foreshadowed. The regional polarization in 1856, shown here, was to be even sharper four years later, as illustrated by Maps 19.3 and 19.4 later in this chapter. © Cengage Learning

Yet the Republicans in 1856 could rightfully claim a "victorious defeat." The new party—a mere two-year-old toddler—had made an astonishing showing against the well-oiled Democratic machine. Whittier exulted:

> Then sound again the bugles,
>   Call the muster-roll anew;
> If months have well-nigh won the field,
>   What may not four years do?

The election of 1856 cast a long shadow forward, and politicians, North and South, peered anxiously toward 1860.

✦ The Dred Scott Bombshell

The **Dred Scott v. Sandford** decision, handed down by the Supreme Court on March 6, 1857, abruptly ended the two-day presidential honeymoon of the unlucky bachelor, James Buchanan. This pronouncement was one of the opening paper-gun blasts of the Civil War.

Basically, the case was simple. Dred Scott, a black slave, had lived with his master for five years in Illinois and Wisconsin Territory. Backed by interested abolitionists, he sued for freedom on the basis of his long residence on free soil.

The Supreme Court proceeded to twist a simple legal case into a complex political issue. It ruled, not surprisingly, that Dred Scott was a black slave and not a citizen, and hence could not sue in federal courts.* The tribunal could then have thrown out the case on these technical grounds alone. But a majority decided to go further, under the leadership of emaciated Chief Justice Roger B. Taney from the slave state of Maryland. A sweeping judgment on the larger issue of slavery in the territories seemed desirable, particularly to forestall arguments by two free-soil justices who were preparing dissenting opinions. The prosouthern majority evidently hoped in this way to lay the odious question to rest.

Taney's thunderclap rocked the free-soilers back on their heels. A majority of the Court decreed that because a slave was private property, he or she could be taken into *any* territory and legally held there in slavery. The reasoning was that the Fifth Amendment clearly forbade Congress to deprive people of their property without due process of law. The Court, to be consistent, went further. The Missouri Compromise, banning slavery north of 36° 30', had been repealed three years earlier by the Kansas-Nebraska Act. But its

---

*This part of the ruling, denying blacks their citizenship, seriously menaced the precarious position of the South's quarter-million free blacks.

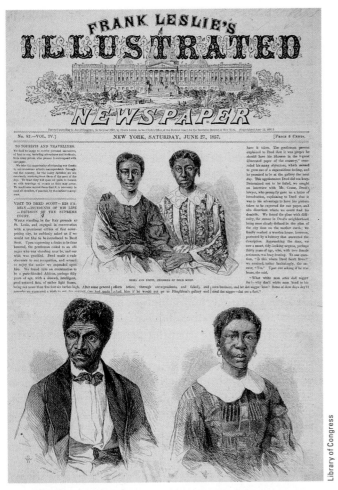

Dred Scott with His Wife and Daughters, 1857 This slave's long legal battle for his freedom, culminating in the Supreme Court's *Dred Scott* decision in 1857, helped to ignite the Civil War. Widespread publicity about the fate of Scott and his family strengthened antislavery sentiment in the North. Articles like this one in *Frank Leslie's Illustrated Newspaper* appealed to the same sentimental regard for the idealized family that Harriet Beecher Stowe so artfully mobilized in *Uncle Tom's Cabin* (see "Examining the Evidence: Harriet Beecher Stowe, *Uncle Tom's Cabin*," p. 398).

Library of Congress

The decision of Chief Justice Roger B. Taney (1777–1864) in the case of *Dred Scott* referred to the status of slaves when the Constitution was adopted:

> **"** They had for more than a century before been regarded as beings of an inferior order; and altogether unfit to associate with the white race, either in social or political relations; and so far inferior that they had no rights which the white man was bound to respect. . . . This opinion was at that time fixed and universal in the civilized portion of the white race. **"**

Taney's statement accurately described historical attitudes, but it deeply offended antislaveryites when applied to conditions in 1857.

spirit was still venerated in the North. Now the Court ruled that the Compromise of 1820 had been unconstitutional all along: Congress had no power to ban slavery from the territories, regardless even of what the territorial legislatures themselves might want.

Southerners were delighted with this unexpected victory. Champions of popular sovereignty were aghast, including Senator Douglas and a host of northern Democrats. Another lethal wedge was thus driven between the northern and southern wings of the once-united Democratic party.

Foes of slavery extension, especially the Republicans, were infuriated by the Dred Scott setback. Their chief rallying cry had been the banishing of bondage from the territories. They now insisted that the ruling of the Court was merely an opinion, not a decision, and no more binding than the views of a "southern debating society." Republican defiance of the exalted tribunal was intensified by an awareness that a majority of its members were southerners and by the conviction that it had debased itself—"sullied the ermine"—by wallowing in the gutter of politics.

Southerners in turn were inflamed by all this defiance. They began to wonder anew how much longer they could remain joined to a section that refused to honor the Supreme Court, to say nothing of the constitutional compact that had established it.

✵ The Financial Crash of 1857

Bitterness caused by the *Dred Scott* decision was deepened by hard times, which dampened a period of feverish prosperity. Then the **panic of 1857** burst about Buchanan's harassed head. The storm was not so bad economically as the panic of 1837, but psychologically it was probably the worst of the nineteenth century.

What caused the crash? Inpouring California gold played its part by helping to inflate the currency. The demands of the Crimean War in Russia (1853–1856) had overstimulated the growing of grain, while frenzied speculation in land and railroads had further ripped the economic fabric. When the collapse came, over five thousand businesses failed within a year. Unemployment, accompanied by hunger meetings in urban areas, was widespread. "Bread or Death" stated one desperate slogan.

The North, including its grain growers, was hardest hit. The South, enjoying favorable cotton prices abroad, rode out the storm with flying colors. Panic conditions seemed further proof that cotton was king and that its economic kingdom was stronger than that of the North. This fatal delusion helped drive the overconfident southerners closer to a shooting showdown.

Financial distress in the North, especially in agriculture, gave a new vigor to the demand for free farms of 160 acres from the public domain. For several decades interested groups had been urging the federal government to abandon its ancient policy of selling the land for revenue. Instead, the argument ran, acreage should be given outright to the sturdy pioneers as a reward for risking health and life to develop it.

A scheme to make outright gifts of homesteads encountered two-pronged opposition. Eastern industrialists had long been unfriendly to free land; some of them feared that their underpaid workers would be drained off to the West. The South was even more bitterly opposed, partly because gang-labor slavery could not flourish on a mere 160 acres. Free farms would merely fill up the territories more rapidly with free-soilers and further tip the political balance against the South. In 1860, after years of debate, Congress finally passed a homestead act—one that made public lands available at a nominal sum of twenty-five cents an acre. But the homestead act was stabbed to death by the veto pen of President Buchanan, near whose elbow sat leading southern sympathizers.

The panic of 1857 also created a clamor for higher tariff rates. Several months before the crash, Congress, embarrassed by a large Treasury surplus, had enacted the **Tariff of 1857**. The new law, responding to pressures from the South, reduced duties to about 20 percent on dutiable goods—the lowest point since the War of 1812. Hardly had the revised rates been placed on the books when financial misery descended like a black pall. Northern manufacturers, many of them Republicans, noisily blamed their misfortunes on the low tariff. As the surplus melted away in the Treasury, industrialists in the North pointed to the need for higher duties. But what really concerned them was their desire for increased protection. Thus the panic of 1857 gave the Republicans two surefire economic issues for the election of 1860: protection for the unprotected and farms for the farmless.

✪ An Illinois Rail-Splitter Emerges

The Illinois senatorial election of 1858 now claimed the national spotlight. Senator Stephen A. Douglas's term was about to expire, and the Republicans decided to run against him a rustic Springfield lawyer, one Abraham Lincoln. The Republican candidate—6 feet 4 inches in height and 180 pounds in weight—presented an awkward but arresting figure. Lincoln's legs, arms, and neck were abnormally long; his head was crowned by coarse, black, and unruly hair; and his face was sad, sunken, and weather-beaten.

Lincoln was no silver-spoon child of the elite. Born in 1809 in a Kentucky log cabin to impoverished parents, he attended a frontier school for not more than a year; being an avid reader, he was mainly self-educated.

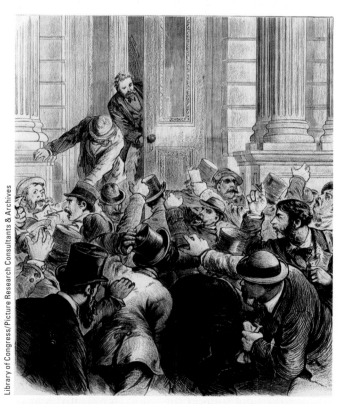

Library of Congress/Picture Research Consultants & Archives

Panic on Wall Street, 1857 The panic of 1857 further burdened President Buchanan, already reeling from the armed clashes in Kansas and the controversy over the *Dred Scott* decision.

In 1832, when Abraham Lincoln (1809–1865) became a candidate for the Illinois legislature, he delivered a speech at a political gathering:

"I presume you all know who I am. I am humble Abraham Lincoln. I have been solicited by many friends to become a candidate for the Legislature. My [Whiggish] politics are short and sweet, like the old woman's dance. I am in favor of a national bank. I am in favor of the internal-improvement system, and a high protective tariff. These are my sentiments and political principles. If elected, I shall be thankful; if not, it will be all the same.**"**

He was elected two years later.

All his life he said, "git," "thar," and "heered." Although narrow-chested and somewhat stoop-shouldered, he shone in his frontier community as a wrestler and weight lifter, and spent some time, among other pioneering pursuits, as a splitter of logs for fence rails. A superb teller of earthy and amusing stories, he would oddly enough plunge into protracted periods of melancholy.

Lincoln's private and professional lives were not especially noteworthy. He married "above himself" socially, into the influential Todd family of Kentucky, and the temperamental outbursts of his high-strung wife, known by her enemies as the "she wolf," helped to school him in patience and forbearance. After reading a little law, he gradually emerged as one of the dozen or so better-known trial lawyers in Illinois, although still accustomed to carrying important papers in his stovepipe hat. He was widely referred to as "Honest Abe," partly because he would refuse cases that he had to suspend his conscience to defend.

The rise of Lincoln as a political figure was less than rocketlike. After making his mark in the Illinois legislature as a Whig politician of the logrolling variety,

he served one undistinguished term in Congress, 1847–1849. Until 1854, when he was forty-five years of age, he had done nothing to establish a claim to statesmanship. But the passage of the Kansas-Nebraska Act in that year lighted within him unexpected fires. After mounting the Republican bandwagon, he emerged as one of the foremost politicians and orators of the Northwest. At the Philadelphia convention of 1856, where John C. Frémont was nominated, Lincoln actually received 110 votes for the vice-presidential nomination.

✯ The Great Debate: Lincoln Versus Douglas

Lincoln, as Republican nominee for the Senate seat, boldly challenged Douglas to a series of joint debates. This was a rash act, because the stumpy senator was probably the nation's most devastating debater. Douglas promptly accepted Lincoln's challenge, and seven meetings—the famed **Lincoln-Douglas debates**—were arranged from August to October 1858.

At first glance the two contestants seemed ill-matched. The well-groomed and polished Douglas, with his bearlike figure and bullhorn voice, presented a striking contrast to the lanky Lincoln, with his baggy clothes and unshined shoes. Moreover, "Old Abe," as he was called in both affection and derision, had a piercing, high-pitched voice and was often ill at ease when he began to speak. But as he threw himself into an argument, he seemed to grow in height, while his glowing eyes lighted up a rugged face. He relied on logic rather than on table-thumping.

The most famous debate came at Freeport, Illinois, where Lincoln nearly impaled his opponent on the horns of a dilemma. Suppose, he queried, the people of a territory should vote slavery down. The Supreme Court in the *Dred Scott* decision had decreed that they could not. Who would prevail, the Court or the people?

Legend to the contrary, Douglas and some southerners had already publicly answered the **Freeport question**. The "Little Giant" therefore did not hesitate to meet the issue head-on, honestly and consistently. His reply to Lincoln became known as the **Freeport Doctrine**. No matter how the Supreme Court ruled, Douglas argued, slavery would stay down if the people voted it down. Laws to protect slavery would have to be passed by the territorial legislatures. These would not be forthcoming in the absence of popular approval, and black bondage would soon disappear. Douglas, in truth, had American history on his side. Where public opinion does not support the federal government, as in the case of Jefferson's embargo (see pp. 216–218), the law is almost impossible to enforce.

The upshot was that Douglas defeated Lincoln for the Senate seat. The "Little Giant's" loyalty to popular

Abraham Lincoln, a Most Uncommon Common Man
This daguerreotype of Lincoln was done by Mathew B. Brady, a distinguished photographer of the era.

Granger Collection

Art Resource, NY

Lincoln and Douglas Debate, 1858 Thousands attended each of the seven Lincoln-Douglas debates. Douglas is shown here sitting to Lincoln's right in the debate at Charleston, Illinois, in September. On one occasion Lincoln quipped that Douglas's logic would prove that a horse chestnut was a chestnut horse.

sovereignty, which still had a powerful appeal in Illinois, probably was decisive. Senators were then chosen by state legislatures; and in the general election that followed the debates, more pro-Douglas members were

Lincoln expressed his views on the relation of the black and white races in 1858, in his first debate with Stephen A. Douglas:

"I, as well as Judge Douglas, am in favor of the race to which I belong, having the superior position. I have never said anything to the contrary, but I hold that notwithstanding all this, there is no reason in the world why the negro is not entitled to all the natural rights enumerated in the Declaration of Independence, the right to life, liberty, and the pursuit of happiness. I hold that he is as much entitled to those rights as the white man. I agree with Judge Douglas he is not my equal in many respects—certainly not in color, perhaps not in moral or intellectual endowment. But in the right to eat the bread, without leave of anybody else, which his own hand earns, he is my equal and the equal of Judge Douglas, and the equal of every living man.**"**

elected than pro-Lincoln members. Yet thanks to inequitable apportionment, the districts carried by Douglas supporters represented a smaller population than those carried by Lincoln supporters. "Honest Abe" thus won a clear moral victory.

Lincoln possibly was playing for larger stakes than just the senatorship. Although defeated, he had shambled into the national limelight in company with the most prominent northern politicians. Newspapers in the East published detailed accounts of the debates, and Lincoln began to emerge as a potential Republican nominee for president. But Douglas, in winning Illinois, hurt his own chances of winning the presidency, while further splitting his splintering party. After his opposition to the Lecompton Constitution for Kansas and his further defiance of the Supreme Court at Freeport, southern Democrats were determined to break up the party (and the Union) rather than accept him. The Lincoln-Douglas debate platform thus proved to be one of the preliminary battlefields of the Civil War.

✦ John Brown: Murderer or Martyr?

The gaunt, grim figure of John Brown of bleeding Kansas infamy now once again took the stage. After studying the tactics of the black rebels Toussaint L'Ouverture (see p. 211) and Nat Turner (see p. 348), he hatched a

Upon hearing of John Brown's execution, escaped slave and abolitionist Harriet Tubman (ca. 1820–1913) paid him the highest tribute for his self-sacrifice:

❝I've been studying, and studying upon it, and its clar to me, it wasn't John Brown that died on that gallows. When I think how he gave up his life for our people, and how he never flinched, but was so brave to the end; its clar to me it wasn't mortal man, it was God in him.**❞**

Not all opponents of slavery, however, shared Tubman's reverence for Brown. Republican presidential candidate Abraham Lincoln dismissed Brown as deluded:

❝[The Brown] affair, in its philosophy, corresponds with the many attempts, related in history, at the assassination of kings and emperors. An enthusiast broods over the oppression of a people till he fancies himself commissioned by Heaven to liberate them. He ventures the attempt, which ends in little else than his own execution.**❞**

daring scheme to invade the South secretly with a handful of followers, call upon the slaves to rise, furnish them with arms, and establish a kind of black free state as a sanctuary. Brown secured several thousand dollars for firearms from northern abolitionists and finally arrived in hilly western Virginia with some twenty men, including several blacks. At scenic **Harpers Ferry**, he seized the federal arsenal in October 1859, incidentally killing seven innocent people, including a free black, and injuring ten or so more. But the slaves, largely ignorant of Brown's strike, failed to rise, and the wounded Brown and the remnants of his tiny band were quickly captured by U.S. Marines under the command of Lieutenant Colonel Robert E. Lee. Ironically, within two years Lee would become the preeminent general in the Confederate army.

"Old Brown" was convicted of murder and treason after a hasty but legal trial. His presumed insanity was supported by affidavits from seventeen friends and relatives, who were trying to save his neck. Actually thirteen of his near relations were regarded as insane, including his mother and grandmother. Governor Wise of Virginia would have been wiser, so his critics say, if he had only clapped the culprit into a lunatic asylum.

But Brown—"God's angry man"—was given every opportunity to pose and to enjoy martyrdom. Though perhaps of unsound mind, he was clever enough to see that he was worth much more to the abolitionist cause dangling from a rope than in any other way. His demeanor during the trial was dignified and courageous, his last words ("this *is* a beautiful country") were to become legendary, and he marched up the scaffold steps without flinching. His conduct was so exemplary, his devotion to freedom so inflexible, that he took on an exalted character, however deplorable his previous record may have been. So the hangman's trap was sprung, and Brown plunged not into oblivion but into world fame. A memorable marching song of the impending Civil War ran,

> *John Brown's body lies a-mould'ring in the grave,*
> *His soul is marching on.*

The effects of Harpers Ferry were inflammatory. In the eyes of the South, already embittered, "Osawatomie Brown" was a wholesale murderer and an apostle of treason. Many southerners asked how they could possibly remain in the Union while a "murderous gang of abolitionists" was financing armed bands to "Brown" them. Moderate northerners, including Republican leaders, openly deplored this mad exploit. But the South naturally concluded that the violent abolitionist view was shared by the entire North, dominated by "Brown-loving" Republicans.

Abolitionists and other ardent free-soilers were infuriated by Brown's execution. Many of them were ignorant of his bloody past and his even more bloody purposes, and they were outraged because the Virginians had hanged so earnest a reformer who was working for so righteous a cause. On the day of his execution, free-soil centers in the North tolled bells, fired guns, lowered flags, and held rallies. Some spoke of "Saint John" Brown, and the serene Ralph Waldo Emerson compared the new martyr-hero with Jesus. The gallows became a cross. E. C. Stedman wrote,

> *And Old Brown,*
> *Osawatomie Brown,*
> *May trouble you more than ever, when you've nailed his*
> *coffin down!*

The ghost of the martyred Brown would not be laid to rest.

✦ The Disruption of the Democrats

Beyond question the presidential election of 1860 was the most fateful in American history. On it hung the issue of peace or civil war.

Deeply divided, the Democrats met in Charleston, South Carolina, with Douglas the leading candidate of the northern wing of the party. But the southern "fire-eaters" regarded him as a traitor, as a result of his unpopular stand on the Lecompton Constitution and

Last Moments of John Brown, by Thomas Hovenden Sentenced to be hanged, John Brown wrote to his brother, "I am quite cheerful in view of my approaching end, being fully persuaded that I am worth inconceivably more to hang than for any other purpose. . . . I count it all joy. 'I have fought the good fight,' and have, as I trust, 'finished my course.'" This painting of Brown going to his execution may have been inspired by the journalist Horace Greeley, who was not present but wrote that "a black woman with a little child stood by the door. He stopped for a moment, and stooping, kissed the child." That scene never took place, as Brown was escorted from the jail only by a detachment of soldiers. But this painting has become famous as a kind of allegorical expression of the pathos of Brown's martyrdom for the abolitionist cause.

the Freeport Doctrine. After a bitter wrangle over the platform, the delegates from most of the cotton states walked out. When the remainder could not scrape together the necessary two-thirds vote for Douglas, the entire body dissolved. The first tragic secession was the secession of southerners from the Democratic National Convention. Departure became habit-forming.

The Democrats tried again in Baltimore. This time the Douglas Democrats, chiefly from the North, were firmly in the saddle. Many of the cotton-state delegates again took a walk, and the rest of the convention enthusiastically nominated their hero. The platform came out squarely for popular sovereignty and, as a sop to the South, against obstruction of the Fugitive Slave Law by the states.

Angered southern Democrats promptly organized a rival convention in Baltimore, in which many of the northern states were unrepresented. They selected as their leader the stern-jawed vice president, John C. Breckinridge, a man of moderate views from the border state of Kentucky. The platform favored the extension of slavery into the territories and the annexation of slave-populated Cuba.

A middle-of-the-road group, fearing for the Union, hastily organized the **Constitutional Union party**, sneered at as the "Do Nothing" or "Old Gentleman's" party. It consisted mainly of former Whigs and Know-Nothings, a veritable "gathering of graybeards." Desperately anxious to elect a compromise candidate, they met in Baltimore and nominated for the presidency John

Bell of Tennessee. They went into battle ringing hand bells for Bell and waving handbills for "The Union, the Constitution, and the Enforcement of the Laws."

✴ A Rail-Splitter Splits the Union

Elated Republicans, scenting victory in the breeze as their opponents split hopelessly, gathered in Chicago in a huge, boxlike wooden structure called the Wigwam. William H. Seward was by far the best known of the contenders. But his radical utterances, including his "irrepressible conflict" speech at Rochester in 1858, had ruined his prospects.* His numerous enemies coined the slogan "Success Rather Than Seward." Lincoln, the favorite son of Illinois, was definitely a "Mr. Second Best," but he was a stronger candidate because he had made fewer enemies. Overtaking Seward on the third ballot, he was nominated amid scenes of the wildest excitement.

The Republican platform had a seductive appeal for just about every important nonsouthern group: for the free-soilers, nonextension of slavery; for the northern manufacturers, a protective tariff; for the immigrants, no abridgment of rights; for the Northwest, a Pacific railroad; for the West, internal improvements at federal

---

*Seward had referred to an "irrepressible conflict" between slavery and freedom, though not necessarily a bloody one.

Lincoln Hits a Home Run in 1860 Currier & Ives, the producer of popular, inexpensive colored prints, portrayed Lincoln's victory over (from left to right) John Bell, Stephen Douglas, and John C. Breckinridge as a baseball game. Baseball developed in New York in the 1840s, and by 1860 the National Association of Baseball Players boasted fifty clubs, several playing regular schedules and charging admission. This cartoon is thought to be the first time baseball was used as a metaphor for politics. Note that Lincoln is beardless. By February 1861, when he left Springfield, Illinois, by train for the White House, he was fully bearded, having followed the advice of an eleven-year-old girl from Westfield, New York, who urged him to grow whiskers because "you would look a great deal better for your face is so thin."

THE NATIONAL GAME. THREE "OUTS" AND ONE "RUN".
ABRAHAM WINNING THE BALL.

Museum of American Political Life

expense; and for the farmers, free homesteads from the public domain. Alluring slogans included "Vote Yourselves a Farm" and "Land for the Landless."

Southern secessionists promptly served notice that the election of the "baboon" Lincoln—the "abolitionist" rail-splitter—would split the Union. In fact, "Honest Abe," though hating slavery, was no outright abolitionist. As late as February 1865, he was inclined to favor cash compensation to the owners of freed slaves. But for the time being, he saw fit, perhaps mistakenly, to issue no statements to quiet southern fears. He had already put himself on record, and fresh statements might stir up fresh antagonisms.

As the election campaign ground noisily forward, Lincoln enthusiasts staged roaring rallies and parades, complete with pitch-dripping torches and oilskin capes. They extolled "High Old Abe," the "Woodchopper of the West," and the "Little Giant Killer," while groaning dismally for "Poor Little Doug." Enthusiastic "Little Giants" and "Little Dougs" retorted with "We want a statesman, not a rail-splitter, as President." Douglas himself waged a vigorous speaking campaign, even in the South, and threatened to put the noose with his own hands around the neck of the first secessionist.

The returns, breathlessly awaited, proclaimed a sweeping victory for Lincoln (see Table 19.1).

✯ The Electoral Upheaval of 1860

Awkward "Abe" Lincoln had run a curious race. To a greater degree than any other holder of the nation's highest office (except John Quincy Adams), he was a minority president. Sixty percent of the voters preferred some other candidate. He was also a sectional president, for in ten southern states, where he was not allowed on the ballot, he polled no popular votes. The election of 1860 was virtually two elections: one in the

TABLE 19.1 Election of 1860			
Candidate	Popular Vote	Percentage of Popular Vote	Electoral Vote
Lincoln	1,865,593	39.79%	180 (every vote of the free states except for 3 of New Jersey's 7 votes)
Douglas	1,382,713	29.40	12 (only Missouri and 3 of New Jersey's 7 votes)
Breckinridge	848,356	18.20	72 (all the cotton states)
Bell	592,906	12.61	39 (Virginia, Kentucky, Tennessee)

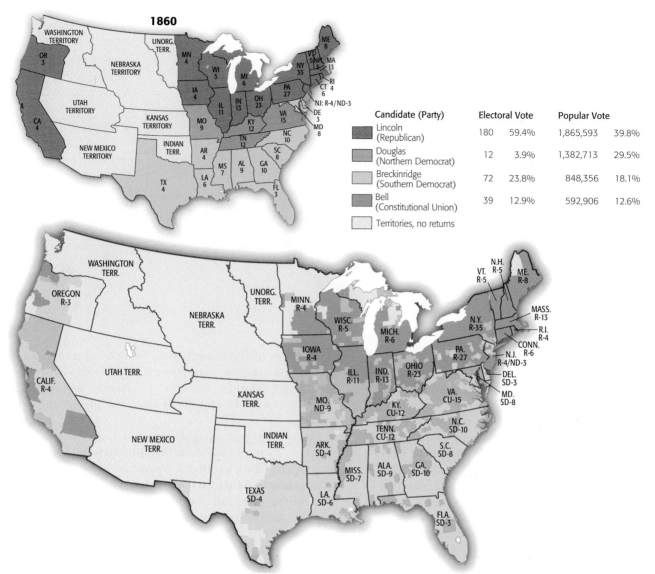

MAP 19.3 Presidential Election of 1860: Electoral Vote by State (top) and Popular Vote by County (bottom) It is a surprising fact that Lincoln, often rated among the greatest presidents, ranks near the bottom in percentage of popular votes. In all the eleven states that seceded, he received only a scattering of one state's votes—about 1.5 percent in Virginia. The vote by county for Lincoln was virtually all cast in the North. The northern Democrat, Douglas, was also nearly shut out in the South, which divided its votes between Breckinridge and Bell. (Note that only citizens of states could vote; inhabitants of territories could not.) © Cengage Learning

North, the other in the South (see Map 19.3). South Carolinians rejoiced over Lincoln's victory; they now had their excuse to secede. In winning the North, the "rail-splitter" had split off the South.

Douglas, though scraping together only twelve electoral votes, made an impressive showing. Boldly breaking with tradition, he campaigned energetically for himself. (Presidential candidates customarily maintained a dignified silence.) He drew important strength from all sections and ranked a fairly close second in the popular-vote column. In fact, the Douglas Democrats and the Breckinridge Democrats together amassed 365,476 more votes than did Lincoln.

A myth persists that if the Democrats had only united behind Douglas, they would have triumphed. Yet the cold figures tell a different story. Even if the "Little Giant" had received all the electoral votes cast for all three of Lincoln's opponents, the "rail-splitter" would have won, 169 to 134 instead of 180 to 123. Lincoln still would have carried the populous states of the

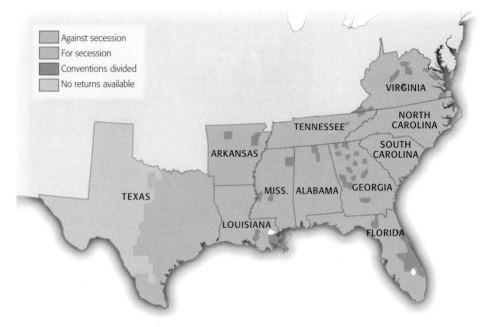

MAP 19.4 Southern Opposition to Secession, 1860–1861 (showing vote by county) This county vote shows the opposition of the anti-planter, antislavery mountain whites in the Appalachian region. There was also considerable resistance to secession in Texas, where Governor Sam Houston, who led the Unionists, was deposed by secessionists.

© Cengage Learning

North and the Northwest. On the other hand, if the Democrats had not broken up, they could have entered the campaign with higher enthusiasm and better organization and might have won.

Significantly, the verdict of the ballot box did not indicate a strong sentiment for secession (see Map 19.4). Breckinridge, while favoring the extension of slavery, was no disunionist. Although the candidate of the "fire-eaters," he polled fewer votes in the slave states than the combined strength of his opponents, Douglas and Bell. He even failed to carry his own Kentucky.

Yet the South, despite its electoral defeat, was not bad off. It still had a five-to-four majority on the Supreme Court. Although the Republicans had elected Lincoln, they controlled neither the Senate nor the House of Representatives. The federal government could not touch slavery in those states where it existed except by a constitutional amendment, and such an amendment could be defeated by one-fourth of the states. The fifteen slave states numbered nearly one-half of the total—a fact not fully appreciated by southern firebrands.

✹ The Secessionist Exodus

But a tragic chain reaction of secession now began to erupt. South Carolina, which had threatened to go out if the "sectional" Lincoln came in, was as good as its word. Four days after the election of the "Illinois baboon" by "insulting" majorities, its legislature voted unanimously to call a special convention. Meeting at Charleston in December 1860, the convention unanimously voted to secede. During the next six weeks, six

other states of the lower South, though somewhat less united, followed the leader over the precipice: Alabama, Mississippi, Florida, Georgia, Louisiana, and Texas. Four more were to join them later, bringing the total to eleven.

With the eyes of destiny upon them, the seven seceders, formally meeting at Montgomery, Alabama, in February 1861, created a government known as the **Confederate States of America**. As their president they chose Jefferson Davis, a dignified and austere recent member of the U.S. Senate from Mississippi. He was a West Pointer and a former cabinet member with wide military and administrative experience; but

The state of South Carolina, leader of the secessionist movement, justified its retreat from the Union in its declaration of independence of December 1860:

❝We affirm that the ends for which this [Federal] government was instituted have been defeated, and the government itself has been made destructive of them by the action of the non-slaveholding states. . . . For twenty five years this agitation has been steadily increasing, until it has now secured to its aid the power of the common government. Observing the forms of the constitution, a sectional party has found within that article establishing the executive department the means of subverting the constitution itself.**❞**

Three days after Lincoln's election, Horace Greeley's influential New York Tribune *(November 9, 1860) declared,*

"If the cotton States shall decide that they can do better out of the Union than in it, we insist on letting them go in peace. The right to secede may be a revolutionary one, but it exists nevertheless.... Whenever a considerable section of our Union shall deliberately resolve to go out, we shall resist all coercive measures designed to keep it in. We hope never to live in a republic, whereof one section is pinned to the residue by bayonets."

After the secession movement got well under way, Greeley's Tribune *changed its tune.*

Jefferson Davis (1808–1889), President of the Confederacy Faced with grave difficulties, he was probably as able a man for the position as the Confederacy could have chosen. Ironically, Davis and Lincoln had both sprung from the same Kentucky soil. The Davis family had moved south from Kentucky, the Lincoln family north. Chicago History Museum

he suffered from chronic ill health, as well as from a frustrated ambition to be a Napoleonic strategist.

The crisis, already critical enough, was deepened by the "lame duck"* interlude. Lincoln, although elected president in November 1860, could not take office until four months later, on March 4, 1861. During this period of protracted uncertainty, when he was still a private citizen in Illinois, seven of the eleven deserting states pulled out of the Union.

President Buchanan, the aging incumbent, has been blamed for not holding the seceders in the Union by sheer force—for wringing his hands instead of secessionist necks. Never a vigorous man and habitually conservative, he was now nearly seventy, and although devoted to the Union, he was surrounded by prosouthern advisers. As an able lawyer wedded to the Constitution, he did not believe that the southern states could legally secede. Yet he could find no authority in the Constitution for stopping them with guns.

"Oh for one hour of Jackson!" cried the advocates of strong-arm tactics. But "Old Buck" Buchanan was not "Old Hickory," and he was faced with a far more complex and serious problem. One important reason why he did not resort to force was that the tiny standing army of some fifteen thousand men, then widely scattered, was urgently needed to control the Indians in the West. Public opinion in the North, at that time, was far from willing to unsheathe the sword. Fighting would merely shatter all prospects of adjustment, and until the guns began to boom, there was still a flickering hope of reconciliation rather than a contested divorce. The weakness lay not so much in Buchanan as in the Constitution and in the Union itself. Ironically,

---

*The "lame duck" period was shortened to ten weeks in 1933 by the Twentieth Amendment (see the Appendix).

when Lincoln became president in March, he essentially continued Buchanan's wait-and-see policy.

✦ The Collapse of Compromise

Impending bloodshed spurred final and frantic attempts at compromise—in the American tradition. The most promising of these efforts was sponsored by Senator John Jordan Crittenden of Kentucky, on whose shoulders had fallen the mantle of a fellow Kentuckian, Henry Clay.

The proposed **Crittenden amendments** to the Constitution were designed to appease the South. Slavery in the territories was to be prohibited north of 36° 30′, but south of that line it was to be given federal protection in all territories existing or "hereafter to be acquired" (such as Cuba). Future states, north or south of 36° 30′, could come into the Union with or without slavery, as they should choose. In short, the slavery supporters were to be guaranteed full rights in the southern territories, as long as they were territories,

One reason why the Crittenden Compromise failed in December 1860 was the prevalence of an attitude reflected in a private letter of Senator James Henry Hammond (1807–1864) of South Carolina on April 19:

"I firmly believe that the slave-holding South is now the controlling power of the world—that no other power would face us in hostility. Cotton, rice, tobacco, and naval stores command the world; and we have sense to know it, and are sufficiently Teutonic to carry it out successfully. The North without us would be a motherless calf, bleating about, and die of mange and starvation.**"**

regardless of the wishes of the majority under popular sovereignty. Federal protection in a territory south of 36° 30′ might conceivably, though improbably, turn the entire area permanently to slavery.

Lincoln flatly rejected the Crittenden scheme, which offered some slight prospect of success, and all hope of compromise evaporated. For this refusal he must bear a heavy responsibility. Yet he had been elected on a platform that opposed the extension of slavery, and he felt that as a matter of principle, he could not afford to yield, even though gains for slavery in the territories might be only temporary. Larger gains might come later in Cuba and Mexico. Crittenden's proposal, said Lincoln, "would amount to a perpetual covenant

of war against every people, tribe, and state owning a foot of land between here and Tierra del Fuego."

As for the supposedly spineless "Old Fogy" Buchanan, how could he have prevented the Civil War by starting a civil war? No one has yet come up with a satisfactory answer. If he had used force on South Carolina in December 1860, the fighting almost certainly would have erupted three months sooner than it did, and under less favorable circumstances for the Union. The North would have appeared as the heavy-handed aggressor. And the crucial Border States, so vital to the Union, probably would have been driven into the arms of their "wayward sisters."

✸ Farewell to Union

Secessionists who parted company with their sister states left for a number of avowed reasons, mostly relating in some way to slavery. They were alarmed by the inexorable tipping of the political balance against them—"the despotic majority of numbers." The "crime" of the North, observed James Russell Lowell, was the census returns. Southerners were also dismayed by the triumph of the new sectional Republican party, which seemed to threaten their rights as a slaveholding minority. They were weary of free-soil criticism, abolitionist nagging, and northern interference, ranging from the Underground Railroad to John Brown's raid. "All we ask is to be let alone," declared Confederate president Jefferson Davis in an early message to his congress.

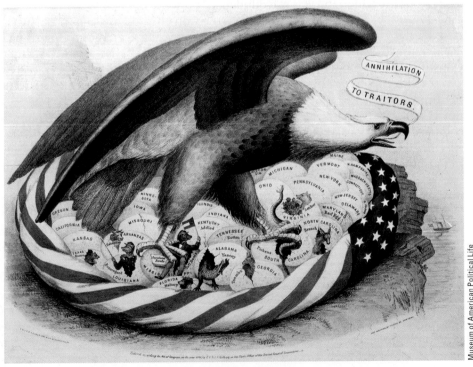

The Eagle's Nest, 1861 The American eagle jealously guards her nest of states and bids defiance to the rebels.

Museum of American Political Life

James Russell Lowell (1819–1891), the northern poet and essayist, wrote in the Atlantic Monthly *shortly after the secessionist movement began,*

❝ The fault of the free States in the eyes of the South is not one that can be atoned for by any yielding of special points here and there. Their offense is that they are free, and that their habits and prepossessions are those of freedom. Their crime is the census of 1860. Their increase in numbers, wealth, and power is a standing aggression. It would not be enough to please the Southern States that we should stop asking them to abolish slavery: what they demand of us is nothing less than that we should abolish the spirit of the age. Our very thoughts are a menace.❞

Regarding the Civil War, the London Times *(November 7, 1861) editorialized,*

❝ The contest is really for empire on the side of the North, and for independence on that of the South, and in this respect we recognize an exact analogy between the North and the Government of George III, and the South and the Thirteen Revolted Provinces.❞

Many southerners supported secession because they felt sure that their departure would be unopposed, despite "Yankee yawp" to the contrary. They were confident that the clodhopping and codfishing Yankee would not or could not fight. They believed that northern manufacturers and bankers, so heavily dependent on southern cotton and markets, would not dare to cut their own economic throats with their own unionist swords. But should war come, the immense debt owed to northern creditors by the South—happy thought—could be promptly repudiated, as it later was.

Southern leaders regarded secession as a golden opportunity to cast aside their generations of "vassalage" to the North. An independent Dixieland could develop its own banking and shipping and trade directly with Europe. The low Tariff of 1857, passed largely by southern votes, was not in itself menacing. But who could tell when the "greedy" Republicans would win control of Congress and drive through their own oppressive

protective tariff? For decades this fundamental friction had pitted the North, with its manufacturing plants, against the South, with its agricultural exports.

Worldwide impulses of nationalism—then stirring in Italy, Germany, Poland, and elsewhere—were fermenting in the South. This huge area, with its distinctive culture, was not so much a section as a subnation. It could not view with complacency the possibility of being lorded over, then or later, by what it regarded as a hostile nation of northerners.

The principles of self-determination—of the Declaration of Independence—seemed to many southerners to apply perfectly to them. Few, if any, of the seceders felt that they were doing anything wrong or immoral. The thirteen original states had voluntarily entered the Union, and now seven—ultimately eleven—southern states were voluntarily withdrawing from it.

Historical parallels ran even deeper. In 1776 thirteen American colonies, led by the rebel George Washington, had seceded from the British Empire by throwing off the yoke of King George III. In 1860–1861, eleven American states, led by the rebel Jefferson Davis, were seceding from the Union by throwing off the yoke of "King" Abraham Lincoln. With that burden gone, the South was confident that it could work out its own peculiar destiny more quietly, happily, and prosperously.

Varying Viewpoints
The Civil War: Repressible or Irrepressible?

Few topics have generated as much controversy among American historians as the causes of the Civil War. Looming over the entire debate is the stark fact the United States was the only slaveowning society that had to fight a war to rid itself of slavery. The very names employed to describe the conflict—notably "Civil War" or "War Between the States" or even "War for Southern Independence"—reveal much about the various authors' points of view. Interpretations of the great conflict have naturally differed according to

section and have been charged with both emotional and moral fervor. Yet despite long and keen interest in the origins of the conflict, the causes of the Civil War remain as passionately debated today as they were a century ago.

The so-called Nationalist School of the late nineteenth century claimed that slavery caused the Civil War. Defending the necessity and inevitability of the war, these northern-oriented historians credited the conflict with ending slavery and preserving the Union. But in the early twentieth century, progressive historians, led by Charles and Mary Beard, presented a more skeptical interpretation. The Beards argued that the war was not fought over slavery per se, but rather was a deeply rooted economic struggle between an industrial North and an agricultural South. Anointing the Civil War the "Second American Revolution," the Beards claimed that the war precipitated vast changes in American class relations and shifted the political balance of power by magnifying the influence of business magnates and industrialists while destroying the plantation aristocracy of the South.

Shaken by the disappointing results of World War I, a new wave of historians argued that the Civil War, too, had actually been a big mistake. Rejecting the nationalist interpretation that the clash was inevitable, James G. Randall and Avery Craven asserted that the war had been a "repressible conflict." Neither slavery nor the economic differences between North and South were sufficient causes for war. Instead Craven and others attributed the bloody confrontation to the breakdown of political institutions, the passion of overzealous reformers, and the ineptitude of a blundering generation of political leaders.

Following the Second World War, however, a neonationalist view regained authority, echoing earlier views in depicting the Civil War as an unavoidable conflict between two societies, one slave and one free. For Allan Nevins and David M. Potter, irreconcilable differences in morality, politics, culture, social values, and economies increasingly eroded the ties between the sections and inexorably set the United States on the road to Civil War.

Eric Foner and Eugene Genovese emphasized each section's nearly paranoid fear that the survival of its distinctive way of life was threatened by the expansion of the other section. In *Free Soil, Free Labor, Free Men* (1970), Foner emphasized that most northerners detested slavery not because it enslaved blacks, but because its existence—and particularly its rapid extension—threatened the position of free white laborers. This "free labor ideology" increasingly became the foundation stone upon which the North claimed its superiority over the South. Eugene Genovese has argued that the South felt similarly endangered. Convinced that the southern labor system was more humane than the northern factory system, southerners saw northern designs to destroy their way of life lurking at every turn—and every territorial battle. The focus on the irreconcilable interests of the free and slave sections as the central cause of the war has been carried into more recent scholarship by historians such as John Ashworth and David L. Lightner.

Some historians have placed party politics at the center of their explanations for the war. For them, no event was more consequential than the breakdown of the Jacksonian party system. When the slavery issue tore apart both the Democratic and the Whig parties, the last ligaments binding the nation together were snapped, and the war inevitably came.

More recently, historians of the "Ethnocultural School," especially Michael Holt, have acknowledged the significance of the collapse of the established parties, but have offered a different analysis of how that breakdown led to war. They have noted that the two great national parties before the 1850s focused attention on issues such as the tariff, banking, and internal improvements, thereby muting sectional differences over slavery. According to this argument, the erosion of the traditional party system was due not to growing differences over slavery, but to a temporary *consensus* between the two parties in the 1850s on almost all national issues *other than* slavery. In this peculiar political atmosphere, the slavery issue rose to the fore, encouraging the emergence of Republicans in the North and secessionists in the South. In the absence of regular, national, two-party conflict over economic issues, purely regional parties (like the Republicans) coalesced. They identified their opponents not simply as competitors for power but as threats to their way of life, even to the life of the Republic itself.

Chapter Review

KEY TERMS

Uncle Tom's Cabin (396)

The Impending Crisis of the South (397)

New England Emigrant Aid Company (398)

Lecompton Constitution (400)

Bleeding Kansas (400)

Dred Scott v. *Sandford* (403)

panic of 1857 (404)

Tariff of 1857 (405)

Lincoln-Douglas debates (406)

Freeport question (406)

Freeport Doctrine (406)

Harpers Ferry (408)

Constitutional Union party (409)

Confederate States of America (412)

Crittenden amendments (413)

PEOPLE TO KNOW

Harriet Beecher Stowe

Henry Ward Beecher

James Buchanan

Charles Sumner

Preston S. Brooks

Dred Scott

Roger B. Taney

Stephen A. Douglas

Abraham Lincoln

John Brown

John C. Breckinridge

John Jordan Crittenden

CHRONOLOGY

1852	Harriet Beecher Stowe publishes *Uncle Tom's Cabin*
1853–1856	Crimean War in Russia
1854	Kansas-Nebraska Act Republican party forms
1856	Buchanan defeats Frémont and Fillmore for presidency Sumner beaten by Brooks in Senate chamber Brown's Pottawatomie Massacre
1856–1861	Civil war in "bleeding Kansas"
1857	*Dred Scott* decision Lecompton Constitution rejected
1857	Panic of 1857 Tariff of 1857 Hinton R. Helper publishes *The Impending Crisis of the South*
1858	Lincoln-Douglas debates
1859	Brown raids Harpers Ferry
1860	Lincoln wins four-way race for presidency South Carolina secedes from Union Crittenden Compromise fails
1861	Seven seceding states form Confederate States of America

TO LEARN MORE

Frederick J. Blue, *Charles Sumner and the Conscience of the North* (1994)

Nicole Etcheson, *Bleeding Kansas: Contested Liberty in the Civil War Era* (2004)

Paul Finkelman, ed., *And His Soul Goes Marching On: Responses to John Brown and the Harpers Ferry Raid* (1995)

Eric Foner, *Free Soil, Free Labor, Free Men: The Ideology of the Republican Party before the Civil War* (1995)

Joan Hedrick, *Harriet Beecher Stowe: A Life* (1994)

Ward M. McAfee, ed., *The Slaveholding Republic* (2001)

Stephen B. Oates, *To Purge This Land with Blood* (1970)

Kenneth M. Stampp, *America in 1857: A Nation on the Brink* (1990)

Harriet Beecher Stowe, *Uncle Tom's Cabin* (1852)

A complete, annotated bibliography for this chapter—along with brief descriptions of the People to Know—may be found on the American Pageant website. The Key Terms are defined in a Glossary at the end of the text.

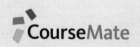

Go to the CourseMate website at **www.cengagebrain.com** for additional study tools and review materials—including audio and video clips—for this chapter.

AP® Review Questions for Chapter 19

1. All of the following are true statements about Harriet Beecher Stowe's novel EXCEPT that
   (A) it helped spark the Civil War.
   (B) it was inspired by the passage of the Fugitive Slave Act.
   (C) Stowe claimed that God wrote the book.
   (D) it sold hundreds of thousands of copies in the United States and beyond.
   (E) it relied on Stowe's many personal experiences and firsthand knowledge of slavery.

2. Why was the Lecompton Constitution considered a sly maneuver?
   (A) It included provisions for allowing slavery in Kansas even if the people voted against slavery.
   (B) It was an attempt to make Kansas a free state, despite earlier agreements that Kansas would be admitted as a slave state.
   (C) It resolved competing land claims in favor of slaveholders.
   (D) It sought to bypass normal preconditions for moving from territory status to statehood.
   (E) It led to the establishment of two different governments in Kansas—one supporting slavery and the other supporting the abolitionist cause.

3. What was Preston Brooks's claim to fame?
   (A) He was a proslavery congressman who staunchly defended his home state of South Carolina's position on including slavery in the new territories.
   (B) He badly beat Senator Charles Sumner over a provocative speech against popular sovereignty and slavery.
   (C) He challenged Sumner to a duel for having insulted his countrymen and a distant cousin.
   (D) He was expelled from the House of Representatives for his violent outbursts.
   (E) He staged an attack on Kansas that came to be known as Bleeding Kansas.

4. The Know-Nothing party, which first appeared on the political scene during the 1856 election, was so named because
   (A) of its hard-line stand supporting new immigrants.
   (B) of the secretive nature of the party.
   (C) it chose as its presidential candidate a man who many joked did not know much about politics.
   (D) it was a band of armed ruffians who secretly staged violent attacks on groups it disliked.
   (E) it was known for planting negative stories about opposing candidates in newspapers and slinging mud behind the scenes.

5. Which of the following was NOT part of the Supreme Court's ruling in the landmark Dred Scott case of 1857?
   (A) A slave could be taken into any state—and remain a slave—regardless of whether the state itself was slave or free.
   (B) The Compromise of 1820 was never constitutional.
   (C) Northern states could be held legally accountable and be required to offer compensation to slaveholders for not returning runaway slaves.
   (D) Dred Scott and his wife were to retain their slave status for life, unless their owner determined to set them free.
   (E) As a slave, Dred Scott could not sue in federal courts.

6. The economic crash of 1857 was caused by all of the following EXCEPT
   (A) inflated currency values.
   (B) feverish land speculation.
   (C) overproduction of grain.
   (D) rapid decline in cotton prices overseas.
   (E) the collapse of hundreds of businesses.

7. Why was Abraham Lincoln nicknamed "Honest Abe"?
   (A) Because he emerged from humble circumstances to champion the cause of the common man
   (B) Because he worked hard, earned an education, and achieved everything on his own merits
   (C) Because, as a lawyer, he would decline cases that went against his conscience
   (D) Because of his impassioned and eloquent response to the Kansas-Nebraska Act
   (E) Because he offered simple, humble statements of his political principles when running for office

8. The major significance of the famed Lincoln-Douglas debates in 1858 was that they
   (A) led to Lincoln's victory against Douglas in the Illinois senate race.
   (B) helped Lincoln's star to rise in the political arena, while Douglas's began to fall.
   (C) led to passage of the Freemont Doctrine.
   (D) were the first time two presidential candidates held a public debate.
   (E) inspired Lincoln's nomination for vice president on the ticket with John Fremont.

9. How did John Brown best serve the antislavery cause?
   (A) Through his execution
   (B) Through his violent raid at Harpers Ferry
   (C) Through his support of Kansas as a free state
   (D) Through his efforts to arm slaves and lead them in a rebellion
   (E) Through his antislavery writings and financial support of northern abolitionists

10. Which of the following is NOT a true statement about the election of Abraham Lincoln in 1860?
    (A) He was not the abolitionist the South thought him to be.
    (B) He was a majority president.
    (C) His election gave South Carolina the excuse it needed to secede.
    (D) His election was due to northern voters.
    (E) He was not the first choice for Republican party candidate.

11. Lincoln's victory should not have caused fear in the South over slavery because
    (A) the Supreme Court was evenly split in terms of North-South political views.
    (B) the nation remained so politically divided that no majority will could have prevailed.
    (C) there were more slave states than free states.
    (D) southern Democrats' control of the House would offset northern Republican control of the Senate.
    (E) it would require a constitutional amendment to end slavery in slave states and there were enough votes to quash such an effort.

12. Which of these states was NOT among the half dozen that joined South Carolina in seceding within just six weeks?
    (A) Alabama
    (B) Mississippi
    (C) Florida
    (D) Missouri
    (E) Texas

13. Lame duck President Buchanan did not move to block southern states from seceding mainly because he
    (A) considered the move a bluff.
    (B) hoped to negotiate a peace with the South.
    (C) did not believe states could secede.
    (D) was a pacifist and did not want to use force.
    (E) did not want the North calling the shots.

14. Which of the following was NOT among southerners' justifications for secession?
    (A) They were exerting their majority political status and clout.
    (B) They were inspired by nationalist movements around the globe.
    (C) They thought they had voluntarily entered the Union and could voluntarily withdraw.
    (D) They saw parallels in their own experience and that of the colonists and King George.
    (E) They feared that the rise of the Republican party signaled their eventual domination by the North.

15. Which of the following events caused the other four?
    (A) Kansas-Nebraska Act
    (B) Formation of the Republican party
    (C) Northern and southern migration to Kansas
    (D) Bleeding Kansas
    (E) Sacking of Lawrence

16. How did sectionalism trump party politics in the years leading up to the Civil War?
    (A) Northerners voted for the Democratic candidate, and southerners voted for the Whig candidate.
    (B) Third parties, like the Know-Nothings, had great success in national elections.
    (C) Presidents took action to delay the war so it wouldn't start during their administrations.
    (D) New parties, including the Republican party, were created.
    (E) Parties split along North-South lines, with two candidates often running for the same office.

Chapter 20

Girding for War: The North and the South

1861–1865

I consider the central idea pervading this struggle is the necessity that is upon us, of proving that popular government is not an absurdity. We must settle this question now, whether in a free government the minority have the right to break up the government whenever they choose. If we fail it will go far to prove the incapability of the people to govern themselves.

ABRAHAM LINCOLN, 7,1861

Abraham Lincoln solemnly took the presidential oath of office on March 4, 1861, after having slipped into Washington at night, partially disguised to thwart assassins. He thus became president not of the *United* States of America, but of the *dis-United* States of America. Seven had already departed; eight more teetered on the edge. The girders of the unfinished Capitol dome loomed nakedly in the background, as if to symbolize the imperfect state of the Union. Before the nation was restored—and the slaves freed at last—the American people would endure four years of anguish and bloodshed, and Lincoln would face tortuous trials of leadership such as have been visited upon few presidents.

✬ The Menace of Secession

Lincoln's inaugural address was firm yet conciliatory: there would be no conflict unless the South provoked it. Secession, the president declared, was wholly impractical, because "physically speaking, we cannot separate."

Here Lincoln put his finger on a profound geographical truth. The North and South were conjoined twins, bound inseparably together. If they had been divided by the Pyrenees or the Danube River, a

sectional divorce might have been more feasible. But the Appalachian Mountains and the mighty Mississippi River both ran the wrong way.

Uncontested secession would create new controversies. What share of the national debt should the South be forced to take with it? What portion of the jointly held federal territories, if any, should the Confederate

Secretary of State William H. Seward (1801–1872) entertained the dangerous idea that if the North picked a fight with one or more European nations, the South would once more rally around the flag. On April Fools' Day, 1861, he submitted to Lincoln a memorandum:

"I would demand explanations from Spain and France, categorically, at once. I would seek explanations from Great Britain and Russia. . . . And, if satisfactory explanations are not received from Spain and France . . . would convene Congress and declare war against them.**"**

Lincoln quietly but firmly quashed Seward's scheme.

Bombardment of Fort Sumter, South Carolina, April 1861 At 4:30 the morning of April 12, a Confederate battery at Fort Johnson opened fire on the Union Forces at Fort Sumter in Charleston Harbor. Residents of Charleston cheered from their rooftops as the beleaguered garrison briefly returned fire, surrendered, and then fled.

states be allotted—areas so largely won with Southern blood? How would the fugitive-slave issue be resolved? The Underground Railroad would certainly redouble its activity, and it would have to transport its passengers only across the Ohio River, not all the way to Canada. Was it conceivable that all such problems could have been solved without ugly armed clashes?

A *united United* States had hitherto been the paramount republic in the Western Hemisphere. If this powerful democracy should break into two hostile parts, the European nations would be delighted. They could gleefully transplant to America their ancient concept of the balance of power. Playing the no-less-ancient game of divide and conquer, they could incite one snarling fragment of the *dis-United* States against the other. The colonies of the European powers in the New World, notably those of Britain, would thus be made safer against the rapacious Yankees. And European imperialists, with no unified republic to stand across their path, could more easily defy the Monroe Doctrine and seize territory in the Americas.

⭐ South Carolina Assails Fort Sumter

The issue of the divided Union came to a head over the matter of federal forts in the South. As the seceding states left, they seized the United States' arsenals, mints, and other public property within their borders. When Lincoln took office, only two significant forts in the South still flew the Stars and Stripes. The more important of the pair was square-walled **Fort Sumter**, in Charleston harbor, with fewer than a hundred men.

Ominously, the choices presented to Lincoln by Fort Sumter were all bad. This stronghold had provisions that would last only a few weeks—until the middle of April 1861. If no supplies were forthcoming, its commander would have to surrender without firing a shot. Lincoln, quite understandably, did not feel that such a weak-kneed course squared with his obligation to protect federal property. But if he sent reinforcements, the South Carolinians would undoubtedly fight back; they could not tolerate a federal fort blocking the mouth of their most important Atlantic seaport.

After agonizing indecision, Lincoln adopted a middle-of-the-road solution. He notified the South Carolinians that an expedition would be sent to *provision* the garrison, though not to *reinforce* it. He promised "no effort to throw in men, arms, and ammunition." But to Southern eyes "provision" still spelled "reinforcement."

A Union naval force was next started on its way to Fort Sumter—a move that the South regarded as an act of aggression. On April 12, 1861, the cannon of the Carolinians opened fire on the fort, while crowds in Charleston applauded and waved handkerchiefs. After a thirty-four-hour bombardment, which took no lives, the dazed garrison surrendered.

The shelling of the fort electrified the North, which at once responded with cries of "Remember Fort Sumter" and "Save the Union." Hitherto countless Northerners had been saying that if the Southern states wanted to go, they should not be pinned to the rest of the nation with bayonets. "Wayward sisters, depart in peace" was a common sentiment, expressed even by the commander of the army, war hero General Winfield Scott, now so feeble at seventy-five that he had to be boosted onto his horse.

But the assault on Fort Sumter provoked the North to a fighting pitch: the fort was lost, but the Union was saved. Lincoln had turned a tactical defeat into a calculated victory. Southerners had wantonly fired upon the glorious Stars and Stripes, and honor demanded an

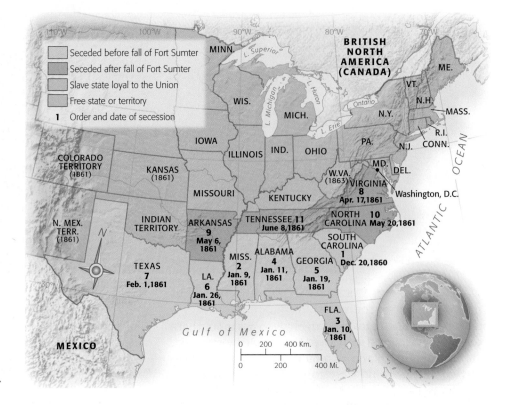

MAP 20.1 Seceding States (with dates and order of secession) Note the long interval—nearly six months—between the secession of South Carolina, the first state to go, and that of Tennessee, the last state to leave the Union. These six months were a time of terrible trial for moderate Southerners. When a Georgia statesman pleaded for restraint and negotiations with Washington, he was rebuffed with the cry, "Throw the bloody spear into this den of incendiaries!" © Cengage Learning

armed response. Lincoln promptly (April 15) issued a call to the states for seventy-five thousand militiamen, and volunteers sprang to the colors in such enthusiastic numbers that many were turned away—a mistake that was not often repeated. On April 19 and 27, the president proclaimed a leaky blockade of Southern seaports.

The call for troops, in turn, aroused the South much as the attack on Fort Sumter had aroused the North. Lincoln was now waging war—from the Southern view an aggressive war—on the Confederacy. Virginia, Arkansas, and Tennessee, all of which had earlier voted down secession, reluctantly joined their embattled sister states, as did North Carolina (see Map 20.1). Thus the seven states became eleven as the "submissionists" and "Union shriekers" were overcome. Richmond, Virginia, replaced Montgomery, Alabama, as the Confederate capital—too near Washington for strategic comfort on either side.

✷ Brothers' Blood and Border Blood

The only slave states left were the crucial **Border States**. This group consisted of Missouri, Kentucky, Maryland, Delaware, and later **West Virginia**—the "mountain white" area that somewhat illegally tore itself from the side of Virginia in mid-1861. If the North had fired the first shot, some or all of these doubtful states probably would have seceded, and the South might well have succeeded. The border group actually

contained a white population more than half that of the entire Confederacy. Maryland, Kentucky, and Missouri would almost double the manufacturing capacity of the South and increase by nearly half its supply of horses and mules. The strategic prize of the Ohio River flowed along the northern border of Kentucky and West Virginia. Two of its navigable tributaries, the Cumberland and Tennessee Rivers, penetrated deep into the heart of Dixie, where much of the Confederacy's grain, gunpowder, and iron was produced. Small wonder that Lincoln reportedly said he *hoped* to have God on his side, but he *had* to have Kentucky.

In dealing with the Border States, President Lincoln did not rely solely on moral suasion but successfully used methods of dubious legality. In Maryland he declared martial law where needed and sent in troops, because this state threatened to cut off Washington from the North. Lincoln also deployed Union soldiers in western Virginia and notably in Missouri, where they fought beside Unionists in a local civil war within the larger Civil War.

Any official statement of the North's war aims was profoundly influenced by the teetering Border States. At the very outset, Lincoln was obliged to declare publicly that he was not fighting to free the blacks. An antislavery declaration would no doubt have driven the Border States into the welcoming arms of the South. An antislavery war was also extremely unpopular in the so-called Butternut region of southern Ohio, Indiana, and Illinois. That area had been settled largely

Abraham Lincoln (1809–1865), Kentucky-born like Jefferson Davis, was aware of Kentucky's crucial importance. In September 1861 he remarked,

❝I think to lose Kentucky is nearly the same as to lose the whole game. Kentucky gone, we cannot hold Missouri, nor, I think, Maryland. These all against us, and the job on our hands is too large for us. We would as well consent to separation at once, including the surrender of this capital [Washington].❞

by Southerners who had carried their racial prejudices with them when they had crossed the Ohio River (see "Makers of America: Settlers of the Old Northwest," pp. 236–237). It was to be a hotbed of pro-Southern sentiment throughout the war. Sensitive to this delicate political calculus, Lincoln insisted repeatedly—even though undercutting his moral high ground—that his paramount purpose was to save the Union at all costs. Thus the war began not as one between slave soil and free soil, but one for the Union—with slaveholders on both sides and many proslavery sympathizers in the North.

Slavery also colored the character of the war in the West. In Indian Territory (present-day Oklahoma), most of the Five Civilized Tribes—the Cherokees, Creeks, Choctaws, Chickasaws, and Seminoles—sided with the Confederacy. Some of these Indians, notably the Cherokees, owned slaves and thus felt themselves to be making common cause with the slaveowning South. To secure their loyalty, the Confederate government agreed to take over federal payments to the tribes and invited the Native Americans to send delegates to the Confederate congress. In return the tribes supplied troops to the Confederate army. Meanwhile, a rival faction of Cherokees and most of the Plains Indians sided with the Union, only to be rewarded after the war with a relentless military campaign to herd them onto reservations or into oblivion.

Unhappily, the conflict between "Billy Yank" and "Johnny Reb" was a brothers' war (see "Makers of America: Billy Yank and Johnny Reb," pp. 422–423). There

Lincoln wrote to the antislavery editor Horace Greeley in August 1862, even as he was about to announce the Emancipation Proclamation,

❝If I could save the Union without freeing any slave, I would do it; and if I could save it by freeing all the slaves, I would do it; and if I could do it by freeing some and leaving others alone, I would also do that.❞

Library of Congress

Friendly Enemies   The man on the right is George Armstrong Custer. The youngest general in the Union army, this brilliant young officer survived the Civil War only to lose his life and that of every soldier under his command to Sioux warriors at the Battle of the Little Bighorn in 1876—"Custer's Last Stand." The man on the left is a Southern soldier and prisoner of war. He and Custer had been classmates at West Point.

were many Northern volunteers from the Southern states and many Southern volunteers from the Northern states. The "mountain whites" of the South sent north some 50,000 men, and the loyal slave states contributed some 300,000 soldiers to the Union. In many a family of the Border States, one brother rode north to fight with the Blue, another south to fight with the Gray. Senator Crittenden of Kentucky, who had fathered the abortive Crittenden Compromise, also had fathered two sons: one became a general in the Union army, the other a general in the Confederate army. Lincoln's own Kentucky-born wife had four brothers who fought for the Confederacy.

✳ The Balance of Forces

When war broke out, the South seemed to have great advantages. The Confederacy could fight defensively behind interior lines. The North had to invade the vast territory of the Confederacy, conquer it, and drag it bodily back into the Union. In fact, the South did not have to win the war in order to win its independence.

The Prussian general Helmuth von Moltke (1800–1891) allegedly remarked that the American Civil War was merely a contest waged by "armed mobs." Whether he meant it or not, the Prussian's famous insult actually contains an important insight. Unlike the professional standing armies of nineteenth-century Europe, the Civil War armies were overwhelmingly amateur and volunteer. Taken from all walks of life, citizen-soldiers gave the Civil War drama its uniquely plebeian cast.

With 2 million men in Union blue and 1 million men in Confederate gray, Civil War soldiers represented a vast cross section of American society. (At nearly 10 percent of the 1860 population, the same rate of mobilization would amount to more than 27 million troops today.) Most soldiers had been farmers or farm laborers. Poor unskilled workers, despite vehement antidraft rhetoric to the contrary, were actually underrepresented. Most troops were native-born, but immigrants did serve in rough proportion to their presence in the general population. Black fighting men accounted for about 10 percent of Union enlistments by war's end (see "Blacks Battle Bondage," pp. 443–444). Perhaps one-third of the soldiers were married. Nearly 40 percent were under twenty-two years of age at the time of enlistment.

Inheritors of the values of Jacksonian mass democracy and Victorian sentiments, Civil War citizen-soldiers brought strong ideological commitments to the struggle. Neither army regulars nor reluctant conscripts, these men fought in the name of country, duty, honor, manhood, and righteousness. Though enemies, Union and Confederate soldiers shared a common commitment to the patriotic "spirit of '76" and the cause of liberty, independence, and republican government. A man's moral obligation to defend his country and preserve his personal reputation provided added motivation. Many interpreted the war as a religious crusade. In short, convictions, not coercion, created Civil War armies.

Despite their similarities, "Billy Yank" (the ordinary Union soldier) and "Johnny Reb" (the typical Confederate) were not necessarily cut from the same cloth. Both armies reflected the societies from which they came. Billy Yank tended to be more literate, intellectual, practical, and efficient, while Johnny Reb was often more jocular, emotional, religious, and personally concerned about the war. Defense of home and hearth meant more to Confederate troops, for the simple reason that most of the fighting occurred on Southern soil. Above all else, the men in gray maintained a distinctive rural individualism and homegrown disrespect for authority. Their counterparts in blue, often familiar with the strict regimen of Northern cities and factories, adapted more quickly to army discipline.

One aspect of soldiering Johnny Reb and Billy Yank shared was the dull routine of camp life. For all its promises of adventure, the life of a Civil War soldier could be downright boring and unpleasant. Men spent fifty days in camp for every one in battle. Reveille, roll call, and drill were daily chores. A soldier's first concern was usually his stomach, even when pork ("sowbelly"), beef ("salt horse"), coffee, and bread (or its unwelcome substitute, "hardtack") were in abundance. Food shortages plagued both armies, especially the Confederates as the war progressed. Uniforms

A Union Private

Collection of Kean E. Wilcox

deteriorated from "finery" to "tatters," as did moral standards. Gambling, drinking, stealing, swearing, and Sabbath-breaking proliferated; even widespread religious revivals could not keep up.

The gravest hardship of all, however, was disease. Germs—especially camp and campaign maladies like dysentery, diarrhea, typhoid, and malaria—took twice as many lives as bullets. By modern standards the mortality rates of wounded soldiers were appallingly high. (World War II marked the first time in American warfare that more soldiers died from combat wounds than from sickness and disease.) Without proper medical understanding of sterilization or sanitation, the risk of sepsis (bacterial infection) accompanied every wound. Head, chest, and stomach wounds were usually considered fatal; arm and leg injuries often resulted in amputation. Only the presence of nurses made life in field hospitals tolerable. Overcoming the vocal hostility of male army doctors and the filth, stench, and agony of these hospitals, some twenty thousand women volunteered as nurses during the war. Working with the maimed and the dying was never pleasant, but female nurses earned the respect of countless wounded soldiers for their dedicated service.

Yet for all its brutality, not even the field hospital could match the traumatic experience of combat. Tension mounted in the final moments before battle, as officers strove to maintain close-order ranks in the face of harrowing enemy gunfire. Artillery shells blanketed the battlefield with a smoky haze. Bullets zinged through the air like a driving rain. Once soldiers joined the action, a rush of adrenaline could transform frightened civilians into frenzied and ferocious fighters. First-timers likened the experience to "seeing the elephant" (an antebellum expression of awe). One sight of mangled limbs or one whiff of decaying flesh was often enough to push men over the edge. "Even when I sleep," a Massachusetts soldier moaned, "I hear the whistling of the shells and the shouts and groans, and to sum it up in two [sic] words it is *horrible*." Given the extraordinary stress of battle, many men avoided combat as much as they could.

Shell-shocked and weary, most soldiers returned home from the war utterly transformed. For nearly a decade and a half, silence reigned, as veterans and civilians entered into a tacit agreement to put the ordeal

A Confederate Soldier

Collection of Jean E. Wilcox

behind them. By 1880 interest revived in the war, and a new battle over its proper meaning commenced. Ignoring the conflict's original significance as a moral victory for slave emancipation, many Americans embraced a new reconciliationist and white supremacist script. In the interest of sectional harmony and national prosperity, Northerners abandoned earlier commitments to black rights. A reunion of sections spelled a division of races. Casting aside their original ideological convictions, many Americans came to regard the conflict as a tragic brothers' war meaningful only for its show of martial valor. Principles that had compelled 3 million men to enlist and caused 620,000 to die were largely forgotten. Instead a sentimental, sanitized, and whitened version of the Civil War became commonplace by the late nineteenth century. Von Moltke's "armed mobs" came to be remembered as the noblest of knights.

423

The Technology of War One of the new machines of destruction that made the Civil War the first mechanized war, this eight-and-a-half-ton federal mortar sat on a railroad flatcar in Petersburg, Virginia, ready to hurl two-hundred-pound missiles as far as two and a half miles. This powerful artillery piece rode on the tracks of a captured Southern railroad—itself another artifact of modern technology that figured heavily in the war. Of the 31,256 miles of railroad track in the United States in 1861, less than 30 percent, or 9,283 miles, were in the Confederate states, soon reduced by Union capture and destruction to 6,000 miles. The Confederate government's failure to understand the military importance of railroads contributed substantially to its defeat.

If it merely fought the invaders to a draw and stood firm, Confederate independence would be won. Fighting on their own soil for self-determination and preservation of their way of life, Southerners at first enjoyed an advantage in morale as well.

Militarily, the South from the opening volleys of the war had the most talented officers. Most conspicuous among a dozen or so first-rate commanders was gray-haired General Robert E. Lee, whose knightly bearing and chivalric sense of honor embodied the Southern ideal. Lincoln had unofficially offered him command of the Northern armies, but when Virginia seceded, Lee felt honor-bound to go with his native state. Lee's chief lieutenant for much of the war was black-bearded Thomas J. ("Stonewall") Jackson, a gifted tactical theorist and a master of speed and deception.

Besides their brilliant leaders, ordinary Southerners were also bred to fight. Accustomed to managing horses and bearing arms from boyhood, they made excellent cavalrymen and foot soldiers. Their high-pitched "rebel yell" ("yeeeahhh") was designed to strike terror into the hearts of fuzz-chinned Yankee recruits. "There is nothing like it on this side of the infernal region," one Northern soldier declared. "The peculiar corkscrew sensation that it sends down your backbone can never be told. You have to feel it."

As one immense farm, the South seemed to be handicapped by the scarcity of factories. Yet by seizing federal weapons, running Union blockades, and developing their own ironworks, Southerners managed to obtain sufficient weaponry. "Yankee ingenuity" was not confined to Yankees.

Nevertheless, as the war dragged on, grave shortages of shoes, uniforms, and blankets disabled the South. Even with immense stores of food on Southern farms, civilians and soldiers often went hungry because of supply problems. "Forward, men! They have cheese in their haversacks," cried one Southern officer as he attacked the Yankees. Much of the hunger was caused by a breakdown of the South's rickety transportation system, especially where the railroad tracks were cut or destroyed by the Yankee invaders.

The economy was the greatest Southern weakness; it was the North's greatest strength. The North was not only a huge farm but a sprawling factory as well (see Table 20.1). Yankees boasted about three-fourths of the nation's wealth, including three-fourths of the thirty thousand miles of railroads.

The North also controlled the sea. With its vastly superior navy, it established a blockade that, though a sieve at first, soon choked off Southern supplies and eventually shattered Southern morale. Its sea power also enabled the North to exchange huge quantities of grain for munitions and supplies from Europe, thus adding the output from the factories of Europe to its own.

The Union also enjoyed a much larger reserve of manpower. The loyal states had a population of some 22 million; the seceding states had 9 million

TABLE 20.1 Manufacturing by Sections, 1860

Section	Number of Establishments	Capital Invested	Average Number of Laborers	Annual Value of Products	Percentage of Total Value
New England	20,671	$ 257,477,783	391,836	$ 468,599,287	24.8%
Middle states	53,387	435,061,964	546,243	802,338,392	42.5
Western states	36,785	194,212,543	209,909	384,606,530	20.4
Southern states	20,631	95,975,185	110,721	155,531,281	8.3
Pacific states	8,777	23,380,334	50,204	71,229,989	3.8
Territories	282	3,747,906	2,333	3,556,197	0.2
TOTAL	140,533	$1,009,855,715	1,311,246	$1,885,861,676	

people, including about 3.5 million slaves. Adding to the North's overwhelming supply of soldiery were ever-more immigrants from Europe, who continued to pour into the North even during the war (see Table 20.2). Over 800,000 newcomers arrived between 1861 and 1865, most of them British, Irish, and German. Large numbers of them were induced to enlist in the Union army. Altogether about one-fifth of the Union forces were foreign-born, and in some units military commands were given in four different languages.

Whether immigrant or native, ordinary Northern boys were much less prepared than their Southern counterparts for military life. Yet the Northern "clodhoppers" and "shopkeepers" eventually adjusted themselves to soldiering and became known for their discipline and determination.

The North was much less fortunate in its higher commanders. Lincoln was forced to use a costly trial-and-error method to sort out effective leaders from the many incompetent political officers, until he finally uncovered a general, Ulysses Simpson Grant, who was determined to slog his way to victory at whatever cost in life and limb.

In the long run, as the Northern strengths were brought to bear, they outweighed those of the South. But when the war began, the chances for Southern independence were unusually favorable—certainly better than the prospects for success of the thirteen colonies in 1776. The turn of a few events could easily have produced a different outcome.

The might-have-beens are fascinating. *If* the Border States had seceded, *if* the uncertain states of the upper Mississippi Valley had turned against the Union, *if* a wave of Northern defeatism had demanded an armistice, and *if* Britain and/or France had broken the Union's naval blockade of Southern ports, the South might well have won. All of these possibilities almost became realities, but none of them actually occurred, and lacking their impetus, the South could not hope to win.

TABLE 20.2 Immigration to United States, 1860–1866

Year	Total	Britain	Ireland	Germany	All Others
1860	153,640	29,737	48,637	54,491	20,775
1861	91,918	19,675	23,797	31,661	16,785
1862	91,985	24,639	23,351	27,529	16,466
1863	176,282	66,882	55,916	33,162	20,322
1864	193,418	53,428	63,523	57,276	19,191
1865*	248,120	82,465	29,772	83,424	52,459
1866	318,568	94,924	36,690	115,892	71,062

*Only the first three months of 1865 were war months.

Dethroning King Cotton

Successful revolutions, including the American Revolution of 1776, have generally succeeded because of foreign intervention. The South counted on it, did not get it, and lost. Of all the Confederacy's potential assets, none counted more weightily than the prospect of foreign intervention. Europe's ruling classes were openly sympathetic to the Confederate cause. They had long abhorred the incendiary example of the American democratic experiment, and they cherished a kind of fellow-feeling for the South's semifeudal, aristocratic social order.

In contrast, the masses of workingpeople in Britain, and to some extent in France, were pulling and praying for the North. Many of them had read *Uncle Tom's Cabin*, and they sensed that the war—though at the outset officially fought only over the question of union—might extinguish slavery if the North emerged victorious. The common folk of Britain could not yet cast the ballot, but they could cast the brick. Their certain hostility to any official intervention on behalf of the South evidently had a sobering effect on the British government. Thus the dead hands of Uncle Tom helped Uncle Sam by restraining the British and French ironclads from piercing the Union blockade. Yet the fact remained that British textile mills depended on the American South for 75 percent of their cotton supplies. Wouldn't silent looms force London to speak? Humanitarian sympathies aside, Southerners counted on hard economic need to bring Britain to their aid. Why did King Cotton fail them?

He failed in part because he had been so lavishly productive in the immediate prewar years of 1857–1860. Enormous exports of cotton in those years had piled up surpluses in British warehouses. When the shooting started in 1861, British manufacturers had on hand a hefty oversupply of fiber. The real pinch did not come until about a year and a half later, when

The American minister to Britain wrote,

"The great body of the aristocracy and the commercial classes are anxious to see the United States go to pieces [but] the middle and lower class sympathise with us [because they] see in the convulsion in America an era in the history of the world, out of which must come in the end a general recognition of the right of mankind to the produce of their labor and the pursuit of happiness."

thousands of hungry operatives were thrown out of work. But by this time Lincoln had announced his slave-emancipation policy, and the "wage slaves" of Britain were not going to demand a war to defend the slaveowners of the South.

The direst effects of the "cotton famine" in Britain were relieved in several ways. Hunger among unemployed workers was partially eased when certain kindhearted Americans sent over several cargoes of foodstuffs. As Union armies penetrated the South, they captured or bought considerable supplies of cotton and shipped them to Britain; the Confederates also ran a limited quantity through the blockade. In addition, the cotton growers of Egypt and India, responding to high prices, increased their output and captured a share of the world cotton market that they held on to well after the war's conclusion. Finally, booming war industries in England, which supplied both the North and the South, relieved unemployment.

King Wheat and King Corn—the monarchs of Northern agriculture—proved to be more potent potentates than King Cotton. During these war years, the North, blessed with ideal weather, produced bountiful crops of grain and harvested them with McCormick's mechanical reaper. In the same period, the British suffered a series of bad harvests. They were forced to import huge quantities of grain from America, which happened to have the cheapest and most abundant supply. If the British had broken the blockade to gain cotton, they would have provoked the North to war and

GARIBALDI GUARD!

PATRIOTI ITALIANI!
HONVEDEK!
AMIS DE LA LIBERTE!
DEUTSCHE FREIHEITS KÆMPFER!

APPEAL!

The aid of every man is required for the service of his ADOPTED COUNTRY! A Regiment of Riflemen, Bersaglieri, Honvedek, Chasseurs, or Scharfschutzen, is now formed under the name of the GARIBALDI GUARD, and encamped near Washington. This Regiment will be increased by order of Government to 1150.

Wanted at once,
250 ABLE-BODIED MEN!
Italians, Hungarians, Germans, and French, Patriots of all Nations,
AROUSE! AROUSE! AROUSE!
The Families of our Soldiers shall be cared for.
PER ORDER,
Col. F. G. D'UTASSY,
Lieut. Col. A. REPETTI,
Quartermaster, CHAS. B. NORTON. Maj. GEO. E. WARING, Jr.
Headquarters, Irving Building, 594 & 596 Broadway.
BAKER & GODWIN, PRINTERS, PRINTING-HOUSE SQUARE, OPPOSITE CITY HALL, NEW YORK.

© Collection of the New York Historical Society

Recruiting Immigrants for the Union Army This poster in several languages appeals to immigrants to enlist. Immigrant manpower provided the Union with both industrial and military muscle.

As the Civil War neared the end of its third year, the London Times *(January 7, 1864) could boast,*

"We are as busy, as rich, and as fortunate in our trade as if the American war had never broken out, and our trade with the States had never been disturbed. Cotton was no King, notwithstanding the prerogatives which had been loudly claimed for him."

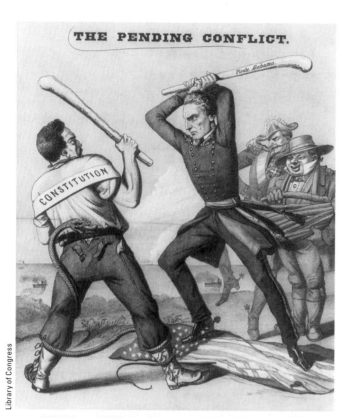

The Pending Conflict, 1863 Great Britain and France look on while the Americans struggle. Despite repeated pleas from Confederate diplomats for recognition and aid, both France and Britain refrained from intervening in the American conflict—not least because of the Union's demonstrated strength on the battlefield and its economic importance to European importers.

would have lost this precious granary. Unemployment for some seemed better than hunger for all. Hence one Yankee journal could exult,

Wave the stars and stripes high o'er us,
Let every freeman sing . . .
Old King Cotton's dead and buried;
*   brave young Corn is King.*

✴ The Decisiveness of Diplomacy

America's diplomatic front has seldom been so critical as during the Civil War. The South never wholly abandoned its dream of foreign intervention, and Europe's rulers schemed to take advantage of America's distress.

The first major crisis with Britain came over the **Trent affair**, late in 1861. A Union warship cruising on the high seas north of Cuba stopped a British mail steamer, the *Trent*, and forcibly removed two Confederate diplomats bound for Europe.

Britons were outraged: upstart Yankees could not so boldly offend the Mistress of the Seas. War preparations buzzed, and red-coated troops embarked for Canada, with bands blaring "I Wish I Was in Dixie." The London Foreign Office prepared an ultimatum demanding surrender of the prisoners and an apology. But luckily, slow communications gave passions on both sides a chance to cool. Lincoln came to see the *Trent* prisoners as "white elephants" and reluctantly released them. "One war at a time," he reportedly said.

Another major crisis in Anglo-American relations arose over the unneutral building in Britain of Confederate commerce-raiders, notably the ***Alabama***. These vessels were not warships within the meaning of loopholed British law because they left their shipyards unarmed and picked up their guns elsewhere. The *Alabama* escaped in 1862 to the Portuguese Azores, and there took on weapons and a crew from two British ships that followed it. Although flying the Confederate flag and officered by Confederates, it was manned by Britons and never entered a Confederate port. Britain was thus the chief naval base of the Confederacy.

The *Alabama* lighted the skies from Europe to the Far East with the burning hulks of Yankee merchantmen. All told, this "British pirate" captured over sixty vessels. Competing British shippers were delighted, while an angered North had to divert naval strength from its blockade for wild-goose chases. The barnacled *Alabama* finally accepted a challenge from a stronger Union cruiser off the coast of France in 1864 and was quickly destroyed.

The *Alabama* was beneath the waves, but the issue of British-built Confederate raiders stayed afloat. Under prodding by the American minister, Charles Francis Adams, the British gradually perceived that allowing such ships to be built was a dangerous precedent that might someday be used against them. In 1863 London openly violated its own leaky laws and seized another raider being built for the South. But despite greater official efforts by Britain to remain truly neutral, Confederate commerce-destroyers, chiefly British-built, captured more than 250 Yankee ships, severely crippling the American merchant marine, which never fully recovered. Glowering Northerners looked farther north and talked openly of securing revenge by grabbing Canada when the war was over.

✴ Foreign Flare-ups

A final Anglo-American crisis was touched off in 1863 by the **Laird rams**—two Confederate warships being constructed in the shipyard of John Laird and Sons in Great Britain. Designed to destroy the wooden ships of the Union navy with their iron rams and large-caliber guns, they were far more dangerous than the swift but lightly armed *Alabama*. If delivered to the South, they probably would have sunk the blockading squadrons and then brought Northern cities under their fire. In retaliation the North doubtless would have invaded Canada, and a full-dress war with Britain would have erupted. But Minister Adams took a hard line, warning that "this is war" if the rams were released. At the last minute, the London government relented and bought the two ships for the Royal Navy. Everyone seemed satisfied—except the disappointed Confederates. Britain also eventually repented its sorry role in the *Alabama* business. It agreed in 1871 to submit the *Alabama* dispute to arbitration, and in 1872 paid American claimants $15.5 million for damages caused by wartime commerce-raiders.

American rancor was also directed at Canada, where despite the vigilance of British authorities, Southern agents plotted to burn Northern cities. One Confederate raid into Vermont left three banks plundered and one American citizen dead. Hatred of England burned especially fiercely among Irish Americans, and they unleashed their fury on Canada. They raised several tiny "armies" of a few hundred green-shirted men and launched invasions of Canada, notably in 1866 and 1870. The Canadians condemned the Washington government for permitting such violations of neutrality, but the administration was hampered by the presence of so many Irish American voters.

As fate would have it, two great nations emerged from the fiery furnace of the American Civil War. One was a reunited United States, and the other was a united Canada. The British Parliament established the **Dominion of Canada** in 1867. It was partly designed to bolster the Canadians, both politically and spiritually, against the possible vengeance of the United States.

Emperor Napoleon III of France, taking advantage of America's preoccupation with its own internal problems, dispatched a French army to occupy Mexico City in 1863. The following year he installed on the ruins of the crushed republic his puppet, Austrian archduke Maximilian, as emperor of Mexico. Both sending the army and enthroning Maximilian were flagrant violations of the Monroe Doctrine. Napoleon was gambling that the Union would collapse and thus America would be too weak to enforce its "hands-off" policy in the Western Hemisphere.

The North, as long as it was convulsed by war, pursued a walk-on-eggs policy toward France. The Washington government gave aid to the resistance movement headed by Mexico's beloved national hero (and the first full-blooded Indian president of Mexico) Benito Juárez. But when the shooting stopped in 1865, Secretary of State Seward, speaking with the authority of nearly a million war-tempered bayonets, prepared to march south. Napoleon realized that his costly gamble was doomed. He reluctantly took "French leave" of his ill-starred puppet in 1867, and Maximilian soon crumpled ingloriously before a Mexican firing squad.

President Davis Versus President Lincoln

The Confederate government, like King Cotton, harbored fatal weaknesses. Its constitution, borrowing liberally from that of the Union, contained one deadly defect. Created by secession, it could not logically deny future secession to its constituent states. President Davis, while making his bow to states' rights, had in view a well-knit central government. But determined states' rights supporters fought him bitterly to the end. The Richmond regime encountered difficulty even in persuading certain state troops to serve outside their own borders. The governor of Georgia, a belligerent states' righter, at times seemed ready to secede from the secession and fight both sides. States' rights were no less damaging to the Confederacy than Yankee firepower.

Sharp-featured Jefferson Davis—tense, humorless, legalistic, and stubborn—was repeatedly in hot water. Although an eloquent orator and an able administrator, he at no time enjoyed real personal popularity and was often at loggerheads with his congress. At times there

Lincoln at Antietam (also known as Sharpsburg), October 1862 Deeply committed to his responsibilities as commander in chief, President Lincoln visited Union forces on the battlefield several times during the war. With him here at Antietam are the detective Allan Pinkerton (on the left), who provided intelligence to the Union army, and General John McClernand, who often accompanied the president on his travels

Library of Congress

was serious talk of impeachment. Unlike Lincoln, Davis was somewhat imperious and inclined to defy rather than lead public opinion. Suffering acutely from neuralgia and other nervous disorders (including a tic), he overworked himself with the details of both civil government and military operations. No one could doubt his courage, sincerity, integrity, and devotion to the South, but the task proved beyond his powers. It was probably beyond the powers of any mere mortal.

Lincoln also had his troubles, but on the whole they were less prostrating. The North enjoyed the prestige of a long-established government, financially stable and fully recognized both at home and abroad. Lincoln, the inexperienced prairie politician, proved superior to the more experienced but less flexible Davis. Able to relax with droll stories at critical times, "Old Abe" grew as the war dragged on. Tactful, quiet, patient, yet firm, he developed a genius for interpreting and leading a fickle public opinion. Holding aloft the banner of Union with inspiring utterances, he demonstrated charitableness toward the South and forbearance toward backbiting colleagues. "Did [Secretary of War Edwin] Stanton say I was a damned fool?" he reportedly replied to a tale-bearer. "Then I dare say I must be one, for Stanton is generally right and he always says what he means."

✯ Limitations on Wartime Liberties

"Honest Abe" Lincoln, when inaugurated, laid his hand on the Bible and swore a solemn oath to uphold the Constitution. Then, feeling driven by necessity, he proceeded to tear a few holes in that hallowed document. He understandably concluded that if he did not do so, and patch the parchment later, there might not be a Constitution of a *united United* States to mend. The "rail-splitter" was no hairsplitter.

But such infractions were not, in general, sweeping. Congress, as is often true in times of crisis, generally accepted or confirmed the president's questionable acts. Lincoln, though accused of being a "Simple Susan Tyrant," did not believe that his ironhanded authority would continue once the Union was preserved. As he pointedly remarked in 1863, a man suffering from "temporary illness" would not persist in feeding on bitter medicines for "the remainder of his healthful life."

Congress was not in session when war erupted, so Lincoln gathered the reins into his own hands. Brushing aside legal objections, he boldly proclaimed a blockade. (His action was later upheld by the Supreme Court.) He arbitrarily increased the size of the Federal army—something that only Congress can do under the Constitution (see Art. I, Sec. VIII, para. 12). (Congress later approved.) He directed the secretary of the Treasury to advance $2 million without appropriation or security

to three private citizens for military purposes—a grave irregularity contrary to the Constitution (see Art. I, Sec. IX, para. 7). He suspended the precious privilege of the **writ of habeas corpus**, so that anti-Unionists might be summarily arrested. In taking this step, he defied a dubious ruling by the chief justice that the safeguards of habeas corpus could be set aside only by the authorization of Congress (see Art. I, Sec. IX, para. 2).

Lincoln's regime was guilty of many other highhanded acts. For example, it arranged for "supervised" voting in the Border States. There the intimidated citizen, holding a colored ballot indicating his party preference, had to march between two lines of armed troops. The federal officials also ordered the suspension of certain newspapers and the arrest of their editors on grounds of obstructing the war.

Jefferson Davis was less able than Lincoln to exercise arbitrary power, mainly because of confirmed states' righters who fanned an intense spirit of localism. To the very end of the conflict, the owners of horse-drawn vans in Petersburg, Virginia, prevented the sensible joining of the incoming and outgoing tracks of a militarily vital railroad. The South seemed willing to lose the war before it would surrender local rights—and it did.

✯ Volunteers and Draftees: North and South

Ravenous, the gods of war demanded men—lots of men. Northern armies were at first manned solely by volunteers, with each state assigned a quota based on population. But in 1863, after volunteering had slackened, Congress passed a federal conscription law for the first time on a nationwide scale in the United States. The provisions were grossly unfair to the poor. Rich boys, including young John D. Rockefeller, could hire substitutes to go in their places or purchase exemption outright by paying $300. "Three-hundred-dollar men" was the scornful epithet applied to these slackers. Draftees who did not have the necessary cash complained that their banditlike government demanded "three hundred dollars or your life."

The draft was especially damned in the Democratic strongholds of the North, notably in New York City. A frightful riot broke out in 1863, touched off largely by underprivileged and antiblack Irish Americans, who shouted, "Down with Lincoln!" and "Down with the draft!" For several days the **New York draft riots** put the city at the mercy of a rampaging, pillaging mob. Scores of lives were lost, and the victims included many lynched blacks. Elsewhere in the North, conscription met with resentment and an occasional minor riot.

More than 90 percent of the Union troops were volunteers, since social and patriotic pressures to enlist were strong. As able-bodied men became scarcer, generous bounties for enlistment were offered by federal, state, and local authorities. An enterprising and money-wise volunteer might legitimately pocket more than $1,000.

With money flowing so freely, an unsavory crew of "bounty brokers" and "substitute brokers" sprang up, at home and abroad. They combed the poorhouses of the British Isles and western Europe, and many an Irishman or German was befuddled with whiskey and induced to enlist. A number of the slippery "bounty boys" deserted, volunteered elsewhere, and netted another handsome haul. The records reveal that one "bounty jumper" repeated his profitable operation thirty-two times. But desertion was by no means confined to "bounty jumpers." The rolls of the Union army recorded about 200,000 deserters of all classes, and the

The New York City Anti-Draft Rioters, 1863 Mostly Irish American mobs convulsed the city for days and were in the end put down only by a merciless application of Federal firepower.

Leg Amputation on the Battlefields of Virginia A surgeon wearing a hat and a sword amputates the leg of a wounded soldier, while an anesthetist (facing the camera) holds a sponge dipped in chloroform over the patient's nose. A surgical assistant ties a tourniquet to stem the flow of blood. Other soldiers, dressed in Zouave uniforms modeled on North African designs, which were popular among some Northern and Southern regiments, watch closely, likely aware of the dangers accompanying such crude surgery. An estimated 30 percent of amputees died from postoperative complications, most often infections.

Confederate authorities were plagued with a runaway problem of similar dimensions.

Like the North, the South at first relied mainly on volunteers. But since the Confederacy was much less populous, it scraped the bottom of its manpower barrel much more quickly (see Table 20.3). Quipsters observed that any man who could see lightning and hear thunder was judged fit for service. The Richmond regime, robbing both "cradle and grave" (ages seventeen to fifty), was forced to resort to conscription as early as April 1862, nearly a year earlier than the Union.

Confederate draft regulations also worked serious injustices. As in the North, a rich man could hire a substitute or purchase exemption. Slaveowners or overseers with twenty slaves might also claim exemption. These special privileges, later modified, made for bad feelings among the less prosperous, many of whom complained that this was "a rich man's war but a poor man's fight." Why sacrifice one's life to save an affluent neighbor's slaves? No large-scale draft riots broke out in the South, as in New York City. But the Confederate conscription agents often found it prudent to avoid those areas inhabited by sharpshooting mountain whites, who were branded "Tories," "traitors," and "Yankee-lovers."

TABLE 20.3	Number of Men in Uniform at Date Given	
Date	**Union**	**Confederate**
July 1861	186,751	112,040
January 1862	575,917	351,418
March 1862	637,126	401,395
January 1863	918,121	446,622
January 1864	860,737	481,180
January 1865	959,460	445,203

A contemporary (October 22, 1863) Richmond diary portrays the ruinous effects of inflation:

"A poor woman yesterday applied to a merchant in Carey Street to purchase a barrel of flour. The price he demanded was $70. 'My God!' exclaimed she, 'how can I pay such prices? I have seven children; what shall I do?' 'I don't know, madam,' said he coolly, 'unless you eat your children.'**"**

✷ The Economic Stresses of War

Blessed with a lion's share of the wealth, the North rode through the financial breakers much more smoothly than the South. Excise taxes on tobacco and alcohol were substantially increased by Congress. An income tax was levied for the first time in the nation's experience, and although the rates were painlessly low by later standards, they netted millions of dollars.

Customs receipts likewise proved to be important revenue-raisers. Early in 1861, after enough antiprotection Southern members had seceded, Congress passed the **Morrill Tariff Act**, superseding the low Tariff of 1857. It increased the existing duties some 5 to 10 percent, boosting them to about the moderate level of the Walker Tariff of 1846. But these modest rates were soon pushed sharply upward by the necessities of war. The increases were designed partly to raise additional revenue and partly to provide more protection for the prosperous manufacturers who were being plucked by the new internal taxes. A protective tariff thus became identified with the Republican party, as American industrialists, mostly Republicans, waxed fat on these welcome benefits.

The Washington Treasury also issued greenbacked paper money, totaling nearly $450 million, at face value. This printing-press currency was inadequately supported by gold, and hence its value was determined by the nation's credit. **Greenbacks** thus fluctuated with the fortunes of Union arms and at one low point were worth only 39 cents on the gold dollar. The holders of the notes, victims of creeping inflation, were indirectly taxed as the value of the currency slowly withered in their hands.

Yet borrowing far outstripped both greenbacks and taxes as a money-raiser. The federal Treasury netted $2,621,916,786 through the sale of bonds, which bore interest and which were payable at a later date. The modern technique of selling these issues to the people

directly through "drives" and payroll deductions had not yet been devised. Accordingly, the Treasury was forced to market its bonds through the private banking house of Jay Cooke and Company, which received a commission of three-eighths of 1 percent on all sales. With both profits and patriotism at stake, the bankers succeeded in making effective appeals to citizen purchasers.

A financial landmark of the war was the **National Banking System**, authorized by Congress in 1863. Launched partly as a stimulant to the sale of government bonds, it was also designed to establish a standard bank-note currency. (The country was then flooded with depreciated "rag money" issued by unreliable bankers.) Banks that joined the National Banking System could buy government bonds and issue sound paper money backed by them. The war-born National Banking Act thus turned out to be the first significant step taken toward a unified banking network since 1836, when the "monster" Bank of the United States was killed by Andrew Jackson. Spawned by the war, this new system continued to function for fifty years, until replaced by the Federal Reserve System in 1913.

An impoverished South was beset by different financial woes. Customs duties were choked off as the coils of the Union blockade tightened. Large issues of Confederate bonds were sold at home and abroad, amounting to nearly $400 million. The Richmond regime also increased taxes sharply and imposed a 10 percent levy on farm produce. But in general the states' rights Southerners were immovably opposed to heavy direct taxation by the central authority: only about 1 percent of the total income was raised in this way.

As revenue began to dry up, the Confederate government was forced to print blue-backed paper money with complete abandon. "Runaway inflation" occurred as Southern presses continued to grind out the poorly backed treasury notes, totaling in all more than $1 billion. The Confederate paper dollar finally sank to the point where it was worth only 1.6 cents when Lee surrendered. Overall, the war inflicted a 9,000 percent inflation rate on the Confederacy, contrasted with 80 percent for the Union.

⭐ The North's Economic Boom

Wartime prosperity in the North was little short of miraculous. The marvel is that a divided nation could fight a costly conflict for four long years and then emerge seemingly more prosperous than ever before.

New factories, sheltered by the friendly umbrella of the new protective tariffs, mushroomed forth. Soaring prices, resulting from inflation, unfortunately pinched the day laborer and the white-collar worker to some extent. But the manufacturers and businesspeople raked in "the fortunes of war."

The Civil War bred a millionaire class for the first time in American history, though a few individuals of extreme wealth could have been found earlier. Many of these newly rich were noisy, gaudy, brassy, and given to extravagant living. Their emergence merely illustrates the truth that some gluttony and greed always

mar the devotion and self-sacrifice called forth by war. The story of speculators and peculators was roughly the same in both camps. But graft was more flagrant in the North than in the South, partly because there was more to steal.

Yankee "sharpness" appeared at its worst. Dishonest agents, putting profits above patriotism, palmed off aged and blind horses on government purchasers. Unscrupulous Northern manufacturers supplied shoes with cardboard soles and fast-disintegrating uniforms of reprocessed or "shoddy" wool rather than virgin wool. Hence the reproachful term "shoddy millionaires" was doubly fair. One profiteer reluctantly admitted that his profits were "painfully large."

Newly invented laborsaving machinery enabled the North to expand economically, even though the cream of its manpower was being drained off to the fighting front. The sewing machine wrought wonders in fabricating uniforms and military footwear.

The marriage of military need and innovative machinery largely ended the production of custom-tailored clothing. Graduated standard measurements

Booth at the Sanitary Fair in Chicago, 1863 The Chicago Sanitary Fair was the first of many such fairs throughout the nation to raise funds for soldier relief efforts. Mainly organized by women, the fair sold captured Confederate flags, battle relics, handicrafts like these potholders (left), and donated items, including President Lincoln's original draft of the Emancipation Proclamation (which garnered $3,000 in auction). When the fair closed, the Chicago headquarters of the U.S. Sanitary Commission had raised $100,000, and its female managers had gained organizational experience that many would put to work in the postwar movement for women's rights.

Chicago History Museum

were introduced, creating "sizes" that were widely used in the civilian garment industry forever after.

Clattering mechanical reapers, which numbered about 250,000 by 1865, proved hardly less potent than thundering guns. They not only released tens of thousands of farm boys for the army but fed them their field rations. They produced vast surpluses of grain that, when sent abroad, helped dethrone King Cotton. They provided profits with which the North was able to buy munitions and supplies from abroad. They contributed to the feverish prosperity of the North—a prosperity that enabled the Union to weather the war with flying colors.

Other industries were humming. The discovery of petroleum gushers in 1859 had led to a rush of "Fifty-Niners" to Pennsylvania. The result was the birth of a new industry, with its "petroleum plutocracy" and "coal oil Johnnies." Pioneers continued to push westward during the war, altogether an estimated 300,000 people. Major magnets were free gold nuggets and free land under the **Homestead Act** of 1862. Strong propellants were the federal draft agents. The only major Northern industry to suffer a crippling setback was the ocean-carrying trade, which fell prey to the *Alabama* and other raiders.

The Civil War was a women's war, too. The protracted conflict opened new opportunities for women. When men departed in uniform, women often took their jobs. In Washington, D.C., five hundred women clerks ("government girls") became government workers, with over one hundred in the Treasury Department alone. The booming military demand for shoes and clothing, combined with technological marvels like the sewing machine, likewise drew countless women into industrial employment. Before the war one industrial worker in four had been female; during the war the ratio rose to one in three.

Other women, on both sides, stepped up to the fighting front—or close behind it. More than four hundred women accompanied husbands and sweethearts into battle by posing as male soldiers. Other women took on dangerous spy missions. One woman was executed for smuggling gold to the Confederacy. Dr. Elizabeth Blackwell, America's first female physician, helped organize the **U.S. Sanitary Commission** to assist the Union armies in the field. The commission trained nurses, collected medical supplies, and equipped hospitals. Commission work helped many women to acquire the organizational skills and the self-confidence that would propel the women's movement forward after the war. Heroically energetic Clara Barton and dedicated Dorothea Dix, superintendent of nurses for the Union army, helped transform nursing from a lowly service into a respected profession—and in the process opened up another major sphere of employment for women in the postwar era. Equally renowned in the South was Sally Tompkins, who ran a Richmond infirmary for wounded Confederate soldiers and was awarded the rank of captain by Confederate president Jefferson Davis. Still other women, North as well as South, organized bazaars and fairs that raised millions of dollars for the relief of widows, orphans, and disabled soldiers.

✶ A Crushed Cotton Kingdom

The South fought to the point of exhaustion. The suffocation caused by the blockade, together with the destruction wrought by invaders, took a terrible toll. Possessing 30 percent of the national wealth in 1860, the South claimed only 12 percent in 1870. Before the war the average per capita income of Southerners (including slaves) was about two-thirds that of Northerners. The Civil War squeezed the average Southern income to two-fifths of the Northern level, where it remained for the rest of the century. The South's bid for independence exacted a cruel and devastating cost.

Transportation collapsed. The South was even driven to the economic cannibalism of pulling up rails from the less-used lines to repair the main ones. Window weights were melted down into bullets; gourds replaced dishes; pins became so scarce that they were loaned with reluctance.

To the brutal end, the South mustered remarkable resourcefulness and spirit. Women buoyed up their menfolk, many of whom had seen enough of war at first hand to be heartily sick of it. A proposal was made by a number of women that they cut off their long hair and sell it abroad. But the project was not adopted, partly because of the blockade. The self-sacrificing women took pride in denying themselves the silks and satins of their Northern sisters. The chorus of a song, "The Southern Girl," touched a cheerful note:

> *So hurrah! hurrah! For Southern Rights, hurrah!*
> *Hurrah! for the homespun dress the Southern ladies wear.*

At war's end the Northern Captains of Industry had conquered the Southern Lords of the Manor. A crippled South left the capitalistic North free to work its own way, with high tariffs and other benefits. The manufacturing moguls of the North, ushering in the full-fledged Industrial Revolution, were headed for increased dominance over American economic and political life. Hitherto the agrarian "slavocracy" of the South had partially checked the ambitions of the rising plutocracy of the North. Now cotton capitalism had lost out to industrial capitalism. The South of 1865 was to be rich in little but amputees, war heroes, ruins, and memories.

Chapter Review

KEY TERMS

Fort Sumter (419)

Border States (420)

West Virginia (420)

Trent affair (427)

Alabama (427)

Laird rams (427)

Dominion of Canada (428)

writ of habeas corpus (429)

New York draft riots (429)

Morrill Tariff Act (431)

greenbacks (431)

National Banking System (431)

Homestead Act (433)

U.S. Sanitary Commission (433)

PEOPLE TO KNOW

Charles Francis Adams

Napoleon III

Maximilian

Jefferson Davis

Elizabeth Blackwell

Clara Barton

Sally Tompkins

CHRONOLOGY

1861	Confederate government formed
	Lincoln takes office (March 4)
	Fort Sumter fired on (April 12)
	Four upper South states secede (April–June)
	Morrill Tariff Act passed
	Trent affair
	Lincoln suspends writ of habeas corpus
1862	Confederacy enacts conscription
	Homestead Act

1862–1864	*Alabama* raids Northern shipping
1863	Union enacts conscription
	New York City draft riots
	National Banking System established
1863–1864	Napoleon III installs Archduke Maximilian as emperor of Mexico
1864	*Alabama* sunk by Union warship

TO LEARN MORE

Daniel Aaron, *The Unwritten War: American Writers and the Civil War* (1973)

David W. Blight, *Race and Reunion: The Civil War in American Memory* (2001)

Richard J. Carwardine, *Lincoln* (2003)

LaWanda Cox, *Lincoln and Black Freedom* (1981)

David H. Donald, *Lincoln* (1995)

———, ed., *Why the North Won the Civil War* (1960)

Drew Gilpin Faust, *The Creation of Confederate Nationalism* (1988)

———, *Mothers of Invention: Women of the Slaveholding South in the American Civil War* (1996)

William Freehling, *The South vs. The South: How Anti-Confederate Southerners Shaped the Course of the Civil War* (2001)

Doris Kearns Goodwin, *Team of Rivals: The Political Genius of Abraham Lincoln* (2005)

Elizabeth D. Leonard, *Yankee Women: Gender Battles in the Civil War* (1994)

Randall M. Miller et al., *Religion and the American Civil War* (1998)

A complete, annotated bibliography for this chapter—along with brief descriptions of the People to Know—may be found on the American Pageant website. The Key Terms are defined in a Glossary at the end of the text.

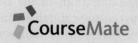 **CourseMate**

Go to the CourseMate website at **www.cengagebrain.com** for additional study tools and review materials—including audio and video clips—for this chapter.

AP® Review Questions for Chapter 20

1. Lincoln feared all of the following possible outcomes if secession were to go unchecked EXCEPT that it would
   - (A) raise questions of how to divide the national debt between the North and South.
   - (B) inhibit industrial development.
   - (C) mean splitting federally owned territories.
   - (D) lead to increased numbers of fugitive slaves.
   - (E) entice Europe to possibly seize American territories.

2. Why is the exchange at Fort Sumter so important?
   - (A) It is considered the start of the Civil War.
   - (B) It was where South Carolina officially seceded.
   - (C) It was the first Southern victory of the Civil War.
   - (D) It marked an act of Southern aggression against the North.
   - (E) It is the site where the Union army first attempted to retake the seceding state of South Carolina and send a message to other states that disunion would not be tolerated.

3. In his efforts to retain the border states within the Union, Lincoln focused his efforts primarily on
   - (A) Maryland.
   - (B) Delaware.
   - (C) West Virginia.
   - (D) Kentucky.
   - (E) Missouri.

4. Which of these is NOT why Lincoln initially said that he was not fighting a war to free the slaves?
   - (A) He did not want to alienate the border states that would be vital to his cause.
   - (B) He feared he would upset other allied states.
   - (C) Members of his family were slaveholders who were on the side of the South.
   - (D) His main objective was keeping the Union together.
   - (E) He sought to negotiate a peace and was willing to compromise on the slavery issue to make it happen, if necessary.

5. All of the following are true statements about soldiers on both sides of the Civil War EXCEPT that
   - (A) Northern soldiers were more intellectual and practical, whereas Southern soldiers were more emotional.
   - (B) Southern soldiers had more difficulty adjusting to military authority than their Northern counterparts.
   - (C) Northern troops were more concerned with defending hearth and home.
   - (D) Southern soldiers had the advantage of fighting defensively, whereas Northerners had to attack on unknown terrain.
   - (E) Northern soldiers tended not to be the natural fighters that Southerners were.

6. Which of the following was the most serious hardship encountered by soldiers on both sides of the Civil War?
   - (A) Food shortages
   - (B) Uniform shortages
   - (C) Boredom
   - (D) Lack of discipline in the camps
   - (E) Disease

7. The South's greatest weakness in the conflict was
   - (A) poor military leadership from the outset.
   - (B) its economy.
   - (C) its lack of arms and weaponry.
   - (D) its minimal control of the seas.
   - (E) its relatively small population.

8. What did the South count on most in its bid to win the Civil War?
   - (A) Foreign intervention
   - (B) The strength of its army
   - (C) Its military leadership
   - (D) World demand for its cotton crops
   - (E) Knowledge of potential battlegrounds

9. The biggest challenge Confederate president Jefferson Davis faced was
   - (A) creating a currency for his new nation.
   - (B) balancing his roles as military and political leader.
   - (C) ongoing tension between states' rights and the need for a unified central government.
   - (D) amassing an army.
   - (E) his lack of popularity.

10. Facing war, Lincoln played fast and loose with the Constitution in all of the following ways EXCEPT that he
    (A) declared a blockade without congressional approval.
    (B) increased the size of the army.
    (C) ordered a $2 million payout to private citizens aiding the military effort.
    (D) suspended freedom of the press by insisting that editors avoid publishing anti-Union articles or editorials.
    (E) suspended the writ of habeas corpus.

11. What was the major spark that triggered the New York draft riots in 1863?
    (A) The beginning of mandatory conscription
    (B) The provision that allowed the rich to hire a substitute when drafted
    (C) The disproportionate number of upstate farmers in the military
    (D) White men's anger at fighting a war over slavery
    (E) The use of bounty brokers to staff the army

12. The North financed its war effort in all of the following ways EXCEPT by
    (A) issuing paper money.
    (B) using excise taxes.
    (C) using tariffs.
    (D) issuing government bonds.
    (E) levying property taxes.

13. The Homestead Act of 1862 promised
    (A) not to tax private property.
    (B) free land to those settling the West.
    (C) leniency to those who fled west to escape the draft.
    (D) free gold to those who mined California.
    (E) oil leases to those settling Pennsylvania.

14. Which of the following was NOT among the official roles women played during the Civil War?
    (A) Soldiers
    (B) Cooks, launderers, and tailors
    (C) Government workers
    (D) Spies
    (E) Nurses

15. The Northern blockade of the South took advantage of the South's shortcomings in all of the following ways EXCEPT that
    (A) it prevented the South from exporting cotton, denying the Confederacy badly needed revenue.
    (B) the South could not receive war supplies from other nations and did not have the industry to produce supplies itself.
    (C) the blockade starved the population because there were no imports and Southern land was badly damaged by battle.
    (D) it stopped the South from building effective warships.
    (E) it stymied Southern naval efforts, as the North gained control of waterways around the South.

16. The Emancipation Proclamation was
    (A) created to free slaves throughout the Union and Confederacy.
    (B) widely criticized by the Northern press.
    (C) a military tactic that strengthened Union morale.
    (D) celebrated by abolitionists.
    (E) unrecognized by Southern slaves.

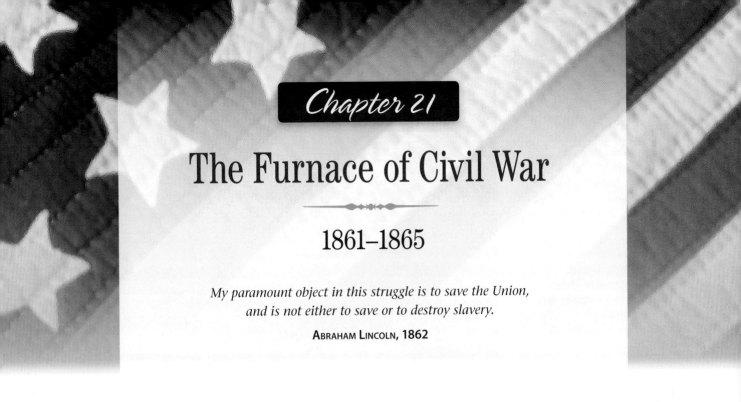

Chapter 21

The Furnace of Civil War

1861–1865

*My paramount object in this struggle is to save the Union,
and is not either to save or to destroy slavery.*

ABRAHAM LINCOLN, 1862

When President Lincoln issued his call to the states for seventy-five thousand militiamen on April 15, 1861, he envisioned them serving for only ninety days. Reaffirming his limited war aims, he declared that he had "no purpose, directly or indirectly, to interfere with slavery in the States where it exists." With a swift flourish of federal force, he hoped to show the folly of secession and rapidly return the rebellious states to the Union. But the war was to be neither brief nor limited. When the guns fell silent four years later, hundreds of thousands of soldiers on both sides lay dead, slavery was ended forever, and the nation faced the challenge of reintegrating the defeated but still recalcitrant South into the Union.

✯ Bull Run Ends the "Ninety-Day War"

Northern newspapers, at first sharing Lincoln's expectation of a quick victory, raised the cry "On to Richmond!" In this yeasty atmosphere, a Union army of some thirty thousand men drilled near Washington in the summer of 1861. It was ill-prepared for battle, but the press and the public clamored for action. Lincoln eventually concluded that an attack on a smaller Confederate force at **Bull Run (Manassas Junction)**, some thirty miles southwest of Washington, might be worth a try. If successful, it would demonstrate the superiority of Union arms. It might even lead to the capture of the Confederate capital at Richmond, one hundred miles to the south. If Richmond fell, secession would be thoroughly discredited, and the Union could

be restored without damage to the economic and social system of the South.

Raw Yankee recruits swaggered out of Washington toward Bull Run on July 21, 1861, as if they were headed for a sporting event. Congressmen and spectators trailed along with their lunch baskets to witness the fun. At first the battle went well for the Yankees. But Thomas J. ("Stonewall") Jackson's gray-clad warriors stood like a stone wall (here he won his nickname), and Confederate reinforcements arrived unexpectedly.

An observer behind the Union lines described the Federal troops' pell-mell retreat from the battlefield at Bull Run:

❝We called to them, tried to tell them there was no danger, called them to stop, implored them to stand. We called them cowards, denounced them in the most offensive terms, put out our heavy revolvers, and threatened to shoot them, but all in vain; a cruel, crazy, mad, hopeless panic possessed them, and communicated to everybody about in front and rear. The heat was awful, although now about six; the men were exhausted—their mouths gaped, their lips cracked and blackened with powder of the cartridges they had bitten off in battle, their eyes staring in frenzy; no mortal ever saw such a mass of ghastly wretches.**❞**

The Army of the Potomac Marching up Pennsylvania Avenue, Washington, D.C., 1861 In this painting Union troops parade before the Battle of Bull Run. Colorfully uniformed, they are a regiment of Zouaves, who adopted the name and style of military dress from a legendarily dashing French infantry unit recruited from Berber tribesmen in North Africa. But bright uniforms were not enough to win battles, and these troops were soon to be routed by the Confederates.

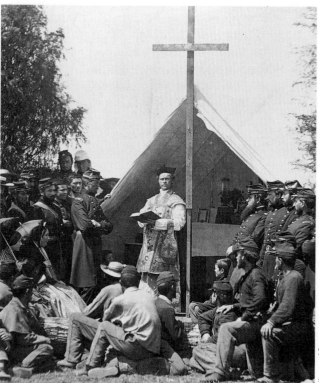

Preparing for Battle These troops of the 69th New York State Militia, a largely Irish regiment, were photographed attending Sunday morning Mass in May 1861, just weeks before the Battle of Bull Run. Because the regiment was camped near Washington, D.C., women were able to visit.

Panic seized the green Union troops, many of whom fled in shameful confusion. The Confederates, themselves too exhausted or disorganized to pursue, feasted on captured lunches.

The "military picnic" at Bull Run, though not decisive militarily, bore significant psychological and political consequences, many of them paradoxical. Victory was worse than defeat for the South, because it inflated an already dangerous overconfidence. Many of the Southern soldiers promptly deserted, some boastfully to display their trophies, others feeling that the war was now surely over. Southern enlistments fell off sharply, and preparations for a protracted conflict slackened. Defeat was better than victory for the Union, because it dispelled all illusions of a one-punch war and caused the Northerners to buckle down to the staggering task at hand. It also set the stage for a war that would be waged not merely for the cause of Union but also, eventually, for the abolitionist ideal of emancipation.

✦ "Tardy George" McClellan and the Peninsula Campaign

Northern hopes brightened later in 1861, when General George B. McClellan was given command of the Army of the Potomac, as the major Union force near Washington was now called. Red-haired and red-mustached, strong and stocky, McClellan was a brilliant, thirty-four-year-old West Pointer. As a serious student of warfare who was dubbed "Young Napoleon," he had seen plenty of fighting, first in the Mexican War and then as an observer of the Crimean War in Russia.

Cocky George McClellan embodied a curious mixture of virtues and defects. He was a superb organizer and drillmaster, and he injected splendid morale into the Army of the Potomac. Hating to sacrifice his troops, he was idolized by his men, who affectionately called him "Little Mac." But he was a perfectionist who seems not to have realized that an army is never ready to the last button and that wars cannot be won without running some risks. He consistently but erroneously believed that the enemy outnumbered him, partly because his intelligence reports from the head of Pinkerton's Detective Agency were unreliable. He was overcautious—Lincoln once accused him of having "the slows"—and he addressed the president in an arrogant tone that a less forgiving person would never have tolerated. Privately the general referred to his chief as a "baboon."

As McClellan doggedly continued to drill his army without moving it toward Richmond, the derisive Northern watchword became "All Quiet Along the Potomac." The song of the hour was "Tardy George" (McClellan). After threatening to "borrow" the army if it was not going to be used, Lincoln finally issued firm orders to advance.

A reluctant McClellan at last decided upon a waterborne approach to Richmond, which lies at the western base of a narrow peninsula formed by the James and York Rivers—hence the name given to this historic encounter: the **Peninsula Campaign** (see Map 21.1). McClellan warily inched toward the Confederate capital in the spring of 1862 with about 100,000

MAP 21.1 Peninsula Campaign, 1862 © Cengage Learning

Abraham Lincoln (1809–1865) treated the demands of George McClellan for reinforcements and his excuses for inaction with infinite patience. One exception came when the general complained that his horses were tired. On October 24, 1862, Lincoln wrote,

❝I have just read your dispatch about sore-tongued and fatigued horses. Will you pardon me for asking what the horses of your army have done since the battle of Antietam that fatigues anything?**❞**

men. After taking a month to capture historic Yorktown, which bristled with imitation wooden cannon, he finally came within sight of the spires of Richmond. At this crucial juncture, Lincoln diverted McClellan's anticipated reinforcements to chase "Stonewall" Jackson, whose lightning feints in the Shenandoah Valley seemed to put Washington, D.C., in jeopardy. Stalled in front of Richmond, McClellan was further frustrated when "Jeb" Stuart's Confederate cavalry rode completely around his army on reconnaissance. Then General Robert E. Lee launched a devastating counterattack—the Seven Days' Battles—June 26–July 2, 1862. The Confederates slowly drove McClellan back to the sea. The Union forces abandoned the Peninsula Campaign as a costly failure, and Lincoln temporarily abandoned McClellan as commander of the Army of the Potomac—though Lee's army had suffered some twenty thousand casualties to McClellan's ten thousand.

Lee had achieved a brilliant, if bloody, triumph. Yet the ironies of his accomplishment are striking. If McClellan had succeeded in taking Richmond and ending the war in mid-1862, the Union would probably have been restored with minimal disruption to the "peculiar institution." Slavery would have survived, at

A Confederate soldier assigned to burial detail after the Seven Days' Battles (1862) wrote,

❝ The sights and smells that assailed us were simply indescribable . . . corpses swollen to twice their original size, some of them actually burst asunder with the pressure of foul gasses. . . . The odors were so nauseating and so deadly that in a short time we all sickened and were lying with our mouths close to the ground, most of us vomiting profusely.**❞**

Civil War Scene (detail)
A Federal brigade repulses a Confederate assault at Williamsburg, Virginia, in 1862, as the Peninsula Campaign presses toward Richmond. General Winfield Scott Hancock commanded the troops. For his success in this action, Hancock earned the nickname "The Superb."

National Museum of American History, Smithsonian Institution, Behring Center

least for a time. By his successful defense of Richmond and defeat of McClellan, Lee had in effect ensured that the war would endure until slavery was uprooted and the Old South thoroughly destroyed. Lincoln himself, who had earlier professed his unwillingness to tamper with slavery where it already existed, now declared that the rebels "cannot experiment for ten years trying to destroy the government and if they fail still come back into the Union unhurt." He began to draft an emancipation proclamation.

Union strategy now turned toward total war (see Map 21.2). As finally developed, the Northern military plan had six components: first, slowly suffocate the South by blockading its coasts; second, liberate the slaves and hence undermine the very economic foundations of the Old South; third, cut the Confederacy in half by seizing control of the Mississippi River backbone; fourth, chop the Confederacy to pieces by sending troops through Georgia and the Carolinas; fifth, decapitate it by capturing its capital at Richmond; and sixth (this was Ulysses Grant's idea especially), try everywhere to engage the enemy's main strength and to grind it into submission.

✴ The War at Sea

The blockade started leakily: it was not clamped down all at once but was extended by degrees. A watertight patrol of some thirty-five hundred miles of coast was impossible for the hastily improvised Northern navy, which counted converted yachts and ferryboats in its fleet. But blockading was simplified by concentrating on the principal ports and inlets where dock facilities were available for loading bulky bales of cotton.

How was the blockade regarded by the naval powers of the world? Ordinarily, they probably would have defied it, for it was never completely effective and was especially sievelike at the outset. But Britain, the greatest maritime nation, recognized it as binding and warned its shippers that they ignored it at their peril. Britain plainly did not want to tie its hands in a future war by insisting that Lincoln maintain impossibly high blockading standards.

Blockade-running was risky but profitable, as the growing scarcity of Southern goods drove prices skyward. The most successful blockade runners were swift, gray-painted steamers, scores of which were specially built in Scotland. A leading rendezvous was the West Indies port of Nassau, in the British Bahamas, where at one time thirty-five of the speedy ships rode at anchor. The low-lying craft would take on cargoes of arms brought in by tramp steamers from Britain, leave with fraudulent papers for "Halifax" (Canada), and then return a few days later with a cargo of cotton. The risks were great, but the profits would mount to 700 percent and more for lucky gamblers. Two successful voyages might well pay for capture on a third. The lush days

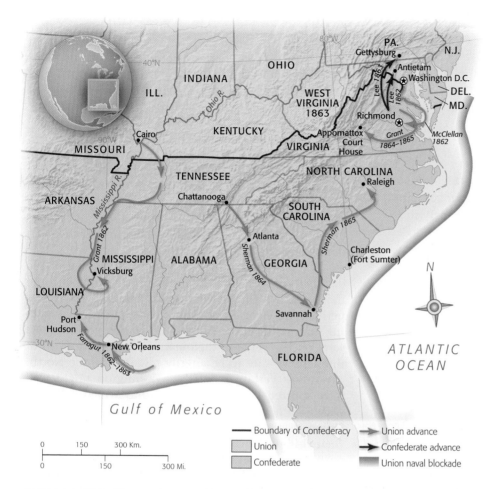

MAP 21.2 Main Thrusts, 1861–1865 Northern strategists at first believed that the rebellion could be snuffed out quickly by a swift, crushing blow. But the stiffness of Southern resistance to the Union's early probes, and the North's inability to strike with sufficient speed and severity, revealed that the conflict would be a war of attrition, long and bloody. © Cengage Learning

of blockade-running finally passed as Union squadrons gradually pinched off the leading Southern ports, from New Orleans to Charleston.

The Northern navy enforced the blockade with high-handed practices. Yankee captains, for example, would seize British freighters on the high seas, if laden with war supplies for the tiny port of Nassau and other halfway stations. The justification was that obviously these shipments were "ultimately" destined, by devious routes, for the Confederacy.

London, although not happy, acquiesced in this disagreeable doctrine of "ultimate destination" or "continuous voyage." British blockaders might need to take advantage of the same far-fetched interpretation in a future war—as in fact they did in the world war of 1914–1918.

The most alarming Confederate threat to the blockade came in 1862. Resourceful Southerners raised and reconditioned a former wooden U.S. warship, the **Merrimack**, and plated its sides with old iron railroad rails. Renamed the *Virginia*, this clumsy but powerful monster easily destroyed two wooden ships of the Union navy in the Virginia waters of Chesapeake Bay; it also threatened catastrophe to the entire Yankee blockading fleet. (Actually the homemade ironclad was not a seaworthy craft.)

A tiny Union ironclad, the **Monitor**, built in about one hundred days, arrived on the scene in the nick of time. For four hours, on March 9, 1862, the little "Yankee cheesebox on a raft" fought the wheezy *Merrimack* to a standstill. Britain and France had already built several powerful ironclads, but the first battle-testing

When news reached Washington that the Merrimack had sunk two wooden Yankee warships with ridiculous ease, President Lincoln, much "excited," summoned his advisers. Secretary of the Navy Gideon Welles (1802–1878) recorded,

❝ The most frightened man on that gloomy day . . . was the Secretary of War [Stanton]. He was at times almost frantic. . . . The *Merrimack*, he said, would destroy every vessel in the service, could lay every city on the coast under contribution, could take Fortress Monroe. . . . Likely the first movement of the *Merrimack* would be to come up the Potomac and disperse Congress, destroy the Capitol and public buildings.❞

of these new craft heralded the doom of wooden warships. A few months after the historic battle, the Confederates destroyed the *Merrimack* to keep it from the grasp of advancing Union troops.

✸ The Pivotal Point: Antietam

Robert E. Lee, having broken the back of McClellan's assault on Richmond, next moved northward. At the **Second Battle of Bull Run** (August 29–30, 1862), he encountered a Federal force under General John Pope. A handsome, dashing, soldierly figure, Pope boasted that in the western theater of war, from which he had recently come, he had seen only the backs of the enemy. Lee quickly gave him a front view, furiously attacking Pope's troops and inflicting a crushing defeat.

Emboldened by this success, Lee daringly thrust into Maryland. He hoped to strike a blow that would not only encourage foreign intervention but also seduce the still-wavering Border State and its sisters from the Union. The Confederate troops sang lustily:

Thou wilt not cower in the dust,
Maryland! my Maryland!
Thy gleaming sword shall never rust,
Maryland! my Maryland!

But the Marylanders did not respond to the siren song. The presence among the invaders of so many blanketless, hatless, and shoeless soldiers dampened the state's ardor.

Events finally converged toward a critical battle at **Antietam** Creek, Maryland. Lincoln, yielding to popular pressure, hastily restored "Little Mac" to active command of the main Northern army. His soldiers

tossed their caps skyward and hugged his horse as they hailed his return. Fortune shone upon McClellan when two Union soldiers found a copy of Lee's battle plans wrapped around a packet of three cigars dropped by a careless Confederate officer. With this crucial piece of intelligence in hand, McClellan succeeded in halting Lee at Antietam on September 17, 1862, in one of the bitterest and bloodiest days of the war.

Antietam was more or less a draw militarily. But Lee, finding his thrust parried, retired across the Potomac. McClellan, from whom much more had been hoped, was removed from his field command for the second and final time. His numerous critics, condemning him for not having boldly pursued the ever-dangerous Lee, finally got his scalp.

The landmark Battle of Antietam was one of the decisive engagements of world history—probably the most decisive of the Civil War. Jefferson Davis was perhaps never again so near victory as on that fateful summer day. The British and French governments were on the verge of diplomatic mediation, a form of interference sure to be angrily resented by the North. An almost certain rebuff by Washington might well have spurred Paris and London into armed collusion with Richmond. But both capitals cooled off when the Union displayed unexpected power at Antietam, and their chill deepened with the passing months.

Bloody Antietam was also the long-awaited "victory" that Lincoln needed for launching his **Emancipation Proclamation**. The abolitionists had long been clamoring for action: Wendell Phillips was denouncing the president as a "first-rate second-rate man." By midsummer of 1862, with the Border States safely in the fold, Lincoln was ready to move. But he believed that to issue such an edict on the heels of a series of military disasters would be folly. It would seem like a confession that the North, unable to conquer the South, was forced to call upon the slaves to murder their masters. Lincoln therefore decided to wait for the outcome of Lee's invasion.

Antietam served as the needed emancipation springboard. The halting of Lee's offensive was just enough of a victory to justify Lincoln's issuing, on September 23, 1862, the preliminary Emancipation Proclamation. This hope-giving document announced that on January 1, 1863, the president would issue a final proclamation.

On the scheduled date, he fully redeemed his promise, and the Civil War became more of a moral crusade as the fate of slavery and the South it had sustained was sealed. The war now became more of what Lincoln called a "remorseless revolutionary struggle." After January 1, 1863, Lincoln said, "the character of the war will be changed. It will be one of subjuga-

The Killing Fields of Antietam These Confederate corpses testify to the awful slaughter of the battle. The twelve-hour fight at Antietam Creek ranks as the bloodiest single day of the war, with more than ten thousand Confederate casualties and even more on the Union side. "At last the battle ended," one historian wrote, "smoke heavy in the air, the twilight quivering with the anguished cries of thousands of wounded men."

tion. . . . The [old] South is to be destroyed and replaced by new propositions and ideas."

✶ A Proclamation Without Emancipation

Lincoln's Emancipation Proclamation of 1863 declared "forever free" the slaves in those Confederate areas still in rebellion. Bondsmen in the loyal Border States were not affected, nor were those in specific conquered areas in the South—all told, about 800,000. The tone of the document was dull and legalistic (one historian has said that it had all the moral grandeur of a bill of lading). But if Lincoln stopped short of a clarion call for a holy war to achieve freedom, he pointedly concluded his historic document by declaring that the proclamation was "an act of justice" and calling for "the considerate judgment of mankind and the gracious favor of Almighty God."

The presidential pen did not formally strike the shackles from a single slave. Where Lincoln could presumably free the slaves—that is, in the loyal Border States—he refused to do so, lest he spur disunion. Where he could not—that is, in the Confederate states—he tried to. In short, where he *could* he would not, and where he *would* he could not. Thus the Emancipation Proclamation was stronger on proclamation than emancipation.

Yet much unofficial do-it-yourself liberation did take place. Thousands of jubilant slaves, learning of the proclamation, flocked to the invading Union armies, stripping already run-down plantations of their work force. In this sense the Emancipation Proclamation was heralded by the drumbeat of running feet. But many fugitives would have come anyhow, as they had from the war's outset. One in seven Southern slaves ran away to Union camps. Their presence in the camps and their perseverance against all odds convinced many Northern soldiers of slavery's evils and helped put emancipation atop Lincoln's agenda. By issuing the proclamation, Lincoln addressed the refugees' plight and strengthened the moral cause of the Union at home and abroad. At the same time, Lincoln's proclamation clearly foreshadowed the ultimate doom of slavery (see Map 21.3). This was legally achieved by action of the individual states and by their ratification of the **Thirteenth Amendment** (see the Appendix) in 1865, eight months after the Civil War had ended. The Emancipation Proclamation also fundamentally changed the nature of the war because it effectively removed any chance of a negotiated settlement. Both sides now knew that the war would be a fight to the finish.

Public reactions to the long-awaited proclamation of 1863 were varied. "God bless Abraham Lincoln," exulted the antislavery editor Horace Greeley in his *New York Tribune*. But many ardent abolitionists

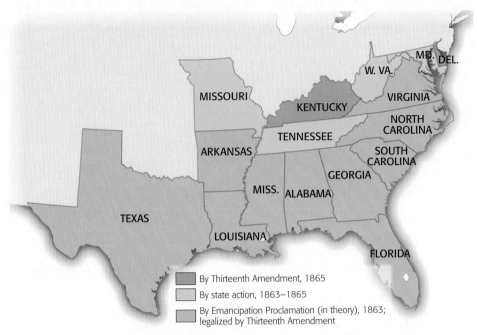

MAP 21.3 Emancipation in the South President Lincoln believed that emancipation of the slaves, accompanied by compensation to their owners, would be fairest to the South. He formally proposed such an amendment to the Constitution in December 1862. What finally emerged was the Thirteenth Amendment of 1865, which freed all slaves *without* compensation. © Cengage Learning

complained that Lincoln had not gone far enough. On the other hand, formidable numbers of Northerners, especially in the "Butternut" regions of the Old Northwest and the Border States, felt that he had gone too far. A cynical Democratic rhymester quipped,

> *Honest old Abe, when the war first began,*
> *Denied abolition was part of his plan;*
> *Honest old Abe has since made a decree,*
> *The war must go on till the slaves are all free.*
> *As both can't be honest, will some one tell how,*
> *If honest Abe then, he is honest Abe now?*

Opposition mounted in the North against supporting an "abolition war"; ex-president Pierce and others felt that emancipation should not be "inflicted" on the slaves. Many Boys in Blue, especially from the Border States, had volunteered to fight for the Union, not against slavery. Desertions increased sharply. The crucial congressional elections in the autumn of 1862 went heavily against the administration, particularly in New York, Pennsylvania, and Ohio. Democrats even carried Lincoln's Illinois, although they did not secure control of Congress.

The Emancipation Proclamation caused an outcry to rise from the South that "Lincoln the fiend" was trying to stir up the "hellish passions" of a slave insurrection. Aristocrats of Europe, noting that the

Abraham Lincoln defended his policies toward blacks in an open letter to Democrats on August 26, 1863:

❝You say you will not fight to free negroes. Some of them seem willing to fight for you; but, no matter. Fight you, then, exclusively to save the Union. I issued the proclamation on purpose to aid you in saving the Union.**❞**

Not everyone in the North welcomed Lincoln's Emancipation Proclamation, as this condemnation from the Cincinnati Enquirer *reveals:*

❝ The hundreds of thousands, if not millions of slaves [the act] will emancipate will come North and West and will either be competitors with our white mechanics and laborers, degrading them by competition, or they will have to be supported as paupers and criminals at the public expense.**❞**

proclamation applied only to rebel slaveholders, were inclined to sympathize with Southern protests. But the Old World working classes, especially in Britain, reacted otherwise. They sensed that the proclamation spelled the ultimate doom of slavery, and many laborers were more determined than ever to oppose intervention. Gradually the diplomatic position of the Union improved.

The North now had much the stronger moral cause. In addition to preserving the Union, it had committed itself to freeing the slaves. The moral position of the South was correspondingly diminished.

✳ Blacks Battle Bondage

As Lincoln moved to emancipate the slaves, he also took steps to enlist blacks in the armed forces. Although some African Americans had served in the Revolution and the War of 1812, the regular army contained no blacks at the war's outset, and the War Department refused to accept those free Northern blacks who tried to volunteer. (The Union navy, however, enrolled many blacks, mainly as cooks, stewards, and firemen.)

But as manpower ran low and emancipation was proclaimed, black enlistees were accepted, sometimes over ferocious protests from Northern as well as Southern whites. By war's end some 180,000 blacks served in the Union army, most of them from the slave states, but

In August 1863 Lincoln wrote to Grant that enlisting black soldiers

"works doubly, weakening the enemy and strengthening us.**"**

In December 1863 he announced,

"It is difficult to say they are not as good soldiers as any.**"**

In August 1864 he said,

"Abandon all the posts now garrisoned by black men, take 150,000 [black] men from our side and put them in the battlefield or cornfield against us, and we would be compelled to abandon the war in three weeks.**"**

many from the free-soil North. Blacks accounted for about 10 percent of the total enlistments in the Union forces on land and sea and included two Massachusetts regiments raised largely through the efforts of the ex-slave Frederick Douglass.

Black fighting men unquestionably had their hearts in the war against slavery that the Civil War had become after Lincoln proclaimed emancipation. Service also offered them a chance to prove their

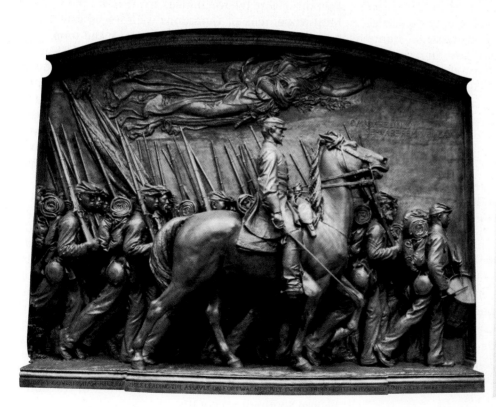

The Fabled 54th Massachusetts Infantry Regiment This bas-relief by famed sculptor Augustus Saint-Gaudens stands today in front of the Massachusetts Statehouse in Boston. It commemorates the all-black volunteer regiment, led by the white Boston patrician Robert Gould Shaw, that suffered heavy casualties during the Union siege of Fort Wagner, South Carolina, in 1863. Nikki Kahn/AP Images

A Bit of War History: Contraband, Recruit, Veteran, by Thomas Waterman Wood, 1865–1866 This painting dramatically commemorates the contributions and sacrifices of the 180,000 African Americans who served in the Union army during the Civil War.

manhood and to strengthen their claim to full citizenship at war's end. Participating in about five hundred engagements, they received a total of twenty-two Congressional Medals of Honor—the highest military award. Their casualties were extremely heavy; more than thirty-eight thousand died, whether from battle, sickness, or reprisals from vengeful masters. Many, when captured, were put to death as slaves in revolt, for not until 1864 did the South recognize them as prisoners of war. In one notorious case, several black soldiers were massacred after they had formally surrendered at Fort Pillow, Tennessee. Thereafter vengeful black units

An affidavit by a Union sergeant described the fate of one group of black Union troops captured by the Confederates:

"All the negroes found in blue uniform or with any outward marks of a Union soldier upon him was killed—I saw some taken into the woods and hung—Others I saw stripped of all their clothing and they stood upon the bank of the river with their faces riverwards and then they were shot—Still others were killed by having their brains beaten out by the butt end of the muskets in the hands of the Rebels."

cried "Remember Fort Pillow" as they swung into battle and vowed to take no prisoners.

For reasons of pride, prejudice, and principle, the Confederacy could not bring itself to enlist slaves until a month before the war ended, and then it was too late. Meanwhile, tens of thousands were forced into labor battalions, the building of fortifications, the supplying of armies, and other war-connected activities. Slaves, moreover, were "the stomach of the Confederacy," for they kept the farms going while the white men fought.

Involuntary labor did not imply slave support for the Confederacy. In many ways the actions of Southern slaves hamstrung the Confederate war effort and subverted the institution of slavery. Fear of slave insurrection necessitated Confederate "home guards," keeping many eligible young white men from the front. Everyday forms of slave resistance, such as slowdowns, strikes, and open defiance, diminished productivity and undermined discipline. When Union troops neared, slave assertiveness increased. As "intelligent contraband," slaves served as Union spies, guides, and scouts or provided shelter to escaped Northern prisoners of war. By war's end nearly half a million slaves took the ultimate risk of revolting "with their feet," abandoning their plantations. Many who remained, especially in the urban South, negotiated new working conditions in factories and on farms. Although they stopped short of violent uprising, slaves contributed powerfully to the collapse of slavery and the disintegration of the antebellum Southern way of life.

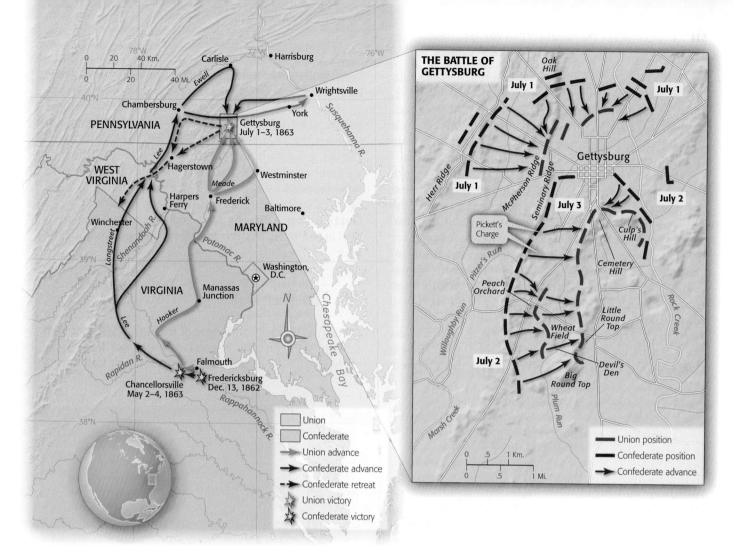

MAP 21.4 The Battle of Gettysburg, 1863 With the failure of Pickett's charge, the fate of the Confederacy was sealed—though the Civil War dragged on for almost two more bloody years. © Cengage Learning

✦ Lee's Last Lunge at Gettysburg

After Antietam, Lincoln replaced McClellan as commander of the Army of the Potomac with General A. E. Burnside, whose ornate side-whiskers came to be known as "burnsides" or "sideburns." Protesting his unfitness for this responsibility, Burnside proved it when he launched a rash frontal attack on Lee's strong position at **Fredericksburg**, Virginia, on December 13, 1862. A chicken could not have lived in the line of fire, remarked one Confederate officer. More than ten thousand Northern soldiers were killed or wounded in "Burnside's Slaughter Pen."

A new slaughter pen was prepared when General Burnside yielded his command to Joseph ("Fighting Joe") Hooker, an aggressive officer but a headstrong subordinate. At Chancellorsville, Virginia, on May 2–4, 1863, Lee daringly divided his numerically inferior force and sent "Stonewall" Jackson to attack the Union flank. The strategy worked. Hooker, temporarily dazed

by a near-hit from a cannonball, was badly beaten but not crushed. This victory was probably Lee's most brilliant, but it was dearly bought. Jackson was mistakenly shot by his own men in the gathering dusk and died a few days later. "I have lost my right arm," lamented Lee. Southern folklore relates how Jackson outflanked the angels while galloping into heaven.

Lee now prepared to follow up his stunning victory by invading the North again, this time through Pennsylvania. A decisive blow would add strength to the noisy peace prodders in the North and would also encourage foreign intervention—still a Southern hope. Three days before the battle was joined, Union general George G. Meade—scholarly, unspectacular, and abrupt—was aroused from his sleep at 2 a.m. with the unwelcome news that he would replace Hooker.

Quite by accident, Meade took his stand atop a low ridge flanking a shallow valley near quiet little **Gettysburg**, Pennsylvania (see Map 21.4). There his 92,000 men in blue locked in furious combat with Lee's 76,000 gray-clad warriors. The battle seesawed across the rolling green slopes for three agonizing days, July 1–3, 1863, and the outcome was in doubt until the very end. The failure of General George Pickett's magnificent but futile charge finally broke the back of the Confederate attack—and broke the heart of the Confederate cause.

Pickett's charge has been called the "high tide of the Confederacy." It defined both the northernmost point reached by any significant Southern force and the last real chance for the Confederates to win the war. As the Battle of Gettysburg raged, a Confederate peace delegation was moving under a flag of truce toward the Union lines near Norfolk, Virginia. Jefferson Davis hoped his negotiators would arrive in Washington from the south just as Lee's triumphant army marched on it from Gettysburg to the north. But the victory at Gettysburg belonged to Lincoln, who refused to allow the Confederate peace mission to pass through Union lines. From now on, the Southern cause was doomed.

Yet the men of Dixie fought on for nearly two years longer, through sweat, blood, and weariness of spirit.

Later in that dreary autumn of 1863, with the graves still fresh, Lincoln journeyed to Gettysburg to dedicate the cemetery. He read a two-minute address, following a two-hour speech by the orator of the day, a former president of Harvard. Lincoln's noble remarks were branded by the London *Times* as "ludicrous" and by Democratic editors as "dishwatery" and "silly." The **Gettysburg Address** attracted relatively little attention at the time, but the president was speaking for the ages.

✴ The War in the West

Events in the western theater of the war at last provided Lincoln with an able general who did not have to be shelved after every reverse. Ulysses S. Grant had been a

Library of Congress

National Archives

General Ulysses S. Grant and General Robert E. Lee   Trained at West Point, Grant (left) proved to be a better general than a president. Oddly, he hated the sight of blood and recoiled from rare beef. Lee (right), a gentlemanly general in an ungentlemanly business, remarked when the Union troops were bloodily repulsed at Fredericksburg, "It is well that war is so terrible, or we should get too fond of it."

Examining the Evidence

Abraham Lincoln's Gettysburg Address

Political speeches are unfortunately all too often composed of claptrap, platitudes, and just plain bunk—and they are frequently written by someone other than the person delivering them. But Abraham Lincoln's address at the dedication of the cemetery at the Gettysburg battlefield on November 19, 1863, has long been recognized as a masterpiece of political oratory and as a foundational document of the American political system, as weighty a statement of the national purpose as the Declaration of Independence (which it deliberately echoes in its statement that all men are created equal) or even the Constitution itself. In just 272 simple but eloquent words that Lincoln himself indisputably wrote, he summarized the case for American nationhood. What were his principal arguments? What values did he invoke? What did he think was at stake in the Civil War? (Conspicuously, he made no direct mention of slavery in this address.) Another speech that Lincoln gave in 1861 offers some clues. He said, "I have often inquired of myself what great principle or idea it was that kept this [nation] together. It was not the mere separation of the colonies from the motherland, but that sentiment in the Declaration of Independence which gave liberty not alone to the people of this country, but hope to the world, for all future time."

John Hay Papers, Manuscript Division, The Library of Congress

447

mediocre student at West Point, distinguishing himself only in horsemanship, although he did fairly well in mathematics. After fighting creditably in the Mexican War, he was stationed at isolated frontier posts, where boredom and loneliness drove him to drink. Resigning from the army to avoid a court-martial for drunkenness, he failed at various business ventures, and when war came, he was working in his father's leather store in Illinois for $50 a month.

Grant did not cut much of a figure. The shy and silent shopkeeper was short, stooped, awkward, stubble-bearded, and sloppy in dress. He managed with some difficulty to secure a colonelcy in the volunteers. From then on, his military experience—combined with his boldness, resourcefulness, and tenacity—catapulted him on a meteoric rise.

Grant's first signal success came in the northern Tennessee theater (see Map 21.5). After heavy fighting, he captured **Fort Henry and Fort Donelson** on the Tennessee and Cumberland Rivers in February 1862. When the Confederate commander at Fort Donelson asked for terms, Grant bluntly demanded "an unconditional and immediate surrender."

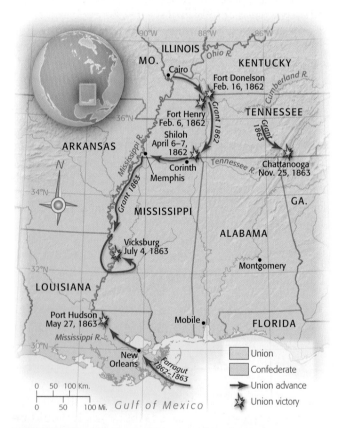

MAP 21.5 The Mississippi River and Tennessee, 1862–1863 © Cengage Learning

Grant's triumph in Tennessee was crucial. It not only riveted Kentucky more securely to the Union but also opened the gateway to the strategically important region of Tennessee, as well as to Georgia and the heart of Dixie. Grant next attempted to exploit his victory by capturing the junction of the main Confederate north-south and east-west railroads in the Mississippi Valley at Corinth, Mississippi. But a Confederate force foiled his plans in a gory battle at **Shiloh**, just over the Tennessee border from Corinth, on April 6–7, 1862. Though Grant successfully counterattacked, the impressive Confederate showing at Shiloh confirmed that there would be no quick end to the war in the West.

Lincoln resisted all demands for the removal of "Unconditional Surrender" Grant, insisting, "I can't spare this man; he fights." When talebearers later told Lincoln that Grant drank too much, the president allegedly replied, "Find me the brand, and I'll send a barrel to each of my other generals." There is no evidence that Grant's drinking habits seriously impaired his military performance.

Other Union thrusts in the West were in the making. In the spring of 1862, a flotilla commanded by David G. Farragut joined with a Northern army to strike the South a blow by seizing New Orleans. With Union gunboats both ascending and descending the Mississippi, the eastern part of the Confederacy was left with a jeopardized back door. Through this narrowing entrance, between **Vicksburg**, Mississippi, and Port Hudson, Louisiana, flowed herds of vitally needed cattle and other provisions from Louisiana and Texas. The fortress of Vicksburg, located on a hairpin turn of the Mississippi, was the South's sentinel protecting the lifeline to the western sources of supply.

General Grant was now given command of the Union forces attacking Vicksburg and in the teeth of grave difficulties displayed rare skill and daring. The siege of Vicksburg was his best-fought campaign of the war. The beleaguered city at length surrendered, on July 4, 1863, with the garrison reduced to eating mules and rats. Five days later came the fall of Port Hudson, the last Southern bastion on the Mississippi. The spinal cord of the Confederacy was now severed, and, in Lincoln's quaint phrase, the Father of Waters at last flowed "unvexed to the sea."

The Union victory at Vicksburg came the day after the Confederate defeat at Gettysburg. The political significance of these back-to-back military successes was monumental. Reopening the Mississippi helped to quell the Northern peace agitation in the "Butternut" area of the Ohio River valley. Confederate control of the Mississippi had cut off that region's usual trade routes down the Ohio-Mississippi River system to New Orleans, thus adding economic pain to that border

In the southern tier of Ohio, Indiana, and Illinois, sympathy for the South combined with hostility to the Northeast to stimulate talk of a "Northwest Confederacy" that would itself secede from the Union and make a separate peace with the Confederacy. These sentiments were fueled by economic grievances stemming from the closure of the Mississippi River to trade, and they gained strength after Lincoln's Emancipation Proclamation. Warned one Ohio congressman in January 1863,

"If you of the East, who have found this war against the South, and for the negro, gratifying to your hate or profitable to your purse, will continue it . . . [be prepared for] eternal divorce between the West and the East."

Another Ohio congressman, giving great urgency to the Union effort to reopen the Mississippi River, declared,

"The erection of the states watered by the Mississippi and its tributaries into an independent Republic is the talk of every other western man."

section's already shaky support for the "abolition war." The twin victories also conclusively tipped the diplomatic scales in favor of the North, as Britain stopped delivery of the Laird rams to the Confederates (see p. 425) and as France killed a deal for the sale of six naval vessels to the Richmond government. By the end of 1863, all Confederate hopes for foreign help were irretrievably lost.

✦ Sherman Scorches Georgia

General Grant, the victor of Vicksburg, was now transferred to the east Tennessee theater, where Confederates had driven Union forces from the battlefield at Chickamauga into the city of Chattanooga, to which they then laid siege. Grant won a series of desperate engagements in November 1863 in the vicinity of besieged Chattanooga, including Missionary Ridge and Lookout Mountain (the "Battle Above the Clouds"). Chattanooga was liberated, the state was cleared of Confederates, and the way was thus opened for an invasion of Georgia. Grant was rewarded by being made general in chief.

Georgia's conquest was entrusted to General William Tecumseh Sherman. Red-haired and red-bearded, grim-faced and ruthless, he captured Atlanta in

September 1864 and burned the city in November of that year. He then daringly left his supply base, lived off the country for some 250 miles, and weeks later emerged at Savannah on the sea. A rousing Northern song ("Marching Through Georgia") said,

> "Sherman's dashing Yankee boys will never reach the coast!"
> So the saucy rebels said—and 't was a handsome boast.

But Sherman's hated "Blue Bellies," sixty thousand strong, cut a sixty-mile swath of destruction through Georgia. They burned buildings, leaving only the blackened chimneys ("Sherman's Sentinels"). They tore up railroad rails, heated them red-hot, and twisted them into "iron doughnuts" and "Sherman's hairpins." They bayoneted family portraits and ran off with valuable "souvenirs." "War . . . is all hell," admitted Sherman later, and he proved it by his efforts to "make Georgia howl." One of the major purposes of **Sherman's march** was to destroy supplies destined for the Confederate army and to weaken the morale of the men at the front by waging war on their homes (see Map 21.6).

Sherman was a pioneer practitioner of "total war." His success in "Shermanizing" the South was attested by increasing numbers of Confederate desertions. Although his methods were brutal, he probably shortened the struggle and hence saved lives. But there can be no doubt that the discipline of his army at times broke down, as roving riffraff (Sherman's "bummers") engaged in an orgy of pillaging. "Sherman the Brute" was universally damned in the South.

After seizing Savannah as a Christmas present for Lincoln, Sherman's army veered north into South Carolina, where the destruction was even more vicious. Many Union soldiers believed that this state, the "hellhole of secession," had wantonly provoked the war. The capital city, Columbia, burst into flames, in all probability the handiwork of the Yankee invader. Crunching

A letter picked up on a dead Confederate in North Carolina and addressed to his "deer sister" concluded that

it was "dam fulishness" trying to "lick shurmin." He had been getting "nuthin but hell & lots uv it" ever since he saw the "dam yanks," and he was "tirde uv it." He would head for home now, but his old horse was "plaid out." If the "dam yankees" had not got there yet, it would be a "dam wunder." They were thicker than "lise on a hen and a dam site ornerier."

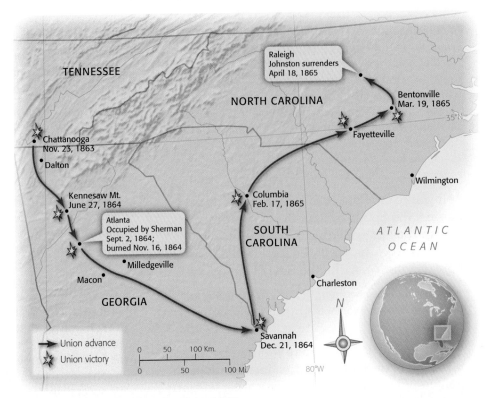

MAP 21.6 Sherman's March, 1864–1865 © Cengage Learning

northward, Sherman's conquering army had rolled deep into North Carolina by the time the war ended.

✷ The Politics of War

Presidential elections come by the calendar and not by the crisis. As fate would have it, the election of 1864 fell most inopportunely in the midst of war.

Political infighting in the North added greatly to Lincoln's cup of woe. Factions within his own party, distrusting his ability or doubting his commitment to abolition, sought to tie his hands or even remove him from office. Conspicuous among his critics was a group led by the overambitious secretary of the Treasury, Salmon Chase. Especially burdensome to Lincoln was the creation of the **Congressional Committee on the Conduct of the War**, formed in late 1861. It was dominated by "radical" Republicans who resented the expansion of presidential power in wartime and who pressed Lincoln zealously on emancipation.

Most dangerous of all to the Union cause were the Northern Democrats. Deprived of the talent that had departed with the Southern wing of the party, those Democrats remaining in the North were left with the taint of association with the seceders. Tragedy befell

the Democrats—and the Union—when their gifted leader, Stephen A. Douglas, died of typhoid fever seven weeks after the war began. Unshakably devoted to the Union, he probably could have kept much of his following on the path of loyalty.

Lacking a leader, the Democrats divided. A large group of "War Democrats" patriotically supported the Lincoln administration, but tens of thousands of "Peace Democrats" did not. At the extreme were the so-called **Copperheads**, named for the poisonous snake that strikes without a warning rattle. Copperheads openly obstructed the war through attacks against the draft, against Lincoln, and especially, after 1863, against emancipation. They denounced the president as the "Illinois Ape" and condemned the "Nigger War." They commanded considerable political strength in the southern parts of Ohio, Indiana, and Illinois.

Notorious among the Copperheads was a sometime congressman from Ohio, Clement L. Vallandigham. This tempestuous character possessed brilliant oratorical gifts and unusual talents for stirring up trouble. A Southern partisan, he publicly demanded an end to the "wicked and cruel" war. The civil courts in Ohio were open, and he should have been tried in them for sedition. But he was convicted by a military tribunal in 1863 for treasonable utterances and was then sentenced

Sherman's March to the Sea, 1863–1864 Sherman's army inflicted cruel destruction along its route, an early instance of a tactic that came to characterize modern warfare, in which civilians are considered legitimate targets.

to prison. Lincoln decided that if Vallandigham liked the Confederates so much, he ought to be banished to their lines. This was done.

Vallandigham was not so easily silenced. Working his way to Canada, he ran for the governorship of Ohio on foreign soil and polled a substantial but insufficient vote. He returned to his own state before the war ended, and although he defied "King Lincoln" and spat upon a military decree, he was not further prosecuted. The strange case of Vallandigham inspired Edward Everett Hale to write his moving but fictional story of Philip Nolan, ***The Man Without a Country*** (1863), which was immensely popular in the North and which helped stimulate devotion to the Union. The fictional Nolan was a young army officer found guilty of participation in the Aaron Burr plot of 1806 (see p. 214). He had cried out in court, "Damn the United States! I wish I may never hear of the United States again!" For this outburst he was condemned to a life of eternal exile on American warships.

✪ The Election of 1864

As the election of 1864 approached, Lincoln's precarious authority depended on his retaining Republican support while spiking the threat from the Peace Democrats and Copperheads.

Fearing defeat, the Republican party executed a clever maneuver. Joining with the War Democrats, it proclaimed itself to be the **Union party** (see Figure 21.1). Thus the Republican party passed temporarily out of existence.

Lincoln's renomination at first encountered surprisingly strong opposition. Hostile factions whipped up considerable agitation to shelve homely "Old Abe" in favor of his handsome nemesis, Secretary of the Treasury Chase. Lincoln was accused of lacking force, of being overready to compromise, of not having won the war, and of having shocked many sensitive souls by his ill-timed and earthy jokes. ("Prince of Jesters," one journal called him.) But the "ditch Lincoln" move

A Study in Black and White Soldiers of the 7th Tennessee Cavalry pose with their slaves—whose bondage the Confederacy fought to perpetuate.

Daguerreotype courtesy of Tom Farish

collapsed, and he was nominated by the Union party without serious dissent.

Lincoln's running mate was ex-tailor Andrew Johnson, a loyal War Democrat from Tennessee who had been a small slaveowner when the conflict began. He was placed on the Union party ticket to "sew up" the election by attracting War Democrats and the voters in the Border States, and, sadly, with no proper regard for the possibility that Lincoln might die in office. Southerners and Copperheads alike condemned both candidates as birds of a feather: two ignorant, third-rate, boorish, backwoods politicians born in log cabins.

Embattled Democrats—regular and Copperhead—nominated the deposed and overcautious war hero General McClellan. The Copperheads managed to force into the Democratic platform a plank denouncing the prosecution of the war as a failure. But McClellan, who

could not otherwise have faced his old comrades-in-arms, repudiated this defeatist declaration.

The campaign was noisy and nasty. The Democrats cried, "Old Abe removed McClellan. We'll now remove Old Abe." They also sang, "Mac Will Win the Union Back." Union party supporters shouted for "Uncle Abe and Andy" and urged, "Vote as you shot." Their most effective slogan, growing out of a remark by Lincoln, was "Don't swap horses in the middle of the river."

Lincoln's reelection was at first gravely in doubt. The war was going badly, and Lincoln himself gave way to despondency, fearing that political defeat was imminent. The anti-Lincoln Republicans, taking heart, started a new movement to "dump" Lincoln in favor of someone else.

But the atmosphere of gloom was changed electrically, as balloting day neared, by a succession of

NORTHERN DEMOCRATS			REPUBLICANS
COPPERHEADS	PEACE DEMOCRATS	WAR DEMOCRATS	

FIGURE 21.1 Union Party, 1864 The blue area represents the Union party. © Cengage Learning

McClellan as Mediator, 1865 This 1864 poster shows Presidents Lincoln and Davis trying to tear the country in half, while former general George McClellan, the candidate of the Democratic party, attempts to mediate.

Northern victories. Admiral Farragut captured Mobile, Alabama, after defiantly shouting the now-famous order, "Damn the torpedoes! Go ahead." General Sherman seized Atlanta. General ("Little Phil") Sheridan laid waste the verdant Shenandoah Valley of Virginia so thoroughly that in his words "a crow could not fly over it without carrying his rations with him."

The president pulled through, but nothing more than necessary was left to chance. At election time many Northern soldiers were furloughed home to support Lincoln at the polls. One Pennsylvania veteran voted forty-nine times—once for himself and once for each absent member of his company. Other Northern soldiers were permitted to cast their ballots at the front.

Lincoln, bolstered by the "bayonet vote," vanquished McClellan by 212 electoral votes to 21, losing only Kentucky, Delaware, and New Jersey (see Map 21.7). But "Little Mac" ran a closer race than the electoral count indicates. He netted a healthy 45 percent of the popular vote, 1,803,787 to Lincoln's 2,206,938, piling up much support in the Southerner-infiltrated states of the Old Northwest, in New York, and also in his native state of Pennsylvania.

One of the most crushing losses suffered by the South was the defeat of the Northern Democrats in 1864. The removal of Lincoln was the last ghost of a hope for a Confederate victory, and the Southern soldiers would wishfully shout, "Hurrah for McClellan!" When Lincoln triumphed, desertions from the sinking Southern ship increased sharply.

✷ Grant Outlasts Lee

After Gettysburg, Grant was brought in from the West over Meade, who was blamed for failing to pursue the defeated but always dangerous Lee. Lincoln needed a general who, employing the superior resources of the North, would have the intestinal stamina to drive ever forward, regardless of casualties. A soldier of bulldog tenacity, Grant was the man for this meat-grinder type of warfare. His overall basic strategy was to assail the

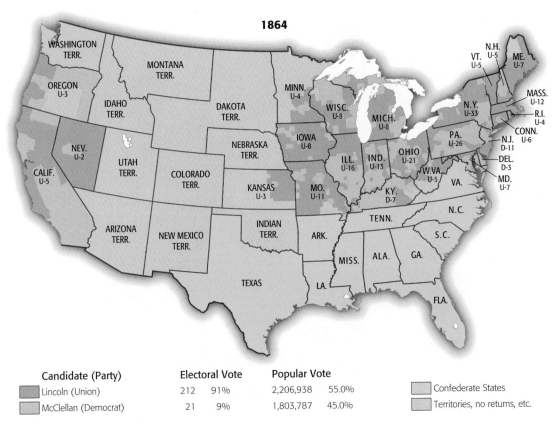

1864

Candidate (Party)	Electoral Vote		Popular Vote	
Lincoln (Union)	212	91%	2,206,938	55.0%
McClellan (Democrat)	21	9%	1,803,787	45.0%

Confederate States
Territories, no returns, etc.

MAP 21.7 Presidential Election of 1864 (showing popular vote by county) Lincoln also carried California, Oregon, and Nevada, but there was a considerable McClellan vote in each. Note McClellan's strength in the Border States and in the southern tier of Ohio, Indiana, and Illinois—the so-called "Butternut" region. © Cengage Learning

enemy's armies simultaneously, so that they could not assist one another and hence could be destroyed piecemeal. His personal motto was "When in doubt, fight." A grimly determined Grant, with more than 100,000 men, struck toward Richmond. He engaged Lee in a series of furious battles in the Wilderness of Virginia, during May and June of 1864, notably in the leaden hurricane of the "Bloody Angle" and "Hell's Half Acre." In this **Wilderness Campaign**, Grant suffered about 50,000 casualties, or nearly as many men as Lee commanded at the start. But Lee lost about as heavily in proportion (see Map 21.8).

In a ghastly gamble, on June 3, 1864, Grant ordered a frontal assault on the impregnable position of Cold Harbor. The Union soldiers advanced to almost certain death with papers pinned on their backs bearing their names and addresses. In a few minutes, about seven thousand men were killed or wounded.

Public opinion in the North was appalled by this "blood and guts" type of fighting. Critics cried that "Grant the Butcher" had gone insane. But Grant's reputation was undeserved, while Lee's was overrated. Lee's rate of loss (at one casualty for every five soldiers) was the highest of any general in the war. By contrast, Grant lost one of ten. Grant had intended to fight battles out in the open, a tactic he had perfected in the West. It was Lee, not Grant, who turned the eastern campaign into a war of attrition fought in the trenches. With fewer men, Lee could no longer seize the offensive, as he had at Chancellorsville or Gettysburg. Lee's new defensive posture in turn forced Grant into some brutal arithmetic. Grant could trade two men for one and still beat the enemy to his knees. "I propose to fight it out on this line," he wrote, "if it takes all summer." It did—and it also took all autumn, all winter, and a part of the spring.

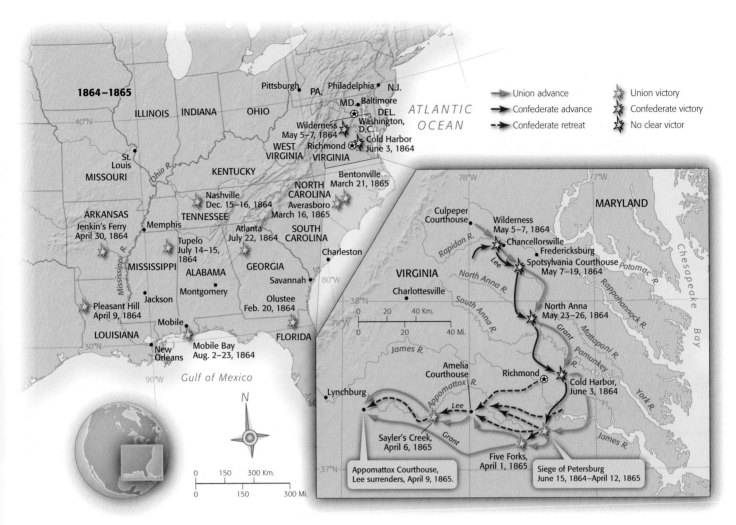

MAP 21.8 Grant's Virginia Campaign, 1864–1865 The Wilderness Campaign pitted soldier against desperate soldier in some of the most brutal and terrifying fighting of the Civil War. "No one could see the fight fifty feet from him," a Union private recalled of his month spent fighting in Virginia. "The lines were very near each other, and from the dense underbrush and the tops of trees came puffs of smoke, the 'ping' of the bullets and the yell of the enemy. It was a blind and bloody hunt to the death, in bewildering thickets, rather than a battle." © Cengage Learning

In February 1865 the Confederates, tasting the bitter dregs of defeat, tried desperately to negotiate for peace between the "two countries." Lincoln himself met with Confederate representatives aboard a Union ship moored at Hampton Roads, Virginia, to discuss peace terms. But Lincoln could accept nothing short of Union and emancipation, and the Southerners could accept nothing short of independence. So the tribulation wore on—amid smoke and agony—to its terrible climax.

The end came with dramatic suddenness. Rapidly advancing Northern troops captured Richmond and cornered Lee at **Appomattox Courthouse** in Virginia, in April 1865. Grant—stubble-bearded and informally dressed—met with Lee on the ninth, Palm Sunday, and granted generous terms of surrender. Among other concessions, the hungry Confederates were allowed to keep their horses for spring plowing.

Tattered Southern veterans—"Lee's Ragamuffins"—wept as they took leave of their beloved commander. The elated Union soldiers cheered, but they were silenced by Grant's stern admonition, "The war is over; the rebels are our countrymen again."

Lincoln traveled to conquered Richmond and sat in Jefferson Davis's evacuated office just forty hours after

The Burning of Richmond, April 1865 The proud Confederate capital, after holding out against repeated Union assaults, was evacuated and burned in the final days of the war.

the Confederate president had left it. "Thank God I have lived to see this," he said. With a small escort of sailors, he walked the blasted streets of the city. Freed slaves began to recognize him, and crowds gathered to see and touch "Father Abraham." One black man fell to his knees before the Emancipator, who said to him, "Don't kneel to me. This is not right. You must kneel to God only, and thank Him for the liberty you will enjoy hereafter." Sadly, as many freed slaves were to discover, the hereafter of their full liberty was a long time coming.

✵ The Martyrdom of Lincoln

On the night of April 14, 1865 (Good Friday), only five days after Lee's surrender, Ford's Theater in Washington witnessed its most sensational drama. A half-crazed, fanatically pro-Southern actor, John Wilkes Booth, slipped behind Lincoln as he sat in his box and shot him in the head. After lying unconscious all night, the Great Emancipator died the following morning. "Now he belongs to the ages," remarked the once-critical Secretary Stanton—probably the finest words he ever spoke.

Lincoln expired in the arms of victory, at the very pinnacle of his fame. From the standpoint of his reputation, his death could not have been better timed if he had hired the assassin. A large number of his countrymen had not suspected his greatness, and many others had even doubted his ability. But his dramatic death helped to erase the memory of his shortcomings and caused his nobler qualities to stand out in clearer relief.

The New York Herald *editorialized on April 16, 1865, that the South had the most to lose from Lincoln's assassination:*

"In the death of President Lincoln we feel the pressure of a heavy national calamity; but the great and irrevocable decree of the loyal States that Union must and shall be preserved will lose nothing of its force, but will be immensely if not terribly strengthened. In striking Abraham Lincoln and his kindly disposed Secretary of State the assassins struck at the best friends in the government to the prostrate rebels of the South."

The full impact of Lincoln's death was not at once apparent to the South. Hundreds of bedraggled ex-Confederate soldiers cheered, as did some Southern civilians and Northern Copperheads, when they learned of the assassination. This reaction was only natural, because Lincoln had kept the war grinding on to the bitter end. If he had only been willing to stop the shooting, the South would have won.

As time wore on, increasing numbers of Southerners perceived that Lincoln's death was a calamity for them. Belatedly they recognized that his kindliness and moderation would have been the most effective shields between them and vindictive treatment by the victors. The assassination unfortunately increased the bitterness in the North, partly because of the fantastic rumor that Jefferson Davis had plotted it.

A few historians have argued that Andrew Johnson, now president-by-bullet, was crucified in Lincoln's

Anne S. K. Brown Military Collection, Brown University Library

President Lincoln's Funeral Procession, New York City, 1865 Lincoln's body traveled by train to lie in state in fourteen cities before arriving at his final resting place of Springfield, Illinois. In New York City, 160,000 mourners accompanied his hearse as the funeral procession slowly made its way down Broadway. Scalpers sold choice window seats for four dollars and up. Blacks were barred from participating, until the mayor changed his mind at the last minute—but only if they marched at the rear.

The American Civil War was rooted in America's "peculiar institution" of slavery as well as uniquely American controversies about westward expansion. But it was also part of a wider phenomenon that transformed many parts of the world in the mid-nineteenth century: nationalism. To be sure, some ancient societies, such as the Greeks and the Hebrews, had a sense of themselves as distinct peoples who shared a common culture and history. But the creation of robust nation-states with strong central governments ruling over large populations that considered themselves part of an enduring community was of decidedly modern origin. Nationalism was anchored in the French and American Revolutions, with their emphasis on popular sovereignty and on a government that expressed the will of a population that saw itself not just as a random assembly of persons, but as a distinctive and coherent "people," often bonded by religion and language. Nationalism also owed much to modern technologies like the steamship, railroad, and telegraph, which extended both the emotional range of fellow feeling and the geographical reach of centralized authority. The convergence of these several nineteenth-century developments, intellectual as well as material, made possible the creation of the "virtual communities" called nations.

In the early nineteenth century, only Britain and France could claim to be nation-states in the modern sense. Central Europe remained a patchwork of major and minor principalities. Italy, in the words of the Austrian diplomat Klemens von Metternich, was merely "a geographic expression," as several small duchies and overgrown city-states uneasily coexisted on the Italian peninsula. Canada, a scattering of disconnected provinces, was more a mapmaker's convention than a functioning political entity. Both Spain and Japan looked united on the map, but both notoriously lacked internal cohesion. And in the United States, sectional and state loyalties continued to compete with notions of a *national* identity.

But within just a dozen years, between 1859 and 1871, Prince Otto von Bismarck created modern Germany; Count Camillo di Cavour united Italy ("We have made Italy; now we must make Italians," quipped one Italian wit); a new Meiji emperor launched Japan on a dramatic program of rapid modernization; the British North America Act of 1867 forged a unified Canada; and the American Civil War, in Abraham Lincoln's words, gave the United States "a new birth of freedom" as a unified country, as well as a significantly invigorated federal government. Before the Civil War, it was said, the United States *were*; after the Civil War, the United States *was*.

Count Camillo di Cavour (1810–1861)
© Hulton-Deutsch Collection/Corbis

Prince Otto von Bismark (1815–1898)
© Bettmann/Corbis

These several consolidations created the model for modern states that has prevailed ever since. The rise of nationalism fostered the growth of unprecedentedly powerful governments able to command deep loyalty from millions of people and consequently to marshal enormous economic and military resources—for good or ill. Nationalism was everywhere accompanied by some degree of political democratization and the expansion of public services, as freshly created or reinvigorated central governments sought to secure the loyalty of peoples newly brought under their sway. Bismarck, for example, supported universal suffrage and social insurance for German workers (establishing precedents that would much later be adopted in the United States). The new Italy and Meiji Japan adopted fairly liberal voting laws and programs for universal education. Britain's Reform Bill of 1867 enfranchised 1.5 million adult, male, urban householders, effectively doubling the British electorate.

In the United States, Civil War–era constitutional amendments at least nominally guaranteed the right to vote to adult African American males, while the federal government adopted ambitious plans to facilitate the construction of transcontinental railroads, distribute public lands under the Homestead Act, and support higher education under the Morrill Land-Grant College Act. The Civil War defined a historic pivot in the role of federal power. Of the twelve amendments to the Constitution passed before 1865, eleven were designed to *limit* the authority of the federal government. Of the fifteen amendments passed since the Civil War, nine contain the phrase "Congress shall have the power to *enforce* this article by appropriate legislation."

The words *nation* and *native* derive from the same Latin root, denoting birth or birthplace. Nationalism is at bottom a sentiment of common feeling or shared identity, generally among people born in the same place. It therefore implies boundaries, territorial as well as psychological. It defines who is included as well as who is excluded. ("No nation imagines itself coterminous with mankind," writes one scholar of nationalism.) It can breed exclusionary and nativist pathologies, as well as chauvinism, jingoism, and imperialism. The United States was no exception to these patterns. Nativists mounted increasingly effective anti-immigrant campaigns in the post–Civil War era, beginning with the Chinese Exclusion Act of 1882 and culminating in the highly restrictionist National Origins Act of 1924. As Germany and Italy acquired colonies in Africa and Japan tightened its grip on Taiwan, Korea, and parts of Manchuria, the United States also joined the imperial scramble, annexing the Philippines, Puerto Rico, Guam, and Samoa before the century's end.

Three Nation Builders: Count Camillo di Cavour (1810–1861), Prince Otto von Bismarck (1815–1898), and Abraham Lincoln (1809–1865) While the two European aristocrats Cavour and Bismarck were creating the new nations of Italy and Germany, respectively, the lowborn Lincoln was preserving American nationhood.

Abraham Lincoln (1809–1865)
Library of Congress

stead. The implication is that if the "rail-splitter" had lived, he would have suffered Johnson's fate of being impeached by the embittered members of his own party, who demanded harshness, not forbearance, toward the South.

The crucifixion thesis does not stand up under scrutiny. Lincoln no doubt would have clashed with Congress; in fact, he had already found himself in some hot water. The legislative branch normally struggles to win back the power that has been wrested from it by the executive in time of crisis. But the sure-footed and experienced Lincoln could hardly have blundered into the same quicksands that engulfed Johnson. Lincoln was a victorious president, and there is no arguing with victory. In addition to his powers of leadership refined in the war crucible, Lincoln possessed in full measure tact, sweet reasonableness, and an uncommon amount of common sense. Andrew Johnson, hot-tempered and impetuous, lacked all of these priceless qualities.

Ford's Theater, with its tragic murder of Lincoln, set the stage for the wrenching ordeal of Reconstruction.

✻ The Aftermath of the Nightmare

The Civil War took a grisly toll in gore, about as much as all of America's subsequent wars combined. Over 600,000 men died in action or of disease, and in all over a million were killed or seriously wounded. The number of dead, amounting to 2 percent of the entire nation's population, greatly exceeded the number of Americans killed in World War II. The modern equivalent would be a loss of some 6 million American lives. To its lasting hurt, the nation lost the cream of its young manhood and potential leadership. In addition, tens of thousands of babies went unborn because potential fathers were at the front.

Direct monetary costs of the conflict totaled about $15 billion. But this colossal figure does not include continuing expenses, such as pensions and interest on the national debt. The intangible costs—dislocations, disunities, wasted energies, lowered ethics, blasted lives, bitter memories, and burning hates—cannot be calculated.

Prisoners from the Front, by Winslow Homer, 1866 This celebrated painting reflects the artist's firsthand observations of the war. Homer brilliantly captured the enduring depths of sectional animosity. The Union officer somewhat disdainfully asserts his command of the situation; the beaten and disarmed Confederates exhibit an out-at-the-elbows pride and defiance.

Grave of William H. Johnson, 1864 Johnson was a free black man who worked as Lincoln's personal valet in Springfield and accompanied him to Washington, D.C. when he assumed the presidency. When lighter-skinned mulatto White House staffers rejected him for his dark skin, Lincoln helped Johnson find other employment in the Treasury and Navy Departments, writing "The bearer of this card, William Johnson (colored), came with me from Illinois, and is a worthy man, as I believe. A. Lincoln." In November 1863 Lincoln requested that Johnson accompany him to deliver his famous address at Gettysburg, where they both contracted smallpox. Lincoln recovered in a few days; Johnson, with a more severe case, died in January 1864. Lincoln arranged for him to be buried at Arlington National Cemetery and wrote the one-word epitaph for his tombstone: "Citizen," a succinct and stinging rebuke of the racist reasoning of the Dred Scott decision.

The greatest constitutional decision of the century, in a sense, was written in blood and handed down at Appomattox Courthouse, near which Lee surrendered. The extreme states' righters were crushed. The national government, tested in the fiery furnace of war, emerged unbroken. Nullification and secession, those twin nightmares of previous decades, were laid to rest.

Beyond doubt the Civil War—the nightmare of the Republic—was the supreme test of American democracy. It finally answered the question, in the words of Lincoln at Gettysburg, whether a nation dedicated to such principles "can long endure." The preservation of democratic ideals, though not an officially announced war aim, was subconsciously one of the major objectives of the North.

Victory for Union arms also provided inspiration to the champions of democracy and liberalism the world over (see "Thinking Globally: The Era of Nationalism," pp. 458–459). The great English **Reform Bill of 1867**, under which Britain became a true political democracy, was passed two years after the Civil War ended. American democracy had proved itself, and its success was an additional argument used by the disfranchised British masses in securing similar blessings for themselves.

The "Lost Cause" of the South was lost, but few Americans today would argue that the result was not for the best. The shameful cancer of slavery was sliced away by the sword, and African Americans were at last in a position to claim their rights to life, liberty, and the pursuit of happiness. The nation was again united politically, though for many generations still divided spiritually by the passions of the war. Grave dangers were averted by a Union victory, including the indefinite prolongation of the "peculiar institution," the unleashing of the slave power on weak Caribbean neighbors, and the transformation of the area from Panama to Hudson Bay into an armed camp, with several heavily armed and hostile states constantly snarling and sniping at one another. America still had a long way to go to make the promises of freedom a reality for all its citizens, black and white. But emancipation laid the necessary groundwork, and a united and democratic United States was free to fulfill its destiny as the dominant republic of the hemisphere—and eventually of the world.

Varying Viewpoints

What Were the Consequences of the Civil War?

With the end of the Civil War in 1865, the United States was permanently altered, despite the reunification of the Union and the Confederacy. Slavery was officially banned, secession was a dead issue, and industrial growth surged forward. For the first time, the United States could securely consider itself a singular nation rather than a union of states. Though sectional differences remained, there would be no return to the unstable days of precarious balancing between Northern and Southern interests. With the Union's victory, power rested firmly with the North, and it would orchestrate the future development of the country. According to historian Eric Foner, the war redrew the economic and political map of the country.

The constitutional impact of the terms of the Union victory created some of the most far-reaching transformations. The first twelve amendments to the Constitution, ratified before the war, had all served to limit government power. In contrast, the Thirteenth Amendment, which abolished slavery, and the revolutionary Fourteenth Amendment, which conferred citizenship and guaranteed civil rights to all those born in the United States, marked unprecedented expansions of federal power.

Historian James McPherson has noted still other ways in which the Civil War extended the authority of the central government. It expanded federal powers of taxation. It encouraged the government to develop the National Banking System, print currency, and conscript an army. It made the federal courts more influential. And through the Freedmen's Bureau, which aided former slaves in the South, it instituted the first federal social welfare agency. With each of these actions, the nation moved toward a more powerful federal government, invested with the authority to protect civil rights, aid its citizens, and enforce laws in an aggressive manner that superseded state powers. A recent book by Drew Gilpin Faust, *Republic of Suffering* (2008), goes further, suggesting that Civil War era experiences with death and tragedy were key to the modernization of America, in terms of both scientific advancement and private belief.

Yet some scholars have disputed whether the Civil War marked an absolute watershed in American history. They correctly note that racial inequality scandalously persisted after the Civil War, despite the abolition of slavery and the supposed protections extended by federal civil rights legislation. Others have argued that the industrial growth of the post–Civil War era had its real roots in the Jacksonian era, and thus cannot be ascribed solely to war. Thomas Cochran has even argued that the Civil War may have retarded overall industrialization rather than advancing it. Regional differences between North and South endured, moreover, even down to the present day.

Even so, the argument that the Civil War launched a modern America remains convincing. The lives of Americans, white and black, North and South, were transformed by the war experience. Industry entered a period of unprecedented growth, having been stoked by the transportation and military needs of the Union army. The emergence of new, national legal and governmental institutions marked the birth of the modern American state. All considered, it is hard to deny that the end of the Civil War brought one chapter of the nation's history to a close, while opening another.

Chapter Review

KEY TERMS

Bull Run (Manassas Junction), Battle of (435)

Peninsula Campaign (437)

Merrimack (439)

Monitor (439)

Bull Run, Second Battle of (440)

Antietam, Battle of (440)

Emancipation Proclamation (440)

Thirteenth Amendment (441)

Fredericksburg, Battle of (445)

Gettysburg, Battle of (445)

Gettysburg Address (446)

Fort Henry and Fort Donelson, Battle of (448)

Shiloh, Battle of (448)

Vicksburg, siege of (448)

Sherman's march (449)

Congressional Committee on the Conduct of the War (450)

Copperheads (450)

The Man Without a Country (451)

Union party (451)

Wilderness Campaign (454)

Appomattox Courthouse (455)

Reform Bill of 1867 (461)

PEOPLE TO KNOW

Thomas J. ("Stonewall") Jackson

George B. McClellan

Robert E. Lee

John Pope

A. E. Burnside

Joseph ("Fighting Joe") Hooker

George G. Meade

George Pickett

Ulysses S. Grant

William Tecumseh Sherman

Salmon Chase

Clement L. Vallandigham

John Wilkes Booth

CHRONOLOGY

1861   First Battle of Bull Run

1862   Grant takes Fort Henry and Fort Donelson
Battle of Shiloh
McClellan's Peninsula Campaign
Seven Days' Battles
Second Battle of Bull Run
Naval battle of *Merrimack* (*Virginia*) and *Monitor*
Battle of Antietam
Preliminary Emancipation Proclamation
Battle of Fredericksburg
Northern army seizes New Orleans

1863   Final Emancipation Proclamation
Battle of Chancellorsville
Battle of Gettysburg
Fall of Vicksburg
Fall of Port Hudson

1864   Sherman's march through Georgia
Grant's Wilderness Campaign
Battle of Cold Harbor
Lincoln defeats McClellan for presidency

1865   Hampton Roads Conference
Lee surrenders to Grant at Appomattox
Lincoln assassinated
Thirteenth Amendment ratified

1867   Reform Bill expands British electorate

TO LEARN MORE

William Blair, *Virginia's Private War: Feeding Body and Soul in the Confederacy, 1861–1865* (1998)

David W. Blight, *Frederick Douglass' Civil War: Keeping Faith in Jubilee* (1989)

Drew Gilpin Faust, *This Republic of Suffering: Death and the American Civil War* (2008)

Joseph Glatthaar, *Forged in Battle: The Civil War Alliance of Black Soldiers and White Officers* (1990)

Allen C. Guelzo, *Lincoln's Emancipation Proclamation: The End of Slavery in America* (2004)

Leon Litwack, *Been in the Storm So Long* (1979)

Robert R. Mackey, *The Uncivil War: Irregular Warfare in the Upper South, 1861–1865* (2004)

Reid Mitchell, *The Vacant Chair: The Northern Soldier Leaves Home* (1993)

Scott Reynolds Nelson and Carol Sheriff, *A People at War: Civilians and Soldiers in America's Civil War, 1854–1877* (2007)

Geoffrey C. Ward, *The Civil War: An Illustrated History* (1990)

Bell I. Wiley, *The Life of Billy Yank* (1952)

———, *The Life of Johnny Reb* (1943)

A complete, annotated bibliography for this chapter—along with brief descriptions of the People to Know—may be found on the American Pageant website. The Key Terms are defined in a Glossary at the end of the text.

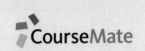

Go to the CourseMate website at **www.cengagebrain.com** for additional study tools and review materials—including audio and video clips—for this chapter.

AP® Review Questions for Chapter 21

1. How did the Battle of Bull Run affect the beginning of the Civil War?
   - (A) It showed the might of the Union army.
   - (B) It forced the North to take the prowess of the Southern military seriously.
   - (C) It gave the South an exaggerated sense of confidence.
   - (D) It was a draw.
   - (E) It hinted that the war would not be over quickly.

2. Union general George McClellan is best remembered for his
   - (A) brilliant sense of timing in battle.
   - (B) unwillingness to risk the lives of his men.
   - (C) slowness to act.
   - (D) preference for attacking by water.
   - (E) lightning-fast attacks.

3. The outcome of the Peninsula Campaign to take Richmond in 1862 is significant because it
   - (A) was the first Southern victory.
   - (B) prolonged the war and began to attach slavery to the cause.
   - (C) was among the most violent conflicts of the war, taking 10,000 Union soldiers' lives and 20,000 Confederates'.
   - (D) was McClellan's shining moment.
   - (E) inspired Union leaders to shift their expectations from a short battle to a long and bloody war.

4. Which of the following was NOT part of Union military strategy against the South?
   - (A) Cause havoc by liberating the slaves
   - (B) Blockade Southern seacoasts
   - (C) Capture the Mississippi
   - (D) Seize Richmond
   - (E) Grind the Confederacy to dust by sending troops through Maryland and Virginia

5. The battle at Antietam is considered a decisive moment in the Civil War for all of the following reasons EXCEPT that
   - (A) the display of Union military might kept France and England from attempting to intervene.
   - (B) McClellan's success was based on discovery of Lee's battle plans.
   - (C) it gave Lincoln the confidence to issue the Emancipation Proclamation.
   - (D) it marked the advent of iron-clad ships.
   - (E) it changed the character and goals of the war.

6. The Emancipation Proclamation of 1863
   - (A) freed all slaves throughout the United States.
   - (B) freed slaves in Confederate and border states.
   - (C) was a symbolic statement of justice.
   - (D) officially and permanently ended slavery.
   - (E) was meant as an appeal to now former slaves to serve in the Union army.

7. How did Southerners manage their slave population during the Civil War?
   - (A) They established home guards to protect against insurrection and flight.
   - (B) They enlisted slaves in the army.
   - (C) They kept potentially unruly slaves in shackles or prisons for much of the war.
   - (D) They used slaves as spies against approaching Union troops.
   - (E) They offered slaves money and better working conditions as incentives to aid the Confederate effort and prevent slave uprisings.

8. The 1863 Battle of Gettysburg
   - (A) ended the Civil War.
   - (B) was considered the "high tide of the Confederacy."
   - (C) was a decisive win for the South.
   - (D) marked General Ulysses S. Grant's first Union victory.
   - (E) enabled Union troops to claim the life of the masterful Confederate general Stonewall Jackson.

9. Which of these battles proved to be General Grant's greatest showing in the war?
   - (A) Shiloh
   - (B) Port Hudson
   - (C) Gettysburg
   - (D) Fort Donelson
   - (E) Vicksburg

10. General William Tecumseh Sherman is most remembered for his
    - (A) rejection of the concept of total war.
    - (B) well-disciplined troops.
    - (C) march to the sea.
    - (D) capture of North Carolina.
    - (E) destruction of Chattanooga, Tennessee.

11. Initially in doubt, Lincoln's reelection was ultimately secured as voting day neared in 1864 by
    (A) a lack of strong competition for the presidency.
    (B) the solid backing of the Copperheads.
    (C) his choice of the popular Andrew Johnson as his running mate.
    (D) a series of Union military victories.
    (E) support from Peace Democrats.

12. What was the Wilderness Campaign?
    (A) Grant's combat strategy focusing on man-to-man confrontations in the Virginia countryside
    (B) Lee's effort to turn the tide of the war back in the South's favor by fighting on familiar terrain
    (C) A series of battles culminating in the fighting at Gettysburg
    (D) Battles between Union forces and Indians on the western frontier
    (E) Grant's strategy to focus on trench warfare

13. Before the war actually ended, initial attempts for a negotiated peace broke down because
    (A) Southerners reviled Lincoln.
    (B) Lincoln was assassinated.
    (C) Jefferson Davis insisted on a place in the reformed Union government.
    (D) the Union insisted that the South bear the entire financial cost of the war.
    (E) the South wanted to retain its independence.

14. Which of the following was NOT an outcome of the Civil War?
    (A) Secession and nullification were put to rest.
    (B) Relationships with Britain and France were stressed.
    (C) A pro-South fanatic shot and killed the president.
    (D) Champions of liberalism and democracy around the world were inspired to further those aims for themselves.
    (E) Slavery, at home and beyond, was ultimately abolished.

15. All of the following opposed the Lincoln administration during the Civil War and the election of 1864 EXCEPT
    (A) Copperheads.
    (B) the Union party.
    (C) Peace Democrats.
    (D) the Congressional Committee on the Conduct of the War.
    (E) General McClellan.

16. The Gettysburg Address and the Declaration of Independence followed a similar line of reasoning because both
    (A) listed grievances against the opposition.
    (B) discussed the permanence of the Union.
    (C) memorialized the men that died for their cause.
    (D) relied on the idea that all men are created equal.
    (E) became landmark documents in American history.

Chapter 22

The Ordeal of Reconstruction

1865–1877

With malice toward none, with charity for all, with firmness in the right as God gives us to see the right, let us strive on to finish the work we are in, to bind up the nation's wounds, to care for him who shall have borne the battle and for his widow and orphan, to do all which may achieve and cherish a just and lasting peace among ourselves and with all nations.

ABRAHAM LINCOLN, SECOND INAUGURAL, MARCH 4, 1865

The battle was done, the buglers silent. Bone-weary and bloodied, the American people, North and South, now faced the staggering challenges of peace. Four questions loomed large. How would the South, physically devastated by war and socially revolutionized by emancipation, be rebuilt? How would liberated blacks fare as free men and women? How would the Southern states be reintegrated into the Union? And who would direct the process of Reconstruction—the Southern states themselves, the president, or Congress?

✴ The Problems of Peace

Other questions also clamored for answers. What should be done with the captured Confederate ringleaders, all of whom were liable to charges of treason? During the war a popular Northern song had been "Hang Jeff Davis to a Sour Apple Tree," and even innocent children had lisped it. Davis was temporarily clapped into irons during the early days of his two-year imprisonment. But he and his fellow "conspirators" were finally released, partly because the odds were that no Virginia jury would convict them. All rebel leaders were finally pardoned by President Johnson as a sort of Christmas present in 1868. But Congress did not remove all remaining civil disabilities until thirty years later and only posthumously restored Davis's citizenship more than a century later.

Dismal indeed was the picture presented by the war-racked South when the rattle of musketry faded.

Not only had an age perished, but a civilization had collapsed, in both its economic and its social structure. The moonlight-and-magnolia Old South, largely imaginary in any case, had forever gone with the wind.

Handsome cities of yesteryear, such as Charleston and Richmond, were rubble-strewn and weed-choked. An Atlantan returned to his once-fair hometown and remarked, "Hell has laid her egg, and right here it hatched."

Economic life had creaked to a halt. Banks and businesses had locked their doors, ruined by runaway inflation. Factories were smokeless, silent, dismantled. The transportation system had broken down completely. Before the war five different railroad lines had converged on Columbia, South Carolina; now the nearest connected track was twenty-nine miles away. Efforts to untwist the rails corkscrewed by Sherman's soldiers proved bumpily unsatisfactory.

Agriculture—the economic lifeblood of the South—was almost hopelessly crippled. Once-white-carpeted cotton fields now yielded a lush harvest of nothing but green weeds. The slave-labor system had collapsed, seed was scarce, and livestock had been driven off by plundering Yankees. Pathetic instances were reported of men hitching themselves to plows, while women and children gripped the handles. Not until 1870 did the seceded states produce as large a cotton crop as that of the fateful year 1860, and much of that yield came from new acreage in the Southwest.

The princely planter aristocrats were humbled by the war—at least temporarily. Reduced to proud poverty, they faced charred and gutted mansions, lost investments, and almost worthless land. Their investments of more than $2 billion in slaves, their primary form of wealth, had evaporated with emancipation.

Beaten but unbent, many high-spirited white Southerners remained dangerously defiant. They cursed the "damnyankees" and spoke of "your government" in Washington instead of "our government." One Southern bishop refused to pray for President Andrew Johnson, though Johnson proved to be in sore need of divine guidance. Conscious of no crime, these former Confederates continued to believe that their view of secession was correct and that the "lost cause" was still a just war. One popular anti-Union song ran,

> I'm glad I fought agin her, I only wish we'd won,
> And I ain't axed any pardon for anything I've done.

Such attitudes boded ill for the prospects of painlessly binding up the Republic's wounds.

★ Freedmen Define Freedom

Confusion abounded in the still-smoldering South about the precise meaning of "freedom" for blacks. Emancipation took effect haltingly and unevenly in different parts of the conquered Confederacy. As Union armies marched in and out of various localities, many blacks found themselves emancipated and then re-enslaved. A North Carolina slave estimated that he had celebrated freedom about twelve times. Blacks from one Texas county fleeing to the free soil of the liberated county next door were attacked by slaveowners as they swam across the river that marked the county line. The next day trees along the riverbank were bent with swinging corpses—a grisly warning to others dreaming of liberty. Other planters resisted emancipation more legalistically, stubbornly protesting that slavery was lawful until state legislatures or the Supreme Court declared otherwise. For many slaves the shackles of bondage were not struck off in a single mighty blow; long-suffering blacks often had to wrench free of their chains link by link.

The variety of responses to emancipation, by whites as well as blacks, illustrated the sometimes startling complexity of the master-slave relationship. Loyalty to the plantation master prompted some slaves to resist the liberating Union armies, while other slaves' pent-up bitterness burst forth violently on the day of liberation. Many newly emancipated slaves, for example, joined Union troops in pillaging their masters' possessions. In one instance a group of Virginia slaves laid twenty lashes on the back of their former master—a painful dose of his own favorite medicine.

Prodded by the bayonets of Yankee armies of occupation, all masters were eventually forced to recognize their slaves' permanent freedom. The once-commanding planter would assemble his former human chattels in front of the porch of the "big house" and announce their liberty. Though some blacks initially responded to news of their emancipation with suspicion and uncertainty, they soon celebrated their newfound freedom. Many took new names in place of the ones given by their masters and demanded that whites formally address them as "Mr." or "Mrs." Others abandoned the coarse cottons that had been their only clothing as slaves and sought

Charleston, South Carolina, in Ruins, April 1865 Rebel troops evacuating Charleston blew up military supplies to deny them to General William Tecumseh Sherman's forces. The explosions ignited fires that all but destroyed the city.

Library of Congress

Tuskegee University Archives

Educating Young Freedmen and Freedwomen, 1870s Freed slaves in the South regarded schooling as the key to improving their children's lives and the fulfillment of a long-sought right that had been denied blacks in slavery. These well-dressed school-children are lined up outside their rural, one-room schoolhouse alongside their teachers, both black and white.

silks, satins, and other finery. Though many whites perceived such behavior as insubordinate, they were forced to recognize the realities of emancipation. "Never before had I a word of impudence from any of our black folk," wrote one white Southerner, "but they are not ours any longer."

Tens of thousands of emancipated blacks took to the roads, some to test their freedom, others to search for long-lost spouses, parents, and children. Emancipation thus strengthened the black family, and many newly freed men and women formalized "slave marriages" for personal and pragmatic reasons, including the desire to make their children legal heirs. Other blacks left their former masters to work in towns and cities, where existing black communities provided protection and mutual assistance. Whole communities sometimes moved together in search of opportunity. From 1878 to 1880, some twenty-five thousand blacks from Louisiana, Texas, and Mississippi surged in a mass exodus to Kansas. The westward flood of these "Exodusters" was stemmed only when steamboat captains refused to transport more black migrants across the Mississippi River.

The church became the focus of black community life in the years following emancipation. As slaves, blacks had worshiped alongside whites, but now they formed their own churches pastored by their own ministers. Black churches grew robustly. The 150,000-member

Houston H. Holloway, age twenty at the time of his emancipation, recalled his feelings upon hearing of his freedom:

❝I felt like a bird out of a cage. Amen. Amen. Amen. I could hardly ask to feel any better than I did that day. . . . The week passed off in a blaze of glory.**❞**

The reunion of long-lost relatives also inspired joy; one Union officer wrote home,

❝Men are taking their wives and children, families which had been for a long time broken up are united and oh! such happiness. I am glad I am here.**❞**

Letter from a Freedman to His Old Master, 1865

What was it like to experience the transition from slavery to freedom? Four million Southern blacks faced this exhilarating and formidable prospect with the end of the war. For historians, recovering the African American perspective on emancipation is challenging. Unlike their white masters, freed blacks left few written records. But one former slave captured in a letter to his "Old Master" (whose surname he bore) the heroic determination of many blacks to build new independent and dignified lives for themselves and their families.

During the war Jourdon Anderson escaped slavery in Tennessee with his wife and two daughters. After relocating to the relative safety of Ohio, he received a communication from his former owner asking him to return. In his bold reply, reportedly "dictated by the old servant" himself, Anderson expressed his family's new expectations for life as free people and an uneasiness about his former master's intentions. He made reference to his "comfortable home," his daughters' schooling, the church that he and his wife were free to attend regularly, and the peace of mind that came with knowing that "my girls [would not be] brought to shame by the violence and wickedness of their young masters." To test the white man's sincerity, Anderson and his wife asked for the astronomical figure of $11,680 in back wages from decades as slaves. He closed by reiterating that "the great desire of my life is to give my children an education and have them form virtuous habits." This rare letter demonstrates that many black correspondents may have been illiterate, but they were hardly inarticulate. And they asserted themselves as parents, workers, and citizens not only from the distance of a former free state like Ohio but also deep within the former slave states of the South. Was the tone of Anderson's letter (and postscript) serious or tongue-in-cheek? What did "freedom" mean for Anderson and other blacks in the months following emancipation? How did the eventual accomplishments of Reconstruction correspond with the initial expectations of people like Anderson and his former owner?

Letter from a Freedman to his Old Master.

The following is a genuine document. It was *dictated* by the old servant, and contains his ideas and forms of expression. [Cincinnati Commercial.

DAYTON, Ohio, August 7, 1865.

To my Old Master, Col. P. H. ANDERSON, *Big Spring, Tennessee.*

SIR: I got your letter and was glad to find that you had not forgotten Jordan, and that you wanted me to come back and live with you again, promising to do better for me than anybody else can. I have often felt uneasy about you. I thought the Yankees would have hung you long before this for harboring Rebs. they found at your house. I suppose they never heard about your going to Col. Martin's to kill the Union soldier that was left by his company in their stable. Although you shot at me twice before I left you, I did not want to hear of your being hurt, and am glad you are still living. It would do me good to go back to the dear old home again and see Miss Mary and Miss Martha and Allen, Esther, Green and Lee. Give my love to them all, and tell them I hope we will meet in the better world, if not in this. I would have gone back to see you all when I was working in the Nashville Hospital, but one of the neighbors told me Henry intended to shoot me if he ever got a chance.

I want to know particularly what the good chance is you propose to give me. I am doing tolerably well here; I get $25 a month, with victuals and clothing; have a comfortable home for Mandy (the folks here call her Mrs. Anderson), and the children, Milly Jane and Grundy, go to school and are learning well; the teacher says Grundy has a head for a preacher. They go to Sunday-School, and Mandy and me attend church regularly. We are kindly treated; sometimes we over-

As to my freedom, which you say I can have, there is nothing to be gained on that score, as I got my free-papers in 1864 from the Provost-Marshal-General of the Department at Nashville. Mandy says she would be afraid to go back without some proof that you are sincerely disposed to treat us justly and kindly—and we have concluded to test your sincerity by asking you to send us our wages for the time we served you. This will make us forget and forgive old sores, and rely on your justice and friendship in the future. I served you faithfully for thirty-two years, and Mandy twenty years, at $25 a month for me, and $2 a week for Mandy. Our earnings would amount to $11,680. Add to this the interest for the time our wages has been kept back and deduct what you paid for our clothing and three doctor's visits to me, and pulling a tooth for Mandy, and the balance will show what we are in justice entitled to. Please send the money by Adams Express, in care of V. Winters, esq., Dayton, Ohio. If you fail to pay us for faithful labors in the past we can have little faith in your promises in the future.

P. S.—Say howdy to George Carter, and thank him for taking the pistol from you when you were shooting at me.

New York Tribune, Tuesday, August 22, 1965

black Baptist Church of 1850 reached 500,000 by 1870, while the African Methodist Episcopal Church quadrupled in size from 100,000 to 400,000 in the first decade after emancipation. These churches formed the bedrock of black community life, and they soon gave rise to other benevolent, fraternal, and mutual aid societies. All these organizations helped blacks protect their newly won freedom.

Emancipation also meant education for many blacks. Learning to read and write had been a privilege generally denied to them under slavery. Freedmen wasted no time establishing societies for self-improvement, which undertook to raise funds to purchase land, build schoolhouses, and hire teachers. One member of a North Carolina education society asserted that "a schoolhouse would be the first proof of their *independence.*" Southern blacks soon found, however, that the demand outstripped the supply of qualified black teachers. They accepted the aid of Northern white women sent by the American Missionary Association, who volunteered their services as teachers. They also turned to the federal government for help. The freed blacks were going to need all the friends—and power—they could muster in Washington.

✸ The Freedmen's Bureau

Abolitionists had long preached that slavery was a degrading institution. Now the emancipators were faced with the brutal reality that the freedmen were overwhelmingly unskilled, unlettered, without property or money, and with scant knowledge of how to survive as free people. To cope with this problem throughout the conquered South, Congress created the **Freedmen's Bureau** on March 3, 1865.

On paper at least, the bureau was intended to be a kind of primitive welfare agency. It was to provide food, clothing, medical care, and education both to freedmen and to white refugees. Heading the bureau was a warmly sympathetic friend of blacks, Union general Oliver O. Howard, who later founded and served as president of Howard University in Washington, D.C.

Women from the North enthusiastically embraced the opportunity to go south and teach in Freedmen's Bureau schools for emancipated blacks. One volunteer explained her motives:

❝I thought I must do something, not having money at my command, what could I do but give myself to the work. . . . I would go to them, and give them my life if necessary.**❞**

The bureau achieved its greatest successes in education. It taught an estimated 200,000 blacks how to read. Many former slaves had a passion for learning, partly because they wanted to close the gap between themselves and whites and partly because they longed to read the Word of God. In one elementary class in North Carolina sat four generations of the same family, ranging from a six-year-old child to a seventy-five-year-old grandmother.

But in other areas, the bureau's accomplishments were meager—or even mischievous. Although the bureau was authorized to settle former slaves on forty-acre tracts confiscated from the Confederates, little land actually made it into blacks' hands. Instead local administrators often collaborated with planters in expelling blacks from towns and cajoling them into signing labor contracts to work for their former masters. Still, the white South resented the bureau as a meddlesome federal interloper that threatened to upset white racial dominance. President Andrew Johnson, who shared the white supremacist views of most white Southerners, repeatedly tried to kill it, and it expired in 1872.

✸ Johnson: The Tailor President

Few presidents have ever been faced with a more perplexing sea of troubles than that confronting Andrew Johnson. What manner of man was this medium-built, dark-eyed, black-haired Tennessean, now chief executive by virtue of the bullet that killed Lincoln?

No citizen, not even Lincoln, has ever reached the White House from humbler beginnings. Born to impoverished parents in North Carolina and orphaned early, Johnson never attended school but was apprenticed to a tailor at age ten. Ambitious to get ahead, he taught himself to read, and later his wife taught him to write and do simple arithmetic. Like many another self-made man, he was inclined to overpraise his maker.

Johnson early became active in politics in Tennessee, where he had moved when seventeen years old. He shone as an impassioned champion of poor whites against the planter aristocrats, although he himself ultimately owned a few slaves. He excelled as a two-fisted stump speaker before angry and heckling crowds, who on occasion greeted his political oratory with cocked pistols, not just cocked ears. Elected to Congress, he attracted much favorable attention in the North (but not the South) when he refused to secede with his own state. After Tennessee was partially "redeemed" by Union armies, he was appointed war governor and served courageously in an atmosphere of danger.

Political exigency next thrust Johnson into the vice presidency. Lincoln's Union party in 1864 needed to

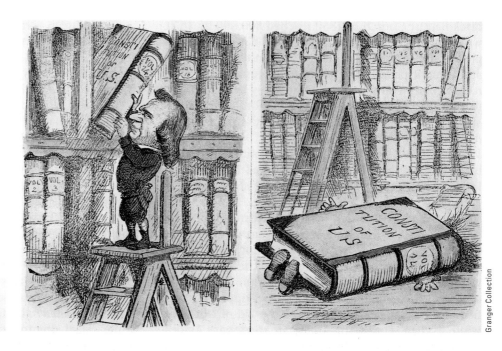

Crushed by the Constitution President Andrew Johnson revered the U.S. Constitution but eventually felt its awesome weight in his impeachment trial.

Granger Collection

attract support from the War Democrats and other pro-Southern elements, and Johnson, a Democrat, seemed to be the ideal man. Unfortunately, he appeared at the vice-presidential inaugural ceremonies the following March in a scandalous condition. He had recently been afflicted with typhoid fever, and although not known as a heavy drinker, he was urged by his friends to take a stiff bracer of whiskey. This he did—with unfortunate results.

"Old Andy" Johnson was no doubt a man of parts—unpolished parts. He was intelligent, able, forceful, and gifted with homespun honesty. Steadfastly devoted to duty and to the people, he was a dogmatic champion of states' rights and the Constitution. He would often present a copy of the document to visitors, and he was buried with one as a pillow.

Yet the man who had raised himself from the tailor's bench to the president's chair was a misfit. A Southerner who did not understand the North, a Tennessean who had earned the distrust of the South, a Democrat who had never been accepted by the Republicans, a president who had never been elected to the office, he was not at home in a Republican White House. Hotheaded, contentious, and stubborn, he was the wrong man in the wrong place at the wrong time. A Reconstruction policy devised by angels might well have failed in his tactless hands.

✯ Presidential Reconstruction

Even before the shooting war had ended, the political war over Reconstruction had begun. Abraham Lincoln

believed that the Southern states had never legally withdrawn from the Union. Their formal restoration to the Union would therefore be relatively simple. Accordingly, Lincoln in 1863 proclaimed his **"10 percent" Reconstruction plan**. It decreed that a state could be reintegrated into the Union when 10 percent of its voters in the presidential election of 1860 had taken an oath of allegiance to the United States and pledged to abide by emancipation. The next step would be formal erection of a state government. Lincoln would then recognize the purified regime.

Lincoln's proclamation provoked a sharp reaction in Congress, where Republicans feared the restoration of the planter aristocracy to power and the possible re-enslavement of blacks. Republicans therefore rammed through Congress in 1864 the **Wade-Davis Bill**. The bill required that 50 percent of a state's voters take the oath of allegiance and demanded stronger safeguards for emancipation than Lincoln's as the price of readmission to the Union. Lincoln "pocket-vetoed" this bill by refusing to sign it after Congress had adjourned. Republicans were outraged. They refused to seat delegates from Louisiana after that state had reorganized its government in accordance with Lincoln's 10 percent plan in 1864.

The controversy surrounding the Wade-Davis Bill had revealed deep differences between the president and Congress. Unlike Lincoln, many in Congress insisted that the seceders had indeed left the Union—had "committed suicide" as republican states—and had therefore forfeited all their rights. They could be readmitted only as "conquered provinces" on such conditions as Congress should decree.

TABLE 22.1 Principal Reconstruction Proposals and Plans

Year	Proposal or Plan
1864–1865	Lincoln's 10 percent proposal
1865–1866	Johnson's version of Lincoln's proposal
1866–1867	Congressional plan: 10 percent plan with Fourteenth Amendment
1867–1877	Congressional plan of military Reconstruction: Fourteenth Amendment plus black suffrage, later established nationwide by Fifteenth Amendment

This episode further revealed differences among Republicans. Two factions were emerging. The majority moderate group tended to agree with Lincoln that the seceded states should be restored to the Union as simply and swiftly as reasonable—though on Congress's terms, not the president's. The minority radical group believed that the South should atone more painfully for its sins. Before the South should be restored, the radicals wanted its social structure uprooted, the haughty planters punished, and the newly emancipated blacks protected by federal power.

Some of the radicals were secretly pleased when the assassin's bullet felled Lincoln, for the martyred president had shown tenderness toward the South. Spiteful "Andy" Johnson, who shared their hatred for the planter aristocrats, would presumably also share their desire to reconstruct the South with a rod of iron.

Johnson soon disillusioned them. He agreed with Lincoln that the seceded states had never legally been outside the Union. Thus he quickly recognized several of Lincoln's 10 percent governments, and on May 29, 1865, he issued his own Reconstruction proclamation (see Table 22.1). It disfranchised certain leading Confederates, including those with taxable property worth more than $20,000, though they might petition him for personal pardons. It called for special state conventions, which were required to repeal the ordinances of secession, repudiate all Confederate debts, and ratify the slave-freeing Thirteenth Amendment. States that complied with these conditions, Johnson declared, would be swiftly readmitted to the Union.

Johnson, savoring his dominance over the high-toned aristocrats who now begged his favor, granted pardons in abundance. Bolstered by the political resurrection of the planter elite, the recently rebellious states moved rapidly in the second half of 1865 to organize governments. But as the pattern of the new governments became clear, Republicans of all stripes grew furious.

✷ The Baleful Black Codes

Among the first acts of the new Southern regimes sanctioned by Johnson was the passage of the iron-toothed **Black Codes**. These laws were designed to regulate the affairs of the emancipated blacks, much as the slave statutes had done in pre–Civil War days. Mississippi passed the first such law in November 1865, and other Southern states soon followed suit. The Black Codes varied in severity from state to state (Mississippi's was the harshest and Georgia's the most lenient), but they had much in common. The Black Codes aimed, first of all, to ensure a stable and subservient labor force. The crushed Cotton Kingdom could not rise from its weeds until the fields were once again put under hoe and plow—and many whites wanted to make sure that they retained the tight control they had exercised over black field hands and plow drivers in the days of slavery.

Dire penalties were therefore imposed by the codes on blacks who "jumped" their labor contracts, which usually committed them to work for the same employer for one year, and generally at pittance wages. Violators could be made to forfeit back wages or could be forcibly dragged back to work by a paid "Negro-catcher." In Mississippi the captured freedmen could be fined and then hired out to pay their fines—an arrangement that closely resembled slavery itself.

Before President Andrew Johnson (1808–1875) softened his Southern policy, his views were radical. Speaking on April 21, 1865, he declared,

❝It is not promulgating anything that I have not heretofore said to say that traitors must be made odious, that treason must be made odious, that traitors must be punished and impoverished. They must not only be punished, but their social power must be destroyed. If not, they will still maintain an ascendancy, and may again become numerous and powerful; for, in the words of a former Senator of the United States, 'When traitors become numerous enough, treason becomes respectable.'**❞**

Early in 1866 one congressman quoted a Georgian:

" The blacks eat, sleep, move, live, only by the tolerance of the whites, who hate them. The blacks own absolutely nothing but their bodies; their former masters own everything, and will sell them nothing. If a black man draws even a bucket of water from a well, he must first get the permission of a white man, his enemy. . . . If he asks for work to earn his living, he must ask it of a white man; and the whites are determined to give him no work, except on such terms as will make him a serf and impair his liberty.**"**

The codes also sought to restore as nearly as possible the pre-emancipation system of race relations. Freedom was legally recognized, as were some other privileges, such as the right to marry. But all the codes forbade a black to serve on a jury; some even barred blacks from renting or leasing land. A black could be punished for "idleness" by being sentenced to work on a chain gang. Nowhere were blacks allowed to vote.

These oppressive laws mocked the ideal of freedom, so recently purchased by buckets of blood. The Black Codes imposed terrible burdens on the unfettered blacks, struggling against mistreatment and poverty to make their way as free people. The worst features of the Black Codes would eventually be repealed, but their revocation could not by itself lift the liberated blacks into economic independence. Lacking capital, and with little to offer but their labor, thousands of impoverished former slaves slipped into the status of sharecropper farmers, as did many landless whites. Luckless sharecroppers gradually sank into a morass of virtual peonage and remained there for generations. Formerly slaves to masters, countless blacks as well as poorer whites in effect became slaves to the soil and to their creditors. Yet the dethroned planter aristocracy resented even this pitiful concession to freedom. Sharecropping was the "wrong policy," said one planter. "It makes the laborer too independent; he becomes a partner, and has a right to be consulted."

The Black Codes made an ugly impression in the North. If the former slaves were being re-enslaved, people asked one another, had not the Boys in Blue spilled their blood in vain? Had the North really won the war?

✦ Congressional Reconstruction

These questions grew more insistent when the congressional delegations from the newly reconstituted Southern states presented themselves in the Capitol in December 1865. To the shock and disgust of the Republicans, many former Confederate leaders were on hand to claim their seats.

The appearance of these ex-rebels was a natural but costly blunder. Voters of the South, seeking able representatives, had turned instinctively to their experienced statesmen. But most of the Southern leaders were tainted by active association with the "lost cause." Among them were four former Confederate generals, five colonels, and various members of the Richmond cabinet and Congress. Worst of all, there was the shrimpy but brainy Alexander Stephens, ex–vice

Sharecroppers Picking Cotton
Although many freed slaves found themselves picking cotton on their former masters' plantations, they took comfort that they were at least paid wages and could work as a family unit. In time, however, they became ensnared in the web of debt that their planter bosses spun to keep a free labor force tightly bound to them.

National Archives

president of the Confederacy, still under indictment for treason.

The presence of these "whitewashed rebels" infuriated the Republicans in Congress. The war had been fought to restore the Union, but not on these kinds of terms. The Republicans were in no hurry to embrace their former enemies—virtually all of them Democrats—in the chambers of the Capitol. While the South had been "out" from 1861 to 1865, the Republicans in Congress had enjoyed a relatively free hand. They had passed much legislation that favored the North, such as the Morrill Tariff, the **Pacific Railroad Act**, and the Homestead Act. Now many Republicans balked at giving up this political advantage. On the first day of the congressional session, December 4, 1865, they banged shut the door in the face of the newly elected Southern delegations.

Looking to the future, the Republicans were alarmed to realize that a restored South would be stronger than ever in national politics. Before the war a black slave had counted as three-fifths of a person in apportioning congressional representation. Now the slave was five-fifths of a person. Eleven Southern states had seceded and been subdued by force of arms. But now, owing to full counting of free blacks, the rebel states were entitled to twelve more votes in Congress, and twelve more presidential electoral votes, than they had previously enjoyed. Again, angry voices in the North raised the cry, Who won the war?

Republicans had good reason to fear that ultimately they might be elbowed aside. Southerners might join hands with Democrats in the North and win control of Congress or maybe even the White House. If this happened, they could perpetuate the Black Codes, virtually re-enslaving blacks. They could dismantle the economic program of the Republican party by lowering tariffs, rerouting the transcontinental railroad, repealing the free-farm Homestead Act, and possibly even repudiating the national debt. President Johnson thus deeply disturbed the congressional Republicans when he announced on December 6, 1865, that the recently rebellious states had satisfied his conditions and that in his view the Union was now restored.

✦ Johnson Clashes with Congress

A clash between president and Congress was now inevitable. It exploded into the open in February 1866, when the president vetoed a bill (later repassed) extending the life of the controversial Freedmen's Bureau.

Aroused, the Republicans swiftly struck back. In March 1866 they passed the **Civil Rights Bill**, which conferred on blacks the privilege of American citizenship and struck at the Black Codes. President Johnson

resolutely vetoed this forward-looking measure on constitutional grounds, but in April congressmen steamrollered it over his veto—something they repeatedly did henceforth. The hapless president, dubbed "Sir Veto" and "Andy Veto," had his presidential wings clipped, as Congress increasingly assumed the dominant role in running the government. One critic called Johnson "the dead dog of the White House."

Republicans now feared that the Southerners might one day win control of Congress and repeal the hated civil rights law. So the lawmakers undertook to rivet the principles of the Civil Rights Bill into the Constitution as the **Fourteenth Amendment**. The proposed amendment, approved by Congress and sent to the states in June 1866 and ratified in 1868, was among the most sweeping amendments ever passed, and proved to be a major pillar of constitutional law ever after. It

An Inflexible President, 1866 This Republican cartoon shows Johnson knocking blacks out of the Freedmen's Bureau by his veto. Library of Congress

(1) conferred civil rights, including citizenship but excluding the franchise, on the freedmen; (2) reduced proportionately the representation of a state in Congress and in the Electoral College if it denied blacks the ballot; (3) disqualified from federal and state office former Confederates who as federal officeholders had once sworn "to support the Constitution of the United States"; and (4) guaranteed the federal debt, while repudiating all Confederate debts. (See the text of the Fourteenth Amendment in the Appendix.)

The radical faction was disappointed that the Fourteenth Amendment did not grant the right to vote, but all Republicans were agreed that no state should be welcomed back into the Union fold without first ratifying the Fourteenth Amendment. Yet President Johnson advised the Southern states to reject it, and all of the "sinful eleven," except Tennessee, defiantly spurned the amendment. Their spirit was reflected in a Southern song:

And I don't want no pardon for what I was or am,
I won't be reconstructed and I don't give a damn.

⭑ Swinging 'Round the Circle with Johnson

As 1866 lengthened, the battle grew between the Congress and the president. The root of the controversy was Johnson's "10 percent" governments that had passed the most stringent Black Codes. Congress had tried to temper the worst features of the codes by extending the life of the embattled Freedmen's Bureau and passing the Civil Rights Bill. Both measures Johnson had vetoed. Now the issue was Southern acceptance of the principles enshrined in the Fourteenth Amendment. The Republicans would settle for nothing less. Indeed, they soon insisted on even more.

The crucial congressional elections of 1866—more crucial than some presidential elections—were fast approaching. Johnson was naturally eager to escape from the clutch of Congress by securing a majority favorable to his soft-on-the-South policy. Invited to dedicate a Chicago monument to Stephen A. Douglas, he undertook to speak at various cities en route in support of his views.

Johnson's famous "swing 'round the circle," beginning in the late summer of 1866, was a seriocomedy of errors. The president delivered a series of "give 'em hell" speeches, in which he accused the radicals in Congress of having planned large-scale antiblack riots and murder in the South. As he spoke, hecklers hurled insults at him. Reverting to his stump-speaking days in Tennessee, he shouted back angry retorts, amid cries of "You be damned" and "Don't get mad, Andy." The dignity of his high office sank to a new low, as the old charges of drunkenness were revived.

As a vote-getter, Johnson was highly successful—for the opposition. His inept speechmaking heightened the cry "Stand by Congress" against the "Tailor of the Potomac." When the ballots were counted, the Republicans had rolled up more than a two-thirds majority in both houses of Congress.

⭑ Republican Principles and Programs

The Republicans now had a veto-proof Congress and virtually unlimited control of Reconstruction policy. But moderates and radicals still disagreed over the best course to pursue in the South.

The radicals in the Senate were led by the courtly and principled idealist Charles Sumner, long since recovered from his prewar caning on the Senate floor, who tirelessly labored not only for black freedom but for racial equality. In the House the most powerful radical was Thaddeus Stevens, crusty and vindictive congressman from Pennsylvania. Seventy-four years old in 1866, he was a curious figure, with a protruding lower lip, a heavy black wig covering his bald head, and a deformed foot. An unswerving friend of blacks, he had defended runaway slaves in court without fee and, before dying, insisted on burial in a black cemetery. His affectionate devotion to blacks was matched by his vitriolic hatred of rebellious white Southerners. A masterly parliamentarian with a razor-sharp mind and withering wit, Stevens was a leading figure on the Joint (House-Senate) Committee on Reconstruction.

Still opposed to rapid restoration of the Southern states, the radicals wanted to keep them out as long as possible and apply federal power to bring about a drastic social and economic transformation in the South. But moderate Republicans, more attuned to the time-honored principles of states' rights and self-government, recoiled from the full implications of the radical program. They preferred policies that restrained the states from abridging citizens' rights, rather than policies that

Representative Thaddeus Stevens (1792–1868), in a congressional speech on January 3, 1867, urged the ballot for blacks out of concern for them and out of bitterness against Southern whites:

❝I am for Negro suffrage in every rebel state. If it be just, it should not be denied; if it be necessary, it should be adopted; if it be a punishment to traitors, they deserve it.❞

Republicans Campaigning in Baton Rouge, Louisiana, 1868 The soldiers' caps and regimental flags demonstrate the continuing federal military presence in the Reconstruction South. Radical Republican congressman Thaddeus Stevens said that Reconstruction must "revolutionize Southern institutions, habits, and manners. . . . The foundation of their institutions . . . must be broken up and relaid, or all our blood and treasure have been spent in vain."

directly involved the federal government in individual lives. The actual policies adopted by Congress showed the influence of both these schools of thought, though the moderates, as the majority faction, had the upper hand. And one thing both groups had come to agree on by 1867 was the necessity to enfranchise black voters, even if it took federal troops to do it.

✦ Reconstruction by the Sword

Against a backdrop of vicious and bloody race riots that had erupted in several Southern cities, Congress passed the **Reconstruction Act** on March 2, 1867 (see Map 22.1). Supplemented by later measures, this drastic legislation divided the South into five military districts, each commanded by a Union general and policed by blue-clad soldiers, about twenty thousand all told. The act also temporarily disfranchised tens of thousands of former Confederates.

Congress additionally laid down stringent conditions for the readmission of the seceded states. The wayward states were required to ratify the Fourteenth Amendment, giving the former slaves their rights as citizens. The bitterest pill of all to white Southerners was the stipulation that they guarantee in their state constitutions full suffrage for their former adult male slaves.

Yet the act, reflecting moderate sentiment, stopped short of giving the freedmen land or education at federal expense. The overriding purpose of the moderates was to create an electorate in Southern states that would vote those states back into the Union on acceptable terms and thus free the federal government from direct responsibility for the protection of black rights. As later events would demonstrate, this approach proved woefully inadequate to the cause of justice for blacks.

The radical Republicans were still worried. The danger loomed that once the unrepentant states were readmitted, they would amend their constitutions so as to withdraw the ballot from blacks. The only ironclad safeguard was to incorporate black suffrage in the federal Constitution. A pattern was emerging: just as the Fourteenth Amendment had constitutionalized the principles of the Civil Rights Bill, now Congress sought to provide constitutional protection for the suffrage provisions in the Reconstruction Act. This goal was finally achieved by the **Fifteenth Amendment**, passed by Congress in 1869 and ratified by the required number of states in 1870 (see the Appendix).

Military Reconstruction of the South not only usurped certain functions of the president as commander in chief but set up a martial regime of dubious legality. The Supreme Court had already ruled, in the case ***Ex parte Milligan*** (1866), that military tribunals

475

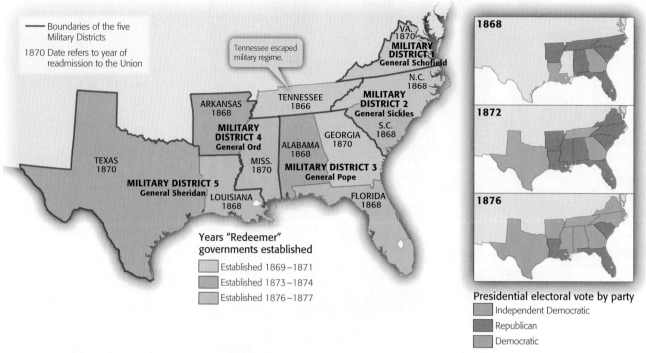

MAP 22.1 Military Reconstruction, 1867 (five districts and commanding generals)
For many white Southerners, military Reconstruction amounted to turning the knife in the wound of defeat. An often-repeated story of later years had a Southerner remark, "I was sixteen years old before I discovered that damnyankee was two words." © Cengage Learning

could not try civilians, even during wartime, in areas where the civil courts were open. Peacetime military rule seemed starkly contrary to the spirit of the Constitution. But the circumstances were extraordinary in the Republic's history, and for the time being the Supreme Court avoided offending the Republican Congress.

Prodded into line by federal bayonets, the Southern states got on with the task of constitution making. By 1870 all of them had reorganized their governments

At a constitutional convention in Alabama, freed people affirmed their rights in the following declaration:

"We claim exactly the same rights, privileges and immunities as are enjoyed by white men—we ask nothing more and will be content with nothing less. . . . The law no longer knows white nor black, but simply men, and consequently we are entitled to ride in public conveyances, hold office, sit on juries and do everything else which we have in the past been prevented from doing solely on the ground of color.**"**

and had been accorded full rights (see Table 22.2). The hated "bluebellies" remained until the new Republican regimes—usually called "radical" regimes—appeared to be firmly entrenched. Yet when the federal troops finally left a state, its government swiftly passed back into the hands of white **Redeemers**, or "Home Rule" regimes, which were inevitably Democratic. Finally, in 1877, the last federal muskets were removed from state politics, and the "solid" Democratic South congealed.

✹ No Women Voters

The passage of the three Reconstruction-era Amendments—the Thirteenth, Fourteenth, and Fifteenth—delighted former abolitionists but deeply disappointed advocates of women's rights. Women had played a prominent part in the prewar abolitionist movement and had often pointed out that both women and blacks lacked basic civil rights, especially the crucial right to vote. The struggle for black freedom and the crusade for women's rights, therefore, were one and the same in the eyes of many women. Yet during the war, feminist leaders such as Elizabeth Cady Stanton and Susan B. Anthony had temporarily suspended their own demands and worked wholeheartedly for the cause of

TABLE 22.2 Southern Reconstruction by State

State	Readmitted to Representation in Congress	Home Rule (Democratic or "Redeemer" Regime) Reestablished	Comments
Tennessee	July 24, 1866		Ratified Fourteenth Amendment in 1866 and hence avoided military Reconstruction*
Arkansas	June 22, 1868	1874	
North Carolina	June 25, 1868	1870	
Alabama	June 25, 1868	1874	
Florida	June 25, 1868	1877	Federal troops restationed in 1877, as result of Hayes-Tilden electoral bargain
Louisiana	June 25, 1868	1877	Same as Florida
South Carolina	June 25, 1868	1877	Same as Florida
Virginia	January 26, 1870	1869	
Mississippi	February 23, 1870	1876	
Texas	March 30, 1870	1874	
Georgia	[June 25, 1868] July 15, 1870	1872	Readmitted June 25, 1868, but returned to military control after expulsion of blacks from legislature

*For many years Tennessee was the only state of the secession to observe Lincoln's birthday as a legal holiday. Many states in the South still observe the birthdays of Jefferson Davis and Robert E. Lee.

black emancipation. The **Woman's Loyal League** had gathered nearly 400,000 signatures on petitions asking Congress to pass a constitutional amendment prohibiting slavery.

Now, with the war ended and the Thirteenth Amendment passed, feminist leaders believed that their time had come. They reeled with shock, however, when the wording of the Fourteenth Amendment, which defined equal national citizenship, for the first time inserted the word *male* into the Constitution in referring to a citizen's right to vote. Both Stanton and Anthony campaigned actively against the Fourteenth

Amendment despite the pleas of Frederick Douglass, who had long supported woman suffrage but believed that this was "the Negro's hour." When the Fifteenth Amendment proposed to prohibit denial of the vote on the basis of "race, color, or previous condition of servitude," Stanton and Anthony wanted the word *sex* added to the list. They lost this battle, too. Fifty years would pass before the Constitution granted women the right to vote.

✶ The Realities of Radical Reconstruction in the South

Blacks now had freedom, of a sort. Their friends in Congress had only haltingly and somewhat belatedly secured the franchise for them. Both Presidents Lincoln and Johnson had proposed to give the ballot gradually to selected blacks who qualified for it through education, property ownership, or military service. Moderate Republicans and even many radicals at first hesitated to bestow suffrage on the freedmen. The Fourteenth Amendment, in many ways the heart of the Republican program for Reconstruction, had fallen short of guaranteeing the right to vote. (It envisioned for blacks the same status as that of women—citizenship without

The prominent suffragist and abolitionist Susan B. Anthony (1820-1906) was outraged over the proposed exclusion of women from the Fourteenth Amendment. In a conversation with her former male allies Wendell Phillips and Theodore Tilton, she reportedly held out her arm and declared,

❝Look at this, all of you. And hear me swear that I will cut off this right arm of mine before I will ever work for or demand the ballot for the negro and not the woman.❞

Freedmen Voting, Richmond, Virginia, 1871 The exercise of democratic rights by former slaves constituted a political and social revolution in the South and was bitterly resented by whites.

Granger Collection

voting rights.) But by 1867 hesitation had given way to a hard determination to enfranchise the former slaves wholesale and immediately, while thousands of white Southerners were being denied the vote. By glaring contrast, most of the Northern states, before ratification of the Fifteenth Amendment in 1870, withheld the ballot from their tiny black minorities. White Southerners naturally concluded that the Republicans were hypocritical in insisting that blacks in the South be allowed to vote.

Having gained their right to suffrage, Southern black men seized the initiative and began to organize politically. Their primary vehicle became the **Union League**, originally a pro-Union organization based in the North. Assisted by Northern blacks, freedmen turned the League into a network of political clubs that educated members in their civic duties and campaigned for Republican candidates. The league's mission soon expanded to include building black churches and schools, representing black grievances before local employers and government, and recruiting militias to protect black communities from white retaliation.

Though African American women did not obtain the right to vote, they too assumed new political roles. Black women faithfully attended the parades and rallies common in black communities during the early years of Reconstruction and helped assemble mass meetings in the newly constructed black churches. They even showed up at the constitutional conventions held throughout the South in 1867, monitoring the proceedings and participating in informal votes outside the convention halls.

But black men elected as delegates to the state constitutional conventions held the greater political authority. They formed the backbone of the black political community. At the conventions, they sat down with whites to hammer out new state constitutions, which most importantly provided for universal male suffrage. Though the subsequent elections produced no black governors or majorities in state senates, black political participation expanded exponentially during Reconstruction. Between 1868 and 1876, fourteen black congressmen and two black senators, Hiram Revels and Blanche K. Bruce, both of Mississippi, served in Washington, D.C. Blacks also served in state governments as lieutenant governors and representatives, and in local governments as mayors, magistrates, sheriffs, and justices of the peace.

The sight of former slaves holding office deeply offended their onetime masters, who lashed out with particular fury at the freedmen's white allies, labeling them **scalawags** and **carpetbaggers**. The so-called scalawags were Southerners, often former Unionists and Whigs. The former Confederates accused them, often with wild exaggeration, of plundering the treasuries of the Southern states through their political influence in the radical governments. The carpetbaggers, on the other hand, were supposedly sleazy Northerners who had packed all their worldly goods into a carpetbag suitcase at war's end and had come south to seek personal power and profit. In fact, most were former Union soldiers and Northern businessmen and professionals who wanted to play a role in modernizing the "New South."

How well or badly did the radical regimes rule? The radical legislatures passed much desirable legislation and introduced many sorely needed reforms. For the first time in Southern history, steps were taken toward establishing adequate public schools. Tax systems were streamlined; public works were launched; and property rights were guaranteed to women. Many welcome reforms were retained by the all-white "Redeemer" governments that later returned to power.

Despite these achievements, graft ran rampant in many "radical" governments. This was especially true in South Carolina and Louisiana, where conscienceless promoters and other pocket-padders used politically inexperienced blacks as pawns. The worst "black-and-white" legislatures purchased, as "legislative supplies," such "stationery" as hams, perfumes, suspenders, bonnets, corsets, champagne, and a coffin. One "thrifty" carpetbag governor in a single year "saved" $100,000 from a salary of $8,000. Yet this sort of corruption was by no means confined to the South in these postwar years. The crimes of the Reconstruction governments were no more outrageous than the scams and felonies being perpetrated in the North at the same time, especially in Boss Tweed's New York.

✸ The Ku Klux Klan

Deeply embittered, some Southern whites resorted to savage measures against "radical" rule. Many whites resented the success and ability of black legislators as much as they resented alleged "corruption." A number of secret organizations mushroomed forth, the most notorious of which was the "Invisible Empire of the South," or **Ku Klux Klan**, founded in Tennessee in 1866. Besheeted nightriders, their horses' hooves muffled, would approach the cabin of an "upstart"

Collection of Thomas H. Gandy & Joan W. Gandy

Congressman John R. Lynch of Mississippi After John Lynch was freed by the Union Army, he got an education at a freedmen's school in Natchez, Mississippi. At age twenty-four, he became speaker of the Mississippi House. In 1872, Lynch joined six other African Americans in Congress, where he made his greatest mark in the long debate over the Civil Rights Act of 1875, barring discrimination in public accommodations. Lynch drew on his own humiliating experiences as a black man in the South to argue for a law prohibiting discrimination on public transportation like trains and at places like inns, restaurants, and theaters. The law passed but was not enforced. It was ruled unconstitutional in 1883.

Tennessee State Museum Collection

The Ku Klux Klan, Tennessee, 1868 This night-riding terrorist has even masked the identity of his horse.

black and hammer on the door. In ghoulish tones one thirsty horseman would demand a bucket of water. Then, under pretense of drinking, he would pour it into a rubber attachment concealed beneath his mask and gown, smack his lips, and declare that this was the first water he had tasted since he was killed at the Battle of Shiloh. If fright did not produce the desired effect, force was employed.

Such tomfoolery and terror proved partially effective. Many ex-bondsmen and white "carpetbaggers," quick to take a hint, shunned the polls. Those stubborn souls who persisted in their "upstart" ways were flogged, mutilated, or even murdered. In one Louisiana parish in 1868, whites in two days killed or wounded two hundred victims; a pile of twenty-five bodies was found half-buried in the woods. By such atrocious practices were blacks "kept in their place"—that is, down. The Klan became a refuge for numerous bandits and cutthroats. Any scoundrel could don a sheet.

Congress, outraged by this night-riding lawlessness, passed the harsh **Force Acts** of 1870 and 1871. Federal troops were able to stamp out much of the "lash law," but by this time the Invisible Empire had already done its work of intimidation. Many of the outlawed groups

The following excerpt is part of a heartrending appeal to Congress in 1871 by a group of Kentucky blacks:

❝We believe you are not familiar with the description of the Ku Klux Klans riding nightly over the country, going from county to county, and in the county towns, spreading terror wherever they go by robbing, whipping, ravishing, and killing our people without provocation, compelling colored people to break the ice and bathe in the chilly waters of the Kentucky River.

"The [state] legislature has adjourned. They refused to enact any laws to suppress Ku-Klux disorder. We regard them [the Ku-Kluxers] as now being licensed to continue their dark and bloody deeds under cover of the dark night. They refuse to allow us to testify in the state courts where a white man is concerned. We find their deeds are perpetrated only upon colored men and white Republicans. We also find that for our services to the government and our race we have become the special object of hatred and persecution at the hands of the Democratic Party. Our people are driven from their homes in great numbers, having no redress only [except] the United States court, which is in many cases unable to reach them.**❞**

A black leader protested to whites in 1868,

❝It is extraordinary that a race such as yours, professing gallantry, chivalry, education, and superiority, living in a land where ringing chimes call child and sire to the Gospel of God—that with all these advantages on your side, you can make war upon the poor defenseless black man.**❞**

continued their tactics in the guise of "dancing clubs," "missionary societies," and "rifle clubs."

White resistance undermined attempts to empower blacks politically. The white South, for many decades, openly flouted the Fourteenth and Fifteenth Amendments. Wholesale disfranchisement of blacks, starting conspicuously about 1890, was achieved by intimidation, fraud, and trickery. Among various underhanded schemes were literacy tests, unfairly administered by whites to the advantage of illiterate whites. In the eyes of white Southerners, the goal of white supremacy fully justified these dishonorable devices.

✦ Johnson Walks the Impeachment Plank

Radicals meanwhile had been sharpening their hatchets for President Johnson. Annoyed by the obstruction of the "drunken tailor" in the White House, they falsely accused him of maintaining there a harem of "dissolute women." Not content with curbing his authority, they decided to remove him altogether by constitutional processes.[*]

As an initial step, Congress in 1867 passed the **Tenure of Office Act**—as usual, over Johnson's veto. Contrary to precedent, the new law required the president to secure the consent of the Senate before he could remove his appointees once they had been approved by that body. One purpose was to freeze into the cabinet the secretary of war, Edwin M. Stanton, a holdover from the Lincoln administration. Although outwardly loyal to Johnson, he was secretly serving as a spy and informer for the radicals.

Johnson provided the radicals with a pretext to begin impeachment proceedings when he abruptly dismissed Stanton early in 1868. The House of Representatives immediately voted 126 to 47 to impeach Johnson

---

[*]For impeachment, see Art. I, Sec. II, para. 5; Art. I, Sec. III, paras. 6, 7; Art. II, Sec. IV, in the Appendix.

Impeachment Drama The impeachment proceedings against President Andrew Johnson, among the most severe constitutional crises in the Republic's history, were high political theater, and tickets were in sharp demand.

for "high crimes and misdemeanors," as required by the Constitution, charging him with various violations of the Tenure of Office Act. Two additional articles related to Johnson's verbal assaults on the Congress, involving "disgrace, ridicule, hatred, contempt, and reproach."

✴ A Not-Guilty Verdict for Johnson

With evident zeal the radical-led Senate now sat as a court to try Johnson on the dubious impeachment charges. The House conducted the prosecution. The trial aroused intense public interest and, with one thousand tickets printed, proved to be the biggest show of 1868. Johnson kept his dignity and sobriety and maintained a discreet silence. His battery of attorneys argued that the president, convinced that the Tenure of Office Act was unconstitutional, had fired Stanton merely to put a test case before the Supreme Court. (That slow-moving tribunal finally ruled indirectly in Johnson's favor fifty-eight years later.) House prosecutors, including oily-tongued Benjamin F. Butler and embittered Thaddeus Stevens, had a harder time building a compelling case for impeachment.

On May 16, 1868, the day for the first voting in the Senate, the tension was electric, and heavy breathing could be heard in the galleries. By a margin of only one vote, the radicals failed to muster the two-thirds majority for Johnson's removal. Seven independent-minded Republican senators, courageously putting country above party, voted "not guilty."

Several factors shaped the outcome. Fears of creating a destabilizing precedent played a role, as did principled opposition to abusing the constitutional mechanism of checks and balances. Political considerations also figured conspicuously. As the vice presidency remained vacant under Johnson, his successor would have been radical Republican Benjamin Wade, the president pro tempore of the Senate. Wade was disliked by many members of the business community for his high-tariff, soft-money, pro-labor views and was distrusted by moderate Republicans. Meanwhile, Johnson indicated through his attorney that he would stop obstructing Republican policies in return for remaining in office.

Diehard radicals were infuriated by their failure to muster a two-thirds majority for Johnson's removal. "The Country is going to the Devil!" cried the crippled Stevens as he was carried from the hall. But the nation, though violently aroused, accepted the verdict with a good temper that did credit to its political maturity. In a less stable republic, an armed uprising might have erupted against the president.

The nation thus narrowly avoided a dangerous precedent that would have gravely weakened one of the three branches of the federal government. Johnson was clearly guilty of bad speeches, bad judgment, and bad temper, but not of "high crimes and misdemeanors." From the standpoint of the radicals, his greatest crime had been to stand inflexibly in their path.

✴ The Purchase of Alaska

Johnson's administration, though enfeebled at home, achieved its most enduring success in the field of foreign relations.

The Russians by 1867 were in a mood to sell the vast and chilly expanse of land now known as Alaska. They had already overextended themselves in North America,

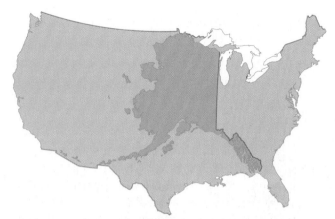

MAP 22.2 Alaska and the Lower Forty-eight States (a size comparison) © Cengage Learning

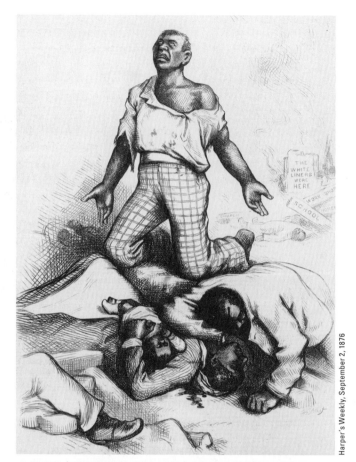

Harper's Weekly, September 2, 1876

Is This a Republican Form of Government? by Thomas Nast, Harper's Weekly, 1876 The nation's most prominent political cartoonist expressed his despair at the tragic way that Reconstruction had ended—with few real gains for the former slaves.

and they saw that in the likely event of another war with Britain, they probably would lose their defenseless northern province to the sea-dominant British. Alaska, moreover, had been ruthlessly "furred out" and was a growing economic liability. The Russians were therefore quite eager to unload their "frozen asset" on the Americans, and they put out seductive feelers in Washington. They preferred the United States to any other purchaser, primarily because they wanted to strengthen the American Republic as a barrier against their ancient enemy, Britain.

In 1867 Secretary of State William Seward, an ardent expansionist, signed a treaty with Russia that transferred Alaska to the United States for the bargain price of $7.2 million (see Map 22.2). But Seward's enthusiasm for these frigid wastes was not shared by his ignorant or uninformed countrymen, who jeered at **Seward's Folly**, "Seward's Icebox," "Frigidia," and "Walrussia."

Then why did Congress and the American public sanction the purchase? For one thing Russia, alone among the powers, had been conspicuously friendly to the North during the recent Civil War. Americans did not feel that they could offend their great and good friend, the tsar, by hurling his walrus-covered icebergs back into his face. Besides, the territory was rumored to be teeming with furs, fish, and gold, and it might yet "pan out" profitably—as it later did with natural resources, including oil and gas. So Congress and the country accepted "Seward's Polar Bear Garden," somewhat derisively but nevertheless hopefully.

★ The Heritage of Reconstruction

Many white Southerners regarded Reconstruction as a more grievous wound than the war itself. It left a

festering scar that would take generations to heal. They resented the upending of their social and racial system, the political empowerment of blacks, and the insult of federal intervention in their local affairs. Yet few rebellions have ended with the victors sitting down to a love feast with the vanquished. Given the explosiveness of the issues that had caused the war, and the bitterness of the fighting, the wonder is that Reconstruction was not far harsher than it was. The fact is that Lincoln, Johnson, and most Republicans had no clear picture at war's end of what federal policy toward the South should be. Policymakers groped for the right policies, influenced as much by Southern responses to defeat and emancipation as by any plans of their own to impose a specific program on the South.

The Republicans acted from a mixture of idealism and political expediency. They wanted both to protect the freed slaves and to promote the fortunes of the Republican party. In the end their efforts backfired badly. Reconstruction conferred only fleeting benefits on blacks and virtually extinguished the Republican party in the South for nearly one hundred years.

Moderate Republicans never fully appreciated the extensive effort necessary to make the freed slaves completely independent citizens, nor the lengths to which Southern whites would go to preserve their system of racial dominance. Had Thaddeus Stevens's radical program of drastic economic reforms and heftier protection of political rights been enacted, things might well have been different. But deep-seated racism, ingrained American resistance to tampering with property rights, and rigid loyalty to the principle of local self-government, combined with spreading indifference in the North to the plight of blacks, formed too formidable an obstacle. Despite good intentions by Republicans, the Old South was in many ways more resurrected than reconstructed, which spelled continuing woe for generations of southern blacks.

The remarkable ex-slave Frederick Douglass (1817?–1895) wrote in 1882,

" Though slavery was abolished, the wrongs of my people were not ended. Though they were not slaves, they were not yet quite free. No man can be truly free whose liberty is dependent upon the thought, feeling, and action of others, and who has himself no means in his own hands for guarding, protecting, defending, and maintaining that liberty. Yet the Negro after his emancipation was precisely in this state of destitution. . . . He was free from the individual master, but the slave of society. He had neither money, property, nor friends. He was free from the old plantation, but he had nothing but the dusty road under his feet. He was free from the old quarter that once gave him shelter, but a slave to the rains of summer and the frosts of winter. He was, in a word, literally turned loose, naked, hungry, and destitute, to the open sky.**"**

Varying Viewpoints
How Radical Was Reconstruction?

Few topics have triggered as much intellectual warfare as the "dark and bloody ground" of Reconstruction. The period provoked questions—sectional, racial, and constitutional—about which people felt deeply and remain deeply divided even today. Scholarly argument goes back conspicuously to a Columbia University historian, William A. Dunning, whose students in the early 1900s published a series of histories of the Reconstruction South. Dunning and his disciples were influenced by the turn-of-the-century spirit of sectional conciliation as well as by current theories about black racial inferiority. Sympathizing with the white South, they wrote about the Reconstruction period as a kind of national disgrace, foisted upon a prostrate region by vindictive and self-seeking radical Republican politicians. If the South had wronged the North by seceding, the North had wronged the South by reconstructing.

A second cycle of scholarship in the 1920s was impelled by a widespread suspicion that the Civil War itself had been a tragic and unnecessary blunder. Attention now shifted to Northern politicians. Scholars like Howard Beale further questioned the motives of the radical Republicans. To Beale and others, the radicals had masked a ruthless desire to exploit Southern labor and resources behind a false front of "concern" for the freed slaves. Moreover, Northern advocacy of black

voting rights was merely a calculated attempt to ensure a Republican political presence in the defeated South. The unfortunate Andrew Johnson, in this view, had valiantly tried to uphold constitutional principles in the face of this cynical Northern onslaught.

Although ignored by his contemporaries, scholar, black nationalist, and founder of the National Association for the Advancement of Colored People W. E. B. Du Bois wrote a sympathetic history of Reconstruction in 1935 that became the basis for historians' interpretations ever since. Following World War II, Kenneth Stampp and others, influenced by the modern civil rights movement, built on Du Bois's argument and claimed that Reconstruction had been a noble though ultimately failed attempt to extend American principles of equity and justice. The radical Republicans and the carpetbaggers were now heroes, whereas Andrew Johnson was castigated for his obstinate racism. By the early 1970s, this view had become orthodoxy, and it generally holds sway today. Yet some scholars, such as Michael Benedict and Leon Litwack, disillusioned with the inability to achieve full racial justice in the 1960s and 1970s, began once more to scrutinize the motives of Northern politicians immediately after the Civil War. They claimed to discover that Reconstruction had never been very radical and that the Freedmen's Bureau and other agencies had merely allowed white planters to maintain their dominance over local politics as well as over the local economy.

More recently, Eric Foner has powerfully reasserted the argument that Reconstruction was a truly radical and noble attempt to establish an interracial democracy. Drawing upon the work of Du Bois, Foner has emphasized the comparative approach to American Reconstruction. Clearly, Foner has admitted, Reconstruction did not create full equality, but it did allow blacks to form political organizations and churches, to vote, and to establish some measure of economic independence. In South Africa, the Caribbean, and other areas once marked by slavery, these opportunities were much harder to come by. Many of the benefits of Reconstruction were erased by whites in the South during the Gilded Age, but in the twentieth century, the constitutional principles and organizations developed during Reconstruction provided the focus and foundation for the post–World War II civil rights movement—which some have called the second Reconstruction. Steven Hahn's *A Nation Under Our Feet: Black Political Struggles in the Rural South from Slavery to the Great Migration* (2003) is the latest contribution to the literature on Reconstruction. Hahn emphasizes the assertiveness and ingenuity of African Americans in creating new political opportunities for themselves after emancipation.

Chapter Review

KEY TERMS

Freedmen's Bureau (469)

"10 percent" Reconstruction plan (470)

Wade-Davis Bill (470)

Black Codes (471)

Pacific Railroad Act (473)

Civil Rights Bill (473)

Fourteenth Amendment (473)

Reconstruction Act (475)

Fifteenth Amendment (475)

Ex parte Milligan (475)

Redeemers (476)

Woman's Loyal League (477)

Union League (478)

scalawags (478)

carpetbaggers (478)

Ku Klux Klan (479)

Force Acts (480)

Tenure of Office Act (480)

Seward's Folly (482)

PEOPLE TO KNOW

Oliver O. Howard

Andrew Johnson

Thaddeus Stevens

Hiram Revels

Edwin M. Stanton

Benjamin Wade

William Seward

TO LEARN MORE

Richard N. Current, *Those Terrible Carpetbaggers* (1988)

Eric Foner, *Reconstruction: America's Unfinished Revolution, 1863–1877* (1988)

———, *Forever Free: The Story of Emancipation and Reconstruction* (2005)

Steven Hahn, *A Nation Under Our Feet: Black Political Struggles in the Rural South from Slavery to the Great Migration* (2003)

James M. McPherson, *Ordeal by Fire: The Civil War and Reconstruction* (1981)

Peggy Pascoe, *What Comes Naturally: Miscegenation Law and the Making of Race in America* (2009)

Michael Perman, *Emancipation and Reconstruction* (rev. ed., 2003)

Lawrence Powell, *New Masters: Northern Planters During the Civil War and Reconstruction* (1980)

Julie Saville, *The Work of Reconstruction* (1994)

David O. Stewart, *The Trial of President Andrew Johnson and the Fight for Lincoln's Legacy* (2009)

Booker T. Washington, *Up from Slavery* (1901)

Heather Andrea Williams, *Self-Taught: African American Education in Slavery and Freedom* (2005)

A complete, annotated bibliography for this chapter—along with brief descriptions of the People to Know—may be found on the American Pageant website. The Key Terms are defined in a Glossary at the end of the text.

CHRONOLOGY

1863 Lincoln announces "10 percent" Reconstruction plan

1864 Lincoln vetoes Wade-Davis Bill

1865 Lincoln assassinated
Johnson issues Reconstruction proclamation
Congress refuses to seat Southern congressmen
Freedmen's Bureau established
Southern states pass Black Codes

1866 Congress passes Civil Rights Bill over Johnson's veto
Congress passes Fourteenth Amendment
Johnson-backed candidates lose congressional election
Ex parte Milligan case
Ku Klux Klan founded

1867 Reconstruction Act
Tenure of Office Act
United States purchases Alaska from Russia

1868 Johnson impeached and acquitted
Johnson pardons Confederate leaders

1870 Fifteenth Amendment ratified

1870–1871 Force Acts

1872 Freedmen's Bureau ended

1877 Reconstruction ends

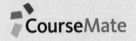 **CourseMate**

Go to the CourseMate website at **www.cengagebrain.com** for additional study tools and review materials—including audio and video clips—for this chapter.

AP® Review Questions for Chapter 22

1. Slaves responded to emancipation during the war years in all of the following ways EXCEPT by
   (A) trying to join the Union army.
   (B) vandalizing their masters' homes and farms.
   (C) changing their names.
   (D) remaining loyal to their masters.
   (E) marrying former mistresses.

2. Who were the Exodusters?
   (A) Former slaves who, after emancipation, vowed never to pick cotton again
   (B) A mass migration of blacks from various Southern states in the late 1870s into Kansas
   (C) Former slaves who spent their postslavery days searching for children or spouses who had been sold away
   (D) Newly freed slaves who founded black churches across the South
   (E) Free blacks who shed their old clothes for fine silks

3. The Freedmen's Bureau
   (A) sold land in the West to newly emancipated slaves.
   (B) negotiated fair labor contracts between newly freed slaves and former masters.
   (C) was established by Congress to provide food, education, and other social services to freedmen.
   (D) was administered in local communities throughout the South by transplanted Washington, D.C., agents.
   (E) lasted just two years before Southerners and President Johnson put an end to it.

4. Before becoming president, Andrew Johnson had been a
   (A) blacksmith.
   (B) student at a prestigious Southern college.
   (C) congressman and governor in South Carolina.
   (D) champion of poor farmers.
   (E) lifelong Republican.

5. Which of the following was NOT a feature of Presidential Reconstruction of the Union?
   (A) The notion that the South had never actually left the Union
   (B) The disenfranchisement of leading Confederates
   (C) The establishment of state conventions that agreed to certain key principles
   (D) The 50 percent Reconstruction plan
   (E) The reorganization of Southern state governments and swift readmission of them to the Union

6. The Black Codes were
   (A) restrictive Southern statutes passed to regulate newly freed slaves.
   (B) harshest in Georgia.
   (C) laws requiring former slaveowners to rehire their slaves as sharecropping farmers.
   (D) laws that safeguarded the new freedoms of emancipated slaves, such as the right to marry and serve on juries.
   (E) state-run efforts to guarantee blacks the right to vote.

7. What single outcome of the war had Northern congressmen wondering who really won?
   (A) The expectation by Southern representatives that they could simply reclaim their seats in Congress
   (B) The election of Jefferson Davis and Andrew Stephens to Southern Senate seats
   (C) The end of the three-fifths compromise
   (D) The imposition of the sharecropping system
   (E) The effort by Southern forces to eliminate the Freedmen's Bureau

8. To secure the gains of the 1866 Civil Rights Bill, Congress sought to pass the Fourteenth Amendment to the Constitution with all of the following terms EXCEPT
   (A) citizenship and civil rights for blacks.
   (B) the right to vote.
   (C) linking the calculation of a state's representation in Congress to whether it offered blacks the ballot.
   (D) disqualifying from federal and state office certain former Confederates.
   (E) the repudiation of Confederate debts.

9. What was the central difference between radical and moderate Republican notions of Reconstruction?
   (A) Radicals wanted rapid restoration of the Southern states.
   (B) Moderates wanted to reinvent the Southern economic system before readmitting southern states.
   (C) Moderates wanted to limit federal intervention in the South.
   (D) Radicals wanted less federal involvement in the South.
   (E) Radicals stood alone in their goal of black enfranchisement.

10. All of the following were tenets of Reconstruction as adopted by Congress EXCEPT
    (A) ratification of the Fourteenth Amendment.
    (B) temporary reorganization of the South into military districts.
    (C) state laws enfranchising former male slaves.
    (D) establishment of new state constitutions and reorganized state governments.
    (E) state-sponsored education and land grants to former slaves.

11. The problem of the Fifteenth Amendment to the Constitution was that it
    (A) granted only property-holding blacks the right to vote.
    (B) inserted the word *male* for the first time into the constitutional definition of citizenship.
    (C) allowed ex-Confederate leaders to vote.
    (D) did not enfranchise women.
    (E) only required that the South allow blacks to vote.

12. Who were the so-called *scalawags* and *carpetbaggers*?
    (A) Scalawags were former slaves elected to office in the Reconstructed South; carpetbaggers were Yankee agents of the Freedmen's Bureau.
    (B) Scalawags were pro-Union Southerners who participated in radical Reconstruction; carpetbaggers were Northerners who moved south seeking profit and power.
    (C) Scalawags were Southerners who sold land to former slaves; carpetbaggers were Northern government officials sent South to ensure that elections were fair and open to everyone.
    (D) Scalawags were Southerners who supported black enfranchisement; carpetbaggers were Northerners who sought to exploit the South's postwar economic crisis for personal gain.
    (E) Scalawags were those who supported Yankee reforms; carpetbaggers were Northern labor activists.

13. White southerners resisted the increased empowerment of blacks in all of the following ways EXCEPT through
    (A) the enactment of the Force Acts of 1870 and 1871.
    (B) the creation of the Ku Klux Klan.
    (C) the establishment of literacy tests as a qualification for voting.
    (D) intimidation and fraud.
    (E) enactment of Black Codes and segregation practices.

14. What was the justification for the impeachment of President Andrew Johnson?
    (A) He kept a harem of women.
    (B) He was often drunk.
    (C) He allegedly violated the Tenure of Office Act.
    (D) He purchased Alaska without the required consent of Congress.
    (E) He had obstructed Reconstruction.

15. Which of the following illustrates an accurate cause-and-effect relationship?
    (A) Carpetbaggers arrive in the South; President Johnson vetoes the Freedmen's Bureau.
    (B) President Johnson violates the Tenure of Office Act and is removed from office by Congress.
    (C) Former Confederates regain political power; radical Republicans exert more influence over Reconstruction.
    (D) The Thirteenth Amendment emancipates slaves and all slaves abandon their former masters.
    (E) Russia aligns itself with the Confederacy, leading Secretary of State Seward to purchase Alaska in a conciliatory move.

16. The initial success of the Reconstruction Act, dividing the South into military districts, faded because
    (A) Northern soldiers attempted to avenge Civil War deaths.
    (B) African Americans were never elected to political office.
    (C) many Southerners resented the continued denial of women's suffrage.
    (D) Black Codes became a part of Southern life after Reconstruction.
    (E) Democrats eventually regained power, leading to an era of "Redemption."

Part Four

Forging an Industrial Society

1865–1909

A nation of farmers fought the Civil War in the 1860s. By the time the Spanish-American War broke out in 1898, America was an industrial nation. For generations Americans had plunged into the wilderness and plowed their fields. Now they settled in cities and toiled in factories. Between the Civil War and the century's end, economic and technological change came so swiftly and massively that it seemed to many Americans that a whole new civilization had emerged.

In some ways it had. The sheer scale of the new industrial society was dazzling. Transcontinental railroads knit the country together from sea to sea. New industries like oil and steel grew to staggering size—and made megamillionaires out of entrepreneurs like oilman John D. Rockefeller and steel maker Andrew Carnegie.

Drawn by the allure of industrial employment, Americans moved to the city, much like their counterparts in industrializing Europe, Russia, and Japan. In 1860 only about 20 percent of the population were city dwellers. By 1900 that proportion doubled, as rural Americans and European immigrants alike flocked to mill town and metropolis in search of steady jobs.

These sweeping changes challenged the spirit of individualism that Americans had celebrated since the seventeenth century. Even on the western frontier, that historic bastion of rugged loners, the hand of government was increasingly felt, as large armies were dispatched to subdue the Plains Indians and federal authority was invoked to regulate the use of natural resources. The rise of powerful monopolies called into question the government's traditional hands-off policy toward business, and a growing band of reformers increasingly clamored for government regulation of private enterprise. The mushrooming cities, with their need for transport systems, schools, hospitals, sanitation, and fire and police protection, required bigger governments and budgets than an earlier generation could have imagined. As never before, Americans struggled to adapt old ideals of private autonomy to the new realities of industrial civilization.

With economic change came social and political turmoil. Labor violence brought bloodshed to places such as Chicago and Homestead, Pennsylvania. Small farmers, squeezed by debt and foreign competition, rallied behind the People's, or "Populist," party, a radical movement of the 1880s and 1890s

Factory Workers, with Railroad Spikes, Harrisburg, Pennsylvania, 1898
Immigrant and native-born workers alike bent their backs to build industrial America. William B. Becker Collection/American Museum of Photography

that attacked the power of Wall Street, big business, and the banks. Anti-immigrant sentiment swelled. Bitter disputes over tariffs and monetary policy deeply divided the country, setting debtors against lenders, farmers against manufacturers, the West and South against the Northeast. And in this unfamiliar era of big money and expanding government, corruption flourished, from town hall to Congress, fueling loud cries for political reform.

The bloodiest conflict of all pitted Plains Indians against the relentless push of westward expansion. As railroads drove their iron arrows through the heart of the West, the Indians lost their land and life-sustaining buffalo herds. By the 1890s, after three decades of fierce fighting with the U.S. Army, the Indians who had once roamed across the vast rolling prairies were struggling to preserve their shattered cultures within the confinement of reservations.

The South remained the one region largely untouched by the Industrial Revolution sweeping the rest of America. A few sleepy southern hamlets did become boomtowns, but for the most part, the South's rural way of life remained unperturbed. The post-emancipation era inflicted new forms of racial injustice on African Americans, the vast majority of whom continued to live in the Old South. State legislatures systematically deprived black Americans of their political rights, including the right to vote. Segregation of schools, housing, and all kinds of public facilities made a mockery of African Americans' Reconstruction-era hopes for equality before the law.

The new wealth and power of industrial America nurtured a growing sense of national self-confidence. Literature flowered, and a golden age of philanthropy dawned. The reform spirit spread. So did a restless appetite for overseas expansion. In a brief war against Spain in 1898, the United States, born in a revolutionary war of independence and long the champion of national self-determination, seized control of the Philippines and itself became an imperial power. Uncle Sam's venture into empire touched off a bitter national debate about America's role in the world and ushered in a long period of argument over the responsibilities, at home as well as abroad, of a modern industrial state.

Curt Teich Postcard Archives, Lake County Museum

Dearborn Street, Chicago Loop, Around 1900 "America is energetic, but Chicago is in a fever," marveled a visiting Englishman about turn-of-the-century Chicago. Street scenes like this were common in America's booming new cities, especially in the "Lord of the Midwest."

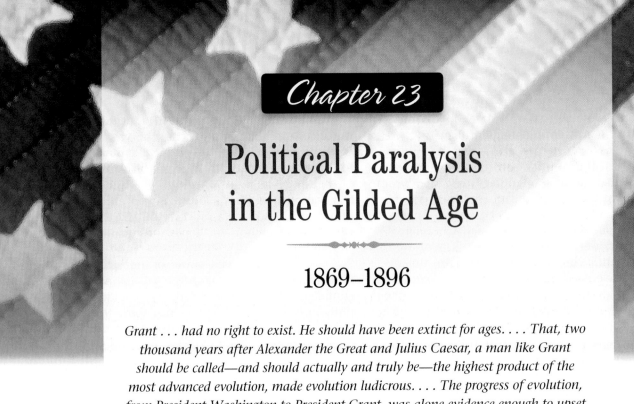

Chapter 23

Political Paralysis in the Gilded Age

1869–1896

Grant . . . had no right to exist. He should have been extinct for ages. . . . That, two thousand years after Alexander the Great and Julius Caesar, a man like Grant should be called—and should actually and truly be—the highest product of the most advanced evolution, made evolution ludicrous. . . . The progress of evolution, from President Washington to President Grant, was alone evidence enough to upset Darwin. . . . Grant . . . should have lived in a cave and worn skins.

HENRY ADAMS, THE EDUCATION OF HENRY ADAMS, 1907

The population of the post–Civil War Republic continued to vault upward by vigorous leaps, despite the awful bloodletting in both Union and Confederate ranks. Census takers reported over 39 million people in 1870, a gain of 26.6 percent over the preceding decade, as the immigrant tide surged again. The United States was now the third-largest nation in the Western world, ranking behind Russia and France.

But the civic health of the United States did not keep pace with its physical growth. The Civil War and its aftermath spawned waste, extravagance, speculation, and graft. Disillusionment ran deep among idealistic Americans in the postwar era. They had spilled their blood for the Union, emancipation, and Abraham Lincoln, who had promised "a new birth of freedom." Instead they got a bitter dose of corruption and political stalemate—beginning with Ulysses S. Grant, a great soldier but an utterly inept politician.

✶ The "Bloody Shirt" Elects Grant

Wrangling between Congress and President Andrew Johnson had soured the people on professional politicians in the Reconstruction era, and the notion still prevailed that a good general would make a good president. Stubbly-bearded General Grant was by far the most popular northern hero to emerge from the war. Grateful citizens of Philadelphia, Washington, and his hometown of Galena, Illinois, passed the hat and in each place presented him with a house. New Yorkers tendered him a check for $105,000. The general, silently puffing on his cigar, unapologetically accepted these gifts as his just deserts for having rescued the Union.

Grant was a hapless greenhorn in the political arena. His one presidential vote had been cast for the Democratic ticket in 1856. A better judge of horse-flesh than of humans, his cultural background was breathtakingly narrow. He once reportedly remarked that Venice (Italy) would be a fine city if only it were drained.

The Republicans, freed from the Union party coalition of war days, enthusiastically nominated Grant for the presidency in 1868. The party's platform sounded a clarion call for continued Reconstruction of the South under the glinting steel of federal bayonets. Yet Grant, always a man of few words, struck a highly popular note in his letter of acceptance when he said, "Let us have peace." This noble sentiment became a leading campaign slogan and was later engraved on his tomb beside the Hudson River.

Expectant Democrats, meeting in their own nominating convention, denounced military Reconstruction but could agree on little else. Wealthy eastern delegates demanded a plank promising that federal war bonds be redeemed in gold—even though many of the bonds had been purchased with badly depreciated paper greenbacks. Poorer midwestern delegates answered with the "Ohio Idea," which called for redemption in greenbacks. Debt-burdened agrarian Democrats thus hoped to keep more money in circulation and keep interest rates lower. This dispute introduced a bitter contest over monetary policy that continued to convulse the Republic until the century's end.

Midwestern delegates got the platform but not the candidate. The nominee, former New York governor Horatio Seymour, scuttled the Democrats' faint hope for success by repudiating the Ohio Idea. Republicans whipped up enthusiasm for Grant by energetically **"waving the bloody shirt"**—that is, reviving gory memories of the Civil War—which became for the first time a prominent feature of a presidential campaign.* "Vote as You Shot" was a powerful Republican slogan aimed at Union army veterans.

Grant won, with 214 electoral votes to 80 for Seymour. But the former general scored a majority of only 300,000 in the popular vote (3,013,421 to 2,706,829). Most white voters apparently supported Seymour, and the ballots of three still-unreconstructed southern states (Mississippi, Texas, and Virginia) were not counted at all. An estimated 500,000 former slaves gave Grant his margin of victory. To remain in power, the Republican party somehow had to continue to control the South—and to keep the ballot in the hands of the grateful freedmen. Republicans could not take future victories "for Granted."

✴ The Era of Good Stealings

A few skunks can pollute a large area. Although the great majority of businesspeople and government officials continued to conduct their affairs with decency and honor, the whole postwar atmosphere stunk of corruption. The Man in the Moon, it was said, had to hold his nose when passing over America. Freewheeling railroad promoters sometimes left gullible bond buyers with only "two streaks of rust and a right of way." Unethical stock-market manipulators were a cinder in the public eye. Too many judges and legislators put

their power up for hire. Cynics defined an honest politician as one who, when bought, would stay bought.

Notorious in the financial world were two millionaire partners, "Jubilee Jim" Fisk and Jay Gould. The corpulent and unscrupulous Fisk provided the "brass," while the undersized and cunning Gould provided the brains. The crafty pair concocted a plot in 1869 to corner the gold market. Their slippery game would work only if the federal Treasury refrained from selling gold. The conspirators worked on President Grant directly and also through his brother-in-law, who received $25,000 for his complicity. For weeks Fisk and Gould

In a famous series of newspaper interviews in 1905, George Washington Plunkitt (1842–1924), a political "boss" in the same Tammany Hall Democratic political "machine" that had spawned William Marcy ("Boss") Tweed, candidly described his ethical and political principles:

❝Everybody is talkin' these days about Tammany men growin' rich on graft, but nobody thinks of drawin' the distinction between honest graft and dishonest graft. There's all the difference in the world between the two. Yes, many of our men have grown rich in politics. I have myself. I've made a big fortune out of the game, and I'm gettin' richer every day, but I've not gone in for dishonest graft—blackmailin' gamblers, saloonkeepers, disorderly people, etc.—and neither has any of the men who have made big fortunes in politics.

"There's an honest graft, and I'm an example of how it works. I might sum up the whole thing by sayin': 'I seen my opportunities and I took 'em.'

"Just let me explain by examples. My party's in power in the city, and it's goin' to undertake a lot of public improvements. Well, I'm tipped off, say, that they're going to lay out a new park at a certain place.

"I see my opportunity and I take it. I go to that place and I buy up all the land I can in the neighborhood. Then the board of this or that makes its plan public, and there is a rush to get my land, which nobody cared particular for before.

"Ain't it perfectly honest to charge a good price and make a profit on my investment and foresight? Of course, it is. Well, that's honest graft.❞

---

*The expression is said to have derived from a speech by Representative Benjamin F. Butler of Massachusetts, who allegedly waved before the House the bloodstained nightshirt of a Klan-flogged carpetbagger.

Can the Law Reach Him? 1872   Cartoonist Thomas Nast attacked "Boss" Tweed in a series of cartoons like this one that appeared in *Harper's Weekly* in 1872. Here Nast depicts the corrupt Tweed as a powerful giant, towering over a puny law force. © Bettmann/Corbis

madly bid the price of gold skyward, so they could later profit from its heightened value. But on "Black Friday" (September 24, 1869), the bubble broke when the Treasury, contrary to Grant's supposed assurances, was compelled to release gold. The price of gold plunged, and scores of honest businesspeople were driven to the wall. A congressional probe concluded that Grant had done nothing crooked, though he had acted stupidly and indiscreetly.

The infamous **Tweed Ring** in New York City vividly displayed the ethics (or lack of ethics) typical of the age. Burly "Boss" Tweed—240 pounds of rascality—employed bribery, graft, and fraudulent elections to milk the metropolis of as much as $200 million. Honest citizens were cowed into silence. Protesters found their tax assessments raised.

Tweed's luck finally ran out. The *New York Times* secured damning evidence in 1871 and courageously published it, though offered $5 million not to do so. Gifted cartoonist Thomas Nast pilloried Tweed mercilessly, after spurning a heavy bribe to desist. The portly thief reportedly complained that his illiterate followers could not help seeing "them damn pictures." New York attorney Samuel J. Tilden headed the prosecution, gaining fame that later paved the path to his presidential nomination. Unbailed and unwept, Tweed died behind bars.

✪ A Carnival of Corruption

More serious than Boss Tweed's peccadilloes were the misdeeds of the federal government. President Grant's cabinet was a rodent's nest of grafters and incompetents. Favor seekers haunted the White House, plying Grant himself with cigars, wines, and horses. His election was a godsend to his in-laws of the Dent family, several dozen of whom attached themselves to the public payroll.

The easygoing Grant was first tarred by the **Crédit Mobilier scandal**, which erupted in 1872. Union Pacific Railroad insiders had formed the Crédit Mobilier construction company and then cleverly hired themselves at inflated prices to build the railroad line, earning dividends as high as 348 percent. Fearing that Congress might blow the whistle, the company furtively distributed shares of its valuable stock to key congressmen. A newspaper exposé and congressional investigation of the scandal led to the formal censure of two congressmen and the revelation that the vice president of the United States had accepted payments from Crédit Mobilier.

The breath of scandal in Washington also reeked of alcohol. In 1874–1875 the sprawling Whiskey Ring robbed the Treasury of millions in excise-tax revenues. "Let no guilty man escape," declared President Grant. But when his own private secretary turned up among the culprits, he volunteered a written statement to the jury that helped exonerate the thief. Further rottenness in the Grant administration came to light in 1876, forcing Secretary of War William Belknap to resign after pocketing bribes from suppliers to the Indian reservations. Grant, ever loyal to his crooked cronies, accepted Belknap's resignation "with great regret."

✪ The Liberal Republican Revolt of 1872

By 1872 a powerful wave of disgust with Grantism was beginning to build up throughout the nation, even before some of the worst scandals had been exposed. Reform-minded citizens banded together to form the Liberal Republican party. Voicing the slogan "Turn the Rascals Out," they urged purification of the Washington administration as well as an end to military Reconstruction.

The Liberal Republicans muffed their chance when their Cincinnati nominating convention astounded the country by nominating the brilliant but erratic Horace Greeley for the presidency. Although Greeley was the fearless editor of the *New York Tribune*, he was dogmatic, emotional, petulant, and notoriously unsound in his political judgments.

More astonishing still was the action of the office-hungry Democrats, who foolishly proceeded to endorse Greeley's candidacy. In swallowing Greeley the Democrats "ate crow" in large gulps, for the eccentric editor had long blasted them as traitors, slave shippers, saloon keepers, horse thieves, and idiots. Yet Greeley pleased the Democrats, North and South, when he pleaded for clasping hands across "the bloody chasm." The Republicans dutifully renominated Grant. The voters were thus presented with a choice between two candidates who had made their careers in fields other than politics and

Can Greeley and the Democrats "Swallow" Each Other? 1872   This cartoon by Thomas Nast is a Republican gibe at the forced alliance between these former foes. General William Tecumseh Sherman wrote from Paris to his brother, "I feel amazed to see the turn things have taken. Grant who never was a Republican is your candidate; and Greeley who never was a Democrat, but quite the reverse, is the Democratic candidate."

who were both eminently unqualified, by temperament and lifelong training, for high political office.

In the mud-spattered campaign that followed, regular Republicans denounced Greeley as an atheist, a communist, a free-lover, a vegetarian, a brown-bread eater, and a cosigner of Jefferson Davis's bail bond. Democrats derided Grant as an ignoramus, a drunkard, and a swindler. But the regular Republicans, chanting "Grant us another term," pulled the president through. The count in the electoral column was 286 to 66, in the popular column 3,596,745 to 2,843,446.

Liberal Republican agitation frightened the regular Republicans into cleaning their own house before they were thrown out of it. The Republican Congress in 1872 passed a general amnesty act, removing political disabilities from all but some five hundred former Confederate leaders. Congress also moved to reduce high Civil War tariffs and to fumigate the Grant administration with mild civil-service reform. Like many American third parties, the Liberal Republicans left some enduring footprints, even in defeat.

✴ Depression, Deflation, and Inflation

Grant's woes deepened in the paralyzing economic **panic of 1873**. Bursting with startling rapidity, the crash was one of those periodic plummets that roller-coastered the economy in this age of unbridled capitalist expansion. Overreaching promoters had laid more railroad track, sunk more mines, erected more factories, and sowed more grainfields than existing markets could bear. Bankers, in turn, had made too many imprudent loans to finance those enterprises. When profits failed to materialize, loans went unpaid, and the whole credit-based house of cards fluttered down. The United States did not suffer alone. Nations worldwide underwent a similar economic collapse in 1873.

Boom times became gloom times as more than fifteen thousand American businesses went bankrupt. In New York City, an army of unemployed riotously battled police. Black Americans were hard hit. The Freedman's Savings and Trust Company had made unsecured loans to several companies that went under. Black depositors who had entrusted over $7 million to the bank lost their savings, and black economic development and black confidence in savings institutions went down with it.

Hard times inflicted the worst punishment on debtors, who intensified their clamor for inflationary policies. Proponents of inflation breathed new life into the issue of greenbacks. During the war $450 million of the "folding money" had been issued, but it had depreciated under a cloud of popular mistrust and dubious legality.* By 1868 the Treasury had already withdrawn $100 million of the "battle-born currency" from circulation, and "hard-money" people everywhere looked forward to its complete disappearance. But now afflicted agrarian and debtor groups—"cheap-money" supporters—clamored for a reissuance of the greenbacks. With a crude but essentially accurate grasp of monetary theory, they reasoned that more money meant cheaper money and, hence, rising prices and easier-to-pay debts. Creditors, of course, reasoning from the same premises, advocated precisely the opposite policy. They had no desire to see the money they had loaned repaid in depreciated dollars. They wanted deflation, not inflation.

The "hard-money" advocates carried the day. In 1874 they persuaded a confused Grant to veto a bill to print more paper money. They scored another victory in the Resumption Act of 1875, which pledged the government to the further withdrawal of greenbacks from circulation and to the redemption of all paper currency in gold at face value, beginning in 1879.

Down but not out, debtors now looked for relief to another precious metal, silver. The "sacred white metal," they claimed, had received a raw deal. In the early 1870s, the Treasury stubbornly and unrealistically maintained that an ounce of silver was worth only one-sixteenth as much as an ounce of gold, though open-market prices for silver were higher. Silver miners thus stopped offering their shiny product for sale to the federal mints. With no silver flowing into the federal coffers, Congress formally dropped the coinage of silver dollars in 1873. Fate then played a sly joke when new silver discoveries later in the 1870s shot production up and forced silver prices down. Westerners from silver-mining states joined with debtors in assailing the "Crime of '73," demanding a return to the "Dollar of Our Daddies." Like the demand for more greenbacks, the demand for the coinage of more silver was nothing more nor less than another scheme to promote inflation.

Hard-money Republicans resisted this scheme and counted on Grant to hold the line against it. He did not disappoint them. The Treasury began to accumulate gold stocks against the appointed day for resumption of metallic-money payments. Coupled with the reduction of greenbacks, this policy was called "contraction." It had a noticeable deflationary effect—the amount of money per capita in circulation actually *decreased* between 1870 and 1880, from $19.42 to $19.37. Contraction probably

---

*The Supreme Court in 1870 declared the Civil War Legal Tender Act unconstitutional. With the concurrence of the Senate, Grant thereupon added to the bench two justices who could be counted on to help reverse that decision, which happened in 1871. This is how the Court grew to its current size of nine justices.

David A. Wells (1828–1898), a leading economist of the era, described the global dimensions of the depression that struck the United States in 1873:

❝Its most noteworthy peculiarity has been its universality; affecting nations that have been involved in war as well as those which have maintained peace; those which have a stable currency, based on gold, and those which have an unstable currency, based on promises which have not been kept; those which live under systems of free exchange of commodities, and those whose exchanges are more or less restricted. It has been grievous in old communities like England and Germany, and equally so in Australia, South Africa, and California, which represent the new; it has been a calamity exceeding[ly] heavy to be borne, alike by the inhabitants of sterile Newfoundland and Labrador, and of the sunny, fruitful sugar-islands of the East and West Indies.**❞**

worsened the impact of the depression. But the new policy did restore the government's credit rating, and it brought the embattled greenbacks up to their full face value. When Redemption Day came in 1879, few greenback holders bothered to exchange the lighter and more convenient bills for gold.

Republican hard-money policy had a political backlash. It helped elect a Democratic House of Representatives in 1874, and in 1878 it spawned the Greenback Labor party, which polled over a million votes and elected fourteen members of Congress. The contest over monetary policy was far from over.

✴ Pallid Politics in the Gilded Age

The political seesaw was delicately balanced throughout most of the **Gilded Age** (a sarcastic name given to the three-decade-long post–Civil War era by Mark Twain in 1873). Even a slight nudge could tip the teeter-totter to the advantage of the opposition party. Every presidential election was a squeaker, and the majority party in the House of Representatives switched six times in the eleven sessions between 1869 and 1891. In only three sessions did the same party control the House, the Senate, and the White House. Wobbling in such shaky equilibrium, politicians tiptoed timidly, producing a political record that was often trivial and petty.

Few significant economic issues separated the major parties. Democrats and Republicans saw very nearly eye-to-eye on questions like the tariff and civil-service reform, and majorities in both parties substantially agreed even on the much-debated currency question. Yet despite their rough agreement on these national matters, the two parties were ferociously competitive with each other. They were tightly and efficiently organized, and they commanded fierce loyalty from their members. Voter turnouts reached heights unmatched before or since. Nearly 80 percent of eligible voters cast their ballots in presidential elections in the three decades after the Civil War. On election days droves of the party faithful tramped behind marching bands to the polling places, and "ticket splitting," or failing to vote the straight party line, was as rare as a silver dollar.

How can this apparent paradox of political consensus and partisan fervor be explained? The answer lies in the sharp ethnic and cultural differences in the membership of the two parties—in distinctions of style and tone, and especially of religious sentiment. Republican voters tended to adhere to those creeds that traced their lineage to Puritanism. They stressed strict codes of personal morality and believed that government should play a role in regulating both the economic and the moral affairs of society. Democrats, among whom immigrant Lutherans and Roman Catholics figured heavily, were more likely to adhere to faiths that took a less stern view of human weakness. Their religions professed toleration of differences in an imperfect world, and they spurned government efforts to impose a single moral standard on the entire society. These differences in temperament and religious values often produced raucous political contests at the local level, where issues like prohibition and education loomed large.

Democrats had a solid electoral base in the South and in the northern industrial cities, teeming with immigrants and controlled by well-oiled political machines. Republican strength lay largely in the Midwest and the rural and small-town Northeast. Grateful freedmen in the South continued to vote Republican in significant numbers. Another important bloc of Republican ballots came from the members of the Grand Army of the Republic (GAR)—a politically potent fraternal organization of several hundred thousand Union veterans of the Civil War.

The lifeblood of both parties was **patronage**— disbursing jobs by the bucketful in return for votes,

The Granger Collection/(inset photo) Collection of Janice L. and David J. Frent

The Political Legacy of the Civil War Union veterans of the Civil War supported Republican candidate Rutherford B. Hayes in 1876. The Grand Army of the Republic (G.A.R.), the Union veterans' organization, voted heavily for the G.O.P. (Grand Old Party) in the post-civil war years.

kickbacks, and party service. Boisterous infighting over patronage beset the Republican party in the 1870s and 1880s. A "Stalwart" faction, led by the handsome and imperious Roscoe ("Lord Roscoe") Conkling, U.S. senator from New York, unblushingly embraced the time-honored system of swapping civil-service jobs for votes. Opposed to the Conklingites were the so-called Half-Breeds, who flirted coyly with civil-service reform, but whose real quarrel with the Stalwarts was over who should grasp the ladle that dished out the spoils. The champion of the Half-Breeds was James G. Blaine of Maine, a radiantly personable congressman with an elastic conscience. But despite the color of their personalities, Conkling and Blaine succeeded only in stalemating each other and deadlocking their party.

★ The Hayes-Tilden Standoff, 1876

Hangers-on around Grant, like fleas urging their ailing dog to live, begged the "Old Man" to try for a third term in 1876. The general, blind to his own ineptitudes, showed a disquieting willingness. But the House, by a lopsided bipartisan vote of 233 to 18, derailed the third-term bandwagon. It passed a resolution that sternly reminded the country—and Grant—of the antidictator implications of the two-term tradition.

With Grant out of the running and with the Conklingites and Blaineites neutralizing each other, the Republicans turned to a compromise candidate, Rutherford B. Hayes, who was obscure enough to be dubbed "The Great Unknown." His foremost qualification was the fact that he hailed from the electorally doubtful but potent state of Ohio, where he had served three terms as governor. So crucial were the "swing" votes of Ohio in the cliffhanging presidential contests of the day that the state produced more than its share of presidential candidates. A political saying of the 1870s paraphrased Shakespeare:

Some are born great,
Some achieve greatness,
And some are born in Ohio.

Pitted against the humdrum Hayes was the Democratic nominee, Samuel J. Tilden, who had risen to fame as the man who bagged Boss Tweed in New York. Campaigning against Republican scandal, Tilden racked up 184 electoral votes of the needed 185, with 20 votes in four states—three of them in the South—doubtful because of irregular returns (see Map 23.1). Surely Tilden could pick up at least one of these, especially in view of the fact that he had polled 247,448 more popular votes than Hayes, 4,284,020 to 4,036,572.

Both parties scurried to send "visiting statesmen" to the contested southern states of Louisiana, South Carolina, and Florida. All three disputed states submitted

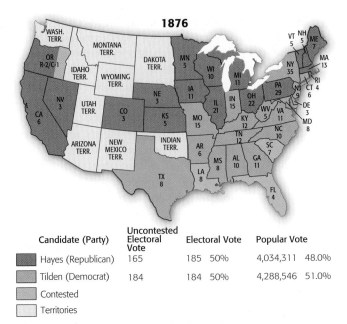

1876

Candidate (Party)	Uncontested Electoral Vote	Electoral Vote		Popular Vote	
Hayes (Republican)	165	185	50%	4,034,311	48.0%
Tilden (Democrat)	184	184	50%	4,288,546	51.0%
Contested					
Territories					

MAP 23.1 Hayes-Tilden Disputed Election of 1876 (with electoral vote by state) Nineteen of the twenty disputed votes composed the total electoral count of Louisiana, South Carolina, and Florida. The twentieth was one of Oregon's three votes, cast by an elector who turned out to be ineligible because he was a federal officeholder (a postmaster), contrary to the Constitution (see Art. II, Sec. I, para. 2). © Cengage Learning

two sets of returns, one Democratic and one Republican. As the weeks drifted by, the paralysis tightened, generating a dramatic constitutional crisis. The Constitution merely specifies that the electoral returns from the states shall be sent to Congress, and in the presence of the House and Senate, they shall be opened by the president of the Senate (see the Twelfth Amendment in the Appendix). But who should count them? On this point the Constitution was silent. If counted by the president of the Senate (a Republican), the Republican returns would be selected. If counted by the Speaker of the House (a Democrat), the Democratic returns would be chosen. How could the impasse be resolved?

★ The Compromise of 1877 and the End of Reconstruction

Clash or compromise was the stark choice. The danger loomed that there would be no president on Inauguration Day, March 4, 1877. "Tilden or Blood!" cried Democratic hotheads, and some of their "Minute Men" began to drill with arms. But behind the scenes, frantically laboring statesmen gradually hammered out an agreement in the Henry Clay tradition—the **Compromise of 1877**.

The election deadlock itself was to be broken by the Electoral Count Act, which Congress passed early

TABLE 23.1	Composition of the Electoral Commission, 1877	
Members	**Republicans**	**Democrats**
Senate (Republican majority)	3	2
House (Democratic majority)	2	3
Supreme Court	3	2
TOTAL	8	7

in 1877. It set up an electoral commission consisting of fifteen men selected from the Senate, the House, and the Supreme Court (see Table 23.1).

In February 1877, about a month before Inauguration Day, the Senate and House met together in an electric atmosphere to settle the dispute. The roll of the states was tolled off alphabetically. When Florida was reached—the first of the three southern states with two sets of returns—the disputed documents were referred to the electoral commission, which sat in a nearby chamber. After prolonged discussion the members agreed, by the partisan vote of eight Republicans to seven Democrats, to accept the Republican returns. Outraged Democrats in Congress, smelling defeat, undertook to launch a filibuster "until hell froze over."

Renewed deadlock was avoided by the rest of the complex Compromise of 1877, already partially concluded behind closed doors. The Democrats reluctantly agreed that Hayes might take office in return for his

withdrawing intrusive federal troops from the two states in which they remained, Louisiana and South Carolina. Among various concessions, the Republicans assured the Democrats a place at the presidential patronage trough and support for a bill subsidizing the Texas and Pacific Railroad's construction of a southern transcontinental line. Not all of these promises were kept in later years, including the Texas and Pacific subsidy. But the deal held together long enough to break the dangerous electoral standoff. The Democrats permitted Hayes to receive the remainder of the disputed returns—all by the partisan vote of 8 to 7. So close was the margin of safety that the explosive issue was settled only three days before the new president was officially sworn into office. The nation breathed a collective sigh of relief.

The compromise bought peace at a price. Partisan violence was averted by sacrificing the civil rights of southern blacks. With the Hayes-Tilden deal, the Republican party quietly abandoned its commitment to racial equality. That commitment had been weakening in any case. Many Republicans had begun to question the worthiness of Reconstruction and were less willing to send dollars and enlisted sons to bolster southern state governments.

The **Civil Rights Act of 1875** was in a sense the last feeble gasp of the congressional radical Republicans. The act supposedly guaranteed equal accommodations in public places and prohibited racial discrimination in jury selection, but the law was born toothless and stayed that way for nearly a century. The Supreme Court pronounced much of the act unconstitutional in the *Civil Rights Cases* (1883). The Court

THE "STRONG" GOVERNMENT 1869–1877. THE "WEAK" GOVERNMENT 1877–1881.

The End of Reconstruction, 1877 President Hayes's "Let 'em Alone" policy replaces the carpetbags and bayonets of the Grant administration, signifying the end of federal efforts to promote racial equality in the South—until the "second Reconstruction" of the civil rights era nearly a century later.

Library of Congress

declared that the Fourteenth Amendment prohibited only *government* violations of civil rights, not the denial of civil rights by *individuals*. When President Hayes withdrew the blue-clad federal troops that were propping up Reconstruction governments, the bayonet-backed Republican regimes collapsed.

✦ The Birth of Jim Crow in the Post-Reconstruction South

The Democratic South speedily solidified and swiftly suppressed the now-friendless blacks. Reconstruction, for better or worse, was officially ended. Shamelessly relying on fraud and intimidation, white Democrats ("Redeemers") reassumed political power in the South and exercised it ruthlessly. Blacks who tried to assert their rights faced unemployment, eviction, and physical harm.

Many blacks (as well as poor whites) were forced into **sharecropping** and tenant farming. Former slaves often found themselves at the mercy of former masters who were now their landlords and creditors. Through the "crop-lien" system, storekeepers extended credit to small farmers for food and supplies and in return took a lien on their harvests. Shrewd merchants manipulated the system so that farmers remained perpetually in debt to them. For generations to come,

southern blacks were condemned to eke out a threadbare living under conditions scarcely better than slavery (see Map 23.2).

With white southerners back in the political saddle, daily discrimination against blacks grew increasingly oppressive. What had started as the informal separation of blacks and whites in the immediate postwar years developed by the 1890s into systematic state-level legal codes of segregation known as **Jim Crow** laws. Southern states also enacted literacy requirements, voter-registration laws, and poll taxes—and tolerated violent intimidation of black voters—to ensure full-scale disfranchisement of the South's freedmen. The Supreme Court validated the South's segregationist social order in the case of ***Plessy v. Ferguson*** (1896). It ruled that "separate but equal" facilities were constitutional under the "equal protection" clause of the Fourteenth Amendment. But in reality the quality of African American life was grotesquely unequal to that of whites. Segregated in inferior schools and separated from whites in virtually all public facilities, including railroad cars, theaters, and even restrooms, blacks were assaulted daily by galling reminders of their second-class citizenship. To ensure the stability of this political and economic "new order," southern whites dealt harshly with any black who dared to violate the South's racial code of conduct. A record number of blacks were lynched during the 1890s, most often for the "crime" of

Jim Crow Justice In 1893 a black man named Henry Smith was burned at the stake in Paris, Texas, for supposedly molesting a four-year-old white girl. Hundreds of gawkers poured into the city from the surrounding county to watch the gruesome spectacle. Public executions like this one, or the more common lynching of black men, were aimed at intimidating African Americans into accepting second-class status in the Jim Crow South.

Library of Congress

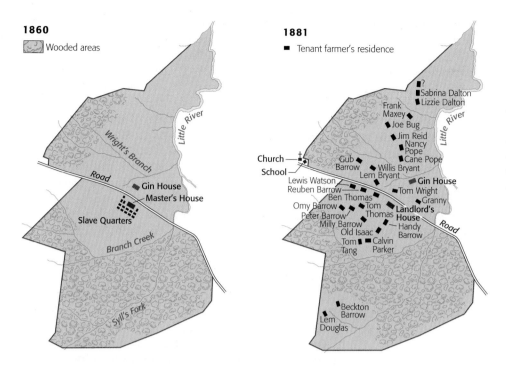

1860

Wooded areas

1881

■ Tenant farmer's residence

MAP 23.2 A Southern Plantation, Before and After the Civil War The emancipated blacks moved out of the slave quarters and into humble cabins dispersed around the plantation. The master had now become the landlord and the employer, and the slaves had become tenant farmers and sharecroppers—but were they better off? © Cengage Learning

TABLE 23.2 Persons in United States Lynched (by race), 1882–2005*			
Year	**Whites**	**Blacks**	**Total**
1882	64	49	113
1885	110	74	184
1890	11	85	96
1895	66	113	179
1900	9	106	115
1905	5	57	62
1910	9	67	76
1915	13	56	69
1920	8	53	61
1925	0	17	17
1930	1	20	21
1935	2	18	20
1940	1	4	5
1945	0	1	1
1950	1	1	2
1965	0	0	0
1996	1	5	6
2000	5	3	8
2005	1	2	3

* Note the predominance of black lynchings after 1890. The worst year was 1892, when 161 blacks and 69 whites were lynched (total 230); the next worst was 1884, when 164 whites and 51 blacks were lynched (total 215). In 1992, the FBI began to collect statistics on hate crimes. From 1996 on, the numbers correspond to all hate crime murders, not limited to lynching.

(Sources: Tuskegee Institute Archives; Federal Bureau of Investigation Hate Crimes Report, relevant years.)

asserting themselves as equals (see Table 23.2). It would take a second Reconstruction, nearly a century later, to redress the racist imbalance of southern society.

✹ Class Conflicts and Ethnic Clashes

The year 1877 marked more than the end of Reconstruction. As the curtains officially closed on regional warfare, they opened on scenes of class struggle. The explosive atmosphere was largely a by-product of the long years of depression and deflation following the panic of 1873. Railroad workers faced particularly hard times, while they watched the railroads continue to rake in huge profits. When the presidents of the nation's four largest railroads collectively decided in 1877 to cut employees' wages by 10 percent, the workers struck back. President Hayes's decision to call in federal troops to quell the unrest brought the striking laborers an outpouring of working-class support. Work stoppages spread like wildfire in cities from Baltimore to St. Louis. When the battling between workers and soldiers ended after several weeks, over one hundred people were dead.

The failure of the great railroad strike exposed the weakness of the labor movement in the face of massive government intervention on the side of the railroads. The federal courts, United States Army, state militias, and local police all lent their muscle to keeping the engines of big business operating at full throttle, and the workers be damned. Meanwhile, racial and ethnic fissures among workers fractured labor unity. Divisions were particularly acute between the Irish and the Chinese in California (see "Makers of America: The Chinese," pp. 500–501). By 1880 the Golden State counted seventy-five thousand Asian newcomers, about 9 percent of its entire population. Mostly poor, uneducated, single males, they derived predominantly from the Taishan district of K'uang-t'ung (Guangdong) province in southern China. They had originally come to America to dig in the goldfields and to sledgehammer the tracks of the transcontinental railroads across the West. When the gold supply petered out and the tracks were laid, many—perhaps half of those who arrived before the 1880s—returned home to China with their meager savings.

Those who remained in America faced extraordinary hardships. They worked at the most menial jobs, often as cooks, laundrymen, or domestic servants. Without women or families, they were deprived of the children who in other immigrant communities eased their parents' assimilation through their exposure to the English language and American customs in school. The phrase "not a Chinaman's chance" emerged in this era to describe the daunting odds against which they struggled.

In San Francisco Irish-born demagogue Denis Kearney incited his followers to violent abuse of the hapless Chinese. The Kearneyites, many of whom were recently arrived immigrants from Europe, hotly resented the competition of cheap labor from the still more recently arrived Chinese. The beef-eater, they claimed, had no chance against the rice-eater in a life-and-death struggle for jobs and wages. The present tens of thousands of Chinese "coolies" were regarded as a menace, the prospective millions as a calamity. Taking to the streets, gangs of Kearneyites terrorized the Chinese by shearing off their precious pigtails. Some victims were murdered outright.

Congress slammed the door on Chinese immigrant laborers when it passed the **Chinese Exclusion Act** in 1882, prohibiting nearly all further immigration from China. The door stayed shut until 1943. Some exclusionists even tried to strip native-born Chinese Americans of their citizenship, but the Supreme Court ruled in *U.S.* v. *Wong Kim Ark* in 1898 that the Fourteenth Amendment guaranteed citizenship to all persons born in the United States. This doctrine of "birthright citizenship" (or *jus soli*, the "right of the soil," as contrasted with *jus sanguinis*, the "right of blood-tie," which based citizenship on the parents' nationality) provided important protections to Chinese Americans as well as to other immigrant communities.

University of California at Berkeley, Bancroft Library

The First Blow at the Chinese Question, 1877
Caucasian workers, seething with economic anxiety and ethnic prejudice, savagely mistreated the Chinese in California in the 1870s.

✪ Garfield and Arthur

As the presidential campaign of 1880 approached, "Rutherfraud" Hayes was a man without a party, denounced and repudiated by the Republican Old Guard. The Republican party sought a new standard-bearer for 1880 and finally settled on a dark-horse candidate, James A. Garfield, from the electorally powerful state of Ohio. His vice-presidential running mate was a notorious Stalwart henchman, Chester A. Arthur of New York.

Energetically waving the bloody shirt, Garfield barely squeaked out a victory over the Democratic candidate and Civil War hero, Winfield Scott Hancock. He polled only 39,213 more votes than Hancock—4,453,295 to 4,414,082—but his margin in the electoral column was a comfortable 214 to 155.

The new president was energetic and able, but he was immediately ensnared in a political conflict between his secretary of state, James G. Blaine, and Blaine's Stalwart nemesis, Senator Roscoe Conkling. Then, as the Republican factions dueled, tragedy struck.

The Office Makes the Man, 1881 Besieged by his former New York cronies, Arthur tries to assert the dignity of his new presidential office.

A disappointed and mentally deranged office seeker, Charles J. Guiteau, shot President Garfield in the back in a Washington railroad station. Garfield lingered in agony for eleven weeks and died on September 19, 1881. Guiteau, when seized, reportedly cried, "I am a Stalwart. Arthur is now President of the United States." The implication was that now the Conklingites would all get good jobs. Guiteau's attorneys argued that he was not guilty because of his incapacity to distinguish right from wrong—an early instance of the "insanity defense." The defendant himself demonstrated his weak grip on reality when he asked all those who had benefited politically from the assassination to contribute to his defense fund. These tactics availed little. Guiteau was found guilty of murder and hanged.

Garfield's death had one positive outcome: it shocked politicians into reforming the shameful spoils system. The unlikely instrument of reform was Chester Arthur. Observers at first underestimated him. His record of cronyism and his fondness for fine wines and elegant clothing (including eighty pairs of trousers) suggested that he was little more than a foppish dandy. But Arthur surprised his critics by prosecuting several fraud cases and giving his former Stalwart pals the cold shoulder.

Disgust with Garfield's murder gave the Republican party itself a previously undetected taste for reform. The medicine finally applied to the long-suffering federal government was the **Pendleton Act** of 1883—the so-called Magna Carta of civil-service reform. It made compulsory campaign contributions from federal employees illegal, and it established the Civil Service Commission to make appointments to federal jobs on the basis of competitive examinations rather than "pull."

Although at first covering only about 10 percent of federal jobs, civil-service reform did rein in the most blatant abuses. Yet like many well-intentioned reforms, it bred unintended problems of its own. With the "plum" federal posts now beyond their reach, politicians were forced to look elsewhere for money, "the mother's milk of politics." Increasingly, they turned to the bulging coffers of the big corporations. A new breed of "boss" emerged—less skilled at mobilizing small armies of immigrants and other voters on election day, but more adept at milking dollars from manufacturers and lobbyists. The Pendleton Act partially divorced politics from patronage, but it helped drive politicians into "marriages of convenience" with big-business leaders (see Figure 23.1).

President Arthur's surprising display of integrity offended too many powerful Republicans. His

Theodore Roosevelt (1858–1919), an ardent civil-service reformer, condemned the patronage system as

❝tending to degrade American politics. . . . The men who are in office only for what they can make out of it are thoroughly unwholesome citizens, and their activity in politics is simply noxious. . . . Decent private citizens must inevitably be driven out of politics if it is suffered to become a mere selfish scramble for plunder, where victory rests with the most greedy, the most cunning, the most brazen. The whole patronage system is inimical to American institutions; it forms one of the gravest problems with which democratic and republican government has to grapple.❞

Between 1800 and 1925, at least 3 million Chinese left their homeland to labor around the globe. The once-great Chinese Empire was disintegrating at the same time that its population was exploding, creating severe land shortages and opening up the unstable country to European imperial powers bent on unlocking the riches of a nation closed to outsiders for centuries. Chinese men, faced with economic hardship and political turmoil in their homeland and lured by labor shortages as far afield as Southeast Asia, Australia, and the Americas, migrated by the tens of thousands to work the plantations and dig the mines that fueled a burgeoning global economy. By 1900 more than 300,000 Chinese had entered the United States to contribute their muscle to building the West, wrenching minerals from stubborn rock and helping to lay the transcontinental railroads that stitched together the American nation (see Table 23.3).

A Chinese Railroad Worker Totes His Tools to Work

Picture Research Consultants & Archives

Although those who set off from China for destinations as diverse as Vietnam, Cuba, Peru, and the United States included a few merchants and artisans, most were unskilled country folk. In some cases families pooled their money to send out a son, but most travelers, desperately poor, obtained their passage through Chinese middlemen, who advanced them ship fare in return for their promise to work off their debts after they landed. This contracting sometimes led to conditions so cruel that the practice was ignominiously called "pig selling."

The first Chinese arrived in Spanish America as early as 1565, but few followed those earliest pioneers. Until the 1848 discovery of gold in California, there were fewer than 50 Chinese living in the United States. But by 1852 at least 25,000 Chinese had arrived in California, which they dubbed the "golden mountain." At that decade's end, Chinese workers made up nearly a quarter of the state's manual laborers, even though they were only a tenth of the population. Employers nationwide viewed the Chinese as cheap labor, recruiting them to cut sugar cane in the South and break strikes in New England shoe factories. A treaty negotiated with China in 1868 by the American diplomat Anson Burlingame guaranteed important civil rights to Chinese immigrants.

The Chinese America of the late nineteenth century was overwhelmingly a bachelor society. Women of good repute rarely made the passage. Of the very few Chinese women who ventured to California at this time, most became prostitutes. Many of them had been deceived by the false promise of honest jobs.

Although a stream of workers returned to their homeland, many Chinese stayed. "Chinatowns" sprang up wherever economic opportunities presented themselves—in railroad towns, farming villages, and cities. Chinese in these settlements spoke their own language, enjoyed the fellowship of their own compatriots, and sought safety from prejudice and violence, never rare in American society. Many immigrant clubs, American adaptations of Chinese traditions of loyalty to clan or region, were established in these communities. Rivaling such clubs and associations were the secret societies known as tongs. The word *tong*—literally, "meeting hall"—acquired a sinister reputation among non-Chinese, for the tongs counted the poorest and shadiest immigrants among their members. These were people without ties to a clan, those individuals most alienated from traditional Chinese organizations and from American society as well.

Mounting anti-Chinese agitation forced the repudiation of the Burlingame Treaty in 1880, and in 1882 the Chinese Exclusion Act barred nearly all Chinese from the United States for six decades. Slowly, however, those men and the few women who remained raised families and reared a new generation of Chinese Americans. They were joined by thousands more immigrants who made the journey illegally or took advantage of the few exceptions permissible under the Exclusion Act. But this second generation still suffered from discrimination, eking out their living in jobs despised by Caucasian laborers or taking daunting risks in small entrepreneurial ventures. Yet many hard-working Chinese did manage to open their own restaurants, laundries, and other small businesses. The enterprises formed a solid economic foundation for their small community and the much larger one that would emerge by the late twentieth century with a huge influx of new immigrants arriving from China.

University of California at Berkeley, Bancroft Library

Chinese Butcher Shop, San Francisco, ca. 1890

TABLE 23.3 Population of Chinese Ancestry in the United States, 1850–2008				
Year	Population	Males per One Female	Percentage U.S.-Born	Total Chinese Immigrants in Preceding Decade*
1850	4,018†	—	—	35
1860	34,933	19	—	41,397
1870	63,199	13	1	64,301
1880	105,465	21	1	123,201
1890	107,488	27	3	61,711
1900	89,863	19	10	14,799
1970††	435,062	N.A.	N.A.	34,764
1980	806,040	N.A.	N.A.	124,326
1990	1,645,472	N.A.	N.A.	346,747
2000	2,432,585	.94	29	419,114
2008	3,077,783	.90	31	631,476

*Includes Chinese immigrants in Hawaii after 1898; by 1970 Hawaii was a state.

†Estimated.

††The passage of the Chinese Exclusion Act in 1882 sharply reduced the Chinese population in the United States. Liberalization of American immigration laws and Chinese policies beginning in the 1970s, however, has led to a great increase in population of Chinese ancestry in the United States.

(Sources: U.S. Census Bureau, relevant years; U.S. Department of Homeland Security, *Statistical Yearbook of the Immigration and Naturalization Service*, 2000.)

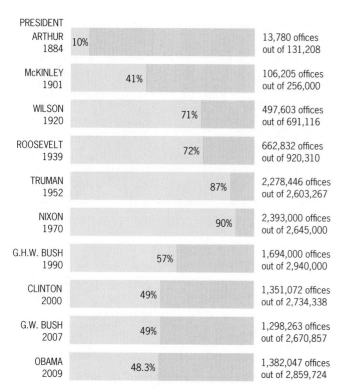

PRESIDENT		
ARTHUR 1884	10%	13,780 offices out of 131,208
McKINLEY 1901	41%	106,205 offices out of 256,000
WILSON 1920	71%	497,603 offices out of 691,116
ROOSEVELT 1939	72%	662,832 offices out of 920,310
TRUMAN 1952	87%	2,278,446 offices out of 2,603,267
NIXON 1970	90%	2,393,000 offices out of 2,645,000
G.H.W. BUSH 1990	57%	1,694,000 offices out of 2,940,000
CLINTON 2000	49%	1,351,072 offices out of 2,734,338
G.W. BUSH 2007	49%	1,298,263 offices out of 2,670,857
OBAMA 2009	48.3%	1,382,047 offices out of 2,859,724

FIGURE 23.1 Civil-Service Employment The proportion of federal jobs that are classified, or subject to rigid civil-service laws and competitive requirements, has greatly increased since Arthur's presidency. The total number of civil-service jobs has remained relatively stable since the 1950s, even as the government has expanded in size and budget. The decline in classified civil-service jobs in recent decades reflects the changes mandated by the Postal Reorganization Act of 1971, which moved U.S. Postal Service employees from competitive to excepted service. Excepted jobs are not subject to rigid civil-service laws passed by Congress. (Sources: U.S. Office of Personnel Management, *Federal Civilian Workforce Statistics—Employment and Trends*, http://www.opm.gov/feddata; and unpublished data.)

"**I Want My Pa!**" Malicious anti-Cleveland cartoon.

Library of Congress

ungrateful party turned him out to pasture, and in 1886 he died of a cerebral hemorrhage.

✶ The Blaine-Cleveland Mudslingers of 1884

James G. Blaine's persistence in pursuit of his party's presidential nomination finally paid off in 1884. The dashing Maine politician, blessed with almost every political asset except a reputation for honesty, was the clear choice of the Republican convention in Chicago. But many reform-minded Republicans gagged on Blaine's candidacy. Blaine's enemies publicized the fishy-smelling "Mulligan letters," written by Blaine to a Boston businessman and linking the powerful politician to a corrupt deal involving federal favors to a

southern railroad. At least one of the damning documents ended with the furtive warning "Burn this letter." Some reformers, unable to swallow Blaine, bolted to the Democrats. They were sneeringly dubbed Mugwumps, a word of Indian derivation meant to suggest that they were "sanctimonious" or "holier-than-thou."*

Victory-starved Democrats turned enthusiastically to a noted reformer, Grover Cleveland. A burly bachelor with a soup-straining mustache and a taste for chewing tobacco, Cleveland was a solid but not brilliant lawyer of forty-seven. He had rocketed from the mayor's office in Buffalo to the governorship of New York and the presidential nomination in three short years. Known as "Grover the Good," he enjoyed a well-deserved reputation for probity in office.

But Cleveland's admirers soon got a shock. Resolute Republicans, digging for dirt in the past of bachelor Cleveland, unearthed the report that he had been involved in an amorous affair with a Buffalo widow. She had an illegitimate son, now eight years old, for whom Cleveland had made financial provision. Democratic elders were demoralized. They hurried to Cleveland and urged him to lie like a gentleman, but their ruggedly honest candidate insisted, "Tell the truth."

The campaign of 1884 sank to perhaps the lowest level in American experience, as the two parties grunted and shoved for the hog trough of office. Few fundamental differences separated them. Even

*Latter-day punsters gibed that the Mugwumps were priggish politicians who sat on the fence with their "mugs" on one side and their "wumps" on the other.

the bloody shirt had faded to a pale pink.* Personalities, not principles, claimed the headlines. Crowds of Democrats surged through city streets, chanting—to the rhythm of left, left, left, right, left—"Burn, burn, burn this letter!" Republicans taunted in return, "Ma, ma, where's my pa?" Defiant Democrats shouted back, "Gone to the White House, ha, ha, ha!"

The contest hinged on the state of New York, where Blaine blundered badly in the closing days of the campaign. A witless Republican clergyman damned the Democrats in a speech as the party of "Rum, Romanism, and Rebellion"—insulting with one swift stroke the culture, the faith, and the patriotism of New York's numerous Irish American voters. Blaine was present at the time but lacked the presence of mind to repudiate the statement immediately. The pungent phrase, shortened to "RRR," stung and stuck. Blaine's silence seemed to give assent, and the wavering Irishmen who deserted his camp helped account for Cleveland's paper-thin plurality of about a thousand votes in New York State, enough to give him the presidency. Cleveland swept the solid South and squeaked into office with 219 to 182 electoral votes and 4,879,507 to 4,850,293 popular votes.

⭐ "Old Grover" Takes Over

Bull-necked Cleveland in 1885 was the first Democrat to take the oath of presidential office since Buchanan, twenty-eight years earlier. Huge question marks hung over his ample frame (5 feet 11 inches, 250 pounds). Could the "party of disunion" be trusted to govern the Union? Would desperate Democrats, ravenously hungry after twenty-four years of exile, trample the frail sprouts of civil-service reform in a stampede to the patronage trough? Could Cleveland restore a measure of respect and power to the maligned and enfeebled presidency?

Cleveland was a man of principles, most of them safely orthodox by the standards of his day. A staunch apostle of the hands-off creed of laissez-faire, the new president caused the hearts of business people and bankers to throb with contentment. He summed up his political philosophy in 1887 when he vetoed a bill to provide seeds for drought-ravaged Texas farmers. "Though the people support the government," he declared, "the government should not support the people." As tactless as

a mirror and as direct as a bulldozer, he was outspoken, unbending, and profanely hot-tempered.

At the outset Cleveland narrowed the North-South chasm by naming to his cabinet two former Confederates. As for the civil service, Cleveland was whipsawed between the demands of the Democratic faithful for jobs and the demands of the Mugwumps, who had helped elect him, for reform. Believing in the merit system, Cleveland at first favored the cause of the reformers, but he eventually caved in to the carpings of Democratic bosses and fired almost two-thirds of the 120,000 federal employees, including 40,000 incumbent (Republican) postmasters, to make room for "deserving Democrats."

Military pensions gave Cleveland some of his most painful political headaches. The politically powerful Grand Army of the Republic (GAR) routinely lobbied hundreds of private pension bills through a compliant

Battling over Lowering the Tariff in the 1880s
Advocates for both higher and lower tariffs claimed to be protecting American workers. In fact, workers were affected differently, depending on their jobs. Some U.S. manufacturing firms benefited from a protective tariff that shielded them from foreign competition, while others suffered from high duties on raw materials. Recognizing this tension, the American Federation of Labor declared neutrality on the tariff question in 1882.

---

*Neither candidate had served in the Civil War. Cleveland had hired a substitute to go in his stead while he supported his widowed mother and two sisters. Blaine was the only Republican presidential candidate from Grant through McKinley (1868 to 1900) who had not been a Civil War officer.

Congress. Benefits were granted to deserters, to bounty jumpers, to men who never served, and to former soldiers who in later years had incurred disabilities in no way connected with war service. A Democrat and a nonveteran, Cleveland was in an awkward position when it came to fighting the pension-grabbers. But the conscience-driven president read each bill carefully, vetoed several hundred of them, and then laboriously penned individual veto messages for Congress.

✵ Cleveland Battles for a Lower Tariff

Cleveland also risked his political neck by prodding the hornet's nest of the tariff issue. During the Civil War, tariff schedules had been jacked up to new high levels, partly to raise revenues for the insatiable military machine. American industry, which was preponderantly in Republican hands, had profited from this protection and hated to see the sheltering benefits reduced in peacetime. But the high duties continued to pile up revenue at the customshouses, and by 1881 the Treasury was running an annual surplus amounting to an embarrassing $145 million. Most of the government's income, in those pre–income tax days, came from the tariff.

Congress could reduce the vexatious surplus in two ways. One was to squander it on pensions and "pork-barrel" bills and thus curry favor with veterans and other self-seeking groups. The other was to lower the tariff—something the big industrialists vehemently opposed. Grover Cleveland, the rustic Buffalo attorney, had known little and cared less about the tariff before entering the White House. But as he studied the subject, he was much impressed by the arguments for downward revision of the tariff schedules. Lower barriers would mean lower prices for consumers and less protection for monopolies. Most important, they would mean an end to the Treasury surplus, a standing mockery of Cleveland's professed belief in fiscal orthodoxy and small-government frugality. After much hesitation Cleveland saw his duty and overdid it.

With his characteristic bluntness, Cleveland tossed an appeal for lower tariffs like a bombshell into the lap of Congress in late 1887. The response was electric. Cleveland succeeded admirably in smoking the issue out into the open. Democrats were deeply frustrated by the obstinacy of their chief. Republicans rejoiced at his apparent recklessness, bellowing loudly that lower tariffs would mean higher taxes, lower wages, and increased unemployment. The old warrior Blaine gloated, "There's one more President for us in [tariff] protection." For the first time in years, a real issue divided the two parties as the 1888 presidential election loomed.

Dismayed Democrats, seeing no alternative, somewhat dejectedly renominated Grover Cleveland in their

Weighing the Candidates, 1888 Novelties like this were widely distributed in late-nineteenth-century political campaigns. This miniature scale could be adjusted in either candidate's favor. Here the Republican Harrison rather improbably outweighs the corpulent Democratic candidate, Grover Cleveland.

Collection of Janice L. and David J. Frent

St. Louis convention. Eager Republicans turned to Benjamin Harrison, whose grandfather was former president William Henry ("Tippecanoe") Harrison. The tariff was the prime issue. The two parties flooded the country with some 10 million pamphlets on the subject.

The specter of a lowered tariff spurred the Republicans to frantic action. In an impressive demonstration of the post–Pendleton Act politics of alliances with big business, they raised a war chest of some $3 million—the heftiest yet—largely by "frying the fat" out of nervous industrialists. The money was widely used to line up corrupt "voting cattle" known as "repeaters" and "floaters." In Indiana, always a crucial "swing" state, votes were shamelessly purchased for as much as $20 each.

On election day Harrison nosed out Cleveland, 233 to 168 electoral votes. A change of about 7,000 ballots in New York would have reversed the outcome. Cleveland actually polled more popular votes, 5,537,857 to 5,447,129, but he nevertheless became the first sitting president to be voted out of his chair since Martin Van Buren in 1840.

✵ The Billion-Dollar Congress

After a four-year famine, the Republicans under Harrison licked their lips hungrily for the bounty of federal offices. They yearned to lavish upon the party faithful the fat surpluses produced by the high tariffs. But in the House of Representatives, they had only three more votes than the necessary quorum of 163 members, and the Democrats were preparing to obstruct all House business by refusing to answer roll calls, demanding roll calls to determine the presence of a quorum, and employing other delaying tactics.

Into this tense cockpit stepped the new Republican Speaker of the House, Thomas B. Reed of Maine. A hulking figure who towered six feet three inches, he was renowned as a master debater. He spoke with a harsh nasal drawl and wielded a verbal harpoon of sarcasm. To one congressman who quoted Henry Clay that he would "rather be right than be president," Reed caustically retorted that he "would never be either." Opponents cringed at the crack of his quip.

Reed soon bent the intimidated House to his imperious will. He counted as present Democrats who had

Thomas B. Reed of Maine, Republican Speaker of the House, 1890 Sometimes referred to as "Czar" Reed, he served as Speaker for six years, dramatically increasing the power of the office in line with his dictum that "the best system is to have one party govern and the other party watch."

not answered the roll and who, rule book in hand, furiously denied that they were legally there. By such tactics "Czar" Reed utterly dominated the "Billion-Dollar" Congress—the first in history to appropriate that sum. Congress showered pensions on Civil War veterans and increased government purchases of silver. To keep the revenues flowing in—and to protect Republican industrialists from foreign competition—the Billion-Dollar Congress also passed the McKinley Tariff Act of 1890, boosting rates to their highest peacetime level ever (an average of 48.4 percent on dutiable goods).

Sponsored in the House by rising Republican star William McKinley of Ohio, the new tariff act brought fresh woes to farmers. Debt-burdened farmers had no choice but to buy manufactured goods from high-priced protected American industrialists, but were compelled to sell their own agricultural products into highly competitive, unprotected world markets. Mounting discontent against the McKinley Tariff caused many rural voters to rise in wrath. In the congressional elections of 1890, the Republicans lost their precarious majority and were reduced to just 88 seats, as compared with 235 Democrats. Even the much-touted McKinley went down to defeat. Ominously for conservatives, the new Congress also included nine members of the Farmers' Alliance, a militant organization of southern and western farmers.

✦ The Drumbeat of Discontent

Politics was no longer "as usual" in 1892, when the newly formed People's party, or "Populists," burst upon the scene. Rooted in the Farmers' Alliance of frustrated farmers in the great agricultural belts of the West and South, the Populists met in Omaha and adopted a scorching platform that denounced "the prolific womb of governmental injustice." They demanded inflation through free and unlimited coinage of silver at the rate of sixteen ounces of silver to one ounce of gold. They further called for a graduated income tax; government ownership of the railroads, telegraph, and telephone; the direct election of U.S. senators; a one-term limit on the presidency; the adoption of the initiative and referendum to allow citizens to shape legislation more directly; a shorter workday; and immigration restriction. As their presidential candidate, the Populists uproariously nominated the eloquent old Greenbacker, General James B. Weaver.

An epidemic of nationwide strikes in the summer of 1892 raised the prospect that the Populists could weld together a coalition of aggrieved workers and indebted farmers in a revolutionary joint assault on the capitalist order. At Andrew Carnegie's Homestead steel plant near Pittsburgh, company officials called in three

Minnesota Farmers Loading a Husker-Shredder, 1890s The purchase of technologically advanced farm equipment increased the productivity of farmers but also saddled them with debt. Many sought debt relief in the 1890s by clamoring for inflationary schemes, including the monetization of silver.

hundred armed Pinkerton detectives in July to crush the defiant **Homestead Strike** by steelworkers angry over pay cuts. Strikers, armed with rifles and dynamite, forced their assailants to surrender after a vicious battle that left ten people dead and some sixty wounded. Troops were eventually summoned, and both the strike and the union were broken. That same month, federal troops bloodily smashed a strike among silver miners in Idaho's fabled Coeur d'Alene district.

The Populists made a remarkable showing in the 1892 presidential election (see Map 23.3). Singing "Good-by, Party Bosses," they rolled up 1,029,846 popular votes and 22 electoral votes for General Weaver. They thus became one of the few third parties in U.S. history to break into the electoral column. But they fell far short of an electoral majority. Industrial laborers, especially in the urban East, did not rally to the Populist banner in appreciable numbers. Populist electoral votes came from only six midwestern and western states, four of which (Kansas, Colorado, Idaho, and Nevada) fell completely into the Populist basket.

The South, although a hotbed of agrarian agitation, proved especially unwilling to throw in its lot with the new party. Race was the reason. The more than 1 million southern black farmers organized in the Colored Farmers' National Alliance shared a host of complaints with poor white farmers, and for a time their common economic goals promised to overcome their racial differences. Recognizing the crucial edge that black votes could give them in the South, Populist leaders like Georgia's Tom Watson reached out to the black community. Watson was a wiry redhead who could "talk like the thrust of a Bowie knife." He declared, "There is no reason why the black man should not understand that the law that hurts me, as a farmer, hurts him, as a farmer." Many blacks were disillusioned enough with

The Homestead Strike, 1892 Three hundred armed Pinkerton detectives floated on barges down the Monongahela River to the site of the Carnegie steel plant at Homestead, Pennsylvania. Met by a defiant and disciplined force of strikers, they were compelled to surrender. Here the Pinkerton men are shown disembarking from their barges after their capitulation, while the jeering strikers ashore exult in their victory.

The Kansas Legislature, 1893 Rifle-bearing Populists seized the Kansas capitol after the election of 1892 to make good their claim that they had won at the polls. Republicans disagreed and eventually prevailed when sergeants at arms, shown here, restored order.

the Republican party to respond. Alarmed, the conservative white "Bourbon" elite in the South played cynically upon historic racial antagonisms to counter the Populists' appeal for interracial solidarity and woo back poor whites.

Southern blacks were heavy losers. The Populist-inspired reminder of potential black political strength led to the near-total extinction of what little African American suffrage remained in the South. White southerners more aggressively than ever used literacy

1892

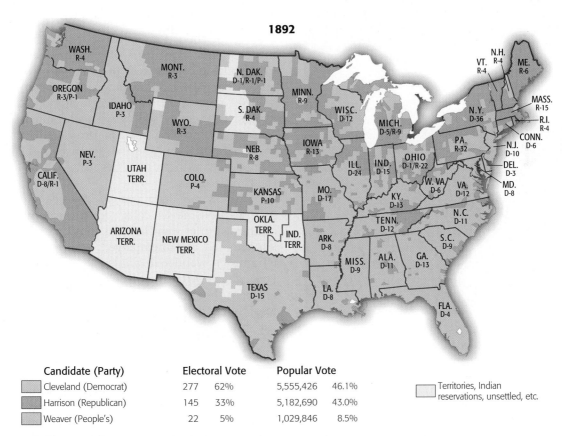

Candidate (Party)	Electoral Vote		Popular Vote	
Cleveland (Democrat)	277	62%	5,555,426	46.1%
Harrison (Republican)	145	33%	5,182,690	43.0%
Weaver (People's)	22	5%	1,029,846	8.5%

Territories, Indian reservations, unsettled, etc.

MAP 23.3 Presidential Election of 1892 (showing vote by county) Note the concentration of Populist strength in the semiarid farming regions of the western half of the country. (Compare this with Map 26.4, showing average annual precipitation with major agricultural products as of 1900, on p. 589.) © Cengage Learning

A popular protest song of the 1890s among western farmers was titled "The Hayseed." One stanza ran,

"I once was a tool of oppression,
And as green as a sucker could be,
And monopolies banded together
To beat a poor hayseed like me."

tests and poll taxes to deny blacks the ballot. The notorious **grandfather clause** exempted from those requirements anyone whose forebear had voted in 1860—when, of course, black slaves had not voted at all. More than half a century would pass before southern blacks could again vote in considerable numbers. Accompanying this disfranchisement were more severe Jim Crow laws, designed to enforce racial segregation in public places, including hotels and restaurants, and

Courtesy of Georgia Archives, Small Print Collection, spc07-038a

Thomas Edward Watson (1865–1922) Populist leader Tom Watson of Georgia began his public career promoting interracial political cooperation, though he sometimes despaired that many poor white farmers preferred to "hug the chains of . . . wretchedness rather than do any experimenting on [the race] question." Watson himself eventually succumbed to racism. In 1913 he proclaimed that "the Negro has no comprehension of virtue, honesty, truth, gratitude, and principle. The South has to lynch him occasionally, and flog him, now and then, to keep him from blaspheming the Almighty by his conduct . . . and color."

backed up by atrocious lynchings and other forms of intimidation.

The conservative crusade to eliminate the black vote also had dire consequences for the Populist party itself. Even Tom Watson abandoned his interracial appeals and, in time, became a vociferous racist himself. After 1896 the Populist party lapsed increasingly into vile racism and staunchly advocated black disfranchisement. Such were the bitterly ironic fruits of the Populist campaign in the South.

Cleveland and Depression

With the Populists divided and the Republicans discredited, Grover Cleveland took office once again in 1893, the only president ever reelected after defeat. He was the same old bull-necked and bullheaded Cleveland, with a little more weight, polish, conservatism, and self-assertiveness. But though it was the same old Cleveland, it was not the same old country. Debtors were up in arms, workers were restless, and the advance shadows of panic were falling. Hardly had Cleveland seated himself in the presidential chair when the devastating depression of 1893 burst about his burly frame. Lasting for about four years, it was the most punishing economic downturn of the nineteenth century. Contributing causes were the splurge of overbuilding and speculation, labor disorders, and the ongoing agricultural depression. Free-silver agitation—the cry to expand the money supply with unlimited coinage of silver—had also damaged American credit abroad, and the usual pinch on American finances had come when European banking houses began to call in loans from the United States.

Distress ran deep and far. About eight thousand American businesses collapsed in six months. Dozens of railroad lines went into the hands of receivers. Soup kitchens fed the unemployed, while gangs of hoboes ("tramps") wandered aimlessly about the country. Local charities did their feeble best, but the federal government, bound by the let-nature-take-its-course philosophy of the times, saw no legitimate way to relieve the suffering masses.

Cleveland, who had earlier been bothered by a surplus, was now burdened with a deepening deficit. The Treasury was required to issue legal tender notes for the silver bullion that it bought. Owners of the paper currency would then present it for gold, and by law the notes had to be reissued. New holders would repeat the process, thus draining away precious gold in an "endless-chain" operation.

Alarmingly, the gold reserve in the Treasury dropped below $100 million, which was popularly regarded as the safe minimum for supporting about $350 million in outstanding paper money. Cleveland saw no alternative but to halt the bleeding away of gold by engineering a repeal of the Sherman Silver Purchase Act of 1890. For this purpose he summoned Congress into an extra session in the summer of 1893.

Unknown to the country, complications threatened from another quarter. A malignant growth had developed on the roof of Cleveland's mouth, and it had to be removed on a private yacht with extreme secrecy. If the president had died under the surgeon's knife, his place would have been taken by the "soft-money" vice president, Adlai E. Stevenson—an eventuality that would have deepened the crisis.

In Congress the debate over the repeal of the silver act was meanwhile running its heated course. A silver-tongued young Democratic congressman from Nebraska, thirty-three-year-old William Jennings Bryan, held the galleries spellbound for three hours as he championed the cause of free silver. The friends of silver announced that "hell would freeze over" before Congress would pass the repeal measure. But an angered Cleveland used his job-granting power to break the filibuster in the Senate. He thus alienated the Democratic silverites like Bryan and disrupted his party at the very outset of his administration.

Repeal of the Sherman Silver Purchase Act only partially stopped the hemorrhaging of gold from the Treasury. In February 1894 the gold reserve sank to a dismaying $41 million. The United States was now in grave danger of going off the gold standard—a move that would render the nation's currency volatile and unreliable as a measure of value and that would also mortally cripple America's international trade. Cleveland floated two Treasury bond issues in 1894, totaling over $100 million, but the "endless-chain" operations continued relentlessly.

Early in 1895 Cleveland turned in desperation to J. P. Morgan, "the bankers' banker" and the head of a Wall Street syndicate. After tense negotiations at the White House, the bankers agreed to lend the government $65 million in gold. They were obviously in business for profit, so they charged a commission amounting to about $7 million. But they did make a significant concession when they agreed to obtain one-half of the gold abroad and take the necessary steps to dam it up in the leaky Treasury. The loan, at least temporarily, helped restore confidence in the nation's finances.

symbolized all that was wicked and grasping in American politics. President Cleveland's secretive dealings with the mighty "Jupiter" Morgan were savagely condemned as a "sellout" of the national government. But Cleveland was certain that he had done no wrong. Sarcastically denying that he was "Morgan's errand boy," Cleveland asserted, "Without shame and without repentance I confess my share of the guilt."

Cleveland suffered further embarrassment with the passage of the Wilson-Gorman Tariff in 1894. The Democrats had pledged to lower tariffs, but by the time their tariff bill made it through Congress, it had been so loaded with special-interest protection that it made scarcely a dent in the high McKinley Tariff rates. An outraged Cleveland grudgingly allowed the bill, which also contained a 2 percent tax on incomes over $4,000, to become law without his signature. When the Supreme Court struck down the income-tax provision in 1895,* the Populists and other disaffected groups found proof that the courts were only the tools of the plutocrats.

Democratic political fortunes naturally suffered in the face of these several setbacks. The tariff dynamite that had blasted the Republicans out of the House in 1890 now dislodged the Democrats, with a strong helping hand from the depression. The revitalized Republicans, singing "Times Are Mighty Hard," won the congressional elections of 1894 in a landslide—244 seats to 105 for the Democrats. The Republicans began to look forward to the presidential race of 1896 with unconcealed glee.

Despite his gruff integrity and occasional courage, Grover Cleveland failed utterly to cope with the serious economic crisis that befell the country in 1893. He was tied down in office by the same threads that held all the politicians of the day to Lilliputian levels. Grant, Hayes, Garfield, Arthur, Harrison, and Cleveland are often referred to as the "forgettable presidents." Bewhiskered and bland in person, they left mostly blanks—or blots—on the nation's political record, as issues like the tariff, the money question, and the rights of labor continued to fester. What little political vitality existed in Gilded Age America was to be found in local settings or in Congress, which overshadowed the White House for most of this period. But before the century ended, down-and-out debtors and disgruntled workers would make one last titanic effort to wring reform out of the political system—in the momentous election of 1896.

✵ Cleveland Breeds a Backlash

The bond deal stirred up a storm. The Wall Street ogre, especially in the eyes of the silverites and other debtors,

---

*It violated the "direct tax" clause. See Art. I, Sec. IX, para. 4 in the Appendix. The Sixteenth Amendment to the Constitution, adopted in 1913, permitted an income tax.

Varying Viewpoints
The Populists: Radicals or Reactionaries?

Taking their cue from contemporary satirical commentaries like Mark Twain and Charles Dudley Warner's *The Gilded Age* (1873), the first historians who wrote about the post–Civil War era judged it harshly. They condemned its politicians as petty and corrupt, lamented the emergence of a new plutocratic class, and railed against the arrogance of corporate power. Such a view is conspicuous in Charles and Mary Beard's *The Rise of American Civilization* (4 vols., 1927–1942), perhaps the most influential American history textbook ever written.

The Beards were leaders of the so-called progressive school of historical writing that flourished in the early years of the twentieth century. Progressive historians, many of whom grew up in the Gilded Age, shared in a widespread disillusionment that the Civil War had failed to generate a rebirth of American idealism. Their political sympathies were chillingly antibusiness and warmly pro-labor, pro-farmer, and pro-reform.

Historians of the progressive persuasion identified Populism as virtually the only organized opposition to the social, economic, and political order that took shape in the last decades of the nineteenth century. The Populists thus became heroes to several generations of writers who bemoaned that order and looked back longingly at Americans' agrarian past. John D. Hicks, *The Populist Revolt* (1931), is the classic portrayal of the Populists as embattled farmers hurling defiance at Wall Street and the robber barons in a last-ditch defense of their simple, honest way of life. Bowed but unbroken by the defeat of their great champion, William Jennings Bryan, in the presidential election of 1896, the Populists, Hicks claimed, left a reforming legacy that flourished again in the progressive era and the New Deal.

Hicks's point of view was the dominant one until the 1950s, when it was sharply criticized by Richard Hofstadter in *The Age of Reform* (1955). Hofstadter charged that the progressive historians had romanticized the Populists, who were best understood not as picturesque protesters, but as "harassed little country businessmen" bristling with provincial prejudices. The city-born-and-bred Hofstadter argued that the Populist revolt was aimed not just at big business and the money power but also somewhat irrationally at urbanism, immigrants, the East, and modernity itself. Hofstadter thus exposed a "dark side" of Populism, which contained elements of backwoods anti-intellectualism, paranoia, and even anti-Semitism.

In the 1960s several scholars, inspired by the work of C. Vann Woodward, as well as by sympathy with the protest movements of that turbulent decade, began to rehabilitate the Populists as authentic reformers with genuine grievances. Especially notable in this vein was Lawrence Goodwyn's *Democratic Promise: The Populist Movement in America* (1976). Goodwyn depicted the Populists as reasonable radicals who were justifiably resentful of their eclipse by urban industrialism and finance capitalism. He also portrayed Populism as the last gasp of popular political participation, a democratic "moment" in American history that expired with the Populists' absorption into the Democratic party.

Two subsequent works, Edward L. Ayers's *Promise of the New South* (1992) and Robert C. McMath's *American Populism* (1993), synthesized many of the older perspectives and presented a balanced view of the Populists as radical in many ways but also limited by their nostalgia for a lost agrarian past. Recently, Eric Rauchway's *Blessed Among Nations* (2006) argued that Populism was a reaction to America's increased reliance on foreign investment. Farmers in southern and western states resented control by foreign capitalists, particularly the British. Although Hofstadter made a similar point fifty years earlier, the impact of the international economy on domestic politics is reemerging as a direction for new research.

Chapter Review

KEY TERMS

"waving the bloody shirt" (489)

Tweed Ring (490)

Crédit Mobilier scandal (490)

panic of 1873 (491)

Gilded Age (492)

patronage (493)

Compromise of 1877 (494)

Civil Rights Act of 1875 (495)

sharecropping (496)

Jim Crow (496)

Plessy v. *Ferguson* (496)

Chinese Exclusion Act (498)

Pendleton Act (499)

Homestead Strike (506)

grandfather clause (508)

PEOPLE TO KNOW

Jay Gould

Horace Greeley

Rutherford B. Hayes

James A. Garfield

Chester Arthur

Grover Cleveland

Thomas B. Reed

Tom Watson

William Jennings Bryan

J. P. Morgan

CHRONOLOGY

1868	Grant defeats Seymour for presidency	**1883**	*Civil Rights Cases* Pendleton Act sets up Civil Service Commission
1869	Fisk and Gould corner gold market		
1871	Tweed scandal in New York	**1884**	Cleveland defeats Blaine for presidency
1872	Crédit Mobilier scandal exposed Liberal Republicans break with Grant Grant defeats Greeley for presidency	**1888**	Harrison defeats Cleveland for presidency
		1890	"Billion-Dollar" Congress McKinley Tariff Act Sherman Silver Purchase Act (repealed 1893)
1873	Panic of 1873		
1875	Whiskey Ring scandal Civil Rights Act of 1875 Resumption Act	**1892**	Homestead steel strike Coeur d'Alene (Idaho) silver miners' strike People's party candidate James B. Weaver wins twenty-two electoral votes Cleveland defeats Harrison and Weaver to regain presidency
1876	Hayes-Tilden election standoff and crisis		
1877	Compromise of 1877 Reconstruction ends Railroad strikes paralyze nation	**1893**	Depression of 1893 begins Republicans regain House of Representatives
1880	Garfield defeats Hancock for presidency	**1895**	J. P. Morgan's banking syndicate loans $65 million in gold to federal government
1881	Garfield assassinated; Arthur assumes presidency	**1896**	*Plessy* v. *Ferguson* legitimizes "separate but equal" doctrine
1882	Chinese Exclusion Act		

TO LEARN MORE

Stephen Cresswell, *Rednecks, Redeemers, and Race: Mississippi after Reconstruction, 1877–1917* (2006)

William Gillette, *Retreat from Reconstruction, 1869–1879* (1979)

Steven Hahn, *A Nation Under Our Feet: Black Political Struggles in the Rural South from Slavery to the Great Migration* (2003)

Michael F. Holt, *By One Vote: The Disputed Presidential Election of 1876* (2008)

Paul Krause, *The Battle for Homestead, 1880–1892: Politics, Culture, and Steel* (1992)

Jackson Lears, *Rebirth of a Nation: The Making of Modern America, 1877–1920* (2009)

Charles Postel, *The Populist Vision* (2007)

Heather Cox Richardson, *The Death of Reconstruction: Race, Labor, and Politics in the Post–Civil War North, 1865–1901* (2001)

Mark W. Summers, *The Era of Good Stealings* (1993)

Alan Trachtenberg, *The Incorporation of America: Culture and Society in the Gilded Age* (1982)

C. Vann Woodward, *Origins of the New South, 1877–1913* (1951)

———, *The Strange Career of Jim Crow* (rev. ed., 1974)

A complete, annotated bibliography for this chapter—along with brief descriptions of the People to Know—may be found on the American Pageant website. The Key Terms are defined in a Glossary at the end of the text.

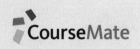

Go to the CourseMate website at **www.cengagebrain.com** for additional study tools and review materials—including audio and video clips—for this chapter.

AP® Review Questions for Chapter 23

1. Despite his status as a military hero, General Ulysses S. Grant proved to be a weak political leader because he
   - (A) was personally honest and corrupt.
   - (B) did not believe in the principles of the Republican party.
   - (C) was unable to get others to follow his lead.
   - (D) had no political experience and was a poor judge of character.
   - (E) lacked political ambition.

2. Which political emotion motivated the Liberal Republican revolt from the regular Republican party in 1872?
   - (A) Dismay at the Republicans' weakness in upholding radical Reconstruction in the South
   - (B) Nostalgia for leadership like that of the martyred Abraham Lincoln
   - (C) Disgust at the corruption and scandals of the Grant administration
   - (D) A fervent passion for reforms on behalf of women and blacks
   - (E) A desire to strengthen the federal government's regulation of big business

3. All of the following were causes of the panic that broke in 1873 in the United States EXCEPT
   - (A) a ripple effect from similar, simultaneous economic panics in Europe and the world.
   - (B) the expansion of more factories, railroads, and mines than existing markets would bear.
   - (C) bank failures resulting from imprudent financial loans made by bankers in support of questionable business ventures.
   - (D) the loss of substantial financial investments by speculators in dubious and unsustainable business ventures.
   - (E) Wall Street's fears about the power of the radical Greenback party.

4. What was a key result of the Republican hard money policies in the mid-1870s?
   - (A) The rise of the American dollar against foreign currencies
   - (B) Damage to the country's credit rating
   - (C) The return to the silver "Dollar of Our Daddies" as the dominant form of U.S. money
   - (D) The defeat of a Democratic House of Representatives in 1874
   - (E) A political turn to the Democrats and the new Greenback Labor party

5. Which development was a critical reason for the extremely high voter turnouts and partisan fervor of the Gilded Age?
   - (A) The radical ideological differences between the Democratic and Republican parties
   - (B) Sharp ethnic and cultural differences in the membership of the Democratic and Republican parties
   - (C) Religious conflict between Catholics and mainline Protestants
   - (D) Political differences over the policy issue of civil service
   - (E) Sectional tensions among the Northeast, Midwest, and South

6. All of the following were among the groups that formed the solid political base of the Republican party in the late nineteenth century EXCEPT
   - (A) northern big cities.
   - (B) Union Civil War veterans of the Grand Army of the Republic.
   - (C) southern black freedmen.
   - (D) the Midwest.
   - (E) the rural and small-town Midwest.

7. What political development resulted from the Compromise of 1877?
   - (A) A renewal of Republican commitment to protect black civil rights in the South
   - (B) The withdrawal of federal troops and abandonment of black rights in the South
   - (C) The election of a Democrat to the presidency
   - (D) Republican support for an inflationary silver-money policy
   - (E) A plan to build the first transcontinental railroad

8. At the end of Reconstruction, southern whites disenfranchised African Americans using all of the following strategies EXCEPT
   - (A) literacy requirements.
   - (B) poll taxes.
   - (C) economic intimidation.
   - (D) lynching.
   - (E) the use of federal troops to discourage African Americans from voting in elections.

9. Which of the following was NOT a cause of labor unrest in the 1870s and 1880s?
   (A) Agitation by communist sympathizers
   (B) Reductions in wages by railroad owners and other industrial employers
   (C) Competition of cheap labor from recently arrived immigrants from China
   (D) Conflict between ethnic groups for unskilled jobs
   (E) Years of depression and deflation that undermined workers' living standards

10. All of the following internal developments during the late nineteenth century in China resulted in Chinese immigration to the United States EXCEPT
   (A) the disintegration of the Chinese Empire.
   (B) severe land shortages.
   (C) the intrusion of European powers.
   (D) the Nationalist Communist Civil War.
   (E) limited economic opportunity and political turmoil.

11. With the passage of the Pendleton Act, prohibiting political contributions from many federal workers, politicians increasingly sought money from
   (A) labor unions.
   (B) farmers and agrarian associations.
   (C) foreign contributors.
   (D) contractors doing business with the federal government.
   (E) large corporations.

12. Grover Cleveland argued for a lower tariff for all of the following reasons EXCEPT
   (A) the failure of high tariffs to raise revenues.
   (B) lower prices for consumers.
   (C) less protection for monopolies.
   (D) the end of the Treasury surplus.
   (E) the need for smaller government.

13. How did the Billion-Dollar Congress quickly dispose of rising government surpluses?
   (A) It provided subsidies to wheat, corn, and cotton farmers.
   (B) It built an expensive new steel navy.
   (C) It expanded pensions for Civil War veterans.
   (D) It cut tariffs and other taxes.
   (E) It increased spending on railroads and other transportation projects.

14. President Cleveland's response to the depression of the 1890s demonstrated that he
   (A) was able to work effectively with J. P. Morgan to address the problems of unemployment.
   (B) understood the problems of urban workers better than those of farmers.
   (C) had a weak grasp of the economic theory that lay behind the demand for free silver.
   (D) was unable to deal effectively with such a massive economic crisis.
   (E) was able to skillfully incorporate some Populist proposals into the Democratic party.

15. The Supreme Court's decision in *Plessy* v. *Ferguson* solidified African Americans' inferior position by
   (A) establishing the principle of "separate but equal."
   (B) allowing the Ku Klux Klan to operate in the South.
   (C) refusing to pass antilynching laws.
   (D) favoring landowners over sharecroppers.
   (E) finding the Civil Rights Act of 1875 unconstitutional.

16. Grover Cleveland's election in 1884 marked a change in nineteenth-century American politics for all of the following reasons EXCEPT that
   (A) he was the first Democrat elected since James Buchanan in 1856.
   (B) he was blunt and tactless, following decades of corruption.
   (C) he was able to narrow the political division between the North and South.
   (D) he favored agricultural over business interests.
   (E) he fired many incumbent Republicans, creating Democratic dominance.

Chapter 24

Industry Comes of Age

1865–1900

The wealthy class is becoming more wealthy; but the poorer class is becoming more dependent. The gulf between the employed and the employer is growing wider; social contrasts are becoming sharper; as liveried carriages appear; so do barefooted children.

HENRY GEORGE, 1879

As the nineteenth century drew to a close, observers were asking, "Why are the best men not in politics?" One answer was that they were being lured away from public life by the lusty attractions of the booming private economy. As America's Industrial Revolution slipped into high gear, talented men ached for profits, not the presidency. They dreamed of controlling corporations, not the Congress. What the nation lost in civic leadership, it gained in an astounding surge of economic growth. As late as 1870, agriculture remained the nation's biggest business. By 1900 it accounted for less than half of the national economy. Until the end of the Civil War, the United States imported more merchandise than it exported. By 1900 it annually delivered more than $600 million worth of manufactured goods to the world's marketplace. Americans did not achieve this economic transformation all by themselves. Foreign investment, labor, trade, and technology made it possible. Although in many ways still a political dwarf, the United States was about to stand up before the world as an industrial colossus—and the lives of millions of working Americans would be transformed in the process.

★ The Iron Colt Becomes an Iron Horse

The government-business entanglements that increasingly shaped politics after the Civil War also undergirded the industrial development of the nation. The unparalleled outburst of railroad construction was a crucial case. When Lincoln was shot in 1865, there were only 35,000 miles of steam railways in the United States, mostly east of the Mississippi. By 1900 the figure had spurted up to 192,556 miles, or more than that for all of Europe combined, and much of the new trackage ran west of the Mississippi (see Figure 24.1).

Transcontinental railroad building was so costly and risky as to require government subsidies, as it had in many other industrializing nations. Everywhere, the construction of railway systems promised greater national unity and economic growth. The extension of rails into thinly populated regions was unprofitable until the areas could be built up, and private promoters were unwilling to suffer heavy initial losses. Congress, impressed by arguments pleading military and postal needs, began to advance liberal loans to two favored cross-continent companies in 1862 and added enormous donations of acreage paralleling the tracks. All told, Washington rewarded the railroads with 155,504,994 acres, and the western states contributed 49 million more—a total area larger than Texas (see Map 24.1).

Grasping railroads tied up even more land than this for a number of years. Land grants to railroads were made in broad belts along the proposed route. Within these belts the railroads were allowed to choose *alternate* mile-square sections in checkerboard fashion. But until they determined the precise location of their tracks and decided which sections were the choicest selections, the railroads withheld *all* the land from other users. President Grover Cleveland put an end to this foot-dragging practice in 1887 and threw open to

CONTINENT AND COUNTRY

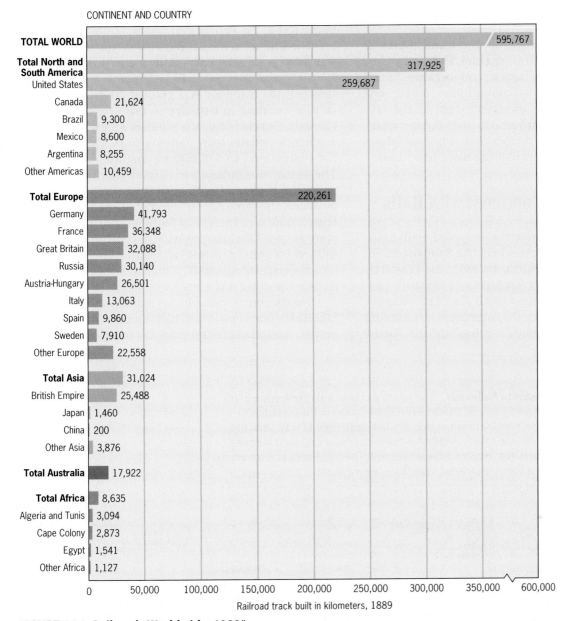

Railroad track built in kilometers, 1889

FIGURE 24.1 Railroads Worldwide, 1889*

*Another calculation of railway track per 10,000 inhabitants in 1904 revealed that the United States was still far out in front, with 26.4 miles of track compared to 15.2 miles for the second-place country, Sweden. Much farther behind were the major western European nations of France (7.3), Germany (6.1), and Great Britain and Ireland (5.4).

(Sources: Henry Poor, *Poor's Manual of the Railroads of the United States for 1891* (1891); Slason Thompson, *Railway Statistics of the United States of America for the Year Ending June 30, 1906, Compared with the Official Reports of 1905 and Recent Statistics of Foreign Railways* (1907).)

settlement the still-unclaimed public portions of the land-grant areas.

Noisy criticism, especially in later years, was leveled at the "giveaway" of so valuable a birthright to greedy corporations. But the government did receive beneficial returns, including long-term preferential rates for postal service and military traffic. Granting land was

also a "cheap" way to subsidize a much-desired transportation system, because it avoided new taxes for direct cash grants. The railroads could turn the land into gold by using it as collateral for loans from private bankers or, later, by selling it. This they often did, at an average price of $3 an acre. Critics were also prone to overlook the fact that the land did not have even that relatively modest value until the railroads had ribboned it with steel.

Frontier villages touched by the magic wand of the iron rail became flourishing cities; those that were bypassed often withered away and became "ghost towns." Little wonder that communities fought one another for the privilege of playing host to the railroads. Ambitious towns customarily held out monetary and other attractions to the builders, who sometimes blackmailed them into contributing more generously.

✦ Spanning the Continent with Rails

Deadlock in the 1850s over the proposed transcontinental railroad was broken when the South seceded, leaving the field to the North. In 1862, the year after the guns first spoke at Fort Sumter, Congress made provision for starting the long-awaited line. One weighty argument for action was the urgency of bolstering the Union, already disrupted, by binding the Pacific

Coast—especially gold-rich California—more securely to the rest of the Republic.

The Union Pacific Railroad—note the word *Union*—was thus commissioned by Congress to thrust westward from Omaha, Nebraska. For each mile of track constructed, the company was granted 20 square miles of land, alternating in 640-acre sections on either side of the track. For each mile the builders were also to receive a generous federal loan, ranging from $16,000 on the flat prairie land to $48,000 for mountainous country. The laying of rails began in earnest after the Civil War ended in 1865, and with juicy loans and land grants available, the "groundhog" promoters made all possible haste. Insiders of the Crédit Mobilier construction company reaped fabulous profits. They slyly pocketed $73 million for some $50 million worth of breakneck construction, spending small change to bribe congressmen to look the other way.

Sweaty construction gangs, containing many Irish "Paddies" (Patricks) who had fought in the Union armies, worked at a frantic pace. On one record-breaking

MAP 24.1 Federal Land Grants to Railroads The heavy red lines indicate areas within which the railroads might be given specific parcels of land. As shown in the inset, land was reserved in belts of various widths on either side of a railroad's right of way. Until the railroad selected the individual mile-square sections it chose to possess, *all* such sections within the belt were withdrawn from eligibility for settlement. The "time zones" were introduced in 1883 (see p. 518), and their boundaries have since been adjusted. © Cengage Learning

PATTERN OF LAND GRANTS

One square mile held by government or sold

Right of way: 100 yards wide

One square mile granted to railroad

Primary federal land grants to railroads

day, a sledge-and-shovel army of some five thousand men laid ten miles of track. A favorite song went like this:

> *Then drill, my Paddies, drill;*
> *Drill, my heroes, drill;*
> *Drill all day,*
> *No sugar in your tay [tea]*
> *Workin' on the U.P. Railway.*

When hostile Indians attacked in futile efforts to protect what once rightfully had been their land, the laborers would drop their picks and seize their rifles. Scores of people—railroad workers and Indians—lost their lives as the rails stretched ever westward. At rail's end, workers tried their best to find relaxation and conviviality in their tented towns, known as "hells on wheels," often teeming with as many as ten thousand men and a sprinkling of painted prostitutes and performers.

Rail laying at the California end was undertaken by the Central Pacific Railroad. This line pushed boldly eastward from boomtown Sacramento, over and through the towering, snow-clogged Sierra Nevada. Four far-seeing men—the so-called Big Four—were the chief financial backers of the enterprise. The quartet included the heavyset, enterprising ex-governor Leland Stanford of California, who had useful political connections, and the burly, energetic Collis P. Huntington, an adept lobbyist. The Big Four cleverly operated through two construction companies, and although they walked away with tens of millions in profits, they kept their hands relatively clean by not becoming involved in the bribing of congressmen.

The Central Pacific, which was granted the same princely subsidies as the Union Pacific, had the same incentive to haste. Some ten thousand Chinese laborers, sweating from dawn to dusk under their basket hats, proved to be cheap, efficient, and expendable (hundreds lost their lives in premature explosions and other mishaps). The towering Sierra Nevada presented a formidable barrier, and the nerves of the Big Four were strained when their workers could chip only a few inches a day tunneling through solid rock, while the Union Pacific was sledgehammering westward across the open plains.

A "wedding of the rails" was finally consummated near Ogden, Utah, in 1869, as two locomotives—"facing on a single track, half a world behind each back"—gently kissed cowcatchers. The colorful ceremony included the breaking of champagne bottles and the driving of a last ceremonial (golden) spike, with ex-governor Stanford clumsily wielding a silver maul. In all, the Union Pacific built 1,086 miles, the Central Pacific 689 miles.

Completion of the transcontinental line—a magnificent engineering feat for that day—was one of America's most impressive peacetime undertakings. It welded the West Coast more firmly to the Union and facilitated a flourishing trade with Asia. It penetrated the arid barrier of the deserts, paving the way for the phenomenal growth of the Great West. Americans

Snow Sheds on the Central Pacific Railroad in the Sierra Nevada Mountains, by Joseph H. Becker, ca. 1869 Formidable obstacles of climate and terrain confronted the builders of the Central Pacific Railroad in the mountainous heights of California. Note the Chinese laborers in the foreground.

Granger Collection

Promoting the Union Pacific Railroad, 1869

Union Pacific Museum Collection

In 1892 James Baird Weaver (1833–1912), nominee of the Populists, wrote regarding the railroad magnates,

> **❝**In their delirium of greed the managers of our transportation systems disregard both private right and the public welfare. Today they will combine and bankrupt their weak rivals, and by the expenditure of a trifling sum possess themselves of properties which cost the outlay of millions. Tomorrow they will capitalize their booty for five times the cost, issue their bonds, and proceed to levy tariffs upon the people to pay dividends upon the fraud.**❞**

New Orleans to San Francisco and was consolidated in the same year.

The last spike of the last of the five transcontinental railroads of the nineteenth century was hammered home in 1893. The Great Northern, which ran from Duluth to Seattle north of the Northern Pacific, was the creation of a far-visioned Canadian American, James J. Hill, a bearlike man who was probably the greatest railroad builder of all. His enterprise was so soundly organized that it rode through later financial storms with flying colors.

Yet the romance of the rails was not without its sordid side. Pioneer builders were often guilty of gross overoptimism. Avidly seeking land bounties and pushing into areas that lacked enough potential population to support a railroad, they sometimes laid down rails that led "from nowhere to nothing." When prosperity failed to smile upon their coming, they went into bankruptcy, carrying down with them the savings of trusting investors. Many of the large railroads in the post–Civil War decades passed through seemingly endless bankruptcies, mergers, or reorganizations.

compared this electrifying achievement with the Declaration of Independence and the emancipation of the slaves; jubilant Philadelphians again rang the cracked bell of Independence Hall.

✴ Binding the Country with Railroad Ties

With the westward trail now blazed, four other transcontinental lines were completed before the century's end. None of them secured monetary loans from the federal government, as did the Union Pacific and the Central Pacific. But all of them except the Great Northern received generous grants of land.

The Northern Pacific Railroad, stretching from Lake Superior to Puget Sound, reached its terminus in 1883. The Atchison, Topeka and Santa Fe, stretching through the southwestern deserts to California, was completed in 1884. The Southern Pacific ribboned from

✴ Railroad Consolidation and Mechanization

The success of the western lines was facilitated by welding together and expanding the older eastern networks, notably the New York Central. The genius in this enterprise was "Commodore" Cornelius Vanderbilt—burly, boisterous, white-whiskered. Having made his millions in steamboating, he daringly turned, in his late sixties, to a new career in railroading. Though ill-educated, ungrammatical, coarse, and ruthless, he was clear-visioned. Offering superior railway service at lower rates, he amassed a fortune of $100 million. His name

The Union Pacific and the Central Pacific Link at Promontory Point, Utah, May 10, 1869 Railroad financiers, dignitaries, spectators, and Chinese (Central Pacific) and Irish (Union Pacific) work gangs witnessed the historic joining that created the nation's first transcontinental railroad. After the two locomotives chugged within a few feet of each other, Central Pacific chief and former California governor Leland Stanford tapped a golden spike into a prepared hole on the last tie with a silver-plated maul. The golden spike was whisked away to be preserved for posterity at the Stanford University Museum, but the iron one that replaced it was hardly ordinary. It was wired to a Union Pacific telegraph line, while a copper plate on the maul was connected to a Central Pacific wire. When they touched, they closed a telegraphic circuit that sent the news to cities all over the country.

is perhaps best remembered through his contribution of $1 million to the founding of Vanderbilt University in Tennessee.

Two significant new improvements proved a boon to the railroads. One was the steel rail, which Vanderbilt helped popularize when he replaced the old iron tracks of the New York Central with the tougher metal. Steel was safer and more economical because it could bear a heavier load. A standard gauge of track width likewise came into wide use during the postwar years, thus eliminating the expense and inconvenience of numerous changes from one line to another.

Other refinements played a vital role in railroading. The Westinghouse air brake, generally adopted in the 1870s, was a marvelous contribution to efficiency and safety. The Pullman Palace Cars, advertised as "gorgeous traveling hotels," were introduced on a considerable scale in the 1860s. Alarmists condemned them as "wheeled torture chambers" and potential funeral pyres, for the wooden cars were equipped with swaying kerosene lamps. Appalling accidents continued to be almost daily tragedies, despite safety devices like the telegraph ("talking wires"), double-tracking, and (later) the block signal.

✴ Revolution by Railways

The metallic fingers of the railroads intimately touched countless phases of American life. For the first time, a sprawling nation became united in a physical sense, bound with ribs of iron and steel. The railroads emerged as the nation's biggest business, employing more people than any other industry and gobbling up nearly 20 percent of investment dollars from foreign and domestic investors alike.

More than any other single factor, the railroad network spurred the amazing economic growth of

517

the post–Civil War years. By stitching North America together from ocean to ocean, the puffing locomotives opened up the West with its wealth of resources. Trains hauled raw materials to factories and sped them back as finished goods for sale across the continent, making the United States the largest integrated national market in the world. The forging of the rails themselves generated the largest single source of orders for the adolescent steel industry.

The screeching iron horse especially stimulated mining and agriculture in the West. It took farmers out to their land, carried the fruits of their toil to market, and brought them their manufactured necessities. Clusters of farm settlements paralleled the railroads, just as earlier they had followed the rivers.

Railways were a boon for cities and played a leading role in the great cityward movement of the last decades of the century. The iron monsters could carry food to enormous concentrations of people and at the same time ensure them a livelihood by providing both raw materials and markets.

Railroad companies also stimulated the mighty stream of immigration. Seeking settlers to whom their land grants might be sold at a profit, they advertised seductively in Europe and sometimes offered to transport the newcomers free to their farms.

The land also felt the impact of the railroad—especially the broad, ecologically fragile midsection of the continent that Thomas Jefferson had purchased from France in 1803. Settlers following the railroads plowed up the tallgrass prairies of Iowa, Illinois, Kansas, and Nebraska and planted well-drained, rectangular cornfields. On the shortgrass prairies of the high plains in the Dakotas and Montana, range-fed cattle rapidly displaced the buffalo, which were hunted to near-extinction. The white pine forests of Michigan, Wisconsin, and Minnesota disappeared into lumber that was rushed by rail to prairie farmers, who used it to build houses and fences.

Time itself was bent to the railroads' needs. Until the 1880s every town in the United States had its own "local" time, dictated by the sun's position. When it was noon in Chicago, it was 11:50 a.m. in St. Louis and 12:18 p.m. in Detroit. For railroad operators worried about keeping schedules and avoiding wrecks, this patchwork of local times was a nightmare. Thus on November 18, 1883, the major rail lines decreed that the continent would henceforth be divided into four "time zones." Most communities quickly adopted railroad "standard" time.

Finally, the railroad, more than any other single factor, was the maker of millionaires. A raw new aristocracy, consisting of "lords of the rail," replaced the old southern "lords of the lash." The multiwebbed lines became the playthings of Wall Street, and colossal wealth was amassed by stock speculators and railroad wreckers.

✦ Wrongdoing in Railroading

Corruption lurks nearby when fabulous fortunes can materialize overnight. The fleecings administered by the railroad construction companies, such as the Crédit Mobilier, were but the first of the bunco games that the railroad promoters learned to play. Methods soon became more refined, as fast-fingered financiers executed multimillion-dollar maneuvers beneath the noses of a bedazzled public. Jay Gould was the most adept of these ringmasters of rapacity. For nearly thirty years, he boomed and busted the stocks of the Erie, the Kansas Pacific, the Union Pacific, and the Texas and Pacific in an incredible circus of speculative skullduggery.

One of the favorite devices of the moguls of manipulation was "stock watering." The term originally referred to the practice of making cattle thirsty by feeding them salt and then having them bloat themselves with water before they were weighed in for sale. Using a variation of this technique, railroad stock promoters grossly inflated their claims about a given line's assets and profitability and sold stocks and bonds far in excess of the railroad's actual value. "Promoters' profits" were often the tail that wagged the iron horse itself. Railroad managers were forced to charge extortionate rates and wage ruthless competitive battles in order to pay off the

William H. Vanderbilt, Robber Baron This 1885 cartoon takes aim at Vanderbilt's notorious comment, "The public be damned!"

exaggerated financial obligations with which they were saddled.

The public interest was frequently trampled underfoot as the railroad titans waged their brutal wars. Crusty old Cornelius Vanderbilt, when told that the law stood in his way, reportedly exclaimed, "Law! What do I care about the law? Hain't I got the power?" On another occasion he supposedly threatened some associates: "I won't sue you, for the law is too slow. I'll ruin you." His son, William H. Vanderbilt, when asked in 1883 about the discontinuance of a fast mail train, reportedly snorted, "The public be damned!"

While abusing the public, the railroaders blandly bought and sold people in public life. They bribed judges and legislatures, employed arm-twisting lobbyists, and elected their own "creatures" to high office. They showered free passes on journalists and politicians in profusion. One railroad man noted in 1885 that in the West "no man who has money, or official position, or influence thinks he ought to pay anything for riding on a railroad."

Railroad kings were, for a time, virtual industrial monarchs. As manipulators of a huge natural monopoly, they exercised more direct control over the lives of more people than did the president of the United States—and their terms were not limited to four years. They increasingly shunned the crude bloodletting of cutthroat competition and began to cooperate with one another to rule the railroad dominion. Sorely pressed to show at least some returns on their bloated investments, they entered into defensive alliances to protect precious profits.

The earliest form of combination was the "pool"—an agreement to divide the business in a given area and share the profits. Other rail barons granted secret rebates or kickbacks to powerful shippers in return for steady and assured traffic. Often they slashed their rates on competing lines, but they more than made up the difference on noncompeting ones, where they might actually charge more for a short haul than for a long one. As a result, small farmers usually paid the highest rates, while large customers got the best deals.

✦ Government Bridles the Iron Horse

It was neither healthy nor politically acceptable that so many people should be at the mercy of so few. Impoverished farmers, especially in the Midwest, began to wonder if the nation had not escaped from the slavery power only to fall into the hands of the money power, as represented by the railroad plutocracy.

But the American people, usually quick to respond to political injustice, were slow to combat economic injustice. Dedicated to free enterprise and to the principle that competition is the soul of trade, they cherished a traditionally keen pride in progress. They remembered that Jefferson's ideals were hostile to government interference with business. Above all, there shimmered the "American dream": the hope that in a catch-as-catch-can economic system, anyone might become a millionaire.

The depression of the 1870s goaded the farmers into protesting against being "railroaded" into bankruptcy. Under pressure from organized agrarian groups like the Grange (Patrons of Husbandry), many midwestern legislatures tried to regulate the railroad monopoly.

The scattered state efforts screeched to a halt in 1886. The Supreme Court, in the famed ***Wabash, St. Louis & Pacific Railroad Company*** v. ***Illinois*** case, decreed that individual states had no power to regulate *inter*state commerce. If the mechanical monster were to be corralled, the federal government would have to do the job.

Stiff-necked President Cleveland did not look kindly on effective regulation. But Congress ignored his grumbling indifference and passed the epochal **Interstate Commerce Act** in 1887. It prohibited rebates and pools and required the railroads to publish their rates openly. It also forbade unfair discrimination against shippers and outlawed charging more for a short haul than for a long one over the same line. Most important, it set up the Interstate Commerce Commission (ICC) to administer and enforce the new legislation.

Despite acclaim, the Interstate Commerce Act emphatically did not represent a popular victory over corporate wealth. One of the leading corporation lawyers of the day, Richard Olney, shrewdly noted that the new commission "can be made of great use to the railroads. It satisfies the popular clamor for a government supervision of railroads, at the same time that such supervision is almost entirely nominal.... The part of wisdom is not to destroy the Commission, but to utilize it."

What the new legislation did do was to provide an orderly forum where competing business interests could resolve their conflicts in peaceable ways. The country could now avoid ruinous rate wars among the railroads and outraged, "confiscatory" attacks on the lines by pitchfork-prodded state legislatures. This was a modest accomplishment but by no means an unimportant one. The Interstate Commerce Act tended to stabilize, not revolutionize, the existing business system.

Yet the act still ranks as a red-letter law. It was the first large-scale attempt by Washington to regulate business in the interest of society at large. It heralded the arrival of a series of independent regulatory commissions in the next century, which would irrevocably commit the government to the daunting task of monitoring and guiding the private economy. It foreshadowed the doom of freewheeling, buccaneering business practices and served full notice that there was a public interest in private enterprise that the government was bound to protect.

✳ Miracles of Mechanization

Postwar industrial expansion, partly a result of the railroad network, rapidly began to assume mammoth proportions. When Lincoln was elected in 1860, the Republic ranked only fourth among the manufacturing nations of the world. By 1894 it had bounded into first place. Why the sudden upsurge?

Liquid capital, previously scarce, was now becoming abundant. The word *millionaire* had not been coined until the 1840s, and in 1861 only a handful of individuals were eligible for this class. But the Civil War, partly through profiteering, created immense fortunes, and these accumulations could now be combined with borrowings from foreign capitalists. Investors from abroad loaned more money to the United States in the postwar period than any country had previously received. Unlike in other countries, in America they mostly put the money into private hands, not public coffers. Investors primarily from Britain, but also from France, Germany, the Netherlands, and Switzerland, sometimes owned all or part of an American business. Other times they simply lent their money to the thousands of European companies set up to manage investment in U.S. industry. Either way, Europeans were usually content to let Americans run the business—until hard times hit and they demanded more say over company operations or government economic policies.

Innovations in transportation fueled growth, too, by bringing the nation's amazingly abundant natural resources—particularly coal, oil, and iron—to the factory door. A shipping system through the Great Lakes carried the rich iron deposits in the Mesabi Range of Minnesota to Chicago and Cleveland for refining. This priceless bonanza, where mountains of red-rusted ore could be scooped up by steam shovels, ultimately

Library of Congress

Thomas Alva Edison in His Lab, 1888 Edison was dubbed the "Wizard of Menlo Park," New Jersey, where he lived and established the first major industrial research laboratory. Edison was not only an ingenious inventor; he also figured out how to apply the principles of mass production to his inventions. Phonographs, telephones, telegraphs, incandescent electric lighting, fluoroscopes, kinetoscopes, and many more technological wonders spread throughout the world following their development in Edison's lab.

Regarding the exploitation of immigrant labor, Ralph Waldo Emerson (1803–1882) wrote in 1860,

❝ The German and Irish millions, like the Negro, have a great deal of guano in their destiny. They are ferried over the Atlantic, and carted over America, to ditch and to drudge, to make corn cheap, and then to lie down prematurely to make a spot of green grass on the prairie. **❞**

became a cornerstone of a vast steel empire. Copper, bauxite, and zinc made similar journeys from mine to manufacture.

The sheer size of the American market encouraged innovators to invent mass-production methods. With cheap transportation crisscrossing the nation and an ever-larger population able and eager to consume, anyone who could make an appealing new product available for a good price in large quantities—and figure out how to market it—thrived. Industrialists continued to refine the pre–Civil War "American System" of using specialized machinery to make interchangeable parts, culminating in 1913 with Henry Ford's fully developed moving assembly line for his Model T (see pp. 231–232 and 711–712).

The captains of industry had a major incentive to invent machines: they made it possible to replace expensive skilled labor with unskilled workers, now cheap and plentiful as a result of massive immigration. Steel, the keystone industry, was built largely on the sweat of low-priced immigrant labor from eastern and southern Europe, working in two 12-hour shifts, seven days a week.

Just as industry served as a hothouse of invention, brilliant ideas gave rise to whole new lines of business. Between 1860 and 1890, some 440,000 patents were issued. Business operations were facilitated by machines such as the cash register, the stock ticker, and the typewriter ("literary piano"), while the refrigerator car, the electric dynamo, and the electric railway speeded urbanization. One of the most ingenious inventions was the telephone, introduced by Alexander Graham Bell in 1876. America was suddenly turned into a nation of "telephoniacs," as a gigantic communications network was built on his invention. The social impact of the telephone further expanded when it lured "number please" women away from the stove to the switchboard. Telephone boys were at first employed as operators, but their profanity shocked patrons.

The most versatile inventor of all was Thomas Alva Edison (1847–1931), who as a boy had been considered so dull-witted that he was taken out of school. His severe deafness enabled him to concentrate without distraction. Edison was a gifted tinkerer and a tireless worker, not a pure scientist. "Genius," he said, "is one percent inspiration and ninety-nine percent perspiration." Wondrous devices poured out of his "invention factory" in New Jersey—the phonograph, the mimeograph, the dictaphone, and the moving picture. He is probably best known for his perfection in 1879 of the electric lightbulb, which turned night into day and transformed ancient human habits as well. People had previously slept an average of nine hours a night; now they slept just a bit more than seven.

✸ The Trust Titan Emerges

Despite pious protests to the contrary, competition was the bugbear of most business leaders of the day. Tycoons like Andrew Carnegie, the steel king; John D. Rockefeller, the oil baron; and J. Pierpont Morgan, the bankers' banker, exercised their genius in devising ways to circumvent competition. Carnegie integrated every phase of his steel-making operation. His miners scratched the ore from the earth in the Mesabi Range; Carnegie ships floated it across the Great Lakes; Carnegie railroads delivered it to the blast furnaces at Pittsburgh. When the molten metal finally poured from the glowing crucibles into the waiting ingot molds, no other hands but those in Carnegie's employ had touched the product. Carnegie thus pioneered the creative entrepreneurial tactic of **vertical integration**, combining into one organization all phases of manufacturing from mining to marketing. His goal was to improve efficiency by making supplies more reliable, controlling the quality of the product at all stages of production, and eliminating middlemen's fees.

Less justifiable on grounds of efficiency was the technique of **horizontal integration**, which simply meant allying with competitors to monopolize a given market. Rockefeller was a master of this stratagem. He perfected a device for controlling bothersome rivals— the **trust**. Stockholders in various smaller oil companies assigned their stock to the board of directors of his Standard Oil Company, formed in 1870. It then consolidated and concerted the operations of the previously competing enterprises. "Let us prey" was said to be Rockefeller's unwritten motto. Ruthlessly wielding vast power, Standard Oil soon cornered virtually the entire

The Octopus, 1904 This cartoon visually captures a feeling of widespread resentment against Standard Oil as a powerful, sprawling "octopus" whose tentacles controlled all branches of government.

world petroleum market. Weaker competitors, left out of the trust agreement, were forced to the wall. Rockefeller's stunning success inspired many imitators, and the word *trust* came to be generally used to describe any large-scale business combination.

The imperial Morgan devised still other schemes for eliminating "wasteful" competition. The depression of the 1890s drove into his welcoming arms many bleeding businesspeople, wounded by cutthroat competition. His prescribed remedy was to consolidate rival enterprises and to ensure future harmony by placing officers of his own banking syndicate on their various boards of directors. These came to be known as **interlocking directorates**.

✴ The Supremacy of Steel

"Steel is king!" might well have been the exultant war cry of the new industrialized generation. The mighty metal ultimately held together the new steel civilization, from skyscrapers to coal scuttles, while providing it with food, shelter, and transportation. Steel making, notably rails for railroads, typified the dominance of "heavy industry," which concentrated on making "capital goods," as distinct from the production of "consumer goods" such as clothes and shoes.

Now taken for granted, steel was a scarce commodity in the wood-and-brick America of Abraham Lincoln. Considerable iron went into railroad rails and bridges, but steel was expensive and was used largely for products like cutlery. The early iron horse snorted exclusively (and dangerously) over iron rails. When in the 1870s "Commodore" Vanderbilt of the New York Central began to use steel rails, he was forced to import them from Britain.

Yet within an amazing twenty years, the United States had outdistanced all foreign competitors and was pouring out more than one-third of the world's supply of steel. By 1900 America was producing as much as Britain and Germany combined.

What wrought the transformation? Chiefly the invention in the 1850s of a method of making cheap steel—the Bessemer process. It was named after a derided British inventor, although an American had stumbled on it a few years earlier. William Kelly, a Kentucky manufacturer of iron kettles, discovered that cold air blown on red-hot iron caused the metal to become white-hot by igniting the carbon and thus eliminating impurities. He tried to apply the new "air boiling" technique to his own product, but his customers decried "Kelly's fool steel," and his business declined. Gradually the Bessemer-Kelly process won acceptance, and these two "crazy men" ultimately made possible the present steel civilization.

✴ Carnegie and Other Sultans of Steel

Kingpin among steelmasters was Andrew Carnegie, an undersized, charming Scotsman. As a towheaded lad of thirteen, he was brought to America by his impoverished parents in 1848 and got a job as a bobbin boy at $1.20 a week. Mounting the ladder of success so fast that he was said to have scorched the rungs, he forged ahead by working hard, doing the extra chore, cheerfully assuming responsibility, and smoothly cultivating influential people.

After accumulating some capital, Carnegie entered the steel business in the Pittsburgh area. A gifted organizer and administrator, he succeeded by picking high-class associates and by eliminating many middlemen. Although inclined to be tough-fisted in business, he was not a monopolist and disliked monopolistic trusts. His remarkable organization was a partnership that involved, at its maximum, about forty "Pittsburgh millionaires." By 1900 he was producing one-fourth of the nation's Bessemer steel, and the partners in these pre–income tax days were dividing profits of $40 million a year as their take-home pay, with the "Napoleon of the Smokestacks" himself receiving a cool $25 million.

Into the picture now stepped the financial giant of the age, J. Pierpont Morgan. "Jupiter" Morgan had made a legendary reputation for himself and his Wall Street banking house by financing the reorganization of railroads, insurance companies, and banks. An impressive

J. P. Morgan (1837–1913) As the most influential banker of his day, Morgan symbolized to many people the power and arrogance of "finance capitalism." The chronic skin disorder on his nose inspired the taunt "Johnny Morgan's nasal organ has a purple hue."

Library of Congress

Andrew Carnegie (1835–1919) wrote in 1889,

❝ The man who dies leaving behind him millions of available wealth, which was his to administer during life, will pass away 'unwept, unhonored, and unsung,' no matter to what uses he leaves the dross which he cannot take with him. Of such as these the public verdict will then be: 'The man who dies thus rich dies disgraced.'❞

figure of a man, with massive shoulders, shaggy brows, piercing eyes, and a bulbous, acne-cursed red nose, he had established an enviable reputation for integrity. He did not believe that "money power" was dangerous, except when in dangerous hands—and he did not regard his own hands as dangerous.

The force of circumstances brought Morgan and Carnegie into collision. By 1900 the canny little Scotsman, weary of turning steel into gold, was eager to sell his holdings. Morgan had meanwhile plunged heavily into the manufacture of steel pipe tubing. Carnegie, cleverly threatening to invade the same business, was ready to ruin his rival if he did not receive his price. The steelmaster's agents haggled with the imperious Morgan for eight agonizing hours, and the financier finally agreed to buy out Carnegie for over $400 million. Fearing that he would die "disgraced" with so much wealth, Carnegie dedicated the remaining years of his life to giving away money for public libraries, pensions for professors, and other such philanthropic purposes—in all disposing of about $350 million.

Morgan moved rapidly to expand his new industrial empire. He took the Carnegie holdings, added others, "watered" the stock liberally, and in 1901 launched the enlarged United States Steel Corporation. Capitalized at $1.4 billion, it was America's first billion-dollar corporation—a larger sum than the total estimated wealth of the nation in 1800. The Industrial Revolution, with its hot Bessemer breath, had come into its own.

✸ Rockefeller Grows an American Beauty Rose

The sudden emergence of the oil industry was one of the most striking developments of the years during and after the Civil War. Traces of oil found on streams had earlier been bottled for back-rub and other patent medicines, but not until 1859 did the first well in Pennsylvania—"Drake's Folly"—pour out its liquid "black gold." Almost overnight an industry was born that was to take more wealth from the earth than all of the gold extracted by the forty-niners and their western successors. Kerosene, derived from petroleum, was the first major product of the infant oil industry. Burned from a cotton wick in a glass chimney lamp, kerosene produced a much brighter flame than whale oil. The oil business boomed; by the 1870s kerosene was America's fourth most valuable export. Whaling, in contrast, the lifeblood of ocean-roaming New Englanders since before the days of *Moby Dick*, swiftly became a sick industry.

But what technology gives, technology takes away. By 1885, 250,000 of Thomas Edison's electric lightbulbs were in use; fifteen years later, perhaps 15 million. The new electric industry rendered kerosene obsolete just

Washington as Seen by the Trusts, 1900 "What a funny little government," John D. Rockefeller observes in this satirical cartoon. His own wealth and power are presumed to dwarf the resources of the federal government.

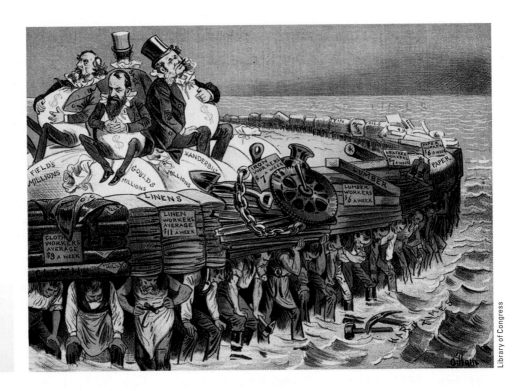

Robber Barons Cyrus Field, Jay Gould, Cornelius Vanderbilt, and Russell Sage Kept Afloat on the Broken Backs of America's Workingmen, 1883

Library of Congress

as kerosene had rendered whale oil obsolete. Only in rural America and overseas did a market continue for oil-fired lamps.

Oil might thus have remained a modest, even a shrinking, industry but for yet another turn of the technological tide—the invention of the automobile. By 1900 the gasoline-burning internal combustion engine had clearly bested its rivals, steam and electricity, as the superior means of automobile propulsion. As the century of the automobile dawned, the oil business got a new, long-lasting, and hugely profitable lease on life.

John D. Rockefeller—lanky, shrewd, ambitious, abstemious (he neither drank, smoked, nor swore)— came to dominate the oil industry. Born to a family of precarious income, he became a successful businessman at age nineteen. One upward stride led to another, and in 1870 he organized the **Standard Oil Company** of Ohio, nucleus of the great trust formed in 1882. Locating his refineries in Cleveland, he sought to eliminate the middlemen and squeeze out competitors.

Pious and parsimonious, Rockefeller flourished in an era of completely free enterprise. So-called piratical practices were employed by "corsairs of finance," and business ethics were distressingly low. Rockefeller, operating "just to the windward of the law," pursued a policy of rule or ruin. "Sell all the oil that is sold in your district" was the hard-boiled order that went out to his local agents. By 1877 Rockefeller controlled 95 percent of all the oil refineries in the country.

Rockefeller—"Reckafellow," as Carnegie had once called him—showed little mercy. A kind of primitive savagery prevailed in the jungle world of big business, where only the fittest survived. Or so Rockefeller believed. His son later explained that the giant American Beauty rose could be produced "only by sacrificing the early buds that grew up around it." His father pinched off the small buds with complete ruthlessness. Employing spies and extorting secret rebates from the railroads, he even forced the lines to pay him rebates on the freight bills of his competitors!

Rockefeller thought he was simply obeying a law of nature. "The time was ripe" for aggressive consolidation, he later reflected. "It had to come, though all we saw at the moment was the need to save ourselves from wasteful conditions. . . . The day of combination is here to stay. Individualism has gone, never to return."

On the other side of the ledger, Rockefeller's oil monopoly did turn out a superior product at a relatively cheap price. It achieved important economies, both at home and abroad, by its large-scale methods of production and distribution. This, in truth, was the tale of the other trusts as well. The efficient use of expensive machinery called for bigness, and consolidation proved more profitable than ruinous price wars.

Other trusts blossomed along with the American Beauty of oil. These included the sugar trust, the tobacco trust, the leather trust, and the harvester trust, which amalgamated some two hundred competitors. The meat industry arose on the backs of bawling western herds, and meat kings like Gustavus F. Swift and Philip Armour took their place among the new royalty. Wealth was coming to dominate the commonwealth.

These untrustworthy trusts, and the "pirates" who captained them, were disturbingly new. They eclipsed an older American aristocracy of modestly successful merchants and professionals. An arrogant class of "new rich" was now elbowing aside the patrician families in the mad scramble for power and prestige. Not surprisingly, the ranks of the antitrust crusaders were frequently spearheaded by the "best men"—genteel old-family do-gooders who were not radicals but conservative defenders of their own vanishing influence.

✴ The Gospel of Wealth

Monarchs of yore invoked the divine right of kings, and America's industrial plutocrats took a somewhat similar stance. Some candidly credited heavenly help. "Godliness is in league with riches," preached the Episcopal bishop of Massachusetts, and hardfisted John D. Rockefeller piously acknowledged that "the good Lord gave me my money." Steel baron Andrew Carnegie agreed that the wealthy, entrusted with society's riches, had to prove themselves morally responsible according to a "Gospel of Wealth." But most defenders of wide-open capitalism relied more heavily on the survival-of-the-fittest theories of English philosopher Herbert Spencer and Yale professor William Graham Sumner. Later mislabeled **Social Darwinists**, these theorists argued that individuals won their stations in life by competing on the basis of their natural talents. The wealthy and powerful had simply demonstrated greater abilities than the poor. Spencer and Sumner owed less to English evolutionary naturalist Charles Darwin, who stressed the adaptation of organisms, than to British laissez-faire economists David Ricardo and Thomas Malthus. In fact, Spencer, not Darwin, coined the phrase "survival of the fittest." "The millionaires are a product of natural selection," Sumner declared. In 1883 he asked, "What do social classes owe each other?" then answered his own question: nothing. Some Social Darwinists later applied this theory to explain why some nations were more powerful than others or had the right to dominate "lesser peoples," often defined by race.

Self-justification by the wealthy inevitably involved contempt for the poor. Many of the rich, especially the newly rich, had pulled themselves up by their own bootstraps; hence they concluded that those who stayed poor must be lazy and lacking in enterprise. The Reverend Russell Conwell of Philadelphia became rich by delivering his lecture "Acres of Diamonds" thousands of times. In it he charged, "There is not a poor person in the United States who was not made poor by his own shortcomings." Such attitudes were a formidable roadblock to social reform.

Plutocracy, like the earlier slavocracy, took its stand firmly on the Constitution. The clause that gave Congress sole jurisdiction over interstate commerce was a godsend to the monopolists; their high-priced lawyers used it time and again to thwart controls by the state legislatures. Giant trusts likewise sought refuge behind the Fourteenth Amendment, which had been originally designed to protect the rights of the ex-slaves as persons. The courts ingeniously interpreted a corporation to be a legal "person" and decreed that, as such, it could not be deprived of its property by a state without "due process of law" (see Amendment XIV, para. 1 in the Appendix). There is some questionable evidence that slippery corporation lawyers deliberately inserted this loophole when the Fourteenth Amendment was being fashioned in 1866.

Great industrialists likewise sought to incorporate in "easy states," like New Jersey, where the restrictions on big business were mild or nonexistent. For example, the Southern Pacific Railroad, with much of its trackage in California, was incorporated in Kentucky.

✴ Government Tackles the Trust Evil

At long last the masses of the people began to mobilize against monopoly. They first tried to control the trusts through state legislation, as they had earlier attempted to curb the railroads. Failing here, as before, they were forced to appeal to Congress. After prolonged pulling and hauling, the **Sherman Anti-Trust Act** of 1890 was finally signed into law.

The Sherman Act flatly forbade combinations in restraint of trade, without any distinction between "good" trusts and "bad" trusts. Bigness, not badness, was the sin. The law proved ineffective, largely because it had only baby teeth or no teeth at all, and because it contained legal loopholes through which clever corporation lawyers could wriggle. But it was unexpectedly effective in one respect. Contrary to its original intent, it was used to curb labor unions or labor combinations that were deemed to be restraining trade.

Industrial millionaires were condemned in the Populist platform of 1892:

❝ The fruits of the toil of millions are boldly stolen to build up colossal fortunes for a few . . . and the possessors of these, in turn despise the Republic and endanger liberty. From the same prolific womb of governmental injustice we breed the two great classes—tramps and millionaires.**❞**

The New Rich and the New Immigrants   A well-to-do family plays chess at its parlor table (left), while a tenement family does "piecework" around its kitchen table— shelling nuts for commercial use (right). The young working girl seems to be "snitching" some nuts for herself. The apparently growing gulf between the rich and the poor deeply worried reformers in the late nineteenth century. They feared that democracy could not survive in the face of such gross inequality.

Early prosecutions of the trusts by the Justice Department under the Sherman Act of 1890, as it turned out, were neither vigorous nor successful. The decisions in seven of the first eight cases presented by the attorney general were adverse to the government. More new trusts were formed in the 1890s under President McKinley than during any other like period. Not until 1914 were the paper jaws of the Sherman Act fitted with reasonably sharp teeth. Until then, there was some question whether the government would control the trusts or the trusts the government.

But the iron grip of monopolistic corporations was being threatened. A revolutionary new principle had been written into the law books by the Sherman Anti-Trust Act of 1890, as well as by the Interstate Commerce Act of 1887. Private greed should henceforth be subordinated to public need.

✷ The South in the Age of Industry

The industrial tidal wave that washed over the North after the Civil War caused only feeble ripples in the backwater of the South. As late as 1900, the South still produced a smaller percentage of the nation's manufactured goods than it had before the Civil War. The plantation system had degenerated into a pattern of absentee landownership. White and black sharecroppers now tilled the soil for a share of the crop, or they

became tenants, in bondage to their landlords, who controlled needed credit and supplies.

Southern agriculture received a welcome boost in the 1880s, when machine-made cigarettes replaced the roll-your-own variety and tobacco consumption shot up. James Buchanan Duke took full advantage of the new technology to mass-produce the dainty "coffin nails." In 1890, in what was becoming a familiar pattern, he absorbed his main competitors into the American Tobacco Company. The cigarette czar later showed such generosity to Trinity College, near his birthplace

Henry W. Grady (1851–1889), editor of the Atlanta Constitution, *urged the new South to industrialize. In a Boston speech in 1889, he described the burial in Georgia of a Confederate veteran:*

❝ The South didn't furnish a thing on earth for that funeral but the corpse and the hole in the ground. . . . They buried him in a New York coat and a Boston pair of shoes and a pair of breeches from Chicago and a shirt from Cincinnati, leaving him nothing to carry into the next world with him to remind him of the country in which he lived, and for which he fought for four years, but the chill of blood in his veins and the marrow in his bones. ❞

A Virginia Tobacco Factory, ca. 1880
The employment of women and children was a common practice in late-nineteenth-century American industry, north as well as south.

in Durham, North Carolina, that the trustees gratefully changed its name to Duke University.

Industrialists tried to coax the agricultural South out of the fields and into the factories, but with only modest success. The region remained overwhelmingly rural. Prominent among the boosters of a "new South" was silver-tongued Henry W. Grady, editor of the *Atlanta Constitution*. He tirelessly exhorted the ex-Confederates to become "Georgia Yankees" and outplay the North at the commercial and industrial game.

Yet formidable obstacles lay in the path of southern industrialization. One was the paper barrier of regional rate-setting systems imposed by the northern-dominated railroad interests. Railroads gave preferential rates to manufactured goods moving southward from the North, but in the opposite direction they discriminated in favor of southern raw materials. The net effect was to keep the South in a kind of servitude to the Northeast—as a supplier of raw materials to the manufacturing metropolis, unable to develop a substantial industrial base of its own.

A bitter example of this economic discrimination against the South was the "Pittsburgh plus" pricing system in the steel industry. Rich deposits of coal and iron ore near Birmingham, Alabama, worked by low-wage southern labor, should have given steel manufacturers there a competitive edge, especially in southern markets. But the steel lords of Pittsburgh brought pressure to bear on the compliant railroads. As a result, Birmingham steel, no matter where it was delivered, was charged a fictional fee, as if it had been shipped from Pittsburgh. This stunting of the South's natural economic advantages throttled the growth of the Birmingham steel industry.

In manufacturing cotton textiles, the South fared considerably better. Southerners had long resented shipping their fiber to New England, and now their cry was "Bring the mills to the cotton." Beginning about 1880, northern capitalists began to erect cotton mills in the South, largely in response to tax benefits and the prospect of cheap and nonunionized labor (see Figure 24.2 and Figure 24.3).

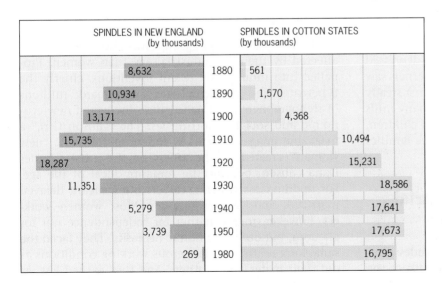

SPINDLES IN NEW ENGLAND (by thousands)		SPINDLES IN COTTON STATES (by thousands)
8,632	1880	561
10,934	1890	1,570
13,171	1900	4,368
15,735	1910	10,494
18,287	1920	15,231
11,351	1930	18,586
5,279	1940	17,641
3,739	1950	17,673
269	1980	16,795

FIGURE 24.2 Cotton Manufacturing Moves South, 1880–1980 Textile manufacturing usually looms large in the early stages of industrial development. In the later stages, it gives way to higher-technology businesses. This trend can be seen here, both in the migration of textile manufacturing to the southern United States and in the decline in the number of spindles in the United States as a whole since the 1930s, as developing Third World countries became major textile producers. (Source: *Historical Statistics of the United States* and *Statistical Abstract of the United States*, relevant years.)

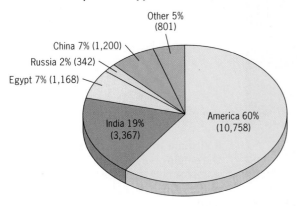

World cotton production, 1903
(Bales of approx. 500 lbs, in thousands)

Other 5%
(801)

China 7% (1,200)

Russia 2% (342)

Egypt 7% (1,168)

India 19%
(3,367)

America 60%
(10,758)

Total: 17,636

FIGURE 24.3 World Cotton Production, 1903 Cotton manufacturing grew in the United States in the early twentieth century, and raw cotton production reached higher levels than anywhere else in the world. (Source: John A. Todd, *The World's Cotton Crops* (London: A. & C. Black, 1915), 395–396.)

The textile mills proved to be a mixed blessing to the economically blighted South. They slowly wove an industrial thread into the fabric of southern life, but at a considerable human cost. Cheap labor was the South's major attraction for potential investors, and keeping labor cheap became almost a religion among southern industrialists. The mills took root in the chronically depressed Piedmont region of southern Appalachia and came to dominate utterly the communities in which they were located.

Rural southerners—virtually all of them white, for blacks were excluded from all but the most menial jobs in the mills—poured out of the hills and hollows to seek employment in the hastily erected company mill towns. Entire families—often derided as "hillbillies" or "lint-heads"—worked from dawn to dusk amid the whirring spindles. They were paid at half the rate of their northern counterparts and often received their compensation in the form of credit at a company store, to which they were habitually in debt. But despite their depressed working conditions and poor pay, many southerners saw employment in the mills as a salvation, the first steady jobs and wages they had ever known. With many mills anxious to tap the cheap labor of women and children, mill work often offered destitute farm-fugitive families their only chance to remain together.

The Impact of the New Industrial Revolution on America

Economic miracles wrought during the decades after the Civil War enormously increased the wealth of the Republic. The standard of living rose sharply, and well-fed American workers enjoyed more physical comforts than their counterparts in any other industrial nation. Urban centers mushroomed as the insatiable factories demanded more American labor and as immigrants swarmed like honeybees to the new jobs (see Map 24.2 and "Makers of America: The Poles," pp. 706–707).

Early Jeffersonian ideals were withering before the smudgy blasts from the smokestacks. As agriculture declined in relation to manufacturing, America could no longer aspire to be a nation of small freehold farms. Jefferson's concepts of free enterprise, with neither help nor hindrance from Washington, were being thrown out the factory window. Tariffs had already provided assistance, but the long arm of federal authority was now committed to decades of corporation curbing and "trust-busting."

Older ways of life also wilted in the heat of the factory furnaces. The very concept of time was revolutionized. Rural American migrants and peasant European immigrants, used to living by the languid clock of nature, now had to regiment their lives by the factory whistle. The seemingly arbitrary discipline of industrial labor did not come easily and sometimes had to be forcibly taught. One large corporation simultaneously instructed its Polish immigrant workers in the English language and in the obligations of factory work schedules:

I hear the whistle. I must hurry.
I hear the five-minute whistle.
It is time to go into the shop. . . .
I change my clothes and get ready to work.
The starting whistle blows.
I eat my lunch.
It is forbidden to eat until then. . . .
I work until the whistle blows to quit.
I leave my place nice and clean.
I put all my clothes in the locker.
I must go home.

Probably no single group was more profoundly affected by the new industrial age than women. Propelled into industry by recent inventions, chiefly the typewriter and the telephone switchboard, millions of stenographers and "hello girls" discovered new economic and social opportunities. The "Gibson Girl," a magazine image of an independent and athletic "new woman" created in the 1890s by the artist Charles Dana Gibson, became the romantic ideal of the age. For middle-class women, careers often meant delayed marriages and smaller families. Most women workers, however, toiled neither for independence nor for glamour, but out of economic necessity. They faced the same long hours and dangerous working conditions as did their mates and brothers, and they earned less, as

MAP 24.2 American Industry in 1900 By the end of the nineteenth century, once-rural America boasted the world's largest industrial output—a development with enormous consequences for politics, diplomacy, and family life. © Cengage Learning

Products manufactured in 20 largest cities

- Clothing
- Flour milling
- Food, beverage, and tobacco processing
- Foundry and machine shop products
- Iron and steel
- Printing and publishing
- Slaughtering and meatpacking
- Textiles
- Mixed or other

Natural resources

- Ag Silver
- Au Gold
- C Coal
- Cu Copper
- Fe Iron ore
- O Oil (petroleum)
- Pb Lead
- Timber Timber

☐ States with 25% or more of employees in manufacturing

wages for "women's jobs" were usually set below those for men's.

The clattering machine age likewise accentuated class division. "Industrial buccaneers" flaunted bloated fortunes, and their rags-to-riches spouses displayed glittering diamonds. Such extravagances evoked bitter criticism. Some of it was envious, but much of it rose from a small but increasingly vocal group of socialists and other radicals, many of whom were recent European immigrants. The existence of an oligarchy of money was amply demonstrated by the fact that in 1900 about one-tenth of the people owned nine-tenths of the nation's wealth.

Women Canning Shrimp, 1893 Long hours, low pay, and wretched working conditions were the common fate of women who labored not for "pin money," but to help support their families. The "family wage" for the workingman was more a hope than a reality.

Library of Congress

A nation of farmers and independent producers was becoming a nation of wage earners. In 1860 half of all workers were self-employed; by the century's end, two of every three working Americans depended on wages. Real wages were rising, and times were good for workers who were working. But with dependence on wages came vulnerability to the swings of the economy and the whims of the employer. The fear of unemployment was never distant. A breadwinner's illness could mean catastrophe for an entire family. Nothing more sharply defined the growing difference between working-class and middle-class conditions of life than the precariousness of the laborer's lot. Reformers struggled to introduce a measure of security—job and wage protection, and provision for temporary unemployment—into the lives of the working class.

Finally, strong pressures for foreign trade developed as the tireless industrial machine threatened to saturate the domestic market. Aided by developments like the laying of a transatlantic telegraph in 1866 and the opening of the Suez Canal in 1869, international trade became ever faster, cheaper, and easier. American products radiated out all over the world—notably the five-gallon kerosene can of the Standard Oil Company. The flag follows trade, and empire tends to follow the flag—a harsh lesson that America was soon to learn.

✸ In Unions There Is Strength

The sweat of the laborer lubricated the vast new industrial machine. Yet the wage workers did not share proportionately with their employers in the benefits of the age of big business.

The worker, suggestive of the Roman galley slave, was becoming a lever-puller in a giant mechanism. Individual originality and creativity were being stifled, and less value than ever before was being placed on manual skills. Before the Civil War, the worker might have toiled

Gibson Girl, 1899 Illustrator Charles Dana Gibson created a sensation with his drawings of healthy, athletic, young women. The image of the "Gibson Girl" inspired new standards of female fashion as the twentieth century opened, and came to symbolize women's growing independence and assertiveness. *Granger Collection*

Library of Congress

Breaker Boys at South Pittson, Pennsylvania, 1911 Photographer Lewis Hine captured the grimness of these mine helpers' lives. For hours they sat on benches above a moving belt, breathing coal dust deep into their lungs and kicking large pieces of coal with their feet, breaking the lumps to uniform size for shipment. Photographs like this one became icons of the reform crusade against child labor, a campaign that succeeded only with the passage of the Fair Labor Standards Act in 1938.

The Photography of Lewis W. Hine

The pell-mell onrush of industrialization after the Civil War spawned countless human abuses, few more objectionable than the employment of children, often in hazardous jobs. For decades reformers tried to arouse public outrage against child labor, and they made significant headway at last with the help of photography—especially the photographs of Lewis W. Hine (1874–1940). A native of Wisconsin, Hine in 1908 became the staff photographer for the National Child Labor Committee, an organization committed to ending child labor. This 1909 photo of young "doffers," whose job it was to remove fully wound bobbins from textile spinning machines, is typical of Hine's work. He shows the boys climbing dangerously on the whirling mechanism, and his own caption for the photo names the mill—"Bibb Mill No. 1, Macon, Georgia"—but not the boys, as if to underline the impersonal, dehumanizing nature of their work and the specific responsibilities of their employer. His other subjects included child workers on Colorado beet farms, in Pennsylvania coal mines and Gulf Coast fish canneries, and in the glass, tobacco, and garment trades. Hine's images contributed heavily to the eventual success of the campaign to end child labor in the New Deal era. He is also celebrated as one of the fathers of documentary photography. Why might Hine's graphic images have succeeded in stirring public opinion more powerfully than factual and statistical demonstrations of the evil

Library of Congress

of child labor? Given Hine's own reform objectives, can his photographs—or any so-called documentary images—be taken at face value as literal, accurate information about the past?

in a small plant whose owner hailed the employee in the morning by first name and inquired after the family's health. But now the factory hand was employed by a corporation—depersonalized, bodiless, soulless, and often conscienceless. The directors knew the worker not, and in fairness to their stockholders, they were not inclined to engage in large-scale private philanthropy.

New machines displaced employees, and though in the long run more jobs were created than destroyed, in the short run the manual worker was often hard hit. A glutted labor market, moreover, severely handicapped wage earners. Employers could take advantage of the vast new railroad network and bring in unemployed workers, from the four corners of the country and beyond, to beat down high wage levels. During the 1880s and 1890s, several hundred thousand unskilled workers a year poured into the country from Europe, creating a labor market more favorable to the boss than the worker.

Individual workers were powerless to battle single-handedly against giant industry. Forced to organize and fight for basic rights, they found the dice heavily loaded against them. The corporation could dispense with the individual worker much more easily than the worker could dispense with the corporation. Employers could pool vast wealth through thousands of stockholders, retain high-priced lawyers, buy up the local press, and put pressure on the politicians. They could import strikebreakers ("scabs") and employ thugs to beat up labor organizers. In 1886 Jay Gould reputedly boasted, "I can hire one-half of the working class to kill the other half."

Corporations had still other weapons in their arsenals. They could call upon the federal courts—presided over by well-fed and conservative judges—to issue injunctions ordering the strikers to cease striking. If defiance and disorder ensued, the company could request the state and federal authorities to bring in troops. Employers could lock their doors against rebellious workers—a procedure called the "lockout"—and then starve them into submission. They could compel them to sign "ironclad oaths" or "yellow-dog contracts,"

The Strike, by Robert Koehler, 1886 Scenes like this were becoming more typical of American life in the late nineteenth century as industrialism advanced spectacularly and sometimes ruthlessly. Here Koehler (1850–1917) shows an entire community of men, women, and children—many of them apparently immigrant newcomers— challenging the power of the "boss." The scene is tense but orderly, though violence seems to be imminent as one striker reaches for a rock.

Deutsches Historisches Museum, Berlin, Germany/AKG, London

both of which were solemn agreements not to join a labor union. They could put the names of agitators on a "black list" and circulate it among fellow employers. A corporation might even own the "company town," with its high-priced grocery stores and "easy" credit. Often the worker sank into perpetual debt—a status that strongly resembled serfdom. Countless thousands of blackened coal miners were born in a company house, nurtured by a (high-priced) company store, and buried in a company graveyard—prematurely dead.

The middle-class public, annoyed by recurrent strikes, grew deaf to the outcry of the worker. American wages were perhaps the highest in the world, although a dollar a day for pick-and-shovel labor does not now seem excessive. Carnegie and Rockefeller had battled their way to the top, and the view was common that the laborer could do likewise. Somehow the strike seemed like a foreign importation—socialistic and hence unpatriotic. Big business might combine into trusts to raise prices, but the worker must not combine into unions

to raise wages. Unemployment seemed to be an act of God, who somehow would take care of the laborer.

✷ Labor Limps Along

Labor unions, which had been few and disorganized in 1861, were given a strong boost by the Civil War. This bloody conflict, with its drain on human resources, put more of a premium on labor; and the mounting cost of living provided an urgent incentive to unionization. By 1872 there were several hundred thousand organized workers and thirty-two national unions, representing such crafts as bricklayers, typesetters, and shoemakers.

The **National Labor Union**, organized in 1866, represented a giant bootstride by workers. One of the earliest national-scale unions to organize in the Americas or Europe, it aimed to unify workers across locales and trades to challenge their ever more powerful bosses. The union lasted six years and attracted the impressive total of some 600,000 members, including the skilled, unskilled, and farmers, though in keeping with the times, it excluded the Chinese and made only nominal efforts to include women and blacks. Black workers organized their own Colored National Labor Union as an adjunct, but their support for the Republican party and the persistent racism of white unionists prevented the two national unions from working together. The National Labor Union agitated for the arbitration of industrial disputes and the eight-hour workday, winning the latter for government workers. But the devastating depression of the 1870s dealt it a knockout blow. Labor was generally rocked back on its heels during the tumultuous years of the depression, but it never completely toppled. Wage reductions in 1877 touched off such disruptive strikes on the railroads that nothing short of federal troops could restore order.

A new organization—the **Knights of Labor**—seized the torch dropped by the defunct National Labor Union (see "Makers of America: The Knights of Labor," pp. 534–535). Officially known as the Noble and Holy Order of the Knights of Labor, it began inauspiciously in 1869 as a secret society, with a private ritual, passwords, and a special handshake. Secrecy, which continued until 1881, would forestall possible reprisals by employers.

The Knights of Labor, like the National Labor Union, sought to include all workers in "one big union." Their slogan was "An injury to one is the concern of all." A welcome mat was rolled out for the skilled and unskilled, for men and women, for whites and blacks, some ninety thousand of whom joined. The Knights barred only "nonproducers"—liquor dealers, professional gamblers, lawyers, bankers, and stockbrokers.

Setting up broad goals, the embattled Knights refused to thrust their lance into politics. Instead they campaigned for economic and social reform, including producers' cooperatives and codes for safety and health. Voicing the war cry "Labor is the only creator of values and capital," they frowned upon industrial warfare while fostering industrial arbitration. The ordinary workday was then ten hours or more, and the Knights waged a determined campaign for the eight-hour stint. A favorite song of these years ran,

Hurrah, hurrah, for labor,
it is mustering all its powers,
And shall march along to victory
with the banner of eight hours.

Under the eloquent but often erratic leadership of Terence V. Powderly, an Irish American of nimble wit and fluent tongue, the Knights won a number of strikes for the eight-hour day. When the Knights staged a successful strike against Jay Gould's Wabash Railroad in 1885, membership mushroomed to about three-quarters of a million workers.

✷ Unhorsing the Knights of Labor

Despite their outward success, the Knights were riding for a fall. They became involved in a number of May Day strikes in 1886, about half of which failed. A focal point was Chicago, home to about eighty thousand Knights. The city was also honeycombed with a few hundred anarchists, many of them foreign-born, who were advocating a violent overthrow of the American government.

Tensions rapidly built up to the bloody **Haymarket Square** episode. Labor disorders had broken out, and on May 4, 1886, the Chicago police advanced on a meeting called to protest alleged brutalities by the authorities. Suddenly a dynamite bomb was thrown that killed or injured several dozen people, including police.

Hysteria swept the Windy City. Eight anarchists were rounded up, although nobody proved that they had anything to do directly with the bomb. But the judge and jury held that since they had preached incendiary doctrines, they could be charged with conspiracy. Five were sentenced to death, one of whom committed suicide, and the other three were given stiff prison terms.

Agitation for clemency mounted. In 1892, some six years later, John P. Altgeld, a German-born Democrat of strong liberal tendencies, was elected governor of Illinois. After studying the Haymarket case exhaustively, he pardoned the three survivors. Violent abuse was showered on him by conservatives, unstinted praise by those who thought the men innocent. He was defeated for reelection and died a few years later in relative obscurity, "The Eagle Forgotten." Whatever the merits of the case, Altgeld displayed courage in opposing what he regarded as a gross injustice.

The Haymarket Square bomb helped blow the props from under the Knights of Labor. They were associated in the public mind, though mistakenly, with the anarchists. The eight-hour movement suffered correspondingly, and subsequent strikes by the Knights met with scant success.

Another fatal handicap of the Knights was their inclusion of both skilled and unskilled workers. Unskilled labor could easily be replaced by strikebreaking "scabs." High-class craft unionists, who enjoyed a semimonopoly of skills, could not readily be supplanted and hence enjoyed a superior bargaining position. They finally wearied of sacrificing this advantage on the altar of solidarity with their unskilled coworkers and sought refuge in a federation of exclusively skilled craft unions—the American Federation of Labor. The desertion of the skilled craft unionists dealt the Knights a body blow. By the 1890s they had melted away to 100,000 members, and these gradually fused with other protest groups of that decade.

It was 1875. The young worker was guided into a room, where his blindfold was removed. Surrounding him were a dozen men, their faces covered by hoods. One of the masked figures solemnly asked three questions: "Do you believe in God?" "Do you gain your bread by the sweat of your brow?" "Are you willing to take a solemn vow, binding you to secrecy, obedience, and mutual assistance?" Yes, came the reply. The men doffed their hoods and joined hands in a circle. Their leader, the Master Workman, declared, "On behalf of the toiling millions of earth, I welcome you to this Sanctuary, dedicated to the service of God, by serving humanity." Then the entire group burst into song:

Storm the fort, ye Knights of Labor,
Battle for your cause;
Equal rights for every neighbor,
Down with tyrant laws!

The carefully staged pageantry then drew to a close. The worker was now a full-fledged member of the Knights of Labor.

He had just joined a loose-knit organization of some 100,000 workingpeople, soon to swell to nearly a million after the Knights led several successful strikes in the 1880s. The first women Knights joined in 1881, when an all-female local was established in the shoe trade in Philadelphia, and one in ten members was a woman by 1885. Women were organizers, too. Fiery Mary Harris ("Mother") Jones got her start agitating for the Knights in the Illinois coalfields. The first all-black local was founded among coal miners in Ottumwa, Iowa. The Knights preached tolerance and the solidarity of all working men and women, and they meant it, but even their inclusionary spirit had its limits. Chinese workers were barred from joining, and the Knights vigorously supported the Chinese Exclusion Act of 1882. They also championed the Contract Labor Law of 1885, which aimed to restrain competition from low-wage immigrant workers—though immigrants, especially the Irish, were themselves disproportionately represented among the Knights' membership.

Terence V. Powderly, born to Irish immigrant parents in Carbondale, Pennsylvania, in 1849, became the Grand Master Workman of the Knights in 1879. Slightly built, with mild blue eyes behind glasses, he had dropped out of school at age thirteen to take a job guarding railroad track switches and rose to mayor of Scranton, Pennsylvania, in the 1870s. In 1894 he became a lawyer—despite the fact that the Knights excluded lawyers from membership. A complex, colorful, and sometimes cynical man, he denounced the "multimillionaires [for] laying the foundation for their colossal fortunes on the bodies and souls of living men." In the eyes of Powderly and his Knights, only the economic and political independence of American workers could preserve republican traditions and institutions from corruption by monopolists and other "parasites."

Powderly denounced "wage-slavery" and dedicated the Knights to achieving the "cooperative commonwealth." Shunning socialism, which advocated government ownership of the means of production, Powderly urged laborers to save enough from their wages to purchase mines, factories, railroads, and stores. They would thereby create a kind of toilers' utopia; because labor would own and operate those enterprises, workers themselves would be owner-producers, and the conflict between labor and capital would evaporate. The Knights actually did operate a few businesses, including coal mines in Indiana, but all eventually failed.

Powderly's vision of the cooperative commonwealth reflected the persistent dream of many nineteenth-century American workers that they would all one day

"Mother Jones"

534

become producers. As expectant capitalists, they lacked "class consciousness"—that is, a sense of themselves as a permanent working class that must organize to coax what benefits it could out of the capitalist system. Samuel Gompers, by contrast, accepted the framework of American capitalism, and his American Federation of Labor sought to work within that framework, not to overturn it. Gompers's conservative strategy, not Powderly's utopian dream, eventually carried the day. The swift decline of the Knights in the 1890s underscored the obsolescence of their unrealistic, even naive, view that a bygone age of independent producers could be restored. Yet the Knights' commitment to unifying all workers in one union—regardless of race, gender, ethnicity, or skill level—provided a blueprint for the eventual success of similarly committed unions like the Congress of Industrial Organizations in the 1930s.

Women Delegates to the 1886 Convention of the Knights of Labor

Samuel Gompers (1850–1924) Gompers (second from the right in the first row), shown here marching in a labor demonstration in Washington, D.C., in 1919, once declared, "Show me the country in which there are no strikes and I'll show you that country in which there is no liberty."

Brown Brothers

✪ The AF of L to the Fore

The elitist **American Federation of Labor**, born in 1886, was largely the brainchild of squat, square-jawed Samuel Gompers. This colorful Jewish cigar maker, born in a London tenement and removed from school at age ten, was brought to America when thirteen. Taking his turn at reading informative literature to fellow cigar makers in New York, he was pressed into overtime service because of his strong voice. Rising spectacularly in the labor ranks, he was elected president of the American Federation of Labor every year except one from 1886 to 1924.

Significantly, the American *Federation* of Labor was just what it called itself—a federation. It consisted of an association of self-governing national unions, each of which kept its independence, with the AF of L unifying overall strategy. No individual laborer could join the central organization.

Gompers adopted a down-to-earth approach, soft-pedaling attempts to engineer sweeping social reform. A bitter foe of socialism, he shunned politics for economic strategies and goals. Gompers had no quarrel with capitalism, but he demanded a fairer share for labor. All he wanted, he said, was "more." Promoting what he called a "pure and simple" unionism, he sought better wages, hours, and working conditions. Unlike the somewhat utopian Knights of Labor, he was not concerned with the sweet by-and-by, but with the bitter here and now. A major goal of Gompers was the "trade agreement" authorizing the **closed shop**—or all-union labor. His chief weapons were the walkout and the boycott, enforced by "We don't patronize" signs. The stronger craft unions of the federation, by pooling funds, were able to amass a war chest that would enable them to ride out prolonged strikes.

The AF of L thus established itself on solid but narrow foundations. Although attempting to speak for all workers, it fell far short of being representative of them. Composed of skilled craftsmen, like the carpenters and the bricklayers, it was willing to let unskilled laborers, including women and especially blacks, fend for themselves. Though hard-pressed by big industry, the federation was basically nonpolitical. But it did attempt to persuade members to reward friends and punish foes at the polls. The AF of L weathered the panic of 1893 reasonably well, and by 1900 it could boast a membership of 500,000. Critics referred to it, with questionable accuracy, as "the labor trust."

Labor disorders continued, peppering the years from 1881 to 1900 with a total of over 23,000 strikes. These disturbances involved 6,610,000 workers, with a total loss to both employers and employees of $450 million. The strikers lost about half their strikes and won or compromised the remainder. Perhaps the gravest weakness of organized labor was that it still embraced only a small minority of all workingpeople—about 3 percent in 1900.

But attitudes toward labor had begun to change perceptibly by 1900. The public was beginning to concede the right of workers to organize, to bargain collectively, and to strike. As a sign of the times, Labor Day was made a legal holiday by act of Congress in 1894. A few enlightened industrialists had come to perceive the wisdom of avoiding costly economic warfare by bargaining with the unions and signing agreements. But the vast majority of employers continued to fight organized labor, which achieved its grudging gains only after recurrent strikes and frequent reverses. Nothing was handed to it on a silver platter. Management still held the whip hand, and several trouble-fraught decades were to pass before labor was to gain a position of relative equality with capital. If the age of big business had dawned, the age of big labor was still some distance over the horizon.

Varying Viewpoints
Industrialization: Boon or Blight?

The capitalists who forged an industrial America in the late nineteenth century were once called captains of industry—a respectful title that bespoke the awe due their wondrous material accomplishments. But these economic innovators have never been universally admired. During the Great Depression of the 1930s, when the entire industrial order they had created seemed to have collapsed utterly, it was fashionable to speak of them as robber barons—a term implying scorn for their highhanded methods. This sneer often issued from the lips and pens of leftist critics like Matthew Josephson, who sympathized with the working classes that were allegedly brutalized by the factory system.

Criticism has also come from writers nostalgic for a preindustrial past. These critics believe that industrialization stripped away the traditions, values, and pride of native farmers and immigrant craftspeople. Conceding that economic development elevated the material standard of living for working Americans, this interpretation contends that the Industrial Revolution diminished their spiritual "quality of life." Accordingly, historians like Herbert Gutman and David Montgomery portray labor's struggle for control of the workplace as the central drama of industrial expansion.

Nevertheless, even these historians concede that class-based protest has never been as powerful a force in the United States as in certain European countries. Many historians believe that this is so because greater social mobility in America dampened class tensions. The French observer Alexis de Tocqueville noted in the 1830s that America had few huge inherited fortunes and that most of its wealthy men were self-made. For two centuries a majority of Americans have believed that greater opportunity distinguished the New World from the Old.

In the 1960s historians led by Stephan Thernstrom began to test this long-standing belief. Looking at such factors as occupation, wealth, and geographic mobility, they tried to gauge the nature and extent of social mobility in the United States. Most of these historians concluded that although relatively few Americans made rags-to-riches leaps like those heralded in the Horatio Alger stories, large numbers experienced small improvements in their economic and social status. Few sons of laborers became corporate tycoons, but many more became line bosses and white-collar clerks. These studies also have found that race and ethnicity often affected one's chances for success. For instance, the children and grandchildren of Jewish immigrants tended to rise faster in the professions than Americans of Italian and Irish descent. Throughout the nineteenth and early twentieth centuries, blacks lagged far behind other groups in almost every category.

In recent years such studies have been criticized by certain historians who point out the difficulties involved in defining social status. For instance, some white-collar clerical workers received lower wages than manual laborers did. Were they higher or lower on the social scale? Furthermore, James Henretta has pointed out that different groups defined success differently: whereas Jewish immigrants often struggled to give their sons professional educations, the Irish put more emphasis on acquiring land and the Italians on building small family-run businesses.

Meanwhile, leftist historians such as Michael Katz have argued that the degree of social mobility in America has been overrated. These historians argue that industrial capitalism created two classes: a working class that sold its labor, and a business class that controlled resources and bought labor. Although most Americans took small steps upward, they generally remained within the class in which they began. Thus, these historians argue, the inequality of a capitalistic class system persisted in America's seemingly fluid society.

Chapter Review

KEY TERMS

Wabash, St. Louis & Pacific Railroad Company v. *Illinois* (519)

Interstate Commerce Act (519)

vertical integration (521)

horizontal integration (521)

trust (521)

interlocking directorates (522)

Standard Oil Company (524)

Social Darwinists (525)

Sherman Anti-Trust Act (525)

National Labor Union (532)

Knights of Labor (533)

Haymarket Square (533)

American Federation of Labor (536)

closed shop (536)

PEOPLE TO KNOW

Cornelius Vanderbilt

Alexander Graham Bell

Thomas Alva Edison

Andrew Carnegie

John D. Rockefeller

Samuel Gompers

CHRONOLOGY

1862 Congress authorizes transcontinental railroad

1866 National Labor Union organized
First working transatlantic telegraph cable

1869 Transcontinental railroad joined near Ogden, Utah
Knights of Labor organized
Suez Canal completed

1870 Standard Oil Company organized

1876 Bell invents telephone

1879 Edison invents electric light

1886 Haymarket Square bombing
Wabash case
American Federation of Labor formed

1887 Interstate Commerce Act

1890 Sherman Anti-Trust Act

1901 United States Steel Corporation formed

TO LEARN MORE

Edward L. Ayers, *The Promise of the New South: Life After Reconstruction* (1992)

David H. Bain, *Empire Express: Building the First Transcontinental Railroad* (1999)

Sven Beckert, *The Monied Metropolis: New York City and the Consolidation of the American Bourgeoisie, 1850–1896* (2001)

Alfred D. Chandler, Jr., *The Visible Hand: The Managerial Revolution in American Business* (1978)

James Green, *Death in the Haymarket: A Story of Chicago, the First Labor Movement, and the Bombing That Divided Gilded Age America* (2006)

Richard Hofstadter, *Social Darwinism in American Thought, 1860–1915* (rev. ed., 1955)

Tera W. Hunter, *To 'Joy My Freedom: Southern Black Women's Lives and Labors After the Civil War* (1997)

Alice Kessler Harris, *Out to Work: A History of Wage-Earning Women in the United States* (1982)

Maury Klein, *The Genesis of Industrial America, 1870–1920* (2007)

David Montgomery, *The Fall of the House of Labor: The Workplace, the State, and American Labor Activism, 1865–1925* (1987)

Daniel T. Rodgers, *The Work Ethic in Industrial America, 1850–1920* (1978)

Richard White, *Railroaded: The Transcontinentals and the Making of Modern America* (2011)

A complete, annotated bibliography for this chapter—along with brief descriptions of the People to Know—may be found on the American Pageant website. The Key Terms are defined in a Glossary at the end of the text.

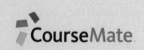

Go to the CourseMate website at www.cengagebrain.com for additional study tools and review materials—including audio and video clips—for this chapter.

AP® Review Questions for Chapter 24

1. All of the following economic developments were significant factors in enabling America to industrialize rapidly EXCEPT
   (A) private foreign investment.
   (B) a plentiful supply of skilled, unskilled, and cheap labor.
   (C) technological innovations.
   (D) increased overseas trade.
   (E) the sale of confiscated Confederate land and property.

2. Which of the following two industries were most significantly expanded as a result of the completion of the transcontinental railroad?
   (A) Textiles and shoemaking
   (B) Mining and agriculture
   (C) Banking and real estate
   (D) Shipping and fishing
   (E) Electricity and telecommunications

3. Which effort represented the first attempt to regulate the monopolizing and pricing practices of the railroad corporations during this period?
   (A) Congressional establishment of the Interstate Commerce Commission
   (B) The U.S. Supreme Court decision of *Wabash, St. Louis, and Pacific Railroad* v. *Illinois*
   (C) An executive order issued by President Cleveland that limited the monopolizing and excessive pricing practices of the railroad corporations
   (D) Congressional legislation aimed at curbing the monopolizing and pricing practices of the railroad corporations
   (E) Laws passed by state legislatures that regulated the monopolizing and pricing practices of the railroad corporations

4. Which of the following was NOT among the common forms of corruption practiced by the wealthy railroad barons?
   (A) Bribing judges and state legislatures
   (B) Requiring their employees to buy railroad stock as a condition of employment
   (C) Providing free railroad passes to journalists and politicians
   (D) Watering down railroad stocks and bonds in order to sell them at inflated prices
   (E) Granting kickbacks to powerful shippers

5. Which of the following best describes the Europeans' approach to ownership or investment in private companies in the United States during this period?
   (A) Appointing European managers to key positions in the company
   (B) Allowing Americans to manage the business unless an economic crisis occurred
   (C) Requiring American banks to issue regular reports on the profitability of their companies
   (D) Steering most of their investment profits back into European investments
   (E) Insisting that the companies employ a percentage of immigrants from the nation owning the company

6. How did the American system of mass manufacture of standardized, interchangeable parts influence the behavior of U.S. capitalists?
   (A) It motivated U.S. capitalists to invest in training their workforce.
   (B) It led U.S. capitalists to hire American workers rather than foreign immigrants.
   (C) It stimulated U.S. capitalists to replace skilled labor with unskilled workers and machinery.
   (D) It caused the building of extremely large factories in dedicated industrial districts.
   (E) It led U.S. capitalists to pay higher wages to retain a stable workforce.

7. What two technological innovations greatly expanded the industrial employment of women in the late nineteenth century?
   (A) Typewriter and telephone
   (B) Electric light and phonograph
   (C) Bessemer steel process and internal combustion engine
   (D) Streetcar and bicycle
   (E) Electric refrigerator and stove

8. All of the following economic strategies were employed by the titans of industry, during this period, to maximize their corporations' profits EXCEPT
   (A) vertical integration of all facets of an industry, from raw materials to final product, within a single company.
   (B) horizontal integration within a single market by securing favorable alliances with potential competitors.
   (C) improving the efficiency of production by making supplies more reliable.
   (D) utilizing technological advances in mechanization and industrial processes to mass-produce products in a cost-effective manner.
   (E) seeking stable labor relations with their workers by permitting collective bargaining with unions.

9. Which of the following best describes the intellectual viewpoint of Andrew Carnegie as expressed in the "Gospel of Wealth"?
    (A) All of the teachings of Jesus should guide a businessman's approach to acquiring and managing his wealth.
    (B) The wealthy should exhibit moral and social responsibility in their use of their God-given money.
    (C) Poor immigrants and ethnic minorities should be provided with substantial government assistance so they can acquire substantial wealth.
    (D) Labor precedes capital in permitting a person to acquire, increase, and maintain wealth.
    (E) A "survival of the fittest" approach to capitalism, emphasizing wealth creation as a result of natural selection

10. Which entity was first prosecuted for alleged restraint-of-trade violations by the U.S. government using the Sherman Anti-Trust Act of 1890?
    (A) Labor unions
    (B) Manufacturing corporations
    (C) State legislatures
    (D) Railroad corporations
    (E) Banking syndicates

11. All of the following were major attractions for potential investors in southern manufacturing industries EXCEPT
    (A) low wages for workers.
    (B) nonunionized labor.
    (C) tax benefits by government.
    (D) plentiful natural resources such as cotton.
    (E) a well-educated and ethnically diverse work force.

12. Despite generally rising wages in the nineteenth century, industrial workers were extremely vulnerable to all of the following EXCEPT
    (A) economic swings and depressions.
    (B) employers' whims.
    (C) new educational requirements for jobs.
    (D) sudden unemployment.
    (E) illness and accident.

13. Which of the following was NOT a strategy utilized by late-nineteenth-century employers to gain leverage over workers seeking to improve their wages and working conditions?
    (A) Closed shop
    (B) Lockouts
    (C) Yellow-dog contracts
    (D) Seeking federal court injunctions against union activity
    (E) Creation of company towns

14. All of the following were reasons that the Knights of Labor ultimately failed to sustain their union independence and membership by the 1890s EXCEPT
    (A) defections by skilled craft unionists to the American Federation of Labor (AFL).
    (B) lack of class consciousness.
    (C) the public's association of the Knights of Labor with the violent activities of anarchists in cities such as Chicago.
    (D) unsuccessful strikes and scant progress in their efforts to secure the eight-hour day.
    (E) racial and gender exclusiveness in their membership.

15. Which of the following was NOT a difference between the Knights of Labor and the American Federation of Labor (AFL)?
    (A) The Knights of Labor included all workers; the AFL only advocated for skilled workers.
    (B) The Knights of Labor welcomed all genders and ethnicities; the AFL excluded women and blacks.
    (C) The Knights of Labor discarded ideas of class in the United States; the AFL worked within those societal limits.
    (D) The Knights of Labor was a huge union, and the AFL was a federation of many specialized unions.
    (E) The Knights of Labor refused to condone striking; the AFL believed that strikes could help the workers' cause.

16. Railroads changed the American landscape in all of the following ways EXCEPT by
    (A) making the United States the single largest integrated national market in the world.
    (B) stimulating mining and agriculture in the West.
    (C) limiting the number of people moving to overcrowded cities.
    (D) employing more people than any other industry.
    (E) displacing buffalo and plowing through the prairies.

Chapter 25

America Moves to the City

1865–1900

What shall we do with our great cities?
What will our great cities do with us . . . ?
[T]he question . . . does not concern the city alone.
The whole country is affected . . . by the condition of its great cities.

LYMAN ABBOTT, 1891

Born in the country, America moved to the city in the decades following the Civil War. By the year 1900, the United States' upsurging population nearly doubled from its level of some 40 million souls enumerated in the census of 1870. Yet in the very same period, the population of American cities *tripled*. By the end of the nineteenth century, four out of ten Americans were city dwellers, in striking contrast to the rustic population of stagecoach days.

This cityward drift affected not only the United States but the entire industrializing world. European peasants, pushed off the land in part by competition from cheap American foodstuffs, were pulled into cities—in both Europe and America—by the new lure of industrial jobs. A revolution in American agriculture thus fed the industrial and urban revolutions in Europe, as well as in the United States.

✵ The Urban Frontier

The growth of American metropolises was spectacular. In 1860 no city in the United States could boast a million inhabitants; by 1890 New York, Chicago, and Philadelphia had vaulted past the million mark. By 1900 New York, with some 3.5 million people, was the second-largest city in the world, outranked only by London. Throughout the world, cities were exploding. London, Paris, Berlin, Tokyo, Moscow, Mexico City, Calcutta, and Shanghai all doubled or tripled in size between 1850 and 1900. The population of Buenos Aires multiplied by more than ten (see Map 25.1).

American cities grew both up and out. The cloud-brushing skyscraper allowed more people and work-places to be packed onto a parcel of land. Appearing first as a ten-story building in Chicago in 1885, the sky-scraper was made usable by the perfecting of the electric elevator. An opinionated Chicago architect, Louis Sullivan (1856–1924), contributed formidably to the further development of the skyscraper with his famous principle that "form follows function." Nesting loftily above city streets in the new steel-skeleton high-rises that Sullivan helped to make popular, many Americans were becoming modern cliff dwellers.

Americans were also becoming commuters, carted daily between home and job on the mass-transit lines that radiated out from central cities to surrounding suburbs. Electric trolleys, powered by wagging antennae from overhead wires, propelled city limits explosively outward. By the end of the century, the nation's first subway opened in Boston; London had led the way by building a subway as early as 1863. The compact and communal "walking city," its boundaries fixed by the limits of leg-power, gave way to the immense and impersonal megalopolis, carved into distinctly different districts for business, industry, and residential neighborhoods—which were in turn segregated by race, ethnicity, and social class.

Rural life could not compete with the siren song of the city (see Figure 25.1). Industrial jobs, above all, drew people off farms in America as well as abroad and into factory centers. But the urban lifestyle also held powerful attractions. The predawn milking of cows had little appeal when compared with the late-night glitter of

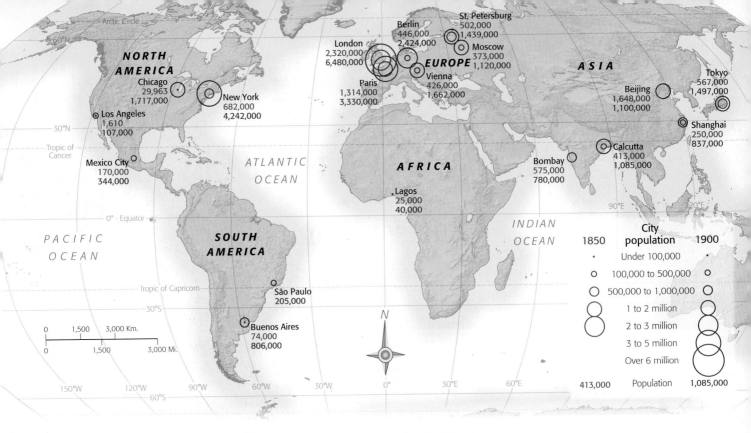

MAP 25.1 Size of World Cities 1850–1900 Sources: United Nations, "World Urbanization Prospects: The 2005 Revision"; Tertius Chandler and Gerald Fox, *3000 Years of Urban Growth* (New York: Academic Press, 1974); U.S. Census; Spencer H. Brown, "Public Health in Lagos, 1850–1900: Perceptions, Patterns, and Perspectives," *International Journal of African Historical Studies* 25, no. 2. (1992): 345; Josephine Olu Abiodun, "The Challenges of Growth and Development in Metropolitan Lagos," in *The Urban Challenge in Africa: Growth and Management of Its Large Cities*, ed. Carole Rakodi (New York: United Nations University Press, 1997), 193–195; United Nations Demographic Yearbook. © Cengage Learning

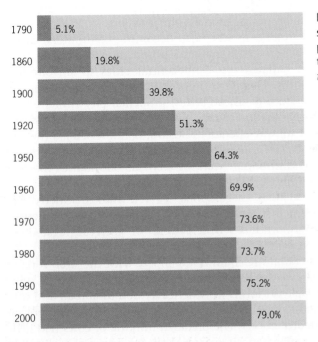

FIGURE 25.1 The Shift to the American City This chart shows the percentage of total population living in locales with a population of twenty-five hundred or more. Note the slowing of the cityward trend from 1970 on. (Sources: *Historical Statistics of the United States*; U.S. Census Bureau.)

city lights, particularly alluring to young adults yearning for independence. Electricity, indoor plumbing, and telephones—whose numbers leapt from some 50,000 in 1880 to over 1 million in 1900—all made life in the big city more enticing. Engineering marvels like the skyscraper and New York's awesome Brooklyn Bridge, a harplike suspension span dedicated in 1883, further added to the seductive glamour of the gleaming cities.

Cavernous department stores such as Macy's in New York and Marshall Field's in Chicago attracted urban middle-class shoppers and provided urban working-class jobs, many of them for women. The bustling emporiums also heralded a dawning era of consumerism and accentuated widening class divisions. When Carrie Meeber, novelist Theodore Dreiser's fictional

Library of Congress

The Brooklyn Bridge   The Brooklyn Bridge opened on May 24, 1883. It had taken thirteen years to build and was the largest suspension bridge in the world, as well as the first made of steel wire. On opening day, an astonishing 1,800 vehicles and 150,300 people made the short but breathtaking trek between the New York City boroughs of Manhattan and Brooklyn. The first person to cross was Emily Warren Roebling, the daughter-in-law of the original designer, John Augustus Roebling, and the wife of his son, Washington Roebling, who had taken over the job when his father died suddenly in 1869. When Washington fell ill himself, Emily learned civil engineering and oversaw much of the remaining work on the bridge.

heroine in *Sister Carrie* (1900), escapes from rural boredom to Chicago just before the turn of the century, it is the spectacle of the city's dazzling department stores that awakens her fateful yearning for a richer, more elegant way of life—for entry into the privileged urban middle class, whose existence she had scarcely imagined in the rustic countryside.

The move to the city introduced Americans to new ways of living. Country dwellers produced little household waste. Domestic animals or scavenging pigs ate food scraps on the farm. Rural women mended and darned worn clothing rather than discard it. Household products were sold in bulk at the local store, without wrapping. Mail-order houses such as Sears and Montgomery Ward, which increasingly displaced the rural "general store" in the late nineteenth century, at first did not list trash barrels or garbage cans in their catalogues. In the city, however, goods came in throwaway

bottles, boxes, bags, and cans. Apartment houses had no adjoining barnyards where residents might toss garbage to the hogs. Cheap ready-to-wear clothing and swiftly changing fashions pushed old suits and dresses out of the closet and onto the trash heap. Waste disposal, in short, was an issue new to the urban age. And the mountains of waste that urbanites generated further testified to a cultural shift away from the virtues of thrift to the conveniences of consumerism.

The jagged skyline of America's perpendicular civilization could not fully conceal the canker sores of a feverish growth. Criminals flourished like lice in the teeming asphalt jungles. Sanitary facilities could not keep pace with the mushrooming population explosion. Impure water, uncollected garbage, unwashed bodies, and droppings from draft animals enveloped many cities in a satanic stench. Baltimore was described as smelling like a billion polecats.

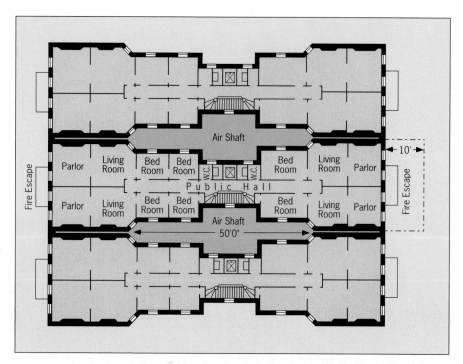

FIGURE 25.2 Dumbbell Tenement
This was the standard architectural plan for the human warehouses on New York's Lower East Side. Despite the innovation of an air shaft to bring light and ventilation to the middle of the building, only one room in each of the apartments was directly exposed to sunlight and open air. All families on a floor shared the toilet ("W.C.") in the hallway.

The cities were monuments of contradiction. They represented "humanity compressed," remarked one observer, "the best and the worst combined, in a strangely composite community." They harbored merchant princes and miserable paupers, stately banks and sooty factories, green-grassed suburbs and treeless ghettos, towering skyscrapers and stinking tenements. The glaring contrasts that assaulted the eye in New York reminded one visitor of "a lady in ball costume, with diamonds in her ears, and her toes out at the boots."

Worst of all were the human pigsties known as slums. They seemed to grow ever more crowded, more filthy, and more rat-infested, especially after the perfection in 1879 of the "dumbbell" tenement (see Figure 25.2). So named because of the outline of its floor plan, the dumbbell was usually seven or eight stories high, with shallow, sunless, and ill-smelling air shafts providing minimal ventilation. Several families were sardined onto each floor of the barracks-like structures, and they shared a malodorous toilet in the hall. In these fetid warrens, conspicuously in New York's "Lung Block," hundreds of unfortunate urbanites coughed away their lives. "Flophouses" abounded where the half-starved and unemployed might sleep for a few cents on verminous mattresses. Small wonder that slum dwellers strove mightily to escape their wretched surroundings—as many of them did. The slums remained foul places, inhabited by successive waves of newcomers. To a remarkable degree, hard-working people moved up and out of them.

Cities were dangerous for everyone. In 1871 two-thirds of downtown Chicago burned in a raging fire that left ninety thousand people homeless and destroyed more than fifteen thousand buildings. Closely packed wooden structures fed the insatiable flames, prompting Chicago and other wary cities to require stone and iron buildings downtown. The wealthiest began to leave the risky cities behind and head for semirural suburbs. These leafy "bedroom communities" eventually ringed the brick-and-concrete cities with a greenbelt of affluence.

✴ The New Immigration

The powerful pull of the American urban magnet was felt even in faraway Europe. A seemingly endless stream of immigrants continued to pour in from the old "mother continent." In each of the three decades from the 1850s through the 1870s, more than 2 million migrants had stepped onto America's shores. By the 1880s the stream had swelled to a rushing torrent, as more than 5 million cascaded into the country. A new high for a single year was reached in 1882, when 788,992 arrived—or more than 2,100 a day (see Figure 25.3).

Until the 1880s most immigrants had come from the British Isles and western Europe, chiefly Germany and Ireland. Also significant were the more than 300,000 Chinese immigrants. Many of these earlier immigrants had faced virulent nativism, especially the Irish and the Chinese. In fact, the latter were legally excluded in 1882 (see p. 498).

But by the last decades of the century, the "old" European immigrants had adjusted well to American

IN THOUSANDS

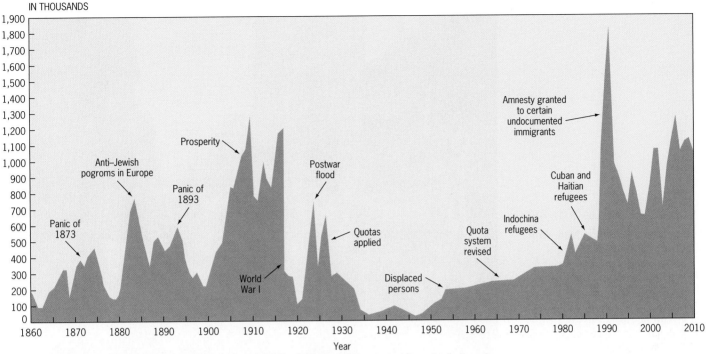

FIGURE 25.3 Annual Immigration, 1860–2010 After 1924 these numbers include only legal, documented immigrants. The 1989 total includes 478,814 people granted permanent residence status under the "amnesty" provisions of the 1986 Immigration Reform and Control Act. The 1990 total includes 880,372 people granted permanent residence under these provisions. The peak came in 1991, when 1,123,162 people were affected by amnesty. (Sources: *Statistical Abstract of the United States,* relevant years; Department of Homeland Security, *Yearbook of Immigration Statistics,* 2009.)

life by building supportive ethnic organizations and melding into established farm communities or urban craft unions. Although many still lived, worked, and worshiped among their own, they were largely accepted as "American" by the native-born.

In the 1880s the character of the immigrant stream changed drastically (see Figure 25.4). The so-called

New Immigrants came from southern and eastern Europe. Among them were Italians, Jews, Croats, Slovaks, Greeks, and Poles. They came from countries with little history of democratic government, where people had grown accustomed to cringing before despotism and where opportunities for advancement were few. These new peoples totaled only 19 percent of the

Million

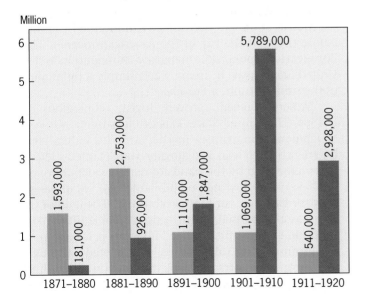

Leading nations of the Old Immigration: England, Ireland, Germany

Leading nations of the New Immigration: Italy, Austria–Hungary, Russia

FIGURE 25.4 Old and New Immigration (by decade, 1871–1920) In the 1880s the sources of immigration to the United States shifted from the British Isles and western Europe to southern and eastern Europe. A century later the old "mother continent" of Europe would account for only 10 percent of immigrants to America (see Figure 42.5 on p. 1000).

Mulberry Street on New York City's Lower East Side, ca. 1900 Population densities in early-twentieth-century American cities were among the highest in the world. Mulberry Street, shown in this photo, was at the heart of New York's "Little Italy" neighborhood.

inpouring immigrants in the 1880s, but by the first decade of the twentieth century, they constituted an astonishing 66 percent of the total inflow. They hived together in cities like New York and Chicago, where the "Little Italys" and "Little Polands" soon claimed more inhabitants than many of the largest cities of the same nationality in the Old World (see "Makers of America: The Italians," pp. 546–547).

Largely illiterate and impoverished, many immigrants at first were content to live within these tightly bound communities based on native language and religion. There they worshiped in Orthodox or Roman Catholic churches or synagogues and in some cases nourished radical political ideas. There, too, they felt sheltered from Americans who revived old nativist fears that had plagued Old Immigrants in the 1840s and 1850s—fears that these New Immigrants would not, or could not, assimilate to life in their new land. The skeptics, who included some immigrants of the earlier wave, began asking whether the nation had become a melting pot or a dumping ground.

✹ Southern Europe Uprooted

Why were these bright-shawled and quaint-jacketed strangers hammering on the gates? In part they left their native countries because Europe seemed to have no room for them. The population of the Old World was growing vigorously. It nearly doubled in the century after 1800, thanks in part to abundant supplies

of fish and grain from America and to the widespread cultivation in Europe of that humble New World transplant, the potato. American food imports and the galloping pace of European industrialization shook the peasantry loose from its ancient habitats and customary occupations, creating a vast, footloose army of the unemployed. Europeans by the millions drained out of the countryside and into European cities. Most stayed there, but some kept moving and left Europe altogether. About 60 million Europeans abandoned the Old Continent in the nineteenth and early twentieth centuries. More than half of them moved to the United States, while their compatriots spread out across the globe to South America, Canada, Africa, and Australia. Masses of people were already in motion in Europe before they felt the tug of the American magnet. This European diaspora, dominated by immigration to the United States, was, in many ways, simply a by-product of the urbanization of Europe.

"America fever" proved highly contagious in Europe. The United States was often painted as a land of fabulous opportunity in the "America letters" sent by friends and relatives already transplanted—letters that were soiled by the hands of many readers. "We eat here every day," wrote one jubilant Pole, "what we get only for Easter in our [native] country." The land of the free was also blessed with freedom from military conscription and institutionalized religious persecution.

Profit-seeking Americans trumpeted throughout Europe the attractions of the new promised land. Industrialists wanted low-wage labor, railroads wanted

Mary Antin (1881–1949), who came to America from Russian Poland in 1894 when thirteen years of age, later wrote in The Promised Land *(1912),*

"So at last I was going to America! Really, really going, at last! The boundaries burst. The arch of heaven soared. A million suns shone out for every star. The winds rushed in from outer space, roaring in my ears, 'America! America!'"

buyers for their land grants, states wanted more population, and steamship lines wanted more human cargo for their holds. In fact, the ease and cheapness of steam-powered shipping greatly accelerated the transoceanic surge.

As the century lengthened, savage persecutions of minorities in Europe drove many shattered souls to American shores. In the 1880s the Russians turned violently upon their own Jews, chiefly in the Polish areas. Tens of thousands of these battered refugees, survivors of centuries of harassment as hated outcasts, fled their burning homes. They made their way to the seaboard cities of the Atlantic Coast, notably New York. Jews had experienced city life in Europe—a circumstance that made them virtually unique among the New Immigrants. Many of them brought their urban skills of tailoring or shopkeeping to American cities. Destitute and devout, eastern European Jews were frequently given a frosty reception not only by old-stock Americans but also by those German Jews who had arrived decades earlier and prospered in the United States, some as garment manufacturers who now employed their coreligionists as cheap labor.

Many of the immigrants never intended to become Americans in any case. A large number of them were single men who worked in the United States for several months or years and then returned home with their hard-earned roll of American dollars. Some 25 percent of the nearly 20 million people who arrived between 1820 and 1900 were "birds of passage" who eventually returned to their country of origin. For them the attraction of the American magnet was never strong.

Even those who stayed in America struggled heroically to preserve their traditional culture. Catholics expanded their parochial-school systems, and Jews established Hebrew schools. Foreign-language newspapers abounded. Yiddish theaters, kosher-food stores, Polish parishes, Greek restaurants, and Italian social clubs all attested to the desire to keep old ways alive. Yet time took its toll on these efforts to conserve the customs of the Old World in the New. The children of the immigrants grew up speaking fluent English, sometimes mocking the broken grammar of their parents. They often rejected the Old Country manners of their mothers and fathers in their desire to plunge headlong into the mainstream of American life.

Reactions to the New Immigration

America's government system, nurtured in wide-open spaces, was ill-suited to the cement forests of the great cities. Beyond minimal checking to weed out criminals

Brown Brothers

Jewish Women Working in a Sweatshop, ca. 1910 Countless immigrant women found their first American employment in shops like this.

Who were the "New Immigrants," these southern and eastern European birds of passage that flocked to the United States between 1880 and 1920? Prominent and typical among them were the Italians, some 4 million of whom sailed to the United States during the four decades of the New Immigration.

They came from the southern provinces of their native land, the heel and toe of the Italian boot. These areas had lagged economically behind the prosperous, industrial region of northern Italy. The north had been the seat of earlier Italian glory, as well as the fountainhead of the successful movement to unify the country in 1860. There industry had been planted and agriculture modernized. Unification raised hopes of similar progress in the downtrodden south, but it was slow in coming. Southern Italian peasants tilled their fields without fertilizer or machinery, using hand plows and rickety hoes that had been passed down for generations.

From such disappointed and demeaned conditions, southern Italians set out for the New World. Most came to the United States, but significant numbers headed for Argentina to work in agriculture. Almost all of them were young men who intended to spend only a few months, stuff their pockets with earnings, and return home. At least half of the Italian immigrants did indeed repatriate—as did comparable numbers of the other New Immigrants, with the conspicuous exception of the Jews, who had fled their native lands to escape religious persecution. Most of the Italian immigrants to the United States sailed through New York harbor, sighting the Statue of Liberty as they debarked from crowded ships. Many soon moved on to other large cities, but so many remained that in the early years of the twentieth century, more Italians resided in New York than in the Italian cities of Florence, Venice, and Genoa combined.

Since the immigrant Italians, with few exceptions, had been peasant farmers in the Old Country, the U.S. government encouraged them to practice their ancestral livelihood here, believing they would more

Italian Immigrants Arriving at Ellis Island, ca. 1910

Brown Brothers

Pietro Learning to Write on Jersey Street "The sons shall teach the fathers," the old saying goes. Many immigrants learned English from their children who attended American schools, like this youngster and parent in early-twentieth-century New Jersey.

Museum of the City of New York The Jacob A. Riis Collection, #160

and the insane, the federal government did virtually nothing to ease the assimilation of immigrants into American society. State governments, usually dominated by rural representatives, did even less. City governments, overwhelmed by the sheer scale of rampant urban growth, proved woefully inadequate to the task.

By default, the business of ministering to the immigrants' needs fell to the unofficial "governments" of the urban political machines, led by "bosses" like New York's notorious Boss Tweed.

Taking care of the immigrants was big business indeed. Trading jobs and services for votes, a powerful

Italian Immigrant Women Doing Piecework at Home in New York, ca. 1910 Culver Pictures

Italian Construction Workers, ca. 1910 Brown Brothers

rapidly assimilate in the countryside than in the ethnic enclaves of the cities. But almost all such ventures failed. The farmers lacked capital, and they were in any case more interested in earning quick money than in permanently sinking roots. Although they huddled in the cities, Italian immigrants did not abandon their rural upbringing entirely. Much to their neighbors' consternation, they often kept chickens in vacant lots and raised vegetables in small garden plots nestled between decaying tenement houses.

Those who bade a permanent farewell to Italy clustered in tightly knit communities that boasted opera clubs, Italian-language newspapers, and courts for playing bocci—a version of lawn bowling imported from the Old Country. Pizza emerged from the hot wood-burning ovens of these Little Italys, its aroma and flavor wafting into the hearts and stomachs of all Americans.

The Italians typically earned their daily bread as industrial laborers—most famously as longshoremen and construction workers. They owed their prominence

in the building trades to the "padrone system." The *padrone*, or labor boss, met immigrants upon their arrival and secured jobs for them in New York, Chicago, the West, or wherever there was an immediate demand for labor. The padrone owed his power to his ability to meet the needs of both Italian newcomers and American bosses, and he often managed to manipulate both for his own gain.

Lacking education, the Italians, as a group, remained in blue-collar jobs longer than some of their fellow New Immigrants. Many Italians, valuing vocation over schooling, sent their children off to work as early in their young lives as possible. Before World War I, less than 1 percent of Italian children enrolled in high school. Over the next fifty years, Italian Americans and their offspring gradually prospered, moving out of the cities into the more affluent suburbs. Many served heroically in World War II and availed themselves of the GI Bill to finance the college educations and professional training their immigrant forebears had lacked.

boss might claim the loyalty of thousands of followers. In return for their support at the polls, the boss provided jobs on the city's payroll, found housing for new arrivals, tided over the needy with gifts of food and clothing, patched up minor scrapes with the law, and helped get schools, parks, and hospitals built in

immigrant neighborhoods. Reformers gagged at this cynical exploitation of the immigrant vote, but the political boss gave valuable assistance that was forthcoming from no other source.

The nation's social conscience, slumbering since the antislavery crusade, gradually awakened to the plight

Manuscript Census Data, 1900

Article I of the Constitution requires that a census of the American people be taken every ten years, in order to provide a reliable basis for congressional apportionment. Early censuses gathered little more than basic population numbers, but over the years the census takers have collected information on other matters as well—including occupational categories, educational levels, and citizenship status—yielding copious raw data for historical analysis. The census of 1890 was the first to use punch cards and electric tabulating machines, which greatly expanded the range of data that could be assembled and correlated—though the basic information was still hand-recorded by individual canvassers who went door-to-door to question household members and fill out the census forms. Those handwritten forms, as much as the aggregate numbers printed in the final census tally, can furnish invaluable insights to the historian. Despite its apparent bureaucratic formality, the form shown here richly details the lives of the residents of a tenement house on New York's Lower East Side in 1900. See in particular the entries for the Goldberg family. In what ways does this document reflect the great demographic changes that swept late-nineteenth-century America? What light does it shed on the character of immigrant "ghettos"? What further use might historians make of information like this?

National Archives

Special Collections and University Archives,
The University of Illinois at Chicago

Hull House   These immigrant children playing games at the settlement house that Jane Addams founded in Chicago were having some fun while also getting instruction from a settlement house worker in how to be a proper American.

of the cities, and especially their immigrant masses. Prominent in this awakening were several Protestant clergymen, who sought to apply the lessons of Christianity to the slums and factories. Noteworthy among them was Walter Rauschenbusch, who in 1886 became pastor of a German Baptist church in New York City. Also conspicuous was Washington Gladden, who took over a Congregational church in Columbus, Ohio, in 1882. Preaching the "social gospel," they both insisted that the churches tackle the burning social issues of the day. The Sermon on the Mount, they declared, was the science of society, and many social gospelers predicted that socialism would be the logical outcome of Christianity. These "Christian socialists" did much to prick callous middle-class consciences, thus preparing the path for the progressive reform movement after the turn of the century.

One middle-class woman who was deeply dedicated to uplifting the urban masses was Jane Addams (1860–1935). Born into a prosperous Illinois family, Addams was one of the first generation of college-educated women. Upon her graduation she sought other outlets for her large talents than could be found in teaching or charitable volunteer work, then the only permissible occupations for a young woman of her social class. Inspired by a visit to England, she acquired the decaying Hull mansion in Chicago in 1889. There she established Hull House, the most prominent (though not the first) American settlement house.

Soft-spoken but tenacious, Addams became a kind of urban American saint in the eyes of many admirers. The philosopher William James told her, "You utter instinctively the truth we others vainly seek." She was a broad-gauge reformer who courageously condemned war as well as poverty, and she eventually won the Nobel Peace Prize in 1931. But her pacifism also earned her the enmity of some Americans, including the Daughters of the American Revolution, who choked on her antiwar views and expelled her from membership in their august organization.

Located in a poor immigrant neighborhood of Greeks, Italians, Russians, and Germans, Hull House offered instruction in English, counseling to help newcomers cope with American big-city life, child-care services for working mothers, and cultural activities for neighborhood residents. Following Jane Addams's lead, women founded **settlement houses** in other cities as well. Conspicuous among the houses was Lillian Wald's Henry Street Settlement in New York, which opened its doors in 1893.

The settlement houses became centers of women's activism and of social reform. The women of Hull House successfully lobbied in 1893 for an Illinois antisweatshop law that protected women workers and prohibited child labor. They were led in this case by the black-clad Florence Kelley, a guerrilla warrior in the urban jungle. Armed with the insights of socialism and endowed with the voice of an actress, Kelley was a lifelong battler for the welfare of women, children, blacks, and consumers. She later moved to the Henry Street Settlement in New York and served for three decades as general secretary of the National Consumers League. The pioneering work of Addams, Wald, and Kelley helped blaze the trail that many women—and some men—later followed into careers in urban reform and the new profession of social work. For these female reformers, and for many other women, the city offered a new kind of frontier opportunity.

More than a million women joined the work force in the single decade of the 1890s. Strict social codes prescribed which women might work and what jobs they might hold. Because employment for wives and mothers was considered taboo, the vast majority of working women were single. Their jobs depended on their race, ethnicity, and class. Black women had few opportunities beyond domestic service. White-collar jobs as social workers, secretaries, department store clerks, and telephone operators were largely reserved for native-born women. Immigrant women tended to cluster in particular industries, as Jewish women did in the garment trades. Although hours were often long, pay low, and advancement limited, a job still bought workingwomen some economic and social independence. After contributing a large share of their earnings to their families, many women still had enough money in their pocketbooks to enter a new urban world of sociability—excursions to amusement parks with friends on days off, Saturday night dances with the "fellas."

✵ Narrowing the Welcome Mat

Antiforeignism, or "nativism," earlier touched off by the Irish and German arrivals in the 1840s and 1850s, bared its ugly face in the 1880s with fresh ferocity. The New Immigrants had come for much the same reasons as the Old—to escape the poverty and squalor of Europe and to seek new opportunities in America. But "nativists" viewed the eastern and southern Europeans as culturally and religiously exotic hordes and often gave them a rude reception. The newest newcomers aroused widespread alarm. Their high birthrate, common among people with a low standard of living and sufficient youth and vigor to pull up stakes, raised worries that the original Anglo-Saxon stock would soon be outbred and outvoted. Still more horrifying was the

In response to nativists who condemned the New Immigrants as despicable human specimens threatening to drag down the American race, the Jewish immigrant playwright Israel Zangwill (1864–1926) celebrated the new superior American emerging out of what he called "the great melting pot" of European races:

❝America is God's crucible, the great melting pot, where all the races of Europe are melting and re-forming! . . . Germans and Frenchmen, Irishmen and Englishmen, Jews and Russians—into the Crucible with you all! God is making the American!❞

prospect that it would be mongrelized by a mixture of "inferior" southern European blood and that the fairer Anglo-Saxon types would disappear. One New England writer cried out in anguish,

> *O Liberty, white Goddess! is it well*
> *To leave the gates unguarded?*

Native-born Americans voiced additional fears. They blamed the immigrants for the degradation of urban government. Some trade unionists assailed the alien arrivals for their willingness to work for "starvation" wages that seemed to them like princely sums and for importing in their intellectual baggage such seemingly dangerous doctrines as socialism, communism, and anarchism. Many business leaders, who had welcomed the flood of cheap manual labor, began to fear that they had embraced a Frankenstein's monster.

Looking Backward Older immigrants, trying to keep their own humble arrival in America "in the shadows," sought to close the bridge that had carried them and their ancestors across the Atlantic.

"Looking Backward" by Joseph Keppler, 1893 Library of Congress

Antiforeign organizations, reminiscent of the "Know-Nothings" of antebellum days, were now revived in a different guise. Notorious among them was the American Protective Association (APA), which was created in 1887 and soon claimed a million members. In pursuing its nativist goals, the APA urged voting against Roman Catholic candidates for office and sponsored the publication of lustful fantasies about runaway nuns.

Organized labor was quick to throw its growing weight behind the move to choke off the rising tide of foreigners. Frequently used as strikebreakers, the wage-depressing immigrants were hard to unionize because of the language barrier. Labor leaders argued, not illogically, that if American industry was entitled to protection from foreign goods, American workers were entitled to protection from foreign laborers.

Congress finally nailed up partial bars against the inpouring immigrants. The first restrictive law, passed in 1882, banged the gate shut in the faces of paupers, criminals, and convicts, all of whom had to be returned at the expense of the greedy or careless shipper. Congress further responded to pained outcries

President Grover Cleveland (1837–1908) declared in 1897,

❝It is said . . . that the quality of recent immigration is undesirable. The time is quite within recent memory when the same thing was said of immigrants who, with their descendants, are now numbered among our best citizens.**❞**

from organized labor when in 1885 it prohibited the importation of foreign workers under contract—usually for substandard wages.

In addition to the first federal restrictions on immigration, the year 1882 brought forth a law to bar completely one ethnic group—the Chinese. Hitherto America, at least officially, had embraced the oppressed and underprivileged of all races and creeds. Hereafter the gates would be padlocked against defective undesirables—plus the Chinese.

In later years other federal laws lengthened the list of undesirables to include the insane, polygamists, prostitutes, alcoholics, anarchists, and people carrying contagious diseases. A proposed literacy test, long a favorite of nativists because it favored the Old Immigrants over the New, met vigorous opposition. It was not enacted until 1917, after three presidents had vetoed it on the grounds that literacy was more a measure of opportunity than of intelligence.

In 1886 the Statue of Liberty arose in New York harbor, a gift from the people of France. On its base were inscribed the words of Emma Lazarus:

> *Give me your tired, your poor*
> *Your huddled masses yearning to breathe free,*
> *The wretched refuse of your teeming shore.*

To many nativists, those noble words described only too accurately the "scum" washed up by the New Immigrant tides. Yet the uprooted immigrants, unlike "natives" lucky enough to have had parents who caught an earlier ship, became American citizens the hard way. They stepped off the boat, many of them full-grown and well muscled, ready to put their shoulders to the nation's industrial wheels. The Republic owes much to these latecomers—for their brawn, their brains, their courage, and the yeasty diversity they brought to American society.

✴ Churches Confront the Urban Challenge

The swelling size and changing character of the urban population posed sharp challenges to American

Lady Liberty Being Readied for Travel A centennial "birthday present" from the French people, the Statue of Liberty arrived from France in 1886.

Musee Carnavalet, Paris/Laurie Platt Winfrey, Inc.

Morning Service at Moody's Church, 1908 Thousands of Chicagoans found the gospel and a helping hand at evangelist Dwight Lyman Moody's church. Although Moody himself died in 1899, his successors continued to attract throngs of worshipers to his church, which could hold up to ten thousand people.

Chicago History Museum

churches, which, like other national institutions, had grown up in the country. Protestant churches, in particular, suffered heavily from the shift to the city, where many of their traditional doctrines and pastoral approaches seemed irrelevant. Some of the larger houses of worship, with their stained-glass windows and thundering pipe organs, were tending to become merely sacred diversions or amusements. Reflecting the wealth of their prosperous parishioners, many of the old-line churches were distressingly slow to raise their voices against social and economic vices. John D. Rockefeller was a pillar of the Baptist Church, J. Pierpont Morgan of the Episcopal Church. Trinity Episcopal Church in New York actually owned some of the city's worst slum property. Cynics remarked that the Episcopal Church had become "the Republican party at prayer." Some religious leaders began to worry that in the age-old struggle between God and the Devil, the Wicked One was registering dismaying gains. The mounting emphasis was on materialism; too many devotees worshiped at the altar of avarice. Money was the accepted measure of achievement, and the new gospel of wealth proclaimed that God caused the righteous to prosper.

Into this spreading moral vacuum stepped a new generation of **liberal Protestants**. With roots in the Unitarian revolt against orthodox Calvinism, liberal ideas came into the mainstream of American Protestantism between 1875 and 1925, despite frequent and bitter controversies with fundamentalists. Entrenched in the leadership and seminaries of the dominant denominations, liberal Protestants adapted religious ideas to modern culture, attempting to reconcile Christianity with new scientific and economic doctrines. They rejected biblical literalism, urging Christians to

view biblical stories as models for Christian behavior rather than as dogma. They stressed the ethical teachings of the Bible and allied themselves with the reform-oriented "social gospel" movement and urban revivalists like Dwight Lyman Moody, a former shoe salesman who captivated audiences with his message of forgiveness. Their optimistic trust in community fellowship and their focus on earthly salvation and personal growth attracted many followers. They helped Protestant Americans reconcile their religious faith with modern, cosmopolitan ways of thinking.

Simultaneously, the Roman Catholic and Jewish faiths were gaining enormous strength from the New Immigration. By 1900 Roman Catholics had become the largest single denomination, numbering nearly 9 million communicants. Cardinal James Gibbons (1834–1921), an urban Catholic leader devoted to American unity, was immensely popular with Roman Catholics and Protestants alike. Acquainted with every president from Johnson to Harding, he employed his liberal sympathies to assist the American labor movement.

By 1890 the variety-loving Americans could choose from 150 religious denominations, 2 of them brand-new. One was the band-playing Salvation Army, whose soldiers without swords invaded America from England in 1879 and established a beachhead on the country's street corners. Appealing frankly to the down-and-outers, the boldly named Salvation Army did much practical good, especially with free soup.

The other important new faith was the Church of Christ, Scientist (Christian Science), founded by Mary Baker Eddy in 1879 after she had suffered much ill health. Preaching that the true practice of Christianity heals sickness, she set forth her views in a book entitled *Science and Health with Key to the Scriptures* (1875), which sold an amazing 400,000 copies before her death. A fertile field for converts was found in America's hurried, nerve-racked, and urbanized civilization, to which Eddy held out the hope of relief from discords and diseases through prayer as taught by Christian Science. By the time she died in 1910, she had founded an influential church that embraced several hundred thousand devoted worshipers.

Urbanites also participated in a new kind of religious-affiliated organization, the Young Men's and Women's Christian Associations. The YMCA and the YWCA, established in the United States before the Civil War, grew by leaps and bounds. Combining physical and other kinds of education with religious instruction, the "Y's" appeared in virtually every major American city by the end of the nineteenth century.

✵ Darwin Disrupts the Churches

The old-time religion received many blows from modern trends, including a booming sale of books on comparative religion and on historical criticism as applied to the Bible. Most unsettling of all were the writings of the English naturalist Charles Darwin. In lucid prose he set forth the sensational theory that higher forms of life had slowly evolved from lower forms, through a process of random biological mutation and adaptation.

Though not the first scientist to propose an evolutionary hypothesis, Darwin broke new ground with his idea of "natural selection." Nature, in his view, blindly selected organisms for survival or death based on random, inheritable variations that they happened to possess. Some traits conferred advantages in the struggle for life, and hence better odds of passing them along to offspring. By providing a material explanation for the evolutionary process, Darwin's theory explicitly rejected the "dogma of special creations," which ascribed the design of each fixed species to divine agency.

Darwin's radical ideas evoked the wrath of scientists and laymen alike. Many zoologists, like Harvard's Louis Agassiz, held fast to the old doctrine of "special creations." By 1875, however, the majority of scientists in America and elsewhere had embraced the theory of organic evolution, though not all endorsed natural selection as its agent. Many preferred an alternative mechanism proposed earlier by the French biologist Jean-Baptiste Lamarck, who argued that traits acquired during the course of an individual's life could shape the future genetic development of a species. Lamarckians briefly tamed the unsettling Darwinian view of chance mutation and competitive inheritance, but Darwin's version would become scientific orthodoxy by the 1920s.

Clergymen and theologians responded to Darwin's theory in several ways. At first most believers joined

As a student at Harvard Medical School, William James (1842-1910) was influenced by Darwinian science. He reviewed Darwin's theory in his first published article in 1865:

❝A doctrine like that of Transmutation of Species . . . cannot but be treated with some respect; and when we find that such naturalists, . . . many of whom but a few days ago were publicly opposing it, are now coming round, one by one, to espouse it, we may well doubt whether it may not be destined eventually to prevail.❞

scientists in rejecting his ideas outright. After 1875, by which time most natural scientists had embraced evolution, the religious community split into two camps. A conservative minority stood firmly behind the Scripture as the infallible Word of God, and they condemned what they thought was the "bestial hypothesis" of the Darwinians. Their rejection of scientific consensus spawned a muscular view of biblical authority that eventually gave rise to fundamentalism in the twentieth century.

Most religious thinkers parted company with the conservatives and flatly refused to accept the Bible in its entirety as either history or science. These "accommodationists" feared that hostility toward evolution would alienate educated believers. Over time an increasing number of liberal thinkers were able to reconcile Darwinism with Christianity. They heralded the revolutionary theory as a newer and grander revelation of the ways of the Almighty. As one commentator observed,

> *Some call it Evolution,*
> *And others call it God.*

Darwinism undoubtedly did much to loosen religious moorings and to promote skepticism among the gospel-glutted. While the liberal efforts at compromise did succeed in keeping many Americans in the pews, those compromises also tended to relegate religious teaching to matters of personal faith, private conduct, and family life. As science began to explain more of the external world, commentators on nature and society increasingly refrained from adding religious perspectives to the discussion.

✵ The Lust for Learning

Public education continued its upward climb. The ideal of tax-supported elementary schools, adopted on a nationwide basis before the Civil War, was still gathering strength. Americans were accepting the truism that a free government cannot function successfully if the people are shackled by ignorance. Beginning about 1870, more and more states were making at least a grade-school education compulsory, and this gain, incidentally, helped check the frightful abuses of child labor.

Spectacular indeed was the spread of high schools, especially by the 1880s and 1890s. Before the Civil War, private academies at the secondary level were common, and tax-supported high schools were rare, numbering only a few hundred. But the concept that a high-school education, as well as a grade-school education, was the birthright of every citizen was now gaining impressive support. By 1900 there were some six thousand high schools. In addition, free textbooks were being provided in increasing quantities by the taxpayers of the states during the last two decades of the century.

Other trends were noteworthy. Teacher-training schools, then called "normal schools," experienced a striking expansion after the Civil War. In 1860 there were only twelve of them, in 1910 over three hundred. Kindergartens, earlier borrowed from Germany, also began to gain strong support. The New Immigration in the 1880s and 1890s brought vast new strength to private Catholic parochial schools, which were fast becoming a major pillar of the nation's educational structure.

Public schools, though showering benefits on children, excluded millions of adults. This deficiency was partially remedied by the Chautauqua movement, a successor to the lyceums, which was launched in 1874 on the shores of Lake Chautauqua, in New York. The organizers achieved gratifying success through nationwide public lectures, often held in tents and featuring well-known speakers, including the witty Mark Twain. In addition, there were extensive Chautauqua courses of home study, for which 100,000 people enrolled in 1892 alone.

Crowded cities, despite their cancers, generally provided better educational facilities than the old one-room, one-teacher red schoolhouse. The success of the public schools is confirmed by the falling of the illiteracy rate from 20 percent in 1870 to 10.7 percent in 1900. Americans were developing a profound faith, often misplaced, in formal education as the sovereign remedy for their ills.

✷ Booker T. Washington and Education for Black People

War-torn and impoverished, the South lagged far behind other regions in public education, and African Americans suffered most severely. A staggering 44

percent of nonwhites were illiterate in 1900. Some help came from northern philanthropists, but the foremost champion of black education was an ex-slave, Booker T. Washington. His classic autobiography, *Up from Slavery* (1900), tells how he slept under a board sidewalk to save pennies for his schooling. Called in 1881 to head the black normal and industrial school at Tuskegee, Alabama, he began with forty students in a tumbledown shanty. Undaunted, he taught black students useful trades so that they could gain self-respect and economic security. Washington's self-help approach to solving the nation's racial problems was labeled "accommodationist" because it stopped short of directly challenging white supremacy. Recognizing the depths of southern white racism, Washington avoided the issue of *social* equality. Instead he grudgingly acquiesced in segregation in return for the right to develop—however modestly and painstakingly—the economic and educational resources of the black community. Economic independence would ultimately be the ticket, Washington believed, to black political and civil rights.

Washington's commitment to training young blacks in agriculture and the trades guided the curriculum

Booker T. Washington (1856–1915) In a famous speech in New Orleans in 1895, Washington grudgingly acquiesced in social separateness for blacks. On that occasion, he told his largely white audience, "In all things that are purely social, we can be as separate as the fingers, yet one as the hand in all things essential to mutual progress."

Tuskegee University Archives

at **Tuskegee Institute** and made it an ideal place for slave-born George Washington Carver to teach and research. After Carver joined the faculty in 1896, he became an internationally famous agricultural chemist who provided a much-needed boost to the southern economy by discovering hundreds of new uses for the lowly peanut (shampoo, axle grease), sweet potato (vinegar), and soybean (paint).

Other black leaders, notably Dr. W. E. B. Du Bois, assailed Booker T. Washington as an "Uncle Tom" who was condemning their race to manual labor and perpetual inferiority. Born in Massachusetts, Du Bois was a mixture of African, French, Dutch, and Indian blood ("Thank God, no Anglo-Saxon," he would add). After a determined struggle, he earned a Ph.D. at Harvard, the first of his race to achieve that goal. ("The honor, I assure you, was Harvard's," he said.) He demanded complete equality for blacks, social as well as economic, and helped found the National Association for the Advancement of Colored People (NAACP) in 1909. Rejecting Washington's gradualism and separatism, he argued that the "talented tenth" of the black community should be given full and immediate access to the mainstream of American life. An exceptionally skilled historian, sociologist, and poet, he died as a self-exile in Africa in 1963,

W. E. B. Du Bois (1868–1963) In 1961, at the end of a long lifetime of struggle for racial justice in the United States, Du Bois renounced his American citizenship at the age of ninety-three and took up residence in the newly independent African state of Ghana.

W. E. B. Du Bois (1868–1963) wrote in his 1903 classic, The Souls of Black Folk,

❝It is a peculiar sensation, this double consciousness, this sense of always looking at one's self through the eyes of others, of measuring one's self through the eyes of others. . . . One ever feels his two-ness—an American, a Negro; two souls, two thoughts, two unreconciled strivings; two warring ideals in one dark body, whose dogged strength alone keeps it from being torn asunder.❞

at the age of ninety-five. Many of Du Bois's differences with Washington reflected the contrasting life experiences of southern and northern blacks.

✴ The Hallowed Halls of Ivy

Colleges and universities also shot up like lusty young saplings in the decades after the Civil War. A college education increasingly seemed indispensable in the scramble for the golden apple of success (see Table 25.1). Even women and African Americans were finding new opportunities for higher education. Women's colleges such as Vassar were gaining ground, and universities open to both genders were blossoming, notably in the Midwest. By 1880 every third college graduate was a woman. By the turn of the century, the black institutes and academies planted during Reconstruction had blossomed into a crop of southern black colleges. Howard University in Washington, D.C., Hampton Institute in Virginia, Atlanta University, and numerous others nurtured higher education for blacks until the civil rights movement of the 1960s made widespread attendance at white institutions possible.

The truly phenomenal growth of higher education owed much to the Morrill Act of 1862. This enlightened law provided a generous grant of public lands to the states for support of education. **Land-grant colleges**, most of which became state universities, in turn bound themselves to provide certain services, such as military training. The Hatch Act of 1887, extending the Morrill Act, provided federal funds for the establishment of agricultural experiment stations in connection with the land-grant colleges. These two pieces of legislation spawned over a hundred colleges and universities, including such institutions as the University of California (1868), the Ohio State University (1870), and Texas A&M (1876).

Private philanthropy richly supplemented government grants to higher education. Many of the new

TABLE 25.1 Educational Levels, 1870–2010

Year	Number Graduating from High School	Number Graduating from College	Median Number of School Years Completed*	High School Graduates as a Percentage of 17-Year-Old Population
1870	16,000	9,371		2.0%
1880	24,000	12,896		2.5%
1890	44,000	15,539		3.5%
1900	95,000	27,410		6.4%
1910	156,000	37,199	8.1†	8.8%
1920	311,000	48,622	8.2†	16.8%
1930	667,000	122,484	8.4†	29.0%
1940	1,221,000	186,500	8.6	50.8%
1950	1,199,700	432,058	9.3	59.0%
1960	1,858,000	392,440	10.5	69.5%
1970	2,889,000	792,316	12.2	76.9%
1980	3,043,000	929,417	12.5	71.4%
1990	2,574,000	1,051,344	12.7	73.4%
2000	2,833,000	1,237,875	NA	69.8%
2005	3,109,000	1,439,264	NA	79.5%
2010 (est.)	3,295,000	1,648,000	NA	82.4%

*People twenty-five years and over.

†1910–1930 based on retrogressions of 1940 data; 1940 was the first year measured. (Source: Folger and Nam, *Education of the American Population*, a 1960 Census Monograph.)

(Sources: *Digest of Education Statistics*, 1992, 2009, a publication of the National Center for Education Statistics; *Statistical Abstract of the United States*, relevant years.)

industrial millionaires, developing tender social consciences, donated immense fortunes to educational enterprises. A philanthropist was cynically described as "one who steals privately and gives publicly." In the twenty years from 1878 to 1898, these money barons gave away about $150 million. Noteworthy among the new private universities of high quality were Cornell (1865) and Leland Stanford Junior (1891), the latter founded in memory of the deceased fifteen-year-old only child of a builder of the Central Pacific Railroad.

Stanford University Under Construction, Late Nineteenth Century

Courtesy Stanford University Archives

The University of Chicago, opened in 1892, speedily forged into a front-rank position, owing largely to the lubricant of John D. Rockefeller's oil millions. Rockefeller died at ninety-seven, after having given some $550 million for philanthropic purposes.

Significant also was the sharp increase in professional and technical schools, where modern laboratories were replacing the solo experiments performed by instructors in front of their classes. Towering among the specialized institutions was Johns Hopkins University, opened in 1876, which maintained the nation's first high-grade graduate school. Several generations of American scholars, repelled by snobbish English cousins and attracted by painstaking Continental methods, had attended German universities. Johns Hopkins ably carried on the Germanic tradition of profusely footnoted tomes. Reputable scholars no longer had to go abroad for a gilt-edged graduate degree. Dr. Woodrow Wilson, among others, received his Ph.D. from Johns Hopkins.

✦ The March of the Mind

Homegrown influences shaped the modern American university as much as German models. Antebellum colleges had stressed the "unity of truth," or the idea that knowledge and morality existed in a single system. Religious instruction in moral philosophy and natural theology served as pillars of the old classical curriculum. In the wake of the Darwinian challenge, when religion and science seemed less compatible, university reformers struggled to reconcile scientific education and religion to preserve the unity of moral and intellectual purpose. When that effort faltered, university educators abandoned moral instruction and divorced "facts" from "values."

Other pressures also helped doom the traditional curriculum. The new industrialization brought insistent demands for "practical" courses and specialized vocational training in the sciences. The elective system, where students selected courses, was gaining popularity. Reformers also emphasized fields of concentration to prepare students for entry into a profession. Specialization, not synthesis, became the primary goal of a university education. The reform spirit received a powerful boost in the 1870s when Dr. Charles W. Eliot, a vigorous young chemist, became president of Harvard College and embarked upon a lengthy career of educational statesmanship. As a sign of the secularizing times, Eliot changed Harvard's motto from *Christo et Ecclesiae* (For Christ and Church) to *Veritas* (Truth).

Medical schools and medical science after the Civil War were prospering. Despite the enormous sale of patent medicines and so-called Indian remedies—"good for man or beast"—the new scientific gains were reflected in improved public health. Revolutionary discoveries abroad, such as those of the French scientist Louis Pasteur and the English physician Joseph Lister, left their imprint on America.* The popularity of heavy whiskers waned as the century ended; such hairy adornments were now coming to be regarded as germ traps. As a result of new health-promoting precautions, including campaigns against public spitting, life expectancy at birth was measurably increased.

One of America's most brilliant intellectuals, the slight and sickly William James (1842–1910), served for thirty-five years on the Harvard faculty. Through his numerous writings, he made a deep mark on many fields. His *Principles of Psychology* (1890) helped to establish the modern discipline of behavioral psychology. In *The Will to Believe* (1897) and *Varieties of Religious Experience* (1902), he explored the philosophy and psychology of religion. In his most famous work, *Pragmatism* (1907), he pronounced America's greatest contribution to the history of philosophy the concept of **pragmatism**—that the truth of an idea was to be tested, above all, by its practical consequences (see "Makers of America: Pioneering Pragmatists," pp. 560–561).

✦ The Appeal of the Press

Books continued to be a major source of edification and enjoyment, for both juveniles and adults. Best sellers of the 1880s were generally old favorites like *David Copperfield* and *Ivanhoe*.

Well-stocked public libraries—the poor person's university—were making encouraging progress, especially in Boston and New York. The magnificent Library of Congress building, which opened its doors in 1897, provided thirteen acres of floor space in the largest and costliest edifice of its kind in the world. A new era was inaugurated by the generous gifts of Andrew Carnegie. This openhanded Scotsman, book-starved in his youth, contributed $60 million for the construction of nearly 1,700 public libraries all over the country, with an additional 750 scattered around the English-speaking world from Great Britain to New Zealand. By 1900 there were about nine thousand free circulating libraries in America, each with at least three hundred books. Roaring newspaper presses, spurred by the invention of the Linotype in 1885, more than kept pace with the demands of a word-hungry public. But the heavy investment in machinery and plant was accompanied by a growing fear of offending advertisers and subscribers. Bare-knuckle editorials were, to an increasing

---

*From Pasteur came the word *pasteurize*; from Lister came *Listerine*.

The "Penny Press" The *Chicago Daily News* was but one of several cheap, mass-circulation newspapers that flourished in the new urban environment of Gilded Age America.

Chicago History Museum

degree, being supplanted by feature articles and non-controversial syndicated material. The day of slashing journalistic giants like Horace Greeley was passing.

Sensationalism, at the same time, was capturing the public taste. The semiliterate immigrants, combined with strap-hanging urban commuters, created a profitable market for news that was simply and punchily written. Sex, scandal, and other human-interest stories burst into the headlines, as a vulgarization of the press accompanied the growth of circulation. Critics now complained in vain of these "presstitutes."

Two new journalistic tycoons emerged. Joseph Pulitzer, Hungarian-born and near-blind, was a leader in the techniques of sensationalism through his ownership of the *St. Louis Post-Dispatch* and *New York World*. His use of colored comic supplements featuring the "Yellow Kid" gave the name **yellow journalism** to his lurid sheets. A close and ruthless competitor was the youthful William Randolph Hearst, who had been expelled from Harvard College for a crude prank. Able to draw on his California father's mining millions, he ultimately built a powerful chain of newspapers, beginning with the *San Francisco Examiner* in 1887.

Unfortunately, the overall influence of Pulitzer and Hearst was not altogether wholesome. Although both championed many worthy causes, both prostituted the press in their struggle for increased circulation; both "stooped, snooped, and scooped to conquer." Their flair for scandal and sensational rumor was happily somewhat offset by the introduction of syndicated material and by the strengthening of the news-gathering Associated Press, which had been founded in the 1840s.

✦ Apostles of Reform

Magazines partially satisfied the public appetite for good reading, notably old East Coast standbys like *Harper's*, the *Atlantic Monthly*, and *Scribner's Monthly* and new western entrants such as the California-based *Overland Monthly*. Possibly the most influential journal of all was the liberal and highly intellectual New York *Nation*, which was read largely by professors, preachers, and publicists as "the weekly Day of Judgment." Launched in 1865 by the Irish-born Edwin L. Godkin, a merciless critic, it crusaded militantly for civil-service reform, honesty in government, and a moderate tariff. The *Nation* attained only a modest circulation—about ten thousand in the nineteenth century—but Godkin believed that if he could reach the right ten thousand leaders, his ideas through them might reach tens of millions.

Another journalist-author, Henry George, was an original thinker who left an enduring mark. Poor in formal schooling, he was rich in idealism and in the milk of human kindness. After seeing poverty at its worst in India and land-grabbing at its greediest in California, he took pen in hand. His classic treatise *Progress and Poverty* undertook to solve "the great enigma of our times"—"the association of progress with poverty." According to George, the pressure of a growing population on a fixed supply of land unjustifiably pushed up property values, showering unearned profits on owners

Henry George (1839–1897) wrote in Progress and Poverty (1879),

❝Our boasted freedom necessarily involves slavery, so long as we recognize private property in land. Until that is abolished, Declarations of Independence and Acts of Emancipation are in vain. So long as one man can claim the exclusive ownership of the land from which other men must live, slavery will exist, and as material progresses on, must grow and deepen!❞

of land. A single 100 percent tax on those windfall profits would eliminate unfair inequalities and stimulate economic growth.

George soon became a most controversial figure. His single-tax idea was so horrifying to the propertied classes that his manuscript was rejected by numerous publishers. Finally brought out in 1879, the book gradually broke into the best-seller lists and ultimately sold some 3 million copies. George also lectured widely in America and Britain, where he left an indelible mark on English Fabian socialism. George's proposals resounded for decades. As late as 1903, a young female follower applied for a patent for "The Landlord's Game," which bore a striking resemblance to Parker Brothers' later Monopoly, released in 1935. In the earlier game, the point was not to amass property, but to expose the unfair advantage enjoyed by the landlord and to show "how the single tax would discourage speculation."

Edward Bellamy, a quiet Massachusetts Yankee, was another journalist-reformer of remarkable power. In 1888 he published a socialistic novel, *Looking Backward*, in which the hero, falling into a hypnotic sleep, awakens in the year 2000. He "looks backward" and finds that the social and economic injustices of 1887 have melted away under an idyllic government, which has nationalized big business to serve the public interest. To a nation already alarmed by the trust evil, the book had a magnetic appeal and sold over a million copies. Scores of Bellamy Clubs sprang up to discuss this mild utopian socialism, and they heavily influenced American reform movements near the end of the century.

✷ The New Morality

Like other radical reformers, Victoria Woodhull shook the pillars of conventional morality when she publicly proclaimed her belief in free love in 1871. Woodhull was a beautiful and eloquent divorcée, sometime stockbroker, and tireless feminist propagandist. Together with her sister, Tennessee Claflin, she published a far-out periodical, *Woodhull and Claflin's Weekly*. The sisters again shocked "respectable" society in 1872 when their journal struck a blow for the new morality by charging that Henry Ward Beecher, the most famous preacher of his day, had for years been carrying on an adulterous affair.

Pure-minded Americans sternly resisted these affronts to their moral principles. Their foremost champion was a portly crusader, Anthony Comstock, who made lifelong war on the "immoral." Armed after 1873 with a federal statute—the notorious "Comstock Law"—this self-appointed defender of sexual purity boasted that he had confiscated no fewer than 202,679 "obscene pictures and photos"; 4,185 "boxes of pills,

powders, etc., used by abortionists"; and 26 "obscene pictures, framed on walls of saloons." His proud claim was that he had driven at least fifteen people to suicide.

The antics of the Woodhull sisters and Comstock exposed to daylight the battle in late-nineteenth-century America over sexual attitudes and the place of women. Switchboards and typewriters in the booming cities became increasingly the tools of women's independence. Young workingwomen headed to dance halls and nightclubs when the day was done, enjoying a new sense of freedom in the cities. This "new morality" began to be reflected in soaring divorce rates, the spreading practice of birth control, and increasingly frank discussion of sexual topics. By 1913, said one popular magazine, the chimes had struck "sex o'clock in America."

The Granger Collection

"Get Thee Behind Me, (Mrs) Satan!" A colorful and charismatic figure, Victoria Claflin Woodhull was the first woman to run for the presidency, in 1872. That same year, noted cartoonist Thomas Nast viciously attacked her for advocating free love.

ineteenth-century Americans, among them proper Bostonians of an intellectual bent, had a habit of joining clubs. Luminaries such as the philosopher Ralph Waldo Emerson, the novelist Nathaniel Hawthorne, and the natural scientist Louis Agassiz regularly met for sumptuous food and social conversation at the Saturday Club. Younger members of Boston's polite society mimicked their elders at a junior edition known simply as "The Club." In a world without academic conferences or professional forums, serious intellectual conversations in the United States tended to occur at private philosophical and literary societies, or simply at regular gatherings in a scholar's home study. One club, founded in Cambridge, Massachusetts, in January 1872, lasted only nine months, but its members left a lasting mark on American intellectual life.

"It was in the earliest Seventies that a knot of us young men in Old Cambridge, calling ourselves, half-ironically, half-defiantly, 'The Metaphysical Club,' ... used to meet, sometimes in my study, sometimes in that of William James," recalled Charles Sanders Peirce in 1907. Peirce's Metaphysical Club was hardly a success by most conventional standards. It kept no records of its proceedings. Its members missed meetings and (except for Peirce) made no mention of its existence in their letters, diaries, or writings. Some of their relatives despised it. A young Henry James (novelist brother of William) griped, "It gives me a headache merely to know of it." But it did boast an impressive roster of

members, including three young men in their early thirties who eventually became foundational figures in their respective fields: the logician and scientist Peirce; the medical doctor, psychologist, and philosopher William James; and the jurist and legal scholar Oliver Wendell Holmes, Jr. With their Harvard friend and fellow philosopher Chauncey Wright, they assembled frequently in their homes and, usually over a bottle of rum, argued over the meaning of life and the nature of the universe. Joined later by the philosophers John Dewey and George Herbert Mead, these thinkers gave earliest expression to a distinctive American philosophy known as "pragmatism."

Pragmatism sprouted in the fertile intellectual soil of the late-nineteenth-century Atlantic world. The ground had already been tilled by the naturalist Charles Darwin, whose revolutionary contributions to evolutionary science greatly influenced the early pragmatists. In place of fixed species, Darwin had posited a natural world of chance, change, and contingency. Thinkers like Peirce and James applied Darwin's insights from biology to fields such as philosophy, logic, and psychology. To them old ways of thinking that assumed absolute truths, sanctioned by religious teaching or idealist philosophy, no longer made sense in the Darwinian age. Instead they welcomed the provisional, fallible nature of experimental knowledge. As James put it, pragmatism "means the open air and possibilities of nature, as against dogma, artificiality,

William James (1842–1910), Physician, Psychologist, and Philosopher Granger Collection

Charles Sanders Peirce (1839–1914), Mathematician and Logician © Bettmann/Corbis

Oliver Wendell Holmes, Jr. (1841–1935), Supreme Court Justice and Scholar Granger Collection

John Dewey (1859–1952), Educator and Philosopher Granger Collection

and the pretence of finality in truth." In short, they embraced uncertainty and developed an entire philosophical system around it. The true value of an idea, said the pragmatists, lay in its ability to solve problems.

While all the pragmatists were far-ranging in their intellectual pursuits, Dewey demonstrated his faith in the unity of theory and practice by becoming a public intellectual and social activist. He founded the Laboratory School at the University of Chicago in 1896 to experiment with an educational philosophy rooted in "learning by doing." He promoted an ethical vision of American society by linking arms with progressive reformers in the 1910s, and he championed democratic ideals by promoting third-party politics in the 1930s and anti-Stalinist agitation in the 1940s. Throughout a prolific career that spanned three generations, Dewey continually stressed the positive virtues of experience, cooperation, and democracy, and he urged philosophers to abandon futile debates about knowledge in favor of tackling the real "problems of men."

Holmes, as a justice on the Massachusetts Supreme Judicial Court for twenty years and on the U.S. Supreme Court for another three decades, similarly followed pragmatism's injunction to evaluate the effects of ideas rather than simply adopt prescriptions from the past. From his personal experience fighting in the Civil War (where he nearly died from his wounds), Holmes acquired a bleak skepticism toward jurisprudence.

While on the bench, he became renowned for his masterfully crafted dissents, most famously asserting the principle of "judicial deference" to legislatures in *Lochner* v. *New York* (1905) and protecting freedom of speech, even freedom for the "opinions that we loathe," in *Abrams* v. *United States* (1919).

Many commentators on pragmatism have considered it the quintessential expression of American practicality. To its critics pragmatism symbolizes the vulgar, can-do attitude and narrow anti-intellectualism of the American middle class. To its celebrants pragmatism offers a needed correction to conventional philosophy by accepting the uncertain and provisional nature of knowledge, reconciling science and culture, and promoting an ethical ideal of democracy. Pragmatism went out of fashion during the Cold War era (ca. 1945–1990), when Americans believed in moral certainties such as the superiority of the United States and the value-free empiricism of science. But it has enjoyed a striking renewal in recent years. As new kinds of uncertainty ranging from terrorist violence to scientific dilemmas raise fresh challenges in the twenty-first century, many modern American intellectuals are harking back to pragmatism. First formulated in the cozy confines of Cambridge's Metaphysical Club more than a century ago, pragmatism offers today's thinkers a philosophy of life built on experimentation, ethical commitment, and open-ended democratic debate.

✦ Families and Women in the City

The new urban environment was hard on families. Paradoxically, the crowded cities were emotionally isolating places. Urban families had to go it alone, separated from clan, kin, and village. As families increasingly became the virtually exclusive arena for intimate companionship and for emotional and psychological satisfaction, they were subjected to unprecedented stress. Many families cracked under the strain. The urban era launched the era of divorce. From the late nineteenth century dates the beginning of the "divorce revolution" that transformed the United States' social landscape in the twentieth century (see Table 25.2).

Urban life also dictated changes in work habits and even in family size. Not only fathers but mothers and even children as young as ten years old often worked, and usually in widely scattered locations. On the farm having many children meant having more hands to help with hoeing and harvesting; but in the city more children meant more mouths to feed, more crowding in sardine-tin tenements, and more human baggage to carry in the uphill struggle for social mobility. Not surprisingly, birthrates were still dropping and family size continued to shrink as the nineteenth century lengthened. Marriages were being delayed, and more couples learned the techniques of birth control. The decline in

In 1906 progressive reformer Jane Addams (1860–1935) argued that granting women the vote would improve the social and political condition of American cities:

"City housekeeping has failed partly because women, the traditional housekeepers, have not been consulted as to its multiform activities. The men have been carelessly indifferent to much of the civic housekeeping, as they have been indifferent to the details of the household. . . . City government demands the help of minds accustomed to detail and a variety of work, to a sense of obligation to the health and welfare of young children, and to a responsibility for the cleanliness and comfort of other people."

family size in fact affected rural Americans as well as urban dwellers, and old-stock "natives" as well as New Immigrants. Women were growing more independent in the urban environment, and in 1898 they heard the voice of a major feminist prophet, Charlotte Perkins Gilman. In that year the freethinking and original-minded Gilman published *Women and Economics*, a classic of feminist literature. A distant relative of Harriet Beecher Stowe and Catharine Beecher, Gilman displayed the restless temperament and reforming zeal characteristic of the remarkable Beecher clan. Strikingly handsome, she shunned traditional feminine frills and instead devoted herself to a vigorous regimen of physical exercise and philosophical meditation.

In her masterwork of 1898, Gilman called on women to abandon their dependent status and contribute to the larger life of the community through productive involvement in the economy. Rejecting all claims that biology gave women a fundamentally different character from men, she argued that "our highly specialized motherhood is not so advantageous as believed." She advocated centralized nurseries and cooperative kitchens to facilitate women's participation in the work force—anticipating by more than half a century the day-care centers and convenience-food services of a later day.

Fiery feminists also continued to insist on the ballot. They had been demanding the vote since before the Civil War, but many high-minded female reformers had temporarily shelved the cause of women to battle for the rights of blacks. In 1890 militant suffragists formed the **National American Woman Suffrage Association (NAWSA)**. Its founders included aging pioneers like Elizabeth Cady Stanton, who had helped

TABLE 25.2 Marriages and Divorces, 1890–2008*			
Year	Marriages	Divorces	Ratio of Divorces to Marriages
1890	570,000	33,461	1:17
1900	709,000	55,751	1:12
1910	948,166	83,045	1:11
1920	1,274,476	170,505	1:7
1930	1,126,856	195,961	1:5
1940	1,595,879	264,000	1:6
1950	1,667,231	385,144	1:4.3
1960	1,523,381	393,000	1:3.8
1970	2,159,000	708,000	1:3
1980	2,390,000	1,189,000	1:2
1990	2,443,000	1,182,000	1:2
2000	2,329,000	NA	NA
2008	2,017,000	NA	NA

*Divorce data have not been collected by the federal government since 1998.

(Sources: *Statistical Abstract of the United States*, relevant years; National Center for Health Statistics, *National Vital Statistics Report*, relevant years.)

MAP 25.2 Woman Suffrage Before the Nineteenth Amendment Dates show when a state or territory adopted woman suffrage. Note the concentration of woman-suffrage states in the West. © Cengage Learning

Full voting rights for women with effective date

Women voting in primaries

Women voting in presidential elections

No voting by women

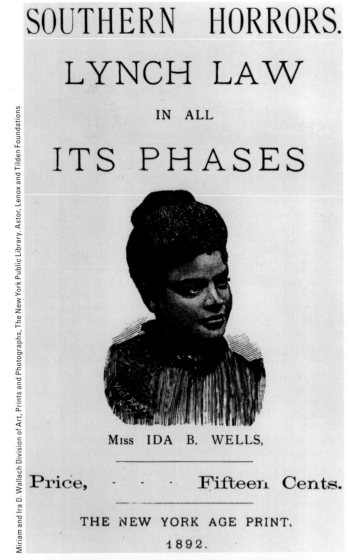

Ida B. Wells (1862–1931) Ida B. Wells courageously and tirelessly crusaded against the lynching of African-Americans. Her sensational pamphlet of 1892 summoned blacks to defend themselves against white violence, declaring that "a Winchester rifle should have a place of honor in every black home."

organize the first women's rights convention in 1848, and her long-time comrade Susan B. Anthony, the radical Quaker spitfire who had courted jail by trying to cast a ballot in the 1872 presidential election.

By 1900 a new generation of women had taken command of the suffrage battle. Their most effective leader was Carrie Chapman Catt, a pragmatic and businesslike reformer of relentless dedication. Significantly, under Catt the suffragists deemphasized the argument that women deserved the vote as a matter of right, because they were in all respects the equals of men. Instead Catt stressed the desirability of giving women

the vote if they were to continue to discharge their traditional duties as homemakers and mothers in the increasingly public world of the city. Women had special responsibility for the health of the family and the education of children, the argument ran. On the farm, women could discharge these responsibilities in the separate sphere of the isolated homestead. But in the city, they needed a voice on boards of public health, police commissions, and school boards.

By thus linking the ballot to a traditional definition of women's role, suffragists registered encouraging gains as the new century opened, despite continuing showers of rotten eggs and the jeers of male critics who insisted that women were made for loving, not for voting. Women were increasingly permitted to vote in local elections, particularly on issues related to the schools. Wyoming Territory—later called "the Equality State"—granted the first unrestricted suffrage to women in 1869. Many western states soon followed Wyoming's example (see Map 25.2). Paralleling these triumphs, most of the states by 1890 had passed laws to permit wives to own or control their property after marriage. City life also fostered the growth of a spate of women's organizations, including the General Federation of Women's Clubs, which counted some 200,000 members in 1900. Meanwhile, in 1893 New Zealand became the first nation to grant women equal suffrage rights, further inspiring American reformers.

The reborn suffrage movement and other women's organizations largely excluded black women from their ranks. Fearful that an integrated campaign would compromise its efforts to get the vote, the National American Woman Suffrage Association limited membership to whites. Black women, however, created their own associations. Journalist and teacher Ida B. Wells inspired black women to mount a nationwide anti-lynching crusade. She also helped launch the black women's club movement, which culminated in the establishment of the National Association of Colored Women in 1896.

✴ Prohibiting Alcohol and Promoting Reform

Alarming gains by Demon Rum spurred the temperance reformers to redoubled zeal. Especially obnoxious to them was the shutter-doored corner saloon, appropriately called "the poor man's club." The barroom helped keep both him and his family poor. Liquor consumption had increased during the nerve-racking days of the Civil War, and immigrant groups, accustomed to alcohol in the Old Country, were hostile to restraints. Whiskey-loving foreigners in Boston would rudely hiss temperance lecturers. Many tipplers charged, with some accuracy, that temperance reform amounted to a middle-class assault on working-class lifestyles.

The National Prohibition party, organized in 1869, polled a sprinkling of votes in some of the ensuing presidential elections. Among the favorite songs of these sober souls were "I'll Marry No Man If He Drinks," "Vote Down the Vile Traffic," and "The Drunkard's Doom." Typical was this:

> Now, all young men, a warning take,
> And shun the poisoned bowl;
> 'Twill lead you down to hell's dark gate,
> And ruin your own soul.

Militant women entered the alcoholic arena, notably when the **Woman's Christian Temperance Union (WCTU)** was organized in 1874. The white ribbon was its symbol of purity; the saintly Frances E. Willard—also a champion of planned parenthood—was its leading spirit. Less saintly was the muscular and mentally deranged "Kansas Cyclone," Carrie A. Nation, whose first husband had died of alcoholism. With her hatchet she boldly smashed saloon bottles and bars, and her "hatchetations" brought considerable disrepute to the prohibition movement because of the violence of her one-woman crusade.

But rum was now on the run. The potent Anti-Saloon League was formed in 1893, with its members singing "The Saloon Must Go" and "Vote for Cold Water, Boys." Female supporters sang "The Lips That Touch Liquor Must Never Touch Mine." Statewide prohibition,

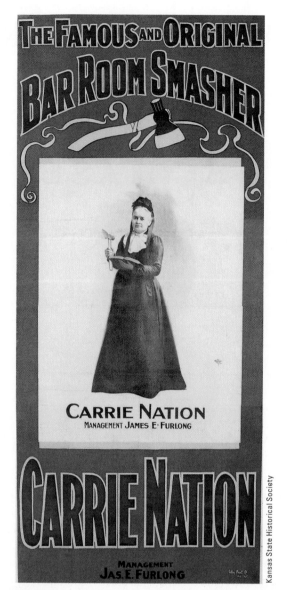

Carrie Nation Advertised as a Lecturer   Nation took her antidrink crusade to several universities, including Harvard and Yale, which she denounced as "hellholes." Predictably, the students greeted her with wild burlesque. "All Nations Welcome but Carrie" became a standard saying in saloons throughout the land.

which had made surprising gains in Maine and elsewhere before the Civil War, was sweeping new states into the "dry" column. The great triumph—but only a temporary one—came in 1919, when the national prohibition amendment (Eighteenth) was attached to the Constitution.

Banners of other social crusaders were aloft. The American Society for the Prevention of Cruelty to Animals (ASPCA) was created in 1866 after its founder had witnessed brutality to horses in Russia. The American Red Cross was launched in 1881, with the dynamic and

Anoka County Historical Society

diminutive five-foot-tall Clara Barton, the "angel" of Civil War battlefields, at the helm.

✹ Postwar Popular Fiction

Not all social activity proved so serious. Post–Civil War Americans devoured millions of "dime novels," usually depicting the wilds of the woolly West. Paint-bedaubed Indians and quick-triggered gunmen like "Deadwood Dick" shot off vast quantities of powder, and virtue invariably triumphed. These lurid "paperbacks" were frowned upon by parents, but goggle-eyed youths read them in haylofts or in schools behind the broad covers of geography books. The king of the dime novelists was Harlan P. Halsey, who made a fortune by dashing off about 650 potboilers, often one in a day.

General Lew Wallace—lawyer, soldier, and author— was a colorful figure. Having fought with distinction in the Civil War, he sought to combat the prevailing wave of Darwinian skepticism with his novel *Ben-Hur: A Tale of the Christ* (1880). A phenomenal success, the book sold an estimated 2 million copies in many languages, including Arabic and Chinese, and later appeared on stage and screen. It was the *Uncle Tom's Cabin* of the anti-Darwinists, who found in it support for the Holy Scriptures.

An even more popular writer was Horatio Alger, a Puritan-reared New Englander, who in 1866 forsook the pulpit for the pen. "Holy Horatio" wrote more than a hundred volumes of juvenile fiction that sold over 17 million copies. His stock formula depicted a poor boy new to the city, who, through a combination of virtue, hard work, and bravery, achieved success, honor, and middle-class respectability—a kind of survival of the purest, especially nonsmokers, nondrinkers, nonswearers, and nonliars. Although accusations of sexual impropriety haunted Alger throughout his life, he implanted in his readers moral lessons and the conviction that there is always room at the top (especially if one is lucky enough to save the life of the boss's daughter and marry her).

✹ Literary Landmarks

Literature and the arts were not immune to the era's sweeping changes. Confronted by new cities and industries, American writers and artists forsook the romantic sentimentality of an earlier age and generated three interrelated currents in the arts: realism, naturalism, and regionalism. Instead of depicting life as it ought to be lived or had supposedly existed in times gone by, realism sought to document contemporary life and society as it actually was, in all its raw and raucous and sometimes even scandalous detail. Naturalism took this fascination with modern life one step further, examining the determinative influence of heredity and social environments in shaping human character. Meanwhile, regionalism aspired to capture the peculiarity, or "local color," of a particular region, before national standardization bleached its variety away. All three movements responded to the Gilded Age's urban, industrial transformation.

Realism quickly came to dominate post–Civil War American literature. Foregoing romantic pageantry and supernatural melodrama, American authors increasingly found their subjects in the coarse human comedy and material drama of the world around them. William Dean Howells (1837–1920), the celebrated "father of American realism," emerged as the era's preeminent advocate of unsentimental literature. A printer's son from Ohio, Howells had scant schoolhouse education, but his busy pen carried him high into the literary circles of the East. In 1871 he became the editor in chief of the prestigious Boston-based *Atlantic Monthly*, where he championed the careers of several young American writers. In no less than thirty-six novels and nearly two hundred books, he wrote about ordinary men and women in familiar surroundings and about contemporary and sometimes controversial social themes. His most famous novel, *The Rise of Silas Lapham* (1885), describes the moral trials of a newly rich paint manufacturer caught up in the caste system of Brahmin Boston. Other well-known works dealt with the once-taboo subject of divorce and the reformers, strikers, and socialists of Gilded Age New York.

Two recipients of Howells's patronage and friendship—Mark Twain and Henry James—carried literary realism to new heights. With his meager formal schooling in frontier Missouri, the mustachioed Twain (1835–1910) typified a new breed of American authors in revolt against the elegant refinements of the old New England school of writing. Christened Samuel Langhorne Clemens, he had served for a time as a Mississippi riverboat pilot and later took his pen name, Mark Twain, from the boatman's cry that meant "two fathoms." After a two-week stint in the local Confederate militia, Twain journeyed westward to Nevada and California, a trip he described, with a mixture of truth and tall tales, in *Roughing It* (1872). One year later, he teamed up with Charles Dudley Warner to write *The Gilded Age*. An acid satire on post–Civil War political corruption and speculative greed, the book gave a name to an era.

Many other books flowed from Twain's busy pen. *The Adventures of Tom Sawyer* (1876) preceded *The Adventures of Huckleberry Finn* (1884), an American masterpiece that defied Twain's own definition of a classic as "a book which people praise and don't read." Over the decades, countless readers have been captivated by Huck's and Jim's search for freedom and friendship across the colorful (and often racist) backdrop of the antebellum Mississippi River valley. Twain's later years

In 1935 Ernest Hemingway (1899–1961) wrote,

"All modern American literature comes from one book by Mark Twain called *Huckleberry Finn*. . . . All American writing comes from that. There was nothing before. There has been nothing as good since."

were soured by bankruptcy growing out of unwise investments, and he was forced to take to the lecture platform and amuse what he called "the damned human race." Journalist, humorist, satirist, and foe of social injustice, he made his most enduring contribution in capturing frontier realism and colloquial humor in the authentic American dialect.

Twain's homegrown vernacular met its match in Henry James's elegantly filigreed prose. Brother of

Collection of the Mark Twain Archives, Elmira College, N.Y.

Mark Twain (1835–1910) Born Samuel Langhorne Clemens, he was not only America's most popular author but also a renowned platform lecturer. This photograph was taken at his house at Quarry Farm, near Elmira, New York, where he wrote major portions of both *The Adventures of Tom Sawyer* and *The Adventures of Huckleberry Finn*.

Harvard philosopher William James, Henry James (1843–1916) was a New Yorker who turned from law to literature and spent most of his life in Europe. Taking as his dominant theme the confrontation of innocent Americans with subtle Europeans, James penned a remarkable number of brilliant realist novels, including *The Portrait of a Lady* (1881) and *The Wings of the Dove* (1902). His book *The Bostonians* (1886) was one of the first novels about the rising feminist movement. James's fiction experimented with point of view and interior monologue, and he frequently made women his central characters, exploring their inner reactions to complex situations with a deftness that marked him as a master of "psychological realism." Long resident in England, he became a British subject shortly before his death.

Like her friend James, Edith Wharton (1862–1937) took a magnifying glass to the inner psychological turmoil and moral shortcomings of post–Civil War high society. Born into money, Wharton spent her years in the blue-blooded social circles of New York, Newport, and Paris. In 1885 she married well but not happily and increasingly turned her energies to writing. Wharton's many novels, including *The House of Mirth* (1905) and *The Age of Innocence* (1920), exposed the futile struggles and interior costs of striving characters stuck on the social ladder.

Wharton's portrayal of upper-crust social strife verged on **naturalism**, a more intense literary response than mainstream realism to the social dislocations and scientific tumult of late-nineteenth-century America. Naturalistic writers sought to apply detached scientific objectivity to the study of human beings—or "human beasts," in French novelist Émile Zola's famous phrase. While realist authors often treated middle- and upper-class characters in everyday settings, naturalistic novelists placed lower-class, marginal characters in extreme or sordid environments, including the urban jungle, where they were subject to the cruel operations of brute instinct, degenerate heredity, and pessimistic determinism.

Stephen Crane (1871–1900), the fourteenth child of a Methodist minister, exemplified this naturalistic urge in his writing. His *Maggie: A Girl of the Streets* (1893), a brutal tale about a poor prostitute driven to suicide, exposed the seamy underside of life in urban, industrial America. The novel proved too grim to find a publisher, so Crane had it printed privately. He rose quickly to prominence with *The Red Badge of Courage* (1895), the stirring story of a bloodied young Civil War recruit ("fresh fish") under the extreme stress of fire. Crane himself had never seen a battle and wrote entirely from printed Civil War records. Sharing the misfortune of his many characters, he died of tuberculosis in 1900, when only twenty-eight.

> *In "The Art of Fiction" (1884), Henry James (1843–1916) articulated the technical goals of realist literature:*
>
> **"**[T]he air of reality . . . seems to me to be the supreme virtue of a novel. . . . [I]t is here that he [the novelist] competes with his brother the painter in *his* attempt to render the look of things, the look that conveys their meaning, to catch the colour, the relief, the expression, the surface, the substance of the human spectacle.**"**

Candid, naturalistic portrayals of contemporary life and social problems were the literary order of the day by the turn of the century. Jack London (1876–1916), famous as a nature writer in such books as *The Call of the Wild* (1903), depicted a future fascistic revolution in *The Iron Heel* (1907), a book that displayed London's socialist leanings. Frank Norris (1870–1902), like London a Californian, wrote *The Octopus* (1901), an earthy saga of the stranglehold in which railroad and corrupt politicians held California wheat ranchers. A sequel, *The Pit* (1903), dealt with the making and breaking of speculators on the Chicago wheat exchange.

Conspicuous among the new naturalistic "social novelists" rising in the literary firmament was Theodore Dreiser (1871–1945), a homely, gangling writer from Indiana. He burst upon the literary scene in 1900 with *Sister Carrie*, a graphic narrative of a poor working girl adapting to urban life in Chicago and New York. She becomes one man's mistress, then elopes with another, and finally strikes out on her own to make a career on the stage. The fictional Carrie's disregard for prevailing moral standards so offended Dreiser's publisher that the book was soon withdrawn from circulation, though it later reemerged as an acclaimed American classic.

Sharing a common documentary impulse with realist and naturalistic fiction, **regionalism** as a movement sought to chronicle the peculiarities of local ways of life before the coming wave of industrial standardization. By the end of the nineteenth century, practically every region of the country had its share of "local colorists." At first blush, these regionalist writers accentuated the differences among still-distant American locales and indulged in a bit of provincial nostalgia. At the same time, however, their work also served to demystify (to some extent) regional differences, especially among national audiences bent on postwar reunification.

Twain, London, and Bret Harte, among other western writers, popularized (and often debunked) the lusty legends of the Old West. A foppishly dressed New Yorker,

Harte (1836–1902) struck it rich in California with gold-rush stories, especially "The Luck of Roaring Camp" (1868) and "The Outcasts of Poker Flat" (1869). Catapulted suddenly into notoriety by those short stories, he never again matched their excellence or their popularity.

Interest in local-color writing about the South also revived in the aftermath of Reconstruction. Two black writers, Paul Laurence Dunbar (1872–1906) and Charles W. Chesnutt (1858–1932), brought their distinctive voices to late-nineteenth-century literature. Dunbar's poetry—particularly his acclaimed *Lyrics of Lowly Life* (1896)—and Chesnutt's fiction—short stories in Howells's *Atlantic Monthly* and *The Conjure Woman* (1899)—embraced the use of black dialect and folklore, previously shunned by black authors, to capture the spontaneity and richness of southern black culture.

Pioneering women also contributed to the post–Civil War southern literary scene. Drawing from her experiences as a young bride and businesswoman in Louisiana, the daring feminist author Kate Chopin (1851–1904) wrote candidly about adultery, suicide, and women's ambitions in *The Awakening* (1899). Largely ignored after her death, Chopin was rediscovered by later readers, who cited her work as suggestive of the feminist yearnings that stirred beneath the surface of "respectability" in the Gilded Age.

Some important authors, of course, defied categorization. The gifted Henry Adams (1838–1918)—son of Charles Francis Adams, grandson of John Quincy Adams, and great-grandson of John Adams—turned unrivaled family connections into a prolific career as a historian, novelist, and critic. In his nine-volume *History of the United States During the Administrations of Jefferson and Madison* (1889–1891), Adams defended his patrician heritage from posthumous attack. Alarmed by modern trends, Adams penned a paean to the bygone beauty and spiritual unity of the High Middle Ages in *Mont-Saint-Michel and Chartres* (1905). Similar anxieties about modernity resurfaced in his best-known work, *The Education of Henry Adams* (1907), an autobiographical account of his own failure to come to grips with the chaotic forces of turn-of-the-century life.

✦ Artistic Triumphs

Realism and regionalism (more so than naturalism) also energized the American art world, much as they did the literary sphere. Philadelphia's native son Thomas Eakins (1844–1916) created a veritable artistic catalogue of his hometown's social, scientific, and sporting life at the end of the nineteenth century. Boston-born Winslow Homer (1836–1910), who as a youth had secretly drawn sketches in school, brought a similar mastery to

the pastoral farms and swelling seas of the Northeast. Earthily American and largely resistant to foreign influences, he reveled in rugged realism and boldness of conception. His oil canvases of the sea and its fisherfolk were striking; probably no American artist has excelled him in portraying the awesome power of the ocean.

Following in the footsteps of the expatriate writers Henry James and Edith Wharton, prominent American painters working in the realist style made their living abroad. James Whistler (1834–1903) did much of his work, including the celebrated portrait of his mother, in England. This eccentric and quarrelsome Massachusetts Yankee had earlier dropped out of West Point after failing chemistry. "Had silicon been a gas," he later jested, "I would have been a major general." Another gifted portrait painter, likewise self-exiled in England, was John Singer Sargent (1856–1925). His flattering but somewhat superficial likenesses of the British nobility and America's nouveau riche were highly prized. Mary Cassatt, an American in exile in Paris, painted sensitive portrayals of modern women and children that earned her a place in the pantheon of the French impressionist painters, whose work revolutionized the European art world after their 1874 debut.

The most gifted sculptor yet produced by America was Augustus Saint-Gaudens (1848–1907). Born in Ireland of an Irish mother and a French father, he became an adopted American. The national urge to commemorate the Civil War brought him a number of famous commissions, including the stirring Robert Gould Shaw Memorial, erected on Boston Common in 1897. It depicts Colonel Shaw, a young white "Boston Brahmin" officer, leading his black troops into battle in the Civil War (see p. 443).

Music, too, was gaining popularity. America of the 1880s and 1890s was assembling high-quality symphony orchestras, notably in Boston, Chicago, and Philadelphia. The famed Metropolitan Opera House of New York was erected in 1883. In its fabled "Diamond Horseshoe," the newly rich, often under the pretense of enjoying the imported singers, would flaunt their jewels, gowns, and furs. While symphonies and operas were devoted to bringing European music to elite American audiences, new strains of homegrown American music were sprouting in the South, another outgrowth of the regionalist trend. Black folk traditions like spirituals and "ragged music" were evolving into the blues, ragtime, and jazz, which would transform American popular music in the twentieth century.

A marvelous invention was the reproduction of music by mechanical means. The phonograph, though a squeakily imperfect instrument when invented by the deaf Edison, had by 1900 reached over 150,000 homes. Americans were rapidly being dosed with "canned

Winslow Homer, Snap the Whip (1872) Among Homer's most famous and controversial paintings, it has been interpreted both as an homage to the innocence of youth and the simplicity of rural life and as a somber allegory about the fragility of human relationships.

music," as the "sitting room" piano increasingly gathered dust.

Wrenching changes to the nation's cities inspired a new generation of architects and planners to reshape American urban space with the **City Beautiful movement**. Its proponents wanted the new American city not just to look beautiful but also to convey a confident sense of harmony, order, and monumentality. To achieve these effects, they copied European styles of beaux arts classicism and planning ideas from the master builder of Paris, Baron Georges-Eugène Haussmann, who in the 1860s had recast the City of Light with grand boulevards, parks, and public buildings. Aiming to assert America's prominence among the greatest urban cultures of the Western world, architects constructed grandiose urban landmarks such as New York's Grand Central Terminal (1913). City planners like Daniel Burnham redesigned Chicago and Washington, D.C., in the belief they could make them perfect progressive cities, inspiring civic virtue in their inhabitants. To this end, they joined contemporary landscape architects and park builders like Frederick Law Olmsted, who sought to foster virtue and egalitarian values with his designs for New York's Central Park (1873) and Boston's "Emerald Necklace" (1896), as well as the campus of Stanford University, which opened in 1891.

Burnham's first major project, which came to symbolize the City Beautiful movement, was his design for the great **World's Columbian Exposition**, held in Chicago in 1893. His imposing landscape of pavilions and fountains honored the four hundredth anniversary

Hamlin Garland (1860–1940), the well-known midwestern novelist and writer of short stories, was immensely impressed by the cultural value of Chicago's Columbian Exposition. He wrote to his aged parents on their Dakota farm,

"Sell the cook stove if necessary and come. You must see this fair."

World's Columbian Exposition, Chicago, 1893 Lagoons helped make the exposition's main buildings, dubbed the "White City," shimmer as the "City Beautiful," in stark contrast to the blocks of dull gray buildings that dominated the real Chicago.

of Columbus's first voyage. This so-called dream of loveliness was visited by 27 million people (roughly equivalent to two-fifths of the nation's population). The Chicago exposition did much to raise American artistic standards and promote city planning, although many fairgoers proved more interested in the contortions of a hootchy-kootchy dancer named "Little Egypt."

✴ The Business of Amusement

Fun and frolic were not neglected by the workaday American. The pursuit of happiness, heralded in the Declaration of Independence, had by century's end become a frenzied scramble. People sought their pleasures fiercely, as they had overrun their continent and built their cities fiercely. And now they had more time to play.

Varied diversions beckoned. The legitimate stage still flourished, as appreciative audiences responded to the lure of the footlights. Vaudeville, with its coarse jokes and graceful acrobats, continued to be immensely popular during the 1880s and 1890s, as were minstrel shows in the South, now performed by black singers and dancers rather than by whites wearing blackface as in the North before the Civil War.

The circus—high-tented and multiringed—finally emerged full-blown. Phineas T. Barnum, the master showman who had early discovered that "the public likes to be humbugged," joined hands with James A. Bailey in 1881 to stage the "Greatest Show on Earth."*

Colorful "Wild West" shows, first performed in 1883, were even more distinctively American. Headed by the knightly, goateed, and free-drinking William F. ("Buffalo Bill") Cody, the troupe included war-whooping Indians, live buffalo, and deadeye marksmen. Among them was the girlish Annie Oakley. Rifle in hand, she could at thirty paces perforate a tossed-up card half a dozen times before it fluttered to the ground (hence the term *Annie Oakley* for a punched ticket and later for a free pass).

Baseball, already widely played before the Civil War, was clearly emerging as the national pastime, if not a national mania. A league of professional players was formed in the 1870s, and in 1888 an all-star

---

*Now Ringling Bros. and Barnum & Bailey Circus.

570

baseball team toured the world, using the pyramids as a backstop while in Egypt. Basketball was invented in 1891 by James Naismith, a YMCA instructor in Springfield, Massachusetts. Designed as an active indoor sport that could be played during the winter months, it spread rapidly and enjoyed enormous popularity in the next century.

A gladiatorial trend toward spectator sports, rather than participative sports, was exemplified by football. This rugged game, with its dangerous flying wedge, had become popular well before 1889, when Yale man Walter C. Camp chose his first "All American" team. The Yale-Princeton game of 1893 drew fifty thousand cheering fans, while foreigners jeered that the nation was getting sports "on the brain."

Even pugilism, with its long background of bare-knuckle brutality, gained a new and gloved respectability in 1892. Agile "Gentleman Jim" Corbett, a scientific boxer, wrestled the world championship from the aging and alcoholic John L. Sullivan, the fabulous "Boston Strong Boy."

Two crazes swept the country in the closing decades of the century. First, croquet became all the rage, though condemned by moralists of the "naughty nineties" because it exposed feminine ankles and promoted flirtation. Second, the low-framed "safety" bicycle came to replace the high-seated model. By 1893 a million bicycles were in use, and thousands of young women, jokesters remarked, were turning to this new "spinning wheel," one that offered freedom, not tedium.

Buffalo Bill Historical Center, Wyoming, Gift of the Coe Foundation

Buffalo Bill's Wild West Show, ca. 1907   By the late 1800s, the "Wild West" was already passing into the realm of myth—and popular entertainment. Famed frontiersman William F. ("Buffalo Bill") Cody (1846–1917) made his fortune showing off his tame cowboys and Indians to enthusiastic urban audiences in Europe as well as the United States. Buffalo Bill's "Wild West"—an extravaganza featuring skilled horsemen from around the globe, including Turks, South American gauchos, Arabs, and Cossacks—was even more motley than the real one.

Cyclists on the Monterey Peninsula, California, 1888 Men and women alike took to the roads on the newfangled "two-wheelers." Bicycling especially appealed to young women eager to escape nineteenth-century strictures against female exercise and bodily exposure.

The land of the skyscraper was plainly becoming more standardized, owing largely to the new industrialization. Although race and ethnicity assigned urban Americans to distinctive neighborhoods and workplaces, to an increasing degree they shared a common popular culture—playing, reading, shopping, and talking alike. As the century drew to a close, the explosion of cities paradoxically made Americans more diverse and more similar at the same time.

Chapter Review

KEY TERMS

New Immigrants (543)
settlement houses (549)
liberal Protestants (552)
Tuskegee Institute (555)
land-grant colleges (555)
pragmatism (557)
yellow journalism (558)
National American Woman Suffrage Association (NAWSA) (562)
Woman's Christian Temperance Union (WCTU) (564)
realism (566)
naturalism (567)
regionalism (567)
City Beautiful movement (569)
World's Columbian Exposition (569)

PEOPLE TO KNOW

Jane Addams
Charles Darwin
Booker T. Washington
W. E. B. Du Bois
Joseph Pulitzer
William Randolph Hearst
John Dewey
Carrie Chapman Catt
Horatio Alger
Mark Twain
Henry James
Winslow Homer
Augustus Saint-Gaudens
Frederick Law Olmsted

CHRONOLOGY

1859 Charles Darwin publishes *On the Origin of Species*

1862 Morrill Act provides public land for higher education

1863 World's first subway system opens in London

1866 American Society for the Prevention of Cruelty to Animals (ASPCA) created

1869 Wyoming Territory grants women right to vote

1871 *Woodhull and Claflin's Weekly* published

1872 Metaphysical Club meets in Cambridge, Massachusetts

1873 Comstock Law
Construction of New York's Central Park officially completed

1874 Woman's Christian Temperance Union (WCTU) organized
Chautauqua education movement launched
Impressionist artists debut in Paris

1876 Johns Hopkins University graduate school established

1879 Henry George publishes *Progress and Poverty*
Dumbbell tenement introduced
Mary Baker Eddy establishes Christian Science
Salvation Army begins work in America

1881 Booker T. Washington becomes head of Tuskegee Institute
American Red Cross founded
Henry James publishes *The Portrait of a Lady*
Barnum and Bailey first join to stage "Greatest Show on Earth"

1882 First immigration-restriction laws passed

1883 Brooklyn Bridge completed
Metropolitan Opera House built in New York

1884 Mark Twain publishes *The Adventures of Huckleberry Finn*

1885 Louis Sullivan builds first skyscraper, in Chicago
Linotype invented

1886 Statue of Liberty erected in New York harbor

1887 American Protective Association (APA) formed
Hatch Act supplements Morrill Act

1888 Edward Bellamy publishes *Looking Backward*
American all-star baseball team tours world

1889 Jane Addams founds Hull House in Chicago

1890 William James publishes *The Principles of Psychology*
National American Woman Suffrage Association (NAWSA) formed

1891 Basketball invented
Stanford University opens

1893 Lillian Wald opens Henry Street Settlement in New York
Anti-Saloon League formed
World's Columbian Exposition held in Chicago
New Zealand grants women right to vote

1895 Stephen Crane publishes *The Red Badge of Courage*

1897 Library of Congress opens
Robert Gould Shaw Memorial erected on Boston Common

1898 Charlotte Perkins Gilman publishes *Women and Economics*

1899 Kate Chopin publishes *The Awakening*

1900 Theodore Dreiser publishes *Sister Carrie*

1907 Henry Adams privately publishes *The Education of Henry Adams*

1910 National Association for the Advancement of Colored People (NAACP) founded

TO LEARN MORE

John Bodnar, *The Transplanted: A History of Immigrants in Urban America* (1985)

Irving Howe, *World of Our Fathers* (1976)

Kenneth T. Jackson, *Crabgrass Frontier: The Suburbanization of America* (1985)

David Levering Lewis, *W. E. B. Du Bois: Biography of a Race, 1868–1919* (1993)

———, *W. E. B. Du Bois: The Fight for Equality and the American Century, 1919–1963* (2000)

Louis Menand, *The Metaphysical Club: A Story of Ideas in America* (2001)

Kathy Peiss, *Cheap Amusements: Working Women and Leisure in Turn-of-the-Century New York* (1986)

Jacob Riis, *How the Other Half Lives* (1890)

Daniel Rodgers, *Atlantic Crossings: Social Politics in a Progressive Age* (1998)

Roy Rosenzweig and Elizabeth Blackmar, *The Park and the People: A History of Central Park* (1992)

Carroll Smith-Rosenberg, *Disorderly Conduct: Visions of Gender in Victorian America* (1985)

Ronald Takaki, *Strangers from a Different Shore: A History of Asian Americans* (1989)

Alan Trachtenberg, *The Incorporation of America: Culture and Society in the Gilded Age* (1982)

A complete, annotated bibliography for this chapter—along with brief descriptions of the People to Know—may be found on the American Pageant website. The Key Terms are defined in a Glossary at the end of the text.

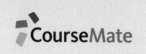

Go to the CourseMate website at **www.cengagebrain.com** for additional study tools and review materials—including audio and video clips—for this chapter.

AP® Review Questions for Chapter 25

1. What was the most important factor that drew rural people off the farms and into the big cities during the period 1865–1900?
   (A) The availability of industrial jobs
   (B) An agricultural system suffering from poor production levels
   (C) The compact and dense nature of those urban communities
   (D) The advent of new housing structures such as dumbbell tenements
   (E) The lure of cultural excitement

2. All of the following characterized the New Immigrants who came to the United States from 1880 to 1900 EXCEPT that
   (A) they were culturally different from previous immigrants to America.
   (B) they attempted to preserve their Old Country culture in America.
   (C) they were subjected to discrimination and violence by nativist Americans because these New Immigrants practiced different religions and some were politically radical.
   (D) they made substantial efforts to convert Americans to Catholicism, Eastern Orthodoxy, or Judaism.
   (E) some New Immigrants emigrated in response to violent religious persecutions organized by government officials and carried out by their countrymen.

3. What vital function did big-city political bosses and their machines perform in order to manage the social and economic demands of the new urban environment?
   (A) They successfully leveraged grant money from the federal government to meet the social and economic needs of urban immigrants.
   (B) They provided jobs and social services to many urban immigrants in exchange for political support that permitted New Immigrants to raise a family, earn a livelihood, and escape abject poverty.
   (C) They successfully lobbied state governments to provide public funds to build an extensive social services network and public housing program in the cities.
   (D) They successfully lobbied state governments to pass political ethics reform legislation to clean up the electoral process in cities.
   (E) They allied with the Protestant churches, the Republican party, and big business to provide jobs, social services, and educational opportunities to the New Immigrants.

4. All of the following characterized the settlement house movement led by leaders like Jane Addams, Lillian Wald, and Florence Kelley EXCEPT that it
   (A) was led mostly by middle-class, reform-minded women and centered in poor immigrant neighborhoods of the city.
   (B) was motivated by a concern that the New Immigrants from eastern and southern Europe required basic education, child-rearing assistance, and learning about American culture in order to assimilate successfully.
   (C) advocated on behalf of social reforms like antisweatshop and child labor laws.
   (D) studiously avoided becoming involved in international efforts to advance worldwide peace and condemn war.
   (E) became a forerunner for the new profession of social work.

5. Which of the following was NOT a reason that many labor unions favored government-imposed restrictions on immigration?
   (A) Immigrants were used by companies as strikebreakers.
   (B) Immigrants were often willing to work for lower wages and in dangerous working conditions.
   (C) Immigrants were sometimes difficult to unionize because of language barriers.
   (D) Union leaders were fearful of some immigrants' embrace of socialism, communism, or anarchism.
   (E) Immigrants were not willing or able to work in factory environments.

6. Which of the following represents the best example of liberal Protestantism's effort to accommodate religion to modern scientific theories such as Darwinism?
   (A) Linking liberal Protestantism to theories of racial superiority and an imperialistic survival of the fittest political dogma
   (B) Attempting to prove that the prayerful dogma of Christian Scientists like Mary Baker Eddy was rooted in scientific fact
   (C) Attempting to demonstrate the scientific superiority of the religious beliefs of Protestantism over those of Catholicism and Judaism
   (D) Proclaiming that Darwinism was an updated, authentic, and grander revelation of the ways of God
   (E) Utilizing Darwinism as an intellectual argument against the effort by liberal Protestant women to become members of the clergy

7. Which were the two major sources of funding for the powerful new American research universities?
   (A) Tuition paid by undergraduate students and fees charged to those served by the universities
   (B) State land grants and wealthy philanthropic industrialists
   (C) The federal government and local communities
   (D) Income from successful patents and corporate research grants
   (E) Churches and numerous private individual donors

8. What was the most important reason why Americans offered growing support for the establishment of a free public education system?
   (A) To combat the growing strength and influence of Catholic parochial schools
   (B) Because Americans accepted the idea that a free government and a republic cannot function effectively without educated citizens
   (C) The folding of private schools because of difficult economic circumstances
   (D) To utilize public schools to identify an intellectual elite
   (E) The decline of the Chautauqua movement

9. Which statement best reflects the different approaches of Booker T. Washington and W. E. B. Du Bois toward black education?
   (A) W. E. B. Du Bois believed that African Americans should develop a talented tenth, while Booker T. Washington emphasized manual labor and industrial training for African Americans.
   (B) W. E. B. Du Bois asserted that African Americans should develop separate black schools and colleges, while Booker T. Washington believed that African Americans should develop a talented tenth.
   (C) W. E. B. Du Bois advocated that African Americans concentrate on manual labor and technical education, while Booker T. Washington emphasized African American access to higher education.
   (D) W. E. B. Du Bois advocated developing separate black colleges and universities, while Booker T. Washington believed that securing access to traditionally white colleges and universities was critical to African American progress.
   (E) Booker T. Washington emphasized education for political action, while W. E. B. Du Bois believed that black education should focus on industrial and technical education.

10. How did American newspaper publishers expand their circulation and public attention in the late nineteenth century?
    (A) By printing hard-hitting editorials about the plight of poor immigrants in the city
    (B) By crusading for social reforms
    (C) By repudiating the tactics of Joseph Pulitzer and William Randolph Hearst
    (D) By focusing on coverage of local community issues and avoiding yellow journalism
    (E) By printing sensationalist stories of sex, corruption, and scandal

11. What development prompted American novelists' turn from romanticism and transcendentalism to rugged social realism?
    (A) The influence of American literature
    (B) The heightened awareness of racial problems
    (C) A higher educational level of their readers
    (D) The materialism and conflicts of the new industrial society
    (E) The growing prominence of women writers

12. By 1900, a new generation of women's suffrage advocates emphasized all the following EXCEPT
    (A) linking the vote to untraditional female family roles such as assuming primary wage-earning responsibilities in the household.
    (B) forming strong alliances with African Americans seeking voting rights.
    (C) the desirability of giving women the vote in order to extend their roles as mothers and homemakers to the public world.
    (D) the need for women living in cities to have political influence on boards of public health, police commissions, and school boards.
    (E) following a state-by-state political strategy to create political momentum on behalf of gaining unrestricted suffrage.

13. The "City Beautiful" movement, exemplified at the 1893 World's Columbian Exposition, fused American and European architecture by
    (A) replicating the designs of ancient buildings in American cities.
    (B) copying beaux arts classicism and incorporating Parisian ideas.
    (C) favoring modern materials, like steel, over older materials.
    (D) crowding buildings into small spaces, foregoing parks and public spaces.
    (E) designing only for the rich and excluding the working class from cities.

14. All of the following are related EXCEPT
    (A) Anthony Comstock's war on the "immoral."
    (B) founding of the Women's Christian Temperance Union.
    (C) establishing the National American Woman Suffrage Association.
    (D) Ida B. Wells's antilynching campaign.
    (E) creating the National Association for the Advancement of Colored People.

Chapter 26

The Great West and the Agricultural Revolution

1865–1896

Up to our own day American history has been in a large degree the history of the colonization of the Great West. The existence of an area of free land, its continuous recession, and the advance of American settlement westward, explain American development.

FREDERICK JACKSON TURNER, 1893

The White Man, who possesses this whole vast country from sea to sea, who roams over it at pleasure, and lives where he likes, cannot know the cramp we feel in this little spot, with the undying remembrance of the fact, which you know as well as we, that every foot of what you proudly call America, not very long ago belonged to the red man.

WASHAKIE (SHOSHONE INDIAN), 1878

*W*hen the Civil War crashed to a close, the frontier line was still wavering westward toward the fabled "100th Meridian," which defines the eastern boundary of the West, America's most arid region (see Map 26.4). A long fringe of settlement, bulging outward here and there, ran roughly north through central Texas and on to the Canadian border. Between this jagged line and the settled areas on the Pacific slope, there were virtually no white people. The few exceptions were the islands of Mormons in Utah, occasional trading posts and gold camps, and several scattered Spanish Mexican settlements throughout the Southwest.

Sprawling in expanse, the Great West was a rough square that measured about a thousand miles on each side. Embracing mountains, plateaus, deserts, and plains, it was the largely parched habitat of the Indian, the buffalo, the wild horse, the prairie dog, and the coyote. Twenty-five years later—that is, by 1890—the entire domain had been carved into states and the four territories of Utah, Arizona, New Mexico, and "Indian

Territory," or Oklahoma. Pioneers flung themselves greedily on this enormous prize, as if to ravish it. Probably never before in human experience had so huge an area been transformed so rapidly.

★ The Clash of Cultures on the Plains

Native Americans numbered about 360,000 in 1860, many of them scattered about the vast grasslands of the trans-Missouri West. But to their eternal misfortune, the Indians stood in the path of the advancing white pioneers. An inevitable clash loomed between an acquisitive, industrializing nation and the Indians' lifeways, highly evolved over centuries to adapt to the demanding environment of the sparsely watered western plains.

Migration and conflict—and sometimes dramatic cultural change—were no strangers in the arid West, even before the whites began to arrive. The Comanches had driven the Apaches off the central plains into

The Buffalo Hunt, by Frederic Remington, 1890 A New Yorker who first went west at the age of nineteen as a cowboy and ranch cook, Remington (1861–1909) became the foremost artist of the vanishing way of life of the old Far West. Once a common sight on the high plains, the kind of buffalo kill that Remington records here was a great rarity by the time he painted this scene in 1890. The once-vast herds of bison had long since been reduced to a pitiful few by the white man's rifles and the increasingly concentrated use of the land by ever more constricted Indians.

Buffalo Bill Historical Center, Cody, Wyoming; Gift of William E. Weiss; 23.62

the upper Rio Grande valley in the eighteenth century. Harried by the Mandans and Chippewas, the Cheyenne had abandoned their villages along the upper reaches of the Mississippi and Missouri Rivers in the century before the Civil War. The Sioux, displaced from the Great Lakes woodlands in the late eighteenth century, emerged onto the plains to prey upon the Crows, Kiowas, and Pawnees. Mounted on Spanish-introduced horses, peoples like the Cheyenne and the Sioux transformed themselves within just a few generations from foot-traveling, crop-growing villagers to wide-ranging nomadic traders and deadly efficient buffalo hunters— so deadly that they threatened to extinguish the vast bison herds that had lured them onto the plains in the first place.

When white soldiers and settlers edged onto the plains in the decades just before the Civil War, they accelerated a fateful cycle that exacerbated already fierce enmities among the Indians and ultimately undermined the foundations of Native American culture. White intruders unwittingly spread cholera, typhoid, and smallpox among the native peoples of the plains, with devastating results. Equally harmful, whites put further pressure on the steadily shrinking bison population by hunting and by grazing their own livestock on the prairie grasses. As the once-mammoth buffalo herds dwindled, warfare intensified among the Plains tribes for ever-scarcer hunting grounds. "I am traveling all over this country, and am cutting the trees of my brothers," an Arikara Indian told a U.S. Army officer along the Platte River in 1835. "I am killing their buf-

falo before my friends arrive so that when they come up, they can find no buffalo."

The federal government tried to pacify the Plains Indians by signing treaties with the "chiefs" of various "tribes" at Fort Laramie in 1851 and at Fort Atkinson in 1853. The treaties marked the beginnings of the **reservation system** in the West. They established

As early as the Coronado expedition in 1541, Spanish explorers marveled at the Plains Indians' reliance on the buffalo:

❝With the skins [the Indians] build their houses; with the skins they clothe and shoe themselves; from the skins they make ropes and also obtain wool. From the sinews they make thread, with which they sew their clothing and likewise their tents. From the bones they shape awls, and the dung they use for firewood, since there is no fuel in all that land. The bladders serve as jugs and drinking vessels. They sustain themselves on the flesh of the animals, eating it slightly roasted and sometimes uncooked. Taking it in their teeth, they pull with one hand; with the other they hold a large flint knife and cut off mouthfuls, swallowing it half chewed, like birds. They eat raw fat, without warming it.❞

One disheartened Indian complained to the white Sioux Commission created by Congress,

❝ Tell your people that since the Great Father promised that we should never be removed we have been moved five times. . . . I think you had better put the Indians on wheels and you can run them about wherever you wish.**❞**

boundaries for the territory of each tribe and attempted to separate the Indians into two great "colonies" to the north and south of a corridor of intended white settlement.

But the white treaty makers misunderstood both Indian government and Indian society. "Tribes" and "chiefs" were often fictions of the white imagination, which could not grasp the fact that many Native Americans, living in scattered bands, recognized only the authority of their immediate families or perhaps a band elder. And the nomadic culture of the Plains Indians was utterly alien to the concept of living out one's life in the confinement of a defined territory.

In the 1860s the federal government intensified this policy and herded the Indians into still-smaller confines, principally the "Great Sioux reservation" in Dakota Territory and Indian Territory in present-day Oklahoma, into which dozens of southern Plains tribes were forced.

The Indians surrendered their ancestral lands only when they had received solemn promises from Washington that they would be left alone and provided with food, clothing, and other supplies. Regrettably, the federal Indian agents were often corrupt. They palmed off moth-eaten blankets, spoiled beef, and other defective provisions on the friendless Indians. One of these cheating officials, on an annual salary of $1,500, returned home after four years with an estimated "savings" of $50,000.

For more than a decade after the Civil War, fierce warfare between Indians and the U.S. Army raged in various parts of the West (see Map 26.1). Army troops, many of them recent immigrants who had, ironically, fled Europe to avoid military service, met formidable adversaries in the Plains Indians, whose superb horsemanship gave them baffling mobility. Fully one-fifth of all U.S. Army personnel on the frontier were African American—dubbed "Buffalo Soldiers" by the Indians, supposedly because of the resemblance of their hair to the bison's furry coat.

✵ Receding Native Population

The Indian wars in the West were often savage clashes. Aggressive whites sometimes shot peaceful Indians on sight, just to make sure they would give no trouble. At Sand Creek, Colorado, in 1864, Colonel J. M. Chivington's militia massacred in cold blood some four hundred Indians who apparently thought they had been promised immunity. Women were shot praying for mercy, children had their brains dashed out, and braves were tortured, scalped, and unspeakably mutilated.

Pawnee Indians in Front of Their Lodge, ca. 1868 The Pawnees of central Nebraska never made war on the United States, which they regarded as an ally in their own struggles against the marauding Sioux.

Cruelty begot cruelty. In 1866 a Sioux war party attempting to block construction of the Bozeman Trail to the Montana goldfields ambushed Captain William J. Fetterman's command of eighty-one soldiers and civilians in Wyoming's Bighorn Mountains. The Indians left not a single survivor and grotesquely mutilated the corpses. One trooper's face was spitted with 105 arrows. George Armstrong Custer, the buckskin-clad "boy general" of Civil War fame, now demoted to colonel and turned Indian fighter, wrote that Fetterman's annihilation "awakened a bitter feeling toward the savage perpetrators." The cycle of ferocious warfare intensified.

The Fetterman massacre led to one of the few—though short-lived—Indian triumphs in the plains wars, the **Battle of the Little Bighorn**. In another Treaty of Fort Laramie, signed in 1868, the government abandoned the Bozeman Trail. The sprawling "Great Sioux

A young lieutenant told Colonel Chivington that to attack the Indians would be a violation of pledges:

"His reply was, bringing his fist down close to my face, 'Damn any man who sympathizes with Indians.' I told him what pledges were given the Indians. He replied that he 'had come to kill Indians, and believed it to be honorable to kill Indians under any and all circumstances.'**"**

reservation" was guaranteed to the Sioux tribes. But in 1874 a new round of warfare with the Plains Indians began when Custer led a "scientific" expedition into the Black Hills of South Dakota (part of the Sioux reservation) and announced that he had discovered gold.

MAP 26.1 Indian Wars, 1860–1890   Surrendering in 1877, Chief Joseph of the Nez Perce declared, "Our chiefs are killed. . . . The old men are all dead. . . . The little children are freezing to death. . . . I want to have time to look for my children. . . . Hear me, my chiefs. My heart is sick and sad. From where the sun now stands I will fight no more forever."

© Cengage Learning

Battle of the Little Big Horn, by Amos Bad Heart Bull This depiction of the battle by an Oglala Sioux tribal historian and artist shows Crazy Horse (in spotted war paint, center) firing on a trooper of Custer's 7th Cavalry. The ground is littered with the bodies of dead soldiers.

Hordes of greedy gold-seekers swarmed into the Sioux lands. The aggrieved Sioux, aided by the Cheyenne and Arapaho Indians, took to the warpath, inspired by the influential and wily Sitting Bull.

Colonel Custer's 7th Cavalry, nearly half of them immigrants, set out to suppress the Indians and to return them to the reservation. Attacking what turned out to be a superior force of some 2,500 well-armed warriors camped along the Little Bighorn River in present-day Montana, the "White Chief with Yellow Hair" and about 250 officers and men were completely wiped out in 1876 when two supporting columns failed to come to their rescue. The Indians' victory was short-lived. In a series of battles across the northern plains in the ensuing months, the U.S. Army relentlessly hunted down the Indians who had humiliated Custer.

One band of Nez Percé Indians in northeastern Oregon were goaded into daring flight in 1877 when U.S. authorities tried to herd them onto a reservation. Chief Joseph finally surrendered his breakaway band of some seven hundred Indians after a tortuous, seventeen-hundred-mile, three-month trek across the Continental Divide toward Canada. There Joseph hoped to rendezvous with Sitting Bull, who had taken refuge north of the border after the Battle of the Little Bighorn. Betrayed into believing they would be returned to their ancestral lands in Idaho, the Nez Percés instead were sent to a dusty reservation in Kansas, where 40 percent of them perished from disease. The survivors were eventually allowed to return to Idaho.

Fierce Apache tribes of Arizona and New Mexico were the most difficult to subdue. Led by Geronimo, whose eyes blazed hatred of the whites, they were pursued into Mexico by federal troops using the sun-flashing heliograph, a communication device that impressed the Indians as "big medicine." Scattered remnants of the warriors were finally persuaded to surrender after the Apache women had been exiled to Florida. The Apaches ultimately became successful farmers in Oklahoma.

This relentless fire-and-sword policy of the whites at last shattered the spirit of the Indians. The vanquished Native Americans were finally ghettoized on reservations, where they could theoretically preserve their cultural autonomy but were in fact compelled to eke out a sullen existence as wards of the government. Their white masters had at last discovered that the Indians were much cheaper to feed than to fight. Even so, for many decades they were almost ignored to death.

The "taming" of the Indians was engineered by a number of factors. Of cardinal importance was the federal government's willingness to back its land claims with military force. Almost as critical was the railroad, which shot an iron arrow through the heart of the

Geronimo (ca. 1823–1909), Also Known by His Apache Name, Goyahkla (One Who Yawns) In 1851 Mexican troops killed Geronimo's mother and wife and three of his children, initiating his lifelong hatred of Mexicans. Ironically, in later life, when he repeatedly fled the intolerable confinement of reservations in the United States, he sought refuge—and freedom—in Mexico. Persuaded at last to surrender to American authorities in 1886, he spent the remainder of his life on reservations in Florida, Alabama, and Oklahoma.

West. Locomotives could bring out unlimited numbers of troops, farmers, cattlemen, sheepherders, and settlers. The Indians were also ravaged by the white people's diseases, to which they showed little resistance, and by their firewater, which they could resist even less. Above all, the virtual extermination of the buffalo doomed the Plains Indians' nomadic way of life.

✪ Bellowing Herds of Bison

Tens of millions of buffalo—described by early Spaniards as "hunchback cows"—blackened the western prairies when white Americans first arrived. These shaggy, lumbering animals were the staff of life for Native Americans (see "Makers of America: The Plains Indians," pp. 582–583). Their flesh provided food; their dried dung provided fuel ("buffalo chips"); their hides provided clothing, lariats, and harnesses.

When the Civil War closed, some 15 million of these meaty beasts were still grazing on the western plains. In 1868 a Kansas Pacific locomotive had to wait eight hours for a herd to amble across the tracks. Much of the food supply of the railroad construction gangs came from leathery buffalo steaks. William "Buffalo Bill" Cody—sinewy, telescope-eyed, and a crack shot—killed over 4,000 animals in eighteen months while employed by the Kansas Pacific.

With the building of the railroad, the massacre of the herds began in deadly earnest. The creatures were slain for their hides, for their tongues or a few other choice cuts, or for sheer amusement. "Sportsmen" on lurching railroad trains would lean out the windows and blaze away at the animals to satisfy their lust for slaughter or excitement. Such wholesale butchery left fewer than a thousand buffalo alive by 1885, and the once-numerous beasts were in danger of complete extinction. The whole story is a shocking example of the greed and waste that accompanied the conquest of the continent.

✪ The End of the Trail

By the 1880s the national conscience began to stir uneasily over the plight of the Indians. Helen Hunt Jackson, a Massachusetts writer of children's literature, pricked the moral sense of Americans in 1881 when she published *A Century of Dishonor*. The book chronicled the sorry record of government ruthlessness and chicanery in dealing with the Indians. Her later novel *Ramona* (1884), a love story about discrimination against California Indians, sold some 600,000 copies and further inspired sympathy for the Indians.

Debate seesawed. Humanitarians wanted to treat the Indians kindly and persuade them thereby to "walk the white man's road." Yet hard-liners insisted on the current policy of forced containment and brutal punishment. Neither side showed much respect for Native American culture. Christian reformers, who often administered educational facilities on the reservations, sometimes withheld food to force the Indians to give up their tribal religions and assimilate to white society. In 1884 these zealous white souls joined with military

© Bettmann/Corbis

National Anthropological Archives, Smithsonian Institution, Washington, D.C.

Civil War veteran and long-time Indian fighter General Philip Sheridan (1831–1888) reflected on the wars against the Indians:

❝We took away their country and their means of support, broke up their mode of living, their habits of life, introduced disease and decay among them, and it was for this and against this they made war. Could anyone expect less?❞

men in successfully persuading the federal government to outlaw the sacred Sun Dance. When the "Ghost Dance" cult later spread to the Dakota Sioux, the army bloodily stamped it out in 1890 at the so-called **Battle of Wounded Knee**. In the fighting thus provoked, an estimated two hundred Indian men, women, and children were killed, as well as twenty-nine invading soldiers.

The misbegotten offspring of the movement to reform Indian policy was the **Dawes Severalty Act** of 1887. Reflecting the forced-civilization views of the reformers, the act dissolved many tribes as legal entities, wiped out tribal ownership of land, and set up individual Indian family heads with 160 free acres. If the Indians behaved themselves like "good white settlers," they would get full title to their holdings, as well as citizenship, in twenty-five years. The probationary period was later extended, but full citizenship was granted to all Indians in 1924.

Former reservation land not allotted to the Indians under the Dawes Act was to be sold to railroads and white settlers, with the proceeds used by the federal government to educate and "civilize" the native peoples. In 1879 the government had already funded the Carlisle Indian School in Pennsylvania, where Native American children, separated from their tribes, were taught English and inculcated with white values and customs. "Kill the Indian and save the man" was the school founder's motto. In the 1890s the government expanded its network of Indian boarding schools and sent "field matrons" to the reservations to teach Native American women the art of sewing and to preach the virtues of chastity and hygiene.

The Dawes Act struck directly at tribal organization and tried to make rugged individualists out of the Indians. This legislation ignored the inherent reliance of traditional Indian culture on tribally held land, literally pulling the land out from under them. By 1900 Indians had lost 50 percent of the 156 million acres

The Indian spokesman Plenty Coups (1848–1932) said in 1909,

❝I see no longer the curling smoke rising from our lodge poles. I hear no longer the songs of the women as they prepare the meal. The antelope have gone; the buffalo wallows are empty. Only the wail of the coyote is heard. The white man's medicine is stronger than ours. . . . We are like birds with a broken wing.❞

Lakotas Receiving Rations at Standing Rock Reservation, ca. 1881 Once the scourge of the plains, the Lakota (part of the Sioux tribes) were reduced by the 1890s to the humiliation of living on government handouts.

The last of the native peoples of North America to bow before the military might of the whites, the Indians of the northern Great Plains long defended their lands and their ways of life against the American cavalry. After the end of the Indian wars, toward the close of the nineteenth century, the Plains tribes struggled on, jealously guarding their communities against white encroachment. Crowded onto reservations, subject to ever-changing federal Indian policies, assailed by corrupt settlers and Indian agents, the Plains Indians have nonetheless preserved much of their ancestral culture to this day.

Before Europeans first appeared in North America in the sixteenth century, the vast plains from northern Texas to Saskatchewan were home to some thirty different tribes. There was no typical Plains Indian; each tribe spoke a distinct language, practiced its own religion, and formed its own government. When members of different bands met on the prairies, communication depended on a special sign language.

Indians had first trod the arid plains to pursue sprawling herds of antelope, elk, and especially buffalo—all important sources of protein. But these early peoples of the plains were not exclusively hunters: the women were expert farmers, coaxing lush gardens of pumpkins, squash, corn, and beans from the dry but fertile soil. Still, the shaggy pelt and heavy flesh of the buffalo constituted the staff of life on the plains. Hunted by men, the great bison were butchered by women, who used every part of the beast. They fashioned horns and hooves into spoons, and intestines into containers. They stretched sinews into strong bowstrings and wove buffalo hair into ropes. Meat not immediately eaten was pounded into pemmican—thin strips of smoked or sun-dried buffalo flesh mixed with berries and stuffed into rawhide bags.

The nomadic Plains Indians sought what shelter they could in small bands throughout the winter, gathering together in summer for religious ceremonies, socializing, and communal buffalo hunts. At first these seasonal migrations required arduous loading and carting. The Indians carried all their possessions or heaped them on wheelless carts called travois, which were dragged by dogs—their only beasts of burden.

A Comanche Village, by George Catlin, 1834

Smithsonian American Art Museum, Washington, DC/Art Resource, NY

Museum of the South Dakota State Historical Society, Pierre SD

(above) A Sioux Carving Horses were essential to the culture of the Plains Indians, and they often carved likenesses of horses killed in battle. Note the red-stained holes depicting this horse's wounds. **(right) A Cheyenne Cradleboard for Carrying a Baby** © Smithsonian Institution/Corbis

Joslyn Art Museum, Omaha, Nebraska

Chan-Chä-Uiá-Teüin, Teton Sioux Woman, by Karl Bodmer, ca. 1830s Bodmer, a German artist, painted this woman's portrait during an expedition to the Great Plains. Her name means "Woman of the Crow Nation," which seems to suggest that she was taken captive from the Sioux's mortal enemies, the Crows.

Then in the sixteenth century, the mounted Spanish *conquistadores* ventured into the New World. Their steeds—some of them escaping to become mustangs, the wild horses of the American West, and others acquired by the Indians in trade—quickly spread over the plains. The horse revolutionized Indian societies, for a time turning the Plains tribes into efficient hunting machines that promised to banish hunger from the prairies. But horse-mounted hunters turned out to be too efficient: overhunting made buffalo ever harder to find. The plains pony also ignited a furious competition for grazing lands, for trade goods, and for ever more horses, so that wars of aggression and of revenge became increasingly bitter and frequent.

The European invasion soon eclipsed the short-lived era of the horse. After many battles the Plains Indians found themselves crammed together on tiny reservations, clinging with tired but determined fingers to their traditions. Although much of Plains Indian culture persists to this day, the Indians' free-ranging way of life has passed into memory. As Black Elk, an Oglala Sioux, put it, "Once we were happy in our own country and we were seldom hungry, for then the two-leggeds and the four-leggeds lived together like relatives, and there was plenty for them and for us. But then the Wasichus [white people] came, and they made little islands for us . . . and always these islands are becoming smaller, for around them surges the gnawing flood of Wasichus."

MAP 26.2 Vanishing Lands Once masters of the continent, Native Americans have been squeezed into just 2 percent of U.S. territory. (From *The New York Times*, June 25, 2000 © 2000 *The New York Times*. All rights reserved. Used by permission and protected by the Copyright Laws of the United States. The printing, copying, redistribution, or retransmission of the Material without express written permission is prohibited.)

they had held just two decades earlier (see Map 26.2). The forced-assimilation doctrine of the Dawes Act remained the cornerstone of the government's official Indian policy for nearly half a century, until the Indian Reorganization Act (the "Indian New Deal") of 1934 partially reversed the individualistic approach and belatedly tried to restore the tribal basis of Indian life (see p. 765).

Under these new federal policies, defective though they were, the Indian population started to mount slowly. The total number had been reduced by 1887 to about 243,000—the result of bullets, bottles, and bacteria—but the census of 2000 counted more than 1.5 million Native Americans, urban and rural.

✷ Mining: From Dishpan to Ore Breaker

The conquest of the Indians and the coming of the railroad were life-giving boons to the mining frontier. The golden gravel of California continued to yield "pay dirt," and in 1858 an electrifying discovery convulsed Colorado. Avid "fifty-niners" or "Pikes Peakers" rushed west to rip at the ramparts of the Rockies. But there were more miners than minerals, and many gold-grubbers, with "Pikes Peak or Bust" inscribed on the canvas of their covered wagons, creaked wearily back with the added inscription, "Busted, by Gosh." Yet countless bearded fortune-seekers stayed on, some to strip away

the silver deposits, others to extract nonmetallic wealth from the earth in the form of golden grain.

"Fifty-niners" also poured feverishly into Nevada in 1859, after the fabulous Comstock Lode had been uncovered. A fantastic amount of gold and silver, worth more than $340 million, was mined by the "Kings of the Comstock" from 1860 to 1890. The scantily populated state of Nevada, "child of the Comstock Lode," was prematurely railroaded into the Union in 1864, partly to provide three electoral votes for President Lincoln.

Smaller "lucky strikes" drew frantic gold- and silver-seekers into Montana, Idaho, and other western states. Boomtowns, known as "Helldorados," sprouted from the desert sands like magic. Every third cabin was a saloon, where sweat-stained miners drank adulterated liquor ("rotgut") in the company of accommodating women. Lynch law and hempen vigilante justice, as in early California, preserved a crude semblance of order in the towns. And when the "diggings" petered out, the gold-seekers decamped, leaving eerily picturesque "ghost towns," such as Virginia City, Nevada, silhouetted in the desert. Begun with a boom, these towns ended with a whimper.

Once the loose surface gold was gobbled up, ore-breaking machinery was imported to smash the gold-bearing quartz. This operation was so expensive that it could ordinarily be undertaken only by corporations pooling the wealth of stockholders. Gradually the age of big business came to the **mining industry**. Dusty,

Hydraulic Mining, Nevada, 1866 Once miners had panned and dredged the most accessible gold from streambeds, they ripped open the earth itself in search of other deposits. High-pressure streams of water, delivered through huge nozzles called "monitors," washed away entire hillsides and created the nightmarish, debris-strewn landscapes that still scar western mountains and foothills.

bewhiskered miners, dishpans in hand, were replaced by impersonal corporations, with their costly machinery and trained engineers. The once-independent gold-washer became just another day laborer.

Yet the mining frontier had played a vital role in conquering the continent. Magnetlike, it attracted population and wealth, while advertising the wonders of the Wild West. Women as well as men found opportunity, running boardinghouses or working as prostitutes. They won a kind of equality on the rough frontier that earned them the vote in Wyoming (1869), Utah (1870), Colorado (1893), and Idaho (1896) long before their sisters in the East could cast a ballot.

The amassing of precious metals helped finance the Civil War, facilitated the building of railroads, and intensified the already bitter conflict between whites and Indians. The outpouring of silver and gold enabled the Treasury to resume specie payments in 1879 and injected the silver issue into American politics. "Silver Senators," representing the thinly peopled "acreage states" of the West, used their disproportionate influence to promote the interests of the silver miners. Finally, the mining frontier added to American folklore and literature, as the writings of Bret Harte and Mark Twain so colorfully attest.

✦ Beef Bonanzas and the Long Drive

When the Civil War ended, the grassy plains of Texas supported several million tough, long-horned cattle.

These scrawny beasts, whose horn spreads sometimes reached eight feet, were killed primarily for their hides. There was no way of getting their meat profitably to market.

The problem of marketing was neatly solved when the transcontinental railroads thrust their iron fingers into the West. Cattle could now be shipped alive to the stockyards, and under "beef barons" like the Swifts and Armours, the highly industrialized meatpacking

Dressed to Kill Cowboys came in all varieties and sizes in the wild and woolly frontier West—and in all kinds of garb as well.

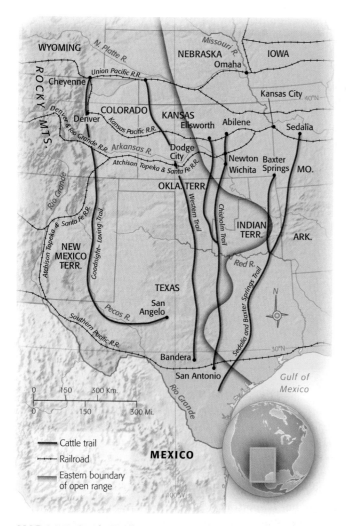

MAP 26.3 Cattle Trails © Cengage Learning

The steer was king in a Cattle Kingdom richly carpeted with grass. As long as lush grass was available, the Long Drive proved profitable—that is, to the luckier cattlemen who escaped Indians, stampedes, cattle fever, and other hazards. From 1866 to 1888, bellowing herds, totaling over 4 million steers, were driven northward from the beef bowl of Texas. The steer was king in a Cattle Kingdom richly carpeted with grass.

What the Lord giveth, the Lord also can taketh away. The railroad made the Long Drive, and the railroad unmade the Long Drive, primarily because the locomotives ran both ways. The same rails that bore the cattle from the open range to the kitchen range brought out the homesteader and the sheepherder. Both of these intruders, sometimes amid flying bullets, built barbed-wire fences that were too numerous to be cut down by the cowboys. Furthermore, the terrible winter of 1886–1887, with blinding blizzards reaching 68 degrees below zero, left thousands of dazed cattle starving and freezing. Overexpansion and overgrazing likewise took their toll, as the cowboys slowly gave way to plowboys.

The only escape for the stockmen was to make cattle-raising a big business and avoid the perils of overproduction. Breeders learned to fence their ranches, lay in winter feed, import blooded bulls, and produce fewer and meatier animals. They also learned to organize. The Wyoming Stock-Growers' Association, especially in the 1880s, virtually controlled the state and its legislature.

This was the heyday of the cowboy. The equipment of the cowhand—from "shooting irons" and ten-gallon hat to chaps and spurs—served a useful, not an ornamental, function. A "genuwine" gun-toting cowpuncher, riding where men were men and smelled like horses, could justifiably boast of his toughness.

These bowlegged Knights of the Saddle, with their colorful trappings and cattle-lulling songs, became part of American folklore. Many of them, perhaps five thousand, were blacks, who especially enjoyed the newfound freedom of the open range.

★ The Farmers' Frontier

Miners and cattlemen created the romantic legend of the West, but it was the sober sodbuster who wrote the final chapter of frontier history. A fresh day dawned for western farmers with the **Homestead Act** of 1862. The new law allowed a settler to acquire as much as 160 acres of land (a quarter-section) by living on it for five years, improving it, and paying a nominal fee of about $30.

The Homestead Act marked a drastic departure from previous policy. Before the act, public land had been sold primarily for revenue; now it was to be given away to

business sprang into existence as a main pillar of the economy. Drawing upon the gigantic stockyards at Kansas City and Chicago, the meatpackers could ship their fresh products to the East Coast in the newly perfected refrigerator cars.

A spectacular feeder of the new slaughterhouses was the "Long Drive" (see Map 26.3). Texas cowboys—black, white, and Mexican—drove herds numbering from one thousand to ten thousand head slowly over the unfenced and unpeopled plains until they reached a railroad terminal. The bawling beasts grazed en route on the free government grass. Favorite terminal points were flyspecked "cow towns" like Dodge City—"the Bibulous Babylon of the Frontier"—and Abilene (Kansas), Ogallala (Nebraska), and Cheyenne (Wyoming). At Abilene order was maintained by Marshal James B. ("Wild Bill") Hickok, a fabulous gunman who reputedly killed only in self-defense or in the line of duty and who was fatally shot in the back in 1876 while playing poker.

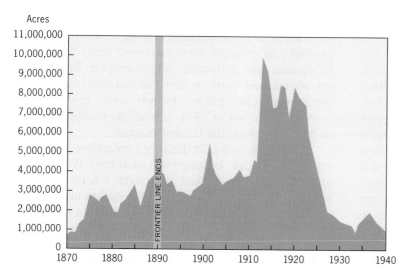

Acres

11,000,000
10,000,000
9,000,000
8,000,000
7,000,000
6,000,000
5,000,000
4,000,000
3,000,000
2,000,000
1,000,000
0

FRONTIER LINE ENDS

1870 1880 1890 1900 1910 1920 1930 1940

FIGURE 26.1 Homesteads from the Public Lands (acreage legally transferred to private ownership) See related Map 26.5 on p. 590.

encourage a rapid filling of empty spaces and to provide a stimulus to the family farm—"the backbone of democracy." The new law was a godsend to a host of farmers who could not afford to buy large holdings. During the forty years after its passage, about half a million families took advantage of the Homestead Act to carve out new homes in the vast open stretches. Yet five times that many families *purchased* their land from the railroads, the land companies, or the states (see Figure 26.1).

The Homestead Act often turned out to be a cruel hoax. The standard 160 acres, quite adequate in the well-watered Mississippi basin, frequently proved pitifully inadequate on the rain-scarce Great Plains. Thousands of homesteaders, perhaps two out of three, were forced to give up the one-sided struggle against drought. Uncle Sam, it was said, bet 160 acres against ten dollars that the settlers could not live on their homesteads for five years. One of these unsuccessful gambles in Greer County, western Oklahoma, inspired a folk song:

> *Hurrah for Greer County! The land of the free,*
> *The land of the bedbug, grasshopper, and flea;*
> *I'll sing of its praises, I'll tell of its fame,*
> *While starving to death on my government claim.*

Naked fraud was spawned by the Homestead Act and similar laws. Perhaps ten times more of the public domain wound up in the clutches of land-grabbing promoters than in the hands of bona fide farmers. Unscrupulous corporations would use "dummy" homesteaders—often their employees or aliens bribed with cash or a bottle of beer—to grab the best properties containing timber, minerals, and oil. Settlers would later swear that they had "improved" the property by erecting a "twelve by fourteen" dwelling, which turned out to measure twelve by fourteen *inches*.

The railways also played a major role in developing the agricultural West, largely through the profitable marketing of crops. Some railroad companies induced Americans and European immigrants to buy the cheap land earlier granted to the railroads by the government. The Northern Pacific Railroad at one time had nearly a thousand paid agents in Europe distributing roseate leaflets in various languages.

Shattering the myth of the Great American Desert opened the gateways to the agricultural West even wider. The windswept prairies were for the most part treeless, and the tough sod had been pounded solid by millions of buffalo hooves. Pioneer explorers and trappers had assumed that the soil must be sterile, simply because it was not heavily watered and did not support immense forests. But once the prairie sod was broken with heavy iron plows pulled by four yokes of oxen—the "plow that broke the plains"—the earth proved astonishingly fruitful. "Sodbusters" poured onto the prairies. Lacking trees for lumber and fuel, they built

In making the arduous journey across the western prairies, many women settlers discovered new confidence in their abilities. Early on in her trek, Mary Richardson Walker (1811–1897) confided in her diary that

"my circumstances are rather trying. So much danger attends me on every hand. A long journey before me, going I know not whither, without mother or sister to attend me, can I expect to survive it all?"

Only a month later, she recorded that

"in the afternoon we rode thirty-five miles without stopping. Pretty well tired out, all of us. Stood it pretty well myself."

homes from the very sod they dug from the ground and burned corncobs for warmth.

Lured by higher wheat prices resulting from crop failures elsewhere in the world, settlers in the 1870s rashly pushed still farther west, onto the poor, marginal lands beyond the 100th meridian. That imaginary line, running north to south from the Dakotas through west Texas, separated two climatological regions—a well-watered area to the east, and a semiarid area to the west (see Map 26.4). Bewhiskered and one-armed geologist John Wesley Powell, explorer of the Colorado River's Grand Canyon and director of the U.S. Geological Survey, warned in 1874 that beyond the 100th meridian so little rain fell that agriculture was impossible without massive irrigation.

Ignoring Powell's advice, farmers heedlessly chewed up the crusty earth in western Kansas, eastern Colorado, and Montana. They quickly went broke as a six-year drought in the 1880s further desiccated the already dusty region. Western Kansas lost half its population between 1888 and 1892. "There is no God west of Salina," one hapless homesteader declared.

In the wake of the devastating drought, the new technique of "dry farming" took root on the plains. Its methods of frequent shallow cultivation supposedly were adapted to the arid western environment, but over time "dry farming" created a finely pulverized surface soil that contributed to the notorious "Dust Bowl" several decades later (see p. 764).

Other adaptations to the western environment were more successful. Tough strains of wheat, resistant to cold and drought, were imported from Russia and blossomed into billowing yellow carpets. Wise farmers abandoned corn in favor of sorghum and other drought-resistant grains. Barbed wire, perfected by Joseph F. Glidden in 1874, solved the problem of how to build fences on the treeless prairies.

Eventually federally financed irrigation projects—on a colossal scale, beyond even what John Wesley Powell had dreamed—caused the Great American Desert to bloom. A century after Powell's predictions, arching dams had tamed the Missouri and Columbia Rivers and had so penned up and diverted the canyon-gnawing Colorado that its mouth in the Gulf of California was dry. More than 45 million acres were irrigated in seventeen western states. In the long run, the hydraulic engineers had more to do with shaping the modern West than all the trappers, miners, cavalrymen, and cowboys ever did (see Map 26.5). As one engineer boasted, "We enjoy pushing rivers around."

✶ The Far West Comes of Age

The Great West experienced a fantastic surge in migration from the 1870s to the 1890s. A parade of new western states proudly joined the Union. Boomtown Colorado, offspring of the Pikes Peak gold rush, was

The Homesteader's Wife, by Harvey Dunn Women as well as men toiled without shade or respite on the sun-scorched and wind-parched Great Plains.

The South Dakota Art Museum

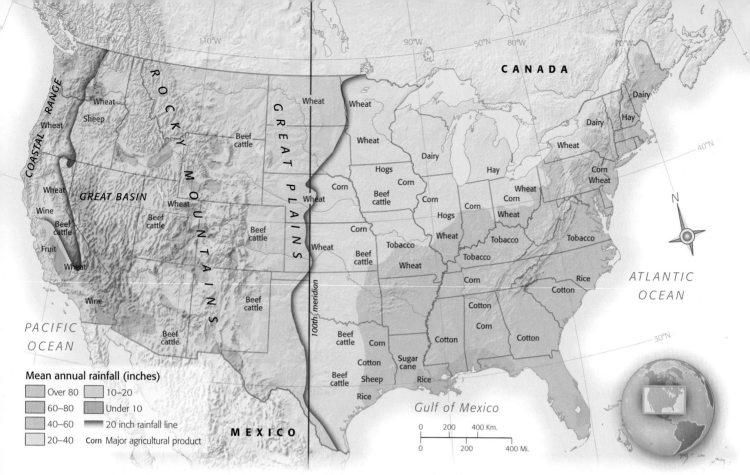

MAP 26.4 Average Annual Precipitation, with Major Agricultural Products, 1900
Northern Hemisphere storms typically circle the globe in a west-to-east direction. Much of the life-nourishing water in these storms is dumped as rainfall on the western slopes of the Pacific coastal ranges and the Rocky Mountains, casting huge "rain shadows" in the Great Basin and in the western Great Plains, up to the line of the 100th meridian. Westward-faring pioneers had to learn new agricultural techniques when they pushed settlement into the drought-prone regions west of the 100th meridian, as reflected in the patterns of crop distribution by 1900. © Cengage Learning

greeted in 1876 as "the Centennial State." In 1889–1890 a Republican Congress, eagerly seeking more Republican electoral and congressional votes, admitted in a wholesale lot six new states: North Dakota, South Dakota, Montana, Washington, Idaho, and Wyoming. The Mormon Church formally—and belatedly, in many Americans' eyes—banned polygamy in 1890, but not until 1896 was Utah deemed worthy of admission. Only Oklahoma, New Mexico, and Arizona remained to be lifted into statehood from contiguous territory on the mainland of North America.

In a last gaudy fling, the federal government made available to settlers vast stretches of fertile plains formerly occupied by the Indians in the district of Oklahoma ("the Beautiful Land"). Scores of overeager and well-armed "sooners," illegally jumping the gun, had entered Oklahoma Territory. They had to be evicted repeatedly by federal troops, who on occasion would

shoot the intruders' horses. On April 22, 1889, all was in readiness for the legal opening, and some 50,000 "boomers" were poised expectantly on the boundary line. At high noon the bugle shrilled, and a horde of "eighty-niners" poured in on lathered horses or careening vehicles. That night a lonely spot on the prairie had mushroomed into the tent city of Guthrie, with over 10,000 people. By the end of the year, Oklahoma boasted 60,000 inhabitants, and Congress made it a territory. In 1907 it became the "Sooner State."

✦ The Fading Frontier

In 1890—a watershed date—the superintendent of the census announced that for the first time in America's experience, a frontier line was no longer discernible. All the unsettled areas were now broken into by isolated

MAP 26.5 Myth and Reality in the West: Percentage of Federal Lands Within Each State, 2004 American folklore pictures the western United States as a land of rugged individualists who tamed the wild region with grit and brawn. The reality is that the federal government has long been by far the West's largest landowner—and that federal projects, especially dam building, have done more to shape the region than all the cowboys and sodbusters there ever were. (Source: Bill Lane Center for the American West, Stanford University.)

© Cengage Learning

bodies of American settlement. The "closing" of the frontier inspired one of the most influential essays ever written about American history—Frederick Jackson Turner's "The Significance of the Frontier in American History" in 1893 (see "Thinking Globally: The Great Frontier," pp. 592–593).

As the nineteenth century neared its sunset, the westward-tramping American people were disturbed to find that their fabled free land was going or had gone. The secretary of war had prophesied in 1827 that five hundred years would be needed to fill the West. But as the nation finally recognized that its land was not inexhaustible, seeds were planted to preserve the vanishing resource. The government set aside land for national parks—first Yellowstone in 1872, followed by Yosemite and Sequoia in 1890.

But the frontier was more than a place; it was also a state of mind and a symbol of opportunity. Its passing ended a romantic phase of the nation's internal development and created new economic and psychological problems.

Traditionally footloose, Americans have been notorious for their mobility. The nation's farmers, unlike the peasants of Europe, have seldom remained rooted to their soil. The land, sold for a profit as settlement closed in, was often the settler's most profitable crop.

Much has been said about the frontier as a "safety valve." The theory is that when hard times came, the unemployed who cluttered the city pavements merely moved west, took up farming, and prospered.

In truth, relatively few city dwellers, at least in the populous eastern centers, migrated to the frontier during depressions. Most of them did not know how to farm; few of them could raise enough money to transport themselves west and then pay for livestock and expensive machinery.

But the safety-valve theory does have some validity. Free acreage did lure to the West a host of immigrant farmers who otherwise might have remained in the eastern cities to clog the job markets and to crowd the festering and already overpopulated slums. And the very *possibility* of westward migration may have induced urban employers to maintain wage rates high enough to discourage workers from leaving. But the real safety valve by the late nineteenth century was in western cities like Chicago, Denver, and San Francisco, where failed farmers, busted miners, and displaced easterners found ways to seek their fortunes. Indeed, after about 1880 the area from the Rocky Mountains to the Pacific Coast was the most urbanized region in America, measured by the percentage of people living in cities.

U.S. history cannot be properly understood unless it is viewed in light of the westward-moving experience. As Frederick Jackson Turner wrote, "American history has been in a large degree the history of the colonization of the Great West." The story of settling and taming the trans-Mississippi West in the late nineteenth century was but the last chapter in the saga of colonizing various American "wests" since Columbus's

Robert Louis Stevenson's Transcontinental Journey, 1879

The celebrated Scottish writer Robert Louis Stevenson, author of such enduring classics as *Treasure Island, Kidnapped*, and *The Strange Case of Dr. Jekyll and Mr. Hyde*, journeyed from Scotland to California in 1879 to rendezvous with his American fiancée, Frances Osbourne. Between New York and San Francisco, Stevenson traveled on the transcontinental railroad line completed just ten years earlier, and he dutifully recorded his impressions of America, the West in particular, as he made his way toward California. Stevenson's account of his trip provides an unusually gifted writer's vivid portrait of the trans-Mississippi West at the close of the era of the Indian wars. Like all travelogues, Stevenson's colorful tale may reveal as much about the traveler as it does about the things he saw. Yet historians frequently make use of such documents to reconstruct the original appearance and texture of places that were once the exotic destinations of adventurous travelers, before they were transformed by the onrush of modernity. In the passages reproduced here, inspired by the view as Stevenson's train passed through Nebraska and Wyoming, what features of the landscape does the author find most remarkable? How does he portray the railroad?

Source: Robert Louis Stevenson, *Across the Plains* (New York: Charles Scribner's Sons, 1897).

THE PLAINS OF NEBRASKA

... We were at sea—there is no other adequate expression—on the plains of Nebraska.... It was a world almost without a feature; an empty sky, an empty earth; front and back, the line of railway stretched from horizon to horizon, like a cue across a billiard-board; on either hand, the green plain ran till it touched the skirts of heaven.... [G]razing beasts were seen upon the prairie at all degrees of distance and diminution; and now and again we might perceive a few dots beside the railroad which grew more and more distinct as we drew nearer till they turned into wooden cabins, and then dwindled and dwindled in our wake until they melted into their surroundings, and we were once more alone upon the billiard-board. The train toiled over this infinity like a snail; and being the one thing moving, it was wonderful what huge proportions it began to assume in our regard....

[That] evening we left Laramie [Wyoming].... And yet when day came, it was to shine upon the same broken and unsightly quarter of the world. Mile upon mile, and not a tree, a bird, or a river. Only down the long, sterile cañons, the train shot hooting and awoke the resting echo. That train was the one piece of life in all the deadly land; it was the one actor, the one spectacle fit to be observed in this paralysis of man and nature. And when I think how the railroad has been pushed through this unwatered wilderness and haunt of savage tribes, and now will bear an emigrant for some £12 from the Atlantic to the Golden Gates; how at each stage of the construction, roaring, impromptu cities, full of gold and lust and death, sprang up and then died away again, and are now but wayside stations in the desert; how in these uncouth places pig-tailed Chinese pirates worked side by side with border ruffians and broken men from Europe, talking together in a mixed dialect, mostly oaths, gambling, drinking, quarrelling and murdering like wolves; how the plumed hereditary lord of all America heard, in this last fastness, the scream of the 'bad medicine waggon' charioting his foes; and then when I go on to remember that all this epical turmoil was conducted by gentlemen in frock coats, and with a view to nothing more extraordinary than a fortune and a subsequent visit to Paris, it seems to me, I own, as if this railway were the one typical achievement of the age in which we live, as if it brought together into one plot all the ends of the world and all the degrees of social rank, and offered to some great writer the busiest, the most extended, and the most varied subject for an enduring literary work....

The Great Frontier

The American pioneers who surged westward in the nineteenth century were part of a great global land grab that changed lives and landscapes on several continents. From the Australian Outback to the Canadian prairies, from the Argentine pampas to the Russian steppes and the African savannas, millions of mostly white settlers poured into vast new territories and claimed them as their own.

Everywhere, the settlers encountered indigenous peoples who had lived on those lands since time immemorial. With their superiority in weaponry, transportation, and political organization, everywhere the newcomers prevailed. By the century's close, they had displaced or destroyed countless native peoples and extended their

dominion over parts of the planet once considered too remote or rugged to be habitable.

The American frontier soon became the stuff of legend, and even the subject of a scholarly explanation of American uniqueness—Frederick Jackson Turner's fabled "frontier thesis," which hailed the gumption and moxie of the pioneers and commended them as the agents of civilization and democracy. Yet far from being unique, those westering Americans had much in common with settlers in sister societies abroad. Argentina had its cowboys (gauchos), and Australia had its colorful backcountry outlaws, such as Ned Kelly, whose exploits rivaled those of Billy the Kid. The Russians and South Africans had their own versions of "Manifest

Destiny," and like the Americans they often cloaked them in the language of racial superiority.

The world's various frontiers also reflected the particularities of geography and history. Australians soon conceded that much of their continent—the world's driest—was too arid for traditional farming. Most of the Outback proved suitable only for enormous "sheep stations," sometimes measuring tens of thousands of acres. Consequently, small-farm homesteading of the American and Canadian type never took root, nor did cities of any consequence emerge in the parched Australian interior.

Canada's westward movement came later than that in the United States and proceeded more peaceably. Only after

Royal Canadian Mounted Police

North-West Mounted Police, ca. 1890   Empowered by an act of Parliament in 1873 to establish Canadian authority and order in the Northwest Territories, this force made frontier settlement somewhat more peaceful in Canada than in the United States. In 1920 the North-West Mounted Police absorbed the Dominion Police and became the famed Royal Canadian Mounted Police, or "Mounties."

Russian Peasants in Siberia, 1910

the Ottawa government promised in 1871 to build a transcontinental railroad connecting eastern Canada to its western provinces did settlement begin in earnest. And unlike in America, where restless pioneers typically struck out on their own and made much mischief among themselves and with the Indians they encountered, in Canada settlers were generally preceded by government authorities—usually the red-jacketed North-West Mounted Police, or "Mounties"—who established at least a semblance of order before large numbers of pioneers appeared on the scene. As a result, Canada's frontier was markedly less violent than America's. Canada, then and now a more law-abiding society than the United States, never had a "Wild West" like that of its southern neighbor.

In Argentina and Russia, inherited patterns of landholding and politics shaped their nineteenth-century frontiers. When Argentina's General Julio Roca vanquished the native Araucanians in 1879, he flung open the horizonless pampas to white settlement. But he

also retained the venerable custom, handed down from Spanish colonial times, of apportioning the land in gigantic *estancias* (ranches) to a few favored fellow soldiers and friends. These lordly landowners then employed wage workers, mostly Italian immigrants, who turned the fertile Argentine interior into a beef bowl and breadbasket to the world. The immigrants themselves, however, had little hope of ever possessing land of their own.

Russia's frontier lay to the east and long felt the heavy hand of the tsar. For centuries autocratic rulers had strongarmed landowning nobles to move their serfs onto the "virgin lands" beyond the settled edge of European Russia. By the nineteenth century, imperial Russia had pushed its frontier onto the rolling steppes of central Asia, home to Tartars, Kalmyks, Kazakhs, and myriad other indigenous peoples. Only military conquest and a strengthened state bureaucracy made possible European settlement in those regions. Between 1867 and 1897, more than a million of the tsar's subjects left for the hinterland. As elsewhere, the railroad

proved essential to the growth of the tsarist empire, especially after the government began construction of the Trans-Siberian line in 1891.

The Dutch-descended Afrikaners, or Boers, in southern Africa found their frontier to the north, and unlike their American counterparts, they made scant claim to be spreading democracy. Rather, they sought to escape British rule in the Cape Colony—in particular, to escape from the threat of racial equality for blacks after Britain abolished slavery in the 1830s. The Afrikaners' "Great Trek" took them into the land of the Zulus, who ferociously resisted the oncoming Boers but eventually, like indigenous peoples everywhere, were forced to submit to white rule.

In the Americas, Australia, Asia, and Africa, the great frontier of the nineteenth century was the companion of conquest. The frontier brought opportunity to some and oppression to others. In many places it nurtured democracy; elsewhere it invigorated autocracy. And everywhere it expanded the domains of European civilization—for better or worse.

day—from the West Indies to the Chesapeake shore, from the valleys of the Hudson and Connecticut Rivers to the valleys of the Tennessee and Ohio Rivers.

And yet the trans-Mississippi West formed a distinct chapter in that saga and retains even to this day much of its uniqueness. There the Native American peoples waged their last and most desperate struggle against colonization, and there most Native Americans live today. There "Anglo" culture collided most directly with Hispanic culture—the historic rival of the Anglo-Americans for dominance in the New World—and the Southwest remains the most Hispanicized region in America. There America faced across the Pacific to Asia, and there most Asian Americans dwell today. There the scale and severity of the environment posed their largest challenges to human ambitions, and there the environment, with its aridity and still-magical emptiness, continues to mold social and political life, and the American imagination, as in no other part of the nation. And in no other region has the federal government, with its vast landholdings, its subsidies to the railroads, and its massive irrigation projects, played so conspicuous a role in economic and social development.

The westward-moving pioneers and the country they confronted have assumed mythic proportions in the American mind. They have been immortalized by such writers as Bret Harte, Mark Twain, Helen Hunt Jackson, and Francis Parkman, and by such painters as George Catlin, Frederic Remington, and Albert Bierstadt. For better or worse, those pioneers planted the seeds of American civilization in the immense western wilderness. The life we live, they dreamed of; the life they lived, we can only dream.

✴ The Farm Becomes a Factory

The situation of American farmers, once jacks-and-jills-of-all-trades, was rapidly changing. They had raised their own food, fashioned their own clothing, and bartered for other necessities with neighbors. Now high prices persuaded farmers to concentrate on growing single "cash" crops, such as wheat or corn, and use their profits to buy foodstuffs at the general store and manufactured goods in town or by mail order. The Chicago firm of Aaron Montgomery Ward sent out its first catalogue—a single sheet—in 1872. Farmers were becoming both consumers and producers in the world economy, as their crops journeyed by rail and ship to distant parts of the globe.

Large-scale farmers, especially in the immense grain-producing areas of the Mississippi Valley, were now both specialists and businesspeople. As cogs in the vast industrial machine, these farmers were intimately tied to banking, railroading, and manufacturing. They had to buy expensive machinery in order to plant and harvest their crops. A powerful steam engine could drag behind it simultaneously the plow, seeder, and harrow. The speed of harvesting wheat was dramatically increased in the 1870s by the invention of the twine binder and then in the 1880s by the "combine"—the combined reaper-thresher, which was drawn by twenty to forty horses and which both reaped and bagged the grain. Widespread use of such costly equipment naturally called for first-class management. But the farmers, often unskilled as businesspeople, were inclined to blame the banks and railroads or the volatility of the global marketplace, rather than their own shortcomings, for their losses.

This amazing **mechanization of agriculture** in the postwar years was almost as striking as the mechanization of industry. In fact, agricultural modernization drove many marginal farmers off the land, thus swelling the ranks of the new industrial work force. As the

Picture Research Consultants & Archives

Grain Harvesting in Washington State Humans, horses, and machines join forces in this turn-of-the-century scene.

rural population steadily decreased, those farmers who remained achieved miracles of production, making America the world's breadbasket and butcher shop. The farm was attaining the status of a factory—an outdoor grain factory. Bonanza wheat farms of the Minnesota–North Dakota area, for example, were enormous. By 1890 at least a half-dozen of them were larger than fifteen thousand acres, with communication by telephone from one part to another. These bonanza farms foreshadowed the gigantic agribusinesses of the next century.

Agriculture was a big business from its earliest days in California's phenomenally productive (and phenomenally irrigated) Central Valley. California farms, carved out of giant Spanish Mexican land grants and the railroads' huge holdings, were from the outset more than three times larger than the national average. The reformer Henry George in 1871 described the Golden State as "not a country of farms but a country of plantations and estates." With the advent of the railroad refrigerator car in the 1880s, California fruit and vegetable crops, raised on sprawling tracts by ill-paid migrant Mexican and Chinese farmhands, sold at a handsome profit in the rich urban markets of the East.

✷ Deflation Dooms the Debtor

Once the farmers became chained to a one-crop economy—wheat or corn—they were in the same leaky boat with the southern cotton growers. As long as prices stayed high, all went well. But when they skidded in the 1880s, bankruptcy fell like a blight on the farm belts.

The grain farmers were no longer the masters of their own destinies. They were engaged in one of the most fiercely competitive of businesses, for the price of their product was determined in a world market by the world output. If the wheat fields of Argentina, Russia, and other foreign countries flourished, the price of the farmers' grain would fall and American sodbusters would face ruin, as they did in the 1880s and 1890s.

Low prices and a deflated currency were the chief worries of the frustrated farmers—North, South, and West. If a family had borrowed $1,000 in 1855, when wheat was worth about a dollar a bushel, they expected to pay back the equivalent of one thousand bushels, plus interest, when the mortgage fell due. But if they let their debt run to 1890, when wheat had fallen to about fifty cents a bushel, they would have to pay back the price of two thousand bushels for the $1,000 they had borrowed, plus interest. This unexpected burden struck them as unjust, though their steely-eyed creditors often branded the complaining farmers as slippery and dishonest rascals.

The deflationary pinch on the debtor flowed partly from the static money supply. There were simply not

A contemporary farm protest song, "The Kansas Fool," ran,

❝ The bankers followed us out west;
And did in mortgages invest;
They looked ahead and shrewdly planned,
And soon they'll have our Kansas land.❞

enough dollars to go around, and as a result, prices were forced down. In 1870 the currency in circulation for each person was $19.42; in 1890 it was only $22.67. Yet during these twenty years, business and industrial activity, increasing manyfold, had intensified the scramble for available currency.

The forgotten farmers were caught on a treadmill. Despite unremitting toil, they operated year after year at a loss and lived off their fat as best they could. In a vicious circle, their farm machinery increased their output of grain, lowered the price, and drove them even deeper into debt. Mortgages engulfed homesteads at an alarming rate; by 1890 Nebraska alone reported more than 100,000 farms blanketed with mortgages. The repeated crash of the sheriff-auctioneer's hammer kept announcing to the world that another sturdy American farmer had become landless in a landed nation.

Ruinous rates of interest, running from 8 to 40 percent, were charged on mortgages, largely by agents of eastern loan companies. The windburned sons and daughters of the sod, who felt that they deserved praise for developing the country, cried out in despair against the loan sharks and the Wall Street octopus.

Farm tenancy rather than farm ownership was spreading like stinkweed. The trend was especially marked in the sharecropping South, where cotton prices also sank dismayingly. By 1880 one-fourth of all American farms were operated by tenants. The United States was ready to feed the world, but under the new industrial feudalism, the farmers were about to sink into a status suggesting Old World serfdom.

✷ Unhappy Farmers

Even Mother Nature ceased smiling, as her powerful forces conspired against agriculture. Mile-wide clouds of grasshoppers, leaving "nothing but the mortgage," periodically ravaged prairie farms. The terrible cotton-boll weevil was also wreaking havoc in the South by the early 1890s.

The good earth was going sour. Floods added to the waste of erosion, which had already washed the topsoil off millions of once-lush southern acres. Expensive fertilizers were urgently needed. A long succession of

Nebraska Homesteaders in Front of Their Sod House, 1887 These two brothers and their families had escaped to Canada from the slave South during the Civil War. Returning to the United States in the 1880s, they took advantage of the Homestead Act to stake out farms in Custer County, Nebraska.

droughts seared the trans-Mississippi West, beginning in the summer of 1887. Whole towns were abandoned. "Going home to the wife's folks" and "In God we trusted, in Kansas we busted" were typical laments of many impoverished farmers, as they fled their weather-beaten shacks and sun-baked sod houses. One irate "poet" snarled,

> *Fifty miles to water,*
> *A hundred miles to wood,*
> *To hell with this damned country,*
> *I'm going home for good.*

To add to their miseries, the soil-tillers were gouged by their government—local, state, and national. Their land was overassessed, and they paid painful local taxes, whereas wealthy easterners could conceal their stocks and bonds in safe-deposit boxes. High protective tariffs in these years poured profits into the pockets of manufacturers. Farmers, on the other hand, had no choice but to sell their low-priced products in a fiercely competitive, unprotected world market, while buying high-priced manufactured goods in a protected home market.

The farmers were also "farmed" by the corporations and processors. They were at the mercy of the harvester trust, the barbed-wire trust, and the fertilizer trust, all of which could control output and raise prices to extortionate levels. Middlemen took a juicy "cut" from the selling price of the goods that the farmers bought, while operators pushed storage rates to the ceiling at grain warehouses and elevators.

In addition, the railroad octopus had the grain growers in its grip. Freight rates could be so high that the farmers sometimes lost less if they burned their corn for fuel than if they shipped it. If they raised their voices in protest, the ruthless railroad operators might let their grain spoil in damp places or refuse to provide them with cars when needed.

Farmers still made up nearly one-half the population in 1890, but they were hopelessly disorganized. The manufacturers and the railroad barons knew how to combine to promote their interests, and so, increasingly, did industrial workers. But the farmers were by nature independent and individualistic—dead set against consolidation or regimentation. No really effective Carnegie or Gompers arose among them to preach the gospel of economic integration and concentration. They never did organize successfully to restrict production until forced to by the federal government nearly half a century later, in Franklin Roosevelt's New Deal days. What they did manage to organize was a monumental political uprising.

✵ The Farmers Take Their Stand

Agrarian unrest had flared forth earlier, in the Greenback movement shortly after the Civil War. Prices sagged in 1868, and a host of farmers unsuccessfully sought relief from low prices and high indebtedness by demanding an inflation of the currency with paper money.

The National Grange of the Patrons of Husbandry—better known as the Grange—was organized in 1867. Its leading spirit was Oliver H. Kelley, a shrewd and energetic Minnesota farmer then working as a clerk in Washington. Kelley's first objective was to enhance the lives of isolated farmers through social, educational, and fraternal activities. Farm men and women, cursed with loneliness in widely separated farmhouses, found the Grange's picnics, concerts, and lectures a godsend. Kelley, a Mason, even found farmers receptive to his mumbo-jumbo of passwords and secret rituals, as well as his four-ply hierarchy, ranging (for men) from Laborer to Husbandman and (for women) from Maid to

Matron. The Grange spread like an old-time prairie fire and by 1875 claimed 800,000 members, chiefly in the Midwest and South. Buzzing with gossip, these calicoed and callous folk often met in red schoolhouses around potbellied stoves.

The Grangers gradually raised their goals from individual self-improvement to improvement of the farmers' collective plight. In a determined effort to escape the clutches of the trusts, they established cooperatively owned stores for consumers and cooperatively owned grain elevators and warehouses for producers. Their most ambitious experiment was an attempt to manufacture harvesting machinery, but this venture, partly as a result of mismanagement, ended in financial disaster.

Embattled Grangers also went into politics, enjoying their most gratifying success in the grain-growing regions of the upper Mississippi Valley, chiefly in Illinois, Wisconsin, Iowa, and Minnesota. There, through state legislation, they strove to regulate railway rates and the storage fees charged by railroads and by the operators of warehouses and grain elevators. Many of the state courts, notably in Illinois, were disposed to recognize the principle of public control of private business for the general welfare. A number of the so-called Granger Laws, however, were badly drawn, and they were bitterly fought through the high courts by the well-paid lawyers of the "interests." Following judicial reverses, most severely at the hands of the Supreme Court in the famous *Wabash* decision of 1886 (see p. 519), the Grangers' influence faded. But their organization has lived on as a vocal champion of farm interests, while brightening rural life with social activities.

Farmers' grievances likewise found a vent in the Greenback Labor party, which combined the inflationary appeal of the earlier Greenbackers with a program for improving the lot of labor. In 1878, the high-water mark of the movement, the Greenback Laborites polled

The Farmers' Grievances This poster from 1875 expresses one of the agrarian radicals' fundamental premises: that all other walks of life were dependent—or even parasitic—on the indispensable work of farmers. In his famous "Cross of Gold" speech in 1896 (see p. 601), Populist presidential candidate William Jennings Bryan put it this way: "Burn down your cities and leave our farms, and your cities will spring up again as if by magic; but destroy our farms and the grass will grow in the streets of every city in the country."

over a million votes and elected fourteen members of Congress. In the presidential election of 1880, the Greenbackers ran General James B. Weaver, an old Granger who was a favorite of Civil War veterans and who possessed a remarkable voice and bearing. He spoke to perhaps half a million citizens in a hundred or so speeches but polled only 3 percent of the total popular vote.

✦ Prelude to Populism

A striking manifestation of rural discontent came through the Farmers' Alliance, founded in Texas in the late 1870s (see p. 505). Farmers came together in the Alliance to socialize, but more importantly to break the strangling grip of the railroads and manufacturers through cooperative buying and selling. Local chapters spread throughout the South and the Great Plains during the 1880s, until by 1890 members numbered more than a million hard-bitten souls.

Unfortunately, the Alliance weakened itself by ignoring the plight of landless tenant farmers, sharecroppers, and farmworkers. Even more debilitating was the Alliance's exclusion of blacks, who counted for nearly half the agricultural population of the South. In the 1880s a separate Colored Farmers' National Alliance emerged to attract black farmers, and by 1890 membership numbered more than 250,000. The long history of racial division in the South, however, made it difficult for white and black farmers to work together in the same organization.

Out of the Farmers' Alliances a new political party emerged in the early 1890s—the People's party. Better known as the **Populists**, these frustrated farmers attacked Wall Street and the "money trust." They called for nationalizing the railroads, telephone, and telegraph; instituting a graduated income tax; and creating a new federal "subtreasury"—a scheme to provide farmers with loans for crops stored in government-owned warehouses, where they could be held until market prices rose. They also wanted the free and unlimited coinage of silver—yet another of the debtors' demands for inflation that echoed continuously throughout the Gilded Age.

Numerous fiery prophets leapt forward to trumpet the Populist cause. The free coinage of silver struck many Populists as a cure-all, especially after the circulation of an enormously popular pamphlet titled *Coin's Financial School* (1894). Written by William Hope Harvey, it was illustrated by clever woodcuts, one of which depicted the gold ogre beheading the beautiful silver maiden. In fiction parading as fact, the booklet showed how the "little professor"—"Coin" Harvey—overwhelmed the bankers and professors of economics with his brilliant arguments on behalf of free silver. Another notorious spellbinder was red-haired Ignatius Donnelly of Minnesota, three times elected to Congress. The queen of the Populist "calamity howlers" was Mary Elizabeth ("Mary Yellin'") Lease, a tall, athletic woman known as the "Kansas Pythoness." She reportedly demanded that Kansans should raise "less corn and more hell." The big-city *New York Evening Post* snarled, "We don't want any more states until we can civilize Kansas." To many easterners, complaint, not corn, was rural America's staple crop.

Yet the Populists, despite their oddities, were not to be laughed away. They were leading a deadly earnest and impassioned campaign to relieve the farmers' many miseries. Smiles faded from Republican and Democratic faces alike as countless thousands of Populists began to sing "Good-bye, My Party, Good-bye." In 1892 the Populists had jolted the traditional parties by winning several congressional seats and polling more than 1 million votes for their presidential candidate, James B. Weaver. Racial divisions continued to hobble the Populists in the South, but in the West their ranks were swelling. Could the People's party now reach beyond its regional bases in agrarian America, join hands with

Kansas State Historical Society

Mary E. Lease (1853–1933) She was so eloquent as to be called the "Patrick Henry in Petticoats."

urban workers, and mount a successful attack on the northeastern citadels of power?

✦ Coxey's Army and the Pullman Strike

The panic of 1893 and the severe ensuing depression strengthened the Populists' argument that farmers and laborers alike were being victimized by an oppressive economic and political system. Ragged armies of the unemployed began marching to protest their plight. In the growing hordes of displaced industrial toilers, the Populists saw potential political allies.

The most famous marcher was "General" Jacob S. Coxey, a wealthy Ohio quarry owner. He set out for Washington in 1894 with a few score of supporters and a swarm of newspaper reporters. His platform included a demand that the government relieve unemployment by an inflationary public works program, supported by some $500 million in legal tender notes to be issued by the Treasury. Coxey himself rode in a carriage with his wife and infant son, appropriately named Legal Tender Coxey, while his tiny "army" tramped along behind, singing,

We're coming, Grover Cleveland,
500,000 strong,
We're marching on to Washington
to right the nation's wrong.

The "Commonweal Army" of Coxeyites finally straggled into the nation's capital, but the invasion took on the aspects of a comic opera when "General" Coxey and his "lieutenants" were arrested for walking on the grass.

Elsewhere, violent flare-ups accompanied labor protests, notably in Chicago. Most dramatic was the crippling **Pullman strike** of 1894. Eugene V. Debs, a charismatic labor leader, had helped organize the American Railway Union of about 150,000 members. The Pullman Palace Car Company, which maintained a model town near Chicago for its employees, was hit hard by the depression and cut wages by about one-third, while holding the line on rent for the company houses. The workers finally struck—in some places overturning Pullman cars—and paralyzed railway traffic from Chicago to the Pacific coast. The American Federation of Labor conspicuously declined to support the Pullman strikers, thus enhancing the AF of L's reputation for "respectability" even while weakening labor's cause by driving a large wedge into the workers' ranks.

The turmoil in Chicago was serious but not yet completely out of hand. At least this was the judgment of Governor John Peter Altgeld of Illinois, a friend of the downtrodden, who had pardoned the Haymarket

After the Pullman strike collapsed, Eugene Debs (1855–1926) said,

❝No strike has ever been lost.❞

In 1897 he declared,

❝The issue is Socialism versus Capitalism. I am for Socialism because I am for humanity.❞

Square anarchists the year before (see p. 533). But U.S. attorney general Richard Olney, an archconservative and an ex–railroad attorney, urged the dispatch of federal troops. His legal grounds were that the strikers were interfering with the transit of the U.S. mail. President Cleveland supported Olney with the ringing declaration, "If it takes the entire army and navy to deliver a postal card in Chicago, that card will be delivered."

To the delight of conservatives, federal troops, bayonets fixed, crushed the Pullman strike. Debs was sentenced to six months' imprisonment for contempt

William B. Becker Collection/American Museum of Photography

Coxey's Army on the March, 1894 This photograph shows two of the banners that Coxey's Army carried. The one in the foreground says "Death to Interest on Bonds," the usual debtors' protest against creditors. The larger one in the background reads "Pittsburg & Allegheny. Work for Americans. More Money, Less Misery, Good Roads," a reference to Coxey's plan to end the depression by employing the jobless to build public works and paying them with greenbacks.

The Pullman Strike, 1894
Illinois National Guardsmen fire on Pullman Company strikers on July 7, 1894. Police clubs and U.S. Army rifles and bayonets finally broke the back of the strike, which halted railroads throughout the country.

of court because he had defied a federal court injunction to cease striking. Ironically, the lean labor agitator spent much of his enforced leisure reading radical literature, which led to his later leadership of the socialist movement in America.

Embittered cries of "government by injunction" now burst from organized labor. This was the first time that such a legal weapon had been used conspicuously by Washington to break a strike, and it was all the more distasteful because defiant workers who were held in contempt could be imprisoned without a jury trial. Signs multiplied that employers were striving to smash labor unions by court action. Nonlabor elements of the country, including the Populists and other debtors, were likewise incensed. They saw in the brutal Pullman episode further proof of an unholy alliance between business and the courts.

✪ Golden McKinley and Silver Bryan

The smoldering grievances of the long-suffering farmers and the depression-plagued laborers gave ominous significance to the election of 1896. Conservatives of all stripes feared an impending upheaval, while down-and-out husbandmen and discontented workers cast about desperately for political salvation. Increasingly, monetary policy—whether to maintain the gold standard or inflate the currency by monetizing silver—loomed as the issue on which the election would turn.

The leading candidate for the Republican presidential nomination in 1896 was former congressman William McKinley of Ohio, sponsor of the ill-starred tariff bill of 1890 (see p. 601). He had established a creditable Civil War record, having risen to the rank of major; he hailed from the electorally potent state of Ohio; and he could point to long years of honorable service in Congress, where he had made many friends with his kindly and conciliatory manner.

As a presidential candidate, McKinley was largely the creature of a fellow Ohioan, Marcus Alonzo Hanna, who had made his fortune in the iron business and now coveted the role of president maker. "I love McKinley," he once said. As a wholehearted Hamiltonian, Hanna believed that a prime function of government was to aid business. Honest, earnest, tough, and direct, he became the personification of big industry in politics. He was often caricatured in cartoons, quite unfairly, as a bloated bully in a loud checkered suit with a dollar sign in each square. He believed that in some measure prosperity "trickled down" to the laborer, whose dinner pail was full when business flourished. Critics assailed this idea as equivalent to feeding the horses in order to feed the sparrows.

The hardheaded Hanna, although something of a novice in politics, organized his preconvention campaign for McKinley with consummate skill and with a liberal outpouring of his own money. The convention steamroller, well lubricated with Hanna's dollars, nominated McKinley on the first ballot in St. Louis in June 1896. The Republican platform cleverly straddled the money question but leaned toward hard-money policies. It declared for the gold standard, even though McKinley's voting record in Congress had been embarrassingly friendly to silver. The platform also condemned hard times and Democratic incapacity, while pouring praise on the protective tariff.

Dissension riddled the Democratic camp. Cleveland no longer led his party. The depression had driven the last nail into his political coffin. Dubbed "the Stuffed Prophet," he was undeniably the most unpopular man in the country. Labor-debtor groups remembered too vividly his intervention in the Pullman strike, the backstairs Morgan bond deal, and especially his stubborn hard-money policies. Ultraconservative in finance, Cleveland now looked more like a Republican than a Democrat on the money issue.

Rudderless, the Democratic convention met in Chicago in July 1896, with the silverites lusting for victory.

Crying for Protection, 1896 Uncle Sam is called on in this cartoon to nurse so-called infant industries—some of which had in fact long since grown into vigorous adulthood.

McKinley Campaign Headquarters, Chicago, 1896 Those few black Americans who could exercise their right to vote in the 1890s still remained faithful to "the party of Lincoln."

Shouting insults at the absent Cleveland, the delegates refused, by a suicidal vote of 564 to 357, to endorse their own administration. They had the enthusiasm and the numbers; all they lacked was a leader.

A new Moses suddenly appeared in the person of William Jennings Bryan of Nebraska. Then only thirty-six years of age and known as "the Boy Orator of the Platte,"* he stepped confidently onto the platform before fifteen thousand people. His masterful presence was set off by a peninsular jaw and raven-black hair. He radiated honesty, sincerity, and energy.

The convention-hall setting was made to order for a magnificent oratorical effort. A hush fell over the delegates as Bryan stood before them. With an organlike voice that rolled into the outer corners of the huge hall, he delivered a fervent plea for silver. Rising to supreme heights of eloquence, he thundered, "We will answer their demands for a gold standard by saying to them: 'You shall not press down upon the brow of labor this crown of thorns, you shall not crucify mankind upon a cross of gold.'"

---

*One contemporary sneered that Bryan, like the Platte River in his home state of Nebraska, was "six inches deep and six miles wide at the mouth."

The Cross of Gold speech was a sensation. Swept off its feet in a tumultuous scene, the Democratic convention nominated Bryan the next day on the fifth ballot. The platform demanded inflation through the unlimited coinage of silver at the ratio of 16 ounces of silver to 1 of gold, though the market ratio was about 32 to 1. This meant that the silver in a dollar would be worth about fifty cents.

Democratic "Gold Bugs," unable to swallow Bryan, bolted their party over the silver issue. A conservative senator from New York, when asked if he was a Democrat still, reportedly replied, "Yes, I am a Democrat still—very still." The Democratic minority, including Cleveland, charged that the Populist-silverites had stolen both the name and the clothes of their party. They nominated a lost-cause ticket of their own, and many of them, including Cleveland, not too secretly hoped for a McKinley victory.

The Populists now faced a dilemma, because the Democratic majority had appropriated their main plank—"16 to 1," that "heaven-born ratio." The bulk of the Populists, fearing a hard-money McKinley victory, endorsed both "fusion" with the Democrats and Bryan for president, sacrificing their identity in the mix. Singing "The Jolly Silver Dollar of the Dads," they became in effect the "Demo-Pop" party, though a handful of the original Populists refused to support Bryan and went down with their colors nailed to the mast.

✴ Class Conflict: Plowholders Versus Bondholders

Mark Hanna smugly assumed that he could make the tariff the focus of the campaign. But Bryan, a dynamo of energy, forced the free-trade issue into the backseat when he took to the stump in behalf of free silver. Sweeping through 27 states and traveling 18,000 miles, he made nearly 600 speeches—36 in one day—and even invaded the East, "the enemy's country." Vachel Lindsay caught the spirit of his oratorical orgy:

> Prairie avenger, mountain lion,
> Bryan, Bryan, Bryan, Bryan,
> Gigantic troubadour, speaking like a siege gun,
> Smashing Plymouth Rock with his boulders
> from the West.*

Free silver became almost as much a religious as a financial issue. Hordes of fanatical free-silverites hailed Bryan as the messiah to lead them out of the wilderness

of debt. They sang, "We'll All Have Our Pockets Lined with Silver" and "No Crown of Thorns, No Cross of Gold."

Bryan created panic among eastern conservatives with his threat of converting their holdings overnight into fifty-cent dollars. The "Gold Bugs" responded with their own free and unlimited coinage of verbiage. They vented their alarm in abusive epithets, ranging from "fanatic" and "madman" to "traitor" and "murderer." "In God We Trust, with Bryan We Bust," the Republicans sneered, while one eastern clergyman cried, "That platform was made in Hell." Widespread fear of Bryan and the "silver lunacy" enabled "Dollar Mark" Hanna, now chairman of the Republican National Committee, to shine as a money-raiser. He "shook down" the trusts and plutocrats and piled up an enormous "slush fund" for a "campaign of education"—or of propaganda, depending on one's point of view. Reminding the voters of Cleveland's "Democratic panic," Republicans appealed to the "belly vote" with their prize slogan, "McKinley and the Full Dinner Pail." The McKinleyites amassed the most formidable political campaign chest thus far in American history. At all levels—national, state, and local—it amounted to about $16 million, as contrasted with about $1 million for the poorer Democrats (roughly "16 to 1"). With some justification, the Bryanites accused Hanna of buying the election and of floating McKinley into the White House on a tidal wave of mud and money.

Bryan's cyclonic campaign began to lose steam as the weeks passed. Fear was probably Hanna's strongest ally, as it was Bryan's worst enemy. Republican businesspeople placed contracts with manufacturers, contingent on the election of McKinley. A few factory owners, with thinly veiled intimidation, paid off their workers and told them not to come to work on Wednesday morning if Bryan won. Reports also circulated that employers were threatening to pay their employees in fifty-cent pieces, instead of in dollars, if Bryan triumphed. Such were some of the "dirty tricks" of the "Stop Bryan, Save America" crusade.

Hanna's campaign methods paid off. On election day McKinley triumphed decisively. The vote was 271 to 176 in the Electoral College and 7,102,246 to 6,492,559 in the popular election. Driven by fear and excitement, an unprecedented outpouring of voters flocked to the polls. McKinley ran strongly in the populous East, where he carried every county of New England, and in the upper Mississippi Valley. Bryan's states, concentrated in the debt-burdened South and the trans-Mississippi West, boasted more acreage than McKinley's but less population (see Map 26.6).

The free-silver election of 1896 was perhaps the most significant political turning point since Lincoln's victories in 1860 and 1864. Despite Bryan's strength in

---

*Reprinted with the permission of Scribner, a division of Simon & Schuster, Inc., from *The Collected Poems of Vachel Lindsay*, Revised Edition by Vachel Lindsay, New York: Macmillan, 1948.

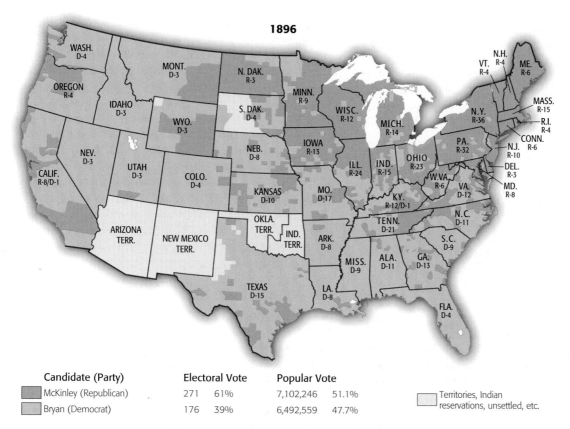

1896

Candidate (Party)	Electoral Vote		Popular Vote	
McKinley (Republican)	271	61%	7,102,246	51.1%
Bryan (Democrat)	176	39%	6,492,559	47.7%

Territories, Indian reservations, unsettled, etc.

MAP 26.6 Presidential Election of 1896 (with electoral vote by state)   This election tolled the death knell of the Gilded Age political party system, with its razor-close elections, strong party loyalties, and high voter turnouts. Bryan's sweep of the southern states and strong showing in the West gave him only 176 electoral votes to McKinley's 271 from the more populous North and East. For years after 1896, Republicans predominated, and citizens showed a declining interest in joining parties and voting. © Cengage Learning

the South and West, the results vividly demonstrated his lack of appeal to the unmortgaged farmer and especially to the eastern urban laborer. Many wage earners in the East voted for their jobs and full dinner pails, threatened as they were by free silver, free trade, and fireless factories. Living precariously on a fixed wage, the factory workers had no reason to favor inflation, which was the heart of the Bryanites' program.

In gold-standard Britain, there was much relief over McKinley's victory. The London Standard *commented,*

❝ The hopelessly ignorant and savagely covetous waifs and strays of American civilization voted for Bryan, but the bulk of the solid sense, business integrity, and social stability sided with McKinley. The nation is to be heartily congratulated.❞

The Bryan-McKinley battle heralded the advent of a new era in American politics. At first glance the election seemed to be the age-old story of the underprivileged many against the privileged few, of the indebted backcountry against the wealthier seaboard, of the country against the city, of the agrarians against the industrialists, of Main Street against Wall Street, of the nobodies against the somebodies. Yet when Bryan made his evangelical appeal to all those supposed foes of the existing social order, not enough of them banded together to form a political majority.

The outcome was instead a resounding victory for big business, the big cities, middle-class values, and financial conservatism. Bryan's defeat marked the last serious effort to win the White House with mostly agrarian votes. The future of presidential politics lay not on the farms, with their dwindling population, but in the mushrooming cities, with their growing hordes of freshly arriving immigrants.

The Grand Old Party's smashing victory of 1896 also heralded a Republican grip on the White House for sixteen consecutive years—indeed, for all but eight of the next thirty-six years. McKinley's election thus imparted a new character to the American political system. The long reign of Republican political dominance that it ushered in was accompanied by diminishing voter participation in elections, the weakening of party organizations, and the fading away of issues like the money question and civil-service reform, which came to be replaced by concern for industrial regulation and the welfare of labor. Scholars have dubbed this new political era the period of the **fourth party system**, signaling a break with the previous "third party system," in place since 1860 and characterized by remarkably high voter turnouts and close contests between Democrats and Republicans.

✦ Republican Stand-pattism Enthroned

An eminently "safe" McKinley took the inaugural oath in 1897. With his impeccable white vest, he seemed never to perspire, even in oppressively muggy Washington. Though a man of considerable ability, he was an ear-to-the-ground politician who seldom got far out

The Sacrilegious Candidate   A hostile cartoonist makes sport of Bryan's notorious Cross of Gold speech in 1896.

Library of Congress

Campaign Gimcracks, 1896   These mechanical cards predicted Republican prosperity with McKinley and economic ruin with Bryan.   Collection of Janice L. and David J. Frent

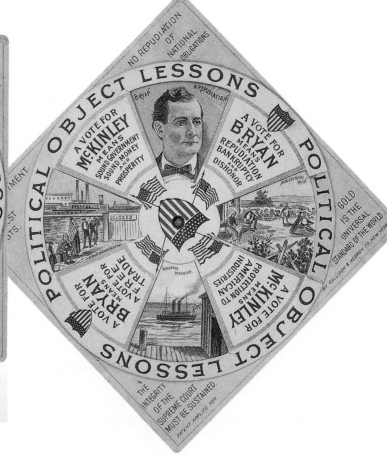

of line with majority opinion. His cautious, conservative nature caused him to shy away from the flaming banner of reform. Business was given a free rein, and the trusts, which had trusted him in 1896, were allowed to develop more mighty muscles without serious restraints.

Almost as soon as McKinley took office, the tariff issue, which had played second fiddle to silver in the "Battle of '96," quickly forced itself to the fore. The current Wilson-Gorman law was not raising enough revenue to cover the annual Treasury deficits, and the Republican trusts thought that they had purchased the right to additional tariff protection by their lush contributions to Hanna's war chest. In due course the Dingley Tariff Bill was jammed through the House in 1897, under the pounding gavel of the rethroned "Czar" Reed. The proposed new rates were high, but not high enough to satisfy the paunchy lobbyists, who once again descended upon the Senate. Over 850 amendments were tacked onto the overburdened bill. The resulting piece of patchwork finally established the average rates at 46.5 percent, substantially higher than the Democratic Wilson-Gorman Act of 1894 and in some categories even higher than the McKinley Act of 1890. (See the chart in the Appendix.)

Prosperity, long lurking around the corner, began to return with a rush in 1897, the first year of McKinley's term. The depression of 1893 had run its course, and farm prices rose. Paint-thirsty midwestern barns blossomed in new colors, and the wheels of industry resumed their hum. Republican politicians, like crowing roosters believing they caused the sun to rise, claimed credit for attracting the sunlight of prosperity.

With the return of prosperity, the money issue that had overshadowed politics since the Civil War gradually faded away. The **Gold Standard Act** of 1900, passed over last-ditch silverite opposition, provided that the paper currency be redeemed freely in gold. Nature and science gradually provided an inflation that the "Gold Bug" East had fought so frantically to prevent. Electrifying discoveries of new gold deposits in Canada's fabled Klondike, as well as in Alaska, South Africa, and Australia, brought huge quantities of gold onto world markets, as did the perfecting of the cheap cyanide process for extracting gold from low-grade ore. Moderate inflation thus took care of the currency needs of an explosively expanding nation, as its circulatory system greatly improved. The tide of "silver heresy" rapidly receded, and the "Popocratic" fish were left gasping high and dry on a golden-sanded beach.

Varying Viewpoints
Was the West Really "Won"?

For more than half a century, the Turner thesis dominated historical writing about the West. In his famous essay of 1893, "The Significance of the Frontier in American History," historian Frederick Jackson Turner argued that the frontier experience molded both region and nation. Not only the West, Turner insisted, but the national character had been uniquely shaped by the westward movement. Pioneers had brought the raw West into the embrace of civilization. And the struggle to overcome the hazards of the western wilderness—including distance, deserts, drought, and Indians—had transformed *Europeans* into tough, inventive, and self-reliant *Americans*.

Turner's thesis raised a question that Americans found especially intriguing in 1893. Just three years earlier, the superintendent of the census declared that the frontier, defined as the boundary of a zone with little or no settled population, had closed forever. What new forces, Turner asked, would shape a distinctive American national character, now that the testing ground of the frontier had been plowed and tamed?

Turner's hypothesis that the American character was forged in the western wilderness is surely among the most provocative statements ever made about the formative influences on the nation's development. But as the frontier era recedes ever further into the past, scholars are less persuaded that Turner's thesis adequately explains the national character. American society is still conspicuously different from European and other cultures, even though Turner's frontier disappeared more than a century ago.

Modern scholars charge that Turner based his thesis on several questionable assumptions. Historian David J. Weber, for example, suggests that the line of the frontier did not define the quavering edge of "civilization," but marked the boundary between diverse cultures, each with its own claims to legitimacy and, indeed, to legitimate possession of the land. The frontier should therefore be understood not as the place where "civilization" triumphed over "savagery," but as the principal site of interaction between those cultures.

Several so-called New Western historians take this argument still further. Scholars such as Patricia Nelson Limerick, Richard White, and Donald Worster suggest that the cultural and ecological damage inflicted by advancing "civilization" must be reckoned with in any final accounting of what the pioneers accomplished. These same scholars insist that the West did not lose its regional identity after the frontier line was no longer recognizable in 1890. The West, they argue, is still a unique part of the national mosaic, a region whose history, culture, and identity remain every bit as distinctive as those of New England or the Old South.

But where Turner saw the frontier as the principal shaper of the region's character, the New Western historians emphasize the effects of ethnic and racial confrontation, topography, climate, and the roles of government and big business as the factors that have made the modern West. The New Western historians thus reject Turner's emphasis on the triumphal civilizing of the wilderness. As they see the matter, European and American settlers did not tame the West, but rather conquered it, by suppressing the Native American and Hispanic peoples who had preceded them into the region. But those conquests were less than complete, so the argument goes, and the West therefore remains, uniquely among American regions, an unsettled arena of commingling and competition among those groups. Moreover, in these accounts the West's distinctively challenging climate and geography yielded to human habitation not through the efforts of heroic individual pioneers, but only through massive corporate—and especially federal government—investments in transportation systems (like the transcontinental railroad) and irrigation projects (like the watering of California's Central Valley). Such developments still give western life its special character today.

Chapter Review

KEY TERMS

reservation system (576)

Little Bighorn, Battle of the (578)

Wounded Knee, Battle of (581)

Dawes Severalty Act (581)

mining industry (584)

Homestead Act (586)

mechanization of agriculture (594)

Populists (598)

Pullman strike (599)

fourth party system (604)

Gold Standard Act (605)

PEOPLE TO KNOW

Frederick Jackson Turner

Jacob S. Coxey

William McKinley

Marcus Alonzo Hanna

TO LEARN MORE

Dee Brown, *Bury My Heart at Wounded Knee: An Indian History of the American West* (1970)

William Cronon, *Nature's Metropolis: Chicago and the Great West* (1991)

Jared Farmer, *On Zion's Mount: Mormons, Indians, and the American Landscape* (2008)

Steven Hahn, *The Roots of Southern Populism: Yeoman Farmers and the Transformation of the Georgia Upcountry, 1850–1890* (1983)

Robert V. Hine, *The American West: A New Interpretive History* (2nd ed., 1984)

Patricia Nelson Limerick, *Legacy of Conquest: The Unbroken Past of the American West* (1987)

Charles Postel, *The Populist Vision* (2007)

Frederick Jackson Turner, "The Significance of the Frontier in American History" (1893)

Louis S. Warren, *Buffalo Bill's America: William Cody and the Wild West Show* (2006)

Elliott West, *The Contested Plains: Indians, Goldseekers, and the Rush to Colorado* (1998)

Richard White, *"It's Your Misfortune and None of My Own": A New History of the American West* (1991)

R. Hal Williams, *Realigning America: McKinley, Bryan, and the Remarkable Election of 1896* (2010)

A complete, annotated bibliography for this chapter—along with brief descriptions of the People to Know—may be found on the American Pageant website. The Key Terms are defined in a Glossary at the end of the text.

CHRONOLOGY

ca. 1700–1800	New Indian peoples move onto Great Plains
1858	Pikes Peak gold rush
1859	Nevada Comstock Lode discovered
1862	Homestead Act
1864	Sand Creek massacre Nevada admitted to Union
1867	National Grange organized
1876	Battle of the Little Bighorn Colorado admitted to Union
1877	Nez Perce war
1881	Helen Hunt Jackson publishes *A Century of Dishonor*
1884	Federal government outlaws Indian Sun Dance
1885	Canadian Pacific Railway, first transcontinental rail line, completed across Canada
1885–1890	Local chapters of Farmers' Alliance formed
1887	Dawes Severalty Act
1889	Oklahoma opened to U.S. citizen settlement
1889–1890	North Dakota, South Dakota, Montana, Washington, Idaho, and Wyoming admitted to Union
1890	Census Bureau declares frontier line ended Emergence of People's party (Populists)
1891	Battle of Wounded Knee Construction of Trans-Siberian Railroad begins
1892	Populist party candidate James B. Weaver polls more than 1 million votes in presidential election
1893	Frederick Jackson Turner publishes "The Significance of the Frontier in American History"
1894	"Coxey's Army" marches on Washington Pullman strike
1896	Utah admitted to Union McKinley defeats Bryan for presidency
1897	Dingley Tariff Act
1900	Gold Standard Act
1907	Oklahoma admitted to Union
1924	Indians granted U.S. citizenship
1934	Indian Reorganization Act

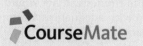
CourseMate

Go to the CourseMate website at **www.cengagebrain.com** for additional study tools and review materials—including audio and video clips—for this chapter.

AP® Review Questions for Chapter 26

1. In post–Civil War America, what was the only reason Indians voluntarily surrendered their ancestral lands?
   (A) Indians chose to migrate further west from their ancestral lands for superior farming.
   (B) Indians received solemn promises from the federal government that they would be left alone and provided with food, clothing, and supplies on their remaining lands.
   (C) Indians lost mobility when white Americans killed their horses.
   (D) Indians were permitted to control the supply of food, buffalo, and other staples within the reservations.
   (E) Indians traded land to whites for rifles, blankets, food, and medicine.

2. What sparked a new round of warfare between the Sioux tribe and the U.S. Army in 1874?
   (A) The massacre of U.S. Army captain William Fetterman and his soldiers by a Sioux war party near the Bozeman Trail
   (B) The start of an effort by Sioux chief Crazy Horse to drive all whites from Montana and the Dakotas
   (C) An expedition by U.S. Army colonel George Custer to Little Big Horn, Montana
   (D) The discovery of gold by Colonel George Custer on Sioux land in the Black Hills
   (E) The announcement of the federal government that it was opening all Sioux lands to settlement

3. All of the following factors contributed to ultimate surrender of the Plains Indians by the 1880s EXCEPT the
   (A) coming of the railroads.
   (B) successive waves of army troops, farmers, cattlemen, sheepherders, and settlers competing for and seizing Plains Indian lands, food and other staples, and natural resources.
   (C) virtual extermination of the buffalo.
   (D) ravaging of the Indian population by white people's diseases.
   (E) failure of Plains Indians to display courage, cunning, and cruelty in warfare.

4. In an effort to assimilate Indians into American society, the Dawes Act did all of the following EXCEPT
   (A) dissolve many tribes as legal entities.
   (B) attempt to make rugged individualists of the Indians.
   (C) abolish tribal ownership of land.
   (D) promise Indians U.S. citizenship in twenty-five years.
   (E) outlaw the Indian Sun (Ghost) Dance.

5. What was the most important role played by the mining frontier?
   (A) Bringing law and order to the West
   (B) Reducing the intensity of conflict between whites and Indians
   (C) Enabling the government to go off the gold standard
   (D) Ensuring that the mining industry would remain in the hands of independent, small businessmen
   (E) Attracting a substantial white population and wealth to the West

6. Which of the following was NOT a serious obstacle or difficulty encountered by families seeking to farm in the frontier West?
   (A) Insufficient quantities of acreage for productive farming in the rain-scarce Great Plains offered for sale through the Homestead Act
   (B) Land-grabbing promoters and speculators obtaining the most attractive land for farming
   (C) Inhospitable soil and inadequate available technology for farming the prairie sod of the Great Plains
   (D) Financial setbacks brought on by periodic severe droughts in the prairie West
   (E) Unscrupulous corporations using dummy homesteaders to obtain the best land

7. Among the following, which group was least likely to migrate to the cattle and farming frontier of the West?
   (A) Eastern city dwellers
   (B) Eastern farmers
   (C) Recent northern European immigrants
   (D) African Americans
   (E) Midwestern farmers

8. Why were Americans disturbed when the superintendent of the census announced in 1890 that a stable frontier line was no longer discernible?
   (A) Americans now knew the Homestead Act would no longer provide them with adequate amounts of cheap, hospitable western lands to farm.
   (B) Americans believed that this declaration meant a renewal of the Indian wars.
   (C) The promise of an endlessly open and vacant West, an element of America's mythological history from its beginnings, was now over.
   (D) Americans feared this development would strengthen the political power of the Populists and radical political parties.
   (E) It meant that a renewal of political tensions and warfare with Mexico was inevitable.

9. How does the safety valve theory of frontier America explain the role of the West in dampening class conflict in the United States?
   (A) Free western land attracted many immigrants to the West who might otherwise have clogged urban eastern job markets and depressed the wages of eastern city dwellers.
   (B) Western farmers tended to be more politically conservative than those in the East and, thus, less apt to support populist or radical appeals to their economic conditions.
   (C) Wealthy western farmers hired many unemployed laborers from eastern cities to reduce unemployment in the East.
   (D) Eastern city dwellers headed to the West for free homesteads during depressions.
   (E) Western cities had less class conflict than those in the East.

10. Which of the following did late-nineteenth-century farmers believe to be most responsible for their difficult economic circumstances?
    (A) Low tariff rates
    (B) Overproduction
    (C) A deflated currency
    (D) An inflated currency
    (E) Excessive government regulation of the economy

11. The Populist party sought to win farmers' and labor's political support by endorsing all of the following EXCEPT
    (A) nationalizing the railroads, telephone, and telegraph.
    (B) a prohibition on court injunctions against labor strikes.
    (C) free coinage of silver.
    (D) low tariff rates.
    (E) a graduated income tax.

12. What was the primary lesson drawn by labor unions, Populists, and debtors from the violent and legal end of the Pullman railway strike?
    (A) Proof of an alliance among big business, the federal government, and the courts against working people
    (B) A strategy by which united working-class action could succeed
    (C) The need for a Socialist party in the United States
    (D) The potential for the federal government to act as an effective counterweight to big business
    (E) That the courts could be relied upon to uphold the rights of workers to strike for better wages and working conditions

13. All of the following characterized the election of 1896 EXCEPT that
    (A) the major political issue of the election was free and unlimited coinage of silver.
    (B) William Jennings Bryan gained the presidential nomination of the Democratic and Populist parties mainly because he eloquently supported farmers' demand for the unlimited coinage of silver.
    (C) it was the last time in American history that a serious effort to win the White House would be made by mostly agrarian votes.
    (D) millions of dollars were raised from trusts and big businessmen by Republican National Committee chairman Mark Hanna to ensure the election of William McKinley and protect big-business interests.
    (E) it ushered in an extended period of increased voter participation, the strengthening of party organizations, and the continued presence of the money question and civil-service reform in the national political discourse.

14. What was the primary cause of the monetary inflation that eventually relieved, but did not end, the social and economic hardships of the late nineteenth century?
    (A) The Gold Standard Act
    (B) McKinley's adoption of the bimetallic standard
    (C) An increase in the international gold supply
    (D) Populist fusion with the Democratic party
    (E) The creation of the Federal Reserve Bank

15. Which of the following was a result of the other four?
    (A) Increase in rural dissent
    (B) High local, state, and national taxes
    (C) Erratic railroad rates
    (D) Creation of the Populist party
    (E) Failure of the Farmers' Alliance

16. All of the following groups populated the American West EXCEPT
    (A) Native Americans.
    (B) "Pikes Peakers."
    (C) women.
    (D) farmers.
    (E) industrialists.

Chapter 27

Empire and Expansion

1890–1909

We assert that no nation can long endure half republic and half empire, and we warn the American people that imperialism abroad will lead quickly and inevitably to despotism at home.

DEMOCRATIC NATIONAL PLATFORM, 1900

*n the years immediately following* the Civil War, Americans remained astonishingly indifferent to the outside world. Enmeshed in struggles over Reconstruction and absorbed in efforts to heal the wounds of civil war, build an industrial economy, make their cities habitable, and settle the sprawling West, most citizens took little interest in international affairs. But the sunset decades of the nineteenth century witnessed a momentous shift in U.S. foreign policy. America's new diplomacy reflected the far-reaching changes that were reshaping agriculture, industry, and the social structure. American statesmen also responded to the intensifying scramble of several other nations for international advantage in the dawning "age of empire." By the beginning of the twentieth century, America had acquired its own empire, an astonishing departure from its venerable anticolonial traditions. The world now had to reckon with a new great power, potentially powerful but with diplomatic ambitions and principles that remained to be defined.

✖ America Turns Outward

Many developments fed the nation's ambition for overseas expansion. Both farmers and factory owners began to look for markets beyond American shores as agricultural and industrial production boomed. Many Americans believed that the United States had to expand or explode. Their country was bursting with a new sense of power generated by the robust growth in population, wealth, and productive capacity—and it was trembling from the hammer blows of labor violence and agrarian unrest. Overseas markets might provide a safety valve to relieve those pressures.

Other forces also whetted the popular appetite for overseas involvement. The lurid "yellow press" of Joseph Pulitzer and William Randolph Hearst described foreign exploits as manly adventures, the kind of dashing derring-do that was the stuff of young boys' dreams. Pious missionaries, inspired by books like the Reverend Josiah Strong's *Our Country: Its Possible Future and Its Present Crisis*, looked overseas for new souls to harvest. Strong trumpeted the superiority of Anglo-Saxon civilization and summoned Americans to spread their religion and their values to the "backward" peoples. He cast his seed on fertile ground. At the same time,

In 1896 the Washington Post *editorialized,*

❝A new consciousness seems to have come upon us—the consciousness of strength—and with it a new appetite, the yearning to show our strength. . . . Ambition, interest, land hunger, pride, the mere joy of fighting, whatever it may be, we are animated by a new sensation. We are face to face with a strange destiny. The taste of Empire is in the mouth of the people even as the taste of blood is in the jungle. It means an Imperial policy, the Republic, renascent, taking her place with the armed nations.**❞**

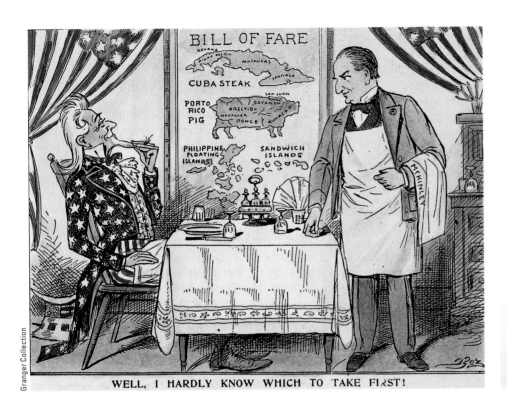

BILL OF FARE

HAVANA

MATANZAS

CUBA STEAK

SANTIAGO

PORTO RICO PIG

SAN JUAN
BAYAMON
ARECIBO
MAYAGUEZ
PONCE
HUMACAO

PHILIPPINE FLOATING ISLANDS

SANDWICH ISLANDS

McKINLEY

WELL, I HARDLY KNOW WHICH TO TAKE FIRST!

Granger Collection

The Imperial Menu A pleased Uncle Sam gets ready to place his order with headwaiter William McKinley. Swallowing some of these possessions eventually produced political indigestion.

aggressive Americans like Theodore Roosevelt and Congressman (later Senator) Henry Cabot Lodge were interpreting Darwinism to mean that the earth belonged to the strong and the fit—that is, to Uncle Sam. This view was strengthened as latecomers to the colonial scramble scooped up leavings from the banquet table of earlier diners. Africa, previously unexplored and mysterious, was partitioned by the Europeans in the 1880s in a pell-mell rush of colonial conquest. In the 1890s Japan, Germany, and Russia all extorted concessions from the anemic Chinese Empire. If America was to survive in the competition of modern nation-states, perhaps it, too, would have to become an imperial power.

The development of a new steel navy also focused attention overseas. Captain Alfred Thayer Mahan's book of 1890, *The Influence of Sea Power upon History, 1660–1783*, argued that control of the sea was the key to world dominance. Mahan helped stimulate the naval race among the great powers that gained momentum around the turn of the century. Red-blooded Americans joined in the demands for a mightier navy and for an American-built isthmian canal between the Atlantic and the Pacific.

America's new international interest manifested itself in several ways. Two-time secretary of state James G. Blaine pushed his **Big Sister policy**, aimed at rallying the Latin American nations behind Uncle Sam's leadership and opening Latin American markets to Yankee traders. Blaine's efforts bore some fruit in 1889,

when he presided over the first Pan-American Conference, held in Washington, D.C., the modest beginnings of an increasingly important series of inter-American assemblages.

A number of diplomatic crises or near-wars also marked the path of American diplomacy in the late 1880s and early 1890s. The American and German navies nearly came to blows in 1889 over the faraway Samoan Islands in the South Pacific, which were formally divided between the two nations in 1899. (German Samoa eventually became an independent republic; American Samoa remains an American possession.) The lynching of eleven Italians in New Orleans in 1891 brought America and Italy to the brink of war, until the United States agreed to pay compensation. In the ugliest affair, American demands on Chile after the deaths of two American sailors in the port of Valparaiso in 1892 made hostilities between the two countries seem inevitable. The threat of attack by Chile's modern navy spread alarm on the Pacific Coast, until the Chileans finally agreed to pay an indemnity. A simmering argument between the United States and Canada over seal hunting near the Pribilof Islands off the coast of Alaska was resolved by arbitration in 1893. The willingness of Americans to risk war over such distant and minor disputes demonstrated the aggressive new national mood.

America's new belligerence combined with old-time anti-British feeling to generate a serious crisis between the United States and Britain in 1895–1896.

The undiplomatic note to Britain by Secretary of State Richard Olney (1835–1917) read,

❝ To-day the United States is practically sovereign on this continent, and its fiat is law upon the subjects to which it confines its interposition. . . . Its infinite resources combined with its isolated position render it master of the situation and practically invulnerable as against any or all other powers.**❞**

The jungle boundary between British Guiana and Venezuela had long been in dispute, but the discovery of gold in the contested area brought the conflict between Britain and Venezuela to a head.

President Cleveland and his pugnacious secretary of state, Richard Olney, waded into the affair with a combative note to Britain invoking the Monroe Doctrine. Not content to stop there, Olney haughtily informed the world's number one naval power that the United States was now calling the tune in the Western Hemisphere.

Unimpressed British officials shrugged off Olney's salvo as just another twist of the lion's tail and replied that the affair was none of Uncle Sam's business. President Cleveland—"mad clear through," as he put it—sent a bristling special message to Congress. He urged an appropriation for a commission of experts, who would run the line where it ought to go. If the British would not accept this rightful boundary, he implied, the United States would fight for it.

The entire country, irrespective of political party, was swept off its feet in an outburst of hysteria. War seemed inevitable. Fortunately, sober second thoughts prevailed on both sides of the Atlantic. A rising challenge from Kaiser Wilhelm's Germany, as well as a looming war with the Dutch-descended Boers in South Africa, left Britain in no mood for war with America. London backed off and consented to arbitration.

The chastened British, their eyes fully opened to the European peril, were now determined to cultivate Yankee friendship. The British inaugurated an era of "patting the eagle's head," which replaced a century or so of America's "twisting the lion's tail." Sometimes called the **Great Rapprochement**—or reconciliation—between the United States and Britain, the new Anglo-American cordiality became a cornerstone of both nations' foreign policies as the twentieth century opened.

✴ Spurning the Hawaiian Pear

Enchanted Hawaii had early attracted the attention of Americans. In the morning years of the nineteenth century, the breeze-brushed islands were a way station and provisioning point for Yankee shippers, sailors, and whalers. In 1820 the first New England missionaries arrived, preaching the twin blessings of Protestant Christianity and protective calico. They came to do good—and did well, as Hawaii became an increasingly important center for sugar production.

Americans gradually came to regard the Hawaiian Islands as a virtual extension of their own coastline. The State Department, beginning in the 1840s, sternly warned other powers to keep their grasping hands off. America's grip was further tightened in 1887 by a treaty with the native government guaranteeing priceless naval-base rights at spacious Pearl Harbor.

But trouble was brewing in the insular paradise. Old World pathogens had scythed the indigenous Hawaiian

They Can't Fight Britain and America waged a war of words during the Venezuelan boundary dispute, but cooler heads prevailed. A new era of diplomatic cooperation between the two former foes dawned, as they saw themselves bound together by ties of language, culture, and mutual economic interest. As the German chancellor Otto von Bismarck reportedly remarked, "The supreme geopolitical fact of the modern era is that the Americans speak English."

Granger Collection

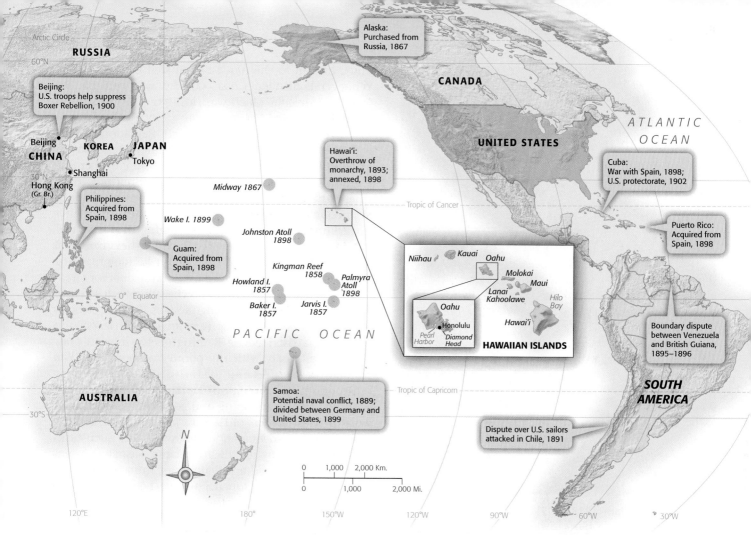

MAP 27.1 United States Expansion, 1857–1917 With the annexation of the Philippines, Hawaii, and Puerto Rico in 1898, the United States became an imperial power.

© Cengage Learning

population down to one-sixth of its size at the time of the first contact with Europeans, leading the American sugar lords to import large numbers of Asian laborers to work the canefields and sugar mills. By century's end, Chinese and Japanese immigrants outnumbered both whites and native Hawaiians, amid mounting worries that Tokyo might be tempted to intervene on behalf of its often-abused nationals. Then sugar markets went sour in 1890 when the **McKinley Tariff** raised barriers against the Hawaiian product. White American planters thereupon renewed their efforts to secure the annexation of Hawaii to the United States. They were blocked by the strong-willed Queen Liliuokalani, who insisted that native Hawaiians should control the islands. Desperate whites, though only a tiny minority, organized a successful revolt early in 1893, openly assisted by American troops, who landed under the unauthorized orders of the expansionist American

minister in Honolulu. "The Hawaiian pear is now fully ripe," he wrote exultantly to his superiors in Washington, "and this is the golden hour for the United States to pluck it."

A treaty of annexation was rushed to Washington, but before it could be railroaded through the Senate, Republican president Harrison's term expired and Democratic president Cleveland came in. Suspecting that his powerful nation had gravely wronged the deposed Queen Liliuokalani and her people, "Old Grover" abruptly withdrew the treaty. A subsequent investigation determined that a majority of the Hawaiian natives opposed annexation. Although Queen Liliuokalani could not be reinstated, the sugarcoated move for annexation had to be temporarily abandoned. The Hawaiian pear continued to ripen until the fateful year of 1898, when the United States acquired its overseas empire (see Map 27.1).

Granger Collection

Queen Liliuokalani (1838–1917) Liliuokalani was the last reigning queen of Hawaii, whose defense of native Hawaiian self-rule led to a revolt by white settlers and to her dethronement. She wrote many songs, the most famous of which was "Aloha Oe," or "Farewell to Thee," played countless times by Hawaiian bands for departing tourists.

✴ Cubans Rise in Revolt

Cuba's masses, frightfully misgoverned, again rose against their Spanish oppressors in 1895. The roots of their revolt were partly economic. Sugar production—the backbone of the island's prosperity—was crippled when the American tariff of 1894 restored high duties on the toothsome product. The desperate insurgents now sought to drive out their Spanish overlords by adopting a scorched-earth policy. The *insurrectos* torched canefields and sugar mills and dynamited passenger trains. Their destructive tactics also menaced American interests on the island.

American sympathies went out to the Cuban underdogs. Sentiment aside, American business had an investment stake of about $50 million in Cuba and an annual trade stake of about $100 million, all of it put at risk by revolutionary upheaval. Moreover, as the calculating Senator Lodge put it, Cuba lay "right athwart the

line" that led to the much-anticipated Panama Canal. Whoever controlled Cuba, said Lodge, "controls the Gulf [of Mexico]." Much was riding on the outcome of events in troubled Cuba.

Fuel was added to the Cuban conflagration in 1896 with the arrival of the Spanish general "Butcher" Weyler. He undertook to crush the rebellion by herding many civilians into barbed-wire reconcentration camps, where they could not give assistance to the armed *insurrectos*. Lacking proper sanitation, these enclosures turned into deadly pestholes; the victims died like dogs.

Atrocities in Cuba were red meat for the sensational new "yellow journalism" of William Randolph Hearst and Joseph Pulitzer. Engaged in a titanic duel for circulation, each attempted to outdo the other with screeching headlines and hair-raising "scoops." Where atrocity stories did not exist, they were invented. Hearst sent the gifted artist Frederic Remington to Cuba to draw sketches, allegedly with the pointed admonition "You furnish the pictures and I'll furnish the war." Among other outrages, Remington depicted Spanish customs officials brutally disrobing and searching an American woman. Most readers of Hearst's *Journal*, their indignation soaring, had no way of knowing that such tasks were performed by female attendants. Hearst also sensationally publicized a private letter from the Spanish minister in Washington, Dupuy de Lôme. The indiscreet epistle, stolen from the mails, described President McKinley in decidedly unflattering terms. The resulting uproar forced Dupuy de Lôme's resignation and further infuriated the American public.

Then early in 1898, Washington sent the battleship *Maine* to Cuba, ostensibly for a "friendly visit" but actually to protect and evacuate Americans if a dangerous flare-up should occur and to demonstrate Washington's concern for the island's stability. Tragedy struck on February 15, 1898, when the **Maine** mysteriously blew up in Havana harbor, with a loss of 260 sailors.

Many Spaniards felt that accusations about their blowing up the Maine *reflected on Spanish honor. One Madrid newspaper spoke up:*

❝ The American jingoes . . . imagine us capable of the most foul villainies and cowardly actions. Scoundrels by nature, the American jingoes believe that all men are made like themselves. What do they know about noble and generous feelings? . . . We should not in any way heed the jingoes: they are not even worth our contempt, or the saliva with which we might honor them in spitting at their faces.❞

Chicago History Museum

The Explosion of the Maine, February 15, 1898 Encouraged and amplified by the "yellow press," the outcry over the tragedy of the *Maine* helped drive the country into an impulsive war against Spain.

Two investigations of the iron coffin ensued, one by U.S. naval officers and the other by Spanish officials. The Spaniards concluded that the explosion had been internal and presumably accidental; the Americans argued that the blast had been caused by a submarine mine. Not until 1976 did U.S. Navy admiral H. G. Rickover confirm the original Spanish finding with overwhelming evidence that the initial explosion had resulted from spontaneous combustion in one of the coal bunkers adjacent to a powder magazine.

But Americans in 1898, now mad for war, blindly embraced the less likely explanation. Lashed to fury by the yellow press, they leapt to the inaccurate conclusion that the Spanish government had been guilty of intolerable treachery. The battle cry of the hour became

Remember the Maine!
To hell with Spain!

Nothing would do but to hurl the "dirty" Spanish flag from the hemisphere.

The national war fever burned ever higher, even though American diplomats had already gained Madrid's agreement to Washington's two basic demands: an end to the reconcentration camps and an armistice with Cuban rebels. The cautious McKinley found himself in a jam. He did not want hostilities, but neither did he want Spain to remain in possession of Cuba. Nor, for that matter, did he want a fully independent Cuba, over which the United States could exercise no control. More impetuous souls denounced the circumspect president as "Wobbly Willie" McKinley. Fight-hungry Theodore Roosevelt reportedly snarled that the "white-livered" occupant of the White House did not have "the backbone of a chocolate éclair." The president, whose shaken nerves required sleeping pills, was even being hanged in effigy.

McKinley, recognizing the inevitable, eventually yielded and gave the people what they wanted. But public pressure did not fully explain McKinley's course. He had little faith in Spain's oft-broken promises. He worried about Democratic reprisals in the upcoming presidential election of 1900 if he continued to appear indecisive in a time of crisis. He also acknowledged America's commercial and strategic interests in Cuba.

On April 11, 1898, McKinley sent his war message to Congress, urging armed intervention to free the oppressed Cubans. The legislators responded uproariously with what was essentially a declaration of war. In a burst of self-righteousness, they likewise adopted the hand-tying **Teller Amendment**. This proviso proclaimed to the world that when the United States had overthrown Spanish misrule, it would give the Cubans their freedom—a declaration that caused imperialistic Europeans to smile skeptically.

✹ Dewey's May Day Victory at Manila

The American people plunged into the war lightheartedly, like schoolchildren off to a picnic. Bands blared incessantly "There'll Be a Hot Time in the Old Town Tonight" and "Hail, Hail, the Gang's All Here," leading some foreigners to believe that those were national anthems.

The war got off to a giddy start for American forces. Even before the declaration of war, on February 25, 1898, while Navy Secretary John D. Long was away from the office, his hot-blooded assistant secretary Theodore Roosevelt took matters into his own hands. Roosevelt cabled Commodore George Dewey, commanding the American Asiatic Squadron at Hong Kong, to descend upon Spain's Philippines in the event of war. "The very devil seemed to possess him," Long later wrote of Roosevelt's actions. But President McKinley subsequently confirmed Roosevelt's instructions, even

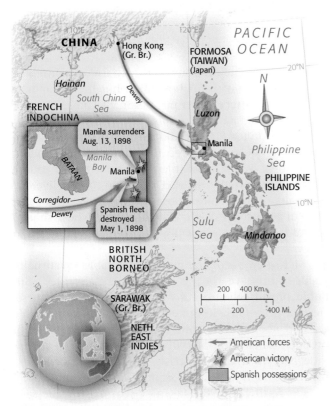

MAP 27.2 Dewey's Route in the Philippines, 1898 © Cengage Learning

though an attack in the distant Far East seemed like a strange way to free nearby Cuba.

Dewey carried out his orders magnificently on May 1, 1898 (see Map 27.2). Sailing boldly with his six warships at night into the fortified harbor of Manila, he trained his guns the next morning on the moldy ten-ship Spanish fleet. The entire collection of antiquated and overmatched vessels was quickly destroyed, with a loss of nearly four hundred Spaniards killed and wounded, and without the loss of a single American life.

Taciturn George Dewey became a national hero overnight. An amateur poet blossomed forth with this:

> *Oh, dewy was the morning*
> *Upon the first of May,*
> *And Dewey was the Admiral,*
> *Down in Manila Bay.*
> *And dewy were the Spaniards' eyes,*
> *Them orbs of black and blue;*
> *And dew we feel discouraged?*
> *I dew not think we dew!*

Yet Dewey was in a perilous position. He had destroyed the enemy fleet, but he could not storm the forts of Manila with his sailors. His nerves frayed, he was forced to wait in the sweltering bay while troop reinforcements were slowly assembled in America. The appearance of German warships in Manila harbor deepened the tension.

Long-awaited American troops, finally arriving in force, captured Manila on August 13, 1898, in collaboration with Filipino insurgents commanded by their well-educated, part-Chinese leader, Emilio Aguinaldo. Dewey, to his later regret, had brought this shrewd and magnetic revolutionary from exile in Asia so that he might weaken Spanish resistance.

These thrilling events in the Philippines had meanwhile focused attention on Hawaii. An impression spread that America needed the archipelago as a coaling and provisioning way station, in order to send supplies and reinforcements to Dewey. McKinley also worried that Japan might grab the Hawaiian Islands while America was distracted elsewhere. A joint resolution of annexation was rushed through Congress and approved by McKinley on July 7, 1898. It granted Hawaiian residents U.S. citizenship; Hawaii received full territorial status in 1900.

✹ The Confused Invasion of Cuba

Shortly after the outbreak of war, the Spanish government ordered a fleet of decrepit warships to Cuba. Panic seized the eastern seaboard of the United States. American vacationers abandoned their seashore cottages, while nervous investors moved their securities

Emilio Aguinaldo (ca. 1869–1964) and Followers, 1900   Aguinaldo had a colorfully checkered career. Exiled from the Philippines by the Spanish in 1897, he was brought back in 1898 to assist the American invasion. A year later he led the Filipino insurrection against the new American rulers. Captured in 1901, he declared his loyalty to the United States. During World War II, he collaborated with the Japanese when they occupied the Philippines. After a lifetime of political intrigue and armed struggle, Aguinaldo died peacefully in Manila in 1964 in his ninety-fifth year.

to inland depositories. The Spanish "armada" eventually wheezed into bottle-shaped Santiago harbor, Cuba, where it was easily blockaded by the much more powerful American fleet.

Sound strategy seemed to dictate that an American army be sent in from the rear to drive out the Spanish ships. Leading the invading force was the grossly overweight General William R. Shafter, a would-be warrior so blubbery and gout-stricken that he had to be carried about on a door. His troops were woefully unequipped for war in the tropics; they had been amply provided with heavy woolen underwear and uniforms designed for subzero operations against the Indians.

The **Rough Riders**, a part of the invading army, now charged onto the stage of history. This colorful regiment of volunteers, short on discipline but long on dash, consisted largely of western cowboys and other hardy characters, with a sprinkling of ex–polo players and ex-convicts. Commanded by Colonel Leonard Wood, the group was organized principally by the glory-chasing Theodore Roosevelt, who had resigned from the Navy Department to serve as lieutenant colonel. He was so nearsighted that as a safeguard he took along a dozen pairs of spectacles, cached in handy spots on his person or nearby.

About the middle of June, a bewildered American army of seventeen thousand men finally embarked at congested Tampa, Florida, amid scenes of indescribable confusion. Shafter's landing near Santiago, thanks to the diversionary tactics of Cuban *insurrectos*, met

little opposition. Brisk fighting broke out on July 1 at El Caney and Kettle Hill, up which Colonel Roosevelt and his horseless Rough Riders charged, with strong support from two crack black regiments. They suffered heavy casualties, but the colorful colonel, having the time of his life, shot a Spaniard with his revolver and rejoiced to see his victim double up like a jackrabbit. He later wrote a book on his exploits, which the famed satirist Finley Peter Dunne's character "Mr. Dooley" remarked ought to have been entitled *Alone in Cubia* [*sic*].

The American army, fast closing in on Santiago, spelled doom for the badly outgunned Spanish fleet. On July 3 the Spaniards dutifully steamed out of the harbor and into the teeth of the waiting American warships. "Don't cheer, men," Captain Philip of the *Texas* admonished his seamen. "The poor devils are dying." Shortly thereafter Santiago surrendered (see Map 27.3).

With a mixture of modesty and immodesty, Colonel Theodore Roosevelt (1858–1919) wrote privately in 1903 of his "Rough Riders,"

❝In my regiment nine-tenths of the men were better horsemen than I was, and probably two-thirds of them better shots than I was, while on the average they were certainly hardier and more enduring. Yet after I had had them a very short while they all knew, and I knew too, that nobody else could command them as I could.**❞**

Colonel Theodore Roosevelt with Some of the "Rough Riders" Roosevelt later described his first encounter with the Spanish enemy: "Soon we came to the brink of a deep valley. There was a good deal of cracking of rifles way off in front of us, but as they used smokeless powder we had no idea as to exactly where they were, or who they were shooting at. Then it dawned on us that we were the target. The bullets began to come overhead, making a sound like the ripping of a silk dress, with sometimes a kind of pop. . . . We advanced, firing at them, and drove them off."

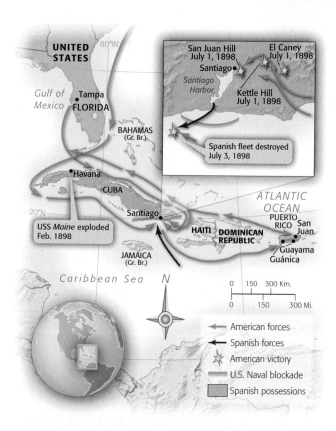

MAP 27.3 The Cuban Campaign, 1898 © Cengage Learning

Hasty preparations were now made for a descent upon Puerto Rico before the war should end. There the American army met even less resistance than in Cuba.

By this time Spain had satisfied its honor. On August 12, 1898, it signed an armistice.

If the Spaniards had held out a few months longer in Cuba, the American army might have melted away. The inroads of malaria, typhoid fever, dysentery, and yellow fever became so severe that hundreds were incapacitated—"an army of convalescents." Others suffered from malodorous canned meat known as "embalmed beef." All told, nearly four hundred men lost their lives to bullets; over five thousand succumbed to bacteria and other causes.

✴ America's Course (Curse?) of Empire

Late in 1898 Spanish and American negotiators met in Paris. War-racked Cuba, as expected, was freed from its Spanish overlords. The Americans had little difficulty in securing the remote Pacific island of Guam, which they had captured early in the conflict from the astonished Spaniards, who, lacking a cable, had not known that a war was on. Spain also ceded Puerto Rico to the United States as payment for war costs. Ironically, the last remnant of Spain's vast New World empire thus became the first territory ever annexed to the United States without the express promise of eventual statehood. In the decades to come, American investment in the island and Puerto Rican immigration to the United States would make this acquisition one of the weightier consequences of this somewhat carefree war (see "Makers of America: The Puerto Ricans," pp. 618–619).

© Bettmann/Corbis

Uncle Sam and People from His Colonies, Postcard, ca. 1900 The acquisition of Puerto Rico, the Philippines, Hawaii, and other Pacific islands brought millions of people of color under the American flag and, as depicted here, the paternal watch of "Uncle Sam." Whether they would eventually become citizens or remain colonial subjects was hotly debated in the United States. Many anti-imperialists opposed colonial expansion precisely because they regarded the exotic new peoples as "unassimilable."

Knottiest of all was the problem of the Philippines, a veritable apple of discord. These lush islands not only embraced an area larger than the British Isles but also contained an ethnically diverse population of some 7 million souls. McKinley was confronted with a devil's dilemma. He did not feel that America could honorably give the islands back to Spanish misrule, especially after it had fought a war to free Cuba. And America would be turning its back upon its responsibilities in a cowardly fashion, he believed, if it simply pulled up anchor and sailed away.

McKinley viewed virtually all the choices open to him as trouble-fraught. The Filipinos, if left to govern themselves, might fall into anarchy. One of the major powers, possibly aggressive Germany or Japan, might then try to seize them. The result could be a major war into which the United States would be sucked. Seemingly the least of the evils consistent with national honor and safety was to acquire all the Philippines and then perhaps give the Filipinos their freedom later.

President McKinley, ever sensitive to public opinion, kept a carefully attuned ear to the ground. The rumble that he heard seemed to call for the entire group of islands. Zealous Protestant missionaries were eager for new converts from Spanish Catholicism,* and the invalid Mrs. McKinley, to whom her husband was devoted, expressed deep concern about the welfare of the Filipinos. Wall Street had generally opposed the war, but awakened by the booming of Dewey's guns, it was clamoring for profits in the Philippines.

A tormented McKinley later claimed that he went down on his knees seeking divine guidance and heard

an inner voice telling him to take all the Philippines and Christianize and civilize them. Accordingly, he decided for outright annexation of the islands. Manila remained a sticking point with the Spaniards because it had been captured the day *after* the armistice was signed, and the city could not therefore properly be claimed among the spoils of war. But the Americans broke the deadlock by agreeing to pay Spain $20 million for the Philippine Islands—the last great Spanish haul from the New World.

The signing of the pact of Paris touched off one of the most impassioned foreign-policy debates in American history. The issue of what to do with the Philippines confronted Americans with fundamental questions about their national identity. Except for glacial Alaska, coral-reefed Hawaii, and a handful of Pacific atolls acquired mostly for whaling stations and guano fertilizer needed

---

*The Philippines had been substantially Christianized by Catholics before the founding of Jamestown in 1607.

President William McKinley (1843–1901) later described his decision to annex the Philippines:

"When next I realized that the Philippines had dropped into our laps, I confess I did not know what to do with them. . . . I went down on my knees and prayed Almighty God for light and guidance. . . . And one night late it came to me this way. . . . That there was nothing left for us to do but to take them all, and to educate the Filipinos, and uplift and civilize and Christianize them and by God's grace do the very best we could by them, as our fellow men, for whom Christ also died. And then I went to bed and went to sleep, and slept soundly."

At dawn on July 26, 1898, the U.S. warship *Gloucester* steamed into Puerto Rico's Guánica harbor, fired at the Spanish blockhouse, and landed some thirty-three hundred troops. Within days the Americans had taken possession of the militarily strategic Caribbean island a thousand miles southeast of Florida. In so doing they set in motion changes on the island that ultimately brought a new wave of immigrants to U.S. shores.

Puerto Rico had been a Spanish possession since Christopher Columbus claimed it for Castile in 1493. The Spaniards enslaved many of the island's forty thousand Taino Indians and set them to work on farms and in mines. Many Tainos died of exhaustion and disease, and in 1511 the Indians rebelled. The Spaniards crushed the uprising, killed thousands of Indians, and began importing African slaves—thus establishing the basis for Puerto Rico's multiracial society.

The first Puerto Rican immigrants to the United States arrived as political exiles in the nineteenth century. From their haven in America, they agitated for the island's independence from Spain. In 1897 Spain finally granted the island local autonomy; ironically, however, the Spanish-American War the following year placed it in American hands. Puerto Rican political émigrés in the United States returned home, but they were soon replaced by poor islanders looking for work.

Changing conditions in Puerto Rico after the U.S. takeover had driven these new immigrants north. Although slow to grant Puerto Ricans U.S. citizenship, the Americans quickly improved health and sanitation on the island, triggering a population surge in the early twentieth century. At the same time, growing monopoly control of Puerto Rico's sugar cane plantations undermined the island's subsistence economy, and a series of hurricanes devastated the coffee plantations that had employed large numbers of people. With almost no industry to provide wage labor, Puerto Rico's unemployment rate soared.

Thus when Congress finally granted Puerto Ricans U.S. citizenship in 1917, thereby eliminating immigration hurdles, many islanders hurried north to find jobs. Over the ensuing decades, Puerto Ricans went to work in Arizona cotton fields, New Jersey soup factories, and

Bildarchiv Preussischer Kulturbesitz/Art Resource, NY

The First Puerto Ricans   The Spanish *conquistadores* treated the native Taino people in Puerto Rico with extreme cruelty, and the Indians were virtually extinct by the mid-1500s.

Utah mines. The majority, however, clustered in New York City and found work in the city's cigar factories, shipyards, and garment industry. Migration slowed somewhat after the 1920s as the Great Depression shrank the job market on the mainland and as World War II made travel hazardous.

When World War II ended in 1945, the sudden advent of cheap air travel sparked an immigration explosion (and set the stage for Leonard Bernstein's great musical production, *West Side Story*, which adapted the story of Romeo and Juliet to the clash of white and Puerto Rican gangs in New York City). As late as the 1930s, the tab for a boat trip to the mainland exceeded the average Puerto Rican's yearly earnings. But with an airplane surplus after World War II, the six-hour flight from Puerto Rico to New York cost under fifty dollars. The Puerto Rican population on the mainland quadrupled between 1940 and 1950 and tripled again by 1960. In 1970, 1.5 million Puerto Ricans lived in the United States, one-third of the island's total population.

U.S. citizenship and affordable air travel made it easy for Puerto Ricans to return home. Thus to a far greater degree than most immigrant groups, Puerto Ricans kept one foot in the United States and the other on their native island. By some estimates 2 million people a year journeyed to and from the island during the postwar period. Puerto Rico's gubernatorial candidates sometimes campaigned in New York for the thousands of voters who were expected to return to the island in time for the election.

Preparing for Carnaval (Carnival) This mask-maker displays an elaborate *máscara de carton* (paper maché mask) made for the annual Puerto Rican festival. Masked figures at *Carnaval* have been part of Puerto Rican culture for more than two hundred years.

This transience worked to keep Puerto Ricans' educational attainment and English proficiency far below the national average. At the same time, the immigrants encountered a deep-seated racism in America unlike anything on their multiracial island. Throughout the postwar years, Puerto Ricans remained one of the poorest groups in the United States, with a median family income below that of African Americans and Mexican Americans.

Still, Puerto Ricans have fared better economically in the United States than on the island, where, in 1970, 60 percent of all inhabitants lived below the poverty line. In recent years Puerto Ricans have attained more schooling, and many have attended college. Invigorated by the civil rights movement of the 1960s, Puerto Ricans also became more politically active, electing growing numbers of congressmen and state and city officials.

Protesting in New York Puerto Ricans demonstrate in April 2001 against U.S. Navy bombing exercises on the Puerto Rican island of Vieques.

to replenish southern soil exhausted by overcultivation, the Republic had hitherto absorbed only contiguous territory on the continent. All previous accessions had been thinly peopled and eligible for ultimate statehood. But in the Philippines, the nation had on its hands a distant tropical area, thickly populated by Asians of a different culture, tongue, and government institutions.

Opponents of annexation argued that such a step would dishonor and ultimately destroy America's venerable commitments to self-determination and anti-colonialism. "Goddamn the United States for its vile conduct in the Philippine Isles!" burst out the usually mild-mannered Professor William James. The Harvard philosopher could not believe that the United States could "puke up its ancient soul in five minutes without a wink of squeamishness." Speaker of the House Thomas "Czar" Reed resigned in protest against America's new imperial adventure. Proponents countered that Philippine annexation would simply continue a glorious history of expansion that had pushed American civilization to the Pacific and now beyond. If Americans were "morally bound to abandon the Philippines," thundered Theodore Roosevelt, "we were also morally bound to abandon Arizona to the Apaches." The **Anti-Imperialist League** sprang into being to fight the McKinley administration's expansionist moves. The organization counted among its members some of the most prominent people in the United States, including the presidents of Stanford and Harvard Universities and the novelist Mark Twain. The anti-imperialist blanket even stretched over such strange

bedfellows as the labor leader Samuel Gompers and the steel titan Andrew Carnegie.

Anti-imperialists raised many objections. The Filipinos thirsted for freedom; to annex them would violate the "consent of the governed" philosophy in the Declaration of Independence and the Constitution. Despotism abroad might well beget despotism at home. Imperialism was costly and unlikely ever to turn a profit. Finally, annexation would propel the United States into the political and military cauldron of East Asia.

Yet the expansionists or imperialists could sing a seductive song. They appealed to patriotism, invoked America's "civilizing mission," and played up possible trade profits. Manila, they claimed, might become another Hong Kong. Rudyard Kipling, the British poet laureate of imperialism, urged America down the slippery path with a quotable poem that he had circulated before publication to Theodore Roosevelt and Henry Cabot Lodge (Roosevelt found it "good sense" but "poor poetry"):

> Take up the White Man's burden—
> Ye dare not stoop to less—
> Nor call too loud on Freedom
> To cloak your weariness.

In short, the wealthy Americans must help to uplift (and exploit) the underprivileged, underfed, and underclad of the world.

Over heated protests, the Senate approved the treaty with Spain with just one vote to spare on February 6, 1899. America was now officially an empire.

The contest over American imperialism took place on the Senate floor as well as around the globe. In 1900 Senator Albert J. Beveridge (1862-1927), Republican from Indiana, returned from an investigative trip to the Philippines to defend its annexation:

❝ The Philippines are ours forever. . . . And just beyond the Philippines are China's illimitable markets. We will not retreat from either. We will not abandon our opportunity in the Orient. We will not renounce our part in the mission of our race: trustee, under God, of the civilization of the world.❞

Two years later Senator George F. Hoar (1826-1904), Republican from Massachusetts, broke with his party to denounce American annexation of the Philippines and other territories:

❝You cannot maintain despotism in Asia and a republic in America. If you try to deprive even a savage or a barbarian of his just rights you can never do it without becoming a savage or a barbarian yourself.❞

✦ Perplexities in Puerto Rico and Cuba

From the outset, the status of Puerto Rico was anomalous—neither a state nor a territory, and with little prospect of eventual independence. The **Foraker Act** of 1900 accorded the Puerto Ricans a limited degree of popular government (and outlawed cockfighting, a favorite island pastime). Congress granted U.S. citizenship to Puerto Ricans in 1917 but withheld full self-rule. Although the American regime worked wondrous improvements in education, sanitation, and transportation, many of the inhabitants still aspired to independence. Great numbers of Puerto Ricans ultimately moved to New York City, where they added to the complexity of the melting pot.

The annexation of Puerto Rico (and the Philippines) posed a thorny legal problem: Did the Constitution follow the flag? Did American laws, including tariff laws and the Bill of Rights, apply with full force to the newly acquired possessions? "Who are we?" a group of Puerto Rican petitioners asked Congress in 1900. "Are we citizens or are we subjects?" Beginning in 1901 with the ***Insular Cases***, a badly divided Supreme Court decreed, in effect, that the flag did outrun the Constitution, and that the outdistanced document did not necessarily extend with full force to the new windfall. Puerto Ricans (and Filipinos) might be subject to American rule, but they did not enjoy all American rights.

Cuba, scorched and chaotic, presented another headache. An American military government, set up under the administrative genius of General Leonard Wood of Rough Rider fame, wrought miracles in government, finance, education, agriculture, and public health. Under his leadership and that of Colonel William C. Gorgas, a frontal attack was launched on yellow fever. Spectacular experiments were performed by Dr. Walter Reed and others upon American soldiers, who volunteered as human guinea pigs, and the stegomyia mosquito was proved to be the lethal carrier. Cleaning up breeding places for mosquitoes wiped out yellow fever in Havana, while dampening the fear of recurrent epidemics in cities of the South and Atlantic seaboard.

The United States, honoring its self-denying Teller Amendment of 1898, withdrew from Cuba in 1902. Old World imperialists could scarcely believe their eyes. But the Washington government could not turn this rich and strategic island completely loose on the international sea; a grasping power like Germany might secure dangerous lodgment near America's soft underbelly. The Cubans were therefore forced to write into their own constitution of 1901 the so-called **Platt Amendment**.

The Cubans loathed the amendment, which served McKinley's ultimate purpose of bringing Cuba under American control. ("Plattism" survives as a colloquial term of derision even in modern-day Cuba.) The newly "liberated" Cubans were forced to agree not to conclude treaties that might compromise their independence (as Uncle Sam saw it) and not to take on debt beyond their resources (as Uncle Sam measured them). They further agreed that the United States might intervene with troops to restore order when it saw fit. Finally, the Cubans promised to sell or lease needed coaling or naval stations, ultimately two and then only one (Guantánamo), to their powerful "benefactor." The United States finally abrogated the amendment in 1934, although Uncle Sam still occupies a twenty-eight-thousand-acre Cuban beachhead at Guantánamo under an agreement that can be revoked only by the consent of both parties (see pp. 779–780).

✴ New Horizons in Two Hemispheres

In essence, the Spanish-American War was a kind of colossal coming-out party. Dewey's thundering guns merely advertised the fact that the nation was already a world power. The war itself was short (113 days), low in casualties, and theatrically successful—despite the

Three years after the Spanish-American War ended, a foreign diplomat in Washington remarked,

"I have seen two Americas, the America before the Spanish American War and the America since."

bungling. Secretary of State John Hay called it a "splendid little war." American prestige rose sharply, and the Europeans grudgingly accorded the Republic more respect. Britain, France, Russia, and other great powers pointedly upgraded their legations in Washington, D.C., which had previously been regarded as a diplomatic backwater.

An exhilarating new martial spirit thrilled America, buoyed along by the newly popular military marching-band music of John Philip Sousa. Most Americans did not start the war with consciously imperialistic motives, but after falling through the cellar door of imperialism in a drunken fit of idealism, they wound up with imperialistic and colonial fruits in their grasp. Captain Mahan's

The New Jingoism An enthusiastic Uncle Sam cheers the U.S. Navy in the "splendid little war" of 1898. Many Americans, however, were less than enthused about America's new imperial adventure.

big-navyism seemed vindicated, energizing popular support for more and better battleships. A masterly organizer, Secretary of War Elihu Root established a general staff for the army and founded the War College in Washington.

One of the most beneficial results of the conflict was the further closing of the "bloody chasm" between North and South. Thousands of patriotic southerners had flocked to the Stars and Stripes, and the gray-bearded General Joseph ("Fighting Joe") Wheeler—a Confederate cavalry hero of about a thousand Civil War skirmishes and battles—was given a command in Cuba. He allegedly cried, in the heat of battle, "To hell with the Yankees! Dammit, I mean the Spaniards."

Even so, the newly imperial nation was not yet prepared to pay the full bill for its new status. By taking on the Philippine Islands, the United States became a full-fledged Far Eastern power. But the distant islands eventually became a "heel of Achilles"—a kind of indefensible hostage given to Japan, as events proved in World War II. Here and elsewhere, the Americans had shortsightedly assumed burdensome commitments that they proved unwilling to defend with appropriate naval and military outlays.

✦ "Little Brown Brothers" in the Philippines

The liberty-loving Filipinos assumed that they, like the Cubans, would be granted their freedom after the Spanish-American War. They were tragically deceived. Washington excluded them from the peace negotiations with Spain and made clear its intention to stay in the Philippines indefinitely. Bitterness toward the occupying American troops erupted into open insurrection on February 4, 1899, under Emilio Aguinaldo. Having plunged into war with Spain to free Cuba, the United States was now forced to deploy some 126,000 troops ten thousand miles away to rivet shackles onto a people who asked for nothing but freedom—in the American tradition.

The poorly equipped Filipino rebels soon melted into the jungle to wage vicious guerrilla warfare. Months earlier, American soldiers thought they were rescuing innocent victims of Spanish tyranny. Now they viewed the Filipinos as dangerous enemies of the United States. This shift contributed to a mounting "race war" in which both sides perpetrated sordid atrocities. Uncle Sam's soldiers adopted the "water cure"—forcing water down victims' throats until they yielded information or died. American-built reconcentration camps rivaled those of "Butcher" Weyler in Cuba. Having begun the Spanish war with noble ideals, America now dirtied its hands. One New York newspaper published a reply to Rudyard Kipling's famous poem:

We've taken up the white man's burden
Of ebony and brown;
Now will you kindly tell us, Rudyard,
How we may put it down?

American Soldier Interrogates Filipino Civilians For three years after its annexation of the Philippine Islands in 1898, the United States fought a savage war to suppress a Filipino rebellion against American rule. More than 200,000 Filipinos perished. There was bitter irony in this clash, as the Americans had claimed to be "liberating" the Filipinos from their oppressive Spanish masters; but the Yankee liberators were sometimes no less oppressive than the Spaniards they had ousted.

Keystone-Mast Collection, UCR/California Museum of Photograph, University of California, Riverside

The Americans broke the back of the Filipino insurrection in 1901, when they cleverly infiltrated a guerrilla camp and captured Aguinaldo. But sporadic fighting dragged on for many dreary months, eventually claiming the lives of 4,234 Americans and as many as 600,000 Filipinos.

Future president William H. Taft, an able and amiable Ohioan who weighed some 350 pounds, became civil governor of the Philippines in 1901. Forming a strong attachment to the Filipinos, he called them his "little brown brothers" and danced light-footedly with the Filipino women. But McKinley's "benevolent assimilation" of the Philippines proceeded with painful slowness. Washington poured millions of dollars into the islands to improve roads, sanitation, and public health. Important economic ties, including trade in sugar, developed between the two peoples. American teachers set up an unusually good school system and helped make English a second language. But all this vast expenditure, which profited America little, was ill-received. The Filipinos hated compulsory Americanization and pined for liberty. They finally got their freedom on the Fourth of July, 1946. In the meantime, thousands of Filipinos emigrated to the United States (see "Makers of America: The Filipinos," pp. 624–625).

✦ Hinging the Open Door in China

Ominous events had meanwhile been brewing in faraway and enfeebled China. After its defeat by Japan in 1894–1895, the imperialistic European powers, notably Russia and Germany, moved in. Like vultures descending upon a wounded animal, they began to tear away valuable leaseholds and economic spheres of influence from the Manchu government.

A growing group of Americans viewed the vivisection of China with alarm. Churches worried about their missionary strongholds. Merchants feared that Europeans would monopolize Chinese markets. An alarmed American public, openly prodded by the press and slyly nudged by certain free-trade Britons, demanded that Washington do something. Secretary of State John Hay, a quiet but witty poet-novelist-diplomat with a flair for capturing the popular imagination, finally decided upon a dramatic move.

In the summer of 1899, Hay dispatched to all the great powers a communication soon known as the **Open Door note**. He urged them to announce that in their leaseholds or spheres of influence they would respect certain Chinese rights and the ideal of fair competition. Tellingly, Hay had not bothered to consult the Chinese themselves.

The phrase *Open Door* quickly caught the American public's fancy. But Hay's proposal caused much squirming in the leading capitals of the world, though all the great powers save Russia, with covetous designs on Manchuria, eventually agreed to it.

Open Door or not, patriotic Chinese did not care to be used as a doormat by the Western powers. In 1900 a superpatriotic group, known as the "Boxers" for their training in the martial arts, broke loose with the cry "Kill Foreign Devils." In what became known as the **Boxer Rebellion**, they murdered more than two hundred foreigners and thousands of Chinese Christians and besieged the foreign diplomatic community in the capital, Beijing (Peking).

By permission of the Houghton Library, Harvard University, ACB 78.1

American Missionary Grace Roberts Teaching in China, 1903 By the turn of the twentieth century, thousands of American men and women had established Christian missions in faraway places such as Hawaii, China, Africa, and Turkey. Missionaries' educational and religious work helped build sentimental, political, and economic ties between Americans and distant nations. At times, however, these close connections led to violent confrontations, such as when the nationalist Boxer rebels attacked missionaries in China in 1900 as symbols of foreign encroachment. Protestant women justified their missionary activities as a logical extension of their traditional female duty to nurture and uplift, but in reality these foreign assignments often propelled them to undertake responsibilities that their stateside mothers and sisters rarely encountered.

At the beginning of the twentieth century, the United States, its imperial muscles just flexed in the war with Spain, found itself in possession of the Philippines. Uncertain of how to manage this empire, which seethed resentfully against its new masters, the United States promised to build democracy in the Philippines and to ready the islanders for home rule. Almost immediately after annexation, the American governor of the archipelago sent a corps of Filipino students to the United States, hoping to forge future leaders steeped in American ways who would someday govern an independent Philippines. Yet this small student group found little favor in their adopted country, although in their native land many went on to become respected citizens and leaders.

Most Filipino immigrants to the United States in these years, however, came not to study but to toil. With Chinese immigration banned, Hawaii and the Pacific Coast states turned to the Philippines for cheap agricultural labor. Beginning in 1906 the Hawaiian Sugar Planters Association aggressively recruited Filipino workers. Enlistments grew slowly at first, but by the 1920s thousands of young Filipino men had reached the Hawaiian Islands and been assigned to sugar plantations or pineapple fields.

Typically a young Filipino wishing to emigrate first made his way to Manila, where he signed a contract with the growers that promised three years' labor in return for transportation to Hawaii, wages, free housing and fuel, and return passage at the end of the contract. Not all of the emigrants returned; there remain in Hawaii today some former field workers still theoretically eligible for free transport back to their native land.

Those Filipinos venturing as far as the American mainland found work less arduous but also less certain than did their countrymen on Hawaiian plantations. Many mainlanders worked seasonally—in winter as domestic servants, busboys, or bellhops; in summer journeying to the fields to harvest lettuce, strawberries, sugar beets, and potatoes. Eventually Filipinos, along with Mexican immigrants, shared the dubious honor of making up California's agricultural work force.

A mobile society, Filipino Americans also were overwhelmingly male; there was only one Filipino woman for every fourteen Filipino men in California in 1930. Thus the issue of intermarriage became acutely sensitive. California and many other states prohibited the marriage of Asians and Caucasians in demeaning laws that remained on the books until 1948. And if a Filipino so much as approached a Caucasian woman, he

Filipino Laborers at Work on a Hawaiian Pineapple Plantation, 1930s

624

Filipino Workers Arriving in Honolulu, 1940s Tags around their necks indicated the plantations to which they had been assigned.

could expect reprisals—sometimes violent. For example, white vigilante groups roamed the Yakima Valley in Washington and the San Joaquin and Salinas Valleys in California, intimidating and even attacking Filipinos whom they accused of improperly accosting white women. In 1930 one Filipino was murdered and others wounded after they invited some Caucasian women to a dance. Undeterred, the Filipinos challenged the restrictive state laws and the hooligans who found in them an excuse for mayhem. But Filipinos, who did not become eligible for American citizenship until 1946, long lacked political leverage.

After World War II, Filipino immigration accelerated. Between 1950 and 1970, the number of Filipinos in the United States nearly doubled, with women and men stepping aboard the new transpacific airliners in roughly equal numbers. Many of these recent arrivals sprang from sturdy middle-class stock and sought in America a better life for their children than the Philippines seemed able to offer. Today the war-torn and perpetually depressed archipelago sends more immigrants to American shores than does any other Asian nation.

Filipino Nurses The nursing shortage in the United States has created many job opportunities for Filipino nurses, who are trained to high medical standards and speak English. A nurse in the United States today can earn more than a physician in the Philippines.

Columbia's Easter Bonnet Many Americans felt a surge of pride as the United States became an imperial power at the dawn of the twentieth century. But then and later, America's world role proved hotly controversial, at home as well as abroad.

A multinational rescue force of some eighteen thousand soldiers arrived in the nick of time and quelled the rebellion. They included several thousand American troops dispatched from the Philippines to protect U.S. rights under the 1844 Treaty of Wanghia (see p. 390) and to keep the Open Door propped open.

The victorious allied invaders acted angrily and vindictively. They assessed prostrate China an excessive

The commercial interests of Britain and America were imperiled by the power grabs in China, and a close concert between the two powers would have helped both. Yet as Secretary of State John Hay (1838–1905) wrote privately in June 1900,

❝Every Senator I see says, 'For God's sake, don't let it appear we have any understanding with England.' How can I make bricks without straw? That we should be compelled to refuse the assistance of the greatest power in the world [Britain], in carrying out our own policy, because all Irishmen are Democrats and some [American] Germans are fools—is enough to drive a man mad.**❞**

indemnity of $333 million, of which America's share was to be $24.5 million. When Washington discovered that this sum was much more than enough to pay damages and expenses, it remitted about $18 million, to be used for the education of a selected group of Chinese students in the United States—a not-so-subtle initiative to further the westernization of Asia.

Secretary Hay let fly another paper broadside in 1900, announcing that henceforth the Open Door would embrace the territorial integrity of China, in addition to its commercial integrity. Those principles helped spare China from possible partition in those troubled years and were formally incorporated into the Nine-Power Treaty of 1922, only to be callously violated by Japan's takeover of Manchuria a decade later (see pp. 731 and 747).

✹ Imperialism or Bryanism in 1900?

President McKinley's renomination by the Republicans in 1900 was a foregone conclusion. He had won a war and acquired rich, though burdensome, real estate; he had safeguarded the gold standard; and he had brought the promised prosperity of the full dinner pail. An irresistible vice-presidential boom developed for Theodore ("Teddy") Roosevelt (TR), the cowboy-hero of the Cuban campaign. Capitalizing on his war-born popularity, he had been elected governor of New York, where the local political bosses had found him headstrong and difficult to manage. They therefore devised a scheme to kick the colorful colonel upstairs into the vice presidency.

This plot to railroad Roosevelt worked beautifully. Gesticulating wildly, he sported a western-style cowboy hat that made him stand out like a white crow at the Republican convention. To cries of "We want Teddy!" he was handily nominated. A wary Mark Hanna reportedly moaned that there would now be only one heartbeat between "that damned cowboy" and the presidency of the United States.

William Jennings Bryan was the odds-on choice of the Democrats, meeting at Kansas City. Their platform proclaimed that the paramount issue was Republican overseas imperialism.

McKinley, the soul of dignity, once again campaigned safely from his front porch. Bryan again took to the stump in a cyclonic campaign. Lincoln, he charged, had abolished slavery for 3.5 million Africans; McKinley had reestablished it for 7 million Filipinos. Roosevelt out-Bryaned Bryan, touring the country with revolver-shooting cowboys. Flashing his monumental teeth and pounding his fist into his palm, Roosevelt denounced all dastards who would haul down Old Glory.

McKinley handily triumphed by a much wider margin than in 1896: 7,218,491 to 6,356,734 popular votes, and 292 to 155 electoral votes. But victory for the Republicans was not a mandate for or against imperialism. If there was any mandate at all it was for the two *P*s: prosperity and protectionism. Meanwhile, the New York bosses gleefully looked forward to watching the nettlesome Roosevelt "take the veil" as vice president.

✦ TR: Brandisher of the Big Stick

Kindly William McKinley had scarcely served another six months when, in September 1901, he was murdered by a deranged anarchist in Buffalo, New York. Roosevelt rode a buckboard out of his campsite in the Adirondacks to take the oath of office, becoming, at age forty-two, the youngest president thus far in American history.

Born into a wealthy and distinguished New York family, Roosevelt, a red-blooded blue blood, had fiercely built up his spindly, asthmatic body by a stern and self-imposed routine of exercise. Educated partly in Europe, he graduated from Harvard with Phi Beta Kappa honors and published, at the age of twenty-four,

Theodore Roosevelt   Roosevelt gives a speech with both voice and body language in North Carolina in 1902.

the first of some thirty volumes of muscular prose. He worked as a ranch owner and cowboy in the Dakotas before pursuing his political career full-time. Barrel-chested, bespectacled, and five feet ten inches tall, with mulelike molars, squinty eyes, droopy mustache, and piercing voice, he was ever the delight of cartoonists.

The Rough Rider's high-voltage energy was electrifying. Believing that it was better to wear out than to rust out, he would shake the hands of some six thousand people at one stretch or ride horseback many miles in a day as an example for portly cavalry officers. Incurably boyish and bellicose, Roosevelt ceaselessly preached the virile virtues and denounced pacifistic "flubdubs" and "mollycoddles." An ardent champion of military and naval preparedness, he adopted as his pet proverb, "Speak softly and carry a big stick, [and] you will go far."

His outsized ego caused it to be said of him that he wanted to be the bride at every wedding and the corpse at every funeral. He loved people and mingled with those of all ranks, from Catholic cardinals to professional prizefighters, one of whom blinded a Rooseveltian eye in a White House bout. "TR" commanded an idolatrous personal following. After visiting him, a journalist wrote, "You go home and wring the personality out of your clothes."

Above all, TR believed that the president should lead, boldly. He had no real respect for the delicate checks and balances among the three branches of the government. The president, he felt, may take any action in the general interest that is not specifically forbidden by the laws of the Constitution.

✦ Building the Panama Canal

Roosevelt soon applied his bullish energy to foreign affairs. The Spanish-American War had reinvigorated interest in the long-talked-about canal across the Central American isthmus, through which only printer's ink had ever flowed. Americans had learned a sobering lesson when the battleship *Oregon*, stationed on the Pacific Coast at the outbreak of war in 1898, took weeks to steam all the way around South America to join the U.S. fleet in Cuban waters. An isthmian canal would plainly augment the strength of the navy by increasing its mobility. Such a waterway would also make easier the defense of such recent acquisitions as Puerto Rico, Hawaii, and the Philippines, while facilitating the operations of the U.S. merchant marine.

Initial obstacles in the path of the canal builders were legal rather than geographical. By the terms of the ancient Clayton-Bulwer Treaty, concluded with Britain in 1850, the United States could not secure exclusive control over an isthmian route. But by 1901 America's

Cutting Through the Continental Divide in Panama The Culebra Cut, the southeastern section of the Panama Canal that extends through the Continental Divide, was later renamed the Gaillard Cut in honor of the U.S. Army Corps of Engineers officer who oversaw this excavation but died shortly before the canal opened in 1914. The cut was one of the greatest engineering feats of its time. Hundreds of drills prepared holes for tons of dynamite, which twice daily blasted the rock so that it could be excavated by steam shovels. Dirt trains, shown in the foreground, then hauled loads of debris to dumps twelve miles away. The summit of Culebra Mountain, through which the cut was made, was lowered from 193 feet to 40 feet above sea level and widened considerably. Library of Congress

British cousins were willing to yield ground. Confronted with an unfriendly Europe and bogged down in the South African Boer War, they consented to the **Hay-Pauncefote Treaty** in 1901. It not only gave the United States a free hand to build the canal but conceded the right to fortify it as well.

But where exactly should the canal be dug? Many American experts favored a route across Nicaragua, but agents of the old French Canal Company were eager to salvage something from their costly failure at S-shaped Panama. Represented by a young, energetic, and unscrupulous engineer, Philippe Bunau-Varilla, the New Panama Canal Company suddenly dropped the price of its holdings from $109 million to the fire-sale price of $40 million.

Congress in June 1902 finally decided on the Panama route. The scene now shifted to Colombia, of which Panama was a restive part. The Colombian senate rejected an American offer of $10 million and annual payment of $250,000 for a six-mile-wide zone across Panama. Roosevelt railed against "those dagoes" who were frustrating his ambitions. Meanwhile, impatient Panamanians, who had rebelled numerous times, were ripe for another revolt. They had counted on a wave of prosperity to follow construction of the canal, and they feared that the United States would now turn to the Nicaraguan route. Scheming Bunau-Varilla was no less disturbed by the prospect of losing the company's $40 million. Working hand in glove with the revolutionists, he helped incite a rebellion on November 3, 1903. U.S. naval forces prevented Colombian troops from crossing the isthmus to quell the uprising.

Roosevelt moved rapidly to make steamy Panama a virtual outpost of the United States. Just three days after the insurrection, he hastily extended the right hand of recognition. Fifteen days later, Bunau-Varilla, who was now the Panamanian minister despite his French citizenship, signed the Hay–Bunau-Varilla Treaty in Washington. The price of the canal strip was left the same, but the zone was widened from six to ten miles. The French company gladly pocketed its $40 million from the U.S. Treasury.

Roosevelt, it seems clear, did not actively plot to tear Panama from the side of Colombia. But the conspirators knew of his angrily expressed views, and they counted on his using the big stick to hold Colombia at

Theodore Roosevelt wrote to a correspondent in February 1904,

❝I have been hoping and praying for three months that the Santo Domingans would behave so that I would not have to act in any way. I want to do nothing but what a policeman has to do. . . . As for annexing the island, I have about the same desire to annex it as a gorged boa-constrictor might have to swallow a porcupine wrong-end-to.❞

bay. The Rough Rider became so indiscreetly involved in the Panama affair as to create the impression that he had been a secret party to the intrigue, and the so-called rape of Panama marked an ugly downward lurch in U.S. relations with Latin America.

Canal construction began in 1904, in the face of daunting difficulties ranging from labor troubles to landslides and lethal tropical diseases. Colonel William C. Gorgas, the quiet and determined exterminator of yellow fever in Havana, ultimately made the Canal Zone "as safe as a health resort." At a cost of some $400 million, an autocratic West Point engineer, Colonel George Washington Goethals, ultimately brought the project to completion in 1914, just as World War I was breaking out.

✦ TR's Perversion of Monroe's Doctrine

Latin American debt defaults prompted further Rooseveltian involvement in affairs south of the border. Nations such as Venezuela and the Dominican Republic were chronically in arrears in their payments to European creditors. Germany actually bombarded a town in delinquent Venezuela in 1903.

Granger Collection

Theodore Roosevelt and His Big Stick in the Caribbean, 1904 Roosevelt's policies seemed to be turning the Caribbean into a Yankee pond.

Roosevelt feared that if the Germans or British got their foot in the door as bill collectors, they might remain in Latin America, in flagrant violation of the Monroe Doctrine. He therefore declared a brazen policy of "preventive intervention," better known as the **Roosevelt Corollary** to the Monroe Doctrine. He announced that in the event of future financial malfeasance by the Latin American nations, the United States itself would intervene, take over the customshouses, pay off the debts, and keep the troublesome Europeans on the other side of the Atlantic. In short, no outsiders could push around the Latin nations except Uncle Sam, Policeman of the Caribbean. This new brandishing of the big stick in the Caribbean became effective in 1905, when the United States took over the management of tariff collections in the Dominican Republic, an arrangement formalized in a treaty with the Dominicans two years later.

TR's rewriting of the Monroe Doctrine probably did more than any other single step to promote the "Bad Neighbor" policy begun in these years. As time wore on, the new corollary was used to justify wholesale interventions and repeated landings of the marines, all of which helped turn the Caribbean into a "Yankee lake." To Latin Americans it seemed as though the revised Monroe Doctrine, far from providing a shield, was a cloak behind which the United States sought to strangle them.

The shadow of the big stick likewise fell again on Cuba in 1906. Revolutionary disorders brought an appeal from the Cuban president, and "necessity being the mother of intervention," U.S. Marines landed. These police forces were withdrawn temporarily in 1909, but in Latin American eyes the episode was but another example of the creeping power of the Colossus of the North.

✸ Roosevelt on the World Stage

Booted and spurred, Roosevelt charged into international affairs far beyond Latin America. The outbreak of war between Russia and Japan in 1904 gave him a chance to perform as a global statesman. The Russian bear, having lumbered across Asia, was seeking to bathe its frostbitten paws in the ice-free ports of China's Manchuria, particularly Port Arthur. In Japanese eyes, Manchuria and Korea in tsarist hands were pistols pointed at Japan's strategic heart. The Japanese responded in 1904 with a devastating surprise pounce on the Russian fleet at Port Arthur. They proceeded to administer a humiliating series of beatings to the inept Russians—the first serious military setback to a major European power by a non-European force since the Turkish invasions of

the sixteenth century. But as the war dragged on, Japan began to run short of men and yen—a weakness it did not want to betray to the enemy. Tokyo officials therefore approached Roosevelt in the deepest secrecy and asked him to help sponsor peace negotiations.

Roosevelt was happy to oblige, as he wanted to avoid a complete Russian collapse so that the tsar's empire could remain a counterweight to Japan's growing power. At Portsmouth, New Hampshire, in 1905, TR guided the warring parties to a settlement that satisfied neither side and left the Japanese, who felt they had won the war, especially resentful. Japan was forced to drop its demands for a cash indemnity and Russian evacuation of Sakhalin Island, though it received some compensation in the form of effective control over Korea, which it formally annexed in 1910.

For achieving this agreement, as well as for helping arrange an international conference at Algeciras, Spain, in 1906 to mediate North African disputes, TR received the Nobel Peace Prize in 1906. But the price of his diplomatic glory was high for U.S. foreign relations. Two historic friendships withered on the windswept plains of Manchuria. U.S. relations with Russia, once friendly, soured as the Russians implausibly accused Roosevelt of robbing them of military victory. Revelations about savage massacres of Russian Jews further poisoned American feeling against Russia. Japan, once America's protégé, felt cheated out of its due compensation. Both newly powerful, Japan and America now became rivals in Asia, as fear and jealousy between them grew. "A subjick race is on'y funny whin it's raaly subjek," said Finley Peter Dunne's Mr. Dooley (see "Thinking Globally: The Age of Empire," pp. 632–633). "About three years ago I stopped laughin' at Japanese jokes."

✸ Japanese Laborers in California

America's Pacific Coast soon felt the effects of the Russo-Japanese War. A new restlessness swept over the rice paddies of Japan, occasioned by the recent conflict's dislocations and tax burdens. A new wave of Japanese immigrants began pouring into the spacious valleys of California. Although Japanese residents never amounted to more than 3 percent of the state's population, white Californians ranted about a new "yellow peril" and feared being drowned in an Asian sea.

A showdown on the influx came in 1906, when San Francisco's school board, coping with the aftermath of a frightful earthquake and fire, ordered the segregation of Chinese, Japanese, and Korean students in a special school to free more space for whites. Instantly the incident boiled into an international crisis. The people of Japan, understandably sensitive on questions of race,

U.S. Army Signal Corps/National Archives

Japanese Workers Building a Road in California, ca. 1910

regarded this discrimination as an insult to them and their beloved children. On both sides of the Pacific, irresponsible war talk sizzled in the yellow press—the real "yellow peril." Roosevelt, who as a Rough Rider had relished shooting, was less happy over the prospect that California might stir up a war that all the other states would have to wage. He therefore invited the entire San Francisco Board of Education, headed by a bassoon-playing mayor under indictment for graft, to come to the White House.

TR finally broke the deadlock, but not until he had brandished his big stick and bared his big teeth. The Californians were induced to repeal the offensive school order and to accept what came to be known as the "Gentlemen's Agreement." By this secret understanding, worked out during 1907–1908, Tokyo agreed to stop the flow of laborers to the American mainland by withholding passports.

Worried that his intercession might be interpreted in Tokyo as prompted by fear, Roosevelt hit upon a dramatic scheme to impress the Japanese with the heft of his big stick. He daringly decided to send the entire battleship fleet on a highly visible voyage around the world. Late in 1907 sixteen sparkling-white, smoke-belching battleships started from Virginia waters. Their commander pointedly declared that he was ready for "a feast, a frolic, or a fight." The Great White Fleet—saluted by cannonading champagne corks—received tumultuous welcomes in Latin America, Hawaii, New Zealand, and Australia (though it ended up having to borrow coal from the British to complete the voyage).

As events turned out, an overwhelming reception in Japan was the high point of the trip. Tens of thousands of kimonoed schoolchildren, trained to wave tiny American flags, movingly sang "The Star-Spangled Banner." In the warm diplomatic atmosphere created by the visit of the fleet, the U.S. signed the **Root-Takahira agreement** with Japan in 1908. It pledged both powers to respect each other's territorial possessions in the Pacific and to uphold the Open Door in China. For the moment, at least, the two rising rival powers had found a means to maintain the peace.

The Age of Empire

*T*he closing years of the nineteenth century witnessed an unprecedented explosion of imperialism, roughly defined as the forcible imposition of one country's rule on the unwilling inhabitants of another. Between 1870 and the outbreak of World War I in 1914, a handful of European states extended their sway over nearly one-quarter of the earth's surface. Other countries followed suit, notably Japan and eventually the United States.

All the imperial powers had in common a heritage of nationalism and a high degree of industrialization. They commanded the elaborate administrative apparatus of large unified states, along with quantities of wealth, technology, and murderous firepower utterly beyond the capacity of the so-called backward peoples they sought to dominate. As a result, imperialism was, from the start, a lopsided game. As one English wit mordantly noted in 1898,

> Whatever happens, we have got
> The Maxim gun, and they have not.

Yet ultimately, even with their enormously disproportionate advantages, the imperial states were unable to sustain the age of imperialism for much more than a century.

In many ways, modern imperialism resembled eighteenth-century mercantilism, as economically advanced states backed away from the free-trade doctrines that had energized the early stages of the Industrial Revolution and sought instead to create what one British imperialist called "a great self-sustaining and self-protecting empire." The new imperialism also differed from older colonialism in that the imperial powers sought not merely to exploit but also to transform, modernize, and "westernize" the "backward" societies under their control.

Imperialists often justified their dominion over less developed societies with high-toned slogans. The British professed to be nobly shouldering "the white man's burden." The French piously invoked their *mission civilisatrice* (civilizing mission). The Germans touted the benefits of spreading their vaunted *Kultur* (culture). The Americans prated about the superiority of the Anglo-Saxons, as the Japanese did about their own "Yamato" race.

These protestations may have been sincere, but other motives more powerfully propelled the imperial enterprise. Prominent among them was the quest for new markets, as maturing industrial economies appeared to be exhausting the possibilities for economic growth at home. The need for reliable sources of products such as cotton, sugar, copper, coffee, and tea also figured conspicuously. An even more compelling incentive was the need to protect the huge investments of capital that built the railroads, highways, bridges, ports, mills, foundries, mines, smelters, and telegraphs of the developing world. By the eve of the First World War, fully one-quarter of Britain's accumulated wealth was invested overseas.

But perhaps the most important factor driving the imperialist venture was simply the competitive nature of the international system itself. In an unstable, unpredictable world inhabited by ambitious and wary powers, no state thought it could afford to cede an advantage, however ill-defined, to any real or imagined rival. Indeed, quite independently of their hard economic value, colonies came to be considered the necessary symbols of great-power status. This perverse logic proved to be a powerful dynamic: once the imperial

A Young Ho Chi Minh Ho Chi Minh (1890–1969) attended the Congress of the Socialist Party in Tours, France, where the French Communist party was created in late December 1920.

Library of Congress

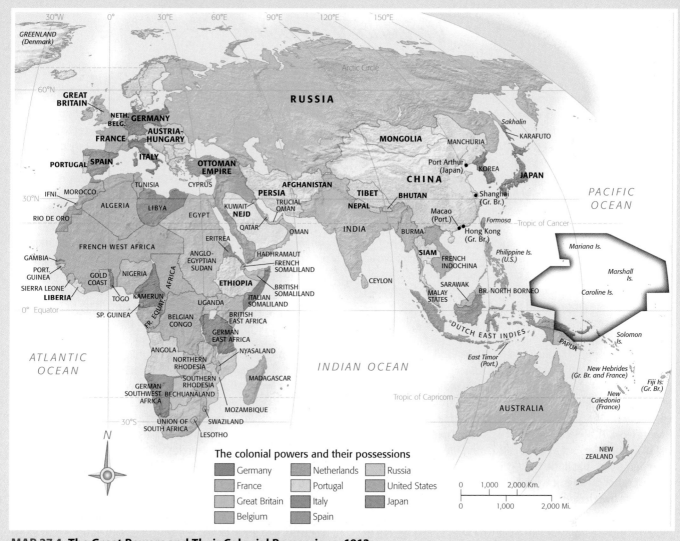

MAP 27.4 The Great Powers and Their Colonial Possessions, 1913 © Cengage Learning

The colonial powers and their possessions

Germany
France
Great Britain
Belgium
Netherlands
Portugal
Italy
Spain
Russia
United States
Japan

race began, it was difficult to stop. As Cecil Rhodes, the fabled British colonizer in southern Africa, once said, "I would annex the planets, if I could. I often think of that."

So when Belgium's King Leopold took an interest in Africa's Congo basin in the 1870s, he touched off a mad imperial scramble that eventually involved Belgium, Britain, Germany, France, Italy, and Portugal. Less than two decades later, with the exceptions of Ethiopia and Liberia, the entire continent, much of it unexplored and of dubious economic value, lay under European domination (see Map 27.4).

In Asia, Germany annexed part of New Guinea in 1884. France completed its annexation of Indochina (present-day Vietnam, Laos, and Cambodia) that same year. Britain acquired Burma (now

Myanmar) in 1885 and parts of Borneo and the Malay Peninsula soon after. Japan closed its grip on Okinawa in 1872, Formosa (Taiwan) in 1895, Port Arthur in 1905, and Korea in 1910. All those powers, in addition to Russia, also had designs on China, which despite its venerable history seemed a poor match for the energetic "nations on the make." In the Open Door notes of 1899 and 1900 (see pp. 623), the United States tried to temper the imperialists' appetites for Chinese territory and concessions, while at the same time America was becoming an imperial power itself with the takeover of the Philippines and Puerto Rico.

The imperialists brought not only their might and their majesty, their capital and their Maxim guns. They also brought their ideas, including concepts

of nationalism, self-determination, and democracy. In 1919 a young Vietnamese nationalist named Nguyen Sinh Cung unsuccessfully petitioned the post–World War I peacemakers at Versailles for his country's right to self-determination. A little more than half a century later, under the name Ho Chi Minh, he secured Vietnam's independence by prevailing in a war first against the French and then against the Americans. By that time the United States had long since voluntarily relinquished the Philippines (in 1946, though Puerto Rico remains an American possession), and virtually all of Africa and Asia had been decolonized. With the handover of Hong Kong (1997) and Macao (1999) to the People's Republic of China, the age of empire effectively ended.

Varying Viewpoints
Why Did America Become a World Power?

American imperialism has long been an embarrassing topic for students of American history, who remember the Republic's own revolutionary origins and anticolonial tradition. Perhaps for that reason, many historians have tried to explain the dramatic overseas expansionism of the 1890s as some kind of aberration—a sudden, singular, and short-lived departure from time-honored American principles and practices. Various explanations have been offered to account for this spasmodic lapse. Scholars such as Julius Pratt pointed to the irresponsible behavior of the yellow press. Richard Hofstadter ascribed America's imperial fling as the "psychic crisis of the 1890s," a crisis brought on, he argued, by the strains of the decade's economic depression and the Populist upheaval. Howard K. Beale emphasized the contagious scramble for imperial possessions by the European powers, as well as Japan, in these years.

In Beale's argument, the United States—and Theodore Roosevelt in particular—succumbed to a kind of international peer pressure: if other countries were expanding their international roles and even establishing colonies around the globe, could the United States safely refrain from doing the same? In Beale's view, Theodore Roosevelt was no simpleminded imperial swashbuckler, but a coolly calculating diplomatic realist who perceived that if the United States did not hold its own against other powers, it would soon risk being pushed around, even in its own hemisphere, despite the Monroe Doctrine.

More recent scholarship by Paul Kramer and others has stressed the degree to which American imperialists turned to European precedents for guidance and inspiration. U.S. colonial officials in the Philippines and Puerto Rico circulated widely in the British colonial world, selectively adapting elements of British imperial policy.

Perhaps the most controversial interpretation of American imperialism has come from a so-called New Left school of writers, inspired by William Appleman Williams (and before him by V. I. Lenin's 1916 book *Imperialism: The Highest Stage of Capitalism*). Historians such as Williams and Walter LaFeber argue that the explanation for political and military expansion abroad is to be found in economic expansion at home. Increasing industrial output, so the argument goes, required ever more raw materials and, especially, overseas markets. To meet those needs, the nation adopted a strategy of "informal empire," shunning formal territorial possessions (with the conspicuous exceptions of Puerto Rico and the Philippines), but seeking economic dominance over foreign markets, materials, and investment outlets. That "revisionist" interpretation, in turn, has been sharply criticized by scholars who point out that foreign trade accounted for only a tiny share of American output and that the diplomacy of this period was far too complex to be reduced to "economic need."

Most recently, historians have highlighted the importance of race and gender in the march toward empire. Roosevelt and other imperialists perceived their world in gendered terms. American society, many feared, was losing touch with the manly virtues. It had grown soft and "feminine" since the closing of the frontier. Imperialists also saw the nations of the world in a strict racial hierarchy, with "primitive" blacks and Indians at the bottom and "civilized" Anglo-Saxons at the top. In this world-view the conquest of "inferior" peoples seemed natural—a tropical tonic to restore the nation's masculine virility. Scholars who emphasize these explanations of imperialism are less likely to see the expansionism of the 1890s as an aberration in American history. Instead, they argue, these overseas adventures were part of a long tradition of race-fueled militarism, from the nation's earliest Indian wars to Cold War engagements in Korea and Vietnam.

Chapter Review

KEY TERMS

Big Sister policy (609)

Great Rapprochement (610)

McKinley Tariff (611)

insurrectos (612)

Maine (612)

Teller Amendment (614)

Rough Riders (615)

Anti-Imperialist League (620)

Foraker Act (620)

Insular Cases (621)

Platt Amendment (621)

Open Door note (623)

Boxer Rebellion (623)

Hay-Pauncefote Treaty (628)

Roosevelt Corollary (630)

Root-Takahira agreement (631)

PEOPLE TO KNOW

Josiah Strong

Alfred Thayer Mahan

James G. Blaine

Richard Olney

Liliuokalani

"Butcher" Weyler

Dupuy de Lôme

George Dewey

Emilio Aguinaldo

William H. Taft

John Hay

Theodore ("Teddy") Roosevelt

CHRONOLOGY

1820	New England missionaries arrive in Hawaii
1889	Samoa crisis with Germany Pan-American Conference
1890	Mahan publishes *The Influence of Sea Power upon History*
1891	New Orleans crisis with Italy
1892	Valparaiso crisis with Chile
1893	Pribilof Islands dispute with Canada White planter revolt in Hawaii Cleveland refuses Hawaii annexation
1895	Cubans revolt against Spain
1895–1896	Venezuelan boundary crisis with Britain
1898	*Maine* explosion in Havana harbor Spanish-American War Teller Amendment Dewey's victory at Manila Bay Hawaii annexed
1899	Senate ratifies treaty acquiring Philippines Aguinaldo launches rebellion against United States in Philippines First American Open Door note
1900	Hawaii receives full territorial status Foraker Act for Puerto Rico Boxer Rebellion and U.S. military expedition to China Second Open Door note McKinley defeats Bryan for presidency

1901	Supreme Court *Insular Cases* Platt Amendment McKinley assassinated; Roosevelt becomes president Filipino rebellion suppressed Hay-Pauncefote Treaty with Britain gives United States exclusive right to build Panama Canal
1902	U.S. troops leave Cuba Colombian senate rejects U.S. proposal for canal across Panama
1903	Panamanian revolution against Colombia Hay–Bunau-Varilla Treaty gives United States control of Canal Zone in newly independent Panama
1904	Roosevelt Corollary to Monroe Doctrine
1904–1914	Construction of Panama Canal
1905	United States takes over Dominican Republic customs service Roosevelt mediates Russo-Japanese peace treaty
1906	San Francisco Japanese education crisis Roosevelt arranges Algeciras Conference
1906–1909	U.S. Marines occupy Cuba
1907	Great White Fleet makes world voyage
1907–1908	"Gentlemen's Agreement" with Japan
1908	Root-Takahira agreement
1917	Puerto Ricans granted U.S. citizenship

TO LEARN MORE

Gail Bederman, *Manliness and Civilization: A Cultural History of Gender and Race in the United States, 1880–1917* (1995)

Robert L. Beisner, *Twelve Against Empire: The Anti-Imperialists, 1898–1900* (1968)

Julia Greene, *The Canal Builders: Making America's Empire at the Panama Canal* (2009)

George C. Herring, *From Colony to Superpower: U.S. Foreign Relations Since 1776* (2008)

Kristin L. Hoganson, *Consumers' Imperium: The Global Production of American Domesticity, 1865–1920* (2007)

William R. Hutchison, *Errand to the World: American Protestant Thought and Foreign Missions* (1987)

Matthew Frye Jacobson, *Barbarian Virtues: The United States Encounters Foreign Peoples at Home and Abroad, 1876–1917* (2000)

Paul A. Kramer, *The Blood of Government: Race, Empire, the United States, and the Philippines* (2006)

Walter LaFeber, *The Cambridge History of American Foreign Relations,* vol. 2: *The American Search for Opportunity, 1865–1913* (1993)

Ernest R. May, *Imperial Democracy: The Emergence of America as a Great Power* (1961)

Louis A. Perez, Jr., *The War of 1898: The United States and Cuba in History and Historiography* (1998)

Emily S. Rosenberg, *Spreading the American Dream: American Economic and Cultural Expansion, 1890–1945* (1982)

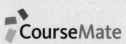

Go to the CourseMate website at **www.cengagebrain.com** for additional study tools and review materials—including audio and video clips—for this chapter.

A complete, annotated bibliography for this chapter—along with brief descriptions of the People to Know—may be found on the American Pageant website. The Key Terms are defined in a Glossary at the end of the text.

AP® Review Questions for Chapter 27

1. Which of the following was the most significant factor in the shift in American foreign policy toward imperialism in the late nineteenth century?
   (A) The popular influence of the yellow press of Joseph Pulitzer and William Randolph Hearst
   (B) The desire for more farmland
   (C) Construction of an American-built isthmian canal between the Atlantic and Pacific Oceans
   (D) A missionary zeal to civilize and bring Christianity to the nonwhite peoples of the South Pacific, Caribbean, and Latin America
   (E) The need for overseas markets for increased industrial and agricultural production

2. What was the primary reason Britain submitted its border dispute with Venezuela to international arbitration?
   (A) The growing tensions with Germany made Britain reluctant to engage in conflict with the United States.
   (B) The discovery of vast gold reserves in India diminished the importance of the British land claims in the jungle boundary between British Guiana and Venezuela.
   (C) Britain feared becoming embroiled in a dangerous land war in South America.
   (D) Doing so would undermine the close relations Spain maintained with the Latin American republics.
   (E) Britain had accepted America's complete political and economic domination over Latin America.

3. Why did the armed American effort to annex Hawaii fail in 1893?
   (A) Queen Liliuokalani and native Hawaiians crushed the revolt by white settlers, large sugar interests, and U.S. army troops supporting annexation.
   (B) It was fiercely opposed by American sugar lords, who feared annexation would eliminate their favored labor and trade arrangements with Hawaii.
   (C) Incoming president Cleveland rejected annexation because he believed native Hawaiians had been wronged by U.S. government support for an armed, sugar interest–supported overthrow of Queen Liliuokalani that enjoyed negligible support among native Hawaiians.
   (D) Protestant missionaries believed annexation would slow the conversion of native Hawaiians and Chinese and Japanese immigrants to Christianity.
   (E) A Japanese threat to declare war on the United States if America annexed Hawaii caused incoming president Cleveland to oppose annexation.

4. What was the most important reason President William McKinley asked Congress to declare war on Spain?
   (A) The business community universally supported the conflict.
   (B) The Spanish government had directly provoked and insulted the United States.
   (C) Spain refused to end the concentration camps and sign an armistice with Cuban rebels.
   (D) McKinley felt that the Teller Amendment would guarantee that the United States would not establish control of Cuba.
   (E) The American public, influenced by the yellow press, and many leading Republicans demanded war in the aftermath of the sinking of the *Maine*.

5. Which statement most accurately characterizes the U.S. Army's performance in Cuba during the Spanish-American War?
   (A) A model of tactical brilliance in an essentially guerrilla campaign
   (B) More successful than that of the U.S. Navy
   (C) Crippled by logistical chaos and disease that killed thousands of soldiers
   (D) Too dependent on the professional military leadership of Colonel Theodore Roosevelt
   (E) Weakened by lingering tensions between former Union and Confederate officers

6. What was the primary argument emphasized by American imperialists who advocated acquisition of the Philippines?
   (A) That annexing the Philippines would continue the glorious tradition of American expansion, pushing American civilization to the Pacific
   (B) The economic potential for the Philippines to advance trade with China and other Asian nations
   (C) The opportunity the Philippines presented for Christian missionary work
   (D) The Filipinos' own preference that their archipelago become an American protectorate
   (E) The potential of the Philippine immigrants to serve as a source for cheap industrial labor

7. Anti-imperialists presented all of the following arguments against acquiring the Philippine Islands EXCEPT that
   (A) it would violate "the consent of the governed" philosophy of the Declaration of Independence.
   (B) despotism abroad might lead to despotism at home.
   (C) the islands were still rightfully Spain's, since they were taken after the armistice had been signed.
   (D) annexation would propel the United States into the political and military cauldron of East Asia.
   (E) imperialism was likely to be more costly than profitable.

8. What was the direct cause of the Filipino insurrection in 1899?
   (A) Spanish citizens living in the Philippines allied with Filipino rebels to restore Spanish political control of the country.
   (B) The United States refused to give the Filipino people their political independence.
   (C) The United States declined to spend any government funds to promote the economic and social development of the Philippines.
   (D) American missionaries tried to convert Catholic Filipinos to Protestantism.
   (E) Japan instigated the insurrection in an effort to establish its geopolitical dominance of the Pacific.

9. Why did many Americans become concerned about the increasing foreign intervention in China at the turn of the twentieth century?
   (A) They feared that U.S. missions would be jeopardized and Chinese markets closed to non-Europeans.
   (B) They feared German military domination of China.
   (C) They desired that the United States should have exclusive trade rights with the Chinese.
   (D) They believed such intervention undermined Chinese sovereignty.
   (E) They opposed the superior racial attitudes and religious proselytizing of Europeans toward the Chinese.

10. What was the primary motivation for the efforts of the United States to secure construction of an isthmian canal across Central America?
    (A) A desire to improve defense by allowing rapid naval movements between two oceans
    (B) The Panamanian Revolution
    (C) America's growing economic interests in Asia
    (D) The desire to ensure that a similar French government effort would not succeed
    (E) The British rejection of the Hay-Pauncefote Treaty

11. What was one key international effect of President Theodore Roosevelt's aggressive involvement and active support for the Panamanian revolt?
    (A) Making other nations reluctant to use the Panama Canal
    (B) Sparking nationalist revolts against American rule in Puerto Rico and the United States
    (C) Allying the United States closely with Britain
    (D) Making all the Central American governments respect the United States
    (E) Increasing anti-American sentiment throughout Latin America

12. Which of the following was NOT a result of President Roosevelt's diplomatic ending of the Russo-Japanese war?
    (A) A dramatic improvement in U.S.-Russian and U.S.-Japan diplomatic relations
    (B) Roosevelt receiving the Nobel Peace Prize in 1906
    (C) Japan feeling cheated out of its due financial compensation
    (D) Russia accusing Roosevelt of robbing it of an impending military victory over Japan
    (E) A cessation of significant Japanese immigration to America's Pacific Coast

13. How did the attitude created by the Venezuelan border dispute indirectly lead to the Spanish-American War?
    (A) The national government realized that all European nations posed threats to the Western Hemisphere.
    (B) The American people were swept off their feet with war hysteria and were disappointed when no such war occurred.
    (C) Americans realized that people in Latin American countries were unable to govern themselves.
    (D) The border dispute led to the creation of the Big Sister policy.
    (E) President McKinley believed that Spanish control in Cuba would eventually lead to similar disputes.

14. How did the United States' position in world affairs change by the beginning of the twentieth century?
    (A) The United States became the most powerful country in the world.
    (B) The United States began to import much more than it exported.
    (C) The United States acquired its own empire, departing from its anticolonial traditions.
    (D) The United States extended humanitarian aid to any place it was necessary.
    (E) The United States tended toward isolationism, remembering Washington's advice.

Part Five

Struggling for Justice at Home and Abroad

1901–1945

*T*he new century brought astonishing changes to the United States. Victory in the Spanish-American War made it clear that the United States was now a world power. Industrialization ushered in giant corporations, sprawling factories, sweatshop labor, and the ubiquitous automobile. A huge wave of immigration was altering the face of the nation, especially the cities, where a majority of Americans lived by 1920. With bigger cities came bigger fears—of crime, vice, poverty, and disease.

Changes of such magnitude raised vexing questions. What role should the United States play in the world? How could the enormous power of industry be controlled? How would the millions of new immigrants make their way in America? What should the country do about poverty, disease, and the continuing plague of racial inequality? All these issues turned on a fundamental point: should government remain narrowly limited in its powers, or did the times require a more potent government that would actively shape society and secure American interests abroad?

The progressive movement represented the first attempt to answer those questions. Reform-minded men and women from all walks of life and from both major parties shared in the progressive crusade for greater government activism. Buoyed by this outlook, Presidents Theodore Roosevelt, William Howard Taft, and Woodrow Wilson enlarged the capacity of government to fight graft, "bust" business trusts, regulate corporations, and promote fair labor practices, child welfare, conservation, and consumer protection. These progressive reformers, convinced that women would bring greater morality to politics, bolstered the decades-long struggle for female suffrage. Women finally secured the vote in 1920 with the ratification of the Nineteenth Amendment.

The progressive-era presidents also challenged America's tradition of isolationism in foreign

Marching for Suffrage   Prominent New York socialite Mrs. Herbert Carpenter, bearing an American flag, marches in a parade for women's suffrage on Manhattan's Fifth Avenue, 1912. © Bettmann/Corbis

policy. They felt the country had a moral obligation to spread democracy and an economic opportunity to reap profits in foreign markets. Roosevelt and Taft launched diplomatic initiatives in the Caribbean, Central America, and East Asia. Wilson aspired to "make the world safe for democracy" by rallying support for American intervention in the First World War.

The progressive spirit waned, however, as the United States retreated during the 1920s into what President Harding called "normalcy." Isolationist sentiment revived with a vengeance. Blessed with a booming economy, Americans turned their gaze inward to baseball heroes, radio, jazz, movies, and the first mass-produced American automobile, the Model T Ford. Presidents Harding, Coolidge, and Hoover backed off from the economic regulatory zeal of their predecessors.

"Normalcy" also had a brutal side. Thousands of suspected radicals were jailed or deported in the red scare of 1919 and 1920. Anti-immigrant passions flared until immigration quotas in 1924 squeezed the flow of newcomers to a trickle. Race riots scorched several northern cities in the summer of 1919, a sign of how embittered race relations had become in the wake of the "great migration" of southern blacks to wartime jobs in northern industry. A reborn Ku Klux Klan staged a comeback, not just in the South but in the North and West as well.

"Normalcy" itself soon proved short-lived, a casualty of the stock-market crash of 1929 and the Great Depression that followed. As Americans watched banks fail, businesses collapse, and millions of people lose their jobs, they asked with renewed urgency what role the government should play in rescuing the nation. President Franklin D. Roosevelt's answer was the "New Deal"—an ambitious array of relief programs, public works, and economic regulations that failed to cure the depression but furnished an impressive legacy of social reforms.

Bound for Guadalcanal, 1942 These troops were headed for one of the bloodiest battles of World War II, in the southwest Pacific's Solomon Islands. America threw some 15 million men and the full weight of its enormous economy into the struggle against German and Japanese aggression. National Archives

Most Americans came to accept an expanded federal government role at home under FDR's leadership in the 1930s, but they still clung stubbornly to isolationism. The United States did little in the 1930s to check the rising military aggression of Japan and Germany. By the early 1940s, events forced Americans to reconsider. Once Hitler's Germany had seized control of most of Europe, Roosevelt, who had long opposed the isolationists, found ways to aid a beleaguered Britain. When Japan attacked the American naval base at Pearl Harbor in December 1941, isolationists at last fell silent. Roosevelt led a stunned but determined nation into the Second World War, and victory in 1945 positioned the United States to assume a commanding position in the postwar world order.

The Great Depression and the Second World War brought to a head a half-century of debate over the role of government and the place of the United States in the world. In the name of a struggle for justice, Roosevelt established a new era of government activism at home and internationalism abroad. The New Deal's legacy set the terms of debate in American political life for the rest of the century.

Chapter 28

Progressivism and the Republican Roosevelt

1901–1912

*When I say I believe in a square deal I do not mean . . . to give every
man the best hand. If the cards do not come to any man, or if they
do come, and he has not got the power to play them, that is his affair.
All I mean is that there shall be no crookedness in the dealing.*

THEODORE ROOSEVELT, 1905

Nearly 76 million Americans greeted the new century in 1900. Almost one in seven of them was foreign-born. In the fourteen years of peace that remained before the Great War of 1914 engulfed the globe, 13 million more migrants would carry their bundles down the gangplanks to the land of promise.

Hardly had the twentieth century dawned on the ethnically and racially mixed American people than they were convulsed by a reform movement, the likes of which the nation had not seen since the 1840s. The new crusaders, who called themselves "progressives," waged war on many evils, notably monopoly, corruption, inefficiency, and social injustice. The progressive army was large, diverse, and widely deployed, but it had a single battle cry: "Strengthen the State." The "real heart of the movement," explained one of the progressive reformers, was "to use government as an agency of human welfare."

✴ Progressive Roots

The groundswell of the new reformist wave went far back—to the Greenback Labor party of the 1870s and the Populists of the 1890s, to the mounting unrest throughout the land as grasping industrialists concentrated more and more power in fewer and fewer hands. An outworn philosophy of hands-off individualism seemed increasingly out of place in the modern machine age. Social and economic problems were now too complex for the intentionally feeble Jeffersonian organs of government. Progressive theorists were insisting that society could no longer afford the luxury of a limitless "let-alone" (laissez-faire) policy. The people, through government, must substitute mastery for drift.

Well before 1900, perceptive politicians and writers had begun to pinpoint targets for the progressive attack. Bryan, Altgeld, and the Populists loudly branded the "bloated trusts" with the stigma of corruption and wrongdoing. In 1894 Henry Demarest Lloyd charged headlong into the Standard Oil Company with his book *Wealth Against Commonwealth*. Eccentric Thorstein Veblen assailed the new rich with his prickly pen in *The Theory of the Leisure Class* (1899), a savage attack on "predatory wealth" and "conspicuous consumption." In Veblen's view the parasitic leisure class engaged in wasteful "business" (or making money for money's sake) rather than productive "industry" (or making goods to satisfy real needs). He urged that social leadership pass from these superfluous titans to truly useful engineers.

Other pen-wielding knights likewise entered the fray. The keen-eyed and keen-nosed Danish immigrant Jacob A. Riis, a reporter for the *New York Sun*, shocked middle-class Americans in 1890 with *How the Other Half Lives*. His account was a damning indictment of the dirt, disease, vice, and misery of the rat-gnawed human rookeries known as New York slums. The book deeply

Picture Research Consultants & Archives

Melting Pot in P.S. 188, 1910 These immigrant children from the Lower East Side of New York are dressed in costumes from their native lands and surround their teacher, adorned as the Statue of Liberty. Schools like this one, flooded with immigrant children who could scarcely speak English, tried to respect their students' ancestral cultures while also cultivating loyalty to their adopted country by teaching American "civics" and appreciation for patriotic symbols and rituals.

influenced a future New York City police commissioner, Theodore Roosevelt. Novelist Theodore Dreiser used his blunt prose to batter promoters and profiteers in *The Financier* (1912) and *The Titan* (1914).

Caustic critics of social injustice issued from several other corners. Socialists, many of whom were European immigrants inspired by the strong movement for state socialism in the Old World, began to register appreciable strength at the ballot box (see "Thinking Globally: 'Why Is There No Socialism in the United States?'" pp. 642–643). High-minded messengers of the **social gospel** promoted a brand of progressivism based on Christian teachings. They used religious doctrine to demand better housing and living conditions for the urban poor. University-based economists urged new reforms modeled on European examples, importing policy ideas from Berlin to Baltimore. Feminists in multiplying numbers added social justice to suffrage on their list of needed reforms. With urban pioneers like Jane Addams in Chicago and Lillian Wald in New York

blazing the way, women entered the fight to improve the lot of families living and working in the festering cities.

✦ Raking Muck with the Muckrakers

Beginning about 1902 the exposing of evil became a flourishing industry among American publishers. A group of aggressive ten- and fifteen-cent popular magazines surged to the front, notably *McClure's*, *Cosmopolitan*, *Collier's*, and *Everybody's*. Waging fierce circulation wars, they dug deep for the dirt that the public loved to hate. Enterprising editors financed extensive research and encouraged pugnacious writing by their bright young reporters, whom President Roosevelt branded as **muckrakers** in 1906. Annoyed by their excess of zeal, he compared the mudslinging magazine dirt-diggers to the figure in Bunyan's *Pilgrim's Progress* who was so intent on raking manure that he could not see the celestial crown dangling overhead.

Room in a Tenement Flat, 1910 Tenement life on the Lower East Side of New York City was exposed by the camera of Jacob Riis, who compiled a large photographic archive of turn-of-the-century urban life. Many families counted themselves lucky to share a single room, no matter how squalid.

Despite presidential scolding, these muckrakers boomed circulation, and some of their most scandalous exposures were published as best-selling books. The reformer-writers ranged far, wide, and deep in their crusade to lay bare the muck of iniquity in American society. In 1902 a brilliant New York reporter, Lincoln Steffens, launched a series of articles in *McClure's* titled "The Shame of the Cities." He fearlessly unmasked the corrupt alliance between big business and municipal government. Steffens was followed in the same magazine by Ida M. Tarbell, a pioneering journalist who published a devastating but factual exposé of the Standard Oil Company. (Her father had been ruined by the oil interests.)

Plucky muckrakers fearlessly tilted their pen-lances at varied targets. They assailed the malpractices of life insurance companies and tariff lobbies. They roasted the beef trust, the "money trust," the railroad barons, and the corrupt amassing of American fortunes. Thomas W. Lawson, an erratic speculator who had

In his muckraker speech (1906), Theodore Roosevelt (1858–1919) said,

"Now, it is very necessary that we should not flinch from seeing what is vile and debasing. There is filth on the floor and it must be scraped up with the muck-rake; and there are times and places where this service is the most needed of all the services that can be performed. But the man who never does anything else, who never thinks or speaks or writes, save of his feats with the muck-rake, speedily becomes, not a help to society, not an incitement to good, but one of the most potent forces for evil."

himself made $50 million on the stock market, laid bare the practices of his accomplices in "Frenzied Finance," a series of articles that appeared in *Everybody's*. Lawson, by fouling his own nest, made many enemies among his rich associates, and he died a poor man.

David G. Phillips shocked an already startled nation by his series in *Cosmopolitan* titled "The Treason of the Senate" (1906). He boldly charged that seventy-five of the ninety senators did not represent the people at all but the railroads and trusts. This withering indictment, buttressed by facts, impressed President Roosevelt. Phillips continued his attacks through novels and was fatally shot in 1911 by a deranged young man whose family he had allegedly maligned.

Some of the most effective fire of the muckrakers was directed at social evils. The ugly list included the immoral "white slave" traffic in women, the rickety slums, and the appalling number of industrial accidents. The sorry subjugation of America's 9 million blacks—of whom 90 percent still lived in the South and one-third were illiterate—was spotlighted in Ray Stannard Baker's *Following the Color Line* (1908). The abuses of child labor were brought luridly to light by John Spargo's *The Bitter Cry of the Children* (1906).

Vendors of potent patent medicines (often heavily spiked with alcohol) likewise came in for bitter criticism. These conscienceless vultures sold incredible quantities of adulterated or habit-forming drugs, while "doping" the press with lavish advertising. Muckraking attacks in *Collier's* were ably reinforced by Dr. Harvey W. Wiley, chief chemist of the Department of Agriculture, who with his famous "Poison Squad" performed experiments on himself.

Full of sound and fury, the muckrakers signified much about the nature of the progressive reform movement. They were long on lamentation but stopped short of revolutionary remedies. To right social wrongs,

Ida Tarbell (1857–1944) in Her Office   Tarbell was the most eminent woman in the muckraking movement and one of the most respected business historians of her generation. In 1904 she earned a national reputation for publishing a scathing history of the Standard Oil Company, the "Mother of Trusts." Two years later she joined Ray Stannard Baker, William Allen White, and other muckrakers in purchasing the *American* magazine, which became a journalistic podium in their campaign for honest government and an end to business abuses.

they counted on publicity and an aroused public conscience, not drastic political change. They sought not to overthrow capitalism but to cleanse it. The cure for the ills of American democracy, they earnestly believed, was more democracy.

In his muckraking classic "The Shame of the Cities" (1904), Lincoln Steffens (1866–1936) decried the great threat posed by New York City's Tammany machine:

“Bribery is no ordinary felony, but treason; . . . 'corruption which breaks out here and there and now and then' is not an occasional offense, but a common practice, and . . . the effect of it is literally to change the form of our government from one that is representative of the people to an oligarchy, representative of special interests.”

✪ Political Progressivism

The question "Who were the progressives?" evokes contradictory answers. Progressive reformers included militarists such as Theodore Roosevelt, who thrilled to the strenuous life, as well as pacifists such as Jane Addams, whose loftiest goals included the abolition of war. Female settlement workers hoping to "Americanize" recent immigrants mobilized alongside labor unionists and enlightened businessmen to strengthen the helping hand of government. In diverse ways, and sometimes with divergent aims, the progressives sought to modernize American institutions to achieve two chief goals: to use the state to curb monopoly power and to improve the common person's conditions of life and labor. Progressives emerged in both major parties, in all regions, and at all levels of government. The truth is that progressivism was less a monolithic minority movement and more a broadly dispersed majority mood. (See Varying Viewpoints, pp. 675–676.)

One of the first objectives of progressives was to regain the power that had slipped from the hands of the people into those of the "interests." These ardent reformers pushed for direct primary elections so as to undercut power-hungry party bosses. They favored the **initiative** so that voters could directly propose legislation themselves, thus bypassing the boss-bought state legislatures. Progressives also agitated for the **referendum**. This device would place laws on the ballot for final approval by the people, especially laws that had been railroaded through a compliant legislature by free-spending agents of big business. The **recall** would enable the voters to remove faithless elected officials, particularly those who had been bribed by bosses or lobbyists.

Rooting out graft also became a prime goal of earnest progressives. A number of the state legislatures passed corrupt-practices acts, which limited the amount of money that candidates could spend for their election. Such legislation also restricted huge gifts from corporations, for which the donors would expect special favors. The secret **Australian ballot** was likewise being introduced more widely in the states to counteract boss rule. Bribery was less feasible when bribers could not tell if they were getting their money's worth from the bribed.

Direct election of U.S. senators became a favorite goal of progressives, especially after the muckrakers had exposed the scandalous intimacy between greedy corporations and Congress. By 1900 the Senate had so many rich men that it was often sneered at as the "Millionaires' Club." Too many of these prosperous solons, elected as they then were by trust-dominated legislatures, heeded the voice of their "masters" rather than the voice of the masses.

"Why Is There No Socialism in the United States?"

The Industrial Revolution that began in Britain in the late eighteenth century had by 1900 utterly transformed life in the Western world and beyond. It also had spawned a powerful theory of history, grounded in the writings of Karl Marx. Marxists believed that history's driving engine was class conflict; that in the industrial era that conflict had been starkly reduced to the contest between capitalists and workers (the *bourgeoisie* and the *proletariat*); and that an inevitable socialist revolution would result in the triumph of the proletariat and the emergence of a classless society. Its organizing principle would be "From each according to his ability, to each according to his needs."

Improbable as it might seem today, many nineteenth-century Marxists expected the first socialist revolution to occur in the United States. Marx himself saw America as the country where capitalism had developed more "shamelessly" than elsewhere, thus setting the stage for the "final conflict" that would yield the socialist utopia. Violent labor upheavals like those at Homestead (see p. 506), Haymarket (see p. 533), and Pullman (see p. 599) seemed to confirm that analysis, and a chorus of European Marxists stepped up their prophecies. Marx's collaborator Friedrich Engels wrote in the aftermath of the Haymarket eruption in May 1886 that in Europe it had taken workers decades to evolve a common "class consciousness," but "on the more favored soil of America, where no medieval ruins bar the way . . . the working class" would do so "within 10 months."

But it was not to be. Twenty years later the head of the German Social Democratic party lamented that "we are waiting for you Americans to do something."

The Americans had done a little something, but amid all the ferment of reform in the progressive era, they remained a sore disappointment to European radicals. Eugene V. Debs organized the Socialist party in 1901 and won 6 percent of the vote in the presidential election of 1912. But the Socialist party remained a tiny, marginal group. It never posed a serious challenge to the major American parties and never remotely approached the stature of Old World working-class parties such as the French Socialists, the Italian Communists, the German Social Democrats, and the British Labour party. At one time or another, most of these European organizations became ruling parties that implemented socialist ideas such as national ownership of core industries, robust support for labor unions, and lavish welfare programs—developments that to this day have had only feeble if any counterparts in the United States.

The failure of Marx's predictions about America occasioned much soul-searching about the plausibility of his entire theory of history. In 1904 a young German scholar named Werner Sombart traveled to the United States—much as Alexis de Tocqueville had nearly seventy-five years earlier—to examine America's puzzling reality firsthand (see "Thinking Globally: Alexis de Tocqueville on Democracy in America and Europe," pp. 252–253). Two years later he published the notable book *Why Is There No Socialism in the United States?* "If Socialism follows as a necessary reaction to capitalism," he asked, why was there no socialist movement worthy of the name in "the country with the most advanced capitalist development, namely the United States?"

Sombart gave several answers:

1. The strikingly egalitarian manners of all Americans. "The bowing and scraping before the 'upper classes,'

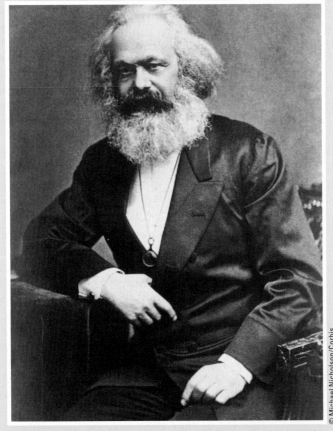

The Prophet of the Class Struggle, Karl Marx (1818–1883)

© Michael Nicholson/Corbis

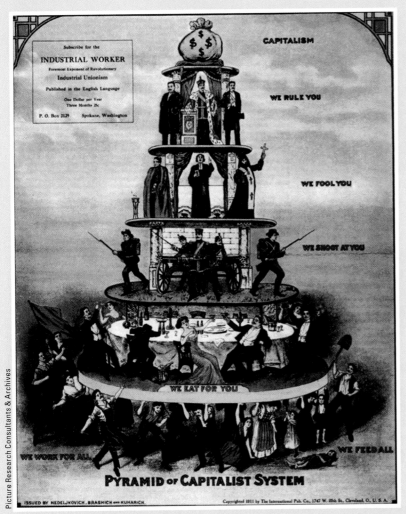

The IWW Seeks Subscribers, 1911 This poster aimed to attract subscribers to *Industrial Worker*, the newspaper of the Industrial Workers of the World (IWW). The IWW was a small but vocal radical labor union that hoped to unify American workers in "one big union," irrespective of their particular jobs, gender, or race. Its motto was "An injury to one is an injury to all." At its peak in 1923, the union claimed 100,000 members, commonly known as Wobblies, and could marshal the support of some 300,000 more, mostly workers on the docks and in mines, lumbering, and textiles.

which produces such an unpleasant impression in Europe, is completely unknown," he noted, reflecting the workers' refusal or inability to consider themselves a class apart.

2. The "safety valve" of the western frontier, which allowed workers to walk away from oppressive employers and strike out on their own. Sombart exaggerated the effects of the frontier (see p. 590), but he did call attention to the remarkable geographic mobility of American workers, which, together with their astonishing racial and ethnic diversity, worked to inhibit their sense of class permanence and class solidarity.

3. The American workers' remarkably high standard of living. "On roast beef and apple pie," he concluded in

a famous sentence, "all socialist utopias have gone to pot."

4. An accident of historical timing. Sombart shared with Tocqueville a deep insight into the American experience. Unlike Europe, where the struggles for political and economic rights went forward in tandem, in America workers had largely achieved full political equality before the onset of America's own Industrial Revolution. They had a stake in the existing political order from the outset and little incentive to overturn it. As another German socialist put it, for the purposes of building class consciousness, "the *struggle* for freedom is very much superior to the effortless possession of a freedom that others have won before." That observation echoed

Tocqueville's celebrated dictum that because the United States never had a feudal phase, it was *born* free, instead of *becoming* so, and was "reaping the fruits of the democratic revolution without having had the revolution itself."

More than a century after Sombart's inquiry, and especially since the collapse of Soviet communism, Marxism stands largely discredited, and some western European societies are edging away from socialist ideas such as national ownership of industries. As one historian has suggested, "One might well ask not 'Why is there no socialism in the United States?' but 'Why has there been no socialist transformation in any advanced capitalist society?'"

Jane Addams and Fellow Pacifists, 1915   Addams cofounded the Women's Peace Party in 1915. Its pacifist platform was said to represent the views of the "mother half of humanity." Although the party initially attracted twenty-five thousand members, America's entry into the war two years later eroded popular support, since pacifist internationalism became suspect as anti-American.

A constitutional amendment to bring about the popular election of senators had rough sledding in Congress, for the plutocratic members of the Senate were happy with existing methods. But a number of states established primary elections in which the voters expressed their preferences for the Senate. The local legislatures, when choosing senators, found it politically wise to heed the voice of the people. Partly as a result of such pressures, the Seventeenth Amendment to the Constitution, approved in 1913, established the direct election of U.S. senators (see the Appendix). But the expected improvement in caliber was slow in coming.

The suffrage campaign of the early twentieth century benefited from a new generation of women who considered themselves "feminists." At a mass meeting in New York in 1914, Marie Jenny Howe (1870–1934), a minister by training as well as a prominent early feminist, proclaimed,

❝We intend simply to be ourselves, not just our little female selves, but our whole big human selves.**❞**

Woman suffrage, the goal of female reformers for many decades, likewise received powerful new support from the progressives early in the 1900s. The political reformers believed that women's votes would elevate the political tone, and the foes of the saloon felt that they could count on the support of enfranchised females. The suffragists, with their cry of "Votes for Women" and "Equal Suffrage for Men and Women," protested bitterly against "Taxation Without Representation." Many of the states, especially the more liberal ones in the West, such as Washington, California, and Oregon, gradually extended the vote to women. But by 1910 nationwide female suffrage was still a decade away, and a suffragist could still be sneeringly defined as "one who has ceased to be a lady and has not yet become a gentleman."

✦ Progressivism in the Cities and States

Progressives scored some of their most impressive gains in the cities. Frustrated by the inefficiency and corruption of machine-oiled city government, many localities followed the pioneering example of Galveston, Texas. In 1901 it had appointed expert-staffed commissions to manage urban affairs. Other communities adopted the city-manager system, also designed to take politics out of municipal administration. Some of these "reforms" obviously valued efficiency more highly than democracy, as control of civic affairs was further removed from the people's hands.

Urban reformers likewise attacked "slumlords," juvenile delinquency, and wide-open prostitution (vice-at-a-price), which flourished in red-light districts unchallenged by bribed police. Public-spirited Americans looked to English and German cities for lessons on how to clean up their water supplies, light their streets, and run their trolley cars. The vogue of public ownership of utilities swept the nation as local governments tried to halt the corrupt sale of franchises.

Progressivism naturally bubbled up to the state level, notably in Wisconsin, which became a yeasty laboratory of reform. The governor of the state, pompadoured Robert M. ("Fighting Bob") La Follette, was an undersized but overbearing crusader who emerged as the most militant of the progressive Republican leaders. After a desperate fight with entrenched monopoly, he reached the governor's chair in 1901. Routing the lumber and railroad "interests," he wrested considerable control from the crooked corporations and returned it to the people. He also perfected a scheme for regulating public utilities, while laboring in close association with experts on the faculty of the state university at Madison.

Other states marched steadily toward the progressive camp, as they undertook to regulate railroads and trusts, chiefly through public utility commissions. Oregon was not far behind Wisconsin, and California made giant bootstrides under the stocky Hiram W. Johnson. Elected Republican governor in 1910, this dynamic prosecutor of grafters helped break the dominant grip of the Southern Pacific Railroad on California politics and then, like La Follette, set up a political machine of his own. Heavily whiskered Charles Evans Hughes, the able and audacious reformist Republican governor of New York, had earlier gained national fame as an investigator of malpractices by gas and insurance companies and by the coal trust.

✵ Progressive Women

Women proved themselves an indispensable part of the progressive army. A crucial focus for women's activism was the settlement house movement (see p. 549). At a time when women could neither vote nor hold political office, settlement houses offered a side door to public life. They exposed middle-class women to the problems plaguing America's cities, including poverty, political corruption, and intolerable working and living conditions. They also gave them the skills and confidence to attack those evils. The women's club movement provided an even broader civic entryway for many middle-class women. Literary clubs, where educated women met to improve themselves with poetry and prose, had existed for decades. But in the late nineteenth and early twentieth centuries, many of these clubs set aside Shakespeare and Henry James for social issues and current events. "Dante has been dead for several centuries," observed the president of the General Federation of Women's Clubs in 1904. "I think it is time that we dropped the study of his *Inferno* and turned our attention to our own."

Nineteenth-century notions of "separate spheres" dictated that a woman's place was in the home, so most female progressives defended their new activities as an extension—not a rejection—of the traditional roles of wife and mother. Thus they were often drawn to moral and "maternal" issues like keeping children out of smudgy mills and sweltering sweatshops, attacking the scourge of tuberculosis bred in airless tenements, winning pensions for mothers with dependent children, and ensuring that only safe food products found their way to the family table. Female activists agitated through organizations like the National Consumers League (1899) and the Women's Trade Union League (1903), as well as through two new federal agencies, the Children's Bureau (1912) and the Women's Bureau (1920), both in the Department of Labor. These wedges into the federal bureaucracy, however small, gave female reformers a national stage for social investigation and advocacy.

Campaigns for factory reform and temperance particularly attracted women foot soldiers. Unsafe and unsanitary sweatshops—factories where workers toiled long hours for low wages—were a public scandal in many cities. Florence Kelley, a former resident of Jane Addams's Hull House, became the State of Illinois's first chief factory inspector and one of the nation's leading advocates for improved factory conditions. In 1899 Kelley took control of the newly founded National Consumers League, which mobilized female consumers to pressure for laws safeguarding women and children in the workplace. In the landmark case ***Muller v. Oregon*** (1908), crusading attorney Louis D. Brandeis persuaded the Supreme Court to accept the constitutionality of laws protecting women workers by presenting evidence of the harmful effects of factory labor on women's weaker bodies. Although this argument calling for special protection for women seemed discriminatory by later standards and closed many "male" jobs to women, progressives at the time hailed Brandeis's achievement as a triumph over existing legal doctrine, which

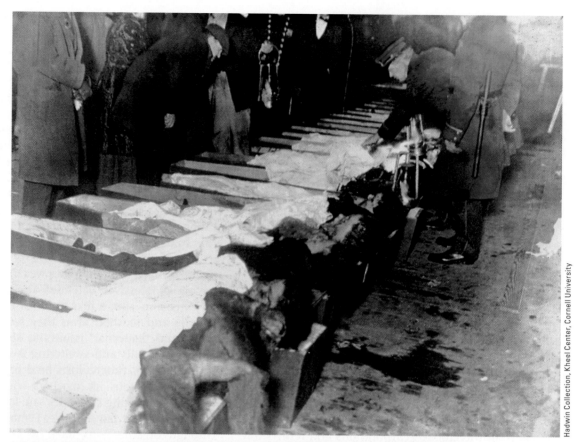

Hadwin Collection, Kheel Center, Cornell University

The Wages of Negligence Officials review the charred remains of some of the survivors of the catastrophic Triangle Shirtwaist Company fire in 1911. Outrage over this calamity galvanized a generation of reformers to fight for better workplace safety rules.

afforded employers total control over the workplace. The American welfare state that emerged from female activism focused more on protecting women and children than on granting benefits to everyone, as was the case in much of western Europe, with its stronger labor movements.

Crusaders for these humane measures did not always have smooth sailing. One dismaying setback came in 1905, when the Supreme Court, in *Lochner v. New York*, invalidated a New York law establishing a ten-hour day for bakers. Yet the reformist progressive wave finally washed up into the judiciary, and in 1917 the Court upheld a ten-hour law for factory workers.

Laws regulating factories were worthless if not enforced, a truth horribly demonstrated by a lethal fire in 1911 at the Triangle Shirtwaist Company in New York City. Locked doors and other flagrant violations of the fire code turned the factory into a death trap. One hundred forty-six workers, most of them young immigrant women, were incinerated or leapt from eighth- and ninth-story windows to their deaths. Lashed by the public outcry, including a massive strike by women in the needle trades, the New York legislature passed much stronger laws regulating the hours and conditions of sweatshop toil. Other legislatures followed, and by 1917 thirty states had put workers' compensation laws on the books, providing insurance to workers injured in industrial accidents. Gradually the concept of the employer's responsibility to society was replacing the old dog-eat-dog philosophy of unregulated free enterprise.

Corner saloons, with their shutter doors, naturally attracted the ire and fire of progressives. Alcohol was intimately connected with prostitution in red-light districts, with the drunken voter, with crooked city officials dominated by "booze" interests, and with the blowsy "boss" who counted poker chips by night and miscounted ballots by day (including the "cemetery vote"). By 1900 cities like New York and San Francisco had one saloon for about every two hundred people.

Antiliquor campaigners received powerful support from several militant organizations, notably the **Woman's Christian Temperance Union (WCTU)**. Founder Frances E. Willard, who would fall to her knees in prayer on saloon floors, mobilized nearly 1 million women to "make the world homelike" and built the

Out of Work and the Reason Why, 1899 This temperance propaganda from an 1899 magazine illustrates the role of women in the temperance movement. Alcohol abuse threatened the stability of the family, still predominantly considered the "woman's sphere" in the late nineteenth century.

WCTU into the largest organization of women in the world. She found a vigorous ally in the Anti-Saloon League, which was aggressive, well organized, and well financed.

Caught up in the crusade, some states and numerous counties passed "dry" laws, which controlled, restricted, or abolished alcohol. The big cities were generally "wet," for they had a large immigrant vote accustomed in the Old Country to the free flow of wine and beer. When World War I erupted in 1914, nearly one-half of the population lived in "dry" territory, and nearly three-fourths of the total area had outlawed saloons. Demon Rum was groggy and about to be floored—temporarily—by the Eighteenth Amendment in 1919.

✦ TR's Square Deal for Labor

Theodore Roosevelt, although something of an imperialistic busybody abroad, was touched by the progressive wave at home. Like other reformers, he feared that the "public interest" was being submerged in the drifting

seas of indifference. Everybody's interest was nobody's interest. Roosevelt decided to make it his. His sportsman's instincts spurred him into demanding a "Square Deal" for capital, labor, and the public at large. Broadly speaking, the president's program embraced three C's: control of the corporations, consumer protection, and conservation of natural resources.

The Square Deal for labor received its acid test in 1902, when a crippling strike broke out in the anthracite coal mines of Pennsylvania. Some 140,000 besooted workers, many of them illiterate immigrants, had long been frightfully exploited and accident-plagued. They demanded, among other improvements, a 20 percent increase in pay and a reduction of the working day from ten to nine hours.

Unsympathetic mine owners, confident that a chilled public would react against the miners, refused to arbitrate or even negotiate. One of their spokesmen, multimillionaire George F. Baer, reflected the high-and-mighty attitude of certain ungenerous employers. Workers, he wrote, would be cared for "not by the labor agitators, but by the Christian men to whom God in His infinite wisdom has given the control of the property interests of this country."

As coal supplies dwindled, factories and schools were forced to shut down, and even hospitals felt the icy grip of winter. Desperately seeking a solution, Roosevelt summoned representatives of the striking miners and the mine owners to the White House. He was profoundly annoyed by the "extraordinary stupidity and bad temper" of the "wooden-headed gentry" who operated the mines. As he later confessed, if it had not been for the dignity of his high office, he would have taken one of them "by the seat of the breeches" and "chucked him out of the window."

Roosevelt finally resorted to his trusty big stick when he threatened to seize the mines and operate

Roosevelt was a charismatic figure who made a powerful impression on his contemporaries. The journalist William Allen White (1868–1944) later wrote of his first meeting with TR in 1897,

❝He sounded in my heart the first trumpet call of the new time that was to be. . . . I had never known such a man as he, and never shall again. He overcame me. And in the hour or two we spent that day at lunch, and in a walk down F Street, he poured into my heart such visions, such ideals, such hopes, such a new attitude toward life and patriotism and the meaning of things, as I had never dreamed men had. . . . After that I was his man.❞

Muller v. Oregon, 1908

Court records provide notably fruitful sources for historians. They not only tell often-colorful stories about the lives of ordinary men and women caught up in the legal system; they also by their very nature testify to the norms and values that lawyers employ to make their cases and that judges invoke to explain their decisions. The case of *Muller* v. *Oregon* (see p. 645) is especially instructive on both counts. The official Supreme

Court records tell how on September 4, 1905, Joe Haselbock, a supervisor in Curt Muller's Grand Laundry in Portland, Oregon, asked an employee, Mrs. E. Gotcher, to remain after hours to do an extra load of laundry. That request violated Oregon's law prohibiting women from working more than ten hours per day. Mrs. Gotcher later complained to the authorities, and Muller was fined $10. Muller refused to pay and took his case all

the way to the U.S. Supreme Court. In its landmark decision (below), the Court upheld the constitutionality of the Oregon statute, and Muller at last had to cough up his fine. On what grounds did the Court justify its ruling? What does Justice David J. Brewer's argument on behalf of the Court's decision suggest about the cultural identity and social role of women in early-twentieth-century American society?

(208 U.S. 412)
CURT MULLER, Plff. in Err.,
v.
STATE OF OREGON.

. . . That woman's physical structure and the performance of material functions place her at a disadvantage in the struggle for subsistence is obvious. This is especially true when the burdens of motherhood are upon her. . . . and as healthy mothers are essential to vigorous offspring, the physical well-being of woman becomes an object of public interest and care in order to preserve the strength and vigor of the race.

Still again, history discloses the fact that woman has always been dependent upon man. He established his control at the outset by superior physical strength, and this control in various forms, with diminishing intensity, has continued to the present. . . . It is still true that in the struggle for subsistence she is not an equal competitor with her brother. . . . Differentiated by these matters from the other sex, she is properly placed in a class by herself, and legislation designed for her protection may be sustained, even when like legislation is not necessary for men, and

could not be sustained. It is impossible to close one's eyes to the fact that she still looks to her brother and depends upon him. . . . The two sexes differ in structure of body, in the functions to be performed by each, in the amount of physical strength, in the capacity for long continued labor, particularly when done standing, the influence of vigorous health upon the future well-being of the race, the self-reliance which enables one to assert full rights, and in the capacity to maintain the struggle for subsistence. This difference justifies a difference in legislation, and upholds that which is designed to compensate for some of the burdens which rest upon her.

We have not referred in this discussion to the denial of the elective franchise in the state of Oregon, for while that may disclose a lack of political equality in all things with her brother, that is not of itself decisive. The reason runs deeper, and rests in the inherent difference between the two sexes, and in the different functions in life which they perform. . . .

---

them with federal troops. Faced with this first-time-ever threat to use federal bayonets against capital, rather than labor, the owners grudgingly consented to arbitration. A compromise decision ultimately gave the miners a 10 percent pay boost and a working day of nine hours.

But their union was not officially recognized as a bargaining agent.

Keenly aware of the mounting antagonisms between capital and labor, Roosevelt urged Congress to create the new Department of Commerce and

Labor. This goal was achieved in 1903. (Ten years later the agency was split in two.) An important arm of the newborn cabinet body was the Bureau of Corporations, which was authorized to probe businesses engaged in interstate commerce. The bureau was highly useful in helping to break the stranglehold of monopoly and in clearing the road for the era of "trust-busting."

⭐ TR Corrals the Corporations

The sprawling railroad octopus sorely needed restraint. The Interstate Commerce Commission, created in 1887 as a feeble sop to the public, had proved woefully inadequate. Railroad barons could simply appeal the commission's decisions on rates to the federal courts—a process that might take ten years.

Spurred by the former-cowboy president, Congress passed effective railroad legislation, beginning with the **Elkins Act** of 1903. This curb was aimed primarily at the rebate evil. Heavy fines could now be imposed both on the railroads that gave rebates and on the shippers that accepted them.

Still more effective was the Hepburn Act of 1906. Free passes, with their hint of bribery, were severely restricted. The once-infantile Interstate Commerce Commission was expanded, and its reach was extended to include express companies, sleeping-car companies, and pipelines. For the first time, the commission was given real molars when it was authorized, on complaint of shippers, to nullify existing rates and stipulate maximum rates.

Railroads also provided Roosevelt with an opportunity to brandish his antitrust bludgeon. *Trusts* had come to be a fighting word in the progressive era. Roosevelt believed that these industrial behemoths, with their efficient means of production, had arrived to stay. He concluded that there were "good" trusts, with public consciences, and "bad" trusts, which lusted greedily for power. He was determined to respond to the popular outcry against the trusts but was also determined not to throw out the baby with the bathwater by indiscriminately smashing all large businesses.

Roosevelt as a trustbuster first burst into the headlines in 1902 with an attack on the Northern Securities Company, a railroad holding company organized by financial titan J. P. Morgan and empire builder James J. Hill. These Napoleonic moguls of money sought to achieve a virtual monopoly of the railroads in the Northwest. Roosevelt was therefore challenging the most regal potentates of the industrial aristocracy.

The railway promoters appealed to the Supreme Court, which in 1904 upheld Roosevelt's antitrust suit and ordered the Northern Securities Company to be dissolved. The *Northern Securities* decision jolted Wall

Library of Congress

Roosevelt Tames the Trusts Legend to the contrary, Roosevelt did not attack all trusts indiscriminately. Rather, he pursued a few high-profile cases against a handful of corporate giants, in order to "tame" other businesses into accepting government regulation.

Street and angered big business but greatly enhanced Roosevelt's reputation as a trust smasher.

Roosevelt's big stick crashed down on other giant monopolies, as he initiated over forty legal proceedings against them. The Supreme Court in 1905 declared the beef trust illegal, and the heavy fist of justice fell upon monopolists controlling sugar, fertilizer, harvesters, and other key products.

Much mythology has inflated Roosevelt's reputation as a trustbuster. The Rough Rider understood the political popularity of monopoly-smashing, but he did not consider it sound economic policy. Combination and integration, he felt, were the hallmarks of the age, and to try to stem the tide of economic progress by political means he considered the rankest folly. Bigness was not necessarily badness, so why punish success? Roosevelt's real purpose in assaulting the Goliaths of industry was symbolic: to prove conclusively that the government, not private business, ruled the country. He believed in regulating, not fragmenting, the big business combines. The threat of dissolution, he felt, might make the sultans of the smokestacks more amenable to federal regulation—as it did.

In truth, Roosevelt never swung his trust-crushing stick with maximum force. In many ways the huge industrial behemoths were healthier—though perhaps more "tame"—at the end of Roosevelt's reign than they had been before. His successor, William Howard Taft, actually "busted" more trusts than TR did. In one celebrated instance in 1907, Roosevelt even gave his personal blessing to J. P. Morgan's plan to have U.S. Steel absorb the Tennessee Coal and Iron Company, without fear of antitrust reprisals. When Taft then launched a suit against U.S. Steel in 1911, the political reaction from TR was explosive.

✴ Caring for the Consumer

Roosevelt backed a noteworthy measure in 1906 that benefited both corporations and consumers. Big meat-packers were being shut out of certain European markets because some American meat—from the small packinghouses, claimed the giants—had been found to be tainted. Foreign governments were even threatening to ban all American meat imports by throwing out the good beef with the bad botulism.

At the same time, American consumers hungered for safer canned products. Their appetite for reform was whetted by Upton Sinclair's sensational novel *The Jungle*, published in 1906. Sinclair, a dedicated Socialist, intended his revolting tract to focus attention on the plight of the workers in the big canning factories, but instead he appalled the public with his description of disgustingly unsanitary food products. (As he put it, he aimed for the nation's heart but hit its stomach.) The book described in noxious detail the filth, disease, and putrefaction in Chicago's damp, ill-ventilated slaughterhouses. Many readers, including Roosevelt, were so sickened that for a time they found meat unpalatable. The president was moved by

the loathsome mess in Chicago to appoint a special investigating commission, whose cold-blooded report almost outdid Sinclair's novel. It related how piles of poisoned rats, rope ends, splinters, and other debris were scooped up and canned as potted ham. A cynical jingle of the time ran,

> *Mary had a little lamb,*
> *And when she saw it sicken,*
> *She shipped it off to Packingtown,*
> *And now it's labeled chicken.*

Backed by a nauseated public, Roosevelt induced Congress to pass the **Meat Inspection Act** of 1906. It decreed that the preparation of meat shipped over state lines would be subject to federal inspection from corral to can. Although the largest packers resisted certain features of the act, they accepted it as an opportunity to drive their smaller, fly-by-night competitors out of business. At the same time, they could receive the government's seal of approval on their exports. As a companion to the Meat Inspection Act, the **Pure Food and Drug Act** of 1906 was designed to prevent the adulteration and mislabeling of foods and pharmaceuticals.

✴ Earth Control

Wasteful Americans, assuming that their natural resources were inexhaustible, had looted and polluted their incomparable domain with unparalleled speed and greed. Western ranchers and timbermen were especially eager to accelerate the destructive process, for they panted to build up the country, and the environmental consequences be hanged. But even before the end of the nineteenth century, far-visioned leaders

Sausage Making, ca. 1906
White-jacketed inspectors like those on the right made some progress in cleaning up the septic slaughterhouses after the passage of the Meat Inspection Act in 1906.

Brown Brothers

saw that such a squandering of the nation's birthright would have to be halted, or America would sink from resource richness to despoiled dearth.

A first feeble step toward conservation had been taken with the Desert Land Act of 1877, under which the federal government sold arid land cheaply on the condition that the purchaser irrigate the thirsty soil within three years. More successful was the Forest Reserve Act of 1891, authorizing the president to set aside public forests as national parks and other reserves. Under this statute some 46 million acres of magnificent trees were rescued from the lumberman's saw in the 1890s and preserved for posterity. The Carey Act of 1894 distributed federal land to the states on the condition that it be irrigated and settled.

A new day in the history of conservation dawned with Roosevelt (see "Makers of America: The Environmentalists," pp. 652–653). Huntsman, naturalist, rancher, lover of the great outdoors, he was appalled by the pillaging of timber and mineral resources. Other dedicated conservationists, notably Gifford Pinchot, head of the federal Division of Forestry, had broken important ground before him. But Roosevelt seized the banner of leadership and charged into the fray with all the weight of his prestige, his energy, his firsthand knowledge, and his slashing invective.

The thirst of the desert still unslaked, Congress responded to the whip of the Rough Rider by passing the landmark Newlands Act of 1902. Washington was authorized to collect money from the sale of public lands in the sun-baked western states and then use these funds for the development of irrigation projects. Settlers repaid the cost of reclamation from their now-productive soil, and the money was put into a revolving fund to finance more such enterprises. The giant Roosevelt Dam, constructed on Arizona's Salt River, was appropriately dedicated by Roosevelt in 1911. Thanks to this epochal legislation, dozens of dams were thrown across virtually every major western river in the ensuing decades.

The Yosemite Museum, Yosemite National Park

High Point for Conservation   Roosevelt and famed naturalist John Muir visit Glacier Point, on the rim of Yosemite Valley, California. In the distance is Yosemite Falls; a few feet behind Roosevelt is a sheer drop of 3,254 feet.

Roosevelt pined to preserve the nation's shrinking forests. By 1900 only about a quarter of the once-vast virgin timberlands remained standing. Lumbermen had already logged off most of the first-growth timber from Maine to Michigan, and the sharp thud of their axes was beginning to split the silence in the great fir forests of the Pacific slope. Roosevelt proceeded to set

In his annual message to Congress in 1907, Roosevelt declared prophetically,

❝We are prone to speak of the resources of this country as inexhaustible; this is not so. The mineral wealth of the country, the coal, iron, oil, gas, and the like, does not reproduce itself, and therefore is certain to be exhausted ultimately; and wastefulness in dealing with it to-day means that our descendants will feel the exhaustion a generation or two before they otherwise would.❞

Gifford Pinchot (1865–1946), a leading conservationist in the Roosevelt administration, wrote,

❝ The object of our forest policy is not to preserve the forests because they are refuges for the wild creatures of the wilderness, but the making of prosperous homes. Every other consideration comes as secondary. . . . The test of utility . . . implies that no lands will be permanently reserves which can serve the people better in any other way.❞

*H*umans have long been awed by nature, but they have also yearned to be its masters. Native American peoples did what they could to shape the natural environment to serve their purposes—burning forests and grasslands, for example, to improve hunting habitats—but they lacked the tools to make Mother Earth bow deeply to their will. The earliest European colonists saw North America as a "howling wilderness" and toiled mightily with ax and plow to tame it. By the mid-nineteenth century, Americans commanded powerful new technologies like the railroad and steam-powered dredges, which promised unbridled dominion over the natural world. Only then did voices begin to be heard in defense of the wounded earth—the faint first stirrings of what would come to be called "environmentalism."

In a pattern that would often be repeated, nature's earliest defenders tended to be well-off townsfolk and city dwellers, like Henry David Thoreau and Ralph Waldo Emerson. The Americans most likely to appreciate the value of the pristine wilderness, it seemed, were those who had ceased to struggle against it. ("Cities, not log cabins, produce Sierra Clubbers," one historian noted.) For the loggers, miners, and farmers who continued to sweat their living out of nature's grudging embrace, concern for environmental niceties often seemed like the sanctimonious piety of a privileged elite.

By the dawn of the twentieth century, many genteel, urban Americans had come to romanticize their pioneer forebears. They reinvented hunting and fishing as sports for the well-to-do, not simply as ways to put food on the table. Preservationists like John Muir waxed lyrical about the mystic allure of unspoiled nature. Seizing the popular mood, Theodore Roosevelt deliberately constructed a public image of himself as a manly outdoorsman—raising cattle in the Dakotas, shooting lions in Africa, rafting down wild rivers in the Amazon basin—and as president he greatly expanded the system of national forests. But Roosevelt was also a pioneer of another sort—as a prominent promoter of the progressive-era "conservation" movement, composed of a loose coalition of scientists, bureaucrats, and businesspeople dependent on stable access to America's rich endowment of natural resources. Progressive conservationists believed that nature must be neither uncritically reverenced nor wastefully exploited, but must instead be efficiently utilized. Thus the same TR who admired the wonders of Yosemite Valley in the company of John Muir also supported the professional forester Gifford Pinchot, who declared that "the object of our forest policy is not to preserve the forests because they are refuges for the wild creatures of the wilderness,

but the making of prosperous homes. . . . Use must be the test by which the forester tries himself."

Pinchot's "rational use" philosophy guided America's natural resource policy until the mid-twentieth century. It justified the systematic harvesting of millions of trees in the sprawling national forests whose boundaries Roosevelt had expanded, and the drowning of vast river valleys behind massive dams that Roosevelt's Reclamation Service helped to build. This attitude toward nature triumphed in the New Deal era of the 1930s, when the federal government initiated colossal projects that undertook nothing less than reengineering the face of the continent—including the Tennessee Valley Authority, the Soil Conservation Service, and the Shelterbelt tree-planting project on the Great Plains. The huge reach of these New Deal projects also introduced millions of Americans to the concept that nature had to be treated with respect, helping to stimulate the post–World War II grassroots environmental movement.

The rise of ecological science in the post–World War II era fundamentally changed the debate about the relation of nature to civilization. Ecologists charged that the apparent "rationality" of the earlier conservationists dangerously neglected the fateful intricacies of biological systems. They called attention to the stunningly complex webs of interrelationships that linked

Gifford Pinchot Going Trout Fishing   The father of the modern Forest Service, Pinchot championed the concept of "rational use" as the guiding principle of the federal government's natural resource management policies.

Lake Powell, Utah Named for the famed explorer John Wesley Powell and formed by one of the several dams on the Colorado River, Lake Powell has been a focus of intense controversy. It drowned the spectacularly beautiful Glen Canyon but created recreational facilities for countless Americans. © Ron Chapple/Corbis

together seemingly unrelated organisms—and to the perils of tampering even slightly with the delicate biological fabrics that nature had taken millennia to weave. Rachel Carson helped to popularize the new outlook in her sensational 1962 exposé, *Silent Spring*, about the far-reaching effects of pesticides on birds, plants, and animals—including humans.

Earth Day, 1999 Some fifteen hundred schoolchildren gathered on the shoreline near Los Angeles to participate in a beach cleanup project. The "O" here represents planet earth; the children inside it represent the North and South American continents. AP Images/Reed Saxon

The advent of ecological studies coincided with a revival of preservationist sentiment, especially in the suburbs, where Americans increasingly dwelled. Hordes of affluent baby boomers took to America's trails, slopes, and waterways—often on public lands like Arizona's wondrous Grand Canyon National Park, or public waters like Utah's shimmering (and man-made) Lake Powell. Membership in environmental organizations such as the Sierra Club and the Audubon Society soared, as a generation infatuated with nature demanded a clean and green world. The first celebration of Earth Day, on April 22, 1970, marked the political maturation of modern-day environmentalism, which wedded scientific analysis with respect for nature's majesty. That same year saw the creation of the federal Environmental Protection Agency (EPA), soon followed by the Endangered Species Act and other legislation designed to regulate the relationship between humans and nature.

At the outset of the twenty-first century, developments like global warming served dramatic notice that planet earth was the biggest ecological system of them all—one that did not recognize national boundaries. Yet while Americans took pride in the efforts they had made to clean up their own turf, who were they, having long since consumed much of their own timberlands, to tell the Brazilians that they should not cut down the Amazon rain forest? Who were they, having tamed virtually all their own free-flowing waters, to tell the Chinese not to dam their rivers? For the peoples of the developing world, struggling to match America's standard of living, environmentalists often seemed like spoiled spoilers, preaching the same privileged pieties that had infuriated generations of working Americans.

Loggers in the State of Washington, 1912 It took the sweat and skill of many men to conquer a giant Douglas fir like this one. An ax-wielding "sniper" had rounded the edges of this log so that a team of oxen, driven by a "bullwhacker," could more easily drag it out of the woods along a "skid road." *Skid road* (sometimes corrupted as *skid row*) was also a name for the often-sleazy sections of logging towns, where loggers spent their time in the off-season.

aside in federal reserves some 125 million acres, or almost three times the acreage thus saved from the saw by his three predecessors. He similarly earmarked millions of acres of coal deposits, as well as water resources useful for irrigation and power. To set a shining example, in 1902 he banned Christmas trees from the White House.

Conservation, including reclamation, may have been Roosevelt's most enduring tangible achievement. He was buoyed in this effort by an upwelling national mood of concern about the disappearance of the frontier—believed to be the source of such national characteristics as individualism and democracy. An increasingly citified people worried that too much civilization might not be good for the national soul. City dwellers snapped up Jack London's *Call of the Wild* (1903) and other books about nature, and urban youngsters

made the outdoor-oriented Boy Scouts of America the country's largest youth organization. Middle-class club-women raised money for nature preserves and organized the Massachusetts—and later National—Audubon Society to save wild native birds by banning the use of plumes to ornament fashionable ladies' hats. The Sierra Club, founded in 1892, dedicated itself to preserving the wildness of the western landscape.

The preservationists lost a major battle in 1913 when the federal government allowed the city of San Francisco to build a dam for its municipal water supply in the spectacular, high-walled **Hetch Hetchy Valley** in Yosemite National Park. The Hetch Hetchy controversy laid bare a deep division between conservationists that persists to the present day. To the preservationists of the Sierra Club, including famed naturalist John Muir, Hetch Hetchy was a "temple" of nature that should

Flooding the Hetch Hetchy Valley to Quench San Francisco's Thirst Preservationists led by John Muir battled for seven years—unsuccessfully—to prevent the building of a dam that would turn this spectacular glacial valley in Yosemite National Park into the Hetch Hetchy Reservoir, which would provide San Francisco with water. Muir observed, "Dam Hetch Hetchy! As well dam for water-tanks the people's cathedrals and churches, for no holier temple has ever been consecrated by the heart of man." Today environmentalists are campaigning to restore the Hetch Hetchy Valley by removing the dam.

The Machine and Nature These hardy sightseers at the Grand Canyon in 1911 ironically and probably unwittingly foreshadowed the mass tourism that arrived with the dawning automobile age. Soon millions of motorized Americans would regularly flee from the cities and suburbs to "get away from it all" in wilderness sites increasingly overrun by their fellow refugees from "civilization."

be held inviolable by the civilizing hand of humanity. But other conservationists, among them President Roosevelt's chief forester, Gifford Pinchot, believed that "wilderness was waste." Pinchot and Roosevelt wanted to *use* the nation's natural endowment intelligently. In their eyes they had to battle on two fronts: against greedy commercial interests that abused nature, as well as against romantic preservationists in thrall to simple "woodman-spare-that-tree" sentimentality.

Under Roosevelt professional foresters and engineers developed a policy of "multiple-use resource management." They sought to combine recreation, sustained-yield logging, watershed protection, and summer stock grazing on the same expanse of federal land.

At first many westerners resisted the federal management of natural resources, but they soon learned how to take advantage of new agencies like the Forest Service and especially the Bureau of Reclamation. The largest ranches and timber companies in particular figured out how to work hand in glove with federal conservation programs devoted to the rational, large-scale, and long-term use of natural resources. The one-man-and-a-mule logger or the one-man-and-a-dog sheepherder had little clout in the new resources bureaucracy. Single-person enterprises were shouldered aside, in the interest of efficiency, by the combined bulk of big business and big government.

✪ The "Roosevelt Panic" of 1907

Roosevelt was handily elected president "in his own right" in 1904 and entered his new term buoyed by his enormous personal popularity—the cuddly "teddy bear" honored one of his bear-hunting exploits (when he saved the life of a cub), and children piped vigorously on whistles modeled on his famous teeth. Yet the conservative Republican bosses considered him as dangerous and unpredictable as a rattlesnake. They grew increasingly restive as Roosevelt in his second term called ever more loudly for regulating corporations, taxing incomes, and protecting workers. Roosevelt, meanwhile, had partly defanged himself after his election in 1904 by announcing that under no circumstances would he be a candidate for a third term. This was a tactical blunder, for the power of the king wanes when the people know he will be dead in four years.

Roosevelt suffered a sharp setback in 1907, when a short but punishing panic descended on Wall Street. The financial flurry featured frightened "runs" on banks, suicides, and criminal indictments against speculators.

The financial world hastened to blame Roosevelt for the storm. It cried that this "quack" had unsettled industry with his boat-rocking tactics. Conservatives damned him as "Theodore the Meddler" and branded the current distress the "Roosevelt panic." The hot-tempered president angrily lashed back at his critics when he accused "certain malefactors of great wealth" of having deliberately engineered the monetary crisis to force the government to relax its assaults on trusts.

Fortunately, the panic of 1907 paved the way for long-overdue fiscal reforms. Precipitating a currency shortage, the flurry laid bare the need for a more elastic medium of exchange. In a crisis of this sort, the hard-pressed banks were unable to increase the volume of money in circulation, and those with ample reserves were reluctant to lend to their less fortunate competitors. Congress in 1908 responded by passing the

Aldrich-Vreeland Act, which authorized national banks to issue emergency currency backed by various kinds of collateral. The path was thus smoothed for the momentous Federal Reserve Act of 1913 (see p. 665).

✦ The Rough Rider Thunders Out

Still warmly popular in 1908, Roosevelt could easily have won a second presidential nomination and almost certainly the election. But he felt bound by his impulsive postelection promise after his victory in 1904.

The departing president thus naturally sought a successor who would carry out "my policies." The man of his choice was amiable, ample-girthed, and huge-framed William Howard Taft, secretary of war and a mild progressive. As an heir apparent, he had often been called upon in Roosevelt's absence to "sit on the lid"—all 350 pounds of him. At the Republican convention of 1908 in Chicago, Roosevelt used his control

Baby, Kiss Papa Good-bye Theodore Roosevelt leaves his baby, "My Policies," in the hands of his chosen successor, William Howard Taft. Friction between Taft and Roosevelt would soon erupt, however, prompting Roosevelt to return to politics and challenge Taft for the presidency.

Granger Collection

of the party machinery—the "steamroller"—to push through Taft's nomination on the first ballot. Three weeks later, in mile-high Denver, in the heart of silver country, the Democrats nominated twice-beaten William Jennings Bryan.

The dull campaign of 1908 featured the rotund Taft and the now-balding "Boy Orator" both trying to don the progressive Roosevelt mantle. The solid Judge Taft read cut-and-dried speeches, while Bryan griped that Roosevelt had stolen his policies from the Bryanite camp. A majority of voters chose stability with Roosevelt-endorsed Taft, who polled 321 electoral votes to 162 for Bryan. The victor's popular count was 7,675,320 to 6,412,294. The election's only surprise came from the Socialists, who amassed 420,793 votes for Eugene V. Debs, the hero of the Pullman strike of 1894 (see pp. 599–600).

Roosevelt, ever in the limelight, left soon after the election for a lion hunt in Africa. His numerous enemies clinked glasses while toasting "Health to the lions," and a few irreverently prayed that some big cat would "do its duty." But TR survived, still bursting with energy at the age of fifty-one in 1909.

Roosevelt was branded by his adversaries as a wild-eyed radical, but his reputation as an eater of errant industrialists now seems inflated. He fought many a sham battle, and the number of laws he inspired was certainly not in proportion to the amount of noise he emitted. He was often under attack from the reigning business lords, but the more enlightened of them knew that they had a friend in the White House. Roosevelt should be remembered first and foremost as the cowboy who started to tame the bucking bronco of adolescent capitalism, thus ensuring it a long adult life.

TR's enthusiasm and perpetual youthfulness, like an overgrown Boy Scout's, appealed to the young of all ages. "You must always remember," a British diplomat cautioned his colleagues, "that the president is about six." He served as a political lightning rod to protect capitalists against popular indignation—and against socialism, which Roosevelt regarded as "ominous." He strenuously sought the middle road between unbridled individualism and paternalistic collectivism. His conservation crusade, which tried to mediate between the romantic wilderness-preservationists and the rapacious resource-predators, was probably his most typical and his most lasting achievement.

Several other contributions of Roosevelt lasted beyond his presidency. First, he greatly enlarged the power and prestige of the presidential office—and masterfully developed the technique of using the big stick of publicity as a political bludgeon. Second, he helped shape the progressive movement and beyond it the liberal reform campaigns later in the century. His Square Deal, in a sense, was the grandfather of the New Deal later launched by his fifth cousin, Franklin D. Roosevelt. Finally, to a greater degree than any of his predecessors, TR opened the eyes of Americans to the fact that they shared the world with other nations. As a great power, they had fallen heir to responsibilities—and had been seized by ambitions—from which there was no escaping.

✸ Taft: A Round Peg in a Square Hole

William Howard Taft, with his ruddy complexion and upturned mustache, at first inspired widespread confidence. "Everybody loves a fat man," the saying goes, and the jovial Taft, with "mirthquakes" of laughter bubbling up from his abundant abdomen, was personally popular. He had graduated second in his class at Yale and had established an enviable reputation as a lawyer and judge, though he was widely regarded as hostile to labor unions. He had been a trusted administrator under Roosevelt—in the Philippines, at home, and in Cuba, where he had served capably as a troubleshooter.

But "good old Will" suffered from lethal political handicaps. Roosevelt had led the conflicting elements of the Republican party by the sheer force of his personality. Taft, in contrast, had none of the arts of a dashing political leader and none of Roosevelt's zest for the fray. Recoiling from the clamor of controversy, he generally adopted an attitude of passivity toward Congress. He was a poor judge of public opinion, and his candor made him a chronic victim of "foot-in-mouth" disease.

"Peaceful Bill" was no doubt a mild progressive, but at heart he was more wedded to the status quo than to change. Significantly, his cabinet did not contain a single representative of the party's "insurgent" wing, which was on fire for reform of current abuses, especially the tariff.

✸ The Dollar Goes Abroad as a Diplomat

Though ordinarily lethargic, Taft bestirred himself to use the lever of American investments to boost American political interests abroad, an approach to foreign policy that his critics denounced as **dollar diplomacy**. Washington warmly encouraged Wall Street bankers to sluice their surplus dollars into foreign areas of strategic concern to the United States, especially in the Far East and in the regions critical to the security of the Panama Canal. By preempting investors from rival powers, such as Germany, New York bankers would thus strengthen American defenses and foreign policies, while bringing further prosperity to their homeland—and to themselves. The almighty dollar thereby supplanted the big stick.

Granger Collection

Ex-President Theodore Roosevelt Watches President Taft Struggle with the Demands of Government, 1910

China's Manchuria was the object of Taft's most spectacular effort to inject the reluctant dollar into the Far Eastern theater. Newly ambitious Japan and imperialistic Russia, recent foes, controlled the railroads of this strategic province. President Taft saw in the Manchurian railway monopoly a possible strangulation of Chinese economic interests and a consequent slamming of the Open Door in the faces of U.S. merchants. In 1909 Secretary of State Philander C. Knox blunderingly proposed that a group of American and foreign bankers buy the Manchurian railroads and then turn them over to China under a self-liquidating arrangement. Both Japan and Russia, unwilling to be jockeyed out of their dominant position, bluntly rejected Knox's overtures. Taft was showered with ridicule.

Another dangerous new trouble spot was the revolution-riddled Caribbean—now virtually a Yankee lake. Hoping to head off trouble, Washington urged Wall Street bankers to pump dollars into the financial vacuums in Honduras and Haiti to keep out foreign funds. The United States, under the Monroe Doctrine, would not permit foreign nations to intervene, and consequently felt obligated to put its money where its mouth was to prevent economic and political instability.

Again necessity was the mother of armed Caribbean intervention. Sporadic disorders in palm-fronded Cuba, Honduras, and the Dominican Republic brought American forces to these countries to restore order and protect American investment. A revolutionary upheaval in Nicaragua, partly fomented by American interests, resulted in the landing of twenty-five hundred marines in 1912. The marines remained in Nicaragua for thirteen years (see Map 29.2 on p. 668).

✦ Taft the Trustbuster

Taft managed to gain some fame as a smasher of monopolies. The ironic truth is that the colorless Taft brought 90 suits against the trusts during his 4 years in office, as compared with some 44 for Roosevelt in 7½ years.

By fateful happenstance the most sensational judicial actions during the Taft regime came in 1911. In that year the Supreme Court ordered the dissolution of the mighty Standard Oil Company, which was judged to be a combination in restraint of trade in violation of the Sherman Anti-Trust Act of 1890. At the same time, the Court handed down its famous "rule of reason." This doctrine held that only those combinations that "unreasonably" restrained trade were illegal. This fineprint proviso ripped a huge hole in the government's antitrust net.

Even more explosively, in 1911 Taft decided to press an antitrust suit against the U.S. Steel Corporation. This initiative infuriated Roosevelt, who had personally been involved in one of the mergers that prompted the suit. Once Roosevelt's protégé, President Taft was increasingly taking on the role of his antagonist. The stage was being set for a bruising confrontation.

✦ Taft Splits the Republican Party

Lowering the barriers of the formidable protective tariff—the "Mother of Trusts"—was high on the agenda of the progressive members of the Republican party, and they at first thought they had a friend and ally in Taft. True to his campaign promises to reduce tariffs, Taft called Congress into special session in March 1909. The House proceeded to pass a moderately reductive bill, but senatorial reactionaries tacked on hundreds of upward tariff revisions. Only items such as hides, sea moss, and canary seed were left on the duty-free list. Much to the dismay of his supporters, Taft signed the **Payne-Aldrich Bill**, rubbing salt in their wounds by proclaiming it "the best bill that the Republican party ever passed."

Taft revealed a further knack for shooting himself in the foot in his handling of conservation. The portly president was a dedicated conservationist, and his contributions—like the establishment of the Bureau of Mines to control mineral resources—actually equaled or surpassed those of Roosevelt. But his praiseworthy accomplishments were largely erased in the public mind by the noisy Ballinger-Pinchot quarrel that erupted in 1910.

When Secretary of the Interior Richard Ballinger opened public lands in Wyoming, Montana, and Alaska to corporate development, he was sharply criticized by Gifford Pinchot, chief of the Agriculture Department's Division of Forestry and a stalwart Rooseveltian. When Taft dismissed Pinchot on the narrow grounds of insubordination, a storm of protest arose from conservationists and from Roosevelt's friends, who were legion. The whole unsavory episode further widened the growing rift between the president and the former president, onetime bosom political partners.

The reformist wing of the Republican party was now up in arms, while Taft was being pushed increasingly into the embrace of the stand-pat Old Guard. By the spring of 1910, the Grand Old Party was split wide-open, owing largely to the clumsiness of Taft. A suspicious Roosevelt returned triumphantly to New York in June 1910 and shortly thereafter stirred up a tempest. Unable to keep silent, he took to the stump at Osawatomie, Kansas, and shocked the Old Guard with a flaming speech. The doctrine that he proclaimed—popularly known as the "New Nationalism"—urged the national government to increase its power to remedy economic and social abuses.

Weakened by these internal divisions, the Republicans lost badly in the congressional elections of 1910. In a victory of landslide proportions, the Democrats emerged with 228 seats, leaving the once-dominant Republicans with only 161. In a further symptom of the reforming temper of the times, a Socialist representative, Austrian-born Victor L. Berger, was elected from Milwaukee.* The Republicans, by virtue of holdovers, retained the Senate, 51 to 41, but the insurgents in their midst were numerous enough to make that hold precarious.

★ The Taft-Roosevelt Rupture

The sputtering uprising in Republican ranks had now blossomed into a full-fledged revolt. Early in 1911 the National Progressive Republican League was formed, with the fiery, white-maned Senator La Follette of Wisconsin its leading candidate for the Republican presidential nomination. The assumption was that Roosevelt, an anti–third termer, would not permit himself to be "drafted."

But the restless Rough Rider began to change his views about third terms as he saw Taft, hand in glove with the hated Old Guard, discard "my policies." In

---

*He was eventually denied his seat in 1919, during a wave of anti-red hysteria.

February 1912 Roosevelt formally wrote to seven state governors that he was willing to accept the Republican nomination. His reasoning was that the third-term tradition applied to three *consecutive elective* terms. Exuberantly he cried, "My hat is in the ring!" and "The fight is on and I am stripped to the buff!"

Roosevelt forthwith seized the Progressive banner, while La Follette, who had served as a convenient pathbreaker, was protestingly elbowed aside. Girded for battle, the Rough Rider came clattering into the presidential primaries then being held in many states. He shouted through half-clenched teeth that the president had fallen under the thumb of the reactionary bosses and that although Taft "means well, he means well feebly." The once-genial Taft, now in a fighting mood, retorted by branding Roosevelt supporters "emotionalists and neurotics."

A Taft-Roosevelt explosion was near in June 1912, when the Republican convention met in Chicago. The Rooseveltites, who were about 100 delegates short of winning the nomination, challenged the right of some 250 Taft delegates to be seated. Most of these contests were arbitrarily settled in favor of Taft, whose supporters held the throttle of the convention steamroller. The Roosevelt adherents, crying "fraud" and "naked theft," in the end refused to vote, and Taft triumphed.

Roosevelt, the supposedly good sportsman, refused to quit the game. Having tasted for the first time the bitter cup of defeat, he was now on fire to lead a third-party crusade.

Chapter Review

KEY TERMS

social gospel (639)
muckrakers (639)
initiative (641)
referendum (641)
recall (641)
Australian ballot (641)
Muller v. *Oregon* (645)
Lochner v. *New York* (645)
Woman's Christian Temperance Union (WCTU) (646)
Elkins Act (649)
Meat Inspection Act (650)
Pure Food and Drug Act (650)
Hetch Hetchy Valley (654)
dollar diplomacy (657)
Payne-Aldrich Bill (658)

PEOPLE TO KNOW

Henry Demarest Lloyd
Thorstein Veblen
Jacob A. Riis
Robert M. ("Fighting Bob") La Follette
Hiram W. Johnson
Florence Kelley
Frances E. Willard
Gifford Pinchot
John Muir

CHRONOLOGY

1892	Sierra Club founded
1899	National Consumers League founded
1901	Commission system established in Galveston, Texas Progressive Robert La Follette elected governor of Wisconsin American Socialist party formed
1902	Lincoln Steffens and Ida Tarbell publish muckraking exposés Anthracite coal strike Newlands Act
1903	Department of Commerce and Labor established Elkins Act Women's Trade Union League founded
1904	*Northern Securities* case Roosevelt defeats Alton B. Parker for presidency
1905	*Lochner* v. *New York*
1906	Hepburn Act Upton Sinclair publishes *The Jungle* Meat Inspection Act Pure Food and Drug Act
1907	"Roosevelt panic"

1908	*Muller* v. *Oregon* Taft defeats Bryan for presidency Aldrich-Vreeland Act
1909	Payne-Aldrich Tariff
1910	Ballinger-Pinchot affair Washington State grants woman suffrage
1911	Triangle Shirtwaist Company fire Standard Oil antitrust case U.S. Steel Corporation antitrust suit California grants woman suffrage
1912	Taft wins Republican nomination over Roosevelt Arizona, Kansas, and Oregon grant woman suffrage Children's Bureau established in Department of Labor
1913	Seventeenth Amendment passed (direct election of U.S. senators) Federal Reserve Act San Francisco decides to build Hetch Hetchy Reservoir
1920	Women's Bureau established in Department of Labor

TO LEARN MORE

Peri E. Arnold, *Remaking the Presidency: Roosevelt, Taft, and Wilson, 1901–1916* (2009)

Nancy Cott, *The Grounding of Modern Feminism* (1987)

Alan Dawley, *Struggles for Justice: Social Responsibility and the Liberal State* (1991)

Glenda Gilmore, *Gender and Jim Crow: Women and the Politics of White Supremacy in North Carolina, 1896–1920* (1996)

Samuel P. Hays, *Conservation and the Gospel of Efficiency* (1959)

Richard Hofstadter, *The Age of Reform* (1955)

T. J. Jackson Lears, *No Place of Grace: Antimodernism and the Transformation of American Culture* (1981)

————, *Rebirth of a Nation: The Making of Modern America, 1877–1920* (2009)

Robyn Muncy, *Creating a Female Dominion in American Reform* (1991)

Kevin P. Murphy, *Political Manhood: Red Bloods, Mollycoddles, and the Politics of Progressive Era Reform* (2008)

Daniel T. Rodgers, *Atlantic Crossings: Social Politics in a Progressive Age* (1998)

Nick Salvatore, *Eugene V. Debs: Citizen and Socialist* (1982)

Kathryn Kish Sklar, *Florence Kelley and the Nation's Work* (1995)

A complete, annotated bibliography for this chapter—along with brief descriptions of the People to Know—may be found on the American Pageant website. The Key Terms are defined in a Glossary at the end of the text.

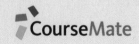

Go to the CourseMate website at **www.cengagebrain.com** for additional study tools and review materials—including audio and video clips—for this chapter.

AP® Review Questions for Chapter 28

1. All of the following were targets of criticism by progressive social critics during the progressive era, 1890–1916, EXCEPT
   - (A) bloated trusts.
   - (B) slum conditions.
   - (C) dangerous and exploitative working hours and conditions in factories.
   - (D) child labor.
   - (E) efforts to assimilate and educate recent immigrants.

2. All of the following political, economic, or social reform initiatives were connected to the progressive movement EXCEPT
   - (A) rooting out graft and corruption in big-city political machines.
   - (B) women's suffrage.
   - (C) a constitutional amendment to guarantee the popular direct election of U.S. senators.
   - (D) a temperance movement aimed at curbing alcohol sales and consumption.
   - (E) nationalizing the railroads and utilities in the United States.

3. How did the muckrakers signify the ideological nature of the progressive reform movement?
   - (A) They proposed detailed, scientific remedies for social problems.
   - (B) They sought to overturn the major features of industrial and finance capitalism.
   - (C) Their reform prescriptions were closely allied with those of the Socialist party.
   - (D) They trusted that media exposures of political corruption and economic exploitation could reform capitalism rather than overthrow it.
   - (E) They looked to start a third political party that would overturn the corrupt and stalemated two-party system.

4. Which statement most accurately characterizes a key belief of advocates of political progressivism during this era?
   - (A) Progressive political reforms such as the secret ballot, referendum and recall, and limits on political contributions from corporate interests would curb the excesses of industrial and finance capitalism and stave off socialism in the United States.
   - (B) Political reforms had to be instituted initially on the federal government level before they could be successfully implemented in states and municipalities.
   - (C) Progressive political reforms should first be developed, implemented, and evaluated in northeastern big cities before being tried in midwestern and western states.
   - (D) Political alliances with socialists and other political radicals should be forged in order to pass these political reforms on the federal, state, and local government level.
   - (E) The achievement of women's suffrage would not significantly aid political progressivism.

5. Why were the settlement house and women's club movements considered crucial centers of female progressive activity?
   - (A) They provided literary and philosophical perspectives on social questions.
   - (B) They broke down the idea that women had special concerns as wives and mothers.
   - (C) They introduced many middle-class women to a broader array of urban social problems and civic concerns.
   - (D) They helped children living in urban slums read classic literature by Dante and Shakespeare.
   - (E) They became launching pads for women seeking political office.

6. What laws or regulations did the tragic Triangle Shirtwaist fire prompt states to pass?
   - (A) Laws requiring mandatory fire escapes for all businesses employing more than ten people
   - (B) Laws prohibiting women from working in the needle trades
   - (C) Antisweatshop and workers' compensation laws for job injuries
   - (D) Zoning regulations governing where dangerous industrial factories could be located
   - (E) Laws guaranteeing unions the right to raise safety concerns

7. The Supreme Court ruling in the business and labor case of *Lochner* v. *New York* did NOT represent a
   (A) legal victory for the efforts of progressives and labor advocates to institute maximum hour laws for workers.
   (B) legal victory for the efforts of business to use the courts to overturn the political successes of progressives and labor advocates to achieve social reforms.
   (C) legal departure from the Court's progressive decision in *Muller* v. *Oregon*, upholding the constitutionality of state laws mandating special protections and work rules for women workers.
   (D) legal victory for the laissez-faire, conservative wing of the Supreme Court.
   (E) setback in the efforts of progressive-era labor advocates and progressives to institute maximum hours and minimum wage laws in the states.

8. What were the Elkins and Hepburn Acts designed to accomplish?
   (A) Regulation of municipal utilities and the end of private utility companies
   (B) Guaranteeing the purity and safety of food and drugs
   (C) Providing federal protection for natural resources
   (D) Improving women's working conditions
   (E) Ending corrupt and exploitative practices by the railroad trusts

9. What was the actual purpose of Teddy Roosevelt's assault on bad trusts?
   (A) To fragment the political power of big business
   (B) To prove that the federal government, and not private business, governed the United States
   (C) To assist labor unions in their organizing efforts
   (D) To halt the trend toward combination and integration in business in the United States
   (E) To uphold the legal right of small business to compete fairly with big business in the United States

10. What was a fundamental belief of the multiple-use conservationists?
    (A) Preserving scenic beauty and natural wonders was incompatible with human activity.
    (B) The environment could be effectively protected and managed without shutting it off to human use.
    (C) Forests and rivers could be used for recreation but not for economic purposes.
    (D) Federal lands should be divided into separate and distinct economically useful areas, recreational areas, and wilderness.
    (E) Cattlemen, lumbermen, and farmers should be entrusted with the development of sustainable use policies.

11. What shortcoming in the U.S. economy did the panic of 1907 reveal?
    (A) The need for substantial reform of U.S. banking and currency policies
    (B) The need to raise tariffs on imported goods
    (C) Insufficient government regulation of corporations
    (D) The need to regulate Wall Street stock trading
    (E) The need for a federally mandated minimum wage for workers

12. Why did Teddy Roosevelt decide to run for the presidency in 1912?
    (A) He believed that President William Howard Taft was discarding Roosevelt's progressive policies.
    (B) President Taft decided not to seek a second term as president.
    (C) Senator Robert LaFollette encouraged him to do so.
    (D) The Socialist party candidate threatened to swing the election to Woodrow Wilson and the Democrats.
    (E) Roosevelt was fiercely opposed to Taft's dollar diplomacy.

13. How did muckrakers in the early twentieth century use tactics employed by the "yellow press" in the late nineteenth century?
    (A) They wrote scandalous articles for widely published magazines revealing the ills in American society.
    (B) They sent reporters and photographers around the country to create news where none existed.
    (C) They used their publications to convince people to recognize wrongdoing in other nations.
    (D) They were single-minded in their focus on reforming the practices of big businesses and trusts.
    (E) They exploited people affected by society's ills for their own gain.

14. Taft's "dollar diplomacy" ultimately failed to change American foreign policy because
    (A) many financial institutions had no desire to become involved in Latin American affairs.
    (B) Latin American nations were too opposed to U.S. intervention to accept financial aid.
    (C) European spheres of influence prevented the United States from purchasing the Manchurian railroads.
    (D) disorder and revolt led to U.S. military intervention in Latin America despite massive financial aid.
    (E) "big-stick diplomacy" was still overwhelmingly favored by many of Taft's closest advisers.

Chapter 29

Wilsonian Progressivism at Home and Abroad

1912–1916

American enterprise is not free; the man with only a little capital is finding it harder and harder to get into the field, more and more impossible to compete with the big fellow. Why? Because the laws of this country do not prevent the strong from crushing the weak.

WOODROW WILSON, THE NEW FREEDOM, 1913

*O*ffice-hungry Democrats—the "outs" since 1897—were jubilant over the disruptive Republican brawl at the convention in Chicago. If they could come up with an outstanding reformist leader, they had an excellent chance to win the White House. Such a leader appeared in Dr. Woodrow Wilson, once a mild conservative but now a militant progressive. Beginning professional life as a brilliant academic lecturer on government, he had risen in 1902 to the presidency of Princeton University, where he had achieved some sweeping educational reforms.

Wilson entered politics in 1910 when New Jersey bosses, needing a respectable "front" candidate for the governorship, offered him the nomination. They expected to lead the academic novice by the nose, but to their surprise, Wilson waged a passionate reform campaign in which he assailed the "predatory" trusts and promised to return state government to the people. Riding the crest of the progressive wave, the "Schoolmaster in Politics" was swept into office.

Once in the governor's chair, Wilson drove through the legislature a sheaf of forward-looking measures that made reactionary New Jersey one of the more liberal states. Filled with righteous indignation, Wilson revealed irresistible reforming zeal, burning eloquence, superb powers of leadership, and a refreshing habit of appealing over the heads of the scheming bosses to the sovereign people. Now a fig-

ure of national eminence, Wilson was being widely mentioned for the presidency.

✦ The "Bull Moose" Campaign of 1912

When the Democrats met at Baltimore in 1912, Wilson was nominated on the forty-sixth ballot, aided by William Jennings Bryan's switch to his side. The Democrats gave Wilson a strong progressive platform to run on; dubbed the **New Freedom** program, it included calls for stronger antitrust legislation, banking reform, and tariff reductions.

Surging events had meanwhile been thrusting Roosevelt to the fore as a candidate for the presidency on a third-party Progressive Republican ticket. The fighting ex-cowboy, angered by his recent rebuff, was eager to lead the charge. A pro-Roosevelt Progressive convention, with about two thousand delegates from forty states, assembled in Chicago during August 1912. Dramatically symbolizing the rising political status of women, as well as Progressive support for the cause of social justice, settlement-house pioneer Jane Addams placed Roosevelt's name in nomination for the presidency. Roosevelt was applauded tumultuously as he cried in a vehement speech, "We stand at Armageddon, and we battle for the Lord!" The hosanna spirit of a religious revival meeting suffused the convention, as the

GOP Divided by Bull Moose Equals Democratic Victory, 1912 Library of Congress

hoarse delegates sang "Onward Christian Soldiers" and "Battle Hymn of the Republic." William Allen White, the caustic Kansas journalist, later wrote, "Roosevelt bit me and I went mad."

Fired-up Progressives entered the campaign with righteousness and enthusiasm. Roosevelt boasted that he felt "as strong as a bull moose," and the bull moose took its place with the donkey and the elephant in the American political zoo. As one poet whimsically put it,

I want to be a Bull Moose,
And with the Bull Moose stand
With antlers on my forehead
And a Big Stick in my hand.

Roosevelt and Taft were bound to slit each other's political throats; by dividing the Republican vote, they virtually guaranteed a Democratic victory. The two antagonists tore into each other as only former friends can. "Death alone can take me out now," cried the once-jovial Taft, as he branded Roosevelt a "dangerous egotist" and a "demagogue." Roosevelt, fighting mad, assailed Taft as a "fathead" with the brain of a "guinea pig."

Beyond the clashing personalities, the overshadowing question of the 1912 campaign was which of two varieties of progressivism would prevail—Roosevelt's **New Nationalism** or Wilson's New Freedom. Both men favored a more active government role in economic and social affairs, but they disagreed sharply over specific strategies. Roosevelt preached the theories spun out by the progressive thinker Herbert Croly in his book *The Promise of American Life* (1910). Croly and TR both favored continued consolidation of trusts and labor unions, paralleled by the growth of powerful regulatory agencies in Washington. Roosevelt and his "bull moosers" also campaigned for woman suffrage and a broad program of social welfare, including minimum wage laws and "socialistic" social insurance. Clearly, the bull moose Progressives looked forward to the kind of activist welfare state that Franklin Roosevelt's New Deal would one day make a reality.

Wilson's New Freedom, by contrast, favored small enterprise, entrepreneurship, and the free functioning of unregulated and unmonopolized markets. The Democrats shunned social-welfare proposals and pinned their economic faith on competition—on the "man on the make," as Wilson put it. The keynote of Wilson's campaign was not regulation but fragmentation of the big industrial combines, chiefly by means of vigorous enforcement of the antitrust laws. The election of 1912 thus offered the voters a choice not merely of policies but of political and economic philosophies—a rarity in U.S. history.

The heat of the campaign cooled a bit when, in Milwaukee, Roosevelt was shot in the chest by a fanatic. The Rough Rider suspended active campaigning for more than two weeks after delivering, with bull moose gameness and a bloody shirt, his scheduled speech.

✴ Woodrow Wilson: A Minority President

Former professor Wilson won handily, with 435 electoral votes and 6,296,547 popular votes. The "third-party" candidate, Roosevelt, finished second, receiving 88 electoral votes and 4,118,571 popular votes. Taft won only 8 electoral votes and 3,486,720 popular votes (see Map 29.1).

The election figures are fascinating. Wilson, with only 41 percent of the popular vote, was clearly a minority president, though his party won a majority in Congress. His popular total was actually smaller than Bryan had amassed in any of his three defeats, despite the increase in population. Taft and Roosevelt together polled over 1.25 million more votes than the Democrats. Progressivism rather than Wilson was the runaway winner. Although the Democratic total obviously included many conservatives in the solid South, the combined progressive vote for Wilson and Roosevelt, totaling 68 percent, far exceeded the tally of the

1912

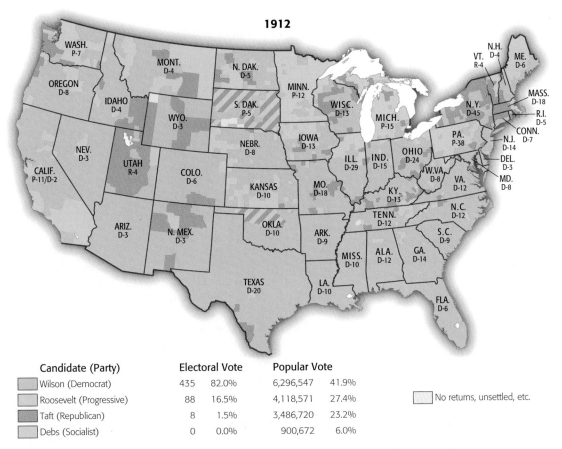

Candidate (Party)	Electoral Vote		Popular Vote	
Wilson (Democrat)	435	82.0%	6,296,547	41.9%
Roosevelt (Progressive)	88	16.5%	4,118,571	27.4%
Taft (Republican)	8	1.5%	3,486,720	23.2%
Debs (Socialist)	0	0.0%	900,672	6.0%

No returns, unsettled, etc.

MAP 29.1 Presidential Election of 1912 (showing votes by county, with electoral vote by state) The Republican split surely boosted Wilson to victory, as he failed to win a clear majority in any state outside the old Confederacy. The election gave the Democrats solid control of the White House and both houses of Congress for the first time since the Civil War. © Cengage Learning

more conservative Taft, who got only 23 percent. To the progressive tally must be added some support for the Socialist candidate, the persistent Eugene V. Debs, who rolled up 900,672 votes, 6 percent of the total cast, or more than twice as many as he had netted four years earlier. Starry-eyed Socialists dreamed of being in the White House within eight years.

Roosevelt's lone-wolf course was tragic both for himself and for his former Republican associates. Perhaps, to rephrase William Allen White, he had bitten himself and gone mad. The Progressive party, which was primarily a one-man show, had no future because it had elected few candidates to state and local offices; the Socialists, in contrast, elected more than a thousand. Without patronage plums to hand out to faithful workers, death by slow starvation was inevitable for the upstart party. Yet the Progressives made a tremendous showing for a hastily organized third party and helped spur the enactment of many of their pet reforms by the Wilsonian Democrats.

As for the Republicans, they were thrust into unaccustomed minority status in Congress for the next six years and were frozen out of the White House for eight years. Taft himself had a fruitful old age. He taught law for eight pleasant years at Yale University and in 1921 became chief justice of the Supreme Court—a job for which he was far more happily suited than the presidency.

✴ Wilson: The Idealist in Politics

(Thomas) Woodrow Wilson, the second Democratic president since 1861, looked like the ascetic intellectual he was, with his clean-cut features, pinched-on eyeglasses, and trim figure. Born in Virginia shortly before the Civil War and reared in Georgia and the Carolinas, the professor-politician was the first man from one of the seceded southern states to reach the White House since Zachary Taylor, sixty-four years earlier.

The impact of Dixieland on young "Tommy" Wilson was profound. He sympathized with the Confederacy's gallant attempt to win its independence, a sentiment that partly inspired his ideal of self-determination for people of other countries. Steeped in the traditions of Jeffersonian democracy, he shared Jefferson's faith in the masses—if they were properly informed.

Son of a Presbyterian minister, Wilson was reared in an atmosphere of fervent piety. He later used the presidential pulpit to preach his inspirational political sermons. A moving orator, Wilson could rise on the wings of spiritual power to soaring eloquence. Skillfully using a persuasive voice, he relied not on arm-waving but on sincerity and moral appeal. As a lifelong student of finely chiseled words, he turned out to be a "phraseocrat" who coined many noble epigrams. Someone has remarked that he was born halfway between the Bible and the dictionary and never strayed far from either.

A profound student of government, Wilson believed that the chief executive should play a dynamic role. He was convinced that Congress could not function properly unless the president, like a kind of prime minister, got out in front and provided leadership. He enjoyed dramatic success, both as governor and as president, in appealing over the heads of legislators to the sovereign people.

Splendid though Wilson's intellectual equipment was, he suffered from serious defects of personality. Though jovial and witty in private, he could be cold and standoffish in public. Incapable of unbending and acting the showman, like "Teddy" Roosevelt, he lacked the common touch. He loved humanity in the mass rather than the individual in person. His academic background caused him to feel most at home with scholars, although he had to work with politicians. An austere and somewhat arrogant intellectual, he looked down his nose through pince-nez glasses upon lesser minds, including journalists. He was especially intolerant of stupid senators, whose "bungalow" minds made him "sick."

Wilson's burning idealism—especially his desire to reform ever-present wickedness—drove him forward faster than lesser spirits were willing to go. His sense of moral righteousness was such that he often found compromise difficult; black was black, wrong was wrong, and one should never compromise with wrong. President Wilson's Scottish Presbyterian ancestors had passed on to him an inflexible stubbornness. When convinced that he was right, the principled Wilson would break before he would bend, unlike the pragmatic Roosevelt.

⭐ Wilson Tackles the Tariff

Few presidents have arrived at the White House with a clearer program than Wilson's or one destined to be

Woodrow Wilson (1856–1924) at Princeton Commencement with Andrew Carnegie, 1906   Before his election to the presidency of the United States in 1912, Wilson (left) served as president of Princeton University (1902–1910) and governor of New Jersey (1910–1912). In all three offices, he undertook substantial reforms. Fighting desperately later for the League of Nations, at the cost of his health, Wilson said, "I would rather fail in a cause that I know some day will triumph than to win in a cause that I know some day will fail."

so completely achieved. The new president called for an all-out assault on what he called "the triple wall of privilege": the tariff, the banks, and the trusts.

He tackled the tariff first, summoning Congress into special session in early 1913. In a precedent-shattering move, he did not send his presidential message over to the Capitol to be read loudly by a bored clerk, as had been the custom since Jefferson's day. Instead he appeared in person before a joint session of Congress and presented his appeal with stunning eloquence and effectiveness.

Moved by Wilson's aggressive leadership, the House swiftly passed the **Underwood Tariff**, which provided for a substantial reduction of rates. When a swarm of lobbyists descended on the Senate seeking to disembowel the bill, Wilson promptly issued a combative message to the people, urging them to hold their elected representatives in line. The tactic worked. The force of public opinion, aroused by the president's oratory, secured late in 1913 final approval of the bill Wilson wanted.

The new Underwood Tariff substantially reduced import fees. It also was a landmark in tax legislation. Under authority granted by the recently ratified Sixteenth Amendment, Congress enacted a graduated income tax, beginning with a modest levy on incomes over $3,000 (then considerably higher than the average family's income). By 1917 revenue from the income tax shot ahead of receipts from the tariff. This gap has since been vastly widened.

Wilson Battles the Bankers

A second bastion of the "triple wall of privilege" was the antiquated and inadequate banking and currency system, long since outgrown by the Republic's lusty economic expansion. The country's financial structure, still creaking along under the Civil War National Banking Act, revealed glaring defects. Its most serious shortcoming, as exposed by the panic of 1907, was the inelasticity of the currency. Banking reserves were heavily concentrated in New York and a handful of other large cities and could not be mobilized in times of financial stress into areas that were badly pinched.

In 1908 Congress had authorized an investigation headed by a mossback banker, Republican senator Aldrich. Three years later Aldrich's special commission recommended a gigantic bank with numerous branches—in effect, a third Bank of the United States.

For their part, Democratic banking reformers heeded the findings of a House committee chaired by Congressman Arsene Pujo, which traced the tentacles of the "money monster" into the hidden vaults of American banking and business. President Wilson's confidant, progressive-minded Massachusetts attorney Louis D. Brandeis, further fanned the flames of reform with his incendiary though scholarly book *Other People's Money and How the Bankers Use It* (1914).

In June 1913, in a second dramatic personal appearance before both houses of Congress, the president delivered a stirring plea for sweeping reform of the banking system. He ringingly endorsed Democratic proposals for a decentralized bank in government hands, as opposed to Republican demands for a huge private bank with fifteen branches.

Again appealing to the sovereign people, Wilson scored another triumph. In 1913 he signed the epochal **Federal Reserve Act**, the most important piece of economic legislation between the Civil War and the New Deal. The new Federal Reserve Board, appointed by the president, oversaw a nationwide system of twelve regional reserve districts, each with its own central bank. Although these regional banks were actually bankers' banks, owned by member financial institutions, the final authority of the Federal Reserve Board guaranteed a substantial measure of public control. The board was also empowered to issue paper money—"Federal Reserve Notes"—backed by commercial paper, such as promissory notes of businesspeople. Thus the amount of money in circulation could be swiftly increased as needed for the legitimate requirements of business.

The Federal Reserve Act was a red-letter achievement. It carried the nation with flying banners through the financial crises of the First World War of 1914–1918. Without it, the Republic's progress toward the modern economic age would have been seriously retarded.

Granger Collection

Reading the Death Warrant This cartoon appeared in a New York newspaper soon after Woodrow Wilson called for dramatic reform of the banking system before both houses of Congress. With the "money trust" of bankers and businessmen cowed, Wilson was able to win popular and congressional support for the Federal Reserve Act of 1913.

✦ The President Tames the Trusts

Without pausing for breath, Wilson pushed toward the last remaining rampart in the "triple wall of privilege"—the trusts. Early in 1914 he again went before Congress in a personal appearance that still carried drama.

Nine months and thousands of words later, Congress responded with the **Federal Trade Commission Act** of 1914. The new law empowered a presidentially appointed commission to turn a searchlight on industries engaged in interstate commerce, such as the meat-packers. The commissioners were expected to crush monopoly at the source by rooting out unfair trade practices, including unlawful competition, false advertising, mislabeling, adulteration, and bribery.

The knot of monopoly was further cut by the **Clayton Anti-Trust Act** of 1914. It lengthened the shopworn Sherman Act's list of business practices that were deemed objectionable, including price discrimination and interlocking directorates (whereby the same individuals served as directors of supposedly competing firms), an end often achieved through **holding companies** (see Figure 29.1).

The Clayton Act also conferred long-overdue benefits on labor. Conservative courts had unexpectedly been ruling that trade unions fell under the antimonopoly restraints of the Sherman Act. A classic case involved striking hatmakers in Danbury, Connecticut, who were assessed triple damages of more than $250,000, which resulted in the loss of their savings and homes. The Clayton Act therefore sought to exempt labor and agricultural organizations from antitrust prosecution, while explicitly legalizing strikes and peaceful picketing.

Union leader Samuel Gompers hailed the act as the Magna Carta of labor because it legally lifted human labor out of the category of "a commodity or article of commerce." But the rejoicing was premature, as conservative judges in later years continued to clip the wings of the union movement.

✦ Wilsonian Progressivism at High Tide

Energetically scaling the "triple wall of privilege," Woodrow Wilson had treated the nation to a dazzling demonstration of vigorous presidential leadership. He proved nearly irresistible in his first eighteen months in office. For once, a political creed was matched by deed, as the progressive reformers racked up victory after victory.

Standing at the peak of his powers at the head of the progressive forces, Wilson pressed ahead with further reforms. The Federal Farm Loan Act of 1916 made credit available to farmers at low rates of interest—as long demanded by the Populists. The Warehouse Act of 1916 authorized loans on the security of staple crops—another Populist idea. Other laws benefited rural America by providing for highway construction and the establishment of agricultural extension work in the state colleges.

Sweaty laborers also made gains as the progressive wave foamed forward. Sailors, treated brutally from cat-o'-nine-tails days onward, were given relief by the La Follette Seaman's Act of 1915. It required decent treatment and a living wage on American merchant ships. One unhappy result of this well-intentioned law was the crippling of America's merchant marine, as freight rates spiraled upward with the crew's wages.

Wilson further helped the workers with the **Workingmen's Compensation Act** of 1916, granting assistance to federal civil-service employees during periods of disability. In the same year, the president approved an act restricting child labor on products flowing into interstate commerce, though the stand-pat Supreme Court soon invalidated the law. Railroad workers, numbering about 1.7 million, were not sidetracked. The **Adamson Act** of 1916 established an eight-hour day for all employees on trains in interstate commerce, with extra pay for overtime.

Wilson earned the enmity of businesspeople and bigots but endeared himself to progressives when in 1916 he nominated for the Supreme Court the prominent reformer Louis D. Brandeis—the first Jew to be called to the high bench. Yet even Wilson's progressivism had its limits, and it clearly stopped short of better treatment for blacks. The southern-bred Wilson actually presided over accelerated segregation in the federal bureaucracy. When a delegation of black leaders personally protested to him, the schoolmasterish president virtually froze them out of his office.

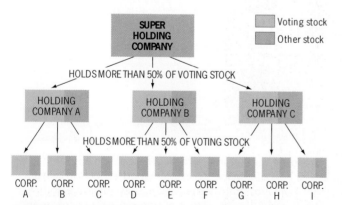

FIGURE 29.1 Organization of Holding Companies Keep in mind that the voting stock of a corporation is often only a fraction of the total stock.

Despite these limitations, Wilson knew that to be reelected in 1916, he needed to identify himself clearly as the candidate of progressivism. He appeased businesspeople by making conservative appointments to the Federal Reserve Board and the Federal Trade Commission, but he devoted most of his energy to cultivating progressive support. Wilson's election in 1912 had been something of a fluke, owing largely to the Taft-Roosevelt split in the Republican ranks. To remain in the White House, the president would have to woo the bull moose voters into the Democratic fold.

✶ New Directions in Foreign Policy

In one important area, Wilson chose not to answer the trumpet call of the bull moosers. In contrast to Roosevelt and even Taft, Wilson recoiled from an aggressive foreign policy. Hating imperialism, he was repelled by TR's big stickism. Suspicious of Wall Street, he detested the so-called dollar diplomacy of Taft.

In office only a week, Wilson declared war on dollar diplomacy. He proclaimed that the government would no longer offer special support to American investors in Latin America and China. Shivering from this Wilsonian bucket of cold water, American bankers pulled out of the Taft-engineered six-nation loan to China the next day.

In a similarly self-denying vein, Wilson persuaded Congress in early 1914 to repeal the Panama Canal Tolls Act of 1912, which had exempted American coastwise shipping from tolls and thereby provoked sharp protests from injured Britain. The president further chimed in with the anti-imperial song of Bryan and other Democrats when he signed the **Jones Act** in 1916. It granted to the Philippines the boon of territorial status and promised independence as soon as a "stable government" could be established. Wilson's racial prejudices, however, made it difficult for him to anticipate anything other than a long political tutelage for the Filipinos. Indeed, not until July 4, 1946—thirty years later—did the United States accept Philippine independence.

Wilson also partially defused a menacing crisis with Japan in 1913. The California legislature, still seeking to rid the Golden State of Japanese settlers, prohibited them from owning land. Tokyo, understandably irritated, lodged vigorous protests. At Fortress Corregidor, in the Philippines, American gunners were put on around-the-clock alert. But when Wilson dispatched Secretary of State William Jennings Bryan to plead with the California legislature to soften its stand, tensions eased somewhat.

Political turmoil in Haiti soon forced Wilson to eat some of his anti-imperialist words. The climax of the disorders came in 1914–1915, when an outraged populace literally tore to pieces the brutal Haitian president.

© Bettmann/Corbis

U.S. Marines in Haiti, 1919 The United States sent the marines to Haiti in 1915 to protect American economic interests. They remained for nineteen years.

In 1915 Wilson reluctantly dispatched marines to protect American lives and property. They remained for nineteen years, making Haiti an American protectorate. In 1916 he stole a page from Roosevelt's corollary to the Monroe Doctrine and concluded a treaty with Haiti providing for U.S. supervision of finances and the police. In the same year, he sent the leathernecked marines to quell riots in the Dominican Republic, and that debt-cursed land came under the shadow of the American eagle's wings for the next eight years. In 1917 Wilson purchased from Denmark the Virgin Islands, in the West Indies, tightening the grip of Uncle Sam in these shark-infested waters. Increasingly, the Caribbean Sea, with its vital approaches to the now-navigable Panama Canal, was taking on the earmarks of a Yankee preserve (see Map 29.2).

✳ Moralistic Diplomacy in Mexico

Rifle bullets whining across the southern border served as a constant reminder that all was not quiet in Mexico. For decades Mexico had been sorely exploited by foreign investors in oil, railroads, and mines. By 1913 American capitalists had sunk about a billion dollars into the underdeveloped but generously endowed country.

But if Mexico was rich, the Mexicans were poor. Fed up with their miserable lot, they at last revolted. Their revolution took an ugly turn in early 1913, when a conscienceless clique (with the support of President Taft's ambassador to Mexico) murdered the popular new revolutionary president and installed General Victoriano Huerta, an Indian, in the president's chair. All this chaos accelerated a massive migration of Mexicans to the United States. More than a million Spanish-speaking newcomers tramped across the southern border in the first three decades of the twentieth century. Settling mostly in Texas, New Mexico, Arizona, and California, they swung picks building highways and railroads or followed the fruit harvests as pickers. Though often segregated in Spanish-speaking enclaves, they helped to create a unique borderland culture that blended Mexican and American folkways.

MAP 29.2 The United States in the Caribbean, 1898–1941   This map explains why many Latin Americans accused the United States of turning the Caribbean Sea into a "Yankee lake." It also suggests that Uncle Sam was much less "isolationist" in his own backyard than he was in faraway Europe or Asia. © Cengage Learning

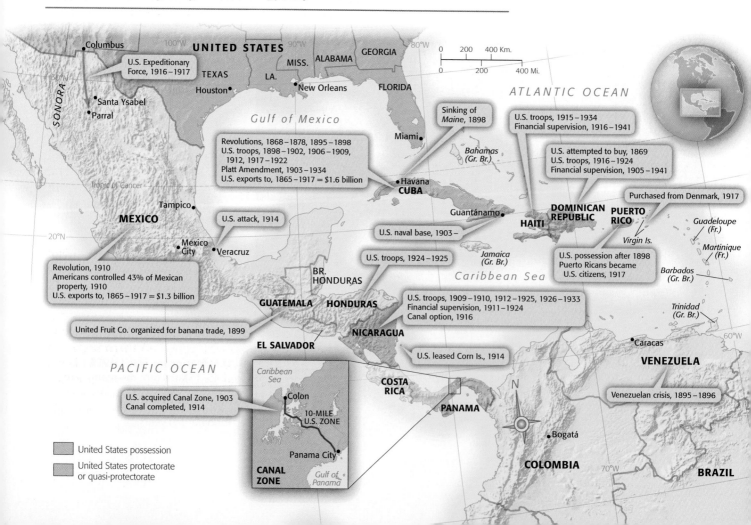

The revolutionary bloodshed also menaced American lives and property in Mexico. Cries for intervention burst from the lips of American jingoes. Prominent among those chanting for war was the influential chain newspaper publisher William Randolph Hearst, whose views presumably were colored by his ownership of a Mexican ranch larger than Rhode Island. Yet once again, President Wilson refused to practice the same old dollar diplomacy of his predecessors, deeming it "perilous" to determine foreign policy "in the terms of material interest."

Wilson strove as best he could to steer a moral course in Mexico. He sent his aggressive ambassador packing, imposed an arms embargo, and refused to recognize officially the murderous government of "that brute" Huerta, even though most foreign powers acknowledged Huerta's bloody-handed regime. "I am going to teach the South American republics to elect good men," the

El Hijo del Ahuizote September 6, 1913

Wilson Confronts Huerta   A Mexican view of the tense standoff between Wilson and the Mexican president, Victoriano Huerta. The artist's rendering seems to reflect the famous observation of long-time Mexican leader Porfirio Diaz: "Poor Mexico! So far from God, so close to the United States."

In October 1913 President Woodrow Wilson (1856–1924) addressed the Southern Commercial Congress in Mobile, Alabama, and drew a connection between the battle against the trusts at home and the travails of countries south of the border:

"We have seen material interests threaten constitutional freedom in the United States. Therefore, we will now know how to sympathize with those in the rest of [Latin] America who have to contend with such powers, not only from within their borders but from outside their borders also."

former professor declared. He put his munitions where his mouth was in 1914, when he allowed American arms to flow to Huerta's principal rivals, white-bearded Venustiano Carranza and the firebrand Francisco ("Pancho") Villa.

The Mexican volcano erupted at the Atlantic seaport of Tampico in April 1914, when a small party of American sailors was arrested. The Mexicans promptly released the captives and apologized, but they refused the affronted American admiral's demand for a salute of twenty-one guns. Wilson, heavy-hearted but stubbornly determined to eliminate Huerta, asked Congress for authority to use force against Mexico. Before Congress could act, Wilson ordered the navy to seize the Mexican port of Veracruz to thwart the arrival of a German steamer carrying Huerta-bound guns and ammunition. Huerta as well as Carranza hotly protested against this high-handed Yankee maneuver.

Just as a full-dress shooting conflict seemed inevitable, Wilson was rescued by an offer of mediation from the ABC Powers—Argentina, Brazil, and Chile. Huerta collapsed in July 1914 under pressure from within and without. He was succeeded by his archrival, Venustiano Carranza, still fiercely resentful of Wilson's military meddling. The whole sorry **Tampico Incident** did not augur well for the future of United States–Mexican relations.

"Pancho" Villa, a combination of bandit and Robin Hood, had meanwhile stolen the spotlight. He emerged as the chief rival to President Carranza, whom Wilson now reluctantly supported. Challenging Carranza's authority while also punishing the gringos, Villa's men ruthlessly hauled sixteen young American mining engineers off a train traveling through northern Mexico in January 1916 and killed them. A month later Villa and his followers, hoping to provoke a war between Wilson and Carranza, blazed across the border into Columbus, New Mexico, and murdered another nineteen Americans.

"Pancho" Villa with His Ragtag Army in Mexico, ca. 1916 His daring, impetuosity, and horsemanship made Villa a hero to the masses of northern Mexico. Yet he proved to be a violent and ineffective crusader against social abuses, and he was assassinated in 1923.

Brown Brothers

General John J. ("Black Jack")* Pershing, a grim-faced and ramrod-erect veteran of the Cuban and Philippine campaigns, was ordered to break up the bandit band. His hastily organized force of several thousand mounted troops penetrated deep into rugged Mexico with surprising speed. They clashed with Carranza's forces and mauled the Villistas but missed capturing Villa himself. As the threat of war with Germany loomed larger, the invading army was withdrawn in January 1917.

✦ Thunder Across the Sea

Europe's powder magazine, long smoldering, blew up in the summer of 1914, when the flaming pistol of a Serb patriot killed the heir to the throne of Austria-Hungary in Sarajevo. An outraged Vienna government, backed by Germany, forthwith presented a stern ultimatum to neighboring Serbia.

An explosive chain reaction followed. Tiny Serbia, backed by its powerful Slav neighbor Russia, refused to bend the knee sufficiently. The Russian tsar began to mobilize his ponderous war machine, menacing Germany on the east, even as his ally, France, confronted Germany on the west. In alarm, the Germans struck suddenly at France through unoffending Belgium; their objective was to knock their ancient enemy out of action so that they would have two free hands to repel Russia. Great Britain, its coastline jeopardized by the assault on Belgium, was sucked into the conflagration on the side of France.

Almost overnight most of Europe was locked in a fight to the death. On one side were arrayed the **Central Powers**: Germany and Austria-Hungary, and later Turkey and Bulgaria. On the other side were the **Allies**: principally France, Britain, and Russia, and later Japan and Italy.

Americans thanked God for the ocean moats and self-righteously congratulated themselves on having had ancestors wise enough to have abandoned the hell pits of Europe. America felt strong, snug, smug, and secure—but not for long.

✦ A Precarious Neutrality

President Wilson's grief at the outbreak of war was compounded by the recent death of his wife. He sorrowfully issued the routine neutrality proclamation and called on Americans to be neutral in thought as well as deed. But such scrupulous evenhandedness proved difficult.

Both sides wooed the United States, the great neutral in the West. The British enjoyed the boon of close cultural, linguistic, and economic ties with America and had the added advantage of controlling most of the transatlantic cables. Their censors sheared away war stories harmful to the Allies and drenched the United States with tales of German bestiality.

The Germans and the Austro-Hungarians counted on the natural sympathies of their transplanted countrymen in America. Including persons with at least one foreign-born parent, people with blood ties to the Central Powers numbered some 11 million in 1914. Some of these recent immigrants expressed noisy sympathy for the fatherland, but most were simply grateful to be so distant from the fray (see Table 29.1).

Most Americans were anti-German from the outset. With his villainous upturned mustache, Kaiser Wilhelm II seemed the embodiment of arrogant autocracy, an impression strengthened by Germany's ruthless strike at neutral Belgium. German and Austrian agents further tarnished the image of the Central Powers in American eyes when they resorted to violence in American factories and ports. When a German operative in 1915 absentmindedly left his briefcase on a New York

---

*So called from his earlier service as an officer with the crack black 10th Cavalry.

TABLE 29.1 Principal Foreign Elements in the United States, Census of 1910

Country of Origin		Foreign-Born	Natives with Two Foreign-Born Parents	Natives with One Foreign-Born Parent	Total
Central Powers {	Germany	2,501,181	3,911,847	1,869,590	8,282,61
	Austria-Hungary	1,670,524	900,129	131,133	2,701,786
Allied Powers {	Great Britain	1,219,968	852,610	1,158,474	3,231,052
	(Ireland)*	1,352,155	2,141,577	1,010,628	4,504,360
	Russia	1,732,421	949,316	70,938	2,752,675
	Italy	1,343,070	695,187	60,103	2,098,360
TOTAL (for all foreign countries, including those not listed)		13,345,545	12,916,311	5,981,526	32,243,282
Percentage of total U.S. population (91,972,266)		14.5	14.0	6.5	35.0

*Ireland was not yet independent.

elevated car, its documents detailing plans for industrial sabotage were quickly discovered and publicized. American opinion, already ill-disposed, was further inflamed against the kaiser and Germany. Yet the great majority of Americans earnestly hoped to stay out of the horrible war.

✵ America Earns Blood Money

When Europe burst into flames in 1914, the United States was bogged down in a worrisome business recession. But as fate would have it, British and French war orders soon pulled American industry out of the morass of hard times and onto a peak of war-born prosperity (see Table 29.2). Part of this boom was financed by American bankers, notably the Wall Street firm of J. P. Morgan and Company, which eventually advanced to the Allies the enormous sum of $2.3 billion during the period of American neutrality. The Central Powers

protested bitterly against the immense trade between America and the Allies, but this traffic did not in fact violate the international neutrality laws. Germany was technically free to trade with the United States. It was prevented from doing so not by American policy but by geography and the British navy. Trade between Germany and America had to move across the Atlantic; but the British controlled the sea-lanes, and they threw a noose-tight blockade of mines and ships across the North Sea,

The Fatherland, *the chief German-American propaganda newspaper in the United States, cried,*

❝We [Americans] prattle about humanity while we manufacture poisoned shrapnel and picric acid for profit. Ten thousand German widows, ten thousand orphans, ten thousand graves bear the legend 'Made in America.'❞

TABLE 29.2 U.S. Exports to Belligerents, 1914–1916

Belligerent	1914	1915	1916	1916 Figure as a Percentage of 1914 Figure
Britain	$594,271,863	$911,794,954	$1,526,685,102	257%
France	159,818,924	369,397,170	628,851,988	393
Italy*	74,235,012	184,819,688	269,246,105	363
Germany	344,794,276	28,863,354	288,899	0.08

*Italy joined the Allies in April 1915.

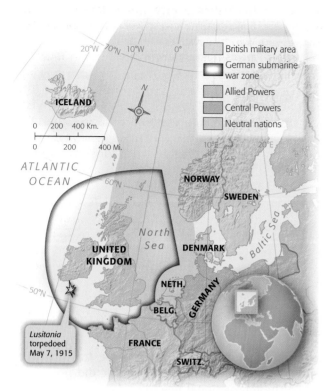

MAP 29.3 British Military Area (declared November 3, 1914) and German Submarine War Zone (declared February 4, 1915) © Cengage Learning

A German U-boat This deadly new weapon rendered useless existing rules of naval warfare, eventually pushing the United States to declare war against Germany in 1917.

gateway to German ports. Over the unavailing protests of American shippers, farmers, and manufacturers, the British began forcing American vessels off the high seas and into their ports. This harassment of American shipping proved highly effective, as trade between Germany and the United States virtually ceased.

Hard-pressed Germany did not tamely consent to being starved out. In retaliation for the British blockade, in February 1915 Berlin announced a submarine war area around the British Isles (see Map 29.3). The submarine was a weapon so new that existing international law could not be made to fit it. The old rule that a warship must stop and board a merchantman could hardly apply to submarines, which could easily be rammed or sunk if they surfaced.

The cigar-shaped marauders posed a dire threat to the United States—so long as Wilson insisted on maintaining America's neutral rights. Berlin officials declared that they would try not to sink *neutral* shipping, but they warned that mistakes would probably occur. Wilson now determined on a policy of calculated risk. He would continue to claim profitable neutral trading rights, while hoping that no high-seas incident would force his hand to grasp the sword of war. Setting his peninsular jaw, he emphatically warned Germany

that it would be held to "strict accountability" for any attacks on American vessels or citizens.

The German submarines (known as **U-boats**, from the German *Unterseeboot*, or "undersea boat") meanwhile began their deadly work. In the first months of 1915, they sank about ninety ships in the war zone. Then the submarine issue became acute when the British passenger liner **Lusitania** was torpedoed and sank off the coast of Ireland on May 7, 1915, with the loss of 1,198 lives, including 128 Americans.

The *Lusitania* was carrying forty-two hundred cases of small-arms ammunition, a fact the Germans used to justify the sinking. But Americans were swept by a wave of shock and anger at this act of "mass murder" and "piracy." The eastern United States, closer to the war, seethed with talk of fighting, but the rest of the country showed a strong distaste for hostilities. The peace-loving Wilson had no stomach for leading a disunited nation into war. He well remembered the mistake

Advertisement from the *New York Herald*, May 1, 1915 Six days later the *Lusitania* was sunk. Note the German warning.

in 1812 of his fellow Princetonian, James Madison. Instead, by a series of increasingly strong notes, Wilson attempted to bring the German warlords sharply to book. Even this measured approach was too much for Secretary of State Bryan, who resigned rather than sign a protestation that might spell shooting. But Wilson resolutely stood his ground. "There is such a thing," he declared, "as a man being too proud to fight." This kind of talk incensed the war-thirsty Theodore Roosevelt. The Rough Rider assailed the spineless simperers who heeded the "weasel words" of the pacifistic professor in the White House.

Yet Wilson, sticking to his verbal guns, made some diplomatic progress. After another British liner, the *Arabic*, was sunk in August 1915, with the loss of two American lives, Berlin reluctantly agreed not to sink unarmed and unresisting passenger ships *without warning.*

This pledge appeared to be violated in March 1916, when the Germans torpedoed a French passenger steamer, the *Sussex*. The infuriated Wilson informed the Germans that unless they renounced the inhuman practice of sinking merchant ships without warning,

"Here's Money for Your Americans. I May Drown Some More." Germany expressed "profound regret" for the deaths of 128 Americans aboard the torpedoed passenger liner *Lusitania* in 1915, but the incident helped feed a mounting anti-German sentiment in the United States.

he would break diplomatic relations—an almost certain prelude to war.

Germany reluctantly knuckled under to President Wilson's *Sussex* ultimatum, agreeing not to sink passenger ships and merchant vessels without giving warning. But the Germans attached a long string to their *Sussex* pledge: the United States would have to persuade the Allies to modify what Berlin regarded as their illegal blockade. This, obviously, was something that Washington could not do. Wilson promptly accepted the German pledge, without accepting the "string." He thus won a temporary but precarious diplomatic victory—precarious because Germany could pull the string whenever it chose, and the president might suddenly find himself tugged over the cliff of war.

✴ Wilson Wins Reelection in 1916

Against this ominous backdrop, the presidential campaign of 1916 gathered speed. Both the bull moose Progressives and the Republicans met in Chicago. The Progressives uproariously renominated Theodore Roosevelt, but the Rough Rider, who loathed Wilson and all his works, had no stomach for splitting the Republicans again and ensuring the reelection of his hated rival. In refusing to run, he sounded the death knell of the Progressive party.

Roosevelt's Republican admirers also clamored for "Teddy," but the Old Guard detested the renegade who had ruptured the party in 1912. Instead they drafted Supreme Court justice Charles Evans Hughes, a cold intellectual who had achieved a solid liberal record when he was governor of New York. The Republican platform condemned the Democratic tariff, assaults on the trusts, and Wilson's wishy-washiness in dealing with Mexico and Germany.

The thick-whiskered Hughes ("an animated feather duster") left the bench for the campaign stump, where he was not at home. In anti-German areas of the country, he assailed Wilson for not standing up to the kaiser, whereas in isolationist areas he took a softer line. This fence-straddling operation led to the jeer "Charles Evasive Hughes."

Hughes was further plagued by Roosevelt, who was delivering a series of skin-'em-alive speeches against "that damned Presbyterian hypocrite Wilson." Frothing for war, TR privately scoffed at Hughes as a "whiskered Wilson"; the only difference between the two, he said, was "a shave."

Wilson, nominated by acclamation at the Democratic convention in St. Louis, ignored Hughes on the theory that one should not try to murder a man who is committing suicide. His campaign was built on the slogan "He Kept Us Out of War."

Theodore Roosevelt, War Hawk The former president clamored for American intervention in the European war, but the country preferred peace in 1916. Ironically, Roosevelt's archrival, Woodrow Wilson, would take the country into the war just months after the 1916 election. Library of Congress

Democratic orators warned that by electing Charles Evans Hughes, the nation would be electing a fight—with a certain frustrated Rough Rider leading the charge. A Democratic advertisement appealing to the American working people read,

You are Working;
—Not Fighting!
Alive and Happy;
—Not Cannon Fodder!
Wilson and Peace with Honor?
or
Hughes with Roosevelt and War?

On election day Hughes swept the East and looked like a surefire winner. Wilson went to bed that night prepared to accept defeat, while the New York newspapers displayed huge portraits of "The President-Elect—Charles Evans Hughes."

But the rest of the country turned the tide. Midwesterners and westerners, attracted by Wilson's progressive reforms and antiwar policies, flocked to the polls for the president. The final result, in doubt for

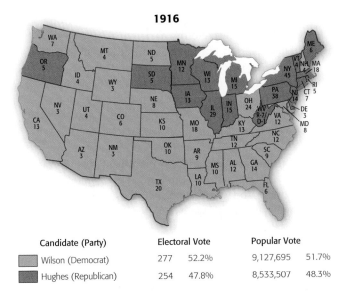

1916

Candidate (Party)	Electoral Vote		Popular Vote	
Wilson (Democrat)	277	52.2%	9,127,695	51.7%
Hughes (Republican)	254	47.8%	8,533,507	48.3%

MAP 29.4 Presidential Election of 1916 (with electoral vote by state) Wilson was so worried about being a lame duck president in a time of great international tensions that he drew up a plan whereby Hughes, if victorious, would be appointed secretary of state, Wilson and the vice president would resign, and Hughes would thus succeed immediately to the presidency. © Cengage Learning

During the 1916 campaign, J. A. O'Leary, the head of a pro-German and pro-Irish organization, sent a scorching telegram to Wilson condemning him for having been pro-British in approving war loans and ammunition traffic. Wilson shot back an answer:

"Your telegram received. I would feel deeply mortified to have you or anybody like you vote for me. Since you have access to many disloyal Americans and I have not, I will ask you to convey this message to them."

President Wilson's devastating and somewhat insulting response probably won him more votes than it lost.

several days, hinged on California, which Wilson carried by some 3,800 votes out of about a million cast.

Wilson barely squeaked through, with a final vote of 277 to 254 in the Electoral College, and 9,127,695 to 8,533,507 in the popular column (see Map 29.4). The prolabor Wilson received strong support from the working class and from renegade bull moosers, whom Republicans failed to lure back into their camp. Wilson had not specifically promised to keep the country out of war, but probably enough voters relied on such implicit assurances to ensure his victory. Their hopeful expectations were soon rudely shattered.

Varying Viewpoints
Who Were the Progressives?

Debate about progressivism has revolved mainly around a question that is simple to ask but devilishly difficult to answer: who were the progressives? It was once taken for granted that progressive reformers were simply the heirs of the Jeffersonian-Jacksonian-Populist reform crusades; they were the oppressed and downtrodden common folk who finally erupted in wrath and demanded their due.

But in his influential *Age of Reform* (1955), Richard Hofstadter astutely challenged that view. Progressive leaders, he argued, were not drawn from the ranks of society's poor and marginalized. Rather, they were middle-class people threatened from above by the emerging power of new corporate elites and from below by a restless working class. It was not economic deprivation, but "status anxiety," Hofstadter insisted, that prompted these people to become reformers. Their psychological motivation, Hofstadter concluded, rendered many of their reform efforts quirky and ineffectual.

By contrast, "New Left" historians, notably Gabriel Kolko, argued that progressivism was dominated by established business leaders who successfully directed "reform" to their own conservative ends. In this view government regulation (as embodied in new agencies like the Federal Reserve Board and the Federal Tariff Commission, and in legislation like the Meat Inspection Act) simply accomplished what two generations of private efforts had failed to do: dampen cutthroat competition, stabilize markets, and make America safe for monopoly capitalism.

Still other scholars, notably Robert H. Wiebe and Samuel P. Hays, argued that the progressives were neither the psychologically or economically disadvantaged nor the old capitalist elite, but were, rather, members of a rapidly emerging, self-confident social class possessed of the new techniques of scientific management, technological expertise, and organizational know-how. This "organizational school" of historians did not see progressivism as a struggle of the "people" against the "interests," as a confused and nostalgic campaign by status-threatened reformers, or as a conservative coup d'état. The progressive movement, in this view, was by and large an effort to rationalize and modernize many social institutions by introducing the wise and impartial hand of government regulation.

This view had much to recommend it. Yet despite its widespread acceptance among historians, it could not adequately account for the titanic political struggles of the progressive era over the very reforms that the "organizational school" regarded as simple adjustments to modernity. It also brushed over the deep philosophical differences that divided progressives themselves—such as between Roosevelt's New Nationalism and Wilson's New Freedom. In addition, the organizational approach did not account for the important role of women in advocating progressive reforms, as demonstrated by Robyn Muncy, Linda Gordon, and Theda Skocpol. Building the American welfare state in the early twentieth century, they have argued, was fundamentally a gendered activity inspired by a "female dominion" of social workers and "social feminists." Scholars such as Daniel T. Rodgers have added that essential inspiration also came from across the Atlantic. In European countries vibrant labor movements sought a welfare state to benefit the working class, whereas in the United States the strength of female reformers promoted welfare programs aimed at protecting women and children. All the same, American programs frequently were modeled after policies adopted in London, Paris, and Berlin.

Chapter Review

KEY TERMS

New Freedom (661)
New Nationalism (662)
Underwood Tariff (664)
Federal Reserve Act (665)
Federal Trade Commission Act (666)
Clayton Anti-Trust Act (666)
holding companies (666)
Workingmen's Compensation Act (666)

Adamson Act (666)
Jones Act (667)
Tampico Incident (669)
Central Powers (670)
Allies (670)
U-boats (672)
Lusitania (672)

PEOPLE TO KNOW

Herbert Croly
Louis D. Brandeis
Victoriano Huerta
Venustiano Carranza

Francisco ("Pancho") Villa
John ("Black Jack") Pershing
Charles Evans Hughes

CHRONOLOGY

1912 Wilson defeats Taft and Roosevelt for presidency

1913 Underwood Tariff Act
Sixteenth Amendment (income tax)
Federal Reserve Act
Huerta takes power in Mexico

1914 Clayton Anti-Trust Act
Federal Trade Commission established
U.S. seizes port of Veracruz, Mexico
World War I begins in Europe

1915 La Follette Seaman's Act
Lusitania torpedoed and sunk by German U-boat
U.S. Marines sent to Haiti
Germany declares submarine war area around British Isles

1916 *Sussex* ultimatum and pledge
U.S. exports to European belligerents skyrocket
Workingmen's Compensation Act
Federal Farm Loan Act
Warehouse Act
Adamson Act
Pancho Villa raids New Mexico
Brandeis appointed to Supreme Court
Jones Act
U.S. Marines sent to Dominican Republic
Wilson defeats Hughes for presidency

1917 United States buys Virgin Islands from Denmark

TO LEARN MORE

Michael C. Adams, *The Great Adventure: Male Desire and the Coming of World War I* (1990)

John W. Chambers, *The Tyranny of Change: America in the Progressive Era, 1900–1917* (rev. ed., 2000)

John Milton Cooper, Jr., *Woodrow Wilson: A Biography* (2009)

————, *The Warrior and the Priest: Woodrow Wilson and Theodore Roosevelt* (1983)

Alexander L. George and Juliette L. George, *Woodrow Wilson and Colonel House* (1956)

Lewis L. Gould, *Four Hats in the Ring: The 1912 Election and the Birth of Modern Politics* (2008)

Henry May, *The End of American Innocence: A Study of the First Years of Our Time* (1959)

Frank A. Ninkovich, *The Wilsonian Century: U.S. Foreign Policy Since 1900* (1999)

Mary Renda, *Taking Haiti: Military Occupation and the Culture of U.S. Imperialism, 1915–1940* (2001)

Edward Stettner, *Shaping Modern Liberalism: Herbert Croly and Progressive Thought* (1993)

Philippa Strum, *Brandeis: Justice for the People* (1985)

Robert W. Tucker, *Woodrow Wilson and the Great War: Reconsidering America's Neutrality, 1914–1917* (2007)

Eileen Welsome, *The General and the Jaguar: Pershing's Hunt for Pancho Villa* (2006)

A complete, annotated bibliography for this chapter—along with brief descriptions of the People to Know—may be found on the American Pageant website. The Key Terms are defined in a Glossary at the end of the text.

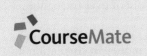

Go to the CourseMate website at **www.cengagebrain.com** for additional study tools and review materials—including audio and video clips—for this chapter.

AP® Review Questions for Chapter 29

1. In 1912, Woodrow Wilson ran for the presidency on a Democratic platform that included support for all of the following EXCEPT
   - (A) antitrust legislation.
   - (B) monetary reform.
   - (C) dollar diplomacy.
   - (D) tariff reductions.
   - (E) support for small business.

2. Which statement best describes the contrasts between Woodrow Wilson's New Freedom progressivism and Theodore Roosevelt's New Nationalism progressivism?
   - (A) Wilson's New Freedom emphasized small enterprise, entrepreneurship, and the free functioning of unregulated and unmonopolized markets; Roosevelt's New Nationalism favored continued consolidation of the trusts and labor unions supplemented by the growth of federal regulatory agencies.
   - (B) Wilson's New Freedom emphasized consolidation of trusts and labor unions; Roosevelt favored advancing small enterprise, entrepreneurship, and the open functioning of unregulated and unmonopolized markets.
   - (C) Wilson's New Freedom favored a broad program of social welfare including minimum wage laws and social insurance; Roosevelt's New Nationalism emphasized a faith in free-market competition, vigorous enforcement of antitrust laws, and shunning of social welfare proposals.
   - (D) Roosevelt's New Nationalism favored placing key industries such as the railroads and utilities under government ownership, while Wilson's New Freedom advocated vigorous regulation of these key private industries.
   - (E) Wilson's New Freedom emphasized the importance of maintaining protectionist high tariffs to protect domestic industry and promote economic growth, while Roosevelt favored lowering tariffs to promote trade and economic expansion.

3. President Woodrow Wilson's political philosophy included all of the following EXCEPT
   - (A) a stubborn commitment to particular progressive principles and an aversion to pragmatic political compromise.
   - (B) scorn for the ability of peoples in other countries to govern themselves.
   - (C) a belief that the president should provide leadership for Congress.
   - (D) a belief that the president should appeal over the heads of legislators to the sovereign people.
   - (E) a belief in the central importance of morality in politics.

4. How did the Underwood Tariff Act reflect President Wilson's progressive goals?
   - (A) The law lowered tariff rates and established the first graduated federal income tax.
   - (B) In addition to lowering tariff rates, the act created an optional retirement system for workers.
   - (C) The act lowered tariff rates and guaranteed equal treatment for men and women in employment.
   - (D) The tariff was used only for increasing government revenue and not to protect American industry from competition.
   - (E) The raising of the tariff provided protection for American farmers against subsidized foreign crop imports.

5. What critical authority was given to the Federal Reserve Board by the Federal Reserve Act of 1913 to permit quasi-public management over the banking and currency system?
   - (A) The power to issue paper money and increase or decrease the amount of money in circulation by altering interest rates
   - (B) The authority to close weak banks
   - (C) The power to take the United States off the gold standard
   - (D) The power to guarantee banking deposits against bank failures
   - (E) The power to collect income taxes directly from employees' paychecks

6. The Federal Trade Commission was established in 1914 to address all of the following practices EXCEPT
   - (A) eliminating unfair and discriminatory trade practices.
   - (B) outlawing unfair business competition and bribery.
   - (C) prohibiting sale of stocks without full disclosure.
   - (D) prohibiting false and misleading advertising.
   - (E) abolishing the mislabeling or adulterating of products.

7. The Clayton Anti-Trust Act of 1914 accomplished all of the following EXCEPT
   - (A) outlawing corporate interlocking directorates.
   - (B) prohibiting price discrimination against different purchasers.
   - (C) exempting labor unions and farm cooperatives from antitrust action.
   - (D) further undercutting the monopolistic practices of big business.
   - (E) providing long-term legal protection for unions to engage in organizing, collective bargaining, and strike activities.

8. What presidential action illustrated the limits of Woodrow Wilson's progressivism?
   - (A) Vetoing the Federal Farm Loan Act
   - (B) Opposing the entry of women into politics
   - (C) Appointing the Jewish Louis D. Brandeis to the U.S. Supreme Court
   - (D) Vetoing legislation to guarantee workers compensation assistance to disabled federal employees
   - (E) Accelerating the segregation of blacks in the federal bureaucracy

9. Which term best characterizes Woodrow Wilson's fundamental overall approach to American foreign policy?
   - (A) Imperialistic
   - (B) Moralistic
   - (C) Realistic
   - (D) Isolationist
   - (E) Balance of power

10. Which of the following represented President Wilson's first direct use of American military forces in revolutionary Mexico?
    - (A) Sending the U.S. armed forces to protect against Mexico's nationalization of American businesses
    - (B) Sending the U.S. Army to prevent Venustiano Carranza from becoming president of Mexico
    - (C) Seizing the Mexican port of Vera Cruz to prevent German delivery of arms to President Huerta
    - (D) Sending the U.S. Army to protect the vast Mexican land holdings of William Randolph Hearst
    - (E) Sending General Pershing into Mexico to capture Mexican revolutionary Pancho Villa following the latter's border raids into New Mexico

11. Which of the following had the most influence on America's growing trading with Britain and its reduction of trade with Germany during the period 1914–1916?
    - (A) The British needed American goods and weapons and the Germans did not.
    - (B) More American sympathized with Britain than with Germany.
    - (C) British agents sabotaged American businesses that traded with Germany.
    - (D) American bankers such as J. P. Morgan were willing to loan money to Britain but not to Germany.
    - (E) The British Navy controlled the Atlantic shipping lanes.

12. Which of the following best characterizes the attitude of the large majority of Americans to the outbreak of World War I in 1914?
    - (A) Most Americans earnestly hoped to remain neutral and stay out of the war.
    - (B) Most Americans favored entering the war in support of the Allies.
    - (C) Most Americans supported the cause of the Central Powers.
    - (D) Most Americans wanted to form a military alliance of neutral nations.
    - (E) Most Americans favored direct U.S. diplomatic mediation of the conflict.

13. What prompted German submarines to begin sinking unarmed and unresisting merchant and passenger ships in the Atlantic during the early years of World War I?
    - (A) The United States' entry into the war in 1917
    - (B) The British naval blockade of Germany
    - (C) A strategic calculation designed to keep the United States out of the war
    - (D) A change in international law permitting this new style of warfare
    - (E) A last-ditch, desperate effort by Germany to win the war

14. What dangerous contingency did Germany attach to its *Sussex* pledge not to attack unarmed neutral shipping during the years of the war?
    - (A) Americans would have to refrain from sailing on British-owned passenger ships.
    - (B) U-boats could capture merchant vessels if the submarines surfaced.
    - (C) The American government would have to guarantee that passenger vessels were not secretly carrying military supplies.
    - (D) The United States would have to persuade the Allies to end their blockade of Germany or unrestricted submarine warfare would resume.
    - (E) Woodrow Wilson would have to seek a fair, negotiated settlement of the war.

15. Which of the following actions was NOT part of Wilson's "moral diplomacy"?
    - (A) Granting the Philippines territorial status
    - (B) Repealing the Panama Canal Tolls Act
    - (C) Rescinding support for American investors in Latin America
    - (D) Convincing the California legislature to soften its anti-Japanese stance
    - (E) Dispatching Marines to Haiti to protect American lives and property

16. Which of the following events is a result of the other four?
    - (A) William Jennings Bryan supports Woodrow Wilson's candidacy
    - (B) Roosevelt's "Bull Moose" party divides traditionally Republican voters
    - (C) Woodrow Wilson wins the presidential election of 1912
    - (D) New Jersey bosses propel Woodrow Wilson to the governorship
    - (E) Woodrow Wilson offers voters a choice in political and economic philosophies

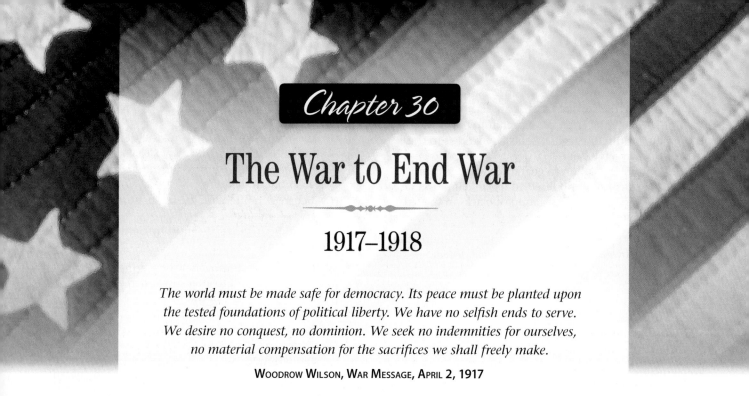

Chapter 30

The War to End War

1917–1918

The world must be made safe for democracy. Its peace must be planted upon the tested foundations of political liberty. We have no selfish ends to serve. We desire no conquest, no dominion. We seek no indemnities for ourselves, no material compensation for the sacrifices we shall freely make.

WOODROW WILSON, WAR MESSAGE, APRIL 2, 1917

Destiny dealt cruelly with Woodrow Wilson. The lover of peace, as fate would have it, was forced to lead a hesitant and peace-loving nation into war. As the last days of 1916 slipped through the hourglass, the president made one final, futile attempt to mediate between the embattled belligerents. On January 22, 1917, he delivered one of his most moving addresses, restating America's commitment to neutral rights and declaring that only a negotiated "peace without victory" would prove durable.

Germany's warlords responded with a blow of the mailed fist. On January 31, 1917, they announced to an astonished world their decision to wage *unrestricted* submarine warfare, sinking *all* ships, including America's, in the war zone.

Why this rash act? War with America was the last thing Germany wanted. But after three ghastly years in the trenches, Germany's leaders decided the distinction between combatants and noncombatants was a luxury they could no longer afford. Thus they jerked on the string they had attached to their *Sussex* pledge in 1916, desperately hoping to bring Britain to its knees before the United States entered the war. Wilson, his bluff called, broke diplomatic relations with Germany but refused to move closer to war unless the Germans undertook "overt" acts against American lives.

War by Act of Germany

To defend American interests short of war, the president asked Congress for authority to arm American merchant ships. When a band of midwestern senators launched a filibuster to block the measure, Wilson denounced them as a "little group of willful men" who were rendering a great nation "helpless and contemptible." But their obstruction was a powerful reminder of the continuing strength of American isolationism.

Meanwhile, the sensational **Zimmermann note** was intercepted and published on March 1, 1917, infuriating Americans, especially westerners. German foreign secretary Arthur Zimmermann had secretly proposed a German-Mexican alliance, tempting anti-Yankee Mexico with veiled promises of recovering Texas, New Mexico, and Arizona.

On the heels of this provocation came the long-dreaded "overt" acts in the Atlantic, where German U-boats sank four unarmed American merchant vessels in the first two weeks of March. As one Philadelphia newspaper observed, "The difference between war and what we have now is that now we aren't fighting back." Simultaneously came the rousing news that a revolution in Russia had toppled the cruel regime of the tsars. America could now fight foursquare for democracy on the side of the Allies, without the black sheep of Russian despotism in the Allied fold.

Subdued and solemn, Wilson at last stood before a hushed joint session of Congress on the evening of April 2, 1917, and asked for a declaration of war. He had lost his gamble that America could pursue the profits of neutral trade without being sucked into the ghastly maelstrom. A myth developed in later years that America was dragged unwittingly into war by munitions makers and Wall Street bankers, desperate to protect their profits and loans. Yet the weapons merchants and financiers were already thriving, unhampered by

PRESIDENT CALLS FOR WAR DECLARATION, STRONGER NAVY, NEW ARMY OF 500,000 MEN, FULL CO-OPERATION WITH GERMANY'S FOES

WAR! Attacks by German submarines finally forced Wilson's hand, and he asked Congress for a declaration of war on April 2, 1917. Four days later, after considerable debate and with fifty-six dissenting votes, Congress obliged the president.

wartime government restrictions and heavy taxation. Their slogan might well have been "Neutrality Forever." The simple truth is that British harassment of American commerce had been galling but endurable; Germany had resorted to the mass killing of civilians. The difference was like that between a gang of thieves and a gang of murderers. President Wilson had drawn a clear, if risky, line against the depredations of the submarine. The German high command, in a last desperate throw of the dice, chose to cross it. In a figurative sense, America's war declaration of April 6, 1917, bore the unambiguous trademark "Made in Germany."

✦ Wilsonian Idealism Enthroned

"It is a fearful thing to lead this great peaceful people into war," Wilson said in his war message. It was fearful indeed, not least of all because of the formidable challenge it posed to Wilson's leadership skills. Ironically, it fell to the scholarly Wilson, deeply respectful of American traditions, to shatter one of the most sacred of those traditions by entangling America in a distant European war.

How could the president arouse the American people to shoulder this unprecedented burden? For more than a century, they had prided themselves on their isolationism from the periodic outbursts of militarized violence that afflicted the Old World. Since 1914 their pride had been reinforced by the bountiful profits gained through neutrality. German U-boats had now roughly shoved a wavering America into the abyss, but ominously, no fewer than six senators and fifty representatives (including the first congresswoman, Jeannette Rankin of Montana) had voted against the war resolution. Wilson could whip up no enthusiasm, especially in the landlocked Midwest, by calling on the nation to fight to make the world safe from the submarine.

To galvanize the country, Wilson would have to proclaim more glorified aims. Radiating the spiritual fervor of his Presbyterian ancestors, he declared the supremely ambitious goal of a crusade "to make the world safe for democracy." Brandishing the sword of righteousness, Wilson virtually hypnotized the nation with his lofty ideals. He contrasted the selfish war aims of the other belligerents, Allied and enemy alike, with America's shining altruism. America, he preached, did not fight for the sake of riches or territorial conquest. The Republic sought only to shape an international order in which democracy could flourish without fear of power-crazed autocrats and militarists.

In Wilsonian idealism the personality of the president and the necessities of history were perfectly matched. The high-minded Wilson genuinely believed in the principles he so eloquently intoned—especially that the modern world could not afford the kind of hyper-destructive war that advanced industrial states were now capable of waging. In this, Wilson's vision was prophetic. In any case, probably no other appeal could have successfully converted the American people from their historic hostility to involvement in European squabbles. Americans, it seemed, could be either isolationists or crusaders, but nothing in between.

Wilson's appeal worked—perhaps too well. Holding aloft the torch of idealism, the president fired up the public mind to a fever pitch. "Force, force to the utmost, force without stint or limit," he cried, while the country responded less elegantly with "Hang the kaiser." Lost on the gale was Wilson's earlier plea for "peace without victory."

✦ Wilson's Fourteen Potent Points

Wilson quickly came to be recognized as the moral leader of the Allied cause. He scaled a summit of inspiring oratory on January 8, 1918, when he delivered his famed **Fourteen Points** Address to an enthusiastic Congress. Although one of his primary purposes was to keep reeling Russia in the war, Wilson's vision inspired all the drooping Allies to make mightier efforts and demoralized the enemy governments by holding out alluring promises to their dissatisfied minorities.

The first five of the Fourteen Points were broad in scope. (1) A proposal to abolish secret treaties pleased liberals of all countries. (2) Freedom of the seas appealed to the Germans, as well as to Americans who distrusted British sea power. (3) A removal of economic barriers among nations had long been the goal of liberal internationalists everywhere. (4) A reduction of armament burdens was gratifying to taxpayers in all countries. (5) An adjustment of colonial claims in the interests of both native peoples and the colonizers was reassuring to the anti-imperialists. Indeed Wilson's pronouncement about colonies was potentially revolutionary. It helped to delegitimize the old empires and opened the road to eventual national independence for millions of "subject peoples."

Other points among the fourteen proved to be no less seductive. They held out the hope of independence ("self-determination") to oppressed minority groups, such as the Poles, millions of whom lay under the heel of Germany and Austria-Hungary. The capstone point, number fourteen, foreshadowed the League of Nations—an international organization that Wilson dreamed would provide a system of collective security. Wilson earnestly prayed that this new scheme would effectively guarantee the political independence and territorial integrity of all countries, whether large or small.

Yet Wilson's appealing points, though raising hopes the world over, were not everywhere applauded. Certain leaders of the Allied nations, with an eye to territorial booty, were less than enthusiastic. Hard-nosed Republicans at home grumbled, and some of them openly mocked the "fourteen commandments" of "God Almighty Wilson."

Anti-German Propaganda   The government relied extensively on emotional appeals and hate propaganda to rally support for the First World War, which most Americans regarded as a distant "European" affair. This poster used gendered imagery to evoke the brutal German violation of Belgian neutrality in August 1914.

Library of Congress

✯ Creel Manipulates Minds

Mobilizing people's minds for war, both in America and abroad, was an urgent task facing the Washington authorities. For this purpose the **Committee on Public Information** was created. It was headed by a youngish journalist, George Creel, who, though outspoken and tactless, was gifted with zeal and imagination. His job was to sell America on the war and sell the world on Wilsonian war aims.

The Creel organization, employing some 150,000 workers at home and overseas, proved that words were indeed weapons. It sent out an army of 75,000 "four-minute men"—often longer-winded than that—who delivered countless speeches containing much "patriotic pep."

Creel's propaganda took varied forms. Posters were splashed on billboards in the "Battle of the Fences," as artists "rallied to the colors." Millions of leaflets and pamphlets, which contained the most pungent Wilsonisms, were showered like confetti upon the world. Propaganda booklets with red-white-and-blue covers were printed by the millions.

Hang-the-kaiser movies, carrying such titles as *The Kaiser, the Beast of Berlin* and *To Hell with the Kaiser*, revealed the helmeted "Hun" at his bloodiest. Arm-waving conductors by the thousands led huge audiences in songs that poured scorn on the enemy and glorified the "boys" in uniform.

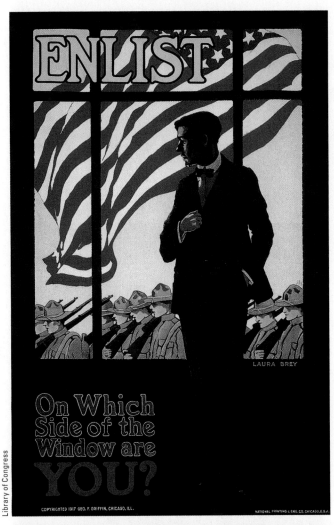

Patriotic Persuasion   Worried about the public's enthusiasm for the war, the government employed all the arts of psychology and propaganda to sustain the martial spirit. The prewar song "I Didn't Raise My Boy to Be a Soldier" was changed to "I Didn't Raise My Boy to Be a Slacker," which in turn inspired the cruel parody "I Didn't Raise My Boy to Be a Sausage."

The entire nation, catching the frenzied spirit of a religious revival, burst into song. This was undoubtedly America's singingest war. Most memorable was George M. Cohan's spine-tingling "Over There":

> *Over there, over there*
> *Send the word, send the word over there,*
> *That the Yanks are coming, the Yanks are coming*
> *The drums rum-tumming ev'rywhere.*

Creel typified American war mobilization, which relied more on aroused passion and voluntary compliance than on formal laws. But he oversold the ideals of Wilson and led the world to expect too much. When the president proved to be a mortal and not a god, the resulting disillusionment both at home and abroad was disastrous.

✴ Enforcing Loyalty and Stifling Dissent

German Americans numbered over 8 million, counting those with at least one parent foreign-born, out of a total population of 100 million. On the whole they proved to be dependably loyal to the United States. Yet rumormongers were quick to spread tales of spying and sabotage; even trifling epidemics of diarrhea were blamed on German agents. A few German Americans were tarred, feathered, and beaten; in one extreme case a German Socialist in Illinois was lynched by a drunken mob.

As emotion mounted, hysterical hatred of Germans and things Germanic swept the nation. Orchestras found it unsafe to present German-composed music, like that of Wagner or Beethoven. German books were removed from library shelves, and German classes were canceled in high schools and colleges. Sauerkraut became "liberty cabbage," hamburger "liberty steak." Even beer became suspect, as patriotic Americans fretted over the loyalty of breweries with names like Schlitz and Pabst.

Both the **Espionage Act** of 1917 and the Sedition Act of 1918 reflected current fears about Germans and antiwar Americans. Especially visible among the nineteen hundred prosecutions pursued under these laws were antiwar Socialists and members of the radical Industrial Workers of the World (IWW). Kingpin Socialist Eugene V. Debs was convicted under the Espionage Act in 1918 and sentenced to ten years in a federal penitentiary. IWW leader William D. ("Big Bill") Haywood and ninety-nine associates were similarly convicted. Virtually any criticism of the government could be censored and punished. Some critics claimed the new laws were bending, if not breaking, the First Amendment. But in *Schenck* v. *United States* (1919), the Supreme Court affirmed their legality, arguing that freedom of speech could be revoked when such speech posed a "clear and present danger" to the nation.

These prosecutions form an ugly chapter in the history of American civil liberty. With the dawn of peace, presidential pardons were rather freely granted, including President Harding's to Eugene Debs in 1921. Yet a few victims lingered behind bars into the 1930s.

✴ The Nation's Factories Go to War

Victory was no foregone conclusion, especially since the Republic, despite ample warning, was caught flat-footedly unready for its leap into global war. The

Socialist Leader Eugene V. Debs Addresses an Antiwar Rally in 1918 For his denunciation of World War I, Debs was convicted under the Espionage Act of 1917 and sent to federal prison. In his courtroom speech defending himself against charges of disloyalty, he passionately declared, "While there is a lower class, I am in it; while there is a criminal element, I am of it; while there is a soul in prison, I am not free." He ran as a presidential candidate in 1920 while still incarcerated in his cell and received nearly a million votes.

pacifistic Wilson had only belatedly backed some mild preparedness measures beginning in 1915, including the creation of a civilian Council of National Defense to study problems of economic mobilization. He had also launched a shipbuilding program (as much to capture the belligerents' war-disrupted foreign trade as to anticipate America's possible entry into the war) and endorsed a modest beefing-up of the army, which with 100,000 regulars then ranked about fifteenth among the armies of the world, in the same category with Persia's. It would take a herculean effort to marshal America's daunting but disorganized resources and throw them into the field quickly enough to bolster the Allied war effort.

Towering obstacles confronted economic mobilizers. Sheer ignorance was among the biggest roadblocks. No one knew precisely how much steel or explosive powder the country was capable of producing. Old ideas also proved to be liabilities, as traditional fears of big government hamstrung efforts to orchestrate the economy from Washington. States' rights Democrats and businesspeople alike balked at federal economic controls, even though the embattled nation could ill afford the freewheeling, hit-or-miss chaos of the peace-time economy.

Late in the war, and after some bruising political battles, Wilson succeeded in imposing some order on this economic confusion. In March 1918 he appointed lone-eagle stock speculator Bernard Baruch to head the **War Industries Board**. Although the War Industries Board had only feeble formal powers, it set a precedent for the federal government to take a central role in economic planning in moments of crisis. It was disbanded just days after the armistice, and Americans returned to their preference for laissez-faire and a weak central government. But in the midst of the Great Depression of the 1930s, policymakers would look back to World War I agencies like this one as models.

✴ Workers in Wartime

Spurred by the slogan "Labor Will Win the War," American workers sweated their way to victory. In part they were driven by the War Department's "work or fight" rule of 1918, which threatened any unemployed male with being immediately drafted—a powerful

Suppressing the Steel Strike: Pittsburgh, 1919 The big steel producers ferociously resisted the unionization of their industry. In Pittsburgh compliant local officials bent to the steel makers' will and issued an order banning all outdoor meetings of strikers. This mounted policeman enforced the order with a flailing billy club. The steelworkers' strike eventually failed, leaving the steel industry un-unionized until the New Deal championed labor's cause in the depression decade of the 1930s.

682

discouragement to go on strike. But for the most part, government tried to treat labor fairly. The **National War Labor Board**, chaired by former president Taft, exerted itself to head off labor disputes that might hamper the war effort. While pressing employers to grant concessions to labor, including high wages and the eight-hour day, the board stopped short of supporting labor's most important demand: a government guarantee of the right to organize into unions.

Fortunately for the Allied cause, Samuel Gompers and his American Federation of Labor (AF of L) loyally supported the war, though some smaller and more radical labor organizations, including the **Industrial Workers of the World**, did not. The IWW, known as the "Wobblies" and sometimes derided as the "I Won't Works," engineered some of the most damaging industrial sabotage, and not without reason. As transient laborers in such industries as fruit and lumber, the Wobblies were victims of some of the shabbiest working conditions in the country. When they protested, many were viciously beaten, arrested, or run out of town.

Mainstream labor's loyalty was rewarded. At war's end, the AF of L had more than doubled its membership, to over 3 million, and in the most heavily unionized sectors—coal mining, manufacturing, and transporta-

tion—real wages (after adjusting for inflation) had risen more than 20 percent over prewar levels. A new day seemed to be dawning for the long-struggling union movement.

Yet labor harbored grievances. Recognition of the right to organize still eluded labor's grasp. Wartime inflation—prices more than doubled between 1914 and 1920—threatened to eclipse wage gains. Not even the call of patriotism and Wilsonian idealism could defuse all labor disputes. Some six thousand strikes, several stained by blood, broke out in the war years. In 1919 the greatest strike in American history rocked the steel industry. More than a quarter of a million steelworkers walked off their jobs in a bid to force their employers to recognize their right to organize and bargain collectively. The steel companies resisted mercilessly. They refused to negotiate with union representatives and brought in thirty thousand African American strikebreakers to keep the mills running. After bitter confrontations that left more than a dozen workers dead, the steel strike collapsed, a grievous setback that crippled the union movement for more than a decade.

The black workers who entered the steel mills in 1919 were but a fraction of the tens of thousands of southern blacks drawn to the North in wartime by the magnet of war-industry employment. These migrants made up the small-scale beginnings of a great northward African American trek that would eventually grow to massive proportions. Their sudden appearance in previously all-white areas sometimes sparked interracial violence. An explosive riot in East St. Louis, Illinois, in July 1917 left nine whites and at least forty blacks dead. An equally gruesome race riot ripped through Chicago. The wartime Windy City was taut with racial tension as a growing black population expanded into white working-class neighborhoods and as African Americans found jobs as strikebreakers in meatpacking plants. Triggered by an incident at a bathing beach in July 1919, a reign of terror descended on the city for nearly two weeks. Black and white gangs roamed Chicago's streets, eventually killing fifteen whites and twenty-three blacks.

✦ Suffering Until Suffrage

Women also heeded the call of patriotism and opportunity. Thousands of female workers flooded into factories and fields, taking up jobs vacated by men who left the assembly line for the frontline. But the war split the women's movement deeply. Many progressive-era feminists were pacifists, inclined to oppose the participation both of America in the war and women in the war effort. This group found a voice in the National Woman's party, led by Quaker activist Alice Paul, which

Chicago History Museum

Chicago Race Riot, 1919 The policeman apparently arrived too late to spare this victim from being pelted by stones from an angry mob.

TABLE 30.1	A Chronology of Women's Right to Vote in National Elections in Selected Nations
1893	New Zealand
1902	Australia (white women only until Aborigines included in 1962)
1906	Finland
1915	Denmark, Iceland
1918	Austria, Canada (women of British and French extraction only until 1950), Germany, Hungary, Poland, Russian Federation, United Kingdom (only women who were married, householders, or university graduates age 30 or over until 1928)
1919	Netherlands, Sweden
1920	United States, Czechoslovakia
1924	Mongolia
1930	South Africa (whites only until 1994), Turkey
1931	Spain (but women lost the vote under the dictator Francisco Franco, 1936–1976)
1934	Brazil, Cuba
1944	France
1945	Italy, Japan
1946	Yugoslavia
1947	Argentina, Mexico, Pakistan
1948	Israel, South Korea
1949	China, Syrian Arab Republic
1950	Haiti, India
1952	Greece, Lebanon
1956	Egypt
1963	Iran
1965	Afghanistan (revoked under Taliban rule, 1996–2001)
1971	Switzerland
1974	Jordan
2005	Kuwait

[Sources: Caroline Daley and Melanie Nolan, eds., *Suffrage and Beyond: International Feminist Perspectives* (1994); http://www.ipu .org/english/issues/wmndocs/suffrage.htm; About.com, Women's History, International Woman Suffrage Timeline, http:// womenshistory.about.com/od/suffrage/a/intl timeline.htm.]

In an open address to Congress in 1917, suffragist Carrie Chapman Catt (1859–1947) capitalized on the idealism of the day and invoked the founding principles of American democracy in arguing the case for women's right to vote:

"How can our nation escape the logic it has never failed to follow, when its last unenfranchised class calls for the vote? Behold our Uncle Sam floating the banner with one hand, 'Taxation without representation is tyranny,' and with the other seizing the billions of dollars paid in taxes by women to whom he refuses 'representation.'. . . Is there a single man who can justify such inequality of treatment, such outrageous discrimination? Not one."

in shaping the peace. The fight for democracy abroad was women's best hope for winning true democracy at home.

War mobilization gave new momentum to the suffrage fight. Impressed by women's war work, President Wilson endorsed woman suffrage as "a vitally necessary war measure." In 1917 New York voted for suffrage at the state level; Michigan, Oklahoma, and South Dakota followed. The next year, governments in Great Britain, Austria, Hungary, and Germany extended the suffrage to women. Not long after, the United States followed suit. In 1920, more than seventy years after the first calls for suffrage at Seneca Falls, the **Nineteenth Amendment** was ratified, giving all American women the right to vote. (See the Appendix and Table 30.1.)

Despite political victory, women's wartime economic gains proved fleeting. Although a permanent Women's Bureau did emerge after the war in the Department of Labor to protect women in the workplace, most women workers soon gave up their war jobs. Meanwhile, Congress affirmed its support for women in their traditional role as mothers when it passed the **Sheppard-Towner Maternity Act** of 1921, providing federally financed instruction in maternal and infant health care. In doing so, it also expanded the responsibility of the federal government for family welfare.

Feminists continued to flex their political muscle in the postwar decade, pressing for more laws to protect women in the workplace and prohibit child labor. Complete success often eluded them in those crusades, but the developments of the World War I era nevertheless foreshadowed a future when women's wage-labor

demonstrated against "Kaiser Wilson" with marches and hunger strikes.

But the larger part of the suffrage movement, represented by the National American Woman Suffrage Association, supported Wilson's war. Leaders echoed Wilson's justification for fighting by arguing that women must take part in the war effort to earn a role

National Archives

Poster Collection, Hoover Institution Archives

In the Trenches and to the Polls Wars often bring opportunities and innovations as well as danger and destruction. As U.S. Army nurses went into harm's way at the fighting front in France, the century-long struggle for women's suffrage intensified on the home front, culminating in the Nineteenth Amendment in 1920.

and political power would reshape the American way of life.

✵ Forging a War Economy

Mobilization relied as much on the heated emotions of patriotism as on the cool majesty of the laws. The largely voluntary character of economic war organization testified to ocean-insulated America's safe distance from the fighting—as well as to the still-modest scale of government powers in the progressive-era Republic. But as the war wore on, government took greater command of the nation's resources to secure an Allied victory.

As the larder of democracy, America had to feed itself and its allies. By a happy inspiration, the man chosen to head the Food Administration was the Quaker-humanitarian Herbert C. Hoover. He was already considered a hero because he had successfully led a massive charitable drive to feed the starving people of war-racked Belgium.

In common with other American war administrators, Hoover preferred to rely on voluntary compliance rather than on compulsory edicts. He deliberately

rejected issuing ration cards, a practice used in Europe. Instead he waged a whirlwind propaganda campaign through posters, billboards, newspapers, pulpits, and movies. To save food for export, Hoover proclaimed wheatless Wednesdays and meatless Tuesdays—all on a voluntary basis. Even children, when eating apples, were urged to be "patriotic to the core."

The country soon broke out in a rash of vegetable "victory gardens," as perspiring patriots hoed their way to victory in backyards and vacant lots. Congress severely restricted the use of foodstuffs for manufacturing alcoholic beverages, and the war-spawned spirit of self-denial helped accelerate the wave of prohibition that was sweeping the country. Many leading brewers were German-descended, and this taint made the drive against alcohol all the more popular. The reformers' dream of a saloonless nation was finally achieved—temporarily—in 1919 with the passage of the Eighteenth Amendment, prohibiting all alcoholic drinks.

Thanks to the fervent patriotic wartime spirit, Hoover's voluntary approach worked. Farm production increased by one-fourth, and food exports to the Allies tripled in volume. Hoover's methods were widely imitated in other war agencies. The Fuel Administration exhorted Americans to save fuel with "heatless Mondays," "lightless nights," and "gasless Sundays." The Treasury Department sponsored huge parades and invoked slogans like "Halt the Hun" to promote four great Liberty Loan drives, followed by a Victory Loan campaign in 1919. Together these efforts netted the then-fantastic sum of about $21 billion, or two-thirds of the current cost of the war to the United States. The remainder was raised by increased taxes, which, unlike the loan subscriptions, were obligatory. (The ultimate bill, including interest and veterans' benefits, mounted to some $112 billion.)

Pressures of various kinds, patriotic and otherwise, were used to sell bonds. The unfortunate German American who could not display a Liberty Bond button might find his or her house bedaubed with yellow paint. A number of reluctant investors in war bonds

were roughly handled. In at least one instance, a man signed for a bond with a rope around his neck.

Despite the Wilson administration's preference for voluntary means of mobilizing the economy, over the course of the war it expanded the federal government in size and power. The War Industries Board issued production quotas, allocated raw materials, and set prices for government purchases. Following indescribable traffic snarls in late 1917, Washington took over the railroads. Time itself came under Uncle Sam's control when the entire country was ordered to observe daylight saving time to extend the workday and save on fuel.

✭ Making Plowboys into Doughboys

Most citizens, at the outset, did not dream of sending a mighty force to France. As far as fighting went, America would use its navy to uphold freedom of the seas. It would continue to ship war materials to the Allies and supply them with loans, which finally totaled nearly $10 billion. But in April and May of 1917, the European associates laid their cards on the table. They confessed that they were scraping the bottom not only of their money chests but, more ominously, of their manpower barrels. A huge American army would have to be raised, trained, and transported, or the whole western front would collapse.

Conscription was the only answer to the need for raising an immense army with all possible speed. Wilson disliked a draft, as did many other Americans with Civil War memories, but he eventually accepted and eloquently supported conscription as a disagreeable and temporary necessity.

The proposed draft bill immediately ran into a barrage of criticism in Congress. A congressman from Missouri, deploring compulsion, cried out in protest that there was "precious little difference between a conscript

THE WOMAN'S LAND ARMY of AMERICA

WOMEN *enlist now and help the* **FARMER** **FIGHT THE FOOD FAMINE**

APPLY: National Office, 19 West 44th Street
New York State Office, 303 Fifth Avenue
OR: Nearest U.S. Employment Bureau office

Library of Congress

Food for Thought Wartime agencies flooded the country with posters like this in 1917–1918, exhorting women on the home front to "grow their own" and thus ease the pressure on food supplies.

Ignoring grisly tales of the agonies of trench warfare, many young American men saw an opportunity for adventure and seized it. Author John Dos Passos (1896–1970) recollected how he felt going off to war in 1917:

❝We had spent our boyhood in the afterglow of the peaceful nineteenth century. . . . What was war like? We wanted to see with our own eyes. We flocked into the volunteer services. I respected the conscientious objectors, and occasionally felt I should take that course myself, but hell, I wanted to see the show.❞

and a convict." Prophets of doom predicted that on draft-registration day, the streets would run red with blood. At length Congress—six weeks after declaring war—grudgingly got around to passing conscription.

The draft act required the registration of all males between the ages of eighteen and forty-five. No "draft dodger" could purchase his exemption or hire a substitute, as in the days of the Civil War, though the law exempted men in key industries, such as shipbuilding.

The draft machinery, on the whole, worked effectively. Registration day proved to be a day of patriotic pilgrimages to flag-draped registration centers, and the sign-up saw no shedding of blood, as some had gloomily predicted. Despite precautions, some 337,000 "slackers" escaped the draft, and about 4,000 conscientious objectors were excused.

Within a few frantic months, the army grew to over 4 million men. For the first time, women were admitted to the armed forces; some 11,000 to the navy and 269 to the marines. African Americans also served in the armed forces, though in strictly segregated units and usually under white officers. Reflecting racial attitudes of the time, military authorities hesitated to train black men for combat, and the majority of black soldiers were assigned to "construction battalions" or put to work unloading ships.

Recruits were supposed to receive six months of training in America and two more months overseas. But so great was the urgency that many doughboys were swept swiftly into battle scarcely knowing how to handle a rifle, much less a bayonet.

✪ Fighting in France—Belatedly

Russia's collapse underscored the need for haste. The communistic Bolsheviks, after seizing power late in 1917, ultimately withdrew their beaten country from the "capitalistic" war early in 1918. This sudden defection released hundreds of thousands of battle-tested Germans from the eastern front facing Russia for the western front in France, where, for the first time in the war, they were developing a dangerous superiority in manpower.

Berlin's calculations as to American tardiness were surprisingly accurate. Germany had counted on knocking out Britain six months after the declaration of unlimited submarine warfare, long before America

Miracles in Shipbuilding

Battling Venereal Disease The American military waged a half-hearted war on rampant venereal disease.

Hulton Archives/Getty Images

Library of Congress

could get into the struggle. No really effective American fighting force reached France until about a year after Congress declared war. Berlin had also reckoned on the inability of the Americans to transport their army, assuming that they were able to raise one. Here again the German predictions were not far from the mark, as shipping shortages plagued the Allies.

Nevertheless, France gradually began to bustle with American doughboys (see Map 30.1). The first trainees to reach the front were used as replacements in the Allied armies and were generally deployed in quiet sectors with the British and French. The newcomers soon made friends with the French girls—or tried to—and one of the most sung-about women in history was the fabled "Mademoiselle from Armentières." One of the printable stanzas ran,

> *She was true to me, she was true to you,*
> *She was true to the whole damn army, too.*

Not surprisingly, American soldiers suffered from high rates of venereal disease, which the army only contributed to by avoiding the subject.

American operations were not confined solely to France; small detachments fought in Belgium, Italy, and notably Russia. The United States, hoping to keep stores of munitions from falling into German hands when Bolshevik Russia quit fighting, contributed some 5,000 troops to an Allied invasion of northern Russia at Archangel. Wilson likewise sent nearly 10,000 troops to Siberia as part of an Allied expedition, which included more than 70,000 Japanese. Major American purposes were to prevent Japan from getting a stranglehold on Siberia, to rescue some 45,000 marooned Czechoslovak troops, and to snatch military supplies from Bolshevik control. Sharp fighting at Archangel and in Siberia involved casualties on both sides, including several hundred Americans. The Bolsheviks long resented these "capitalistic" interventions, which they regarded as high-handed efforts to suffocate their infant communist revolution in its cradle.

✦ America Helps Hammer the "Hun"

The dreaded German drive on the western front exploded in the spring of 1918. Spearheaded by about half a million troops, the enemy rolled forward with terrifying momentum. So dire was the peril that the Allied nations for the first time united under a supreme commander, the quiet French marshal Foch, whose axiom was "To make war is to attack." Until then the Allies had been fighting imperfectly coordinated actions.

At last the ill-trained "Yanks" were coming—and not a moment too soon. Late in May 1918, the German juggernaut, smashing to within forty miles of Paris,

MAP 30.1 Major U.S. Operations in France, 1918 One doughboy recorded in his diary his baptism of fire at St. Mihiel: "Hiked through dark woods. No lights allowed, guided by holding on the pack of the man ahead. Stumbled through underbrush for about half mile into an open field where we waited in soaking rain until about 10:00 P.M. We then started on our hike to the St. Mihiel front, arriving on the crest of a hill at 1:00 A.M. I saw a sight which I shall never forget. It was the zero hour and in one instant the entire front as far as the eye could reach in either direction was a sheet of flame, while the heavy artillery made the earth quake."

© Cengage Learning

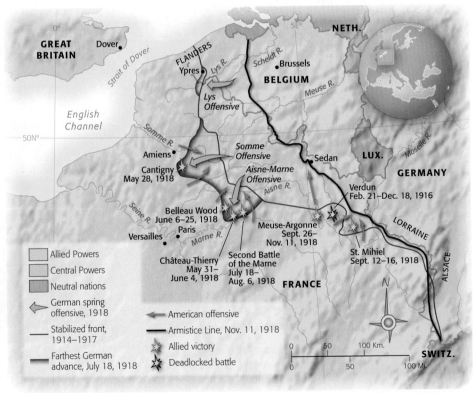

"Mademoiselle from Armentières"

Some familiar songs, such as Julia Ward Howe's stirring Civil War–era melody "Battle Hymn of the Republic," were penned by known composers and have well-established scores and lyrics. But many ballads have no specific author. Songwriters may fit new verses to known tunes, but the songs essentially grow out of the soil of popular culture and take on a life of their own. "Yankee Doodle Dandy," for example, originated during the seventeenth-century English Civil War, was adapted by the American revolutionaries more than a century later, and was parodied by Southerners during the American Civil War:

> Yankee Doodle had a mind
> To whip the Southern "traitors,"
> Because they didn't choose to live
> On codfish and potaters.

"Stagger Lee," or "Stagolee," a blues ballad supposedly based on a murder in Memphis in the 1930s, has been played in countless renditions, with its homicidal subject variously portrayed as a ruthless badman or a civil rights hero.

This process of accretion and adaptation can furnish valuable clues to historians about changing sentiments and sensibilities, just as the ballads themselves give expression to feelings not always evident in the official record. Folklorist Alan Lomax spent a lifetime tracking down American ballads, documenting layers of life and experience not usually excavated by traditional scholars. In the case of the First World War's most notorious song, "Mademoiselle from Armentières" (or "Hinky Dinky, Parley-Voo?"), he compiled from various sources more than six hundred soldier-authored stanzas, some of which are reproduced here (others he delicately described as "not mailable"). What fresh—and irreverent—perspectives do they reveal about the soldier's-eye view of military life?

> Mademoiselle from Armentières,
> She hadn't been kissed in forty years.
>
> She might have been young for all we knew,
> When Napoleon flopped at Waterloo. . . .

> You'll never get your Croix de Guerre,
> If you never wash your underwear. . . .
>
> The French, they are a funny race,
> They fight with their feet and save their face.
>
> The cootie [louse] is the national bug of France.
> The cootie's found all over France,
> No matter where you hang your pants. . . .
>
> Oh, the seventy-seventh went over the top,
> A sous lieutenant, a Jew, and a Wop. . . .
>
> The officers get all the steak,
> And all we get is the belly-ache.
>
> The general got a Croix de Guerre,
> The son-of-a-gun was never there. . . .
>
> There's many and many a married man,
> Wants to go back to France again.
>
> 'Twas a hell of a war as we recall,
> But still 'twas better than none at all.

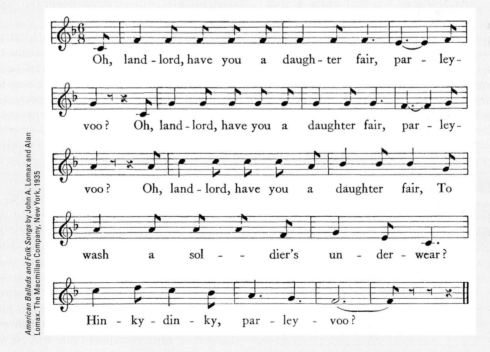

American Ballads and Folk Songs by John A. Lomax and Alan Lomax. The Macmillan Company, New York, 1935

Oh, land-lord, have you a daugh-ter fair, par-ley-voo? Oh, land-lord, have you a daughter fair, par-ley-voo? Oh, land-lord, have you a daughter fair, To wash a sol-dier's un-der-wear? Hin-ky-din-ky, par-ley-voo?

Source: From John A. Lomax and Alan Lomax, *American Ballads and Folksongs*, pp. 558–560. Reprinted by permission of Odyssey Productions, Inc.

Gassed, by John Singer Sargent The noted artist captures the horror of trench warfare in World War I. The enemy was often distant and unseen, and death came impersonally from gas or artillery fire. American troops, entering the line only in the war's final days, were only briefly exposed to this kind of brutal fighting.

threatened to knock out France. Newly arrived American troops, numbering fewer than thirty thousand, were thrown into the breach at **Château-Thierry**, right in the teeth of the German advance. This was a historic moment—the first significant engagement of American troops in a European war. Battle-fatigued French soldiers watched incredulously as the roads filled with endless truckloads of American doughboys, singing New World songs at the top of their voices, a seemingly inexhaustible flood of fresh and gleaming youth. With their arrival it was clear that a new American giant had arisen in the West to replace the dying Russian titan in the East.

American weight in the scales was now being felt on both sides of the conflict (see Figure 30.1). By July 1918 the awesome German drive had spent its force, and keyed-up American men participated in a Foch counteroffensive in the Second Battle of the Marne.

This engagement marked the beginning of a German withdrawal that was never effectively reversed. In September 1918 nine American divisions (about 243,000 men) joined four French divisions to push the Germans from the St. Mihiel salient, a German dagger in France's flank.

The Americans, dissatisfied with merely bolstering the British and French, had meanwhile been demanding a separate army. General John J. ("Black Jack") Pershing was finally assigned a front of eighty-five miles, stretching northwestward from the Swiss border to meet the French lines.

As part of the last mighty Allied assault, involving several million men, Pershing's army undertook the **Meuse-Argonne offensive**, from September 26 to November 11, 1918. One objective was to cut the German railroad lines feeding the western front. This battle, the most gargantuan thus far in American history, lasted forty-seven days and engaged 1.2 million American troops. With especially heavy fighting in the rugged Argonne Forest, the killed and wounded mounted to 120,000, or 10 percent of the Americans involved. The slow progress and severe losses from machine guns resulted in part from inadequate training, in part from dashing open-field tactics, with the bayonet liberally employed. Tennessee-bred Alvin C. York, a member of an antiwar religious sect, became a hero when he single-handedly killed 20 Germans and captured 132 more. Victory was in sight—and fortunately so. The slowly advancing American armies in France were eating up their supplies so rapidly that they were in grave danger of running short. But the battered Germans were ready to stagger out of the trenches and cry *"Kamerad"* (Comrade). Their allies were deserting them, the

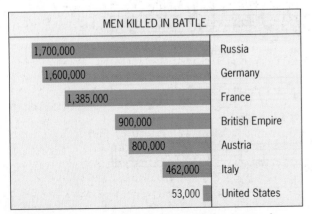

MEN KILLED IN BATTLE	
1,700,000	Russia
1,600,000	Germany
1,385,000	France
900,000	British Empire
800,000	Austria
462,000	Italy
53,000	United States

FIGURE 30.1 Approximate Comparative Losses in World War I

British blockade was causing critical food shortages, and the sledgehammer blows of the Allies pummeled them relentlessly. Propaganda leaflets, containing seductive Wilsonian promises, rained down upon their crumbling lines from balloons, shells, and rockets.

★ The Fourteen Points Disarm Germany

Berlin was now ready to hoist the white flag. Warned of imminent defeat by the generals, it turned to the presumably softhearted Wilson in October 1918, seeking a peace based on the Fourteen Points. In stern responses the president made it clear that the kaiser must be thrown overboard before an armistice could be negotiated. War-weary Germans, whom Wilson had been trying to turn against their "military masters," took the hint. The kaiser was forced to flee to Holland, where he lived out his remaining twenty-three years, "unwept, unhonored, and unhung."

The exhausted Germans were through. They laid down their arms at eleven o'clock on the eleventh day of the eleventh month of 1918, and an eerie, numbing silence fell over the western front. War-taut America burst into a delirium of around-the-clock rejoicing, as the war to end wars had ended. But the costs exceeded comprehension: nearly 9 million soldiers had died, and more than 20 million had suffered grievous wounds. To make matters worse, some 30 million people perished

Theodore Roosevelt (1858–1919) favored the Germans' unconditional surrender. Referring to Wilson's practice of drafting diplomatic notes on his own typewriter, Roosevelt telegraphed several senators (October 24, 1918),

> **❝**Let us dictate peace by the hammering guns and not chat about peace to the accompaniment of clicking typewriters. The language of the fourteen points and the subsequent statements explaining or qualifying them are thoroughly mischievous.**❞**

in a worldwide influenza pandemic in 1918–1919. Over 550,000 Americans—more than ten times the number of U.S. combat casualties—died from the flu.

The United States' main contributions to the ultimate victory had been foodstuffs, munitions, credits, oil for this first mechanized war, and manpower—but

© Bettmann/Corbis

Home from the War, 1919 Most black troops in World War I were denied combat duty and served as laborers and stevedores, but this wounded veteran had seen some tough fighting—though in a segregated unit, the 369th Colored Infantry Regiment, also known as the "Hell-fighters of Harlem." Segregation followed black servicemen even into death. When Congress appropriated money in 1930 to send "Gold Star Mothers" to visit the graves of their slain soldier-sons in France, it provided for separate ships, hotels, and trains for African American women. Several black mothers, preferring "to remain at home and retain our honor and self-respect," reluctantly refused to make the trip.

VELL, IT DIDN'T PAY

NOT THIS TIME

German "Repentance," 1918 A prophetic reflection of the view that the failure to smash Germany completely would lead to another world war. Library of Congress not battlefield victories. The Yanks fought only two major battles, at St. Mihiel and the Meuse-Argonne, both in the last two months of the four-year war, and they were still grinding away in the Meuse-Argonne, well short of their objectives, when the war ended. It was the *prospect* of endless U.S. troop reserves, rather than America's actual military performance, that eventually demoralized the Germans.

Ironically enough, General Pershing in some ways depended more on the Allies than they depended on him. His army purchased more of its supplies in Europe than it shipped from the United States. Fewer than five hundred of Pershing's artillery pieces were of American manufacture. Virtually all of his aircraft were provided by the British and French. Britain and France transported a majority of the doughboys to Europe. The United States, in short, was no arsenal of democracy in this war; that role awaited it in the next global conflict, two decades later.

✵ Wilson Steps Down from Olympus

Woodrow Wilson had helped to win the war. What part would he now play in shaping the peace? Expectations ran extravagantly high. As the fighting in Europe crashed to a close, the American president towered at the peak of his popularity and power. In lonely huts in the mountains of Italy, candles burned before poster-portraits of the revered American prophet. In Poland starry-eyed university students would meet in the streets, clasp hands, and utter only one word: "Wilson." No other man had ever occupied so dizzy a pinnacle as moral leader of the world. Wilson also had behind him the prestige of victory and the economic resources of the mightiest nation on earth. But at this fateful moment, his sureness of touch deserted him, and he began to make a series of tragic fumbles.

Under the slogan "Politics Is Adjourned," partisan political strife had been kept below the surface during the war crisis. Hoping to strengthen his hand at the Paris peace table, Wilson broke the truce by personally appealing for a Democratic victory in the congressional elections of November 1918. But the maneuver backfired when voters instead returned a narrow Republican majority to Congress. Having staked his reputation on the outcome, Wilson went to Paris as a diminished leader. Unlike all the parliamentary statesmen at the table, he did not command a legislative majority at home.

Wilson's decision to go in person to Paris to help make the peace infuriated Republicans. At that time no president had traveled to Europe, and Wilson's journey looked to his critics like flamboyant grandstanding. He further ruffled Republican feathers when he snubbed the Senate in assembling his peace delegation and neglected to include a single Republican senator in his official party. The logical choice was the new chairman of the Senate Committee on Foreign Relations, slender and aristocratically bewhiskered Henry Cabot Lodge of Massachusetts, a Harvard Ph.D. But including Lodge would have been problematic for the president. The senator's mind, quipped one critic, was like the soil of his native New England: "naturally barren but highly cultivated." Wilson loathed him, and the feeling was hotly reciprocated. An accomplished author, Lodge had been known as the "scholar in politics" until Wilson came on the scene. The two men were at daggers drawn, personally and politically.

✵ An Idealist Amid the Imperialists

Woodrow Wilson, the great prophet arisen in the West, received tumultuous welcomes from the masses of France, England, and Italy late in 1918 and early in 1919. They saw in his idealism the promise of a better world. But the statesmen of France and Italy were careful to keep the new messiah at arm's length from worshipful crowds. He might so arouse the people as to prompt them to overthrow their leaders and upset finespun imperialistic plans.

The Paris Conference of great and small nations fell into the hands of an inner clique, known as the Big Four. Wilson, representing the richest and freshest great power, more or less occupied the driver's seat. He was joined by genial Premier Vittorio Orlando of Italy and brilliant Prime Minister David Lloyd George of Britain. Perhaps the most realistic of the quartet was cynical, hard-bitten Premier Georges Clemenceau of France, the seventy-eight-year-old "organizer of victory" known as "the Tiger."

Speed was urgent when the conference opened on January 18, 1919. Europe seemed to be slipping into anarchy; the red tide of communism was licking westward from Bolshevist Russia.

The English science fiction writer H. G. Wells (1866–1946), soon a strong proponent of the League of Nations, spoke for many Europeans when he praised Woodrow Wilson in 1917:

❝In all the world there is no outstanding figure to which the world will listen, there is no man audible in all the world, in Japan as well as Germany and Rome as well as Boston—except the President of the United States.**❞**

National Archives

Wilson in Dover, England, 1919 Hailed by many Europeans in early 1919 as the savior of the Western world, Wilson was a fallen idol only a few months later, when Americans repudiated the peace treaty he had helped to craft.

Wilson's ultimate goal was a world parliament to be known as the **League of Nations**, but he first bent his energies to preventing any vengeful parceling out of the former colonies and protectorates of the vanquished powers. (He was less attentive to the fate of colonies belonging to the victorious French and English.) Wilson tried to force through a compromise between naked imperialism and Wilsonian idealism. The victors would not take possession of the conquered territory outright, but would receive it as trustees of the League of Nations. Strategic Syria, for example, was awarded to France, and oil-rich Iraq went to Britain. In practice this half-loaf solution was little more than the old prewar colonialism, thinly disguised, although in the decades to come, anticolonial independence movements would wield the Wilsonian ideal of self-determination against their imperial occupiers.

Meanwhile, Wilson had been serving as midwife for the League of Nations, which he envisioned as containing an assembly with seats for all nations and a council to be controlled by the great powers. He gained a signal victory over the skeptical Old World diplomats in February 1919, when they agreed to make the League Covenant, Wilson's brainchild, an integral part of the final peace treaty. At one point he spoke with such ardor for his plan that even the hard-boiled newspaper reporters forgot to take notes.

✦ Hammering Out the Treaty

Domestic duties now required Wilson to make a quick trip to America, where ugly storms were brewing in the Senate. Certain Republican senators, Lodge in the lead, were sharpening their knives for Wilson. To them the League was either a useless "sewing circle" or an overpotent "super-state." Their hard core was composed of a dozen or so militant isolationists, led by Senators

William Borah of Idaho and Hiram Johnson of California, who were known as **irreconcilables** or "the Battalion of Death."

Thirty-nine Republican senators or senators-elect—enough to defeat the treaty—proclaimed that the Senate would not approve the League of Nations in its existing imperfect form. These difficulties delighted

Granger Collection

Pilgrim Landing in America, 1919

693

Wilson's Allied adversaries in Paris. They were now in a stronger bargaining position because Wilson would have to beg them for changes in the covenant that would safeguard the Monroe Doctrine and other American interests dear to the senators.

As soon as Wilson was back in Paris, the hardheaded Clemenceau pressed French demands for the German-inhabited Rhineland and the Saar Valley, a rich coal area. Faced with fierce Wilsonian opposition to this violation of self-determination, France settled for a compromise whereby the Saar basin would remain under the League of Nations for fifteen years, and then a popular vote would determine its fate.* In exchange for dropping its demands for the Rhineland, France got the Security Treaty, in which both Britain and America pledged to come to its aid in the event of another German invasion. The French later felt betrayed when this pact was quickly pigeonholed by the U.S. Senate, which shied away from all entangling alliances.

Wilson's next battle was with Italy over Fiume, a valuable seaport inhabited by both Italians and Yugoslavs. When Italy demanded Fiume, Wilson insisted that the seaport go to Yugoslavia and appealed over the heads of Italy's leaders to the country's masses. The maneuver fell flat. The Italian delegates went home in a huff, while the Italian masses turned savagely against Wilson.

Another crucial struggle was with Japan over China's Shandong (Shantung) Peninsula and the German islands in the Pacific, which the Japanese had seized during the war. Japan was conceded the strategic Pacific islands under a League of Nations mandate,† but Wilson staunchly opposed Japanese control of Shandong as a violation of self-determination for its 30 million Chinese residents. But when the Japanese threatened to walk out, Wilson reluctantly accepted a compromise whereby Japan kept Germany's economic holdings in Shandong and pledged to return the peninsula to China at a later date. The Chinese were outraged by this imperialistic solution, while Clemenceau jeered that Wilson "talked like Jesus Christ and acted like Lloyd George."

✦ The Peace Treaty That Bred a New War

A completed **Treaty of Versailles**, after more weeks of wrangling, was handed to the Germans in June 1919—almost literally on the point of a bayonet. Excluded from the settlement negotiations at Paris, Germany had

capitulated in the hope that it would be granted a peace based on the Fourteen Points. A careful analysis of the treaty shows that only about four of the twenty-three original Wilsonian points and subsequent principles were fully honored. Vengeance, not reconciliation, was the treaty's dominant tone. Loud and bitter cries of betrayal burst from German throats—charges that Adolf Hitler would soon reiterate during his meteoric rise to power.

Wilson, of course, was guilty of no conscious betrayal. But the Allied powers were torn by conflicting aims, many of them sanctioned by secret treaties. There had to be compromise at Paris, or there would be no agreement. Faced with hard realities, Wilson was forced to compromise away some of his less cherished Fourteen Points in order to salvage the more precious League of Nations. He was much like the mother who had to throw her sickly younger children to the pursuing wolves to save her sturdy firstborn.

A troubled Wilson was not happy with the results. Greeted a few months earlier with frenzied acclaim in Europe, he was now a fallen idol, condemned alike by disillusioned liberals and frustrated imperialists. He was keenly aware of some of the injustices that had been forced into the treaty. But he was hoping that the League of Nations—a potent League with America as a leader—would iron out the inequities.

Yet the loudly condemned treaty had much to commend it. Not least among its merits was its liberation of millions of minority peoples, such as the Poles, from the yoke of imperial dynasties. Wilson's disappointments and his critics to the contrary, the settlement was almost certainly a fairer one because he had gone to Paris.

✦ The Domestic Parade of Prejudice

Returning for the second and final time to America, Wilson sailed straight into a political typhoon. Isolationists raised a whirlwind of protest against the treaty, especially against Wilson's commitment to usher the United States into his newfangled League of Nations. Invoking the revered advice of Washington and Jefferson, they wanted no part of any "entangling alliance."

Nor were the isolationists Wilson's only problem. Critics showered the Treaty of Versailles with abuse from all sides.

Rabid Hun-haters, regarding the pact as not harsh enough, voiced their discontent. Principled liberals, like the editors of the New York *Nation*, thought it too harsh—and a gross betrayal to boot. German Americans, Italian Americans, and others whom Wilson termed "hyphenated Americans" were aroused because the peace settlement was not sufficiently favorable to their native lands.

---

*The Saar population voted overwhelmingly to rejoin Germany in 1935.
†In due time the Japanese illegally fortified these islands—the Marshalls, Marianas, and Carolines—and used them as bases against the United States in World War II.

Contentious Nuptials Woodrow Wilson's visionary effort to end more than a century of American aloofness from world affairs met vigorous opposition from traditional isolationists, especially in the U.S. Senate. Senators eventually refused to ratify the Versailles Treaty, shattering Wilson's dream of making the United States a more engaged international actor.

Irish Americans, traditional twisters of the British lion's tail, also denounced the League. They felt that with the additional votes of the five overseas British dominions, it gave Britain undue influence, and they feared that it could be used to force the United States to crush any rising for Irish independence. Crowds of Irish American zealots hissed and booed Wilson's name.

⭐ Wilson's Tour and Collapse (1919)

Despite mounting discontent, the president had reason to feel optimistic. When he brought home the treaty, with the "Wilson League" firmly riveted in as Part I, a strong majority of the people still seemed favorable. At this time—early July 1919—Senator Lodge had no real hope of defeating the Treaty of Versailles. His strategy was merely to amend it in such a way as to "Americanize," "Republicanize," or "senatorialize" it. The Republicans could then claim political credit for the changes.

Lodge effectively used delay to muddle and divide public opinion. He read the entire 264-page treaty aloud in the Senate Foreign Relations Committee and held protracted hearings in which people of various nationalities aired their grievances.

Wilson fretted increasingly as the hot summer of 1919 wore on. The bulky pact was bogged down in the Senate, while the nation was drifting into confusion and apathy. He therefore decided to take his case to the country in a spectacular speechmaking tour. He would appeal over the heads of the Senate to the sovereign people—as he often had in the past.

The strenuous barnstorming campaign was undertaken in the face of protests by physicians and friends. Wilson had never been robust; he had entered the White House nearly seven years before with a stomach pump and with headache pills for his neuritis. His frail body had begun to sag under the strain of partisan strife, a global war, and a stressful peace conference. But he declared that he was willing to die, like the soldiers he had sent into battle, for the sake of the new world order.

The presidential tour, begun in September 1919, got off to a rather lame start. The Midwest received Wilson lukewarmly, partly because of strong German American influence. Trailing after him like bloodhounds came two "irreconcilable" senators, Borah and Johnson, who spoke in the same cities a few days later. Hat-tossing crowds answered their attacks on Wilson, crying, "Impeach him, impeach him!"

But the reception was different in the Rocky Mountain region and on the Pacific Coast. These areas, which had elected Wilson in 1916, welcomed him with heartwarming outbursts. The high point—and the breaking point—of the return trip was at Pueblo, Colorado, September 25, 1919. Wilson, with tears coursing down his cheeks, pleaded for the League of Nations as the only real hope of preventing future wars. That night he collapsed from physical and nervous exhaustion.

Wilson was whisked back in the "funeral train" to Washington, where several days later a stroke paralyzed one side of his body. During the next few weeks, he lay in a darkened room in the White House, as much a victim of the war as the unknown soldier buried at Arlington. For more than seven months, he did not meet with his cabinet.

⭐ Defeat Through Deadlock

Senator Lodge, coldly calculating, was now at the helm. After failing to amend the treaty outright, he finally came up with fourteen formal reservations to it—a sardonic slap at Wilson's Fourteen Points. These safeguards reserved the rights of the United States under the Monroe Doctrine and the Constitution and otherwise sought to protect American sovereignty. Senator Lodge and other critics were especially alarmed by Article X of the League because it *morally* bound the

United States to aid any member victimized by external aggression. A jealous Congress wanted to reserve for itself the constitutional war-declaring power.

Wilson, hating Lodge, saw red at the mere suggestion of the Lodge reservations. He was quite willing to accept somewhat similar reservations sponsored by his faithful Democratic followers, but he insisted that the Lodge reservations "emasculated" the entire pact.

Although too feeble to lead, Wilson was still strong enough to obstruct. When the day finally came for the voting in the Senate, he sent word to all true Democrats to vote *against* the treaty with the odious Lodge reservations attached. Wilson hoped that when these were cleared away, the path would be open for ratification without reservations or with only some mild Democratic ones.

Loyal Democrats in the Senate, on November 19, 1919, blindly did Wilson's bidding. Combining with the "irreconcilables," mostly Republicans, they rejected the treaty with the Lodge reservations appended, 55 to 39.

The nation was too deeply shocked to accept the verdict as final. About four-fifths of the senators professed to favor the treaty, with or without reservations, yet a simple majority could not agree on a single proposition. So strong was public indignation that the Senate was forced to act a second time. In March 1920 the treaty was brought up again, with the Lodge reservations tacked on.

There was only one possible path to success. Unless the Senate approved the pact with the reservations, the entire document would be rejected. But the sickly Wilson, still sheltered behind drawn curtains and blind to disagreeable realities, again sent word to all loyal Democrats to vote down the treaty with the obnoxious reservations. He thus signed the death warrant of the treaty as far as America was concerned. On March 19, 1920, the treaty netted a simple majority but failed to get the necessary two-thirds majority by a count of 49 yeas to 35 nays.

Who defeated the treaty? The Lodge-Wilson personal feud, traditionalism, isolationism, disillusionment, and partisanship all contributed to the confused picture. But Wilson himself must bear a substantial share of the responsibility. He asked for all or nothing—and got nothing. One Democratic senator angrily charged that the president had strangled his own brainchild with his own palsied hands rather than let the Senate straighten its crooked limbs.

✹ The "Solemn Referendum" of 1920

Wilson had his own pet solution for the deadlock, and this partly explains why he refused to compromise on Lodge's terms. He proposed to settle the treaty issue in the forthcoming presidential campaign of 1920 by appealing to the people for a "solemn referendum." This was sheer folly, for a true mandate on the League in the noisy arena of politics was clearly an impossibility.

Jubilant Republicans gathered in Chicago in June 1920 with wayward bull moosers back in the corral (after Theodore Roosevelt's death in 1919) and the senatorial Old Guard back in the saddle. The convention devised a masterfully ambiguous platform that could appeal to both pro-League and anti-League sentiment in the party. The nominee would run on a teeter-totter rather than a platform.

As the leading presidential contestants jousted with one another, the political weathervane began to veer toward genial Senator Warren G. Harding of Ohio. A group of Senate bosses, meeting rather casually in the historic "smoke-filled" Room 404 of the Hotel Blackstone, informally decided on the affable and malleable Ohioan. Their fair-haired boy was a prosperous, back-slapping, small-town newspaper editor of the "folksy" type, quite the opposite of Wilson, who had earlier noted the senator's "disturbingly dull" mind. For vice president the party nominated frugal, grim-faced Governor Calvin ("Silent Cal") Coolidge of Massachusetts, who had attracted conservative support by breaking a police strike in Boston.

Meeting in San Francisco, Democrats nominated earnest Governor James M. Cox of Ohio, who strongly supported the League. His running mate was Assistant Navy Secretary Franklin D. Roosevelt, a young, handsome, vibrant New Yorker.

Democratic attempts to make the campaign a referendum on the League were thwarted by Senator Harding, who issued muddled and contradictory statements on the issue from his front porch. Pro-League and anti-League Republicans both claimed that Harding's election would advance their cause, while the candidate suggested that if elected he would work for a vague Association of Nations—*a* league but not *the* League.

With newly enfranchised women swelling the vote totals, Harding was swept into power with a prodigious plurality of over 7 million votes—16,143,407 to 9,130,328 for Cox, the largest victory margin to that date in a presidential election. The electoral count was 404 to 127. Eugene V. Debs, federal prisoner number 9653 at the Atlanta Penitentiary, rolled up the largest vote ever for the left-wing Socialist party—919,799.

Public desire for a change found vent in a resounding repudiation of "high-and-mighty" Wilsonism. People were tired of professional highbrowism, star-reaching idealism, bothersome do-goodism, moral overstrain, and constant self-sacrifice. Eager to lapse back into "normalcy," they were willing to accept a second-rate president—and they got a third-rate one.

Although the election could not be considered a true referendum, Republican isolationists successfully turned Harding's victory into a death sentence for the

League. Politicians increasingly shunned the League as they would a leper. When the legendary Wilson died in 1924, admirers knelt in the snow outside his Washington home. His "great vision" of a league for peace had perished long before.

✦ The Betrayal of Great Expectations

America's spurning of the League was tragically short-sighted. The Republic had helped to win a costly war, but it foolishly kicked the fruits of victory under the table. Whether a strong international organization would have averted World War II in 1939 will always be a matter of dispute. But there can be no doubt that the orphaned League of Nations was undercut at the start by the refusal of the mightiest power on the globe to join it. The Allies themselves were largely to blame for the new world conflagration that flared up in 1939, but they found a convenient justification for their own short-comings by pointing an accusing finger at Uncle Sam.

The ultimate collapse of the Treaty of Versailles must be laid, at least in some degree, at America's door-step. This complicated pact, tied in with the four other peace treaties through the League Covenant, was a top-heavy structure designed to rest on a four-legged table.

The fourth leg, the United States, was never put into place. This rickety structure teetered for over a decade and then crashed in ruins—a debacle that played into the hands of the German demagogue Adolf Hitler.

No less ominous events were set in motion when the Senate spurned the Security Treaty with France. The French, fearing that a new generation of Germans would follow in their fathers' goose steps, undertook to build up a powerful military force. Predictably resenting the presence of strong French armies, Germany began to rearm illegally. The seething cauldron of uncertainty and suspicion brewed an intoxicant that helped inflame the fanatical following of Hitler.

The United States, as the tragic sequel proved, hurt its own cause when it buried its head in the sand. Granted that the conduct of its Allies had been disillusioning, it had its own ends to serve by carrying through the Wilsonian program. It would have been well advised if it had forthrightly assumed its war-born responsibilities and had resolutely embraced the role of global leader proffered by the hand of destiny. In the interests of its own security, if for no other reason, the United States should have used its enormous strength to shape world-shaking events. Instead it permitted itself blithely to drift toward the abyss of a second and even more bloody international disaster.

Varying Viewpoints
Woodrow Wilson: Realist or Idealist?

*A*s the first president to take the United States into a foreign war, Woodrow Wilson was obliged to make a systematic case to the American people to justify his unprecedented European intervention. His ideas have largely defined the character of American foreign policy ever since—for better or worse.

"Wilsonianism" comprised three closely related principles: (1) the era of American isolation from world affairs had irretrievably ended; (2) the United States must infuse its own founding political and economic ideas—including democracy, the rule of law, free trade, and national self-determination (or anticolonialism)—into the international order; and (3) American influence could eventually steer the world away from rivalry and warfare and toward a cooperative and peaceful international system, maintained by the League of Nations or, later, the United Nations.

Whether that Wilsonian vision constituted hard-nosed realism or starry-eyed idealism has excited scholarly debate for nearly a century. "Realists," such as George F. Kennan and Henry Kissinger, insist that Wilson was anything but a realist. They criticize the president as a naive, impractical dreamer who failed to understand that the international order was, and

always will be, an anarchic, unruly arena, outside the rule of law, where only military force can effectively protect the nation's security. In a sharp critique in his 1950 study, *American Diplomacy*, Kennan condemned Wilson's vision as "moralism-legalism." In this view Wilson dangerously threatened to sacrifice American self-interests on the altar of his admirable but ultimately unworkable ideas.

Wilson's defenders, including his biographers Arthur S. Link and Thomas J. Knock, argue that Wilson's idealism was in fact a kind of higher realism, recognizing as it did that armed conflict on the scale of World War I could never again be tolerated and that some framework of peaceful international relations simply had to be found. The development of nuclear weapons in a later generation gave this argument more force. This "liberal" defense of Wilsonianism derives from the centuries-old liberal faith that, given sufficient intelligence and will-power, the world can be made a better place. Realists reject this notion of moral and political progress as hopelessly innocent, especially as applied to international affairs.

Some leftist scholars, such as William Appleman Williams, have argued that Wilson was in fact a realist of another kind: a subtle and wily imperialist whose stirring rhetoric cloaked a grasping ambition to make the United States the world's dominant economic power. Sometimes called "the imperialism of free trade," this strategy allegedly sought not to decolonialize the world and open up international commerce for the good of peoples elsewhere, but to create a system in which American economic might would irresistibly prevail. Wilson's defenders, however, would claim that in a Wilsonian world, *all* parties would be better off because of free trade and international competition.

Still other scholars, especially John Milton Cooper, Jr., have emphasized the absence of economic factors in shaping Wilson's diplomacy. Isolationism, so this argument goes, held such sway over American thinking precisely because the United States had such a puny financial stake abroad—no hard American economic interests were mortally threatened in 1917, nor for a long time thereafter. In these circumstances

Wilson—and the Wilsonians who came after him, such as Franklin D. Roosevelt—had no choice but to appeal to abstract ideals and high principles. The "idealistic" Wilsonian strain in American diplomacy, in this view, may have been an unavoidable heritage of America's historically isolated situation. If so, it was Wilson's genius to make practical use of those ideas in his bid for popular support of his diplomacy.

Finally, a new generation of scholars has begun to explore the influence of Wilsonian ideals on social movements outside the United States and Europe. Erez Manela has argued that emerging anticolonial and nationalist movements appropriated Wilsonian ideals and adapted them to their own political ends, challenging forms of colonialism that Wilson himself failed to criticize. In this view the legacy of Wilsonian foreign policy may have been felt most strongly outside the United States.

Chapter Review

KEY TERMS

Zimmermann note (678)

Fourteen Points (680)

Committee on Public Information (680)

Espionage Act (681)

Schenck v. *United States* (681)

War Industries Board (682)

National War Labor Board (682)

Industrial Workers of the World (683)

Nineteenth Amendment (684)

Sheppard-Towner Maternity Act (684)

Château-Thierry, Battle of (690)

Meuse-Argonne offensive (690)

League of Nations (693)

irreconcilables (693)

Versailles, Treaty of (694)

PEOPLE TO KNOW

Arthur Zimmermann

George Creel

Eugene V. Debs

William D. ("Big Bill") Haywood

Bernard Baruch

Herbert C. Hoover

Henry Cabot Lodge

David Lloyd George

TO LEARN MORE

Christopher Capozzola, *Uncle Sam Wants You: World War I and the Making of the Modern American Citizen* (2008)

John W. Chambers, *To Raise an Army: The Draft Comes to Modern America* (1987)

Alan Dawley, *Changing the World: American Progressives in War and Revolution* (2003)

Ernest Freeberg, *Democracy's Prisoners: Eugene V. Debs, the Great War, and the Right to Dissent* (2008)

Paul Fussell, *The Great War and Modern Memory* (1975)

Maurine W. Greenwald, *Women, War, and Work* (1980)

Ellis Hawley, *The Great War and the Search for Modern Order* (rev. ed., 1997)

Jennifer Keene, *Doughboys, the Great War, and the Remaking of America* (2001)

David M. Kennedy, *Over Here: The First World War and American Society* (rev. ed., 2005)

Thomas J. Knock, *To End All Wars: Woodrow Wilson and the Quest for a New World Order* (1992)

Erez Manela, *The Wilsonian Moment: Self-Determination and the International Origins of Anticolonial Nationalism* (2007)

Paul L. Murphy, *World War I and the Origin of Civil Liberties in the United States* (1979)

A complete, annotated bibliography for this chapter—along with brief descriptions of the People to Know—may be found on the American Pageant website. The Key Terms are defined in a Glossary at the end of the text.

CHRONOLOGY

1915	Council of National Defense established
1917	Germany resumes unrestricted submarine warfare
	Zimmermann note
	Railroads placed under federal control
	United States enters World War I
	Espionage Act of 1917
	Wilson calls for "peace without victory"
	Bolshevik Revolution
1918	Wilson proposes Fourteen Points
	Sedition Act of 1918
	Battle of Château-Thierry
	Second Battle of the Marne
	Meuse-Argonne offensive

1918–1919	Armistice ends World War I
	Worldwide influenza pandemic
1919	Paris Peace Conference and Treaty of Versailles
	Wilson's pro-League tour and collapse
	Eighteenth Amendment (prohibition of alcohol) passed
	First Senate defeat of Versailles Treaty
1920	Final Senate defeat of Versailles Treaty after reconsideration
	Nineteenth Amendment (woman suffrage) passed
	Harding defeats Cox for presidency

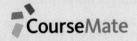 **CourseMate**

Go to the CourseMate website at **www.cengagebrain.com** for additional study tools and review materials—including audio and video clips—for this chapter.

AP® Review Questions for Chapter 30

1. All of the following were factors contributing to the entrance of the United States into World War I in 1917 EXCEPT
   (A) the interception and publication of the Zimmerman note.
   (B) the resumption of unrestricted submarine warfare by Germany against all American vessels in the Atlantic war zone.
   (C) President Wilson's moralistic and idealistic approach to America's role in shaping a democratic world order.
   (D) the revolutionary overthrow of the tsarist regime in Russia, which allowed America to fully champion democracy with its support of the Allies.
   (E) the clamoring for war from munitions makers, bankers, and Wall Street financiers seeking to protect their loans and profits.

2. Which of the following did NOT represent one of Wilson's Fourteen Points upon which he based America's foreign policy in World War I?
   (A) Reduction of armaments
   (B) An international guarantee of freedom of religion
   (C) An abolition of secret treaties
   (D) A new international organization to guarantee collective security
   (E) The principle of national self-determination for subject peoples

3. Which of the following best characterizes the U.S. government's approach to civil liberties during World War I?
   (A) Threatened by President Wilson but protected by the courts
   (B) Limited civil liberties offered by the U.S. government, but no one imprisoned for his or her ideological convictions
   (C) Protected for everyone except German-Americans
   (D) Violated mostly in the western United States
   (E) Severely damaged by the political pressures of loyalty and conformity

4. Which of the following best describes America's preparedness for entry into World War I?
   (A) Well prepared militarily and industrially thanks to the foresight of Woodrow Wilson
   (B) Well prepared militarily but not industrially
   (C) Well prepared industrially but not militarily
   (D) Well prepared for land combat but not for naval warfare
   (E) Poorly prepared militarily and industrially to leap into a global war

5. Which of the following provided the critical political momentum for women achieving the constitutional right to vote in the United States?
   (A) The labor contributions and political support of working women for the war effort
   (B) The marches and hunger strike of the National Women's Party
   (C) The peace movement led by progressive-era feminists
   (D) Political support from allied African Americans
   (E) The joint support of organized labor and big business for women's suffrage

6. Organized labor held all of the following grievances during and shortly after World War I EXCEPT
   (A) the inability to gain the legal right to organize and collectively bargain with employers.
   (B) war-spawned inflation.
   (C) suppression of the American Federation of Labor.
   (D) violence against workers by employers.
   (E) the use of African Americans as strikebreakers.

7. Which of the following resulted from the movement of tens of thousands of southern African Americans to the North during World War I?
   (A) Improved race relations in the South
   (B) An outbreak of racial violence in the North
   (C) Fewer blacks willing to be used as strikebreakers
   (D) The development of a new black middle class
   (E) A new congressional push for federal civil rights legislation protecting African Americans seeking employment and fair housing

8. The United States used all of the following methods to support the war effort EXCEPT
   (A) placing significant public pressure on some people to buy war bonds.
   (B) having heatless Mondays to conserve fuel.
   (C) establishing widespread government control of wages and prices.
   (D) instituting Daylight Savings Time to extend the work day.
   (E) government assumption of management and operation of the railroads.

9. Which of the following was NOT true of the U.S. armed forces during World War I?
   (A) An expansive conscription law, passed in 1917, allowed the U.S. Army to grow to over 4 million men.
   (B) For the first time in U.S. history, women were admitted to and served with distinction in the armed forces of the United States.
   (C) All conscientious objectors were required to serve in the U.S. armed forces.
   (D) African Americans served in strictly segregated units under mainly white officers.
   (E) The urgent need for manpower meant that many young American recruits received insufficient and inadequate training before being thrust into battle.

10. Why did the Germans gain an immense military advantage during the first months of fighting in 1918?
    (A) The Germans had discovered how to use tanks and poison gas effectively.
    (B) The Austrian army was able to switch from the Italian front to the western front.
    (C) The Bolsheviks took Russia out of the war, allowing German troops to go to the western front.
    (D) The Germans had seized the two strategic points of Verdun and Ypres.
    (E) The brilliant German generals Hindenburg and Ludendorff had taken effective control of the German government.

11. The main contributions to the Allied victory in World War I included all of the following EXCEPT
    (A) battlefield victories.
    (B) foodstuffs.
    (C) oil.
    (D) munitions.
    (E) financial credit.

12. At the Paris Peace Conference, President Wilson sought all of the following EXCEPT
    (A) preventing a seizure of territory by the victors.
    (B) an immediate end to the European colonial empires in Africa and Asia.
    (C) a world parliament of nations to provide collective security.
    (D) national self-determination for smaller European nations.
    (E) free trade and freedom of the seas.

13. What was the primary argument of Senate opponents such as Senator Henry Cabot Lodge against the League of Nations as proposed in the Treaty of Versailles?
    (A) The League of Nations failed to provide enough German financial reparations to the United States.
    (B) The League of Nations violated Wilson's own Fourteen Points.
    (C) The League of Nations stripped Congress of its constitutional war-declaring powers.
    (D) The League of Nations would not provide political sovereignty to oppressed colonial peoples.
    (E) The League of Nations would isolate the United States from postwar world affairs.

14. What political goal were Republican isolationists able to achieve with the election in 1920 of Warren Harding?
    (A) A political mandate for international arms reduction
    (B) A guarantee of U.S. military withdrawal from Latin America
    (C) A crusade against Bolshevik communism
    (D) A victory for U.S. intervention on behalf of oppressed colonial peoples
    (E) The death sentence for the League of Nations

15. Which traditionally American ideal did Wilson rely upon when he decided to tour the country to garner support for the League of Nations?
    (A) Wilson believed in direct democracy and thought the people should vote on whether or not to ratify the treaty.
    (B) Members of Congress are meant to represent the people; if Wilson could convince the people, Congress would have to follow.
    (C) The American people expect their representatives to come directly to them to explain their actions.
    (D) Wilson supported the progressive idea that the people should be more involved in state and local government matters.
    (E) Wilson thought he owed the people an explanation for taking away Congress's power to declare war.

16. Americans rallied to support a previously divisive war in all of the following ways EXCEPT that
    (A) the Industrial Workers of the World supported the war.
    (B) people responded to Hoover's requests without rationing.
    (C) Americans invested $21 billion in the war effort.
    (D) people across the nation sang their support for the war.
    (E) eligible men recognized their patriotic duty to register for the draft.

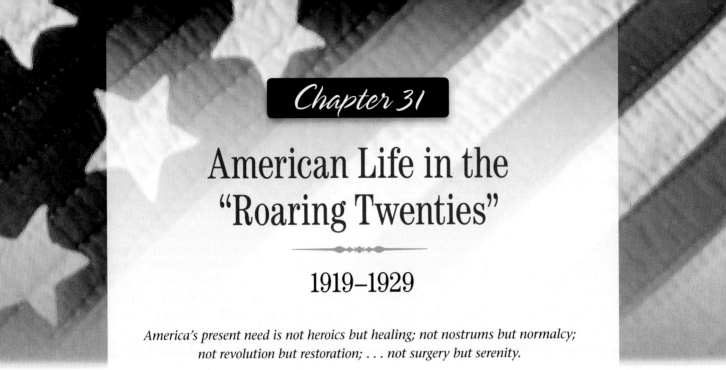

Chapter 31

American Life in the "Roaring Twenties"

1919–1929

America's present need is not heroics but healing; not nostrums but normalcy; not revolution but restoration; . . . not surgery but serenity.

WARREN G. HARDING, 1920

*B**loodied by the war* and disillusioned by the peace, Americans turned inward in the 1920s. Shunning diplomatic commitments to foreign countries, they also denounced "radical" foreign ideas, condemned "un-American" lifestyles, and clanged shut the immigration gates against foreign peoples. They partly sealed off the domestic economy from the rest of the world and plunged headlong into a dizzying decade of homegrown prosperity.

The boom of the golden twenties showered genuine benefits on Americans, as incomes and living standards rose for many. But there seemed to be something incredible about it all, even as people sang,

My sister she works in the laundry,
My father sells bootlegger gin,
My mother she takes in the washing,
My God! how the money rolls in!

New technologies, new consumer products, and new forms of leisure and entertainment made the twenties roar. Yet just beneath the surface lurked widespread anxieties about the future and fears that America was losing sight of its traditional ways.

✦ Seeing Red

Hysterical fears of red Russia continued to color American thinking for several years after the Communists came to power in the **Bolshevik Revolution** of 1917, which spawned a tiny Communist party in America. Tensions were heightened by an epidemic of strikes that convulsed the Republic at war's end, many of them the result of high prices and frustrated union-organizing drives. Upstanding Americans jumped to the conclusion that labor troubles were fomented by bomb-and-whisker Bolsheviks. A general strike in Seattle in 1919, though modest in its demands and orderly in its methods, prompted a call from the mayor for federal troops to head off "the anarchy of Russia." Fire-and-brimstone evangelist Billy Sunday struck a responsive chord when he described a Bolshevik as "a guy with a face like a porcupine and a breath that would scare a pole cat. . . . If I had my way, I'd fill the jails so full of them that their feet would stick out the window."

The big **red scare** of 1919–1920 resulted in a nationwide crusade against left-wingers whose Americanism was suspect. Attorney General A. Mitchell Palmer, who "saw red" too easily, earned the title of the "Fighting Quaker" by his excess of zeal in rounding up suspects. They ultimately totaled about six thousand. This drive to root out radicals was redoubled in June 1919, when a bomb shattered both the nerves and the Washington home of Palmer. The "Fighting Quaker" was thereupon dubbed the "Quaking Fighter."

An author-soldier (Arthur Guy Empey, 1883–1963) applauded the "deportation delirium" when he wrote,

"I believe we should place them [the reds] all on a ship of stone, with sails of lead, and that their first stopping place should be hell.**"**

Other events highlighted the red scare. Late in December 1919, a shipload of 249 alleged alien radicals was deported on the *Buford* (the "Soviet Ark") to the "workers' paradise" of Russia. One zealot cried, "My motto for the Reds is S.O.S.—ship or shoot." Hysteria was temporarily revived in September 1920, when a still-unexplained bomb blast on Wall Street killed thirty-eight people and wounded more than a hundred others.

Various states joined the pack in the outcry against radicals. In 1919–1920 a number of legislatures, reflecting the anxiety of "solid" citizens, passed **criminal syndicalism laws**. These anti-red statutes, some of which were born of the war, made unlawful the mere *advocacy* of violence to secure social change. Critics protested that mere words were not criminal deeds, that there was a great gulf between throwing fits and throwing bombs, and that "free screech" was for the nasty as well as the nice. Violence was done to traditional American concepts of free speech as IWW members and other radicals were vigorously prosecuted. The hysteria went so far that in 1920 five members of the New York legislature, all lawfully elected, were denied their seats simply because they were Socialists.

The red scare was a godsend to conservative businesspeople, who used it to break the backs of the fledgling unions. Labor's call for the "closed," or all-union, shop was denounced as "Sovietism in disguise." Employers, in turn, hailed their own antiunion campaign for the "open" shop as the **American plan**.

Anti-redism and antiforeignism were reflected in a notorious case regarded by liberals as a "judicial lynching." Nicola Sacco, a shoe-factory worker, and Bartolomeo Vanzetti, a fish peddler, were convicted in 1921 of the murder of a Massachusetts paymaster and his guard. The jury and judge were prejudiced in some degree against the defendants because they were Italians, atheists, anarchists, and draft dodgers.

Liberals and radicals the world over rallied to the defense of the two aliens doomed to die. The case dragged on for six years until 1927, when the condemned men were electrocuted. Communists and other radicals were thus presented with two martyrs in the "class struggle," while many American liberals hung their heads. The evidence against the accused, though damaging, betrayed serious weaknesses. If the trial had been held in an atmosphere less charged with anti-redism, the outcome might well have been only a prison term.

✦ Hooded Hoodlums of the KKK

A new **Ku Klux Klan**, spawned by the postwar reaction, mushroomed fearsomely in the early 1920s. Despite the familiar sheets and hoods, it more closely resembled the antiforeign "nativist" movements of the 1850s than the antiblack nightriders of the 1860s. It was antiforeign, anti-Catholic, antiblack, anti-Jewish,

Bomb Blast on Wall Street, September 1920 The target of this terrorist attack seemed to be the offices of the haughty financier J. P. Morgan, but no person or group claimed responsibility for the blast, and the victims were random financial district employees, not the moguls of Wall Street. The bombing fed the anti-radical, anti-immigrant mood of the day. Federal Hall, where George Washington was inaugurated, can be seen at the right.

© Bettmann/Corbis

Klanswomen on Parade, 1928 Founded in the Reconstruction era, the Ku Klux Klan enjoyed a remarkable resurgence in the 1920s. Here women members, unmasked and unapologetic, march down Pennsylvania Avenue under the shadow of the Capitol dome.

Hiram Wesley Evans (1881–1966), imperial wizard of the Ku Klux Klan, in 1926 poignantly described the cultural grievances that fueled the Klan and lay behind much of the Fundamentalist revolt against "Modernism":

❝Nordic Americans for the last generation have found themselves increasingly uncomfortable and finally deeply distressed. . . . One by one all our traditional moral standards went by the boards, or were so disregarded that they ceased to be binding. The sacredness of our Sabbath, of our homes, of chastity, and finally even of our right to teach our own children in our own schools fundamental facts and truths were torn away from us. Those who maintained the old standards did so only in the face of constant ridicule. . . . We found our great cities and the control of much of our industry and commerce taken over by strangers. . . . We are a movement of the plain people, very weak in the matter of culture, intellectual support, and trained leadership. . . . This is undoubtedly a weakness. It lays us open to the charge of being 'hicks' and 'rubes' and 'drivers of second-hand Fords.'❞

antipacifist, anti-Communist, anti-internationalist, anti-evolutionist, antibootlegger, antigambling, anti-adultery, and anti–birth control. It was also pro–Anglo-Saxon, pro-"native" American, and pro-Protestant. In short, the besheeted Klan betokened an extremist, ultraconservative uprising against many of the forces of diversity and modernity that were transforming American culture.

As reconstituted, the Klan spread with astonishing rapidity, especially in the Midwest and the **Bible Belt** South where Protestant Fundamentalism thrived. At its peak in the mid-1920s, it claimed about 5 million dues-paying members and wielded potent political influence. It capitalized on the typically American love of on-the-edge adventure and in-group camaraderie, to say nothing of the adolescent ardor for secret ritual. The "Knights of the Invisible Empire" included among their officials Imperial Wizards, Grand Goblins, King Kleagles, and other horrendous "kreatures." The most impressive displays were "konclaves" and huge flag-waving parades. The chief warning was the blazing cross. The principal weapon was the bloodied lash, supplemented by tar and feathers. Rallying songs were "The Fiery Cross on High," "One Hundred Percent American," and "The Ku Klux Klan and the Pope" (against kissing the Pope's toe). One brutal slogan was "Kill the Kikes, Koons, and Katholics."

This reign of hooded horror, so repulsive to the best American ideals, collapsed rather suddenly in the late 1920s. Decent people at last recoiled from the orgy of ribboned flesh and terrorism, while scandalous embezzling by Klan officials launched a congressional investigation. The bubble was punctured when the movement was exposed as a vicious racket based on a $10 initiation fee, $4 of which was kicked back to local organizers as an incentive to recruit. The KKK was an alarming manifestation of the intolerance and prejudice plaguing people anxious about the dizzying pace of social change in the 1920s. Despite the Klan's decline, civil rights activists fought in vain for legislation making lynching a federal crime, as lawmakers feared alienating southern white voters.

✳ Stemming the Foreign Flood

Isolationist America of the 1920s, ingrown and provincial, had little use for the immigrants who began to flood into the country again as peace settled soothingly on the war-torn world. Some 800,000 stepped ashore in 1920–1921, about two-thirds of them from southern

The Granger Collection, New York

The Only Way to Handle It Isolationists and nativists succeeded in damming up the flow of immigrants to the United States in the early 1920s. The Immigration Act of 1924 placed strict quotas on European immigrants and completely shut out the Japanese.

and eastern Europe. The "one-hundred-percent Americans," recoiling at the sight of this resumed "New Immigration," once again cried that the famed poem at the base of the Statue of Liberty was all too literally true: they claimed that a sickly Europe was indeed vomiting on America "the wretched refuse of its teeming shore."

Congress temporarily plugged the breach with the Emergency Quota Act of 1921. Newcomers from Europe were restricted in any given year to a definite quota, which was set at 3 percent of the people of their nationality who had been living in the United States in 1910. This national-origins system was relatively favorable to the immigrants from southern and eastern Europe, for by 1910 immense numbers of them had already arrived.

This stopgap legislation of 1921 was replaced by the **Immigration Act of 1924**. Quotas for foreigners were cut from 3 percent to 2 percent. The national-origins base was shifted from the census of 1910 to that of 1890, by which time comparatively few southern Europeans had arrived.* Great Britain and Northern Ireland, for example, could send 65,721 a year as against 5,802 for Italy. Southern Europeans bitterly denounced the device as unfair and discriminatory—a triumph for the "nativist" belief that blue-eyed and fair-haired northern Europeans were of better blood. The purpose was clearly to freeze America's existing racial composition, which was largely northern European. A flagrantly discriminatory section of the Immigration Act of 1924 slammed the door absolutely against Japanese immigrants. Mass "Hate America" rallies erupted in Japan, and one Japanese superpatriot expressed his outrage by committing suicide near the American embassy in Tokyo. Exempt from the quota system were Canadians and Latin Americans, whose proximity made them easy to attract for jobs when times were good and just as easy to send back home when they were not.

The quota system effected a pivotal departure in American policy. It claimed that the nation was filling up and that a "No Vacancy" sign was needed. Immigration henceforth dwindled to a mere trickle. By 1931, probably for the first time in the American experience, more foreigners left than arrived. Quotas thus caused America to sacrifice something of its tradition of freedom and opportunity, as well as its future ethnic diversity (see Figure 31.1).

The Immigration Act of 1924 marked the end of an era—a period of virtually unrestricted immigration that in the preceding century had brought some 35

---

*Five years later the Immigration Act of 1929, using 1920 as the quota base, virtually cut immigration in half by limiting the total to 152,574 a year. In 1965 Congress abolished the national-origins quota system.

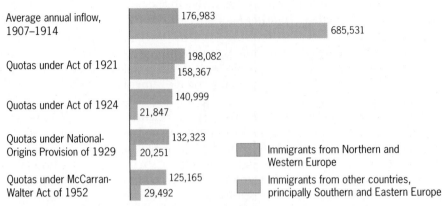

FIGURE 31.1 Annual Immigration and the Quota Laws The national-origins quota system was abolished in 1965. Legislation in that year capped the level of immigration at 170,000 per year but made exceptions for children, spouses, and parents of persons already arrived. It also restricted immigration from any single country to 20,000 people per year. The immigration laws were again significantly revised in 1986, and changed twice more in 1990 and 1996. In the twenty-first century, immigration laws remain highly controversial. (See pp. 902 and 1000.)

million newcomers to the United States, mostly from Europe. The immigrant tide was now cut off, but it left on American shores by the 1920s a patchwork of ethnic communities separated from each other and from the larger society by language, religion, and customs. Many of the most recent arrivals, including the Italians, Jews, and Poles, lived in isolated enclaves with their own houses of worship, newspapers, and theaters (see "Makers of America: The Poles," pp. 706–707). Efforts to organize labor unions repeatedly foundered on the rocks of ethnic differences. Immigrant workers on the same shop floor might share a common interest in wages and working conditions, but they often had no common language with which to forge common cause. Indeed cynical employers often played upon ethnic rivalries to keep their workers divided and powerless. Ethnic variety thus undermined class and political solidarity. It was an old American story, but one that some reformers hoped would not go on forever.

Immigration restriction did not appeal to all reformers. Particularly opposed was the chorus of "cultural pluralists" who had long criticized the idea that an American "melting pot" would eliminate ethnic differences. Two intellectuals, the philosopher Horace Kallen and the critic Randolph Bourne, championed alternative conceptions of the immigrant role in American society. At a time when war hysteria demanded the "one-hundred-percent Americanization" of German and Austrian immigrants, Kallen defended the newcomers' right to practice their ancestral customs. In Kallen's vision the United States should provide a protective canopy for ethnic and racial groups to preserve their cultural

uniqueness. Like instruments in a symphony orchestra, each immigrant community would harmonize with the others while retaining its own singular identity.

If Kallen stressed the preservation of identity, Bourne advocated greater cross-fertilization among immigrants. Cosmopolitan interchange, Bourne believed, was destined to make America "not a nationality but a transnationality, a weaving back and forth, with the other lands, of many threads of all sizes and colors." In this view the United States should serve as the vanguard of a more international and multicultural age.

Kallen's pluralism and Bourne's cosmopolitanism attracted a handful of other intellectuals to the defense of ethnic diversity, including progressives like John Dewey, Jane Addams, and Louis Brandeis. Vastly outnumbered in the debate over immigration restriction in the 1920s, these early proponents of "cultural pluralism" planted the seeds for the blooming of "multiculturalism" in the last quarter of the twentieth century.

✷ The Prohibition "Experiment"

One of the last peculiar spasms of the progressive reform movement was prohibition, loudly supported by crusading churches and by many women. The arid new order was authorized in 1919 by the **Eighteenth Amendment** (see the Appendix), as implemented by the **Volstead Act** passed by Congress later that year. Together these laws made the world "safe for hypocrisy."

The legal abolition of alcohol was especially popular in the South and West. Southern whites were eager

No More Moonshine Federal agents gloat over a captured still in Dayton, Ohio, in 1930. "Moonshiners," or makers of illegal liquor, enjoyed a boom during prohibition, though zealous G-men (government agents) put the owner of this makeshift distillery out of business—at least temporarily.

to keep stimulants out of the hands of blacks, lest they burst out of "their place." In the West prohibition represented an attack on all the vices associated with the ubiquitous western saloon: public drunkenness, prostitution, corruption, and crime. But despite the overwhelming ratification of the "dry" amendment, strong opposition persisted in the larger eastern cities. For many "wet" foreign-born people, Old World styles of sociability were built around drinking in beer gardens and corner taverns. Yet most Americans now assumed that prohibition had come to stay. Everywhere carousers indulged in last wild flings, as the nation prepared to enter upon a permanent "alcoholiday."

But prohibitionists were naive in the extreme. They overlooked the tenacious American tradition of strong drink and of weak control by the central government, especially over private lives. They forgot that the federal authorities had never satisfactorily enforced a law where the majority of the people—or a strong minority—were hostile to it. They ignored the fact that one cannot make a crime overnight out of something that millions of people have never regarded as a crime. Lawmakers could not legislate away a thirst.

Peculiar conditions hampered the enforcement of prohibition. Profound disillusionment over the aftermath of the war raised serious questions as to the wisdom of further self-denial. Slaking thirst became a cherished personal liberty, and many ardent wets believed that the way to bring about repeal was to violate the law on a large enough scale. Hypocritical, hip-flasked legislators spoke or voted dry while privately drinking wet. ("Let us strike a blow for liberty" was an ironic toast.) Frustrated soldiers, returning from France, complained that prohibition had been "put over" on them while they were "over there." Grimy workers bemoaned the loss of their cheap beer, while pointing out that the idle rich could buy all the illicit alcohol they wanted. Flaming youth of the jazz age thought it "smart" to swill bootleg liquor—"liquid tonsillectomies." Millions of older citizens likewise found forbidden fruit fascinating, as they engaged in "bar hunts."

Prohibition might have started off on a better foot if there had been a larger army of enforcement officials.

Automaker Henry Ford (1863–1947), an ardent prohibitionist, posted this notice in his Detroit factory in 1922:

"From now on it will cost a man his job . . . to have the odor of beer, wine or liquor on his breath, or to have any of these intoxicants on his person or in his home. The Eighteenth Amendment is a part of the fundamental laws of this country. It was meant to be enforced. Politics has interfered with the enforcement of this law, but so far as our organization is concerned, it is going to be enforced to the letter."

The Poles were among the largest immigrant groups to respond to industrializing America's call for badly needed labor after the Civil War. Between 1870 and World War I, some 2 million Polish-speaking peasants boarded steamships bound for the United States. By the 1920s, when antiforeign feeling led to restrictive legislation that choked the immigrant stream to a trickle, Polish immigrants and their American-born children began to develop new identities as Polish Americans.

The first Poles to arrive in the New World had landed in Jamestown in 1608 and helped to develop that colony's timber industry. Over the ensuing two and a half centuries, scattered religious dissenters and revolutionary nationalists also made their way from Poland to America. During the Revolution about one hundred Poles, including two officers recruited by Benjamin Franklin, served in the Continental Army.

But the Polish hopefuls who poured into the United States in the late nineteenth century came primarily to stave off starvation and to earn money to buy land. Known in their homeland as *za chlebem* (for bread) emigrants, they belonged to the mass of central and eastern European peasants who had been forced off their farms by growing competition from the large-scale, mechanized agriculture of western Europe and the United States. An exceptionally high birthrate among the Catholic Poles compounded this economic pressure, creating an army of the land-poor and landless, who left their homes seasonally or permanently in search of work. In 1891 farmworkers and unskilled laborers in the United States earned about $1 a day, more than eight times as much as agricultural workers in the Polish province of Galicia. Such a magnet was irresistible.

These Polish-speaking newcomers emigrated not from a unified nation, but from a weakened country that had been partitioned in the eighteenth century by three great European powers: Prussia (later Germany), Austria-Hungary, and Russia. The Prussian Poles, driven from their homeland in part by the anti-Catholic policies that the German imperial government pursued in the 1870s, arrived in America first. Fleeing religious persecution as well as economic turmoil, many of these early immigrants came to the United States intending to stay. By contrast, most of those who came later from Austrian and Russian Poland simply hoped to earn enough American dollars to return home and buy land.

Some of the Polish peasants learned of America from propaganda spread throughout Europe by agents for U.S. railroad and steamship lines. But many more were lured by glowing letters from friends and relatives already living in the United States. The first wave of Polish immigrants had established a thriving network of self-help and fraternal associations organized around Polish Catholic parishes. Often Polish American entrepreneurs helped their European compatriots make travel arrangements or find jobs in the United States. One of the most successful of these, the energetic Chicago grocer Anton Schermann, is credited with "bringing over" 100,000 Poles and causing the Windy City to earn the nickname the "American Warsaw."

Most of the Poles arriving in the United States in the late nineteenth century headed for booming industrial cities such as Buffalo, Pittsburgh, Detroit, Milwaukee, and Chicago. In 1907 four-fifths of the men toiled as unskilled laborers in coal mines, meatpacking factories, textile and steel mills, oil refineries, and garment-making shops. Although married women usually stayed home and contributed to the family's earnings by taking in laundry and boarders, children and single girls often joined their fathers and brothers on the job.

Culver Pictures

Polish Coal Miners, ca. 1905   It was common practice in American mines to segregate mining crews by ethnicity and race.

Solidarity Still, 1981 Many Polish Americans continue to take a keen interest in the fate of their ancestral land. In the 1980s many of them supported a challenge to the communist government led by a renegade trade union federation called Solidarity. Thousands rallied in Chicago, the home of the largest Polish community in the United States, to protest against Polish prime minister General Wojciech Jaruzelski (mocked here leashed to Soviet leader Leonid Brezhnev), who had imposed martial law and ordered the mass arrest of Solidarity activists.

By putting the whole family to work, America's Polish immigrants saved tidy sums. By 1901 about one-third of all Poles in the United States owned real estate, and they sent so much money to relatives in Austria and Russia that American and European authorities fretted about the consequences: in 1907 a nativist U.S. immigration commission groused that the huge outflow of funds to eastern Europe was weakening the U.S. economy.

When an independent Poland was created after World War I, few Poles chose to return to their Old World homeland. Instead, like other immigrant groups in the 1920s, they redoubled their efforts to integrate into American society. Polish institutions like churches and fraternal organizations, which had served to perpetuate a distinctive Polish culture in the New World, now facilitated the transformation of Poles into Polish Americans. When Poland was absorbed into the communist bloc after World War II, Polish Americans clung still more tightly to their American identity, pushing for landmarks like Chicago's Pulaski Road to memorialize their culture in the New World.

But the state and federal agencies were understaffed, and their snoopers, susceptible to bribery, were underpaid. The public was increasingly distressed as scores of people, including innocent bystanders, were killed by quick-triggered dry agents.

Prohibition simply did not prohibit. The old-time "men only" corner saloons were replaced by thousands of "speakeasies," each with its tiny grilled window through which the thirsty spoke softly before the barred door was opened. Hard liquor, especially the cocktail, was drunk in staggering volume by both men and women. Largely because of the difficulties of transporting and concealing bottles, beverages of high alcoholic content were popular. Foreign rum-runners, often from the West Indies, had their inning, and countless cases of liquor leaked down from Canada. The zeal of American prohibition agents on occasion strained diplomatic relations with Uncle Sam's northern neighbor.

"Home brew" and "bathtub gin" became popular, as law-evading adults engaged in "alky cooking" with toy stills. The worst of the homemade "rotgut" produced blindness, even death. The affable bootlegger worked in silent partnership with the friendly undertaker.

Yet the "noble experiment" was not entirely a failure. Bank savings increased, and absenteeism in industry decreased, presumably because of the newly sober ways of formerly soused barflies. On the whole, probably less alcohol was consumed than in the days before prohibition, though strong drink continued to be available. As the legendary tippler remarked, prohibition was "a darn sight better than no liquor at all."

✸ The Golden Age of Gangsterism

Prohibition spawned shocking crimes. The lush profits of illegal alcohol led to bribery of the police, many of whom were induced to see and smell no evil. Violent wars broke out in the big cities between rival gangs— often rooted in immigrant neighborhoods—who sought to corner the rich market in booze. Rival triggermen used their sawed-off shotguns and chattering "typewriters" (machine guns) to "erase" bootlegging competitors who were trying to "muscle in" on their "racket." In the gang wars of the 1920s in Chicago, about five hundred mobsters were murdered. Arrests were few and convictions were even fewer, as the button-lipped gangsters covered for one another with the underworld's code of silence.

Chicago was by far the most spectacular example of lawlessness. In 1925 "Scarface" Al Capone, a grasping and murderous booze distributor, began six years of gang warfare that netted him millions of blood-spattered dollars. He zoomed through the streets in an

Gangster Al Capone Fishing in Florida Capone may have looked like any Chicago businessman on vacation, but his business was bigger and nastier than most, as he often eliminated his competition by murder. He was reported as saying, "Everybody calls me a racketeer. I call myself a businessman. When I sell liquor, it's bootlegging. When my patrons serve it on a silver tray on Lake Shore Drive, it's hospitality." He was finally jailed in 1932 for falsifying his income-tax returns.

armor-plated car with bulletproof windows. A Brooklyn newspaper quipped,

> *And the pistols' red glare,*
> *Bombs bursting in air*
> *Give proof through the night*
> *That Chicago's still there.*

Capone, though branded "Public Enemy Number One," could not be convicted of the cold-blooded massacre, on St. Valentine's Day in 1929, of seven disarmed members of a rival gang. But after serving most of an eleven-year sentence in a federal penitentiary for income-tax evasion, he was released as a syphilitic wreck.

Gangsters rapidly moved into other profitable and illicit activities: prostitution, gambling, and narcotics. Honest merchants were forced to pay "protection money" to the organized thugs; otherwise their windows would be smashed, their trucks overturned, or their employees or themselves beaten up. **Racketeers** even invaded the ranks of local labor unions as organizers and promoters. Organized crime had come to be one of the nation's most gigantic businesses. By 1930 the annual "take" of the underworld was estimated to be from $12 billion to $18 billion—several times the income of the Washington government.

Criminal callousness sank to new depths in 1932 with the kidnapping for ransom, and eventual murder, of the infant son of aviator-hero Charles A. Lindbergh. The entire nation was inexpressibly shocked and saddened, causing Congress in 1932 to pass the so-called Lindbergh Law, making interstate abduction in certain circumstances a death-penalty offense.

✴ Monkey Business in Tennessee

Education in the 1920s continued to make giant bootstrides. More and more states were requiring young people to remain in school until age sixteen or eighteen, or until graduation from high school. The proportion of seventeen-year-olds who finished high school almost doubled in the 1920s, to more than one in four.

The most revolutionary contribution to educational theory during these yeasty years was made by mild-mannered Professor John Dewey, who served on the faculty of Columbia University from 1904 to 1930. By common consent one of America's few front-rank philosophers, he set forth the principles of "learning by doing" that formed the foundation of so-called progressive education, with its greater "permissiveness." He believed that the workbench was as essential as the blackboard, and that "education for life"

should be a primary goal of the teacher. (For more on Dewey, see "Makers of America: Pioneering Pragmatists," pp. 560–561.)

Science also scored wondrous advances in these years. A massive public-health program, launched by the Rockefeller Foundation in the South in 1909, had virtually wiped out the ancient affliction of hookworm by the 1920s. Better nutrition and health care helped to increase the life expectancy of a newborn infant from fifty years in 1901 to fifty-nine years in 1929.

Yet both science and progressive education in the 1920s were subjected to unfriendly fire from the newly organized Fundamentalists. These devoted religionists charged that the teaching of Darwinian evolution was destroying faith in God and the Bible, while contributing to the moral breakdown of youth in the jazz age. Numerous attempts were made to secure laws prohibiting the teaching of evolution, "the bestial hypothesis," in the public schools, and three southern states adopted such shackling measures. The trio of states included Tennessee, in the heart of the so-called Bible Belt South, where the spirit of evangelical religion was still robust.

The Battle over Evolution Opponents of Darwin's theories set up shop at the opening of the famed "Monkey Trial" in Dayton, Tennessee, in 1925. The trial was an early battle in an American "culture war" that is still being waged more than seventy-five years later.

The stage was set for the memorable "Monkey Trial" at the hamlet of Dayton, in eastern Tennessee, in 1925. A likable high-school biology teacher, John T. Scopes, was indicted for teaching evolution. Batteries of newspaper reporters, armed with notebooks and cameras, descended upon the quiet town to witness the spectacle. Scopes was defended by nationally known attorneys, while former presidential candidate William Jennings Bryan, an ardent Presbyterian Fundamentalist, joined the prosecution. Taking the stand as an expert on the Bible, Bryan was made to appear foolish by the famed criminal lawyer Clarence Darrow. Five days after the trial was over, Bryan died of a stroke, no doubt brought on by the wilting heat and witness-stand strain.

This historic clash between theology and biology proved inconclusive. Scopes, the forgotten man of the drama, was found guilty and fined $100. But the supreme court of Tennessee, while upholding the law, set aside the fine on a technicality.* The Fundamentalists at best won only a hollow victory, for the absurdities of the trial cast ridicule on their cause. Yet even though increasing numbers of Christians were coming to reconcile the revelations of religion with the findings of modern science, **Fundamentalism**, with its emphasis on a literal reading of the Bible, remained a vibrant force in American spiritual life. It was especially strong in the Baptist Church and in the rapidly growing Churches of Christ, organized in 1906.

⭐ The Mass-Consumption Economy

Prosperity—real, sustained, and widely shared—put much of the "roar" into the twenties. The economy kicked off its war harness in 1919, faltered a few steps in the recession of 1920–1921, and then sprinted forward for nearly seven years. Both the recent war and Treasury Secretary Andrew Mellon's tax policies favored the rapid expansion of capital investment. Ingenious machines, powered by relatively cheap energy from newly tapped oil fields, dramatically increased the productivity of the laborer. Assembly-line production reached such perfection in Henry Ford's famed Rouge River plant near Detroit that a finished automobile emerged every ten seconds.

Great new industries suddenly sprouted forth. Supplying electrical power for the humming new machines became a giant business in the 1920s. Above all, the automobile, once the horseless chariot of the rich, now became the carriage of the common citizen. By 1930 Americans owned almost 30 million cars.

The nation's deepening "love affair" with the automobile headlined a momentous shift in the character of the economy. American manufacturers seemed to have mastered the problems of production; their worries now focused on consumption. Could they find the mass markets for the goods they had contrived to spew forth in such profusion?

Responding to this need, a new arm of American commerce came into being: advertising. By persuasion and ploy, seduction and sexual suggestion, advertisers sought to make Americans chronically discontented with their paltry possessions and want more, more, more. A founder of this new "profession" was Bruce Barton, prominent New York partner in a Madison Avenue firm. In 1925 Barton published a best seller, *The Man Nobody Knows*, setting forth the provocative thesis that Jesus Christ was the greatest adman of all time. "Every advertising man ought to study the parables of Jesus," Barton preached. "They are marvelously condensed, as all good advertising should be." Barton even had a good word to say for Christ's executive ability:

Brown Brothers

Babe Ruth: The "Sultan of Swat"

---

*The Tennessee law was not formally repealed until 1967.

"He picked up twelve men from the bottom ranks of business and forged them into an organization that conquered the world."

Sports became big business in the consumer economy of the 1920s. Ballyhooed by the "image makers," home-run heroes like George H. ("Babe") Ruth were far better known than most statesmen. The fans bought tickets in such numbers that Babe's hometown park, Yankee Stadium, became known as "the house that Ruth built." In 1921 the slugging heavyweight champion, Jack Dempsey, knocked out the dapper French light heavyweight Georges Carpentier. The Jersey City crowd in attendance had paid more than a million dollars—the first in a series of million-dollar "gates" in the golden 1920s.

Buying on credit was another innovative feature of the postwar economy. "Possess today and pay tomorrow" was the message directed at buyers. Once-frugal descendants of Puritans went ever deeper into debt to own all kinds of newfangled marvels—refrigerators, vacuum cleaners, and especially cars and radios—*now*. Prosperity thus accumulated an overhanging cloud of debt, and the economy became increasingly vulnerable to disruptions of the credit structure.

✳ Putting America on Rubber Tires

A new industrial revolution slipped into high gear in America in the 1920s. Thrusting out steel tentacles, it changed the daily life of the people in unprecedented ways. Machinery was the new messiah—and the automobile was its principal prophet.

Of all the inventions of the era, the automobile cut the deepest track. It heralded an amazing new industrial system based on assembly-line methods and mass-production techniques.

Americans adapted rather than invented the gasoline engine; Europeans can claim the original honor. By the 1890s a few daring American inventors and promoters, including Henry Ford and Ransom E. Olds (Oldsmobile), were developing the infant automotive industry. By 1910 sixty-nine car companies rolled out a total annual production of 181,000 units. The early contraptions were neither speedy nor reliable. Many a stalled motorist, profanely cranking a balky automobile, had to endure the jeer "Get a horse" from the occupants of a passing dobbin-drawn carriage.

An enormous industry sprang into being, as Detroit became the motorcar capital of America. The mechanized colossus owed much to the stopwatch efficiency techniques of Frederick W. Taylor, a prominent inventor, engineer, and tennis player, who sought to eliminate wasted motion. His epitaph reads "Father of **Scientific Management**."

From the Collections of The Henry Ford

Henry Ford in His First Car, Built in 1896 Ford has been called the "Father of the Traffic Jam."

Best known of the new crop of industrial wizards was Henry Ford, who more than any other individual put America on rubber tires. His high and hideous Model T ("Tin Lizzie") was cheap, rugged, and reasonably reliable, though rough and clattering. The parts of Ford's "flivver" were highly standardized, but the behavior of this rattling good car was so eccentric that it became the butt of numberless jokes.

Lean and silent Henry Ford, who was said to have wheels in his head, erected an immense personal empire on the cornerstone of his mechanical genius, though his associates provided much of the organizational talent. Ill-educated, this multimillionaire mechanic was socially and culturally narrow. "History is bunk," he once testified. But he dedicated himself with one-track devotion to the gospel of standardization. After two early failures, he grasped and applied fully the technique of the moving assembly line—**Fordism**. He is

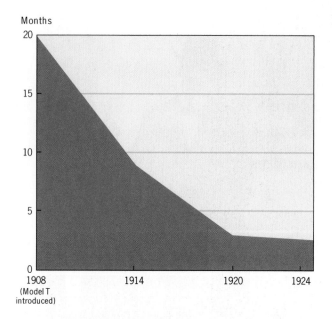

FIGURE 31.2 The Cost of a Model T Ford, 1908–1924
Henry Ford's mass-production techniques cut the costs of
production dramatically and put the automobile within reach
of the workingperson's purse. (Cost is shown in months of
labor for an employee at the average national wage.)

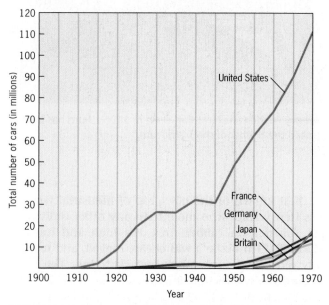

**FIGURE 31.3 International Comparison of Number of
Automobiles**

enamored, though their workers resented those "American methods."

The flood of Fords was phenomenal. In 1914 the "Automobile Wizard" turned out his 500,000th Model T. By 1930 his total had risen to 20 million, or, on a bumper-to-bumper basis, more than enough to encircle the globe. A national newspaper and magazine poll conducted in 1923 revealed Ford to be the people's choice for the presidential nomination in 1924. By 1929, when the great bull market collapsed, 26 million motor vehicles were registered in the United States. This figure, averaging 1 for every 4.9 Americans, represented far more automobiles than existed in all the rest of the world (see Figure 31.3).

✪ The Advent of the Gasoline Age

The impact of the self-propelled carriage on various aspects of American life was tremendous. A gigantic new industry emerged, dependent on steel but displacing steel from its kingpin role. Employing directly or indirectly about 6 million people by 1930, it was a major wellspring of the nation's prosperity. Thousands of new jobs, moreover, were created by supporting industries. The lengthening list would include rubber, glass, and fabrics, to say nothing of highway construction and thousands of service stations and garages. America's standard of living, responding to this infectious vitality, rose to an enviable level.

New industries boomed lustily; older ones grew sickly. The petroleum business experienced an explosive development. Hundreds of oil derricks shot up in California, Texas, and Oklahoma, as these states expanded wondrously and the wilderness frontier became an industrial frontier. The once-feared railroad octopus, on the other hand, was hard hit by the competition of passenger cars, buses, and trucks. An age-old story was repeated: one industry's gains were another industry's pains.

Other effects were widely felt. Speedy marketing of perishable foodstuffs, such as fresh fruits, was accelerated. A new prosperity enriched outlying farms, as city dwellers were provided with produce at attractive prices. Countless new roads ribboned out to meet the demand of the American motorist for smoother and faster highways, often paid for by taxes on gasoline. The era of mud ended as the nation made haste to construct the finest network of hard-surfaced roadways in the world. Lured by sophisticated advertising, and encouraged by tempting installment-plan buying, countless Americans with shallow purses acquired the habit of riding as they paid.

Zooming motorcars were agents of social change. At first a luxury, they rapidly became a necessity. Essentially devices for needed transportation, they soon

supposed to have remarked that the purchaser could have his automobile in any color he desired—just as long as it was black. So economical were his methods that in the mid-1920s he was selling the Ford roadster for $260—well within the purse of a thrifty worker (see Figure 31.2). Before long, Fordism caught fire outside the United States. German engineers were particularly

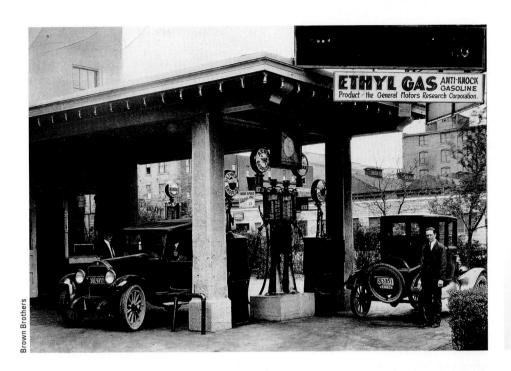

Brown Brothers

Gas Station, 1923 Gas stations like this one began to appear about 1913. Before that the nation's handful of automobile owners bought fuel from their local oil companies and stored it in tanks in their own yards.

developed into a badge of freedom and equality—a necessary prop for self-respect. To some, ostentation seemed more important than transportation. Leisure hours could now be spent more pleasurably, as tens of thousands of cooped-up souls responded to the call of the open road on joyriding vacations. Women were further freed from clinging-vine dependence on men. Isolation among the sections was broken down, and the less attractive states lost population at an alarming rate. By the late 1920s, Americans owned more automobiles than bathtubs. "I can't go to town in a bathtub," one homemaker explained.

Other social by-products of the automobile were visible. Autobuses made possible the consolidation of schools and to some extent of churches. The sprawling suburbs spread out still farther from the urban core, as America became a nation of commuters.

The demon machine, on the other hand, exacted a terrible toll by catering to the American mania for speed. Citizens were becoming statistics. Not counting the hundreds of thousands of injured and crippled, the one millionth American had died in a motor vehicle accident by 1951—more than all those killed on all the battlefields of all the nation's wars to that date. "The public be rammed" seemed to be the motto of the new age.

Virtuous home life partially broke down as joyriders of all ages forsook the parlor for the highway. The morals of flaming youth sagged correspondingly—at least in the judgment of their elders. What might young people get up to in the privacy of a closed-top Model T? An Indiana juvenile court judge voiced parents' worst fears when he condemned the automobile as "a house of prostitution on wheels." Even the celebrated crime

Picture Research Consultants & Archives

The Modern Woman in the Driver's Seat As part of its effort to sell to a mass market, the Ford Motor Company used advertising to convey that driving an automobile was respectable for women. A woman who drove was not only modern, but she also better fulfilled her traditional duties as a household manager.

waves of the 1920s and 1930s were aided and abetted by the motorcar, for gangsters could now make quick getaways.

Yet no sane American would plead for a return of the old horse and buggy, complete with fly-breeding manure. The automobile contributed notably to improved air and environmental quality, despite its later notoriety as a polluter. Life might be cut short on the highways, and smog might poison the air, but the automobile brought more convenience, pleasure, and excitement into more people's lives than almost any other single invention.

✸ Humans Develop Wings

Gasoline engines also provided the power that enabled humans to fulfill the age-old dream of sprouting wings. After near-successful experiments by others with heavier-than-air craft, the Wright brothers, Orville and Wilbur, performed "the miracle at Kitty Hawk," North Carolina.

On a historic day—December 17, 1903—Orville Wright took aloft a feebly engined plane that stayed airborne for 12 seconds and 120 feet. Thus the air age was launched by two obscure Ohio bicycle repairmen.

As aviation gradually got off the ground, the world slowly shrank. The public was made increasingly air-minded by unsung heroes—often martyrs—who appeared as stunt fliers at fairs and other public gatherings. Airplanes—"flying coffins"—were used with marked success for various purposes during the Great War of 1914–1918. Shortly thereafter private companies began to operate passenger lines with airmail contracts, which were in effect a subsidy from Washington. The first transcontinental airmail route was established from New York to San Francisco in 1920.

In 1927 modest and skillful Charles A. Lindbergh, the so-called Flyin' Fool, electrified the world with the first solo west-to-east conquest of the Atlantic. Seeking a prize of $25,000, the lanky stunt flier courageously piloted his single-engine plane, the *Spirit of St. Louis*, from New York to Paris in a grueling thirty-three hours and thirty-nine minutes.

Lindbergh's exploit swept Americans off their feet. Fed up with the cynicism and debunking of the jazz age, they found in this wholesome and handsome youth a genuine hero. They clasped the soaring "Lone Eagle" to their hearts much more warmly than the bashful young man desired. "Lucky Lindy" received an uproarious welcome in the "hero canyon" of lower Broadway, as eighteen hundred tons of ticker tape and other improvised confetti showered upon him. Lindbergh's achievement—it was more than a "stunt"—did

Lucky Lindy Charles A. Lindbergh (1902–1974) stands in front of the aircraft that made him famous. The first person to fly solo across the Atlantic, Lindbergh became an acclaimed celebrity—perhaps the first media-made "hero" of the twentieth century. His shining reputation later lost some of its luster when he voiced anti-Semitic sentiments and opposed American entry into World War II, though he went on to fly several combat missions in the war against Japan.

Picture Research Consultants & Archives

much to dramatize and popularize flying, while giving a strong boost to the infant aviation industry.

The impact of the airship was tremendous. It provided the restless American spirit with yet another dimension. At the same time, it gave birth to a giant new industry. Unfortunately, the accident rate in the pioneer stages of aviation was high, though hardly more so than on the early railroads. But by the 1930s and 1940s, travel by air on regularly scheduled airlines was significantly safer than on many overcrowded highways.

Humanity's new wings also increased the tempo of an already breathless civilization. The floundering railroad received another setback through the loss of passengers and mail. A lethal new weapon was given to the gods of war, and with the coming of city-busting aerial bombs, people could well debate whether the conquest of the air was a blessing or a curse. The Atlantic Ocean was shriveling to about the size of the Aegean Sea in the days of Socrates, while isolation behind ocean moats was becoming a bygone dream.

✸ The Radio Revolution

The speed of the airplane was far eclipsed by the speed of radio waves. Guglielmo Marconi, an Italian, invented wireless telegraphy in the 1890s, and his brainchild was used for long-range communication during World War I.

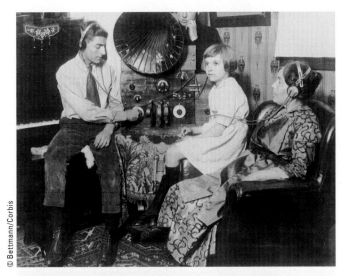

Family "Listening In" to the Radio, 1922 The Lacambanne family of San Francisco gathered in their parlor to listen to a concert broadcast over the radio. In the early years, when only a handful of households could afford a radio, listening brought family and neighbors together to share a common experience.

© Bettmann/Corbis

Radio came in with a bang in the winter of 1921–1922. A San Francisco newspaper reported a discovery that countless citizens were making:

❝ There is radio music in the air, every night, everywhere. Anybody can hear it at home on a receiving set, which any boy can put up in an hour. **❞**

Next came the voice-carrying radio, a triumph of many minds. A red-letter day was posted in November 1920, when the Pittsburgh radio station KDKA broadcast the news of the Harding landslide. Later miracles were achieved in transatlantic wireless phonographs, radiotelephones, and television. The earliest radio programs reached only local audiences. But by the late 1920s, technological improvements made long-distance broadcasting possible, and national commercial networks drowned out much local programming. Meanwhile, advertising "commercials" made radio another vehicle for American free enterprise, as contrasted with the government-owned systems of Europe.

While other marvels of the era—like the automobile—were luring Americans away from home, the radio was drawing them back. For much of the decade, family and neighbors gathered around a household's sole radio as they once had around the toasty hearth. Radio knitted the nation together. Various regions heard voices with standardized accents, and countless millions "tuned in" to perennial comedy favorites like "Amos 'n' Andy." Programs sponsored by manufacturers and distributors of brand-name products, like the "A&P Gypsies" and the "Eveready Hour," helped to make radio-touted labels household words and purchases.

Educationally and culturally, the radio made a significant contribution. Sports were further stimulated. Politicians had to adjust their speaking techniques to the new medium, and millions rather than thousands of voters heard their promises and pleas. A host of listeners swallowed the gospel of their favorite newscaster or were even ringside participants in world-shaking events. Finally, the music of famous artists and symphony orchestras was beamed into countless homes.

✸ Hollywood's Filmland Fantasies

The flickering movie was the fruit of numerous geniuses, including Thomas A. Edison. As early as the 1890s, this novel contraption, though still in crude form, had attained some popularity in the naughty peep-show penny arcades. The real birth of the movie came in 1903, when the first story sequence reached

In the face of protests against sex in the movies, the industry appointed a "movie czar," Will H. Hays (1879-1954), who issued the famous "Hays Code" in 1934. As he stated in a speech,

" This industry must have toward that sacred thing, the mind of a child, toward that clean virgin thing, that unmarked slate, the same responsibility, the same care about the impressions made upon it, that the best clergyman or the most inspired teacher of youth would have. **"**

the screen. This breathless melodrama, *The Great Train Robbery*, was featured in the five-cent theaters, popularly called "nickelodeons." Spectacular among the first full-length classics was D. W. Griffith's *Birth of a Nation* (1915), which glorified the Ku Klux Klan of Reconstruction days and defamed both blacks and Northern carpetbaggers. White southerners reputedly fired guns at the screen during the attempted "rape" scene. African Americans were outraged at the film and angrily organized protest marches, petition campaigns, and public hearings.

A fascinating industry was thus launched. Hollywood, in southern California, quickly became the movie capital of the world, for it enjoyed a maximum of sunshine and other advantages. Early producers featured nudity and heavy-lidded female vampires ("vamps"), and an offended public forced the screen magnates to set up their own rigorous code of censorship. The motion picture really arrived during World War I, when it was used as an engine of anti-German propaganda. Specially prepared "hang the kaiser" films aided powerfully in selling war bonds and in boosting morale.

A new era began in 1927 with the success of the first "talkie"—*The Jazz Singer*, starring the white performer Al Jolson in blackface. The age of the "silents" was ushered out as theaters everywhere were "wired for sound." At about the same time, reasonably satisfactory color films were being produced.

Movies eclipsed all other new forms of amusement in the phenomenal growth of their popularity. Movie "stars" of the first pulchritude commanded much larger salaries than the president of the United States, in some cases as much as $100,000 for a single picture. Many actors and actresses were far more widely known than the nation's political leaders.

Critics bemoaned the vulgarization of popular tastes wrought by the new technologies of radio and motion pictures. But the effects of the new mass media were not all negative. The insularity of ethnic communities eroded as the immigrants' children, especially, forsook the neighborhood vaudeville theater for the downtown movie palace or turned away from Grandma's Yiddish storytelling to tune in "Amos 'n' Andy." If some of the rich diversity of the immigrants' Old Country cultures was lost, the standardization of tastes and of language hastened entry into the American mainstream—and set the stage for the emergence of a working-class political coalition that, for a time, would overcome the divisive ethnic differences of the past.

✷ The Dynamic Decade

Far-reaching changes in lifestyles and values paralleled the dramatic upsurge of the economy. The census of 1920 revealed that for the first time most Americans no longer lived in the countryside but in urban areas. Women continued to find opportunities for employment in the cities, though they tended to cluster in a few low-paying jobs (such as retail clerking and office typing) that became classified as "women's work." An organized birth-control movement, led by the fiery feminist Margaret Sanger, openly championed the

Margaret Sanger (1879–1966) in Boston, 1929 Forbidden to speak on the inflammatory topic of birth control, a defiant Sanger covered her mouth and "lectured" in Boston by writing on a blackboard. Since 1912 Sanger had devoted herself to promoting birth control and establishing contraceptive clinics throughout the United States.

© Bettmann/Corbis

The Jazz Singer, 1927

The Jazz Singer was the first feature-length "talkie," a motion picture in which the characters actually spoke, and its arrival spelled the end for "silent" films, where the audience read subtitles with live or recorded music as background. Although moviegoers flocked to The Jazz Singer to hear recorded sound, when they got there they found a movie concerned with themes of great interest to the urban, first- or second-generation immigrant audiences who were Hollywood's major patrons. The Jazz Singer told the story of a poor, assimilating Jewish immigrant torn between following his father's wish that he train as an Orthodox cantor and his own ambition to make a success of himself as a jazz singer, performing in the popular blackface style. The movie's star, Al Jolson, was himself an immigrant Jew who had made his name as a blackface performer. White actors had gradually taken over the southern black minstrel show during the nineteenth century. By the early twentieth century, Jewish entertainers had entirely monopolized these roles. Jolson, like other Jewish blackface performers, used his ability to impersonate a black person to force his acceptance into mainstream white American society. This use of blackface seems ironic, since black Americans in the 1920s were struggling with their own real-life battles against Jim Crow–era segregation, a blatant form of exclusion from American society. Besides the novelty of being a "talkie," what may have made The Jazz Singer a box office hit in 1927? How might different types of viewers in the audience have responded to the story? What does the popularity of blackface reveal about racial attitudes at the time?

The Kobal Collection/The Picture Desk

The Flapper New dance styles, like the "Charleston," flamboyantly displayed the new social freedom of the "flapper," whose dress and antics frequently flummoxed the guardians of respectability.

use of contraceptives. Alice Paul's National Woman's party began in 1923 to campaign for an Equal Rights Amendment to the Constitution. (The campaign was still stalled short of success nearly nine decades later.) To some defenders of traditional ways, it seemed that the world had suddenly gone mad.

Even the churches were affected. The Fundamentalist champions of the old-time religion lost ground to the Modernists, who liked to think that God was a "good guy" and the universe a pretty chummy place.

Some churches tried to fight the Devil with worldly weapons. Competing with joyriding automobiles and golf links, they turned to quality entertainment of their own, including wholesome moving pictures for young people. One uptown house of the Lord in New York advertised on a billboard, "Come to Church: Christian Worship Increases Your Efficiency."

Even before the war, one observer thought the chimes had "struck sex o'clock in America," and the 1920s witnessed what many old-timers regarded as a veritable erotic eruption. Advertisers exploited sexual allure to sell everything from soap to car tires. Once-modest maidens now proclaimed their new freedom as "flappers" in bobbed tresses and dresses. Young women appeared with hemlines elevated, stockings rolled, breasts taped flat, cheeks rouged, and lips a "crimson gash" that held a dangling cigarette. Thus did the "flapper" symbolize a yearned-for and devil-may-care independence (some said wild abandon) in some American women. Still more adventuresome females shocked their elders when they sported the new one-piece bathing suits.

Justification for this new sexual frankness could be found in the recently translated writings of Dr. Sigmund Freud. This Viennese physician appeared to argue that sexual repression was responsible for a variety of nervous and emotional ills. Thus not pleasure alone but also health demanded sexual gratification and liberation.

Many taboos flew out the window as sex-conscious Americans let themselves go. As unknowing Freudians, teenagers pioneered the sexual frontiers. Glued together in rhythmic embrace, they danced to jazz music squeaking from phonographs. In an earlier day, a kiss had been the equivalent of a proposal of marriage. But in the new era, exploratory young folk sat in darkened movie houses or took to the highways and byways in automobiles. There the youthful "neckers" and "petters" poached upon the forbidden territory of each other's bodies.

If the flapper was the goddess of the "era of wonderful nonsense," jazz was its sacred music. With its virtuoso wanderings and tricky syncopation, jazz moved

The Guardian of Morality Women's new one-piece bathing suits were a sensation in the 1920s. Here a check is carefully made to ensure that not too much leg is showing.

Not all Americans welcomed the rising popularity of jazz music. For some stuffy traditionalists, including clergyman and writer Henry van Dyck (1852–1933), jazz symbolized the excessive liberation and dangerous exuberance of modern society:

"As I understand it, [jazz] is not music at all. It is merely an irritation of the nerves of hearing, a sensual teasing of the strings of physical passion. . . . '[J]azz' is an unmitigated cacophony, a combination of disagreeable sounds in complicated discords, a willful ugliness and a deliberate vulgarity.**"**

up from New Orleans along with the migrating blacks during World War I. Tunes like W. C. Handy's "St. Louis Blues" (1914) became instant classics, as the wailing saxophone became the trumpet of the new era. Black performers such as Handy, "Jelly Roll" Morton, Louis Armstrong, and Joe "King" Oliver gave birth to jazz, but the entertainment industry soon spawned all-white bands—notably Paul Whiteman's. Caucasian impresarios cornered the profits, though not the creative soul, of America's most native music.

A new racial pride also blossomed in the northern black communities that burgeoned during and after the war. Harlem in New York City, counting some 150,000 African American residents in the 1920s, was one of the largest black communities in the world. Harlem sustained a vibrant, creative culture that nourished poets like Langston Hughes, whose first volume of verses, *The Weary Blues*, appeared in 1926. Harlem in the 1920s also spawned a charismatic political leader, Marcus Garvey. The Jamaican-born Garvey

Library of Congress

Marcus Garvey (1887–1940) In 1920 Garvey, the Jamaican-born founder of the United Negro Improvement Association, advocated a constitution to protect the rights of black Americans. By that year his nationalist self-help organization boasted eleven hundred branches in forty countries in the Americas and Africa. Most of those branches were located in the United States, his base of operations until 1927.

Stock Montage

King Oliver's Creole Jazz Band, Early 1920s Joe "King" Oliver arrived in Chicago from New Orleans in 1918. His band became the first important black jazz ensemble and made Chicago's Royal Garden Café a magnet for jazz lovers. Left to right: Honoré Dutrey, trombone; Baby Dodds, drums; "King" Oliver, cornet; Lil Hardin, piano; Bill Johnson, banjo; and Johnny Dodds, clarinet. Kneeling in the foreground is the young Louis Armstrong.

founded the **United Negro Improvement Association (UNIA)** to promote the resettlement of American blacks in their own "African homeland." Within the United States, the UNIA sponsored stores and other businesses, like the Black Star Line Steamship Company, to keep blacks' dollars in black pockets. Most of Garvey's enterprises failed financially, and Garvey himself was convicted in 1927 for alleged mail fraud and deported by a nervous U.S. government. But the race pride that Garvey inspired among the 4 million blacks who counted themselves UNIA followers at the movement's height helped these newcomers to northern cities gain self-confidence and self-reliance. And his example proved important to the later founding of the Nation of Islam (Black Muslim) movement.

✦ Cultural Liberation

Likewise in literature and the arts, an older era seemed to have ground to a halt with the recent war. By the dawn of the 1920s, most of the custodians of an aging genteel culture had died—Henry James in 1916, Henry Adams in 1918, and William Dean Howells ("the Dean of American literature") in 1920. A few novelists who had been popular in the previous decades continued to thrive, notably the well-to-do, cosmopolitan New Yorker Edith Wharton and the Virginia-born Willa Cather, esteemed for her stark but sympathetic portrayals of pioneering on the prairies.

But in the decade after the war, a new generation of writers and artists burst upon the scene. Many of them hailed from ethnic and regional backgrounds different from that of the Protestant New Englanders who traditionally had dominated American cultural life. The newcomers exhibited the energy of youth, the ambition of excluded outsiders, and in many cases the smoldering resentment of ideals betrayed. Animated by the spark of the international modernist movement (see "Thinking Globally: Modernism," pp. 722-723), they bestowed on American culture a new vitality, imaginativeness, and artistic daring.

Central to **modernism** was its questioning of social conventions and traditional authorities, considered outmoded by the accelerating changes of twentieth-century life. No one personified this iconoclasm better than H. L. Mencken, the "Bad Boy of Baltimore." As the era's most influential critic, Mencken promoted modernist causes in politics and literature. Little escaped his acidic wit. In his columns for the *Baltimore Sun*, he assailed marriage, patriotism, democracy, prohibition, Rotarians, and other sacred icons of the middle-class American "booboisie." The provincial South he contemptuously dismissed as "the Sahara of the Bozart" (a bastardization of *beaux arts*, French for

H. L. Mencken's (1880-1956) obituary of his old nemesis, William Jennings Bryan, seethed with contempt for the American heartland:

❝Out where the grass grows high, and the horned cattle dream away the lazy days, and men still fear the powers and principalities of the air—out there between the corn-rows he held his old puissance to the end. There was no need of beaters to drive in his game. The news that he was coming was enough. For miles the flivver dust would choke the roads.❞

the "fine arts"), and he scathingly attacked hypocritical do-gooders as "Puritans." Puritanism, he jibed, was "the haunting fear that someone, somewhere, might be happy."

The war had jolted many young writers out of their complacency about traditional values and literary standards. With their pens they probed for new codes of morals and understanding, as well as fresh forms of expression. F. Scott Fitzgerald, a handsome Minnesota-born Princetonian then only twenty-four years old, became an overnight celebrity when he published *This Side of Paradise* in 1920. The book became a kind of Bible for the young. It was eagerly devoured by aspiring flappers and their ardent wooers, many of whom affected an air of bewildered abandon toward life. Catching the spirit of the hour (often about 4 A.M.), Fitzgerald found "all gods dead, all wars fought, all faiths in man shaken." He followed this melancholy success with *The Great Gatsby* (1925), a brilliant commentary on the illusory American ideal of the self-made man. Midwesterner James Gatz reinvented himself as tycoon Jay Gatsby, only to be destroyed by the power of those with established wealth and social standing. Theodore Dreiser's masterpiece of 1925, *An American Tragedy*, similarly explored the pitfalls of social striving, as it dealt with the murder of a pregnant working girl by her socially ambitious young lover.

Ernest Hemingway, who had seen action on the Italian front in 1917, was among the writers most affected by the war. He responded to pernicious propaganda and the overblown appeal to patriotism by devising his own lean, word-sparing but word-perfect style. Hemingway wrote on the "iceberg" principle: "There is seven-eighths of it under water for every part that shows." His hard-boiled realism typified postwar writing. In *The Sun Also Rises* (1926), he told of disillusioned, spiritually numb American expatriates in Europe. In *A Farewell to Arms* (1929), he turned his own war story into one of the finest novels in any language about the war experience. Hemingway's literary successes and

Stock Montage

F. Scott Fitzgerald and His Wife, Zelda The Fitzgeralds are shown here in the happy, early days of their stormy marriage.

flamboyant personal life made him one of the most famous writers in the world. He won the Nobel Prize in literature in 1954—and blew out his brains with a shotgun blast in 1961.

Hemingway, Fitzgerald, and many other American writers and painters formed an artistic **"Lost Generation"** as expatriates in postwar Europe. They found shelter and inspiration in the Paris salon of their brainy and eccentric countrywoman, Gertrude Stein. A literary innovator in her own right, Stein had studied at Radcliffe College at Harvard University under the famed philosopher William James; her early works apply his theory of "stream of consciousness" to literature. Hobnobbing in Paris with the iconoclastic artists Pablo Picasso and Henri Matisse, Stein wrote radically experimental poetry and prose, including *Three Lives* (1909), *Tender Buttons* (1914), and, most famously, *The Autobiography of Alice B. Toklas* (1933), named for her lifelong partner.

Stein joined fellow American poets Ezra Pound and T. S. Eliot in the vanguard of modernist literary

innovation. These "high modernists" experimented with the breakdown of traditional literary forms and exposed the losses associated with modernity. They wrote in a self-consciously internationalist mode, haughtily rejecting the parochialism they found at home. Pound, a brilliantly erratic Idahoan who permanently deserted America for Europe, rejected what he called "an old bitch civilization, gone in the teeth" and proclaimed his doctrine: "Make It New." Pound strongly influenced the Missouri-born and Harvard-educated Eliot, who took up residence (and eventual citizenship) in England. In *The Waste Land* (1922), Eliot produced one of the most impenetrable but influential poems of the century. Composed of discontinuous segments, multiple perspectives, and arcane allusions, the poem depicts the fragmentation and frightening desolation of postwar society. Much more accessible was the poetry of fellow Harvard graduate e.e. cummings, who relied on unorthodox diction and peculiar typesetting to produce startling poetical effects.

Not all literary efforts of the era proved so radical. Many American writers continued to employ a familiar regionalist style that was by turns celebratory and critical. Robert Frost, a San Francisco–born poet, wrote hauntingly about the nature and folkways of his adopted New England. Ever-popular Carl Sandburg extolled the working classes of Chicago in strong, simple cadences. Other regionalist writers caustically probed Middle American small-town life. Sherwood Anderson dissected various fictional personalities in *Winesburg, Ohio* (1919), finding them all in some way warped by their cramped psychological surroundings. Sinclair Lewis, a hotheaded, heavy-drinking journalist from Sauk Centre, Minnesota, sprang into prominence in 1920 with *Main Street*, the best-selling story of one woman's unsuccessful revolt against provincialism. In *Babbitt* (1922) he affectionately pilloried George F. Babbitt, a prosperous, vulgar, middle-class real estate broker who slavishly conforms to the respectable materialism of his group. The word *Babbittry* was quickly coined to describe his all-too-familiar lifestyle.

William Faulkner, a dark-eyed, pensive Mississippian, focused on the displacement of the agrarian Old South by a rising industrial order. His life's work offered a fictional chronicle of an imaginary, history-rich Deep

In a score of novels, William Faulkner (1897–1962) explored the collective psychology of his native South, where the pressures of historical memory continually reverberated in the present. As he wrote in Requiem for a Nun *(1951),*

❝ The past is never dead. It's not even past.❞

"On or about" February 1913, to adapt a phrase from the British novelist Virginia Woolf, "the human character changed."* In that month, New York's 69th Regiment Armory hosted the International Exhibition of Modern Art. The event marked America's introduction to avant-garde European modernism and the arrival, so to speak, of a world-shattering cultural idiom. Nearly 1,250 works of art were displayed, including contributions by Vincent van Gogh, Edward Munch, Pablo Picasso, and some three hundred other European and American artists. Though scandalized critics considered many modernist works an affront to prim-and-proper Victorian values, captivated Americans visited the exhibition in droves. By the traveling show's end, upwards of half a million attendees had been exposed to modernist styles in New York, Chicago, and Boston.

Almost a full century after the Armory Show, modernism remains difficult to define. Not to be confused with modernization—that is, society's transformation from a traditional, agricultural basis to an urban, industrial, bureaucratic order—modernism can best be understood as an artistic or cultural response to the advent of modernity. Whether celebrating or criticizing twentieth-century life as new, complex, and demanding, all modernists revolted against nineteenth-century realism, formalism, and reverence for tradition. They sought to overthrow the smug Victorian mentality, with its comforting belief in abso-

lute "truth" in a stable, predictable, middle-class world. Modernists insisted instead on a radical, post-Darwinian appreciation of random chance, incessant change, contingency, uncertainty, and fragmentation. Having blasted the nineteenth-century intellectual order to pieces, modernists were in no rush to put the resulting fragments back together again. Instead, they turned inward, exploring the subconscious and humanity's supposedly animal nature in search of a more authentic, reintegrated self.

The 1913 New York exhibition symbolized two important facets of turn-of-the-century modernism: its global scope and its self-conscious sense of discontinuity with the past. Originating in the urban, bohemian circles of late-nineteenth-century Europe, especially Paris's Latin Quarter in the 1870s and 1880s, modernism soon colonized the globe. Many credited avant-garde European artists with leading this full-frontal assault on the tastes and values of the nineteenth-century bourgeoisie. Closer to home, American modernism claimed domestic roots, particularly in the pragmatic philosophy of William James and John Dewey (see "Makers of America: Pioneering Pragmatists," pp. 560–561). At its core, the modernist movement also emphasized a deep,

self-conscious break from history. Rejecting the authority of tradition, modernists extolled novel ways of thinking. They brought this iconoclastic fervor to art, music, literature, and architecture.

Of all modernism's cultural expressions, art was the most striking—and controversial. A vanguard of French symbolists, dadaists, and surrealists aimed to replace representation in art with pure abstraction. Picasso's cubist paintings, for instance, experimented with abstract multiperspectival techniques, setting up visual obstacles meant to disorient the viewer and isolate the individual's subjective consciousness. Marcel Duchamp's *Nude Descending a Staircase* (1912), the highlight of the Armory Show, offered a

*Woolf's original remark referred to December 1910, when a similar exhibition of postimpressionist art toured London.

Nude Descending a Staircase No. 2, by Marcel Duchamp, 1912 This painting, now permanently displayed at the Philadelphia Museum of Art, caused a scandal both in Paris, where it was originally shown, and at the fabled New York Armory Show in 1913. Duchamp shattered convention by evoking motion with repeated superimposed images, and by rendering the human body with stark, angular lines.

The Darwin D. Martin House Buffalo, New York, by Frank Lloyd Wright Completed in 1905, the Martin House is one of Wright's masterworks and an outstanding example of the "prairie style." Architects of the Prairie School sought to create an indigenous American modern architectural form, free of inherited design ideas and based on simple, horizontal lines and native craftsmanship.

bewildering, ambulatory succession of superimposed images. One critic likened it to "an explosion in a shingle factory." Modernist music also proved riotous, quite literally in the case of the May 1913 Paris premiere of Igor Stravinsky's *Rite of Spring*, which provoked fistfights in the aisles. Stravinsky and Arnold Schoenberg introduced elements of dissonance and atonality in their music, often alienating listeners with their uncompromising technical experimentation.

Modernist literary pioneers adapted analogous experimental techniques to their own craft. Like their fellow artists, writers sought to debunk the notions of order, sequence, and unity and capture in words the fragmentary nature of modern life. Abandoning the omniscient third-person narrator, modernist writers often wrote in the first person, endowing their narrators with a less than complete (and not entirely trustworthy) vision of events. To add to the disorientation, authors like William Faulkner sometimes employed unsettling shifts in perspective among multiple narrators or across wide swaths of time. The overall effect served to focus attention on each character's unique individual consciousness. The newfangled findings of psychological sci-

ence aided this pursuit. Some authors, including the flamboyantly idiosyncratic American Gertrude Stein, imported their "stream of consciousness" technique from the psychologist and philosopher William James (Stein's professor at Radcliffe). Others, including Eugene O'Neill, borrowed from the Viennese psychiatrist Sigmund Freud to explore their characters' subconscious and base motivations.

Architecture also reinvented itself as modern in the twentieth century. Here, American architects took the lead, especially Louis Sullivan and Frank Lloyd Wright operating in the nation's heartland. Sullivan coined the phrase "form follows function" (modernism's great credo) and practically invented the modern skyscraper in turn-of-the-century Chicago. Wright advanced the unorthodox theory that buildings should grow organically from their sites, incorporate indigenous materials, and not slavishly imitate classical and European importations. He designed open-plan "prairie-style" structures to fit the environment of the American Midwest. After 1918, an interwar European elite called for the rejection of architectural tradition, the elimination of ornament, and the outward expression of structure. German "Bauhaus"

(translated as "House of Building") architects Walter Gropius and Ludwig Mies van der Rohe joined the Swiss urbanist Le Corbusier in imagining the egalitarian possibilities of modernist buildings as "machines for living in." Around midcentury, fellow "international style" architects began to erect giant skyscrapers free of applied ornament. These steel-and-glass utopias, self-consciously engineered to promote global (rather than local) tastes and to signal a complete break from the past, symbolized for many the archetypal modernist structure.

The enduring presence of modernist buildings in American cities and towns suggests that modernism's impact on the American cultural landscape lasted considerably longer than the Armory Show's four-week run in 1913. Historians continue to debate the movement's full scope, timing, and legacy. At its most narrow, modernism can be seen as a small-scale movement confined to early-twentieth-century developments in literature and the arts. At its most broad, as Virginia Woolf claimed, modernism might represent nothing short of a complete cultural revolution, unfolding from its earliest stages into the dominant artistic and intellectual sensibility of the twentieth-century West.

South county he named "Yoknapatawpha." In powerful books like *The Sound and the Fury* (1929) and *As I Lay Dying* (1930), Faulkner peeled back layers of time and consciousness from the constricted souls of his ingrown southern characters. In contrast to Hemingway's spare prose, Faulkner experimented with multiple narrators, complex structure, and "stream of consciousness" techniques. His extended meditation on "the ragtag and bob-ends of old tales and talkings" culminated in what some readers consider his greatest work, *Absalom, Absalom!* (1936).

Though novelists and poets dominated modernist literary output in the 1920s, American composers and playwrights also made important contributions on the stage. Jerome Kern and Oscar Hammerstein's *Show Boat* debuted on Broadway in 1927 as the first true American "musical play." Eugene O'Neill, a restless Princeton dropout, emerged as America's first world-class playwright. In plays like *Strange Interlude* (1928), O'Neill laid bare Freudian notions of sex and the subconscious in a

Langston Hughes (1902–1967) celebrated Harlem's role in energizing a generation of artists and writers in his poem "Esthete in Harlem" (1930):

"Strange,
That in this nigger place
I should meet life face to face;
When, for years, I had been seeking
Life in places gentler-speaking,
Until I came to this vile street
And found Life stepping on my feet!"*

succession of dramatic soliloquies. A prodigious playwright, he authored more than a dozen productions in the 1920s and garnered the Nobel Prize in literature in 1936, six years after Sinclair Lewis had been named the first American winner .

O'Neill arose from New York's Greenwich Village, which before and after the war was a seething cauldron of writers, painters, musicians, actors, and other would-be artists. After the war a black cultural renaissance also took root uptown in Harlem, led by such gifted writers as Claude McKay, Langston Hughes, and Zora Neale Hurston, and by jazz artists like Louis Armstrong and Eubie Blake. In an outpouring of creative expression called the **Harlem Renaissance**, they proudly exulted in their black culture and argued for a "New Negro" who was a full citizen and a social equal to whites. Adopting modernist techniques, Hughes and Hurston captured the oral and improvisational traditions of contemporary blacks in dialect-filled poetry and prose.

✦ Wall Street's Big Bull Market

Signals abounded that the economic joyride might end in a crash; even in the best years of the 1920s, several hundred banks failed annually. This something-for-nothing craze was well illustrated by real estate speculation, especially the fantastic Florida boom that culminated in 1925. Numerous underwater lots were sold to eager purchasers for preposterous sums. The whole wildcat scheme collapsed when the peninsula was devastated by a West Indian hurricane, which belied advertisements of a "soothing tropical wind."

Granger Collection

Langston Hughes (1902–1967)   Raised in the Midwest, Hughes arrived in New York City in 1921 to attend Columbia University. He spent most of his life in Harlem, making it so much the center of his prolific and versatile literary career that he was often introduced as "the Poet Laureate of Harlem."

---

*"Esthete in Harlem," from *The Collected Poems of Langston Hughes* by Langston Hughes, edited by Arnold Rampersad with David Roessel, Associate Editor. Copyright ©1994 by the Estate of Langston Hughes. Used by permission of Alfred A. Knopf, a division of Random House, Inc. and Harold Ober Associates Incorporated.

Calvin Coolidge Presides over the "Jazz Age"
Coolidge's hands-off policies were sweet music to big business.

The stock exchange provided even greater sensations. Speculation ran wild, and an orgy of boom-or-bust trading pushed the market up to dizzy peaks. "Never sell America short" and "Be a bull on America" were favorite catchwords, as Wall Street bulls gored one another and fleeced greedy lambs. The stock market became a veritable gambling den.

As the 1920s lurched forward, everybody seemed to be buying stocks "on margin"—that is, with a small down payment. Barbers, stenographers, and elevator operators cashed in on "hot tips" picked up while on duty. One valet was reported to have parlayed his wages into a quarter of a million dollars. "The cash register crashed the social register," as rags-to-riches Americans reverently worshiped at the altar of the ticker-tape machine. So powerful was the intoxicant of quick profits that few heeded the warnings raised in certain quarters that this kind of tinsel prosperity could not last forever.

Little was done by Washington to curb money-mad speculators. In the wartime days of Wilson, the national debt had rocketed from the 1914 figure of $1,188,235,400 to the 1921 peak of $23,976,250,608. Conservative principles of money management pointed to a diversion of surplus funds to reduce this financial burden.

A businesslike move toward economic sanity was made in 1921, when a Republican Congress created the Bureau of the Budget. The bureau's director was to assist the president in preparing careful estimates of receipts and expenditures for submission to Congress as the annual budget. This new reform, long overdue, was designed in part to prevent haphazardly extravagant appropriations.

The burdensome taxes inherited from the war were especially distasteful to Secretary of the Treasury Mellon, as well as to his fellow millionaires. Their theory was that such high levies forced the rich to invest in tax-exempt securities rather than in the factories that provided prosperous payrolls. The Mellonites also argued, with considerable persuasiveness, that high taxes not only discouraged business but, in so doing, also brought a smaller net return to the Treasury than moderate taxes.

Seeking to succor the "poor" rich people, Mellon helped engineer a series of tax reductions from 1921 to 1926. Congress followed his lead by repealing the excess-profits tax, abolishing the gift tax, and reducing excise taxes, the surtax, the income tax, and estate taxes. In 1921 a wealthy person with an income of $1 million had paid $663,000 in income taxes; in 1926 the same person paid about $200,000. Secretary Mellon's spare-the-rich policies thus shifted much of the tax burden from the wealthy to the middle-income groups.

Mellon, lionized by conservatives as the "greatest secretary of the Treasury since Hamilton," remains a controversial figure. True, he reduced the national debt by $10 billion—from about $26 billion to $16 billion. But foes of the emaciated multimillionaire charged that he should have bitten an even larger chunk out of the debt, especially while the country was pulsating with prosperity. He was also accused of indirectly encouraging the bull market. If he had absorbed more of the national income in taxes, there would have been less money left for frenzied speculation. His refusal to do so typified the single-mindedly probusiness regime that dominated the political scene throughout the postwar decade.

Chapter Review

KEY TERMS

Bolshevik Revolution (700)

red scare (700)

criminal syndicalism laws (701)

American plan (701)

Ku Klux Klan (701)

Bible Belt (702)

Immigration Act of 1924 (703)

Eighteenth Amendment (704)

Volstead Act (704)

racketeers (708)

Fundamentalism (710)

Scientific Management (711)

Fordism (711)

United Negro Improvement Association (UNIA) (720)

modernism (720)

"Lost Generation" (721)

Harlem Renaissance (724)

PEOPLE TO KNOW

A. Mitchell Palmer

Nicola Sacco

Bartolomeo Vanzetti

Horace Kallen

Randolph Bourne

Al Capone

John T. Scopes

Frederick W. Taylor

Henry Ford

Charles A. Lindbergh

Sigmund Freud

H. L. Mencken

F. Scott Fitzgerald

Ernest Hemingway

T. S. Eliot

William Faulkner

Langston Hughes

TO LEARN MORE

Casey Nelson Blake, *Beloved Community: The Cultural Criticism of Randolph Bourne, Van Wyck Brooks, Waldo Frank, and Lewis Mumford* (1990)

Clare Corbould, *Becoming African Americans: Black Public Life in Harlem, 1919–1939* (2009)

Nancy Cott, *The Grounding of Modern Feminism* (1987)

John Higham, *Strangers in the Land: Patterns of American Nativism, 1860–1925* (1955)

Edward J. Larsen, *Summer for the Gods: The Scopes Trial and America's Continuing Debate over Science and Religion* (1997)

William Leuchtenburg, *The Perils of Prosperity, 1914–1932* (1958)

David Levering Lewis, *When Harlem Was in Vogue* (1981)

Michael Lienesch, *In the Beginning: Fundamentalism, the Scopes Trial, and the Making of the Antievolution Movement* (2007)

Nancy MacLean, *Behind the Mask of Chivalry: The Making of the Second Ku Klux Klan* (1993)

Roland Marchand, *Advertising the American Dream: Making Way for Modernity, 1920–1940* (1985)

Craig Monk, *Writing the Lost Generation: Expatriate Autobiography and American Modernism* (2008)

Mae M. Ngai, *Impossible Subjects: Illegal Aliens and the Making of Modern America* (2004)

Daniel Okrent, *Last Call: The Rise and Fall of Prohibition* (2010)

Christine Stansell, *American Moderns: Bohemian New York and the Creation of a New Century* (1999)

Jan Voogd, *Race Riots and Resistance: The Red Summer of 1919* (2008)

A complete, annotated bibliography for this chapter—along with brief descriptions of the People to Know—may be found on the American Pageant website. The Key Terms are defined in a Glossary at the end of the text.

CHRONOLOGY

1903	Wright brothers fly first airplane First story-sequence motion picture
1908	Henry Ford introduces Model T
1914	W. C. Handy's "St. Louis Blues" debuts
1917	Bolshevik Revolution in Russia
1919	Eighteenth Amendment (prohibition) Volstead Act Seattle general strike Anderson publishes *Winesburg, Ohio*
1919–1920	"Red scare"
1920	Radio broadcasting begins Fitzgerald publishes *This Side of Paradise* Lewis publishes *Main Street*
1921	Sacco-Vanzetti trial Emergency Quota Act Bureau of the Budget created
1922	Lewis publishes *Babbitt* Eliot publishes *The Waste Land*

1923	Equal Rights Amendment (ERA) proposed
1924	Immigration Act of 1924
1925	Scopes trial Florida real estate boom Fitzgerald publishes *The Great Gatsby* Dreiser publishes *An American Tragedy*
1926	Hughes publishes *The Weary Blues* Hemingway publishes *The Sun Also Rises*
1927	Lindbergh flies solo across Atlantic First talking motion picture, *The Jazz Singer* *Show Boat* opens on Broadway Sacco and Vanzetti executed
1928	Eugene O'Neill's *Strange Interlude* debuts on Broadway
1929	Faulkner publishes *The Sound and the Fury* Hemingway publishes *A Farewell to Arms*
1932	Al Capone imprisoned

Go to the CourseMate website at **www.cengagebrain.com** for additional study tools and review materials—including audio and video clips—for this chapter.

AP® Review Questions for Chapter 31

1. Responding to continuing upheavals in the postwar world order and to significant social changes that upended traditional American culture and values, most Americans in the 1920s did all of the following EXCEPT
   - (A) denounce radical foreign political ideas.
   - (B) condemn un-American lifestyles.
   - (C) struggle to achieve economic prosperity.
   - (D) shun diplomatic commitments to foreign countries.
   - (E) support severe restrictions on immigration.

2. How did the business sector use the red scare to its advantage in the 1920s?
   - (A) It established the closed shop throughout the nation.
   - (B) It cooperated with federal and state governments to break the backs of fledgling unions.
   - (C) It generally accepted the rights of the unions to organize and collectively bargain in order to gain labor peace.
   - (D) It secured passage of a federal law making most union-organizing activity illegal.
   - (E) Businesspeople refused to hire any socialists, communists, or other workers advocating radical ideologies.

3. Which of the following was most important in prompting Americans to support the Immigration Act of 1924?
   - (A) Increased migration of blacks to the North
   - (B) A nativist belief that northern Europeans were culturally superior to the waves of eastern and southern Europeans who had arrived in America over the last forty years
   - (C) A desire to abolish the quota system in the United States
   - (D) A desire to halt immigration from Latin America
   - (E) Fierce economic competition for jobs between northern Europeans, on the one hand, and eastern and southern Europeans, on the other

4. Which of the following would a cultural pluralist such as Horace Kallen, Randolph Bourne, or Louis Brandeis support?
   - (A) An American melting pot cultural ideology that advocated eliminating ethnic differences
   - (B) Tighter legal restrictions on immigration from all parts of Europe
   - (C) Greater cross-fertilization among all immigrants to promote a cosmopolitan interchange of customs, cultural ideas, and traditions
   - (D) Requiring that all recent immigrants display the American flag outside their homes to demonstrate their 100 percent Americanization
   - (E) Forbidding immigrants to celebrate publicly their respective cultural and religious holidays in the United States

5. Which of the following represented a key obstacle to working-class solidarity and union organizing in the United States during this period?
   - (A) Employers' devious use of ethnic tensions and rivalries among workers to thwart union activities and working-class solidarity
   - (B) The absence of a progressive reform impulse in America
   - (C) The growing influence of communists and other radicals in the labor movement
   - (D) The general satisfaction of most workers with the wages, benefits, and working conditions provided by their employers
   - (E) The hostility of the Catholic Church to social reform

6. All of the following undermined the effective enforcement of prohibition laws against alcohol EXCEPT
   - (A) historically weak central government control over the private spheres of Americans' lives.
   - (B) a libertine and iconoclastic postwar cultural milieu that crossed social and economic class lines.
   - (C) the fierce hostility of the majority—or a strong minority—of Americans to prohibition of alcohol.
   - (D) alcohol smuggling and distribution operations sponsored in Canada and the West Indies by organized crime syndicates.
   - (E) overwhelming popular opposition to prohibition in the South and the West.

7. According to John Dewey, the primary goal of progressive education should be to
   - (A) instill discipline and character in young people.
   - (B) emphasize the liberal arts over the natural sciences in teaching curricula.
   - (C) undermine students' naïve religious beliefs.
   - (D) develop specialized functional skills for employment.
   - (E) educate students for life through active, participatory learning methods.

8. Which of the following was NOT an outcome of the 1925 Scopes Monkey Trial?
   - (A) Fundamentalist religion continuing to be a vibrant force in American spiritual life
   - (B) A hollow victory for the Fundamentalist cause because the scientific absurdities of their position were revealed
   - (C) A complete legal vindication of a teacher's right to teach evolution in the public schools of Tennessee
   - (D) The final appearance in the influential civic life of former presidential candidate William Jennings Bryan
   - (E) A progressive reconciling of the theological beliefs of religion with the findings of modern science by increasing numbers of mainline Christians

9. How did American businesses in the 1920s attempt to meet the challenge of developing enormous universal markets for their mass-produced goods?
   (A) They developed a wide range of products.
   (B) They nurtured the birth and development of consumer advertising.
   (C) They engaged in fierce price competition wars.
   (D) They introduced direct selling through catalogues and door-to-door solicitations.
   (E) They offered government-backed guarantees on product performance.

10. What dark cloud hung over the economic prosperity enjoyed by Americans in the 1920s?
    (A) An enormous amount of American consumer debt
    (B) The inability of American business to produce sufficient numbers of products to meet increasing consumer demand
    (C) A takeover by political radicals in the union movement that threatened labor-business peace
    (D) Superfluous government spending that threatened to crowd out private investment in the booming economy
    (E) An excessive level of savings by Americans that dampened consumer spending

11. All of the following were an outgrowth of the automobile revolution EXCEPT
    (A) the consolidation of schools.
    (B) the increased dependence of women on men.
    (C) the spread of suburbs.
    (D) a loss of population in less attractive states.
    (E) altered youthful sexual behavior.

12. What did the 1920 census reveal about the lives of Americans?
    (A) For the first time in the nation's history, most men worked in manufacturing.
    (B) For the first time in the nation's history, most adult women were employed outside the home.
    (C) For the first time in the nation's history, more Americans lived in the cities than in the countryside.
    (D) For the first time in the nation's history, most Americans lived in the trans-Mississippi West.
    (E) For the first time in the nation's history, most American families had fewer than four children.

13. What did many Americans point to in order to justify their new sexual frankness?
    (A) The increased consumption of alcohol
    (B) The decline of Fundamentalism
    (C) The rise of the women's movement
    (D) The theories of Sigmund Freud
    (E) The influence of erotically explicit movies

14. Which socioeconomic group bore the heaviest tax burden in the 1920s due to the tax policies of Secretary of the Treasury Andrew Mellon?
    (A) Middle-income groups
    (B) The wealthy
    (C) The working class
    (D) The business community
    (E) The estates of those deceased

15. All of the following works of literature examined the values of 1920s America EXCEPT
    (A) *The Great Gatsby*.
    (B) *The Sun Also Rises*.
    (C) *Babbitt*.
    (D) *The Clansman*.
    (E) *The Sound and the Fury*.

16. How did the cultural liberation of the 1920s extend to African Americans, especially in northern cities?
    (A) The first "talkies" featured white actors in "black face."
    (B) Marcus Garvey created the United Negro Improvement Association.
    (C) Writers and artists displayed racial pride and asserted their self-worth.
    (D) *Birth of a Nation* became a national sensation.
    (E) White Americans patronized Harlem jazz clubs.

Chapter 32

The Politics of Boom and Bust

1920–1932

We in America today are nearer to the final triumph over poverty than ever before in the history of any land. We have not yet reached the goal—but . . . we shall soon, with the help of God, be in sight of the day when poverty will be banished from this nation.

HERBERT HOOVER, 1928

Three Republican presidents—Warren G. Harding, Calvin Coolidge, and Herbert Hoover—steered the nation on the roller-coaster ride of the 1920s, a thrilling ascent from the depths of post–World War I recession to breathtaking heights of prosperity, followed by a terrifying crash into the Great Depression. In a retreat from progressive reform, Republicans sought to serve the public good less by direct government action and more through cooperation with big business. Some corrupt officials served themselves as well, exploiting public resources for personal profit. Meanwhile, the United States retreated from its brief internationalist fling during World War I and resumed with a vengeance its traditional foreign policy of military unpreparedness and political isolationism.

✹ The Republican "Old Guard" Returns

Warren G. Harding, inaugurated in 1921, *looked* presidential. With erect figure, broad shoulders, high forehead, bushy eyebrows, and graying hair, he was one of the best-liked men of his generation. An easygoing, warm-handed backslapper, he exuded graciousness and love of people. So kindly was his nature that he would brush off ants rather than crush them.

Yet the charming, smiling exterior concealed a weak, inept interior. With a mediocre mind, Harding quickly found himself beyond his depth in the presidency. "God! What a job!" was his anguished cry on one occasion.

Harding, like Grant, was unable to detect moral halitosis in his evil associates, and he was soon surrounded by his poker-playing, shirt-sleeved cronies of the "Ohio Gang." "A good guy," Harding was "one of the boys." He hated to hurt people's feelings, especially those of his friends, by saying no, and designing political leeches capitalized on this weakness. The difference between George Washington and Warren Harding, ran a current quip, was that while Washington could not tell a lie, Harding could not tell a liar. He "was not a bad man," said one Washington observer. "He was just a slob."

Candidate Harding, who admitted his scanty mental furnishings, had promised to gather about him the "best minds" of the party. Charles Evans Hughes—masterful, imperious, incisive, brilliant—brought to the position of secretary of state a dominating if somewhat conservative leadership. The new secretary of the Treasury was a lean and elderly Pittsburgh aluminum king, Andrew W. Mellon, multimillionaire collector of the paintings that are now displayed in Washington as his gift to the nation. Chubby-faced Herbert Hoover, famed feeder of the Belgians and wartime food administrator, became secretary of commerce. An energetic businessman and engineer, he raised his second-rate cabinet post to first-rate importance, especially in drumming up foreign trade for U.S. manufacturers.

But the "best minds" of the cabinet were largely offset by two of the worst. Senator Albert B. Fall of New Mexico, a scheming anticonservationist, was appointed secretary of the interior. As guardian of the nation's natural resources, he resembled the wolf hired to protect the sheep. Harry M. Daugherty, a small-town lawyer but a big-time crook in the "Ohio Gang," was supposed to prosecute wrongdoers as attorney general.

⬟ GOP Reaction at the Throttle

Well-intentioned but weak-willed, Harding was a perfect "front" for enterprising industrialists. A McKinley-style old order settled back into place with a heavy thud at war's end, crushing the reform seedlings that had sprouted in the progressive era. A nest-feathering crowd moved into Washington and proceeded to hoodwink Harding, whom many regarded as an "amiable boob."

This new Old Guard hoped to improve on the old business doctrine of laissez-faire. Their plea was not simply for government to keep its hands off business, but for government to help guide business along the path to profits. They subtly and effectively achieved their ends by putting the courts and the administrative bureaus into the safekeeping of fellow stand-patters for the duration of the decade.

The Supreme Court was a striking example of this trend. Harding lived less than three years as president, but he appointed four of the nine justices. Several of his choices were or became deep-dyed reactionaries, and they buttressed the dike against popular currents for nearly two decades. Harding's fortunate choice for chief justice was ex-president Taft, who not only performed his duties ably but surprisingly was more liberal than some of his cautious associates.

In the first years of the 1920s, the Supreme Court axed progressive legislation. It killed a federal child-labor law, stripped away many of labor's hard-won gains, and rigidly restricted government intervention in the economy. In the landmark case of **Adkins v. Children's Hospital** (1923), the Court reversed its

Justice Oliver Wendell Holmes (1841–1935), wryly dissenting in the Adkins *case, said,*

"It would need more than the Nineteenth Amendment to convince me that there are no differences between men and women, or that legislation cannot take those differences into account."

own reasoning in *Muller* v. *Oregon* (see p. 645), which had declared women to be deserving of special protection in the workplace, and invalidated a minimum-wage law for women. Its strained ruling was that because women now had the vote (Nineteenth Amendment), they were the legal equals of men and could no longer be protected by special legislation. The contradictory premises of the *Muller* and *Adkins* cases framed a debate over gender differences that would continue for the rest of the century: were women sufficiently different from men that they merited special legal and social treatment, or were they effectively equal in the eyes of the law and therefore undeserving of special protections and preferences? (An analogous debate over racial differences haunted affirmative-action policies later in the century.)

Corporations, under Harding, could once more relax and expand. Antitrust laws were often ignored, circumvented, or feebly enforced by friendly prosecutors in the attorney general's office. The Interstate Commerce Commission, to single out one agency, came to be dominated by men who were personally sympathetic to the managers of the railroads. Harding reactionaries might well have boasted, "We care not what laws the Democrats pass as long as we are permitted to administer them."

Government for Sale This 1924 cartoon satirizing the corruption of the Harding administration shows the sale of the Capitol, the White House, and even the Washington Monument.

Big industrialists, striving to reduce the rigors of competition, now had a free hand to set up trade associations. Cement manufacturers, for example, would use these agencies to agree upon standardization of products, publicity campaigns, and a united front in dealing with the railroads and labor. Although many of these associations ran counter to the spirit of existing antitrust legislation, their formation was encouraged by Secretary Hoover. His sense of engineering efficiency led him to condemn the waste resulting from cutthroat competition, and his commitment to voluntary cooperation led him to urge businesses to regulate themselves rather than be regulated by big government.

✶ The Aftermath of War

Wartime government controls on the economy were swiftly dismantled. The War Industries Board disappeared with almost indecent haste. With its passing, progressive hopes for more government regulation of big business evaporated.

Washington likewise returned the railroads to private management in 1920. Reformers had hoped that wartime government operation of the lines might lead to their permanent nationalization. Instead Congress passed the Esch-Cummins Transportation Act of 1920, which encouraged private consolidation of the railroads and pledged the Interstate Commerce Commission to guarantee their profitability. The new philosophy was not to save the country from the railroads, as in the days of the Populists, but to save the railroads for the country.

The federal government also tried to pull up anchor and get out of the shipping business. The Merchant Marine Act of 1920 authorized the Shipping Board, which controlled about fifteen hundred vessels, to dispose of much of the hastily built wartime fleet at bargain-basement prices. The board operated the remaining vessels without conspicuous success. Under the La Follette Seaman's Act of 1915, American shipping could not thrive in competition with foreigners, who all too often provided their crews with wretched food and starvation wages.

Labor, suddenly deprived of its wartime crutch of friendly government support, limped along badly in the postwar decade. A bloody strike in the steel industry was ruthlessly broken in 1919, partly by exploiting ethnic and racial divisions among the steelworkers and partly by branding the strikers as dangerous "reds." The Railway Labor Board, a successor body to the wartime labor boards, ordered a wage cut of 12 percent in 1922, provoking a two-month strike. It ended when Attorney General Daugherty, who fully shared Harding's big-business bias, clamped on the strikers one of the most

sweeping injunctions in American history. Unions wilted in this hostile political environment, and membership shriveled by nearly 30 percent between 1920 and 1930.

Needy veterans were among the few nonbusiness groups to reap lasting gains from the war. Congress in 1921 generously created the Veterans Bureau, authorized to operate hospitals and provide vocational rehabilitation for the disabled.

Veterans quickly organized into pressure groups. The American Legion had been founded in Paris in 1919 by Colonel Theodore Roosevelt, Jr. Legionnaires met periodically to renew old hardships and let off steam in good-natured horseplay. The legion soon became distinguished for its militant patriotism, rock-ribbed conservatism, and zealous antiradicalism.

The legion also became notorious for its aggressive lobbying for veterans' benefits. The chief grievance of the former "doughboys" was monetary—they wanted their "dough." The former servicemen demanded "adjusted compensation" to make up for the wages they had "lost" when they turned in their factory overalls for military uniforms during the Great War.

Critics denounced this demand as a holdup "bonus," but the millions of veterans deployed heavy political artillery. They browbeat Congress into passing a bonus bill in 1922, which Harding promptly vetoed. Re-forming their lines, the repulsed veterans gathered for a final attack. In 1924 Congress again hoisted the white flag and passed the Adjusted Compensation Act. It gave every former soldier a paid-up insurance policy due in twenty years—adding about $3.5 billion to the total cost of the war. Penny-pinching Calvin Coolidge sternly vetoed the measure, but Congress overrode him, leaving the veterans with their loot.

✶ America Seeks Benefits Without Burdens

Making peace with the fallen foe was the most pressing problem left on Harding's doorstep. The United States, having rejected the Treaty of Versailles, was still technically at war with Germany, Austria, and Hungary nearly three years after the armistice. Peace was finally achieved by lone-wolf tactics. In July 1921 Congress passed a simple joint resolution that declared the war officially ended.

Isolation was enthroned in Washington. The Harding administration, with the Senate "irreconcilables" holding a hatchet over its head, continued to regard the League of Nations as a thing unclean. Harding at first refused even to support the League's world health program. But the new world body was much too important to be completely ignored. "Unofficial observers" were

"I Sympathize Deeply with You, Madam, but I Cannot Associate with You," 1923 President Harding's secretary of state, Charles Evans Hughes, broke the news to a desperate, war-tattered Europe that America was going, and staying, home.

Granger Collection

the initiative. He was prodded by businesspeople unwilling to dig deeper into their pockets for money to finance the ambitious naval building program started during the war. A deadly contest was shaping up with Britain and Japan, which watched with alarm as the oceans filled with American vessels. Britain still commanded the world's largest navy, but the clatter of American riveters proclaimed that the United States would soon overtake it.

Public agitation in America, fed by these worries, brought about the headline-making Washington "Disarmament" Conference in 1921–1922. Invitations went to all the major naval powers—except Bolshevik Russia, whose government the United States refused officially to recognize. The double agenda included naval disarmament and the situation in the Far East.

At the outset Secretary Hughes startled the delegates, who were expecting the usual diplomatic fence-straddling, with a comprehensive, concrete plan for declaring a ten-year "holiday" on the construction of battleships and even for scrapping some of the huge dreadnoughts already built. He proposed that the scaled-down navies of America and Britain should enjoy parity in battleships and aircraft carriers, with Japan on the small end of a 5:5:3 ratio. This arrangement sounded to the sensitive Japanese ambassador like "Rolls-Royce, Rolls-Royce, Ford."

Complex bargaining followed in the wake of Hughes's proposals. The Five-Power Naval Treaty of 1922 embodied Hughes's ideas on ship ratios, but only after face-saving compensation was offered to the insecure Japanese (see Figure 32.1). The British and Americans both conceded that they would refrain from fortifying their Far Eastern possessions, including the Philippines. The Japanese were not subjected to such restraints in their possessions. In addition, a Four-Power Treaty replaced the twenty-year-old Anglo-Japanese alliance. The new pact bound Britain, Japan, France, and the United States to preserve the status quo in the Pacific—another concession to the jumpy Japanese. Finally, the Washington Conference gave chaotic China—"the Sick Man of the Far East"—a shot in the arm with the **Nine-Power Treaty** of 1922, whose

sent to its seat in Geneva, Switzerland, to hang around like detectives shadowing a suspected criminal.

Harding could not completely turn his back on the outside world, especially the Middle East, where a sharp rivalry developed between America and Britain for oil-drilling concessions. Remembering that the Allies had floated to victory on a flood of oil, experts recognized that liquid "black gold" would be as necessary as blood in the battles of tomorrow. Secretary Hughes eventually secured for American oil companies the right to share in the exploitation of the sandy region's oil riches.

Disarmament was one international issue on which Harding, after much indecision, finally seized

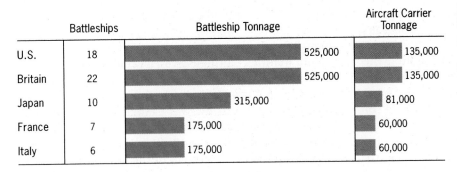

	Battleships	Battleship Tonnage	Aircraft Carrier Tonnage
U.S.	18	525,000	135,000
Britain	22	525,000	135,000
Japan	10	315,000	81,000
France	7	175,000	60,000
Italy	6	175,000	60,000

FIGURE 32.1 Limits Imposed by Washington Conference, 1921–1922 The pledge of the British and Americans to refrain from fortifying their Far Eastern possessions, while Japan was allowed to fortify its possessions, was the key to the naval-limitation treaty. The United States and Great Britain thus won a temporary victory but later paid a horrendous price when they had to dislodge the well-entrenched Japanese from the Pacific in World War II.

signatories agreed to nail wide-open the Open Door in China.

When the final gavel banged, the Hardingites boasted with much fanfare—and some justification—of their globe-shaking achievement in disarmament. But their satisfaction was somewhat illusory. No restrictions had been placed on small warships, and the other powers churned ahead with the construction of cruisers, destroyers, and submarines, while penny-pinching Uncle Sam lagged dangerously behind. Congress also pointedly declared that it was making no commitment to the use of armed force or any kind of joint action when it ratified the Four-Power Treaty. These reservations, in effect, rendered the treaty a dead letter. Ominously, the American people seemed content to rely for their security on words and wishful thinking rather than on weapons and hardheaded realism.

A similar sentimentalism welled up later in the decade, when Americans clamored for the "outlawry of war." The conviction spread that if quarreling nations would only take the pledge to foreswear war as an instrument of national policy, swords could be beaten into plowshares. Calvin Coolidge's secretary of state, Frank B. Kellogg, who later won the Nobel Peace Prize for his role, was lukewarm about the idea. But after petitions bearing more than 2 million signatures cascaded into Washington, he signed with the French foreign minister in 1928 the famed **Kellogg-Briand Pact**. Officially known as the Pact of Paris, it was ultimately ratified by sixty-two nations.

This new parchment peace was delusory in the extreme. Defensive wars were still permitted, and what scheming aggressor could not cook up an excuse of self-defense? Lacking both muscles and teeth, the pact was a diplomatic derelict—and virtually useless in a showdown. Yet it accurately—and dangerously—reflected the American mind in the 1920s, which was all too willing to be lulled into a false sense of security. This mood took even deeper hold in the ostrich-like neutralism of the 1930s.

Hiking the Tariff Higher

A comparable lack of realism afflicted foreign economic policy in the 1920s. Businesspeople, shortsightedly obsessed with the dazzling prospects in the prosperous home market, sought to keep that market to themselves by flinging up insurmountable tariff walls around the United States. They were spurred into action by their fear of a flood of cheap goods from recovering Europe, especially during the brief but sharp recession of 1920–1921.

In 1922 Congress passed the comprehensive **Fordney-McCumber Tariff Law**. Glib lobbyists once more descended upon Washington and helped boost schedules from the average of 27 percent under Wilson's Underwood Tariff of 1913 to an average of 38.5 percent, which was almost as high as Taft's Payne-Aldrich Tariff of 1909. (See the Appendix.) Duties on farm produce were increased, and the principle was proclaimed that the general rates were designed to equalize the cost of American and foreign production. A promising degree of flexibility was introduced for the first time, when the president was authorized, with the advice of the fact-finding Tariff Commission, to reduce or increase duties by as much as 50 percent.

Presidents Harding and Coolidge, true to their big-industry sympathies, were far more friendly to tariff increases than to reductions. In six years they authorized thirty-two upward changes, including on their list vital commodities like dairy products, chemicals, and pig iron. During the same period, the White House ordered only five reductions. These included mill feed and such trifling items as bobwhite quail, paintbrush handles, phenol, and cresylic acid.

The high-tariff course thus charted by the Republican regimes set off an ominous chain reaction. European producers felt the squeeze, for the American tariff walls prolonged their postwar chaos. An impoverished Europe needed to sell its manufactured goods to the United States, particularly if it hoped to achieve economic recovery and to pay its huge war debt to Washington. America needed to give foreign nations a chance to make a profit from it so that they could buy its manufactured articles and repay debts. International trade, Americans were slow to learn, is a two-way street. In general, they could not sell to others in quantity unless they bought from them in quantity—or lent them more U.S. dollars.

Erecting tariff walls was a game that two could play. The American example spurred European nations, throughout the feverish 1920s, to pile up higher barriers themselves. These artificial obstacles were doubly bad: they hurt not only American-made goods but the products of European countries as well. The whole vicious circle further deepened the international economic distress, providing one more rung on the ladder by which Adolf Hitler scrambled to power.

The Stench of Scandal

The loose morality and get-rich-quickism of the Harding era manifested themselves spectacularly in a series of scandals.

Early in 1923 Colonel Charles R. Forbes, onetime deserter from the army, was caught with his hand in the till and resigned as head of the Veterans Bureau. An appointee of the gullible Harding, he and his accomplices looted the government to the tune of about $200 million, chiefly in connection with the building of

Washington Officials Trying to Outpace the Teapot Dome Scandal, ca. 1922

veterans' hospitals. He was sentenced to two years in a federal penitentiary.

Most shocking of all was the **Teapot Dome scandal**, an affair that involved priceless naval oil reserves at Teapot Dome (Wyoming) and Elk Hills (California). In 1921 the slippery secretary of the interior, Albert B. Fall, induced his careless colleague, the secretary of the navy, to transfer these valuable properties to the Interior Department. Harding indiscreetly signed the secret order. Fall then quietly leased the lands to oilmen Harry F. Sinclair and Edward L. Doheny, but not until he had received a bribe ("loan") of $100,000 from Doheny and about three times that amount in all from Sinclair.

Teapot Dome, no tempest in a teapot, finally came to a whistling boil. Details of the crooked transaction gradually began to leak out in March 1923, two years after Harding took office. Fall, Sinclair, and Doheny were indicted the next year, but the case dragged through the courts until 1929. Finally Fall was found guilty of taking a bribe and was sentenced to one year in jail. By a curious quirk of justice, the two bribe givers were acquitted while the bribe taker was convicted, although Sinclair served several months in jail for having "shadowed" jurors and for refusing to testify before a Senate committee.

The oily smudge from Teapot Dome polluted the prestige of the Washington government. Right-thinking citizens wondered what was going on when public officials could sell out the nation's vital resources, especially those reserved for the U.S. Navy. The acquittal of Sinclair and Doheny undermined faith in the courts, while giving further currency to the cynical sayings "You can't

put a million dollars in jail" and "In America everyone is assumed guilty until proven rich."

Still more scandals erupted. Persistent reports as to the underhanded doings of Attorney General Daugherty prompted a Senate investigation in 1924 of the illegal sale of pardons and liquor permits. Forced to resign, the accused official was tried in 1927 but was released after a jury twice failed to agree. During the trial Daugherty hid behind the trousers of the now-dead Harding by implying that persistent probing might uncover crookedness in the White House.

Harding was mercifully spared the full revelation of these iniquities, though his worst suspicions were aroused. While news of the scandals was beginning to break, he embarked upon a speechmaking tour across the country all the way to Alaska. On the return trip, he died in San Francisco, on August 2, 1923, of pneumonia and thrombosis. His death may have been hastened by a broken heart resulting from the disloyalty of designing friends. Mourning millions, not yet fully aware of the graft in Washington, expressed genuine sorrow.

The brutal fact is that Harding was not a strong enough man for the presidency—as he himself privately admitted. Such was his weakness that he tolerated people and conditions that subjected the Republic to its worst disgrace since the days of President Grant.

✸ "Silent Cal" Coolidge

News of Harding's death was sped to Vice President Coolidge, then visiting at his father's New England farmhouse. By the light of two kerosene lamps, the elder Coolidge, a justice of the peace, used the old family Bible to administer the presidential oath to his son.

This homespun setting was symbolic of Coolidge. Quite unlike Harding, the stern-faced Vermonter, with his thin nose and tightly set lips, embodied the New England virtues of honesty, morality, industry, and frugality. As a youth, his father reported, he seemed to get more sap out of a maple tree than did any of the other boys. Practicing a rigid economy in both money and words, "Silent Cal" came to be known in Washington conversational circles for his brilliant flashes of silence. His dour, serious visage prompted the acid observation that he had been "weaned on a pickle."

Coolidge seemed to be a crystallization of the commonplace. Painfully shy, he was blessed with only mediocre powers of leadership. He would occasionally display a dry wit in private, but his speeches, delivered in a nasal New England twang, were invariably boring. A staunch apostle of the status quo, he was no knight in armor riding forth to tilt at wrongs. His only horse, in fact, was an electric-powered steed on which he took his exercise. True to Republican philosophy, he became

Calvin Coolidge, Gentleman Angler Coolidge "was a real conservative, a fundamentalist in religion, in the economic and social order, and in fishing," said his successor, Herbert Hoover, who had a fly fisherman's disdain for Coolidge's bait-fishing tactics—and for his predecessor's laissez-faire politics as well.

AP/Wide World

the "high priest of the great god Business." He believed that "the man who builds a factory builds a temple" and that "the man who works there worships there."

The hands-off temperament of "Cautious Cal" Coolidge suited the times perfectly. His thrifty nature caused him to sympathize fully with Secretary of the Treasury Mellon's efforts to reduce both taxes and debts. No foe of industrial bigness, he let business have its head. "Coolidge luck" held during his five and a half prosperity-blessed years.

Ever a profile in caution, Coolidge slowly gave the Harding regime a badly needed moral fumigation. Teapot Dome had scalded the Republican party badly, but so transparently honest was the vinegary Vermonter that the scandalous oil did not rub off on him. The public, though at first shocked by the scandal, quickly simmered down, and an alarming tendency developed in certain quarters to excuse some of the wrongdoers on the grounds that "they had gotten away with it." Some critics even condemned the government prosecutors for continuing to rock the boat. America's moral sensibility was evidently being dulled by prosperity.

✯ Frustrated Farmers

Sun-bronzed farmers were caught squarely in a boom-or-bust cycle in the postwar decade. While the fighting had raged, they had raked in money hand over gnarled

fist; by the spring of 1920, the price of wheat had shot up to an incredible $3 a bushel. But peace brought an end to government-guaranteed high prices and to massive purchases by other nations, as foreign production reentered the stream of world commerce.

Machines also threatened to plow the farmers under an avalanche of their own overabundant crops. The gasoline-engine tractor was working a revolution on American farms. This steel mule was to cultivation and sowing what the McCormick reaper was to harvesting. Blue-denimed farmers no longer had to plod after the horse-drawn plow with high-footed gait. They could sit erect on their chugging mechanized chariots and turn under and harrow many acres in a single day. They could grow bigger crops on larger areas, using fewer horses and hired hands. The wartime boom had encouraged them to bring vast new tracts under cultivation, especially in the "wheat belt" of the upper Midwest. But such improved efficiency and expanded agricultural acreage helped to pile up more price-dampening surpluses. A withering depression swept through agricultural districts in the 1920s, when one farm in four was sold for debt or taxes. As a plaintive song of the period ran,

No use talkin', any man's beat,
With 'leven-cent cotton and forty-cent meat.

Schemes abounded for bringing relief to the hard-pressed farmers. A bipartisan "farm bloc" from the

Library of Congress

Have you placed a Sentimental Value on your Horses out of proportion to the work they are able to perform?

BAILOR MOTOR CULTIVATORS

Mechanizing Agriculture Just as the automobile replaced the horse on city streets, so did the gas-engine tractor replace horses and mules on the nation's farms in the 1920s. American farmers owned ten times more tractors in 1930 than they did in 1920. The smoke-belching tractors bolstered productivity but also increased the farmers' debt burden, as the Great Depression made tragically clear.

agricultural states coalesced in Congress in 1921 and succeeded in driving through some helpful laws. Noteworthy was the Capper-Volstead Act, which exempted farmers' marketing cooperatives from antitrust prosecution. The farm bloc's favorite proposal was the **McNary-Haugen Bill**, pushed energetically from 1924 to 1928. It sought to keep agricultural prices high by authorizing the government to buy up surpluses and sell them abroad. Government losses were to be made up by a special tax on the farmers. Congress twice passed the bill, but frugal Coolidge twice vetoed it. Farm prices stayed down, and farmers' political temperatures stayed high, reaching a fever pitch in the election of 1924.

✪ A Three-Way Race for the White House in 1924

Self-satisfied Republicans, chanting "Keep Cool and Keep Coolidge," nominated "Silent Cal" for the presidency at their convention in Cleveland in the simmering summer of 1924. Squabbling Democrats had more difficulty choosing a candidate when they met in New York's sweltering Madison Square Garden. Reflecting many of the cultural tensions of the decade, the party was hopelessly split between "wets" and "drys," urbanites and farmers, Fundamentalists and Modernists, northern liberals and southern stand-patters, immigrants and old-stock Americans. In one symptomatic spasm of discord, the conventioneers failed by just one vote to pass a resolution condemning the Ku Klux Klan.

Deadlocked for an unprecedented 102 ballots, the convention at last turned wearily, sweatily, and unenthusiastically to John W. Davis. A wealthy corporation lawyer connected with the Wall Street banking house of J. P. Morgan and Company, the polished nominee was no less conservative than cautious Calvin Coolidge.

The field was now wide-open for a liberal candidate. The white-pompadoured Senator Robert ("Fighting Bob") La Follette from Wisconsin, perennial aspirant to the presidency and now sixty-nine years of age, sprang forward to lead a new Progressive party. He gained the endorsement of the American Federation of Labor and enjoyed the support of the shrinking Socialist party, but his major constituency was made up of the price-pinched farmers. La Follette's new Progressive party, fielding only a presidential ticket, with no candidates for local office, was a head without a body. It proved to be only a shadow of the robust Progressive coalition of prewar days. Its platform called for government ownership of railroads and relief for farmers, lashed out at monopoly and antilabor injunctions, and urged a constitutional amendment to limit the Supreme Court's power to invalidate laws passed by Congress.

La Follette turned in a respectable showing, polling nearly 5 million votes. But "Cautious Cal" and the oil-smeared Republicans slipped easily back into office, overwhelming Davis, 15,718,211 to 8,385,283. The electoral count stood at 382 for Coolidge, 136 for Davis, and 13 for La Follette, all from his home state of Wisconsin (see Map 32.1). As the so-called conscience of the callous 1920s, La Follette injected a badly needed liberal tonic into a decade drugged on prosperity. But

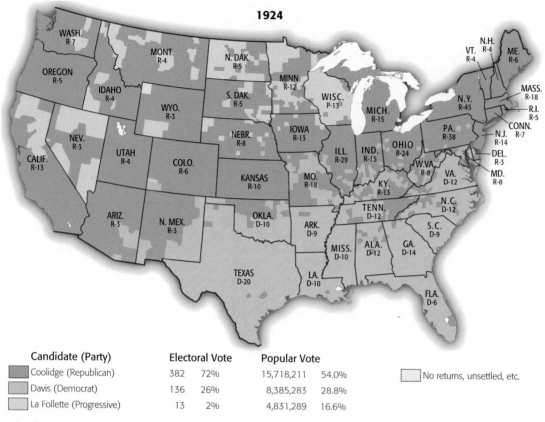

Candidate (Party)	Electoral Vote		Popular Vote	
Coolidge (Republican)	382	72%	15,718,211	54.0%
Davis (Democrat)	136	26%	8,385,283	28.8%
La Follette (Progressive)	13	2%	4,831,289	16.6%

No returns, unsettled, etc.

MAP 32.1 Presidential Election of 1924 (showing popular vote by county) Note the concentration of La Follette's votes in the old Populist strongholds of the Midwest and the mountain states. His ticket did especially well in the grain-growing districts battered by the postwar slump in agricultural prices. © Cengage Learning

times were too good for too many for his reforming message to carry the day.

✷ Foreign-Policy Flounderings

Isolation continued to reign in the Coolidge era. Despite presidential proddings, the Senate proved unwilling to allow America to adhere to the World Court—the judicial arm of the still-suspect League of Nations. Coolidge only halfheartedly—and unsuccessfully—pursued further naval disarmament after the loudly trumpeted agreements worked out at the Washington Conference in 1922.

A glaring exception to the United States' inward-looking indifference to the outside world was the armed interventionism in the Caribbean and Central America. American troops were withdrawn (after an eight-year stay) from the Dominican Republic in 1924, but they remained in Haiti from 1914 to 1934. President Coolidge in 1925 briefly removed American bayonets from troubled Nicaragua, where they had glinted

intermittently since 1909, but in 1926 he sent them back, five thousand strong, and they stayed until 1933. American oil companies clamored for a military expedition to Mexico in 1926 when the Mexican government began to assert its sovereignty over oil resources. Coolidge kept cool and defused the Mexican crisis with some skillful diplomatic negotiating. But his mailed-fist tactics elsewhere bred sore resentments south of the Rio Grande, where angry critics loudly assailed "*yanqui* imperialism."

Overshadowing all other foreign-policy problems in the 1920s was the knotty issue of international debts, a complicated tangle of private loans, Allied war debts, and German reparations payments (see Figure 32.2). Almost overnight, World War I had reversed the international financial position of the United States. In 1914 America had been a debtor nation to the sum of about $4 billion; by 1922 it had become a creditor nation to the sum of about $16 billion. The almighty dollar rivaled the pound sterling as the financial giant of the world. American investors loaned some $10 billion to foreigners in the 1920s, though even this huge river

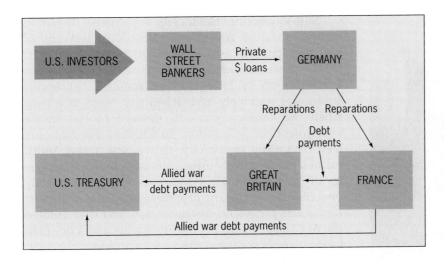

FIGURE 32.2 Aspects of the Financial Merry-go-round, 1921–1933 Great Britain, with a debt of over $4 billion owed to the U.S. Treasury, had a huge stake in proposals for inter-Allied debt cancellation, but France's stake was even larger. Less prosperous than Britain in the 1920s and more battered by the war, which had been fought on its soil, France owed nearly $3.5 billion to the United States and additional billions to Britain.

of money could not fully refloat the war-shelled world economy. Americans, bewitched by lucrative investment opportunities in their domestic economy, did not lend nearly so large a fraction of their national income overseas as had the British in the prewar period.

The key knot in the debt tangle was the $10 billion that the U.S. Treasury had loaned to the Allies during and immediately after the war. Uncle Sam held their IOUs—and he wanted to be paid. The Allies, in turn, protested that the demand for repayment was grossly unfair. The French and the British pointed out, with much justice, that they had held up a wall of flesh and bone against the common foe until America the Unready had finally entered the fray. America, they argued, should write off its loans as war costs, just as the Allies had been tragically forced to write off the lives of millions of young men. The debtors also complained that the real effect of their borrowed dollars had been to fuel the boom in the already roaring wartime economy in America, where nearly all their purchases had been made. And the final straw, protested the Europeans, was that America's postwar tariff walls made it almost impossible for them to sell their goods to earn the dollars to pay their debts.

✷ Unraveling the Debt Knot

America's tightfisted insistence on getting its money back helped to harden the hearts of the Allies against conquered Germany. The French and the British demanded that the Germans make enormous reparations payments, totaling some $32 billion, as compensation for war-inflicted damages. The Allies hoped to settle their debts to the United States with the money received from Germany. The French, seeking to extort lagging reparations payments, sent troops into Germany's industrialized Ruhr Valley in 1923.

Berlin responded by permitting its currency to inflate astronomically. At one point in October 1923, a loaf of bread cost 480 million marks, or about $120 million in preinflation money. German society teetered on the brink of mad anarchy, and the whole international house of financial cards threatened to flutter down in colossal chaos.

Sensible statesmen now urged that war debts and reparations alike be drastically scaled down or even canceled outright. But to Americans such proposals smacked of "welshing" on a debt. "We went across, but they won't come across," cried a prominent politician. Scroogelike, Calvin Coolidge turned aside suggestions of debt cancellation with a typically terse question: "They hired the money, didn't they?" The Washington administration proved especially unrealistic in its dogged insistence that there was no connection whatever between debts and reparations.

Reality finally dawned in the **Dawes Plan** of 1924. Negotiated largely by Charles Dawes, about to be nominated as Coolidge's running mate, it rescheduled German reparations payments and opened the way for further American private loans to Germany. The whole financial cycle now became still more complicated, as U.S. bankers loaned money to Germany, Germany paid reparations to France and Britain, and the former Allies paid war debts to the United States. Clearly the source of this monetary merry-go-round was the flowing well of American credit. When that well dried up after the great crash in 1929, the jungle of international finance quickly turned into a desert. President Herbert Hoover declared a one-year debt moratorium in 1931, and before long all the debtors had defaulted—except "honest little Finland," which struggled along making payments until the last of its debt was discharged in 1976.

The United States never did get its money, but it harvested a bumper crop of ill will. Irate French crowds on occasion attacked American tourists, and

A German Woman Burns Near-worthless Paper Currency for Cooking Fuel, 1923 The memory of the hyper-inflation of the 1920s haunted Germans well into the twenty-first century.

throughout Europe Uncle Sam was caricatured as Uncle Shylock, greedily whetting his knife for the last pound of Allied flesh. The bad taste left in American mouths by the whole sorry episode contributed powerfully to the storm-cellar neutrality legislation passed by Congress in the 1930s.

✫ The Triumph of Herbert Hoover, 1928

Poker-faced Calvin Coolidge, the tight-lipped "Sphinx of the Potomac," bowed out of the 1928 presidential race when he announced, "I do not choose to run." His logical successor was super-Secretary (of Commerce) Herbert Hoover, unpopular with the political bosses but the much-admired darling of the masses, who asked, "Hoo but Hoover?" He was nominated on a platform that clucked contentedly over both prosperity and prohibition.

Still-squabbling Democrats nominated Alfred E. Smith, four-time governor of New York and one of the most colorful personalities in American politics. He was a wisecracking, glad-handing liberal who suffered from several fatal political handicaps. "Al(cohol)" Smith was soakingly and drippingly "wet" at a time when the country was still devoted to the "noble experiment" of prohibition. To a nation that had only recently moved to the city, native New Yorker Smith seemed too abrasively urban. He was a Roman Catholic in an overwhelmingly Protestant—and unfortunately prejudiced—land. Many dry, rural, and Fundamentalist Democrats gagged on his candidacy, and they saddled the wet Smith with a dry running mate and a dry platform. Jauntily sporting a brown derby and a big cigar, Smith, "the Happy Warrior," tried to carry alcohol on one shoulder and water on the other. But his effort was doomed from the start.

Radio figured prominently in this campaign for the first time, and it helped Hoover more than Smith. The New Yorker had more personal sparkle, but he could not project it through the radio (which in his Lower East Side twang he pronounced "radd-dee-o," grating on the ears of many listeners). Iowa-born Hoover, with his double-breasted dignity, came out of the microphone better than he went in. Decrying un-American "socialism" and preaching "rugged individualism," he sounded both grassrootish and statesmanlike.

Chubby-faced, ruddy-complexioned Herbert Hoover, with his painfully high starched collar, was a living example of the American success story and an intriguing mixture of two centuries. As a poor orphan boy who had worked his way through Stanford University, he had absorbed the nineteenth-century copybook maxims of industry, thrift, and self-reliance. As a fabulously successful mining engineer and a brilliant businessman, he had honed to a high degree the efficiency doctrines of the progressive era.

A small-town boy from Iowa and Oregon, he had traveled and worked abroad extensively. Long years of self-imposed exile had deepened his determination, abundantly supported by national tradition, to avoid foreign entanglements. His experiences abroad had further strengthened his faith in American individualism, free enterprise, and small government.

With his unshaken dignity and Quaker restraint, Hoover was a far cry from the typical backslapping politician. Though a citizen of the world and laden with international honors, he was quite shy, standoffish, and stiff. Personally colorless in public, he had been accustomed during much of his life to giving orders to subordinates and not to soliciting votes. Never before elected to public office, he was thin-skinned in the face of criticism, and he did not adapt readily to the necessary give-and-take of political accommodation.

His real power lay in his integrity, his humanitarianism, his passion for assembling the facts, his efficiency, his talents for administration, and his ability to inspire loyalty in close associates. They called him "the Chief."

As befitted America's newly mechanized civilization, Hoover was the ideal businessperson's candidate. A self-made millionaire, he recoiled from anything suggesting socialism, paternalism, or "planned economy." Yet as secretary of commerce, he had exhibited some progressive instincts. He endorsed labor unions and supported federal regulation of the new radio broadcasting industry. He even flirted for a time with the idea of government-owned radio, similar to the British Broadcasting Corporation (BBC).

As bands blared Smith's theme song, "The Sidewalks of New York," the campaign sank into the sewers beneath the sidewalks. Despite the best efforts of Hoover and Smith, below-the-belt tactics were employed to a disgusting degree by lower-level campaigners. Religious bigotry raised its hideous head over Smith's Catholicism. An irresponsible whispering campaign claimed that "A Vote for Al Smith Is a Vote for the Pope" and that the White House, under Smith, would become a branch of the Vatican—complete with "Rum, Romanism, and Ruin." Hoover's attempts to quash such rumors were in vain.

The proverbially solid South—"100 percent American" and a stronghold of Protestant Ku Klux Klanism—shied away from "city slicker" Al Smith. It might have accepted a Catholic, or a wet, or the descendant of Irish grandparents, or an urbanite. But a concoction of Catholicism, wettism, foreignism, and liberalism brewed on the sidewalks of New York was too bitter a dose for southern stomachs. Smith's theme song was a constant and rasping reminder that his upbringing had not been convincingly American.

Hoover triumphed in a landslide. He bagged 21,391,993 popular votes to 15,016,169 for his embittered opponent, while rolling up an electoral count of 444 to 87. A huge Republican majority was returned to the House of Representatives. Tens of thousands of dry southern Democrats—"Hoovercrats"—rebelled against Al Smith, and Hoover proved to be the first Republican candidate in fifty-two years, except for Harding's Tennessee victory in 1920, to carry a state that had seceded. He swept five states of the former Confederacy, as well as all of the Border States (see Map 32.2).

Herbert Hoover on the Road "Whistle-stop" campaigns, with candidates speaking from the rear platforms of trains, were a standard feature of American politics before the advent of television. Herbert Hoover here greets a crowd in Newark, New Jersey, during the 1928 campaign.

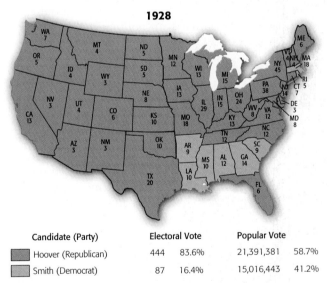

1928

Candidate (Party)	Electoral Vote		Popular Vote	
Hoover (Republican)	444	83.6%	21,391,381	58.7%
Smith (Democrat)	87	16.4%	15,016,443	41.2%

MAP 32.2 Presidential Election of 1928 (with electoral vote by state) Smith, despite his defeat, managed to poll almost as many votes as the victorious Coolidge had in 1924. By attracting to the party an immense urban or "sidewalk" vote, the breezy New Yorker foreshadowed Roosevelt's New Deal victory in 1932, when the Democrats patched together the solid South and the urban North. A cruel joke had the Catholic Smith cabling the Pope a single word after the election: "Unpack." © Cengage Learning

✹ President Hoover's First Moves

Prosperity in the late 1920s smiled broadly as the Hoover years began. Soaring stocks on the bull market continued to defy the laws of financial gravitation. But two immense groups of citizens were not getting their share of the riches flowing from the national cornucopia: the unorganized wage earners and especially the disorganized farmers.

Hoover's administration, in line with its philosophy of promoting self-help, responded to the outcry of the wounded farmers with legislative aspirin. The **Agricultural Marketing Act**, passed by Congress in June 1929, was designed to help the farmers help themselves, largely through producers' cooperatives. It set up the Federal Farm Board, with a revolving fund of half a billion dollars at its disposal. Money was lent generously to farm organizations seeking to buy, sell, and store agricultural surpluses.

In 1930 the Farm Board itself created both the Grain Stabilization Corporation and the Cotton Stabilization Corporation. The prime goal was to bolster sagging prices by buying up surpluses. But the two agencies were soon suffocated by an avalanche of farm produce, as wheat dropped to fifty-seven cents a bushel and cotton to five cents a pound.

Farmers had meanwhile clutched at the tariff as a possible straw to help keep their heads above the waters of financial ruin. During the recent presidential campaign, Hoover, an amateur in politics, had been stampeded into a politically unwise pledge. He had promised to call Congress into special session to consider agricultural relief and, specifically, to bring about "limited" changes in the tariff. These hope-giving assurances no doubt won many votes for Hoover in the midwestern farm belt.

The **Hawley-Smoot Tariff** of 1930 followed the well-worn pattern of Washington horse trading. It started out in the House as a fairly reasonable protective measure, designed to assist the farmers. But by the time the high-pressure lobbyists had pushed it through the Senate, it had acquired about a thousand amendments. It thus turned out to be the highest protective tariff in the nation's peacetime history. The average duty on nonfree goods was raised from 38.5 percent, as established by the Fordney-McCumber Act of 1922, to nearly 60 percent.

To angered foreigners, the Hawley-Smoot Tariff was a blow below the trade belt. It seemed like a declaration of economic warfare on the entire outside world. It reversed a promising worldwide trend toward reasonable tariffs and widened the yawning trade gaps. It plunged both America and other nations deeper into the terrible depression that had already begun. It increased international financial chaos and forced the United States further into the bog of economic isolationism. And economic isolationism, both at home and abroad, was playing directly into the hands of a hate-filled German demagogue, Adolf Hitler.

✹ The Great Crash Ends the Golden Twenties

When Herbert Hoover confidently took the presidential oath on March 4, 1929, there were few black clouds on the economic horizon. The "long boom" seemed endless, with the painful exception of the debt-blanketed farm belt. America's productive colossus—stimulated by the automobile, radio, movies, and other new industries—was roaring along at a dizzy speed that suggested a permanent plateau of prosperity. Few people sensed that it might smother its own fires by pouring out too much.

The speculative bubble was actually near the bursting point. Prices on the stock exchange continued to spiral upward and create a fool's paradise of paper profits, despite Hoover's early but fruitless efforts to curb speculation through the Federal Reserve Board. A few prophets of disaster were bold enough to sound warnings but were drowned out by the mad chatter of the ticker-tape machine.

A catastrophic crash came in October 1929. It was partially triggered by the British, who raised their interest rates in an effort to bring back capital lured abroad by American investments. Foreign investors and wary domestic speculators began to dump their "insecurities," and an orgy of selling followed. Tension built up to the panicky **Black Tuesday** of October 29, 1929, when 16,410,030 shares of stocks were sold in a save-who-may scramble. Wall Street became a wailing wall as gloom and doom replaced boom, and suicides increased alarmingly. A "sick joke" of the time had hotel room clerks ask registrants, "For sleeping or jumping?"

Losses, even in blue-chip securities, were unbelievable. By the end of 1929—two months after the initial crash—stockholders had lost $40 billion in paper values, or more than the total cost of World War I to the United States (see Figure 32.3).

The stock-market collapse heralded a business depression, at home and abroad, that was the most prolonged and prostrating in American or world experience. No other industrialized nation suffered so severe a setback. By the end of 1930, more than 4 million workers in the United States were jobless; two years later the figure had about tripled. Hungry and despairing workers pounded pavements in search of nonexistent jobs

Pride Goes Before a Fall The great crash of 1929 humbled many a high-flying investor. The desperate curbside seller of this brand-new Chrysler Model 75 paid $1,550 for it just months before.

("We're firing, not hiring"). Where employees were not discharged, wages and salaries were often slashed. A current jingle ran,

> *Mellon pulled the whistle,*
> *Hoover rang the bell*
> *Wall Street gave the signal*
> *And the country went to hell.*

The misery and gloom were incalculable, as forests of dead chimneys stood stark against the sky. Over five thousand banks collapsed in the first three years of the depression, carrying down with them the life savings of tens of thousands of ordinary citizens. Countless

thousands of honest, hard-working people lost their homes and farms to the forecloser's hammer. Breadlines formed, soup kitchens dispensed food, and apple sellers stood shivering on street corners trying to peddle their wares for five cents. Families felt the stress, as jobless fathers nursed their guilt and shame at not being able to provide for their households. Breadless breadwinners often blamed themselves for their plight, despite abundant evidence that the economic system, not individual initiative, had broken down. Mothers meanwhile nursed fewer babies, as hard times reached even into the nation's bedrooms, precipitating a decade-long dearth of births. As cash registers gathered cobwebs, the

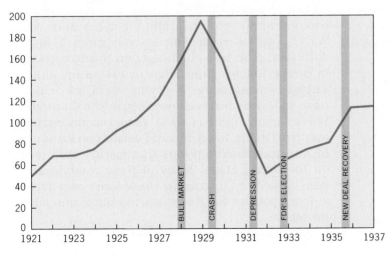

FIGURE 32.3 Index of Common Stock Prices (1926 = 100)

The Unemployed, by John Langley Howard, 1937 In this painting Howard soberly evokes the dispirited state of millions of unemployed Americans during the depression.

song "My God, How the Money Rolls In" was replaced with "Brother, Can You Spare a Dime?"

⭐ Hooked on the Horn of Plenty

What caused the Great Depression? One basic explanation is overproduction by both farm and factory. Ironically, the depression of the 1930s was one of abundance, not want. It was the "great glut" or the "plague of plenty."

The nation's ability to produce goods had clearly outrun its capacity to consume or pay for them. Too

The Depression spectacle of want in the shadow of surplus moved an observer to write in Current History *(1932),*

❝We still pray to be given each day our daily bread. Yet there is too much bread, too much wheat and corn, meat and oil and almost every commodity required by man for his subsistence and material happiness. We are not able to purchase the abundance that modern methods of agriculture, mining and manufacture make available in such bountiful quantities. Why is mankind being asked to go hungry and cold and poverty stricken in the midst of plenty?❞

much money was going into the hands of a few wealthy people, who in turn invested it in factories and other agencies of production. Not enough was going into salaries and wages, where revitalizing purchasing power could be more quickly felt.

Other maladies were at work. Overexpansion of credit through installment-plan buying overstimulated production. Paying on so-called easy terms caused many consumers to dive in beyond their depth. Normal technological unemployment, resulting from new laborsaving machines, also added its burden to the abnormal unemployment of the "threadbare thirties."

This already bleak picture was further darkened by economic anemia abroad. Britain and the Continent had never fully recovered from the upheaval of World War I. Depression in America was given a further downward push by a chain-reaction financial collapse in Europe, following the failure in 1931 of a prominent Vienna banking house. A drying up of international trade, moreover, had been hastened by the shortsighted Hawley-Smoot Tariff of 1930. European uncertainties over reparations, war debts, and defaults on loans owed to America caused tensions that reacted unfavorably on the United States. Many of these conditions had been created or worsened by Uncle Sam's own narrow-visioned policies, but it was now too late to unscramble the omelet.

As if man-made disasters were not enough, a terrible drought scorched the Mississippi Valley in 1930.

"Hooverville" in Seattle, 1934
In the early years of the depression, desperate, homeless people constructed shacks out of scavenged materials. These shantytowns sprang up in cities across the country.

Thousands of farms were sold at auction for taxes, though in some cases kind neighbors would intimidate prospective buyers, bid one cent, and return the property to its original owner. Farm tenancy or rental—a species of peonage—was spreading at an alarming rate among both whites and blacks.

By 1930 the depression had become a national calamity. Through no fault of their own, a host of industrious citizens had lost everything. They wanted to work—but there was no work. The insidious effect of all this dazed despair on the nation's spirit was incalculable and long-lasting. America's "uniqueness" no longer seemed so unique or its Manifest Destiny so manifest. Hitherto the people had grappled with storms, trees, stones, and other physical obstacles. But the depression was a baffling wraith they could not grasp. Initiative and self-respect were stifled, as panhandlers begged for food or "charity soup." In extreme cases "ragged individualists" slept under "Hoover blankets" (old newspapers), fought over the contents of garbage cans, or cooked their findings in old oil drums in tin-and-paper shantytowns cynically named **Hoovervilles**. The very foundations of America's social and political structure trembled.

⭐ Rugged Times for Rugged Individualists

Hoover's exalted reputation as a wonder-worker and efficiency engineer crashed about as dismally as the stock market. He doubtless would have shone in the prosperity-drenched Coolidge years, when he had foreseen the abolition of poverty and poor-houses. But damming the Great Depression proved to be a task beyond his engineering talents.

The perplexed president was impaled on the horns of a cruel dilemma. As a deservedly famed humanitarian, he was profoundly distressed by the widespread misery about him. Yet as a "rugged individualist," deeply rooted in an earlier era of free enterprise, he shrank from the heresy of government handouts. Convinced that industry, thrift, and self-reliance were the virtues that had made America great, President Hoover

Wall Streeter Martin Devries, observing President Herbert Hoover's struggle to keep his footing as the tidal wave of the Great Depression washed over him, decided he was a good man stuck in the wrong place, at the wrong time:

❝Hoover happened to be in a bad spot. The Depression came on, and there he was. If Jesus Christ had been there, he'd have had the same problem. It's too bad for poor old Herbie that he happened to be there. This was a world-wide Depression. It wasn't Hoover's fault. In 1932 . . . , a monkey could have been elected against him, no question about it.**❞**

Home Relief Station, by Louis Ribak, 1935–1936 Destitute and despairing, millions of hard-working Americans like these had to endure the degradation and humiliation of going on relief as the pall of depression descended over the land.

Whitney Museum of American Art

feared that a government doling out doles would weaken, perhaps destroy, the national fiber.

As the depression nightmare steadily worsened, relief by local government agencies broke down. Hoover was finally forced to turn reluctantly from his doctrine of log-cabin individualism and accept the proposition that the welfare of the people in a nationwide catastrophe is a direct concern of the national government.

The president at last worked out a compromise between the old hands-off philosophy and the "soul-destroying" direct dole then being used in England. He would assist the hard-pressed railroads, banks, and rural credit corporations, in the hope that if financial health were restored at the top of the economic pyramid, unemployment would be relieved at the bottom on a trickle-down basis.

Herbert Hoover (1874–1964) spoke approvingly in a campaign speech in 1928 of "the American system of Rugged Individualism." In 1930 he referred to Cleveland's 1887 veto of a bill to appropriate seed grain for the drought-stricken farmers of Texas:

"I do not believe that the power and duty of the General Government ought to be extended to the relief of individual suffering. . . . The lesson should be constantly enforced that though the people support the Government the Government should not support the people.**"**

Partisan critics sneered at the "Great Humanitarian"—he who had fed the faraway Belgians but would not use federal funds to feed needy Americans. Hostile commentators remarked that he was willing to lend government money to the big bankers, who allegedly had plunged the country into the mess. He would likewise lend money to agricultural organizations to feed pigs—but not people. Pigs, the cynics of the time noted, had no character to undermine.

Much of this criticism was unfair. Although continued suffering seemed to mock the effectiveness of Hoover's measures, his efforts probably prevented a more serious collapse than did occur. And his expenditures for relief, revolutionary for that day, paved the path for the enormous federal outlays of his New Deal successor, Franklin Roosevelt. Hoover proved that the old bootstrap-pulling techniques would no longer work in a crisis of this magnitude, especially when people lacked boots.

✦ Hoover Battles the Great Depression

President Hoover, in line with his "trickle-down" philosophy, at last recommended that Congress vote immense sums for useful public works. Though at heart an antispender, he secured from Congress appropriations totaling $2.25 billion for such projects.

Most imposing of the public enterprises was the gigantic Hoover Dam on the Colorado River. Voted by

Lampooning Hoover, 1932

The pages of *The American Pageant* are filled with political cartoons that provide pungent commentary on historical events. With one image rather than many words, a cartoonist can convey a point of view much the way an editorial writer does. This cartoon appeared in the *Washington Daily News* on July 25, 1932, three and a half months before Republican president Hoover lost the presidential election to his Democratic challenger, Franklin D. Roosevelt. The cartoonist foretells Hoover's defeat in November and departure from the White House the following March (not January, as at present) and expresses his support for the Home Loan Bank Bill. With this proposal Hoover sought to come to the aid of home mortgage lenders in order to forestall them from foreclosing on homeowners. The cartoonist jokes that Hoover supported this bill because he identified with homeowners about to lose their homes, but he also cleverly insinuates that Hoover's banking reform was motivated by electoral opportunism. Surely Hoover sought to win public support in return for his new banking program as he battled for reelection, but the Home Loan Bank Bill also reflected Hoover's growing recognition that the federal government had to take direct action to remedy flaws that had precipitated the crisis of the Great Depression. As Hoover later recorded in his memoirs, "All this seems dull economics, but the poignant American drama revolving around the loss of the old homestead had a million repetitions straight from life, not because of the designing villain but because of a fault in our financial system." How does the cartoonist use caricature to make his point? What accounts for the political cartoon's special power? Are there limitations to this genre? Find another cartoon in this book and subject it to similar analysis.

FDR Library

Congress in the days of Coolidge, it was begun in 1930 under Hoover and completed in 1936 under Roosevelt. It succeeded in creating a huge man-made lake for purposes of irrigation, flood control, and electric power.

But Hoover sternly fought all schemes that he regarded as "socialistic." Conspicuous among them was the Muscle Shoals Bill, designed to dam the Tennessee River and ultimately embraced by Franklin Roosevelt's Tennessee Valley Authority. Hoover emphatically vetoed this measure, primarily because he opposed the government's selling electricity in competition with its own citizens in private companies.

Early in 1932 Congress, responding to Hoover's belated appeal, established the **Reconstruction Finance Corporation (RFC)**. With an initial working capital of half a billion dollars, this agency became a government lending bank. It was designed to provide indirect relief by assisting insurance companies, banks, agricultural organizations, railroads, and even hard-pressed state and local governments. But to preserve individualism and character, there would be no loans to individuals from this "billion-dollar soup kitchen."

"Pump-priming" loans by the RFC were no doubt of widespread benefit, though the organization was established many months too late for maximum usefulness. Projects that it supported were largely self-liquidating, and the government as a banker actually profited to the tune of many millions of dollars. Giant corporations so obviously benefited from this assistance that the RFC was dubbed—rather unfairly—"the millionaires' dole." The irony is that the thrifty and individualistic Hoover had sponsored the project, though with initial reluctance. It actually had a strong New Dealish flavor.

Hoover's administration also provided some indirect benefits for labor. After stormy debate, Congress passed the **Norris–La Guardia Anti-Injunction Act** in 1932, and Hoover signed it. The measure outlawed "yellow-dog" (antiunion) contracts and forbade the federal courts to issue injunctions to restrain strikes, boycotts, and peaceful picketing.

The truth is that Herbert Hoover, despite criticism of his "heartlessness," did inaugurate a significant new policy. In previous panics the masses had been forced to "sweat it out." Slow though Hoover was to abandon this nineteenth-century bias, by the end of his term he had started down the road toward government assistance for needy citizens—a road that Franklin Roosevelt would travel much farther.

Hoover's woes were increased by a hostile Congress. At critical times during his first two years, the Republican majority proved highly uncooperative. Friction worsened during his last two years. A depression-cursed electorate, rebelling in the congressional elections of 1930, so reduced the Republican majority that Democrats controlled the new House and almost controlled the Senate. Insurgent Republicans could—and did—combine with opposition Democrats to harass Hoover. Some of the president's troubles were deliberately manufactured by Congress, which, in his words, "played politics with human misery."

✦ Routing the Bonus Army in Washington

Many veterans of World War I were numbered among the hard-hit victims of the depression. Industry had secured a "bonus"—though a dubious one—in the Hawley-Smoot Tariff. So the thoughts of the former soldiers naturally turned to what the government owed them for their services in 1917–1918, when they had "saved" democracy. A drive developed for the premature payment of the deferred bonus voted by Congress in 1924 and payable in 1945.

Thousands of impoverished veterans, both of war and of unemployment, were now prepared to move on Washington, there to demand of Congress the immediate payment of their *entire* bonus. The "Bonus Expeditionary Force" (BEF), which mustered about twenty thousand souls, converged on the capital in the summer of 1932. These supplicants promptly set up unsanitary public camps and erected shacks on vacant lots—a gigantic "Hooverville." They thus created a menace to the public health, while attempting to intimidate Congress by their presence in force. After the pending bonus bill had failed in Congress by a narrow margin, Hoover arranged to pay the return fare of about six thousand bonus marchers. The rest refused to decamp, though ordered to do so.

Following riots that cost two lives, Hoover responded to the demands of the Washington authorities by ordering the army to evacuate the unwanted guests. Although Hoover charged that the **Bonus Army** was led by riffraff and reds, in fact only a sprinkling of them were former convicts and communist agitators. The eviction was carried out by General Douglas MacArthur with bayonets and tear gas, and with far more severity than Hoover had planned. A few of the former soldiers were injured as the torch was put to their pathetic shanties in the inglorious "Battle of Anacostia Flats." An eleven-month-old "bonus baby" allegedly died from exposure to tear gas.

This brutal episode brought down additional abuse on the once-popular Hoover, who by now was the most loudly booed man in the country. The Democrats, not content with Hoover's vulnerable record, employed professional "smear" artists to drive him from office. Cynics sneered that the "Great Engineer" had in a few months "ditched, drained, and damned the country." The existing panic was unfairly branded "the Hoover

© Bettmann/Corbis

The Bonus Army in Washington, D.C., 1932 World War I veterans from Muncie, Indiana, were among many contingents to set up camp in the capital during the summer of 1932, determined to remain there until they received full payment of their promised bonuses.

depression." In truth, Hoover had been oversold as a wizard, and the public grumbled when his magician's wand failed to produce rabbits. The time was ripening for the Democratic party—and Franklin D. Roosevelt— to cash in on Hoover's calamities.

✦ Japanese Militarists Attack China

The Great Depression, which brewed enough distress at home, added immensely to difficulties abroad. Militaristic Japan stole the Far Eastern spotlight. In September 1931 the Japanese imperialists, noting that the Western world was badly mired in a depression, lunged into Manchuria. Alleging provocation, they rapidly overran the coveted Chinese province and proceeded to bolt shut the Open Door in the conquered area.

America had a strong sentimental stake in China but few significant economic interests. In fact, American commercial ties with Japan far outweighed those with China. Yet most Americans were stunned by this act of naked aggression. It flagrantly violated the League of Nations covenant, as well as various other international agreements solemnly signed by Tokyo, not to mention the American sense of fair play. Indignant Americans, though by no means a majority, urged strong measures ranging from boycotts to blockades. Possibly a tight blockade by the League,

backed by the United States, would have brought Japan sharply to book.

But the League was handicapped in taking two-fisted action by the nonmembership of the United States. Washington flatly rebuffed initial attempts in 1931 to secure American cooperation in applying economic pressure on Japan. Washington and Secretary of State Henry L. Stimson in the end decided to fire only paper bullets at the Japanese aggressors. The so-called Stimson doctrine, proclaimed in 1932, declared that the United States would not recognize any territorial acquisitions achieved by force. Righteous indignation—or a preach-and-run policy—would substitute for solid initiatives.

Hoover later wrote of his differences with Secretary of State Stimson over economic boycotts,

❝I was soon to realize that my able Secretary was at times more of a warrior than a diplomat. To him the phrase 'economic sanctions' was the magic wand of force by which all peace could be summoned from the vasty deep. . . . Ever since Versailles I had held that 'economic sanctions' meant war when applied to any large nation.❞

Japanese Aggression in Manchuria This American cartoon lambastes Japan for disregarding international treaty agreements when it seized Manchuria in 1931. The next year the Japanese would set up the puppet state of Manchukuo.

This verbal slap on the wrist from America did not deter the march of the Japanese militarists. Smarting under a Chinese boycott, they bombed Shanghai in 1932, with shocking losses to civilians. Outraged Americans launched informal boycotts of Japanese goods, chiefly dime-store knickknacks. But there was no real sentiment for armed intervention among a depression-ridden people, who remained strongly isolationist during the 1930s.

In a broad sense, collective security died and World War II was born in 1931 on the windswept plains of Manchuria. The League members had the economic and naval power to halt Japan but lacked the courage to act. One reason—though not the only one—was that they could not count on America's support. Even so, the Republic came closer to stepping into the chill waters of internationalism than American prophets would have dared to predict in the early 1920s.

✶ Hoover Pioneers the Good Neighbor Policy

Hoover's arrival in the White House brought a more hopeful turn to relations with America's southern neighbors. The new president was deeply interested in the often-troubled nations below the Rio Grande. Shortly after his election in 1928, he had undertaken a goodwill tour of Latin America—on a U.S. battleship.

World depression softened an age-old aggressive attitude in the United States toward weak Latin neighbors. Following the stock-market collapse of 1929, Americans had less money to invest abroad. As millions of dollars' worth of investments in Latin America went sour, many Yankees felt as though they were more preyed upon than preying. So-called economic imperialism became much less popular in the United States than it had been in the golden twenties.

As an advocate of international goodwill, Hoover strove to abandon the interventionist twist given to the Monroe Doctrine by Theodore Roosevelt. In 1932 he negotiated a new treaty with the French-speaking Republic of Haiti, and this pact, later supplanted by an executive agreement, provided for the complete withdrawal of American platoons by 1934. Further pleasing omens came early in 1933, when the last marine "leathernecks" sailed away from Nicaragua after an almost continuous stay of some twenty years.

Herbert Hoover, the engineer in politics, thus happily engineered the foundation stones of the Good Neighbor policy. Upon them rose an imposing edifice in the days of his successor, Franklin Roosevelt.

Chapter Review

KEY TERMS

Adkins v. *Children's Hospital* (729)
Nine-Power Treaty (731)
Kellogg-Briand Pact (732)
Fordney-McCumber Tariff Law (732)
Teapot Dome scandal (733)

McNary-Haugen Bill (735)
Dawes Plan (737)
Agricultural Marketing Act (740)
Hawley-Smoot Tariff (740)
Black Tuesday (740)
Hoovervilles (743)

Reconstruction Finance Corporation (RFC) (746)
Norris–La Guardia Anti-Injunction Act (746)
Bonus Army (746)

PEOPLE TO KNOW

Bonus Army
Warren G. Harding
Albert B. Fall
Calvin Coolidge

John W. Davis
Robert M. ("Fighting Bob") La Follette
Albert E. Smith

CHRONOLOGY

1919 American Legion founded
Chicago race riot

1920 Esch-Cummins Transportation Act
Merchant Marine Act

1921 Veterans Bureau created
Capper-Volstead Act

1922 Five-Power Naval Treaty signed
Four-Power and Nine-Power Treaties on the Far East
Fordney-McCumber Tariff Law

1923 *Adkins* v. *Children's Hospital*
Teapot Dome scandal
Harding dies; Coolidge assumes presidency

1924 Adjusted Compensation Act for veterans
Dawes Plan for international finance
U.S. troops leave Dominican Republic
Coolidge wins three-way presidential election

1926 U.S. troops occupy Nicaragua

1928 Kellogg-Briand Pact
Hoover defeats Smith for presidency
Hoover makes goodwill tour of Latin America

1929 Agricultural Marketing Act sets up Federal Farm Board
Stock-market crash

1930 Hawley-Smoot Tariff

1931 Japanese invade Manchuria

1932 Reconstruction Finance Corporation (RFC) established
Norris–La Guardia Anti-Injunction Act
"Bonus Army" dispersed from Washington, D.C.

TO LEARN MORE

Liaquat Ahamed, *Lords of Finance: The Bankers Who Broke the World* (2009)

Michael A. Bernstein, *The Great Depression: Delayed Recovery and Economic Change in America, 1929–1939* (1987)

John D. Hicks, *Republican Ascendancy, 1921–1933* (1960)

Robert McElvaine, *The Great Depression: America, 1929–1941* (rev. ed., 1993)

Burl Noggle, *Into the Twenties: The United States from Armistice to Normalcy* (1974)

Emily Rosenberg, *Financial Missionaries to the World: The Politics and Culture of Dollar Diplomacy, 1900–1930* (1999)

Peter Temin, *Did Monetary Factors Cause the Great Depression?* (1976)

Joan Hoff Wilson, *American Business and Foreign Policy, 1920–1933* (1971)

———, *Herbert Hoover, Forgotten Progressive* (1975)

Robert H. Zieger, *American Workers, American Unions, 1920–1985* (1986)

A complete, annotated bibliography for this chapter—along with brief descriptions of the People to Know—may be found on the American Pageant website. The Key Terms are defined in a Glossary at the end of the text.

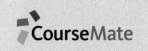

Go to the CourseMate website at **www.cengagebrain.com** for additional study tools and review materials—including audio and video clips—for this chapter.

AP® Review Questions for Chapter 32

1. All of the following characterize Warren G. Harding's weaknesses as president EXCEPT
   (A) a lack of political experience.
   (B) a mediocre mind.
   (C) an inability to detect moral weaknesses and ethical lapses in his associates.
   (D) an unwillingness to hurt people's feelings by saying no.
   (E) administrative and executive management shortcomings.

2. Which of the following best describes the Republican economic policies implemented under President Warren G. Harding?
   (A) A continuation of the same laissez-faire doctrine as practiced under President William McKinley's Republican administration
   (B) A modification in laissez-faire economic doctrine that included using the courts and administrative agencies to maximize the profits of the business sector
   (C) The institution of many government regulatory schemes to curb the exploitative economic and labor relations practices of big business
   (D) The development and implementation of economic policies that aided small business at the expense of big business
   (E) The use of antitrust and regulatory powers to increase competition in business

3. Which of the following best characterizes U.S. Supreme Court decisions in the 1920s?
   (A) Extremely hostile to progressive social reform legislation enacted during the progressive era
   (B) Generally hostile to progressive social reforms with the exception of maintaining workplace protections for women
   (C) Attempting to strike a fair balance between labor and business over collective bargaining, union organizing, and right-to-strike legal issues
   (D) Upholding antitrust and government regulatory schemes designed to expand government intervention in the economy
   (E) Demonstrating a consistent willingness to stand by recent court precedent, as in, for example, the ruling in the landmark *Adkins* case

4. What was the primary motivation for President Harding's willingness to seize the initiative on the issue of international disarmament?
   (A) He feared renewed war in Europe.
   (B) He recognized that Japan and the United States might enter a dangerous arms race.
   (C) Businesspeople were unwilling to help pay for a larger United States Navy.
   (D) He did not want the League of Nations to take the lead on this problem.
   (E) American public opinion strongly supported peacemaking efforts.

5. All of the following were long-term effects of the Fordney-McCumber and Hawley-Smoot Tariff laws EXCEPT that the tariffs
   (A) lowered the price paid by Americans for domestic manufactured goods.
   (B) raised the price paid by Americans for imported agricultural foodstuffs.
   (C) shrank international trade and made it impossible for Europe to repay American war loans.
   (D) directly contributed to the plunging of America and the rest of the world into a severe economic depression by the end of the 1920s.
   (E) closed the wide balance of trade gaps in the world and helped maintain the peace on the European and Asian continents.

6. The Teapot Dome and other government scandals during the Harding administration prompted all of the following EXCEPT
   (A) criminal prosecutions against corrupt members of the Harding administration.
   (B) a display of strong leadership by President Harding to root out public corruption, sponsor government ethics reform legislation, and cooperate with Senate investigations of his administration.
   (C) a significant drop in the public confidence and trust in the federal government.
   (D) a marked deterioration in the health of President Harding.
   (E) resignations of many key members of the Harding administration, including the secretary of interior and the attorney general of the United States.

7. How did the McNary-Haugen bill, passed by Congress and vetoed by President Coolidge, seek to assist American farmers?
   (A) It restricted the amount of crops farmers could plant in order to drive up prices.
   (B) It required the federal government to buy farm surpluses and sell them abroad.
   (C) It provided federal support for agricultural equipment and seeds.
   (D) It blocked the import of certain cheaper agricultural commodities from Europe and Latin America.
   (E) It provided federal loans for agricultural equipment and seeds.

8. Senator Robert LaFollette's Progressive party advocated all of the following EXCEPT
   (A) government ownership of railroads.
   (B) economic relief for farmers.
   (C) opposition to antilabor injunctions.
   (D) opposition to monopolies.
   (E) increased power and authority for the U.S. Supreme Court.

9. Which of the following arguments was advanced by America's European allies to try to persuade the United States that they should not have to repay loans issued by America to them during World War I?
   (A) The United States had owed these European nations about $4 billion before the war.
   (B) The total debt owed the U.S. government did not represent a significant sum of dollars.
   (C) Since European nations had paid a much heavier price in lost lives, it was only fair for the United States to write off the debt.
   (D) Since the United States was making so much money from Mexican and Middle Eastern oil resources, it did not need the dollars owed it by these European allies.
   (E) Because Germany was not paying its reparations to the allied European nations, they could not afford to pay off the debt to the United States.

10. What did the Dawes Plan of 1924 depend on to successfully address the problem of war debt and war reparations?
    (A) The long-term availability of free-flowing American credit
    (B) Full repayment of inter-Allied debt by Great Britain and France
    (C) Cancellation of all German reparation payments to Great Britain and France
    (D) Private U.S. bank loans to Great Britain and France
    (E) Repeal of high tariffs on British, French, and German industrial and agricultural goods

11. All of the following were political liabilities for New York Democratic governor Al Smith in his unsuccessful, path-breaking run for the presidency in 1928 EXCEPT Smith's
    (A) Catholic religion.
    (B) support for the repeal of prohibition.
    (C) big-city background.
    (D) failure to win the support of American labor.
    (E) radio speaking skill.

12. Which of the following was NOT a cause of the Great Depression?
    (A) The drying up of international trade expedited by enactment of the Hawley-Smoot Tariff of 1930
    (B) Continued agricultural and industrial overproduction
    (C) Rampant unchecked stock speculation culminating in the great crash of 1929
    (D) The prolonged economic anemia experienced by Britain and European nations
    (E) Superfluous government spending to stimulate job creation in the American economy

13. Which of the following best describes President Hoover's approach to the Great Depression?
    (A) Leave the economy alone to work itself out of trouble
    (B) Nationalize major industries
    (C) Encourage the states to stimulate spending
    (D) Work for the breakup of business monopolies
    (E) Offer limited federal assistance to businesses, banks, agricultural organizations, and state and local governments but not to individuals

14. Which of the following most limited the ability of the League of Nations to reverse Japan's invasion and occupation of Manchuria?
    (A) The United States was not a member of the League of Nations.
    (B) Japan left the League following Japan's invasion and occupation of Manchuria.
    (C) China did not desire the League to become involved in the war with Japan.
    (D) League members lacked the economic and naval power to halt Japanese aggression in Manchuria.
    (E) The outlawing of war and other provisions in the Kellogg-Briand Pact

15. Which 1920s president is most closely related to President Grover Cleveland's 1887 idea, "Though the people support the government, the government should not support the people"?
    (A) Woodrow Wilson
    (B) Warren Harding
    (C) Calvin Coolidge
    (D) Herbert Hoover
    (E) Franklin D. Roosevelt

16. America abandoned its policy of isolationism in the 1920s in all of the following ways EXCEPT by
    (A) providing benefits and insurance for American soldiers in World War I.
    (B) entering into the Nine Power Treaty, affirming the Open Door in China.
    (C) signing the Kellogg Briand Pact, outlawing war.
    (D) creating the Dawes Plan and assisting Germany with reparations.
    (E) hosting the Washington "Disarmament" Conference of 1921–1922.

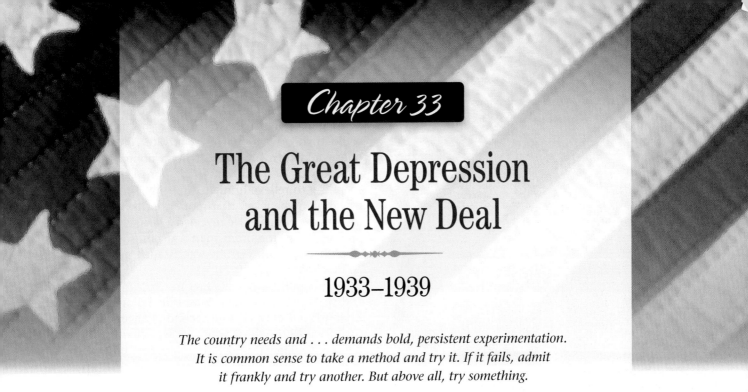

Chapter 33

The Great Depression and the New Deal

1933–1939

*The country needs and . . . demands bold, persistent experimentation.
It is common sense to take a method and try it. If it fails, admit
it frankly and try another. But above all, try something.*

FRANKLIN D. ROOSEVELT, CAMPAIGN SPEECH, 1932

Voters were in an ugly mood as the presidential campaign of 1932 neared. Countless factory chimneys remained ominously cold, while more than 11 million unemployed workers and their families sank ever deeper into the pit of poverty. Herbert Hoover may have won the 1928 election by promising "a chicken in every pot," but three years later that chicken seemed to have laid a discharge slip in every pay envelope.

Hoover, sick at heart, was renominated by the Republican convention in Chicago without great enthusiasm. The platform indulged in extravagant praise of Republican antidepression policies, while halfheartedly promising to repeal national prohibition and return control of liquor to the states.

The rising star of the Democratic firmament was Governor Franklin Delano Roosevelt of New York, a fifth cousin of Theodore Roosevelt. Like the Rough Rider, he had been born to a wealthy New York family, had graduated from Harvard, had been elected as a kid-gloved politician to the New York legislature, had served as governor of the Empire State, had been nominated for the vice presidency (though not elected), and had served capably as assistant secretary of the navy. Although both men were master politicians, adept with the colorful phrase, TR was pugnacious and confrontational, while FDR was suave and conciliatory—qualities that appealed strongly to a people traumatized by one of the greatest crises in American history.

✷ FDR: Politician in a Wheelchair

Infantile paralysis, while putting steel braces on Franklin Roosevelt's legs, put additional steel into his soul. Until 1921, when the dread disease struck, young Roosevelt—tall (six feet two inches), athletic, and handsome—impressed observers as charming and witty, yet at times as a superficial and arrogant "lightweight." But suffering humbled him to the level of common clay. In courageously fighting his way back from complete helplessness to a hobbling mobility, he schooled himself in patience, tolerance, compassion, and strength of will. He once remarked that after trying for two years to wiggle one big toe, all else seemed easy.

Another of Roosevelt's great personal and political assets was his wife, Eleanor. The niece of Theodore Roosevelt, she was Franklin Roosevelt's distant cousin as well as his spouse. Tall, ungainly, and toothy, she overcame the misery of an unhappy childhood and emerged as a champion of the dispossessed—and, ultimately, as the "conscience of the New Deal." FDR's political career was as much hers as it was his own. She traveled countless miles with him or on his behalf in all his campaigns, beginning with his run for the New York legislature before World War I, later considering herself "his legs." But Mrs. Roosevelt also marched to her own drummer. As a young woman she had worked in a New York settlement house, and later on she joined

AP Images

Eleanor Roosevelt (1884–1962)   Roosevelt was America's most active First Lady and commanded enormous popularity and influence during FDR's presidency. Here she emerges, miner's cap in hand, from an Ohio coal mine.

the Women's Trade Union League (see p. 645) and the League of Women Voters. When she and Franklin moved into the White House, she brought an unprecedented number of women activists with her to Washington. This network of reformers helped make her the most active First Lady in history.

Through her lobbying of her husband, her speeches, and her syndicated newspaper column, Eleanor Roosevelt powerfully influenced the policies of the national government. Always she battled for the impoverished and the oppressed. At one meeting in Birmingham, Alabama, she confounded local authorities and flouted the segregation statutes by deliberately straddling the aisle separating the black and white seating sections. Sadly, her personal relationship with her husband was often rocky, due to his infidelities. Condemned by conservatives and loved by liberals, she was one of the most controversial—and consequential—public figures of the twentieth century.

Franklin Roosevelt's political appeal was amazing. His commanding presence and his golden speaking voice, despite a sophisticated accent, combined to make him the premier American orator of his generation. He could turn on his charm in private conversations as one would turn on a faucet. As a popular depression governor of New York, he had sponsored heavy state spending to relieve human suffering. Though favoring frugality, he believed that money, rather than humanity, was expendable. He revealed a deep concern for the plight of the "forgotten man"—a phrase he used in a 1932 speech—although he was assailed by the rich as a "traitor to his class."

Exuberant Democrats met in Chicago in June 1932 and speedily nominated Roosevelt. Fellow New Yorker Al Smith felt entitled to a second chance, and a beautiful friendship wilted when he was elbowed aside for Roosevelt. The Democratic platform promised not only a balanced budget but sweeping social and economic reforms. Roosevelt flew daringly through stormy weather to Chicago, where he smashed precedent by accepting the nomination in person. He electrified the delegates and the public with these words: "I pledge you, I pledge myself to a new deal for the American people."

✴ Presidential Hopefuls of 1932

In the campaign that followed, Roosevelt seized the offensive with a slashing attack on the Republican Old Dealers. He was especially eager to prove that he was not an invalid ("Roosevelt Is Robust") and to display his magnificent torso and radiant personality to as many voters as possible.

Roosevelt consistently preached a New Deal for the "forgotten man," but he was annoyingly vague and somewhat contradictory. Many of his speeches were "ghostwritten" by the "Brains Trust" (popularly the **Brain Trust**), a small group of reform-minded intellectuals. They were predominantly youngish college professors who, as a kind of kitchen cabinet, later

> *In his successful campaign for the governorship of New York in 1928, Franklin Roosevelt (1882–1945) had played down alleged Democratic "socialism":*
>
> **❝**We often hear it said that government operation of anything under the sun is socialistic. If that is so, our postal service is socialistic, so is the parcel post which has largely taken the place of the old express companies; so are the public highways which took the place of the toll roads.**❞**

authored much of the **New Deal** legislation. Roosevelt rashly promised a balanced budget and berated heavy Hooverian deficits, amid cries of "Throw the Spenders Out!" and "Out of the Red with Roosevelt." All of this was to make ironic reading in later months.

The high spirits of the Democrats found expression in the catchy air "Happy Days Are Here Again." This theme song fit FDR's indestructible smile, his jauntily angled cigarette holder, his breezy optimism, and his promises to do something, even at the risk of bold experimentation.

Grim-faced Herbert Hoover remained in the White House, conscientiously battling the depression through short lunches and long hours. Out on the firing line, his supporters halfheartedly assured half-listening voters, "The Worst Is Past," "It Might Have Been Worse,"

The Vanquished and the Victor A dour Hoover and an ebullient Roosevelt ride to the inauguration ceremonies on March 4, 1933. This magazine cover was never published, presumably because of the editors' sensitivity about the attempted assassination of Roosevelt when he was riding in an open car in Florida on February 15, 1933, less than three weeks earlier. The attempt on Roosevelt's life ended in the death of Chicago mayor Anton J. Cermak.

and "Prosperity Is Just Around the Corner." Hoover never ceased to insist that the uncertainty and fear produced by Roosevelt's impending victory plunged the nation deeper into the depression.

With the campaign going badly for the Republicans, a weary and despondent Hoover was persuaded to take to the stump. He stoutly reaffirmed his faith in American free enterprise and individual initiative, and gloomily predicted that if the Hawley-Smoot Tariff was repealed, grass would grow "in the streets of a hundred cities." Such down-at-the-mouthism contrasted sharply with Roosevelt's tooth-flashing optimism and sparkling promises.

✦ Hoover's Humiliation in 1932

Hoover had been swept into office on the rising tide of prosperity; he was swept out of office by the receding tide of depression. The flood of votes totaled 22,809,638 for Roosevelt and 15,758,901 for Hoover; the electoral count stood at 472 to 59. In all, the loser carried only six rock-ribbed Republican states.

One striking feature of the election was the beginning of a distinct shift of blacks, traditionally grateful to the Republican party of Lincoln, over to the Roosevelt camp. As the "last hired and first fired," black Americans had been among the worst sufferers from the depression. Beginning with the election of 1932, they became, notably in the great urban centers of the North, a vital element in the Democratic party.

Hard times unquestionably ruined the Republicans, for the electoral upheaval in 1932 was as much anti-Hoover as it was pro-Roosevelt. Democrats had only to harness the national grudge and let it pull them to victory. An overwhelming majority of Democrats appear to have voiced a demand for change: *a* new deal rather than *the* New Deal, for the latter was only a gleam in the eyes of its sponsors. Any upstanding Democratic candidate probably could have won.

The preinauguration lame duck period now ground slowly to an end. Hoover, though defeated and repudiated, continued to be president for four long months, until March 4, 1933. But he was helpless to embark upon any long-range policies without the cooperation of Roosevelt—and the victorious president-elect proved rather uncooperative. Hoover at length succeeded in arranging two meetings with him to discuss the war-debt muddle. But Roosevelt, who airily remarked to the press, "It's not my baby," fought shy of assuming responsibility without authority. As Hoover privately confessed, he was trying to bind his successor to an anti-inflationary policy that would have made impossible many of the later New Deal experiments. But in politics the winner, not the loser, calls the tune.

With Washington deadlocked, the vast and vaunted American economic machine clanked to a virtual halt. One worker in four tramped the streets, feet weary and hands idle. Banks were locking their doors all over the nation, as people nervously stuffed paper money under their mattresses. Hooverites, then and later, accused Roosevelt of deliberately permitting the depression to worsen so that he could emerge the more spectacularly as a savior.

✦ FDR and the Three R's: Relief, Recovery, Reform

Great crises often call forth gifted leaders, and the hand of destiny tapped Roosevelt on the shoulder. On a dreary Inauguration Day, March 4, 1933, his vibrant voice, broadcast nationally from a bulletproof stand, provided the American people with inspirational new hope. He denounced the "money changers" who had brought on the calamity and declared that the government must wage war on the Great Depression as it would wage war on an armed foe. His clarion note was

Unemployed and Frustrated Democratic candidate Franklin Roosevelt offered hope, if few concrete plans, to the millions struggling to cope with the Great Depression.

© 1930 Detroit News/Picture Research Consultants & Archives

One Chinese observer of America, No-Yong Park (1899–1976), born in Manchuria and educated in the United States, remained optimistic about America even in the depths of the Great Depression. He wrote in An Oriental View of American Civilization *(1934),*

"Of all the peoples of the world, Americans, to my mind, are the most progressive. They are the ones who live in the future tense. Their mind and soul are always bent for the future. They never move backward and always march forward.**"**

"Let me assert my firm belief that the only thing we have to fear is fear itself."

Roosevelt moved decisively. Now that he had full responsibility, he boldly declared a nationwide banking holiday, March 6–10, as a prelude to opening the banks on a sounder basis. He then summoned the overwhelmingly Democratic Congress into special session to cope with the national emergency. For the so-called **Hundred Days** (March 9–June 16, 1933), members hastily cranked out an unprecedented basketful of remedial legislation (see Table 33.1). Some of it derived from earlier progressivism, but these new measures mostly sought to deal with a desperate emergency.

Roosevelt's New Deal programs aimed at three R's—relief, recovery, and reform. Short-range goals were relief and immediate recovery, especially in the first two years. Long-range goals were permanent recovery and reform of current abuses, particularly those that had produced the boom-or-bust catastrophe. The three-R objectives often overlapped and got in one another's way. But amid all the topsy-turvy haste, the gigantic New Deal program lurched forward.

Firmly ensconced in the driver's seat, President Roosevelt cracked the whip. A green Congress so fully shared the panicky feeling of the country that it was ready to rubber-stamp bills drafted by White House advisers—measures that Roosevelt called "must legislation." More than that, Congress gave the president extraordinary blank-check powers: some of the laws it passed expressly delegated legislative authority to the chief executive. One senator complained that if FDR asked Congress "to commit suicide tomorrow, they'd do it."

Roosevelt was delighted to exert executive leadership, and Congress responded to it, although he did not always know precisely where he was going. He was inclined to do things by intuition—off the cuff. He was like the quarterback, as he put it, whose next play depends on the outcome of the previous play. So desperate was the mood of an action-starved public that

TABLE 33.1 Principal New Deal Acts During the Hundred Days Congress, 1933* (items in parentheses indicate secondary purposes)

Recovery	Relief	Reform
FDR closes banks, March 6, 1933		
Emergency Banking Relief Act, March 9, 1933		
(Beer Act)	(Beer Act)	Beer and Wine Revenue Act, March 22, 1933
(CCC)	Unemployment Relief Act, March 31, 1933, creates Civilian Conservation Corps (CCC)	
FDR orders gold surrender, April 5, 1933		
FDR abandons gold standard, April 19, 1933		
(FERA)	Federal Emergency Relief Act, May 12, 1933, creates Federal Emergency Relief Administration (FERA)	
(AAA)	Agricultural Adjustment Act (AAA), May 12, 1933	
(TVA)	(TVA)	Tennessee Valley Authority Act (TVA), May 18, 1933
		Federal Securities Act, May 27, 1933
Gold-payment clause repealed, June 5, 1933		
(HOLC)	Home Owners' Refinancing Act, June 13, 1933, creates Home Owners' Loan Corporation (HOLC)	
National Industrial Recovery Act, June 16, 1933, creates National Recovery Administration (NRA), Public Works Administration (PWA)	(NRA, PWA)	(NRA)
(Glass-Steagall Act)	(Glass-Steagall Act)	Glass-Steagall Banking Reform Act, June 16, 1933, creates Federal Deposit Insurance Corporation

*For later New Deal measures, see p. 758.

any movement, even in the wrong direction, seemed better than no movement at all.

The frantic Hundred Days Congress passed many essentials of the New Deal "three R's," though important long-range measures were added in later sessions. These reforms owed much to the legacy of the pre–World War I progressive movement. Many of them were long overdue, sidetracked by the war in Europe and the Old Guard reaction of the 1920s. In an explosive burst of pent-up energy, New Dealers raided file cabinets full of old pamphlets on German social insurance, English housing and garden cities, Danish agricultural recovery, and American World War I collectivization. In time they embraced progressive ideas such as unemployment insurance, old-age insurance, minimum-wage regulations, the conservation and development of natural resources, and restrictions on child labor. They also invented some new schemes, such as the Tennessee

Valley Authority (see p. 765). Soon depression-weary Europeans would come to the United States to marvel at the exciting din of reform activity under way. No longer would America look as backward in the realm of social welfare as it once had.

✯ Roosevelt Manages the Money

Banking chaos cried aloud for immediate action. Congress pulled itself together and in an incredible eight hours had the Emergency Banking Relief Act of 1933 ready for Roosevelt's busy pen. The new law invested the president with the power to regulate banking transactions and foreign exchange and to reopen solvent banks.

Roosevelt, the master showman, next turned to the radio to deliver the first of his thirty famous "fireside chats." As some 35 million people hung on his soothing

The Champ: FDR Chatting with Reporters Roosevelt mastered the press as few presidents before or since have been able to do. He was also ingenious in finding opportunities to converse with reporters in situations where he could conceal his physical limitations.

words, he gave assurances that it was now safer to keep money in a reopened bank than "under the mattress." Confidence returned with a gush, and the banks began to unlock their doors.

The Hundred Days, or Emergency, Congress buttressed public reliance on the banking system by enacting the memorable **Glass-Steagall Banking Reform Act**. This measure provided for the Federal Deposit Insurance Corporation, which insured individual deposits up to $5,000 (later raised). Thus ended the disgraceful epidemic of bank failures, which dated back to the "wildcat" days of Andrew Jackson (see Figure 33.1).*

Roosevelt moved swiftly elsewhere on the financial front, seeking to protect the melting gold reserves and to prevent panicky hoarding. He ordered all private holdings of gold to be surrendered to the Treasury in exchange for paper currency and then took the nation off the gold standard. The Emergency Congress responded to his recommendation by canceling the gold-payment clause in all contracts and authorizing repayment in paper money. A "managed currency" was well on its way.

---

*When FDR was inaugurated in 1933, not a single Canadian bank had failed.

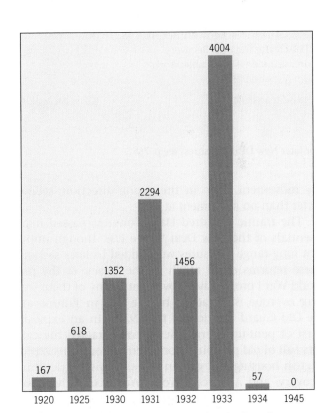

FIGURE 33.1 Bank Failures Before and After the Glass-Steagall Banking Reform Act of 1933

The goal of Roosevelt's "managed currency" was inflation, which he believed would relieve debtors' burdens and stimulate new production. Roosevelt's principal instrument for achieving inflation was gold buying. He instructed the Treasury to purchase gold at increasing prices, ratcheting the dollar price of gold up from $21 an ounce in 1933 to $35 an ounce in early 1934, a price that held for nearly four decades. This policy did increase the amount of dollars in circulation, as holders of gold cashed it in at the elevated prices. But this inflationary result also provoked the wrath of "sound-money" critics, who gagged on the "baloney dollar." The gold-buying scheme came to an end in February 1934, when FDR returned the nation to a limited gold standard for purposes of international trade only. Thereafter (until 1971—see p. 922), the United States pledged itself to pay foreign bills, if requested, in gold at the rate of one ounce of gold for every $35 due. But domestic circulation of gold continued to be prohibited, and gold coins became collectors' items.

✦ Creating Jobs for the Jobless

Overwhelming unemployment, even more than banking, clamored for prompt remedial action. One out of every four workers was jobless when FDR took his inaugural oath—the highest level of unemployment in the nation's history, before or since. Roosevelt had no hesitancy about using federal money to assist the unemployed and at the same time to "prime the pump" of industrial recovery. (A farmer has to pour a little water into a dry pump—that is, "prime it"—to start the flow.)

The Hundred Days Congress responded to Roosevelt's spurs when it created the **Civilian Conservation Corps (CCC)**, which proved to be perhaps the most popular of all the New Deal "alphabetical agencies." This law provided employment in fresh-air government camps for about 3 million uniformed young men, many of whom might otherwise have

© Bettmann/Corbis

CCC Workers in Alaska, 1939   These Tlingit carvers in Alaska's southeastern panhandle were part of a CCC project to restore totem poles. Here they stand with a pole carved in the likeness of Abraham Lincoln.

One desperate man wrote to a newspaper in 1932,

❝I am forty-eight; married twenty-one years; four children, three in school. For the last eight years I was employed as a Pullman conductor. Since September, 1930, they have given me seven months part-time work. Today I am an object of charity. . . . My small, weak, and frail wife and two small children are suffering and I have come to that terrible place where I could easily resort to violence in my desperation.**❞**

been driven by desperation into criminal habits. Their work was useful—including reforestation, firefighting (forty-seven lost their lives), flood control, and swamp drainage. The recruits were required to help their parents by sending home most of their pay. Both human resources and natural resources were thus conserved, though there were minor complaints of "militarizing" the nation's youth. Critics charged that CCC "soldiers" would later claim pensions for exposure to poison ivy.

The first major effort of the new Congress to grapple with the millions of adult unemployed was the Federal Emergency Relief Act. Its chief aim was immediate relief rather than long-range recovery. The resulting Federal Emergency Relief Administration (FERA) was handed over to zealous Harry L. Hopkins, a painfully thin, shabbily dressed, chain-smoking New York social worker who had earlier won Roosevelt's friendship and who became one of his most influential advisers. Hopkins's agency in all granted about $3 billion to the

TABLE 33.2 Later Major New Deal Measures, 1933–1939
(items in parentheses indicate secondary purposes)

Recovery	Relief	Reform
(CWA)	FDR establishes Civil Works Administration (CWA), November 9, 1933	
Gold Reserve Act, January 30, 1934, authorizes FDR's devaluation, January 31, 1934		
		Securities and Exchange Commission (SEC) authorized by Congress, June 6, 1934
(Reciprocal Trade Agreements Act)	(Reciprocal Trade Agreements Act)	Reciprocal Trade Agreements Act, June 12, 1934 (see p. 780)
		Indian Reorganization Act, June 18, 1934
(FHA)	National Housing Act, June 28, 1934, authorizes Federal Housing Administration (FHA)	(FHA)
(Frazier-Lemke Act)	Frazier-Lemke Farm Bankruptcy Act, June 28, 1934	
(Resettlement Administration)	FDR creates Resettlement Administration, April 30, 1935	
(WPA)	FDR creates Works Progress Administration (WPA), May 6, 1935, under act of April 8, 1935	
(Wagner Act)	(Wagner Act)	Wagner Act (National Labor Relations Act), July 5, 1935
		Social Security Act, August 14, 1935
		Public Utility Holding Company Act, August 26, 1935
(Soil Conservation Act)	Soil Conservation and Domestic Allotment Act, February 29, 1936	
(USHA)	(USHA)	United States Housing Authority (USHA) established by Congress, September 1, 1937
(Second AAA)	Second Agricultural Adjustment Act, February 16, 1938	
(Fair Labor Standards Act)	(Fair Labor Standards Act)	Fair Labor Standards Act (Wages and Hours Bill), June 25, 1938
		Reorganization Act, April 3, 1939
		Hatch Act, August 2, 1939

states for direct dole payments or preferably for wages on work projects.*

Immediate relief was also given to two large and hard-pressed special groups by the Hundred Days Congress. One section of the Agricultural Adjustment Act (AAA) made available many millions of dollars to help farmers meet their mortgages. Another law created the

Home Owners' Loan Corporation (HOLC). Designed to refinance mortgages on nonfarm homes, it ultimately assisted about a million badly pinched households. The agency not only bailed out mortgage-holding banks, it also bolted the political loyalties of relieved middle-class homeowners securely to the Democratic party.

Harassed by the continuing plague of unemployment, FDR himself established the Civil Works Administration (CWA) late in 1933 (see Table 33.2). As a branch of the FERA, it also fell under the direction of

*A boast attributed to Hopkins in 1938 was "We will spend and spend, tax and tax, and elect and elect."

Hopkins. Designed to provide purely temporary jobs during the cruel winter emergency, it served a useful purpose. Tens of thousands of jobless were employed at leaf raking and other make-work tasks, which were dubbed "boondoggling." As this kind of labor put a premium on shovel-leaning slow motion, the scheme was widely criticized. "The only thing we have to fear," scoffers remarked, "is work itself."

✶ A Day for Every Demagogue

Direct relief from Washington to needy families helped pull the nation through the ghastly winter of 1933–1934. But the disheartening persistence of unemployment and suffering demonstrated that emergency relief measures had to be not only continued but supplemented. One danger signal was the appearance of various demagogues, notably a magnetic "microphone messiah," Father Charles Coughlin, a Catholic priest in Michigan who began broadcasting in 1930 and whose slogan was "Social Justice." His anti–New Deal harangues to some 40 million radio fans finally became so anti-Semitic, fascistic, and demagogic that he was silenced in 1942 by his ecclesiastical superiors.

Also notorious among the new brood of agitators were those who capitalized on popular discontent to make pie-in-the-sky promises. Most conspicuous

Huey Long (1893–1935) Long pursued progressive policies as governor of Louisiana, even while he ruled the state with a dictatorial hand. A flamboyant and unpredictable populist, he set the orthodox political establishment on its ear, especially after he became a U.S. senator in 1930. Long's admirers called him the "Kingfish"; Franklin Roosevelt called him "one of the two most dangerous men in the country." (The other, said Roosevelt, was General Douglas MacArthur.)

Library of Congress

In 1935 Father Charles Coughlin (1891–1979) single-handedly defeated President Roosevelt's effort to win Senate ratification of a treaty providing for American membership in the World Court, a judicial body of limited authority established by the League of Nations. What FDR saw as a symbolic embrace of international responsibility Coughlin convinced his radio listeners was a conspiracy of international moneyed interests against American sovereignty:

❝Our thanks are due to Almighty God in that America retains her sovereignty. Congratulations to the aroused people of the United States who, by more than 200,000 telegrams containing at least 1,000,000 names, demanded that the principles established by Washington and Jefferson shall keep us clear from foreign entanglements and European hatreds.❞

of these individuals were Dr. Francis E. Townsend, a retired California physician who promised everyone over sixty $200 a month, and Senator Huey P. ("Kingfish") Long of Louisiana, who was said to have more brass than a government mule. He used his abundant rabble-rousing talents to publicize his "Share Our Wealth" program, which promised to make "Every Man a King." Every family was to receive $5,000, supposedly at the expense of the prosperous. H. L. Mencken called Long's chief lieutenant, former clergyman Gerald L. K. Smith, "the gutsiest, goriest, loudest and lustiest, the deadliest and damndest orator ever heard on this or any other earth, the champion boob-bumper of all time." Fear of Long's becoming a fascist dictator ended when he was shot by an assassin in the Louisiana state capitol in 1935.

Father Coughlin and Huey Long frightened many Americans because they raised troubling questions about the link between fascism and economic crisis. Danger seemed to be lurking ominously in many corners of the world. Authoritarian rule was strengthening in Japan, while Adolf Hitler was acquiring absolute authority in Germany. Some even worried that Franklin Roosevelt himself would turn into a dictator.

Partly to quiet the groundswell of unrest that might lead to a political explosion, Congress authorized the Works Progress Administration (WPA) in 1935. The objective was employment on useful projects. Launched under the supervision of the ailing but energetic Hopkins, this remarkable agency ultimately spent about $11 billion on thousands of public buildings, bridges, and hard-surfaced roads. Not every WPA project strengthened the infrastructure: for instance, one controlled crickets in Wyoming, while another

WPA Mural, by Victor Arnautoff (1896–1979), 1934 *The Pedestrian Scene*, painted on a wall of Coit Tower in San Francisco, was one of a series of murals commissioned by the federal government to employ artists during the Great Depression.

built a monkey pen in Oklahoma City. John Steinbeck, future Nobel Prize novelist, counted dogs in his California county. One of the most well-loved WPA programs was the Federal Art Project, which hired artists to create posters and murals—many still adorning post office walls. Critics sneered that WPA meant "We Provide Alms." But the fact is that over a period of eight years, nearly 9 million people were given jobs, not handouts. The WPA nourished much precious talent, preserved self-respect, and fostered the creation of more than a million pieces of art, many of them publicly displayed.

✷ New Visibility for Women

Just over a decade after the ratification of the Nineteenth Amendment, American women began to carve a larger space for themselves in the nation's political and intellectual life. First Lady Eleanor Roosevelt may have been the most visible woman in the Roosevelt White House, but she was hardly the only female voice. Secretary of Labor Frances Perkins (1880–1965) burst through the gender barrier when she became America's first woman cabinet member. Mary McLeod Bethune (1875–1955), director of the Office of Minority Affairs

in the National Youth Administration, served as the highest-ranking African American in the Roosevelt administration.

Women also made important contributions in the social sciences, especially in the relatively new and open field of anthropology. Ruth Benedict (1887–1948) carried on the work of her mentor, Franz Boas (1858–1942), by developing the "culture and personality movement" in the 1930s and 1940s. Benedict's landmark work, *Patterns of Culture* (1934), established the study of cultures as collective personalities. Each culture, like each individual, had its own "more or less consistent pattern of thought and action." One of Benedict's students, Margaret Mead (1901–1978), drew from her own scholarly studies of adolescence among Pacific island peoples to advance bold new ideas about sexuality, gender roles, and intergenerational relationships. With thirty-four books and a curatorship at the American Museum of Natural History in New York City to her credit, Mead helped popularize cultural anthropology and achieved a celebrity status rare among social scientists.

Pearl S. Buck (1892–1973) won similar acclaim as a novelist. Raised in China by Presbyterian missionary parents, Buck introduced American readers to Chinese

AP Photo

Frances Perkins (1880–1965) at the Site of the Golden Gate Bridge Project, 1935 The first woman cabinet member, Perkins served as secretary of labor under Roosevelt. She was subjected to much undeserved criticism from male businessmen, laborites, and politicians. They sneered that FDR "kept her in labor" for many years.

peasant society. Her best-selling novel, *The Good Earth* (1931), earned her the Nobel Prize for literature in 1938, making her the third American (after Sinclair Lewis and Eugene O'Neill) to win the award. A prolific author all her life, Buck also used her fame to advance humanitarian causes.

✵ Helping Industry and Labor

A daring attempt to stimulate a nationwide comeback was initiated when the Emergency Congress authorized the **National Recovery Administration (NRA)**. This ingenious scheme was by far the most complex and far-reaching effort by the New Dealers to combine immediate relief with long-range recovery and reform. Triple-barreled, it was designed to assist industry, labor, and the unemployed.

Individual industries—over two hundred in all—were to work out codes of "fair competition," under which hours of labor would be reduced so that employment could be spread over more people. A ceiling was placed on the maximum hours of labor; a floor was placed under wages to establish minimum levels.

Labor, under the NRA, was granted additional benefits. Workers were formally guaranteed the right to organize and bargain collectively through representatives *of their own choosing*—not through handpicked agents of the company's choosing. The hated "yellow-dog," or antiunion, contract was expressly forbidden, and certain safeguarding restrictions were placed on the use of child labor.

Industrial recovery through the NRA's "fair competition" codes would at best be painful, for these called for self-denial by both management and labor. Patriotism was aroused by mass meetings and monster parades, which included 200,000 marchers on New York City's Fifth Avenue. A handsome blue eagle was designed as the symbol of the NRA, and merchants subscribing to a code displayed it in their windows with the slogan "We Do Our Part." A newly formed professional football team was christened the Philadelphia

Moorland-Spingarn Research Center, Howard University, Washington, D.C.

Mary McLeod Bethune (1875–1955) The daughter of ex-slaves and founder of a college in Florida, Bethune became the highest-ranking African American in the Roosevelt administration when she was appointed director of the Office of Minority Affairs in the National Youth Administration (NYA). From this base she organized the "Black Cabinet" to make sure blacks benefited from the New Deal programs along with whites. Here she is picketing against segregated hiring practices at the Peoples Drug Store chain, one of the earliest targets of the black civil rights movement.

Eagles. Such was the enthusiasm for the NRA that for a brief period, there was a marked upswing in business activity, although Roosevelt had warned, "We cannot ballyhoo our way to prosperity."

But the high-flying eagle gradually fluttered to earth. Too much self-sacrifice was expected of labor,

industry, and the public for such a scheme to work. Critics began to brand the NRA "National Run Around" and "Nuts Running America," symbolized by what Henry Ford called "that damn Roosevelt buzzard." A new "age of chiselry" dawned as certain unscrupulous businesspeople ("chiselers") publicly displayed the blue bird in their windows but secretly violated the codes. Complete collapse was imminent when, in 1935, the Supreme Court shot down the dying eagle in the famed *Schechter* "sick chicken" decision. The learned justices unanimously held that Congress could not "delegate legislative powers" to the executive. They further declared that congressional control of interstate commerce could not properly apply to a local fowl business, like that of the Schechter brothers in Brooklyn, New York. Roosevelt was incensed by this "horse and buggy" interpretation of the Constitution, but actually the Court helped him out of a bad jam.

The same act of Congress that hatched the NRA eagle also authorized the Public Works Administration (PWA), likewise intended both for industrial recovery and for unemployment relief. The agency was headed by the secretary of the interior, acid-tongued Harold L. Ickes, a free-swinging former bull mooser. Long-range recovery was the primary purpose of the new agency, and in time over $4 billion was spent on some thirty-four thousand projects, which included public buildings, highways, and parkways. One spectacular achievement was the Grand Coulee Dam on the Columbia River—the largest structure erected by humans since the Great Wall of China. In the depths of the depression, the grand dam seemed the height of folly. It made possible the irrigation of millions of acres of new farmland—at a time when the government was desperately trying to reduce farm surpluses. It created more electrical power than the entire Tennessee Valley Authority—in a region with little industry and virtually no market for additional power. But with the outbreak of World War II and then postwar prosperity, the dam would come to seem a stroke of genius, transforming the entire region with abundant water and power.

Special stimulants aided the recovery of one segment of business—the liquor industry. The imminent repeal of the prohibition amendment afforded an opportunity to raise needed federal revenue and at the same time to provide a measure of employment. Prodded by Roosevelt, the Hundred Days Congress, in one of its earliest acts, legalized light wine and beer with an alcoholic content (presumably nonintoxicating) not exceeding 3.2 percent by weight, and levied a tax of $5 on every barrel so manufactured. Disgruntled drys, unwilling to acknowledge the breakdown of law and order begotten by bootlegging, damned Roosevelt as "a 3.2 percent American." Prohibition was officially

Grand Coulee Dam on the Columbia River, Washington State The Grand Coulee Dam was one of the most ambitious projects of the New Deal's Public Works Administration. It is one of the few man-made constructions visible from outer space, the largest concrete structure in the United States, and the central facility in the Columbia Basin Project, which generates electricity for the Pacific Northwest and provides irrigation for half a million acres of Columbia Valley farmland—services that have transformed the life of the region.

repealed by the Twenty-first Amendment late in 1933 (see the Appendix), and the saloon doors swung open.

✴ Paying Farmers Not to Farm

Ever since the war-boom days of 1918, farmers had suffered from low prices and overproduction, especially in grain. During the depression, conditions became desperate as innumerable mortgages were foreclosed, as corn was burned for fuel, and as embattled farmers tried to prevent the shipment of crops to glutted markets. In Iowa several volatile counties were placed under martial law.

A radical new approach to farm recovery was embraced when the Emergency Congress established the **Agricultural Adjustment Administration (AAA)**. Through "artificial scarcity" this agency was to establish "parity prices" for basic commodities. "Parity" was the price set for a product that gave it the same real value, in purchasing power, that it had enjoyed during the period from 1909 to 1914. The AAA would eliminate price-depressing surpluses by paying growers to reduce their crop acreage. The millions of dollars needed for these payments were to be raised by taxing processors of farm products, such as flour millers, who in turn would shift the burden to consumers.

Unhappily, the AAA got off to a wobbly start. It was begun after much of the cotton crop for 1933 had been planted, and balky mules, trained otherwise, were forced to plow under countless young plants. Several million squealing pigs were purchased and slaughtered. Much of their meat was distributed to people on relief, but some of it was used for fertilizer. This "sinful" destruction of food, at a time when thousands of citizens were hungry, increased condemnation of the American economic system by many left-leaning voices.

"Subsidized scarcity" did have the effect of raising farm income, but the whole confused enterprise met with acid criticism. Farmers, food processors, consumers, and taxpayers were all to some degree unhappy. Paying the farmers not to farm actually increased unemployment, at a time when other New Deal agencies were striving to decrease it. When the Supreme Court finally killed the AAA in 1936 by declaring its regulatory taxation provisions unconstitutional, foes of the plow-under program rejoiced loudly.

Quickly recovering from this blow, the New Deal Congress hastened to pass the Soil Conservation and Domestic Allotment Act of 1936. The withdrawal of acreage from production was now achieved by paying farmers to plant soil-conserving crops, like soybeans, or to let their land lie fallow. With the emphasis thus

on conservation, the Supreme Court placed its stamp of approval on the revamped scheme.

The Second Agricultural Adjustment Act of 1938, passed two years later, was a more comprehensive substitute, although it continued conservation payments. If growers observed acreage restrictions on specified commodities like cotton and wheat, they would be eligible for parity payments. Other provisions of the new AAA were designed to give farmers not only a fairer price but a more substantial share of the national income. Both goals were partially achieved.

✸ Dust Bowls and Black Blizzards

Nature meanwhile had been providing some unplanned scarcity. Late in 1933 a prolonged drought struck the states of the trans-Mississippi Great Plains. Rainless weeks were followed by furious, whining winds, while the sun was darkened by millions of tons of powdery topsoil torn from homesteads in an area that stretched from eastern Colorado to western Missouri—soon to be dubbed the **Dust Bowl**. Despondent citizens sat on front porches with protective masks on their faces, watching their farms swirl by. A seven-year-old boy in Kansas suffocated. Overawed victims of the Dust Bowl disaster predicted the end of the world or the second coming of Christ.

An Okie Family Hits the Road in the 1930s to Escape the Dust Bowl

Library of Congress

Novelist John Steinbeck (1902–1968) relates in his novel The Grapes of Wrath *(1939) that when the "Okies" and "Arkies" reached California, they found the big growers unwilling to pay more than twenty-five cents an hour for work in the fields. One owner mutters,*

❝A Red is any son-of-a-bitch that wants thirty cents an hour when we're paying twenty-five!❞

Drought and wind triggered the dust storms, but they were not the only culprits. The human hand had also worked its mischief. High grain prices during World War I had enticed farmers to bring countless acres of marginal land under cultivation. Worse, dry-farming techniques and mechanization had revolutionized Great Plains agriculture. The steam tractor and the disk plow tore up infinitely more sod than a team of oxen ever could, leaving the powdery topsoil to be swept away at nature's whim (see Map 33.1).

Burned and blown out of the Dust Bowl, tens of thousands of refugees fled their ruined acres. In five years about 350,000 Oklahomans and Arkansans—"Okies" and "Arkies"—trekked to southern California in "junkyards on wheels." Undeterred by signs saying "KEEP OUT," many found a new home in the San Joaquin Valley, which shared much in common with the southern plains—arid climate, cotton growing, new-found oil deposits, and abundant land. Yet the transition was cruel. Food, shelter, and clothing were scarce; the winter months, without work and heat, proved nearly unendurable for the migrants. The dismal story of these human tumbleweeds was realistically portrayed in John Steinbeck's best-selling novel *The Grapes of Wrath* (1939), which proved to be the *Uncle Tom's Cabin* of the Dust Bowl.

Zealous New Dealers, sympathetic toward the soil-tillers, made various other efforts to relieve their burdens. The Frazier-Lemke Farm Bankruptcy Act, passed in 1934, made possible a suspension of mortgage foreclosures for five years, but it was voided the next year by the Supreme Court. A revised law, limiting the grace period to three years, was unanimously upheld. In 1935 the president set up the Resettlement Administration, charged with the task of removing near-farmless farmers to better land. And more than 200 million young trees were successfully planted on the bare prairies as windbreaks by the young men of the Civilian Conservation Corps, even though one governor jeered at trying to "grow hair on a bald head."

Native Americans also felt the far-reaching hand of New Deal reform. Commissioner of Indian Affairs John

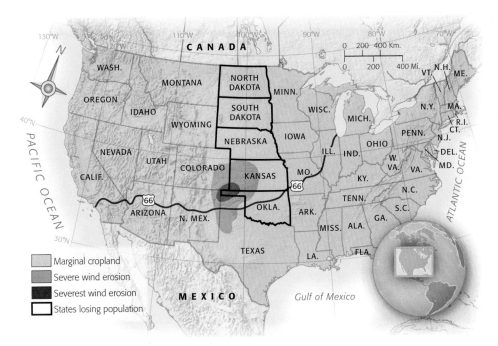

MAP 33.1 The Extent of Erosion in the 1930s Note the extensive wind erosion in the western Oklahoma panhandle region, which was dubbed the "Dust Bowl" in the 1930s. Mechanized farmers had "busted" the sod of the southern plains so thoroughly that they literally broke the back of the land. Tons of dust blew out of the Dust Bowl in the 1930s and blotted the sun from the skies as far away as New York. A Kansas newspaperman reported in 1935 that in his dust-darkened town, "Lady Godiva could ride through streets without even the horse seeing her." © Cengage Learning

Collier ardently sought to reverse the forced-assimilation policies in place since the Dawes Act of 1887 (see p. 581). Inspired by a sojourn among the Pueblo Indians in Taos, New Mexico, Collier promoted the Indian Reorganization Act of 1934 (the "Indian New Deal"). The new law encouraged tribes to establish local self-government and to preserve their native crafts and traditions. The act also helped to stop the loss of Indian lands and revived tribes' interest in their identity and culture. Yet not all Indians applauded it. Some denounced the legislation as a "back-to-the-blanket" measure that sought to make museum pieces out of Native Americans. Seventy-seven tribes refused to organize under its provisions, though nearly two hundred others did establish tribal governments.

✵ Battling Bankers and Big Business

Reformist New Dealers were determined from the outset to curb the "money changers" who had played fast and loose with gullible investors before the Wall Street crash of 1929. The Hundred Days Congress passed the "Truth in Securities Act" (Federal Securities Act), which required promoters to transmit to investors sworn information regarding the soundness of their stocks and bonds. An old saying was thus reversed to read "Let the seller beware," although the buyer might never read the fine print.

In 1934 Congress took further steps to protect the public against fraud, deception, and inside manipulation. It authorized the Securities and Exchange Commission (SEC), which was designed as a watchdog administrative agency. Stock markets henceforth were to operate more as trading marts and less as gambling casinos.

New Dealers likewise directed their fire at public utility holding companies, those supercorporations. Citizens had seen one of these incredible colossi collapse during the spring of 1932, when Chicagoan Samuel Insull's multibillion-dollar financial empire crashed. Possibilities of controlling, with a minimum of capital, a half-dozen or so pyramided layers of big business suggested to Roosevelt "a ninety-six-inch dog being wagged by a four-inch tail." The Public Utility Holding Company Act of 1935 finally delivered a "death sentence" to this type of bloated growth, except where it might be deemed economically needful.

✵ The TVA Harnesses the Tennessee

Inevitably, the sprawling electric-power industry attracted the fire of New Deal reformers. Within a few decades, it had risen from nothingness to a behemoth with an investment of $13 billion. As a public utility, it reached directly and regularly into the pocketbooks of millions of consumers for vitally needed services. Ardent New Dealers accused it of gouging the public with excessive rates, especially since it owed its success to having secured, often for a song, priceless water-power sites from the public domain.

The tempestuous Tennessee River provided New Dealers with a rare opportunity. With its tributaries, the river drained a badly eroded area about the size of

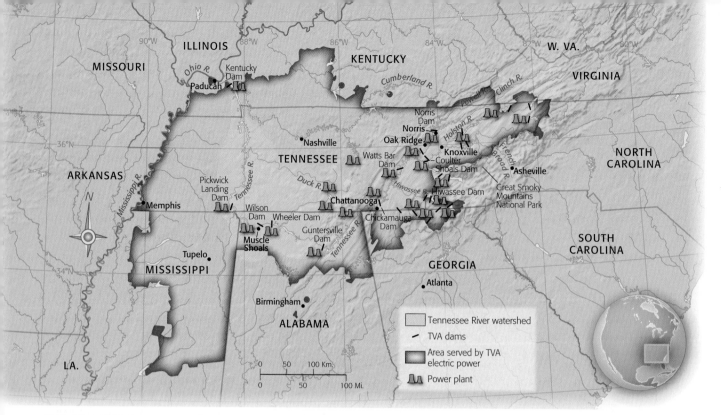

MAP 33.2 TVA Area More than twenty dams were constructed on the river's tributaries as part of a massive project to control flooding, generate hydroelectric power, and revitalize the Tennessee Valley region, while also creating jobs for the unemployed. The shaded area represents the area served by TVA electric power. © Cengage Learning

England, and one containing some 2.5 million of the most poverty-stricken people in America. The federal government already owned valuable properties at Muscle Shoals, where it had erected plants for needed nitrates in World War I. By developing the hydroelectric potential of the entire area, Washington could combine the immediate advantage of putting thousands of people to work and a long-term project for reforming the power monopoly.

An act creating the **Tennessee Valley Authority (TVA)** was passed in 1933 by the Hundred Days Congress. This far-ranging enterprise was largely a result of the steadfast vision and unflagging zeal of Senator George W. Norris of Nebraska, after whom one of the mighty dams was named. From the standpoint of "planned economy," the TVA was by far the most revolutionary of all the New Deal schemes.

This new agency was determined to discover precisely how much the production and distribution of electricity cost, so that a "yardstick" could be set up to test the fairness of rates charged by private companies. Utility corporations lashed back at this entering wedge of government control, charging that the low cost of TVA power was due to dishonest bookkeeping and the absence of taxes. Critics complained that the whole dream was "creeping socialism in concrete."

But the New Dealers, shrugging off such outcries, pointed a prideful finger at the amazing achievements of the TVA. The gigantic project brought to the area not only full employment and the blessings of cheap electric power (see Figure 33.2), but low-cost housing, abundant cheap nitrates, the restoration of eroded soil, reforestation, improved navigation, and flood control. Rivers ran blue instead of brown, and a once-poverty-cursed area was being transformed into one of the most flourishing regions in the United States.

Foreigners were greatly impressed with the possibilities of similar schemes in their own lands, and exulting New Dealers agitated for parallel enterprises in the valleys of the Columbia, Colorado, and Missouri Rivers. Federally built dams one day would span all those waterways, impounding more than 30 percent of the total annual runoff from the "roof of America" in the Rocky Mountains. Hydroelectric power from those dams would drive the growth of the urban West, and the waters they diverted would nurture agriculture in the previously bone-dry western deserts. But conservative reaction against the "socialistic" New Deal would confine the TVA's brand of federally guided resource management and comprehensive regional development to the Tennessee Valley (see Map 33.2).

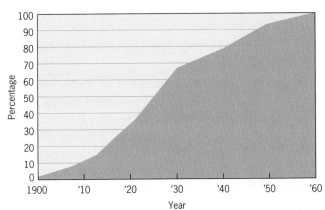

FIGURE 33.2 Occupied Households with Electric Service, 1900–1960 Well into the twentieth century, a majority of American households had no electrical service. The New Deal's Rural Electrification Agency and projects like the Tennessee Valley Authority (TVA) helped make electricity available to almost all Americans by 1960. African American leader Andrew Young later claimed that the TVA created the economic underpinnings of the civil rights movement: "It was the presence of the cheap electricity, lower interest rates, water projects, that laid the foundation for the New South."

✵ Housing and Social Security

The New Deal had meanwhile framed sturdy new policies for housing construction. To speed recovery and better homes, Roosevelt set up the Federal Housing Administration (FHA) as early as 1934. The building industry was to be stimulated by small loans to householders, both for improving their dwellings and for completing new ones. So popular did the FHA prove to be that it was one of the few "alphabetical agencies" to outlast the age of Roosevelt.

Congress bolstered the program in 1937 by authorizing the United States Housing Authority (USHA), an agency designed to lend money to states or communities for low-cost construction. Although units for about 650,000 low-income people were started, new building fell tragically short of needs. New Deal efforts to expand the project collided with brick-wall opposition from real estate promoters, builders, and landlords ("slumlords"), to say nothing of anti–New Dealers who attacked what they considered down-the-rathole spending. Nonetheless, for the first time in a century, the slum areas in America ceased growing and even shrank.

Incomparably more important was the success of New Dealers in the field of unemployment insurance and old-age pensions. Their greatest victory was the epochal **Social Security Act** of 1935—one of the most complicated and far-reaching laws ever to pass Congress. To cushion future depressions, the measure provided for federal-state unemployment insurance. To provide security for old age, specified categories of retired workers were to receive regular payments from Washington. These payments ranged from $10 to $85 a month (raised periodically) and were financed by a payroll tax on both employers and employees. Provision was also made for the blind, the physically handicapped, delinquent children, and other dependents.

Republican opposition to the sweeping new legislation was bitter. "Social Security," insisted Hoover, "must be builded upon a cult of work, not a cult of leisure." The GOP national chairman falsely charged that every worker would have to wear a metal dog tag for life.

Social Security was largely inspired by the example of some of the more highly industrialized nations of Europe. In the agricultural America of an earlier day, there had always been farm chores for all ages, and the large family had cared for its own dependents. But in an urbanized economy, at the mercy of boom-or-bust cycles, the government was now recognizing its responsibility for the welfare of its citizens. By 1939 over 45 million people were eligible for Social Security benefits. In subsequent years further categories of workers were added, including, belatedly, farm and domestic workers. For decades millions of poor men and women were excluded from Social Security. In contrast to Europe, where welfare programs generally were universal, American workers had to be employed and in certain kinds of jobs to get coverage.

✵ A New Deal for Labor

The NRA blue eagles, with their call for collective bargaining, had been a godsend to organized labor. As New Deal expenditures brought some slackening of unemployment, labor began to feel more secure and hence more self-assertive. A rash of walkouts occurred in the summer of 1934, including a paralyzing general strike in San Francisco (following a "Bloody Thursday"), which was broken only when outraged citizens resorted to vigilante tactics.

When the Supreme Court axed the blue eagle, a Congress sympathetic to labor unions undertook to fill the vacuum. The fruit of its deliberations was the National Labor Relations Act of 1935, more commonly known as the **Wagner Act**, after its congressional sponsor, New York senator Robert F. Wagner. This trailblazing law created a powerful new National Labor Relations Board for administrative purposes and reasserted the right of labor to engage in self-organization and to bargain collectively through representatives of its own choice. Considered the Magna Carta of American labor, the Wagner Act proved to be a major milestone for American workers.

Under the encouragement of a highly sympathetic National Labor Relations Board, a host of unskilled workers began to organize themselves into effective unions. The leader of this drive was beetle-browed, domineering, and melodramatic John L. Lewis, boss of the United Mine Workers. In 1935 he succeeded in forming the Committee for Industrial Organization (CIO) within the ranks of the skilled-craft American Federation of Labor. But skilled workers, ever since the days of the ill-fated Knights of Labor in the 1880s, had shown only lukewarm sympathy for the cause of unskilled labor, especially blacks. In 1936, following inevitable friction with the CIO, the older federation suspended the upstart unions associated with the newer organization.

Undaunted, the rebellious CIO moved on a concerted scale into the huge automobile industry. Late in 1936 the workers resorted to a revolutionary technique (earlier used in both Europe and America) known as the sit-down strike: they refused to leave the factory building of General Motors at Flint, Michigan, and thus prevented the importation of strikebreakers. Conservative respecters of private property were scandalized. The CIO finally won a resounding victory when its union, after heated negotiations, was recognized by General Motors as the sole bargaining agency for its employees.

Unskilled workers now pressed their advantage. The United States Steel Company, hitherto an impossible

A worker at a Chevrolet plant in Flint, Michigan, wrote after the United Auto Workers–CIO victory in 1937,

“ The inhuman high speed is *no more.* We now have a voice, and have slowed up the speed of the line. And [we] are now treated as human beings, and not as part of the machinery. The high pressure is taken off. . . . It proves clearly that united we stand, divided or alone we fall.**”**

nut for labor to crack, averted a costly strike when it voluntarily granted rights of unionization to its CIO-organized employees. But the "little steel" companies fought back savagely. Citizens were shocked in 1937 by the Memorial Day massacre at the plant of the Republic Steel Company in South Chicago. In a bloody fracas, police fired upon pickets and workers, leaving the area strewn with several score dead and wounded.

A better deal for labor continued when Congress, in 1938, passed the memorable **Fair Labor Standards Act** (Wages and Hours Bill). Industries involved in interstate commerce were to set up minimum-wage and maximum-hour levels. The eventual goals were forty cents an hour (later raised) and a forty-hour week. Labor by children under sixteen (under eighteen if the occupation was dangerous) was forbidden. These

General Motors Sit-down Strikers, Flint, Michigan, 1937 Strikers like these sometimes kept their spirits up with the song "Sit Down":

When the boss won't talk
Don't take a walk;
Sit down, sit down.

Granger Collection

Labor Triumphant   After generations of struggle, organized labor made dramatic gains in membership and bargaining power during the New Deal years.

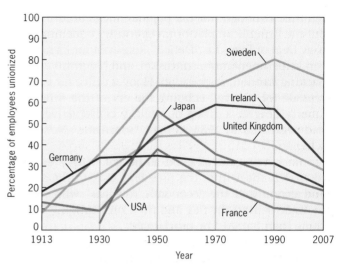

FIGURE 33.3 Labor Union Membership in Selected Countries, 1913–2007   In the United States, the percentage of the labor force that was unionized increased until 1954, when it began a long-term decline. In the 1990s it had a brief rise with the organization of service and government workers, only to decline again until it reached a low of 12 percent in 2006. In 2007 unionization grew by .1 percent, adding 311,000 workers, which brought total union membership to 15.7 million, the highest in many years. Note the different fortunes of organized labor in other countries in the face of the Great Depression, World War II, postwar prosperity, and deindustrialization.

Sources: James C. Docherty, *Historical Dictionary of Organized Labor*, 2nd ed., pp. 408–415 and 420–421. Copyright © 2004. Reprinted by permission of Scarecrow Press; Organisation for Economic Co-Operation and Development, online OECD Employment database.

reforms were bitterly though futilely opposed by many industrialists, especially by those southern textile manufacturers who had profited from low-wage labor. But the exclusion of agricultural, service, and domestic workers meant that blacks, Mexican Americans, and women—who were concentrated in these fields—did not benefit from the act.

In later New Deal days, labor unionization thrived (see Figure 33.3). "Roosevelt wants you to join a union" was the rallying cry of professional organizers. The president received valuable support at ballot-box time from labor leaders and many appreciative workingpeople. One mill worker remarked that Roosevelt was "the only man we ever had in the White House who would know that my boss is a s.o.b."

The CIO surged forward, breaking completely with the AF of L in 1938. On that occasion the *Committee for Industrial Organization* was formally reconstituted as the ***Congress of Industrial Organizations*** (the new **CIO**), under the visionary though high-handed presidency of John L. Lewis. By 1940 the CIO could

claim about 4 million members in its constituent unions, including some 200,000 blacks. Nevertheless, bitter and annoying jurisdictional feuding involving strikes continued with the AF of L. At times labor seemed more bent on costly civil war than on its age-old war with management.

✷ Landon Challenges "the Champ"

As the presidential campaign of 1936 neared, the New Dealers were on top of the world. They had achieved considerable progress, and millions of "reliefers" were grateful to their bountiful government. The exultant Democrats renominated Roosevelt on a platform squarely endorsing the New Deal.

The Republicans were hard-pressed to find someone to feed to "the Champ." They finally settled on the colorless but homespun and honest governor of the Sunflower State of Kansas, Alfred M. Landon. Landon himself was a moderate who accepted some New Deal reforms, although not the popular Social Security Act. But the Republican platform vigorously condemned the New Deal of Franklin "Deficit" Roosevelt for its radicalism, experimentation, confusion, and "frightful waste." Backing Landon, ex-president Hoover called for a "holy crusade for liberty," echoing the cry of the American Liberty League, a group of wealthy conservatives who had organized in 1934 to fight "socialistic" New Deal schemes.

Roosevelt gave as good as he got. Angry enough to stretch sheet iron, the president took to the stump and denounced the "economic royalists" who sought to "hide behind the flag and the Constitution." "I welcome their hatred," he proclaimed.

A landslide overwhelmed Landon, as the demoralized Republicans carried only two states, Maine and Vermont. This dismal showing caused political wiseacres to make the old adage read, "As Maine goes, so goes Vermont."* The popular vote was 27,752,869 to 16,674,665; the electoral count was 523 to 8—the most lopsided in 116 years. A good-humored newspaper columnist quipped, "If Landon had given one more speech, Roosevelt would have carried Canada, too." Democratic majorities, riding in on Roosevelt's magic coattails, were again returned to Congress. Jubilant Democrats could now claim more than two-thirds of the seats in the House and a like proportion in the Senate.

The battle of 1936, perhaps the most bitter since Bryan's defeat in 1896, partially bore out Republican charges of class warfare. Even more than in 1932, the needy economic groups were lined up against the so-called greedy economic groups. CIO units contributed generously to FDR's campaign chest. Many left-wingers turned to Roosevelt, as the customary third-party protest vote sharply declined. Blacks, several million of whom had also appreciated welcome relief checks, had by now largely shaken off their traditional allegiance to the Republican party. To them, Lincoln was "finally dead."

FDR won primarily because he appealed to the "forgotten man," whom he never forgot. Some of the president's support was only pocketbook-deep: "reliefers" were not going to bite the hand that doled out the government checks. No one, as Al Smith remarked, "shoots at Santa Claus." But Roosevelt in fact had forged a powerful and enduring coalition of the South: blacks, urbanites, and the poor. He proved especially effective in marshaling the support of the multitudes of "New Immigrants"—mostly the Catholics and Jews who had swarmed into the great cities since the turn of

*Maine, which traditionally held its state elections in September, was long regarded as a political weathervane, hence the expression "As Maine goes, so goes the nation."

> *Three days before the 1936 election, Roosevelt took the moral high ground in his speech at New York's Madison Square Garden:*
>
> **"**I should like to have it said of my first Administration that in it the forces of selfishness and of lust for power met their match. I should like to have it said of my second Administration that in it these forces met their master.**"**

the century. These once-scorned newcomers, with their now-numerous sons and daughters, had at last come politically of age. In the 1920s one out of every twenty-five federal judgeships went to a Catholic; Roosevelt appointed Catholics to one out of every four.

✴ Nine Old Men on the Bench

Bowing his head to the sleety blasts, Roosevelt took the presidential oath on January 20, 1937, instead of the traditional March 4. The Twentieth Amendment to the Constitution had been ratified in 1933. (See the Appendix.) It swept away the postelection lame duck session of Congress and shortened by six weeks the awkward period before inauguration.

Flushed with victory, Roosevelt interpreted his reelection as a mandate to continue New Deal reforms. But in his eyes, the cloistered old men on the supreme bench, like fossilized stumbling blocks, stood stubbornly in the pathway of progress. In nine major cases involving the New Deal, the Roosevelt administration had been thwarted seven times. The Court was ultraconservative, and six of the nine oldsters in black were over seventy. As luck would have it, not a single member had been appointed by FDR in his first term.

Roosevelt, his "Dutch up," viewed with mounting impatience what he regarded as the obstructive conservatism of the Court. Some of these Old Guard appointees were hanging on with a senile grip, partly because they felt it their patriotic duty to curb the "socialistic" tendencies of that radical in the White House. Roosevelt believed that the voters in three successive elections—the presidential elections of 1932 and 1936 and the midterm congressional elections of 1934—had returned a smashing verdict in favor of his program of reform. Democracy, in his view, meant rule by the people. If the American way of life was to be preserved, Roosevelt argued, the Supreme Court ought to get in line with the supreme court of public opinion.

Roosevelt finally hit upon a Court scheme that he regarded as "the answer to a maiden's prayer." In fact, it proved to be one of the most costly political misjudgments of his career. When he sprang his brainstorm on a shocked nation early in 1937, he caught the country and Congress completely by surprise. Roosevelt bluntly asked Congress for legislation to permit him to add a new justice to the Supreme Court for every member over seventy who would not retire. The maximum membership could then be fifteen. Roosevelt pointed to the necessity of injecting vigorous new blood, for the Court, he alleged, was far behind in its work. This charge, which turned out to be false, brought heated accusations of dishonesty. At best Roosevelt was headstrong and not fully aware of the fact that the Court, in popular thinking, had become something of a sacred cow.

✷ The Court Changes Course

Congress and the nation were promptly convulsed over Roosevelt's **Court-packing plan** to expand the Supreme Court. Franklin "Double-crossing" Roosevelt was vilified for attempting to break down the delicate checks and balances among the three branches of the government. He was accused of grooming himself as a dictator by trying to browbeat the judiciary. In the eyes of countless citizens, mostly Republicans but including many Democrats, basic liberties seemed to be in jeopardy. "God Bless the Supreme Court" was a fervent prayer.

The Court had meanwhile seen the ax hanging over its head. Whatever his motives, Justice Owen J. Roberts, formerly regarded as a conservative, began to vote on the side of his liberal colleagues. "A switch in time saves nine" was the classic witticism inspired by this ideological change. By a five-to-four decision, the Court, in March 1937, upheld the principle of a state minimum wage for women, thereby reversing its stand on a different case a year earlier. In succeeding decisions, a Court more sympathetic to the New Deal upheld the National Labor Relations Act (Wagner Act) and the Social Security Act. Roosevelt's "Court-packing" was further undermined when Congress voted full pay for justices over seventy who retired, whereupon one of the oldest conservative members resigned, to be replaced by a New Dealer, Justice Hugo Black.

Congress finally passed a court reform bill, but this watered-down version applied only to lower courts. Roosevelt, the master politician, thus suffered his first major legislative defeat at the hands of his own party in Congress. Americans have never viewed lightly a president's tampering with the Supreme Court, no matter how popular their chief executive may be. Yet in losing this battle, Roosevelt incidentally won his campaign. The Court, as he had hoped, became markedly more friendly to New Deal reforms. Furthermore, a succession of deaths and resignations enabled him in time to make nine appointments to the tribunal—more than any of his predecessors since George Washington. The clock "unpacked" the Court.

Granger Collection

The Response to Roosevelt's "Court-Packing" Plan, 1937
Even the Democratic donkey kicked up a storm in opposition to President Roosevelt's plan to expand the Supreme Court to as many as fifteen judges.

Yet in a sense, FDR lost both the Court battle and the war. He so aroused conservatives of both parties in Congress that few New Deal reforms were passed after 1937, the year of the fight to "pack" the bench. With this catastrophic miscalculation, he squandered much of the political goodwill that had carried him to such a resounding victory in the 1936 election.

✵ Twilight of the New Deal

Roosevelt's first term, from 1933 to 1937, did not banish the depression from the land. Unemployment stubbornly persisted in 1936 at about 15 percent, down from the grim 25 percent of 1933 but still miserably high (see Figure 33.4). Despite the inventiveness of New Deal programs and the billions of dollars in "pump priming," recovery had been dishearteningly modest, though the country seemed to be inching its way back to economic health.

Then, in 1937, the economy took another sharp downturn, a surprisingly severe depression-within-the-depression that the president's critics quickly dubbed

the "Roosevelt recession." In fact, government policies had caused the nosedive, as new Social Security taxes began to bite into payrolls and as the administration cut back on spending out of continuing reverence for the orthodox economic doctrine of the balanced budget.

Only at this late date did Roosevelt at last frankly and deliberately embrace the recommendations of the British economist John Maynard Keynes. The New Deal had run deficits for several years, but all of them had been rather small and none was intended. Now, in April 1937, Roosevelt announced a bold program to stimulate the economy by planned deficit spending. Although the deficits were still undersized for the herculean task of conquering the depression, this abrupt policy reversal marked a major turning point in the government's relation to the economy. **Keynesianism**—the use of government spending and fiscal policy to "prime the pump" of the economy and encourage consumer spending—became the new economic orthodoxy and remained so for decades.

Roosevelt had meanwhile been pushing the remaining reform measures of the New Deal. Early in 1937 he urged Congress—a Congress growing more

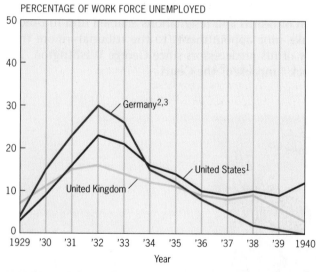

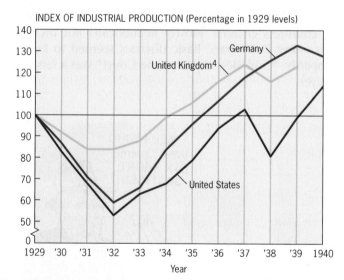

FIGURE 33.4 Economic Impact of the Great Depression on the United States, the United Kingdom, and Germany, 1929–1940

[1]Federal Emergency Relief Administration workers are counted as employed.

[2]Figure shows registered unemployment in Germany in 1929; industrial unemployment, as reported by unions, was 13.1 percent.

[3]Unemployment ceased to be an issue in Germany by 1939 with the mobilization for war. The labor force was actually augmented by the often-forced importation of foreign workers and the use of prison labor. Those who were unemployed suffered from a disability of some kind.

[4]This is an average of the industrial indexes in the United Kingdom for the first six months of 1939 only. Thereafter, no figures are available until 1946.

[Sources: *United States Historical Statistics*, vol. 2; *Statistical Yearbook of the League of Nations* (1938–1939 and 1941–1942); *International Historical Statistics, 1750–2005: Europe; State, Economy, and Society in Western Europe, 1815–1975*, vol. 2.]

A basic objective of the New Deal was featured in Roosevelt's second inaugural address (1937):

❝I see one-third of a nation ill-housed, ill-clad, ill-nourished. . . . The test of our progress is not whether we add more to the abundance of those who have much; it is whether we provide enough for those who have too little.**❞**

conservative—to authorize a sweeping reorganization of the national administration in the interests of streamlined efficiency. But the issue became tangled up with his presumed autocratic ambitions in regard to the Supreme Court, and he suffered another stinging defeat. Two years later, in 1939, Congress partially relented and in the Reorganization Act gave him limited powers for administrative reforms, including the key new Executive Office in the White House.

The New Dealers were accused of having the richest campaign chest in history, and in truth government relief checks had a curious habit of coming in bunches just before ballot time. To remedy such practices, Congress adopted the much-heralded Hatch Act of 1939. This act barred federal administrative officials, except the highest policy-making officers, from active political campaigning and soliciting. It also forbade the use of government funds for political purposes, as well as the collection of campaign contributions from people receiving relief payments. The Hatch Act was broadened in 1940 to place limits on campaign contributions and expenditures, but such clever ways of getting

around it were found that on the whole the legislation proved disappointing.

By 1938 the New Deal had clearly lost most of its early momentum. Magician Roosevelt could find few dazzling new reform rabbits to pull out of his tall silk hat. In the congressional elections of 1938, the Republicans, for the first time, cut heavily into the New Deal majorities in Congress, though failing to gain control of either house. The international crisis that came to a boil in 1938–1939 shifted public attention away from domestic reform and no doubt helped save the political hide of the Roosevelt "spendocracy." The New Deal, for all practical purposes, had shot its bolt.

✦ New Deal or Raw Deal?

Foes of the New Deal condemned its alleged waste, incompetence, confusion, contradictions, and cross-purposes, as well as the chiseling and graft in the alphabetical agencies—"alphabet soup," sneered Al Smith. Roosevelt had done nothing, cynics said, that an earthquake could not have done better. Critics deplored the employment of "crackpot" college professors, leftist "pinkos," and outright Communists. Such subversives, it was charged, were trying to make America over in the Bolshevik-Marxist image under "Rooseveltski." The Hearst newspapers lambasted,

> *The Red New Deal with a Soviet seal*
> *Endorsed by a Moscow hand,*
> *The strange result of an alien cult*
> *In a liberty-loving land.*

Whitney Museum of American Art

Employment Agency, by Isaac Soyer, 1937 Millions of jobless Americans felt the despair Soyer captured in this painting, as depression-era unemployment reached levels never seen before or since in American history.

Roosevelt was further accused by conservatives of being Jewish ("Rosenfield") and of tapping too many bright young Jewish leftists ("The Jew Deal") for his "Drain Trust."

Hardheaded businesspeople, who "had met a payroll," were shocked by the leap-before-you-look, try-anything-once spirit of Roosevelt, the jolly improviser. They accused him of confusing noise and movement with progress. Others appreciated the president's do-something approach. Humorist Will Rogers, the rope-twirling "poet lariat" of the era, remarked that if Roosevelt were to burn down the Capitol, people would say, "Well, we at least got a fire started, anyhow."

"Bureaucratic meddling" and "regimentation" were also bitter complaints of anti–New Dealers; in truth, bureaucracy did blossom. The federal government, with its hundreds of thousands of employees, became incomparably the largest single business in the country, as the states faded further into the background.

Promises of budget balancing, to say nothing of other promises, had flown out the window—so foes of the New Deal pointed out. The national debt had stood at the already enormous figure of $19,487,000,000 in 1932 and had skyrocketed to $40,440,000,000 by 1939. America was becoming, its critics charged, a "handout state" trying to squander itself into prosperity—*U.S.* stood for "unlimited spending." Such lavish benefactions were undermining the old virtues of thrift and initiative. Ordinary Americans, once self-reliant citizens, were getting a bad case of the "gimmies": their wishbones were becoming larger than their backbones. In the nineteenth century, hard-pressed workers went west; now they went on relief.

Business was bitter. Accusing the New Deal of fomenting class strife, conservatives insisted that the laborer and the farmer—especially the big operator—were being pampered. Why "soak the successful"? Countless businesspeople, especially Republicans, declared that they could pull themselves out of the depression if they could only get the federal government—an interventionist big government—off their backs. Private enterprise, they charged, was being stifled by "planned economy," "planned bankruptcy," "creeping socialism," and the philosophy "Washington can do it better," with a federal pill for every ill. States' rights were being ignored, while the government was competing in business with its own citizens, under a "dictatorship of do-gooders."

The aggressive leadership of Roosevelt—"one-man supergovernment"—also came in for denunciation. Heavy fire was especially directed at his attempts to browbeat the Supreme Court and to create a "dummy Congress." Roosevelt had even tried in the 1938 elections, with backfiring results, to "purge" members of Congress who would not march in lockstep with him.

The three senators whom he publicly opposed were all triumphantly reelected.

The most damning indictment of the New Deal was that it had failed to cure the depression. Afloat in a sea of red ink, some argued, it had merely administered aspirin, sedatives, and Band-Aids. Many economists came to believe that better results would have been achieved by much greater deficit spending. Despite some $20 billion poured out in six years of deficit spending and lending, of leaf raking and pump priming, the gap was not closed between production and consumption. There were even more mountainous farm surpluses under Roosevelt than under Hoover. Millions of dispirited men and women were still unemployed in 1939, after six years of drain, strain, and pain. Not until World War II blazed forth in Europe was the unemployment headache solved.

★ FDR's Balance Sheet

New Dealers staunchly defended their record. Admitting that there had been some waste, they pointed out that relief—not economy—had been the primary object of their multifront war on the depression. Conceding also that there had been some graft, they argued that it had been trivial in view of the immense sums spent and the obvious need for haste.

Apologists for Roosevelt further declared that the New Deal had relieved the worst of the crisis in 1933. It promoted the philosophy of "balancing the human budget" and accepted the principle that the federal government was morally bound to prevent mass hunger and starvation by "managing" the economy. The Washington regime was to be used, not feared. The collapse of America's economic system was averted, a fairer distribution of the national income was achieved, and the citizens were enabled to regain and retain their self-respect. "Nobody is going to starve" was Roosevelt's promise.

Though hated by business tycoons, FDR should have been their patron saint, so his admirers claimed. He deflected popular resentments against business and may have saved the American system of free enterprise. Roosevelt's quarrel was not with capitalism but with capitalists; he purged American capitalism of some of its worst abuses so that it might be saved from itself. He may even have headed off a more radical swing to the left by a mild dose of what was mistakenly reviled as "socialism." The head of the American Socialist party, when once asked if the New Deal had carried out the Socialist program, reportedly replied that it had indeed—on a stretcher. Nor, Roosevelt's defenders claimed, did the New Deal bankrupt the United States: the sensational increase in the national debt was caused

FDR Library

Our Skipper This pro-FDR cartoon depicts a confident Roosevelt ignoring his critics while heading cheerily toward economic recovery. In fact, FDR's New Deal brought neither the recovery he promised nor the ruin his detractors prophesied. The depression dragged on with only periodic improvement for nearly eight years under his leadership, until the cataclysmic emergency of World War II finally banished unemployment from the land.

by World War II, not the New Deal. The national debt was only $40 billion in 1939 but $258 billion in 1945.

Roosevelt, like Jefferson, provided bold reform without a bloody revolution—at a time in history when some foreign nations were suffering armed uprisings and when many Europeans were predicting either communism or fascism for America. He was upbraided by the left-wing radicals for not going far enough, by the right-wing radicals for going too far. Choosing the middle road, he has been called the greatest American conservative since Hamilton. He was in fact Hamiltonian

in his espousal of big government, but Jeffersonian in his concern for the "forgotten man." Demonstrating anew the value of powerful presidential leadership, he exercised that power to relieve the erosion of the nation's greatest physical resource—its people. He helped preserve democracy in America in a time when democracies abroad were disappearing down the sinkhole of dictatorship. And in playing this role, he unwittingly girded the nation for its part in the titanic war that loomed on the horizon—a war in which democracy the world over would be at stake.

Varying Viewpoints
How Radical Was the New Deal?

The Great Depression was both a great calamity and a great opportunity. How effectively Franklin Roosevelt responded to the calamity and what use he made of the opportunity are the two great questions that have animated historical debate about the New Deal.

Some historians have actually denied that there was much of a connection between the depression and the New Deal. Arthur M. Schlesinger, Jr., for example, who believed in "cycles" of reform and reaction in American history, wrote that "there would very likely have been some sort of New Deal in the 1930s even without the Depression." But most of the first generation of historians who wrote about the New Deal (in the 1940s, 1950s, and early 1960s) agreed with Carl Degler's judgment that the New Deal was "a revolutionary response to a revolutionary situation." In this view, though Roosevelt never found a means short of war to bring about economic recovery,

he shrewdly utilized the stubborn economic crisis as a means to enact sweeping reforms.

Some leftist scholars writing in the 1960s, however, notably Barton J. Bernstein, charged that the New Deal did not reach far enough. This criticism echoed the socialist complaint in the 1930s that the depression represented the total collapse of American capitalism and that the New Deal had muffed the chance truly to remake American society. Roosevelt had the chance, these historians argued, to redistribute wealth, improve race relations, and bring the giant corporations to heel. Instead, said these critics, the New Deal simply represented a conservative holding action to shore up a sagging and corrupt capitalist order.

Those charges against the New Deal stimulated another generation of scholars in the 1970s, 1980s, and 1990s to look closely at the concrete institutional, attitudinal, and economic circumstances in which the New Deal unfolded. Historians such as James Patterson, Alan Brinkley, Kenneth Jackson, Harvard Sitkoff, and Lizabeth Cohen—sometimes loosely referred to as the "constraints school"—concluded that the New Deal offered just about as much reform as circumstances allowed and as the majority of Americans wanted. The findings of these historians are impressive: the system of checks and balances limited presidential power; the disproportionate influence of southern Democrats in Congress stalled attempts to move toward racial justice; the federal system, in fact, inhibited all efforts to initiate change from Washington.

Most important, a majority of the American people at the time wanted to reform capitalism, not overthrow it. Industrial workers, for example, were not hapless pawns upon whom the New Deal was foisted, frustrating their yearning for more radical change. Instead, as David Kennedy has argued, they sought security and self-determination in ways quite compatible with the New Deal's programs for unemployment insurance, old-age pensions, and guarantees of labor's right to organize.

Most recently, scholars such as Alice Kessler-Harris, Linda Gordon, and Suzanne Mettler have argued that the New Deal had a more radical effect on men than on women. Social Security, for example, was designed to assist male breadwinners, who were then expected to share their benefits with their dependent wives and children. In addition, married women were rarely favored for government jobs in agencies such as the WPA. As a result, many women found themselves cast ever more firmly in the traditional role of wife and mother. At the time, however, most people believed that these were fair, if unequal, solutions to the catastrophic Great Depression.

Perhaps William Leuchtenburg summed it up best when he described the New Deal as a "half-way revolution," neither radical nor conservative, but accurately reflecting the American people's needs and desires in the 1930s—and for a long time thereafter. The great "New Deal coalition" that dominated American politics for nearly four decades after Roosevelt's election in 1932 represented a broad consensus in American society about the opportunities and legitimate limits of government efforts to shape the social and economic order.

Chapter Review

KEY TERMS

Brain Trust (752)

New Deal (753)

Hundred Days (754)

Glass-Steagall Banking Reform Act (756)

Civilian Conservation Corps (CCC) (757)

National Recovery Administration (NRA) (761)

Agricultural Adjustment Administration (AAA) (763)

Dust Bowl (764)

Tennessee Valley Authority (TVA) (766)

Social Security Act (767)

Wagner Act (767)

Fair Labor Standards Act (768)

Congress of Industrial Organizations (CIO) (769)

Court-packing plan (771)

Keynesianism (772)

PEOPLE TO KNOW

Franklin Delano Roosevelt

Eleanor Roosevelt

Harry L. Hopkins

Father Charles Coughlin

Francis E. Townsend

Huey P. ("Kingfish") Long

Frances Perkins

Mary McLeod Bethune

Robert F. Wagner

CHRONOLOGY

1932	Roosevelt defeats Hoover for presidency
1933	Bank holiday
	Emergency Banking Relief Act
	Beer and Wine Revenue Act
	Hundred Days Congress enacts AAA, TVA, HOLC, NRA, and PWA
	Federal Securities Act
	Glass-Steagall Banking Reform Act
	CWA established
	Twentieth Amendment (changed calendar of congressional sessions and date of presidential inauguration)
	Twenty-first Amendment (prohibition repealed)
	Nazis legally come to power in Germany with passage of Enabling Act
1934	Gold Reserve Act
	Securities and Exchange Commission authorized
	Indian Reorganization Act
	FHA established
	Frazier-Lemke Farm Bankruptcy Act
1935	WPA established
	Wagner Act
	Resettlement Administration
	Social Security Act
	Public Utility Holding Company Act
	Schechter "sick chicken" case
	CIO organized
1936	Soil Conservation and Domestic Allotment Act
	Roosevelt defeats Landon for presidency
1937	USHA established
	Roosevelt announces "Court-packing" plan
1938	Second AAA
	Fair Labor Standards Act
1939	Reorganization Act
	Hatch Act

TO LEARN MORE

Alan Brinkley, *The End of Reform: New Deal Liberalism in Depression and War* (1995)

———, *Voices of Protest: Huey Long, Father Coughlin, and the Great Depression* (1982)

Lizabeth Cohen, *Making a New Deal: Industrial Workers in Chicago, 1919–1939* (rev. ed., 2008)

Blanche Wiesen Cook, *Eleanor Roosevelt: A Life* (1992).

Michael Denning, *The Cultural Front: The Laboring of American Culture in the Twentieth Century* (1996)

James N. Gregory, *American Exodus: The Dustbowl Migration and Okie Culture in California* (1989)

Robin D. G. Kelley, *Hammer and Hoe: Alabama Communists During the Great Depression* (1990)

David M. Kennedy, *Freedom from Fear: The American People in Depression and War* (1999)

Alice Kessler-Harris, *In Pursuit of Equity: Men, Women, and the Quest for Economic Citizenship in Twentieth-Century America* (2001)

Neil M. Maher, *Nature's New Deal: The Civilian Conservation Corps and the Roots of the American Environmental Movement* (2008)

Lois Scharf, *Eleanor Roosevelt: First Lady of American Liberalism* (1987)

Jeff Shesol, *Supreme Power: Franklin Roosevelt vs. the Supreme Court* (2010)

Nick Taylor, *American-Made: The Enduring Legacy of the WPA: When FDR Put the Nation to Work* (2008)

Studs Terkel, *Hard Times: An Oral History of the Great Depression* (1970)

Wendy Wall, *Inventing the "American Way": The Politics of Consensus from the New Deal to the Civil Rights Movement* (2008)

A complete, annotated bibliography for this chapter—along with brief descriptions of the People to Know—may be found on the American Pageant website. The Key Terms are defined in a Glossary at the end of the text.

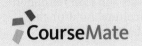

Go to the CourseMate website at **www.cengagebrain.com** for additional study tools and review materials—including audio and video clips—for this chapter.

AP® Review Questions for Chapter 33

1. Which of the following represents a specific promise made by Franklin Roosevelt in the presidential campaign of 1932, concerning how he would attack the Great Depression?
   (A) Roosevelt promised to nationalize all banks and major industries.
   (B) Roosevelt promised to mobilize America's youth in wartime.
   (C) Roosevelt pledged to continue the economic policies undertaken by President Hoover.
   (D) Roosevelt promised to experiment with bold new government programs for economic and social reform while balancing the federal budget.
   (E) Roosevelt promised to engage in Keynesian deficit spending by the U.S. government to stimulate the economy.

2. Which of the following best describes President Roosevelt's first Hundred Days in office?
   (A) A flood of social and economic relief, recovery, and reform New Deal legislation passed by a highly supportive Congress eager to assist the new president
   (B) Cautious and gradual legislative efforts by President Roosevelt and Congress to address the severe social and economic problems caused by the Great Depression
   (C) A do-nothing Congress blocking nearly every relief, recovery, and reform proposal sent by President Roosevelt for congressional consideration
   (D) President Roosevelt "going over the heads of Congress" to appeal for Americans to prod a reluctant Congress to adopt his relief, recovery, and reform proposals
   (E) President Roosevelt and Congress failing to come to a political consensus concerning how to address the social and economic ills spawned by the Great Depression

3. President Roosevelt responded to the public uncertainty and grave concerns about the soundness of the American financial system by doing all of the following EXCEPT
   (A) closing all American banks for a week, shortly after taking office, in order to reorganize them on a sounder basis.
   (B) securing congressional passage of the Glass-Steagall Banking Reform Act.
   (C) creating the Federal Deposit Insurance Corporation to insure all individual deposits initially up to $5,000.
   (D) nationalizing several major banks tottering on the brink of failure and bringing them under the management of the Federal Reserve Board.
   (E) using his masterful communication skills to deliver one of his famous radio fireside chats to assure Americans that federal legislation had now placed banks and their depositors' funds on solid footing.

4. Which controversial New Deal program prompted critics to brand it as a dangerous example of government control of industry and creeping socialism?
   (A) The Tennessee Valley Authority
   (B) The Federal Housing Administration
   (C) The Agricultural Adjustment Act
   (D) The Civilian Conservation Corps
   (E) The Federal Emergency Relief Administration

5. What demagogic promise did Senator Huey P. Long make to gain a large national following in the early to mid-1930s?
   (A) Senator Long promised to nationalize all banks and public utility companies.
   (B) Senator Long promised to assess a special tax on Jews for causing the Great Depression.
   (C) Senator Long promised to help farmers and workers organize collectively to resist the power of corporations.
   (D) Senator Long promised to provide the unemployed and elderly with a $200-a-month social security payment.
   (E) Senator Long promised to "share our wealth" by raising taxes on the rich and giving every family $5,000.

6. What was the primary reason for the failure of the National Recovery Administration (NRA) to spark a significant industrial recovery?
   (A) Business and organized labor resisted regulation by the agency.
   (B) The fair competition wages and maximum hours labor codes required too much self-sacrifice on the part of industry, labor, and the public.
   (C) Harold Ickes, the head of the agency, proved to be an incompetent administrator.
   (D) The NRA failed to provide enough protection for organized labor to bargain fairly with management.
   (E) The agency did not have enough power to control business.

7. How did the first Agricultural Adjustment Act propose to solve the farm problem?
   (A) By reducing agricultural production through government payments to reduce crop acreage
   (B) By subsidizing American farmers' exports overseas
   (C) By providing financial incentives to farmers to move from private farming to farm cooperatives
   (D) By providing government-financed price supports to guarantee a minimum price for farmers' goods in domestic agricultural markets
   (E) By offering financial grants and loan restructuring assistance from the Agricultural Adjustment Administration to help farmers pay their mortgages

8. What was the purpose of the Federal Securities Act and the Securities Exchange Commission?
   (A) To halt the sale of stocks on the margin (i.e., with borrowed funds)
   (B) To force stockbrokers to register with the federal government
   (C) To prevent interlocking directorates and business pyramiding schemes
   (D) To provide full disclosure of information and prevent insider trading and other fraudulent practices
   (E) To enable the Chicago Board of Trade to compete with the New York Stock Exchange

9. What was the most important difference between the American Social Security system established by the New Deal and most European social welfare systems?
   (A) The American Social Security system was opposed by large sectors of the public, while most European social welfare systems enjoyed overwhelming popular support.
   (B) The American Social Security system, in contrast to most European social welfare systems, did not permit the Social Security number to be used for identification and security purposes.
   (C) The American Social Security system, as opposed to its European social welfare counterparts, did not address the issue of single mothers in the home with dependent children.
   (D) When it was established in 1935, the American Social Security system, unlike most concurrent European social welfare systems, failed to include disability insurance and state-federal unemployment insurance benefits for eligible workers.
   (E) As opposed to most European social welfare systems, American workers had to be employed to obtain Social Security benefits.

10. The Wagner or National Labor Relations Act of 1935 accomplished all of the following EXCEPT
   (A) helping spur the creation and the development of the unskilled industrial workers' union, the Congress of Industrial Workers.
   (B) ushering in a decade of peace and stability in organized labor-business relations.
   (C) giving organized labor the legal authority to bargain collectively.
   (D) being vehemently opposed by the American Federation of Labor because of its weak protections for organized labor.
   (E) establishing the powerful National Labor Relations Board to mediate and arbitrate disputes between labor and business.

11. All of the following characterized President Roosevelt's Supreme Court–packing scheme in 1937 EXCEPT that
   (A) it was motivated by President Roosevelt's frustration over many of his New Deal programs being declared unconstitutional.
   (B) it represented a nakedly political attempt to overturn the constitutional checks and balances among the three branches of government.
   (C) the scheme was dropped when Justice Roberts began to vote on the side of four of his colleagues and upheld the constitutionality of New Deal programs.
   (D) it had an adverse effect on President Roosevelt's efforts to pass other New Deal social and economic reforms in 1937.
   (E) it raised the political ire and fierce opposition of only Republicans.

12. Which of the following represents the consensus assessment of the historical legacy of Roosevelt's New Deal by most historians?
   (A) The programs of the New Deal ended the Great Depression and spurred the American economic recovery in the 1940s.
   (B) The New Deal provided moderate social and economic reform to millions of Americans and probably staved off the rise of socialism or reactionary fascism in the United States.
   (C) The New Deal crippled the American system of free enterprise for many years with its socialistic undermining of capitalism.
   (D) The New Deal would have been more effective if President Roosevelt had demonstrated powerful presidential leadership.
   (E) The New Deal represented an unsuccessful attempt to create a centrally planned economy by an elitist dictatorship of left-wing do-gooders.

13. In which of the following pairs is the New Deal program properly categorized?
   (A) Social Security Act; Reform
   (B) Emergency Banking Act; Recovery
   (C) Securities and Exchange Commission; Relief
   (D) Agricultural Adjustment Act; Reform
   (E) Gold Reserve Act; Relief

14. In addition to improving people's economic circumstances, Franklin Roosevelt attempted to increase certain groups' stature in the United States by
   (A) increasing the number of justices to make the Supreme Court seem more democratic.
   (B) creating a "Brains Trust" of advisers from business and elite educational institutions.
   (C) appointing the first female cabinet member in U.S. history.
   (D) supporting Eleanor Roosevelt's work with underrepresented groups.
   (E) establishing the "Black Cabinet," ensuring blacks' participation in the New Deal.

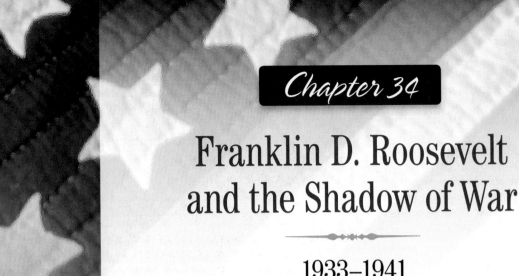

Chapter 34

Franklin D. Roosevelt and the Shadow of War

1933–1941

The epidemic of world lawlessness is spreading. When an epidemic of physical disease starts to spread, the community approves and joins in a quarantine of the patients in order to protect the health of the community against the spread of the disease. . . . There must be positive endeavors to preserve peace.

FRANKLIN D. ROOSEVELT, CHICAGO "QUARANTINE SPEECH," 1937

*A*mericans in the 1930s tried to turn their backs on the world's problems. Their president at first seemed to share these views. The only battle Roosevelt sought was against the depression. America had its own burdens to shoulder, and the costs of foreign involvement, whether in blood or treasure, simply seemed too great.

But as the clouds of war gathered over Europe, Roosevelt eventually concluded that the United States could no longer remain aloof. Events gradually brought the American people around to his thinking: no nation was safe in an era of international anarchy, and the world could not remain half-enchained and half-free.

✷ The London Conference

The sixty-six-nation **London Economic Conference**, meeting in the summer of 1933, revealed how thoroughly Roosevelt's early foreign policy was subordinated to his strategy for domestic economic recovery. The delegates to the London Conference hoped to organize a coordinated international attack on the global depression. They were particularly eager to stabilize the values of the various nations' currencies and the rates at which they could be exchanged. Exchange-rate stabilization was essential to the revival of world trade, which had all but evaporated by 1933.

Roosevelt at first agreed to send an American delegation to the conference, including Secretary of State Cordell Hull. But the president soon began to have second thoughts about the conference's agenda. He wanted to pursue his gold-juggling and other inflationary policies at home as a means of stimulating American recovery. An international agreement to maintain the value of the dollar in terms of other currencies might tie his hands, and at bottom Roosevelt was unwilling to sacrifice the possibility of domestic recovery for the sake of international cooperation. While vacationing on a yacht along the New England coast, he dashed off a radio message to London, scolding the conference for attempting to stabilize currencies and essentially declaring America's withdrawal from the negotiations.

Roosevelt's bombshell announcement yanked the rug from under the London Conference. The delegates adjourned empty-handed, amid cries of American bad faith. Whether the conference could have arrested the worldwide economic slide is debatable, but Roosevelt's every-man-for-himself attitude plunged the planet even deeper into economic crisis. The collapse of the London Conference also strengthened the global trend toward extreme nationalism, making international cooperation ever more difficult as the dangerous decade of the 1930s unfolded. Reflecting the powerful persistence of American isolationism, Roosevelt's action played directly into the hands of the power-mad dictators who were determined to shatter the peace of the world. Americans themselves would eventually pay a high price for the narrow-minded belief that the United States could go it alone in the modern world.

✴ Freedom for (from?) the Filipinos and Recognition for the Russians

Roosevelt matched isolationism from Europe with withdrawal from Asia. The Great Depression burst the fragile bubble of President McKinley's imperialistic dream in the Far East. With the descent into hard times, American taxpayers were eager to throw overboard their expensive tropical liability in the Philippine Islands. Organized labor demanded the exclusion of low-wage Filipino workers, and American sugar producers clamored for the elimination of Philippine competition.

Remembering its earlier promises of freedom for the Philippines, Congress passed the Tydings-McDuffie Act in 1934. The act provided for the independence of the Philippines after a twelve-year period of economic and political tutelage—that is, by 1946. The United States agreed to relinquish its army bases, but naval bases were reserved for future discussion—and retention.

Just Another Customer, 1933 The United States recognizes the Soviet Union.

Jack Beers/The Dallas Morning News

In truth, the American people were not so much giving freedom to the Philippines as they were freeing themselves *from* the Philippines. With a selfish eye to their own welfare, and with apparent disregard for the political situation in Asia, they proposed to leave the Philippines to their fate, while imposing upon the Filipinos economic terms so ungenerous as to threaten the islands with economic prostration. Once again, American isolationists rejoiced. Yet in Tokyo, Japanese militarists were calculating that they had little to fear from an inward-looking America that was abandoning its principal possession in Asia.

At the same time, Roosevelt made at least one internationalist gesture when he formally recognized the Soviet Union in 1933. Over the noisy protests of anti-communist conservatives, as well as Roman Catholics offended by the Kremlin's antireligious policies, Roosevelt extended the hand of diplomatic recognition to the sixteen-year-old Bolshevik regime. He was motivated in part by the hope for trade with Soviet Russia, as well as by the desire to bolster the Soviet Union as a friendly counterweight to the possible threat of German power in Europe and Japanese power in Asia.

✴ Becoming a Good Neighbor

Closer to home, Roosevelt inaugurated a refreshing new era in relations with Latin America. He proclaimed in his inaugural address, "I would dedicate this nation to the policy of the Good Neighbor." Taken together, Roosevelt's noninvolvement in Europe and withdrawal from Asia, along with this brotherly embrace of his New World neighbors, suggested that the United States was giving up its ambition to be a world power and would content itself instead with being merely a regional power, its interests and activities confined exclusively to the Western Hemisphere.

Old-fashioned intervention by bayonet in the Caribbean had not paid off, except in an evil harvest of resentment, suspicion, and fear. The Great Depression had cooled off Yankee economic aggressiveness, as thousands of investors in Latin American securities became sackholders rather than stockholders. There were now fewer dollars to be protected by the rifles of the hated marines.

With war-thirsty dictators seizing power in Europe and Asia, Roosevelt was eager to line up the Latin Americans to help defend the Western Hemisphere. Embittered neighbors would be potential tools of transoceanic aggressors. President Roosevelt made clear at the outset that he was going to renounce armed intervention, particularly the vexatious corollary to the Monroe Doctrine devised by his cousin Theodore Roosevelt. Late in 1933, at the Seventh Pan-American

Conference in Montevideo, Uruguay, the U.S. delegation formally endorsed nonintervention.

Deeds followed words. The last marines departed from Haiti in 1934. The same year, after military strongman Fulgencio Batista had come to power, restive Cuba was released from the worst hobbles of the Platt Amendment, under which America had been free to intervene, although the United States retained its naval base at Guantánamo (see p. 621). The tiny country of Panama received a similar uplift in 1936, when Washington partially relaxed its grip on the isthmus nation.

The hope-inspiring **Good Neighbor policy**, with the accent on consultation and nonintervention, received its acid test in Mexico. When the Mexican government seized Yankee oil properties in 1938, American investors vehemently demanded armed intervention to repossess their confiscated businesses. But Roosevelt successfully resisted the badgering, and a settlement was finally threshed out in 1941, even though the oil companies lost much of their original stake.

Spectacular success crowned Roosevelt's Good Neighbor policy. His earnest attempts to usher in a new era of friendliness, though hurting some U.S. bondholders, paid rich dividends in goodwill among the peoples to the south. No other citizen of the United States has ever been held in such high esteem in Latin America during his lifetime. Roosevelt was cheered with tumultuous enthusiasm when, as a "traveling salesman for peace," he journeyed to the special Inter-American Conference at Buenos Aires, Argentina, in 1936. The Colossus of the North now seemed less a vulture and more an eagle.

✴ Secretary Hull's Reciprocal Trade Agreements

Intimately associated with Good Neighborism, and also popular in Latin America, was the reciprocal trade policy of the New Dealers. Its chief architect was idealistic Secretary of State Hull, a high-minded Tennessean of the low-tariff school. Like Roosevelt, he believed that trade was a two-way street, that a nation can sell abroad only as it buys abroad, that tariff barriers choke off foreign trade, and that trade wars beget shooting wars.

Responding to the Hull-Roosevelt leadership, Congress passed the **Reciprocal Trade Agreements Act** in 1934. Designed in part to lift American export trade from the depression doldrums, this enlightened measure was aimed at both relief and recovery. At the same time, it activated the low-tariff policies of the New Dealers. (See the tariff chart in the Appendix.)

The Reciprocal Trade Agreements Act avoided the dangerous uncertainties of a wholesale tariff revision; it merely whittled down the most objectionable schedules of the Hawley-Smoot law by amending them. Roosevelt was empowered to lower existing rates by as much as 50 percent, provided that the other country involved was willing to respond with similar reductions. The resulting pacts, moreover, were to become effective without the formal approval of the Senate. This novel feature not only ensured speedier action but sidestepped the twin evils of high-stakes logrolling and high-pressure lobbying in Congress.

Secretary Hull, whose zeal for reciprocity was unflagging, succeeded in negotiating pacts with twenty-one countries by the end of 1939. During these same years, U.S. foreign trade increased appreciably, presumably in part as a result of the Hull-Roosevelt policies. Trade agreements undoubtedly bettered economic and political relations with Latin America and proved to be an influence for peace in a war-bent world.

The Reciprocal Trade Agreements Act was a landmark piece of legislation. It reversed the traditional high-protective-tariff policy that had persisted almost unbroken since Civil War days and that had so damaged the American and international economies following World War I. It also paved the way for the American-led free-trade international economic system that took shape after World War II, a period that witnessed the most robust growth in the history of international trade.

✴ Storm-Cellar Isolationism

Post-1918 chaos in Europe, followed by the Great Depression, spawned the ominous spread of totalitarianism. The individual was nothing; the state was everything. The communist USSR led the way, with the crafty and ruthless Joseph Stalin finally emerging as dictator. In 1936 he began to purge his communist state of all suspected dissidents, ultimately executing hundreds of thousands and banishing millions to remote Siberian forced-labor camps. Blustery Benito Mussolini, a swaggering Fascist, seized the reins of power in Italy during 1922. And Adolf Hitler, a fanatic with a toothbrush mustache, plotted and harangued his way into control of Germany in 1933 with liberal use of the "big lie."

Hitler was the most dangerous of the dictators, because he combined tremendous power with impulsiveness. A frustrated Austrian painter, with hypnotic talents as an orator and a leader, he had secured control of the Nazi party by making political capital of the Treaty of Versailles and Germany's depression-spawned unemployment. He was thus a misbegotten child of the shortsighted postwar policies of the victorious Allies, including the United States. The desperate German people had fallen in behind the new Pied Piper, for they saw no other hope of escape from the plague of economic chaos and national disgrace. Hitler withdrew Germany from the League of Nations in 1933 and began clandestinely (and illegally) rearming. In 1936 the Nazi Hitler and the Fascist Mussolini allied themselves in the **Rome-Berlin Axis**.

International gangsterism was likewise spreading in the Far East, where imperial Japan was on the make. Like Germany and Italy, Japan was a so-called have-not power. Like them, it resented the ungenerous Treaty of Versailles. Like them, it demanded additional space for its teeming millions, cooped-up in their crowded island nation.

Japanese navalists were not to be denied. Determined to find a place in the Asiatic sun, Tokyo gave notice in 1934 of the termination of the twelve-year-old Washington Naval Treaty. A year later at London, the Japanese torpedoed all hope of effective naval disarmament. Upon being denied complete parity, they walked out of the multipower conference and accelerated their construction of giant battleships. By 1935 Japan, too, had quit the League of Nations. Five years later it joined arms with Germany and Italy in the Tripartite Pact.

Jut-jawed Mussolini, seeking both glory and empire in Africa, brutally attacked Ethiopia in 1935 with bombers and tanks. The brave defenders, armed with spears and ancient firearms, were speedily crushed. Members of the League of Nations could have caused Mussolini's war machine to creak to a halt—if they had only dared to embargo oil. But when the League quailed rather than risk global hostilities, it merely signed its own death warrant.

Isolationism, long festering in America, received a strong boost from these alarms abroad. Though disapproving of the dictators, Americans still believed that

Adolf Hitler Reviewing Troops, Berlin, 1939 Egging his people on with theatrical displays of pomp and ceremony, Hitler had created a vast military machine by 1939, when he started World War II with a brutal attack against Poland.

Hugo Jaeger/Time & Life Pictures/Getty Images

The Wages of Despair Disillusioned and desperate, millions of Germans in the 1930s looked to Adolf Hitler as their savior from the harsh terms of the Treaty of Versailles, which had concluded World War I. This Nazi poster reads, "Our Last Hope: Hitler."

Page 792 in the Poster Collection, Hoover Institution Archives

The thirst of Benito Mussolini (1883–1945) for national glory in Ethiopia is indicated by his remark in 1940:

❝ To make a people great it is necessary to send them to battle even if you have to kick them in the pants. ❞ (The Italians were notoriously unwarlike.)

In 1934 Mussolini proclaimed in a public speech,

❝ We have buried the putrid corpse of liberty. ❞

their encircling seas conferred a kind of mystic immunity. They were continuing to suffer the disillusionment born of their participation in World War I, which they now regarded as a colossal blunder. They likewise nursed bitter memories of the ungrateful and defaulting debtors. As early as 1934, a spiteful Congress passed the **Johnson Debt Default Act**, which prevented debt-dodging nations from borrowing further in the United States. If attacked again by aggressors, these delinquents could "stew in their own juices."

Mired down in the Great Depression, Americans had no real appreciation of the revolutionary forces being harnessed by the dictators. The "have-not" powers were out to become "have" powers. Americans were not so much afraid that totalitarian aggression would cause trouble as they were fearful that they might be drawn into it. Strong nationwide sentiment welled up for a constitutional amendment to forbid a declaration of war by Congress—except in case of invasion—unless there was a favorable popular referendum. With a mixture of seriousness and frivolity, a group of Princeton University students began to agitate in 1936 for a bonus to be paid to the Veterans of Future Wars (VFW) while the prospective frontliners were still alive.

✦ Congress Legislates Neutrality

As the gloomy 1930s lengthened, an avalanche of lurid articles and books condemning the munitions manufacturers as war-fomenting "merchants of death" poured from American presses. A Senate committee, headed by Senator Gerald Nye of North Dakota, was appointed in 1934 to investigate the "blood business." By sensationalizing evidence regarding America's entry into World War I, the senatorial probers tended to shift the blame away from the German submarines onto the American bankers and arms manufacturers. Because the munitions makers had obviously made money out of the war, many a naive citizen leaped to the illogical conclusion that these soulless scavengers had *caused* the war in order to make money. This kind of reasoning

suggested that if the profits could only be removed from the arms traffic—"one hell of a business"—the country could steer clear of any world conflict that might erupt in the future.

Responding to overwhelming popular pressure, Congress made haste to legislate the nation out of war. Action was spurred by the danger that Mussolini's Ethiopian assault would plunge the world into a new bloodbath. The **Neutrality Acts of 1935, 1936, and 1937**, taken together, stipulated that *when the president proclaimed* the existence of a foreign war, certain restrictions would automatically go into effect. No American could legally sail on a belligerent ship, sell or transport munitions to a belligerent, or make loans to a belligerent.

This head-in-the-sand legislation in effect marked an abandonment of the traditional policy of freedom of the seas—a policy for which America had professedly fought two full-fledged wars and several undeclared wars. The Neutrality Acts were specifically tailored to keep the nation out of a conflict like World War I. If they had been in effect at that time, America probably would not have been sucked in—at least not in April 1917. Congress was one war too late with its legislation. What had seemed dishonorable to Wilson seemed honorable and desirable to a later disillusioned generation.

"The Only Way We Can Save Her," 1939 Even as war broke out in Europe, many Americans continued to insist on the morality of U.S. neutrality.

Storm-cellar neutrality proved to be tragically shortsighted. America falsely assumed that the decision for peace or war lay in its own hands, not in those of the satanic forces already unleashed in the world. Prisoner of its own fears, it failed to recognize that it might have used its enormous power to shape international events. Instead it remained at the mercy of events controlled by the dictators.

Statutory neutrality, though of undoubted legality, was of dubious morality. America served notice that it would make no distinction whatever between brutal aggressors and innocent victims. By striving to hold the scales even, it actually overbalanced them in favor of the dictators, who had armed themselves to the teeth. By declining to use its vast industrial strength to aid its democratic friends and defeat its totalitarian foes, it helped goad the aggressors along their blood-spattered path of conquest.

✴ America Dooms Loyalist Spain

The Spanish Civil War of 1936–1939—a proving ground and dress rehearsal in miniature for World War II—was a painful object lesson in the folly of neutrality-by-legislation. Spanish rebels, who rose against the left-leaning republican government in Madrid, were headed by fascistic General Francisco Franco. Generously aided by his fellow conspirators Hitler and Mussolini, he undertook to overthrow the established Loyalist regime, which in turn was assisted on a smaller scale by the Soviet Union. This pipeline from communist Moscow chilled the natural sympathies of many Americans, especially Roman Catholics, for the republican Loyalists. But other Americans burned with passion to defend the struggling republic against Franco's fascist coup. Some three thousand young men and women headed to Spain to fight as volunteers in the **Abraham Lincoln Brigade**.

Washington continued official relations with the Loyalist government. But Congress, with the encouragement of Roosevelt and with only one dissenting vote, amended the existing neutrality legislation so as to apply an arms embargo to both Loyalists and rebels. "Roosevelt," remarked the dictator Franco, "behaved in the manner of a true gentleman." FDR later regretted being so gentlemanly.

Uncle Sam thus sat on the sidelines while Franco, abundantly supplied with arms and men by his fellow dictators, strangled the republican government of Spain. The democracies, including the United States, were so determined to stay out of war that they helped to condemn a fellow democracy to death. In so doing they further encouraged the dictators to take the dangerous road that led over the precipice to World War II.

Canute Frankson (1890–194?), an African American member of the Abraham Lincoln Brigade, explained why he went to Spain to fight against the fascist Franco in 1937:

❝Since this is a war between whites who for centuries have held us in slavery, and have heaped every kind of insult and abuse upon us, segregated and Jim-crowed us; why [am] I, a Negro . . . in Spain today? Because we are no longer an isolated minority group fighting hopelessly against an immense giant. . . . Because if we crush Fascism here we'll save our people in America, and in other parts of the world from the vicious persecution, wholesale imprisonment, and slaughter which the Jewish people . . . are suffering under Hitler's Fascist heels. . . . We will build us a new society—a society of peace and plenty. There will be no color line, no jim-crow trains, no lynching. That is why, my dear, I'm here in Spain.❞

Such peace-at-any-price-ism was further cursed with illogic. Although determined to stay out of war, America declined to build up its armed forces to a point where it could deter the aggressors. In fact, it allowed its navy to decline in relative strength. It had been led to believe that huge fleets caused huge wars; it was also trying to spare the complaining taxpayer during the grim days of the Great Depression. When President Roosevelt repeatedly called for preparedness, he was branded a warmonger. Not until 1938, the year before World War II exploded, did Congress come to grips with the problem when it passed a billion-dollar naval construction act. The calamitous story was repeated of too little, too late.

America's policy toward Spain "had been a grave mistake," Franklin D. Roosevelt (1882–1945) told his cabinet in early 1939:

❝ The policy we should have adopted was to forbid the transportation of munitions of war in American bottoms [ships]. This could have been done and Loyalist Spain would still have been able to come to us for what she needed to fight for her life against Franco—to fight for her life and for the lives of some of the rest of us as well, as events will very likely prove.❞

✦ Appeasing Japan and Germany

Sulfurous war clouds had meanwhile been gathering in the tension-taut Far East. In 1937 the Japanese militarists, at the Marco Polo Bridge near Beijing (Peking), touched off the explosion that led to an all-out invasion of China. In a sense this attack was the curtain-raiser of World War II.

Roosevelt shrewdly declined to invoke the recently passed neutrality legislation by refusing to call the China incident an officially declared war. If he had put the existing restrictions into effect, he would have cut off the trickle of munitions on which the Chinese were desperately dependent. The Japanese, of course, could continue to buy mountains of war supplies in the United States.

In Chicago—unofficial isolationist "capital" of America—President Roosevelt delivered his sensational **Quarantine Speech** in the autumn of 1937. Alarmed by the recent aggressions of Italy and Japan, he called for "positive endeavors" to "quarantine" the aggressors—presumably by economic embargoes.

The speech triggered a cyclone of protest from isolationists and other foes of involvement; they feared that a moral quarantine would lead to a shooting quarantine. Startled by this angry response, Roosevelt retreated and sought less direct means to curb the dictators.

America's isolationist mood intensified, especially in regard to China. In December 1937 Japanese aviators bombed and sank an American gunboat, the *Panay*, in Chinese waters, with a loss of two killed and thirty wounded. In the days of 1898, when the *Maine* went down, this outrage might have provoked war. But after Tokyo hastened to make the necessary apologies and pay a proper indemnity, Americans breathed a deep sigh of relief. Japanese militarists were thus encouraged to vent their anger against the "superior" white race by subjecting American civilians in China, both male and female, to humiliating slappings and strippings.

Adolf Hitler meanwhile grew louder and bolder in Europe. In 1935 he had openly flouted the Treaty of Versailles by introducing compulsory military service in Germany. The next year he brazenly marched into the demilitarized German Rhineland, likewise contrary to the detested treaty, while France and Britain looked on in an agony of indecision. Lashing his following to a frenzy, Hitler undertook to persecute and then exterminate the Jewish population in the areas under his control. In the end he wiped out about 6 million innocent victims, mostly in gas chambers. Calling upon his people to sacrifice butter for guns, he whipped the new German air force and mechanized ground divisions into the most devastating military machine the world had yet seen.

Suddenly, in March 1938, Hitler bloodlessly occupied German-speaking Austria, his birthplace. The democratic powers, wringing their hands in despair, prayed that this last grab would satisfy his passion for conquest.

But like a drunken reveler calling for madder music and stronger wine, Hitler could not stop. Intoxicated by his recent gains, he began to make bullying demands for the German-inhabited Sudetenland of neighboring Czechoslovakia. The leaders of Britain and France, eager to appease Hitler, sought frantically to bring the dispute to the conference table. President Roosevelt, also deeply alarmed, kept the wires hot with personal messages to both Hitler and Mussolini urging a peaceful settlement.

A conference was finally held in Munich, Germany, in September 1938. The Western European democracies, badly unprepared for war, betrayed Czechoslovakia to Germany when they consented to the shearing away of the Sudetenland. They hoped—and these hopes were shared by the American people—that the concessions at the conference table would slake Hitler's thirst for power and bring "peace in our time." Indeed Hitler publicly promised that the Sudetenland "is the last territorial claim I have to make in Europe."

Appeasement of the dictators, symbolized by the ugly word *Munich*, turned out to be merely surrender on the installment plan. It was like giving a cannibal a finger in the hope of saving an arm. In March 1939, scarcely six months later, Hitler suddenly erased the rest of Czechoslovakia from the map, contrary to his solemn vows. The democratic world was again stunned.

✦ Hitler's Belligerency and U.S. Neutrality

Joseph Stalin, the sphinx of the Kremlin, was a key to the peace puzzle. In the summer of 1939, the British and French were busily negotiating with Moscow, hopeful of securing a mutual-defense treaty that would halt Hitler. But mutual suspicions proved insuperable. Then the Soviet Union astounded the world by signing, on August 23, 1939, a nonaggression treaty with the German dictator.

The notorious **Hitler-Stalin pact** meant that the Nazi German leader now had a green light to make war on Poland and the Western democracies, without fearing a stab in the back from the Soviet Union—his Communist arch-foe. Consternation struck those wishful thinkers in Western Europe who had fondly hoped that Hitler might be sicced upon Stalin so that the twin menaces would bleed each other to death. It was as plain as the mustache on Stalin's face that the wily Soviet dictator was plotting to turn his German

The Granger Collection, New York

Poland Falls to the Nazi Juggernaut, 1939 After swallowing Austria and Czechoslovakia in 1938, Hitler launched all-out war on Poland in September 1939, and the Nazi war machine seemed unstoppable.

accomplice against the Western democracies. The two warring camps would then kill each other off—and leave Stalin bestriding Europe like a colossus.

With the signing of the Nazi-Soviet pact, World War II was only hours away. Hitler now demanded from neighboring Poland a return of the areas wrested from Germany after World War I. Failing to secure satisfaction, he sent his mechanized divisions crashing into Poland at dawn on September 1, 1939.

Britain and France, honoring their commitments to Poland, promptly declared war. At long last they perceived the folly of continued appeasement. But they were powerless to aid Poland, which succumbed in three weeks to Hitler's smashing strategy of terror. Stalin, as prearranged secretly in his fateful pact with Hitler, came in on the kill for his share of old Russian Poland. Long-dreaded World War II was now fully launched, and the long truce of 1919–1939 had come to an end.

President Roosevelt speedily issued the routine proclamations of neutrality. Americans were overwhelmingly anti-Nazi and anti-Hitler; they fervently hoped that the democracies would win; they fondly believed that the forces of righteousness would triumph, as in 1918. But they were desperately determined to stay out: they were not going to be "suckers" again.

Neutrality promptly became a heated issue in the United States. Ill-prepared Britain and France urgently needed American airplanes and other weapons, but the Neutrality Act of 1937 raised a sternly forbidding hand. Roosevelt summoned Congress in special session, shortly after the invasion of Poland, to consider lifting the arms embargo. After six hectic weeks of debate, a makeshift law emerged.

The **Neutrality Act of 1939** provided that henceforth the European democracies might buy American war materials, but only on a "cash-and-carry basis." This meant that they would have to transport the munitions in their own ships, after paying for them in cash. America would thus avoid loans, war debts, and the torpedoing of American arms-carriers. While Congress thus loosened former restrictions in response to interventionist cries, it added others in response to isolationist fears. Roosevelt was now also authorized to proclaim danger zones into which American merchant ships would be forbidden to enter.

This unneutral neutrality law unfortunately hurt China, which was effectively blockaded by the Imperial Japanese Navy. But despite its defects, it clearly favored the European democracies against the dictators. As the British and French navies controlled the Atlantic, the European aggressors could not send their ships to buy America's munitions. The United States not only improved its moral position but simultaneously helped its economic position. Overseas demand for war goods brought a sharp upswing from the recession of 1937–1938 and ultimately solved the decade-long unemployment crisis (see Figure 33.4 on p. 772).

President Roosevelt was roused at 3 A.M. on September 1, 1939, by a telephone call from Ambassador William Bullitt (1891–1967) in Paris:

"Mr. President, several German divisions are deep in Polish territory. . . . There are reports of bombers over the city of Warsaw."

FDR replied,

"Well, Bill, it has come at last. God help us all."

The Fall of France

The months following the collapse of Poland, while France and Britain marked time, were known as the "phony war." An ominous silence fell on Europe, as Hitler shifted his victorious divisions from Poland for a knockout blow at France. Inaction during this anxious period was relieved by the Soviets, who wantonly attacked neighboring Finland in an effort to secure strategic buffer territory. The debt-paying Finns, who had a host of admirers in America, were speedily granted $30 million by an isolationist Congress for *nonmilitary* supplies. But despite heroic resistance, Finland was finally flattened by the Soviet steamroller.

An abrupt end to the "phony war" came in April 1940 when Hitler, again without warning, overran his weaker neighbors Denmark and Norway. Hardly pausing for breath, the next month he attacked the Netherlands and Belgium, followed by a paralyzing blow at France. By late June France was forced to surrender, but not until Mussolini had pounced on its rear for a jackal's share of the loot. In a pell-mell but successful evacuation from the French port of Dunkirk, the British managed to salvage the bulk of their shattered and partially disarmed army. The crisis providentially brought forth an inspired leader in Prime Minister Winston Churchill, the bulldog-jawed orator who

Hitler Swaggers into Paris, 1940   The fall of France to German forces in June 1940 was a galling blow to French pride and convinced many Americans that their country must mobilize to defeat the Nazi menace.

Hulton-Deutsch/Corbis

Adolf Hitler (1889–1945) promised to win his fellow Germans Lebensraum, or "living space," and to win it by war if necessary. In his eyes, his nationalist and racist crusade justified every violent means at hand. As he told his commanders,

❝When you start a war, what matters is not who is right, but who wins. Close your hearts to pity. Act with brutality. Eighty million Germans must get what is their due. Their existence must be made secure. The stronger man is in the right.**❞**

nerved his people to fight off the fearful air bombings of their cities.

France's sudden collapse shocked Americans out of their daydreams. Stouthearted Britons, singing "There'll Always Be an England," were all that stood between Hitler and the death of constitutional government in Europe. If Britain went under, Hitler would have at his disposal the workshops, shipyards, and slave labor of Western Europe. He might even have the powerful British fleet as well. This frightening possibility, which seemed to pose a dire threat to American security, steeled the American people to a tremendous effort.

Roosevelt moved with electrifying energy and dispatch. He called upon an already debt-burdened nation to build huge airfleets and a two-ocean navy, which could also check Japan. Congress, jarred out of its apathy toward preparedness, within a year appropriated

President Roosevelt made a compelling case against the isolationists in a speech at the University of Virginia on June 10, 1940:

❝Some indeed still hold to the now somewhat obvious delusion that we of the United States can safely permit the United States to become a lone island, a lone island in a world dominated by the philosophy of force. Such an island may be the dream of those who still talk and vote as isolationists. Such an island represents to me and to the overwhelming majority of Americans today a helpless nightmare of a people without freedom—the nightmare of a people lodged in prison, handcuffed, hungry, and fed through the bars from day to day by the contemptuous, unpitying masters of other continents.**❞**

Public-Opinion Polling in the 1930s

In 1936 the prominent news publication *Literary Digest* made a monumental gaffe when it relied on public-opinion polling data to forecast a victory for the Republican candidate, Alf Landon, over the incumbent, Franklin D. Roosevelt. As it happened, Roosevelt racked up a monstrous majority, winning the electoral votes of all but two states. The *Digest's* error had been to compile its polling lists from records of automobile registration and telephone directories—unwittingly skewing its sample toward relatively well-off voters in an era when fewer than half of American families owned either a car or a telephone. The *Digest's* embarrassing mistake ended an era of informal polling techniques, as new, scientifically sophisticated polling organizations founded by George Gallup and Elmo Roper forged to the fore. From this date forward, polling became a standard tool for marketers and advertisers—as well as for political strategists and historians. Yet controversy has long clouded the relationship between pollsters and politicians, who are often accused of abdicating their roles as leaders and slavishly deferring to public opinion, rather than trying to shape it. Franklin Roosevelt confronted this issue in the 1930s, as polls seemed to confirm the stubborn isolationism of the American people, even as the president grew increasingly convinced that the United States must play a more active international role. What do the poll results below suggest about Roosevelt's handling of this issue? About the reliability of polling data? What are the legitimate political uses of public-opinion polls? How valuable are they to the historian?

[1.] (U.S. Oct 3 '39) Do you think the United States should do everything possible to help England and France win the war, except go to war ourselves? (AIPO)

Yes 62%   No 38%

[2.] (U.S. Oct 3 '39) If it appears that Germany is defeating England and France, should the United States declare war on Germany and send our army and navy to Europe to fight? (AIPO)

	Yes	No
National total	29%	71%
BY GEOGRAPHICAL SECTION		
New England	33%	67%
Middle Atlantic	27	73
East central	25	75
West central	26	74
South.	47	53
West	28	72
(Jan 30 '40) National total	23%	77%

[3.] (U.S. May 29 '40) If the question of the United States going to war against Germany came up for a national vote to go to war (go into the war or stay out of the war)? (AIPO)

Yes 16%   No 84%
(June 11 '40) . . . . Go in 19%   Stay out 81%

[4.] (U.S. Aug 5 '41) Should the United States go to war now against Japan? (AIPO)

	Yes	No	No opinion
	22%	78% = 100%	11%
(Oct 22 '41)	13	74	13

[5.] (U.S. Sept 17 '41) Should the United States go into the war now and send an army to Europe to fight? (AIPO)

Yes 9%   No 87%   No opinion 4%

[6.] (U.S. Nov 5 '41) If, in trying to defeat Germany, it becomes necessary to send a large American army to Europe, would you favor this step? (AIPO)

Yes 47%   No 46%   No opinion 7%

Source: From Hadley Cantril, ed., *Public Opinion, 1935–1946* (Princeton, N.J.: Princeton University Press, 1951).

---

the astounding sum of $37 billion. This figure was more than the total cost of fighting World War I and about five times larger than any New Deal annual budget.

Congress also passed a conscription law, approved September 6, 1940. Under this measure—America's first peacetime draft—provision was made for training each year 1.2 million troops and 800,000 reserves. The act was later adapted to the requirements of a global war.

The Latin American bulwark likewise needed bracing. The Netherlands, Denmark, and France, all crushed under the German jackboot, had orphaned colonies in the New World. Would these fall into German hands?

At the Havana Conference of 1940, the United States agreed to share with its twenty New World neighbors the responsibility of upholding the Monroe Doctrine. This ancient dictum, hitherto unilateral, had been a bludgeon brandished only in the hated Yankee fist. Now multilateral, it was to be wielded by twenty-one pairs of American hands—at least in theory.

✹ Refugees from the Holocaust

Aroused by Adolf Hitler, the ancient demon of anti-Semitism brutally bared its fangs. During the late nineteenth century, Jewish communities in Eastern Europe were frequent victims of pogroms, mob attacks approved or condoned by local authorities. In modern Germany primeval violence reappeared with shocking efficiency on the night of November 9, 1938. Instigated by a speech by Nazi propagandist Joseph Goebbels, mobs ransacked more than seven thousand Jewish shops and almost all of the country's synagogues. At least ninety-one Jews lost their lives, and about thirty thousand were sent to concentration camps in the turbulent wake of **Kristallnacht**, the "night of broken glass."

Many Jews attempted to escape from Hitler's racist juggernaut. To take one poignant case, in May 1939, 937 passengers, almost all of them Jewish refugees, boarded the ship *St. Louis* in Hamburg and departed for Havana. When they reached Cuba, however, most were denied entry for lack of a valid Cuban visa. The *St. Louis* then sailed to Miami, which proved no more hospitable. President Roosevelt briefly showed some interest in accepting the beleaguered passengers, but restrictive immigration laws, together with opposition from southern Democrats and Secretary of State Cordell Hull, convinced him otherwise. After being turned away one last time in Canada, the *St. Louis* eventually deposited its passengers in England, France, Belgium, and the Netherlands, where many of them subsequently perished under the Nazi heel.

After reports of the Nazi genocide began to be verified in 1942, Roosevelt created the **War Refugee Board**, which saved thousands of Hungarian Jews from deportation to the notorious death camp at Auschwitz. But all told, only 150,000 Jews, mostly Germans and Austrians, found refuge in the United States. By the end of the war, some 6 million Jews had been murdered in the Holocaust.

Shattered Jewish Storefronts in Berlin This photo was taken after the attacks of Kristallnacht on November 9, 1938.

Bildarchiv Preussicher Kulterbesitz/Art Resource, NY

Albert Einstein Arriving in America, 1933 Sadly, the United States admitted only a trickle of Jewish refugees, while the Holocaust engulfed European Jewry.

✦ Bolstering Britain

Before the fall of France in June 1940, Washington had generally observed a technical neutrality. But now, as Britain alone stood between Hitler and his dream of world domination, the wisdom of neutrality seemed increasingly questionable. Hitler launched air attacks against Britain in August 1940, preparatory to an invasion scheduled for September. For months the Battle of Britain raged in the air over the British Isles. The Royal Air Force's tenacious defense of its native islands eventually led Hitler to postpone his planned invasion indefinitely.

During the precarious months of the Battle of Britain, debate intensified in the United States over what foreign policy to embrace. Radio broadcasts from London brought the drama of the nightly German air raids directly into millions of American homes. Sympathy for Britain grew, but it was not yet sufficient to push the United States into war.

Roosevelt faced a historic decision: whether to hunker down in the Western Hemisphere, assume a "Fortress America" defensive posture, and let the rest of the world go it alone; or to bolster beleaguered Britain by all means short of war itself. Both sides had their advocates.

Supporters of aid to Britain formed propaganda groups, the most potent of which was the Committee to Defend America by Aiding the Allies. Its argument was double-barreled. To interventionists it could appeal for direct succor to the British by such slogans as "Britain Is Fighting Our Fight." To isolationists it could appeal for assistance to the democracies by "All Methods Short of War," so that the terrible conflict would be kept in faraway Europe.

The isolationists, both numerous and sincere, were by no means silent. Determined to avoid American bloodshed at all costs, they organized the America First

Committee and proclaimed, "England Will Fight to the Last American." They contended that America should concentrate what strength it had to defend its own shores, lest a victorious Hitler, after crushing Britain, plot a transoceanic assault. Their basic philosophy was "The Yanks Are Not Coming," and their most effective speechmaker was the famed aviator Colonel Charles A. Lindbergh, who, ironically, had narrowed the Atlantic in 1927.

Britain was in critical need of destroyers, for German submarines were again threatening to starve it out with attacks on shipping. Roosevelt moved boldly when, on September 2, 1940, he agreed to transfer to Great Britain fifty old-model, four-funnel destroyers left over from World War I. In return, the British promised to hand over to the United States eight valuable defensive base sites, stretching from Newfoundland to South America. These strategically located outposts

Pro-British Propaganda This patriotic poster was put out by the Committee to Defend America by Aiding the Allies.

were to remain under the Stars and Stripes for ninety-nine years.

Transferring fifty destroyers to a foreign navy was a highly questionable disposal of government property, despite a strained interpretation of existing legislation. The exchange was achieved by a simple presidential agreement, without so much as a "by your leave" to Congress. Applause burst from the aid-to-Britain advocates, many of whom had been urging such a step. But condemnation arose from America Firsters and other isolationists, as well as from anti-administration Republicans. Some of them approved the transfer but decried Roosevelt's secretive and arbitrary methods. Yet so grave was the crisis that the president was unwilling to submit the scheme to the uncertainties and delays of a full-dress debate in the Congress.

Shifting warships from a neutral United States to a belligerent Britain was, beyond question, a flagrant violation of neutral obligations—at least neutral obligations that had existed before Hitler's barefaced aggressions rendered foolish such old-fashioned concepts of fair play. Public-opinion polls demonstrated that a majority of Americans were determined, even at the risk of armed hostilities, to provide the battered British with "all aid short of war."

✴ Shattering the Two-Term Tradition

A distracting presidential election, as fate decreed, came in the midst of this crisis. The two leading Republican aspirants were round-faced and flat-voiced Senator Robert A. Taft of Ohio, son of the ex-president, and the energetic boy wonder, lawyer-prosecutor Thomas E. Dewey of New York. But in one of the miracles of American political history, the Philadelphia convention was swept off its feet by a colorful latecomer, Wendell L. Willkie, a German-descended son of Hoosier Indiana. This dynamic lawyer—tousled-headed, long-lipped, broad-faced, and large-framed—had until recently been a Democrat and the head of a huge public utility corporation. A complete novice in politics, he had rocketed from political nothingness in a few short weeks. His great appeal lay in his personality, for he was magnetic, transparently trustful, and honest in a homespun, Lincolnesque way.

With the galleries in Philadelphia wildly chanting "We Want Willkie," the delegates finally accepted this political upstart as the only candidate who could possibly beat Roosevelt. The Republican platform condemned FDR's alleged dictatorship, as well as the costly and confusing zigzags of the New Deal. Willkie, an outspoken liberal, was opposed not so much to the New Deal as to its extravagances and inefficiencies. Democratic critics branded him "the rich man's Roosevelt" and "the simple barefoot Wall Street lawyer."

While the rumor pot boiled, Roosevelt delayed to the last minute the announcement of his decision to challenge the sacred two-term tradition. Despite what he described as his personal yearning for retirement, he avowed that in so grave a crisis he owed his experienced hand to the service of his country and humanity. The Democratic delegates in Chicago, realizing that only with "the Champ" could they defeat Willkie, drafted him by a technically unanimous vote. "Better a Third Term Than a Third-Rater" was the war cry of many Democrats.

Burning with sincerity and energy, Willkie launched out upon a whirlwind, Bryanesque campaign in which he delivered over five hundred speeches. At times his voice became a hoarse croak. The country was already badly split between interventionists and isolationists, and Willkie might have widened the breach dangerously by a violent attack on Roosevelt's aid-to-Britain policies. But seeing eye-to-eye with FDR on the necessity of bolstering the beleaguered democracies, he refrained from assailing the president's interventionism, though objecting to his methods.

In the realm of foreign affairs, there was not much to choose between the two candidates. Both promised to stay out of the war; both promised to strengthen the nation's defenses. Yet Willkie, with a mop of black hair in his eyes, hit hard at Rooseveltian "dictatorship" and the third term. His enthusiastic followers cried, "Win with Willkie," "No Fourth Term Either," and "There's No Indispensable Man."

Roosevelt, busy at his desk with mounting problems, made only a few speeches. Stung by taunts that he was leading the nation by the back door into the European slaughterhouse, he repeatedly denied any such intention. His most specific statement was at Boston, where he emphatically declared, "Your boys are not going to be sent into any foreign wars"—a pledge that later came back to plague him. He and his supporters vigorously defended the New Deal, as well as all-out preparations for the defense of America and aid to the Allies.

Roosevelt triumphed, although Willkie ran a strong race. The popular total was 27,307,819 to 22,321,018, and the electoral count was 449 to 82 (see Map 34.1). This contest was much less of a walkaway than in 1932 or 1936; Democratic majorities in Congress remained about the same.

Jubilant Democrats hailed their triumph as a mandate to abolish the two-term tradition. But the truth is that Roosevelt won in spite of the third-term handicap. Voters generally felt that should war come, the experienced hand of the tried leader was needed at the helm. Less appealing was the completely inexperienced hand of the well-intentioned Willkie, who had never held public office.

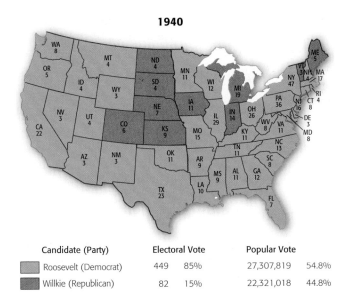

1940

Candidate (Party)	Electoral Vote		Popular Vote	
Roosevelt (Democrat)	449	85%	27,307,819	54.8%
Willkie (Republican)	82	15%	22,321,018	44.8%

MAP 34.1 Presidential Election of 1940 (with electoral vote by state) Willkie referred to Roosevelt only as "the third-term candidate." On election eve FDR hinted that communists and fascists were among Willkie's supporters. Despite these campaign conflicts, the two men respected each other. FDR later asked Willkie to serve as his emissary abroad and even suggested that they run together on a coalition ticket in 1944. © Cengage Learning

The time-honored argument that one should not change horses in the middle of a stream was strong, especially in an era of war-pumped prosperity. Roosevelt might not have won if there had not been a war crisis. On the other hand, he probably would not have run if foreign perils had not loomed so ominously. In a sense, his opponent was Adolf Hitler, not Willkie.

✵ A Landmark Lend-Lease Law

By late 1940 embattled Britain was nearing the end of its financial tether; its credits in America were being rapidly consumed by insatiable war orders. But Roosevelt, who had bitter memories of the wrangling over the Allied debts of World War I, was determined, as he put it, to eliminate "the silly, foolish, old dollar sign." He finally hit on the scheme of lending or leasing American arms to the reeling democracies. When the shooting was over, to use his comparison, the guns and tanks could be returned, just as one's next-door neighbor would return a garden hose when a threatening fire was put out. But isolationist Senator Taft (who was reputed to have the finest mind in Washington until he made it up) retorted that lending arms was like lending chewing gum: "You don't want it back." Who wants a chewed-up tank?

The **Lend-Lease Bill**, patriotically numbered 1776, was entitled "An Act Further to Promote the Defense of the United States." Sprung on the country after the election was safely over, it was praised by the administration as a device that would keep the nation out of the war rather than drag it in. The underlying concept was "Send guns, not sons" or "Billions, not bodies." America, so President Roosevelt promised, would be the "arsenal of democracy." It would send a limitless supply of arms to the victims of aggression, who in turn would finish the job and keep the war on

No to Lend-Lease Members of the Massachusetts Woman's Political Club presented President Roosevelt with a petition protesting adoption of the Lend-Lease Bill and picketed the White House. They feared that America's increasing involvement with the Allied cause would eventually draw their sons into battle—as it did, despite the president's assurances to the contrary.

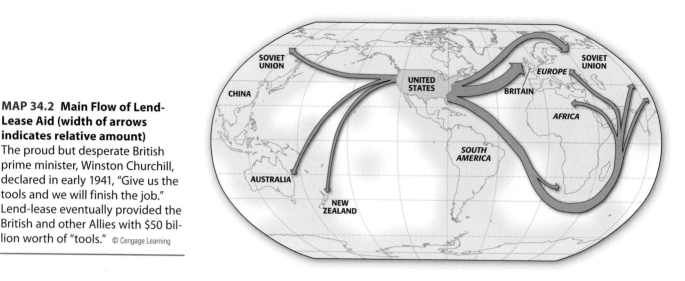

MAP 34.2 Main Flow of Lend-Lease Aid (width of arrows indicates relative amount) The proud but desperate British prime minister, Winston Churchill, declared in early 1941, "Give us the tools and we will finish the job." Lend-lease eventually provided the British and other Allies with $50 billion worth of "tools." © Cengage Learning

their side of the Atlantic. Accounts would be settled by returning the used weapons or their equivalents to the United States when the war was ended.

Lend-lease was heatedly debated throughout the land and in Congress. Most of the opposition came, as might be expected, from isolationists and anti-Roosevelt Republicans. The scheme was assailed as "the blank-check bill" and, in the words of isolationist Senator Burton Wheeler, as "the new Triple-A [Agricultural Adjustment Act] bill"—a measure designed to "plow under every fourth American boy." Nevertheless, lend-lease was finally approved in March 1941 by sweeping majorities in both houses of Congress.

Lend-lease was one of the most momentous laws ever to pass Congress; it was a challenge hurled squarely into the teeth of the Axis dictators. America pledged itself, to the extent of its vast resources, to bolster those nations that were indirectly defending it by fighting aggression. When the gigantic operation ended in 1945, America had sent about $50 billion worth of arms and equipment—much more than the cost to the country of World War I—to those nations fighting aggressors (see Map 34.2). The passing of lend-lease was in effect an economic declaration of war; now a shooting declaration could not be very far around the corner.

By its very nature, the Lend-Lease Bill marked the abandonment of any pretense of neutrality. It was no destroyer deal arranged privately by President Roosevelt. The bill was universally debated, over drugstore counters and cracker barrels, from California all the way to Maine, and the sovereign citizen at last spoke through convincing majorities in Congress. Most people probably realized that they were tossing the old concepts of neutrality out the window. But they also recognized that they would play a suicidal game if they bound themselves by the oxcart rules of the nineteenth century—especially while the Axis aggressors

themselves openly spurned international obligations. Lend-lease would admittedly involve a grave risk of war, but most Americans were prepared to take that chance rather than see Britain collapse and then face the diabolical dictators alone.

Lend-lease had the somewhat incidental result of gearing U.S. factories for all-out war production. The enormously increased capacity thus achieved helped save America's own skin when, at long last, the shooting war burst around its head.

Hitler evidently recognized lend-lease as an unofficial declaration of war. Until then Germany had avoided attacking U.S. ships; memories of America's decisive intervention in 1917–1918 were still fresh in German minds. But after the passing of lend-lease, there was less point in trying to curry favor with the United States. On May 21, 1941, the *Robin Moor*, an unarmed American merchantman, was torpedoed and destroyed by a German submarine in the South Atlantic, outside a war zone. The sinkings had started, but on a limited scale.

✵ Charting a New World

Two globe-shaking events marked the course of World War II before the assault on Pearl Harbor in December 1941. One was the fall of France in June 1940; the other was Hitler's invasion of the Soviet Union, almost exactly one year later, in June 1941.

The scheming dictators Hitler and Stalin had been uneasy yoke-fellows under the ill-begotten Nazi-Soviet pact of 1939. As masters of the double cross, neither trusted the other. They engaged in prolonged dickering in a secret attempt to divide potential territorial spoils between them, but Stalin balked at dominant German control of the Balkans. Hitler thereupon decided to crush his coconspirator, seize the oil and other resources of the Soviet Union, and then have two free hands to snuff out Britain. He assumed that his invincible armies would subdue Stalin's "Mongol half-wits" in a few short weeks.

Out of a clear sky, on June 22, 1941, Hitler launched a devastating attack on his Soviet neighbor. This timely assault was an incredible stroke of good fortune for the democratic world—or so it seemed at the time. The two fiends could now slit each other's throats on the icy steppes of Russia. Or they would if the Soviets did not quickly collapse, as many military experts predicted.

Sound American strategy seemed to dictate speedy aid to Moscow while it was still afloat. Roosevelt immediately promised assistance and backed up his words by making some military supplies available. Several months later, interpreting the lend-lease law to mean that the defense of the USSR was now essential for the defense of the United States, he extended $1 billion in lend-lease—the first installment on an ultimate total of $11 billion. Meanwhile, the valor of the red army, combined with the white paralysis of an early Russian winter, had halted Hitler's invaders at the gates of Moscow.

With the surrender of the Soviet Union still a dread possibility, the drama-charged Atlantic Conference was held in August 1941. British prime minister Winston Churchill, with cigar embedded in his cherubic face,

Unexpected Guest, 1941   Stalin joins the democracies, Britain and America. Library of Congress

Senator (later president) Harry S Truman (1884–1972) expressed a common reaction to Hitler's invasion of the Soviet Union in 1941:

❝If we see that Germany is winning, we ought to help Russia, and if we see Russia is winning, we ought to help Germany, and that way let them kill as many as possible.**❞**

secretly met with Roosevelt on a warship off the foggy coast of Newfoundland. This was the first of a series of history-making conferences between the two statesmen for the discussion of common problems, including the menace of Japan in the Far East.

The most memorable offspring of this get-together was the eight-point **Atlantic Charter**. It was formally accepted by Roosevelt and Churchill and endorsed by the Soviet Union later that year. Suggestive of Wilson's Fourteen Points, the new covenant outlined the aspirations of the democracies for a better world at war's end. Arguing for the rights of individuals rather than nations, the Atlantic Charter laid the groundwork for later advocacy on behalf of universal human rights.

Many were surprised by how specific the document was. Opposing imperialistic annexations, the charter promised that there would be no territorial changes contrary to the wishes of the inhabitants (self-determination). It further affirmed the right of a people to choose their own form of government and, in particular, to regain the governments abolished by the dictators. Among various other goals, the charter declared for disarmament and a peace of security, pending a "permanent system of general security" (a new League of Nations).

Liberals the world over took heart from the Atlantic Charter, as they had taken heart from Wilson's comparable Fourteen Points. It was especially gratifying to subject populations, like the Poles, who were then ground under the iron heel of a conqueror. But the agreement was roundly condemned in the United States by isolationists and others hostile to Roosevelt. What right, they charged, had "neutral" America to confer with belligerent Britain on common policies? Such critics missed the point: the nation was in fact no longer neutral.

✴ U.S. Destroyers and Hitler's U-boats Clash

Lend-lease shipments of arms to Britain on British ships were bound to be sunk by German wolf-pack submarines. If the intent was to get the munitions to England, not to dump them into the ocean, the freighters would have to be escorted by U.S. warships. Britain simply did not have enough destroyers. The dangerous possibility of being "convoyed into war" had been mentioned in Congress during the lengthy debate on lend-lease, but administration spokespeople had brushed the idea aside. Their strategy was to make only one commitment at a time.

Roosevelt made the fateful decision to convoy in July 1941. By virtue of his authority as commander in chief of the armed forces, the president issued orders to the navy to escort lend-lease shipments as far as Iceland. The British would then shepherd them the rest of the way.

Inevitable clashes with submarines ensued on the Iceland run, even though Hitler's orders were to strike at American warships only in self-defense. In September 1941 the U.S. destroyer *Greer*, provocatively trailing a German U-boat, was attacked by the undersea craft, without damage to either side. Roosevelt then proclaimed a shoot-on-sight policy. On October 17 the escorting destroyer *Kearny*, while engaged in a battle with U-boats, lost eleven men when it was crippled but not sent to the bottom. Two weeks later the destroyer *Reuben James* was torpedoed and sunk off southwestern Iceland, with the loss of more than a hundred officers and enlisted men.

Neutrality was still inscribed on the statute books, but not in American hearts. Congress, responding to public pressures and confronted with a shooting war, voted in mid-November 1941 to pull the teeth from the now-useless Neutrality Act of 1939. Merchant ships could henceforth be legally armed, and they could enter the combat zones with munitions for Britain. Americans braced themselves for wholesale attacks by Hitler's submarines.

✦ Surprise Assault on Pearl Harbor

The blowup came not in the Atlantic, but in the faraway Pacific. This explosion should have surprised no close observer, for Japan, since September 1940, had been a formal military ally of Nazi Germany—America's shooting foe in the North Atlantic.

Japan's position in the Far East had grown more perilous by the hour. It was still mired down in the costly and exhausting "China incident," from which it could extract neither honor nor victory. Its war machine was fatally dependent on immense shipments of steel, scrap iron, oil, and aviation gasoline from the United States. Such assistance to the Japanese aggressor was highly unpopular in America. But Roosevelt had resolutely held off an embargo, lest he goad the

Tokyo warlords into a descent upon the oil-rich but defense-poor Dutch East Indies.

Washington, late in 1940, finally imposed the first of its embargoes on Japan-bound supplies. This blow was followed in mid-1941 by a freezing of Japanese assets in the United States and a cessation of all shipments of gasoline and other sinews of war. As the oil gauge dropped, the squeeze on Japan grew steadily more nerve-racking. Japanese leaders were faced with two painful alternatives. They could either knuckle under to the Americans or break out of the embargo ring by a desperate attack on the oil supplies and other riches of Southeast Asia.

Final tense negotiations with Japan took place in Washington during November and early December of 1941. The State Department insisted that the Japanese clear out of China, but to sweeten the pill offered to renew trade relations on a limited basis. Japanese imperialists, after waging a bitter war against the Chinese for more than four years, were unwilling to lose face by withdrawing at the behest of the United States. Faced with capitulation or continued conquest, they chose the sword.

Officials in Washington, having "cracked" the top-secret code of the Japanese, knew that Tokyo's decision was for war. But the United States, as a democracy committed to public debate and action by Congress, could not shoot first. Roosevelt, misled by Japanese ship movements in the Far East, evidently expected the blow to fall on British Malaya or on the Philippines. No one in high authority in Washington seems to have believed that the Japanese were either strong enough or foolhardy enough to strike Hawaii.

But the paralyzing blow struck **Pearl Harbor**, while Tokyo was deliberately prolonging negotiations in Washington. Japanese bombers, winging in from distant aircraft carriers, attacked without warning on the "Black Sunday" morning of December 7, 1941. It was a date, as Roosevelt told Congress, "which will live in infamy." About three thousand casualties were inflicted on American personnel, many aircraft were destroyed, the battleship fleet was virtually wiped out when all eight of the craft were sunk or otherwise

Roosevelt's war message to Congress began with these famous words:

❝Yesterday, December 7, 1941—a date which will live in infamy—the United States of America was suddenly and deliberately attacked by naval and air forces of the Empire of Japan.❞

U.S. Army

The Battleship *West Virginia* The shocking Japanese attack on Pearl Harbor on December 7, 1941, propelled the United States into World War II. One of the first ships to be hit, the USS *West Virginia* quickly sank at its mooring, taking at least seventy sailors down with it. By September 1944 the *West Virginia* had been repaired and was back in service.

immobilized, and numerous small vessels were damaged or destroyed. Fortunately for America, the three priceless aircraft carriers happened to be outside the harbor.

An angered Congress the next day officially recognized the war that had been "thrust" upon the United States. The roll call in the Senate and House fell only one vote short of unanimity. Germany and Italy, allies of Japan, spared Congress the indecision of debate by declaring war on December 11, 1941. This challenge was formally accepted on the same day by a unanimous vote of both Senate and House. The unofficial war, already of many months' duration, was now official.

✴ America's Transformation from Bystander to Belligerent

Japan's hara-kiri gamble in Hawaii paid off only in the short run. True, the Pacific fleet was largely destroyed or immobilized, but the sneak attack aroused and united America as almost nothing else could have done. To the very day of the blowup, a strong majority

of Americans still wanted to keep out of war. But the bombs that pulverized Pearl Harbor blasted the isolationists into silence. The only thing left to do, growled isolationist Senator Wheeler, was "to lick hell out of them."

But Pearl Harbor was not the full answer to the question of why the United States went to war. This treacherous attack was but the last explosion in a long chain reaction. Following the fall of France, Americans were confronted with a devil's dilemma. They desired above all to stay out of the conflict, yet they did not want Britain to be knocked out. They wished to halt Japan's conquests in the Far East—conquests that menaced not only American trade and security but international peace as well. To keep Britain from collapsing, the Roosevelt administration felt compelled to extend the unneutral aid that invited attacks from German submarines. To keep Japan from expanding, Washington undertook to cut off vital Japanese supplies with embargoes that invited possible retaliation. Rather than let democracy die and dictatorship rule supreme, most citizens were evidently determined to support a policy that might lead to war. It did.

Chapter Review

KEY TERMS

London Economic Conference (778)

Good Neighbor policy (780)

Reciprocal Trade Agreements Act (780)

Rome-Berlin Axis (781)

Johnson Debt Default Act (782)

Neutrality Acts of 1935, 1936, and 1937 (782)

Abraham Lincoln Brigade (783)

Quarantine Speech (784)

Appeasement (784)

Hitler-Stalin pact (784)

Neutrality Act of 1939 (785)

Kristallnacht (788)

War Refugee Board (788)

Lend-Lease Bill (791)

Atlantic Charter (793)

Pearl Harbor (794)

PEOPLE TO KNOW

Benito Mussolini

Adolf Hitler

Francisco Franco

Cordell Hull

Wendell L. Willkie

CHRONOLOGY

1933
FDR torpedoes London Economic Conference
United States recognizes Soviet Union
FDR declares Good Neighbor policy toward Latin America
Hitler becomes German chancellor
Germany quits League of Nations

1934
Tydings-McDuffie Act provides for Philippine independence on July 4, 1946
Reciprocal Trade Agreements Act
U.S. Marines vacate Haiti

1935
Nuremberg Laws implemented against German Jews
Mussolini invades Ethiopia
U.S. Neutrality Act of 1935
Japan quits League of Nations

1936
U.S. Neutrality Act of 1936
Mussolini and Hitler form Rome-Berlin Axis
Stalin begins Great Purge
German troops invade Rhineland

1936–1939 Spanish Civil War

1937
U.S. Neutrality Act of 1937
Panay incident
Japan invades China

1938
Hitler seizes Austria
Munich Conference
Kristallnacht in Germany

1939
Hitler seizes all of Czechoslovakia
Nazi-Soviet pact
World War II begins in Europe with Hitler's invasion of Poland
U.S. Neutrality Act of 1939

1940
Fall of France
Hitler invades Denmark, Norway, Netherlands, and Belgium
United States invokes first peacetime draft
Havana Conference
Battle of Britain
Bases-for-destroyers deal with Britain
FDR defeats Willkie for presidency

1941
Lend-Lease Act
Hitler attacks Soviet Union
Atlantic Charter
Japan attacks Pearl Harbor

TO LEARN MORE

Peter N. Carroll, *The Odyssey of the Abraham Lincoln Brigade: Americans in the Spanish Civil War* (1994)

Robert Dallek, *Franklin D. Roosevelt and American Foreign Policy, 1932–1945* (1995)

Justus D. Doenecke, *Storm on the Horizon: The Challenge to American Intervention, 1939–1941* (2000)

Irwin F. Gellman, *Good Neighbor Diplomacy: United States Policies in Latin America, 1933–1945* (1979)

Akira Iriye, *The Globalizing of America, 1913–1945* (1993)

Manfred Jonas, *Isolationism in America, 1935–1941* (1966)

Primo Levi, *Survival in Auschwitz: The Nazi Assault on Humanity* (1961)

B. J. C. McKercher, *Transition of Power: Britain's Loss of Global Pre-eminence to the United States, 1930–1945* (1999)

Edward S. Miller, *Bankrupting the Enemy: The U.S. Financial Siege of Japan Before Pearl Harbor* (2007)

Gordon W. Prange, *At Dawn We Slept: The Untold Story of Pearl Harbor* (1981)

David Reynolds, *From Munich to Pearl Harbor: Roosevelt's America and the Origins of the Second World War* (2001)

Dominic Tierney, *FDR and the Spanish Civil War: Neutrality and Commitment in the Struggle That Divided America* (2007)

A complete, annotated bibliography for this chapter—along with brief descriptions of the People to Know—may be found on the American Pageant website. The Key Terms are defined in a Glossary at the end of the text.

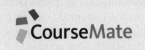

Go to the CourseMate website at **www.cengagebrain.com** for additional study tools and review materials—including audio and video clips—for this chapter.

AP® Review Questions for Chapter 34

1. Why did President Franklin Roosevelt undermine the goals of the London Economic Conference, causing it to collapse?
   (A) Its members insisted on the rigid adherence to the gold standard.
   (B) Any agreement to stabilize national currencies might hurt America's recovery from depression.
   (C) Any agreement emanating from the conference would necessarily involve the United States militarily with the League of Nations.
   (D) The delegates refused to work on reviving trade.
   (E) It was dominated by British and Swiss bankers.

2. Which of the following represented a partial motivation for President Roosevelt's decision to recognize the Soviet Union diplomatically?
   (A) It was an effort to gain political support from American Catholics.
   (B) It was a diplomatic reward to the Soviet Union for modifying its repressive communist policies.
   (C) President Roosevelt hoped that diplomatic recognition of the Soviet Union would serve as a diplomatic counterweight to the rising power of Japan and Germany.
   (D) It was an attempt to win favor with American liberals and leftists.
   (E) It was an effort to open opportunities for American investment in Siberian oil fields.

3. All of the following marked President Roosevelt's Good Neighbor Policy toward Latin America EXCEPT
   (A) withdrawal of American troops from Haiti.
   (B) repeal of most of America's interventionist rights in Cuba granted by the Platt Amendment.
   (C) partial release of the American political and military stranglehold over Panama.
   (D) a formal endorsement of nonintervention in Latin American affairs at the Seventh Pan-American Conference in 1933.
   (E) using the threat of armed intervention to uphold American oil companies' interests in Mexico.

4. Which of the following best characterizes the foreign trade policy of President Franklin Roosevelt?
   (A) Lowering U.S. tariffs to increase trade
   (B) Increasing U.S. tariffs to protect American industry and agriculture
   (C) Seeking formal consultation with and approval by the U.S. Senate before proceeding with reciprocal trade agreements with other nations
   (D) Continuing the same tariff rates and schedules of the Hawley-Smoot law
   (E) Postponing any adjustments on trade policy until after the onset of World War II

5. Passage of the Neutrality Acts of 1935, 1936, and 1937 and the overall congressional efforts to maintain U.S. neutrality in Europe resulted in all of the following EXCEPT
   (A) abandonment of the traditional policy of freedom of the seas.
   (B) a decline in the U.S. Navy and other armed forces.
   (C) prohibiting the U.S. government from making a critical distinction between aggressor nations and the countries victimized by unprovoked aggression.
   (D) spurring aggressor nations to become bolder on their paths of conquest.
   (E) balancing the scales between dictators and U.S. allies by trading with neither.

6. What was one critical byproduct of America's neutrality policy during the Spanish Civil War in 1936–1939?
   (A) It facilitated a fascist victory in Spain by General Franco that encouraged dictators in Germany and Japan to undertake further military aggression in Europe and Asia.
   (B) It permitted the Loyalists to win the Spanish Civil War.
   (C) It cemented a long-term political friendship and alliance between Roosevelt and Franco while they were both in power.
   (D) It did nothing to prevent Hitler from ultimately conquering Spain.
   (E) It prevented the Soviet Union from providing any military assistance to the Loyalist cause.

7. What did Britain and France hope would result from the signing of the Munich agreement with Adolf Hitler in March 1938?
   (A) Britain and France hoped they could prevent a European war by consenting to Germany's military occupation and political incorporation of the Czech Sudetenland.
   (B) Britain and France hoped they could break the alliance between Hitler and Mussolini.
   (C) Britain and France hoped that this political concession would prompt Hitler to reverse his persecution of Jews in Germany and Austria.
   (D) Britain and France hoped that the Munich agreement would persuade Germany to withdraw from and restore political sovereignty to Austria.
   (E) Britain and France hoped that the United States would soon sign a military alliance pact tying the defense of Britain and France to America.

8. Which of the following best characterizes the efforts made by the U.S. government in the late 1930s and early 1940s to save Jewish refugees from the Holocaust?
   - (A) Very limited U.S. government assistance to save a relatively small number of European Jews from the Holocaust
   - (B) A substantial military, diplomatic, and economic effort to accept as many Jews as possible from occupied Europe
   - (C) An effective use of secret diplomacy and covert intelligence operations to smuggle substantial numbers of Jews out of Nazi-occupied Europe
   - (D) Collaborating closely with Jewish rescue organizations to accept large numbers of beleaguered Jewish refugees such as those stranded on the ship *St. Louis*
   - (E) Amending America's restrictive immigration laws so that large numbers of Jewish refugees could legally emigrate from Nazi-occupied Europe to the United States

9. What event prompted the American government to take immediate steps to upgrade its military preparedness for war and abandon the pretense of neutrality in Europe?
   - (A) Germany's invasion and occupation of Denmark and Norway
   - (B) Germany's invasion and occupation of Poland
   - (C) France falling to Germany
   - (D) Italy's initial participation in the invasion of France by Germany
   - (E) The overrunning of Belgium and the Netherlands by Nazi Germany

10. Which of the following best characterizes the attitude of a strong majority of the American public at the end of 1940 toward America's proper role concerning the war in Europe?
    - (A) Solid support for the viewpoint of the America First Committee
    - (B) Solid support for a declaration of war against Germany to save Britain
    - (C) Solid support to send a large American expeditionary force to help Britain stave off Nazi Germany
    - (D) Solid support for shipping Britain everything except military weapons
    - (E) Solid support for providing Britain with all economic and military aid short of war

11. All of the following characterized the lend-lease program of 1941 EXCEPT that it
    - (A) increased the likelihood that America would be brought into the war on behalf of the Allies.
    - (B) represented another privately arranged executive deal between Roosevelt and Churchill, such as the destroyers-for-bases trade.
    - (C) was a direct political and military challenge to the Axis dictators.
    - (D) catalyzed American factories to prepare for all-out war production.
    - (E) signaled the end of any expectation that American neutrality in the war in Europe could be maintained.

12. All of the following contributed to Japan's belief by 1941 that it had no alternative to going to war with the United States EXCEPT
    - (A) President Roosevelt's absolute insistence that Japan withdraw from China.
    - (B) successive U.S. government-imposed embargoes in 1940 and 1941 on Japan-bound supplies, including steel, scrap iron, oil, and aviation gasoline.
    - (C) a freezing of Japanese assets in the United States in mid-1941.
    - (D) Japan's knowledge that U.S. intelligence officials had cracked the top-secret code of the Japanese, revealing Japan's war plans.
    - (E) America's continuing efforts to become the dominant naval, economic, and geopolitical power in the Pacific and Southeast Asia.

13. What did all of the United States' Neutrality Acts before 1940 have in common?
    - (A) The government forbade all trade with belligerent nations throughout the 1930s.
    - (B) The United States refused to make loans to any nation involved in war.
    - (C) Congress had final say over U.S. involvement with warring nations.
    - (D) All of the Neutrality Acts favored the nations that would make up the AXIS powers.
    - (E) The United States insisted upon freedom of the seas, as it did before World War I.

14. Which of the following does NOT indicate that the United States was actively involved in World War II before the attack on Pearl Harbor?
    - (A) U.S. naval forces engaged in battle with German submarines in 1941.
    - (B) Officials in Washington studied and "cracked" Japan's secret code.
    - (C) Roosevelt and Churchill created the Atlantic Charter, detailing the postwar world.
    - (D) Roosevelt proclaimed that the United States would be the "Arsenal of Democracy."
    - (E) Anti-Nazi and anti-Hitler Americans believed that the democracies would triumph.

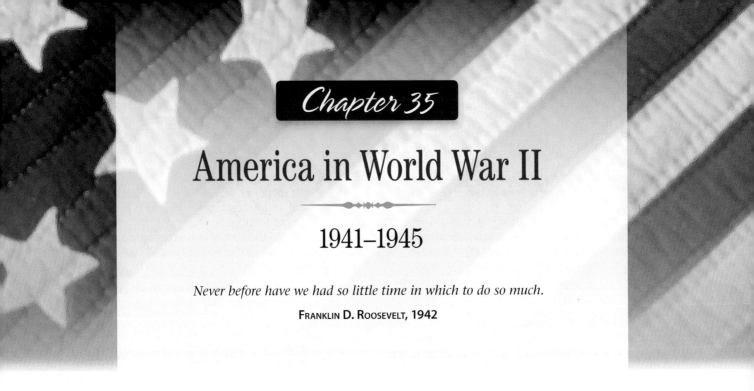

Chapter 35

America in World War II

1941–1945

Never before have we had so little time in which to do so much.

FRANKLIN D. ROOSEVELT, 1942

The United States was plunged into the inferno of World War II with the most stupefying and humiliating military defeat in its history. In the dismal months that ensued, the democratic world teetered on the edge of disaster.

Japan's fanatics forgot that whoever stabs a king must stab to kill. A wounded but still potent American giant pulled itself out of the mud of Pearl Harbor, grimly determined to avenge the bloody treachery. "Get Japan first" was the cry that rose from millions of infuriated Americans, especially on the Pacific Coast. These outraged souls regarded America's share in the global conflict as a private war of vengeance in the Pacific, with the European front a kind of holding operation.

But Washington, in the so-called **ABC-1 agreement** with the British, had earlier and wisely adopted the grand strategy of "getting Germany first." If America diverted its main strength to the Pacific, Hitler might crush both the Soviet Union and Britain and then emerge unconquerable in Fortress Europe. But if Germany was knocked out first, the combined Allied forces could be concentrated on Japan, and its daring game of conquest would be up. Meanwhile, just enough American strength would be sent to the Pacific to prevent Japan from digging in too deeply.

The get-Germany-first strategy was the solid foundation on which all American military strategy was built. But it encountered much ignorant criticism from two-fisted Americans who thirsted for revenge against Japan. Aggrieved protests were also registered by short-handed American commanders in the Pacific and by Chinese and Australian allies. But President Roosevelt, a competent strategist in his own right, wisely resisted these pressures.

✪ The Allies Trade Space for Time

Given time, the Allies seemed bound to triumph. But would they be given time? True, they had on their side the great mass of the world's population, but the wolf is never intimidated by the number of the sheep. The United States was the mightiest military power on earth—potentially. But wars are won with bullets, not blueprints. Indeed America came perilously close to losing the war to the well-armed aggressors before it could begin to throw its full weight onto the scales.

Time, in a sense, was the most needed munition. Expense was no limitation. The overpowering problem confronting America was to retool itself for all-out war production, while praying that the dictators would not meanwhile crush their adversaries who still remained in the field—notably Britain and the Soviet Union. Haste was all the more imperative because the highly skilled German scientists might turn up with unbeatable secret weapons, including rocket bombs and perhaps even atomic arms.

America's task was far more complex and backbreaking than during World War I. It had to feed, clothe, and arm itself, as well as transport its forces to regions as far separated as Britain and Burma. More than that, it had to send a vast amount of food and munitions to its hard-pressed allies, who stretched all the way from the USSR to Australia. Could the American people, reputedly "gone soft," measure up to this herculean task? Was democracy "rotten" and "decadent," as the dictators sneeringly proclaimed?

⭐ The Shock of War

National unity was no worry, thanks to the electrifying blow by the Japanese at Pearl Harbor. American Communists had denounced the Anglo-French "imperialist" war before Hitler attacked Stalin in 1941, but they now clamored for an unmitigated assault on the Axis powers. The handful of strutting pro-Hitlerites in the United States melted away, while millions of Italian Americans and German Americans loyally supported the nation's war program. In contrast to World War I, when the patriotism of millions of immigrants was hotly questioned, World War II actually speeded the assimilation of many ethnic groups into American society. Immigration had been choked off for almost two decades before 1941, and America's ethnic communities were now composed of well-settled members, whose votes were crucial to Franklin Roosevelt's

Brown Brothers

Enemy Aliens When the United States suddenly found itself at war with Germany, Italy, and Japan in December 1941, noncitizen German, Italian, and Japanese immigrants became "enemy aliens" and were required to register with the authorities. Several hundred resident Germans and Italians were detained in internment camps, but the harshest treatment was meted out to the Japanese, some 110,000 of whom, noncitizens and citizens alike, were eventually interned. Ironically, the two Japanese American Boy Scouts posting this notice in Los Angeles would soon be on their way to a government detention camp.

American song titles after Pearl Harbor combined nationalism with unabashed racism: "We Are the Sons of the Rising Guns," "Oh, You Little Son of an Oriental," "To Be Specific, It's Our Pacific," "The Sun Will Soon Be Setting on the Land of the Rising Sun," "The Japs Don't Stand a Chinaman's Chance," and "We're Gonna Find a Fellow Who Is Yellow and Beat Him Red, White, and Blue."

Monica Sone (b. 1919), a college-age Japanese American woman in Seattle, recorded the shock she and her brother felt when they learned of Executive Order No. 9066, which authorized the War Department to remove Japanese—aliens and citizens alike—from their homes:

❝In anger, Henry and I read and reread the Executive Order. Henry crumbled the newspaper in his hand and threw it against the wall. 'Doesn't my citizenship mean a single blessed thing to anyone? Why doesn't somebody make up my mind for me? First they want me in the army. Now they're going to slap an alien 4-C on me because of my ancestry. . . .' Once more I felt like a despised, pathetic two-headed freak, a Japanese and an American, neither of which seemed to be doing me any good.❞

Democratic party. Consequently, there was virtually no government witch-hunting of minority groups, as had happened in World War I.

A painful exception was the plight of some 110,000 Japanese Americans, concentrated on the Pacific Coast (see "Makers of America: The Japanese," pp. 800-801). The Washington top command, fearing that they might act as saboteurs for Japan in case of invasion, forcibly herded them together in concentration camps, though about two-thirds of them were American-born U.S. citizens. This brutal precaution, authorized under **Executive Order No. 9066**, was both unnecessary and unfair, as the loyalty and combat record of Japanese Americans proved to be admirable. But a wave of post–Pearl Harbor hysteria, backed by the long historical swell of anti-Japanese prejudice on the West Coast, temporarily robbed many Americans of their good sense—and their sense of justice. The internment camps deprived these uprooted Americans of dignity and basic rights; the internees also lost hundreds of millions of dollars in property and foregone earnings. The wartime Supreme Court in 1944 upheld the constitutionality of the Japanese relocation in *Korematsu v. U.S.* But more than four decades later, in 1988, the

In 1853 the American commodore Matthew Perry sailed four gunboats into Japan's Uraga Bay and demanded that the nation open itself to diplomatic and commercial exchange with the United States. Perry's arrival ended two centuries of Japan's self-imposed isolation and eventually led to the overthrow of the last Japanese shogun (military ruler) and the restoration of the emperor. Within two decades of Perry's arrival, Japan's new "Meiji" government had launched the nation on an ambitious program of industrialization and militarization designed to make it the economic and political equal of the Western powers.

As Japan rapidly modernized, its citizens increasingly took ship for America. A steep land tax imposed by the Meiji government to pay for its reforms drove more than 300,000 Japanese farmers off their land. In 1884 the Meiji government permitted Hawaiian planters to recruit contract laborers from among this displaced population. By the 1890s many Japanese were sailing beyond Hawaii to the ports of Long Beach, San Francisco, and Seattle.

Between 1885 and 1924, roughly 200,000 Japanese migrated to Hawaii, and around 180,000 more ventured to the U.S. mainland. They were a select group: because the Meiji government saw overseas Japanese as representatives of their homeland, it strictly regulated emigration. Thus Japanese immigrants to America arrived with more money than their European counterparts. Also, because of Japan's system of compulsory education, Japanese immigrants on average were better educated and more literate than European immigrants.

Women as well as men migrated. The Japanese government, wanting to avoid the problems of an itinerant bachelor society that it observed among the Chinese in the United States, actively promoted women's migration. Although most Japanese immigrants were young men in their twenties and thirties, thousands of women also ventured to Hawaii and the mainland as contract laborers or "picture brides," so called because their courtship had consisted exclusively of an exchange of photographs with their prospective husbands.

Like many Chinese and European immigrants, most Japanese who came to America expected to stay only temporarily. They planned to work hard for wages that were high by Japanese standards and then to return home and buy land. In Hawaii most Japanese labored on the vast sugar cane plantations. On the mainland they initially found migratory work on the railroads or in fish, fruit, or vegetable canneries. A separate Japanese economy of restaurants, stores, and boardinghouses soon sprang up in cities to serve the immigrants' needs.

From such humble beginnings, many Japanese—particularly those on the Pacific Coast—quickly moved into farming. In the late nineteenth century, the spread of irrigation shifted California agriculture from grain to fruits and vegetables, and the invention of the refrigerated railcar opened hungry new markets in the East. The Japanese, with centuries of experience in intensive farming, arrived just in time to take advantage of these developments. As early as 1910, Japanese farmers produced 70 percent of California's strawberries, and by 1940 they

Campaign Against the Japanese, Hollywood, California, 1923 Long before Japanese Americans were interned during World War II as a security risk, they faced intense discrimination throughout the United States.

grew 95 percent of the state's snap beans and more than half of its tomatoes. One Japanese farmer, known as the Potato King, sent his children to Harvard and Stanford and died in 1926 with an estate valued at $15 million.

But the very success of the Japanese proved a lightning rod for trouble. On the West Coast, Japanese immigrants had long endured racist barbs and social segregation. Increasingly, white workers and farmers, jealous of Japanese success, pushed for immigration restrictions. Bowing to this pressure, President Theodore Roosevelt in 1908 negotiated the "Gentlemen's Agreement," under which the Japanese government voluntarily agreed to limit emigration. In 1913 the California legislature denied Japanese immigrants already living in the United States the right to own land.

Legally barred from becoming citizens, Japanese immigrants (the "Issei," from the Japanese word for *first*) became more determined than ever that their American-born children (the "Nissei," from the Japanese word for *second*) would reap the full benefits of their birthright. Japanese parents encouraged their children to learn English, to excel in school, and to get a college education. Many Nissei grew up in two worlds, a fact they often recognized by Americanizing their Japanese names. Although education and acculturation did not protect the Nissei from the hysteria of World War II, those assets did give them a springboard to success in the postwar era.

Japanese American Evacuees, 1942 After the U.S. Army's Western Defense Command ordered the forced evacuation of all Japanese and Japanese Americans living on the Pacific Coast, families had no choice but to pack up whatever they could carry and move to the "relocation centers" hastily erected farther inland.

Three Boys at Manzanar, by Toyo Miyatake (1895–1979) Miyatake was an acclaimed Japanese American photographer with his own studio in Los Angeles before he and his family were evacuated to the Manzanar internment camp. He was determined to pursue his craft there, at first working secretly and then with the knowledge of the authorities. His pictures are the only photographic records of daily camp life taken by an internee. The guards allowed him to step outside the barbed-wire fence to take this photograph.

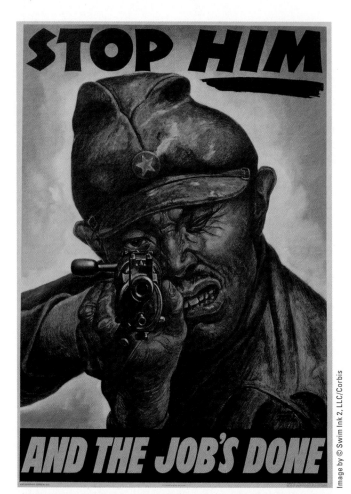

Anti-Japanese Poster, World War II Government propaganda during the war exploited racial stereotypes, often depicting Japanese people with big teeth and poor vision.

U.S. government officially apologized for its actions and approved the payment of reparations of $20,000 to each camp survivor.

The war prompted other changes in the American mood. Many programs of the once-popular New Deal—including the Civilian Conservation Corps, the Works Progress Administration, and the National Youth Administration—were wiped out by the conservative Congress elected in 1942. Roosevelt declared in 1943 that "Dr. New Deal" was going into retirement, to be replaced by "Dr. Win-the-War." His announcement acknowledged not only the urgency of the war effort but the power of the revitalized conservative forces in the country. The era of New Deal reform was over.

World War II was no idealistic crusade, as World War I had been. The Washington government did make some effort to propagandize at home and abroad with the Atlantic Charter, but the accent was on action. Opinion polls in 1942 revealed that nine out of ten

Americans could cite no provisions of the Atlantic Charter. A majority then, and a near-majority two years later, confessed to having "no clear idea what the war is about." All Americans knew was that they had a dirty job on their hands and that the only way out was forward. They went about their bloody task with astonishing efficiency.

✷ Building the War Machine

The war crisis caused the drooping American economy to snap to attention. Massive military orders—over $100 billion in 1942 alone—almost instantly soaked up the idle industrial capacity of the still-lingering Great Depression. Orchestrated by the **War Production Board (WPB)**, American factories poured forth an avalanche of weaponry: 40 billion bullets, 300,000 aircraft, 76,000 ships, 86,000 tanks, and 2.6 million machine guns. Miracle-man shipbuilder Henry J. Kaiser was dubbed "Sir Launchalot" for his prodigies of ship construction; one of his ships was fully assembled in fourteen days, complete with life jackets and coat hangers.

The War Production Board halted the manufacture of nonessential items such as passenger cars. It assigned priorities for transportation and access to raw materials. When the Japanese invasion of British Malaya and the Dutch East Indies snapped America's lifeline of natural rubber, the government imposed a national speed limit and gasoline rationing in order to conserve rubber and built fifty-one synthetic-rubber plants. By war's end they were far outproducing the prewar supply.

Farmers, too, rolled up their sleeves and increased their output. The armed forces drained the farms of workers, but heavy new investment in agricultural machinery and improved fertilizers more than made up the difference. In 1944 and 1945, blue-jeaned farmers hauled in record-breaking billion-bushel wheat harvests.

These wonders of production also brought economic strains. Full employment and scarce consumer goods fueled a sharp inflationary surge in 1942. The **Office of Price Administration (OPA)** eventually brought ascending prices under control with extensive regulations. Rationing held down the consumption of critical goods such as meat and butter, though some "black marketeers" and "meatleggers" cheated the system. The **National War Labor Board (NWLB)** imposed ceilings on wage increases.

Labor unions, whose membership grew from about 10 million to more than 13 million workers during the war, fiercely resented the government-dictated wage ceilings. Despite the no-strike pledges of most of the major unions, a rash of labor walkouts plagued the war effort. Prominent among the strikers were the United

Mine Workers, who several times were called off the job by their crusty and iron-willed chieftain, John L. Lewis.

Threats of lost production through strikes became so worrisome that Congress, in June 1943, passed the **Smith-Connally Anti-Strike Act**. This act authorized the federal government to seize and operate tied-up industries. Strikes against any government-operated industry were made a criminal offense. Under the act, Washington took over the coal mines and, for a brief period, the railroads. Yet work stoppages, although dangerous, actually accounted for less than 1 percent of the total working hours of the United States' wartime laboring force—a record better than blockaded Britain's. American workers, on the whole, were commendably committed to the war effort.

✴ Manpower and Womanpower

The armed services enlisted nearly 15 million men in World War II and some 216,000 women, who were employed for noncombat duties. Best known of these "women in arms" were the **WACs (Women's Army Corps)**, **WAVES (Women Accepted for Volunteer Emergency Service)** (navy), and **SPARs (U.S. Coast Guard Women's Reserve)**. As the draft net was tightened after Pearl Harbor, millions of young men were plucked from their homes and clothed in "GI" (government issue) outfits. As the arsenal of democracy, the United States exempted certain key categories of industrial and agricultural workers from the draft, in order to keep its mighty industrial and food-producing machines humming.

But even with these exemptions, the draft left the nation's farms and factories so short of personnel that new workers had to be found. An agreement with Mexico in 1942 brought thousands of Mexican agricultural workers, called *braceros*, across the border to harvest the fruit and grain crops of the West. The **Bracero program** outlived the war by some twenty years, becoming a fixed feature of the agricultural economy in many western states.

Even more dramatic was the march of women onto the factory floor. More than 6 million women took up jobs outside the home; over half of them had never before worked for wages. Many of them were mothers, and the government was obliged to set up some 3,000 day-care centers to care for "Rosie the Riveter's" children while she drilled the fuselage of a heavy bomber or joined the links of a tank track. When the war ended, Rosie and many of her sisters were in no hurry to put down their tools. They wanted to keep on working and often did. The war thus foreshadowed an eventual revolution in the roles of women in American society.

Yet the war's immediate impact on women's lives has frequently been exaggerated. The great majority of American women—especially those with husbands present in the home or with small children to care for—did not work for wages in the wartime economy but continued in their traditional roles. In both Britain and the Soviet Union, a far greater percentage of women, including mothers, were pressed into industrial employment

OURS...to fight for

Freedom of Speech *Freedom of Worship*

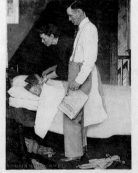

Freedom from Want *Freedom from Fear*

Library of Congress

The Four Freedoms, by Norman Rockwell In his January 6, 1941, speech to Congress requesting lend-lease aid to the Allies, President Roosevelt spoke eloquently of the "four freedoms" then threatened by Nazi and Japanese aggression. They are here given pictorial representation by Norman Rockwell, probably the most popular and best-loved American artist of the time.

Poster appeals and slogans urging women to enlist in the WACs (Women's Army Corps) were "Speed Them Back, Join the WAC," "I'd Rather Be with Them—Than Waiting for Them," "Back the Attack, Be a WAC! For America Is Calling," and (a song throwback to World War I) "The WACs and WAVES Will Win the War, Parlez Vous."

War Workers More than 6 million women—more than 3 million of them homemakers who had never before worked for wages—entered the work force during World War II. In contrast to the experience of women workers in World War I, many of these newly employed women continued as wage workers after the war ended.

as the gods of war laid a much heavier hand on those societies than they did on the United States. A poll in 1943 revealed that a majority of American women would not take a job in a war plant if it were offered.

At war's end, two-thirds of women war workers left the labor force. Many of them were forced out of their jobs by employers and unions eager to reemploy returning servicemen. But half of them told census takers that they quit their jobs voluntarily because of family obligations. The immediate postwar period witnessed not a permanent widening of women's employment opportunities, but a widespread rush into suburban domesticity and the mothering of the "baby boomers," who were born by the tens of millions in the decade and a half after 1945. America was destined to experience a thoroughgoing revolution in women's status later in the postwar period, but that epochal change was only beginning to gather momentum in the war years.

✹ Wartime Migrations

The war also proved to be a demographic cauldron, churning and shifting the American population. Many of the 15 million men and women in uniform, having seen new sights and glimpsed new horizons, chose not to go home again at war's end. War industries sucked people into boomtowns like Los Angeles, Detroit, Seattle, and Baton Rouge. California's population grew by nearly 2 million. The South experienced especially dramatic changes. Franklin Roosevelt had called the South "the nation's number one economic problem" in 1938; when war came, he seized the opportunity to accelerate the region's economic development. The states of the old Confederacy received a disproportionate share of defense contracts, including nearly $6 billion of federally financed industrial facilities. Here were the seeds of the postwar blossoming of the "Sunbelt" (see Map 35.1).

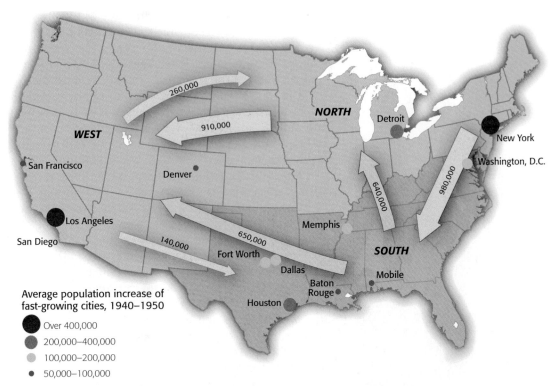

MAP 35.1 Internal Migration in the United States During World War II Few events in American history have moved the American people about so massively as World War II. The West and the South boomed, and several war-industry cities grew explosively. A majority of migrants from the South were blacks; 1.6 million African Americans left the region in the 1940s. (Source: United States Department of Labor, Bureau of Labor Statistics.) © Cengage Learning

Despite this economic stimulus in the South, some 1.6 million blacks left the land of their ancient enslavement to seek jobs in the war plants of the West and North. Forever after, race relations constituted a national, not a regional, issue. Explosive tensions developed over employment, housing, and segregated facilities. Black leader A. Philip Randolph, head of the Brotherhood of Sleeping Car Porters, threatened a massive "Negro March on Washington" in 1941 to demand equal opportunities for blacks in war jobs and in the armed forces. Roosevelt's response was to issue an executive order forbidding discrimination in defense industries. In addition, the president established the **Fair Employment Practices Commission (FEPC)** to monitor compliance with his edict. Blacks were also drafted into the armed forces, though they were still generally assigned to service branches rather than combat units and subjected to petty degradations such as segregated blood banks for the wounded. But in general the war helped to embolden blacks in their long struggle for equality. They rallied behind the slogan "Double V"—victory over the dictators abroad and over

racism at home. Membership in the National Association for the Advancement of Colored People (NAACP) shot up almost to the half-million mark, and a new militant organization committed to nonviolent "direct

An African American soldier angrily complained about segregation in the armed forces during World War II:

❝Why is it we Negro soldiers who are as much a part of Uncle Sam's great military machine as any cannot be treated with equality and the respect due us? The same respect which white soldiers expect and demand from us? . . . There is great need for drastic change in this man's Army! How can we be trained to protect America, which is called a *free* nation, when all around us rears the ugly head of segregation?**❞**

Segregation in the Military   A white officer reviews the 99th Pursuit Squadron, the famed "Tuskegee Airmen." They flew more than sixteen hundred fighter-support missions in North Africa and compiled an outstanding record, never losing a bomber to enemy aircraft. But these fliers were among the few African Americans who saw combat duty in World War II, when a still strictly segregated military assigned most blacks to construction, longshoreman, and mess-hall service.

action," the **Congress of Racial Equality (CORE)**, was founded in 1942.

The northward migration of African Americans accelerated after the war, thanks to the advent of the mechanical cotton picker—an invention whose impact rivaled that of Eli Whitney's cotton gin. Introduced in 1944, this new mechanical marvel did the work of fifty people at about one-eighth the cost. Overnight, the Cotton South's historic need for cheap labor disappeared. Their muscle no longer required in Dixie, some 5 million black tenant farmers and sharecroppers headed north in the three decades after the war. Theirs was one of the great migrations in American history, comparable in size to the immigrant floods from Ireland, Italy, and Poland. Within a single generation, a near-majority of African Americans gave up their

historic homeland and their rural way of life. By 1970 half of all blacks lived outside the South, and *urban* had become almost a synonym for *black*. The speed and scale of these changes jolted the migrants and sometimes convulsed the communities that received them.

The war also prompted an exodus of Native Americans from the reservations. Thousands of Indian men and women found war work in the major cities, and thousands more answered Uncle Sam's call to arms. More than 90 percent of Indians resided on reservations in 1940; six decades later more than half lived in cities, with a large concentration in southern California.

Some twenty-five thousand Native American men served in the armed forces. Comanches in Europe and Navajos in the Pacific made especially valuable contributions as "**code talkers**." They transmitted radio messages in their native languages, which were incomprehensible to the Germans and the Japanese.

The sudden rubbing against one another of unfamiliar peoples produced some distressingly violent friction. In 1943 young "zoot-suit"–clad Mexicans and Mexican Americans in Los Angeles were viciously attacked by Anglo sailors who cruised the streets in taxicabs searching for victims. Order was restored only after the Mexican ambassador made an emotional plea, pointing out that such outbreaks were grist for Nazi propaganda mills. At almost the same time, an even more brutal race riot that killed twenty-five blacks and nine whites erupted in Detroit.

Navajo Code Talkers, 1943   One of the best-kept secrets of World War II was the use of the Navajo language in a Marine Corps code designed to confuse the Japanese. Two marines in the leatherneck unit made up of Native Americans from Arizona and New Mexico transmitted in code during the battle for Bougainville Island in the South Pacific in 1943.

"Let John Henry Go" This image from the cover of the National Urban League's publication *Opportunity* reflects the rising militancy of African Americans in the World War II era. That militancy helped to energize the civil rights movement in the postwar years.

✦ Holding the Home Front

Despite these ugly episodes, Americans on the home front suffered little from the war, compared to the peoples of the other fighting nations. By war's end much of the planet was a smoking ruin. But in America the war invigorated the economy and lifted the country out of a decade-long depression. The gross national product vaulted from less than $100 billion in 1940 to more than $200 billion in 1945. Corporate profits rose from about $6 billion in 1940 to almost twice that amount four years later. ("If you are going to try to go to war in a capitalist country," said Secretary of War Henry Stimson, "you have to let business make money out of the process, or business won't work.") Despite wage ceilings, overtime pay fattened pay envelopes. Disposable personal income, even after payment of wartime taxes, more than doubled. On December 7, 1944, the

third anniversary of Pearl Harbor, Macy's department store rang up the biggest sales day in its history. Americans had never had it so good—and they wanted it a lot better. When price controls were finally lifted in 1946, America's pent-up lust to consume pushed prices up 33 percent in less than two years. The rest of the world, meanwhile, was still clawing its way out from under the rubble of war.

The hand of government touched more American lives more intimately during the war than ever before. The war, perhaps even more than the New Deal, pointed the way to the post-1945 era of big-government interventionism. Every household felt the constraints of the rationing system. Millions of men and women worked for Uncle Sam in the armed forces. Millions more worked for him in the defense industries, where their employers and unions were monitored by the FEPC and the NWLB, and their personal needs were cared for by government-sponsored housing projects, day-care facilities, and health plans. The Office of Scientific Research and Development channeled hundreds of millions of dollars into university-based scientific research, establishing the partnership between the government and universities that underwrote America's technological and economic leadership in the postwar era.

The flood of war dollars—not the relatively modest rivulet of New Deal spending—at last swept the plague of unemployment from the land. War, not enlightened social policy, cured the depression. As the postwar economy continued to depend dangerously on military spending for its health, many observers looked back to the years 1941–1945 as the origins of a "warfare-welfare state."

The conflict was phenomenally expensive. The wartime bill amounted to more than $330 billion—ten times the direct cost of World War I and twice as much as *all* previous federal spending since 1776. Roosevelt would have preferred to follow a pay-as-you-go policy to finance the war, but the costs were simply too gigantic. The income-tax net was expanded to catch about four times as many people as before, and maximum tax rates rose as high as 90 percent. But despite such drastic measures, only about two-fifths of the war costs were paid from current revenues. The remainder was borrowed. The national debt skyrocketed from $49 billion in 1941 to $259 billion in 1945 (see Figure 35.1). When production finally slipped into high gear, the war was costing about $10 million an hour. This was the price of victory over such implacable enemies.

✦ The Rising Sun in the Pacific

Early successes of the efficient Japanese militarists were breathtaking: they realized that they would have to

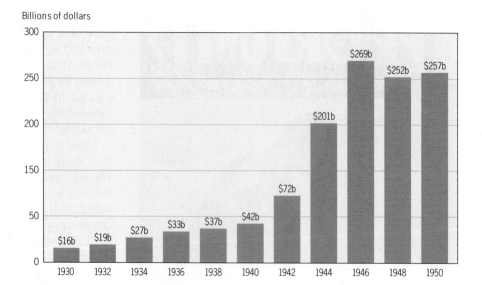

Billions of dollars

FIGURE 35.1 The National Debt, 1930–1950 Contrary to much popular mythology, it was World War II, not the New Deal, that first ballooned the national debt. The debt accumulated to still greater amounts in the 1980s and 1990s, and exploded with the onset of the "Great Recession" in 2008 (see Figure 40.1 on p. 952). (Source: *Historical Statistics of the United States*.)

win quickly or lose slowly. Seldom, if ever, has so much territory been conquered so rapidly with so little loss.

Simultaneously with the assault on Pearl Harbor, the Japanese launched widespread and uniformly successful attacks on various Far Eastern bastions. These included the American outposts of Guam, Wake, and the Philippines. In a dismayingly short time, the Japanese invader seized not only the British-Chinese port of Hong Kong but also British Malaya, with its critically important supplies of rubber and tin.

Nor did the Japanese tide stop there. The overambitious soldiers of the emperor, plunging into the snake-infested jungles of Burma, cut the famed Burma Road. This was the route over which the United States had been trucking a trickle of munitions to the armies of the Chinese generalissimo Jiang Jieshi (Chiang Kai-shek), who was still resisting the Japanese invader in China. Thereafter, intrepid American aviators were forced to fly a handful of war supplies to Jiang "over the hump" of the towering Himalaya mountains from the India-Burma theater. Meanwhile, the Japanese had lunged southward against the oil-rich Dutch East Indies. The jungle-matted islands speedily fell to the assailants after the combined British, Australian, Dutch, and American naval and air forces had been smashed at an early date by their numerically superior foe.

Better news came from the Philippines, which succeeded dramatically in slowing down the mikado's warriors for five months. The Japanese promptly landed a small but effective army, and General Douglas MacArthur, the eloquent and egotistical American commander, withdrew to a strong defensive position at Bataan, not far from Manila. There about twenty thousand American troops, supported by a much larger

force of ill-trained Filipinos, held off violent Japanese attacks until April 9, 1942. The defenders, reduced to eating mules and monkeys, heroically traded their lives for time in the face of hopeless odds. They grimly joked while vainly hoping for reinforcements:

> *We're the battling bastards of Bataan;*
> *No Mamma, no Papa, no Uncle Sam.*

Before the inevitable American surrender, General MacArthur was ordered by Washington to depart secretly for Australia, there to head the resistance against the Japanese. Leaving by motorboat and airplane, he proclaimed, "I shall return." After the battered remnants of his army had hoisted the white flag, they were treated with vicious cruelty in the infamous eighty-mile Bataan Death March to prisoner-of-war camps—the first in a series of atrocities committed by both sides in the unusually savage Pacific war. The island fortress of Corregidor, in Manila harbor, held out until May 6, 1942, when it too surrendered and left Japanese forces in complete control of the Philippine archipelago (see Map 35.2).

✴ Japan's High Tide at Midway

The aggressive warriors from Japan, making hay while the Rising Sun shone, pushed relentlessly southward. They invaded the turtle-shaped island of New Guinea, north of Australia, and landed on the Solomon Islands, from which they threatened Australia itself. Their onrush was finally checked by a crucial naval battle fought in the Coral Sea, in May 1942. An American carrier task force, with Australian support, inflicted heavy

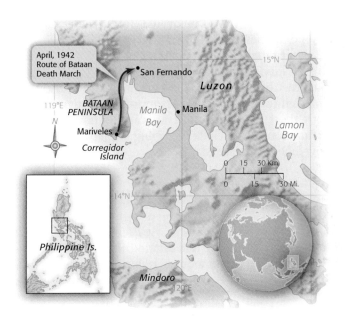

MAP 35.2 Corregidor and Bataan © Cengage Learning

Hell in the Pacific Assaulting Japanese island fortresses in the Pacific was a bloody, costly business. These American soldiers perished as they stepped ashore at Buna beach in New Guinea in 1942. Their damaged landing craft wallows in the surf behind them. Appearing in *Life* magazine on September 20, 1943, nearly two years after Pearl Harbor, this was the first photograph of dead GIs that the War Department allowed to be published.

losses on the victory-flushed Japanese. For the first time in history, the fighting was all done by carrier-based aircraft, and neither fleet saw or fired a shot directly at the other.

Japan next undertook to seize Midway Island, more than a thousand miles northwest of Honolulu. From this strategic base, it could launch devastating assaults on Pearl Harbor and perhaps force the weakened American Pacific fleet into destructive combat—possibly even compel the United States to negotiate a cease-fire in the Pacific. The epochal **Battle of Midway** was fought on June 3–6, 1942. Admiral Chester W. Nimitz, a high-grade naval strategist, directed a smaller but skillfully maneuvered carrier force, under Admiral Raymond A. Spruance, against the powerful invading fleet. The fighting was all done by aircraft, and the Japanese broke off action after losing four vitally important carriers.

Midway was a pivotal victory. Combined with the Battle of the Coral Sea, the U.S. success at Midway halted Japan's juggernaut. But the thrust of the Japanese into the eastern Pacific did net them America's fog-girt islands of Kiska and Attu, in the Aleutian archipelago, off Alaska. This easy conquest aroused fear of an invasion of the United States from the northwest. Much American strength was consequently diverted to the defense of Alaska, including the construction of the "Alcan" Highway through Canada.

Yet the Japanese imperialists, overextended in 1942, suffered from "victory disease." Their appetites

were bigger than their stomachs. If they had only dug in and consolidated their gains, they would have been much more difficult to dislodge once the tide turned.

American Leapfrogging Toward Tokyo

Following the heartening victory at Midway, the United States for the first time was able to seize the initiative in the Pacific. In August 1942 American ground forces gained a toehold on Guadalcanal Island, in the Solomons, in an effort to protect the lifeline from America to Australia through the southwest Pacific. An early naval defeat inflicted by the Japanese shortened American supplies dangerously, and for weeks the U.S. troops held on to the malarial island by their fingernails. After several desperate sea battles for naval control, the Japanese troops evacuated Guadalcanal in February 1943. Japanese losses were 20,000, compared to 1,700 for the Americans. That casualty ratio of more than ten to one, Japanese to American, persisted throughout the Pacific war.

American and Australian forces, under General MacArthur, meanwhile had been hanging on courageously to the southeastern tip of New Guinea, the last buffer protecting Australia. The scales of war gradually began to tip as the American navy, including submarines, inflicted lethal losses on Japanese supply ships and troop carriers. Conquest of the north coast of New Guinea was completed by August 1944, after General MacArthur had fought his way westward through tropical jungle hells. This hard-won victory was the first leg of his long return journey to the Philippines.

The U.S. Navy, with marines and army divisions doing the meat-grinder fighting, had meanwhile been "leapfrogging" the Japanese-held islands in the Pacific. Old-fashioned strategy dictated that the American forces, as they drove toward Tokyo, should reduce the fortified Japanese outposts on their flank. This course would have taken many bloodstained months, for the holed-in defenders were prepared to die to the last man in their caves. The new strategy of island hopping called for bypassing some of the most heavily fortified Japanese posts, capturing nearby islands, setting up airfields on them, and then neutralizing the enemy bases through heavy bombing. Deprived of essential supplies from the homeland, Japan's outposts would slowly wither on the vine—as they did.

Brilliant success crowned the American attacks on the Japanese island strongholds in the Pacific, where Admiral Nimitz skillfully coordinated the efforts of naval, air, and ground units. In May and August of 1943, Attu and Kiska in the Aleutians were easily retaken. In November 1943 "bloody Tarawa" and Makin, both in the Gilbert Islands, fell after suicidal resistance. In January and February 1944, the key outposts of the Marshall Islands group succumbed after savage fighting.

Especially prized were the Marianas, including America's conquered Guam. From bases in the Marianas, the United States' new B-29 superbombers could carry out round-trip bombing raids on Japan's home islands. The assault on the Marianas opened on June 19, 1944, with what American pilots called the "Great Marianas Turkey Shoot." A combination of the combat superiority of the recently developed American "Hellcat" fighter plane and the new technology of the antiaircraft proximity fuse destroyed nearly 250 Japanese aircraft, with a loss of only 29 American planes. The following day, in the Battle of the Philippine Sea, U.S. naval forces sank several Japanese carriers. The

Japanese navy never recovered from these massive losses of planes, pilots, and ships.

After fanatical resistance, including a mass suicide leap of surviving Japanese soldiers and civilians from "Suicide Cliff" on Saipan, the major islands of the Marianas fell to the U.S. attackers in July and August 1944. With these unsinkable aircraft carriers now available, virtual round-the-clock bombing of Japan began in November 1944 (see Map 35.3).

✦ The Allied Halting of Hitler

Early setbacks for America in the Pacific were paralleled in the Atlantic. Hitler had entered the war with a formidable fleet of ultramodern submarines, which ultimately operated in "wolf packs" with frightful effect, especially in the North Atlantic, the Caribbean, and the Gulf of Mexico. During ten months of 1942 more than 500 merchant ships were reported lost—111 in June alone—as ship destruction far outran construction.

The tide of subsea battle turned with agonizing slowness. Old techniques, such as escorting convoys of merchant vessels and dropping depth bombs from destroyers, were strengthened by air patrol, the newly invented technology of radar, and the bombing of submarine bases. "Keep 'Em Sailing" was the motto of oil-begrimed merchant seamen, hundreds of whom perished as unsung heroes in icy seas. Eventually Allied antisubmarine tactics improved substantially, thanks especially to British code breakers, who had cracked the Germans' "Enigma" codes and could therefore pinpoint the locations of the U-boats lurking in the North Atlantic.

Not until the spring of 1943 did the Allies clearly have the upper hand against the U-boat. If they had not won the Battle of the Atlantic, Britain would have been forced under, and a second front could not have been launched from its island springboard. Victory over the undersea raiders was nerve-rackingly narrow. When the war ended, Hitler was about to mass-produce a fearsome new submarine—one that could remain underwater indefinitely and cruise at seventeen knots when submerged.

British prime minister Winston Churchill (1874–1965) observed in a speech in May 1943,

❝ The proud German Army has by its sudden collapse, sudden crumbling and breaking up . . . once again proved the truth of the saying, 'The Hun [German] is always either at your throat or at your feet.' ❞

MAP 35.3 United States Thrusts in the Pacific, 1942–1945
American strategists had to choose among four proposed plans for waging the war against Japan:

1. Defeating the Japanese in China by funneling supplies over the Himalayan "hump" from India.
2. Carrying the war into Southeast Asia (a proposal much favored by the British, who could thus regain Singapore).
3. Heavy bombing of Japan from Chinese air bases.
4. "Island hopping" from the South Pacific to within striking distance of the Japanese home islands. This strategy, favored by General Douglas MacArthur, was the one finally emphasized. © Cengage Learning

Meanwhile, the turning point of the land-air war against Hitler had come late in 1942. The British had launched a thousand-plane raid on Cologne in May. In August 1942 they were joined by the American air force and were cascading bombs on German cities. The Germans under Marshal Erwin Rommel—the "Desert Fox"—had driven eastward across the hot sands of North Africa into Egypt, perilously close to the Suez Canal. A breakthrough would have spelled disaster for the Allies. But late in October 1942, British general Bernard Montgomery delivered a withering attack at El Alamein, west of Cairo. With the aid of several hundred hastily shipped American Sherman tanks, he speedily drove the enemy back to Tunisia, more than a thousand miles away.

On the Soviet front, the unexpected successes of the red army gave a new lift to the Allied cause. In September 1942 the Russians stalled the German steamroller at rubble-strewn Stalingrad, graveyard of Hitler's hopes. More than a score of invading divisions, caught in an icy noose, later surrendered or were "mopped up." In November 1942 the resilient Russians unleashed a crushing counteroffensive, which was never seriously reversed. A year later Stalin had regained about two-thirds of the blood-soaked Soviet motherland wrested from him by the German invader.

✴ A Second Front from North Africa to Rome

Soviet losses were already staggering in 1942: millions of soldiers and civilians lay dead, and Hitler's armies had overrun most of the western USSR. Anglo-American losses at this time could be counted only in the thousands. By war's end, the grave had closed over some 20 million Soviets, and a great swath of their country, equivalent in the United States to the area from Chicago to the Atlantic seaboard, had been laid waste. Small wonder that Kremlin leaders clamored for a second front to divert the German strength westward.

Many Americans, including FDR, were eager to begin a diversionary invasion of France in 1942 or 1943. They feared that the Soviets, unable to hold out forever against Germany, might make a separate peace as they had in 1918 and leave the Western Allies to face Hitler's fury alone. Roosevelt rashly promised the Soviets in early 1942 that he would open a second front on the European continent by the end of the year—a promise that proved utterly impossible to keep.

British military planners, remembering their appalling losses in 1914–1918, were not enthusiastic about a frontal assault on German-held France. It might end in disaster. They preferred to attack Hitler's Fortress Europe through the "soft underbelly" of the Mediterranean. Faced with British boot-dragging and a woeful lack of resources, the Americans reluctantly agreed to postpone a massive invasion of Europe.

An assault on French-held North Africa was a compromise second front, and a far cry from what the badly battered Soviets were demanding. The highly secret attack, launched in November 1942, was headed by a gifted and easy-smiling American general, Dwight D. ("Ike") Eisenhower, a master of organization and conciliation. As a joint Allied operation ultimately involving some 400,000 men (British, Canadian, French, and chiefly American) and about 850 ships, the invasion was the mightiest waterborne effort up to that time in history. After savage fighting, the remnants of the German-Italian army were finally trapped in Tunisia and surrendered in May 1943.

Women at War Members of the Women's Army Corps disembark in North Africa in 1944. (Note: "Auxillary" was dropped from the name in 1943.)

© Bettmann/Corbis

New blows were now planned by the Allies. At Casablanca, in newly occupied French Morocco, President Roosevelt, who had boldly flown the Atlantic, met in a historic conference with Winston Churchill in January 1943. The Big Two agreed to step up the Pacific war, invade Sicily, increase pressure on Italy, and insist upon an "unconditional surrender" of the enemy, a phrase earlier popularized by General Ulysses S. Grant during the Civil War. Such an unyielding policy would presumably hearten the ultrasuspicious Soviets, who professed to fear separate Allied peace negotiations. It would also forestall charges of broken armistice terms, such as had come after 1918. Paradoxically, the tough-sounding unconditional surrender declaration was an admission of the weakness of the Western Allies. Still unable in 1943 to mount the kind of second front their Soviet partner desperately demanded, the British and the Americans had little but words to offer Stalin.

"Unconditional surrender" proved to be one of the most controversial moves of the war. The main criticism was that it steeled the enemy to fight to a last-bunker resistance, while discouraging antiwar groups in Germany from revolting. Although there was some truth in these charges, no one can prove that "unconditional surrender" either shortened or lengthened the war. But this is known: by helping to destroy the German government utterly, the harsh policy forced a thorough postwar reconstruction.

The Allied forces, victorious in Africa, now turned against the not-so-soft underbelly of Europe. Sicily fell in August 1943 after sporadic but sometimes bitter resistance. Shortly before the conquest of the island, Mussolini was deposed, and Italy surrendered unconditionally soon thereafter, in September 1943. President Roosevelt, referring to the three original Axis countries—Germany, Italy, and Japan—joked grimly that it was now one down and two to go.

But if Italy dropped out of the war, the Germans did not drop out of Italy. Hitler's well-trained troops stubbornly resisted the Allied invaders now pouring into the toe of the Italian boot. They also unleashed their fury against the Italians, who had turned their coats and declared war on Germany in October 1943. "Sunny Italy" proceeded to belie its name, for in the snow-covered and mud-caked mountains of its elongated peninsula occurred some of the filthiest, bloodiest, and most frustrating fighting of the war.

For many months Italy appeared to be a dead end, as the Allied advance was halted by a seemingly impregnable German defense centered on the ancient monastery of Monte Cassino. After a touch-and-go assault on the Anzio beachhead, Rome was finally taken on June 4, 1944. The tremendous cross-channel invasion of France begun two days later turned Italy into a kind of sideshow, but the Allies, limited in manpower,

The Big Two British Prime Minister Winston Churchill and U.S. President Franklin D. Roosevelt meet at the Casablanca conference in Morocco, January 1943. The two leaders had a remarkable personal relationship that shaped the outcome of World War II and the course of history. They met in person nine times over the course of the war. "It is fun to be in the same decade with you," FDR cabled to Churchill after one of their meetings. As for Churchill, who was desperate for American aid in the struggle against Hitler, he once commented that "No lover ever studied the whims of his mistress as I did those of Franklin Roosevelt."

continued to fight their way slowly and painfully into northern Italy. On May 2, 1945, only five days before Germany's official surrender, several hundred thousand Axis troops in Italy laid down their arms and became prisoners of war. While the Italian second front opened the Mediterranean and diverted some German divisions from the blazing Soviet and French battle lines, it also may have delayed the main Allied invasion of Europe, from England across the English Channel to France, by many months—allowing more time for the Soviet army to advance into Eastern Europe.

✮ D-Day: June 6, 1944

The Soviets had never ceased their clamor for an all-out second front, and the time rapidly approached for Churchill, Roosevelt, and Stalin to meet in person to coordinate the promised effort. Marshal Joseph Stalin, with a careful eye on Soviet military operations, balked at leaving Moscow. President Roosevelt, who jauntily remarked in private, "I can handle that old buzzard," was eager to confer with him. The president seemed confident that Rooseveltian charm could woo the hardened conspirator of the Kremlin from his nasty communist ways.

Tehran, the capital of Iran (Persia), was finally chosen as the meeting place. To this ancient city Roosevelt riskily flew, after a stopover conference in Cairo with Britain's Churchill and China's Jiang Jieshi regarding the war against Japan. At Tehran the discussions among Stalin, Roosevelt, and Churchill—from November 28 to December 1, 1943—progressed smoothly. Perhaps the most important achievement was agreement on broad plans, especially those for launching Soviet attacks on Germany from the east simultaneously with the prospective Allied assault from the west.

Preparations for the cross-channel invasion of France were gigantic. Britain's fast-anchored isle virtually groaned with munitions, supplies, and troops, as nearly 3 million fighting men were readied. Because the United States was to provide most of the Allied warriors, the overall command was entrusted to an American, General Eisenhower. He had already distinguished himself in the North African and Mediterranean campaigns, not only for his military capacity but also for his gifts as a conciliator of clashing Allied interests.

French Normandy, less heavily defended than other parts of the European coast, was pinpointed for the invasion assault. On **D-Day**, June 6, 1944, the enormous operation, which involved some forty-six hundred vessels, unwound. Stiff resistance was encountered from the Germans, who had been misled by a feint into expecting the blow to fall farther north. The Allies had already achieved mastery of the air over France. They were thus able to block reinforcements by crippling the railroads, while worsening German fuel shortages by bombing gasoline-producing plants.

The Allied beachhead, at first clung to with fingertips, was gradually enlarged, consolidated, and reinforced. After desperate fighting, the invaders finally broke out of the German iron ring that enclosed the Normandy landing zone. Most spectacular were the lunges across France by American armored divisions, brilliantly commanded by blustery and profane General George S. ("Blood 'n' Guts") Patton. The retreat of the German defenders was hastened when an American-French force landed in August 1944 on the southern coast of France and swept northward. With the assistance of the French "underground," Paris was liberated in August 1944, amid exuberant manifestations of joy and gratitude.

Allied forces rolled irresistibly toward Germany, and many of the Americans encountered places, like

Allies Landing in Normandy, June 6, 1944 Nine-foot ocean swells on invasion day made loading the assault landing craft, such as the one pictured here, treacherous business. Many men were injured or tossed into the sea as the bathtublike amphibious vessels bobbed wildly up and down alongside the troop transports. As the vulnerable boats churned toward the beach, some officers led their tense, grim-faced troops in prayer. One major, recalling the remarkable Battle of Agincourt in 1415, quoted from Shakespeare's Henry V: "He that outlives this day, and comes safe home / Will stand a tip-toe when this day is named."

Château-Thierry, familiar to their fathers in 1918. "Lafayette, we are here again," quipped some of the American soldiers. The first important German city (Aachen) fell to the Americans in October 1944, and the days of Hitler's "thousand-year Reich" were numbered (see Map 35.4).

✪ FDR: The Fourth-Termite of 1944

The presidential campaign of 1944, which was bound to divert energy from the war program, came most awkwardly as the awful conflict roared to its climax. But the normal electoral processes continued to function, despite some loose talk of suspending them "for the duration."

Victory-starved Republicans met in Chicago with hopeful enthusiasm. They quickly nominated the short, mustachioed, and dapper Thomas E. Dewey, popular vote-getting governor of New York. Regarded as a liberal, he had already made a national reputation as a prosecutor of grafters and racketeers in New York City. His shortness and youth—he was only forty-two—had caused one veteran New Dealer to sneer that

the candidate had cast his diaper into the ring. To offset Dewey's mild internationalism, the convention nominated for the vice presidency a strong isolationist, handsome and white-maned Senator John W. Bricker of Ohio. Yet the platform called for an unstinted prosecution of the war and for the creation of a new international organization to maintain peace.

FDR, aging under the strain, was the "indispensable man" of the Democrats. No other major figure was available, and the war was apparently grinding to its finale. He was nominated at Chicago on the first ballot by acclamation. But in a sense he was the "forgotten man" of the convention, for in view of his age, an unusual amount of attention was focused on the vice presidency.

The scramble for the vice-presidential plum turned into something of a free-for-all. Henry A. Wallace, onetime "plow 'em under" secretary of agriculture, had served four years as vice president and desired a renomination. But conservative Democrats distrusted him as an ill-balanced and unpredictable liberal. A "ditch Wallace" move developed tremendous momentum, despite the popularity of Wallace with large numbers of voters and many of the delegates. With Roosevelt's

MAP 35.4 World War II in Europe and North Africa, 1939–1945 © Cengage Learning

blessing, the vice-presidential nomination finally went to smiling and self-assured Senator Harry S Truman of Missouri ("the new Missouri Compromise"). Hitherto inconspicuous, he had recently attained national visibility as the efficient chairman of a Senate committee conducting an investigation of wasteful war expenditures. Nobody had much against him or on him.

✴ Roosevelt Defeats Dewey

A dynamic Dewey took the offensive, for Roosevelt was too consumed with directing the war to spare much time for speechmaking. The vigorous young "crime buster," with his beautiful baritone voice and polished diction, denounced the tired and quarrelsome "old men" in Washington. He proclaimed repeatedly that after "twelve long years" of New Dealism, it was "time for a change." As for the war, Dewey would not alter the basic strategy but would fight it better—a type of "me-tooism" ridiculed by the Democrats. The fourth-term issue did not figure prominently, now that the ice had been broken by Roosevelt's third term. But "Dewey-eyed" Republicans half-humorously professed to fear fifth and sixth terms by the "lifer" in the White House.

In the closing weeks of the campaign, Roosevelt left his desk for the stump. He was stung by certain Republican charges, including criticism that he had sent a U.S. Navy destroyer to retrieve his pet Scottie dog, Fala. He was also eager to show himself, even in chilling rains, to spike well-founded rumors of failing health.

Substantial assistance came from the new political action committee of the CIO, which was organized to get around the law banning the direct use of union funds for political purposes. Zealous CIO members, branded as communists by the Republicans, rang countless doorbells and asked, with pointed reference to the recent depression, "What were you doing in 1932?" At times Roosevelt seemed to be running again against Hoover. As in every one of his previous three campaigns, FDR was opposed by a majority of the newspapers, which were owned chiefly by Republicans.

Roosevelt, as customary, won a sweeping victory: 432 to 99 in the Electoral College; 25,606,585 to 22,014,745 in the popular vote. Elated, he quipped that "the first twelve years are the hardest."

Roosevelt won primarily because the war was going well. A winning pitcher is not ordinarily pulled from the game. Foreign policy was a decisive factor with untold thousands of voters, who concluded that Roosevelt's experienced hand was needed in fashioning a future organization for world peace. The dapper Dewey, cruelly dubbed "the little man on top of the wedding cake," had spoken smoothly of international cooperation, but his isolationist running mate, Bricker, had implanted serious doubts. The Republican party was still suffering from the taint of isolationism fastened on it by the Hardingites.

✯ The Last Days of Hitler

By mid-December 1944, the month after Roosevelt's fourth-term victory, Germany seemed to be wobbling on its last legs. The Soviet surge had penetrated eastern Germany. Allied aerial "blockbuster" bombs, making the "rubble bounce" with around-the-clock attacks, were falling like giant explosive hailstones on cities, factories, and transportation arteries. The German western front seemed about to buckle under the sledgehammer blows of the United States and its Allies.

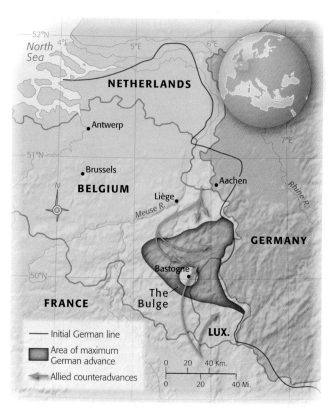

MAP 35.5 Battle of the Bulge, December 1944–January 1945 © Cengage Learning

American and Soviet Soldiers Meet in Germany, 1945
Such friendly sights soon became rare as mutual suspicion deepened.

Hitler then staked everything on one last throw of his reserves. Secretly concentrating a powerful force, he hurled it, on December 16, 1944, against the thinly held American lines in the heavily befogged and snow-shrouded Ardennes Forest. His objective was the Belgian port of Antwerp, key to the Allied supply operation. Caught off guard, the outmanned Americans were driven back, creating a deep "bulge" in the Allied line. The ten-day penetration was finally halted after the 101st Airborne Division had stood firm at the vital bastion of Bastogne. The commander, Brigadier General A. C. McAuliffe, defiantly answered the German demand for surrender with one word: "Nuts." Reinforcements were rushed up, and the last-gasp Hitlerian offensive was at length bloodily stemmed in the Battle of the Bulge (see Map 35.5).

In March 1945, forward-driving American troops reached Germany's Rhine River, where, by incredibly good luck, they found one strategic bridge undemolished. Pressing their advantage, General Eisenhower's troops reached the Elbe River in April 1945. There, a short distance south of Berlin, American and Soviet advance guards dramatically clasped hands amid cries of *"Amerikanskie tovarishchi"* (American comrades). The conquering Americans were horrified to find blood-spattered and still-stinking concentration camps, where

Franklin Roosevelt at Tehran, 1943

In late 1943 the "Big Three" wartime leaders—British prime minister Winston Churchill, American president Franklin Roosevelt, and Soviet leader Joseph Stalin—gathered together for the first time. They met amid growing Soviet frustration with the British and Americans for their failure thus far to open a "second front" against Germany in Western Europe, while the Soviets continued to suffer horrendous losses in the savage fighting in Eastern Europe. American military planners were eager to open a second front as soon as possible, but the British, who would necessarily have to supply most of the troops until America was fully mobilized, balked. Tension among the three leaders over the second-front plan—codenamed OVERLORD, the operation that resulted in the Anglo-American invasion of Normandy on "D-Day," June 6, 1944—is evident in this report of their discussions in the Iranian city of Tehran on November 28, 1943. The excerpts printed here are actually taken from two separate accounts: one composed by the American diplomat and Roosevelt's official translator Charles Bohlen, the other written by a military officer on behalf of the United States Joint Chiefs of Staff. Both versions were published in *Foreign Relations of the United States*, a compilation of American diplomatic records since 1861. The Soviets and the British also kept their own records of the Tehran meetings, giving historians remarkably rich sources with which to reconstruct the crucial negotiations and decisions that shaped wartime diplomacy. Why might the history of diplomacy be so lavishly documented? At this meeting, what were the principal objectives that each leader pursued? How did each man address his task? In what ways was the future of the war—and the postwar world—here foreshadowed?

FIRST PLENARY MEETING, NOVEMBER 28, 1943, 4 P.M., CONFERENCE ROOM, SOVIET EMBASSY

Bohlen Minutes

SECRET

THE PRESIDENT said as the youngest of the three present he ventured to welcome his elders. He said he wished to welcome the new members to the family circle and tell them that meetings of this character were conducted as between friends with complete frankness on all sides with nothing that was said to be made public. . . .

Chief of Staff Minutes

MARSHAL STALIN asked who will be the commander in this Operation Overlord. (THE PRESIDENT and PRIME MINISTER interpolated this was not yet decided.) MARSHAL STALIN continued, "Then nothing will come out of these operations." . . .

THE PRESIDENT said we again come back to the problem of the timing for OVERLORD. It was believed that it would be good for OVERLORD to take place about 1 May, or certainly not later than 15 May or 20 May, if possible.

THE PRIME MINISTER said that he could not agree to that. . . .

. . . He said he (the Prime Minister) was going to do everything in the power of His Majesty's Government to begin OVERLORD at the earliest possible moment. However, he did not think that the many great possibilities in the Mediterranean should be ruthlessly cast aside as valueless merely on the question of a month's delay in OVERLORD.

MARSHAL STALIN said all the Mediterranean operations are diversions. . . .

THE PRESIDENT said he found that his staff places emphasis on OVERLORD. While on the other hand the Prime Minister and his staff also emphasize OVERLORD, nevertheless the United States does not feel that OVERLORD should be put off.

THE PRESIDENT questioned whether it would not be possible for the ad hoc committee to go ahead with their deliberations without any further directive and to produce an answer by tomorrow morning.

MARSHAL STALIN questioned, "What can such a committee do?" He said, "We Chiefs of State have more power and more authority than a committee. General Brooke cannot force our opinions and there are many questions which can be decided only by us." He said he would like to ask if the British are thinking seriously of OVERLORD only in order to satisfy the U.S.S.R.

THE PRIME MINISTER replied that if the conditions specified at Moscow regarding OVERLORD should exist, he firmly believed it would be England's duty to hurl every ounce of strength she had across the Channel at the Germans.

THE PRESIDENT observed that in an hour a very good dinner would be awaiting all and people would be very hungry. He suggested that the staffs should meet tomorrow morning and discuss the matter. . . .

Source: FDR Library

The Horror of the Holocaust Although the outside world had some knowledge of the Nazi death camps before the war's end, the full revelation of Hitler's atrocities as the Allies overran Germany in the spring of 1945 stunned and sickened the invading troops. At General Eisenhower's orders, German civilians were compelled to view the evidence of the Nazi regime's genocidal crimes—though these witnesses at Buchenwald tried to look the other way, as many had done during the war itself.

the German Nazis had engaged in the scientific mass murder of "undesirables," including an estimated 6 million Jews. The Washington government had long been informed about Hitler's campaign of genocide against the Jews and had been reprehensibly slow to take steps against it. Roosevelt's administration had bolted the door against large numbers of Jewish refugees, and his military commanders declined even to bomb the rail lines that carried the victims to the camps. But until the war's end, the full dimensions of the "Holocaust" had not been known. When the details were revealed, the whole world was aghast.

The vengeful Soviets, clawing their way forward from the east, reached Berlin in April 1945. After desperate house-to-house fighting, followed by an orgy of pillage and rape, they captured the bomb-shattered city. Adolf Hitler, after a hasty marriage to his mistress, committed suicide in an underground bunker on April 30, 1945.

Tragedy had meanwhile struck the United States. President Roosevelt, while relaxing at Warm Springs, Georgia, suddenly died from a massive cerebral hemorrhage on April 12, 1945. The crushing burden of twelve depression and war years in the White House had finally taken its toll. Knots of confused, leaderless citizens gathered to discuss the future anxiously, as a bewildered, unbriefed Vice President Truman took the helm.

On May 7, 1945, what was left of the German government surrendered unconditionally. May 8 was officially proclaimed **V-E (Victory in Europe) Day** and was greeted with frenzied rejoicing in the Allied countries.

✵ Japan Dies Hard

Japan's rickety bamboo empire meanwhile was tottering to its fall. American submarines—"the silent service"—were sending the Japanese merchant marine to the bottom so fast they were running out of prey. All told, these "undersea craft" destroyed 1,042 ships, or about 50 percent of Japan's entire life-sustaining merchant fleet.

Giant bomber attacks were more spectacular. Launched from Saipan and other captured Mariana Islands, they were reducing the enemy's fragile cities to cinders. The massive firebomb raid on Tokyo, March 9–10, 1945, was annihilating. It destroyed over 250,000 buildings, gutted a quarter of the city, and killed an estimated 83,000 people—a loss comparable to that later inflicted by the atomic bombs.

General MacArthur was also on the move. Completing the conquest of jungle-draped New Guinea, he headed northwest for the Philippines, en route to Japan, with 600 ships and 250,000 men. In a scene well staged for the photographers, he splashed ashore at Leyte Island on October 20, 1944, with the summons, "People of the Philippines, I have returned. . . . Rally to me."

Japan's navy—still menacing—now made one last-chance effort to destroy MacArthur by wiping out his transports and supply ships. A gigantic clash at Leyte Gulf, fought on the sea and in the air, was actually three battles (October 23–26, 1944). The Americans won all of them, though the crucial engagement was almost lost when Admiral William F. ("Bull") Halsey was decoyed away by a feint.

Japan was through as a sea power: it had lost about sixty ships in the greatest naval battle of all time. American fleets, numbering more than four thousand vessels, now commanded the western Pacific. Several battleships, raised from the mud of Pearl Harbor, were exacting belated but sweet revenge.

Overrunning Leyte, MacArthur next landed on the main Philippine island of Luzon in January 1945. Manila was his major objective; the ravaged city fell in March, but the Philippines were not conquered until July. Victory was purchased only after bitter fighting against holed-in Japanese, who took a toll of over sixty thousand American casualties.

America's steel vise was tightening mercilessly around Japan. The tiny island of Iwo Jima, needed as a haven for damaged American bombers returning from Japan, was captured in March 1945. This desperate twenty-five-day assault cost over four thousand American dead.

Okinawa, a well-defended Japanese island, was next on the list: it was needed for closer bases from which to blast and burn enemy cities and industries. Fighting dragged on from April to June of 1945. Japanese soldiers, fighting with incredible courage from their caves, finally sold Okinawa for fifty thousand American casualties, while suffering far heavier losses themselves.

The U.S. Navy, which covered the invasion of Okinawa, sustained severe damage. Japanese suicide pilots ("kamikazes") in an exhibition of mass hara-kiri for their god-emperor, crashed their bomb-laden planes onto the decks of the invading fleet. All told, the death squads sank over thirty ships and badly damaged scores more.

✴ The Atomic Bombs

Strategists in Washington were meanwhile planning an all-out invasion of the main islands of Japan—an invasion that presumably would cost hundreds of thousands of American (and even more Japanese) casualties. Tokyo, recognizing imminent defeat, had secretly sent peace feelers to Moscow, which had not yet entered the Far Eastern war. The Americans, having broken the secret Japanese radio codes, knew of these feelers. But bomb-scorched Japan still showed no outward willingness to surrender *unconditionally* to the Allies.

National Archives

The Flag Raising at Iwo Jima   Atop Mount Suribachi, press photographer Joe Rosenthal snapped this dramatic picture, probably the most famous of the war.

Hiroshima, Japan, August 1945 The almost incomprehensibly destructive power of history's first atomic bomb is vividly evident in this photograph. The single bomb killed an estimated 130,000 Japanese, many of whom succumbed months after the blast to agonizing deaths from exposure to radiation.

The **Potsdam conference**, held near Berlin in July 1945, sounded the death knell of the Japanese. There President Truman, still new on his job, met in a seventeen-day parley with Joseph Stalin and the British leaders. The conferees issued a stern ultimatum to Japan: surrender or be destroyed. American bombers showered the dire warning on Japan in tens of thousands of leaflets, but no encouraging response was forthcoming.

America had a fantastic ace up its sleeve. Early in 1940, after Hitler's wanton assault on Poland, Roosevelt was persuaded by American and exiled scientists, notably German-born Albert Einstein, to push ahead with preparations for unlocking the secret of an atomic bomb. Congress, at Roosevelt's blank-check request, blindly made available nearly $2 billion. Many military minds were skeptical of this "damned professor's nonsense," but fears that the Germans might first acquire such an awesome weapon provided a powerful spur to action. Ironically, Germany eventually abandoned its own atomic project as too costly. And as it happened, the war against Germany ended before the American weapon was ready. In a cruel twist of fate, Japan—not Germany, the original target—suffered the fate of being the first nation subjected to atomic bombardment.

What was called the **Manhattan Project** pushed feverishly forward, as American know-how and industrial power were combined with the most advanced scientific knowledge. Much technical skill was provided by British and refugee scientists, who had fled to America to escape the torture chambers of the dictators. Finally, in the desert near Alamogordo, New Mexico, on July 16, 1945, the experts detonated the first awesome and devastating atomic device.

With Japan still refusing to surrender, the Potsdam threat was fulfilled. On August 6, 1945, a lone American bomber dropped one atomic bomb on the city of Hiroshima, Japan. In a blinding flash of death, followed by a funnel-shaped cloud, about 180,000 people were left killed, wounded, or missing. Some 70,000 of them died instantaneously. Sixty thousand more soon perished from burns and radiation disease.

The scientific director of the Manhattan Project, J. Robert Oppenheimer (1904–1967), recalled his reaction as he witnessed the detonation of the first atomic bomb at the Trinity test site in Alamogordo, New Mexico, in July 1945. He was not only awed by the extraordinary force of this new weapon. He also feared the power to do harm that it gave to humans:

"I remembered the line from the Hindu scripture, the Bhagavad-Gita: 'Now I am become Death, the destroyer of Worlds.'"

Two days later, on August 8, Stalin entered the war against Japan, exactly on the deadline date previously agreed upon with his allies. Soviet armies speedily overran the depleted Japanese defenses in Manchuria and Korea in a six-day "victory parade" that involved several thousand Russian casualties. Stalin was evidently determined to be in on the kill, lest he lose a voice in the final division of Japan's holdings.

Fanatically resisting Japanese, though facing atomization, still did not surrender. American aviators, on August 9, dropped a second atomic bomb on the city of Nagasaki. The explosion took a horrible toll of about eighty thousand people killed or missing. (See "Varying Viewpoints," p. 825.) The Japanese nation could endure no more. On August 10, 1945, Tokyo sued for peace on one condition: that Hirohito, the bespectacled Son of Heaven, be allowed to remain on his ancestral throne as nominal emperor. Despite their "unconditional surrender" policy, the Allies accepted this condition on August 14, 1945. The Japanese, though losing face, were able to save both their exalted ruler and what was left of their native land.

The formal end came, with dramatic force, on September 2, 1945. Official surrender ceremonies were conducted by General MacArthur on the battleship *Missouri* in Tokyo Bay. At the same time, Americans at home hysterically celebrated **V-J (Victory in Japan) Day** after the most horrible war in history had ended in mushrooming atomic clouds.

✴ The Allies Triumphant

World War II proved to be terribly costly. American forces suffered some 1 million casualties, more than one-third of which were deaths. Compared with other wars, the proportion killed by wounds and disease was sharply reduced, owing in part to the use of blood

AP Photo

The Japanese Surrender   Representatives of the Japanese government arrived to sign the surrender document on the deck of the battleship *Missouri* in Tokyo harbor, September 2, 1945. General Douglas MacArthur then made a conciliatory address, expressing hope "that from this solemn occasion a better world shall emerge . . . a world founded on faith and understanding." A Japanese diplomat attending wondered "whether it would have been possible for us, had we been victorious, to embrace the vanquished with a similar magnanimity." Soon thereafter General MacArthur took up his duties as director of the U.S. occupation of Japan.

America and the World in Depression and War: A Study in Contrasts

The Great Depression of the 1930s was a monstrous, planetary-scale economic hurricane that wreaked havoc around the globe. All nations were walloped by its destructive force, but two were especially hard hit: the United States and Germany. In both countries production of goods declined by nearly 50 percent, and unemployment approached 25 percent. Also in both countries the depression discredited existing political regimes and created opportunities for new leadership to emerge. Fatefully, Germany got Adolf Hitler, while the United States got Franklin D. Roosevelt.

Roosevelt and Hitler were of the same generation, both born in the 1880s. They came to power within weeks of each other—Hitler as Germany's chancellor on January 30, 1933, and Roosevelt as U.S. president on March 4, 1933. Both achieved office through democratic elections, though democracy soon withered under one's hand and flourished under the other's.

Roosevelt's entire presidency unfolded under the looming threat, and eventually the armed challenge, of Hitler's Nazi regime. FDR's record, as well as the very character of American democracy in the mid-twentieth century, can only be properly understood in that larger context.

Consider: In the spring of 1933, Roosevelt was coaxing legislation out of the Hundred Days Congress, forging labor unions and sundry ethnic and racial minorities into a long-lasting Democratic party coalition, and making innovative use of the radio to outflank the hostile media magnates who controlled the nation's newspapers. In those same months, Hitler was dissolving German labor unions and ruthlessly censoring the German press. Soon he declared the Nazis the only legal political party in Germany and proceeded to impose on the German people a reign of terror cruelly enforced by the Gestapo, the Nazis' grimly efficient secret police.

A year later, while Roosevelt worried about a possible political challenge from the swashbuckling Louisiana senator Huey P. Long, Hitler dispatched with his main Nazi rival, Ernst Röhm, by ordering his execution.

The following year, 1935, Roosevelt shepherded his sweeping reform program through Congress, notably including the Social Security Act, which helped to usher millions of Americans into the mainstream of American life, especially members of the great immigrant communities that had arrived a generation or so earlier. "We are going to make a country," Roosevelt said, "in which no one is left out." That same year Hitler codified the Nazis' viciously anti-Semitic policies in the notorious Nuremberg Laws, stripping German Jews of their citizenship, barring them from the professions and military service, and prohibiting marriage between Jews and "Aryans" (defined by the Nazis as a master race of non-Jewish Caucasians, especially those having Nordic features)—all gruesome steps on the

road to the genocidal war-time Holocaust, which would eventually murder some 6 million Jews.

Meanwhile, Hitler was relentlessly building his war machine, while FDR's America clung stubbornly to its traditional isolationism. And when the great conflict of World War II finally erupted, Hitler's Germany and Roosevelt's America fought decidedly different wars. Indeed the United States' experience in the war stands in vivid contrast to the experience of *all* other combatants, including not only Germany but also America's allies in the "Grand Alliance."

Hitler's vaunted "thousand-year Reich" lay in smoldering ruins at war's end, his people dazed, demoralized, and starving. The strutting Führer had brewed a catastrophe so vast that its conclusion seemed to sunder the web of time itself. Germans remember the moment of their surrender on May 7, 1945, as the *Stunde null*, or "zero hour," when history's clock came to a fearful halt. Elsewhere, even America's main wartime partners, Great Britain and the

Franklin Delano Roosevelt, Thirty-second President of the United States

FDR Library

TABLE 35.1 The Comparative Costs of World War II

Country	Military Deaths	Civilian Deaths	Government Expenditures	Damage to Civilian Property
China	2,000,000	7,750,000		
France	250,000	350,000		
Poland	123,000	6,000,000		
USSR	10,000,000	17,000,000	$192 billion	$128 billion
United Kingdom	300,000	60,600	$120 billion	$5 billion
United States	405,399	6*	$317 billion	
Germany (including Austria)	3,500,000	1,600,000	$272 billion	$50–$75 billion
Italy	242,000	60,000	$94 billion	
Japan	2,000,000	650,000		

*In the forty-eight states; additional civilian deaths occurred in Hawaii, Alaska, and the Philippines.

Sources: World War II casualty estimates vary widely. The figures here are largely taken from David M. Kennedy, ed., *The Library of Congress World War II Companion;* I. C. B. Dear, ed., *The Oxford Companion to the Second World War*; Louis L. Snyder, *Historical Guide to World War II*; and John Ellis, *World War II: A Statistical Survey.*

Soviet Union, had paid a far greater price in blood and treasure than the United States. Uniquely among all the belligerents in World War II—perhaps uniquely in the history of warfare—the United States had managed to grow its civilian economy even while waging a hugely costly war. In Germany, Britain, and the Soviet Union, the civilian standard of living had gone down by approximately one-third. In the United States, the civilian economy had actually expanded by 15 percent, preparing the way for phenomenal prosperity in the postwar decades.

And though 405,399 brave American service members died in World War II, proportionate to population American losses were about one-third those of Britain and about one-sixtieth those of the Soviet Union, where some 10 million soldiers and a staggering 17 million civilians perished (see Table 35.1). By glaring contrast, in the forty-eight continental American states that had a star on the flag in 1945, the U.S. civilian death toll due to enemy action was just six persons, all of them the victims of a crude Japanese balloon-borne firebomb that exploded in their faces near the hamlet of Bly, Oregon, on May 5, 1945.

For all the misery that depression and war visited upon the United States, Americans could count their blessings that fortune had spared them the enormous deprivations and horrors that were all too common elsewhere. Yet some observers worried that America was now assuming leadership in a world where the depths of other peoples' wounds and woes could scarcely be imagined.

U.S. Army Center of Military History

German Chancellor Adolf Hitler

V-J Day: Crowds Cheering at Times Square, by Edward Dancig, 1947 Russian-born American artist Edward Dancig captured the feelings of triumph and relief that Americans felt at the end of World War II. His painting shows the V-J (Victory in Japan) Day celebration of August 15, 1945, in New York's Times Square.

D. Wigmore Fine Art Ltd

This complex conflict was the best-fought war in America's history. Though unprepared for it at the outset, the nation was better prepared than for the others, partly because it had begun to buckle on its armor about a year and a half before the war officially began. It was actually fighting German submarines in the Atlantic months before the explosion in the Pacific at Pearl Harbor. In the end the United States showed itself to be resourceful, tough, adaptable—able to accommodate itself to the tactics of an enemy who was relentless and ruthless.

American military leadership proved to be of the highest order. A new crop of war heroes emerged in brilliant generals like Eisenhower, MacArthur, and Marshall (chief of staff) and in imaginative admirals like Nimitz and Spruance. President Roosevelt and Prime Minister Churchill, as kindred spirits, collaborated closely in planning strategy. "It is fun to be in the same decade with you," FDR once cabled Churchill.

Industrial leaders were no less skilled, for marvels of production were performed almost daily. Assembly lines proved as important as battle lines, and victory went again to the side with the most smokestacks. The enemy was almost literally smothered by bayonets, bullets, bazookas, and bombs. Hitler and his Axis co-conspirators had chosen to make war with machines, and the ingenious Yankees could ask for nothing better. They demonstrated again, as they had in World War I, that the American way of war was simply more—more men, more weapons, more machines, more technology, and more money than any enemy could hope to match. From 1940 to 1945, the output of American factories was simply phenomenal. As Winston Churchill remarked, "Nothing succeeds like excess."

Hermann Goering, a Nazi leader, had sneered, "The Americans can't build planes—only electric iceboxes and razor blades." Democracy had given its answer, as the dictators, despite long preparation, were overthrown and discredited. It is true that an unusual amount of direct control was exercised over the individual by the Washington authorities during the war emergency. But the American people preserved their precious liberties without serious impairment.

plasma and "miracle" drugs, notably penicillin. Yet heavy though American losses were, the Soviet allies suffered casualties many times greater—more than 25 million people killed. In grim testimony to the nature of modern warfare, World War II was the first war that killed more civilians than armed combatants (see "Thinking Globally: America and the World in Depression and War: A Study in Contrasts," pp. 822–823).

America was fortunate in emerging with its mainland virtually unscathed. Two Japanese submarines, using shells and bombers, had rather harmlessly attacked the California and Oregon coast, and a few Japanese fire-bomb balloons had drifted across the Pacific, killing six civilians in Oregon. But that was about all. Much of the rest of the world was utterly destroyed and destitute. America alone was untouched and healthy—oiled and muscled like a prize bull, standing astride the world's ruined landscape.

Varying Viewpoints
The Atomic Bombs: Were They Justified?

No episode of the World War II era has provoked sharper controversy than the atomic bombings of Japan in August 1945. Lingering moral misgivings about the nuclear incineration of Hiroshima and Nagasaki have long threatened to tarnish America's crown of military victory. Some critics have accused the United States of racist motives because the bombs were dropped on a nonwhite people. Other commentators note that the Japanese were already reeling on the verge of collapse by 1945, and therefore history's most awful weapons—especially the second bomb, on Nagasaki—were unnecessary to bring the war to a conclusion. Still other scholars, notably Gar Alperovitz, have further charged that the atomic attacks on Hiroshima and Nagasaki were not the last shots of World War II, but the first salvos in the emerging Cold War. Alperovitz argues that President Truman willfully ignored Tokyo's attempts to negotiate a surrender in the summer of 1945 and rejected all alternatives to dropping the bomb because he wanted to intimidate and isolate the Soviet Union. He unleashed his horrible new weapons, so this argument goes, not simply to defeat Japan, but to end the Far Eastern conflict before the Soviets could enter it, and thereby freeze them out of any role in formulating postwar reconstruction policy in Asia.

Each of these accusations has been vigorously rebutted. Richard Rhodes's exhaustive history of the making of the atomic bomb emphasizes that the Anglo-American atomic project began as a race against the Germans, who were known to be actively pursuing a nuclear weapons program. (Unknown to the Americans, Germany effectively terminated its effort in 1942, just as the Anglo-American project went into high gear.) From the outset both British and American planners believed that the bomb, if successful, would be not just another weapon, but *the* ultimate instrument of destruction that would decisively deliver victory into the hands of whoever possessed it. They consequently assumed that it would be used at the earliest possible moment. There is, therefore, no credible reason to conclude that German cities would not have suffered the fate of Hiroshima and Nagasaki if nuclear weapons had become available sooner or if the European phase of the war had lasted longer.

It is true that American intelligence sources in the early summer of 1945 reported that some Japanese statesmen were trying to enlist the still-neutral Russians' good offices to negotiate a surrender. But as R. J. C. Butow's fine-grained study of Japan's decision to surrender demonstrates, it was unclear whether those initiatives had the full backing of the Japanese government. Moreover, the Japanese clung to several unac-

ceptable conditions, including protection for their imperial system of government, the right to disarm and repatriate their own troops, no military occupation of the home islands, no international trials of alleged war criminals, and possible retention of some of their conquered territories. All this flew squarely in the face of America's repeatedly declared intention to settle for nothing less than *unconditional* surrender. As for the Nagasaki bomb (dropped on August 9), Butow also notes that it conclusively dispelled the Japanese government's original assessment that the Hiroshima attack (on August 6) was a one-time-only stunt, with little likelihood of further nuclear strikes to follow. (Even then, some diehard military officers, refusing to acknowledge defeat, tried, on the night of August 14, to storm the Imperial Palace to seize the recording of the emperor's surrender announcement before it could be broadcast the following day.)

Could the use of the atomic bombs have been avoided? Studies by Martin J. Sherwin, Barton J. Bernstein, and McGeorge Bundy have shown that few policymakers at the time seriously asked that question. As Winston Churchill later wrote, "The decision whether or not to use the atomic bomb to compel the surrender of Japan was never even an issue. There was unanimous, automatic, unquestioned agreement around our table; nor did I ever hear the slightest suggestion that we should do otherwise." In fact, the "decision" to use the bomb was not made in 1945, but in 1942, when the United States committed itself to a crash program to build—and use—a nuclear weapon as swiftly as possible. Intimidating the Soviets might have been a "bonus" to using the bomb against Japan, but influencing Soviet behavior was never the *primary* reason for the fateful decision. American leaders wanted to end the war as soon as possible. To that end they had always assumed the atomic bomb would be dropped as soon as it was available. That moment came on August 6, 1945.

Doubt and remorse about the atomic conclusion of World War II have plagued the American conscience ever since. Less often remarked on are the deaths of four times more Japanese noncombatants than died at Hiroshima and Nagasaki in the so-called conventional firebombing of some five dozen Japanese cities in 1945. Those deaths suggest that the deeper moral question should perhaps be addressed not to the particular technology of nuclear weaponry and the fate of those two unfortunate Japanese cities, but to the quite deliberate decision, made by several combatants—including the Germans, the British, the Americans, and the Japanese themselves—to designate civilian populations as legitimate military targets.

Chapter Review

KEY TERMS

ABC-1 agreement (791)

Executive Order
No. 9066 (792)

War Production Board
(WPB) (802)

Office of Price Administration (OPA) (802)

National War Labor Board
(NWLB) (802)

Smith-Connally Anti-Strike
Act (803)

WACs (Women's Army
Corps) (803)

WAVES (Women Accepted
for Volunteer Emergency
Service) (803)

SPARs (U.S. Coast Guard
Women's Reserve) (803)

Bracero program (803)

Fair Employment Practices
Commission (FEPC) (805)

Congress of Racial Equality
(CORE) (806)

code talkers (806)

Midway, Battle of (809)

D-Day (813)

V-E (Victory in Europe)
Day (818)

Potsdam conference (820)

Manhattan Project (820)

V-J (Victory in Japan)
Day (821)

PEOPLE TO KNOW

Douglas MacArthur

Chester Nimitz

Dwight D. "Ike" Eisenhower

Harry S Truman

Albert Einstein

CHRONOLOGY

1941
United States declares war on Japan
Germany declares war on United States
Randolph plans black march on
Washington
Fair Employment Practices Commission
(FEPC) established
Roosevelt delivers "Four Freedoms" speech

1942
Japanese Americans sent to internment
camps
Japan conquers the Philippines
Battle of the Coral Sea
Battle of Midway
United States invades North Africa
Congress of Racial Equality (CORE)
founded

1943
Allies hold Casablanca conference
Allies invade Italy
Smith-Connally Anti-Strike Act
"Zoot-suit" riots in Los Angeles
Race riot in Detroit
Japanese driven from Guadalcanal
Tehran conference

1944
Korematsu v. *U.S.*
D-Day invasion of France
Battle of the Marianas
Roosevelt defeats Dewey for presidency

1944–1945 Battle of the Bulge

1945
Roosevelt dies; Truman assumes presidency
Germany surrenders
Battles of Iwo Jima and Okinawa
Potsdam conference
Atomic bombs dropped on Hiroshima and
Nagasaki
Yalta conference
Japan surrenders

TO LEARN MORE

Kai Bird and Martin J. Sherwin, *American Prometheus: The Triumph and Tragedy of J. Robert Oppenheimer* (2005)

John M. Blum, *V Was for Victory: Politics and American Culture During World War II* (1976)

Roger Daniels, *Prisoners Without Trial: Japanese Americans in World War II* (1993)

Norman Davies, *No Simple Victory: World War II in Europe, 1939–1945* (2007)

John W. Dower, *War Without Mercy: Race and Power in the Pacific War* (1986)

Sherna Gluck, *Rosie the Riveter Revisited: Women, the War, and Social Change* (1988)

David M. Kennedy, *Freedom from Fear: The American People in Depression and War, 1929–1945* (1999)

Kevin Allen Leonard, *The Battle for Los Angeles: Racial Ideology and World War II* (2006)

Nelson Lichtenstein, *Labor's War at Home: The CIO in World War II* (1982)

Sean L. Malloy, *Atomic Tragedy: Henry L. Stimson and the Decision to Use the Bomb against Japan* (2008)

Richard Rhodes, *The Making of the Atomic Bomb* (1986)

Ronald H. Spector, *Eagle Against the Sun: The American War with Japan* (1985)

Ronald T. Takaki, *Double Victory: A Multicultural History of America in World War II* (2000)

Isabel Wilkerson, *The Warmth of Other Suns: The Epic Story of America's Great Migration* (2010)

A complete, annotated bibliography for this chapter—along with brief descriptions of the People to Know—may be found on the American Pageant website. The Key Terms are defined in a Glossary at the end of the text.

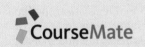

Go to the CourseMate website at **www.cengagebrain.com** for additional study tools and review materials—including audio and video clips—for this chapter.

AP® Review Questions for Chapter 35

1. What was the fundamental strategic decision of World War II that was made by President Roosevelt and British prime minister Churchill at the very beginning of the war?
   (A) Roosevelt and Churchill decided to plan for a second front in Western Europe as soon as possible.
   (B) Roosevelt and Churchill chose to force Italy out of the war first by immediately attacking the soft underbelly of Europe.
   (C) Roosevelt and Churchill decided to arouse the American people to support an idealistic Wilsonian crusade for democracy.
   (D) Roosevelt and Churchill prioritized the war in Europe and placed the Pacific war against Japan on the back burner.
   (E) Roosevelt and Churchill agreed to fight an equally vigorous naval war against Japan and a land war against Germany and Italy.

2. All of the following were true of the experience of Japanese Americans in the United States during World War II EXCEPT that
   (A) Japanese Americans, concentrated on the West Coast, were forcibly relocated into internment camps in America during the course of World War II.
   (B) millions of dollars of property and monetary assets belonging to Japanese Americans were seized and expropriated by the U.S. government during World War II.
   (C) many Japanese Americans demonstrated their loyalty to the United States and bravery on the battlefield fighting on behalf of America during World War II.
   (D) German American and Italian American citizens received much harsher treatment from the U.S government than did Japanese American citizens of the United States.
   (E) near the conclusion of World War II, the U.S. Supreme Court declared internment of Japanese Americans to be unconstitutional and ordered them freed from internment camps.

3. How was inflation kept in check by the U.S. government despite the demands of the wartime economy?
   (A) The U.S government directed production to whatever goods were in most demand.
   (B) The U.S. government prosecuted war profiteers and black marketers who tried to earn windfall profits.
   (C) The U.S. government permitted large numbers of illegal migrants to enter the work force.
   (D) The U.S. government sharply constricted the flow of credit from the Federal Reserve Board.
   (E) The U.S. government imposed wage and price controls throughout the U.S. economy.

4. All of the following characterized labor relations with business and government during World War II EXCEPT
   (A) a substantial increase in union membership.
   (B) several strikes by the United Mine Workers that periodically disrupted coal production.
   (C) congressional passage of a federal law authorizing the federal government to seize and operate any industry paralyzed by union strikes.
   (D) relatively few work stoppages undertaken by organized labor, particularly compared with their counterparts in Britain.
   (E) a takeover by radical elements in several prominent labor unions to demand an end to government-dictated wage ceilings.

5. What was one outcome of the employment of more than 6 million women in American industry during World War II?
   (A) The passage of congressional legislation that guaranteed equal pay for men and women
   (B) A greater percentage of American women being employed in war industries than anywhere else in the world
   (C) The wartime establishment of child-care centers by the government
   (D) Employers and unions encouraging women to remain in the labor force at the war's end
   (E) A majority of women war workers remaining in the labor force at the war's conclusion

6. All of the following characterized the experience of African Americans during World War II EXCEPT
   (A) fighting in integrated combat units.
   (B) rallying behind the "Double V" slogan (victory over dictators abroad and racism at home).
   (C) migrating to northern and western cities in large numbers.
   (D) forming a new civil rights organization, the Congress of Racial Equality (CORE).
   (E) serving with distinction in the Army Air Corps.

7. What crucial strategic mistake did the Japanese make in 1942 that doomed their attempt to control most of the Pacific?
   (A) The Japanese failed to take the Philippines.
   (B) The Japanese unsuccessfully attacked the oil-rich Dutch East Indies.
   (C) The Japanese overextended themselves at Midway and in the Battle of the Coral Sea instead of digging in and consolidating their previous gains.
   (D) The Japanese sent their submarine force on a suicide mission at the battle of Corregidor.
   (E) The Japanese attacked Alaska and Australia.

8. Which of the following best characterizes the primary U.S. strategy in its war against Japan?
   (A) The United States invaded Japanese strongholds in Southeast Asia such as British Malaya.
   (B) The United States launched heavy bombings of Japan from Chinese air bases.
   (C) The United States fortified China by transporting supplies from India over the Himalayan hump.
   (D) The United States engaged in island hopping across the South Pacific, while bypassing Japanese strongholds.
   (E) The United States outmaneuvered the Japanese naval flanks in New Guinea and Alaska.

9. Which of the following is NOT true about the European theater of war from 1941 to 1945?
   (A) Until spring 1943, probably Hitler's greatest hope for defeating Britain and winning the war was that German U-boats would destroy Allied shipping.
   (B) Hitler's advance in the European theater of war crested beginning with the Battle of Stalingrad in the fall and winter of 1942–1943, after which Nazi Germany's fortunes gradually declined.
   (C) As a substitute for opening a major second front in France, the Americans and British decided to attack Hitler's forces first in North Africa and Italy.
   (D) President Roosevelt fulfilled his promise to the Soviets to open a second front in Western Europe by the end of 1942.
   (E) One key impact of the Allied Italian front was that it probably delayed the D-Day invasion and allowed the Soviet Union to advance further into Eastern Europe.

10. What effect did Roosevelt's and Churchill's declaration in January 1942 that the Allies would demand the absolute and unconditional surrender of Germany have on the ultimate course of the war?
    (A) It guaranteed that Germany would have to be totally reconstructed and politically reorganized after the war.
    (B) It clearly shortened the duration of the war.
    (C) It may have prevented a separate peace from being struck between Hitler and Stalin.
    (D) It encouraged anti-Hitler resisters in Germany to try to overthrow the Nazis.
    (E) It steeled the resolve of Mussolini and fascist Italian forces to continue to resist the Allies until 1945.

11. What was the most significant development in the Democratic convention of 1944?
    (A) Roosevelt's third-term liberal vice president, Henry Wallace, was dumped by Roosevelt in favor of Senator Harry Truman.
    (B) Roosevelt's appearance at the Democratic convention revealed how physically frail he was.
    (C) Party leaders developed a campaign that downplayed the New Deal's success.
    (D) There was growing Democratic resistance to Roosevelt's pursuit of a fourth term.
    (E) The issue of civil rights came to the fore as the dominant concern of the party.

12. What was the outcome of the Potsdam conference in July 1945?
    (A) The political fate of Eastern Europe was determined by President Truman, Joseph Stalin, and the British leaders.
    (B) France and China were brought into the conference as part of the Big Five.
    (C) It was concluded that the Soviet Union would enter the war in the Pacific.
    (D) It was Franklin Roosevelt's last wartime meeting with Churchill and Stalin.
    (E) An ultimatum was issued to Japan to surrender or be destroyed.

13. Historians have offered all of the following scholarly criticisms of the momentous decision to drop the atomic bombs on Nagasaki and Hiroshima EXCEPT that
    (A) cultural racism against a nonwhite people on the part of American leaders propelled the decision-making process concerning the dropping of the atomic bombs on Japan.
    (B) the Japanese were already reeling and close to collapsing by August 1945, making the dropping of the atomic bombs unnecessary.
    (C) the dropping of the atomic bombs on Hiroshima and Nagasaki was aimed at developing strategic leverage over the Soviet Union in the emerging Cold War.
    (D) the United States' insistence on accepting nothing less than unconditional surrender ignored the very real possibility of negotiating a Japanese surrender through Russian mediation.
    (E) vigorous dissent from high levels of the American government was ignored and repudiated by President Truman.

14. World War II integrated Native Americans into daily life and the war effort in all of the following ways EXCEPT
    (A) working in war industries.
    (B) joining the military.
    (C) being appointed to government offices.
    (D) moving off of reservations and into cities.
    (E) transmitting messages as "code talkers."

15. One way in which World War II affected the United States and its allies differently was that
    (A) the U.S. economy prospered while its allies suffered financially.
    (B) the United States, unlike its allies, suffered thousands of civilian deaths.
    (C) American citizens failed to support the war or aid the troops.
    (D) Britain and the USSR fought wars on two fronts while the United States focused on one.
    (E) the United States was unwilling to demand unconditional surrender from its enemies.

Part Six

Making Modern America

1945 to the Present

World War II broke the back of the Great Depression in the United States and also ended the century-and-a-half-old American tradition of isolationism in foreign affairs. Alone among the warring powers, the United States managed to emerge from the great conflict physically unscarred, economically healthy, and diplomatically strengthened. Yet if Americans faced a world full of promise at the war's end, it was also a world full of dangers, none more disconcerting than Soviet communism. These two themes of promise and menace mingled uneasily throughout the nearly five decades of the Cold War era, from the end of World War II in 1945 to the collapse of the Soviet Union in 1991.

At home unprecedented prosperity in the postwar quarter-century nourished a robust sense of national self-confidence and fed a revolution of rising expectations. Invigorated by the prospect of endlessly spreading affluence, Americans in the 1940s, 1950s, and 1960s had record numbers of babies, aspired to ever-higher standards of living, generously expanded the welfare state (especially for the elderly), widened opportunities for women, welcomed immigrants, and even found the will to grapple at long last with the nation's grossest legacy of injustice, its treatment of African Americans. With the exception of Dwight Eisenhower's presidency in the 1950s, Americans elected liberal Democratic presidents (Harry Truman in 1948, John F. Kennedy in 1960, and Lyndon Johnson in 1964). The Democratic party, the party of the liberal New Deal at home and of an activist foreign policy abroad, comfortably remained the nation's majority party. Americans trusted their government and had faith in the American dream that their children would lead a richer life than their parents had done. Anything and everything seemed possible.

The rising curve of ascending expectations, propelled by exploding economic growth, bounded upward throughout the 1950s. It peaked in the 1960s, an exceptionally stormy decade during which faith in government, in the wisdom of American foreign policy, and in the American dream itself, began to sour. Lyndon Johnson's "Great Society" reforms, billed as the completion of the unfinished work of the New Deal, foundered on the rocks of fiscal limitations and stubborn racial

A Suburban Society   In the phenomenally affluent post-WWII years, newly prosperous Americans flocked to spanking-new suburban housing developments. By the twentieth century's end, a majority of Americans were suburbanites. J. R. Eyerman/Time & Life Pictures/Getty Images

resentments. Johnson, the most ambitious reformer in the White House since Franklin Roosevelt, eventually saw his presidency destroyed by the furies unleashed over the Vietnam War.

When economic growth flattened in the 1970s, the horizon of hopes for the future seemed to vanish as well. The nation entered a frustrating period of stalled expectations, increasingly rancorous racial tensions, disillusion with government, and political stalemate. Yet in one important arena progress continued. As "second-wave feminism" gathered steam, women burst through barriers that had long excluded them from traditional male domains from the factory floor and U.S. Army to the Ivy League.

Beginning in 1968, Americans stopped sending New Deal–style liberals to the White House, electing moderate Republicans (Richard Nixon in 1968 and 1972, succeeded by the unelected Gerald Ford after Watergate), moderate southern Democrats (Jimmy Carter in 1976 and Bill Clinton in 1992 and 1996), and conservative Republicans (Ronald Reagan in 1980 and 1984, George H. W. Bush in 1992, and George W. Bush in 2000 and 2004). Throughout these years, Democrats usually remained in control of both houses of Congress, until the "Republican revolution" of 1994 put a new generation of conservative legislators in power. Only with popular discontent over the Iraq War did the Democrats narrowly regain control of both houses in 2006, and the White House in 2008, with the election of the nation's first African American president, Barack Obama. Then in 2010 newly energized conservative Republicans once again won a majority of seats in the House, and political gridlock ensued. As the twenty-first century lengthened, the nation seemed increasingly polarized, unable to reconcile progressive ambitions for more social provision and economic and environmental regulation with conservative demands for lower taxes and smaller government.

Abroad the fierce competition with the Soviet Union, and after 1949 with communist China as well, colored almost every aspect of America's foreign relations and shaped domestic life, too. Unreasoning fear of communists at home unleashed the destructive force of McCarthyism in the 1950s—a modern-day witch hunt in which careers were capsized and lives ruined by reckless accusations of communist sympathizing. The FBI encroached on

The End of an Era? As surely as victory in World War II restored confidence and prosperity to a people demoralized by the Great Depression, the terrorist attacks of September 11, 2001, struck electric fear into the American people—and menaced their historical commitment to an open society and individual liberties. Photo by Spencer Platt/ Getty Images

sacred American liberties in its zeal to uncover communist "subversives."

The Cold War remained cold, in the sense that no shooting conflict broke out between the great-power rivals. But the United States did fight two shooting wars in the Cold War era, in Korea in the 1950s and Vietnam in the 1960s. Vietnam, the only foreign war in which the United States has ever been defeated, cruelly convulsed American society, ending not only Lyndon Johnson's presidency but the thirty-five-year era of the Democratic party's political dominance as well. Vietnam also touched off the most vicious inflationary cycle in American history, and embittered and disillusioned an entire generation.

Uncle Sam in the Cold War era built a fearsome—and expensive—arsenal of nuclear weapons, great air and missile fleets to deliver them, a two-ocean navy, and, for a time, a large army raised by conscription. When the Cold War ended, Americans turned to the promise of an information age in a global economy. But terrorist attacks on American soil in 2001 shifted the country's attention back to national defense and international military strategy, launching two wars (in Iraq and Afghanistan) and fundamentally transforming both foreign and domestic politics. The "Great Recession" that walloped the global economy in 2008 and hit America with special force further intensified partisan divisions and perhaps spelled an end to an era of expanding personal opportunity, government-sponsored social provision, and American global hegemony.

Chapter 36

The Cold War Begins

1945–1952

The United States stand at this moment at the summit of the world.

WINSTON CHURCHILL, 1945

*T*he *American people,* 140 million strong, cheered their nation's victories in Europe and Asia at the conclusion of World War II. But before the shouting had even faded, many Americans began to worry about their future. Four fiery years of global war had not entirely driven from their minds the painful memories of twelve desperate years of the Great Depression. Still more ominously, victory celebrations had barely ended before America's crumbling relations with its wartime ally, the Soviet Union, threatened a new and even more terrible international conflict.

✯ Postwar Economic Anxieties

The decade of the 1930s had left deep scars. Joblessness and insecurity had pushed up the suicide rate and dampened the marriage rate. Babies went unborn as pinched budgets and sagging self-esteem wrought a sexual depression in American bedrooms. The war had banished the blight of depression, but would the respite last? Grim-faced observers were warning that the war had only temporarily lifted the pall of economic stagnation and that peace would bring the return of hard times. Homeward-bound GIs, so the gloomy predictions ran, would step out of the army's chow lines and back into the breadlines of the unemployed.

The faltering economy in the initial postwar years threatened to confirm the worst predictions of the doomsayers who foresaw another Great Depression. Real gross national product (GNP) slumped sickeningly in 1946 and 1947 from its wartime peak. With the removal of wartime price controls, prices giddily levitated by 33 percent in 1946–1947. An epidemic of strikes swept the country. During 1946 alone some 4.6 million laborers laid down their tools, fearful that soon they could barely afford the autos and other goods they were manufacturing.

The growing muscle of organized labor deeply annoyed many conservatives. They had their revenge against labor's New Deal gains in 1947, when a Republican-controlled Congress (the first in fourteen years) passed the **Taft-Hartley Act** over President Truman's vigorous veto. Labor leaders condemned the Taft-Hartley Act as a "slave-labor law." It outlawed the "closed" (all-union) shop, made unions liable for damages that resulted from jurisdictional disputes among themselves, and required union leaders to take a noncommunist oath.

Taft-Hartley was only one of several obstacles that slowed the growth of organized labor in the years after World War II. In the heady days of the New Deal, unions had spread swiftly in the industrialized Northeast, especially in huge manufacturing industries like steel and automobiles. But labor's postwar efforts to organize in the historically antiunion regions of the South and West proved frustrating. The CIO's **Operation Dixie**, aimed at unionizing southern textile workers and steelworkers, failed miserably in 1948 to overcome lingering fears of racial mixing. And workers in the rapidly growing service sector of the economy—many of them middle-aged women, often working only part-time in small shops, widely separated from one another—proved much more difficult to organize than the thousands of assembly-line workers who in the 1930s had poured into the auto and steel unions.

© Bettmann/Corbis

Going to College on the GI Bill Financed by the federal government, thousands of World War II veterans crowded into college classrooms in the late 1940s. Universities struggled to house these older students, many of whom already had families. Pennsylvania State College resorted to setting up hundreds of trailers.

Union membership would peak in the 1950s and then begin a long, unremitting decline.

The Democratic administration meanwhile took some steps of its own to forestall an economic downturn. It sold war factories and other government installations to private businesses at fire-sale prices. It secured passage of the **Employment Act of 1946**, making it government policy "to promote maximum employment, production, and purchasing power." The act created a three-member Council of Economic Advisers to provide the president with the data and the recommendations to make that policy a reality.

Most dramatic was the passage of the Servicemen's Readjustment Act of 1944—better known as the GI Bill of Rights, or the **GI Bill**. Enacted partly out of fear that the employment markets would never be able to absorb 15 million returning veterans at war's end, the GI Bill made generous provisions for sending the former soldiers to school. In the postwar decade, some 8 million veterans advanced their education at Uncle Sam's expense. The majority attended technical and vocational schools, but colleges and universities were crowded to the blackboards as more than 2 million ex-GIs stormed the halls of higher learning. The total eventually spent for education was some $14.5 billion in taxpayer dollars. The act also enabled the Veterans Administration (VA) to guarantee about $16 billion in loans for veterans to buy homes, farms, and small businesses. By raising educational levels and stimulating the construction industry, the GI Bill powerfully nurtured the robust and long-lived economic expansion that eventually took hold in the late 1940s and that profoundly shaped the entire history of the postwar era.

✬ The Long Economic Boom, 1950–1970

Gross national product began to climb haltingly in 1948. Then, beginning about 1950, the American economy surged onto a dazzling plateau of sustained growth that was to last virtually uninterrupted for two decades. America's economic performance became the envy of the world. National income nearly doubled in the 1950s and almost doubled again in the 1960s, shooting through the trillion-dollar mark in 1973. Americans, some 6 percent of the world's people, were enjoying about 40 percent of the planet's wealth.

Nothing loomed larger in the history of the post–World War II era than this fantastic eruption of affluence. It did not enrich all Americans, and it did not touch all people evenly, but it transformed the lives of a majority of citizens and molded the agenda of politics and society for at least two generations. Prosperity underwrote social mobility; it paved the way for the eventual success of the civil rights movement; it funded vast new welfare programs, like Medicare; and it gave Americans the confidence to exercise unprecedented international leadership in the Cold War era.

As the gusher of postwar prosperity poured forth its riches, Americans drank deeply from the gilded goblet. Millions of depression-pinched souls sought to make up for the sufferings of the 1930s. They determined to "get theirs" while the getting was good. A people who had once considered a chicken in every pot the standard of comfort and security now hungered for two cars in every garage, swimming pools in their backyards, vacation homes, and gas-guzzling recreational vehicles. The size of the "middle class," defined as households earning between $3,000 and $10,000 a year, doubled from pre–Great Depression days and included 60 percent of the American people by the mid-1950s. By the end of that decade, the vast majority of American families owned their own cars and washing machines, and nearly 90 percent owned a television set—a gadget invented in the 1920s but virtually unknown until the late 1940s. In another revolution of sweeping consequences, almost 60 percent of American families owned their own homes by 1960, compared with less than 40 percent in the 1920s.

Of all the beneficiaries of postwar prosperity, none reaped greater rewards than women. More than ever, urban offices and shops provided a bonanza of employment for female workers. The great majority of new jobs created in the postwar era went to women, as the service sector of the economy dramatically outgrew the old industrial and manufacturing sectors. Women accounted for a quarter of the American work force at the end of World War II and for nearly half the labor pool five decades later. Yet even as women continued their march into the workplace in the 1940s and 1950s, popular culture glorified the traditional feminine roles of homemaker and mother. The clash between the demands of suburban housewifery and the realities of employment eventually sparked a feminist revolt in the 1960s.

✦ The Roots of Postwar Prosperity

What propelled this unprecedented economic explosion? The Second World War itself provided a powerful stimulus. While other countries had been ravaged by years of fighting, the United States had used the war crisis to fire up its smokeless factories and rebuild its depression-plagued economy. Invigorated by battle, America had almost effortlessly come to dominate the ruined global landscape of the postwar period.

Ominously, much of the glittering prosperity of the 1950s and 1960s rested on the underpinnings of colossal military budgets, leading some critics to speak of a "permanent war economy" (see Figure 36.1). The economic upturn of 1950 was fueled by massive

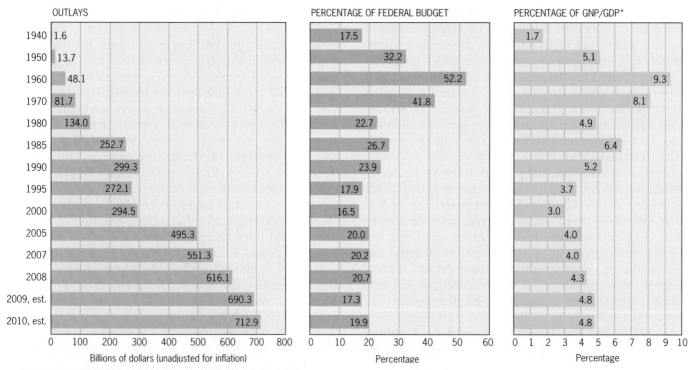

FIGURE 36.1* National Defense Budget, 1940–2010

*Gross *national* product (GNP) was used before 1960. It includes income from overseas investment and excludes profits generated in the United States but accruing to foreign accounts. Gross *domestic* product (GDP), used thereafter, excludes overseas profits owed to American accounts but includes the value of all items originating in the United States, regardless of the destination of the profits. Until recent years those factors made for negligible differences in the calculation of *national* and *domestic* product, but most economists now prefer the latter approach.

(Sources: *Statistical Abstract of the United States, 2010,* from US Office of Management and Budget (Congressional Budget Office), *Budget of the United States Government, Historical Tables,* annual. http://whitehouse.gov/omb/budget/fy2009/budget.html.)

Advertising Prosperity, 1956

This Ford advertisement in a popular magazine encouraged readers to buy a second car. By the mid-1950s, once manufacturers had met the demand for cars, homes, appliances, and other consumer goods that a decade and a half of depression and world war had pent up, they worried about how to keep expanding their markets. "Planned obsolescence"—changing design frequently enough to necessitate replacement purchasing—was one strategy. Altering expectations about what consumers needed was another. This advertisement suggests that the up-to-date family, living in its modern-style suburban home, had no choice but to own two cars, one for the male breadwinner's business, the other for the wife's "ferrying the family." What kinds of gender role prescriptions are reinforced in this advertisement? What assumptions has Ford made about prospective buyers of its cars? How much can mass advertising tell us about the actual values of Americans living at a particular time?

The only problem in posing this picture was getting the two Fords to stand still.

Seven good reasons for two FORDS

To free their family from one-car captivity the Bremers got two Fords: a Country Sedan and a Thunderbird—the car that inspired the styling and performance of all '56 Fords.

"We saw the need for a second car even before our first youngster arrived. If you're married you know why. The five children just made two Fords *more* necessary. I need a car for business. My wife needs one for ferrying the family.

"*Why are they Fords?* In the first place, you can't beat Ford's looks at *twice* the price. You get extra zip in a Ford V-8, too. That's why it's the world's best seller! It's a good investment, too. Nothing at the price keeps its value like a Ford. And, of course, you don't need children to appreciate the extra safety of Ford Lifeguard Design," says Mr. Bremer.

SEE YOUR LOCAL FORD DEALER

The Country Sedan, one of six Ford do-it-alls, has 4-doors, lots of room. And its 202-h.p. V-8 is the most powerful standard "8" in its field.

The Ford Thunderbird inspired the styling for *all* Fords. And you can have its own 225-h.p. Special V-8 in most of them.

Join the 300,000 TWO FORD families!

appropriations for the Korean War, and defense spending accounted for some 10 percent of the GNP throughout the ensuing decade. Pentagon dollars primed the pumps of high-technology industries such as aerospace, plastics, and electronics—areas in which the United States reigned supreme over all foreign competitors. The military budget also financed much scientific research and development ("R and D"—hence the name of one of the most famous "think tanks," the Rand Corporation). More than ever before, unlocking the secrets of nature was the key to unleashing economic growth.

Cheap energy also fed the economic boom. American and European companies controlled the flow of abundant petroleum from the sandy expanses of the Middle East, and they kept prices low. Americans doubled their consumption of inexpensive and seemingly inexhaustible oil in the quarter-century after the war. Anticipating a limitless future of low-cost fuels, they flung out endless ribbons of highways, installed air-conditioning in their homes, and engineered a sixfold increase in the country's electricity-generating capacity between 1945 and 1970. Spidery grids of electrical cables carried the pent-up power of oil, gas, coal, and falling water to activate the tools of workers on the factory floor.

With the forces of nature increasingly harnessed in their hands, workers chalked up spectacular gains in productivity—the amount of output per hour of work. In the two decades after the outbreak of the Korean War in 1950, productivity increased at an average rate of more than 3 percent per year. Gains in productivity were also enhanced by the rising educational level of the work force. By 1970 nearly 90 percent of the school-age population was enrolled in educational institutions—a dramatic contrast with the opening years of the century, when only half of this age group had attended school. Better educated and better equipped, American workers in 1970 could produce nearly twice as much in an hour's labor as they had in 1950. Productivity was the key to prosperity. Rising productivity in the 1950s and 1960s virtually doubled the average American's standard of living in the postwar quarter-century.

Also contributing to the vigor of the postwar economy were some momentous changes in the nation's basic economic structure. Conspicuous was the accelerating shift of the work force out of agriculture, which achieved productivity gains virtually unmatched by any other economic sector. The family farm nearly became an antique artifact as consolidation produced giant agribusinesses able to employ costly machinery. Thanks largely to mechanization and to rich new fertilizers—as well as to government subsidies and price supports—one farmworker by the century's end could produce food for over fifty people, compared with about fifteen people in the 1940s. Farmers whose

Agribusiness Expensive machinery of the sort shown here made most of American agriculture a capital-intensive, phenomenally productive big business by the twenty-first century—and sounded the death knell for many small-scale family farms.

forebears had busted sod with oxen or horses now plowed their fields in air-conditioned tractor cabs, listening on their stereophonic radios to weather forecasts or the latest Chicago commodities market quotations. Once the mighty backbone of the agricultural Republic, and still some 15 percent of the labor force at the end of World War II, farmers made up a slim 2 percent of working Americans by the turn of the twenty-first century—yet they fed much of the world.

✪ The Smiling Sunbelt

The convulsive economic changes of the post-1945 period shook and shifted the American people, amplifying the population redistribution set in motion by World War II. As immigrants and westward-trekking pioneers, Americans had always been a people on the move, but they were astonishingly footloose in the postwar years. For some three decades after 1945, an average of 30 million people changed residences every year. Families especially felt the strain, as distance divided parents from children, and brothers and sisters from one another. One sign of this sort of stress was the phenomenal popularity of advice books on child-rearing, especially Dr. Benjamin Spock's *The Common Sense Book of Baby and Child Care*. First published in 1945, it instructed millions of parents during the ensuing decades in the kind of homely wisdom that was once transmitted naturally from grandparent to parent, and from parent to child. In fluid postwar neighborhoods, friendships were also hard to sustain. Mobility could exact a high human cost in loneliness and isolation.

Especially striking was the growth of the **Sunbelt**—a fifteen-state area stretching in a smiling crescent from Virginia through Florida and Texas to Arizona and California. This region increased its population at a rate nearly double that of the old industrial zones of the Northeast (the "Frostbelt"). In the 1950s California alone accounted for one-fifth of the entire nation's population growth and by 1963 had outdistanced New York as the most populous state—a position it still holds in the early years of the twenty-first century, with more than 36 million people, or more than one out of every eight Americans.

The South and Southwest were a new frontier for Americans after World War II. These modern pioneers came in search of jobs, a better climate, and lower taxes. Jobs they found in abundance, especially in the California electronics industry, in the aerospace complexes in Florida and Texas, and in the huge military installations that powerful southern congressional representatives secured for their districts (see Map 36.1).

A Niagara of federal dollars accounted for much of the Sunbelt's prosperity, though, ironically, southern and western politicians led the cry against government spending. By the early twenty-first century, states in the South and West were annually receiving some $444 billion more in federal funds than those in the Northeast and Midwest. A new economic war between the states seemed to be shaping up. Northeasterners and their allies from the hard-hit heavy-industry region of the Ohio Valley (the "Rustbelt") tried to rally political support with the sarcastic slogan "The North shall rise again."

These dramatic shifts of population and wealth further broke the historic grip of the North on the nation's political life. Every elected occupant of the White House from 1964 to 2008 hailed from the Sunbelt, and the region's congressional representation rose as its population grew.

✦ The Rush to the Suburbs

In all regions America's modern migrants—if they were white—fled from the cities to the burgeoning new suburbs (see "Makers of America: The Suburbanites," pp. 836–837). While other industrial countries struggled to rebuild their war-ravaged cities, government policies in the United States encouraged movement away from urban centers. Federal Housing Administration (FHA) and Veterans Administration (VA) home-loan guarantees made it more economically attractive to own a home in the suburbs than to rent an apartment in the city. Tax deductions for interest payments on home mortgages provided additional financial incentive. And government-built highways that sped commuters from suburban homes to city jobs further facilitated this mass migration. By 1960 one in every four Americans

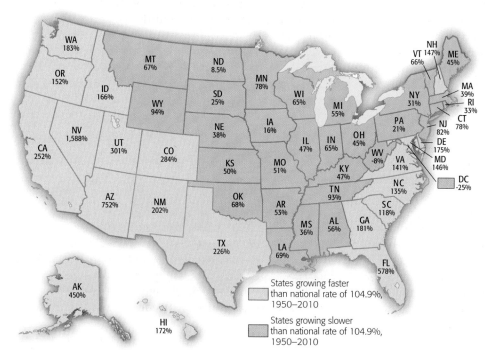

MAP 36.1 Distribution of Population Increase, 1950–2008 States with figures higher than 102 percent were growing faster than the national average between 1950 and 2008. Note that much of the growth was in the "Sunbelt," a loose geographical concept, as some Deep South states had very little population growth, whereas the mountain and Pacific states were booming. (Sources: *Statistical Abstract of the United States* and U.S. Census, relevant years.) © Cengage Learning

Few images evoke more vividly the prosperity of the postwar era than aerial photographs of sprawling suburbs. Neat rows of look-alike tract houses, each with a driveway and lawn and here and there a backyard swimming pool, came to symbolize the capacity of the economy to deliver the "American dream" to millions of families.

Suburbanization was hardly new. Well-off city dwellers had beaten paths to leafy outlying neighborhoods since the nineteenth century. But after 1945 the steady flow became a stampede. The baby boom, new highways, government guarantees for mortgage lending, and favorable tax policies all made suburbia blossom.

Who were the Americans racing to the new postwar suburbs? War veterans led the way in the late 1940s, aided by Veterans Administration mortgages that featured tiny down payments and low interest rates. The general public soon followed. The Federal Housing Administration (FHA) offered insured mortgages with low down payments and 2 to 3 percent interest rates on thirty-year loans. With deals like this, it was hardly surprising that American families flocked into "Levittowns," built by William and Alfred Levitt, and other similar suburban developments.

People of all kinds found their way to suburbia, heading for neighborhoods that varied from the posh to the plain. Yet for all this diversity, the overwhelming majority of suburbanites were white and middle-class. In 1967 sociologist Herbert Gans published *The Levittowners*, based on his own move to a Levitt-built community outside Philadelphia. He described suburban families in tract developments as predominantly third- or fourth-generation Americans with some college education and at least two children.

Men tended to work in either white-collar jobs or upper-level blue-collar positions such as foremen. Women usually worked in the home, so much so that suburbia came to symbolize the domestic confinement that feminists in the 1960s and 1970s decried in their campaign for women's rights.

The house itself became more important than ever as postwar suburbanites built their leisure lives around television, home improvement projects, and barbecues on the patio. The center of family life shifted to the fenced-in backyard, as neighborly city habits of visiting on the front stoop, gabbing on the sidewalk, and strolling to local stores disappeared. Institutions that had thrived as social centers in the city—churches, women's clubs, fraternal organizations, and taverns—had a tougher time attracting patrons in the privatized world of postwar suburbia.

Life in the suburbs was a boon to the automobile, as parents jumped behind the wheel to shuttle children, groceries, and golf clubs to and fro. The second car, once an unheard-of luxury, became a practical "necessity" for suburban families constantly "on the go." A car culture sprang up with new destinations, like drive-thru restaurants and drive-in movies. Roadside shopping centers edged out downtowns as places to shop. Meanwhile, the new interstate highway system enabled breadwinners to live farther and farther from their jobs and still commute to work daily.

Many suburbanites continued to depend on cities for jobs, though by the 1980s the suburbs themselves became important sites of employment. Wherever they worked, suburbanites turned their backs on the city and its problems. They fought to maintain their communities as secluded retreats, independent municipalities with their own taxes, schools, and zoning restrictions designed to keep out public housing and the poor. Even the naming of towns and streets reflected a pastoral ideal. Poplar Terrace and Mountainview Drive were popular street names; East Paterson, New Jersey, was renamed Elmwood Park in 1973. With a majority of Americans living in suburbs by the 1980s, cities lost their political clout. Bereft of state and federal aid, cit-

Drive-in Café in Los Angeles, the Mother and Model of All Suburbias

Aerial View of the On-ramps to a Typical New Interstate Highway, 1950s

ies festered with worsening social problems: poverty, drug addiction, and crime.

Middle-class African Americans began to move to the suburbs in substantial numbers by the 1980s, but even that migration failed to alter dramatically the racial divide of metropolitan America. Black suburbanites settled in towns like Rolling Oaks outside Miami or Brook Glen near Atlanta—black middle-class towns in white-majority counties. By the end of the twentieth century, suburbia as a whole was more racially diverse than at midcentury. But old patterns of urban "white flight" and residential segregation endured.

Buyers Line Up for a Levittown Home, 1951   Mass construction techniques and a New Deal-inspired revolution in home mortgage financing made first-time homeowners out of millions of Americans in the post-World War II years.

dwelt in suburbia, and a half-century later, more than half the nation's population did.

The construction industry boomed in the 1950s and 1960s to satisfy this demand. Pioneered by innovators like the Levitt brothers, whose first **Levittown** sprouted on New York's Long Island in the 1940s, builders revolutionized the techniques of home construction. Erecting hundreds or even thousands of dwellings in a single project, specialized crews working from standardized plans laid foundations, while others raised factory-assembled framing modules, put on roofs, strung wires, installed plumbing, and finished the walls in record time and with cost-cutting efficiency. Snooty critics wailed about the aesthetic monotony of the suburban "tract" developments, but eager home buyers nevertheless moved into them by the millions.

"White flight" to the leafy green suburbs left the inner cities—especially those in the Northeast and Midwest—black, brown, and broke. Migrating blacks from the South filled up the urban neighborhoods that were abandoned by the departing white middle class (see "Makers of America: The Great African American Migration," pp. 870–871). In effect, the incoming blacks imported the grinding poverty of the rural South into the inner cores of northern cities. Taxpaying businesses fled with their affluent customers from downtown shops to suburban shopping malls (another post–World War II invention).

Government policies sometimes aggravated this spreading pattern of residential segregation. FHA administrators, citing the "risk" of making loans to blacks and other "unharmonious racial or nationality groups," often refused them mortgages for private home purchases, thus limiting black mobility out of the inner cities and driving many minorities into public housing projects. Even public housing programs frequently followed a so-called neighborhood composition rule, which effectively built housing for blacks in neighborhoods that were already identified as predominantly black—thus solidifying racial separation.

✹ The Postwar Baby Boom

Of all the upheavals in postwar America, none was more dramatic than the **baby boom**—the huge leap in the birthrate in the decade and a half after 1945. Confident young men and women tied the nuptial knot in record numbers at war's end, and they began immediately to fill the nation's empty cradles. They thus touched off a demographic explosion that added more than 50 million bawling babies to the nation's population by the end of the 1950s. The soaring birthrate finally crested in 1957 and was followed by a deepening birth dearth. By 1973 fertility rates had dropped below the point necessary to maintain existing population figures without further immigration.

This boom-or-bust cycle of births begot a bulging wave along the American population curve. As the oversize postwar generation grew to maturity, it was destined—like the fabled pig passing through the python—to strain and distort many aspects of American life. Elementary-school enrollments, for example, swelled to nearly 34 million pupils in 1970. Then began a steady decline, as the onward-marching age group left in its wake closed schools and unemployed teachers.

The maturing babies of the postwar boom sent economic shock waves undulating through the decades. As tykes and toddlers in the 1940s and 1950s, they made up a lucrative market for manufacturers of canned food and other baby products. As teenagers in the 1960s, the same youngsters spent an estimated $20 billion a year for clothes and recorded rock music—and their sheer numbers laid the basis of the much-ballyhooed "youth culture" of that tumultuous decade. In the 1970s the consumer tastes of the aging baby boomers changed again, and the most popular jeans maker began marketing pants with a fuller cut for those former "kids" who could no longer squeeze into their size-thirty Levi's. In the 1980s the horde of baby boomers bumped and jostled one another in the job market, struggling to get a foothold on the crowded ladder of social mobility. As the boomers entered middle age, a "secondary boom" of children peaked in the early 1990s—a faint demographic echo of the postwar population explosion. The impact of the huge postwar generation will continue to ripple through American society well into the twenty-first century, when its members pass eventually into retirement, placing enormous strains on the Social Security system.

✹ Truman: The "Gutty" Man from Missouri

Presiding over the opening of the postwar period was an "accidental president"—Harry S Truman. "The moon, the stars, and all the planets" had fallen on him, he remarked when he was called upon to shoulder the dead Roosevelt's awesome burdens of leadership. Trim and owlishly bespectacled, with his graying hair and friendly, toothy grin, Truman was called "the average man's average man." Even his height—five feet eight inches—was average. The first president in many years without a college education, he had farmed, served as an artillery officer in France during World War I, and failed as a haberdasher. He then tried his hand at precinct-level Missouri politics, through which he rose from a judgeship to the U.S. Senate. Though a protégé of a notorious political machine in Kansas City, he had managed to keep his own hands clean.

The problems of the postwar period were staggering, and the suddenly burdened new president at first approached his tasks with humility. But gradually he evolved from a shrinking pipsqueak into a scrappy little cuss, gaining confidence to the point of cockiness. When the Soviet foreign minister complained, "I have never been talked to like that in my life," Truman shot back, "Carry out your agreements and you won't get talked to like that." Truman later boasted, "I gave him the one-two, right to the jaw."

A smallish man thrust suddenly into a giant job, Truman permitted designing old associates of the "Missouri gang" to gather around him and, like Grant, was stubbornly loyal to them when they were caught with cream on their whiskers. On occasion he would send critics hot-tempered and profane "s.o.b." letters. Most troubling, in trying to demonstrate to a skeptical public his decisiveness and power of command, he was inclined to go off half-cocked or stick mulishly to a wrongheaded notion. "To err is Truman," cynics jibed.

But if he was sometimes small in the small things, he was often big in the big things. He had down-home authenticity, few pretensions, rock-solid probity, and a lot of that old-fashioned character trait called moxie. Not one to dodge responsibility, he placed a sign on his White House desk that read, "The buck stops here." Among his favorite sayings was "If you can't stand the heat, get out of the kitchen."

✴ Yalta: Bargain or Betrayal?

Vast and silent, the Soviet Union continued to be the great enigma. The conference at Tehran in 1943, where Roosevelt first met Joseph Stalin man to man, had cleared the air somewhat, but much remained unresolved—especially questions about the postwar fates of Germany, Eastern Europe, and Asia.

The **Yalta conference**, the final fateful conference of the Big Three, took place in February 1945. At this former tsarist resort on the relatively warm shores of the Black Sea, Stalin, Churchill, and the fast-failing Roosevelt reached momentous agreements, after pledging their faith with vodka. Final plans were laid for smashing the buckling German lines and assigning occupation zones in Germany to the victorious powers. Stalin agreed that Poland, with revised boundaries, should have a representative government based on free elections—a pledge he soon broke. Bulgaria and Romania were likewise to have free elections—a promise also flouted. The Big Three further announced plans for fashioning a new international peacekeeping organization—the United Nations.

Of all the grave decisions at Yalta, the most controversial concerned the Far East. The atomic bomb had not yet been tested, and Washington strategists expected frightful American casualties in the projected assault on Japan. From Roosevelt's standpoint it seemed highly desirable that Stalin should enter the Asian war,

The Big Three From left to right, Churchill, Roosevelt, and Stalin sit somberly at their fateful meeting at Yalta in February 1945. Roosevelt was only weeks away from death.

Granger Collection

pin down Japanese troops in Manchuria and Korea, and lighten American losses. But Soviet casualties had already been enormous, and Moscow presumably needed inducements to bring it into the Far Eastern conflagration.

Horse trader Stalin was in a position at Yalta to exact a high price. He agreed to attack Japan within three months after the collapse of Germany, and he later redeemed this pledge in full. In return, the Soviets were promised the southern half of Sakhalin Island, lost by Russia to Japan in 1905, and Japan's Kurile Islands as well. The Soviet Union was also granted joint control over the railroads of China's Manchuria and special privileges in the two key seaports of that area, Dairen and Port Arthur. These concessions evidently would give Stalin control over vital industrial centers of America's weakening Chinese ally.

As it turned out, Moscow's muscle was not necessary to knock out Japan. Critics charged that Roosevelt had sold Jiang Jieshi (Chiang Kai-shek) down the river when he conceded control of Manchuria to Stalin. The consequent undermining of Chinese morale, so the accusation ran, contributed powerfully to Jiang's overthrow by the communists four years later. The critics also assailed the "sellout" of Poland and other Eastern European countries.

Roosevelt's defenders countered that Stalin, with his mighty red army, could have secured much more of China if he wished and that the Yalta conference really set limits on his ambitions. Apologists for Roosevelt also contended that if Stalin had kept his promise to support free elections in Poland and the liberated Balkans, the sorry sequel would have been different. Actually, Soviet troops had then occupied much of Eastern Europe, and a war to throw them out was unthinkable.

The fact is that the Big Three at Yalta were not drafting a comprehensive peace settlement; at most they were sketching general intentions and testing one another's reactions. Later critics who howled about broken promises overlooked that fundamental point. In the case of Poland, Roosevelt admitted that the Yalta agreement was "so elastic that the Russians can stretch it all the way from Yalta to Washington without ever technically breaking it." More specific understandings among the wartime allies—especially the two emerging superpowers, the United States and the Soviet Union—awaited the arrival of peace.

✴ The United States and the Soviet Union

History provided little hope that the United States and the Soviet Union would reach cordial understandings about the shape of the postwar world. Mutual suspicions were ancient, abundant, and abiding. Commu-nism and capitalism were historically hostile social philosophies. The United States had refused officially to recognize the Bolshevik revolutionary government in Moscow until it was sixteen years old, in 1933. Soviet skepticism toward the West was nourished by the British and American delays in opening up a second front against Germany, while the Soviet army paid a grisly price to roll the Nazi invaders back across Russia and Eastern Europe. Britain and America had also frozen their Soviet "ally" out of the project to develop atomic weapons, further feeding Stalin's mistrust. The Washington government rubbed salt in Soviet wounds when it abruptly terminated vital lend-lease aid to a battered USSR in 1945 and spurned Moscow's plea for a $6 billion reconstruction loan—while approving a similar loan of $3.75 billion to Britain in 1946.

Different visions of the postwar world also separated the two superpowers. Stalin aimed above all to guarantee the security of the Soviet Union. The USSR had twice in the twentieth century been stabbed in its heartland by attacks across the windswept plains of Eastern Europe. Stalin made it clear from the outset of the war that he was determined to have friendly governments along the Soviet western border, especially in Poland. By maintaining an extensive Soviet sphere of influence in Eastern and Central Europe, the USSR could protect itself and consolidate its revolutionary base as the world's leading communist country.

To many Americans, that "sphere of influence" looked like an ill-gained "empire." Doubting that Soviet goals were purely defensive, they remembered the earlier Bolshevik call for world revolution. Stalin's emphasis on "spheres" also clashed with Franklin Roosevelt's Wilsonian dream of an "open world," decolonized, demilitarized, and democratized, with a strong international organization to oversee global peace.

Even the ways in which the United States and the Soviet Union resembled each other were troublesome. Both countries had been largely isolated from world affairs before World War II—the United States through choice, the Soviet Union through rejection by the other powers. Both nations also had a history of conducting a kind of "missionary" diplomacy—of trying to export to all the world the political doctrines precipitated out of their respective revolutionary origins.

Unaccustomed to their great-power roles, unfamiliar with or even antagonistic to each other, and each believing in the universal applicability of its own particular ideology, America and the USSR suddenly found themselves staring eyeball-to-eyeball over the prostrate body of a battered Europe—a Europe that had been the traditional center of international affairs. In these circumstances some sort of confrontation was virtually unavoidable. The wartime "Grand Alliance" of the United States, the Soviet Union, and Britain had been a misbegotten child of necessity, kept alive only until the

The Communist Menace   First appearing in the *New York Daily News* on January 6, 1946, this map reflected Americans' rising anxiety after World War II that the Soviet Union was an aggressively expansionist power, relentlessly gobbling up territory and imposing its will across both Europe and Asia.

mutual enemy was crushed. When the hated Hitler fell, suspicion and rivalry between communistic, despotic Russia and capitalistic, democratic America were all but inevitable. In a fateful progression of events, marked often by misperceptions as well as by genuine conflicts of interest, the two powers provoked each other into a tense standoff known as the **Cold War**. Enduring four and a half decades, the Cold War not only shaped Soviet-American relations; it overshadowed the entire postwar international order in every corner of the globe. The Cold War also molded societies and economies and the lives of individual people all over the planet.

✖ Shaping the Postwar World

Despite these obstacles, the United States did manage at war's end to erect some of the structures that would support Roosevelt's vision of an open world. At the **Bretton Woods Conference** in Bretton Woods, New Hampshire, in 1944, the Western Allies established the International Monetary Fund (IMF) to encourage world trade by regulating currency exchange rates. They also founded the International Bank for Reconstruction and Development (World Bank) to promote economic growth in war-ravaged and underdeveloped areas. In contrast to its behavior after World War I, the United States took the lead in creating these important international bodies and supplied most of their funding. The stubborn Soviets declined to participate (see "Thinking Globally: The Era of Globalization," pp. 842–843).

As flags wept at half-mast, the United Nations Conference opened on schedule, April 25, 1945, despite Roosevelt's dismaying death thirteen days earlier. Unlike Woodrow Wilson, Roosevelt had shrewdly moved to establish the new international body before the war's conclusion, so as to capitalize on the wartime spirit of cooperation and insulate planning for the United Nations from the potentially divisive issue of the peace settlement. Meeting at the San Francisco War Memorial Opera House, representatives from fifty nations fashioned the United Nations Charter.

Woodrow Wilson had envisioned a world order organized around the principles of self-determination and free trade—a world "made safe for democracy." But Wilson's dream perished in the turbulent aftermath of World War I. The United States retreated into a selfish and short-sighted isolationism: hiking tariffs to record levels, refusing to join the new League of Nations, and stoutly asserting its neutrality, even as the Great Depression plunged the planet into economic chaos and World War II eventually wreathed the globe in fire and destruction.

Franklin Roosevelt had served Wilson as assistant secretary of the navy. He had shared his chief's idealistic goals, as well as Wilson's bitter disappointment when they failed to be achieved. FDR also believed that many of the ills that beset the world in the post–World War I era could have been avoided if only the United States had played an international role commensurate with its power and its own highest ideals. He resolved not to squander another opportunity for American international leadership.

So on August 9, 1941, as much of Europe writhed under the Nazi jackboot, President Roosevelt rendezvoused with British prime minister Winston Churchill aboard two warships anchored off the coast of Newfoundland. After three days of talks, they publicly announced their vision of the postwar world. What came to be called the "Atlantic Charter" proclaimed for all nations the rights to self-determination and free access to trade. It also foresaw the creation of a new international organization to replace the defunct League of Nations. And it declared that a postwar peace must ensure "freedom from fear and want" for all individuals, everywhere—the first time global economic prosperity was formally declared to be an objective of any country's foreign policy. Roosevelt and

United Nations, 1947 by Henry Rowland Eveleigh

UNITED NATIONS

Great Hopes for World Peace with the United Nations, 1947 The achievements of the new international regime were dramatic. International trade doubled in the 1950s and again in the 1960s. By century's end, the volume of global commerce was ten times larger than in 1950 (see Table 36.1). Increased trade fueled postwar recovery in Europe and Japan and set several underdeveloped countries—notably Taiwan, Singapore, South Korea, India, and China—on the path to modernization and prosperity.

Churchill had drafted the charter for a new era in American diplomacy and for a new phase of world history as well.

After World War II, the United States, victorious and robust at the end of a conflict that had laid waste all the traditional great powers, was uniquely positioned to shape the world order

after World War II. To a remarkable degree, it followed the Wilsonian principles embodied in the Atlantic Charter. It gave birth to an array of multilateral institutions to promote trade and international investment, support the rule of law, and nurture democracy. They included the World Bank, to fund post-

TABLE 36.1 International Trade, 1948–2008

	1948	1953	1963	1973	1983	1993	2003	2008
Total volume of world trade (in billions of U.S. dollars)	59	84	157	579	1,838	3,676	7,377	15,717
Total volume of U.S. exports (in billions of U.S. dollars)	13	12	22	71	202	457	728	1,305
Share of world exports (%)								
United States	22	19	15	12	11	13	10	8
Europe	35	39	48	51	43	45	46	41
Africa	7	6	6	5	4	3	2	3
Middle East	2	3	3	4	7	4	4	7
Asia	14	13	12	15	19	26	26	28
GATT/WTO members	63	69	75	84	77	89	94	93

(Sources: All data except total volume of U.S. exports are from World Trade Organization, *International Trade Statistics*, 2009. U.S. export data for 1948–1993 are from *United States Historical Statistics of the United States*, vol. 5; data for 2003 and 2008 are from Foreign Exports Division, U.S. Census Bureau. Because different organizations rely on different methodologies for estimating total exports, WTO estimates used to compute the U.S. share of world exports differ slightly from those presented in this table.)

war reconstruction; the International Monetary Fund (IMF), to stabilize world currencies; and the General Agreement on Tariffs and Trade (GATT), to lower barriers to international commerce. In the ensuing decades, 102 nations, accounting for 80 percent of world trade, signed GATT (succeeded by the World Trade Organization, or WTO, in the 1990s). The United States also took the lead in founding and funding the United Nations (U.N.), which worked to arbitrate international disputes, improve standards of living worldwide, and encourage decolonization, particularly in Asia and Africa.

As Roosevelt and Churchill anticipated, the benefits of trade extended far beyond rising incomes. As goods flowed across borders, so too did advances in medicine and nutrition. Since 1950 the average life expectancy worldwide has increased by twenty years, with the biggest gains in the developing world.

Rising prosperity and improved standards of living also strengthened the middle classes in developing countries, with democracy often following in the footsteps of globalization. The number of electoral democracies increased from 44 in 1950 to 120 in 2000. Recent studies confirm that states with open trade policies are three times more likely to protect civil liberties than those without such policies.

For some four decades, the full effects of this liberalized world order were muffled by the Cold War. Eastern Europe and the Soviet Union in particular were conspicuous nonparticipants in the emerging global economy, and the United States often supported repressive, undemocratic regimes simply to keep them out of the Soviet camp. But the end of the Cold War and the dissolution of the Soviet bloc in the early 1990s unleashed the full force of globalization. International trade, investment, and migration exploded. More than fifty new electoral democracies, notably in Eastern Europe, Asia, and Latin America, emerged in the last decade of the twentieth century.

Global trade, already at record levels, doubled between 1990 and 2003.

Despite these gains, problems persist. Critics decry the job insecurity, exploitative labor practices, inflationary pressures, widening income disparities both within and between nations, and environmental degradation that have accompanied worldwide industrial growth. Many African nations have proved chronically unable to overcome political instability, systemic poverty, and devastating epidemics. Africa's woes, and those of many Middle Eastern states as well, demonstrate that many parts of the world are still very far from safe for democracy. Yet the liberalized world order that the United States took the lead in building after World War II left an impressive legacy of international stability, burgeoning prosperity, and freedom from fear and want for millions of human beings—a lasting testament to Wilson's vision and to Roosevelt's leadership.

In June 1946 Bernard Baruch (1870–1965), in presenting his plan for the control of atomic energy to the United Nations, said,

"We are here to make a choice between the quick and the dead. That is our business. Behind the black portent of the new atomic age lies a hope which, seized upon with faith, can work our salvation. If we fail, then we have damned every man to be the slave of fear. Let us not deceive ourselves; we must elect world peace or world destruction.**"**

The **United Nations (U.N.)** was a successor to the old League of Nations, but it differed from its predecessor in significant ways. Born in a moment of idealism and designed to prevent another great-power war, the League had adopted rules denying the veto power to any party to a dispute. The U.N., by contrast, more realistically provided that no member of the Security Council, dominated by the Big Five powers (the United States, Britain, the USSR, France, and China), could have action taken against it without its consent. The League, in short, presumed great-power conflict; the U.N. presumed great-power cooperation. Both approaches had their liabilities. The U.N. also featured the General Assembly, which could be controlled by smaller countries. In contrast to the chilly American reception of the League in 1919, the Senate overwhelmingly approved the U.N. Charter on July 28, 1945, by a vote of 89 to 2—not least because it provided safeguards for American sovereignty and freedom of action.

The United Nations, setting up its permanent glass home in New York City, had some gratifying initial successes. It helped preserve peace in Iran, Kashmir, and other trouble spots. It played a large role in creating the new Jewish state of Israel. The U.N. Trusteeship Council guided former colonies to independence. Through such arms as UNESCO (United Nations Educational, Scientific, and Cultural Organization), FAO (Food and Agricultural Organization), and WHO (World Health Organization), the U.N. brought benefits to peoples the world over.

The fearsome new technology of the atom put to an early test the spirit of cooperation on which the U.N. had been founded. The new organization failed badly. U.S. delegate Bernard Baruch called in 1946 for a U.N. agency, free from the great-power veto, with worldwide authority over atomic energy, weapons, and research. The Soviet delegate countered that the possession of nuclear weapons should simply be outlawed by every nation. President Truman said that it would be folly to "throw away our gun until we are sure the rest of the world can't arm against us." The suspicious Soviets felt the same way and used their veto power to scuttle the proposals. A priceless opportunity to tame the nuclear monster in its infancy was lost. The atomic clock ticked ominously on for the next forty-five years, shadowing all relations between the Soviet Union and the United States and threatening the very future of the human race.

✦ The Problem of Germany

Hitler's ruined Reich posed especially thorny problems for all the wartime Allies. They agreed only that the cancer of Nazism had to be cut out of the German

The Nuremberg War Crimes Trial, 1946 Of the Nazi defendants pictured here, from left to right in the first row, Hermann Goering committed suicide during the trial; Rudolf Hess was sentenced to life in prison and died of an apparent suicide in his cell in 1987; Joachim von Ribbentrop, Wilhelm Keitel, and Ernest Kaltenbrunner were executed; in the second row, Karl Doenitz was sentenced to ten years in prison; Erich Raeder was sentenced to life in prison but released in 1955; Baldur von Schirach was sentenced to twenty years in prison; and Fritz Sauckel was executed.

© Bettmann/Corbis

MAP 36.2 Postwar Partition of Germany Germany lost much of its territory in the east to Poland and the Soviet Union. The military occupation zones were the bases for the formation of two separate countries in 1949, when the British, French, and American zones became West Germany, and the Soviet zone became East Germany. (The two Germanys were reunited in 1990.) Berlin remained under joint four-power occupation from 1945 to 1990 and became a focus and symbol of Cold War tensions.

© Cengage Learning

body politic, which involved punishing Nazi leaders for war crimes. The Allies joined in trying twenty-two top culprits at the **Nuremberg war crimes trial** during 1945–1946. Accusations included committing crimes against the laws of war and humanity and plotting aggressions contrary to solemn treaty pledges.

Justice, Nuremberg-style, was harsh. Twelve of the accused Nazis swung from the gallows, and seven were sentenced to long jail terms. "Foxy Hermann" Goering, whose blubbery chest had once blazed with ribbons, cheated the hangman a few hours before his scheduled execution by swallowing a hidden cyanide capsule. The trials of several small-fry Nazis continued for years. Legal critics in America and elsewhere condemned these proceedings as judicial lynchings, because the victims were tried for offenses that had not been clear-cut crimes when the war began.

Beyond punishing the top Nazis, the Allies could agree on little about postwar Germany. Some American Hitler-haters, noting that an industrialized Germany had been a brutal aggressor, at first wanted to dismantle German factories and reduce the country to a potato patch. The Soviets, denied American economic assistance, were determined to rebuild their shattered land by extracting enormous reparations from the Germans. Both these desires clashed headlong with the reality that an industrial, healthy German economy was indispensable to the recovery of Europe. The Americans soon came to appreciate that fact. But the Soviets, deeply fearful of another blitzkrieg, resisted all efforts to revitalize Germany.

Along with Austria, Germany had been divided at war's end into four military occupation zones, each assigned to one of the Big Four powers (France, Britain, America, and the USSR) (see Map 36.2). The Western Allies refused to allow Moscow to bleed their zones of the reparations that Stalin insisted he had been promised at Yalta. They also began to promote the idea of a reunited Germany. The communists responded by tightening their grip on their Eastern zone. Before long, it was apparent that Germany would remain indefinitely divided. West Germany eventually became an independent country, wedded to the West. East Germany, along with other Soviet-dominated Eastern European

Former British prime minister Winston Churchill (1874–1965), in a highly controversial speech at Fulton, Missouri (March 1946), warned of Soviet expansionism:

❝From Stettin in the Baltic to Trieste in the Adriatic an iron curtain has descended across the Continent.❞

Berlin, 1948 Grateful city residents watch a U.S. airplane fly in much-needed supplies.

Harry Redl/Time & Life Pictures/Getty Images

countries, such as Poland and Hungary, became nominally independent "satellite" states, bound to the Soviet Union. Eastern Europe virtually disappeared from Western sight behind the "iron curtain" of secrecy and isolation that Stalin clanged down across Europe from the Baltic to the Adriatic. The division of Europe would endure for more than four decades.

With Germany now split in two, there remained the problem of the rubble heap known as Berlin. Lying deep within the Soviet zone, this beleaguered isle in a red sea had been broken, like Germany as a whole, into sectors occupied by troops of each of the four victorious powers. In 1948, following controversies over German currency reform and four-power control, the Soviets abruptly choked off all rail and highway access to Berlin. They evidently reasoned that the Allies would be starved out.

Berlin became a hugely symbolic issue for both sides. At stake was not only the fate of the city but a test of wills between Moscow and Washington. The Americans organized the gigantic **Berlin airlift** in the midst of hair-trigger tension. For nearly a year, flying

some of the very aircraft that had recently dropped bombs on Berlin, American pilots ferried thousands of tons of supplies a day to the grateful Berliners, their former enemies. Western Europeans took heart from this vivid demonstration of America's determination to honor its commitments in Europe. The Soviets, their bluff dramatically called, finally lifted their blockade in May 1949. In the same year, the governments of the two Germanys, East and West, were formally established. The Cold War had icily congealed.

✴ The Cold War Congeals

A crafty Stalin also probed the West's resolve at other sensitive points, including oil-rich Iran. Seeking to secure oil concessions similar to those held by the British and Americans, Stalin in 1946 broke an agreement to remove his troops from Iran's northernmost province, which the USSR had occupied, with British and American approval, during World War II. Instead he used the troops to aid a rebel movement. Truman sent off a stinging protest, and the Soviet dictator backed down.

Moscow's hard-line policies in Germany, Eastern Europe, and the Middle East wrought a psychological Pearl Harbor. The eyes of Americans were jarred wide-open by the Kremlin's apparent unwillingness to continue the wartime partnership. Any remaining goodwill from the period of comradeship-in-arms evaporated in a cloud of dark distrust. "I'm tired of babying the Soviets," Truman remarked privately in 1946, as attitudes on both sides began to harden frostily.

Truman's piecemeal responses to various Soviet challenges took on intellectual coherence in 1947, with the formulation of the **containment doctrine**. Crafted by a brilliant young diplomat and Soviet specialist, George F. Kennan, this concept held that Russia, whether tsarist or communist, was relentlessly expansionary. But the Kremlin was also cautious, Kennan argued, and the flow of Soviet power into "every nook and cranny available to it" could be stemmed by "firm and vigilant containment."

Truman embraced Kennan's advice when he formally and publicly adopted a "get-tough-with-Russia" policy in 1947. His first dramatic move was triggered by word that heavily burdened Britain could no longer bear the financial and military load of defending Greece against communist pressures. If Greece fell, Turkey would presumably collapse, and the strategic eastern Mediterranean would pass into the Soviet orbit.

In a surprise appearance, the president went before Congress on March 12, 1947, and requested support for what came to be known as the **Truman Doctrine**. Specifically, he asked for $400 million to bolster Greece and Turkey, which Congress quickly granted. More generally, he declared that "it must be the policy of the United States to support free peoples who are resisting attempted subjugation by armed minorities or by outside pressures"—a sweeping and open-ended commitment of vast and worrisome proportions. Critics then and later charged that Truman had overreacted by promising unlimited support to any tinhorn despot who claimed to be resisting "Communist aggression." Critics also complained that the Truman Doctrine needlessly polarized the world into pro-Soviet and pro-American camps and unwisely construed the Soviet threat as primarily military in nature. Apologists for Truman have explained that it was Truman's fear of a revived isolationism that led him to exaggerate the Soviet threat and to pitch his message in the charged language of a holy global war against godless communism—a description of the Cold War that straightjacketed future policymakers who would seek to tone down Soviet-American competition and animosity.

Truman found support for casting the Cold War as a battle between good and evil from theologians like the influential liberal Protestant clergyman Reinhold Niebuhr (1892–1971). For over five decades after World War I, Niebuhr crusaded against what he perceived as

In February 1946 Kremlin specialist George F. Kennan (1904–2005) sent his landmark "Long Telegram" to the State Department. In the eight-thousand-word, eighteen-page message, Kennan assessed the Soviet threat and called for a new kind of response, which would eventually become known as the "containment doctrine":

❝In summary, we have here a political force [Stalin's regime] committed fanatically to the belief that with [the] US there can be no permanent *modus vivendi*, that it is desirable and necessary that the internal harmony of our society be disrupted, our traditional way of life be destroyed, the international authority of our state be broken, if Soviet power is to be secure.❞

the drift away from Christian foundations. A vocal enemy of fascism, pacifism, and communism in the 1940s and 1950s, Niebuhr divided the world into two polarized camps: the "children of light" and the "children of darkness." For Niebuhr, Christian justice, including force if necessary, required a "realist" response to "children of darkness" like Hitler and Stalin.

A threat of a different sort loomed in Western Europe—especially France, Italy, and Germany. These key nations were still suffering from the hunger and economic chaos spawned by war. They were in grave danger of being taken over from the inside by Communist parties that could exploit these hardships.

President Truman responded with a bold policy. In a commencement address at Harvard University on June 5, 1947, Secretary of State George C. Marshall invited the Europeans to get together and work out a *joint* plan for their economic recovery. If they did so, then the United States would provide substantial financial assistance. This forced cooperation constituted a powerful nudge on the road to the eventual creation of the European Community (EC).

The democratic nations of Europe rose enthusiastically to the life-giving bait of the so-called **Marshall Plan**. They met in Paris in July 1947 to thrash out the details. There Marshall offered the same aid to the Soviet Union and its allies, if they would make political reforms and accept certain outside controls. In fact, the Americans worried that the Russian bear might hug the Marshall Plan to death, and therefore made the terms deliberately difficult for the USSR to accept. Nobody was surprised when the Soviets walked out, denouncing the "Martial Plan" as one more capitalist trick.

The Granger Collection, New York

Where To? 1947 As this satirical view of the Truman Doctrine shows, not all Americans were sure where the country's new foreign policy was taking them.

MAP 36.3 United States Foreign Aid, Military and Economic, 1945–1954 Marshall Plan aid swelled the outlay for Europe. Note the emphasis on the "developed" world, with relatively little aid going to "developing." © Cengage Learning

The Marshall Plan called for spending $12.5 billion over four years in sixteen cooperating countries (see Map 36.3). Congress at first balked at this mammoth sum. It looked even more huge when added to the nearly $2 billion the United States had already contributed to European relief through the United Nations Relief and Rehabilitation Administration (UNRRA) and the hefty American contributions to the United Nations, IMF, and World Bank. But a Soviet-sponsored communist coup in Czechoslovakia finally awakened the legislators to reality, and they voted the initial appropriations in April 1948. Congress evidently concluded that if Uncle Sam did not get the Europeans back on their feet, they would never get off his back.

Truman's Marshall Plan was a spectacular success. American dollars pumped reviving blood into the economic veins of the anemic Western European nations. Within a few years, most of them were exceeding their prewar outputs, as an "economic miracle" drenched Europe in prosperity. The Communist parties in Italy and France lost ground, and these two keystone countries were saved from the westward thrust of communism.

A resolute Truman made another fateful decision in 1948. Access to Middle Eastern oil was crucial to the European recovery program and, increasingly, to the health of the U.S. economy, given finite American oil reserves. Yet the Arab oil countries adamantly opposed the creation of the Jewish state of Israel in the British mandate territory of Palestine. Should Israel be born, a Saudi Arabian leader warned Truman, the Arabs "will lay siege to it until it dies of famine." Defying Arab wrath as well as the objections of his own State and Defense Departments and the European Allies, all of

The Marshall Plan Turns Enemies into Friends The poster in this 1950 photograph in Berlin reads, "Berlin Rebuilt with Help from the Marshall Plan."

Soviet Magazine, *Krokodil*

American Motor of the Latest Type   In this Russian cartoon, the conquering Truman uses U.S. moneybags to induce dollar-hungry European nations to draw the American capitalistic chariot.

the air force (a recognition of the rising importance of airpower). The uniformed heads of each service were brought together as the Joint Chiefs of Staff.

The National Security Act also established the National Security Council (NSC) to advise the president on security matters and the Central Intelligence Agency (CIA) to coordinate the government's foreign fact gathering. The "Voice of America," authorized by Congress in 1948, began beaming American radio broadcasts behind the iron curtain. In the same year, Congress resurrected the military draft, providing for the conscription of selected young men from nineteen to twenty-five years of age. The forbidding presence of the Selective Service System shaped millions of young people's educational, marital, and career plans in the following quarter-century. One shoe at a time, a war-weary America was reluctantly returning to a war footing.

The Soviet threat was also forcing the democracies of Western Europe into an unforeseen degree of unity. In 1948 Britain, France, Belgium, the Netherlands, and Luxembourg signed a path-breaking treaty of defensive alliance at Brussels. They then invited the United States to join them.

The proposal confronted the United States with a historic decision. America had traditionally avoided entangling alliances, especially in peacetime (if the Cold War could be considered peacetime). Yet American participation in the emerging coalition could serve many purposes: it would strengthen the policy of containing the Soviet Union; it would provide a framework for the reintegration of Germany into the European family; and it would reassure jittery Europeans that a traditionally isolationist Uncle Sam was not about to abandon them to the marauding Russian bear—or to a resurgent and domineering Germany.

The Truman administration decided to join the European pact, called the **North Atlantic Treaty Organization (NATO)** in recognition of its transatlantic character. With white-tie pageantry, the NATO treaty was signed in Washington on April 4, 1949. The twelve original signatories pledged to regard an attack on one as an attack on all and promised to respond with "armed force" if necessary. Despite last-ditch howls from immovable isolationists, the Senate approved the treaty on July 21, 1949, by a vote of 82 to 13. Membership was boosted to fourteen in 1952 by the inclusion of Greece and Turkey, to fifteen in 1955 by the addition of West Germany.

The NATO pact was epochal. It marked a dramatic departure from American diplomatic convention, a gigantic boost for European unification, and a significant step in the militarization of the Cold War. NATO became the cornerstone of all Cold War American policy toward Europe. With good reason pundits summed

them afraid to antagonize the oil-endowed Arabs, Truman officially recognized the state of Israel on the day of its birth, May 14, 1948. Humanitarian sympathy for the Jewish survivors of the Holocaust ranked high among his reasons, as did his wishes to preempt Soviet influence in the Jewish state and to retain the support of American Jewish voters. Truman's policy of strong support for Israel would vastly complicate U.S. relations with the Arab world in the decades ahead.

✸ America Begins to Rearm

The Cold War, the struggle to contain Soviet communism, was not war, yet it was not peace. The standoff with the Kremlin banished the dreams of tax-fatigued Americans that tanks could be beaten into automobiles.

The Soviet menace spurred the unification of the armed services as well as the creation of a huge new national security apparatus. Congress in 1947 passed the National Security Act, creating the Department of Defense. The department was to be housed in the sprawling Pentagon building on the banks of the Potomac and to be headed by a new cabinet officer, the secretary of defense. Under the secretary, but now without cabinet status, were the civilian secretaries of the navy, the army (replacing the old secretary of war), and

Reaching Across the Atlantic in Peacetime, 1948 When the United States joined with the Western European powers in the North Atlantic Alliance, soon to be called the North Atlantic Treaty Organization, it overcame its historic isolationism in the wake of wars. By 1955 former enemy West Germany would be admitted to NATO to help defend Western Europe against Soviet aggression.

Granger Collection

up NATO's threefold purpose: "to keep the Russians out, the Germans down, and the Americans in."

✷ Reconstruction and Revolution in Asia

Reconstruction in Japan was simpler than in Germany, primarily because it was largely a one-man show. The occupying American army, under the supreme Allied commander, five-star general Douglas MacArthur, sat in the driver's seat. In the teeth of violent protests from Soviet officials, MacArthur went inflexibly ahead with his program for the democratization of Japan. Following the pattern in Germany, top Japanese "war criminals" were tried in Tokyo from 1946 to 1948. Eighteen of them were sentenced to prison terms, and seven were hanged.

General MacArthur, as a kind of Yankee mikado, enjoyed stunning success. The Japanese cooperated to an astonishing degree. They saw that good behavior and the adoption of democracy would speed the end of the occupation—as it did. A MacArthur-dictated constitution was adopted in 1946. It renounced militarism, provided for women's equality, and introduced Western-style democratic government—paving the way for a phenomenal economic recovery that within a few decades made Japan one of the world's mightiest industrial powers.

If Japan was a success story for American policymakers, the opposite was true in China, where a bitter civil war had raged for years between Nationalists and communists. Washington had halfheartedly supported the Nationalist government of Generalissimo Jiang Jieshi in his struggle with the communists under Mao Zedong (Mao Tse-tung). But ineptitude and corruption within the generalissimo's regime gradually began to corrode the confidence of his people. Communist armies swept south overwhelmingly, and late in 1949 Jiang was forced to flee with the remnants of his once-powerful force to the last-hope island of Formosa (Taiwan).

The collapse of Nationalist China was a depressing defeat for America and its allies in the Cold War—the

In August 1949 Secretary of State Dean Acheson (1893–1971) explained publicly why America had "dumped" Jiang Jieshi:

❝ The unfortunate but inescapable fact is that the ominous result of the civil war in China was beyond the control of the government of the United States. Nothing that this country did or could have done within the reasonable limits of its capabilities could have changed that result; nothing that was left undone by this country has contributed to it. It was the product of internal Chinese forces, forces which this country tried to influence but could not. **❞**

worst to date. At one fell swoop, nearly one-fourth of the world's population—some 500 million people—was swept into the communist camp. The so-called fall of China became a bitterly partisan issue in the United States. The Republicans, seeking "goats" who had "lost China," assailed President Truman and his bristly mustached, British-appearing secretary of state, Dean Acheson. They insisted that Democratic agencies, wormy with communists, had deliberately withheld aid from Jiang Jieshi so that he would fall. Democrats heatedly replied that when a regime has forfeited the support of its people, no amount of outside help will save it. Truman, the argument ran, did not "lose" China, because he never had China to lose. Jiang himself had never controlled all of China.

More bad news came in September 1949 when President Truman shocked the nation by announcing that the Soviets had exploded an atomic bomb—approximately three years earlier than many experts had thought possible. American strategists since 1945 had counted on keeping the Soviets in line by threats of a one-sided aerial attack with nuclear weapons. But atomic bombing was now a game that two could play.

To outpace the Soviets in nuclear weaponry, Truman ordered the development of the "H-bomb" (hydrogen bomb)—a city-smashing thermonuclear weapon that was a thousand times more powerful than the atomic bomb. J. Robert Oppenheimer, former scientific director of the Manhattan Project and current chair of the Atomic Energy Commission, led a group of scientists in opposition to the crash program to design thermonuclear weapons. The H-bomb, these scientists

warned, was so deadly that "it becomes a weapon which in practical effect is almost one of genocide." Famed physicist Albert Einstein, whose theories had helped give birth to the atomic age, declared that "annihilation of any life on earth has been brought within the range of technical possibilities."

But Einstein and Oppenheimer, the nation's two most famous scientists, could not persuade Truman, anxious over communist threats in East Asia. The United States exploded its first hydrogen device on a South Pacific atoll in 1952. Not to be outdone, the Soviets countered with their first H-bomb explosion in

The Hydrogen Bomb, 1954
This test blast at Bikini Atoll in the Marshall Islands was so powerful that one Japanese fisherman was killed and all twenty-two of his crewmates were seriously injured by radioactive ash that fell on their vessel some eighty miles away. Fishing boats a thousand miles from Bikini later brought in radioactively contaminated catches.

1953, and the nuclear arms race entered a perilously competitive cycle. Nuclear "superiority" became a dangerous and delusive dream, as each side tried to outdo the other in the scramble to build more destructive weapons. If the Cold War should ever blaze into a hot war, there might be no world left for the communists to communize or the democracies to democratize—a chilling thought that constrained both camps. Peace through mutual terror brought a shaky stability to the superpower standoff.

✷ Ferreting Out Alleged Communists

One of the most active Cold War fronts was at home, where a new anti-red chase was in full cry. Many nervous citizens feared that communist spies, paid with Moscow gold, were undermining the government and treacherously misdirecting foreign policy. In 1947 Truman launched a massive "loyalty" program. The attorney general drew up a list of ninety supposedly disloyal

Richard Nixon, Red-hunter Congressman Nixon examines the microfilm that figured as important evidence in Alger Hiss's conviction for perjury in 1950.

organizations, none of which was given the opportunity to prove its innocence. The Loyalty Review Board investigated more than 3 million federal employees, some 3,000 of whom either resigned or were dismissed, none under formal indictment.

Individual states likewise became intensely security-conscious. Loyalty oaths in increasing numbers were demanded of employees, especially teachers. The gnawing question for many earnest Americans was, Could the nation continue to enjoy traditional freedoms—especially freedom of speech, freedom of thought, and the right of political dissent—in a Cold War climate?

In 1949 eleven communists were brought before a New York jury for violating the Smith Act of 1940, the first peacetime antisedition law since 1798. Convicted of advocating the overthrow of the American government by force, the defendants were sent to prison. The Supreme Court upheld their convictions in *Dennis* v. *United States* (1951).

The House of Representatives in 1938 had established the **House Un-American Activities Committee (HUAC)** to investigate "subversion." In 1948 committee member Richard M. Nixon, an ambitious red-catcher, led the chase after Alger Hiss, a prominent ex–New Dealer and a distinguished member of the "eastern establishment." Accused of being a communist agent in the 1930s, Hiss demanded the right to defend himself. He dramatically met his chief accuser before HUAC in August 1948. Hiss denied everything but was caught in embarrassing falsehoods, convicted of perjury in 1950, and sentenced to five years in prison.

Was America really riddled with Soviet spies? Soviet agents did infiltrate certain government agencies, though without severely damaging consequences, and espionage may have helped the Soviets to develop an atomic bomb somewhat sooner than they would have otherwise. Truman's loyalty program thus had a basis in reality. But for many ordinary Americans, the hunt for communists was not just about fending off the military threat of the Soviet Union. Unsettling dangers lurked closer to home. While men like Nixon and Senator Joseph McCarthy led the search for communists in Washington, conservative politicians at the state and local levels discovered that all manner of real or perceived social changes—including declining religious sentiment, increased sexual freedom, and agitation for civil rights—could be tarred with a red brush. Anticommunist crusaders ransacked school libraries for "subversive" textbooks and drove debtors, drinkers, and homosexuals, all alleged to be security risks, from their jobs.

Some Americans, including President Truman, realized that the red hunt was turning into a witch hunt. In 1950 Truman vetoed the McCarran Internal Security Bill, which among other provisions authorized the president to arrest and detain suspicious people during an "internal security emergency." Critics protested that the bill smacked of police-state, concentration-camp tactics. But the congressional guardians of the Republic's liberties enacted the bill over Truman's veto.

The stunning success of the Soviet scientists in developing an atomic bomb was attributed by many to the cleverness of communist spies in stealing American secrets. Notorious among those who had allegedly "leaked" atomic data to Moscow were two American citizens, Julius and Ethel Rosenberg. They were convicted in 1951 of espionage and went to the electric chair in 1953—the only people in American history ever executed in peacetime for espionage. Their sensational trial and electrocution, combined with sympathy for their two orphaned children, began to sour some sober citizens on the excesses of the red-hunters.

✺ Democratic Divisions in 1948

Attacking high prices and "High-Tax Harry" Truman, the Republicans had won control of Congress in the congressional elections of 1946. Their prospects had seldom looked rosier as they gathered in Philadelphia to choose their 1948 presidential candidate. They noisily renominated warmed-over New York governor Thomas E. Dewey, still as debonair as if he had stepped out of a bandbox.

Also gathering in Philadelphia, Democratic politicos looked without enthusiasm on their hand-me-down president and sang, "I'm Just Mild About Harry." But their "dump Truman" movement collapsed when war hero Dwight D. Eisenhower refused to be drafted. The peppery president, unwanted but undaunted, was then chosen in the face of vehement opposition by southern delegates, who had been alienated by his strong stand in favor of civil rights for blacks, especially his decision in 1948 to desegregate the military.

Truman's nomination split the party wide-open. Embittered southern Democrats from thirteen states, like their fire-eating forebears of 1860, next met in their own convention, in Birmingham, Alabama, with Confederate flags brashly in evidence. Amid scenes of heated defiance, these "Dixiecrats" nominated Governor J. Strom Thurmond of South Carolina on a States' Rights party ticket.

To add to the confusion within Democratic ranks, former vice president Henry A. Wallace threw his hat into the ring. Having parted company with the administration over its get-tough-with-Russia policy, he was nominated at Philadelphia by the new Progressive party—a bizarre collection of disgruntled former New

Harry S. Truman Library

The Harried Piano Player, 1948 Besieged by the left and right wings of his own party, and by a host of domestic and foreign problems, Truman was a long shot for reelection in 1948. But the scrappy president surprised his legions of critics by handily defeating his opponent, Thomas E. Dewey.

Dealers, starry-eyed pacifists, well-meaning liberals, and communist-fronters.

Wallace, a vigorous if misguided liberal, assailed Uncle Sam's "dollar imperialism" from the stump. This so-called Pied Piper of the Politburo took an apparently pro-Soviet line that earned him drenchings with rotten eggs in hostile cities. But to many Americans, Wallace raised the only hopeful voice in the deepening gloom of the Cold War.

With the Democrats ruptured three ways and the Republican congressional victory of 1946 just past, Dewey's victory seemed assured. Succumbing to overconfidence engendered by his massive lead in public-opinion polls, the cold, smug Dewey confined himself to dispensing soothing-syrup trivialities like "Our future lies before us."

The seemingly doomed Truman, with little money and few active supporters, had to rely on his "gut-fighter" instincts and folksy personality. Traveling the country by train to deliver some three hundred "give 'em hell" speeches, he lashed out at the Taft-Hartley "slave-labor" law and the "do-nothing" Republican Congress, while whipping up support for his program of civil rights, improved labor benefits, and health

That Ain't the Way I Heard It! Truman wins.

As Truman's Fair Deal was rebuffed by a hostile Congress, critics like the conservative New York Daily News *gloated that the odious New Deal was finally vanquished:*

"The New Deal is kaput like the Thirty Years' War or the Black Plague or other disasters. . . . [Its demise] is like coming out of the darkness into sunlight. Like feeling clean again after a long time in the muck."

insurance. "Pour it on 'em, Harry!" cried increasingly large and enthusiastic crowds, as the pugnacious president rained a barrage of verbal uppercuts on his opponent.

On election night the *Chicago Tribune* ran off an early edition with the headline "DEWEY DEFEATS TRUMAN." But in the morning, it turned out that "President" Dewey had embarrassingly snatched defeat from the jaws of victory. Truman had swept to a stunning triumph, to the complete bewilderment of politicians, pollsters, prophets, and pundits. Even though Thurmond took away 39 electoral votes in the South, Truman won 303 electoral votes, primarily from the South, Midwest, and West. Dewey's 189 electoral votes came principally from the East. The popular vote was 24,179,345 for Truman, 21,991,291 for Dewey, 1,176,125 for Thurmond, and 1,157,326 for Wallace. To make the victory sweeter, the Democrats regained control of Congress as well.

Truman's victory rested on farmers, workers, and blacks, all of whom were Republican-wary. Republican

In his inaugural address in January 1949, President Harry S Truman (1884–1972) said,

"Communism is based on the belief that man is so weak and inadequate that he is unable to govern himself, and therefore requires the rule of strong masters. . . . Democracy is based on the conviction that man has the moral and intellectual capacity, as well as the inalienable right, to govern himself with reason and justice."

overconfidence and Truman's lone-wolf, never-say-die campaign also won him the support of many Americans who admired his "guts." No one wanted him, someone remarked, except the people. Dewey, in contrast, struck many voters as arrogant, evasive, and wooden. When Dewey took the platform to give a speech, said one commentator, "he comes out like a man who has been mounted on casters and given a tremendous shove from behind."

Smiling and self-assured, Truman sounded a clarion note in the fourth point of his inaugural address, when he called for a "bold new program" (known thereafter as "Point Four"). The plan was to lend U.S. money and technical aid to underdeveloped lands to help them help themselves. Truman wanted to spend millions to keep underprivileged peoples from becoming communists rather than spend billions to shoot them after they had become communists. This farseeing program was officially launched in 1950, and it brought badly needed assistance to impoverished countries, notably in Latin America, Africa, the Near East, and the Far East.

At home Truman outlined a sweeping **Fair Deal** program in his 1949 message to Congress. It called for improved housing, full employment, a higher minimum wage, better farm price supports, new TVAs, and an extension of Social Security. But most of the Fair Deal fell victim to congressional opposition from Republicans and southern Democrats. The only major successes came in raising the minimum wage, providing for public housing in the Housing Act of 1949, and extending old-age insurance to many more beneficiaries in the Social Security Act of 1950.

✦ The Korean Volcano Erupts

Korea, the Land of the Morning Calm, heralded a new and more disturbing phase of the Cold War—a shooting phase—in June 1950. When Japan collapsed in

1945, Soviet troops had accepted the Japanese surrender north of the thirty-eighth parallel on the Korean peninsula, and American troops had done likewise south of that line. Both superpowers professed to want the reunification and independence of Korea, a Japanese colony since 1910. But, as in Germany, each helped to set up rival regimes above and below the parallel.

By 1949, when the Soviets and Americans had both withdrawn their forces, the entire peninsula was a bristling armed camp, with two hostile regimes eyeing each other suspiciously. Secretary of State Acheson seemed to wash his hands of the dispute early in 1950, when he declared in a memorable speech that Korea was outside the essential United States defense perimeter in the Pacific.

The explosion came on June 25, 1950. Spearheaded by Soviet-made tanks, North Korean army columns rumbled across the thirty-eighth parallel. Caught flat-footed, the South Korean forces were shoved back southward to a dangerously tiny defensive area around Pusan, their weary backs to the sea.

President Truman sprang quickly into the breach. The invasion seemed to provide devastating proof of a fundamental premise in the "containment doctrine" that shaped Washington's foreign policy: that even a slight relaxation of America's guard was an invitation to communist aggression somewhere.

The Korean invasion prompted a massive expansion of the American military. A few months before, Truman's National Security Council had issued its famous **National Security Council Memorandum Number 68 (NSC-68)**, recommending that the United States quadruple its defense spending. Ignored at first because it seemed politically impossible to implement, NSC-68 got a new lease on life from the Korean crisis. "Korea saved us," Secretary of State Acheson later commented. Truman now ordered a massive military buildup, well beyond what was necessary for Korea. Soon the United States had 3.5 million men under arms and was spending $50 billion per year on the defense budget—some 13 percent of the GNP.

NSC-68 was a key document of the Cold War period, not only because it marked a major step in the militarization of American foreign policy, but also because it vividly reflected the sense of almost limitless possibility that pervaded postwar American society. NSC-68 rested on the assumption that the enormous American economy could bear without strain the huge costs of a gigantic rearmament program. Said one NSC-68 planner, "There was practically nothing the country could not do if it wanted to do it."

Truman took full advantage of a temporary Soviet absence from the United Nations Security Council on June 25, 1950, to obtain a unanimous condemnation of North Korea as an aggressor. (Why the Soviets were absent remains controversial. Scholars once believed that the Soviets were just as surprised as the Americans by the attack. It now appears that Stalin had given his reluctant approval to North Korea's strike plan but believed that the fighting would be brief and that the United States would take little interest in it.) The Security Council also called upon all U.N. members, including the United States, to "render every assistance" to restore peace. Two days later, without consulting Congress, Truman ordered American air and naval units to support South Korea. Before the week was out, he also ordered General Douglas MacArthur's Japan-based occupation troops into action alongside the beleaguered South Koreans. So began the ill-fated **Korean War**.

Officially, the United States was simply participating in a United Nations "police action." But in fact, the United States made up the overwhelming bulk of the U.N. contingents, and General MacArthur, appointed U.N. commander of the entire operation, took his orders from Washington, not from the Security Council.

✠ The Military Seesaw in Korea

Rather than fight his way out of the southern Pusan perimeter, MacArthur launched a daring amphibious landing behind the enemy's lines at Inchon. This bold gamble on September 15, 1950, succeeded brilliantly; within two weeks the North Koreans had scrambled back behind the "sanctuary" of the thirty-eighth parallel. Truman's avowed intention was to restore South Korea to its former borders, but the pursuing South Koreans had already crossed the thirty-eighth parallel, and there seemed little point in permitting the North Koreans to regroup and come again. The U.N. General Assembly tacitly authorized a crossing by MacArthur, whom President Truman ordered northward, provided that there was no intervention in force by the Chinese or Soviets (see Map 36.4).

The Americans thus raised the stakes in Korea, and in so doing they quickened the fears of another potential player in this dangerous game. The Chinese communists had publicly warned that they would not sit idly by and watch hostile troops approach the strategic Yalu River boundary between Korea and China. But MacArthur pooh-poohed all predictions of an effective intervention by the Chinese and reportedly boasted that he would "have the boys home by Christmas."

MacArthur erred badly. In November 1950 tens of thousands of Chinese "volunteers" fell upon his rashly overextended lines and hurled the U.N. forces reeling

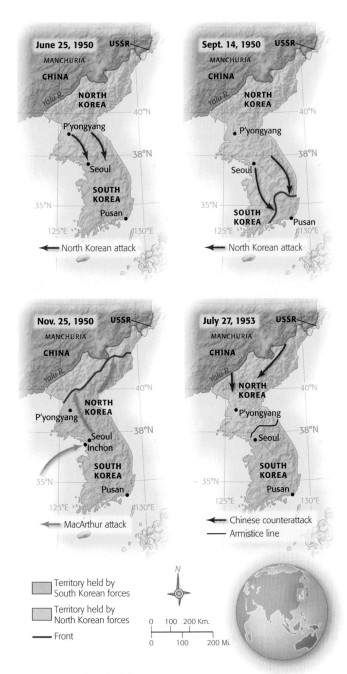

MAP 36.4 The Shifting Front in Korea © Cengage Learning

Truman Takes the Heat

back down the peninsula. The fighting now sank into a frostbitten stalemate on the icy terrain near the thirty-eighth parallel.

An imperious MacArthur, humiliated by this rout, pressed for drastic retaliation. He favored a blockade of the Chinese coast and bombardment of Chinese bases in Manchuria. He even suggested that the United States use nuclear weapons on the advancing Chinese and their supply lines. But Washington policymakers, with anxious eyes on Moscow, refused to enlarge

the already costly conflict. The chairman of the Joint Chiefs of Staff declared that a wider clash in Asia would be "the wrong war, at the wrong place, at the wrong time, and with the wrong enemy." Europe, not Asia, was the administration's first concern; and the USSR, not China, loomed as the more sinister foe.

Two-fisted General MacArthur felt that he was being asked to fight with one hand tied behind his back. He sneered at the concept of a "limited war" and insisted that "there is no substitute for victory." Truman bravely resisted calls for nuclear escalation, a rare example of a military commander refusing to use the most powerful weapons at his disposal. When MacArthur began to criticize the president's policies publicly, Truman had no choice but to remove the insubordinate MacArthur from command on April 11, 1951. MacArthur, a legend in his own mind, returned to an uproarious welcome, whereas Truman was condemned as a "pig," an "imbecile," a "Judas," and an appeaser of "Communist Russia and Communist China." In July 1951 truce discussions began in a rude field tent near the firing line but were almost immediately snagged on the issue of prisoner exchange. Talks dragged on unproductively for nearly two years while men continued to die.

Varying Viewpoints
Who Was to Blame for the Cold War?

Whose fault was the Cold War? (And, for that matter, who should get credit for ending it?) For two decades after World War II, American historians generally agreed that the aggressive Soviets were solely responsible. This "orthodox" or "official" appraisal squared with the traditional view of the United States as a virtuous, innocent land with an idealistic foreign policy. This point of view also justified America's Cold War containment policy, which cast the Soviet Union as the aggressor that must be confined by an ever-vigilant United States. America supposedly had only defensive intentions, with no expansionary ambitions of its own.

In the 1960s a vigorous revisionist interpretation flowered, powerfully influenced by disillusion over U.S. involvement in Vietnam. The revisionists stood the orthodox view on its head. The Soviets, they argued, had only defensive intentions at the end of World War II; it was the Americans who had behaved provocatively by brandishing their new atomic weaponry. Some of these critics pointed an accusing finger at President Truman, alleging that he abandoned Roosevelt's conciliatory approach to the Soviets and adopted a bullying attitude, emboldened by the American atomic monopoly.

More radical revisionists like Gabriel and Joyce Kolko even claimed to have found the roots of Truman's alleged belligerence in long-standing American policies of economic imperialism—policies that eventually resulted in the tragedy of Vietnam (see pp. 874–875). In this view the Vietnam War followed logically from America's insatiable "need" for overseas markets and raw materials. Vietnam itself may have been economically unimportant, but, so the argument ran, a communist Vietnam represented an intolerable challenge to American hegemony. Revisionists cited their own version of the "domino theory," which war apologists used to defend America's military actions in Vietnam. According to the domino theory, if the United States declined to fight in Vietnam, other countries would lose their faith in America's will (or their fear of American power) and would tumble one after the other like "dominoes" into the Soviet camp. Revisionists stressed what they saw as the *economic necessity* behind the domino theory: losing in Vietnam, they claimed, would unravel the American economy.

In the 1970s a "postrevisionist" interpretation emerged that is widely agreed upon today. Historians such as John Lewis Gaddis and Melvyn Leffler pooh-pooh the economic determinism of the revisionists, while frankly acknowledging that the United States did have vital security interests at stake in the post–World War II era. The postrevisionists analyze the ways in which inherited ideas (like isolationism) and the contentious nature of postwar domestic politics, as well as miscalculations by American leaders, led a nation in search of security into seeking not simply a sufficiency but a "preponderance" of power. The American *overreaction* to its security needs, these scholars suggest, exacerbated U.S.-Soviet relations and precipitated the four-decade-long nuclear arms race that formed the centerpiece of the Cold War.

In the case of Vietnam, the postrevisionist historians focus not on economic necessity, but on a failure of political intelligence, induced by the stressful conditions of the Cold War, that made the dubious domino theory seem plausible. Misunderstanding Vietnamese intentions, exaggerating Soviet ambitions, and fearing to appear "soft on communism" in the eyes of their domestic political rivals, American leaders plunged into Vietnam, sadly misguided by their own Cold War obsessions.

Most postrevisionists, however, still lay the lion's share of the blame for the Cold War on the Soviet Union. By the same token, they credit the Soviets with ending the Cold War—a view hotly disputed by Ronald Reagan's champions, who claim that it was his anti-Soviet policies in the 1980s that brought the Russians to their knees (see pp. 946–947). The great unknown, of course, is the precise nature of Soviet thinking in the Cold War years. Were Soviet aims predominantly defensive, or did the Kremlin incessantly plot world conquest? Was there an opportunity for reconciliation with the West following Stalin's death in 1953? Should Mikhail Gorbachev or Ronald Reagan be remembered as the leader who ended the Cold War? With the opening of Soviet archives, scholars are eagerly pursuing answers to such questions.

Chapter Review

KEY TERMS

Taft-Hartley Act (830)

Operation Dixie (830)

Employment Act
of 1946 (831)

GI Bill (831)

Sunbelt (835)

Levittown (838)

baby boom (838)

Yalta conference (839)

Cold War (841)

Bretton Woods
Conference (841)

United Nations (U.N.) (844)

Nuremberg war crimes
trial (845)

Berlin airlift (846)

containment doctrine (846)

Truman Doctrine (846)

Marshall Plan (847)

North Atlantic Treaty Organization (NATO) (849)

House Un-American
Activities Committee
(HUAC) (852)

Fair Deal (854)

National Security Council
Memorandum Number
68 (NSC-68) (855)

Korean War (855)

PEOPLE TO KNOW

Benjamin Spock

Joseph Stalin

Jiang Jieshi

George F. Kennan

Reinhold Niebuhr

George C. Marshall

CHRONOLOGY

1944	Servicemen's Readjustment Act (GI Bill) Bretton Woods economic conference
1945	Spock publishes *The Common Sense Book of Baby and Child Care* Yalta conference United States ends lend-lease to USSR United Nations established
1945–1946	Nuremberg war crimes trial in Germany
1946	Employment Act creates Council of Economic Advisers Iran crisis Kennan's "Long Telegram" lays out "containment doctrine"
1946–1948	Tokyo war crimes trials
1947	Truman Doctrine Marshall Plan Taft-Hartley Act National Security Act creates Department of Defense, National Security Council (NSC), and Central Intelligence Agency (CIA)
1948	Israel founded; United States recognizes it "Voice of America" begins radio broadcasts behind iron curtain Alger Hiss case begins Truman defeats Dewey for presidency
1948–1949	Berlin blockade
1949	NATO established Communists defeat Nationalists in China Soviets explode their first atomic bomb
1950	American economy begins postwar growth McCarthy red hunt begins McCarran Internal Security Bill passed by Congress over Truman's veto
1950–1953	Korean War
1951	Truman fires MacArthur Rosenbergs convicted of treason
1952	United States explodes first hydrogen bomb
1957	Postwar peak of U.S. birthrate
1973	U.S. birthrate falls below replacement level

TO LEARN MORE

Dean Acheson, *Present at the Creation* (1969)

Lizabeth Cohen, *A Consumers' Republic: The Politics of Mass Consumption in Postwar America* (2003)

John Lewis Gaddis, *The Cold War: A New History* (2005)

Herbert J. Gans, *The Levittowners* (1967)

David Halberstam, *The Coldest Winter: America and the Korean War* (2007)

Kenneth T. Jackson, *Crabgrass Frontier: The Suburbanization of the United States* (1985)

Kevin Kruse and Thomas Sugrue, eds., *The New Suburban History* (2006)

Marvyn P. Leffler, *A Preponderance of Power: National Security, the Truman Administration, and the Cold War, 1945–1950* (1980)

Ellen Schrecker, *Many Are the Crimes* (1998)

Bruce Schulman, *From Cotton Belt to Sunbelt: Federal Policy, Economic Development, and the Transformation of the South* (1991)

A complete, annotated bibliography for this chapter—along with brief descriptions of the People to Know—may be found on the American Pageant website. The Key Terms are defined in a Glossary at the end of the text.

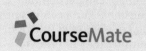

Go to the CourseMate website at **www.cengagebrain.com** for additional study tools and review materials—including audio and video clips—for this chapter.

AP® Review Questions for Chapter 36

1. In an effort to forestall an economic downturn, the Truman administration did all of the following EXCEPT
   (A) create the President's Council of Economic Advisers.
   (B) sell war factories and other government installations to private businesses at very low prices.
   (C) pass the Employment Act, which made it government policy to promote maximum employment.
   (D) pass the Service Readjustment Act, known as the GI Bill of Rights.
   (E) continue wartime wage and price controls.

2. Which of the following was NOT a demographic characteristic of the post–World War II era in the United States?
   (A) The vast expansion of the homeowning middle class
   (B) A dramatically decreased number of American farms and farmers, accompanied by expansions in agricultural output and productivity
   (C) A massive migration of Americans from the cities to the suburbs
   (D) Substantial growth in the population and prosperity of the Sunbelt region of the United States
   (E) Urban-suburban integration of blacks and whites in major metropolitan areas

3. Which of the following was NOT among the key decisions made by Roosevelt, Stalin, and Churchill at the Yalta conference?
   (A) The Soviet Union would attack Japan within three months in exchange for territorial concessions.
   (B) The Soviet Union would sponsor free elections in Poland, Bulgaria, and Romania.
   (C) Occupation zones in Germany would be assigned to each of the victorious great powers.
   (D) The Soviets and Americans would militarily withdraw from Europe after a peace treaty was signed.
   (E) A new international peacekeeping organization, the United Nations, would be established.

4. One of the most significant structural differences between the old League of Nations and the new United Nations was that the United Nations
   (A) did not attempt to include all the independent nations of the world in its membership.
   (B) gave a veto in the powerful Security Council to the five great powers.
   (C) did not try to address the question of colonialism.
   (D) developed its own independent military force controlled by the Security Council.
   (E) established a powerful independent executive branch in the Secretary General.

5. Which of the following best describes the implementation of the containment doctrine, as developed by George F. Kennan and advanced by President Truman?
   (A) The Soviet Union should be gradually forced to surrender its sphere of influence in Eastern Europe through American and Western European military support of democratic uprisings in Eastern Europe.
   (B) The Soviet Union should be prevented from trading with nations in Africa and Asia.
   (C) The West and the Soviet Union should seek to contain the spread of nuclear weapons.
   (D) Possible Soviet expansion into Greece and Turkey should be blocked by providing firm but not aggressive military, diplomatic, and economic assistance to these two unstable European nations.
   (E) The Soviet Union should be prohibited from joining the European Community (EC) in order to contain and ultimately reduce its economic power.

6. Critics of the Truman Doctrine assailed it for all of the following reasons EXCEPT that
   (A) the Truman Doctrine was an overly sweeping and open-ended commitment of interventionism that could not be militarily or economically sustained for the long term.
   (B) Truman's promise of unlimited support for any peoples resisting communist aggression would be used by anticommunist despots seeking to claim American assistance against supposed Soviet-backed communist insurgencies.
   (C) the Truman Doctrine recklessly polarized the world into pro-Soviet and pro-American camps.
   (D) the Truman Doctrine construed the Soviet threat as primarily military in nature and did not emphasize economic assistance and development as an important bulwark against communism.
   (E) the Truman Doctrine would spark a revival of strident America First Committee–style isolationism in the United States.

7. All of the following were characteristics of President Truman's Marshall Plan EXCEPT that
   (A) the United States offered generous and liberal terms to the Soviet Union in an effort to entice the USSR to accept Marshall Plan economic aid.
   (B) Congress initially balked at, but ultimately approved, spending $12.5 billion over four years for military and economic assistance to sixteen cooperating countries in Europe.
   (C) the Marshall Plan was a tremendous success in reviving the anemic postwar economies of Western Europe.
   (D) as a result of European prosperity sparked by Marshall Plan aid, the Communist parties in Italy and France faltered during the immediate postwar years and these two nations remained solidly in the pro-American European camp.
   (E) relatively little Marshall Plan aid was sent to so-called Third World nations or less developed countries (sometimes called Third World countries).

8. American membership in the North Atlantic Treaty Organization did all of the following EXCEPT
   (A) strengthen the containment of the Soviet Union.
   (B) bring West Germany into the anticommunist alliance.
   (C) reduce America's defense expenditures, since the United States would now get help from Western European countries and Canada.
   (D) unify European and U.S. interests, reassuring Europeans that the United States would not abandon them.
   (E) boldly move away from U.S. isolationism.

9. Which of the following was NOT true of the new Japanese government installed by General Douglas MacArthur in 1946?
   (A) The Japanese government joined an American military alliance to prevent the spread of communism in East Asia.
   (B) The Japanese government pledged itself to providing for women's equality.
   (C) Japan was now governed under the principles of a Western-style democratic constitution dictated by MacArthur.
   (D) The constitution and policies of the postwar Japanese government helped pave the way for a spectacular postwar economic recovery.
   (E) The Japanese government renounced militarism.

10. Which of the following was NOT among the features of the increasing domestic anticommunist uproar of the late 1940s?
    (A) The Federal Bureau of Investigation successfully prevented the Soviets from stealing American atomic secrets.
    (B) Two American citizens, Julius and Ethel Rosenberg, were executed as Soviet spies.
    (C) The House Un-American Activities Committee (HUAC), featuring Congressman Richard Nixon as its most prominent member, conducted a controversial investigation designed to prove that Alger Hiss of the State Department was a communist agent.
    (D) Conservative local politicians used communism to attack changes in American sexual and cultural values.
    (E) Teachers and other employees in many states were forced to sign loyalty oaths.

11. All of the following characterized the NSC-68 document EXCEPT that
    (A) it reflected the American belief in the limitless capabilities of the American economy and society to meet America's foreign policy and national security challenges.
    (B) it called for a massive increase in military spending and the militarization of American foreign policy.
    (C) the Korean crisis gave NSC-68 the necessary political impetus and political cover for its successful policy implementation under the Truman administration.

    (D) in contrast to the multifaceted containment policy outlined by George Kennan, NSC-68 emphasized military action in foreign policy over diplomatic and economic initiatives.
    (E) the national security and military spending prescriptions contained in NSC-68 were embraced by the midwestern isolationist wing of the Republican party.

12. What caused President Harry Truman to relieve General Douglas MacArthur from command of the United Nations troops in Korea in April of 1951?
    (A) MacArthur continued to lose crucial battles.
    (B) MacArthur crossed the 38th parallel and entered North Korea.
    (C) The Chinese entered the Korean War after MacArthur said they would not.
    (D) MacArthur began to openly defy Truman's orders on military policy in Korea.
    (E) MacArthur announced he would run for president of the United States in 1952.

13. How does the 1950s baby boom continue to affect the United States today?
    (A) The baby boom eventually contributed to an even larger population explosion when "baby boomers" had children of their own.
    (B) As "baby boomers" reach retirement age, the number of people eligible for Social Security puts a huge strain on the system.
    (C) People moved to urban areas to start families, leading to constant overpopulation.
    (D) Adults born in the 1950s have a great deal of influence over pop culture and fashion in the twenty-first century.
    (E) The generation born after World War II directly benefited from the GI Bill, creating a large, patriotic demographic group.

14. The United States' move away from isolationism as it emerged as a superpower after World War II is evident in all of the following EXCEPT in
    (A) the United Nations making its permanent home in New York City.
    (B) the United States' instrumental role in creating and funding the International Monetary Fund and the World Bank.
    (C) the Marshall Plan positioning the United States as the financial savior of Western Europe.
    (D) Truman's policy of strong support for Israel despite domestic and international objections.
    (E) the National Security Act establishing a National Security Council to advise the president on security matters.

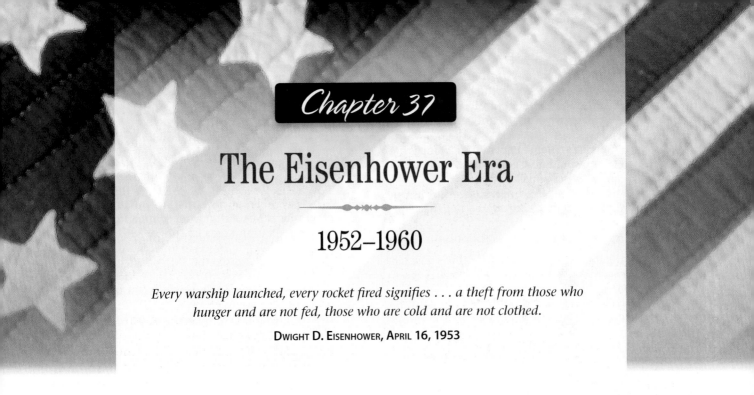

Chapter 37

The Eisenhower Era

1952–1960

Every warship launched, every rocket fired signifies . . . a theft from those who hunger and are not fed, those who are cold and are not clothed.

DWIGHT D. EISENHOWER, APRIL 16, 1953

In President Dwight D. Eisenhower, the man and the hour met. Americans yearned for a period of calm in which they could pursue without distraction their new visions of consumerist affluence. The nation sorely needed a respite from twenty years of depression and war. Yet the American people unexpectedly found themselves in the early 1950s dug into the frontlines of the Cold War abroad and dangerously divided at home over the explosive issues of communist subversion and civil rights. They longed for reassuring leadership. "Ike" seemed ready both to reassure and to lead.

⋇ Affluence and Its Anxieties

The continuing post–World War II economic boom wrought wondrous changes in American society in the 1950s. Prosperity triggered a fabulous surge in home construction, as a nation of renters became a nation of homeowners. One of every four homes standing in America in 1960 had been built during the 1950s, and 83 percent of those new homes were in suburbia.

More than ever, science and technology drove economic growth. The invention of the transistor in 1948 sparked a revolution in electronics, and especially in computers. The first electronic computers assembled in the 1940s were massive machines with hundreds of miles of wiring and thousands of fickle cathode ray tubes. Transistors and, later, printed circuits on silicon wafers made possible dramatic miniaturization and phenomenal computational speed. Computer giant International Business Machines (IBM) expanded robustly, becoming the prototype of the "high-tech" corporation in the dawning "information age." Eventually personal computers and even inexpensive pocket calculators contained more computing power than room-size early models. Computers transformed age-old business practices like billing and inventory control and opened genuine new frontiers in areas like airline scheduling, high-speed printing, and telecommunications.

Aerospace industries also grew fantastically in the 1950s, thanks both to Eisenhower's aggressive buildup of the Strategic Air Command and to a robustly expanding passenger airline business—as well as to connections between military and civilian aircraft production. In 1957 the Seattle-based Boeing Company brought out the first large passenger jet, the "707." Its design owed much to the previous development of SAC's long-range strategic bomber, the B-52. Two years later Boeing delivered the first presidential jet, a specially modified 707, to its first user, Dwight D. Eisenhower. "Air Force One" dazzled him with its speed and comfort.

The nature of the work force was also changing. A quiet revolution was marked in 1956 when "white-collar" workers for the first time outnumbered "blue-collar" workers, signaling the passage from an industrial to a postindustrial, or service-based, economy. Keeping pace with that fundamental transformation, organized labor withered along with the smokestack industries that had been its sustenance. Union membership as a

© Bettmann/Corbis

An Early Computer, ca. 1950 Just a few decades later, technological improvements would bring the computing power of this bulky behemoth to the user's desktop.

World War II ended, many women, including those who had worked in war plants, returned to highly conventional female roles as wives and mothers—the remarkably prolific mothers of the huge "baby-boom" generation. A "cult of domesticity" emerged in popular culture to celebrate those eternal feminine functions. When 1950s television programs like "Ozzie and Harriet" or "Leave It to Beaver" depicted idyllic suburban families with a working husband, two children, and a wife who did not work outside the home, they did so without irony; much of white, middle-class America really did live that way. But as the 1950s progressed, another quiet revolution was gaining momentum that was destined to transform women's roles and even the character of the American family.

Of some 40 million new jobs created in the three decades after 1950, more than 30 million were in clerical and service work. Women filled the huge majority of these new positions. They were the principal employment beneficiaries of the postwar era, creating an extensive "pink-collar ghetto" of occupations that came to be dominated by women (see Figure 37.1).

Exploding employment opportunities for women in the 1950s unleashed a groundswell of social and psychological shocks that mounted to tidal-wave proportions in the decades that followed. From one perspective women's surge into the workplace was nothing new, only a return to the days when the United States was an agricultural nation, and men and women alike toiled on the family farm. But the urban age was not the agricultural age, and women's new dual role as *both* workers *and* homemakers raised urgent questions about family life and traditional definitions of gender differences.

Feminist Betty Friedan gave focus and fuel to women's feelings in 1963 when she published **_The Feminine Mystique_**, a runaway best seller and a classic of

percentage of the labor force peaked at about 35 percent in 1954 and then went into steady decline (see p. 769). Some observers concluded that the union movement had played out its historic role of empowering workers and ensuring economic justice, and that unions would eventually disappear altogether in the postindustrial era.

The surge in white-collar employment opened special opportunities for women (see Table 37.1). When

TABLE 37.1 Occupational Distribution of Workingwomen, 1900–2000*

	1900	1920	1940	1960	1980	2000
Total white-collar workers†	17.8%	38.8%	44.9%	52.5%	65.6%	73.0%
Clerical workers	4.0	18.7	21.5	28.7	30.5	36.7
Manual workers	27.8	23.8	21.6	18.0	14.8	8.7
Farmworkers	18.9	13.5	4.0	1.8	1.0	0.3
Service workers‡	35.5	23.9	29.4	21.9	18.1	18.0

*Major categories; percentage of all women workers in each category, calculated at fourteen and older until 1970 and then sixteen and older.
†Includes clerical, sales, professional, and technical workers, managers, and officials.
‡Includes domestic servants.

(Sources: *Historical Statistics of the United States* and *Statistical Abstract of the United States*, relevant years.)

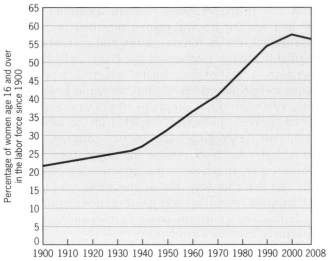

FIGURE 37.1 Women in the Labor Force, 1900–2008
(Sources: *Historical Statistics of the United States* and *Statistical Abstract of the United States*, relevant years.)

feminist protest literature that launched the modern women's movement. Friedan spoke in rousing accents to millions of able, educated women who applauded her indictment of the stifling boredom of suburban housewifery. Many of those women were already working for wages, but they were also struggling against the guilt and frustration of leading an "unfeminine" life as defined by the postwar "cult of domesticity."

✷ Consumer Culture in the Fifties

The 1950s witnessed a huge expansion of the middle class and the blossoming of a consumer culture. Diner's Club introduced the plastic credit card in 1949, just one year after the first "fast-food"–style McDonald's hamburger stand opened in San Bernardino, California. In 1955 Disneyland opened its doors in Anaheim, California. Easy credit, high-volume "fast-food" production, and new forms of leisure marked an emerging affluent lifestyle that soon moved beyond America's borders. Manufacturers, retailers, and advertisers spread American-style consumer capitalism throughout much of the noncommunist world.

Crucial to the development of that lifestyle was the rapid rise of the new technology of television. Only 6 TV stations were broadcasting in 1946; a decade later 442 stations were operating. TV sets were rich people's novelties in the 1940s, but 7 million sets were sold in 1951. By 1960 virtually every American home had one, in a stunning display of the speed with which new technologies can pervade and transform modern societies (see Figure 37.2).

Attendance at movies sank as the entertainment industry changed its focus from the silver screen to the picture tube. By the mid-1950s, advertisers annually spent $10 billion to hawk their wares on television, while critics fumed that the wildly popular new mass medium was degrading the public's aesthetic, social, moral, political, and educational standards. To the

The Booming Service Sector
Services displaced manufacturing as the most dynamic area of the economy in the post–World War II era, and women made up a majority of new workers in the nation's offices and classrooms and on sales floors and hospital wards.

The Original Golden Arches, 1955 Maurice and Richard McDonald replaced their original drive-in hamburger stand in San Bernardino, California, with this double-arched design in 1953. McDonald's soon became one of the largest franchised restaurant chains in the world and a global symbol of American consumerism.

question "Why is television called a medium?" pundits replied, "Because it's never rare or well done."

Even religion capitalized on the powerful new electronic pulpit. "Televangelists" like the Baptist Billy Graham, the Pentecostal Holiness preacher Oral Roberts, and the Roman Catholic Fulton J. Sheen took to the airwaves to spread the Christian gospel. Television also catalyzed the commercialization of professional sports, as viewing audiences that once numbered in the stadium-capacity thousands could now be counted in the couch-potato millions.

Sports also reflected the shift in population toward the West and South. In 1958 baseball's New York Giants moved to San Francisco, and the Brooklyn Dodgers abandoned Flatbush for Los Angeles. Those moves touched off a new westward and southward movement of sports franchises. Shifting population and spreading affluence led eventually to substantial expansion of the major baseball leagues and the principal football and basketball leagues as well.

Popular music was dramatically transformed in the fifties. The chief revolutionary was Elvis Presley, a white singer born in 1935 in Tupelo, Mississippi. Fusing black rhythm and blues with white bluegrass and country styles, Elvis created a new musical idiom known forever after as **rock 'n' roll**. Rock was "crossover" music, carrying its heavy beat and driving rhythms across the cultural divide that separated black and white musical traditions. Listening and dancing to rock 'n' roll became a rite of passage for millions of young people around the world, from Japan to working-class Liverpool, England, where Elvis's music inspired teenagers John Lennon and Paul McCartney to form a band that would become the Beatles.

Traditionalists were repelled by Presley, and they found much more to upset them in the affluent fifties. Movie star Marilyn Monroe, with her ingenuous smile and mandolin-curved hips, helped to popularize—and commercialize—new standards of sensuous sexuality. So did *Playboy* magazine, whose first issue Monroe graced in 1953. As the decade closed, Americans were well on their way to becoming free-spending

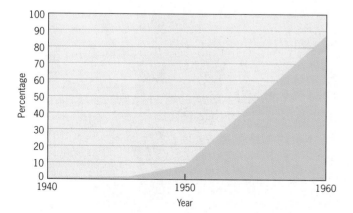

FIGURE 37.2 Households with Television Sets, 1946–1960 Note the rapid adoption of this new device, a harbinger of the viral spread of technologies like cell phones and the Internet later in the century.

The King With his fleshy face, pouting lips, and antic, sexually suggestive gyrations, Elvis Presley became the high priest of rock 'n' roll in the 1950s, to the chagrin of parents everywhere. Bloated by fame, fortune, and drugs, he died in 1977 at the age of forty-two.

consumers of mass-produced, standardized products, which were advertised on the electronic medium of television and often sold for their alleged sexual allure.

Many critics lamented the implications of this new consumerist lifestyle. Harvard sociologist David Riesman portrayed the postwar generation as a pack of conformists in *The Lonely Crowd* (1950), as did William H. Whyte, Jr., in *The Organization Man*. Novelist Sloan Wilson explored a similar theme in *The Man in the Gray Flannel Suit* (1955). Harvard economist John Kenneth Galbraith questioned the relation between private wealth and the public good in a series of books beginning with *The Affluent Society* (1958). The postwar explosion of prosperity, Galbraith claimed, had produced a troublesome combination of private opulence amid public squalor. Americans had televisions in their homes but garbage in their streets. They ate rich food but breathed foul air. But Galbraith's call for social spending to match private purchasing fell on mostly deaf ears in the giddily affluent 1950s.

✪ The Advent of Eisenhower

Democratic prospects in the presidential election of 1952 were blighted by the military deadlock in Korea, Truman's clash with MacArthur, war-bred inflation, and whiffs of scandal from the White House. Dispirited

Democrats nominated a reluctant Adlai E. Stevenson, the eloquent and idealistic governor of Illinois. Republicans enthusiastically chose war hero General Dwight D. Eisenhower on the first ballot. "Ike's" running mate was California senator Richard M. Nixon, who had gained notoriety as a relentless red-hunter.

Eisenhower was already the most popular American of his time, as "I Like Ike" buttons everywhere testified. Striking a grandfatherly, nonpartisan pose, Eisenhower left the rough campaigning to Nixon, who relished bare-knuckle political combat. The vice-presidential candidate lambasted his opponents with charges that they had cultivated corruption, caved in on Korea, and coddled communists. He particularly blasted the cerebral Stevenson as "Adlai the appeaser," with a "Ph.D. from [Secretary of State] Dean Acheson's College of Cowardly Communist Containment."

Nixon himself faltered late in the campaign amid accusations that he had accepted illegal donations. Responding with a self-pitying live address on television, Nixon denied the charges and solemnly declared that the only campaign gift he had ever received was the family cocker spaniel, Checkers. The shameless and mawkish **Checkers Speech** saved Nixon's spot on the ticket and spotlighted a fundamental change in American politics. Television was now a formidable political tool that, much more than radio, allowed candidates to bypass traditional party machinery and speak directly to voters.

The Republicans' Choice, 1952 Nominee Eisenhower and his vice-presidential running mate, Nixon, greet the delegates.

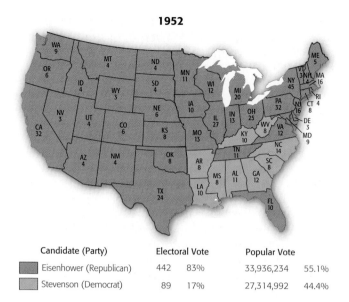

1952

Candidate (Party)	Electoral Vote		Popular Vote	
Eisenhower (Republican)	442	83%	33,936,234	55.1%
Stevenson (Democrat)	89	17%	27,314,992	44.4%

MAP 37.1 Presidential Election of 1952 (with electoral vote by state) A Democrat quipped that "if the voters liked the Republicans the way they liked Ike, the two-party system would be in bad shape." Fortunately for Democrats, Eisenhower scored a personal, not a party, victory. Republicans won minuscule majorities in Congress, which disappeared in the congressional elections two years later. © Cengage Learning

Soon even Eisenhower was reluctantly appearing in short, tightly scripted televised "spots" that foreshadowed the future of political advertising. Devoid of substance, they vastly oversimplified complicated economic and social issues. They amounted, as one critic observed, to "selling the President like toothpaste." And given television's origins in entertainment and advertising, political messages would be increasingly tuned to the standards of show business and commercialism.

The outcome of the presidential election of 1952 was never really in doubt. Given an extra prod by Eisenhower's last-minute pledge to go personally to Korea to end the war, the voters overwhelmingly declared for Ike. He garnered 33,936,234 votes to Stevenson's 27,314,992, ringing up 442 electoral votes to 89 for his opponent (see Map 37.1). Ike also managed to pull enough Republican legislators into office on his military coattails to gain GOP control of the new Congress by a hairbreadth.

True to his campaign pledge, president-elect Eisenhower undertook a flying three-day visit to Korea in December 1952. But even a glamorous Ike could not immediately budge the peace negotiations off dead center. Seven long months later, after Eisenhower had hinted that he might use atomic weapons, an armistice was finally signed. (Subsequent inquiries suggested that Ike's hints were so artfully veiled that the Chinese

never understood them. They agreed to end the war for reasons of their own, especially its burdensome financial costs.)

The brutal and futile fighting had lasted three years. About fifty-four thousand Americans lay dead, joined by perhaps more than a million Chinese, North Koreans, and South Koreans. Tens of billions of American dollars had been poured down the Asian sinkhole. Yet this terrible toll in blood and treasure bought only a return to the conditions of 1950: Korea remained divided at the thirty-eighth parallel, Communist in the North, Western-looking in the South. Americans took what little comfort they could from the fact that communism had been "contained" and that the bloodletting had been "limited" to something less than full-scale global war. The shooting had ended, but the Cold War still remained frigidly frozen.

As a military commander, Eisenhower had cultivated a leadership style that self-consciously projected an image of sincerity, fairness, and optimism. He had been widely perceived during World War II as an "unmilitary" general, and in the White House he similarly struck the pose of an "unpolitical" president, serenely above the petty partisan fray. He also shrewdly knew that his greatest "asset" was his enjoyment of the "affection and respect of our citizenry," as he confided to his diary in 1949.

Ike thus seemed ideally suited to soothe the anxieties of troubled Americans, much as a distinguished and well-loved grandfather brings stability to his family.

U.S. Army Photograph

Korean War Scene A grief-stricken American soldier whose buddy has been killed is being comforted, while a medical corpsman fills out casualty tags.

He played this role well as he presided over a decade of shaky peace and shining prosperity. Yet critics charged that he unwisely hoarded the "asset" of his immense popularity, rather than spend it for a good cause (especially civil rights), and that he cared more for social harmony than for social justice.

✴ The Rise and Fall of Joseph McCarthy

One of the first problems Eisenhower faced was the swelling popularity and swaggering power of an obstreperous anticommunist crusader, Wisconsin Republican senator Joseph R. McCarthy. Elected to the Senate on the basis of a trumped-up war-hero record, McCarthy had crashed into the limelight in February 1950 when he accused Secretary of State Dean Acheson of knowingly employing 205 Communist party members. Pressed to reveal the names, McCarthy later conceded that there were only 57 genuine communists and in the end failed to root out even one. Some of McCarthy's Republican colleagues nevertheless realized the partisan usefulness of this kind of attack on the Democratic administration. Ohio's Senator John Bricker reportedly said, "Joe, you're a dirty s.o.b., but there are

In a moment of high drama during the Army-McCarthy hearings, attorney Joseph Welch (1890–1960) reproached McCarthy in front of a huge national television audience for threatening to slander a young lawyer on Welch's staff:

❝Until this moment, Senator, I think I never really gauged your cruelty or your recklessness. Little did I dream you could be so cruel as to do an injury to that lad. . . . If it were in my power to forgive you for your reckless cruelty, I would do so. I like to think that I am a gentleman, but your forgiveness will have to come from someone other than me. . . . Have you no decency, sir, at long last? Have you left no sense of decency?**❞**

times when you've got to have an s.o.b. around, and this is one of them."

McCarthy's rhetoric grew bolder and his accusations spread more wildly after the Republican victory in 1952. McCarthy saw the red hand of Moscow everywhere. The Democrats, he charged, "bent to whispered pleas from the lips of traitors." Incredibly, he even denounced General George Marshall, former army chief of staff and ex–secretary of state, as "part of a conspiracy so immense and an infamy so black as to dwarf any previous venture in the history of man."

McCarthy—and what became known as **McCarthyism**—flourished in the seething Cold War atmosphere of suspicion and fear. The senator was neither the first nor the most effective red-hunter, but he was surely the most ruthless, and he did the most damage to American traditions of fair play and free speech. The careers of countless officials, writers, and actors were ruined after "Low-Blow Joe" had "named" them, often unfairly, as communists or communist sympathizers. Politicians trembled in the face of such onslaughts, especially when opinion polls showed that a majority of the American people approved of McCarthy's crusade.

Eisenhower privately loathed McCarthy but publicly tried to stay out of his way, saying, "I will not get in the gutter with that guy." Trying to appease the brash demagogue from Wisconsin, Eisenhower allowed him, in effect, to control personnel policy at the State Department. One baleful result was severe damage to the morale and effectiveness of the professional foreign service. In particular, McCarthyite purges deprived the government of a number of Asian specialists who might have counseled a wiser course in Vietnam in the fateful decade that followed. McCarthy's extreme antics also

Senator McCarthy Extinguishes the Torch of Liberty While preaching patriotism, McCarthy irresponsibly menaced American traditions of civil liberties.

damaged America's international reputation for fair and open democracy at a moment when it was important to keep Western Europe on the United States' side in an intensifying Cold War.

McCarthy finally bent the bow too far when he attacked the U.S. Army. The embattled military men fought back in thirty-five days of televised hearings in the spring of 1954. The political power of the new broadcast medium was again demonstrated by the **Army-McCarthy hearings**, as up to 20 million Americans at a time watched in fascination while a boorish, surly McCarthy publicly cut his own throat by parading his essential meanness and irresponsibility. A few months later, the Senate formally condemned him for "conduct unbecoming a member." Three years later, unwept and unsung, McCarthy died of chronic alcoholism. But "McCarthyism" has passed into the English language as a label for the dangerous forces of unfairness and fear that a democratic society can unleash only at its peril.

✦ Desegregating American Society

America counted some 15 million black citizens in 1950, two-thirds of whom still made their homes in the South. There they lived bound by the iron folkways of a segregated society. A rigid set of antiquated rules known as **Jim Crow** laws governed all aspects of their existence, from the schoolroom to the restroom. Every day of their lives, southern blacks dealt with a bizarre array of separate social arrangements that kept them insulated from whites, economically inferior, and politically powerless. Blacks in the South not only attended segregated schools but were compelled to use separate public toilets, drinking fountains, restaurants, and waiting

The New York Times Co./Getty Images

The Face of Segregation These women in the segregated South of the 1950s were compelled to enter the movie theater through the "Colored Entrance." Once inside, they were restricted to a separate seating section, usually in the rear of the theater.

rooms. Trains and buses had "whites only" and "colored only" seating. Only about 20 percent of eligible southern blacks were registered to vote, and fewer than 5 percent were registered in some Deep South states like Mississippi and Alabama. As late as 1960, white southern sensibilities about segregation were so tender that television networks blotted out black speakers at the national political conventions for fear of offending southern stations.

Where the law proved insufficient to enforce this regime, vigilante violence did the job. Six black war veterans, claiming the rights for which they had fought overseas, were murdered in the summer of 1946. A Mississippi mob lynched black fourteen-year-old Emmett Till in 1955 for allegedly leering at a white woman. It is small wonder that a black clergyman declared that "everywhere I go in the South the Negro is forced to choose between his hide and his soul."

Segregation tarnished America's international image, much as McCarthyism did. After the war African

A black woman described the day-in, day-out humiliations of life in the Jim Crow South:

❝You could not go to a white restaurant; you sat in a special place at the movie house; and Lord knows, you sat in the back of the bus. It didn't make any difference if you were rich or poor, if you were black you were nothing. You might have a hundred dollars in your pocket, but if you went to the store you would wait at the side until all the clerks got through with all the white folks, no matter if they didn't have change for a dollar. Then the clerk would finally look at you and say, 'Oh, did you want something? I didn't see you there.'**❞**

American entertainers like Paul Robeson and Josephine Baker toured widely in Europe and Latin America, informing audiences about the horrors of Jim Crow and raising doubts about America's reputation as the beacon of freedom against Soviet communism. In response, the State Department confiscated Robeson's passport, but it had to find other ways to silence Baker, who had assumed French citizenship. Intellectuals poured on criticism as well. Swedish scholar Gunnar Myrdal published his landmark book, *An American Dilemma*, exposing the scandalous contradiction between "The American Creed"—allegiance to the values of "progress, liberty, equality, and humanitarianism"—and the nation's shameful treatment of black citizens.

International pressure combined with grassroots and legal activism to propel some racial progress in the North after World War II. In a growing number of northern cities and states, African Americans battled for—and won—equal access to public accommodations like restaurants, hotels, theaters, and beaches. Jackie Robinson cracked baseball's color barrier when the Brooklyn Dodgers signed him in 1947. The National Association for the Advancement of Colored People (NAACP) pushed the Supreme Court in 1950 to rule in *Sweatt* v. *Painter* that separate professional schools for blacks failed to meet the test of equality. The national conscience was slowly awakening from its centuries-long slumber, but black suffering still continued, especially in the South.

Increasingly, however, African Americans refused to suffer in silence (see "Makers of America: The Great African American Migration," pp. 870–871). On a chilly day in December 1955, Rosa Parks, a college-educated black seamstress, made history in Montgomery, Alabama. She boarded a bus, took a seat in the "whites only" section, and refused to give it up. Her arrest for violating the city's Jim Crow statutes sparked a year-long black boycott of city buses and served notice throughout the South that blacks would no longer submit meekly to the absurdities and indignities of segregation.

The **Montgomery bus boycott** also catapulted to prominence a young pastor at Montgomery's Dexter Avenue Baptist Church, the Reverend Martin Luther King, Jr. Barely twenty-seven years old, King seemed an unlikely champion of the downtrodden and disfranchised. Raised in a prosperous black family in Atlanta and educated partly in the North, he had for most of his life been sheltered from the grossest cruelties of segregation. But his oratorical skill, his passionate devotion to biblical and constitutional conceptions of justice, and his devotion to the nonviolent principles of India's Mohandas Gandhi were destined to thrust him to the forefront of the black revolution that would soon pulse across the South and the rest of the nation.

✶ Seeds of the Civil Rights Revolution

When President Harry Truman heard about the lynching of black war veterans in 1946, he exclaimed, "My God! I had no idea it was as terrible as that." The horrified Truman responded by commissioning a report titled "To Secure These Rights." Following the report's recommendations, Truman in 1948 ended segregation in federal civil service and ordered "equality of treatment and opportunity" in the armed forces. Yet Congress stubbornly resisted passing civil rights legislation, and Truman's successor, Dwight Eisenhower, showed no real interest in racial issues. It was the Supreme Court that assumed political leadership in the civil rights struggle.

Chief Justice Earl Warren, former governor of California, shocked traditionalists with his active judicial intervention in previously taboo social issues. Publicly snubbed and privately scorned by President Eisenhower, Warren courageously led the Court to address urgent issues that Congress and the president preferred to avoid, as "Impeach Earl Warren" signs blossomed along the nation's highways.

The unanimous decision of the Warren Court in **Brown v. Board of Education of Topeka, Kansas** in May 1954 was epochal. In a forceful opinion, the learned justices ruled that segregation in the public schools was "inherently unequal" and thus unconstitutional. The uncompromising sweep of the decision startled conservatives like an exploding time bomb, for it reversed the Court's earlier declaration of 1896 in *Plessy* v. *Ferguson* (see p. 496) that "separate but equal" facilities were allowable under the Constitution. That

Joseph E. Lowery (b. 1921), a Methodist minister and civil rights activist in Mobile, Alabama, reflected on the powerful message of the 1955 Montgomery bus boycott for blacks:

❝You see, what the bus thing did was simply more than withholding patronage from the bus; it was restoring a sense of dignity to the patrons, as best expressed by an oft-quoted black woman in Montgomery who said, 'Since I've been walking, my feet are tired, but my soul's rested.' . . . [P]rior to the bus boycotts, the determination of our freedom rested with the courts. With the bus boycott, we determined it. . . . The court could say what it liked, we weren't gon' ride—in the back of the bus. We'd walk.**❞**

Integration in Little Rock, Arkansas, 1957 Fifteen-year-old Elizabeth Eckford endured scathing insults from white students and parents as she attempted to enter Little Rock's Central High School. The showdown at Little Rock was a replay of nineteenth-century confrontations over "states' rights," and forced a reluctant Eisenhower administration to assert the supremacy of federal power.

doctrine was now dead. Desegregation, the justices insisted, must go ahead with "all deliberate speed."

The Border States generally made reasonable efforts to comply with this ruling, but in the Deep South diehards organized "massive resistance" against the Court's annulment of the sacred principle of "separate but equal." More than a hundred southern congressional representatives and senators signed the "Declaration of Constitutional Principles" in 1956, pledging their unyielding resistance to desegregation. Several states diverted public funds to hastily created "private" schools, for there the integration order was more difficult to apply. Throughout the South white citizens' councils, sometimes with fire and hemp, thwarted attempts to make integration a reality. Ten years after the Court's momentous ruling, fewer than 2 percent of the eligible blacks in the Deep South were sitting in classrooms with whites.

President Eisenhower remained reluctant to promote integration. He shied away from employing his vast popularity and the prestige of his office to educate white Americans about the need for racial justice. His personal attitudes may have helped to restrain him. He had grown up in an all-white town, spent his career in a segregated army, and advised against integration of the armed forces in 1948. He complained that the Supreme Court's decision in *Brown* v. *Board of Education* had upset "the customs and convictions of at least two generations of Americans," and he steadfastly refused to issue a public statement endorsing the Court's conclusions. "I do not believe," he explained, "that prejudices, even palpably unjustifiable prejudices, will succumb to compulsion."

But in September 1957, Ike was forced to act. Orval Faubus, the governor of Arkansas, mobilized the National Guard to prevent nine black students from enrolling in Little Rock's Central High School. Confronted with a direct challenge to federal authority, Eisenhower sent troops to escort the children to their classes.

In the same year, Congress passed the first Civil Rights Act since Reconstruction days. Eisenhower characteristically reassured a southern senator that the legislation represented "the mildest civil rights bill possible." It set up a permanent Civil Rights Commission to investigate violations of civil rights and authorized federal injunctions to protect voting rights.

Blacks meanwhile continued to take the civil rights movement into their own hands. Martin Luther King, Jr., formed the Southern Christian Leadership Conference (SCLC) in 1957. It aimed to mobilize the vast power of the black churches on behalf of black rights. This was an exceptionally shrewd strategy, because the churches were the largest and best-organized black institutions that had been allowed to flourish in a segregated society.

More spontaneous was the "sit-in" movement launched on February 1, 1960, by four black college freshmen in Greensboro, North Carolina. Without a detailed plan or institutional support, they demanded service at a whites-only Woolworth's lunch counter. Observing that "fellows like you make our race look bad," the black waitress refused to serve them. But they kept their seats and returned the next day with nineteen classmates. The following day, eighty-five students joined in; by the end of the week, a thousand. The sit-in movement rolled swiftly across the South, swelling into a wave of wade-ins, lie-ins, and pray-ins to compel equal treatment in restaurants, transportation, employment, housing, and voter registration. In April 1960

The great social upheavals of World War II continued to transform America well after the guns had fallen silent in 1945. Among the groups most affected by the war were African Americans. Predominantly a rural, southern people before 1940, African Americans were propelled by the war into the cities of the North and West, and by 1970 a majority lived outside the states of the old Confederacy. The results of that massive demographic shift were momentous, for African Americans and for all of American society.

So many black southerners took to the roads during World War II that local officials lost track of their numbers. Black workers on the move crowded into boardinghouses, camped out in cars, and clustered in the juke joints of roadside America en route to their new lives.

Southern cotton fields and tobacco plantations had historically yielded slender sustenance to African American farmers, most of whom struggled to make ends meet as tenants or sharecroppers. The Great Depression dealt black southerners yet another blow, for when New Deal farm programs paid growers to leave their land fallow, many landlords simply pocketed the money and evicted their tenants—white as well as black—from their now-idle fields. As the Depression deepened, dispossessed former tenants and sharecroppers toiled as seasonal farmworkers or languished without jobs, without shelter, and without hope.

The spanking-new munitions plants and bustling shipyards of wartime America at first offered little solace to African Americans, particularly in the South. In 1940 and 1941, the labor-hungry war machine soaked up unemployed white workers but commonly denied jobs to blacks. When the army constructed a training camp near Petersburg, Virginia, it imported white carpenters from all parts of the United States, rather than employ the hundreds of skilled black carpenters who lived nearby. Fed up with such injustices, many African Americans headed for shipyards, factories, foundries, and fields on the Pacific Coast or north of the Mason-Dixon line, where their willing hands found more work awaiting them.

Angered by the racism that was depriving their people of a fair share of jobs, black leaders cajoled President Roosevelt into issuing an executive order in June 1941 declaring that "there shall be no discrimination in the

The Granger Collection, New York

The Migration of the Negro, by Jacob Lawrence, 1940–1941 Artist Jacob Lawrence depicted the migration of southern blacks to the North during and after World War II in a series of paintings. The first panel of the series bears the description "During the World War there was a great migration north by southern Negroes."

The Home Front Though often confronted by prejudice and discrimination, many African American migrants from the rural South found their first industrial jobs in wartime defense plants during World War II.

Detroit Race Riot, 1943 A black passenger is dragged from a streetcar.

employment of workers in defense industries or government because of race, creed, color, or national origin." Roosevelt's action was a tenuous, hesitant step. Yet in its way Executive Order 8802 amounted to a second Emancipation Proclamation, as the federal government for the first time since Reconstruction had committed itself to ensuring justice for African Americans.

The entire nation was now forced to face the evil of racism, as bloody wartime riots in Detroit, New York, Philadelphia, and other cities tragically demonstrated. But for the first time, large numbers of blacks secured a foothold in the industrial economy, and they were not about to give it up.

By war's end the great wartime exodus had scattered hundreds of thousands of African Americans to new regions and new ways of life—a second black diaspora comparable in its scale and consequence to the original black dispersal out of Africa. In the postwar decades, blacks continued to pour out of the South in search of economic opportunity and political freedom. In western and northern cities, blacks now competed for housing and jobs, and they also voted—many of them for the first time in their lives.

As early as 1945, NAACP leader Walter White concluded that the war "immeasurably magnified the Negro's awareness of the disparity between the American profession and practice of democracy." After the war, he predicted, African Americans would be "convinced that whatever betterment of their lot is achieved must come largely from their own efforts." The wartime migration thus set the stage for the success of the civil rights movement that began to stir in the late 1940s and the 1950s. With their new political base outside the Old South, and with new support from the Democratic party, African Americans eventually forced an end to the hated segregationist practices that had kept them from enjoying full rights as citizens.

Martin Luther King, Jr., and His Wife, Coretta, Arrested King and his wife were arrested for the first time in Montgomery, Alabama, in 1955 while organizing the bus boycott.

southern black students formed the **Student Nonviolent Coordinating Committee** (**SNCC**, pronounced "snick") to give more focus and force to these efforts. Young and impassioned, SNCC members would eventually lose patience with the more stately tactics of the SCLC and the even more deliberate legalisms of the NAACP.

✦ Eisenhower Republicanism at Home

The balding, sixty-two-year-old General Eisenhower had entered the White House in 1953 pledging his administration to a philosophy of "dynamic conservatism." "In all those things which deal with people, be liberal, be human," he advised. But when it came to "people's money, or their economy, or their form of government, be conservative." This balanced, middle-of-the-road course harmonized with the depression-daunted and war-weary mood of the times. Some critics called Eisenhower's presidency a case of "the bland leading the bland."

Above all, Eisenhower strove to balance the federal budget and guard the Republic from what he called "creeping socialism." The former supreme Allied commander put the brakes on Truman's enormous military buildup, though defense spending still soaked up some 10 percent of the GNP. True to his small-government philosophy, Eisenhower supported the transfer of control over offshore oil fields from the federal government to the states. Ike also tried to curb the TVA (see p. 766) by encouraging a private power company to build a generating plant to compete with the massive public utility spawned by the New Deal. Eisenhower's secretary of health, education, and welfare condemned the free distribution of the Salk antipolio vaccine as "socialized medicine."

Eisenhower responded to the Mexican government's worries that illegal Mexican immigration to the United States would undercut the *bracero* program of legally imported farmworkers inaugurated during

Operation Wetback Thousands of illegal Mexican immigrants were forcibly repatriated to Mexico in the federal government's 1954 roundup operation, which was promoted in part by the Mexican government. The man in this photograph is being pulled across the border by a Mexican official, while an American spectator tries to pull him back into the United States.

J. R. Eyerman/Time & Life Pictures/Getty Images

Drive-in Movie Theater, Utah, 1958 Going to the movies became one more thing Americans could do in their cars in the 1950s. Here moviegoers watch Charlton Heston as Moses in the Academy Award–winning motion picture *The Ten Commandments*. It was the last film made by famed director Cecil B. DeMille.

World War II (see p. 803). In a massive roundup of illegal immigrants, dubbed **Operation Wetback** in reference to the migrants' watery route across the Rio Grande, as many as 1 million Mexicans were apprehended and returned to Mexico in 1954.

In yet another of the rude and arbitrary reversals that long have afflicted the government's relations with Native Americans, Eisenhower also sought to cancel the tribal preservation policies of the "Indian New Deal," in place since 1934 (see p. 765). He proposed to "terminate" the tribes as legal entities and to revert to the assimilationist goals of the Dawes Severalty Act of 1887 (see p. 581). Most Indians resisted termination, and the policy was abandoned in 1961.

Eisenhower obviously could not unscramble all the eggs that had been fried by New Dealers and Fair Dealers for twenty long years. He pragmatically accepted and thereby legitimated many New Dealish programs, stitching them permanently into the fabric of American society. As he told his brother, "Should

any political party attempt to abolish Social Security, unemployment insurance, and eliminate labor and farm programs, you would not hear of that party again in our political history."

In some ways Eisenhower even did the New Deal one better. In a public works project that dwarfed anything the New Dealers had ever dreamed of, Ike backed the **Federal Highway Act of 1956**, a $27 billion plan to build forty-two thousand miles of sleek, fast motorways. The former general believed that such roads were essential to national defense, allowing U.S. troops to mobilize anywhere in the country in the event of a Soviet invasion. Beyond being a defense strategy, laying down these modern, multilane roads created countless construction jobs and speeded the suburbanization of America. The Highway Act offered juicy benefits to the trucking, automobile, oil, and travel industries, while at the same time robbing the railroads, especially passenger trains, of business. The act also exacerbated problems of air quality and energy consumption, and it had especially disastrous consequences for cities, whose once-vibrant downtowns withered away while shopping malls and other sites of leisure and consumption flourished in the far-flung suburbs.

✦ A "New Look" in Foreign Policy

The 1952 Republican platform called for a "new look" in foreign policy. It condemned mere "containment" of communism as "negative, futile, and immoral." Incoming secretary of state John Foster Dulles promised not merely to stem the red tide but to "roll back" its gains and "liberate captive peoples." At the same time, the new administration promised to balance the budget by cutting military spending.

How were these two contradictory goals to be reached? Dulles answered with a **policy of boldness**

Hungarian Uprising, October 26, 1956 Soviet tanks rolled through the streets of Budapest to crush an anticommunist uprising against the Soviets, who had controlled Hungary since World War II. This demonstration of brute force against a grassroots democratic movement turned many communist sympathizers in the West definitively against the Soviet Union.

Keystone/Getty Images

in early 1954. Eisenhower would relegate the army and the navy to the backseat and build up an airfleet of superbombers (called the Strategic Air Command, or SAC) equipped with city-flattening nuclear bombs. These fearsome weapons would inflict "massive retaliation" on the Soviets or the Chinese if they got out of hand. The advantages of this new policy were thought to be its paralyzing nuclear impact and its cheaper price tag when compared with conventional forces—"more bang for the buck." At the same time, Eisenhower sought a thaw in the Cold War through negotiations with the new Soviet leaders who came to power after dictator Joseph Stalin's death in 1953.

In the end, the touted "new look" proved illusory. A new Soviet premier, the burly apparatchik Nikita Khrushchev, rudely rejected Ike's call in 1955 for an "open skies" mutual inspection program over both the Soviet Union and the United States. In 1956 the Hungarians rose up against their Soviet masters and felt badly betrayed when the United States turned a deaf ear to their desperate appeals for aid. The brutally crushed **Hungarian uprising** revealed the sobering truth that America's mighty nuclear sledgehammer was too heavy a weapon to wield in such a relatively minor crisis. The rigid futility of the "massive retaliation" doctrine was thus starkly exposed. To his dismay, Eisenhower also discovered that the aerial and atomic hardware necessary for "massive retaliation" was staggeringly expensive.

✦ The Vietnam Nightmare

Western Europe, thanks to the Marshall Plan and NATO, seemed reasonably secure by the early 1950s, but Southeast Asia was a different can of worms. In Vietnam and elsewhere, nationalist movements had sought for years to throw off the yoke of French colonial rule. The legendary Vietnamese leader, goateed Ho Chi Minh, had tried to appeal personally to Woodrow Wilson in Paris as early as 1919 to support self-determination for the peoples of Southeast Asia. Franklin Roosevelt had likewise inspired hope among Asian nationalists.

But Cold War events dampened the dreams of anticolonial Asian peoples. Their leaders—including Ho Chi Minh—became increasingly communist while the United States became increasingly anticommunist. By 1954 American taxpayers were financing nearly 80 percent of the costs of a bottomless French colonial war in Indochina. The United States' share amounted to about $1 billion a year.

Despite this massive aid, French forces continued to crumble under pressure from Ho Chi Minh's nationalist guerrilla forces, called the Viet Minh. In March

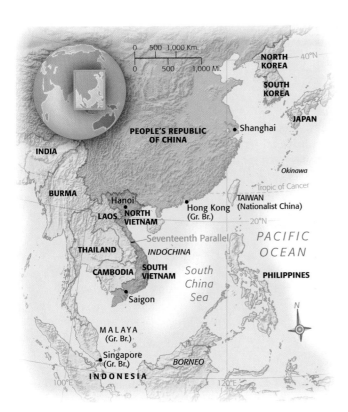

**MAP 37.2 East and Southeast Asia,
1955–1956** © Cengage Learning

1954 a key French garrison was trapped hopelessly in the fortress of Dien Bien Phu in the northwestern corner of Vietnam. The new "policy of boldness" was now put to the test. Secretary Dulles, Vice President Nixon, and the chairman of the Joint Chiefs of Staff favored intervention with American bombers to help bail out the beleaguered French. But Eisenhower, wary about another war in Asia so soon after Korea and correctly fearing British nonsupport, held back.

The **Battle of Dien Bien Phu** proved a victory for the nationalists, and a multination conference in Geneva roughly halved Vietnam at the seventeenth parallel (see Map 37.2). The victorious Ho Chi Minh in the north consented to this arrangement on the assurance that Vietnam-wide elections would be held within two years. In the south a pro-Western government under Ngo Dinh Diem was soon entrenched at Saigon. The Vietnamese never held the promised elections, primarily because the communists seemed certain to win, and Vietnam remained a dangerously divided country.

The United States did not sign the Geneva accords, though Eisenhower promised economic and military aid to the autocratic Diem regime, provided that it undertook certain social reforms. Change came at a snail's pace, but American aid continued, as communist guerrillas heated up their campaign against Diem.

The Americans had evidently backed a losing horse but could see no easy way to call off their bet.

✴ Cold War Crises in Europe and the Middle East

The United States had initially backed the French in Indochina in part to win French approval of a plan to rearm West Germany. Despite French fears, the Germans were finally welcomed into the NATO fold in 1955, with an expected contribution of half a million troops. In the same year, the Eastern European countries and the Soviets signed the Warsaw Pact, creating a red military counterweight to the newly bolstered NATO forces in the West.

Despite these hardening military lines, the Cold War seemed to be thawing a bit in 1955. In May the Soviets rather surprisingly agreed to end their occupation of Austria. A summit conference in Geneva in July produced little progress on the burning issues, but it bred a conciliatory "spirit of Geneva" that caused a modest blush of optimism to pass over the face of the Western world. Hopes rose further the following year when Soviet Communist party boss Khrushchev publicly denounced the bloody excesses of Joseph Stalin, the dictator dead since 1953.

Violent events late in 1956 ended the post-Geneva lull. When the liberty-loving Hungarians struck for their freedom, they were ruthlessly overpowered by Soviet tanks, while the Western world looked on in horror.

Fears of Soviet penetration into the oil-rich Middle East further heightened Cold War tensions. The government of Iran, supposedly influenced by the Kremlin, began to resist the power of the gigantic Western companies that controlled Iranian petroleum. In response, the American Central Intelligence Agency (CIA) helped to engineer a coup in 1953 that installed the youthful shah of Iran, Mohammed Reza Pahlevi, as a kind of dictator. Though successful in the short run in securing Iranian oil for the West, the American intervention left a bitter legacy of resentment among many Iranians. More than two decades later, they took their revenge on the shah and his American allies (see pp. 936–938).

The **Suez crisis** proved far messier than the swift stroke in Iran. President Nasser of Egypt, an ardent Arab nationalist, was seeking funds to build an immense dam on the upper Nile for urgently needed irrigation and power. America and Britain tentatively offered financial help, but when Nasser began to flirt openly with the communist camp, Secretary of State Dulles dramatically withdrew the dam offer. Nasser promptly regained face by nationalizing the Suez Canal, owned chiefly by British and French stockholders.

Egyptian President Gamal Abdel Nasser, 1954 Shown here greeting exuberant supporters after his election as the first president of the new Egyptian republic, Nasser was long a thorn in the flesh of American and European policymakers anxious to protect the precious oil resources of the Middle East. "Nassarism," his version of pan-Arabism, won a great following in the Arab world during the 1950s and 1960s.

AP Images

Nasser's action placed a razor's edge at the jugular vein of Western Europe's oil supply. America's jittery French and British allies, deliberately keeping Washington in the dark and coordinating their blow with one from Israel, staged a joint assault on Egypt late in October 1956.

For a breathless week, the world teetered on the edge of the abyss. The French and British, however, had made a fatal miscalculation—that the United States would supply them with oil while their Middle Eastern supplies were disrupted, as an oil-rich Uncle Sam had done in the two world wars. But to their unpleasant surprise, a furious President Eisenhower resolved to let them "boil in their own oil" and refused to release emergency supplies. The oilless allies resentfully withdrew their troops, and for the first time in history, a United Nations police force was sent to maintain order.

The Suez crisis also marked the last time in history that the United States could brandish its "oil weapon." As recently as 1940, the United States had produced two-thirds of the world's oil, while a scant 5 percent of the global supply flowed from the Middle East. But by 1948 the United States had become a net oil importer. Its days as an "oil power" clearly were numbered as the economic and strategic importance of the Middle East oil region grew dramatically.

The U.S. president and Congress proclaimed the Eisenhower Doctrine in 1957, pledging U.S. military and economic aid to Middle Eastern nations threatened by communist aggression. The real threat to U.S. interests in the Middle East, however, was not communism but nationalism, as Nasser's wild popularity among the masses of all Arab countries demonstrated. The poor, sandy sheikdoms increasingly resolved to reap for themselves the lion's share of the enormous oil wealth that Western companies pumped out of the scorching Middle Eastern deserts. In a portentous move, Saudi Arabia, Kuwait, Iraq, and Iran joined with Venezuela in 1960 to form the **Organization of Petroleum Exporting Countries (OPEC)**. In the next two decades, OPEC's stranglehold on the Western economies would tighten to a degree that even Nasser could not have imagined.

⭐ Round Two for Ike

The election of 1956 was a replay of the 1952 contest, with President Eisenhower pitted once more against Adlai Stevenson. The Democrats were hard-pressed to find issues with which to attack the genial general in a time of prosperity and peace, and the voters made it clear that they still liked Ike. Eisenhower piled up an enormous majority of 35,590,472 popular votes to Stevenson's 26,022,752; in the Electoral College, the count was even more unbalanced at 457 for Republicans to 73 for Democrats. Eisenhower made deeper inroads into the traditional bastion of Democratic strength, the once-solid South, than he had in 1952. Louisiana went Republican for the first time since 1876, during

Reconstruction days. But the general's coattails were not so stiff or broad as in 1952. He failed to win for his party either house of Congress—the first time since Zachary Taylor's election in 1848 that a winning president had headed such a losing ticket.

In fragile health, Eisenhower began his second term as a part-time president. Critics charged that he kept his hands on his golf clubs, fly rod, and shotgun more often than on the levers of power. But in his last years in office, Ike rallied himself to do less golfing and more governing.

A key area in which the president bestirred himself was labor legislation. Congressional investigations produced scandalous revelations of gangsterism, fraud, and brass-knuckles tactics in many American unions, especially the Teamsters. The AF of L–CIO, born of a merger of the two giants in 1955, expelled the Teamsters in 1957 for choosing leaders like two-fisted James R. "Jimmy" Hoffa. Convicted of jury tampering, Hoffa served part of his sentence before disappearing without a trace—evidently the victim of gangsters he had

The Helicopter Era, 1957   President Eisenhower was routinely criticized by liberals, as in this Herblock cartoon in the *Washington Post*, for his apparent indifference to many seething social problems of the day. His failure to employ his vast prestige on behalf of civil rights was especially conspicuous.   *The Helicopter Era. A 1957 Herblock Cartoon, copyright by The Herb Block Foundation*

crossed. To counter such corruption, Eisenhower persuaded Congress to pass the Landrum-Griffin Act in 1959. The act was designed to bring labor leaders to book for financial shenanigans and bullying tactics, but it also expanded some of the antilabor strictures of the earlier Taft-Hartley Act (see p. 830).

Soviet scientists astounded the world on October 4, 1957, by lofting into orbit around the globe a beep-beeping "baby moon" (*Sputnik I*) weighing 184 pounds. A month later they topped their own ace by sending aloft a larger satellite (*Sputnik II*) weighing 1,120 pounds and carrying a dog.

This amazing breakthrough rattled American self-confidence. It cast doubts on America's vaunted scientific superiority and raised some sobering military questions. If the Soviets could fire heavy objects into outer space, they certainly could reach America with intercontinental ballistic missiles (ICBMs).

"Rocket fever" swept the nation. Eisenhower established the National Aeronautics and Space Administration (NASA) and directed billions of dollars to missile development. After humiliating and well-advertised failures—notably the Vanguard missile, which blew up on national television just a few feet above the ground in 1957—in February 1958 the United States managed to put into orbit a grapefruit-sized satellite weighing 2.5 pounds. By the end of the decade, several satellites had been launched, and the United States had successfully tested its own ICBMs.

The **Sputnik** success led to a critical comparison of the American educational system, which was already under fire as too easygoing, with that of the Soviet Union. A strong move now developed in the United States to replace "frills" with solid subjects—to substitute square roots for square dancing. Congress rejected demands for federal scholarships, but late in 1958 the National Defense and Education Act (NDEA) authorized $887 million in loans to needy college students and in grants for the improvement of teaching the sciences and languages.

✪ The Continuing Cold War

The fantastic race toward nuclear annihilation continued unabated. Humanity-minded scientists urged that nuclear tests be stopped before the atmosphere became so polluted as to produce generations of deformed mutants. The Soviets, after completing an intensive series of exceptionally "dirty" tests, proclaimed a suspension in March 1958 and urged the Western world to follow. Beginning in October 1958, Washington did halt both underground and atmospheric testing. But attempts to regularize such suspensions by proper inspection sank on the reef of mutual mistrust.

Thermonuclear suicide seemed nearer in July 1958, when both Egyptian and communist plottings threatened to engulf Western-oriented Lebanon. After its president had called for aid under the Eisenhower Doctrine, the United States boldly landed several thousand troops and helped restore order without taking a single life.

The burly Khrushchev, seeking new propaganda laurels, was eager to meet with Eisenhower and pave the way for a "summit conference" with Western leaders. Despite grave misgivings as to any tangible results, the president invited him to America in 1959. Arriving in New York, Khrushchev appeared before the U.N. General Assembly and dramatically resurrected the ancient Soviet proposal of complete disarmament. But he offered no practical means of achieving this end.

A result of this tour was a meeting at Camp David, the presidential retreat in Maryland. Khrushchev emerged saying that his ultimatum for the evacuation of Berlin would be extended indefinitely. The relieved world gave prayerful but premature thanks for the "spirit of Camp David."

The Camp David spirit quickly evaporated when the follow-up Paris "summit conference," scheduled for May 1960, turned out to be an incredible fiasco. Both Moscow and Washington had taken a firm stand on the burning Berlin issue, and neither could risk backing down publicly. Then, on the eve of the conference, an American U-2 spy plane was shot down deep in the heart of Russia. After bungling bureaucratic denials in Washington, "honest Ike" took the unprecedented step of assuming personal responsibility. Khrushchev stormed into Paris filling the air with invective, and the conference collapsed before it could get off the ground. The concord of Camp David was replaced with the grapes of wrath.

✸ Cuba's Castroism Spells Communism

Latin Americans bitterly resented Uncle Sam's lavishing of billions of dollars on Europe, while doling out only millions to its poor relations to the south. They also chafed at Washington's continuing habit of intervening in Latin American affairs—as in a CIA-directed coup that ousted a leftist government in Guatemala in 1954. On the other hand, Washington continued to support—even decorate—bloody dictators who claimed to be combating communists.

Most ominous of all was the communist beachhead in Cuba. Iron-fisted dictator Fulgencio Batista, in power since the 1930s, had encouraged huge investments of American capital, and Washington in turn had given him some support. But early in 1959, black-bearded Fidel Castro engineered a revolution that ousted

Batista. Castro then denounced the Yankee imperialists and began to expropriate valuable American properties in pursuing a land-distribution program. Washington, finally losing patience, released Cuba from "imperialistic slavery" by cutting off the heavy U.S. imports of Cuban sugar. Castro retaliated with further wholesale confiscations of Yankee property and in effect made his left-wing dictatorship an economic and military satellite of Moscow, to the Kremlin's delighted surprise. An exodus of anti-Castro Cubans headed for the United States, especially Florida. Nearly 1 million arrived between 1960 and 2000. Washington broke diplomatic relations with Castro's government early in 1961 and imposed a strict embargo on trade with Cuba. Strengthened by the Helms-Burton Act in 1996, the embargo has remained in place, even since Castro's departure from power in 2008.

Americans talked seriously of invoking the Monroe Doctrine before the Soviets set up a communist base only ninety miles from their shores. Khrushchev angrily proclaimed that the Monroe Doctrine was dead and indicated that he would shower missiles upon the United States if it attacked his new friend Castro.

✸ Kennedy Challenges Nixon for the Presidency

Republicans approached the presidential campaign of 1960 with Vice President Nixon as their heir apparent. To many he was a gifted party leader, to others a ruthless opportunist. The "old" Nixon had been a no-holds-barred campaigner, adept at skewering Democrats and left-wingers. The "new" Nixon was represented as a mature, seasoned statesman. He had gained particular notice in a finger-pointing **kitchen debate** with Khrushchev in Moscow in 1959, where Nixon extolled the virtues of American consumerism over Soviet economic planning. The next year he handily won the Republican nomination. His running mate was patrician Henry Cabot Lodge, Jr., of Massachusetts (grandson of Woodrow Wilson's arch-foe).

By contrast, the Democratic race for the presidential nomination started as a free-for-all. John F. Kennedy—a youthful, dark-haired millionaire senator from Massachusetts—won impressive victories in the primaries. He then scored a first-ballot triumph in Los Angeles over his closest rival, Senator Lyndon B. Johnson, the Senate majority leader from Texas. A disappointed South was not completely appeased when Johnson accepted second place on the ticket in an eleventh-hour marriage of convenience. Kennedy's challenging acceptance speech called upon the American people for sacrifices to achieve their potential greatness, which he hailed as the New Frontier.

Bigotry inevitably showed its snarling face. Senator Kennedy was a Roman Catholic, the first to be nominated since Al Smith's ill-starred campaign in 1928. Smear artists revived the ancient charges about the Pope's controlling the White House. Kennedy pointed to his fourteen years of service in Congress, denied that he would be swayed by Rome, and asked if some 40 million Catholic Americans were to be condemned to second-class citizenship from birth.

Kennedy's Catholicism aroused misgivings in the Protestant, Bible Belt South, which was ordinarily Democratic. "I fear Catholicism more than I fear communism," declaimed one Baptist minister in North Carolina. But the religious issue largely canceled itself out. If many southern Democrats stayed away from the polls because of Kennedy's Catholicism, northern Democrats in unusually large numbers supported Kennedy because of the bitter attacks on their Catholic faith.

Kennedy charged that the Soviets, with their nuclear bombs and circling Sputniks, had gained on America in prestige and power. Nixon retorted that the nation's prestige had not slipped, although Kennedy was causing it to do so by his unpatriotic talk.

Television may well have tipped the scales. Nixon agreed to meet Kennedy in four so-called debates. The

Candidate John F. Kennedy (1917–1963), in a speech to a Houston group of Protestant ministers (September 12, 1960), declared,

"I believe in an America where the separation of church and state is absolute—where no Catholic prelate would tell the President, should he be a Catholic, how to act, and no Protestant minister would tell his parishioners for whom to vote . . . and where no man is denied public office because his religion differs from the President who might appoint him or the people who might elect him."

contestants crossed words in millions of living rooms before audiences estimated at 60 million or more. Nobody "won" the debates. But Kennedy at least held his own and did not suffer by comparison with the more "experienced" Nixon. The debates once again demonstrated the importance of image over substance in the television age. Many viewers found Kennedy's glamour and vitality far more appealing than Nixon's tired and pallid appearance.

Kennedy squeezed through by the rather comfortable margin of 303 electoral votes to 219,* but with the breathtakingly close popular margin of only 118,574 votes out of over 68 million cast (see Map 37.3). He was the first Roman Catholic and the youngest person to date to be elected president. Like Franklin Roosevelt, Kennedy ran well in the large industrial centers, where he had strong support from workers, Catholics, and African Americans. (He had solicitously telephoned the pregnant Coretta King, whose husband, Martin Luther King, Jr., was then imprisoned in Georgia for a sit-in.) Although losing a few seats, the Democrats also swept both houses of Congress by wide margins.

✬ An Old General Fades Away

President Eisenhower continued to enjoy extraordinary popularity to the final curtain. Despite Democratic jibes about "eight years of golfing and goofing," of "putting and puttering," Eisenhower was universally admired and respected for his dignity, decency, sincerity, goodwill, and moderation.

Pessimists had predicted that Eisenhower would be a seriously crippled "lame duck" during his second

Cornell Capa/Magnum Photos

John F. Kennedy Campaigning for the Presidency, 1960 At right is his wife, Jacqueline Kennedy.

---

*Six Democratic electors in Alabama, all eight unpledged Democratic electors in Mississippi, and one Republican elector in Oklahoma voted for Senator Harry F. Byrd, who ran as an independent.

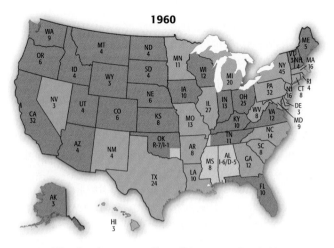

1960

Candidate (Party)	Electoral Vote		Popular Vote	
Kennedy (Democrat)	303	56.50%	34,266,731	49.7%
Nixon (Republican)	219	40.75%	34,108,157	49.5%
Byrd (Independent)	15	2.75%	501,643	0.7%

MAP 37.3 Presidential Election of 1960 (with electoral vote by state) Kennedy owed his hairbreadth triumph to his victories in twenty-six of the forty largest cities—and to Lyndon Johnson's strenuous campaigning in the South, where Kennedy's Catholicism may have been a hotter issue than his stand on civil rights. © Cengage Learning

After campaigning with promises to reduce the defense budget, President Dwight Eisenhower (1890–1969) presided over unprecedented increases in military spending. In his Farewell Address on January 17, 1961, he sagely but ironically warned against the menace his own policies had nurtured:

❝ This conjunction of an immense military establishment and a large arms industry is new in the American experience. . . . In the councils of government, we must guard against the acquisition of unwarranted influence, whether sought or unsought, by the military-industrial complex.❞

term, owing to the barrier against reelection erected by the Twenty-second Amendment, ratified in 1951. (See the Appendix.) In truth, he displayed more vigor, more political know-how, and more aggressive leadership during his last two years as president than ever before. For an unprecedented six years, from 1955 to 1961, Congress remained in Democratic hands, yet Eisenhower exerted unusual control over the legislative branch. He wielded the veto 169 times, and only twice was his nay overridden by the required two-thirds vote.

America was fabulously prosperous in the Eisenhower years, despite pockets of poverty and unemployment, recurrent recessions, and perennial farm problems. To the north the vast St. Lawrence waterway project, constructed jointly with Canada and completed in 1959, had turned the cities of the Great Lakes into bustling ocean seaports. "Old Glory" could now proudly display fifty stars. Alaska attained statehood in 1959, as did Hawaii. Alaska, though gigantic, was thinly populated and noncontiguous, but these objections were overcome in a Democratic Congress that expected Alaska to vote Democratic. Hawaii had ample population (largely of Asian descent), advanced democratic institutions, and more acreage than the mainland states of Rhode Island, Delaware, or Connecticut. As the first noncontiguous states to join the Union, Alaska and Hawaii helped turn America's face toward the Pacific and East Asia.

Though a crusading general, Eisenhower as president mounted no moral crusade for civil rights. This was perhaps his greatest failing. Yet he was no bigot, and he had done far more than grin away problems and tread water. As a Republican president, he had further woven the reforms of the Democratic New Deal and Fair Deal into the fabric of national life. As a former general, he had exercised wise restraint in his use of military power and had soberly guided foreign policy away from countless threats to peace. The old soldier left office crestfallen at his failure to end the arms race with the Soviets. Yet he had ended one war and avoided all others. As the decades lengthened, appreciation of him grew.

✪ A Cultural Renaissance

America's unprecedented global power in the heady post–World War II decades was matched by its new international ascendancy in the arts. Shedding the national inferiority complex that had vexed previous generations, American creative genius exerted a powerful worldwide influence in painting, architecture, and literature.

New York became the art capital of the world after World War II, as well-heeled Americans supported countless painters and sculptors. The open and tradition-free American environment seemed especially congenial to the experimental mood of much modern art. Jackson Pollock pioneered **abstract expressionism** in the 1940s and 1950s, flinging paint on huge flats stretched across his studio floor. Realistic representation went out the window, as artists like Pollock and Willem de Kooning strove to create spontaneous "action paintings" that expressed the painter's individuality and made the viewer a creative participant in defining the painting's meaning. Mark Rothko and his fellow "color field"

The Shopping Mall as New Town Square, 1960

In this photograph, Democratic presidential candidate John F. Kennedy is shown campaigning at the Bergen Mall in Paramus, New Jersey, in 1960. The Bergen Mall opened in 1957, at a time when similar shopping centers were popping up in suburbanizing metropolitan areas all over the United States. Real estate developers watched Americans flee cities for suburbs, and they followed the money, locating shopping centers strategically at new highway intersections or along the busiest thoroughfares. As suburbanites increasingly found branches of their favorite department and chain stores closer to home during the 1950s and 1960s, they found it less and less necessary to go downtown. Shopping centers for their part went out of their way to sell themselves as modern-style downtowns worthy of being the public core of new suburban communities, even though legally they were privately owned space. They provided the full range of shops and services once found in city centers, including restaurants, post offices, Laundromats, banks, and even chapels. They offered entertainment, from movie theaters and skating rinks to free open-air concerts, carnivals, and exhibitions. They made auditoriums available for community meetings. And they attracted public events like Kennedy on the stump. Just four years earlier, a regional shopping center would have been a rare campaign stop for a presidential candidate. Look closely at this photograph. What kind of audience greeted candidate Kennedy at the Bergen Mall? How different might the crowd have looked in a more socially diverse urban center like Manhattan or in nearby Newark, the largest city in New Jersey at the time? What did it mean for sites of consumption, such as privately owned shopping centers, to take on the roles and responsibilities previously associated with urban streets, squares, and parks? How might current struggles of downtown merchants against big-box chain stores like Wal-Mart be related to this history?

Courtesy of the Newark Public Library

Jackson Pollock Flinging Paint on a Canvas, 1950 Promoters of the avant-garde lauded Pollock's paintings, but some critics dismissed them as meaningless explosions of formless energy.

© Rudolph Burckhardt/Sygma/Corbis

employed plain geometric forms and basic building materials like brick and concrete to make beautiful, simple buildings, such as the serene, seaside Salk Institute (1965) in La Jolla, California. Eero Saarinen, the son of a Finnish immigrant, contributed a number of imaginative structures, including the sleek TWA Flight Center (1962) at New York's JFK Airport and the lofty Gateway Arch (1965) in St. Louis. Chinese-born I. M. Pei designed numerous graceful buildings on several college campuses, as well as the dramatic East Wing of the National Gallery of Art (1978) in Washington and the angular John F. Kennedy Library (1979) in Boston.

Postwar America reaped its greatest cultural harvest in the field of literature. In fiction writing some of the prewar masters continued to ply their trade, notably Ernest Hemingway in *The Old Man and the Sea* (1952). A Nobel laureate in 1954, Hemingway was dead by his own duck gun in 1961. John Steinbeck, another prewar writer who persisted in graphic portrayals of American society, such as *East of Eden* (1952) and *Travels with Charley* (1962), received the Nobel Prize for literature in 1962, the seventh American to be so honored.

painters likewise dispatched with figurative representation, enveloping whole canvases with bold, shimmering swaths of color. Other artists creatively exploited more familiar forms. "Pop" (short for popular) artists in the 1960s, notably Andy Warhol, canonized on canvas mundane items of consumer culture like soup cans and soda bottles. Roy Lichtenstein parodied old-fashioned comic strips, and Claes Oldenburg surprised viewers with exotic versions of everyday objects, such as giant plastic sculptures of pillow-soft telephones.

American architecture also reached new heights in the postwar era. While a residential building boom erected vast tracts of look-alike, ranch-style houses across the suburban landscape, ultra-modern skyscrapers arose in the nation's urban centers. Conceived in the modernist or **"International Style,"** these massive corporate high-rises were essentially giant steel boxes wrapped in glass. Classic examples of this "curtain-wall" design include the United Nations headquarters (1952) and the Seagram Building (1957) in New York City and, later, the Sears Tower (1974) in Chicago and the John Hancock Tower (1976) in Boston.

Other postwar architectural achievements transcended the stark steel-and-glass box. Old master Frank Lloyd Wright continued to produce strikingly original designs, conspicuously in the round-walled Guggenheim Museum (1959) in New York. Louis Kahn

Ernest Hemingway (1899–1961) Celebrated both for his writing and his colorful, swashbuckling lifestyle, Hemingway poses here with a dead leopard in 1953.

AP Photo/National Portrait Gallery/Earl Theisen

Curiously, World War II did not inspire the same kind of literary outpouring that World War I had. Searing realism, the trademark style of war writers in the 1920s, characterized the earliest novels that portrayed soldierly life in World War II, such as Norman Mailer's *The Naked and the Dead* (1948) and James Jones's *From Here to Eternity* (1951). But as time passed, realistic war writing fell from favor. Authors tended increasingly to write about the war in fantastic and even psychedelic prose. Joseph Heller's *Catch-22* (1961) dealt with the improbable antics and anguish of American airmen in the wartime Mediterranean. A savage satire, it made readers hurt when they laughed. The supercharged imagination of Kurt Vonnegut, Jr., poured forth works of puzzling complexity in sometimes impenetrably inventive prose, including the dark comedy war tale *Slaughterhouse Five* (1969).

More than the war itself, the fruits of victory at home captured America's literary imagination at mid-century. Postwar pens reacted to the nation's newly affluent, exuberantly consumerist society in two typical ways. One group of countercultural "Beat" writers rejected modern American life outright, seeking romantic self-expression in stridently nonconformist lifestyles (see "Makers of America: The Beat Generation," pp. 884–885).

A larger group of mainstream writers tackled the realities and dilemmas of postwar American society head on. Pennsylvania-born John Updike celebrated the feats and failings of ordinary, small-town America in sensual detail in his four-part "Rabbit" series, starting with *Rabbit, Run* (1960). Updike explicitly addressed suburban, middle-class infidelity in *Couples* (1968). Massachusetts-bred John Cheever, "the Chekhov of the exurbs," similarly chronicled suburban manners and morals in short stories such as "The Swimmer" (1964) and novels like *The Wapshot Chronicle* (1957). Gore Vidal penned a series of intriguing historical novels, as well as several impish and always iconoclastic works, including *Myra Breckinridge* (1968), about a reincarnated transsexual. Together these writers constituted the rear guard of an older, WASP (white Anglo-Saxon Protestant) elite that had long dominated American writing.

Poets were often highly critical, even deeply despairing, about the conformist character of midcentury American life. Older poets were still active, including cantankerous Ezra Pound, jailed after the war in a U.S. Army detention center near Pisa, Italy, for alleged collaboration with the Fascists. Connecticut insurance executive Wallace Stevens and New Jersey pediatrician William Carlos Williams continued after 1945 to pursue second careers as prolific poets of world-class stature.

But younger poets increasingly came to the fore during the postwar period. In short lyric meditations,

In his poem "A Supermarket in California" (1956), Allen Ginsburg (1926–1997) fantasized about meeting nineteenth-century American poet Walt Whitman amidst the lavish consumerism (and spiritual emptiness) of a postwar supermarket:

"I saw you, Walt Whitman, childless, lonely old grubber, poking among the meats in the refrigerator and eyeing the grocery boys.

I heard you asking questions of each: Who killed the pork chops? What price bananas? Are you my Angel?

I wandered in and out of the brilliant stacks of cans following you, and followed in my imagination by the store detective.

We strode down the open corridors together in our solitary fancy tasting artichokes, possessing every frozen delicacy, and never passing the cashier."

they experimented with a frank, "confessional" style, revealing personal experiences with sex, drugs, and madness. Inspired by the Beat poets, Robert Lowell helped inaugurate this trend with his psychologically intense *Life Studies* (1959). Descended from a long line of patrician New Englanders, Lowell sought to apply the wisdom of the Puritan past to the perplexing present in allegorical poems like *For the Union Dead* (1964). Troubled Sylvia Plath crafted the moving verses of *Ariel* (published posthumously in 1966) and a disturbing autobiographical novel, *The Bell Jar* (1963), but her career was cut short when she took her own life in 1963. Along with Plath, Anne Sexton attended Lowell's Boston poetry seminar. She produced brooding autobiographical poems, including *To Bedlam and Part Way Back* (1960), until her death by apparent suicide in 1974. Another brilliant poet of the period, John Berryman, ended his prolific career in 1972 by leaping from a Minneapolis bridge onto the frozen bank of the Mississippi River. Writing poetry seemed to be a dangerous pursuit in modern America. The life of the poet, it was said, began in sadness and ended in madness.

Playwrights were also acute observers of postwar American social mores. Tennessee Williams wrote a series of blistering dramas about psychological misfits struggling to hold themselves together amid the disintegrating forces of modern life. Noteworthy were *A Streetcar Named Desire* (1947) and *Cat on a Hot Tin Roof* (1955), each delivering powerful critiques of the contemporary restrictions placed on women's lives. Arthur Miller brought to the stage searching probes of

"I saw the best minds of my generation," Beat poet Allen Ginsberg (1926–1997) proclaimed, "destroyed by madness, starving hysterical naked, dragging themselves through the negro streets at dawn looking for an angry fix, angelheaded hipsters burning for the ancient heavenly connection to the starry dynamo in the machinery of night. . . ." Ginsberg's famous opening lines of "Howl" (1955) introduced the **Beat Generation** to the literary world. The poem's unruly verse and riotous content encapsulated the Beat Generation's contempt for the listless, middle-class suburban conformity they saw in World War II–weary America. Striving for liberation, these social drifters advocated free-form experimentation in life as well as literature: marching to one's own "beat." At once "beaten down" by the relentless, everyday pressures of bourgeois existence, these bohemian hedonists also deemed themselves capable of "beatitude," or blessedness.

Jack Kerouac (1922–1969) coined the term that defined this "generation" (more accurately, a small coterie) of alternative poets and personalities. Born Jean-Louis Lebris Kerouac to working-class, French-Canadian parents in Lowell, Massachusetts, he grew up speaking Quebecois French instead of English and hardly seemed the likely voice of a new literary generation. But a football scholarship to Columbia University sent him to New York City in the early 1940s, where he met the charismatic Neal Cassady, who introduced him to a shadowy underworld of hobos, jazz musicians, drug addicts, and petty criminals located around Times Square. Drifting in and out of school and employment, Kerouac eventually joined Cassady on a series of wild transcontinental road trips between 1947 and 1950.

These wanderings became the substance of Kerouac's landmark novel *On the Road* (1957), a sort of pocket bible for social rebels in the late 1950s. Legendarily written on a 120-foot roll of teletype paper over the course of only twenty days, the book recounted the impulsive, and ultimately disappointing, adventures of Kerouac and Cassady (fictionalized as Sal Paradise and Dean Moriarty) among the outcasts and eccentrics they encountered

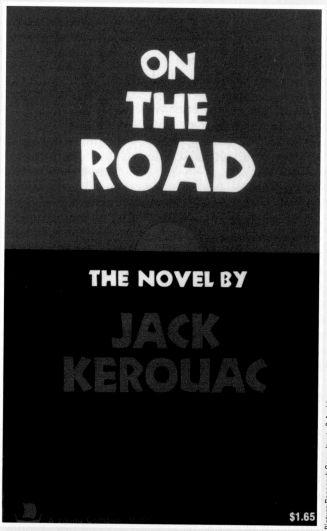

"Beat" Author Jack Kerouac at Work, 1950 A generation of "hipsters" and wannabe nonconformists took Kerouac's impulsive writings to be almost sacred texts and tried to conform their lifestyles to his errant ways.

Private Collection/ Picture Research Consultants & Archives

The Cover of Kerouac's Celebrated Novel Hailed as an homage to unfettered spontaneity, *On the Road* was actually the product of several years of writing, revising, and editing.

Picture Research Consultants & Archives

A Gaggle of Beats From left to right, Bob Donlin, Neal Cassady, Allen Ginsberg, Robert LaVinge, and Lawrence Ferlinghetti stand outside Ferlinghetti's famed City Lights Bookstore in San Francisco, California, 1956.

along the way. Kerouac called his nonstop, drug-fueled writing technique "spontaneous prose" and conceptualized it as the literary equivalent of jazz improvisation or bebop. Though the book made him an instant literary celebrity, Kerouac's alcoholic lifestyle eventually killed him at the relatively young age of forty-seven.

Bearded and bespectacled Allen Ginsberg, the Beat Generation's most eloquent spokesman, lasted longer on the literary scene. Raised in New Jersey by a school teacher father and a Russian émigré mother who suffered from bouts of mental illness, Ginsberg made his way to nearby Columbia in the 1940s and fell in with the seedy Times Square circle, where he made friends with Kerouac, Cassady, and other Beat figures. After an eight-month confinement in a psychiatric institution, Ginsberg relocated to San Francisco's bohemian North Beach neighborhood. A 1955 public reading of Ginsberg's epic poem "Howl" launched a literary renaissance in the city, centered on Lawrence Ferlinghetti's City Lights Bookstore. Ginsberg's poem eulogized his peers. Its long, tumbling poetic line recalled Walt Whitman's exuberant voice and recounted the Beat poet's experiences with homosexual sex, psychedelic drugs, and spiritual illumination. Ferlinghetti's publication of *Howl and Other Poems* in 1956 led to a highly publicized San Francisco obscenity trial, which brought national media attention to Beat culture and scored a victory for First Amendment freedom of expression.

Tall and bleak William S. Burroughs (1914–1997), though a decade older than Kerouac and Ginsberg, contributed the third great work of Beat literature in *Naked Lunch* (1962). Scion of a wealthy St. Louis family, Burroughs developed an unhealthy penchant for guns and petty crime as a maladjusted youth. After graduating from Harvard, he landed in New York City and befriended Kerouac, Ginsberg, and other Beats. The circle of friends fell in trouble with the law when one of them slayed an unwanted sexual partner; Burroughs and Kerouac were material witnesses to the crime. Later, a drunken Burroughs shot dead his common-law wife in Mexico City. Drug addict, fugitive, and homosexual, he resettled in Morocco and wrote *Naked Lunch*, a disjointed tale of urban junkies and extreme sexual practices that satirized Cold War conformity, anxiety, and psychiatric science. *Newsweek* called Burroughs's work "a masterpiece, but a totally insane and anarchic one." Its controversial publication spurred an obscenity trial in Massachusetts and made Burroughs an early icon of postmodernism (see Chapter 42, pp. 1007–1010).

As the latest in America's tradition of "protest" cultures, the writers of the Beat Generation enjoyed their moment in the sun in the late 1950s. To literature, they contributed a new style of free-form narration. Beyond the page, they promoted interest in bebop jazz and eastern religious mysticism, particularly Zen Buddhism. By the early 1960s, much of their energy had dissipated. Later generations often remembered not the Beats' literary achievements or spiritual aspirations, but their ostentatious embrace of cool jazz, snapping fingers, goatees, berets, and bad coffeehouse poetry. (San Francisco columnist Herb Caen coined the sneering term *beatnik* in 1958, linking Cold War anxiety over the recent Sputnik launch with disapproval of the Beats' antisocial and delinquent tendencies.) Nonetheless, many features of the Beat spirit lived on in the countercultural "hippie" movement of the 1960s, including sexual liberation, alternative spirituality, experimentation with drugs, and an emphasis on spontaneity, authenticity, and extreme sensation. Long after hippies had passed out of fashion, youngsters in America and around the world continued to find inspiration in the writings of Kerouac, Ginsberg, Burroughs, and their fellow Beats.

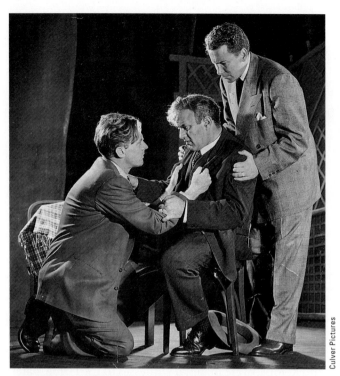

Culver Pictures

Death of a Salesman   First performed in 1949, Arthur Miller's play probed the psychic costs of failure in a society that held out the promise of "success" to all. The play especially resonated with audiences in the booming 1950s and quickly took its place as an American classic. This scene from the original Broadway production shows Arthur Kennedy as Biff Loman (left) confronting his father, Willy, played by Lee J. Cobb (seated), while his brother, Happy, portrayed by Cameron Mitchell, looks on. Not shown here is Willy's compassionate wife, Linda, brilliantly acted by Mildred Dunnock.

American values, notably *Death of a Salesman* (1949), a tragic indictment of the American dream of material success, and *The Crucible* (1953), which treated the Salem witch trials as a dark parable warning against the dangers of McCarthyism. Lorraine Hansberry offered an affecting, realistic portrait of African American life in *A Raisin in the Sun* (1959). In the 1960s Edward Albee

Arthur Miller (1915–2005) challenged America's blind faith in postwar material success in his masterpiece Death of a Salesman *(1949). Early in the play, Miller's protagonist, Willy Loman, offers the era's customary advice on success in business to his son Biff:*

❝[T]he man who makes an appearance in the business world, the man who creates personal interest, is the man who gets ahead. Be liked and you will never want.**❞**

exposed the rapacious underside of middle-class life in *Who's Afraid of Virginia Woolf?* (1962).

Still, the realist novel remained the preferred genre for chroniclers of the postwar literary scene. With no shortage of ambition, a number of authors set out to produce "the great American novel." In the same mold as Mark Twain's *Adventures of Huckleberry Finn* and F. Scott Fitzgerald's *Great Gatsby*, many of these works took the form of a *Bildungsroman* (German for "formation novel"), or a tale chronicling the education and maturation of a young protagonist. New York novelist and infamous recluse J. D. Salinger painted an unforgettable portrait of adolescent angst, alienation, and rebellion in *The Catcher in the Rye* (1951). Ralph Ellison depicted the African American's often tortured quest for personal identity in *Invisible Man* (1952), a haunting novel narrated by a nameless black person who finds that none of his supposed supporters—white philanthropists, black nationalists, and Communist party members—can see him as a real man. Chicagoan Saul Bellow concocted a more readily recognizable Everyman in *The Adventures of Augie March* (1953), a coming-of-age tale about a young man buffeted by fate and struggling to make sense of the chaotic modern world. Alabama novelist Harper Lee drew from the Southern Gothic tradition to tell of racial injustice and the loss of youthful innocence in *To Kill a Mockingbird* (1960), one of the most widely read novels in all of American literature.

As these works attested, underrepresented groups gained new prominence in midcentury literary circles. Black authors built on the earlier achievements of the Harlem Renaissance. A decade before Ellison's emergence, Richard Wright had found literary acclaim with his chilling portrait of a black Chicago killer in *Native Son* (1940). The book made Wright the first African American best seller, and he followed its success with the semi-autobiographical and highly influential *Black Boy* (1945). Later, James Baldwin won plaudits as a novelist and essayist, particularly for his sensitive reflections on the racial question in *The Fire Next Time* (1963). Black nationalist LeRoi Jones, who changed his name to Imamu Amiri Baraka, crafted powerful plays like *Dutchman* (1964).

The South boasted its own literary renaissance, led by veteran Mississippi author William Faulkner, a Nobel recipient in 1950. Distancing themselves from an earlier "Lost Cause" literature that had glorified the antebellum South, **Southern Renaissance** writers brought a new critical appreciation to the region's burdens of history, racism, and conservatism. After taking his stand with fellow conservative "agrarian" writers in the 1930s, Tennesseean Robert Penn Warren immortalized Louisiana politico Huey Long in *All the King's Men* (1946). Fellow Mississippians Walker Percy and Eudora Welty grasped the falling torch from the failing Faulkner, who died in 1962. Along with Georgian Flannery O'Connor, these later Southern Renaissance writers perceptively tracked the changes reshaping the postwar South, while also exploring universal themes of yearning, failure, success, and sorrow. Virginian William Styron confronted the harsh history of his home state in a controversial fictional representation of an 1831 slave rebellion, *The Confessions of Nat Turner* (1967).

Especially bountiful was the harvest of books by Jewish novelists. Some critics quipped that a knowledge of Yiddish was becoming necessary to understand much of the dialogue presented in modern American novels. Many Jewish writers found their favorite subject matter in the experience of lower- and middle-class Jewish immigrants. Bernard Malamud rendered a touching portrait of a family of New York Jewish storekeepers in *The Assistant* (1957). Malamud also explored the mythic qualities of the culture of baseball in *The Natural* (1952). Philip Roth wrote comically about young New Jersey suburbanites in *Goodbye, Columbus* (1959) and penned an uproarious account of a sexually obsessed middle-aged New Yorker in *Portnoy's Complaint* (1969). Saul Bellow contributed masterful sketches of Jewish urban and literary life, following the landmark achievement of *Augie March* with *Herzog* (1962). Bellow won the Nobel Prize for literature in 1976, becoming the eighth American so honored in the previous half-century.

Chapter Review

KEY TERMS

The Feminine Mystique (861)
rock 'n' roll (863)
Checkers Speech (864)
McCarthyism (866)
Army-McCarthy hearings (867)
Jim Crow (867)
Montgomery bus boycott (868)
Brown v. *Board of Education of Topeka, Kansas* (868)
Student Nonviolent Coordinating Committee (SNCC) (872)
Operation Wetback (873)
Federal Highway Act of 1956 (873)

policy of boldness (874)
Hungarian uprising (874)
Dien Bien Phu, Battle of (875)
Suez crisis (875)
Organization of Petroleum Exporting Countries (OPEC) (876)
Sputnik (877)
kitchen debate (878)
abstract expressionism (880)
International Style (882)
Beat Generation (884)
Southern Renaissance (886)

PEOPLE TO KNOW

Dwight D. ("Ike") Eisenhower
Richard M. Nixon
Betty Friedan
Elvis Presley
Joseph McCarthy
Rosa Parks
Martin Luther King, Jr.
Earl Warren
John Foster Dulles
Nikita Khrushchev
Ho Chi Minh

Gamal Abdel Nasser
Fidel Castro
John F. Kennedy
Lyndon B. Johnson
Jackson Pollock
Andy Warhol
Eero Saarinen
Jack Kerouac
Allen Ginsberg
Arthur Miller
Ralph Ellison

TO LEARN MORE

Glenn Altschuler, *All Shook Up: How Rock 'N' Roll Changed America* (2003)
Stephen Ambrose, *Eisenhower: The President* (1984)
Laura A. Belmonte, *Selling the American Way: U.S. Propaganda and the Cold War* (2010)
James Campbell, *This Is the Beat Generation: New York, San Francisco, Paris* (2001)
Lizabeth Cohen, *A Consumers' Republic: The Politics of Mass Consumption in Postwar America* (2003)

Mary Dudziak, *Cold War Civil Rights* (2000)
John Egerton, *Speak Now Against the Day: The Generation Before the Civil Rights Movement in the South* (1994)
Tom Engelhardt, *The End of Victory Culture* (1995)
Melvyn Leffler, *For the Soul of Mankind: The United States, the Soviet Union, and the Cold War* (2007)
Elaine May, *Homeward Bound: American Families in the Cold War Era* (1988)

David Nichols, *A Matter of Justice: Eisenhower and the Beginning of the Civil Rights Revolution* (2007)

Thomas Sugrue, *The Origins of the Urban Crisis: Race and Inequality in Postwar Detroit* (1996)

Theodore White, *Making of the President, 1960* (1961)

A complete, annotated bibliography for this chapter—along with brief descriptions of the People to Know—may be found on the American Pageant website. The Key Terms are defined in a Glossary at the end of the text.

CHRONOLOGY

1951	Salinger publishes *The Catcher in the Rye*
1952	Eisenhower defeats Stevenson for presidency Ellison publishes *Invisible Man* United Nations headquarters open in New York City
1953	CIA-engineered coup installs shah of Iran Joseph Stalin dies Miller's *The Crucible* debuts on Broadway Bellow publishes *The Adventures of Augie March*
1954	French defeated at Dien Bien Phu in Vietnam Army-McCarthy hearings *Brown v. Board of Education* Nasser becomes prime minister of Egypt CIA-sponsored coup in Guatemala
1955	Montgomery bus boycott by blacks begins; emergence of Martin Luther King, Jr. Geneva summit meeting on Vietnam Soviet Union withdraws troops from Austria Warsaw Pact signed AF of L merges with CIO Tennessee Williams's *Cat on a Hot Tin Roof* first performed
1956	Soviets crush Hungarian revolt Suez crisis Eisenhower defeats Stevenson for presidency Ginsberg publishes *Howl and Other Poems*

1957	Little Rock school desegregation crisis Civil Rights Act passed Southern Christian Leadership Conference (SCLC) formed Eisenhower Doctrine Soviet Union launches Sputnik satellites Kerouac publishes *On the Road*
1958	U.S. troops sent to Lebanon NDEA authorizes loans and grants for science and language education Galbraith publishes *The Affluent Society*
1958–1959	Berlin crisis
1959	Castro seizes power in Cuba Landrum-Griffin Act Alaska and Hawaii attain statehood Guggenheim Museum opens in New York City
1960	Sit-in movement for civil rights begins U-2 incident sabotages Paris summit OPEC formed Kennedy defeats Nixon for presidency Updike publishes *Rabbit, Run* Lee publishes *To Kill a Mockingbird*
1961	Heller publishes *Catch-22*
1962	TWA Flight Center opens in New York
1963	Plath publishes *The Bell Jar*

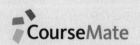

Go to the CourseMate website at **www.cengagebrain.com** for additional study tools and review materials—including audio and video clips—for this chapter.

AP® Review Questions for Chapter 37

1. Which of the following was NOT true of the changing nature of work in the 1950s?
   (A) Science and technology drove economic growth.
   (B) There were fewer jobs in the military-related aerospace industry.
   (C) White-collar workers were surpassing blue-collar workers in numbers.
   (D) Labor unions reached a peak and then began to decline.
   (E) Job opportunities were opening to women in the white-collar work force.

2. Which of the following best summarizes the fundamental criticism directed against the new popular mass media culture of the early post–World War II era offered by social critics such as David Riesman and William H. Whyte, Jr.?
   (A) Affluence tended to erode Americans' moral character.
   (B) Americans had become affluent conformists unable to think for themselves.
   (C) The wealth produced by the new mass economy was unevenly distributed.
   (D) The openly sexual displays of figures like Elvis Presley and Marilyn Monroe were morally dangerous.
   (E) Americans were becoming too soft to be able to fight the Cold War effectively.

3. What campaign pledge did Republican presidential candidate Dwight Eisenhower make that sealed his 1952 election victory over Democratic candidate Adlai Stevenson?
   (A) Eisenhower promised to use atomic weapons to end the Korean War.
   (B) Eisenhower pledged that he would order a naval blockade of the China coast and bomb Manchuria to end the Korean War.
   (C) Eisenhower promised to open peace negotiations over Korea with Chinese leader Mao Zedong.
   (D) Eisenhower affirmed that he would order the United Nations troops to invade North Korea.
   (E) Eisenhower promised to personally travel to Korea to end the war.

4. All of the following were true about the rise and fall of the notorious anticommunist crusader Senator Joseph McCarthy EXCEPT that
   (A) Senator McCarthy first rose to national prominence by publicly charging that scores of known communists were working for the U.S. State Department.
   (B) Senator McCarthy outrageously charged that General George Marshall, a former secretary of state and World War II military hero, was part of a pro-communist conspiracy to betray America.
   (C) as a result of Senator McCarthy's purges against Asian experts in the State Department, the department lost a number of Asian specialists who might have counseled a wiser course in Vietnam.
   (D) President Eisenhower, at an early stage during Senator McCarthy's political rise, publicly denounced McCarthy's slanderous and demagogic attacks against Americans loyally working for the U.S. government.
   (E) Senator McCarthy's fall from political power and influence was hastened when he foolishly and ineptly attempted to attack the U.S. Army during the televised Army-McCarthy hearings in the spring of 1954.

5. In an effort to overturn Jim Crow laws and the segregated system they had created, African Americans used all of the following strategies EXCEPT
   (A) economic boycotts.
   (B) legal attacks on the underpinning of segregation in the courts.
   (C) appeals to foreign governments to pressure the United States to establish racial justice.
   (D) mobilization of African American churches on behalf of civil rights.
   (E) use of the nonviolent tactics of Mohandas Gandhi.

6. What prompted the U.S. Supreme Court to advance the cause of civil rights in the 1950s, beginning with the landmark 1954 decision in *Brown* v. *Board of Education*?
   (A) The Court believed that it was the only branch of government with the constitutional authority to do so.
   (B) The Court was dominated and heavily influenced by New Deal liberals appointed by President Roosevelt.
   (C) President Eisenhower had requested the Court to intervene in the matter of civil rights.
   (D) Congress and the presidency had largely abdicated their responsibility by taking a hands-off approach to civil rights.
   (E) The Court sought to ensure that its earlier historical precedents in the area of civil rights, such as *Plessy* v. *Ferguson*, were upheld.

7. Which federal public works program promoted by President Eisenhower was far larger and more expensive than any program of Roosevelt's New Deal?
   - (A) The interstate highway system
   - (B) The Grand Coulee dam project
   - (C) The St. Lawrence seaway
   - (D) The airport construction project
   - (E) The public housing system

8. Which of the following represented the strategic military policy underlying President Eisenhower's and Secretary of State John Foster Dulles's "new look" foreign policy in the 1950s?
   - (A) The dismantling of the military-industrial complex
   - (B) Massive new military spending
   - (C) Greater reliance on air power and the deterrent power of nuclear weapons than on the army and navy
   - (D) A buildup of unconventional and guerrilla-warfare forces
   - (E) The rapid deployment of the navy and marines to trouble spots

9. Which of the following international crises amply demonstrated the futility of the stated Eisenhower administration policy of massive retaliation and the limitations on its ability to roll back communist geopolitical gains?
   - (A) The Hungarian revolt in 1956
   - (B) The Suez crisis of 1956
   - (C) The CIA-sponsored coup in Iran in 1953
   - (D) The CIA-directed coup against the elected government of Guatemala in 1954
   - (E) The American U-2 spy plane incident

10. Which of the following was NOT an American government response to the launching of *Sputnik* by the Soviet Union in 1957?
    - (A) Spending millions of dollars to improve American science and language education principally through the National Defense Education Act
    - (B) The establishment of the National Aeronautics and Space Administration (NASA)
    - (C) The directing of billions of public dollars to missile and satellite development
    - (D) A sober reassessment by U.S. policymakers of America's vaunted scientific and military superiority and dominance
    - (E) Passage of the Landrum-Griffin Act

11. By the end of the 1950s, Latin American anger toward the United States had intensified because Washington had done all of the following EXCEPT
    - (A) extend massive aid to Europe and little to Latin America.
    - (B) continue to intervene in Latin American affairs.
    - (C) support repressive right-wing dictators who claimed to be fighting communism.
    - (D) provide diplomatic support and economic assistance to Fidel Castro's revolutionary government in Cuba.
    - (E) initiate a CIA-directed coup in Guatemala.

12. Which factor do some historians believe tipped the electoral scales for Senator John F. Kennedy against Vice President Richard Nixon in the presidential election of 1960?
    - (A) Kennedy's age
    - (B) Kennedy's religion
    - (C) Kennedy's political experience as a senator and congressman
    - (D) Kennedy's televised debates with Richard Nixon
    - (E) President Eisenhower's heavy loss of popularity in his last two years in office

13. All of the following American writers portrayed varying and illuminating aspects of African American life and identity in postwar America EXCEPT
    - (A) Richard Wright.
    - (B) James Baldwin.
    - (C) Arthur Miller.
    - (D) Lorraine Hansberry.
    - (E) LeRoi Jones.

14. Which of the following is NOT an effect of television on American culture?
    - (A) Shrinking attendance at movies
    - (B) Increased influence of advertising
    - (C) The rise of "televangelists"
    - (D) The creation of rock 'n' roll music
    - (E) Commercialization of professional sports

15. The Suez crisis marked a turning point in American foreign policy because
    - (A) the United States pulled funding promised to Egypt for a dam on the upper Nile.
    - (B) the United States engineered a coup, placing Shah Mohammed Reza Pahlevi in power.
    - (C) it marked the last time that the United States could use its oil as a "weapon."
    - (D) Western involvement in the Middle East led to the creation of OPEC.
    - (E) the United States pledged to aid Middle Eastern nations threatened by communism.

Chapter 38

The Stormy Sixties

1960–1968

Let the word go forth from this time and place, to friend and foe alike, that the torch has been passed to a new generation of Americans.

JOHN F. KENNEDY, INAUGURAL, 1961

Complacent and comfortable as the 1950s closed, Americans elected in 1960 a young, vigorous president who pledged "to get the country moving again." Neither the nation nor the new president had any inkling as the new decade opened just how action-packed it would be, both at home and abroad. The 1960s would bring a sexual revolution, a civil rights revolution, the emergence of a "youth culture," a devastating war in Vietnam, and the beginnings, at least, of a feminist revolution. By the end of the stormy sixties, many Americans would yearn nostalgically for the comparative calm of the fifties.

★ Kennedy's "New Frontier" Spirit

Hatless and topcoatless in the twenty-two-degree chill, John F. Kennedy delivered a stirring inaugural address on January 20, 1961. Tall, elegantly handsome, speaking crisply and with staccato finger jabs at the air, Kennedy personified the glamour and vitality of the new administration. The youngest president ever elected, he assembled one of the youngest cabinets, including his thirty-five-year-old brother, Robert F. Kennedy, as attorney general. "Bobby," the president quipped, would find "some legal experience" useful when he began to practice law. The new attorney general set out, among other reforms, to recast the priorities of the FBI. The bureau deployed nearly a thousand agents on "internal security" work but targeted only a dozen against organized crime and gave virtually no attention to civil rights violations. Robert Kennedy's efforts were stoutly resisted by J. Edgar Hoover, who had served as FBI director longer than the new attorney general had been alive. Business whiz Robert S. McNamara left the presidency of the Ford Motor Company to take over the Defense Department. Along with other youthful, talented advisers, these appointees made up an inner circle of "the best and the brightest" men around the president.

From the outset Kennedy inspired high expectations, especially among the young. His challenge of a **New Frontier** quickened patriotic pulses. He brought a warm heart to the Cold War when he proposed the **Peace Corps**, an army of idealistic and mostly youthful volunteers to bring American skills to underdeveloped countries. He summoned citizens to service with his clarion call to "ask not what your country can do for you: ask what you can do for your country."

Himself Harvard-educated, Kennedy and his Ivy League lieutenants (heavily from Harvard) radiated confidence in their abilities. The president's personal grace and wit won him the deep affection of many of his fellow citizens. A journalist called Kennedy "the most seductive man I've ever met. He exuded a sense of vibrant life and humor that seemed naturally to bubble

Richard Goodwin (b. 1931), a young Peace Corps staffer, eloquently summed up the buoyantly optimistic mood of the early 1960s:

"For a moment, it seemed as if the entire country, the whole spinning globe, rested, malleable and receptive, in our beneficent hands."

President John F. Kennedy and His Wife, Jacqueline Bouvier Kennedy Shown here leaving the White House to attend a series of inaugural balls in January 1961, the young and vibrant first couple brought beauty, style, and grace to the presidency.

© Bettmann/Corbis

up out of him." In an unprecedented gesture, he invited white-maned poet Robert Frost to speak at his inaugural ceremonies. The old Yankee versifier shrewdly took stock of the situation. "You're something of Irish and I suppose something of Harvard," he told Kennedy—and advised him to be more Irish than Harvard.

✴ The New Frontier at Home

Kennedy came into office with fragile Democratic majorities in Congress. Southern Democrats threatened to team up with Republicans and ax New Frontier proposals such as medical assistance for the aged and increased federal aid to education. Kennedy won a first round in his campaign for a more cooperative Congress when he forced an expansion of the all-important House Rules Committee, dominated by conservatives who could have bottled up his entire legislative program. Despite this victory, the New Frontier did not expand swiftly. Key medical and education bills remained stalled in Congress.

Another vexing problem was the economy. Kennedy had campaigned on the theme of revitalizing the economy after the recessions of the Eisenhower years. His administration helped negotiate a noninflationary wage agreement in the steel industry in early 1962. The assumption was that the companies, for their part, would keep the lid on prices. But almost immediately steel management announced significant price

increases, thereby seemingly demonstrating bad faith. The president erupted in wrath. "My father always told me that all businessmen were sons of bitches," he said, "but I never believed him till now." He called the "big steel" men onto the Oval Office carpet and unleashed his Irish temper. Overawed, the steel operators backed down.

The steel episode provoked fiery attacks by big business on the New Frontier, but Kennedy soon appealed to believers in free enterprise when he announced his support of a general tax-cut bill. He rejected the advice of those who wished greater government spending and instead chose to stimulate the economy by slashing taxes and putting more money directly into private hands. When he announced his policy before a big business group, one observer called it "the most Republican speech since McKinley."

Kennedy's New Frontier vision also extended to the "final frontier." Early in his term, the president promoted a multibillion-dollar project dedicated, as he put it, to "landing a man on the Moon and returning him safely to earth." When skeptics objected that the money could be better spent elsewhere, Kennedy summoned stirring rhetoric of rising to challenges and expanding human possibilities. In reality, the moon shot was a calculated plan to restore America's prestige in the space race, severely damaged by the Soviet Sputnik successes (see p. 877). Twenty-four billion dollars later, in July 1969, two NASA astronauts triumphantly planted their footprints—and the American flag—on

On the Moon This moon's-eye view of the earth greeted the first men to land on the lunar surface. (right) Astronaut Edwin ("Buzz") Aldrin descends from the spacecraft. As he stepped onto the moon's surface, his companion, Neil Armstrong, said, "That's one small step for man; one giant leap for mankind."

the moon's dusty surface. As people around the globe huddled around televisions to watch the **Apollo** mission live, the world had never seemed so small and interconnected, nor the United States so dominant.

✴ Rumblings in Europe

A few months after settling into the White House, the new president met Soviet premier Khrushchev at Vienna in June 1961. The tough-talking Soviet leader adopted a belligerent attitude, threatening to make a treaty with East Germany and cut off Western access to Berlin. Though visibly shaken, the president refused to be bullied.

The Soviets backed off from their most bellicose threats but suddenly began to construct the **Berlin Wall** in August 1961. A barbed-wire and concrete barrier, it was designed to plug the heavy population drain from East Germany to West Germany through the Berlin funnel. But to the free world, the "Wall of Shame" looked like a gigantic enclosure around a concentration camp. The wall stood for almost three decades as an ugly scar symbolizing the post–World War II division of Europe into two hostile camps.

Kennedy meanwhile turned his attention to Western Europe, now miraculously prospering after the tonic of Marshall Plan aid and the growth of the American-encouraged **European Economic Community (EEC)**, the free-trade area that later evolved into the European Union. He finally secured passage of the Trade Expansion Act in 1962, authorizing tariff cuts of up to 50 percent to promote trade with EEC countries. This act led to the so-called Kennedy Round of tariff negotiations, concluded in 1967, and to a significant expansion of European-American trade. These liberalized trade policies inaugurated a new era of such robustly invigorated international commerce that a new word was coined to describe it: *globalization*.

But not all of Kennedy's ambitious designs for Europe were realized. American policymakers were dedicated to an economically and militarily united "Atlantic Community," with the United States the dominant partner. But they found their way blocked by towering, stiff-backed Charles de Gaulle, president of France. With a haughty "*non*," de Gaulle vetoed the British application for Common Market membership in 1963, fearing that the British "special relationship" with the United States would make Britain a Trojan horse for deepening American control over European

The Berlin Wall, 1961–1989 The wall separating East and West Berlin stood for nearly thirty years as a hated symbol of the division of Europe into democratic and communist camps. (left) East German soldiers stand guard as the concrete wall is constructed, November 20, 1961. (right) Demonstrators celebrating the impending reunification of East and West Germany begin to tear down the wall in 1989.

affairs. De Gaulle deemed the Americans unreliable in a crisis, so he tried to preserve French freedom of action by developing his own small atomic force. Despite the perils of nuclear proliferation or Soviet domination, de Gaulle demanded an independent Europe, free of Yankee influence.

✴ Foreign Flare-ups and "Flexible Response"

Special problems for U.S. foreign policy emerged from the worldwide decolonization of European overseas possessions after World War II. Sparsely populated Laos, freed of its French colonial overlords in 1954, was festering dangerously by the time Kennedy came into office. The Eisenhower administration had drenched this jungle kingdom with dollars but failed to cleanse the country of an aggressive communist element. A red Laos, many observers feared, would be a river on which

the influence of Communist China would flood into all of Southeast Asia.

As the Laotian civil war raged, Kennedy's military advisers seriously considered sending in American troops. But the president found that he had insufficient forces to put out the fire in Asia and still honor his commitments in Europe. Kennedy thus sought a diplomatic escape hatch in the fourteen-power Geneva conference, which imposed a shaky peace on Laos in 1962.

These "brushfire wars" intensified the pressure for a shift away from Secretary Dulles's dubious doctrine of "massive retaliation." Kennedy felt hamstrung by the knowledge that in a crisis, he had the Devil's choice between humiliation and nuclear incineration. With Defense Secretary McNamara, he pushed the strategy of "flexible response"—that is, developing an array of military "options" that could be precisely matched to the gravity of the crisis at hand. To this end Kennedy increased spending on conventional military forces and bolstered the Special Forces (Green Berets). They were an elite antiguerrilla outfit trained to survive on snake meat and to kill with scientific finesse.

✸ Stepping into the Vietnam Quagmire

The doctrine of "flexible response" seemed sane enough, but it contained lethal logic. It potentially lowered the level at which diplomacy would give way to shooting. It also provided a mechanism for a progressive, and possibly endless, stepping-up of the use of force. Vietnam soon presented grisly proof of these pitfalls.

The corrupt, right-wing government of Ngo Dinh Diem in Saigon, despite a deluge of American dollars, had ruled shakily since the partition of Vietnam in 1954 (see p. 875). Anti-Diem agitators noisily threatened to topple the pro-American government from power. In a fateful decision late in 1961, Kennedy ordered a sharp increase in the number of "military advisers" (U.S. troops) in South Vietnam.

American forces allegedly entered Vietnam to foster political stability—to help protect Diem from the communists long enough to allow him to enact basic social

Backbone The United States supports South Vietnam.
Wil-Jo Associates

reforms favored by the Americans. But the Kennedy administration eventually despaired of the reactionary Diem and encouraged a successful coup against him in November 1963. Ironically, the United States thus contributed to a long process of political disintegration that its original policy had meant to prevent. Kennedy still told the South Vietnamese that it was "their war," but he had made dangerously deep political commitments. By the time of his death, he had ordered more than fifteen thousand American men into the far-off Asian slaughter pen. A graceful pullout was becoming increasingly difficult (see Map 38.1).

"Modernization theory" provided the theoretical underpinnings for an activist U.S. foreign policy in the "underdeveloped" world. Its proponents believed that the traditional societies of Asia, Africa, and Latin America could develop into modern industrial and democratic nations by following the West's own path. Noted economic historian Walt Whitman Rostow, one of the most influential modernization theorists, charted the route from traditional society to "the age of high mass-consumption" in his book *The Stages of Economic Growth* (1960). Though it would later come under attack for its Eurocentric bias, modernization theory offered a powerful intellectual framework for policymakers ensnared in the Cold War. Rostow himself served as an influential adviser to the Kennedy and Johnson administrations.

✸ Cuban Confrontations

Although the United States regarded Latin America as its backyard, its southern neighbors feared and resented the powerful Colossus of the North. In 1961 Kennedy extended the hand of friendship with the Alliance for Progress (*Alianza para el Progreso*), hailed as a Marshall Plan for Latin America. A primary goal was to help the Good Neighbors close the gap between the callous rich and the wretched poor, and thus quiet communist agitation. But results were disappointing; there was little alliance and even less progress. American handouts had little positive impact on Latin America's immense social problems.

President Kennedy also struck below the border with the mailed fist. He had inherited from the Eisenhower administration a CIA-backed scheme to topple Fidel Castro from power by invading Cuba with anticommunist exiles. On April 17, 1961, some twelve hundred exiles landed at Cuba's Bay of Pigs. When the ill-starred **Bay of Pigs invasion** bogged down, Kennedy stood fast in his decision to keep hands off, and the bullet-riddled band of anti-Castroites surrendered. President Kennedy assumed full responsibility for the

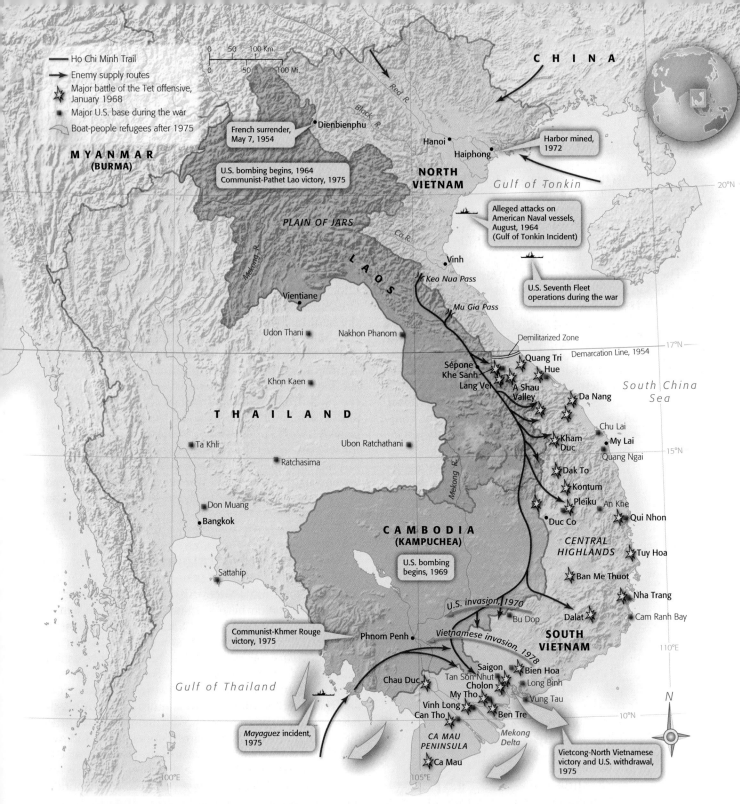

MAP 38.1 Vietnam and Southeast Asia, 1954–1975   Le Ly Hayslip (b. 1949) was born in a peasant village in South Vietnam, just south of Da Nang. In her memoir, *When Heaven and Earth Changed Places*, she describes the trauma endured by ordinary Vietnamese as a result of America's fight against the Viet Cong: "In 1963—the year the Viet Cong came to my village—American warplanes bombed Man Quang. It was at noon, just when the children were getting out of school. My aunt Thu and her pregnant daughter-in-law were making lunch for her husband and four grandchildren when the air-raid signal blared. They all jumped under the wooden table and sheltered the pregnant woman with their bodies—even the little kids. A bomb fell in Aunt Thu's front yard. . . . Hot shrapnel tore through everyone except the pregnant woman. Aunt Thu and one of her grandchildren were killed. The passing fragment left only a weeping hole where her generous heart had been." © Cengage Learning

Failed Bay of Pigs Invasion, 1961 Cuban soldiers demonstrate a beach gun they used against a brigade of ex-Cubans who furtively invaded Cuba as agents of the United States. The debacle was one of several unsuccessful American attempts to overthrow Cuban leader Fidel Castro.

failure, remarking that "victory has a hundred fathers, and defeat is an orphan."

The Bay of Pigs blunder, along with continuing American covert efforts to assassinate Castro and overthrow his government, naturally pushed the Cuban leader even further into the Soviet embrace. Wily Chairman Khrushchev lost little time in taking full advantage of his Cuban comrade's position just ninety miles off Florida's coast. In October 1962 the aerial photographs of American spy planes revealed that the Soviets were secretly and speedily installing nuclear-tipped missiles in Cuba. The Soviets evidently intended to use these devastating weapons to shield Castro and to blackmail the United States into backing down in Berlin and other trouble spots.

Kennedy and Khrushchev now began a nerve-racking game of "nuclear chicken." The president flatly rejected air force proposals for a "surgical" bombing strike against the missile-launching sites. Instead, on October 22, 1962, he ordered a naval "quarantine" of Cuba and demanded immediate removal of the threatening weaponry. He also served notice on Khrushchev that any attack on the United States from Cuba would be regarded as coming from the Soviet Union and would trigger nuclear retaliation against the Russian heartland.

For an anxious week, Americans waited while Soviet ships approached the patrol line established by the U.S. Navy off the island of Cuba. Seizing or sinking a Soviet vessel on the high seas would unquestionably be regarded by the Kremlin as an act of war. The world teetered breathlessly on the brink of global atomization. Only in 1991 did the full dimensions of this nuclear peril become known, when the Russians revealed that their ground forces in Cuba already had operational nuclear weapons at their disposal and were authorized to launch them if attacked.

In this tense eyeball-to-eyeball confrontation, Khrushchev finally flinched. On October 28 he agreed to a partially face-saving compromise, by which he would pull the missiles out of Cuba. The United States in return agreed to end the quarantine and not invade the island. The American government also quietly signaled that it would remove from Turkey some of its own missiles targeted at the Soviet Union.

Fallout from the **Cuban missile crisis** was considerable. A disgraced Khrushchev was ultimately hounded out of the Kremlin and became an "unperson." Hardliners in Moscow, vowing never again to be humiliated in a nuclear face-off, launched an enormous program of military expansion. The Soviet buildup reached a crescendo in the next decade, stimulating, in turn, a vast American effort to "catch up with the Russians." The Democrats did better than expected in the midterm elections of November 1962—allegedly because the Republicans were "Cubanized." Kennedy, apparently sobered by the appalling risks he had just run, pushed harder for a nuclear test-ban treaty with the Soviet Union. After prolonged negotiations in Moscow, a pact prohibiting trial nuclear explosions in the atmosphere was signed in late 1963. Another barometer indicating a thaw in the Cold War was the installation (August 1963) of a Moscow-Washington "hot line," permitting immediate teletype communication in case of a crisis.

Most significant was Kennedy's speech at American University in Washington, D.C., in June 1963. The president urged Americans to abandon a view of the Soviet Union as a Devil-ridden land filled with fanatics and instead to deal with the world "as it is, not as it might have been had the history of the last eighteen years been different." Kennedy thus tried to lay the foundation for a realistic policy of peaceful coexistence with the Soviet Union. Here were the modest origins of the policy that later came to be known as "détente" (French for "relaxation of tension").

★ The Struggle for Civil Rights

Kennedy had campaigned with a strong appeal to black voters, but he proceeded gingerly to redeem his promises. Although he had pledged to eliminate racial discrimination in housing "with a stroke of the pen," it took him nearly two years to find the right pen. Civil rights groups meanwhile sent thousands of pens to the White House in an "Ink for Jack" protest against the president's slowness.

Political concerns stayed the president's hand on civil rights. Elected by a wafer-thin margin, and with shaky control over Congress, Kennedy needed the support of southern legislators to pass his economic and social legislation, especially his medical and educational bills. He believed, perhaps justifiably, that those measures would eventually benefit black Americans at least as much as specific legislation on civil rights. Bold moves for racial justice would have to wait.

But events soon scrambled these careful calculations. After the wave of sit-ins that surged across the South in 1960, groups of **Freedom Riders** fanned out to end segregation in facilities serving interstate bus passengers. A white mob torched a Freedom Ride bus near Anniston, Alabama, in May 1961, and Attorney General Robert Kennedy's personal representative was beaten unconscious in another anti–Freedom Ride riot in Montgomery. When southern officials proved unwilling or unable to stem the violence, Washington dispatched federal marshals to protect the Freedom Riders.

Reluctantly but fatefully, the Kennedy administration had now joined hands with the civil rights movement. Because of that partnership, the Kennedys proved ultrawary about the political associates of Martin Luther King, Jr. Fearful of embarrassing revelations that some of King's advisers had communist affiliations, Robert Kennedy ordered FBI director J. Edgar Hoover

to wiretap King's phone in late 1963. But for the most part, the relationship between King and the Kennedys was a fruitful one. Encouraged by Robert Kennedy, and with financial backing from Kennedy-prodded private foundations, SNCC and other civil rights groups inaugurated the **Voter Education Project** to register the South's historically disfranchised blacks. Because of his support for civil rights, President Kennedy told a group of black leaders in 1963, "I may lose the next election . . . I don't care."

Integrating southern universities threatened to provoke wholesale slaughter. Some desegregated painlessly, but the University of Mississippi ("Ole Miss") became a volcano. A twenty-nine-year-old air force veteran, James Meredith, encountered violent opposition when he attempted to register in October 1962. In the end President Kennedy was forced to send in four hundred federal marshals and three thousand troops to enroll Meredith in his first class—in colonial American history.

In the spring of 1963, Martin Luther King, Jr., launched a campaign against discrimination in Birmingham, Alabama, the most segregated big city in America. Although blacks constituted nearly half of the city's population, they made up fewer than 15 percent of the city's voters. Previous attempts to crack the city's rigid racial barriers had produced more than fifty cross burnings and eighteen bomb attacks since 1957. "Some of the people sitting here will not come back alive from this campaign," King advised his organizers. Events soon confirmed this grim prediction of violence. Watching developments on television screens, a horrified world saw peaceful civil rights marchers repeatedly repelled by police with attack dogs and electric cattle

Freedom Ride, 1961 Rampaging whites near Anniston, Alabama, burned this bus carrying an interracial group of Freedom Riders on May 14, 1961.

© Bettmann/Corbis

Hosing Down Civil Rights Demonstrators, Birmingham, Alabama, 1963

prods. Most fearsome of all were the high-pressure water hoses directed at the civil rights demonstrators. They delivered water with enough force to knock bricks loose from buildings or strip bark from trees at a distance of one hundred feet. Water from the hoses bowled little children down the street like tumbleweeds.

Jolted by these vicious confrontations, President Kennedy delivered a memorable televised speech to the nation on June 11, 1963. In contrast to Eisenhower's cool aloofness from the racial question, Kennedy called the situation a "moral issue" and committed his personal and presidential prestige to finding a solution.

Drawing on the same spiritual traditions as Martin Luther King, Jr., Kennedy declared that the principle at stake "is as old as the Scriptures and is as clear as the American Constitution." He called for new civil rights legislation to protect black citizens. In August King led more than 200,000 black and white demonstrators on a peaceful **March on Washington** in support of the proposed legislation. In an electrifying speech from the Lincoln Memorial, King declared, "I have a dream that my four little children will one day live in a nation where they will not be judged by the color of their skin, but by the content of their character."

Martin Luther King, Jr., Addresses the March on Washington, August 1963 This was the occasion of King's famous "I Have a Dream" speech, in which he declared, "When the architects of our great republic wrote the magnificent words of the Constitution and the Declaration of Independence, they were signing a promissory note to which every American was to fall heir. This note was a promise that all men, yes, black men as well as white men, would be guaranteed the inalienable rights of life, liberty, and the pursuit of happiness."

*In his civil rights address of June 11, 1963, President
John F. Kennedy (1917-1963) said,*

"If an American, because his skin is dark, cannot eat lunch in a restaurant open to the public; if he cannot send his children to the best public school available; if he cannot vote for the public officials who represent him; if, in short, he cannot enjoy the full and free life which all of us want, then who among us would be content to have the color of his skin changed and stand in his place?"

Still the violence continued. On the very night of Kennedy's stirring television address, a white gunman shot down Medgar Evers, a black Mississippi civil rights worker. In September 1963 an explosion blasted a Baptist church in Birmingham, killing four black girls who had just finished their lesson called "The Love That Forgives." By the time of Kennedy's death, his civil rights bill was making little headway, and frustrated blacks were growing increasingly impatient.

The Killing of Kennedy

Violence haunted America in the mid-1960s, and it stalked onto center stage on November 22, 1963. While riding in an open limousine in downtown Dallas, Texas, President Kennedy was shot in the brain by a concealed rifleman and died within seconds. As a stunned nation grieved, the tragedy grew still more unbelievable. The alleged assassin, a furtive figure named Lee Harvey Oswald, was himself shot to death in front of television cameras by a self-appointed avenger, Jack Ruby. So bizarre were the events surrounding the two murders that even an elaborate official investigation conducted by Chief Justice Warren could not quiet all doubts and theories about what had really happened.

Vice President Johnson was promptly sworn in as president on a waiting airplane and flown back to Washington with Kennedy's body. Although he mistrusted "the Harvards," Johnson retained most of the bright Kennedy team. The new president managed a dignified and efficient transition, pledging continuity with his slain predecessor's policies.

For several days the nation was steeped in sorrow. Not until then did many Americans realize how fully their young, vibrant president and his captivating wife had cast a spell over them. Chopped down in his prime after only slightly more than a thousand days in the White House, Kennedy was acclaimed more for the ideals he had enunciated and the spirit he had kindled than for the concrete goals he had achieved. He had laid one myth to rest forever—that a Catholic could not be trusted with the presidency of the United States.

In later years revelations about Kennedy's womanizing and allegations about his involvement with organized crime figures tarnished his reputation. But despite those accusations, his apparent vigor, charisma, and idealism made him an inspirational figure for the generation of Americans who came of age in the 1960s—including Bill Clinton, who as a boy had briefly met President Kennedy and would himself be elected president in 1992.

The LBJ Brand on the Presidency

The torch passed to craggy-faced Lyndon Baines Johnson, a Texan who towered six feet three inches. The new president hailed from the populist hill country west of Austin, Texas, whose people had first sent him to Washington as a twenty-nine-year-old congressman in 1937. Franklin D. Roosevelt was his political "Daddy," Johnson claimed, and he had supported New Deal measures down the line. But when LBJ lost a Senate race in 1941, he learned the sobering lesson that liberal political beliefs did not necessarily win elections in Texas. He trimmed his sails to the right and squeezed himself into a Senate seat in 1948 with a questionable eighty-seven-vote margin—hence the ironic nickname "Landslide Lyndon."

Entrenched in the Senate, Johnson developed into a masterful wheeler-dealer. He became the Democratic majority leader in 1954, wielding power second only to that of Eisenhower in the White House. He could move mountains or checkmate opponents as the occasion demanded, using what came to be known as the "Johnson treatment"—a flashing display of backslapping, flesh-pressing, and arm-twisting that overbore friend and foe alike. His ego and vanity were legendary. On a visit to the Pope, Johnson was presented with a precious fourteenth-century painting from the Vatican art collection; in return, LBJ gave the Pope a bust—of LBJ!

As president, Johnson quickly shed the conservative coloration of his Senate years to reveal the latent liberal underneath. "No memorial oration or eulogy," Johnson declared to Congress, "could more eloquently honor President Kennedy's memory than the earliest possible passage of the Civil Rights Bill for which he fought so long." After a lengthy conservative filibuster, Congress at last passed the landmark **Civil Rights Act of 1964**. The act banned racial discrimination in most private facilities open to the public, including theaters, hospitals, and restaurants. It strengthened the federal government's power to end segregation in

200,000 Join Orderly March in Capital for Civil Rights; Kennedy Sees Negro Gain

LEADERS OF RALLY URGE ACTION 'NOW'

Ask Laws Against Inequity
—Picnic Air Prevails as
Crowds Clap and Sing

Continued From Page 1, Col. 8

would speed the legislation, which faces a filibuster by Southerners.

Senator Everett McKinley Dirksen of Illinois, the Republican leader, said he thought the demonstration would be neither an advantage nor a disadvantage to the prospects for the civil rights bill.

The human tide that swept over the Mall between the shrines of Washington and Lincoln fell back faster than it came on. As soon as the ceremony broke up this afternoon, the exodus began. With astounding speed, the last buses and trains cleared the city by mid-evening.

At 9 P.M. the city was as calm as the waters of the Reflecting Pool between the two memorials.

At the Lincoln Memorial early in the afternoon, in the midst of a songfest before the addresses, Josephine Baker, the singer, who had flown from her home in Paris, said to the thousands stretching down both sides of the Reflecting Pool:

"You are on the eve of a complete victory. You can't go wrong. The world is behind

LEADERS MEET WITH KENNEDY: From left Whitney M. Young Jr., of National Urban League; the Rev. Dr. Martin Luther King Jr., Southern Christian Leadership Conference; John Lewis, partly hidden, Student Nonviolent Coordinating Committee; Rabbi Joachim Prinz, American Jewish Congress; the Rev. Dr. Eugene Carson Blake, United Presbyterian Church in U.S.A.; A. Philip Randolph, Negro American Labor President; Walter P. Reuther, the United Automobile Workers President Johnson, almost hidden, and Roy Wilkins, N.J. Kennedy and Mr. Johnson met with leaders of the civil at the White H se after the ceremonies at the Linco

President Meets March Chiefs; Urges Bipartisan Aid on Rights

Continued From Page 1, Col. 7

canapes and sandwiches by Filipino mess boys.

Several of the march leaders had not eaten during a long, exhausting day.

The leaders, a mixed Negro and white group for whom A. Philip Randolph served as spokesman, made it plain in a news conference after their meeting with the President that they were exhilarated and encouraged by the day's events.

Mr. Randolph, president of the Brotherhood of Sleeping Car Porters, called the march "one of the biggest, most creative and constructive demonstrations ever held in the history of our nation" and one of which "every American could be proud."

march." He said he hoped there need be no more all-Negro protest marches or demonstrations.

Mr. Randolph said the march also demonstrated "unity among leadership of the Negroes." But at the White House news conference there was what appeared to be some subtle jockeying for position among them.

Mr. Blake referred, for instance, to Dr. King as "clearly the religious leader of this demonstration."

Randolph Lauds Wilkins

Almost immediately, Mr. Randolph introduced Mr. Wilkins as "the acknowledged leader of the civil rights movement in America."

When it came time to introduce Dr. King, Mr. Randolph termed him "the moral leader of the nation."

March a Big Boost for Bill, Kennedy Tells 10 Leaders

Continued From Page 1

ministration "will continue its efforts to obtain increased employment and to eliminate discrimination in employment practices," two of the prime goals of the march.

The statement did not say specifically whether the President intends to alter his program by writing in a specific Fair Employment Practice Commission section which they demanded.

"We have witnessed today in Washington tens of thousands of Americans—both Negro and white —exercising their right to assemble peacefully and direct the widest possible attention to a great national issue, Kennedy said.

He added, "The gains of 1963 will never be reversed" in the field of Negro rights.

JUBILANT AT PEACE

The Negro leadership obviously was jubilant over the fact that no outbreak occurred at the program. "Today we had a peaceful demonstration, an orderly demonstration," said march leader A. Philip Randolph.

"An historic occasion was written today that will have its lasting effect on history," Randolph added.

The Rev. Martin Luther King Jr., called by Randolph, "the moral leader of our nation," said it was "one of the greatest days of America . . . it was one of the greatest — if not the greatest — march of all times."

That summation came following a full day of activity that began at 8 a.m. (Atlanta time) on Capitol Hill in a series of meetings with congressional leaders.

First the civil rights leaders walked into Senate majority leader Mike Mansfield's office about 10 minutes early, and emerged saying they had stressed the need for a Fair Employment Practices Act.

Mansfield said, however, that no promises were asked and none given during the 40-minute session.

The crucial visit—to Republican leaders Everett Dirksen and Charles Halleck in Dirksen's office—was a bit more brief.

DIRKSEN UNYIELDING

Wilkins said Dirksen told them he had not changed his mind about Title II of the President's bill, the public accommodations section. He opposes it. Dirksen added he supports the rest of the President's civil rights bill, Wilkins said.

As for Halleck, whose control of Republican House votes could make or break the bill, he was "very friendly" on civil rights, Wilkins said.

Again, however, there were no specific promises about either House or Senate passage, the Negro leaders said. Without sizable Republican support, the administration cannot override the Southern Democratic objections.

ASSURED BY McCORMICK

On to House Speaker John McCormick's office went the marchers for a 50-minute session where

"be assured us that if FEPC and Title 3 [allowing the Justice department to institute civil rights suits] are put into the package, these two measures will get through the house."

Randolph, president of the AFL-CIO Brotherhood of Sleeping Car Porters and originator of the march, added that the meeting with McCormick was "very encouraging to the committee."

Randolph made his brief comment to newsmen on the House steps and then joined the other march leaders in a limousine parade back to the Washington Monument to lead the walk to the Lincoln Memorial.

PREDICTS PASSAGE

Inside the Capitol, McCormick admitted reporters and predicted "a bill will pass," although he did not know whether the controversial FEPC and public accommodations sections would be passed.

McCormick said United Auto Workers Union president Walter Reuther brought up a possible increase in the minimum wage from $1.25 to $2.

Asked whether the giant march would hurt or help in seeking passage of the civil rights bill, McCormick replied, "I think if the demonstration is done in an orderly way it will be helpful. They've got a serious task today" keeping the march orderly and peaceful.

SKIRT CAPITOL AREA

Somewhat to everyone's surprise, the marchers generally stayed away from the Capitol area. Most congressmen said they had not been approached for appointments, and the corridors were generally bare. Many Capitol workers took off for the day.

But precautions had been taken anyway. There was such a force

of uniformed officers on hand to cope with any possible trouble that one senator was prompted to comment: "It almost looks like we had a military coup d'etat during the night."

It was almost certain, however, that there would be post mortems for weeks of what effect the march had on Congress.

10-DAY RECESS

There will be plenty of time for assessment and reassessment of the march, since Congress has decided to take a 10-day Labor Day recess.

Rep. Emanuel Celler, D-NY, chairman of the House Judiciary Committee, said ... hoped to begin committee ... on the bill this week but that it must be postponed until after the recess.

Celler joined McCormick in predicting passage of some sort of FEPC law—the one thing that most speakers at the giant rally stressed most.

Dr. King Names Ex-Red Cross Official as Aide

A former official of the American Red Cross has been appointed special assistant to Dr. Martin Luther King Jr. president of the Southern Christian Leadership Conference.

SCLC announced the appointment of Harry G. Boyte, 52, of Atlanta, who served 17 years with the Red Cross.

Boyte was born in Charlotte, N.C. He joined the Red Cross in 1942 and subsequently became administrative assistant chief of personnel.

Atlanta Constitution

*T*he day after the March on Washington of August 28, 1963 (see p. 897), newspapers all over the country carried reports of this historic assembly of more than 200,000 people to demand civil rights and equal job opportunities for African Americans. Although the basic outlines of the story were the same in most papers, ancillary articles, photographs, and editorials revealed deep-seated biases in coverage. Shown here are continuations from the front-page stories in the *New York Times*, a bastion of northeastern liberalism (above), and the *Atlanta Constitution*, a major southern newspaper (right). While the *Times* called the march "orderly" in its headline, the *Constitution*'s story in its right columns highlighted the potential for violence and the precautions taken by police. The article read: "There was such a force of uniformed officers on hand to cope with any possible trouble that one senator was prompted to comment: 'It almost looks like we had a military coup d'état during the night.'" In addition to stressing the march's potential for disruption, the *Constitution* ran an advertisement right below the March on Washington story for a National Ku Klux Klan Rally two days hence, featuring prominent speakers and a cross burning. This comparison of newspaper coverage of a controversial event serves as a reminder that press reporting must always be scrutinized for biases when it is used as historical evidence. What other differences in coverage separated these two newspapers? What factors contribute to press biases?

(top) *New York Times*; (above) *Atlanta Constitution*

schools and other public places. Title VII of the act barred employers from discriminating based on race or national origin in hiring and empowered the Equal Employment Opportunity Commission (EEOC, a body Kennedy had created in 1961) to enforce the law. When conservatives tried to derail the legislation by adding a prohibition on sexual, as well as racial, discrimination, the tactic backfired. The bill's opponents cynically calculated that liberals would not be able to support a bill that threatened to wipe out laws that singled out women for special protection because of their sex. But the act's Title VII passed with the sexual clause intact. It soon proved to be a powerful instrument of federally enforced gender equality, as well as racial equality. Johnson struck another blow for women and minorities in 1965 when he issued an executive order requiring all federal contractors to take **affirmative action** against discrimination.

Johnson also rammed Kennedy's stalled tax bill through Congress and added proposals of his own for a billion-dollar "War on Poverty." Johnson voiced special concern for Appalachia, where the sickness of the soft-coal industry had left tens of thousands of mountain folk on the human slag heap.

Johnson dubbed his domestic program the **Great Society**—a sweeping set of New Dealish economic and welfare measures aimed at transforming the American way of life. Public support for LBJ's antipoverty war was aroused by Michael Harrington's *The Other America* (1962), which revealed that in affluent America 20 percent of the population—and over 40 percent of the black population—suffered in poverty.

✴ Johnson Battles Goldwater in 1964

Johnson's nomination by the Democrats in 1964 was a foregone conclusion; he was chosen by acclamation in Atlantic City as his birthday present. Thanks to the tall Texan, the Democrats stood foursquare on their most liberal platform since Truman's Fair Deal days. The Republicans, convening in San Francisco's Cow Palace, nominated box-jawed Senator Barry Goldwater of Arizona, a bronzed and bespectacled champion of rock-ribbed conservatism. The American stage was thus set for a historic clash of political principles.

Goldwater's forces had galloped out of the Southwest to ride roughshod over the moderate Republican "eastern establishment." Insisting that the GOP offer "a choice not an echo," Goldwater attacked the federal income tax, the Social Security system, the Tennessee Valley Authority, civil rights legislation, the nuclear test-ban treaty, and, most loudly, the Great Society. His fiercely dedicated followers proclaimed, "In Your Heart You Know He's Right," which prompted the Democratic

Negative Campaigning This infamous "attack ad" was televised only once as a paid political advertisement, but it signaled the emergence of a newly noxious style of political campaigning. The ad showed a child dreamily pulling petals from a flower. Suddenly her voice gave way to that of a man reciting an ominous countdown, followed by an exploding nuclear bomb and a throaty voice warning "Vote for President Johnson on November 3. The stakes are too high for you to stay home." The ad implied that a Goldwater presidency would risk nuclear Armageddon. Controversy forced the ad's sponsors to take it off the air, but it was repeatedly reshown in news coverage of the controversy itself—raising serious questions about the very definition of "news."

1964

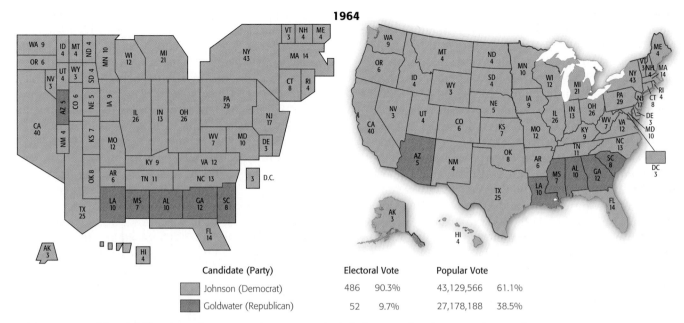

Candidate (Party)	Electoral Vote		Popular Vote	
Johnson (Democrat)	486	90.3%	43,129,566	61.1%
Goldwater (Republican)	52	9.7%	27,178,188	38.5%

MAP 38.2 Presidential Election of 1964 In the map on the left the size of each state is distorted according to its weight in the Electoral College. In New Orleans, toward the end of the campaign, a gutsy Johnson displayed his commitment to civil rights when he told a story about an old senator who once said of his Deep South constituents, "I would like to go back down there and make them just one more Democratic speech. . . . The poor old State, they haven't heard a Democratic speech in 30 years. All they hear at election time is Negro, Negro, Negro!" Johnson's open voicing of sentiments like this contributed heavily to his losses in the traditionally Democratic "solid South." © Cengage Learning

response, "In Your Guts You Know He's Nuts." Goldwater warmed right-wing hearts when he proclaimed that "extremism in the defense of liberty is no vice. And . . . moderation in the pursuit of justice is no virtue."

Democrats gleefully exploited the image of Goldwater as a trigger-happy cowboy who would "Barry us" in the debris of World War III. Johnson cultivated the contrasting image of a resolute statesman by seizing upon the Tonkin Gulf episode early in August 1964. Unbeknownst to the American public or Congress, U.S. Navy ships had been cooperating with South Vietnamese gunboats in provocative raids along the coast of North Vietnam. Two of these American destroyers were allegedly fired upon by the North Vietnamese on August 2 and 4, although exactly what happened still remains unclear. Later investigations strongly suggested that the North Vietnamese fired in self-defense on August 2 and that the "attack" of August 4 never happened. Johnson later reportedly wisecracked, "For all I know, the Navy was shooting at whales out there."

Johnson nevertheless promptly called the attack "unprovoked" and moved swiftly to make political hay out of this episode. He ordered a "limited" retaliatory air raid against the North Vietnamese bases, loudly proclaiming that he sought "no wider war"—thus implying that the truculent Goldwater did. Johnson also used the

incident to spur congressional passage of the all-purpose Tonkin Gulf Resolution. With only two dissenting votes in both houses, the lawmakers virtually abdicated their war-declaring powers and handed the president a blank check to use further force in Southeast Asia. The Tonkin Gulf Resolution, Johnson boasted, was "like grandma's nightshirt—it covered everything."

The towering Texan rode to a spectacular victory in November 1964. The voters were herded into Johnson's column by fondness for the Kennedy legacy, faith in Great Society promises, and fear of Goldwater. A stampede of 43,129,566 Johnson votes trampled the Republican ticket with its 27,178,188 supporters. The tally in the Electoral College was 486 to 52 (see Map 38.2). Goldwater carried only his native Arizona and five other states—all of them, significantly, in the traditionally Democratic but now racially restless South. Johnson's record-breaking 61 percent of the popular vote swept lopsided Democratic majorities into both houses of Congress.

✴ The Great Society Congress

Johnson's huge victory temporarily smashed the conservative congressional coalition of southern Democrats and northern Republicans. A wide-open legislative road stretched before the Great Society programs, as the president skillfully ringmastered his two-to-one Democratic majorities. Congress poured out a flood of legislation, comparable only to the output of the New Dealers in the Hundred Days Congress of 1933. Johnson, confident that a growing economy gave him ample fiscal and political room for maneuver, delivered at last on long-deferred Democratic promises of social reform.

Escalating the War on Poverty, Congress doubled the appropriation of the Office of Economic Opportunity to $2 billion and granted more than $1 billion to redevelop the gutted hills and hollows of Appalachia. Johnson also prodded Congress into creating two new cabinet offices: the Department of Transportation and the Department of Housing and Urban Development (HUD), to which he named the first black cabinet secretary in the nation's history, respected economist Robert C. Weaver. Other noteworthy laws established the National Endowments for the Arts and the Humanities, designed to lift the level of American cultural life.

Even more impressive were the Big Four legislative achievements that crowned LBJ's Great Society program: aid to education, medical care for the elderly and indigent, immigration reform, and a new voting rights bill.

Johnson neatly avoided the thorny question of separation of church and state by channeling educational aid to students, not schools, thus allowing funds to flow to hard-pressed parochial institutions. (Catholic John F. Kennedy had not dared to touch this prickly issue.) With a keen eye for the dramatic, LBJ signed the education bill in the humble one-room Texas schoolhouse he had attended as a boy.

Medicare for the elderly, accompanied by Medicaid for the poor, became a reality in 1965. Like the New Deal's Social Security program, Medicare and Medicaid created "entitlements." That is, they conferred rights on certain categories of Americans virtually in perpetuity, without the need for repeated congressional approval. These programs were part of a spreading "rights revolution" that materially improved the lives of millions of Americans—but also eventually undermined the federal government's financial health.

Immigration reform was the third of Johnson's Big Four feats. The Immigration and Nationality Act of 1965 abolished at last the "national-origins" quota system that had been in place since 1921 (see p. 703). The act also doubled (to 290,000) the number of immigrants allowed to enter annually, while for the first time setting limits on immigrants from the Western Hemisphere (120,000). The new law further provided for the admission of close relatives of United States citizens, outside those numerical limits. To the surprise of many of the act's architects, more than 100,000 persons per year took advantage of its "family unification" provisions in the decades after 1965, and the immigrant stream swelled beyond expectations. Even more surprising to the act's sponsors, the sources of immigration soon shifted heavily from Europe to Latin America and Asia, dramatically changing the racial and ethnic composition of the American population.

Great Society programs came in for rancorous political attack in later years. Conservatives charged that the billions spent for "social engineering" had simply been flushed down the waste pipe. Yet the poverty rate declined measurably in the ensuing decade (see Figure

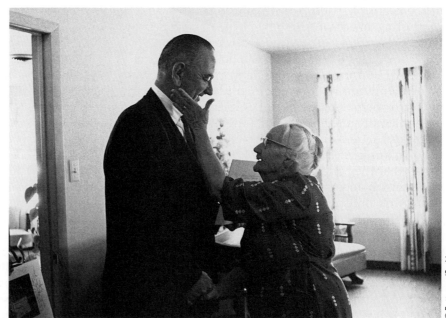

Giving Thanks for Medicare An elderly woman showed her gratitude to President Lyndon B. Johnson for his signing of the Medicare bill in April 1965, providing basic medical care for the aged. In tribute to former president Truman's unsuccessful effort to pass a national medical insurance program twenty years earlier, Johnson flew to Truman's Missouri home to sign the bill that he claimed would deliver "care for the sick and serenity for the fearful." No one acknowledged that Truman's earlier plan had been much more comprehensive or that Johnson, then a young Texas congressman, had opposed it.

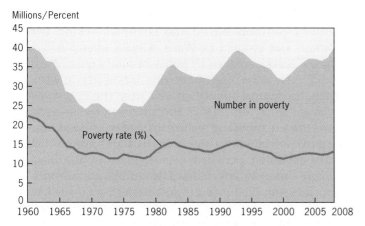

Millions/Percent

FIGURE 38.1 Poverty in the United States, 1960–2011
In 2000 the poverty rate fell to 11.3 percent, its lowest level since 1979. In the "Great Recession" of the early twenty-first century, it ticked upward again, to 15.1 percent in 2011. The absolute numbers refer to those people who live in families whose total income is lower than a set "poverty threshold," which is tied to the consumer price index, so it varies with inflation. The "poverty rate" means the percentage of all Americans living below that threshold. (Source: U.S. Bureau of the Census, http://www.census.gov/hhes/www/poverty/histpov/hstpov2.html.)

38.1). Medicare made especially dramatic reductions in the incidence of poverty among America's elderly. Other antipoverty programs, among them Project Head Start, sharply improved the educational performance of underprivileged youth. Infant mortality rates also fell in minority communities as general health conditions improved. Lyndon Johnson was not fully victorious in the war against poverty, but he did win several noteworthy battles.

✦ Battling for Black Rights

With the last of his Big Four reforms, the Voting Rights Act of 1965, Johnson made heartening headway against one of the most persistent American evils, racial discrimination. In Johnson's native South, the walls of segregation were crumbling, but not fast enough for long-suffering African Americans. The Civil Rights Act of 1964 gave the federal government more muscle to enforce school-desegregation orders and to prohibit racial discrimination in all kinds of public accommodations and employment. But the problem of voting rights remained. In Mississippi, which had the largest black minority of any state, only about 5 percent of eligible blacks were registered to vote. The lopsided pattern was similar throughout the South. Ballot-denying devices like the poll tax, literacy tests, and barefaced intimidation still barred black people from the political

process. Mississippi law required the names of prospective black registrants to be published for two weeks in local newspapers—a device that virtually guaranteed economic reprisals, or worse.

Beginning in 1964, opening up the polling booths became the chief goal of the black movement in the South. The Twenty-fourth Amendment, ratified in January 1964, abolished the poll tax in federal elections. (See the Appendix.) Blacks joined hands with white civil rights workers—many of them student volunteers from the North—in a massive voter-registration drive in Mississippi during the **Freedom Summer** of 1964. Singing "We Shall Overcome," they zealously set out to soothe generations of white anxieties and black fears.

But events soon blighted bright hopes. In late June 1964, one black and two white civil rights workers disappeared in Mississippi. Their badly beaten bodies were later found buried beneath an earthen dam. FBI investigators eventually arrested twenty-one white Mississippians, including the local sheriff, in connection with the killings. But white juries refused to convict the whites for these murders. In August an integrated **Mississippi Freedom Democratic party** delegation was denied its seat at the national Democratic convention. Only a handful of black Mississippians had succeeded in registering to vote.

Early in 1965 Martin Luther King, Jr., resumed the voter-registration campaign in Selma, Alabama, where blacks made up 50 percent of the population but only 1 percent of the voters. State troopers with tear gas and whips assaulted King's demonstrators as they marched peacefully to the state capital at Montgomery. A Boston Unitarian minister was killed, and a few days later a white Detroit woman was shotgunned to death by Klansmen on the highway near Selma.

As the nation recoiled in horror before these violent scenes, President Johnson, speaking in soft southern accents, delivered a compelling address on television. What happened in Selma, he insisted, concerned all Americans, "who must overcome the crippling legacy of bigotry and injustice." Then, in a stirring adaptation of the anthem of the civil rights movement, the president concluded, "And we shall overcome." Following words with deeds, Johnson speedily shepherded through Congress the landmark **Voting Rights Act of 1965**, signed into law on August 6. It outlawed literacy tests and sent federal voter registrars into several southern states.

The passage of the Voting Rights Act, exactly one hundred years after the conclusion of the Civil War, climaxed a century of awful abuse and robust resurgence for African Americans in the South. "Give us the ballot," said Martin Luther King, Jr., "and the South will never be the same again." He was right. The act did not end discrimination and oppression overnight, but

Confrontation at the Edmund Pettus Bridge, Selma, Alabama, 1965 Named for a Confederate general, the Edmund Pettus Bridge became the scene of a violent clash in March, 1965. Moments after this photo was taken, Alabama state troopers, wielding billy clubs and lobbing tear gas canisters, assaulted peaceful civil rights demonstrators marching to the Alabama state capital in Montgomery. Dozens of demonstrators were hospitalized. Heavy media coverage of this and similar events helped stir the nation's conscience about civil rights and led to passage of the historic Voting Rights Act in 1965.

it placed an awesome lever for change in blacks' hands. Black southerners now had power and began to wield it without fear of reprisals. White southerners began to court black votes and business as never before. In the following decade, for the first time since emancipation, African Americans began to migrate *into* the South.

✹ Black Power

The Voting Rights Act of 1965 marked the end of an era in the history of the civil rights movement—the era of nonviolent demonstrations, focused on the South, led by peaceful moderates like Martin Luther King, Jr., and aimed at integrating blacks into American society. As

if to symbolize the turn of events, just five days after President Johnson signed the landmark voting law, a bloody riot erupted in Watts, a black ghetto in Los Angeles. Blacks enraged by police brutality burned and looted their own neighborhoods for nearly a week. When the smoke finally cleared over the Los Angeles basin, thirty-one blacks and three whites lay dead, more than a thousand people had been injured, and hundreds of buildings stood charred and gutted. The Watts explosion heralded a new phase of the black struggle—increasingly marked by militant confrontation, focusing on northern and western cities, led by radical and sometimes violent spokespersons, and often aiming not at interracial cooperation but at black separatism.

The pious Christian moderation of Martin Luther King, Jr., came under heavy fire from this second wave of younger black leaders, who privately mocked the dignified Dr. King as "de Lawd." Deepening division among black leaders was highlighted by the career of Malcolm X. Born Malcolm Little, he was at first inspired by the militant black nationalists in the Nation of Islam. Like

Malcolm X The charismatic black leader was a hypnotizing speaker who could rivet and arouse crowds with his call for black separatism. At the end of his life, Malcolm began to temper his separatist creed.

the Nation's founder, Elijah Muhammed (born Elijah Poole), Malcolm changed his surname to advertise his lost African identity in white America. A brilliant and charismatic preacher, Malcolm X trumpeted black separatism and inveighed against the "blue-eyed white devils." Eventually Malcolm distanced himself from Elijah Muhammed's separatist preachings and moved toward mainstream Islam. (By the 1990s Islam was among America's fastest-growing religions and counted some 2 million African American converts—or "reverts," as Muslims described it—in its ranks.) In early 1965 he was cut down by rival Nation of Islam gunmen while speaking to a large crowd in New York City.

The militant **Black Panther party** meanwhile brandished weapons in the streets of Oakland, California, even while it was establishing children's breakfast programs. Then in 1966 Trinidad-born Stokely Carmichael, a leader of the Student Nonviolent Coordinating Committee (SNCC), began to preach the doctrine of **Black Power**, which, he said, "will smash everything Western civilization has created." Some advocates of Black Power insisted that they simply intended the slogan to describe a broad-front effort to exercise the political and economic rights gained by the civil rights movement and to speed the integration of American society. But other African Americans, recollecting previous black nationalist movements like that of Marcus Garvey earlier in the century (see pp. 719–720), breathed a vibrant separatist meaning into the concept of Black Power. They emphasized African American distinctiveness, promoted "Afro" hairstyles and dress, shed their "white" names for new African identities, and demanded black studies programs in schools and universities.

Ironically, just as the civil rights movement had achieved its greatest legal and political triumphs, more city-shaking riots erupted in the black ghettos of several American cities. A bloody outburst in Newark, New Jersey, in the summer of 1967 took twenty-five lives. Federal troops restored order in Detroit, Michigan, after forty-three people died in the streets. As in Los Angeles, black rioters torched their own neighborhoods, attacking police officers and even firefighters, who had to battle both flames and mobs howling "Burn, baby, burn."

These riotous outbursts angered many white Americans, who threatened to retaliate with their own "backlash" against ghetto arsonists and killers. Inner-city anarchy baffled many northerners, who had considered racial problems a purely "southern" question. But black concerns had moved north—as had nearly half the nation's black people. In the North the Black Power movement now focused less on civil rights and more on economic demands. Black unemployment, for example, was nearly double that for whites. These oppressive new problems seemed even less likely to be solved peaceably than the struggle for voting rights in the South.

Despair deepened when the magnetic and moderate voice of Martin Luther King, Jr., was forever silenced by a sniper's bullet in Memphis, Tennessee, on April 4, 1968. A martyr for justice, he had bled and died against the peculiarly American thorn of race. The killing of King cruelly robbed the American people of one of the most inspirational leaders in their history—at a time when they could least afford to lose him. This outrage triggered a nationwide orgy of ghetto-gutting and violence that cost over forty lives.

Rioters noisily made news, but thousands of other blacks quietly made history. Their voter registration in the South shot upward, and by the late 1960s several hundred blacks held elected office in the Old South. Cleveland, Ohio, and Gary, Indiana, elected black mayors. By 1972 nearly half of southern black children sat in integrated classrooms. Actually, more schools in the South were integrated than in the North. About a

---

Dr. Martin Luther King, Jr. (1929–1968) and Malcolm X (1925–1965) not only differed in the goals they held out to their fellow African Americans—King urging racial integration and Malcolm X black separatism—but also in the means they advocated to achieve them. In his famous "I Have a Dream" speech during the interracial March on Washington on August 28, 1963, King proclaimed to a quarter of a million people assembled at the Lincoln Memorial,

❝In the process of gaining our rightful place we must not be guilty of wrongful deeds. Let us not seek to satisfy our thirst for freedom by drinking from the cup of bitterness and hatred. . . . We must not allow our creative protest to degenerate into physical violence. Again and again we must rise to the majestic heights of meeting physical force with soul force.❞

About three months later, Malcolm X angrily rejected King's "peaceful, turn-the-other-cheek revolution":

❝Revolution is bloody, revolution is hostile, revolution knows no compromise, revolution overturns and destroys everything that gets in its way. And you, sitting around here like a knot on the wall, saying, 'I'm going to love these folks no matter how much they hate me,' . . . Whoever heard of a revolution where they lock arms . . . , singing 'We shall overcome?' You don't do that in a revolution. You don't do any singing, you're too busy swinging.❞

third of black families had risen economically into the ranks of the middle class—though an equal proportion remained below the "poverty line." King left a shining legacy of racial progress, but he was cut down when the job was far from completed.

Combating Communism in Two Hemispheres

Violence at home eclipsed Johnson's legislative triumphs, while foreign flare-ups threatened his political life. Discontented Dominicans rose in revolt against their military government in April 1965. Johnson speedily announced that the Dominican Republic was the target of a Castro-like coup by "Communist conspirators," and he dispatched American troops, ultimately some twenty-five thousand, to restore order. But the evidence of a communist takeover was fragmentary at best. Johnson was widely condemned, at home and in Latin America, for his temporary reversion to the officially abandoned "gunboat diplomacy."

At about the same time, Johnson was sinking deeper into the monsoon mud of Vietnam. Guerillas loyal to the North Vietnamese communists, called Viet Cong, attacked an American air base at Pleiku, South Vietnam, in February 1965. The president immediately ordered retaliatory bombing raids against military installations in North Vietnam and for the first time ordered attacking U.S. troops to land. By the middle of March 1965, the Americans had "Operation Rolling Thunder" in full swing—regular full-scale bombing attacks against North Vietnam. Before 1965 ended, some 184,000 American troops were involved, most of them slogging through the jungles and rice paddies of South Vietnam searching for guerrillas.

Johnson had now taken the first fateful steps down a slippery path. He and his advisers believed that a fine-tuned, step-by-step "escalation" of American force would drive the enemy to defeat with a minimum loss of life on both sides. But the enemy matched every increase in American firepower with more men and more wiliness in the art of guerrilla warfare.

The South Vietnamese themselves were meanwhile becoming spectators in their own war, as the fighting became increasingly Americanized. Corrupt and collapsible governments succeeded each other in Saigon with bewildering rapidity. Yet American officials continued to talk of defending a faithful democratic ally. Washington spokespeople also defended America's action as a test of Uncle Sam's "commitment" and of the reliability of his numerous treaty pledges to resist communist encroachment. Persuaded by such panicky thinking, Johnson steadily raised the military stakes in Vietnam. By 1968 he had poured more than half a million troops into Southeast Asia, and the annual bill for the war was exceeding $30 billion. Yet the end was nowhere in sight.

Vietnam Vexations

America could not defeat the enemy in Vietnam, but it seemed to be defeating itself. World opinion grew

The Mechanized War High technology and modern equipment, such as this helicopter, gave the Americans in Vietnam a huge military advantage. But unaccompanied by a clear political purpose and a national will to win, technological superiority was insufficient to achieve final victory.

AP Images

increasingly hostile; the blasting of an underdeveloped country by a mighty superpower struck many critics as obscene. Several nations expelled American Peace Corps volunteers. The ever-censorious Charles de Gaulle withdrew France from NATO in 1966 and ordered all American troops out of the country, reportedly prompting Johnson to ask if that included the thousands buried in Normandy.

Overcommitment in Southeast Asia also tied America's hands elsewhere. Attacked by Soviet-backed Egypt, Jordan, and Syria, a beleaguered Israel stunned the world with a military triumph in June 1967. When the smoke cleared after the **Six-Day War**, Israel expanded to control new territories in the Sinai Peninsula, the Golan Heights, the Gaza Strip, and the West Bank of the Jordan River, including Jerusalem (see Map 40.2 on p. 948). The Israeli victory brought some 1 million resentful Palestinian Arabs under direct Israeli control, while another 350,000 Palestinian refugees fled to neighboring Jordan. The Israelis eventually withdrew from the Sinai after signing a peace treaty with Egypt, but they refused to relinquish the other areas without a treaty and began moving Jewish settlers into the heavily Arab district of the West Bank. The Six-Day War markedly intensified the problems of the already volatile Middle East, leading to an in tractable stand-off between the Israelis and Palestinians, now led by Yasir Arafat (1929–2004), head of the Palestine Liberation Organization (PLO). For decades a return to the "pre-1967 boundaries" would be a key negotiating aim for Palestinians. The Middle East became an ever more dangerously packed powder keg that the war-plagued United States proved powerless to defuse.

Domestic discontent festered as the Vietnamese entanglement dragged on. Antiwar demonstrations had begun on a small scale with campus "teach-ins" in 1965, and gradually these protests mounted to tidal-wave proportions. As the long arm of the military draft dragged more and more young men off to the Southeast Asian slaughter pen, resistance stiffened. Thousands of draft registrants fled to Canada; others publicly burned their draft cards. Hundreds of thousands of marchers filled the streets of New York, San Francisco, and other cities, chanting, "Hell no, we won't go" and "Hey, hey, LBJ, how many kids did you kill today?" Many Americans felt pangs of conscience at the spectacle of their countrymen burning peasant huts and blistering civilians with ghastly napalm.

Opposition in Congress to the Vietnam involvement centered in the influential Senate Committee on Foreign Relations, headed by Senator William Fulbright of Arkansas. A constant thorn in the side of the president, he staged a series of widely viewed televised hearings in 1966 and 1967, during which prominent personages aired their views, largely antiwar. Gradually the public

The Vietnam Quagmire Marine PFC Phillip Mark Wilson of Wolfforth, Texas, carries a rocket launcher across a stream near the "demilitarized zone" (DMZ) that separated North and South Vietnam. Wilson was killed in action soon after this photo was taken, just five days after his 21st birthday.

Larry Burrows/Time & Life Pictures/Getty Images

came to feel that it had been deceived about the causes and "winnability" of the war. A yawning "credibility gap" opened between the government and the people. New flocks of antiwar "doves" were hatching daily.

Even within the administration, doubts were deepening about the wisdom of the war in Vietnam. When Defense Secretary McNamara expressed increasing discomfiture at the course of events, he was quietly eased out of the cabinet. (Years later McNamara wrote that "we were wrong, terribly wrong," about Vietnam.) By early 1968 the brutal and futile struggle had become the longest and most unpopular foreign war in the nation's history. The government had failed utterly to explain to the people what was supposed to be at stake in Vietnam. Many critics wondered if any objective could be worth the vast price, in blood and treasure, that America was paying. Casualties, killed and wounded, already exceeded 100,000. More bombs had been dropped on Vietnam than on all enemy territory in World War II.

The war was also ripping apart the fabric of American society and even threatening to shred the Constitution. In 1967 President Johnson ordered the CIA, in clear violation of its charter as a *foreign* intelligence agency, to spy on domestic antiwar activists. He also encouraged the FBI to turn its counterintelligence program, code-named "Cointelpro," against the peace movement. "Cointelpro" subverted leading "doves" with false accusations that they were communist sympathizers. These clandestine tactics made the FBI look like a totalitarian state's secret police rather than a guardian of American democracy.

As the war dragged on, evidence mounted that America had been entrapped in an Asian civil war, fighting against highly motivated rebels who were striving to overthrow an oppressive regime. Yet Johnson clung to his basic strategy of ratcheting up the pressure bit by bit. He stubbornly assured doubting Americans that he could see "the light at the end of the tunnel." But to growing numbers of Americans, it seemed that Johnson was bent on "saving" Vietnam by destroying it.

✴ Vietnam Topples Johnson

Hawkish illusions that the struggle was about to be won were shattered by a blistering communist offensive launched in late January 1968, during Tet, the Vietnamese New Year. At a time when the Viet Cong were supposedly licking their wounds, they suddenly and simultaneously mounted savage attacks on twenty-seven key South Vietnamese cities, including the capital, Saigon. Although eventually beaten off with heavy losses, they demonstrated anew that victory could not be gained by Johnson's strategy of gradual escalation. The Tet offensive ended in a military defeat but a political victory for the Viet Cong. With an increasingly insistent voice, American public opinion demanded a speedy end to the war. Opposition grew so vehement that President Johnson could feel the very foundations of government shaking under his feet. He was also

President Lyndon Johnson Haunted by Specters of Vietnam, 1967

Paul Szep/Getty Images

suffering through hells of personal agony over American casualties. He wept as he signed letters of condolence and slipped off at night to pray with monks at a small Catholic church in Washington.

American military leaders responded to the Tet attacks with a request for 200,000 more troops. The size of the request staggered many policymakers. Former secretary of state Dean Acheson reportedly advised the president that "the Joint Chiefs of Staff don't know what they're talking about."

The president meanwhile was being sharply challenged from within his own party. Eugene McCarthy, a little-known Democratic senator from Minnesota, had emerged as a contender for the 1968 Democratic presidential nomination. The soft-spoken McCarthy, a sometime poet and devout Catholic, gathered a small army of antiwar college students as campaign workers. Going "clean for Gene," with shaven faces and shortened locks, they helped him gain an impressive 41.4 percent of the Democratic vote in the New Hampshire primary on March 12, 1968. Although still second to Johnson's 49.6 percent, McCarthy's showing was devastating for the president. Johnson's star fell further four days later when Senator Robert F. Kennedy, now a senator from New York and an outspoken dove on the war, threw his hat into the ring. The charismatic and handsome Kennedy, heir to his murdered brother's mantle of leadership, stirred a passionate response among workers, African Americans, Latinos, and young people.

These startling events abroad and at home were not lost on LBJ. In a bombshell address on March 31, 1968, he announced on nationwide television that he would freeze American troop levels and scale back the bombing. Then, in a dramatic plea to unify a dangerously divided nation, Johnson startled his vast audience by firmly declaring that he would not be a candidate for the presidency in 1968.

Johnson's "abdication" had the effect of preserving the military status quo. He had held the "hawks" in check, while offering himself as a sacrifice to the militant "doves." The United States could thus maintain the maximum *acceptable* level of military activity in Vietnam with one hand, while trying to negotiate a settlement with the other. North Vietnam shortly agreed to commence negotiations in Paris. But progress was glacially slow, as prolonged bickering developed over the very shape of the conference table.

✴ The Presidential Sweepstakes of 1968

The summer of 1968 was one of the hottest political seasons in the nation's history. Johnson's heir apparent for the Democratic nomination was his liberal vice

© Bettmann/Corbis

The Siege of Chicago, 1968
Antiwar protesters staged demonstrations in the streets of Chicago during the Democratic National Convention in August 1968. Some 2,500 members of the radical Youth International Party (known as the Yippies) planned a peaceful "festival of light" across the street from the convention hall, but instead found themselves drawn into a melee with the police and National Guardsmen. The confrontation in Chicago badly tarnished Democratic candidate Hubert Humphrey's presidential campaign. His Republican opponent, Richard Nixon, won the presidency with calls for an "honorable peace" in Vietnam and "law and order" at home.

president, Hubert H. Humphrey, a former pharmacist, college professor, mayor, and U.S. senator from Minnesota. Senators McCarthy and Kennedy meanwhile dueled in several state primaries, with Kennedy's bandwagon gathering ever-increasing speed. But on June 5, 1968, the night of an exciting victory in the California primary, Kennedy was shot to death by a young Arab immigrant resentful of the candidate's pro-Israel views.

Angry antiwar zealots, deprived by an assassin's bullet of their leading candidate, streamed menacingly into Chicago for the Democratic convention in August 1968. Mayor Richard Daley responded by arranging for barbed-wire barricades around the convention hall ("Fort Daley"), as well as thousands of police and National Guard reinforcements. Some militant demonstrators baited the officers in blue by calling them "pigs," chanting "Ho, Ho, Ho Chi Minh," shouting obscenities, and hurling bags and cans of excrement at the police lines. As people the world over watched on television, the exasperated "peace officers" broke into a "police riot," clubbing and manhandling innocent and guilty alike. Acrid tear gas fumes hung heavy over the city even as Humphrey steamrollered to the nomination on the first ballot.

The Humphrey forces blocked the McCarthyites' attempt to secure an antiwar platform plank and hammered into place their own declaration that armed force would be relentlessly applied until the enemy showed more willingness to negotiate.

Scenting victory over the badly divided Democrats, the Republicans convened in plush Miami Beach,

Florida, where former vice president Richard M. Nixon arose from his political grave to win the nomination. As a "hawk" on Vietnam and a right-leaning middle-of-the-roader on domestic policy, Nixon pleased the Goldwater conservatives and was acceptable to party moderates. He appealed to white southern voters and to the "law-and-order" element when he tapped as his vice-presidential running mate Maryland's Governor Spiro T. Agnew, noted for his tough stands against dissidents and black militants. The Republican platform called for victory in Vietnam and a strong anticrime policy.

Adding color and confusion to the campaign was a "spoiler" third-party ticket—the American Independent party—headed by a scrappy ex-pugilist, George C. Wallace, former governor of Alabama. In 1963 he had stood in the doorway to prevent two black students from entering the University of Alabama. "Segregation now! Segregation tomorrow! Segregation forever!" he shouted. Wallace jabbed repeatedly at "pointy-headed bureaucrats," and he taunted hecklers as "bums" in need of a bath. Speaking behind a bulletproof screen, he called for prodding the blacks into their place, with bayonets if necessary. He and his running mate, former air force general Curtis LeMay, also proposed smashing the North Vietnamese to smithereens by "bombing them back to the Stone Age."

Between the positions of the Republicans and the Democrats on Vietnam, there was little choice. Both candidates were committed to carrying on the war until the enemy settled for an "honorable peace," which

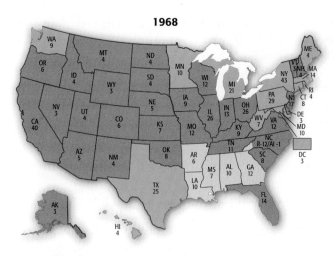

1968

Candidate (Party)	Electoral Vote		Popular Vote	
Nixon (Republican)	301	56.1%	31,785,480	43.4%
Humphrey (Democrat)	191	35.5%	31,275,166	42.7%
Wallace (American Independent)	46	8.4%	9,906,473	13.5%

MAP 38.3 Presidential Election of 1968 (with electoral vote by state) George Wallace won in five states, and he denied a clear majority to either of the two major-party candidates in twenty-five other states. A shift of some fifty thousand votes might well have thrown the election into the House of Representatives, giving Wallace the strategic bargaining position he sought. © Cengage Learning

seemed to mean an American victory. The millions of "doves" had no place to roost, and many refused to vote at all. Humphrey, scorched by the LBJ brand, went down to defeat as a loyal prisoner of his chief's policies.

Nixon, who had lost a cliffhanger to Kennedy in 1960, won one in 1968. He garnered 301 electoral votes, with 43.4 percent of the popular tally (31,785,480), as compared with 191 electoral votes and 42.7 percent of the popular votes (31,275,166) for Humphrey (see Map 38.3). Unlike most new presidents, Nixon faced congressional majorities of the opposing party in both houses. He carried not a single major city, thus attesting to the continuing urban strength of the Democrats, who also won about 95 percent of the black vote. Nixon had received no clear mandate to do anything. He was a minority president who owed his election to divisions over the war and protest against the unfair draft, crime, and rioting.

As for Wallace, he won an impressive 9,906,473 popular votes and 46 electoral votes, all from five states of the Deep South, four of which the Republican Goldwater had carried in 1964. Wallace remained a formidable force, for he had amassed the largest third-party popular vote in American history to that point and was the last third-party candidate to win any electoral votes. (In 1992 Ross Perot enjoyed a greater popular-vote margin but won no states; see p. 996.) Wallace had also resoundingly demonstrated the continuing power of "populist" politics, which appealed to voters' fears and resentments rather than to the better angels of their nature. His candidacy foreshadowed a coarsening of American political life that would take deep root in the ensuing decades.

✦ The Obituary of Lyndon Johnson

Talented but tragedy-struck Lyndon Johnson returned to his Texas ranch in January 1969 and died there four years later. His party was defeated, and his "me-too" Hubert Humphrey was repudiated. Yet Johnson's legislative leadership for a time had been remarkable. No president since Lincoln had worked harder or done more for civil rights. None had shown more compassion for the poor, blacks, and the ill-educated.

But by 1966 Johnson was already sinking into the Vietnam quicksands. Great Society programs began to wither on the vine, as soaring war costs sucked tax dollars into the military machine. His effort to provide both guns and butter prevented him from delivering either in sufficient quantity. The War on Poverty met resistance that was as stubborn as the Viet Cong and eventually went down to defeat. Great want persisted alongside great wealth.

Johnson had crucified himself on the cross of Vietnam. The Southeast Asian quagmire engulfed his noblest intentions. Committed to some degree by his two predecessors, he had chosen to defend the American foothold and enlarge the conflict rather than be run out. He was evidently persuaded by his brightest advisers, both civilian and military, that massive aerial bombing and limited troop commitments would make a "cheap" victory possible. His decision not to escalate the fighting further offended the "hawks," and his refusal to back off altogether antagonized the "doves." Like the Calvinists of colonial days, luckless Lyndon Johnson was damned if he did and damned if he did not.

✦ The Cultural Upheaval of the 1960s

The struggles of the 1960s against racism, poverty, and the war in Vietnam had momentous cultural consequences. The decade came to be seen as a watershed dividing two distinct eras in terms of values, morals, and behavior.

Everywhere in 1960s America, a newly negative attitude toward all kinds of authority took hold. Disillusioned by the discovery that American society was not free of racism, sexism, imperialism, and oppression, many young people lost their traditional moral rudders. Neither families nor churches nor schools seemed to be able to define values and shape behavior with the certainty of shared purpose that many people believed had once existed. The nation's mainline Protestant denominations, which had dominated American religious life for centuries, lost their grip in the 1960s, as weekly churchgoing declined from 48 percent in the late 1950s to 41 percent in the early 1970s. The liberal Protestant churches suffered the most. They increasingly ceded religious authority to conservative evangelicals while surrendering cultural authority to secular professionals and academic social scientists. A new cultural divide began to take shape, as educated Americans became increasingly secular and the less

educated became more religious. Religious upheaval even churned the tradition-bound Roman Catholic Church, among the world's oldest and most conservative institutions. Clerics abandoned their Roman collars and Latin lingo, folk songs replaced Gregorian chants, and meatless Fridays became ancient history. No matter what the topic, conventional wisdom and inherited ideas came under fire. "Trust no one over thirty" was a popular sneer of rebellious youth.

Skepticism about authority had deep historical roots in American culture, and it had even bloomed in the supposedly complacent and conformist 1950s. "Beat" poets like Allen Ginsberg and iconoclastic novelists like Jack Kerouac had voiced dark disillusion with the materialistic pursuits and "establishment" arrogance of the Eisenhower era. In movies like *Rebel Without a Cause* (1955), the attractive young actor James Dean expressed the restless frustration of many young people.

The disaffection of the young reached crisis proportions in the tumultuous 1960s. One of the first organized protests against established authority broke out at the University of California at Berkeley in 1964, in the aptly named Free Speech Movement. Students objected to an administrative ban on the use of campus space for political debate. During months of protest, they accused the Cold War "megaversity" of promoting corporate interests rather than humane values. But in only a few years, the clean-cut Berkeley activists and their sober-minded sit-ins would seem downright quaint. Fired by outrage against the war in Vietnam, some sons and daughters of the middle class became radical political rebels. Others turned to mind-bending drugs, tuned in to "acid rock," and dropped out of "straight" society. Still others "did their own thing" in communes or "alternative" institutions. Patriotism became a dirty word. Beflowered women in trousers and long-haired men with earrings heralded the rise of a self-conscious "counterculture" stridently opposed to traditional American ways.

Social upheaval in the 1960s was far from an American-only phenomenon. As people born in the wake of World War II came of age across the world, they questioned established authority everywhere. Waves of protests and calls for individual rights and political freedom spread like wildfire. The year 1968 was so stormy that it became synonymous with unrest in many languages. In May of that year, leftist French students organized city-crippling strikes against their country's antiquated university system. Joined by millions of workers, they nearly toppled the government. The global spirit of protest—against the Vietnam War, racial injustice, and the strictures of bourgeois society—spread from Berkeley, California, to Columbia University in New York, to West Berlin, and even to

The Free Speech Movement, Berkeley, California, 1964
The Free Speech Movement on the campus of the University of California at Berkeley marked the first of the large-scale student mobilizations that rocked campuses across the country throughout the rest of the 1960s. Here a student schooled in passive resistance is dragged by police to a waiting bus.

Paris, 1968 Protests ripped through the world in 1968. In Paris student battles with campus authorities and police triggered a massive nationwide labor strike and nearly brought down the French government.

Communist China. In Czechoslovakia, deep within the Soviet bloc, Western-inspired reformers launched the liberating program that became known as the "Prague Spring" in January 1968. For eight months political freedom blossomed, until ruthlessly mowed down by Soviet tanks. Despite backlashes—by university presidents, conservative politicians, and communist leaders—the genie of cultural and political protest was out of the bottle.

The 1960s also witnessed a "sexual revolution," though its novelty and scale are often exaggerated. Without doubt, the introduction of the birth-control pill in 1960 made unwanted pregnancies much easier to avoid and sexual appetites easier to satisfy. The Mattachine Society, founded in Los Angeles in 1951, was a pioneering advocate for gay rights, as gay men and lesbians increasingly demanded sexual tolerance. A brutal attack on gay men by off-duty police officers at New

The First Gay Pride Parade, New York City, 1970 On the first anniversary of homosexuals' celebrated resistance to police harassment at the Stonewall Inn, on June 27, 1969, two hundred men and women marched from Greenwich Village to Central Park, initiating a tradition that now has spread to many other American cities and around the globe, attracting thousands of paraders, onlookers, and even prominent politicians.

York's Stonewall Inn in 1969 proved a turning point, when the victims fought back in what became known as the **Stonewall Rebellion**. Widening worries in the 1980s about sexually transmitted diseases like genital herpes and AIDS (acquired immunodeficiency syndrome) finally slowed, but did not reverse, the sexual revolution.

Launched in youthful idealism, many of the cultural "revolutions" of the 1960s sputtered out in violence and cynicism. **Students for a Democratic Society (SDS)**, once at the forefront of the antipoverty and antiwar campaigns, had by decade's end spawned an underground terrorist group called the Weathermen. Peaceful civil rights demonstrations had given way to blockbusting urban riots. What started as apparently innocent experiments with drugs like marijuana and LSD had fried many youthful brains and spawned a loathsome underworld of drug lords and addicts.

Straight-laced guardians of respectability denounced the self-indulgent romanticism of the "flower children" as the beginning of the end of modern civilization. Sympathetic observers hailed the "greening" of America—the replacement of materialism and imperialism by a new consciousness of human values. The upheavals of the 1960s could be largely attributed to the three P's: the youthful population bulge, protest against racism and the Vietnam War, and the apparent permanence of prosperity. As the decade flowed into the 1970s, the flower children grew older and had children of their own, the civil rights movement fell silent, the war ended, and economic stagnation blighted the bloom of prosperity. Young people in the 1970s seemed more concerned with finding a job in the system than with tearing the system down. But if the "counterculture" had not managed fully to replace older values, it had weakened their grip, perhaps permanently.

Varying Viewpoints
The Sixties: Constructive or Destructive?

The 1960s were convulsed by controversy, and they have remained controversial ever since. Conflicts raged in that turbulent decade between social classes, races, sexes, and generations. More than three decades later, the shock waves from the 1960s still reverberate through American society. The "Contract with America" that swept conservative Republicans to power in 1994 amounted to nothing less than a wholesale repudiation of the government activism that marked the sixties and a resounding reaffirmation of the "traditional values" that sixties culture supposedly trashed. Liberal Democrats, on the other hand, continue to press affirmative action for women and minorities, protection for the environment, an expanded welfare state, and sexual tolerance—all legacies of the stormy sixties.

Four issues dominate historical discussion of the 1960s: the struggle for civil rights, the Great Society's "War on Poverty," the Vietnam War and the antiwar movement, and the emergence of the "counterculture."

Although most scholars praise the civil rights achievements of the 1960s, they disagree over the civil rights movement's turn away from nonviolence and its embrace of separatism and Black Power. The Freedom Riders and Martin Luther King, Jr., find much more approval in most history books than do Malcolm X and the Black Panther party. But some scholars, notably William L. Van Deburg in *New Day in Babylon: The Black Power Movement and American Culture, 1965–1975* (1992), argue that the "flank effect" of radical Black Power advocates like Stokely Carmichael actually enhanced the bargaining position of moderates like Dr. King. Deburg

also suggests that the enthusiasm of Black Power advocates for African American cultural uniqueness reshaped both black self-consciousness and the broader culture, as it provided a model for the feminist and multiculturalist movements of the 1970s and later.

Johnson's War on Poverty has found its liberal defenders in scholars like Allen Matusow (*The Unraveling of America*, 1984) and John Schwarz (*America's Hidden Success*, 1988). Schwarz demonstrates, for example, that Medicare and Social Security reforms virtually eliminated poverty among America's elderly. But the Great Society has also provoked strong criticism from writers such as Charles Murray (*Losing Ground*, 1984) and Lawrence Meade (*Beyond Entitlements*, 1986). As those conservative critics see the poverty issue, the Great Society was part of the problem, not part of the solution. In their view the War on Poverty did not simply fail to eradicate poverty among the so-called underclass; it actually deepened the dependency of the poor on the welfare state and even generated a multigenerational "cycle" of poverty. In this argument Johnson's Great Society stands indicted of creating in effect a permanent welfare class.

For many young people of the 1960s, the antiwar movement protesting America's policy in Vietnam provided their initiation into politics and their introduction to "movement culture," with its sense of community and shared purpose. But scholars disagree over the movement's real effectiveness in checking the war. Writers like John Lewis Gaddis (*Strategies of Containment*, 1982) explain America's eventual withdrawal from Vietnam essentially without reference to the protesters in the streets. Others, like Todd Gitlin (*The Sixties: Years of Hope, Days of Rage*, 1987), insist that mass protest was the force that finally pressed the war to a conclusion.

Debate over the counterculture not only pits liberals against conservatives but also pits liberals against radicals. A liberal historian like William O'Neill (*Coming Apart*, 1971) might sympathize with what he considers some of the worthy values pushed by student activists, such as racial justice, non-violence, and the antiwar movement, but he also claims that much of the sixties "youth culture" degenerated into hedonism, arrogance, and social polarization. In contrast, younger historians such as Michael Kazin and Maurice Isserman argue that cultural radicalism and political radicalism were two sides of the same coin. Many young people in the sixties made little distinction between the personal and the political. As Sara Evans demonstrates in *Personal Politics* (1980), "the personal *was* the political" for many women. She finds the roots of modern feminism in the sexism women activists encountered in the civil rights and antiwar movements.

Although scholars rightly see the 1960s as a liberal decade, some have also started to focus on the other side of the political spectrum. Historians like Lisa McGirr (*Suburban Warriors*, 2001) argue that even though Barry Goldwater lost in a landslide in 1964, the conservative movement he kick-started laid the foundation for later successes by Ronald Reagan and both George Bushes. Rebecca Klatch shows in *A Generation Divided* (1999) how the New Right fed off the New Left, reshaping American politics in profound ways. Liberal policies toward minorities, women, and the poor fueled the fires of traditionalists who wanted a return to "the good old days." And the hedonistic counterculture sparked a religious revival that led to politically powerful groups like the Moral Majority by the 1970s.

While critics may argue over the "good" versus the "bad" sixties, there is no denying the degree to which that tumultuous time, for better or worse, shaped the world in which we now live.

Chapter Review

KEY TERMS

New Frontier (889)

Peace Corps (889)

Apollo (891)

Berlin Wall (891)

European Economic
  Community (EEC) (891)

Bay of Pigs invasion (893)

Cuban missile crisis (895)

Freedom Riders (896)

Voter Education
  Project (896)

March on Washington (897)

Civil Rights Act
  of 1964 (898)

affirmative action (900)

Great Society (900)

Freedom Summer (903)

Mississippi Freedom
  Democratic party (903)

Voting Rights Act
  of 1965 (903)

Black Panther party (905)

Black Power (905)

Six-Day War (907)

Stonewall Rebellion (913)

Students for a Democratic
  Society (SDS) (913)

PEOPLE TO KNOW

Robert F. Kennedy

Robert S. McNamara

Ngo Dinh Diem

James Meredith

Lee Harvey Oswald

Malcolm X

Eugene McCarthy

George C. Wallace

CHRONOLOGY

1957	European Economic Community (EEC, Common Market) created by Treaty of Rome
1961	Berlin Wall built Alliance for Progress Bay of Pigs invasion Kennedy sends "military advisers" to South Vietnam
1962	Pressure from Kennedy results in rollback of steel prices Trade Expansion Act Laos neutralized Cuban missile crisis
1963	France vetoes British membership in EEC Anti-Diem coup in South Vietnam Civil rights march in Washington, D.C. Kennedy assassinated; Johnson assumes presidency
1964	Twenty-fourth Amendment (abolishing poll tax in federal elections) ratified "Freedom Summer" voter registration in South Gulf of Tonkin Resolution Johnson defeats Goldwater for presidency War on Poverty begins Civil Rights Act
1965	Great Society legislation Voting Rights Act U.S. troops occupy Dominican Republic
1965–1968	Race riots in U.S. cities
1966	France withdraws from NATO
1967	Six-Day War between Israel and Egypt
1968	North Vietnamese army launches Tet offensive in South Vietnam Worldwide protests Martin Luther King, Jr., and Robert Kennedy assassinated Prague Spring crushed by Soviet army Nixon defeats Humphrey and Wallace for presidency
1969	Stonewall Inn riot in New York City Astronauts land on moon

TO LEARN MORE

Dan Carter, *The Politics of Rage: George Wallace, the Origins of the New Conservatism, and the Transformation of American Politics* (1995)

Robert Dallek, *An Unfinished Life: John F. Kennedy, 1917–1963* (2003)

Alex Haley, *The Autobiography of Malcolm X* (1966)

Maurice Isserman and Michael Kazin, *America Divided: The Civil War of the 1960s* (2000)

Robert F. Kennedy, *Thirteen Days* (1969)

G. Calvin Mackenzie and Robert Weisbrot, *The Liberal Hour: Washington and the Politics of Change in the 1960s* (2008)

Lisa McGirr, *Suburban Warriors: The Origins of the New American Right* (2001)

James Miller, *"Democracy Is in the Streets": From Port Huron to the Siege of Chicago* (1987)

Ann Moody, *Coming of Age in Mississippi* (1968)

Bruce Schulman, *Lyndon B. Johnson and American Liberalism* (1994)

Thomas J. Sugrue, *Sweet Land of Liberty: The Forgotten Struggle for Civil Rights in the North* (2008)

Jeremi Suri, *Power and Protest: Global Revolution and the Rise of Détente* (2003)

A complete, annotated bibliography for this chapter—along with brief descriptions of the People to Know—may be found on the American Pageant website. The Key Terms are defined in a Glossary at the end of the text.

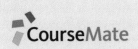

Go to the CourseMate website at **www.cengagebrain.com** for additional study tools and review materials—including audio and video clips—for this chapter.

AP® Review Questions for Chapter 38

1. When he assumed office in 1961, which economic strategy did President Kennedy employ to try to stimulate the sluggish national economy?
   (A) A massive foreign-aid program
   (B) Large-scale government spending programs
   (C) A general tax cut
   (D) Reducing expenditures on the space program
   (E) Raising tariffs on imported goods

2. Political instability and armed conflict in which of the following nations offered the first pivotal test of the Kennedy administration's new national security strategy of flexible response?
   (A) Cuba
   (B) Laos
   (C) Vietnam
   (D) Thailand
   (E) Cambodia

3. The results of the Cuban missile crisis included all the following EXCEPT
   (A) U.S. agreement to abandon the American base at Guantanamo Bay and return this property to Cuba.
   (B) the removal of Nikita Khrushchev from power in the Soviet Union.
   (C) a U.S. promise not to invade Cuba.
   (D) an ambitious program of military expansion by the Soviet Union.
   (E) withdrawal of U.S. missiles in Turkey.

4. What event during the 1960s marked the beginning of closer cooperation and a strategic partnership between the Kennedy administration and the civil rights movement?
   (A) President Kennedy sending federal marshals in the summer of 1961 to protect the Freedom Riders
   (B) Attorney General Robert Kennedy ordering the FBI to remove the wiretap from Martin Luther King, Jr.'s, phone
   (C) The Kennedy administration securing passage of the Voting Rights Act
   (D) The journeying of Robert Kennedy and President Kennedy to the South to support the registration of black voters
   (E) The issuance of an executive order by President Kennedy requiring the desegregation of all public schools in the nation

5. What was the political purpose of the 1963 March on Washington led by Martin Luther King, Jr.?
   (A) To galvanize popular support behind the voting rights bill
   (B) To mobilize popular support behind the civil rights bill that would end segregation and eliminate racial discrimination in public facilities and employment
   (C) To mobilize opposition to growing U.S. involvement in Vietnam
   (D) To organize popular support for a massive public works employment program
   (E) To organize popular support behind the fair housing bill

6. What was the political result of the Gulf of Tonkin Resolution of 1964?
   (A) The United States declared war on North Vietnam.
   (B) Congress handed the president a blank check to use further force in Vietnam.
   (C) The military was given the authority to use tactical nuclear weapons.
   (D) Congress maintained its war-declaring power.
   (E) The goals of American military involvement became clear.

7. Which of the following represents the consensus assessment of most historians about the accomplishments of Lyndon Johnson's Great Society programs?
   (A) Billions of dollars had been spent for social engineering that produced negligible favorable social or economic results for needy Americans.
   (B) The failures of Great Society programs proved that poverty could not be successfully addressed with public funds.
   (C) The Great Society programs achieved some noteworthy accomplishments in expanding education and health care for vulnerable, poor, and underserved Americans.
   (D) Rampant waste, fraud, and abuse undermined the success of nearly all Great Society programs.
   (E) The Great Society programs actually increased the poverty rate in America.

8. Which of the following represented a singular political achievement for women during the 1960s in the area of civil rights?
   (A) Title VII of the Civil Rights Act of 1964 included a provision that prohibited sexual discrimination in public facilities and employment.
   (B) The Voting Rights Act of 1965 barred continuing voting rights discrimination against women.
   (C) The Violence Against Women Act provided billions of dollars to enhance the investigation and prosecution of crimes against women and provided restitution funds to women.
   (D) Title IX barred discrimination against women in all educational activities, including academics, athletics, and extracurricular activities.
   (E) Women were provided greater access to educational and employment opportunities through affirmative-action policies undertaken during the Johnson administration.

9. The Watts riot in 1965 marked all of the following EXCEPT
   (A) the start of a more militant and confrontational phase of the civil rights movement.
   (B) a shift of focus away from the South and toward northern and western cities by many African Americans seeking racial justice during this period.
   (C) the development of a radicalized wing of the civil rights movement emphasizing black separatism.
   (D) the overheated frustrations of African Americans experiencing regular police brutality while living in an economically deprived inner-city neighborhood.
   (E) the beginning of a strategic reversal involving the acceptance of targeted violence by previously moderate civil rights leaders like Martin Luther King, Jr.

10. Which of the following political events started to educate the public about U.S. involvement in Vietnam and stimulate growing public opposition in the late 1960s to American policy in Southeast Asia?
    (A) The televised congressional hearings on President Johnson's Vietnam policy, held by Senator William Fulbright's Foreign Relations Committee
    (B) Vice President Humphrey's public break with the Vietnam policy of Lyndon Johnson
    (C) The televised congressional hearings about President Johnson's Vietnam policy, held by Richard Russell's Armed Services Committee
    (D) Senator Eugene McCarthy's insurgent presidential campaign of 1968 against President Johnson for the Democratic presidential nomination
    (E) The entrance of Senator Robert F. Kennedy as an antiwar candidate into the 1968 presidential campaign

11. Which startling event galvanized vehement public opposition to the Vietnam War and placed increasing public pressure on President Johnson to end the war quickly?
    (A) The Tet offensive
    (B) The revelation of the secret bombing of Cambodia
    (C) The resignation of Defense Secretary Robert McNamara
    (D) The revelation that the Tonkin Gulf attacks had been provoked by U.S. military forces
    (E) The public revelation of the FBI's Cointelpro counterintelligence campaign against the domestic peace movement

12. All of the following are examples of the revolutionary cultural upheavals of the 1960s EXCEPT the
    (A) greater freedom women and men felt to satisfy their sexual desires because of the introduction of the birth control pill.
    (B) birth of the gay and lesbian liberation movement to demand equal rights and protection from the law.
    (C) evolution and devolution of Students for a Democratic Society (SDS) as a political force in the 1960s.
    (D) student Free Speech Movement that emerged at the University of California at Berkeley in 1964.
    (E) rise in the influence of mainstream liberal Protestant churches and the concurrent decline of the conservative evangelical movement during the 1960s.

13. President Johnson's Great Society programs have been compared to the New Deal because both
    (A) were created by Democratic presidents.
    (B) emphasized education and equality.
    (C) led to the creation of legislation aimed at massive economic reform.
    (D) aimed to alleviate suffering during an economic downturn.
    (E) successfully met all of their stated goals.

14. The year 1968 is often referred to as a defining moment in U.S. history for all of the following reasons EXCEPT that
    (A) race riots took place across the country, spoiling the dreams of civil rights activists.
    (B) important leaders were assassinated, creating political and social upheaval.
    (C) the Republicans regained control of the White House after years of Democratic rule.
    (D) events in and concerning the Vietnam War expanded a growing antiwar movement.
    (E) President Johnson refused to run for reelection, affecting U.S. politics and the progression of the Vietnam War.

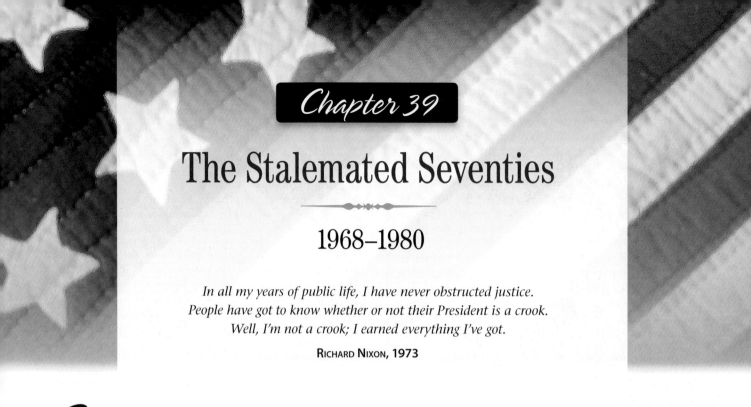

Chapter 39

The Stalemated Seventies

1968–1980

In all my years of public life, I have never obstructed justice.
People have got to know whether or not their President is a crook.
Well, I'm not a crook; I earned everything I've got.

RICHARD NIXON, 1973

As the 1960s lurched to a close, the fantastic quarter-century economic boom of the post–World War II era also showed signs of petering out. By increasing their productivity, American workers had doubled their average standard of living in the twenty-five years since the end of World War II. Now, fatefully, productivity gains slowed to the vanishing point. The entire decade of the 1970s did not witness a productivity advance equivalent to even one year's progress in the preceding two decades. At the new rate, it would take five hundred more years to bring about another doubling of the average worker's standard of living. The median income of the average American family stagnated in the two decades after 1970 and failed to decline only because of the addition of working wives' wages to the family income (see Figure 39.1). The rising baby-boom generation now faced the depressing prospect of a living standard that would be lower than that of their parents. As the postwar wave of robust economic growth crested by the early 1970s, at home and abroad the "can-do" American spirit gave way to an unaccustomed sense of limits.

★ Sources of Stagnation

What caused the sudden slump in productivity? Some observers cited the increasing presence in the work force of women and teenagers, who typically had fewer skills than adult male workers and were less likely to take the full-time, long-term jobs where skills might be developed. Other commentators blamed declining investment in new machinery, the heavy costs of compliance

with government-imposed safety and health regulations, and the general shift of the American economy from manufacturing to services, where productivity gains were allegedly more difficult to achieve and measure. Yet in the last analysis, much mystery attends the productivity slowdown, and economists have wrestled inconclusively with the puzzle.

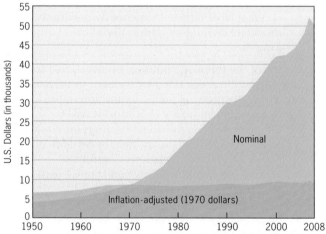

FIGURE 39.1 Median Household Income, 1970–2008
During the long post–World War II economic boom (from about 1950 to 1970), family incomes increased dramatically, but after 1970 "real," or inflation-adjusted, incomes stagnated. Prosperity in the late 1990s led to a slight upward trend, though adjusted median family income began to decline in the early years of the twenty-first century. (Sources: U.S. Census Bureau, Historical Income Tables—Households, 2007; U.S. Census Bureau *Consumer Income Report*, relevant years; *Statistical Abstract of the United States*, 2010.)

New York Daily World

THE NIXON WAVE

The Nixon Wave   During Richard Nixon's presidency, Americans experienced the first serious inflation since the immediate post–World War II years. The inflationary surge grew to tidal-wave proportions by the late 1970s, when the consumer price index rose at an annual rate of more than 10 percent.

The Vietnam War also precipitated painful economic distortions. The disastrous conflict in Southeast Asia drained tax dollars from needed improvements in education, deflected scientific skill and manufacturing capacity from the civilian sector, and touched off a sickening spiral of inflation. Sharply rising oil prices in the 1970s also fed inflation, but its deepest roots lay in deficit spending in the 1960s—especially Lyndon Johnson's insistence on simultaneously fighting the war in Vietnam and funding Great Society programs at home, all without a tax increase to finance the added expenditures. Both military spending and welfare spending are inherently inflationary (in the absence of offsetting tax collections), because they put dollars into people's hands without adding to the supply of goods that those dollars can buy.

Whatever its cause, the effects of inflation were deeply felt. Prices increased astonishingly throughout the 1970s. The cost of living tripled in the dozen years after Richard Nixon's inauguration, in the longest and steepest inflationary cycle in American history.

Other weaknesses in the nation's economy were also laid bare by the abrupt reversal of America's financial fortunes in the 1970s. The competitive advantage of many major American businesses had been so enormous after World War II that they had small incentive to modernize plants and seek more efficient methods of production. The defeated German and Japanese people had meanwhile clawed their way out of the ruins of war and built wholly new factories with the most up-to-date technology and management techniques. By the 1970s their efforts paid handsome rewards, as they came to dominate industries like steel, automobiles, and consumer electronics—fields in which the United States had once been unchallengeable.

The poor economic performance of the 1970s hung over the decade like a pall. It frustrated both policymakers and citizens who keenly remembered the growth and optimism of the quarter-century since World War II. The overachieving postwar generation had never met a problem it could not solve. But now a stalemated, unpopular war and a stagnant, unresponsive economy heralded the end of the self-confident postwar era. With it ended the liberal dream, vivid since New Deal days, that an affluent society could spend its way to social justice.

✵ Nixon "Vietnamizes" the War

Inaugurated on January 20, 1969, Richard Nixon urged the American people, torn with dissension over Vietnam and race relations, to "stop shouting at one another." Yet the new president seemed an unlikely conciliator of the clashing forces that appeared to be ripping apart American society. Solitary and suspicious by nature, Nixon could be brittle and testy in the face of opposition. He also harbored bitter resentments against the "liberal establishment" that had cast him into the political darkness for much of the preceding decade. Yet Nixon brought one hugely valuable asset with him to the White House—his broad knowledge and thoughtful expertise in foreign affairs. With calculating shrewdness he applied himself to putting America's foreign-policy house in order.

The first burning need was to quiet the public uproar over Vietnam. President Nixon's announced policy, called **Vietnamization**, was to withdraw the 540,000 U.S. troops in South Vietnam over an extended period. The South Vietnamese—with American money, weapons, training, and advice—could then gradually take over the burden of fighting their own war.

The so-called **Nixon Doctrine** thus evolved. It proclaimed that the United States would honor its existing defense commitments but that in the future, Asians and others would have to fight their own wars without the support of large bodies of American ground troops.

Nixon sought not to end the war, but to win it by other means, without the further spilling of American blood. But even this much involvement was distasteful to the American "doves," many of whom demanded a withdrawal that was prompt, complete, unconditional, and irreversible. Antiwar protesters staged a massive national Vietnam moratorium in October 1969, as nearly 100,000 people jammed Boston Common and some 50,000 filed by the White House carrying lighted candles.

Undaunted, Nixon launched a counteroffensive by appealing to the **silent majority** who presumably supported the war. Though ostensibly conciliatory, Nixon's appeal was in fact deeply divisive. His intentions soon became clear when he unleashed tough-talking Vice President Agnew to attack the "nattering nabobs of negativism" who demanded a quick withdrawal from Vietnam. Nixon himself in 1970 sneered at the student antiwar demonstrators as "bums."

By January 1970 the Vietnam conflict had become the longest in American history and, with 40,000 killed and over 250,000 wounded, the third most costly foreign war in the nation's experience. It had also become grotesquely unpopular, even among troops in the field. Because draft policies largely exempted college students and men with critical civilian skills, the armed forces in Vietnam were largely composed of the least privileged young Americans. Especially in the war's early stages, African Americans were disproportionately represented in the army and accounted for a disproportionately high share of combat fatalities. Black and white soldiers alike fought not only against the Vietnamese enemy but also against the coiled fear of floundering through booby-trapped swamps and steaming jungles, often unable to distinguish friend from foe among the Vietnamese peasants. Drug abuse, mutiny, and sabotage dulled the army's fighting edge. Morale appeared

Vietnam Vets Protest the War, 1971 Public opinion gradually but inexorably turned against the war. In 1965 polls showed that only 15 percent of Americans favored withdrawal from Vietnam. But by 1969, 69 percent of those interviewed indicated that they considered the war a "mistake," and by 1970 a majority supported withdrawal of U.S. troops. In this demonstration on April 23, 1971, eight hundred veterans threw away their Purple Hearts, Bronze Stars, Silver Stars, and other military honors in front of the U.S. Capitol in protest against a war they no longer could support.

A Marine Corps officer expressed the disillusion that beset many American troops in Vietnam:

"For years we disposed of the enemy dead like so much garbage. We stuck cigarettes in the mouths of corpses, put *Playboy* magazines in their hands, cut off their ears to wear around our necks. We incinerated them with napalm, atomized them with B-52 strikes, shoved them out the doors of helicopters above the South China Sea. . . . All we did was count, count bodies. Count dead human beings. . . . That was our fundamental military strategy. Body count. And the count kept going up."

to have plummeted to rock bottom when rumors filtered out of Vietnam that soldiers were "fragging" their own officers—murdering them with fragmentation grenades.

Domestic disgust with the war was further deepened in 1970 by revelations of the **My Lai Massacre**, in which American troops had murdered innocent women and children in the village of My Lai two years earlier. Increasingly desperate for a quick end to the demoralizing conflict, Nixon widened the war in 1970 by ordering an attack on Vietnam's neighbor, Cambodia.

✪ Cambodianizing the Vietnam War

For several years the North Vietnamese and Viet Cong had been using Cambodia, bordering South Vietnam on the west, as a springboard for troops, weapons, and supplies. Suddenly, on April 29, 1970, without consulting Congress, Nixon ordered American forces to join with the South Vietnamese in cleaning out the enemy sanctuaries in officially neutral Cambodia.

Angry students nationwide responded to the Cambodian invasion with rock throwing, window smashing, and arson. At **Kent State University** in Ohio, jumpy members of the National Guard fired into a noisy crowd, killing four and wounding many more; at historically black Jackson State College in Mississippi, the highway patrol discharged volleys at a student dormitory, killing two students. The nation fell prey to turmoil as rioters and arsonists convulsed the land.

Nixon withdrew the American troops from Cambodia on June 29, 1970, after only two months. But in America the Cambodian invasion deepened the bitterness between "hawks" and "doves," as right-wing groups physically assaulted leftists. Disillusionment with "whitey's war" increased ominously among African Americans in the armed forces. The Senate (though not the House) overwhelmingly repealed the Gulf of Tonkin blank check that Congress had given Johnson in 1964 and sought ways to restrain Nixon. The youth of America, still aroused, were only slightly mollified when the government reduced draft calls and shortened the period of draftability, on a lottery basis, from eight years to one year. They were similarly pleased, though not

The War at Home, Spring 1970 President Nixon's order to invade Cambodia sparked angry protests on American campuses. At Kent State University in Ohio, the nation watched in horror as four student demonstrators were shot by jittery National Guardsmen.

pacified, when the Twenty-sixth Amendment in 1971 lowered the voting age to eighteen (see the Appendix).

New combustibles fueled the fires of antiwar discontent in June 1971, when a former Pentagon official leaked to the *New York Times* the **Pentagon Papers**, a top-secret Pentagon study that documented the blunders and deceptions of the Kennedy and Johnson administrations, especially the provoking of the 1964 North Vietnamese attack in the Gulf of Tonkin.

✴ Nixon's Détente with Beijing (Peking) and Moscow

As the antiwar firestorm flared ever higher, Nixon concluded that the road out of Vietnam ran through Beijing and Moscow. The two great communist powers, the Soviet Union and China, were clashing bitterly over their rival interpretations of Marxism. In 1969 they had even fought several bloody skirmishes along the "inner border" that separated them in Asia. Nixon astutely perceived that the Chinese-Soviet tension afforded the United States an opportunity to play off one antagonist against the other and to enlist the aid of both in pressuring North Vietnam into peace.

Nixon's thinking was reinforced by his national security adviser, Dr. Henry A. Kissinger. Bespectacled and German-accented, Kissinger had reached America as a youth when his parents fled Hitler's anti-Jewish

Cold War? Not for Some Library of Congress

persecutions. In 1969 the former Harvard professor had begun meeting secretly on Nixon's behalf with North Vietnamese officials in Paris to negotiate an end to the war in Vietnam. He was meanwhile preparing the president's path to Beijing and Moscow.

Nixon, heretofore an uncompromising anticommunist, announced to a startled nation in July 1971 that he had accepted an invitation to visit Communist China the following year. He made his historic journey in February 1972, enjoying glass-clinking toasts and walks on the fabled Great Wall of China. He capped his visit with the Shanghai Communiqué, in which the two nations agreed to "normalize" their relationship. An important part of the accord was America's acceptance of a "one-China" policy, implying a lessened American commitment to the independence of Taiwan.

Nixon next traveled to Moscow in May 1972 to play his "China card" in a game of high-stakes diplomacy in the Kremlin. The Soviets, hungry for American foodstuffs and alarmed over the possibility of intensified rivalry with an American-backed China, were ready to deal. Nixon's visits ushered in an era of **détente**, or relaxed tension, with the two communist powers and produced several significant agreements in 1972,

including a three-year arrangement by which the food-rich United States agreed to sell the Soviets at least $750 million worth of wheat, corn, and other cereals.

More important, the United States and the USSR agreed to an anti–ballistic missile (ABM) treaty, which limited each nation to two clusters of defensive missiles, and to a series of arms-reduction negotiations known as SALT (Strategic Arms Limitation Talks), aimed at freezing the numbers of long-range nuclear missiles for five years. The ABM and SALT accords constituted long-overdue first steps toward slowing the arms race. Yet even though the ABM treaty forbade elaborate defensive systems, the United States forged ahead with the development of "MIRVs" (multiple independently targeted reentry vehicles), designed to overcome any defense by "saturating" it with large numbers of warheads, several to a rocket. Predictably, the Soviets proceeded to "MIRV" their own missiles, and the arms race ratcheted up to a still more perilous plateau, with over sixteen thousand nuclear warheads deployed by both sides by the end of the 1980s.

Nixon's détente diplomacy did, to some extent, deice the Cold War. Yet Nixon remained staunchly anticommunist when the occasion seemed to demand it. He strongly opposed the election of the outspoken Marxist Salvador Allende to the presidency of Chile in 1970. His administration slapped an embargo on the Allende regime, and the Central Intelligence Agency worked covertly to undermine the legitimately elected leftist president. When Allende died during a Chilean army attack on his headquarters in 1973, many observers smelled a Yankee rat—an impression that deepened when Washington warmly embraced Allende's successor, military dictator General Augusto Pinochet. Even so, by checkmating and coopting the two great communist powers, the president had cleverly set the stage for America's exit from Vietnam, although the concluding act in that wrenching tragedy remained to be played.

✵ A New Team on the Supreme Bench

Nixon had lashed out during the campaign at the "permissiveness" and "judicial activism" of the Supreme Court presided over by Chief Justice Earl Warren. Following his appointment in 1953, the jovial Warren had led the Court into a series of decisions that drastically affected sexual freedom, the rights of criminals, the practice of religion, civil rights, and the structure of political representation. The decisions of the Warren Court reflected its deep concern for the individual, no matter how lowly.

In *Griswold* v. *Connecticut* (1965), the Court struck down a state law that prohibited the use of contraceptives, even among married couples. The Court pro-

Balancing Act Nixon treads delicately between the two communist superpowers in 1973, holding some of the wheat with which he enticed both into détente.

Picture Research Consultants & Archives

SAVE Our Republic
IMPEACH EARL WARREN

FOR INFORMATION
WRITE . . .
THOMAS HILL 385 CONCORD AVE BELMONT, MASS.

The Embattled Warren Court The United States Supreme Court, presided over by Chief Justice Earl Warren, made historic decisions in areas ranging from criminal justice to civil rights and political representation. Its achievements provoked often ferocious conservative backlash, as seen in this billboard advertisement calling for Warren's impeachment.

claimed (critics said "invented") a "right of privacy" that soon provided the basis for decisions protecting women's abortion rights.

In 1963 the Court held (*Gideon* v. *Wainwright*) that all criminal defendants were entitled to legal counsel, even if they were too poor to afford it. More controversial still were decisions in two cases—*Escobedo* (1964) and *Miranda* (1966)—that ensured the right of the accused to remain silent and enjoy other protections. The latter case gave rise to the **Miranda warning** that arresting police officers must read to suspects. These several court rulings sought to prevent abusive police tactics, but they appeared to conservatives to coddle criminals and subvert law and order.

Conservatives also objected to the Court's views on religion. In two stunning decisions, *Engel* v. *Vitale* (1962) and *School District of Abington Township* v. *Schempp* (1963), the justices argued that the First Amendment's separation of church and state meant that public schools could not require prayer or Bible reading. Social conservatives raised anew the battle cry "Impeach Earl Warren" (see p. 868).

From 1954 on, the Court came under relentless criticism, the bitterest since New Deal days. But for better or worse, the black-robed justices were grappling with stubborn social problems spawned by midcentury tensions, even—or especially—if duly elected legislatures failed to do so.

Fulfilling campaign promises, President Nixon undertook to change the Court's philosophical complexion. Taking advantage of several vacancies, he sought appointees who would strictly interpret the Constitution, cease "meddling" in social and political questions, and not coddle radicals or criminals. The Senate in 1969 speedily confirmed his nomination of white-maned Warren E. Burger of Minnesota to succeed the retiring Earl Warren as chief justice. Before the end of 1971, the Court counted four conservative Nixon appointments out of nine members.

Yet Nixon was to learn the ironic lesson that many presidents have learned about their Supreme Court appointees: once seated on the high bench, the justices are fully free to think and decide according to their own beliefs, not according to the president's expectations. The Burger Court that Nixon shaped proved reluctant to dismantle the "liberal" rulings of the Warren Court; it even produced the most controversial judicial opinion of modern times, the momentous *Roe* v. *Wade* decision in 1973, which legalized abortion (see p. 932).

✷ Nixon on the Home Front

Surprisingly, Nixon presided over significant expansion of the welfare programs that conservative Republicans routinely denounced. He approved increased appropriations for entitlements like Food Stamps, Medicaid, and Aid to Families with Dependent Children (AFDC), while adding a generous new program, Supplemental Security Income (SSI), to assist the indigent aged, blind, and disabled. He signed legislation in 1972 guaranteeing automatic Social Security cost-of-living increases to protect the elderly against the ravages of inflation when prices rose more than 3 percent in any year. Ironically, this "indexing" actually helped to fuel the inflationary fires that raged out of control later in the decade.

Amid much controversy, Nixon in 1969 implemented his so-called Philadelphia Plan, requiring construction-trade unions to establish "goals and timetables" for the hiring of black apprentices. Nixon may have been motivated in part by a desire to weaken the forces of liberalism by driving a wedge between blacks and trade unions. But whatever his reasoning, the president's new policy had far-reaching implications. Soon extended to all federal contracts, the **Philadelphia Plan** in effect required thousands of employers to meet hiring quotas or to establish "set-asides" for minority subcontractors.

Nixon's Philadelphia Plan drastically altered the meaning of "affirmative action." Lyndon Johnson had intended affirmative action to protect *individuals* against discrimination. Nixon now transformed and escalated affirmative action into a program that conferred privileges on certain *groups*. The Supreme Court went along with Nixon's approach. In *Griggs* v. *Duke Power Co.* (1971), the black-robed justices prohibited intelligence tests or other devices that had the effect of excluding minorities or women from certain jobs. The Court's ruling strongly suggested to employers that the only sure protection against charges of discrimination was to hire minority workers—or admit minority students—in proportion to their presence in the population.

Together the actions of Nixon and the Court opened broad employment and educational opportunities for minorities and women. They also opened a Pandora's box of protest from critics who assailed the new style of affirmative action as "reverse discrimination," imposed by executive order and judicial decision, not by democratically elected representatives. Yet

Author Rachel Carson (1907–1964) Some call her the mother of the modern conservation movement because of the impact of her 1962 book, *Silent Spring*.

Alfred Eisenstadt/Time Life Pictures/Getty Images

what other remedy was there, defenders asked, to offset centuries of prejudice and opportunity denied?

Among Nixon's legacies was the creation in 1970 of the **Environmental Protection Agency (EPA)**, which climaxed two decades of mounting concern for the environment. Scientist and author Rachel Carson gave the environmental movement a huge boost in 1962 when she published *Silent Spring*, an enormously effective piece of latter-day muckraking that exposed the poisonous effects of pesticides. On April 22, 1970, millions of environmentalists around the world celebrated the first **Earth Day** to raise awareness and to encourage their leaders to act. In the wake of what became a yearly event, the U.S. Congress passed the Clean Air Act of 1970 and the Endangered Species Act of 1973. The EPA now stood on the frontline of the battle for ecological sanity and made notable progress in reducing automobile emissions and cleaning up befouled waterways and toxic waste sites.

The federal government also expanded its regulatory reach on behalf of workers and consumers. Late in 1970 Nixon signed the Occupational Safety and Health Administration (OSHA) into law, creating an agency dedicated to improving working conditions, preventing work-related accidents and deaths, and issuing safety standards. The Consumer Product Safety Commission (CPSC) followed two years later, holding companies to account for selling dangerous products. Together these three mega-agencies gave the federal government far more direct control over business operations than in years past, drawing the ire of many big companies, which chastised the overbearing "national nanny."

Worried about creeping inflation (then running at about 5 percent), Nixon overcame his distaste for economic controls and imposed a ninety-day wage and price freeze in 1971. To stimulate the nation's sagging exports, he next stunned the world by taking the United States off the gold standard and devaluing the dollar. These moves effectively ended the "Bretton Woods" system of international currency stabilization that had functioned for more that a quarter of a century after World War II (see p. 841).

Elected as a minority president, with only 43 percent of the vote in 1968, Nixon devised a clever but cynical plan—called the **southern strategy**—to achieve a solid majority in 1972. Appointing conservative Supreme Court justices, soft-pedaling civil rights, and opposing school busing to achieve racial balance were all parts of the strategy.

✴ The Nixon Landslide of 1972

But as fate would have it, the southern strategy became superfluous as foreign policy dominated the

Fritz Behrendt

presidential campaign of 1972. Vietnam continued to be the burning issue. Nearly four years had passed since Nixon had promised, as a presidential candidate, to end the war and "win" the peace. Yet in the spring of 1972, the fighting escalated anew to alarming levels when the North Vietnamese, heavily equipped with foreign tanks, burst through the demilitarized zone (DMZ) separating the two Vietnams. Nixon reacted promptly by launching massive bombing attacks on strategic centers in North Vietnam, including Hanoi, the capital. Gambling heavily on foreign forbearance, he also ordered the dropping of contact mines to blockade the principal harbors of North Vietnam. Either Moscow or Beijing, or both, could have responded explosively, but neither did, thanks to Nixon's shrewd diplomacy.

The continuing Vietnam conflict spurred the rise of South Dakota senator George McGovern to the 1972 Democratic nomination. McGovern's promise to pull the remaining American troops out of Vietnam in ninety days earned him the backing of the large antiwar element in the party. But his appeal to racial minorities, feminists, leftists, and youth alienated the traditional working-class backbone of his party. Moreover, the discovery shortly after the convention that McGovern's running mate, Missouri senator Thomas Eagleton, had undergone psychiatric care—including electroshock therapy—forced Eagleton's ouster from the ticket and virtually doomed the Democrats' hopes of recapturing the White House.

Nixon's campaign emphasized that he had wound down the "Democratic war" in Vietnam from some

540,000 troops to about 30,000. His candidacy received an added boost just twelve days before the election when the high-flying Dr. Kissinger announced that "peace is at hand" in Vietnam and that an agreement would be reached in a few days.

Nixon won the election in a landslide. His lopsided victory encompassed every state except Massachusetts and the nonstate District of Columbia (which was granted electoral votes by the Twenty-third Amendment in 1961—see Appendix). He piled up 520 electoral votes to 17 for McGovern and a popular majority of 47,169,911 to 29,170,383 votes. McGovern had counted on a large number of young people's votes, but less than half the 18–21 age group even bothered to register to vote.

The dove of peace, "at hand" in Vietnam just before the balloting, took flight after the election. Fighting on both sides escalated again, and Nixon launched a furious two-week bombing of North Vietnam in an iron-handed effort to force the North Vietnamese back to the conference table. This merciless pounding drove the North Vietnamese negotiators to agree to a cease-fire in the Treaty of Paris on January 23, 1973, nearly three months after peace was prematurely proclaimed.

Nixon hailed the face-saving cease-fire as "peace with honor," but the boast rang hollow. The United States was to withdraw its remaining 27,000 or so troops and could reclaim some 560 American prisoners of war. The North Vietnamese were allowed to keep some 145,000 troops in South Vietnam, where they still occupied about 30 percent of the country. The shaky "peace" was in reality little more than a thinly disguised American retreat.

The Secret Bombing of Cambodia and the War Powers Act

The constitutionality of Nixon's continued aerial battering of Cambodia had meanwhile been coming under increasing fire. In July 1973 America was shocked to learn that the U.S. Air Force had secretly conducted some thirty-five hundred bombing raids against North Vietnamese positions in Cambodia, beginning in March 1969 and continuing for some fourteen months prior to the open American incursion in May 1970. The most disturbing feature of these sky forays was that while they were going on, American officials, including the president, had sworn that Cambodian neutrality was being respected. Countless Americans began to wonder what kind of representative government they had if the United States had been fighting a war they knew nothing about.

Defiance followed secretiveness. After the Vietnam cease-fire in January 1973, Nixon brazenly continued large-scale bombing of communist forces in order to help the rightist Cambodian government, and he repeatedly vetoed congressional efforts to stop him. The years of bombing inflicted grisly wounds on Cambodia, blasting its people, shredding its economy, and revolutionizing its politics. The long-suffering Cambodians soon groaned under the sadistic heel of Pol Pot, a murderous tyrant who dispatched as many as 2 million of his people to their graves. He was forced from power, ironically enough, only by a full-dress Vietnamese invasion in 1978, followed by a military occupation that dragged on for a decade.

Congressional opposition to the expansion of presidential war-making powers by Johnson and Nixon led to the **War Powers Act** in November 1973. Passed over Nixon's veto, it required the president to report to Congress within forty-eight hours after committing troops to a foreign conflict or "substantially" enlarging American combat units in a foreign country. Such a limited authorization would have to end within sixty days unless Congress extended it for thirty more days.

The War Powers Act was but one manifestation of what came to be called the "New Isolationism," a mood of caution and restraint in the conduct of the nation's foreign affairs after the bloody and futile misadventure in Vietnam. Meanwhile, the draft ended in January 1973, although it was retained on a standby basis. Future members of the armed forces were to be volunteers, greatly easing anxieties among draft-age youth.

The Arab Oil Embargo and the Energy Crisis

The long-rumbling Middle East erupted anew in October 1973, when the rearmed Syrians and Egyptians unleashed surprise attacks on Israel in an attempt to regain the territory they had lost in the Six-Day War of 1967. With the Israelis in desperate retreat, Kissinger, who had become secretary of state in September, hastily flew to Moscow in an effort to restrain the Soviets, who were arming the attackers. Believing that the Kremlin was poised to fly combat troops to the Suez area, Nixon placed America's nuclear forces on alert and ordered a gigantic airlift of nearly $2 billion in war materials to the Israelis. This assistance helped save the day, as the Israelis aggressively turned the tide and threatened Cairo itself before American diplomacy brought about an uneasy cease-fire to what became known as the Yom Kippur War.

America's policy of backing Israel against its oil-rich neighbors exacted a heavy penalty. Late in October 1973, the OPEC nations announced an embargo on oil shipments to the United States and several European allies supporting Israel, especially the Netherlands. What was more, the oil-rich Arab states cut their oil production, further ratcheting up pressure on the entire West, whose citizens suffered a long winter of lowered thermostats and speedometers. Lines at gas stations grew longer as tempers grew shorter. The shortage triggered a major economic recession not just in America but also in France and Britain. Although the latter two countries had not supported Israel and had thus been exempted from the embargo, in an increasingly globalized, interconnected world, all nations soon felt the crunch.

The "energy crisis" suddenly energized a number of long-deferred projects. Congress approved a costly Alaska pipeline and a national speed limit of fifty-five miles per hour to conserve fuel. Agitation mounted for heavier use of coal and nuclear power, despite the environmental threat they posed.

The five months of the Arab "blackmail" embargo in 1974 clearly signaled the end of an era—the era of

The Washington Post *(July 19, 1973) carried this news item:*

"American B-52 bombers dropped about 104,000 tons of explosives on Communist sanctuaries in neutralist Cambodia during a series of raids in 1969 and 1970. . . . The secret bombing was acknowledged by the Pentagon the Monday after a former Air Force major . . . described how he falsified reports on Cambodian air operations and destroyed records on the bombing missions actually flown."

Uncle Sam's Bed of Nails
The oil crises of the 1970s tortured the American economy.

cheap and abundant energy. A twenty-year surplus of world oil supplies had masked the fact that since 1948 the United States had been a net importer of oil. American oil production peaked in 1970 and then began an irreversible decline. Blissfully unaware of their dependence on foreign suppliers, Americans, like revelers on a binge, had more than tripled their oil consumption since the end of World War II. The number of automobiles increased 250 percent between 1949 and 1972, and Detroit's engineers gave nary a thought to building more fuel-efficient engines.

By 1974 America was oil-addicted and extremely vulnerable to any interruption in supplies. That stark fact would deeply color the diplomatic and economic history of the next three decades and beyond, as the Middle East loomed ever larger on the map of America's strategic interests. OPEC approximately quadrupled its price for crude oil after lifting the embargo in 1974. Huge new oil bills wildly disrupted the U.S. balance of international trade and added further fuel to the already raging fires of inflation. The United States took the lead in forming the International Energy Agency in 1974 as a counterweight to OPEC, and various sectors of the economy, including Detroit's carmakers, began their slow, grudging adjustment to the rudely dawning age of energy dependency. But full reconciliation to that uncomfortable reality was a long time coming.

✦ Watergate and the Unmaking of a President

Nixon's electoral triumph in 1972 was almost immediately sullied—and eventually undone—by the so-called **Watergate** scandal. On June 17, 1972, five men were arrested in the Watergate apartment-office complex in Washington after a bungled effort to plant electronic "bugs" in the Democratic party's headquarters. They were soon revealed to be working for the Republican Committee to Re-Elect the President—popularly known as CREEP. The Watergate break-in turned out to be just one in a series of Nixon administration "dirty tricks" that included forging documents to discredit Democrats, using the Internal Revenue Service to harass innocent citizens named on a White House "enemies list," burglarizing the office of the psychiatrist who had treated the leaker of the Pentagon Papers, and perverting the FBI and the CIA to cover the tricksters' tracks.

Meanwhile, the moral stench hanging over the White House worsened when Vice President Agnew was forced to resign in October 1973 for taking bribes

Oil Shock   When OPEC dramatically jacked up oil prices in the 1970s, many Americans—as represented by the Henry Kissinger figure in this cartoon—were slow to realize that an era of low energy prices had ended forever.

Nixon, the "Law-and-Order-Man" New York Newsday

from Maryland contractors while governor and also as vice president. In the first use of the Twenty-fifth Amendment (see the Appendix), Nixon nominated and Congress confirmed Agnew's successor, a twelve-term congressman from Michigan, Gerald ("Jerry") Ford.

Amid a mood of growing national outrage, a select Senate committee conducted widely televised hearings about the Watergate affair in 1973–1974. Nixon indignantly denied any prior knowledge of the break-in and any involvement in the legal proceedings against the burglars. But John Dean III, a former White House lawyer with a remarkable memory, accused top White House officials, including the president, of obstructing justice by trying to cover up the Watergate break-in and silence its perpetrators. Then another former White House aide revealed that a secret taping system had recorded most of Nixon's Oval Office conversations. Now Dean's sensational testimony could be checked against the White House tapes, and the Senate committee could better determine who was telling the truth. But Nixon, stubbornly citing his "executive privilege," refused to hand over the tapes. Then, on October 20, 1973, he ordered the "Saturday Night Massacre," firing his own special prosecutor appointed to investigate the Watergate scandal, as well as his attorney general and deputy attorney general because they had refused to go along with firing the prosecutor.

Responding at last to the House Judiciary Committee's demand for the Watergate tapes, Nixon agreed in the spring of 1974 to the publication of "relevant" portions of the tapes, with many sections missing (including Nixon's frequent obscenities, which were excised with the phrase "expletive deleted"). But on July 24, 1974, the president suffered a disastrous setback when the Supreme Court unanimously ruled that "executive privilege" gave him no right to withhold evidence relevant to possible criminal activity. Skating on thin ice over hot water, Nixon reluctantly complied.

Seeking to soften the impact of inevitable disclosure, Nixon now made public three subpoenaed tapes of conversations with his chief aide on June 23, 1972. Fatally for his own case, one of them—the notorious **"smoking gun" tape** (see p. 927)—revealed the president giving orders, six days after the Watergate break-in, to

Smoking Pistol Exhibit A The tape-recorded conversations between President Nixon and his top aide on June 23, 1972, proved mortally damaging to Nixon's claim that he had played no role in the Watergate cover-up.

The "Smoking Gun" Tape, June 23, 1972, 10:04–11:39 A.M.

The technological capability to record Oval Office conversations combined with Richard Nixon's obsession with documenting his presidency to give the public—and the Senate committee investigating his role in the break-in of the Democratic National Committee headquarters in the Watergate Office Tower—rare access to personal conversations between the president and his closest advisers. This tape, which undeniably exposed Nixon's central role in constructing a "cover-up" of the Watergate break-in, was made on Nixon's first day back in Washington after the botched burglary of June 17, 1972. In this conversation with White House Chief of Staff H. R. Haldeman, Nixon devised a plan to block a widening FBI investigation by instructing the director of the CIA to deflect any further FBI snooping on the grounds that it would endanger sensitive CIA operations. Nixon refused to turn over this and other tapes to Senate investigators until so ordered by the Supreme Court on July 24, 1974. Within four days of its release on August 5, Nixon was forced to resign. After eighteen months of protesting his innocence of the crime and his ignorance of any effort to obstruct justice, Nixon was finally undone by the evidence in this incriminating "smoking gun" tape. While tapes documented two straight years of Nixon's Oval Office conversations, other presidents, such as Franklin Roosevelt, John F. Kennedy, and Lyndon Baines Johnson, recorded important meetings and crisis deliberations. Since Watergate, however, it is unlikely that any president has permitted extensive tape recording, depriving historians of a unique insight into the inner workings of the White House. Should taped White House discussions be part of the public record of a presidency, and if so, who should have access to them? What else might historians learn from a tape like this one, besides analyzing the Watergate cover-up?

Haldeman: . . . yesterday, they concluded it was not the White House, but are now convinced it is a CIA thing, so the CIA turn off would . . .

President: Well, not sure of their analysis, I'm not going to get that involved. I'm (unintelligible).

Haldeman: No, sir. We don't want you to.

President: You call them in

President: Good. Good deal! Play it tough. That's the way they play it and that's the way we are going to play it.

Haldeman: O.K. We'll do it.

President: Yeah, when I saw that news summary item, I of course knew it was a bunch of crap, but I thought ah, well it's good to have them off on this wild hair thing because when they start bugging us, which they have, we'll know our little boys will not know how to handle it. I hope they will though. You never know. Maybe, you think about it. Good!

President: When you get in these people when you . . . get these people in, say: "Look, the problem is that this will open the whole, the whole Bay of Pigs thing, and the President just feels that" ah, without going into the details . . . don't, don't lie to them to the extent to say there is no involvement, but just say this is sort of a comedy of errors, bizarre, without getting into it, "the President believes that it is going to open the whole Bay of Pigs thing up again. And, ah because these people are plugging for, for keeps and that they should call the FBI in and say that we wish for the country, don't go any further into this case," period!

Source: Nixon Presidential Materials Project, National Archives and Record Administration

use the CIA to hold back an inquiry by the FBI. Nixon's own tape-recorded words convicted him of having been an active party to the attempted cover-up. The House Judiciary Committee proceeded to draw up articles of impeachment, based on obstruction of justice, abuse of the powers of the presidential office, and contempt of Congress.

The public's wrath proved to be overwhelming. Republican leaders in Congress concluded that the guilty and unpredictable Nixon was a loose cannon on the deck of the ship of state. They frankly informed the president that his impeachment by the full House and removal by the Senate were foregone conclusions and that he would do best to resign.

Left with no better choice, Nixon choked back his tears and announced his resignation in a dramatic television appearance on August 8, 1974. Few presidents had flown so high, and none had sunk so low. In his Farewell Address, Nixon admitted having made some "judgments" that "were wrong" but insisted that he had always acted "in what I believed at the time to be the best interests of the nation." Unconvinced, countless Americans would change the song "Hail to the Chief" to "Jail to the Chief."

The nation had survived a wrenching constitutional crisis, which proved that the impeachment machinery forged by the Founding Fathers could work when public opinion overwhelmingly demanded that it be implemented. The principles that no person is above the law and that presidents must be held to strict accountability for their acts were strengthened. The United States of America, on the eve of its two-hundredth birthday as a republic, had eventually cleaned its own sullied house, giving an impressive demonstration of self-discipline and self-government to the rest of the world.

✵ The First Unelected President

Gerald Rudolph Ford, the first man to be made president solely by a vote of Congress, entered the besmirched White House in August 1974 with serious handicaps. He was widely—and unfairly—suspected of being little more than a dim-witted former college football player. President Johnson had sneered that "Jerry" was so lacking in brainpower that he could not walk and chew gum at the same time. Worse, Ford had been selected, not elected, vice president, following Spiro Agnew's resignation in disgrace. The sour odor of illegitimacy hung about this president without precedent.

Then, out of a clear sky, Ford granted a complete pardon to Nixon for any crimes he may have committed as president, discovered or undiscovered. Democrats were outraged, and lingering suspicions about the circumstances of the pardon cast a dark shadow over

Ford's prospects of being elected president in his own right in 1976.

Ford at first sought to enhance the so-called détente with the Soviet Union that Nixon had crafted. In July 1975 President Ford joined leaders from thirty-four other nations in Helsinki, Finland, to sign several sets of historic accords. One group of agreements officially wrote an end to World War II by finally legitimizing the Soviet-dictated boundaries of Poland and other Eastern European countries. In return, the Soviets signed a "third basket" of agreements, guaranteeing more liberal exchanges of people and information between East and West and protecting certain basic "human rights." The Helsinki accords kindled small dissident movements in Eastern Europe and even in the USSR itself, but the Soviets soon poured ice water on these sputtering flames of freedom.

Western Europeans, especially the West Germans, cheered the Helsinki conference as a milestone of détente. But in the United States, critics increasingly charged that détente was proving to be a one-way street. American grain and technology flowed across the Atlantic to the USSR, and little of comparable importance flowed back. Moscow also continued its human rights violations, including restrictions on Jewish emigration, which prompted Congress in 1974 to add punitive restrictions to a U.S. Soviet trade bill. Despite these difficulties, Ford at first clung stubbornly to détente. But the American public's fury over Moscow's double-dealing so steadily mounted that by the end of his term, the president was refusing even to pronounce the word *détente* in public. The thaw in the Cold War was threatening to prove chillingly brief.

✵ Defeat in Vietnam

Early in 1975 the North Vietnamese gave full throttle to their long-expected drive southward. President Ford urged Congress to vote still more weapons for Vietnam, but his plea was in vain, and without the crutch of massive American aid, the South Vietnamese quickly and ingloriously collapsed.

The dam burst so rapidly that the remaining Americans had to be frantically evacuated by helicopter, the last of them on April 29, 1975. Also rescued were about 140,000 South Vietnamese, most of them so dangerously identified with the Americans that they feared a bloodbath by the victorious communists. Ford compassionately admitted these people to the United States, where they added further seasoning to the melting pot. Eventually some 500,000 arrived (see "Makers of America: The Vietnamese," pp. 930–931).

America's longest, most frustrating war thus ended not with a bang but a whimper. In a technical sense,

Passing the Buck A satirical view of where responsibility for the Vietnam debacle should be laid. *Who Lost Vietnam?* FEIFFER © JULES FEIFFER

the Americans had not lost the war; their client nation had. The United States had fought the North Vietnamese to a standstill and had then withdrawn its troops in 1973, leaving the South Vietnamese to fight their own war, with generous shipments of costly American aircraft, tanks, and other munitions. The estimated cost to America was $118 billion in current outlays, together with some 56,000 dead and 300,000 wounded. The people of the United States had in fact provided just about everything, except the will to win—and that could not be injected by outsiders.

Technicalities aside, America had lost more than a war. It had lost face in the eyes of foreigners, lost its own self-esteem, lost confidence in its military prowess, and lost much of the economic muscle that had made possible its global leadership since World War II.

Americans reluctantly came to realize that their power as well as their pride had been deeply wounded in Vietnam and that recovery would be slow and painful.

✴ Feminist Victories and Defeats

As the army limped home from Vietnam, there was little rejoicing on the college campuses, where demonstrators had once braved tear gas and billy clubs to denounce the war. The antiwar movement, like many of the other protest movements that convulsed the country in the 1960s, had long since splintered and stalled. One major exception to this pattern stood out: American feminists, although they had their differences, showed vitality and momentum. They won legislative

The Abortion Wars Pro-choice and pro-life demonstrators brandish their beliefs. By the end of the twentieth century, the debate over abortion had become the most morally charged and divisive issue in American society since the struggle over slavery in the nineteenth century.

Diana Walker/Getty Images

At first glance the towns of Westminster and Fountain Valley, California, seem to resemble other California communities nearby. Tract homes line residential streets; shopping centers flank the busy thoroughfares. But these are no ordinary American suburbs. Instead they make up "Little Saigons," vibrant outposts of Vietnamese culture in the contemporary United States. Shops offer exotic Asian merchandise; restaurants serve such delicacies as lemongrass chicken. These neighborhoods, living reminders of America's anguish in Vietnam, are a rarely acknowledged consequence of that sorrowful conflict.

Before South Vietnam fell in 1975, few Vietnamese ventured across the Pacific. Indeed, throughout most of American history until the mid-twentieth century, the bulk of U.S. immigrants had come from Europe, with the notable exception of the Chinese and, to a lesser extent, the Japanese (see pp. 500–501 and pp. 800–801). This trend began to change in the 1960s, as people from South America and Asia began arriving in greater numbers. The war-weary Vietnamese were at the forefront of this new immigration, so much so that in 1966 the U.S. Immigration authorities designated "Vietnamese" as a separate category of newcomers. Most early immigrants were the wives and children of U.S. servicemen.

As the communists closed in on Saigon in the mid-1970s, many Vietnamese, particularly those who had worked closely with American or South Vietnamese authorities, feared for their lives. Gathering together as many of their extended-family members as they could, thousands of Vietnamese prepared to flee the country. In a few hectic days in 1975, some 140,000 Vietnamese escaped before the approaching communist gunfire, a few dramatically clinging to the bottoms of departing U.S. helicopters. From Saigon they were conveyed to military bases in Guam and the Philippines. Another 60,000 less fortunate Vietnamese escaped at the same time over land and sea to Hong Kong and Thailand, where they waited nervously for permission to move on.

To accommodate the refugees, the U.S. government set up camps across the United States. Arrivals were crowded into army barracks affording little room and less privacy. These were boot camps not for military service but for assimilation into American society. A rigorous program trained the Vietnamese in English, forbade children from speaking their native language in the classroom, and even immersed them in American slang. Many resented this attempt to mold them, to strip them of their culture.

Their discontent boiled over when authorities prepared to release the refugees from camps and board them with families around the nation. The resettlement officials had decided to find a sponsor for each Vietnamese family—an American family that would provide food, shelter, and assistance for the refugees until they could fend for themselves. But the Vietnamese people cherish their traditional extended families—grandparents, uncles, aunts, and cousins living communally with parents and children. Few American sponsors would accommodate a large extended family; fewer Vietnamese families would willingly separate.

The refugees were dispersed to Iowa, Illinois, Pennsylvania, New York, Washington, and California. But

The Last Days of Saigon   Violence often attended the frantic American evacuation from Vietnam in 1975.

and judicial victories and provoked an intense rethinking of gender roles. (On the roots of this movement, see "Makers of America: The Feminists," pp. 934–935.)

Thousands of women marched in the Women's Stride for Equality on the fiftieth anniversary of woman suffrage in 1970. In 1972 Congress passed Title IX of the Education Amendments, prohibiting sex discrimination in any federally assisted educational program or activity. Perhaps this act's biggest impact was to create opportunities for girls' and women's athletics at schools and colleges, giving birth to a new "Title IX generation" that would reach maturity in the 1980s

Lawrence Migdale

Preserving the Past A Vietnamese American boy learns classical calligraphy from his grandfather.

the settlement sites, many of them tucked away in rural districts, offered scant economic opportunities. The immigrants, who had held mainly skilled or white-collar positions in Vietnam, bristled as they were herded into menial labor. As soon as they could, they relocated, hastening to established Vietnamese enclaves around San Francisco, Los Angeles, and Dallas.

Soon a second throng of Vietnamese immigrants pushed into these Little Saigons. Fleeing from the ravages of poverty and from the oppressive communist government, these stragglers had crammed themselves and their few possessions into little boats, hoping to reach Hong Kong or get picked up by foreign ships. Eventually many of these "boat people" reached the United States. Usually less educated than the first arrivals and receiving far less resettlement aid from the U.S. government, they were, however, more willing to start at the bottom. Today these two groups total more than half a million people. Differing in experience and expectations, the Vietnamese share a new home in a strange land. Their uprooting is an immense, unreckoned consequence of America's longest war.

Christopher Morris/Black Star/Stockphoto.com

Boat People Vietnamese refugees flee to freedom.

and 1990s and help professionalize women's sports as well. The **Equal Rights Amendment (ERA)** to the Constitution won congressional approval in 1972. It declared, "Equality of rights under the law shall not be denied or abridged by the United States or by any State on account of sex." Twenty-eight of the necessary

thirty-eight states quickly ratified the amendment, first proposed by suffragists in 1923. Hopes rose that the ERA might soon become the law of the land.

Even the Supreme Court seemed to be on the movement's side. In *Reed* v. *Reed* (1971) and *Frontiero* v. *Richardson* (1973), the Court challenged sex discrimination in legislation and employment. And in the landmark case of **Roe v. Wade** (1973), the Court struck down laws prohibiting abortion, arguing that a woman's decision to terminate a pregnancy was protected by the constitutional right of privacy.

But the feminist movement soon faced a formidable backlash. In 1972 President Nixon vetoed a proposal to set up nationwide public day care, saying it would weaken the American family. Antifeminists blamed the women's movement for the rising divorce rate, which tripled between 1960 and 1976. And the Catholic Church and the religious right organized a powerful grassroots movement to oppose the legalization of abortion.

For many feminists the most bitter defeat was the death of the ERA. Antifeminists, led by conservative activist Phyllis Schlafly, argued that the ERA would remove traditional protections that women enjoyed by forcing the law to see them as men's equals. They

Antifeminist Phyllis Schlafly (b. 1924) Schlafly traveled the country promoting her "STOP ERA" campaign. She argued that ratification of the Equal Rights Amendment would undermine the American family by violating "the right of a wife to be supported by her husband," requiring women to serve in combat, and legalizing homosexual marriage.

Joan Roth/Getty Images

further believed that the amendment would threaten the basic family structure of American society. Schlafly charged that the ERA's advocates were just "bitter women seeking a constitutional cure for their personal problems." In 1979 Congress extended the deadline for ratification of the amendment, but opponents dug in their heels. The ERA died in 1982, three states short of success.

✦ The Seventies in Black and White

Although the civil rights movement had fractured, race remained an explosive issue in the 1970s. The Supreme Court in *Milliken* v. *Bradley* (1974) blindsided school integrationists when it ruled that desegregation plans could not require students to move across school-district lines. The decision effectively exempted suburban districts from shouldering any part of the burden of desegregating inner-city schools, thereby reinforcing "white flight" from cities to suburbs. By the same token, the decision distilled all the problems of desegregation into the least prosperous districts, often pitting the poorest, most disadvantaged elements of the white and black communities against one another.

Affirmative-action programs also remained highly controversial. White workers who were denied advancement and white students who were refused college admission continued to raise the cry of "reverse discrimination," charging that their rights had been violated by employers and admissions officers who put more weight on racial or ethnic background than on ability or achievement.

One white Californian, Allan Bakke, made headlines in 1978 when the Supreme Court, by the narrowest of margins (five to four) upheld his claim that his application to medical school had been turned down because of an admissions program that favored minority applicants. In a tortured decision reflecting the troubling moral ambiguities and insoluble political complexities of this issue, the Court ordered the University of California at Davis medical school to admit Bakke and declared that preference in admissions could not be given to members of any group, minority or majority, on the basis of ethnic or racial identity alone. Yet at the same time, the Court said that racial factors might be taken into account in a school's overall admissions policy for purposes of assembling a diverse student body. Among the dissenters on the sharply divided bench was the Court's only black justice, Thurgood Marshall. He warned in an impassioned opinion that the denial of racial preferences might sweep away years of progress by the civil rights movement. But many conservatives cheered the decision as affirming the principle that justice is colorblind.

A Sad Day for Old Glory   In 1976, America's bicentennial year, anti-busing demonstrators convulsed Boston, the historic "cradle of liberty." White disillusionment with the race-based policies that were a legacy of Lyndon Johnson's "Great Society" programs of the 1960s helped to feed the conservative, antigovernment movement that elected Ronald Reagan in 1980.

Inspired by the civil rights movement, Native Americans in the 1970s gained remarkable power through using the courts and well-planned acts of civil disobedience. But while blacks had fought against segregation, Indians used the tactics of the civil rights movement to assert their status as separate semi-sovereign peoples. Indian activists captured the nation's attention by seizing the island of Alcatraz in 1970 and the village of Wounded Knee, South Dakota, in 1972. A series of victories in the courts consolidated the decade's gains. In the case of *United States* v. *Wheeler* (1978), the Supreme Court declared that Indian tribes possessed a "unique and limited" sovereignty, subject to the will of Congress but not to individual states.

✦ The Bicentennial Campaign

America's two-hundredth birthday, in 1976, fell during a presidential election year—a fitting coincidence for a proud democracy. President Gerald Ford energetically sought the Republican nomination in his own right and defeated challenger Ronald Reagan, former actor and governor of California, who ran as a more conservative candidate.

The Democratic standard-bearer was fifty-one-year-old James Earl ("Jimmy") Carter, Jr., a dark-horse candidate who galloped out of obscurity during the long primary-election season. A peanut farmer and former Georgia governor who insisted on the humble "Jimmy" as his first name, this born-again Baptist touched many people with his down-home sincerity. He ran against the memory of Nixon and Watergate as much as he ran against Ford. His most effective campaign pitch was his promise "I'll never lie to you." Untainted by ties with a corrupt and cynical Washington, he attracted voters as an outsider who would clean the disorderly house of "big government."

Carter squeezed out a narrow victory on election day, with 51 percent of the popular vote. The electoral count stood at 297 to 240. The winner swept every state except Virginia in his native South. Especially important were the votes of African Americans, 97 percent of whom cast their ballots for Carter.

Carter enjoyed hefty Democratic majorities in both houses of Congress. Hopes ran high that the stalemate of the Nixon-Ford years between a Republican White House and a Democratic Capitol Hill would now be ended. At first Carter enjoyed notable success, as Congress granted his requests to create a new cabinet-level Department of Energy and to cut taxes. The new president's popularity remained exceptionally high during his first few months in office, even when he courted public disfavor by courageously keeping his campaign promise to pardon some ten thousand draft evaders of the Vietnam War era.

But Carter's honeymoon did not last long. An inexperienced outsider, he had campaigned against the Washington "establishment" and never quite made the transition to being an insider himself. He repeatedly rubbed congressional fur the wrong way, especially by failing to consult adequately with the leaders. Critics charged that he isolated himself in a shallow pool of fellow Georgians, whose ignorance of the ways of Washington compounded the problems of their greenhorn chief.

✦ Carter's Humanitarian Diplomacy

As a committed Christian, President Carter displayed from the outset an overriding concern for "human rights" as the guiding principle of his foreign policy. In the African nations of Rhodesia (later Zimbabwe) and South Africa, Carter and his eloquent U.N. ambassador, Andrew Young, championed the oppressed black majority.

The president's most spectacular foreign-policy achievement came in September 1978 when he invited President Anwar Sadat of Egypt and Prime Minister

*G*well-to-do housewife and mother of seven, Elizabeth Cady Stanton (1815–1902) was an unlikely revolutionary. Yet this founding mother of American feminism devoted seven decades of her life to the fight for women's rights.

Young Elizabeth Cady drew her inspiration from the fight against slavery. In 1840 she married fellow abolitionist Henry Stanton. Honeymooning in London, they attended the World Anti-Slavery Convention, where women were forced to sit in a screened-off balcony above the convention floor. This insult awakened Stanton to the cause that would occupy her life. With Lucretia Mott and other female abolitionists, Stanton went on to organize the Seneca Falls Convention in 1848. There she presented her Declaration of Sentiments, modeled on the Declaration of Independence and proclaiming that "all men *and women* are created equal." She demanded for women the right to own property, to enter the professions, and, most daring of all, to vote.

As visionaries of a radically different future for women, early feminists encountered a mountain of hostility and tasted bitter disappointment. Stanton failed in her struggle to have women included in the Fourteenth Amendment to the U.S. Constitution, which granted African Americans equal citizenship. She died before seeing her dream of woman suffrage realized in the Nineteenth Amendment (1920). Yet by imagining women's emancipation as an expansion of America's founding principles of citizenship, Stanton charted a path that other feminists would follow a century later.

Historians use the terms "first wave" and "second wave" to distinguish the women's movement of the nineteenth century from that of the late twentieth century. The woman most often credited with launching the "second wave" is Betty Friedan (1921–2006). Growing up in Peoria, Illinois, she had seen her mother grow bitter over sacrificing a journalism career to raise her family. Friedan, a suburban housewife, went on to write the 1963 best seller *The Feminine Mystique*, exposing the quiet desperation of millions of housewives trapped in the "comfortable concentration camp" of the suburban home. The book struck a resonant chord and catapulted its author onto the national stage. In 1966 Friedan cofounded the National Organization for Women (NOW), the chief political arm and more moderate wing of second-wave feminism.

Elizabeth Cady Stanton (1815–1902) and Two of Her Sons, 1848 In the same year this photo was taken, Stanton delivered her Declaration of Sentiments to the first Woman's Rights Convention in Seneca Falls, New York.

Elizabeth Cady Stanton Trust/Picture Research Consultants & Archives

Just as first-wave feminism grew out of abolitionism, the second wave drew ideas, leaders, and tactics from the civil rights movement of the 1960s. Civil rights workers and feminists alike focused on equal rights. NOW campaigned vigorously for the Equal Rights Amendment, which fell just three states short of ratification in 1982. But second-wave feminism knew no national boundaries. In the late 1960s, activists around the world resurrected the tradition of International Women's Day, which first-wave feminists had marked through the 1920s. March 8 became an

Menachem Begin of Israel to a summit conference at Camp David, the woodsy presidential retreat in the Maryland highlands. Skillfully serving as go-between, Carter persuaded the two visitors to sign an accord (September 17, 1978) that held considerable promise

of peace. Israel agreed in principle to withdraw from territory conquered in the 1967 war, and Egypt in return promised to respect Israel's borders. Both parties pledged themselves to sign a formal peace treaty within three months.

Marching for Women's Rights, 1977 A multiethnic and multiracial group of women, accompanied by noted "second-wave" feminists Bella Abzug (in hat) and Betty Friedan (far right), helped to carry a torch from Seneca Falls, New York, birthplace of the feminist movement, to Houston, Texas, site of the National Women's Conference.

international day of celebration and awareness of the continued inequality and violence that many women faced around the globe.

Second-wave feminism also had an avowedly radical wing, supported by younger women who were eager to challenge almost every traditional male and female gender role and to take the feminist cause to the streets. Among these women was Robin Morgan (b. 1941). As a college student in the 1960s, Morgan was active in civil rights organizations that provided her with a model for crusading against social injustice. They also exposed her to the same sexism that plagued society at large. Women in the movement who protested against gender discrimination met ridicule, as in SNCC leader Stokely Carmichael's famous retort, "The only position for women in SNCC is prone." Morgan went on to found WITCH (Women's International Terrorist Conspiracy from Hell), made famous by its protest at the 1968 Miss America pageant in Atlantic City, New Jersey. There demonstrators crowned a sheep Miss America and threw symbols of women's oppression—bras, girdles, and dishcloths—into trash cans. (Contrary to news stories, they did not burn the bras.)

As the contrast between WITCH and NOW suggests, second-wave feminism was a remarkably diverse movement. Feminists disagreed over many issues—from pornography and marriage to how much to expect from government, capitalism, and men. Some feminists placed a priority on gender equality—for example, full female service in the military. Others defended a feminism of gender difference—such as maternity leave and other special protections for women in the workplace.

Still, beyond these differences feminists had much in common. Most advocated a woman's right to choose in the battle over abortion rights. Most regarded the law as the key weapon against gender discrimination. By the early twenty-first century, radical and moderate feminists alike could take pride in a host of achievements that had changed the landscape of gender relations beyond what most people could have imagined at midcentury. Yet like Elizabeth Cady Stanton, second-wave feminists also shared the burden of understanding that the goals of genuine equality would take more than a lifetime to achieve.

The president crowned this diplomatic success by resuming full diplomatic relations with China in early 1979 after a nearly thirty-year interruption. Carter also successfully pushed through two treaties to turn over the Panama Canal to the Panamanians. Although these treaties were decried by conservatives such as Ronald Reagan—who stridently declared, "We bought it, we paid for it, we built it, and we intend to keep it!"—the United States gave up control of the canal on December 31, 1999.

Celebrating the Camp David Agreement, September 1978 Anwar Sadat of Egypt (left) and Menachem Begin of Israel (right) join U.S. president Jimmy Carter in confirming the historic accord that brought the hope of peace to the war-torn Middle East.

Black Star/Stockphoto.com

Despite these dramatic accomplishments, trouble stalked Carter's foreign policy. Overshadowing all international issues was the ominous reheating of the Cold War with the Soviet Union. Détente fell into disrepute as thousands of Cuban troops, assisted by Soviet advisers, appeared in Angola, Ethiopia, and elsewhere in Africa to support revolutionary factions. Arms-control negotiations with Moscow stalled in the face of this Soviet military meddling.

✷ Economic and Energy Woes

Adding to Carter's mushrooming troubles was the failing health of the economy. A stinging recession during Ford's presidency had brought the inflation rate down slightly to just under 6 percent, but from the moment Carter took over, prices resumed their dizzying ascent, driving the inflation rate well above 13 percent by 1980 (see Figure 39.2). The soaring bill for imported oil plunged America's balance of payments deeply into the red (an unprecedented $40 billion in 1978).

The "oil shocks" of the 1970s taught Americans a painful but necessary lesson: that they could never again seriously consider a policy of economic isolation, as they had tried to do in the decades between the two world wars. For most of American history, foreign trade had accounted for no more than 10 percent of gross national product (GNP). But huge foreign-oil bills drove that figure steadily upward in the 1970s and thereafter. By century's end, some 27 percent of GNP depended on foreign trade. Unable to dominate international trade and finance as easily as they once had, Americans would have to master foreign languages and study foreign cultures if they wanted to prosper in the rapidly globalizing economy.

Historical Double Take Many Americans who looked back reverently to Theodore Roosevelt's "Rough Rider" diplomacy were outraged at the Panama "giveaway." But the Carter administration, looking to the future, argued persuasively that relinquishing control of the canal would be healthy for U.S.–Latin American relations. © Valtman/Rothco

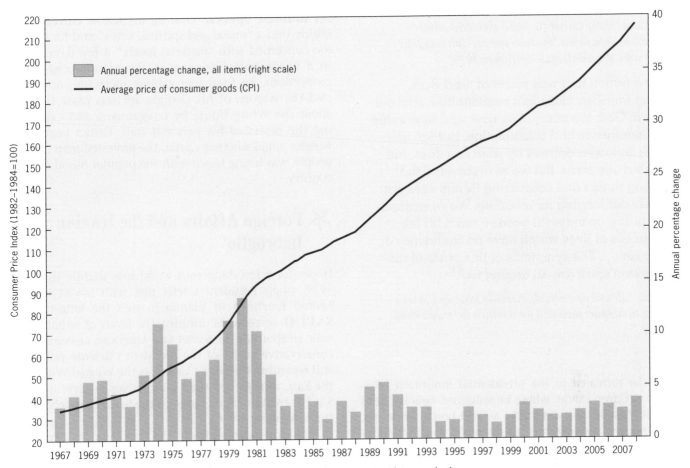

FIGURE 39.2 The History of the Consumer Price Index, 1967–2008 This graph shows both the annual percentage rate of inflation and the cumulative shrinkage of the dollar's value since 1967. (By 2008 it took more than six dollars to buy what one dollar had purchased in 1967.) (Sources: Bureau of Labor Statistics and *Statistical Abstract of the United States*, relevant years.)

Yawning deficits in the federal budget, reaching nearly $60 billion in 1980, further aggravated the U.S. economy's inflationary ailments. The elderly and other Americans living on fixed incomes suffered from the shrinking dollar. People with money to lend pushed interest rates ever higher, hoping to protect themselves from being repaid in badly depreciated dollars. The "prime rate" (the rate of interest that banks charge their very best customers) vaulted to an unheard-of 20 percent in early 1980. The high cost of borrowing money shoved small businesses to the wall and strangled the construction industry, which was heavily dependent on loans to finance new housing and other projects.

Carter diagnosed America's economic disease as stemming primarily from the nation's costly dependence on foreign oil. Unfortunately, his legislative proposals for energy conservation in 1977 ignited a blaze of indifference among the American people, who had already forgotten the long gasoline lines of 1973.

Events in Iran jolted Americans out of their complacency about energy supplies in 1979. The imperious Mohammed Reza Pahlevi, installed as shah of Iran with help from America's CIA in 1953, had long ruled his oil-rich land with a will of steel. His repressive regime was finally overthrown in January 1979. Violent revolution was spearheaded in Iran by Muslim fundamentalists who fiercely resented the shah's campaign to westernize and secularize his country. Denouncing the United States as the "Great Satan" that had abetted the shah's efforts, these extremists engulfed Iran in chaos in the wake of his departure. The crippling upheavals soon spread to Iran's oil fields. As Iranian oil stopped flowing into the stream of world commerce, shortages appeared, and OPEC again seized the opportunity to hike petroleum prices. Americans once more found themselves waiting impatiently in long lines at gas stations or buying gasoline only on specified days.

As the oil crisis deepened, President Carter sensed the rising temperature of popular discontent. In July

President Jimmy Carter (b. 1924) delivered what became known as his "malaise speech" (although he never used the word) on television in 1979:

"In a nation that was proud of hard work, strong families, close-knit communities, and our faith in God, too many of us now tend to worship self-indulgence and consumption. Human identity is no longer defined by what one does, but by what one owns. But we've discovered that owning things and consuming things does not satisfy our longing for meaning. We've learned that piling up material goods cannot fill the emptiness of lives which have no confidence or purpose. . . . The symptoms of this crisis of the American spirit are all around us."

In time cultural conservatives would take up Carter's theme to support their call for a return to "traditional values."

1979 he retreated to the presidential mountain hideaway at Camp David, where he remained largely out of public view for ten days. Like a royal potentate of old, summoning the wise men of the realm for their counsel in a time of crisis, Carter called in over a hundred leaders from all walks of life to give him their views. Meanwhile, the nation waited anxiously for the results of these extraordinary deliberations.

When Carter came down from the mountaintop on July 15, 1979, he stunned a perplexed nation with his **malaise speech**, chiding his fellow citizens for falling into a "moral and spiritual crisis" and for being too concerned with "material goods." A few days later, in a bureaucratic massacre of almost unprecedented proportions, he fired four cabinet secretaries and circled the wagons of his Georgia advisers more tightly about the White House by reorganizing and expanding the power of his personal staff. Critics began to wonder aloud whether Carter, the professed man of the people, was losing touch with the popular mood of the country.

✦ Foreign Affairs and the Iranian Imbroglio

Hopes for a less dangerous world rose slightly in June 1979, when President Carter met with Soviet leader Leonid Brezhnev in Vienna to sign the long-stalled **SALT II** agreements, limiting the levels of lethal strategic weapons in the Soviet and American arsenals. But conservative critics of the president's defense policies, still regarding the Soviet Union as the Wicked Witch of the East, unsheathed their long knives to carve up the SALT II treaty when it came to the Senate for debate in the summer of 1979.

Political earthquakes in the petroleum-rich Persian Gulf region finally buried all hopes of ratifying the SALT II treaty. On November 4, 1979, a mob of rabidly anti-American Muslim militants stormed the United States embassy in Tehran, Iran, and took all of its occupants hostage. The captors then demanded that the American authorities ship back to Iran the exiled shah,

Europeans are Skeptical about US-USSR SALT II Talks As President Carter and Soviet leader Leonid Brezhnev prepared to meet for arms-reduction talks in Vienna in June 1979, a German newspaper cartoonist questioned the depth of their commitment to genuine disarmament.

Behrendt/Frankfurter Allgemeine Zeitung

who had arrived in the United States two weeks earlier for medical treatment.

World opinion hotly condemned the diplomatic felony in Iran, while Americans agonized over both the fate of the hostages and the stability of the entire Persian Gulf region, so dangerously close to the Soviet Union. The Soviet army then aroused the West's worst fears on December 27, 1979, when it blitzed into the mountainous nation of Afghanistan, next door to Iran, and appeared to be poised for a thrust at the oil jugular of the gulf.

President Carter reacted vigorously to these alarming events. He slapped an embargo on the export of grain and high-technology machinery to the USSR and called for a boycott of the upcoming Olympic Games in Moscow. He proposed the creation of a "Rapid Deployment Force" to respond to suddenly developing crises in faraway places and requested that young people (including women) be made to register for a possible military draft. The president proclaimed that the United States would "use any means necessary, including force," to protect the Persian Gulf against Soviet incursions. He grimly conceded that he had misjudged the Soviets, and the SALT II treaty became a dead letter in the Senate. Meanwhile, the Soviet army met unexpectedly stiff resistance in Afghanistan and bogged down in a nasty, decade-long guerrilla war that came to be called "Russia's Vietnam."

The **Iranian hostage crisis** was Carter's—and America's—bed of nails. The captured Americans languished in cruel captivity, while the nightly television news broadcasts in the United States showed humiliating scenes of Iranian mobs burning the American flag and spitting on effigies of Uncle Sam.

Carter at first tried to apply economic sanctions and the pressure of world public opinion against the Iranians, while waiting for the emergence of a stable government with which to negotiate. But the political turmoil in Iran rumbled on endlessly, and the president's frustration grew. Carter at last ordered a daring rescue mission. A highly trained commando team penetrated deep into Iran's sandy interior. Their plan required ticktock-perfect timing to succeed, and when equipment failures prevented some members of the team from reaching their destination, the mission had to be scrapped. As the commandos withdrew in the dark desert night, two of their aircraft collided, killing eight of the would-be rescuers.

This disastrous failure of the rescue raid proved anguishing for Americans. The episode seemed to underscore the nation's helplessness and even incompetence in the face of a mortifying insult to the national honor. The stalemate with Iran dragged on throughout the rest of Carter's term, providing an embarrassing backdrop to the embattled president's struggle for reelection.

Henri Bureau/Sygma/© Bettmann/Corbis

Iranians Denounce President Jimmy Carter, November 1979 Scenes like this one appeared almost nightly on American television during the 444 days of the Iranian hostage crisis, humiliating Carter and angering American citizens.

Chapter Review

KEY TERMS

Vietnamization (917)

Nixon Doctrine (917)

silent majority (918)

My Lai Massacre (918)

Kent State University (919)

Pentagon Papers (919)

détente (920)

Miranda warning (921)

Philadelphia Plan (921)

Environmental Protection
Agency (EPA) (922)

Earth Day (922)

southern strategy (922)

War Powers Act (924)

Watergate (925)

"smoking gun" tape (926)

Equal Rights Amendment
(ERA) (931)

Roe v. *Wade* (932)

malaise speech (938)

SALT II (938)

Iranian hostage crisis (939)

PEOPLE TO KNOW

Henry A. Kissinger

Warren E. Burger

Rachel Carson

George McGovern

Gerald ("Jerry") Ford

John Dean III

James Earl ("Jimmy")
Carter, Jr.

Leonid Brezhnev

CHRONOLOGY

1968   My Lai Massacre
WITCH protests Miss America pageant in
Atlantic City, New Jersey

1970   Nixon orders invasion of Cambodia
Kent State and Jackson State incidents
Environmental Protection Agency (EPA)
created
Clean Air Act

1971   Pentagon Papers published

1972   Twenty-sixth Amendment (lowering voting
age to eighteen) passed
Nixon visits China and Soviet Union
Shanghai Communiqué begins "normaliza-
tion" of U.S.-Chinese relations
ABM and SALT I treaties ratified
Nixon defeats McGovern for presidency
Equal Rights Amendment passes Congress
(not ratified by states)
Title IX of Education Amendments passed

1973   Treaty of Paris enacts cease-fire in Vietnam
and U.S. withdrawal
Agnew resigns; Ford appointed vice
president
War Powers Act
Yom Kippur War
OPEC oil embargo
Endangered Species Act
Chilean president Salvador Allende killed in
CIA-backed coup
Frontiero v. *Richardson*
Roe v. *Wade*

1973–1974   Watergate hearings and investigations

1974   Nixon resigns; Ford assumes presidency
OPEC ends embargo, increases oil prices
International Energy Agency formed
Milliken v. *Bradley*

1975   Helsinki accords
South Vietnam falls to communists

1976   Carter defeats Ford for presidency

1978   Camp David accords between Egypt and
Israel
United States v. *Wheeler*

1979   Iranian revolution and oil crisis
SALT II agreements signed (never ratified by
Senate)
Soviet Union invades Afghanistan

1979–1981   Iranian hostage crisis

1980   U.S. boycotts Summer Olympics in Moscow

TO LEARN MORE

Stephen Ambrose, *Nixon: The Triumph of a Politician, 1962–1972* (1989)

Carl Bernstein and Bob Woodward, *All the President's Men* (1974)

James Bill, *The Eagle and the Lion* (1987)

Robert Dallek, *Nixon and Kissinger: Partners in Power* (2007)

Alice Echols, *Daring to Be Bad: Radical Feminism in America, 1967–1975* (1989)

David Greenberg, *Nixon's Shadow: The History of an Image* (2003)

Linda Greenhouse, *Becoming Justice Blackmun: Harry Blackmun's Supreme Court Journey* (2005)

Walter LaFeber, *Inevitable Revolutions: The United States in Central America*, 2nd ed., (1993)

Matthew D. Lassiter, *The Silent Majority: Suburban Politics in the Sunbelt South* (2007)

Rick Perlstein, *Nixonland: The Rise of a President and the Fracturing of America* (2008)

Bruce Schulman, *The Seventies: The Great Shift in American Culture, Society, and Politics* (2001)

, and Julian Zelizer, eds., *Rightward Bound: Making America Conservative in the 1970s* (2008)

Jeremi Suri, *Henry Kissinger and the American Century* (2007)

Bob Woodward and Scott Armstrong, *The Brethren: Inside the Supreme Court* (1979)

A complete, annotated bibliography for this chapter—along with brief descriptions of the People to Know—may be found on the American Pageant website. The Key Terms are defined in a Glossary at the end of the text.

Go to the CourseMate website at **www.cengagebrain.com** for additional study tools and review materials—including audio and video clips—for this chapter.

AP® Review Questions for Chapter 39

1. All of the following were sources of the economic stagnation that plagued America in the 1970s EXCEPT
   - (A) a drastic decline in worker productivity.
   - (B) inflationary and unsustainable government spending on military and social welfare matters.
   - (C) sharply rising oil and energy prices that fed spiraling inflation.
   - (D) the loss of the competitive advantage historically held by American business in key sectors of the economy like steel, automobiles, and consumer electronics.
   - (E) steep tax increases in the 1960s and early 1970s to fund increased domestic and military spending.

2. President Richard Nixon's Vietnam policy included all of the following EXCEPT
   - (A) the congressionally unauthorized extension of the war to Cambodia.
   - (B) a gradual handover of the ground war to the South Vietnamese.
   - (C) massive bombing campaigns in Vietnam, Cambodia, and Laos.
   - (D) creating a draft lottery and reducing draft calls.
   - (E) steadily increasing American troop commitments in Vietnam.

3. Which of the following best characterizes President Nixon's policy of détente?
   - (A) It was designed to improve relations between the Soviet Union and China.
   - (B) It was aimed at ending the political division of Germany and Korea.
   - (C) It found support in the Democratic party but not in the Republican party.
   - (D) It ushered in an era of relaxed bilateral tensions between the United States and the two leading communist powers, China and the Soviet Union.
   - (E) It was shaped by President Nixon's chief foreign policy adviser, Spiro Agnew.

4. Which of the following was NOT a decision issued by the U.S. Supreme Court during the Warren Court era?
   - (A) The Court upheld a married couple's right to use contraceptives based on a constitutional right to privacy.
   - (B) The Court held that all defendants in serious criminal cases were entitled to legal counsel, even if they were too poor to afford it.
   - (C) The Court guaranteed the right of the accused to remain silent and to enjoy other constitutional protections against self-incrimination.
   - (D) The Court cited the First Amendment in prohibiting required prayers and Bible reading in the public schools.
   - (E) The Court upheld the right of state legislatures to disregard the one-man, one-vote principle in apportioning legislative districts.

5. Why did the creation of the Environmental Protection Agency (EPA) and the Occupational Safety and Health Administration (OSHA) arouse such bitter opposition among many businesspeople?
   - (A) The actions of these new federal agencies undermined strong efforts that businesses were already making to protect the environment and worker safety.
   - (B) The work of these two agencies directly involved the federal government in many aspects of business decision making.
   - (C) These two federal agencies were financed by new corporate taxes.
   - (D) These two businesses operated under laws passed by an antibusiness administration.
   - (E) Richard Nixon appointed environmentalist Rachel Carson to lead the EPA and labor and consumer activist Ralph Nader to head OSHA.

6. The list of illegal activities perpetrated by the law-and-order Nixon administration that were uncovered in the Watergate scandal included all of the following EXCEPT
   - (A) breaking into the Democratic party headquarters in order to bug it to gain information about Democrats' plans for the 1972 presidential campaign.
   - (B) using the Internal Revenue Service to harass political enemies of Nixon.
   - (C) forging documents to discredit prominent Democratic politicians.
   - (D) bribing U.S. Supreme Court justices to write favorable judicial opinions.
   - (E) using the FBI and the CIA to conceal and cover up previous crimes of the Nixon administration.

7. What legal claim did President Nixon unsuccessfully make to the U.S. Supreme Court to resist the efforts of the Watergate special prosecutor and Congress to obtain his taped conversations with aides in the White House?
   - (A) Executive privilege (presidential confidentiality) allowed him to withhold the tapes.
   - (B) Releasing the tapes would violate his right to privacy.
   - (C) Releasing the tapes would violate his Fifth Amendment protection against self-incrimination.
   - (D) The president has absolute sovereign immunity in all criminal investigations.
   - (E) Release of the tapes would interfere with his constitutional right to make foreign policy as commander in chief.

8. Which was the most controversial action of Gerald Ford's presidency?
   (A) Pardoning Richard Nixon for any known or unknown crimes Nixon had committed during his presidency
   (B) Signing the Helsinki accords with the Soviet Union
   (C) Frantically evacuating the last Americans and Vietnamese by helicopter during the fall of South Vietnam to the communists
   (D) Arranging the deal whereby Nixon resigned as president
   (E) Pardoning Vietnam War draft resisters and evaders

9. Which was NOT among the notable achievements of the feminist movement in America during the 1970s?
   (A) Congressional passage of Title IX, prohibiting sex discrimination in any federally funded education program or activity, including intercollegiate and interscholastic athletics
   (B) The Supreme Court decision in *Roe* v. *Wade*, holding that state laws prohibiting abortion were unconstitutional because they violated a woman's constitutional right to privacy
   (C) Supreme Court decisions expanding women's legal protections in the areas of sex discrimination in legislation and employment
   (D) A major rethinking of traditional gender roles in American society that helped catapult millions of American women into the workplace
   (E) The ratification of the Equal Rights Amendment (ERA) constitutionally guaranteeing women equality of rights under law in all fifty states

10. Which of the following most accurately describes the key holding of the Supreme Court in the *Bakke* case?
    (A) The white Californian, Allan Bakke, who challenged the constitutionality of the medical admissions program at the University of California at Davis should have been awarded a minority preference in admissions because he was Jewish.
    (B) Public universities could impose racial quotas, but private universities were barred from doing so.
    (C) All forms of affirmative action in university admissions constituted unconstitutional reverse discrimination.
    (D) It was legally permissible for universities to establish minority-based educational programs and housing arrangements.
    (E) Racial quotas were unconstitutional, but race could be taken into account as one plus factor in university admissions.

11. The presidency of Jimmy Carter was undermined by all of the following EXCEPT
    (A) the inflationary oil shocks of the 1970s.
    (B) the ominous reheating of the Cold War with the Soviets.
    (C) the Iranian hostage crisis.
    (D) an overreliance on a small circle of Georgia advisers for political advice.
    (E) armed conflict in the Middle East between Israel and Egypt.

12. What was the guiding principle of President Carter's foreign policy?
    (A) Isolationism
    (B) Containment
    (C) Unilateralism
    (D) Human rights
    (E) Rolling back communism in developing nations (sometimes called Third World nations)

13. How did the Watergate scandal prove that the United States Constitution could work effectively in a crisis?
    (A) States were able to influence the national government to remove corrupt officials.
    (B) Two branches of government investigated and punished abuses of power in the third.
    (C) Congress approved an amendment prohibiting taping systems in the White House.
    (D) The two-party system survived Nixon's attempt to harm the Democratic party.
    (E) All presidents since Nixon have exercised limited powers.

14. The energy crises of 1973 and 1979 were similar in all of the following ways EXCEPT that
    (A) both resulted from actions taken by OPEC.
    (B) both were indirectly caused by American interference in the Middle East.
    (C) both led to long lines at gas stations and restrictions on fuel purchases.
    (D) both signaled the end of an era of cheap and abundant energy sources.
    (E) both coincided with economic downturns.

Chapter 40

The Resurgence of Conservatism

1980–1992

It will be my intention to curb the size and influence of the federal establishment and to demand recognition of the distinction between the powers granted to the federal government and those reserved to the states or to the people.

RONALD REAGAN, INAUGURAL, 1981

"*It's morning in America*" was the slogan of Republican candidate Ronald Reagan in his 1984 presidential campaign. Certainly the 1980s were a new day for America's conservative right. Census figures confirmed that the average American was older than in the stormy sixties and much more likely to live in the South or West, the traditional bastions of the "Old Right," where many residents harbored suspicions of federal power. The conservative cause drew added strength from the emergence of a "New Right" movement, partly in response to the countercultural protests of the 1960s. Spearheading the New Right were evangelical Christian groups such as the Moral Majority, dedicated believers who enjoyed startling success as political fund-raisers and organizers.

Many New Right activists were far less agitated about economic questions than about cultural concerns—the so-called social issues. They denounced abortion, pornography, homosexuality, feminism, and affirmative action. They championed prayer in the schools and tougher penalties for criminals. Together the Old and New Right added up to a powerful political combination, devoted to changing the very character of American society.

★ The Election of Ronald Reagan, 1980

Ronald Reagan was well suited to lead the gathering conservative crusade. Reared in a generation whose

values were formed well before the upheavals of the 1960s, he naturally sided with the New Right on social issues. In economic and social matters alike, he denounced the activist government and failed "social engineering" of the 1960s. Just as his early political hero, Franklin Roosevelt, had championed the "forgotten man" against big business, Reagan championed the "common man" against big government. He condemned federal intervention in local affairs, favoritism for minorities, and the elitism of arrogant bureaucrats. He aimed especially to win over from the Democratic column working-class and lower-middle-class white voters by implying that the Democratic party had become the party of big government and the exclusive tool of its minority constituents.

Though Reagan was no intellectual, he drew on the ideas of a small but influential group of thinkers known as "neoconservatives." Their ranks included Norman Podhoretz, editor of *Commentary* magazine, and Irving Kristol, editor of *The Public Interest*. Reacting against what they saw as the excesses of 1960s liberalism, the neoconservatives championed free-market capitalism liberated from government restraints, and they took tough, harshly anti-Soviet positions in foreign policy. They also questioned liberal welfare programs and affirmative-action policies and called for the reassertion of traditional values of individualism and the centrality of the family.

An actor-turned-politician, Reagan enjoyed enormous popularity with his crooked grin and aw-shucks manner. The son of a ne'er-do-well, impoverished Irish

President Ronald Reagan Older than any man previously elected to the presidency, Reagan displayed youthful vigor both on the campaign trail and in office.

© Bettmann/Corbis

American father with a fondness for the bottle, he had grown up in a small Illinois town. Reagan got his start in life in the depressed 1930s as a sports announcer for an Iowa radio station. Good looks and a way with words landed him acting jobs in Hollywood, where he became a B-grade star in the 1940s. He displayed a flair for politics as president of the Screen Actors Guild in the McCarthy era of the early 1950s, when he helped purge communists and other suspected "reds" from the film industry. In 1954 he became a spokesman for General Electric and began to abandon his New Deal-ish political views and increasingly to preach a conservative, antigovernment line. Reagan's growing skill at promoting the conservative cause inspired a group of wealthy California businessmen to help him launch his political career as governor of California from 1966 to 1974.

By 1980 the Republican party was ready to challenge the Democrats' hold on the White House. Bedeviled abroad and becalmed at home, Jimmy Carter's administration struck many Americans as bungling and befuddled. Carter's inability to control double-digit inflation was especially damaging. Frustrated critics bellyached loudly about the Georgian's alleged mismanagement of the nation's affairs.

Disaffection with Carter's apparent ineptitude ran deep even in his own Democratic party, where an "ABC" (Anybody but Carter) movement gathered steam. The liberal wing of the party found its champion in Senator Edward Kennedy of Massachusetts, the last survivor of the assassin-plagued Kennedy brothers. He and Carter slugged it out in a series of bruising primary elections, while delighted Republicans decorously proceeded to name Reagan their presidential nominee. In the end Kennedy's candidacy fell victim to the country's conservative mood and to lingering suspicions about a 1969 automobile accident on Chappaquiddick Island, Massachusetts, in which a young woman assistant was drowned when Kennedy's car plunged off a bridge. A badly battered Carter, his party divided and in disarray, was left to do battle with Reagan.

The Republican candidate proved to be a formidable campaigner. Using his professional acting skills to great advantage, Reagan attacked the incumbent's fumbling performance in foreign policy and blasted the "big-government" philosophy of the Democratic party (a philosophy that Carter did not fully embrace). Galloping inflation, sky-high interest rates, and a faltering economy also put the incumbent president on the defensive. Carter countered ineffectively with charges that Reagan was a trigger-happy cold warrior who might push the country into nuclear war.

Carter's spotty record in office was no defense against Reagan's popular appeal. On election day the Republican rang up a spectacular victory, bagging over 51 percent of the popular vote, while 41 percent went to Carter. Reflecting a small but vocal protest against both candidates, nearly 7 percent of the electorate voted for liberal Republican congressman John Anderson, who ran as an independent. The electoral count stood at 489 for Reagan and 49 for Carter, making him the first elected president to be unseated by voters since Herbert Hoover in 1932 (see Map 40.1). Equally startling, the Republicans gained control of the Senate for the first time in twenty-six years. Leading Democratic

In a speech to the National Association of Evangelicals on March 8, 1983, President Ronald Reagan (1911–2004) defined his stand on school prayer:

❝ The Declaration of Independence mentions the Supreme Being no less than four times. 'In God We Trust' is engraved on our coinage. The Supreme Court opens its proceedings with a religious invocation. And the Members of Congress open their sessions with a prayer. I just happen to believe the schoolchildren of the United States are entitled to the same privileges as Supreme Court Justices and Congressmen. ❞

1980

Candidate (Party)	Electoral Vote		Popular Vote	
Reagan (Republican)	489	90.9%	43,899,248	50.8%
Carter (Democrat)	49	9.1%	35,481,435	41.0%
Anderson (Independent)			5,719,437	6.6%

MAP 40.1 Presidential Election of 1980 (with electoral vote by state) This map graphically displays Reagan's land-slide victory over both Carter and Anderson. © Cengage Learning

federal government. He sought nothing less than the dismantling of the welfare state and the reversal of the political evolution of the preceding half-century. Assembling a conservative cabinet of "the best and the rightest," he took dead aim at what he regarded as the bloated federal budget. "Government is not the solution to our problem," he declared. "Government is the problem." Years of New Deal–style tax-and-spend programs, Reagan jested, had created a federal government that reminded him of the definition of a baby as a creature who was all appetite at one end, with no sense of responsibility at the other.

On his conservative crusade for smaller government, less bureaucracy, and freer markets, Reagan found common cause with the new leader of America's oldest ally, Great Britain. Conservative Margaret Thatcher became Britain's first female prime minister in 1979. With a mandate to improve her nation's economy, which had suffered through the 1970s as the United States had, she embarked on a mission to reduce the power of labor unions and government involvement in business, two of Reagan's chief goals. The philosophic kinship between "Ronnie and Maggie," as the press dubbed the two heads of state, went beyond

liberals, including George McGovern, had been targeted for defeat by well-heeled New Right groups. They went down like dead timber in the conservative windstorm that swept the country.

Carter showed dignity in defeat, delivering a thoughtful Farewell Address that stressed his efforts to scale down the deadly arms race, to promote human rights, and to protect the environment. In one of his last acts in office, he signed a bill preserving some 100 million acres of Alaska land for national parks, forests, and wildlife refuges. An unusually intelligent, articulate, and well-meaning president, he had been hampered by his lack of managerial talent and had been badly buffeted by events beyond his control, such as the soaring price of oil, runaway inflation, and the galling insult of the hostages still held in Iran. Though unsuccessful in the White House, Carter earned much admiration in later years for his humanitarian and human rights activities. He received the Nobel Peace Prize in 2002.

✯ The Reagan Revolution

Reagan's arrival in Washington was triumphal. The Iranians contributed to the festive mood by releasing the hostages on Reagan's Inauguration Day, January 20, 1981, after 444 days of captivity.

The new president, a hale and hearty sixty-nine-year-old, was devoted to fiscal fitness and a leaner

Coming Home After more than a year in captivity in Iran, these hostages were released on the very day of Ronald Reagan's presidential inauguration.

© Bettmann/Corbis

economics. Emboldened by each other, they strengthened the Anglo-American alliance through muscular foreign policy against a number of foes, especially the Soviet bloc. Their common refrain was that free markets made free peoples and that shrinking government meant keeping their nations safer from communism.

By the early 1980s, this antigovernment message found a receptive audience in the United States. In the two decades since 1960, federal spending had risen from about 18 percent of gross national product to nearly 23 percent. At the same time, the composition of the federal budget had been shifting from defense to entitlement programs, including Social Security and Medicare (see the chart in the Appendix). In 1973 the budget of the Department of Health, Education, and Welfare surpassed that of the Department of Defense. Citizens increasingly balked at paying the bills for further extension of government "benefits." After four decades of advancing New Deal and Great Society programs, a strong countercurrent took hold. Californians staged a "tax revolt" in 1978 (known by its official ballot title of **Proposition 13**) that slashed property taxes and forced painful cuts in government services. The California "tax quake" jolted other state capitals and even rocked the pillars of Congress in faraway Washington, D.C. Ronald Reagan had ridden this political shock wave to presidential victory in 1980 and now proceeded to rattle the "welfare state" to its very foundations.

Reagan pursued his smaller-government policies with near-religious zeal and remarkable effectiveness.

The Triumph of the Right, 1980 Republican conservatives scored a double victory in 1980, winning control of both the White House and the Senate. Aided by conservative Democratic "boll weevils," they also dominated the House of Representatives, and a new era of conservatism dawned in the nation's capital. Jim Borgman. Reprinted with permission of Universal Press Syndicate. All rights reserved.

He proposed a new federal budget that necessitated cuts of some $35 billion, mostly in social programs like food stamps and federally funded job-training centers. Reagan worked naturally in harness with the Republican majority in the Senate, but to get his way in the Democratic House, he undertook some old-fashioned politicking. He enterprisingly wooed a group of mostly southern conservative Democrats (dubbed **boll weevils**), who abandoned their own party's leadership to follow the president. The new president seemed strong and motivated, all the more so after a failed assassination attempt in March 1981 brought an outpouring of sympathy and support.

✷ The Battle of the Budget

Swept along on a tide of presidential popularity, Congress swallowed Reagan's budget proposals. The new president's triumph amazed political observers, especially defeated Democrats. He had descended upon Washington like an avenging angel of conservatism, kicking up a blinding whirlwind of political change. His impressive performance demonstrated the power of the presidency with a skill not seen since Lyndon Johnson's day. Out the window went the textbooks that had concluded, largely on the basis of the stalemated 1970s, that the Oval Office had been eclipsed by a powerful, uncontrollable Congress.

Reagan hardly rested to savor the sweetness of his victory. The second part of his economic program called for substantial reductions in marginal tax rates over a period of three years. Many Democrats, the president quipped, had "never met a tax they didn't hike." Thanks largely to Reagan's skill as a television performer and the continued defection of the "boll weevils" from the Democratic camp, the president again had his way. In late 1981 Congress approved a set of far-reaching tax reforms that lowered individual tax rates, reduced federal estate taxes, and created new tax-free savings plans for small investors. Reagan's **supply-side economics** advisers assured him that the combination of budgetary discipline and tax reduction would stimulate new investment, boost productivity, foster dramatic economic growth, and eventually even reduce the federal deficit.

But at first "supply-side" economics seemed to be a beautiful theory mugged by a gang of brutal facts, as the economy slid into its deepest recession since the 1930s. Unemployment reached nearly 11 percent in 1982, businesses folded, and several bank failures jolted the nation's entire financial system. The automobile industry, once the brightest jewel in America's industrial crown, turned in its dimmest performance in history. Battling against Japanese imports, major automakers reported losses in the hundreds of millions of dollars. Fuming and frustrated Democrats angrily charged that the president's budget cuts slashed especially cruelly at the poor and the handicapped and that his tax cuts favored the well-to-do. In reality, the anti-inflationary "tight money" policies that led to the so-called "Reagan recession" of 1981–1982 had been launched by the Federal Reserve Board in 1979, on Carter's watch.

Ignoring the yawping pack of Democratic critics, President Reagan and his economic advisers serenely waited for their supply-side economic policies (**Reaganomics**) to produce the promised results. The supply-siders seemed to be vindicated when a healthy economic recovery finally got under way in 1983. Yet the economy of the 1980s was not uniformly sound. For the first time in the twentieth century, income gaps widened between the richest and the poorest Americans. The poor got poorer and the very rich grew fabulously richer, while middle-class incomes largely stagnated. Symbolic of the new income stratification was the emergence of "yuppies," or young, urban professionals. Sporting Rolex watches and BMW sports cars, they made a near-religion out of conspicuous consumption. Though something of a stereotype and numbering only about 1.5 million people, yuppies showcased the values of materialism and the pursuit of wealth that came to symbolize the high-rolling 1980s.

Some economists located the sources of the economic upturn neither in the president's budget cuts and tax reforms nor in the go-get-'em avarice of the yuppies. It was massive military expenditures, they argued, that constituted the real foundation of 1980s prosperity. Reagan cascaded nearly $2 trillion dollars onto the Pentagon in the 1980s, asserting the need to close a "window of vulnerability" in the armaments race with the Soviet Union. Ironically, this conservative president thereby plunged the government into a red-ink bath of deficit spending that made the New Deal look downright stingy. Federal budget deficits topped $100 billion in 1982, and the government's books were nearly $200 billion out of balance in every subsequent year of the 1980s. Massive government borrowing to cover those deficits kept interest rates high, and high interest rates in turn elevated the value of the dollar to record altitudes in the international money markets. The soaring dollar was good news for American tourists and buyers of foreign cars, but it dealt crippling blows to American exporters, as the American international trade deficit reached a record $152 billion in 1987. The masters of international commerce and finance for a generation after World War II, Americans suddenly became the world's heaviest borrowers in the global economy of the 1980s.

✦ Reagan Renews the Cold War

Hard as nails toward the Soviet Union in his campaign speeches, Reagan saw no reason to soften up after he checked in at the White House. He claimed that the Soviets were "prepared to commit any crime, to lie, to cheat," in pursuit of their goals of world conquest. He denounced the Soviet Union as the "focus of evil in the modern world."

Reagan believed in negotiating with the Soviets—but only from a position of overwhelming strength. Accordingly, his strategy for dealing with Moscow was simple: by enormously expanding U.S. military capabilities, he could threaten the Soviets with a fantastically expensive new round of the arms race. The American economy, theoretically, could better bear this new financial burden than could the creaking Soviet system. Desperate to avoid economic ruin, Kremlin leaders would come to the bargaining table and sing Reagan's tune.

This strategy resembled a riverboat gambler's ploy. It wagered the enormous sum of Reagan's defense budgets on the hope that the other side would not call Washington's bluff and initiate a new cycle of arms competition. Reagan played his trump card in this risky game in March 1983, when he announced his intention to pursue a high-technology missile-defense system called the **Strategic Defense Initiative (SDI)**, popularly known as Star Wars. The plan called for orbiting battle stations in space that could fire laser beams or other

Star Wars Fantasies President Reagan's Strategic Defense Initiative (popularly known as Star Wars) evoked extravagant hopes for an impermeable defensive shield, but its daunting physical and engineering requirements also occasioned much ridicule in the scientific community.

The Hartford Courant

forms of concentrated energy to vaporize intercontinental missiles on liftoff. Reagan described SDI as offering potential salvation from the nuclear nightmare by throwing an "astrodome" defense shield over American cities. Most scientists considered this an impossible goal. But the deeper logic of SDI lay in its fit with Reagan's overall Soviet strategy. By pitching the arms contest onto a stratospheric plane of high technology and astronomical expense, it would further force the Kremlin's hand.

Relations with the Soviets further nosedived in late 1981, when the government of Poland, needled for over a year by a popular movement of workingpeople organized into a massive union called "Solidarity," clamped martial law on the troubled country. Reagan saw the heavy fist of the Kremlin inside this Polish iron glove, and he imposed economic sanctions on Poland and the USSR alike.

Dealing with the Soviet Union was additionally complicated by the inertia and ill health of the aging oligarchs in the Kremlin, three of whom died between late 1982 and early 1985. Relations grew even more tense when the Soviets, in September 1983, blasted from the skies a Korean passenger airliner that had inexplicably violated Soviet airspace. Hundreds of civilians, including many Americans, plummeted to their deaths in the frigid Sea of Okhotsk. By the end of 1983, all arms-control negotiations with the Soviets were broken off. The deepening chill of the Cold War was further felt in 1984, when USSR and Soviet-bloc athletes boycotted the Olympic Games in Los Angeles.

✦ Troubles Abroad

The volatile Middle Eastern pot continued to boil ominously. Israel badly strained its bonds of friendship with the United States by continuing to allow new settlements to be established in the occupied territory of the Jordan River's West Bank (see Map 40.2). Israel further raised the stakes in the Middle East in June 1982 when it invaded neighboring Lebanon, seeking to suppress once and for all the guerrilla bases from which Palestinian fighters harassed beleaguered Israel. The Palestinians were bloodily subdued, but Lebanon, already pulverized by years of episodic civil war, was plunged into armed chaos. President Reagan was obliged to send American troops to Lebanon in 1983 as part of an international peacekeeping force, but their presence did not bring peace. A suicide bomber crashed an explosives-laden truck into a United States Marine barracks on October 23, 1983, killing more than two hundred marines. President Reagan soon thereafter withdrew the remaining American troops, while

miraculously suffering no political damage from this horrifying and humiliating attack. His mystified Democratic opponents began to call him the "Teflon president," to whom nothing hurtful could stick.

Central America, in the United States' own backyard, also rumbled menacingly. A leftist revolution had deposed the long-time dictator of Nicaragua in 1979. President Carter had tried to ignore the hotly anti-American rhetoric of the revolutionaries, known as **Sandinistas**, and to establish good diplomatic relations with them. But cold warrior Reagan took their rhetoric at face value and hurled back at them some hot language of his own. He accused the Sandinistas of turning their country into a forward base for Soviet and Cuban military penetration of all of Central America. Brandishing photographs taken from high-flying spy planes, administration spokespeople claimed that Nicaraguan leftists were shipping weapons to revolutionary forces in tiny El Salvador, torn by violence since a coup in 1979.

Reagan sent military "advisers" to prop up the pro-American government of El Salvador. He also provided covert aid, including the CIA-engineered mining of harbors, to the rebel **contras** opposing the anti-American government of Nicaragua. Reagan flexed his military muscles elsewhere in the turbulent Caribbean. In a dramatic display of American might, in October 1983 he dispatched a heavy-firepower invasion force to the island of Grenada, where a military coup had killed the prime minister and brought Marxists to power. Swiftly overrunning the tiny island and ousting the insurgents, American troops vividly demonstrated Reagan's determination to assert the dominance of the United States in the Caribbean, just as Theodore Roosevelt had done (see Map 40.3).

✦ Round Two for Reagan

A confident Ronald Reagan, bolstered by a buoyant economy at home and by the popularity of his defiant posture abroad, met little opposition in his bid for a second White House term in 1984. His opponent was Democrat Walter Mondale, who made history by naming as his vice-presidential running mate Congresswoman Geraldine Ferraro of New York. She was the first woman ever to appear on a major-party presidential ticket. But even this dramatic gesture could not salvage Mondale's candidacy, which was fatally tainted by his service as vice president in the deeply discredited Carter administration. On election day Reagan walked away with 525 electoral votes to Mondale's 13, winning everywhere except in Mondale's home state of Minnesota and the District of Columbia. Reagan also over-

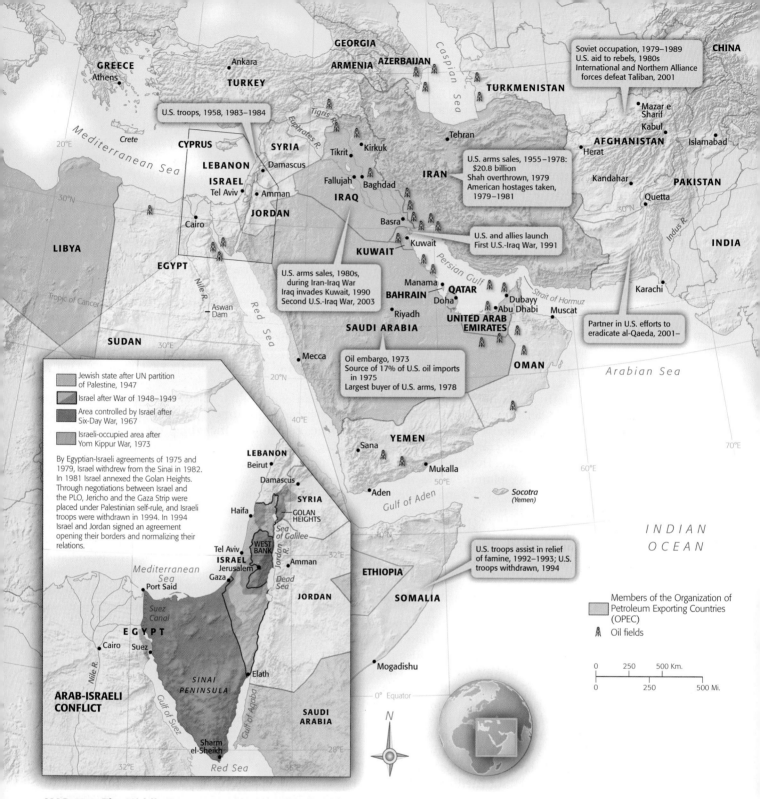

MAP 40.2 The Middle East A combination of political instability and precious petroleum resources has made the region from Egypt to Afghanistan an "arc of crisis." © Cengage Learning

Labels and callouts on map:

U.S. troops, 1958, 1983–1984

Soviet occupation, 1979–1989
U.S. aid to rebels, 1980s
International and Northern Alliance forces defeat Taliban, 2001

U.S. arms sales, 1955–1978:
$20.8 billion
Shah overthrown, 1979
American hostages taken, 1979–1981

U.S. and allies launch
First U.S.-Iraq War, 1991

U.S. arms sales, 1980s, during Iran-Iraq War
Iraq invades Kuwait, 1990
Second U.S.-Iraq War, 2003

Partner in U.S. efforts to eradicate al-Qaeda, 2001–

Oil embargo, 1973
Source of 17% of U.S. oil imports in 1975
Largest buyer of U.S. arms, 1978

U.S. troops assist in relief of famine, 1992–1993; U.S. troops withdrawn, 1994

Members of the Organization of Petroleum Exporting Countries (OPEC)

Oil fields

Inset map legend:

Jewish state after UN partition of Palestine, 1947

Israel after War of 1948–1949

Area controlled by Israel after Six-Day War, 1967

Israeli-occupied area after Yom Kippur War, 1973

By Egyptian-Israeli agreements of 1975 and 1979, Israel withdrew from the Sinai in 1982. In 1981 Israel annexed the Golan Heights. Through negotiations between Israel and the PLO, Jericho and the Gaza Strip were placed under Palestinian self-rule, and Israeli troops were withdrawn in 1994. In 1994 Israel and Jordan signed an agreement opening their borders and normalizing their relations.

ARAB-ISRAELI CONFLICT

whelmed Mondale in the popular vote—52,609,797 to 36,450,613.

Shrinking the federal government and reducing taxes had been the main objectives of Reagan's first term; foreign-policy issues dominated the news in his second term. The president soon found himself contending for the world's attention with a charismatic new Soviet leader, Mikhail Gorbachev, installed as chairman of the Soviet Communist party in March 1985. Gorbachev was personable, energetic, imaginative, and committed to radical reforms in the Soviet Union. He announced two policies with remarkable, even revolutionary, implications. **Glasnost**, or "openness," aimed to ventilate the secretive, repressive stuffiness of Soviet society by introducing free speech and a measure of political liberty. **Perestroika**, or "restructuring," was intended to revive the moribund Soviet economy by adopting many of the free-market practices—such as the profit motive and an end to subsidized prices—of the capitalist West.

Both glasnost and perestroika required that the Soviet Union shrink the size of its enormous military machine and redirect its energies to the dismal civilian economy. That requirement, in turn, necessitated an end to the Cold War. Gorbachev accordingly made warm overtures to the West, including an announcement in April 1985 that the Soviet Union would cease to deploy intermediate-range nuclear forces (INF) targeted at Western Europe, pending an agreement on their complete elimination. He pushed this goal when he met with Ronald Reagan at the first of four summit meetings, in Geneva in November 1985. A second summit meeting, in Reykjavik, Iceland, in October 1986, broke down when a furious Reagan stormed out, convinced that Gorbachev had come to end plans for the beloved SDI. But at a third summit, in Washington, D.C., in December 1987, the two leaders at last signed the **Intermediate-Range Nuclear Forces (INF) Treaty**, banning all of these missiles from Europe. Reagan and Gorbachev capped their new friendship in May 1988 at a final summit in Moscow. There Reagan, who had entered office condemning the "evil empire" of Soviet communism, warmly praised Gorbachev. Reagan, the consummate cold warrior, had been flexible and savvy enough to seize a historic opportunity to join with the Soviet chief to bring the Cold War to a kind of conclusion. For this, history would give both leaders high marks.

Reagan made other decisive moves in foreign policy. His administration provided strong backing in February 1986 for Corazon Aquino's ouster of dictator Ferdinand Marcos in the Philippines. Reagan also ordered a lightning air raid against Libya in 1986, in retaliation for alleged Libyan sponsorship of terrorist attacks, including a bomb blast in a West Berlin discotheque that killed a U.S. serviceman.

MAP 40.3 Central America and the Caribbean This region, so important to the United States throughout its history, remained a hotbed of unrest through the last years of the Cold War and beyond. © Cengage Learning

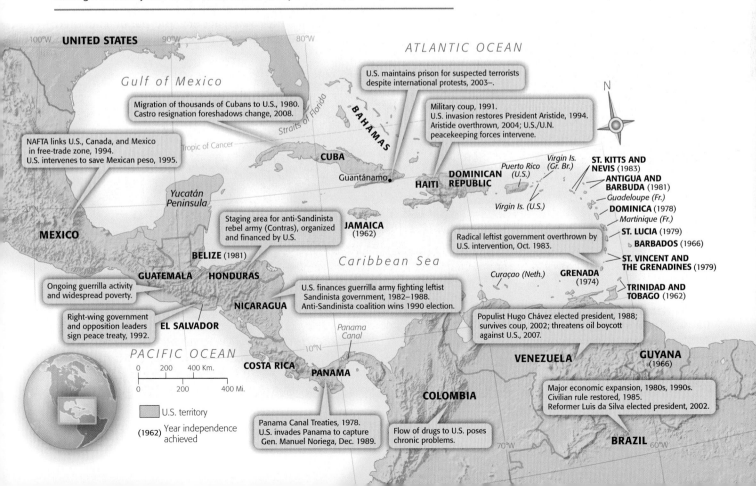

East Meets West President Reagan greets Soviet leader Mikhail Gorbachev at a summit meeting in Moscow in May 1988.

✵ The Iran-Contra Imbroglio

Two foreign-policy problems seemed insoluble to Reagan: the continuing captivity of a number of American hostages, seized by Muslim extremist groups in bleeding, battered Lebanon; and the continuing grip on power of the left-wing Sandinista government in Nicaragua. The president repeatedly requested that Congress provide military aid to the contra rebels fighting against the Sandinista regime. Congress repeatedly refused, and the administration grew increasingly frustrated, even obsessed, in its search for a means to help the contras.

Unknown to the American public, some Washington officials saw a possible linkage between the two thorny problems of the Middle Eastern hostages and the Central American Sandinistas. In 1985 American diplomats secretly arranged arms sales to Iran, which

was mired in a devastating territorial war with neighboring Iraq. In return, the Iranians helped obtain the release of at least one American hostage held by Middle Eastern terrorists. Meanwhile, the money Iran paid for the American weapons was diverted to the contras in Nicaragua. These actions brazenly violated a congressional ban on military aid to the Nicaraguan rebels—not to mention Reagan's repeated vow that he would never negotiate with terrorists. Washington also continued to support Iraqi dictator Saddam Hussein, to whom it sold weapons used against Iran.

News of these secret dealings broke in November 1986 and ignited a firestorm of controversy. President Reagan claimed he was innocent of wrongdoing and ignorant of his subordinates' activities. Reviving a refrain from the Watergate era, the public clamored to know "what the president knew and when he knew

Contra Rebel Troops Head for Battle These rebels were long-seasoned and battle-scarred veterans of Nicaragua's civil war by the time this photograph was taken in 1987.

On March 4, 1987, President Ronald Reagan somewhat confusingly tried to explain his role (or lack of role) in the arms-for-hostages deal with Iran:

"A few months ago I told the American people I did not trade arms for hostages. My heart and my best intentions still tell me that is true, but the facts and the evidence tell me it is not.**"**

it." Although Reagan was never found to have lied outright, a congressional committee condemned the "secrecy, deception, and disdain for the law" displayed by administration officials and concluded that "if the president did not know what his national security advisers were doing, he should have."

The **Iran-Contra affair** cast a dark shadow over the Reagan record on foreign policy, tending to obscure the president's outstanding achievement in establishing a new relationship with the Soviets. Out of the several Iran-Contra investigations, a picture emerged of Reagan as a lazy, perhaps even senile, president who napped through meetings and paid little or no attention to the details of policy. Reagan's critics pounced on this portrait as proof that the movie-star-turned-politician was a mental lightweight who had merely acted his way through the role of the presidency without really understanding the script. But despite these damaging revelations, Reagan remained among the most popular and beloved presidents in modern American history.

✴ Reagan's Economic Legacy

Ronald Reagan had taken office vowing to invigorate the American economy by rolling back government regulations, lowering taxes, and balancing the budget. He did ease many regulatory rules, and he pushed major tax reform bills through Congress in 1981 and 1986. But a balanced budget remained grotesquely out of reach. Supply-side economic theory had promised that lower taxes would actually *increase* government revenue because they would stimulate the economy as a whole. But, in fact, the combination of tax reduction and huge increases in military spending opened a vast "revenue hole" of $200 billion annual deficits. In his eight years in office, President Reagan added nearly $2 trillion to the national debt—more than all of his predecessors combined, including those who had fought protracted global wars (see Figure 40.1).

The staggering deficits of the Reagan years assuredly constituted a great economic failure. And because

so much of the Reagan-era debt was financed by foreign lenders, especially the Japanese, the deficits virtually guaranteed that future generations of Americans would either have to work harder than their parents, lower their standard of living, or both to pay their foreign creditors when the bills came due.

But if the deficits represented an economic failure, they also constituted, strangely enough, a kind of political triumph. Among the paramount goals of Reagan's political life was his ambition to slow the growth of government, and especially to block or even repeal the social programs launched in the era of Lyndon Johnson's Great Society. By appearing to make new social spending both practically and politically impossible for the foreseeable future, the deficits served exactly that purpose. They achieved, in short, Reagan's highest political objective: the containment of the welfare state. Ronald Reagan thus ensured the long-term perpetuation of his dearest political values to a degree that few presidents have managed to achieve. For better or worse, the consequences of "Reaganomics" would be large and durable.

Yet another legacy of the 1980s was a sharp reversal of a long-term trend toward a more equitable distribution of income and an increasing squeeze on the middle class. In the early 1990s, median household income (in 1993 dollars) actually declined, from about $33,500 in 1989 to about $31,000 in 1993 (see Figure 40.2). Whether that disturbing trend should be attributed to Reagan's policies or to more deeply running economic currents remained controversial.

✴ The Religious Right

Religion pervaded American politics in the 1980s. Especially conspicuous was a coalition of conservative, evangelical Christians known as the religious right. In 1979 the Reverend Jerry Falwell, an evangelical minister from Lynchburg, Virginia, founded a political organization called the **Moral Majority**. Falwell preached with great success against sexual permissiveness, abortion, feminism, and the spread of gay rights. In its first two years, the Moral Majority registered between 2 million and 3 million voters. Using radio, direct-mail marketing, and cable TV, "televangelists" reached huge audiences in the 1980s, collected millions of dollars, and became aggressive political advocates of conservative causes.

Members of the religious right were sometimes called "movement conservatives," a term that recalls the left-wing protest movements of the 1960s. In many ways the religious right of the 1980s was a reflection of, or answer to, sixties radicalism. Feminists in the 1960s declared that "the personal was political." The

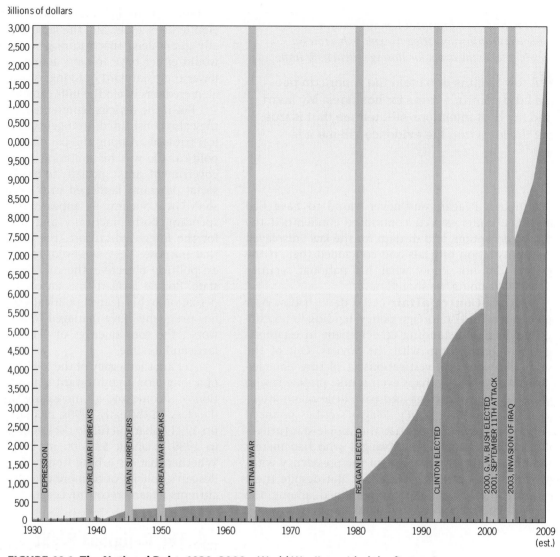

FIGURE 40.1 The National Debt, 1930–2009 World War II provided the first major boost to the national debt. The policies of the Reagan and George H. W. Bush administrations, 1981–1993, explosively expanded the debt to the $4 trillion level. By the 1990s, 14 percent of federal revenues went to interest payments on the debt. The budget surpluses created by the booming economy of the second Clinton administration (1997–2001) raised the prospect that the debt might be paid off. But the combination of the George W. Bush tax cuts and increased military spending sent the debt soaring again after 2001. Those tax cuts, combined with the revenue losses and stimulus expenditures occasioned by the "Great Recession" that began in 2008, kicked the debt up to unprecedented peacetime levels, approaching 100 percent of GDP. Real-time updates of the public debt are available from the Department of the Treasury's Bureau of the Public Debt, at http://www.publicdebt. treas.gov. (Sources: *Historical Statistics of the United States* and *Statistical Abstract of the United States*, relevant years; Office of Management and Budget Historical Tables.)

religious right did the same. What had in the past been personal matters—gender roles, homosexuality, and prayer—became the organizing ground for a powerful political movement. Like advocates of multiculturalism and affirmative action, the religious right practiced a form of "identity politics." But rather than defining themselves as Latino voters or gay voters, they declared themselves Christian or pro-life voters. The New Right also mimicked the New Left in some of its tactics. If the left had consciousness-raising sessions, the right had prayer meetings. Adherents articulated their positions in a language of rights and entitlements, as in the

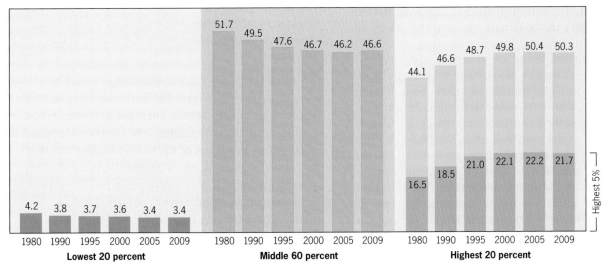

FIGURE 40.2 Share of Income Received by Families, by Quintile, 1980–2009 Since 1980 the incomes of the lowest 20 percent and the middle 60 percent have been shrinking, while the incomes of the highest 20 percent, and particularly the top 5 percent, have climbed steadily. (Source: *Statistical Abstract of the United States*, 2010; U.S. Census Bureau *Consumer Income Report*, relevant years.)

"right-to-life" (or anti-abortion) movement. They even mirrored the tactics of civil disobedience. Protesters in the 1960s blocked entrances to draft offices; protesters in the 1980s blocked entrances to abortion clinics.

Several leaders of the religious right fell from grace in the latter part of the decade. One tearfully admitted to repeated trysts with prostitutes. Another went to prison following revelations of his own financial and sexual misconduct. But such scandals would not shake the faith of America's conservative Christians or diminish the new political clout of activist, evangelical religionists.

✦ Conservatism in the Courts

If the budget was Reagan's chief weapon in the war against the welfare state, the courts became his principal instrument in the "cultural wars" demanded by the religious right. By the time he left office, Reagan had appointed a near-majority of all sitting judges. Equally important, he had named three conservative-minded justices to the U.S. Supreme Court. They included Sandra Day O'Connor, a brilliant, public-spirited Arizona judge. When she was sworn in on September 25, 1981, she became the first woman to ascend to the high bench in the Court's nearly two-hundred-year history.

Reaganism repudiated two great icons of the liberal political culture: affirmative action and abortion. The Court showed its newly conservative colors in 1984, when it decreed, in a case involving Memphis firefighters, that union rules about job seniority could outweigh affirmative-action concerns in guiding promotion policies in the city's fire department. In two cases in 1989 (*Ward's Cove Packing* v. *Antonia* and *Martin* v. *Wilks*), the Court made it more difficult to prove that an employer practiced racial discrimination in hiring and made it easier for white males to argue that they were the victims of reverse discrimination by employers who

The Moral Majority, 1981 Television evangelist and religious leader the Reverend Jerry Falwell mobilized his national Moral Majority organization in support of Ronald Reagan's presidential campaign in 1980 and a conservative social agenda.

Eve Arnold/Magnum Photos, Inc.

followed affirmative-action practices. Congress passed legislation in 1991 that partially reversed the effects of those decisions.

The contentious issue of abortion also reached the Court in 1989. In the case of *Roe* v. *Wade* in 1973, the Supreme Court had prohibited states from making laws that interfered with a woman's right to an abortion during the early months of pregnancy. For nearly two decades, that decision had been the bedrock principle on which "pro-choice" advocates built their case for abortion rights. It had also provoked bitter criticism from Roman Catholics and various "right-to-life" groups, who wanted a virtually absolute ban on all abortions. In *Webster* v. *Reproductive Health Services*, the Court in July 1989 did not entirely overturn *Roe*, but it seriously compromised *Roe*'s protection of abortion rights. By approving a Missouri law that imposed certain restrictions on abortion, the Court signaled that it was inviting the states to legislate in an area in which *Roe* had previously forbidden them to legislate. The Court renewed that invitation in *Planned Parenthood* v.

"WELL, IT'S ABOUT TIME"

The Justice Is a Lady, 1981 Herblock hails Sandra Day O'Connor's appointment to the Supreme Court. *The Justice Is a Lady, A 1981 Herblock Cartoon, copyright by The Herb Block Foundation*

> *Speaking to the National Association of Evangelicals, President Ronald Reagan said the following about abortion:*
>
> "More than a decade ago, a Supreme Court decision [*Roe* v. *Wade*, 1973] literally wiped off the books of fifty states statutes protecting the rights of unborn children. Abortion on demand now takes the lives of up to 1½ million unborn children a year. Human life legislation ending this tragedy will some day pass the Congress, and you and I must never rest until it does. Unless and until it can be proven that the unborn child is not a living entity, then its right to life, liberty, and the pursuit of happiness must be protected."

Casey in 1992, when it ruled that states could restrict access to abortion as long as they did not place an "undue burden" on the woman. Using this standard, the Court held that Pennsylvania could not compel a wife to notify her husband about an abortion but could require a minor child to notify parents, as well as other restrictions.

Right-to-life advocates were at first delighted by the *Webster* decision. But the Court's ruling also galvanized pro-choice organizations into a new militancy. Bruising, divisive battles loomed as state legislatures across the land confronted abortion. This painful cultural conflict over the unborn was also part of the Reagan era's bequest to the future.

✦ Referendum on Reaganism in 1988

Republicans lost control of the Senate in the off-year elections of November 1986. Hopes rose among Democrats that the "Reagan Revolution" might be showing signs of political vulnerability at last. The newly Democratic majority in the Senate flexed its political muscles in 1987 when it rejected an ultraconservative nominee for the Supreme Court.

Democrats also relished the prospect of making political hay out of both the Iran-Contra affair and disquieting signs of economic trouble. The "double mountain" of deficits—the federal budget deficit and the international trade deficit—continued to grow ominously. Falling oil prices blighted the economy of the Southwest, slashing real estate values and undermining hundreds of savings and loan (S&L) institutions. The damage to the S&Ls was so massive that a federal rescue operation was eventually estimated to carry a price tag of well over $500 billion. Meanwhile, many American banks found themselves holding near-worthless loans they had unwisely foisted upon Third World countries, especially in Latin America. In 1984 it took federal assistance to save Continental Illinois Bank from a catastrophic failure. More banks and savings institutions were folding than at any time since the Great Depression of the 1930s. A wave of mergers, acquisitions, and leveraged buyouts washed over Wall Street, leaving many brokers and traders megarich and many companies saddled with megadebt. A cold spasm of fear struck the money markets on **Black Monday**, October 19, 1987, when the leading stock-market index plunged 508 points—the largest one-day decline in history to that point. This crash, said *Newsweek* magazine, heralded "the final collapse of the money culture . . . , the death knell of the 1980s." But as Mark Twain famously commented about his own obituary, this announcement proved premature.

Hoping to cash in on these ethical and economic anxieties, a pack of Democrats—dubbed the "Seven Dwarfs" by derisive Republicans—chased after their party's 1988 presidential nomination. The handsome and charismatic Democratic front-runner, former Colorado senator Gary Hart, was forced to drop out of the race in May 1987 after charges of sexual misconduct. African American candidate Jesse Jackson, a rousing speechmaker who hoped to forge a "rainbow coalition" of minorities and the disadvantaged, campaigned energetically. But the Democratic nomination in the end went to the coolly cerebral governor of Massachusetts, Michael Dukakis. Republicans nominated Reagan's vice president, George H. W. Bush, who ran largely on the Reagan record of tax cuts, strong defense policies, toughness on crime, opposition to abortion, and a long-running if hardly robust economic expansion. Dukakis made little headway exploiting the ethical and economic sore spots and came across to television viewers as almost supernaturally devoid of emotion. On election day the voters gave him just 41,016,429 votes to 47,946,422 for Bush. The Electoral College count was 111 to 426.

Hollywood director Oliver Stone's (b. 1946) film Wall Street *both romanticized and vilified the business culture of the 1980s. The character of Gordon Gekko, inspired by real-life corporate raider Ivan Boesky, captured the spirit of the times:*

❝Ladies and gentlemen, greed is good. Greed works, greed is right. . . . Greed for life, money, love, knowledge, has marked the upward surge of mankind—and greed, mark my words, will save the malfunctioning corporation called the U.S.A.**❞**

✷ George H. W. Bush and the End of the Cold War

George Herbert Walker Bush was born with a silver ladle in his mouth. His father had served as a U.S. senator from Connecticut, and young George had enjoyed a first-rate education at Yale. After service in World War II, he had amassed a modest fortune of his own in the oil business in Texas. His deepest commitment, however, was to public service; he left the business world to serve briefly as a congressman and then held various posts in several Republican administrations, including emissary to China, ambassador to the United Nations, director of the Central Intelligence Agency, and vice president. He capped this long political career when he was inaugurated president in January 1989, promising to work for "a kinder, gentler America."

In the first months of the Bush administration, the communist world commanded the planet's fascinated attention. Everywhere in the communist bloc, it seemed, the season of democracy had arrived.

In China hundreds of thousands of prodemocracy demonstrators thronged through Beijing's Tiananmen Square in the spring of 1989. They proudly flourished a thirty-foot-high "Goddess of Democracy," modeled on the Statue of Liberty, as a symbol of their aspirations.

But in June of that year, China's aging and autocratic rulers brutally crushed the prodemocracy movement. Tanks rolled over the crowds, and

George Herbert Walker Bush (b. 1924) Campaigning, October 1988 Bush soundly defeated Democratic candidate Michael Dukakis in the November 1988 election.

Tiananmen Square, Beijing, China, June 1989 The Chinese communist state mobilized all its forces against students demonstrating for a more democratic China.

AP Images

machine-gunners killed hundreds of protesters. World opinion roundly condemned the bloody suppression of the prodemocracy demonstrators. President Bush joined in the criticism. Yet despite angry demands in Congress for punitive restrictions on trade with China, the president insisted on maintaining normal relations with Beijing.

Stunning changes also shook Eastern Europe. Long oppressed by puppet regimes propped up by Soviet guns, the region was revolutionized in just a few startling months in 1989. The Solidarity movement in Poland led the way when it toppled Poland's communist government in August. With dizzying speed, communist regimes collapsed in Hungary, Czechoslovakia, East Germany, and even hyperrepressive Romania. In December 1989, jubilant Germans danced atop the hated Berlin Wall, symbol of the division of Germany and all of Europe into two armed and hostile camps. The wall itself soon came down, heralding the imminent end of the forty-five-year-long Cold War. Chunks of the wall's

Fallen Idol Romanians toppled this statue of Vladimir Lenin in 1990, symbolically marking the collapse of the Marxian dream that had agitated the world for more than a century.

Gao Gross/Image Works/Getty Images

MAP 40.4 The End of the Cold War Changed the Map of Europe © Cengage Learning

concrete became instant collectors' items—gray souvenirs of a grim episode in Europe's history. With the approval of the victorious Allied powers of World War II, the two Germanys, divided since 1945, were at last reunited in October 1990.

Most startling of all were the changes that rolled over the heartland of world communism, the Soviet Union itself. Mikhail Gorbachev's policies of glasnost and perestroika had set in motion a groundswell that surged out of his control. Old-guard hard-liners, in a last-gasp effort to preserve the tottering communist system, attempted to dislodge Gorbachev with a military coup in August 1991. With the support of Boris Yeltsin, president of the Russian Republic (one of the several republics that composed the Union of Soviet Socialist Republics, or USSR), Gorbachev foiled the plotters. But his days were numbered. In December 1991 Gorbachev resigned as Soviet president. He had become a leader without a country as the Soviet Union dissolved into its component parts, some fifteen republics loosely confederated in the **Commonwealth of Independent States (CIS)**, with Russia the most powerful state and Yeltsin the dominant leader. To varying degrees, all the new governments in the CIS repudiated communism and embraced democratic reforms and a free-market economy (see Map 40.4).

These developments astonished the "experts," who had long preached that the steely vise-grip of communist rule never could be peacefully broken. Yet suddenly and almost miraculously, the totalitarian tonnage of communist oppression had been rendered politically weightless. Most spectacularly, the demise of the Soviet Union wrote a definitive finish to the Cold War era. More than four decades of nail-biting tension between two nuclear superpowers, the Soviet Union and the United States, evaporated when the USSR dismantled itself. With the Soviet Union swept into the dustbin of history and communism all but extinct, Bush spoke hopefully of a "new world order," where democracy would reign and diplomacy would supersede weaponry. Some observers even saw in these developments "the end of history," in the sense that democracy, victorious in its two-century-long struggle against foes on the left and right, had no ideological battles left to fight.

Exultant Americans joked that the USSR had become the "USS *were*." But the disintegration of the Soviet Union was no laughing matter. Rankling questions remained. For example, who would honor arms-control agreements with the United States? Which of the successor states of the former Soviet Union would take command of the formidable Soviet nuclear arsenal? (A partial answer was provided in early 1993, when

In his state of the union address on January 31, 1990, President George H. W. Bush (b. 1924) declared,

" The events of the year just ended, the revolution of '89, have been a chain reaction, changes so striking that it marks the beginning of a new era in the world's affairs. "

Just six months later, speaking at Stanford University, Soviet president Mikhail Gorbachev (b. 1931) said,

" The Cold War is now behind us. Let us not wrangle over who won it. It is in the common interest of our two countries and nations not to fight this trend toward cooperation, but rather to promote it. "

President Bush, in one of his last official acts, signed the START II accord with Russian president Boris Yeltsin, committing both powers to reduce their long-range nuclear arsenals by two-thirds within ten years.)

Throughout the former Soviet empire, waves of nationalistic fervor and long-suppressed ethnic and racial hatreds rolled across the vast land as communism's roots were wrenched out. A particularly nasty conflict erupted in the Russian Caucasus in 1991, when the Chechnyan minority tried to declare their independence from Russia, prompting President Yeltsin to send in Russian troops. Ethnic warfare flared in other disintegrating communist countries as well, notably in misery-drenched Yugoslavia, racked by vicious "ethnic cleansing" campaigns against various minorities.

The end of the Cold War also proved a mixed blessing for the United States. For nearly half a century, the containment of Soviet communism had been the paramount goal of U.S. foreign policy. Indeed the Cold War era had been the only lengthy period in American history when the United States had consistently pursued an internationalist foreign policy. With the Soviet threat now canceled, would the United States revert to its traditional isolationism? What principles would guide American diplomacy now that "anticommunism" had lost its relevance?

The Soviet-American rivalry, with its demands for high levels of military preparedness, had also deeply shaped and even invigorated the U.S. economy. Huge economic sectors such as aerospace were heavily sustained by military contracts. The economic cost of beating swords into plowshares became painfully apparent in 1991 when the Pentagon announced the closing of thirty-four military bases and canceled a $52 billion order for a navy attack plane. More closings and cancellations followed. Communities that had been drenched with Pentagon dollars now nearly dried up, especially in hard-hit southern California, where scores of defense plants shut their doors and unemployment soared. The problems of weaning the U.S. economy from its decades of dependence on defense spending tempered the euphoria of Americans as they welcomed the Cold War's long-awaited finale.

Elsewhere in the world, democracy marched triumphantly forward. The white regime in South Africa took a giant step toward liberating that troubled land from its racist past when in 1990 it freed African leader Nelson Mandela, who had served twenty-seven years

The Agony of Yugoslavia, 1992 These Bosnian refugees from the town of Jajce illustrate the plight of millions of Yugoslavians as their country slid into vicious interethnic battles in the wake of the Cold War's conclusion.

Black Star/Stockphoto.com

in prison for conspiring to overthrow the government. Four years later Mandela was elected South Africa's president. Free elections in Nicaragua in February 1990 removed the leftist Sandinistas from power. Two years later peace came at last to war-ravaged El Salvador.

✴ The Persian Gulf Crisis

Sadly, the end of the Cold War did not mean the end of all wars. President Bush flexed the United States' still-intimidating military muscles in tiny Panama in December 1989, when he sent airborne troops to capture dictator and drug lord Manuel Noriega.

Still more ominous events in the summer of 1990 severely tested Bush's dream of a democratic and peaceful new world order. On August 2 Saddam Hussein, the brutal and ambitious ruler of Iraq, sent his armies to overrun Kuwait, a tiny, oil-rich desert sheikdom on Iraq's southern frontier.

Oil fueled Saddam's aggression. Financially exhausted by its eight-year war with Iran, which had ended in a stalemate in 1988, Iraq needed Kuwait's oil to pay its huge war bills. Saddam's larger design was ironfisted control over the entire Persian Gulf region. With his hand thus firmly clutching the world's economic jugular vein, he dreamed of dictating the terms of oil supplies to the industrial nations, and perhaps of totally extinguishing the Arabs' enemy, Israel.

Ironically, the United States and its allies had helped supply Saddam with the tools of aggression. He was widely known to be a thug and assassin who intimidated his underlings by showing them the bodies of his executed adversaries hanging on meat hooks. But in the 1980s, American enmity for Islamic-fundamentalist Iran was intense, and Saddam was at war with Iran. Assuming that "the enemy of my enemy is my friend," American policymakers helped build Saddam's military machine into a formidable force.

On August 2, 1990, Saddam's army roared into Kuwait. The speed and audacity of the invasion was stunning, but the world responded just as swiftly. The United Nations Security Council unanimously condemned the invasion on August 3 and demanded the immediate and unconditional withdrawal of Iraq's troops. When an economic embargo failed to squeeze the Iraqis into compliance by November, the Security Council delivered an ultimatum to Saddam to leave Kuwait by January 15, 1991, or U.N. forces would "use all necessary means" to expel his troops. For perhaps the first time in the post–World War II era, the U.N. seemed to be fulfilling its founders' dreams that it could preserve international order by putting guns where its mouth was. It also put them where the world's critical oil supply was.

In a logistical operation of astonishing complexity, the United States spearheaded a massive international military deployment on the sandy Arabian Peninsula. As the January 15 deadline approached, some 539,000 U.S. soldiers, sailors, and pilots—many of them women and all of them members of the new, post-Vietnam, all-volunteer American military—swarmed into the Persian Gulf region. They were joined by nearly 270,000 troops, pilots, and sailors from twenty-eight other countries in the coalition opposed to Iraq. When all diplomatic efforts to resolve the crisis failed, the U.S. Congress voted regretfully on January 12 to approve the use of force. On January 16 the time bomb of war ticked off its last beats.

The United States and its U.N. allies unleashed a hellish air attack against Iraq. For thirty-seven days, warplanes pummeled targets in occupied Kuwait and in Iraq itself, in an awesome display of high-technology, precision-targeting modern warfare. Iraq responded to this pounding by launching several dozen "Scud" short-range ballistic missiles against military and civilian targets in Saudi Arabia and Israel. These missile attacks claimed several lives but did no significant military damage.

Yet if Iraq made but a feeble military response to the air campaign, the allied commander, the beefy and blunt American general Norman ("Stormin' Norman") Schwarzkopf, took nothing for granted. Saddam, who had threatened to wage "the mother of all battles," had the capacity to inflict awful damage. Iraq had stockpiled tons of chemical and biological weapons, including poison gas and the means to spread epidemics of anthrax. Saddam's tactics also included ecological warfare as he released a gigantic oil slick into the Persian Gulf to forestall amphibious assault and ignited hundreds of oil-well fires, whose smoky plumes shrouded the ground from aerial view. Faced with these horrifying tactics, Schwarzkopf's strategy was starkly simple: soften the Iraqis with relentless bombing, then suffocate them on the ground with a tidal-wave rush of troops and armor.

On February 23 the dreaded and long-awaited land war began. Dubbed **Operation Desert Storm**, it lasted only four days—the "hundred-hour war" (see Map 40.5). With lightning speed the U.N. forces penetrated deep into Iraq, outflanking the occupying forces in Kuwait and blocking the enemy's ability either to retreat or to reinforce. Allied casualties were amazingly light, whereas much of Iraq's remaining fighting force was quickly destroyed or captured. On February 27 Saddam accepted a cease-fire, and Kuwait was liberated.

Most Americans cheered the war's rapid and enormously successful conclusion. Many people echoed President Bush's sentiments when he declared, "By God,

The Highway of Death The allied coalition wreaked gruesome destruction on Iraqi forces fleeing back to Iraq after their defeat in Kuwait in 1991.

© Peter Turnley/Corbis

we've kicked the Vietnam Syndrome once and for all!" But when the smoke cleared, Saddam Hussein had survived to menace the world another day. America and its allies had agreed to the liberation of Kuwait, but Bush, fearing that a full assault on Baghdad would cost many lives and much public support, stopped well short of overthrowing the tyrant Saddam. The perpetually troubled Middle East knew scarcely less trouble after Desert Storm had ceased to thunder, and the United States, for better or worse, found itself even more deeply ensnared in the region's web of mortal hatreds and intractable conflicts.

MAP 40.5 Operation Desert Storm: The Ground War, February 23–27, 1991 © Cengage Learning

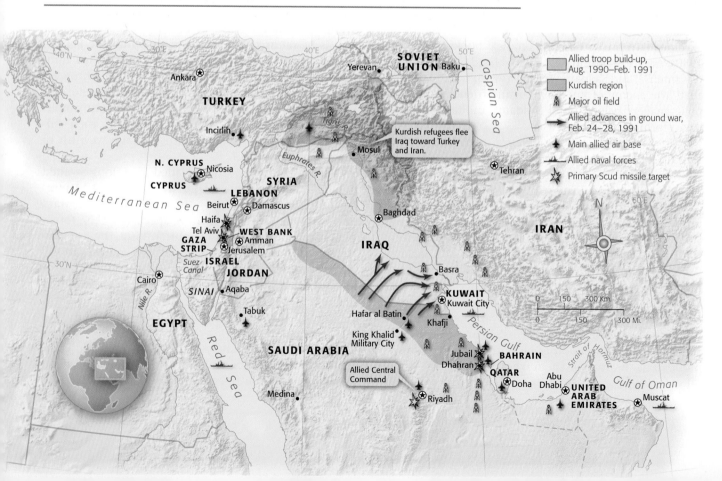

� Bush on the Home Front

George H. W. Bush partly redeemed his pledge to work for a "kinder, gentler America" when he signed the **Americans with Disabilities Act (ADA)** in 1990, a landmark law prohibiting discrimination against the 43 million U.S. citizens with physical or mental disabilities. The president also signed a major water projects bill in 1992 that fundamentally reformed the distribution of subsidized federal water in the West. The bill put the interests of the environment ahead of agriculture, especially in California's heavily irrigated Central Valley, and made much more water available to the West's thirsty cities.

The new president continued to aggravate the explosive "social issues" that had so divided Americans throughout the 1980s, especially the nettlesome questions of affirmative action and abortion. In 1990 Bush's Department of Education challenged the legality of college scholarships targeted for racial minorities. Bush repeatedly threatened to veto civil rights legislation that would make it easier for employees to prove discrimination in hiring and promotion practices. (He grudgingly accepted a watered-down civil rights bill in 1991.)

Most provocatively, in 1991 Bush nominated for the Supreme Court the conservative African American jurist Clarence Thomas, a stern critic of affirmative action. Thomas's nomination was loudly opposed by liberal groups, including organized labor, the National Association for the Advancement of Colored People (NAACP), and the National Organization for Women (NOW). Reflecting irreconcilable divisions over affirmative action and abortion, the Senate Judiciary Committee concluded its hearings on the nomination with a divided 7–7 vote and forwarded the matter to the full Senate without a recommendation.

Then, just days before the Senate was scheduled to vote in early October 1991, a press leak revealed that Anita Hill, a law professor at the University of Oklahoma, had accused Thomas of sexual harassment. The Senate Judiciary Committee was forced to reopen its hearings. For days a prurient American public sat glued to their television sets as Hill graphically detailed her charges of sexual improprieties and Thomas angrily responded. In the end, by a 52–48 vote, the Senate confirmed Thomas as the second African American ever to sit on the supreme bench (Thurgood Marshall was the first). While many Americans hailed Hill as a heroine for focusing the nation's attention on issues of sexual harassment, Thomas maintained that Hill's widely publicized, unproved allegations amounted to "a high-tech lynching for uppity blacks who in any way deign to think for themselves, to do for themselves."

The furor over Thomas's confirmation suggested that the social issues that had helped produce three Republican presidential victories in the 1980s were losing some of their electoral appeal. Many women, enraged by the all-male judiciary committee's behavior in the Thomas hearings, grew increasingly critical of the president's uncompromising stand on abortion. A "gender gap" opened between the two political parties, as pro-choice women grew increasingly cool toward the strong anti-abortion stand of the Republicans.

© Ron Sachs/CNP/Corbis

President George H. W. Bush Signs the Americans with Disabilities Act on the South Lawn of the White House, July 26, 1990

Still more damaging to President Bush's political health was the economy, which sputtered and stalled almost from the outset of his administration. By 1992 the unemployment rate exceeded 7 percent. It approached 10 percent in the key state of California, ravaged by defense cutbacks. The federal budget deficit continued to mushroom cancerously, topping $250 billion in each of Bush's years as president. In a desperate attempt to stop the hemorrhage of red ink, Bush agreed in 1990 to a budget increase that included $133 billion in new taxes.

Bush's 1990 tax and budget package added up to a political catastrophe. In his 1988 presidential campaign, Bush had belligerently declared, "Read my lips—no new taxes." Now he had flagrantly broken that campaign promise.

Varying Viewpoints
Where Did Modern Conservatism Come From?

Ronald Reagan's election surprised many historians. Reflecting a liberal political outlook that is common among academic scholars, they were long accustomed to understanding American history as an inexorable, almost evolutionary, unfolding of liberal principles, including the quests for economic equality, social justice, and active government. That point of view animated the enormously popular writings of the so-called progressive historians, such as Charles and Mary Beard, earlier in the century (see "Varying Viewpoints: The Populists: Radicals or Reactionaries?" on p. 510). For the Beards, "conservatives" were the rich, privileged elites bent on preserving their wealth and power and determined to keep government impotent, but doomed in the end to give way to the forces of liberal democracy.

Even the "New Left" revisionists of the 1960s, while critical of the celebratory tone of their progressive forebears, were convinced that the deepest currents of American history flowed leftward. But whether they were liberal or revisionist, most scholars writing in the first three post–World War II decades dismissed conservatism as an obsolete political creed. The revisionists were much more interested in decrying liberalism's deficiencies than in analyzing conservatism's strengths. Liberals and revisionists alike abandoned the Beards' image of powerful conservative elites and offered instead a contemptuous portrait of conservatives as fringe wackos—paranoid McCarthyites or racist demagogues who, in the words of the liberal critic Lionel Trilling, trafficked only in "irritable mental gestures which seem to resemble ideas." Such an outlook is conspicuous in books such as Daniel Bell's *The Radical Right* (1963) and Richard Hofstadter's *The Paranoid Style in American Politics* (1965).

Yet what flowed out of the turbulent decade of the 1960s was not a strengthened liberalism, but a revived conservatism. Ronald Reagan's huge political success compelled a thorough reexamination of the tradition of American conservatism and the sources of its modern resurgence.

Historians such as Leo Ribuffo and Alan Brinkley have argued that characters once dismissed as irrational crackpots or colorful irrelevancies—including religious fundamentalists and depression-era figures like Huey Long and Father Charles Coughlin—articulated values deeply rooted and widely shared in American culture. Those conservative spokespersons, whatever their peculiarities, offered a vision of free individuals, minimal government, and autonomous local communities that harked back to many of the themes of "civic republicanism" in the era of young nationhood.

But modern conservatism, however deep its roots, is also a product of the recent historical past. As scholars like Thomas Sugrue and Thomas Edsall have shown, the economic stagnation that set in after 1970 made many Americans insecure about their futures and receptive to new political doctrines. At the same time, as the commentator Kevin Phillips has stressed, "social issues," with little or no apparent economic content, became increasingly prominent, as movements for sexual liberation, legal abortion, and women's rights sharply challenged traditional beliefs. Perhaps most important, the success of the civil rights movement thrust the perpetually agonizing question of race relations to the very center of American political life. Finally, the failure of government policies in Vietnam, runaway inflation in the 1970s, and the disillusioning Watergate episode cast doubt on the legitimacy, the efficacy, and even the morality of "big government."

Many modern conservatives, including the pundit George Will, stress the deep historical roots of American conservatism. In their view, as Will once put it, it took sixteen years to count the ballots from the 1964 (Goldwater versus Johnson) election, and Goldwater won after all. But that argument is surely overstated. Goldwater ran against the legacy of the New Deal and was overwhelmingly defeated. Reagan ran against the consequences of the Great Society and won decisively. Many conservatives, in short, apparently acknowledge the legitimacy of the New Deal and the stake that many middle-class Americans feel they have in its programs of Social Security, home mortgage subsidies, farm price supports, and similar policies. But they reject the philosophy of the Great Society, with its more focused attack on urban poverty and its vigorous support of affirmative action. Modern conservatism springs less from a repudiation of government per se and more from a disapproval of the particular priorities and strategies of the Great Society. The different historical fates of the New Deal and the Great Society suggest the key to the rise of modern conservatism.

Chapter Review

KEY TERMS

Proposition 13 (945)

boll weevils (945)

supply-side economics (945)

Reaganomics (946)

Strategic Defense Initiative (SDI) (946)

Sandinistas (947)

contras (947)

glasnost (949)

perestroika (949)

Intermediate-Range Nuclear Forces (INF) Treaty (949)

Iran-Contra affair (951)

Moral Majority (951)

Black Monday (955)

Commonwealth of Independent States (CIS) (957)

Operation Desert Storm (959)

Americans with Disabilities Act (ADA) (961)

PEOPLE TO KNOW

Ronald Reagan

Margaret Thatcher

Mikhail Gorbachev

Saddam Hussein

Jerry Falwell

Sandra Day O'Connor

George H. W. Bush

Boris Yeltsin

Nelson Mandela

Manuel Noriega

Norman ("Stormin' Norman") Schwarzkopf

Clarence Thomas

CHRONOLOGY

1980	Reagan defeats Carter for presidency
1981	Iran releases American hostages "Reaganomics" spending and tax cuts passed Solidarity movement in Poland O'Connor appointed to Supreme Court (first woman justice)
1981–1991	United States aids anti-leftist forces in Central America
1982	Recession hits U.S. economy Israel invades Lebanon
1983	Reagan announces SDI plan (Star Wars) U.S. marines killed in Beirut, Lebanon U.S. invasion of Grenada
1984	Reagan defeats Mondale for presidency Soviet Union boycotts Summer Olympics in Los Angeles
1985	Gorbachev comes to power in Soviet Union, announces glasnost and perestroika First Reagan-Gorbachev summit meeting in Geneva
1986	Reagan administration backs Aquino in Philippines Iran-Contra affair revealed Second Reagan-Gorbachev summit meeting in Reykjavik, Iceland

1987	Stock market plunges 508 points Third Reagan-Gorbachev summit meeting in Washington, D.C.; INF treaty signed
1988	Fourth Reagan-Gorbachev summit meeting in Moscow Bush defeats Dukakis for presidency
1989	Chinese government suppresses prodemocracy demonstrators in Tiananmen Square *Webster* v. *Reproductive Health Services* Eastern European countries oust communist governments Berlin Wall torn down
1990	Iraq invades Kuwait East and West Germany unite Americans with Disabilities Act (ADA)
1991	Persian Gulf War Thomas appointed to Supreme Court Gorbachev survives coup attempt, resigns as Soviet president Soviet Union dissolves; republics form Commonwealth of Independent States
1992	Twenty-seventh Amendment (prohibiting congressional pay raises from taking effect until an election seats a new session of Congress) ratified *Planned Parenthood* v. *Casey*

TO LEARN MORE

Robert Collins, *Transforming America: Politics and Culture During the Reagan Years* (2007)

Donald T. Critchlow, *The Conservative Ascendancy: How the GOP Right Made Political History* (2007)

Barbara Ehrenreich, *The Worst Years of Our Lives: Irreverent Notes from a Decade of Greed* (1990)

Irving Kristol, *Reflections of a Neoconservative* (1983)

Walter LaFeber, *Inevitable Revolutions* (2nd ed., 1993)

Melvyn Leffler, *For the Soul of Mankind: The United States, the Soviet Union, and the Cold War* (2007)

William Martin, *With God on Our Side: The Rise of the Religious Right in America* (1996)

Richard L. Pacelle, Jr., *The Transformation of the Supreme Court's Agenda: From the New Deal to the Reagan Administration* (1991)

Kevin Phillips, *The Politics of Rich and Poor: Wealth and the American Electorate in the Reagan Aftermath* (1990)

Paul C. Roberts, *The Supply-Side Revolution* (1984)

Daniel T. Rodgers, *Age of Fracture* (2011)

Jonathan M. Schoenwald, *A Time for Choosing: The Rise of Modern American Conservatism* (2001)

John W. Sloan, *The Reagan Effect: Economics and Presidential Leadership* (1999)

David A. Stockman, *The Triumph of Politics: Why the Reagan Revolution Failed* (1986)

Gil Troy, *Morning in America: How Ronald Reagan Invented the 1980s* (2007)

Sean Wilentz, *The Age of Reagan: A History, 1974–2008* (2008)

A complete, annotated bibliography for this chapter—along with brief descriptions of the People to Know—may be found on the American Pageant website. The Key Terms are defined in a Glossary at the end of the text.

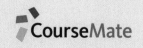

Go to the CourseMate website at **www.cengagebrain.com** for additional study tools and review materials—including audio and video clips—for this chapter.

AP® Review Questions for Chapter 40

1. Which of the following issues was NOT an important concern that the New Right hoped to constrict or eliminate through legal action?
   (A) Divorce
   (B) Pornography
   (C) Homosexuality
   (D) Abortion
   (E) Affirmative action

2. All of the following contributed to Ronald Reagan's landslide electoral victory over President Carter in 1980 EXCEPT
   (A) the Carter administration's inability to control double-digit inflation and sky-high interest rates.
   (B) a divided Democratic party, unhealed following the unsuccessful Democratic nomination challenge of Senator Edward Kennedy.
   (C) Ronald Reagan's ability to employ his well-honed acting skills to communicate effectively with the American public.
   (D) President Carter's decision to preserve some 100 million acres of Alaska land for national parks, forests, and wildlife refuges during an energy crisis.
   (E) Public frustration over President Carter's supposed mismanagement of foreign affairs such as the protracted Iranian hostage crisis.

3. Which of the following was Ronald Reagan's overall key domestic goal as president?
   (A) Dismantling the welfare state by reducing or eliminating entitlement and discretionary social welfare programs in order to reduce the size of government
   (B) Removing government interference in people's private lives in such areas as abortion and pornography
   (C) Reducing the growth of military spending in order to balance the federal budget
   (D) Developing and implementing a federally mandated reform of public education
   (E) Advancing big-business interests over organized labor in order to stimulate economic growth and reduce wage inflation

4. What were the initial results in 1982 of President Reagan's supply-side economic plan of deep federal budget cuts and substantial tax reductions?
   (A) A sharp recession and rise in unemployment
   (B) A reduced federal budget deficit
   (C) An international trade surplus for the United States
   (D) An economic boom
   (E) Record corporate profits for major industries like the automobile industry

5. Which of the following most accurately characterizes the economic results produced by Reaganomics in the 1980s?
   (A) For the first time in the twentieth century, income widened between the richest and poorest Americans.
   (B) Middle-class incomes rose.
   (C) The poor made substantial economic gains.
   (D) The economy was uniformly healthy.
   (E) The majority of Americans were middle class.

6. All of the following were examples of Ronald Reagan's determination to renew the Cold War during his first presidential term EXCEPT
   (A) denouncing the Soviet Union in political speeches as "the focus of evil in the modern world."
   (B) President Reagan's pursuit of a high-technology missile-defense system known as Star Wars.
   (C) President Reagan's strong support for the political and economic efforts of the independent Polish labor movement, Solidarity.
   (D) President Reagan spawning a new arms race with the Soviet Union by substantially increasing America's nuclear arms arsenal and military capabilities around the world.
   (E) American military forces ousting from power an insurgent group of Marxists who had taken over the tiny Caribbean island of Grenada.

7. What did the Iran-Contra affair essentially involve?
   (A) The United States hiring Iranian militants to fight for the right-wing Nicaraguan contra rebels against the left-wing Sandinista government in Nicaragua
   (B) The United States selling arms to Iran in exchange for hostages and diverting the profits to illegally fund the Nicaraguan contras
   (C) The United States selling arms to both sides in the Iran-Iraq war
   (D) The United States secretly recognizing the Iranian regime while claiming to be boycotting it
   (E) The United States persuading the Iranian government to directly fund the contra rebels by unfreezing Iranian assets in the United States and presenting Iranian leader Ayatollah Khomeini with gifts such as a birthday cake

8. Which of the following demonstrates most vividly how President Reagan, during his second term, departed from the militantly anti-Soviet stance of his first term?
   (A) President Reagan joining with Soviet leader Mikhail Gorbachev to end Soviet-American political and military conflicts in less developed countries
   (B) President Reagan acquiescing in Eastern Europe continuing to be a legitimate sphere of influence for the Soviet Union
   (C) President Reagan negotiating and signing arms control agreements with the new Soviet leader Mikhail Gorbachev
   (D) President Reagan making the Soviet Union a major trading partner of the United States
   (E) President Reagan's decision to abandon his high-technology, antimissile defense system, the Strategic Defense Initiative (SDI)

9. Which of the following most accurately describes the Supreme Court decisions in *Webster* v. *Reproductive Health Services* and *Planned Parenthood* v. *Casey*?
   (A) The Court severely restricted legal abortion to the first two months of pregnancy.
   (B) The Court permitted states to put some restrictions on abortion, while fundamentally upholding the abortion rights decision of *Roe* v. *Wade*.
   (C) The Court overturned *Roe* v. *Wade*.
   (D) The Court declared that the issue of legalized abortion should be completely determined by the states.
   (E) The Court declared that the constitutional right to life trumped the constitutional right of privacy, and all abortions, except when the mother's life is in danger, are illegal.

10. All of the following were consequences of the end of the Cold War EXCEPT that
    (A) long-suppressed ethnic hatreds flared in the former Soviet republics.
    (B) communist regimes were overthrown in Poland, Hungary, Romania, Bulgaria, Czechoslovakia, and East Germany.
    (C) long-suppressed ethnic hatreds flared in the former communist nations of Eastern Europe.
    (D) the entire European continent enjoyed an extended period of political stability.
    (E) unemployment increased in aerospace and defense industries and community dislocations occurred because of Pentagon budget cuts.

11 Which of the following reasons prompted President George H. W. Bush to organize America's European and Arab allies into a political and military coalition that ultimately ousted Iraqi forces from Kuwait in 1991?
   (A) President Bush feared that Iraqi leader Saddam Hussein's larger goal was to assume control over the entire oil-producing and economically vital Persian Gulf region.
   (B) President Bush believed that re-establishing the sovereignty of Kuwait was critical to his overall policy of creating pro-Western capitalist democracies throughout the Middle East.
   (C) President Bush believed that ousting Iraq from Kuwait would guarantee Israel's security in the face of growing military threats from the Arab states.
   (D) President Bush was confident that rolling back the Iraqi forces from Kuwait would prompt a successful Kurdish and Shi'ite uprising in Iraq leading to the overthrow of Saddam Hussein.
   (E) President Bush desired to use the Persian Gulf crisis as a way to guarantee permanent military bases in the Middle East.

12. What domestic achievement represented a partial redemption of President George H. W. Bush's 1988 campaign pledge to work for a "kinder, gentler America"?
    (A) The nomination and confirmation of progressive African American judge Clarence Thomas to succeed retiring liberal African American justice Thurgood Marshall on the U.S. Supreme Court
    (B) The signing of the Americans with Disabilities Act (ADA) in 1990 to prohibit discrimination against U.S citizens with physical or mental disabilities
    (C) President Bush's Department of Education challenging the legality of college scholarships for racial minorities
    (D) President Bush signing into law a massive public works employment program to reduce high unemployment in the United States
    (E) President Bush agreeing in 1990 to a federal budget increase that included $133 million in new taxes

13 Which statement about the Persian Gulf War is NOT true?
   (A) President George H. W. Bush declared that the United States "kicked the Vietnam syndrome."
   (B) Saddam Hussein was removed from power.
   (C) The Persian Gulf War grew out of a unanimous Security Council resolution.
   (D) The Persian Gulf War lasted for less than two months.
   (E) The Persian Gulf War was a response to Iraq's invasion of Kuwait.

14. Reagan's theory of "supply-side" economics, also referred to as the "trickle-down" theory, is most closely related to the policies of
    (A) George H. W. Bush.
    (B) Richard Nixon.
    (C) Lyndon Johnson.
    (D) Franklin Roosevelt.
    (E) Herbert Hoover.

Chapter 41

America Confronts the Post–Cold War Era

1992–2011

There is nothing wrong with America that cannot be cured with what is right in America.

WILLIAM J. CLINTON, INAUGURAL, 1993

The collapse of the Soviet Union and the democratization of its client regimes in Eastern Europe ended the four-decade-old Cold War and left the United States the world's sole remaining superpower. Americans welcomed these changes but seemed unsure how to exercise their unprecedented economic and military might in this new international scenario. The culture wars that had started in the 1960s fed ferociously partisan political squabbles that distracted the nation from the urgent task of clearly defining its role in the dawning age of globalization. In 2000 George W. Bush won a bitterly contested presidential election that left the nation more rancorously divided than ever, until the spectacular terrorist attacks on September 11, 2001, called forth, at least temporarily, a resurgent sense of national unity. Bush responded to the 9/11 attacks by invading the terrorist haven of Afghanistan. Amidst roiling controversy over his claims that Iraq possessed **weapons of mass destruction (WMD)** and had ties to terrorists, Bush proceeded to invade Iraq as well. After the failure to find WMD and over four thousand American battle deaths in the prolonged Iraq War, a war-weary country, nostalgic for the prosperity and peace of the 1990s, made history by electing the first African American president, Barack Obama. The new president inherited a crushing economic crisis, soon dubbed "The Great Recession." Its scale was exceeded in modern times only by the Great Depression of the 1930s. And like Franklin Roosevelt in the depression era, Obama seized the occasion to pursue major reforms in health care and financial regulation. But unlike FDR, Obama triggered a powerful Republican backlash that erased the Democratic majority in the House of Representatives in the congressional elections of 2010.

✯ Bill Clinton: The First Baby-Boomer President

As the last decade of the twentieth century opened, the slumbering economy, the widening gender gap, and the rising anti-incumbent spirit spelled opportunity for Democrats, frozen out of the White House for all but four years since 1968. Governor William Jefferson ("Bill") Clinton of Arkansas weathered blistering accusations of womanizing and draft evasion to emerge as his party's standard-bearer. He selected a fellow forty-something southern white male Protestant moderate, Senator Albert Gore of Tennessee, as his vice-presidential running mate.

Clinton claimed to be a "new" Democrat, chastened by the party's long exile in the political wilderness. With other centrist Democrats, he had formed the **Democratic Leadership Council** to point the party away from its traditional antibusiness, dovish, champion-of-the-underdog orientation and toward progrowth, strong defense, and anticrime policies. Clinton campaigned especially vigorously on promises to stimulate the economy, reform the welfare system, and overhaul the nation's health-care apparatus.

Trying to wring one more win out of the social issues that had underwritten two Reagan and one Bush presidential victories, the Republicans emphasized "family values" and, as expected, nominated George H. W. Bush and Vice President J. Danforth Quayle for a second term. But Bush's listless campaign could not keep pace with the super-energetic and phenomenally articulate Clinton. Bush claimed credit for ending the Cold War and trumpeted his leadership role in the Persian Gulf War. But pocketbook problems as the economy dipped into recession swayed more voters than pride in past foreign policy.

At Clinton's campaign headquarters, a simple sign reminded staffers of his principal campaign theme: "It's the economy, stupid." Reflecting pervasive economic unease and the virulence of the throw-the-bums-out national mood, nearly 20 percent of voters cast their ballots for independent presidential candidate H. Ross Perot, a bantamweight, jug-eared Texas billionaire who harped incessantly on the problem of the federal deficit and made a boast of the fact that he had never held any public office.

Perot's colorful presence probably accounted for the record turnout on election day, when some 100 million voters—55 percent of those eligible—went to the polls. The final tally gave Clinton 44,909,889 popular votes and 370 votes in the Electoral College. He was the first baby boomer to ascend to the White House, a distinction reflecting the electoral profile of the population,

1992

Candidate (Party)	Electoral Vote		Popular Vote	
Clinton (Democrat)	370	68.8%	44,908,233	43.0%
Bush (Republican)	168	31.2%	39,102,282	37.4%
Perot (Independent)	0	0.0%	19,741,048	18.9%

MAP 41.1 Presidential Election of 1992 (with electoral vote by state) © Cengage Learning

Presidential Campaign Debate, 1992 George Bush, Ross Perot, and Bill Clinton squared off at the University of Richmond (Virginia) on October 16, 1992. The telegenic Clinton handily dominated the televised debates, especially in the "talk-show" format used on this occasion.

70 percent of whom had been born after World War II. Bush polled some 39,104,545 popular votes and 168 electoral votes. Perot won no electoral votes but did gather 19,742,267 popular votes—the strongest showing for an independent or third-party candidate since Theodore Roosevelt ran on the Bull Moose ticket in 1912 (see Map 41.1). Democrats also racked up clear majorities in both houses of Congress, which seated near-record numbers of new members, including thirty-nine African Americans, nineteen Hispanic Americans, seven Asian Americans, one Native American, and forty-eight women, six of them in the Senate. Clinton also seized the opportunity in 1993 to nominate Ruth Bader Ginsburg to the Supreme Court, where she joined Sandra Day O'Connor to make a pair of women justices.

✦ A False Start for Reform

Badly overestimating his electoral mandate for liberal reform, the young president made a series of costly blunders upon entering the White House. He stirred a hornet's nest of controversy by advocating an end to the ban on gays and lesbians in the armed services. Confronted with fierce opposition, the president finally had to settle for a **"Don't Ask, Don't Tell"** policy that quietly accepted gay and lesbian soldiers and sailors without officially acknowledging their presence in the military. (Congress finally repealed the discriminatory policy in 2010.)

Even more damaging to Clinton's political standing, and to his hopes for lasting liberal achievement, was the fiasco of his attempt to reform the nation's health-care system. In a dramatic but personally and politically risky move, the president appointed his wife, nationally prominent lawyer and children's advocate Hillary Rodham Clinton, as the director of a task force charged with redesigning the medical-service industry. Their stupefyingly complicated plan was dead on arrival when it was presented to Congress in October 1993. The First Lady was doused with a torrent of abuse, although she eventually rehabilitated herself sufficiently to win election as a U.S. senator from New York in 2000—the first First Lady ever to hold elective office—and later became President Obama's secretary of state. President Clinton had better luck with a deficit-reduction bill in 1993, which combined with an increasingly buoyant economy by 1996 to shrink the federal deficit to its lowest level in more than a decade. By 1998 Clinton's policies seemed to have caged the ravenous deficit monster, as Congress argued over the unfamiliar question of how to manage federal budget *surpluses*.

Despite these successes, a sour antigovernment mood persisted. A huge explosion destroyed a federal office building in Oklahoma City in 1995, taking 168 lives, in retribution for a 1993 standoff in Waco, Texas, between federal agents and a fundamentalist sect known as the Branch Davidians. That showdown had ended in the destruction of the sect's compound and the deaths of many Branch Davidians, including women and children. Events like the **Oklahoma City bombing** brought to light a lurid and secretive underground of paramilitary private "militias" composed of alienated citizens armed to the teeth and ultrasuspicious of all government.

Even many law-abiding citizens shared to some degree in the antigovernment attitudes that drove the militia members to murderous extremes. Thanks largely to the disillusioning agony of the Vietnam War and the naked cynicism of Richard Nixon in the Watergate scandal, the confidence in government that had come naturally to the generation that had licked the Great Depression and won the Second World War was in short supply by century's end. Reflecting that pervasive disenchantment with politics and politicians, several states passed term-limit laws for elected officials, although the Supreme Court ruled in 1995 that the restrictions did not apply to federal officeholders.

AP Images

Bombing of Federal Building in Oklahoma City, 1995 A truck bomb killed 168 people in this federal office building in the worst act of terrorism in the United States until September 11, 2001. Convicted in 2001 for the attack, antigovernment militant Timothy McVeigh became the first person executed by the federal government in nearly forty years.

✵ The Politics of Distrust

Clinton's failed initiatives and widespread antigovernment sentiment afforded Republicans a golden opportunity in 1994, and they seized it aggressively. Led by outspoken Georgia Representative Newt Gingrich, Republicans offered voters a **Contract with America** that promised an all-out assault on budget deficits and radical reductions in welfare programs. Their campaign succeeded fabulously, as a conservative tornado roared across the land in the 1994 congressional elections. Republicans picked up eleven new governorships, eight seats in the Senate, and fifty-three seats in the House (where Gingrich became Speaker), giving them control of both chambers of the federal Congress for the first time in forty years.

But if President Clinton had overplayed his mandate for liberal reform in 1993, the congressional Republicans soon proceeded to overplay their mandate for conservative retrenchment. In 1996 the new Congress achieved a major conservative victory when it compelled a reluctant Clinton to sign the **Welfare Reform Bill**, which made deep cuts in welfare grants and required able-bodied welfare recipients to find employment. The new welfare law also tightly restricted welfare benefits for legal and illegal immigrants alike, reflecting a rising tide of anti-immigrant sentiment as the numbers of newcomers climbed toward an all-time high. Old-line liberal Democrats howled with pain at the president's alleged betrayal of his party's heritage. But Clinton's acceptance of the welfare reform package was part of his shrewd political strategy of accommodating the electorate's conservative mood by moving to his right.

Many Americans gradually came to feel that the Gingrich Republicans were bending their conservative bow too far, especially when the new Speaker advocated provocative ideas like sending the children of welfare families to orphanages. In a tense confrontation between the Democratic president and the Republican Congress, the federal government was actually forced to shut down for several days at the end of 1995 until a budget package was agreed upon. These outlandishly partisan antics bred a backlash that helped President Clinton rebound from his political near-death experience.

As the 1996 election approached, the Republicans chose Kansas senator Robert Dole as their presidential candidate. A decorated World War II veteran, Dole ran a lackluster campaign. Clinton, buoyed by a healthy economy and by his artful trimming to the conservative wind, breezed to an easy victory, with 47,401,898 popular votes to Dole's 39,198,482 (see Map 41.2). The Reform party's egomaniacal leader, Ross Perot, ran a sorry third, picking up less than half the votes he had garnered in 1992. Clinton won 379 electoral votes, Dole only 159. But Republicans remained in control of Congress.

1996

Candidate (Party)	Electoral Vote		Popular Vote	
Clinton (Democrat)	379	70.4%	47,401,054	49.2%
Dole (Republican)	159	29.6%	39,197,350	40.7%
Perot (Independent)	0	0.0%	8,085,285	8.4%

MAP 41.2 Presidential Election of 1996 (with electoral vote by state) The "solid South," once a safe Democratic stronghold, had by century's end largely become Republican territory. © Cengage Learning

✵ Clinton Again

As Clinton began his second term—the first Democratic president since Franklin Delano Roosevelt to be reelected—the heady promises of far-reaching reform with which he had entered the White House four years earlier were no longer heard. Still facing Republican majorities in both houses of Congress, he proposed only modest legislative goals, even though soaring tax revenues generated by the prosperous economy produced in 1998 a balanced federal budget for the first time in three decades.

Clinton cleverly managed to put Republicans on the defensive by claiming the political middle ground. He now warmly embraced the landmark Welfare Reform Bill of 1996 that he had initially been slow to endorse. Juggling the political hot potato of affirmative action, Clinton pledged to "mend it, not end it." When voters in California in 1996 approved Proposition 209, prohibiting affirmative-action preferences in government and higher education, the number of minority students in the state's public universities temporarily plummeted. A federal appeals court decision, *Hopwood* v. *Texas*, had a similar effect in Texas. Clinton criticized these broad assaults on affirmative action but stopped short of trying to reverse them, aware that public support for affirmative action, especially among white Americans, had diminished since the 1970s.

Clinton's major political advantage continued to be the roaring economy, which by 2000 had sustained the

Protesting NAFTA, 1993 These members of the Teamsters Union feared that the adoption of the North American Free Trade Agreement would mean the replacement of high-paying American jobs with low-wage, nonunion Mexican labor. More than a decade later, the treaty still rankled. Policymakers disagreed about whether NAFTA had been damaging to American workers. In the 2008 election, the Republicans endorsed it, while the Democrats attacked it.

longest period of growth in American history, driven by the Federal Reserve Board's low-interest, easy-money policies and by the explosive growth of new Internet ("dot-com") businesses. While unemployment crept down to 4 percent and employers scrambled madly for workers, inflationary pressure remained remarkably low.

Prosperity did not make Clinton immune to controversy over trade policy. During his first term, he had shown political courage by supporting the **North American Free Trade Agreement (NAFTA)**, creating in 1993 a free-trade zone encompassing Mexico, Canada, and the United States. In doing so, he bucked the opposition of protectionists in his own party, especially labor leaders fearful of losing jobs to low-wage Mexican workers. Clinton took another step in 1994 toward a global free-trade system when he vigorously promoted the creation of the **World Trade Organization (WTO)**, the successor to the General Agreement on Tariffs and Trade (GATT) and a cherished goal of free-trade advocates since the end of the Second World War.

Simmering discontent over trade policy boiled over in 1999 when Clinton hosted the meeting of the WTO in Seattle. The city's streets filled with protesters railing against what they viewed as the human and environmental costs of economic "globalization."

✴ Problems Abroad

The end of the Cold War dismantled the framework within which the United States had conducted foreign policy for nearly half a century. Clinton groped for a diplomatic formula to replace anticommunism as the basic premise of American diplomacy.

Absorbed by domestic issues, President Clinton at first seemed uncertain and even amateurish in his conduct of foreign policy. He followed his predecessor's lead in dispatching American troops as part of a peacekeeping mission to Somalia. But after Somali rebels killed more than a dozen Americans, the president quietly withdrew the U.S. units in March 1994, without having accomplished any clearly defined goal. Burned in Somalia, Washington stood on the sidelines in 1994 when catastrophic ethnic violence in the central African country of Rwanda resulted in the deaths of half a million people.

Clinton also struggled to define a policy with respect to China, which was rapidly emerging as an economic and political powerhouse. Clinton soft-pedaled his earlier criticism of the Beijing regime on human rights issues and instead began seeking improved trade relations with that robustly industrializing country and potential market bonanza. By 2000 Clinton was crusading for a controversial China trade bill. Congress passed it in May 2000, making the Asian giant a full-fledged trading partner of the United States.

Other problems boiled up in the tormented Balkans in southeastern Europe. As vicious ethnic conflict raged through Bosnia, the Washington government dithered until finally deciding to commit American troops to a NATO peacekeeping contingent in late 1995. Yet NATO's expansion to include the new member states of Poland, Hungary, and the Czech Republic in 1997, and its continuing presence in Bosnia, failed to pacify the Balkans completely. When Serbian president Slobodan Milošević in 1999 unleashed a new round of "ethnic cleansing" in the region, this time against ethnic Albanians in the province of Kosovo, U.S.-led NATO forces launched an air war against Serbia. The bombing campaign eventually forced Milošević to accept a NATO peacekeeping force on the ground in Kosovo. Milošević was arrested in 2001 and put on trial before the International Criminal Court in The Hague, where he died in 2006 before the trial was completed.

The Middle East remained a major focus of American diplomacy right up to the end of Clinton's tenure. In 1993 Clinton presided over a historic meeting at the White House between Israeli premier Yitzhak Rabin and Palestine Liberation Organization (PLO) leader Yasir Arafat. They agreed in principle on self-rule for the Palestinians within Israel. But hopes flickered two years later when Rabin fell to an assassin's bullet. Clinton and his second-term secretary of state, Madeleine Albright, spent the rest of the 1990s struggling in vain to broker the permanent settlement that continued to elude Israelis and Palestinians. Arafat died in 2004 with his dream of creating a Palestinian state still unrealized.

In his final year as president, Clinton stepped up his efforts to leave a legacy as an international peacemaker. Along with his work in the Middle East, he sought to bring peace to Northern Ireland and the Korean peninsula, and he traveled to India and Pakistan in hopes of reducing the rivalry between the two nuclear powers of southern Asia. But the guiding principles of American foreign policy in the post–Cold War era remained ill-defined and elusive.

✴ Scandal and Impeachment

Scandal had dogged Bill Clinton from the beginning of his presidency. Critics brought charges of everything from philandering to illegal financial transactions.

Allegations of corruption stemming from a real estate deal called **Whitewater** while he was governor of Arkansas triggered an investigation by a special prosecutor, but no indictment ever materialized.

All the previous scandals were overshadowed by the revelation in January 1998 that Clinton had engaged in a sexual affair with a young White House intern, Monica Lewinsky, and then blatantly lied about it when testifying under oath in another woman's civil suit accusing him of sexual harassment. Caught in his bold lie, the president made a humiliating confession, but his political opponents smelled blood in the water. In September 1998 the special prosecutor investigating Whitewater, who had broad powers to investigate *any* evidence of presidential malfeasance, presented a stinging report, including lurid sexual details, to the Republican-controlled House of Representatives. That report presented eleven possible grounds for impeachment, all related to lying about the **Lewinsky affair**.

The House quickly cranked up the rusty machinery of impeachment. As an acrid partisan atmosphere enveloped the Capitol, House Republicans in December 1998 passed two articles of impeachment against the president: perjury before a grand jury and obstruction of justice. Crying foul, the Democratic minority

Intifada Against Israeli Control, 1994 Beginning in 1987, Palestinians living in the Israeli-controlled territories of the West Bank and Gaza rose up in protest. As the stalemate dragged on, the likelihood of Middle East peace receded, despite repeated international diplomatic efforts to reach a settlement. These young Palestinians in East Jerusalem wave Palestine Liberation Organization (PLO) flags outlawed by Israel.

© Bettmann/Corbis

Michael Dougan

The Legacy of Impeachment
Time magazine's cartoonist asked how future generations would judge the Clinton impeachment episode— and how it might be treated in history textbooks.

charged that, however deplorable Clinton's personal misconduct, sexual transgressions did not rise to the level of "high crimes and misdemeanors" prescribed in the Constitution (see Art. II, Sec. IV in the Appendix). The House Republican managers (prosecutors) of impeachment for the Senate trial replied that perjury and obstruction were grave public issues and that nothing less than the "rule of law" was at stake.

As cries of "honor the Constitution" and "sexual McCarthyism" filled the air, the nation debated whether the president's peccadilloes amounted to high crimes or low follies. Most Americans apparently leaned toward the latter view. In the 1998 midterm elections, voters reduced the House Republicans' majority, causing fiery House speaker Newt Gingrich to resign his post. Although Americans held a low opinion of Clinton's slipshod personal morals, most liked the president's political and economic policies and wanted him to stay in office.

In early 1999, for the first time in 130 years, the nation witnessed an impeachment proceeding in the U.S. Senate. Dusting off ancient precedents from Andrew Johnson's trial, the one hundred senators solemnly heard arguments in the case. With the facts widely known and the two parties' political positions firmly locked in, the trial's outcome was a foregone conclusion. On the key obstruction of justice charge, five northeastern Republicans joined all forty-five Democratic senators in voting not guilty. The fifty Republican votes for conviction fell far short of the constitutionally required two-thirds majority. The vote on the perjury charge was forty-five guilty, fifty-five not guilty.

✦ Clinton's Legacy and the 2000 Election

Beyond the obvious stain of impeachment, Clinton's legacy was mixed. His sound economic policies encouraged growth and trade in a rapidly globalizing post–Cold War world. Yet as a "New Democrat" and avowed centrist, Clinton did more to consolidate than to reverse the Reagan-Bush revolution against New Deal liberalism that for half a century had provided the compass for the Democratic party and the nation. Further, by setting such a low standard in his personal conduct, he replenished the sad reservoir of public cynicism about politics that Vietnam and Watergate had created a generation before.

Nonetheless, as the end of the Clinton term and the beginning of the new millennium approached, the Democrats stayed on their political course and nominated loyal vice president Albert Gore for president. Gore faced the tricky challenge of linking himself to Clinton-era peace and prosperity while at the same time distancing himself from his boss's personal foibles. He chose as his running mate Connecticut senator Joseph Lieberman, an outspoken Clinton critic and the first Jew nominated to a major national ticket. Their Republican challenger, George W. Bush, won the nomination on the strength of his father's name and his years as governor of Texas. Bush surrounded himself with Washington insiders, including vice-presidential nominee Richard Cheney, and, in a clear jab at Clinton, promised to "restore dignity to the White House."

Rosy estimates that the federal budget would produce a surplus of some $2 trillion in the coming decade set the stage for the presidential contest. Echoing the Republican creed of smaller government, Bush argued for returning the budget surplus to "the people" through massive tax cuts and for promoting private-sector programs, such as school vouchers and a reliance on "faith-based" institutions to help the poor. Gore proposed smaller tax cuts, targeted at middle- and lower-class people, and strengthening Social Security. In an era of peace, foreign policy figured hardly at all in the campaign, although Bush struck a moderate note when he urged that America should act like "a humble nation."

Pollsters predicted a close election, but none foresaw the epochal cliffhanger that the election would become. On election day the country split nearly evenly between the two candidates, and it was soon clear that Florida's electoral votes would determine the winner. Television news programs announced that Bush had won the Sunshine State, and Al Gore called the Texas governor to concede defeat. Yet just an hour later, Gore's camp decided that Florida was too close to call, and the vice president—in perhaps the most awkward phone call in modern politics—phoned back to retract his concession.

What ensued was a five-week political standoff over how to count the votes in Florida. Democrats argued that some ballots were confusing or had been misread by machines and asked for recounts by hand in several counties. Republicans claimed that such recounts would amount to "changing the rules in the middle of

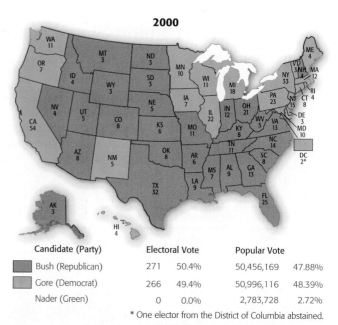

2000

Candidate (Party)	Electoral Vote		Popular Vote	
Bush (Republican)	271	50.4%	50,456,169	47.88%
Gore (Democrat)	266	49.4%	50,996,116	48.39%
Nader (Green)	0	0.0%	2,783,728	2.72%

* One elector from the District of Columbia abstained.

MAP 41.3 Presidential Election of 2000 (with electoral vote by state) Although Democrat Albert Gore won the popular election by half a million votes, George W. Bush's contested 537-vote advantage in Florida gave him a slight lead in the Electoral College. The 2.7 million popular votes won by Green party candidate and consumer activist Ralph Nader almost surely deprived Gore of victory, casting Nader in the role of spoiler. Bush's failure to win the popular vote inspired critics to protest at his inauguration with placards reading "Hail to the Thief." © Cengage Learning

the game" and thus thwart the rule of law. After weeks of legal bickering with the presidency in the balance, the Supreme Court finally intervened. By a five-to-four vote along partisan lines, the Court reasoned that since neither Florida's legislature nor its courts had established a uniform standard for evaluating disputed ballots, the hand counts amounted to an unconstitutional breach of the Fourteenth Amendment's equal protection clause.

That ruling gave Bush the White House but cast a dark shadow of illegitimacy over his presidency. Bush officially won Florida by 537 votes out of 6 million cast, and he squeaked by in the Electoral College, 271 to 266 (see Maps 41.3 and 41.4). The national popular vote went decisively to Gore, 50,999,897 to 50,456,002. For the first time since 1888, a candidate won the White House with fewer popular votes than his opponent. Calls to abolish the Electoral College, however, were few and muted (see Art. V of the Constitution).

★ Bush Begins

As the son of the forty-first president ("41"), George W. Bush ("43") became the first presidential offspring

2000

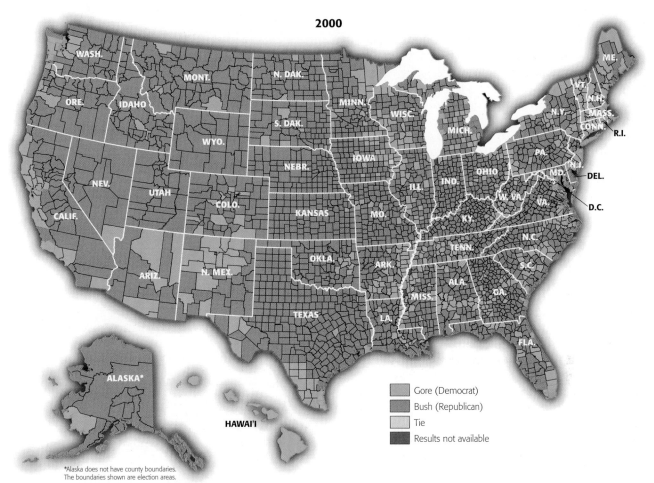

Gore (Democrat)
Bush (Republican)
Tie
Results not available

Alaska does not have county boundaries. The boundaries shown are election areas.

MAP 41.4 America in Red and Blue   This map showing the vote by county in the hotly contested 2000 presidential election vividly illustrates the geography of modern America's political divisions. Democratic candidate Albert Gore won a popular majority by carrying just 676 mostly urban counties, heavily populated by union members, minorities, and prosperous, educated white-collar workers. Republican George W. Bush won the election by taking 2,477 mostly rural counties, where feelings about "social issues" such as abortion and gun control ran high and shaped solid conservative constituencies. (Source: Adapted from VNS Graphic by Stanford Kay-Newsweek.) © Cengage Learning

since John Quincy Adams to reach the White House. Raised largely in Texas, the younger Bush publicly distanced himself from his family's privileged New England heritage and affected the chummy manner of a self-made good ol' boy—though he held degrees from Yale and Harvard. (His adversaries sniped that he had been born on third base and claimed to have hit a triple.) He promised to bring to Washington the conciliatory skills he had honed as the Republican governor of Texas, where he had worked well with the Democratic majority in the state's legislature.

But as president, Bush soon proved to be more of a divider than a uniter, less a "compassionate conservative" than a crusading ideologue. Religious traditionalists cheered but liberals jeered when he withdrew American support from international health programs

that sanctioned abortion, advocated federally financed faith-based social-welfare initiatives, and sharply limited government-sponsored research on embryonic stem cells, which many scientists believed held the key to conquering diseases such as Parkinson's and Alzheimer's. He pleased corporate chieftains but angered environmentalists by challenging scientific findings on groundwater contamination and global warming, repudiating the **Kyoto Treaty** limiting greenhouse gas emissions (negotiated by the Clinton administration but never ratified by the Senate), advocating new oil exploration in the Arctic National Wildlife Refuge on Alaska's ecologically fragile north coast, and allowing Vice President Cheney to hammer out his administration's energy policy in behind-closed-doors meetings with representatives of several giant oil companies. Even many fiscal

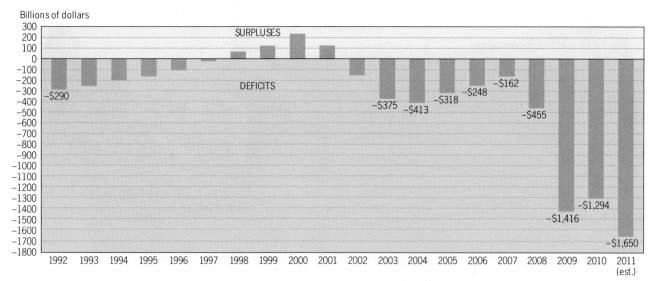

Billions of dollars

FIGURE 41.1 Deficits into Surpluses and Back Again In 1998 the U.S. budget deficit became a surplus for the first time in decades. But by 2002 the government was back in deficit, due to President Bush's tax cuts, a weak economy, and mushrooming defense spending on the Iraq War. Following the onset of the "Great Recession" in 2008, deficits ballooned to historic highs. (Source: Office of Management and Budget, *Historical Tables: Budget of the United States Government, Fiscal Year 2009.*)

conservatives thought him reckless when he pressed ahead with a whopping $1.3 trillion tax cut. Together with a softening economy and the increasing costs of war in Iraq, the tax cut turned the federal budget surpluses of the late 1990s into yawning deficits, reaching more than $400 billion in 2004 (see Figure 41.1).

✵ Terrorism Comes to America

On September 11, 2001, the long era of America's impregnable national security violently ended. On a balmy late-summer morning, suicidal terrorists slammed two hijacked airliners, loaded with passengers and jet fuel, into the twin towers of New York City's World Trade Center. They flew a third plane into the military nerve center of the Pentagon, near Washington, D.C., killing 189 people. Heroic passengers forced a fourth hijacked aircraft to crash in rural Pennsylvania, killing all 44 aboard but depriving the terrorists of an additional weapon of mass destruction. As the two giant New York skyscrapers thunderously collapsed, some three thousand innocent victims perished, including people of many races and faiths from more than sixty countries, as well as hundreds of New York's police- and fire-department rescue workers. A stunned nation blossomed with flags, as grieving and outraged Americans struggled to express their sorrow and solidarity in the face of the catastrophic terrorism of **9/11**.

President Bush responded with a sober and stirring address to Congress nine days later. His solemn demeanor and the gravity of the situation helped to

The Toll of Terror Grief overcame this exhausted firefighter during the search for survivors in the wreckage of New York City's World Trade Center.

© David Turnley/Corbis

dissipate the cloud of illegitimacy that had shadowed his presidency since the disputed election of 2000. While emphasizing his respect for the Islamic religion and Muslim people, he identified the principal enemy as Osama bin Laden, head of a shadowy terrorist network known as **Al Qaeda** ("the base" in Arabic). A wealthy extremist exiled from his native Saudi Arabia, bin Laden was associated with earlier attacks on American embassies in East Africa and on the USS *Cole* in Yemen. He had taken refuge in landlocked Afghanistan, ruled by Islamic fundamentalists called the Taliban. (Ironically, the United States had indirectly helped bring the Taliban to power by supporting religious rebels resisting the Soviet invasion of Afghanistan in the 1980s.) Bin Laden was known to harbor venomous resentment toward the United States for its growing military presence in the Middle East (especially on the sacred soil of the Arabian Peninsula) and its unyielding support for Israel in the face of intensifying Palestinian nationalism. Bin Laden also fed on worldwide resentment of America's enormous economic, military, and cultural power. Ironically, America's most conspicuous strengths had made it a conspicuous target.

When the Taliban refused to hand over bin Laden, Bush ordered a massive military campaign against Afghanistan. Within three months American and Afghan rebel forces had overthrown the Taliban but failed to find bin Laden, and Americans continued to live in fear of future attacks. Confronted with this unconventional, diffuse menace, antiterrorism experts called for a new kind of "asymmetrical warfare," employing not just traditional military muscle but also counter-insurgency tactics like innovative intelligence gathering, training of local police forces, economic reprisals, infiltration of suspected organizations, and even assassinations.

The terrorists' blows diabolically coincided with the onset of a recession. The already gathering economic downturn worsened as edgy Americans shunned air travel and the tourist industry withered. In this anxious atmosphere, Congress in October 2001 rammed through the **USA Patriot Act.*** The act permitted extensive telephone and e-mail surveillance and authorized the detention and deportation of immigrants suspected of terrorism. Just over a year later, Congress created the new cabinet-level **Department of Homeland Security** to protect the nation's borders and ferret out potential attackers. The Justice Department meanwhile rounded up hundreds of immigrants and held them without habeas corpus (formal charges in an open court). The Bush administration further called for trying suspected terrorists before military tribunals, where the usual rules of evidence and procedure did not apply. As hundreds of Taliban fighters captured in Afghanistan languished in legal limbo and demoralizing isolation in the **Guantánamo Detention Camp** on the American military base at Guantánamo, Cuba, public-opinion polls showed Americans sharply divided on whether the terrorist threat fully warranted such drastic encroachments on America's venerable tradition of protecting civil liberties.

---

*The act's official name is Uniting and Strengthening America by Providing Appropriate Tools Required to Intercept and Obstruct Terrorism.

The Attacks Seen Around the World The attacks of September 11, 2001, became events of international, not just American, significance, as revealed in the newspapers on display in Sofia, Bulgaria.

Liberty or Death Critics of the USA Patriot Act feared the extinction of cherished civil liberties, including the right to protest against the government's policies.

Catastrophic terrorism posed an unprecedented challenge to the United States. The events of that murderous September morning reanimated American patriotism, but they also brought a long chapter in American history to a dramatic climax. All but unique among modern peoples, Americans for nearly two centuries had been spared from foreign attack on their homeland. That unusual degree of virtually cost-free national security had undergirded the values of openness and individual freedom that defined the distinctive character of American society. Now American security and American liberty alike were dangerously imperiled.

✺ Bush Takes the Offensive Against Iraq

On only its second day in office, the Bush administration warned that it would not tolerate Iraq's continued defiance of United Nations weapons inspections, mandated after Iraq's defeat in the 1991 Persian Gulf War. Iraqi dictator Saddam Hussein, after playing hide-and seek with the inspectors for years, expelled them from his country in 1998, inducing President Clinton, with congressional approval, to declare that Saddam's removal ("regime change") was an official goal of U.S. policy. But no sustained military action against Iraq had followed.

Now, in the context of the new terrorist threat, the Bush administration focused on Iraq with a vengeance.

In January 2002, just weeks after the September 11 attacks, Bush claimed that Iraq, along with Iran and North Korea, constituted an "axis of evil" that gravely menaced American security. Iran and North Korea were both known to be pursuing nuclear weapons programs, and Iran had long supported terrorist operations in the Middle East. But Iraqi tyrant Saddam Hussein, defeated but not destroyed by Bush's father in 1991, became the principal object of the new president's wrath. The elder Bush had carefully assembled a broad international coalition to fight the 1991 Persian Gulf War. He had also spoken so often of "prudence" that late-night television comedians had mocked him for it. In contrast, his son was brashly determined to break with long-standing American traditions and wage a preemptive war against Iraq—and to go it alone if necessary. The younger Bush thus cast off his appeal for America to be a "humble nation" and stood revealed as a plunger, a daring risk-taker willing to embrace bold, dramatic policies, foreign as well as fiscal. In that spirit Bush began laying plans for a war against Iraq.

Itching for a fight, and egged on by hawkish Vice President Cheney and other "neoconservative" advisers, Bush accused the Iraqi regime of all manner of wrongdoing: oppressing its own people; frustrating the weapons inspectors; developing nuclear, chemical, and

---

In his 2002 state of the union address, President George W. Bush (b. 1946) declared:

❝Iraq continues to flaunt its hostility toward America and to support terror. The Iraqi regime has plotted to develop anthrax, and nerve gas, and nuclear weapons for over a decade. This is a regime that has already used poison gas to murder thousands of its own citizens—leaving the bodies of mothers huddled over their dead children. This is a regime that agreed to international inspections—then kicked out the inspectors. This is a regime that has something to hide from the civilized world.

"States like these, and their terrorist allies, constitute an axis of evil, arming to threaten the peace of the world. By seeking weapons of mass destruction, these regimes pose a grave and growing danger. They could provide these arms to terrorists, giving them the means to match their hatred. They could attack our allies or attempt to blackmail the United States. In any of these cases, the price of indifference would be catastrophic.❞

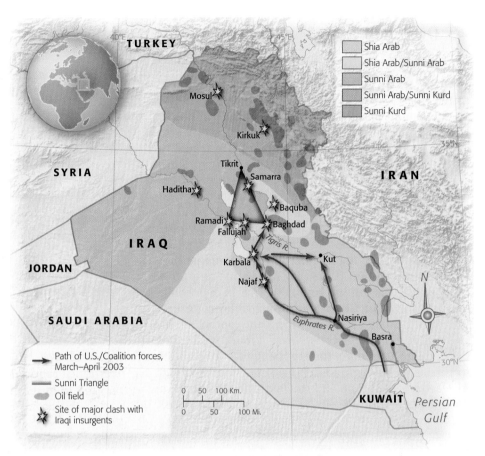

MAP 41.5 Iraq in Transition
Carved out of the old Ottoman Empire after World War I, Iraq has long been a combustible compound of rivalrous ethnic and religious groups. Saddam Hussein's dictatorial regime imposed a brutal peace on the country for twenty-four years following his ascent to power in 1979, but after the American invasion in 2003, old feuds resumed, exacerbated by stinging resentment against the occupying forces. © Cengage Learning

biological weapons of mass destruction referred to as "WMD"; and supporting terrorist organizations like Al Qaeda. Perhaps most controversially, he also suggested that a liberated, democratized Iraq might provide a beacon of hope to the Islamic world and thereby begin to improve the political equation in the volatile Middle East. To skeptical observers, including America's usually reliable European allies, the very multiplicity of Bush's reasons for war cast doubt on his case, and his ambition to create a democracy in long-suffering Iraq, burdened with centuries of internecine conflict, seemed naively utopian. Secretary of State Colin Powell urged caution, warning about the long-term consequences for the United States of invading and occupying an unstable, religiously and culturally divided nation of 25 million people. "You break it, you own it," he told the president.

Heavy majorities in both houses of Congress nevertheless passed a resolution in October 2002 authorizing the president to employ armed force to defend against Iraqi threats to America's national security and to enforce United Nations resolutions regarding Iraq. A month later the U.N. Security Council voted unanimously to give Iraq "a final opportunity to comply with its disarmament obligations." There followed a months-long cat-and-mouse game. U.N. weapons inspectors returned to Iraq. Saddam once again harassed and blocked them. No weapons of mass destruction were found. The inspectors

Ethnic and religious groups by percent of total population (c. 25,000,000)

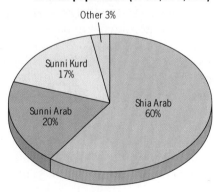

asked for more time. The United Nations declined to authorize the use of force to compel compliance.

In this tense and confusing atmosphere, Bush, with Britain his only major ally, launched the long-anticipated invasion of Iraq on March 19, 2003. Saddam Hussein's vaunted military machine collapsed almost immediately. In less than a month, Baghdad had fallen and Saddam had been driven from power and hounded into hiding. (He was found and arrested some nine months later and executed in 2006.) From the deck of a U.S. aircraft carrier off the California coast, speaking beneath a banner declaring "Mission Accomplished," Bush triumphantly announced on May 1, 2003, that "major combat operations in Iraq have ended" (see Map 41.5).

✦ Owning Iraq

President Bush's words soon came back to haunt him. "Neoconservative" pundits in Washington had predicted that American soldiers would be greeted as liberators and that Saddam's ouster would lead to flowering democracy across the Middle East. In reality post-Saddam Iraq quickly devolved into a seething cauldron of violence. The country's largest ethnic groups, Sunni and Shia Muslims, clashed violently, especially in the capital city of Baghdad. Both groups attacked American forces, especially after the U.S. decision to disband the Iraqi army, which deprived Iraq of an effective indigenous police force. A locally grown insurgency quickly spread, and occupying Iraq became ever more perilous for American troops. Hatred for Americans only worsened with revelations in April 2004 that Iraqi prisoners in Baghdad's **Abu Ghraib prison** had been tortured and humiliated by their American captors. Amid this chaos, jihadist terrorists from around the region flooded into Iraq, often fueling the intra-Iraqi conflicts to further their own radical Islamist vision. Although Al Qaeda had had no link to Iraq under Saddam, as Bush had falsely alleged, the organization certainly

In his 1998 book, A World Transformed, *former president George H. W. Bush (b. 1924) explained his rationale for not driving Saddam Hussein from power during the 1991 Persian Gulf War. His words made sobering reading in the context of his son's subsequent invasion of Iraq:*

❝ Trying to eliminate Saddam . . . would have incurred incalculable human and political costs. . . . The coalition would instantly have collapsed, the Arabs deserting it in anger and other allies pulling out as well. Under the circumstances, there was no viable 'exit strategy' we could see, violating another of our principles. Furthermore, we had been self-consciously trying to set a pattern for handling aggression in the post–Cold War world. Going in and occupying Iraq, thus unilaterally exceeding the United Nations' mandate, would have destroyed the precedent of international response to aggression that we hoped to establish.❞

© Bettmann/Corbis

On the Fiery Ground in Basra, Iraq, 2004 These British soldiers are running from a gasoline bomb detonated during a protest by Iraqi job seekers who claimed that they had been promised employment in the security services. The British, who had invaded Iraq alongside the United States, oversaw the southern Iraq city of Basra, a role that proved so unpopular with British voters that Prime Minister Tony Blair was eventually forced to resign.

moved in afterward. These three battles—Shia-Sunni ethnic violence, counter-occupation insurgency, and jihadist terrorism—fed a spiraling maelstrom of bloodshed. By the end of 2006, more Americans had died in Iraq than in the attacks of September 11 (see "Thinking Globally: America Through Foreign Eyes: Hyperpower or Hapless Power?" pp. 980–981).

Almost from the outset of the intervention, American forces began preparing to withdraw. In the summer of 2004, the American military ceded political power and limited sovereignty to an interim Iraqi government. National elections followed in early 2005, and millions of Iraqis voted for a national assembly to draft a constitution. After a referendum vote on the constitution in October 2005, another round of elections chose parliamentary representatives, a prime minister, and a president. But under the seeming stability of Iraq's new democratic government lay deep, violent tensions. Sunni Muslims, the minority that had held power under Saddam Hussein, one of their own, feared reprisals and repressions under a majority Shia government. Sunnis largely boycotted the first election and tried unsuccessfully to block the ratification of the constitution. Unsuccessful at the ballot box, many Sunnis turned to bombings and political assassinations.

✴ Reelecting George W. Bush

Americans had rarely been as divided as they were in the first years of the twenty-first century. Civil libertarians worried that the government was trampling on personal freedoms in the name of fighting terrorism. Revelations in 2002 about flagrant corporate fraud fed rampant popular disillusion with the business community. Cultural tensions brewed over the rights of gay and lesbian Americans when leaders in San Francisco and Massachusetts permitted same-sex couples to marry in 2004. Affirmative action continued to spark sharp debate, as the Supreme Court permitted some preferential treatment in admitting minority undergraduate and law students to the University of Michigan in 2003.

Amid this division George W. Bush positioned himself to run for reelection. He proclaimed that his tax cuts had spurred economic growth. Targeting what he called "the soft bigotry of low expectations," he championed the **No Child Left Behind Act** of 2002, which mandated sanctions against schools that failed to meet federal performance standards. He played to cultural conservatives in opposing stem cell research (see p. 973) and called for a constitutional amendment to ban gay marriage. But most of all, he promoted himself as a stalwart leader in wartime, warning the country not to "change horses midstream."

After a bruising round of primary elections, the embattled Democrats chose lanky and long-jawed Massachusetts senator John Kerry to represent their ticket. Kerry pushed progressive visions of government and counted on his Vietnam War record to counter charges that he would be weak in the face of terrorism. But that plan backfired as Kerry fell under attack for his very public opposition to Vietnam once he had returned from battle in the early 1970s. In spite of increased public misgivings about the war in Iraq, Bush nailed down a decisive victory in November 2004. He received the first popular vote majority by a presidential candidate in more than a decade—60,639,281 to 57,355,978—and won the Electoral College, 286 to 252, if by only one state (this time Ohio). This time his victory was clear, constitutional, and uncontested.

✴ Bush's Second Term

Reelection, George W. Bush announced, gave him "political capital," which he intended to spend on an aggressive domestic agenda. The appointment of two new conservative Supreme Court justices (John G. Roberts and Samuel A. Alito, Jr.) upon the retirement of Sandra Day O'Connor and the death of Chief Justice William Rehnquist seemed to bode well for his ambitions. But Bush soon overplayed his hand. Attacking the core of New Deal liberalism, he proposed a radical program to privatize much of Social Security. A massive outcry led by the American Association of Retired Persons (AARP) and other liberal groups reminded Americans how much they loved Social Security, warts and all. Bush's proposal faded away within six months of his reelection. The same fate befell a proposed constitutional amendment to ban same-sex marriage, which had been a major "values" issue in the 2004 campaign.

The president also took (faulty) aim at the contentious issue of immigration reform. Here he parted company with the conservative wing of his party, many of whom wanted to deport the nearly 12 million undocumented people in the United States. His compromise plan to establish a guest-worker program and a "path to citizenship" for the undocumented ended up pleasing no one. Congress rejected it in the summer of 2007, and the issue was dead for the rest of Bush's term (see p. 1000).

Every second-term president since the 1960s had seen scandal mar his later years in office. Nixon had Watergate, Reagan had Iran-contra, and Clinton had Lewinsky. The Bush White House was no exception, but this time the accusations were political, not personal. In the fall of 2005, Vice President Dick Cheney's chief of staff was convicted of perjury in an investigation into the source of a leak that had exposed the identity of an undercover CIA agent as political retaliation against her antiwar husband. Then in December of that year, journalists discovered that the government was

America Through Foreign Eyes: Hyperpower or Hapless Power?

*W*hen the Soviet Union disintegrated in 1991, the Cold War concluded at last. So did an era in the history of American foreign policy, and in the history of the international order. For nearly half a century following World War II, the confrontation with the Soviets had deeply shaped Americans' conception of themselves—their national identity—as well as their role and reputation in the wider world. In the long twilight struggle against Soviet communism, they had accumulated unprecedented economic, military, and cultural might, and had taken virtuous pride in themselves as the global champions of democracy, justice, and human rights. Now, as the sole surviving "superpower," they faced no counterbalancing regime and, apparently, no check on their national ambitions. The United States seemed to wield all but limitless power to mold the international environment as it wished. Not since the days of ancient Rome did any people bestride the world so unopposed.

Not everyone welcomed the emergence of this international colossus. Australians grumbled that the United States was a "tall poppy" that needed to be cut down to size. French foreign minister Hubert Védrine coined a new term when he described the United States in 1999 not merely as a superpower but as a "hyper power," one "that is dominant or predominant in all categories," including not only the traditional domains of politics, economics, and the military, but even including "attitudes, concepts, languages, and modes of life." He called upon Europeans to create an alternative to the American "steamroller," to "work in favor of real multilateralism against unilateralism, for balanced multipolarism against unipolarism, for cultural diversity against uniformity." In the parlance of international relations, Védrine was promoting a "balancing" strategy to cope with U.S. power, rather than the "bandwagon" strategy of simply submitting to American hegemony and making the most of it. Notably, he was not proposing outright opposition.

As the last days of the twentieth century slipped through the hourglass, American power surely looked formidable. The United States was the world's third most populous nation (after China and India), enjoyed the world's largest economy (more than three times larger than second-ranked Japan), was the acknowledged global leader in high-tech information and biomedical innovations, and spent more on its armed forces than the rest of the world *combined*. Yet the realities of American power were somewhat less imposing. Uncle Sam struggled to find solid footing in the post–Cold War international arena. Washington in the 1990s badly botched a peacekeeping mission in lawless Somalia; stood by helplessly as genocidal militias murdered nearly a million Rwandans; dithered over how to stabilize chaotic Haiti; fumbled indecisively as nationalist and sectarian violence convulsed the former Balkan nation of Yugoslavia; found

AP Images

Torture at Abu Ghraib Prison, Baghdad, 2003   Revelations that American soldiers had brutally tortured Iraqi prisoners contributed to condemnation of the nation's disregard for human rights and growing disquiet about America's unilateral policing of the world.

no effective response to terrorist attacks on New York City's World Trade Center, the destroyer USS *Cole*, and American embassies in Kenya and Tanzania; and notoriously failed to bring any conclusion to the decades-old confrontation between Israelis and Palestinians, who erupted in a bloody intifada (rebellion) against the Jewish state in 2000.

The barbarous Al Qaeda assault that finally toppled the twin towers of the World Trade Center on September 11, 2001, momentarily brought an outpouring of sympathy from an astonished and outraged world—and also brought a dramatic shift in American foreign policy. Even *Le Monde*, France's leading newspaper, declared that in this dangerous hour "Nous sommes tous Américains" (We are all Americans). For the first time in history, the North Atlantic Treaty Organization (NATO) invoked the treaty's Article Five, confirming that an attack on one member was an attack on all members.

But such sentiments proved short-lived. When President George W. Bush in 2002 asserted a new right of preemptive war and then proceeded to invade Iraq for what looked to many observers like the most dubious of reasons, anti-American sentiment swelled the world over. In February 2002 some 10 million people in sixty countries demonstrated against the impending U.S. invasion of Iraq. Exacerbated by Washington's rejection of the Kyoto Treaty dealing with global warming, and by several American states' continuing embrace of the death penalty (which had largely disappeared in Europe and elsewhere), America's standing deteriorated even among its traditional allies and sank to rock-bottom lows in Islamic countries. Simmering resentment over the detention of hundreds of captured Afghans at the U.S. military base in Guantánamo, Cuba; revelations about human rights abuses inflicted by American troops on Iraqi prisoners at Baghdad's Abu Ghraib prison; and "rendition" by American

agents of suspected terrorists to the notoriously cruel security services of other countries further drained the depleted reservoirs of America's moral and political capital. The election of Barack Obama in 2008 briefly burnished the American image once more, but in the eyes of many global citizens, America was no longer a "City on a Hill" to be admired and emulated.

Once a moral beacon and political inspiration to a suffering world, the United States in the early twenty-first century had come to be regarded by millions of people the world over as a moral scourge and a political and military danger (see Table 41.1). Recapturing its stature as a legitimate world leader, rebuilding its alliances, restructuring the myriad multilateral institutions it had worked so hard to build in the Cold War era, and recapturing a sense of itself as a just and humane society were tasks that urgently confronted the Republic as the new century advanced.

TABLE 41.1 World Public Opinion of the United States

Question: Do you have a very favorable, somewhat favorable, somewhat unfavorable, or very unfavorable opinion of the United States? (percent favorable)

	2000	2002	2003	2004	2005	2006	2007	2008	2009	2010
Britain	83%	75%	70	58%	55%	56%	51%	53%	69%	65%
France	62	63	43	37	43	39	39	42	75	73
Germany	78	61	45	38	41	37	30	31	64	63
Spain	50	—	38	—	41	23	34	33	58	61
Russia	37	61	36	47	52	43	41	46	44	57
Indonesia	75	61	15	—	38	30	29	37	63	59
Pakistan	23	10	13	21	23	27	15	19	16	17
Jordan	—	25	1	5	21	15	20	19	25	21
Turkey	52	30	15	30	23	12	9	12	14	17
Nigeria	46	—	61	—	—	62	70	64	79	81
Japan	77	72	—	—	—	63	61	50	59	66
India	—	54	—	—	71	56	59	66	76	66
China	—	—	—	—	42	47	34	41	47	58

(Source: From Pew Global Attitudes Report 2010, "Obama More Popular Abroad Than at Home, Global Image of U.S. Continues to Benefit." Reprinted by permission of Pew Research Center.)

After the Levees Broke in New Orleans, August 2005 When ferocious Hurricane Katrina hammered the Gulf Coast, it overtaxed a deficient levee system and unleashed floodwaters into New Orleans, submerging 80 percent of the city and destroying more than a quarter-million of its homes. Many families unable or unwilling to flee the city sought refuge in the Superdome, where water, food, and other supplies were soon in very short supply. Experts predicted that it would be years before the city fully recovered, if ever.

© Bettmann/Corbis

conducting illegal wiretap surveillance on American citizens inside the United States in violation of federal law. Perhaps the most tragic and avoidable of Bush's missteps came in the botched response to the deadly **Hurricane Katrina**, which devastated New Orleans and much of the Gulf Coast in late August 2005, flooding 80 percent of the historic city and causing over 1,300 deaths and $150 billion in damages. The Federal Emergency Management Agency (FEMA) proved pathetically inept in New Orleans, and Bush came in for still more criticism. A consensus began to build that Bush was a genial personality but an impetuous, unreflective, and frequently feckless leader, a president in over his head in a sea of complex problems that he seemed incapable of mastering.

✴ Midterm Elections of 2006

As charges of dictatorial power-grabbing, cronyism, and incompetence mounted during Bush's second term, Republicans fell victim in the midterm elections of 2006 to the same anti-incumbency sentiment they had ridden to power twelve years earlier. Democrats narrowly regained control of both houses of Congress for the first time since they had lost them to the Gingrich revolution in 1994 (see p. 968). California Democrat Nancy Pelosi became the first woman to serve as Speaker of the House.

The biggest factor in the Democratic sweep was the perceived mishandling of the war in Iraq. Prewar claims about WMD and Iraq's connections to Al Qaeda and 9/11 had all proved false. By late 2005 polls revealed that a majority of Americans considered the war a mistake. Even more felt that the Bush administration, particularly the Defense Department under Secretary Donald Rumsfeld, had badly mismanaged events on the ground. Rumsfeld resigned after the Republicans' "thumping" in the 2006 midterm elections. But Iraq still knew no peace, and the death toll, Iraqi and

Pismestrovic, Klene Zeitung, Cartoon Arts International, Inc.

European Disapproval of the Iraq War, 2007

American alike, continued to rise. The Bush administration attempted to assert greater control in early 2007 with a "surge" of twenty thousand additional troops. The surge brought a modest measure of stability to Iraq, but as the 2008 election cycle got under way, public opinion nevertheless solidified even more strongly against the war. President Bush's approval ratings sank below 30 percent. Candidate Barack Obama's promise to conclude the war in timely fashion gave him a powerful lift in the upcoming presidential election.

✖ The Presidential Election of 2008

With neither the sitting president nor vice president running, the 2008 election was truly "open" for the first time in eighty years. The Democratic race soon tightened into a fiercely fought contest between the forty-six-year-old, first-term Illinois senator Barack Obama and the precampaign favorite, former First Lady and sitting New York senator Hillary Rodham Clinton. Obama narrowly prevailed, surviving Clinton's attacks on his inexperience. Son of a black Kenyan father and a white Kansan mother and raised in Hawaii and Indonesia, Obama had a cosmopolitan background well suited to the age of globalization. He promised gridlock-weary voters a "postpartisan" politics that would end the divisive battles of the Bush years. To strengthen his national security credentials, he picked foreign-policy-savvy Delaware senator Joseph Biden as his running mate.

In keeping with the country's anti-Bush mood, Republicans nominated long-time Arizona senator John McCain, aged seventy-two, a self-styled "maverick" and a Vietnam War hero who had endured years of torture as a prisoner of war. He had a record of supporting bipartisan legislation on such issues as normalizing relations with North Vietnam, campaign finance, and immigration reform. McCain picked Sarah Palin as his running mate. The former beauty queen, small-town mayor, self-proclaimed "hockey-mom," and staunch abortion rights opponent had served only twenty-one months as Alaska's governor. As McCain hoped, the telegenic Palin galvanized the conservative Republican base. But when interview gaffes exposed her weak grasp of the issues, Palin became fodder for late-night television comedians and, polls showed, at least as much a liability as an asset to the Republican ticket.

Armed with an unprecedented war chest of nearly $700 million, mostly raised from small donors via the Internet, Obama seized the advantage in both the "air war" (television) and the "ground war" (door-to-door campaigning by his legions of volunteers). His poise and gravitas in televised debates favorably impressed many voters, and his campaign slogan, "Yes we can," excited widespread hope and enthusiasm. Then, just six weeks before election day, a sudden economic maelstrom gave his campaign a buoyant boost.

The American housing price bubble, fed by years of the Federal Reserve System's easy-money policies and the private banking system's lax lending practices,

The New First Family President-elect Barack Obama, wife Michelle, and daughters Sacha and Malia, on election night 2008 in Chicago's Grant Park.

©JIM BOURG /Reuters/Corbis

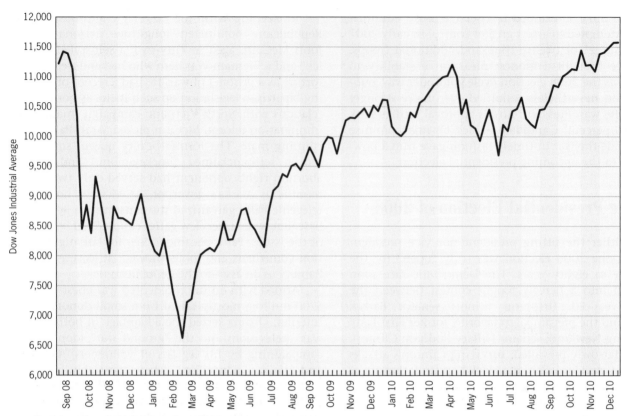

FIGURE 41.2 The Great Recession Takes Hold The financial turmoil that rocked the world in 2008 sent stock market values plummeting. (Source: Data from *http://www.nyse.tv/dow-jones-industrial-average-history-djia.htm.)*

burst at last. The long era of cheap and abundant credit, when bankers had stuffed their balance sheets with complex and highly risky loans, shivered to an alarmingly abrupt halt. By 2008 the collapse in real estate values was generating a tsunami of mortgage defaults, especially among "subprime" borrowers whose escalating mortgage payments stretched them to the breaking point. Bankers and other lenders watched in horror as countless homeowners defaulted and the worth of mortgage-backed securities sank precipitously. Aggressive "**deleveraging**" set in worldwide, as financial institutions from Tokyo to New York to London scrambled to reduce their debt loads by selling assets (at ever-declining prices). But some debts could not be unloaded at any price, and credit markets soon froze everywhere. Following the collapse of the venerable Wall Street firm of Lehman Brothers in September 2008, stocks fell into a deep swoon. The gravest financial hurricane since the Great Depression of the 1930s was gathering ever-increasing force (see Figure 41.2).

In contrast to the infamous 1929 crash that heralded the onset of the Great Depression, it took days, not years, for a terrified Bush administration to intervene on a gigantic scale. The federal government nationalized the country's two biggest mortgage companies, the

Federal National Mortgage Association ("Fannie Mae") and the Federal Home Mortgage Corporation ("Freddie Mac"), and effectively took over the world's biggest insurance company, the American International Group (AIG). Treasury secretary Henry Paulson next persuaded Congress to create the Troubled Assets Relief Program (TARP), authorizing a whopping $700 billion to buy "toxic" assets and inject cash directly into the nation's biggest banks and corporations. (Despite public outrage over TARP's original cost, estimates are that after loans are repaid it will have cost taxpayers about $30 billion—arguably a bargain price to pay for rescuing the nation's financial and business system and staving off a repeat of the Great Depression.)

Candidate Obama seized the political opportunity presented by the mounting economic crisis and declared that electing McCain would amount to a "third Bush term" and lead to further financial turmoil. Obama called for reviving the faltering economy with bold public investments in alternative energy and infrastructure repair. McCain derided such ideas as "socialism."

Unsettled by the galloping economic calamity, voters delivered a historic victory to Barack Obama. He garnered 53 percent of the popular vote, prevailing even in such traditional Republican strongholds as Virginia,

2008

Candidate (Party)	Electoral Vote		Popular Vote	
Obama (Democrat)	365	68%	69,498,459	52.9%
McCain (Republican)	173	32%	59,948,283	45.6%

MAP 41.6 Presidential Election of 2008   A record voter turnout, swelled by millions of young new voters, African Americans, and Latinos, gave Senator Barack Obama an Electoral College landslide and the Democratic party solid control of both houses of Congress. Obama redrew the electoral map by taking nine states won by George W. Bush in 2004.

© Cengage Learning

Asked by an interviewer in February 2009, just one month into his presidency, if he felt "burdened" by the welter of problems he faced, President Obama (b. 1961) replied:

"I think that we are at an extraordinary moment that is full of peril but full of possibility and I think that's the time you want to be president. . . . [T]here's something about this country where hard times, big challenges bring out the best in us. This is when the political system starts to move effectively. This is when people start getting out of the petty and the trivial debates. This is when the public starts paying attention. . . . [W]hen things are going well . . . they've got better things to do than to think about public policy. . . ."

Nevada, and Colorado, and won the Electoral College 365 to 173 (see Map 41.6). Democrats also enlarged their majorities in the House and the Senate. In further contrast with the famously rocky transition from depression-era president Herbert Hoover to Franklin Roosevelt, the outgoing Bush and incoming Obama administrations conspicuously cooperated to ensure continuity and consistency in combating the economic crisis.

Obama's election opened a new chapter in the long-vexed history of American race relations. It also confronted the nation's first African American president with the daunting challenge of governing a country embroiled in two wars even as it sank into the deepest economic abyss since the 1930s. "Black Man Given Nation's Worst Job," jibed the satirical magazine, *The Onion.*

✵ Obama in the White House

Inspired by Barack Obama's vision of "hope," a vast and exuberant crowd gathered in Washington, D.C., to celebrate his inauguration. Youthful energy was in the air, though in his inaugural address Obama struck a sober note by calling on Americans to "put away childish things" and embrace "a new era of responsibility."

Obama's solemn tone was fitting. Even as he spoke, home construction was grinding to a halt, mortgage

foreclosures were soaring, and countless businesses were shutting their doors. Most alarmingly, the economy was shedding a sickening 700,000 jobs a month. The unemployment rate climbed above 10 percent—the highest level since the early 1980s and perhaps heralding a return to the catastrophic joblessness of the Great Depression of the 1930s.

Obama strongly counterpunched against the deepening crisis. In his first hundred days he pushed through a series of major initiatives that included a new round of help for troubled banks, tax and mortgage relief, and a huge "stimulus" bill—the **American Relief and Recovery Act**—that contained nearly a trillion dollars of tax cuts, as well as new spending for jobs, infrastructure projects, and relief to state and local governments. The government also shored up bankrupt automakers General Motors and Chrysler, as well as threatened banks and insurance companies. The nonpartisan Congressional Budget Office later estimated that those measures saved up to 3 million jobs, helping substantially to arrest the economy's freefall.

By the summer of 2009, the worst of the panic was over and the economy began to expand once more. Economists tempered their comparisons with the Great Depression and gave the less frightening label "Great Recession" to the turmoil. But the economy had been badly wounded and continued to suffer. Hopes for a rapid recovery proved false, and the first steps toward growth were feeble and faltering. The unemployment rate stayed stuck above 9 percent. As millions of Americans lost jobs and homes, and many more succumbed to anxiety and fear, the effects of the Great Recession wormed their way deeply into the American psyche, and would not be quickly dislodged. Psychology and economics intersected, as newly anxious consumers cut back on spending, further burdening an already sluggish recovery.

Even while pursuing economic recovery, President Obama also sought to achieve the long-sought liberal goal of health-care reform. When attempts to enlist Republican support bogged down in congressional haggling, he had to rely on Democrats alone to pass a landmark health bill, the **Patient Protection and Affordable Care Act**, in March 2010. The new health-care law (derided by critics as "Obamacare") mandated all Americans to purchase health insurance starting in 2014, required states to establish "exchanges" whereby individuals and small businesses could purchase health-care insurance at competitive rates, prohibited insurers from denying coverage to anyone with a preexisting medical condition, and allowed children up to the age of twenty-six to remain covered by their parent's health plans. The price of the bill was estimated at $940 billion over ten years, but experts also predicted that the bill's cost-cutting measures would reduce the federal deficit by more than $1 trillion over twenty years.

Scarcely pausing, Obama soon followed his health-care success with the 2010 **Wall Street Reform and Consumer Protection Act**, which pointed the way to a major overhaul of the nation's financial regulatory system. The act aimed to curb the risky, high-flying practices that had contributed to the debacle of 2008 with new controls on banks, investment houses, and stock markets, and with new truth-in-lending rules to protect consumers.

✷ A Sea of Troubles

Yet Obama had unusual difficulty reaping the political rewards of these legislative achievements. He seemed caught between an anvil and a boulder. Because his measures only halted, but did not reverse, the economy's decline, critics on the left condemned him as too timid. Because federal budget deficits ballooned dramatically on his watch (thanks not only to his own initiatives but also to the Bush-era tax cuts combined with declining tax revenues in the midst of the downturn), critics on the right excoriated him as a big-government spendthrift. The conjunction of expanding federal programs and mounting deficits tapped into a deep vein of American wariness of "big government." Starting with vehement attacks on the health-care bill in the summer of 2009, angry protesters accused the Obama administration of promoting "socialism" and "unconstitutional" controls over individual lives. Calling themselves the "Tea party" after the American Revolutionary Patriots, these noisy citizens combined a knack for street-theater demonstrations with nonstop Internet and media fulminations against the president and his policies. Some critics groused that the "Tea party" was not a genuine grassroots movement but an "astro-turf" phenomenon—a fake populist uprising shrewdly manipulated by the usual behind-the-scenes bigshots.

Heartened by the Tea party's mobilization, Republicans determined to fight the administration tooth and nail, steadfastly repudiating Obama's promise of a postpartisan politics. The president did succeed in appointing two new Supreme Court Justices, Sonia Sotomayor (the Court's first Hispanic) in 2009 and Elena Kagan in 2010, bringing the number of female justices to three. But other efforts, like a "cap-and-trade" bill to curb greenhouse gases and reduce global warming, fell victim to the fervent minority's opposition, and gridlock returned to Washington.

As the Great Recession continued to weigh heavily upon the land, Obama's approval ratings steadily slipped, and his party slid downhill with him. In the midterm elections of 2010, Republicans gained six seats in the Senate and a whopping sixty-three seats in the House, enough to give them majority control of the lower chamber when the new Congress convened in 2011. President Obama glumly acknowledged his party's "shellacking," but then surprisingly proceeded to wring several major accomplishments out of the postelection "lame-duck" session in December 2010, including an $858 billion package that extended unemployment benefits as well as the Bush-era tax cuts, the repeal of "Don't Ask Don't Tell," and a renewed nuclear arms reduction treaty (New START, or Strategic Arms Reduction Treaty) with Russia. But he fell short of passing the DREAM Act (Development, Relief and Education for Alien Minors Act), which would have created a path to citizenship for undocumented youths who either graduated from college or served in the U.S. armed forces. The vexed issue of immigration reform, especially with respect to the nation's 12 million "illegals," also waited for resolution another day.

✷ Wars, Oil Spills, and Political Backlash

Along with economic problems, Obama also inherited America's wars in Iraq and Afghanistan, as well as a raft of other headaches. The new president sought to wind down the Iraq War while leaving behind a reasonably stable country. Shortly after taking office, Obama announced that American combat operations in Iraq would end in summer 2010 and that all American combat troops would be withdrawn by 2011. Despite

The End of Osama bin Laden   President Barack Obama and his national security team huddle in the White House Situation Room to watch live updates on the mission to kill Osama bin Laden, May 2, 2011. Nearly ten years after the murderous attacks of September 11, 2001, rough justice was meted out to the terrorist mastermind. Much commentary on this photograph has focused on the presence of women in the room and on the President's lack of macho swagger, even as American forces closed in on the nation's most hated foe.

continuing violence and the agonizingly slow birth of a viable Iraqi government, the deadline for ending American-led operations was met. Still, about 50,000 American troops remained in the country to protect U.S. bases and support Iraqi security efforts.

Afghanistan was a thornier nettle to grasp. Obama had declared the Afghan war necessary to defeat Al Qaeda and prevent future terrorism. But Afghan *jihadi* (militant Islamic) fighters grew stronger against an Afghan government plagued by incompetence and corruption. More ominously, the Taliban and Al Qaeda found refuge across the border in unstable but nuclear-armed Pakistan, posing the danger of an expanded conflict there as well.

Pressed by some to deepen the American commitment, and by others to seek a way out of the increasingly costly conflict, Obama chose to do both. In December 2009 he declared that American troops would begin withdrawing by 2011—but that in order to achieve that goal he was deploying an additional thirty thousand U.S. soldiers to combat the insurgency. He

ordered changes in strategy and appointed a new U.S. commander, General David Petraeus. But casualties increased and frustration with the nearly decade-long conflict grew, with no satisfactory exit in sight.

Obama soon faced an unprecedented environmental calamity as well. On April 20, 2010, the BP (formerly British Petroleum) energy corporation's Deepwater Horizon oil platform in the Gulf of Mexico exploded, killing seventeen workers and spewing oil from its deep well nearly two miles below the ocean floor. Over the next four months the American public watched helplessly as nearly 5 billion gallons of oil poured into the Gulf of Mexico, fouling beaches and killing wildlife from Louisiana to Florida. For four months BP futilely attempted to stop the gusher of oil, as anger mounted against both the oil giant's and the federal government's inability to contain the disaster. By the time the well was finally capped in August 2010, it had become the worst oil disaster in U.S. history.

When American forces dramatically concluded a ten-year manhunt and killed Osama bin Laden in May

2011, the president's poll ratings got a brief upward bump. But the lift proved vanishingly brief. As the accumulated federal debt approached its legal limit of $14.3 trillion in the summer of 2011, the Republican Tea Party faction seized the occasion to play a game of fiscal "chicken" with the White House. Raising the debt ceiling had historically been a routine matter, but led by the eighty-five freshmen elected in 2010, House Republicans stubbornly refused to lift the debt limit until the president agreed to a long-term deficit-reduction plan that called for huge spending cuts and few if any tax increases. Heartened by their triumph, Republicans looked to the upcoming 2012 presidential election with increasing hope for victory—though the spectacle of protracted wrangling and partisan intransigence while the nation's credit rating, and the health of the global economy, hung in the balance deeply disillusioned many Americans of both parties. Some critics began to question the soundness of the American political system itself.

Meanwhile, dramatic demographic changes were altering the political landscape, with consequences that both parties struggled to understand (see Map. 41.7). And as so often in the past, economic anxieties stoked anti-immigrant sentiment. In April 2010 Arizona enacted a harsh statute requiring state and local police to help enforce federal immigration laws. Although a federal judge put the statute on hold, Arizona's action was applauded in many other places, especially those with substantial Latino immigrant populations. As Latinos replaced African Americans as the country's largest minority, much of the nation's political future hinged on their sense of belonging and their stake in the future of the republic.

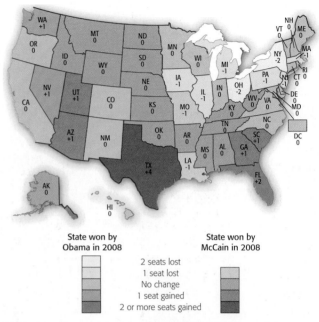

State won by Obama in 2008

State won by McCain in 2008

2 seats lost
1 seat lost
No change
1 seat gained
2 or more seats gained

MAP 41.7 Demography Is (Political) Destiny The United States is one of the few nations with a constitutionally mandated census, a provision reflecting the Founders' expectation that the country's population would grow and spread out, and their commitment to maintaining fair and proportional representation in the federal electoral system. Thus, every ten years congressional districts are redrawn; some states gain and some states lose representation in the House and the Electoral College. This map, showing the reapportionment resulting from the 2010 census, clearly shows the continuing shift of the nation's population and political center of gravity southward and westward. Note that Texas is the biggest gainer from the 2010 census, and that for the first time since becoming a state in 1850, California will gain no congressional seats or electoral college votes. © Cengage Learning

Chapter Review

KEY TERMS

weapons of mass destruction (WMD) (965)

Democratic Leadership Council (965)

"Don't Ask, Don't Tell" (966)

Oklahoma City bombing (967)

Contract with America (968)

Welfare Reform Bill (968)

North American Free Trade Agreement (NAFTA) (969)

World Trade Organization (WTO) (969)

Whitewater (970)

Lewinsky affair (970)

Kyoto Treaty (973)

9/11 (974)

Al Qaeda (975)

USA Patriot Act (975)

Department of Homeland Security (975)

Guantánamo Detention Camp (975)

Abu Ghraib prison (978)

No Child Left Behind Act (979)

Hurricane Katrina (982)

deleveraging (984)

American Relief and Recovery Act (985)

Patient Protection and Affordable Care Act (986)

Wall Street Reform and Consumer Protection Act (986)

PEOPLE TO KNOW

William Jefferson ("Bill")
Clinton
H. Ross Perot
Hillary Rodham Clinton

Newt Gingrich
Robert Dole
John McCain
Sarah Palin

Monica Lewinsky
George W. Bush
Richard Cheney
John Kerry

Nancy Pelosi
Barack Obama
Joseph R. ("Joe") Biden

CHRONOLOGY

1992 Clinton defeats Bush and Perot for presidency

1993 NAFTA signed

1994 Republicans win majorities in both houses of Congress

1996 Welfare Reform Bill becomes law
Clinton defeats Dole for presidency

1998 Clinton-Lewinsky scandal
U.S. and Britain launch military strikes against Iraq
House of Representatives impeaches Clinton

1999 Senate acquits Clinton on impeachment charges
Kosovo crisis; NATO warfare with Serbia
Protest in Seattle against World Trade Organization

2000 U.S. normalizes trade relations with China
George W. Bush wins presidency in Electoral College; Albert Gore takes popular vote

2001 Terrorists attack New York City and Washington, D.C., on September 11
U.S. invades Afghanistan
Congress passes USA Patriot Act

2002 Congress passes No Child Left Behind Act
Bush labels Iraq, Iran, and North Korea "axis of evil"
Congress authorizes use of force against Iraq

2002 U.N. Security Council demands that Iraq comply with weapons inspections
Republicans regain Senate

2003 U.S. invades Iraq
Saddam Hussein captured in Iraq
Supreme Court narrowly approves affirmative action

2004 Gay marriage controversy erupts
Iraqi interim government installed
Bush defeats Kerry for presidency

2005 Iraq elects permanent government but quickly descends into sectarian conflict

2006 Saddam Hussein executed

2007 U.S. troop surge in Iraq

2008 Barack Obama elected 44th president of the United States

2009 American Relief and Recovery Act passed

2010 BP Deepwater Horizon oil platform explodes in Gulf of Mexico
Patient Protection and Affordable Care Act passed
Wall Street Reform and Consumer Protection Act passed
"Don't Ask, Don't Tell" policy repealed
New START treaty approved

TO LEARN MORE

John Cassidy, *How Markets Fail: The Logic of Economic Calamities* (2009)
Alan Dershowitz, *Supreme Injustice: How the High Court Hijacked Election 2000* (2001)
Elizabeth Drew, *Showdown: The Struggle Between the Gingrich Congress and the Clinton White House* (1997)
Dave Eggers, *Zeitoun* (2009)
Lloyd C. Gardner, *The Long Road to Baghdad: A History of U.S. Foreign Policy from the 1970s to the Present* (2010)
Joe Klein, *The Natural* (2002)

George Packer, *The Assassins' Gate: America in Iraq* (2005)
Richard Posner, *An Affair of State: The Investigation, Impeachment, and Trial of President Clinton* (1999)
Jack Rakove, *The Unfinished Election of 2000* (2001)
Thomas Ricks, *Fiasco: The American Military Adventure in Iraq* (2006)
James Stewart, *Blood Sport* (1996)
Bob Woodward, *Bush at War* (2002); *Plan of Attack* (2004); *State of Denial: Bush at War, Part III* (2006)
———, *The Choice* (1996)

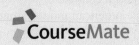 Go to the CourseMate website at **www.cengagebrain.com** for additional study tools and review materials—including audio and video clips—for this chapter.

A complete, annotated bibliography for this chapter—along with brief descriptions of the People to Know—may be found on the American Pageant website. The Key Terms are defined in a Glossary at the end of the text.

AP® Review Questions for Chapter 41

1. What prompted the first wave of heavy criticism and verbal abuse to be hurled at First Lady Hillary Rodham Clinton during the onset of the Clinton administration?
   - (A) Mrs. Clinton's decision to run for the U.S. Senate in the state of New York
   - (B) Mrs. Clinton not publicly criticizing her husband's sexual affairs
   - (C) Mrs. Clinton advocating too strongly for the role of women in the administration
   - (D) Mrs. Clinton developing an excessively complex health-care plan that was quickly dropped by Congress
   - (E) Mrs. Clinton claiming that the political problems that she and her husband encountered were the result of "a vast right-wing conspiracy"

2. Which of the following represented a significant political victory for President Clinton at the beginning of the Clinton administration?
   - (A) Congressional passage of the 1993 deficit-reduction bill
   - (B) An end to the ban on gays and lesbians in the military
   - (C) Congressional passage of health-care reform
   - (D) Congressional approval of a campaign finance reform bill
   - (E) Congressional passage of a middle-class tax cut

3. Which of the following events is most indicative of a deep dissatisfaction with the government?
   - (A) The bombing of a federal office building in Oklahoma City
   - (B) Appointing the second woman to the Supreme Court
   - (C) Republicans creating the Contract with America
   - (D) Repealing term limits for federal officials
   - (E) Federal agents storming the Branch Davidian compound in Waco

4. Which of the following political decisions by President Clinton aroused the hostility and ire of many liberals in his own party?
   - (A) President Clinton's signature of the welfare reform bill that included work requirements and time limits for welfare benefits
   - (B) President Clinton's appointment of Ruth Bader Ginsburg to the U.S. Supreme Court
   - (C) President Clinton signing a bill to restrict teenagers' access to abortion
   - (D) President Clinton's support of the North American Free Trade Agreement (NAFTA) with Canada and Mexico
   - (E) President Clinton's decision to put his wife Hillary Rodham Clinton in charge of health-care reform

5. What action during the first year of the Republican-led Congress led to an emerging public consensus that the Republicans had overreached with their conservative policies?
   - (A) The shutdown of the federal government during a dispute between the Republican congressional leadership and President Clinton over the federal budget
   - (B) The passage of the Welfare Reform Bill
   - (C) The passage of a bill to limit unfunded mandates on state and local governments
   - (D) The impeachment of President Clinton for lying about his sexual affairs
   - (E) The ethics investigation into activities of Speaker of the House Newt Gingrich

6. Which of the following was NOT among the areas where President Clinton's foreign policy stumbled in the first years of his presidency?
   - (A) Human rights and trade with China
   - (B) American troops in Somalia
   - (C) Intervening in the Rwandan genocide
   - (D) Ending ethnic conflict in the Balkans
   - (E) Developing strong relations with America's allies Germany and France

7. What was the primary political legacy of President Clinton, according to some historians?
   - (A) President Clinton revived the vigorous liberal traditions of the Democratic party.
   - (B) President Clinton established a firm direction for American foreign policy after the Cold War.
   - (C) President Clinton consolidated the Reagan-Bush revolution by encouraging reduced expectations of government.
   - (D) President Clinton restored faith in elected officials if not in big government.
   - (E) President Clinton turned the Democratic party away from the historic commitments to racial and social justice.

8. What did the U.S. Supreme Court cite as its reasoning for taking the unprecedented action of prohibiting further recounting of Florida's popular vote and awarding the 2000 election to George W. Bush?
   - (A) The Court's fear that the election would be thrown into the House of Representatives
   - (B) The corruption and incompetence of Florida election authorities
   - (C) A legal finding that Florida's inconsistent standards for evaluating the disputed ballots violated the equal protection clause of the Constitution
   - (D) Clear evidence that the votes would have favored Bush even if they had all been counted
   - (E) Political pressure from the American military that feared a foreign attack if no president had been named

9. Which of the following was NOT among the polarizing conservative policies pursued by President George W. Bush when he assumed the presidency?
   (A) Passing the No Child Left Behind education reform law
   (B) Sharply cutting taxes
   (C) Withdrawing American support from international family planning programs that permitted abortion
   (D) Refusing to permit government-sponsored embryonic stem cell research
   (E) Repudiating the Kyoto Treaty on greenhouse gases and opening Alaska to more oil exploration

10. All of the following constituted U.S. government responses to terrorist attacks on September 11, 2001, EXCEPT
   (A) passage of the USA-Patriot Act, which provided for, among other things, the extensive telephone and e-mail surveillance of Americans suspected of ties to terrorism.
   (B) the indefinite detention and deportation of immigrants suspected of terrorism.
   (C) a sustained effort to try suspected terrorists before military tribunals rather than before civilian courts.
   (D) the creation of a cabinet-level Department of Homeland Security to protect the nation's borders and identify potential attackers.
   (E) suspension of Americans' First Amendment right to protest against government policies.

11. What did the U.S. military encounter in Iraq after ousting Saddam Hussein from power?
   (A) The abuse of American prisoners by the remnants of Hussein's army
   (B) A warm reception from the Iraqi people
   (C) A confident new democratic Iraq
   (D) An invasion of Iraq by militant Arab states
   (E) Violent resistance from Iraqi insurgents and foreign militants drawn to the country

12. What revelation in 2004 concerning the Iraq War prompted a deep escalation of anti-American sentiment in Iraq and throughout the Arab world?
   (A) The revelation that some American soldiers had humiliated and abused Iraqi captives in the Abu Ghraib prison
   (B) The news that Al Qaeda members captured in Iraq began leading a guerrilla movement
   (C) The revelation that American military forces in Iraq were receiving intelligence and interrogation assistance from the Mossad, the Israeli intelligence agency
   (D) The information that the new Iraqi government was relying heavily on former Sunni members of Saddam Hussein's government
   (E) The revelation that the United States had bombed substantial civilian districts in Baghdad

13. George W. Bush successfully won reelection in 2004 over Senator John Kerry by claiming all of the following EXCEPT that he
   (A) was a strong leader in the war on terrorism and Kerry would be a weak and indecisive commander in chief.
   (B) enjoyed nearly universal support among foreign leaders, including the political leadership of U.S. allies in Germany and France, while Kerry could not win the confidence of these foreign leaders.
   (C) had started to reform and improve public education in America with the passage and implementation of the No Child Left Behind Act.
   (D) cultivated his conservative base by resisting full-scale embryonic stem cell research and calling for a constitutional amendment to ban gay marriage.
   (E) had passed enormous tax cuts to return money to individual taxpayers, while Kerry was likely to raise taxes on middle-class Americans.

14. The most important issue in the presidential election of 2008 was
   (A) the economic crisis.
   (B) U.S. intervention in the Middle East.
   (C) health care.
   (D) education.
   (E) Don't Ask, Don't Tell.

15. The "Tea party" movement that emerged in 2008 shares all of the following qualities with the Patriots after whom they named themselves EXCEPT that
   (A) both believe they are fighting against an oppressive government.
   (B) both oppose any new taxes levied on the people, directly or indirectly.
   (C) both are small, local groups without a wide support base.
   (D) both use extreme measures to make their point.
   (E) both believe their ideas and actions are essential to improving Americans' lives.

Chapter 42

The American People Face a New Century

As our case is new, so we must think anew and act anew. We must disenthrall ourselves, and then we shall save our country.

ABRAHAM LINCOLN, 1862

Well beyond its two-hundredth birthday as the twenty-first century entered its second decade, the United States was both an old and a new nation. It boasted one of the longest uninterrupted traditions of democratic government of any country on earth. Indeed, it had pioneered the techniques of mass democracy and was, in that sense, the oldest modern polity. As one of the earliest countries to industrialize, America had also dwelt in the modern economic era longer than most nations. But the Republic was in many ways still youthful as well. Innovation, entrepreneurship, and risk-taking—all characteristics of youth—were honored national values.

America's twenty-first century began much like the twentieth, as society continued to be rejuvenated by fresh waves of immigrants, full of energy and ambition. The U.S. economy, despite the impact of the "Great Recession," remained an important engine of world economic growth. American inventions—especially computer and communications technologies—continued to transform the face of global society. Consumers from Berlin to Beijing seemed to worship the icons of American culture—downing soft drinks and donning blue jeans, watching Hollywood films and television series, listening to rock or country music, even adopting indigenous American sports like baseball and basketball. In the realm of consumerism, American products appeared to have Coca-Colonized the globe.

The history of American society also seemed to have increased global significance as the third millennium of the Christian era opened. Americans were a pluralistic people who had struggled for centuries to offer opportunity, tolerance, and justice to many different religious, ethnic, and racial groups. Their historical trials and triumphs could offer valuable lessons to the rapidly internationalizing planetary society that was emerging at the dawn of the twenty-first century.

Much history remained to be made as the country entered its third century of nationhood. The great social experiment of American democracy was far from completed as the United States faced its future. Astonishing breakthroughs in science and technology, especially in genetics, bioengineering, and communications, presented Americans with stunning opportunities as well as wrenching ethical choices. Global climate change made the responsible stewardship of a fragile planet more urgent than ever. Inequality and prejudice continued to challenge Americans to close the gap between their most hallowed values and the stark realities of modern life. The terrorist attacks of September 11, 2001, violently heralded a new era of fear and anxiety. And the severe economic crisis that convulsed the nation and the world in 2008 demonstrated that free-market capitalism could still produce abundant misery as well as material abundance.

But men and women make history only within the framework bequeathed to them by earlier generations. For better or worse, they march forward along time's path bearing the burdens of the past. Knowing when they have come to a truly new turn in the road, when they can lay part of their burden down and when they cannot, or should not—all this constitutes the sort of wisdom that only historical study can engender.

✴ Economic Revolutions

When the twentieth century opened, United States Steel Corporation was the flagship business of America's booming industrial revolution. A generation later, General Motors, annually producing millions of automobiles, became the characteristic American corporation, signaling the historic shift to a mass consumer economy that began in the 1920s and flowered fully in the 1950s. Following World War II, the rise of International Business Machines (IBM) and, later, Microsoft Corporation symbolized yet another momentous transformation, to the fast-paced "information age," when the storing, organizing, and processing of data became an industry in its own right.

The pace of the information age soon accelerated. As the twenty-first century opened, the phenomenal growth of the Internet heralded an explosive communications revolution. New corporate giants like Google redefined the ways that people knew about the world, while social networking services like Facebook and Twitter redefined the ways they knew each other. Businesspeople could now instantaneously girdle the planet with transactions of prodigious scope and serpentine complexity. Japanese bankers might sell wheat contracts in Chicago and simultaneously direct the profits to buying oil shipments from the Persian Gulf offered by a broker in Amsterdam. Peoples from all corners of the planet were rocketing down the "information superhighway" toward the uncharted terrain of an electronic global village, where traditional geographic, social, and political boundaries could be vaulted with the tap of a keypad.

But the very speed and efficiency of the new communications tools threatened to wipe out entire occupational categories, and even ways of life. Postal carriers, travel agents, store clerks, bank tellers, stockbrokers, and all kinds of other workers whose business it was to mediate between product and client were in danger of becoming road kill on the information superhighway. White-collar jobs in financial services and high-tech engineering, once thought securely anchored in places like Chicago, Los Angeles, and New York, could now be "outsourced" to countries such as Ireland and India, where employees could help keep a company's global circuits firing twenty-four hours a day.

Increasingly, scientific research was the motor that propelled the economy, and new scientific knowledge raised new moral dilemmas and provoked new political arguments. When scientists first unlocked the secrets of molecular genetic structure in the 1950s, the road lay open to breeding new strains of high-yield, pest- and weather-resistant crops; to curing hereditary diseases; and also, unfortunately, to unleashing genetic mutations that might threaten the complex balance of the wondrous biosphere in which humankind was delicately suspended. As the curtain rose on the new century, scientists stood at the threshold of a revolution in biological engineering. The Human Genome Project established the DNA sequencing of the thirty thousand human genes, pointing the way to radical new medical therapies—and to mouthwatering profits

© Bettmann/Corbis

Outsourcing Jobs to India Sophisticated computer technology has allowed developing countries like India to attract Western employers seeking lower labor costs. India's educated and English-speaking work force has made it particularly suitable for international call centers and computer programming.

for bioengineering firms. Startling breakthroughs in the cloning of animals raised thorny questions about the legitimacy of applying cloning technology to human reproduction. Research into human stem cells held out the promise of cures for afflictions like Parkinson's disease and Alzheimer's. But some religious groups protested that harvesting stem cells involved the destruction of human life in embryonic form—just one example of the many ways that Americans continued to struggle with the ethical implications of their vast new technological powers.

Other unprecedented ethical questions also clamored for resolution. What principles should govern the allocation of human organs for lifesaving transplants? Was it wise in the first place to spend money on such costly procedures rather than devote society's resources to improved sanitation, maternal and infant care, and nutritional and health education? How, if at all, should society regulate the increasingly lengthy and often painful process of dying? (See "Makers of America: Scientists and Engineers," pp. 994–995.)

✵ Affluence and Inequality

Americans were still an affluent people at the beginning of the twenty-first century. Median household income reached $49,400 in 2011. Even those Americans with incomes below the government's official poverty level (defined in 2010 as $22,314 for a family of four) enjoyed a standard of living higher than that of two-thirds of the rest of humankind.

Americans were no longer the world's wealthiest people, as they had been in the quarter-century

TABLE 42.1 Widening Income Inequality

Share of Aggregate Income	1980	1990	2000	2008
Lowest fifth	4.2	3.8	3.6	3.4
Second fifth	10.2	9.6	8.9	8.6
Third fifth	16.8	15.9	14.8	14.7
Fourth fifth	24.7	24.0	23.0	23.2
Highest fifth	44.1	46.6	49.8	50.3
Top 5%	16.5	18.5	22.1	21.7

During the last two decades of the twentieth century, the top fifth of the country's households made significant gains in income, while everyone else lost ground.

(Source: *Statistical Abstract of the United States,* 2010; U.S. Census Bureau *Current Population Reports.*)

after World War II. Citizens of several other countries enjoyed higher average per capita incomes, and many nations boasted more equitable distributions of wealth. In an unsettling reversal of long-term trends in American society, during the last two decades of the twentieth century, the rich got fabulously richer, while the poor got an ever-shrinking share of the pie. The richest 20 percent of Americans in 2009 raked in half the nation's income, while the poorest 20 percent received a little over 3 percent (see Table 42.1). The gap between rich and poor began to widen in the 1980s and widened further thereafter. That trend was evident in many industrial societies, but it was most pronounced in the United States. Between 1968 and 2009, the share of the

Two Nations? While decaying neighborhoods and legions of the homeless blighted American cities in the early twenty-first century, affluent Americans lived the good life in booming suburbs and in the more suburbanized cities of the Sunbelt, such as this development of million-dollar homes around a country club in Las Vegas, Nevada.

	U.S.	CANADA	GERMANY	JAPAN	SWEDEN	HONG KONG	UK	KOREA	ITALY	FRANCE	CZECH	SPAIN
Income Inequality (Gini Index)	45.0	32.1	27.0	37.6	23.0	53.3	34.0	31.4	32.0	32.7	26.0	32.0
Unemployment Rate	9.7	8.0	7.4	5.1	8.3	4.3	7.9	3.3	8.4	9.5	7.1	20.0
Level of Democracy	8.18	9.08	8.38	8.08	9.50	5.92	8.16	8.11	7.83	7.77	8.19	8.16
Life Expectancy at Birth	78.37	81.38	80.07	82.25	81.07	82.04	80.05	79.05	81.77	81.19	77.19	81.17
Food Insecurity	16	8	4	9	6	6	9	11	15	10	14	14
Prison Population Rate	743	117	85	59	78	141	154	98	113	96	214	159
Student Math Scores	487	527	513	529	494	555	492	546	483	497	493	483
Student Science Scores	502	529	520	539	495	549	514	538	489	498	500	488

■ Best   ■ Worse   ■ Worst

FIGURE 42.1 How the United States Measures Up Once the undisputed world leader in countless areas of human endeavor, the United States looked to be falling behind on several crucial counts in the early twenty-first century.

nation's income that flowed to the top 20 percent of its households swelled from 40 percent to 50.3 percent. Even more striking, in the same period the top 5 percent of income earners saw their share of the national income grow from about 15 percent to a remarkable 21.7 percent. The Welfare Reform Bill of 1996, restricting access to social services and requiring able-bodied welfare recipients to find work, weakened the financial footing of many impoverished families still further, and the Great Recession added to their ranks.

Widening inequality could be measured in other ways as well. In the 1970s chief executives typically earned forty-one times as much as the average worker in their corporations; by the early 2000s, they earned 245 times as much. Prior to the passage of the Obama health-care bill in 2010, 50 million people had no medical insurance. At the same time, some 46.2 million people remained mired in poverty in 2011 (the largest number in more than 50 years). They represented 15.1 percent of all Americans (approximately 12.3 percent of whites, 25.8 percent of African Americans, 25.3 percent of Latinos, and 12.5 percent of Asians), a depressing indictment of the inequities afflicting an affluent and allegedly egalitarian republic (for comparative data, see Figure 42.1).

What caused the widening income gap? Some critics pointed to the tax and fiscal policies of the Reagan and both Bush (father and son) presidencies, which favored the wealthy (see Table 42.2). But deeper-running historical currents probably played a more powerful role, as suggested by the similar experiences of other industrialized societies. Among the most conspicuous

causes were intensifying global economic competition; the shrinkage in high-paying manufacturing jobs for semiskilled and unskilled workers; the greater economic rewards commanded by educated workers in high-tech industries; the decline of unions; the growth of part-time and temporary work; the rising tide of relatively low-skill immigrants; and the increasing tendency of

TABLE 42.2 Who Pays Federal Income Taxes? (share of U.S. income tax, by income percentile)

Income Group (base income shown as of 2007)	1994	2007
Top 1% (above $410,096)	28.7%	40.4%
Top 5% (above $160,041)	47.4	60.6
Top 10% (above $113,018)	59.1	71.2
Top 25% (above $66,532)	79.5	86.6
Top 50% (above $32,879)	95.2	97.1
Bottom 50% (below $32,879)	4.8	2.9

Because the United States has long had a "progressive" income tax system, in which tax obligations are distributed according to ability to pay, widening income inequality was reflected in a redistribution of tax burdens. In the booming 1990s, the rich did indeed get richer—but they also paid an increasing fraction of the total federal tax take. These figures help explain why tax cuts benefit the wealthy more than middle-income earners and the poor.

(Source: Internal Revenue Service data, Tax Foundation; http://www.taxfoundation.org/news/show/250.html.)

Subatomic particles and space-bound satellites do not respect political boundaries. Disease-carrying viruses spread across the globe. Radio waves and Internet communications reach every corner of planet Earth. At first glance science, technology, and medicine appear to be quintessentially international phenomena. Scientists often pride themselves on the universal validity of scientific knowledge and the transnational character of scientific networks. In a world marked by political divisions, science evidently knows no bounds.

But a closer look reveals that national context does influence the character of scientific enterprise. American scientists have repeatedly made significant contributions to the life of the nation. They, in turn, have been shaped by its unique historical circumstances—especially America's intensifying concerns about national security in the twentieth century. Once marginal players in global intellectual life, American scientists now stand at the forefront of worldwide scientific advancement. In many ways the rise of American science has kept pace with the arrival of the United States as a world power.

Nowhere was this trend more evident than in the story of "Big Science." The unusual demands of America's national security state during World War II and the Cold War required vast scientific investments. The result was Big Science, or multidisciplinary research enterprises of unparalleled size, scope, and cost. Big Science and Big Technology meant big bucks, big machines, and big teams of scientists and engineers. The close link between government and science was not new—precedents stretched as far back as the founding of the National Academy of Sciences during the Civil War. But the depression-era Tennessee Valley Authority (TVA) and the wartime Manhattan Project ushered in ventures of colossal scale and ambition. As the head of the TVA wrote in 1944, "There is almost nothing, however fantastic, that (given competent organization) a team of engineers, scientists, and administrators cannot do today."

Cold War competition with the Soviets translated into huge government investments in physics, chemistry, and aerospace. The equation was simple: national security depended on technological superiority, which entailed costly facilities for scientific research and ambitious efforts to recruit and train scientists. In the 1950s defense projects employed two-thirds of the nation's scientists and engineers. Laboratories, reactors, accelerators, and observatories proliferated. After the Soviets launched the world's first artificial satellite (*Sputnik I*) in 1957, the international space race became America's top

Launching *Apollo 11* NASA flight directors monitor the launch of the *Apollo 11* lunar landing mission from the Manned Spacecraft Center in Houston, Texas, in July 1969.

scientific priority. To land astronauts on the moon, the National Aeronautics and Space Administration (NASA) spent a whopping $25.4 billion over eleven years on Project Apollo. Another massive aerospace mission, President Reagan's controversial Strategic Defense Initiative (or "Star Wars"), consumed somewhere between $32 billion and $71 billion between 1984 and 1994.

In America's burgeoning "research universities," the federal government found willing partners in the promotion of the scientific enterprise. University-employed scientists, largely paid by government grants, concentrated on basic research, accounting for over 75 percent of the estimated $51.9 billion spent on basic science in 2008. Meanwhile, private industry spent additional billions on applied research and product development.

For consumers of air bags, smart phones, and other high-tech gadgets, these investments yielded rich rewards as innovative technologies dramatically improved the quality of life. Over the course of the twentieth century, American corporations spearheaded a global revolution in communications and information technology. American Telephone and Telegraph (AT&T) and Radio Corporation of America (RCA) attended the birth of telephones, radio, and television. Apple, International Business Machines (IBM), and Microsoft introduced personal computers. Government and industry scientists together invented the Internet.

Twentieth-century advances in medical science and technology have also revolutionized American lives. Thanks to new drugs, devices, and methods of treatment, the average life expectancy in the United States leapt from 47.3 years in 1900 to 77.9 years in 2007. In the first half of the twentieth century, physicians discovered hormones and vitamins, introduced penicillin and other antibiotics, and experimented with insulin therapy for diabetes and radiation therapy for cancer. More recently, cutting-edge medical science has nurtured in-vitro fertilization; developed respirators, artificial hearts, and other medical devices; and largely contained the AIDS epidemic.

Much of the optimism for future medical breakthroughs centers on the $3 billion Human Genome Project, which completed its mapping and sequencing of all the genetic material in the human body in 2003. Deemed the "holy grail" of genomics research, the project promised countless benefits, including new diagnoses for genetic defects, innovative therapies, and untold commercial applications. Coordinated by the Department of Energy and the National Institutes of Health, the project engaged thousands of scientists in universities and laboratories across the nation and around the globe.

To achieve such innovation, Big Science typically demands complex teams of scientists, engineers, and technicians. When traditional channels of recruitment came up short, scientific institutions increasingly recruited foreigners, women, and minorities (see Figure 42.2). Immigrants and exiles played key roles in the development of the atomic bomb and Cold War weaponry. Long relegated to junior positions as assistants and technicians, women and minorities have recently made significant gains in the "white man's world" of science. In 2007 women represented 27 percent of

Percent

FIGURE 42.2 Demographic Profile of Women, Minorities, and the Foreign-Born in Nonacademic Science and Engineering Occupations, 1980–2000 (Source: *Science and Engineering Indicators, 2002,* http://www.nsf.gov/statistics/seind02/c3/fig03-13.htm.)

employed doctoral scientists and engineers in the United States, African Americans 5 percent, and Hispanics 4 percent, while the foreign-born accounted for 24 percent.

Despite these stunning achievements, evidence suggests that the United States might be losing its preeminence in science. After dominating the intellectual world from the 1960s through the 1990s, American scientists are now winning fewer prizes and patents and publishing fewer scientific papers than their peers in Europe and Asia. Experts predict that current school-age Americans will not be able to meet the rising demand for scientific expertise. Moreover, fewer foreigners will arrive to fill the gap, as international competition for their labor heats up in places like Brazil, China, and India. For the United States to retain preeminence in science in the twenty-first century, it must continue to welcome all talent to the field. That means attracting both foreign-born scientists and young American students whose brainpower has long helped make the nation a scientific power.

A Scientist Working in Her Lab This medical school professor researching pancreatic regeneration was part of the surge of women pursuing scientific careers, particularly in the biological sciences. By 2004 as many women as men enrolled in medical schools, and minority enrollment climbed as well. In that year 7 percent of entering medical students were Latino, and 6.5 percent were African American.

educated men and women to marry one another and both work, creating households with very high incomes. Educational opportunities also had a way of perpetuating inequality, starting with the underfunding of many schools in poor urban areas and the soaring cost of higher education. A 2004 study revealed that at the 146 most selective colleges, 74 percent of the students came from families with incomes in the top 25 percent, compared to 3 percent of the students from the bottom income quartile.

✦ The Feminist Revolution

All Americans were caught up in the great economic changes of the late twentieth century, but no group was more profoundly affected than women. When the century opened, women made up about 20 percent of all workers. Over the next five decades, they increased their presence in the labor force at a fairly steady rate, except for a temporary spurt during World War II. Then, beginning in the 1950s, women's entry into the workplace accelerated dramatically. By the 1990s nearly half of all workers were women, and the majority of working-age women held jobs outside the home. Most astonishing was the upsurge in employment among mothers. In 1950 nearly 90 percent of mothers with children under the age of six did not work for pay. But half a century later, a majority of women with children as young as one year old were wage earners (see Table 42.3). Women now brought home the bacon and then cooked it, too. By 2008 American women participated in the work force in higher numbers than in almost all industrialized countries except Russia and China (see Figure 42.3).

Beginning in the 1960s, many all-male strongholds, including Yale, Princeton, West Point, and even,

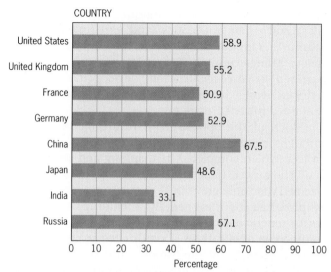

FIGURE 42.3 Women in the Work Force Globally, 2008 (Source: The World Bank, *World Development Indicators.*)

belatedly, southern military academies like the Citadel and Virginia Military Institute, opened their doors to women. By the twenty-first century, women were piloting airliners, orbiting the earth, governing states and cities, and writing Supreme Court decisions.

Yet despite these gains, many feminists remained frustrated. Women continued to receive lower wages—80 cents on the dollar in 2009—compared with men doing the same full-time work. They also tended to concentrate in a few low-prestige, low-paying occupations (the "pink-collar ghetto"). Although they made up more than half the population, women in 2009 accounted for just 32 percent of lawyers and judges (up from 5 percent in 1970) and 32 percent of physicians (up from 10 percent in 1970). Overt sexual discrimination explained some of this occupational segregation, but most of it seemed attributable to the greater burdens of parenthood on women than on men. Women were far more likely than men to interrupt their careers to bear and raise children, and even to choose less demanding career paths to allow for fulfilling those traditional roles. Discrimination and a focus on children also helped account for the persistence of a "gender gap" in voting behavior. Women continued to vote in greater numbers than men for Democratic candidates, who were often perceived as being more willing to favor government support for health and child care, education, and job equality, as well as being more vigilant to protect abortion rights.

As the revolution in women's status rolled on in the 2000s, men's lives changed as well. Some employers provided paternity leave in addition to maternity leave, in recognition of the shared obligations of the two-worker household. More men assumed traditional female responsibilities such as cooking, laundry, and

TABLE 42.3 Working Women: Labor Force Participation Rates for Wives and Mothers, 1950–2007*				
Year	Married	Married, with Children	Married, with Children Ages 6–17	Married, with Children Under Age 6
1950	23.8%	NA	28.3%	11.9%
1960	30.5	NA	39.0	18.6
1970	40.8	39.7	49.2	30.3
1980	50.1	54.1	61.7	45.1
1990	58.2	66.3	73.6	58.9
2000	62.0	70.6	77.2	62.8
2007	61.6	69.3	76.2	61.5

*Percent of women in each specific category in the labor force.

(Source: *Statistical Abstract of the United States,* relevant years.)

A New World for Women Revolutionary changes in the economy and in social values opened new career opportunities for women, even as many of them continued to perform their traditional duties as mothers and homemakers. Here U.S. Air Force Major General Margaret H. Woodward (top left) is shown at her desk as Joint Force Air Component Commander. Drew Gilpin Faust (bottom right) became the first woman to serve as president of Harvard University in 2007. Women athletes also came into their own in the wake of the feminist revolution. Venus and Serena Williams (top right) enthralled the tennis world as individual champions and as a doubles team beginning in the late 1990s.

child care. Recognizing the new realities of the modern American household, Congress passed a Family Leave Bill in 1993, mandating job protection for working fathers as well as mothers who needed to take time off from work for family-related reasons.

✷ New Families and Old

The traditional nuclear family, once prized as the foundation of society and the nursery of the Republic, suffered heavy blows in modern America. By the 1990s one out of every two marriages ended in divorce. Seven times more children were affected by divorce than at the beginning of the twentieth century. Kids who commuted between separated parents were commonplace. The old ideal of a family with two parents, only one of whom worked, was now a virtually useless way to picture the typical American household.

Traditional families were not only falling apart at an alarming rate but were also increasingly slow to form in the first place. The proportion of adults living alone tripled in the four decades after 1950, and by the 1990s nearly one-third of women aged twenty-five to twenty-nine had never married. In the 1960s, 5 percent of all births were to unmarried women, but three decades later one out of four white babies, one out of three Latino babies, and two out of three African American babies were born to single mothers. Every fourth child in America was growing up in a household that lacked two parents. The collapse of the traditional family contributed heavily to the pauperization of many women and children, as single parents (usually mothers) struggled to keep their households economically

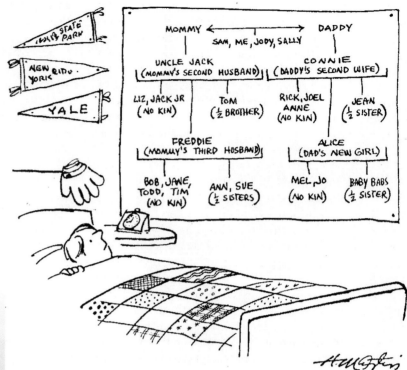

The Modern Family Tree High divorce rates and the increasing number of "blended families" in modern American society could make for confusing "family trees." Reproduced with permission of Punch Ltd., www.punch.co.uk

afloat. Single parenthood outstripped race and ethnicity as the most telling predictor of poverty in America.

Child-rearing, the family's foremost function, was being increasingly assigned to "parent-substitutes" at day-care centers or schools—or to television and DVD players, the modern age's "electronic baby-sitters." Estimates were that the average child by age sixteen had watched up to fifteen thousand hours of TV—more time than was spent in the classroom. Parental anxieties multiplied with the advent of the Internet—an electronic cornucopia where youngsters could "surf" through poetry and problem sets as well as pornography.

But if the *traditional* family was increasingly rare, the family itself remained a bedrock of American society in the early twenty-first century, as viable families now assumed a variety of forms. Children in households led by a single parent, stepparent, or grandparent, as well as children with gay or lesbian parents, encountered a degree of acceptance that would have been unimaginable a generation earlier. Even the notion of gay marriage, which emerged as a major public controversy when the Massachusetts Supreme Judicial Court ruled it legal in 2003, signaled that the idea of marriage retained its luster. Teenage pregnancy, a key source of single parenthood, was also on the decline after the mid-1990s. Even divorce rates appeared to ebb a bit, with 3.4 divorces per thousand people in 2008, down from 5.3 per thousand in 1981. The family was not evaporating, but evolving into multiple forms.

✵ The Aging of America

Old age was more and more likely to be a lengthy experience for Americans, who were living longer than ever before. A person born at the dawn of the century could expect to survive less than fifty years, whereas someone born in 2000 could anticipate a life span of seventy-seven years. (The figures were slightly lower for nonwhites, reflecting differences in living standards, especially diet and health care.) The census of 1950 recorded that women for the first time made up a majority of Americans, thanks largely to greater female longevity. Miraculous medical advances lengthened and strengthened lives. Noteworthy were the development of antibiotics after 1940 and Dr. Jonas Salk's discovery in 1953 of a vaccine against a dreaded crippler, polio.

Longer lives spelled more elderly people. One American in eight was over sixty-five years of age in 2009, and projections were that one of every five people would be in the "sunset years" by 2050, as the median age rose toward forty. This aging of the population raised a host of political, social, and economic questions. Older Americans formed a potent electoral bloc that aggressively lobbied for government favors and achieved real gains for senior citizens. The share of GNP spent on health care for people over sixty-five more than doubled in the three decades after the enactment of Medicare in 1965. This growth in medical payments for the old far outstripped the growth of educational expenditures for the young, with corresponding consequences for the social and economic status of both populations. As late as the 1960s, nearly a quarter of Americans over the age of sixty-five lived in poverty; three decades later only about one in ten did. The figures for young people moved in the reverse direction: whereas 15 percent of children were living in poverty in the 1970s, nearly 21 percent were impoverished in 2008.

These triumphs for senior citizens also brought fiscal strains, especially on the Social Security and Medicare systems. Social Security was established in 1935 to provide income for retired workers. Before that time, most workers continued to toil after age sixty-five. By century's end only a small minority did (about 15 percent of men and 8 percent of women), and a majority of the elderly population relied primarily on Social Security checks for their living expenses. Contrary to popular mythology, Social Security payments to retirees did not represent reimbursement for contributions that the elderly had made during their working lives. In fact, the payments of current workers into the Social Security system funded the benefits to the current generation of retirees. By the time the new century opened, those benefits had risen

so high, and the ratio of active workers to retirees had dropped so low, that drastic adjustments were necessary. The problem intensified as the soaring rise of health-care costs, especially prescription drugs and long-term nursing care, threatened to bankrupt the Medicare system on which most senior citizens relied.

At the beginning of the new century, as the huge wave of post–World War II baby boomers approached retirement age, it seemed that the "unfunded liability"— the difference between what the government had promised to pay to the elderly and the taxes it expected to take in—might rise above $7 trillion, a sum that threatened to inflict fiscal ruin on the Republic unless fundamental reforms were adopted. Yet because of the electoral power of older Americans, Social Security and Medicare reform remained the "third rail" of American politics, which politicians touched only at their peril (see Figure 42.4).

Courtesy of the Honolulu Marathon

Senior Power Living longer and living healthier, older Americans coalesced into one of America's most politically powerful interest groups in the early twenty-first century.

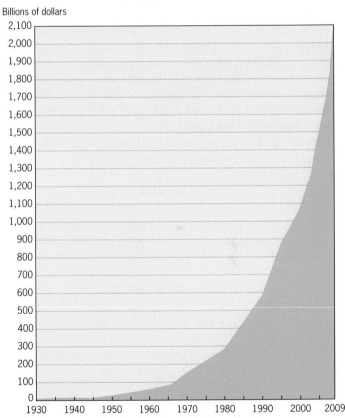

Billions of dollars

FIGURE 42.4 Government Expenditures for Social Welfare, 1930–2009 "Social welfare" includes unemployment and old-age insurance, health care, and veterans' benefits. The skyrocketing costs from the mid-1960s onward reflect new commitments made through Great Society programs and the increasing size (and political clout) of the elderly population, who were the main beneficiaries of expensive programs like Medicare. The steep rise after 1970 is also explained by the galloping inflation of the 1970s. (Sources: *Statistical Abstract of the United States*, 2010; Office of Management and Budget, Historical Tables http://www.whitehouse.gov/omb/budget/Historicals/.)

⭐ The New Immigration

Newcomers continued to come ashore in waves that numbered nearly 1 million persons per year from the 1980s into the early twenty-first century—the largest inflow of immigrants in America's experience. In striking contrast to the historic pattern of immigration, Europe contributed far fewer people than did Asia and Latin America (see Figure 42.5). And unlike their predecessors, many of the new immigrants settled not only in traditional ethnic enclaves in cities and towns but also in the sprawling suburbs of places like Los Angeles, Dallas, and Atlanta, where many of the new jobs were to be found.

What prompted this new migration to America? The truth is that the newest immigrants came for many of the same reasons as the old. They typically left countries where populations were growing rapidly and where agricultural and industrial revolutions were shaking people loose from old habits of life—conditions almost identical to those in nineteenth-century Europe. And they came to America, as previous immigrants had done, in search of jobs and economic opportunity. Some came with skills and even professional degrees, from India or Taiwan or the former Soviet Union, and they found their way into middle-class jobs. But most came with fewer skills and less education, seeking work as janitors, nannies, farm laborers, lawn cutters, or restaurant workers.

The Southwest, from Texas to California, felt the immigrant impact especially sharply, as Mexican migrants—by far the largest contingent of modern immigrants—concentrated heavily in that region. By the turn of the century, Latinos made up nearly one-third of the population in Texas, Arizona, and California and 40 percent in New Mexico—amounting to a demographic *reconquista* of the lands lost by Mexico in the war of 1846–1848 (see "Makers of America: The Latinos," pp. 1002–1003).

The size and geographic concentration of the Latino population in the Southwest had few precedents in the history of American immigration. Most previous groups had been so thinly scattered across the land that they had little choice but to learn English and make their way in the larger American society, however much they might have longed to preserve their native language and customs. But it seemed possible that Mexican Americans might succeed in creating a truly bicultural zone in the booming southwestern states, especially since their mother culture lay accessible just next door. Some old-stock Americans worried about the capacity of the modern United States to absorb these new immigrants. The Immigration Reform and Control Act of 1986 attempted to choke off illegal entry by penalizing employers of undocumented aliens and by granting amnesty to many of those already here. But immigrants just kept coming, legal and illegal alike, as political leaders struggled in vain to devise an

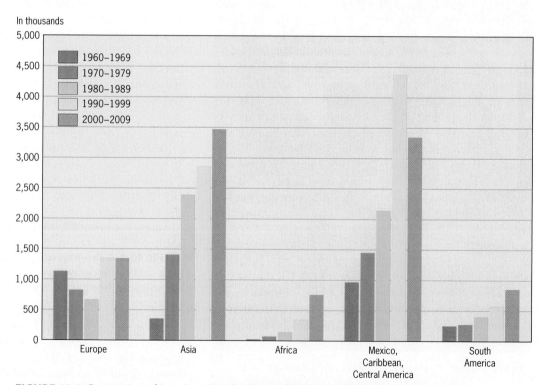

FIGURE 42.5 Recent Legal Immigration by Area of Origin, 1961–2009 (Source: *Yearbook of Immigration Statistics*, 2009, Department of Homeland Security.)

"I CAN TELL BY THE COLOR OF YOUR SKIN YOU'RE NOT FROM AROUND HERE, ARE YOU?"

ARIZONA DOING THE JOB THE FEDS WON'T DO!

Immigration Confrontation When Arizona Governor Jan Brewer signed a tough new bill in 2010 authorizing local police to crack down on illegal immigrants, the national debate over immigration policy grew still more bitterly divisive. Champions of the bill hailed Arizona for taking a stand in the void left by federal inaction. Critics denounced it as an invitation to the harassment of all Hispanics—indeed, all people of color—regardless of their citizenship status.

immigration system that was fair, realistic, and true to the nation's traditions.

Yet the fact was that foreign-born people accounted for only about 13 percent of the American population in 2007, a far smaller proportion than the historical high point of nearly 15 percent recorded in the census of 1910, but evidence nonetheless that American society continued to welcome—and need—newcomers. Somewhat inconsistently, critics charged both that immigrants robbed citizens of jobs and that they dumped themselves on the welfare rolls at the taxpayers' expense. But studies showed that immigrants took jobs scorned by Americans and that they paid more dollars in federal taxes (withholding and Social Security taxes, as well as excise taxes) than they claimed for welfare payments. The story was different at the state level, where expenditures for immigrant education and health care often exceeded the net tax contribution of the immigrants themselves. Yet the infusion of young immigrants and their offspring was just what the country needed when faced with the challenges of an aging population. A more urgent worry was that unscrupulous employers might take cruel advantage of alien workers, who often had scant knowledge of their legal rights.

Debates over immigration were complicated by the problem of illegal immigrants. The intensity mounted in 2006, when xenophobic pundits and politicians fanned the old flames of anxiety that millions of undocumented workers were usurping American tax dollars and privileges. Immigrant sympathizers argued that unlawful aliens had to be legalized so that they could receive the same protections as other workers. Amid this chaos President George W. Bush and a bipartisan group of legislators proposed a law to establish a guest-worker program for undocumented workers and create a path to citizenship, albeit after paying a fine. Anti-immigrant forces condemned the plan as "amnesty." Business interests protested that it put too great a burden on employers to verify the right to work. And immigrant rights advocates claimed that it would create "second-class citizens." In the end, the compromise bill pleased no one and fell into the dustbin. But the debate over immigration only grew more bitter. Legislators in Arizona, provoked by continuing immigrant flows over the state's long desert border with Mexico, passed a harsh anti-immigrant law in 2010 requiring local police to detain people if there was "reasonable suspicion" that they were illegal. Critics complained that the law amounted to unfair "racial profiling," and that the state was unconstitutionally usurping federal responsibility for controlling immigration. The matter seemed destined for eventual adjudication by the United States Supreme Court. Later in that same year, Congress rejected the DREAM Act (Development, Relief and Education for Alien Minors), which would have provided a path to citizenship for undocumented youth who either finished college or served in the U.S. military.

*T*oday Mexican food is handed through fast-food drive-up windows in all fifty states, Spanish-language broadcasts fill the airwaves, and the Latino community has its own telephone book, the *Spanish Yellow Pages*. Latinos send representatives to Congress and mayors to city halls, record hit songs, paint murals, and teach history. Latinos, among the fastest-growing segments of the U.S. population, include Puerto Ricans, frequent voyagers between their native island and northeastern cities; Cubans, many of them refugees from the communist dictatorship of Fidel Castro, concentrated in Miami and southern Florida; and Central Americans, fleeing the ravages of civil war in Nicaragua and El Salvador.

But the most populous group of Latinos derives from Mexico (see Figure 42.6). The first significant numbers of Mexicans began heading for *El Norte* ("the North") around 1910, when the upheavals of the Mexican Revolution stirred and shuffled the Mexican population into more or less constant flux. Their northward passage was briefly interrupted during the Great Depression, when thousands of Mexican nationals were deported. But immigration resumed during World War II, and since then a steady flow of legal immigrants has passed through border checkpoints, joined by countless millions of their undocumented countrymen and countrywomen stealing across the southwestern frontier on moonless nights.

For the most part, these Mexicans came to work in the fields, following the ripening crops northward to Canada through the summer and autumn months. In winter many headed back to Mexico, but some gathered instead in the cities of the Southwest—El Paso, Los Angeles, Houston, and San Bernardino. There they found regular work, even if lack of skills and racial discrimination often confined them to manual labor. City jobs might pay less than farm labor, but the work was steady and offered the prospect of a stable home. Houses may have been shabby in the barrios, but these Mexican neighborhoods provided a sense of togetherness, a place to raise a family, and the chance to join a mutual aid society. Such societies, or *mutualistas*, sponsored baseball leagues, helped the sick and disabled, and defended their members against discrimination.

Mexican immigrants lived so close to the border that their native country acted like a powerful magnet, drawing them back time and time again. Until tighter border controls were put in place after the terrorist attacks of September 2001, Mexicans frequently returned to see relatives or visit the homes of their youth, and relatively few became U.S. citizens. Indeed, in many Mexican American communities, it was a badge of dishonor to apply for U.S. citizenship.

The Mexican government, likewise influenced by the proximity of the two countries, intervened in the daily lives of its nationals in America, sometimes discouraging them from becoming citizens of their adopted country. As Anglo reformers attempted to Americanize the immigrants in the 1910s and 1920s, the Mexican consulate in Los Angeles launched a Mexicanization

Demonstrating for Immigrant Rights, Los Angeles, 2007 Latinos march in downtown Los Angeles in support of legalizing undocumented parents who have children born in the United States. U.S. law gives the right of citizenship to anyone born on American soil ("jus soli"), but not necessarily to the parents of that child.

© Bettmann/Corbis

Mexican American Farmworkers Pitting Apricots in Fruit Groves near Los Angeles, 1924

FIGURE 42.6 Sources of Latino Population in the United States, 2008   (Source: U.S. Census Bureau; Pew Hispanic Center, *Statistical Portrait of Hispanics in the United States, 2008.*)

Puerto Rican
8.9%
(4.2 million)

Cuban
3.5%
(1.6 million)

Central/South American or other Latino
21.9%
(10.3 million)

Mexican
65.7%
(30.7 million)

program. The consulate sponsored parades on Cinco de Mayo ("Fifth of May"), celebrating Mexico's defeat of a French army at the Battle of Puebla in 1862, and opened special Spanish-language schools for children. Since World War II, the American-born generation has carried on the fight for political representation, economic opportunity, and cultural preservation.

Fresh arrivals from Mexico and from the other Latin American nations daily swell Latino communities across America. The census of 2000 revealed that Latinos had become the largest minority group in the United States, surpassing African Americans. As the United States moves through the twenty-first century, it is taking on a pronounced Spanish accent, and increasingly Latinos are making themselves a force to be reckoned with in American politics, culture, and the economy.

Young Latina Activists in East Boston, 2004
Latinos have become increasingly influential voters, courted by Democratic and Republican candidates alike.

✵ Beyond the Melting Pot

Thanks both to continued immigration and to their own high birthrate, Latinos were becoming an increasingly important minority. The United States by 2008 was home to about 47 million of them. They included some 31 million Chicanos, or Mexican Americans, mostly in the Southwest, as well as 4 million Puerto Ricans, chiefly in the Northeast, and more than 1 million Cubans in Florida (where it was jokingly said that Miami had become the most "Anglo" city in Latin America).

Flexing their political muscles, Latinos elected mayors of Miami, Denver, San Antonio, and Los Angeles. After years of struggle, the United Farm Workers Organizing Committee (UFWOC), headed by the soft-spoken and charismatic César Chávez, succeeded in improving working conditions for the mostly Chicano "stoop laborers" who followed the cycle of planting and harvesting across the American West. Latino influence was destined to grow, as suggested by the increasing presence of Spanish-language ballots and television broadcasts. Latinos, newly confident and organized, became the nation's largest ethnic minority, outnumbering even African Americans, in 2003. Indeed by the early twenty-first century, the Chicano population of America's largest state, California, led the Anglo population, making the state a patchwork of minorities with no single ethnic majority. In 2003 most newborns in California were Latino, a powerful harbinger of the state's demographic future—and the nation's. By 2010, the Census Bureau counted four "majority-minority" states (all of them in the booming West), where no ethnic group commanded a majority: Texas, New Mexico, California, and Hawaii. Nationwide, the birthrate for nonwhites in 2010 was poised to eclipse the white birthrate for the first time in history.

Asian Americans also made great strides. By the 1980s they were America's fastest-growing minority, numbering nearly 15 million by 2008. Once feared and hated as the "yellow peril" and consigned to the most menial and degrading jobs, citizens of Asian ancestry were now counted among the most prosperous Americans. Their rising political influence was heralded in the 1998 election of Oregon's Taiwan-born David Wu as the first Chinese American to serve in the House of Representatives.

Indians, the original Americans, numbered more than 2.5 million in the 2010 census. Half of them had left their reservations to live in cities. Meanwhile, unemployment and alcoholism had blighted reservation life. Many tribes took advantage of their special legal status as independent nations to open bingo halls and gambling casinos for the general public on reservation lands, but the cycle of discrimination and poverty proved hard to break.

✵ Cities and Suburbs

America's "alabaster cities" of song and story grew more sooty and less safe in the closing decades of the twentieth century. Crime was the great scourge of urban life. The rate of violent crimes committed in cities

The Oldest Americans
Members of the Cheyenne River Sioux Tribe celebrate the opening of the Smithsonian Institution's National Museum of the American Indian in Washington, D.C., 2004.

AP Photo/Pablo Martinez Monsivais

reached an all-time high in the drug-infested 1980s and then leveled off in the early 1990s. The number of violent crimes even began to decline substantially in many areas after 1995. Nevertheless, murders, robberies, and rapes remained shockingly common not only in cities but also in suburbs and rural areas. America imprisoned a larger fraction of its citizens than almost any other country in the world, and some desperate citizens resorted to armed vigilante tactics to protect themselves.

The migration from cities to the suburbs was so swift and massive that by the mid-1990s a majority of Americans were suburban dwellers (see Figure 42.7). Jobs, too, became suburbanized. The nation's rather brief "urban age" lasted little more than seven decades after 1920, and with its passing many observers saw a new fragmentation and isolation in American life. Some affluent suburban neighborhoods walled themselves off behind elaborate security systems in "gated communities," making it harder, perhaps, to sustain a sense of a larger and inclusive national community. By the first decade of the twenty-first century, the suburban rings around big cities such as New York, Chicago, Houston, and Washington, D.C., were becoming more racially and ethnically diverse, though individual schools and towns were often homogeneous.

Suburbs grew fastest in the West and Southwest. In the outer orbits of Los Angeles, San Diego, Las Vegas, and Phoenix, builders of roads, water mains, and schools could barely keep up with the new towns sprouting across the hardscrabble landscapes. Newcomers came not only from nearby cities but from other regions of the United States as well. A momentous shift of the American population was under way, as inhabitants from the Northeast and the Rustbelt Midwest moved southward and westward to job opportunities and the sun. The Great Plains, where 60 percent of all counties were losing population as the twentieth century ended, faced the sharpest decline, hollowing out the traditional American heartland. By the early twenty-first century, the Great Plains contained fewer people than the Los Angeles basin, despite being five times the size of the entire state of California.

Some major cities exhibited signs of renewal. Commercial redevelopment gained ground in cities such as New York, Boston, Chicago, San Francisco, and even the classic "city without a center," Los Angeles. Well-to-do residents reclaimed once-fashionable neighborhoods and sent real estate values soaring. But these latter-day urban homesteaders struggled to make their cities genuine centers of residential integration. Cities stubbornly remained as divided by wealth and race as the suburban social landscape surrounding them.

Minority America

Racial and ethnic tensions also exacerbated the problems of American cities. These stresses were especially evident in Los Angeles, which, like New York a century earlier, was a magnet for minorities, especially immigrants from Asia and Latin America. When in 1992 a mostly white jury exonerated white Los Angeles police officers who had been videotaped ferociously beating a black suspect, the minority neighborhoods of South Central Los Angeles erupted in rage. Arson and looting

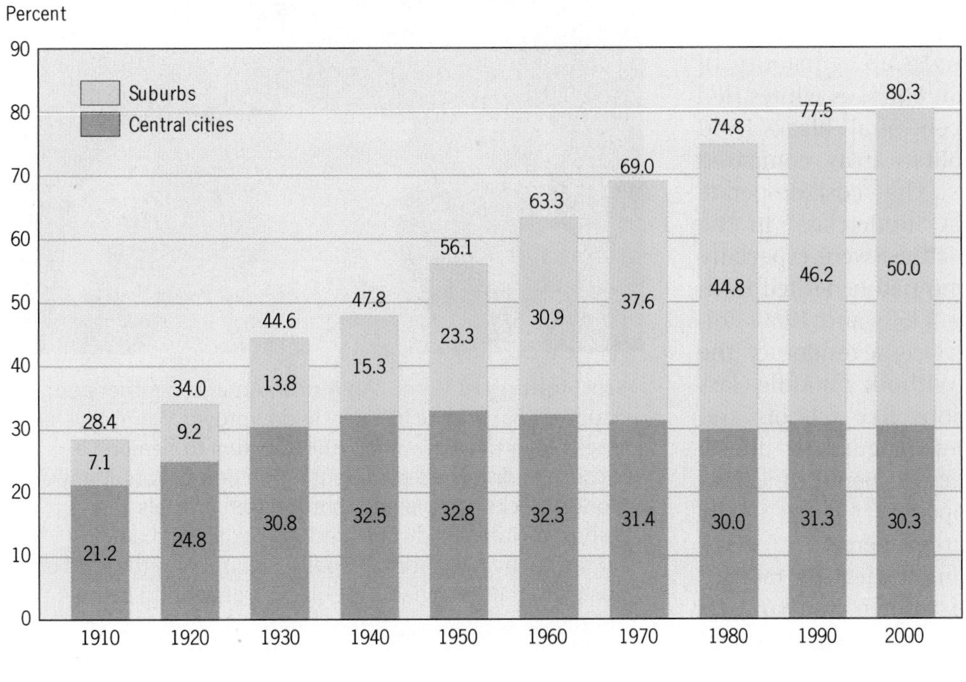

FIGURE 42.7 Percent of Total Population Living in Metropolitan Areas and in Their Central Cities and Suburbs, 1910–2000 (Source: U.S. Census Bureau, Decennial Census of Population, 1910 to 2000, compiled in *Demographic Trends in the 20th Century*, no. 2002.)

laid waste entire city blocks, and scores of people were killed. In a sobering demonstration of the complexity of modern American racial rivalries, many black rioters vented their anger at the white police and the judicial system by attacking Asian shopkeepers, who in turn formed armed patrols to protect their property. A decade later many a burned-out lot remained abandoned and weed-choked in neighborhoods still plagued by gang violence and the demoralizing effects of grinding poverty.

The Los Angeles riots vividly testified to black skepticism about the American system of justice. Just three years later, again in Los Angeles, the televised spectacle of former football "hero" O. J. Simpson's murder trial fed white disillusionment with the state of race relations. After months of testimony that seemed to point to Simpson's guilt, the jury acquitted him, presumably because certain Los Angeles police officers involved in the case had been shown to harbor racist sentiments. In a later civil trial, another jury unanimously found Simpson liable for the "wrongful deaths" of his former wife and another victim. (In 2008 Simpson was sentenced to thirty-three years in jail for unrelated felony convictions.) The reaction to the Simpson verdicts revealed the yawning chasm that separated white and black America, as most whites continued to believe Simpson guilty, while a majority of African Americans told pollsters that the original not-guilty verdict was justified. Similarly, complaints by African Americans that they had been unlawfully kept from the polls during the 2000 presidential election in Florida reflected the conviction of many blacks that they were still facing a Jim Crow South of systematic racial disfranchisement.

American cities have always held an astonishing variety of ethnic and racial groups, but by the late twentieth century, minorities made up a majority of the population of many American cities, as whites fled to the suburbs. In 2002, 52 percent of all blacks lived in central cities within metropolitan areas, compared with only 21 percent of whites. The most desperate black ghettos, housing a hapless "underclass" in the inner core of the old industrial cities, were especially problematic. Successful blacks who had benefited from the civil rights revolution of the 1950s and 1960s followed whites to the suburbs, leaving a residue of the poorest poor in the old ghettos. Without a middle class to sustain community institutions like schools and small businesses, the inner cities, plagued by unemployment and drug addiction, seemed bereft of leadership, cohesion, resources, and hope.

Single women headed about 45 percent of black families in 2009, more than three times the rate for whites. Many African American women, husbandless and jobless, struggled to feed their children. As social

scientists increasingly emphasized the importance of the home environment for success in school, it became clear that many fatherless, impoverished African American children seemed consigned to suffer from educational handicaps that were difficult to overcome.

Some segments of the African American community did prosper in the wake of the civil rights gains of the 1950s and 1960s, although they still had a long hill to climb before reaching full equality. By 2009, 43 percent of all black families (compared to 68 percent of all white families) had incomes of at least $50,000, qualifying them (barely) as middle class. Blacks continued

Luis Alvariz/AP Wide World Photos

Still Fighting to Vote An African American father and daughter participate in a rally in downtown Miami several weeks after the November 2000 election to demand a recount of dismissed presidential election ballots. Many Florida blacks complained that election officials had disproportionately disqualified their votes and unfairly turned them away from the polls, resurrecting the kind of obstacles that long had kept blacks from voting in the South.

to make headway in political life. The number of black elected officials had risen above the nine thousand mark, including more than three dozen members of Congress and the mayors of several large cities, not to mention President Barack Obama.

By the early twenty-first century, blacks had also dramatically advanced into higher education, though the educational gap between blacks and whites stubbornly persisted. In 2009, 12.7 percent of blacks over age twenty-five had a bachelor's degree, compared to 19.3 percent of whites and 21 percent of non-Hispanic whites. The political assault against affirmative action in California and elsewhere in the 1990s only compounded the obstacles to advanced training for many young African Americans. But defenders of affirmative action chalked up a major victory in 2003 when the Supreme Court in a key case involving the University of Michigan affirmed that achieving racial diversity on college campuses was a legitimate means to secure a more equitable society. The Court preserved affirmative action in university admissions as long as schools avoided using quotas, point systems, or other mechanistic ways of diversifying their student bodies, though it remained uneasy about letting such programs endure indefinitely. Justice Sandra Day O'Connor said, "We expect that twenty-five years from now, the use of racial preferences will no longer be necessary."

✵ E Pluribus Plures

Controversial issues of color and culture also pervaded the realm of ideas in the late twentieth century. Echoing early-twentieth-century "cultural pluralists" like Horace Kallen and Randolph Bourne, many intellectuals after 1970 embraced the creed of "multiculturalism." The new mantra celebrated diversity for its own sake and stressed the need to preserve and promote, rather than squash, a variety of distinct ethnic and racial cultures in the United States.

The nation's classrooms became battlegrounds for the debate over America's commitment to pluralism. Multiculturalists attacked the traditional curriculum as "Eurocentric" and advocated greater focus on the achievements of African Americans, Latinos, Asian Americans, and Native Americans. In response, critics charged that too much stress on ethnic difference would come at the expense of national cohesion and an appreciation of common American values.

The Census Bureau further enlivened the debate when in 2000 it allowed respondents to identify themselves with more than one of the six standard racial categories (black, white, Latino, American Indian, Asian, and Native Hawaiian or other Pacific Islander). Signifying a mounting revolution in attitudes toward

In 1990 the African American intellectual Shelby Steele (b. 1946) declared in his provocative book, The Content of Our Character,

❝What is needed now is a new spirit of pragmatism in racial matters where blacks are seen simply as American citizens who deserve complete fairness and in some cases developmental assistance, but in no case special entitlements based on color. We need deracinated social policies that attack poverty rather than black poverty and that instill those values that make for self-reliance.❞

race, nearly 7 million Americans chose to describe themselves as biracial or multiracial. As recently as the 1960s, interracial marriage was still illegal in sixteen states. But by the early twenty-first century, many Americans, including such celebrities as golfer Tiger Woods and actress Rosario Dawson, were proclaiming their mixed heritage as a point of pride.

✵ The Postmodern Mind

Despite the mind-sapping chatter of the "boob tube" and the distractions of the Internet, Americans in the early twenty-first century read more, listened to more music, and were better educated than ever before. Colleges awarded some 3 million degrees annually, and more than one person in five in the twenty-five- to thirty-four-year-old age group boasted a college bachelor's degree in 2009. (Nearly one in three had an associate's degree.) The swelling ranks of educated people lifted the economy to more advanced levels while creating more consumers of "high culture." Each year millions of Americans visited museums and patronized hundreds of opera companies and symphony orchestras—as well as countless popular music groups.

Commentators often described these contemporary Americans as living in a "postmodern" age, though few could agree on precisely what that term meant. But whatever else it denotes, *postmodernism* generally refers to a distrust of rational, scientific descriptions of the self or the world, and the insistence that human beliefs and realities are socially "constructed." In place of modernism's faith in certainty, objectivity, and unity, postmodernism stresses skepticism, relativity, and multiplicity. Postmodernism has enormously influenced contemporary philosophy, social theory, art, architecture, and literature, among other fields.

Postmodern architecture made the most visible footprint on the American cultural landscape. Rejecting

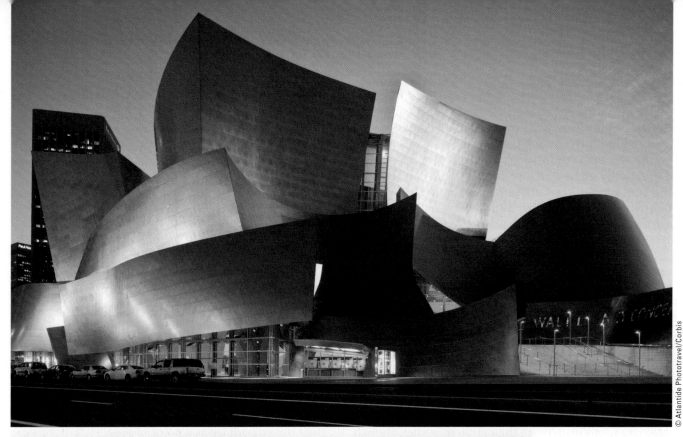

Architect Frank Gehry's Walt Disney Concert Hall, Los Angeles, California, Completed in 2003

the austere functionalism that had dominated architecture for much of the last century, postmodernists such as Robert Venturi and Michael Graves revived the decorative details of earlier historical styles. Modernists had valued minimalism and an absence of ornament—"Less is more," the renowned German architect Ludwig Mies van der Rohe proclaimed. But postmodernists celebrated a playful eclecticism of architectural elements—"Less is a bore," as Venturi put it. The flight from stark modernism took especially fanciful forms in Frank Gehry's use of luminous, undulating sheets of metallic skin in the widely hailed Guggenheim Museum (1997) in Bilbao, Spain, and the Walt Disney Concert Hall (2003) in Los Angeles.

The postmodern sensibility carried over into other art forms. Classical music composers like John Adams and John Zorn broke down boundaries between "high"

The term postmodernism *often means different things to different people. Choreographer Twyla Tharp (b. 1941) captured some of the trouble in defining a term that resists easy definition:*

❝ There's this expression called postmodernism, which is kind of silly, and destroys a perfectly good word called modern, which now no longer means anything.❞

and "low" styles and blended diverse musical genres and traditions in an experimental mix. Choreographers such as Steve Paxton and Twyla Tharp paired everyday movements with classical techniques and gave contemporary dancers license to improvise. Hip-hop artists from Biz Markie to Jay-Z "sampled" beats from other sound recordings, and lyrical MCs overlaid them with complex "rapping" schemes. Born in America's urban ghettos in the 1970s, hip-hop blossomed into a mainstream cultural phenomenon, both nationally and internationally. "Mash-up" artists also gained popularity, cleverly fusing fragments from songs of different musical genres or remixing one song's vocal track over another song's instrumentals.

Visual artists also felt the eclectic urge. Cindy Sherman, Jenny Holzer, and Kara Walker combined old and new media to confront, confound, and even offend the viewer. Jeff Koons and Shepard Fairey borrowed industrial materials and pop culture imagery to blur the hidebound distinction between highbrow and lowbrow cultures. Their pastiches of disparate fragments, often presented in ironic fashion, came to symbolize postmodern art.

Postmodern literature, like art, had deep roots in the second half of the twentieth century. After World War II, authors like William S. Burroughs, Kurt Vonnegut, and Thomas Pynchon pioneered the use of nonlinear narratives, pastiche forms, parody, and paradox in their fiction. A newer generation of writers, including

Kara Walker Stands Before her Painting, Gone, An Historical of a Civil War as it Occurred Between the Dusky Thighs of One Young Negress and Her Heart, 1994 Walker has daringly adapted the venerable technique of cut-paper silhouettes to explore modern themes of racial identity and historical revisionism. Here she contrasts the romantic image of the antebellum South captured in Margaret Mitchell's celebrated novel and film *Gone with the Wind* with the perspective of an enslaved black woman.

Michael Chabon, Jeffrey Eugenides, and Zadie Smith, adapted these techniques for contemporary audiences. Among these "post-postmodernists," David Foster Wallace playfully lampooned North America's dystopian future in *Infinite Jest* (1996), complete with calendar years named after corporate sponsors. Colson Whitehead ruminated on modern racial uplift among rival schools of elevator operators in *The Intuitionist* (1999). Jonathan Franzen satirized dysfunctional midwestern families to great critical acclaim in *The Corrections* (2001) and *Freedom* (2010).

Other major works of contemporary fiction, especially from the pens of female and minority authors, complemented postmodernism's ethos of pluralism and cultural diversity. Toni Morrison wove a bewitching portrait of maternal affection in *Beloved* (1987) and in 1993 became the first African American woman to win the Nobel Prize for literature. E. Annie Proulx won widespread acclaim with her comical yet tender portrayal of a struggling family in *The Shipping News* (1993). Her moving tale of homoerotic love between two cowboys in "Brokeback Mountain" (1997) reached

Latinos Breaking in Los Angeles Breakdancing emerged among African Americans in New York in the late twentieth century to become an integral part of hip-hop culture.

In her touching novel The Joy Luck Club *(1989), Amy Tan (b. 1952) explored the complex dilemmas of growing up as a Chinese American:*

"'A girl is like a young tree,' [my mother] said. 'You must stand tall and listen to your mother standing next to you. That is the only way to grow strong and straight. But if you bend to listen to other people, you will grow crooked and weak. . . .' Over the years I learned to choose from the best opinions. Chinese people had Chinese opinions. American people had American opinions. And in almost every case, the American version was much better. It was only later that I discovered there was a serious flaw with the American version. There were too many choices, so it was easy to get confused and pick the wrong thing.**"**

a mass audience in 2005 as an award-winning motion picture. James Welch, Leslie Marmon Silko, Joy Harjo, and Sherman Alexie contributed to a Native American literary renaissance that sought to recover the tribal past while reimagining its present.

Immigration in the new century also began to yield its own rich cultural harvest. Asian American authors flourished, among them playwright David Hwang, novelist Amy Tan, and Chinese-born Ha Jin, who wrote evocatively about his country of origin in novels like *Waiting* (1999) and *War Trash* (2004). Jhumpa Lahiri's *Interpreter of Maladies* (1999) and *Unaccustomed Earth* (2008) explored the sometimes painful relationship between immigrant Indian parents and their American-born children. Latino writers made their mark as well. Junot Diaz's Pulitzer Prize–winning *The Brief Wondrous Life of Oscar Wao* (2007) brilliantly bridged the worlds of the Dominican Republic and New Jersey in a dazzling concoction of street-smart Spanglish.

On the stage, contemporary political themes and social commentary predominated. The AIDS epidemic inspired Tony Kushner's sensationally inventive *Angels in America* (1991), as well as Jonathan Larson's Tony Award–winning musical *Rent* (1996). Eve Ensler espoused feminist empowerment (and an end to violence against women) with comic intimacy in her *Vagina Monologues* (1996). Cuban American Nilo Cruz won a Pulitzer Prize in 2003 for *Anna in the Tropics*, about immigrant cigar makers confronting the tide of mechanization in 1929 Tampa. Tracy Letts peeled back the hypocrisies of middle-American family life in *August: Osage County* (2007). Lynn Nottage's deeply moving *Ruined* (2008), about a young African rape

victim, found hope and redemption even amidst the brutal chaos of the Congo's eternal wars.

Film, the most characteristic American art form, continued to flourish, as pioneering directors such as George Lucas, Steven Spielberg, James Cameron, and Spike Lee were followed by a wave of even bolder young iconoclasts, including Quentin Tarantino, the Coen brothers, and Kathryn Bigelow. Tarantino's *Pulp Fiction* (1994) and David Lynch's *Mulholland Drive* (2001), notable for their unconventional storylines, cinematic allusions, and dark comedic stylings, were prime examples of postmodern film. On the television screen, documentaries thrived, as innovative filmmakers such as Ken Burns chronicled great American themes like the history of baseball, jazz, the national parks, the Civil War, and World War II. Cable television entered a golden era, as high-quality dramas such as *The Sopranos* (1999–2007) and *The Wire* (2002–2008) enjoyed commercial and critical success.

✴ The New Media

By the early twenty-first century, the Internet had dramatically transformed daily life for most Americans. First created by the government for Cold War intelligence sharing, the World Wide Web spread like wildfire through American homes, schools, and offices during the mid-1990s. The percentage of households with Internet access skyrocketed from 18 percent in 1997 to about 70 percent in 2009. In rapidly increasing numbers, Americans turned to the Internet to communicate, shop, work, and electronically bond with family, friends, and lovers. The "dot-com" explosion of Internet-based high-tech companies drove the tremendous economic boom of the late 1990s.

Even as the "dot-com bubble" began to deflate, the Internet demonstrated its staying power. Many online start-up companies failed, but those that survived often became giants in retail (Amazon.com), information gathering (Google), and even finance (E*Trade). The Internet reshaped the traditional corporate world as well, as almost every business, group, or organization—from used-car dealers to sports teams to college arts groups—had its own Web site.

Fulfilling the promises of its early boosters, the Internet seemed to have a democratizing effect, spreading power and information among more and more Americans. Young people in particular flocked to social-networking sites like Facebook and Twitter to make connections, often with people in foreign countries. YouTube allowed everyday users to post home videos online for the whole world to see. And millions of people around the globe started a media revolution with their "Weblogs," or "blogs." "Bloggers" lent their

Tahrir (Liberation) Square, Cairo, Egypt, January 31, 2011 A man takes pictures with his cell phone amid the uprisings that ousted Egypt's president. Social media fueled the "Arab Spring" protests that swept across the Middle East in early 2011.

voices to issues from foreign policy to college life, offering their beliefs and opinions without fear (and often without research). As the "blogosphere" grew, it posed a major challenge to the traditional media—newspapers especially—that had shaped Americans' understanding of the news for hundreds of years. Supporters argued that this "new Media" added fresh voices and new perspectives, but opponents questioned bloggers' expertise and accused them of spreading misinformation.

Blogs were not the only threat the Internet posed to the "mainstream media." Americans became ever less willing to read the morning paper or watch the evening network news shows when they could access a welter of information on their computer screens. Cable news had challenged the old system since the 1980s, but the spread of the Internet made the twenty-four-hour news cycle a reality. Consumer demand pushed daily newspapers to offer their reporting online, often for free. Subscription rates plummeted, and ad sales—the engine that drives print journalism—fell off markedly. As with railroads and the telegraph in the nineteenth century, and radio and television in the twentieth century, computers and the Internet drove major readjustments in modern American economic, social, and cultural life.

✦ The American Prospect

The American spirit pulsed with vitality in the early twenty-first century, but grave problems continued to plague the Republic. Women still fell short of first-class economic citizenship, and American society groped for ways to adapt the traditional family to the new realities of women's work outside the home. A generation after the civil rights triumphs of the 1960s, full equality remained an elusive dream for countless Americans of color. Powerful foreign competitors challenged America's premier economic status. As manufacturing jobs disappeared, and as corporate giants like Enron and Lehman Brothers collapsed, many Americans began to fear their economy as a treacherous landscape, even as it offered some of them astounding prosperity. The alarmingly unequal distribution of wealth and income threatened to turn America into a society of haves and have-nots, mocking the ideals of democracy and breeding seething resentments along the economic frontier that divided rich from poor.

Environmental worries also clouded the country's future. Coal-fired electrical-generating plants helped form acid rain and measurably contributed to the greenhouse effect, an ominous warming in the planet's temperature. The unsolved problem of radioactive waste disposal hampered the development of nuclear power plants. The planet was being drained of oil. Disastrous accidents like the explosion of BP's Deepwater Horizon oil-drilling rig off the Louisiana coast in 2010, which spilled millions of barrels of oil into nearby coastal waters and threatened the Gulf of Mexico's rich but fragile ecosystem, dramatically underscored the risks of mankind's increasingly desperate quest for fossil fuels.

By the early twenty-first century, the once-lonely cries for alternative fuel sources had given way to public fascination with solar power and windmills, methane fuel, electric "hybrid" cars, and the pursuit of an affordable hydrogen fuel cell. Energy conservation remained another crucial but elusive strategy—much-heralded at the politician's rostrum, but too rarely embodied in public policy, as witnessed in the Bush administration's rejection of the Kyoto Treaty on global warming in 2001 and the disappointing failure of the Copenhagen Climate Conference in 2009.

As the human family grew at an alarming rate on a shrinking globe, new challenges still faced America and its historical beliefs. The task of cleansing the earth of its abundant pollutants—including nuclear weapons—was one urgent mission confronting the American people in the new century. Another was seeking ways to resolve the ethnic and cultural conflicts that erupted with renewed virulence around the globe in the wake of the Cold War's end. At the same time, new opportunities beckoned in outer space and on inner-city streets, at the artist's easel and in the concert hall, at the inventor's bench and in the scientist's laboratory, and in the unending quest for social justice, individual fulfillment, and international peace.

The terrorist attack on America on September 11, 2001, posed yet another challenge to the United States. Shielded for nearly two centuries against assaults on its soil, it would now have to preserve its security in a world made smaller by global communication and transportation, without altering its fundamental democratic values and way of life. The great danger posed by terrorism was not that Al Qaeda or other foreign enemies would seize control of the country or any portion of its territory. It was, rather, that in fighting terrorism, Americans would so compromise their freedoms at home and so isolate the country internationally that it would lose touch with its own guiding principles. Wars in Afghanistan and Iraq made these difficulties clear. The challenge was to enhance national security without eroding democratic liberties, to protect the country's borders without preventing the arrival of desirable immigrants, and to use military force wisely without undermining America's standing in the world.

In facing those challenges, the world's oldest republic had an extraordinary tradition of resilience and resourcefulness to draw on. Born as a revolutionary force in a world of conservatism, the United States stood in the twenty-first century as a conservative force in a world of revolution. It had long held aloft the banner of liberal democracy in a world racked by revolutions of the right and left, including fascism, Nazism, and communism. Yet through it all, much that was truly revolutionary also remained a part of America's liberal democratic heritage, as its people pioneered in revolutions against colonialism, racism, sexism, ignorance, and poverty.

The dream of "making the world safe for democracy," articulated nearly a century earlier by Woodrow Wilson at the end of the First World War, gained a new poignancy after September 11, 2001, when Americans expressed a yearning for greater equality, opportunity, and democracy in the Middle East—all in the hope of diminishing the root causes of international terrorism. The capacity to nurture progress abroad, however, depended on the ability of Americans to improve their own country, and to do so in the midst of new threats to their own security. As Wilson wrote in 1893, long before he became president, "Democratic institutions are never done; they are like living tissue, always a-making. It is a strenuous thing, this of living the life of a free people."

TO LEARN MORE

Nancy Altman, *The Battle for Social Security: From FDR's Vision to Bush's Gamble* (2005)

Margot Canaday, *The Straight State: Sexuality and Citizenship in Twentieth-Century America* (2009)

John Cassidy, *How Markets Fail: The Logic of Economic Calamities* (2009)

Gail Collins, *When Everything Changed: The Amazing Journey of American Women from 1960 to the Present* (2009)

Steven Connor, ed., *The Cambridge Companion to Postmodernism* (2004)

David Dent, *In Search of Black America: Discovering the African American Dream* (2000)

Barbara Ehrenreich, *Nickel and Dimed: On (Not) Getting By in America* (2001)

Bill Ong Hing, *Defining America Through Immigration Policy* (2004)

David A. Hollinger, *Postethnic America: Beyond Multiculturalism*, rev. ed. (2005)

Paul Krugman, *The Great Unraveling: Losing Our Way in the New Century* (2003)

Michael Lewis, *The Big Short: Inside the Doomsday Machine* (2010)

Katherine Newman, *A Different Shade of Gray: Midlife and Beyond in the Inner City* (2003)

George Sanchez, *Becoming Mexican American* (1989)

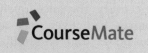

Go to the CourseMate website at **www.cengagebrain.com** for additional study tools and review materials—including audio and video clips—for this chapter.

A complete, annotated bibliography for this chapter—along with brief descriptions of the People to Know—may be found on the American Pageant website. The Key Terms are defined in a Glossary at the end of the text.

AP® Review Questions for Chapter 42

1. All of the following proved to be characteristics of the new information age EXCEPT
   - (A) instant global communications.
   - (B) high-tech computer and media businesses.
   - (C) the decline of traditional occupations mediating between products and clients.
   - (D) an end to the boom-and-bust capitalist business cycle.
   - (E) outsourcing of white-collar jobs to Third World countries.

2. Which of the following most accurately characterizes the rise of Big Science in the post–World War II era?
   - (A) A resolution of questions concerning the ethical implications of scientific research
   - (B) Large expenditures on failed research initiatives
   - (C) A close alliance of the federal government, defense-oriented industries, and American research universities
   - (D) An emphasis on individual scientific genius and entrepreneurship
   - (E) A belief that knowledge should be advanced without government involvement and interference

3. The gap between rich and poor Americans widened in the 1980s and 1990s for all of the following reasons EXCEPT
   - (A) intensifying global competition.
   - (B) the decline of unions.
   - (C) the tax policies of the Carter and Clinton administrations.
   - (D) the growth of part-time and temporary work.
   - (E) the greater economic rewards for education.

4. Despite numerous victories of feminists in the 1990s and 2000s, women continued to feel frustrated by their level of workplace progress for all of the following reasons EXCEPT that they
   - (A) continued to bear more of the burdens of parenthood than men.
   - (B) were paid less than men for performing corresponding jobs.
   - (C) remained concentrated in traditionally feminine occupations.
   - (D) continued to be legally barred from holding high-level, high-prestige positions.
   - (E) continued to bear the greatest responsibilities for the welfare of children.

5. By the 2000s, the traditional nuclear family unit was undergoing severe strain for all of the following reasons EXCEPT that
   - (A) the divorce rate had increased.
   - (B) the number of single-parent-, stepparent-, grandparent-, and gay and lesbian-led households had risen.
   - (C) parent-substitutes, such as child-care centers, schools, television, and the Internet, had assumed a key role in child-rearing.
   - (D) the family no longer served many of its traditional social functions.
   - (E) the Family and Medical Leave Act of 1993 encouraged many mothers to seek part-time work outside the home.

6. Why did Latinos maintain their linguistic and cultural identities better than most previous immigrant groups?
   - (A) The Latino population was so thinly scattered across the country.
   - (B) Bilingual education laws meant that Latinos did not have to learn English and American culture to assimilate.
   - (C) The large numbers of Latinos and the regional geographic concentration of Latinos in America facilitated the maintenance of their native languages and cultures.
   - (D) Latinos had a stronger desire to preserve their cultures than previous groups possessed.
   - (E) Latinos remained politically loyal to the Latin American nations from which they emigrated.

7. Which of the following is true about the DREAM Act?
   - (A) It would have required all illegal immigrants to send their kids to public schools.
   - (B) It would prevent illegal immigrants from returning to their country of origin.
   - (C) It states that a majority of illegal immigrants claim welfare benefits at taxpayers' expense.
   - (D) It blames illegal immigrants for a disproportionate share of crime in the United States.
   - (E) It would have provided a path to citizenship for undocumented young people who graduated from college or joined the military.

8. Which of the following was NOT a sign of increased diversity in America?
   - (A) President Bush developed a controversial plan for a path to citizenship for illegal immigrants.
   - (B) Critics argued that immigrants steal Americans' jobs and exploit the welfare system.
   - (C) Asian Americans rose to become among the most prosperous citizens in the United States.
   - (D) Native Americans moved off of their reservations and into cities.
   - (E) By 2008 the United States was home to 47 million Latino immigrants.

9. Which of the following proves that African Americans became a force in politics by the beginning of the twenty-first century?
   - (A) They relied on racial solidarity.
   - (B) They learned how to mobilize bloc voting.
   - (C) The number of African American elected officials surpassed nine thousand.
   - (D) African American representatives continued to come from areas dominated by African Americans.
   - (E) They made key alliances with city political bosses and urban political machines.

10. What important legal boost was given by the U.S. Supreme Court in 2003 to African Americans' goal of achieving access to higher education?
    - (A) Racial discrimination in awarding financial aid was illegal.
    - (B) Formerly all-white universities had to provide compensation for past discrimination.
    - (C) Affirmative action in admissions was legitimate as long as rigid quotas or point systems were not used.
    - (D) Racially oriented African American studies programs were constitutional.
    - (E) Rigid quotas and point systems constructed for admissions programs were constitutional as long as they were developed to correct past discrimination at a college or university.

11. What was one reasonable charge that critics of multiculturalism in American education made about its possible impact on American society?
    - (A) Multiculturalism distorts the political, economic, and social achievements of minorities.
    - (B) Multiculturalism places too much emphasis on the influence of white ethnic groups on the development of American society and culture.
    - (C) Multiculturalism may lead to ethnic violence and possibly civil war in America.
    - (D) Multiculturalism may lead to the development of socialism in the United States.
    - (E) Multiculturalism may cause a loss of national cohesion and appreciation of shared American values.

12. All of the following represent postmodernism EXCEPT
    - (A) Frank Gehry's architecture.
    - (B) Walt Disney's animation.
    - (C) Cindy Sherman's artwork.
    - (D) Kurt Vonnegut's literature.
    - (E) Twyla Tharp's choreography.

13. Which of the following best characterizes one key overall effect of the electronic New Media in the early twenty-first century?
    - (A) The New Media had been used to reinforce the existing political and economic power structure.
    - (B) Access to the New Media has been restricted to those with extensive education and training in their use.
    - (C) The New Media has not influenced the operations and daily news cycle maintained by traditional media outlets, such as the television networks and newspapers.
    - (D) The New Media has had a democratizing effect for ordinary citizens who desire to obtain and disseminate information and to influence opinion about a wide variety of topics.
    - (E) The New Media has established rigorous journalistic standards for the reporting of news and information.

14. All of the following offer evidence that the United States has evolved socially and politically EXCEPT that
    - (A) many Americans identify themselves as biracial or multiracial.
    - (B) America is now the conservative force in a world of revolution.
    - (C) incidents like the Los Angeles riots of 1992 continue to occur.
    - (D) women are a major force in education, the military, and athletics.
    - (E) people of all races, genders, and socioeconomic classes attain college degrees.

15. In which of the following pairs is the second event a result of the first?
    - (A) Massive layoffs in science-related industries → The trend toward outsourcing
    - (B) Increasing social equality → Increasing economic equality
    - (C) Baby boomers reach retirement age → Greater availability of Social Security
    - (D) Rise of the Internet → Decline of traditional news outlets like daily newspapers
    - (E) Increased number of resident aliens → Laws targeting illegal immigrants

DOCUMENTS

Declaration of Independence

In Congress, July 4, 1776

The Unanimous Declaration of the Thirteen United States of America

[Bracketed material in color has been inserted by the authors. For adoption background see pp. 137–139.]

When, in the course of human events, it becomes necessary for one people to dissolve the political bonds which have connected them with another, and to assume, among the powers of the earth, the separate and equal station to which the laws of nature and of nature's God entitle them, a decent respect to the opinions of mankind requires that they should declare the causes which impel them to the separation.

We hold these truths to be self-evident: That all men are created equal; that they are endowed by their Creator with certain unalienable rights; that among these are life, liberty, and the pursuit of happiness; that, to secure these rights, governments are instituted among men, deriving their just powers from the consent of the governed; that whenever any form of government becomes destructive of these ends, it is the right of the people to alter or to abolish it, and to institute new government, laying its foundation on such principles, and organizing its powers in such form, as to them shall seem most likely to effect their safety and happiness. Prudence, indeed, will dictate that governments long established should not be changed for light and transient causes; and accordingly all experience hath shown that mankind are more disposed to suffer, while evils are sufferable, than to right themselves by abolishing the forms to which they are accustomed. But when a long train of abuses and usurpations, pursuing invariably the same object, evinces a design to reduce them under absolute despotism, it is their right, it is their duty, to throw off such government, and to provide new guards for their future security. Such has been the patient sufferance of these colonies; and such is now the necessity which constrains them to alter their former systems of government. The history of the present King of Great Britain is a history of repeated injuries and usurpations, all having in direct object the establishment of an absolute tyranny over these states. To prove this, let facts be submitted to a candid world.

He has refused his assent to laws, the most wholesome and necessary for the public good. [See royal veto, p. 115.]

He has forbidden his governors to pass laws of immediate and pressing importance, unless suspended in their operation till his assent should be obtained; and, when so suspended, he has utterly neglected to attend to them.

He has refused to pass other laws for the accommodation of large districts of people [by establishing new countries], unless those people would relinquish the right of representation in the legislature, a right inestimable to them, and formidable to tyrants only.

He has called together legislative bodies at places unusual, uncomfortable, and distant from the depository of their public records, for the sole purpose of fatiguing them into compliance with his measures. [e.g., removal of Massachusetts Assembly to Salem, 1774.]

He has dissolved representative houses repeatedly, for opposing, with manly firmness, his invasions on the rights of the people. [e.g., Virginia Assembly, 1765.]

He has refused for a long time, after such dissolutions, to cause others to be elected; whereby the legislative powers, incapable of annihilation, have returned to the people at large for their exercise; the state remaining, in the mean time, exposed to all the dangers of invasions from without and convulsions within.

He has endeavored to prevent the population [populating] of these states; for that purpose obstructing the laws for naturalization of foreigners; refusing to pass others to encourage their migration hither, and raising the conditions of new appropriations of lands. [e.g., Proclamation of 1763, p. 111.]

He has obstructed the administration of justice, by refusing his assent to laws for establishing judiciary powers.

He has made judges dependent on his will alone, for the tenure of their offices, and the amount and payment of their salaries. [See Townshend Acts, p. 118.]

He has erected a multitude of new offices, and sent hither swarms of officers to harass our people and eat out their substance. [See enforcement of Navigation Laws, p. 121.]

He has kept among us, in times of peace, standing armies, without the consent of our legislatures. [See pp. 116, 119.]

He has affected to render the military independent of, and superior to, the civil power.

He has combined with others to subject us to a jurisdiction foreign to our constitution, and unacknowledged by our laws, giving his assent to their acts of pretended legislation:

> For quartering large bodies of armed troops among us [See Boston Massacre, p. 119];
>
> For protecting them, by a mock trial, from punishment for any murders which they should commit on the inhabitants of these states [See 1774 Acts, p. 122];
>
> For cutting off our trade with all parts of the world [See Boston Port Act, p. 122];
>
> For imposing taxes on us without our consent [See Stamp Act, pp. 115–117];
>
> For depriving us, in many cases, of the benefits of trial by jury;
>
> For transporting us beyond seas, to be tried for pretended offenses;
>
> For abolishing the free system of English laws in a neighboring province [Quebec], establishing therein an arbitrary government, and enlarging its boundaries, so as to render it at once an example and fit instrument for introducing the same absolute rule into these colonies [Quebec Act, p. 122];
>
> For taking away our charters, abolishing our most valuable laws, and altering fundamentally the forms of our governments [e.g., in Massachusetts, p. 122];
>
> For suspending our own legislatures, and declaring themselves invested with power to legislate for us in all cases whatsoever [See Stamp Act repeal, pp. 117–118.]

He has abdicated government here, by declaring us out of his protection and waging war against us. [Proclamation, pp. 133.]

He has plundered our seas, ravaged our coasts, burned our towns, and destroyed the lives of our people. [e.g., the burning of Falmouth (Portland), p. 133.]

He is at this time transporting large armies of foreign mercenaries [Hessians, p. 133] to complete the works of death, desolation, and tyranny already begun with circumstances of cruelty and perfidy scarcely paralleled in the most barbarous ages, and totally unworthy the head of a civilized nation.

He has constrained our fellow-citizens, taken captive on the high seas [by impressment], to bear arms against their country, to become the executioners of their friends and brethren, or to fall themselves by their hands.

He has excited domestic insurrection among us [i.e., among slaves], and has endeavored to bring on the inhabitants of our frontiers the merciless Indian savages, whose known rule of warfare is an undistinguished destruction of all ages, sexes, and conditions.

In every stage of these oppressions we have petitioned for redress in the most humble terms; our repeated petitions have been answered only by repeated injury. [e.g., pp. 132–134.] A prince, whose character is thus marked by every act which may define a tyrant, is unfit to be the ruler of a free people.

Nor have we been wanting in our attentions to our British brethren. We have warned them, from time to time, of attempts by their legislature to extend an unwarrantable jurisdiction over us. We have reminded them of the circumstances of our emigration and settlement here. We have appealed to their native justice and magnanimity; and we have conjured them, by the ties of our common kindred, to disavow these usurpations, which would inevitably interrupt our connections and correspondence. They, too, have been deaf to the voice of justice and of consanguinity [blood relationship]. We must, therefore, acquiesce in the necessity which denounces [announces] our separation, and hold them, as we hold the rest of mankind, enemies in war, in peace friends.

We, therefore, the representatives of the United States of America, in General Congress assembled, appealing to the Supreme Judge of the world for the rectitude of our intentions, do, in the name and by the authority of the good people of these colonies, solemnly publish and declare, That these United Colonies are, and of right ought to be, FREE AND INDEPENDENT STATES; that they are absolved from all allegiance to the British crown, and that all political connection between them and the state of Great Britain is, and ought to be, totally dissolved; and that, as free and independent states, they have full power to levy war, conclude peace, contract alliances, establish commerce, and do all other acts and things which independent states may of right do. And for the support of this declaration, with a firm reliance on the protection of Divine Providence, we mutually pledge to each other our lives, our fortunes, and our sacred honor.

[Signed by]

JOHN HANCOCK [President]
[and fifty-five others]

Constitution of the
United States of America

[Boldface headings and bracketed explanatory matter and marginal comments (both in color) have been inserted for the reader's convenience. Passages that are no longer operative are printed in italic type.]

Article I. **PREAMBLE**

Section I. We the people of the United States, in order to form a more perfect union, establish justice, insure domestic tranquility, provide for the common defense, promote the general welfare, and secure the blessings of liberty to ourselves and our posterity, do ordain and establish this CONSTITUTION for the United States of America.

Section II. *Legislative Department*

Congress

Legislative power vested in a two-house Congress. All legislative powers herein granted shall be vested in a Congress of the United States, which shall consist of a Senate and a House of Representatives.

House of Representatives

1. The people elect representatives biennially. The House of Representatives shall be composed of members chosen every second year by the people of the several States, and the electors [voters] in each State shall have the qualifications requisite for electors of the most numerous branch of the State Legislature.

2. Who may be representatives. No person shall be a Representative who shall not have attained the age of twenty-five years, and been seven years a citizen of the United States, and who shall not, when elected, be an inhabitant of that State in which he shall be chosen.

See 1787 compromise, pp. 170–172.

See 1787 compromise, pp. 170–172.

3. Representation in the House based on population; census. Representatives and direct taxes[1] shall be apportioned among the several States which may be included within this Union, according to their respective numbers, *which shall be determined by adding to the whole number of free persons, including those bound to service for a term of years* [apprentices and indentured servants], *and excluding Indians not taxed, three-fifths of all other persons* [slaves].[2] The actual enumeration [census] shall be made within three years after the first meeting of the Congress of the United States, and within every subsequent term of ten years, in such manner as they shall by law direct. The number of Representatives shall not exceed one for every thirty thousand, but each State shall have at least one Representative; *and until such enumeration shall be made, the State of New Hampshire shall be entitled to choose three, Massachusetts eight, Rhode Island and Providence Plantations one, Connecticut five, New York six, New Jersey four, Pennsylvania eight, Delaware one, Maryland six, Virginia ten, North Carolina five, South Carolina five, and Georgia three.*

---

[1]Modified in 1913 by the Sixteenth Amendment re income taxes (see p. 665).

[2]The word *slave* appears nowhere in the original, unamended Constitution. The three-fifths rule ceased to be in force when the Thirteenth Amendment was adopted in 1865 (see p. 66 and amendments below).

4. Vacancies in the House are filled by election. When vacancies happen in the representation from any State, the Executive authority [governor] therefore shall issue writs of election [call a special election] to fill such vacancies.

5. The House selects its Speaker; has sole power to vote impeachment charges (i.e., indictments). The House of Representatives shall choose their Speaker and other officers; and shall have the sole power of impeachment.

See Chase and Johnson trials, pp. 210, 481; Nixon trial preliminaries, pp. 925–928; and discussion of Clinton's impeachment, pp. 970–971.

Section III.   Senate

1. Senators represent the states. The Senate of the United States shall be composed of two Senators from each State, *chosen by the legislature thereof,*[1] for six Years; and each Senator shall have one vote.

2. One-third of senators chosen every two years; vacancies. *Immediately after they shall be assembled in consequence of the first election, they shall be divided as equally as may be into three classes. The seats of the Senators of the first class shall be vacated at the expiration of the second year, of the second class at the expiration of the fourth year, and of the third class at the expiration of the sixth year,* so that one-third may be chosen every second year; *and if vacancies happen by resignation or otherwise, during the recess of the legislature of any State, the Executive* [governor] *thereof may make temporary appointments until the next meeting of the legislature, which shall then fill such vacancies.*[2]

3. Who may be senators. No person shall be a Senator who shall not have attained to the age of thirty years, and been nine years a citizen of the United States, and who shall not, when elected, be an inhabitant of that State for which he shall be chosen.

4. The vice president presides over the Senate. The Vice President of the United States shall be President of the Senate, but shall have no vote, unless they be equally divided [tied].

5. The Senate chooses its other officers. The Senate shall choose their other officers, and also a President *pro tempore,* in the absence of the Vice President, or when he shall exercise the office of the President of the United States.

See Chase and Johnson trials, pp. 210, 481; and discussion of Clinton's impeachment, pp. 970–971.

6. The Senate has sole power to try impeachments. The Senate shall have the sole power to try all impeachments. When sitting for that purpose, they shall be on oath or affirmation. When the President of the United States is tried, the Chief Justice shall preside[3]: and no person shall be convicted without the concurrence of two-thirds of the members present.

7. Penalties for impeachment conviction. Judgment in cases of impeachment shall not extend further than to removal from office, and disqualification to hold and enjoy any office of honor, trust or profit under the United States: but the party convicted shall nevertheless be liable and subject to indictment, trial, judgment and punishment, according to law.

Section IV.   Election and Meetings of Congress

1. Regulation of elections. The times, places and manner of holding elections for Senators and Representatives shall be prescribed in each State by the legislature thereof; but the Congress may at any time by law make or alter such regulations, except as to the places of choosing Senators.

2. Congress must meet once a year. The Congress shall assemble at least once in every year, and such meeting *shall be on the first Monday in December, unless they shall by law appoint a different day.*[4]

---

[1] Repealed in favor of popular election in 1913 by the Seventeenth Amendment.
[2] Changed in 1913 by the Seventeenth Amendment.
[3] The vice president, as next in line, would be an interested party.
[4] Changed in 1933 to January 3 by the Twentieth Amendment (see p. 770 and below).

Section V. Organization and Rules of the Houses

1. Each house may reject members; quorums. Each house shall be the judge of the elections, returns and qualifications of its own members, and a majority of each shall constitute a quorum to do business; but a smaller number may adjourn from day to day, and may be authorized to compel the attendance of absent members, in such manner, and under such penalties, as each house may provide.

See "Bully" Brooks case, pp. 400–401.

2. Each house makes its own rules. Each house may determine the rules of its proceedings, punish its members for disorderly behavior, and with the concurrence of two-thirds, expel a member.

3. Each house must keep and publish a record of its proceedings. Each house shall keep a journal of its proceedings, and from time to time publish the same, excepting such parts as may in their judgment require secrecy; and the yeas and nays of the members of either house on any question shall, at the desire of one-fifth of those present, be entered on the journal.

4. Both houses must agree on adjournment. Neither house, during the session of Congress, shall, without the consent of the other, adjourn for more than three days, nor to any other place than that in which the two houses shall be sitting.

Section VI. Privileges of and Prohibitions upon Congressmen

1. Congressional salaries; immunities. The Senators and Representatives shall receive a compensation for their services, to be ascertained by law and paid out of the treasury of the United States. They shall in all cases except treason, felony and breach of the peace, be privileged from arrest during their attendance at the session of their respective houses, and in going to and returning from the same; and for any speech or debate in either house, they shall not be questioned in any other place [i.e., they shall be immune from libel suits].

2. A congressman may not hold any other federal civil office. No Senator or Representative shall, during the time for which he was elected, be appointed to any civil office under the authority of the United States, which shall have been created, or the emoluments whereof shall have been increased, during such time; and no person holding any office under the United States shall be a member of either house during his continuance in office.

Section VII. Method of Making Laws

See 1787 compromise, pp. 171–172.

1. Money bills must originate in the House. All bills for raising revenue shall originate in the House of Representatives; but the Senate may propose or concur with amendments as on other bills.

Nixon, more than any predecessors, "impounded" billions of dollars voted by Congress for specific purposes, because he disapproved of them. The courts generally failed to sustain him, and his impeachment foes regarded wholesale impoundment as a violation of his oath to "faithfully execute" the laws.

2. The president's veto power; Congress may override. Every bill which shall have passed the House of Representatives and the Senate, shall, before it become a law, be presented to the President of the United States; if he approve he shall sign it, but if not he shall return it with his objections to that house in which it shall have originated, who shall enter the objections at large on their journal, and proceed to reconsider it. If after such reconsideration two-thirds of that house shall agree to pass the bill, it shall be sent, together with the objections, to the other house, by which it shall likewise be reconsidered, and, if approved by two-thirds of that house, it shall become a law. But in all such cases the votes of both houses shall be determined by yeas and nays, and the names of the persons voting for and against the bill shall be entered on the journal of each house respectively. If any bill shall not be returned by the President within ten days (Sundays excepted) after it shall have been presented to him, the same shall be a law, in like manner as if he had signed it, unless the Congress by their adjournment prevent its return, in which case it shall not be a law [this is the so-called pocket veto].

3. All measures requiring the agreement of both houses go to president for approval. Every order, resolution, or vote to which the concurrence of the Senate and House of Representatives may be necessary (except on a question of adjournment) shall be presented to the President of the United States; and before the same shall take effect, shall be approved by him, or being disapproved by him, shall be repassed by two-thirds of the Senate and House of Representatives, according to the rules and limitations prescribed in the case of a bill.

Section VIII.   **Powers Granted to Congress**

Congress has certain enumerated powers:

1. It may lay and collect taxes. The Congress shall have power to lay and collect taxes, duties, imposts, and excises, to pay the debts and provide for the common defense and general welfare of the United States; but all duties, imposts and excises shall be uniform throughout the United States;

2. It may borrow money. To borrow money on the credit of the United States;

3. It may regulate foreign and interstate trade. To regulate commerce with foreign nations, and among the several States, and with the Indian tribes;

For 1798 naturalization see p. 196.

4. It may pass naturalization and bankruptcy laws. To establish an uniform rule of naturalization, and uniform laws on the subject of bankruptcies throughout the United States;

5. It may coin money. To coin money, regulate the value thereof, and of foreign coin, and fix the standard of weights and measures;

6. It may punish counterfeiters. To provide for the punishment of counterfeiting the securities and current coin of the United States;

7. It may establish a postal service. To establish post offices and post roads;

8. It may issue patents and copyrights. To promote the progress of science and useful arts by securing for limited times to authors and inventors the exclusive right to their respective writings and discoveries;

9. It may establish inferior courts. To constitute tribunals inferior to the Supreme Court;

See Judiciary Act of 1789, p. 182.

10. It may punish crimes committed on the high seas. To define and punish piracies and felonies committed on the high seas [i.e., outside the three-mile limit] and offenses against the law of nations [international law];

11. It may declare war; authorize privateers. To declare war,[1] grant letters of marque and reprisal,[2] and make rules concerning captures on land and water;

12. It may maintain an army. To raise and support armies, but no appropriation of money to that use shall be for a longer term than two years;[3]

13. It may maintain a navy. To provide and maintain a navy;

14. It may regulate the army and navy. To make rules for the government and regulation of the land and naval forces;

15. It may call out the state militia. To provide for calling forth the militia to execute the laws of the Union, suppress insurrections, and repel invasions;

See Whiskey Rebellion, pp. 185–186.

16. It shares with the states control of militia. To provide for organizing, arming, and disciplining the militia, and for governing such part of them as may be employed in the service of the United States, reserving to the States respectively the appointment of the officers, and the authority of training the militia according to the discipline prescribed by Congress;

17. It makes laws for the District of Columbia and other federal areas. To exercise exclusive legislation in all cases whatsoever, over such district (not exceeding ten miles square) as may, by cession of particular States, and the acceptance of Congress, become the seat of government of the United States,[1] and to exercise like

---

[1]Note that presidents, though they can provoke war (see the case of Polk, pp. 369–370) or wage it after it is declared, cannot declare it.

[2]Papers issued private citizens in wartime authorizing them to capture enemy ships.

[3]A reflection of fear of standing armies earlier expressed in the Declaration of Independence.

authority over all places purchased by the consent of the legislature of the State, in which the same shall be, for the erection of forts, magazines, arsenals, dock-yards, and other needful buildings;—and

Congress has certain implied powers:

This is the famous "elastic clause"; See p. 185.

18. It may make laws necessary for carrying out the enumerated powers. To make all laws which shall be necessary and proper for carrying into execution the foregoing powers, and all other powers vested by this Constitution in the government of the United States, or in any departure or officer thereof.

Section IX.   Powers Denied to the Federal Government

See 1787 slave compromise, p. 172.

1. Congressional control of slave trade postponed until 1808. *The migration or importation of such persons as any of the States now existing shall think proper to admit shall not be prohibited by the Congress prior to the year 1808; but a tax or duty may be imposed on such importation, not exceeding $10 for each person.*

See Lincoln's unlawful suspension, p. 429.

2. The writ of habeas corpus[2] may be suspended only in cases of rebellion or invasion. The privilege of the writ of habeas corpus shall not be suspended, unless when in cases of rebellion or invasion the public safety may require it.

3. Attainders[3] and ex post facto laws[4] forbidden. No bill of attainder or ex post facto law shall be passed.

4. Direct taxes must be apportioned according to population. No capitation [head or poll tax] or other direct, tax shall be laid, unless in proportion to the census or enumeration herein before directed to be taken.[5]

5. Export taxes forbidden. No tax or duty shall be laid on articles exported from any State.

6. Congress must not discriminate among states in regulating commerce. No preference shall be given by any regulation of commerce or revenue to the ports of one State over those of another; nor shall vessels bound to, or from, one State, be obliged to enter, clear, or pay duties in another.

See Lincoln's unlawful infraction, p. 429.

7. Public money may not be spent without congressional appropriation; accounting. No money shall be drawn from the treasury, but in consequence of appropriations made by law; and a regular statement and account of the receipts and expenditures of all public money shall be published from time to time.

8. Titles of nobility prohibited; foreign gifts. No title of nobility shall be granted by the United States; and no person holding office of profit or trust under them, shall, without the consent of Congress, accept of any present, emolument, office, or title, of any kind whatever, from any king, prince, or foreign state.

Section X.   Powers Denied to the States

Absolute prohibitions on the states:

On contracts see Fletcher v. Peck, *p. 238.*

1. The states are forbidden to do certain things. No State shall enter into any treaty, alliance, or confederation; grant letters of marque and reprisal [i.e., authorize privateers]; coin money; emit bills of credit [issue paper money]; make anything but

---

[1]The District of Columbia, ten miles square, was established in 1791 with a cession from Virginia (see p. 183).

[2]A writ of habeas corpus is a document that enables a person under arrest to obtain an immediate examination in court to ascertain whether he or she is being legally held.

[3]A bill of attainder is a special legislative act condemning and punishing an individual without a judicial trial.

[4]An ex post facto law is one that fixes punishments for acts committed before the law was passed.

[5]Modified in 1913 by the Sixteenth Amendment (see p. 742 and amendments below).

gold and silver coin a [legal] tender in payment of debts; pass any bill of attainder,[1] ex post facto,[1] or law impairing the obligation of contracts, or grant any title of nobility.

Conditional prohibitions on the states:

Cf. Confederation chaos, pp. 164–165.

2. The states may not levy duties without the consent of Congress. No State shall, without the consent of Congress, lay any imposts or duties on imports or exports, except what may be absolutely necessary for executing its inspection laws: and the net produce of all duties and imposts, laid by any State on imports or exports, shall be for the use of the treasury of the United States; and all such laws shall be subject to the revision and control of the Congress.

3. Certain other federal powers are forbidden the states except with the consent of Congress. No State shall, without the consent of Congress, lay any duty of tonnage [i.e., duty on ship tonnage], keep [nonmilitia] troops or ships of war in time of peace, enter into any agreement or compact with another State, or with a foreign power, or engage in war, unless actually invaded, or in such imminent danger as will not admit of delay.

Article II. *Executive Department*

Section I. President and Vice President

1. The president is the chief executive; term of office. The executive power shall be vested in a President of the United States of America. He shall hold his office during the term of four years,[2] and, together with the Vice President, chosen for the same term, be elected as follows:

See 1787 compromise, pp. 171–172.

See 1876 Oregon case, p. 494.

2. The president is chosen by electors. Each State shall appoint, in such manner as the legislature thereof may direct, a number of electors, equal to the whole number of Senators and Representatives to which the State may be entitled in the Congress; but no Senator or Representative, or person holding an office of trust or profit under the United States, shall be appointed an elector.

A majority of the electoral votes needed to elect a president. *The electors shall meet in their respective States, and vote by ballot for two persons, of whom one at least shall not be an inhabitant of the same State with themselves. And they shall make a list of all the persons voted for, and of the number of votes for each; which list they shall sign and certify, and transmit sealed to the seat of government of the United States, directed to the President of the Senate. The President of the Senate shall, in the presence of the Senate and House of Representatives, open all the certificates, and the votes shall be counted. The person having the greatest number of votes shall be the President, if such number be a majority of the whole number of electors appointed; and if there be more than one who have such majority, and have an equal number of votes, then the House of Representatives shall immediately*

See Burr-Jefferson disputed election of 1800, pp. 203–204.

choose by ballot one of them for President; and if no person have a majority, then from the five highest on the list the said house shall in like manner choose the President. But in choosing the President the votes shall be taken by States, the representation from each State having one vote; a quorum for this purpose shall consist of a member or members from two-thirds of the States, and a majority of all the States shall be necessary to a choice. In every case, after the choice of the President, the person having the greatest number of votes of the electors shall

See Jefferson as vice president in 1796, p. 194.

be the Vice President. But if there should remain two or more who have equal votes, the Senate shall choose from them by ballot the Vice President.[3]

---

[1]For definitions see footnotes 3 and 4 on preceding page.
[2]No reference to reelection; for anti–third term Twenty-second Amendment, see below.
[3]Repealed in 1804 by the Twelfth Amendment (for text see below).

3. Congress decides time of meeting of Electoral College. The Congress may determine the time of choosing the electors and the day on which they shall give their votes; which day shall be the same throughout the United States.

To provide for foreign-born people, like Alexander Hamilton, born in the British West Indies.

4. Who may be president. No person except a natural-born citizen, *or a citizen of the United States at the time of the adoption of this Constitution,* shall be eligible to the office of President; neither shall any person be eligible to that office who shall not have attained to the age of thirty-five years, and been fourteen years a resident within the United States [i.e., a legal resident].

Modified by Twentieth and Twenty-fifth Amendments below.

5. Replacements for president. In case of the removal of the President from office or of his death, resignation, or inability to discharge the powers and duties of said office, the same shall devolve on the Vice President, and the Congress may by law provide for the case of removal, death, resignation, or inability, both of the President and Vice President, declaring what officer shall then act as President, and such officer shall act accordingly, until the disability be removed, or a President shall be elected.

6. The president's salary. The President shall, at stated times, receive for his services a compensation, which shall neither be increased or diminished during the period for which he shall have been elected, and he shall not receive within that period any other emolument from the United States, or any of them.

7. The president's oath of office. Before he enter on the execution of his office, he shall take the following oath or affirmation:—"I do solemnly swear (or affirm) that I will faithfully execute the office of the President of the United States, and will to the best of my ability preserve, protect and defend the Constitution of the United States."

Section II. **Powers of the President**

See cabinet evolution, p. 182.

1. The president has important military and civil powers. The President shall be commander in chief of the army and navy of the United States, and of the militia of the several States, when called into the actual service of the United States; he may require the opinion, in writing, of the principal officer in each of the executive departments, upon any subject relating to the duties of their respective offices, and he shall have power to grant reprieves and pardons for offenses against the United States, except in cases of impeachment.[1]

For president's removal power, see pp. 480–481.

2. The president may negotiate treaties and nominate federal officials. He shall have power, by and with the advice and consent of the Senate, to make treaties, provided two-thirds of the Senators present concur; and he shall nominate, and by and with the advice and consent of the Senate, shall appoint ambassadors, other public ministers and consuls, judges of the Supreme Court, and all other officers of the United States, whose appointments are not herein otherwise provided for, and which shall be established by law: but the Congress may by law vest the appointment of such inferior officers, as they think proper, in the President alone, in the courts of law, or in the heads of departments.

3. The president may fill vacancies during Senate recess. The President shall have power to fill up all vacancies that may happen during the recess of the Senate, by granting commissions which shall expire at the end of their next session.

Section III. **Other Powers and Duties of the President**

For president's personal appearances, see p. 665.

Messages; extra sessions; receiving ambassadors; execution of the laws. He shall from time to time give to the Congress information of the state of the Union, and recommend to their consideration such measures as he shall judge necessary and expedient; he may, on extraordinary occasions, convene both houses, or either of

---

[1]To prevent the president's pardoning himself or his close associates, as was feared in the case of Richard Nixon. See p. 928.

them, and in case of disagreement between them, with respect to the time of adjournment, he may adjourn them to such time as he shall think proper; he shall receive ambassadors and other public ministers; he shall take care that the laws be faithfully executed, and shall commission all the officers of the United States.

Section IV.   **Impeachment**

See discussion of Presidents Johnson, pp. 480–481; Nixon, pp. 925–928; and Clinton, pp. 970–971.

Civil officers may be removed by impeachment. The President, Vice President and all civil officers[1] of the United States shall be removed from office on impeachment for, and on conviction of, treason, bribery, and other high crimes and misdemeanors.

Article III.   *Judicial Department*

Section I.   **The Federal Courts**

See Judiciary Act of 1789, p. 182.

The judicial power belongs to the federal courts. The judicial power of the United States shall be vested in one Supreme Court, and in such inferior courts as the Congress may from time to time ordain and establish. The judges, both of the Supreme and inferior courts, shall hold their offices during good behavior, and shall, at stated times, receive for their services a compensation which shall not be diminished[2] during their continuance in office.

Section II.   **Jurisdiction of Federal Courts**

1. Kinds of cases that may be heard. The judicial power shall extend to all cases, in law and equity, arising under this Constitution, the laws of the United States, and treaties made, or which shall be made, under their authority;—to all cases affecting ambassadors, other public ministers and consuls;—to all cases of admiralty and maritime jurisdiction;—to controversies to which the United States shall be a party;—to controversies between two or more States;—*between a State and citizens of another State*[3];—between citizens of different States;—between citizens of the same State claiming lands under grants of different States, and between a State, or the citizens thereof, and foreign states, citizens or subjects.

2. Jurisdiction of the Supreme Court. In all cases affecting ambassadors, other public ministers and consuls, and those in which a State shall be a party, the Supreme Court shall have original jurisdiction.[4] In all the other cases before mentioned, the Supreme Court shall have appellate jurisdiction,[5] both as to law and fact, with such exceptions, and under such regulations, as the Congress shall make.

3. Trial for federal crime is by jury. The trial of all crimes, except in cases of impeachment, shall be by jury; and such trial shall be held in the State where the said crimes shall have been committed; but when not committed within any State, the trial shall be at such place or places as the Congress may by law have directed.

---

[1] i.e., all federal executive and judicial officers, but not members of Congress or military personnel.

[2] In 1978, in a case involving federal judges, the Supreme Court ruled that diminution of salaries by inflation was irrelevant.

[3] The Eleventh Amendment (see below) restricts this to suits by a state against citizens of another state.

[4] i.e., such cases must originate in the Supreme Court.

[5] i.e., it hears other cases only when they are appealed to it from a lower federal court or a state court.

Section III.   Treason

See Burr trial, p. 215.

1. Treason defined. Treason against the United States shall consist only in levying war against them, or in adhering to their enemies, giving them aid and comfort. No person shall be convicted of treason unless on the testimony of two witnesses to the same overt act, or on confession in open court.

2. Congress fixes punishment for treason. The Congress shall have power to declare the punishment of treason, but no attainder of treason shall work corruption of blood, or forfeiture except during the life of the person attained.[1]

Article IV.   *Relations of the States to One Another*

Section I.   Credit to Acts, Records, and Court Proceedings

Each state must respect the public acts of the others. Full faith and credit shall be given in each State to the public acts, records, and judicial proceedings of every other State.[2] And the Congress may by general laws prescribe the manner in which such acts, records, and proceedings shall be proved [attested], and the effect thereof.

Section II.   Duties of States to States

1. Citizenship in one state is valid in all. The citizens of each State shall be entitled to all privileges and immunities of citizens in the several States.

This stipulation is sometimes openly flouted. In 1978 Governor Jerry Brown of California, acting on humanitarian grounds, refused to surrender to South Dakota an American Indian, Dennis Banks, who was charged with murder in an armed uprising.

Basis of fugitive-slave laws; see pp. 385–386.

2. Fugitives from justice must be surrendered by the state to which they have fled. A person charged in any State with treason, felony, or other crime, who shall flee from justice, and be found in another State, shall on demand of the executive authority [governor] of the State from which he fled, be delivered up, to be removed to the State having jurisdiction of the crime.

3. Slaves and apprentices must be returned. *No person held to service or labor in one State, under the laws thereof, escaping into another, shall, in consequence of any law or regulation therein, be discharged from such service or labor, but shall be delivered up on claim of the party to whom such service or labor may be due.*[3]

Section III.   New States and Territories

e.g., Maine (1820); see p. 234.

1. Congress may admit new states. New States may be admitted by the Congress into this Union; but no new State shall be formed or erected within the jurisdiction of any other State; nor any State be formed by the junction of two or more States, or parts of States, without the consent of the legislatures of the States concerned as well as of the Congress.[4]

2. Congress regulates federal territory and property. The Congress shall have power to dispose of and make all needful rules and regulations respecting the territory or other property belonging to the United States; and nothing in this Constitution shall be so construed as to prejudice any claims of the United States, or of any particular State.

Section IV.   Protection to the States

See Cleveland and the Pullman strike, p. 599.

United States guarantees to states representative government and protection against invasion and rebellion. The United States shall guarantee to every

---

[1] i.e., punishment only for the offender; none for his or her heirs.

[2] e.g., a marriage in one is valid in all.

[3] Invalidated in 1865 by the Thirteenth Amendment (for text see below).

[4] Loyal West Virginia was formed by Lincoln in 1862 from seceded Virginia. This act was of dubious constitutionality and was justified in part by the wartime powers of the president. See pp. 420–421.

State in this Union a republican form of government, and shall protect each of them against invasion; and on application of the legislature, or of the executive [governor] (when the legislature cannot be convened), against domestic violence.

Article V.   *The Process of Amendment*

The Constitution may be amended in four ways. The Congress, whenever two-thirds of both houses shall deem it necessary, shall propose amendments to this Constitution, or, on the application of the legislature of two-thirds of the several States, shall call a convention for proposing amendments, which, in either case, shall be valid to all intents and purposes, as part of this Constitution, when ratified by the legislatures of three-fourths of the several States, or by conventions in three-fourths thereof, as the one or the other mode of ratification may be proposed by the Congress; provided *that no amendments which may be made prior to the year one thousand eight hundred and eight shall in any manner affect the first and fourth clauses in the ninth section of the first article;*[1] and that no State, without its consent, shall be deprived of its equal suffrage in the Senate.

Article VI.   *General Provisions*

This pledge honored by Hamilton, pp. 182–183.

1. The debts of the Confederation are taken over. All debts contracted and engagements entered into, before the adoption of this Constitution, shall be as valid against the United States under this Constitution, as under the Confederation.

2. The Constitution, federal laws, and treaties are the supreme law of the land. This Constitution, and the laws of the United States which shall be made in pursuance thereof; and all treaties made, or which shall be made, under the authority of the United States, shall be the supreme law of the land; and the judges in every State shall be bound thereby, anything in the Constitution or laws of any State to the contrary notwithstanding.

3. Federal and state officers bound by oath to support the Constitution. The Senators and Representatives before mentioned, and the members of the several State legislatures, and all executive and judicial officers, both of the United States and of the several States, shall be bound by oath or affirmation to support this Constitution; but no religious test shall ever be required as a qualification to any office or public trust under the United States.

Article VII.   *Ratification of the Constitution*

See 1787 irregularity, pp. 172–174.

The Constitution effective when ratified by conventions in nine states. The ratification of the conventions of nine States shall be sufficient for the establishment of this Constitution between the States so ratifying the same.

Done in Convention by the unanimous consent of the States present, the seventeenth day of September in the year of our Lord one thousand seven hundred and eighty-seven and of the Independence of the United States of America the twelfth. In witness whereof we have hereunto subscribed our names.

[Signed by]

G° WASHINGTON

Presidt and Deputy from Virginia

[and thirty-eight others]

---

[1]This clause, regarding slave trade and direct taxes, became inoperative in 1808.

AMENDMENTS TO THE CONSTITUTION

Amendment I. *Religious and Political Freedom*

For background of Bill of Rights, see pp. 181–182.

Congress must not interfere with freedom of religion, speech or press, assembly, and petition. Congress shall make no law respecting an establishment of religion,[1] or prohibiting the free exercise thereof; or abridging the freedom of speech, or of the press; or the right of the people peaceably to assemble, and to petition the government for a redress of grievances.

Amendment II. *Right to Bear Arms*

The people may bear arms. A well-regulated militia being necessary to the security of a free State, the right of the people to keep and bear arms [i.e., for military purposes] shall not be infringed.[2]

Amendment III. *Quartering of Troops*

See Declaration of Independence and British quartering above.

Soldiers may not be arbitrarily quartered on the people. No soldier shall, in time of peace, be quartered in any house without the consent of the owner, nor in time of war, but in a manner to be prescribed by law.

Amendment IV. *Searches and Seizures*

A reflection of colonial grievances against the crown.

Unreasonable searches are forbidden. The right of the people to be secure in their persons, houses, papers, and effects, against unreasonable searches and seizures, shall not be violated, and no [search] warrants shall issue but upon probable cause, supported by oath or affirmation, and particularly describing the place to be searched, and the persons or things to be seized.

Amendment V. *Right to Life, Liberty, and Property*

When witnesses refuse to answer questions in court, they routinely "take the Fifth Amendment."

The individual is guaranteed certain rights when on trial and the right to life, liberty, and property. No person shall be held to answer for a capital, or otherwise infamous crime, unless on a presentment [formal charge] or indictment of a grand jury, except in cases arising in the naval forces, or in the militia, when in actual service in time of war or public danger; nor shall any person be subject for the same offense to be twice put in jeopardy of life or limb; nor shall be compelled in any criminal case to be a witness against himself, nor be deprived of life, liberty, or property, without due process of law; nor shall private property be taken for public use [i.e., by eminent domain] without just compensation.

Amendment VI. *Protection in Criminal Trials*

See Declaration of Independence above.

An accused person has important rights. In all criminal prosecutions, the accused shall enjoy the right to a speedy and public trial, by an impartial jury of the State and district wherein the crime shall have been committed, which district shall

---

[1] In 1787 "an establishment of religion" referred to an "established church," or one supported by all taxpayers, whether members or not. But the courts have often acted under this article to keep religion, including prayers, out of the public schools.

[2] The courts long held that the right to bear arms was a limited right linked to the maintenance of militias. But in the case of *District of Columbia v. Heller* in 2008, the Supreme Court defined the right to bear arms as an individual right, not contingent on "participation in some corporate body." Yet the Court still left the door open to some kinds of gun-control legislation.

have been previously ascertained by law, and to be informed of the nature and cause of the accusation; to be confronted with the witnesses against him; to have compulsory process [subpoena] for obtaining witnesses in his favor, and to have the assistance of counsel for his defense.

Amendment VII. *Suits at Common Law*

The rules of common law are recognized. In suits at common law, where the value in controversy shall exceed twenty dollars, the right of trial by jury shall be preserved, and no fact tried by a jury shall be otherwise re-examined in any court of the United States, than according to the rules of the common law.

Amendment VIII. *Bail and Punishments*

Excessive fines and unusual punishments are forbidden. Excessive bail shall not be required, nor excessive fines imposed, nor cruel and unusual punishment inflicted.

Amendment IX. *Concerning Rights Not Enumerated*

The Ninth and Tenth Amendments were bulwarks of southern states' rights before the Civil War.

The people retain rights not here enumerated. The enumeration in the Constitution, of certain rights, shall not be construed to deny or disparage others retained by the people.

Amendment X. *Powers Reserved to the States and to the People*

A concession to states' rights, p. 183.

Powers not delegated to the federal government are reserved to the states and the people. The powers not delegated to the United States by the Constitution, nor prohibited by it to the States, are reserved to the States respectively, or to the people.

Amendment XI. *Suits Against a State*

The federal courts have no authority in suits by citizens against a state. The judicial power of the United States shall not be construed to extend to any suit in law or equity, commenced or prosecuted against one of the United States by citizens of another State, or by citizens or subjects of any foreign state. [Adopted 1798.]

Amendment XII. *Election of President and Vice President*

Forestalls repetition of 1800 electoral dispute, pp. 203–204.

See 1876 disputed election. pp. 494–496.

See 1824 election, pp. 246–248.

1. Changes in manner of electing president and vice president; procedure when no presidential candidate receives electoral majority. The electors shall meet in their respective States, and vote by ballot for President and Vice President, one of whom, at least, shall not be an inhabitant of the same state with themselves; they shall name in their ballots the person voted for as President, and in distinct ballots the person voted for as Vice President, and they shall make distinct lists of all persons voted for as President, and of all persons voted for as Vice President, and of the number of votes for each, which lists they shall sign and certify, and transmit sealed to the seat of government of the United States, directed to the President of the Senate;—the President of the Senate shall, in the presence of the Senate and House of Representatives, open all the certificates and the votes shall be counted;—the person having the greatest number of votes for President shall be the President, if such number be a majority of the whole number of electors appointed; and if no person have such majority, then from the persons having the highest numbers not exceeding three on the list of those voted for as President, the House of

Representatives shall choose immediately, by ballot, the President. But in choosing the President, the votes shall be taken by States, the representation from each State having one vote; a quorum for this purpose shall consist of a member or members from two-thirds of the States, and a majority of all the States shall be necessary to a choice. And if the House of Representatives shall not choose a President whenever the right of choice shall devolve upon them, before *the fourth day of March*[1] next following, then the Vice President shall act as President, as in the case of the death or other constitutional disability of the President.

2. Procedure when no vice presidential candidate receives electoral majority. The person having the greatest number of votes as Vice President, shall be the Vice President, if such number be a majority of the whole number of electors appointed; and if no person have a majority, then from the two highest numbers on the list the Senate shall choose the Vice President; a quorum for the purpose shall consist of two-thirds of the whole number of Senators, and a majority of the whole number shall be necessary to a choice. But no person constitutionally ineligible to the office of President shall be eligible to that of Vice President of the United States. [Adopted 1804.]

Amendment XIII.   *Slavery Prohibited*

For background see pp. 441–443.

Slavery forbidden. 1. Neither slavery[2] nor involuntary servitude, except as a punishment for crime whereof the party shall have been duly convicted, shall exist within the United States, or any place subject to their jurisdiction.

2. Congress shall have power to enforce this article by appropriate legislation. [Adopted 1865.]

Amendment XIV.   *Civil Rights for Ex-slaves,[3] etc.*

For background see pp. 473–474.

For corporations as "persons," see p. 525.

Abolishes three-fifths rule for slaves, Art. I., Sec. II, para. 3.

1. Ex-slaves made citizens; U.S. citizenship primary. All persons born or naturalized in the United States, and subject to the jurisdiction thereof, are citizens of the United States and of the State wherein they reside. No State shall make or enforce any law which shall abridge the privileges or immunities of citizens of the United States; nor shall any State deprive any person of life, liberty, or property, without due process of law; nor deny to any person within its jurisdiction the equal protection of the laws.

2. When a state denies citizens the vote, its representation shall be reduced. Representatives shall be apportioned among the several States according to their respective numbers, counting the whole number of persons in each State, excluding Indians not taxed. But when the right to vote at any election for the choice of Electors for President and Vice President of the United States, Representatives in Congress, the executive and judicial officers of a State, or the members of the legislature thereof, is denied to any of the male inhabitants of such State, being twenty-one years of age and citizens of the United States, or in any way abridged, except for participation in rebellion, or other crime, the basis of representation therein shall be reduced in the proportion which the number of such make citizens shall bear to the whole number of male citizens twenty-one years of age in such State.[4]

Leading ex-Confederates denied office. See p. 474.

3. Certain persons who have been in rebellion are ineligible for federal and state office. No person shall be a Senator or Representative in Congress, or Elector of President and Vice President, or hold any office, civil or military, under the

---

[1] Changed to January 20 by the Twentieth Amendment (for text see below).

[2] The only explicit mention of slavery in the Constitution.

[3] Occasionally an offender is prosecuted under the Thirteenth Amendment for keeping an employee or other person under conditions approximating slavery.

[4] The provisions concerning "male" inhabitants were modified by the Nineteenth Amendment, which enfranchised women. The legal voting age was changed from twenty-one to eighteen by the Twenty-sixth Amendment.

United States, or under any State, who, having previously taken an oath, as a member of Congress, or as an officer of the United States, or as a member of any State legislature, or as an executive or judicial officer of any State, to support the Constitution of the United States, shall have engaged in insurrection or rebellion against the same, or given aid or comfort to the enemies thereof. But Congress may, by a vote of two-thirds of each house, remove such disability.

The ex-Confederates were thus forced to repudiate their debts and pay pensions to their own veterans, plus taxes for the pensions of Union veterans, their conquerors.

4. Debts incurred in aid of rebellion are void. The validity of the public debt of the United States, authorizing by law, including debts incurred for payment of pensions and bounties for services in suppressing insurrection or rebellion, shall not be questioned. But neither the United States nor any State shall assume or pay any debt or obligation incurred in aid of insurrection or rebellion against the United States, or any claim for the loss or emancipation of any slave; but all such debts, obligations, and claims shall be held illegal and void.

5. Enforcement. The Congress shall have power to enforce, by appropriate legislation, the provisions of this article. [Adopted 1868.]

Amendment XV. *Suffrage for Blacks*

For background see p. 475.

Black males are made voters. 1. The right of the citizens of the United States to vote shall not be denied or abridged by the United States or by any State on account of race, color, or previous condition of servitude.

2. The Congress shall have power to enforce this article by appropriate legislation. [Adopted 1870.]

Amendment XVI. *Income Taxes*

For background see p. 665.

Congress has power to lay and collect income taxes. The Congress shall have power to lay and collect taxes on incomes, from whatever source derived, without apportionment among the several States, and without regard to any census or enumeration. [Adopted 1913.]

Amendment XVII. *Direct Election of Senators*

Senators shall be elected by popular vote. 1. The Senate of the United States shall be composed of two Senators from each State, elected by the people thereof, for six years; and each Senator shall have one vote. The electors in each State shall have the qualifications requisite for electors of [voters for] the most numerous branch of the State legislatures.

2. When vacancies happen in the representation of any State in the Senate, the executive authority of such State shall issue writs of election to fill such vacancies: Provided, that the Legislature of any State may empower the executive thereof to make temporary appointments until the people fill the vacancies by election as the Legislature may direct.

3. This amendment shall not be so construed as to affect the election or term of any Senator chosen before it becomes valid as part of the Constitution. [Adopted 1913.]

Amendment XVIII. *National Prohibition*

For background see pp. 704–705.

The sale or manufacture of intoxicating liquors is forbidden. 1. *After one year from the ratification of this article the manufacture, sale, or transportation of intoxicating liquors within, the importation thereof into, or the exportation thereof from the United States and all territory subject to the jurisdiction thereof, for beverage purposes, is hereby prohibited.*

2. *The Congress and the several States shall have concurrent power to enforce this article by appropriate legislation.*

3. *This article shall be inoperative unless it shall have been ratified as an amendment to the Constitution by the legislatures of the several States, as provided by the Constitution, within seven years from the date of the submission thereof to the States by the Congress.* [Adopted 1919; repealed 1933 by Twenty-first Amendment.]

Amendment XIX. *Woman Suffrage*

For background see pp. 683–684.

Women guaranteed the right to vote. 1. The right of citizens of the United States to vote shall not be denied or abridged by the United States or by any State on account of sex.

2. Congress shall have power to enforce this article by appropriate legislation. [Adopted 1920.]

Amendment XX. *Presidential and Congressional Terms*

Shortens lame duck periods by modifying Art. I, Sec. IV, para. 2.

1. Presidential, vice presidential, and congressional terms of office begin in January. The terms of the President and Vice President shall end at noon on the 20th day of January, and the terms of Senators and Representatives at noon on the 3d day of January, of the years in which such terms would have ended if this article had not been ratified; and the terms of their successors shall then begin.

2. New meeting date for Congress. The Congress shall assemble at least once in every year, and such meeting shall begin at noon on the 3d day of January, unless they shall by law appoint a different day.

3. Emergency presidential and vice presidential succession. If, at the time fixed for the beginning of the term of the President, the President-elect shall have died, the Vice President–elect shall become President. If a President shall not have been chosen before the time fixed for the beginning of his term, or if the President-elect shall have failed to qualify, then the Vice President–elect shall act as President until a President shall have qualified; and the Congress may by law provide for the case wherein neither a President-elect nor a Vice President–elect shall have qualified, declaring who shall then act as President, or the manner in which one who is to act shall be selected, and such persons shall act accordingly until a President or Vice President shall have qualified.

4. The Congress may by law provide for the case of the death of any of the persons from whom the House of Representatives may choose a President whenever the right of choice shall have devolved upon them, and for the case of the death of any of the persons from whom the Senate may choose a Vice President whenever the right of choice shall have devolved upon them.

5. Sections 1 and 2 shall take effect on the 15th day of October following the ratification of this article.

6. This article shall be inoperative unless it shall have been ratified as an amendment to the Constitution by the Legislatures of three-fourths of the several States within seven years from the date of its submission. [Adopted 1933.]

Amendment XXI. *Prohibition Repealed*

For background see pp. 762–763.

1. Eighteenth Amendment repealed. The eighteenth article of amendment to the Constitution of the United States is hereby repealed.

2. Local laws honored. The transportation or importation into any State, Territory, or Possession of the United States for delivery or use therein of intoxicating liquors, in violation of the laws thereof, is hereby prohibited.

3. This article shall be inoperative unless it shall have been ratified as an amendment to the Constitution by conventions in the several States, as provided in the Constitution, within seven years from the date of the submission thereof to the States by the Congress. [Adopted 1933.]

Amendment XXII.

Sometimes referred to as the anti–Franklin Roosevelt amendment.

Anti–Third Term Amendment

1. Presidential term is limited. No person shall be elected to the office of President more than twice, and no person who has held the office of President, or acted as President, for more than two years of a term to which some other person was elected President shall be elected to the office of President more than once. But this article shall not apply to any person holding the office of President when this article was proposed by the Congress [i.e., Truman], and shall not prevent any person who may be holding the office of President, during the term within which this article becomes operative [i.e., Truman] from holding the office of President or acting as President during the remainder of such term.

2. This article shall be inoperative unless it shall have been ratified as an amendment to the Constitution by the legislatures of three-fourths of the several States within seven years from the date of its submission to the States by the Congress. [Adopted 1951.]

Amendment XXIII.

Designed to give the District of Columbia three electoral votes and to quiet the century-old cry of "No taxation without representation." Yet the District of Columbia still has only one nonvoting member of Congress.

District of Columbia Vote

1. Presidential electors for the District of Columbia. The District, constituting the seat of government of the United States, shall appoint in such manner as the Congress shall direct:

A number of electors of President and Vice President equal to the whole number of Senators and Representatives in Congress to which the District would be entitled if it were a State, but in no event more than the least populous State; they shall be in addition to those appointed by the States, but they shall be considered for the purposes of the election of President and Vice President, to be electors appointed by a State; and they shall meet in the District and perform such duties as provided by the twelfth article of amendment.

2. Enforcement. The Congress shall have the power to enforce this article by appropriate legislation. [Adopted 1961.]

Amendment XXIV.

Designed to end discrimination against poor people, including southern blacks who were often denied the vote through inability to pay poll taxes. See p. 903.

Poll Tax

1. Payment of poll tax or other taxes not to be prerequisite for voting in federal elections. The right of citizens of the United States to vote in any primary or other election for President or Vice President, for electors for President or Vice President, or for Senator or Representative in Congress, shall not be denied or abridged by the United States or any State by reason of failure to pay any poll tax or other tax.

2. Enforcement. The Congress shall have the power to enforce this article by appropriate legislation. [Adopted 1964.]

Amendment XXV.

Gerald Ford was the first "appointed president." See pp. 926, 928.

Presidential Succession and Disability

1. Vice president to become president. In case of the removal of the President from office or of his death or resignation, the Vice President shall become President.[1]

2. Successor to vice president provided. Whenever there is a vacancy in the office of the Vice President, the President shall nominate a Vice President who shall take office upon confirmation by a majority vote of both Houses of Congress.

---

[1]The original Constitution (Art. II, Sec. I, para. 5) was vague on this point, stipulating that "the powers and duties" of the president, but not necessarily the title, should "devolve" on the vice president. President Tyler, the first "accidental president," assumed not only the powers and duties but the title as well.

3. Vice president to serve for disabled president. Whenever the President transmits to the President pro tempore of the Senate and the Speaker of the House of Representatives his written declaration that he is unable to discharge the powers and duties of his office, and until he transmits to them a written declaration to the contrary, such powers and duties shall be discharged by the Vice President as Acting President.

4. Procedure for disqualifying or requalifying president. Whenever the Vice President and a majority of either the principal officers of the executive departments or of such other body as Congress may by law provide, transmit to the President pro tempore of the Senate and the Speaker of the House of Representatives their written declaration that the President is unable to discharge the powers and duties of his office, the Vice President shall immediately assume the powers and duties of the office as Acting President.

Thereafter, when the President transmits to the President pro tempore of the Senate and the Speaker of the House of Representatives his written declaration that no inability exists, he shall resume the powers and duties of his office unless the Vice President and a majority of either the principal officers of the executive department[s] or of such other body as Congress may by law provide, transmit within four days to the President pro tempore of the Senate and the Speaker of the House of Representatives their written declaration that the President is unable to discharge the powers and duties of his office. Thereupon Congress shall decide the issue, assembling within forty-eight hours for that purpose if not in session. If the Congress, within twenty-one days after receipt of the latter written declaration, or, if Congress is not in session, within twenty-one days after Congress is required to assemble, determines by two-thirds vote of both Houses that the President is unable to discharge the powers and duties of his office, the Vice President shall continue to discharge the same as Acting President; otherwise, the President shall resume the powers and duties of his office. [Adopted 1967.]

Amendment XXVI. *Lowering Voting Age*

A response to the current revolt of youth. See p. 919.

1. Ballot for eighteen-year-olds. The right of citizens of the United States, who are eighteen years of age or older, to vote shall not be denied or abridged by the United States or any state on account of age.

2. Enforcement. The Congress shall have the power to enforce this article by appropriate legislation. [Adopted 1971.]

Amendment XXVII. *Restricting Congressional Pay Raises*

Reflects anti-incumbent sentiment of early 1990s. First proposed by James Madison in 1789; took 203 years to be ratified.

Congress not allowed to increase its current pay. No law varying the compensation for the services of the Senators and Representatives shall take effect, until an election of Representatives shall have intervened. [Adopted 1992.]

TABLES

Table A.1 Presidential Elections*

Election	Candidates	Parties	Popular Vote	Electoral Vote
1789	GEORGE WASHINGTON	No party designation		69
	JOHN ADAMS			34
	MINOR CANDIDATES			35
1792	GEORGE WASHINGTON	No party designation		132
	JOHN ADAMS			77
	GEORGE CLINTON			50
	MINOR CANDIDATES			5
1796	JOHN ADAMS	Federalist		71
	THOMAS JEFFERSON	Democratic-Republican		68
	THOMAS PINCKNEY	Federalist		59
	AARON BURR	Democratic-Republican		30
	MINOR CANDIDATES			48
1800	THOMAS JEFFERSON	Democratic-Republican		73
	AARON BURR	Democratic-Republican		73
	JOHN ADAMS	Federalist		65
	CHARLES C. PINCKNEY	Federalist		64
	JOHN JAY	Federalist		1
1804	THOMAS JEFFERSON	Democratic-Republican		162
	CHARLES C. PINCKNEY	Federalist		14
1808	JAMES MADISON	Democratic-Republican		122
	CHARLES C. PINCKNEY	Federalist		47
	GEORGE CLINTON	Democratic-Republican		6
1812	JAMES MADISON	Democratic-Republican		128
	DEWITT CLINTON	Federalist		89
1816	JAMES MONROE	Democratic-Republican		183
	RUFUS KING	Federalist		34
1820	JAMES MONROE	Democratic-Republican		231
	JOHN Q. ADAMS	Independent Republican		1
1824	JOHN Q. ADAMS (Min.)[†]	Democratic-Republican	108,740	84
	ANDREW JACKSON	Democratic-Republican	153,544	99
	WILLIAM H. CRAWFORD	Democratic-Republican	46,618	41
	HENRY CLAY	Democratic-Republican	47,136	37
1828	ANDREW JACKSON	Democratic	647,286	178
	JOHN Q. ADAMS	National Republican	508,064	83
1832	ANDREW JACKSON	Democratic	687,502	219
	HENRY CLAY	National Republican	530,189	49
	WILLIAM WIRT	Anti-Masonic	33,108	7
	JOHN FLOYD	National Republican		11
1836	MARTIN VAN BUREN	Democratic	765,483	170
	WILLIAM H. HARRISON	Whig		73
	HUGH L. WHITE	Whig	739,795	26
	DANIEL WEBSTER	Whig		14
	W. P. MANGUM	Whig		11

* Candidates receiving less than 1 percent of the popular vote are omitted. Before the Twelfth Amendment (1804), the Electoral College voted for two presidential candidates, and the runner-up became vice president. Basic figures are taken primarily from *Historical Statistics of the United States, Colonial Times to 1970* (1975), pp. 1073–1074, and *Statistical Abstract of the United States,* relevant years.

† "Min." indicates minority president—one receiving less than 50 percent of all popular votes.

Presidential Elections (continued)

Election	Candidates	Parties	Popular Vote	Electoral Vote
1840	WILLIAM H. HARRISON	Whig	1,274,624	234
	MARTIN VAN BUREN	Democratic	1,127,781	60
1844	JAMES K. POLK (Min.)†	Democratic	1,338,464	170
	HENRY CLAY	Whig	1,300,097	105
	JAMES G. BIRNEY	Liberty	62,300	0
1848	ZACHARY TAYLOR	Whig	1,360,967	163
	LEWIS CASS	Democratic	1,222,342	127
	MARTIN VAN BUREN	Free Soil	291,263	0
1852	FRANKLIN PIERCE	Democratic	1,601,117	254
	WINFIELD SCOTT	Whig	1,385,453	42
	JOHN P. HALE	Free Soil	155,825	0
1856	JAMES BUCHANAN (Min.)*	Democratic	1,832,955	174
	JOHN C. FRÉMONT	Republican	1,339,932	114
	MILLARD FILLMORE	American	871,731	8
1860	ABRAHAM LINCOLN (Min.)*	Republican	1,865,593	180
	STEPHEN A. DOUGLAS	Democratic	1,382,713	12
	JOHN C. BRECKINRIDGE	Democratic	848,356	72
	JOHN BELL	Constitutional Union	592,906	39
1864	ABRAHAM LINCOLN	Union	2,206,938	212
	GEORGE B. MC CLELLAN	Democratic	1,803,787	21
1868	ULYSSES S. GRANT	Republican	3,013,421	214
	HORATIO SEYMOUR	Democratic	2,706,829	80
1872	ULYSSES S. GRANT	Republican	3,596,745	286
	HORACE GREELEY	Democratic Liberal Republican	2,843,446	66
1876	RUTHERFORD B. HAYES (Min.)*	Republican	4,036,572	185
	SAMUEL J. TILDEN	Democratic	4,284,020	184
1880	JAMES A. GARFIELD (Min.)*	Republican	4,453,295	214
	WINFIELD S. HANCOCK	Democratic	4,414,082	155
	JAMES B. WEAVER	Greenback-Labor	308,578	0
1884	GROVER CLEVELAND (Min.)*	Democratic	4,879,507	219
	JAMES G. BLAINE	Republican	4,850,293	182
	BENJAMIN F. BUTLER	Greenback-Labor	175,370	0
	JOHN P. ST. JOHN	Prohibition	150,369	0
1888	BENJAMIN HARRISON (Min.)*	Republican	5,447,129	233
	GROVER CLEVELAND	Democratic	5,537,857	168
	CLINTON B. FISK	Prohibition	249,506	0
	ANSON J. STREETER	Union Labor	146,935	0
1892	GROVER CLEVELAND (Min.)*	Democratic	5,555,426	277
	BENJAMIN HARRISON	Republican	5,182,690	145
	JAMES B. WEAVER	People's	1,029,846	22
	JOHN BIDWELL	Prohibition	264,133	0
1896	WILLIAM MC KINLEY	Republican	7,102,246	271
	WILLIAM J. BRYAN	Democratic	6,492,559	176
1900	WILLIAM MC KINLEY	Republican	7,218,491	292
	WILLIAM J. BRYAN	Democratic; Populist	6,356,734	155
	JOHN C. WOOLLEY	Prohibition	208,914	0
1904	THEODORE ROOSEVELT	Republican	7,628,461	336
	ALTON B. PARKER	Democratic	5,084,223	140
	EUGENE V. DEBS	Socialist	402,283	0
	SILAS C. SWALLOW	Prohibition	258,536	0

* "Min." indicates minority president—one receiving less than 50 percent of all popular votes.

Presidential Elections (continued)

Election	Candidates	Parties	Popular Vote	Electoral Vote
1908	WILLIAM H. TAFT	Republican	7,675,320	321
	WILLIAM J. BRYAN	Democratic	6,412,294	162
	EUGENE V. DEBS	Socialist	420,793	0
	EUGENE W. CHAFIN	Prohibition	253,840	0
1912	WOODROW WILSON (Min.)*	Democratic	6,296,547	435
	THEODORE ROOSEVELT	Progressive	4,118,571	88
	WILLIAM H. TAFT	Republican	3,486,720	8
	EUGENE V. DEBS	Socialist	900,672	0
	EUGENE W. CHAFIN	Prohibition	206,275	0
1916	WOODROW WILSON (Min.)*	Democratic	9,127,695	277
	CHARLES E. HUGHES	Republican	8,533,507	254
	A. L. BENSON	Socialist	585,113	0
	J. F. HANLY	Prohibition	220,506	0
1920	WARREN G. HARDING	Republican	16,143,407	404
	JAMES M. COX	Democratic	9,130,328	127
	EUGENE V. DEBS	Socialist	919,799	0
	P. P. CHRISTENSEN	Farmer-Labor	265,411	0
1924	CALVIN COOLIDGE	Republican	15,718,211	382
	JOHN W. DAVIS	Democratic	8,385,283	136
	ROBERT M. LA FOLLETTE	Progressive	4,831,289	13
1928	HERBERT C. HOOVER	Republican	21,391,993	444
	ALFRED E. SMITH	Democratic	15,016,169	87
1932	FRANKLIN D. ROOSEVELT	Democratic	22,809,638	472
	HERBERT C. HOOVER	Republican	15,758,901	59
	NORMAN THOMAS	Socialist	881,951	0
1936	FRANKLIN D. ROOSEVELT	Democratic	27,752,869	523
	ALFRED M. LANDON	Republican	16,674,665	8
	WILLIAM LEMKE	Union	882,479	0
1940	FRANKLIN D. ROOSEVELT	Democratic	27,307,819	449
	WENDELL L. WILLKIE	Republican	22,321,018	82
1944	FRANKLIN D. ROOSEVELT	Democratic	25,606,585	432
	THOMAS E. DEWEY	Republican	22,014,745	99
1948	HARRY S TRUMAN (Min.)*	Democratic	24,179,345	303
	THOMAS E. DEWEY	Republican	21,991,291	189
	J. STROM THURMOND	States' Rights Democratic	1,176,125	39
	HENRY A. WALLACE	Progressive	1,157,326	0
1952	DWIGHT D. EISENHOWER	Republican	33,936,234	442
	ADLAI E. STEVENSON	Democratic	27,314,992	89
1956	DWIGHT D. EISENHOWER	Republican	35,590,472	457
	ADLAI E. STEVENSON	Democratic	26,022,752	73
1960	JOHN F. KENNEDY (Min.)*†	Democratic	34,226,731	303
	RICHARD M. NIXON	Republican	34,108,157	219
1964	LYNDON B. JOHNSON	Democratic	43,129,566	486
	BARRY M. GOLDWATER	Republican	27,178,188	52
1968	RICHARD M. NIXON (Min.)*	Republican	31,785,480	301
	HUBERT H. HUMPHREY, JR.	Democratic	31,275,166	191
	GEORGE C. WALLACE	American Independent	9,906,473	46
1972	RICHARD M. NIXON	Republican	47,169,911	520
	GEORGE S. MC GOVERN	Democratic	29,170,383	17

* "Min." indicates minority president—one receiving less than 50 percent of all popular votes.
† Six Democratic electors in Alabama, all eight unpledged Democratic electors in Mississippi, and one Republican elector in Oklahoma voted for Senator Harry F. Byrd.

Presidential Elections (continued)

Election	Candidates	Parties	Popular Vote	Electoral Vote
1976	JIMMY CARTER	Democratic	40,828,657	297
	GERALD R. FORD	Republican	39,145,520	240
1980	RONALD W. REAGAN	Republican	43,899,248	489
	JIMMY CARTER	Democratic	35,481,435	49
	JOHN B. ANDERSON	Independent	5,719,437	0
1984	RONALD W. REAGAN	Republican	52,609,797	525
	WALTER MONDALE	Democratic	36,450,613	13
1988	GEORGE BUSH	Republican	47,946,422	426
	MICHAEL DUKAKIS	Democratic	41,016,429	111
1992	WILLIAM CLINTON (Min.)*	Democratic	44,909,889	370
	GEORGE BUSH	Republican	39,104,545	168
	H. ROSS PEROT	Independent	19,742,267	0
1996	WILLIAM CLINTON (Min.)*	Democratic	47,401,898	379
	ROBERT DOLE	Republican	39,198,482	159
	H. ROSS PEROT	Reform	7,874,283	0
2000	GEORGE W. BUSH (Min.)*	Republican	50,456,002	271
	ALBERT GORE, JR.	Democratic	50,999,897	266
	RALPH NADER	Green	2,783,728	0
2004	GEORGE W. BUSH	Republican	60,693,281	286
	JOHN KERRY	Democratic	57,355,978	252
	RALPH NADER	Green	405,623	0
2008	BARACK OBAMA	Democratic	65,980,131	364
	JOHN MC CAIN	Republican	57,779,170	174

* "Min." indicates minority president—one receiving less than 50 percent of all popular votes.

Table A.2 Presidents and Vice Presidents

Term	President	Vice President
1789–1793	George Washington	John Adams
1793–1797	George Washington	John Adams
1797–1801	John Adams	Thomas Jefferson
1801–1805	Thomas Jefferson	Aaron Burr
1805–1809	Thomas Jefferson	George Clinton
1809–1813	James Madison	George Clinton (d. 1812)
1813–1817	James Madison	Elbridge Gerry (d. 1814)
1817–1821	James Monroe	Daniel D. Tompkins
1821–1825	James Monroe	Daniel D. Tompkins
1825–1829	John Quincy Adams	John C. Calhoun
1829–1833	Andrew Jackson	John C. Calhoun (resigned 1832)
1833–1837	Andrew Jackson	Martin Van Buren
1837–1841	Martin Van Buren	Richard M. Johnson
1841–1845	William H. Harrison (d. 1841) John Tyler	John Tyler
1845–1849	James K. Polk	George M. Dallas
1849–1853	Zachary Taylor (d. 1850) Millard Fillmore	Millard Fillmore
1853–1857	Franklin Pierce	William R. D. King (d. 1853)

Presidents and Vice Presidents (continued)

Term	President	Vice President
1857–1861	James Buchanan	John C. Breckinridge
1861–1865	Abraham Lincoln	Hannibal Hamlin
1865–1869	Abraham Lincoln (d. 1865) Andrew Johnson	Andrew Johnson
1869–1873	Ulysses S. Grant	Schuyler Colfax
1873–1877	Ulysses S. Grant	Henry Wilson (d. 1875)
1877–1881	Rutherford B. Hayes	William A. Wheeler
1881–1885	James A. Garfield (d. 1881) Chester A. Arthur	Chester A. Arthur
1885–1889	Grover Cleveland	Thomas A. Hendricks (d. 1885)
1889–1893	Benjamin Harrison	Levi P. Morton
1893–1897	Grover Cleveland	Adlai E. Stevenson
1897–1901	William McKinley	Garret A. Hobart (d. 1899)
1901–1905	William McKinley (d. 1901) Theodore Roosevelt	Theodore Roosevelt
1905–1909	Theodore Roosevelt	Charles W. Fairbanks
1909–1913	William H. Taft	James S. Sherman (d. 1912)
1913–1917	Woodrow Wilson	Thomas R. Marshall
1917–1921	Woodrow Wilson	Thomas R. Marshall
1921–1925	Warren G. Harding (d. 1923) Calvin Coolidge	Calvin Coolidge
1925–1929	Calvin Coolidge	Charles G. Dawes
1929–1933	Herbert Hoover	Charles Curtis
1933–1937	Franklin D. Roosevelt	John N. Garner
1937–1941	Franklin D. Roosevelt	John N. Garner
1941–1945	Franklin D. Roosevelt	Henry A. Wallace
1945–1949	Franklin D. Roosevelt (d. 1945) Harry S Truman	Harry S Truman
1949–1953	Harry S Truman	Alben W. Barkley
1953–1957	Dwight D. Eisenhower	Richard M. Nixon
1957–1961	Dwight D. Eisenhower	Richard M. Nixon
1961–1965	John F. Kennedy (d. 1963) Lyndon B. Johnson	Lyndon B. Johnson
1965–1969	Lyndon B. Johnson	Hubert H. Humphrey, Jr.
1969–1974	Richard M. Nixon	Spiro T. Agnew (resigned 1973); Gerald R. Ford
1974–1977	Gerald R. Ford	Nelson A. Rockefeller
1977–1981	Jimmy Carter	Walter F. Mondale
1981–1985	Ronald Reagan	George Bush
1985–1989	Ronald Reagan	George Bush
1989–1993	George Bush	J. Danforth Quayle III
1993–1997	William Clinton	Albert Gore, Jr.
1997–2001	William Clinton	Albert Gore, Jr.
2001–2005	George W. Bush	Richard Cheney
2005–2009	George W. Bush	Richard Cheney
2009–	Barack Obama	Joseph Biden

Table A.3 Admission of States   (See Table 9.3 on p. 193 for order in which the original thirteen entered the Union.)

Order of Admission	State	Date of Admission	Order of Admission	State	Date of Admission
14	Vermont	Mar. 4, 1791	33	Oregon	Feb. 14, 1859
15	Kentucky	June 1, 1792	34	Kansas	Jan. 29, 1861
16	Tennessee	June 1, 1796	35	W. Virginia	June 20, 1863
17	Ohio	Mar. 1, 1803	36	Nevada	Oct. 31, 1864
18	Louisiana	April 30, 1812	37	Nebraska	Mar. 1, 1867
19	Indiana	Dec. 11, 1816	38	Colorado	Aug. 1, 1876
20	Mississippi	Dec. 10, 1817	39	N. Dakota	Nov. 2, 1889
21	Illinois	Dec. 3, 1818	40	S. Dakota	Nov. 2, 1889
22	Alabama	Dec. 14, 1819	41	Montana	Nov. 8, 1889
23	Maine	Mar. 15, 1820	42	Washington	Nov. 11, 1889
24	Missouri	Aug. 10, 1821	43	Idaho	July 3, 1890
25	Arkansas	June 15, 1836	44	Wyoming	July 10, 1890
26	Michigan	Jan. 26, 1837	45	Utah	Jan. 4, 1896
27	Florida	Mar. 3, 1845	46	Oklahoma	Nov. 16, 1907
28	Texas	Dec. 29, 1845	47	New Mexico	Jan. 6, 1912
29	Iowa	Dec. 28, 1846	48	Arizona	Feb. 14, 1912
30	Wisconsin	May 29, 1848	49	Alaska	Jan. 3, 1959
31	California	Sept. 9, 1850	50	Hawaii	Aug. 21, 1959
32	Minnesota	May 11, 1858			

Table A.4 Estimates of Total Costs and Number of Battle Deaths of Major U.S. Wars[1]

War	Total Costs[2] (millions of dollars)	Original Costs (millions of dollars)	Number of Battle Deaths
Iraq War (2003–)	N/A	$806,000[3]	3,489[4]
Afghan War (2001–)	N/A	$444,000[5]	1,419[6]
Vietnam Conflict	$352,000	140,600	47,355[7]
Korean Conflict	164,000	54,000	33,629
World War II	664,000	288,000	291,557
World War I	112,000	26,000	53,402
Spanish-American War	6,460	400	385
Civil War { Union only	12,952	3,200	140,414
Civil War { Confederacy (est.)	N.A.	1,000	94,000
Mexican War	147	73	1,733
War of 1812	158	93	2,260
American Revolution	190	100	6,824

[1]Deaths from disease and other causes are not shown. In earlier wars especially, owing to poor medical and sanitary practices, nonbattle deaths substantially exceeded combat casualties.
[2]The difference between total costs and original costs is attributable to continuing postwar payments for items such as veterans' benefits, interest on war debts, and so on.
[3]Through 2011
[4]Through October 6, 2011
[5]Through 2011
[6]Through October 6, 2011
[7]1957–1990

(Sources: *Historical Statistics of the United States, Statistical Abstract of the United States,* relevant years, *The World Almanac and Book of Facts, 1986, Congressional Research Service,* Department of Defense, and Congressional Research Service Reports.)

GLOSSARY OF KEY TERMS

9/11 (2001): Common shorthand for the terrorist attacks that occurred on September 11, 2001, in which nineteen militant Islamist men hijacked and crashed four commercial aircraft. Two planes hit the Twin Towers of the World Trade Center in New York City, causing them to collapse. One plane crashed into the Pentagon in Washington, D.C., and the fourth, overtaken by passengers, crashed into a field in rural Pennsylvania. Nearly 3,000 people were killed in the worst case of domestic terrorism in American history. (974)

"10 percent" Reconstruction plan (1863): Introduced by President Lincoln, it proposed that a state be readmitted to the Union once 10 percent of its voters had pledged loyalty to the United States and promised to honor emancipation. (470)

ABC-1 agreement (1941): An agreement between Britain and the United States developed at a conference in Washington, D.C., between January 29–March 27, 1941, that should the United States enter World War II, the two nations and their allies would coordinate their military planning, making a priority of protecting the British Commonwealth. That would mean "getting Germany first" in the Atlantic and the European theater and fighting more defensively on other military fronts. (791)

Abraham Lincoln Brigade: Idealistic American volunteers who served in the Spanish Civil War, defending Spanish republican forces from the fascist General Francisco Franco's nationalist coup. Some 3,000 Americans served alongside volunteers from other countries. (783)

abstract expressionism: An experimental style of mid-twentieth-century modern art exemplified by Jackson Pollock's spontaneous "action paintings," created by flinging paint on canvases stretched across the studio floor. (880)

Abu Ghraib prison: A detention facility near Baghdad, Iraq. Under Saddam Hussein, the prison was the site of infamous torturing and execution of political dissidents. In 2004, during the U.S. occupation of Iraq, the prison became the focal point of a prisoner-abuse and torture scandal after photographs surfaced of American soldiers mistreating, torturing, and degrading Iraqi war prisoners and suspected terrorists. The scandal was one of several dark spots on the public image of the Iraq War and led to increased criticism of Secretary of Defense Donald Rumsfeld. (978)

Acadians: French residents of Nova Scotia, many of whom were uprooted by the British in 1755 and scattered as far south as Louisiana, where their descendants became known as "Cajuns." (104)

Acoma, Battle of (1599): Fought between Spaniards under Don Juan de Oñate and the Pueblo Indians in present-day New Mexico. Spaniards brutally crushed the Pueblo peoples and established the territory as New Mexico in 1609. (21)

Act of Toleration (1649): Passed in Maryland, it guaranteed toleration to all Christians but decreed the death penalty for those, like Jews and atheists, who denied the divinity of Jesus Christ. Ensured that Maryland would continue to attract a high proportion of Catholic migrants throughout the colonial period. (32)

Adamson Act (1916): This law established an eight-hour day for all employees on trains involved in interstate commerce, with extra pay for overtime. It was the first federal law regulating the hours of workers in private companies, and was upheld by the Supreme Court in *Wilson v. New* (1917). (666)

***Adkins v. Children's Hospital* (1923):** A landmark Supreme Court decision reversing the ruling in *Muller v. Oregan*, which had declared women to be deserving of special protection in the workplace. (729)

admiralty courts: Used to try offenders for violating the various Navigation Acts passed by the crown after the French and Indian War. Colonists argued that the courts encroached on their rights as Englishmen since they lacked juries and placed the burden of proof on the accused. (116)

affirmative action: Program designed to redress historic racial and gender imbalances in jobs and education. The term grew from an executive order issued by John F. Kennedy in 1961 mandating that projects paid for with federal funds could not discriminate based on race in their hiring practices. In the late 1960s, President Nixon's Philadelphia Plan changed the meaning of affirmative action to require attention to certain groups, rather than protect individuals against discrimination. (900)

***The Age of Reason* (1794):** Thomas Paine's anticlerical treatise that accused churches of seeking to acquire "power and profit" and to "enslave mankind." (307)

Agricultural Adjustment Administration (AAA) (1933): A New Deal program designed to raise agricultural prices by paying farmers not to farm. It was based on the assumption that higher prices would increase farmers' purchasing power and thereby help alleviate the Great Depression. (763)

Agricultural Marketing Act (1929): This act established the Federal Farm Board, a lending bureau for hard-pressed farmers. The act also aimed to help farmers help themselves through new producers' cooperatives. As the depression worsened in 1930, the Board tried to bolster falling prices by buying up surpluses, but it was unable to cope with the flood of farm produce to market. (740)

Al Qaeda: Arabic for "The Base," an international alliance of anti-Western Islamic fundamentalist terrorist organizations founded in the late 1980s. Founded by veterans of the Afghan struggle against the Soviet Union, the group was headed by Osama Bin Laden and has taken responsibility for numerous terrorist attacks, especially after the late 1990s. Al Qaeda organized the attacks of September 11, 2001, in the United States, from its headquarters in Taliban-controlled Afghanistan. Since the U.S-led invasion of Afghanistan in 2001 and the launch of the "Global War on Terror," the group has been weakened, but still poses significant threats around the world. (975)

Alabama (1862–1864): British-built and manned Confederate warship that raided Union shipping during the Civil War. One of many built by the British for the Confederacy, despite Union protests. (427)

Alamo: Fortress in Texas where four hundred American volunteers were slain by Santa Anna in 1836. "Remember the Alamo" became a battle cry in support of Texan independence. (266)

Albany Congress (1754): Intercolonial congress summoned by the British government to foster greater colonial unity and assure Iroquois support in the escalating war against the French. (106)

Alien Laws (1798): Acts passed by a Federalist Congress raising the residency requirement for citizenship to fourteen years and granting the president the power to deport dangerous foreigners in times of peace. (196)

Allies: Great Britain, Russia, and France, later joined by Italy, Japan, and the United States, formed this alliance against the Central Powers in World War I. (670)

American Anti-Slavery Society (1833–1870): Abolitionist society founded by William Lloyd Garrison, who advocated the immediate abolition of slavery. By 1838, the organization had more than 250,000 members across 1,350 chapters. (351)

American Colonization Society: Reflecting the focus of early abolitionists on transporting freed blacks back to Africa, the organization established Liberia, a West-African settlement intended as a haven for emancipated slaves. (349)

American Federation of Labor: A national federation of trade unions that included only skilled workers, founded in 1886. Led by Samuel Gompers for nearly four decades, the AFL sought to negotiate with employers for a better kind of capitalism that rewarded workers fairly with better wages, hours, and conditions. The AFL's membership was almost entirely white and male until the middle of the twentieth century. (536)

American plan: A business-oriented approach to worker relations popular among firms in the 1920s to defeat unionization. Managers sought to strengthen their communication with workers and to offer benefits like pensions and insurance. They insisted on an "open shop" in contrast to the mandatory union membership through the "closed shop" that many labor activists had demanded in the strike wave after World War I. (701)

American Relief and Recovery Act: Among the earliest initiatives of the Obama Administration to combat the Great Recession. It was based on the economic theories of John Maynard Keynes that called for increased government spending to offset decreased private spending in times of economic downturn. The Act was controversial from the outset, passing with no Republican votes in the House, and only three in the Senate, and helping to foster the "Tea Party" movement to curb government deficits, even while critics on the Left argued that the Act's $787 billion appropriation was not enough to turn the economy around. (985)

"The American Scholar" (1837): Ralph Waldo Emerson's address at Harvard College, in which he declared an intellectual independence from Europe, urging American scholars to develop their own traditions. (328)

American System (1820s): Henry Clay's three-pronged system to promote American industry. Clay advocated a strong banking system, a protective tariff, and a federally funded transportation network. (231)

American Temperance Society: Founded in Boston in 1826 as part of a growing effort of nineteenth-century reformers to limit alcohol consumption. (316)

Americans with Disabilities Act (ADA, 1990): Landmark law signed by President George H. W. Bush that prohibited discrimination against people with physical or mental handicaps. It represented a legislative triumph for champions of equal protections to all. (961)

Amistad (1839): Spanish slave ship dramatically seized off the coast of Cuba by the enslaved Africans aboard. The ship was driven ashore in Long Island and the slaves were put on trial. Former president John Quincy Adams argued their case before the Supreme Court, securing their eventual release. (348)

Ancient Order of Hibernians (mid-nineteenth century): Irish semi-secret society that served as a benevolent organization for downtrodden Irish immigrants in the United States. (281)

Anglo-American Convention (1818): Signed by Britain and the United States, the pact allowed New England fishermen access to Newfoundland fisheries, established the northern border of Louisiana territory and provided for the joint occupation of the Oregon Country for ten years. (239)

Antietam, Battle of (September 1862): Landmark battle in the Civil War that essentially ended in a draw but demonstrated the prowess of the Union army, forestalling foreign intervention and giving Lincoln the "victory" he needed to issue the Emancipation Proclamation. (440)

antifederalists: Opponents of the 1787 Constitution, they cast the document as antidemocratic, objected to the subordination of the states to the central government, and feared encroachment on individuals' liberties in the absence of a bill of rights. (173)

Anti-Imperialist League (1898–1921): A diverse group formed in order to protest American colonial oversight in the Philippines. It included university presidents, industrialists, clergymen, and labor leaders. Strongest in the Northeast, the Anti-imperialist League was the largest lobbying organization on a U.S. foreign-policy issue until the end of the nineteenth century. It declined in strength after the United States signed the Treaty of Paris (which approved the annexation of the Philippines), and especially after hostilities broke out between Filipino nationalists and American forces. (620)

Anti-Masonic party (established c. 1826): First founded in New York, it gained considerable influence in New England and the mid-Atlantic during the 1832 election, campaigning against the politically influential Masonic order, a secret society. Anti-Masons opposed Andrew Jackson, a Mason, and drew much of their support from evangelical Protestants. (258)

antinomianism: Belief that the elect need not obey the law of either God or man; most notably espoused in the colonies by Anne Hutchinson. (45)

Apollo (1961–1975): Program of manned space flights run by America's National Aeronautics and Space Administration (NASA). The project's highest achievement was the landing of Apollo 11 on the moon on July 20, 1969. (891)

***Appeal to the Colored Citizens of the World* (1829):** Incendiary abolitionist track advocating the violent over-throw of slavery. Published by David Walker, a Southern-born free black. (352)

Appeasement (1938): The policy followed by leaders of Britain and France at the 1938 conference in Munich. Their purpose was to avoid war, but they allowed Germany to take the Sudetenland from Czechoslovakia. (784)

Appomattox Courthouse: Site where Robert E. Lee surrendered to Ulysses S. Grant in April 1865 after almost a year of brutal fighting throughout Virginia in the "Wilderness Campaign." (455)

Armed Neutrality (1780): Loose alliance of nonbelligerent naval powers, organized by Russia's Catherine the Great, to protect neutral trading rights during the war for American independence. (146)

Arminianism: Belief that salvation is offered to all humans but is conditional on acceptance of God's grace. Different from Calvinism, which emphasizes predestination and unconditional election. (87)

Army-McCarthy Hearings (1954): Congressional hearings called by Senator Joseph McCarthy to accuse members of the army of communist ties. In this widely televised spectacle, McCarthy finally went too far for public approval. The hearings exposed the Senator's extremism and led to his eventual disgrace. (867)

Aroostook War (began 1839): Series of clashes between American and Canadian lumberjacks in the disputed territory of northern Maine, resolved when a permanent boundary was agreed upon in 1842. (363)

Articles of Confederation (1781): First American constitution that established the United States as a loose confederation of states under a weak national Congress, which was not granted the power to regulate commerce or collect taxes. The Articles were replaced by a more efficient Constitution in 1789. (163)

The Association (1774): Non-importation agreement crafted during the First Continental Congress calling for the complete boycott of British goods. (123)

assumption: Transfer of debt from one party to another. In order to strengthen the union, the federal government assumed states' Revolutionary War debts in 1790, thereby tying the interests of wealthy lenders with those of the national government. (183)

Atlantic Charter (1941): Meeting on a warship off the coast of Newfoundland in August 1941, Franklin Roosevelt and British Prime Minister Winston Churchill signed this covenant outlining the future path toward disarmament, peace, and a permanent system of general security. Its spirit would animate the founding of the United Nations and raise awareness of the human rights of individuals after World War II. (793)

Australian ballot: A system that allows voters privacy in marking their ballot choices. Developed in Australia in the 1850s, it was introduced to the United States during the progressive era to help counteract boss rule. (641)

***Awful Disclosures* (1836):** Maria Monk's sensational expose of alleged horrors in Catholic convents. Its popularity reflected nativist fears of Catholic influence. (284)

Aztecs: Native American empire that controlled present-day Mexico until 1521, when they were conquered by Spanish Hernán Cortés. The Aztecs maintained control over their vast empire through a system of trade and tribute, and came to be known for their advances in mathematics and writing, and their use of human sacrifices in religious ceremonies. (6)

baby boom (1946–1964): Demographic explosion from births to returning soldiers and others who had put off starting families during the war. This large generation of new Americans forced the expansion of many institutions such as schools and universities. (838)

Bacon's Rebellion (1676): Uprising of Virginia back-country farmers and indentured servants led by planter Nathaniel Bacon; initially a response to Governor William Berkeley's refusal to protect backcountry settlers from Indian attacks, the rebellion eventually grew into a broader conflict between impoverished settlers and the planter elite. (62)

Bank of the United States (1791): Chartered by Congress as part of Alexander Hamilton's financial program, the bank printed paper money and served as a depository for Treasury funds. It drew opposition from Jeffersonian Republicans, who argued that the bank was unconstitutional. (185)

Bank War (1832): Battle between President Andrew Jackson and Congressional supporters of the Bank of the United States over the bank's renewal in 1832. Jackson vetoed the Bank Bill, arguing that the bank favored moneyed interests at the expense of western farmers. (259)

Barbados slave code (1661): First formal statute governing the treatment of slaves, which provided for harsh punishments against offending slaves but lacked penalties for the mistreatment of slaves by masters. Similar statutes were adopted by Southern plantation societies on the North American mainland in the 17th and 18th centuries. (33)

Bay of Pigs invasion (1961): CIA plot in 1961 to overthrow Fidel Castro by training Cuban exiles to invade and supporting them with American air power. The mission failed and became a public relations disaster early in John F. Kennedy's presidency. (893)

Beat Generation: A small coterie of mid-twentieth-century bohemian writers and personalities, including Jack Kerouac, Allen Ginsberg, and William S. Burroughs, who bemoaned bourgeois conformity and advocated free-form experimentation in life and literature. (884)

Berlin airlift (1948): Year-long mission of flying food and supplies to blockaded West Berliners, whom the Soviet Union cut off from access to the West in the first major crisis of the Cold War. (846)

Berlin Wall: Fortified and guarded barrier between East and West Berlin erected on orders from Soviet Premier Nikita Khrushchev in 1961 to stop the flow of people to the West. Until its destruction in 1989, the wall was a vivid symbol of the divide between the communist and capitalist worlds. (891)

Bible Belt: The region of the American South, extending roughly from North Carolina west to Oklahoma and Texas, where Protestant Fundamentalism and belief in literal interpretation of the Bible were traditionally strongest. (702)

Big Sister policy (1880s): A foreign policy of Secretary of State James G. Blaine aimed at rallying Latin American nations behind American leadership and opening Latin American markets to Yankee traders. The policy bore fruit in 1889, when Blaine presided over the First International Conference of American States. (609)

Bill of Rights (1791): Popular term for the first ten amendments to the U.S. Constitution. The amendments secure key rights for individuals and reserve to the states all powers not explicitly delegated or prohibited by the Constitution. (182)

Black Belt: Region of the Deep South with the highest concentration of slaves. The "Black Belt" emerged in the nineteenth century as cotton production became more profitable and slavery expanded south and west. (347)

Black Codes (1865–1866): Laws passed throughout the South to restrict the rights of emancipated blacks, particularly with respect to negotiating labor contracts. Increased Northerners' criticisms of President Andrew Johnson's lenient Reconstruction policies. (471)

Black Hawk War (1832): Series of clashes in Illinois and Wisconsin between American forces and Indian chief Black Hawk of the Sauk and Fox tribes, who unsuccessfully tried to reclaim territory lost under the 1830 Indian Removal Act. (258)

Black Legend: False notion that Spanish conquerors did little but butcher the Indians and steal their gold in the name of Christ. (22)

Black Monday: October 19, 1987. Date of the largest single-day decline in the Dow Jones Industrial Average until September 2001. The downturn indicated instability in the booming business culture of the 1980s but did not lead to a serious economic recession. (955)

Black Panther party: Organization of armed black militants formed in Oakland, California, in 1966 to protect black rights. The Panthers represented a growing dissatisfaction with the non-violent wing of the civil rights movement, and signaled a new direction to that movement after the legislative victories of 1964 and 1965. (905)

Black Power: Doctrine of militancy and separatism that rose in prominence after 1965. Black Power activists rejected Martin Luther King's pacifism and desire for integration. Rather, they promoted pride in African heritage and an often militant position in defense of their rights. (905)

Black Tuesday (1929): The dark, panicky day of October 29, 1929 when over 16,410,000 shares of stock were sold on Wall Street. It was a trigger that helped bring on the Great Depression. (740)

Bleeding Kansas (1856–1861): Civil war in Kansas over the issue of slavery in the territory, fought intermittently until 1861, when it merged with the wider national Civil War. (400)

blue laws: Also known as sumptuary laws, they are designed to restrict personal behavior in accord with a strict code of morality. Blue laws were passed across the colonies, particularly in Puritan New England and Quaker Pennsylvania. (55)

boll weevils: Term for conservative southern Democrats who voted increasingly for Republican issues during the Carter and Reagan administrations. (945)

Bolshevik Revolution (1917): The second stage of the Russian Revolution in November 1917 when Vladimir Lenin and his Bolshevik party seized power and established a communist state. The first stage had occurred the previous February when more moderate revolutionaries overthrew the Russian Czar. (700)

Bonus Army (1932): Officially known as the Bonus Expeditionary Force (BEF), this rag-tag group of 20,000 veterans marched on Washington to demand immediate payment of bonuses earned during World War I. General Douglas MacArthur dispersed the veterans with tear gas and bayonets. (746)

Border States: Five slave states—Missouri, Kentucky, Maryland, Delaware, and West Virginia—that did not secede during the Civil War. To keep the states in the Union, Abraham Lincoln insisted that the war was not about abolishing slavery but rather protecting the Union. (420)

Boston Massacre (1770): Clash between unruly Bostonian protestors and locally stationed British redcoats, who fired on the jeering crowd, killing or wounding eleven citizens. (118)

Boston Tea Party (1773): Rowdy protest against the British East India Company's newly acquired monopoly on the tea trade. Colonists, disguised as Indians, dumped 342 chests of tea into Boston harbor, prompting harsh sanctions from the British Parliament. (121)

Boxer Rebellion (1900): An uprising in China directed against foreign influence. It was suppressed by an international force of some eighteen thousand soldiers, including several thousand Americans. The Boxer Rebellion paved the way for the revolution of 1911, which led to the establishment of the Republic of China in 1912. (623)

***Bracero* program (1942):** Program established by agreement with the Mexican government to recruit temporary Mexican agricultural workers to the United States to make up for wartime labor shortages in the Far West. The program persisted until 1964, by when it had sponsored 4.5 million border crossings. (803)

Brain Trust: Specialists in law, economics, and welfare, many of them young university professors, who advised President Franklin D. Roosevelt and helped develop the policies of the New Deal. (752)

breakers: Slave drivers who employed the lash to brutally "break" the souls of strong-willed slaves. (346)

Bretton Woods Conference (1944): Meeting of Western allies to establish a postwar international economic order to avoid crises like the one that spawned World War II. Led to the creation of the International Monetary Fund (IMF) and the World Bank, designed to regulate currency levels and provide aid to underdeveloped countries. (841)

Brook Farm (1841–1846): Transcendentalist commune founded by a group of intellectuals, who emphasized living plainly while pursuing the life of the mind. The community fell into debt and dissolved when their communal home burned to the ground in 1846. (320)

***Brown* v. *Board of Education of Topeka, Kansas* (1954):** Landmark Supreme Court decision that overturned *Plessy* v. *Ferguson* (1896) and abolished racial segregation in public schools. The Court reasoned that "separate" was inherently "unequal," rejecting the foundation of the Jim Crow system of racial segregation in the South. This decision was the first major step toward the legal end of racial discrimination and a major accomplishment for the Civil Rights Movement. (868)

Buena Vista, Battle of (1847): Key American victory against Mexican forces in the Mexican-American War. Elevated General Zachary Taylor to national prominence and helped secure his success in the 1848 presidential election. (371)

buffer: In politics, a territory between two antagonistic powers, intended to minimize the possibility of conflict between them. In British North America, Georgia was established as a buffer colony between British and Spanish territory. (38)

Bull Run (Manassas Junction), Battle of (July 1861): First major battle of the Civil War and a victory for the South, it dispelled Northern illusions of swift victory. (435)

Bunker Hill, Battle of (June 1775): Fought on the outskirts of Boston, on Breed's Hill, the battle ended in the colonial militia's retreat, though at a heavy cost to the British. (133)

Burned-Over District: Popular name for Western New York, a region particularly swept up in the religious fervor of the Second Great Awakening. (309)

Cahokia (c. 1100 A.D.): Mississippian settlement near present-day East St. Louis, home to as many as 25,000 Native Americans. (8)

California Bear Flag Republic (1846): Short-lived California republic, established by local American settlers who revolted against Mexico. Once news of the war with Mexico reached the Americans, they abandoned the Republic in favor of joining the United States. (371)

California gold rush (beginning in 1849): Inflow of thousands of miners to Northern California after news reports of the discovery of gold at Sutter's Mill in January of 1848 had spread around the world by the end of that year. The onslaught of migrants prompted Californians to organize a government and apply for statehood in 1849. (380)

Calvinism: Dominant theological credo of the New England Puritans based on the teachings of John Calvin. Calvinists believed in predestination—that only "the elect" were destined for salvation. (41)

Camp followers: Women and children who followed the Continental Army during the American Revolution, providing vital services such as cooking and sewing in return for rations. (128)

Canadian Shield: First part of the North American landmass to emerge above sea level. (4)

capitalism: Economic system characterized by private property, generally free trade, and open and accessible markets. European colonization of the Americas, and in particular, the discovery of vast bullion deposits, helped bring about Europe's transition to capitalism. (16)

caravel: Small regular vessel with a high deck and three triangular sails. Caravels could sail more closely into the wind, allowing European sailors to explore the Western shores of Africa, previously made inaccessible due to prevailing winds on the homeward journey. (11)

***Caroline* (1837):** Diplomatic row between the United States and Britain. Developed after British troops set fire to an American steamer carrying supplies across the Niagara River to Canadian insurgents, during Canada's short-lived insurrection. (362)

carpetbaggers: Pejorative used by Southern whites to describe Northern businessmen and politicians who came to the South after the Civil War to work on Reconstruction projects or invest in Southern infrastructure. (478)

Central Powers: Germany and Austria-Hungary, later joined by Turkey and Bulgaria, made up this alliance against the Allies in World War I. (670)

charter: Legal document granted by a government to some group or agency to implement a stated purpose, and spelling out the attending rights and obligations. British colonial charters guaranteed inhabitants all the rights of Englishmen, which helped solidify colonists' ties to Britain during the early years of settlement. (27)

Château Thierry, Battle of (1918): The first significant engagement of American troops in World War I—and, indeed, in any European war. To weary French soldiers, the American doughboys were an image of fresh and gleaming youth. (690)

Checkers Speech (1952): Nationally televised address by vice-presidential candidate Richard Nixon. Using the new mass medium of television shortly before the 1952 election, the vice presidential candidate saved his place on the ticket by defending himself against accusations of corruption. (864)

Chesapeake **affair (1807):** Conflict between Britain and the United States that precipitated the 1807 embargo. The conflict developed when a British ship, in search of deserters, fired on the American *Chesapeake* off the coast of Virginia. (216)

Chinese Exclusion Act (1882): Federal legislation that prohibited most further Chinese immigration to the United States. This was the first major legal restriction on immigration in U.S. history. (498)

City Beautiful movement: A turn-of-the-century movement among progressive architects and city planners, who aimed to promote order, harmony, and virtue while beautifying the nation's new urban spaces with grand boulevards, welcoming parks, and monumental public buildings. (569)

civic virtue: Willingness on the part of citizens to sacrifice personal self-interest for the public good. Deemed a necessary component of a successful republic. (159)

civil law: Body of written law enacted through legislative statutes or constitutional provisions. In countries where civil law prevails, judges must apply the statutes precisely as written. (171)

Civil Rights Act of 1875: The last piece of federal civil rights legislation until the 1950s, the law promised blacks equal access to public accommodations and banned racism in jury selection, but the Act provided no means of enforcement and was therefore ineffective. In 1883, the Supreme Court declared most of the Act unconstitutional. (495)

Civil Rights Act of 1964: Federal law that banned racial discrimination in public facilities and strengthened the federal government's power to fight segregation in schools. Title VII of the act prohibited employers from discriminating based on race in their hiring practices, and empowered the Equal Employment Opportunity Commission (EEOC) to regulate fair employment. (898)

Civil Rights Bill (1866): Passed over Andrew Johnson's veto, the bill aimed to counteract the Black Codes by conferring citizenship on African Americans and making it a crime to deprive blacks of their rights to sue, testify in court, or hold property. (473)

Civilian Conservation Corps (CCC) (1933): A government program created by Congress to hire young unemployed men to improve the rural, out-of-doors environment with such work as planting trees, fighting fires, draining swamps, and maintaining National Parks. The CCC proved to be an important foundation for the post–World War II environmental movement. (757)

Clayton Anti-Trust Act (1914): Law extending the antitrust protections of the Sherman Anti-Trust Act and exempting labor unions and agricultural organizations from antimonopoly constraints. The act conferred long-overdue benefits on labor. (666)

Clayton-Bulwer Treaty (1850): Signed by Great Britain and the United States, it provided that the two nations would jointly protect the neutrality of Central America and that neither power would seek to fortify or exclusively control any future isthmian waterway. Later revoked by the Hay-Pauncefote Treaty of 1901, which gave the United States control of the Panama Canal. (389)

clipper ships (1840s–1850s): Small, swift vessels that gave American shippers an advantage in the carrying trade. Clipper ships were made largely obsolete by the advent of sturdier, roomier iron steamers on the eve of the Civil War. (301)

closed shop: A union-organizing term that refers to the practice of allowing only unionized employees to work for a particular company. The AFL became known for negotiating closed-shop agreements with employers, in which the employer would agree not to hire non-union members. (536)

Code talkers: Native American men who served in the military by transmitting radio messages in their native languages, which were undecipherable by German and Japanese spies. (806)

Cohens v. Virginia **(1821):** Case that reinforced federal supremacy by establishing the right of the Supreme Court to review decisions of state supreme courts in questions involving the powers of the federal government. (238)

Cold War (1946–1991): The 45-year-long diplomatic tension between the United States and the Soviet Union that divided much of the world into polarized camps, capitalist against communist. Most of the international conflicts during that period, particularly in the developing world, can be traced to the competition between the United States and the Soviet Union. (841)

Columbian Exchange: The transfer of goods, crops, and diseases between New and Old World societies after 1492. (14)

Committee on Public Information (1917): A government office during World War I known popularly as the Creel Committee for its chairman George Creel, it was dedicated to winning everyday Americans' support for the war effort. It regularly distributed prowar propaganda and sent out an army of "four-minute men" to rally crowds and deliver "patriotic pep." (680)

committees of correspondence (1772 and after): Local committees established across Massachusetts, and later in each of the thirteen colonies, to maintain colonial opposition to British policies through the exchange of letters and pamphlets. (120)

common law: Laws that originate from court rulings and customs, as opposed to legislative statutes. The United States Constitution grew out of the Anglo-American common law tradition and thus provided only a general organizational framework for the new federal government. (171)

Common Sense **(1776):** Thomas Paine's pamphlet urging the colonies to declare independence and establish a republican government. The widely read pamphlet helped convince colonists to support the Revolution. (135)

Commonwealth of Independent States (CIS): Organization formed from the former republics of the Soviet Union in 1991. (957)

Commonwealth v. Hunt (1842): Massachusetts Supreme Court decision that strengthened the labor movement by upholding the legality of unions. (292)

Compromise of 1850: Admitted California as a free state, opened New Mexico and Utah to popular sovereignty, ended the slave trade (but not slavery itself) in Washington, D.C., and introduced a more stringent fugitive slave law. Widely opposed in both the North and South, it did little to settle the escalating dispute over slavery. (384)

Compromise of 1877: The agreement that finally resolved the 1876 election and officially ended Reconstruction. In exchange for the Republican candidate, Rutherford B. Hayes, winning the presidency, Hayes agreed to withdraw the last of the federal troops from the former Confederate states. This deal effectively completed the southern return to white-only, Democratic-dominated electoral politics. (494)

compromise Tariff of 1833: Passed as a measure to resolve the nullification crisis, it provided that tariffs be lowered gradually, over a period of ten years, to 1816 levels. (256)

Confederate States of America (1861–1865): Government established after seven Southern states seceded from the Union. Later joined by four more states from the Upper South. (412)

Congregational Church: Self-governing Puritan congregations without the hierarchical establishment of the Anglican Church. (73)

Congress of Industrial Organizations (CIO): A New Deal-era labor organization that broke away from the American Federation of Labor (AFL) in order to organize unskilled industrial workers regardless of their particular economic sector or craft. The CIO gave a great boost to labor organizing in the midst of the Great Depression and during World War II. In 1955, the CIO merged with the AFL. (769)

Congress of Racial Equality (CORE) (1942): Nonviolent civil rights organization founded in 1942 and committed to the "Double V"—victory over fascism abroad and racism at home. After World War II, CORE would become a major force in the civil rights movement. (806)

Congress of Vienna (1814–1815): Convention of major European powers to redraw the boundaries of continental Europe after the defeat of Napoleonic France. (227)

Congressional Committee on the Conduct of the War (1861–1865): Established by Congress during the Civil War to oversee military affairs. Largely under the control of Radical Republicans, the committee agitated for a more vigorous war effort and actively pressed Lincoln on the issue of emancipation. (450)

conquistadores: Sixteenth-century Spaniards who fanned out across the Americas, from Colorado to Argentina, eventually conquering the Aztec and Incan empires. (16)

Conscience Whigs (1840s and 1850s): Northern Whigs who opposed slavery on moral grounds. Conscience Whigs sought to prevent the annexation of Texas as a slave state, fearing that the new slave territory would only serve to buttress the Southern "slave power." (372)

Constitutional Union party (1860): Formed by moderate Whigs and Know-Nothings in an effort to elect a compromise candidate and avert a sectional crisis. (409)

containment doctrine: America's strategy against the Soviet Union based on ideas of George Kennan. The doctrine declared that the Soviet Union and communism were inherently expansionist and had to be stopped from spreading through both military and political pressure. Containment guided American foreign policy throughout most of the Cold War. (846)

Contract with America (1994): Multi-point program offered by Republican candidates and sitting politicians in the 1994 midterm election. The platform proposed smaller government, Congressional ethics reform, term limits, great emphasis on personal responsibility, and a general repudiation of the Democratic party. This articulation of dissent was a significant blow to the Clinton Administration and led to the Republican party's takeover of both houses of Congress for the first time in half a century. (968)

contras: Anti-Sandinista fighters in the Nicaraguan civil war. The Contras were secretly supplied with American military aid, paid for with money the United States clandestinely made selling arms to Iran. (947)

Convention of 1800: Agreement to formally dissolve the United States' treaty with France, originally signed during the Revolutionary War. The difficulties posed by America's peacetime alliance with France contributed to Americans' longstanding opposition to entangling alliances with foreign powers. (196)

conversion: Intense religious experience that confirmed an individual's place among the "elect," or the "visible saints." Calvinists who experienced conversion were then expected to lead sanctified lives to demonstrate their salvation. (41)

Copperheads: Northern Democrats who obstructed the war effort by attacking Abraham Lincoln, the draft and, after 1863, emancipation. (450)

Corps of Discovery (1804–1806): Team of adventurers, led by Meriwether Lewis and William Clark, sent by Thomas Jefferson to explore Louisiana Territory and find a water route to the Pacific. Louis and Clark brought back detailed accounts of the West's flora, fauna, and native populations, and their voyage demonstrated the viability of overland travel to the West. (213)

corrupt bargain: Alleged deal between presidential candidates John Quincy Adams and Henry Clay to throw the election, to be decided by the House of Representatives, in Adams' favor. Though never proven, the accusation became the rallying cry for supporters of Andrew Jackson, who had actually garnered a plurality of the popular vote in 1824. (246)

cotton gin (1793): Eli Whitney's invention that sped up the process of harvesting cotton. The gin made cotton cultivation more profitable, revitalizing the Southern economy and increasing the importance of slavery in the South. (287)

coureurs de bois: Translated as "runners of the woods," they were French fur-trappers, also known as **"voyageurs"** (travelers), who established trading posts throughout North America. The fur trade wreaked havoc on the health and folkways of their Native American trading partners. (99)

Court-packing plan (1937): Franklin Roosevelt's politically motivated and ill-fated scheme to add a new justice to the Supreme Court for every member over seventy who would not retire. His objective was to overcome the Court's objections to New Deal reforms. (771)

Crédit Mobilier scandal (1872): A construction company was formed by owners of the Union Pacific Railroad for the purpose of receiving government contracts to build the railroad at highly inflated prices—and profits. In 1872 a scandal erupted when journalists discovered that the Crédit Mobilier Company had bribed congressmen and even the Vice President in order to allow the ruse to continue. (490)

Creole (1841): American ship captured by a group of rebelling Virginia slaves. The slaves successfully sought asylum in the Bahamas, raising fears among Southern planters that the British West Indies would become a safe haven for runaway slaves. (362)

criminal syndicalism laws (1919–1920): Passed by many states during the Red Scare of 1919–1920, these nefarious laws outlawed the mere advocacy of violence to secure social change. Stump speakers for the International Workers of the World, or IWW, were special targets. (701)

Crittenden amendments (1860): Proposed in an attempt to appease the South, the failed Constitutional amendments would have given federal protection for slavery in all territories south of 36°30' where slavery was supported by popular sovereignty. (413)

Cuban missile crisis (1962): Standoff between John F. Kennedy and Soviet Premier Nikita Khrushchev in October 1962 over Soviet plans to install nuclear weapons in Cuba. Although the crisis was ultimately settled in America's favor and represented a foreign policy triumph for Kennedy, it brought the world's superpowers perilously close to the brink of nuclear confrontation. (895)

cult of domesticity: Pervasive nineteenth-century cultural creed that venerated the domestic role of women. It gave married women greater authority to shape home life but limited opportunities outside the domestic sphere. (294)

Dartmouth College v. Woodward (1819): Supreme Court case that sustained Dartmouth University's original charter against changes proposed by the New Hampshire state legislature, thereby protecting corporations from domination by state governments. (238)

Daughters of Liberty: Patriotic groups that played a central role in agitating against the Stamp Act and enforcing non-importation agreements. (See also **Sons of Liberty**) (117)

Dawes Plan (1924): An arrangement negotiated in 1924 to reschedule German reparations payments. It stabilized the German currency and opened the way for further American private loans to Germany. (737)

Dawes Severalty Act (1887): An act that broke up Indian reservations and distributed land to individual households.

Leftover land was sold for money to fund U.S. government efforts to "civilize" Native Americans. Of 130 million acres held in Native American reservations before the Act, 90 million were sold to non-Native buyers. (581)

D-Day (1944): A massive military operation led by American forces in Normandy beginning on June 6, 1944. The pivotal battle led to the liberation of France and brought on the final phases of World War II in Europe. (813)

Declaration of Independence (July 4, 1776): Formal pronouncement of independence drafted by Thomas Jefferson and approved by Congress. The declaration allowed Americans to appeal for foreign aid and served as an inspiration for later revolutionary movements worldwide. (137)

Declaration of the Rights of Man (1789): Declaration of rights adopted during the French Revolution. Modeled after the American Declaration of Independence. (139)

Declaratory Act (1766): Passed alongside the repeal of the Stamp Act, it reaffirmed Parliament's unqualified sovereignty over the North American colonies. (118)

deism: Eighteenth-century religious doctrine that emphasized reasoned moral behavior and the scientific pursuit of knowledge. Most deists rejected biblical inerrancy and the divinity of Christ, but they did believe that a Supreme Being created the universe. (307)

deleveraging: The inverse of "leveraging," whereby businesses increase their financial power by borrowing money (debt) in addition to their own assets (equity). In times of uncertainty or credit tightening, the same businesses seek to improve their debt-to-equity ratios by shedding debt through the sale of assets purchased with borrowed money. (984)

Democratic Leadership Council: Non-profit organization of centrist Democrats founded in the mid-1980s. The group attempted to push the Democratic party toward pro-growth, strong defense, and anticrime policies. Among its most influential early members was Bill Clinton, whom it held up as an example of "third way" politics. (965)

Department of Homeland Security: Cabinet-level agency created in 2003 to unify and coordinate public safety and anti-terrorism operations within the federal government. (975)

détente: From the French for "reduced tension," the period of Cold War thawing when the United States and the Soviet Union negotiated reduced armament treaties under Presidents Nixon, Ford, and Carter. As a policy prescription, détente marked a departure from the policies of proportional response, mutually assured destruction, and containment that had defined the earlier years of the Cold War. (920)

Dien Bien Phu, Battle of (1954): Military engagement in French colonial Vietnam in which French forces were defeated by Viet Minh nationalists loyal to Ho Chi Minh. With this loss, the French ended their colonial involvement in Indochina, paving the way for America's entry. (875)

disestablished: To separate an official state church from its connection with the government. Following the

Revolution, all states disestablished the Anglican Church, though some New England states maintained established Congregational Churches well into the nineteenth century. (158)

dollar diplomacy: Name applied by President Taft's critics to the policy of supporting U.S. investments and political interests abroad. First applied to the financing of railways in China after 1909, the policy then spread to Haiti, Honduras, and Nicaragua. President Woodrow Wilson disavowed the practice, but his administration undertook comparable acts of intervention in support of U.S. business interests, especially in Latin America. (657)

Dominion of Canada (established 1867): Unified Canadian government created by Britain to bolster Canadians against potential attacks or overtures from the United States. (428)

Dominion of New England (1686–1689): Administrative union created by royal authority, incorporating all of New England, New York, and East and West Jersey. Placed under the rule of Sir Edmund Andros who curbed popular assemblies, taxed residents without their consent, and strictly enforced Navigation Laws. Its collapse after the Glorious Revolution in England demonstrated colonial opposition to strict royal control. (49)

Don't Ask, Don't Tell: From 1993 to 2010, the policy affecting homosexuals in the military. It emerged as a compromise between the standing prohibition against homosexuals in the armed forces and President Clinton's push to allow all citizens to serve regardless of sexual orientation. Military authorities were forbidden to ask about a service member's orientation, and gay service personnel could be discharged if they publicly revealed their homosexuality. At President Obama's urging, Congress repealed DADT in 2010, permitting gays to serve openly in uniform. (966)

***Dred Scott* v. *Sandford* (1857):** Supreme Court decision that extended federal protection to slavery by ruling that Congress did not have the power to prohibit slavery in any territory. Also declared that slaves, as property, were not citizens of the United States. (403)

Dust Bowl: Grim nickname for the Great Plains region devastated by drought and dust storms during the 1930s. The disaster led to the migration into California of thousands of displaced "Okies" and "Arkies." (764)

Earth Day (1970): International day of celebration and awareness of global environmental issues launched by conservationists on April 22, 1970. (922)

ecological imperialism: Historians' term for the spoliation of western natural resources through excessive hunting, logging, mining, and grazing. (277)

Edict of Nantes (1598): Decree issued by the French crown granting limited toleration to French Protestants. Ended religious wars in France and inaugurated a period of French preeminence in Europe and across the Atlantic. Its repeal in 1685 prompted a fresh migration of Protestant Huguenots to North America. (98)

Eighteenth Amendment (1919): Ratified in 1919, this Constitutional amendment prohibited the manufacture, sale, and transportation of alcoholic beverages. It ushered in the era known as Prohibition. (704)

Elkins Act (1903): Law passed by Congress to impose penalties on railroads that offered rebates and customers who accepted them. The law strengthened the Interstate Commerce Act of 1887. The Hepburn Act of 1906 added free passes to the list of railroad no-no's. (649)

Emancipation Proclamation (1863): Declared all slaves in rebelling states to be free but did not affect slavery in nonrebelling Border States. The Proclamation closed the door on possible compromise with the South and encouraged thousands of Southern slaves to flee to Union lines. (440)

Embargo Act (1807): Enacted in response to British and French mistreatment of American merchants, the Act banned the export of all goods from the United States to any foreign port. The embargo placed great strains on the American economy while only marginally affecting its European targets, and was therefore repealed in 1809. (217)

Employment Act of 1946: Legislation declaring that the government's economic policy should aim to promote maximum employment, production, and purchasing power, as well as to keep inflation low. A general commitment that was much shorter on specific targets and rules than its liberal creators had wished. The Act created the Council of Economic Advisers to provide the president with data and recommendations to make economic policy. (831)

***encomienda*:** Spanish government's policy to "commend," or give, Indians to certain colonists in return for the promise to Christianize them. Part of a broader Spanish effort to subdue Indian tribes in the West Indies and on the North American mainland. (17)

English Civil War (1642–1651): Armed conflict between royalists and parliamentarians, resulting in the victory of pro-Parliament forces and the execution of Charles I. (48)

Environmental Protection Agency (EPA): A governmental organization signed into law by Richard Nixon in 1970 designed to regulate pollution, emissions, and other factors that negatively influence the natural environment. The creation of the EPA marked a newfound commitment by the federal government to actively combat environmental risks and was a significant triumph for the environmentalist movement. (922)

Equal Rights Amendment (ERA): Equal Rights Amendment, which declared full constitutional equality for women. Although it passed both houses of Congress in 1972, a concerted grassroots campaign by anti-feminists led by Phyllis Schlafly persuaded enough state legislatures to vote against ratification. The amendment failed to become part of the Constitution. (931)

Era of Good Feelings (1816–1824): Popular name for the period of one-party, Republican, rule during James Monroe's presidency. The term obscures bitter conflicts over internal improvements, slavery, and the national bank. (232)

Erie Canal (completed 1825): New York state canal that linked Lake Erie to the Hudson River. It dramatically lowered shipping costs, fueling an economic boom in upstate

New York and increasing the profitability of farming in the Old Northwest. (298)

Espionage Act (1917): A law prohibiting interference with the draft and other acts of national "disloyalty." Together with the Sedition Act of 1918, which added penalties for abusing the government in writing, it created a climate that was unfriendly to civil liberties. (681)

European Economic Community (EEC): Free trade zone in Western Europe created by Treaty of Rome in 1957. Often referred to as the "Common Market," this collection of countries originally included France, West Germany, Italy, Belgium, the Netherlands, and Luxembourg. The body eventually expanded to become the European Union, which by 2005 included 27 member states. (891)

Ex parte Milligan (1866): Civil War Era case in which the Supreme Court ruled that military tribunals could not be used to try civilians if civil courts were open. (475)

excise tax: Tax on goods produced domestically. Excise taxes, particularly the 1791 tax on whiskey, were a highly controversial component of Alexander Hamilton's financial program. (184)

Executive Order No. 9066 (1942): Order of President Franklin D. Roosevelt authorizing the War Department to remove Japanese "enemy aliens" to isolated internment camps. Immigrants and citizens alike were sent away from their homes, neighbors, schools, and businesses. The Japanese internment policy was held to be constitutional by the United States Supreme Court in *Korematsu* v. *U.S.* (1944). (792)

factory girls: Young women employed in the growing factories of the early nineteenth century, they labored long hours in difficult conditions, living in socially new conditions away from farms and families. (293)

Fair Deal: President Truman's extensive social program introduced in his 1949 message to Congress. Republicans and Southern Democrats kept much of his vision from being enacted, except for raising the minimum wage, providing for more public housing, and extending old-age insurance to many more beneficiaries under the Social Security Act. (854)

Fair Employment Practices Commission (FEPC) (1941): Threatened with a massive "Negro March on Washington" to demand equal job opportunities in war jobs and in the military, Franklin D. Roosevelt's administration issued an executive order forbidding racial discrimination in all defense plants operating under contract with the federal government. The FEPC was intended to monitor compliance with the Executive Order. (805)

Fair Labor Standards Act (1938): Important New Deal labor legislation that regulated minimum wages and maximum hours for workers involved in interstate commerce. The law also outlawed labor by children under sixteen. The exclusion of agricultural, service, and domestic workers meant that many blacks, Mexican Americans, and women—who were concentrated in these sectors—did not benefit from the act's protection. (768)

Fallen Timbers, Battle of (1794): Decisive battle between the Miami confederacy and the U.S. Army. British forces refused to shelter the routed Indians, forcing the latter to attain a peace settlement with the United States. (191)

Farewell Address (1796): George Washington's address at the end of his presidency, warning against "permanent alliances" with other nations. Washington did not oppose all alliances, but believed that the young, fledgling nation should forge alliances only on a temporary basis, in extraordinary circumstances. (193)

Federal Highway Act of 1956: Federal legislation signed by Dwight D. Eisenhower to construct thousands of miles of modern highways in the name of national defense. Officially called the National Interstate and Defense Highways Act, this bill dramatically increased the move to the suburbs, as white middle-class people could more easily commute to urban jobs. (873)

Federal Reserve Act (1913): An act establishing twelve regional Federal Reserve Banks and a Federal Reserve Board, appointed by the president, to regulate banking and create stability on a national scale in the volatile banking sector. The law carried the nation through the financial crises of the First World War of 1914–1918. (665)

Federal Style: Early national style of architecture that borrowed from neoclassical models and emphasized symmetry, balance, and restraint. Famous builders associated with this style included Charles Bulfinch and Benjamin Latrobe. (324)

Federal Trade Commission Act (1914): A banner accomplishment of Woodrow Wilson's administration, this law empowered a standing, presidentially appointed commission to investigate illegal business practices in interstate commerce like unlawful competition, false advertising, and mislabeling of goods. (666)

The Federalist (1788): Collection of essays written by John Jay, James Madison, and Alexander Hamilton and published during the ratification debate in New York to lay out the Federalists' arguments in favor of the new Constitution. Since their publication, these influential essays have served as an important source for constitutional interpretation. (175)

federalists: Proponents of the 1787 Constitution, they favored a strong national government, arguing that the checks and balances in the new Constitution would safeguard the people's liberties. (173)

The Feminine Mystique (1963): Best-selling book by feminist thinker Betty Friedan. This work challenged women to move beyond the drudgery of suburban housewifery and helped launch what would become second-wave feminism. (861)

Fifteenth Amendment (ratified 1870): Prohibited states from denying citizens the franchise on account of race. It disappointed feminists who wanted the Amendment to include guarantees for women's suffrage. (475)

"Fifty-four forty or fight" (1846): Slogan adopted by mid-nineteenth-century expansionists who advocated the occupation of Oregon territory, jointly held by Britain and the United States. Though President Polk had pledged to seize all of Oregon, to 54° 40', he settled on the forty-ninth parallel as a compromise with the British. (367)

First Anglo-Powhatan War (1614): Series of clashes between the Powhatan Confederacy and English settlers in Virginia. English colonists torched and pillaged Indian villages, applying tactics used in England's campaigns against the Irish. (29)

First Continental Congress (1774): Convention of delegates from twelve of the thirteen colonies that convened in Philadelphia to craft a response to the Intolerable Acts. Delegates established Association, which called for a complete boycott of British goods. (122)

***Fletcher v. Peck* (1810):** Established firmer protection for private property and asserted the right of the Supreme Court to invalidate state laws in conflict with the federal Constitution. (238)

Florida Purchase Treaty (Adams-Onís Treaty) (1819): Under the agreement, Spain ceded Florida to the United States, which, in exchange, abandoned its claims to Texas. (240)

Foraker Act (1900): Sponsored by Senator Joseph B. Foraker, a Republican from Ohio, this accorded Puerto Ricans a limited degree of popular government. It was the first comprehensive congressional effort to provide for governance of territories acquired after the Spanish American War, and served as a model for a similar act adopted for the Philippines in 1902. (620)

Force Acts (1870–1871): Passed by Congress following a wave of Ku Klux Klan violence, the acts banned clan membership, prohibited the use of intimidation to prevent blacks from voting, and gave the U.S. military the authority to enforce the acts. (480)

Force Bill (1833): Passed by Congress alongside the Compromise Tariff, it authorized the president to use the military to collect federal tariff duties. (256)

Fordism: A system of assembly-line manufacturing and mass production named after Henry Ford, founder of the Ford Motor Company and developer of the Model T car. (711)

Fordney-McCumber Tariff Law (1922): A comprehensive bill passed to protect domestic production from foreign competitors. As a direct result, many European nations were spurred to increase their own trade barriers. (732)

Fort Henry and Fort Donelson, Battle of (February 1862): Key victory for Union General Ulysses S. Grant, it secured the North's hold on Kentucky and paved the way for Grant's attacks deeper into Tennessee. (448)

Fort Stanwix, Treaty of (1784): Treaty signed by the United States and the pro-British Iroquois granting Ohio country to the Americans. (149)

Fort Sumter: South Carolina location where Confederate forces fired the first shots of the Civil War in April of 1861, after Union forces attempted to provision the fort. (419)

Fourteen Points (1918): Woodrow Wilson's proposal to ensure peace after World War I, calling for an end to secret treaties, widespread arms reduction, national self-determination, and a new league of nations. (680)

Fourteenth Amendment (ratified 1868): Constitutional amendment that extended civil rights to freedmen and prohibited states from taking away such rights without due process. (473)

fourth party system (1896–1932): A term scholars have used to describe national politics from 1896–1932, when Republicans had a tight grip on the White House and issues such as industrial regulation and labor concerns became paramount, replacing older concerns such as civil service reform and monetary policy. (604)

Fredericksburg, Battle of (December 1862): Decisive victory in Virginia for Confederate Robert E. Lee, who successfully repelled a Union attack on his lines. (445)

Free Soil party (1848–1854): Antislavery party in the 1848 and 1852 elections that opposed the extension of slavery into the territories, arguing that the presence of slavery would limit opportunities for free laborers. (379)

Freedmen's Bureau (1865–1872): Created to aid newly emancipated slaves by providing food, clothing, medical care, education, and legal support. Its achievements were uneven and depended largely on the quality of local administrators. (469)

Freedom Riders (1961): Organized mixed-race groups who rode interstate buses deep into the South to draw attention to and protest racial segregation, beginning in 1961. This effort by northern young people to challenge racism proved a political and public relations success for the Civil Rights Movement. (903)

Freedom Summer (1964): A voter registration drive in Mississippi spearheaded by a coalition of civil rights groups. The campaign drew the activism of thousands of black and white civil rights workers, many of whom were students from the north, and was marred by the abduction and murder of three such workers at the hands of white racists. (903)

Freeport Doctrine (1858): Declared that since slavery could not exist without laws to protect it, territorial legislatures, not the Supreme Court, would have the final say on the slavery question. First argued by Ste1phen Douglass in 1858 in response to Abraham Lincoln's "Freeport Question." (406)

Freeport question (1858): Raised during one of the Lincoln-Douglas debates by Abraham Lincoln, who asked whether the Court or the people should decide the future of slavery in the territories. (406)

French and Indian War (Seven Years' War) (1754–1763): Nine-year war between the British and the French in North America. It resulted in the expulsion of the French from the North American mainland and helped spark the Seven Years' War in Europe. (104)

Fugitive Slave Law (1850): Passed as part of the Compromise of 1850, it set high penalties for anyone who aided escaped slaves and compelled all law enforcement officers to participate in retrieving runaways. Strengthened the antislavery cause in the North. (385)

Fundamental Orders (1639): Drafted by settlers in the Connecticut River Valley, document was the first "modern constitution" establishing a democratically controlled government. Key features of the document were borrowed for Connecticut's colonial charter and later, its state constitution. (47)

Fundamentalism: A Protestant Christian movement emphasizing the literal truth of the Bible and opposing religious modernism, which sought to reconcile religion and science. It was especially strong in the Baptist Church and the Church of Christ, first organized in 1906. (710)

funding at par: Payment of debts, such as government bonds, at face value. In 1790, Alexander Hamilton proposed that the federal government pay its Revolutionary war debts in full in order to bolster the nation's credit. (183)

Gadsden Purchase (1853): Acquired additional land from Mexico for $10 million to facilitate the construction of a southern transcontinental railroad. (392)

Gag Resolution: Prohibited debate or action on antislavery appeals. Driven through the House by pro-slavery Southerners, the gag resolution passed every year for eight years, eventually overturned with the help of John Quincy Adams. (256)

Gettysburg Address (1863): Abraham Lincoln's oft-quoted speech, delivered at the dedication of the cemetery at Gettysburg battlefield. In the address, Lincoln framed the war as a means to uphold the values of liberty. (446)

Gettysburg, Battle of (July 1863): Civil War battle in Pennsylvania that ended in Union victory, spelling doom for the Confederacy, which never again managed to invade the North. Site of General George Pickett's daring but doomed charge on the Northern lines. (445)

Ghent, Treaty of (1815): Ended the War of 1812 in a virtual draw, restoring prewar borders but failing to address any of the grievances that first brought America into the war. (227)

GI Bill (1944): Known officially as the Servicemen's Readjustment Act and more informally as the GI Bill of Rights, this law helped returning World War II soldiers reintegrate into civilian life by securing loans to buy homes and farms and set up small businesses and by making tuition and stipends available for them to attend college and job training programs. The Act was also intended to cushion the blow of 15 million returning servicemen on the employment market and to nurture the postwar economy. (831)

Gibbons v. Ogden (1824): Suit over whether New York State could grant a monopoly to a ferry operating on interstate waters. The ruling reasserted that Congress had the sole power to regulate interstate commerce. (238)

Gilded Age (1877–1896): A term given to the period 1865–1896 by Mark Twain, indicating both the fabulous wealth and the widespread corruption of the era. (492)

Glasnost: Meaning "openness," a cornerstone along with *Perestroika* of Soviet president Mikhail Gorbachev's reform movement in the USSR in the 1980s. These policies resulted in greater market liberalization, access to the West, and ultimately the end of communist rule. (949)

Glass-Steagall Banking Reform Act (1933): A law creating the Federal Deposit Insurance Corporation, which insured individual bank deposits and ended a century-long tradition of unstable banking that had reached a crisis in the Great Depression. (756)

Glorious (or Bloodless) Revolution (1688): Relatively peaceful overthrow of the unpopular Catholic monarch, James II, replacing him with Dutch-born William III and Mary, daughter of James II. William and Mary accepted increased Parliamentary oversight and new limits on monarchical authority. (50)

Gold Standard Act (1900): An act that guaranteed that paper currency would be redeemed freely in gold, putting an end to the already dying "free silver" campaign. (605)

Goliad: Texas outpost where American volunteers, having laid down their arms and surrendered, were massacred by Mexican forces in 1836. The incident, along with the slaughter at the Alamo, fueled American support for Texan independence. (266)

Good Neighbor policy: A departure from the Roosevelt Corollary to the Monroe Doctrine, the Good Neighbor Policy stressed nonintervention in Latin America. It was begun by Herbert Hoover but associated with Franklin D. Roosevelt. (780)

grandfather clause: A regulation established in many southern states in the 1890s that exempted from voting requirements (such as literacy tests and poll taxes) anyone who could prove that their ancestors ("grandfathers") had been able to vote in 1860. Since slaves could not vote before the Civil War, these clauses guaranteed the right to vote to many whites while denying it to blacks. (508)

Great Awakening (1730s and 1740s): Religious revival that swept the colonies. Participating ministers, most notably Jonathan Edwards and George Whitfield, placed an emphasis on direct, emotive spirituality. A Second Great Awakening arose in the nineteenth century. (87)

Great Compromise (1787): Popular term for the measure which reconciled the New Jersey and Virginia plans at the constitutional convention, giving states proportional representation in the House and equal representation in the Senate. The compromise broke the stalemate at the convention and paved the way for subsequent compromises over slavery and the Electoral College. (170)

Great Migration (1630–1642): Migration of seventy thousand refugees from England to the North American colonies, primarily New England and the Caribbean. The twenty thousand migrants who came to Massachusetts largely shared a common sense of purpose—to establish a model Christian settlement in the new world. (43)

Great Rapprochement: After decades of occasionally "twisting the lion's tail," American diplomats began to cultivate close, cordial relations with Great Britain at the end of the nineteenth century—a relationship that would intensify further during World War I. (610)

Great Society (1964–1968): President Lyndon Johnson's term for his domestic policy agenda. Billed as a successor to the New Deal, the Great Society aimed to extend the postwar prosperity to all people in American society by promoting civil rights and fighting poverty. Great

Society programs included the War on Poverty, which expanded the Social Security system by creating Medicare and Medicaid to provide health care for the aged and the poor. Johnson also signed laws protecting consumers and empowering community organizations to combat poverty at grassroots levels. (900)

Greek Revival: Inspired by the contemporary Greek independence movement, this building style, popular between 1820 and 1850, imitated ancient Greek structural forms in search of a democratic architectural vernacular. (324)

greenbacks: Paper currency issued by the Union Treasury during the Civil War. Inadequately supported by gold, greenbacks fluctuated in value throughout the war, reaching a low of 39 cents on the dollar. (431)

Greenville, Treaty of (1795): Under the terms of the treaty, the Miami Confederacy agreed to cede territory in the Old Northwest to the United States in exchange for cash payment, hunting rights, and formal recognition of their sovereign status. (191)

Guadalupe Hidalgo, Treaty of (1848): Ended the war with Mexico. Mexico agreed to cede territory reaching northwest from Texas to Oregon in exchange for $18.25 million in cash and assumed debts. (372)

Guantánamo Detention Camp: Controversial prison facility constructed after the U.S.-led invasion of Afghanistan in 2001. Located on territory occupied by the U.S. military, but not technically part of the United States, the facility serves as an extra-legal holding area for suspected terrorists. (975)

Haitian Revolution (1791-1804): War incited by a slave uprising in French-controlled Saint Domingue, resulting in the creation of the first independent black republic in the Americas. (211)

Half-Way Covenant (1662): Agreement allowing unconverted offspring of church members to baptize their children. It signified a waning of religious zeal among second and third generation Puritans. (73)

Harlem Renaissance: A creative outpouring among African-American writers, jazz musicians, and social thinkers, centered around Harlem in the 1920s, that celebrated black culture and advocated for a "New Negro" in American social, political, and intellectual life. (724)

Harpers Ferry: Federal arsenal in Virginia seized by abolitionist John Brown in 1859. Though Brown was later captured and executed, his raid alarmed Southerners who believed that Northerners shared in Brown's extremism. (408)

Hartford Convention (1814–1815): Convention of Federalists from five New England states who opposed the War of 1812 and resented the strength of Southern and Western interests in Congress and in the White House. (228)

Hawley-Smoot Tariff (1930): The highest protective tariff in the peacetime history of the United States, passed as a result of good old-fashioned horse trading. To the outside world, it smacked of ugly economic warfare. (740)

Haymarket Square (1886): A May Day rally that turned violent when someone threw a bomb into the middle of the meeting, killing several dozen people. Eight anarchists were arrested for conspiracy contributing to the disorder, although evidence linking them to the bombing was thin. Four were executed, one committed suicide, and three were pardoned in 1893. (533)

Hay-Pauncefote Treaty (1901): A treated signed between the United States and Great Britain, giving Americans a free hand to build a canal in Central America. The treaty nullified the Clayton-Bulwer Treaty of 1850, which prohibited the British or U.S. from acquiring territory in Central America. (628)

headright system: Employed in the tobacco colonies to encourage the importation of indentured servants, the system allowed an individual to acquire fifty acres of land if he paid for a laborer's passage to the colony. (61)

Hessians: German troops hired from their princes by George III to aid in putting down the colonial insurrection. This hardened the resolve of American colonists, who resented the use of paid foreign fighters. (133)

Hetch Hetchy Valley: The federal government allowed the city of San Francisco to build a dam here in 1913. This was a blow to preservationists, who wished to protect the Yosemite National Park, where the dam was located. (654)

Hitler-Stalin pact (1939): Treaty signed on August 23, 1939 in which Germany and the Soviet Union agreed not to fight each other. The fateful agreement paved the way for German aggression against Poland and the Western democracies. (784)

holding companies: A company that owns part or all of the other companies' stock in order to extend monopoly control. Often, a holding company does not produce goods or services of its own but only exists to control other companies. The Clayton Anti-Trust Act of 1914 sought to clamp down on these companies when they obstructed competition. (666)

Homestead Act (1862): A federal law that gave settlers 160 acres of land for about $30 if they lived on it for five years and improved it by, for instance, building a house on it. The act helped make land accessible to hundreds of thousands of westward-moving settlers, but many people also found disappointment when their land was infertile or they saw speculators grabbing up the best land. (433, 586)

Homestead Strike (1892): A strike at a Carnegie steel plant in Homestead, P.A., that ended in an armed battle between the strikers, three hundred armed "Pinkerton" detectives hired by Carnegie, and federal troops, which killed ten people and wounded more than sixty. The strike was part of a nationwide wave of labor unrest in the summer of 1892 that helped the Populists gain some support from industrial workers. (506)

Hoovervilles: Grim shantytowns where impoverished victims of the Great Depression slept under newspapers and in makeshift tents. Their visibility (and sarcastic name) tarnished the reputation of the Hoover administration. (743)

horizontal integration: The practice perfected by John D. Rockefeller of dominating a particular phase of the production process in order to monopolize a market, often by forming trusts and alliances with competitors. (521)

House of Burgesses: Representative parliamentary assembly created to govern Virginia, establishing a precedent for government in the English colonies. (32)

House Un-American Activities Committee (HUAC): Investigatory body established in 1938 to root out "subversion." Sought to expose communist influence in American government and society, in particular through the trial of Alger Hiss. (852)

Hudson River school (mid-nineteenth century): American artistic movement that produced romantic renditions of local landscapes. (325)

Huguenots: French Protestant dissenters, the Huguenots were granted limited toleration under the Edict of Nantes. After King Louis XIV outlawed Protestantism in 1685, many Huguenots fled elsewhere, including to British North America. (98)

Hundred Days (1933): The first hundred days of Franklin D. Roosevelt's administration, stretching from March 9 to June 16, 1933, when an unprecedented number of reform bills were passed by a Democratic Congress to launch the New Deal. (754)

Hungarian uprising (1956): Series of demonstrations in Hungary against the Soviet Union. Soviet Premier Nikita Khrushchev violently suppressed this pro-Western uprising, highlighting the limitations of America's power in Eastern Europe. (874)

Hurricane Katrina (2005): The costliest and one of the deadliest hurricanes in the history of the United States, killing nearly 2000 Americans. The storm ravaged the Gulf Coast, especially the city of New Orleans, in late August of 2005. In New Orleans, high winds and rain caused the city's levees to break, leading to catastrophic flooding, particularly centered on the city's most impoverished wards. A tardy and feeble response by local and federal authorities exacerbated the damage and led to widespread criticism of the Federal Emergency Management Agency (FEMA). (982)

Immigration Act of 1924: Also known as the "National Origins Act," this law established quotas for immigration to the United States. Immigrants from Southern and Eastern Europe were sharply curtailed, while immigrants from Asia were shut out altogether. (703)

***The Impending Crisis of the South* (1857):** Antislavery tract, written by white Southerner Hinton R. Helper, arguing that nonslaveholding whites actually suffered most in a slave economy. (397)

impressment: Act of forcibly drafting an individual into military service, employed by the British navy against American seamen in times of war against France, 1793–1815. Impressment was a continual source of conflict between Britain and the United States in the early national period. (216)

Incas: Highly advanced South American civilization that occupied present-day Peru until it was conquered by Spanish forces under Francisco Pizarro in 1532. The Incas developed sophisticated agricultural techniques, such as

terrace farming, in order to sustain large, complex societies in the unforgiving Andes Mountains. (6)

indentured servants: Migrants who, in exchange for transatlantic passage, bound themselves to a colonial employer for a term of service, typically between four and seven years. Their migration addressed the chronic labor shortage in the colonies and facilitated settlement. (61)

Indian Removal Act (1830): Ordered the removal of Indian Tribes still residing east of the Mississippi to newly established Indian Territory west of Arkansas and Missouri. Tribes resisting eviction were forcibly removed by American forces, often after prolonged legal or military battles. (258)

Industrial Revolution: Shift toward mass production and mechanization that included the creation of the modern factory system. (285)

Industrial Workers of the World (1905): The IWW, also known as the "Wobblies," was a radical organization that sought to build "one big union" and advocated industrial sabotage in defense of that goal. At its peak in 1923, it could claim 100,000 members and could gain the support of 300,000. The IWW particularly appealed to migratory workers in agriculture and lumbering and to miners, all of whom suffered from horrific working conditions. (683)

initiative: A progressive reform measure allowing voters to petition to have a law placed on the general ballot. Like the referendum and recall, it brought democracy directly "to the people," and helped foster a shift toward interest-group politics and away from old political "machines." (641)

***Insular Cases* (1901–1904):** Beginning in 1901, a badly divided Supreme Court decreed in these cases that the Constitution did not follow the flag. In other words, Puerto Ricans and Filipinos would not necessarily enjoy all American rights. (621)

***insurrectos*:** Cuban insurgents who sought freedom from colonial Spanish rule. Their destructive tactics threatened American economic interests in Cuban plantations and railroads. (612)

interlocking directorates: The practice of having executives or directors from one company serve on the Board of Directors of another company. J. P. Morgan introduced this practice to eliminate banking competition in the 1890s. (522)

Intermediate-Range Nuclear Forces (INF) Treaty (1987): Arms limitation agreement settled by Ronald Reagan and Mikhail Gorbachev after several attempts. The treaty banned all intermediate-range nuclear missiles from Europe and marked a significant thaw in the Cold War. (949)

International Style: Archetypal, post-World War II modernist architectural style, best known for its "curtain-wall" designs of steel-and-glass corporate high-rises. (882)

Interstate Commerce Act (1887): Congressional legislation that established the Interstate Commerce Commission, compelled railroads to publish standard rates, and prohibited rebates and pools. Railroads quickly became adept at using the Act to achieve their own ends, but the Act gave the government an important means to regulate big business. (519)

"Intolerable Acts" (1774): Series of punitive measures passed in retaliation for the Boston Tea Party, closing the Port of Boston, revoking a number of rights in the Massachusetts colonial charter, and expanding the Quartering Act to allow for the lodging of soldiers in private homes. In response, colonists convened the First Continental Congress and called for a complete boycott of British goods. (122)

Iran-Contra Affair (1987): Major political scandal of Ronald Reagan's second term. An illicit arrangement of selling "arms for hostages" with Iran and using money to support the contras in Nicaragua, the scandal deeply damaged Reagan's credibility. (951)

Iranian hostage crisis: The 444 days, from November 1979 to January 1981, in which American embassy workers were held captive by Iranian revolutionaries. The Iranian Revolution began in January 1979 when young Muslim fundamentalists overthrew the oppressive regime of the American-backed shah, forcing him into exile. Deeming the United States "the Great Satan," these revolutionaries triggered an energy crisis by cutting off Iranian oil. The hostage crisis began when revolutionaries stormed the American embassy, demanding that the United States return the shah to Iran for trial. The episode was marked by botched diplomacy and failed rescue attempts by the Carter Administration. After permanently damaging relations between the two countries, the crisis ended with the hostages' release the day Ronald Reagan became president, January 20, 1981. (939)

Iroquois Confederacy (late 1500s): Bound together five tribes—the Mohawks, the Oneidas, the Onondagas, the Cayugas, and the Senecas—in the Mohawk Valley of what is now New York State. (36)

irreconcilables: Led by Senators William Borah of Idaho and Hiram Johnson of California, this was a hard-core group of militant isolationists who opposed the Wilsonian dream of international cooperation in the League of Nations after World War I. Their efforts played an important part in preventing American participation in the international organization. (693)

Jamestown (1607): First permanent English settlement in North America founded by the Virginia Company. (27)

Jay's Treaty (1794): Negotiated by Chief Justice John Jay in an effort to avoid war with Britain, the treaty included a British promise to evacuate outposts on U.S. soil and pay damages for seized American vessels, in exchange for which Jay bound the United States to repay pre-Revolutionary war debts and to abide by Britain's restrictive trading policies toward France. (193)

jeremiad: Often-fiery sermons lamenting the waning piety of parishioners first delivered in New England in the mid-seventeenth century; named after the doom-saying Old Testament prophet Jeremiah. (73)

Jim Crow: System of racial segregation in the American South from the end of Reconstruction until the mid-twentieth century. Based on the concept of "separate but equal" facilities for blacks and whites, the Jim Crow system sought to prevent racial mixing in public, including restaurants, movie theaters, and public transportation. An informal system, it was generally perpetuated by custom, violence, and intimidation. (496, 867)

Johnson Debt Default Act (1934): Steeped in ugly memories of World War I, this spiteful act prevented debt-ridden nations from borrowing further from the United States. (782)

joint-stock company: Short-term partnership between multiple investors to fund a commercial enterprise; such arrangements were used to fund England's early colonial ventures. (27)

Jones Act (1916): Law according territorial status to the Philippines and promising independence as soon as a "stable government" could be established. The United States did not grant the Philippines independence until July 4, 1946. (667)

Judiciary Act of 1789: Organized the federal legal system, establishing the Supreme Court, federal district and circuit courts, and the office of the attorney general. (182)

Judiciary Act of 1801: Passed by the departing Federalist Congress, it created sixteen new federal judgeships ensuring a Federalist hold on the judiciary. (208)

Kanagawa, Treaty of (1854): Ended Japan's two-hundred year period of economic isolation, establishing an American consulate in Japan and securing American coaling rights in Japanese ports. (391)

Kansas-Nebraska Act (1854): Proposed that the issue of slavery be decided by popular sovereignty in the Kansas and Nebraska territories, thus revoking the 1820 Missouri Compromise. Introduced by Stephen Douglass in an effort to bring Nebraska into the Union and pave the way for a northern transcontinental railroad. (394)

Kellogg-Briand Pact (1928): A sentimental triumph of the 1920s peace movement, this 1928 pact linked sixty-two nations in the supposed "outlawry of war." (732)

Kent State University (shooting 1970): Massacre of four college students by National Guardsmen on May 4, 1970, in Ohio. In response to Nixon's announcement that he had expanded the Vietnam War into Cambodia, college campuses across the country exploded in violence. On May 14 and 15, students at historically black Jackson State College in Mississippi were protesting the war as well as the Kent State shooting when highway patrolmen fired into a student dormitory, killing two students. (919)

Keynesianism: An economic theory based on the thoughts of British economist John Maynard Keynes, holding that central banks should adjust interest rates and governments should use deficit spending and tax policies to increase purchasing power and hence prosperity. (772)

King George's War (1744–1748): North American theater of Europe's War of Austrian Succession that once again pitted British colonists against their French counterparts in the North. The peace settlement did not involve any territorial realignment, leading to conflict between New England settlers and the British government. (102)

King Philip's War (1675–1676): Series of assaults by Metacom, King Philip, on English settlements in New England. The attacks slowed the westward migration of New England settlers for several decades. (48)

King William's War (1689–1697): War fought largely between French trappers, British settlers, and their respective Indian allies from 1689–1697. The colonial theater of the larger War of the League of Augsburg in Europe. (100)

kitchen debate (1959): Televised exchange in 1959 between Soviet Premier Nikita Khrushchev and American Vice President Richard Nixon. Meeting at the American National Exhibition in Moscow, the two leaders sparred over the relative merits of capitalist consumer culture versus Soviet state planning. Nixon won applause for his staunch defense of American capitalism, helping lead him to the Republican nomination for president in 1960. (878)

Knights of Labor: The second national labor organization, organized in 1869 as a secret society and opened for public membership in 1881. The Knights were known for their efforts to organize all workers, regardless of skill level, gender, or race. After the mid-1880s their membership declined for a variety of reasons, including the Knights' participation in violent strikes and discord between skilled and unskilled members. (533)

Know-Nothing party (1850s): Nativist political party, also known as the American party, which emerged in response to an influx of immigrants, particularly Irish Catholics. (284)

Korean War (1950–1953): First "hot war" of the Cold War. The Korean War began in 1950 when the Soviet-backed North Koreans invaded South Korea before meeting a counter-offensive by UN Forces, dominated by the United States. The war ended in stalemate in 1953. (855)

Kristallnacht: German for "night of broken glass," it refers to the murderous pogrom that destroyed Jewish businesses and synagogues and sent thousands to concentration camps on the night of November 9, 1938. Thousands more attempted to find refuge in the United States, but were ultimately turned away due to restrictive immigration laws. (788)

Ku Klux Klan: An extremist, paramilitary, right-wing secret society founded in the mid-nineteenth century and revived during the 1920s. It was anti-foreign, anti-black, anti-Jewish, anti-pacifist, anti-communist, anti-internationalist, anti-evolutionist, and anti-bootlegger, but pro-Anglo-Saxon and pro-Protestant. Its members, cloaked in sheets to conceal their identities, terrorized freedmen and sympathetic whites throughout the South after the Civil War. By the 1890s, Klan-style violence and Democratic legislation succeeded in virtually disenfranchising all Southern blacks. (479, 701)

Kyoto Treaty: International treaty to limit greenhouse gas emissions. It was negotiated and opened for signatories in 1997, and took effect in 2005. Although signed by 169 (of 192) countries, the Bush Administration rejected the plan as too costly in 2001. (973)

Laird rams (1863): Two well-armed ironclad warships constructed for the Confederacy by a British firm. Seeking to avoid war with the United States, the British government purchased the two ships for its Royal Navy instead. (427)

Land Act of 1820: Fueled the settlement of the Northwest and Missouri territories by lowering the price of public land. Also prohibited the purchase of federal acreage on credit, thereby eliminating one of the causes of the Panic of 1819. (234)

Land Ordinance of 1785: Provided for the sale of land in the Old Northwest and earmarked the proceeds toward repaying the national debt. (165)

land-grant colleges: Colleges and universities created from allocations of public land through the Morrell Act of 1862 and the Hatch Act of 1887. These grants helped fuel the boom in higher education in the late nineteenth century, and many of today's public universities derive from these grants. (555)

League of Nations (1919): A world organization of national governments proposed by President Woodrow Wilson and established by the Treaty of Versailles in 1919. It worked to facilitate peaceful international cooperation. Despite emotional appeals by Wilson, isolationists' objections to the League created the major obstacle to American signing of the Treaty of Versailles. (693)

Lecompton Constitution (1857): Proposed Kansas constitution, whose ratification was unfairly rigged so as to guarantee slavery in the territory. Initially ratified by proslavery forces, it was later voted down when Congress required that the entire constitution be put up for a vote. (400)

Leisler's Rebellion (1689–1691): Armed conflict between aspiring merchants led by Jacob Leisler and the ruling elite of New York. One of many uprisings that erupted across the colonies when wealthy colonists attempted to recreate European social structures in the New World. (76)

Lend-Lease Bill (1941): Based on the motto, "Send guns, not sons," this law abandoned former pretenses of neutrality by allowing Americans to sell unlimited supplies of arms to any nation defending itself against the Axis Powers. Patriotically numbered 1776, the bill was praised as a device for keeping the nation out of World War II. (791)

Levittown: Suburban communities with mass-produced tract houses built in the New York and Philadelphia metropolitan areas in the 1950s by William Levitt and Sons. Typically inhabited by white middle-class people who fled the cities in search of homes to buy for their growing families. (838)

Lewinsky affair (1998–1999): Political sex scandal that resulted in Bill Clinton's impeachment and trial by Congress. In 1998, Clinton gave sworn testimony in a sexual harassment case that he had never engaged in sexual activity with a White House intern named Monica Lewinsky. When prosecutors discovered evidence that the President had lied under oath about the affair, to which Clinton admitted, Republicans in Congress began impeachment proceedings. Although Clinton was ultimately not convicted by the Senate, the scandal put a lasting blemish on his presidential legacy. (970)

Lexington and Concord, Battles of (April 1775): First battles of the Revolutionary War, fought outside of Boston.

The colonial militia successfully defended their stores of munitions, forcing the British to retreat to Boston. (124)

Liberal Protestants: Members of a branch of Protestantism that flourished from 1875 to 1925 and encouraged followers to use the Bible as a moral compass rather than to believe that the Bible represented scientific or historical truth. Many Liberal Protestants became active in the "social gospel" and other reform movements of the era. (552)

The Liberator **(1831–1865):** Antislavery newspaper published by William Lloyd Garrison, who called for the immediate emancipation of all slaves. (350)

Liberia: West-African nation founded in 1822 as a haven for freed blacks, fifteen thousand of whom made their way back across the Atlantic by the 1860s. (349)

Liberty party (1840–1848): Antislavery party that ran candidates in the 1840 and 1844 elections before merging with the Free Soil party. Supporters of the Liberty party sought the eventual abolition of slavery, but in the short term hoped to halt the expansion of slavery into the territories and abolish the domestic slave trade. (367)

limited liability: Legal principle that facilitates capital investment by offering protection for individual investors, who, in cases of legal claims or bankruptcy, cannot be held responsible for more than the value of their individual shares. (290)

Lincoln-Douglas debates (1858): Series of debates between Abraham Lincoln and Stephen Douglass during the U.S. Senate race in Illinois. Douglass won the election but Lincoln gained national prominence and emerged as the leading candidate for the 1860 Republican nomination. (406)

Little Bighorn, Battle of (1876): A particularly violent example of the warfare between whites and Native Americans in the late nineteenth century, also known as "Custer's Last Stand." In two days, June 25 and 26, 1876, the combined forces of over 2,000 Sioux, Cheyenne, and Arapaho Indians defeated and killed more than 250 U.S. soldiers, including Colonel George Custer. The battle came as the U.S. government tried to compel Native Americans to remain on the reservations and Native Americans tried to defend territory from white gold-seekers. This Indian advantage did not last long, however, as the union of these Indian fighters proved tenuous and the United States Army soon exacted retribution. (578)

Lochner v. *New York* **(1905):** A setback for labor reformers, this 1905 Supreme Court decision invalidated a state law establishing a ten-hour day for bakers. It held that the "right to free contract" was implicit in the due process clause of the Fourteenth Amendment. (645)

London Economic Conference (1933): A sixty-nation economic conference organized to stabilize international currency rates. Franklin Roosevelt's decision to revoke American participation contributed to a deepening world economic crisis. (778)

Long Island, Battle of (August 1776): Battle for the control of New York. British troops overwhelmed the colonial militias and retained control of the city for most of the war. (144)

loose construction: Legal doctrine which holds that the federal government can use powers not specifically granted or prohibited in the Constitution to carry out its constitutionally mandated responsibilities. (238)

"Lost Generation": A creative circle of expatriate American artists and writers, including Ernest Hemingway, F. Scott Fitzgerald, and Gertrude Stein, who found shelter and inspiration in post-World War I Europe. (721)

Louisiana Purchase (1803): Acquisition of Louisiana territory from France. The purchase more than doubled the territory of the United States, opening vast tracts for settlement. (213)

Loyalists: American colonists who opposed the Revolution and maintained their loyalty to the King; sometimes referred to as "Tories." (139)

Lusitania: British passenger liner torpedoed and sank by Germany on May 7, 1915. It ended the lives of 1,198 people, including 128 Americans, and pushed the United States closer to war. (672)

lyceum: (From the Greek name for the ancient Athenian school where Aristotle taught.) Public lecture hall that hosted speakers on topics ranging from science to moral philosophy. Part of a broader flourishing of higher education in the mid-nineteenth century. (314)

Macon's Bill No. 2: Aimed at resuming peaceful trade with Britain and France, the act stipulated that if either Britain or France repealed its trade restrictions, the United States would reinstate the embargo against the nonrepealing nation. When Napoleon offered to lift his restrictions on British ports, the United States was forced to declare an embargo on Britain, thereby pushing the two nations closer toward war. (218)

Maine **(1898):** American battleship dispatched to keep a "friendly" watch over Cuba in early 1898. It mysteriously blew up in Havana harbor on February 15, 1898, with a loss of 260 sailors. Later evidence confirmed that the explosion was accidental, resulting from combustion in one of the ship's internal coal bunkers. But many Americans, eager for war, insisted that it was the fault of a Spanish submarine mine. (612)

Maine Law of 1851: Prohibited the manufacture and sale of alcohol. A dozen other states followed Maine's lead, though most statutes proved ineffective and were repealed within a decade. (317)

malaise speech (1979): National address by Jimmy Carter in July 1979 in which the President chided American materialism and urged a communal spirit in the face of economic hardships. Although Carter intended the speech to improve both public morale and his standings as a leader, it had the opposite effect and was widely perceived as a political disaster for the embattled president. (938)

The Man Without a Country **(1863):** Edward Everett Hale's fictional account of a treasonous soldier's journeys in exile. The book was widely read in the North, inspiring greater devotion to the Union. (451)

Manhattan Project (1942): Code name for the American commission established in 1942 to develop the atomic bomb. The first experimental bomb was detonated on July 16, 1945, in the desert of New Mexico. Atomic bombs were then dropped on two cities in Japan in hopes of bringing the war to an end: Hiroshima on August 6, 1945, and Nagasaki on August 9, 1945. (820)

Manifest Destiny (1840s and 1850s): Belief that the United States was destined by God to spread its "empire of liberty" across North America. Served as a justification for mid-nineteenth-century expansionism. (366)

***Marbury* v. *Madison* (1803):** Supreme Court case that established the principle of "judicial review"—the idea that the Supreme Court had the final authority to determine constitutionality. (209)

March on Washington (1963): Massive civil rights demonstration in August 1963 in support of Kennedy-backed legislation to secure legal protections for American blacks. One of the most visually impressive manifestations of the Civil Rights Movement, the march was the occasion of Martin Luther King's famous "I Have a Dream" speech. (897)

market revolution: Eighteenth- and nineteenth-century transformation from a disaggregated, subsistence economy to a national commercial and industrial network. (302)

Marshall Plan (1948): Massive transfer of aid money to help rebuild postwar Western Europe, intended to bolster capitalist and democratic governments and prevent domestic communist groups from riding poverty and misery to power. The plan was first announced by Secretary of State George Marshall at Harvard's commencement in June 1947. (847)

Mason-Dixon line: Originally drawn by surveyors to resolve the boundaries between Maryland, Delaware, Pennsylvania and Virginia in the 1760s, it came to symbolize the North-South divide over slavery. (353)

Massachusetts Bay Colony (founded in 1630): Established by non-separating Puritans, it soon grew to be the largest and most influential of the New England colonies. (43)

Mayflower Compact (1620): Agreement to form a majoritarian government in Plymouth, signed aboard the *Mayflower*. Created a foundation for self-government in the colony. (43)

McCarthyism: A brand of vitriolic, fear-mongering anti-communism associated with the career of Senator Joseph McCarthy. In the early 1950s, Senator McCarthy used his position in Congress to baselessly accuse high-ranking government officials and other Americans of conspiracy with communism. The term named after him refers to the dangerous forces of unfairness and fear wrought by anti-communist paranoia. (866)

McCormick reaper (1831): Mechanized the harvest of grains, such as wheat, allowing farmers to cultivate larger plots. The introduction of the reaper in the 1830s fueled the establishment of large-scale commercial agriculture in the Midwest. (295)

***McCulloch* v. *Maryland* (1819):** Supreme Court case that strengthened federal authority and upheld the constitutionality of the Bank of the United States by establishing

that the State of Maryland did not have power to tax the bank. (238)

McKinley Tariff (1890): Shepherded through Congress by President William McKinley, this tariff raised duties on Hawaiian sugar and set off renewed efforts to secure the annexation of Hawaii to the United States. (611)

McNary-Haugen Bill (1924–1928): A farm-relief bill that was championed throughout the 1920s and aimed to keep agricultural prices high by authorizing the government to buy up surpluses and sell them abroad. Congress twice passed the bill, but President Calvin Coolidge vetoed it in 1927 and 1928. (735)

Meat Inspection Act (1906): A law passed by Congress to subject meat shipped over state lines to federal inspection. The publication of Upton Sinclair's novel, *The Jungle,* earlier that year so disgusted American consumers with its description of conditions in slaughterhouses and meat-packing plants that it mobilized public support for government action. (650)

mechanization of agriculture: The development of engine-driven machines, like the combine, which helped to dramatically increase the productivity of land in the 1870s and 1880s. This process contributed to the consolidation of agricultural business that drove many family farms out of existence. (594)

mercantilism: Economic theory that closely linked a nation's political and military power to its bullion reserves. Mercantilists generally favored protectionism and colonial acquisition as means to increase exports. (114)

***Merrimack* and *Monitor* (1862):** Confederate and Union ironclads, respectively, whose successes against wooden ships signaled an end to wooden warships. They fought an historic, though inconsequential battle in 1862. (439)

***mestizos*:** People of mixed Indian and European heritage, notably in Mexico. (20)

Meuse-Argonne offensive (1918): General John J. "Black Jack" Pershing led American troops in this effort to cut the German railroad lines supplying the western front. It was one of the few major battles that Americans participated in during the entire war, and was still underway when the war ended. (690)

middle passage: Transatlantic voyage slaves endured between Africa and the colonies. Mortality rates were notoriously high. (66)

middlemen: In trading systems, those dealers who operate between the original producers of goods and the retail merchants who sell to consumers. After the eleventh century, European exploration was driven in large part by a desire to acquire alluring Asian goods without paying heavy tolls to Muslim middlemen. (11)

midnight judges (1801): Federal justices appointed by John Adams during the last days of his presidency. Their positions were revoked when the newly elected Republican Congress repealed the Judiciary Act. (208)

Midway, Battle of (1942): A pivotal naval battle fought near the island of Midway on June 3–6, 1942. The victory halted Japanese advances in the Pacific. (809)

mining industry: After gold and silver strikes in Colorado, Nevada, and other western territories in the second half of the nineteenth century, fortune seekers by the thousands rushed to the West to dig. These metals were essential to U.S. industrial growth and were also sold into world markets. After surface metals were removed, people sought ways to extract ore from underground, leading to the development of heavy mining machinery. This, in turn, led to the consolidation of the mining industry, because only big companies could afford to buy and build the necessary machines. (584)

minstrel shows: Variety shows performed by white actors in black-face. First popularized in the mid-nineteenth century. (325)

Miranda warning: A statement of an arrested person's constitutional rights, which police officers must read during an arrest. The warning came out of the Supreme Court's decision in *Miranda* v. *Arizona* in 1966 that accused people have the right to remain silent, consult an attorney, and enjoy other protections. The Court declared that law enforcement officers must make sure suspects understand their constitutional rights, thus creating a safeguard against forced confessions and self-implication. (921)

Mississippi Freedom Democratic party (1964): Political party organized by civil rights activists to challenge Mississippi's delegation to the Democratic National Convention, who opposed the civil rights planks in the party's platform. Claiming a mandate to represent the true voice of Mississippi, where almost no black citizens could vote, the MFDP demanded to be seated at the convention but were denied by party bosses. The effort was both a setback to civil rights activism in the south and a motivation to continue to struggle for black voting rights. (903)

Missouri Compromise (1820): Allowed Missouri to enter as a slave state but preserved the balance between North and South by carving free-soil Maine out of Massachusetts and prohibiting slavery from territories acquired in the Louisiana Purchase, north of the line of 36°30′. (235)

Model Treaty (1776): Sample treaty drafted by the Continental Congress as a guide for American diplomats. Reflected the Americans' desire to foster commercial partnerships rather than political or military entanglements. (145)

modernism: In response to the demanding conditions of modern life, this artistic and cultural movement revolted against comfortable Victorian standards and accepted chance, change, contingency, uncertainty, and fragmentation. Originating among avant-garde artists and intellectuals around the turn of the twentieth century, modernism blossomed into a full-fledged cultural movement in art, music, literature, and architecture. (720)

Molasses Act (1737): Tax on imported molasses passed by Parliament in an effort to squelch the North American trade with the French West Indies. It proved largely ineffective due to widespread smuggling. (85)

Molly Maguires (1860s–1870s): Secret organization of Irish miners that campaigned, at times violently, against poor working conditions in the Pennsylvania mines. (281)

Monitor: See *Merrimack*. (439)

Monroe Doctrine (1823): Statement delivered by President James Monroe, warning European powers to refrain from seeking any new territories in the Americas. The United States largely lacked the power to back up the pronouncement, which was actually enforced by the British, who sought unfettered access to Latin American markets. (242)

Montgomery bus boycott (1955): Protest, sparked by Rosa Parks's defiant refusal to move to the back of the bus, by black Alabamians against segregated seating on city buses. The bus boycott lasted from December 1, 1955, until December 26, 1956, and became one of the foundational moments of the Civil Rights Movement. It led to the rise of Martin Luther King, Jr., and ultimately to a Supreme Court decision opposing segregated busing. (868)

Moral Majority: Political action committee founded by evangelical Reverend Jerry Falwell in 1979 to promote traditional Christian values and oppose feminism, abortion, and gay rights. The group was a major linchpin in the resurgent religious right of the 1980s. (951)

Mormons: Religious followers of Joseph Smith, who founded a communal, oligarchic religious order in the 1830s, officially known as the Church of Jesus Christ of Latter-Day Saints. Mormons, facing deep hostility from their non-Mormon neighbors, eventually migrated west and established a flourishing settlement in the Utah desert. (310)

Morrill Tariff Act (1861): Increased duties back up to 1846 levels to raise revenue for the Civil War. (431)

muckrakers: Bright young reporters at the turn of the twentieth century who won this unfavorable moniker from Theodore Roosevelt, but boosted the circulations of their magazines by writing exposés of widespread corruption in American society. Their subjects included business manipulation of government, white slavers, child labor, and the illegal deeds of the trusts, and helped spur the passage of reform legislation. (639)

Muller v. *Oregon* (1908): A landmark Supreme Court case in which crusading attorney (and future Supreme Court Justice) Louis D. Brandeis persuaded the Supreme Court to accept the constitutionality of limiting the hours of women workers. Coming on the heels of *Lochner* v. *New York*, it established a different standard for male and female workers. (645)

My Lai Massacre (1968): Military assault in a small Vietnamese village on March 16, 1968, in which American soldiers under the command of 2nd Lieutenant William Calley murdered hundreds of unarmed Vietnamese civilians, mostly women and children. The atrocity produced outrage and reduced support for the war in America and around the world when details of the massacre and an attempted cover-up were revealed in 1971. (918)

Narrative of the Life of Frederick Douglass (1845): Vivid autobiography of the escaped slave and renowned abolitionist Frederick Douglass. (352)

Nat Turner's rebellion (1831): Virginia slave revolt that resulted in the deaths of sixty whites and raised fears among white Southerners of further uprisings. (348)

National American Woman Suffrage Association (NAWSA): An organization founded in 1890 to demand the vote for women. NAWSA argued that women should be allowed to vote because their responsibilities in the home and family made them indispensable in the public decision-making process. During World War I, NAWSA supported the war effort and lauded women's role in the Allied victory, which helped to finally achieve nationwide woman suffrage in the Nineteenth Amendment (1920). (562)

National Banking System (1863): Network of member banks that could issue currency against purchased government bonds. Created during the Civil War to establish a stable national currency and stimulate the sale of war bonds. (431)

National Labor Union (1866–1872): This first national labor organization in U.S. history was founded in 1866 and gained 600,000 members from many parts of the workforce, although it limited the participation of Chinese, women, and blacks. The organization devoted much of its energy to fighting for an eight-hour workday before it dissolved in 1872. (532)

National Recovery Administration (NRA) (1933): Known by its critics as the "National Run Around," the NRA was an early New Deal program designed to assist industry, labor, and the unemployed through centralized planning mechanisms that monitored workers' earnings and working hours to distribute work and established codes for "fair competition" to ensure that similar procedures were followed by all firms in any particular industrial sector. (761)

National Security Council Memorandum Number 68 (NSC-68) (1950): National Security Council recommendation to quadruple defense spending and rapidly expand peace-time armed forces to address Cold War tensions. It reflected a new militarization of American foreign policy but the huge costs of rearmament were not expected to interfere with what seemed like the limitless possibilities of postwar prosperity. (855)

National War Labor Board (1918): This wartime agency was chaired by former President Taft and aimed to prevent labor disputes by encouraging high wages and an eight-hour day. While granting some concessions to labor, it stopped short of supporting labor's most important demand: a government guarantee of the right to organize into unions. (682)

National War Labor Board (NWLB): Established by President Franklin D. Roosevelt to act as an arbitration tribunal and mediate disputes between labor and management that might have led to war stoppages and thereby undermined the war effort. The NWLB was also charged with adjusting wages with an eye to controlling inflation. (802)

naturalism: An offshoot of mainstream realism, this late-nineteenth-century literary movement purported to apply detached scientific objectivity to the study of human characters shaped by degenerate heredity and extreme or sordid social environments. (567)

Navigation Laws: Series of laws passed, beginning in 1651, to regulate colonial shipping; the acts provided that only English ships would be allowed to trade in English and colonial ports, and that all goods destined for the colonies would first pass through England. (49)

Neutrality Act of 1939: This act stipulated that European democracies might buy American munitions, but only if they could pay in cash and transport them in their own ships. The terms were known as "Cash-and-Carry." It represented an effort to avoid war debts and protect American arms-carriers from torpedo attacks. (785)

Neutrality Acts of 1935, 1936, and 1937: Short-sighted acts passed in 1935, 1936, and 1937 to prevent American participation in a European War. Among other restrictions, they prevented Americans from selling munitions to foreign belligerents. (782)

Neutrality Proclamation (1793): Issued by George Washington, it proclaimed America's formal neutrality in the escalating conflict between England and France, a statement that enraged pro-French Jeffersonians. (190)

New Deal: The economic and political policies of Franklin Roosevelt's administration in the 1930s, which aimed to solve the problems of the Great Depression by providing relief for the unemployed and launching efforts to stimulate economic recovery. The New Deal built on reforms of the progressive era to expand greatly an American-style welfare state. (753)

New England Confederation (1643): Weak union of the colonies in Massachusetts and Connecticut led by Puritans for the purposes of defense and organization, an early attempt at self-government during the benign neglect of the English Civil War. (48)

New England Emigrant Aid Company (founded 1854): Organization created to facilitate the migration of free laborers to Kansas in order to prevent the establishment of slavery in the territory. (398)

New Freedom (1912): Platform of reforms advocated by Woodrow Wilson in his first presidential campaign, including stronger antitrust legislation to protect small business enterprises from monopolies, banking reform, and tariff reductions. Wilson's strategy involved taking action to increase opportunities for capitalist competition rather than increasing government regulation of large trusts. (661)

New Frontier (1961–1963): President Kennedy's nickname for his domestic policy agenda. Buoyed by youthful optimism, the program included proposals for the Peace Corps and efforts to improve education and health care. (889)

New Harmony (1825–1827): Communal society of around one thousand members, established in New Harmony, Indiana by Robert Owen. The community attracted a hodgepodge of individuals, from scholars to crooks, and fell apart due to infighting and confusion after just two years. (320)

New Immigrants: Immigrants from southern and eastern Europe who formed a recognizable wave of immigration from the 1880s until 1924, in contrast to the immigrants from western Europe who had come before them. These new immigrants congregated in ethnic urban neighborhoods, where they worried many native-born Americans, some of whom responded with nativist anti-immigrant campaigns and others of whom introduced urban reforms to help the immigrants assimilate. (543)

New Jersey Plan (1787): "Small-state plan" put forth at the Philadelphia convention, proposing equal representation by state, regardless of population, in a unicameral legislature. Small states feared that the more populous states would dominate the agenda under a proportional system. (170)

new lights: Ministers who took part in the revivalist, emotive religious tradition pioneered by George Whitefield during the Great Awakening. (88)

New Nationalism (1912): State-interventionist reform program devised by journalist Herbert Croly and advocated by Theodore Roosevelt during his Bull Moose presidential campaign. Roosevelt did not object to continued consolidation of trusts and labor unions. Rather, he sought to create stronger regulatory agencies to insure that they operated to serve the public interest, not just private gain. (662)

New Orleans, Battle of (January 1815): Resounding victory of American forces against the British, restoring American confidence and fueling an outpouring of nationalism. Final battle of the War of 1812. (226)

New York draft riots (1863): Uprising, mostly of working-class Irish-Americans, in protest of the draft. Rioters were particularly incensed by the ability of the rich to hire substitutes or purchase exemptions. (429)

New York slave revolt (1712): Uprising of approximately two dozen slaves that resulted in the deaths of nine whites and the brutal execution of twenty-one participating blacks. (67)

Nine-Power Treaty (1922): Agreement coming out of the Washington "Disarmament" Conference of 1921–1922 that pledged Britain, France, Italy, Japan, the United States, China, the Netherlands, Portugal, and Belgium to abide by the Open Door Policy in China. The Five-Power Naval Treaty on ship ratios and the Four-Power Treaty to preserve the status quo in the Pacific also came out of the conference. (731)

Nineteenth Amendment (1920): This Constitutional amendment, finally passed by Congress in 1919 and ratified in 1920, gave women the right to vote over seventy years after the first organized calls for woman's suffrage in Seneca Falls, New York. (684)

Nixon Doctrine: President Nixon's plan for "peace with honor" in Vietnam. The doctrine stated that the United States would honor its existing defense commitments but, in the future, countries would have to fight their own wars. (917)

No Child Left Behind Act (2001): An education bill created and signed by the George W. Bush administration. Designed to increase accountability standards for primary and secondary schools, the law authorized several federal programs to monitor those standards and increased choices for parents in selecting schools for their children. The program was highly controversial, in large part because it linked results on standardized to federal funding for schools and school districts. (979)

noche triste **(June 30, 1520):** "Sad night", when the Aztecs attacked Hernán Cortés and his forces in the Aztec capital, Tenochitlán, killing hundreds. Cortés laid siege to the city the following year, precipitating the fall of the Aztec Empire and inaugurating three centuries of Spanish rule. (19)

nonimportation agreements (1765 and after): Boycotts against British goods adopted in response to the Stamp Act and, later, the Townshend and Intolerable Acts. The agreements were the most effective form of protest against British policies in the colonies. (117)

Non-Intercourse Act (1809): Passed alongside the repeal of the Embargo Act, it reopened trade with all but the two belligerent nations, Britain and France. The Act continued Jefferson's policy of economic coercion, still with little effect. (218)

Norris-La Guardia Anti-Injunction Act (1932): This law banned "yellow-dog," or anti-union, work contracts and forbade federal courts from issuing injunctions to quash strikes and boycotts. It was an early piece of labor-friendly federal legislation. (746)

North American Free Trade Agreement (NAFTA) (1993): Free trade zone encompassing Mexico, Canada, and the United States. A symbol of the increased reality of a globalized market place, the treaty passed despite opposition from protectionists and labor leaders. (969)

North Atlantic Treaty Organization (NATO): Military alliance of Western European powers and the United States and Canada established in 1949 to defend against the common threat from the Soviet Union, marking a giant stride forward for European unity and American internationalism. (849)

Northwest Ordinance (1787): Created a policy for administering the Northwest Territories. It included a path to statehood and forbade the expansion of slavery into the territories. (166)

Nullification Crisis (1832–1833): Showdown between President Andrew Jackson and the South Carolina legislature, which declared the 1832 tariff null and void in the state and threatened secession if the federal government tried to collect duties. It was resolved by a compromise negotiated by Henry Clay in 1833. (255)

Nuremberg war crimes trial (1946): Highly publicized proceedings against former Nazi leaders for war crimes and crimes against humanity as part of the Allies denazification program in postwar Germany. The trials led to several executions and long prison sentences. (845)

Office of Price Administration (OPA) (1941–1947): A critically important wartime agency charged with regulating the consumer economy through rationing scarce supplies, such as automobiles, tires, fuel, nylon, and sugar, and by curbing inflation by setting ceilings on the price of goods. Rents were controlled as well in parts of the country overwhelmed by war workers. The OPA was extended after World War II ended to continue the fight against inflation, but was abolished in 1947. (802)

Oklahoma City bombing (1995): Truck-bomb explosion that killed 168 people in a federal office building on

April 19, 1995. The attack was perpetrated by right-wing and anti-government militant Timothy McVeigh, later executed by the U.S. government for the crime. (967)

old lights: Orthodox clergymen who rejected the emotionalism of the Great Awakening in favor of a more rational spirituality. (88)

Old Northwest: Territories acquired by the federal government from the states, encompassing land northwest of the Ohio River, east of the Mississippi River, and south of the Great Lakes. The well-organized management and sale of the land in the territories under the land ordinances of 1785 and 1787 established a precedent for handling future land acquisitions. (165)

Olive Branch Petition (July 1775): Conciliatory measure adopted by the Continental Congress, professing American loyalty and seeking an end to the hostilities. King George rejected the petition and proclaimed the colonies in rebellion. (133)

Oneida Community: One of the more radical utopian communities established in the nineteenth century, it advocated "free love," birth control, and eugenics. Utopian communities reflected the reformist spirit of the age. (320)

Open Door note (1899–1900): A set of diplomatic letters in which Secretary of State John Hay urged the great powers to respect Chinese rights and free and open competition within their spheres of influence. The notes established the "Open Door Policy," which sought to ensure access to the Chinese market for the United States, despite the fact that the U.S. did not have a formal sphere of influence in China. (623)

Operation Desert Storm (1991): U.S.-led multi-country military engagement in January and February of 1991 that drove Saddam Hussein's Iraqi army out of neighboring Kuwait. In addition to presaging the longer and more protracted Iraq War of the 2000s, the 1991 war helped undo what some called the "Vietnam Syndrome," a feeling of military uncertainty that plagued many Americans. (959)

Operation Dixie (1948): Failed effort by the CIO after World War II to unionize southern workers, especially in textile factories. (830)

Operation Wetback (1954): A government program to roundup and deport as many as one million illegal Mexican migrant workers in the United States. The program was promoted in part by the Mexican government and reflected burgeoning concerns about non-European immigration to America. (873)

Opium War (1839–1842): War between Britain and China over trading rights, particularly Britain's desire to continue selling opium to Chinese traders. The resulting trade agreement prompted Americans to seek similar concessions from the Chinese. (390)

Orders in Council (1806–1807): Edicts issued by the British Crown closing French-owned European ports to foreign shipping. The French responded by ordering the seizure of all vessels entering British ports, thereby cutting off American merchants from trade with both parties. (216)

Organization of Petroleum Exporting Countries (OPEC): Cartel comprising Middle Eastern states and Venezuela first organized in 1960. OPEC aimed to control access to and prices of oil, wresting power from Western oil companies and investors. In the process, it gradually strengthened the hand of non-Western powers on the world stage. (876)

Ostend Manifesto (1854): Secret Franklin Pierce administration proposal to purchase or, that failing, to wrest militarily Cuba from Spain. Once leaked, it was quickly abandoned due to vehement opposition from the North. (390)

Pacific Railroad Act (1862): Helped fund the construction of the Union Pacific transcontinental railroad with the use of land grants and government bonds. (473)

panic of 1819: Severe financial crisis brought on primarily by the efforts of the Bank of the United States to curb overspeculation on western lands. It disproportionately affected the poorer classes, especially in the West, sowing the seeds of Jacksonian Democracy. (233)

panic of 1837: Economic crisis triggered by bank failures, elevated grain prices, and Andrew Jackson's efforts to curb overspeculation on western lands and transportation improvements. In response, President Martin Van Buren proposed the "Divorce Bill," which pulled treasury funds out of the banking system altogether, contracting the credit supply. (264)

panic of 1857: Financial crash brought on by gold-fueled inflation, overspeculation, and excess grain production. Raised calls in the North for higher tariffs and for free homesteads on western public lands. (404)

panic of 1873: A world-wide depression that began in the United States when one of the nation's largest banks abruptly declared bankruptcy, leading to the collapse of thousands of banks and businesses. The crisis intensified debtors' calls for inflationary measures such as the printing of more paper money and the unlimited coinage of silver. Conflicts over monetary policy greatly influenced politics in the last quarter of the nineteenth century. (491)

Paris, Treaty of (1783): Peace treaty signed by Britain and the United States ending the Revolutionary War. The British formally recognized American independence and ceded territory east of the Mississippi while the Americans, in turn, promised to restore Loyalist property and repay debts to British creditors. (151)

Patent Office: Federal government bureau that reviews patent applications. A patent is a legal recognition of a new invention, granting exclusive rights to the inventor for a period of years. (290)

Patient Protection and Affordable Care Act (2010): Also known, somewhat derisively, as "Obamacare," the Act extended health care insurance to some 30 million Americans, marking a major step toward achieving the century-old goal of universal health care coverage for all citizens. (986)

Patriots: colonists who supported the American Revolution; they were also known as "Whigs." (139)

patronage: A system, prevalent during the Gilded Age, in which political parties granted jobs and favors to party regulars who delivered votes on election day. Patronage was both an essential wellspring of support for both parties and a source of conflict within the Republican party. (207)

patronage: Practice of rewarding political support with special favors, often in the form of public office. Upon assuming office, Thomas Jefferson dismissed few Federalist employees, leaving scant openings to fill with political appointees. (493)

patroonships: Vast tracts of land along the Hudson River in New Netherlands granted to wealthy promoters in exchange for bringing fifty settlers to the property. (51)

Paxton Boys (1764): Armed march on Philadelphia by Scotts-Irish frontiersmen in protest against the Quaker establishment's lenient policies toward Native Americans. (80)

Payne-Aldrich Bill (1909): While intended to lower tariff rates, this bill was eventually revised beyond all recognition, retaining high rates on most imports. President Taft angered the progressive wing of his party when he declared it "the best bill that the Republican party ever passed." (658)

Peace Corps: A federal agency created by President Kennedy in 1961 to promote voluntary service by Americans in foreign countries. The Peace Corps provides labor power to help developing countries improve their infrastructure, health care, educational systems, and other aspects of their societies. Part of Kennedy's New Frontier vision, the organization represented an effort by postwar liberals to promote American values and influence through productive exchanges across the world. (889)

Pearl Harbor (1941): An American naval base in Hawaii where Japanese warplanes destroyed numerous ships and caused 3,000 casualties on December 7, 1941—a day that, in President Roosevelt's words, was to "live in infamy." The attack brought the United States into World War II. (794)

peculiar institution: Widely used term for the institution of American slavery in the South. Its use in the first half of the 19th century reflected a growing division between the North, where slavery was gradually abolished, and the South, where slavery became increasingly entrenched. (234)

Pendleton Act (1883): Congressional legislation that established the Civil Service Commission, which granted federal government jobs on the basis of examinations instead of political patronage, thus reigning in the spoils system. (499)

Peninsula Campaign (1862): Union General George B. McClellan's failed effort to seize Richmond, the Confederate Capital. Had McClellan taken Richmond and toppled the Confederacy, slavery would have most likely survived in the South for some time. (437)

Pentagon Papers: Secret U.S. government report detailing early planning and policy decisions regarding the Vietnam War under Presidents Kennedy and Johnson. Leaked to the *New York Times* in 1971, it revealed instances of governmental secrecy, lies, and incompetence in the prosecution of the war. (919)

Pequot War (1636–1638): Series of clashes between English settlers and Pequot Indians in the Connecticut River valley. Ended in the slaughter of the Pequots by the Puritans and their Narragansett Indian allies. (47)

Perestroika: Meaning "restructuring," a cornerstone along with *Glasnost* of Soviet president Mikhail Gorbachev's reform movement in the USSR in the 1980s. These policies resulted in greater market liberalization, access to the West, and ultimately the end of communist rule. (949)

pet banks: Popular term for pro-Jackson state banks that received the bulk of federal deposits when Andrew Jackson moved to dismantle the Bank of the United States in 1833. (262)

Philadelphia Plan (1969): Program established by Richard Nixon to require construction trade unions to work toward hiring more black apprentices. The plan altered Lyndon Johnson's concept of "affirmative action" to focus on groups rather than individuals. (921)

Pinckney's Treaty (1795): Signed with Spain which, fearing an Anglo-American alliance, granted Americans free navigation of the Mississippi and the disputed territory of Florida. (193)

plantation: Large-scale agricultural enterprise growing commercial crops and usually employing coerced or slave labor. European settlers established plantations in Africa, South America, the Caribbean, and the American South. (12)

Platt Amendment (1901): Following its military occupation, the United States successfully pressured the Cuban government to write this amendment into its constitution. It limited Cuba's treaty-making abilities, controlled its debt, and stipulated that the United States could intervene militarily to restore order when it saw fit. (621)

Plessy v. Ferguson **(1896):** An 1896 Supreme Court case that upheld the constitutionality of segregation laws, saying that as long as blacks were provided with "separate but equal" facilities, these laws did not violate the Fourteenth Amendment. This decision provided legal justification for the Jim Crow system until the 1950s. (496)

policy of boldness (1954): Foreign policy objective of Dwight Eisenhower's Secretary of State John Foster Dulles, who believed in changing the containment strategy to one that more directly engaged the Soviet Union and attempted to roll back communist influence around the world. This policy led to a build-up of America's nuclear arsenal to threaten "massive retaliation" against communist enemies, launching the Cold War's arms race. (874)

Pontiac's uprising (1763): Bloody campaign waged by Ottawa chief Pontiac to drive the British out of Ohio Country. It was brutally crushed by British troops, who resorted to distributing blankets infected with smallpox as a means to put down the rebellion. (109)

Pony Express (1860–1861): Short-lived, speedy mail service between Missouri and California that relied on lightweight riders galloping between closely placed outposts. (301)

Poor Richard's Almanack **(1732–1758):** Widely read annual pamphlet edited by Benjamin Franklin. Best known for its proverbs and aphorisms emphasizing thrift, industry, morality, and common sense. (91)

Popé's Rebellion (1680): Pueblo Indian rebellion that drove Spanish settlers from New Mexico. (21)

popular sovereignty: (in the context of the slavery debate) Notion that the sovereign people of a given territory should decide whether to allow slavery. Seemingly a compromise, it was largely opposed by Northern abolitionists who feared it would promote the spread of slavery to the territories. (378)

Populists: Officially known as the People's party, the Populists represented Westerners and Southerners who believed that U.S. economic policy inappropriately favored Eastern businessmen instead of the nation's farmers. Their proposals included nationalizing the railroads, creating a graduated income tax, and most significantly the unlimited coinage of silver. (598)

Potsdam conference (1945): From July 17 to August 2, 1945, President Harry S Truman met with Soviet leader Joseph Stalin and British leaders Winston Churchill and later Clement Attlee (when the Labour party defeated Churchill's Conservative party) near Berlin to deliver an ultimatum to Japan: surrender or be destroyed. (820)

pragmatism: A distinctive American philosophy that emerged in the late nineteenth century around the theory that the true value of an idea lay in its ability to solve problems. The pragmatists thus embraced the provisional, uncertain nature of experimental knowledge. Among the most well-known purveyors of pragmatism were John Dewey, Oliver Wendell Holmes, Jr., and William James. (557)

predestination: Calvinist doctrine that God has foreordained some people to be saved and some to be damned. Though their fate was irreversible, Calvinists, particularly those who believed they were destined for salvation, sought to lead sanctified lives in order to demonstrate to others that they were in fact members of the "elect." (41)

primogeniture: Legal principle that the oldest son inherits all family property or land. Landowner's younger sons, forced to seek their fortunes elsewhere, pioneered early exploration and settlement of the Americas. (27)

privateers: Privately owned armed ships authorized by Congress to prey on enemy shipping during the Revolutionary War. Privateers, more numerous than the tiny American Navy, inflicted heavy damages on British shippers. (149)

Proclamation of 1763: Decree issued by Parliament in the wake of Pontiac's uprising, prohibiting settlement beyond the Appalachians. Contributed to rising resentment of British rule in the American colonies. (111)

Proposition 13 (1978): A successful California state ballot initiative that capped the state's real estate tax at 1 percent of assessed value. The proposition radically reduced average property tax levels, decreasing revenue for the state government and signaling the political power of the "tax revolt," increasingly aligned with conservative politics. (945)

proprietary colonies: Colonies—Maryland, Pennsylvania, and Delaware—under the control of local proprietors, who appointed colonial governors. (92)

Protestant Reformation (16th Century): Movement to reform the Catholic Church launched in Germany by Martin Luther. Reformers questioned the authority of the Pope, sought to eliminate the selling of indulgences, and encouraged the translation of the Bible from Latin, which few at the time could read. The reformation was launched in England in the 1530s when King Henry VIII broke with the Roman Catholic Church. (24)

Pullman strike (1894): An 1894 strike by railroad workers upset by drastic wage cuts. The strike was led by socialist Eugene Debs but not supported by the American Federation of Labor. Eventually President Grover Cleveland intervened and federal troops forced an end to the strike. The strike highlighted both divisions within labor and the government's new willingness to use armed force to combat work stoppages. (599)

Pure Food and Drug Act (1906): A law passed by Congress to inspect and regulate the labeling of all foods and pharmaceuticals intended for human consumption. This legislation, and additional provisions passed in 1911 to strengthen it, aimed particularly at the patent medicine industry. The more comprehensive Food, Drug, and Cosmetic Act of 1938 largely replaced this legislation. (650)

Puritans: English Protestant reformers who sought to purify the Church of England of Catholic rituals and creeds. Some of the most devout Puritans believed that only "visible saints" should be admitted to church membership. (42)

Quakers: Religious group known for their tolerance, emphasis on peace, and idealistic Indian policy, who settled heavily in Pennsylvania in the seventeenth and eighteenth centuries. (53)

Quarantine Speech (1937): An important speech delivered by Franklin Roosevelt in which he called for "positive endeavors" to "quarantine" land-hungry dictators, presumably through economic embargos. The speech flew in the face of isolationist politicians. (784)

Quartering Act (1765): Required colonies to provide food and quarters for British troops. Many colonists resented the act, which they perceived as an encroachment on their rights. (116)

Quebec Act (1774): Allowed the French residents of Québec to retain their traditional political and religious institutions, and extended the boundaries of the province southward to the Ohio River. Mistakenly perceived by the colonists to be part of Parliament's response to the Boston Tea Party. (122)

Québec, Battle of (1759): Historic British victory over French forces on the outskirts of Québec. The surrender of Québec marked the beginning of the end of French rule in North America. (107)

Queen Anne's War (1702–1713): Second in a series of conflicts between the European powers for control of North America, fought between the English and French colonists in the North, and the English and Spanish in Florida.

Under the peace treaty, the French ceded Acadia (Nova Scotia), Newfoundland, and Hudson Bay to Britain. (100)

racketeers: People who obtain money illegally by fraud, bootlegging, gambling, or threats of violence. Racketeers invaded the ranks of labor during the 1920s, a decade when gambling and gangsterism were prevalent in American life. (708)

radical Whigs: Eighteenth-century British political commentators who agitated against political corruption and emphasized the threat to liberty posed by arbitrary power. Their writings shaped American political thought and made colonists especially alert to encroachments on their rights. (113)

Reaganomics: Informal term for Ronald Reagan's economic policies, which focused on reducing taxes, social spending, and government regulation, while increasing outlays for defense. (946)

realism: Mid-nineteenth-century movement in European and American literature and the arts that sought to depict contemporary life and society as it actually was, in all its unvarnished detail. Adherents eschewed the idealism and nostalgia of the earlier romantic sensibility. (566)

recall: A progressive ballot procedure allowing voters to remove elected officials from office. (641)

Reciprocal Trade Agreements Act (1934): This act reversed traditional high-protective-tariff policies by allowing the president to negotiate lower tariffs with trade partners, without Senate approval. Its chief architect was Secretary of State Cordell Hull, who believed that tariff barriers choked off foreign trade. (780)

Reconstruction Act (1867): Passed by the newly elected Republican Congress, it divided the South into five military districts, disenfranchised former confederates, and required that Southern states both ratify the Fourteenth Amendment and write state constitutions guaranteeing freedmen the franchise before gaining readmission to the Union. (475)

Reconstruction Finance Corporation (RFC) (1932): A government lending agency established under the Hoover administration in order to assist insurance companies, banks, agricultural organizations, railroads, and local governments. It was a precursor to later agencies that grew out of the New Deal and symbolized a recognition by the Republicans that some federal action was required to address the Great Depression. (746)

red scare (1919–1920): A period of intense anti-communism lasting from 1919 to 1920. The "Palmer raids" of Attorney General A. Mitchell Palmer resulted in about six thousand deportations of people suspected of "subversive" activities. (700)

Redeemers: Southern Democratic politicians who sought to wrest control from Republican regimes in the South after Reconstruction. (476)

referendum: A progressive reform procedure allowing voters to place a bill on the ballot for final approval, even after being passed by the legislature. (641)

Reform Bill of 1867: Granted suffrage to all male British citizens, dramatically expanding the electorate. The success of the American democratic experiment, reinforced by the Union victory in the Civil War, was used as one of the arguments in favor of the Bill. (461)

regionalism: A recurring artistic movement that, in the context of the late nineteenth century, aspired to capture the peculiarities, or "local color," of America's various regions in the face of modernization and national standardization. (567)

regulars: Trained professional soldiers, as distinct from militia or conscripts. During the French and Indian War, British generals, used to commanding experienced regulars, often showed contempt for ill-trained colonial militiamen. (106)

Regulator movement (1768–1771): Eventually violent uprising of backcountry settlers in North Carolina against unfair taxation and the control of colonial affairs by the seaboard elite. (80)

Reign of Terror (1793–1794): Ten-month period of brutal repression when some 40,000 individuals were executed as enemies of the French Revolution. While many Jeffersonians maintained their faith in the French Republic, Federalists withdrew their already lukewarm support once the Reign of Terror commenced. (190)

rendezvous: The principal marketplace of the Northwest fur trade, which peaked in the 1820s and 1830s. Each summer, traders set up camps in the Rocky Mountains to exchange manufactured goods for beaver pelts. (277)

republican motherhood: Ideal of family organization and female behavior after the American Revolution that stressed the role of women in guiding family members toward republican virtue. (159)

republicanism: Political theory of representative government, based on the principle of popular sovereignty, with a strong emphasis on liberty and civic virtue. Influential in eighteenth-century American political thought, it stood as an alternative to monarchical rule. (113)

reservation system: The system that allotted land with designated boundaries to Native American tribes in the West, beginning in the 1850s and ending with the Dawes Severalty Act of 1887. Within these reservations, most land was used communally, rather than owned individually. The U.S. government encouraged and sometimes violently coerced Native Americans to stay on the reservations at all times. (576)

responsorial: Call and response style of preaching that melded Christian and African traditions. Practiced by African slaves in the South. (348)

Revolution of 1800: Electoral victory of Democratic Republicans over the Federalists, who lost their Congressional majority and the presidency. The peaceful transfer of power between rival parties solidified faith in America's political system. (204)

Roanoke Island (1585): Sir Walter Raleigh's failed colonial settlement off the coast of North Carolina. (25)

rock 'n' roll: "Crossover" musical style that rose to dominance in the 1950s, merging black rhythm and blues with white bluegrass and country. Featuring a heavy beat and driving rhythm, rock 'n' roll music became a defining feature of the 1950s youth culture. (863)

Roe v. Wade (1973): Landmark Supreme Court decision that forbade states from barring abortion by citing a woman's constitutional right to privacy. Seen as a victory for feminism and civil liberties by some, the decision provoked a strong counter-reaction by opponents to abortion, galvanizing the Pro-Life movement. (932)

romanticism: Early-nineteenth-century movement in European and American literature and the arts that, in reaction to the hyper-rational Enlightenment, emphasized imagination over reason, nature over civilization, intuition over calculation, and the self over society. (326)

Rome-Berlin Axis (1936): Nazi Germany, under Adolf Hitler, and Fascist Italy, led by Benito Mussolini, allied themselves together under this nefarious treaty. The pact was signed after both countries had intervened on behalf of the fascist leader Francisco Franco during the Spanish Civil War. (781)

Roosevelt Corollary (1904): A brazen policy of "preventive intervention" advocated by Theodore Roosevelt in his Annual Message to Congress in 1904. Adding ballast to the Monroe Doctrine, his corollary stipulated that the United States would retain a right to intervene in the domestic affairs of Latin American nations in order to restore military and financial order. (630)

Root-Takahira agreement (1908): Signed on November 30, 1908, the United States and Japan agreed to respect each other's territorial possessions in the Pacific and to uphold the Open Door in China. The Agreement was credited with easing tensions between the two nations, but it also resulted in a weakened American influence over further Japanese hegemony in China. (631)

Rough Riders (1898): Organized by Theodore Roosevelt, this was a colorful, motley regiment of Cuban war volunteers consisting of western cowboys, ex-convicts, and effete Ivy Leaguers. Roosevelt emphasized his experience with the regiment in subsequent campaigns for Governor of New York and Vice-President under William McKinley. (615)

Royal African Company: English joint-stock company that enjoyed a state-granted monopoly on the colonial slave trade from 1672 until 1698. The supply of slaves to the North American colonies rose sharply once the company lost its monopoly privileges. (66)

royal colonies: Colonies where governors were appointed directly by the King. Though often competent administrators, the governors frequently ran into trouble with colonial legislatures, which resented the imposition of control from across the Atlantic. (92)

Rush-Bagot agreement (1817): Signed by Britain and the United States, it established strict limits on naval armaments in the Great Lakes, a first step in the full demilitarization of the U.S.-Canadian border, completed in the 1870s. (230)

Russo-American Treaty (1824): Fixed the line of 54°40' as the southernmost boundary of Russian holdings in North America. (243)

Salem witch trials (1692–1693): Series of witchcraft trials launched after a group of adolescent girls in Salem, Massachusetts, claimed to have been bewitched by certain older women of the town. Twenty individuals were put to death before the trials were put to an end by the Governor of Massachusetts. (74)

SALT II: Strategic Arms Limitation Treaty agreement between Soviet leader Leonid Brezhnev and American president Jimmy Carter. Despite an accord to limit weapons between the two leaders, the agreement was ultimately scuttled in the U.S. Senate following the Soviet invasion of Afghanistan in 1979. (938)

salutary neglect (1688–1763): Unofficial policy of relaxed royal control over colonial trade and only weak enforcement of Navigation Laws. Lasted from the Glorious Revolution to the end of the French and Indian War in 1763. (50)

San Jacinto, Battle of (1836): Resulted in the capture of Mexican dictator Santa Anna, who was forced to withdraw his troops from Texas and recognize the Rio Grande as Texas's Southwestern border. (267)

Sandinistas: Leftwing anti-American revolutionaries in Nicaragua who launched a civil war in 1979. (947)

Saratoga, Battle of (October 1777): Decisive colonial victory in upstate New York, which helped secure French support for the Revolutionary cause. (145)

scalawags: Derogatory term for pro-Union Southerners whom Southern Democrats accused of plundering the resources of the South in collusion with Republican governments after the Civil War. (478)

Schenck v. United States (1919): A Supreme Court decision that upheld the Espionage and Sedition Acts, reasoning that freedom of speech could be curtailed when it posed a "clear and present danger" to the nation. (681)

Scientific Management: A system of industrial management created and promoted in the early twentieth century by Frederick W. Taylor, emphasizing stopwatch efficiency to improve factory performance. The system gained immense popularity across the United States and Europe. (711)

Second Anglo-Powhatan War (1644–1646): Last-ditch effort by the Indians to dislodge Virginia settlements. The resulting peace treaty formally separated white and Indian areas of settlement. (29)

Second Battle of Bull Run (August 1862): Civil War battle that ended in a decisive victory for Confederate General Robert E. Lee, who was emboldened to push further into the North. (440)

Second Continental Congress (1775–1781): Representative body of delegates from all thirteen colonies. Drafted the Declaration of Independence and managed the colonial war effort. (132)

Second Great Awakening (early nineteenth century): Religious revival characterized by emotional mass "camp meetings" and widespread conversion. Brought about a democratization of religion as a multiplicity of denominations vied for members. (308)

Sedition Act (1798): Enacted by the Federalist Congress in an effort to clamp down on Jeffersonian opposition, the law made anyone convicted of defaming government officials or interfering with government policies liable to imprisonment and a heavy fine. The act drew heavy criticism from Republicans, who let the act expire in 1801. (196)

"Self-Reliance" (1841): Ralph Waldo Emerson's popular lecture-essay that reflected the spirit of individualism pervasive in American popular culture during the 1830s and 1840s. (276)

Separatists: Small group of Puritans who sought to break away entirely from the Church of England; after initially settling in Holland, a number of English Separatists made their way to Plymouth Bay, Massachusetts in 1620. (42)

settlement houses: Mostly run by middle-class native-born women, settlement houses in immigrant neighborhoods provided housing, food, education, child care, cultural activities, and social connections for new arrivals to the United States. Many women, both native-born and immigrant, developed life-long passions for social activism in the settlement houses. Jane Addams's Hull House in Chicago and Lillian Wald's Henry Street Settlement in New York City were two of the most prominent. (549)

Seventh of March speech (1850): Daniel Webster's impassioned address urging the North to support of the Compromise of 1850. Webster argued that topography and climate would keep slavery from becoming entrenched in Mexican Cession territory and urged Northerners to make all reasonable concessions to prevent disunion. (383)

Seward's Folly (1867): Popular term for Secretary of State William Seward's purchase of Alaska from Russia. The derisive term reflected the anti-expansionist sentiments of most Americans immediately after the Civil War. (482)

Shakers (established c. 1770s): Called "Shakers" for their lively dance worship, they emphasized simple, communal living and were all expected to practice celibacy. First transplanted to America from England by Mother Ann Lee, the Shakers counted six thousand members by 1840, though by the 1940s the movement had largely died out. (320)

sharecropping: An agricultural system that emerged after the Civil War in which black and white farmers rented land and residences from a plantation owner in exchange for giving him a certain "share" of each year's crop. Sharecropping was the dominant form of southern agriculture after the Civil War, and landowners manipulated this system to keep tenants in perpetual debt and unable to leave their plantations. (496)

Shays's Rebellion (1786): Armed uprising of western Massachusetts debtors seeking lower taxes and an end to property foreclosures. Though quickly put down, the insurrection inspired fears of "mob rule" among leading Revolutionaries. (167)

Sheppard-Towner Maternity Act (1921): Designed to appeal to new women voters, this act provided federally financed instruction in maternal and infant health care and expanded the role of government in family welfare. (684)

Sherman Anti-Trust Act (1890): A law that forbade trusts or combinations in business, this was landmark legislation because it was one of the first Congressional attempts to regulate big business for the public good. At first the law was mostly used to restrain trade unions as the courts tended to side with companies in legal cases. In 1914 the Act was revised so it could more effectively be used against monopolistic corporations. (525)

Sherman's march (1864–1865): Union General William Tecumseh Sherman's destructive march through Georgia. An early instance of "total war," purposely targeting infrastructure and civilian property to diminish morale and undercut the Confederate war effort. (449)

Shiloh, Battle of (April 1862): Bloody Civil War battle on the Tennessee-Mississippi border that resulted in the deaths of more than 23,000 soldiers and ended in a marginal Union victory. (448)

silent majority: Nixon Administration's term to describe generally content, law-abiding middle-class Americans who supported both the Vietnam War and America's institutions. As a political tool, the concept attempted to make a subtle distinction between believers in "traditional" values and the vocal minority of civil rights agitators, student protesters, counter-culturalists, and other seeming disruptors of the social fabric. (918)

Six-Day War (1967): Military conflict between Israel and its Arab neighbors, including Syria, Egypt, and Jordan. The war ended with an Israeli victory and territorial expansion into the Sinai Peninsula, the Golan Heights, the Gaza Strip, and the West Bank. The 1967 war was a humiliation for several Arab states, and the territorial disputes it created formed the basis for continued conflict in the region. (907)

Slave Codes: Set of laws defining racial slavery beginning in 1662, including establishing the hereditary nature of slavery, and legally limiting the rights and learning of slaves. (66)

Smith-Connally Anti-Strike Act (1943): Passed amidst worries about the effects that labor strikes would have on war production, this law allowed the federal government to seize and operate plants threatened by labor disputes. It also criminalized strike action against government-run companies. (803)

"smoking gun" tape: Recording made in the Oval Office in June 1972 that proved conclusively that Nixon knew about the Watergate break-in and endeavored to cover it up. Led to complete break-down in Congressional support for Nixon after the Supreme Court ordered he hand the tape to investigators. (926)

Social Darwinists: Believers in the idea, popular in the late nineteenth century, that people gained wealth by "survival of the fittest." Therefore, the wealthy had simply won a natural competition and owed nothing to the poor, and indeed service to the poor would interfere with this organic process. Some social Darwinists also applied this theory to whole nations and races, explaining that powerful peoples were naturally endowed with gifts that allowed them to gain superiority over others. This theory provided one of the popular justifications for U.S. imperial ventures like the Spanish-American war. (525)

social gospel: A reform movement led by Protestant ministers who used religious doctrine to demand better housing and living conditions for the urban poor. Popular at the turn of the twentieth century, it was closely linked to the settlement house movement, which brought middle-class, Anglo-American service volunteers into contact with immigrants and working people. (639)

Social Security Act (1935): A flagship accomplishment of the New Deal, this law provided for unemployment and old-age insurance financed by a payroll tax on employers and employees. It has long remained a pillar of the "New Deal Order." (767)

Society of the Cincinnati (established 1783): Exclusive, hereditary organization of former officers in the Continental Army. Many resented the pretentiousness of the order, viewing it as a vestige of pre-Revolutionary traditions. (158)

Sons of Liberty: Patriotic groups that played a central role in agitating against the Stamp Act and enforcing non-importation agreements. (See also **Daughters of Liberty**) (117)

South Carolina slave revolt (Stono River) (1739): Uprising, also known as the Stono Rebellion, of more than fifty South Carolina blacks along the Stono River. The slaves attempted to reach Spanish Florida but were stopped by the South Carolina militia. (67)

Southern Renaissance: A literary outpouring among mid-twentieth-century southern writers, begun by William Faulkner and marked by a new critical appreciation of the region's burdens of history, racism, and conservatism. (886)

southern strategy (1972): Nixon reelection campaign strategy designed to appeal to conservative whites in the historically Democratic south. The President stressed law and order issues and remained noncommittal on civil rights. This strategy typified the regional split between the two parties as white Southerners became increasingly attracted to the Republican party in the aftermath of the Civil Rights Movement. (922)

Spanish Armada (1588): Spanish fleet defeated in the English Channel in 1588. The defeat of the Armada marked the beginning of the decline of the Spanish Empire. (25)

SPARs (U.S. Coast Guard Women's Reserve): See **WAACs (Women's Army Auxiliary Corps)**. (803)

Specie Circular (1836): U.S. Treasury decree requiring that all public lands be purchased with "hard," or metallic, currency. Issued after small state banks flooded the market with unreliable paper currency, fueling land speculation in the West. (262)

spoils system: Policy of rewarding political supporters with public office, first widely employed at the federal level by Andrew Jackson. The practice was widely abused by unscrupulous office seekers, but it also helped cement party loyalty in the emerging two-party system. (251)

spot resolutions (1846): Measures introduced by Illinois congressman Abraham Lincoln, questioning President James K. Polk's justification for war with Mexico. Lincoln requested that Polk clarify precisely where Mexican forces had attacked American troops. (370)

Sputnik (1957): Soviet satellite first launched into Earth orbit on October 4, 1957. This scientific achievement marked the first time human beings had put a man-made object into orbit and pushed the USSR noticeably ahead of the United States in the Space Race. A month later, the Soviet Union sent a larger satellite, *Sputnik II*, into space, prompting the United States to redouble its space exploration efforts and raising American fears of Soviet superiority. (877)

squatters: Frontier farmers who illegally occupied land owned by others or not yet officially opened for settlement. Many of North Carolina's early settlers were squatters, who contributed to the colony's reputation as being more independent-minded and "democratic" than its neighbors. (35)

Stamp Act Congress (1765): Assembly of delegates from nine colonies who met in New York City to draft a petition for the repeal of the Stamp Act. Helped ease sectional suspicions and promote intercolonial unity. (117)

stamp tax (1765): Widely unpopular tax on an array of paper goods, repealed in 1766 after mass protests erupted across the colonies. Colonists developed the principle of "no taxation without representation" that questioned Parliament's authority over the colonies and laid the foundation for future revolutionary claims. (116)

Standard Oil Company (1870–1911): John D. Rockefeller's company, formed in 1870, which came to symbolize the trusts and monopolies of the Gilded Age. By 1877 Standard Oil controlled 95% of the oil refineries in the U.S. It was also one of the first multinational corporations, and at times distributed more than half of the company's kerosene production outside the U.S. By the turn of the century it had become a target for trust-busting reformers, and in 1911 the Supreme Court ordered it to break up into several dozen smaller companies. (524)

Stonewall Rebellion (1969): Uprising in support of equal rights for gay people sparked by an assault by off-duty police officers at a gay bar in New York. The rebellion led to a rise in activism and militancy within the gay community and furthered the sexual revolution of the late 1960s. (913)

Strategic Defense Initiative (SDI): Reagan administration plan announced in 1983 to create a missile-defense system over American territory to block a nuclear attack. Derided as "Star Wars" by critics, the plan typified Reagan's commitment to vigorous defense spending even as he sought to limit the size of government in domestic matters. (946)

Student Nonviolent Coordinating Committee (SNCC): Youth organization founded by southern black students in 1960 to promote civil rights. Drawing on its members' youthful energies, SNCC in its early years coordinated demonstrations, sit-ins, and voter registration drives. (872)

Students for a Democratic Society (SDS): A campus-based political organization founded in 1961 by Tom Hayden that became an iconic representation of the New Left. Originally geared toward the intellectual promise of "participatory democracy," SDS emerged at the forefront of the civil rights, antipoverty, and antiwar movements during the 1960s. (913)

Suez crisis (1956): International crisis launched when Egyptian president Gamal Abdel Nasser nationalized the Suez Canal, which had been owned mostly by French and British stockholders. The crisis led to a British and French attack on Egypt, which failed without aid from the United States. The Suez crisis marked an important turning point in the post-colonial Middle East and highlighted the rising importance of oil in world affairs. (875)

Sugar Act (1764): Duty on imported sugar from the West Indies. It was the first tax levied on the colonists by the crown and was lowered substantially in response to widespread protests. (115)

Sunbelt: The fifteen-state crescent through the American South and Southwest that experienced terrific population and productivity expansion during World War II and particularly in the decades after the war, eclipsing the old industrial Northeast (the "Frostbelt"). (835)

supply-side economics: Economic theory that underlay Ronald Reagan's tax and spending cuts. Contrary to Keynesianism, supply-side theory declared that government policy should aim to increase the supply of goods and services, rather than the demand for them. It held that lower taxes and decreased regulation would increase productivity by providing increased incentives to work, thus increasing productivity and the tax base. (945)

Taft-Hartley Act (1947): Republican-promoted, anti-union legislation passed over President Truman's vigorous veto that weakened many of labor's New Deal gains by banning the closed shop and other strategies that helped unions organize. It also required union leaders to take a noncommunist oath, which purged the union movement of many of its most committed and active organizers. (830)

Tallmadge amendment (1819): Failed proposal to prohibit the importation of slaves into Missouri territory and pave the way for gradual emancipation. Southerners vehemently opposed the amendment, which they perceived as a threat to the sectional balance between North and South. (234)

Tammany Hall (established 1789): Powerful New York political machine that primarily drew support from the city's immigrants, who depended on Tammany Hall patronage, particularly social services. (281)

Tampico Incident (1914): An arrest of American sailors by the Mexican government that spurred Woodrow Wilson to dispatch the American navy to seize the port of Veracruz in April 1914. Although war was avoided, tensions grew between the United States and Mexico. (669)

tariff: Tax levied on imports. Traditionally, manufacturers support tariffs as protective and revenue-raising measures, while agricultural interests, dependent on world markets, oppose high tariffs. (184)

Tariff of 1816: First protective tariff in American history, created primarily to shield New England manufacturers from the inflow of British goods after the War of 1812. (231)

Tariff of 1842: Protective measure passed by Congressional Whigs, raising tariffs to pre-Compromise of 1833 rates. (361)

Tariff of 1857: Lowered duties on imports in response to a high Treasury surplus and pressure from Southern farmers. (405)

Tariff of Abominations (1828): Noteworthy for its unprecedentedly high duties on imports. Southerners vehemently opposed the Tariff, arguing that it hurt Southern farmers, who did not enjoy the protection of tariffs, but were forced to pay higher prices for manufactures. (254)

Teapot Dome scandal (1921): A tawdry affair involving the illegal lease of priceless naval oil reserves in Teapot Dome, Wyoming and Elk Hills, California. The scandal, which implicated President Harding's Secretary of the Interior, was one of several that gave his administration a reputation for corruption. (733)

Teller Amendment (1898): A proviso to President William McKinley's war plans that proclaimed to the world that when the United States had overthrown Spanish misrule, it would give Cuba its freedom. The amendment testified to the ostensibly "anti-imperialist" designs of the initial war plans. (614)

Tennessee Valley Authority (TVA) (1933): One of the most revolutionary of the New Deal public works projects, the TVA brought cheap electric power, full employment, low-cost housing, and environmental improvements to Americans in the Tennessee Valley. (766)

Tenure of Office Act (1867): Required the President to seek approval from the Senate before removing appointees. When Andrew Johnson removed his secretary of war in violation of the act, he was impeached by the house but remained in office when the Senate fell one vote short of removing him. (480)

Thirteenth Amendment (1865): Constitutional amendment prohibiting all forms of slavery and involuntary servitude. Former Confederate States were required to ratify the amendment prior to gaining reentry into the Union. (441)

three-fifths compromise (1787): Determined that each slave would be counted as three-fifths of a person for the purpose of apportioning taxes and representation. The compromise granted disproportionate political power to Southern slave states. (172)

three-sister farming: Agricultural system employed by North American Indians as early as 1000 A.D.; maize, beans, and squash were grown together to maximize yields. (8)

Tippecanoe, Battle of (1811): Resulted in the defeat of Shawnee chief Tenskwatawa, "the Prophet" at the hands William Henry Harrison in the Indiana wilderness. After the battle, the Prophet's brother, Tecumseh, forged an alliance with the British against the United States. (219)

Tordesillas, Treaty of (1494): Signed by Spain and Portugal, dividing the territories of the New World. Spain received the bulk of territory in the Americas, compensating Portugal with titles to lands in Africa and Asia. (15)

Townshend Acts (1767): External, or indirect, levies on glass, white lead, paper, paint and tea, the proceeds of which were used to pay colonial governors, who had previously been paid directly by colonial assemblies. Sparked another round of protests in the colonies. (118)

Trail of Tears (1838–1839): Forced march of 15,000 Cherokee Indians from their Georgia and Alabama homes to Indian Territory. Some 4,000 Cherokee died on the arduous journey. (258)

transcendentalism (mid-nineteenth century): Literary and intellectual movement that emphasized individualism and self-reliance, predicated upon a belief that each person possesses an "inner-light" that can point the way to truth and direct contact with God. (327)

transportation revolution: Term referring to a series of nineteenth-century transportation innovations—turnpikes, steamboats, canals, and railroads—that linked local and regional markets, creating a national economy. (302)

Trent affair (1861): Diplomatic row that threatened to bring the British into the Civil War on the side of the Confederacy, after a Union warship stopped a British steamer and arrested two Confederate diplomats on board. (427)

Trenton, Battle of (December 1776): George Washington surprised and captured a garrison of sleeping German Hessians, raising the morale of his crestfallen army and setting the stage for his victory at Princeton a week later. (144)

triangular trade: Exchange of rum, slaves, and molasses between the North American Colonies, Africa, and the West Indies. A small but immensely profitable subset of the Atlantic trade. (83)

Tripolitan War (1801–1805): Four-year conflict between the American Navy and the North-African nation of Tripoli over piracy in the Mediterranean. Jefferson, a staunch noninterventionist, reluctantly deployed American forces, eventually securing a peace treaty with Tripoli. (210)

Truman Doctrine (1947): President Truman's universal pledge of support for any people fighting any communist or communist-inspired threat. Truman presented the doctrine to Congress in 1947 in support of his request for $400 million to defend Greece and Turkey against Soviet-backed insurgencies. (846)

trust: A mechanism by which one company grants control over its operations, through ownership of its stock, to another company. The Standard Oil Company became known for this practice in the 1870s as it eliminated its competition by taking control of smaller oil companies. (521)

turnpike: Privately funded, toll-based public road constructed in the early nineteenth century to facilitate commerce. (296)

Tuscarora War (1711–1713): Began with an Indian attack on Newbern, North Carolina. After the Tuscaroras were defeated, remaining Indian survivors migrated northward, eventually joining the Iroquois Confederacy as its sixth nation. (38)

Tuskegee Institute: A normal and industrial school led by Booker T. Washington in Tuskegee, Alabama. It focused on training young black students in agriculture and the trades to help them achieve economic independence. Washington justified segregated, vocational training as a necessary first step on the road to racial equality, although critics accused him of being too "accomodationist." (555)

Tweed Ring: A symbol of Gilded Age corruption, "Boss" Tweed and his deputies ran the New York City Democratic party in the 1860s and swindled $200 million from the city through bribery, graft, and vote-buying. Boss Tweed was eventually jailed for his crimes and died behind bars. (490)

U.S. Sanitary Commission (established 1861): Founded with the help of Elizabeth Blackwell, the government agency trained nurses, collected medical supplies, and equipped hospitals in an effort to help the Union Army. The commission helped professionalize nursing and gave many women the confidence and organizational skills to propel the women's movement in the postwar years. (433)

U-boats: German submarines, named for the German _Unterseeboot,_ or "undersea boat," proved deadly for Allied ships in the war zone. U-boat attacks played an important role in drawing the United States into the First World War. (672)

Uncle Tom's Cabin (1852): Harriet Beecher Stowe's widely read novel that dramatized the horrors of slavery. It heightened Northern support for abolition and escalated the sectional conflict. (396)

Underground Railroad: Informal network of volunteers that helped runaway slaves escape from the South and reach free-soil Canada. Seeking to halt the flow of runaway slaves to the North, Southern planters and congressmen pushed for a stronger fugitive slave law. (382)

Underwood Tariff (1913): This tariff provided for a substantial reduction of rates and enacted an unprecedented, graduated federal income tax. By 1917, revenue from the income tax surpassed receipts from the tariff, a gap that has since been vastly widened. (664)

Union League: Reconstruction-Era African American organization that worked to educate Southern blacks about civic life, built black schools and churches, and represented African American interests before government and employers. It also campaigned on behalf of Republican candidates and recruited local militias to protect blacks from white intimidation. (478)

Union party (1864): A coalition party of pro-war Democrats and Republicans formed during the 1864 election to defeat anti-war Northern Democrats. (451)

Unitarians: Believe in a unitary deity, reject the divinity of Christ, and emphasize the inherent goodness of mankind. Unitarianism, inspired in part by Deism, first caught on in New England at the end of the eighteenth century. (307)

United Nations (U.N.): International body formed in 1945 to bring nations into dialogue in hopes of preventing further world wars. Much like the former League of Nations in ambition, the UN was more realistic in recognizing the authority of the Big Five Powers in keeping peace in the world. Thus, it guaranteed veto power to all permanent members of its Security Council—Britain, China, France, the Soviet Union, and the United States. (844)

United Negro Improvement Association (UNIA): A black nationalist organization founded in 1914 by the Jamaican-born Marcus Garvey in order to promote resettlement of African Americans to their "African homeland" and to stimulate a vigorous separate black economy within the United States. (720)

USA Patriot Act (2001): Legislation passed shortly after the terrorist attacks of September 11, 2001, that granted broad surveillance and detention authority to the government. (975)

Valley Forge (1777–1778): Encampment where George Washington's poorly equipped army spent a wretched, freezing winter. Hundreds of men died and more than a thousand deserted. The plight of the starving, shivering soldiers reflected the main weakness of the American army—a lack of stable supplies and munitions. (128)

V-E (Victory in Europe) Day: The source of frenzied rejoicing, May 8, 1945 marked the official end to the war in Europe, following the unconditional surrender of what remained of the German government. (818)

Versailles, Treaty of (1919): World War I concluded with this vengeful document, which secured peace but imposed sharp terms on Germany and created a territorial mandate system to manage former colonies of the world powers. To Woodrow Wilson's chagrin, it incorporated very few of his original Fourteen Points, although it did include the League of Nations that Wilson had long sought. Isolationists in the United States, deeply opposed to the League, led the opposition to the Treaty, which was never ratified by the Senate. (694)

vertical integration: The practice perfected by Andrew Carnegie of controlling every step of the industrial production process in order to increase efficiency and limit competition. (521)

Vicksburg, siege of (1863): Two-and-a-half month siege of a Confederate fort on the Mississippi River in Tennessee. Vicksburg finally fell to Ulysses S. Grant in July of 1863, giving the Union Army control of the Mississippi River and splitting the South in two. (448)

Vietnamization: Military strategy launched by Richard Nixon in 1969. The plan reduced the number of American combat troops in Vietnam and left more of the fighting to the South Vietnamese, who were supplied with American armor, tanks, and weaponry. (917)

Virginia and Kentucky resolutions (1798–1799): Statements secretly drafted by Jefferson and Madison for the legislatures of Kentucky and Virginia. Argued that states were the final arbiters of whether the federal government overstepped its boundaries and could therefore nullify, or refuse to accept, national legislation they deemed unconstitutional. (198)

Virginia Company: English joint-stock company that received a charter from King James I that allowed it to found the Virginia colony. (27)

Virginia Plan: "Large state" proposal for the new constitution, calling for proportional representation in both houses of a bicameral Congress. The plan favored larger states and thus prompted smaller states to come back with their own plan for apportioning representation. (170)

Virginia Statute for Religious Freedom (1786): Measure enacted by the Virginia legislature prohibiting state support for religious institutions and recognizing freedom of worship. Served as a model for the religion clause of the first amendment to the Constitution. (158)

V-J (Victory in Japan) Day: August 15, 1945 heralded the surrender of Japan and the final end to World War II. (821)

Volstead Act (1919): A federal act enforcing the Eighteenth Amendment, which prohibited the manufacture, sale, and transportation of alcoholic beverages. (704)

Voter Education Project (1962–1968): Effort by SNCC and other civil rights groups to register the South's historically disenfranchised black population. The project typified a common strategy of the civil rights movement, which sought to counter racial discrimination by empowering people at grassroots levels to exercise their civic rights through voting. (896)

Voting Rights Act of 1965: Legislation pushed through Congress by President Johnson that prohibited ballot-denying tactics, such as literary tests and intimidation. The Voting Rights Act was a successor to the Civil Rights Act of 1964 and sought to make racial disenfranchisement explicitly illegal. (903)

voyageurs: See *coureurs de bois.* (99)

WAACs (Women's Army Auxiliary Corps), WAVES (Women Accepted for Volunteer Emergency Service), and SPARs (U.S. Coast Guard Women's Reserve: The women's branches of the U.S. Army, Navy, and Coast Guard, established during World War II to employ women in noncombatant jobs. Women now participated in the armed services in ways that went beyond their traditional roles as nurses. (803)

***Wabash, St. Louis & Pacific Railroad Company* v. *Illinois* (1886):** A Supreme Court decision that prohibited states from regulating the railroads because the Constitution grants Congress the power to regulate interstate commerce. As a result, reformers turned their attention to the federal government, which now held sole power to regulate the railroad industry. (519)

Wade-Davis Bill: Passed by Congressional Republicans in response to Abraham Lincoln's "10 percent plan," it required that 50 percent of a state's voters pledge allegiance to the Union, and set stronger safeguards for emancipation. Reflected divisions between Congress and the President, and between radical and moderate Republicans, over the treatment of the defeated South. (470)

Wagner Act (1935): Also known as the National Labor Relations Act, this law protected the right of labor to organize in unions and bargain collectively with employers, and established the National Labor Relations Board to monitor unfair labor practices on the part of employers. Its passage marked the culmination of decades of labor protest. (767)

Walker Tariff (1846): Revenue-enhancing measure that lowered tariffs from 1842 levels thereby fueling trade and increasing Treasury receipts. (367)

Wall Street Reform and Consumer Protection Act (2010): Also known as the Dodd-Frank Act, after its Democratic sponsors, Connecticut Senator Christopher Dodd and Massachusetts Representative Barney Frank. In an effort to avoid another financial crisis like the Great Recession, the Act updated many federal regulations affecting the financial and banking systems, and created some new agencies such as the Bureau of Consumer Financial Protection. (986)

Wanghia, Treaty of (1844): Signed by the U.S. and China, it assured the United States the same trading concessions granted to other powers, greatly expanding America's trade with the Chinese. (390)

war hawks (1811–1812): Democratic-Republican Congressmen who pressed James Madison to declare war on Britain. Largely drawn from the South and West, the war hawks resented British constraints on American trade and accused the British of supporting Indian attacks against American settlements on the frontier. (219)

War Industries Board (1917): Headed by Bernard Baruch, this federal agency coordinated industrial production during World War I, setting production quotas, allocating raw materials, and pushing companies to increase efficiency and eliminate waste. Under the economic mobilization of the War Industries Board, industrial production in the United States increased 20 percent during the war. (682)

War of 1812 (1812–1815): Fought between Britain and the United States largely over the issues of trade and impressment. Though the war ended in a relative draw, it demonstrated America's willingness to defend its interests militarily, earning the young nation newfound respect from European powers. (224)

War of Jenkins's Ear (began in 1739): Small-scale clash between Britain and Spain in the Caribbean and in the buffer colony, Georgia. It merged with the much larger War of Austrian Succession in 1742. (101)

War Powers Act (1973): Law passed by Congress in 1973 limiting the President's ability to wage war without Congressional approval. The act required the President to notify Congress within 48 hours of committing troops to a foreign conflict. An important consequence of the Vietnam War, this piece of legislation sought to reduce the President's unilateral authority in military matters. (924)

War Production Board (WPB): Established in 1942 by executive order to direct all war production, including procuring and allocating raw materials, to maximize the nation's war machine. The WPB had sweeping powers over the U.S. economy and was abolished in November 1945 soon after Japan's defeat. (802)

War Refugee Board (1944): A United States agency formed to help rescue Jews from German-occupied territories and to provide relief to inmates of Nazi concentration camps.

The agency performed noble work, but it did not begin operations until very late in the war, after millions had already been murdered. (788)

Watergate: Series of scandals that resulted in President Richard Nixon's resignation in August 1974 amid calls for his impeachment. The episode sprang from a failed burglary attempt at Democratic party headquarters in Washington's Watergate Hotel during the 1972 election. (925)

WAVES (Women Accepted for Volunteer Emergency Service): See **WAACs (Women's Army Auxiliary Corps)**.

"Waving the bloody shirt": The use of Civil War imagery by political candidates and parties to draw votes to their side of the ticket. (489)

weapons of mass destruction (WMD): Refers to weapons—nuclear, biological, and chemical—that can kill large numbers of people and do great damage to the built and natural environment. The term was used to refer to nuclear weapons during the Cold War. The Bush administration's claim that Saddam Hussein had developed WMD provided the rationale for the United States's invasion of Iraq in 2003. These weapons were never found after the invasion. (965)

Welfare Reform Bill (1996): Legislation that made deep cuts in welfare grants and required able-bodied welfare recipients to find employment. Part of Bill Clinton's campaign platform in 1992, the reforms were widely seen by liberals as an abandonment of key New Deal/Great Society provisions to care for the impoverished. (968)

West Africa Squadron (established 1808): British Royal Navy force formed to enforce the abolition of the slave trade in 1807. It intercepted hundreds of slave ships and freed thousands of Africans. (344)

West Virginia (admitted to the Union 1863): Mountainous region that broke away from Virginia in 1861 to form its own state after Virginia seceded from the Union. Most of the residents of West Virginia were independent farmers and miners who did not own slaves and thus opposed the Confederate cause. (420)

Whiskey Rebellion (1794): Popular uprising of whiskey distillers in southwestern Pennsylvania in opposition to an excise tax on whiskey. In a show of strength and resolve by the new central government, Washington put down the rebellion with militia drawn from several states. (185)

Whitewater: A series of scandals during the Clinton Administration that stemmed from a failed real estate investment from which the Clintons were alleged to have illicitly profited. The accusations prompted the appointment of a special federal prosecutor, though no indictments. (970)

Wilderness Campaign (1864–1865): A series of brutal clashes between Ulysses S. Grant's and Robert E. Lee's armies in Virginia, leading up to Grant's capture of Richmond in April of 1865. Having lost Richmond, Lee surrendered to Grant at Appomattox Courthouse. (454)

Wilmot Proviso (1846): Amendment that sought to prohibit slavery from territories acquired from Mexico. Introduced by Pennsylvania congressman David Wilmot, the failed amendment ratcheted up tensions between North and South over the issue of slavery. (376)

Woman's Loyal League (1863–1865): Women's organization formed to help bring about an end to the Civil War and encourage Congress to pass a constitutional amendment prohibiting slavery. (477)

Woman's Rights Convention at Seneca Falls (1848): Gathering of feminist activists in Seneca Falls, New York, where Elizabeth Cady Stanton read her "Declaration of Sentiments," stating that "all men and women are created equal." (318)

Women's Christian Temperance Union (WCTU): Founded in Ohio in the 1870s to combat the evils of excessive alcohol consumption, the WCTU went on to embrace a broad reform agenda, including campaigns to abolish prostitution and gain the right to vote for women. (646, 564)

Workingmen's Compensation Act: Passed under Woodrow Wilson, this law granted assistance to federal civil-service employees during periods of disability. It was a precursor to labor-friendly legislation passed during the New Deal. (666)

World Trade Organization (WTO) (1995): An international body to promote and supervise liberal trade among nations. The successor to the General Agreement on Tariffs and Trade, it marked a key world trade policy achievement of the Clinton Administration. (969)

World's Columbian Exposition (1893): Held in Chicago, Americans saw this World's Fair as their opportunity to claim a place among the world's most "civilized" societies, by which they meant the countries of western Europe. The Fair honored art, architecture, and science, and its promoters built a mini-city in which to host the fair that reflected all the ideals of city planning popular at the time. For many, this was the high point of the "City Beautiful" movement. (569)

Wounded Knee, Battle of (1890): A battle between the U.S. Army and the Dakota Sioux, in which several hundred Native Americans and 29 U.S. soldiers died. Tensions erupted violently over two major issues: the Sioux practice of the "Ghost Dance," which the U.S. government had outlawed, and the dispute over whether Sioux reservation land would be broken up because of the Dawes Act. (581)

writ of habeas corpus: Petition requiring law enforcement officers to present detained individuals before the court to examine the legality of the arrest. Protects individuals from arbitrary state action. Suspended by Lincoln during the Civil War. (429)

XYZ Affair (1797): Diplomatic conflict between France and the United States when American envoys to France were asked to pay a hefty bribe for the privilege of meeting with the French foreign minister. Many in the U.S. called for war against France, while American sailors and privateers waged an undeclared war against French merchants in the Caribbean. (195)

Yalta conference (1945): Meeting of Franklin Roosevelt, Winston Churchill, and Joseph Stalin, in February 1945 at an old Tsarist resort on the Black Sea, where the Big Three leaders laid the foundations for the postwar division of power in Europe, including a divided Germany and territorial concessions to the Soviet Union. (839)

Yamasee Indians: Defeated by the south Carolinans in the war of 1715–1716. The Yamasee defeat devastated the last of the coastal Indian tribes in the Southern colonies. (38)

yellow journalism: A scandal-mongering practice of journalism that emerged in New York during the Gilded Age out of the circulation battles between Joseph Pulitzer's *New York World* and William Randolph Hearst's *New York Journal*. The expression has remained a pejorative term referring to sensationalist journalism practiced with unethical, unprofessional standards. (558)

Yorktown, Battle of (October 1781): George Washington, with the aid of the French Army, besieged Cornwallis at Yorktown, while the French naval fleet prevented British reinforcements from coming ashore. Cornwallis surrendered, dealing a heavy blow to the British war effort and paving the way for an eventual peace. (150)

Zenger trial (1734–1735): New York libel case against John Peter Zenger. Established the principle that truthful statements about public officials could not be prosecuted as libel. (92)

Zimmermann note (1917): German foreign secretary Arthur Zimmerman had secretly proposed a German-Mexican alliance against the United States. When the note was intercepted and published in March 1917, it caused an uproar that made some Americans more willing to enter the war. (678)

Practice Material for the AP U.S. History Examination
Document-Based Questions (DBQ)

PART ONE: Founding the New Nation, c. 33,000 B.C.E.–1783 C.E.

DBQ 1
The Transformation of Colonial Virginia, 1606–1700

Directions: In this DBQ, you must compose an essay that uses both your interpretation of Documents A–H and your own outside knowledge of the period mentioned in this question.

Over the course of the seventeenth century, the settlers in England's Virginia colony faced a number of hardships. Examine the challenges the Virginians faced and the ways in which their efforts changed the colony socially and economically over the century.

Use these documents and your knowledge of the period from 1606 to 1700 to compose your answer.

Document A: Michael Drayton, "Ode to the Virginian Voyage," 1606

You brave heroic minds,
Worthy your country's name,
That honour still pursue,
Go and subdue!
Whilst loit'ring hinds
Lurk here at home with shame.

Britons, you stay too long;
Quickly aboard bestow you,
. . . .
And cheerfully at sea
Success you still entice
To get the pearl and gold,
And ours to hold
Virginia,
Earth's only paradise!

Where nature hath in store
Fowl, venison, and fish,
And the fruitful'st soil,
Without your toil,
Three harvests more,
All greater than your wish.

And the ambitious vine
Crowns with his purple mass,
The cedar reaching high
To kiss the sky,
The cypress, pine,
And useful sassafras;

To whose the golden age
Still nature's laws doth give;
No other cares that tend
But them to defend
From winter's age,
That long there doth not live.

. . . .
In kenning [appearance] of the shore,
Thanks to God first given,
O you, the happiest men,
Be frolic then!
Let cannons roar
Frighting the wide heaven.

And in regions far
Such heroes bring ye forth,
As those from whom we came;
And plant our name
Under that star
Not known unto our north.

Document B
Source: George Percy, *A Discourse on the Plantation of Virginia*, c. 1612.

Our men were destroyed with cruel diseases as swellings, burning fevers, and by wars, and some departed suddenly, but for the most part they died of mere famine. There were never Englishmen left in a foreign country in such misery as we were in this new discovered Virginia.

Document C

Source: Early tobacco advertisement.

Life is a Smoke!—If this be true, Tobacco will thy Life renew; Then fear not Death, nor killing Care, Whil'ß we have beft Virginia here.

Document D: Richard Frethorne, letter to his father and mother, 20 March and 2 & 3 April 1623

Source: Susan Kingsbury, ed., *The Records of the Virginia Company of London* (Washington, D.C.: Government Printing Office, 1935), 4: 58–62.

LOVING AND KIND FATHER AND MOTHER:

This is to let you understand that [this] country . . . causeth much sickness, [including] the scurvy and [dysentery] and diverse other diseases, which maketh the body very poor and weak. And when we are sick there is nothing to comfort us[.] As for deer or venison I never saw any since I came into this land. There is indeed some fowl, but we are not allowed to go and get it, but must work hard both early and late for a mess of water gruel and a mouthful of bread and beef. A mouthful of bread . . . must serve for four men which is most pitiful. . . . [P]eople cry out day and night—Oh! That they were in England[;] to be in England again. . . . [We] live in fear of the enemy every hour, yet we have had a combat with them . . . and we took two alive and made slaves of them. . . . [W]e are in great danger; for our plantation [Martin's Hundred] is very weak by reason of the death and sickness of our company [of men], and yet we are but 32 to fight against 3000 if they should come. And the [nearest] help that we have is ten mile of us, and when the rogues overcame this place [earlier] they slew 80 persons. . . .

Document E

Source: Father Andrew White, blank contract for indentured servant, 1635.

This indenture made the _____ day of_____ in the_____ yeere of our Soveraigne Lord King Charles, &c. betweene _____ of the one party, and _____ on the other party, Witnesseth, that the said _____ doth hereby covenant promise, and grant, to and with the said _____ his Executors and Assignes, to serve him from the day of the date hereof, until his first and next arrivall . . . and after for and during the tearme of yeeres, _____ in such service and imployment, as he the said _____ or his assignes shall there imploy him, according to the custome of the Countrey in the like kind. In consideration whereof, the said _____ doth promise and grant, to and with the said _____ to pay for his passing, and to find him with Meat, Drinke, Apparell and Lodging, with other necessaries during the said terme; and at the end of the said terme, to give him one whole yeeres provision of Corne, and fifty acres of Land, according to the order of the country.

Document F: Earthenware vessels made at Jamestown between 1625 and 1640

Source: John Cotter and J. Paul Hudson, *New Discoveries at Jamestown*, National Park Service, 1957.

Document G
Source: Report of Governor William Berkeley of Virginia to the Crown, 1671.

Question: What number of planters, servants, and slaves; and how many parishes are there in your plantation?

Answer: We suppose, and I am very sure we do not much miscount, that there is in Virginia above forty thousand persons, men, women, and children, and of which there are two thousand black slaves, six thousand Christian servants [indentured] for a short time. The rest are born in the country or have come in to settle and seat, in bettering their condition in a growing country.

Question: What number of English, Scots, or Irish have for these seven years last past come yearly to plant and inhabit within your government; as also what blacks or slaves have been brought in within the said time?

Answer: Yearly, we suppose there comes in, of servants, about fifteen hundred, of which most are English, few Scotch, and fewer Irish, and not above two or three ships of Negroes in seven years.

Document H: Virginia statutes pertaining to slavery passed by the Virginia Assembly, 1639–1691

January 1639/40 - ALL persons except negroes to be provided with arms and ammunition . . . at pleasure of the Governor and Council.

December 1662 - Be it therefore enacted . . . , that all children borne in this country shalbe held bond or free only according to the condition of the mother. . . .

September 1667 - It is enacted . . . that the conferring of baptisme doth not alter the condition of the person as to his bondage or ffreedome. . . .

April 1691 - WHEREAS many times negroes, mulattoes, and other slaves unlawfully absent themselves from their masters and mistresses service, and lie hid and lurk in obscure places killing hoggs and committing other injuries to the inhabitants of this dominion, . . . Be it enacted . . . , that the sherrife [shall] apprehend such negroes, mulattoes, and other slaves, . . . and in case any negroes, mulattoes or other slaves or slaves . . . shall resist, runaway, or refuse to deliver and surrender him or themselves to any person or persons. . . , it shall . . . be lawfull for such person and persons to kill and distroy such negroes, mulattoes, and other slave or slaves. . . .

Provided that where any negroe or mulattoe slave or slaves shall be killed in pursuance of this act, the owner or owners of such negro or mulatto slave shall be paid for such negro or mulatto slave four thousand pounds of tobacco by the publique. . . .

Be it enacted . . . , whatsoever English or other white man or woman being free shall intermarry with a negroe, mulatto, or Indian man or woman bond or free shall within three months after such marriage be banished and removed from this dominion forever. . . .

DBQ 2
English-Indian Relations, 1600–1700

Directions: In this DBQ, you must compose an essay that uses both your interpretation of Documents A–H and your own outside knowledge of the period mentioned in this question.

> Discuss the nature of the relationship between the Indians and the English along the Atlantic seaboard in the years 1600 to 1700 and to what extent that relationship changed over the seventeenth century.

> Use these documents and your knowledge of the period from 1600 to 1700 to compose your answer.

Document A
Source: Proceedings of the Virginia House of Burgesses, 1619.

> Be it enacted by this present Assembly that for laying a surer foundation of the conversion of the Indians to Christian religion, each town, city, borough, and particularly plantation do obtain unto themselves, by just means, a certain number of the natives' children to be educated by them in true religion and a civil course of life of which children the most towardly [promising] boys in wit and graces of nature to be brought up by them in the first elements of literature, so as to be fitted for the college intended for them; that from thence they may be sent to that work of conversion.

Document B
Source: Report of Edward Waterhouse, 1622, from the records of the Virginia Company of London.

> On Friday morning (the fatal day) the 22nd of March [1622] as also in the evening, as in other days before, they came unarmed into our houses, without bows or arrows, or other weapons, with deer, turkeys, fish, furs, and other provisions to sell and truck with us for glass, beads, and other trifles; yea, in some places, sat down at breakfast with our people at their tables, whom immediately with their own tools and weapons, either laid down, or standing in their houses, they basely and barbarously murdered, not sparing either age or sex, man, woman, or child.

Document C: Matthaes Merian, An Indian Massacre of 1622, in *de Bry's America*, 1628

Library of Congress

Document D: The Book of the General Lawes and Libertyes Concerning the Inhabitants of the Massachusets . . . ,1647

> Nor shall any man within this Jurisdiction . . . amend, repair, or cause to be amended or repaired any gun . . . belonging to any Indian. . . . Nor shall sell or give to any Indian . . . any such gun, . . . or any militarie weapons . . . upon [pain] of ten pounds fine, . . . and that the court of Assistants shall have power to increase the Fine; or to impose [corporal] punishment. . . .

> It is ordered . . . that in all places, the English . . . shall keep their cattle from destroying the Indians corn, in any ground where they have right to plant; and if any of their corn be destroyed for want of fencing, or herding; the town shall make satisfaction. . . . Provided that the Indians shall make proof that the cattle of such a town, farm, or person did the damage.

> And it is farther ordered and decreed by this Court; that no Indian shall at any time powaw, or performe outward worship to their false gods: or to the devil in any part of our Jurisdiction. . . .

Document E

Source: Report of Plymouth Colonial Officials, 1675.

Not to look back further than the troubles that were between the Colony of New Plymouth and Philip, sachem [chieftain] of Mount Hope in the year 1671, it may be remembered that . . . [he] was . . . the offending party; and that Plymouth had just cause to take up arms against him; and it was then agreed that he should pay that colony a certain sum of money, in part of their damage and charge by him occasioned; and he then not only renewed his ancient covenant of friendship with them; but made himself and his people absolute subjects to our Sovereign Lord King Charles the Second. . . .

But sometime last winter the Governor of Plymouth was informed by Sassamon, a faithful Indian, that the said Philip was undoubtedly endeavoring to raise new troubles, and was endeavoring to engage all the sachems round about in a war against us. . . .

Document F: John Easton, deputy governor of Rhode Island, *A Relation of the Indian War*, 1675

Philip charged it to be dishonesty in us to put off the Hearing the just Complaints, therefore we consented to hear them. They said thay had bine the first in doing Good to the English, and the English the first in doing Rong; said when the English first came, their King's Father was as a great Man, and the English as a littell Child; he constrained other Indians from ronging the English, and gave them Corn and shewed them how to plant. . . . And another Greavance was, if 20 of their honest Indians testified that a Englishman had dun them Rong, it was as nothing; and if but one of their worst Indians testified against any Indian or their King, when it pleased the English it was sufficient. . . . Another Grievance, the English Catell and Horses still increased; [and] they could not keep their Corn from being spoiled, they never being used to fence, and thought when the English bought Land of them they would have kept their Catell upon their owne Land. Another Grievance, the English were so eager to sell the Indians [liquor]. . . .

Document G

Source: Report of the Royal Commission to the Crown, 1677.

The people [became] jealous [of] Governor [Berkeley of Virginia] for the lucre of beaver and otter trade, etc., with the Indians, rather sought to protect the Indians than them, since after public proclamations prohibiting all trade with the Indians (they complain), he privately gave commission to some of his friends to truck with them, and that those persons furnished the Indians with powder, shot, etc., so that they were better provided than His Majesty's subjects.

The peoples of Charles City County (near Merchants Hope) being [denied] a commission by the Governor, although he was truly informed . . . of several formidable bodies of Indians coming down on the heads of the James River within fifty or sixty miles of the English plantations . . . they begin to beat up drums for volunteers to go out against the Indians, and so continued sundry days drawing into arms, the magistrates being either so remiss or of the same faction that they suffered the disaster without contradiction or endeavoring to prevent so dangerous a beginning. . . .

Document H: "A Treaty between the Agents of Massachusett's Bay, New-Plymuth, and Connecticut, and the Sachems [Chieves] of the Five Nations, at Albany, in the Year 1689"

Source: Hyser and Arndt, *Voices of the American Past*, I, 22–23.

We patiently bore many Injuries from the French, from one Year to another, before we took up the Axe against them. . . . We assure you, that we are resolved never to drop the Axe, the French never shall see our Faces in Peace, we shall never be reconciled as long as one Frenchman is alive. We shall never make Peace, though our Nation should be ruined by it, and every one of us cut in Pieces. Our Brethren of the three Colonies may depend on this.

. . .

[W]e are resolved to look on your enemies as ours. . . . Brethren your War is our War, for we will live and dye with you. . . .

DBQ 3
The American Revolution, 1750–1776

Directions: In this DBQ, you must compose an essay that uses both your interpretation of Documents A–I and your own outside knowledge of the period mentioned in this question.

> To what extent was the conflict between Great Britain and her North American colonies economic in origin rather than rooted in political and social controversies and differences?

> Use these documents and your knowledge of the period from 1750 to 1776 to compose your answer.

Document A: James Otis, Speech on Writs of Assistance, 24 February 1761

Source: Henry Commager, ed., *Documents of American History*, 9th ed., 45–47.

[The] writ . . . being general, is illegal. It is a power that places the liberty of every man in the hands of every petty officer. . . . I admit that special writs of assistance, to search special places, may be granted to certain persons on oath; but I deny that the [general] writ . . . can be granted, for I beg leave to make some observations on the [general] writ itself. In the first place, the writ is universal . . . so that it is directed to every subject in the King's dominions. Every one with this writ may be a tyrant. . . . In the next place, it is perpetual. . . . A man is accountable to no person for his doings. . . . Writs in their nature are temporary things. When the purposes for which they are issued are answered, they exist no more; but these live forever; no one can be called to account. [R]eason and the constitution are both against this [general] writ.

Document B: Stamp Act Resolutions, 1765, issued by the Stamp Act Congress

Source: *Enduring Voices: Document Sets to Accompany the Enduring Vision*, 40–41.

II. That His majesty's liege [loyal] subjects in these colonies are intitled [sic] to all of the inherent rights and liberties of his natural born subjects within the kingdom of Great Britain.

III. That it is inseparably essential to the freedom of a people, and the undoubted right of Englishmen, that no taxes be imposed on them but with their own consent, given personally or by their representatives.

IX. That the duties imposed by several late Acts of Parliament, from the peculiar circumstances of these colonies, will be extremely burthensome and grievous; and from the scarcity of specie, the payment of them absolutely impracticable.

XI. That the restrictions imposed by several late Acts of Parliament on the trade of these colonies will render them unable to purchase the manufactures of Great Britain.

Document C: Charleston, South Carolina, Sons of Liberty, 1766

Source: *Enduring Voices: Document Sets to Accompany the Enduring Vision*, 48.

1. Christopher Gadsden, merchant
2. William Johnson, blacksmith
3. Joseph Veree, carpenter. . .
7. George Flagg, painter and glazier [works on windows]. . .
9. John Hall, coachmaker. . .
11. Robert Jones, sadler. . .
19. William Trusler, butcher
21. Alexander Alexander, schoolmaster
22. Edward Weyman, clerk of St. Philip's Church, and glass grinder

Document D: Gottfreid Achenwall, "The Pattern of Colonial Commerce," interview with Benjamin Franklin, July 1766, in Gottingen, Germany
Source: *American Spirit*, 11th ed., 94–96.

The colonies are generally restricted in all their foreign trade, and even more in their shipping in all sorts of ways. Nevertheless the continental colonies particularly maintain a considerable shipping trade of their own. . . . Many products, particularly those for shipbuilding and raw materials for manufactures: mast trees, ship timber, iron, copper, . . . cotton, indigo, tobacco, skins and furs, they may not export. These are reserved for the British realm, must be brought by British merchants, and carried by British ships and sailors. In areas where an English company has the exclusive trade, they may not trade, for example, with the East Indies. . . . Trade with the Spanish in America is a mere contraband trade. . . . But the colonist risks it because he can bring back specie, which is so rare in the colonies. . . . In general, no foreign nation is permitted to go to the colonies to buy products and carry them away, much less to send their own goods over; both export and import remain a privilege for British subjects or especially for inhabitants of England.

Document E: John Dickinson, *Letters from an American Farmer*, II, 1767–1768

Great-Britain has prohibited the manufacturing of iron and steel in these colonies, without any objection being made to her right of doing it. The like right she must have to prohibit any other manufacture among us. Thus she is possessed of an undisputed precedent on that point. . . .

Here then, my dear country men ROUSE yourselves, and behold the ruin hanging over your heads. If you ONCE admit, that Great-Britain may lay duties upon her exportations to us, for the purpose of levying money on us only, she then will have nothing to do, but to lay those duties on the articles which she prohibits us to manufacture—and the tragedy of American liberty is finished. . . . If Great-Britain can order us to come to her for necessaries we want, and can order us to pay what taxes she pleases before we take them away, or when we land them here, we are as abject slaves as France and Poland. . . .

Document F: Samuel Adams, "Declaration of Rights," Massachusetts Committee of Correspondence, 20 November 1772
Source: *Annals of America*, vol. 2, 217–220.

By the charter of this province, [there] shall be liberty of conscience allowed in the worship of God to all Christians, except Papists. . . .

All persons born in the British American colonies are, by the laws of God and nature and by the common law of England . . . well-entitled to all the natural, essential, inherent, and inseparable rights, liberties, and privileges of subjects born in Great Britain. . . .

Document G: "Declaration of Colonial Rights and Grievances," 1 October 1774, First Continental Congress
Source: *Enduring Voices: Document Sets to Accompany the Enduring Vision*, 41–43.

[The] inhabitants of the English colonies in North America, by the immutable laws of nature, the principles of the English Constitution, and the several charters or compacts, have the following rights:

1. They are entitled to life, liberty, and property. . . .
5. That the respective colonies are entitled to the common law of England. . .
8. That they have a right peaceably to assemble, consider their grievances, and petition the king; and that all prosecutions, prohibitory proclamations and commitments for the same are illegal.
9. That keeping a standing army in these colonies in time of peace, without the consent of the legislature of that colony, in which the army is kept is against the law.

Document H: America in flames

Document I: "Proceedings in the Convention of Virginia Relating to the Proclamation of Lord Dunmore," 25 January 1776

Source: *Annals of America*, vol. 2, 383–385

[Lord Dunmore, the royal governor of Virginia,] has offered freedom to the servants and slaves of those he is pleased to term rebels, arming them against their masters, and destroying the peace and happiness of His Majesty's good and faithful whose property is rendered insecure and whose lives are exposed to the dangers of a general insurrection. . . .

Whereas Lord Dunmore, by his proclamation dated . . . the 7th day of November 1775, has offered freedom to such able-bodied slaves as are willing to join him and take up arms against the good people of this colony. . . , it is enacted that all Negro or other slaves conspiring to rebel or make insurrection shall suffer death and be excluded all benefit of clergy—we think it proper to declare that all slaves who have been, or shall be seduced by [Dunmore's] proclamation . . . to desert their master's service, and take up arms against the inhabitants of this colony shall be liable to . . . punishment. . . .

PART TWO: Building the New Nation, 1776–1860

DBQ 4
Thomas Jefferson and Philosophical Consistency, 1790–1809

Directions: In this DBQ, you must compose an essay that uses both your interpretation of Documents A–I and your own outside knowledge of the period mentioned in this question.

> Although Thomas Jefferson and Alexander Hamilton fought bitterly over issues of constitutional interpretation in the 1790s, the policies of the Jeffersonian Republican presidents Jefferson and Madison in the years 1801–1817 often reflected the beliefs of the Federalist Hamilton. To what extent is this an accurate statement?
>
> Use these documents and your knowledge of the period from 1790 to 1809 to compose your answer.

Document A: Thomas Jefferson, "Opinion on the Constitutionality of a National Bank, 15 February 1791"

I consider the foundation of the Constitution as laid on this ground: That "all powers not delegated to the United States, by the Constitution, nor prohibited by it to the States, are reserved to the States or to the people." [Xth amendment.] To take a single step beyond the boundaries thus specially drawn around the powers of Congress, is to take possession of a boundless field of power, no longer susceptible of any definition.

The incorporation of a bank, and the powers assumed by this bill, have not, in my opinion, been delegated to the United States, by the Constitution.

Document B: Alexander Hamilton, Tully No. III, 28 August 1794
Source: *Annals of America*, vol. 3, 561–563.

Government is frequently and aptly classed under two descriptions—a government of *force*, and a government of *laws*. The first is the definition of despotism; the last of liberty. But how can a government of laws exist when laws are disrespected and disobeyed? Government supposes control. It is that *power* by which individuals in society are kept from doing injury to each other, and are brought to cooperate to a common end. The instruments by which it must act are either the *authority* of the laws or *force*. If the first be destroyed, the last must be substituted, and where this becomes the ordinary instrument of government, there is an end to liberty!

. . .

Fellow Citizens: you are told that it will be intemperate to urge the execution of the laws which are resisted. What? Will it be indeed intemperate in your chief magistrate, sworn to uphold the Constitution, charged faithfully to execute the laws, and authorized to employ for that purpose force when the ordinary means fail—will it be intemperate in him to exert that force when the Constitution and the laws are opposed by force?

Document C: James Madison, "Virginia Resolutions," 1798

That this Assembly doth explicitly and peremptorily declare, that it views the powers of the federal government, as resulting from the compact, to which the states are parties; as limited by the plain sense and intention of the instrument constituting the compact; as no further valid than they are authorized by the grants enumerated in that compact; and that in case of a deliberate, palpable, and dangerous exercise of other powers, not granted by the said compact, the states who are parties thereto, have the right, and are in duty bound, to interpose for arresting the progress of the evil, and for maintaining within their respective limits, the authorities, rights and liberties appertaining to them.

That the General Assembly doth also express its deep regret, that a spirit has in sundry instances, been manifested by the federal government, to enlarge its powers by forced constructions of the constitutional charter which defines them.

Document D: Thomas Jefferson, Annual Message, 8 December 1801

When we consider that this government is charged with the external and mutual relations only of these states; that the states themselves have principal care of our persons, our property, and our reputation, constituting the great field of human concerns, we may well doubt whether our organization is not too complicated, too expensive; whether offices or officers have not been multiplied unnec-essarily, and sometimes injuriously to the service they were meant to promote. I will cause to be laid before you an essay toward a statement of those who, under public employment of various kinds, draw money from the treasury or from our citizens. Time has not permitted a perfect enumeration, the ramifications of office being too multiplied and remote to be completely traced in a first trial. Among those who are dependent on executive discretion, I have begun the reduction of what was deemed necessary. The expenses of diplomatic agency have been considerably diminished. The inspectors of internal revenue who were found to obstruct the accountability of the institution, have been discontinued.

Document E

Source: Four Barbary States of North Africa, c. 1805. (See text p. 211 for full-size map.)

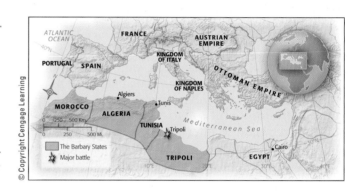

Document F: Isaac Cruikshank, "The Happy Effects of That Grand System of Shutting Ports Against the English," 1808

Source: Catalogue of prints and drawings in the British Museum. Division I, political and personal satires, v. 8, no. 11039. Published by Walker, 1808 Octr.15, London. Forms part of the British Cartoon Prints Collection.

Document G: John Adams to Benjamin Waterhouse, 11 March 1812
Source: *Annals of America*, vol. 4, 312.

If I had a vote I should give it to Mr. Madison at the next election, because I know of no man who would do better. At present the general government are approaching nearer and nearer to my system. They are restoring the taxes that ought never to have been repealed. They are doing something by sea. . . . That is the only arm that can protect us and preserve the Union. This object I have pursued with unabated zeal for six and thirty years.

Document H: John Randolph, Virginia Jeffersonian Republican Congressman, speech in Congress, on the 1816 tariff bill
Source: *Annals of America*, vol. 4, 427–428.

[We] have . . . proof that the present government have renounced the true republican principles of Jefferson's administration on which they raised themselves to power, and that they have taken up, in their stead, those of John Adams. . . . [T]heir principle now is old Federalism, vamped up into something bearing the superficial appearance of republicanism. . . . I will not agree to lay a duty on the cultivators of the soil to encourage exotic man-ufacturers; because, after all, we should only get much worse things at a much higher price, and, we, the cultivators of the country, would in the end pay for all.

Document I: John Calhoun, Jeffersonian Republican congressman from South Carolina, speech before Congress, 4 February 1817
Source: *Annals of America*, vol. 4, 457–461.

[To] what can we direct our resources and attention more important than internal improvements? What can add more to the wealth, the strength, and the political prosperity of our country? . . . It was sufficient to observe that every branch of the national industry—agricultural, manufacturing and commercial—was greatly stimulated and rendered by [them] more productive. . . . Let it not be said that internal improvements may be wholly left to the enterprise of the states and individuals. . . . [Many] of the improvements contemplated . . . are on too great a scale for the resources of the states or individuals. . . . They required the resources and the general superintendence of [the national] govern-ment to effect and complete them. . . . [On] this subject of national power, what . . . can tend more powerfully to produce [national unity] than over-coming the effects of distance? . . . Such, then, being the obvious advantages of internal improve-ments, why . . . should . . . some members [have] constitutional objections[?] [I am] no advocate for refined arguments on the Constitution. The instru-ment was not intended as a thesis for the logician to exercise his ingenuity on. It ought to be con-strued with good, plain sense. . . .

DBQ 5
The Changing Place of Women, 1815–1860

Directions: In this DBQ, you must compose an essay that uses both your interpretation of Documents A–I and your own outside knowledge of the period mentioned in this question.

> Evaluate how and why the antebellum market revolution and Second Great Awakening affected the evolution of women's role in the family, workplace, and society in the years 1815–1860.

> Use these documents and your knowledge of the period from 1815 to 1860 to compose your answer.

Document A
Source: Charles G. Finney, comments on a convert in New York, memoir, 1831.

> A Christian woman persuaded [Mrs. M] to come see me. She had been a gay, worldly woman, and very fond of society. She afterward told me that when I first came there, she greatly regretted it, and feared there would be a revival; and a revival would greatly interfere with the pleasures and amuse-ments that she had promised herself that winter. [But] after considerable conversation and prayer, her heart broke down and she settled into a joyous faith. . . . From that moment, she was out-spoken in her religious convictions, and zealous for the con-version of her friends.

Document B: "Selling a Mother from Her Child"
Source: *Antislavery Almanac,* 1840.

SELLING A MOTHER FROM HER CHILD.
" ' Do you *often* buy the wife without the husband ?' ' Yes, *very often* ; and *frequently*, too, they sell me the mother while they keep her children. I have often known them take away the infant from its mother's breast, and keep it, while they sold her.' "—*Prof. Andrews, late of the University*

Document C: E. L. F. [possibly Eliza Lee Follen], "What Have Women to Do with Slavery: A Dialogue," *The Liberator*, 1 November 1839

Mrs. A. Is it possible, my dear Harriet, that . . . you have actually joined the Anti-Slavery Society? . . . I thought your mother did not approve of your engaging in this matter.

Harriet. She did not, but then she wished me to act according to my own sense of right; she says I am of an age to decide for myself upon questions of right and wrong.

Mrs. A. I am sorry that my sister has been so weakly indulgent to you; I doubt not that in a short time I shall hear that she also has turned abolitionist, and . . . she will sign the petitions of Congress with other misguided women.

Harriet. I cannot help hoping that your fears may be realized. But . . . I thought you told me that you were convinced that slavery is sinful. . . .

Mrs. A. . . . I [am]; but I do not approve of the doings of the abolitionists . . . ; and most of all . . . I disapprove of women's meddling with such things. . . . It is evident, my dear, that men are appointed by Providence to make and administer the laws; it is a violation of the Divine Order when women interfere in politics. . . . [Slavery] is a politi-cal question—and . . . there is a great impropriety in women's meddling with the subject.

Harriet. I do not see why . . . women, with the strength and the enlightening power of truth on their side, may not do something to overthrow it.

Document D: Harriet Farley, "Slave Labor vs. Free Labor," *Lowell Offering*, **December 1840**

"She has worked in a factory, is sufficient to damn to infamy the most worthy and virtuous girl." [italics in original]

So says Mr. Orestes A. Brownson. . . . I assert that it is not true, . . . and he may now see what will probably appear to him quite as marvellous . . . , that a factory girl is not afraid to oppose herself to the Editor of the Boston Quarterly Review. True, he has upon his side fame, learning, and great talent; but I have what is better . . . and that is truth. . . .

And whom has Mr. Brownson slandered? [Thousands of] girls who generally come from quiet country homes, where their minds and manners have been formed under the eyes of the worthy sons of the Pilgrims, and their virtuous partners, and who return again to become the wives of the free intelligent yeomanry of New England and the mothers of quite a portion of our future republicans. . . .

[We] are collected [in the factories], namely, to get money, as much of it and as fast as we can; and it's because our toil is so unremitting, that the wages of factory girls are higher than those of females engaged in most other occupations. It is these wages which . . . have drawn so many worthy, virtuous, intelligent, and well-educated girls to Lowell . . . ; and strange would it be, if in money loving New England, one of the most lucrative female employments should be rejected because it is so toilsome, or because some people are prejudiced against it. Yankee girls have too much *independence* for *that*. . . .

There are among us all sorts of girls. . . . The Improvement Circles, the Lyceum and Institute, the social religious meetings, the Circulating and other libraries, can bear testimony that the little time they have is spent in a better manner. Our well filled churches and lecture halls and the high character of our clergymen and lecturers, will testify that the state of morals and intelligence is not low.

Document E

Source: Editorial from *Godey's Lady's Book*, magazine, 1845.

The mass of mankind are very ignorant and wicked. Wherefore is this? Because the mother, whom God constituted the first teacher of every human being, has been degraded by men from her high office; or, what is the same thing, been denied those privileges of education which only can enable her to discharge her duty to her children with discretion and effect. . . . If half the effort and expense had been directed to enlighten and improve the minds of females which have been lavished on the other sex, we should now have a very different state of society.

Document F

Source: Dorothea Dix to the Massachusetts legislature, report, 1843.

I proceed, gentlemen, briefly to call your attention to the present state of insane persons confined within this Commonwealth in cages, closets, cellars, stalls, pens! Chained, naked, beaten with rods, and lashed into obedience!

Document G: Sarony and Major, "The Happy Mother," 1846

Library of Congress

Document H

Source: "Bloomer costume," *Harper's New Monthly Magazine*, 1851. (See text p. 319 for full-size illustration.)

Document I

Source: Petition to the Massachusetts legislature, 1853.

We deem the extension to woman of all civil rights a measure of vital importance to the welfare and progress of the state. On every principle of natural justice, as well as by the nature of our institutions, she is as fully entitled as man to vote and to be eligible to office. . . . Ours is a government professedly resting on the consent of the governed. Woman is surely as competent to give that consent as man. Our Revolution claimed that taxation and representation should be coextensive. While the property and labor of women are subject to taxation, she is entitled to a voice in fixing the amount of taxes and the use of them, when collected, and is entitled to a voice in the laws that regulate punishments.

PART THREE: Testing the New Nation, 1820–1877

DBQ 6
Slavery and Sectional Attitudes, 1830–1860

Directions: In this DBQ, you must compose an essay that uses both your interpretation of Documents A–I and your own outside knowledge of the period mentioned in this question.

> In the years 1830–1860, many northern Americans came to see slavery as an evil, while many southerners defended the institution as a positive good. Why did the North and South come to such different views of slavery in the years prior to the Civil War?
>
> Use these documents and your knowledge of the period from 1830 to 1860 to compose your answer.

Document A
Source: Governor George McDuffie to the South Carolina legislature, 1835.

> In all respects the comforts of our slaves are greatly superior to those of the English [factory] operatives, or the Irish and continental peasantry, to say nothing of the millions of paupers crowded together in those loathsome receptacles of starving humanity, the public poorhouses. . . . From this excess of labor, this actual want, and these distressing cares, our slaves are entirely exempted.

Document B
Source: William Harper, *Memoir on Slavery*, 1837.

> Supposing finally that the abolitionists should effect their purpose. What would be the result? The first and most obvious effect would be to put an end to the cultivation of our great Southern staple [cotton]. . . . The cultivation of the great staple crops cannot be carried on in any portion of our country where there are not slaves.

Document C
Source: *The American Anti-Slavery Almanac for 1838*, N. Southard, Editor.

TEARING UP FREE PAPERS.
In the Southern States, every colored person is presumed to be a slave, till proved to be free; and they are often robbed of the proof.

Courtesy of the John Hay Library at Brown University

Document D: Henry Highland Garnet, "Address to the Slaves of the United States of America," National Negro Convention, Buffalo, New York, 1843
Source: Manning Marable and Leith Mullings, eds., *Let Nobody Turn Us Around*, 60.

SLAVERY! How much misery is comprehended in that single word. What mind is there that does not shrink from its direful effects? Unless the image of God be obliterated from the soul, all men cherish the love of Liberty. . . . In every man's mind the good seeds of liberty are planted, and he who brings his fellow down so low, as to make him contented with a condition of slavery, commits the highest crime against God and man. Brethren, your opponents aim to do this. They endeavor to make you as much like brutes as possible. . . .

TO SUCH DEGRADATION IT IS SINFUL IN THE EXTREME FOR YOU TO MAKE VOLUNTARY SUBMISSION. The divine commandments you are in duty bound to reference and obey. If you do not obey them, you will surely meet with the displeasure of the Almighty. . . . The forlorn condition in which you are placed does not destroy your moral obligation to God.

Document E: "Harvesting Cotton," Currier and Ives print

A COTTON PLANTATION ON THE MISSISSIPPI.

Library of Congress

Document F
Source: Abraham Lincoln, speech, Peoria, Illinois, October 1854.

Already the liberal party throughout the world express the apprehension "that the one retrograde institution in America is undermining the principles of progress and fatally violating the noblest political system the world ever saw." This is not the taunt of enemies but the warning of friends. Is it quite safe to disregard it, to despise it? . . .

In our greedy chase to make profit of the Negro, let us beware lest we "cancel and tear in pieces" even the white man's charter of freedom.

Document G: A Catechism for Slaves, 1854
Source: Belmonte, *Speaking of America*, vol. I, 272 (Frederick Doulgass's Paper, 2 June 1854, from *The Southern Episcopalian* [Charleston, South Carolina, April 1854]).

Q: Who gave you a master and mistress?
A: God gave them to me.

Q: Who says you must obey them?
A: God says I must.

Q: What book tells you these things?
A: The Bible.

Q: How does God do all his work?
A: He always does it right.

Q: Does God love to work?
A: Yes, God is always at work.

Q: Do the angels work?
A: Yes, they do what God tells them.

. . . .

Q: What does God say about your work?
A: That they who will not work shall not eat.

. . . .

Q: What makes you lazy?
A: My wicked heart.

Q: How do you know your heart is wicked?
A: I feel it every day.

Q: Who teaches you so many wicked things?
A: The Devil.

Q: Must you let the Devil teach you?
A: No, I must not.

Document H
Source: Poster for *Uncle Tom's Cabin*, c. 1860.

Granger Collection

Document I: Stephen F. Hale, commissioner from Alabama, to Governor Beriah Magoffin of Kentucky, 27 December 1860, encouraging Kentucky to secede
Source: Excerpted from Charles B. Dew, *Apostles of Disunion*, 92–98.

African slavery has not only become one of the fixed domestic institutions of the Southern States, but forms an important element of their political power, and constitutes the most valuable species of their property, worth, according to recent estimates, not less than $4,000,000,000; forming, in fact, the basis upon which rests the prosperity and wealth of most of these States, and supplying the commerce of the world with its richest freights, and furnishing the manufactories of two continents with raw material, and their operatives with bread. It is upon this gigantic interest, this peculiar institution, that the Northern States and their people have been waging an unrelenting and fanatical war for the last quarter century. . . .

[Abraham Lincoln] stands forth as the representative of the fanaticism of the North, which, . . . acknowledges allegiance to a higher law than the Constitution striking down the sovereignty and equality of the States, and resting its claims to popular favor upon one dogma—the equality of the races, white and black.

Therefore . . . the election of Mr. Lincoln cannot be regarded otherwise than a solemn declaration, on the part of a great majority of the Northern people, of hostility to the South . . . ; nothing less than . . . [inaugurating] all the horrors of a Santo Domingo servile insurrection, consigning her citizens to assassinations and her wives and daughters to pollution and violation to gratify the lust of half-civilized Africans.

DBQ 7
Abraham Lincoln and the Struggle for Union and Emancipation, 1861–1865

Directions: In this DBQ, you must compose an essay that uses both your interpretation of Documents A–L and your own outside knowledge of the period mentioned in this question.

In a letter to newspaperman Horace Greeley on August 22, 1862, Abraham Lincoln explained, "If I could save the Union without freeing any slave I would do it; and if I could save it by freeing all the slaves, I would do it; and if I could do it by freeing some and leaving others, I would also do that." A month later, however, Lincoln issued the Emancipation Proclamation, making the abolition of slavery, as well as the preservation of the Union, a war aim. Discuss the relationship between Lincoln's goals of preserving the Union and freeing the slaves.

Use these documents and your knowledge of the period from 1861 to 1865 to compose your answer.

Document A
Source: Abraham Lincoln to Congress, March 1862.

I recommend the adoption of a joint resolution by your honorable bodies, which shall be substantially as follows: Resolved, that the United States ought to cooperate with any state which may adopt gradual abolishment of slavery, giving to such state pecuniary aid, to be used by such state, in its discretion, to compensate for the inconveniences, public and private, produced by such change of system. . . . The Federal government would find its highest interest in such a measure as one of the most efficient means of self preservation.

Document B
Source: Abraham Lincoln to a Committee of Religious Denominations of Chicago, 13 September 1862.

I will also concede that emancipation would help us in Europe, and convince them that we are incited by something more than ambition. . . . [U]nquestionably, it would weaken the rebels by drawing off their laborers, which is of great importance; but I am not so sure we could do much with the blacks. If we were to arm them, I fear that in a few weeks the arms would be in the hands of the rebels; and, indeed, thus far we have not had arms enough to equip our white troops.

Document C: Jefferson Davis to the Confederate Congress, 14 January 1863

We may well leave it to the instincts of that common humanity which a beneficent Creator has implanted in the breasts of our fellow-men of all countries to pass judgment on [the Emancipation Proclamation] by which several millions of human beings of an inferior race, peaceful and contented laborers in their sphere, are doomed to extermination, while at the same time they are encouraged to a general assassination of their masters. . . . Our own detestation of those who have attempted the most execrable measure recorded in the history of guilty man is tempered by profound contempt for the impotent rage which it discloses. . . .

This proclamation is also an authentic statement by the Government of the United States of its inability to subjugate the South by force of arms, and as such must be accepted by neutral nations, which no longer find any justification in withholding our just claims to formal recognition.

Document D: Breaking That "Backbone"
Source: Published by Currier & Ives, Nassau St., N.Y. (1862 or 1863).

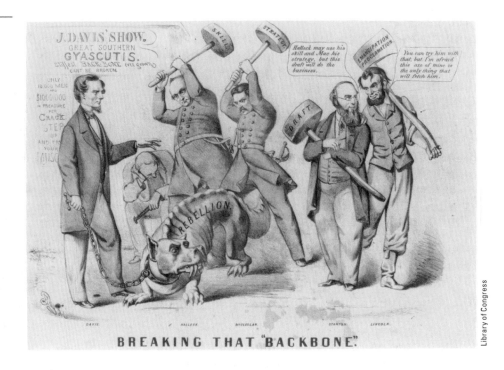

BREAKING THAT "BACKBONE."

Library of Congress

Document E: "The Emancipation Proclamation. Speeches of the Hon. Albert Andrus, of Franklin, and Hon. William H. Brand, of Madison, delivered in the [New York] Assembly, on the evening of March 4th, 1863, . . ."
Source: African American Pamphlet Collection (Library of Congress).

[Albert Andrus]: The great question before the House now is, whether the President acted wisely, or whether he has the right, under the Constitution of the United States, to issue [the] proclamation of emancipation. . . . [T]here is no power given in the Constitution for the President or Congress to abolish a state institution. . . . But, Sir, there is a war power given to the commander-in-chief of the army and navy in extreme cases which would justify him in resorting to every means in his power for the salvation of our country.

I consider that the southern people have forfeited all rights and protection under the constitution. . . . When, Sir, I consider that those rebellious states, without good cause or provocation, have ruthlessly and wickedly undertaken to overthrow the best government that God ever gave to man . . . I am free to say that in my opinion the emancipation measure should have a fair trial.

[William Brand]: But, Sir, the lives and property, including slaves, of all true union men and women should be protected . . . , provided they will lay down their arms and return and become loyal subjects to the Government as it was, and the Constitution as it is.

Document F
Source: Recruiting Poster for the 54th Massachusetts Regiment, 1863.

Massachusetts Historical Society

Document G

Source: Lincoln to members of the Democratic Party, speech, 26 August 1863.

You say you will not fight to free negroes. Some of them seem willing to fight for you, but, no matter. Fight you, then, exclusively to save the Union. I issued the proclamation on purpose to aid you in saving the Union.

Document H

Source: Thomas Buckner on anti-Negro rioting in Detroit, self-published pamphlet, 1863.

The present state of affairs in relation to the colored people is one of great perplexity, and it is not only so on account of the South but also in the North. . . .

On the one hand, they are being mobbed, and everything that is sacred to a people to make a country or home dear are denied them in many of the large Northern cities. On the other hand, they are marching off to the call of the government as if they were sharing all the blessings of the most favored citizens!

Document J

Source: Abraham Lincoln, Second Inaugural Address, March 1865.

One-eighth of the whole population were colored slaves, not distributed generally over the Union, but localized in the southern part of it. These slaves constituted a peculiar and powerful interest. All knew that this interest was somehow the cause of the war. To strengthen, perpetuate, and extend this interest was the object for which the insurgents would rend the Union even by war, while the government claimed no right to do more than to restrict the territorial enlargement of it.

Neither party expected for the war the magnitude or the duration which it has already attained. Neither anticipated that the cause of the conflict might cease with or even before the conflict itself should cease. Each looked for an easier triumph and a result less fundamental and astounding.

Document I: The Old Union Wagon

Source: Entry 1863 -15. Library of Congress Rare Books and Special Collections Division, Washington, D.C.

Document K: Frederick Douglass, "Oration in Memory of Abraham Lincoln," 14 April 1876, delivered at the Unveiling of the Freedmen's Monument in Memory of Abraham Lincoln, recounting Lincoln during the Civil War

[W]e are here to express, as best we may, by appropriate forms and ceremonies, our grateful sense of the vast, high, and preeminent services rendered to ourselves, to our race, to our country, and to the whole world by Abraham Lincoln. . . .

It must be admitted, truth compels me to admit, even here in the presence of the monument we have erected to his memory, Abraham Lincoln was not, in the fullest sense of the word, either our man or our model. . . .

He was preeminently the white man's President, entirely devoted to the welfare of white men. He was ready and willing at any time during the first years of his administration to deny, postpone, and sacrifice the rights of humanity in the colored people to promote the welfare of the white people of this country. . . .

Our faith in him was often taxed and strained to the uttermost, but it never failed. . . .

[U]nder his wise and beneficent rule we saw ourselves gradually lifted from the depths of slavery to the heights of liberty and manhood. . . .

Viewed from the genuine abolition ground, Mr. Lincoln seemed tardy, cold, dull, and indifferent; but measuring him by the sentiment of his country, a sentiment he was bound as a statesman to consult, he was swift, zealous, radical, and determined. . . .

[B]ecause of his fidelity to union and liberty, he is doubly dear to us, and his memory will be precious forever.

Document L: National picture. Behold oh! America, your sons. The greatest among men / L. Kurz; lith. by Chas. Shober, Chicago
Source: Entry 1865 -8. Library of Congress Prints and Photographs Division, Washington, D.C.

PART FOUR: Forging an Industrial Society, 1865–1909

DBQ 8
The Role of Capitalists, 1875–1900

Directions: In this DBQ, you must compose an essay that uses both your interpretation of Documents A–J and your own outside knowledge of the period mentioned in this question.

> Historians have often portrayed the capitalists who shaped post–Civil War industrial America as either admirable "captains of industry" or corrupt "robber barons." Evaluate which of these is a more accurate characterization of these capitalists.
>
> Use these documents and your knowledge of the period from 1875 to 1900 to compose your answer.

Document A
Source: Henry George, *Progress and Poverty,* 1879.

> The wealthy class is becoming more wealthy; but the poorer class is becoming more dependent. The gulf between the employed and the employer is growing wider; social contrasts are becoming sharper; as liveried carriages appear; so do barefooted children.

Document B
Source: C. D. Warner, "The South Revisited," *Harper's New Monthly Magazine*, March 1887.

> When we come to the New Industrial South, the change is marvelous. . . . Instead of a South devoted to agriculture . . . we find a South wide awake to business, excited and even astonished at the development of its own immense resources, . . . eagerly laying lines of communication, rapidly opening mines, building furnaces, foundries, and all sorts of shops for utilizing the native riches. . . .
>
> The South is manufacturing a great variety of things needed in the house, on the farm, and in the shops, for home consumption, and already sends to the North and West several manufactured products. . . .
>
> When I have been asked what impressed me the most in this hasty tour, I have always said that the most notable thing was that everybody was at work. . . . [E]very man, woman, and child was actively employed, and in most cases there were fewer idlers than in many Northern towns. . . .
>
> It cannot be too strongly impressed upon the public mind that the South . . . is marching with the North in the same purpose of wealth by industry.

Document C
Source: Andrew Carnegie, *Gospel of Wealth,* 1889.

> This, then, is held to be the duty of the man of wealth: . . . to consider all surplus revenues which come to him simply as trust funds, which he is called upon to administer, and strictly bound as a matter of duty to administer in the manner which, in his judgment, is best calculated to produce the most beneficial results for the community—the man of wealth thus becoming the mere agent and trustee for his poorer brethren, bring to their service his superior wisdom, experience, and ability to administer, doing for them better than they would or could do for themselves. . . .

Document D
Source: The Robber Barons of Today, 1889.

Document E

Source: James B. Weaver, Populist presidential candidate, *A Call to Action,* 1892.

The trust is organized commerce with the Golden Rule excluded and the trustees exempted from the restraints of conscience.

The main weapons of the trust are threats, intimidation, bribery, fraud, wreck, and pillage. Take one well-authenticated instance in the history of the Oat Meal Trust as an example. In 1887 this trust decided that a part of their mills should stand idle. They were accordingly closed. This resulted in the discharge of a large number of laborers who had to suffer in consequence. . . .

The most distressing feature of this war of the trusts is the fact that they control the articles which the plain people consume in their daily life. It cuts off their accumulations and deprives them of the staff upon which they fain would lean in their old age.

Document F: The Breakers, Vanderbilt "summer cottage," Newport, Rhode Island, c. 1904. Built 1893–1895 by Cornelius Vanderbilt, II

Photo Courtesy of The Preservation Society of Newport County

Document G

Source: E. Levasseur, "The Concentration of Industry, and Machinery in the United States," *Annals of the American Academy of Political and Social Science,* March 1897.

In the Senate inquiry of 1883, [on] education and labor, a weaver . . . said that he had worked seventeen years in England, and that conditions were much better than in America. The manufacturers there were not so desirous as they are here of working their men like horses or slaves. . . .

The manufacturers judge that the movement to [mechanize] has been advantageous to workmen . . . because the level of salaries has been raised, . . . because they purchase more with the same sum, and . . . because their task has become less onerous, the machine doing nearly everything which requires great strength. . . .

The laboring classes do not share this optimism. They reproach the machine with exhausting the physical powers of the laborer; . . . They reproach it with demanding such continued attention that it enervates, and of leaving no respite to the laborer, through the continuity of its movement. . . . They reproach the machine with degrading man by transforming him into a machine . . . [and] with diminishing the number of skilled workers, permitting . . . the substitution of unskilled workers and lowering the average level of wages.

Document H: Clement Studebaker, manufacturer of horse-drawn vehicles, testimony to Chicago Conference on Trusts, 1899

Source: *Annals of America,* vol. 12, 298.

No true monopoly is possible in this country except that enjoyed by virtue of a patent granted by the United States. If those who undertake to inaugurate trusts had a monopoly of the trust business there would be cause for alarm. But anyone can go into the trust . . . business who is able to find others who will join him. Herein is the safety of society. Combinations of capital build railroads and decrease the cost of travel and transportation. Some part of their saving they keep as profit, but whenever they undertake to keep so much of it from the public as to give them unusually large returns on their capital, a rival road springs up, and down goes the cost to the customer.

Trusts have undertaken to enfold producers so as to limit competition, but in vain. . . . Whenever . . . great companies give evidence of making large profits, some powerful rival comes to the field, and competition proceeds to regulate prices on a lower plane.

Document I: John D. Rockefeller, testimony to the United States Industrial Commission, before the House of Representatives, 1899

Source: *Annals of America*, vol. 12, 314–315.

I ascribe the success of the Standard [Oil Company] to its consistent policy to make the volume of business large through the merits and cheapness of its products. It has spared no expense in finding, securing, and utilizing the best and cheapest methods of manufacturing. It has sought for the best superintendents and workmen and paid the best wages. . . . It has not only sought markets for its principal products but for all possible byproducts. . . . It has not hesitated to invest millions of dollars in methods of cheapening the gathering and distribution of oil by pipelines, special cars, tank steamers, and tank wagons. . . .

It is too late to argue about advantages of industrial combinations. They are a necessity.

Their chief advantages are: (1) command of necessary capital; . . . (4) economy in the business; (5) improvements and economies which are derived from knowledge of many interested persons of wide experience; (6) power to give the public improved products at less prices and still make a profit for stockholders. . . .

Document J

Source: Breaker Boys at Woodward Coal Mining, Kingston, Pennsylvania, c. 1900.

Library of Congress

DBQ 9
The Farmers' Movement, 1870–1900

Directions: In this DBQ, you must compose an essay that uses both your interpretation of Documents A–I and your own outside knowledge of the period mentioned in this question.

> **Why did farmers express discontent during 1870–1900, and what impact did their new attitudes and actions have on national politics?**
>
> Use these documents and your knowledge of the period from 1870 to 1900 to compose your answer.

Document A
Source: The Farmers' Grievances, 1875. (See text p. 597 for full-size illustration.)

Granger Collection

Document B
Source: Booker T. Washington to George Washington Cable, 8 October 1889.

When the [Civil] War ended the colored people had nothing much on which to live. . . . They had to get the local merchant or someone else to supply the food for the family to eat while the first crop was being made. For every dollar's worth of provisions so advanced the local merchant charged from 12 to 30 percent interest. In order to be sure that he secured his principal and interest a mortgage or lien was taken on the crop. . . . Of course the farmers could pay no such interest and the end of the first year found them in debt—the 2nd year they tried again, but there was the old debt and the new interest to pay, and in this way the "mortgage system" has gotten a hold on everything that it seems impossible to shake off. Its evils have grown instead of decreasing, until it is safe to say that 5/6 of the colored farmers mortgage their crops every year. . . . [In] most every case mules, cows, wagons, plows and often all household furniture [are also] covered by the lien. . . .

Many of the colored farmers have almost given up hope. . . .

Document C
Source: Mary E. Lease, lawyer, speech, 1890.

The great common people of this country are slaves, and monopoly is the master. The West and South are bound and prostrate before the manufacturing East.

The parties lie to us and the political speakers mislead us. We were told two years ago to go to work and raise a big crop, that was all we needed. We went to work and plowed and planted; the rains fell, the sun shone, nature smiled, and we raised the big crop that they told us to; and what came of it? Eight-cent corn, ten-cent oats, two-cent beef, and no price at all for butter and eggs—that's what came of it.

We want money, land, and transportation. We want the abolition of the national banks, and we want the power to make loans direct from the government. We want the accursed foreclosure system wiped out. Land equal to a tract thirty miles wide and ninety miles long has been foreclosed and bought in my loan companies of Kansas in a year.

Document D

Source: Presidential Election of 1892. (See text p. 507 for full-size map.)

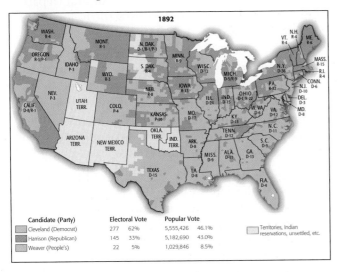

Document E

Source: Richard Olney, future United States Attorney General, to Charles E. Perkins, president of the Chicago and Burlington Railroad, letter, 1892.

The [Interstate Commerce] Commission, as its functions have now been limited by the courts, is, or can be made of great use to the railroads. It satisfies the popular clamor for a government supervision of railroads, at the same time that supervision is almost entirely nominal. Further, the older such a commission gets to be, the more inclined it will be found to take the business and railroad view of things. It thus becomes a sort of barrier between railroad corporations and the people and a sort of protection against hasty and crude legislation hostile to railroad interests. . . . The part of wisdom is not to destroy the Commission but to utilize it.

Document F

Source: F. B. Tracy, "Why the Farmers Revolted," *Forum*, October 1893.

Nothing has done more to injure the [western] region than these freight rates. The railroads have retarded its growth as much as they first hastened it. The rates are often four times as large as Eastern rates. . . .

These freight rates have been especially burdensome to the farmers, who are far from their selling and buying markets. . . .

Another fact which has incited the farmer against corporations is the bold and unblushing participation of the railways in politics. . . . [The] railroads have secured an iron grip upon legislatures. . . .

Closely connected . . . are the money grievances. As . . . the farmer could not make payments on his land . . . he found that he could not sell his produce at a profit . . . [and] that the rate of interest was rapidly rising. . . .

Disaster always follows the exaction of such exorbitant rates of interest, and want or eviction quickly came. . . . Like a lightning flash, the idea of political action ran through the alliances. A few farmers' victories in county campaigns the previous year became a promise of broader conquest, and with one bound the Farmers' Alliance went into politics all over the West.

Document G: Leading Economic Sectors, 1849 and 1899

Source: *Historical Statistics of the United States; Statistical Abstract of the United States,* relevant years; and Bureau of Economic Analysis.

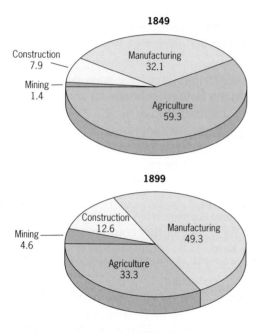

1849

Construction 7.9
Manufacturing 32.1
Mining 1.4
Agriculture 59.3

1899

Construction 12.6
Manufacturing 49.3
Mining 4.6
Agriculture 33.3

Document H: "Government Crop Report"

Source: *New York Times,* 13 June 1894.

[C]rop reports received by the Agricultural Department as made public to-day show the following results by States:

New-Jersey[sic]—Excessive rains and cool nights were injurious to all crops; locusts very destructive; much corn and potatoes replanted. . . .

South Carolina—Cotton shows slight improvement, but remains small; corn beginning to suffer from drought; . . . forage drops generally are drying up, . . . drought becoming serious.

Georgia—All crops at a standstill from drought; even corn begins to wither. . . .

Alabama—Drought continues . . . cotton and corn drying up in places. . . .

Mississippi—Cool and dry; unfavorable for all crops; corn small . . . cotton full of lice; potatoes not producing well. . . .

Tennessee—tobacco drying from drought. . . .

Illinois—Drought beginning to injuriously affect crops. . . .

Wisconsin—Rain needed; some damage by frost first of last week. . . .

Minnesota—Drought continues and late-sown grain, grass, gardens, and small fruit suffering; clinch and potato bug ravages increasing.

Nebraska—Local rains have greatly improved crops; corn prospects generally very good; small grain will be short; pastures recovering.

Document I

Source: *London Standard,* commenting on William Jennings Bryan's defeat in the presidential election, 1896.

The complete rejection of Bryan's tempting program, addressed to indolence, incapacity, and cupidity, shows that these qualities are less widely distributed in the United States than Bryan would have us believe. . . . The hopelessly ignorant and savagely covetous waifs and strays of American civilization voted for Bryan, but the bulk of the solid sense, business, integrity, and social stability sided with McKinley. The nation is to be heartily congratulated.

PART FIVE: Struggling for Justice at Home and Abroad, 1901–1945

DBQ 10

Progressivism and Its Antecedents, 1880–1920

Directions: In this DBQ, you must compose an essay that uses both your interpretation of Documents A–K and your own outside knowledge of the period mentioned in this question.

> **To what extent was the Progressive Movement (1900–1920) an extension of reformers' ideas and programs of the late nineteenth century?**
>
> Use these documents and your knowledge of the period from 1880 to 1920 to compose your answer.

Document A: Theodore Roosevelt, "Public Office and Private Gain," 1885

Source: *Annals of America*, vol. 11, 76–77.

In the three [sessions of the New York legislature] of which I have been a member, I have sat with bankers and bricklayers, with merchants and mechanics, with lawyers, . . . [and] saloon keepers. . . . Among my colleagues there were many very good men; there was a still more numerous class of men who were neither very good or very bad, but went one way or the other, according to the strength of the various conflicting influences acting around, behind, and upon them; and finally there were many very bad men. . . .

It is from [the] great cities that the worst legislators come. It is true that there are always among them a few cultivated and scholarly men who are well educated and who stand on a higher and broader intellectual and moral plane . . . , but the bulk are very low indeed. They are usually foreigners of little or no education, with exceedingly misty ideas as to morality, and possessed of an ignorance so profound [which] has at times [had] serious effects upon our laws. . . . [It is] so difficult to procure the passage of good laws or prevent the passage of bad ones. . . .

Document B: Preamble and Declaration of Principles of the Great and Growing Order of Workingmen, the Knights of Labor, 1886

The alarming development and aggressiveness of great capitalists and corporations, unless checked, will inevitably lead to the pauperization and hopeless degradation of the toiling classes. It is imperative . . . that a check be placed on unjust accumulation, and the power for evil of aggregated wealth. . . .

We declare to the world that our aims are: . . .

2. To secure to the worker the full enjoyment of the wealth they create [and] sufficient leisure to develop their intellectual, moral, and social faculties. . . .

In order to secure these results we demand of the State: . . .

4. The public lands, the heritage of the people, be reserved for actual settlers, not another acre for railroads or speculators. . . .

6. The adoption of measures providing for the health and safety of those engaged in mining, manufacturing, and the building industries, and indemnification to those engaged therein for injuries suffered through lack of necessary safeguards. . . .

11. The prohibition by law of the employment of children under fifteen years of age in workshops, mines and factories. . . .

13. That a graduated income tax be levied. . . .

16. That the importation of foreign labor under contract be prohibited. . . .

And while making the foregoing demands upon the State and national government, we will endeavor to associate our own labors to:

20. To secure for both sexes equal pay for equal work.

21. To shorten the hours of labor by a general refusal to work more than eight hours.

Document C: Shooting craps in the hall of the Newsboys' Lodging House
Source: Jacob Riis (1849–1914). Library of Congress Prints and Photographs Division, Washington, D.C.

Library of Congress

Document D: Henry Demarest Lloyd, *Wealth Against Commonwealth*, 1894

If our civilization is destroyed, . . . it will not be by [the] barbarians from below. Our barbarians come from above. Our great money-makers have sprung in one generation into seats of power kings do not know. The forces and the wealth are new, and have been the opportunity of new men. Without restraints of culture, experience, the pride, or even the inherited caution of class or rank, these men, intoxicated, think they are the wave instead of the float, and that they have created the business which has created them. . . . They claim a power without control, exercised through forms which make it secret, anonymous, and perpetual. The possibilities of its gratification have been widening before them without interruption since they began, and even at a thousand millions they will feel no satiation and will see no place to stop. They are gluttons of luxury and power, rough, unsocialized, believing that mankind must be kept terrorized. Powers of pity die out of them, because they work through agents and die in their agents, because what they do is not for themselves.

Document E: Samuel Jones, mayor of Toledo, Ohio, 1897–1904, "The New Patriotism: A Golden-Rule Government for Cities," *Municipal Affairs*, September 1899
Source: *Annals of America*, vol. 12, 316–321.

We have cities in which a few are wealthy, a few are in what may be called comfortable circumstances, vast numbers are propertyless, and thousands are in pauperism and crime. . . . [T]he inequalities that characterize our rich and poor [do not] represent the ideas that the founders of this republic saw when they wrote that "All men are created equal." . . .

Political parties are a curse to every department of our municipal government; the prime purpose of their existence is to capture the offices and administer every function of government [only for] the interest of the party. . . .

[C]ities have [financed] humanizing and educating influences [such] as children's playgrounds, free [bath houses], free music in the parks for people, and in some instances . . . free lectures and free concerts for the winter evenings. . . .

We are coming to understand that every public utility and necessity to the public welfare should be publicly owned, publicly operated, and publicly paid for. Among the properties that according to any scientific conception of the purpose of government should be so owned are waterworks, heating and lighting plants, street railways, telephones, . . . telegraphs, parks, playgrounds. . . .

Document F: [Anti-trust cartoons]: The little boy [Common People] and the big boys [Trusts] prepare for the baseball season

Source: Library of Congress Print and Photographs Division, Washington, D.C.

Document G: Niagara Movement's Declaration of Principles, 1905, Buffalo, New York

The members of the conference . . . congratulate the Negro-Americans on certain undoubted evidences of progress in the last decade particularly . . . the buying of property, the checking of crime, the uplift in home life, the advance in literature and art, and the demonstration of constructive and executive ability in the conduct of great religious, economic and educational institutions.

We believe in manhood suffrage. . . .

We believe also in protest against the curtailment of our civil [and political] rights. All American citizens have the right to equal treatment in places of public entertainment. . . .

We especially complain against the denial of equal opportunities to us in economic life; in the rural districts of the South this amounts to peonage and virtual slavery. . . .

We urge an increase in public high school facilities in the South, where the Negro-Americans are almost wholly without such provisions.

We demand upright judges in courts, juries selected without discrimination on account of color. . . .

Any discrimination based simply on race or color is barbarous, we care not how hallowed it be by custom, expediency or prejudice. . . .

We protest against the "Jim Crow" car, since [it renders] us open to insults and discomfort and [crucifies] wantonly our manhood, womanhood and self-respect. . . .

Of the above grievances we do not hesitate to . . . complain loudly and insistently. To ignore, overlook, or apologize for these wrongs is to prove ourselves unworthy of freedom. Persistent manly agitation is the way to liberty. . . .

Document H: Strikes, Ladies Tailors, New York, February 1910, Picket Girls on Duty

Source: George Grantham Bain Collection, Library of Congress.

Document I: 1912 Democratic Party Platform

The expanding organization of industry makes it essential that there should be no abridgment of the right of the wage earners and producers to organize for the protection of wages and the improvement of labor conditions, to the end that such labor organizations and their members should not be regarded as illegal combinations in restraint of trade.

We pledge the Democratic party to the enactment of a law creating a department of labor, represented separately in the President's cabinet. . . .

We congratulate the country upon the triumph of two important reforms demanded in the last national platform, namely, the amendment of the Federal Constitution authorizing an income tax, and the amendment providing for the popular election of senators, and we call upon the people of all the States to rally to the support of the pending propositions and secure their ratification.

We favor the immediate downward revision of the existing high, and in many cases prohibitive, tariff duties, insisting that material reductions be speedily made upon the necessaries of life. Articles entering into competition with trust-controlled products and articles of American manufacture which are sold abroad more cheaply than at home should be put upon the free list.

Document J: "Comstockery in America"
Source: Margaret Sanger, July 1915, *The Woman Rebel*

[The Comstock laws] were passed [in 1873] and executed ostensibly to prevent the passage of obscene literature through the U.S. mails. . . . Anthony Comstock [US Post Office Inspector and Secretary for the Society for the Suppression of Vice] then became the official guardian of American morality. . . .

There have been many publications during these years which have been suppressed by the orders of Comstock . . .[;] one of the latest, and most flagrant . . . was in the suppression and confiscation of the monthly publication, "The Woman Rebel." This was a working woman's paper, the first of its kind ever issued in America. [It] claimed that one of the working woman's greatest enslavements was her ignorance of the means to control the size of her family. The editor [Sanger] promised to defy the existing law. . . .

[The issues of *The Woman Rebel* were suppressed] and three indictments . . . covering twelve counts, were returned against me [Sanger], as the editor [by a federal grand jury]. All the indictments were returned and counts were made on all articles which discussed the idea of the Working Woman keeping down the number of her family.

Document K: Keating-Owen Child Labor Act of 1916

AN ACT To prevent interstate commerce in the products of child labor, and for other purposes.

Be it enacted by the Senate and House of Representatives of the United States of America in Congress assembled, That no producer, manufacturer, or dealer shall ship or deliver for shipment in interstate or foreign commerce, any article or commodity the product of any mine or quarry situated in the United States, [where] children under the age of sixteen years have been employed or permitted to work, or any article or commodity the product of any mill, cannery, workshop, factory, or manufacturing establishment, situated in the United States [where] children under the age of fourteen years have been employed or permitted to work, or children between the ages of fourteen years and sixteen years have been employed or permitted to work more than eight hours in any day, or more than six days in any week, or after the hour of seven o'clock [PM], or before the hour of six o'clock [AM].

DBQ 11
The United States as World Power, 1895–1920

Directions: In this DBQ, you must compose an essay that uses both your interpretation of Documents A–I and your own outside knowledge of the period mentioned in this question.

> **Which factor, self-interest or idealism, was more important in driving American foreign policy in the years 1895–1920?**
>
> Use these documents and your knowledge of the period from 1895 to 1920 to compose your answer.

Document A
Source: *Washington Post* editorial, 1896.

A new consciousness seems to have come upon us—the consciousness of strength—and with it a new appetite, the yearning to show our strength. . . . Ambition, interest, land hunger, pride, the mere joy of fighting, whatever it may be, we are animated by a new sensation. We are face to face with a strange destiny. The taste of Empire is in the mouth of the people even as the taste of blood is in the jungle. It means an Imperial policy, the Republic renascent, taking her place with the armed nations.

Document B
Source: Senator Albert J. Beveridge, speech, Indianapolis, 16 September 1898.

[T]oday we are raising more than we can consume. Today we are making more than we can use. Today our industrial society is congested; there are more workers than there is work; there is more capital than there is investment. . . . Therefore we must find new markets for our produce, new occupation for our capital, new work for our labor. . . .

The commercial supremacy of the Republic means that this Nation is to be the sovereign factor in the peace of the world. For the conflicts of the future are to be conflicts of trade—struggles for markets—commercial wars for existence. . . . We cannot fly from our world duties; it is ours to execute the purpose of a fate that has driven us to be greater than our small intentions. We cannot retreat from any soil where Providence has unfurled our banner; it is ours to save that soil for liberty and civilization.

Document C
Source: William Graham Sumner, university professor, essay in *War and Other Essays*, 1919 (first published in 1898).

There is not a civilized nation which does not talk about its civilizing mission just as grandly as we do. . . . We assume that what we like and practice, and what we think better, must come as a welcome blessing to Spanish-Americans and Filipinos. This is grossly and obviously untrue. . . . They like their own ways, and if we appear amongst them as rulers, there will be social discord. . . . [The] reason why liberty, of which we Americans talk so much, is a good thing is that it means leaving people to live out their own lives in their own way, while we do the same.

Document D: Edward D. Whitney, "Meaning of the Decisions in the Insular Cases"
Source: *New York Times*, 16 June 1901.

Congress may extend or withhold the Constitution over the territory under its control. . . . [The cases decide] that the provinces ceded by Spain are not part of "the United States" as that phrase is used in the Constitution. . . . This much is agreed upon by a majority of the [Supreme] court. . . . The treaty-making power may bring foreign countries into the ownership and possession of the United States, but it can not incorporate them as part of the United States, because an act of this fundamental importance requires the assent, not only of the President and the Senate, but also of the House of Representatives. . . .

The most important indirect result . . . is that the [Puerto] Ricans and Filipinos do not become citizens of the United States under the Fourteenth Amendment, nor is Congress obliged to extend our . . . naturalization laws over these islands.

Document E

Source: American Missionary Grace Roberts Teaching in China, 1903. (See text p. 623 for full-size photograph.)

By permission of the Houghton Library, Harvard University, ACB 78.1

Document F

Source: President Theodore Roosevelt, annual message to Congress, December 6, 1904.

Our interests and those of our southern neighbors are in reality identical. They have great natural riches, and if within their borders the reign of law and justice obtains, prosperity is sure to come to them. While they thus obey the primary laws of civilized society, they may rest assured that they will be treated by us in a spirit of cordial and helpful sympathy. We would interfere with them only in the last resort, and then only if it became evident that their inability or unwillingness to do justice at home and abroad had violated the rights of the United States or had invited foreign aggression to the detriment of the entire body of American nations.

Document G

Source: United States Expansion, 1857–1917. (See text p. 611 for full-size map.)

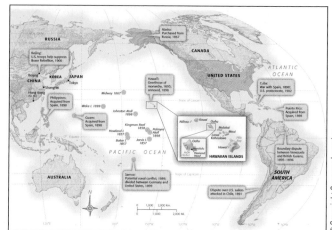

© Copyright Cengage Learning

Document H
Source: President Woodrow Wilson to Congress, 2 April 1917.

I officially laid before you [in February, 1917] the extraordinary announcement of the Imperial German Government that . . . it was [Germany's] purpose to put aside all restraints of law and humanity and use its submarines to sink every vessel that sought to approach either the ports of Great Britain . . . or any of the ports controlled by the enemies of Germany. . . .

It is a war against all nations. . . . Our motive will not be revenge or the victorious assertion of the physical might of the nation, but only the vindication of right, of human right, of which we are only a single champion. . . .

It is a fearful thing to lead this great peaceful people into war . . . , [but] the right is more precious than peace, and we shall fight for the things which we have always carried nearest our hearts— for democracy, for the right of those who submit to authority to have a voice in their own Governments, for the rights and liberties of small nations, for a universal dominion of right by such a concert of free peoples as shall bring peace and safety to all nations and make the world itself at last free.

Document I: "Can He Produce the Harmony?"
Source: Reprinted from *The Brooklyn Citizen* in *Review of Reviews*, Vol. 59, No. 6. February 1919. The Ohio State University Cartoon Research Library.

© George Matthew Adams

CAN HE PRODUCE THE HARMONY?
From the *Citizen* (Brooklyn, N. Y.)

DBQ 12

Analyzing the Causes and Effects of the Great Depression, 1919–1939

Directions: In this DBQ, you must compose an essay that uses both your interpretation of Documents A–J and your own outside knowledge of the period mentioned in this question.

Analyze the causes of the Great Depression and its effects on American society.

Use these documents and your knowledge of the period from 1919 to 1939 to compose your answer.

Document A
Source: National Bureau of Economic Research.

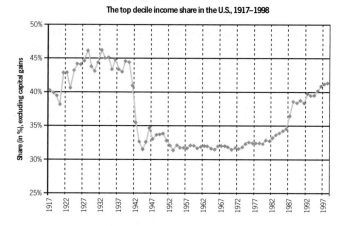

The top decile income share in the U.S., 1917–1998

Document B: Hawthorne Daniel, "Living and Dying on the Installment Plan," 1926
Source: *World's Work*, January 1926, 329 (reprinted in *The Roaring Twenties: An Eyewitness History* by Tom Streissguth, *Facts on File, Inc.*).

So popular has installment buying become, with purchasers as well as manufacturers and merchants, that it is possible today to buy almost everything from candy to private yachts on the deferred payment plan. Within the last twenty years, and particularly within the last six, installment buying has grown like a mushroom, and now there are few things besides carfare, meals at restaurants, and theatre tickets that cannot be paid for at so much down and so much periodically . . . since the country really has more money than it needs, the additional cost to the purchase has not yet caused any vital difficulties.

Document C: "Bankers v. Panic," 1929
Source: *Time Magazine*, 4 November 1929.

Promptly at 10 a. m. on Thursday Oct. 24, sounded the gong of the New York Stock Exchange and 6,000 shares of Montgomery Ward changed hands at 83—its 1929 high having been 156.

For so many months so many people had saved money and borrowed money and borrowed on their borrowings to possess themselves of the little pieces of paper by virtue of which they became partners in U. S. Industry. Now they were trying to get rid of them even more frantically than they had tried to get them. Stocks bought without reference to their earnings were being sold without reference to their dividends. At around noon there came the no-bid menace. Even in a panic-market, someone must buy the "dumped" shares, but stocks were dropping from 2 to 10 points between sales—losing from 2 to 10 points before a buyer could be found for them. Sound stocks at shrunk prices—and nobody to buy them. It looked as if U. S. Industries' little partners were in a fair way to bankrupt the firm.

Document D: Herbert Hoover, Statement on the Tariff Bill, 15 June 1930

I SHALL approve the tariff bill. This legislation has now been under almost continuous consideration by Congress for nearly 15 months. It was undertaken as the result of pledges given by the Republican Party at Kansas City. Its declarations embraced these obligations:

"The Republican Party believes that the home market built up under the protective policy belongs to the American farmer, and it pledges its support of legislation which will give this market to him to the full extent of his ability to supply it. . . .

"There are certain industries which cannot now successfully compete with foreign producers because of lower foreign wages and a lower cost of living abroad. . . .

The complaints from some foreign countries that these duties have been placed unduly high can be remedied, if justified, by proper application to the Tariff Commission. . . . It is urgent that the uncertainties in the business world which have been added to by the long-extended debate of the measure should be ended. They can be ended only by completion of this bill. Meritorious demands for further protection to agriculture and labor which have developed since the tariff of 1922 would not end if this bill fails of enactment. Agitation for legislative tariff revision would necessarily continue before the country. Nothing would contribute to retard business recovery more than this continued agitation.

Document E

Source: *Daily Telegram* by Will Rogers, 26 November 1930.

Some of the writers are having a little trouble scraping up a reason for Thanksgiving this year. Some think we ought to skip a year and put on a big one in '31.

The original idea of the day was to give thanks for a "bountiful harvest." Well, the "bountiful harvest" is the very thing that's the matter with us. Too much wheat, too much corn, too much cotton, too much beef, too much production of everything.

So we are going through a unique experience. We are the first nation to starve to death in a storehouse that's overfilled with everything we want.

Document F: Unemployment statistics, 1929–1941

Source: U.S. Bureau of the Census, *Historical Statistics of the United States, Colonial Times to 1970* (Washington, D.C., 1975).

UNEMPLOYMENT: 1929 TO 1941	
Year	Percentage of Labor Force
1929	3.2%
1930	8.7%
1931	15.9%
1932	23.6%
1933	24.9%
1934	21.7%
1935	20.1%
1936	16.9%
1937	14.3%
1938	19.0%
1939	17.2%
1940	14.6%
1941	9.9%

Document G: Electoral College maps, 1928 and 1932

Election of 1928 Electoral College Map

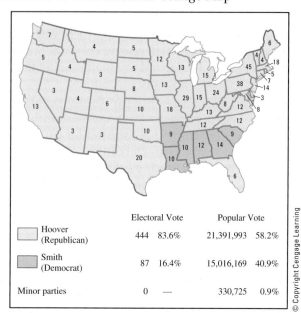

	Electoral Vote		Popular Vote	
Hoover (Republican)	444	83.6%	21,391,993	58.2%
Smith (Democrat)	87	16.4%	15,016,169	40.9%
Minor parties	0	—	330,725	0.9%

© Copyright Cengage Learning

Election of 1932 Electoral College Map

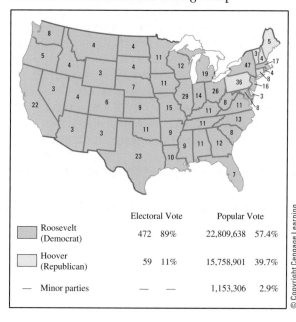

	Electoral Vote		Popular Vote	
Roosevelt (Democrat)	472	89%	22,809,638	57.4%
Hoover (Republican)	59	11%	15,758,901	39.7%
— Minor parties	—	—	1,153,306	2.9%

© Copyright Cengage Learning

Document H: Political cartoon by John Tinney McCutcheon

Source: *Chicago Tribune*, 1932.

The Granger Collection, New York

Document I: John Maynard Keynes, "An Open Letter to President Roosevelt"

Source: *New York Times*, 31 December 1933.

The object of recovery is to increase the national output and put more men to work. In the economic system of the modern world, output is primarily produced *for sale*; and the volume of output depends on the amount of purchasing power, compared with the prime cost of production, which is expected to come in the market. Broadly speaking, therefore, an increase of output depends on the amount of purchasing power, compared with the prime cost of production, which is expected to come on the market. Broadly speaking, therefore, an increase of output cannot occur unless by the operation of one or other of three factors. Individuals must be induced to spend more out of their existing incomes; or the business world must be induced, either by increased confidence in the prospects or by a lower rate of interest, to create additional current incomes in the hands of their employees, which is what happens when either the working or the fixed capital of the country is being increased; or public authority must be called in aid to create additional current incomes through the expenditure of borrowed or printed money. In bad times the first factor cannot be expected to work on a sufficient scale. The second factor will come in as the second wave of attack on the slump *after* the tide has been turned by the expenditures of public authority. It is, therefore, only from the third factor that we can expect the initial major impulse.

Document J: Social Security poster, 1935
Source: FDR Presidential Library.

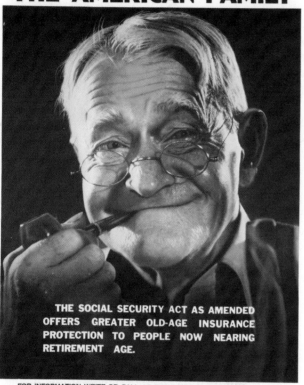

MORE SECURITY FOR THE AMERICAN FAMILY

THE SOCIAL SECURITY ACT AS AMENDED OFFERS GREATER OLD-AGE INSURANCE PROTECTION TO PEOPLE NOW NEARING RETIREMENT AGE.

FOR INFORMATION WRITE OR CALL AT THE NEAREST FIELD OFFICE OF THE **SOCIAL SECURITY BOARD**

Document K: Excerpt from John Steinbeck, *The Grapes of Wrath*, 1939
Source: Chapter 19, 316–319.

Now farming became industry. . . . And it came about that owners no longer worked on their farms. They farmed on paper; and they forgot the land, the smell, the feel of it, and remembered only that they owned it, remembered only what they gained and lost by it. And some of the farms grew so large that one man could not even conceive of them any more, so large that it took batteries of bookkeepers to keep track of interest and gain and loss. . . . And the owners not only did not work the farms any more, many of them had never seen the farms they owned. . . .

And the dispossessed, the migrants, flowed into California, two hundred and fifty thousand, and three hundred thousand. Behind them new tractors were going on the land and the tenants were being forced off. And new waves were on the way, new waves of the dispossessed and the homeless, hardened, intent, and dangerous. . . .

And a homeless hungry man, driving the roads with his wife beside him and his thin children in the back seat, could look at the fallow fields which might produce food but not profit and that man could know how a fallow field is a sin and the unused land a crime against the thin children. . . . And in the south he saw the golden oranges hanging on the trees, the little golden oranges on the dark green trees; and guards with shotguns patrolling the lines so a man might not pick an orange for a thin child, oranges to be dumped if the price was low. . . .

He drove his old car to Hooverville . . . for there was a Hooverville on the edge of every town.

PART SIX: Making Modern America, 1945 to the Present

DBQ 13
The Cold War, 1941–1953

Directions: In this DBQ, you must compose an essay that uses both your interpretation of Documents A–I and your own outside knowledge of the period mentioned in this question.

From 1941 to 1945, the United States and the Soviet Union were allies in the fight to eliminate German Nazism and Japanese militarism. By 1953, however, they had become implacable enemies in the Cold War. Analyze the reasons why this had occurred.

Use these documents and your knowledge of the period from 1941 to 1953 to compose your answer.

Document A: Joint Message of Assistance to the Soviet Union from President Roosevelt and Prime Minister Churchill, 15 August 1941

Source: *Peace and War, United States Foreign Policy 1931–1941* (Washington, D.C.: Printing Office, 1943).

We have taken the opportunity . . . to consult together as to how best our two countries can help your country in the splendid defense that you are making against the Nazi attack. We are at the moment cooperating to provide you with the very maximum of supplies that you most urgently need. Already many shiploads have left our shores and more will leave in the immediate future. . . .

The war goes on upon many fronts and before it is over there may be further fighting fronts that will be developed. Our resources though immense are limited, and it must become a question as to where and when those resources can best be used to further [to] the greatest extent our common effort. . . .

We realize fully how vitally important to the defeat of Hitlerism is the brave and steadfast resistance of the Soviet Union and we feel therefore that we must not in any circumstances fail to act quickly and immediately in this matter on planning the program for the future allocation of our joint resources.

Document B: Joseph Stalin, memorandum to aides, 13 August 1942

Source: Memorandum in Russian from Joseph Stalin about opening a second front in Europe during World War II, with English translation of same, 13 August 1942 (W. Averell Harriman Papers) Library of Congress.

I ascertained that the Prime Minister of Great Britain, Mr. Churchill, considered the organization of a second front in Europe in 1942 to be impossible.

. . .

[T]he organization of a second front in Europe had as its object the withdrawal of [German] forces from the Eastern front to the West, and the creation in the West of a serious base of resistance to the German-Fascist forces and the affording of relief by this means to the situation of the Soviet forces on the Soviet-German front in 1942. . . .

It is easy to grasp that the refusal of the government of Great Britain to create a second front in 1942 in Europe inflicts a moral blow to the whole of Soviet public opinion. . . .

It appears to me and my colleagues that the most favorable conditions exist . . . for the creation of a second front in Europe [in 1942], inasmuch as almost all the forces of the [German] army, and the best forces . . . have been withdrawn to the Eastern front. . . . I was however unfortunately unsuccessful in convincing [Mr. Churchill], while Mr. [Averell] Harriman, the representative of the President of the U.S.A., fully supported [Churchill] in the negotiations held in Moscow.

Document C: "Roosevelt, Stalin, and Churchill on Portico of Russian Embassy in Teheran [Iran], During Conference—Nov. 28–Dec. 1, 1943"
Source: U.S. Army Signal Corps. Portraits of the Presidents and First Ladies, 1789–Present, American Memory collections, Library of Congress.

Library of Congress

Document D: Vera Micheles Dean, *Our Russian Ally*, "Does the U. S. Get Along with Russia?"
American Historical Association, G.I. Roundtable Series pamphlets, January 1945.

Many people in the United States have been critical of Communist propaganda abroad, of Russia's policy toward religion, and of the anticapitalist features of Soviet economy. . . . Since 1941, when both the United States and Russia entered the war, our relations have been marked by increasing understanding and mutual desire to work together both in time of war and in the postwar period. . . .

The process of leveling off differences between Russia and the Western world will proceed [all] the more rapidly if Russia participates freely and equally in the life of the international community. It will be further helped if the Western world seeks to understand Russia and its policy in terms of Russia's basic national interests. Participation in international agencies would afford the Russians an opportunity to share the experience of Western countries. Most Russians have been acquainted with the West only through Soviet publications, which until the German invasion sought to decry conditions in "bourgeois" countries.

Document E: Memorandum from William Leahy, Roosevelt's Chief of Staff, to Secretary of State Edward Stettinius, 11 May 1945

The following message, sent by Prime Minister Churchill to Foreign Secretary Anthony Eden, is quoted for your information:

1. I consider the Polish deadlock can probably only be resolved at a conference between the three heads of governments. . . .

2. The Polish question may be easier to settle when set in relation to the now numerous outstanding questions of the utmost gravity which require urgent settlement with the Russians. . . . [T]he [sweeping] tide of Russian domination [over Eastern Europe is] an event which, if it occurred, would be one of the most melancholy in history. . . . Poland would be completely engulfed and buried deep in Russian occupied lands. . . . [T]he territories under Russian control would include the Baltic provinces, [much of Germany], all [of] Czechoslovakia, a large part of Austria, the whole of Yugoslavia, Hungary, [Romania], Bulgaria until Greece in her present tottering condition is reached. . . . If the red section was deleted, the document would be shortened to 171 words. The position of Turkey and Constantinople will certainly come . . . into discussion.

   . . .

4. It is just about time that these formidable issues were examined between the principal powers. . . . If they are not settled before the United States armies withdraw from Europe and the Western World folds up its war machines, there are no prospects of a satisfactory solution and very little of preventing a third world war. . . . I am against weakening our claim against Russia on behalf of Poland in any way.

Document F: Dean Acheson, Secretary of State under Truman, *Present at the Creation: My Years at the State Department,* **1969**
Source: http://www.mtholyoke.edu/acad/intrel/acheson.htm.

The Iranian crisis of 1945–46 revolved [around] whether the Soviet Union would withdraw its troops from northern Iran as it had agreed to do [six months after the end of hostilities] in 1942 and 1943. In 1942 the Soviet Union and Great Britain had put troops into northern and southern Iran, respectively, to block a possible German move and to protect Iranian oil.

Meanwhile, the Soviet Government had been arming a separatist movement (the Tudeh Party) in Azerbaijan, and when it staged a revolt against the Shah in November 1945 [they] refused to allow his troops access to the province to suppress it. The crisis was on. . . . The date for troop withdrawal passed without action.

[The United States and Britain] sent a favorable response to [the Iranian prime minister's] request for our strong support should the Soviet Union object to Iranian troops entering Azerbaijan. When the troops arrived they were wildly welcomed, and the separatist regime collapsed. . . .

With the crisis over, [the American] Ambassador . . . cabled on December 17, 1946, that in the Iranian view the quick collapse of the Tudeh Party was due to the conviction of everyone—the Russians, the Iranians, and the Azerbaijanis—that the United States was not bluffing but solidly supporting Iranian sovereignty. . . .

Document G

Library of Congress

Document H: Plans for NATO unveiled, Leslie Gilbert Illingworth, London *Daily Mail,* **20 March 1949**
Source: British Cartoon Archive, Templeman Library, University of Kent, http://library.kent.ac.uk/cartoons.

Daily Mail, 20 March 1949/The British Cartoon Archive, University of Kent

Document I: Report on the Conference of the leaders of the People's Democracies and the Soviet Union, 9 to 12 January 1951, Moscow
Source: http://www.gwu.edu/%7Ensarchiv/NSAEBB/NSAEBB14/doc4.htm.

Comrade Stalin opened the conference with the following remarks:

The opinion arose in recent times that the United States is an invincible power and is prepared to initiate a third world war. As it turns out, however . . . the U.S. [is] unprepared to initiate a third world war. . . .

The U.S. is bogged down in Asia and will remain pinned down there for several years.

The fact that the U.S. will be tied down in Asia for the next two or three years constitutes a very favorable circumstance for us, for the world revolutionary movement. . . .

Our task consists of using the two-to-three years at our disposal in order to create a modern and powerful military force. . . . You in the People's Democracies must, within two to three years, create modern and powerful armies that must be combat-ready by the end of the three-year period.

. . .

Why is this necessary? This is necessary in view of the imperialists' way of thinking: they are in the habit of attacking unarmed or weakly armed countries in order to liquidate them, but they keep away from well armed countries.

DBQ 14
Conformity and Turbulence, 1950–1970

Directions: In this DBQ, you must compose an essay that uses both your interpretation of Documents A–J and your own outside knowledge of the period mentioned in this question.

Historians tend to portray the 1950s as a decade of prosperity, conformity, and consensus, and the 1960s as a decade of turbulence, protest, and disillusionment. Do you agree or disagree with this view? In answering this question, address to what extent these two decades differed from each other politically and socially.

Use these documents and your knowledge of the period from 1950 to 1970 to compose your answer.

Document A
Source: Moving to the Suburbs, 1954.

Document B
Source: Senator McCarthy Extinguishes the Torch of Liberty, mid-1950s.

Document C
Source: "The Changing American Market," *Fortune*, 1955.

All history can show no more portentous economic phenomenon than today's American market.... It is enabling Americans to raise their standard of living every year while other countries have trouble maintaining theirs....

The most important change of the past few years . . . is the rise of the great mass into a new moneyed middle class. . . . It is like no other middle class in history. . . . [They] buy the same things—the same staples, the same appliances, the same cars, the same furniture, and much the same recreation. . . . The marketer who designs for his product to appeal to the whole group has hit the new mass market. . . .

[On] the whole people seem more inclined to spend than they ever have been. . . . [The] nation is, or is pretty close to being depression-proof [due to consumer spending]. . . .

Document D
Source: Elvis Presley, mid-1950s. (See text p. 864 for full-size photograph.)

Charles Trainor/Time & Life Pictures/Getty Images

Document E
Source: Integration at Little Rock, 1957.

Will Counts, The Arkansas Democrat-Gazette, Inc., courtesy Vivian Counts and Indiana University Archives

Document F: John F. Kennedy, Address to the Economic Club of New York, 14 December 1962
Source: http://www.americanrhetoric.com/speeches/jfkeconomicclubaddress.html.

In the last two years we have made significant strides. Our gross national product has risen eleven percent, while inflation has been arrested. Employment has been increased by one-point-three million jobs. Profits, personal income, living standards—all are setting new records. Most of the economic indicators for this quarter are up and the prospects are for further expansion in the next quarter. But we must look beyond the next quarter, or the last quarter, or even the last two years. For we can and must do better, much better than we've been doing for the last five-and-a-half years.

This economy is capable of producing, without strain, 30 to 40 billion [dollars] more than we are producing today. Business earnings could be seven to eight billion higher than they are today. Utilization of existing plant and equipment could be much higher—and, if it were, investment would rise. We need not accept an unemployment rate of five percent or more, such as we have had for 60 out of the last 61 months. There is no need for us to be satisfied with a rate of growth that keeps good men out of work and good capacity out of use.

Document G
Source: Malcolm X, "Message to the Grass Roots," speech, Detroit, Michigan, 10 November 1963.

Revolution is bloody, revolution is hostile, revolution knows no compromise, revolution overturns and destroys everything that gets in its way. And you, sitting around here like a knot on the wall, saying, "I'm going to love these folks no matter how much they hate me.". . . Whoever heard of a revolution where they lock arms . . . singing "We shall overcome"? You don't do that in a revolution. You don't do any singing, you're too busy swinging.

Document H
Source: Betty Friedan, *The Feminine Mystique*, 1963.

The problem lay buried, unspoken, for many years in the minds of American women. It was a strange stirring, a sense of dissatisfaction, a yearning that women suffered in the middle of the twentieth century in the United States. Each suburban wife struggled with it alone. As she made the beds, shopped for groceries, matched slipcover material, ate peanut butter sandwiches with her children, chauffeured Cub Scouts and Brownies, lay beside her husband at night—she was afraid to ask even of herself the silent question—"Is this all?"

Document I
Source: President Lyndon Johnson, speech at Johns Hopkins University, 7 April 1965.

Why are we in South Viet-Nam?

We are there because we have a promise to keep. Since 1954 every American President has offered support to the people of South Viet-Nam. . . . [We] have made a national pledge to help South Viet-Nam defend its independence. . . .

To dishonor that pledge, to abandon this small and brave nation to its enemies, and to the terror that must follow, would be an unforgivable wrong.

We are also there to strengthen world order. Around the globe from Berlin to Thailand are people whose well[-]being rests in part on the belief they can count on us if they are attacked. To leave Vietnam to its fate would shake the confidence of all these people in the value of an American commitment and in the value of America's word.

Document J
Source: The Siege of Chicago, 1968.

© Bettmann/Corbis

DBQ 15
Assessing Ronald Reagan's Presidency, 1980–1989

Directions: In this DBQ, you must compose an essay that uses both your interpretation of Documents A–J and your own outside knowledge of the period mentioned in the question.

Evaluate the effectiveness of the Reagan administration's responses to the domestic and international challenges of the 1980s.

Use these documents and your knowledge of the period from 1980 to 1989 to compose your answer.

Document A: Ronald Reagan's Neshoba County Fair Speech, 3 August 1980
Source: http://neshobademocrat.com.

I know, people have been telling me that Jimmy Carter has been doing his best. And that's our problem. The President lately has been saying that I am irresponsible. And you know, I'll admit to that if he'll confess he's responsible. We've had the New Deal, and then Harry Truman gave us the Fair Deal, and now we have a misdeal. . . .We know that an administration for three and a half years, that told us when they took office that it was going to reduce inflation to less than four percent and reduce unemployment to less than four percent, has betrayed the people with an inflation rate that they hope that they might get back down to 10 percent after it having reached 18 at the beginning of the year. . . . But probably the worst thing is what had been done to this county on the international scene. This once proud country, this country that all the world turned to and looked to as the shelter, as the safety and as the anchor to windward. Today, our friends don't know whether they can trust us, and certainly our enemies have no respect for us. . . . I believe in state's rights; I believe in people doing as much as they can for themselves at the community level and at the private level. And I believe that we've distorted the balance of our government today by giving powers that were never intended in the constitution to that federal establishment.

Document B: Ronald Reagan, Inaugural Address, 20 January 1981
Source: http://www.presidency.ucsb.edu.

For decades we have piled deficit upon deficit, mortgaging our future and our children's future for the temporary convenience of the present. To continue this long trend is to guarantee tremendous social, cultural, political, and economic upheavals. . . .

In this present crisis, government is not the solution to our problem; government is the problem. From time to time we've been tempted to believe that society has become too complex to be managed by self-rule, that government by an elite group is superior to government for, by, and of the people. Well, if no one among us is capable of governing himself, then who among us has the capacity to govern someone else? All of us together, in and out of government, must bear the burden. The solutions we seek must be equitable, with no one group singled out to pay a higher price. . . .

And as we renew ourselves here in our own land, we will be seen as having greater strength throughout the world. We will again be the exemplar of freedom and a beacon of hope for those who do not now have freedom.

Document C: United States National Debt and Unemployment Rate Chart, 1981–1988

Source: *Economic Report of the President, 1990.*

Year	Unemployment Rate	National Debt	% Increase National Debt
1981	7.5%	994,300,000,000	9.4%
1982	9.5%	1,136,800,000,000	14.3%
1983	9.5%	1,371,200,000,000	20.6%
1984	7.4%	1,564,100,000,000	14.1%
1985	7.1%	1,817,000,000,000	16.2%
1986	6.9%	2,120,100,000,000	16.7%
1987	6.1%	2,345,600,000,000	10.6%
1988	5.4%	2,600,800,000,000	10.9%

Document D: "The Education of David Stockman"

Source: *Atlantic Monthly*, December 1981.

While ideology would guide Stockman in his new job, he would be confronted with a large and tangible political problem: how to resolve the three-sided dilemma created by Ronald Reagan's contradictory campaign promises. In private, Stockman agreed that his former congressional mentor, John Anderson, running as an independent candidate for President in 1980, had asked the right question: How is it possible to raise defense spending, cut income taxes, and balance the budget, all at the same time? . . .

But Stockman was confident, even cocky, that he and some of his fellow conservatives had the answer. It was a theory of economics—the supply-side theory—that promised an end to the twin aggravations of the 1970s: high inflation and stagnant growth in America's productivity. . . . "The whole thing is premised on faith," Stockman explained. "On a belief about how the world works."

Document E: Ronald Reagan, "Speech to the National Association of Evangelicals," 3 March 1983

. . . But if history teaches anything, it teaches that simple-minded appeasement or wishful thinking about our adversaries is folly. It means the betrayal of our past, the squandering of our freedom. So, I urge you to speak out against those who would place the United States in a position of military and moral inferiority. . . . So, in your discussions of the nuclear freeze proposals, I urge you to beware the temptation of pride—the temptation of blithely declaring yourselves above it all and label both sides equally at fault, to ignore the facts of history and the aggressive impulses of an evil empire, to simply call the arms race a giant misunderstanding and thereby remove yourself from the struggle between right and wrong and good and evil. . . . I believe we shall rise to the challenge. I believe that communism is another sad, bizarre chapter in human history whose last pages even now are being written.

Document F: Star Wars political cartoon by Steve Greenberg

Source: *Seattle Post-Intelligencer*, 1985. Reprinted in Charles Brooks, ed., *Best Political Cartoons of the Year, 1986 Edition*, 82.

Steve Greenberg, Seattle Post-Intelligencer, 1985

Document G: Senator Edward Kennedy, "Robert Bork's America"
Source: *Congressional Record*, 23 June 1987.

Robert Bork's America is a land in which women would be forced into back-alley abortions, blacks would sit at segregated lunch counters, rogue police could break down citizens' doors in midnight raids, schoolchildren could not be taught about evolution, writers and artists would be censored at the whim of government, and the doors of the federal courts would be shut on the fingers of millions of citizens for whom the judiciary is often the only protector of the individual rights that are the heart of our democracy. America is a better and freer nation than Robert Bork thinks. Yet in the current delicate balance of the Supreme Court, his rigid ideology will tip the scales of justice against the kind of country America is and ought to be. The damage that President Reagan will do through this nomination, if it is not rejected by the Senate, could live on far beyond the end of his presidential term. President Reagan is still our President. But he should not be able to reach out from the muck of Irangate, reach into the muck of Watergate, and impose his reactionary vision of the Constitution on the Supreme Court and on the next generation of Americans. No justice would be better than this injustice.

Document H: "If Papa Won't Preach It, Young Ron Reagan Will, with a TV Pitch Promoting Safe Sex"
Source: *People Magazine*, 13 July 1987.

The young man talking into the TV camera has a message his parents might not want to hear. "The U.S. government is not moving fast enough to stop the spread of AIDS," he says. "If you don't think enough is being done, write to your congressman—or to someone higher up." Suddenly, the war against AIDS has an unlikely but famous foot soldier: Ron Jr. . . . As Ron sees it, his father is getting bad counsel from "people who just think about image and votes." At his request, the script for the public-service announcement was changed slightly from its original form—"write your congressman, or my father"—to deflect the focus from the President. Instead, Ron Jr. points the finger at some of the President's supporters. He is particularly annoyed with Secretary of Education William Bennett, who advocates restricting AIDS education in the schools.

Document I
Source: *Report of the Congressional Committees Investigating the Iran-Contra Affair*, "Introduction to the Iran-Contra Minority Report," 17 November 1987.

President Reagan and his staff made mistakes in the Iran-contra affair. It is important at the outset, however, to note that the President himself has already taken the hard step of acknowledging his mistakes and reacting precisely to correct what went wrong. . . . The bottom line, however, is that the mistakes of the Iran-contra affair were just that—mistakes in judgment, and nothing more. . . . President Reagan has been praised by his supporters as a "communicator" and criticized by his opponents as an ideologue. The mistakes of the Iran-Contra Affair, ironically, came from a lack of communication and an inadequate appreciation of the importance of ideas.

Document J: "Evolution of Reagan" by Joe Majeski
Source: *Times Leader (PA)*, 1988. Reprinted in Charles Brooks, ed. *Best Editorial Cartoons of the Year, 1989 edition*, 45.

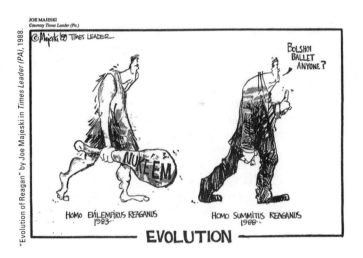

"Evolution of Reagan" by Joe Majeski in *Times Leader (PA)*, 1988.

Free-Response Essay Questions

PART ONE: Founding the New Nation, ca. 33,000 B.C.E.–1783 C.E.

1. Analyze the effects of the Columbian exchange on Europeans and native North Americans from 1492 to 1607.

2. Evaluate the extent of settlement and influence of three of these groups of non-English settlers in North America before 1775.
    French
    Dutch
    Scots-Irish
    German
    African

3. Explain the theory of mercantilism and the role it played in prompting Americans to rebel in 1776.

PART TWO: Building the Nation, 1776–1860

4. To what extent did European events influence the course of American development between 1795 and 1810? Assess with respect to three of the following.
    XYZ Affair
    Alien and Sedition Acts
    Louisiana Purchase
    Embargo of 1807

5. Analyze the social changes that gave rise to mass democracy in the United States between 1820 and 1840. Include the roles of three of the following in this process.
    John Marshall
    Henry Clay
    Andrew Jackson
    William Henry Harrison

6. Analyze the ways in which the "transportation revolution" (1820–1860) affected economic relationships among the Northeast, the South, and the West.

PART THREE: Testing the New Nation, 1820–1877

7. Evaluate the relative importance of three of the following in precipitating the secession crisis of 1860–1861. Please confine your response to the years 1846–1861.
    Slavery
    Westward expansion
    Bad leadership
    States' rights

8. What geographic and strategic advantages did the South possess at the outset of the Civil War? Why were these not sufficient to prevail in the struggle?

9. To what extent did the constitutional amendments ratified during Reconstruction (Thirteenth, Fourteenth, and Fifteenth) bring political and economic equality to the former slaves by 1900?

PART FOUR: Forging an Industrial Society, 1865–1909

10. Analyze the part played by immigration in transforming the urban social fabric of the United States between 1870 and 1900.

11. Assess the roles played by three of the following in the social-class conflicts that characterized the late nineteenth century.
    Tom Watson
    W. E. B. Du Bois
    Mary Harris "Mother" Jones
    Ida B. Wells

12. Analyze and explain the role played by railroads in the rapid economic growth of late-nineteenth-century America.

PART FIVE: Struggling for Justice at Home and Abroad, 1901–1945

13. Explain how the presidential candidates in the election of 1912 demonstrated the contrasting political interests and ideas of the early 1900s.

14. Explain the role of new ideas and technologies in creating political and social tension during the 1920s.

15. Analyze the long-term significance of the New Deal for three of the following groups.
    Industrial workers
    Retired workers
    Women
    Farmers and farm workers

PART SIX: Making Modern America, 1945 to the Present

16. Compare and contrast the effects of United States involvement in the Korean War (1950–1953) and the Vietnam War (1964–1973) on two of the following.
    Civil Liberties
    Presidential Politics
    Cold War Foreign Policy

17. Assess the role played by television in shaping political events between 1950 and 1965. Include analysis of its significance in at least three of the following events.
    "Checkers" speech (1952)
    Army-McCarthy hearings (1954)
    Presidential election debates (1960)
    Birmingham civil rights protest (1963)

18. "Unlike William Clinton whose presidency was tarnished by domestic issues, but redeemed by a restrained foreign policy, George W. Bush's presidency was fortified by domestic issues, but discredited by an aggressive foreign policy." Assess the validity of this statement with specific reference to the years 1992–2008.

INDEX

Hard-money advocates, 492, 602
Harjo, Joy, 1010
Harlem, 53, 719
Harlem Renaissance, 724
Harmar, Josiah, 191
Harper's (Harper's New Monthly Magazine), 319, 558
Harpers Ferry, Virginia, Brown, John at, 407–408
Harrington, Michael, 900
Harrison, Benjamin, 504, 611
Harrison, William Henry, 220, 233, 360, 361, 504; election of 1836 and, 263; election of 1840 and, 270–271; Tippecanoe battle and, 220; War of 1812 and, 225, 230
Hart, Gary, 955
Harte, Bret, 567–568, 585, 594
Hartford, 46
Hartford Convention (1814–1815), 228–229
Harvard University, 73, 90, 314, 557
Harvester trust, 524
Harvesting (Krans), 320
Harvey, William Hope, 598
Hatch Act (1887), 555
Hatch Act (1939), 758, 773
Haussmann, Georges-Eugène, 569
Havana, 107, 612
Havana Conference (1940), 788
Hawaii, 880; acquisition of, 610–611, 611 (map), 614; immigrant workers in, 611, 624; Japanese immigrants in, 800; Pearl Harbor attack in, 798; revolt of whites in, 611
Hawaiian Sugar Planters Association, 624
"Hawks" (Vietnam War), 910, 919
Hawley-Smoot Tariff (1930), 740, 742, 780
Hawthorne, Nathaniel, 72, 320, 328, 331, 560
Hay, John, 621, 623, 626
Hay-Bunau-Varilla Treaty (1902), 628
Hayes, Rutherford B., 496, 498; election of 1876 and, 493, 494–495, 494 (map); railroad strike and, 497
Haymarket Square episode, 533, 599, 642
Hayne, Robert Y., 256
Hay-Pauncefote Treaty (1901), 389, 628
Hays, Samuel P., 675
Hays Code, 716
Hayslip, Le Ly, 894 (map)
Haywood, William D. ("Big Bill"), 681
H-bomb, 851–852
Headright system, 61
Head Start, 903
Health, in Chesapeake, 60
Health care: Clinton and, 967; costs of, 999; Obama policies toward, 986, 993. *See also* Disease; Medical care
Hearst, William Randolph, 558, 608, 612, 669
Hebrew schools, 545
Hegemony, of United States, 980
Helicopters, Eisenhower and, 877
Heller, Joseph, 883
Hell Gate, 53
"Hello girls," 528
Helms-Burton Act (1996), 878
Helper, Hinton R., 397
Helsinki accords (1975), 928
Hemings, Madison, 205
Hemings, Sally, Jefferson and, 203, 205
Hemingway, Ernest, 566, 720–721, 882

Henretta, James, 537
Henry VII (England, r. 1485–1509), 26
Henry VIII (England, r. 1509–1547), 26, 41; Catholic Church and, 24
Henry, Patrick, 123, 142, 169, 173, 175
Henry Street Settlement, 549
Hepburn Act (1906), 649
Herblock (cartoonist), 954
Hermitage (Nashville, Tennessee), 251
Herzog (Bellow), 887
Hess, Rudolf, 844
Hessians, in American Revolution, 125, 133, 143, 144, 147
Hetch Hetchy Valley, flooding of, 654–655
Hewitt, Nancy, 333
Heyrman, Christine, 95
Hiawatha (Iroquois), 8, 36
Hickok, James B., 586
Hicks, Edward, 54
Hicks, John D., 510
"High crimes and misdemeanors," 481
High culture, 1007
Higher education, 313–314; blacks in, 1007; for women, 313, 314. *See also* Universities and colleges
High Federalists, 194
High-rise buildings, 882
High schools, 554, 709
High-tech industries, 834, 991
Highways. *See* Roads and highways
Hill, Anita, 961
Hill, James J., 516, 649
Hillbillies, 528
"Hindrances to Revivals" (Finney), 309
Hine, Lewis, photography of, 530, 531
Hip-hop, 1008
Hippies, 885
Hirohito (Japan), 821
Hiroshima, atomic bombing of, 820, 825
Hispanics: in Southwest, 594; on Supreme Court, 986. *See also* Latinos
Hispaniola, 14, 15, 17
Hiss, Alger, 852
History and historians: on American and French Revolutions, 189; on American Revolution, 152–153; in antebellum period, 332; on antebellum reformers, 333; on atomic bomb use, 825; on causes of Civil War, 415–416; on Cold War, 857; on colonial society, 95–96; consensus view of, 153, 178; on consequences of Civil War, 462; constraints school of, 776; crucifixion thesis of, 457–460; on distinctiveness of America, 57–58; global view of, 153; on imperialism, 634; imperial school of, 153; on industrialization, 537; on Jacksonian democracy, 273–274; leftist school of, 537, 697–698, 775; on modern conservatism, 962; Nationalist school of, 177, 415–416; on nature of slavery, 357–358; neonationalist school of, 416; on New Deal, 775–776; New Left school of, 634, 675; New Western, 605–606; in 1960s, 913–914; organizational school of, 675–676; on Populists, 510; progressive school of, 153, 177–178, 510; on progressivism, 675–676; "realist," 697; on Reconstruction, 483–484; revisionist school of, 634, 857, 962; revolutionary and counterrevolutionary views of Constitution, 177–178; social

movements and, 153; of technology, 292; transatlantic view of, 153; on Turner's thesis, 605–606; on U.S. imperialism, 634; Whig view of history, 152; on Wilson, 697–698; on woman suffrage movement, 333. *See also* specific historians and movements
History of the United States During the Administrations of Jefferson and Madison (Adams), 568
History of the United States of America (Bancroft), 152
Hitler, Adolf, 694, 697, 740, 781, 786; appeasement of, 784; Great Depression and, 822; Jewish policies of, 784; last days of, 816–818; lend-lease and, 792; Spanish Civil War and, 783; suicide by, 818; in World War II, 811, 824
Hitler-Stalin pact (1939), 784–785
Hoar, George F., 620
Hoban, James, 230
Hoboes ("tramps"), 508
Ho Chi Minh, 632, 633, 874
Hoffa, James R. ("Jimmy"), 877
Hofstadter, Richard, 273, 510, 634, 675, 962
Hog industry, 295
Holding companies, 666, 765
Holidays, colonial, 95
Holland, 25; Separatists from, 42; Texas and, 363; William III from, 50. *See also* Dutch
Holloway, Houston H., 467
Hollywood, movie industry in, 716
Holmes, Oliver Wendell (father), 324, 328
Holmes, Oliver Wendell, Jr. (son), 560, 561, 729
Holocaust: refugees from, 788; in World War II, 816–818, 822
Holt, Michael, 416
Holton, Woody, 153, 178
Holzer, Jenny, 1008
Home brew, 708
Home front: in World War I, 680–686; in World War II, 807, 871
Homeland Security, Department of, 975
Home Loan Bank bill, 745
Home loans, 835
Home Owner's Loan Corporation (HOLC), 755, 758
Home Owner's Refinancing Act (1933), 755
Homer, Winslow, 312, 460, 568, 569
Home rule, for American colonists, 146
Home Rule regimes, in South, 476
Homestead act (1860), 405
Homestead Act (1862), 433, 459, 473, 586–587, 596
Homesteading, 586–588, 587, 588
Homestead Strike, 505–506, 642
Homosexuals. *See* Gays and lesbians
Honduras, dollar diplomacy in, 658
Hone, Philip, 265, 291, 324
Hong Kong, 162, 390, 633, 808
Hooker, Joseph ("Fighting Joe"), 445
Hookworms, eradication of, 709
Hoover, Herbert, 637, 739, 746–747, 744, 745, 767, 770; election of 1928 and, 738–739, 739 (map); election of 1932 and, 753; as Food Administration head, 685; Good Neighbor policy of, 748; Great Depression policies of, 743–746; as Secretary of Commerce, 728, 729
Hoover, J. Edgar, 889, 896

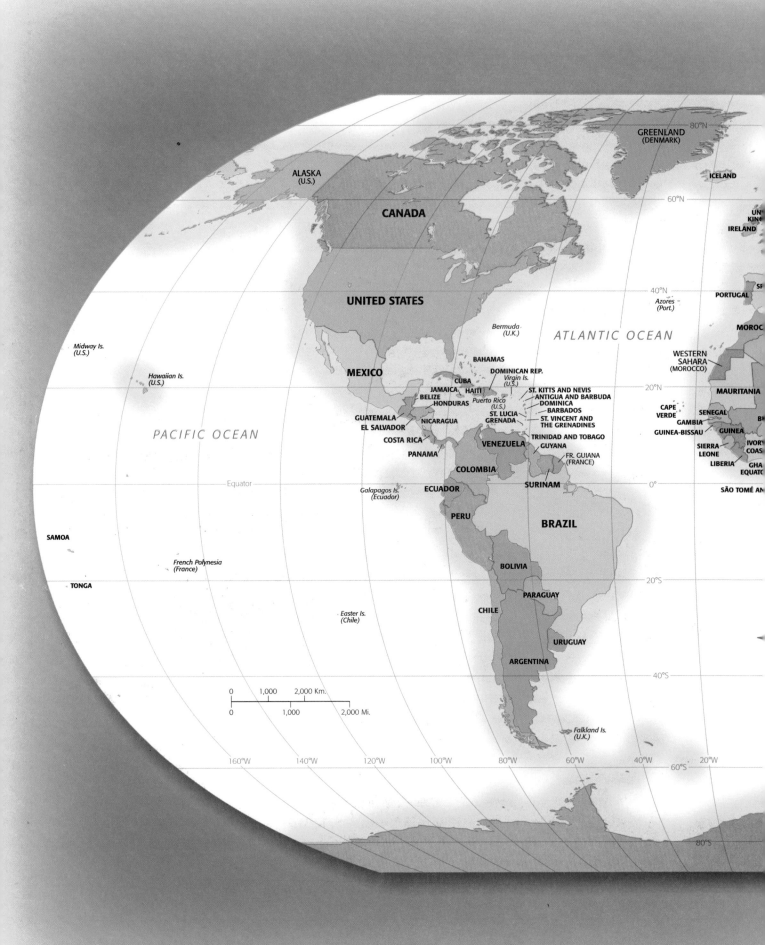